D1103918

Ellicott's Bible Commentary

In One Volume

A verse-by-verse explanation
by Charles John Ellicott

Condensed and Edited by Donald N. Bowdle, Ph.D., Th.D.

 ZONDERVAN
PUBLISHING HOUSE
OF THE ZONDERVAN CORPORATION
GRAND RAPIDS, MICHIGAN 49506

PREFACE

Charles John Ellicott, eminent Anglican divine in the conservative tradition, was born at Whitwell, near Stamford, Rutlandshire, England, on April 25, 1819. He was educated at Oakham, Stamford and St. John's College (Cambridge), where in 1845 he was elected Fellow. Ordained dean that same year, and priest in 1846, the young clergyman and scholar served from 1848 to 1861 as professor of divinity in King's College, London, and until 1858 as rector of Pilton, Rutlandshire. In 1859 he was invited as Hulsean Lecturer at Cambridge University, his addresses appearing in published form as *Historical Lectures on the Life of Our Lord Jesus Christ.* The following year he was appointed Hulsean Professor of Divinity at that institution.

Ellicott resigned both professorships in 1861, accepting the post of Dean of Exeter. Subsequently he was named Bishop of Gloucester and Bristol (1863-1897) and of Gloucester (1897-1905). During those forty-two years of episcopate, Ellicott helped to establish several significant memorials, among them the Gloucester Theological College and the Church Aid Society in Bristol.

A linguist, exegete, and historian of the first rank, Bishop Ellicott served on numerous commissions for ecclesiastical polity and scholarly publication. He was secretary to the Lambeth Conferences of 1867, 1878, and 1888; he chaired the committee producing the English Revised Version of the New Testament (1870-1881), missing only 2 of 407 sessions; he published a series of *Critical and Grammatical Commentaries* on most of the Pauline Epistles; and he authored several important works, such as *The Being of God, Modern Unbelief, The History and Obligation of the Sabbath, Aids to the Faith,* and *Christus Comprobatur.* His long and prolific life came to an end on October 15, 1905.

Nearly a full century ago, Ellicott published his *Commentary on the Whole Bible.* Offered originally in eight large volumes, that set was comprised not only of his own incisive comments, but of those complementary insights of twenty-nine other eminent scholars in the field. Among that notable roster were F. W. Farrar, C. D. Ginsburg, W. F. Moulton, Alfred Plummer, E. H. Plumptre, William Sanday, R. Payne Smith, and H. D. M. Spence.

According to the preface of that original publication, all of the compilers laboring therein believed the Holy Scriptures to be in fact the Word of God. They were committed to a policy of complete honesty in treating the text: meeting difficulties fairly, removing some of those difficulties where such could be done, and simply leaving others "where it did not appear that God had yet vouchsafed to us the means of doing more than modifying them, or reducing their gravity and magnitude."

It is entirely appropriate that a popular abridgment of that highly significant work now should appear. This present volume represents the careful analysis, critical selection, and condensation of nearly 5,000 pages of text. In every case I have allowed the writers to speak for themselves, foregoing any attempt at conciliation of divergent viewpoints and inserting only that transitional material necessary in compensation for alterations in original commentary. I have, however, modernized the language, checked statements of archeological and manuscript natures against the best and most recent scholarship, and enlarged the number of cross-references throughout, believing that this would enhance the functionality of an abridged edition.

The reader is asked to remember and appreciate the inherent limitations of a one-volume commentary. The very nature and scope of this smaller production precluded a veritable wealth of truths and applications. My criteria of selectivity— since such were necessarily imposed upon me for this present purpose—were: 1) original languages and manuscript evidence, to clarify the text; 2) historical and archeological detail, to locate the text; 3) classical allusions, to illustrate the text; 4) Messianic prophecy and fulfillment, to vindicate the text; and 5) evangelistic application, to render relevant all that the text has promised. Furthermore, in the absence of introductions to the several biblical books, I commend to the reader those helpful volumes by conservative and evangelical scholars like Edward J. Young, Merrill F. Unger, Everett F. Harrison, J. Barton Payne, H. E. Dana, Merrill C. Tenney, and Robert Gundry.

I have pursued this pleasant but demanding project with a sense of privilege and responsibility. "Ellicott" has been my constant companion for nearly three years, finding urgent place in a multifarious routine, whether in Richmond, Princeton, New York City, Toronto, St. Louis, the shores of Chesapeake Bay, or certainly Cleveland. But every effort has rendered this undertaking a spiritual experience as well as an academic engagement.

To fail to acknowledge the many hands that helped would, on my part, be inexcusable. For this opportunity of ministry through the printed page my sincere thanks are due: Dr. Charles W. Conn and Dr. Ray H. Hughes, who recommended me for the project; Dr. Pat Zondervan, who extended the invitation and became a warm, personal friend; Mr. Al Bryant, who graciously extended deadlines to accommodate my other obligations; my colleagues and students at Lee College, who shared my enthusiasm; my children, Keven and Karen, who somehow seemed to understand what it was all about; and my wife, who typed those endless pages of manuscript—I don't know how anyone could put out a book without Nancy!

DONALD N. BOWDLE
LEE COLLEGE
Cleveland, Tenn.

CONTENTS

ABOUT THE EDITOR

Donald N. Bowdle is a native of Easton, Maryland, and an ordained minister in the Church of God. He holds the B.A. degree *magna cum laude* in religion and history from Lee College, and graduate degrees of M.A. and Ph.D. in New Testament language and literature from Bob Jones University, Th.M. in ancient and medieval church history from Princeton Theological Seminary, and Th.D. in American church history from Union Theological Seminary in Virginia.

At Princeton he was awarded a Samuel Robinson Foundation Scholarship, and at Union the Robert C. and Sadie G. Anderson Foundation Scholarship for Graduate Study. Bowdle has taught European and American history at Virginia Commonwealth University in Richmond, and continues as book reviewer for the influential *Richmond Times-Dispatch,* with more than sixty published reviews to date, and as regular contributor to the Quarterly *Religious and Theological Abstracts.*

A popular speaker at educational conferences and ministerial retreats, Bowdle has addressed numerous large and significant conventions, including those of Church of God National Youth and Christian Education in Los Angeles and the interdenominational National Sunday School Association in Milwaukee. His pulpit ministry is well-known both throughout his own communion and to Presbyterian congregations in Virginia, West Virginia, North Carolina, and Tennessee.

Dr. Bowdle presently serves as Professor of History and Religion, and is Chairman of the Department of History, at Lee College, Cleveland, Tennessee, where his peers have elected him to *Who's Who in American Education, Outstanding Educators of America, Outstanding Young Men of America*, and *Personalities of the South.* He is an active member of the Southern Historical Association, the American Society of Church History, the Society of Biblical Literature, the Evangelical Theological Society, the society for Pentecostal Studies, and the Academy of Christians in the Professions.

GENESIS

1

The Creative Week (1:1-2:3)

(1) In the beginning.—Not, as in John 1:1, "from eternity," but in the beginning of this sidereal system, of which our sun, with its attendant planets, forms a part. As there never was a time when God did not exist, and as activity is an essential part of His being (John 5:17), so, probably, there was never a time when worlds did not exist; and in the process of calling them into existence when and how He willed, we may well believe that God acted in accordance with the working of some universal law, of which He is Himself the Author. It was natural with John, when placing the same words at the commencement of his gospel, to carry our minds back to a more absolute conceivable "beginning," when the work of creation had not begun, and when in the whole universe there was only God.

God.—Heb., **Elohim.** A word plural in form, but joined with a singular verb, except when it refers to the false gods of the heathen, in which case if takes a plural verb. Its root meaning is "strength," "power"; and the form **Elohim** is not to be regarded as a **pluralis majestatis**, but as embodying the effort of early human thought in feeling after the Deity, and arriving at the conclusion that the Deity was one. Thus, in the name **Elohim** it included in one Person all the powers, mights, and influences by which the world was first created and is now governed and maintained. Christians may also well see in this a foreshadowing of the plurality of persons in the divine Trinity; but its primary lesson is that, however diverse may seem the working of the powers of nature, the Worker is one and His work one.

Created.—Creation, in its strict sense of producing something out of nothing, contains an idea so noble and elevated that naturally human language could only gradually rise up to it. It is quite possible, therefore, that the word **bârâ**, "he created," may originally have signified to hew stone or fell timber; but as a matter of fact it is a rare word, and employed chiefly or entirely in connection with the activity of God. As, moreover, "the heaven and the earth" can only mean the totality of all existent things, the idea of creating them out of nothing is contained in the very form of the sentence.

The heaven and the earth.—The normal phrase in the Bible for the universe (Deut. 32:1; Ps. 148:13; Isa. 1:2). To the Hebrew this consisted of our one planet and the atmosphere surrounding it, in which he beheld the sun, moon, and stars. But it is one of the more than human qualities of the language of the Holy Scriptures that, while written by men whose knowledge was in accordance with their times, it does not contradict the increased knowledge of later times. Contemporaneous with the creation of the earth was the calling into existence, not merely perhaps of our solar system but of that sidereal universe of which we form so small a part; but naturally in the Bible our attention is confined to that which chiefly concerns ourselves.

(2) And the earth.—The conjunction "and" negates the well-meant attempt to harmonize geology and Scripture by taking verse 1 as a mere heading; the two verses go together, and form a general summary of creation, which is afterwards divided into its several stages.

Was is not the copula, but the substantive verb "existed," and expresses duration of time. After creation, the earth existed as a shapeless and empty waste.

Without form, and void.—Literally, **tohu** and **bohu**, which words are both substantives, and signify "wasteness" and "emptiness." The similarity of their forms, joined with the harshness of their sound, made them pass almost into a proverb for everything that was dreary and desolate (Isa. 34:10; Jer. 4:23). It expresses here the state of primeval matter immediately after creation, when as yet there was no cohesion between the separate particles.

Darkness.—This agrees with the previous representation of the chaos out of which the earth was to be shaped. It existed at present only as an incoherent waste of emptiness.

The deep.—Heb., **Tehom.** This word, from a root signifying confusion or disturbance, is poetically applied to the ocean, as in Ps. 42:7, from the restless motion of its waves, but is used here to describe the chaos as a surging mass of shapeless matter.

The Spirit of God.—Heb., "a wind of God," i.e., a mighty wind, as rendered by the Targum and most Jewish interpreters. This unseen material force, wind (John 3:8), has always suggested to the human mind the thought of the divine agency, which, equally unseen, is mightier in its working. When, then, creation is ascribed to the wind (Job 26:13; Ps. 104:30), we justly see, not the mere instrumental force employed, but

1

rather that divine operative energy which resides especially in the Third Person of the Holy Trinity. But we must be on our guard against the common error of commentators, who read into the text of these ancient documents perfect doctrines which were not revealed in their fullness until the Gospel was given. It is a marvelous fact that Genesis contains the germ of almost every evangelical truth, but it contains it in a suggestive and not a completed form. So here this mighty energizing wind suggests to us the thought of the Holy Ghost, and is far more eloquent in its original simplicity than when we read into it a doctrine not made known until revelation was perfected in Christ (John 7:39).

Moved.—Heb., "fluttered lovingly." (See Deut. 32:11.) This word also would lead the mind up to the thought of the agency of a Person. In Syriac the verb is a common one for the incubation of birds; and, in allusion to this place, it is metaphorically employed, both of the waving of the hand of the priest over the cup in consecrating the wine for the Eucharist, and of that of the patriarch over the head of a bishop at his consecration. Two points must be noticed: the first, that the motion was not self-originated, but was external to the chaos; the second, that it was a gentle and loving energy, which tenderly and gradually, with fostering care, called forth the latent possibilities of a nascent world.

The Creative Days

(3) And God said.—There could be no voice and sound, nor was there any person to whom God addressed this word of power. The phrase, then, is metaphorical, and means that God enacted for the universe a law; and we find the command similarly given ten times. The beauty and sublimity of the language here used has often been noticed: God makes no preparation, He employs no means, needs no secondary agency. He speaks, and it is done. His word alone contains all things necessary for the fulfillment of His will. So in the cognate languages the word **Emir**, ruler, is literally, "speaker." The Supreme One speaks: with the rest, to hear is to obey. God, then, by speaking, gives to nature a universal and enduring law. His commands are not temporary, but eternal; and whatever secondary causes were called into existence when the Elohim, by a word, created light, those

same causes produce it now, and will produce it until God recalls His word. We have, then, here nature's first universal law. What is it?

Let there be light: and there was light.—The sublimity of the original is lost in our language by the cumbrous multiplication of particles. Light is not itself a substance, but is a condition or state of matter; and this primeval light was probably electric, arising from the condensation and friction of the elements as they began to arrange themselves in order. And this, again, was due to what is commonly called the law of gravitation, or of the attraction of matter.

(4) And God saw.—This contemplation indicates, first, lapse of time; and next, that the judgment pronounced was the verdict of the divine reason.

That it was good.—As light was a necessary result of motion in the world-mass, so was it indispensable for all that was to follow, inasmuch as neither vegetable nor animal life can exist without it. But the repeated approval by the Deity of each part and portion of this material universe (comp. Ps. 104:31) asserts that this world is a noble home for man, and life a blessing, in spite of its solemn responsibilities.

And God divided. . . .—The first three creative days are all days of order and distribution, and have been called "the three separations." But while on the first two days no new thing was created, but only the chaotic matter (described in verse 2) arranged, on day three there was the introduction of vegetable life. The division on the first day does not imply that darkness has a separate and independent existence, but that there were now periods of light and darkness; and thus by the end of the first day our earth must have advanced far on its way towards its present state. It is even more probable that the ultimate results of each creative word are summed up in the account given of it. The separations must have begun immediately after the "wind of Elohim" began to brood upon and move the chaotic mass.

(5) God called the light Day. . . Night.—Before this distinction of night and day was possible there must have been outside the earth, not as yet the sun, but a bright phosphorescent mass, such as now enwraps that luminary; and, secondly, the earth must have begun to revolve upon its axis. Consequent upon this would be, not merely alternate periods of light and darkness, but also of heat and cold, from which would result important effects upon the formation of the earth's crust. Moreover, in thus giving "day" and "night" names, God ordained language, and that vocal sounds should be the symbols of things. This law already looks forward to the existence of man, the one being on earth who calls things by their names.

And the evening and the morning.—The word "evening" means a "mixture." It is no longer the opaque darkness of a world without light, but the intermingling of light and darkness (comp. Zech. 14:6, 7). This is followed by a "morning," that is, a "breaking forth" of light. Evening is placed first because there was a progress from a less to a greater brightness and order and beauty. The Jewish method of calculating the day from sunset to sunset was not the cause, but the result of this arrangement.

The first day.—A creative day is not a period of twenty-four hours, but an **aeon**, or period of indefinite duration, as the Bible itself teaches us. For in 2:4 the six days of this narrative are described as and summed up in one day, creation being there regarded, not in its successive stages, but as a whole. So by the common consent of commentators, the seventh day, or day of God's rest, is that age in which we are now living, and which will continue until the consummation of all things. So in Zech. 14:7 the whole gospel dispensation is called "one day"; and constantly in Hebrew, as probably in all languages, "day" is used in a very indefinite manner, as, for instance, in Deut. 9:1. As Augustine pointed out, there was no sun then and "it is very difficult for us to imagine what sort of days these could be" (**De Civ. Dei,** 11:6, 7). It must further be observed that this knowledge of the stages of creation could only have been given by revelation, and that the agreement of the Mosaic record with geology is so striking that there is no real difficulty in believing it to be inspired.

(6) A firmament.—If, as geologists tell us, the earth at this stage was an incandescent mass, this expanse would be the ring of equilibrium, where the heat supplied from below was exactly equal to that given off by radiation into the cold ether above. And gradually this would sink lower and lower, until finally it reached the surface of the earth; and at this point the work of the second day would be complete.

(7) God made the firmament.—This wide open expanse upon earth's surface, supplied by the chemistry of nature—that is, of God—

with that marvelous mixture of gases which form atmospheric air, was a primary necessity for man's existence and activity. In each step of the narrative it is ever man that is in view; and even the weight of the superincumbent atmosphere is indispensable for the health and comfort of the human body, and for the keeping of all things in their place on earth. And in this secondary sense it may still rightly be called the firmament.

The waters which were under the firmament. . .the waters which were above the firmament.—This is a popular description of what we see daily. The atmosphere is the receptacle of the waters evaporated from the earth and ocean, and by means of electrical action it keeps these aqueous particles in a state of repulsion, and forms clouds, which the winds carry in their bosom. So full of thoughtful contrivance and arrangement are the laws by which rain is formed and the earth watered, that they are constantly referred to in the Bible as the chief natural proof of God's wisdom and goodness. (See Acts 14:17). The use, however, of popular language and ideas is confessedly the method of Holy Scripture, and we must not force upon the writer knowledge which man was to gain for himself. Even if the writer supposed that the rains were poured down from an upper reservoir, it would be no more an argument against his being inspired than Mark's expression, "The sun did set" (Mark 1:32), disproves the inspiration of the gospels. For the attainment of all such knowledge God has provided another way.

(8) God called the firmament (the expanse) **Heaven.**—This is a Saxon word, and means "something heaved up." In verse 1, "the heaven" may include the abysmal regions of space; here it means the atmosphere around our earth. The work of the second day is not described as being good, although the LXX adds this usual formula. Probably, however, the work of the second and third days is regarded as one. In both there was a separation of waters; but it was only when the open expanse reached the earth's surface, and reduced its temperature, that water could exist in any other form than that of vapor. But no sooner did it exist in a fluid form than the pressure of the atmosphere would make it seek the lowest level. The cooling, moreover, of the earth's surface would produce cracks and fissures, into which the waters would descend, and when these processes were well advanced,

3

then at the end of the third day "God saw that it was good."

(9) Unto one place.—The ocean bed. We must add the vast depth of the ocean to the height of the mountains before we can rightly estimate the intensity of the forces at work on the third day. Vast, too, as the surface of the ocean may appear compared with the dry land, it is evidently only just sufficient to supply the rain necessary for vegetation.

Let the dry land appear.—Simple as this might appear, it yet required special provision on the part of the Creator; for otherwise the various materials of the earth would have arranged themselves in concentric strata, according to their density, and upon them the water would have reposed evenly, and above it the air. But geologists tell us that these strata have been broken up and distorted from below by volcanic agencies, while the surface has been furrowed and worn by the denuding power of water. This was the third day's work.

(11) Let the earth bring forth grass.—The second creative act was the introduction of life, first vegetable, and then animal; and for this nothing less than an Almighty power would suffice. Three stages of it are enumerated. The first is **deshe**, not "grass," but a mere greenness, without visible seed or stalk. Far higher in the scale are the seed-bearing plants which follow, among which the most important are the cerealia; while in the third class, vegetation reaches its highest development in the tree with woody stem, and the seed enclosed in an edible covering. But as far from there being anything in the creative record to require us to believe that the development of vegetation was not gradual, it is absolutely described as being so; and with that first streak of green God gave also the law of vegetation, and under His fostering hand all in due time came to pass which that first bestowal of vegetable life contained. It is the constant rule of Holy Scripture to include in a narrative the ultimate as well as the immediate results of an act; and moreover, in the record of these creative days we are told what on each day was new, while the continuance of all that preceded is understood. When, then, on the third day, "God said, Let the earth bring forth grass . . . herb yielding seed . . . tree," He gave the perfect command, but the complete fulfillment of that command would be gradual, as the state of the earth and the necessities of the living creatures brought forth upon it re-

quired. For in God's work there is always a fitness, and nothing with Him is hurried or premature.

(14) Let there be lights (luminaries) **in the firmament** (or expanse) **of the heaven.**—In Hebrew the word for light is ór, and for luminary, **ma-ór,** a light-bearer. The light was created on the first day, and its concentration into great centers must at once have commenced; but the great luminaries did not appear in the open sky until the fourth day. With this begins the second triad of the creative days. Up to this time there had been arrangement chiefly; heat and water had had their periods of excessive activity, but with the introduction of vegetation there came also the promise of things higher and nobler than mechanical laws. Now, this fourth day seems to mark two things: first, the surface of the earth has become so cool as to need heat given it from without; and secondly, there was now a long pause in creation. No new law in it is promulgated, no new factor introduced; only the atmosphere grows clearer, the earth more dry; vegetation does its part in absorbing gases; and day by day the sun shines with more unclouded brilliancy, followed by the mild radiance of the moon, and finally, by the faint gleamings of the stars.

Let them be for signs—i.e., marks, means of knowing. This may be taken as qualifying what follows, and would then mean, Let them be means for distinguishing seasons, days, and years.

Seasons.—Not spring, summer, and the like, but regularly recurring periods, like the three great festivals of the Jews. In old time men depended, both in agriculture, navigation, and daily life, upon their own observation of the setting and rising of the constellations. Even now as of old, days, years and seasons depend upon the motion of the heavenly orbs.

(15) To give light.—This was to be henceforward the permanent arrangement for the bestowal of that which is an essential condition for all life, vegetable and animal. As day and night began on the first day, it is evident that very soon there was a concentrating mass of light and heat outside the earth, and as the expanse grew clear its effects must have become more powerful. There was daylight, then, long before the fourth day; but it was only then that the sun and moon became fully formed and constituted as they are at present, and shone regularly and clearly in the bright sky.

(16) He made the stars also.—The He-

4

brew is, "God made two great lights . . . to rule the night; and also the stars." The real sense is that the stars were to rule the night equally with the moon. Besides this, there was no place where the stars—by which the planets are chiefly meant—could be so well mentioned as here. At the end of the fourth day the distribution of land and water, the state of the atmosphere, the alternation of day and night, of seasons and years, and the astronomical relations of the sun, moon and planets (with the stars) to the earth were all settled and fixed, much as they are at present.

(20) Let the waters. . .in the open firmament.—The days of the second creative triad correspond to those of the first. Light was created on the first day, and on the fourth it was gathered into light-bearers; on the second day air and water were called into being, and on the fifth day they were peopled with life; lastly, on the third day the dry land appeared, and on the sixth day it became the home of animals and man.

Bring forth abundantly the moving creature that hath life.—Literally, "let the waters swarm a swarm of living soul." But the word "soul" properly signifies "breath," and thus, after the long pause of the fourth day, during which vegetation was advancing under the ripening effects of solar heat, we now hasten onward to another creative act, by which God called into being creatures which live by breathing. And as vegetation began with a green tinge upon the rocks, so doubtless animal life began in the most rudimentary manner, and advanced through animalcules and insects up to fish and reptiles. The main point noticed in the text as to the living things produced on this day is their fecundity. They are all those creatures which multiply in masses. It does not, however, follow that the highest forms of fish and reptiles were reached before the lowest form of land animal was created. All that we are taught is that the Infusoria and Ovipara preceded the Mammalia.

And fowl that may fly.—Heb., "and let fowl," or winged creatures, "fly above the earth." This includes all creatures that can wing their way in the air.

(21) God created great whales.—Whales, strictly speaking, are mammals, and belong to the creation of the sixth day. But **tannin**, the word used here, means any "long" creature, and is used of serpents in Exod. 7:9, 10 (where, however, it may mean a crocodile), and in Deut. 32:33; of the crocodile in Ps. 74:13, Isa. 51:9, Ezek. 29:3; and

of sea monsters generally in Job 7:12. It thus appropriately marks the great Saurian age. The use, too, of the verb **bârâ**, "he created," is no argument against its meaning "to produce out of nothing," because it belongs not to these monsters, which may have been "evolved," but to the whole verse, which describes the introduction of animal life.

After their kind.—This suggests the belief that the various genera and species of birds, fishes, and insects were from the beginning distinct, and will continue so, even if there be some amount of free play in the improvement and development of existing species.

(22) Be fruitful, and multiply.—This blessing shows that the earth was replenished with animal life from a limited number of progenitors, and probably from a small number of centers, both for the flora and for the fauna.

(23) The fifth day.—Upon the work of the first four days geology is virtually silent, and the theories respecting the physical formation of the world belong to other sciences. But as regards the fifth day, its testimony is ample. We learn that this fifth day covers a vast space of time, and it is probable that the introduction of the various genera and species was gradual. God does nothing in haste, and our conceptions of His marvelous working are made more clear and worthy of His greatness by the evidence which geology affords.

(24) Let the earth bring forth.—Neither this, nor the corresponding phrase in verse 20, necessarily imply spontaneous generation, though such is its literal meaning. It need mean no more than that land animals, produced on the dry ground, were now to follow upon those produced in the waters. However produced, we believe that the sole active power was the creative will of God, but of His **modus operandi** we know nothing.

On this sixth creative day there are four words of power. By the first, the higher animals are summoned into being; by the second, man; the third provides for the continuance and increase of the beings which God had created; the fourth assigns the vegetable world both to man and animals as food.

The creation of man is thus made a distinct act; for though created on the sixth day, because he is a land animal, yet it is in the latter part of the day, and after a pause of contemplation and counsel. The reason for this is that in man's creation we have a far greater advance in the work of the Almighty than at any previous stage. For up to this time all has been "law," and the highest point reached was "instinct"; we now have freedom, reason, intellect, speech. The evolutionist may give us many interesting theories about the upgrowth of man's physical nature, but the introduction of this moral and mental freedom places as wide a chasm in his way as the first introduction of vegetable, and then of animal life.

The living creature, or rather, "the creature that lives by breathing," is divided into three classes. The first is **behemah**, "cattle": literally, the "dumb" brute, but especially used of the larger ruminants, which were soon domesticated, and became man's speechless servants. Next comes the "creeping thing," or rather, "moving thing," from a verb translated "moveth" in verse 21. It probably signifies the whole multitude of small animals, and not reptiles particularly. Strictly the word refers rather to their number than to their means of locomotion, and means a "swarm." The third class is the "beast of the earth," the wild animals that roam over a large extent of country, including the carnivora. The narrative of the flood proves conclusively that there were no carnivora in the ark; and immediately afterwards beasts that kill men were ordered to be destroyed (9:5, 6). It is plain that from the first these beasts lay outside the covenant. In spite of their presence, all was good.

(26) Let us make man.—The making of man is so ushered in as to show that at length the work of creation had reached its perfection and ultimate goal. More truly and more reverently we may say that this first chapter of Genesis is the chapter of mysteries, and just as "the wind of God" in verse 2 was the pregnant germ which grew into the revelation of the Holy Ghost, so in Elohim, the many powers concentrated in one being, lies the germ of the doctrine of a plurality of persons in the divine Unity. It is not a formal proof of the Trinity, nor do believers in the inspiration of Holy Scripture so use it. What they affirm is, that from the very beginning the Bible is full of such germs, and that no one of them remains barren, but all develop, and become Christian truths. There is in this first book a vast array of figures, types, indications, yearnings, hopes, fears, promises, and express predictions, which advance onward like an ever-deepening river, and when they all find

a logical fulfillment in one way, the conclusion is that that fulfillment is not only true, but was intended.

Man.—Hebrew, **Adam.** It is hopeless to attempt any derivation of the name, as it must have existed before any of the verbs and nouns from which commentators attempt to give it a meaning; and the **adâmâh**, or "tilled ground," of which we shall soon hear so much, evidently had its name from Adam.

In our image, after our likeness.—The human body is after God's image only as being the means whereby man attains to dominion: for dominion is God's attribute, inasmuch as He is sole Lord. Man's body, therefore, as that of one who rules, is erect, and endowed with speech, that he may give the word of command. The soul is, first, in God's "image." This, as suggesting an external likeness, may refer to man's reason, free will, self-consciousness, and so on. But it is, secondly, in God's "likeness," which implies something closer and more inward. It refers to man's moral powers, and especially to his capacity of attaining unto holiness. Now man has lost neither of these two. (Comp. 4:6; I Cor. 11:7; James 3:9.) Both were weakened and defiled by the fall, but were still retained in a greater or less degree. In the man Christ Jesus both were perfect; and fallen man, when newly created in Christ, attains actually to that perfection which was his only potentially at his first creation, and to which Adam never did attain.

Let them have dominion.—The plural here shows that we have to do not with Adam and Eve, but with the human race generally. This, too, agrees with the whole bearing of the first chapter, which deals in a large general way with genera and species, and not with individuals. This is important as an additional proof that God's likeness and image belong to the whole species man, and could not therefore have been lost by the fall.

(27) Created.—This significant verb is thrice repeated with reference to man. It indicates, first, that man has that in him which was not a development or evolution, but something new. He is, in fact, the most perfect work of the creative energy, and differs from the animals not only in degree, but in kind, though possessing, in common with them, an organized body. And next, it indicates the rejoicing of the Deity at the completion of His purpose.

(29) Every herb bearing seed. . .every tree.—Of the three classes of plants enumerated in verse 11, the two most perfect kinds are given to man for his food. The fundamental supply for the maintenance of animal life was the blade and leaf and that of human life the perfected seed and ripe fruit. Man is thus from the first pointed out as of a higher organization than the animal; and the fact that his food is such as requires preparation and cooking has been the basis, not merely of most of the refinements of life, but even of the close union of the family. For what would become of it without the common meal?

But undoubtedly the food originally assigned to man was vegetable; nor was expression permission given to eat flesh until after the flood. Nevertheless the dominion given to man, in verse 28, over fish, bird, and animal, made it lawful for him to use them for his food; and the skins with which Adam and Eve were clothed on their expulsion from Paradise prove that animals had been already killed. We may well believe that until the flood the descendants of Seth partook of flesh rarely, and only at a sacrifice, but that after the flood a more free use of it was permitted. (Comp. 9:3.)

(31) Behold, it was very good.—This final blessing of God's completed work on the Friday must be compared with the final words of Christ spoken of the second creation, upon the same day of the week, when He said "It is finished." Next we must notice that this world was only "good" until man was placed upon it, but then became "very good." This verdict, too, had respect to man as a species, and is not therefore annulled by the fall. In spite, therefore, of the serious responsibilities attendant upon the bestowal of free will on man, we believe that the world is still for purposes of mercy, and that God not only rejoiced at first, but "shall rejoice in his works" (Ps. 104:31).

2

The Sabbath

(1) Were finished.—The first three verses of this chapter form part of the previous narrative, and contain its divine purpose. For the great object of this hymn of creation is to give the sanction of the Creator to the Sabbath. Hence the ascribing of rest to Him who wearies not, and hence also the description of the several stages of creation as days. Labor is, no doubt, ennobled by creation being described as work done by God; but the higher purpose of this Scripture was that for which appeal is made to it in the Fourth Commandment, namely, to ennoble man's weekly rest.

The host of them.—The word translated "host" does not refer to military arrangement, but to numbers gathered in crowds. This crowded throng of heaven sometimes means the angels, as in I Kings 22:19; more often the stars. Here it is the host both of heaven and earth, and signifies the multitudes of living creatures which people the land, and seas, and air.

(2) God ended his work.—Not all work (see John 5:17), but the special work of creation. The laws given in these six days still continue their activity; they are still maintained, and there may even be with them progress and development. There is also something special on this seventh day; for in it the work of redemption was willed by the Father, wrought by the Son, and applied by the Holy Ghost. But there is no creative activity, as when vegetable or animal life began, or when a free agent first walked erect upon a world given him to subdue.

(3) Sanctified it.—That is, separated it from ordinary uses, and hallowed it. Legal observance of the Sabbath did not begin till the days of Moses (Exod. 31:13, 35:2); but this blessing and sanctification were given prior to any covenant with man, and by Elohim, the God of nature, and not Jehovah, the God of grace. The weekly rest, therefore, is universal, permanent, and independent of the Mosaic law.

Which God created and made.—Literally, "created to make." God created the world in order to make and form and fashion it. There is a work of completion which follows upon creation, and this may still be going on, and be perfected only when there is a new heaven and a new earth.

The Generations of the Heavens and of the Earth (2:4-4:26)

"The Book of Genesis," or generation, is the title given by Matthew to his gospel. This title, however, does not mean a genealogical list of a person's ancestors, but the register of his posterity. As applied to the "heavens and the earth," it signifies the history of what followed upon their creation.

(4) In the day.—Viewed in its several stages, and with reference to the weekly

7

rest, there were six days of creation, which are here described as one day, because they were but divisions in one continuous act.

The Lord God.—Jehovah-Elohim.

(5) And every plant. . . The more correct rendering is, "There was no shrub of the field (no wild shrub) as yet on the earth, and no herb of the field had as yet sprung up." The purpose of the writer is to prepare for the planting of the paradise. To understand these opening words, we must bear in mind that the object of the narrative is not now the formation of the world, but man's relation to Jehovah, and thus the long stages of creation appear but as one day's work.

(6) A mist.—There was already preparation for the divine method of watering the earth, and making it capable of producing food for man. But, as we gather from chapter 1, vast periods of indefinite length intervened between the first rain and the creation of man; and in each of them numerous series of animals were introduced, adapted each to the geologic condition of its time. All this now is rapidly passed over, and three points only lightly touched: namely, first, the earth saturated with vapor, and unfit for man; secondly, the vapor condensing into rain, and the earth growing fit for man; thirdly, man.

(7) And the Lord God formed man of the dust of the ground.—Literally, "formed the man (adam) dust from the ground." In this section the prominent idea is not that of producing out of nothing, but of "forming," that is, shaping and moulding. So in verse 19 Jehovah forms the animals, and in verse 8 He plants a garden. As Elohim is almighty power, so Jehovah is wisdom and skill, and His works are full of contrivance and design. As regards man's body, Jehovah forms it "dust from the ground": The **adâmâh,** or fruitful arable soil, so called from Adam, for whose use it was specially fitted, and by whom it was first tilled. But the main intention of the words is to point out man's feebleness. He is made not from the rocks, nor from ores of metal, but from the light, shifting particles of the surface, blown about by every wind. Yet, frail as is man's body, God— . . . **breathed into his nostrils the breath of life.**—The life came not as the result of man's bodily organization, nor as derived by evolution from any other animal, but as a gift direct from God.

And man became a living soul.—The word translated "soul" contains no idea of a spiritual existence. For in 1:20, "creature that hath life," and in verse 24, "the living

creature," are literally, "living soul." Really the word refers to the breathing, or in some way extracting oxygen from the atmospheric air. And whatever superiority over other animals may be possessed by man comes from the manner in which this living breath was bestowed upon him, and not from his being "a living soul"; for that is common to all alike.

The whole of this second narrative is pre-eminently anthropomorphic. In the previous history Elohim commands and it is done. Here He forms and builds, and plants, and breathes into His work, and is the companion and friend of the creature He has made. It thus sets before us the love and tenderness of Jehovah, who provides for man a home, fashions for him a wife to be his partner and helpmate, rejoices in his intellect, and brings the lower world to him to see what he will call them, and even after the Fall provides the poor outcasts with clothing. It is a picture fitted for the infancy of mankind, and speaking the language of primeval simplicity. But its lesson is for all times. For it proclaims the love of God to man, his special pre-eminence in the scale of being, and that Elohim, the Almighty Creator, is Jehovah-Elohim, the friend and counselor of the creature whom He has endowed with reason and free will.

(8) The Lord God planted a garden.—It was a separate plot of ground, fenced off from the rest of Eden, and planted with trees and herbs that were of choicer kinds, more fit for food, and more beautiful in foliage and blossom, than elsewhere. The word Paradise, usually applied to it, is a Persian name for an enclosed park, such as the kings of Persia used for hunting.

Eastward in Eden.—This does not mean in the eastern portion of Eden, but that Eden itself was to the east of the regions known to the Israelites. The "Eden," that is, pleasure-ground, occurs elsewhere, but for regions not identical with that in which the Paradise was situated (II Kings 19:12; Isa. 37:12; 51:3; Ezek. 27:23; Amos 1:5). Of its site no certain conclusions have been established, and probably the Flood so altered the conformation of the ground as to make the identification of the four rivers impossible. But there can be no doubt that an eastern district of Asia is meant, and that the details at the time the narrative was written were sufficient to indicate with sufficient clearness where and what the region was.

(9) Every tree that is pleasant to the

sight, and good for food.—Two trees in the center of the garden had marvelous qualities; for "the tree of life" had the power of so renewing man's physical energies that his body, though formed of the dust of the ground, and therefore naturally mortal, would, by its continual use, live on for ever. The other, "the tree of knowledge of good and evil," must have acquired this name after the fall. As long as Adam and Eve were in their original innocence they had no knowledge of evil, nor could any mere mental development bestow it upon them. They must either feel it in themselves, or see it in others, before they could know it. We conclude, then, that this was the tree to which God's command, that they should not eat of it (comp. 3:3), was attached; and only by the breach of that command would man attain to this higher knowledge, with all the solemn responsibilities attached to it. Besides this, each tree had a symbolic meaning, and especially the tree of life (Rev. 2:7, 22:2).

(10) A river went out of Eden.—The idea is that of a stream rising in Eden, and flowing through the Paradise, and at some distance outside of it divided into four great rivers. This has made many suppose that the site of Paradise was in the Persian Gulf, in a region now submerged; and the Babylonian legends actually place it there, at Eridu, at the junction of the Tigris and Euphrates. The two other rivers they suppose to have been the Indus and the Nile, represented by the two coasts of the Persian Gulf.

(11, 12) The name of the first is Pison.—"The full-flowing" (Gesenius), or "free streaming" (Fürst). As two of the four rivers of Paradise rise in Armenia, so we must probably seek the other two there.

Compasseth.—This word, without strictly meaning "to go around," gives the idea of a devious course (comp. I Sam. 7:16; S. of Sol. 3:3), as if the river had not reached a level plain.

Havilah may mean "sandy land" (Delitzsch), or "circuit region." There seems to have been more than one country of this name. But we know of no such river, rising in Armenia or elsewhere, which answers to this description now. Besides gold of great purity, pronounced emphatically "good," this land produced "bdellium," a scented gum, to which manna is compared (Num. 11:7), though the meaning even there is uncertain.

The onyx stone.—The root signifies something "pale," while the onyx has its name from its markings resembling those of the human nail.

(13) Gihon, "the river that bursts forth," has been supposed to be the Nile, because it is said to wind about Ethiopia (Cush). According to this view, there was originally no break between Asia and Africa, and the Nile, entering Abyssinia from Arabia, took thence a northerly course, and traversed Egypt. But Cush is now known to have signified at this period the southern half of Arabia, and it was not until later times that the name was carried by colonists to Abyssinia. Moreover Gihon, in Arabic Jaihan, is a common name among the Arabs for a river, and perhaps the Oxus is here meant, which flowed northward from Armenia into the Caspian.

(14) Of the "Hiddekel" and "Euphrates" there is no doubt: the former is the Tigris, or Tigres, which is a mere Grecizing of its Oriental name. The Samaritan Codex reads "the Dekel," that is, it has the article instead of the Hebrew Kheth. Tigris is said to mean an arrow. The Samaritan reading is probably right.

Euphrates.—No description is given of this as being the largest and best known of Asiatic rivers. Hence, probably, the Pison and Gihon were but small streams. "Euphrates" is the Greek manner of pronouncing the Hebrew **Phrath**, the first syllable being simply a help in sounding the double consonant. In Accadian it is called **Purrat**, and means "the curving water," being so named from its shape.

(15) And the Lord God took the man (the adam), **and put him into the garden of Eden.**—The narrative now reverts to verse 8, but the word transplated "put" is not the same in both places. Here it literally means "He made him rest," that is, He gave it to him as his permanent and settled dwelling.

To dress it and to keep it.—The first word literally means "to work it"; for though a paradise, yet the garden had to be tilled and planted. Seeds must be sown and cultivated plots kept in order; but all this really added to Adam's happiness, because the **adâmâh,** as yet uncursed, responded willingly to the husbandman's care. The other word, "to keep it," implies, however, some difficulty and danger. Though no unpropitious weather, nor blight nor mildew, spoiled the crop, yet apparently it had to be guarded against the incursion of wild animals and birds, and protected even against

9

the violence of winds and the burning heat of the sun.

(16, 17) The Lord God commanded.—Probation is the law of man's moral condition now, and it began in Paradise, only the conditions there were different.

In the day. . . . —The law of man's mortal life came into existence with the eating of the forbidden fruit. Contemporaneously with that act, man passed from the paradisiacal state, with the possibility of living for ever, into the mortal state, with the certainty sooner or later of dying. It was a new condition and constitution of things which then commenced, and to which not Adam only, but also his posterity was subject. And thus this command resembles the words of Elohim in the first chapter. By them the fundamental laws of the material universe were given and established for all time; and the word of Jehovah-Elohim equally here was a law, not for the day only on which Adam broke the command, but for all men everywhere as long as the world shall last.

(18) It is not good . . . —In these words we have the divine appointment of marriage, and also the declaration that the female is subsequent in order of production to the male, and formed from him. The happiness of marriage is based, not upon the woman being just the same thing as the man, but upon her being one in whom he sees his image and counterpart.

(19 Out of the ground.—The **adâmâh;** thus the physical constituents of the animals are the same as those of the body of man. The real point of the narrative is the insight it gives us into Adam's intellectual condition, his study of the animal creation, and the nature of the employment in which he spent his time. Then finally, at the end of verse 20, after numerous animals had passed before him, comes the assertion, with cumulative force, that woman alone is a meet companion for man.

(20) And Adam gave names.—Throughout this chapter Adam is but once mentioned as a proper name; and the regular phrase in the Hebrew is "the adam," that is, the man, except in the last clause of this verse. In verse 23 there is a different word for man, namely, **ish.** As he pursues his occupations in the garden, new animals and birds from time to time come under his notice, and these he studies, and observes their ways and habits, and so at length gives them appellations. Most of these titles would be imitations of their cries, or would be taken from some marked feature in their

form or plumage, or mode of locomotion. Adam is thus found possessed of powers of observation and reflection upon the natural objects round him.

But for Adam.—In this one place there is no article, and our version may be right in regarding it as a proper name. While thus he could tame many, and make them share his dwelling, he found among them no "counterpart of himself," capable of answering his thoughts and of holding with him rational discourse.

(21) And the Lord God caused a deep sleep (comp. Job. 4:13, where it is the same word) **to fall upon Adam.**—Heb., the man.

One of his ribs.—The word is never translated "rib" except in this place, but always "side," "flank." Woman was not formed out of one of man's many ribs of which he would not feel the loss. She is one side of man, and though he may have several sides to his nature and character, yet without woman one integral portion of him is wanting.

Closed up the flesh instead thereof.—A cavity was prevented by drawing the flesh on the two edges close together. Metaphysically it means that man has no compensation for what was abstracted from him, except in the woman, who is the one side of his nature which he has lost.

(22) Made he a woman.—Heb., "he built up into a woman." Her formation is described as requiring both time and care on the heavenly Artificer's part. Thus woman is no casual or hasty production of nature, but is the finished result of labor and skill. Finally, she is brought with special honor to the man as the Creator's last and most perfect work. Every step and stage in the description is intended for the ennoblement of marriage. Woman is not made from the **adâmâh,** but from the **adam.** The anthropomorphic language of these early chapters is part of that condescension to human weakness which makes it the rule everywhere for inspiration to use popular language. The whole narrative has a nobler meaning, and the practical result of its teaching was that neither woman nor marriage ever sank into that utter degradation among the Jews which elsewhere aided so greatly in corrupting morals and men.

(23) This is now.—Literally, "this stroke," or "beat of the foot" in keeping time. It means, therefore, "this time," or colloquially, "at last." At last, on waking from his trance, he found one standing by him in whom he recognized a second self, and he welcomed her joyfully, and exclaimed, "This **at last** is bone of my bones, and flesh of my flesh": that is, she is man's counterpart, not merely in feeling and sense—his flesh—but in his solid qualities. In several of the Semitic dialects "bone" is used for "self." Thus "bone of my bones" means "my very own self," while "flesh of my flesh" adds the more tender and gentle qualities.

She shall be called Woman (Ishah), because she was taken out of Man (Ish).—Adam, who knew that he was an **Ish** called the woman a "female Ish." The words of our version, "man" and "woman" (perhaps womb-man), represent with sufficient accuracy the relation of the words in the original.

(24) Therefore shall a man leave . . .—These are evidently the words of the narrator. Adam names this new product of creative power, as he had named others, but he knew nothing about young men leaving their father's house for the wife's sake. Moreover, in Matt. 19:5, our Lord quotes these words as spoken by God, and the simplest interpretation of this declaration is that the inspired narrator was moved by the Spirit of God to give this solemn sanction to marriage, founded upon Adam's words. The great and primary object of this part of the narrative is to set forth marriage as a divine ordinance.

The Temptation and Fall

(25) They were both naked.—This is the description of perfect childlike innocence, and belongs naturally to beings who as yet knew neither good nor evil. It is not, however, the conclusion of the marriage section, where it would be indelicate, but the introduction to the account of the temptation, where it prepares the way for man's easy fall. Moreover, there is a play upon words in the two verses. Man is **arom** = naked; the serpent is **arum** = crafty. Thus in guileless simplicity our first parents fall in with the tempting serpent, who, in obvious contrast with their untried innocence, is described as a being of special subtlety.

3

(1) Now the serpent.—Literally, "And." The Hebrew language, however, is very poor in particles, and the intended contrast would be made plainer by rendering "Now

they were both naked (**arumim**) . . . but the serpent was subtil (**arum**), more than every beast of the field." This quality of the serpent was in itself innocent, and even admirable, and accordingly the LXX "prudent"; but it was made use of by the tempter to deceive Eve; for, it has been remarked, she would not be surprised on finding herself spoken to by so sagacious a creature. If this be so, it follows that Eve must have dwelt in Paradise long enough to have learned something of the habits of the animals around her.

And he said unto the woman.—The leading point of the narrative is that the temptation came upon man from without, and through the woman. Such questions, therefore, as whether it were a real serpent or Satan under a serpent-like form, whether it spoke with a real voice, and whether the narrative describes a literal occurrence or is allegorical, are better left unanswered. God has given us the account of man's temptation and fall, and the entry of sin into the world, in this actual form; and the more reverent course is to draw from the narrative the lessons it was evidently intended to teach us, and not enter upon too curious speculations. We are dealing with records of a vast antiquity and we cannot expect to find them as easy to understand as the pages of modern history.

Yea, hath God said . . . ?—There is a tone of surprise in these words, as if the tempter could not bring himself to believe that such a commandment had been given. Can it really be true, he asks, that Elohim has subjected you to such a prohibition? How unworthy and wrong of Him! Neither the serpent nor the woman use the title—common throughout this section—of Jehovah-Elohim, a sure sign that there was a thoughtful purpose in giving this appellation to the Deity. It is the impersonal God of creation to whom the tempter refers, and the woman follows his guidance, forgetting that it was Jehovah, the loving personal Being in covenant with them, who had really given them the command.

(5) Ye shall be as gods.—Rather, "as God," as Elohim Himself, in the particular quality of knowing good and evil. It was a high bait which the tempter offered; and Eve, who at first had answered rightly, and who as yet knew nothing of falsehood, dallied with the temptation, and was lost. But we must not comment too severely upon her conduct. It was no mean desire which led her astray: she longed for more knowledge and greater perfection; she wished even to rise above the level of her nature; but the means she used were in violation of God's command, and so she fell.

(6) And when the woman saw ... she took.—Heb., "And the woman saw ... and she took. . . ." In this, the original form of the narrative, we see the progress of the temptation detailed in a far more lively manner than in our version. To this combined influence of her senses without and her ambition within she was unable to offer that resistance which would have been possible only by a living faith in the spoken word of God. She eats, therefore, and gives to her husband—so called here for the first time—and he eats with her. She is pictured to us as more quick and observant, more open to impressions, more curious and full of longings than the man, whose passive behavior is as striking as the woman's eagerness and excitability.

(7) The eyes of them both were opened.—This consciousness of guilt came upon them as soon as they had broken God's commandment by eating of the forbidden fruit; and it is evident from the narrative that they ate together; for otherwise Eve would have been guilty of leading Adam into sin after her understanding had been enlightened to perceive the consequences of her act. But manifestly her deed was not without his cognizance and approval, and he had shared, in his own way, her ambition of attaining to the God-like. But how miserably was this proud desire disappointed! Their increased knowledge brought only shame. Their minds were awakened and enlarged, but the price they paid for it was their innocence and peace.

They sewed fig leaves together.—The word signifies the common fig-tree (**Ficus carica**), one of the earliest plants subjected to man's use. More remarkable is the word "sewed." The Syriac translator felt the difficulty of supposing Eve acquainted with the art of needlework, and renders it, "they stuck leaves together." But the word certainly implies something more elaborate than this. Probably some time elapsed between their sin and its punishment; and thus there was not merely that first hasty covering of themselves which has made commentators look about for a leaf large enough to encircle their bodies, but respite sufficient to allow of something more careful and ingenious; and Eve may have used her first advance in intellect for the adornment of her person. During this delay they would

have time for reflection, and begin to understand the nature of the change that had taken place in their condition.

Aprons.—More correctly, "girdles."

(8) And they heard the voice of the Lord God walking in the garden.—Jehovah appears here as the owner of the Paradise, and as taking in it His daily exercise; for the verb is in the reflexive conjugation, and means "walking for pleasure." The time is "the cool (literally, **the wind**) of the day," the hour in a hot climate when the evening breeze sets in, and men, rising from their noontide slumber, go forth for labor or recreation. In this description the primary lesson is that hitherto man had lived in close communion with God. His intellect was undeveloped; his mental powers still slumbered; but nevertheless there was a deep spiritual sympathy between him and his Maker. It is the nobler side of Adam's relationship to God before the fall.

Hid themselves from the presence of the Lord God.—This does not imply a visible appearance, for the whole narrative is anthropomorphic. Next, we find in their conduct an attempt to escape from the further result of sin. The first result was shame, from which man endeavored to free himself by covering his person; the second was fear, and this man would cure by departing still farther from God. But the voice of Jehovah reaches him, and with rebuke and punishment gives also healing and hope.

(11) Who told thee that thou wast naked?—Adam had given as his excuse that which was really the consequence of his sin; but by this question God awakens his conscience, and makes him feel that what he had described as a want or imperfection was really the result of his own act. And as long as a man feels sorrow only for the results of his actions there is no repentance, and no wish to return to the divine presence. God, therefore, in order to win Adam back to better thoughts, carries his mind from the effect to the sin that had caused it.

(12, 13) She gave me ...—It is a mistake to suppose that Adam wished to shift the blame, first upon Eve, and then upon God, who had given her to him; rather, he recapitulates the history, as if, in his view, it was a matter of course that he should act as he had done and as if he had no sense that there was any blame whatever attaching to any one. His conscience still seems utterly unmoved. Far nobler is the woman's answer. She acknowledges that she had been led astray, and, under the influence of the serpent's deceit, had broken God's commandment.

(14, 15) Unto the serpent.—As the serpent had tempted our first parents purposely and consciously in order to lead them into sin, he stood there without excuse, and received a threefold penalty. The outward form of the condemnation is made suitable to the shape which the tempter had assumed; but the true force and meaning, especially in the last and most intense portion of the sentence, belong, not to the animal, but to Satan himself. The serpent is but the type: diabolic agency the reality. First, therefore, the serpent is condemned to crawl. The meaning is that henceforward the serpent's crawling motion is to be to it a mark of disgrace, and to Satan a sign of meanness and contempt. Secondly, to "lick the dust," because his mean devices lead, as in this place, only to the manifestation of God's glory. In the **Paradise Lost** Milton has made Satan a hero, though fallen; really he is a despicable and mean-spirited foe, whose strength lies in man's moral feebleness. Finally, there is perpetual enmity between the serpent and man. The adder in the path bites man's heel, and is crushed beneath his tramp. It has been noticed that in spite of the beauty and gracefulness of many of the species, man's loathing of them is innate.

Her seed ... shall bruise thy head.—We have here the sum of the whole matter, and the rest of the Bible does but explain the nature of this struggle, the persons who wage it, and the manner and consequences of the victory. Here, too, we learn the end and purpose for which the narrative is cast in its present form. It pictures to us man in a close and loving relation, not to an abstract deity, but to a personal and covenant Jehovah. Meanwhile, in accordance with the universal law that free will goes hand in hand with responsibility, an easy and simple trial is provided for man's obedience. He fails, and henceforward he must wage a sterner conflict, and attain to victory only by effort and suffering. In this struggle man is finally to prevail, but not unscathed. And his triumph is to be gained not by mere human strength, but by the coming of One who is "the Woman's Seed"; and round this promised Deliverer the rest of Scripture groups itself. Leave out these words, and all the inspired teaching which follows would be an ever-widening river without a fountainhead. But necessarily with the fall came

the promise of restoration. Grace is no afterthought, but enters the world side by side with sin. Upon this foundation the rest of Holy Scripture is built, till revelation at last reaches its cornerstone in Christ. The outward form of the narrative affords endless subjects for curious discussion; its inner meaning and true object being to lay the broad basis of all future revealed truth.

Like a large proportion of the words used in Genesis, the verb is rare, being found only twice elsewhere in Scripture. In Job 9:17 the meaning seems plainly to be "to break," but in Ps. 139:11, where, however, the reading is uncertain, the sense required is "to cover" or "veil." The translation of the King James Version may be depended upon as correct, in spite of its not being altogether applicable to the attack of a natural serpent upon a wayfarer's heel.

(16) Unto the woman he said.—The woman is not cursed as the serpent was, but punished as next in guilt; and the retribution is twofold. First, God greatly multiplies "her sorrow and her conception," that is, her sorrow generally, but especially in connection with pregnancy, when with anguish and peril of life she wins the joy of bringing a man into the world. But also "thy desire shall be to thy husband." In the sin she had been the prime actor, and the man had yielded her too ready an obedience. Henceforward she was to live in subjection to him; yet not unhappily, because her inferiority was to be tempered by a natural longing for the married state and by love toward her master. Among the heathen the punishment was made very bitter by the degradation to which woman was reduced; among the Jews the wife, though she never sank so low, was nevertheless purchased of her father, was liable to divorce at the husband's will, and was treated as in all respects his inferior. In Christ the whole penalty, as Paul teaches, has been abrogated (Gal. 3:28), and the Christian woman is no more inferior to the man than is the Gentile to the Jew, or the bondman to the free.

(17, 18) Unto Adam (without the article, and therefore a proper name) **he said.**—Instead of protecting his wife and shielding her from evil, Adam had passively followed her lead in disobeying God's command; and therefore "the ground," the **adâmâh** out of which Adam had been formed, instead of being, as heretofore, his friend and willing subject, becomes unfruitful, and must be forced by toil and labor to yield its produce. Left to itself, it will no longer bring forth choice trees laden with generous fruit, such as Adam found in the garden, but the natural tendency will be to degenerate, till "thorns" only "and thistles" usurp the ground. In the renewed earth the golden age of "Paradise will return, and the tendency of nature will no longer be to decay and degeneration, but to the substitution unceasingly of the nobler and the more beautiful in the place of that which was worthless and mean (Isa. 55:13).

(19) Dust thou art . . .—It appears from this that death was man's normal condition. The body of Adam, composed of particles of earth, was capable of division, and our first parents in Paradise were assured of an unending existence by a special gift, typified by the tree of life. But now this gift was withdrawn, and henceforward the sweat of man's brow was in itself proof that he was returning to his earth: for it told of exhaustion and waste.

(20) Adam called his wife's name Eve.— Heb., **Chavvah**; in Greek, **Zoë**. It has been debated whether this name is a substantive, **Life** (LXX.), or a participle, **Life-producer** (Symm). Adam's condition was now one of death, but his wife thereby attained a higher value in his sight. Through her alone could human life be continued, and the "woman's seed" be obtained who was to raise up man from his fall. While, then, woman's punishment consists in the multiplication of her "sorrow and conception," she becomes thereby only more precious to man; and while "her desire is to her husband," Adam turns from his own punishment to look upon her with more tender love. Adam throws no blame either on Eve or on his Maker, because he does not feel himself to blame. He rather means, "How could I err in following one so noble, and in whom I recognize Thy best and choicest gift?" And so here he turns to her and calls her **Chavvah**, his compensation for his loss, and the antidote for the sentence of death.

(21) Coats of skins.—Animals, therefore, were killed even in Paradise; nor is it certain that man's diet was until the Flood entirely vegetarian (see note on 1:29). Until sin entered the world no sacrifices could have been offered; and if, therefore, these were skins of animals offered in sacrifice, as many suppose, Adam must in some way, immediately after the Fall, have been taught that without shedding of blood is no remission of sin, but that God will accept a vicarious sacrifice. We see in this arrival at the idea of sacrifice a rapid development in

Adam of thought and intellect, yet it may not have been entirely spontaneous, but the effect of divinely-inspired convictions rising up within his soul. It shows also that the innocence of our first parents was gone. In his happy state Adam had studied the animals, and tamed them and made them his friends; now a sense of guilt urges him to inflict upon them pain and suffering and death. But in the first sacrifice was laid the foundation of the whole Mosaical dispensation, as in verse 15 that of the Gospel.

(22) As one of us.—See note on 1:26. All those qualities which constitute man's likeness to God—free will, self-dependence, the exercise of reason and of choice—had been developed by the Fall, and Adam was now a very different being from what he had been in the days of his simple innocency.

Lest he put forth his hand.—Adam had exercised the power of marring God's work, and if an unending physical life were added to the gift of free will now in revolt against God, his condition and that of mankind would become most miserable. Man is still to attain to immortality, but it must now be through struggle, sorrow, penitence, faith, and death.

(23) To till the ground.—This is the same word as that rendered "dress" in 2:15. Adam's task is the same, but the conditions are altered.

(24) So he drove out the man.—This implies displeasure and compulsion. Adam departed unwillingly from his happy home, and with the consciousness that he had incurred the divine anger. It was the consequence of his sin, and was a punishment, even if necessary for his good under the changed circumstances produced by his disobedience.

He placed.—Literally, "caused to dwell." The return to Paradise was closed for ever.

At the east of the garden of Eden.— Adam still had his habitation in the land of Eden, and probably in the immediate neighborhood of Paradise. (Comp. 4:16.)

Cherubims.—The cherub was a symbolical figure, representing strength and majesty. The ordinary derivation, from a root signifying to "carve, grave" and especially to "plough," compared with Exod. 25:20, suggests that the cherubim were winged bulls, probably with human heads, like those brought from Nineveh. We must not confound them with the four living creatures of Ezekiel's vision (Ezek. 1:5), which are the "beasts" of the Revelation of John.

The office of the cherub here is to guard the Paradise, lest man should try to force an entrance back.

4

The Founding of the Family, and Commencement of the Non-Paradisiacal Life

(1) **She . . . bare Cain, and said . . .** —In this chapter we have the history of the founding of the family of Cain, a race godless and wanton, but who, nevertheless, far outstripped the descendants of Seth in the arts of civilization. To tillage and a pastoral life they added metallurgy and music; and the knowledge not only of copper and its uses, but even of iron (verse 22), must have given them a command over the resources of nature so great as to have vastly diminished the curse of labor, and made their lives easy and luxurious.

I have gotten a man from the Lord.— Rather, "who is Jehovah." It is inconceivable that **eth** should have here a different meaning from that which it has in 1:1. It there gives emphasis to the object of the verb: "God created **eth** the heaven and **eth** the earth," that is, "even the heaven and even the earth." So, also here, "I have gotten a man **eth** Jehovah," "even Jehovah." The objection that this implies too advanced a knowledge of Messianic ideas is unfounded. It is we who read backward, and put our ideas into the words of the narrative. These words were intended to lead on to those ideas, but they were at present only as the germ, or as the filament in the acorn which contains the oak tree. If there is one thing certain, it is that religious knowledge was given gradually, and that the significance of the name Jehovah was revealed by slow degrees. (See note on verse 26.) Eve attached no notion of divinity to the name; still less did she foresee that by the superstition of the Jews the title "Lord" would be substituted for it. We distinctly know that Jehovah was not even the patriarchal name of the Deity (Exod. 6:3), and still less could it have been God's title in Paradise. But Eve had received the promise that her seed should crush the head of her enemy, and to this promise her words referred, and the title in her mouth meant probably no more than "the coming One." Apparently, too, it was out of Eve's words

that this most significant title of the covenant God arose.

Further, Eve calls Cain "a man," Heb., **ish**, a being. (See note on 2:23.) As Cain was the first infant, no word as yet existed for child. But in calling him "a being, even the future one," a lower sense, often attached to these words, is not to be altogether excluded. It has been said that Eve, in the birth of this child, saw the remedy for death. Death might slay the individual, but the existence of the race was secured. Her words therefore might be paraphrased: "I have gained a man, who is the pledge of future existence." Mankind is thus that which shall exist. Now, it is one of the properties of Holy Scripture that words spoken in a lower and ordinary sense are often prophetic: so that even supposing that Eve meant no more than this, it would not exclude the higher interpretation. Finally, in Christ alone man does exist and endure. He is the perfect man—man's highest level; so that even thus there would be a presage of immortality for man in the saying, "I have gained a man, even he that shall become." Grant that it was then but an indefinite yearning: it was one, nevertheless, which all future inspiration was to make distinct and clear; and now, under the guidance of the Spirit, it has become the especial title of the Second Person in the Holy Trinity.

(2) **Abel.**—**Hebel** means a thing "unstable, not abiding," like a breath or vapor. Now, we can scarcely suppose that Eve so called her child from a presentiment of evil or a mere passing depression of spirits; more probably it was a title given to him after his untimely death. Giving names to children would become usual only when population increased; and it was not till a religious rite was instituted for their dedication to God that they had names given to them in their infancy. Even then Esau was changed to Edom, and Jacob to Israel, while previously such names as Eber and Peleg, and earlier still Jabal and Jubal, must have been given to those who bore them from what they became. Probably, therefore, it was only after Abel's death that his sorrowing relatives called him the "Breath" that had passed away.

Abel was a keeper of sheep, but Cain was a tiller of the ground.—As Adam was 130 years old when Seth was born (5:3), there was a long period for the increase of Adam's family (comp. verses 14-17), and also for the development of the characters

15

of these his two eldest sons. In the one we seem to see a rough, strong nature, who took the hard work as he found it, and subdued the ground with muscular energy; in the other a nature more refined and thoughtful, and making progress upward. Adam had already tamed animals in Paradise: to these Abel devotes himself, tends them carefully, and gains from them ample and easy means of sustenance, higher in kind even than the fruits of Paradise. Round these two the other sons and daughters of Adam group themselves, and Cain seems already to have had a wife when he murdered his brother (verse 17).

(3, 4) In process of time.—Heb., "at the end of days": not at the end of a week, or a year, or of harvest-time, but of a long indefinite period, shown by the age of Adam at the birth of Seth to have been something less than 130 years.

An offering.—Heb., "a thank-offering, a present." We must be careful not to introduce here any of the later Levitical ideas about sacrifice. All that we know about this offering is that it was an act of worship, and apparently something usual. Now, each brought of his own produce, and one was accepted and one rejected. Why? We are expressly told in Heb. 11:4 that Abel's was the more excellent sacrifice, because it was offered "in faith." It was the state of their hearts that made the difference; though, as the result of unbelief, Cain's may have been a scanty present of common produce, and not of first-fruits, while Abel brought "firstlings, and of the fat thereof," the choicest portion. Abel may also have shown a deeper faith in the promised Deliverer by offering an animal sacrifice: and certainly the acceptance of his sacrifice quickened among men the belief that the proper way of approaching God was by the death of a victim.

The Lord had respect.—Heb., "looked upon," showed that He had seen it. The brothers were aware that God was pleased with the one and displeased with the other. More important is it to notice, first, that God's familiar presence was not withdrawn from man after the fall. He talked with Cain as kindly as with Adam of old. And secondly, in these, the earliest, records of mankind religion is built upon love, and the Deity appears as man's personal friend. This negates the scientific theory that religion grew out of dim fears and terror at natural phenomena, ending gradually in the evolution of the idea of a destructive and dangerous power outside of man, which man must propitiate as best he could.

(5) Cain was very wroth.—Heb., "it burned to Cain exceedingly": that is, his heart was full of hot indignant feelings, because of the preference shown to his younger brother.

(7) If thou doest well.—Literally, the words mean, "If thou doest well, is there not lifting up?" It had just been said that his countenance fell; and this "lifting up" is often elsewhere applied to the countenance. (Comp. Job 10:15; 11:15.) "Instead, then, of thy present gloomy despondent mood, in which thou goest about with downcast look, thou shalt lift up thy head, and have peace and good temper beaming in thine eyes as the result of a quiet conscience." The second half of the verse means: "If thou doest not well, sin croucheth at the door, that is, lies dangerously near thee, and puts thee in peril. Beware, therefore, and stand on thy guard; and then **his** desire shall be unto thee, and thou shalt rule over **him**. At present thou are vexed and envious because thy younger brother is rich and prosperous, while thy tillage yields thee but scanty returns. Do well, and the divine blessing will rest on thee, and thou wilt recover thy rights of primogeniture, and thy brother will look up to thee in loving obedience."

We have in this verse proof of a struggle in Cain's conscience. Jehovah would not have remonstrated thus kindly with him had he been altogether reprobate. Possibly, too, for a time he prevailed over his evil tempers. It is a gratuitous assumption that the murder followed immediately upon the sacrifice. The words of the Almighty rather show that repentance was still possible, and that Cain might still recover the divine favor.

(8) And Cain talked with Abel his brother.—Heb., "And Cain said unto Abel his brother." To this the Samaritan Pentateuch, the LXX, the Syriac, and the Vulgate add, "Let us go out into the field." The authority of the versions is very great. If we could, with the King James Version, translate "Cain talked with Abel," this would imply that Cain triumphed for a time over his angry feelings, and resumed friendly intercourse with his brother. But such a rendering is impossible, as also is one that has been suggested, "Cain told it unto Abel his brother": that is, told all that had passed between him and Jehovah. Either, therefore, we must accept the addition of the versions, or regard the passage as at present beyond our powers.

It came to pass, when they were in the field.—the open, uncultivated land, where Abel's flocks would find pasture. We cannot suppose that this murder was premeditated. Cain did not even know what a human death was. Possibly Abel's flocks had trespassed on Cain's land, and when he went to remonstrate, his envy was stirred at the sight of his brother's affluence. A quarrel ensued, and Cain, in that fierce anger, to fits of which he was liable (verse 5), tried to enforce his mastery by blows, and before he well knew what he was doing, he had shed his brother's blood, and stood in terror before the first human corpse.

(9) And the Lord said unto Cain, Where is Abel thy brother?—It is the beauty of these early narratives that the dealings of the Deity with mankind are all clothed in an anthropomorphic form, for the reasons of which see note on 2:7. It seems, then, that Cain at first went away, scarcely conscious of the greatness of his crime. He had asserted his rights, had suppressed the usurpation of his privileges by the younger son, and if he had used force it was his brother's fault for resisting him. But Cain could not quiet his conscience; remorse tracked his footsteps. Where is Abel, thy brother? But the strong-willed man resists. What has he to do with Abel? Is he "his brother's keeper"?

(10) Thy brother's blood crieth unto me.—The sight he has seen of death cleaves to him, and grows into a terror; and from above the voice of Jehovah tells him that the blood he has shed calls aloud for vengeance. Thus with the first shedding of human blood that ominous thought sprang up, divinely bestowed, that the earth will grant no peace to the wretch who has stained her fair face with the life stream of man. But the blood of Jesus "speaketh better things than that of Abel" (Heb. 12:24). The voice of one cried for justice and retribution: the other for reconciliation and peace.

(11, 12) And now (because of thy crime) art thou cursed from the earth.—Heb., "from the adâmâh," or cultivated ground. Cain was the first human being on whom a curse was inflicted, and it was to rise up from the ground, the portion of the earth won and subdued by man, to punish him. Restless and uneasy, and haunted by the memory of his crime, he shall become a wanderer, not merely in the adâmâh, his native soil, but in the earth. Poverty must necessarily be the lot of one thus roaming, not in search of a better lot, but under the compulsion of an evil conscience.

(13, 14) My punishment (or "my iniquity") is greater than I can bear.—Literally, "than can be borne," or "forgiven." It is in accordance with the manner of the Hebrew language to have only one word for an act and its result. The full meaning, therefore, is, "My sin is past forgiveness, and its result is an intolerable punishment." This latter idea seems foremost in Cain's mind, and is dwelt upon in verse 14. He there complains that he is driven, not "from the face of the earth," which was impossible, but from the adâmâh, his dear native soil, banished from which he must go into the silence and solitude of an earth unknown and untracked. And next, "from thy face shall I be hid." Naturally, Cain had no idea of an omnipresent God, and away from the adâmâh he supposed that it would be impossible to enjoy divine favor and protection. Without this there would be no safety for him anywhere, so that he must rove about perpetually, and "every one that findeth me shall slay me." In the adâmâh Jehovah would protect him; away from it, men, unseen by Jehovah, might do as they liked. But who were these men? Some commentators answer, Adam's other sons, especially those who had attached themselves to Abel. But others, with more probability, think that Cain's was a vain apprehension. How could he know that Adam and his family were the sole inhabitants of the earth?

(15) The Lord said unto him, Therefore.—Most of the versions have "Not so," which requires only a slight and probable change of the Hebrew text.

Sevenfold.—Cain's punishment was severe, because his crime was the result of bad and violent passions, but his life was not taken because the act was not premeditated. Murder was more than he had meant. But as any one killing him would mean murder, therefore the vengeance would be sevenfold: that is, complete, seven being the number of perfection. In this we have the germ of the merciful law which set cities of refuge apart for the involuntary manslayer.

The Lord set a mark upon Cain.—This rendering suggests an utterly false idea. Cain was not branded nor marked in any way. What the Hebrew says is, "And Jehovah set," that is, appointed, "unto Cain a sign, that no one finding him should slay him." In a similar manner God appointed the rainbow as a sign unto Noah that mankind should never again be destroyed by a

17

flood. Probably the sign here was also some natural phenomenon, the regular recurrence of which would assure Cain of his security, and so pacify his excited feelings.

(16) Cain went out from the presence of the Lord.—Adam and his family probably worshiped with their faces toward the Paradise, and Cain, on migrating from the whole land of Eden, regarded himself as beyond the range of the vision of God. (See note on verse 14.)

The Land of Nod.—i.e., of wandering. Read without vowels, the word becomes India. All that is certain is that Cain emigrated into Eastern Asia, and as none of Noah's descendants, in the table of nations in chap. 10, are described as having traveled eastward, many regard the Mongol race as the offspring of Cain.

Cain and His Descendants

(17) Cain knew his wife.—As a rule, only the eldest son is mentioned in the genealogies, and Abel's birth is chronicled chiefly because of its tragical end, leading to the enactment of the merciful law which followed and to the sundering of the human race. One of Adam's daughters apparently clave unto her brother, in spite of the solemn decree of banishment passed upon him, probably, by his father, and followed him in his wanderings as his wife, and bare him a son, whom they called "Enoch." Now this name, in Hebrew **Chanoch**, is of the utmost importance in estimating Cain's character. It means "train" in Prov. 22:6 ("Train up a child"), but is used in Deut. 20:5 of the "dedication" of a house; and thus Cain also calls his city Enoch, "dedicated." We see in it a purpose that the child should be a trained and consecrated man; and Cain must have now put off those fierce and violent habits which had led him into so terrible a crime. We may add that this prepares our minds for the rapid advance of the Cainites in the arts of civilization, and for the very remarkable step next taken by Cain.

He builded a city.—Cain appears as a wise ruler, like Nimrod subsequently, rather than as a religious man. His purpose was much the same as that of the builders of the Tower of Babel, who wanted to keep mankind together that they might form a powerful community. It is worth notice that in the line of Seth, the name of the seventh and noblest of that race, is also Enoch, whose training was a close walk with God.

(18) Unto Enoch was born Irad.—Cain was building a city, "'Ir," and it was this probably which suggested the name "'Irad." Possibly 'Irad means "citizen"; but these names have been so corrupted by transcribers that we cannot feel sure of them. Methusael, Enoch, and Lamech (Heb., **Lemech**), have a certain degree of similitude with those in the line of the Sethites, whence many commentators have assumed that the two lists are variations of the same original record. But it is usually a similarity of sound only with a diversity of meaning. Thus Mehujael, "smitten of God," answers to Mahalaleel, "glory to God"; Methusael, "God's hero," to Methuselah, "the armed warrior." Even when the names are the same, their history is often most diverse. Thus in the Cainite line Enoch is "initiation" into city life, in the Sethite into a life of holiness; and the Cainite polygamist Lemech, rejoicing in the weapons invented by his son, is the very opposite of the Sethite Lemech, who calls his son Noah, "quiet, rest."

(19-22) Lamech took unto him two wives.—Whether polygamy began with Lamech is uncertain, but it is in keeping with the insolent character of the man. Jabal, Adah's eldest son, took to a nomadic life, whence his name, which means "wanderer," and was looked up to by the nomad tribes as their founder. The difference between their mode of life and that of Abel was that they perpetually changed their habitation, while he remained in the neighborhood of Adam's dwelling. The younger, "Jubal," that is, the **music-player**, "was the father of all such as handle the harp and organ." Of these instruments, the **kinnôr**, always translated "harp" in our version, was certainly a stringed instrument—a guitar or lyre. The other, in Hebrew **'ugab**, is mentioned only in Job. 21:12; 30:31; Ps. 150: 4. It was a small wind instrument, a reed or pipe.

The son of Zillah attained to higher distinction. He is the first "sharpener (or hammerer) of every instrument of copper and iron." Copper is comparatively soft, and is easily beaten to an edge; but it was long before men learned the art of mixing with it an alloy of tin, and so producing the far harder substance, bronze. The alloy to which we give the name of brass was absolutely unknown to the ancients. The discovery of iron marks a far greater advance in metallurgy, as the ore has to be smelted, and the implement produced is more precious. The name of this hero is Tubal-cain, in Persian the word Tubal means "copper." Cain is a distinct name from that of Adam's first-born, and means, in most Semitic languages, "smith"; thus Tubal-cain probably signifies "coppersmith."

The sister of Tubal-cain was Naamah.— The same as Naomi (Ruth 1:2), and meaning "beauty," "loveliness." As women are not generally mentioned in the genealogies, and as no history follows of this personage, her name must be given as an indication that a great advance had been made, not only in the arts, but also in the elegancies of life. Women could not have been mere drudges and household slaves, nor men coarse and boorish, when Naamah's beauty was so highly appreciated.

(23, 24) Lamech said ... —Following quickly upon music, we have poetry, but it is in praise of ferocity, and gives utterance to the pride of one who, by means of the weapons forged by his son, had taken violent revenge for an attack made upon him. It is intended to show that, side by side with progress in the material arts, moral degradation was going on. Cain's own act is spoken of, not as a sin to be ashamed of, but as a deed of ancient heroism: not comparable, however, with the glory of Lamech, whose wrath shall be tenfold. With this boastful poem in praise of armed violence and bloodshed, joined with indications of luxury and a life of pleasure, the narrator closes the history of the race of Cain.

Substitution of Seth for Abel

(25) Seth.—Heb., **Sheth**, that is, "appointed," "substituted": he was thus specially designated as the son who was to be the chief over Adam's family.

(26) He called his name Enos.—Heb., **Enosh**, that is "man." We thus find language growing. Up to this time there had been two names for man: Adam and Ish, "a being." (See note on 2:23.) We have now Enosh, which, according to Fürst and others, signifies "mortal." Most probably it is the generic word for man.

Then began men to call upon the name of the Lord (Jehovah).—That is, the notion of divinity began now to be attached to this name, and even in their worship men called upon God as Jehovah. Eve, as we have seen, attached no such idea to it; and when, in 4:3, we read that Cain and Abel brought an offering to Jehovah, these are the words of the narrator, who in the story of the Fall

had expressly styled the Deity Jehovah-Elohim, that is, Jehovah-God, or more exactly, "the coming God," in order to show that Elohim and Jehovah are one. Two hundred and thirty-five years had elapsed between the birth of Cain and that of Enos, and men had learned a truer appreciation of the promise given to their primal mother, in 3:15, than she herself had when she supposed that her first child was to win back for her the Paradise. It was long afterwards, in the days of Moses, that it became the personal name of the covenant God of the Jews.

5

Patriarchal Genealogy From Adam to Noah

(1) This is the book of the generations of Adam.—See note on 2:4.

In the likeness of God.—Man is now a fallen being, but these words are repeated to show that the divine likeness was not therefore lost, nor the primeval blessing bestowed at his creation revoked. As man's likeness to God does not mainly consist in moral innocence (see note on 1:26), it was not affected by the entrance into the world of sin, except as far as sin corrupted the vessel in which this great gift was deposited. (Comp. II Cor. 4:7.)

(3) In his own likeness, after his image.— That is, Adam handed down to his posterity that divine likeness which he had himself received.

(5) The days that Adam lived were nine hundred and thirty years.—The numbers in the Bible are involved in great difficulty, owing to the Hebrew method of numeration being to attach numerical values to letters, and add them together; and as the words thus formed are unmeaning, they easily become corrupted. Hence there is a great discrepancy in the numbers as specified by the three main authorities, the Hebrew text making the length of time from the expulsion from Paradise to the Flood 1656 years. (See note on 11:10.) Hence many have supposed that in the early Biblical genealogies races or dynasties were meant, or that at a time when there were only engraved cylinders or marks scratched on stones or impressed on bricks as modes of writing, a few names only were selected, each one of whom, by the length of years assigned to him, represented an indefinitely protracted period. In proof that there was something artificial in these genealogies, they point to the fact that the **tôldôth** of Adam are arranged in ten generations, and that the same number of generations composes the **tôldôth** of Shem (11:10-26); while in our Lord's genealogy names are confessedly omitted in order to produce three series, each of fourteen names. It is also undeniable that in Hebrew genealogies it was the rule to omit names. Thus the genealogy of Moses contains only four individuals: Levi, Kohath, Amram, Moses (I Chron. 6:1-3); while for the same period there are eleven descents given in the genealogy of Jehoshuah (ibid, 7:23-27). All this is sufficient to convince every thoughtful person that we must not use these genealogies for chronological purposes. They were not drawn up with any such intention, but to trace the line of primogeniture, and show whose was the birthright. But the longevity of the antediluvian race does not depend upon these genealogies alone, but is part of the very substance of the narrative. We learn, however, from 6:3 that it did not prove a blessing, and we possibly are to understand that a change took place at the time of the Flood in man's physical constitution, by which the duration of his life was gradually limited to 120 years. (On the names in verses 9ff., see note on 4:18.)

(24) Enoch walked with God.—This is translated in the LXX, "Enoch pleased God," whence comes the "testimony" quoted in Heb. 11:5. Really it gives the cause of which the Greek phrase is the effect; for it denotes a steady continuance in well-doing, and a life spent in the immediate presence of and in constant communion with God. (See note on 4:18.)

God took him.—Instead of the mournful refrain "and he died," coming like a surprise at the end of each of these protracted lives, we have here an early removal into another world, suggesting already that long life was not the highest form of blessing; and this removal is without pain, decay, or death into the immediate presence of God. Thus one of Adam's posterity after the fall succeeded in doing, though, doubtless, not without special help and blessing from the Almighty, that wherein Adam in Paradise had failed. We learn, too, from Jude 14, 15, that Enoch's was a removal from prevailing evil to happiness secured. Already, probably, the intermarriages between the Cainites and Sethites had begun, and with it the corruption of mankind. Enoch's translation

took place about the middle of the antediluvian period.

(29) He called his name Noah.—This is the first recorded instance, since the days of Eve, of a child being named at his birth, and in both cases the name ended in disappointment. Noah brought no rest, but in his days came the Flood to punish human sin. We have already noticed that this longing of Lamech for comfort is in strong contrast with the arrogance of his namesake of the race of Cain. (Comp. 4:18.)

The ground (adâmâh) which the Lord hath cursed.—It is usual to style this section Elohistic, because it so evidently takes up the narrative at 2:3. Yet, first, the writer distinctly refers to 3:17, where it is Jehovah -Elohim who curses the ground; and next he uses the name Jehovah as equivalent to God, according to what we are told in 4:26. Here, then, as in several other places, the idea that Genesis can be arranged in two portions, distinguished as Elohistic or Jehovistic, according to the name of God employed in them, entirely breaks down. It is remarkable, also, that the word for "toil" in Lamech's distich is the same as that rendered "sorrow" in 3:16, 17, and that it occurs only in these three places.

(32) And Noah begat Shem, Ham, and Japheth.—From them have sprung the three great lines into which the human family is divided. Shem means "name"—that is, fame, glory; and he, as the owner of the birthright, was the progenitor of our Lord. Ham, the "dark-colored," was the ancestor of the Egyptians, Cushites, and other black races of Arabia and Africa. Japheth, the "widener," but according to others the "fair," though the youngest son, was the ancestor of most of the races of Europe, as well as of some of the chief nations of Asia.

6

(1) When men (the adam) **began to multiply.**—The multiplication of the race of Adam was probably comparatively slow. Each patriarch begat "sons and daughters," and as we find Cain building a city, he must have seen, at all events, the possibility of a considerable population settling around him. It was probably, as we saw above, about the time of Enoch that the corruption of the family of Adam began to become general.

(2) The sons of God ... —The literal translation of this verse is, "And the sons of the Elohim saw the daughters of the adam that they were good (beautiful); and they took to them wives whomsoever they chose." Of the sons of Elohim there are three principal interpretations: the first, that of the Targums and the chief Jewish expositors, that they were nobles and men of high rank; the second, that they were angels. Jude, in Jude 6, and Peter, in II Peter 2:4 seem to favor this interpretaton, possibly as being the translation of the LXX. according to several MSS. But even if this is their meaning, which is very uncertain, they use it only as an illustration; and a higher authority says that the angels neither marry nor are given in marriage. The third, and most generally accepted interpretation in modern times, is that the sons of the Elohim were the Sethites, and that when they married for mere lust of beauty, universal corruption soon ensued. But no modern commentator has shown how such marriages could produce "mighty men . . . men of renown"; or how strong warriors could be the result of the intermarriage of pious men with women of an inferior race such as the Cainites are assumed to have been.

The Jewish interpreters, who well understood the uses of their own language, are right in the main point that the phrase "sons of the Elohim" conveys no idea of moral goodness or piety. Elohim constantly means "mighty ones."

Who, then, are these "mighty ones"? Before answering this question, let me call attention to the plain teaching of the narrative as to what is meant by the "daughters of men." It says: "When the adam began to multiply, and daughters were born unto them, the sons of Elohim saw the daughters of the adam . . . and took them wives," etc. But according to every right rule of interpretation, the "daughters of the adam" in verse 1 must be the same as the "daughters of the adam" in verse 2, whom the sons of the Elohim married. Now, it seems undeniable that the adam here spoken of were the Sethites. The phrase occurs in the history of Noah, just after giving his descent from Adam; Cain is absolutely passed over, even in the account of the birth of Seth, who is described as Adam's first-born, such as legally he was. The corruption described is that of the Sethites; for the Cainites have already been depicted as violent and lustful, and their history has been brought to an end. Moreover, in verse 3, "the adam with whom God will not always strive" is certainly the family of Seth, who, though the

chosen people and possessors of the birthright, are nevertheless described as falling into evil ways; and their utter corruption finally is the result of the depravation of their women by a race superior to themselves in muscular vigor and warlike prowess.

Where, then, shall we find these men? Certainly among the descendants of Cain. In 4:17-24, we find Cain described as the founder of civil institutions and social life: the name he gives to his son testifies to his determination that his race shall be trained men. They advance rapidly in the arts, become rich, refined, luxurious, but also martial and arrogant. To the simple "daughters of the adam," these men, enriched by the possession of implements of metal, playing sweet music on harp and pipe, and rendered invincible by the deadly weapons they had forged, must have seemed indeed as very "sons of the Elohim." The Sethites could not have taken the Cainite women according to their fancy in the way described, protected as they were by armed men; but the whole phrase, "whomsoever they would," reeks of that arrogancy and wantonness of which the polygamist Lamech had set so notable an example. And so, not by the women corrupting nobler natures, but by these strong men acting according to their lust, the race with the birthright sank to the Cainite level, and God had no longer a people on earth worthy of His choice.

(3) And the Lord said.—As the Sethites are now the fallen race, it is their covenant Jehovah who determines to reduce the extreme duration of human life to that which, under the most favorable sanitary influences, might still be its normal length.

My spirit shall not always strive with man.—The meaning of this much-contested clause is really settled by the main purpose and context of the verse, which is the divine determination to shorten human life. Whether, then, God's spirit be the animating breath spoken of in 2:7 and 7:22, whereby human life is sustained, or the spiritual part of men, his conscience and moral sense—God's best gift to him—in the opposition to his flesh, the struggle henceforward is not to be indefinitely prolonged. In the first case, the struggle spoken of is that between the elements of life and death in the body; in the second, it refers to the moral probation to which man is subject. The versions generally take the former meaning, and translate "shall not dwell," or "abide"; but there is much in favor of the rendering "shall strive," though the verb more exactly means "to rule," "preside over," "sit as judge." Literally, then, it signifies that the divine gift of life shall not rule in man "for ever"; that is, for a period so protracted as was antediluvian life. (Comp. Deut. 15:17, etc.)

With man.—Heb., "with the adam": spoken with special reference to the Sethites.

For that he also is flesh.—If Abraham brought these records with him from Ur, we have an explanation of the acknowledged fact that Aramaisms do occur in the earlier portions of the Bible. Man is "also" flesh, that is, his body is of the same nature as those of the animals, and in spite of his noble gifts and precedence, he must submit to a life of the same moderate duration as that allotted them.

(4) Giants.—Heb., **Nephilim**, mentioned again in Num. 13:33, and apparently a race of great physical strength and stature. Nothing is more probable than that, at a time when men lived for centuries, human vigor should also show itself in producing not merely individuals, but a race of more than ordinary height. They were apparently of the Cainite stock, and the text carefully distinguishes them from the offspring of the mixed marriages.

The same became mighty men.—Gibborim, "mighty men" (see 10:8), has nothing to do with stature, but means heroes, warriors. It is also generally used in a good sense. The children of these mixed marriages were a race of brave fighting men, who by their martial deeds won for themselves reputation.

(5) And God saw.—Really, "And Jehovah saw."

Imagination.—More exactly, "form," "shape." Thus every idea or embodied thought, which presented itself to the mind through the working of the heart—that is, the whole inner nature of man—"was only evil continually"—Heb., "all the day," from morning to night, without reproof of conscience or fear of the divine justice. A more forcible picture of complete depravity could scarcely be drawn; and this corruption of man's inner nature is ascribed to the overthrow of moral and social restraints.

(6) And it repented the Lord.—If we begin with the omniscience and omnipotence of God as our postulates, everything upon earth must be predestined and immutably foreordained. If we start with man's free will, everything will depend upon hu-

man choice and action. Both these sides must be true, though our mental powers are too limited to combine them. In Holy Scripture the latter view is kept more prominently in the foreground, because upon it depends human responsibility. Thus, here, the overwhelming of mankind by a flood, and the subsequent abbreviation of life, is set before our eyes as painful to the Deity, and contrary to His goodwill toward men, but as necessitated by the extreme depravity of even the chosen Sethite race.

(7) I will destroy.—Heb., "delete," "rub out."

From the face of the earth.—Heb., the **adâmâh,** the tilled ground which man had subdued and cultivated.

Both man, and beast.—The animal world was to share in this destruction because its fate is bound up with that of man (Rom. 8:19-22).

(8) But Noah found grace.—This is the first place where grace is mentioned in the Bible, and with these words ends the **Tôldôth Adam.** It has traced man from his creation until his wickedness was so great that the divine justice demanded his punishment. But it concludes with words of hope. Jehovah's purpose was not extermination, but regeneration; and with Noah a higher and better order of things was to begin.

The Generations of Noah (6:9-9:28)

(9) Noah was a just man and perfect in his generations.—"Just" is literally, "righteous," one whose actions were sufficiently upright to exempt him from the punishment inflicted upon the rest of mankind. "Perfect" means "sound," "healthy," and conveys no idea of sinlessness. It answers to the Latin **integer,** whence our word integrity, and not to **perfectus.**

Generations (dôrôth) is not the same word as at the beginning of the verse (tôldôth), but simply means "his contemporaries." And this he was because—

Noah walked with God.—See Note on 5:22.

(11) The earth.—This is the larger word, and it occurs no less than six times in these three verses, thus indicating a more widespread calamity than if **adâmâh** only had been used, as in verse 7. But the earth that "was corrupt before God" was not the whole material globe, but that part which man, notably the **gibborim** of verse 4, had "filled with violence."

(12) All flesh had corrupted his way upon

the earth.—These material things were incapable alike of moral good or evil, but man had made them the instruments of working his carnal will, and because of the associations connected with them they must be effaced, or "rubbed out." (See note on verse 7.)

(13) The end of all flesh is come before me.—A metaphor taken from the customs of earthly kings. Before an order is executed the decree is presented to the sovereign, that it may finally be examined, and if approved, receive the sign manual, upon which it becomes law.

(14) Make thee an ark.—**Têbah,** a word so archaic that scholars neither know its derivation nor even to what language it belongs. It is certain, however, that it was an oblong box, not capable of sailing, but intended merely to float.

Of gopher wood.—This is also a word which occurs nowhere else, but means the cypress, a tall, upright evergreen tree, of great durability, and in ancient days much valued for shipbuilding.

Rooms.—Literally, "nests," small cells or cabins, arranged in three tiers, so that the interlacing of the timbers might aid in holding the whole structure together.

Pitch.—That is, "natural bitumen." The Ark therefore must have been built in some country where this natural product is easily obtainable, as in Assyria.

(15) Cubits.—The cubit is the length of the arm from the elbow to the tip of the middle finger. As, further, it was regarded as one-fourth of a man's height, we may safely compute it at eighteen inches, except where the sacred or longer cubit is expressly mentioned. Thus the Ark was 450 feet long, 75 broad, and 45 in depth.

(16) A window.—It was evidently a means, not merely of lighting the ark, but also of ventilating it. If the **zohar** was an open space one cubit in height, running around the Ark, and formed by not boarding over the upright beams, it would have given a sufficient supply of air, and being protected by the overhanging eaves of the roof—for the Ark had no deck—would not have admitted any serious amount of rain.

Above.—Or, "upward." Thou shalt finish it (the Ark, as is shown by the gender) from beneath, working upward till the last cubit, which is not to be finished, but left open for ventilation and light.

The door was to be at the side, and probably extended throughout the three sto-ries, two-thirds of which, however, might be closed as soon as the lower stories had received their freightage of provisions.

(17) A flood.—**Mabbul,** another archaic word. It is used only of the deluge, except in Ps. 29:10, where, however, there is an evident allusion to the Flood of Noah.

Every thing that is in the earth shall die.—This by no means involves the theory of a universal deluge. The writer described with perfect truthfulness that of which he was either an eyewitness, or of which he had received the knowledge by tradition; or lastly, that he recorded in his own language the impressions divinely inspired in his mind by God.

"We have no right to force upon him, and upon the scene so vividly described, our modern notions of our modern knowledge of the earth, so much beyond any knowledge he could have possessed or any conception he could have formed." (Lange.) The narrative itself repeatedly negates the theory that the Flood extended itself to any great distance beyond the regions then occupied by man. Moreover, it is in exact accordance with the use of words in Holy Scripture that the large term, "the earth," is limited to the earth as known to Noah and his contemporaries. We shall also discover in what follows reason for believing that the account originally came from one who was an eyewitness; and the extreme antiquity of the language is a proof that it was committed to writing at a time long anterior to the age of Moses.

(18) My covenant.—There had been no covenant with Adam or with the Sethites, but in the higher state of things which began with Noah, man was to hold a more exactly defined relation to God; and though they had begun to attach the notion of Deity to the name Jehovah in the days of Enos (4:26), yet it was not until the time of Moses that it became the distinct title of God in covenant with man. Of this relation a necessary result was revelation, as in no other way could there be a communication between the two contracting parties. Hence the Bible is called "The Old and New Covenant," or "The Old and New Testament," the Greek term being of wider meaning than either word with us, and signifying either an agreement between the living or the document by which a testator disposes of his property after his death (Heb. 9:16, 17). The title of covenant is more applicable to the Scriptures of the prior dispensation, which contain a series of such relations, all preparing for the last and best and most perfect, which was a Testament ratified in the blood of Christ.

(19-22) Of every living thing of all flesh, two . . . — The vast size of the Ark and the wide terms used of the animals to be collected into it, make it evident that Noah was to save not merely his domestic cattle, but many wild species of beasts, birds, and creeping things. But the terms are conditioned by the usual rules for the interpretation of the language of Holy Scripture, and by the internal necessities of the event itself. Thus the animals in the Ark could not have been more in number than four men and four women could attend to. Next the terms exclude the carnivora (see also note on 6:5).

7

(1) Come thou.—The task of building the Ark is over, and after a week, to be spent in collecting animals and birds, Noah is to take up his abode in it. Many commentators suppose that 120 years were spent in the work; but this view arises from an untenable interpretation of 6:3, which really fixes the future duration of human life.

(2) Of every clean beast thou shalt take to thee by sevens.—Heb., "seven seven." If "seven pairs" be the right interpretation, only a few species could have been included, as to attend properly to so large a number of animals would have been beyond the power of Noah and his sons. But which were the clean beasts? There can be no reference here to the Levitical law, which had respect to human food; nor to animals tamed and untamed, as all alike are called cattle; but probably the clean cattle were such as from the days of Adam and Abel had been offered in sacrifice. Thus provision was made for Noah's sacrifice on his egress from the Ark, and also for his possession of a small herd of such animals as would be most useful to him amid the desolation which must have existed for a long time after the Flood. The clean beasts would therefore be oxen, sheep, goats; the unclean, camels, horses, asses, and such other animals as stood in some relation to man. Of birds, the dove would especially be clean.

There is nothing improbable in Moses having two records of the Flood before him, and while the division of Genesis into Elohistic and Jehovistic portions usually breaks down, there is a **primâ facie** appearance of the combination of the two narra-

tives in the present history, or, at least, in this one section (7:1-6).

(4) Forty days.—Henceforward forty became the sacred number of trial and patience, and, besides the obvious places in the Old Testament, it was the duration both of our Lord's fast in the wilderness and of His sojourn on earth after the Resurrection.

Every living substance.—The word "living" is found neither in the Hebrew nor in the ancient versions, and limits the sense unnecessarily. The word is rare, being found only thrice, namely, here, in verse 23, and in Deut. 11:6. It means "whatever stands erect." Thus God "destroys"—Heb., "blots out" (see note on 6:7)—not man and beast only, but the whole existent state of things—"from the face of the earth"—Heb., **the adâmâh,** the cultivated and inhabited ground. This section is much more limited in the extent which it gives to the Flood, not including reptiles, or rather, small animals, among those saved in the ark, and confining the overflow of the waters to the inhabited region.

(10) After seven days.—Said, in Jewish tradition, to have been the seven days of mourning for Methuselah, who died in the year of the Flood.

(11) In the second month.—That is, of the civil year, which commenced in Tisri, at the autumnal equinox. The Flood thus began toward the end of October, and lasted till the spring. The ecclesiastical year began in Abib, or April; but it was instituted in remembrance of the deliverance from Egypt (Exod. 12:2; 23:15), and can have no place here. The year was evidently the lunar year of 360 days, for the waters prevail for 150 days (chap. 7:24), and then abate for 150 days (8:3). Now, as the end of the first period of 150 days is described in 8:4 as the seventeenth day of the seventh month, whereas the Flood began on the seventeenth of the second month, it is plain that the 150 days form five months of thirty days each.

The fountains of the great deep broken up (Heb., **cloven**), **and the windows (lattices) of heaven were opened.**—The words at least suggest the idea of a great cosmic catastrophe, by which some vast body of water was set loose. Without some such natural convulsion it is very difficult to understand how the Ark, a vessel incapable of sailing, could have gone against the current up to the water-shed of Ararat. As the annual evaporation of the earth is also a comparatively fixed quantity, the concentrated downpour of it for forty days and night would scarcely have produced a Flood as vast as the deluge of Noah evidently was. It is thus probable that there was, besides the rains, some vast displacement of water which helped in producing these terrific effects.

(14) Every beast.—Heb., "every living thing" (as in 8:1).

(16) The Lord (Jehovah) shut him in.—The assigning to Jehovah of this act of personal care for Noah is very remarkable.

(17-19) The waters increased ... —The swelling of the Flood is told with great power in these verses, but every stage and detail has reference to the Ark, as if the author of the narrative was one of those on board. First, the "waters increased," and raised up the Ark till it floated. Next, "they became strong and increased exceedingly"— the word rendered "prevailed" really signifying the setting in of mighty currents (see note on 8:1), as the water sought the lower ground—and at this stage the Ark began to move. Finally, they "became strong exceedingly, exceedingly," rushing along with ever-increasing force, and carrying the Ark high above every hill in its course. Of these it is said—

All the high hills, that were under the whole heaven, were covered.—Many regard it as a proof of the deluge having been universal. But omitting the well-known fact that in the Bible the word "all" means much less than with us, we must also remember that the Hebrew language has a very small vocabulary, and "the whole heaven" means simply "the whole sky." Far and wide, in every direction, to the utmost reach of the beholder's gaze, no mountain was in sight. All was a surging waste of flood. The mountains were those of the Noachian world, as limited as the Roman world of Luke 2:1, or even more so.

(20) Fifteen cubits upward.—This apparently was the draught of the Ark, computed after it had settled in the region of Ararat. Fifteen cubits would be about twenty-two feet, and as the Ark floated onward without interruption until it finally grounded, there must have been this depth of water even on the highest summit in its course. But as they would be seeking the lower grounds during the whole forty days, it is difficult to understand how they could cover any of the heights to the depth of twenty-two feet, unless there were some cosmic convulsion (see note on verse 11), and in this way there would be no difficulty in the Ark being

carried against the current of the Tigris and Euphrates up to the high lands of Armenia.

(23) Every living substance.—"Every thing that stood erect" (See note on verse 4.)

(24) Prevailed.—Heb., "were strong," as in verse 18. The rains lasted forty days; for one hundred and ten more days they still bore up the Ark, and then it grounded. But though still mighty, they had by this time "abated" (see 8:3), inasmuch as, instead of covering the hills to the depth of nearly four fathoms, the Ark now had touched dry land. Again, then, the narrative seems to give the personal experiences of someone in the Ark.

8

(1) The waters assuaged.—Heb., "became still." It is plain from this that the "strength" of the waters, described in 7:24, has reference to the violent currents which still existed up to the end of the one hundred and fiftieth day, after which they ceased.

A wind (comp. the creative wind in 1:2) began to blow as soon as the rains ceased, or even before, as must necessarily have been the case with so vast a disturbance of the atmosphere; but its special purpose of assuaging the waters only began when the downpour was over. This wind would affect the course of the Ark, but scarcely so strongly as the currents of the water.

(3) The waters returned from off the earth.—This backward motion of the waters also seems to indicate that a vast wave from the sea had swept over the land, in addition to the forty days of rain.

Were abated.—Heb., "decreased." Those in the Ark would notice the changing current, and would know, by their being aground, that the Flood was diminishing. But it was not till the first day of the tenth month that the tops of the mountains were seen. This slow abatement of the waters and their stillness, described in verse 1, makes it probable that the Ark had grounded on some land-locked spot.

(4) The seventh month, on the seventeenth day of the month.—As each month had thirty days, this makes exactly 150 days (see 7:11). The seventh civil month would be Abib. "On the 17th day of Abib the ark rested on Mount Ararat; on the 17th day of Abib, the Israelites passed over the Red Sea; on the 17th day of Abib, Christ, our Lord, rose

25

again from the dead." (Speaker's Commentary.)

Ararat.—If in 11:2 the King James Version is right in saying that the descendants of Noah traveled "from the east" to Shinar, this could not be the Ararat of Armenia. The rendering, however, "from the east," is by no means certain, and many translate "eastward," and even the King James Version renders the word "east," that is, eastward, in 13:11. In II Kings 19:37 "Ararat" is translated Armenia. But the inspired narrative says that it rested "upon the mountains of Ararat," upon some chain of hills there, and seventy-three days afterward Noah found himself surrounded by an amphitheater of mountains, the word used in verse 5 being emphatic, and signifying "the tops of the mountains became distinctly visible," and not that they had just begun to emerge. For, doubtless, after so vast a flood, mists and vapors would for a long time prevail and shut out the surrounding world from Noah's view.

(5) Seen.—See note on verse 4.

(6) Noah opened the window.—Not the **zohar** of 6:16, but an aperture. He had waited forty days after seeing the heights around him rising clearly into the air, and then, impatient of the slow subsidence of the waters, Noah at last sent forth a raven to bring him some news of the state of the earth. This bird was chosen as one strong of flight, and also, perhaps, because it was anciently regarded as prophetic of the weather. Besides this, it is easily tamed, and as Noah retained its mate he had security for its return. And so it seems to have done, for it is described as going "forth to and fro." Each night it returned to the Ark.

(8, 9) He sent forth a dove . . . —From the nature of its food, the raven had not brought back to Noah any special information; but as the dove feeds on vegetable products, he hopes that he shall learn by her means what is the state of "the ground," the low-lying **adâmâh**. But as this species of bird does not fly far from its home, except when assembled in vast numbers, it quickly returned, finding water all around. This proves that the Ark had not settled upon a lofty eminence; for as it had been already aground 120 days, and as within another fortnight the waters had "abated from off the earth," it could only have been in some valley or plain among the mountains of Ararat that the waters were thus "on the face of the whole earth," the larger word, yet which certainly does not mean here the whole world, but only a very small region in the immediate neighborhood of the Ark.

(10-12) Again he sent forth the dove . . . —When after another week's delay, Noah again sent forth the dove, it remained away until "the time of evening," finding both food and ground on which it could alight near the Ark. It was not till nightfall that it came home, bringing to him "an olive leaf plucked off," or, possibly, "a fresh olive leaf." The olive tree, which grows abundantly in Armenia, is said to vegetate under water; but what Noah wanted to learn was, not whether the topmost boughs were emerging from the Flood, but whether the soil beneath was becoming free from water. Now, after a seven day's interval, when Noah again sent forth the dove, she did not return, "because the ground was dry." It is thus plain that the olive tree had had plenty of time on some of the higher lands, while the flood was subsiding, to sprout new leaves. From this event the olive leaf, thus sent by the regenerated earth to Noah in proof that she was ready to yield herself to him, has been ever since, among all mankind, the symbol of peace.

(13) The first day of the month.—This was exactly one month after the day on which Noah, for the third time, sent out the dove (verse 12). It was thus very slowly that the earth returned to its normal state. The intervals of seven days between the sending forth of the birds prove that the division of time into weeks was fully established, and also suggests that religious observances were connected with it.

The covering of the ark.—The word is elsewhere used of the covering of skins for the Tabernacle (Exod. 26:14; Num. 4:25), and it has probably a similar meaning here.

No one can read the narrative without noticing that Noah is not only described as shut up within the Ark, but as having very slight means of observing what was going on around. Had there been a deck, Noah would have known exactly the state of the Flood, whereas, peeping only through the **zohar**, he seems to have been able to see but little, possibly because his sight was obstructed by the overhanging eaves of the roof. Thus the freshly-plucked olive leaf was like a revelation to him. But when these skins were taken off, there were numerous apertures through which he could obtain an uninterrupted view, and he "looked, and, behold, the face of the **adâmâh** was dry."

(14) In the second month, on the seven and twentieth day of the month.—That is, fifty-seven days after Noah removed the covering, and a year and eleven days after the Flood began. The word rendered "dried" at the end of this verse is different from that translated "dried up" and "dry" in verse 13, and marks a further stage in the process. It should be translated, "was thoroughly dry."

(15-19) Go forth . . . —The vast extent of the Flood, and the total destruction of all that had existed before, is indicated by the repetition of the primeval command, in 1:22, "to be fruitful and multiply upon the earth." Whatever the Flood may have been with respect to the whole globe, it was to Noah and his race absolutely a new beginning of things.

(20) Noah builded an altar unto the Lord (Jehovah).—One result of the Flood was to sweep away all traces of the earthly paradise and of the subsequent abode of Adam; and it is probable also that Noah was removed far away from his previous home by the floating of the Ark. Thus to him and his family it was a new earth, with no holy places, no spots hallowed by the past history of man. He therefore determines to consecrate the earth to Jehovah, who had been the object of the worship of his family since the days of Enos, and therefore builds an altar, the first mentioned in the Bible. By so doing he provided for future generations a central spot and sanctuary, around which their religious ideas would group themselves. The animals offered were probably the seventh of all clean kinds (see note on 7:2). With Noah's burnt offerings we must not connect any of the later Levitical ideas. Apparently it was a simple thank offering, the dominant thought of which was hallowing man's future life by beginning it with worship.

(21) A sweet savour.—Heb., "a smell of satisfaction." The idea is not so much that the sacrifice gave God pleasure as that it caused Him to regard man with complacency. The anger at sin which had caused the Flood was over now, and there was peace between heaven and earth.

Said in his heart.—Heb., "to his heart": that is, "Jehovah determined with Himself, came to the settled purpose" (Comp. 17:17.)

For the imagination of man's heart is evil from his youth.—See 6:5. There seems at first sight to be an inconsistency between the two passages. For in the former place man's inborn sinfulness is described as an aggravation of his offense, while here it is used as a reason for mercy. But it is a characteristic of the Bible that it states the two sides of every principle with abrupt simplicity, and most heresies have arisen from seizing upon one side only, and omitting the other from view. Man is one whose every imagination of the heart is only evil continually. (Comp. Matt. 15:19.) In the antediluvian world, with death indefinitely postponed, these imaginations had been unrestrained, and had therefore led to habitual and inveterate sin; and so justice at last had smitten it. But when man strives against them, and sin is the result of infirmity, then mercy heals and grace strengthens the penitent. When man, therefore, began his renewed life by hallowing it with religion, God saw therein the pledge of a struggle on his part after holiness, and the proof that the world would never again become totally corrupt. In this changed state of things human weakness was a reason only for mercy, and God gave the promise that as long as the world shall last, so a total destruction of man and his works upon it shall never again take place by the same agency.

(22) While the earth remaineth . . . —The verse describes those great alterations upon which the well-being of the earth depends, whether considered absolutely, as of light and darkness, cold and heat, or with reference to man's labors, as of sowing and harvesting; or relatively with respect to vegetation, winter being earth's time of rest, and summer that of its activity.

As regards these promises, Delitzsch considers that they probably came to Noah as strong inward convictions in answer to his prayers during the sacrifice.

9

(1) God blessed Noah.—The blessing bestowed upon Noah, the second father of mankind, is exactly parallel to that given to our first father in Gen. 1:28, 29; 2:16, 17, with a significant addition growing out of the history of the past. There is the same command to fill the world with human life, and the same promise that the fear of man shall rest upon the whole animated creation; but this grant of dominion is so extended that the animals are now given to man for his food. But just as there was a restriction as regards Adam's food, the fruit of the tree of knowledge being refused him, so now there is a prohibition against the eating of blood. The addition is the sanctity given to human life, with the evident object of guarding against such a disruption of the human race as was the result of Cain's murder of Abel. Thus, then, man starts afresh upon his task of subjugating the earth, with increased dominion over the animal world, and with his own life more solemnly guarded and made secure.

(4) But flesh ... —The words are remarkable. "Only flesh in its soul, its blood, ye shall not eat." The King James Version is probably right in taking **blood** as in apposition to **soul**, which word means here the principle of animation, or that which causes an animal to live. This is God's special gift; for He alone can bestow upon that aggregation of solids and fluids which we call a body the secret principle of life. Of this hidden life the blood is the representative, and while man is permitted to have the body for his food, as being the mere vessel which contains this life, the gift itself must go back to God, and the blood as its symbol be treated with reverence.

(5) Your blood of your lives ... —As it is, then, the support of man's life, an animal which sheds it becomes guilty, and must be slain; and still more must those animals be destroyed which prey upon man. Thus there is a command given for the extirpation of the carnivora at the time when the more peaceful animals had just been saved. The last clause literally is ... "at the hand of man, at the hand of one that is his brother, will I require the soul of man." This has nothing to do with the avenger of blood. The near kinsman is here the murderer, and the commandment requires that even such an one should not be spared.

(6) By man ... —This penalty of life for life is not to be left to natural law, but man himself, in such a manner and under such safeguards as the civil law in each country shall order, is to execute the divine command. And thus protected from violence, both of man and beast, and with all such terrible crimes forbidden as had polluted Adam's beginning, Noah in peace and security is to commence afresh man's great work upon earth.

(9) I, behold, I establish my covenant ... —The covenant between God and man is thus solemnly introduced as Elohim's personal act. No covenant is mentioned as existing between Elohim and the antediluvian world; but distinctly now there is a step onward in all respects, and man, in the renovated earth after the Flood, is brought nearer to God by being admitted into covenant with Him. And not only is man

included in the covenant, but, first, those animals which had been with Noah in the Ark; and, secondly, those which had not been admitted there. For the words of verse 10 are: "From all that go out of the ark unto every beast of the earth" (the larger world). Plainly, the words imply the existence of a larger world-sphere than that in connection with Noah, and give the assurance that not only those now providentially preserved, but the animals everywhere, shall never again be in danger of a similar extinction.

(12) This is the token of the covenant. —The word rendered "token" really means "sign," and is a term that has met with very unfortunate treatment in our version, especially in the New Testament, where—as, for instance, in John's gospel—it is too frequently translated "miracle." Its meaning will best be seen by examining some of the places where it occurs: e.g., Gen. 17:11; Exod. 3:12; 12:13; 13:16; Num. 17:10; Josh. 2:12; Job 21:29; Pss. 65:8, 86:17, 135:9; Isa. 44:25. In the majority of these places the sign, or token, is some natural occurrence, but in its higher meaning it is a proof or indication of God's immediate working. We may dismiss, then, all such curious speculations as that no rain fell before the Flood, or that some condition was wanting necessary for producing this glorious symbol. What Noah needed was a guarantee and a memorial which, as often as rain occurred, would bring back to his thoughts the divine promise; and such a memorial was best taken from the natural accompaniments of rain.

Promises are revocable, and their fulfillment may depend upon man's co-agency; a covenant is irrevocable, and under no circumstances will the earth again be destroyed by water. (Comp. note on 17:2.)

(18) Ham is the father of Canaan. Though human life had thus begun again upon a firmer footing, yet evil and discord were soon to reappear, though in a milder form. No brother sheds a brother's blood, but in the next generation sin breaks forth afresh, and the human family is disunited thereby, the descendants of Canaan taking the place of the Cainites—without, indeed, their striking gifts, but nevertheless as a race foremost in trade and commerce. After enumerating the three sons of Noah, we are told: "Of"—more correctly, "from"—"them was the whole earth overspread," that is, "peopled."

(20, 21) Noah began to be an husband-

man.—Rather, "Noah, being a husbandman" (Heb., "a man of the **adâmâh**"), "began to plant a vineyard." Noah had always been a husbandman: it was the cultivation of the vine, still abundant in Armenia, that was new. Scarcely aware, perhaps, of the intoxicating qualities of the juice which he had allowed to ferment, he drank to excess, and became the first example of the shameful effects of intemperance.

(21) He was uncovered is, literally, "he uncovered himself." It was no accident, but a willful breach of modesty.

(22, 23) Ham . . . saw . . . and told.—The sin lay not in seeing, which might be unintentional, but in telling, especially if his purpose was to ridicule his father. His brothers, with filial piety, "took a garment," the loose outer robe or cloak enveloping the whole body, and with reverent delicacy walked backwards, and laid it upon their father's person.

(24) Noah . . . knew what his younger son had done unto him.—Heb., "his son, the little one." This can only mean his youngest son. So it is applied to Benjamin in 42:34; 43:29, and to David in I Sam. 16:11, where the words literally are, "there remaineth yet the little one." Now Ham was not the youngest son, but Japheth; and it is not Ham who is cursed, but Canaan. So far from Ham being accursed, his descendants were building mighty cities, such as Egyptian Thebes, Nineveh, and Babylon, were rearing palaces, digging canals, organizing governments, and founding empires at a time when the descendants of Japheth were wandering over Europe with no better weapons than implements of flint and bone. The application of the curse to Ham seems to have been suggested to commentators by the degradation of the African race in modern times, and especially by the prevalence of Negro slavery: but anciently the converse was the case, and for centuries the Egyptians, a Hamite race, made the Israelites serve them.

We must not extend, therefore, to Ham the curse pronounced upon Canaan. But what had Canaan done to deserve it? As "the son, the little one," was not Ham, so certainly it was not Japheth, but probably it was Canaan. He was the youngest son of Ham, and in Hebrew "son" is occasionally used for grandson (Gen. 29:5, 31:55), and so he might be described as Noah's youngest son, being the youngest member of his family. Origen quotes a tradition that Canaan was the first who saw Noah's ex-

posure, and that he told it to his father. Aben Ezra says that Canaan had done worse than mock, though the Scripture does not in words reveal his crime. With some such surmise we must be content; and the meaning seems to be, "Noah awoke from his wine, and knew what (Canaan) his youngest son (or grandson) had done unto him; and it was a deed so shameless that he said, 'Cursed be Canaan.' "

(25) Cursed be Canaan.—The prophecy of Noah takes the form of a poem, like Lamech's boast in chapter 4. In it Ham is passed over in silence, as though his unfilial conduct, recorded in verse 22, made him unworthy of a blessing, while it was not so wicked as to bring on him a curse. The whole weight of Noah's displeasure falls on Canaan, whose degraded position among the nations is thrice insisted upon.

A servant of servants.—That is, the most abject of slaves. This was fulfilled in the conquest of Canaan by Joshua, but the race had nevertheless a great future before it. The Hittites were one of the foremost nations of antiquity, and the Sidonians, Tyrians, and Phoenicians were such famous traders, that Canaanite is in our version translated "merchant," without even a note in the margin (e.g., Prov. 31:24). But the whole race was enslaved by one of the most terrible and degrading forms of idolatry, and as Shem's blessing is religious, so possibly is Canaan's curse.

(26) Blessed be the Lord God.—The greatness of Shem's blessing is shown by its taking the form of a hymn of praise to Jehovah, the personal God; and the patriarch's fervent outburst of thanksgiving was a presage of the hallelujahs that were to arise unto God from all mankind for the birth of that son of Shem in whom all nations were to be blessed.

(27) God shall enlarge Japheth.—First, the Deity is here "Elohim," following upon "Jehovah" in the preceding verse, and that with extraordinary exactness. Jehovah has never been the special name of the Deity worshiped by the race of Japheth. But it soon became the proper title of God in covenant with the race of Shem. It is plainly impossible to divide this most ancient poem into Elohistic and Jehovistic sections, and the theory, however plausible occasionally, fails in a crucial place like this. Next, there is a play upon the name of Japheth, or rather, **Yepheth**, our translators having made the same mistake as in changing Hebel into Abel. The Hebrew is "God enlarge

29

the enlarger" (not "God shall enlarge"). While, then, it is the special blessing of Shem that through him the voice of thanksgiving is to ascend to Jehovah, the God of grace; it is Elohim, the God of nature and of the universe, who gives to Japheth wide extension and the most numerous posterity.

He shall dwell in the tents of Shem.— (Rather, "let him dwell"). In one sense Shem now dwells in the tents of Japheth: for the Jews, the noblest representatives of Shem, dwell dispersed in Aryan countries. But the religious privileges of their race now belong to the family of Japheth. Carried by Jewish missionaries, like Paul, throughout the Roman world, they have become the property of the leading members of the Aryan race; and thus Japheth takes possession of the tents which by right of primogeniture belong to Shem. For "to dwell in the tents of Shem" is not so much to share them as to own them; and if the Jews retain some degree of faith, it has lost with them all expansive power; while the right interpretation of their Scriptures, and as well the maintenance as the propagation of the religion of their Messiah, are now in the hands of the descendants of Japheth. Yet Shem does not lose all pre-eminence: for again we read—

Canaan shall be his servant (rather, "their").—If Shem loses the foremost place of primogeniture, he is still a brother, and Canaan but a slave.

(29) All the days of Noah.—While Noah attained to the same age as the antediluvian patriarchs, 950 years, human life was fast diminishing. The whole life-time of Shem was 600 years; that of Peleg, a few generations afterward, only 239. After him only one man, Terah, is described as living more than 200 years, and of his age there is great doubt. (See note on 11:32.) Thus before Shem's death the age of man was rapidly shortening, and things were settling down to that condition in which they are set before us in profane literature.

10

The Ethnological Table (10:1-11:9)

(1) These are the generations (the **tôldôth) of the sons of Noah.**—The importance of this "table of the nations" can scarcely be overestimated. Its position is very remarkable. It stands at the end of grand traditional records of the mighty past, but belongs to a period long subsequent, giving us a picture of the division of the world at a time when nations and kingdoms had become settled, and their boundaries fixed; and it couples this with the confusion of tongues, difference of language being the great factor in this breaking up of the human race. Now, it is important to remember that it is not a genealogical table. It concerns peoples, and not individuals, and no names are mentioned which were not represented by political organizations. Generally even the names are not those of men, but of tribes or nations. We must also bear in mind that it works **backward**, and not forward. Taking the nations at some particular time, it groups them together, and classifies them according to the line to which they belonged.

As regards the order, it begins with Japheth, the youngest son—for never was there a translation more opposed to the undeviating rule of such sentences than that of our version in 10:21. "Shem ... the brother of Japheth the elder," instead of "Shem, the elder brother of Japheth." But Japheth is here placed first because so little was known of the nations sprung from him. It gives, moreover, the mere first division into main lines, and then, in spite of the grand future that awaited his descendants, it dismisses them in brief haste to their homes on the Black and Mediterranean seas. It next takes Ham. Now, Ham was to the family of Noah what Cain was to that of Adam: first in all worldly accomplishments, last in all the gifts of piety. Settling upon the Nile, the Tigris, and Euphrates, his progeny raised up mighty cities, while Japhethites were wandering in barbarous hordes over Europe, and the Shemites were pasturing their cattle upon the chalkdowns of Syria; whence, nevertheless, they soon came to do battle with the Hamites for the possession of Mesopotamia. Of the Hamites it brings the history down to the time of their settlement in Canaan, but as it mentions Sodom and Gomorrah as still standing, the document must be prior to the time of the destruction of those cities, eighteen centuries and more before Christ; while, as it describes the Canaanites as even then in possession of Palestine, and as formed into tribes in much the same way as just before the time of Moses, it is evident that a much longer period must have elapsed between the Flood and the birth of Abraham than is supposed. As the line of Shem was to be traced in subsequent **tôldôth**, it is not carried down as far as that of Ham, but stops at a great dividing line, at which the family breaks up into the race of Joktan and that of Peleg. To the former it ascribes thirteen nations, while the race of Peleg is left for future histories. The names of the Joktanite tribes also indicate the lapse of a lengthened period of time, as they abound in Arabic pecularities.

(1) Shem, Ham, and Japheth.—This is the undeviating arrangement of the three brothers. (See note on 9:24; 10:21.)

(2) The sons of Japheth.—Of these, seven main divisions are enumerated, some of which are subsequently subdivided:

1. **Gomer.**—Their original settlement was between Magog and Madai, that is, between the Scythians and the Medes. After remaining some time on the Caspian and Black Seas, on which latter they have left their name in the Crimea, a powerful branch of them struck across the center of Russia and skirted the Baltic. Generally they are the race to which the name is given of Celts.

2. **Magog.**—The Russians are their modern representatives.

3. **Madai.**—The Medes, who dwelt to the south and southwest of the Caspian.

4. **Javan.**—That is, Ionia, the land of the Greeks.

5. **Tubal.**—The Tibareni, on the south-east of the Black Sea.

6. **Meshech,**—a people of Colchis and Armenia.

7. **Tiras,**—the Thracians. This would make the Scandinavian race the modern representatives of Tiras.

In this enumeration the race of Japheth is described as occupying Asia Minor, Armenia, the countries to the west as far as the Caspian Sea, and thence northward to the shores of the Black Sea. Subsequently it spread along the northern shores of the Mediterranean and over all Europe. But though unnoticed by the writer, its exten-ion was equally remarkable toward the east. Parthia, Bactria, the Punjab, India, are equally Japhethite with Germany, Greece, and Rome; and in Sanscrit literature the Aryan first showed that genius, which, omit-ing the greatest of all books, the Semitic Bible, has made this race the foremost writers in the world.

(6) Ham.—Many derive this word from a Hebrew root, and explain it as signifying "hot," "sunburned," and so swarthy. Ja-pheth they connect with a word signifying "to be fair"; and so Ham is the progenitor of dark races, Japheth of those of a fair complexion, while the olive-colored spring from Shem. More probably it is "Chemi," the old name of Egypt "the land of Ham" (Ps. 78:51), called by Plutarch Chemia, and was taken from the "black" color of the soil.

The Hamites are grouped in three principal divisions:

1. **Cush.**—The home of the Cushites was on the Tigris and Euphrates, where Nimrod raised them to great power. Thence they spread into the southern peninsula of Arabia, and crossing the Red Sea at a later date, colonized Nubia and Abyssinia. Their high rank in old time is marked by the place held by them in the **Iliad** of Homer.

2. **Mizraim.**—Egypt. In form the word is a dual, and may point to the division of the country into Upper and Lower Egypt.

3. **Phut.**—The Lybians of North Africa.

4. **Canaan.**—See note on verses 15-19.

(8) Cush began Nimrod.—This does not mean that Nimrod was the son of Cush, but only that Cush was his ancestor. In the days of Nimrod population had become numer-ous, and whereas each tribe and family had hitherto lived in independence, subject only to the authority of the natural head, he was able, by his personal vigor, to reduce sever-al tribes to obedience, to prevail upon them to build and inhabit cities, and to consoli-date them into one body politic.

He began to be a mighty one.—Heb., **gibbor** = warrior. (See note on 6:4.)

(9) He was a mighty hunter.—When men were still leading a pastoral life, and were but poorly armed, the war with wild beasts was a most important and dangerous occu-pation. He next undertook the more serious duty of introducing order and rule among men who had hitherto lived in scattered groups without control, and without the means of suppressing feuds and of punish-ing deeds of violence.

(10) The beginning of his kingdom.—Nimrod's empire began with the cities enu-merated in this verse, and thence extended into Assyria, as is mentioned in verse 11. First, then, he established his sovereignty "in the land of Shinar": "that is, in Baby-lonia, the lower portion of Mesopotamia, as distinguished from Assyria, the upper por-tion. It is called "Sumir" in the cuneiform inscriptions. In Micah 5:6 Babylonia is called "the land of Nimrod." He had there four cities.

(11, 12) Out of that land went forth

Asshur.—So the LXX., Syriac, and Vulg.; but the Targum and most modern authorities rightly translate, "Out of that land he went forth into Assyria." We have here nothing to do with Asshur the son of Shem (see verse 22), but are occupied with Nimrod and the Hamites, who, after firmly establishing themselves in Babylonia, subsequently extended their influence northward. It is not necessary to suppose that this spread of Hamite civilization northward was the work of Nimrod personally; if done by his successors, it would, in Biblical language, be ascribed to its prime mover.

(13, 14) With Mizraim are connected seven inferior African races.

The Philistim.—The word Philistine means "emigrant," and is translated "alien, foreigner," by the LXX. We are here told that they came into Palestine as colonists from the Casluhim; but in Jer. 47:4; Amos 9:7, they are described as a colony from Caphtor. Probably the first Philistine settlers in Gerar (Gen. 26:1), and in the towns conquered by Judah (Judges 1:18), were Casluchians; but afterward, at the time when they struggled with Israel for empire, in the days of Samson, Eli, and Saul, there had been a second and larger immigration from Crete. As they seem to have spoken a Semitic tongue, they had apparently adopted the language of the Canaanites among whom they had settled, and especially of the Avim (Deut. 2:23).

(15-18) Canaan.—The meaning of this name is uncertain, as, most probably, it is a Hamitic word: if derived from a Semitic root, it may mean the "lowland." Though the Canaanites spoke a Semitic tongue at the time when we find them in Palestine, yet the assertion of the Bible that they were Hamites is confirmed by the testimony of profane writers, who say that their original home was on the Indian Ocean. They had probably been driven there by the pressure of Semitic races, with whose language they had already become familiar; and when, farther, they found a Semitic people thinly spread over Palestine, they may, while absorbing them, have been confirmed in the use of their tongue. So, subsequently, Abraham gave up Syriac for Hebrew; and though these are kindred dialects, yet they are often remote enough from one another (see Gen. 31:47). On the other hand, the whole character of the Canaanite religion and thought was Hamitic, and while they were active in commercial pursuits, and in culture far in advance of the Greeks, to whom they gave their alphabet, they were intensely sensuous in their worship and voluptuous in their manners. They are divided into eleven tribes:

Sidon.—This is remarkable as being the only town mentioned in the account either of Mizraim or of Canaan. All the rest are apparently the names of tribes still wandering about; and thus we gain a clearer idea both of the antiquity of this early record, and also of the great advance made by Nimrod in founding so many cities. Sidon, situated on the seashore, about thirty miles north of Tyre, thus early became a settled community and the seat of social life, because of its advantage for fishing (from which its name is derived), and also for commerce.

Heth.—The Kheta, or Hittites, a powerful race, whose language and monuments have recently become the object of careful study. They seem subsequently to have possessed not only Syria, but also a large portion of Asia Minor. (See note on 23:3.)

The Jebusite.—This race held the territory afterward occupied by Benjamin, and retained Jerusalem until the time of David (II Sam. 5:6-9. See note on 14:18.)

The Amorite.—Or rather, "Emorite," that is, mountaineer. Next to the Kheta, or Hittites, they were the most powerful race in Palestine, holding the hill country of Judea, where they had five kings (Josh. 10:5), and a large district on the eastern side of the Jordan (II Sam. 9:10).

The Hivite.—At Sichem (34:2), at Gibeon (Josh. 9:7), and near Hermon and Lebanon (Josh. 11:3; Judges 3:3).

Afterward were the families of the Canaanites spread abroad.—This may mean either that they spread inward, or may refer to the numerous colonies of the Tyrians or the Mediterranean. While in Babylonia the Hamites are described as black, this branch was called Phoenicians, from their ruddy color, in contrast with the olive-colored Semitic stock. As they came by sea from the Indian Ocean, their earliest settlement was on the coast, and thus Sidon is called "the first-born" of Ham. Thence they advanced into the interior, and though few in number, absorbed by their superior culture the inhabitants of Palestine. It is probably this expansion inward which is here referred to.

(19, 20) The border ... —The boundaries given are Sidon in the north, Gerar and Gaza in the south and southwest, and from there to the Dead Sea.

(21-23) Shem ... the brother of Japheth

the elder.—Really, "the elder brother of Japheth." Though the rules of Hebrew grammar will admit of no other rendering, it is remarkable that both the Syriac and the Vulgate make the same mistake as our own version. In designating Shem as "the father of all the children of Eber," attention is called to the fact that the descendants of Peleg, his elder son, are omitted from this table, and reserved for the **Tôldôth Shem.** (See note on 11:10.)

Elam.—"The primitive inhabitants of Elam were a race closely allied to the Accadians, and spread over the whole range of country which stretched from the southern shores of the Caspian to the Persian Gulf." The Semitic Asshur expelled a Hamite race from Assyria. See chap. 14 on the conquests of the Elamite Chedorlaomer.

Asshur.—This Semitic stock seems to have been the first to settle on the Tigris, as the Hamites were the first to settle on the Euphrates. Finally, as we have seen (verse 11), they conquered the whole country.

Aram.—As Asshur means "plain," so Aram means "highland." It was originally the name of the Lebanon ranges, and thus Damascus is called Aram in II Sam. 8:5. Subsequently the race so extended itself as to possess Mesopotamia, a lowland country, but called, as early as Gen. 24:10, "Aram of the two rivers." The greatness of Aram will be best seen by examining those places in our version where Syria and Syrian are spoken of, and which, in the Hebrew, are really Aram.

(24) Arphaxad begat Salah.—Heb., **Shelah.** The rest of the chapter is devoted to giving an account of the settlements of the Joktanite Arabs.

(25) Peleg; for in his days was the earth divided.—This may refer to the breaking up of the race of Shem into separate nations, which severally occupied a distinct region; and so, while Joktan took Arabia, and in course of time expelled the Hamites from that country, Asshur, Aram, and Peleg occupied the regions on the north and northwest.

(26-31) Joktan.—"The little one," as being a younger son. Of the thirteen divisions of his family, few are of any importance, though several of the names are curious from their connection with the Arabic language. The Joktanite country was Arabia Felix, or Yemen. As the people led a pastoral life without founding cities, the traces of their tribal names are insignificant.

(32) After their generations.—Heb., "according to their **Tôldôth.**" This makes it probable that each family preserved in some way an historical record of its descent; and as this table is called the **Tôldôth of the Sons of Noah,** it was probably formed by a comparison of numerous **Tôldôth,** each showing the descent of various members of the three great families into which the sons of Noah were divided.

11

(1) The whole earth.—That is, "all mankind." After giving the connection of the various races of the then known world, we go back to the reason of this dispersion, which is found in the confusion of tongues.

Of one language, and of one speech.—Literally, "of one lip, and of words one": that is, both the pronunciation and the vocabulary were identical.

(2) As they journeyed.—The word literally refers to the pulling up of the tent pegs, and sets the human family before us as a band of nomads, wandering from place to place, and shifting their tents as their cattle needed fresh pasture.

From the east.—So all the versions. Mount Ararat was to the northwest of Shinar, and while so lofty a mountain could not have been the spot where the Ark rested, yet neither could any portion of Armenia or of the Carduchian Mountains be described as to the east of Babylonia. The Bible elsewhere seems to point to Armenia as the cradle of the human race. Most modern commentators, therefore, translate "eastward," and such certainly is the meaning of the word in 13:11, where also the versions, excepting our own, render "from the east."

Land of Shinar.—See note on 10:10. The whole of Chaldea is a level plain, and the soil immensely rich, as it is an alluvial deposit, which still goes on forming at the head of the Persian Gulf.

(3) Let us make brick, and burn them throughly.—Heb., "for a burning." Bricks in the East usually are simply dried in the sun, and this produces a sufficiently durable building material. It marks a great progress in the arts of civilization that these nomads had learned that clay when burned becomes insoluble; and their buildings with "slime," or native pitch, for cement would be virtually indestructible.

(4) A tower, whose top may reach unto heaven.—The Hebrew is far less hyperbolical: namely, "whose head (or top) is in the heavens," or skies, like the walls of the Canaanite cities (Deut. 1:28). The object of the builders was twofold: first, they wished to have some central beacon which might guide them in their return from their wanderings; and secondly, they had a distinctly ambitious object, for by remaining as one nation they would be able to reduce to obedience all the tribes now perpetually wandering away from them, and so would "make them a name." But we undoubtedly find a political purpose of preventing that dispersion of mankind which God had commanded (1:28), and of using the consequent aggregation of population for the attaining to empire. There was probably some one able and ambitious mind at the bottom of this purpose, and doubtless it had very many advantages: for it is what is now called centralization.

(5-7) The Lord came down.—The narrative is given in that simple anthropological manner usual in the Book of Genesis, which so clearly sets before us God's loving care of man, and here and in 28:21 the equity of divine justice. For Jehovah is described as a mighty king, who, hearing in His upper and heavenly dwelling of man's ambitious purpose, determines to go and inspect the work in person, that having seen, he may deal with the offenders justly. Having, then, inspected the tower and the city nestling around it, the Deity affirms that this centralization is injurious to man's best interests, and must be counteracted by an opposite principle, namely, the tendency of mankind to make constant changes in language, and thereby to break up into different communities, kept permanently apart by the use of different tongues. Already there are thoughts among them of universal empire, and if thus the spread of mankind be hindered, and its division into numerous nations, each contributing its share to the progress and welfare of the world, be stopped, man will remain a poor debased creature, and will fail utterly in accomplishing the purpose for which he was placed upon earth. "Go to," therefore, He says, in irony of their twice-repeated phrase, "we will go down, and make their speech unintelligible to one another." Now, though there is no assertion of a miracle here, yet we may well believe that there was an extraordinary quickening of a natural law which existed from the first. This, however, is but a secondary question, and the main fact is the statement that the divine means

for counteracting man's ambitious and ever-recurring dream of universal sovereignty is the law of diversity of speech. To this day diversity of language is a powerful factor in keeping nations apart, or in preventing portions of the same kingdom from agreeing heartily together. And thus at Babel the first attempt to bind the human family into one whole came to an ignominious end.

(8) The Lord (Jehovah) **scattered them abroad from thence upon the face of all the earth: and they left off to build the city.**— And so the divine purpose of occupying the world was carried into effect.

(9) Therefore is the name of it called Babel.—(See 10:10.) Man calls his projected bity Bab-el, "the gate"—that is, the court— "of God"; God calls it Babble; for in all languages indistinct and confused speech is represented by the action of the lips in producing the sound of **b**. The exact Hebrew word for this was **balbal**—the Greek verb, **bambaino**; the Latin, **balbutio**; and a man who stammered was called **balbus**. The town, then, keeps its first name, but with a contemptuous meaning attached to it.

The Tôldôth Shem

(10-26) These are the generations of Shem.—Here also, as in chap. 5, there is a very considerable divergence between the statements of the Hebrew, the Samaritan, and the Septuagint texts. According to the Hebrew, the total number of years from Shem to the birth of Abram was 390, but scholars have long acknowledged that these genealogies were never intended for chronological purposes, and that so to employ them leads only to error.

Like the genealogy of Seth, in chap. 5, the Tôldôth Shem also consists of ten generations, and thus forms, according to Hebrew ideas respecting the number ten, a perfect representation of the race.

Nahor, "panting, earnest struggle," indicates, most probably, the commencement of that seeking after a closer communion with God which made his descendants withdraw from contact with the rest and form a separate community, distinguished by its firm hold of the doctrine of the unity of the Godhead. From the words of Joshua (Josh. 24:2) it is plain, not only that idolatry was generally practiced among the descendants of Shem, but that even Nahor and Terah were not free from its influence. Yet, probably, the monotheism of Abraham was preceded by an effort to return to the purer doctrine of their ancestors in Nahor's time, and the gods which they still worshiped were the teraphim, regarded both by Laban and Rachel (31:30, 34) as a kind of inferior household genius, which brought good luck to the family.

Terah, "wandering," indicates the commencement of that separation from the rest caused by religious differences, which ended in the migration of Abram into Canaan.

In Abram, "high-father," we have a prophetic name, indicative of the high purpose for which the father of the faithful was chosen. There is a difficulty about the date of his birth. We read that "Terah lived seventy years, and begat Abram, Nahor, and Haran"; and in verse 32 that "the days of Terah were two hundred and five years." But Stephen says that Terah died in Haran before Abram's migration (Acts 7:4), and in 12:4 we are told that Abram was seventy-five years of age when he departed from that country. Either, therefore, Terah was a hundred and thirty years old when Abram was born—and Abram was a younger, and not the older son—or the Samaritan text is right in making the total age of Terah a hundred and forty-five years. The latter is probably the true solution: first, because Nahor died at the age of a hundred and forty-eight, and it is not probable that Terah outlived him by too much; for human life, as we have seen, was progressively shortening after the Flood: and secondly, because Abram, in 17:17, speaks of it as almost an impossibility for a man to have a son when he is a hundred years old. Had he been born when his father was a hundred and thirty, he could scarcely have spoken in this way.

The Tôldôth Terah

(27) Now these are the generations.—This **tôldôth,** which extends to 25:11, is one of the most interesting in the Book of Genesis, as it gives us the history of the patriarch Abraham, in whom God was pleased to lay the foundation of the intermediate dispensation and of the Jewish Church, by whose institutions and psalmists and prophets the light of true religion was to be maintained, and the way prepared for the coming of Christ. But though Abraham is the central figure, yet the narrative is called the **Tôldôth Terah.** It connects Abraham with the past, and shows that, through Terah and the **tôldôth** which ended in him, he was the representative of Shem.

Terah begat Abram.—Commentators, in their endeavor to make Stephen's assertion in Acts 7:4 agree with the numbers of the Hebrew text, have supposed that Abram was not the eldest son, and that the first place was given him because of his spiritual pre-eminence. But this is contrary to the rules of the Hebrew language, and the failure of the attempt to deprive Shem of his birthright by a mistranslation of 10:21 confirms Abram's claim to the same prerogative.

(28) Haran died before his father.—Heb., "in the presence of his father." This is the first recorded instance of a premature death caused by natural decay.

In Ur of the Chaldees.—"Ur-Casdim," the city of Mugheir. Abraham migrated from a town which was then a famous seat of learning, and where even the ordinary transactions of life were recorded on tablets of terra cotta. Very probably, therefore, he carried with him bricks and cylinders inscribed with these ancient records. We are no longer, therefore, surprised at the striking similarity between the narratives in the Book of Genesis prior to the migration of Abraham and those preserved in the cuneiform inscriptions. But the believer in inspiration cannot fail to be struck also at their dissimilarity. The cuneiform inscriptions are polytheistic, acknowledging twelve superior gods, and of gods inferior a countless multitude. The Semitic race is accused of adding to these a number of goddesses. Of all this there is no trace in the Biblical records; nor is there in the whole Chaldean literature anything so grand and divine as the thoughts expressed in the opening words of Genesis: "In the beginning God created the heaven and the earth."

As Ur is an Accadian word, we must reject all Semitic interpretations of its meaning. It was a walled town, and the great port for the commerce of the Persian Gulf, while around it lay a marvelously rich country, said to be the original home of the wheat plant, and famous for its dates and other fruits. Its being called Ur-Casdim, "Ur of the Chaldees," shows that they had already won it from the Accadians when Terah dwelt there. Its subsequent name, Mugheir, probably means "mother of bitumen"—that is, producer of it.

(29) Iscah.—Not the same as Sarai, for we learn in 20:12 that she was Abraham's half-sister—that is, a daughter of Terah by another wife. Marriages between near relatives seem to have been allowed at this time, and were perhaps even common for religious reasons (see 24:3, 4; 28:1, 2), but not marriages between those actually by the same mother.

(31) They went forth with them.—This may possibly mean that they went forth in one body; but the phrase is strange, and the Samaritan, followed by the LXX and Vulgate, by a slight transposition of the letters reads, "And he (Terah) brought them forth."

Haran.—The Charran of Acts 7:4. The name must not be confounded with that of Haran, the father of Lot, as really it is in the Heb. **Kharan**, and was so called in Accadian times, in which language the word means "road," being the key of the highway from the east to the west. It was both a very early and a very late outpost of Chaldean power.

Terah's migration was partly perhaps a movement of a tribe of the Semites northward (see note on verse 28), but chiefly it had a religious motive: for Ur was the special seat of the worship of the moon-god, Sin; and though Terah had not attained to the purity of Abraham's faith, yet neither was he altogether an idolater. But why did they intend "to go into the land of Canaan"? As Abram subsequently continued this migration in simple dependence upon God's guidance (12:1), it was probably the divine rather than the human purpose that is here expressed. We gather also that the divine summons came to Abram in Ur (see 15:7; Neh. 9:7; Acts 7:2), but we learn in 12:1 that his final destination was not then definitely told him.

(32) The days of Terah.—See note on verse 26. According to the Samaritan text, Abram left Haran in the same year as that in which Terah died. Nahor had probably joined Terah about this time, as we find him subsequently settled in Haran (24:10); and moreover, Abram is expressly commanded to leave "his kindred and his father's house," whereas all those who are mentioned by name as going with Terah shared in Abram's subsequent migration. (See verse 31.)

12

(1) Now the Lord had said unto Abram.—Heb., "And Jehovah said unto Abram." There is no new beginning; but having briefly sketched the family from which Abram sprang, and indicated that he had inherited from them the right of primogeni-

ture, the narrative next proceeds to the primary purpose of the **Tôldôth Terah,** which is to show how in Abram Jehovah prepared for the fulfillment, through Israel, of the protevangelium contained in the promise made to Eve at the fall (3:15).

Thy country.—A proof that Abram and his father were no new settlers at Ur, but that the race of Shem had at this time long held sway there, as is now known to have been the case.

Thy kindred.—This rendering is supported by 43:7; but it more probably means "thy birthplace." It is the word translated "nativity" in 11:28, where its meaning is settled by the prefixed "land"; and the sense is probably the same here. If so, the command certainly came to Abram at Ur, though most of the versions suppose that it happened at Haran.

A land that I will shew thee.—In 11:31 it is expressly said that the land was Canaan, but possibly this knowledge was concealed from the patriarch himself for a time, and neither he nor Terah knew on leaving Ur what their final destination would be.

(2, 3) Thou shalt be a blessing.—More correctly, "Be thou a blessing." The promises made to Abram are partly personal and partly universal, embracing the whole world. In return for all that he abandons he is to become the founder of a powerful nation, who will honor his name, and teach the inheritors of their spiritual privileges to share in their veneration for him. But in the command to "be" or "become a blessing," we reach a higher level, and it is the glory of Abram's faith that it was not selfish, and in return for his consenting to lead the life of a stranger, he was to be the means of procuring religious privileges, not only for his own descendants, but also "for all families of the earth."

I will bless ... —These words indicate relations mysteriously close between Jehovah and Abram, whereby the friends and enemies of the one become so equally to the other. But in the second clause the King James version has not noticed an essential difference between the verbs used. They occur together again in Exod. 22:28, and are there more correctly rendered by "revile" and "curse." The one word signifies to treat lightly and contemptuously, the other to pronounce a curse, usually in a judicial manner. We might, therefore, translate, "I will curse—pass a sentence of rejection upon—him that speaketh lightly of, or revileth thee."

In thee shall all families of the earth be blessed.—Henceforward Abram and the nation sprung from him were to be the intermediaries between God and mankind, and accordingly revelation was virtually confined to them. But though the knowledge of God's will was to be given through them, it was for the benefit of all the families of every race and kindred distributed throughout the habitable world, the adâmâh (Rom. 3:29; 10:12, etc.).

(4) Abram ... departed out of Haran.—The command given him in Ur may have been repeated in Haran; but more probably Abram had remained there only on account of Terah.

(5) Their substance that they had gathered.—Not cattle only, but wealth of every kind. As we have no data about the migration of Terah, except that it was after the death of Haran, and that Haran left children, we cannot tell how long the family rested at their first halting place, but it was probably a period of several years; and as Abram was "very rich in silver and in gold," he had apparently engaged there in trade, and thus possibly knew the course which the caravans took.

The souls that they had gotten.—Heb., "had made." These were Abram's dependents and slaves (comp. 14:14), though the word "slave" suggests a different relation to us than that which existed between Abram and his household. Their descendants were most certainly incorporated into the Israelitish nation, and we have direct testimony that Abram gave them careful religious training (18:19). Thus the Jewish traditions record a fact, and by acknowledging Abram's household as proselytes admit their claim to incorporation with the race.

Into the land of Canaan they came.—Three hundred miles separated him from Canaan. The ford by which he crossed the Euphrates was probably that at Jerabolus, the ancient Carchemish. The difficulty of passing so great a river with so much substance and people, and cattle would give fresh importance to his title of "the Hebrew," **the passer over,** already his by right of descent from Eber, so named from the passage of the Tigris. From Carchemish Abram's route would lie to the southwest, by Tadmor and Damascus. Only about a year elapsed between Abram's departure from Kharan and his settlement in Canaan.

(6) The place of Sichem.—Heb., "Shechem." This word signifies "shoulder," and was the name of the ridge uniting Mounts Ebal and Gerizim, the summits of which are about two miles apart.

The plain of Moreh.—Heb., "the oak of Moreh." It was here that Jacob buried the strange gods brought by his household from Haran (35:4), and here, too, Joshua set up the stone of testimony (Josh. 24:26; Judges 9:6); but as in Deut. 11:30 the oaks (wrongly translated in most places as "plains") are described in the plural, it is probable that the word is to be taken as a collective for an oak grove. Such shady spots were favorite places for the tents of the wandering patriarchs.

The Canaanite was then in the land.—This is no sign of post-Mosaic authorship, nor a later interpolation, as if the meaning were that the Canaanite was there at that time, but is so no longer. What really is meant is that Abram on his arrival found the country no longer in the hands of the old Semitic stock, but occupied by the Canaanites, who seem to have gained the ascendancy, not so much by conquest as by gradual and peaceful means. We gather from the Egyptian records that this had taken place not very long before Abram's time.

(7) The Lord appeared unto Abram.—This is the first time that any appearance of the Deity is mentioned. Always previously the communications between God and man had been direct, without the intervention of any visible medium. But from now on we read repeatedly of a divine appearance, and this visible manifestation is subsequently connected with the phrase "an angel of Jehovah" (see 16:7; 22:11, etc.), and less frequently "an angel of God" (21:17; Judges 6:20; 13:9). There is a question whether this was a created angel or an anticipation of the incarnation of Christ.

There builded he an altar unto the Lord.—By doing so he took possession of the land for Jehovah, and consecrated it to Him. The altar would, further, be a place of public worship and of sacrifice. In a similar spirit Noah had taken possession of the renovated earth (8:20).

(8) He removed.—It was the usual condition of the nomad life, and Abram's wealth in cattle would make frequent changes necessary. His first long halt was in the hill country between Beth-el and Hai, or rather Ai, as in Josh. 8:1-3. Here, too, Abram made open profession of his faith, and worshiped with his household at an altar dedicated to Jehovah.

(9) Toward the south.—The Negeb, or dry land.

Abram's Visit to Egypt

(10) There was a famine in the land.—This famine must have happened within a few years after Abram reached Canaan; for he was seventy-five years of age on leaving Haran, and as Ishmael, his son by an Egyptian slave-woman, was thirteen years old when Abram was ninety-nine, only about eight years are left for the events recorded in chaps. 12-16. As rain falls in Palestine only at two periods of the year, the failure of either of these seasons would be immediately felt, especially in a dry region like the Negeb, and at a time when, with no means of bringing food from a distance, men had to depend upon the annual products of the land. As Egypt is watered by the flooding of the Nile, caused by the heavy rains which fall in Abyssinia, it probably had not suffered from what was a mere local failure in South Palestine; and Abram, already far on his way to Egypt, was forced by the necessity of providing fodder for his cattle to run the risk of proceeding there. In Canaan he had found a thinly scattered Canaanite population for whom probably he would have been a match in war; in Egypt he would find a powerful empire, and would be at the mercy of its rulers. It is proof of Abram's faith that in this necessity he neither retraced his steps (Heb. 11:15), nor sought a new home. For he went to Egypt with no intention of settling, but only "to sojourn there," to remain there for a brief period, after which, with returning rains he would go back to Canaan.

(11-13) Thou art a fair woman.—From 20:13 it appears that on leaving Haran Abram and Sarai had agreed upon adopting this expedient, which seems to us so strangely contrary to the faith which the patriarch was at that very time displaying. Perhaps Abram may have depended upon Sarai's cleverness to help herself out of the difficulty; but such a mixture of faith and weakness, of trust in God in abandoning so much and trust in worldly policy for preservation in a foreseen danger, cannot but make us feel how much of infirmity there was even in a character otherwise so noble.

(13) My sister.—True literally, as Sarai was Terah's daughter (20:12), but absolutely false, as it implied that she was wholly his sister, and therefore not his wife.

(14, 15) Pharaoh is not the name of a person, but was the title borne by all the Egyptian monarchs.

(15) The princes ... commended her before Pharaoh.—In the days of Abram Canaan was the highway to Egypt, and so large an immigration of men of the Semitic stock found their way there that they overspread the whole Delta, and finally, under the name of Hyksos, made themselves masters of the throne of Pharaohs, and retained their supremacy for several centuries. To keep out these hordes, Amenemhai had built a chain of fortresses, with a connecting wall. On arriving at this wall, so powerful a sheik, with so large a following, would be interrogated by the Egyptian scribes, and a report sent to the Pharaoh.

(16) He entreated Abram well.—It was usual to give the relatives a sum of money when taking a daughter or sister to wife. The presents here show that Pharaoh fully believed that he was acting lawfully, while the largeness of them proves that Sarai, in spite of her years, was looked upon as a valuable acquisition.

(19) So I might have taken her to me to wife.—The Hebrew is, "and I took her to me to wife": that is, I took her with the intention of making her my wife. During the interval before the marriage Pharaoh and his household were visited with such marked troubles that he became alarmed, and possibly Sarai then revealed to him her true relationship to Abram. We find in Esth. 2:12 that in the case of maidens there was a probation of twelve months duration before the marriage took place, and Sarai was probably saved by some such formality. The conduct of Pharaoh is upright and dignified; nor ought we to disbelieve his assurance that he had acted upon the supposition that Sarai might lawfully be his. The silence of Abram seems to indicate his consciousness that Pharaoh had acted more righteously than himself.

13

Abram's Return From Egypt and His Separation From Lot

(1-4) He went on his journeys.—The Vulgate very reasonably translates, "by the same route by which he had come."

(5, 6) Lot.—He, too, had possibly received presents in Egypt, for we find him rivaling his uncle in wealth; and, like Abram, he was the chief of a powerful clan.

The repetition that "the land was not able to bear them," and that "they could not dwell together," implies that the difficulty had long been felt before it led to an open rupture.

(7) The Perizzite.—As the Canaanites devoted their main strength to a maritime life and trade, they would not attempt to extirpate these natives, but would be content with driving them into the interior. As thus some districts would be occupied by the dominant Canaanites, and others by these aborigines, two such large clans as those of Abram and Lot would find it difficult to discover unoccupied land enough to provide pasture for their cattle. The land must have been thinly peopled for it to have been possible for them to do this, even when they had arranged to dwell apart.

(8, 9) Let there be no strife.—It is evident that Lot was beginning to take part with his herdmen, and regard himself as an injured man. But Abram meets him with the utmost generosity, acknowledges that their growth in wealth rendered a separation necessary, and gives him his choice. And Lot accepts it. Instead of feeling that it was due to his uncle's age and rank to yield to him the preference, he greedily accepts the offer, selects the region that seemed to offer the greatest earthly advantages, but finds in the long run that it has perils which far outweigh its promises of wealth and pleasure.

(10) The plain of Jordan.—This word **Ciccar**, literally means the "circuit" and is the proper name of the Jordan Valley, and especially of the Plain of Jericho. It is now called the Ghor, or "depression." Most of the valley lies below the level of the Mediterranean, the Sea of Galilee being about 682 feet below it, and the Dead Sea no less than 1,292 feet. As the watershed to the south rises to a level of 200 feet above the Mediterranean, all egress for the waters is thereby cut off, and here are numerous proofs that at some distant period the whole valley, about 150 miles in length, was a succession of large lakes. But even in Abram's days the Jordan poured down a far larger volume of water than at present; for by the loss of its forests the climate of Palestine has become much more dry than of old, and regions once fertile are now barren. And as the supply of water has become less than that lost by evaporation, the Dead Sea has gradually receded, and left around it arid wastes covered over with incrustations of salt.

As the garden of the Lord.—This "barren tract" was once the Ciccar, and the traces of ancient irrigation and aqueducts attest its former fertility. It was upon this district, "well watered everywhere," that Lot gazed so covetously, and its richness is indicated by a double comparison: for, first, it was like Jehovah's garden in Eden, watered by its four rivers; and next, it was like Egypt, rendered fertile by artificial means.

As thou comest unto Zoar.—This makes no sense whatsoever. No person on the route to Egypt could possibly take Zoar in his way; and of the five cities of the plain this was the least like Paradise. The Syriac has preserved the right reading, namely, Zoan. This city was situated on the eastern side of the Tanaitic branch of the Nile, at the head of a fertile plain, called "the field of Zoan" in Ps. 78:12. Through this rich and well-watered region Lot had lately traveled in Abram's company, and the luxuriant vegetation there made it not unworthy to be compared with Paradise.

(11) Lot journeyed east.—This is the word translated "eastward" in 2:8, and "from the east" in 11:2. Here it can only mean "toward the east."

(12, 13) Lot dwelled in the cities of the plain.—Heb., "of the Ciccar." Not as yet within their walls, but in their neighborhood, and evidently with a longing "toward Sodom," where, in chapter 19, we find him sitting in the gate as a citizen, and with his tent changed to a house. While, then, Abram continued to lead a hardy life as a stranger upon the bracing hills, Lot sighed for the less self-denying habits of the city.

(14) The Lord said unto Abram.—The departure of Lot was certainly a great grief to Abram; for he lost thereby the companionship of the relative who had shared his abandonment of his country, and whom, probably, in his childless state, he had regarded as his heir. Jehovah, therefore, consoles him by a more definite promise of the possession of the whole land of which he had so generously given Lot the choice, and by the assurance that his own seed should be numerous as the dust of the earth. We may also feel sure that as Lot was deteriorating, so Abram was drawing nearer to God, and walking more closely with Him; and hence the fuller assurance of the divine blessing.

(18) The plain of Mamre.—(Heb., "oaks of Mamre.") Mamre was an Amorite, then living, and as he was confederate with Abram, it was apparently with the consent of the Amorites, and by virtue of the treaty entered into with them, that Abram made this oak-grove one of his permanent stations.

Hebron.—That is, "alliance." Hebron was perhaps so called from the confederacy formed between Abram and the Amorites. (Comp. 10:16.)

14

Invasion of the Jordan Valley by Chedorlaomer, King of Elam

(1) It came to pass.—Connected with the settlement of Lot in the Jordan Valley is one of the most remarkable episodes in the whole Bible. The way in which the patriarch is described in it, as "Abram the Hebrew," seems certainly to suggest that we have to do here with a narrative of foreign origin.

Its incorporation with the history admirably sets forth the consequences of Lot's choice in the troubles, and even ruin, which overtook him, the bravery and power of Abram, and his generosity to the rescued kings. It is also most interesting, as showing Abram's relation to the Amorites, among whom he lived, and the existence in Palestine of a Semitic population, who still worshiped "the most high God," and over whom one of the noblest figures in the Old Testament was king. The narrative is Jehovistic, for Abram calls God **Jehovah El Elion,** but is, nevertheless, of such ancient date as to forbid the acceptance of the theory which regards the occurrence of the name Jehovah as a proof of later authorship.

Shinar.—See on 10:10.

(2) Bera king of Sodom.—The failure of the attempt to explain the names of these five kings, and of the cities over which they ruled (with one or two exceptions), by the help of the Hebrew language makes it probable that the inhabitants of the Ciccar were of some Hamite stock who had colonized this region from the east. They do not seem to have had much affinity either with the Amorites or with the Jebusites, their neighbors.

(3) All these were joined together.—Were united in a confederacy, and so formed a pentapolis, or group of five allied towns, like the Philistine league with its five lords (I Sam. 6:16-18).

The vale of Siddim.—The name **sidd** is still given by the Arabs to the cliffs or banks of marl which run along the southern

edge of the plain of Jericho; and with this agrees Aben-Ezra's explanation, who derives the word from the Hebrew **sid,** "chalk."

Which is the salt sea.—Probably "the vale of Siddim" was the name of the whole district in which these sidds, or bluffs, are situated.

(4) They served.—That is, "paid a yearly tribute," that they might be exempt from Chedorlaomer's marauding expeditions (see II Kings 18:7). There must, therefore, have been envoys going from time to time to and from the Jordan Valley to Shinar.

(5) The Rephaims.—From this wide dispersion of them we may safely conclude that they belonged to the earlier settlers in the land, and that only their rulers, like Og (Josh. 9:10), were Amorites.

(10) The vale of Siddim was full of slime-pits.—That is, of holes from which bitumen had been excavated, and the places from where it had been dug out, and which are often very deep, formed dangerous impediments in the way of the defeated side.

(13) Abram the Hebrew.—That is, "the immigrant" (from beyond the Euphrates), but also his patronymic from Eber, who in like manner had crossed the Tigris. It was, no doubt, the usual title of Abram among the Canaanites, and has been preserved from the original document, from which also probably was taken the exact description of Lot in verse 12.

(14) Abram . . . armed . . .—As Abram's cattle would often be exposed to danger from the Amalekites, who throughout the Biblical history appear as a race of inveterate plunderers, there is no reason to doubt that these men were trained and practiced in the use of weapons. This large number of servants born in his house, and of an age capable of undergoing the fatigues of a rapid pursuit, added to the older men left to defend and take care of the cattle, proves that Abram was the chieftain of a powerful tribe.

Dan.—Dan is about 140 miles from Hebron, where Abram began his march. (See Laish, at the source of the Jordan; Judges 18:29.)

(15) Hobah . . . on the left hand of Damascus.—That is, "to the north," as the Hebrews looked eastward in defining the quarters of the heaven. The victory had thus been followed up with great energy, the pursuit having lasted, according to Josephus, the whole of the next day and night after that on which the attack was made. At Hobah the mountains cease, and the great plain of Damascus begins, and further pursuit was therefore useless.

(17) The valley of Shaveh.—That is, the valley of the plain. It was the place where Absalom erected his pillar (II Sam. 18:18), and lay on the northern side of Jerusalem, probably where the Kedron valley widens out. Its other name, "the king's dale," may have been given it from this meeting of the kings of Salem and Sodom with the victorious Abram; but Onkelos, with far greater probability, considers that it was so called because upon this level ground the kings of Judah in subsequent times assembled and exercised their forces.

(18) Melchizedek king of Salem.—We may feel certain that the place was really Jerusalem (Ps. 76:2); for it lay on Abram's route homeward, and was within a reasonable distance of Sodom.

In Melchizedek we have a type of Christ (Ps. 110:4; Heb. 5:6, 10; 7:1-21), and so venerable is his character and aspect that Jewish tradition identified him with the patriarch Shem, thus reconciling also to themselves his superiority over their forefather Abraham. But this idea is contradicted by Heb. 7:3. He was more probably the king of some Semitic race who still occupied Salem, but from whom it was at a subsequent period wrested by the Jebusites (Judges 19:10, 11).

The typical value of Melchizedek's priesthood lies not merely in his being "king of righteousness and king of peace," but even more in his priesthood being universal, limited by no external ordinances, and attached to no particular race or people. Moreover, he is a king-priest (Ps. 110), and by taking precedence over Abram, and blessing him, and receiving of him tithes, he became the representative of a higher priesthood than any that could spring from Abram's loins.

Bread and wine.—The representatives of food of all kinds, both liquid and solid. Though the primary object of this offering was the refreshing of the bodies of Abram's men, and of the prisoners wearied with their long march to and fro, yet we cannot but recognize in it a foreshowing of the bestowal by Christ, the antitype, upon His Church of the spiritual food of His most blessed Body and Blood.

Priest of the most high God.—Heb., of **El'elyon.** The mention of the term "priest" (used here for the first time) shows that some sort of sacrificial worship existed at Salem. Sacrifice had, however, been prac-

ticed before; for Abel had acted as a priest when offering his firstlings, and Abram at the various altars which he built. Apparently, however, Melchizedek had been set apart for the priesthood in some more definite way. Melchizedek is described as a priest of **El'elyon,** thus claiming that Jehovah was that Supreme Deity whom Melchizedek served, though without the special knowledge of Him which the patriarch possessed.

(20) He gave him tithes.—Abram thus consecrated the war by a thank offering to God, who had given him the victory. But he also, by paying tithes, acknowledged the priesthood of Melchizedek, and that the God whom he served was the true God. (See Heb. 7:4-11.)

(21) Give me the persons.—To this day it is the rule among the Arabs that, if a camp be plundered, anyone who recovers the booty gives up only the persons, and takes the rest for himself. But Abram, with noble generosity, will accept nothing. The "lifting up of the hand" to give solemnity to an oath is mentioned here for the first time.

15

Jehovah's Covenant With Abram

(1) The word of the Lord came unto Abram.—This phrase, used so often afterward to signify revelation, occurs here for the first time. Up to this time Abram had received only general promises of offspring, and of the land being the possession of his seed. The time had come when the patriarch needed and obtained more formal assurances, first, of the bestowal upon him of offspring (verses 1-6), and, secondly, of the future possession of Palestine (verses 18-21).

(2) Lord God.—Not "Jehovah Elohim," but "Lord Jehovah," "Lord" being the ordinary title of respect. Usually Jehovah takes the vowels of **'donai,** "lord," but as the two words occur here together, it takes the vowels of **Elohim,** therefore our translation, in obedience to a superstition of the Jews (4:1).

What wilt thou give me?—There is a slight tone of complaint in these words. Jehovah promised Abram a "reward great exceedingly." He answers that no reward can really be great as long as he has no heir.

The steward of my house is generally explained as meaning "the son of possession," that is, the possessor, owner of my house when I die.

(3) One born in my house.—The Hebrew is, "the son of my house," my house-son, not born of me, but the chief of the house next to myself, and its representative.

(5) He brought him forth.—Abram feels himself led forth from the tent into the open space around, and is there commanded to count the stars. As a matter of fact, the stars visible to the naked eye are not very numerous, but they have always been a received metaphor for an infinite multitude, probably because, as men gaze, they perpetually see the faint radiance of more and more distant constellations. Thus they cannot be counted, and Abram's seed was to be countless, because of the vastness of its number.

(6) He believed in the Lord (in Jehovah) . . .—We have here the germ of the doctrine of free justification. Abram was both a holy man and one who proved his faith by his works; but nevertheless the inspired narrator inserts this reflection, not after the history of the offering of Isaac, but in the account of this vision, where all that Abram did was to believe, and for that belief's sake was accounted righteous before God. For the definite conclusions deduced from this verse by Paul see Rom. 4. The quotation there is from the LXX, and gives the general sense, but the correct rendering of the Hebrew is that given here.

(8) Whereby shall I know that I shall inherit it?—Abram now asks this question, not from want of faith, but from a desire for a more direct confirmation of the promise and fuller knowledge of the details.

(9, 10) Take me an heifer . . .—This form of making a covenant was probably that usual in Babylonia, and thus Abram received the assurance of his inheritance by means of a ceremony with which he was familiar. But in most ancient languages men are said "to cut" or "strike" a covenant, because the most solemn formula involved either the cutting of victims in two, or striking them dead, as was the Roman manner. The severing of the bodies was not, as some suppose, to represent the two parties; but, as explained in Jer. 34:18-20, it set forth the penalty of perjury, and was usually accompanied by the imprecation upon the covenant-breaker of a destruction as complete as that which had befallen the slaughtered animals. There is no mention in this place of a sacrifice, although the animals are those subsequently set apart for sacrifice by the Levitical law.

(12) Lo, an horror of great darkness fell upon him.—The terror was not mental so much as bodily, caused by a deep gloom settling around him, such as would be the effect of an eclipse of the setting sun, and shutting all mortal things away from his view.

(13) Four hundred years.—The exact duration of the sojourn in Egypt was 430 years (Exod. 12:40, 41), and with this agrees the genealogy of Jehoshua (l Chron. 7:23-27).

(15) Thou shalt go to thy fathers in peace.—Abram's ancestors had died in Babylonia, but the phrase, used here for the first time, evidently involves the thought of the immortality of the soul. The body may be buried far away, but the soul joins the company of its forefathers in some separate abode, not to be absorbed, but still to enjoy a personal existence. (Comp. chap. 25:8.) A similar, but more exact, distinction between the body and the spirit is drawn in Eccl. 12:7.

(17) A smoking furnace.—The word really means the circular firepot which Orientals use in their houses to sit around for purposes of warmth. This one was wreathed in smoke, out of which shot "a burning lamp" (Heb., "a torch of flame"). For not two symbols, but only one, passed between the divided carcases. Abram had probably passed between them immediately after arranging them, and now Jehovah does the same. Fire is the recognized symbol of the Deity, as in the burning bush, the pillar of fire, the lightnings on Mount Sinai, etc.

(18) The river of Egypt.—That is, the Nile. In the Hebrew the Wady-el-Arish, on the southern border of Simeon, is always distinguished from the Nile, though the distinction is neglected in the King James version. The word used here signifies a river that flows constantly; and Abram's posterity are to be found a kingdom conterminous with the Nile and the Euphrates, that is, with Egypt and Babylonia. If these bounds are large and vague, we must also remember that they are limited by the names of the ten nations which follow. Between the Nile and the Euphrates, the territories of these ten tribes is alone definitely bestowed upon Abram.

16

The Son of the Bondwoman

(1) Now Sarai.—The history of Abram is given in a succession of brief narratives, written possibly by the patriarch himself; and though papyrus was known at Ur, yet the absence of any convenient writing material for ordinary use would oblige men in those ancient days to content themselves with short inscriptions, like those tablets of clay brought from Ur. The narrator would naturally make but few alterations in such precious documents, and hence a certain amount of recapitulation, like that which we find in the Books of Samuel, where again we have not a narrative from one pen, but the arrangement of materials already ancient. As, however, the divine object was the revealing to mankind of the way by which God would raise up man from the Fall, the narrator would be guided by inspiration in his choice of materials, and in the omission of such things as did not fall in with this purpose; and the evident reverence with which he deals with these records is a warrant to us of their genuineness. Such additions as the remark that the "Valley of Shaveh" was many centuries later called "the King's Dale" (14:17; II Sam. 18:18) are generally acknowledged to have been the work of Ezra and the men of the Great Synagogue, after the return from the exile.

Hagar.—She was an Egyptian woman who had escaped to Abram when he was in the Negeb, and had then received the appellation, which virtually means "run-away."

(2) That I may obtain children by her.—As then the children of a woman bestowed by her mistress upon the husband were regarded as belonging to the wife (30:3), Sarai, despairing of bearing a son herself, as she was now seventy-five, and had been in Canaan ten years, concluded that her heir was to be born of a substitute.

As regards the morality of the act, we find that marriage with one wife was the original law (2:24), and that when polygamy was introduced it was coupled by the inspired narrator with violence and licence (4:19). Monogamy was the rule, as we see in the households of Noah, Terah, Isaac, and others; but many, like Esau and Jacob, allowed themselves a greater latitude. In so doing, their conduct falls below the level of Christian morality, but every one's actions are strongly influenced by the general views of the people among whom he lives; and in Abram's case it must be said in his defense that, with so much depending on his having offspring, he took no steps to obtain another wife, but remained content with the barren Sarai. When he did take Hagar it was at his wife's request, and for a reason which

seemed to them adequate, and even religious.

(4) Her mistress was despised.—Hagar, we are told in verse 3, was to be, not Abram's concubine, but his wife. She was to be Sarai's representative, and though now she would hold the highest place in the household next to Sarai, because of this relation to Abram, yet she would continue to be Sarai's maid. But no sooner had she conceived, than, proud of her superiority over her mistress, she wished to overthrow this arrangement, and, at all events, acted as if she was Abram's wife absolutely, and thrust Sarai aside.

(6) Sarai dealt hardly with her.—"Sarai humbled her," that is, reduced her to her original condition. It was quite right that as Hagar had abused her elevation, Abram should make her yield to Sarai all due respect and submission; but in making her resume her old position as a slave, Sarai was possibly dealing unkindly with her (but see note on verse 9).

(7) The angel of the Lord.—Heb., **of Jehovah.** (See note on 12:7.)

In the way to Shur.—Hagar evidently fled by the usual route leading from Hebron past Beer-sheba to Egypt. The wilderness was that of Paran, in which Kadesh was situated. The fountain by which Hagar was sitting was on the road to Shur, which is a desert on the eastern side of Egypt.

(8) Whence camest thou?—It is noteworthy that in these divine communications God's knowledge of all the circumstances is not presumed, but the person visited is led on to tell them. This adds much to the freshness and poetry of the narrative. Here, however, in the address, **Hagar, Sarai's maid,** the angel, at least, shows that he is aware who she is, and also reminds her of what she had forgotten, that in bestowing her upon Abram Sarai did not cease to be her mistress.

(9) Submit thyself.—Heb., "humble thyself." It is the verb translated "dealt hardly" in verse 6. The angel therefore commands her to take the position which Sarai was forcing upon her; and by so doing proves to us that there had been no personal maltreatment.

(11) Ishmael.—That is, "God heareth." Like Samuel, Ishmael received his name from the events of his mother's life, and not from anything in his own.

(12) He will be a wild man.—Heb., "he will be a wild-ass man," i.e., the wild ass of the Arabian deserts. It is the very type of the Bedouin Arabs, whose delight is to rove at will over the desert, and who despise the ease and luxury of a settled life.

(14) Beer-lahai-roi.—That is, "Well of the living-seeing" (of God), the well where God has been seen, and the beholder still lives. It became afterward a favorite dwelling place of Isaac (25:11).

17

Confirmation of the Covenant by the Sacrament of Circumcision

(1) Abram was ninety years old and nine.—Thirteen years, therefore, had passed by since the birth of Ishmael, who doubtless during this time had grown very dear to the childless old man, as we gather from the wish expressed in verse 18.

I am the Almighty God.—Heb., **El shaddai.** The word is archaic, but there is no doubt that it means "strong so as to overpower." Besides its use in Genesis we find it employed as the name of Deity by Balaam (Num. 24:4, 16); by Naomi (Ruth 1:20); and in the Book of Job, where it occurs thirty-one times. In Exod. 6:3 it is said, with evident reference to this place, that El shaddai was the name of God revealed to the patriarchs, but that He was not known to them by His name Jehovah. Here, nevertheless, in a passage said by commentators to be Elohistic, we read that "Jehovah appeared to Abram, and said to him I am El shaddai." But the very gist of the passage is the identification of Jehovah and El shaddai, and the great object of the manifest care with which Moses distinguishes the divine names seems to be to show, that though Jehovah became the special name of Elohim in His covenant relation to Israel after the Exodus, yet that the name was one old and primeval (4:26), and that the God of revelation, under various titles, was ever one and the same.

(2) I will make my covenant.—In 15:18 the Heb. word for "make" is "cut," and refers to the severing of the victims; here it is "give," "place," and implies that it was an act of grace on God's part (comp. note on 9:9). Abram had now waited twenty-five years after leaving Ur-Chasdim, and fourteen or fifteen years since the ratification of the solemn covenant between him and Jehovah (15:18); but the time had at length arrived for the fulfillment of the promise, and in token thereof Abram and Sarai were to change their names, and all the males be

44

brought near to God by a solemn sacrament.

(4) Of many nations.—This is a feeble rendering of a remarkable phrase. Literally the word signifies a confused noise like the din of a populous city. Abram is to be the father of a thronging crowd of nations. And so in verse 5.

(5) Abram.—That is, "high father."

Abraham = "Father of a multitude," **raham** being an Arabic word, perhaps current in Hebrew in ancient times. By some commentators the stress is thrown upon the insertion of the letter "h," as being the representative of the name Yahveh or Hehveh. (Compare the change of Oshea into Jehoshua, Num. 13:16.)

(10) Shall be circumcised.—Circumcision was just as appropriate a sign of the covenant if borrowed from institutions already existing as if then used for the first time. It is an acknowledged fact that the Bible is always true to the local coloring. Chaldaean influence is predominant in those early portions of Genesis which we owe to Abram, a citizen of Ur of the Chaldees; his life and surroundings subsequently are those of an Arab sheik; while Egyptian influence is strongly marked in the latter part of Genesis, and in the history of the Exodus from that country. In this fact we have a sufficient answer to the theories which would bring down the composition of the Pentateuch to a late period: for the author would certainly have written in accordance with the facts and ideas of his own times.

The fitness of circumcision to be a sign of entering into a covenant, and especially into one to which children were to be admitted, consisted in its being a representation of a new birth by the putting off of the old man, and the dedication of the new man unto holiness. The flesh was cast away that the spirit might grow strong; and the change of name in Abram and Sarai was typical of this change of condition. They had been born again, and so must again be named. And though women could not indeed be admitted directly into the covenant, yet they shared in its privileges by virtue of their consanguinity to the men, who were as sponsors for them; and thus Sarai changes her name equally with her husband.

(13) He that is born in thy house ...—Two things follow from this wide extension of the rite of circumcision: the first, that all members of Abram's household, being thus sharers in the covenant, were also numbered as belonging to the nations that sprang from him. The second point is, that as all who were circumcised were regarded as Israelites, so also circumcision was confined to the Israelites. It was not a catholic ordinance intended, like baptism, for all people and all times. Nor was it primarily a religious institution. The bought slave was circumcised first, and instructed afterward. No profession of faith was required, but he was admitted to the privilege in right of his master. The reason of this was that it was an admission into the Jewish nation first, and by consequence only into the church. It is one of the many points which distinguish slavery, as practiced among the Jews, from the degrading form of it which existed in modern times, that from the days of Abram onward the slave by being circumcised was proclaimed to be one of the same race and nation as his master, and thereby entitled to share in his national and religious privileges.

(14) Shall be cut off from his people.— The punishment seems to have been that of excommunication or outlawry, to which other penalties might have been attached by custom; but the main point was that one uncircumcised (as subsequently one who violated the principles of the Mosaic law) forfeited his privileges as a member of the Jewish nation, could claim no protection from the elders for life and property, and could not take his place at the gate of the city.

(15) Sarai.— Probably "princely," an adjective of the same form as **shaddai**, verse 1; while "Sarah" means princess. The change of name shows that she was admitted to the covenant. (Comp. verse 10.)

(16) A son ... of her.— This is the first place where it was definitely promised that Abram's heir should be Sarah's own son. This must be remembered in estimating the conduct of Abram and Sarah in the matter of Hagar. They had long waited, and hoped, before taking measures of their own for the fulfilment of the promise.

(17) Abraham ... laughed.— The Jewish interpreters regard Abraham's laugh as one of joy, and Sarah's (18:12) as one of unbelief. We may, however, well doubt whether there really was this difference between them; but our Lord confirms the view that joy was uppermost in Abraham's heart (John 8:56). Still with belief there was surprise, and the feeling that what was promised was so strange as to be well-nigh incredible. Really, the idea brought out by

this double laughter is that Isaac's birth was contrary to nature.

(18) O that Ishmael ... —For thirteen years Ishmael had been the "son of the house" (15:3), and regarded probably as the true heir. Mingled then with Abraham's joy there was also the pain, natural to a father, of knowing that this transference of the promise to Sarah's child meant the deposition and disappointment of one who for so long had held the post of honor. While the birthright and religious pre-eminence is justly given to the son of the freewoman, there is a large earthly blessing for the handmaid's son.

(19) Thou shalt call his name Isaac.— That is, "he laughs." The name was to be a perpetual memorial that Isaac's birth was naturally such an impossibility as to excite ridicule.

(25) Ishmael ... was thirteen years old.— Hence the Mohammedans defer circumcision to the thirteenth year.

18

Visit of Angels to Abraham at Mamre; and Overthrow of Sodom

(1) And the Lord (Jehovah) **appeared unto him.**—This familiar intercourse, and clear revelation of Jehovah to Abraham, follows upon his closer relation to God by virtue of the sacrament of circumcision.

(2) Three men.—One was "the angel of Jehovah," who came as the manifestation of Deity to Abraham, and the other two were his companions, commissioned by him afterward to execute judgment on the cities of the plain. The number three pointed also to the Trinity of Persons in the Godhead. But we must be careful not to use it as a proof of this doctrine, lest the inference should be drawn of a personal appearance of the Father and of the Holy Ghost.

(3) My Lord.—Heb., **'donai**, a term of simple respect, just as the bowing toward the earth is exactly what an Arab sheik would do now to a passing traveler. Abraham's conduct is marked by all the stately courtesy usual among Orientals. It was only afterward that he knew that he was entertaining angels unawares (Heb. 13:2).

(4) Wash your feet.—This is the first necessity of Oriental hospitality (Judges 19:21), not merely because the feet, protected only by sandals, are soiled by the dirt of the roads, but because it cools the whole body, and allays the feverishness caused by the heat of traveling.

(6) Three measures.—Heb., "three seahs," the seah being a little more than a peck. Cakes such as those here described, baked amid the embers on the hot hearthstone, are considered a delicacy (I Kings 19:6). Abraham's calf, "tender and good," shows that he regarded his visitors as persons of more than ordinary high rank; and the quantity of food cooked seems to show that the three travelers had numerous attendants.

(8) And they did eat.—The Targum of Jonathan and other Jewish authorities translate "and they made show of eating," lest it should seem as though angels ate (Judges 13:16). There is the same mystery as regards our risen Lord (Luke 24:43).

(12) Sarah laughed.—See note on 17:17. The laughter of both the husband and wife brings into prominence the inconceivable character of the fact. Sarah's conduct has been unjustly condemned. Although Abraham may have begun to guess that his visitors were more than men, she probably had no such suspicions. Sitting inside the tent, and catching their words only occasionally, listening perhaps, now only because she heard her own name mentioned, when she hears them talk of her having a child she naturally laughs, thinking possibly that they did not know how old she was.

(14) Is any thing too hard for the Lord.—Heb., "Is anything too wonderful for Jehovah?" At last it is made evident that the travelers are messengers from God; but, until this declaration, there could have been, at most, only a dim feeling that the visitation was more than human. Though the angel does not claim for himself divinity, yet the narrator prefixes to his words, "And Jehovah said." In some ineffable way there was an identity between Jehovah and the angel.

(15) Sarah denied.—With strange inconsistency Sarah knows that the speaker is divine, and that he preceived the thoughts that passed "within herself" in the retirement of the tent, and yet denies; but it was the inconsistency of fright.

(16) The men . . . looked toward Sodom.—This visitation of God combined mercy and love for Abraham, and through him for all mankind, with the punishment of men whose wickedness was so universal that there were none left among them to bear witness for God, and labor for a better state of things.

(19) For I know him, that he will.—It gives God's foreknowledge of the purpose for which He had called Abraham as the reason for thus revealing to him the method of the divine justice. And this purpose was, that from Abraham should spring a nation whose institutions were to be fraught with divine truth, whose prophets were to be the means of revealing God's will to man, and of whom, as concerning the flesh, the Messiah should come.

(21) I will go down.—God examines before He punishes (see note on 11:5) with the same care and personal inspection as the most conscientious earthly judge.

(22) Abraham stood yet before the Lord (before Jehovah).—The two angels went on their way in form as men, toward Sodom, but the one who was a manifestation of Jehovah (verses 13, 17) remained behind.

(23) Abraham drew near.—As Jewish commentators remark, this word is especially used of prayer, and Abraham's intercession is unspeakably noble. Nor must we suppose that he thought only of Lot. Neither must we suppose that Abraham adroitly began with a large number, with the intention of lessening it. It was the readiness with which each prayer was heard which made him in his earnestness continue his entreaties. It thus illustrates the principle that the faith of the believer grows strong as he feels that his prayers are accepted, and he ventures finally to offer petitions, nothing wavering, which at an earlier stage would have seemed to him to ask more than he might venture to hope from the divine goodness.

(33) The Lord (Jehovah) went his way.—The purpose of the revelation was fulfilled. Besides the primary object of making known the perfect justice of God's dealings with men, it further showed that the Gentile world was both subject to Jehovah's dominion, and that there was mercy for it as well as for the covenant people. Such, in future times, was also the lesson of the Book of Jonah.

19

(1) Lot sat in the gate of Sodom.—He had therefore become a citizen of Sodom, probably after the deliverance from the Elamite invasion. Meanwhile all intercourse between Abraham and him apparently had ceased, and he had lost all share in the covenant of circumcision.

(3) He pressed upon them greatly.—This he did as knowing the licentiousness of the people; but the angels do not readily accept his hospitality, as they had done that of Abraham, because his character had deteriorated.

(8) I have two daughters.—It is plain from Judges 19:24 that this proposal was not viewed formerly with the horror which it seems to deserve. Lot was bound by the laws of hospitality to do his utmost to protect his guests, yet he was also bound as a father equally to protect his daughters to the last extremity. The difficulty arises from the high character given of Lot by Peter (II Pet. 2:7, 8): but Lot was righteous only relatively; and though his soul was daily vexed by what he saw, it was not vexed enough to make him quit such evil surroundings, and return to the healthy and virtuous life of the mountains. And, when finally he sought refuge in them, as it was not of his own free will, but on compulsion (verse 30), he found there no peace, but shared, even if unknowingly, in deeds of horrible lust. The warning of his fall is that men who part with religious privileges for the sake of worldly advantage are in danger of sinking into moral degradation, and of losing, with their faith and hope, not only their self-respect and happiness, but even that earthly profit for the sake of which they sacrificed their religion.

(9) He will needs be a judge.—Heb., "is ever acting as a judge." This suggests that Lot had previously reproved the men of Sodom, and agrees with II Pet. 2:8.

(11) Blindness.—This word occurs elsewhere only in II Kings 6:18, and in both cases it is plain that actual blindness is not meant. The men were unaware that anything had happened to them. The people of Sodom thought they saw the door. The word really means a disturbance of vision caused by the eye not being in its proper connection with the brain. And so the men of Sodom seemed always just upon the point of reaching the door, but always failed, they knew not how, but as they always supposed by one another's fault. It is a strange picture of men given over to unbelief and sin, and who "seeing see not," because they reject the true light.

(14) Which married his daughters.—Lot had other daughters, besides the two which escaped with him.

(16) And while he lingered.—Lot still clung to his wealth, and could not make up his mind to leave it, and so at length the angels took him by the hand and compelled him to leave the doomed city.

(17) Look not behind thee.—This was not merely to prevent delay, but also showed that God demanded of them a total abandonment in heart and will of the condemned cities, and hence the severity with which the violation of the command was visited.

Plain.—The Ciccar or circle of Jordan. So also in verses 25, 28, 29, see note on 13:10.

(19) Lest some evil.—Heb., "lest the evil," lest the threatened calamity overtake me and I die.

(24) The Lord (Jehovah) **rained ... from the Lord** (from Jehovah).—Calvin takes it as an emphatic reiteration of its being Jehovah's act. Jehovah had mysteriously manifested Himself upon earth by the visit of the three angels to Abraham, but His activity on earth is one with His willing in heaven.

Brimstone and fire.—Though God used natural agencies in the destruction of the Ciccar cities, yet what was in itself a catastrophe of nature became miraculous by the circumstances which surrounded it. It was thus made the means not merely of executing the divine justice, of strengthening Abraham's faith, and of warning Lot, but also of giving moral and religious instruction throughout all time. As for the catastrophe itself, it was not a mere thunderstorm which set the earth, saturated with naphtha, on fire; but, in a region where earthquakes are still common, there was apparently an outburst of volcanic violence, casting forth blazing bitumen and brimstone. This falling down upon the houses, and upon the soil charged with combustible matter, caused a conflagration so sudden and widespread that few or none could escape. Sulphur and niter are still found as natural products on the shores of the Dead Sea.

(26) His wife looked back from behind him.—In Oriental countries it is still the rule for the wife to walk behind her husband. The earthquake heaped up a mighty mass of rock-salt, which lies in solid strata round the Dead Sea, and Lot's wife was entangled in the convulsion and perished, leaving the hill of salt, in which she was enclosed, as her memorial.

(27) Abraham gat up early in the morning.—This was necessary, because he had a walk of some miles before he reached "the place where he stood before Jehovah" on the previous evening; and probably the mighty forces which overthrew the cities had been some hours at work when he

47

reached the head of the ravine through which the terrible scene became visible. Naturally his anxiety to know the result of his intercession, and the fate of his brother's son, would urge him to be on foot at the early dawn.

(28) Lo, the smoke of the country ("land") **went up as the smoke of a furnace.**— The violence of the fire is indicated by the last word, which is not the ordinary word for a "furnace," but means a kiln, such as that used for burning chalk into lime, or for melting ores of metal.

(30) He feared to dwell in Zoar.—Though this little place had been granted him for an asylum, yet, terrified at the sight of the smoking valley, and remembering that he had been originally commanded to go to the mountains, he summons up his courage and proceeds there.

(31) The first-born said unto the younger.— Several modern commentators see in this recital a mark of Jewish hatred toward the Moabites and Ammonites, and an attempt to brand their origin with shame. We find in Deut. 2:9-19 no trace of the existence of this hostility, but, on the contrary, the relationship of these two nations to Israel is used as a ground for kindly feelings; and in the story of Ruth the Moabitess, and the friendship which existed between the kings of Moab and David, we have proof that such feelings existed.

(32) That we may preserve seed of our father.—This was a very strong feeling in ancient times, and affords the sole excuse for the revolting conduct of these women. The utter degradation of Lot and his family is the most painful part of his story, which thus ends in his intense shame.

(37, 38) Moab ... Ben-ammi.—Both these names suggest an incestuous origin, but the latter in a less repulsive way. "Son of my people" means one born of intercourse with her own kin and family.

20

Abraham's Denial of His Wife at Gerar

(1) Abraham journeyed from thence.— That is, from Mamre, where he had so long halted, and which seems to have continued to be one of his homes. As he had been commanded to traverse the whole land (13:17, 18), we need seek no reasons for his removal. It was the rule of his life to move

from place to place, both on account of his cattle, and also because by so doing he was taking possession of the country. There were, nevertheless, certain places which were his headquarters, such as Bethel, Mamre, and Beer-sheba.

The south country.—It is a proper name, the Negeb; see note on 12:9.

(2) She is my sister.—Twenty years before, Abraham had acted in the same way in Egypt, and Pharaoh had rebuked him, but sent him away with large presents. We learn from this chapter, verse 13, that the false representation which twice brought them into trouble was habitual with the two; nor does Abraham ever seem conscious that he was acting in it wrongfully. But Holy Scripture neither represents its heroes as perfect, nor does it raise them disproportionately above the level of their own times. Its distinguishing feature rather is that it always insists upon a perpetual progress upward, and urges men onward to be better and holier than those that went before.

(3) God (Elohim) **came ...** —With the same care in the application of the names, it is necessarily Elohim who appears to a heathen king; and had the title Jehovah been used it would have been a violation of the narrator's rule. In 12:17 it is Jehovah who plagues Pharaoh for Sarah's sake. But equally here, verse 18, it is Jehovah who protects Sarah from Abimelech; in both cases it being the covenant-God, who saves his people from injury.

Thou art but a dead man.—Heb., "thou diest," or "art dying." Abimelech was already suffering from the malady spoken of in verse 17, when Elohim appeared to him and warned him that death would be the result of perseverance in retaining Sarah. It was this malady which was the cause of the abstention spoken of in verses 4 and 6.

(4) A righteous nation.—There is an allusion here to the fate of Sodom. Though the malady was confined to Abimelech and his household, yet he sees destruction threatening his whole people, who, compared with the inhabitants of the Ciccar cities, were righteous.

(5) In the integrity of my heart ... —Not only does Abimelech assert this, but Elohim (see verse 6) admits the plea. But the words mean no more than that he was not consciously violating any of his own rules of morality. The inner light is but a faint and inconstant glimmering, but Christ is the true light; for only by Him does the law of nature become a clear rule for human guidance (John 1:9; Rom. 2:14, 15; Matt. 6:23).

(7) He is a prophet.—The word prophet is used here in its old sense of "spokesman" (comp. Exod. 7:1, with 4:16), and especially of such an one as mediates between God and man. There was a true feeling that God in His own nature is beyond the reach of man (Job 9:32, 33, 16:21; I Tim. 6:16); and this in heathen nations led to men peopling their heavens with a multitude of minor deities. Not only Abraham, but the patriarchs generally are called "Christs and prophets" (Ps. 105:15), as being speakers for God to man, and for man to God, until the true Christ and prophet came. Abimelech, moreover, is thus taught that he does not himself hold a near relation to God, but requires someone to speak for him; perhaps, too, he would gather from it that he had need of fuller instruction, and that he ought to try to attain to a higher level, and that Abraham would become a prophet to him in its other sense of being a teacher.

(10) What sawest thou?—Abimelech first denies by indignant questions that he had been guilty of any wrong toward Abraham, and then asks what he had seen in the conduct of himself and people to justify such mistrust of them. Throughout, the king speaks as a man conscious that his citizens so respected the rights of a stranger and of marriage, that Sarah would have been perfectly safe had Abraham openly said that she was his wife.

(11) Surely the fear of God ... — Abraham's general condemnation of the people had some excuse in the widespread depravity of the nations in Canaan, but was nevertheless unjust. Both in Egypt and in Gerar the standard of morality was higher than Abraham supposed. His difficulty was the result of his own imperfect faith; but the fact that this trickery was arranged between man and wife when starting on their long wanderings, proves that they rather overrated than underrated the risks that lay before them. The expedient was indeed a sorry one, and shows that Abraham's faith was not yet that of a martyr.

(12) Not the daughter of my mother.—This disproves the notion that Sarah was the same as Iscah (11:29). Sarah was apparently Abraham's half-sister, being Terah's daughter by another wife; and we gather from her calling her child Sarai—that is, "princely" (see 17:15)—that she was not a

concubine, but belonged to some noble race.

(14) Abimelech ... gave them unto Abraham.—Pharaoh's presents were given when he took Sarah, and though he did not exact them back, yet he bade Abraham "go his way" in displeasure. More generously, the Philistine gave presents on restoring Sarah, and granted her husband permission to dwell in his land wherever it pleased him. He also acknowledged thereby that he had done Abraham a wrong.

(16) A thousand pieces of silver.—Heb., "a thousand of silver." This was the total value of Abimelech's present, and not an additional gift. A thousand shekels would be a large sum at a time when silver was scarce and dear.

He is to thee a covering of the eyes.—This speech of Abimelech is full of difficulty. It begins with a touch of irony in calling Abraham "thy brother." The correct rendering probably is, "And unto Sarah he said, Behold, I have given thy brother (a gift worth) a thousand (pieces) of silver: behold, it shall be to thee for a covering of the eyes to all that are with thee (that is,—so large a compensation for the wrong done thee in taking thee from thy husband, will be a proof to all thy friends and attendants that thou hast not been disgraced, but treated with honor); and in respect of all that has happened thou art thus righted."

(17) Abraham prayed ... —As Abimelech had now made liberal compensation, it became the duty of Abraham to intercede for him. The malady seems to have been one confined to Abimelech, as its object was to protect Sarah; but in some way it so affected the whole household as to produce general barrenness.

21

Birth of Isaac, and Rejection of Ishmael

(1) And the Lord (Jehovah) **visited Sarah as he had said.**—See 17:19, where it is Elohim who gives the promise. So here in verse 2 the name Elohim is interchanged with Jehovah.

(3) Abraham called the name of his son.—We have here two things contrary to subsequent usage: for, first, the father names the child, and not the mother; and, secondly, he names him at his birth, instead of waiting until his circumcision. The child really was named by God (chap. 17:19), and Abraham only acknowledges that the son born was the promised Isaac.

Isaac.—This name not only recorded the fact of the laughter of the father (17:17) and of the mother (18:12), but was a standing memorial that Isaac's birth was contrary to nature.

(6, 7) God hath made me to laugh.— Sarah's laugh was one of mingled emotions. Joy was uppermost in the mind. Doubtless she called to mind the feelings with which she listened to the announcement of her bearing a son, made by those whom she then regarded as mere passing wayfarers (18:12), but whom she had now long known to be the messengers of God.

(9) Mocking.—What exactly Ishmael was doing is not said, but we may feel sure that Sarah was not without good reason for her conduct; for Paul bears witness that Ishmael persecuted Isaac (Gal. 4:29). When we consider that Ishmael had been the heir for fourteen years, and that he now fell back into an inferior positon, we cannot be surprised if at this banquet in his rival's honor he gave way to spiteful feelings, and by word and gesture derided and ridiculed him. Hagar too had probably never regarded Sarah with much affection since her forced return, and now that her son was disinherited, her bitterness would grow more intense.

(10) Bondwoman.—Heb., ammâh. This word is rightly translated "handmaid." The rendering "bondwoman" unduly depresses Hagar's condition, and with it that of the Jewish Church in the allegory contained in Gal. 4:22-31.

(12) In Isaac shall thy seed be called.— Heb., "in Isaac there shall be called to thee a seed": that is, the seed that shall especially be accounted thine, and which, as such, shall inherit the promises, will be that sprung from Isaac.

(13) The son of the bondwoman.—Heb., "of the handmaid." Hagar is never acknowledged as Abraham's wife, though her child, as Abraham's son, receives a noble promise for the father's sake.

(14) The wilderness of Beer-sheba.—As yet this region had no name (see verse 31). It lay about twenty Roman miles or more below Hebron, and was the most southerly part of Palestine.

(15) She cast the child under one of the shrubs.—The act was one of despair. Ishmael, though seventeen years of age, had not yet come to his strength, and at a time when human life was so prolonged that forty was

the usual age for marriage, was probably not as capable of bearing fatigue as a young man nearly grown up would be in our days. He thus became exhausted, and apparently fainted; and his mother, after trying in vain to support him, cast him down in anguish, and abandoned herself to her grief.

(17) The angel of God.—In 16:7 it was "the angel of Jehovah" which appeared unto Hagar; here it is the angel of Elohim. It is impossible not to be struck with this exact use of the names of Deity. Hagar was then still a member of Abraham's family; here she is so no longer; and it is Elohim, and not Jehovah, the covenant God of the chosen race, who saves her.

(20) And dwelt in the wilderness.—He sought no refuge in Egypt, where so large a Semitic population was gathering, nor in any Canaanite town, but took to the wandering life in the desert, such as is still usual with the Arabs.

(21) A wife out of the land of Egypt.— However natural this might be on Hagar's part, it would nevertheless strengthen the heathen element in Ishmael and his descendants. We find, nevertheless, that he was subsequently on friendly terms with Isaac (25:9; 28:8, 9).

Abimelech's Covenant With Abraham

(22) Abimelech and Phichol.— Abimelech, that is, "Father King," was the title not only of the king of Gerar, but of the kings of the Philistines generally. In like manner Phichol, "mouth of all," seems to have been the official designation of the prime minister, and commander-in-chief. This visit of the king and his vizier appears to have taken place some considerable time after the beginning of the sojourn of Abraham at Gerar; for the friendly feelings which then existed had evidently given way to a coolness, occasioned by the quarrels between their herdsmen. In this narrative, Abraham appears as a chieftain powerful enough for a king to wish to make an alliance with him.

(26) I wot not.—This explains the reason of Abimelech's visit. The king's herdsmen had robbed Abraham of a well, a species of property jealously defended in the East because of its great value, and Abraham in some way had made his displeasure felt. Abimelech, ever friendly toward Abraham, by whose nobleness of character he had been greatly impressed, comes to learn the cause of the coolness, and to enter into a more close and lasting alliance with the patriarch.

(33) And called there on the name of the Lord, the everlasting God.—Heb., "on the name of Jehovah, El'olam" (comp. 4:26). In 14:22 Abraham claimed for Jehovah that he was **El'elyon**, the supreme God; in 17:1, Jehovah reveals Himself as **El shaddai**, the almighty God; and now Abraham claims for Him the attribute of eternity. As he advanced in holiness, Abraham also grew in knowledge of the manifold nature of the Deity, and we also more clearly understand why the Hebrews called God, not El, but Elohim. In the plural appellation all the divine attributes were combined. El might be **'elyon**, or **shaddai**, or **'olam**; Elohim was all in one.

22

The Offering of Isaac on Mount Moriah

(1) God did tempt Abraham.—Heb., "proved" him, put his faith and obedience to the proof. In the midst of this tranquil evening of his days came the severest trial of all; for he was commanded to slay his son. The trial was twofold. For, first, human sacrifice was abhorrent to the nature of Jehovah, and Abraham's clear duty would be to prove the command. Could such a deed really be enjoined upon him by God? Now no subjective proof would be sufficient. In later times many an Israelite was moved by deep religious fanaticism to give his first-born in the hope of appeasing the anger of God at his sin (Mic. 6:7); but instead of peace it brought only a deeper condemnation upon his soul. Had Abraham been moved only by an internal and subjective impulse, his conduct would have deserved and met with similar condemnation. But when, upon examination, he became convinced that the command came from outside himself, and from the same God with whom on former occasions he had so often held converse, then the antecedents of his own life required of him obedience. But even when satisfied of this, there was, secondly, the trial of his faith. A command which he had tested, not only subjectively by prayer, but objectively by comparison with the manner of previous revelations, bade him with his own hand destroy the son in whom "his seed was to be called." His love for his child, his previous

faith in the promise, the religious value and worth of Isaac as the appointed means for the blessing of all mankind—this, and more besides, stood arrayed against the command. But Abraham, in spite of all, obeyed, and in proportion to the greatness of the trial was the greatness of the reward. If the act had possessed no typical value, it would have been difficult for us to reconcile to our consciences a command which might have seemed, indirectly at least, to have authorized human sacrifices. But there was in it the setting forth of the mystery of the Father giving the Son to die for the sins of the world; and therein lies both the value and the justification of Abraham's conduct and of the divine command.

(2) Thine only son Isaac.—The words in the original are more emphatic, being, "Take, I pray, thy son, thine only son, whom thou lovest, even Isaac." If childlessness had been so unendurable to Abraham (15:2), what would it be now, after so many years of enjoyment of a son, and after giving up Ishmael for his sake (17:18)?

The land of Moriah.—Moriah may mean "Jah is provider." If this is the meaning, the name would be derived from this event, and would signify the place where "Jehovah will Himself provide the sacrifice." As Abraham and Isaac reached the spot on the third day, and evidently at an early hour, Gerizim is too remote from Beer-sheba for this to be possible. Even Jerusalem is distant enough. We may notice also, that Moriah is described as "a land," in some part of which Abraham was to be shown the special mountain intended for the sacrifice.

Offer him there for a burnt offering.—In the epistle to the Hebrews (11:17-19) the victory of Abraham's faith is described as consisting in the belief, that even though Isaac were killed, nevertheless the promise would still in some divine manner be fulfilled in him.

(4) Afar off.—In Isaac thus carrying the wood on which he was to be sacrificed, the Church Fathers discerned a type of Christ carrying His cross (John 19:17).

(8) God will provide himself a lamb.—Heb., "the lamb." We learn from Heb. 11:17-19, that Abraham expected that he was to consummate the sacrifice, but that Isaac would be restored to him from the dead, and the promise that his seed was to be born of him so fulfilled. The bestowal of Isaac had been so extraordinary, that Abraham would not feel staggered at what otherwise would have seemed incredible. Apparently, therefore, he meant Isaac by "the lamb," thus showing that it was not he who chose the victim, but God.

(9) Abraham ... bound Isaac.—Jewish commentators agree that this was done with Isaac's consent, nor could it well have been otherwise. Thus his youthful faith was tried equally with that of his father, his future life sanctified, and himself ennobled by being made a type of Christ (I Pet. 2:23).

(11) The angel of the Lord.—Up to this point, the narrative had been Elohistic, but it is the angel of Jehovah who interferes to stop the sacrifice (see note on 16:7).

(13) A burnt offering in the stead of his son.—We have here the fact of substitution, and the doctrine of a vicarious sacrifice. The ram took Isaac's place, and by its actual death completed the typical representation of the Saviour's death on Calvary. And while it would have been most painful for Isaac to have actually died by his father's hand, the doctrine of the possibility of a vicarious sacrifice would have been even less clearly taught thereby. He therefore rises again to life from the altar, and the ram dies in his stead, and by the two combined the whole mystery is set forth of God giving His Son to die for mankind, and of life springing from His death.

(14) Jehovah-jireh.—That is, "Jehovah will provide." In verse 8 Abraham had said **Elohim-jireh,** "God will provide." He now uses Jehovah as the equivalent of Elohim. It is added that hence arose a proverb, "In the mount of the Lord it shall be seen," or rather, "In the mount of Jehovah it shall be provided."—The verb literally means "to see," or, "to see to a thing," and the sense of the proverb plainly is that in man's necessity God will Himself see to it, and provide due help and deliverance. The Samaritan, Syriac and Vulgate have a better reading, namely, "In the mount Jehovah will provide." The two renderings, besides their general proverbial sense, point onward to the providing upon this very spot of the sacrifice that was to take away the sins of the world (comp. Isa. 53:5).

But when and how did this grow into a proverb? and who added this note? It may have been inserted by Moses when he arranged these marvelous documents; less probably by Ezra and the men of the Great Synagogue, when they collected and revised the several books of Holy Scripture after the exile. In either case, the proverb is a national testimony to the genuineness of the record, and proves that the facts narrated in

it were so impressed upon the memory of Abraham's descendants, as to shape their thoughts and language.

(16) By myself have I sworn, saith the Lord (Jehovah).—This solemn interposition of an oath (Heb. 6:17), of which the present is the sole instance in Holy Scripture, plainly indicates that this trial of Abraham's faith was of no common kind, and that its typical teaching is of no ordinary value. He is thus the highest and most perfect example of faith, and by his offering of his son the Church received the assurance that the Son of God incarnate in the flesh would upon that very mountain offer the sacrifice divinely necessary for the pardon of man's sins.

23

Death and Burial of Sarah

(1) Sarah was an hundred and seven and twenty years old.—Sarah is the only woman whose age at her death is mentioned in the Bible, an honor doubtless given her as the ancestress of the Hebrew race (Isa. 51:2). As she was ninety at Isaac's birth, he would now have been thirty-seven years of age.

(2) Kirjath-arba; the same is Hebron.—This was a very ancient city, built seven years before Zoan in Egypt (Num. 13:22), probably by a tribe of Semites on their way to the Delta. It lies upon the very border of the Negeb of Judah, about twenty-two miles south of Jerusalem. Originally it was named Kirjath-arba, and though Arba is called "the father of Anak" (Josh. 15:13), yet the literal meaning "City of Four" (arba being the Hebrew numeral "four"), coupled with the fact that Hebron means "alliance" (13:18), suggests that its building was the result of the union of four families; and afterward, from the name of the city, Arba may have been used often as a proper name. At the conquest of Palestine there were descendants of Anak still dwelling there, and apparently they had restored the old title, but were expelled by Caleb (Josh. 15:14), who took it as his possession, and seems to have given its name to a grandchild as a memorial of his victory (I Chr. 2:42).

(3) Abraham stood up from before his dead.—His first care on arriving at Hebron had been to prostrate himself in Sarah's tent, and give utterance to his grief. Only after this he rises to prepare for her burial.

The sons of Heth.—Up to this time we have read only of Amorites, Mamre and his brothers, at Hebron. It now appears that it was the property of the Hittites, a race who, while the Israelites sojourned in Egypt, became so powerful as to contend for empire with the Egyptians themselves. Their capital was Emesa in Northern Syria. (See note on 10:15.)

(4) A possession of a burying place.— While strangers might pasture their cattle upon the open downs, yet the consent of the natives seems to have been necessary before Abraham could occupy any spot permanently (15:13; 20:15). Thus, in spite of his power and wealth, Abraham, as regards his legal position toward the inhabitants, was but a stranger and sojourner (Heb. 11:9), and could secure a resting place for his dead only by their consent.

(6) In the choice of our sepulchres.—The interview between Abraham and the Hittites is marked by the utmost courtesy on both sides, but it is a mistake to suppose that this acceptance of the patriarch's proposal contained the idea that he might select a sepulcher without paying for it. The payment, in true Oriental fashion, is kept in the background, but is presupposed on both sides.

(9) The cave of Machpelah.—That is, the "double cave," consisting probably of an outer and an inner compartment.

(10) And Ephron dwelt among . . . —At these assemblies held at the gate of the city every free-born citizen had a right to be present, and matters were settled by common consent.

(15) The land is worth . . . —The money amounts to about $1,000, no mean price, considering the high value of silver in those days.

(16) Abraham weighed . . . current money with the merchant.—Shekel literally means weight, and money was not coined until long afterward. In the last clause, by inserting "money" our vision antedates facts. According to the Hebrew, it was the silver that was current with the merchants. The metal was probably made into small bars, marked by the refiner to indicate their quality: and Abraham weighed out to Ephron about 200 ounces of silver in bars of the quality usual in trade.

24

Marriage of Isaac and Rebekah

(1) Abraham was old.—As Isaac was thirty-seven years of age when Sarah died

(23:1), and forty at his marriage (25:20), Abraham, who was a centenarian at Isaac's birth, would now be nearly 140. As he lived to be 175 (25:7), he survived Isaac's marriage thirty-five years, and lived to see Esau and Jacob nearly grown up.

(2) Unto his eldest servant of his house.— Heb., "his servant, the elder of his house." It is the name of an office; and though one holding so confidential a post would be a man of ripe years, yet it is not probable that Abraham would send anyone who was not still vigorous on so distant a journey. Eliezer of Damascus had held a similar office fifty-five years previously (15:2), but this was probably a younger man.

Put . . . thy hand under my thigh.—As Jacob requires that Joseph should swear to him in the same manner (47:29), this form of oath was evidently regarded as a very solemn one. The meaning of it has been much discussed, but we find the thigh in 46:26; Exod. 1:5—in both which places it is rendered "loins"—used as the source of posterity. Probably, therefore, it is a euphemistic manner of describing the circumcised member, which was to be touched by the hand placed beneath the thigh; and thus the oath was really by the holy covenant between Abraham and God, of which circumcision was the symbol.

(6) Beware thou that thou bring not my son thither again.—The betrothal of Isaac and Rebekah is told with the utmost exactness of detail, because it contained two principles of primary importance to Abraham's posterity: the first, that they were not to allow themselves to be merged among the Canaanites, but remain a distinct people. And secondly, that under no circumstances might they return to Mesopotamia, but must cling devotedly to the land of which God had promised them the possession.

(10) And the servant.—Why did not Isaac go himself in search of a wife? We must not conclude from his inactivity that the matter had not his full concurrence; but he was the heir, and according to Oriental manners it was fit that the choice should be left to a trusty deputy. What is unusual in the narrative is the distance to which the servant was sent, and the limitation of his choice to a particular family; but both these peculiarities arose from the religious considerations involved.

For all the goods of his master were in his hand.—Rather, "with every good thing of his master's in his hand." It was necessary not only that the servant should take with him such a convoy as would ensure his safety and that of the bride on their return, but also such rich presents as would adequately represent Abraham's wealth and power.

Mesopotamia.—Heb., **Aram-Naharaim:** that is, that part of Syria which lies between the Tigris and Euphrates. It was a mountainless region, except toward the north.

(16) The damsel.—This word (Heb., Na'ar) is of the common gender in the Pentateuch, except in Deut. 22:19, where it has the feminine termination. In the rest of the Bible the gender is always marked. We have herein another of the many linguistic proofs of the extreme antiquity of the Pentateuch, and it is the more interesting because it is found in a Jehovistic section. (See note on 43:8.)

(21) And the man wondering at her ... —The servant, we may well believe, was astonished at the exactness and quickness with which his prayer was being answered, but this is not the point to which the rest of the verse refers; rather, it sets him before us as keenly observing all she said and did, and carefully coming to the conclusion that the comely and generous maiden was the destined bride of the son of his lord.

(22) Earring.—Really "nose-ring"; for in verse 47 the man places it on her nose, wrongly translated "face" in our version. (See Ezek. 16:12; Prov. 11:22.) It was hung not from the central cartilage of the nose, but from the left nostril, the flesh of which was pierced for that purpose. Its weight, about a quarter of an ounce, would make it not more disfiguring than many of the personal ornaments worn at the present time.

(24) Bethuel the son of Milcah, which she bare unto Nahor.—Not only on the father's side, but also on the mother's, she was Isaac's cousin, Milcah being the daughter of Haran, Abraham's brother.

(28) The damsel ran, and told (them of) her mother's house.—The wife of a sheik has a separate tent (verse 67), and the result of polygamy is to make each family hold closely together. Naturally, too, the maiden would first show her mother and the women presents of so special a meaning. We even find Laban, the brother, acting as Rebekah's representative; and it is only when the final decision has to be given that Bethuel is allowed to have any voice in the matter (verse 50).

(31) Come in, thou blessed of the Lord.— This hospitality was in the East almost a matter of course, though Laban's earnest-

ness may have been increased by the sight of his sister's golden ornaments. More remarkable is it that Laban addresses the servant as "blessed of Jehovah," for we learn in Josh. 24:2 that the monotheism of Nahor and his family was by no means pure. Still, neither were they idolaters, and the "other gods" whom they served were probably teraphim, as certainly were the gods of Laban mentioned in 31:30.

(53) Jewels of silver, and jewels of gold.— Heb., "vessels." In ancient times a wife had to be bought (34:12), and the presents given were not mere ornaments and jewelry, but articles of substantial use and value. These went partly to the bride, and partly to her relatives: and they are described here as going exclusively to the brother and mother. Possibly, polygamy had led to the custom of the purchase-presents going to the mother's tent.

(58) Wilt thou go with this man?—A woman in the East has little choice in the matter of her marriage, and here, moreover, everything was so plainly providential, that Rebekah, like her father and brother (verse 50), would have felt it wrong to make difficulties, and she expressed her readiness to go at once, though she will never see her relatives again. Of course there would be some little delay for preparation, but none for leave-taking.

(62) The well Lahai-roi.—Hagar's well (16:14), situated in the "south country," that is, the Negeb (see 12:9). The oasis around it became Isaac's favorite residence (25:11), and was in the neighborhood of Beer-sheba, where Abraham was dwelling when Sarah died at Hebron (23:2). The journey of the servant would take some months, and during this time Abraham's herds would be shifted from station to station, but it would be known where he was from the period of the year. As Isaac was at the station most remote from Charran, Rebekah would have visited all his homes before arriving at Beer-lahai-roi.

(64) She lighted off.—Heb., "fell": descended hastily from her camel. It is still the custom in the East for an inferior when meeting a superior to dismount, and advance on foot. Rebekah, therefore, would have been thought bold and disrespectful had she not acknowledged the superiority of her lord. Besides beauty, we have already seen in her kindliness of heart, activity, and courageous submission to the guidance of Providence; we now see her modesty and courtesy toward her husband.

(65) She took a veil, and covered herself.—Brides are usually taken to the bridegroom enveloped in a veil, which covers the whole body, and is far larger than that ordinarily worn. By wrapping herself in this veil Rebekah notified that she was the bride. After marriage it was seldom worn at this early period, and so both the Egyptians and Abimelech saw Sarah's beauty.

25

Abraham's Marriage With Keturah

(1) Then again Abraham took a wife.—The position of Keturah was entirely distinct from that of Hagar. The latter was Sarah's representative; and her son, if Sarah had remained barren, would have been the heir. Keturah was a secondary wife, whose children from the first held an inferior position in the household. So Bilhah and Zilpah became the substitutes of Rachel and Leah, and therefore their children ranked side by side with Reuben and Joseph, though not altogether on the same level. They were patriarchs, and the progenitors of tribes, even if the tribes sprung from them held a lower rank.

(2) Midian is the one son of Keturah who had a great future before him, for his race became famous traders (37:28); and as they are called "Medanites" there in the Hebrew, in verse 36, it is probable that Medan and Midian coalesced into one tribe. Jethro, the father-in-law of Moses, belonged to them (Exod. 2:15, 16), and, enriched by commerce, they became so powerful as to be dangerous neighbors to the Israelites. (Judges 6; 7; 8.)

(6) The east country.—By this is meant Arabia and Southern Mesopotamia, where, by their superior vigor and organization, the descendants of Abraham were able to establish their supremacy over the natives. The Bedouin still follow Abraham's practice. When their children are grown up, they give each of the younger sons his share of their goods (Luke 15:12), whereupon they move to a distance, and leave the eldest brother in quiet possession of the home.

(7) An hundred threescore and fifteen years.—As Abraham was seventy-five years of age when he left Haran (12:4), his sojourn in Canaan lasted just a century, one quarter of which was spent in the long trial of his faith before Isaac was granted to him.

As, however, Esau and Jacob were born when Isaac was sixty years of age (25:26), they would be fifteen at Abraham's death, and probably had often seen their grandfather, and received his blessing.

(8) Abraham ... was gathered to his people.—Upon the belief in a future life implied in these words, see note on 15:15, and comp. Heb. 11:16.

(9) His sons Isaac and Ishmael.—Isaac was now seventy-five years of age, and Ishmael eighty-nine, and the two old men, with their enmity long over, met as friends at their father's burial. While Keturah's sons were apparently sent far away into Arabia, Ishmael at Paran (21:21) would be at no very great distance from the well Lahai-roi, which was Isaac's favorite residence.

(11) God blessed his son Isaac.—With this general summary the Tôldôth Terah concludes, and no portion of Holy Scripture is more interesting or valuable; for in it the broad foundation is laid for the fulfillment of the protevangelium contained in 3:15, the progenitor of the chosen race is selected and proved on trial, and the preparation made for the giving of the Law, and for the growing light of prophecy, by the nearness wherewith Abraham walked with God.

The Tôldôth Ishmael

(12) These are the generations of Ishmael.—Following the usual rule of this book, Ishmael is not dismissed from the divine presence without a short record of his history, after which he falls into the background, and the historian proceeds with his main subject, which is the preparation for the forming of that race and nation of whom, according to the flesh, Christ came. These brief notices, moreover, of personages not in the direct line of Christ's ancestry have their value in God's great purpose that the Jewish Messiah should be the Redeemer of the Gentiles also (Rom. 10:12); and consequently from the first their history was not alien from God's counsels.

(13-15) The sons of Ishmael.—The abode of the twelve tribes sprung from Ishmael was the northern part of Arabia, whence gradually they extended their influence, and apparently soon absorbed the Joktanites (10:26-30), themselves a kindred Semitic race. These genealogies would be inexplicable if we did not remember that successive waves of people occupied these lands, and that while the old names remained, the dominant race was new. So the rapid growth of individuals into tribes (as of Midian, 25:2) was the result of races of higher civilization and greater energy subduing feeble and less highly-developed tribes. Hence in verse 16 the sons of Ishmael are called "princes."

(18) He died.—But the Hebrew is, "he fell"—that is, his lot fell; he settled there.

In the presence of.—This means "to the east" of all his brethren.

The Tôldôth Isaac (25:19-35:29)
The Birth of Isaac's Sons

(19) Abraham begat Isaac.—The tôldôth in its original form gave probably a complete genealogy of Isaac, tracing up his descent to Shem, and showing thereby that the right of primogeniture belonged to him; but the inspired historian uses only so much of this as is necessary for tracing the development of the divine plan of human redemption.

(20) The Syrian.—Really, "the Aramean," or descendant of Aram. (See 10:22, 23.) The name of the district also correctly is "Paddan-Aram," the region immediately in the neighborhood of Charran.

(21) Isaac entreated the Lord.—This barrenness lasted twenty years (verse 26), and must have greatly troubled Isaac; but it would also compel him to dwell much in thought upon the purpose for which he had been given to Abraham, and afterward rescued from death upon mount Jehovah-Jireh. And when offspring came, in answer to his earnest pleading of the promise, the delay would serve to impress upon both parents the religious significance of their existence as a separate race and family, and the necessity of training their children worthily.

(22) The children struggled together.—Two dissimilar nations sprang from Abraham, but from mothers totally unlike; so, too, from the peaceful Isaac two distinct races of men were to take their origin, but from the same mother, and the contest began while they were yet unborn.

(23) And the Lord said unto her.—The answer is in the form of poetry. It shows that even in their earliest childhood her sons would be unlike in character and unfriendly in disposition; upon this follows their development into hostile nations, and the prediction that the son who started with the advantages of the birthright, the stronger physical nature, and superior strength in

men and arms (32:6), would, nevertheless, finally hold the inferior position.

(25) Red.—A secondary reason for the name Edom. (See verse 30.)

All over like an hairy garment.—It appears that Esau's body was entirely covered with red down, which developed in time into hair as coarse as that of a kid (27:16), and betokened a strong and vigorous, but sensual nature.

Esau.—The Jewish commentators form this name from the verb "to make," and render it "well-made"; but the usual explanation is "hairy," from a word now extant only in Arabic.

(26) His hand took hold on Esau's heel.—Jacob appeared without delay, following immediately upon his brother. This is expressed by the metaphorical phrase that his hand had hold on Esau's heel—that is, there was absolutely no interval between them.

His name was called Jacob.—The name signifies "one who follows at another's heels." It was Esau who first put upon it a bad meaning (27:36), and this bad sense has been riveted to it by Jacob's own unworthy conduct. It is constantly so used even in the Bible. Thus, in Hosea 12:3 the Hebrew has "he Jacobed," literally, "heeled"—that is, overreached, got the better by cunning of—"his brother in the womb." This is the meaning put upon the name by Esau, and in Jer. 9:4 and elsewhere; but it is not well-rendered by our word "supplant," which contains a different metaphor, the **planta** being the sole of the foot; whereas to be at a person's heel is to be his determined pursuer, and one who on overtaking throws him down.

Development of the Characters
of Esau and Jacob.
Esau Sells His Birthright

(27) The boys grew.—With advancing years came also the formation of their characters. Esau became a skillful hunter, a "man of the field." But "Jacob was a plain man."

Dwelling in tents.—Both Jacob and Esau had tents for their abode, but Jacob stayed at home, following domestic occupations, and busied about the flocks and cattle. Thus the struggle between the twins led also to a divergence of feeling on the part of the parents.

(29, 30) Jacob sod pottage.—The diverse occupations of the two youths led, in course of time, to an act fatal to Esau's character and well-being. Coming home one day weary, and fainting with hunger, he found Jacob preparing a pottage of lentils. No sooner did the savoury smell reach him than he cried out in haste, "Let me swallow, I pray, of the red, this red." The verb expresses extreme eagerness, and he adds no noun whatever, but points to the steaming dish. And Jacob, seeing his brother's greediness and ravenous hunger, refuses to give him food until he has parted with the high and sacred prerogative which made him the inheritor of the divine promise.

Therefore was his name called Edom.— Esau may have been called Edom, that is, "Rufus," the red one, before, but after this act it ceased to be a mere allusive by-name, and became his ordinary appellation.

(34) He did eat and drink, and rose up, and went his way.—These words graphically describe Esau's complete indifference to the spiritual privileges of which he had denuded himself. There is no regret, no sad feeling that he had prolonged his life at too high a cost. And if Jacob is cunning, and mean in the advantage he took of his brother, still he valued these privileges, and in the sequel he had his reward and his punishment. He was confirmed in the possession of the birthright, and became the progenitor of the chosen race, and of the Messiah; but henceforward his life was full of danger and difficulty. He had to flee from his brother's enmity, and was perpetually the victim of fraud and the most cruel deceit. But gradually his character ripened for good. He ceased to be a scheming, worldly-minded Jacob, and became an Israel, and in his pious old age we see a man full of trust and faith in God, unworldly and unselfish, and animated by tender and loving feeling. Purified from his early infirmities, and with all his better nature strengthened and sanctified by sorrow, he shows himself worthy of his second name, and becomes "a prince with God."

26

Adventures of Isaac at Gerar

(2) The Lord appeared unto him.—Only one other time does Jehovah manifest Himself to Isaac (verse 24), and sixty years had now passed since the revelations recorded in chap. 22. Excepting to Abraham, it was only at rare and distant intervals that God spake to the patriarchs. The greater part of their lives was spent under the control of the same ordinary Providence as that which governs our actions now; but on special occasions God was pleased to confirm their faith in Him in a way not necessary now that we have had made known to us the whole counsel of God.

(7) He said, She is my sister.—We have already seen that Abraham at Gerar showed no consciousness of having done wrong in denying his wife (20:2); and we now find Isaac imitating his example with even less reason for his conduct. The circumstances are, however, different. It is the people who inquire about Isaac's relation to Rebekah, and though she was "fair to look upon," yet no annoyance followed upon his denial of her. The king after "a long time" detects their intimacy; but there are no presents, and no marks of respect to Rebekah, and no friendship. It is only after long quarrels, during which Isaac is obliged to withdraw to a long distance from Gerar, that finally peace is made between them.

(8) Abimelech.—Upon this title of the Philistine monarchs see note on 21:22. As eighty years had elapsed since Abraham's sojourn in Gerar, it is highly improbable that the same king was still reigning; but both king and people maintain on this occasion the good character previously deserved.

(12) Isaac sowed in that land.—The tendency, both with Abraham and Isaac, had long been to remain in the region about Beersheba. Isaac had been driven there by the famine, by which he had probably lost most of his cattle, and many even of his people. His large harvest recouped him for his losses, and made him once more a prosperous man; and in due time Beer-sheba was again his home, and with settled habits agriculture was sure to begin.

(15) The wells.—In the East the digger of a well is regarded as a public benefactor; but the Philistines stopped those that Abraham had dug, probably because they regarded his possession of them, though confirmed by the covenant between him and Abimelech (21:32), as an intrusion upon their rights as the people of the country. Envious, too, at the rapid increase of an alien's wealth, they determined to drive Isaac away; and for this no expedient would be more effectual than the preventing him from procuring water for his cattle. Following upon this came an express command of the king to depart, which Isaac obeyed; for he had sought refuge there because of the

57

famine, and had no right to continue at Gerar, if the people refused their hospitality.

(18-22) Isaac digged again the wells ... —This activity of Isaac called forth anew the opposition of the Philistines. His first well was in the wady of Gerar, and was the more valuable because it was not the mere remains of the water of the torrent, but was fed by a spring, as we learn from its being called "a well of living water." But though Isaac had a right to these wells by reason of the old covenant between his father and the king, yet when his claim was resisted he abandoned the well, but in token of displeasure called it Esek, "contention." When compelled to resign his next well he called it by a harsher name—Sitnah, "enmity"; for their opposition was developing into bitter persecution. And now, wearied with the strife, he withdrew far away, and the Philistines, having gained their end, followed him no farther. In quiet, therefore, he again dug a well, and called it Rehoboth, "wide open spaces." It lies to the south of Beer-sheba, about forty miles away from Gerar.

(23-25) He went up from thence to Beer-sheba.—This was a very serious act on Isaac's part. He does not go back to the well Lahai-Roi, where he had so long resided, but to Beer-sheba, his father's favorite home. It was a claim on his part to the rights and inheritance of Abraham, and the claim was admitted. The same night Jehovah appears to him, bids him put away his fears, and renews to him the promises which were his by the right of his birth.

My servant Abraham.—A title of high honor and significance, given to Moses repeatedly, to Joshua (Josh. 24:29), to Israel (Isa. 41:8), and to the Messiah (Isa. 52:13). It means God's prime minister and vicegerent.

Digged a well signifies the re-opening of the well which Abraham had dug, but which had become stopped up by violence or neglect.

(26) Abimelech went to him.—The return of Isaac to Beer-sheba was a matter of serious importance also to Abimelech. The Philistines were themselves an alien race, and an alliance between Isaac and Ishmael, and others of the Semitic stock, might end in their expulsion from the country. Abraham had also been confederate with the Amorites (14:13), and on friendly terms with the Hittites (23:6), the two most powerful races of Canaan, and they might be ready to aid his son. When, then, Isaac thus

retraced his steps, Abimelech, uncertain of Isaac's purpose, determined to offer peace and friendship, and to propose the renewal of the old covenant which had existed between Abraham and the people of Gerar.

(27) Wherefore come ye to me?—Isaac's return had brought matters to a crisis, and the king must now decide whether there was to be peace or war.

(28, 29) The Lord was with thee ... blessed of the Lord.—This use of the word "Lord," that is, Jehovah, is remarkable. In 21:22, 23 Abimelech uses the term Elohim, "God," in accordance with the careful discrimination in the use of the names of the Deity often previously referred to. By the long residence, first of Abraham and then of Isaac, in their territory, the Philistines would indeed have become better acquainted with the religion of the patriarchs. The king did not use any generic or heathen names of the Deity, but that whereby the patriarchs worshiped their covenant God, and his so doing was probably intended as an act of homage to Him.

(33) Therefore the name of the city is Beer-sheba unto this day.—There was no city at this time at Beer-sheba, but one is mentioned at the conquest of Canaan by Joshua (Josh. 15:28). This note, as is the case generally with those which speak of a thing existing "unto this day," was added by Ezra and the men of the Great Synagogue, after the return from Babylon (comp. 22:14); and its meaning is that, whereas Abraham's name had been forgotten while the place lay desolate, this remarkable coincidence of the water being again found, just when the covenant had been confirmed by the customary sevenfold sacrifice, so impressed the minds of the people that the title of Beer-sheba never again passed into oblivion.

Esau's Marriage with Canaanitish Women

(34) Esau was forty years old.—He was therefore of exactly the same age as Isaac was when, sixty years before, he married Rebekah. But by thus intermarrying with idolaters Esau violated the great principle laid down by Abraham (24:3), forfeited thereby his birthright, and, as such marriages were illegal, is even called a fornicator in Heb. 12:16. His conduct was regarded by his parents with "grief of mind"—Heb., "bitterness of spirit": that is, with mingled anger and sorrow. As this conduct of Esau prepares the mind for his final rejection and loss of the birthright, the place of these two verses would rightly be at the beginning of chap 27. The Jews arrange them as a separate section.

27

Jacob by Subtlety Obtains the First-born's Blessing

(1) **It came to pass.**—The importance of this chapter is manifest. Just as in Abraham's life the decision had to be made which of the two sons, Ishmael and Isaac, was to be the heir of the promise, so, here again, there is the same divine election (Rom. 9:10-13): but while Abraham obeyed, though with heavy heart (21:11), Isaac even struggled against God's will, and his assent was obtained by human craft working tortuously to effect that which God would have wrought in His own better way.

Isaac was old.—Isaac was now 117 years of age, but he lived to be 180 (35:28). Probably, therefore, his failing eyesight was the result of some acute disorder, which so enfeebled his general health that he had grown despondent, and thought his death near. But he recovered, and attained to a good old age. Moreover, the term "old" is used in a general sense in the Old Testament, and thus Samuel is described as old in I Sam. 8:1, when we should have spoken of him as at most middle-aged.

(4) **Savoury meat.**—On the rare occasions on which an Arab sheik tastes flesh, it is flavored with almonds, pistachio nuts and raisins. It would thus not be easy for Isaac to distinguish the taste of the flesh of a kid from that of an antelope.

That my soul may bless thee.—We gather from the solemn blessing given to his sons by Jacob (chap. 49) that this was a prophetic act by which the patriarchs, under the influence of the Spirit, and in expectation of death, decided to which son should belong the birthright. Here Isaac resisted the Spirit; for the clear warning had been given that "the elder should serve the younger" (25:23). Isaac may have been moved to this act by indignation at the manner in which Esau had been induced to sell the birthright, and in annulling that sale he would have been within his rights; but he was not justified in disregarding the voice of prophecy, nor in his indifference to Esau's violation of the Abrahamic law in marrying

heathen women. And thus he becomes the victim of craft and treachery, while Jacob is led on to a deed which was the cause of endless grief to him and Rebekah, and has stained his character forever.

(5) **Rebekah heard.**—Had her faith been pure and exalted, she would have known that God would fulfill His word without her help; but all alike act from unworthy motives, and all have their need of punishment. But here the fault began with Isaac, and Rebekah probably considered that she was preventing a grievous wrong.

(13) **Upon me be thy curse.**—No curse followed upon their conduct; but on the contrary, Isaac acknowledged the substantial justice of the act of Rebekah and her son, and confirmed Jacob in the possession of the blessing (verse 33). It seems strange, nevertheless, that neither of them had any scruples at the immorality of the deed, but apparently thought that as the end was right they were justified in using falsehood and treachery.

(15) **Goodly raiment.**—It has been supposed that the elder son held a sort of priestly office in the household, and as Isaac's sight was growing dim, that Esau ministered for him at sacrifices. Evidently the clothing was something special, and such as was peculiar to Esau.

(20) **Because the Lord thy God brought it to me.**—Jacob does not keep up his acting well here, for it was not in accordance with Esau's character to see anything providential in his success in hunting. This may have helped to arouse Isaac's suspicions, who immediately proceeds to examine him.

(29) **Let people serve thee.**—Heb., "peoples." Up to this point the blessing had been general, but now Isaac bestows the birthright, carrying with it widespread dominion, precedence over all other members of the family, and special blessedness. The phrases "thy brethren" and "thy mother's son" include all nations sprung from Abraham, and all possible offshoots from Isaac's own descendants.

Cursed ... and blessed.—This is a special portion of the blessing given to Abraham (12:3); but Isaac stops short with this, and does not bestow the greater privilege that "in him should all families of the earth be blessed" (12:3; 22:18; 26:4). The reason for this may be that it was a blessing which God must grant, and not man; or he may have had misgivings that it was more than Esau was worthy to receive; or, finally, his whole conduct being wrong, he could see

59

and value only the earthly and lower prerogatives of the birthright. Subsequently he bestows the Abrahamic blessing upon Jacob in general terms (28:4); but this, its highest privilege, is confirmed to Jacob by Jehovah Himself (ibid. verse 14).

(33) **Isaac trembled very exceedingly.**—This was not from mere vexation at having been so deceived, and made to give the blessing contrary to his wishes. What Isaac felt was that he had been resisting God. In spite of the prophecy given to the mother, and Esau's own irreligious character and heathen marriages, he had determined to bestow on him the birthright by an act of his own will; and he had failed. But he persists no longer in his sin. Acknowledging the divine purpose, he has no word of blame for Rebekah and Jacob, but confirms to Jacob the possession of the birthright, and declares, "Yea, he shall be blessed."

(36) **Is not he rightly named Jacob?**—In thus playing upon his brother's name, Esau has had a lasting revenge; for the bad sense which he for the first time put upon the word Jacob has adhered to it, no doubt, because Jacob's own conduct made it only too appropriate. Its right meaning is "one who follows close upon another's heels." (See note on 25:26.)

(39) **Isaac his father answered.**—Unwillingly, and only after repeated entreaty and earnest expostulation, and even tears, upon Esau's side, does Isaac bring himself to the effort to lessen in any way the painful consequences to his favorite son of his brother having robbed him of the blessing. Plainly, he felt that he had endeavored to do what was wrong, and was afraid lest he should still be found resisting God's will.

Thy dwelling shall be the fatness.—Most modern expositors consider that the preposition should not be translated "of," but "from," that is:—"Behold thy dwelling shall be away from the fat places of the earth," etc. By this rendering the parts of the blessing agree together. Idumaea, though not destitute of fruitful tracts, and even famous for its orchards, was, as a whole, sterile and unproductive, and the people were restless and unquiet. Moreover, Isaac had already given the corn land and vineyards to Jacob (verse 37), and had no second gift of them in his power. Esau was to inhabit a land which by its barrenness would force him to a life of adventure, military service, and freebooting.

(40) **When thou shalt have the dominion.**—

The prophecy of Edom's subjection to his brother was literally fulfilled, and Idumaea was for ages a mere dependency upon Judah; but in the days first of Joram, and then of Ahaz, it revolted, and recovered its freedom. It was again conquered by Hyrcanus, the nephew of Judas Maccabaeus; nor was its subject condition altered by the fact that the dynasty of the Herods was of Edomite extraction. In troubled times, then, it broke the yoke from its neck; but generally Edom served his brother.

Jacob is Sent Away by His Father and Mother to Haran

(42) **These words of Esau.**—Though spoken "in his heart," Esau had evidently made no secret of his evil purpose, and Rebekah therefore determines to send Jacob to her father's house, not merely for safety, but that he might take a wife from among his own kindred.

(44) **A few days.**—Like Esau (verse 41), Rebekah expected that Isaac's end was near. Really Jacob was absent for forty years and while Isaac lived to see him return, Rebekah saw him again no more.

(46) **Rebekah said to Isaac.**—With this begins a new act. In the previous five verses we had the general results of Rebekah's guile: we have now the special consequence of Jacob's departure for Haran. Upon Rebekah's communication to Isaac follows his decision in the next chapter. In the Hebrew there is no break from the beginning of chap. 27, to the end of verse 9 of chap. 28.

28

(1) **Isaac called Jacob.**—Though Rebekah's primary motive was her concern for Jacob's safety, yet we must not imagine that his marriage was a mere pretext. On the contrary, now that he was acknowledged as the first-born, both he and she would have been abandoning his high position had they not arranged for the fulfillment of his duty in this respect. What is remarkable is the frankness of Isaac's conduct. There is no attempt to substitute Esau for Jacob, nor to lessen the privileges of the latter, but with hearty cheerfulness he blesses the younger son, and confirms him in the possession of the whole Abrahamic blessing.

(2) **Padan-aram.**—See note on 25:20. Throughout this verse Isaac shows a much

more intimate acquaintance with the family at Haran than was possessed by Abraham. (Comp. 24:4.) It was this greater knowledge which made Isaac send Jacob in person, and not a deputy. With a few trusty attendants he would journey till he reached the usual caravan route which led through Damascus to Haran, and would then attach himself to some trading company for escort and society.

(3) **God Almighty.**—Heb., **El Shaddai.** As it was Isaac's purpose in this blessing to confirm Jacob in the possession of the promises made to Abraham, he is careful to use the same title as that borne by God in the covenant whereby the land of Canaan was given to his seed, and of which the sacrament of circumcision was the seal. (See 17:1.)

Esau Marries a Daughter of Ishmael

(6) **When Esau.**—The solemn transfer of the birthright to Jacob, and Isaac's complete assent thereto, must have been the cause of no little grief to Esau, and evidently it made him feel that he had greatly contributed to this result by his own illegitimate marriages. When, then, he sees Jacob sent away to obtain a wife, in accordance with the rule established by Abraham, he determines also to conform to it, and marries a daughter of Ishmael.

Jacob's Dream

(10) **And Jacob.**—Henceforward his fortunes solely occupy the inspired narrator, though Isaac had still sixty-three years to live. (See note on 11:27.)

(11) **He lighted upon a certain place.**—As it lay twelve miles north of Jerusalem, in the mountains of Ephraim, Jacob had already been on the route at least four days (see note on 22:4); thus, meditating much and praying much, he had in those four days drawn near to God, and is at last accepted. The interest in Jacob's life lies in the gradual improvement and progress of his character. Religion was always a reality with him; but at first it was of a low type, and marred by duplicity and earthly scheming. His schemes succeed, but bring with them sorrow and trial; and trial purifies him, and gradually he advances into a religion of unselfish and holy piety.

He took of the stones ... —Jewish commentators identify the place with Mount Moriah, and say that the stone which Jacob placed under his head was one of those which had formed the altar upon which Isaac had been bound for sacrifice.

(12) **Behold a ladder ...** —Isaac had confirmed Jacob in the possession of the blessing before he started on his long journey, but it was necessary that he should also have the divine ratification of his appointment; for the chief privilege was the covenant with God previously confirmed to Isaac, his father (17:19-21). In his sleep he sees a ladder, or staircase, rising from the ground at his side, and reaching up to heaven. It tells him that heaven and earth are united, and that there is a way from one to the other. Upon these stairs "messengers of Elohim are ascending and descending," carrying up to God men's prayers, and the tale of their wants and sorrows, of their faith and hope and trust; and bringing down to them help and comfort and blessing. The covenant God is seen stationed at the head of this pathway between earth and heaven. But besides this, the value of Jacob in Jehovah's sight arises now from his being the appointed ancestor of the Messiah, in whom all the families of the earth were to be blessed (verse 14). Christ, too, is the Way symbolized by this ladder (John 14:6), and the bridge of union between the material and the spiritual world (I Tim. 2:5). Our Lord, accordingly, Himself claims that "the angels of God ascend and descend upon Him" (John 1:51).

(16) **Surely the Lord** (Jehovah) **is in this place.**—Jacob was not unaware of the omnipresence of the Deity: what astonished him was that Jehovah should thus reveal Himself far away from the shrines where He was worshiped. First Abraham and then Isaac, had for so long made Beer-sheba their home, that Jacob probably knew little about the sanctity of the spot, and felt himself far away from all the religious associations of his youth, and from that "presence of Jehovah" which in antediluvian times had also been supposed to be confined to certain localities (4:16). But one great object of the dream was to show that Jehovah watches over the whole earth, and that messengers to and fro come from Him and return unto Him.

(19) **Beth-el ... Luz.**—In Josh. 16:1, 2, we find that Luz and Beth-el were distinct places, though near one another; and with this agrees the present passage. For plainly, Jacob and his attendants did not go inside the city, but slept on the open ground.

Probably at the time of Joshua's conquest Beth-el was rather a holy place than a town; and when Ephraim seized upon Luz and put the people to the sword (Judges 1:23-25), the victors transferred the name of Beth-el to it. Thus the spot where Jacob slept would not be the town of Beth-el, but some place a mile or two away from it.

(20-22) Then shall the Lord (Jehovah) **be my God.**—This is a false translation, and gives a wrong sense. Jacob, in his vow, which implies no doubt on his part, but is his acceptance of the terms of the covenant, says: "If Elohim will be with me, and will protect me on this journey that I go, and will give me bread to eat and clothing to wear, and if I come again in peace to my father's house, and Jehovah will be my Elohim, then this stone which I have set up as a pillar shall be Beth-Elohim; and of all that thou shalt give me I will surely pay thee tithes." Verse 20 and 21 are a recapitulation of the mercies of which he was to be the recipient, while in verse 22 Jacob states what shall be his vow of gratitude.

But what was a Beth-Elohim? Jacob apparently meant a place where prayer and offerings would be acceptable, because God had manifested Himself there; and His vow signified that if, preserved by Jehovah's care, he was permitted to visit the place again, he would consecrate it to Jehovah's service, and spend there in sacrifice, or in some other way to His honor, the tithe of whatever property he might have acquired.

29

Marriage of Jacob With Leah and Rachel

(1) Jacob went on his journey.—Confirmed in the possession of the birthright by God as well as man, and encouraged by the promise of the divine presence, and of a safe return home, he casts no wistful glances back, but pursues his journey under the exhilarating influence of hope.

The people of the east.—Usually the Arabians are designated by this phrase, but it here signifies the tribes who inhabited northern Mesopotamia.

(2) A great stone was upon the well's mouth.—The region around Haran, though fertile, is very dry, and the chief use of the stone was to prevent the well from being choked with sand. Besides this, the stone may have marked that the well was private property: for, as we have seen in the account of the covenants of Abraham and Isaac with Abimelech, no possession was more valued than that of wells. It is probable that Laban had at least a first claim upon its enjoyment.

(5) Laban the son of Nahor.—Laban was really the son of Bethuel and grandson of Nahor; but Nahor was the founder of the family, as being the original immigrant from Ur, who came to supply Abraham's place on his departure.

(9) Rachel came with her father's sheep.—As forty years at least elapsed between this meeting of Jacob and Rachel and the birth of Benjamin, she must have been a mere child at this time.

(12) Her father's brother.—Really his nephew; but terms of relationship are used in a very indefinite way in Hebrew. (Comp. verses 5, 15; 13:8, etc.)

(17) Leah was tender eyed.—Leah, whose name signifies "languor, weariness," had dull bleared eyes. Probably she suffered, as so many do in that hot sandy region, from some form of ophthalmia. Rachel (Heb., "the ewe") was, on the contrary, "beautiful and well favoured" (Heb., "beautiful in form and beautiful in look"). Yet it was not Rachel, with her fair face and well-proportioned figure, and her husband's lasting love, that was the mother of the progenitor of the Messiah, but the weary-eyed Leah.

(18) I will serve thee seven years for Rachel thy younger daughter.—Wives had to be purchased in the East (24:53), and as Jacob had brought no rich presents, such as Abraham had sent when seeking a wife for his son, he had only his personal services to offer.

(19) It is better that I give her to thee.—It is still the custom among the Arabs to prefer a relative as the husband of a daughter, and on giving a moderate dowry the elder cousins can claim the elder daughters in marriage, and the younger the younger. Thus Jacob, as the second son, had a claim upon Rachel. As Jacob offered seven years' service for Rachel, and gave a second seven years' service for her after he had been tricked into taking Leah, we may conclude that the length of time was not unreasonable.

(23) He took Leah his daughter.—As the bride is taken to the bridegroom's house closely veiled (see note on 24:65), and as probably there was some similarity in voice and form between the two sisters, this deception was quite easy. But Leah must have been a party to the fraud, and therefore Jacob's dislike of her was not altogether without reason.

(26) It must not be so done in our country.—We have seen that it is still customary for the elder cousin to take the elder daughter, and the younger the younger. But Laban affirms that if the elder daughter be not claimed, it was the rule in Haran for her to take precedence over her sisters. Apparently Leah loved Jacob (30:15), and Laban wanted a continuance of his service, and so this unscrupulous plot was arranged between them upon a pretext which, if not false, was yet overstrained. Jacob plainly had no idea of such a custom, and would not have given seven years' service for Leah.

(28) Fulfil her week.—The marriage festival seems to have lasted a week, as was the custom in later times (Judges 14:12), and to have forsaken Leah during this period would have been to offer her an insult which her brothers must have avenged. Appeased, therefore, by the promise of Rachel as soon as the seven days are over, Jacob rather than quarrel with the whole family, submits to the wrong.

(28) He gave him Rachel ... to wife also.—After the monogamy of Abraham, and the stricter monogamy of Isaac, how came Jacob to marry two wives? Probably, even after Leah had been forced upon him, Jacob regarded Rachel as his own, and as polygamy was not actually forbidden, considered that he was only acting justly by her and himself in marrying her. He had seen Esau blamed, not for marrying two wives, but for taking Hittites; and his love for Rachel would make him need but little argument. The only other alternative, namely, to have divorced Leah, would have been worse, and happily divorce was not a practice as yet introduced.

Birth of Jacob's Eleven Sons, and His Daughter

(31) Leah was hated.—We must not often this down too much; for plainly Leah was not the object of love at all. It was her fruitfulness which gave her value in her husband's eyes, and when this ceased, Jacob utterly neglected her (30:15).

(32-35) She called his name Reuben.—There is something very touching in the history of these four births. When the first child is born, Leah joyfully calls him "Reuben," that is, "See a son!" and fondly hopes that now she is a mother her husband will love her. And the mention of her "affliction" shows that, while she loved Jacob tenderly, he was to her more than unloving. Her second son she calls "Simeon," that is "hearing," and, disappointed in her first hope, regards the child as a gift of Jehovah to compensate for the lack of affection for which she so longed. Her third son she calls "Levi," that is, "joined," still hoping that as in her tent alone there were children to play around the father, he would be more united to her. But her hope remains unfulfilled. And when her fourth son is born, she calls him "Judah," that is, "praise." Throughout, in the midst of her melancholy, there is a tone of fervent piety, and that not merely to God, but to the covenant Jehovah. And now slowly she parts with her hope of human affection, and finds comfort in Jehovah alone. "This time," she says, "I will praise Jehovah." And it was this son of the despised one, whose birth called forth from her this hymn of simple thanksgiving, who was foreordained to be the ancestor of the promised seed.

30

(1) Give me children, or else I die.—There is an Oriental proverb that a childless person is as good as dead; and this was probably Rachel's meaning, and not that she should die of vexation. Great was the affliction to a Hebrew woman of being barren (I Sam. 1:10).

(3) Behold my maid Bilhah.—Rachel had little excuse for this action; for there was no religious hope involved, as when Sarah gave Hagar to Abraham (16:2), but solely vexation at her own barrenness, and envy of her sister. All that can be said in her defense is, that the custom existed, and, perhaps because it was distasteful to the wife, was looked upon as meritorious (verse 18).

She shall bear upon my knees.—It appears that there was a custom of placing the new-born child upon the knees, first of the father, who, by accepting it, acknowledged the infant as his own; and secondly, upon those of the mother. In this case, as Bilhah's children were regarded as legally born of Rachel, they would be placed upon Rachel's knees.

(6) God hath judged me.—Rachel has no misgivings herself as to the rectitude of her conduct, and by the name she gives the child, she affirms that God also had given a decision in her favor; for "Dan" means "judging." While, too, Leah had spoken of Jehovah, Rachel speaks of Elohim, not merely because she could not expect a child of Bilhah to be the ancestor of the Messiah, but because she was herself half an idolater (31:19). When, however, she has a child of her own, she, too, taught by long trial, speaks of Jehovah (verse 24).

(8) With great wrestlings.—Rachel's was a discreditable victory, won by making use of a bad custom, and it consisted in weaning her husband still more completely from the unloved Leah. Now that Bilhah and children were added to the attractiveness of her tent, her sister, she boasts, will be thought of no more.

(9-13) Leah ... took Zilpah ...—By ceasing to bear, Leah had lost her one hold upon her husband's affection, and to regain it she follows Rachel's example. The struggle of these two women for the husband gives us a strange picture of manners and morals, but must not be judged by our standard. Leah herself regards the bestowal of her handmaid upon Jacob as a deserving act of self-sacrifice (verse 18). The names, moreover, which she gives Zilpah's children show that the happier frame of mind to which she had attained when she called her fourth son Judah, "praise," remained unbroken. With regard to the meaning of the word "Gad," all the versions render it "prosperity, good fortune." Zilpah's other son is called Asher, that is, "happy."

Mandrakes.—Heb., "love-apples," the size of a small plum, round, yellow, and full of soft pulp. In the East the mandragora has been, and is, the subject of many superstitions, and its Hebrew name arose from the popular belief that it was a specific against barrenness. Rachel, therefore, who still yearned for children of her own, was anxious to obtain some of the fruit, and Leah consents only upon the proffered condition that Jacob shall spend the night in her tent.

(18) Issachar.—Heb., "there is hire." In her eyes the birth of her fifth son was a divine reward for the self-sacrifice involved in giving her maid to Jacob, and which had been followed by years of neglect of herself. As, too, it is said that "God hearkened unto Leah," we may feel sure that she had prayed for God's blessing upon her reunion with her husband. The shame really was that she should have been forced thus to buy her husband's attentions.

(20) Zebulun.—The substantive **zebul** is not uncommon, and means "dwelling, station."

As a woman's value in the East rises with each son, Leah now hoped for more love from her husband. Nor does she seem to have been disappointed.

(21) Dinah.—That is, "judgment." The birth of Dinah is chronicled because it led to Simeon and Levi forfeiting the birthright. Jacob had other daughters (37:35; 46:7), but the birth of a girl is regarded in the East as a misfortune; no feast is made, and no congratulations offered to the parents.

(22-24) God remembered Rachel.—Rachel's long barrenness had probably humbled and disciplined her; and, cured of her former petulance, she trusts no longer to "love-apples," but looks to God for the great blessing of children. He hearkens to her prayer, and remembers her. The name Joseph may signify "he adds," which is the meaning made prominent by Rachel. As Joseph was born six or seven years before Jacob left Padan-aram, Rachel had been barren for twenty-six years. In her joy at Joseph's birth there is no trace of the ungenerous triumph over Leah so marked in her rejoicing at the birth of the sons of Bilhah; and in her trust that "Jehovah would add to her another son," she evidently had in mind the covenant promises, which a son of her own womb might now inherit. As a matter of fact, the long struggle for supremacy lay between the houses of Joseph and Judah; and Judah finally prevailed.

Jacob Serves Laban Six Years for Wages

(25) Jacob said unto Laban, Send me away.—After Jacob had served Laban fourteen years for his two daughters, he continued with him for twenty years without any settled hire, receiving merely maintenance for himself and family. Jacob desired to return to his father, if for no other reason, yet because now it was time to provide for his children, and at Isaac's death he was joint heir of his property.

(32) The speckled and spotted cattle (sheep).—In the East sheep are generally white, and goats black or brown. Jacob therefore, proposes that all such shall belong to Laban, but that the particolored should be his hire. By "speckled" are meant those sheep and goats that had small spots upon their coats, and by "spotted," those that had large patches of another color. Besides these, Jacob is to have all "brown cattle," that is, "sheep." In verse 35 we have another word, "ring-straked," that is, having the colors in stripes. This is never the case with sheep, but goats often have their coats thus definitely marked.

(35) And he removed.—Jacob was to make the selection at once, but the next day Laban was to look over all those put aside, and if he found among them any white sheep, or black or brown goats, he was to regard them as stolen,—that is, not merely might he take them back, but require the usual fine or compensation.

(36) He set three days' journey betwixt himself and Jacob.—This means that Laban required that there should be an interval of between thirty and forty miles between "himself," that is, his flocks, and those of Jacob. His wealth in sheep and goats must have been enormous to require so large a separate feeding-ground; and this we learn from verse 30 had been the result of Jacob's care.

(37) And Jacob took him rods ... — Jacob's plan was to place before the ewes and she-goats at breeding time objects of a speckled color, and as he put them at their watering-place, where everything was familiar to them, they would, with the usual curiosity of these animals, gaze upon them intently, with the result that many of them would bear speckled young (see note on 31:4).

(40) Jacob ... set the faces of the flocks toward ... —As the speckled lambs and kids would for some time remain with Laban's flocks, this may perhaps mean that, when driving them to water, Jacob placed all the striped kids and dark lambs together, that, by being in a mass, they might work upon the imagination of the ewes and she-goats. Finally, after these had conceived he drove the parti-colored young away to his own flocks.

(43) The man increased exceedingly. — Wool, as the chief material for clothing, is a very valuable commodity in the East, and by the sale of it Jacob would obtain means for the purchase of male and female servants and camels. The latter were especially valuable for purposes of commerce, in which Jacob evidently was actively engaged, and from which probably came his chief gains.

31

Jacob's Flight—The Pursuit of Him by Laban, and Their Reconciliation

(3) The Lord said unto Jacob.—This is probably the revelation, more exactly described in verses 10-13, as given to Jacob in a dream.

(4) Jacob sent and called Rachel and Leah ... —Jacob's speech to his wives consists of three parts: first, he tells them of the change in Laban's manner toward him, and his consequent fear of violence; he next justifies his own conduct toward their father, and accuses him of repeated injustice; finally, he announces to them that he had received the divine command to return to Canaan. As regards the second point, Jacob had undoubtedly used stratagems to increase his wages, and of this his wives must have been well aware. On the other hand, we learn that Laban had openly violated the terms of the bargain; and, whereas, all the parti-colored kids and lambs were to belong to Jacob, no sooner did they increase beyond expectation, than Laban, first, would give him only the speckled, the most common kind, and, finally, only the ring-straked, which were the most rare. Of course Jacob would keep all the sheep and goats which he had once made over to the charge of his sons; it would be the additions to them from Laban's flocks which were thus diminished.

It was at the breeding time (verse 10) that Jacob saw the vision, with its twofold lesson: the first, that the multiplication of his wages had been God's gift, and not the result of his own artifices; the second, that this bestowal of wealth was to enable him to return to Canaan. His wives heartily concurred in his purpose, but it was not till the time of sheep-shearing came (verse 19) that he effected his escape. It is not easy to calculate the interval between this and the time when they began their journey.

(7) Ten times.—That is, a good many times.

(10) Rams.—Heb., "he-goats." The King James Version has made the alteration, because the word rendered "cattle" is really "sheep" (and so in verses 8, 12, etc.); but, like our word "flock," it also included goats.

(12) Grisled.—That is, covered with spots like hail stones.

(19) Laban went to shear his sheep.—The sheep shearing was a joyous time, when the hard toil of the shearers was relieved by feasting (I Sam. 25:8). But why was not Jacob present? Probably, as the result of the growing estrangement between them, caused by the too rapid increase of Jacob's riches, Laban and his sons had gradually taken the management of their flocks into their own hands.

Images.—Heb., **teraphim**, called Laban's gods in verse 30, and we find that their worship continued throughout the Old Testament history. We gather that they had a head shaped like that of a man, but, probably, a dwarf trunk (verse 34), which proves that they, in this case, were of no great size. In the history of the thorough reformation carried out by King Josiah we find the mention of teraphim among the things put away (II Kings 23:24). We learn, nevertheless, from Zech. 10:2, that they were still used for divination; and from Hos. 3:4 that both pillars and teraphim had long been objects of ordinary superstition among the ten tribes. As Nebuchadnezzar divines by them (Ezek. 21:21) they were possibly of Chaldaean origin; and, probably, were not so much worshiped as used for consultation. Here Rachel stole them upon the supposition that they would bring prosperity to her and her husband.

(21) The river.—The Euphrates.

Mount Gilead.—Gilead, "the region of rock," was the mountainous frontier between the Aramean and Canaanite races.

(23) His brethren.—As Jacob, who had no relatives with him except his sons, applies this term in verse 46 to his followers, it is, probably an honorable way of describing retainers, who were freemen and of a higher class than men-servants.

Seven days' journey.—The hill, which subsequently was called Mount Gilead, lay to the south of the Jabbok; but as Mahanaim, reached some days after the meeting with Laban, is to the north of that river, the word Gilead was evidently applied to the whole of the region of chalk cliffs on the east of the Jordan. This is made certain by the fact that Laban overtook Jacob in seven days. But as the distance from Haran to the most northerly part of this country (afterward assigned to the half-tribe of Manasseh) was fully three hundred miles, it would require hard riding on the part of Laban and his brethren to enable them to overtake Jacob, even on the borders of this region. Thus Jacob had reached Canaanite ground—a matter of considerable importance—before his father-in-law overtook him.

(26-30) Laban said...—Laban reproaches Jacob, first, for carrying away his daughters secretly, which was an affront to them (verse 26) and an injury to his own feelings (verse 28); secondly, he tells him that he should have punished him but for the divine warning; lastly, he accuses him of stealing his teraphim.

(31, 32) Jacob answered.—Jacob gives the true reason for his flight; after which, indignant at the charge of theft, he returns, in his anger, as rash an answer about the teraphim as Joseph's brethren subsequently did about the stolen cup (44:9).

(34) The camel's furniture.—That is, the camel's saddle. It is now made of wickerwork, and is protected by curtains and a canopy. Probably Rachel's was far simpler; and as the teraphim seem to have had heads shaped like those of a man, and dwarf bodies, they would easily be crammed under it.

(36) Jacob was wroth.—Naturally he regarded the accusation about the teraphim as a mere device for searching his goods, and when nothing was found gave free vent to his indignation.

(42) The fear of Isaac.—That is, the object of Isaac's worship. The reason given by the Jewish commentators for this remarkable way of describing the Deity whom Isaac served is that, as his father was still alive, Jacob would have been wanting in reverence, if he had spoken of God as "Isaac's God," even though Jehovah had condescended so to call Himself (28:13).

(43) Laban answered...—Laban does not attempt any reply to Jacob's angry invectives, but answers affectionately. He proposes that they should make a covenant, by which Jacob should bind himself to deal kindly with his daughters, and to take no other wife; while he promises for himself that he would do Jacob no wrong.

(47) Jegar-sahadutha.—These are two Syriac words of the same meaning as Gal-eed, "Heap of Witness." A Syriac (or Aramaic) dialect was most probably the ordinary language of the people in Mesopotamia.

(49) Mizpah.—That is, "Watchtower." In the reason given for the name Laban calls Jacob's God "Jehovah," an appellation which he must have learned from Jacob and which proves not merely that he had some knowledge of Hebrew but that he and Jacob had talked together upon religious subjects, and that he was not a mere idolater, though he did call the teraphim his gods.

(53) Judge.—The verb is plural, "be judges." We ought, therefore, to translate "the gods of their father." Apparently, he thought that Abraham took one of Terah's Elohim, and Nahor another. His views were thus polytheistic, and so, generally, the ancients regarded the gods as local beings, with powers limited to certain districts. Jacob swears by the one Being who was the sole object of Isaac's worship. (See note on 20:13.)

32

(1) Jacob went on his way.—Jacob now takes his journey through the country that was to be the heritage of his seed, and doubtless he was harassed by many anxious thoughts; for Esau might prove a fiercer foe than Laban. It was fit therefore that he should receive encouragement, and so after some days, probably after about a week's journey southward, he has a vision of "angels of God."

Angels of God.—As Jacob on his road to Padan-aram had been assured of God's watchful care of him by the vision of the angels ascending and descending the stairs, so now also in a dream he sees the angels encamped on each side of him, to assure him of protection against his brother.

(2) Mahanaim.—That is, "the two camps," his own and that of the angels; or, possibly, two camps of angels, one on either side of him.

Jacob's Reconciliation With Esau (32:3-33:16)

(3) Jacob sent messengers.—As Jacob traveled homeward to Hebron the news somehow reached him that Esau, at the head of a large body of retainers, was engaged in an expedition against the Horites, a miserable race of cave men, utterly unable to cope with Esau and his trained servants. We learn from 36:6 that Esau's home was still with Isaac at Hebron. He seems also to have taken a Horite wife (36:5), and being thus connected with the country, upon Isaac's death he willingly left it, and it then became "the country," Heb. "the field of Edom." Its other name, "Seir," i.e., rough, hairy, shows that it was then covered with forests, and the term "field" that it was an uncultivated region. It was entirely in the spirit of the adventurous Esau to make this expedition, and on his

father's death to prefer this wild land to the peaceful pastures at Hebron.

(9) Jacob said.—Jacob's prayer, the first recorded in the Bible, is remarkable for combining great earnestness with simplicity. After addressing God as the Elohim of his fathers, he draws closer to Him as the Jehovah who had personally commanded him to return to his birthplace (31:13). And next, while acknowledging his own unworthiness, he shows that already he had been the recipient of the divine favor, and prays earnestly for deliverance, using the touching words "and smite me, mother upon children." His mind does not rest upon his own death, but upon the terrible picture of the mother, trying with all a mother's love to protect her offspring, and slain upon their bodies. In Hosea 10:14 this is spoken of as the most cruel and pitiable of the miseries of war. But finally he feels that this sad end is impossible; for he has God's promise that his seed shall be numerous as the sand of the sea. In prayer to man it may be ungenerous to remind another of promises made and favors expected, but with God each first act of grace and mercy is the pledge of continued favor.

(13) He lodged there.—That is, at Mahanaim. On the first news of Esau's approach in so hostile a manner, Jacob had divided his possessions into two main divisions, in the hope of saving at least one. He now, quieted by his prayer, makes more exact arrangements, selects a present for Esau of five hundred and fifty head of cattle, sends them forward with intervals between, that repeated impressions might soften his brother's fierce mood, sees all his followers safely across the Jabbok, and remains alone behind to pray. As he thus placed everything in Esau's power, faith seems to have regained the ascendancy over his fears, though he still takes every prudent measure for the safety of those whom he loved.

(20) I will appease him.—The Heb. literally is, "I will cover his face." The covering of the face of the offended person, so that he could no longer see the offense, became the usual legal word for making an atonement (Lev. 9:7, etc.).

(22) The ford Jabbok.—The boundary between the tribes of Manasseh and Gad. It flows through a deep ravine, with so rapid a current as to make the crossing of it a matter of difficulty. This ravine, or wady, has a width of from four to six miles.

(24) There wrestled.—This verb, **abak,**

67

occurs only here, and without doubt it was chosen because of its resemblance to the name Jabbok. Its probable derivation is from a word signifying "dust," or because, as was the custom in Greece, they rubbed their bodies with it.

A man.—Such he seemed to be to Jacob; but Hosea (12:4) calls him an angel; and, in verse 30, Jacob recognizes in him a manifestation of the Deity. It was one of the many signs indicative of a more complete manifestation by the coming of the Word in the flesh.

(25) The hollow of Jacob's thigh was out of joint.—The hollow is in Hebrew the pan or socket into which the end of the thigh bone is inserted, and the verb more probably signifies that it was sprained from the over-tension of the muscles in the wrestling. But, in spite of his sprained tendons, Jacob still resisted, and could not be thrown down, and the angel, unable to gain any further advantage, at last acknowledges Jacob's superiority, and at sunrise craves permission to depart.

(26) Let me go ... —Heb., "send me away, for the gleam of morning has gone up." The asking of permission to depart was the acknowledgment of defeat. The struggle must end at daybreak, because Jacob must now take up his day's work; and the wrestling had been for the purpose of giving him courage, and enabling him to meet danger and difficulty in the power of faith.

Except thou bless me.—The vanquished must yield the spoil to the victor; and Jacob, who had gradually become aware that the being who was wrestling with him was something more than man, asks of him, as his ransom, a blessing.

(28) Israel.—That is, "a prince of God," or "one powerful with God." (See note on 17:15.) Esau had given a bad meaning to the name of Jacob, nor had it been undeserved. But a change has now come over Jacob's character, and he is henceforth no longer the crafty schemer who was ever plotting for his own advantage, but one humble and penitent, who can trust himself and all he has in God's hands.

(29) Wherefore ... —In the blessing which followed there was a clear proof that Jacob's opponent was a divine personage.

(30) Peniel.—Elsewhere "Penuel," and so probably it should be read here. It means, "the face of God." For the rest of the verse see note on 16:13.

(32) The sinew which shrank.—It was probably the large tendon which takes its origin from the spinal cord, and extends down the thigh to the ankle. By the Greeks it was named **tendo Achillis**, because it reaches the heel. Jewish commentators notice that this was the second special ordinance imposed upon the race of Abraham, circumcision having been enjoined upon them by God, while this grew out of an historical event in the life of their progenitor, to the reality of which it bears remarkable testimony.

33

(3) He passed over before them.—While providing some small chance of escape for his wives and children, arranged according to their rank, Jacob manfully went first and placed himself entirely in Esau's power. He endeavored, nevertheless, by his sevenfold obeisance in acknowledgment of Esau's superiority, to propitiate him; for the cause of the quarrel had been Jacob's usurpation of Esau's right of precedence as the first born. This bowing in the East is made by bending the body forward with the arms crossed, and the right hand held over the heart.

(4) Esau ran to meet him.—Whatever may have been Esau's intention when he started, no sooner does he see his brother than the old times of their childhood return to his heart, and he is overcome with love; nor does he ever seem afterward to have wavered in his fraternal affection.

(10) For therefore I have seen thy face.—The behavior of Esau is very generous. He wished to spare his brother so large a present, and therefore leads the conversation to it, knowing, of course, what was the meaning of the five herds, as their drivers had delivered to him Jacob's message. To have refused it, however, would have been a mark of hostility, especially as Jacob represented it as the gift of an inferior for the purpose of obtaining the favor of one from whom he had feared danger.

(14) Unto Seir.—This implies a purpose of visiting Esau in his new acquisition, not carried out probably because Esau did not as yet settle there, but returned to Hebron to his father.

Jacob's Settlement in Canaan—Dinah's Wrong, and the Fierce Vengeance of Simeon and Levi (33:17-34:31)

(17) Succoth.—That is, "booths," in the tribe of Gad, on the east of the Jordan, in the corner formed by that river and the Jabbok. He not only put up some protection, probably wattled enclosures made with branches of trees, for his cattle, but built a house for himself—something, that is, more solid than a tent: and there he lay until he was healed of his lameness. The strained sinew would require some months of perfect rest before Jacob could move about: but it was healed, for "Jacob came whole and sound to the city of Shechem."

(18) In the land of Canaan.—Jacob therefore had now crossed the river Jordan, and so far completed his homeward journey. Probably as soon as he had recovered from his lameness he visited his father, but as his possessions were large, and Esau was the chief at Hebron, there was no room at present for him to dwell there, nor in fact was this possible until Isaac's death.

(19) He bought ...—Abraham had been obliged to buy land for a burial place, and we find even then that the field he wanted had an owner who could give him a title to its possession. Jacob a century later finds it necessary to buy even the ground on which to pitch a tent, though his cattle might still roam freely about for pasture. In this, the first parcel of ground possessed by Jacob, the embalmed body of Joseph was buried (Josh. 24:32; see also John 4:5).

An hundred pieces of money.—Heb., "a hundred **kesitas.**" The etymology of the word is uncertain, and apparently all knowledge of its meaning had at an early period passed away.

(20) He erected there an altar.—Abraham had already built an altar in this neighborhood (12:7), and Jacob now followed his example—partly as a thank-offering for his safe return, partly also as taking possession of the country; but chiefly as a profession of faith, and public recognition of the new relation in which he stood to God. This especially appears in his calling the altar "El, the Elohim of Israel."

34

(1) Dinah ... went out to see the daughters of the land.—Jacob evidently remained at Succoth only until he was **shalem**, sound and whole from his sprain, and Dinah's visit was one of curiosity, for she went "to see the daughters of the land," that is, she wanted to see what the native women were like, and how they dressed themselves. Josephus says that she took the opportunity of a festival at Shechem: but as neither her father nor brothers knew of her going, but were with their cattle as usual, it is probable that with one or two women only she slipped away from her father's camp and paid the penalty of her girlish curiosity. It is probable that her dishonor took place within a few weeks after Jacob's arrival there.

(7) He had wrought folly in Israel.—The great anger of Jacob's sons agrees as completely with the general harshness of their characters as the silence of the father with his habitual thoughtfulness: but it was aroused by a great wrong. The use, however, of the term **Israel**, to signify the family of Jacob as distinguished from his person belongs to the age of Moses, and is one of the proofs of the arrangement of these records having been his work. In selecting them, and weaving them together into one history, he would add whatever was necessary, and in the latter half of this verse we apparently have one such addition.

(21) Let us take their daughters ...—In a young community, such as this of the Hivites at Shechem appears to have been, the addition of a large number of women was a valuable increase of their strength, and one that brought the promise also of future extension. Jacob's men were also chiefly of the Semitic stock, and therefore possessed of high physical and mental endowments: and as they were rich in cattle and other wealth, their incorporation with the people of Shechem would raise it to a high rank among the petty states of Canaan. There was much plausibility, therefore, in Hamor's proposal and arguments.

(25) Simeon and Levi, Dinah's brethren.—As born of the same mother, they, with Reuben and Judah, were especially bound to espouse their sister's cause, but the method they took was cruel in the extreme. And it seems that these two were the leaders in the plot, having probably excluded Reuben from it, as a man of feeble character and opposed to bloodshed (37:22); and Judah, as one too honorable to take part in so nefarious a transaction. Long afterward Jacob speaks of it in terms of the strongest reprobation (49:5-7).

(29) Their little ones.—Heb., "their **taf.**" The LXX has altered the order here, but otherwise translates correctly "their persons," that is, their property in men servants and maid servants, as opposed to to their cattle and their wealth in goods. In 50:8 the LXX translates "clan," and in verse

21 "household." The slaves thus seized would form the most valuable part probably of the spoil.

(30) Ye have troubled me.—Jacob's timidity led him to think first of the danger that would result from the conduct of his sons, and only afterward of the cruelty and treacherousness of their deed.

35

Jacob Returns to Beth-el and Hebron. Death of Isaac

(1) Arise, go up to Beth-el.—The position of Jacob at Shechem had become dangerous; for though the first result of the high-handed proceeding of Simeon and Levi was to strike the natives with terror (verse 5), yet reprisals might follow if they had time to learn the comparatively small number of Jacob's followers. It was necessary, therefore, to remove; but besides this, Beth-el was the goal of the patriarch's journeyings. He had made a solemn vow there on his journey to Padan-aram, and though forty-two years had elapsed, it had not been forgotten (see 31:13); and the divine command to go thither was the outward authorization of what his own conscience dictated.

(2) Strange gods.—Besides Rachel's teraphim, many, probably, of the persons acquired by Jacob at Haran were idolaters, and had brought their gods with them. Besides these, the numerous men and women who formed the **"tafs"** of the Shechemites were certainly worshipers of false deities. The object, then, of this reformation was not merely to raise Jacob's own family to a higher spiritual state, but also to initiate the many heathen belonging to their households into the true religion. Outward rites of purification and changes of garment were to accompany the religious teaching given, because of their symbolical value. This reformation is interesting as being the first of a long series of such acts constantly recurring in the history of Israel; and especially it is parallel to the sanctification of the people at Sinai. Also, symbolical washings were enjoined (Exod. 19:10-14). These subsequently were still practiced under the Law, and grew into the baptism by which we are now admitted into the Church of Christ.

(4) Earrings.—Earrings seem to have been worn not so much for ornament as for superstitious purposes, being regarded as talismans or amulets. Hence it was from their earrings that Aaron made the golden calf (Exod. 32:2-4).

(7) El-beth-el.—That is, "the God of the house of God"; the God into whose house he had been admitted, and seen there the wonders of His providence.

(8) Deborah.—As she was at Hebron with Rebekah when Jacob journeyed to Haran, he must have somehow gone there before this, have seen his father, and told him of his fortunes. Apparently Rebekah was then dead, and Jacob brought back Deborah with him. How dear she was to them is shown by their calling the tree under which she was buried "the oak of weeping."

(9) When he came out of Padan-aram.—At Beth-el Jacob, when going forth, had seen the dream which assured him of divine protection: at Beth-el, on his return, God renews the covenant, confirms to him the name of Israel, and transfers to him the promises of a numerous seed and of the possession of the land. It was the ratification to him of the inheritance of all the hopes and assurances given to Abraham.

(11) God Almighty.—Heb., **El-shaddai**, the name by which God had entered into the covenant with Abraham (17:1).

(13) God went up from him.—This formula, used before in chaps. 17:22; 18:33, shows that this manifestation of God's presence was more solemn than any of those previous occasions upon which the deity had revealed Himself to Jacob. It was, in fact, the acknowledgment of the patriarch as the heir of the Abrahamic covenant.

(15) Jacob called . . .—See 28:19. The name had, of course, remained unknown and unused, as what then passed had been confined to Jacob's own inward consciousness. He now teaches the name to his family, explains the reason why he first gave it, and requires them to employ it. But with so grand a beginning the town was debased to unholy uses, and from being Beth-el, "the house of God," it became Beth-aven, "the house of iniquity" (Hos. 10:5).

(16) Ephrath (the fruitful) and **Beth-lehem** (the house of bread) have virtually the same meaning, but the latter name would be given to the town only when its pastures had given place to arable lands, where corn was sown for bread.

(18) Ben-oni . . . Benjamin.—Rachel, in her dying moments, names her child "the son of my sorrow." Jacob's name, "son of the right hand," was probably given not merely that the child might bear no ill-

70

omened title, but to mark his sense of the value and preciousness of his last born son.

(20) That is the pillar of Rachel's grave unto this day.—This is a later addition, but whether inserted by Moses or Ezra we cannot tell. Its site was known in the days of Samuel (I Sam. 10:2); and as the pillar would be a mass of unwrought stone, with which the natives would have no object in interfering, its identification upon the conquest of Canaan would not be difficult.

(21) The tower of Edar.—The word used often means a beacon hill, a hill on which a tower for observation is erected. Until Esau, with his possessions, withdrew to Seir, there would be no room for Jacob and his flocks and herds at Hebron, but he would at Eder be so near his father as to be able often to visit him. And thus his exile was now over, and he was at last at home.

(22) Reuben.—Again another grief for Jacob to mar his return home, and this time it arises from the sin of his first born, who thereby forfeits the birthright. It was the thought of these miseries, following upon his long years of exile, which made Jacob speak so sorrowfully of his experience of life before Pharaoh (chap. 47:9).

36

The Tôldôth Esau

(1) The generations of Esau.—This **tôldôth** consists of chaps. 36-37:1. It begins with an enumeration of Esau's wives, in which the names are different from those given in chaps. 26:34; 28:9. Next we have the genealogy of Esau, upon the same principle as that whereby the **tôldôth** Ishmael was inserted immediately after the history of Abraham's death (25:12-18); but this is followed, in verses 20-30, by a genealogy of the Horite inhabitants of Mount Seir. Among these Esau dwelt as the predominant power, but nevertheless on friendly terms. We next have a list of kings who are said to have reigned in Edom "before there reigned any king over the children of Israel." Of these Edomite kings, it is remarkable that they do not succeed one another by hereditary succession, nor have they the same capital, but seem to belong to a time of anarchy, like that which existed in Israel under the Judges. During this period the Edomites and Horites were fused together, chiefly by conquest (Deut. 2:12, 22). Finally, we have a list of the eleven dukes of Edom, "after their places." As these dukes represented tribes or clans, this catalogue is geographical, and as such it is described in verse 43, and was intended to give the political arrangement of the land at the later date when this addition was made, and when considerable changes had taken place since the time of the first settlement.

These last two documents, forming verses 31-43, were probably added at the time when the Books of Samuel were composed; but as we find the list of the kings given also in I Chron. 1:43-50, and as at that date great activity existed in completing the canon of Holy Scripture, some suppose that the lists in both places are by the same hand. It is entirely wrong to describe them as interpolations; for it was the rule to add to and complete genealogies; and besides there existed in the Jewish Church a living authority in the prophets who had the right and power to make necessary additions to the divine record. It is to the "schools of the prophets" that we owe, under God's providence, the existence of most of the Old Testament Scriptures, and the preservation of all of them; and they did not preserve them for the sake of the authors, but for the sake of what was written. And there is nothing derogatory to the authority or inspiration of Holy Scripture in believing that the prophets were from time to time moved by the Spirit to add to what had been written.

(2) Adah the daughter of Elon the Hittite.—In chap. 26:34, she is called "Bashemath the daughter of Elon the Hittite." As Adah means "ornament," and Bashemath "sweet-scented," both may possibly have been terms of endearment, arising from modifications of her Hittite name.

Aholibamah the daughter of Anah the daughter of Zibeon the Hivite.—It seems certain that Aholibamah was a Horite, and therefore, entirely distinct from Judith. Judith (26:34), the first wife, apparently had no children and hence arose the temptation to Esau to marry some one besides. Now we see the reason for giving the genealogy of the Horites, and also why Esau took the Horite land for a possession. In some expedition into the country of Seir, Esau had married the daughter of one of the dukes there, and through her had acquired a right to ducal rank.

Excepting the Semites, no race in Palestine stands as high as the Hittites, and no race as low as the Horites. The meanness of the Horites is not a deduction merely from their having dwelt in caves, for the country is so admirably adapted to this mode of living that it still exists there; but they are omitted from the table of nations in chap. 10, and seem generally to have been a feeble aboriginal race.

(5) In the land of Canaan.—We find Esau with a band of armed men in Seir on Jacob's return from Padan-aram, but he still had his home at Hebron with his father until Isaac's death, twenty-two years later. Evidently he had taken Aholibamah home, and she had borne him three sons. After Isaac's death the land of Seir had so great attractions for him that he migrated there with his share of Isaac's wealth, and left Hebron to Jacob, who now moved down from the town of Eder, and took possession of the homestead of his fathers. Thus the inheritance of the birthright came finally to Jacob by Esau's own act, and would doubtless have come to him; only his father's blessing and the transference to him of the Abrahamic promises would have been given him, not at the time of Isaac's temporary illness, but on his deathbed.

(8) Mount Seir.—The land of Idumea extends from the southern extremity of the Dead Sea to the Gulf of Elath, and consists of a chain of mountains running parallel to the Akaba, or continuation of the deep depression through which the Jordan flows till it loses itself in the Dead Sea. The border of it was distant only some fifty or sixty miles from Hebron, so that Esau's transference of himself there was an easy matter.

(12) Amalek.—The Amalekites constituted one of the most widely spread races of antiquity, occupying the whole country from Shur, on the borders of Egypt, to Havilah, in Arabia Felix. But probably there was a fusion of some of the Horites with the Amalekites, just as the Kenezites, under Caleb, were fused into the tribe of Judah. Of the Amalekites in Seir, Amalek, the grandson of Esau, was probably the founder; for in verse 16 he is called a "duke," and therefore one district of the country would belong to his descendants, in the same manner as each son of Jacob had a territory called after his name. There is no difficulty in the absence of their names from chap. 10. They were regarded by Israel, not as a nation, but as a hateful horde of plunderers.

37

(1) And Jacob . . . —This verse is not the beginning of a new section, but the conclusion of the **Tôldôth Esau.**

The Tôldôth Jacob

Joseph Is Sold by His Brethren Into Egypt

(2) The generations of Jacob.—This **Tôldôth** extends to the end of Genesis, and is the history of the removal, through Joseph's instrumentality, of the family of Jacob from Canaan into Egypt, as a step preparatory to its growth into a nation.

Joseph being seventeen years old.—He was born about seven years before Jacob left Haran, and as the journey home probably occupied two full years, he would have dwelt in Isaac's neighborhood for seven or eight years. Isaac's life was prolonged for about twelve years after the sale of Joseph by his brethren.

And the lad was with the sons of Bilhah, and with the sons of Zilpah.—As the youngest son it was his duty to wait upon his brothers, just as David had to look after the sheep while his brothers went to the festival; and was also sent to the camp to attend to them (1 Sam. 16:11; 17:17, 18). The sons of Jacob were dispersed in detachments over the large extent of country occupied by Jacob's cattle, and Joseph probably after his mother's death, when he was about nine years old, would be brought up in the tent of Bilhah, his mother's handmaid. He would naturally, therefore, go with her sons, with whom were also the sons of the other handmaid. They do not seem to have taken any special part in Joseph's sale.

(3) He was the son of his old age.—The epithet is intelligible if Jacob had waited twenty-seven years after his marriage with Rachel, before Joseph was born. There would then be a considerable interval between him and the other sons; and though Rachel had a second son some years afterward, yet Joseph would continue to be the son long looked for, whose birth had given him so great happiness; whereas his joy at Benjamin's coming was bought at the terrible price of the mother's death.

A coat of many colours.—Two explanations are given of this phrase; the first, that it was a long garment with sleeves or fringes; the other, that it was composed of patchwork of various colors. The latter is the more probable interpretation. Some have thought that Jacob by this dress marked out Joseph as the future head of the family, in the place of Reuben, supposing it to indicate the priestly office borne by the first-born; but this is doubtful, and it was Judah to whom Jacob gave the right of primogeniture.

(5) Joseph dreamed a dream.—As being from time to time used by God for providential purposes, dreams are occasionally described as a lower kind of prophecy (Num. 12:6-8; Deut. 13:1; 1 Sam. 28:15). In the life of Joseph they form the turning point in his history, and it is to be noticed that while revelations were frequently made to Jacob, we have henceforward no record of any such direct communication from God to man until the time of Moses. The utmost granted to Joseph was to dream dreams; and after this the children of Israel in Egypt were left entirely to natural laws and influences. (Comp. note on 26:2.)

(7) Stood upright.—Heb., "took its station." It implies that the sheaf took the position of chief. We gather from this dream that Jacob practiced agriculture, not occasionally, as had been the case with Isaac (26:12), but regularly, as seems to have been usual also at Haran (30:14).

(10) His father rebuked him.—In making the sun and moon bow down before him, Joseph's dream seemed to violate the respect due to parents. As Jacob probably regarded his son's dreams as the result of his letting his fancy dwell upon ideas of self-exaltation, he rightly rebuked him; while, nevertheless, "observed the saying," (Comp. note on Luke 2:51.)

(12) Shechem.—Jacob's sons seem to have retained Shechem, by right of their high-handed proceedings related in 34:27-29. It gives us a great idea of Jacob's wealth and power, that while dwelling a little to the north of Hebron, he should send part of his cattle so far away as to Shechem, a distance of sixty miles.

(17) Dothan.—This town was twelve miles north of Shechem, and is famous as being the place where Elisha struck the Syrian army with blindness (II Kings 6:13-23). It is situated in a small but fertile valley, and Jacob's sons, having exhausted the produce of the larger plain round Shechem, had moved northward there.

(19) This dreamer.—Heb., "this lord of dreams," a phrase expressive of contempt.

(20) Into some pit.—Heb., "into one of the pits," that is, cisterns dug to catch and preserve the rain water. In summer they are dry, and a man thrown into one of them would have very little chance of escape, as

they are not only deep, but narrow at the top. The Jewish interpreters accuse Simeon of being the prime mover in the plot, and say that this was the reason why Joseph cast him into prison (42:24). We learn from 42:21 that Joseph begged hard for mercy, and to be spared so painful a death, but that his brothers would not hear.

Though never represented in the Scriptures as a type of Christ, yet the whole of the Old Testament is so full of events and histories, which reappear in the gospel narrative, that the Church Fathers have never hesitated in regarding Joseph, the innocent delivered to death, but raised later to glory, as especially typifying to us our Lord. Pascal (**Pensées**, ii.9. 2) sums up the points of resemblance—in his father's love for him, his being sent to see after the peace of his brethren, their conspiring against him, his being sold for twenty pieces of silver, his rising from his humiliation to be the lord and saviour of those who had wronged him; and with them the saviour also of the world. As too, he was in prison with two malefactors, so was our Lord crucified between two thieves; and as one of these was saved and one left to his condemnation, so Joseph gave deliverance to the chief butler, but, to the chief baker punishment. Joseph's history is likewise a vindication of God's providential dealings with men. He is innocent, and pure in life, but wronged again and again; yet every wrong was but a step in the pathway of his exaltation.

(25) A company of Ishmeelites.—Dothan was situated on the great caravan line by which the products of India and Western Asia were brought to Egypt. As the eastern side of Canaan is covered by the great Arabian desert, the caravans had to travel in a northwesterly direction until, having forded the Euphrates, they could strike across from Tadmor to Gilead. Probably these merchants belonged to some branch of the Canaanites, who were the great traders of ancient times, and which Ishmael and Midian had compelled to submit to their sway. (But see note on 25:2.) Really Ishmeelites, Midianites, and Medanites are all one and the same, if we regard them as bearing the names only politically.

(28) Twenty pieces of silver.—Twenty shekels of silver were computed, in Lev. 27:5, as the average worth of a male slave under twenty. It would be about $20 in money.

(29) Reuben returned.—Reuben, between the casting of Joseph into the pit and evening meal, had apparently gone a long round to fetch in the more distant cattle, and probably had remained away as long as possible, in order to feel sure that his brethren would on his return be at their dinner. He hoped thus to be able to go alone to the cistern, and rescue Joseph, and send him away home before the rest could interfere.

(34) Many days.—Jacob mourned for Joseph not merely during the usual period, but as long as to move even the hearts of those who had wronged him. We learn how long and intense Jacob's sorrow was from 45:26-28.

(35) Into the grave.—Heb., **Sheol**, which, like Hades in Greek, means the place of departed spirits. (Comp. note on 15:15.)

(36) Captain of the guard.—Heb., "chief of the slaughterers." The king's bodyguard, whose business it would be to execute condemned criminals.

38

Family History of Judah

This episode is no interruption of the narrative, for, as we have seen, the **Tôldôth Jacob** is the history generally of Jacob's posterity, and especially of the next great event in their development into a nation, namely the descent into Egypt. Two main reasons may be assigned therefore for giving this history of Judah's life; the first, that it shows the great risk of utter contamination incurred by the patriarchs in living among the Canaanites; the second, and more important, that Judah was invested by his father with the rights of primogeniture, and therefore that this history belongs to the genealogy of the Messiah.

(1) At that time.—This does not mean at the time of Joseph's sale; for as there was only an interval of twenty-two years between that event and the descent into Egypt, this period is scarcely long enough for the events recorded in this chapter. The chronology gives time for Judah to have been Joseph's senior by twenty years, and the events recorded here probably began soon after his father's arrival at the tower of Eder.

Adullamite.—The town of Adullam, near which was David's famous cave, lay in the great valley of Elah, which formed the highway from Hebron to the country of the Philistines. Judah "went down" there because it was toward the sea, and the road is an actual descent from the hill country of Judah into the Shephelah, or lowland, in which Adullam was situated. The sons of Jacob often, probably, with a few retainers, made expeditions in search of pastures for their cattle; and Hirah, apparently, had shown Judah hospitality on some such journey, and finally a friendship had grown up between them.

(8) Go in unto thy brother's wife.—We learn from this that the law of the Levirate, by which the brother of the dead husband was required to marry the widow, was of far more ancient date than the law of Moses. Its object, first of all, was to prevent the extinction of any line of descent, a matter of great importance in those genealogical days; and, secondly, it was an obstacle to the accumulation of landed property in few hands, as the son first born after the Levirate marriage inherited the property of his deceased uncle, while the second son was the representative of the real father. The Mosaic Law did not institute, but regulated the custom, confining such marriages to cases where the deceased brother had died without children, and permitting the brother to refuse to marry the widow, under a penalty, nevertheless, of disgrace. Onan, by refusing to take Tamar, may have been actuated by the selfish motive of obtaining for himself the rights of primogeniture, which would otherwise have gone to his eldest son, as the heir of his uncle Er.

(12) Timnath.—Timnath was on the Philistine border, beyond Bethshemesh. It lay only about seven miles beyond Adullam. For sheepshearing, see note on 31:19.

(15) Because she covered her face.—The Jewish commentators all agree that this was not the custom of harlots; and as Judah, in verse 21, calls her **kedeshah**, one consecrated, he probably thought that she was a woman performing the vow required of every female votary of the Phoenician Venus (Astarte), once in her lifetime (Herod. i.199). Hence the hire was a kid to be sacrificed to the goddess. As for Tamar, her object was to assert her claim to the inheritance of Er. Lange considers that the wickedness of Er had caused him, equally with Onan, to neglect her, and that consequently there was no real incest. This is made probable by her immediate conception.

(18) Thy bracelets.—Heb., "thy cord." Judah evidently suspended his signet around his neck by a cord. Probably each man of distinction had his emblem, and in chap. 49 Jacob seems to refer to them. Thus Judah's emblem was a lion, Zebulun's a ship, Issachar's an ass, etc.

Thy staff.—The staff in ancient times was elaborately adorned. It is from these staves that the scepters of kings, and the batons of field marshals, etc., are derived.

(23) Lest we be shamed.—Judah regards what he had done as shameful, and having his friend's testimony, if needed, to prove that he had performed what he promised, he bears with the loss of his signet and staff, rather than let the people know that he had been guilty of an act which they too would condemn.

(24) Let her be burnt.—As being by law the wife of Shelah, Tamar was condemned by Judah in right of his position, as head of the family, to the punishment usual for adultery. In subsequent times, this penalty was limited to one who had married mother and daughter (Lev. 20:14); or to the daughter of a priest guilty of unchastity (ibid. 21:9). On this account, the Jewish expositors argue that Tamar belonged to a priestly family, and some even think that she was descended from Melchisedek.

(25, 26) She sent ... —The Talmud praises Tamar for so acting, as to bring no public disgrace upon Judah; and he acknowledges that he was most to blame, because the cause of her crime was his own failure to act justly by her.

39

Joseph's Fortunes in the House of Potiphar

(1) Potiphar ... bought him.—Having given the genealogy of Judah's house, which, owing to the sins of Reuben, Simeon, and Levi, was now to be the Messianic line, and invested with the inheritance of the Abrahamic promises, the history reverts to Joseph, because it was through him that Israel was to be transplanted into Egypt. His life there is divided into two main portions, during the first of which, for thirteen years, he was a slave; while during the second, for seventy years, he was governor over all the land of Egypt.

(2) The Lord.—Heb., "Jehovah." In the history of Joseph there is the greatest possible precision in the use of divine names. Wherever, as here, the writer speaks in his own person, he uses the name Jehovah, which is a strong argument for the Mosaic authorship of this narrative, as while the

whole color of this **Tôldôth** is strongly Egyptian, the word Jehovah was not specifically the name, in the family of Abraham, for God in covenant with man until the time of the Exodus (Exod. 6:3). Excepting one place (49:18) the name of the Deity everywhere is either El or Elohim. Very probably Joseph had left memorials of his life behind him, in which naturally he used only the general term God. In framing these into a history, the writer carefully shows that it was the covenant Jehovah who guarded and kept his innocent worshiper.

(4) He served him.—Rather, "he ministered to him" (Num. 3:6), as the word is used not so much of work as of office. His office is explained more exactly in the next verse, where we read that "he made him overseer," or his deputy. In the Egyptian monuments we often find an overseer with writing materials keeping an account of all expenditure and of the labor done.

(7) His master's wife.—Egyptian women did not live in seclusion, nor did they go veiled. The story of an innocent youth slandered by an unchaste woman whom he has repulsed became a favorite subject with classical authors.

(14) He hath brought in.—The wife ascribes it as a fault to Potiphar, that, by buying a foreign slave, he had exposed her to insult. And so in verse 17.

(20) Prison.—It is supposed to mean a round or arched tower. As the king's prisoners were confined there, it was a portion of Potiphar's official residence, as he was captain of the royal bodyguard (see note on 40:3). We learn from Ps. 105:18 that Joseph's treatment in the prison at first was very severe; but as Potiphar in 40:4 is said to have entrusted Joseph with the charge of the chief butler and baker, he must soon have been convinced of his innocence.

40

Joseph Interprets the Dreams of the Chief Butler and Baker

(1) Butler.—Heb., "one who gives to drink," cupbearer. We learn in verse 11 that it was grape wine which he gave the king to drink.

Baker.—There is proof from the monuments that they had carried the art of making confectionery to great perfection.

(3, 4) In the house of the captain of the

guard.—That is, of Potiphar. As he is said to have charged Joseph with the care of these two high officials, he must, before this, have become aware of his innocence. But as the wife in ancient times in Egypt was endowed with all the husband's property, and was a formidable person, Potiphar may not have wished to offend her.

(8) There is no interpreter.—In Egypt it was the business of men trained for the purpose, called in 41:8, "magicians" and "wise men," to interpret dreams, and to such the butler and baker could have no access from their prison. But Joseph denies that art and training can really avail, and claims that the interpretation belongs to God.

(11) Into Pharaoh's hand.—Heb., "I placed the cup upon Pharaoh's palm," i.e., the hollow produced by bending the fingers inward. Egyptian cups had no stems, but were flat bowls or saucers, held in the very way which the cupbearer describes.

(15) I was stolen.—Joseph here speaks only generally, as his purpose was to arouse the sympathy of the Egyptian by making him know that he was free born, and reduced to slavery by fraud. It would have done harm rather than good to have said that his sale was owing to family feuds; and, moreover, noble-minded men do not willingly reveal that which is to the discredit of their relatives.

Land of the Hebrews.—Jacob and his race had settled possessions in Canaan at Hebron, Shechem, Beer-sheba, etc. The term Hebrew, moreover, was an old one; for in the ancient record of the invasion of Palestine by Chedorlaomer, we saw that Abram was described as "the Hebrew" (14:13). But Joseph did not mean that the land of Canaan belonged to them, but that he was stolen from the settlements of these "immigrants," and from the land wherein they sojourned.

(16, 17) Three white baskets.—Most commentators agree in rendering it "baskets of white bread." The "bakemeats" were all preparations of pastry and confectionery, as throughout the Bible "meat" does not mean flesh, but food. (Comp. notes on Luke 24:41; John 21:5.)

(19) Shall Pharaoh lift up thy head from off thee.—In verse 13 the "lifting up of the butler's head" meant his elevation to his former rank. Here there is the significant addition "from off thee," implying that he would be beheaded, and his body publicly exposed to ignominy.

41

Joseph Interprets Pharaoh's Dreams; He Is Made Governor of Egypt, and Marries There

(1) Pharaoh dreamed.—After two years spent in the prison, the time has now come for Joseph's elevation to power; and it is to be noticed that this was not brought about by those arts by which men usually attain to greatness, such as statesmanship, or military skill; nor was it by accident, but according to the Biblical rule, by the direct intervention of Providence. Just as centuries afterward, Daniel rose to high office at Babylon by God making known to him the dream of Nebuchadnezzar; so here, the transplantation of Israel into Egypt is brought about by the revelation to Joseph of "what was to be hereafter."

The river.—The Pharaoh in whose reign Joseph became governor of Egypt is generally supposed to have been Apophis, the most famous of the shepherd kings. But some, however, decide in favor of King Amenemha III, the greatest monarch of the noble twelfth dynasty, and the last king of all Egypt.

(2) Kine.—The cow was regarded by the Egyptians as the symbol of the earth, and of agriculture; and naturally both the kine and the ears of wheat rose out of the river, because as no rain falls in Egypt, its fertility depends entirely upon the overflow of the Nile.

(8) Magicians.—The word used here probably means the "sacred scribes" who were skilled in writing and reading hieroglyphics. But in ancient times the possession of real knowledge was generally accompanied by a claim to an occult and mysterious acquaintance with the secrets of the gods and of nature. And as the people regarded the knowledge which such scribes really possessed as more than human, the claim was easily maintained, or, rather, grew naturally out of the superstition for the multitude. So, too, the "wise men" were men educated and trained, but probably the profession of magic, of divination, and astrology was that which gained for them wealth and honor, and not the possession of whatever real science existed at that time in Egypt.

(14) He shaved himself.—Herodotus (2:36) mentions that the Egyptians allowed their hair and beards to grow only when in mourning; whereas in Palestine the beard was regarded as a manly ornament. On Egyptian monuments only captives and men of low condition are represented with beards. In the prison, therefore, Joseph would leave his beard untrimmed, but when summoned into the king's presence, he would shave it off.

(19) Poor and very ill favored and lean-fleshed.—Pharaoh, in his recital, describes his dreams at greater length than is the case in the narrative (verses 2-7), and also mentions the impressions made upon his imagination by what he had seen.

(34) Take up the fifth part of the land.—Heb., "let him fifth the land," that is, exact a fifth part of the produce. It has been supposed that it had been usual in Egypt to pay to the king a tithe of the crop, and the doubling of the tax would not press very heavily on the people in these years of extraordinary abundance. As the reason of the enactment would be made known, it would also induce all careful people to store up a portion of their own superabundance for future need. Subsequently, a fifth of the produce was fixed by Joseph permanently as the king's rent.

(38) In whom the Spirit of God is.—Joseph from the first declared that he neither claimed for himself, nor possessed any art of divination, but that "Elohim would answer (that which would be for) the peace of Pharaoh" (verse 16). And not only does Pharaoh now recognize the truth of Joseph's words, but sees also in him the instrument by which Elohim had spoken. But besides the interpretation of the dreams, Joseph had given the king wise and prudent advice, and he justly felt that one so gifted by God, and so intelligent in counsel, was the person best fitted to carry Egypt through the years of trouble in store for her.

(40) Over my house.—The chief over the palace was in ancient times next in power to the sovereign.

(42) Vestures of fine linen.—In the East it is usual on all occasions of showing the royal favor, to give changes of raiment: but there is here the further signification, that as this fine white linen was the special dress of the king and the priests, the bestowal of it indicated Joseph's admission into the ruling classes of Egypt. Probably as he married a priest's daughter, he was himself also previously enrolled among the ranks of the priesthood.

(45) Zaphnath-paaneah.—This word is Egyptian; it means "food of the living," in

the sense of "he who feeds the world." There is no authority for the supposition that the name means "revealer of secrets."

On.—This is also an Egyptian word, signifying the sun, where in Hebrew the name of this city was Beth-shemesh, "house of the sun"; in Greek, Heliopolis. It was famous for its temple of Ra, the sun, destroyed at an early period by the Persians, but still remarkable for its ruins. It is situated about six miles northeast of Cairo.

A difficulty has been felt by some that Joseph, a worshiper of the one God, should ally himself with an idolater. The elevation of a slave to high rank is not an uncommon occurrence in the East. Joseph would rightly regard the whole matter as providential, and though he might not know for what exact purpose, as regards his race, he was thus exalted, there was noble work for him to do in saving Egypt from perishing by famine. The narrative throughout represents him as remaining true to the religion of his family, but probably on public occasions he would be required to attend at the religious solemnities of the Egyptian gods. We must remember, however, that their worship had not degenerated as yet into the miserable idolatry of later times, and that the Egyptian creed contained much primeval truth, though in a corrupted form. Pharaoh himself, in verses 38, 39, speaks as one who acknowledged a supreme God, and Joseph throughout freely called him Elohim. As for Asenath, no doubt Joseph would teach her higher views of the Deity, and make her acquainted with the religious hopes and destinies of the Abrahamic race.

(51) Manasseh.—That is, "causing to forget." Joseph has been blamed for forgetting "his father's house," but the phrase means that now that he was married and had a child, he ceased to suffer from homesickness, and became contented with his lot. He pined no longer for the open downs of Canaan as he had done in the prison; but his love for his father was as warm as ever.

(52) Ephraim.—That is, "fruitfulness." The dual ending probably intensifies the meaning.

(54) "The Dearth."—As the Nile at this early period was not assisted and regulated in its overflow by dams and canals, famines were much more common in Egypt than when subsequently the kings had done so much to provide against this danger. As, too, this dearth was "in all lands," in Arabia, Palestine, Ethiopia, etc., there was evidently a long period of excessive drought.

42
First Visit of Joseph's Brethren
to Egypt

(6) Joseph's brethren came and bowed down themselves before him. —Throughout the land of Egypt Joseph would sell by deputy, and only give general directions; but the arrival of so large a party as Joseph's ten brethren, each probably with several attendants, would be reported to the governor in person, as certainly was the case with Abraham when he went into Egypt (12:14, 15). Such visits would happen only occasionally, and the arrival of foreigners was always a matter looked upon with suspicion, especially upon the Arabian frontier.

(7) Joseph . . . spake roughly unto them. — Joseph has been accused of harshness in his treatment of his brethren, and still more so of his father in forcing him to send away Benjamin. The latter was, no doubt, the result of his great longing to see his only brother, and he may not have known how dear he was to Jacob, or have reflected upon the pain which his father would feel in parting with him. Still it was but a temporary separation, to prepare for a happy reunion. As regards his half-brethren, Joseph was obliged to prove them, and he did nothing to them which they did not richly deserve. Possibly his first emotion toward them was one of indignation, but it melted away, when, even in but one of them, he saw proof that they were not entirely destitute of better feeling (see verses 22, 24).

(8) Joseph knew. —As this is twice repeated, some suppose that Joseph (in verse 7) had only a suspicion, from their dress and appearance, that these Canaanites were his brethren; but when they spake the Hebrew tongue (comp. verse 23), every doubt was removed. They would not recognize him, as he used the Egyptian language, was clad in a white linen dress, and being but seventeen when sold, had during the twenty years of separation changed in appearance much more than they had.

(15) By the life of Pharaoh. —It was common in ancient times to swear by the king's life (see I Sam. 17:55; II Sam. 14:19), and even by the life of Jehovah (ibid. 15:21; II Kings 2:2, 4, 6). It is only in the stricter morality of the Gospel that such oaths are forbidden (Matt. 5:33-37).

(20) Bring your youngest brother. — Besides his desire to be reunited to his brother, Joseph reasonably felt that the possession of Benjamin would be the best means of inducing his father also to come to him. While substituting a much milder proposal for his former one, that nine should remain in prison, and the tenth go to fetch Benjamin, Joseph nevertheless takes care to make his brethren feel that he was in earnest.

(21) We are verily guilty. —Though they were now suffering unjustly, it brought back to their mind their former sin; and the fact that it was so fresh in their memories is a sign of the reality of their repentance.

(24) He turned . . . and wept. —There was no bitterness in Joseph's heart, and at their first word of regret he melted. But lest he should lose Benjamin he overcame his feelings, and commanded that Simeon should be bound, choosing him, probably, as the one chiefly guilty of the wrong done him. As soon as the rest had departed, he would probably make his imprisonment as easy as possible, especially as he was detained, not as an evildoer, but as a hostage.

(25) To restore every man's money into his sack. —It is evident that each one had made his own separate purchase for his own household. The restoration of the money frightened Joseph's brethren, as they saw in it a pretext for their detention on their next visit. But Joseph could not have meant thus to alarm them, as their fear would act as an obstacle to their coming again accompanied by Benjamin. It is more likely that he intended it as an encouragement, and sign of secret good will.

(37) Slay my two sons. —Reuben does not suppose that Jacob would really put his grandchildren to death, but simply means to offer his father a strong assurance that Benjamin would run no danger. It was but feeble talk, in agreement with the general weakness of Reuben's character.

(38) Then shall ye bring down my gray hairs with sorrow to the grave. —Jacob, both here and in 47:9, speaks as one on whom sorrow had pressed very heavily. Probably by this time he had lost Leah as well as Rachel, but the blow that had struck him utterly down had evidently been the loss of Joseph, in whom Rachel had still seemed to live on for him. And therefore now he clung the more warmly to Benjamin, and it is plain that the father's deep sorrow for the loss of the petted son had softened the hearts of his brethren.

43

The Second Visit to Egypt

(7) The man asked us straitly.—In 42:13 they appear rather as volunteering a statement of their family relations than as having it wrung from them by cross-examination. But really this history must be taken as explaining and supplementing the former.

(8) The lad.—Benjamin was now between twenty and thirty years of age. The term "lad" in Judah's mouth is one of affection, but even in itself it suits very well to a youth of this age. Rebekah (in 24:16) is called in the Hebrew "a lad" (see note there), and so is Shechem in 34:19. The assertion, therefore, that Benjamin is here represented as a mere boy, is disproved by the use of the word in the Hebrew.

Our little ones.—Heb., "our **tafs**," that is, our households. (See note on 34:29.)

(9) Then let me bear the blame for ever.— This is much more manly and therefore more persuasive than Reuben's talk about pledging the lives of his children. For it was real, nor would it be a slight matter to stand in his father's presence all the rest of his life as one guilty of a grievous crime.

(11) The best fruits.—The smallness of the present does not so much show that Jacob had very simple ideas respecting the greatness of the king of Egypt, as that there was a scarcity even of these fruits. Probably the trade in them had ceased, and therefore even a moderate quantity would be welcome.

(23) Your God ... —Either Joseph had instructed his steward what to say, or he had trained his household generally in the truths of his religion. The word for "treasure" means "hidden treasure," or as we call it a "windfall." By bringing out Simeon he would remove their worst fears, and so at last they consent to go in.

(28) They bowed down.—This was the literal fulfillment of the first dream concerning the eleven sheaves making obeisance. As their business in Egypt was to buy corn, there was a fitness also in their being represented as sheaves.

(32) By himself ... by themselves.— These caste distinctions were common in ancient times. Joseph probably had his food served separately because of his high rank; but the word "abomination" shows that eating with foreigners was shunned by the Egyptians for religious considerations. He-

rodotus (2:41) says that the Greeks were equally the objects of their dislike, and that the use even of a Greek knife would render food, otherwise clean, polluted in the eyes of the Egyptians.

(33) They sat.—The Egyptians are always represented on the monuments as sitting at their meals. The brethren, on finding themselves placed according to their age, must have supposed that Joseph possessed powers of divination, especially as the giving of due precedence was and is looked upon in the East as a matter of high importance.

(34) Messes.—A portion of food from that prepared for the chief is regarded in the East as a mark both of honor and friendship, and the largeness of Benjamin's mess marked him out as the special object of Joseph's regard. It has been supposed that Joseph intended to try his brethren by this preference, and see if they were still envious. More probably it was dictated simply by his love.

44

The Cup is Placed in Benjamin's Riding Bag

(2) Put my cup ... —Rather, "bowl," as it signifies a large round vessel from which the wine was poured into the drinking cups. Joseph's purpose apparently was to detain no one but Benjamin, and it was only when Judah spoke so nobly, and pointed out that Jacob's heart would be broken with grief if he lost the one remaining son of Rachel, made more dear to him by his brother's fate, that he determined to give a home to them all. He naturally supposed that his father had long since ceased to grieve for himself, and probably even hoped to prevail upon him subsequently to join him in Egypt. But when Judah offered himself for slavery rather than that his father should suffer the grief of seeing them return without Benjamin, Joseph understood that Jacob's anguish would be great beyond endurance, and he also became aware that his brethren were no longer as heartless as they had shown themselves of old.

(5) Whereby ... he divineth.—Cup divination was common in Egypt in ancient times, and was a kind of clairvoyance, the bowl being partly filled with water, and the eye of the diviner fixed upon some one point in it till, wearied with gazing, a state of half stupor was induced, during which

79

the mind, freed from the control of reason, acted in a manner parallel to its operation in dreams. In verse 15, Joseph asserts that he practiced this art, and innocently. The genuine piety and goodness of Joseph would not raise him above the reach of the superstitions of his time.

(9) Let him die.—Joseph's brethren, conscious of their innocence, deny the theft, and, like Jacob when accused of stealing the teraphim (31:32), declare that the guilty person shall die, and the rest be made slaves; readily too they consent to be searched, and take their traveling-bags from off the asses on which they were riding. The steward, who knew where the bowl was, answers that only the man in whose bag it is found shall be punished, and that not by death but by slavery. When the bowl was found in Benjamin's possession all hope was gone, and they rent their clothes in uncontrollable grief.

(17) God forbid.—Had they been as hardhearted as when they sold Joseph into slavery, they would readily have gone away, leaving their brother to his fate. But they had changed, and therefore they earnestly exerted themselves for his deliverance, though they must have felt it to be an almost hopeless task. They would feel sure of Benjamin's innocence, but they would also remember that the previous day Joseph had shown him the utmost honor; and this would be a proof to them that for some reason or other the Egyptian governor had taken a fancy to him, and determined to have him in his service; and that therefore he had contrived this wicked scheme.

(18) Then Judah came near.—The power of Judah's speech lies in the facts themselves, which gain in pathos from being simply told; but the ending is grand because of the speaker's magnanimity.

45

Joseph Is Reconciled to His Brethren, and Encourages Them and His Father to Make Egypt Their Home

(1) Joseph could not refrain himself.—The picture which Judah had drawn of his father's love for Benjamin, the thought that by separating them he might have made his father die of grief, and the sight of his brethren, and especially of Judah offering to endure a life of slavery in order that Benjamin might go free, overpowered Joseph's

feelings, and he commanded all his attendants to quit the apartment in order that there might be no restraint upon himself or his brethren when he made known to them that he was the brother whom they had so cruelly years ago condemned to be a slave.

(4) I am Joseph your brother.—There is much force in the assurance that he was still their brother. For they stood speechless in terrified surprise at finding that the hated dreamer, upon the anguish of whose soul they had looked unmoved, was now the ruler of a mighty empire. But with magnanimous gentleness he bids them neither to grieve nor be angry with themselves; for behind their acts there had been a watchful Providence guiding all things for good.

(7) To preserve you a posterity in the earth.—Heb., "To put for you a remnant in the land," that is, to preserve a remainder for you, as the word is translated in II Sam. 14:7. During the seven years' famine many races probably dwindled away, and the Hebrews, as mere sojourners in Canaan, would have been in danger of total extinction.

(8) A father.—This was a not uncommon title of the chief minister or vizier of Oriental kings.

(10) The land of Goshen.—This land, also called "the land of Rameses" (47:11), probably from the city "Raamses," which the Israelites were compelled to build there (Exod. 1:11), was situated on the eastern bank of the Nile, and apparently commencing a little to the north of Memphis extended to the Mediterranean, and to the borders of the Philistines' land (Exod. 13:17). It probably was an unsettled district, but rich in pastures, and belonged in a loose way to Egypt. Here the Israelites were constantly joined by large numbers of Semitic immigrants, who were enrolled in their "tafs," and swelled the rapidly increasing number of their dependents. For, as we have seen before, not merely the lineal descendants of Abraham were circumcised, but all his household and his slaves; and being thus admitted into the covenant became members of the Jewish church and nation (17:23).

(24) See that ye fall not out by the way.—Heb., "do not get angry on the journey." Joseph feared that they might reproach one another for their treatment of him, and try to throw the blame on the one or two chiefly guilty, and that so quarrels might ensue. This is the meaning given to the passage in all the versions, and agrees with Joseph's efforts to quiet their fears, and convince them of his good intentions.

(26) Jacob's heart fainted.—Heb., "grew cold." This was not the effect of incredulity or suspicion, but of surprise. It is only when he sees the wagons, and other clear proofs of the fact, that life returns to his benumbed faculties, and he becomes capable of joy.

46

Emigration of Israel and His Sons Into Egypt

(1) Israel ... came to Beer-sheba.— Though Jacob, in the first tumult of his joy, had determined upon hastening to Egypt, yet many second thoughts must have made him hesitate. He would call up to mind the boding prophecy in 15:13, that the descendants of Abraham were to be reduced to slavery, and suffer affliction in a foreign land for four hundred years. It might even be a sin, involving the loss of the Abrahamic covenant, to quit the land of Canaan, which Abraham had expressly forbidden Isaac to abandon (24:8). Isaac, too, when going into Egypt, had been commanded to remain in Palestine (26:2). Jacob therefore determines solemnly to consult God before finally taking so important a step, and no place could be more suitable than Beer-sheba, as both Abraham and Isaac had built altars there for Jehovah's worship (21:33, 26:25), and, moreover, it lay upon the route from Hebron to Egypt.

(3) I am God, the God of thy father.— Heb., "I am the El, the Elohim of thy father." This is the last revelation given to Jacob, nor is any other supernatural event recorded until the vision of the burning bush (Exod. 3:4). It is brief, clear, and decisive, and every clause is weighty. Jacob is to migrate into Egypt, his race is to grow there into a nation, so that the stay there would be long; God's presence and blessing will accompany and remain with them, and finally will bring them back to the promised land. For himself, too, there is the promise that Joseph will tend his sick bed and be with him at his death.

(4) Joseph shall put his hand upon thine eyes.—Both among the Jews and Greeks it was the duty of those nearest in blood to close the eyes of a deceased relative. The promise conveyed the assurance that Jacob

would die peacefully, surrounded by his friends. For the fulfillment see 50:1.

(6) Their goods.—The patriarchs would leave their household stuff behind, but all valuables, and the records of their house, and their tôldôth, they would carefully carry with them.

Genealogical Table of the Israelites

(8) These are the names of the children of Israel, which came into Egypt. This document, consisting of verses 8-27, is one that would be of the highest importance to the Israelites, when taking possession of Canaan, being as it were their title-deed to the land. Accordingly we find that it is drawn up in a legal manner representing as sons some who were really grandsons, but who took as heads of families the place usually held by sons. We next find that it represents them as all born in Canaan, not in a natural sense, but as the rightful heirs of the country. The genealogical table of the twelve patriarchs is given three times in Holy Scripture: here, in Num. 26, and in 1 Chron. 1-8. See also Exod. 6:14-16, where only Reuben, Simeon, and Levi are given.

Excepting Benjamin, the other genealogies do not offer any great difficulties; for variations in the spelling of names are too common to cause surprise, and names would be omitted whenever in later times the family had ceased to have a representative. Thus, probably, no member of the tribe of Dan returned from the Captivity with an authenticated genealogy, and therefore no mention of them is made in the book of Chronicles. The utter confusion in the genealogy of Benjamin is the natural result of the ruinous war narrated in Judges 20:21; but when that tribe produced a king, the utmost care would be taken to remedy, as far as possible, the destruction of documents caused by that struggle; and the genealogy in 1 Chron. 8 is the royal pedigree of King Saul.

(26) All the souls were threescore and six.—This total is obtained by omitting Jacob, Joseph, and Joseph's two sons. If we include these, the whole number becomes threescore and ten, as in verse 27. In the LXX the names of five grandsons are added to verse 20, and thus the total is made seventy-five as quoted by Stephen in Acts 7:14.

Arrival of Jacob in Egypt

(28) To direct his face unto Goshen.—

Joseph does not bring his brethren into the narrow and populous Nile Valley which formed Egypt proper, because they could not have maintained there an isolated mode of life. But this was indispensable for them if they were to multiply into a nation fit to be the guardians and depositories of a growing revelation, until the fullness of the time should come, when the world would be ready to receive the perfect knowledge of God's will. As the Egyptians were an agricultural people, and hated sheep and shepherds (verse 34), the Israelites would run no danger of being absorbed by them as long as they continued to devote themselves to their old pursuits. As Goshen was admirably suited for a pastoral life, they would remain there as distinct and separate from the rest of mankind as they had been in Canaan.

47

Joseph Presents His Father and Brethren to Pharaoh

(1) Behold, they are in the land of Goshen.—Though Joseph had all along wished this to be the dwelling place of his brethren, yet it was necessary to obtain Pharaoh's permission; and at present Joseph mentions only that they had halted there. In verse 4 they ask for the necessary consent.

(3) Also our fathers.—Joseph had instructed them to add this (46:34), because occupations were hereditary among the Egyptians, and thus Pharaoh would conclude that in their case also no change was possible in their mode of life.

(7) Jacob blessed Pharaoh.—The presentation of Jacob to Pharaoh seems to have been a much more solemn matter than that of Joseph's brethren. Pharaoh looks upon them with interest as the brothers of his vizier, grants their request for leave to dwell in Goshen, and even empowers Joseph to make the ablest of them chief herdsman over the royal cattle. But Jacob had attained to an age which gave him great dignity: for to an Egyptian 120 was the utmost limit of longevity. Jacob was now 130, and Pharaoh treats him with the greatest honor, and twice accepts his blessing. More must be meant by this than the usual salutation in which each one presented to the king prayed for the prolongation of his life. Pharaoh probably bowed before Jacob as a saintly personage, and received a formal benediction.

(9) Few and evil.—Evil certainly: for from the time when he deceived his father, Jacob's life had been one of great anxiety and care, in addition to his many sorrows. All these troubles had fallen upon him, and made his days evil; but they were few only in comparison with those of his father and grandfather. In Pharaoh's eyes Jacob had lived beyond the usual span of human existence; but to himself he seemed prematurely old. His end came after seventeen years of peaceful decay spent under Joseph's loving care.

(11) The land of Rameses.—See note on 45:10. Though the LXX takes "land of Rameses" as equivalent to Goshen, it was more probably some special district of it, for, as we have seen, Goshen was a territory of vast extent. It deserved its description as "the best of the land."

Joseph's Policy in Egypt

(16) Give your cattle.—As the people were in want of food, and their land incapable of cultivation as long as the Nile ceased to overflow, this was a merciful arrangement, by which the owners were delivered from a burden, and also a portion of the cattle saved for the time when they would be needed again for agricultural purposes.

(17) Horses ... flocks ... herds ... asses.—The mention of horses is a most important fact in settling the much-debated question as to the dynasty under which Joseph became governor of Egypt. When Abram went there, horses do not seem as yet to have been known (see note on 12:16), but oxen and asses were common, and the former indigenous in the country. The horse was introduced by the Hyksos, and the first representation of one is drawing the war chariot of the king who expelled them. The "flocks" are expressly said in the Hebrew to be "sheep." This, too, is important; for while goats were indigenous in Egypt, sheep do not appear in the most ancient monuments, though they were introduced at an earlier date than horses.

(20) So the land became Pharaoh's.—Joseph has been accused of reducing a free people to slavery by his policy. Undoubtedly he did vastly increase the royal power; but from what we read of the vassalage under which the Egyptians lived to a multitude of petty sovereigns, and also to their wives, their priests, and their embalmers, an increase in the power of the king, so as to make it predominant, would be to their advantage.

(21) He removed them to cities.—Joseph's object in this measure was most merciful. As the corn was stored up in the cities, the people would be sure of nourishment only if they were in the immediate neighborhood of the food. As a consequence, possibly, of Joseph's policy, the number of cities in the Valley of the Nile became so enormous that Herodotus computes them at 20,000.

(23) Lo, here is seed for you.—As Joseph would give them seed wherewith to sow their fields only when the famine was nearly over, these arrangements seem to have been completed shortly before the end of the seventh year; and then, with seed it would be necessary also to supply them with oxen to plough the soil, and swine wherewith to trample in the seed. A fifth part of the produce would be a very moderate rent.

(25) Thou hast saved our lives.—The people were more than satisfied with Joseph's regulations; and if he had made them dependent upon the Pharaoh, apparently he had broken the yoke of the smaller lords, the hereditary princes of the districts into which Egypt was parceled out; and they were more likely to be well-treated by the ruler of the whole land than by men of inferior rank.

Israel in Egypt

(29) The time drew nigh that Israel must die.—At last Jacob feels his end approaching, though apparently he was not as yet in immediate danger of death. But there was a wish over which he had long pondered; and desiring to have his mind set at rest, he sends for Joseph, and makes him promise that he will bury him in the cave at Machpelah.

Put ... thy hand under my thigh.—See note on 24:2.

(31) Israel bowed himself upon the bed's head.—The LXX, followed by the epistle to the Hebrews (11:21) and the Syriac, read, "on the top of his staff." The word in the Hebrew, without vowels, may mean either "bed" or "staff." The points indicating the vowels were added in later times, and while valuable as representing a very ancient tradition, are nevertheless not final authority. The rendering, however, of the King James Version is the most satisfactory.

48

The Blessing of Manasseh and Ephraim, and the Recognition of Them by Jacob As Heads of Tribes

(1) His two sons.—The purpose of the genealogy given in chap. 46 was the recognition of those of Jacob's descendants who were to hold the high position of heads of "families." In this chapter a still more important matter is settled; for Jacob, exercising to the full his rights as the father and head of the Israelite race, and moved thereto both by his love for Rachel, the high rank of Joseph, and also by the spirit of prophecy, bestows upon Joseph two tribes. No authority less than that of Jacob would have sufficed for this, and therefore the grant is carefully recorded, and holds its right place immediately before the solemn blessing given by the dying patriarch to his sons.

(3) God Almighty.—Heb., **El Shaddai.** The act recorded in this chapter is grounded by Jacob upon the promise made to him at Bethel on his return from Padan-aram; and it was under the old covenant name by which God had revealed Himself to Abram (17:1) that he was there made the heir of the Abrahamic promises. (See note on 35:11.)

(5) As Reuben and Simeon, they shall be mine.—That is, Ephraim shall be regarded as my first-born, and Manasseh as my second son. This was undoubtedly the case; for though "Judah prevailed above his brethren, and of him came the prince (and of him the Messiah), yet the birthright was Joseph's" (1 Chron. 5:2). The legal right of the first-born was a double share of the father's goods. This was bestowed upon Joseph in giving him two tribes, and to the other sons but one. It was in a spiritual sense, and with reference to the promise that all mankind should be blessed in Jacob's seed, that the birthright was Judah's. As Joseph was the son of the chief and best-beloved wife, he had a sort of claim to the birthright; but in agreement with the law afterward specially enacted (Deut. 21:15-17), Jacob acknowledges that the right had belonged to Reuben, but excludes him from the possession of it as the penalty of his great and terrible sin. Simeon and Levi are next passed over, because of their cruelty, and so Judah takes Reuben's place.

(14) Guiding his hands wittingly.—The LXX, Syriac, and Vulgate translate, "placing his hands crosswise."

83

(15, 16) He blessed Joseph, and said.—In Jacob's blessing there is a threefold appellation of the Deity, and a threefold blessing given to Joseph's sons. God is, first, the Elohim before whom his fathers had walked. Next, He is the Elohim who, as a shepherd, had watched over Jacob all his life long. But, thirdly, He is that divine Presence which had been, and still was, Jacob's "goël," redeeming and rescuing him from all evil. The word "goël" is here used for the first time. Moreover, the verb is present, "the angel that redeemeth me from all evil." Jacob recognized a divine Presence which constantly guarded him, and which was ever his Redeemer and Saviour.

(19) His younger brother shall be greater.—In the final numbering of the tribes on the plains of Moab, the tribe of Manasseh had 52,700 souls, and that of Ephraim only 32,500 (Num. 26:34, 37). It was the division of the tribe of Manasseh into two portions which made it politically insignificant, while Ephraim obtained a commanding position in the land of Canaan; and as Joshua was an Ephraimite, it naturally held the rank of foremost tribe during his days, and claimed it always afterward. The influence also of the tribe would be strengthened by the ark being placed in one of its towns.

(22) One portion.—Heb., "one Shechem." In favor of this being the town of Shechem is the fact that it did belong to Jacob (37:12, where see note); also that Joseph's embalmed body was deposited there (see Josh. 24:32); and lastly, the testimony of John 4:5, where a parcel of ground at Sychar, close to Shechem, is identified with the ground given by Jacob to Joseph. But what is meant by "Jacob having taken it out of the hand of the Amorite by his sword and his bow"? Shechem was strictly a town of the Hivites, but as they were but a feeble tribe, the term Amorite may be used to give greater glory to the exploit. In 15:16, the Amorites, literally "mountaineers," are described as owners of the whole country, and probably it was a term loosely applied to all the inhabitants of the uplands, though occasionally used with a more definite meaning (15:21). It is quite possible that, after the inhumane treatment of the Hivites at Shechem, the Amorites did gather themselves together to avenge the wrong, but were deterred by the threatening position taken up by Jacob, or even repulsed in an attack. The latter supposition would best harmonize with the fact that "a mighty terror fell upon all the cities round about" (35:5), and also with the exultant spirit in which Jacob, a pre-eminently peaceful and timid man, here alludes to the one military exploit of his life.

49

The Blessing of the Twelve Tribes

(1) That which shall befall you.—This dying song of Jacob has been regarded alike by Jews and Christians as a prophetic hymn spoken by the patriarch under the influence of the Holy Spirit. By many modern commentators, however, it has been placed in David's time, and even ascribed to Nathan, partly on the ground that it is too spirited to have been the composition of one lying in the last decrepitude of old age, but chiefly because, in the description given of Judah, it is supposed to refer to the elevation of David to the royal dignity. But if it was thus written by a member of David's court, we should reasonably expect an exact knowledge of the state of things in David's time. For this, in fact, is the argument upon which these critics depend, that the internal evidence shows that it belongs to David's reign. Now so far is this from being true, that not only is the whole exceedingly general, containing scarcely more than faint and dim hopes and anticipations, but, except in the matter of Judah's pre-eminence, there is no knowledge whatsoever of the arrangements of David's time. Generally we may affirm that the sole argument for Jacob's blessing having been written in historic times is the position given to Judah. Everything beside negates this view; and we may reasonably ascribe the high rank of Judah to the fact that after the setting aside of Reuben, Simeon and Levi, he became the first-born.

In the last days.—The phrase is often opposed to "the beginning of days," and is constantly used of the times of the Messiah. Here these "after days" apparently commence with the conquest of Canaan, but look onward to the advent of Christ.

(3) The excellency ... —We must here supply, "And therefore to thee as the first-born belonged," first, "the excellency of dignity," that is, the priesthood; and secondly, "the excellency of power," that is, the kingly office. As a matter of history, no king, judge, or prophet is recorded as having sprung from the tribe of Reuben.

84

(4) Thou shalt not excel.—That is, thou shalt not have that excellency which was thine by right of birth.

(5) Simeon and Levi are brethren.—That is, they are alike in character and disposition. Despising the feeble Reuben, they seem to have been close friends and allies, and probably tried to exercise a tyrannical authority over their younger brethren, Judah being the only one near them in age.

(6) Unto their assembly, mine honour, be not thou united.—In the first clause Jacob bids his "soul," his true self, not to enter their alliance; here, after the manner of the parallelism of Hebrew poetry, he intensifies the meaning.

(7) I will divide them ... —This prediction was equally fulfilled in the fact that neither of the tribes of Simeon and Levi possessed any political importance in Israel. But in every other respect the fulfillment was utterly diverse. In Levi's case the curse was changed into a blessing by the faithfulness of the tribe upon a very trying occasion (Exod. 32:26-28); and we learn from it the great lesson that the divine rewards and punishments, even when specified in prophecy, are nevertheless conditional upon human conduct. Of this diversity of fulfillment there is not the slightest indication in Jacob's blessing, while in that of Moses the lot of Levi is described in terms of the highest praise, and that of Simeon is passed over in inglorious silence.

(8) Judah, thou art he whom thy brethren shall praise.—Judah had received his name, Praise, because at his birth Leah had praised Jehovah (29:35). It is now to have another justification in the noble history of his race, which, taking the foremost place by reason of the disqualification of Reuben, Simeon, and Levi, finally was destined to win freedom and empire for Israel.

(9) Judah is a lion's whelp.—The sons of Jacob had each his signet, and Judah's was so large as to be worn by him attached to a cord fastened round his neck (38:18). Probably his emblem was a lion. Using then his self-chosen emblem, Jacob compares him, first, to a "lion's whelp," full of activity and enterprise, and which, after feasting upon its prey, "goes up" to its mountain lair, calm and fearless in the consciousness of its strength. But as Judah is a young lion in his activity and fearlessness, so is he "a lion" full-grown and majestic in his repose, which Jacob's words literally describe. For the "stooping down" is the bending of the limbs

together before the lion "couches," that is, down in his den.

(10) The sceptre shall not depart from Judah. The staff, adorned with carvings, and handed down from father to son, soon became the emblem of authority (see note on 38:18). It probably indicates here tribal rather than royal rank, and means that Judah would continue, until the time indicated, to be a self-governed and legally-constituted tribe.

Nor a lawgiver from between his feet.—Most modern critics translate "ruler's staff," but "lawgiver" has the support of all the ancient versions. "Ruler's staff" has the parallelism in its favor, but the ancient versions must not be lightly disregarded, and, besides, everywhere else the word means law-giver (see Deut. 33:21; Judges 5:14; Isa. 33:22). "From between his feet" means, "from among his descendants." The Targum of Onkelos renders, "from his children's children."

Until Shiloh come.—Many modern critics translate, "until he come to Shiloh," but this is to be rejected, first, as being contrary to all the ancient versions; and, secondly, as turning sense into nonsense. The town of Shiloh was in the tribe of Ephraim, and we know of no way in which Judah ever went there. The Ark was for a time at Shiloh, but the place lost all importance and sank into utter obscurity after its destruction by the Philistines, long before Judah took the leading part in the commonwealth of Israel.

Shiloh.—There are several interpretations of this word, depending upon different ways of spelling it. All the versions excepting the Vulgate read Sheloh; and to this we must add that Sheloh is the reading even of several Hebrew MSS. Sheloh literally means, "Whose it is." The form is quite in its place in the mouth of Jacob, who had lived so long in a land where an Aramaic dialect was spoken.

Ezekiel 21:27 (Heb., 32), quotes Jacob's words, using however the Hebrew idiom, "Until he come, whose is the right." And Paul (Gal. 3:19) refers to it in the words, "Until the seed come to whom it is promised," where the latter words seem to be a free rendering of the phrase in the LXX, "for whom it is laid up."

The passage has always been regarded as Messianic, not merely by Christians, but by the Jews, all whose ancient writers, including the Talmud, explain the name Shiloh, or Sheloh, of the Messiah. But the Targum of Onkelos would of itself be a sufficient

85

proof. as we have there not the opinions or knowledge of one man. but the traditional explanation of the Pentateuch. handed down orally from the time of Ezra. and committed to writing probably in the first century of the Christian era. The objection has. indeed. been made in modern times that the patriarchs had no Messianic expectations. With those who believe in prophecy such an objection can have no weight; but independently of this. the promise made to Abraham. and solemnly confirmed to Jacob. that in his seed all the kindreds of the earth should be blessed. was preeminently Messianic: as was also the name Jehovah: for that name was the embodiment of the promise made to Eve. and beginning with her cry of hope that she had gotten the Coming One. had become by the time of Enoch the symbol of the expectation of mankind that God would appear on earth in human nature to save them.

Unto him shall the gathering of the people be.—The word "gathering" means "obedience." as is proved by the other place where it occurs (Prov. 30:17). For "people" the Heb. has "peoples." Not Israel only. "the people." but all nations are to obey Him "whose is the kingdom."

(11) Binding his foal ... —Having declared the spiritual prerogative of Judah. the patriarch now foretells that his land would be so rich in vineyards that the traveler would tie his ass to the vine. as the tree abundant everywhere. The abundance of grapes is next hyperbolically described as so great that their juice will be used like water for the commonest purposes.

(12) His eyes shall be red with wine.—The words do not refer to Judah's person. but describe the prosperity of his descendants. whose temporal welfare will show itself in their bright and healthy countenances.

(13) Zebulun ... —The territory of the tribe lay upon the inland Sea of Gennesaret. but did not extend to the shore of the Mediterranean. It is very possible that. living in the neighborhood of the Phoenicians. they took part in maritime pursuits: and thus the general meaning of the blessing may be that Zebulun would be a tribe, not of agriculturists, but of traders.

(14) Issachar.—The description of Issachar's lot is derived partly from the cognizance he had chosen for his signet, and partly from his personal character. He had taken for his symbol the ass—a very noble, active, spirited, and enduring animal in the

East. His real character was slothful, inactive. and commonplace. Jacob therefore likens him to a "strong ass"; he is thus fit only to be a drudge. and with the laziness of a cart horse lies down "between two burdens." More exactly it means the pens in which the cattle were folded during the nights of summer. Thus Issachar, stretched at ease between his cattle pens, gives us the idea of a tribe occupied with pastoral pursuits, and destitute of all higher aspirations.

(15) A servant unto tribute.—Heb., "taskwork." The picture is that of a race settled in a rich agricultural country, and content to endure a great deal of injustice because their condition as a whole was prosperous.

(16, 17) Dan.—In passing on to the sons of the handmaids it was necessary to assure them of an independent rank among their brethren. The four tribes descended from them always held an inferior position, but Jacob by his words to Dan prevented their ever becoming subject states. He says that Dan shall judge his people as a distinct and separate tribe, possessed of all those rights of self-government and tribal independence which this rank implied. It seems also that Dan's symbol was a serpent, and from this Jacob prophesies that though too weak a tribe to take the foremost place in war, yet that Dan should not be without military importance: and this was especially the case in the days of Samson.

(18) I have waited for thy salvation, O Lord (Jehovah).—Among the many explanations hazarded of this ejaculation the most probable is that the thought of the serpent wounding his prey in the heel carried the mind of the patriarch back to the Fall of man, and the promise made to Eve. And thus it is a profession of faith, naturally called out by this chain of ideas, in the advent in due time of the promised Deliverer, and of which the accomplishment had become united in thought with the name of Jehovah.

(19) Gad. —Jacob connects it with the root **gadad**, "to gather in troops." Thus, then, "A troop" or "throng of plunderers shall throng upon him, but he shall throng upon their heel." Settling upon the east of the Jordan he shall be exposed to many sudden incursions of plunderers, but, though ever unready, he shall gather his forces and repel them, and follow with avenging energy upon their rear.

(20) Asher.—The territory of this tribe, extending along the coast from Mount Carmel to Lebanon, was very productive. Zebulun, the trading tribe, could reach the sea only through their possessions.

(21) Naphtali.—Naphtali, contrary to Gad, is light and active, moving rapidly like "a hind let loose"; or, literally, "sent forth," like the scouts or van of an army. And thus he brings back "goodly words," that is, trustworthy intelligence to guide the army in its motions.

(22-26) Joseph.—The blessing of Joseph is, in many particulars, the most remarkable of all. Jacob throughout it seems struggling with himself, and anxious to bestow more than was in his power. Jacob magnifies again and again, but in obscure terms, his blessing upon Joseph which, when analyzed, amounts simply to excessive fruitfulness, with no Messianic or spiritual prerogative. Beginning with this, Jacob next dwells upon Joseph's trials, and upon the manliness with which he had borne and overcome them; and then magnifies the blessedness of the earthly lot of his race, won for them by the personal worth of Joseph with a description of which Jacob ends his words.

(26) The blessings of thy father.—The chief spiritual blessing was bestowed upon Judah, while for Joseph there was only earthly prosperity. Most modern commentators adopt the reading of the Samaritan Pentateuch, supported by the Samaritan Targum and the LXX, "The blessings of thy father are mightier than the blessings of the ancient mountains, than the desire (or beauty) of the everlasting hills."

Him that was separate from his brethren.—Many see in this an allusion to the sovereignty over the ten tribes being finally attained to by Ephraim, but probably the meaning is that Joseph was the noblest and highest in rank among Jacob's children.

(27) Benjamin.—With this description of their ancestor agrees the character of his race, which was the most spirited and warlike of all the tribes of Israel.

(28) These are the twelve tribes.—As we have seen in the case of Dan, Jacob had the further object of forming his descendants into twelve separate communities. From this position Levi naturally was excluded, when selected for the priesthood, and room was thus made for the bestowal of two of these communities upon the descendants of Joseph. Only in case of war they were to combine under the chieftainship of Judah. In the Book of Judges, however, we find the tribes as separate in matters of war as of peace, and by the time of Saul the need of a

closer union had been felt, and tribal independence had been found to lead only to anarchy.

50
Burial of Jacob, and Happy Old Age of Joseph

(2) The physicians embalmed Israel.—The command given first by Jacob to Joseph (47:29, 30), and then urged earnestly upon all his sons, and with the reminder that the cave of Machpelah had been purchased and belonged to him by right (49:29-32), made it especially necessary that the patriarch's body should be prepared for so long a journey. It was also usual at that period to embalm the dead. The embalmers are not generally called physicians, but probably what is meant is that the embalming of Jacob's body was superintended by the physicians attached to Joseph's household. Egypt was famous for its physicians, who were in advance of those of other countries.

(3) Forty days.—The usual period of mourning among the Israelites was thirty days (Num. 20:29; Deut. 34:8). Probably, therefore, the forty days spent in the embalming were included in the "threescore and ten days," during which the Egyptians mourned for Jacob.

(4) Joseph spake unto the house of Pharaoh.—It may seem at first sight strange that Joseph should make his request through mediators, but probably no one in the attire of mourning might enter the royal presence. (Comp. Esth. 4:2.) The dress of a mourner was squalid, his beard unshorn, his hair in disorder, and while these outward signs of grief were maintained, he was also expected to confine himself to his own house.

(9) A very great company.—These were the chief officers of Pharaoh's household, and also of the districts into which Egypt was divided, of which each had its separate governor. Of the Israelites only the men of rank, Jacob's own sons, and the officers of his house took part in the funeral procession, while their "little ones"—Heb., their **"tafs,"** translated here in the LXX "their clans," and signifying the great body of their dependents—remained with their cattle in the land of Goshen.

(10) Beyond Jordan.—It is certain that the route taken by Joseph lay to the east of the Dead Sea; for Goren-Atad is placed by Jerome at Beth-Hoglah, which lay between the Jordan and Jericho, and Joseph could have gone there only by traveling through the territories of Moab and Ammon. While therefore "beyond Jordan" would naturally mean "on the east of Jordan," it may here express the fact that Joseph had just crossed the Jordan when the lamentation was made.

(15) Joseph will peradventure ... —Heb., "What if Joseph should hate us, etc." They had not seen any change in his treatment of them, but if it were the case that he cherished feelings of revenge, they felt that they were now in his power.

(16, 17) Thy father did command ... —Many Jewish expositors consider that this was untrue, and that Jacob was never made aware of the fact that his brethren had sold Joseph into slavery. It is, however, probable, from 49:6, that Jacob not only knew of it, but saw in Simeon and Levi the chief offenders. But besides the father's authority the message brings a twofold influence to bear upon Joseph: for first it reminds him that they were his brethren, and next, that they shared the same religious faith—no slight band of union in a country where the religion was so unlike their own.

(20) Ye thought ... God meant.—The verb in the Heb. is the same, and contrasts man's purpose with God's purpose. In 45:7 Joseph had already pointed out that the divine providence had overruled the evil intentions of his brethren for good. At the end of the verse "much people," or "a great people," means the Egyptians.

(24) God will ... bring you out of this land.—This is, first, a proof of Joseph's faith, commended in Heb. 11:22; and, secondly, it is a preparation for the next book (Exodus). Joseph's faith thus unites the two books together.

(26) A coffin.—Joseph orders that his embalmed body should be placed in some part of Goshen, from where it would be easy to remove it when the time of deliverance had arrived. And his wish was fulfilled; for "Moses took the bones of Joseph with him" (Exod. 13:19), and Joshua buried them in Shechem, in the piece of ground which Jacob had given to him (Josh. 24:32).

With the death of Joseph ends the preparation for the formation of a chosen race. Abraham and Lot, Esau and Jacob had been compelled to separate; but now, under Joseph, they had been placed in a large, fertile, and well-nigh uninhabited region. The few who dwelt there were, as far as we can judge, of the Semitic stock, and whatever immigrants came from time to time were also of the same race, and were soon enrolled in the **"taf"** of some noble or chief. And thus all was ready for their growth into a nation; and when we next read of them they had multiplied into a people so vast that Egypt was afraid of them.

EXODUS

The Multiplication of the Israelites in Egypt, and Their Oppression by a New King

(1) Now these are the names. The history begins properly with verse 7. Verses 1-6 form the connecting link between Genesis and Exodus, and would not have been needed unless Exodus had been introduced as a distinct work, since they are little more than a recapitulation of what had been already stated and stated more fully in Genesis. Compare verses 1-5 with Gen. 46:8-27, and verse 6 with Gen. 50:26.

Every man and his household.—"A household," in the language of the East, includes not only children and grandchildren, but retainers also—"servants born in the house"—like those of Abraham (Gen. 14:14). The number of each "household" may thus have been considerable.

(5) All the souls . . . were seventy souls.—Comp. Gen. 46:8-27. The number is made up as follows:—Jacob himself, 1; his sons, 12; his daughter, Dinah, 1; his grandsons, 51; his granddaughter, Serah, 1; his great-grandsons, 4—Total, 70. His daughters, except Dinah, and his sons' daughters, except Serah, spoken of in Gen. 46:7, are not included. If his female descendants were, at the time of his descent into Egypt, as numerous as the males, the entire number of those who "came out of his loins" must have been 132. To form a calculation of the number of persons who entered Egypt with him, we must add the wives of his sons and grandsons, and the husbands of his daughters and granddaughters. A further liberal allowance must be made also for retainers. It is not perhaps surprising that Kurtz, taking all these classes into account, should calculate that those who entered Egypt with Jacob amounted to "several thousands."

(7) The children of Israel were fruitful.—A "great" multiplication is evidently intended. On the actual extent of the multiplication and the time that it occupied, see the comment on 12:37-41.

The land—i.e., where they dwelt—Goshen (Gen. 47:4-6)—which seems to have been the more eastern portion of the Delta.

(8) There arose up a new king.—Probably Seti I, the father of Rameses II, and the son of Rameses I. Seti, though not the actual founder of the nineteenth dynasty, was the originator of its greatness.

Which knew not Joseph.—It seems to be implied that, for some considerable time after his death, the memory of the benefits conferred by Joseph upon Egypt had protected his kinsfolk. But, in the shifts and changes incident to politics—especially to Oriental politics—this condition of things had passed away. The "new king" felt under no obligation to him, perhaps was even ignorant of his name. He viewed the political situation apart from all personal predilections, and saw a danger in it.

(9) More and mightier than we.—The more to impress his counselors, and gain their consent to his designs, the king exaggerates. Ancient Egypt must have had a population of seven or eight millions, which would imply nearly two millions of adult males, whereas the adult male Israelites, near a century later, were no more than six hundred thousand (12:37).

(10) When there falleth out any war.—The Egyptians were in general an aggressive people—a terror to their neighbors, and seldom the object of attack. But about the beginning of the nineteenth dynasty a change took place.

It was not likely that the Hebrews would have any real sympathy with an attacking nation, whether Arabs, Philistines, Syrians, or Hittites; but they might regard an invasion as affording them a good opportunity of striking a blow for freedom, and, therefore, attack the Egyptians simultaneously with their other foes. The Egyptians themselves would perhaps suppose a closer connection between them and the other Eastern races than really existed.

Get them up out of the land.—The Pharaohs of the nineteenth dynasty were excessively jealous of the withdrawal from Egypt of any of their subjects, and endeavored both to hinder and to recover them. Immigration was encouraged, emigration sternly checked. The loss of the entire nation of the Hebrews could not be contemplated without extreme alarm.

(11) To afflict them.—This was the object of the whole proceeding. It was hoped that severe labor under the lash would produce so much suffering that the number of Israelites would be thinned, and their multiplication stopped. Humanly speaking, the scheme was one likely to be successful.

They built for Pharaoh treasure cities.—By "treasure cities" we are to understand "magazines"—i.e., strongholds, where munitions of war could be laid up for use in case of an invasion. (In I Kings 9:19, and II Chron. 8:4, the same expression is translated "cities of store.") The Pharaohs of the nineteenth dynasty gave great attention to the guarding of the northeastern frontier in this way.

Pithom.—This city is reasonably identified with the "Patumus" of Herodotus (2:158), which was in Lower Egypt. It was, as the name implies, a city of the sun god, and was probably not very far from Heliopolis, the main seat of the sun god's worship.

Raamses.—Pi-Ramesu, the city of Rameses, was the ordinary seat of the Court during the earlier part of the nineteenth dynasty. It appears to have been a new name for Tanis, or for a suburb of Tanis, which overshadowed the old city. Rameses II claims to have built the greater part of it; but it was probably begun by his father, Seti, who made the defense of the northeastern frontier one of his main cares.

(12) The more they afflicted them, the more they multiplied and grew.—This result was not natural. It can only be ascribed to God's superintending providence. Naturally, severe and constant labor exhausts a nation, and causes its numbers to diminish.

(22) Ye shall cast into the river.—Infanticide, so shocking to Christians, has prevailed widely at different times and places, and been regarded as a trivial matter. In Sparta, the State decided which children should live and which should die. At Athens a law of Solon left the decision to the parent. At Rome, the rule was that infants were made away with, unless the father interposed, and declared it to be his wish that a particular child should be brought up. The Syrians offered unwelcome children in sacrifice to Moloch; the Carthaginians to Melkarth. Heathen nations do not generally regard human life as sacred. On the contrary, they hold that considerations of expediency justify the sweeping away of any life that inconveniences the State. Hence infanticide is introduced by Plato into his model republic (**Rep.** 5.9). The condemnation to death of all male Hebrew children by Pharaoh is thus in no respect improbable. Perhaps the children were viewed as offerings to the Nile, or to Savak, the crocodile-headed god, of whom each crocodile was an emblem. As the Nile swarmed with crocodiles throughout its whole course, the bodies were sure to be devoured.

2

The Birth, Education and Early Life of Moses

(1) A man of the house of Levi.—Note the extreme simplicity of this announcement; and compare it with the elaborate legends wherewith Oriental religions commonly surrounded the birth of those who were considered their founders, as Thoth, Zoroaster, Orpheus. Even the name of the man is here omitted as unimportant. It is difficult to conceive any one but Moses making such an omission.

A daughter of Levi.—i.e., a woman of the same tribe as himself, a descendant of Levi—not a daughter in the literal sense, which the chronology makes impossible.

(3) An ark of bulrushes.—Literally, "a chest of the papyrus plant." The words used are both of Egyptian origin. The papyrus plant was a material frequently used by the Egyptians for boats and even larger vessels.

Slime and . . . pitch.—By "slime" seems to be meant bitumen, or mineral pitch, as in Gen. 11:3; by "pitch," the ordinary vegetable pitch of commerce. Mineral pitch, though not a product of Egypt, was imported into the country from Mesopotamia, and was largely used for embalming.

In the flags.—A rank aquatic vegetation abounds on the Lower Nile, and in all the backwaters and marshy tracts connected with it. Jochebed placed her child "in the flags," that the ark might not float away down the river, and so be lost to her sight.

(4) His sister.—Presumably Miriam, the only sister of Moses mentioned elsewhere (15:20, 21; Num. 26:59). To have taken the part which is assigned her in this chapter, she must have been a girl of some fourteen or fifteen years of age, and possessed of much quickness and intelligence.

(5) The daughter of Pharaoh came down to wash herself.—This would be quite in accordance with Egyptian ideas. Women were allowed great liberty in Egypt, and moved about much as they pleased. Cleanliness was especially regarded; and the Nile water was considered healthy and fructifying.

(10) He became her son.—Possibly by a formal act of adoption; but we have at present no evidence that adoption was an Egyptian custom. Perhaps the writer means simply that she brought him up as if he had been her son, gave him a son's education, and a son's privileges.

She called his name Moses.—The name was derived from an Egyptian verb, meaning "to produce," "to draw forth"; and the princess justified her imposition of the name by a reference to this etymology. Owing to the existence of a cognate verb in Hebrew, it was possible to transfer her explanation into the Hebrew language exactly and literally.

(11) In those days.—Notes of time are used with considerable latitude by the sacred writers. According to the tradition followed by Stephen (Acts 7:23), Moses was "full forty years old" when he took the step here indicated. We might have expected him to have come forward sooner; but there may have been difficulties in his so doing.

He went out unto his brethren.—It is probable that Pharaoh's daughter had never concealed from Moses that he was not her own child, but one of the oppressed race. It is not a mere visit that is here spoken of, but a complete withdrawal from the palace, and renunciation of his position at the court. (See Heb. 11:24, 25.) It is the first sign of that strong sympathy and tender affection for his people which characterizes him throughout the narrative, and culminates in the pathetic cry, "Forgive them; and if not, blot me out of thy book" (32:32).

He spied an Egyptian smiting a Hebrew.—Probably a taskmaster chastising one of the laborers, whom he accused of idling. Stephen regards the act as one of "oppression" and "wrongdoing" (Acts 7:24). Moses must certainly have viewed it in this light, or he would not have been so moved to indignation as to kill the Egyptian. Though not a cruel nation, the Egyptians, no doubt, like other slave drivers, occasionally abused their power, and treated the unfortunate laborers with cruelty.

(12) He slew the Egyptian.—Jewish commentators gloss over the act, or even eulogize it as patriotic and heroical. But it was clearly the deed of a hasty and undisciplined spirit. The offense did not deserve death, and if it had, Moses had neither legal office nor divine call, justifying him in making himself an executioner. The result was, that, by his one wrong act, Moses put it out of his power to do anything toward alleviating the sufferings of his brethren for forty years.

(14) Who made thee a prince and a judge over us?—As the reputed son of a princess, Moses would be in some way a "prince." But no one had given him jurisdiction over the Hebrews. He had not really interfered as one who claimed authority, but as any man of position and education naturally interferes to stop a quarrel. That fatal error laid Moses open to attack, and deprived him of the influence as a peacemaker which he might otherwise have exercised over his countrymen.

(15) When Pharaoh heard . . . he sought to slay Moses.—The administration of justice was one of the chief duties of the royal office; and the crime committed by Moses was one to be punished by death. There was nothing to reduce it from murder to manslaughter. And the motives which extenuate it in the eyes of moderns—patriotic zeal and hatred of oppression—would not have commanded the sympathies of a Pharaoh.

Dwelt in the land of Midian.—The Midian of this book seems to be the southeastern portion of the Sinaitic peninsula, not the opposite Arabian coast, where were the main settlements of the nation.

(16) The priest of Midian.—Reuel may have been both "priest" and "prince," like Melchizedek (Gen. 14:18). In 18:12, Jethro is represented as exercising priestly functions. The Midianites, descendants of Abraham by Keturah, worshiped the true God, and seem to have been at this time a religious people. The name Reuel, or Raguel, means "friend of God."

(17) The shepherds came.—Those of the neighborhood. The rule of the desert is that those who come to a well take their turns in the use of the water in the order of their arrival. But these rude shepherds declined to wait for their turn.

(21) Moses was content to dwell with the man.—Reuel must have been so pleased with the manner and appearance of Moses that he invited him to take service with him—perhaps to share his tent. Moses consented, and in course of time took to wife Zipporah, one of Reuel's daughters. Marriage with the Midianites was allowed, even under the Law. It has been conjectured that Reuel might have communicated to Moses traditions or even documents concerning their common ancestor, Abraham, and his family.

(23) In process of time.—As Moses was now eighty years old (7:7), and only forty

91

when he left Egypt, the Pharaoh from whom he fled must have reigned above forty years. Between the beginning of the eighteenth and the close of the nineteenth dynasty, two kings only seem to have reigned as long as this—Thotmes III and Rameses II. The choice of the Pharaoh from whom Moses fled thus lies between these two.

Their cry came up unto God.—"Exceeding bitter cries" always find their way to the ears of God. The existing oppression was such that Israel cried to God as they had never cried before, and so moved Him to have compassion on them. The miraculous action, begun in chap. 3, is the result of the cries and groans here mentioned.

3

(1) Jethro, his father-in-law.—Rather, "his relation by marriage." The word is one of wide use. He was probably Reuel's son, and Moses' brother-in-law. His father having died, he had succeeded to his father's position, and was at once priest and sheikh of the tribe.

To the backside of the desert.—Heb., "behind the desert"—i.e., to the fertile tract which lay behind the sandy plain stretching from the Sinaitic range to the shore of the Elanitic gulf.

(2) The angel of the Lord.—Heb., "an angel of Jehovah." In verse 4 the angel is called both "Jehovah" and "Elohim," so it is concluded, with reason, that it was the Second Person of the Trinity who appeared to Moses.

(4) When the Lord saw ... God called.—Heb., "When Jehovah saw, Elohim called." The theory of two authors of Exodus, one Jehovistic and the other Elohistic, is completely refuted by this passage; for it is impossible to ascribe one clause of a sentence to one author, and the next to another. If originally the same term had been used in both places, a reviser would not have altered one without altering both.

(5) Put off thy shoes.—Egyptians before the time of Moses, and Orientals generally, in ancient (as in modern) times, removed their sandals (or their shoes) from their feet on entering any place to which respect was due, as a temple, a palace, and even the private house of a great man. It is worthy of notice that God Himself orders this mark of respect to be shown to the place which

His Presence has hallowed. On the reverence due to holy places, see the note on Gen. 28:16.

(6) The God of Abraham.—Primarily, no doubt, the meaning was, "the God who was worshiped by Abraham, Isaac, and Jacob"; but the form of the expression, "the God of Abraham," etc., indicated the continued existence of the patriarchs after death, since He can only be the God of existent, and not of non-existent things. (See note on Matt. 22:32.)

(8) A good land and a large.—The land promised to Abraham (Gen. 15:18) well deserves this description. Besides Philistia, and Palestine on both sides of the Jordan, it included almost the whole of Syria from Galilee on the south, to Amanus, Taurus, and the Euphrates on the north and northeast. This tract of country is 450 miles long, and from sixty to a hundred and twenty miles broad. Its area is not much less than 50,000 square miles. Although some parts are unproductive, it is, on the whole, a region of great fertility, quite capable of forming the seat of a powerful empire.

A land flowing with milk and honey.—This expression, here used for the first time, was already, it is probable, a proverbial one, denoting generally, richness and fertility. (See Num: 13:27).

(11) Who am I, that I should go?—The men most fit for great missions are apt to deem themselves unfit. In Moses' case, though there were some manifest grounds of fitness—e.g., his Egyptian training and learning, his familiarity with the court, his knowledge of both nations and both languages—yet, on the other hand, there were certain very marked (apparent) disqualifications. Forty years of exile, and of a shepherd's life had at once unfitted him for dealing with a court, and made him a stranger to his brethren. Want of eloquence seemed to be a fatal defect in one who must work mainly by persuasion. Even his age (eighty) might well have seemed to him unsuitable.

(13) What is his name?—In Egypt, and wherever polytheism prevailed, every god had, as a matter of course, a name. Among the Israelites up to this time God had been known only by titles, as **El** or **Elohim**, "the Lofty One"; **Shaddai**, "the Powerful"; **Jahveh**, or **Jehovah**, "the Existent." These titles were used with some perception of their meaning; no one of them had as yet passed into a proper name. Moses, imagining that the people might have become so far Egyptianized as to be no longer content with this state of things, asks God by what name he shall speak of Him to them. Who shall he say has appeared to him?

(14) I AM THAT I AM.—It is generally assumed that this is given to Moses as the full name of God. But perhaps it is rather a deep and mysterious statement of His nature. "I am that which I am." My nature cannot be declared in words, cannot be conceived of by human thought. I exist in such sort that my whole inscrutable nature is implied in my existence. I exist, as nothing else does—necessarily, eternally, really. If I am to give myself a name expressive of my nature, as far as language can be, let me be called "I AM."

Say . . . I AM hath sent me unto you.—I AM, assumed as a name, implies (1) an existence different from all other existence. "I am, and there is none beside me" (Isa. 45:6); (2) an existence out of time, with which time has nothing to do (John 8:58); (3) an existence that is real, all other being shadowy; (4) an independent and unconditioned existence, from which all other is derived, and on which it is dependent.

(15) The Lord God of your fathers.—Heb., "Jehovah, God of your fathers." The "I AM" of the preceding verse ('ehyeh) is modified here into Jahveh, or Jehovah, by a substitution of the third Person for the first. The meaning of the name remains the same. Jehovah (rendered "Lord") is the predominant name of God throughout the rest of the Old Testament.

(16) The elders of Israel.—Not so much the old men generally, as the rulers—those who bore authority over the rest—men of considerable age, no doubt, for the most part. The Hebrews, even during the oppression, enjoyed some kind of internal organization and native government.

(18) Three days' journey.—The necessity for withdrawing to so great a distance arose from the remarkable peculiarity in the Egyptian religion, the worship of animals. Cows, or at any rate, white cows, were sacred throughout the whole of Egypt, and to kill them was regarded as a crime of the deepest kind. Sheep were sacred to the inhabitants of one nome or canton, goats to those of another (Herod. 2:42). Unless the Hebrews retired to a place where there were no Egyptians, they would be unable to perform their sacred rites without danger of disturbance, and even bloodshed. (See note on 8:26.)

(22) Every woman shall borrow.—Rather, "shall ask." That there was really no pretense of "borrowing," appears from 12:33-36, where we find that the "jewels" were not asked for until the very moment of departure, when the Israelites were being "thrust forth," and the people were eager for them to be gone, certainly neither expecting nor wishing to see them again. Asking for presents is a common practice in the East, and persons who were leaving their homes to set out on a long journey through a strange country would have abundant excuse, if any had been needed, for soliciting aid from their rich neighbors.

4

(1) They will say, The Lord hath not appeared.—It is probable that the people would have said this if Moses had not had any credentials to produce. It is even possible that they did say it. There had been no appearance of Jehovah to any one for more than four hundred years, and they might well think that the age of miracles was past. Miracles cluster around certain crises in God's dealings with man, ceasing altogether between one crisis and another. They were suspended for above 500 years between the time of Daniel and the appearance of the angel to Zacharias.

(2) A rod.—Most commentators regard the "rod" of Moses as his shepherd's crook, and this is certainly possible; but the etymology of the word employed seems rather to point to an ordinary staff, or walking stick.

(4) Take it by the tail.—Those who venture to handle poisonous snakes generally take hold of them by the neck, in which case they are unable to bite. To test the faith and courage of Moses, the command is given him to lay hold of **this** serpent "by the tail."

(5) That they may believe . . .—These are God's words to Moses, in continuation of those which form the first portion of the preceding verse. The clause describing the action of Moses in verse 4 is parenthetic. The words give divine sanction to the view that the power of working miracles is given to men, primarily and mainly, for its evidential value, to accredit them as God's messengers. Without the gift of miracles neither would Moses have persuaded the Israelites, nor would the apostles have converted the world.

(6) His hand was leprous as snow.—The

worst form of leprosy was called by the Greeks, "the white disease." When it is fully developed, the whole skin appears glossy white, and every hair is "white like wool." This form is said to be absolutely incurable.

(9) Shall become blood.—The signs were, no doubt, selected primarily for facility of exhibition; but they may also have been intended to be significant. The change of a rod into a serpent showed that a feeble implement might become a power to chastise and to destroy. That of a healthy into a leprous hand, and the reverse, indicated that Moses' mission was both to punish and to save; while the change of the water into blood suggested—albeit vaguely— the conversion of that peace and prosperity which Egypt was enjoying into calamity, suffering, and bloodshed.

(10) I am not eloquent.—Moses, still reluctant, raises a new objection. He is not gifted with facility of speech. Words do not come readily to him; perhaps, when they come, he has a difficulty in uttering them. According to a Jewish tradition, he was unable to pronounce the labials, **b, f, m, p, v.** According to his own expressions at the end of the verse, he was "heavy" or "slow of speech," and "heavy" or "slow of tongue."

(12) I will be with thy mouth.—To suggest words (see Matt. 10:19, 20), and assist utterance. Comp. the reluctance of Jeremiah and God's dealings with him (Jer. 1:6-9).

(13) Send, I pray thee, by the hand of him whom thou wilt send.—A curt, impatient, and scarcely reverent speech. Moses means that he will undertake the task if God insists; but that God would do far better to send another. Hence the "anger of the Lord" against him (verse 14), which led to Aaron's association with him as joint leader of the people.

(16) Instead of God.—God did not speak to Aaron directly, but only through Moses. Aaron was to recognize in Moses God's mouthpiece, and to consider what Moses told him as coming from God. Moses had still, therefore, the higher position.

(18) Jethro said, Go in peace.—Jethro's character is altogether one of which kindness and peacefulness are the main elements. He is sort of a second Melchizedek, both priest and king, a worshiper of the true God, and one in whose presence both Moses and Aaron are content to play a secondary part (18:9, 12). But he never asserts himself; he is always kind, gentle, acquiescent, helpful. He might easily have made a difficulty at the present point of the narrative, have demurred to the weakening of the tribe by the withdrawal of an important member from it, have positively refused to allow the departure of Zipporah and her children. But his words are simply "Go in peace." He consents, and does not mar the grace of his act by any show of reluctance. He later receives them back, and protects them (18:2).

(20) The rod of God.—An emphatic phrase. God's endowment of the rod with miraculous power had made it "the rod of God." It was the instrument by means of which most of the plagues and the other miracles were wrought (7:20; 8:6, 17; 9:23; 10:13; 14:16; 17:5; Num. 20:9; etc.).

(21) I will harden his heart.—The hardening of Pharaoh's heart has been the subject of much controversy. It is ascribed to God in this place, and again in 7:3; 9:12; 10:1, 20, 27; 14:4, 8; to Pharaoh in 8:15, 32; and 9:34; to the action of the heart itself in 7:13, 22; 9:7, 35. Three different modes of operation may be meant. Each term has a period during which it is predominant. In the narrative of what happened, the action of the heart is itself predominant in the first period; that of Pharaoh on his heart in the second; that of God in the third. We may suppose that, at first, Pharaoh's nature was simply not impressed, and that then his heart is said to have "hardened itself," or "remained hard"; that after a while he began to be impressed; but that by an effort of his will controlled himself, and determined that he would not yield: thus "hardening his own heart"; finally, that after he had done this twice (8:15, 32), God stepped in and "smote him with a spirit of blindness and infatuation," as a judgment upon him (9:12), thus, finally, "hardening" him (comp. Rom. 9:18). Pharaoh's time of probation being past, God used him as a mere means of showing forth His glory. There is nothing in this contrary to the general teaching of the Scriptures, or to the divine perfection.

(22) Israel is my son.—Compare Hosea 11:1. This tender relation, now first revealed, is not a mere metaphor, meaning "as dear to me as a son," but a reality. The Israel of God enjoys the sonship of adoption by being taken into the True Son, and made one with Him (Rom. 8:14-17).

My first-born.—Admitted to sonship in the Messiah before the other nations of the earth.

(24) The Lord met him.—God met Moses, i.e., visited him with a sharp attack of illness, which threatened to be fatal. Both he and his wife seem at once to have concluded that the visitation was a punishment, on account of their having neglected to circumcise their newborn son. Perhaps Moses had an intimation from God to that effect.

(25) At his feet.—Moses' feet, undoubtedly. The action was petulant and reproachful. Zipporah regarded the bloody rites of her husband's religion as cruel and barbarous, and cast the foreskin of her son at his feet, as though he were a Moloch requiring a bloody offering.

(26) So he let him go.—God let Moses go) i.e., allowed him to recover—accepted Zipporah's act as sufficient, albeit tardy, reparation, and spared the life of her husband.

Then she said.—Zipporah had called him "a bloody husband" on account of the circumcisions—of Gershom in Midian many years previously, and now of Eliezer. We learn from 18:2, 3, that Zipporah and her boys were sent back to Jethro by Moses, probably at this time. Moses was in haste, and the child could not have traveled conveniently for some days.

The Return to Egypt

(31) The people believed.—The Israelites in Egypt, though suffering under severe oppression, had an organization of their own, jurisdiction attaching probably to the heads of tribes, or of chief families. Moses and Aaron could have no power to convene them; but they invited them to a conference, and the elders came. The narrative is very much compressed. The elders heard the words, and saw the signs first. Then they must have summoned an assembly of the people, after working hours, and the people must have been addressed and shown the signs. The effect was to convince them also, and to induce them to accept Moses and Aaron for the national leaders.

5

First Application of Moses to Pharaoh, and Increase of the Oppression

(1) Went in.—The Court, according to Ps. 78:12, 43, was held at Zoan (i.e., Tanis). This was the ordinary residence of Rameses II and his son Menephthah.

They they may hold a feast unto me.—God's entire purpose is not at once revealed to Pharaoh. He is tried with a moderate demand, which he might well have granted. By refusing it he showed himself harsh, unkind, and inconsiderate, so tempting God to lay upon him a greater burden.

(2) Who is the Lord?—The king means to say, that, whoever Jehovah is, He can have no authority over **him**, as He is not one of **his** gods. The Egyptians were accustomed to the idea of local gods, and quite expected every nation to have a deity or several deities of its own; but they regarded the powers of each as circumscribed, certainly not extending beyond the race or nation to which the god belonged.

(5) And Pharaoh said.—Pharaoh turns to the officers of his court and reproaches them with allowing the Hebrews to be idle. They have time to hold meetings (4:30, 31), and listen to inflammatory harangues, and depute leaders to make inconvenient proposals—why are they not kept closer to their tasks? Some change of system is required.

(7) Let them go and gather straw.—This requirement would more than double the people's toils. They would have to disperse themselves over the harvest fields, often lying at a considerable distance from the brick fields, to detach the straw from the soil, gather it into bundles, and convey it to the scene of their ordinary labors. Having done this they were then required to complete the ordinary "tale."

(12) Stubble instead of straw.—Heb., "stubble for the straw." Reaping in Egypt was effected by cutting off the ears only from the stalks, and thus a tall stubble was left in the fields. This appears not to have been valued by the cultivators, and whoever wished was allowed to collect it. After collecting it, and bringing it to the brick fields in bundles, they would have to chop it small before it would be fit for use.

(15) The officers ... came and cried unto Pharaoh.—The Egyptian monarchs were accessible to all. It was a part of their duty to hear complaints personally; and they, for the most part, devoted to this employment the earlier hours of each day (see Herod. 2:173).

(17) Ye are idle.—Idleness was regarded by the Egyptians as one of the worst sins. It had to be specially disclaimed in the final judgment before Osiris. Men sometimes disclaimed it in the epitaphs which they placed upon their tombs. Pharaoh had already made the charge, by implication, against Moses and Aaron (verse 4).

(22) Moses returned unto the Lord.—He could find nothing to say to the officers. The course of events had as much disappointed him as it had them. All that he could do was to complain to God, with a freedom which seems to us almost to border in irreverence, but which God excused in him, since it had its root in his tender love for his people. Moses might perhaps have borne with patience a mere negative result—the postponement of any open manifestation of the divine power—but the thought that he had increased the burdens and aggravated the misery of his countrymen was more than he could bear without complaining.

6

God's Renewal and Enlargement of His Promises

(1) Now shalt thou see.—Moses' complaint was that God delayed. The answer is an assurance that there will be no more delay; the work is about to begin, and Moses will behold it. He will then cease to doubt.

With a strong hand shall he let them go.—i.e., through the compulsion which my strong hand will exert on him.

(3) I appeared ... by the name of God Almighty.—For the name "El Shaddai," see Gen. 17:1. Its primary idea is, no doubt, that of "overpowering strength." The primary idea of "Jehovah" is, on the contrary, that of absolute, eternal, unconditional, independent existence. Both names were probably of a great antiquity, and widely spread among Semitic races; but, at different times and in different places, special stress was laid on the one or on the other. To the early patriarchs God revealed Himself as "El Shaddai," because He desired to impress upon them His ability to fulfill the promises which He had made to them; to Moses and Israel generally, at the date of the Exodus, He insisted on His name Jehovah, because they were in the closest contact with polytheism, and had themselves, in many cases, fallen into polytheism (Josh. 24:14), against which this name was a standing protest since "the Existent" must mean "the Self-Existent," and so "the Only Existent." (See Deut. 4:39.)

(4) The land of Canaan.—Canaan proper was the tract between Sidon and Gaza (Gen. 10:19), which is now counted as "Palestine." The region promised to Abra-

ham, however, and included in a larger sense of the word "Canaan," was much more extensive, reaching as it did from the Nile to the Euphrates (Gen. 15:18). This vast territory was actually possessed by Israel under David and Solomon (I Kings 4:21-24). But Abraham, Isaac, and Jacob were occupants of Canaan merely by sufferance: they were allowed to dwell in it because it was not half peopled. The ownership was recognized as belonging to the Canaanite nations, Hittites and others (Gen. 20:15; 23:3-20).

(6) I will redeem you.—The idea of God purchasing, or redeeming, Israel is here brought forward for the first time. The redemption was accomplished in the long series of wonders, culminating in the tenth plague, and by being led through the Red Sea. (See 15:13-16.) The delivery from Pharaoh typified **our** deliverance from the power of Satan; the bringing forth from Egypt **our** deliverance from the power of sin.

(7) I will take you to me for a people.—Comp. 19:15, 16; Deut. 7:6. The selection of Israel as a "peculiar people" did not involve the abandonment of all other nations, as we see by the instances of Balaam, Ruth, Job, Nebuchadnezzar, Darius the Mede, Cyrus, and others, but "in every nation those that feared him and worked righteousness" were accepted with Him (Acts 10:35). The centurion of the gospels (Matt. 8:5-13, Luke 7:2-10) and Cornelius in the Acts (Acts 10:1-33) carry the same principle into gospel times.

(9) They hearkened not.—The second message was received in quite a different spirit from the first. Then "the people believed, and bowed their knees and worshipped" (4:31). Now they could not even be induced to listen.

The Second Message to Pharaoh

(11) Speak unto Pharaoh.—The second message was an advance upon the first. The first asked only for permission to enter the wilderness, much of which was within the limits of Egypt; the second was a demand that the Israelites should be allowed "to go out of the land."

(12) How then shall Pharaoh hear me?—This time the objection comes from Moses. His double rejection by Pharaoh (5:1-4) and by Israel (6:9), had thrown him back into utter despondency. All that diffidence and distrust of himself which he had shown in

his earlier communications with Jehovah
(3:11, 4:1, 10, 13) revived, and he despaired
of success in his mission.

Uncircumcised lips.—Some argue from
this expression that Moses was "tongue-
tied." He had some difficulty of utterance
but whether or not it was a physical impediment remains uncertain. (See note on 4:10.)
"Uncircumcised" is used, according to the
Hebrew idiom, for any imperfection which
interferes with efficiency. An "uncircumcised ear," is explained in Jer. 6:10 to be an
ear that "cannot hearken"; and an "uncircumcised heart" (Lev. 26:41) is a heart that
fails to understand.

The Family of Moses

**(14) These be the heads of their fathers'
houses.**—Genealogies have always had a
special interest for the Semitic races. The
descent of a man who aspired to be a leader
would be a subject of curiosity, with a
Semitic people, to all those who submitted
themselves to his guidance; and Moses naturally inserts his at the point where, fully
accepting the post of leader, he came forward and began his struggle with Pharaoh
for the emancipation of his nation.

Attempts have been made to show that
the present genealogy is complete, and that
Moses was Levi's great-grandson. But in
Joshua's case there were ten generations (at
least) between him and Jacob (I Chron.
7:23-27); so that three generations only between Jacob and Moses are scarcely possible. The Israelites were in the habit of
constructing their genealogies by omitting
some of the links, as we see plainly in the
genealogy of Ezra (Ezra 7:1-5) and in Matthew's genealogy of our Lord (Matt. 1:8). In
this present genealogy four or five (perhaps
more) names are probably omitted between
Amram, the son of Kohath, and Amram,
the father of Moses.

(17) The sons of Gershon.—From this
point the genealogy is no longer a recapitulation, but an original historical document
of first-rate importance, which is confirmed
by Numbers (Num. 3:18-33) and Chronicles
(I Chron. 6:17-19).

(20) The years of the life of Amram.—
The long lives of Levi, Kohath, and Amram, the father of Moses, are not recorded
for any chronological purpose, but to show
that the blessing of God rested in a special
way on the house of Levi, even before it
became the priestly tribe.

**(23) Elisheba, daughter of Amminadab,
sister of Naashon.**—Amminadab and
Naashon were among the ancestors of David (Ruth 4:19, 20; I Chron. 2:10-15), and
their names are consequently found in the
genealogies of our Lord (Matt. 1:4; Luke
3:32, 33).

(26) Their armies.—This expression is
here used of the Israelites for the first time.
It seems to refer to the organization of a
quasi-military character, which enabled
them at last to leave Egypt, not a disorderly
mob, but "harnessed," or "in military array" (13:18).

The Second Message to Pharaoh
(resumed)

(28-30) These verses are most closely connected with chap. 7. They are a recapitulation of main points in chap. 6, rendered
necessary by the long parenthesis (verses
14-27), and serve to unite chap. 7 with the
previous narrative. They contain no new
information.

7

**(1) See, I have made thee a god to
Pharaoh.**—This is God's answer to the objection of Moses (6:12). The force of it
would seem to be: "Thou art not called on
to speak, but to act. In action thou wilt be
to Pharaoh as a god—powerful, wonder-
working, irresistible; it is Aaron who will
have to speak to him, and **he** is eloquent"
(4:14).

(3) I will harden Pharaoh's heart.—See
note on 4:21.

**(5) The Egyptians shall know that I am
the Lord.**—Heb., "that I am Jehovah." No
doubt this was one of the main lessons
intended to be taught by the whole series of
miraculous events connected with the Exodus. Egypt was the greatest monarchy in
the whole world. She was now at the height
of her glory. Among existent polytheisms,
hers was the most famous; and her gods
must have seemed, not only to herself, but
to all the surrounding nations, the most
powerful. To discredit them was to throw
discredit upon polytheism generally, and to
exalt the name of Jehovah above that of all
the deities of the nations. (Comp. 14:11-16.)

(11) The magicians of Egypt.—Magic was
widely practiced in Egypt, and consisted
mainly in the composition and employment
of charms which were believed to exert a
powerful effect both over man and over the

brute creation. Charms were also regarded as potent in this life to produce or remove disease, and avert the attacks of noxious animals. Some Egyptian works are mere collections of magical receipts, and supply strange prescriptions which are to be used, and mystic words which are to be uttered. A Jewish tradition, accepted by the Apostle Paul (II Tim. 3:8), spoke of two magicians as the special opponents of Moses, and called them "Jannes and Jambres." It has been supposed by some that the magicians were really in possession of supernatural powers, obtained by a connection with evil spirits; but, on the whole, it is perhaps most probable that they were merely persons acquainted with many secrets of nature not generally known, and trained in tricks of sleight-of-hand and conjuring.

(13) He hardened Pharaoh's heart.—This is a mis-translation. The verb is intransitive, and "Pharaoh's heart" is its nominative case. Translate, "Pharaoh's heart hardened itself." It is essential to the idea of a final **penal** hardening that in the earlier stages Pharaoh should have been left to himself.

The First Plague

(14-21) The water turned to blood: The present miracle is to be done on the largest possible scale, in the sight of all the Egyptians, and not as a sign, but as a "judgment." The judgment strikes the Egyptians two severe blows. (1) It involves an insult to their religion, and brings it into discredit, since the Nile-god, Hapi, was a main object of worship, closely connected with Osiris. (2) It is a great physical affliction. They are accustomed to use the Nile water for drinking, for ablutions, for the washing of their clothes, and for culinary purposes; they have great difficulty in procuring any other. Again, their fish are killed. Fish was one of their principal foods, perhaps the main food of the common people; and the river was the chief source from which the fish supply was obtained. The punishment is retaliatory: for as they had made the Nile the means of destroying Hebrew infants (1:22), so that Hebrew parents had loathed to drink of it, as though stained with the blood of their children, so is it now made by means of blood undrinkable for themselves. The plague lasts seven days (verse 25), a longer time than any other; and if not so destructive as the later ones, was perhaps of all the most nauseous and disgusting.

(20) In the sight of Pharaoh, and in the sight of his servants.—If the occasion was one of a Nile festival, Pharaoh would have "gone out to the water" (verse 15) accompanied by all the great officers of the Court, by a large body of the priests, and vast numbers of the people. If it was a mere occasion of bathing, he would have had with him a pretty numerous train of attendants. In either case considerable publicity was given to the miracle.

(22) The magicians ... did so with their enchantments.—The act of the magicians must have been a poor imitation of the action of Moses and Aaron. The magicians could not act on this large scale. They could only operate, or seem to operate, on some small quantity of water, obtained probably in the way noticed in verse 24. They turned the liquid of a red color, or by sleight of hand substituted blood for it. The result was subjected to no test, and was perhaps not even done in the presence of any hostile witness.

8

The Second Plague

(1-4) The second infliction upon Egypt was an innumerable multitude of frogs which came up out of the river and infested the cities, the houses, the sleeping apartments, the beds, the ovens, and the kneading-troughs. There was no escaping them. Here, again, the infliction was double. (1) Frogs were sacred animals to the Egyptians, who regarded them as symbols of procreative power, and associated them especially with the goddess Heka, whom they represented as frog-headed. Sacred animals might not be intentionally killed; and even their involuntary slaughter was not unfrequently punished with death. To be plagued with a multitude of frogs which might not be put to death, yet on which it was scarcely possible not to tread, was a severe trial to the religious feelings of the people, and tended to bring the religion itself into contempt. (2) The visitation was horrible to the senses—nauseous, disgusting. The frogs were hideous to the eye, grating to the ear, repulsive to the touch. Their constant presence everywhere rendered them a continual torment. If other later plagues were more injurious, the plague of frogs was perhaps of all the most loathsome.

(7) The magicians did so.—All that the writer means to express is that they **seemed**

to Pharaoh and to the Court to do on a small scale what Moses and Aaron had done on the largest possible scale. They would have shown their own power and the power of their gods far more satisfactorily had they succeeded in taking the frogs away.

(8) Pharaoh called for Moses.—This was the first sign of yielding. Pharaoh had borne the infliction of the water turned to blood without flinching, probably because individually he had suffered but little from it. But he suffered from the frogs as much as any one else (verses 3, 4). As far as words could go, the concession was complete.

(13, 14) The frogs died.—God, who knew the heart of Pharaoh, and its insincerity, or at any rate its changefulness, took the plague of frogs away in a manner that made its removal almost as bad as its continuance.

(15) He hardened his heart.—Hitherto Pharaoh's nature had not been impressed; his heart had remained dull, callous, hard. Now an impression had been made (verse 8), and he must have yielded, if he had not called in his own will to efface it. Herein was his great guilt. (See note on chap. 4:21.)

The Third Plague

(16, 17) It is disputed whether this plague was one of lice or of mosquitoes. Josephus and the Jewish commentators generally take the former view, while the latter is supported by the LXX and Vulgate, by the authorities of Philo, Origen, and Augustine in ancient, and Gesenius, Keil, and Kalisch in modern times. The word used **(kinnim)** is reasonably regarded as formed by **onomatopoeia**, from the sharp tingling sound given out by the insect when on the wing. The trouble caused to the Egyptians of the Delta by mosquitoes is noticed by Herodotus (2:95). They are said to attack not only the exposed parts of the skin, but especially the ears, the nostrils, and eyes, where they do great damage.

It is noticed that the third plague, whatever it was, came without warning. It was God's judgment on Pharaoh for hardening his heart and breaking his promise (verse 15); and he was not given the option of avoiding it by submission to God's will.

(18) The magicians did so.—i.e., tried to do so. Mosquitoes were things too delicate to be caught, and manipulated, and produced at a given moment by sleight of hand. The magicians tried to produce a counterfeit of the miracle, but could not.

(19) Pharaoh's heart was hardened.—The mosquitoes did not impress Pharaoh as the frogs had done (verses 8-15). Probably the visitation affected him but little, since he would possess mosquito curtains, and could inhabit the loftier parts of his palace, which would be above the height whereto the mosquito ascends (Herod. 2:95).

The Fourth Plague

(20, 21) There is, again, a doubt as to the nature of the fourth plague. It is suggested that the plague was really one of the "kakerlaque," a kind of beetle, which is injurious both to the persons of men, to the furniture and fittings of houses, and to the crops in the fields. Like all beetles, it was sacred, and might not be destroyed, being emblematic of the sun-god, Ra, especially in his form of Khepra, or "the creator." Egyptians were obliged to submit to such a plague without attempting to diminish it, and would naturally view the infliction as a sign that the sun-god was angry with them. The plague was thus an advance on previous plagues, and if less disgusting than some others, was far more injurious.

(22) I will sever in that day the land of Goshen.—This was a new feature, and one calculated to make a deep impression both on king and people. Nature had put no severance between it and the regions where Egyptians dwelt; so the severance to be made would be a manifest miracle.

(25) Pharaoh called for Moses.—Pharaoh suffered from the kakerlaque equally with his subjects, **more** than his subjects. He therefore gave way before this plague almost at once, and without waiting for any remonstrance on the part of the magicians or others, "called for Moses."

(26) It is not meet so to do.—Pressed to remain "in the land," and sacrifice, Moses deemed it right to explain to the king why this was impossible. The Israelites would have to "sacrifice the abomination of the Egyptians"—i.e., animals of which the Egyptians abominated the killing; and if they did this in the presence of Egyptians, a riot would be certain to break out. The sacrificial animals of the Hebrews—sheep, goats, and cattle—were all of them sacred animals, either to the Egyptians generally, or to the inhabitants of certain districts.

(29) Let not Pharaoh deal deceitfully any more.—God's servants must rebuke even kings when they openly break the moral law (I Sam. 13:23; 15:16-23; II Sam. 12:7-12; I

Kings 21:20-22; Matt. 14:4, etc.). Pharaoh had promised unconditionally to let the people go if the frogs were removed (verse 8), and had then flagrantly broken his word. Moses was right to rebuke his "deceit."

9

The Fifth Plague

(1-3) The nature of the fifth plague is manifest, and admits of no dispute. It was a "rinderpest," or murrain upon cattle; which, however, unlike most similar disorders, attacked the greater number of the domesticated animals—horses, asses, camels, oxen, and sheep. Thus the Egyptian losses were very heavy, and the king, no doubt, suffered with the rest, for the Egyptian monarchs were large cattle owners (Gen. 47:6, 17). The Pharaoh was, however, less impressed by this plague than by the fourth, and made no sign of submission.

(4) **The Lord shall sever.**—Comp. 8:22. Apparently Israel had been subjected to the first, second, and third plagues, which caused annoyance only, and not loss. Their exemption began with the fourth plague, and then probably continued without intermission, though it is not always mentioned.

(5) **The Lord appointed a set time.**—As murrain is not uncommon in Egypt, especially in the Delta, and the coming affliction might therefore be ascribed by the Egyptians to natural causes, God took care to mark its miraculous character by appointing a time, by exempting the cattle of Israel, and by making the disease fatal to **all** the cattle of the Egyptians that were left "in the field."

The Sixth Plague

(8-10) Here, again, there is little question of what the plague was. Doubts may be entertained as to its exact character, and its proper medical designation, but all agree that it was a severe cutaneous disorder, accompanied by pustules or ulcers. It was not announced beforehand to the Egyptians, nor were they allowed the opportunity of escaping it. Like the third plague, it was altogether of the nature of a judgment; and the judgment was a severe one. Now, for the first time, was acute suffering inflicted on the persons of men; now, for the first time, was it shown how Jehovah could smite with a terrible disease; and if with a disease, why not with death?

(10) **A boil breaking forth with blains.**—Heb., "an inflammation, producing pustules." Diseases of this character are not uncommon in Egypt (comp. Deut. 28:27), but they are not often very severe; nor do they attack indifferently man and beast. The miraculous character of the plague was shown by its being announced beforehand; by its severity (verse 11); by its universality (verse 11); and by its extension to animals.

(12) **The Lord hardened the heart of Pharaoh.**—The judicial punitive hardening of Pharaoh's heart by God now began. Pharaoh had twice hardened himself—i.e., resisted an impression made upon him, and crushed his inclination to yield to it (8:15, 32). (See note on 4:21; see also Rom. 1:28.)

The Seventh Plague

(13-19) This plague presents to us several new features. (1) It is ushered in with an unusually long and exceedingly awful message (verses 13-19). (2) It is the first plague that attacks human life (verse 19). (3) It is more destructive than any previous plague to property (verse 25). (4) It is accompanied with terrible demonstrations (verse 23). (5) It is made to test the degree of faith to which the Egyptians have attained, by means of a revelation of the way whereby it may be escaped (verse 20). Though the plagues do not form a regularly ascending series, each transcending the last, yet there is a certain progression observable. The earlier ones cause annoyance rather than injury; those which follow cause loss of property; then God's hand is laid on men's persons, so as to hurt, but not to kill; lastly, life itself is attacked. The seventh plague was peculiarly astonishing and alarming to the Egyptians, because hail and thunder, even rain, were rare phenomena in their country; and a thunderstorm accompanied by such features as characterized this one was absolutely unknown. The hailstones must have been of an enormous size and weight to kill men and cattle. It is not surprising that the visitation brought down the pride of Pharaoh more than any preceding one, and made him for the time being consent unconditionally to the people's departure (verse 28).

(29) **That thou mayest know how that the earth is the Lord's.**—Comp. verse 15. It was the general belief of the Egyptians, as of most ancient nations, that each country had its own god or gods. Pharaoh had already admitted Jehovah's power (8:8), and now

regarded Him as the God of the Hebrews (8:28). God desired to have it generally acknowledged that He was the God of the whole earth.

(31) The flax and the barley was smitten.—The flax is "bolled"—i.e., forms its seed-vessel—toward the end of January or beginning of February and the barley comes into ear about the same time. The wheat is a full month later than the barley in Egypt, and does not come into ear until March. These facts fix the date of this plague, and help to fix the dates both of the earlier and the later ones.

(34) Pharaoh . . . sinned yet more, and hardened his heart.—As Pharaoh had never been so much moved previously, so it now required a greater effort of his will to "harden his heart" than it had ever done before; and thus he now "sinned yet more" than he had as yet sinned.

10

The Eighth Plague

(1-4) The nature of the visitation is uncontested and incontestable—it was a terrible invasion of locusts. Locusts are an occasional, though not a frequent, scourge in Egypt. They are not bred there, and necessarily arrive from some foreign country. When they descend, their ravages are as severe as elsewhere. They fly across the country, darkening the air with their compact ranks, which are undisturbed by the constant attacks of crows and vultures, and making a strange whizzing sound, like that of fire, or many distant wheels. Where they alight they devour every green thing, even stripping the trees of their leaves. They always enter Egypt either from the south or from the east, and necessarily come with a wind, since they cannot possibly fly any considerable distance without one. After the loss of their cattle by murrain and hail, and the ruin of the flax and barley crops by the latter agency, nothing was wanting to complete the desolation of the country and the impoverishment of its inhabitants but the ruin of the wheat and doora ("rie") crops, which the locusts speedily effected.

(1) I have hardened . . . the heart of his servants.—They, too, had first hardened their own hearts (9:34), and so deserved a penal hardening. A certain amount of responsibility rested on **them**. Had they allowed the miracles to have their full natural

effect upon their minds, they would have been convinced that resistance was useless, and would have impressed their views upon the Pharaoh. Even in the most absolute governments public opinion has weight, and the general sentiment of the Court almost always carries the sovereign with it. There is nothing derogatory to the divine nature in a penal hardening being, as it were, utilized to increase the glory of God, and affect for good future generations of His people.

(5) They shall eat the residue of that which is escaped . . . every tree.—Comp. 9:32. The description of Joel has never been surpassed (Joel 1:7; 2:3).

(7) Let the men go.—Though the heart of Pharaoh remained hard, the plagues had a certain effect on the minds of the Egyptians. First, the magicians were impressed (8:19). Then a certain number of the people feared (9:20). Now the very officers of the Court, those who were in the closest contact with the king, believed that the words of Moses would come true, and counseled the king to yield. The word used, which is not that of verse 11, would cover women and children.

(9) With our flocks and with our herds.—The family of Jacob brought numerous flocks and herds into Egypt (Gen. 47:1). These had, no doubt, increased, notwithstanding the oppression, and at the time of the Exodus must have been numerous. The requirement to "take a lamb for an house" (12:3) on the institution of the Passover involved the killing, on a single day, of 200,000 lambs. Even after this the flocks and herds which went out with them (12:38) were "very much cattle."

(10) Evil is before you.—You contemplate doing me a mischief, by depriving me of the services of so large a body of laborers.

(11) That ye did desire.—There was no ground for this reproach. Moses and Aaron had always demanded the release of the entire nation ("let my **people** go").

(14) The locusts went up over all the land of Egypt.—It is not, perhaps, certain that this is intended literally, since universal expressions are continually used by the sacred writers where something less than universality is meant. Perhaps the visitation was confined to the Delta and the vicinity of Memphis. Even so, it would have covered an area of 7,000 square miles.

(16) Pharaoh called for Moses and Aaron in haste.—The expression "hasted to call" is new, and marks extreme urgency. The visitation of the locusts was felt as far more severe than any previous one. It entirely destroyed all the remaining harvest, both of grain and fruit, and must have produced a terrible famine, had it not been for the Egyptian institution of granaries (Gen. 41:35, 48).

I have sinned ... —Comp. 9:27. This confession is an improvement upon the former one, as acknowledging a double fault, and as free from any attempt to put the blame, either wholly or in part, upon others. It was probably sincere at the time; but the feeling from which it sprang was short-lived.

(19) The Red sea.—Heb., "the sea of weeds," or "of rushes." The Red Sea probably acquired this name among the Hebrews from the fact that in the time of Moses its northwestern recess communicated with a marshy tract, extending as far as the Bitter Lakes, and abounding in aquatic plants of a luxuriant growth. (Comp. 2:3, where the same term designates the water plants of the Nile.)

The Ninth Plague

(21-23) The ninth plague, like the third and sixth, was sent without any previous warning. It consisted in a "thick darkness," which may have been brought about by means of the "Wind of the Desert," which frequently blows about the time of the vernal equinox, and brings with it such clouds of a fine impalpable sand that the light of the sun is obscured, and an effect produced which some travelers have compared to "the most gloomy night." Such a preternatural continuance of absolutely impenetrable "blackness of darkness" would cause to any man a feeling of intense alarm and horror (verses 21, 23). To the Egyptians it would be peculiarly painful and terrible. Ra, the sun-god, was among the principal objects of their worship, especially in the Delta where Heliopolis and Pithom were cities dedicated to him. Darkness was a creation of Set—the Evil Principle, the destroyer of Osiris—and of Apophis, the Great Serpent, the impeder of souls in the lower world. It would have seemed to the Egyptians that Ra was dead, that Set had triumphed over his brother, that Apophis had encircled the world with his dark folds, and plunged it in eternal night. Hence Pharaoh's early call for Moses, and permission that the people should depart, with their families (verse 24);

a concession which, however, was marred by the proviso, "Only let your flocks and herds be stayed."

(26) Our cattle also shall go with us.—Once more Moses rejects the proffered compromise—rejects it absolutely and altogether. The cattle shall **all** go with the people. And why? First, because it is theirs and not Pharaoh's; secondly, because it is God's. The festival to be held in the wilderness is altogether a new thing; its ritual has not at present been laid down. The people will only be told "with what they must serve the Lord" when they are come to the place where they are to serve Him: i.e., to Sinai (3:12).

(29) The division between chaps. 10 and 11 is unfortunate. The interview between Pharaoh and Moses was not yet over. It is continued in verses 4-8 of the next chapter, and only terminates when the prophet "went out from Pharaoh in a great anger." Verses 1-3 of chap. 11 are parenthetic.

11

Announcement of the Tenth Plague

(1) And the Lord said.—A revelation was made to Moses before his present interview with Pharaoh began. The insertion is needed in order to explain the confidence of Moses in regard to the last plague (verse 5), and the effect it would have on the Egyptians (verse 8).

(2) Let every man borrow.—See the comment on 3:22.

(3) The man Moses.—It is difficult to imagine anyone but Moses giving him so bald and poor a designation. To other writers he is a "prophet" (Deut. 34:10; Luke 24:27; Acts 3:22, 7:37), or "a man of God" (Deut. 33:1; Josh. 14:6; Ps. 90, Title; Ezra 3:2), or "the servant of the Lord" (Josh 1:1; Heb. 3:5); never simply "the man."

(4) And Moses said.—In continuation of the speech recorded in 10:29, face to face with Pharaoh, Moses makes his last appeal—utters his last threats. Hardened as his heart is, Pharaoh is yet to be allowed "a place for repentance." God announces to him, by the mouth of Moses, the coming destruction of the first-born. If Pharaoh had even now relented, it was not too late. But he had "hardened himself," and then "been hardened," until, practically, the time for relenting was gone by. He remained obdurate, and "would not let the children of Israel go out of his land" (verse 10).

(5) All the first-born ... shall die.—The Heb. word translated **first-born** is applied only to males; the eldest **son** should be cut off. In Egypt, as in most other countries, the law of primogeniture prevailed—the eldest son was the hope, stay, and support of the household, his father's companion, his mother's joy, the object of his brothers' and sisters' reverence. The first-born of the Pharaoh bore the title of "hereditary crown prince," and succeeded his father, unless he died or was formally set aside during his father's lifetime. Among the nobles, estates were inherited, and sometimes titles descended to the first-born. No greater affliction can be conceived, short of destruction of the people, than the sudden death in every family of him round whom the highest interests and fondest hopes clustered.

All the first-born of beasts.—The aggravation of the calamity by its extension to beasts is remarkable, and is probably to be connected with the Egyptian animal-worship.

(8) In a great anger.—Heb., "in heat of anger": i.e., burning with indignation. Moses had not shown this in his speech, which had been calm and dignified; but he here records what he had felt. For once his acquired "meekness" failed, and the hot natural temper of his youth blazed up. His life had been threatened—he had been ignominiously dismissed—he had been deprived of his right of audience for the future (10:28). Under such circumstances, he did well to be angry.

12

Institution of the Passover

(1) In the land of Egypt.—This section (verses 1-28) has the appearance of having been written independently of the previous narrative—earlier, probably, and as a part of the Law rather than of the history. It throws together instructions on the subject of the Passover which must have been given at different times (comp. verses 3, 12, 17).

(2) The beginning of months.—It was this month which was now made, by God's command, the first month of the Hebrew year; but as yet it had not the name Nisan: it was called Abib (13:4), the month of "greenness." Henceforth the Hebrews had two years, a civil and a sacred one (Joseph., **Ant. Jud.**, 1:3, §3). The civil year began with Tisri (see 23:16), in the autumn, at the

close of the harvest; the sacred year began with Abib (called afterward Nisan), six months earlier.

(3) A lamb.—The requirement indicates a social condition in which there was no extreme poverty. All Israelites are supposed either to possess a lamb or to be able to purchase one.

(5) Without blemish.—Natural piety teaches that we must not "offer the blind, the lame, or the sick for sacrifice" (Mal. 1:8). We must give to God of our best. The Law emphasized this teaching, and here, on the first occasion when a sacrifice was formally appointed, required it to be absolutely without blemish of any kind. Afterward the requirement was made general (Lev. 22:19-25). It was peculiarly fitting that the Paschal offering should be without defect of any kind, as especially typifying "the Lamb of God," who is "holy, harmless, undefiled"—a "lamb without spot."

(7) The two side posts and on the upper door post.—The idea seems to have been that the destroying influence, whatever it was, would enter the house by the door. The sight of the bloody stains above the door and on either side would prevent its entering.

(8) Unleavened bread ... bitter herbs.—As partaking of the lamb typified feeding on Christ, so the putting away of leaven and eating unleavened bread signified the putting away of all defilement and corruption before we approach Christ to feed on Him (I Cor. 5:8). The bitter herbs probably represented "self-denial" or "repentance."

(9) His head with his legs ...—The lamb was to be roasted whole: "not a bone of it was to be broken" (verse 46).

The purtenance thereof.—Heb., "its inside." The entrails were taken out, carefully cleansed, and then replaced.

(10) Ye shall let nothing of it remain.—That there might be neither profanation nor superstitious use of what was left.

(11) Thus shall ye eat it.—The injunctions which follow are not repeated in any later part of the Law, and were not generally regarded as binding at any Passover after the first. They all had reference to the impending departure of the Israelites, who were to eat the Passover prepared as for a journey. Some such attitude befits Christians at all times, since they know not when the summons may come to them requiring them to leave the Egypt of this world and start for the heavenly country.

It is the Lord's passover.—The word

"passover" (**pesakh**) is here used for the first time. It is supposed by some to be of Egyptian origin, and to signify primarily "a spreading out of wings, so as to protect." But the meaning "pass over" is still regarded by many of the best Hebraists as the primary and most proper sense, and the word itself as Semitic.

(**12**) **Against all the gods of Egypt I will execute judgment.**—The death of all the first-born beasts would have been felt by the Egyptians as a heavy judgment upon their gods. Some of their sacred animals were regarded as actual reincarnations of deity; and if any of these perished, as is likely, the threat would have been executed to the letter.

(**14**) **Ye shall keep it a feast ... by an ordinance for ever.**—The Passover is continued in the Eucharist (I Cor. 5:7, 8).

(**15**) **Seven days.**—That the division of time into periods of seven days each was recognized in the family of Abraham appears from Gen. 29:27. According to some, God established the division by an express command to our first parents in Paradise that they should keep the seventh day holy (see Gen. 2:3); but this is greatly questioned by others, who regard Gen. 2:3 as **anticipatory**, and think the Sabbath was not instituted until the giving of the manna (Exod. 16:23). The injunction here given, if it belongs to the time of the tenth plague, would be the first preliminary note of warning with respect to the Sabbath, raising an expectation of it, and preparing the way for it, leading up to the subsequent revelations in the wilderness of Sin and at Sinai.

(**19**) **A stranger**—i.e., a foreigner in blood. (See note on Gen. 17:13.) When the "exclusiveness" of the Hebrews is made a charge against them, justice requires us to remember that from the first it was open to those who were not of Hebrew blood to share in the Hebrew privileges by accepting the covenant of circumcision, and joining themselves to the nation. It was in this way that the Kenites, and even the Gibeonites, became reckoned to Israel. It is probable that many of the "six hundred thousand" mentioned in verse 37 were so admitted to Israel.

The First Passover Kept

(**23**) **The destroyer.**—The "plague" of verse 13 is here called "the destroyer," as again in Heb. 11:28. Jehovah seems to have employed an angel, or "angels" (Ps. 78:49)

as His agents to effect the actual slaying of the first-born. (Comp. II Sam. 24:16; I Chron. 21:15; II Kings 19:35; Heb. 1:14.)

The Tenth Plague

(**29, 30**) The nature of the tenth plague is indubitable, but as to the exact agency which was employed there may be different views. The visitation is ordinarily ascribed to God Himself (4:23, 11:4, 12:12, 27, 29, 13:15, etc.), but in verse 23 to "the destroyer." This expression points to angelic agency. That agency, however, does not exclude a further natural one. As in II Sam. 24 the seventy thousand whom the destroying angel killed (verse 16) are said to have been slain by a pestilence (verse 15), so it may have been here. Pestilence often rages in Egypt in the spring of the year, and carries off thousands in a short space. As with so many of the other plagues, God may here too have employed a natural agency. None the less would the plague have been miraculous in its intensity and in its selection of victims.

(**30**) **Not a house where there was not one dead.**—To judge Scripture fairly, we must make allowance for the hyperbole of Oriental thought and expression, which causes the substitution of universal terms for general ones, and the absence of qualifying clauses. The meaning is that in the great majority of houses there was one dead.

The Dismissal of the Israelites

(**32**) **And bless me also.**—Here Pharaoh's humiliation reaches its extreme point. He is reduced by the terrible calamity of the last plague not only to grant all the demands made of him freely, and without restriction, but to crave the favor of a blessing from those whom he had despised, rebuked (5:4), thwarted, and finally driven from his presence under the threat of death (10:28). Those with whom were the issues of life and death must, he felt, have the power to bless or curse effectually.

(**35**) **They borrowed.**—See note on 3:22.

The Departure of Israel,
Their Numbers and the Time
of the Egyptian Sojourn

(**37-41**) The two principal statements of this passage are that the sojourn of the Israelites in Egypt lasted four hundred and thirty years, and that at the time of the departure the number of the "men" was six hundred thousand. This latter statement is confirmed, and even enlarged, by the more accurate estimate of Numbers 1 and 2, which goes into particulars with respect to the several tribes, and makes the exact amount of the adult male population, exclusive of the Levites, to be 603,550 (2:32). It would follow that the nation, at the time of its departure, was one of more than two million souls.

Two difficulties are raised with respect to this estimate: (1) Could the Israelites possibly have increased during their sojourn in Egypt from the "seventy souls" who went down with Jacob to two million? But it is reasonable that "several thousands" (see note on 1:5) could so multiply during the course of 430 years. (2) Is it conceivable that such a multitude, with their flocks and herds, could have departed Egypt on one day, and marched in a body through the narrow wadys of the Sinaitic region to the plain in front of Sinai? But we must remember that as far as Marah the country was perfectly open, and allowed of any extension of the line of march on either flank. After this, probably the host spread itself out, and proceeded to the rendezvous in front of the Ras Sufsafeh by several routes, of which Moses traces only the one which he himself followed. All that the narrative requires is that the **main body** of the people should have been encamped in front of Sinai, have heard the Decalogue delivered, and consented to the covenant.

(37) From Rameses to Succoth.—The difference between the Raamses of 1:11 and the Rameses of this passage is merely one of "pointing." Succoth has been identified with an Egyptian town called Thukot; but it is probably a Semitic word, signifying "tents" or "booths." The district fifteen miles southeast of Tanis was the first stopping place of the Israelites.

(38) A mixed multitude went up also with them.—Nothing is told us of the component elements of this "mixed multitude." We hear of them as "murmuring" in Num. 11:4, so that they seem to have remained with Israel. Some may have been Egyptians impressed by the recent miracles; some foreigners held to servitude, like the Israelites, and glad to escape from their masters.

(40) Was four hundred and thirty years.—The genealogy of Joshua (I Chron. 7:22-27), which places him in the eleventh generation from Jacob, accords well with this term of

years. The other genealogies are more or less abbreviated.

Further Directions Respecting the Passover

(43-51) This is the ordinance.—These directions, together with those which follow with respect to the sanctification of the first-born (13:1-16), seem to have been given to Moses at Succoth, and were consequently recorded at this point of the narrative. They comprise three principal points:— (1) The exclusion of all uncircumcised persons from the Passover (verse 43); (2) the admission of all full proselytes (verses 48, 49); and (3) the injunction that no bone of the lamb should be broken (verse 46).

(46) Neither shall ye break a bone thereof.—In the case of all other victims, the limbs were to be separated from the body. Here the victim was to be roasted whole, and to remain whole, as a symbol of unity, and a type of Him through whom men are brought into unity with each other and with God. (See John 19:33-36.)

13

Sanctification of the Firstborn, and Law of Redemption

(2) Sanctify unto me all the first-born.—It was a reasonable demand that the existing first-born of Israel, spared by God when the Egyptian first-born were destroyed, should be regarded from then on as His, and set apart for His service. The extension of the demand to existing beasts was also reasonable, since they too had been spared.

(3) Remember this day.—Remembrance was secured in four ways:—(1) By the month being made to begin the ecclesiastical year; (2) by the institution of the Passover; (3) by the seven days of unleavened bread; and (4) by the redemption, and the inquiries it would necessitate (verses 14, 15).

(4) The month Abib.—See note on 12:2. It retained its name until the Babylonian captivity, when the Babylonian name Nisan superseded the original one (Neh. 2:1; Esther 3:7).

(5) The Canaanites, and the Hittites ...—The full number of the Canaanitish nations was seven, five of which are here enumerated. The other two were the Perizzites and the Girgashites, which seem to have been the least important. The most important were the Canaanites, Hittites, and Amorites; and these are consequently almost always placed first. At the time of the Exodus, and for many centuries afterward, the actually most powerful nation would seem to have been that of the Hittites. (See Josh. 1:4; I Kings 10:29; II Kings 7:6.)

A land flowing with milk and honey.—See note on 3:8.

(9) It shall be for a sign unto thee upon thine hand, and for a memorial between thine eyes.—These phylacteries consist of small strips of parchment, on which are written certain passages from the Law—viz., Exod. 13:2-10; Deut. 6:4-9; 11:13-21—and which are then folded tight, placed in small boxes, and attached by bands to the left wrist and the forehead at the hours of prayer. It is well known that a similar custom prevailed in Egypt. But the adoption of Egyptian customs, **purged from their superstition**, is quite in the spirit of the Mosaic institutions, and in no way reprehensible. If the Israelites were addicted to wearing amulets, like the Egyptians, it would have been a wise proviso to substitute for the magic charms of sorcerers the solemn words of the Law, and in this way to turn a current superstition to a good account.

(13) All the first-born of man among thy children shalt thou redeem.—This was declared in anticipation of the arrangement afterward to be made, whereby the tribe of Levi was taken in lieu of the first-born for the service of the sanctuary (Num. 3:40-45), and an obligation was imposed on Israelites of other tribes to "redeem" their sons by a payment of five shekels for each to the priests (Num. 18:15, 16).

The Direction of the March

(17) God led them not through the way of the land of the Philistines.—In verses 17-19 the writer interposes some parenthetic remarks, which are not a continuation of the narrative interrupted (12:42), but rather reflections that occur to him. The starting point of the journey being Tanis or Rameses, in the Eastern Delta, not far from the sea, he sees that the shortest, and apparently the easiest, route for the Israelites to have pursued would have been that which led along the coast, from Tanis to Pelusium, from there to Gaza, Ascalon, and Ashdod, the chief towns of the Philistines. The distance along this line was not more than

about 200 miles, and might have been accomplished in a fortnight. He anticipates an inquiry. Why did they not pursue this route? The reply is, that such was not the will of God.

When they see war.—The Philistines must be viewed as one of the most warlike people of the time. In Joshua's time they already possessed their five strong fortresses—Gaza, Ascalon, Ashdod, Gath, and Ekron (Josh. 13:3); and during the period of the judges they raised themselves to the leading position in the Palestinian region. Palestine derives its name from them, and would not have obtained the name unless they had been a very remarkable race. We can well understand that the Israelites after four centuries of slavery would have been an ill match for the Philistines, and that, if defeated or intimidated, they might have felt that no course was open to them but a return to Egypt.

(18) But God led the people about.—Or, "led the people a circuit"—took them, not by the direct route, but by the way of the Red Sea and the wilderness of Sinai to the Transjordanian region, the land of the Amorites, and so across Jordan to Canaan proper.

The children of Israel went up harnessed out of the land of Egypt.—The best explanation is, that the word here means "organized," "in military order." It was clearly necessary, to prevent confusion, that a military order should have been adopted, and there are indications that during the year of contention with Pharaoh such an organization was introduced and proceeded with. (See chaps. 4:29, 31; 6:26; 12:3, 21, 51.) It must have been brought to a high pitch of perfection for the Exodus to have taken place, as it seems to have done, without serious confusion or entanglement.

The Journey Resumed

(20) They took their journey from Succoth, and encamped in Etham.—The exact position of both Succoth and Etham are uncertain, and can only be conjectured; but they probably lay to the southeast of Tanis, between that city and the Bitter Lakes.

(21) The Lord went before them.—In verses 17, 18 the writer has declared that "God led the people"; he now explains how. From Succoth certainly, probably from Rameses, He moved in front of the host in the form of a pillar, which had the appearance of smoke by day and of fire by night.

The pillar was at once a signal and a guide. When it moved, the people moved; when it stopped, they encamped (40:36-38); where it went, they followed. It was altogether of a miraculous and abnormal character.

(22) He took not away.—Comp. 40:38; Num. 9:16, 10:34. The cloud probably disappeared at Abel-shittim (Num. 33:49).

14

The Pursuit by Pharaoh and the Passage of the Red Sea

(2) Speak unto the children of Israel, that they turn.—The march of the Israelites had been hitherto almost due southeast. They had reached the edge of the desert (13:20), near the head of the Bitter Lakes. At this point an express command was given them to "turn." "The sea" of this verse can scarcely be different from "the Red Sea" of 13:18, the only sea previously mentioned by the writer. To reach this sea it was necessary that they should deflect their course to the right, from southeast to south, so keeping within the limits of Egypt, and placing the Bitter Lakes on their left hand.

Pi-hahiroth . . . Migdol . . . Baal-zephon.— These places cannot be identified. They were Egyptian towns or villages of no importance, near the head of the Gulf of Suez, situated on its western shores. The accumulation of names indicates an accurate acquaintance with Egyptian topography, such as no Israelite but one who had accompanied the expedition is likely to have possessed.

(5) The heart of Pharaoh and of his servants was turned against the people.—No doubt the change began as soon as Israel began its march. The emigration left Eastern Egypt a solitude, suspended all the royal works that were in progress, threw the whole course of commerce and business into disorder. Beforehand, neither the king nor the people had understood what the loss of six hundred thousand laborers—some of them highly skilled—would be. When Israel was gone they realized it; consequently both king and people regretted what they had done.

(13, 14) Fear ye not, stand still.—As long as we have means of resistance put in our power, with a reasonable prospect of success, it is our duty to use them—to exert ourselves to the uttermost, to make all possible efforts. God, for the most part, "helps those who help themselves." But there are occasions when we can do nothing—when all must be left to Him. (Comp. II Chron. 20:17.) Under these circumstances, our duty and our true wisdom is to wait patiently, quietly, courageously. Moses, probably, did not yet know how God would effect Israel's deliverance, but he was confident that, in one way or another, it would be effected.

(15-18) Wherefore criest thou unto me?— The Israelites were to strike their tents at once, and prepare for a forward movement. Moses was to descend to the edge of the sea, with his rod in his hand, and to stretch it out over the sea, and then await the consequences, which would be a "division" of the waters—the sea-bed would for a certain space become dry, and Israel would be able to cross to the other side (verse 16); the Egyptians would follow, and then destruction would come upon them, and God would "get himself honour upon Pharaoh, and upon all his host" (verses 17, 18). The exact mode of the destruction was not announced.

(19, 20) The angel of God, which went before the camp of Israel.—The angel is distinguished from the cloud, and represented as antedating its movements and directing them. It is clear that the object of the movement now made was double: to check and trouble the Egyptians by involving them in "cloud and darkness"; and to cheer and assist the Israelites by affording them abundant light for all their necessary arrangements.

(21) The Lord caused the sea to go back by a strong east wind.—If we imagine the Bitter Lakes joined to the Red Sea by a narrow and shallow channel, and a southeast wind blowing strongly up this channel, we can easily conceive that the water in the Bitter Lakes might be driven northward, and held there, while the natural action of the ebb tide withdrew the Red Sea water to the southward. A portion of the channel might in this way have been left dry, and have so continued until the wind changed and the tide began to flow. It is true that Scripture does not speak of the ebb and flow of the tide, since in them there was nothing unusual. Whether the whole effect was purely natural, or whether (as in so many other cases) God used the force of nature as far as it could go, and further supernaturally increased its force, we are not told. (See Ps. 78:13.)

(23) All Pharaoh's horses, his chariots, and his horsemen.—The chariot and cavalry force alone entered the sea, not the infantry. (Comp. verse 28 and 15:1.) The point is of importance as connected with the question whether the Pharaoh himself perished. If all his force entered, he could not well have stayed behind; if only a portion, he might have elected to remain with the others. Menephthah, the probable Pharaoh of the Exodus, was apt to consult his own safety. We know that he reigned at least five more years.

(31) Israel saw that great work.—The destruction of the Pharaoh's chariot force and cavalry in the Red Sea secured the retreat of Israel, and saved them from any further molestation at the hands of the Egyptians. The spirit of the nation was effectually broken for the time; and it was not until after several reigns, and an interval of anarchy, that there was a revival. The episode in the life of the nation begun by the descent of Jacob into Egypt now terminated, and a fresh beginning was made. In the open air of the desert, cut off from all other races, admitted to close communion with Jehovah, the people entered upon that new and higher existence which culminated in the teaching of the prophets, in the noble struggles of Ezra and Nehemiah, and in the memorable stand on behalf of religious truth and national independence which was made by the Maccabees.

15

The Song of Moses

(1) Then sang Moses and the children of Israel.—The ode divides itself into two portions (verses 1-12 and verses 13-18): the first retrospective, and anthropomorphic, the second prospective.

(3) The Lord is his name.—In the very name, Jehovah, is implied all might, all power, and so necessarily the strength to prevail in battle. The name, meaning "the Existent," implies that nothing else has any real existence independently of Him; and if no existence, then necessarily no strength.

(11) Who is like unto thee . . . among the gods?—It had been a main object of the entire series of miraculous visitations to show that Jehovah was "exalted far above all other gods." (See 7:5; 14:4, 18.) Moses now emphasizes the contrast by adducing three points on which Jehovah is unapproachable—holiness, awesomeness, and miraculous power. (Comp. Ps. 86:8.)

(13-18) This stanza of the ode involves a change of attitude, and deals with new matters. The poet's eye fixes itself upon the future. He speaks of: the guidance of God, lately begun, and about to continue until Canaan is reached; the enemies of Israel, and the effect which the miraculous deliverance of Israel from Egypt will have upon them; and the people brought into the "land of their inheritance" and securely established there under the ordering of divine Providence. Then, with an ascription of glory which may be compared with the Doxology attached to the Lord's Prayer in Matthew (6:13), he terminates his composition. Comp. Pss. 10:16; 29:10; 145:13; 146:10.

(20) Miriam the prophetess.—In Miriam (see 2:3-8; Num. 12:1-15; Micah 6:4) we have the first of that long series of religious women presented to us in Holy Scripture, who are not merely pious and God-fearing, but exercise a quasi-ministerial office. Examples of other "prophetesses" will be found in Judg. 4:4; II Kings 22:14; Isa. 8:3; Luke 2:36. In the early Christian Church there was an order of "deaconesses" (Rom. 16:1).

Timbrels and with dances.—By "timbrels" are meant tambourines, favorite instruments in Egypt, and usually played by women there. The combination of music with song in religious worship, here for the first time brought before us, became the fixed rule of the Tabernacle service from the time of David (II Sam. 6:15; I Chron. 23:5; 25:1-6), and was adopted into the Temple service from its first establishment (II Chron. 5:12). Sanctioned under the new covenant by the general praise of psalmody, and by the representations given in the Apocalypse of the Church triumphant in heaven (Rev. 5:8; 14:2, 3), it has always maintained itself in the Christian Church. Dancing, on the contrary, has never found an entrance into Christian ceremony. The reason of this is to be found in the abuses which, through human infirmity, became by degrees connected with the practice, causing it to become unfit for a religious purpose.

The Journey From the Red Sea to Elim

(22) So Moses brought Israel.—The regular narrative is here resumed from 14:31, and the Israelites are brought two stages upon their journey toward Sinai (3:12)— first to Marah (verse 23), and next to Elim (verse 27). It is uncertain at what exact point of the coast they emerged from the sea-bed, but it can scarcely have been at any great distance from the modern Suez.

(25) The Lord shewed him a tree.— Perhaps in ancient times there were forms of vegetable life in the peninsula which do not now exist there. Moses would scarcely have been "shown a tree" unless the tree had some virtue of its own; but, on the other hand, the tree alone is scarcely to be credited with the entire effect. As in so many other instances, God seems to have made use of nature, as far as nature could go, and then to have superadded His own omnipotent energy in order to produce the required effect. (Compare our blessed Lord's method in working His miracles.)

He made for them a statute and an ordinance.—God took advantage of the occasion to draw a lesson from it. He promised that, as He had healed the waters, so, if the Israelites would henceforth faithfully keep His commandments, He would "heal" **them** (verse 26), keeping them free from all the diseases of Egypt, and from the far greater evil involved in their own corrupted nature and infirmity.

16

The Journey From Elim— The Manna Given

(1) They took their journey from Elim.— The stay at Elim was probably for some days. "Sin" was reached exactly one month after the departure from Egypt, yet there had been only five camping places between Sin and Rameses, and one journey of three days through a wilderness (15:22). Long rests are thus clearly indicated. The places named were the headquarters of the camp on each occasion, but the entire host must have always covered a vast tract, and the flocks and herds must have been driven into all the neighboring valleys where there was pasture. This line of march is indicated in Num. 33:10, 11.

(2) The whole congregation . . . murmured.—This is the third "murmuring." The first was at Pi-hahiroth, on the appearance of the host of Pharaoh (14:11, 12); the second was at Marah, when the water proved undrinkable (15:24); the third, in the wilderness of Sin, was brought about by no special occurrence—unless it were the exhaustion of the supplies of grain which had

been brought out of Egypt—but seems to have resulted from a general dissatisfaction with the conditions of life in the wilderness, and with the prospects which lay before them.

(3) By the hand of the Lord.—There is, perhaps, an allusion to the last of the plagues. "Would that we had not been spared, but had been smitten, as the Egyptians were! A sudden death would have been far better than a long and lingering one."

When we did eat bread to the full.—It was the habit of the Egyptians to feed well those whom they employed in forced labors (Herod. 2:125). The remembrance of the past abundance intensified the pain felt at the present want.

(4) That I may prove them.—Human life is a probation. God proves and tries those **most** whom He takes to Himself for His "peculiar people." The Israelites were tested, both in the wilderness and afterward throughout their career as a nation, by a number of positive precepts, whereof this concerning the manna was one. Christians are tested by positive precepts with respect to common worship, prayer, and sacraments —the object being in all cases to see whether men "will walk in God's law or no." Men are apt to prefer their own inventions to the simple rule of following at once the letter and the spirit of God's commandments.

(5) They shall prepare.—On the method of preparation see Num. 11:8.

It shall be twice as much.—Some suppose this to be a command—"Ye shall gather twice as much"; but it is more natural to take it as an announcement of a fact—"You will find that what you have gathered turns out to be twice as much." A miraculous doubling of the quantity seems to be intended. (Comp. verse 22.)

(10) The glory of the Lord appeared in the cloud.—There can be no reasonable doubt that the "pillar of the cloud" is meant. It was before this that they had been required to appear (verse 9), and from this almost certainly that some bright radiance was now made to stream forth. The object was at once to rebuke their murmurings, and to uphold the authority of Moses and Aaron.

(13) At even the quails came up.—The common quail is abundant in the East, and regularly migrates from Syria and Arabia in the autumn of the year for the purpose of wintering in Central Africa, then it returns in immense masses in the spring. Exhausted after a long flight over the Red Sea, the flocks drop to the ground as soon as they reach the coast, and it is then easy either to take the birds with the hand or to kill them with sticks. The flesh of the quail is regarded as a delicacy throughout the East, though if too many are eaten it is said to be unwholesome.

(14) A small round thing, as small as the hoar frost.—What the manna was has been much disputed. There are two natural substances, quite distinct, with which it has been compared, and by some persons identified. But the manna of Scripture in its most important characteristics is altogether **sui generis**. For (1) it was adapted to be men's principal nourishment, and served the Israelites as such for forty years; (2) it was supplied in quantities far exceeding anything that is recorded of the natural substances compared with it; (3) it continued through the whole year; (4) for forty years it fell regularly for six nights following, and ceased upon the seventh night; (5) it "bred worms" if kept to a second day, when gathered on five days out of the six, but when gathered on the sixth day continued good throughout the seventh, and bred no worms. The manna of Scripture must therefore be regarded as a miraculous substance, created **ad hoc**, and not as a natural product. It pleased the Creator, however, to proceed on the lines of Nature, so to speak, and to assimilate His new to certain of His old creations.

(15) It is manna.—This is certainly a wrong translation. The words of the original, **man hu**, must either be rendered, as in the LXX and the Vulgate, "What is this?" or, as by Gesenius, Kurtz, and others, "This is a gift."

(20) It bred worms.—On the Sabbath it bred no worms (verse 24), so that we must view the result spoken of as a punishment for disobedience, not as produced naturally. Neither of the natural mannas is subject to any rapid decomposition.

(23) Bake ... seethe.—These directions imply a different substance from any of the natural forms of manna. The heavenly "gift" could be either made into a paste and baked, or converted into a porridge.

(25) Today is a sabbath,—That is to say, **a rest**. By these words the Sabbath was either instituted, or re-instituted, and became from that time on binding on the Israelites. Its essential character of a weekly "rest" was at once assigned to it—(1) by its name; (2) by God's resting on it from His

self-imposed task of giving the manna; and (3) by the rest which the absence of manna on the seventh day imposed on the people. Thus the way was prepared for the stringent law of Sabbath observance laid down in the fourth commandment. (See note on Gen. 2:2, 3.)

(28) How long refuse ye to keep my commandments?—The people had already broken one of the positive precepts with respect to the manna (see verse 20); now they broke another—in the spirit, at any rate—since they would have gathered had they found anything to gather.

(31) It was like coriander seed.—The appearance of the manna is compared above to hoar frost (verse 14); here, and in Num. 11:7, to coriander seed. The former account describes its look as it lay on the ground, the latter its appearance after it was collected and brought in. The coriander seed is a small round grain of a whitish or yellowish gray.

(32-35) And Moses said ... Fill an omer.— This narrative, which must belong to a later date than any other part of Exodus, since it assumes that the Tabernacle is set up (verse 34), seems to have been placed here on account of its subject matter. The writer wishes to conclude the history of the manna.

(33) Lay it up before the Lord.— According to the writer of the epistle to the Hebrews, the Ark of the Covenant contained three things only—the tables, the pot of manna, and Aaron's rod that budded (Heb. 9:4). The deposit of the manna in so sacred a place may be accounted for by its typifying "the true bread from heaven" (John 6:32).

(35) The children of Israel did eat manna forty years.—Moses may have added this verse to the present chapter shortly before his death. He does not say that it had ceased to be given. We know that in fact it did not cease till the Jordan was crossed by the Israelites under Joshua, and Canaan was actually reached (Josh. 5:10-12).

(36) Now an omer.—An omer was about three English pints.

17

The Murmuring at Rephidim and the Fight With Amalek

(1) After their journeys.—We find from Num. 33:12, 13, that Rephidim was reached from the wilderness of Sin by three journeys —from Sin to Dophkah, from Dophkah to Alush, and from Alush to Rephidim. The distance by the route which we have supposed the Israelites to have taken is about fifty miles.

Rephidim means "resting places," and is the most fertile spot in the whole peninsula, where there is usually abundant water, rich vegetation, and numerous palm trees.

(2) The people did chide.—Water is scanty along the route by which Rephidim was reached. Such a supply as the people may have brought with them from Elim would have been exhausted. They would have looked forward to replenishing their waterskins. They would be suffering both from thirst and disappointment. The needs of their children and their cattle (verse 3) would be an aggravation of their pain.

(5) Take with thee of the elders—as witnesses. Each miracle had an educational value, and was designed to call forth, exercise, and so strengthen the faith of the people.

(6) The rock in Horeb must necessarily designate some particular rock of the Horeb region already known to Moses during his previous stay in these parts.

(8) Then came Amalek.—The Amalekites had not been previously (except in the anticipatory notice of Gen. 14:7) mentioned as a nation. Their name marks them for descendants of Amalek, the grandson of Esau (Gen. 36:12, 16). Though Edomites, they are always regarded as a distinct race, and one especially hostile to Israel (verse 16). Their present hostility was not altogether unprovoked. No doubt they regarded the Sinaitic region as their own, and as the most valuable portion of their territory, since it contained their summer and autumn pastures. Naturally, they would resent the occupation. They would not understand that it was only temporary.

(9) Moses said unto Joshua.—This is the first mention of Joshua. He was an Ephraimite, the son of a man called Nun, and the tenth in descent from Joseph (see note on 6:16), in the prime of life—about 45 years old—and probably known as possessing military capacity. His actual name at the time was Hoshea, which might have been viewed as a good omen, since the word meant "Saviour." Moses afterward changed his name to Jehoshua (Num. 13:16), which became by contraction Joshua. We find him, later in Exodus, acting as Moses' personal attendant, or "min-

ister" (24:13, 32:17, 33:11), accompanying him to the top of Sinai, and placed by him in charge of the first "Tabernacle." Afterwards he, with Caleb, was the only one of the spies who brought back a true report of Canaan (Num. 14:6-9). His choice as leader to succeed Moses resulted naturally from his antecedents, and is related in Num. 27:18-23.

(10) Hur.—According to Jewish tradition (Joseph., **Ant. Jud.**, 3: 2, §4) Hur was the husband of Miriam, and so the brother-in-law of Moses and Aaron. He was a descendant of Judah (I Chron. 2:3-20). Moses left him joint regent with Aaron when he ascended up into Sinai (24:14).

(11) When Moses held up his hand ... Israel prevailed, etc.—In order to teach the lesson of the value of intercessory prayer, God made the fortunes of the fight to vary according as Moses "held up his hand," or allowed it to sink down. It is not probable that the Israelites were **directly** affected by the bodily movements of Moses, or indeed could discern them, but Moses, Aaron, and Hur were struck by the fact that the fluctuations in the battle coincided with the motions of Moses' hands.

(14) Write this for a memorial in a book.— Heb., "in the book." That "books" existed long prior to Moses is implied in his quotation of them (Gen. 5:1; Num. 21:14), and has been abundantly proved by the discoveries made of Egyptian papyri dating from a time long anterior to the Jewish lawgiver. The expression used in the present place, "**the** book," is remarkable, and seems to imply that a book already existed at the date of the engagement, in which God's dealings with His people were entered from time to time. This book was probably the germ of the existing Pentateuch, which was composed in many portions, and at intervals, as occasion arose.

I will utterly put out the remembrance of Amalek.—The extermination of Amalek, here prophesied, was afterward laid as a positive command upon the Israelites (Deut. 25:19), and was accomplished in party by Saul and David (I Sam. 14:48; 15:7; 27:8; 30:17; II Sam. 8:12), but finally and completely in the reign of Hezekiah (I Chron. 4:43). Amalek's sin was, that after all the signs and wonders which had shown the Israelites to be God's peculiar people, he braved God's displeasure by attacking them (Deut. 25:18).

(15) And called the name of it Jehovah-nissi.—When an altar was built as a memorial, the purpose would be helped by a name, which would tend to keep the event commemorated in remembrance. Jehovah-nissi—"the Lord is my banner"—would tell to all who heard the word that here there had been a struggle, and that a people which worshiped Jehovah had been victorious.

18

The Visit of Jethro

(1) Jethro, the priest of Midian, Moses' father in law.—On Jethro's probable relationship to Moses, see note on 3:1. On the priesthood of Reuel, which Jethro seems to have inherited, see note on 2:16.

(2) After he had sent her back.—Moses had sent Zipporah back to her own relatives, either in anger, on account of the scene described in 4:24-26, or simply that he might not be encumbered with wife and children during the dangers and troubles which he anticipated in Egypt. Jethro assumed that, as the main troubles were now over, he would be glad to have his wife and children restored to him.

(3) Gershom.—See note on 2:22.

(4) Eliezer.—Eliezer is supposed to have been the boy whom Zipporah circumcised in the wilderness (4:25).

(5) Where he encamped at the mount of God.—It is quite possible that "the mount of God" may be here used, in a broad sense, of the entire Sinaitic mountain region, as "wilderness" is earlier used in the broad sense of the infertile region between Egypt and Palestine. Or the movement described in 19:1, 2 may have taken place before Jethro's arrival, though not related until after it. We must bear in mind that Exodus was probably composed in detached portions, and arranged afterward. The present chapter has every appearance of being one such detached portion.

(10, 11) Jethro said, Blessed be the Lord.—Heb., "Jehovah." The Midianites, descendants of Abraham by Keturah, acknowledged the true God, and the Israelites could rightfully join with them in acts of worship. But it is scarcely likely that they knew God among themselves as "Jehovah." Jethro, however, understanding Moses to speak of the supreme God under that designation, adopted it from him, blessed His name, and expressed his conviction that Jehovah was exalted above all other gods. The pure monotheism of later times scarcely existed as yet.

(13) Moses sat to judge the people.—The office of prince, or ruler, was in early times regarded as including within it that of judge. Rulers in these ages were sometimes even called "judges," as were those of Israel from Joshua to Samuel. Moses, it would seem, had, from the time that he became chief of his nation, undertaken the hearing of all complaints and the decision of all causes. He held court days from time to time, when the host was stationary, and judged all the cases that were brought before him. No causes were decided by anyone else.

(14) Why sittest thou thyself alone?—The emphatic word is "alone." Why dost thou not, Jethro means, devolve a part of the duty upon others?

(15, 16) Moses assigns two reasons for his conduct. (1) The people want decisions which they can feel to have divine sanction. (2) He does not simply judge, but he takes the opportunity to educate and instruct the people in delivering his judgments.

(24, 25) Moses hearkened.—The appointment of judges, according to Jethro's advice, was not made until after the giving of the Law and the setting up of the Tabernacle. (See Deut. 1:9-15.)

19

The Manifestation of God
to the People on Mount Sinai

(2) They were departed from Rephidim.—The march to "the wilderness of Sinai" must have been about eighteen to twenty-five miles. It is a plain two miles long by half a mile wide, enclosed between two precipitous mountain ranges of black and yellow granite, having at its end the prodigious mountain block of Ras Sufsafeh, nearly flat, and covered with stunted tamarisk bushes. No spot in the whole peninsula is so well supplied with water.

(4) I bare you on eagles' wings.—Comp. Deut. 32:11. When its young are first fledged, the eagle is said to assist them in their flight by flying beneath them, so that they may settle upon its wings or back, if necessary. God means that He has bestowed upon His people the same tender and powerful care, has borne them up mightily when they might have fallen, supported their first flight as fledglings, and so saved them from disaster.

(5) A peculiar treasure.—The Hebrew signifies "to earn," or "acquire," and means primarily some valuable possession which the owner has gotten by his own exertions. God views the Israelites as made His own by the long series of mighty works done for their deliverance, whereby He is sometimes said to have "redeemed" (6:6; 15:13; or "purchased" them (15:16).

Above all people: for all the earth is mine.—While claiming a peculiar right in Israel, God does not mean to separate Himself from the other nations, to cease to care for them, or give them up to their own devices. He is always "the Most High **over all the earth**" (Ps. 83:18).

(6) A kingdom of priests.—They were kings as lords over themselves, equals one to another, owing allegiance to God only. They were priests, as entitled to draw near to God in prayer without an intermediary, to bring Him their offerings, pay Him their vows, and hold communion with Him in heart and soul. The same privileges are declared by Peter (I Pet. 2:9) and John (Rev. 1:6) to belong to all Christians, who in this respect as in so many others, are now "the Israel of God" (Gal. 6:16).

An holy nation.—It is not the duty of personal, but the privilege of official, holiness that is here intended. Personal holiness was the natural and fitting outcome from this official holiness; but it is not here spoken of.

(7) Moses ... called for the elders.—The "elders" formed the usual channel of communication between Moses and the people, reporting his words to them, and theirs to him. (See 4:29; 12:21; 17:5, 6; 18:12; 24:14; etc.) On their position and authority, see note on 3:16.

(9) Lo, I come unto thee in a thick cloud.—It is absolutely necessary that He should be closely veiled when he draws near to men, for otherwise they could not endure for a moment "the brightness of His presence." (See 40:35; II Chron. 5:14; 7:2.) If even the light that remained on Moses' face after conversation with God required him from that day on to wear a veil before the people (34:33-35), how much more needful must it be that God should cover His face when He condescends to converse with men! In the present case, it would seem to have been "the pillar of the cloud" that had guided Israel, which served Him for a covering, and out of which He spoke to Moses and the people.

That the people may hear ... and believe thee for ever.—God's purpose in manifesting Himself to the people was twofold:—(1) To impress them with the awful sense of His presence, and through them, their descendants; (2) to make them more ready to submit to Moses, and "believe him for ever." On the whole, it must be said that the purpose was accomplished.

(10) Go unto the people, and sanctify them.—The approaching manifestation required, above all things, that the people should be "sanctified." Sanctification is twofold—outward and inward. The real essential preparation for approach to God is inward sanctification; but no external command can secure this. Moses was therefore instructed to issue directions for outward purification; and it was left to the spiritual insight of the people to perceive and recognize that such purity symbolized and required internal purification as its counterpart. The external purification was to consist in three things—(1) Ablution, or washing of the person; (2) washing of clothes; and (3) abstinence from sexual intercourse (verse 15).

(11) Against the third day.—There is no special "significance" in this mention of "the third day." The important point is that the purification was to continue through two entire days—one day not being sufficient. This taught the lesson that man's defilement is, in the sight of God, very great.

(12) Thou shalt set bounds.—Here was another formal and mechanical direction, having for its object to deepen and intensify the lesson of God's unapproachable majesty and holiness. Moses was required to "set bounds to the people," i.e., to make a substantial fence between the camp and the base of Sinai, which should prevent both animals and men from coming in contact with the mountain. Modern travelers generally observe how abruptly the rocky precipice of Ras Sufsafeh rises from the plain in front of it, so that in many places it is quite possible to stand on the plain and yet touch the mountain.

(13) There shall not an hand touch it.—This translation gives an entirely wrong sense. The meaning is, beyond all doubt, "There shall not a hand touch **him**," i.e., the transgressor. To stop him and seize him, another person must have transgressed the bounds, and so have repeated the act which was forbidden. This course was to be avoided, and punishment was to be inflicted on the transgressor by stoning him, or transfixing him with arrows, from within the barrier.

They shall come up to the mount.—Rather, "into the mount." The word "they" in this present place is emphatic, and refers to certain privileged persons, as Moses and Aaron (verse 24), not to the people generally.

(16-20) Thunders and lightnings, and a thick cloud.—Compare with this description that of Deut. (4:11,12), which is fuller in some respects. As awful a manifestation has never been made at any other place or time, nor will be until the consummation of all things. To regard it as a mere "storm of thunder and lightning," or as "an earthquake with volcanic eruptions," is to miss altogether the meaning of the author, and to empty his narrative of all its natural significance.

The voice of the trumpet.—The trumpet's blare is the signal of a herald calling attention to a proclamation about to be made. At the last day the coming of Christ is to be announced by "the trump of God" (I Thess. 4:16). In the Apocalypse angels are often represented as sounding with trumpets (Rev. 8:7, 8, 10, 12; 9:1, 14; etc.) when some great event is about to occur.

(17) At the nether part of the mount.—In the plain directly in front of the Ras Sufsafeh, and almost under it.

God's Warning to the People Against a Too Near Approach

(21-25) It is evident from this concluding paragraph of the chapter that the first warning was insufficient. An intention to "break through, to gaze," must have been entertained by many. To this intention the existing priesthood, whatever it was, were parties (verse 22). It always grates upon men's feelings to be told that they are less holy than others; and we can easily understand that those who had hitherto acted as priests to the nation would resent their exclusion from "holy ground" to which the sons of Amram were about to be admitted. Even of the people there may have been many who participated in the feeling, and thought that Moses and Aaron were "taking too much upon them, seeing that the whole congregation" was holy. Hence, a further very stringent command was required.

(22) The priests.—This has been called an anachronism, since the Levitical priesthood was not as yet instituted. But the Israelites, like all other ancient tribes or races, must

have had priests long before this, appointed upon one principle or another. It is a reasonable conjecture that hitherto the heads of families had exercised sacerdotal functions.

20

The Ten Commandments

(1) All these words.—In Scripture the phrase used to designate the Ten Commandments is "the **Ten Words**" (34:28; Deut. 4:13; 10:4). It has been universally recognized, both by the Jewish and Christian Churches, that they occupy a unique position among the utterances which constitute God's revelation to man. Alone uttered publicly by God in the ears of the people, alone inscribed on stone by the finger of God Himself, alone, of all commands, deposited in the **penetrale** of worship—the Ark—they formed the germ and basis, the very pith and kernel of the covenant which God, through Moses, made with man, and which was to continue for more than thirteen hundred years the exposition of His will to the human race. They enunciate a morality infinitely above that of all the wisest of mankind to whom revelation was unknown. There is no compendium of morality in Confucianism, in Buddhism, in the religion of Zoroaster, or of Egypt, or of Greece or Rome, which can be put in competition with the Decalogue.

(2) I am the Lord thy God.—The binding nature of commands upon the conscience depends upon the authority of the person who issues them. That there might be no dispute as to what the authority was in the case of the Decalogue, God prefaced the commands themselves by this distinct statement.

(3) Before me.—God does not suppose that the Israelites, after all that He had done for them, would discard Him, and substitute other gods in His place, but fears the syncretism which would unite His worship with that of other deities. All polytheisms were syncretic, and readily enlarged their pantheons, since, when once the principle of unity is departed from, whether the plurality be a little greater or a little less cannot much matter. Israel, in later years, fell into the same error, and, without intending to apostatize from Jehovah, added on the worship of Baal, Ashtoreth, Moloch, Chemosh, Remphan, etc. It is this form of polytheism against which the first commandment is directed. It asserts the **sole** claim of Jehovah to our religious regards.

(4) Thou shalt not make unto thee any graven image.—What the second commandment forbade was the worship of God under a material form. It asserted the spirituality of Jehovah. While in the rest of the ancient world there was scarcely a single nation or tribe which did not "make to itself" images of the gods, and regard the images themselves with superstitious veneration, in Judaism alone was this seductive practice disallowed. God would have no likeness made of Him, no representation that might cloud the conception of His entire separation from matter, His purely spiritual essence.

(5) A jealous God.—i.e., jealous of His own honor, one who will not see "His glory given to another" (Isa. 42:8; 48:11), or allow rivals to dispute His sole and absolute sovereignty. (Comp. 34:14; Deut. 4:24; 5:9; 6:15; Josh. 24:19.) **Visiting the iniquity of the fathers upon the children.**—The knowledge that their sins will put their children at a disadvantage is calculated to check men in their evil courses more than almost anything else. Still, the penalty upon the children is not final or irreversible. Under whatever disadvantages they are born, they may struggle against them, and lead good lives, and place themselves, even in this world, on a level with those who were born under every favorable circumstance. It is needless to say that, as respects another world, their parents' iniquities will not be visited on them.

(6) Shewing mercy unto thousands.—Rather, "to the thousandth generation," as is distinctly expressed in Deut. 7:9. God's mercy infinitely transcends His righteous anger. Sin is visited on three, or at most four, generations. Righteousness is remembered, and advantages descendants, for ever.

(7) Thou shalt not take the name of the Lord thy God in vain.—The Hebrew is ambiguous, as is to some extent the English translation. Our Lord's comment in the Sermon on the Mount favors the view that false swearing alone was actually forbidden by the Law, since He proceeds to condemn profane swearing on His own authority: "But I say unto you" (Matt. 5:34). False swearing is among the greatest insults that man can offer to God, and, as being such, is naturally forbidden in the first table, which teaches us our duty to God. It is also

destructive of civil society; and hence it is again forbidden in the second table (verse 16), which defines our duties to our neighbor.

(8) Remember the sabbath day.—We cannot conclude that the Sabbath was a primitive institution, which the Israelites were bound to have held in perpetual remembrance, since the reference may be merely to the injunction recently given in connection with the gathering of the manna. The Sabbath had certainly been at that time solemnly instituted, if not earlier. (See note on 16:25.)

To keep it holy.—It has been already noted that the rest of Sabbath was to be a "holy rest" (16:23); but it is not quite clear what was intended by this. Probably there were always some whom natural piety taught that, in the absence of their ordinary employments, it was intended they should devote themselves to prayer and communion with God—to meditation on "high and holy themes," such as His mercies in past time, His character, attributes, revelations of Himself, government of the world, dealings with men and nations. Thus only could the day be really "kept holy," with a positive, and not a mere negative, holiness.

(9) Six days shalt thou labor.—The intention of the clause is prohibitory rather than mandatory—"thou shalt not work more than six days out of the seven."

(10) In it thou shalt not do any work.—Some exceptions were allowed, as the work of the priests and Levites in the Temple on the Sabbath, attendance on and care of the sick, rescue of a beast that was in peril of its life, etc. (See Matt. 12:5, 11.) But the tendency was to press the negative aspect to an extreme, and to ignore the positive one. Our Lord's practice was pointedly directed against the overstrained theory of Sabbath observance which was current in His day, and was clearly intended to vindicate for His disciples a liberty which ecclesiastical authority was disposed to deny them.

(11) For in six days the Lord made heaven and earth.—God might have created all things on one day had He so pleased; but, having the institution of the Sabbath in view, He prefigured it by spreading His work over six days, and then resting on the seventh. His law of the Sabbath established a conformity between the method of His own working and that of His reasonable creatures, and taught men to look on work, not as an aimless, indefinite, incessant, weary round, but as leading on to an end, a

115

rest, a fruition, a time for looking back, and seeing the result and rejoicing in it. Each Sabbath is such a time, and is a type and foretaste of that eternal "sabbatizing" in another world which "remaineth for the people of God" (Heb. 4:9).

(12) Honour thy father and thy mother.— Of all our duties to our fellowmen, the first and most fundamental is our duty toward our parents, which lies at the root of all our social relations, and is the first of which we naturally become conscious. Honor, reverence, and obedience are due to parents from the position in which they stand to their children. The divine legislation of Sinai is in full accord, here as elsewhere, with the voice of reason and conscience, affirming broadly the principles of parental authority and filial submission, but leaving the mode in which the principles should be carried out to the discretion of individuals or communities.

That thy days may be long upon the land.—The fifth commandment (as all allow) is "the first commandment **with promise**" (Eph. 6:2); but the promise may be understood in two quite different senses. (1) It may be taken as guaranteeing national permanence to the people among whom filial respect and obedience is generally practiced; or (2) it may be understood in the simpler and more literal sense of a pledge that obedient children shall, as a general rule, receive for their reward the blessing of long life.

(13) Thou shalt not kill.—From the peculiar duties owed by children to their parents, the divine legislator went on to lay down those general duties which men owe to their fellowmen. And of these the first is that of respecting their life. When God "set a mark upon Cain" (Gen. 4:15), he marked thereby His abhorrence of the murderer. The "seven precepts of Noah" included one which distinctly forbade the taking of human life (Gen. 9:6). The Mosaic legislation on the point was different from others principally by the care it took to distinguish between actual murder, manslaughter (21:13), death by misadventure (Num. 35:23), and justifiable homicide (22:2). Before it made these distinctions, however, the great principle of the sanctity of human life had to be broadly laid down; and so the law was given in the widest possible terms — "Thou shalt not kill." Exceptions were reserved until later.

(14) Thou shalt not commit adultery.— Next to the duty of respecting a man's life is

placed that of respecting his domestic peace and honor. Adultery is an invasion of the household, a destruction of the bond which unites the family, a dissolution of that contract which is the main basis of social order. The Mosaic enactments on the subject are peculiar chiefly in the absolute equality on which they place the man and the woman. Adulterers are as hateful as adulteresses, and are as surely to be put to death (Lev. 20:10; Deut. 22:22-24; etc.).

(15) Thou shalt not steal.—Our third duty toward our neighbor is to respect his right to his property. The framers of Utopias, both ancient and modern, have imagined communities in which private property should not exist. But such a condition of things has never yet been realized in practice. In the laws of all known States private property has been recognized, and social order has been, in a great measure, based upon it. Here, again, law has but embodied natural instinct.

(16) Thou shalt not bear false witness against thy neighbour.—Our fourth duty to our neighbor is not to injure his character. False witness is, of course, worse when given in a court of justice; and this offense has generally been made punishable by law. It was peculiar to the Hebrew legislation that it not only forbade and punished (Deut. 19:16-20) false testimony of this extreme kind, but denounced also the far commoner, yet scarcely less injurious, practice of spreading untrue reports about others, thus injuring them in men's esteem.

(17) Thou shalt not covet.—This command seems to have been added in order to teach the general principle that the Law of God is concerned, not with acts and words only, but with the thoughts of the heart. Rightly understood, the seventh and eighth commandments contain the tenth, which strikes at covetousness and lustful desire (Comp. Matt. 5:27, 28.) But ancient moralists did not usually recognize this; thought unless carried out into acts, was regarded as "free."

At the People's Request, Moses Becomes Their Intermediary

(18-21) The delivery of the Ten Commandments by a voice manifestly superhuman impressed the people with an awful fear. From Deuteronomy we learn that they retired within their tents (Deut. 5:30), having first sent a deputation to Moses, with a request that he would thereafter act as their intermediary. It pleased God to assent to this proposal; and the remainder of the Law was communicated by God to Moses, and by Moses to the Israelites.

The Book of the Covenant

(22-26) In the remainder of chap. 20, and in the three chapters which follow, we have a series of laws delivered by God to Moses, immediately after the delivery of the Decalogue, which constituted the second stage of the revelation, and stood midway between the first great enunciation of abstract principles in the Ten Commandments and the ultimate minute and complicated elaboration of rules to meet all cases which fills the three Books of Leviticus, Numbers, and Deuteronomy. This intermediate revelation appears to have been at once committed to writing, and in its written shape was known as the "Book of the Covenant" (24:7), and regarded with special veneration.

The "Book of the Covenant" is no mere tentative sketch; but a very wonderful condensation of the essence of all the more important matters which Moses afterward put forth by divine inspiration in the long space of nearly forty years.

Laws Concerning Religion

(23) Ye shall not make with me gods of silver.—The animal worship of the Egyptians had no attractions for the Hebrews; they did not offer to images of stone or marble, like the Assyrians or the Greeks; much less was it their habit to "bow down to stocks," like so many of the heathen nations around them. The "molten image," generally completed by a certain amount of graving, was the form of idol which had most charms for them, and the more precious the material the more satisfied were they to worship it. But notice the prohibition regarding "hewn stone" in verse 25.

21

Laws Concerning the Rights of Persons

(2) If thou buy an Hebrew servant.—In any consideration of the rights of persons, those of the slave class naturally presented themselves first of all, since they were the most liable to infraction. Slaves might be either natives or foreigners. A Hebrew could become a slave—(1) through crime

(22:3); (2) through indebtedness (Lev. 25:39); (3) through his father's right to sell him (Neh. 5:5). Foreign slaves might be either prisoners taken in war, or persons bought of their owners (Lev. 25:45). The rights of Hebrew slaves are here specially considered.

Six years he shall serve.—The Hebrew was not to be retained in slavery for a longer space than six years. If a jubilee year occurred before the end of the six years, then he regained his freedom earlier (Lev. 25:39-41); but in no case could he be retained more than six years in the slave condition, except by his own consent, formally given (verse 5). This law was an enormous advance upon anything previously known in the slave legislation of the most civilized country.

(6) His master shall bring him unto the judges.—In order to mark that thereafter the volunteer bondman became attached to the household, he was to be physically attached to the house by having an awl forced through his ear, and then driven into the door or doorpost. Hence "opening the ear" became a synonym for assigning a man to the slave condition.

(12-14) He that smiteth a man, so that he die.—For every case of homicide the same penalty would not be fitting. Accordingly we have here, first, the assignment of the death penalty for homicide of the first degree, i.e., murder; and secondly, the provision of a refuge for homicide of the second degree, i.e., manslaughter, or death by misadventure. The death penalty for murder had already received divine sanction in the injunctions given to Noah (Gen. 9:6). Tradition, backed up by conscience, had made it an almost universal law. The Sinaitic legislation adopted the law into the national code, and lent it additional force by the proviso, which we know to have been carried out in practice (I Kings 2:28-34), that the murderer was even to be torn from God's altar, if he took refuge there.

(15-17) And he that smiteth his father ...—With homicide are joined some other offenses, regarded as of a heinous character, and made punishable by death: viz., (1) striking a parent; (2) kidnapping; and (3) cursing a parent. The immediate sequence of these crimes upon murder, and their punishment by the same penalty, marks strongly God's abhorrence of them.

(18, 19) Severe assault, endangering life, but not actually taking it, is placed under the same head with homicide, as approaching to it, but is not to be punished in the same way. The law imposed a fine, which was to be fixed at such an amount as would at once compensate the sufferer for the loss of his time (verse 19), and defray the cost of his cure.

(20) And if a man smite his servant.— The Mosaic Law, unlike most other codes, proceeded to forbid the homicide of slaves. Hitherto, throughout the East, and also in many parts of the West, slaves had been regarded as so absolutely their master's property that he was entitled to do as he pleased with them. Now, for the first time— as far as we know—was the life of the slave protected.

(22, 24) Life for life, eye for eye.—It is a reasonable conjecture that the law of retaliation was much older than Moses, and accepted by him as tolerable rather than devised as rightful. The law itself was widely spread. Theoretically, retaliation is the most exact and strictest justice; but in practice difficulties arise, causing the rule to be discarded as soon as civilization reaches a certain point, and tending generally to the substitution of a money compensation, to be paid to the injured party by the injurer. The present passage sanctioned the law of retaliation in principle, but authorized its enforcement in a single case only. In a later part of the Mosaic code the application was made universal (Lev. 24:17-21; Deut. 19:21).

(26, 27) The eye ... tooth.—An exception to the law of retaliation is made here. If the injurer is a free man and the injured person a slave, the marked social inequality of the parties would make exact retaliation an injustice. The master who inflicts any such permanent damage—from the least to the greatest—loses all property in his slave, and is bound at once to emancipate him. The loss of an eye is viewed as the greatest permanent injury to the person; the loss of a tooth as the least.

(28-32) Injuries to the person might arise either from man or from animals. In the case of a slave, compensation was fixed at what was regarded as the standard price of a slave (Lev. 25:44-46; 27:3), which was about thirty silver shekels.

Laws Concerning the Rights of Property

(33-36) The legislation first treats loss due to carelessness.

22

(1-4) Theft is here treated of with great brevity, only three kinds being distinguished—(1) Housebreaking; (2) stealing without conversion of the property; (3) stealing with conversion. The main principle of punishment laid down is the exaction from the offender of double (verse 4). When, however, there has been conversion of the property, the penalty is heavier. Incidentally it is enacted that the burglar may be resisted by force (verse 2), and that to kill him shall be justifiable homicide; and further, it is recorded that a thief unable to make the legal restitution shall become a slave in order to pay his debt (verse 3).

Verses 5, 6 deal with trespass, verses 6-13 with embezzlement and negligence, and verses 14, 15 with indiscretion in borrowing and lending.

Miscellaneous Laws

(16-31) The remainder of the chapter contains law which it is impossible to bring under any general head. Moses may have recorded them in the order in which they were delivered to him; or have committed them to writing as they afterward occurred to his memory.

(28) Thou shalt not revile the gods.—It is best to translate by "God," and to understand the entire passage as intended to connect the sin of cursing a ruler with that of reviling God, the ruler being regarded as God's representative.

23

(1-19) The "miscellaneous laws" are here continued. From verse 1 to verse 9 no kind of sequence in the laws can be traced; from verse 10 to the first clause of verse 19 there is, on the contrary, a certain connection, since the laws enunciated are concerned with ceremonial observance. The closing law, however, is not ceremonial, but the prohibition of a practice considered to be cruel. On the whole, it may be said that the Book of the Covenant maintains its unsystematic character to the close.

Ceremonial Laws

(10, 11) Six years ... the seventh year.— The Sabbatical year which is here commanded was an institution wholly unknown to any nation but the Hebrews. It is most extraordinary that any legislator should have been able to induce a people to accept such a law. It is questionable whether, under a primitive agricultural system, when rotation of crops was unknown, the lying of the land fallow during one year in seven would not have been an economical benefit. Still the enactment was no doubt unpopular: it checked the regular course of agriculture, and seemed to rob landowners of one-seventh of their natural gains. Accordingly, we find that it was very irregularly observed (II Chron. 36:21). After the Captivity, however, the observance became regular, and classical writers notice the custom as one existing in their day. The object of the law was threefold—(1) to test obedience; (2) to give an advantage to the poor and needy, to whom the crop of the seventh year belonged (verse 11); and (3) to allow an opportunity, once in seven years, for prolonged communion with God and increased religious observances. (See Deut. 1:10-13.)

(14-17) The first great festival—the Passover festival—had been already instituted 12:3-20; 13:3-10). It pleased the divine Legislator at this time to add to that festival two others, and to make all three equally obligatory. There is some reason to suppose that, in part, the "feast of harvest" and the "feast of ingathering" already existed. Whatever the previous practice, these three festival-seasons were now laid down as essential parts of the Law, and continued—supplemented by two others—the national festivals as long as Israel was a nation. Such institutions exerted a political as well as a religious influence, and helped toward national unity. This was especially the case when, as in the present, they were expressly made gatherings of the whole nation to a single center.

(15) The feast of unleavened bread.—See 2:15-20.

None shall appear before me empty.—Viewed religiously, the festivals were annual national thanksgivings for mercies received, both natural and miraculous—the first for the beginning of harvest and the deliverance out of Egypt; the second for the completion of the grain harvest and the passage of the Red Sea; the third for the final gathering in of the fruits and the many mercies of the wilderness. The law here laid down with respect to the first feast is afterward extended to the other two (Deut. 16:16).

(16) The feast of harvest.—It was calculated that the grain harvest would be completed fifty days after it had begun. On this fiftieth day (Pentecost) the second festival was to begin by the offering of two loaves made of the new wheat just gathered in.

The feast of ingathering.—Elsewhere commonly called "the feast of tabernacles" (Lev. 23:34; Deut. 16:13, 16; 31:10; II Chron. 8:13; Ezra 3:4; Zech. 14:16-19, etc.). Like the feast of unleavened bread, this lasted a week. It corresponded to a certain extent with modern "harvest festivals," but was more prolonged and of a more distinctly religious character. The time fixed for it was the week beginning with the fifteenth and terminating with the twenty-first of the month Tisri, corresponding to our October. The vintage and the olive harvest had by that time been completed, and thanks were given for God's bounties through the whole year. At the same time the sojourn in the wilderness was commemorated; and as a memorial of that time those who attended the feast dwelt during its continuance in booths made of branches of trees. (See Lev. 23:40; Neh. 8:14-17.)

The Promises of God to Israel, if the Covenant Is Kept

(20-33) The Book of the Covenant terminates, very appropriately, with a series of promises. If Israel will keep His covenant, they will enjoy the following blessings:—(1) the guidance and protection of His angel until Canaan is reached; (2) God's help against their adversaries, who will, little by little, be driven out; (3) the ultimate possession of the entire country between the Mediterranean and the Red Sea on the one hand, the Desert and the Euphrates on the other; (4) a blessing upon their flocks and herds; and (5) a blessing upon themselves, whereby they will escape sickness and enjoy a long term of life. All these advantages, however, are conditional upon obedience, and may be forfeited.

(20) I send an Angel before thee.—Most commentators see in the promise the first mention of the "Angel of the Covenant," who is reasonably identified with the Second Person of the Holy Trinity, the Eternal Son and Word of God. When the promise is retracted on account of the sin of the golden

119

calf, it is in the words, "I will not go up with thee" (33:3).

(21) My name is in him.—God and His name are in Scripture almost convertible terms. He is never said to set His name in a man.

(28) I will send hornets.—Heb., "the hornet." (Comp. Josh. 24:12, where "the hornet" is said to have been sent.) Probably the Egyptians are the hornets intended. It was they who, under Rameses III, broke the power of the Hittites and other nations of Palestine, while the Israelites were sojourners in the wilderness. Possibly the term was chosen in reference to the hieroglyphic sign for "king" in Egypt, which was the figure of a bee or wasp.

(31) Thy bounds.—This was exactly the extent to which the dominions of Israel reached under Solomon, as we see from the description in Kings and Chronicles (I Kings 4:21, 24; II Chron. 9:26). It had, according to Moses (Gen. 15:18), been already indicated with tolerable precision in the original promise made to Abraham.

24

The Ratification of the Covenant

(4) Moses wrote.—Comp. 17:14. The familiarity of Moses with writing is throughout presumed in the Pentateuch. One "learned in all the wisdom of the Egyptians" under the nineteenth dynasty could not well be ignorant of this ordinary Egyptian accomplishment.

(5) Burnt offerings ... peace offerings.—Burnt offerings were at once expiatory and signs of self-dedication. Peace offerings were indications of man's gratitude for mercies received. Both were now offered together, to mark (1) Israel's thankfulness for being taken into covenant, and (2) Israel's determination to consecrate itself wholly to the service of God.

(7) The book of the covenant—i.e., the book which he had written overnight, the collection of laws and promises which we have in 20:22-23:33.

(8) And Moses took the blood, and sprinkled it ... —Half of the blood had been sprinkled upon the altar, which symbolized Jehovah; the other half was now sprinkled upon the people, or, rather upon their representatives—the elders and others who stood nearest to Moses. Thus the two parties to the covenant, sprinkled with the blood of the same sacrifices, were brought into sacramental union. (See Heb. 9:19.)

(9) Then went up.—It pleased God to terminate the whole transaction by a closing scene of extraordinary grandeur, beauty, and spiritual significance. A sacrificial meal was always regarded as a religious act—an act done "before God" (18:12), involving communion with Him. God willed now to signalize this sacrificial feast above all others by making His presence not only felt but **seen.** As Moses, Aaron with his two sons, and the elders were engaged in the feast (verse 11), a vision of marvelous splendor broke upon them. God showed Himself to them—not, as before, amid thunders and lightnings, and a thick cloud, and fire, and smoke, and earthquake (19:16, 18), but in His loveliness. They "saw God," and were neither hurt nor even terrified; they could while seeing Him, still eat and drink—they felt themselves like guests at His board, as if He were banqueting with them. It is impossible to doubt that we have here a precious forecast of the Christian's highest privilege—the realization of the presence of God in the sacred feast of the Holy Communion.

(10) They saw the God of Israel.—Probably, in human form, as Isaiah saw Him (Isa. 6:1-5), and Ezekiel (Ezek. 1:26) and even Nebuchadnezzar (Dan. 3:25).

The Second Ascent of Moses Into Mount Sinai

(12-18) The great work still remained to be done. A series of laws had been laid down for the nation and accepted with unanimity (verses 3, 7). It was necessary for the sustentation of the religious life of the people that a sacred polity should be instituted, a form of worship set up, and regulations established with regard to all the externals of religion—holy persons, holy places, rites, ceremonies, vestments, incense consecration. Full and complete knowledge of all the details is elaborately set forth in chaps. 25-30, and again in chaps. 35-40, which from then on constituted the essentials of the external worship of Israel. The Decalogue and the Book of the Covenant had no doubt a considerable share in forming the character of the Hebrew nation, but a larger share must be assigned to the ritual and ceremonial which Moses was now instructed to set up, and which forms the main subject of the remainder of the Book.

(12) And I will give thee tables of stone ... —It is remarkable that these are no expressly said, either here or in 31:18, to have contained the Ten Commandments. The fact, however, is distinctly stated in Deut. 5:22; and with respect to the second tables, the same is affirmed in Exod. 34:28. The fiction of a double decalogue is thus precluded.

25

The Gifts Which Might Be Given for the Tabernacle and the Priests' Dresses

(2) Speak unto the children of Israel that they bring me an offering.—God, being about to command the construction of a dwelling for Himself, such as the circumstances of the case allowed, prefaced His directions concerning its materials and form by instructing Moses to invite the people to contribute from their stores, as an offering to Himself, the various substances which were suitable for the dwelling and its appurtenances. The erection of sanctuaries is one of the fittest occasions for man to show his gratitude to God by giving to Him of His own, largely and liberally. (See chap. 36.)

The Sanctuary and Its Contents

(8) Let them make me a sanctuary.—The enumeration of the gifts (verses 3-7) has been subordinate to this. As they are still in a nomadic condition, a building, in the ordinary sense of the word, would have been unsuitable. They must soon have left it or have foregone their hopes of Palestine. God therefore devised for them a structure in harmony with their condition—a "tent-temple"—modeled on the ordinary form of the better Oriental tents, but of the best materials and of an unusual size—yet still portable. It is this structure, with its contents and its adjuncts, which forms the main subject of the rest of the Book of Exodus, and which is now minutely and elaborately described in six consecutive chapters (chaps. 25-30).

That I may dwell among them.—Compare chaps. 29:42-46; 40:34-38. Though God "dwelleth not in temples made with hands" (Acts 7:48), is not confined to them, cannot be comprehended within them, yet since it pleases Him to manifest Himself especially in such abodes, He may be well said to "dwell there" in a peculiar manner. His dwelling with Israel was not purely spiritual. From time to time He manifested Himself sensibly in the Holy of Holies, where He dwelt continually, and might be consulted by the temporal ruler of the nation.

(9) The pattern.—It has been maintained that God showed to Moses a series of visions in which the forms were represented to the eye of the mind. The entire analogy of the divine dealings is in favor of this view.

The Ark

(10) They shall make an ark.—Arôn is properly a chest or coffer of small dimensions, used to contain money or other valuables (II Kings 12:9, 10; II Chron. 25:8-11, etc.). In one place it is applied to a mummy-case (Gen. 50:26). Here it designates a wooden chest three feet nine inches long, two feet three inches broad, and two feet three inches deep. The primary object of the Ark was to contain the two tables of stone, written with the finger of God, which Moses was to receive before he came down from the mount. (See 24:12, and comp. 25:16.)

(12) In the four corners thereof.—Literally, "at the four feet thereof." The rings were to be affixed, not at the four upper corners of the chest, but at the four bottom corners, in order that the Ark, when carried on men's shoulders, might be elevated above them, and so, be in no danger of coming in contact with the bearers' persons. (See II Sam. 6:6, 7.)

(16) The testimony which I shall give thee.—The two tables of stone were called "the Testimony" as being God's witness against sin (Deut. 31:26). Since it contained them, the Ark was called "the ark of the testimony."

The Mercy Seat

(17) A mercy seat.—Kapporeth has never any other meaning than that of "covering" or "expiating sins."

Of pure gold.—It was intended to show by this lavish outlay, that the "mercy seat" was that object in which the accessories of worship culminated, the crowning glory of the material Tabernacle.

(18) Two cherubims.—(See Gen. 3:24.) Not all angels are cherubim. The cherubim constitute a select class, very near to God, very powerful, very resolute, highly fitted to act as guards. It is probably with this spe-

121

cial reference that the cherubic figures were selected to be placed upon the mercy seat—they guarded the precious deposit of the two tables, toward which they looked (verse 20). Some hold that the proper figure of a cherub is that of a bull or ox, and think that the cherubim of the tabernacle were winged bulls, not unlike the Assyrian. But the predominant opinion seems to be that they were simply human figures with the addition of a pair of wings. In this case they would bear a considerable resemblance to the figures of Ma, or Truth, so often seen inside Egyptian arks.

(19) Of the mercy seat shall ye make the cherubims.—The meaning seems to be that the cherubims were not to be detached images, made separately, and then fastened to the mercy seat, but to be formed out of the same mass of gold with the mercy seat, and so to be part and parcel of it.

(20) The cherubims shall stretch forth their wings on high.—The two wings of both cherubs were to be elevated and advanced so as to overshadow the mercy seat, and, as it were, protect it.

(22) There will I meet with thee.—The place of the **Shechinah**, or visible manifestation of God's presence, was to be between the two cherubim over the mercy seat. There God would meet His people, "to speak there unto them" (29:42), either literally, as when He answered inquiries of the high priest by Urim and Thummim, or spiritually, as when He accepted incense, and the blood of offerings, and prayers, offered to Him by the people through their appointed representatives, the priests. It was for the purpose of thus "meeting" His people that the entire Tabernacle was designed, and hence its ordinary name was "the Tent of Meeting," unhappily rendered in the King James Version by the "tabernacle of the congregation." (See 27:21.)

The Table of Shewbread

(23-30) Thou shalt also make a table.—The Ark and mercy seat, which covered it, constituted the entire furniture of the inner sanctuary, or "Holy of Holies" (40:20, 21). When this had been shown to Moses the next thing to be done was to set before him the furniture of the outer sanctuary, or holy place. This consisted of three articles—(1) the table of showbread, described in this passage; (2) the golden candlestick, described in verses 31-40; and (3) the altar of incense, described in 30:1-10. The "table of

shewbread" was a receptacle for the twelve loaves which were to be "set continually before the Lord" (Lev. 24:8) as a thank offering on the part of His people—a perpetual acknowledgment of His perpetual protection and favor. It was to be just large enough to contain the twelve loaves, set in two rows, being a yard long, and a foot and one half broad. The vessels belonging to the table (verse 29) were not placed on it.

(30) Thou shalt set upon the table shewbread before me alway.—For a detailed account of the arrangement of the showbread see Lev. 24:5-9. The Hebrew expression translated "shewbread" is literally, "bread of face," or "bread of presence"—bread, that is, which was set forth always before the presence of God.

The Golden Candlestick

(31-39) It was composed of a straight stem, rising perpendicularly from a base, and having on either side of it three curved arms or branches, all of them in the same plane, and all rising to the same level. The stem and arms were ornamented with representations of almond flowers, pomegranates, and lily blossoms, repeated as there was room for them, the top ornament being in every case a lily blossom, which held a hemispherical lamp. The form and ornamentation of the base are unknown. The special object of the candlestick seems to have been to give light by night. Its lamps were to be lighted at even (30:8) by the High Priest, and were to burn from evening to morning (27:21), when they were to be "dressed," or trimmed (30:7), and "extinguished."

26

The Tabernacle

(1-37) The sacred tent which was to form the "House of God," or Temple, for Israel during the continuance of the people in the wilderness, and which in point of fact served them for a national sanctuary until the construction of the first temple by Solomon, is described in this chapter with a minuteness which leaves little to be desired. It is called "the dwelling," and "the tent" (verse 36)—the former from its purpose, as being the place where God "dwelt" in a peculiar manner (25:22); the latter from its shape and general construction, which resembled those of other tents of the period.

The necessary foundation was a framework of wood. This consisted of five "pillars," or tent poles, in front (verse 37), graduated in height to suit the slope of the roof, and doubtless five similar ones at the back, though these are not mentioned. A ridge pole must have connected the two central tent poles, and over this ridge pole the covering of the tent, which was of goat's hair (verse 7), was no doubt strained in the ordinary way by means of cords and "pins," or tent pegs (35:18). Thus an oblong square space was roofed over, which seems to have been sixty feet long by thirty broad. Within this "tent" was placed the "dwelling." The "dwelling" was a space forty-five feet long by fifteen broad, enclosed on three sides by walls of boards (verses 18-25), and opening in front into a sort of porch formed by the projection of the "tent" beyond the "dwelling." Toward the open air this porch was closed, wholly or partially, by a curtain (verse 36). The "dwelling" was roofed over by another "curtain," or "hanging," of bright colors and rich materials (verses 1-6). It was divided into two portions, called respectively "the Holy Place," and the "Holy of Holies"—the former toward the porch, the latter away from it. These two places were separated by a veil hung upon four pillars (verses 31, 32). (See Lev. 16:2-34; Heb. 9:7.) Their relative size is uncertain; but it may be suspected that the Holy of Holies was the smaller of the two, and conjectured that the proportion was as one to two, the Holy of Holies being a square of fifteen feet, and the Holy Place an oblong, thirty feet long by fifteen. The whole structure was placed within an area called "the Court of the Tabernacle," which is described in the next chapter.

27

The Altar of Burnt Offering

(1) Of shittim wood.—What was here directed to be made was rather an "altar-case" than an altar, and the true altar was the earth with which, at each halt in the wilderness, the "case" of shittim wood covered with bronze was filled.

(2) The horns of it.—Horns were, as far as is known, peculiar to Israelite altars. Originally, they would seem to have been mere ornaments at the four upper corners, but ultimately they came to be regarded as essential to an altar, and the virtue of the

altar was thought to lie especially in them. The victims were bound to them (Ps. 118:27); criminals clung to them (I Kings 1:50; 2:28); and the blood of sin offerings was smeared upon them for purposes of expiation (29:12; Lev. 8:15; 9:9, etc.).

The Court of the Tabernacle

(9-18) Almost every ancient temple stood within a sacred enclosure, which isolated it from the common working world, and rendered its religious character more distinctly apparent. An open space of this kind, always desirable, was absolutely necessary where the sanctuary itself was covered in, since it would have been intolerable to kill and burn victims in a confined and covered space. The altar which has been described (verses 1-8) was necessarily placed outside the tabernacle, and formed the chief furniture of the court.

28

The Designation of Aaron and His Sons for the Priestly Office, With Directions for Their Ministerial Apparel

(1) Take thou unto thee Aaron thy brother.—Perhaps in consequence of his original reluctance and want of faith (3:11; 4:10-13), perhaps on account of Aaron's elder birth (7:7), it pleased God to commit the office of ministering to Him in the tabernacle, not to Moses and his descendants, but to Aaron and those sprung from his loins. In this way Aaron and his sons were "drawn near" to Moses in respect of rank, position, and dignity.

That he may minister to me in the priest's office.—The actual investiture of Aaron with the priestly office did not take place until some time after the tabernacle was completed. It is related in Lev. 8; and his first priestly acts are recorded in the following chapter (Lev. 9:8-22).

(2) Holy garments.—Though holiness is, strictly speaking, a personal quality, yet all nations have felt it right to regard as "holy," in a certain modified sense, all those material objects which are connected with religion and employed in the worship of God. Hence we hear, both in Scripture and elsewhere, of "holy places," "holy vessels," "holy books," "holy garments."

For glory and for beauty.—These words

have great force. God would have His priests richly, as well as decently, appareled to give to the service of the sanctuary the highest artistic, as well as the highest spiritual, perfection. God's regard for "beauty" is here brought prominently before us, and no honest exegesis can ignore the pregnant fact that when God was pleased to give directions for His worship upon earth, they were made subservient, not only to utility and convenience, but to beauty. Beauty, it would seem, is not a thing despised by the Creator of the universe.

(4) These are the garments.—The garments peculiar to the high priest are taken first, and described with great elaboration in thirty-six verses (4-39). The most conspicuous was the breastplate, described in verses 13-30, and here mentioned first of all. Next to this came the peculiar vestment called the "ephod," a sort of jerkin or waistcoat, upon which the breastplate was worn (described in verses 6-12). Under the ephod was the long robe of blue, called "the robe of the ephod," which may be considered as the main garment, and which is described in verses 31-35. Upon his head the high priest wore a "mitre" or turban (described in verses 36-38); and inside his "robe" he wore a linen shirt or tunic, secured by a girdle (verse 39). Underneath the tunic he wore linen drawers (verses 42, 43). Nothing is said as to any covering for his feet; but it is probable that they were protected by sandals.

(5) They shall take gold, and blue—i.e., the necessary gold, blue, etc., for the construction of the vestments. It is to be noted that the materials are the same as those employed for the veil and curtains of the sanctuary (26:1, 31, 36), but with the further addition of gold and precious stones (verses 9, 17-21).

(29) Aaron shall bear the names ... upon his heart.—Comp. verse 12. The high priest was to be wholly identified with the people; to be one with them in affection no less than in action; to bear their names on his shoulders, as supporting them and wrestling for them, while he also bore their names on his heart, as loving them and feeling for them. Thus he was continually to present before God a twofold "memorial" of His people, and to make a sort of double appeal, on the one hand, to God's power, and, on the other hand, to His mercy and loving-kindness.

(30) Thou shalt put in the breastplate of judgment the Urim and the Thummim.— Comp. Lev. 8:8. The words "Urim and Thummim" mean literally, "lights and perfections." The question arises, what do these two words, as here used, designate? Some small objects which the bag of the breastplate could hold, and with which the people had long been familiar, can alone answer the requirements of the case. Probability seems on the whole to be in favor of a connection between divination by teraphim and consultation of God by Urim and Thummim (Judges 17:5; 18:14, 17, 20; Hosea 3:4), whence it is reasonable to conclude that the Urim and Thummim were small images, by which God had been consulted in the past, and by which Moses was now authorized to state that He would be consulted in the future. How the consultation was made, and the decision given, is a question still more obscure than that which has been just considered, and one which seems to admit of no solution.

(35) And his sound shall be heard.—The great object of the bells was to make known to the people, by a sensible manifestation, every movement of their representative, every act that he performed on their behalf. The bells enabled them to follow in their thoughts the entire service that he was engaged in, to join their prayers and praises with his, and to offer to God a common worship. So important was this union of priest and people in the worship of God regarded, that death was denounced on the high priest who should minister in the sanctuary without this essential garment.

(40) For glory and for beauty.—It is certainly remarkable that as plain a dress as that of the ordinary priests—a white tunic, a girdle, which may or may not have been embroidered, and a plain white close-fitting cap—should be regarded as sufficing "for glory and for beauty." White robes, however, are in Scripture constantly represented as eminently glorious (Dan. 7:9; Mark 9:3; John 20:12; Acts 1:10; Rev. 4:4; 6:11; 7:9-14; 15:6; etc.).

(41) Thou shalt put them upon Aaron ... and his sons.—Moses was by these words commanded to take the part in the consecration of Aaron and his sons which he is related to have taken in Lev. 8:6-30.

And shalt anoint them.—See 29:7-9.

29

The Form of Consecration for the Priests

(1) This is the thing that thou shalt do

unto them to hallow them.—The consecration of the priests had been commanded
in the preceding chapter (28:41). The method of it is now laid down. It consists of five
things:—(1) Ablution (verse 4); (2) Investi-
tute (verses 5-9); (3) Chrism, or anointing
(verse 7); (4) Sacrifice (verses 10-23); and
(5) Filling the hand (verse 24). All of these
were symbolical acts, typical of things spiritual—ablution, of the putting away of impurity; investiture, of being clothed with
holiness; unction, of the giving of divine
grace, etc.; the entire consecration forming
an acted parable, very suggestive and full of
instruction to such as understood its meaning.

**(10) Aaron and his sons shall put their
hands upon the head of the bullock.**—By
this symbolical action, which was commanded in the case of every sin offering
(Lev. 4:4, 15, 24, 29, 33; 16:21; etc.), the
offerer identified himself with the animal,
and transferred to it the guilt of his own
sins and imperfections. The animal thereby
became accursed, and its death paid the
penalty due to the sins laid upon it, and set
free those who had committed them. Similarly, Christ, our sin offering, was "made a
curse for us" (Gal. 3:13).

**(15) Put their hands upon the head of the
ram.**—Again identifying themselves with
the animal, as in verse 10, but with a
different purpose from their former one.
Then they transferred their sins to the victim; now they claimed a part in the victim's
dedication to God, offering themselves with
it, and becoming, themselves, "a sweet savour, an offering made by fire unto the
Lord" (verse 18).

(19) The other ram.—Comp. verses 1 and
5. This ram is called in Leviticus (8:22)
"the ram of consecration." It formed by far
the most peculiar part of the whole ceremony. Consecrated to God by the act of sacrifice, its blood was used, together with the
holy oil, for the consecration of Aaron and
his sons (verses 20, 21); while at the same
time its most sacred parts were placed on
their hands by Moses, that with them they
might perform their first sacerdotal act, and
so be inaugurated into their office (verses
22-24). This last was not only the crowning
act of the ceremony, but also its most
essential feature—the act which imparted to
Aaron and his sons the priestly character.

The Law of the Daily Sacrifice, and
the Promise of God's Presence

(38-42) The consecration of the altar,

which took place during the consecration of
the priests, was to be followed immediately
by the establishment of the daily sacrifice.
Two lambs were to be offered every day,
partly in expiation of the daily sins of the
nation, but mainly as a sign that the nation
daily renewed its self-dedication to Jehovah. Meat and drink offerings were signs of
the gratitude due to God for His perpetual
mercies, and acknowledgments of His protecting care and loving-kindness. Incense
was a figure of the perpetual prayer that it
behooved the nation to send up to the
Throne of Grace for a continuance of the
divine favor. (See 30:7, 8.)

**(45) I will dwell among the children of
Israel.**—It must not be supposed that the
fulfillment of this promise was effected by
the mere presence of the Shechinah within
the Tabernacle (verse 42). It pledged God to
a perpetual supervision, care, and tender
protection of His people, such as we find
actually exercised in the history of the nation.

30

The Altar of Incense

(3) Thou shalt overlay it with pure gold.—
Next to the Ark of the covenant the most
holy article of furniture contained either in
the sanctuary or in its court was the altar of
incense. It symbolized prayer in its general
use (Ps. 141:2; Luke 1:10), and it symbolized expiation in the purpose whereto it was
to be applied on certain occasions, as when
the high priest had sinned in his official
capacity (Lev. 4:3-12), or when the whole
congregation had sinned through inadver-
tence (ibid. verses 13-21). It was, therefore,
"most holy to the Lord." Hence, its materials were to be the same with those of the
Ark of the covenant, and its place was to be
directly opposite the Ark, near to it, but on
the outer side of the veil (40:5).

**(10) Aaron shall make an atonement
upon the horns of it once in a year.**—This
passage seems to determine the sense of
Lev. 16:18. Once in the year, on the great
day of atonement, the high priest, after
entering within the veil and sprinkling the
blood of the offerings upon the mercy seat
(Lev. 16:14, 15), was to "go out unto the
altar that was before the Lord, and put of
the blood of the bullock, and of the blood
of the goat, upon the horns of the altar
round about, and sprinkle of the blood upon
it with his finger seven times," and so

"cleanse it, and hallow it," and "make an atonement for it" (ibid. verses 18, 19).

The Brazen Laver

(19) Aaron and his sons shall wash their hands and their feet.—Washing the hands symbolized purity in act; washing the feet, holiness in all their walk and conversation.

(20) That they die not.—Comp. 28:35, 43. It is not easy to see why the death penalty was threatened against neglect of certain ceremonial observances, and not of others. Ablution, however, was so easy, and probably so long-established a practice, that to omit it would imply intentional disrespect toward God. (See Heb. 12:14.)

31

The Appointment of Bezaleel and Aholiab

(1-11) The instructions needed for the making of the tabernacle, its furniture, and the priests' dresses, were now complete. Moses was sufficiently informed, by what he had heard and seen, both as to the "Tent of Meeting" itself, and as to all its appurtenances and paraphernalia. But Moses was not himself an artist. It was therefore necessary that the manual work of carrying out the instructions given him should be entrusted to others. God saw fit to mark the importance of the work by taking the direct appointment of the persons to be employed upon Himself. He knew to whom He had given the highest artistic power, and who at the same time that they possessed it would work in the most religious spirit. He accordingly named two persons, Bezaleel and Aholiab, as those to whom the superintendence of the whole business should be given. Bezaleel was to be leader and chief, Aholiab assistant. Bezaleel's task was to be general, Aholiab's, apparently, special (38:23). Both, however, were to receive the special assistance of God's Holy Spirit for the due execution of their respective tasks (verses 3-6).

The Law of the Sabbath Declared Anew Under a Penal Sanction

(12-17) The worship of the tabernacle was so closely connected with Sabbatical observance (Lev. 19:30), that no surprise can be felt at a recurrence to the subject in the present place. Hitherto the Sabbath had been, in the main, a positive enactment intended to test obedience (16:23); now it was elevated into a sacramental sign between God and His people (verse 13). Having become such a sign, it was necessary to be guarded by a new sanction, and this was done by assigning the death penalty to any infraction of the law of Sabbath observance (verses 14, 15).

(13) It is a sign between me and you.—Circumcision had been given as a covenant sign to Abraham and his descendants (Gen. 17:9-13); but its adoption by many of the heathen nations had rendered it no longer a distinguishing mark by which God's people could be certainly known from others. Thus a new "sign" was needed. The observance of one day in seven as a day of holy rest became from that day on the distinguishing sign, and proved effectual. It was not likely to be adopted, and in point of fact was not adopted, by any of the heathen. We find it in the latest time of the Jewish nation still regarded as the special mark and badge of a Jew.

The Two Tables Given

(18) The termination and crown of the entire conference which Moses had held with God on Mount Sinai for forty days and forty nights (24:18) was the committal to his hands of the two tables of testimony which had been promised before the ascent into the mount was made (ibid. verse 12), and which were presupposed in the entire arrangement of the sanctuary.

Written with the finger of God.—Comp. 24:12, where God speaks of "commandments which **I** have written." We must understand that the tables were inscribed by some supernatural process, and not by any human hand. The exact nature of the supernatural process is not revealed to us.

32

The Idolatry of the Golden Calf

(1) When the people saw that Moses delayed to come down.—After seven chapters of directions, which belong to the Mosaic or Levitical Law, the writer here resumes his historical narrative. Leaving Moses still in the mount, he returns to the plain at its base in order to relate the events which had occurred there during Moses' absence.

Up, make us gods.—Rather, "make us a god." The religious condition of the Israelites during the sojourn in Egypt has been so entirely passed over in the previous narrative, that this request comes upon us as a surprise and a shock. True, there have been warnings against idolatry, reiterated warnings (20:4, 5, 23; 23:32, 33), but no tendency toward it has manifested itself, no hint has been given that it was an immediate and pressing danger. When, however, we carefully scrutinize the rest of Scripture, we find reason to believe that a leaning toward idolatry had, in point of fact, shown itself among the people while they were in Egypt, and had even attained some considerable development. (See Lev. 17:7; Josh. 24:14; Ezek. 20:8; 23:3.) This tendency had been checked by the series of extraordinary manifestations which had accompanied the Exodus. Now, however, in the absence of Moses, in the uncertainty which prevailed as to whether or not he still lived, and in the withdrawal from the camp of that divine Presence which had until now gone before them, the idolatrous instinct once more came to the front. The cry was raised, "make us a god"—make us something to take the place of the pillar of the cloud, something visible, tangible, on which we can believe the divine Presence to rest, and which may "go before us" and conduct us.

This Moses, the man that brought us up ... —Contemptuous words, showing how shortlived is human gratitude, and even human respect. An absence of less than six weeks, and a belief that he was no more, had sufficed to change the great deliverer into "this Moses, the man who brought us up."

(2) And Aaron said ... Break off the golden earrings.—It is a reasonable conjecture that Aaron thought to prevent the projected idolatry by this requirement. Not having the courage to meet the demand of the people with a direct negative, he may have aimed at diverting them from their purpose by requiring a sacrifice which they would be unwilling to make, viz., the personal ornaments of their wives and children. The women might reasonably have been expected to resist, and the men to yield before such resistance; but the event proved otherwise.

(4) A molten calf.—The "molten calf," which had no exact counterpart in Egypt, perhaps points back to an older idolatry,

such as is glanced at in Josh. 24:14, where the Israelites are warned to "put away the gods which their fathers served on the other side of the flood," i.e., of the Euphrates. Certainly the bull form was more distinctive of the Babylonian and Assyrian than of the Egyptian worship, and it may be suspected that the emigrants from Chaldsea had clung through all their wanderings to the mystic symbolism which had been elaborated in that primeval land, and which they would contrast favorably with the coarse animal worship of Egypt. In Chaldea, the bull, generally winged and human-headed, represented the combination of wisdom, strength, and omnipresence, which characterizes divinity; and this combination might well have seemed to carnal minds no unapt symbol of Jehovah.

(5) Aaron ... built an altar before it.—Having once yielded to the popular cry, Aaron was carried on from one compliance to another. Perhaps he flattered himself that by heading the movement he could control it, and hinder it from becoming downright apostasy from Jehovah. In his view no doubt the calf was an emblem of Jehovah, and the worship paid it was the worship of Jehovah. Hence the festival which he proclaimed was to be "a feast to Jehovah." But how little able he was to guide events, or to hinder the worst evils of idolatry from speedily manifesting themselves, appears from verses 6 and 25.

God's Offer to Moses

(9) It is a stiff-necked people.—This phrase afterward so common (33:3, 5; 34:9; Deut. 9:6, 13; 10:16; II Chron. 30:8; 36:13; Ps. 75:5; Jer. 17:23; Acts 7:51), occurs here for the first time. It is generally explained as "obstinate," but rather means "perverse," the metaphor being taken from the horse that stiffens his neck against the pull of the rein, and will not be guided by the rider.

(10) I will make of thee a great nation.—i.e., I will put thee in the place of Abraham, make thee the father of the faithful, destroy all existing Israelites but thee and thine, and proceed de novo to raise up a "great nation" out of thy loins. Moses was tried by an offer which would have exalted him at the expense of the people. He was allowed to see that he might either sacrifice the people and obtain his own aggrandizement, or deny himself and save them. That he chose the better part redounds to his undying glory.

Moses' Reply, and God's "Repentance"

(11-13) Moses has three arguments: (1) God had done so much for His people, that surely He will not now make all of none effect (verse 11); (2) their destruction will give a triumph to the Egyptians (verse 12); (3) it will nullify the promises made to Abraham, Isaac, and Jacob (Gen. 15:5; 17:2-6; 26:3-5; 28:14-15; 35:11). To these arguments he adds entreaties that God will be merciful, and change His purpose (verse 12).

(14) The Lord repented of the evil.— Moses' intercession was effectual. God first announced a (conditional) purpose, and then announced a different one. The mode of speech is anthropomorphic.

The Descent of Moses From Sinai, and the Suppression of the Idolatry

(15) The tables were written on both their sides.—It has been calculated that the 172 words of the Decalogue could easily have been inscribed in letters of a fair size on the four surfaces indicated, if the tablets were 27 inches long by 18 inches broad, and that two tablets of this size would readily have been conveyed in a man's two hands (Keil).

(16) The tables were the work of God.— The natural meaning of the words is that God Himself fashioned them. This was not the case with the second tables (34:1, 4).

The writing was the writing of God.—See note on 31:18.

(17) When Joshua heard.—Joshua's presence with Moses in the mount has not been indicated since 24:13. But it would seem that when Moses was summoned up into the cloud (24:16) his faithful "minister" remained where he was, waiting for his master. He may have found shelter in some "cleft of the rock"; and the manna may have fallen about him and sufficed for his sustenance during the forty days and nights of his master's absence.

The noise of the people as they shouted.— "Shouting" was a feature of idolatrous rites (I Kings 18:28; Acts 19:34; Herod. 2:60, etc.), and was in part a cause, in part a result, of the physical excitement which prevailed during such orgies. Moses, forewarned of the actual state of affairs (verses 7, 8), had probably a shrewd suspicion of the real nature of the sounds. He contented himself, however, with negativing his minister's conjecture.

(19) He cast the tables out of his hands.—

Comp. Deut. 9:17. In righteous indignation, but perhaps with some revival of the hot temper which had led him astray in his younger days (2:12).

(22-24) Aaron's conduct was really without excuse; but he attempts two pleas—the first insufficient, the second false and fatuous. (1) The people compelled him. (2) He threw the gold into the furnace, and "it came out a calf." In Deuteronomy, Moses informs us that Aaron's whole conduct so angered God that God would have destroyed him but for his own intercession (Deut. 9:20).

(26) Then Moses stood in the gate of the camp.—The crowning step was now to be taken. Though the idol had been seized and its destruction begun, though Aaron had been rebuked and put to shame, yet the revel continued. Once launched on an evil course, the bulk of the people persisted in it. Moses felt that God was openly insulted by such conduct, against which death was pronounced by the Law (22:20), and which might at any moment provoke God to destroy the whole people (verse 10). He therefore proceeded to suppress the idolatry by a stern act of judicial severity.

Moses' Intercession on Behalf of the People

(32) If thou wilt forgive their sin.— Supply after the word "sin," "well and good," "I am content," or some such phrase. Similar instances of **aposiopesis** will be found in Dan. 3:15; Luke 13:9; 19:42; John 6:62; Rom. 9:22. The usage is common among Orientals.

Blot me, I pray thee, out of thy book.— Comp. Rom. 9:1-3. Moses seems to have risen to the same height of self-abnegation as Paul, and to have willed to be "accursed from God for his brethren, his kinsmen according to the flesh." As his sacrifice could not have redeemed them (Ps. 49:7), God did not accept it in the literal sense; but the offer may have availed much toward the pardon of the people, and toward lightening the chastisement which they received (verses 34, 35).

(33) Whosoever hath sinned against me, him will I blot out.—Comp. Ezek. 18:4: "The soul that sinneth, it shall die." A mere man cannot take other men's sins on him, cannot relieve them of the penalties attached to sin, the worst of which is the depravation of the soul itself. Sin persisted in blots out from God's book by the absolute contradiction that there is between evil and good. Even Christ's merits cannot avail the sinner who does not put away his sin, detest it, abhor it, revolt from it. Only One who can implant a principle of life in man can save from death.

(34) In the day when I visit . . . their sin upon them.—All sin is followed by suffering; the sequence is inevitable. God had now consented to spare His people, and to take them back into favor; but they were not to expect that matters would be with them as if their sin had not taken place. It would still be "visited upon them"—not, indeed, by instant death, but still in some way or other. The weary waiting in the wilderness for forty years may have been a part of the punishment (Num. 14:33); but it may also have been inflicted on different persons in many different ways.

33

The Humiliation of the People at the Threat of God's Withdrawal

(1-6) If God consented at all to renew His covenant with the people, after they had so flagrantly broken it, the terms of which He would renew it were, in strict justice, purely optional. In the "Book of the Covenant" He had promised to go up with them by an angel, in whom was His name (23:20-23): i.e., by His Son, the Second Person in the Holy Trinity. He now, to mark His displeasure, withdrew this promise, and substituted for the divine presence that of a mere angel (verses 2, 3). Dimly the people felt the importance of the change, the vast difference between the angelic and the divine, and "mourned" their loss (verse 4).

Moses Establishes a Temporary Tabernacle

(7-11) Months would necessarily elapse before the Tabernacle could be constructed according to the pattern which he had seen in the mount. During this interval Moses determined to make use of one of the existing tents as a "house of prayer," severing it from the others and giving it the name "Tent of Meeting," which was afterward appropriated to the Tabernacle. It would seem that he selected his own tent for the purpose—probably because it was the best that the camp afforded—and contented himself with another. God deigned to ap-

prove his design, and descended in the cloudy pillar on the tent each time Moses entered it.

(11) Face to face.—Comp. Num. 12:8; Deut. 34:10. This is clearly spoken of as a privilege peculiar to Moses; but in what exactly the peculiarity consisted is not apparent. Some special closeness of approach is no doubt meant—some nearness such as had been enjoyed by no mortal previously. In later times, Isaiah (Isa. 6:1-5) and Ezekiel (Ezek. 1:28) were perhaps equally favored.

Moses Obtains a Renewal of God's Promise to Go Up With the People

(12-17) The self-humiliation of the people (verses 4-6) had appeased God's anger. He was now ready to be entreated. Moses therefore renews his supplications on their behalf, and especially prays for a revocation of the threatened withdrawal of the divine Presence, and substitution for it of a mere angel. Taking advantage of his privilege to speak to God as friend with friend (verse 11), he ventures to expostulate, uses familiar terms, and persists until he at last obtains a distinct declaration that his request is granted (verse 17).

(12) I know thee by name.—God had shown this knowledge when He called Moses out of the burning bush (3:4), and again, probably, when he "called unto him out of the midst of the cloud" (24:16); but the exact phrase had not been used previously. It implies a high degree of divine favor. God "knows by name" only those whom He greatly regards.

(13) Consider that this nation is thy people.—Moses glances back at God's words recorded in 32:7, and reminds God that the Israelites are not merely his (Moses') people, but also, in a higher sense, God's people. As such, God had acknowledged them (3:7, 10; 5:1; 6:7; 7:4; etc.).

Moses's Request to See God's Glory, and God's Reply to It

(18-23) "Shew me," Moses said, "I beseech thee, thy glory." God could not grant his request in full, for it is impossible as long as we are in the flesh that we should look on God and live. "No man hath seen God at any time" (John 1:18). But He granted all that could be granted. He made "all his goodness pass before" Moses; He gave him a fresh revelation of His name

129

(34:6, 7); and He even let him see some actual portion of His "glory"—as much as mortal man could possibly behold—more than any son of man had ever beheld before—more, probably, than any other son of man will ever behold until the consummation of all things (verses 22, 23).

34

Preparations for a Renewal of the Covenant

(1) **Hew thee two tables.**—Something is always lost by sin, even when it is forgiven. The first tables were "the work of God" (32:16), the second were hewn by the hand of Moses.

Of stone.—Literally, "of stones"—hewn, i.e., out of two separate stones, which could not be said of the first tables, since none knew how God fashioned them.

I will write.—It is quite clear that the second tables, equally with the first, were inscribed "with the finger of God." (Comp. Deut. 4:13; 10:2, 4.) It is also quite clear that exactly the same words were written on each.

Moses Allowed to See God's Glory

(5-8) The present ascent of Moses to the top of Sinai had two objects:—(1) the repair of the loss occasioned by his breaking the first tables; and (2) the accomplishment of the promise made to him that (under certain restrictions) he should "see God's glory." Combined with this promise were two minor ones—that God would make His "goodness" pass before him, and that He would reveal to him afresh His name. The revelation of the name is recorded in verses 6, 7, the manifestation of the glory in verse 5. How Moses was enabled to see God's goodness pass before him is not stated. (Comp. note on 33:19.)

(6) **The Lord passed by before him.**—In this brief phrase we have the entire historical narrative of the manifestation to Moses of God's glory. For details we must refer to the terms of the promise (33:21-23), which are also characterized by brevity. This was so brilliant a vision that it left a permanent light upon his countenance, which he was obliged ordinarily to conceal from the people by means of a veil (verses 29-35).

The Lord, The Lord God. . . .—The new "name" of God is not a "name," as we

understand the expression; it is rather a description of His nature by means of a series of epithets. At the bush He had revealed His eternal, self-existent character, in the descent on Sinai (19:16-19; 20:18-21) He had shown His terribleness; now, in the act of pardoning His people and taking them once more into favor, He made known His attribute of mercy.

The Covenant Renewed, and the Decalogue a Second Time Given

(9) **If now I have found grace in thy sight.**—Rather, "Since now, etc." The evidences of God's favor toward him—which Moses had now experienced, emboldened him to prefer fresh requests on behalf of the people. God has promised to go up in the midst of them; will He not also promise to forgive their iniquity and sin if they offend Him in the way, and permanently to attach them to Himself by making them "His inheritance"? God does not directly answer these prayers, but indirectly accepts them by renewing His covenant with Israel (verses 10, 27).

(12-26) This passage may be compared with chap. 23. It repeats, with some enlargements, the enactments there made, and traces in detail the evil consequences which would follow from a neglect of the enactments.

(17) **Thou shalt make thee no molten gods.**—It is just possible that the Israelites when they worshiped the golden calf may have conceived that they were not breaking the second commandment, which forbad the adoration of any "graven image." An express law was therefore made against "molten images."

(27) **Write thou these words.**—This express command accounts for the assignment of so much space to what is mainly repetition. The requirement of the repetition can only be explained by the importance of the laws laid down under the circumstances of the Hebrew nation, and the power of repetition to enforce upon the conscience what is pressed upon it by reiteration.

(28) **He was there with the Lord forty days and forty nights.**—We learn from Deuteronomy 9:18, 19 that this long time was required for an earnest and prolonged intercession by Moses on behalf of his nation, which ultimately prevailed with God and induced Him to put away His "anger and hot displeasure."

He wrote upon the tables.—The Hebrew

idiom allows us to regard Jehovah as the nominative to the verb "wrote"; and it is necessary to do so in order to bring the passage into agreement with 34:1, and with Deut. 10:2, 4. Thus the second tables are to be viewed as "written with the finger of God" no less than the first (31:18; 32:16).

The Descent of Moses From Mount Sinai With the Second Tables

(29) The skin of his face shone.—That an actual physical phenomenon is intended appears from the entire narrative, as well as from Paul's comment upon it in II Cor. 3:7-18. According to some commentators, a radiance like that here described was a part of man's original heritage, a feature of that "image of God" wherein he was created (Gen. 1:27). The gift was forfeited by the Fall, and will not be restored generally until the time of the restitution of all things. But meanwhile, from time to time, it pleases God to restore to certain of His saints the physical glory, which is the symbol of internal purity and holiness, as to Moses on this occasion and afterward to Elijah on the mount of transfiguration (Luke 9:31), and to Stephen when he pleaded before the Sanhedrin (Acts 6:15). A glory of the kind, but of surpassing brilliancy, belonged to the human nature of our blessed Lord, who concealed it ordinarily, but allowed it to appear temporarily at the transfiguration, and permanently after His ascension (Rev. 1:16; 10:1; 21:23; 22:5). The grant of the privilege to Moses was perhaps necessary to support his authority among a people of such materialistic leanings as the Israelites.

35

Iteration of the Law Concerning the Sabbath

(1-3) Moses, being about to require the people to engage in the work, first, of constructing the materials for the Tabernacle, and then of uprearing the Tabernacle itself, prefaced his requirements by a renewed promulgation of the law of the Sabbath, with additional particularity, and with a new sanction. (See 31:12-17.)

The Zeal of the People in Offering and Assisting in the Work

(21) They came, every one whose heart stirred him up.—All classes came. And the great majority gave freely—to the utmost of their power. "A willing heart" (verse 5; also 25:2) was the **sine qua non** of an acceptable offering. Still it is implied, both here and in verses 22, 29, that there were some whose hearts did not stir them up. Enough and to spare, was, however, contributed, and at last the people had to be "restrained from bringing" (36:6). Compare the liberality shown when David was collecting materials for the Temple (I Chron. 29:6-9); and, again, when Zerubbabel was about to rear up the second Temple on the return from the Captivity (Ezra 2:68-70; Neh. 7:70-72).

36

The Construction of the Tabernacle

(8-36) This passage follows 26:1-32.

(37, 38) These verses correspond in the main to verses 36, 37 of chap. 26, which they presuppose and confirm, adding, however, one new fact, viz., that the capitals of the five pillars were overlaid with gold. Either God had given no order on this point, or Moses had omitted to record it. (See also 38:19.)

37

(1-24) This passage corresponds with verses 10-39 of chap. 25, and contains an account of the construction of the holy furniture: (1) of the Holy of Holies: the ark (verses 1-5) and the mercy seat (verses 6-9); (2) of the Holy Place: the table of shewbread (verses 10-16) and the golden candlestick (verses 17-24).

(25-29) And he made ...—The order of the instructions given on Mount Sinai is here departed from. The present passage corresponds with verses 1-5, 22-25, 34, 35 of chap. 30, with which it is in the closest agreement.

38

(1) He made the altar.—From the furniture of the sanctuary, the transition is natural to the furniture of the court in which it stood. This is now described. It consisted of the brazen altar, or altar of burnt offering (verses 1-7), and the great brazen laver (verse 8). (See 27:1-8.)

(9-20) The construction of the court follows upon that of the furniture which it contained. The passage runs parallel with 27:9-19.

The Sum of the Gold, Silver, and Bronze Employed in the Tabernacle

(24) The gold of the offering, was twenty and nine talents.—The gold talent has been estimated as equal to 10,000 shekels. In this case the gold employed in the Tabernacle would have been worth about $400,200. The amount was remarkable, and indicated at once the liberal spirit which animated the people and the general feeling that a lavish expenditure was required by the occasion. There is no difficulty in supposing that the Israelites possessed at the time gold to the (highest) value estimated, since they had carried with them out of Egypt, besides their ancestral wealth, a vast amount of gold and silver ornaments, freely given to them by the Egyptians (3:22; 12:35, 36).

(25) The silver . . . was an hundred talents.—The silver talent contained 3,000 shekels. The value of the silver contributed would have been $538,000, or a little under. It was contributed by "them that were numbered of the congregation," each of whom paid a bekah, or half a shekel. (See 30:12-16.)

(26) For every one that went to be numbered.—It is remarkable that the principle of compulsory payment toward the fabric of the sanctuary should have received a sanction at the very time when the greatest stress was laid upon the greater acceptableness of voluntary offerings. (See 25:2; 35:5, 21-29.) Whatever may be thought of the expediency of levying church rates, they are clearly defensible in principle, both from the standpoint of the Old Testament and of the New (Matt. 17:24-27).

Six hundred thousand and three thousand and five hundred and fifty.—The identity of this number with that which is given in Num. 1:46, as arrived at "in the second year, on the first day of the second month" (Num. 1:1), is best explained by regarding both passages as having reference to the same transaction. The taking of the census occupied several months, during which the money was gradually collected, the sockets, etc., made, and the Tabernacle set up. The registration was deferred, and took place on a single day, when Moses and Aaron went around the tribes, received the results from their hands, and entered them in a book. It

appears from Num. 1:47 that the Levites were not counted in the sum total, no atonement money being taken from them.

(29) Seventy talents.—No great quantity was needed, since bronze was required only for the laver, for the altar of burnt offering and its vessels, for the sockets of the Tabernacle gate, for those of the court, and for the "pins," or pegs, both of the court and the Tabernacle.

39

The Making of the Holy Garments

(1-31) This section corresponds to 28:5-40, but does not follow exactly the same order.

(25) Bells of pure gold.—On the object of the bells, see note on 28:35.

The Presentation of the Work to Moses, and His Approval of It

(33-43) It is probable that the various parts of the work were presented to Moses for inspection as they were completed; that if they did not satisfy him, they might be altered and amended at once. Moses alone had seen "the pattern in the mount," and Moses alone could say if the work came up to the required standard. We are not told that anything was rejected; and it is quite possible that all the portions of the work were satisfactorily rendered at their first attempt by the several workmen; for the workmen, it must be remembered, besides receiving instructions from Moses, were divinely assisted in the production of their several works (36:2). Being satisfied, Moses expressed his own and God's approval by blessing those who had worked so faithfully.

40

The Instructions for the Uprearing of the Tabernacle

(1-8) Though the work was now complete, and all the parts of the Tabernacle made ready, Moses did not at once proceed to erect it. As when he first went up into Sinai (24:16), so now he waited for a divine summons, a distinct command fixing the time for him to do that which he knew that he had to do. God fixed for the erection "the first day of the first month" (verse 2)—i.e., the New Year's Day of the first year of freedom. At the same time He gave directions fixing the order in which all should be done, and determining the position of the various articles of furniture which the Tabernacle and its court were to contain (verses 4-8).

The Instructions for the Consecration of the Tabernacle and the Priests

(9-15) Instructions for the consecration of the Tabernacle, its furniture and its vessels, by anointing, and for the consecration of Aaron and his sons by ablution, anointing, and investiture, were attached to those given concerning the setting up of the Tabernacle, and are here recorded, although their execution appears to have been delayed to a later date. (See Lev. 8:1-13.) Moses perhaps found that there was not time for the completion of the ceremony on the day of the erection of the Tabernacle, and therefore deferred a part of it.

The Uprearing of the Tabernacle

(17) On the first day of the month . . . the tabernacle was reared up.—The Tabernacle was so constructed as to be capable of being rapidly both put together and taken to pieces. The erection of the framework, and the stretching upon it of the fine linen and goat's-hair coverings must have been the main difficulty. The first erection was completed in less than a day.

The Descent of the Glory of God Upon the Tabernacle

(34) Then a cloud.—Heb., "the cloud," i.e., the same cloud that had accompanied the host and directed their journeys from Succoth (13:20-22).

Covered the tent.—The cloud rested on the tent outside; the "glory of God," —some ineffably brilliant appearance—entered inside, and "filled" the entire dwelling. It pleased God thus to manifest His intention of making good His promise to go with the people in person (33:17). (Comp. the effect of the "glory" when it descended on Solomon's Temple, I Kings 8:11; II Chron. 5:14; 7:2.)

LEVITICUS

The name Leviticus, that is, the Levitical book, as this portion of the Pentateuch is called in our Bibles, is taken from the Greek (LXX) Version of the Old Testament, where it is so called because it treats of the sacrificial ordinances and the services performed by the Levites.

(1) And the Lord called ... and spake.— At the end of the previous book we are told that when the tent of meeting was completed, the Lord showed His approbation of it by covering the outside of the edifice with a heaven-sent cloud, and by filling the inside with His glory (Exod. 40:34-38). He therefore, who had filled the sanctuary with his glory, now "called unto Moses," thus indicating by "And he called," which is one word in the original, the intimate connection between the two books. The ancient Jewish synagogue already pointed out the fact that this unusual phrase, "And he called unto Moses," is used as an introductory formula on the three different occasions when the Lord made a special communication to this great lawgiver. Thus when the Lord first communicated to Moses that He was about to deliver the Israelites from Egypt, "He called unto him" from the burning bush (Exod. 3:4). When the Lord was about to give Moses the Ten Commandments for the people of Israel, "He called unto him" from the top of Sinai (Exod. 19:3, 20); and now when the Lord is about to give to His chosen people, through His servant Moses, the laws by which their divine worship is to be regulated, "He called unto him" from the tent of meeting (Lev. 1:1).

(3) If his offering be a burnt sacrifice.— First in order comes the burnt offering, which is divided into burnt offering from the cattle (verses 3-9), and burnt offering from the flock (verses 10-13). The ox takes precedence because it is the more costly and more important sacrifice. It had to be without disease or blemish of any kind. To offer a defective sacrifice was an insult and a deception. Hence the exclamation of the prophet in Mal. 1:14. The offerer is to bring the animal to "the entrance of the tent of meeting," as it should be rendered, that is, to the front of the Tabernacle where the brazen altar stood (Exod. 40:6).

Of his own voluntary will.—In Lev. 22:19, 20, 21 it is explicitly declared, "ye shall offer for your acceptance a male without blemish of the beeves, of the sheep or of the goats, but whatsoever hath a blemish that ye shall not offer, for it shall not be acceptable for you." The phrase "for your acceptance," or "acceptable for you," is used only in connection with burnt offerings and peace offerings, but never with sin offerings.

(4) And he shall put his hand.—The officer indicated thereby both the surrender of his ownership of the victim, and the transfer to it of the feelings by which he was influenced in performing this act of dedication to the Lord. From the practice which obtained during the second Temple, we know that the offerer himself laid both his hands between the two horns of the animal while alive, and that no proxy could do it. If several offered one sacrifice, each one laid his hand separately on the victim, confessing his sins.

To make atonement for him.—As the imposition of hands, confession, repentance, and prayer accompanied this sacrifice, and, moreover, as these acts secure for the offerer acceptance with God, hence expiatory virtue is here and elsewhere ascribed to this burnt offering (14:20; 16:24; Micah 6:6; Job 1:5; 42:8), which belongs more particularly to sin and trespass offerings (Lev. 4:20, 26, 31, 35; 5:16, 18; 7:7, etc.).

(10) Of the flocks.—Bullocks of course could only be offered by the wealthy. Hence the law now provides for those who could not afford so costly a sacrifice. They are to bring a lamb of the first year, which was the ordinary burnt offering in the time of Christ, and not a goat. The directions given with regard to the burnt offering from bullocks equally apply to the burnt offering from the flock (verses 10-13). They are therefore not repeated.

(14) Be of fowls.—The fowls here are in contrast to the cattle in verse 2. And as the quadrupeds there are immediately defined to consist of bullocks, sheep and goats, so the generic term "winged creature" is here restricted to the dove and pigeon. It will thus be seen that five different kinds are allowed for the burnt offering, viz., the bullock, lamb, goat, dove and pigeon, the same that Abram was commanded to offer (Gen. 15:9).

Of turtledoves.—Though in the case of the burnt offering, as well as of the sin offering, pigeons were permitted to those who were too poor to offer quadrupeds, yet in certain other cases birds were prescribed for all irrespective of their circumstances. To supply the demand for them, dealers in these birds sat about with them in cages on stalls in the Temple court (Matt. 21:12; John 2:16, etc.).

(15) And the priest.—It was probably out of consideration for the feelings of the poor offerer, and to increase the importance of the otherwise small offering, that the priest himself brought the victim to the altar and slew it instead of the worshiper performing these acts, as in the case of quadrupeds. The imposition of hands upon the victim was dispensed with, both because the bird was too small for this ceremony, and because the offerer brought it in his hands to the place of sacrifice, thus conveying by this act the idea involved in the imposition of hands.

2

(1) A meat offering.—The meat offerings which come next in the legal enumeration, and which occupy the whole of the present chapter, consisted of three kinds. The first is fine flour with oil and frankincense (verses 1-3). The flour was of wheat (Exod. 29:2), and was double the value of the ordinary barley flour (II Kings 7:1, 16, 18), and because of its use at the sacrifices formed part of the Temple stores (I Chron. 9:29; 23:29).

Shall pour oil upon it.—The offerer is here commanded to put oil into this preparation in order to make it more palatable to the priests who were to eat part of it. The frankincense was designed to counteract the offensive smell arising from the quantity of the flesh burned there, as is evident from the following verse, where it is stated that it is wholly to be burned.

(2) Memorial.—So called because it was designed to bring the worshiper into the grateful remembrance of God, and to remind him, as it were, of His promise to accept the service of His people rendered to Him in accordance with His command (Cf. Ps. 20:3; Acts 10:4.)

(4) A meat offering baken in the oven.—The second kind of meat offering consisted of preparations baked with oil in the oven, or in the pan, or cooked in a pot (verses 4-10). Whichever of the three cereal preparations is preferred, the offerer is to present it to the priest, who is to take it to the altar. Verses 9 and 10, which conclude the law

about the bloodless offerings, resume and expand the directions given in verses 1 and 2.

(13) The salt of the covenant of thy God.—From its antiseptic and savory qualities, salt became the symbol of hospitality, friendship, durability, fidelity. "To eat bread and salt together" is, in the East, an expression for a league of mutual amity. When the Arabs make a covenant together, they put salt on the blade of a sword, from which every one puts a little into his mouth. This constitutes for them blood relations, and they remain faithful to each other even when in danger of life. Hence the expression "a covenant of salt," which also occurs in Num. 18:19, and II Chron. 13:5, denotes an indissoluble alliance, an everlasting covenant.

(14) And if thou offer.—The third kind of meat offering (verses 14-16) is of the firstfruits. These verses should properly come immediately after verse 12, since verse 13 concludes the directions about the different kinds of bloodless offerings, with general remarks applying to all animal sacrifices. Parched or roasted corn, as here described, was, and still is, a favorite article of food in the East (Lev. 23:14; Josh. 5:11; Ruth 2:14; I Sam. 17:17; 25:18; II Sam. 17:28;). The regulations about it are the same as those given with regard to the other two kinds of bloodless offerings.

3

(1) A sacrifice of peace offering.—The peace offering of which this chapter treats consisted of two kinds, the peace offering from the herd (verses 1-5), and the peace offering from the flock (verses 6-15). As in the case of the burnt offering (1:3), the ox is mentioned first, because it is most costly and more important.

(3) The fat.—That is, the best or choicest part. Hence the expression is also used for the best produce of the ground (Gen. 45:18; Num. 18:12). As the most valuable part of the animal, the fat belonged to God, and therefore had a peculiar sanctity, for which reason it was not allowed to be eaten (Lev. 3:17; 7:23).

(6) Of the flock.—That is, of sheep or goats; they too might be either male or female, provided only that they were without organic defects.

(17) A perpetual statute for your generations throughout all your dwellings.—

(Comp. Lev. 23:14, 21, 31.) The law not to eat fat of cattle, sheep, or goats is to be binding upon the Israelites throughout all their future generations, and is applicable to any place where they may dwell. For the import of this statute see 7:23-25.

4

(2) If a soul shall sin.—It will be seen that while the three previous kinds of offerings, viz., the burnt offering (1:1-17), the meat offering (2:1-16), and the peace offering (3:1-17), are spoken of as familiarly known and practiced among the Israelites before the giving of the Law, the sin offering and the trespass offering are here introduced as a new injunction.

Through ignorance.—He did it inadvertently, and at the time of its committal did not know that it was a transgression, but recognized it as a sin after he did it. (Comp. verses 13, 22, 27; 5:18; 22:14.)

(3) The priest that is anointed.—To illustrate this law, the conduct of the high priest is adduced as the first instance, to show when and how this exalted functionary is to bring the sin offering in question. By this the Levitical law indicates that even the chief of the priesthood was but a frail being like the rest of the people, and was exposed to the same infirmities as the laity, thus precluding the assumption of spiritual superiority. Therefore the remark of the apostle in Heb. 7:27, 28. The high priest is called "the anointed priest," because, like Aaron, he alone was anointed when he succeeded to the high office, while the ordinary priests were simply consecrated. Their anointing descended with them to all futurity by virtue of being the descendants of Aaron. (See 8:12.)

According to the sin of the people.—That is, he having in ignorance committed the same sin as the common people, to which he is as liable as they.

(4) Unto the door of the tabernacle of the congregation.—Better, "unto the entrance of the tent of meeting." The regulations about the bringing of the sin offering up to the sprinkling of the blood are the same as those about the other sacrifices.

(6) Before the Lord.—As the Lord was enthroned on the mercy seat between the cherubim (Exod. 25:22) in the holy of holies, the phrase "before the Lord" is used for the place in front of the holy of holies, where the altar of incense, the showbread,

and the golden candlestick stood (Exod. 27:21; 28:35; 30:8; 34:34; etc.), and toward which the blood was sprinkled.

Before the veil of the sanctuary.—This phrase is simply explanatory of the former phrase. As the veil separated the holy of holies, where the Shechinah dwelt, from the holy place, the words are simply used as another expression for "before the Lord."

(12) Without the camp.—During the time of the second Temple there were three places for burning: one place was in the court of the sanctuary, where they burned the sacrifices which were unfit and rejected; the second place was in the mountain of the house called **Birah**, where were buried those sacrifices which met with an accident after they had been carried out of the court; and the third place was without Jerusalem, called the place of ashes. It is this place to which the apostle refers in Heb. 13:11, 12.

(13) And if the whole congregation.—As the whole Church, in its corporate body, is no more exempt from human frailty than its highest spiritual chief, the law now prescribes the sin offering for the congregation (verses 13-21). The case here assumed is that of the whole congregation having ignorantly committed some act which at the time of its committal they believed to be lawful, but which they afterward discovered to be sinful.

(15) And the elders of the congregation shall lay their hands.—As the whole congregation could not lay their hands on the victim, their representatives had to perform this act. (See verse 4.) But as the elders also were far too many to do it, since they were seventy in number, it was ordained during the second Temple that three of their members should lay their hands upon the sacrifice. Besides this sin offering there was only one other congregational offering upon which there was this laying of hands: i.e., the scapegoat (Lev. 16:21).

(16-21) The rest of the regulations are exactly the same as those prescribed in the sin offering for the high priest himself in verses 5-12.

(22) When a ruler hath sinned.—The third instance adduced is that of a ruler sinning inadvertently (verses 22-26). As the word here translated "ruler" is used for a king (I Kings 11:34; Ezek. 34:24; 46:2), the head of a tribe (Num. 1:4-16), or the division of a tribe (Num. 34:18), opinions differ as to the exact position of the personage here meant.

(27) And if any one of the common

people.—The fourth instance adduced (verses 27-35) is that of "any one of the people of the land," as this phrase is rendered in Lev. 20:2, 4; II Kings 9:18, 19; 16:15. That is, any member of the congregation, whether he be a private Israelite, ordinary priest, or Levite, in contradistinction to the aforementioned high priest and ruler.

(29-31) And he shall lay.—It is supposed by some that these words are designedly used in connection with the least costly sin offering, to indicate that the humblest gift of the humblest person, if sincerely offered, is as acceptable to God as the most costly offering of the most exalted in the land.

5

(1) And hear the voice of swearing.—The lawgiver proceeds to set forth in verses 1-13 the trespass offering which every Israelite is to bring when he has violated certain precepts here specified. The first instance adduced is that of failing to come forward as witness after the judicial adjuration has been uttered. It was the duty of every member of the community to aid the authorities in maintaining the integrity of the divine law. Hence, when an offense was committed which the constituted tribunals were unable to bring home to the offender for want of evidence, a solemn adjuration was addressed by the judge to individual members, to a district, or to the whole community. If after such an adjuration, anyone who was cognizant of the offense failed to come forward to testify what he knew, he was considered in the sight of God as participating in the transgression which he had thus concealed. An instance of this adjuration is recorded in Matt. 26:63.

(2) Or if a soul touch any unclean thing.—The second instance adduced which requires this sacrifice is the case of any one touching the dead body of a clean animal, or the living or dead body of an unclean animal or reptile.

(3) Or if he touch the uncleanness of man.—The sundry classes of defilement which a human being might contract and impart to others by contact are set forth in Lev. 12-15.

(4) Pronouncing with his lips.—That is, if he uttered an oath in thoughtlessness or in passion, without his heart realizing it, that he will do this or that.

(5) And it shall be, when ...—When he feels that he has been guilty of one of these sins specified in verses 1-4, he must confess the offense which he has committed.

(6) And he shall bring his trespass offering ... a lamb or a kid of the goats.—The first thing to be noticed is that the sacrifice is here called "trespass offering." In the verse before us, and in the rest of this section, viz., verses 7-13, which treat of this sacrifice, no distinction is made between the ranks of the offenders. There is no special legislation for the high priest, the whole congregation, or the prince, as in the case with the sin offering, which is described in the former chapter. The spiritual officer and temporal sovereign are here on a level with the ordinary layman. There is no scale in the sacrifices corresponding to the position of the sinner. They are all alike to bring the same victim. It is implied that, apart from the minor deviations here specified, the sacrificial rites were to be the same as those in connection with the sin offering.

(7) And if he be not able to bring.—The only exception to this general rule was poverty. The poor man who was unable to bring a sheep or she-goat, might bring two turtledoves, as these were plentiful and cheap in Palestine. (See 1:14.)

(11) But if he be not able.—The benign consideration for the poor, and the desire not to penalize them too heavily for their frailties, are here still more evinced in the statute before us. If anyone is so impoverished that the offering of two birds would press too heavily upon him, he might bring the tenth part of an ephah of fine flour, a little less than half a gallon.

(15) In the holy things of the Lord.—That is, inadvertently keeping back the things which belong to the sanctuary, and to the service of the Lord, as, for instance, the tithes, the firstfruits, or not consecrating or redeeming his first-born (Exod. 28:38; Num. 5:6-8).

A ram without blemish.—For committing any of these transgressions presumptuously, the transgressor incurred the punishment of excision (Num. 15:30; Heb. 10:28); but when they were done unawares, he was to bring a ram as a sacrifice. The sacrifice for a trespass in holy things, though ignorantly committed, was more costly than for the sin of ignorance mentioned in verse 6.

(17) And if a soul sin.—To guard the Israelites most effectually against making profane use of anything dedicated to the sanctuary and its service, it is here further enacted in verses 17-19, that a trespass offering is to be brought when a man only suspects that he had used things which belonged to the Lord, though he can no longer remember what particular holy property it was, which he used for his own purpose.

(18) And he shall bring a ram.—Under such circumstances of suspense and feelings of guilt, he is to bring the same victim as in the former instance.

With thy estimation.—That is, according to thy i.e., Moses' valuation, the ram is to be worth two shekels. (See verse 15.)

And wist it not.—As the case is a doubtful one, he is exempt from the additional fifth part which the transgressor had to pay who indisputably committed this offense in ignorance. (See verse 16.)

6

(1) And the Lord spake.—Like 5:14, which begins with the same introductory formula, this is a further communication made to the lawgiver wherein other instances are specified which require a trespass offering.

(2) And commit a trespass against the Lord.—It will be seen that the trespass against God is, strictly speaking, a violation of the rights of a neighbor's property. As fraud and plunder are most subversive of social life, a crime of this sort is described as an insult to God, who is the founder and sovereign ruler of His people.

(5) And shall add the fifth part more thereto.—It will be seen that in Exod. 22:1-9, when a person was guilty of any of the offenses here specified, the offender was condemned to make a fourfold restitution, while in the passage before us the penalty is reduced to the restitution of the principal with the addition of a fifth part. The reason for this difference is that the law in Exodus deals with a culprit who is convicted of his crime in a court of justice by means of witnesses, while the law before us deals with an offender who voluntarily confesses his offense.

(8) And the Lord spake unto Moses, saying.—Until this time the law pointed out to the people under what circumstances and how they are to bring their sacred oblations. Now directions are given to the priests how to conduct the sacrificial service of the people.

(14) And this is the law of the meat offering.—In 2:1-3, where this meat offering is spoken of, the people are told of what it is to consist, and what portion of it was the prerogative of the officiating priest. In the

section before us (6:14-18) additional directions are given to the priests about the eating of the portions which belong to them and about the treatment of the residue.

(19) And the Lord spake unto Moses.—The new law, which is here introduced with this special formula (see verse 8), gives directions about the meat offering which the high priest is to bring on his consecration to the pontifical office.

(24) And the Lord spake unto Moses.—This introduces a more expanded law than the one contained in 4:1-5, giving more precise directions to the priests about the sin offering of the laity.

(26) Shall eat it.—God gave the sin offering as food for the priests to bear the iniquity of the congregation, and to make atonement for them (10:17). It constituted a part of their livelihood (Ezek. 44:28, 29). The officiating priest to whom fell this prerogative could invite not only his family but other priests and their sons to partake of it. Covetous priests abused this gift (Hos. 4:8).

7

(1) Likewise this is the law ...—Just as 6:24-30 contains additional regulations addressed to the priest about the rites of the sin offering, so 7:1-10 gives more precise instructions about the trespass offering, supplementing 5:1-13, also designed for the guidance of the priest.

(11) And this is the law of the sacrifice of peace offerings.—Here we have more specific and fuller directions given to the priests with regard to the peace offerings, about which orders had previously been given to the people (3:1-15).

(22) And the Lord spake unto Moses.—This formula introduces a fresh and supplementary communication made to the lawgiver, containing explanations and restrictions of the precept laid down in 3:17 about the fat and blood of animals.

(28) And the Lord spake unto Moses.—With this formula, additional precepts are introduced, regulating God's portion of the peace offering.

(37) This is the law ...—This and the following verse sum up the whole sacrificial law contained in chaps. 1-8.

8

(1) And the Lord spake unto Moses.—As

the consecration of Aaron and his sons to the priesthood was to be accompanied by different kinds of sacrifices, it was first of all necessary to define the ritual of each sacrifice (chaps. 1-7). The lawgiver now proceeds to record the communication which he received from the Lord respecting the appointment to the sacerdotal office, thus resuming the narrative which was broken off at the end of Exodus.

(5) This is the thing which the Lord commanded.—That is, these are the instructions which are given in Exod. 29:1-37, and which Moses now published to the assembled representatives of the people.

(10) And Moses took the anointing oil.—Having invested the high priest with the visible emblems of his office and holiness, Moses now acts in accordance with the directions given in Exod. 30:26-30; 40:9-11.

(12) And he poured of the anointing oil upon Aaron's head.—This profuse pouring of oil (see Exod. 29:7; Ps. 133:2) was repeated at the consecration of every successor to the high priesthood, while the common priests were simply marked with the finger on their forehead on their first installation. Tradition informs us that during the second Temple, the person who anointed the high priest first threw oil upon his head, and then drew with his finger the sign of the letter **Caph**, being the initial of **Cohen**, i.e., priest, between the eyebrows of the newly-consecrated pontiff.

(14) And he brought the bullock for the sin offering.—Though duly consecrated, Aaron and his sons had first to be purged of their sins before they could begin their priestly functions in the sanctuary. Hence, Moses, as the mediator of the covenant delegated by God to perform the act of consecration, also performed the sacrificial rites, while the installed priests stood as penitent sinners by the side of the sin offering which was now offered for the first time. For the laying on of the hands by the offerer on the victim, see 1:4.

9

(1) Moses called Aaron and his sons, and the elders.—That is, the same elders, the representative of the people, who were called to attest the imposing ceremony of consecration (See 8:3), are now also summoned to witness how the newly-installed priests entered upon the active duties of their ministrations. Like newly-born children

who remain seven days in a state of uncleanness and enter into the covenant privileges of the congregation on the eighth day, so the newly-created priests after a purging of seven days began their sacred duties and partook of their privileges on this symbolical day.

(2) A young calf for a sin offering.—Before they could mediate for the forgiveness of the people, Aaron and his sons had first to bring a sin offering for themselves, in expiation probably for the feeling of pride which they might have fostered at having been so highly distinguished and chosen to be the mediators of the people. This sin offering, however, showed him that, though a high priest, he was beset with the same infirmities, and stood in need of the same atonement, as the people whom he represented. As this is the only instance in which a calf is appointed for a sin offering, and as the offerer who is ordered to bring this exceptional sacrifice is Aaron, Jewish tradition will have it that it was designed to refer to the sin of the golden calf which he made for the people. (Exod. 32:4-6.) This sense seems to derive support from verse 7.

(7) And Moses said unto Aaron.—Though he was now the duly-installed high priest, yet he did not approach the altar till he was solemnly called upon by Moses to do it, thereby showing the authorized representatives of the people that Aaron did not take this honor to himself, but that it was the call of God by Moses. Hence, the remark of the apostle in Heb. 5:4, 5.

(15) And he brought the people's offering.—Being reconciled to God by the atoning sacrifice which he offered for his own share in the sin, Aaron was now qualified to offer the sin offering of the people.

(22) And Aaron lifted up his hand.—Having now completed the rites of the various sacrifices, and while still standing on the elevation leading to the altar, Aaron with uplifted hands solemnly pronounces upon the assembled people the priestly benediction prescribed in Num. 6:24-26. As the Lord separated the tribe of Levi to bless the people in His name (Deut. 10:8; 21:5), the descendants of Aaron to this day pronounce this benediction upon the congregation in the synagogue at certain periods of the year.

(24) And there came a fire.—In this manner God afterward testified His acceptance of the sacrifice of Gideon (Judges 6:20, 21); of Elijah (I Kings 18:38); and the sacrifices

139

of Solomon at the dedication of the Temple (II Chron. 7:1, 2).

10

(1) And Nadab and Abihu.—Immediately after the divine manifestation of God's acceptance of the services connected with the institution of the priesthood, and while the congregation is still giving utterance to their profound expressions of thankfulness and joy, the assembled people see a most daring act of sacrilege committed by two of the five newly-installed priests, and have to witness the most awful punishment which befalls the offenders. The offenders are the two eldest sons of Aaron, who had received the high distinction to be invited to accompany their father and Moses to the summit of the hallowed mount (Exod. 24:1); the lesson to the Israelites was that the priests, though mediators between God and the people, are beset with the same infirmities as the laity, and must not presume upon their office.

Took either of them his censer.—The sin of Nadab and Abihu was of a complicated nature, and involved and consisted of several transgressions:—(1) They each took **his** own censer, and not the sacred utensil of the sanctuary. (2) They both offered it together, whereas the incense was only to be offered by one. (3) They presumptuously encroached upon the functions of the high priest; for according to the Law the high priest alone burned incense **in a censer.** (4) They offered the incense at an unauthorized time, since it was apart from the morning and evening sacrifice.

And offered strange fire.—They filled their vessels with common fire instead of taking it from the holy fire of the altar, which was always to be used in burning incense. (See 9:24; 16:12.) Ancient tradition says that Nadab and Abihu had partaken too freely of the drink offering, and performed their service in a state of intoxication, when they were incapacitated to distinguish between what was legal and illegal. Others, however, suppose that the phrase "strange fire" denotes not offered according to the prescribed Law, just as "strange incense" is used in the sense of incense not prepared in the manner ordered by the Law (Exod. 30:9).

(2) And there went out fire from the Lord.—By fire they sinned, and by fire they died. The divine fire which issued forth to consume the sacrifices as a token of accep-

tance, now descended as the avenger of sin to consume the sacrificers, just as the same Gospel is to one a savour of life unto life, and to another a savour of death unto death. (See II Cor. 2:16.)

And devoured them.—That is, slay them, since we are told in verse 5 that not only were their bodies in a perfect state of preservation, but even their garments were not burned. The word "consume," however, is used here, to keep up the connection between this verse and 9:24.

(8) And the Lord spake unto Aaron.—As half of the staff of the priesthood had thus been struck down, and the other half were not allowed to mourn over the departed (verse 6), the chief of the survivors might have thought that God was altogether displeased with the newly-created pontificate. To comfort him, therefore, as well as to restore the prestige of this sacred office in the eyes of the spiritual functionaries, the Lord, who previously made all such communications to Moses, now honors Aaron with speaking to him immediately.

(9) Do not drink wine.—As the command that the priests are to abstain from any intoxicating liquors when performing their sacred functions follows so closely upon the death of Nadab and Abihu, the opinion existed as early at least as the time of Christ that there is a connection between the specific sin and the general law, that the two sons of Aaron drank wine to excess when they offered strange fire, and that the present prohibition is based upon that circumstance. See the apostle's injunctions, accordingly, in I Tim. 3:2, 3.

(10) And that ye may put difference.—The motive here assigned for their abstinence from intoxicating liquor is, that by keeping sober they might be able to discriminate between the legal and illegal points in the prescribed observances which required the greatest care. (See Ezek. 44:23.)

(11) And that ye may teach.—The priests were not only to keep sober to be able to decide the questions of ritual, but they were to teach the people, since the ceremonial law affected domestic life and social intercourse (Deut. 33:10; Mal. 2:7). For a prophet's charging them with neglect, see Ezek. 22:26.

(16) And Moses diligently sought the goat.—That is, the flesh of the goat of the sin offering which was offered by the nation on the eighth day. (See 9:15.)

And, behold, it was burnt.—Being overwhelmed with grief at the loss of their brothers, Eleazar and Ithamar could not eat, and as none but priests were allowed to partake of the flesh of the sin offering, they burned it on the altar, to prevent its corruption. They did this all the more readily since the flesh of Aaron's sin offering was just before this burned without the camp. (See 9:11.)

(19) And Aaron said.—Though, according to verse 16, Moses only blamed Eleazar and Ithamar for this transgression of the law, yet there can hardly be any doubt that Aaron was included in this censure, and that the lawgiver abstained from expressing his anger against the pontiff because of the supreme dignity of his office, which he would not lower in the sight of the people. Aaron, however, was fully sensible of this, and replies to the charge brought against his sons.

While he, Eleazar, and Ithamar were duly performing the sacrificial rites, Nadab and Abihu, his other two sons, transgressed, and were suddenly struck down dead, thus overwhelming the survivors with sorrow, and rendering them unfit to partake of the sacrifices. Aaron submits that, unfitted as they thus were by mourning and the sense of their own sinfulness, if they had partaken of this solemn meal it would not have been acceptable to the Lord.

(20) And ... he was content.—Moses acknowledged Aaron's plea to be just, and that he had himself spoken hastily. This is a remarkable instance of Moses' humility, and of the human side of his nature as a lawgiver. (See also Num. 32:6; etc.) Therefore Jewish tradition from time immemorial ascribes the mistake to Moses, and not to Aaron.

11

(1) And the Lord spake unto Moses and to Aaron.—Lest the rebuke which Moses publicly administered to the priests (see 10:16) should diminish their influence with the people to whom they had to teach the laws of clean and unclean things laid down in the following chapters, the Lord here honors Aaron as well as Moses, by making this communication to them conjointly.

(2) These are the beasts ... —The dietary laws, which stand first in the general precepts about clean and unclean things, are given in accordance with the Hebrew division of the animal kingdom into four principal classes:—(1) the land animals (verses 3-8), (2) the water animals (verses 9-12), (3) the birds of the air (verses 13-19), and (4) the swarming animals (verses 20-23). Note the parallel regulations in Deut. 14:4, 5.

(29) These also shall be unclean.—As verses 24-28 have been occupied with the discussion of the defilement caused by the carcasses of unclean quadrupeds, which belong to the first class of the animal kingdom, the Lawgiver now enumerates those "creeping things" of the fourth class, which likewise cause defilement by touching them. Verses 29ff. are a resumption of verse 20.

(43) Ye shall not make your selves abominable.—Not only is it disgusting to eat these abominable creatures, but their carcasses defile and debar him who comes in contact with them from entering into the sanctuary and from partaking of the sacrificial meal.

(44) For I am the Lord your God.—As the Lord who is their God is Himself holy, His people, in order to enjoy perfect communion with Him, must also be holy. Hence they must abstain from all these objects of defilement which mar that holy communion. Cf. I Peter 1:15, 16.

(46) This is the law of the beasts.—This is a recapitulation of the different classes of animals proscribed in the dietary laws. In this summary they are not enumerated in the same order in which they are discussed. The same is the case in the summary of the sacrificial law. (See 7:37, 38.)

12

(1) And the Lord spake unto Moses.—The laws of defilement contracted from without by eating or coming in contact with unclean objects are naturally followed by precepts about defilement arising from within the human body itself.

(2) If a woman have conceived seed.—This general statement is afterward specified by the phrases "and born a man child," and "bear a maid child," here and in verse 5. Thus the regulations about impurity naturally begin with the beginning of life.

(6) And when the days ... —Having described in the previous verses the conditions of defilement arising from childbirth, the legislator now prescribes the offerings to be brought for the purification of the woman.

(8) And if she be not able.—As a merciful provision for those who were too poor to bring a lamb, the law permits them to bring a turtledove or a pigeon for a burnt offering, provided only it is the same kind of bird as the one brought for a sin offering. (See 1:14.) It was therefore the poor woman's sacrifice which the mother of our Lord offered, when, in accordance with this commutation, she offered a pair of turtledoves or two young pigeons, on presenting herself for purification at the Temple with the child Jesus, on the expiration of the prescribed term of uncleanness (Luke 2:24), and the priest, after sprinkling her with the blood of the humble sacrifice, declared her cleansed.

13

(1) And the Lord spake unto Moses and Aaron.—As laws of leprosy chiefly concerned the priests who had to examine the symptoms and to decide whether they indicated the distemper or not, the Lord addressed the regulations to Aaron as well as to Moses. The leprosy discussed in this and the following chapters consists of three general classes: viz., (1) leprosy of man (13:2-46); (2) leprosy of garments (13:47-59); and (3) leprosy of houses (14:33-57).

In discussing the leprosy of man, the lawgiver enumerates six different circumstances under which it may develop itself. These are, consecutively, verses 2-8, 9-17, 18-26, 29-37, 38, 39, and 40-44.

(45) His clothes shall be rent.—As leprosy was regarded as a visitation from God for sin committed by the person thus afflicted, the patient is to rend his garments like one mourning for the dead. (See 21:10.)

And he shall put a covering upon his upper lip.—To veil the beard, which was the pride of the Oriental, was also a sign of mourning. (Comp. Ezek. 24:17, 22; Micah 3:7.)

And shall cry, Unclean.—As leprosy was most defiling, and as the very entrance of a leper into a house rendered everything in it unclean, the person thus afflicted had to warn off the passers by, lest they should approach him, and by contact with him become defiled. In some instances this was done by a herald, who preceded the leper.

(46) He shall dwell alone.—In consequence of his extreme defilement, the leper had to live in seclusion outside the camp or city (Num. 5:1-4; 12:10-15; II Kings 7:3; etc.). He forfeited both the right of inher-

itance and of disposing of his property, for he was considered a dead man. Leprosy was regarded as an awful punishment from the Lord (II Kings 5:7; II Chron. 26:20), which they invoked upon all their mortal enemies (II Sam. 3:29; II Kings 5:27).

(47) The garment also that.—The same phrase, "plague of leprosy," is used both in the case of garments and of human beings, and the symptoms and working of leprous garments and those of leprous men are identical. Neither the regulations here laid down, nor the further development of them regard leprosy as contagious. This is evident from the fact that the priest was in constant and close contact with the leper, and that the leper who was **entirely** covered was pronounced clean, and could mix with the community (see verses 12, 13.)

14

(2) This shall be the law of the leper.—That is, the manner in which an Israelite cured of his leprosy shall be purified and restored to the communion of the sanctuary on the day when he is pronounced clean.

He shall be brought unto the priest.—He is to be conducted from his place of seclusion (see 13:46) to an appointed place on the borders of the camp. It was this coming to the priest to which Christ referred when He said to the leper whom He had healed, "Go . . . show thyself to the priest, and offer the gift that Moses commanded" (Matt. 8:4).

(24-29) And the priest shall take the lamb.—The ritual for the poor man's sacrifices, however, is the same as that which is prescribed for the rich man. The solemnity and imposing nature of the service is not diminished, as both rich and poor are alike in the presence of the Lord. Hence the directions in verses 24-29 in connection with the humbler sacrifices are simply a repetition of those ordained in verses 12-18, to be observed in the case of the more costly offerings.

(33) And the Lord spake unto Moses and unto Aaron.—While the law about the cleansing of restored lepers was addressed to Moses alone (see verse 1), the regulations about leprous houses, like those with regard to leprous garments and persons, are for the same reason delivered to Moses and Aaron conjointly. (See 13:1.)

(34) When ye be come into the land of

Canaan.—We have here the first of four instances in Leviticus of a law being given prospectively, having no immediate bearing on the condition of the people of Israel (see 19:23; 23:10; 25:2). This may be the reason why it is separated from the law of leprous men and garments, which we should naturally expect it would follow, instead of being preceded by the law of cleansing, and why it occupies the position of an appendix.

(49-53) And he shall take to cleanse the house.—The same rites are prescribed for cleansing the house which were performed in cleansing the healed leper (see verses 3-7), with the exception of the sacrifices which the man brought afterward, and which were necessarily absent in the case of the restored leprous house.

15

(1) And the Lord spake unto Moses and to Aaron.—This chapter, which lays down the laws of uncleanness arising from issues, discusses two diseased (verses 2-15 and 25-30), and three natural secretions (verses 16-18 and 19-24).

16

(1) And the Lord spake unto Moses.—As the observance of the minute regulations given in the preceding chapters about the daily sacrifices and purifications would necessarily be tainted with many imperfections and shortcomings, both on the part of the mediating priests and the offering laity, a general Day of Atonement enacted in this chapter is therefore an appropriate conclusion of the laws of purification in the preceding chapters. It is an annual supplement and completion of all the ordinances which were daily practiced, and the design of which was to obtain atonement and reconciliation.

(2) That he come not at all times.—Moses is to warn his brother Aaron, the high priest, that if he wishes to escape a fate similar to that of his two sons, he is not to presume to enter the Holy of Holies except on one day of the year, the Day of Atonement.

Into the holy place.—This is here more minutely defined by "within the veil," thus showing that the Holy of Holies is meant. In the succeeding portions of this chapter,

however, the expression "holy" is used for "Holy of Holies" without this adjunct. (See verses 3, 16, 17, 20, 27.)

For I will appear in the cloud.—That is, because the Lord appeared over the mercy seat and between the cherubim in the bright luminous cloud which constituted the symbol of His divine presence (see Exod. 25:22), therefore even the high priest must not approach it except on the occasion here prescribed.

(3) With a young bullock for a sin offering—which had to be of the second year (see Exod. 29:1), and which the high priest had to buy with his own money. It was to be his own property because the victim was to expiate his own sins, since he, like the meanest sinner, required divine mercy and forgiveness, though, owing to his high office, he had to bring a more costly sacrifice.

(5) Two kids of the goats.—(See 4:23.) These two goats, which were the sin offering for the people, and the ram, which was their burnt offering, were purchased with the money of the public some time before the Day of Atonement.

(8) And Aaron shall cast lots.—The lots consisted of two small tablets which at an earlier time were of box or ebony wood, but which during the later part of the second Temple were made of gold, and were kept in a wooden chest. On the one was engraved the words "For Jehovah," and on the other "For Azazel," the expression in the original which is translated "scapegoat" in the King James Version. The high priest, after shaking the chest, put both his hands into the urn and simultaneously took out the two tablets, one in each hand. Hereupon he put the tablet which he had in his right hand upon the goat that was standing on his right side, while the tablet in his left hand he put on the goat on his left side. If the tablet with the inscription "For Jehovah" was in his right hand the chief priest who stood at the right of the pontiff exclaimed "Hold up thy right hand on high!" and if it happened to be in the left hand, the chief of the principal household, who stood on his left, called out to him "Hold up thy left hand." Hereupon the high priest laid the two lots on the two goats, the one in the right hand on the goat at his right, and the one in the left hand on the animal at his left, exclaiming at the same time, "To the Lord a sin offering!"

And the other lot for the scapegoat.—The word Azazel, which only occurs in this chapter, probably denotes the utterly banished demon, the prince of the evil spirits, who with his legions occupies the desert regions and desolated places. (Comp. Isa. 13:21; 34:14; Matt. 12:43; Luke 11:24; Rev. 18:2.) As the removal or pardon of sin is often represented in the Bible by its being banished into the uttermost parts of the earth and seas (Micah 7:19; Ps. 103:12), nothing could be more striking or convey to the people the idea of absolute forgiveness better than this symbolical act of sending the goat laden with the sins of the congregation to the wilderness, the abode of the prince of darkness, back to the author of all sin.

(20) And when he hath made an end. — Having finished the expiation for himself, his fellow priests, and the sanctuary with its utensils, the goat destined by lot for Azazel, which was standing in the court before the Lord, was now brought to the high priest, that he might complete the sin offering for the Israelites.

(21) Putting them upon the head of the goat.—By this imposition of hands, and the confession, the high priest transferred the sins of the nation to the goat. He then turned to the people, and declared, "Ye shall be clean."

(29) And this shall be a statute for ever.— Literally, "a statute of eternity," that is, an everlasting ordinance. That which is contained in verses 29, 30 is binding upon the Israelites as long as they exist, and is to be observed by them annually.

In the seventh month, on the tenth day.— This month, which is called **Tishri**, corresponds to September, and is the month of great festivals. On the first is the Feast of Trumpets (see 23:24), on the tenth the Day of Atonement, and on the fourteenth begins the Feast of Tabernacles which lasts eight days.

17

(1) And the Lord spake unto Moses.— The Day of Atonement was instituted to purge, in a special manner, the whole community from all their sins, and present them a holy nation before the Lord once a year. It is now followed by regulations concerning everyday life, the observance of which is to foster the holiness secured on that particular day. This chapter concerns offering the blood of slain beasts (verses 3-7), bringing sacrifices to the appointed sanctuary (verses 8, 9), and abstaining from all eating of blood (verses 10-16).

18

(1) And the Lord spake unto Moses.— Unlike the preceding divine communications, which treated of the ritual and ceremonial pollutions, the enactments which Moses is here commanded to communicate to the children of Israel affect their moral life—precepts which form the basis of domestic purity, and which are the foundation of human happiness. Here are treated incestuous marriages (verses 6-18), unlawful lusts (verses 19, 20, 22, 23), and child sacrifice (verse 21).

(2) I am the Lord your God.—The Lord is their recognized and sole sovereign; the children of Israel are therefore bound to obey His precepts, and not be led astray by the customs or statutes which prevailed among the people whose country they are to possess. Moreover, as He is holy, the Israelites, by faithfully obeying His sacred laws, will attain to that holiness which will bring them in communion with Him in whose image they were created. This phrase, which is so emphatically repeated twice more in this chapter (verses 4, 30), has been used only once before in this book. (See 11:44.)

(24) Defile not ye yourselves.—The lawgiver who solemnly introduced these precepts by five verses of preamble at the beginning of the chapter (verses 1-5), now concludes by an equally solemn appeal to God's people sacredly to observe them in all their integrity, since the violation of them (verses 6-23) has branded those nations with infamy, and brought about their national destruction, and expulsion from the very land which is now to be given to the Israelites.

19

(1) And the Lord spake unto Moses.— The prohibitions in the preceding chapter, which are designed to regulate the moral conduct of relations and connections toward each other in their family circles, are now followed by precepts which affect the Israelite's life in all its bearings, both toward God and man. The precepts in this chapter are divided into sixteen groups, eight of which end with the emphatic reiteration, "I am the Lord your God" (verses 2-4, 10, 25, 31, 34, 36), and eight with the shorter formula, "I am the Lord" (verses 12, 14, 16, 18, 28, 30, 32, 37).

(2) Speak unto all the congregation of the

children of Israel.—The importance which the Lawgiver Himself attaches to this epitome of the whole Law, as this section is called, may be seen from the fact that God commands Moses to address these precepts "to all **the congregation** of the children of Israel"—a phrase which occurs nowhere else in Leviticus in this formula, and which is only to be found once more in the whole Pentateuch (Exod. 12:3), at the institution of the Passover, the great national festival which commemorates the redemption of the Israelites from Egypt.

(23) And when ye shall come.—This is the second of the four instances in Leviticus of a law being given prospectively having no immediate bearing on the condition of the people of Israel (viz., 14:34; 19:23; 23:10; 25:2).

20

(1) And the Lord spake unto Moses.—It is difficult to account for the position of this chapter. If chap. 20 contains the penalties attached to the sins enumerated in chap. 18, we should expect it immediately to follow that chapter. It may, however, be that before enacting these severe punishments, the Lawgiver wanted to appeal to the high calling of the nation, to qualify them by the sublime precepts laid down in chap. 19 for obedience to the laws in chap. 18, and that in the chapter before us the civil punishments are set forth as an alternative for those who will not be guided by the spiritual sentiments enunciated in chap. 19.

(7) Sanctify yourselves therefore, and be ye holy.—It is only by keeping the divine ordinances that the Israelites will attain to that state of holiness which will not only arm them to resist the abominable rites and idolatrous practices denounced in the foregoing verses, but which will enable them to reflect the holiness of their Lord.

(22) Ye shall therefore keep all my statutes.—Like the prohibitions (see 18:26-30), the penalties here enacted for transgressing them conclude with an appeal to the Israelites to keep the divine precepts, and not to be guilty of the crimes for which the former inhabitants of the land have been cast out.

(26) And have severed you from other people.—God has separated them from the rest of the nations to be His holy people, and to be an example to them. The Mosaic doctrine of the separation of Israel, so far

from tending to produce and harbor in the Jews contracted views of God's mercy, and a contempt for all other nations, has taught them to look upon themselves as simply having gone first to the mountain of the Lord, and that all other nations are to follow, and to become with them children of God.

21

(1) And the Lord said unto Moses.—The laws about the purity and holiness of the Jewish community, and of every individual lay member, enacted in 11:1-20:27, are now followed by statutes respecting the purity and holiness of the priesthood who minister in holy things in behalf of the people, and who, by virtue of their high office, were to be models of both ceremonial and moral purity.

(16) And the Lord spake unto Moses.—In the preceding part of this chapter the priests were warned against coming into contact with the dead, and forbidden voluntarily to disfigure themselves or to disqualify themselves and their descendants for their sacred office by illegal alliances. The legislator, therefore, now passes on to other blemishes, which, though not voluntarily contracted, likewise disqualify the priests for performing sacerdotal duties in the sanctuary.

22

(1) And the Lord spake unto Moses.—In this chapter the laws regulating the conduct of the priests in their holy ministrations are continued. As the last chapter concluded with the permission to disqualified priests to eat of the sacrifices, this chapter opens with conditions under which even the legally qualified priests must not partake of the offerings.

(3) That soul shall be cut off from my presence.—This phrase, with the expression "from my presence," does not occur again in the Pentateuch when the Lord threatens with the penalty of excision. In Leviticus, where, besides the passage before us, the penalty is enacted six times, the formula is always, "the soul shall be cut off from his people" (7:20, 21, 25, 27; 19:8; 23:29). Its exceptional form here may therefore have reference to the peculiar circumstances. If the priest ventures to approach the altar presumptuously to partake in a defiled state of the holy sacrifices, God Himself will banish him from His presence as He did Nadab and Abihu.

(17) And the Lord spake unto Moses.— The laws about the physical features and ceremonial purity of the priests, who are to be devoted to the services of the altar, are now followed by kindred precepts about the animals which are to be offered upon the altar.

(33) That brought you out.—By this signal act of redemption from bondage, and by choosing them as His peculiar people, God has a special claim upon His redeemed people that they should keep His commandments. (See 11:45.)

23

(1) And the Lord spake unto Moses.— The regulations about the holiness of the sanctuary and the sacrifices, the holiness of the priests and the people, are now followed by statutes about holy seasons.

(3) Six days shall work be done.— Recurring every week, and being the most important as well as the oldest of all festivals, the sabbath introduces the holy seasons.

(4) These are the feasts of the Lord.—The following are the festivals proper as distinguished from the sabbath: (1) Passover (verses 4-14); (2) Pentecost (verses 15-22); (3) New Year (verses 23-25); (4) Day of Atonement (verses 26-32); (5) Tabernacles (verses 33-36a); and (6) the concluding festival (verse 36b). See Exod. 23; Lev. 16.

(10) When ye be come into the land.— This is the third of the four instances in Leviticus where a law is given prospectively, having no immediate bearing on the condition of the people of Israel. (See 19:23.)

(37) To offer an offering.—On these festivals sacrifices are to be offered as prescribed in Num. 28 and 29.

(38) Beside the sabbaths.—The sacrifices ordered for each of these festivals are to be in addition to the sacrifices appointed to each weekly sabbath in the year; so that when one of these festivals falls on a sabbath, the sacrifices due to the latter are not set aside by the former. Both must be offered in their proper order.

Beside your gifts.—Nor are they to interfere with the voluntary offerings which each individual brought privately (Deut. 16:10,

17), or with the performance of vows (Deut. 12:6-12).

(39) Also in the fifteenth day.—After the list of festivals discussed in this chapter has been summed up in verses 37 and 38, the next five verses return to the Feast of Tabernacles. The regulations are supplementary to those given before, and embody a separate enactment.

24

(1) And the Lord spake unto Moses.— The regulations about the annual festivals and the ritual connected with them are now followed by directions with regard to the daily service and its ritual.

(5) And bake twelve cakes.—This order is about the preparation of the showbread, and the use to be made of it.

(10) The son of an Israelitish woman, whose father was an Egyptian.—This incident, which is so difficult to connect satisfactorily with the preceding legislation, brings before us a picture of the camp life of the Israelites in the wilderness. According to tradition, the father of this blasphemer was the taskmaster under whom Shelomith's husband worked in Egypt, that he had injured Shelomith and then smote her husband, that this was the Egyptian whom Moses slew (Exod. 2:12) for the injuries he had thus inflicted both upon the Hebrew and his wife, and that the culprit before us is the son of the outraged Shelomith by the slain Egyptian.

This son of the Israelitish woman and a man of Israel strove together.—This semi-Egyptian contended with this Danite that he had a right from the side of his mother to encamp among the children of Dan, while the Danite disputed this, maintaining that a son could only pitch his tent by the standard of his father's name (Num. 2:2).

(11) Blasphemed the name of the Lord, and cursed.—Being vexed with the divine enactments which excluded him from encamping in the tribe of his mother, he both cursed God who gave such law, and reviled the judges who pronounced judgment against him. The expression, "the Name," which later was commonly used instead of the ineffable Jehovah (see also verse 16), has been substituted here for the Tetragrammaton by a transcriber who out of reverence would not combine cursing with it. The same shyness on the part of copyists has been the cause of inserting the word Lord (**Adonai**) and God (**Elohim**) for Jehovah in various passages of the Old Testament. During the second Temple, however, this passage was rendered, "he pronounced the Name and cursed." Hence it was enacted that the simple pronunciation of the Tetragrammaton was criminal.

(15) Whosoever curseth his God.—As Moses had to appeal to God for direction, the Lord has not only declared what should be done with this particular offender, but lays down a general law for the punishment of blasphemers.

(17) And he that killeth a man.—The enactment that in case of blaspheming no difference is to be made between a non-Israelite and Israelite, is now followed by other laws respecting murder and personal injury which have been given before (Exod. 21:12, etc.), but which are here repeated in order to show that, like blasphemy, they apply alike to Gentile and Jew. It may also be that the repetition here of the law of murder is designed to draw a distinction between the judicial sentence of death carried out by the community, and the illegal taking away of life by individuals.

25

(1) And the Lord spake unto Moses.—This chapter should properly have followed chap. 23, since the institutions of the sabbatical year, and the jubilee which it discusses, are closely connected with the regulations about the festivals laid down in that chapter. The isolation of these ordinances from the rest of the festivals cannot be satisfactorily explained on any other principle than that which the authorities during the second Temple laid down, viz., that many of the sections are transposed, and that "there is no strict sequence in the Law."

(2) When ye come into the land.—This is the fourth instance in Leviticus of a law being given prospectively which had not immediate bearing on the condition of Israel. (See 14:34; 19:23; 23:10.)

Then shall the land keep a sabbath.—The septennial sabbath is to be to the land what the weekly sabbath is to the whole earth. Just as the seventh day is dedicated to God in recognition of His being the Creator of the world, so the seventh year is to be consecrated to Him in acknowledgment that He is the owner of the land. Therefore, like the weekly sabbath (Exod. 20:10; Lev. 23:3;

Deut. 5:14), the seventh year sabbath is belonging "unto the Lord." (See verse 4.)

(4) The seventh year shall be a sabbath of rest.—Like the weekly sabbath, the seventh year is to be the Lord's sabbath. The soil is therefore to have a perfect rest.

(8) Number seven sabbaths of years.—The seven days of each week stand for so many years, so that seven weeks of years make forty-nine years. Hence the explanation in the next clause: "Seven times seven years." The observance of the jubilee, like that of the sabbatical year, was only to become obligatory when the Israelites had taken possession of the promised land (see verse 2).

(9) In the day of atonement shall ye make the trumpet sound.—On the close of the great Day of Atonement, when the Hebrews realized that they had peace of mind, that their heavenly Father had annulled their sins, and that they had become reunited to Him through His forgiving mercy, every Israelite was called upon to proclaim throughout the land, by nine blasts of the cornet, that he too had given the soil rest, that he had freed every encumbered family estate, and that he had given liberty to every slave, who was now to rejoin his kindred. Inasmuch as God has forgiven his debts, he also is to forgive his debtors.

(10) It shall be a jubilee.—This is an abbreviation of the fuller form, "a year of jubilee," used in the other passages of this chapter (see verses 13, 28, 40, 50, 52, 54), and denotes "a year proclaimed by the blast of the horn," since the word **yôbel** signifies both ram's horn and the sound emitted from it.

(21) It shall bring forth fruit for three years.—This special blessing will be manifested in the abundant crop of the harvest preceding the sabbatical year. Just as at the institution of the weekly Sabbath, when God required abstention from labor, He sent down a double portion of manna every sixth day to make up for the day of rest (Exod. 16:22-27), so He will exercise a special providence every sixth year by blessing the soil with a treble crop to compensate for giving the land a septennial sabbath.

(23) The land shall not be sold for ever.—That is, no plot of the land of Israel must be absolutely alienated from the original proprietor, who has been driven by poverty to sell his patrimony.

For the land is mine.—The reason for his prohibition absolutely to cut off the patri-

147

mony from the family, is that God claims to be the supreme owner of the land (Exod. 15:17; Isa. 14:2, 25; Jer. 2:7; Ps. 10:16), and as the Lord of the soil He prescribes conditions on which he allotted it to the different tribes of Israel.

(24) Ye shall grant a redemption for the land.—The land is not even to remain with the purchaser in the year of jubilee, but the buyer is to grant every opportunity to the seller to redeem it before that time.

(25) And if any of his kin come to redeem it, then shall he redeem.—If he has thus been compelled by pressure of poverty to sell part of his land, then it is the duty of the nearest relative to redeem the property which his impoverished relative has been obliged to sell. The expression "redeemer" is applied in Hebrew to one who, by virtue of being the nearest of kin, had not only to redeem the patrimony of the family, but to marry the childless widow of his brother (Ruth 3:13), and avenge the blood of his relative (Num. 35:19-28; Deut. 19:6-12).

(28) Then that which is sold.—In the case that the vendor is unable to return to the purchaser the probable value of the crops between the contemplated redemption and the jubilee year, the land thus sold is to continue with the purchaser until jubilee, when it is to revert to the vendor without any repayment whatever. The design of this law was to secure to each family a permanent interest in the soil, and to prevent the accumulation of land on the part of the greedy few who are ever anxious to join field to field, thus precluding the existence of landless beggars and too extensive landed proprietors.

(29) A dwelling house in a walled city.—It is, however, quite different in the case of houses in walled cities. These are not the creation of God (see verse 30).

(32) Notwithstanding the cities of the Levites, and the houses.—The houses which belong to the Levites, in the forty-eight cities given to them (see Num. 35:1-8; Josh. 21:1-3); are to be exempt from this general law of house property.

May the Levites redeem at any time.—Having the same value to the Levites as landed property has to the other tribes, and being all that they possessed, these houses are to be subject to the jubilee laws for fields, and hence may be redeemed at any time.

(35) And if thy brother be waxen poor.—This part of the jubilee laws which relates to the manumission of the Israelites who

through poverty are compelled to sell themselves as bondsmen (verses 39-55) is introduced by a pathetic appeal to the benevolence of the people to bestow brotherly help to the poor (verses 35-38).

(42) For they are my servants.—This is a clue to the whole system of Hebrew servitude. These poverty-stricken men, who are driven to sell themselves to their fellow Israelites, God claims as His servants. God is their Lord as well as their master's Lord. He delivered them both alike from bondage to serve Him. There is, therefore, no difference between bond and free.

(48) He may be redeemed again.—The law which applies to a heathen who sold himself to a Hebrew is reversed in this case. While the heathen cannot be redeemed, and is to remain a bondman for ever, the Israelite who sells himself to a heathen may be redeemed.

26

(1) Ye shall make you no idols.—The first two verses of this chapter are still a part of the previous section in the Hebrew original. By separating them from their proper position, and making them begin a new chapter, both the logical sequence and the import of these two verses are greatly obscured. As verses 47-55 legislated for cases where Israelites are driven by extreme poverty to sell themselves to a heathen, and when they may be compelled to continue in this service to the year of jubilee, and thus be obliged to witness idolatrous practices, the Lawgiver solemnly repeats the two fundamental precepts of Judaism, which they might be in danger of neglecting, viz., to abstain from idol worship and to keep the Sabbath, which are two essential commandments of the Decalogue. The same two commandments, but in reverse order, are also joined together in 19:3, 4.

(3) If ye walk in my statutes.—Having set forth the ceremonial and moral injunctions which are necessary for the development and maintenance of holiness and purity in the commonwealth, the legislator now concludes by showing the happiness which will accrue to the Israelites from a faithful observance of these laws, and the punishments which await them if they transgress these divine ordinances.

(13) I have broken the bands of your yoke.—The promises thus made to the Israelites of the extraordinary fertility of their land, of peace within and immunity from war without, and of the divine presence constantly sojourning among them, if they will faithfully obey the commandments of the Lord, now conclude with the oft-repeated solemn appeal to the obligation they are under to the God who had so marvelously delivered them from cruel bondage and made them His servants.

(14) But if ye will not hearken unto me.—The glowing promises of blessings for obedience are now followed by a catalog of calamities of the most appalling nature, which will overtake the Israelites if they disobey the divine commandments. There are five degrees of punishment: verses 14-17, 18-20, 21, 22, 23-26, 27-33.

(44) And yet for all that.—Even if it be so that they remain exiles in foreign lands for a long time, this is no proof that God has finally cast them off, has given them over to destruction, and abrogated His covenant with them. He is always their God, and will keep His covenant for ever.

27

(1) And the Lord spake unto Moses.—As various allusions are made throughout this book to vows, thus legally acknowledging the existence of the ancient practice of votive offerings (7:16; 22:18, 21, 23; 23:38), the Levitical code, which is pre-eminently designed to uphold the holiness of the sanctuary and its sacrifices, as well as the holiness of the priests and the people, would be incomplete without defining the nature and obligation of these self-imposed sacrifices.

NUMBERS

1

(1) In the tabernacle of the congregation.—
The tabernacle of the congregation, or "tent
of meeting," so called because it was there
that God met with Moses (17:4; Exod.
25:22), had been set up one month previously (Exod. 40:17), nearly a year after the
Exodus.

(3) From twenty years old and upward.—
The result of the previous numbering
(Exod. 30:12; 38:26), which was made about
six months earlier, and which was probably
obtained by counting the number of half-
shekels which were paid, as Ithamar appears to have done (Exod 38:21), exactly
corresponds with the result of the present
census (verse 46). But the complete census,
or numbering and enrollment of the persons
according to tribes, families, and fathers'
houses, appears to have been deferred until
after the erection of the tabernacle, toward
the construction of which the atonement
money had been paid. If the whole was
done in obedience to the command contained in Exod. 30:12, and was regarded as
one transaction, those only would be numbered on the second occasion who had
already paid their atonement money.

(4) Every one head ... —There were
many heads of fathers' houses in each tribe;
but it appears from verse 16 (7:10, 11) that
in each case the tribal "prince" was selected
to preside over the census.

(16) Heads of thousands in Israel.—
Comp. Exod. 18:21, 25, where rulers, or
princes of thousands, are the highest class of
officers recommended by Jethro, and appointed by Moses. See also 10:4.

(18) Declared their pedigrees.—The people appear to have been enrolled by their
polls, i.e., individually, under three heads—
(1) according to the tribe to which they
belonged; (2) according to the family,
which, as it appears from 3:22, included in
some cases two or three thousand persons;
and (3) according to their father's house.
The importance of this enrollment, as affording the means of tracing the genealogy of
Christ, must not be overlooked.

**(27) Threescore and fourteen thousand
and six hundred.**—The superiority of Judah
in point of numbers over all the other tribes
deserves notice in connection with the
blessing pronounced on that tribe by Jacob
in Gen. 49:8. In like manner it should be

observed that the number of the tribe of
Ephraim (verse 33) exceeded that of the
tribe of Manasseh (verse 35). (See Gen.
48:19, 20.)

**(46) Six hundred thousand and three
thousand and five hundred and fifty.**—It is
obvious that the odd numbers were not
reckoned. In 11:21, as in Exod. 12:37, the
whole number is reckoned roughly at six
hundred thousand.

(48) For the Lord had spoken ... —It is
true that the Levites were not included in
the earlier numbering, and consequently
that they must have been exempted by divine direction. It does not appear, however,
that there is a reference to any previous
command respecting the Levites, or that the
specific destination of the Levites had been
previously declared.

(50) The tabernacle of testimony.—The
testimony (sometimes described as the two
tables of the testimony—(Exod. 31:18;
34:29), denotes in the first instance the
tables of the law which were directed to be
placed in the Ark (Exod. 25:16, 21). Hence
the Ark is described as the Ark of the
testimony (Exod. 25:22; 26:33), and the
Tabernacle as the Tabernacle of the testimony (Exod. 38:21), and the tent is called
the tent of the testimony (9:15). Also the
veil which separated the holy place from
the most holy is called the veil of the
testimony (Lev. 24:3).

2

(17) In the midst of the camp.—The area
of the camp has been computed at about
three square miles. The form of encampment was probably circular. The word **ma-
haneh** (camp) here denotes evidently the
whole of the four united camps or hosts. As
the tent of meeting was compassed about by
the four camps when stationary, so it was
placed in the center when they were in
motion, having the camps of Judah and
Reuben before it, and those of Ephraim and
Dan behind it. The placement of the tribes
was evidently determined in accordance
with their mutual relationship. Thus, the
eastern camp was composed exclusively of
the descendants of the sons of Leah; the
southern of those of the two remaining sons
of Leah (the tribe of Levi being encamped
around the Tabernacle) and a son of Zilpah,
Leah's handmaid; the western of those of
one of the sons and of the two grandsons of
Rachel; and the northern of those of the two

sons of Bilhah and of the remaining son of Zilpah. If this arrangement is examined, it will be found that, if allowance is made for the separation of the tribe of Levi, none could have been made in which the relationship by birth would be more closely adhered to. (We may learn from this arrangement that the ties of nature should strengthen those of Christian communion.) It is deserving of notice that when the lots of the several tribes were finally determined, we find that the temporary association established during their encampments in the wilderness was to a great extent preserved.

(32) These are those which were numbered.—The number of the Israelites was very large, considering in how short time and under what adverse circumstances the small company which went down into Egypt had multiplied into 600,000 men capable of bearing arms, independently of the tribe of Levi.

3

(1) These also are the generations of Aaron and Moses ... —The name of Aaron is placed first, not only because he was the elder brother, but also because the ministry of Moses was restricted to his own person, and his sons are merely classed among the rest of the Levitical families in I Chron. 23:14; whereas the office of Aaron was perpetuated in the persons of his descendants. Therefore we find no mention made in this place of the sons of Moses, but only of those of Aaron. The word "generations" here, as in the book of Genesis (e.g., 6:9; 25:19) and elsewhere, is used to denote the "history"; and in this sense the present and the following chapters pertain as much to Moses as to Aaron. Or the reference may be to the fact that Moses and Aaron were made the heads of the whole tribe of Levi, and therefore that the Levitical families generally are traced equally to both.

(9) They are wholly given unto him.—In 8:16 the Levites are represented as "wholly given" to the Lord instead of the first-born; and in verse 19 of that chapter, as in verse 12 of this chapter, they are represented as being given by Him to Aaron and his sons. The tribe of Levi had proved themselves the most zealous for the honor of the Lord at the time of the worship of the golden calf (Exod. 32:26-29), and it was then that Moses gave them the charge to consecrate

themselves to the Lord. There was, therefore, a special reason for the selection of this tribe, independently of the fact that Moses and Aaron (and consequently the priests, as the descendants of Aaron) belonged to it.

(32) And Eleazar the son of Aaron the priest ... —In virtue, as it should seem, of the descent of Moses and Aaron from Kohath, the Kohathites had the most honorable portion of the service of the Tabernacle assigned to them; and therefore, as the priests belonged to the Amramites, one of the four families of the Kohathites, Eleazar, the eldest surviving son of Aaron, was chosen to have the oversight over the whole body of the Levites.

(39) Twenty and two thousand.—The total of the three items—viz., 7,500, 8,600, and 6,200—amounts to 22,300. It appears, however, from verse 46 that the total is correctly given as 22,000, inasmuch as the number of the first-born, 22,273, exceeded that of the Levites by 273. If the numbers were denoted, as it has been commonly supposed, by the letters of the alphabet, it is quite possible that one letter may have been substituted by the scribe for another.

(41) And thou shalt take the Levites for me (I am the Lord) ... —The assertions which have been frequently made respecting the transference of the priesthood of the first-born to the Levites appear to be altogether without foundation. For (1) the priesthood which was exercised in patriarchal times was not restricted to the first-born, but appears to have been common to the head of every family. (2) This priesthood was exercised previously to the Exodus, and consequently previously to the command given to Moses to sanctify the first-born. And (3) the priesthood, which belonged not to the first-born exclusively, but to the Israelites at large, was from that time on strictly confined to the family of Aaron, who inherited it not as the substitutes of the first-born, but in the place of the whole nation.

(43) Twenty and two thousand two hundred and threescore and thirteen.—The extremely small number of the first-born in proportion to a male population of 600,000 of twenty years of age and upward—i.e., to a population of about 1,000,000 males—has been a fruitful source of difficulty, and, in some cases, a ground for the rejection of the historical truth of the narrative, which involves, it has been alleged, the incredible conclusion that there was only **one** first-

151

born to **forty-four** males. It might suffice to reply that it is difficult, if not impossible, to conceive that a writer who has recorded, or, according to the theory in question, **invented** so many complicated calculations, should have inserted among them one which is fraught with so much apparent improbability. Some have urged that by the first-born in every **family** we are to understand the first-born in every **household**, including the children of concubines and slaves.

4

(2) Of the sons of Kohath ... —Kohath appears to have been the second son of Levi (3:17), but the Kohathites here stand first because Moses and Aaron belonged to them, and it was their office to bear the Ark.

(3) From thirty years old and upward even until fifty years old.—The previous census of the Levites was from a month old. The present census was with a view to the discharge of duties requiring a considerable amount of physical strength, and therefore the prescribed age for entering upon these duties was fixed at this time at thirty, and limited to fifty. It has been supposed by some that five years were spent in preparation for the service, and that it is in this way that the apparent discrepancy between this verse and 8:24, where the age for entering upon the service is fixed at twenty-five, is to be reconciled.

(5) Aaron shall come, and his sons ... —Under ordinary circumstances the high priest himself only might enter the most holy place on one day in the year. At the time of the moving of the camp, however, the divine Presence seems to have departed from the Holy of Holies, and to have ascended in the cloud which gave the signal for the removal.

(15) But they shall not touch any holy thing, lest they die.—The word which is rendered "any holy thing" may here, as elsewhere, denote "the sanctuary." This injunction is repeated in 18:3. We find in II Sam. 6:6, 7 an instance of the fatal result of the violation of this command by Uzzah, who being, as is most probable, a Levite, and of the family of Kohath, ought to have been acquainted with the law respecting the removal of the Ark. It is obvious that the Kohathites, as the immediate assistants of the priests, in regard to the vessels of the

sanctuary, were especially exposed to the risk of violating the law by touching the most holy things.

(48) Eight thousand and five hundred and fourscore.—This number of men between the ages of twenty and fifty bears a just proportion to that of all the males from a month old and upward—viz., 22,000.

5

This chapter contains laws for the preservation of sanctity among the people in the midst of whom Jehovah was pleased to dwell. For issuance of the laws in detail, comp. Lev. 1-3, 13, 14, passim.

6

(2) When either man or woman shall separate themselves to vow a vow ... — Comp. Lev. 27:2. The vows here referred to were made for a specific period. At a later time, however, some were consecrated or set apart as Nazirites during the entire period of their lives, as in the case of Samson, Samuel, and John the Baptist. This consecration, however, appears to have been made rather as the result of divine revelation than of arbitrary appointment on the part of their parents. The meaning of the word "Nazirite" (Hebrew **nazir**) is contained in the concluding words of the verse—to "separate (i.e., himself) unto Jehovah"— where the cognate verb is used. The law of the Nazirite was more strict than that which was placed upon the priests, thus typifying the entire surrender of the heart and life to God, and freedom from the distraction of earthly ties. The ideal of this separation, however, was not that of a life of monastic seclusion, but of action, and of uninterrupted devotion to the divine service.

(23) On this wise ye shall bless the children of Israel.—The occasions on which this blessing was used are not recorded. The blessing itself, which marks in a special manner the spiritual character of the chosen people, consists of three double clauses. In each of these three clauses the sacred name Jehovah is repeated, and there is a rising gradation in the blessing invoked, until it culminates in that peace which is the highest of those gifts that God can bestow and that man can possess. There has been commonly recognized in this blessing an allusion to the doctrine of the Trinity. Mention is made in Lev. 9:22 of a blessing pronounced by Aaron upon the people, but no form of words is found there.

7

(1) On the day that Moses had fully set up the tabernacle.—The Tabernacle was set up on the first day of the **first** month of the second year (Exod. 40:17), and the events recorded in this and the preceding chapters appear to have taken place on and after the first day of the **second** month of that year (1:1). The account of the setting up of the Tabernacle and the altar, etc., is contained in Exod. 40:17-33, and the account of the anointing and consecration is contained in Lev. 8:10, 11. It appears from a comparison of Exod. 40:17 with Num. 10:11 that fifty days intervened between the erection of the Tabernacle and the beginning of the march from Sinai.

(12) And he that offered his offering the first day . . . —It should be observed that the order in which the offerings were made for dedication of the altar is not that of chap. 1, but that observed in the encampments, as prescribed in chap. 2.

(13) And his offering was one silver charger . . . —The offerings of the twelve princes, or rather of the tribes which the princes represented, was the same in each case. The repetition of the description of the offerings, which occupies the remaining portion of this chapter, may serve to denote the special regard which God has to the offerings of His people, as may be learned from the notice which our Lord took of the offerings which were made for the Temple service, and His commendation of that of the poor widow who cast her two mites into the treasury (Mark 12:41-44).

(89) To speak with him.—i.e., with God. Inasmuch as the tent of meeting took its name from the promise made to Moses (Exod. 25:22) that God would meet with him there, it was not necessary to supply the divine name. The terms in which the promise is expressed seem to denote that it was in the Holy of Holies that God met with Moses.

8

(5) And the Lord spake unto Moses.—As Moses had already officiated in the consecration of the priests (Lev. 8), so now, notwithstanding the fact that Aaron and his sons were already consecrated, he is commanded to officiate at the cleansing of the Levites.

(10) Shall put their hands upon the Levites.—The same phrase is here used as in verse 12, and elsewhere, of the offerer who was required to lay his hand upon the victim which he offered in sacrifice. By this symbolical act the obligation which rested upon the whole nation in regard to the dedication of the first-born was transferred to the Levites, who were thereafter to be dedicated to the service of the Lord, and given over to the priests as the representatives of the Lord.

(16) Instead of such as open every womb, even instead of the firstborn of all the children of Israel.—It is difficult to determine whether the second clause is to be regarded as an exact equivalent, or as a limitation of the first. If an exact equivalent, a different meaning must be assigned to the "first-born" from that which it commonly bears in the Pentateuch, where it appears to be restricted to the first-born son on the father's side. (Comp. Exod. 13:2.)

(19) That there be no plague among the children of Israel.—The appointment of the Levites in the place of the first-born was calculated to insure the reverent and orderly discharge of the duties of the sanctuary, and to operate as a safeguard against those sins of omission and commission into which the first-born would have been more likely to be betrayed, and which would have provoked the divine wrath against the Israelites generally.

9

(1) In the first month of the second year.—The celebration of the Passover, as recorded in this chapter, preceded in order of time the numbering of the people recorded in chap. 1, and the other events which were connected with it. No provision had hitherto been made for the celebration of the Passover in the wilderness. A special injunction was, therefore, required for this purpose. Had it not been for the rebellion of the people, the next Passover after the original Egyptian Passover would have been celebrated in the land of Canaan, and it was for that one only that provision had been made (Exod. 12:25).

(6) And there were certain men . . . — While reference would naturally be made to Moses on all doubtful occasions, none

153

would be so likely to have recourse to him with the inquiry contained in verse 7 as those who had been employed by his direction (Lev. 10:4) in the burial of Nadab and Abihu. The law contained in Lev. 7:21 appears to have been understood to refer to all sacrificial meals. The legal uncleanness which disqualified the Israelites for participation in the Passover may be regarded as typical of the moral and spiritual disqualifications which render men unfit for participation in the Lord's Supper.

(15) The cloud covered the tabernacle ... —The account of the cloud covering the Tabernacle is repeated in this place, inasmuch as the history which follows relates the removal of the Tabernacle under the guidance of the same cloud which covered it at its erection. Comp. Ps. 78:14; Neh. 9:12; Isa. 4:5.

(22) Or a year.—If the rendering of the King James Version, "a year," is correct, as it probably is, it will follow that these words could not have been written until after the first arrival at Kadesh (13:26), and probably not until after the end of the wanderings in the wilderness. The elaborate manner in which the statement is made and repeated in almost identical terms shows the great importance which the writer ascribed to the divine guardianship which was exercised over the Israelites, and to their submission to the miraculous guidance which was given to them.

10

(11) On the twentieth day of the second month.—It appears from Exod. 19:1 that the Israelites encamped before Mount Sinai in the third month of the preceding year, and, as is generally supposed, on the first day of the month. In this case the encampment at the foot of Mount Sinai had lasted eleven months and nineteen days. No day of the month, however, is specified in Exod. 19:1, and no **certain** reliance can be placed upon the Jewish tradition that the Law was delivered fifty days after the Exodus. There is the same omission of the day of the month in Num. 9:1 and 20:1.

(12) And the cloud rested in the wilderness of Paran.—The fact is here mentioned by way of anticipation (see verse 33). Comp. Deut. 1:19. The wilderness is supposed to have been bounded by the land of Canaan on the north, by the valley of Arabah on the east, and by the desert of

Sinai on the south. Its western boundary appears to have been the Wady-el-Arish, which divides the wilderness into two parts, of which the western part is sometime known as the wilderness of Shur. The sojourn of the Israelites was confined to the eastern part.

(17) And the tabernacle was taken down ... —The order of precedence as regards the twelve tribes which were encamped on the four sides of the Tabernacle is clearly laid down in chap. 2, where it is ordered that the camp of the Levites should set forward "in the midst of the camps" (verse 17). The precise position which the three bodies of Levites—the Gershonites, Merarites, and Kohathites—were to occupy in the marches is defined in this chapter.

(33) Three days' journey.—The place at which the first protracted halt was made appears to have been either at Taberah, which means "burning," or at Kibroth hattaavah, "the graves of lust." (Comp. 11:3, 34; 33:16).

11

(1) And consumed them that were in the uttermost parts of the camp.—Most commentators have remarked, and justly, upon the great severity of the divine judgments which were inflicted after the giving of the Law, as compared with those which were inflicted before it. Reference may be made in illustration of this point to Exod. 14:11-14; 15:24, 25; 16:2-8; 17:3-7. The writer of the epistle to the Hebrews argues from the just recompense of reward which every transgression and disobedience received under the Law, the impossibility of the escape of those who neglect the great salvation of the Gospel. (See Heb. 2:2, 3. Comp. also Heb. 10:28, 29; 12:25.)

(4) And the mixed multitude.—These were, in many cases, probably, children of Hebrew women by Egyptian fathers. This mixed multitude appears to have been quite large, and they may have become, as the Gibeonites at a later period, servants to the Israelites, as hewers of wood and drawers of water (Deut. 29:11). It is probable that this mixed multitude may have partaken even more largely than the Israelites of the fish and vegetables of Egypt, and they appear to have instigated the Israelites to repine at the deprivations to which they were exposed in the wilderness. There is no mention in Exod. 16:3 of weeping, but the same craving after the fleshpots of Egypt was probably manifested in the same manner in both cases.

(7) And the manna was ... —The design of the description of the manna in this place (comp. Exod. 16:14, 31) was probably to exhibit in its just light the sinfulness of the Israelites in repining at the merciful provision which God had made for the supply of their wants. The dissatisfaction of the Israelites with the sweet bread of heaven, and their craving after the more savory and more stimulating food of Egypt, may be regarded as typical of man's natural repugnance to the spiritual food which is provided in the Gospel, and his restless cravings after the pleasures of the world.

(13) Whence should I have flesh ...?— Moses does not justify the murmuring of the people, and was doubtless conscious of their sinfulness. At the same time, he displays a spirit of discontent, and almost of despair at God's dealings with himself; and he appears to treat the demand of the Israelites for flesh as one which was not altogether unreasonable.

(16) Seventy men of the elders of Israel .. —Frequent mention is made in Scripture of the number "seventy"—a number which is composed of the two sacred numbers "seven" and "ten"—the former being the seal of the covenant, and the latter probably denoting perfection. The seventy who were chosen on the present occasion may have consisted of some of those who were appointed as judges at the suggestion of Jethro (Exod. 18:25, 26), but there is no evidence of their identity with any persons previously selected.

(21) Six hundred thousand footmen.—In :46 the number is stated to be 603,550; but here, as elsewhere, a round number is mentioned.

(28) My lord Moses, forbid them.—The motive which prompted Joshua in making his request appears to have been similar to that which led John to forbid the man to cast out devils who did not follow with the apostles (Mark 9:38, 39; Luke 9:49, 50). But as the man did not cast out devils in his own name, but in that of Christ, so in this case Eldad and Medad prophesied in virtue of the spirit which rested upon them from above, of which the Holy Ghost, not Moses, was the giver. The motives which deterred Eldad and Medad from going to the tent of meeting are unknown. The history teaches the freeness and the sovereignty of the Holy Spirit's influences, as afterward did that of

Cornelius, when the Holy Ghost fell upon him and upon those who were with him, previous to the reception of baptism, and they spoke with tongues and magnified God (Acts 10:44-48).

(32) Ten homers.—The "homer," which was equal to ten ephahs, or a hundred omers, appears to have contained between five and six bushels, according to the Rabbinists.

(33) With a very great plague.—The noun, **maccah**, plague, is cognate to the verb which is rendered "smote." It is frequently used of a stroke inflicted by God, as, e.g., pestilence or any epidemic sickness. A surfeit on quail, such as that in which the Israelites had indulged, especially under the circumstances in which they were placed, would naturally produce a considerable amount of sickness. Here, then, as in the account of the plagues of Egypt and in other parts of the sacred history, the natural and the supernatural are closely combined.

12

(1) And Miriam and Aaron spake against Moses.—Miriam appears to have been the leader in this insurrection against the authority of Moses. Her name occurs before that of Aaron, either as the nearer or as the more prominent subject; and the verb which is rendered "spake" is in the feminine gender. Moreover, the judgment which was inflicted (verse 10) fell upon Miriam, not upon Aaron, who seems to have yielded to the suggestions of Miriam, as he had previously done to the request of the Israelites in regard to the golden calf.

Because of the Ethiopian woman whom he had married.—It seems probable that Zipporah was dead, and that Moses had married one of the African Cushites who had accompanied the Israelites in their march out of Egypt, or one of the Cushites who dwelt in Arabia, and who were found at this time in the neighborhood of Sinai. A similar marriage had been contracted by Joseph, and such marriages were not forbidden by the Law, which prohibited marriage with the Canaanites (Exod. 34:16).

(2) Hath the Lord indeed spoken only by Moses?—There is probably a reference in these words to the facts related in Exod. 4:10-16, where Moses speaks of his own slowness of speech (verse 10), and where it is said of Aaron, "And he shall be thy spokesman unto the people" (verse 16).

Miriam also is spoken of in Exod. 15:20 as "the prophetess." "Such is the depravity of human nature," writes Calvin, "that they not only abuse the gifts of God towards the brother whom they despise, but by an ungodly and sacrilegious glorification extol the gifts themselves in such a manner as to hide the Author of the gifts."

(3) Now the man Moses was very meek ... —These words have been urged by some as an argument against the Mosaic authorship of the Pentateuch generally, or of the Book of Numbers in particular, but whether they may or may not have been inserted by a later writer, this influence is altogether unfounded. It is possible that the writer of Deut. 34:10 may have inserted these words in this place. On the other hand, there is no necessity for such a supposition. An objective statement, such as that contained in these words, is perfectly consistent with true humility and with a deep sense of sinfulness and frailty.

(7) My servant Moses ... —Reference is made to these words in Heb. 3:5, 6. The whole of the Mosaic economy or dispensation, or the house of Israel, is spoken of as God's house. A contrast is drawn between the vocation of Moses as a servant **in** the house of God and that of Christ as a Son **over** His own house.

(10) And the cloud departed ... —The withdrawal of the cloud was the visible token of the divine displeasure. The word **sar,** "departed," which is here used, is an entirely different word from that which occurs in 9:17. The "lifting up" of the cloud was the signal for the breaking up of the camp and the resumption of the march; the "withdrawal" of the cloud was the token of the withdrawal of the divine presence and direction.

And Aaron looked upon Miriam ... — Or, "and Aaron turned towards Miriam"— i.e., directed his attention to her, etc. This may have been the first case in which Aaron was required to carry into execution the laws laid down in Lev. 13, 14, respecting the inspection of the leper; and the duties which devolved upon him must have been doubly painful from the fact that the leper stood in a near relationship to himself, and that he had been a participator in the sin which had called for so severe a punishment.

13

(1) And the Lord spake unto Moses ...

—There is no inconsistency between this statement and that which is contained in Deut. 1:22, where the sending of the spies is represented as having originated with the people. It is there said that the saying pleased Moses well; but it would be wholly inconsistent with the character and conduct of Moses to suppose that in a matter of such importance he should have acted in accordance with the suggestion of the people, or upon his own judgment, without seeking direction from God. The command which was given to Moses must not be regarded as implying of necessity that the expedition of the spies was, in the first instance, ordained by God, any more than the command which was afterward given to Balaam to accompany the messengers of Balak was any indication that God originally commanded, or approved of his journey.

(2) Every one a ruler among them.—A comparison of the names which follow with those which are given in 1:5-15 will show that the persons selected were not the tribal princes who are mentioned in connection with the census. The tribe of Levi, as in the former case, is not represented, as the Levites were to have no inheritance in the land and the number of twelve, as in chap. 1, is made up by the division of the tribe of Joseph into the two tribes of Ephraim and Manasseh.

(16) And Moses called Oshea ... —It is not distinctly stated that the change of name took place at this time. It may have taken place at an earlier period, and have been confirmed on the present occasion, as in the case of "Israel" (Gen. 32:28; 35:10), and of "Bethel" (Gen. 28:19; 35:15). On the other hand, it is quite possible that the name may have been anticipatorily adopted in Exod. 17:9, 13; 24:13; 32:17, 33:11, and Num. 11:28. The original name Hoshea mean "help," or "salvation." The name Joshua, or Jehoshua, means "Jehovah is help," or "salvation."

(17) Get you up this way southward.— The southern part of Palestine was known by the name of "the Negeb." It formed the transition from the desert to the more highly cultivated land, and was more fitted for grazing than for agricultural purposes.

Into the mountain.—The word which is used here commonly denotes the hill country, i.e., the mountainous part of Palestine which was inhabited by the Hittite, Jebusites, and Amorites. It is called "the mount of the Amorites" in Deut. 1:7, inasmuch as the Amorites were the strongest of the Canaanite tribes.

(18) And see the land.—Or, "inspect the land." The same word is used of the inspection of the leper by the priest in Lev. 13:3, 5, 6, 10, 13, etc.

(20) Now the time . . . —The first grapes ripen in Palestine as early as August, or even July, although the vintage does not take place until September or October.

(21) From the wilderness of Zin.—The name of the wilderness of Zin, in which Kadesh was situated, appears to have been given to the northern or northeastern part of the wilderness of Paran. Comp. 20:1; 27:14; 33:36; 34:3, 4; Deut. 32:51; Josh. 15:1, 3.

Unto Rehob, as men come to Hamath.—Or, near Dan-Laish, the northern boundary of the land assigned to the Israelites (Num. 34:8).

(23) Upon a staff.—The arrangement referred to in the text was probably made, not because the weight was too great for one person to carry, but in order to prevent the grapes from being crushed. The pomegranates and figs, which are still some of the most important fruits of Hebron, were probably carried on the same pole. This incident has obvious reference to the homeward journey of the spies. As the grapes of Eschol were to the Israelites both a pledge and a specimen of the fruits of Canaan, so the communion which believers have with God on earth is a pledge as well as a foretaste of the blessedness of heaven.

(25) After forty days.—This time allowed a full and careful exploration of the land.

(28) Nevertheless the people be strong . . . —The spies adopted the words of Exod. 3:8, "flowing with milk and honey," as descriptive of the fertility of the land of Canaan, but at the same time they discouraged the hearts of their brethren by their description of the strength of the fortified cities and the gigantic stature of the inhabitants.

(30) And Caleb stilled the people.—The fact that Caleb alone is mentioned in this place is by no means inconsistent with the statement which is contained in 14:6-9, from which it appears that Joshua and Caleb concurred in exhorting the people to go up and take possession of the land of promise. It appears, moreover, from Deut. 1:29, etc., that Moses also remonstrated earnestly with the people, and yet neither here nor in the following chapter is mention made of that remonstrance.

(32) A land that eateth up the inhabitants thereof.—The allusion is to the strife and discord which prevailed among the various tribes who contended for its possession. (Comp. Lev. 26:38.)

Men of great stature.—Such persons did undoubtedly exist in the land of Canaan, but there is no evidence that the inhabitants generally were of extraordinary size.

(33) And there we saw the giants.—The same word, **nephilim**, is found in Gen. 6:4.

14

(2) And all the children of Israel murmured.—On the present occasion their murmuring was not against Moses and Aaron only, (see Exod. 16:2, 3), but they openly rebelled against Jehovah Himself, to whom they ascribed, in the way of reproach, their exodus from the land of Egypt.

(3) And wherefore hath the Lord brought us unto this land . . . ?—The destruction which the Israelites apprehended at this time was not a destruction by famine or drought, but by the sword of the Amorites and of the children of the Anakim. (Comp. Deut. 1:27, 28.)

(12) And will make of thee a greater nation and mightier than they.—A similar promise had been given to Moses on occasion of the rebellion at Sinai, and Moses on that occasion interceded with God on behalf of His people in like manner as at this time (Exod. 32:10-12).

(13, 14) And Moses said unto the Lord . . . —Reference may be made to the following passages in illustration of the argument by which Moses enforced his intercessory prayer on behalf of Israel:—Deut. 32:26, 27; Josh. 7:9; Isaiah 48:9, 11; Ezek. 36:22, 23.

(21-23) But as truly as I live . . . —Some have explained the words **these ten times** by adding to the eight murmurings which are recorded—(1) at the Red Sea (Exod. 14:11, 12); (2) at Marah (Exod. 15:23); (3) in the wilderness of Sin (Exod. 16:2); (4) at Rephidim (Exod. 17:2); (5) at Horeb (Exod. 32); (6) at Taberah (Num. 11:1); (7) at the graves of lust (Num. 11:4); and (8) at Kadesh (Num. 14)—the transgressions of certain individuals—(1) in keeping the manna until the morning of the day after that on which it was gathered (Exod. 16:20); and (2) in going out to gather the manna on the seventh day, when none fell (Exod. 16:27). It is more probable, however, that the number ten is used here, as elsewhere (comp. Gen. 31:7), as denoting a full measure.

The persons to whom the penalty applied are specified in verse 29: viz., those who were included in the first census. The principal exceptions to the threat of exclusion from the land of promise are specified in verses 30 and 31: viz., Joshua and Caleb, and the generation which had not reached twenty years of age at the Exodus. The other exception, or exceptions, if such there were, belonged to the tribe of Levi, which was not included in the census which was first taken, nor represented by the spies.

(24) And his seed shall possess it.—It appears from Joshua 14:6-14 that Moses had especially promised Hebron to Caleb, and that the mountainous country which the Anakim inhabited, and which only he and Joshua of the twelve spies believed that the Israelites were able to take possession of, was afterward allotted to him by Joshua "for an inheritance."

(28) As ye have spoken in mine ears, so will I do unto you.—The Israelites had exclaimed in their sinful murmuring against God, "Would God we had died in the wilderness" (verse 2); And God declared in His wrathful displeasure that the judgment which they had thus invoked should be inflicted upon them, and that their carcasses should fall in the wilderness.

(34) Even forty days, each day for a year.—The numbering which is recorded in chap. 26 took place after the death of Aaron, which happened on the first day of the fifth month of the fortieth year after the Exodus (33:38). Therefore it follows that the year and a half which elapsed since the Exodus must be included in the forty years of shepherd life in the wilderness.

(42) Go not up, for the Lord is not among you.—Moses had already received the command which is contained in verse 25. He knew, therefore, that the Israelites would not have the guidance of the cloud, the visible token of the divine presence.

15

(1, 2) And the Lord spake unto Moses, saying ... —We learn from Deut. 1:46 that the Israelites "abode in Kadesh many days," and from Deut. 2:1 that afterward they "turned," in obedience to the command given in the preceding chapter of this book, and "took their journey into the wilderness by the way of the Red Sea." It

appears, further, from Num. 20:1 that in the first month of the fortieth year they came again into the desert of Zin, and "abode in Kadesh."

In regard to the transactions recorded in this and in the four following chapters we have no certain chronological data. The fact that additional laws were given during the long period of the wanderings in the wilderness furnished a practical proof of the continuance of the covenant which had been made with Israel at Sinai. The levitical law had been given under the presumption that they would obey Him who gave it, and that they would be soon afterward in Canaan, when they would be able to comply with that law. (Comp. Deut. 4:14.) But they murmured against God at Kadesh-barnea, and thus they forfeited the **privileges of obedience**. They had kept one Passover at Mount Sinai, but there is no evidence that they were ever permitted to keep another Passover during the whole term of their wanderings. They themselves felt and acted as men under a ban.

The words which follow were evidently addressed to those of the Israelites who were under twenty years of age at the time of the Exodus. (Comp. Exod. 29; Lev. 4, 23.)

(32) And while the children of Israel were in the wilderness ... —It is probable that the incident which is recorded here is designed to illustrate the presumptuous sins which were to be punished by death. The observance of the Sabbath was obligatory in the wilderness as well as in the land of Canaan (comp. Exod. 16:27-30), and the punishment of death had already been denounced against those who profaned it by doing any work thereon (see Exod. 31:15; 35:2), but the manner in which death was to be inflicted does not appear to have been declared.

(38) That they make them fringes ... —The outer garment of the Jews was a four-cornered cloth, which was also used by the poor as a quilt or bedspread (Exod. 22:26, 27). It appears to have been commonly used with a hole in the center, through which the head was put, so that one-half covered the front and the other the back of the body. These tassels, or fringes, were enlarged by the Pharisees to exhibit their punctilious fulfillment of the Law (Matt. 23:5). Great sanctity was attached to these fringes or tassels, and for this cause the woman with the issue of blood desired to touch a **kraspedon** of our Saviour's garment (Matt. 9:20).

16

(1) Now Korah, the son of Izhar ...—The rebellion of Korah, Dathan, and Abiram is the only important event which is recorded in connection with the protracted wandering in the desert. The time and place of its occurrence cannot be positively determined. The circumstances out of which it appears to have arisen render it probable that it took place during one of the early years of the wanderings in the wilderness, either during the abode at Kadesh or subsequently to the departure from it. The leaders of the rebellion, among whom Korah holds the most conspicuous place (comp. 16:1; 26:9; Jude 11), belonged to the tribes of Levi and Reuben. Korah, as the descendant of Izhar, the brother of Amram, who was the father of Moses and Aaron, may well be supposed to have been jealous of the peculiar prerogatives of the priestly family. Dathan and Abiram, on like grounds, may be supposed to have been discontented on account of the transference of the birthright, and the consequent loss of the leadership which had been possessed by their tribe, and which was now held by the tribe of Judah. It is possible that they may have regarded the priesthood also as among the prerogatives of the first-born which should have descended to them. No further mention is made of the name of On, nor is he expressly included in the account of the final punishment.

(2) And they rose up ...—i.e., in rebellion.

Two hundred and fifty princes ...—It has been inferred from 27:3, where it is stated that Zelophehad, the Manassite, did not take part in the rebellion, that these princes, or chief men of the congregation, belonged to the other tribes of Israel as well as that of Levi. They are called Korah's company because he was their leader, and it is probable from verse 8 that a large number of them belonged to the tribe of Levi.

(6) Take you censers.—The offering of incense was the peculiar prerogative and the holiest function of the priesthood. The destruction of Nadab and Abihu ought to have served as a warning to Korah and his company not to provoke a similar exhibition of the divine displeasure.

(7) Ye take too much upon you ...

—Moses here adopts the language of Korah in verse 3. The meaning appears to be, as more fully explained in verses 9, 10, that it ought to have sufficed Korah and the other Levites that they had been chosen from among their brethren to discharge the inferior offices of the sanctuary. As the other Levites who belonged to Korah's company sought the priesthood, so Korah may have aimed at the high priesthood.

(19) All the congregation.—It is evident from these words that there was a general disposition on the part of the people to favor the insurrection of Korah against Moses and Aaron.

(28) To do all these works.—i.e., to bring the people out of the land of Egypt, to exchange the first-born for the Levites, to consecrate Aaron and his sons to the priesthood, and generally to declare the will of the Lord to the people.

(32) And the earth opened her mouth ...—Had this verse stood alone it might have been inferred that Korah and his family shared the fate of Dathan and Abiram and their families and households. In regard to the sons of Korah, however, there is direct evidence that they did not share in the punishment of Dathan and Abiram (see verse 27). In regard to Korah there is ground for the belief that he perished by fire with the 250 men who offered incense with him. It is true, indeed, that in 26:10 Korah is mentioned in conjunction with Dathan and Abiram; but in the other places in which reference is made to the conspiracy, the fate of the chief conspirators is separated. (Comp. Deut. 11:6; Ps. 106:17.)

(41) But on the morrow ...—It is difficult to conceive of a more striking illustration of the depravity of the human heart than is afforded by this outbreak of the same spirit of rebellion which had been so signally punished on the preceding day. (Comp. 20:3.)

17

(3) And thou shalt write Aaron's name upon the rod of Levi.—Aaron was descended from the **second** son of Levi. He was not, therefore, the natural, but the divinely-appointed head of his father's house, and therefore it would not have sufficed for the purpose contemplated to have inscribed the name of Levi upon the rod. Aaron was constituted the head alike of the priests and

159

of the Levites, into which two classes the tribe of Levi was divided.

(8) Behold, the rod of Aaron for the house of Levi was budded ... —The budding of Aaron's rod was the divinely appointed proof of the establishment of the priesthood in his person and in his posterity. The miraculous shooting forth of Aaron's dry rod may be regarded as a type of the mode of the Spirit's operation in the Church, and more especially in the work of the ministry; "Not by might, nor by power, but by my spirit, saith the Lord of hosts" (Zech. 4:6).

And yielded almonds.—The word **shaked** (almond tree) is a cognate form of the verb **shakad**—"to keep watch." The name is supposed to have been given to the almond tree because it blossoms at a time when vegetation is lying in the sleep of winter.

(10) Bring Aaron's rod again before the testimony.—It is not stated here that the rod was put within the Ark. Nor is it so stated in Exod. 16:33 with regard to the pot of manna. Neither of these was within the Ark when it was brought into Solomon's temple (I Kings 8:9); but this statement is by no means inconsistent with that contained in Heb. 9:4, inasmuch as the assertion that there was nothing but the tables of the law in the Ark at that time does not prove that there were not other things in it at an earlier period, and may be thought to suggest the inference that such was actually the case.

(12, 13) And the children of Israel spake unto Moses ... —The true answer to their inquiry whether they were doomed utterly to perish, in which the priesthood of Christ is typically set forth as bearing the iniquity of the sanctuary, and thus making reconciliation for the sins and securing the acceptance of the imperfect service of His people.

18

(7) And within the veil.—The reference appears to be to the whole of the priestly duties which were discharged by Aaron and his sons, from those connected with the altar of burnt offering to those which were performed in the most holy place.

(19) It is a covenant of salt.—i.e., an indissoluble covenant. (See note on Lev. 2:13; also II Chron. 13:5.)

(20) Thou shalt have no inheritance ...

—Aaron is addressed in this verse as the representative of the priesthood. He himself did not enter into the land of Canaan.

I am thy part and thine inheritance ... —All that are admitted into the number of Christ's royal priesthood have God for their portion and inheritance—in life, in death, and throughout eternity. (Comp. Pss. 73:26; 142:5.)

(21) All the tenth in Israel.—The reference here is to the first tithe, or tenth of the whole of the produce of the land. Verse 24 assigns the reason why the Levites were to have no inheritance among the children of Israel.

(25) And the Lord spake unto Moses ... —The law respecting the Levitical dues was given to Aaron, and communicated through Him to the people. The law respecting the tithe which the Levites were to give to the priests (the tithe of the tithe), in which Aaron's family were directly concerned, was communicated to Moses, and by him to the Levites.

19

(2) This is the ordinance of the law ... —The extraordinary mortality which the Israelites had sustained (16:49) may have called for some special rites of purification from the defilement caused by contact with the dead. This institution was one which admitted of observance in the wilderness under circumstances in which other requirements of the Levitical law could not be observed.

(6) And the priest shall take cedar wood, and hyssop, and scarlet.—Cedar wood may be regarded as the emblem of fragrance and incorruption; hyssop as the emblem of purification; and scarlet (or crimson) wool or cloth may be regarded as emblematic both of sin, which is compared to it in Isa. 1:18, and also of the blood, which is the life, the shedding of which was needful in order to receive the remission of sin. All of these were used in the purification of the leper (Lev. 14:4.) In both cases there appears to be a typical reference to the sprinkling of the blood of Christ. (See Heb. 9:13, 14.)

(10) And it shall be unto the children of Israel, and unto the stranger ... —So the promise of the remission of sins through Christ Jesus was not only to the Jews and to their children, but also to all that were afar off. (See Acts 2:39.)

160

20

(1) Then came ... —The interval of time between the events related in the preceding chapters and in this chapter is unknown.

In the first month.—It has been commonly supposed that the reference is to the first month of the fortieth year, when the Israelites are thought to have arrived for the second time at Kadesh. Some, however, are of the opinion that the journey is the same as that which is mentioned in 12:16, and in Deut. 1:19; and that the arrival at Kadesh was on the first month of the third year, i.e., the year which followed the departure from Sinai, which departure took place on the twentieth day of the second month, in the second year after the Exodus.

And the people abode in Kadesh.—It is evident that the sojourn in Kadesh was a protracted one, whether Kadesh did, or did not serve as the headquarters of the people from the second or third year of the Exodus until that in which they entered into the land of Canaan.

(12) And the Lord spake unto Moses and Aaron.—We read in Ps. 106:33 that the Israelites "provoked (literally, **made to rebel**) his spirit, so that he spake unadvisedly with his lips." Whatever was the nature of the sin thus committed, it is clear that Aaron was a participator in it with Moses. It has been thought that the sin of Moses and Aaron consisted in arrogating to themselves the honor which was due only to God, "Must **we** fetch you water?" but the personal pronoun does not occur in the Hebrew, as it might, and probably would, have occurred, if intended to be emphatic. The more probable explanation appears to be that, notwithstanding the miraculous supply of water which had begun at Rephidim, and which had been subsequently continued, Moses and Aaron distrusted the word and power (verse 12) of God, and that they yielded to the impulse of impatience and anger, as betrayed both by the language which they used and by the double smiting of the rock, to which Moses had been commanded only to speak. To what degree Aaron was concerned in these sins can be inferred only from the facts that he, as well as Moses, was charged with the sin of unbelief, and that the punishment of exclusion from the land of Canaan was inflicted upon both.

(13) And he was sanctified in them.—It has been supposed that the place derived its name of Kadesh (or, more fully, Kadesh-barnea, 32:8) from the cognate verb, which is rendered **sanctify** in this and the preceding verse. It was in Kadesh that the sentence of exclusion had been pronounced upon the people generally (14:22, 23), and upon Moses and Aaron in particular, and it was thus that the Lord sanctified Himself in dealing with the transgressors.

(14) Thus saith thy brother Israel.—The Edomites, as the descendants of Esau, who received the name of Edom (Gen. 25:30), were closely connected with the descendants of Jacob.

(26) And strip Aaron of his garments.—Thus the same hands which had invested Aaron with the sacred garments were employed in divesting him of them, and, in both cases, in obedience to the express command of God. The removal of the priestly robes from Aaron may be regarded as typical of the future disannulling of his priesthood when a priest after the order of Melchizedek should arise. (Comp. Heb. 7, 8.)

(28) And Aaron died there in the top of the mount.—The date of Aaron's death, as we learn from 33:38, 39 was the first day of the fifth month, in the fortieth year after the Exodus, and his age a hundred and twenty-three years.

21

(4) Because of the way.—Better, "in (or, on) the way." In addition to all the hardships and dangers of the journey, they were conscious that they were turning their backs upon the land of Canaan, because of Edom's refusal (20:21), instead of marching by a direct course into it.

(9) And Moses made a serpent of brass.—The old serpent was the cause of death, temporal and spiritual. Christ Jesus, "in the likeness of sinful flesh" (Rom. 8:3), was made sin for us (II Cor. 5:21), and thus fulfilled, as He Himself explained to Nicodemus, the type of the brazen serpent (John 3:14, 15.) This serpent was preserved by the Israelites, and taken into Canaan, and was ultimately destroyed by King Hezekiah, after it had become an object of idolatrous worship (II Kings 18:4).

(14, 15) The book of the wars of the Lord.—Nothing is known about this book. The last days of Moses may have been a suitable time for the beginning of such a work. The history of the journey from Kadesh to the **Arboth Moab** was not written by Moses until after the defeat of the two kings of the Amorites, and the subjugation of the land on the east of the Jordan.

22

(3) And Moab was sore afraid of the people.—There was no ground for this apprehension, inasmuch as the divine command given to Moses was "Distress not the Moabites, neither contend with them in battle" (Deut. 2:9). It does not appear, however, that Balak was aware of the prohibition; and the recent conquests of the Israelites naturally filled the Moabites with alarm, especially inasmuch as when the Israelites sent to the king of Moab to ask permission to pass through his land he did not consent (Judg. 11:17).

(5) Balaam the son of Beor.—It has been thought that Balaam belonged to a family in which the magical art was hereditary. He is described in Josh. 13:22 as "the soothsayer" i.e., one of that class of persons who were not to be tolerated among the Israelites, and who are spoken of as "an abomination unto the Lord" (Deut. 18:10-12).

To Pethor, which is by the river of the land ...—Pethor was in Mesopotamia (23:7), where Lot, from whom the Moabites were descended, had dwelt (Gen. 12:5). "The river" is the Euphrates here, as elsewhere. (See e.g., Gen. 15:18; 31:21; Exod. 23:31; II Chron. 9:26.)

(6) Curse me this petple.—Balak undoubtedly believed in the efficacy of Balaam's magical incantations. It is deserving of observation, moreover, that, as has been remarked by Keil, "it is frequently celebrated as a great favor displayed toward Israel that the Lord did not hearken to Balaam, but turned the curse into a blessing" (Deut. 23:5; Josh. 24:10; Neh. 13:2).

(8) As the Lord shall speak unto me.—It appears from this verse, as from verses 18, 19, that the name of Jehovah was known to Balaam.

(14) Balaam refuseth to come with us.—It does not appear that Balaam had told the messengers of Balak the ground of the divine prohibition; viz., "for they are blessed." Balak accordingly entertained the hope that stronger inducements would prevail with Balaam.

(20) Rise up, and go with them.—There is no real inconsistency with verse 12. The absolute and immutable prohibition had reference to the cursing. The going with the messengers, which was forbidden in mercy at first, was commanded in judgment at last. God often punishes disobedience to His declared will by permitting the transgressors to "eat the fruit of their own way, and to be filled with their own devices" (Prov. 1:31).

(28) And the Lord opened the mouth of the ass.—The real question at issue is not whether the recorded results might have been accomplished on the supposition that the incidents are to be explained subjectively, but what is the interpretation which the narrative itself suggests, and which the words of II Pet. 2:16 require? In regard to the narrative itself, there is no intimation given that its respective portions are to be differently interpreted; nor is it possible, without doing violence to its obvious meaning, to interpret some parts of it objectively and other parts subjectively; while in regard to the testimony of Peter, it would be impossible to conceive of a statement couched in terms more directly suggestive of a literal fact than the following—"The dumb ass, speaking with man's voice, forbade the madness of the prophet." In regard to the objections which have been raised to the literal interpretation, grounded on the absence of any expression of surprise on the part of Balaam, and of any allusion to the effect produced upon the Moabitish princes and Balaam's servants, it will suffice to observe (1) that here, as elsewhere, no just inference can be drawn from the silence of Scripture; and (2) that, as in the case of those who were with Paul as he went to Damascus (Acts 9), we have no means of determining, on the assumption of the presence of witnesses throughout the miraculous occurrences described, what amount of those occurrences they may have seen and heard.

(35) Go with the man: but only the word that I shall speak unto thee ...—The command contained in verse 20 is here repeated, and the unrighteous prophet is punished by being constrained to reap the fruit of his own perversity. It should be observed that here, as elsewhere, the angel who speaks to Balaam identifies himself with Him who sent him: "The word that I shall speak unto thee, that thou shalt speak." (Comp. verse 20, where God Himself is represented as delivering to Balaam the same injunction.)

23

(5) The Lord put a word in Balaam's

mouth.—"God, who had opened the mouth of the ass in a manner contrary to her nature, now opens Balaam's mouth in a manner contrary to his own will" (Bishop Wordsworth).

(11) Thou hast blessed them altogether.—Hebrew, "Thou hast blessed, to bless": an emphatic mode of stating that Balaam had continued to give utterance to nothing but blessings.

(14) The field of Zophim.—The spot seems to be identified with that from which Moses afterward surveyed the promised land (Deut. 3:27), and which is described in Deut. 34:1 as "the mountain of Nebo," or Mount Nebo. It is possible, however, that Pisgah may have had more than one of such summits.

(19) Neither the son of man, that he should repent.—The adoption of these words, with slight variation, by Samuel (I Sam. 15:29) affords evidence of his familiarity with this portion of the Pentateuch.

(22) God brought them out of Egypt.—Literally, "is bringing them." The use of the participle denotes the continuance of the action. He who brought them forth out of Egypt was still conducting them on their march. There is an obvious allusion in these words to those of Balak in 22:5: "Behold, there is a people come out from Egypt." Seeing that the people did not come out of Egypt in obedience to their own caprice, but under divine guidance, it was vain for Balak to resist them on their course, seeing that to contend with them was to contend against God.

(23) Surely there is no enchantment against Jacob ... —The Israelites had no need of augury and divination, seeing that God revealed to them His acts, His counsel, and His will. "What is here affirmed of Israel," says Hengstenberg, "applies to the Church of all ages, and also to every individual believer. The Church of God knows from His own Word what God does, and what it has to do in consequence. The wisdom of this world resembles augury and divination. The Church of God, which is in possession of His word, has no need of it." (**History of Balaam and His Prophecies**, p. 441.)

(27) Peradventure it will please God ... —Balak appears to be satisfied that Balaam was hindered by God from uttering the curses which he desired him to pronounce upon Israel (comp. 24:11). Or the words may have been spoken ironically.

(2) And the spirit of God came upon him.—In regard to the two former utterances, it is said that Jehovah put a word in the mouth of Balaam (23:5, 15). In the present case the Spirit of God came upon (or, over) Him. The same expression is used of the messengers of Saul (I Sam. 19:20), and of Saul himself (verse 23). The prophecy of Caiaphas (John 11:51) affords another instance of the sovereign power of the Spirit as displayed through the medium of wicked men.

(3) The man whose eyes are open.—The meaning of this verse is sufficiently explained by that which follows. Balaam appears to have been thrown into an ecstatic state, as was Saul, and as were many of the ancient prophets; and while the eye of the outer senses was closed, the eye of the inner senses was preternaturally opened. (Comp. I Sam. 19:24; Ezek. 1:28; Dan. 8:17, 18; Rev. 1:17.)

(7) He shall pour the water out of his buckets.—The nation is personified as a man carrying two buckets full of water, which was the type and leading source of blessing and prosperity in the East. This is a beautiful image of the true Israel "pouring out the living waters of salvation, the pure streams of the Spirit, and making the wilderness of the world to rejoice and be glad" (Bishop Wordsworth).

His king shall be higher than Agag ... —Agag appears to have been the title (**nomen digitatis**) of the Amalekite kings, as "Pharaoh" of the Egyptian and "Abimelech" of the Philistine kings. The reference does not seem to be to any particular king, but to the kingdom which should hereafter be established in Israel—to the kings, generally, which should come out of the loins of Abraham (Gen. 17:6, 35:11).

(9) Blessed is he that blesseth thee ... —Compare the original blessing which was pronounced upon Abraham by the Lord (Gen. 12:3), and which was afterward adopted by Isaac in the blessing which he pronounced upon Jacob (Gen. 27:29).

(14) I will advertise thee ... —The word which is here employed generally means to "advise." The announcement which Balaam made to Balak virtually included advice, inasmuch as it foretold the supremacy of Israel over all their foes, and, consequently, implied the folly of opposition to their progress. It is not stated whether it was or was not at this time that Balaam "taught

Balac to cast a stumbling block before the children of Israel, to eat things sacrificed unto idols, and to commit fornication" (Rev. 2:14).

(17) I shall see him ... —The reference cannot be to Israel, whose armies were encamped before the eyes of Balaam. His words must be understood as having reference to One whom he beheld with the eyes of his mind, not with his bodily sight. This is obvious from the words which follow. Balaam beholds in vision a Star and a Sceptre, not as having already appeared, but as about to appear in the future.

There shall come a Star out of Jacob ... —The verb is in the prophetic past or historic tense of prophecy, denoting the certainty of the event predicted. If there is any ambiguity in the first symbol it is removed in the second. A star is a fitting image of an illustrious king or ruler, and the mention of the "sceptre" in the words which follow (comp. Gen. 49:10) shows that it is so employed in the present instance. Ibn Ezra interprets these words of David (II Sam. 8), but he says that many interpret them of the Messiah. The words of the Magi, "We have seen his star in the East" (Matt. 2:2), appear to have reference to this prophecy.

(20) And when he looked on Amalek ... —Some understand the allusion to be to the fact that the Amalekites were the first nation which attacked Israel when they had come out of Egypt (Exod. 17:8). It is possible, however, that there may be a reference both to time and rank. (Comp. Amos 6:1.)

(21, 22) And he looked on the Kenites ... —Another rendering of verse 22, and one which appears to be more agreeable to the context in which it stands, is the following:—"For surely the Kenites shall not be destroyed until Asshur shall carry thee into captivity." (Comp. Judg. 1:16.) This version has the support of the Targum of Palestine and other authorities. If this interpretation of the text is received, the antithesis between the doom of the Amalekites and the deliverence of the Kenites corresponds to the attitude assumed by those tribes respectively in regard to Israel.

(24) And ships shall come from the coast of Chittim.—The Chittim (or, Kittim) are said to have migrated from Phoenicia to Cyprus (see Josephus, "Antiq." i. 6, 1). The name probably applies to the islands and coasts of the Mediterranean generally. The rendering of the Vulgate is **Italia**, and in

Dan. 11:30, which is obviously founded upon this verse, the Vulgate identifies the Kittim with the Romans.

And he also shall perish for ever.—i.e., the victorious power which was to afflict Asshur (the Eastern Shemites) and Eber (the Western Shemites). "The overthrow of this last power of the world," says Keil, "concerning which the prophet Daniel was the first to receive and proclaim new revelations, belongs to 'the end of the days,' in which the star out of Jacob is to rise upon Israel as 'a bright morning-star'" (Rev. 22:16).

25

(9) Twenty and four thousand.—In 1 Cor. 10:8 the number of those who "fell in one day" is said to have been "three and twenty thousand." It has been supposed that a thousand were put to death by the judges, and that these were not included in Paul's enumeration. Presuming, however, that there has been no error in either place on the part of the scribes in recording the numbers, the words "in one day" may account for the apparent discrepancy.

(11) Phinehas, the son of Eleazar, the son of Aaron the priest ... —The description of Phinehas, as in verse 7, is repeated in full, as if to denote that he was not a private individual, but one invested with putlic authority.

(12) My covenant of peace.—Phinehas, as one who was zealous for the honor of God and of the house of the Lord, was a fitting type of Christ, in whom the prediction of the Psalmist received its accomplishment, "The zeal of thine house hath eaten me up" (Ps. 69:9; John 2:17). The covenant of grace is described in Isa. 54:10 and Mal. 2:5 as the covenant of peace (Comp. Ps. 89:28, 29.)

(13) Even the covenant of an everlasting priesthood.—Phinehas succeeded his father Eleazar as high priest (Judg. 20:28). After a temporary interruption in the succession, which existed in the time of Eli, and continued until the time of David, when there appears to have been a joint high-priesthood, the office was restored by Solomon to Zadok, the descendant of Phinehas, and so continued until the gradual dissolution of the Jewish state. Christ's priesthood is "an unchangeable priesthood" (Heb. 7:24).

26

(1) And it came to pass after the plague ... —The plague probably destroyed the remnant of the generation which had come out of Egypt, and which had been numbered in the wilderness of Sinai.

(2) Take the sum ... —The same command had been given to Moses and Aaron (1:2, 3). In that case a man taken out of every tribe, the head of his father's house, was appointed to assist Moses and Aaron in taking the census. It is probable that the same arrangement was made in the present instance, though it is not recorded.

Note that Reuben has decreased by 2,770 from the former census (1:21), Simeon by 37,100, and Gad by 5,150. No doubt recent sin and association could account for this (see verses 9, 10; also 12:10; 16:1; 25:14). Note, too, the present decrease of 8,000 by Ephraim, and comp. note on 1:27.

(53-56) Unto these the land shall be divided ... —The general apportionment of the land, as regarded the relative position of each tribe, was to be decided by lot, which was commonly looked upon as the determination of God Himself, and in this instance was undoubtedly so. The extent of territory was to be determined by the number of names—i.e., of persons—in each tribe, and each inheritance was to bear the name of the ancestor of the tribe.

(64) But among these ... —Thus the prediction contained in 14:29-32 was fulfilled. The fact that the fulfillment of this prediction is stated after verse 62, which contains the result of the census as regards the Levites, viewed in connection with the statement contained in verse 65, might seem to favor the inference that the sentence of exclusion was applicable to the tribe of Levi as well as to the other tribes. On the other hand, the second clause of verse 62 may be alleged in support of the opposite view.

27

(3) Our father died in the wilderness. —In obedience to the directions contained in the preceding chapter (verses 52-56), the land of Canaan was to be portioned out in accordance with the results of the census which had recently been taken among the males who were older than twenty years of age; and consequently the daughters of Zelophehad would not have shared in the

inheritance. Keil quotes several instances in which the sons of mothers who possessed landed property were received through that inheritance into the family of their mothers, and included in the tribe to which the mothers belonged. In this case the desire of the daughters of Zelophehad was that their father's name should be perpetuated—i.e., that their sons should be enrolled as descendants of Zelophehad, and should succeed to that portion of the land which, under ordinary circumstances, would have fallen to his sons, had he left any behind him. (See verses 5-11 and chap. 36.)

(12) Get thee up into this mount Abarim.—The position of this command, in immediate connection with the answer returned to the request of the daughters of Zelophehad, is remarkable. They were to enter into the land of promise, and their descendants were to inherit it. The great lawgiver himself was to be excluded on account of his transgression. He does not, however, shrink from recording the sentence of exclusion in immediate connection with an incident which brings out that exclusion into greater prominence. The fulfillment of the announcement made to Moses is related in Deut. 32:48-52.

And see the land which I have given unto the children of Israel.—The law led men to "see the promises afar off, and to embrace them" (Heb. 11:13), and it brought them to the borders of Canaan, but could not bring them into it: that was reserved for Joshua, the type of Jesus. It must not be overlooked, however, that, although he was shut out during his lifetime from entering into the land of Canaan, Moses was permitted to stand with Elijah upon the Mount of Transfiguration (Matt. 17:3).

(16) Let the Lord ... —We have a remarkable instance here of the true greatness of Moses. Instead of indulging in excessive grief, or in unavailing remorse, the mind of Moses was intently fixed upon the welfare of those for whose sake he had been willing that his own name should be blotted out of the Book (Exod. 32:32); and instead of appointing one of his own family, or the man of his own choice, as his successor, he commits the matter to God, and prays that He will appoint one who would be a true shepherd to the flock.

(18) And lay thine hand upon him.—It is to be observed that the spiritual qualifications of Joshua did not supersede the necessity of an outward consecration to his office. Nay, more; it seems that special qualifications for the office were bestowed in connection with the imposition of the hands of Moses (See Deut. 34:9).

(21) After the judgment of Urim ... — See note on Exod. 28:30.

28

(1) And the Lord spake unto Moses ... —The sacrificial laws had been to a great extent in abeyance during the wanderings of the Israelites in the wilderness. It was needful, therefore, that before the entrance into the land of Canaan those laws should be promulgated afresh. (See Exod. 12, 39, 42; Lev. 23.)

29

(1) And in the seventh month ... —This chapter contains an account of the days which were to be observed as religious ordinances in the seventh or Sabbatical month—a month which contained more of those days than any other month in the year. (See Lev. 16, 23.)

30

(2) If a man vow a vow unto the Lord ... —It is natural to suppose that at the expiration of the protracted wanderings in the wilderness the pious Israelites would be desirous of testifying their gratitude by dedicating themselves, or some portion of their substance beyond that which the law demanded, to the service of the Lord. And hence, although some regulations respecting vows had already been made (see Lev. 27), it was needful that before their entrance into the land of Canaan some additions should be made to the law which pertained to the nature and obligation of vows. The sacred character of a vow is enforced and timely caution given that it was better for them not to vow than to vow and not to pay. (Comp. Eccles. 5:2-5.)

31

(1) Avenge the children of Israel of the Midianites.—The time had now come for the fulfillment of the command which had already been given (see 25:16-18), after which Moses was to be gathered unto his people, as it had been revealed to him (27:13). After Balaam had been dismissed by Balak, he appears to have gone, not to the Moabites, but to the Midianites; and it was in consequence of the counsel which he gave to the Midianites (25:5) that the Israelites were reduced into the idolatrous and lascivious worship of Baal Peor. It is possible, also, that the Midianites, as the descendants of Abraham, may have possessed clearer light and greater privileges than the Moabites. They may have had many men as enlightened as Jethro among them, and consequently they may have incurred the greater guilt. But the Moabites were not left unpunished (see Deut. 23:3, 4).

(8) Balaam also the son of Beor they slew with the sword.—The death of Balaam by the sword of the Israelites presents a strange and instructive contrast to the prayer which he uttered that he might die the death of the righteous (23:10). If, as some think, we are to understand Micah 6:8 as containing the actual words which were addressed by Balaam to Balak, few men possessed a clearer perception of moral truth. And yet, notwithstanding the light which Balaam possessed, the sublimity of the prophecies which he uttered, and the purity of the motives by which he professed to be actuated, he loved the wages of unrighteousness, gave himself up to do Satan's bidding in casting a stumbling block before the children of Israel, and miserably perished among the enemies of God and of His people. There is a striking and instructive contrast between Balaam and Moses, both of whom had visions of Christ and prophesied of Him, while one loved the wages of unrighteousness, and the other did all for God's glory.

32

(5) Bring us not over Jordan.—These words have been understood by Moses as a request that the conquest of the western side of the Jordan might be left to the other tribes, and that the Reubenites and Gadites might be permitted at once to establish themselves in the land which had been already subjugated. Their language indicated a selfish consideration of their own interests and was calculated to discourage and dishearten their brethren; consequently their proposal was strongly reproved by Moses until certain conditions had been met (see verses 20-24). It is deserving of notice that the tribes of Reuben and Gad and the half tribe of Manasseh (see verses 33 and 39) were among the first who were taken into captivity by the king of Assyria (I Chron. 5:26).

33

(1) These are the journeys of the children of Israel ... —The word which is rendered "journey" appears to denote primarily "the breaking up" of the encampments, which lasted for different periods, and which, during the protracted wanderings in the wilderness, may have been of the average duration of a year. The list of the encampments is expressly said to have been written by Moses, and it served as a permanent memorial, on the one hand, of the sin and rebellion of the nation, and, on the other hand, of the faithfulness and longsuffering of God in leading and sustaining His people throughout their sojourn in the wilderness. See Exod. 12-15. (But comp. verses 30-33 with Deut. 10:6, 7, where the reference is to the final breaking up of the encampment at Kadesh at the expiration of the forty years of wandering in the wilderness.)

(56) Moreover it shall come to pass ... —It must be borne in mind that the idolatrous inhabitants of Canaan were never wholly exterminated, and the pernicious influence which they exercised was felt throughout the whole of the history of the Israelites until the judgments threatened against them were finally executed in the Assyrian and Babylonian captivites.

34

(2, 3) When ye come ... —It was important for the Israelites to be taught that, while divinely commissioned to exterminate the idolatrous inhabitants of the land of Canaan, they had no commission to make aggressive wars upon the surrounding nations which were beyond the confines of the land which was allotted to them.

The land of the Israelites was to extend toward the south as far as the wilderness of Zin, which was to divide their territory from that of the Edomites. The boundary line was to go in a southwesterly direction from the southern point of the Dead Sea, as far as the height of Akrabbim, and was to be continued from this point in a westerly direction as far as Kadesh-barnea, which was at the western extremity of the desert of Zin. It ran along the valleys which form a natural division between the cultivated land and the desert, from the Arabah on the east to the Mediterranean on the west, the Brook of Egypt—i.e., the Wady-el-Arish—forming the western boundary until it reached the sea. From Mount Hor, a peak near the Mediterranean, and on the northwest within sight of Sidon, the boundary line crossed the northern portion of the Lebanon range. From Riblah on the northeast the boundary went southward by the side of the lake of Chinnereth, or Sea of Galilee, from where the eastern boundary was the Jordan down to the Dead Sea. This was to be the Land of the Israelites, according to its borders on every side.

(18) And ye shall take one prince of every tribe ... —In addition to Eleazar the high priest, and Joshua the commander of the army, one chief man, or prince, was to be selected out of each of the ten tribes which were interested in the division, as at the first census one out of each tribe was associated with Moses and Aaron (1:4), and as was **probably** the case at the second census under Moses and Eleazar. (Comp. 27:2.) Security was thus afforded for the equity and impartiality of the allotment; the position of the territory only, and not its dimensions, being determined by lot. With the exception of Caleb, the names of the princes selected for this purpose are not mentioned elsewhere.

35

(2) Cities to dwell in.—The object of the dispersion of the Levites throughout the other tribes seems to have been primarily with a view to the instruction of their brethren in the law of the Lord (Deut. 33:10). It is probable that the Levites also discharged all those other functions which are now discharged by the learned professions.

(6-8) And among the cities which ye shall give ... —It had already been announced in general terms that a place should be appointed where any one could flee who had unintentionally smitten a man so that he died, and had not lain in wait with a view to commit murder (Exod. 21:12, 13). In the verses which follow, the law is delivered at length, and is repeated and further expanded in Deut. 19:1-13. Levitical cities were especially consecrated to the Lord (see Josh. 20:7), and it was to the priests and

Levites that the people looked as administrators of justice.

(12) And they shall be unto you cities for refuge ... —The avenger (Heb., **goel**) was the near kinsman whose office it was to redeem the person or inheritance of his kinsman, if that kinsman was reduced by poverty to sell himself into slavery, or to sell his inheritance; and also to avenge his blood in the event of his being slain. (See Lev. 25:25-55.) The law of the **goel**, as contained in this chapter, served to keep in check the excited passions of the close relatives of the man who had been slain, and to secure for him a fair and impartial trial. Christ, as our "Redeemer" (Heb., **goel**), ever lives (Job 19:25). He has redeemed the persons and the inheritance of His people by His death; and He will, in the last great day, ransom them from the power of the grave, redeem them from death (Hos. 13:4), and avenge their blood on them that dwell on the earth (Rev. 6:10).

(14) Ye shall give three cities on this side Jordan.—Moses himself appointed the three cities on the east of the Jordan—viz., Bezer, in the country of the Reubenites; Ramoth in Gilead, in the country of the Gadites; and Golan in Bashan, in the country of the Manassites (Deut. 4:43). The three cities on the west of the Jordan were not appointed until the land had been allotted among the nine tribes and a half (Josh. 20:7), when the original appointment of Moses in regard to the three cities of the east of the Jordan was confirmed (Josh. 20:8). It is supposed that the six cities were so selected that no one should be above thirty miles from the nearest city of refuge.

(25) And he shall abide in it unto the death of the high priest.—Although the death which had been occasioned was accidental, not intentional, nevertheless the shedding of blood demanded expiation. The manslayer was, therefore, required to remain an exile from his own home until the death of the high priest. As the high priest, by reason of the anointing with the holy oil, became qualified to act as the representative of the nation, and in that capacity acted as their mediator on the great day of atonement, so the death of the high priest assumed a symbolical or representative character, and became a type of that of the great High Priest who, through the eternal Spirit, offered Himself without spot to God, and who by His death made a propitiation for the sins of the world.

(26) But if the slayer shall at any time come without the border of the city ... —As the bodily safety of the Israelite who had slain a man depended upon his strict observance of the law which required him to remain within the city of refuge until the death of the high priest, so in the same way the spiritual safety of the believer depends upon his exclusive reliance upon the merits and efficacy of the atoning death and righteousness of Christ.

36

(8, 9) And every daughter, that possesseth an inheritance ... —The particular direction which was given in the case of the daughters of Zelophehad (27:1-11) is extended in these verses into a general and permanent law that no heiress in Israel should marry out of her father's tribe, in order that the inheritance might not be transferred from one tribe to another, and thus, in process of time, the division of the land among the tribes, which was made under divine direction, be materially changed.

DEUTERONOMY

1

Introduction

(1) These be the words which Moses spake unto all Israel.—The first two verses and the three that follow form a kind of double introduction to the book, and perhaps more especially to the first portion of it, which ends with 4:40. The first two verses state that the substance of this book was first delivered to Israel by Moses between Sinai and Kadesh-barnea. The further introduction shows the words to have been redelivered in the plains of Moab, and preserved in their later rather than their earlier form. The very name Deuteronomy implies the repetition of a law previously given. (See note on 17:18.) This introduction to Deuteronomy seems the work of one who had known the wilderness, and yet wrote from Palestine. Joshua, the next writer to Moses, and possibly also his amanuensis, may have prefixed it to the book. If he did not, it is wholly impossible to say who did.

(2) Kadesh-barnea.—In the regular narrative of the Exodus we read of the place to which the twelve spies returned as Kadesh (Num. 13:26), and of the place at which the period of unrecorded wandering closed (Num. 20:1), in the first month of the fortieth year, as Kadesh. The name "Kadesh-barnea" first appears in Moses' speech (Num. 32:8), where he refers to the sending of the twelve spies. And with the exception of three places where the name is used in describing boundaries, Kadesh-barnea is always found in speeches. This first chapter of Deuteronomy is the only one which contains the name both with and without the appendage -barnea, which connects it with the wanderings of Israel (verse 2). Upon the whole, it seems most likely that only one place or district is intended by the name.

(3) And it came to pass in the fortieth year, in the eleventh month.—The "and" is the real beginning of Deuteronomy, and connects it with the previous books. The moral of these words has been well pointed out by Jewish writers. It was but eleven days' journey from Sinai to Kadesh-barnea — the place from where Israel should have begun the conquest of the Promised Land; but not only eleven days of the second year of the Exodus, but eleven months of the fortieth year found them still in the wilder-

ness. "We see that they could not enter in because of unbelief" (Heb. 3:19).

(3, 4) Moses spake unto the children of Israel ... after he had slain Sihon ... and Og.—The conquest of these two kings and their territories was one of the exploits of the fortieth year (see Num. 21:21-35) and the last exploit of Moses' life. In the period of repose that followed he found a suitable time to exhort the children of Israel, "according unto all that the Lord had given him in commandment unto them." From 34:8, we learn that "the children of Israel wept for Moses thirty days." These days would seem to be the last month of the fortieth year, for "on the tenth day of the first month" (probably of the next year, Josh. 4:19) they passed over Jordan. Thus the **last delivery** of the discourses recorded in Deuteronomy would seem to lie within a single month.

(5) To declare.—The emphatic reiteration of what had been already received from God and delivered to Israel may be intended. But the etymological relationships of the word also suggest the idea of writing. It would seem, then, that at this period Moses began to put the discourses and laws that he had delivered into a permanent form, arranging and writing them with the same motive which influenced the Apostle Peter (II Pet. 1:15).

In this discourse the history of Israel, from the time of their departure from Sinai, is briefly recapitulated with a short practical exhortation. This portion of history comprises three periods of the Exodus: (1) The march from Sinai to Kadesh-barnea, with the sending of the twelve spies and its results, related more at length in Num. 10:11; 14:45. The characteristic feature of this period is **failure** on the part of both leaders and people to rise to their high calling. (2) The thirty-seven and a half years that follow are a period of disgrace, as appears by the absence of all note of time or place in the direct narrative between Num. 14 and 20 and in chaps. 32, 33. This long wandering was also a period of training and discipline. (3) The fortieth year of the Exodus, in which Israel reached the banks of Jordan. The sentence of death pronounced against their elder generation having been executed, a new life was now begun.

(37) Also the Lord was angry with me for your sakes.—Here, again, Moses combines his own rejection, an event of the fortieth year of the Exodus, with the rejection of the people in the second year. The reason was the same—**unbelief.** As the spies presumed to investigate the route and order of the conquest, a matter of divine guidance, so Moses presumed to alter the prescribed order for the miracle in Kadesh. Like transgressions incurred like penalties. The fault for which the people had suffered could not be overlooked in the leader.

2

(5) I have given mount Seir unto Esau.— It is worthy of notice that the development of Ishmael preceded that of Isaac, and the inheritance of Esau was won earlier than that of Jacob. (Comp. Gen. 25:16 with 35:23-26, and Gen. 36:31 wih 37:1.) Isaac and Israel were still strangers and sojourners, while the Ishmaelites were princes, with towns and castles, and the Edomites dukes and kings.

(14) Thirty and eight years; until all . . . —The observation indicates an intimate knowledge of the incidents of the Exodus. It is quite natural to suppose that, as the survivors of that generation became fewer, those who remained would become marked men. Every man of the twelve tribes who passed the census at Sinai was doomed. The fortieth year of the Exodus had more than half expired when they came to the brook Zered. All who remained alive in that year knew that they had a short time to live. Probably more notice was taken of the last few deaths than of all the rest of the six hundred thousand put together.

(21) The Lord destroyed them before them.—It is noticeable that the conquest of Canaan is here brought into the domain of common history by comparison with the conquests of gigantic races accomplished by Edom, Moab, and Ammon. The value of this analogy to Moses and Israel is plain. If the children of Lot, Ishmael, and Esau— who were but Gentiles, although they were Abraham's seed—were able to dispossess these gigantic races, how much more would Israel be able to dispossess the Canaanites under the personal guidance of Jehovah?

(30) The Lord thy God hardened his spirit, and made his heart obstinate.— Jehovah gave the strength to Sihon, as He had done to Pharaoh, and as He does to all. Sihon was responsible for using the strength which God gave him in opposition to the divine purposes. To "harden" a man's spirit is not necessarily a moral process any more

than the hardening of steel. "Made obstinate" is the same verb used in Joshua 1:6, "Be of a good courage." An unyielding spirit and a courageous heart are good or bad according to the use made of them. Sihon used them badly, Joshua used them well. God's gifts were the same to both. (See also Josh. 11:20.)

3

(11) Of the remnant of giants.—i.e., of the nation of Rephaim in these parts. (See note on Gen. 14:5.)

(14) Jair took . . . unto this day.—The last words of this chapter seem to point to a later hand, as of Joshua, describing the completion of the conquest. The expression "unto this day" is characteristically common in Joshua, or in the editorial notes inserted throughout that book.

(23-28) And I besought the Lord at that time.—Two things Moses is recorded to have asked for himself in the story of the Exodus. The first is written in Exod. 33:18, "I beseech thee shew me thy glory." The second is before us here: ". . . I pray thee, let me go over, and see the good land beyond Jordan." It would seem that Moses desired not so much to view the land (which, indeed, was granted him), but to see the greatness of Jehovah manifested in the conquest, as he had seen it in the victories over Og and Sihon. While we cannot allow for a moment that "the old fathers looked only for transitory promises," yet it is impossible not to feel in this prayer of Moses the pressure of the veil which hung over the unseen world before the coming of our Saviour, who "brought life and immortality to light through the Gospel." Moses evidently did not realize that he might see the works of Jehovah and His glory still more clearly in the other world.

(26) Let it suffice thee.—"Far more than this is reserved for thee; plentiful goodness is hidden for thee." And so indeed it proved. For on some goodly mountain (Hermon or "Lebanon") Moses and Elias stood with the Saviour of the world, and spoke of a far more glorious conquest than Joshua's, even "his decease, which he should fulfill at Jerusalem" (Luke 9:31).

(29) So we abode in the valley over against Beth-peor.—Moses' burial place, as it appears by 34:6. It is a significant finishing touch to the scene described above. This verse also concludes the recapitulation of

Israel's journey from Horeb (1:6) to the banks of Jordan, with which this first discourse of Moses begins. The remainder, contained in chap. 4, is the practical part of the discourse.

4

(1) Now therefore hearken.—The whole point of the exhortation in this chapter is the same which we find in Joshua's address to the people (Josh. 24), that they should serve Jehovah. And the ground of the exhortation is His revelation of Himself in Horeb as their God.

(2) Ye shall not add unto the word.—"The word," not "the words." The "word" is the substance of the Law. The "words" in which it is expressed may be more or less. The law of Moses contains in it the germ of all revelation to the very end.

(5) That ye should do so in the land.—It should never be forgotten that there is a special connection between the Law of Moses and the land of Canaan. It cannot be kept in many of its precepts, except by a chosen people in a protected land.

(9) Only take heed to thyself.—The exhortation contained in the following verses lays special emphasis on one point—the worship of the invisible Jehovah without images. This more than anything else would tend to separate the religion of Israel from that of all other nations. It is worth while to observe that we cannot find any trace of a system of national education in Israel until many years later. When education is purely parental, it is likely to be neglected in many instances.

(10) The day that thou stoodest before the Lord thy God in Horeb.—The Church of Israel dated from Sinai, as the Church of Christ does from Pentecost. It is noticeable that the giving of the Law appears to have taken place about fifty days after the Passover in Egypt. Jewish writers associate the Feast of Pentecost with the memory of the event. A similar association, and a contrast between the first and last Pentecost, appears to have been present in Paul's mind in II Cor. 3.

Gather me the people together.—The Greek here might be paraphrased according to New Testament language, "Form a Church of this people." The "day of the assembly" alluded to in this and other passages (as 10:4) may be similarly paraphrased as "the day of the Church." It

seems to be the source of the expression used by Stephen, "the Church in the wilderness" (Acts 7:38). Thus the analogy between Israel's receiving the **letter** of the law at Sinai, and the gift of the Holy Spirit in Jerusalem is brought out.

(27) And the Lord shall scatter you.—Our familiarity with this fact in history must not blind us to its force when uttered as a prophecy. (Comp. 30:1-5.) The fact that the Jews were taken captive for idolatry, and dispersed for the rejection of JESUS, is a remarkable proof that the real reason why they were brought into Canaan and kept there, was to be witnesses for Jehovah. The cause of a people and its idols is so constantly identified in the Old Testament, that those who are in bondage to a nation may naturally be described as in bondage to its gods. Captivity was the means of eradicating idolatry from Israel rather than encouraging it.

(32) For ask now ... whether there hath been any such thing.—The same argument is afterward employed by Paul (Rom. 11:29) for the restoration of Israel: "for the gifts and calling of God are without repentance," i.e., irrevocable. He did not go and take Him a nation out of the midst of another nation in order to abandon them at last. He never did so much in the way of personal and visible intervention for any people; and He will not forsake the work of His own hands. Moses had proved the truth of what he says here in many scenes of sin and peril averted by his own intercession. (See especially Num. 14:11-21, and comp. I Sam. 12:22.)

The Appointment of Three Cities of Refuge

(41) Then Moses severed.—The word "then" appears to be a note of time. It would seem that the appointment of the three cities of refuge on the eastern side of Jordan actually followed this discourse.

Second Discourse

(44-49) These words form an introduction to the second discourse, which occupies the larger portion of the book—from 5:1 to the end of chap. 26. There is no real break between. The present introduction differs from what we find in 1:1. There is no intimation that this portion of Deuteronomy was a repetition of what had been delivered between Sinai and Kadesh-

171

barnea. What follows is said to have been spoken in the land of Sihon and Og, after the conquest by Israel. The whole passage (verses 44-49) may be editorial, and added by Joshua in Canaan. But there is no necessity for this view.

5

This chapter contains a recapitulation of the Decalogue itself and of the circumstances of its delivery. The repetition of the Ten Commandments is the true beginning of the Deuteronomy, as their first delivery is the beginning of the Law itself. (See Exod. 20.)

(12-15) The language of this commandment is identical with the form it takes in Exodus only as far as the 13th and 14th verses are concerned; and even here the special mention of the ox and the ass is confined to Deuteronomy. The introduction and the close of the command, which gives the reason for it, are different here. The reason drawn from the creation is not mentioned; the reason drawn from the Exodus is. This fact illustrates the observation that in Deuteronomy we find "the Gospel of the Pentateuch." If for the Exodus of Israel we substitute here "the exodus of Christ, which He accomplished at Jerusalem," not so much by His death as by His **resurrection**, we have a reason for keeping not the **Sabbath**, but the **Lord's Day**.

(28-31) And the Lord heard the voice of your words ... —The divine comment on the words of the people is recorded only in Deuteronomy; but in order to obtain a complete record of it we must refer to 18:18, 19. It will appear by comparison of the two passages that the promise of the Prophet like unto Moses was given at this time. It is not a little remarkable that He who gave the Law from Sinai "in blackness and darkness and tempest" should, on that very day, acknowledge the need of a different form of teaching for His people, and should promise it then and there. But it must not be forgotten that the Angel of the covenant and the Prophet like unto Moses are one. He who gave the Law on Sinai died under it on Calvary, and provided for its observance forever. (See Heb. 8:10.)

6

First Portion of the Commentary on the Law

(1) These are the commandments, the statutes, and the judgments, which the Lord ... commanded ... that ye might do them in the land.**—After the Decalogue itself has been recapitulated, Moses proceeds to apply its principles to the conduct of Israel in the Promised Land. The first part of the application is more general, and concerns the relation of Israel to Jehovah, who has brought them from Egypt through the wilderness to the Promised Land. This portion concludes with chap. 11. The precepts that follow are particular, and concern the land of Israel viewed as the seat of (1) the **worship** and (2) the **kingdom** of Jehovah. But the whole discourse, from 4:44 to the end of chap. 26, is presented to us as one unbroken whole.

(4, 5) Hear, O Israel ... —These two verses are called by our Lord "the first and great commandment" in the Law. (See Mark 12:29, 30.) The first words of the Talmud concern the hours when this form should be recited in daily morning or evening prayer—"Hear, O Israel: Jehovah our God is one Jehovah." The unity of Jehovah, as opposed to the belief in "gods many and lords many," is the keynote of the Jewish faith. "**We** worship one God in Trinity, and Trinity in Unity." But this truth, though visible in the Old Testament by the light of the New, was not explicitly revealed until it came forth in history, when the Father sent the Son to be the Saviour of the world, and both sent the Holy Spirit to represent Him in the Church.

(13) Thou shalt fear the Lord thy God, and serve him.—i.e., Him only, as translated by the LXX, and cited by our Lord in His temptation. It is remarkable that all His answers to the tempter were taken not only from Deuteronomy, but from one and the same portion of Deuteronomy—chaps. 5-10, inclusive—the portion which applies the principles of the Decalogue to Israel's life. (See verse 16, and 8:3; 10:20.)

7

(1) When the Lord thy God shall bring thee into the land ... —The former chapter applies the Decalogue to the love of Jehovah and of His word, and to faith in Him as the God of Israel; and thus it may be regarded as an expansion of the first commandment. The exhortation in this chapter concerns the treatment of idolaters in the conquest of Canaan, and the avoidance of all such intercourse or union with them as might tend to turn Israel from Jehovah. Obviously, this may be connected both with the first and with the second commandment.

(7) The Lord did not ... choose you, because ye were more.—The danger lest Israel's peculiar relation to the Most High should beget national pride is so obvious, that Moses takes special pains to counteract it by asserting God's sovereignty in the choice.

Ye were the fewest of all people.—It may be observed that the development of the Moabites, Ammonites, Ishmaelites, and Edomites (all, like Israel, descended from Terah), was far more rapid than that of the chosen line and their territorial conquests much earlier. The Scripture is throughout consistent in representing Israel's development as due to the special providence of God.

8

The Remembrance of the Exodus

(2) And thou shalt remember.—The whole of the remainder of this exhortation, to the end of chap. 10, is chiefly taken up with this topic. Israel must remember (1) the leading of Jehovah, and (2) their own rebellious perversity in the journey through the wilderness. The same recollection is made the occasion for a separate note of praise in Ps. 136:16.

The way which the Lord thy God led thee these forty years.—Not so much the literal journey, but "the way"; i.e., the manner. The details of the actual journey are of course included, but only as incidents of "the way." In the Acts of the Apostles the Christian life is in several passages called "the way." In all these things the Israelites were types of us.

(3) That man doth not live by bread only, but by every word that proceedeth out of the mouth of the Lord.—Not here alone, but throughout the Law, as in the Gospel, we are taught that life is to do the will of God. The special interest of these words arises from our Lord's use of them in the hour of temptation. He also was led forty days (each day for a year of the Exodus) in the wilderness, living upon the word of God. At the end of that time it was proposed to Him to create bread for Himself. But He had learned the lesson which Israel was to learn; and so, even when God permitted Him to hunger, He still refused to live by His own word. He preferred that of His Father.

(4) Thy raiment waxed not old upon thee.—The Jewish commentators say that it grew with their growth, from childhood to manhood. We cannot say that anything miraculous is certainly intended, though it is not impossible. It may mean that God in His providence directed them to clothe themselves in a manner suitable to their journey and their mode of life, just as He taught them how to make and clothe His own tabernacle with various fabrics and coverings of skin.

Neither did thy foot swell.—Just as those who were to die in the wilderness could not live, so those who were to enter Canaan were preserved in health through the journey there. It seems allowable to point out the spiritual interpretation of the passage also. If "the way" that God leads any of His children through this present evil world should seem long, and should entail constant need of renewal and cleansing in His sight, He provides us with "raiment that waxes not old," in the everlasting righteousness of His Son; and He also says of those who wait on the Lord that they shall "walk, and not faint" (Isa. 40:31).

9

Exhortation to Remember
the Sins of the Exodus

(1) Hear, O Israel.—A fresh portion of the exhortation begins here. The cause of Israel's conquest of Canaan is not to be sought in their own merit, but in the choice of Jehovah.

(2) Whom thou knowest.—The pronoun is emphatic. The twelve spies, two of whom were still living, had seen them (Num. 13:33), and their fame was doubtless notorious. It seems to have been a common saying, possibly among the Anakim themselves, "Who will stand up to the children of Anak?" No one could be found to face them.

(9) I neither did eat bread nor drink water.—This fact is not related in Exodus concerning the first forty days which Moses spent in Mount Sinai "with his minister Joshua." It might be supposed or implied, but it is not recorded.

(17) I ... brake them before your eyes.—This shows that the act was deliberate on

Moses' part. He did not simply drop the tables in his passion before they reached the camp; he deliberately broke the material covenant in the face of the people, who had broken the covenant itself. When we remember the effect of hastily touching not the tables of the Law themselves, but the mere chest that contained them, then we may well believe that the breaking of these two tables was an act necessary for the safety of Israel. In Exod. 33:7 we read that Moses placed the temporary tabernacle outside the camp at the same time. The two actions seem to have had the same significance, and to have been done for the same reason.

(18) And I fell down before the Lord, as at the first, forty days and forty nights.— Moses, during the first ascent, received the pattern of the Tabernacle and the directions for the priesthood, which he did not deliver to Israel until after he descended from Sinai the second time. (See Exod. 24:18 to 31, and 35:1, etc.) During the first forty days, Joshua was with Moses in the mount (probably to help in taking the pattern for the Tabernacle); during the second forty Moses was alone.

(21) I took your sin . . . and I cast the dust thereof into the brook.—The stream from the rock in Horeb not only gave Israel drink, but bore away their "sin" upon its waters. "And that Rock was Christ." This identification of the sin with the material object is in harmony with the Law in Leviticus, where "sin" and "sin-offering"— "trespass" and "trespass-offering"—are respectively denoted by a single word.

(26) I prayed therefore . . . and said.— The words that follow are similar to those which are recorded in Exod. 32:11-13. Moses appears to be alluding to his first intercession here, before he descended from Sinai for the first time. Few of the words used by Moses in the second forty days are found in Exodus. (See Exod. 34:9.)

10

(1) At that time the Lord said unto me.— The command to make the Ark was given in the former period of forty days (Exod. 25:10); the command to hew the two tables was given after Moses had seen the glory of God (Exod. 33) from the cleft in the rock, but before the forty days spent in intercession.

(2) And I will write on the tables.—It is a common error to suppose that **Moses wrote** the Law the second time. The mistake arises from the change of person in Exod. 34:28, where the same pronoun "he" refers first to Moses, and then to Jehovah. But there is no doubt as to the fact or its spiritual meaning. The tables of stone represent the "fleshy tables of the heart," as Paul teaches us in II Cor. 3:3. The Ark and the Tabernacle which received the Law are a figure of God's human temple, and of the renewed heart of man.

(4) In the day of the assembly.—Or, in New Testament language, "the day of the Church." The Pentecost of the Old Testament was the day when "the letter" was given; the Pentecost of the New Testament was the day of the "Spirit that giveth life." Each of these aspects of God's covenant produced a Church after its kind.

(6, 7) These verses are among the most difficult in Deuteronomy. The main point is that Israel re-visited in their journey around the land of Edom four places where they had previously encamped, and among them Mosera, or Moseroth, the district in which Mount Hor, where Aaron died, was situated. There is no impossibility in this; in fact, it is highly probable, and would partly account for the statement in Num. 21:4, that "the soul of the people was much discouraged because of the way." It was just about this time that the fiery serpents came.

11

(6) What he did unto Dathan and Abiram . . . —See Num. 16. It is impossible to separate the rebellion of Korah from that of Dathan and Abiram, and seeing that the whole point of Korah's rebellion was the priesthood, it is difficult to see how the writer of Deuteronomy could be ignorant of any priesthood save that of the whole tribe of Levi. The object of Korah's rebellion was to abolish the distinction between a Kohathite and a priest.

(10) Not as the land of Egypt.—But much better. And Egypt was praised above all lands, as it is said (Gen. 13:10), "As the garden of the Lord, like the land of Egypt." And the land of Goshen, where Israel dwelt, is called "the best of the land of Egypt" (Gen. 47:6). And even this was not as good as the land of Israel.

(14) The first rain (after sowing), **the latter rain** (just before harvest). In the ninth month and the first month respectively. (See Ezra 10:9, 13, and Joel 2:23.)

(18) Therefore shall ye lay up these my words.—The same injunctions are found above (6:6-9). The Jewish commentator remarks, somewhat sadly, here, that they would remember them in their captivity, if not before.

(31) For ye shall pass over Jordan.—Here ends the first portion of the exposition of the Decalogue—that which sets forth the relation of the people brought out of Egypt to Jehovah. The following chapters set forth the laws of the land of Israel—first, as the seat of worship of Jehovah; secondly, as the seat of His kingdom; thirdly, as the area of operation of certain rules of behavior, intended to form a distinctive character for His people. The land is considered as the seat of Jehovah's worship from 12:1 to 16:17, inclusive.

12

(2) Ye shall utterly destroy.—First of all these requirements constitute the destruction of every vestige of idolatry. In the land of Jehovah there must be no trace of any other god but Him. But Israel disobeyed the order. They did not themselves yield to idolatry in Joshua's time. The Canaanites being left undisturbed after they ceased to resist openly, and their objects of worship being left unmolested, there were constant temptations to idolatry, to which Israel yielded. And thus it was not until the times of Hezekiah and Josiah that these laws were carried out. But this does not prove the law to have come into existence then.

(5) But unto the place which the Lord your God shall choose out of all your tribes.—The form of the order proves its antiquity. No one who was acquainted with the removal of that "place" from Shiloh to Nob, from Nob to Gibeon, from Gibeon to Jerusalem, could have written with such utter unconsciousness of later history as these words imply. It is noticeable that in the reading of this precept in the times of our Lord, the Jews seem to have arrived at the same state of unconsciousness. They could not conceive of the presence or worship of Jehovah anywhere but at Jerusalem. (See on this topic Stephen's speech in Acts 7, and the incidental proofs it contains of God's presence with Israel **in many places**, in reply to the accusation made against

Stephen of preaching the destruction of the one idolized seat of worship at Jerusalem.)

(8) Ye shall not do after all the things that we do here this day.—Here is another precept strongly marked with the condition of Israel in the wilderness. It has been too much overlooked by recent commentators that the law of Moses has a **prophetic side**. It was given to him and to Israel at a time when they were not in a position to keep it. It was the law of the land which God would give them. In many ways its observance depended on the completion of the conquest of the land, and upon the quietness of the times in which they lived. This prophetic aspect was certainly not unrecognized by the Jews (see Lev. 23:37-43; Neh. 8:17).

(11) Then there shall be a place.—See II Sam. 7:1. The building of Jerusalem and of the Temple brought with it in due time the accomplishment of the law which is appended to the prophecy.

(16) Ye shall pour it upon the earth.—This act was a necessary part of every slaughter of an animal for food. The blood, which is the life, must be poured upon the earth for God, whether the victim was consigned to the altar or not. It was a continual reminder of the necessity for the sacrifice of the death of Christ, to be continued until He should come. Thus the act was, in a sense, sacramental.

(32) What thing soever I command you.—No later writer could put these words into the mouth of Moses, if he had altered the precepts of Moses to any appreciable extent.

13

(1) If there arise.—Three cases of instigation to idolatry are considered in this chapter:—(1) The false prophet (verses 1-5; comp. Elijah, I Kings 18). (2) A private individual (verses 6-11; comp. Jehu and Jehoiada, II Kings 10:19-27; 11:18, and Asa, II Chron. 15:13). (3) A city (verses 12-18; comp. Ai and Gibeah, Judg. 7, 20, 21, and Hos. 9:9; 10:9). In every case the penalty is the same—death without mercy.

(6) If thy brother.—The law may seem harsh, but its principle is reproduced in the Gospel (Matt. 10:37; Luke 14:26). It is impossible to deny or escape the identity of the Lord Jesus with the Jehovah of the Old Testament. He does not always put the execution of His judgments into human hands, but He is the same forever.

175

14

(1) Ye are the children of the Lord.—This fact is made the foundation of all the laws of ceremonial and moral holiness in the Pentateuch, more especially in the Book of Leviticus, where these laws are chiefly to be found. (Comp. Lev. 11.)

(2) For thou art an holy people.—This verse is repeated from 7:6. In the former passage, the principle is made the ground for destroying all monuments of idolatry in the land of Israel. Here it is made the basis of outward personal dignity and purity. This recalls the arrangement of the Book of Leviticus somewhat forcibly. The laws of ceremonial holiness stand first in that book, before the law of yearly atonement. Then follow the laws of moral holiness. But the principle and ground of all these laws is the same: "Ye shall be holy, for I am holy, and ye are mine."

(22) Thou shalt truly tithe.—The Talmud and Jewish interpreters in general are agreed in the view that the tithe mentioned in this passage, both here and in verse 28, and also the tithe described in 26:12-15, are all one thing—"the second tithe," and entirely distinct from the ordinary tithe assigned to the Levites for their subsistence in Num. 18:21, and by them tithed again for the priests (Num. 18:26). The tithe described in Numbers was called "the first tithe," and was not considered sacred. The second tithe, on the contrary, was always regarded as a holy thing.

15

The Law here is an extension of that which we find in Exod. 21 and Lev. 25.

16

Verses 1-8. The Passover
(See Exod. 12.)

Verses 9-12. The Feast of Weeks,
or Pentecost

See Exod. 23:16; 34:18-23; Lev. 23:15-22; Num. 28:26-31. The feast itself is ordained in Exodus; the **time** is given in Leviticus; and the sacrifices in Numbers.

Verses 13-15. The Feast of
Tabernacles

For details of the observance see the passages already referred to in Exodus, Leviticus and Numbers, but more especially Lev. 23:33-43.

The eighth day (Lev. 23:36; Num. 29:12) is treated apart from the first seven days of the Feast of Tabernacles, somewhat in the same way as the Passover is always distinguished in the Pentateuch from the six days which followed it, and which are called the Feast of Unleavened Bread. The reason for the distinction in that case becomes clear in the fulfillment of the feast by our Lord. The Passover is His sacrifice and death. We keep the Feast of Unleavened Bread by serving Him in "sincerity and truth." The Feast of Tabernacles has not yet been fulfilled by our Lord like the two other great feasts of the Jewish calendar. Unfulfilled prophecies regarding it may be pointed out as in Zech. 14. Our Lord refused to signalize that feast by any public manifestation (John 7:2-10). There may, therefore, be some reason for separating the eighth and last day of the Feast of Tabernacles from the former seven, which will appear in its fulfillment in the kingdom of God. It is remarkable that the dedication of Solomon's temple, the beginning of the second temple, and the dedication of the wall of Jerusalem, all occurred about the time of the Feast of Tabernacles.

17

(1) Thou shalt not sacrifice . . . —The law concerning the purity of victims is given in full in Lev. 22:17-25. It takes place there among the special laws of holiness. The same principle appears to unite the several topics treated here in Deuteronomy, as the holy days, the administration of justice, the absence of groves and images, with such a precept as this regarding the perfection of sacrifices. The holiness of the God of Israel necessitates them all. Truth, justice, and purity are demanded in all that come nigh Him.

Verses 2-7. Every Idolater to be
Stoned (Comp. chap. 13.)

(3) Either the sun, or moon, or any of the host of heaven.—This is the oldest and simplest, and apparently most innocent form of idolatry. If this were punishable with death, obviously no grosser form of idolatry could be spared. The Book of Job, which knows no other idolatry, admits this to be a denial of "the God that is above" (Job 31:26-28).

(7) The evil.—Comp. I Cor. 5:13. The phrase is of frequent occurrence in Deuteronomy, and if we are to understand that in all places where it occurs "the evil" is to be understood of an individual, and to be taken in the masculine gender, the fact seems to deserve notice in considering the phrase "deliver us from evil" in the Lord's Prayer. There is really no such thing as wickedness in the world apart from some wicked being or person. We are also reminded of the famous argument of Augustine that evil has no existence except as a corruption of good, or a creature's perverted will.

Verses 8-20. The Supremacy in Israel of the Written Law of God

(8) Into the place which the Lord thy God shall choose.—This implies what was afterward ordered before Moses' death, that the standard copy of the Law would be kept beside the Ark of the Covenant, in the sacred place (31:26).

(9) The priests the Levites, and ... the judge.—The order agrees exactly with the constitution which Moses left behind him at his death. This has been already indicated in Num. 27:15-21. The priests are the custodians of the Law; the judge or chief magistrate is the executor of it. The principle is not altered by the substitution of a king for the judge, or by the addition of a prophet. (Comp. Mal. 2:7, 8; and our Lord's application, Matt. 23:2, 3.)

(9-11) And they shall shew thee the sentence of judgment ... —The four English verbs have only three equivalents in Hebrew, viz., **tell**, **teach**, and **say**. This was the function of the priest and of the judge. It is not sufficiently observed that this defines the relation between the Church and the Bible from the time the Law was delivered to the Church, and that the relation between the Church and the Bible is the same to this day. The only authority wherewith the Church (of Israel, or of Christ) can "bind" or "loose" is the written Law of God. The binding (or forbidding) and loosing (or permitting) of the rabbis—the authority which our Lord committed to His Church—was only the application of His written Word.

Nor does the varying relation between the executive and legislative authority alter the principle. Where the Law of Jehovah is the law of the land, death may be the penalty of disobedience. Where it is only the law of the Christian community, exclusion may be the extreme penalty that is possible. But still the relation between the written Word and the ministers of the Church is the same. The Church is the witness and keeper of Holy Writ, and can only show it from the sentence of judgment. The sentence is an application of the Law, not a mere invention of the authorities themselves.

Verses 14-20. The Law of the Kingdom

(14) When thou art come unto the land.— These are not the words of a legislator who is already in the land. Those who say that this law dates from later times must be prepared to assert that this clause is expressly framed to suit the lips of Moses, and is thus far a deliberate forgery.

I will set a king over me, like as all the nations.—There is an evident allusion to this phrase in I Sam. 8:20, "That we also may be like all the nations." It is noticeable that Moses in this place says nothing in disapproval of the design. In fact his words might easily have been cited by the people in support of their proposal. Looked at this way, the citation of the words of Deuteronomy in Samuel is perfectly natural. But if we suppose (with some modern writers) that the passage in Deuteronomy was constructed from that in Samuel, there remains precisely the same unconsciousness of the locality of the place which Jehovah should choose in Palestine as appears in every reference to it in this book. In Moses this is perfectly natural. But that any later writer should be so totally regardless of the claims of Judah, David, and Jerusalem, and say nothing either for or against them, is inconceivable.

(18) He shall write him a copy of this law.—This phrase is the source of the Greek title of the book, **Deuteronomion**, or in English, Deuteronomy. The word appears also in Josh. 8:32. The English conveys the right sense of the word, which primarily denotes repetition. In Hebrew it is **Mishneh**, the name later given to the "text" of the Talmud, of which the idea is to repeat the law; though it is a somewhat peculiar repetition, in which minutia are chiefly dealt with, and weightier matters left out. See traces of this direction in Joash (II

Chron. 23:11); Jehoshaphat (II Chron. 17:9); and Josiah (II Chron. 34:18).

(20) To the end that he may prolong his days in his kingdom, he, and his children.— The striking fact that no dynasty except that of David ever continued for more than five generations, and only two dynasties for more than two generations, while David's dynasty was perpetual by promise, could hardly have escaped notice, if known to the writer of this book.

18

Verses 1-5. The Priests' Due
(Comp. Num. 18:18-21.)

(5) To stand to minister in the name of the Lord.—This is the office of the priests. The Levites are said, "to stand before the congregation to minister unto them" (Num. 16:9). If the writer of Deuteronomy knew no distinction between priest and Levite, it is difficult to see how the Jews could have derived the distinctive privileges of the priests from these enactments.

(6-8) And if a Levite come.—The Levites with the priests were to receive forty-eight cities in Israel, with the suburbs (Num. 35:7). There was as yet no provision made by which all could serve in turn at the tabernacle. When David divided them all into courses, priests, Levites, singers (and porters?) alike, there was no longer any need for this provision. The institutions of David prove its antiquity. The only case in history that illustrates it is that of the child Samuel (see I Sam. 2).

(9-14) Certain forms of idolatry to be avoided, especially unlawful means of communication with the unseen world.

Verses 15-20. The One Mediator

The connection between these verses and the preceding is well illustrated by the questions in Isa. 8:19 and Luke 24:5.

(15) The Lord thy God will raise up unto thee a Prophet.—Namely, Him of whom Peter spoke in Acts 3:22-26. "Unto you first God, having raised up his Son Jesus, sent him to bless you." It must not be forgotten that the prophetic office is still continued to our risen Lord. There would be no need to look downward, to consult dead relatives, or seek knowledge from spirits, even if they were accessible. The Holy Spirit, our Comforter and Advocate on earth, and the

Prophet, our Advocate that speaks from heaven, are enough for all human need.

(20) That prophet shall die.—Comp. the case of Hananiah (Jer. 28).

19

Here a fresh section of the laws begins.
The Cities of Refuge
(Comp. Num. 35:9; Josh. 20.)

(8, 9) If the Lord thy God enlarge thy coast ... thou shalt add three cities.—i.e., thou shalt add three to the six, making nine in all. There is no trace of this ever having been done in the history of Israel. The comments of Jewish writers show that nothing is known of the fact in their literature. Thus the Jews take the passage as prophetic of their ultimate restoration.

20

Laws of Warfare

(1) When thou goest out to battle.—i.e., generally; not only in the immediate conquest of Canaan. Yet it may be observed that in the writings of Moses it is foreseen that the completion of the conquest will be gradual, and that Israel will have to go to battle many times before all enemies are overcome. (See Ps. 20:7.)

21

Here again, in chaps. 21 and 22, we are reminded that the Law of Jehovah was also the civil and criminal law of Israel.

(23) He that is hanged is accursed of God.—In the LXX it is, "Cursed of God is every one that hangeth upon a tree," and is cited in this form by Paul (Gal. 3:13). We cannot see why he should be pronounced cursed, except for the sake of that which was designed by the determined counsel and foreknowledge of God, that His Son Jesus Christ should bear our sins in His own body on the tree, and redeem us from the curse of the Law, by being "made a curse for us." There is no doubt as to the shame of the punishment which our Lord endured and despised.

Thou shalt in any wise bury him that day.—This is another law remarkably and providentially fulfilled in our Lord's death

We do not read that the robbers who were crucified with Him were buried, though their bodies were removed from the cross. It is not improbable that this law was also intended to prevent the barbarous practice of leaving men impaled on sharp stakes or suspended upon crosses from day to day until they died from pain and thirst. It certainly is a disgrace to the divine image to treat it in this manner.

22

(21) She hath wrought folly in Israel. — This expression appears for the first time in Gen. 34:7, shortly after the bestowal of the name "Israel" (Gen. 32). It would almost appear that the name entailed a higher standard of behavior upon Jacob's family after the hand of the Holy One had been laid upon their father. A separate code of rules was binding upon the chosen people from the very beginning of their history. Hardly any point is made of more importance, from the birth of Isaac downward, than the purity of the chosen seed.

(24) His neighbour's wife. — It is evident from the language of this precept that a betrothed virgin in Israel is regarded as a "wife." This illustrates the language of Matt. 1.

23

The old heading of this chapter, "Who may or may not enter into the congregation," supplies a good connection with what goes before. From the law of marriage in the Church of Israel it is a natural step to the children of Israel, the members of this Church.

(14) For the Lord thy God walketh in the midst of ... thee. — This is a most beautiful argument for purity in every sense. It was evidently present in Paul's mind in II Cor. 6:16-7:1.

(19, 20) Usury. — See Exod. 22:25; Lev. 25:35, 36. Some writers on this law have thought that it forbids the putting out of money to interest. But it is noticeable that in both the passages referred to the loan is supposed to be made to a "poor man" in "real distress." Usury in such cases means oppression; and so it is proved to be by the examples given in Neh. 5:2-5, 10-12. The Mosaic law against usury does not belong to commerce with other nations; it is part of the poor law of the land of Israel.

24

Verses 1-4. Divorce

(1) Let him write her a bill of divorcement. — "Moses, because of the hardness of your hearts, suffered you to put away your wives," is the divine comment upon this. It is a distinct concession to the weakness of Israel—not the ideal standard of the Law, but the highest which it was found practicable to enforce. (See Matt. 19:2 seq.) There are many other particular enactments in the Law of Moses of which the same thing may be said. The ideal standard of morality has never varied. There is no higher ideal than that of the Pentateuch. But the Law which was actually enforced, in many particulars fell short of that ideal.

Various Precepts of Humanity
Verse 5-end of chap. 25.

(17-22) The stranger, the fatherless, and the widow—are the subject of all the laws in these verses. For verses 17, 18, see Exod. 22:22-24. As to the harvest, see Lev. 23:22.

In a special way and for some special reason, all through the Old Testament, "the Lord careth for the stranger." What the reason is, if we had the Old Testament only, we might find it hard to discover. But when we open the New Testament, we may see that this is one aspect of the love of God the Father to His Son Jesus Christ, who was one day to come among us as "a stranger," when there was "no room for him in the inn." His coming forth as a stranger could not be unnoticed. And, therefore, the name and mention of the stranger all through the Old Testament is like a path strewn with flowers, in expectation of the coming one that is greatly beloved.

25

(1) They shall justify the righteous, and condemn the wicked. — See Exod. 23:7; Prov. 17:15. It should be noticed that "justify" is here used forensically, not meaning to make righteous, but to "treat as righteous." Those who object to this sense in Paul's epistles will find it hard to put any other sense upon the word in the rest of Holy Scripture.

(4) Thou shalt not muzzle the ox.—We have a comment on these words from Paul in two places (I Cor. 9:9, and I Tim. 5:18). It is not only written for the sake of the oxen, but to prove that the "labourer is worthy of his hire"; "they that preach the Gospel should live of the Gospel."

(5) If brethren dwell together.—The object of the law was held to be attained if the family of the dead man was perpetuated, and did not become extinct. Therefore the marriage specified was not necessarily between the brother and the brother's wife, but might be between other representatives of the two persons in question. (See Ruth 4.) The law is older than Moses. We first hear of it in the household of Judah the son of Jacob (Gen. 38:8). The violation of the law then was punished with death, not with disgrace only.

But that which makes the law most memorable is the teaching elicited from the lips of our Saviour by the question which the Sadducees raised upon it (Matt. 22:24). It is worthwhile to observe that the law itself demands that in some sense there should be a resurrection. Boaz puts it thus (Ruth 4:5), "to raise up the name of the dead upon his inheritance." Why should the name of the dead be kept up, if the dead has passed out of existence? We may well believe that this law was partly intended (like baptism for the dead, or like giving children the names of their departed progenitors) for the express purpose of keeping alive the hope of resurrection in the minds of the chosen people.

(16) An abomination unto the Lord.—See Prov. 11:1; Amos 8:4-8. The protection of the poor is the chief practical end in this; rich men can take care of themselves. Poor men are doubly robbed by short weight and measure, because they cannot protect themselves against it. The injustice tends to perpetuate their poverty.

(17-19) At the end of all the precepts of humanity, the extermination of that people which is presented to us as the incarnation of inhumanity is decreed. These details are not given in Exod. 17. The decree was carried in several stages: by Barak and Gideon (Judg. 5:14; 6:3; 7:12; etc.), by Saul and Samuel (I Sam. 15), by David (I Sam. 27:8, 9; 30:17), by the Simeonites (I Chron. 4:42, 43), and lastly by Esther, who exterminated the Agagites in Haman's house. No doubt any remnant of Amalek in the Persian empire under Mordecai would have shared Haman's fate.

180

26

Verses 1-11. Presentation of the Firstfruits

(1) When thou art come in.—From the words of verse 11, "thou shalt rejoice," the Jews gather that the thanksgiving to be said over the firstfruits (in verses 5-10) must be said at some time between the close of the feast of unleavened bread on the twenty-first day of the first month (the "solemn assembly" of Deut. 16:8) and the Feast of Tabernacles.

(5) A Syrian ready to perish.—The reference is to Jacob, especially when pursued by Laban, who would have taken from him his all, except for the divine mercy and protection. We may also recall his danger from Esau (Gen. 32; 33), from the Shechemites (34; 35), and from the famine, until he heard of Joseph.

(6, 7) See Exod. 2:25; 3:9; and 6:5, 6 for the source of this confession. Samuel in his famous speech (I Sam. 12:8) takes up the language of this passage.

Verses 12-15. Declaration of the Tithe

(12) The third year, which is the year of tithing.—See 14:28, 29. In the third and sixth years, the second tithe, which in other years was eaten by the owners (in kind or value) at Jerusalem, was given to the poor and was called the poor's tithe. Thus the words "and hast given it unto the Levite," are applied to the first tithe, which was never omitted, and which is prescribed by Num. 18. The words that follow, "the stranger, the fatherless, and the widow," are interpreted of the poor's tithe. The prescribed confession is not to be made until **all the tithe** has been given, both first and second, i.e., the annual tithe to the Levites, and the second, which was in these years devoted to the poor. According to Jewish usage, this confession would be offered on Passover eve of the fourth year.

Verses 16-19. Close of the Exhortation

(16) This day the Lord thy God hath commanded thee.—These words are not to be taken as part of the service described in the previous verses, but as the words of Moses in bringing his exhortation to a close. If, as some would have us believe, the Book of Deuteronomy draws these things from the prophets, rather than the prophets from Moses, how is it that there is not the faintest allusion in Deuteronomy to Jerusalem, which in the days of the prophets had become the center of all these hopes?

27

The Law to Be Established in Canaan As the Law of the Land

(3) **Thou shalt write upon them all the words of this law, when thou art passed over, that thou mayest go in.**—Again it is evident that the "going in" to the land and the "passing over" Jordan are not identical. The "Law of God" was to be set up in the heart of the country, as soon as Israel had entered it, in order that they might complete the conquest of it. It is abundantly clear that Israel's title to Canaan was dependent upon their maintaining the Law of Jehovah as the law of the land.

For the fulfillment of this precept, see Josh. 8:32-35. The words of this verse are an additional reason for the view that the Law was set up on Ebal immediately after the capture of Ai, without waiting for the completion of the conquest.

(26) **Cursed be he that confirmeth not all the words of this law to do them.**—From this verse Paul reasons that "as many as are of the works of the law are under a curse" (Gal. 3:10). For no man can do all of them. And therefore it is impossible to secure the blessing of Gerizim except through Him who bare the curse of Ebal. "Christ hath redeemed us from the curse of the law, being made a curse for us, as it is written, cursed is every one that hangeth on a tree" ibid., 3:13).

28

Sanctions of the Law in Deuteronomy. The Blessing and the Curse

Almost every specific portion of the Law in Scripture has a passage of this kind at the end. The code in Exod. 21-23 ends with a declaration of rewards and punishments (Exod. 23:20-33). The laws of holiness, ceremonial and moral, in Leviticus, are closed by chapter 26. This Book of Deuteronomy, more profound and more spiritual in its teaching, and more earnest in its exhortation than all the rest of the Law, closes with this denunciation—the most tremendous in

all Scripture—of the consequences of disobedience in detail. The Sermon on the Mount, the law of the New Testament, closes with a passage that astonished the hearers by its authority (Matt. 7:21-27). The exhortations of our Lord's ministry, both public and private, have a similar close: for Israel in Matt. 23, for the disciples in Matt. 25. And the epistle to the Hebrews, the last appeal to the Jewish nation in God's Word, has a similar passage in chap. 12, before the final exhortations and salutations. Finally, the Apocalypse itself puts the same kind of close to all Scripture in 22:10-19.

We may divide this chapter into four parts. First, the blessings of obedience to the nation as God's people (verses 1-14). Secondly, the curses of disobedience (verses 15-48). Thirdly, the prophecy of the conquest of Israel by a strange nation, and the miseries of the siege of the capital (verses 49-57). Fourthly, the continued and protracted misery of the rejected nation (verses 58-68).

The remarkably prophetic character of this chapter is beyond question. It must be observed, moreover, as a most significant fact, that this chapter does not form the close of the Pentateuch. Another covenant is made with Israel after this. And Moses departed with words of blessing on his lips. (See note on 29:1.)

(9) **The Lord shall establish thee an holy people.**—i.e., shall "maintain" thee in that position or shall "raise thee up" into it, and exalt thee to it, in its fullest sense. The word here employed has branched out into two lines of thought. In Jewish literature it has taken the sense of permanence and perpetuity. Through the LXX it has given birth to the New Testament word for "resurrection." (See 18:18, and comp. Acts 3:26; II Sam. 7:12; I Chron. 17:11.)

(32) **Thy sons and thy daughters.**—The language of this verse is perhaps the most pathetic piece of description in the whole chapter. Many of the nations bordering on Israel were accustomed when they made inroads to take away, not only the cattle, but also the children for slaves. Another equally pathetic passage in Jeremiah touches on the same thing (see Jer. 31:15-17).

(36) **Thee, and thy king which thou shalt set over thee.**—Comp. 17:14. The former passage is not the only one in which Moses shows his foreknowledge that Israel would have a king. But could any later writer have concealed his knowledge that there were

two kingdoms, or have avoided all allusion to the throne of David in passages like these?

Several kings went into captivity. Jehoahaz was taken to Egypt; Jeconiah and Zedekiah to Babylon. Hoshea's fate is not recorded in Scripture; but he was taken (apparently) with Samaria by the Assyrians.

(49) The Lord shall bring a nation against thee.—In this instance the Chaldaeans were intended, "that bitter and hasty nation" (Hab. 1:6).

As swift as the eagle flieth.—The eagles of Rome may be alluded to here. And of the Chaldaeans it is said, "They shall fly as the eagle that hasteth to eat" (Hab. 1:8).

(52) And he shall besiege thee in all thy gates.—The siege of the last two "de-fenced cities" by Nebuchadnezzar's army is mentioned in Jer. 34:7. (Comp. II Chron. 36:17; Lam. 5:12.) The siege and capture of Jotapata by the Romans, in spite of all the efforts of the Jews to defend it, is especially recorded by Josephus.

(53) Thou shalt eat the fruit of thine own body.—This is especially confirmed in the siege of Samaria by the Syrians (II Kings 6:26-29; but see note on verse 56), and also in Jerusalem when besieged by Nebuchadnezzar. (See Lam. 2:20; 4:10.)

(56) The tender and delicate woman.—This was fulfilled to the very letter in the case of Mary of Beth-ezob in the siege of Jerusalem by Titus. The story is told with horrible minuteness by Josephus, and again by Eusebius in his Church History. The secrecy of the deed was one of its horrors.

(64) And the Lord shall scatter thee among all people.—Fulfilled, literally, in this last (Roman) dispersion.

Thou shalt serve other gods.—We do not know of Israel's falling into actual idolatry in dispersion, except in Egypt (Jer. 44:17), and possibly in Babylon (Ezek. 14:22, 23; comp. 33:25). But they were slaves to the worshipers of other gods.

29

The Second Covenant

(1) These are the words of the covenant.—The position of Deut. 29 and 30 is analogous to that of Lev. 27. The tremendous curse of the Sinaitic covenant is not the end of God's dealings with the chosen people. After that, there is still another covenant ("in the land of Moab"), to the force of which there is no limit (see verse 15). The

gifts and calling of God are irrevocable. Nothing can destroy the relation between Jehovah and Israel. Their resurrection as a nation may well be described by the words of Moses in Ps. 90.

Beside the covenant which he made with them in Horeb.—It should be carefully noted that the formal repetition of the Law in Moses' second great discourse in this book opens with these words (5:2), "the Lord our God made a covenant with us in Horeb." There is no real break in Deuteronomy from 5:1 to the end of chap. 26. And chaps. 27 and 28 are the "sanction" of that covenant.

(2) And Moses called unto all Israel, and said unto them.—The point set before them is one simple thing, to accept Jehovah as their God. All this is closely reproduced in Josh. 24.

(13) That he may establish thee to day for a people unto himself.—It must be carefully observed that this is the aspect of the covenant which makes Jehovah responsible for the fulfillment of the whole. The people's part, as described in this verse, is only to accept the position. And thus the covenant of Deut. 29 is brought into the closest similarity with that which is called the New Covenant in Jer. 31:31 and Heb. 8:8, the form of which is "I will" be to them a God, and "they shall" be to me a people. In Deuteronomy the first half of the New Covenant appears here in chap. 29. The second part appears in 30:6-8.

(29) The secret things belong unto the Lord our God.—Moses was delivering to Israel not law only but prophecy. We may be certain that there was more in this latter portion of his prophecy than he could understand. May not this be one of the occasions concerning which the apostle says of the prophets, that they "searched what or what manner of time the spirit of Christ which was in them did signify"? All those curses were to come upon Israel, and yet, after that, there was still a covenant with them, embracing every generation to the world's end. Must not Moses have longed to know what would befall his people in the latter days? And if we ourselves, "upon whom the ends of the world are come," do not yet see the future of Israel distinctly, are not the words appropriate still? (See I Pet. 1:10-12; I Cor. 10:11; comp. Ps. 119:166.)

30

(5) Into the land which thy fathers pos-

sessed.—It is difficult to interpret these words of any land except Palestine. Comp Jer. 29:13, 14, for their fulfillment in the first restoration, from Babylon.

(8) And thou shalt return and ... do all his commandments.—It is certain that the laws of Deuteronomy have never been kept perfectly. The minute observances of the Talmudical system took the heart and spirit out of the Law of Moses. Christians do not profess to obey any commandments but those which are called moral. If the Law itself is to be fulfilled, a restoration of Israel would seem to be necessary.

(14) But the word is very nigh unto thee.—Here the difference between the Jewish and the Christian commentator is very striking. What could more clearly prove that the covenant of chaps. 28 and 29 was meant to present the way of salvation from a different point of view to the Sinaitic covenant, and was "beside the covenant which he made with them in Horeb" (29:1)? We are not to suppose there was ever a different way of salvation. The Decalogue itself begins (like the New Covenant) with "I am the Lord thy God." But, unlike the New Covenant, it makes no provision whereby Israel may keep the laws arising out of the relationship. The New Covenant not only asserts the relationship, but also provides the means whereby men may walk worthy of it. See Lev. 18:5; Rom. 10:6ff. It is only in the power of this principle that Moses, in the exhortation which he founds on this statement of the way of righteousness through faith, could say as he did in verse 19, "therefore choose life."

31

Moses Resigns His Charge

(3) The Lord thy God, he will go over before thee ... Joshua, he shall go over before thee.—Can it be accidental that Jehovah and Joshua are spoken of in exactly the same language, and that there is no distinguishing conjunction between them, the "and" of the English Version being supplied? The prophetical truth of this identification is too remarkable to be missed.

(16) Behold, thou shalt sleep with thy fathers ... —This prophecy that the children of Israel would forsake Jehovah and break His covenant is remarkable, when we consider His dealings with them as a nation. When He chose Israel to be His peo-

ple, He knew the risk of doing so, and He provided for it beforehand. Not less when He said, "Let us make man in our image, **after our likeness,**" did He provide the means of forming in us the divine character by all that Christ has done. The Fall is recorded in the third chapter of Genesis. Redemption and restoration are exhibited in type and symbol in the second chapter. God brought Israel into Canaan in full foreknowledge of what the people would become when there.

(24) When Moses had made an end of writing.—This means the completion of the books of Moses as he delivered them to Israel; not merely Deuteronomy, as in verse 9, but the whole, including the song mentioned in verse 22. The song was probably the end of the book as delivered to them by Moses.

32

Verses 1-43. The Song of Moses

(4) He is the Rock ... —No such combination of all the words for "uprightness," "sincerity," "equity," and "reliability" is to be found elsewhere in all Scripture. This is the character of the **Rock**. This name of God (**Tzur**) is one of the characteristics of the song. So exclusively is the term in Hebrew used in this sense, that no man is ever described by it in the Old Testament. And the LXX, in this song and in many other places, does not translate it at all, but gives it as **God**. In other places the word **Petra** (never Petros) is employed. This fact indicates that the Petra of Matt. 16:18 could only have been understood by Jews as denoting Deity, and that it not only referred to Christ, but to **Christ as God**. No other interpretation will suit the language of Holy Scripture.

Verses 44ff. Joshua Takes Up the History

(44) He, and Hoshea the son of Nun.— Why should Joshua be called Hoshea in this place? His name was apparently changed to Joshua at the time when he entered the Promised Land with the eleven others who searched it out (Num. 13:8, 16). Now that he is about to lead Israel to the conquest, we are once more reminded of his change of name, and that the "salavation of Jehovah" was to be manifested through him.

Possibly the change of name was also at this time confirmed to him.

It is possible that this mention of Hoshea may be Joshua's first mention of himself in the sacred writings. After the close of the song, the remainder of Deuteronomy is not covered by Moses' signature. It belongs to Joshua, or else the author is unknown.

(49) Get thee up into this mountain Abarim.—See Num. 27:12. The same command was given there, and was answered by Moses with the prayer for a successor, which was granted. All that is narrated between that passage and this may be considered as preliminary to Moses' departure.

Mount Nebo.—The particular peak of the "Abarim," where Moses was to die, was not mentioned before. The rugged summit of Mount Nebo rises abruptly 4,000 feet above the plain and still retains its name, with unchanged meaning, in the Arabic **Neba**, or "height."

(50, 51) And die in the mount ... as Aaron thy brother died in mount Hor ... because ye trespassed against me.—It may be asked why Moses and Aaron should both have been made to ascend a mountain to die. A clue to the reason may be found in the words and act which constituted their transgression. They were bidden to speak to the rock in Kadesh, and they struck it. The words which Moses used on that occasion were, "Hear now, ye rebels; must we fetch you water **out of this cliff (Selagh)**?" The last words of the sentence are emphatic; and the rock is described as a **cliff**, not by the name given to the Rock in Horeb (**Tzur**). This view harmonizes with the spiritual significance of the act. The smitten Rock in Horeb was Christ; the cliff not to be smitten in Kadesh pointed also to Christ, ascended now, needing only the prayer of faith to call down all that He will give. And so Moses himself taught in some of his latest words.

33

Moses' Last Blessing

(1) Moses the man of God blessed the children of Israel.—The title "man of God" is here used for the first time. Its counterpart is to be found in 34:5: "Moses the 'servant of Jehovah' died." The more any man is a "servant to Jehovah," the more is he a "man of Elohim" to his fellowmen. After Moses, Elijah and Elisha are more

184

especially described by this title ("man of God") in the Old Testament.

(7) And this (he said) **of Judah.**—Many prayers in Old Testament history were heard from Judah's lips. The prayers of David, Solomon, Asa, Jehoshaphat, Hezekiah, Manasseh, and Daniel were all "the voice of Judah." The last line of Old Testament history is a prayer of Judah by the mouth of Nehemiah, "Remember me, O my God, for good." And, best of all, every prayer of our Lord's is "the voice of Judah" also.

(8) And of Levi.—Next to Joseph, this tribe has the largest share in Moses' last words, as we might naturally expect, it being his own tribe. The "character of the priest" is the principal subject.

(11) Bless, Lord, his substance.—This petition is consistent with the enactment that Levi should have no land. But a blessing on his substance means a blessing to the whole land of Israel. Levi's substance was Israel's tithe.

(12) And of Benjamin.—It is generally agreed that this blessing points to the site of the place which Jehovah chose out of all the tribes of Israel, **Jerusalem, in the tribe of Benjamin.**

34

Death of Moses

(5) So Moses the servant of the Lord died ... —It is extraordinary, when we consider the story of Moses' last days, how wholly self is cast aside. There is no anxiety about the unseen world, and no positive expression of hope. (Paul says far more than Moses about his prospects in the life to come.) To Moses, death is a source of anxiety on account of his people, and a source of pain to himself, because he cannot go over Jordan and see the works of Jehovah on the other side. Beyond this, his reticence is absolute, and his calm silence is sublime. But he died in the company of Jehovah, and may well have felt that he would not lose His presence in the other world. Jehovah was with him, and he feared no evil.

(6) And he buried him.—Moses is alone in this honor. The Son of God was buried by sinful men. Moses was buried by Jehovah.

But no man knoweth of his sepulchre.—The contention between Michael and the devil about the body of Moses (Jude 9) was, in fact, a struggle for his body. Moses was to be raised from the dead, and Satan resisted his resurrection. When the contest took place we cannot say. But Moses, who died and was buried, and Elijah, who was translated, "appeared in glory" on the holy mount, and the New Testament gives no hint of difference between them. We do not know how Moses could have appeared as a disembodied spirit so as to be seen of men.

(10) And there arose not a prophet since in Israel like unto Moses, whom the Lord knew face to face.—Probably these words are later than the time of Joshua, when longer experience gave men the power to see how far inferior the prophets were to their great predecessor in this respect. The difference is most clearly set forth in Num. 12:7, 8.

THE BOOK OF JOSHUA

1

Verses 1-9. Joshua's Commission

(1) After the death of Moses ... the Lord spake unto Joshua ... Moses' minister.— Joshua's commission was the first of its kind, but not the last. No man before Joshua had received orders to regulate his conduct by the words of a written book. Abraham and his household had kept God's laws. Moses had acted by divine commission. But Abraham and Moses received their orders from the mouth of Jehovah. Joshua and all his successors must fulfill the orders of "this book of the law." Thus Joshua was Moses' minister in more than one sense. He was Moses' confidential agent and personal attendant while he lived, and afterward the executor of that which Moses had written. But the position of Joshua, though at first unique and without precedent, was the position designed for all his successors, more especially for that great personage whose name Joshua was the first to bear. (See Exod. 17:9, 14; Ps. 40:7; Rom. 15:8.)

(3) Every place that the sole of your foot shall tread upon, that have I given unto you.—The conquest of Canaan was the special duty assigned to Joshua by the word of Moses. But the conquest of Canaan, as effected by Joshua, must be carefully defined. It was a limited conquest, and he was a representative conqueror. He took a certain number of strongholds throughout the country, and utterly crushed the armies that were opposed to him in the field. He established the people of Israel in the position that he had won. He then divided to the tribes of Israel the whole territory, conquered and unconquered alike. The conquest which Joshua began for the people must be carried out in detail by the several tribes themselves. (See 12:9-24; 13:1-7.)

(5) I will not fail thee, nor forsake thee.— Comp. Gen. 28:15; Heb. 13:5.

(8) Thou shalt meditate therein day and night ... then thou shalt make thy way prosperous.—Moses was the prophet "whom the Lord knew face to face," but Joshua and all his successors, from the least to the greatest, find their blessing and their portion in the careful study and fulfillment of the written word of God. (See Ps. 1:1, 2.) God's Word, from its first appearance as a collective book, occupies the same position. It is supreme. It is set above Joshua. It is

never superseded. And its authority is independent of its quantity, in every stage, from the completion of the law of Moses to the completion of the entire book.

Verses 10-15. Joshua's First Orders

(10) Then Joshua commanded the officers of the people.—Joshua's first orders to the people were to prepare for the passage of Jordan within three days. We may compare this event, in its relation to Joshua, with the giving of the Law from Sinai to Moses. Both were preceded by a three days' notice and a sanctification of the people. Both were means employed by God to establish the leaders whom He had chosen in the position which He designed for them. (Comp. Exod. 19:9, 11 with Josh. 1:11; 3:7; 4:14.)

2

The Spies and Rahab

(1) Joshua ... sent out of Shittim.—That is, he sent the spies before the people left the place where they had been encamped for some months (Num. 22:1; 33:49). Shittim was the last stage of the Exodus under Moses. Probably the sending of these two spies was simultaneous with the issue of the general orders to Israel to prepare for the passage of Jordan within three days. The three days of 1:11 and 2:22 appear to be the same period of time.

Two men to spy.—The sending of these spies should be compared, as to the general effect and character of the measure, with other similar events. There are three instances of sending spies in reference to Canaan—viz., (1) the sending of the twelve by Moses from Kadesh-barnea; (2) the instance before us; (3) the sending of men to view Ai. The present instance is the only one in which the measure had a good effect. (See Deut. 1:22; and 7:2, 3.)

Into an harlot's house, named Rahab.— The attempts to show that Rahab was **not** "an harlot" are not justified by the word used in Hebrew, or in the Greek of the LXX, in Heb. 11:31, or in James 2:25. But there is no harm in supposing that she was also an innkeeper, which the Targum calls her in every place; indeed, it is very probable that the spies would resort to a place of public entertainment as most suitable for ascertaining the state of the public mind.

(4) There came men unto me, but I wist

not whence they were.—Here is a falsehood which evidently left no stain on Rahab's conscience, although all falsehood is sin. The divine standard of sin and holiness never varies; but the standard of man's conscience, even when faith is a dominant principle in the character, may vary to a considerable degree. Here, as elsewhere, the application of the Law brings the discovery of sin.

(9-11) She said unto the men, I know that the Lord hath given you the land ... —The words of this confession are memorable in every way. Note the fulfillment of the prophetic song of Moses, which is partly repeated here (Exod. 15:15, 16). But especially observe the expression of Rahab's own belief, "Jehovah, your God, he is God in heaven above and in earth beneath." Rahab's confession is one of a series. The Egyptians, Philistines, Syrians, Assyrians, Babylonians, Persians, were all in turn brought to the same acknowledgment by their contact with Israel. The reason is stated in Josh. 4:24.

(18) The window which thou didst let us down by.—It seems almost needless to observe that the scarlet line and the cord by which the men were lowered are not the same thing, but described by different words in the original. It would have been preposterous to require Rahab to display in her window the means by which the spies had escaped. It would at once have declared the tale to all beholders—the very thing Rahab was pledged not to do. The "line of scarlet thread" and the "stalks of flax" on the roof were probably parts of the same business, and thus there would be nothing unusual in what was exhibited at the window, although it would be a sufficient token to those who were in the secret, to enable them to identify the house.

(19) Whosoever shall go out ... —Comp. Exod. 12:22 (the account of the Passover). What the blood was to the houses of Israel in Egypt, that the scarlet line in the window was to the house of Rahab. Both alike prefigured the blood of Christ.

3

The Passage of Jordan

(2-6) The priests are to bear the Ark. This was usually the duty of the Levites of the family of Kohath; but both at the passage of Jordan and the taking of Jericho, the priests were employed as bearers. The people must be sanctified, as they were in preparation for the giving of the Law at Sinai (in Exod. 19). And the Ark itself takes, in some sense, a fresh position. Up to this time, during the whole of the Exodus, they had been led by the pillar of cloud and fire. It had been a visible token of God's presence especially granted to Moses, and with him it had disappeared. The Ark was now to be the only leader, and therefore it must be placed in a somewhat more conspicuous position.

It may be of use to consider here what was the actual significance of the position assigned to the Ark in Joshua. The central thing, the only thing not of human workmanship, that remained in the Ark, was "the law written with the finger of God." The Israelites marched into Jordan led by the written law of God. As soon as the army of Joshua reached the center of Canaan, this same law was written on great stones in the heart of the country and became the law of the land. Was it not the direct object of the conquest of Canaan, that God's law should not only have a people to obey it, but a country in which its working might be exhibited to the nations as the law of the land?

(7) The Lord said unto Joshua, This day will I begin to magnify thee ... —It is here stated that the passage of Jordan was to be to Joshua what the giving of the Law at Sinai was to Moses, "that the people may hear when I speak with thee, and believe thee for ever" (Exod. 19:9). But the power which establishes Joshua is the work of the written instead of the spoken Word.

(11) The ark of the covenant.—The ten commandments are presented throughout this narrative as a covenant. So Exod. 34:28, "the words of the covenant, the ten commandments." It must be remembered that a promise precedes all the commandments: "I am Jehovah thy God." The "ten words" that follow are the testimony to His character who commanded the covenant.

(16) Very far from the city Adam, that is beside Zaretan.—For Zaretan see 1 Kings 4:12; 7:46. Adam, as the name of a city, does not occur elsewhere. Zaretan was beneath Jezreel, but has not been identified. Adam has been thought to be at the ford Damieh, thirty miles away.

4

(3) Out of the midst of Jordan ... twelve

stones.—Comp. verse 9. It would seem that we are to understand two monuments to have been set up, one on either side of the river, to mark the place where the Israelites crossed. The western monument was in Gilgal, the other on the opposite side, at the edge of the overflow, where the priests had stopped. The words "in the midst" do not necessarily mean more than "within."

May not the Ark standing in the midst of Jordan represent that suspension of the power of death which is effected by the interposition of our Saviour, and fills the interval between the reign of death "from Adam to Moses," and the "second death" that is to come?

(10) According to all that Moses commanded Joshua.—It would seem that the passage of Jordan had been made the subject of some directions by Moses, though nothing is written concerning the manner of it in the Pentateuch. It is noticeable that if Israel had gone into the land when Moses brought them to the frontier of Kadesh-barnea, in the second year of the Exodus, they would have had no occasion to pass the Jordan at all. When the route was changed we cannot say, unless the compassing of the land of Edom (Num. 21), when they left Kadesh the second time, because they were not permitted to cross that territory, marks the decision.

(14) All the days of his life.—This ends the section, as appears by comparison with 3:7. Observe that Joshua's position, as equal to Moses in the respect of the people, dates from the passage of Jordan, a fact not to be forgotten in considering his Antitype.

Events at Gilgal

(19) On the tenth day of the first month.—This is probably the forty-first year after they left Egypt. Exactly forty years before, on the tenth day of the first month (Exod. 12:3), they had been commanded to take them "a lamb for an house," that they might keep the Passover. The forty years of the Exodus were now complete, and on the selfsame day they passed over the last barrier and entered the Promised Land.

5

(1) The Amorites . . . and . . . Canaanites.—Two principal nations seem to be here mentioned as representatives of the rest.

(4) The cause why Joshua did circum-

cise.—The period of wandering, between the departure from Kadesh-barnea and the return to Kadesh (thirty-seven and a half years), is a kind of blank in the story of the Exodus. The five chapters which belong to it in the Book of Numbers (15-19) contain no note of progress as to time or place. The people had "turned back in their hearts to Egypt" (Acts 7:39; Num. 14:4), and were bearing the reproach of their apostasy all those years, "the reproach of Egypt." Suffering under the "breach of promise" of Jehovah (Num. 14:34), they appear to have omitted the sign of the covenant, as though they were no longer the people of God. The passage of Jordan was the practical proof of Israel's restoration to divine favor, and they were brought into covenant with Him once more. Comp. Col. 2:11.

(10) The passover.—This is the third Passover in Israel's history. The first two were kept under Moses: (1) in Egypt, when the Lord delivered them; (2) at Sinai, when He had "brought them unto Himself"; (3) on the other side of Jordan under Joshua. Observe the connection between the Passover and circumcision. The law in Exod. 12:48 is, "no uncircumcised person shall eat thereof." Therefore, while they wandered in the wilderness, this uncircumcised generation could not keep the Passover.

(12) The manna ceased on the morrow after they had eaten of the old corn of the land.—On the fourteenth day was the Passover; on the fifteenth, Israel ate of the produce of the land. From that day the manna fell no more—i.e., on the sixteenth day of the first month of the year of their entering the land of Canaan. Thirty-nine years and eleven months it had fallen, except on the Sabbath (see Exod. 16:1, 7, 13, 14).

The Conquest of Canaan

(13) At this point begins the second great division of the book. The Passage of Jordan was the great event of the first portion, and for that Joshua received special directions from Jehovah. A vision now appears to him to inaugurate his second great enterprise which was to put the inhabitants of Canaan to the sword. The character of this vision should be carefully noted, as it is of the utmost importance to the interpretation of the book.

(13) There stood a man over against him with his sword draw in his hand.—This should be compared with the vision which

Moses saw at Horeb (Exod. 3). The equality of the two visions is proved by the use of the same command on both occasions (Exod. 3:5; Jose. 5:15). But the actual appearances must be contrasted. The bush burning presents to us the figure of suffering Israel in the furnace; the man with the drawn sword is the sign of victory. Jehovah no longer suffers with and in His people, but He stands forth to lead them with the drawn sword.

(14) And he said, Nay; but as captain of the host of the Lord am I now come.—The wars of Israel in Canaan are always presented by the Old Testament as "the wars of the Lord." It would be well to remember this aspect of the story. The conquest of Canaan is too often treated as an enterprise of the Israelites, carried out with great cruelties, for which they claimed the divine sanction. The Old Testament presents the matter in an entirely different light. The war is a divine enterprise, in which human instruments are employed, but so as to be entirely subordinate to the divine will. Jehovah is not for Israel, nor for Israel's foes. He fights for His own right hand, and Israel is but a fragment of His army.

6

(1) Now Jericho ... —This verse should be read parenthetically, and verses 2-5 should be taken as the orders given to Joshua by the captain of the Lord's host.

(7) Pass on, and compass the city.—The meaning of this proceeding becomes clearer when we remember that the center of the procession is the written Law of God. The Ark is the vessel that contains it. The armed men that precede it are its executioners. The priests who blow the trumpets are its heralds. The whole Law of Moses is but the expansion of the Decalogue; and the Pentateuch contains an ample statement of the transgressions which had brought the inhabitants of Canaan under the ban of the divine law. The seven days' march around Jericho, in absolute silence, was well calculated to impress on the inhabitants the lesson of "the forbearance of God." For several generations the long-suffering of God had waited. In the first year of the Exodus He had threatened the Amorites, bringing the sword of Israel to their borders; and then He had drawn back His hand from them, and given them forty years' respite more. But now the long-suffering of God had waited long enough.

(25) And Joshua saved Rahab the harlot alive.—See Matt. 1:5; Heb. 11:31; James 2:25.

(26) Cursed be the man ... that ... buildeth this city Jericho.—The curse of Joshua was not incurred until Hiel the Bethelite built the city in the reign of Ahab. The curse, fulfilled upon Hiel and his family, appears to have been finally removed by the intercession of Elisha (II Kings 2:18-22) at the request of the inhabitants.

7

(2) Joshua sent men from Jericho to Ai.—The next step after the capture of Ai, before the further conquest of the country, was to set up the Ten Commandments in Mount Ebal, in the heart of the country, and to pronounce there the blessing and the curse which are the sanction of the Law of God. It may well be that the course of the first military operations was directed to this end. The capture of Ai would put the Israelites in possession of the main road running north and south through Palestine, and enable them to reach the center immediately. Thus the character of the war, which was no mere human enterprise, is maintained; and it is probable that the divine reason for the movement is that which we are intended to observe. For the first mention of Ai, see Gen. 12:8.

(3) Make not all the people to labour thither.—In these words we see, by a sort of side glance, the (not unnatural) comment of Israel on the seven days' march around Jericho. They thought it useless labor, and were unable to appreciate the lesson which it taught. (See note on 2:1.)

(6) Joshua rent his clothes ... —The words of Joshua and his behavior on this occasion are consistent with all that we read of him and confirm the notion that he was not a man of a naturally daring and adventurous spirit, but inclined to distrust his own powers; and yet he was utterly indomitable and unflinching in the discharge of his duty—a man of moral rather than physical courage.

(11) They have also transgressed my covenant.—The law is again brought prominently forward in this scene. God made Israel the executioners of His wrath against the idolaters. They must have no other gods but Him, and they must not treat the things

189

that had been defiled by association with idolatry as their own spoil. The words which especially apply to this are to be found in Deut. 7:25, 26. But the whole spoil of Canaan was not so treated; concerning that of Jericho, however, there had been express orders, possibly because the city was especially defiled with idolatry. God had proclaimed it abomination. It was **chê-rem**—"devoted" or "accursed"—and no Israelite was to appropriate any of it, under penalty of becoming **chêrem** himself, and making his household **chêrem**. This Achan had done.

(14) The tribe which the Lord taketh.—There is nothing in the language of the passage, when closely considered, which would lead us to suppose that the discovery of the criminal was by casting lots. The parallel passage (I Sam. 10:20, 21) shows that the oracle of God was consulted. So it was, perhaps, in the case of Achan. We seem to see the High Priest of Israel asking counsel as it had been foretold in Num. 27:21, and the elders of Israel standing by, at the door of the Tabernacle of the congregation. The representatives of the tribes enter the sacred enclosure in succession, and pass before the High Priest in awful silence, broken only by the voice of Jehovah, who pronounces at intervals the names Judah, Zarhite, Zabdi, Carmi, Achan. It must have been a terrible ordeal. All who were present must have received a lesson, which it was impossible to forget, as to the reality of the covenant of God. The arrest of Jordan, the overthrow of Jericho, and the discovery of Achan, are all manifestations of power proceeding from the same source.

(24) And . . . all that he had.—The severity of the punishment must be estimated by the relation of Achan's crime to the whole plan of the conquest of Canaan. If the destruction of the Canaanites was indeed the execution of the divine vengeance, it must be kept entirely clear of all baser motives, lest men should say that Jehovah gave His people license to deal with the Canaanites as it seemed best for themselves. I Sam. 15; Esther 8:11; 9:5-10, 15, 16 illustrate the same principle.

The valley of Achor.—See I Chron. 2:7. The valley of Achor is a pass leading from Gilgal towards the center of the country, or, as it might be represented, from Jericho towards Jerusalem—i.e., from the city of destruction to the city of God. So it was to Israel in the conquest.

190

8

(3) And Joshua chose out thirty thousand mighty men.—The aim of Joshua was to isolate the town of Ai, taking it in front and flank; but there was another town immediately in the rear, less than two miles off. It was necessary, therefore, to employ a sufficient body of men to close the communications between Bethel and Ai from the first.

(17) There was not a man left in Ai or Beth-el.—The road past Beth-el to Ai had been left open. It passes the north end of two ravines in which Joshua's ambush was posted. At the same time, it would have been easy to conceal a chain of sentinels that could observe it and tell the 35,000 men in ambush what was going on, so that if any attempt had been made by the men of Beth-el to protect Ai, it could easily have been frustrated. But no one suspected any danger, and therefore no such attempt was made. The men of Beth-el and Ai took the road that was left open to them and pursued the Israelites, probably down the ancient way past Michmash toward the Shebarim, leaving Beth-el and Ai both unprotected. After they had gone some distance, about a mile or a mile and a half from Ai, this road would bring them past the lower end of the ravine in which the ambush was posted. A second chain of outposts would easily take the signal from Joshua when this point had been passed, and then all was over with the town of Ai. The name "Ai" means "heap" (of ruins, apparently). It is curious that we do not hear of the capture of Beth-el at this time (see 12:16; Judg. 1:22).

Jericho and Ai are the only cities of Canaan of which the capture by Joshua is recorded in the narrative, as it was in fact, a specimen of the whole conquest of the Canaanite cities. Two campaigns in like manner are recorded as specimens of Joshua's battles with the enemy in the open field. In the capture of Jericho and in the southern campaign, the hand of God is more especially manifested. In the capture of Ai and in the northern campaign, the labor of Israel in the conflict is more prominent. The whole work is thus presented to us in a twofold aspect, as the work of Israel and the work of God.

The Law Set Up in the Heart of the Country

(30) Then Joshua built.—By the capture

of Ai, Joshua had obtained command over the road to Shechem. We hear of no strong place north of Beth-el in that part of the country. The confederacy of the southern kings had its center far to the south of this, and there was a considerable distance between Shechem and the strong places to the north. It is in keeping with the purpose of the conquest of Canaan that the Law of the God of Israel should be as soon as possible proclaimed and set up in the heart of the country, to be from that day forward the law of the land. For the enactment that was here carried out, see Deut. 11:26-30; 27:2, etc. Observe that the command required the work to be done as soon after the passing of Jordan as possible.

9

Preparations of the Canaanites for War

(1, 2) These verses record the general preparation of the natives of Canaan for the last struggle with Joshua.

The Gibeonites Make Peace With Joshua

(3) The inhabitants of Gibeon.—Hivites, as appears by verse 7. Gibeon was one member of a tetrapolis, or community of four cities, as is seen in verse 17. Their deception of Joshua and the Israelites on this occasion is a curious compensation for what was done by Simeon and Levi to the Hivites long before, when Jacob first came to Shechem from Padan-Aram (see Gen. 34). On that occasion, the inhabitants of a single city of the Hivites were put to the sword by Israel, by means of a strategem; on this occasion, a stratagem saved four Hivite cities from destruction by Israel's sword.

(19) We have sworn unto them ... therefore we may not touch them.—Although the covenant was obtained from the Israelites by false pretenses, yet, being made in the name of Jehovah, it could not be broken; it was His covenant. We should notice that the Law of Jehovah had raised the tone of morality in this particular.

(23) Bondmen, and hewers of wood and drawers of water for the house of my God.— The precedent established in regard to the Gibeonites appears to have been followed by Solomon in his dealings with all the remnant of the doomed nations of Canaan who were not destroyed. (See I Kings 9:20,

21; II Chron. 8:7, 8.) It is thought that they are to be recognized in the Nethinim of Ezra and Nehemiah (see note on Ezra 2:43). The existence of this large body of Canaanites should be remembered in considering the edict of the Law of Moses, that the seven nations were to be destroyed. The sentence was clearly not executed on the mass of the non-resisting population.

10

Conquest of the Southern Confederacy of the Nations of Canaan

(1) Adoni-zedec king of Jerusalem.—We may compare this name (Lord of Righteousness) with Melchizedek (King of Righteousness). (See Gen. 14:18; Heb. 7:1.) The similarity of the names makes it probable that the Salem of Gen. 14:18 is Jerusalem. The title Lord or King of Righteousness may have belonged to the king of Jerusalem, not only as a local title, but also in relation to the surrounding tribes, over whom he may have been a suzerain.

(4) Come up ... that we may smite Gibeon.—It is remarkable that we do not read of one direct attack upon Joshua and his army in all the wars of Canaan. The Canaanites seem to have acted strictly upon the defensive; and this fact tallies with what we read of the alarm and depression that spread among them at the passage of Jordan by Israel. In the present instance it was thought necessary to smite Gibeon, not only to make an example of the inhabitants, but also because of its importance as a stronghold in the hands of Israel. The position of the Hivite tetrapolis was strong enough to command the country. The fact that a man of Gibeon was afterward selected to reign over Israel, and that the Tabernacle was stationed there, so that Gibeon became a sort of metropolis during the latter portion of Saul's reign, is a significant comment upon this. (See I Sam. 6:21; 7:1; 10:24-26.)

(12-15) The whole of this paragraph appears to be a quotation from the Book of Jasher. That book is mentioned also in II Sam. 1:18, where the lament of David over Saul and Jonathan appears to be a citation from it. We may compare Num. 21:14 and 27, where reference is made to poetical passages either current among the people (as national ballads) or actually written. The name Jasher (upright) is not taken as the name of an author, and what it refers to no

191

one knows. From the fact that all the passages cited in this way are more or less poetical, we may infer that there was a poetical literature among the Hebrews (partly written, partly unwritten) from which the inspired writers occasionally made extracts. The songs of Moses, including the Ninetieth Psalm, belong to this literature.

(12) And he said in the sight of Israel, Sun, stand thou still ... —We do not seem to gain anything by supposing that the miracle was only apparent—i.e., that the light of the sun and moon was retained in its position, while the heavenly bodies themselves maintained their actual course. Nor, again, can we accept the view of some, that it was the **night**, not the **day**, that was especially prolonged. The word used for the sun's standing still is peculiar, and signifies to be "dumb" or "silent." We may compare with this metaphor the words of Ps. 19:3, 4. Joshua's command was that the sun should for the time silence that penetrating voice, and be dumb from those all-prevailing words.

How the miracle was done we are not informed. But if we understand the narrative literally, the problem is, How to suspend the motion of the earth upon its axis, and the motion of the moon around the earth, for twelve hours, the earth being free to move around the sun, and the moon free to revolve upon her axis, if these motions are independent of the others. Yet, the presumption against a miracle of this kind is not a reasonable presumption. The presumption that the sun will rise tomorrow, and that the day will be of a given length, is not based upon reason at all, however strongly it may be felt by mankind. But many who do not doubt that the Creator **could** perform the miracle, nevertheless hesitate to believe that He **would** have done such a thing under the stated circumstances and for the proposed end. The answer to this objection is that the history of the chosen people in Holy Scripture is a series of miracles. At the same time, if anyone finds it easier to believe that the motions of the earth, sun, and moon were continued, and the light only was arrested in its course, the Scripture does not forbid that view.

(14) And there was no day like that before it or after it.—These words are meaningless, unless the writer intended to convey the idea that there was really a great miracle.

(19) For the Lord your God hath delivered them into your hand.—The extermination of each particular army or nation was to be determined (as to time and circumstances) by the mandate of Jehovah, whose guidance Israel must follow on all occasions. (See Deut. 7:1, 2, 16, 22.) The present occasion was one for pursuit and slaughter without respite or delay. But though the army, as an army, was annihilated, a remnant of fugitives escaped into fortified places.

11

Joshua's Northern Campaign

(1) Jabin king of Razor, in upper Galilee, seems to have been in northern Palestine what Adonizedec, king of Jerusalem, was in the south. For the strength of this monarchy see Judg. 4, 5. From its formidable character when it recovered strength in the days of the judges, we may gather some notion of what it was at first.

(5) The waters of Merom.—The most northerly of the three lakes on the course of the Jordan.

(7) Suddenly.—The command of Jehovah is the authority for the act (verse 6). On this occasion, as in the former campaign which began at Gibeon, Joshua surprised his adversaries by the rapidity of his movements.

(8) Misrephoth-maim is thought to be the same as Zarephath, near Sidon.

(18) A long time.—See note on 14:7, 10. The war seems to have lasted seven years, a long time when compared with the disconnected raids and single campaigns which made up the greater part of ancient warfare, when there were no standing armies.

(20) It was of the Lord to harden their hearts ... —i.e., render them obstinate. These words go to prove that the conquest of Canaan was not intended to be a massacre of the unresisting inhabitants.

(22) Only in ... Gath.—(See Judg. 1:10.) Goliath of Gath and his gigantic relatives (I Sam. 17; II Sam. 21) seem to have been a part of this remnant.

12

Summary of the Conquered Territory

The third great division of the book (comp. note on 5:13) begins here, with a summary of the conquered territory according to kings.

(6) Them did Moses the servant of the Lord ... smite.—The continuity of the work of Moses and Joshua should be noticed. The land which God gave to Israel is made up of two portions: (1) a territory on the east of Jordan conquered by Moses, and given by him to two and a half tribes, as the "portion of the law-giver"; (2) a territory on the west of Jordan, of larger extent, conquered by Joshua, and given to nine and a half tribes. But the conquest of Canaan is one enterprise, begun by Moses and finished by Joshua. And the land of Israel is one country, though divided by Jordan into two portions. The analogy between the work of Moses and Joshua in this literal conquest, and the work of Moses and the true Joshua in respect of the inheritance of the Church of God, which was partly won before the passage of Jordan—i.e., before the death of Christ—but much more afterward, is too plain to be overlooked.

(7) And these are the kings of the country which Joshua ... smote.—There are two kings reckoned to Moses, and thirty-one to Joshua, making a total of thirty-three. Yet the two slain by Moses are individually represented as far greater than any who are named in this book. And in the Psalms, in more than one place, we have "Sihon king of the Amorites, and Og the king of Bashan" expressed by name, and the rest only summarized, as "all the kingdoms of Canaan" (Pss. 135:11, 12; 136:19, 20).

(16) The town of Bethel, on the borders of Benjamin and Ephraim, which passed from the one tribe to the other (Josh. 18:22; I Kings 12:29), seems to mark the geographical transition in this list from the territory conquered in the southern campaign of Joshua to that which he conquered in his northern campaign.

13

Verses 1-14. Description of the Territory to Be Divided

(1) Joshua was old and stricken in years.—Rather, "he had aged, and was advanced in days." Old is too absolute a word. He did not live beyond a hundred and ten years (24:29), and this was not a great age for the time. But in several instances the Hebrew word here employed is used not so much in respect of the number of years men lived, but rather in regard to the weakening of the vital powers. (Comp. Gen. 27:1; 1 Kings 1:15, etc.) The hardships and anxieties of his life had aged him.

(1, 7) There remaineth yet very much land to be possessed ... Now therefore divide this land.—The land had still to be "inherited"—i.e., not overrun, or conquered, as far as it could be said to be conquered by defeating the armies that took the field; all this was done already, but the land had not passed out of the hands of its actual possessors into the hands of Israel. It is remarkable that we have here a distinct order given to Joshua to divide to Israel land which was **not yet conquered.** We may say, then, that while the list of kings in chap. 12 represents the territory in that aspect in which it was conquered, by the reduction of a number of fortified posts and strongholds, and the subjugation of all the principal rulers of the country, the description of its boundaries in chap. 13 represents it as not yet conquered—viz., as still containing several nations whom the Israelites must dispossess when God gave them the opportunity and ordered them to drive them out.

It is important to mark clearly the distinction between the work done by Joshua and the work left for Israel. Joshua overthrew the ruling powers of Palestine, destroyed the kingdoms, defeated the armies, and captured the fortresses to such an extent as to give Israel a firm foothold in the country. But he did not exterminate the population from every portion even of that territory which he distributed to the several tribes. And there were several nations—of whom the Philistines and Phoenicians were the chief—whom he left entirely intact. The purpose of this is explained in Judg. 2:20-23 and 3:1-4. The work done by Joshua was thus distinctly limited.

The work left for Israel was partly similar to that which Joshua had done, and partly different. It was the same when any great war broke out between Israel and the unconquered nations. But for the most part it was entirely different, and was the completion of the conquest of the land in detail throughout the several towns and villages. The rules laid down in the law of Moses were to be the guiding principle for Israel, as also for Joshua. The seventh and twelfth chapters of Deuteronomy gave them clearly: (1) Utter extermination of the nations "when Jehovah should deliver them up"—i.e., not at the pleasure of Israel, but at the divine decree. (2) The destruction of all traces of idolatry in the conquered territory. (3) No covenant or treaty was to be made between Israel and the nations of Canaan, and all intermarriage was prohibited.

Had rules 2 and 3 been faithfully observed, there would have been constant outbreaks of hostility, terminating in the further and more rapid extermination of the enemies of Israel, or else in their absolute submission to Israelitish law; and thus the entire conquest would have been completed in a comparatively short time. But, in fact, the second and third rules were constantly broken. Mixed marriages were common, and idolatry was maintained instead of being destroyed. Therefore Israelites and Canaanites were mingled together, and it became impossible to carry out rule 1; for one set of inhabitants could not be exterminated without inflicting serious injury upon the other.

When we consider these rules, it is impossible not to be struck with the wisdom of them when regarded as a means to the proposed end. We are also able to understand more clearly why so much stress was laid upon the necessity of adherence to the **Book of the Law** in Joshua's commission (1:6-8).

(If the authorship of Deuteronomy belonged to the late date which some claim for it, how could we account for the insertion of a law which was never kept, and could not be kept at the time when some suppose it was written? From the days of Solomon and following, the relation of the remnant of the conquered Canaanites to Israel was fixed. The Phoenicians and Philistines maintained a separate national existence to the last.)

Verses 15-33. Description of the Territory Distributed by Moses on the East of Jordan

(21) The princes of Midian ... —This verse supplies a further reason for hostilities between Midian and Israel. The Midianites were "dukes of Sihon," and a part of his government. Through them he appears to have exercised his dominion over the conquered territory which he had taken from Moab. This land Israel had now, in turn, taken from him. But in order to complete its subjugation, the removal of Sihon's dukes, the princes or kings of Midian, was also necessary. This was brought about in

the manner described in Num. 22-25, and 31. The relation between Midian and Moab which is **implied**, but not explained in Numbers, is explained by the apparently casual remark in this place. It is another example of undesigned agreement between Joshua and the Pentateuch.

14

Division of the Territory on the West of Jordan to Nine Tribes and a Half

Here begins the fourth great division of the book (comp. notes on 5:13 and chap. 12); and here we enter upon the record of the third portion of Joshua's great work. He had (1) to bring Israel over Jordan; (2) to conquer the land; (3) to divide it among the tribes.

(1) Eleazar ... and Joshua.—Not Joshua and Eleazar, observe. (Comp. Num. 27; Deut. 17.) In these passages we see delineated the nature of the government established in Israel by Moses to continue until there was a king. The priest had the legislative authority, the executive power rested with the judge. Of these judges, Joshua stands first; those who followed, until Samuel, held the same relation to the priest. Joshua was also a prophet. Samuel (a prophet likewise) established a third power in the constitution, and made the supreme executive power continuous and hereditary, giving to Israel a form of government by prophet, priest and king. For the present, however, Eleazar and Joshua were the rulers.

And the heads of the fathers of the tribes of the children of Israel.—These men are all named in Num. 34:16-28: one from every tribe, in addition to Eleazar and Joshua. The names were then given by God to Moses, as the narrative states in verses 16-19. It is remarkable that before the land was conquered, in view of all the battles that were to be fought before it could be divided, the names of the men who were to divide it should be revealed. Man could not have arranged it so. With the single exception of Caleb, we know nothing of these twelve commissioners except their names.

(2-5) The argument of these verses can only mean that the tribal inheritances were to be twelve in number, and therefore the Levites were excluded from any distinct territorial position, for the children of Joseph were to be two tribes. Thus there are two ways of counting Jacob's sons, each making twelve; and these two seem to be recognized as distinct in Exod. 28.

Inheritance of Judah

(6) Caleb the son of Jephunneh.—Caleb was the commissioner appointed from the tribe of Judah to divide the land (Num. 34:19). His coming forward on this occasion to ask for his own inheritance first of all might appear to savor of self-interest, if the post of honor for which he applied had not been also the most dangerous and difficult position in the inheritance of his tribe. He applied for the territory of the gigantic sons of Anak, whom he undertook to drive out in the strength of Jehovah. Therefore "Joshua blessed him" and gave him Hebron for his inheritance.

(7, 10) Forty years old was I ... and I am this day fourscore and five years old.—In this speech we have the only direct evidence as to the duration of the wars of Canaan under Joshua. The spies were sent from Kadesh-barnea in the second year of the Exodus, about thirty-eight and a half years before the passage of Jordan (see Deut. 2:14). Thus Caleb would be 78 years old when they crossed the Jordan. He was 85 when they began to divide the country. Therefore the conquest itself must have extended over a period of seven years. It is clear that the record of the capture of Jericho and Ai, with the two campaigns of Joshua against the southern and northern confederacies, does not give **all** the details of the war.

(15) Kirjath-arba.—See note on Gen. 23:2.

15

(1) This then was the lot.—The question arises at this point how the position of the tribes of Judah, Ephraim, and Manasseh was determined. As to the remaining seven, see note on 18:5-10. It is noticeable that Hebron appears to have been promised to Caleb (14:12), and Shechem assigned to Joseph by Jacob (Gen. 48:21, 22; Josh. 24:32). This necessarily brought the tribe of Judah into the south, the neighborhood of Hebron, and Ephraim (with his brother Manasseh) into the center of the country.

(13-19) And unto Caleb ... —This paragraph occurs also in Judg. 1:10-15, with some slight variations. Which is its original

place? It seems hardly possible to make the narrative in Judg. 1 a mere repetition of an earlier story, because it is presented as a part of that which happened after Joshua's death. It would seem, then, that the entire conquest of the Anakim was not effected at once, but begun by Caleb and Joshua in Joshua's lifetime, and completed by the tribe of Judah, under the leadership of Caleb, after Joshua's death. Ahiman, Sheshai, and Talmai are thought to be the names of three clans of the Anakim. (See note on Judg. 1:10; and comp. Num. 13:22.) Upon the whole, it seems reasonable to conclude that the proceedings by which Caleb secured his inheritance, and fulfilled the promise of 14:12, have been recorded here for the sake of completeness, though not necessarily belonging to this time.

(31) Ziklag.—It is noticeable that Ziklag became the property of the kings of Judah by the gift of Achish, who bestowed it on David (I Sam. 27:6), not by the gift of Joshua to Judah. The partial character of the conquest and the division of unconquered territory to the tribes is thus illustrated.

(63) Could not drive them out.—It is observable that the failure of the three great tribes of Judah and Joseph (Ephraim and Manasseh) to clear the inheritance assigned to them is especially noticed in the Book of Joshua—viz., Judah in this place, and Ephraim and Manasseh in 16:10 and 17:11, 12. A list of the failures of all the tribes is given in Judg. 1.

16

Inheritance of Joseph

(1) The lot of the children of Joseph.— The order of precedence among the tribes of Israel was always Judah first and the sons of Joseph second. (See I Chron. 5:2.) Accordingly in the division of the land of Canaan under Joshua, there are three successive stages: **first**, the settlement of the tribe of Judah in the strongholds of the south of Palestine; **second**, the establishment of Ephraim and Manasseh in the center of the country, and in some strong positions toward the north; **third**, the settlement of the remaining tribes, so as to fill up the gaps left between Judah and Joseph, and also upon the outskirts of their territory, so as to be, as it were, under the shadow of their wings.

In the inheritance of Ephraim and Manasseh we observe some features which distinguish this description from that of Judah's inheritance in chap. 15. The boundaries of the territory are given, but there is no catalogue of cities. There is also another peculiarity: the tribe of Ephraim is interlocked with the tribe of Manasseh, and the tribe of Manasseh again with Issachar and Asher, by the possession of cities in the territory of these other tribes. This fact would manifestly tend to produce a **solidarity** among the several tribes, and to prevent disunion by creating common interests. The interest of the stronger tribes would be served by completing the conquest of the territory assigned to the weaker.

17

(2) Shechem.—It is noteworthy that according to the boundary of Ephraim and Manasseh, described in chap. 16, the town of Shechem appears to have lain within the border of Manasseh, but as "the separate cities" of Ephraim were among the inheritance of Manasseh (16:9), this may have been the case with Shechem, the first metropolis of the Israelites in Palestine. Territorially, the tribe of Manasseh had the largest share of Palestine.

(14, 15) The request and the answer are both characteristic. Joshua's own greatness was emphatically of that kind which is proved by deeds, and not by words. The arrogance of the Ephraimites, on the other hand, may be abundantly illustrated from Old Testament history. They were constantly asserting their right to the supremacy in Israel, without exhibiting any qualification for it.

But the incident in this chapter is the key to several difficulties in the Book of Joshua. It is plain, from what is here stated, that a large portion of the center of Palestine consisted of uncleared forest: that the cities and inhabitants of that district were far fewer than those of the valley of Esdraelon, or of the territory assigned to Judah on the south. And this fact justifies the strategy of the attack of Israel under Joshua upon the center of the country, so that the forces of the Canaanites were necessarily divided, and the Israelites could strike first with their whole force at the southern armies, and then turn around upon their enemies in the north. It helps to explain the ease with which they set up the law on Ebal at the

beginning of the invasion, and the selection of Shechem for the capital afterward.

18

(1) At Shiloh.—Shiloh was about ten miles due south of Shechem, in the territory of Ephraim. As soon as the position of Ephraim, Joshua's tribe, was settled in the central part of the country, the tabernacle was set up there. For the situation of Shiloh, see Judg. 21:19.

(5-10) They shall divide it into seven parts.—Joshua ordered that the rest of the territory should be surveyed, and divided, according to the number of the cities, into seven portions, which were then to be allotted according to the instructions given by Moses. The several tribes were not permitted to choose their own portions. Num. 26:54, 55 implies that there must be unequal portions of territory for larger and smaller tribes, but that the particular position of each tribe must be settled by the lot, whereof "the whole disposing is of the Lord." We are not told how this rule was carried out in the case of Judah, Ephraim, and Manasseh, who received their inheritance first. Possibly a sufficient extent of territory was surveyed at first to provide three large allotments. The three tribes might then cast lots, first between Judah and Joseph for the northern or southern portions, and then between Ephraim and Manasseh for the two sections of the northern territory.

The Inheritance of Benjamin

(11) The lot of the tribe of the children of Benjamin.—It was by no accident that their lot came forth between Judah and Joseph. No wiser method could have been devised to secure a united Israel than thus to make Benjamin the link between the two most powerful and naturally rival tribes. In the story of Joseph, the brethren are reconciled through the mutual affection of Judah and Joseph for Benjamin as their father's youngest and best-loved son.

The position thus given to Benjamin under Joshua was still further developed by circumstances. The tribe was almost exterminated in the time of the judges; the survivors were united in marriage with women of Ephraim and Manasseh. On the other hand, the city of Jerusalem, although assigned by Joshua to Benjamin, was first a joint possession of Judah and Benjamin

(I Chron. 8:28, 32; Judg. 1:8, 21), then the royal city of the kings of the house of Judah. The selection of the first king of Israel from Benjamin, and the ultimate planting of the religious and political center of all the tribes on the confines of Judah and Benjamin in Jerusalem, would have been schemes of man's devising. They were really links in the long chain of God's providential dealing with the chosen people.

(22) **Beth-el** seems to have passed into the hands of Ephraim without question when the tribe of Benjamin was all but exterminated. In the division of the kingdoms, though the tribe of Benjamin followed the house of Judah, the town of Bethel was regarded as part of the kingdom of Israel, and Jeroboam's southern boundary. He set up two golden calves, one in Bethel and the other in Dan, at the northern and southern extremities of his kingdom.

(28) **Jebusi, which is Jerusalem.**— Jerusalem is always thought of as the capital of Judah. But it was originally a Benjamite city. No later writer than Joshua would be likely to have placed it in the territory of Benjamin.

19

Inheritance of Simeon

(1) **Their inheritance was within the inheritance of the children of Judah.**—The southern part of the inheritance of Judah was given up to Simeon. (See Judg. 1:3, 17.) In this fact a prophecy was fulfilled, for the effect of the allotment was to separate Simeon from the tribes with whom he had been united in the journey through the wilderness (viz., Reuben and Gad), who had cast off Simeon, and united themselves with the half tribe of Manasseh instead. Being also separated from Levi, Simeon was still further isolated, with the result that in the final separation of Israel and Judah, after Solomon's death, the tribe of Simeon, though adhering to the kingdom of the ten tribes (for the children of Simeon were counted strangers in Judah—II Chron. 15:9), was separated from the territory of that kingdom by the whole breadth of the kingdom of Judah. Thus were Jacob's words brought to pass, which he spoke on his deathbed regarding Simeon and Levi (Gen. 49:7).

(9) **The part of the children of Judah was too much for them.**—In Judg. 1 we read

that Judah invoked the assistance of Simeon to complete the conquest of his inheritance, and also assisted Simeon to conquer his. This fact illustrates the character of the conquest of Canaan by Joshua, and shows that when his work was done, something was still left for the individual tribes to do.

Inheritance of Zebulun

(15) **Beth-lehem.**—The other Bethlehem is called in Judg. (17:7, 19:1) and Ruth (1:1), Bethlehem-Judah; and in Micah (5:2), Bethlehem-Ephratah. Bethlehem-Judah is designated Bethlehem only when it is impossible to mistake it for Bethlehem of Zebulun (e.g., Ruth 1:19; I Sam. 16:4).

Inheritance of Issachar

(17) **The fourth lot ... to Issachar.**— These two tribes were located next to the house of Joseph on the north. It should be remembered that Issachar and Zebulun had been associated with Judah to form the same camp and division of the army in the wilderness. This association, lasting forty years, must have created many ties between these two tribes and their leader Judah. It was no ordinary wisdom that placed the descendants of Rachel (Ephraim, Benjamin, and Manasseh) between Judah on the south and Judah's two associates on the north—to cement the union of all Israel, and as far as possible to prevent discord.

With regard to Judah and Zebulun, it is noticeable that we find their union reproduced in the earthly history of our Lord. Mary, who was of the house of David, and Joseph of the same lineage, are found dwelling in Nazareth, in the tribe of Zebulun. Thus the north and the south alike had "part in David" and inheritance in David's Son.

Inheritances of Asher and Naphtali

(24-39) Asher and Naphtali had been associated with Dan in the Exodus, and with him had encamped on the north side of the Tabernacle, and had brought up the rear. These two, each dissociated from his own brother (viz., Asher from Gad and Naphtali from Dan), are paired together in their inheritance in Palestine. The tribe of Asher was more akin to the house of Judah, for Zilpah, the mother of Asher, was Leah's handmaid; and the tribe of Naphtali to the house of Joseph, for Bilhah, Naphtali's

197

mother, was Rachel's handmaid. But in all cases the lot of the inheritance of the tribe seems to have fallen in such a way as to favor the construction of a united Israel.

Inheritance of Dan

(40) The seventh lot . . . of the children of Dan.—Dan was the most numerous tribe, next to Judah, in each census taken during the Exodus. (See Num. 1 and 26.) This tribe had also had a post of honor in being commander of the rear guard during the march. A similar post is here assigned to Dan in Palestine, viz., next to Judah, on the side of the Philistine territory. The Philistines were the most powerful and warlike of the unconquered nations of Palestine. The wisdom of guarding Israel on their frontier by the two strongest of the tribes is manifest. It was Samson, a Danite, who began to deliver Israel from them, and David completed the work. Though there were Philistine wars in the time of the later kings, they never had dominion over Israel after David's time.

20

The Inheritance of Levi

(2) Appoint out for you cities of refuge.— The law in Num. 35 appointed that the Levites should have six cities of refuge and forty-two others. This connection is not always observed, but it has an important bearing on the institution here described. See notes on Num. 35:25, 26; and comp. Deut. 19.

21

The Rest of the Levitical Cities

(9-19) It is worthy of notice that, with the exception of a single city in the tribe of Simeon (Ain, verse 16), all the priestly cities are so arranged as to fall ultimately within the kingdom of Judah, of which the capital was Jerusalem, the city which the Lord had chosen out of all the tribes of Israel to put His name there. The Levites also left their cities and their suburbs in the reign of Jeroboam (II Chron. 11:14) and came over to Judah. But the fact that all the priests, with one exception, were already settled in that kingdom, must have been a

great attraction. When these facts are observed, it is hardly possible not to be struck with the undesigned agreement between the Book of Joshua and the later history, as well as with the divine foresight which arranged the distribution of the people thus.

(27-30) Each of the four divisions of the house of Levi (the priests, the Kohathites, the Gershonites, the Merarites) is made a bond to cement three of the twelve tribes together. Sometimes the association is obvious. In this case the two sides of Jordan are bound together by the Gershonites.

(34-38) In the case of the Gershonites, two tribes on the west of Jordan united to one on the east. The Merarites are employed to connect two tribes on the east of Jordan with one upon the west, and the southeast of the Israelitish territory with the north. It is interesting to observe that Joshua's work of dividing the land of Canaan was so much directed to preserve the union of the several parts. The name of Levi ("joined") thus received a spiritual emphasis. He was divided in Israel that he might be a bond of union, bringing the tribes of Israel together and joining all of them to their God.

(43) And the Lord gave unto Israel.— Although the conquest of Canaan was not completed in the time of Joshua, as it was afterward under David, yet we see by this statement that the expectations of Israel were abundantly satisfied. They received all that they hoped for.

22

Dismissal of the Two and a Half Tribes to Their Inheritance on the East of Jordan

(7) When Joshua sent them away also unto their tents, then he blessed them.—It is noteworthy that of all the tribes of Israel who followed Joshua, and remained with him, this half tribe of Manasseh alone is mentioned as receiving a special blessing. The conduct of the two and a half tribes in choosing their inheritance on the east of Jordan has been regarded as laying them open to some blame. Historically, this is incorrect. God delivered the land of Sihon and Og to Israel; someone must inherit it. Again, the true eastern boundary of Palestine is not the Jordan, but the mountain range of Gilead, which parts it from the desert that lies beyond. Really the two and a half tribes were as much in Palestine as the rest, only their position does not take advantage of that wonderful miracle by which Jordan was driven back, and the Israelites were enabled to strike at the heart of their Canaanitish foes. They themselves, however, were compelled to cross the Jordan before they could obtain the nest which they seemed to have won before they crossed it. In the spiritual world these two and a half tribes answer to the people who received their inheritance from Moses (i.e., from the law); the others are those who received nothing until they followed Joshua, i.e., the Captain of salvation, Jesus Christ, who gives rest to all. When He came, His own people were divided, like the tribe of Manasseh. Some could not forsake Moses, a sacrifice which they thought He required of them; some gave up all, and followed Him.

(11) Have built an altar.—As appears by verse 28, it was a representation of the altar of Jehovah, a copy of the one altar which He had given to Israel for sacrifice. The design was to set up on the east of Jordan a likeness of that altar which was established on the west, that the tribes on the other side of Jordan might appeal to it as a proof that they also were the people of Jehovah.

(12) To go up to war against them.— There is no more striking proof of Israel's obedience to the Law and veneration for it in the days of Joshua than this. A single altar to Jehovah, besides the one in Shiloh, is sufficient cause for war against the builders of it. (Comp. Jer. 11:13.)

(26) An altar.—Rather, "the altar," i.e., the pattern or copy of the altar of Jehovah, to prove that the two and a half tribes had the same right to approach Him as all the rest.

(27) Ye have no part in the Lord.—The person who made it the law of Israel to have no part in Jehovah was "Jeroboam the son of Nebat, who made Israel to sin" by setting up the calves, and thus diverting the stream of national worshipers from Jerusalem, the place chosen by the Lord. But Joshua's efforts under the direction of Jehovah for the establishment of national unity in Israel are proved by the narrative in this chapter to have taken considerable effect. At whatever cost, it was felt that the unity of national worship must be maintained. Rebellion "against Jehovah" is treated by the heads of Israel (verse 19) as rebellion "against us." (See Judg. 12:4.)

23

Joshua's Last Charge

(2) And said unto them . . . —The address which follows should be contrasted with that in chap. 24. The first is suited to men of education, authority, and position in Israel, and concerns the duty of the rulers; the second contains one plain lesson for all the people, and makes no demand upon their intellect, nor does it require any position of influence or authority to carry out the instructions which it gives.

(6) Be ye therefore very courageous to keep and to do all that is written in the book of the law of Moses.—As Joshua was the servant of the Law himself, so must his successors be. No higher position was attainable than this. It has been the same with the successors of the greater Joshua. With them, and with those who follow them, nothing can ever supersede the authority of **the written word**.

(7) Come not among these nations.—i.e., do not mix with them. (See 13:2-7, for the rules to be observed in dealing with the nations.) It must always be remembered that, in proposing the extermination of the seven nations, Jehovah reserved to Himself the ordering of the details of the conquest and extermination. He did not propose to deliver them all to Israel at once, for reasons set forth in Judg. 2, 3. Meanwhile, it was a trial of Israel's faith and obedience to live among idolaters without making any peace with them, or lending any countenance to their idolatry.

24

(1, 2) Joshua gathered all the tribes . . . —In the speech that now follows Joshua briefly recapitulates the national history; he had not thought this necessary for the rulers. The simple lesson which Joshua's words are intended to enforce is the duty of **serving Jehovah**, and **serving Him alone**. It is the first great lesson of the old covenant. "I am Jehovah, thy God; thou shalt have no other gods before me." The Ark of this covenant had brought them over Jordan into the Promised Land.

(14) Fear the Lord.—It should be remembered that, throughout the whole of this passage, "Lord" stands for JEHOVAH, the covenant God of Israel.

(15) As for me and my house, we will serve the Lord.—For Joshua himself the service of Jehovah on earth was nearly over. He pledges his "house" to the same service. It is a singular fact that no descendant of the great conqueror, no member of his household, is named in the Bible. In the genealogies of Ephraim in I Chron. 7, Joshua's name is the last in his own line. The silence of Scripture under this head is profoundly significant. It is one more analogy between the Joshua of the Old Testament and his great Antitype in the Gospel: "whose house are we, if we hold fast the confidence and the rejoicing of the hope firm unto the end" (Heb. 3:6). The house of Joshua embraces all the faithful servants of the Lord.

(16-21) Jehovah will not consent to be served as one God among many. This was the thing which Israel was doing at the moment, which they meant to do, and did do, with rare intervals, down to the Babylonish captivity, when the evil spirit of (literal) idolatry was expelled for evermore. Israel always maintained the worship of Jehovah (except in **very evil** times) as the national Deity, but did not abstain from the recognition and partial worship of other national deities of whom they were afraid, and whom they thought it necessary to propitiate. Therefore Joshua's argument is perfectly intelligible, and was entirely necessary for those times.

(26) And Joshua wrote these words in the book of the law of God.—Primarily "these words" appear to refer to the transaction of the covenant (verse 25). But it must be observed that this is also the second signature among the sacred writers of the Old Testament. The first is that of Moses (Deut. 31:9). The next signature after Joshua's is that of Samuel (I Sam. 10:25). We have here a clue to the authorship of the Old Testament and to the view of the writers who succeeded Moses in what they did. They did not look upon themselves as writers of distinct books, but as authorized to add their part to the book already written, to write what was assigned to them "in the book of the law of God." The unity of Holy Scripture is thus seen to have been an essential feature of the Bible from the very first.

(32) The bones of Joseph ...—It may be that this fact helped to fix the position of Ephraim and Manasseh in the center of the country.

(33) And Eleazar the son of Aaron died.—Eleazar the priest and Joshua the son of Nun were the Aaron and Moses of this period. It is fitting that the Book of Joshua should close with the death of Eleazar, for when Joshua was given as a shepherd to Israel, in answer to the prayer of Moses, Eleazar was also given to Joshua for a counselor (Num. 27:21). It is rather singular that nothing but this has been recorded of Eleazar's personal history. Everything stated about him in his lifetime is official. Not a word that he uttered has been preserved.

Phinehas his son.—Although Phinehas himself was "zealous for his God," we can hardly say that the people served Jehovah all the days of Phinehas (see Judg. 20:28). With Eleazar and Joshua the spirit of strict obedience to the Law seems to have, in a great measure, passed away.

JUDGES

1

(1) **Now.**—The "now" should rather be rendered "And," as in Lev. 1:1; Num. 1:1; Josh. 1:1; I Sam. 1:1; II Sam. 1:1; I Kings 1:1. The word connects this book with the last, "as a link in the chain of books which relate in unbroken connection the sacred history of the world from the Creation to the Exile" (Bertheau).

After the death of Joshua.—In these first words we are met by a difficulty, for there can be little reasonable doubt that most of the events narrated from this verse to 2:5 took place **before** the death of Joshua, whose death and burial are accordingly mentioned in 2:8, 9. The whole passage (1:1 to 2:5) evidently describes the first movements of the Israelites after their establishment on the western side of the Jordan (see Josh. 18:1-3; 21:43; 22:32; 24:28), for it is inconceivable that the Israelites should have remained inactive during the long life of Joshua, who attained the age of 110 years. We suppose that these words were left unaltered as a general description of the book when the prefatory matter and appendix (chaps. 17-21) were attached to it.

Asked the Lord.—If the narrative of this chapter is retrospective, the high priest must have been Eleazar, the son of Aaron (Josh. 14:1); if not, it must have been his son Phinehas (Josh. 24:33). This method of inquiring of God was done in the absence of any authoritative declaration on the part of a prophet (see note on Exod. 28:30). The Urim and Thummim was **not** the jewelled "breastplate of judgment," but something which was put "in it." It is probably useless to inquire as to the method by which the will of God was revealed by the Urim and Thummim.

(2) **Judah shall go up.**—Judah is chosen from the eminence and power of the tribe, which was also the most numerous at both of the censuses taken in the wilderness (Num. 1:26; 26:19-22). Jacob's blessing on the tribe is given in Gen. 49:8. (Comp. Num. 34:19; Josh. 15:1.) In the arrangement of the camp, Judah was stationed at the east, with Issachar and Zebulon, and always started first on the march (Num. 2:3-9), with its lion-standard, which was a symbol of its lion-courage (Gen. 49:9; Rev. 5:5). The same answer is given by Urim in 20:18.

(3) **Unto Simeon his brother.**—Both Judah and Simeon were sons of Leah. It was natural that the two tribes should help one another, because their lots were conterminous (see Josh. 19:1, 9). The tribe of Simeon was remarkable for its fierce valor (I Chron. 4:24-37, 38-43). It is omitted in the blessing of Moses (Deut. 33; see Num. 25:14). They seem to have melted away among the nomad tribes of the south, but we see them showing a last flash of vitality in the days of Hezekiah (I Chron. 4:41).

(4) **The Canaanites and the Perizzites.**—See Gen. 13:7; 34:30. The former seem to have been "lowlanders" (Num. 13:29; Josh. 11:3; 17:16). The latter were the mountain and forest tribes (Josh. 11:3; 17:15). Their antiquity and importance appear from the allusions to them in Gen. 13:7; 34:30; I Kings 9:20. The name itself seems to mean "open villages" (I Sam. 6:18; Deut. 3:5), and may imply that they were agriculturists. The name does not occur in the genealogy of nations in Gen. 10.

(6) **Cut off his thumbs and his great toes.**—The cutting off of his thumbs would prevent him from ever again drawing a bow or wielding a sword. The cutting off of his great toes would deprive him of that speed which was so essential for an ancient warrior. Either of these mutilations would be sufficient to rob him of his throne, since ancient races never tolerated a king who had any personal defects. This kind of punishment was not uncommon in ancient days. The peculiar appropriateness of the punishment in this instance arose from the Lex talionis, or "law of equivalent punishment," which Moses had tolerated as the best means to limit intensity of those blood-feuds (Lev. 24:19, 20; Deut. 19:21; comp. Judg. 15:10, 11), which, "because of the hardness of their hearts," he was unable entirely to abolish.

(7) **They brought him to Jerusalem.**—This notice may be prospective, i.e., it may refer to a time subsequent to the conquest of Jerusalem mentioned in the next verse. (See Josh. 12:8-10; 15:63.) The name Jerusalem is used by anticipation, for it seems to have been called Jebus until the days of David (see 19:10). As it is also called Jebusi (i.e., "the Jebusite") in Josh. 15:8; 18:16, probably the name of the town comes from that of the tribe, and the derivation of it is unknown.

(9) **In the mountain, and in the south, and in the valley.**—These are three marked regions of Palestine: the "hill country" (**ha-**

Har, Josh. 9:1), in which were Hebron and Debir (verses 10, 11); the south or **Negeb** (Josh. 15:21), in which were Arad and Zephath; and the valley, or rather lowlands (**Shephelah**, Josh. 11:16; 15:33), in which were the three Philistian towns of Gaza, Askelon, and Ekron (verse 18). The **Har** is the central or highland district of Palestine, which runs through the whole length of the country, broken only by the plain of Jezreel. The **Negeb**, derived from a root which means "dry," was the region mainly occupied by the tribe of Simeon. The **Shephelah**, or low maritime plains, is Palestine proper, i.e., the region of Philistia, the seacoast south of the Plain of Sharon.

(10) That dwelt in Hebron.—See Josh. 10:36, 37. Hebron is midway between Jerusalem and Beersheba, and twenty miles from either. The first name of the city, which is one of the most ancient in the world (Num. 13:22), was Mamre (Gen. 13:18), from the name of its chief (ibid. 14:24). It was a city of refuge (Josh. 21:11-13). This assault may be identical with those touched upon in Josh. 11:21; 14:6-15; 15:13, 14. On Kirjath-arba, see Gen. 23:2.

Sheshai, and Ahiman, and Talmai.—Possibly the names of three clans of the Anakim (Num. 13:22, 23). The Anakim are connected with the Nephilim.

(19) Chariots of iron.—See 4:3; Josh. 11:6-9; 17:16; I Sam. 13:5. The phrase means either "chariots with iron-bound wheels" or "**scythed** chariots." We see a reason for the partial failure of the Israelites in the fact that at this time they had not attained to the same level of civilization as the Canaanites in arts and arms. This advantage could only have been rendered unavailing by more faith and faithfulness than they showed in their conduct.

(21) The children of Benjamin did not drive out the Jebusites.—Jerusalem was on the borders of Judah (Josh. 16:8) and Benjamin (Josh. 18:28). It belongs more properly to the latter, but the conquest of Zion by David (II Sam. 5:7) naturally caused its closer identification with Judah. The Jebusites were tolerated inhabitants ever after this conquest, and had their own prince (II Sam. 24:18). We even find traces of them after the exile (Ezra 9:1). Jerusalem is a remarkable exception to the rule that the Israelites conquered "the hill-country," but not the plain.

Unto this day.—The assignment of Jerusalem to Benjamin shows that this narrative, though not contemporaneous, is older than the conquest of Jerusalem by David.

(22) Beth-el.—The position of this town on the "highway" between Hebron and Shechem—the main thoroughfare of Palestine (20:31; 21:19)—gave it great importance, as did also its sacred connection with events in the life of Abraham (Gen. 12:8, 9; 13:3, 4) and Jacob (Gen. 28:10-17). Bethel belonged properly to Benjamin (Josh. 18: 21, 22), but possibly, as in the case of Jerusalem, the border of Ephraim and Benjamin separated the upper from the lower town.

(26) Into the land of the Hittites.—Probably the inhabitants of Bethel belonged to this tribe of Canaanites. In Josh. 1:4 their name is used for all the inhabitants of Canaan, but probably it means the coast dwellers. They are often conjecturally classed with the inhabitants of Citium, in Cyprus. They first appear as "children of Heth" in Gen. 23:20.

(28) Did not utterly drive them out.—This is mentioned by way of blame, as the cause of their future sins and disasters (2:2; Josh. 16:10; 17:13). As to the morality of these exterminating wars, we must bear in mind that men and nations must alike be judged by the moral standard of their own day, not by the advanced morality of later ages. We learn from unanimous testimony that the nations of Canaan had sunk to the lowest and vilest depths of moral degeneracy. When nations have fallen thus low, the cup of their iniquity is full; they are practically irreclaimable. To mingle with them would inevitably be to learn their works, for their worst abominations would find an ally in the natural weakness and corruption of the human heart. The Israelites therefore believed that it was their positive duty to destroy them, and the impulse which led them to do so was one which sprang from their best and not from their worst instincts.

2

(1) An angel of the Lord.—The words "Maleak Jehovah" are used of Haggai, in Hag. 1:13; of prophets in Isa. 42:19; Mal. 3:1; of priests in Mal. 2:7. Therefore from very ancient times these words have been interpreted as, "a messenger of the Lord." No indications are given of anything especially miraculous. On the other hand, it

seems probable that by "the angel of the Lord" the writer meant "the captain of the Lord's host," who appeared to Joshua at Jericho (Josh. 5:13-15; see Gen. 16:7; 22:11; Exod. 3:2, 6, 14; Num. 22:22, etc.). Against this conclusion may be urged the fact that in no other instance does an angel appear to, or preach to, multitudes. Angels are sent to individuals, but prophets to nations.
I will never break my covenant with you.—See Gen. 17:7; Deut. 29:12; Ps. 89:28, 34; Luke 1:54, 55, etc., Exod. 3:6-8.

(2) And ye shall make no league.—This is the condition of the Covenant, quoted from Deut. 7:2; 12:2, 3. Comp. Exod. 23:31-33; 34:12, 13.

(3) I will not drive them out.—The withdrawal of the conditional promises in Exod. 23:31.

(6-10) This passage strongly tends to support the view that the events of the previous chapter, and the message at Bochim, occurred before Joshua's death. See note on 1:1 and comp. Josh. 24:28-33. It is usually supposed that Joshua was about eighty at the time of the conquest of Canaan, because that was the age of his comrade Caleb (Josh. 14:7); if so, he had lived thirty years after the conquest. The gradual tendency to deteriorate after the removal of a good ruler is but too common (Acts 20:29; Phil. 2:12).

(11) Baalim.—Baal means "lord," or "possessor," and in its idolatrous sense was applied especially to the sun that was worshiped as the great nature-power, under a multitude of different names and attributes. Baal worship was evidently Phoenician. The splendor of the worship, as well as its sensual and orgiastic character, made it very attractive to the backsliding Israelites.

(12) Forsook the Lord God of their fathers.—(Deut. 31:16, 17.) It seems, however, that the sin of the Israelites was a breach rather of the second than of the first commandment. It was not so much a worshiping of other gods as a worshiping of Jehovah under false symbols adopted from the surrounding nations by a spurious syncretism. Similarly, the calf worship of the northern tribes was originally intended to be an adoration of Jehovah, under the form of cherubic symbols, but naturally lapsed with dangerous facility into actual Baal-worship (Exod. 32:5; I Kings 22:6).

(13) Ashtaroth.—The plural of the feminine word Ashtareth, or Astarte, "the goddess of the Sidonians" (I Kings 11:5), the Phoenician Venus—is identified sometimes with the moon, and sometimes with the planet Venus. She is called the "queen of heaven" in Jer. 7:18; 44:17, and was called Baalti ("my lady") by the Phoenicians. The worship of Baalim and Ashtaroth naturally went hand in hand.

(16) The Lord raised up judges.—This is the keynote to the book. The word for judges is **Shophetim.** The ordinary verb "to judge," in Hebrew, is not **Shaphât,** but day-yân. Evidently their deliverers are of higher rank than the mere tribe magistrates mentioned in Exod. 18:26; Deut. 1:16, etc. Of the judges in this book some—e.g., Tola, Ibzan, Elon, and Abdon—are not said to have performed any warlike deeds. They may, however, have been warriors, like Jair, whose exploits are preserved only in tradition. Samuel, though not himself a fighter, yet roused the military courage of his people. They received no salary, imposed no tributes, made no laws, but merely exercised, for the deliverance of Israel, the personal ascendency conferred upon them by "the Spirit of God." The judges of Israel, at any rate in their true ideal, were not only military deliverers, but also supporters of divine law and order. The abeyance of normally constituted authority during this period is seen in the fact that one of the judges is the son of a "stranger" (11:2), another a woman (4:4), and not one of them (in this book) of priestly or splendid birth.

(18) It repented the Lord.—i.e., Jehovah was grieved. The simple anthropomorphism of early ages never hesitates to describe the ways and thoughts of Jehovah by the analogy of human lives; nor is it easy to see how the sacred writers could have otherwise expressed their meaning. Yet they were, even in using this language, perfectly aware that it was only an imperfect and approximate method of explaining God's dealings with man. Note in Num. 23:19, Job. 23:13, Mal. 3:6, the language of calm and unmetaphorical instruction.

(19) Stubborn.—They are called "stiffnecked" in Exod. 32:9; Deut. 10:16; Acts 7:51. The prophets and sacred writers are always careful to impress upon the Jews that they are chosen by God's free grace to work out His purpose, and that their selection for this service was in no sense due to any merits of their own (Isa. 45:2; Ps. 81:11, 12; Matt. 23:37; Acts 7:51). It is to be noted that in the Bible there is none of the extravagant national self-satisfaction which defaces so much of the Talmud.

(22) That through them I may prove

Israel.—Yet in this as in all God's punishments there was an element of mercy mingled with the judgment, as we see from Exod. 23:29, 30; Deut. 7:22. If in one point of view the non-extermination of Canaan at first led the Israelites into temptation and brought down retributive punishments upon them, yet out of these evils God raised good: "They learned by perpetual struggle to defend their new home, and the free exercise of their religion, and so they prepared for coming generations a sacred place where that religion and national culture might develop. During the long pause of apparent inaction a hidden movement was going on, and the principles and truths so marvellously brought to light were taking firm root" (Ewald).

3

(1) As many of Israel as had not known all the wars of Canaan.—This expression clearly implies the generation after that of Joshua. "The wars of Canaan" are equivalent to "the wars of the Lord," and refer to the struggles of the actual conquest.

(5) Dwelt among the Canaanites . . . —At this verse begins the second great section of the book (3:5-chap. 16), which has been summarized as a history of sin repeating itself, with constant attendance of divine grace. This beginning of intermarriages shows that we are now a generation removed from the days of Joshua.

(8) Chushan-rishathaim king of Mesopotamia.—His invasion, like that of Chedorlaomer, king of Elam, and Amraphel, king of Shinar, was from the south. Therefore it is repelled by Othniel, whose inheritance was in the tribe of Judah. We find no other invaders from the far east till the close of the monarchy.

(9) Othniel.—The name means "lion of God."

(10) The Spirit of the Lord came upon him.—This expression constantly recurs in this book (6:34; 11:29; 13:25). The Jews, however, placed Othniel highest among the judges, and applied to him the words of Cant. 4:7, "Thou art all fair . . .; there is no spot in thee," because he alone of the judges is represented as irreproachable. Further than this, they followed some dim traditional data in identifying him with Jabez (1 Chron. 4:10), and regarding him as a learned teacher of the Law. (See 1:13.)

(11) The land had rest forty years.—Many questions have been raised, such as—Do the forty years **include** or **exclude** the period of servitude? Is forty meant to be an exact or a general number? Are the various periods of rest and servitude continuous and successive, or do they refer to different parts of the Holy Land, and do they synchronize? The chronological data of the Book of Judges is not sufficiently definite to enable us to construct a system out of it.

Died.—Probably during the forty years, unless we suppose that he attained a most unusual age. After this event the tribe of Judah sinks into the background until the days of David.

(12) Did evil again.—Literally, "added to do evil," with special reference to idolatry, as in 2:11, etc.

Strengthened Eglon the king of Moab.—See 1 Sam. 12:9. Eglon was a successor of Balak (Num. 22-24).

(15) Ehud the son of Gera.—The name Gera was hereditary in the tribe of Benjamin (see II Sam. 19:18; I Chron. 8:1-7), and the Jews so constantly omit steps in their genealogies that we can never be sure that "son" means more than "descendant." (See Gen. 46:21; I Chron. 8:3.) Ehud seems to be another form of Abihud (I Chron. 8:1-8). Jerome explains it to mean "one who praises" or "is praised." Josephus calls him a young man.

(16) Upon his right thigh.—This would avert all suspicion. Doubtless the war-cloak was flung in folds over the left shoulder, and Eglon, unaware that the bearer of the tribute was left-handed, would see that the side at which arms were usually worn was covered with a flowing robe, and would not suspect the dagger hidden at the right side. Daggers were often, however, worn at the right side, when a sword was slung to the left. Amasa fell by a similar act of treachery by Joab (II Sam. 20:9, 10).

(22) And the dirt came out.—The meaning of this clause is excessively doubtful, because the Hebrew word rendered "dirt" occurs here only. The Vulgate and Gesenius hold to an alternative rendering, "it came out at the fundament." The Jews were themselves uncertain of the meaning. Ewald renders it, "he rushed out into the gallery," which runs round the roof. He refers to Ezek. 42:5.

(28) Took the fords of Jordan.—This was a matter of extreme importance. The fords of Jordan were few, and far distant from each other (Josh. 2:7). The steep ravine through which it flows forms a natural

Theology - with a view!
History - high view!
JUDGES 3:28-4:6

barrier to Western Palestine, and by securing the fords they cut off from the Moabites all chance of succor. The vehement rapidity of Ehud's movements had rendered their escape impossible.

(31) Shamgar.—He is mentioned here alone, and alluded to in 5:6. We know nothing of Shamgar's tribe or family, but, as neither his name nor that of his father is Jewish, it has been conjectured that he may have been a Kenite. Shamgar means "name of a stranger."

Six hundred men.—It has been most needlessly assumed that he slew them single-handed, and not, as is probable, at the head of a band of peasants armed with the same rude weapons as himself. Nothing is more common in Scripture, as in all literature, than to say that a leader personally did what was done under his leadership, e.g., "Saul has slain his thousands, and David his ten thousands" (I Sam. 18:7).

With an ox goad.—In the East they are sometimes formidable implements, eight feet long, pointed with a strong sharp iron head. The use of them—since whips were not used for cattle—is alluded to in I Sam. 13:21; Acts. 9:5. Being disarmed, the Israelites would be unable to find any more effective weapon (5:6, 8). Disarmament was the universal policy of ancient days (I Sam. 13:19); and this reduced the Israelites to the use of inventive skill in very simple weapons (I Sam. 17:40, 43). Samson had nothing better than the jawbone of an ass (15:15).

He also delivered Israel.—Josephus (**Antt.** 5:4, §3), following some Jewish **hagadah**, says that Shamgar was chosen judge, but died in the first year of his office. This may have been a mere inference, from his being passed over in 4:1. He does not mention his deed of prowess.

4

(2) Jabin king of Canaan.—The name means "he is wise." It may have been a dynastic name, like Abimelech, Melchizedek, Pharaoh, Hadad, Agag, etc., or of some great tribe or nation of the Canaanites. In Josh. 11:1 Jabin is called king of Hazor, and sends messages to all the other Canaanite princes.

Sisera.—It is again a curious, though it may be an unimportant circumstance, that in I Sam. 12:9 the prophet mentions Sisera **before** Eglon. There are difficulties in whatever scheme of chronology we adopt. Si-

multaneous struggles may have been going on in the south against the Philistines and in the north against the Canaanites (see 5:6). We must remember, however, the antiquity and the fragmentary nature of the records, which were written with other and far higher views than that of furnishing us with an elaborate consecutive history.

Harosheth.—The name means "wood-cutting." We may conjecture that the town (lying in "Galilee of the Gentiles") was named from the fact that Sisera made the subject Israelites serve as "hewers of wood" in the cedar-woods and fir-woods of Lebanon.

(4) Deborah, a prophetess.—She can be compared to Miriam (Exod. 15:20), Huldah (II Kings 22:14), Noadiah (Neh. 6:14), Anna (Luke 2:36), etc. Her name means "bee." She is the only female judge, or, indeed, female ruler of any kind in Jewish history, except the Phoenician murderess, Athaliah. She is also the only judge to whom the title "prophet" is expressly given. "Prophetess" implies the possession of poetic as well as of prophetic gifts (Exod. 15:20); and we see her right to such a title, both in her predictions (4:9), in her lofty courage (5:7), and the splendor of her inspired song (chap. 5).

She judged Israel.—It is uncertain whether Deborah was of the tribe of Ephraim or Issachar (5:15). We see from verse 5 that up to this time her functions had mainly consisted of peaceful arbitration and legal decision (Deut. 17:8).

(6) Barak ... Kedesh-naphtali.—"Barak" means "lightning" (Jos., **Antt.**); "Kedesh" means a **holy** city. There were, therefore, many towns of this name. This sanctuary of Naphtali was a Levitical refuge city in Galilee (Josh. 19:35-37; 20:7; 21:32). The fact that the fame of Barak had penetrated from the northern city to the southern limits of Ephraim shows that he must have been a man of great worth.

Mount Tabor.—The broad flat top of this strong, beautiful, and easily fortified mountain (which is nearly a mile in circumference) would serve the double purpose of a watch-post and a stronghold. It was in the district of Issachar, about six miles from Nazareth, and its peculiarities attracted notice in very early days (see Josh. 19:22; Ps. 89:12; Jer. 46:18). It was long regarded as the scene of the Transfiguration, but it must yield this glory to Mount Hermon. But the sacred character of the hill seems to be distinctly intimated in Deut. 33:19.

(7) To the river Kishon.—This word rendered "river" means rather "a torrent bed." The river is always prominently mentioned in connection with this great victory (Ps. 83:9), because the overwhelming defeat of Canaan was due in great measure to the providential swelling of the torrent waters, which turned its banks into a morass and rendered the iron chariots worse than useless. It rises partly in Mount Tabor and flows into the Bay of Acre, under Mount Carmel. (Comp. I Kings 18:40.) The plain of Jezreel (Esdraelon), through which it flows has been in all ages the battlefield of Palestine.

(8) If thou wilt go with me.—The enterprise seemed so daring and so hopeless, that if not for his own sake, yet for the sake of his army, Barak felt how much would be gained by the presence of the inspired prophetess.

(9) Of a woman.—To enter into the force of this we must remember the humble and almost downtrodden position of women in the East, so that it could hardly fail to be a humiliation to a great warrior to be told that the chief glory would fall to a woman. He may have supposed that the woman was Deborah herself; but the woman was not the great prophetess, but Jael, the wife of the nomad chief (Jos. **Antt.** 5:5 §4). Compare the feeling implied in 9:24.

(14) Went down from mount Tabor.—As he had neither cavalry nor chariots, it required no little faith in Barak to abandon his strong post and assume the aggressive against the kind of forces which struck most terror into the Israelites (Heb. 11:32). If the beginning of the battle was at Taanach, the Israelites had to march thirteen miles along the caravan road. Probably the Canaanites watched this bold and unexpected movement with much astonishment.

(17) Fled away on his feet to the tent of Jael.—Women had separate tents (Gen. 18:6), and these were regarded as inviolably secure. He thought that there he would lie unsuspected till the pursuers passed (comp. Gen. 24:67). The "peace" enabled Sisera boldly to appeal to these nomads for the sacred duty of protection. Three days must have elapsed since the battle before it would be possible for Sisera to fly on foot from the Kishon to the nomad's terebinth. It may well be conceived that the unfortunate general arrived there in miserable plight—a starving and ruined fugitive.

(21) Heber's wife.—This addition, being needless, might be regarded as emphatic,

and as involving an element of condemnation by calling prominent attention to the "peace between Jabin . . . and the house of Heber" (verse 17). It may, however, be due to the ancient character of the narrative.

A nail of the tent.—Probably one of the great tent pegs used to fasten down the cords which keep the tent in its place (Exod. 27:19; Isa. 22:23; 54:2, etc.). Josephus says an iron nail, but there is nothing to show whether it was of iron or of wood, and the LXX, by rendering it **passalon** ("a wooden plug"), seem to have understood the latter.

An hammer.—The ponderous wooden mallet kept in every tent to beat down the cord pegs. The word is **Makkebeth**, from which is derived the word **Maccabee.** The warrior-priests, to whom that title was given, were the "hammers" of their enemies.

(23) So God subdued.—This attribution of the deliverance of Israel to God's providence and aid does not necessarily involve the least approval of the false and cruel elements which stained the courage and faith of Jael. Though God overrules even criminal acts to the fulfillment of His own purposes, the crimes themselves meet with their own just condemnation and retribution. At the same time, Jael must not be classed with women actuated only by a demoniacal thirst for vengeance, but rather with women like Judith, who regarded themselves as the champions of a great and good cause.

5

The song of Deborah is one of the grandest outbursts of impassioned poetry in the Bible. (Comp. Exod. 15; Num. 21:27-30; Deut. 32; I Sam. 18:7; II Sam. 1.) It is a song of victory. The peculiar splendor and intensity of the poetic passion which breathes throughout the ode, the archaic simplicity of its structure, and the fact that it refers to many circumstances not preserved in the parallel prose narrative, leave little or no doubt as to its perfect genuineness.

It has been arranged in various ways, but the arrangement adopted by Ewald, with some modifications, seems to be the most satisfactory. It consists of a prelude, followed by three main sections, each divisible into three unequal strophes, and ends with a triumphant aspiration, as follows:

The Prelude (2, 3) 1. The Significance of

the Victory (4-11). (a.) Israel's Glorious Redemption of Old (4, 5). (b.) Israel's Recent Degeneracy (6-8). (c.) The Crisis of Deliverence (9-11).
Second Prelude (12). 2. The Muster and the Battle (13-21). (a.) The Gathering of the Loyal (13-15a). (b.) The Malingerers and the Brave (15b-18). (c.) The Victory (19-22).
3. The Issues of the Victory (24-30). (a.) The Faithless City (23). (b.) The Avenger (24-27). (c.) The Mother's Frustrated Hope (28-30). The Cry of Triumph (31).

6

(1) Midian.—Midian was the son of Abraham and Keturah (Gen. 25:2), and from him descended the numerous and wealthy nomadic tribes which occupied the plains east of Moab (Num. 31:32-39). The name belongs, properly, to the tribes on the southeast of the Gulf of Akabah (I Kings 11:18). Moses himself had lived for forty years among them (Exod. 3:1; 18:1); but the Israelites had been bidden to maintain deadly hostility against the nation because of the shameful worship of Baal-peor, to which, under the instigation of Balaam, the Midianites had tempted them (Num. 25:1-18).

(2) The hand of Midian prevailed.—See 3:10. This oppression is wholly different from that with which we have been dealing in the last chapter. That was the last great attempt of the old inhabitants to recover their lost country; this is a foreign invasion.

(4) They encamped against them.—It is not implied that there were any battles. The Israelites were too wretched and helpless to offer any resistance. (See Heb. 11:38.) These Arabs would swarm over the Jordan, at the fords of Bethshean, about harvest time, and would sweep away the produce of the rich plain of Jezreel and the whole Shephelah, even as far south as Gaza. (Comp. the Scythian invasion, alluded to in Zeph. 2:5, 6.)

(10) The gods of the Amorites.—See Josh. 24:15; I Kings 21:26. As the Amorites seem to have been the highlanders of Palestine, and the most powerful of all the Canaanitish tribes, their name is sometimes used for that of all Canaanites (Josh. 24:15). No deliverance can be promised till repentance has begun. When the warnings of the prophet are heeded, the mission of the deliverer begins.

(11) There came an angel of the Lord.—

We cannot suppose, as some have done, that a prophet is intended, like the one in verse 8. There the word is **Nabi**, here it is **Maleak-Jehovah**, as in 2:1. (Note "Lord" in verse 14.)

(12) The Lord is with thee, thou mighty man of valour.—It was at once a salutation and a blessing. (Comp. Josh. 1:5; Luke 1:28). The address seems to show that Gideon, whose name means "hewer," had already distinguished himself by bravery in war. Only the second and third of the three epochs of his life are narrated; but we see from scattered glimpses that he and his brothers had possibly taken part already in some battle on Mount Tabor—possibly even (so scanty are all our details, and so little certain is the chronology) in the struggle against the Canaanites (4:6; 8:18).

(15) Wherewith shall I save Israel?—We repeatedly find this preliminary diffidence of humility in those whom God selects for His service. (Comp. Exod. 4:1-13; I Sam. 9:21; Isa. 6:5; Jer. 1:6, 7, etc.)

(22) When Gideon perceived.—The last sign gave him a deeper sense than before of the grandeur of the messenger who had come to him.

(26) Build an altar ...—The Jews point out the peculiar features of this burnt offering: (1) it was not at Shiloh; (2) it was not offered by a priest; (3) it was offered at night; and (4) the fire was kindled with the unhallowed materials of an idol. The divine command was, of course, more than sufficient to justify these merely ritual irregularities; and, indeed, it is clear that in these rude times, when the country was in the hands of the heathen, the Levitic order of worship became, for the time, impossible in many particulars.

(27) Ten men of his servants.—This shows Gideon's independent position, and also that he had tried to keep his own household free from the guilt of idolatry amid the all but universal defection.

(28) Arose early in the morning.—The habits of Orientals are early, and Baal-worship may well have involved some adoration of the rising sun.

(31) He that will plead for him, let him be put to death.—These words of Joash were extraordinarily bold and cunning. Possibly the brave act of his son may have roused his conscience, and Gideon may have told him that he had acted under divine guidance. But he saves his son's life, not by excusing his act, but by feigning such a zeal for Baal as to denounce it as a

207

blasphemous impiety to suppose that Baal
will not avenge his own insult—an impiety
so monstrous, that the man who was guilty
of it should be put to death at once. Thus
he made Baal-worship a plea for **not** avenging the insult offered to Baal. He was well
aware that if he thus gained time, the fact
that Baal did **not** interfere to protect himself from such fearful outrage would weigh
powerfully with all his worshipers.

(36) If thou wilt save Israel.—This diffidence and hesitation show the seriousness
of the crisis. Gideon saw that by human
strength alone he would be utterly helpless
to repel the countless hosts of the
marauders. He had already shown his faith,
but now he needed fresh encouragement in
his dangerous task.

7

(1) Jerubbaal, who is Gideon.—Jerubbaal
means "Baal's antagonist" (see note on
6:32). Abraham, Sarah, Jacob, Joseph, Esther, Daniel, Paul, etc., are other instances of
Scriptural characters who have two names.

**(2) The people that are with thee are too
many for me.**—This must have put the faith
of Gideon to a severe trial, since the Midianites were 135,000 in number (8:10), and
Gideon's forces only 32,000 (verse 4).

(3) Whosoever is fearful and afraid.—
This proclamation is in exact accordance
with Deut. 20:8. It is there founded on the
psychological observation that cowardice is
exceedingly contagious, so that the presence
of timid men in an army is a source of
direct danger. The same rule was rigidly
observed by the faithful Judas Maccabeus
(I Macc. 3:56). In this instance there was
the further reason given in verse 2.

(4) The people are yet too many.—A
fresh trial of faith, but small numbers were
essential for the method of victory by which
God intended that the deliverance should be
achieved.

**(5) Every one that lappeth of the water
with his tongue.**—Greater self-control
would be shown by stooping and drinking
the water out of the hand than by flinging
themselves at full length to drink, which
would be the natural instinct of a thirsty
man.

As a dog lappeth.—Some commentators
think that this is an allusion to Egyptian
dogs, who, out of fear for the Nile crocodiles, only venture to lap the water while
they are running along the banks.

(14) This is nothing else save the sword

of Gideon.—The sort of dread which re
vealed itself by this instant interpretation of
the dream shows that Israel was formidable
even in its depression, doubtless because the
nations around were well aware of the di
vine aid by which they had so often struck
terror into their enemies. This would give
additional force to the promise which Gide
on had already received (verse 9).

(16) Into three companies.—See 9:43
This division of the attacking force was a
common stratagem. We find it in Job. 1:17
I Sam. 11:11; and II Sam. 18:2. (Comp
Gen. 14:15.)

A trumpet.—Hearing the sound of three
hundred rams' horns, the Midianites would
naturally suppose that they were being at
tacked by three hundred companies.

(19) The middle watch.—The Jew
formerly divided the night, from 6 p.m. to
a.m. into three watches (Exod. 14:24;
Sam. 11:11). The subsequent division into
four watches of three hours each was bor
rowed from the Romans (Matt. 14:25; Mar
6:48). At the beginning of the middle
watch—i.e., soon after 10 at night—would
be the time at which the host would b
buried in their first sleep.

They had but newly set the watch.—
Literally, "scarcely." The attack took plac
at the moment of confusion caused by chang
ing the watch.

(20) The trumpets in their right hands ..
—Thus the three hundred of Gideon wer
comparatively defenseless, though, if they
had any armor at all, doubtless they coul
still hold the shield on the left arm, whil
the sword was girded on the thigh. Th
effect of the sudden crash and glare an
shout upon the vast unwieldy host of th
Bedouins may be imagined. Startled fro
sleep in a camp which, like Oriental camp
must have been most imperfectly protecte
and disciplined, they would see on ever
side blazing torches, and hear on every sid
the rams' horns and the terrible shout of th
Israelites. The instant result was a wil
panic. (See Ps. 83:13, 14; Isa. 9:4; 10:26.)

(23) Out of Naphtali.—Doubtless thes
pursuers were some of those who had le
Gideon's camp before the victory. Those o
Naphtali and Asher might pursue the flyin
Midianites northward, and those of Manas
seh might pursue those who fled southwar
to the lower fords.

8

(1) The men of Ephraim.—The arroganc

of this tribe was derived partly from its strength, and partly from the memories of their ancestor Joseph, and from the almost regal influence which had been so long exercised by their tribesman, Joshua. This arrogance was destined to bring on them a terrible humiliation (12:1). The complaint was fiercely urged that they had proved both their power and their fidelity to the national cause. What they wanted was the acknowledgement of their claims by all the tribes.

(4) And Gideon came to Jordan.—This verse resumes the narrative of 7:23. The intermediate verses are an episode, and they are only here introduced by anticipation, in order to close the notice about the tribe of Ephraim.

(5) Unto the men of Succoth.—The name Succoth means "booths," and the place was so named, or renamed, because of the "booths" which had been erected there by Jacob on his return from Padan-aram (Gen. 33:17; Josh. 13:27). It was situated in the tribe of Gad. (See Pss. 60:6, 108:7.)

(6) Are the hands of Zebah and Zalmunna now in thine hand?—The general meaning is: "Are you so completely victor as to secure us from the vengeance of these kings?" (Comp. I Kings 20:11.) We do not now whether the tone of the elders of Succoth was one of derision or only of cowardice. In any case, they were guilty of inhumanity, want of faith, want of courage, and want of patriotism.

(7) And Gideon said.—Notice in this verse the mixture of heroic faith and barbarous severity. It was this courage and faith (Heb. 11:32) which ennobled Gideon and made him an example for all time. The ruthlessness of the punishment which he threatened to inflict belongs to the wild times in which he lived, and the very partial spiritual enlightenment of an imperfect dispensation (Matt. 5:21; 19:8; Acts. 17:30). It has usually been supposed that they were scourged with thorns, which would be terrible enough; but the verb here used is stronger, and seems to imply that they were "put under harrows" after thorns and briers had been scattered over them. That Gideon should inflict a retribution so awful cannot be surprising if we remember that David seems to have done the same (II Sam. 12:31; I Chron. 20:3; Amos 1:3). In this case, however, the torture was more terrible, because it was inflicted not on aliens, but on Israelites.

(8) He went up thence to Penuel.—

Penuel was also in the tribe of Gad, on the heights above the Jordan Valley, on the southern bank of the Jabbok. The name means "face of God," from Jacob's vision (Gen. 32:30). It is again mentioned as a fortified town in I Kings 12:25.

(11) By the way of them that dwelt in tents.—He seems to have taken a wide circuit, through some nomad district, leaving the main road, so as once more to make up for his inferior numbers (for there were still 15,000 left of these children of the East) by surprise and stratagem. Nobah was in Manasseh (Num. 32:42), and Jogbehah in Gad (Num. 32:34).

The host was secure.—They would have thought it most unlikely that the Israelites, with their mere handful of men, would pursue so large an army for so long a distance. They fancied themselves beyond the reach of pursuit because they miscalculated the energy and powers of Gideon, who, not improbably, once more attacked them by night.

(17) Beat down the tower.—The importance of the place led to its refortification by Jeroboam (I Kings 12:25).

(18) Resembled the children of a king.—We learn from this reference that Gideon added to his other gifts that tall, commanding presence which always carried weight in early days (I Sam. 10:24; 16:6, 7).

(20) And he said unto Jether.—Gideon, as the last survivor of all his kingly brothers, would hold himself justified in putting his captives to death. Jether also would inherit the duties of goel (Num. 35:12; II Sam. 2:22, etc.), and Gideon desired both to train the boy to fearlessness against the enemies of Israel (Josh. 10:24, 25), to give him prestige, and to add to the disgrace of the Midianite kings.

(22) Then the men of Israel.—Here begins the phase of the life of Gideon which was characterized by his noblest act—the refusal of the kingdom—and his most questionable act—the setting up of a schismatic worship.

(27) Put it in his city, even in Ophrah.—This gives us a clue to Gideon's motive in making the ephod. Shiloh, the national sanctuary, was in the precincts of the fierce tribe of Ephraim, and Gideon may have been as anxious as Jeroboam later was to keep some direct hold on the nation's worship, as one of the secrets of political power. It was the endeavor to secure and perpetuate by unworthy political expedients a

209

power which he had received by divine appointment.

Went thither a whoring after it.—As to the nature of the schismatic service we are told nothing further. The strange narrative of chap. 18 shows us the decadence and disintegration of the national worship at this period, and it is far from improbable that Gideon may have associated his worship with an unauthorized priesthood and modes of divination, if not with teraphim, etc. (17:5; Hosea 3:4).

(28) Thus was Midian subdued.—This verse closes the second great epoch of Gideon's life. The remaining verses of the chapter furnish us with a few notices of the third and last period of his life.

(29) Jerubbaal.—The sudden reversion to this name may be significant. Baal had failed to "plead," but nevertheless Gideon was not safe from idolatrous tendencies.

9

(1) And Abimelech.—For the name as a dynastic title, see Gen. 20; Ps. 34 (title). This narrative of the rise and fall of Abimelech, "the bramble king," is singularly vivid in many of its details, while at the same time material facts are so briefly touched upon that parts of the story must remain obscure. The general bearing of this graphic episode is to illustrate the slow, but certain, working of divine retribution. The two main faults of the last phase of Gideon's career had been his polygamy and his dangerous tampering with unauthorized, if not idolatrous, worship. The retribution for both errors falls on his house. The agents of their overthrow are the kinsmen of his base-born son by a Canaanite mother.

(5) Slew his brethren ... —This is the first mention in Scripture of the hideous custom, which is so common among all Oriental despots, of anticipating conspiracies by destroying all their brothers and near kinsmen. There is little affection and much jealousy in polygamous households. Abimelech by this vile wickedness set a fatal precedent, which was followed again and again in the kingdom of Israel by Baasha (I Kings 15:29), Zimri (I Kings 16:11), Jehu (II Kings 10:7), and probably by other kings (II Kings 15); and by Athaliah (II Kings 11:1) in the kingdom of Judah. Herod also put to death most of his kinsmen, and some of his sons.

(6) Made Abimelech king.—He was the

first Israelite who ever bore that name. It does not appear that his royalty was recognized beyond the limits of Ephraim. Gideon had not only refused the title of king, but even the title of ruler (8:23).

(8) The trees went forth.—As in this chapter we have the first Israelite "king" and the first massacre of brethren, so here we have the first fable. Though there are many "fables" and parables in Scripture, there is only one other "fable," and that is one closely akin to this (II Kings 14:9). Paul, however, in I Cor. 12:14-19, evidently refers to an ancient fable. A "fable" is a fanciful story to inculcate prudential morality. In the Bible "trees" seem to be more favorite **dramatis personae** than the talking birds and beasts of other nations. The scenery immediately around Jotham would furnish the most striking illustration of his words, for it is more umbrageous than any other in Palestine, and Shechem seems to rise out of a sea of living verdure. The aptitude for keen and proverbial speech seems to have been hereditary in his family (Joash, 6:31; Gideon, 8:2).

(14) Unto the bramble.—Despairing of their best, they avail themselves of the unscrupulous ambition of their worst. There seems to be an echo of this fable in Aesop's fable of the fox and the thorn, where the fox is badly rent by taking hold of the thorn to save himself from a fall, and the thorn asks him what else he could expect.

(15) Put your trust in my shadow.—The mean leaves and bristling thorns of the rhamnus could afford no shadow to speak of, and even such as they could afford would be dangerous; but the fable is full of fine and biting irony.

If not.—The bramble is not only eager to be king, but has spiteful and dangerous threats—the counterpart of those, doubtless, which had been used by Abimelech—to discourage any withdrawal of the offer.

(20) Let fire come out.—The malediction is that they may perish by mutual destruction. It was exactly fulfilled (verses 45-49).

(21) Went to Beer.—Since Beer means a "well," it was naturally a very common name in Palestine. Probably Jotham would be safe anywhere in the territories of Judah or Benjamin (see Josh. 9:17), without going to the Beer of Num. 21:16, on the frontiers of Moab, an ancient sanctuary on the other side of the Jordan.

(38) Where is now thy mouth ...?— "Mouth" here means "boastfulness." This is usually taken as a bitter taunt, as though

Zebul could now safely throw off his deceitful acquiescence in Gaal's plans. It may be so, for the narrative gives us no further details; but unless Zebul was in some way secured by his own adherents from Gaal's immediate vengeance, it seems better to take it as a sort of expostulation against Gaal's past rashness.

(54) A woman slew him.—He did not, however, escape the taunt (II Sam. 11:21). We see also from the narrative of the death of Saul in II Sam. 1:9; I Sam. 31:4, how sensitive the ancients were about the manner of their death. It was a similar feeling which made Deborah exult in the death of Sisera by the hand of a woman, and the Jews in the murder of Holofernes by Judith. It is remarkable that both of the first two Israelite kings die by suicide to avoid a death of greater shame.

(56, 67) Thus.—These impressive verses give the explanation of the whole narrative. They are inserted to show that God punishes both individual and national crimes, and that men's pleasant vices are made the instruments to scourge them. The murderer of his brothers "on one stone" (verse 5) is slain by a stone flung on his head, and the treacherous idolaters are treacherously burned in the temple of their idol.

10

(1) After Abimelech.—This is merely a note of time. Abimelech is not counted among the judges, though it is not improbable that, evil as was the episode of his rebellions, he may have kept foreign enemies in check.

Tola.—This is the name of a son of Issachar (Gen. 46:13). It means "worm," and may, like Puah, be connected with the trade in purple dyes. He seems to have been the only judge furnished by this indolent tribe, unless Deborah is an exception. Josephus omits his name.

(3) Jair, a Gileadite.—In Num. 32:41 we are told of a Jair, the son of Manasseh, who "took the small towns" of Gilead, and called them Havoth-jair. This earlier Jair plays a splendid part in Jewish legend, which is alluded to only in Scripture (see Deut. 3:14). In what relation the Jair of these verses stood to him we cannot, in the uncertain data of the chronology, decide. The Jair of Num. 32:41 was descended from Judah on the father's side, and on the

mother's was a great-grandson of Manasseh.

(6) Did evil again.—Literally, "added to do evil": "joining new sins to their old ones," as the Vulg. paraphrases it (2:11; 3:7; etc.).

Served Baalim, and Ashtaroth.—See 2:19. Seven kinds of idols are mentioned, in obvious symmetry with the seven retributive oppressions in verses 11, 12.

(13) I will deliver you no more.—A threat which, as the sequel proves, was (as in other passages of Scripture) to be understood conditionally (Jer. 18:7, 8).

(16) They put away the strange gods.—The moment the sincerity of their repentance was proved, God hears them (I Sam. 7:3; II Chron. 15:8).

11

(1) Gilead begat Jephthah.—We are here met by the same questions as those which concern Tola and Jair. That Gilead is a proper name, not the name of the country mythically personified, may be regarded as certain. But is this Gilead the son of Machir, the son of Manasseh, or some later Gilead? or does "begat" mean "was the ancestor of"? The answer to these questions depends mainly upon the insoluble problem of the chronology. The obscure genealogy of I Chron. 7:14, 17 seems to show that the family of Manasseh had Syrian (Aramean) connections, and Jephthah's mother may have been an Aramitess from the district of Tob. The name Jephthah means "he opens" (the womb).

(2) They thrust out Jephthah.—This was in perfect accordance with the Law (Deut. 23:2, 3), and with family rules and traditions. Abraham had sent the son of Hagar and the sons of Keturah to found other settlements (Gen. 21:10; 25:6).

(3) Dwelt in the land of Tob.—A Syrian district on the northeast of Peraea (II Sam. 10:6). It is referred to in I Macc. 5:13; II Macc. 12:17.

Went out with him.—Jephthah simply became a sort of Syrian freebooter. His half-heathen origin, no doubt, influenced his character unfavorably, as it had done that of Abimelech.

(5) When the children of Ammon made war.—The allusion is to some special threat of invasion at the close of the eighteen years of oppression (10:9).

(11) The people made him head and

211

captain.—The people ratified the promise of the elders, and solemnly inaugurated him as both the civil and military leader of the Trans-jordanic tribes.

Before the Lord in Mizpeh.—Some have supposed that this must mean that the oath was taken before the Tabernacle or Ark, or Urim and Thummim, because the phrase has this meaning elsewhere (see 20:26; 21:2; Exod. 34:34; Josh. 18:8). There are, indeed, no limits to the possible irregularities of these disturbed times, during which the priests seem to have sunk into the completest insignificance. The Ark may therefore have been transferred for a time to Mizpah, in Benjamin (20:1), as tradition says. But "before Jehovah" probably means nothing more than by some solemn religious utterance or ceremony; and Mizpah in Gilead had its own sacred associations (Gen. 31:48, 49).

(13) Because Israel took away my land.—This was a plausible plea, but was not in accordance with facts. The Israelites had been distinctly forbidden to war against the Moabites and Ammonites (Deut. 2:9, 19); but when Sihon, king of the Amorites, had refused them permission to pass peaceably through his land, and had even come out to battle against them, they had defeated him and seized his territory. It was quite true that a large district in this territory had originally belonged to Moab and Ammon, and had been wrested from them by Sihon (Num. 21:21-30; Josh. 13:25); but that was a question with which the Israelites had nothing to do, and it was absurd to expect that they would shed their blood to win settlements for the sole purpose of restoring them to nations which regarded them with the deadliest enmity. The area in dispute was occupied by Gad and Reuben.

(14, 15) And Jephthah sent messengers again.—Jephthah disputes the king of Ammon's facts, and supports his denial of them by historical retrospect (verses 16-24).

(26) Three hundred years.—The chronology of the Jews is confessedly loose and uncertain, and it seems quite possible that "three hundred years" may be a marginal gloss which has crept into the text. The words not only create an immense chronological difficulty, but are quite needless to Jephthah's argument. If, however, in spite of these difficulties, the clause is genuine, and if there has not been one of the clerical errors which are so common where numerals are concerned, it seems possible that 300 years may be counted inclusively, **e.g.**, 100

full years since the death of Joshua an nominal completion of the conquest o Canaan, with parts of a century before an after it. Certainly this is a recognized mod of reckoning time among the Jews. Whatev er explanation we may adopt, there is noth ing but conjecture to go upon.

(27) The Lord the Judge be judge thi day.—An appeal to the arbitrament of Je hovah to decide on the justice of an appea to arms. (Comp. Gen. 16:5; 18:25; 31:53; Sam. 24:15.) These verses contain a deepl interesting specimen of what may be calle ancient diplomacy, and very powerful an straightforward it is—at once honest, con ciliatory, and firm.

(29) The Spirit of the Lord came upo Jephthah.—A weaker expression is use than that which is applied to Gideon i 6:34. It implies that he was endowed wit the courage and wisdom without which suc cess would have been impossible. Th phrase no more involves a complete inspi ration of Jephthah than it does in the cas of Samson; nor is it meant to imply th least approval of many of his subsequen actions. It furnished the power which h needed to work out the deliverance—an that only. To hold up characters like Jeph thah and Samson as religious example except (as is done in Heb. 11:32) in the on special characteristic of faith displayed a memorable crises, is to sacrifice the whol spirit of Scripture to the misinterpretatio of a phrase.

(31) Whatsoever cometh forth.—The vie held of this passage, from early Jewish day down to the Middle Ages, and still held b nearly all unbiased commentators, is tha Jephthah, ignorant as he was—being a ma of semi-heathen parentage, and long famil iarized with heathen surroundings— contemplated a human sacrifice. To say tha he imagined that an animal would "com forth of the doors of his house to meet him" on his triumphant return is a notio which even Augustine ridicules. Jephtha left God, as it were, to choose His ow victim, and probably anticipated that i would be some slave. The notion of huma sacrifice was all but universal among an cient nations, and it was especially preva lent among the Syrians, among whom Jeph thah had lived for so many years, an among the Phoenicians, whose gods ha been recently adopted by the Israelite (10:6). Further than this, it was the peculia worship of the Moabites and Ammonites

gainst whom Jephthah was marching to
attle.

The great lesson which had been taught
o Abraham at Jehovah-jireh was that the
ery notion of human sacrifice was abhor-
ent. It had been expressly forbidden in the
.aw (Lev. 18:21; Deut. 12:31, etc.). Yet
ven in the wilderness Israel had been
:uilty of Moloch-worship (Ezek. 20:26; Jer.
9:1; Moloch, Amos 5:26; Acts 7:43; see
.lso II Chron. 28:3; 33:6). The possibility of
ephthah's being guilty of so rash and evil a
ow cannot be excluded by the phrase that
the Spirit of the Lord came upon him."
he phrase must not be interpreted of high
r permanent spiritual achievement, but of
livine strength granted for a particular end.

(35) I cannot go back.—See note on
Num. 30:3. Jephthah had not understood
ntil now the horror of human sacrifice.
he Hebrews had the most intense feeling
bout the awfulness of breaking an oath or
ow, and they left no room for any mental
eservations (Lev. 27:28, 29).

**(36) Do to me according to that which
ath proceeded out of thy mouth.**—While
ephthah must not be judged for that terri-
le ignorance of God's nature which led
im to offer a sacrifice, we may well rejoice
n the gleam of sunlight which is flung upon
he sacred page by his faithfulness in not
;oing back from his vow, though it were to
is own hurt (Ps. 15:4), and in the beautiful
levotion of his daughter, cheerfully ac-
quiescing in her own sacrifice for the good
f her country.

(37) And bewail my virginity.—The
hought which was so grievous to the He-
rew maiden was not death, but to die
nwedded and childless. The absence of
notherhood cut off from her, and, in this
nstance, from her house, the hopes which
rophecy had cherished.

12

(1) And didst not call us.—The tribe of
phraim throughout the Book of Judges is
epresented in a most unenviable light—
lothful and acquiescent in time of oppres-
ion, and turbulently arrogant when others
ave taken the initiative and won the victo-
y (Josh. 17:14-18; Judg. 8:1). They brought
n their own heads the terrible disgrace and
umiliation which Jephthah inflicted on
hem. See note on 8:1.

(3) Wherefore then are ye come up . . . ?—
ephthah's answer is as moderate as Gide-

on's (8:2, 3), though it does not display the
same happy tact, and refers to topics which
could not but be irritating. Whether it was
made in a conciliatory spirit or not, we
cannot tell. Certainly if Ephraim persisted
in aggressive violence after these explanations, they placed themselves so flagrantly
in the wrong that civil war became inevitable.

**(4) Ye Gileadites are fugitives of
Ephraim.**—It is possible that fierce jealousies may have sprung up between the
Eastern Manassites and their tribal brethren
of the West, and that these may have mainly originated in the fact that the Eastern
Manassites less and less acknowledged the
lead of Ephraim, but changing their character and their habits, threw in their lot more
and more with the pastoral tribes of Reuben
and Gad. The taunt sounds as if it had
sprung from a schism in clanship, a contemptuous disclaimer on the part of
Ephraim of any ties with this Eastern half-
tribe.

(6) And he said Sibboleth.—The word
Shibboleth, meaning "a ford," has become a
proverb for the minute differences which
religious parties thrust into exaggerated
prominence and defend with deadly ferocity. In this instance, however, the defective
pronunciation was not the reason for putting men to death, but only the sign that the
man was an Ephraimite. (See Milton's interesting lines. **Samson Agonistes.** 282-289.)

**For he could not frame to pronounce it
right.**—This is a most singular circumstance, and it is one which, if it stood alone,
would have decisive weight in the question
of chronology. Nothing is more natural or
more analogous with common linguistic
phenomena than that differences of dialect
and pronunciation should develop themselves between tribes divided by the deep
barrier of the Jordan Valley; and these
differences would arise all the more rapidly
if the Eastern tribes were powerfully subjected to Syrian and other foreign influences. (Comp. Neh. 13:24.) Still, it must
have required a certain lapse of time before
a difference so marked as the inability of
the Western tribes to pronounce the letter
sh could have arisen.

(7) Judged Israel.—The word implies that
he was one of the recognized **Shophetim,**
but there are no details to show in the case
of any of the judges either what were the
limits of their jurisdiction or what amount
of authority it implied.

(8) Ibzan.—Nothing more is known of

213

Ibzan than is detailed in these three verses.

Of Bethlehem.—Bethlehem is usually assumed to be Bethlehem in Judah. But Judah seems at this epoch to have stood entirely aloof from the general life of the nation. There was a Bethlehem in Zebulon (Josh. 19:15), and as the next judge was a Zebulonite (verse 11), and that tribe had been recently powerful and prominent (4:10; 5:18), it may be the town here intended.

(11) Elon.—The name means "a terebinth." Orientals to this day are often named after trees.

(13) Abdon.—The name means "servant." Some suppose that he is the unknown Bedan of I Sam. 12:11.

Hillel.—The first occurrence of a name ("praising") afterward destined to be so famous in the annals of Jewish theology. Hillel, the rival of Shammai, shortly before our Lord's day, may be regarded, with all his faults, as by far the greatest and best of the rabbis.

13

The narrative of the next four chapters is in great measure biographical. It treats the background of Samson's birth (chap. 13); and illustrates his dedication to God as the source of his strength (chaps. 14, 15), and his own personal sins and follies as the source of his ruin (chap. 16). Samson shows greater personal prowess than any of the judges, but a less noble personal character.

(1) Did evil again.—See note on 10:6.

Of the Philistines.—See note on Gen. 10:14.

Forty years.—These terminated with the battle of Ebenezer (I Sam. 7:13). The Ark had been taken and sent back about twenty years before this battle, and the acts of Samson probably fall within those twenty years, so that Eli died about the time that Samson came of age.

(3) The angel of the Lord.—See note on 2:1.

(4, 5) The law of the Nazarite is laid down in Num. 6. Samson is the first recorded Nazarite. Both the mother and the nation were impressed with his separated character.

(5) Shall begin to deliver.—The weaknesses of Samson rendered him unfit to achieve that complete deliverance which was carried out by Samuel.

(24) Samson.—The name means "sunny." The connection of "the sun" with strength

was natural (5:31; Ps. 19:5, 6). The rabbis say that he was "named after the name of God, who is called sun and shield of Israel" (Ps. 84:11).

The child grew, and the Lord blessed him.—God has many different kinds of blessings, and those here alluded to appear to be the gifts of health, strength, courage, etc. These blessings by no means place Samson on a level with Samuel (I Sam. 2:21-26; 3:19) or John the Baptist (Luke 1:80), both of whom were Nazarites.

(25) Began to move him.—The word implies vehement and overwhelming impulses to noble deeds, which, however, only came over him "at times" (14:6; 15:14; 16:20).

14

(1) Of the daughters of the Philistines.—This was against the spirit of the law, which forbad intermarriages with Canaanites (Exod. 34:16; Deut. 7:3, 4). The sequel showed the wisdom of the law (II Cor. 6:14).

(3) Of the uncircumcised Philistines.—This on the lips of Israelites was a term of peculiar hatred (I Sam. 17:36). How repugnant such a marriage would be in the eyes of Manoah and his wife we may see from the story of Simeon, Levi, and the Shechemites (Gen. 34).

(4) That it was of the Lord.—All that can be meant is that in this marriage God was overruling the course of events to the furtherance of His own designs. He makes even the weakness and the fierceness of man redound to His praise. (Comp. Josh. 11:10; II Chron. 25:20.) See the same phrase in the story of Rehoboam's folly (I Kings 12:15).

(5) The vineyards of Timnath.—All this part of Palestine, and especially the neighboring valley of Sorek (16:4), was famous for its vines (Isa. 5:2; Jer. 2:21). The hills of Judah, which at that time were laboriously terraced up to the summit, were peculiarly favorable for vineyards (Gen. 49:11).

(8) A swarm of bees and honey in the carcase of the lion.—The word "carcase" here means "skeleton." The fierce sun of the East dries up all the animal moisture of a dead body, and reduces it to a skeleton with extreme rapidity, and bees have no dislike to dried bones as a place in which to swarm.

(9) He took thereof in his hands.—Unless he considered that a skeleton could not be regarded as a dead body, he could not have done this without breaking the express conditions of his Nazarite vow (Num. 6:6).

(12) I will not put forth a riddle unto you.—**Chidah**, "a riddle," comes from **chud**, "to knot." The use of riddles at feasts is of great antiquity among the Jews (I Kings 10:1, etc.). Jewish legends have much to tell us of the riddles which passed between Solomon and the Queen of Sheba, and between Solomon and Hiram (Jos., Antt. 8:5, §3); and large sums often depended on the discovery of the answer.

Sheets.—It means shirts of fine linen, such as are worn only by the wealthy (Isa. 3:23; Mark 14:51). Samson's offer was fair enough, for if defeated, each paranymph (see Matt. 9:15) would only have to provide one "sheet" and one robe, whereas Samson, if they guessed his riddle, would have to provide thirty.

(17) She told the riddle.—Perhaps she might have done so in any case, but she now had the excuse of violent menaces.

(18) If ye had not plowed with my heifer.—Many commentators read in this proverbial phrase an implication that Samson suspected his wife of adultery. (See verse 20; and comp. 15:6 with Gen. 38:24.)

(19) To Ashkelon.—Probably he seized the opportunity of some great feast to Dagon, or even of another marriage festival, since the linen robes and rich garments would not be such as would be worn every day.

15

(1) I will go in to my wife.—Uxoriousness was the chief secret of the weakness and ruin of Samson, as it was afterward of a very different type of man, Solomon.

(2) Verily thought ... utterly hated.—As Samson had left his wife in anger immediately after the wedding feast, the father might have reasonably supposed that he meant finally to desert her.

Her younger sister.—The father sought in this way to repair the wrong he had inflicted, and to offer some equivalent for the dower which he had wrongly appropriated.

(3) Now.—He means that his second act of vengeance will at least have more excuse than his assault on the Askelonites.

(4) Put a firebrand in the midst.—The firebrands were pieces of resinous wood, like Gideon's torches (7:20), which were loosely trailed between the tails of the

jackals ("foxes"). The object of tying **two** together was to impede their motion a little, so that they might not dart away so violently as to extinguish the torch. To burn the crops of an Arab is to this day the deadliest of all injuries. (Comp. II Sam. 14:30.)

(9) Then the Philistines went up.—They "went up" in hostile array against the hill-country of Judea (to "the rock of Etam") to take vengeance for the dreadful injury which Samson had inflicted on them.

(10) Why are ye come up against us?—Samson was not of the tribe of Judah, which seems to have been living in contented servitude.

(11) What is this that thou hast done unto us?—The abject condition into which the Lion Tribe had sunk can best be estimated by this reproach against the national hero, and still more by their baseness in betraying him. He finds no sympathy.

(15) A new jawbone.—Literally, "a moist jawbone"—i.e., the jawbone of an animal recently dead, and before the bone had become brittle. In this instance, at any rate, Samson might feel himself absolved from the rule of ceremonial cleanness, which forbad him as a Nazarite to touch carcasses.

Slew a thousand men.—The expression (whether due to poetry or not) is to be taken generally, like "Saul has slain his thousands, and David his ten thousands." A supernatural awe was doubtless attached by this time to Samson's name and person. The very fact that, though armed only with this wretched weapon of offense, he yet dared to rush upon the Philistines would make them fly in wilder panic (Josh. 23:10). The Philistines, dull and superstitious, seem to have been peculiarly liable to these panics (I Sam. 14:4-18).

(20) And he judged Israel.—Probably, as Jephthah had done, with the sort of vague prerogatives of a military hero. Why the verse is found here, as though to close the narrative (comp. 12:7, etc.), and is again repeated in 16:31, we cannot say.

16

(1) Then went Samson to Gaza.—The narrative is brief and detached. Gaza is near the sea, and was the chief town of the Philistines, in the very heart of their country.

(3) Went away with them, bar and all.—The bar was the bar which fastened the two valves together. Gaza, as we see from the site of its walls, had several gates. The site of the gate traditionally pointed out is on the southeast. It may have been the smaller gate, by the side of the main gate, which he thus tore up.

That is before Hebron.—It is not implied that Samson walked with the gates and bars on his shoulders nine miles to Hebron; but probably to a hill in the direction of Hebron, from which the hills of Hebron are visible. In this narrative it is distinctly implied that the strength of Samson was a supernatural gift, arising from his dedication to God. The carrying away the gate of his enemies would be understood in the East as a very peculiar insult.

(4) He loved a woman.—Delilah was not, as Milton represents, his wife. Josephus (**Antt.** 5:8, §11) says that she was one who played the harlot among the Philistines, and the Church Fathers all speak of her in similar terms. Nor is it at all clear—as is generally assumed (Milton, for example)— that she was a Philistine.

In the valley of Sorek.—Sorek was not in the Philistine district, but was near Samson's native town of Zorah (13:2). See note on 14:5.

Delilah.—The "tender" or "delicate."

(5) The lords of the Philistines.—The five "satraps" of the Pentapolis: Gaza, Ashdod, Ashkelon, Gath, and Ekron (see 3:3). If she was what Josephus asserts, the Philistines might both get access to her, and tempt the greed of an unprincipled and degraded mind. Had she been of their own race, threats would probably have been even more effectual with her than with the lady of Timmah. The LXX here begin to call the Philistines "aliens."

Wherein his great strength lieth.—They attributed his strength to some amulet which might be removed.

(6) And wherewith thou mightest be bound.—The narrative, if taken as a full account of all that took place, would leave in the mind an impression of almost incredible fatuity on the part of Samson. If Delilah spoke thus plainly at once, however, we can only imagine that she was professing to treat the whole matter as a jest. It is only by supposing such in this instance that we can retain credit for even the most ordinary sense on the part of the Danite hero. But his fault was not stupidity—it was sensual infatuation; and in the ruin and shame which this sensual weakness brought upon him, and the way in which, step by step, it led

him to forfeit the great gift of God, lies the chief moral of the story.

(7) Green withs.—The number seven is used as the sacred number implying perfectness; and it is one of the signs that even thus early Samson is playing about on the confines of his secret.

(11) That never were occupied.— "Occupied" is an old word for "used." Here, again, Samson distantly touches on the consecration which is the secret of his strength.

(13) If thou weavest the seven locks of my head with the web.—With almost incredible levity and folly, Samson here goes to the verge of the true secret, and allows his sacred hair to be woven in a harlot's loom.

(16) His soul was vexed.—He at last reveals the secret. Even the dangerous use which Delilah had made of his last revelation did not rouse his mind from its besotted stupefaction. If he thrice proved his vast strength, he also thrice proved his immense folly. The hair of Samson was no magical amulet. It was only a sign of dedication to God. While he kept his vow the strength remained; it only departed when the vow was shamefully broken.

(20) And he wist not that the Lord was departed from him.—A deeply tragic clause. Men do not know how much they are changed "when the Lord departs from them" until they feel the effects of that departure in utter shame and weakness. Samson's strength was in no sense in his hair, but only in the dedication to God of which it was the symbol.

(21) He did grind in the prison house.— To blind a man was the most effectual humiliation (II Kings 25:7). To grind was the degrading work of slaves and females (Exod. 11:5; Isa. 47:2). The end of Samson was mournful; "his whole powerful life was only like a light, blazing up brightly at moments, and shining afar, but often dimmed, and utterly extinguished before its time" (Ewald).

(26) That I may feel the pillars.—The temple of Dagon (from **Dag,** "fish"), had a flat roof; but further than this we are unable to conjecture what was its architecture. The more distinguished people were with the lords in the house itself; the common people were on the flat roof.

(28) O Lord God ... O God.—Three names of God—Adonai, Jehovah, Elohim.

That I may be at once avenged of the

Philistines.—Again we see that Samson stood at a comparatively low level of spiritual enlightenment as well as of moral purity. One cannot help feeling that Milton has read into the hero's character an austere grandeur which it did not possess.

(31) His brethren and all the house of his father.—Probably Manoah and his wife were dead. The religious terror caused by the catastrophe may well have prevented the people of Gaza from offering any opposition to the removal of his body.

17

The two narratives which occupy the five remaining chapters of the Book of Judges are disconnected from one another and from what precedes. They are, in fact, two Appendices, which serve the purpose of showing the social anarchy, religious confusion, and moral degradation to which tribes and individuals were liable during this period. In date they belong to an earlier time than most of the preceding chapters. The first narrative (chaps. 17, 18) still bears on the fortunes of Dan, the tribe of Samson; and in both the narratives the tribe of Judah—which has been almost unnoticed in the body of the book—occupies an important position (17:9; 18:12; 19:1, 2, 10; 20:18). These chapters belong, in fact, mainly to the annals of Dan and Judah. It is somewhat remarkable that both of them turn on the fortunes of a Levite of Bethlehem-Judah (17:7; 19:1).

(1) A man of mount Ephraim.—Most of the idolatrous violations of the second commandment occurred in the northern kingdom (Gideon, 8:27; Micah, chap. 17; Jeroboam, I Kings 12, 13). These apostasies were not a worship of other gods, but a worship of the true God under unauthorized conditions, and with forbidden images. Scripture does not deem it necessary to say anything more about Micah.

(3) To make a graven image and a molten image.—In the universal decadence of religion, the people, untaught by a careless priesthood, had become ignorant of the second commandment. The word used for a graven image is **pesel**, and for a molten image is **massecah**. They are the very words used in the curse against idolaters in Deut. 27:15. It is impossible to determine whether the graven and molten image consisted of one or of two silver "calves," like that of

the wilderness, and those later set up by Jeroboam at Dan and Bethel. This, however, was a form which the violation of the second commandment was constantly liable to take, and it probably involved much less blame than other violations of it—not, as is often stated, because the Israelites had become familiar with the worship of Apis and Mnevis in Egypt, but because the calf was a recognized cherubic emblem, and had consequently been deliberately sanctioned in the symbolism of the Temple. See Exod. 20:4, 23; 32:4, 5; I Kings 7:25, etc.)

(5) Had an house of gods.—It is quite clear that Micah did not abandon the worship of God under the names of Jehovah and Elohim, by which He was known to the Israelites. How he co-ordinated this worship with his grossly idolatrous symbols, or whom those symbols were intended to represent, it is impossible to say. The fact remains that in the Beth-Micah we find "a house of gods"—"a whole chapel of idols"—consecrated to Jehovah as a pious act (17:2, 5, 13; 18:6).

And teraphim.—These were Syrian images (Gen. 31:19), the use of which among the Israelites seems to have lasted for a long period, until it was put down by King Josiah in his great reformation (II Kings 23:4; Ezek. 21:26; Hosea 3:4; Zech. 10:2).

(6) In those days there was no king.—This shows that these narratives were written, or more probably edited, in the days of the monarchy. (See 18:1; 19:1; 21:25.)

Did that which was right in his own eyes.—The notice is added to show why there was no authoritative interference of prince or ruler to prevent idolatrous or lawless proceedings. (See Deut. 12:8.)

(7) A young man.—Later on in the story we, as it were incidentally, make the astonishing discovery that this young man was no other than a grandson of Moses. (See 18:30.)

(13) I have a Levite to my priest.—It is at least doubtful whether the priestly functions expected of him in this instance included sacrifice; but, in any case, Micah could hardly have been unaware that the Levites were incapable of priestly functions (Num. 16:10), or of the fact that the authorized worship of the nation was to be confined to the place which God should choose, which in this instance was Shiloh. In any case, however, the passage furnishes us with a fresh proof of the utter neglect of the Mosaic Law, as represented in the Book of Leviticus, from a very early period. His "house of God" seems to have resembled the high places, which even the faithful kings of Israel were unable or unwilling to clear away.

18

(1) Unto that day all their inheritance had not fallen unto them.—The Danites' inheritance is described in Josh. 19:40-46. The inheritance had been assigned to them; but they had not been able to conquer it, owing to the opposition of the Philistines and the Amorites. The failure of the Danites to conquer their allotment, and the low condition to which they dwindled, are the more remarkable because in the wilderness they were the strongest of all the tribes, numbering 62,700, and because they received the smallest assignment of land of all the tribes.

(3) What makest thou in this place?—The accent of extreme surprise in the spies' queries shows that they knew Jonathan, and did not expect to find a Judaean Levite in Ephraim, much less in Micah's "spurious Shiloh."

(7) Laish.—It is four miles from Caesarea Philippi, and was the northernmost city of Palestine (20:1). It is sometimes called "el-Leddan," because it is at the source of the Leddan, the chief stream of the Jordan. The name "Dan" in Gen. 14:14 may have been altered from Laish at a later date (Ewald).

(10) God hath given it into your hands.—Of this they feel confident, from the interpretation which they put upon the oracular response given them by Jonathan in verse 6.

(11) Appointed.—This was not a mere raid of warriors, but the migration of a section from the tribe, accompanied by their wives and children, and carrying their possessions with them (verse 21).

(20) The priest's heart was glad.—The disgraceful alacrity with which he sanctions the theft, and abandons for self-interest the cause of Micah, is very unworthy of a grandson of Moses.

(27) Burnt the city with fire.—Probably the notion that such conduct was cruel and unjustifiable never occurred to them; nor must we judge them by the standard of Christian times. But Dan was no gainer. His name disappears from the records of I Chron. 4:1, and he is not mentioned among

the elected tribes in Rev. 7. It has been conjectured, from II Chron. 2:14, that the cause of their disappearance from Israelite records—the latest mention of them as a tribe being in I Chron. 27:22—was due to their intermarriages with the Phoenicians.

(28) In the valley that lieth by Beth-rehob.—At the foot of the lowest range of Lebanon, and at the sources of the Jordan (Num. 13:21), north of Lake Huleh. The name means "house of spaciousness."

(30) Set up the graven image.—If this **pesel** was in the form of a calf, the tradition of this cult may have given greater facility to the daring innovation of Jeroboam (I Kings 12:30). In any case, it would make the inhabitants more ready to accept a cherubic symbol of Jehovah; for we may fairly assume that the "image" was not dissociated from the worship of God, whether as Elohim or Jehovah. Whether this, or rather the smallness of Dan, is the reason for its exclusion from Rev. 7:4 must remain uncertain. The Fathers thought, for this reason, that Antichrist would spring from the tribe of Dan.

Jonathan, the son of Gershom, the son of Manasseh.—The extreme reluctance to admit this fact—the disgrace involved against the memory of Moses by this rapid and total degeneracy of his grandson—is probably the reason why up to this point in the narrative the name has been withheld. There can, however, be no doubt that Jonathan was the young Levite who has all along been spoken of. The reading of "Manasseh" for "Moses" is by the confession of the Jews themselves due to the same cause. Without the points the names only differ by the letter **n**. But in the Masoretic text the **n** is not boldly inserted, but is timidly and furtively suspended. This was done to conceal from the uninitiated the painful fact.

There is no reason why Jonathan should not have been the actual grandson of Moses, since he is contemporary with Phinehas (20:28), who was, without any question, the actual grandson of Aaron. This rapid degeneracy may perhaps account for the obscuration of the family of Moses, which never seems to have subsequently risen into any importance, and of which no more names are preserved. Jonathan's name is excluded, perhaps deliberately, from Chron. 23:15, 16. It is probably from a similar dislike to reveal the disgrace which thus fell on the family of the great lawgiver that Josephus entirely omits the story. It is impossible that he should not have been perfectly acquainted with it. But the identity of Jonathan with Shebuel in I Chron. 23:16 is asserted in the Targum.

Until the day of the captivity of the land.—"The captivity" no doubt means, in the light of verse 30, the Philistine captivity, which resulted from their terrible sack of Shiloh after the battle of Aphek (I Sam. 4:11, 22). It is called "a captivity" in the passage which so graphically describes the scene in Ps. 78:58-61.

(31) All the time that the house of God was in Shiloh.—i.e., until Samuel's early manhood, when the Philistines sacked Shiloh, to which place the Ark and Tabernacle never returned (I Sam. 3:31; 4:3; 6:21; 7:1). This verse may probably have been added by a later hand to prevent any mistake in the interpretation of the former. It may have been written in Saul's reign, when the Tabernacle and ephod had been removed to Nob for greater safety. The last mention of the town of Dan is in II Chron. 16:4.

19

In this chapter we see the unutterable depth of profligacy and shamelessness into which some of the Israelites had sunk. At the same time, we see that the moral sense of the nation was still sufficiently keen to be aroused by the glare of unnatural illumination thus flung upon their consciences. This narrative, like the former, belongs to the period between the death of Joshua and the rise of the greater Judges.

(1) Took to him a concubine.—Such connections were not legally forbidden; yet it is probable that in the case of all but princes or eminent men they were looked on with moral disapprobation. She is called "a wife or concubine"—i.e., a wife with inferior rights for herself and her children.

(7) His father in law urged him.—Considering the remorselessly savage revenge which is permitted to an Eastern husband in punishment of unfaithfulness, the father might well desire to be thoroughly assured that the Levite was not dissembling, and did not desire to inflict some sanguinary retribution on his wife.

(11) The day was far spent.—Jerusalem is only two hours distant from Bethlehem. The father of the woman, by his unwise neglect to speed the parting guest, had greatly added to the perils of their journey in a half-conquered country, and in such wild times.

This city of the Jebusites.—Their complete and undisturbed possession shows that this narrative falls at an early date (1:7, 8, 11, 21; Josh. 15:63). The travelers would reach the town from Bethlehem at about five o'clock.

(12) To Gibeah.—This is the "Gibeah of Saul," where the first king of Israel was born (I Sam. 11:4). It was one of the fourteen cities of Benjamin (Josh. 18:28), and only involved a journey of four miles more.

(13) Or in Ramah.—This town is only two miles beyond Gibeah. The Levite is naturally anxious to push on homeward as fast as he can. Perhaps he knew that Gibeah did not bear a good character, and that it would be better to get as far as Ramah if possible. In countries where there are no public inns, each town and village gets a character of its own from the reports of travelers.

(22) Sons of Belial.—It is only by a deeply-rooted misconception that Belial is written with a capital. The word is not the name (as is supposed) of an evil spirit, but an ordinary noun, "sons of worthlessness," i.e., "worthless fellows." (See Deut. 13:14; Ps. 18:4.) Later (comp. II Cor. 6:15) it became a kind of proper name. We cannot wonder that the intense horror excited by this scene of infamy lasted for centuries afterward (Hosea 9:9; 10:9).

(30) The verse shows that the Levite had successfully gauged the depths of moral indignation that still lay in the hearts of his countrymen. The story of the deed thrilled through all Palestine, and awoke a determined desire for retribution upon the guilty inhabitants of Gibeah. The whole nation felt the stain and shame.

20

(1) In Mizpeh.—This Mizpeh is not the same as the one mentioned in 11:11, but is that from which the traveler gains his first glimpse of Jerusalem. It was the scene of great gatherings of the tribes in the days of Samuel (I Sam. 7:5; 10:17) and of Solomon (II Chron. 1:3), and even after the captivity (II Kings. 25:23).

(2) Four hundred thousand.—Here we learn the interesting fact that in their struggles against the Canaanites the number of the people had been diminished one-third—

i.e., to a far greater extent than they had been diminished by the wanderings in the wilderness. (See Num. 1:46.)

(5) Thought to have slain me.—Obviously some circumstances of the assault have been omitted in 19:22-25. The Levite colors the whole story in the way most favorable to himself.

(13) The children of Benjamin would not hearken.—That they should have preferred a destructive civil war to the giving up their criminals illustrates the peculiarly fierce character of the tribe (Gen. 49:27). Their determination was to hold out against united Israel.

(18) Judah ... first.—This is remarkable as indicating that the Urim and Thummim were something more than a pair of lots, and that the questions with which God was consulted by its means were other than those which admitted a mere positive or negative answer.

(27) Enquired of the Lord.—It is clear that the nation had been thoroughly and beneficially humiliated by these two terrible reverses, and that their approach to Jehovah on this occasion was far more solemn and devout than it had been at first. **Was there.**—i.e., at Bethel, though Bethel has not been mentioned, owing to the erroneous rendering of the name by "House of God" in verses 18-26.

(28) Phinehas.—The fact that the high priest is still the grandson of Aaron is an important note of time, and proves decisively that this narrative, like the last, is anterior to much that has been recorded in the earlier chapters. (See note on 21:16.)

(29) Set liers in wait.—This exceedingly simple and primitive stratagem had also been successful against Ai (Josh. 8:4) and against Shechem (9:43). Here, as in verses 22, 23, the narrative follows a loose order, the general fact being sometimes stated by anticipation, and the details subsequently filled in.

(48) As well the men of every city, as the beast.—The whole tribe (with the exception of 600 fugitives) was placed under the ban of extirpation, as though they had been Canaanites, just as mercilessly as Sihon and his people (Deut. 2:34; 13:15, 16), or Jericho (Josh. 6:17, 21), or Ai (Josh. 8:25, 26). Their feelings were doubtless exasperated by the fearful destruction which Benjamin had inflicted upon them, as well as by religious horror at the conduct of the tribe. The good side of the deed lies in its motive: it expressed an intense horror against moral

pollution. The evil side lay in its ruthless savagery. In both aspects it agrees both with the recorded and the traditional character of Phinehas (Num. 25:8; 31:6).

21

(3) Why is this come to pass ...?—This is not so much an inquiry into the cause which was indeed too patent, but a wail of regret, implying a prayer to be enlightened as to the best means of averting the calamity. The repetition of the name "Israel" three times shows that the nation had not yet lost its sense of corporate unity, often as that unity had been torn apart by their civil dissensions. Their wild justice is mingled with a still wilder mercy.

(8) There came none to the camp from Jabesh-gilead.—For some reason with which we are unacquainted, there seems to have been a bond of intense sympathy between the inhabitants of this town and Benjamin. If their abstinence from the assembly of vengeance was not due to this, we must suppose that the sort of companionship in misery caused by these wild events itself created a sense of union between these communities. (See I Sam. 11; 31; II Sam. 2.) Jabesh recovered from the extermination now inflicted on its innabitants.

(12) Unto the camp to Shiloh.—The Israelites, now that the war with Benjamin was over, appear to have moved their stationary camp to Shiloh, the normal and more central seat of the tabernacle at this period (18:31).

(15) The Lord had made a breach.—The breach had been caused by their own headstrong fury and unreasoning passion, even though it had been in a righteous cause; but in the Hebrew conception the results even of man's sin and follies are referred to Jehovah as overruled by Him (Amos 3:6; Isa. 45:7).

(16) How shall we do ...?—They want to keep their vow in the letter, while they break it in the spirit. Their want of moral enlightenment revealed itself in this way and still more in having ever taken this horrible oath, which involved the butchery of innocent men, and of still more innocent women and children. What the Israelites should have done was not to bathe their hands in more rivers of fraternal blood, but to pray to God to forgive the brutal vehemence which disgraced a cause originally righteous, and to have allowed the remnant of the Benjamites to intermarry with them once more. As all these events took place under the guidance of Phinehas, they give us a high estimate indeed of the zeal which was his noblest characteristic (Ps. 106:30). Yet a very low estimate of his state of spiritual insight. But why should we suppose that the grandson of Aaron, in such times as these—when all was anarchy, idolatry, and restlessness, against which he either did not strive or strove most ineffectually—should stand on so much higher a level than his schismatical and semi-idolatrous cousin, the wandering grandson of Moses?

(17) That a tribe be not destroyed.— Benjamin never quite recovered from this crushing blow. Even though it furnished the second judge (Ehud) and the first king (Saul) to Israel, and was advantageously situated, and was often honored by the residence of Samuel, it became a mere satellite to the more powerful tribe of Judah. Perhaps in the quiescence and permanence derived from the close association with its powerful neighbor we see in part the fulfillment of the blessing in Deut. 3:12.

(19) A place which is on the north side of Beth-el . . . —This elaborate description of the site of Shiloh, a place which is so often mentioned elsewhere without any addition, is extremely curious. There can be little doubt that it is due to the marginal gloss of some Masoretic scribe. It was spoken at Shiloh itself, and the site was well known to all Israel. But by the time the story was committed to writing in the days of the kings, or finally edited in the days of Ezra, Shiloh had long been desolate, and probably the very site was unknown to thousands. This very valuable and interesting description has alone enabled us to identify the modern site. There seems to have been no regular town at Shiloh; at least, no extensive ruins are traceable. It was probably a community which was mainly connected with the service of the Tabernacle.

(25) In those days . . . —This verse, already occurring in 17:6; 18:1; 19:1, is here added once more by way of apology for the lawless crimes, terrible disasters, evaded vows, and unhallowed excesses of retribution, which it has been the painful duty of the sacred historian thus faithfully and impartially to narrate. Out of these depths the subsequent judges, whose deeds have been recorded in the earlier chapters, partially raised their countrymen, until the dread lessons of calamity had been fully learned, and the nation was ripe for the heroic splendor and more enlightened faithfulness of the earlier monarchy.

THE BOOK OF RUTH

1

(1) When the judges ruled.—This note of time is by no means definite. Some have proposed to connect the famine with the ravages of the Midianites (Judg. 6:1); or, supposing the genealogy to be complete (which is more likely, however, to be abridged, in the earlier generations), and since Boaz was the son of Salmon (Salma, I Chron. 2:11) and Rachab (Matt. 1:5), whom there can be no reasonable grounds for supposing to be other than the Rahab of Jericho, the events must be placed comparatively early in the period of the judges.

Beth-lehem.—Judah is added by way of distinction from the Bethlehem in the tribe of Zebulun (Josh. 19:15).

Moab.—The land of Moab seems to have been of exceptional richness and fertility (see Isa. 16; Jer. 48). It was divided from the land of Israel by the Dead Sea, and on the north by the river Arnon, the old boundary between Moab and the Amorites (Num. 21:13). The journey of the family from Bethlehem would probably first lead them near Jericho, and so across the fords of the Jordan into the territory of the tribe of Reuben. Through the hilly country of this tribe, another long journey would bring them to the Arnon, the frontier river.

How far Elimelech was justified in fleeing, even under the pressure of the famine, from the land of Jehovah to a land where Chemosh was worshiped and the abominations of Baal-peor practiced, may well be doubted, even though God overruled it all for good. It was disobeying the spirit of God's Law, and holding of little value the blessings of the land of promise.

(2) Naomi.—The name is derived from the Hebrew root meaning "to be pleasant" (see verse 20, where Mara means "bitter"). Mahlon and Chilion mean "sickness" and "wasting"; it may be in reference to their premature death, the names being given by reason of their feeble health.

(4) They took them wives.—This seems to have been after the father's death. The fault of settling on a heathen soil, begun by the father, is carried on by the sons in marrying heathen women, for such we cannot doubt they must have been. This act was to incur a further risk of being involved in idolatry.

Ruth.—This name will mean either "comeliness" or "companion," according to the spelling of which we suppose the present name to be a contraction. The Syriac spelling supports the latter view. Ruth was the wife of Mahlon (4:10), apparently the elder son.

(5) And . . . died.—Clearly as quite young men. Some see in the death of Elimelech and his sons God's punishment for the disregard of His law. Thus Naomi is left alone, as one on whom comes suddenly the loss of children and widowhood.

(6) That she might return.—The three women actually began the journey; and when the start was made, Naomi urged her companions to return. Then, as with Pliable in the **Pilgrim's Progress,** so with Orpah: the dangers and difficulties of the way were too much for her affection.

The Lord had visited his people.—The famine had ceased, and Naomi's heart yearns for the old home. Perhaps, too, the scenes where everything reminded her of her husband and sons, filled her with sadness (for it would appear that she set out immediately after her son's death), and perhaps, too, her conscience smote her of distrusting the mercies of the God of Israel.

(15) Her gods.—Naomi doubtless views the Moabite idols as realities, whose power is, however, confined to the land of Moab. She is not sufficiently enlightened in her religion to see in the Lord more than the God of Israel.

(16) Intreat me not.—Ruth's nobleness is proof against all. The intensity of her feeling comes out all the more strongly now that she pleads alone.

(17) The Lord do so to me.—Ruth clinches her resolutions with a solemn oath, in which, if we are to take the words literally, she swears by the name of the God of Israel. With this Naomi yields; after so solemn a protest she can urge no more.

(19) They went.—The journey for two women apparently alone was long and toilsome, and not free from danger. Two rivers, Arnon and Jordan, had to be forded or otherwise crossed; and the distance of actual journeying cannot have been less than fifty miles.

(22) Barley-harvest.—God had restored plenty to His people, and the wayfarers thus arrive to witness and receive their share of the blessing. The barley harvest was the earliest (Exod. 9:31, 32), and would ordinarily fall about the end of April.

2

(1) Boaz.—See note on 1:1. According to the line, however, given in 4:18 seq., Boaz is grandson of the Nahshon who was prince of the tribe of Judah during the wanderings in the desert, and son of Salmon and Rahab of Jericho. (Salmon has been supposed by some to be one of the spies whom Joshua sent to Jericho.) It may be noted that the difficulty of date may be lessened by supposing that in the last two generations we have children of their fathers' old age.

(2) Let me now go.—The character of Ruth comes out strongly here. Energy, honesty of purpose, and loyalty are alike evinced here.

(3) Her hap was to light on.—Literally, "her hap happened." A chance in outward appearance, yet a clear shaping of her course by unseen hands. Her steps were divinely guided to a certain field, that God's good purposes should be worked out.

(4) The Lord be with you.—There is a trace here of the good feeling prevailing between Boaz and his servants. Though he has come to his field to supervise the work, it is not in a faultfinding spirit, but with true courtesy and friendliness; nor is it a frivolous jesting manner that he displays, but with gravity and soberness he presents a true gentleman in his relationship with his inferiors.

(8) My daughter.—This address suggests that Boaz was no longer a young man; clearly the account he had heard of Ruth, both from his servant and from general report, as well as her appearance and behavior, and doubtless a feeling of pity at her condition, had prepossessed him in her favor.

(10) A stranger.—A foreigner. Note, however, that the Moabite language, though having its own peculiarities, really differed but little from Hebrew, as may be seen, for instance, from the famous inscription of King Mesha discovered in the land of Moab in 1868.

(17) Beat out.—That is, she threshed it herself, so as to save the labor of carrying away the straw. She then found she had an ephah, that is, rather more than four pecks.

(19) Blessed be he that did take knowledge of thee.—Naomi easily perceives that the quantity of corn brought home is unusually large, and that therefore some special kindness must have been shown. Her own, therefore, as well as her daughter's thanks are due to this benefactor.

3

(1) Rest.—Although Naomi had already (1:12) repudiated any thought of marriage for herself, still she felt it her duty to do what she could to provide a home for the daughter-in-law who had so loyally followed her, lest her own death should leave her young companion especially unprotected and friendless. But there is clearly a second thought. The marriage of Boaz and Ruth will not only insure rest for the latter, but will also raise up the seed of her dead son and preserve the family name.

(3-5) The plan suggested by Naomi seems strange, yet some thoughts may give a certain coloring to it. (1) Naomi seems to have believed that Boaz was the nearest kinsman (the **goel,** or redeemer), being ignorant of the yet nearer one (verse 12). Consequently, according to Israelite law (Deut. 25:5 seq.), it would be the duty of Boaz to marry Ruth to raise up seed to the dead. (2) The general tone of Naomi's character is clearly shown in this book to be that of a God-fearing woman, so that it is certain that, however curious in its external form, there can be nothing counseled here which really is repugnant to God's law, or shocking to a virtuous man such as Boaz, otherwise Naomi would simply have been most completely frustrating her own purpose. (3) Her knowledge by long intimacy of Ruth's character, and doubtless also of that of Boaz by report, would enable her to feel sure that no ill effects could accrue.

(4) Uncover his feet.—We are told that the custom still prevails in Palestine of owners of crops sleeping on their threshing floors, lying with the clothes on, but with their feet covered with a mantle.

(5) I will do.—Ruth's obedience here is an intelligent obedience. She knew in what relation Boaz stood to her family, and the duties attaching to the relationship (2:20; 3:9). Thus with obedient trust, implicitly but not blindly, she follows her mother-in-law's orders; strong in conscious innocence she risks the obloquy that may attend her duty.

(10) Blessed be thou of the Lord.—This answer of Boaz's is in itself a sufficient proof of the view he took of her conduct, and of the integrity of his own. The Targum on verse 15 supposes that to Ruth, the distant ancestress of the Saviour, was vouchsafed the knowledge, as in its fullness to the Virgin hereafter, of the birth of the Messiah through her. Origen compares

Ruth to the Gentile Church, the engrafted wild olive.

(14) One could know another.—i.e., before daylight, in the early dusk. Thus it is of Ruth, not of himself, that Boaz is here thinking. A sensible man like Boaz knows "that we must not only keep a good conscience, but keep a good name; we must avoid not only sin but scandal" (Henry).

4

(1) Such a one.—This phrase is used like the English so-and-so, such-and-such, of names which it is thought either unnecessary or undesirable to give. Why the name is not recorded here does not appear: possibly it was not known to the writer, or it may have been thought unworthy of recording, since he neglected his plain duty in refusing to raise up seed to the dead. We know nothing of this unnamed person except the fact of the offering of the redemption set before him, and his refusal of it, an offer which involved the glory of being the ancestor of the Christ.

(3) Naomi ... selleth ...—Naomi, as the representative of the dead Elimelech, had, as far as it was possible for an Israelite to part with a family estate, sold the land to obtain in some way the means of living. In the year of Jubilee, the property would return to the family, on which it was, so to speak, settled, but Boaz proposes to the **Goel** that he should redeem the property at once.

(5) What day ...—When the person had been bought out to whom Naomi had sold the land until the year of Jubilee should restore it to her family, there remained Naomi's own claim on the land, and afterward that of Ruth, as the widow of the son of Elimelech. But further, this last carried with it the necessity of taking Ruth to wife, so that a child might be born to inherit, as the son of Mahlon, Mahlon's inheritance.

(6) Lest I mar ...—The redemption of the land would involve the spending of money, drawn away from the **Goel's** own estate; but the land thus acquired would not belong to the **Goel** himself, but to the son he should have by Ruth, who would yet be, in the eyes of the law, the son of Mahlon. It would, therefore, be like mortgaging one's own estate, and that for the benefit of another. Josephus and the Targum explain it by saying that he already had a wife, and feared the discord that might arise.

(7) Plucked off his shoe.—The idea of this act apparently is that the man resigns the right of walking on the land as master, in favor of him to whom he gives the shoe. A similar but not identical custom is prescribed in Deut. 25:9.

(11) The Lord ...—In this way is the nuptial blessing invoked. (See Gen. 35:16, 19; 38:29; Jer. 31:15; Matt. 2:18.)

(17) Obed.—i.e., a serving one.

(18-22) This short genealogy, abruptly added, may be due to a later hand, it being thought necessary to connect David's line fully with Judah. (See Gen. 46:12; Exod. 6:23; Num. 1:7; I Chron. 2:9, 11; Matt. 1:3, 5.)

FIRST SAMUEL

1

Somewhere about the year 1140 B.C. (or, as some suppose, thirty years earlier), the Levitical family of Elkanah, of the house of Kohath, lived in Ramathaim-zophim, a little city of Benjamin, built on the slopes of Mount Ephraim. The supposed date of the Trojan War coincides with this period of Jewish history. We may then fairly assume that the events related in the Homeric epic took place during the time treated of in these Books of Samuel.

(1) His name was Elkanah.—Elkanah, the father of the future prophet-judge, was a Levite of the family of Kohath (compare the genealogy given here with I Chron. 6:22). He is here termed an Ephrathite: that is, an Ephraimite. Some have found a difficulty in reconciling the Levitical descent of Samuel with his dedication to the Lord by his mother, supposing that in the case of a Levite this would be unnecessary; but the dedication of Samuel, it should be remembered, was a life-long one, whereas the Levitical service only began when the Levite was twenty-five years old; and even then the service was not continuous.

(2) And he had two wives.—The primeval divine ordination gave its sanction alone to monogamy. The first to have violated God's original ordinance appears to have been Lamech, of the family of Cain (Gen. 4:19). The practice apparently had become general throughout the East when the Mosaic Law was formulated. In this divine code it is noticeable that while polygamy is accepted as a custom prevailing everywhere, it is never approved. The laws of Moses simply seek to restrict and limit it by wise and humane regulations.

Hannah . . . Peninnah.—Hannah signifies grace or favor and has always been a favorite name among the women of the East. The traditional mother of the Virgin Mary was named Anna. (See Luke 2:36.) Peninnah is translated by some scholars "coral"; according to others it signifies "pearl."

(3) Went up out of his city yearly.—The Hebrew expression rendered "yearly" is found in Exodus 13:10, and there refers to the Feast of Unleavened Bread, the Passover. There is little doubt but that this great national festival is here referred to. It was the Passover that the whole family was accustomed to keep at the sanctuary of the

Eternal. The writer places in strong contrast the piety and devotion which evidently still existed in the family life of many in Israel with the fearful disorders and crime which disfigured the priestly life in those days. There were not a few, doubtless, in Israel who, like Elkanah and his house, honored the name of the Lord, while the recognized rulers and religious guides of the people, like the sons of Eli the high priest, too often lived in open and notorious sin.

Unto the Lord of hosts.—It is estimated that this title of God—"Lord of Hosts," or "Jehovah Sabaoth"—occurs 260 times in the Old Testament, but it is not found in any of the books written or compiled before this time. In the New Testament it is used only once (see Jas. 5:4). The glorious title, with which Isaiah, who uses it some sixty times, and Jeremiah some eighty times, have especially made us familiar, represented Jehovah, the Eternal One, as ruler over the heavenly hosts: that is, over the angels and the stars.

It is especially noteworthy that here in these Books of Samuel, which tell of the establishment of an earthly sovereignty over the tribes, this stately title of the real King in Israel, which afterward became so general, first appears. It was the solemn protest of Samuel and his school against any eclipsing of the mighty but invisible sovereignty of the Eternal by the passing splendors and the outward pomp of an earthly monarchy set up over the people. It told also the strange and alien peoples that the God who loved Israel was, also, the star ruler, the Lord of the whole universe, visible and invisible.

In Shiloh.—That is, "rest." This sacred city was situated in Ephraim. It became the sanctuary of Israel in the time of Joshua, who pitched the tent of the Tabernacle there. Shiloh, as the permanent seat of the Ark and the Tabernacle, was the religious center of Israel during the whole period of the judges. On rare occasions the sacred tent, and all or part of the holy furniture, seems to have been temporarily moved to such places as Mizpah and Bethel, but its regular home was Shiloh. At the time of the birth of Samuel, and during his younger days, the high priest resided there, and the religious families of the people were in the habit of making an annual pilgrimage to this, the central sanctuary of the worship of Jehovah.

The priests of the Lord.—Hophni and Phinehas are here alluded to especially by name: first, because of their rank and connection with the high priest Eli, to whose high dignity one of the brothers would probably succeed; secondly, because these unhappy men figured in one of the great historical disasters of the people; thirdly, because the writer, out of many servants of the sanctuary, chose two prominent figures to illustrate the terrible state of corruption into which the priesthood had fallen.

(7) And as he did so year by year.—That is, Elkanah, on the occasion of every yearly visit to the national sanctuary, was in the habit of publicly giving the childless Hannah the double gift, to show his undiminished love; while the happier mother of his children, jealous of her rival, every year chose this solemn occasion of offering thank offerings before the Tabernacle, especially to taunt the childless wife, no doubt referring the absence of children, which among the mothers of Israel was considered so deep a calamity, to the special anger of God.

(9) Now Eli the priest sat upon a seat.—Eli, the high priest of Israel at this time, was a descendant of Ithamar, the younger son of Aaron (see I Chron. 24:3). The circumstances which led to the transfer of the dignity from the line of Eleazar, who succeeded his father Aaron in the office, are unknown. It has been suggested that at the death of the last high priest of the line of Eleazar, Ozi, there was no son of sufficient age and experience to succeed, and so the office passed to the next of kin, Eli, a son of the house of Ithamar. (See Josephus, **Ant.** 5, 2, §5.) The seat upon which Eli is represented as usually sitting (see 4:18) was evidently a chair or throne of state, where the high-priestly judge sat at certain times to administer justice and to transact business. The Hebrew word rendered here "post," and the expression "doors of the house" (3:15), seem to suggest that now a permanent home had been erected for the sanctuary; something of a building, possibly of stone, surrounding the Tabernacle had been built.

(11) And she vowed a vow.—The vow of Hannah contained two solemn promises. The one pledged the son she prayed for to the service of the Eternal all the days of his life. The other promised that he should be a Nazarite.

These strange restrictions and customs had an inner significance. The abstinence from wine and strong drink signified that the Nazarite determined to avoid all sensual

indulgence which might cloud the mind and render the man unfit for prayer to, and work for, the Lord; the avoiding contact with the dead was a perpetual outward protest that the power of the solemn vow renounced all moral defilement, that he gave up every thing which could stain and soil the life consecrated to the Eternal's service; the untouched hair, which here is especially mentioned, was a public protest that the consecrated one had determined to refrain from intercourse with the world, and to devote the whole strength and fullness of life to the Lord's work.

(13) Now Hannah, she spake in her heart.—Eli was watching the worshipers and was struck with dismay at her silent earnestness, such heartfelt prayer being apparently not usual at that time, and remembering the condition of the moral life in the precincts of the sanctuary over which he ruled with so weak and vacillating a rule, and how sadly frequent were disorders at the sacrificial meal, at once suspected that the weeping, praying one was a drunken woman. He, however, quickly atoned for his unworthy suspicion.

(20) And called his name Samuel.—The words translated "because I have asked him of the Lord" do not explain the meaning of the name "Samuel." They simply give the reason for his mother so calling him. The name Sh'muel (Samuel) is formed from the Hebrew words **Sh'mua El**, "heard of God."

(28) I have lent him to the Lord.—The rendering of the Hebrew here "I have lent" is false (See Exod. 12:36.) The sense is: "The Lord gave him to me, and now I have returned him whom I obtained by prayer to the Lord, as one asked or demanded."

2

(1-10) The Song of Hannah. Hannah had had personal experience of the gracious government of the kind, all-pitiful God; her own mercies were a pledge to her of the gracious way in which the nation itself was led by Jehovah, a sign by which she discerned how the Eternal not only always delivered the individual sufferer who turned to Him, but would also at all times be ready to succour and deliver His people.

These true, beautiful thoughts the Spirit of the Lord first planted in Hannah's heart, and then gave her lips grace and power to utter them in the sublime language of her hymn, which became one of the loved songs of the people, and as such was handed down from generation to generation in Israel, in the very words which first fell from the blessed mother of the child-prophet.

(1) Mine horn is exalted.—The image "horn" is taken from oxen and those animals whose strength lies in their horns. It is a favorite Hebrew symbol, and one that had become familiar to them from their long experience—dating from remote patriarchal times—as a shepherd-people.

(2) Neither is there any rock.—This was a favorite simile among the inspired song writers of Israel. The image, doubtless, is a memory of the long desert wandering. The steep precipices and the strange fantastic rocks of Sinai, standing up in the midst of the shifting desert sands, supplied an ever-present picture of unchangeableness, of majesty, and of security. The term rock, as applied to God, is first found in the Song of Moses (Deut. 32:4, 15, 18, 30, 31, 37), where the juxtaposition of rock and salvation in verse 15 seems to indicate that Hannah was acquainted with this song or national hymn of Moses. The same phrase is frequent in the Psalms.

(5) The barren hath born seven.—Here the thought of the inspired singer reverts to herself, and the imagery is drawn from the story of her own life. Seven children are mentioned as the full number of the divine blessing in children (see Ruth 4:15; Jer. 15:9). There is a curious Jewish legend which relates how for each boy child that was born to Hannah, two of Peninnah's died.

(6-9) The reign of a divine Law administered by the God to whom Hannah prayed is universal, and guides with a strict unerring justice what are commonly called the ups and downs, the changes and chances, of this mortal life.

(10) His king ... of his anointed.—Even Jewish expositors have generally interpreted these words as a prophecy of King Messiah. The words received a partial fulfillment in the splendid reigns of David and Solomon; but the pious Jew looked on the golden halo which surrounded these great reigns as but a pale reflection of the glory which would accompany King Messiah when He should appear. This is the first passage in the Old Testament which speaks of "His Anointed," or "His Messiah." The LXX renders the words **"Christou autou."**

This song was soon evidently well-known in Israel. The imagery, and in several passages the very words, are reproduced in the Psalms.

(11) The life of the dedicated child Samuel was a different one; he lived under the shadow of the sanctuary, ministering with his child powers before the altar of the Invisible, and trained, we may well assume, in all the traditions and learning of Israel by the old high priest. The word "minister" is the official term used to signify the duties performed by priests and Levites in connection with the service of God.

(12) Sons of.—The word Belial is printed here and in 1:16, as though Belial were the name of some pagan deity, but it simply signifies "worthlessness." "Sons of Belial" signifies, then, merely "sons of worthlessness," worthless, good-for-nothing men. Comp. II Cor. 6:15.

They knew not the Lord.—The whole conduct of these high priestly officials showed they were utter unbelievers. They used their sacred position merely as affording an opportunity for their selfish extortions; and, as is so often the case now, as it was then, their unbelief was the source of their moral worthlessness (see verse 22). Hophni and Phinehas are true examples of the grasping and worldly clergy of all ages.

(13) The priest's custom.—That is to say, the custom or practice introduced under these robber-priests, who were not content with the modest share of the offerings assigned to them by the Law of Moses. (See Lev. 7:31, 35; Deut. 18:3.)

(16, 17) The solemn ritual of the sacrifice was not only transgressed by these covetous, greedy, ministering priests, but the worshipers were compelled by force to yield to these new lawless customs, probably introduced by these sons of the high priest Eli. Religion was being brought into general disrepute through the conduct of its leading ministers.

(18) Ministered ... being a child.—A striking contrast is intended to be drawn here between the covetous, self-seeking ministrations of the worldly priests and the quiet service of the boy devoted by his pious mother and father to the sanctuary service.

(20) And Eli blessed ... —The blessing of Eli, his training of Samuel, his sorrow at his priestly sons' wickedness, his passionate love for his country, all indicate that the influence of the weak but loving high priest was ever exerted to keep the faith of the people pure, and the life of Israel white before the Lord. There were evidently two

227

parties at Shiloh, the headquarters of the national religion: the reckless, unbelieving section, headed by Hophni and Phinehas; and the God-fearing, law-loving partisans of the old divine Law, under the influence of the weak, but religious, Eli. These latter kept the lamp of the loved faith burning—though but dimly—among the covenant people until the days when the strong hand of Samuel took the helm of government in Israel.

(22) The women that assembled.—These women were evidently in some way connected with the service of the Tabernacle; possibly they assisted in the liturgical portion of the sanctuary worship. (Comp. Ps. 68:25.) Here, as so often in the world's story, immorality follows on unbelief. In Ps. 78:60-64, the punishment of the guilty priests and the forsaking of the defiled sanctuary is recorded.

(25) They hearkened not ... because the Lord would slay them.—Here the mysteries connected with God's foreknowledge and man's free will are touched upon. The Lord's resolution to slay them was founded on the eternal foreknowledge of their persistence in wrong-doing. This is spoken of in Exod. 4:21 as "hardening the heart." (See note on 3:14.)

(27) There came a man of God.—Of this messenger of the Highest, whom, from his peculiar title, and also from the character of his communication, we must regard as one of the order of prophets, we know nothing. He appears suddenly on the scene at Shiloh, nameless and—as far as we know—homeless, delivers his message of doom, and disappears. Until the sudden appearance of this "man of God," no mention of a prophet in the story of Israel had been made since the days of Deborah.

Did I plainly appear ... ?—The interrogations in this divine message do not ask a question with a view to a reply, but simply emphatically appeal to Eli's conscience. To these questions respecting well-known facts the old man would reply with a silent "Yes."

(29) Wherefore kick ye at my sacrifice.—The image is one drawn from the pastoral life of the people: the ox or ass overfed, pampered, and indulged, becomes unmanageable, and refuses obedience to his kind master. See Deut. 32:15.

And honourest thy sons above me.—Although Eli knew well what was right, yet foolish fondness for his sons seems in part to have blinded his eyes to the enormity of

their wickedness. It is also probable that he was influenced not by feelings of weak affection, but by unwillingness to divert from his own family the rich source of wealth which proceeded from the offerings of the pilgrims from all parts of the land. These considerations induced him to maintain these bad and covetous men as his acknowledged representatives in the national sanctuary of Shiloh. Eli then allowed things, which gradually grew worse and worse, to drift, and merely interfered with a weak rebuke; but the day of reckoning was at hand.

(31) I will cut off thine arm.—"The arm" signifies power and strength. (See for the figure Job 22:9; Ps. 37:17.)

And there shall not be an old man in thine house.—No one more in thy house shall attain to old age; sickness or the sword shall early consume its members. This strange denunciation is emphasized by being repeated in the next verse, and in different words again in verse 33.

(32) And thou shalt see an enemy.—The reference is no doubt to the capture of the Ark by the Philistines in the battle where his sons were slain. The earthly habitation of the Eternal was there robbed of its glory and pride, for the ark of the covenant was the heart of the sanctuary.

(34) In one day they shall die both of them.—See for a literal fulfillment the recital in 4:11. This foreshadowing of terrible calamity which was to befall Israel was to be a sign to Eli that all the awful predictions concerning the fate of his doomed house would be carried out to the bitter end.

(35) A faithful priest.—Many of the conditions are fairly fulfilled by Samuel, to whom naturally our thoughts at once turn. He occupies a foremost place in the long Jewish story, and immediately succeeded Eli in most of his important political life in Israel. He was also eminently and consistently faithful to his master and God during his whole life. (For his numerous posterity, see 1 Chron. 6:33; 25:4, 5.) Samuel, though a Levite, was not of the sons of Aaron; yet he seems, even in Eli's days, to have ministered as a priest before the Lord, the circumstances of his early connection with the sanctuary being exceptional. The Aaronic priesthood fell for a long time into such disrepute that it had to beg for honor and support from him (verse 36), and became dependent on the new order of things instituted by Samuel.

Some commentators, with a singular confusion of ideas, see a reference to Christ in the "faithful priest," forgetting that this "faithful priest" who was to arise in Eli's place was to walk **before** the Lord's Christ, or Anointed One.

3

(1) Was precious in those days.—That is, "rare." "The word of the Lord" is the will of the Lord announced by a prophet, seer, or man of God. Between the days of Deborah and the nameless man of God who came with the awful message to Eli, no inspired voice seems to have spoken to the chosen people.

The "open vision" refers to such manifestations of the divinity as were promised to Abraham, Moses, Joshua, and Manoah, and in this chapter to Samuel. There may possibly be some reference to the appearance of divine glory which was connected with the Urim and Thummim which were worn by the high priest. This significant silence on the part of the invisible King the writer dwells on as a result of the deep corruption into which the priests and, through their evil example, a large portion of the nation had fallen.

(3, 4) The high priest slept in one of the chambers adjacent to the sanctuary, and the attendant ministers in another. In the center, on the left of the entrance, stood the seven-branched candlestick, now mentioned for the last time, superseded in the reign of Solomon by the ten separate candlesticks, but revived after the Captivity. The only light of the Tabernacle during the night, it was solemnly lighted every evening and extinguished just before morning, when the doors were opened.

The Lord called Samuel.—It seems probable that the voice came from out of the "visible glory," the Shekinah, which on that solemn night of the calling of the child-prophet no doubt rested on its chosen earthly throne—the mercy-seat of God—which formed the top of the Ark, and which was overshadowed by the outspread wings of the golden Cherubim. Josephus tells us that Samuel, when the Lord first called him, was twelve years old. This was the age of the child Jesus when He disputed with the doctors in the Temple.

(9-10) And the Lord came, and stood.—The question is naturally asked, **What** came and stood before the boy's couch? As a rule, we find that generally, when the Lord

was pleased to take some form, the form is specified. Was it not this Shekinah which filled the chamber of the child, and from out of **this** came the voice of the Eternal, and spoke to Samuel?

(11) The ears of every one that heareth it shall tingle.—The calamity which is here referred to was the capture of the Ark of the Covenant. Neither the death of the warrior priests, Hophni and Phinehas, nor the crushing defeat of the Hebrew army, would have so powerfully affected the people; but that the sacred symbol of the presence and protection of the invisible King should be allowed to fall into the hands of the uncircumcised Philistines, the hereditary foes of the chosen race, was a calamity unparalleled in their annals. It seemed to say that God had indeed forsaken them. The expression is a singular one, and recurs in II Kings 21:12, and Jer. 19:3, on the occasion of the destruction of Jerusalem by Nebuchadnezzar.

(14) Shall not be purged with sacrifice.—A great theological truth is contained in these few words. In the sacrificial theory of the Mosaic Law we see there was a limit to the efficacy of sacrifice after a certain point in sin and evil example had been reached. Did not men like Eli, sure of divine love, look to some other means of deliverance after the earthly penalty had been paid? Did they not anticipate, "as in a glass darkly," the blood of another Victim, which should cleanse the repentant and sorrowing sinner from all sin?

(20) A prophet of the Lord.—Then from the northern to the southern cities of the land the fame of Samuel was established. The minds of all the people were thus gradually prepared when the right moment came to acknowledge Samuel as a God-sent chieftain. On this rapid and universal acknowledgment of the young prophet it has been observed that the people, in spite of their disruption, yet formed religiously one unit.

4

(1) And the word of Samuel.—The compiler of the book, in his relation of the young prophet's error, touches upon an important feature of his great life. Anarchy and confusion had long prevailed throughout the tribes, and none of the hero Judges who had as yet been raised to power had succeeded in restoring the stern, rigid form of theocracy which had made the Israel of Moses and Joshua so great and powerful. A terrible picture of the corruption of the priesthood is presented to us during the last period of Eli's reign. We can well imagine what the ordinary life of many among the people, with such an example from their religious guides and temporal governors, must have been. Individual instances of piety, not infrequent of themselves, would have been totally insufficient to preserve the nation from the decay which always follows corruption. In this period of moral degradation the Philistines, part of the original inhabitants of the land, a warlike and enterprising race, taking advantage of the internal jealousies and the weaknesses of Israel, made themselves supreme in many portions of the land, treating the former conquerors often with harshness, and even with contempt.

Samuel grew up to manhood in the midst of this state of things. The boy prophet, as he passed out of childhood into manhood, does not appear at first to have recognized the depth of moral degradation into which Israel had sunk, or to have seen that it was utterly hopeless to attempt to free the people from the yoke of the Philistine foes until something like a pure national religion was restored. The first call to arms, therefore, resulted in utter disaster, and the defeat at Aphek—the result of the summons of Samuel—was the prelude to the crushing blow to the pride of Israel which soon after deprived them of their leaders, their choicest warriors, and, above all, of their loved and cherished Ark of the Covenant.

(3) It may save us.—It was a curious delusion, this baseless hope of the elders, that the unseen God was inseparably connected with that strange and beautiful symbol of His presence. One of the greatest of Samuel's successors, Jeremiah, presses home the same truth the people were so slow in learning (Jer. 7:4, 5, 7). They had been disloyal to their King, His sanctuary had become infamous as the center of vice, His ministers were chiefly known as the prominent examples of covetousness and immorality, and the Ark had become only a symbol of the broken covenant. It was in vain that the grand battle hymn of Israel was raised as in the old days when the Ark set forward (Num. 10:35).

See Ps. 78:59-61, where the crushing defeat of Aphek and the signal victory of the Philistines is recounted in detail. (For the fate of Shiloh, see Jer. 7:12; 26:9.)

(11) And the ark of God was taken.—The bare fact, without comment or note, is given of this, the greatest calamity that had yet happened to Israel. All the people would know by this terrible sign that their invisible King had withdrawn His countenance from them; but the loss of the Ark to the heathen taught another lesson, not merely for the Israel of the days of Eli and Samuel—the eternal truth that "the living God does not bind His presence to a dead thing" (Erdman).

The two sons of Eli ... were slain.—See note on 2:34.

(12) And there ran a man of Benjamin.—The Rabbinical tradition relates that this messenger was Saul, who snatched from Goliath the tables of the Law taken out of the Ark, in order to save them. The whole of this account is so vivid and full of detail that it must have come from some eyewitness—probably Samuel himself. Swift runners were employed to carry news in wartime in the East. In the sacred story we possess several important instances of such messages: e.g., II Sam. 2:18; 18:21-27; Comp. Phidippides (Herodotus, 6.105, 6). The rent clothes and the earth upon the head were the usual indications that the news brought by the messenger were tidings of evil.

(16) I fled to-day out of the army.—The words of the runner were remembered. The whole vivid scene was evidently related by a bystander; some have even suggested that it was Samuel who stood by Eli's side.

(18) He fell from off the seat backward.—The compiler of these books was actuated by no feeling of friendship to the high priest Eli. In composing this history of the events which led to the elevation of Samuel to the judgeship, he simply puts together the materials he possessed of the records of these days, and gives us a vivid picture of the calamities of the rule of Eli. As he never spares his weakness, or attempts to veil his blind nepotism, we feel here the perfect truth of this touching incident which closed the old man's life. He loved the Ark, because of its close connection with his God, better, after all, than his two sons.

(21, 22) The glory is departed from Israel.—This singular and circumstantial account is introduced from the records of that sad time solely for the purpose of showing how deeply the heart of Israel was penetrated with a love for their God, His Tabernacle, and its sacred contents. "The wife of this deeply corrupt man shows how penetrated the whole people then was with the sense of the value of its covenant with God." (Von Gerlach)

The meaning of the term I-chabod is much disputed. The best rendering seems to be "Alas! the glory."

5

(2) They brought it into the house of Dagon.—In Ashdod the Philistines placed the Ark in the temple of the popular Philistine god, Dagon. This was their vengeance for the slaughter of the 3,000 Philistine worshipers in the temple of the same deity at Gaza, not many years before, by the blind Hebrew champion Samson. (See Judg. 16:23-30.)

(3) Dagon was fallen upon his face.—This Dagon was one of the chief Philistine deities, and had temples not only in Ashdod and in Gaza, but also in the cities of Philistia. The idol had a human head and hands, and the body of a fish. The derivation is from **Dag**, a fish, which represents the sea from which the Philistines drew their wealth and power. The Philistine federation seems to have been a powerful one, and owing to the disinclination of the Israelites to maritime pursuits and foreign commerce (the foreign commercial expeditions of King Solomon were apparently quite exceptional) held in their hands a large proportion of the Mediterranean trade. This strange image the men of Ashdod, on the morrow of their triumphal offering of the Ark of the Lord before the idol shrine, found prostrate on the temple floor, before the desecrated sacred coffer of the Israelites. (Comp. verse 5 with Zeph. 1:9.)

(6) But the hand of the Lord was heavy upon them of Ashdod.—A painful and distressing sickness, in the form, perhaps, of tumors (the word **emerods** should be spelled **hemorrhoids**) broke out among the inhabitants of the Philistine city in which was situated the idol temple, where was placed the Ark of the Covenant.

(11) Send away the ark.—The constitution of Philistia was oligarchical. The lords of the Philistines were a long time before they could make up their minds to get rid of this deadly trophy of their victory. To see the historical sacred treasure of Israel, so long veiled in awful mystery, at the feet of their fish-god idol, was a perpetual renewal for Philistia of the glorious triumph of Aphek, which avenged so many years of bitter humiliation. The plague and misery which afflicted the cities of Philistia in the day when the sacred Ark dwelt an unhonored guest in their midst suggest many and grave thoughts.

6

(2) Diviners.—These men, who in one form or other dabbled in occult science, and perhaps here and there were aided by evil and unclean spirits, but who more frequently traded on the credulity and superstition of their fellows, occupied a considerable position among the nations of antiquity. We hear of them frequently among the Israelites, who seem to have adopted this class of advisers from the heathen nations around them. Isaiah (3:2) especially mentions them, and reckons these diviners among the leading orders of the State.

(3) Send it not empty.—The advice was to propitiate with gifts the powerful Hebrew Deity, whom they imagined was offended and angry at the insult offered Him—the being placed in an inferior position in the Dagon temple.

(4) Five golden emerods, and five golden mice.—It was a general custom in the nations of antiquity to offer to the deity, to whom sickness or recovery from sickness was ascribed, likenesses of the diseased parts. This is the first mention of the plague of "mice" in the Hebrew text. In these warm countries which border the Mediterranean, vast quantities of these mice from time to time seem to have appeared and devoured the crops. Aristotle and Pliny both mention their devastations. In Egypt this visitation was so dreaded that the mouse seems to have been the hieroglyphic for destruction.

(6) As the Egyptians and Pharaoh hardened their hearts.—These constant references to the story of Moses and the Exodus (comp. 4:5-9) are indications that the deep impression those events had made on the surrounding nations; therefore the value they set on the Ark, which they looked upon as the visible symbol of the mighty Hebrew God.

(9) It was a chance that happened to us.—The priests and diviners were not certain whether the plague had been sent by the offended God of Israel or had visited Philistia in the ordinary course of nature. This strange experiment would satisfy the minds of the Philistine people. If the cows, contrary to their expectation, kept on the road to Beth-shemesh, this would be a sign that they were guided by a divine power, and that the scourge from which they were suffering came from the angry Israelite Deity. If, on the other hand, the animals, left to themselves, returned to their own stalls, then the Philistines might safely retain the Ark, being confident that their late sufferings were simply the results of natural causes.

(19) They had looked into the ark.—The favorite Rabbinical explanation of the original is that the chief men of the city, most of whom were priests and Levites, after the festive rejoicings which accompanied the sacrificial feast celebrating the Ark's joyful return, heated with wine, lost all sense of reverence and determined to use this opportunity of gazing into that sacred chest of which they had heard so much and into which no profane eye in Israel had ever peered. Perhaps they excused themselves by a desire to learn if the Philistines had violated the secrets of the holy chest.

Even he smote of the people fifty thousand and threescore and ten men.—Here it is perfectly clear that the present Hebrew text is corrupt. The system of writing letters for numbers constantly has occasioned great discrepancies in the several versions. The number of stricken ones, 50,070, is simply inconceivable. Beth-shemesh was never a large or important place; there were, in fact, no great cities in Israel; the population was always a scattered one, the people living generally on their farms. Josephus, **Ant.** 6.1, §4, in his account of this occurrence speaks of the smitten as numbering seventy. This is probably the correct number.

(20) Who is able to stand?—The men of the priestly city of Beth-shemesh strangely connected their invisible King with that golden Ark, which, sacred though it was, was but a lifeless chest of wood and gold. Yet through their superstition we can discern a deep consciousness of sin and shortcoming, which argued well for the future reformation of the religious life of the people—a grand work which Samuel the prophet labored so faithfully and so successfully to bring about.

7

(1) The ark of the Lord.—Kirjath-jearim, the home of the Ark for nearly fifty years, was probably selected as the resting place of the sacred emblem as being the nearest large city to Beth-shemesh then in the hands of the Israelites. It was neither a priestly nor a Levitical city, but it no doubt had preserved something of its ancient character of sanctity even among the children of Israel. In old days, before the Hebrew invasion, it was a notable "high place" and a seat of worship of Baal.

Samuel—who, though he is not named in this transaction, was, no doubt, the director—would, of course, have endeavored to find a man of the tribe of Levi for the sacred trust (see II Sam. 6:3). Here the Ark remained until King David brought it from "the house on the hill," in "the city of woods," first to the home of Obed-edom, and then to his own royal Zion (II Sam. 6. See Ps. 132:6).

(2) And all the house of Israel lamented after the Lord.—This "lamenting" or "hungering after the Lord" was a gradual result of Samuel's unwearied labors. The assertion of 3:19, that "none of his words fell to the ground," especially belongs to this period of restless activity. Slowly, but surely, the heart of the people, roused by his loving but passionate appeals, returned to their eternal Friend. Sick of crime and folly, gradually they began to hate their impurity and moral degradation. By degrees they began to loathe their idolatry. And when Samuel, after his twenty years of faithful restless work among them, summoned them boldly to declare their abhorrence of the strange Philistine gods, and the life taught and lived by the Philistine peoples, the heart of all Israel responded with intense gladness to the summons.

(3) The strange gods.—"Baalim" (verse 4), plural form of Baal, refers to the numerous images of Baal which existed, as does the plural form Ashtaroth to those of the female goddess Astarte. They were both favorite Phoenician deities, representing the productive power of nature, and were generally worshiped throughout the East, usually with a wild and wanton worship.

Prepare your hearts.—It was, indeed, a desperate venture to which the prophet summoned unarmed and undisciplined Israel. Samuel challenged Israel to bid defiance to the most cherished institutions of their oppressors. If defeated, then Israel would bring upon their devoted heads utter misery and ruin. For twenty years the great patriot-statesman had labored for this end. He had succeeded at last in opening the eyes of Israel to see the real cause of their misfortunes

He had made them as a nation hunger for the lost presence of the Eternal, who had loved them in past days with so great a love.

(5) Mizpeh.—The name signifies a "watch-tower," a place where an outlook could be kept against an advancing enemy. The assembly of the tribes at Mizpah (in Benjamin) marked a new departure for Israel. It was the result of more than twenty years of toil undertaken by the greatest reformer and statesman the chosen race ever knew. The great gathering belonged to religion and to war. Its first object was solemnly to assure the Lord that the heart of His people, so long estranged from Him, was again His. Its second was to implore that Jehovah might again restore a repentant and sorrowful people to the land of their inheritance. The solemn pouring out of water before the Lord symbolized, to a people trained so carefully to watch the meaning and signification of symbols and imagery, the heart and whole inner life poured out before the Lord; the fasting represented the repentant humble sinner bowed down in grief before the one true God.

(8) Cease not to cry unto the Lord our God for us.—Once more, as in old days, the glorious Arm fought with no earthly weapons for the people: an awful thunderstorm burst over the combatant hosts, the storm probably beating in the faces of the advancing Philistines. The tribes welcomed it as the answer to their prophet's prayer. Josephus tells us of an earthquake which added fresh horrors to the scene of battle. The dismayed Philistines fled, and the rout was complete; the defeated army hurried panic-stricken over the same ground in the neighborhood of Aphek, illustrious twenty years before for their signal victory. The scene of carnage now received the significant name of Eben-ezer, or "The Stone of Help."

(13) So the Philistines were subdued.—The work of Samuel had been thorough. It was no mere solitary victory, this success of Israel at Eben-ezer, but was the sign of a new spirit in Israel, which animated the nation during the lifetime of Samuel, and the reigns of David and Solomon and the great Hebrew kings. The petty jealousies had disappeared, and had given place to a great national desire for unity. And the Philistines never entirely recovered their supremacy in Canaan.

From the days of Samuel a new order—that of the Prophets, whose exact functions with regard to the ritual of the worship of the Eternal was undefined—was acknowledged by the people as the regular medium of communication with the Jewish king of Israel.

(15) And Samuel judged Israel all the days of his life.—Probably for at least twenty years after the decisive battle of Ebenezer Samuel, as "judge," exercised the chief authority in Israel. The time at length arrived when, convinced by clear divine monition that it was best for the people that a king should rule over them, Samuel the seer, then advanced in years, voluntarily laid down his high office in favor of the new king, Saul; but his influence remained, and his authority, whenever he chose to exercise it, seems to have continued undiminished, and on momentous occasions (see, e.g., 15:33) we find king and nation submitting to his counsel and expressed will.

(16) To Beth-el, and Gilgal, and Mizpeh, and judged Israel.—These centers were all situated in the tribe of Benjamin. The power of Samuel, if not exclusively, was chiefly exercised among the southern tribes. Religion at an early date became corrupted in the north of the Promised Land, and the restoration of faith and purification of life—the result of the great work of Samuel—was so much less marked in the northern than in the southern tribes, that when the strong hand of Solomon was removed, a formal secession from the southern league at once took place. This was followed by a rapid deterioration both in faith and practice in the northern kingdom of Israel.

8

(1) When Samuel was old.—We are not able with any precision to fix the dates of Samuel's life. When the Israelite victory at Ebenezer took place, Samuel the judge was probably nearly fifty years of age. Another considerable lapse of time must be assumed between the throwing off the Philistine yoke and the request of the people for an earthly king. Seventy years of age is a likely supposition.

(2) They were judges in Beer-sheba.—It is probable that at the time when old age was beginning to enfeeble the strength of Samuel, and many of the duties devolved upon his worthless sons, the Philistines recovered much of their lost power over the southern districts of Israel. The names of these sons are especially significant of the

233

holy atmosphere their father lived in. Joel signifies Jehovah is God; and Abiah, Jehovah a Father. But the glorious traditions of Samuel were quickly forgotten by these unworthy men.

(3) Took bribes, and perverted judgment.—This sin, at all times a fatally common one in the East, was especially denounced in the Law. (See Exod. 23:6-8; Deut. 16:19.) It is strange that the same ills that ruined Eli's house, owing to the evil conduct of his children, now threatened Samuel. The prophet-judge, however, acted differently to the high priestly judge. The sons of Samuel were evidently, through their father's action in procuring the election of Saul, quickly deposed from their authority. The punishment seems to have been successful in correcting the corrupt tendencies of these men, for we hear later of the high position occupied at the court of David by the distinguished descendants of the noble and disinterested prophet. (See I Chron. 6:33; 25:4, 5, respecting Heman, the grandson of Samuel.)

(6) The thing displeased Samuel.—It is clear that it was perfectly justifiable in the elders of the people to come to the resolution contained in their petition to Samuel. The Deuteronomy directions contained in 17:14-20 are clear and explicit in this matter of an earthly king for the people, and Moses evidently had looked forward to this alteration in the constitution when he framed the Law. The displeasure of the prophet-judge, however, was very natural.

(7) Hearken unto the voice of the people.—Israel's desire was the deliberate abandonment by the Eternal God of His first intention as regarded Israel, the deliberate lowering of the grand ideal once formed for His chosen people. Here we see how sadly possible it is for man in the exercise of his perfect free will to mar the glorious work arranged for him by his God.

(11) And he said, This will be the manner of the king that shall reign over you.—In this whole transaction of the appointment of an earthly king in Israel, we must not forget that although under the present circumstances of Israel it was the best course to pursue, and, as such, received the divine sanction, yet it was giving up the old grand ideal of a nation dwelling on earth ruled over directly by a King whose throne and home were in the eternal heavens. The glorious hope had to be given up, because Israel had been tried and found unworthy

to share in the undreamed-of blessings of such a government.

He will take your sons.—Here follows a graphic picture of the changed life of the people under a despotic monarch. The old pastoral life would give way to a very different way of living: the court, the cities, the prospect of war. All these heavy burdens would become the heritage of Israel if they chose to imitate in their government the nations of the world.

(18) The Lord will not hear you in that day.—After the separation of the north and the south, when King Solomon was dead, a large proportion of the northern sovereigns fulfilled in their lives and government of the realm the dark forebodings of the seer. The northern tribes broke with all the hallowed associations connected with the Ark and Temple, and set up a rival and semi-idolatrous religion in some of their own popular centers. One wicked dynasty succeeded another, until the cup of iniquity was filled and Israel carried away captive.

(20) Like all the nations.—There is something strangely painful in these terms with which the elders urged their request. The wish "to be like other nations" seems to have been very strong with them. They forgot, or chose to ignore, the solitary position of lofty pre-eminence God had given them among the nations. They had, it is true, failed to comprehend it in past, as in present days, but this haste to give up their lofty privileges, and to descend from the pedestal on which their God had set them, was in the eye of one like Samuel a strange inexplicable foolishness.

(22) Hearken unto their voice.—For the third time (see verses 7 and 9) God had allowed His servant to remonstrate, well knowing all the time what would be the result of his remonstrances. So now, with the selfsame words with which He had spoken to Samuel when at the first he laid the petition of Israel before the eternal throne, He finally directs him respecting the course of action he was to pursue on this momentous occasion.

9

(1, 2) Here begins a short account of the family of this man chosen for so high an office, and after a word or two of personal description there follows a relation of the circumstances under which he met Samuel.

Saul, a man in the prime of manhood, distinguished among his fellowmen by his great stature, and for his grace and manly beauty, was the son of a noble and opulent Benjamite of Gibeah, a small city in the south of the Land of Promise. (Comp. Gen. 46:21; I Sam. 9:1; 10:21; 14:51; I Chron. 7:6-8; 9:35.)

The whole of this chapter and part of the following is full of picturesque details of the pastoral life of the people. In many of the little pictures we see how strongly at this early period the religion of the Eternal colored almost all parts of the everyday life of Israel.

(10) Unto the city.—The name of the city where Samuel and Saul first met in this strange way is not given. Still, the impression which the narrative leaves on the mind is that it was Samuel's usual residence—Ramah. We know Samuel had built an altar to the Lord at Ramah (7:17); on the day of Saul's arrival there was a great sacrifice taking place on the altar of the high place of the city. Again, in this nameless city the seer had a house of his own (see verses 18 and 25). Samuel, too, was known to Saul's servant as dwelling in this place.

(15) Had told Samuel in his ear.—Literally, "had uncovered the ear of Samuel." The image is taken from the action of pushing aside the headdress, in order the more conveniently to whisper some words into the ear. This is one of the few more direct intimations in the sacred records of one of the ways in which the Spirit of God communicated divine thoughts to the human spirit. Here the Eternal Spirit is represented as whispering in the ear of man.

(22) And Samuel took Saul.—The seer gave Saul no answer to his question (verse 21), in which the young man's wonderment was expressed that one so insignificant should be chosen for so high a destiny. Samuel merely wished, in the first instance, to awaken new and grander thoughts and aspirations in this young heart, and without reply he proceeded to conduct his guests to the scene of the sacrifice on the high place. In the guest chamber, where thirty of the most distinguished persons present at the solemn sacrifice were assembled, Samuel places Saul and his companion, no doubt to their great surprise, in the principal seats.

Not only was Saul thus highly honored in public as the future king, but his servant also. If, as tradition tells us, this servant was

Doeg the Edomite, he, too, on this occasion had a foretaste of his future position, an earnest of the rank and power which he would receive when he would be one of Saul's great officers of state.

(25) And when they were come down.—After the public sacrificial meal at which such signal honors had been shown to the Benjamite stranger and his servant, the prophet-judge detained Saul from continuing his journey homeward, and persuaded him to remain as his guest that night at Ramah. He conducted him to the flat roof of his house, often the favorite locality in the East for quiet conversation or rest, and where frequently the honored guest was lodged for the night: there the prophet had a long interview with his young guest. The solemn words of the old man that evening referred, no doubt, to the sad religious and political decline of the people of God. It has been suggested that this conversation was the connecting link between that on the height (verses 19, 20) and the communication which Samuel made to Saul the following morning.

(27) That I may shew thee the word of God.—The meaning of all that had happened to Saul on the day before was now to be revealed. The prophet directs that the servant should be sent on alone, that he might in all solemn confidence impart to Saul "the word of God," that is, all that the God of Israel had revealed to him, the seer, concerning Saul's appointment. It would have been interesting to have learned something of Saul's state of mind when this startling revelation of the choice of God was first made to him. The writer here is silent, but in the next chapter (verse 6) we read that the Spirit of the Lord was especially promised to this chosen one. When new duties are imposed by God, He never forgets to bestow the gift of new powers.

10

(1) Then Samuel took a vial of oil.—The vial was a narrow-necked vessel, from which the oil flowed in drops. It was, of course, no common oil which the prophet used on this momentous occasion, but the oil of holy ointment, the sacred anointing oil which was used at the consecration of the priests, and also of the Tabernacle and the sacred vessels. (See Exod. 29:7;

30:23-33; etc.) The solemn anointing took place in the ceremony of consecration in the case of some, but not of all, the Hebrew sovereigns. Founders of dynasties or those irregularly advanced to the throne were so anointed.

(2) When thou art departed from me today, then . . . —Here follows Samuel's careful description of the three signs which should meet the future king as he went from Ramah to his father's home in Benjamin. Each of these tokens, which were to strengthen the young Saul's faith, contained a solemn lesson, the deep meaning of which, as his life went on, the future sovereign would be able to ponder over. Each of the three signs from heaven met him at one of the sacred spots which were so plentifully dotted over these southern districts of Canaan. At the sepulchre of Rachel, men should meet him on his homeward journey with the news that the lost asses which he had gone to seek were found again. This showed him that henceforth in his new life he was to dismiss all lower cares, and give himself up alone to higher and more important matters. Further on in his journey, three men on a pilgrimage to the great Beth-el sanctuary would meet him, and would offer him some of the loaves which they proposed offering at Beth-el. The signification of this peculiar gift was that some portion of the products of the soil, which had hitherto been appropriated exclusively to the service and support of the sanctuary, in future should be devoted to the maintenance of the anointed of the Lord. The third sign which he should perceive would meet him as he approached his home. A number of prophets belonging to one of the "schools" of the prophets founded by Samuel would meet him. They would be plunged in prophetic raptures and a new and mighty influence would come upon Saul himself. The new influence would be the Spirit of the Lord, and from that moment he would be a changed man. He must remember that in a moment the same divine power might wing away from him its solemn flight; that was the lesson of the third sign which was to meet him on his homeward journey.

(5) A company of prophets.—These evidently belonged to one of those seminaries termed "schools of the prophets," founded by Samuel for the training of young men. The foundation of these schools in different parts of the country was one of the greatest of the works of this noble, patriotic man.

These schools seem to have flourished during the whole period of the monarchy, and in no small measure contributed to the moral and mental development of the people. Some of the youth of Israel who received in these schools their training became public preachers of the Word; for after all, this, rather than foretelling future events, was the grand duty of the prophet's calling.

It is a grave mistake to conclude that **all**, or even the greater part, of these young men trained in the "schools of the prophets" were **inspired** in the usual sense of the word. The aim of these institutions, beside high mental culture, seems to have been to train the youth of Israel to love, and then live, noble pure lives. It was owing to these great educational institutions which Samuel founded that the Israelites became a highly trained and literary people.

We understand very little respecting this state of ecstasy—what produced it, and how it affected those who had fallen into this strange condition. The object of the musical teaching of the schools of the prophets was, no doubt, to enable those who had studied in the seminaries to guide and direct the religious gatherings of the people, into which —as we know from the subsequent Temple service, the model of all popular sacred gatherings for worship—music and psalmody entered so largely.

(8, 9) Samuel had bidden the future king to advance along the paths of glory and difficulty which lay before him in all confidence and trust, acting in each emergency according to the dictates of his own heart— only in **one** thing he must be ever on his guard. In his future great work for the regeneration and advancement of Israel, he must, for the sake of the faith of Israel, be on his guard against infringing the sacred privileges of the religion of the Eternal. In the plenitude of his kingly power, the day would come when the temptation would assault him to disregard the ancient sanctity of the sacrifice, and to assume as king, functions which belonged alone to men like Samuel set apart for the sacred office, and thus publicly to dishonor the commandments of God, and by his reckless example of unbelief in revelation to weaken the faith of the people. (See 13:8ff.)

The "heart" is mentioned as changed by God, because, according to the conception of the divine writings, the heart is represented as the center of the whole mental and physical life—of will, desire, thought, perception, and feeling. It was one thing for Samuel the seer to put before the young Benjamite the brilliant destiny which lay before him, but it required a higher influence to transform Saul into a fit and worthy recipient of such honors and powers.

Of the first two signs which were to meet him no further details are given; we are simply told that in the order predicted by Samuel Saul came across them. The third alone gives occasion for a special mention, because it had a great effect on the life of the future king.

(20) The tribe of Benjamin was taken.— The words "unto the Lord" (verse 17) probably signify that the mysterious Urim and Thummim, by which inquiry was made of the Eternal, had been brought there by the high priest, or, on the supposition that the office was then vacant, by the priest who temporarily replaced him. How the "lots" were taken is not said; usually it was by throwing tablets (Josh. 18:6, 8), but sometimes by drawing from a vessel or urn, as in Num. 33:54. The latter, from the Hebrew word used, was probably the method employed on this occasion.

"It is to be noted that for the full and auspicious acknowledgment of Saul as king, his mysterious interview with the seer did not alone suffice. Publicly, in solemn national assembly, it was necessary for the Spirit of the Eternal to choose him out, and to make him known as the Eternal's man." (Ewald)

(25) Wrote it in a book.—The "Law of the Kingdom" related to the divinely established right and duties of the God-appointed king, and also clearly set forth the limitations of his power. (See note on 8:6; comp. Deut. 17:14-20.) This sacred document contained, too, no doubt, the exact details of the singular story of the choice of the first king of Israel. We may, therefore, fairly conclude that from the record laid up among the sacred archives in the sanctuary, the compiler or redactor of this "Book of Samuel" derived his intimate knowledge of every little fact connected with the divine choice of Saul.

We find here, in this writing of Samuel, the first trace of literary composition among the Israelites since the days of Moses. The great revival in letters which began shortly after the days of Saul was due, most probably, to the influence of Samuel and those great schools of the prophets which he had established in the land.

And Samuel sent all the people away.— Throughout the remainder of the great seer's life, whenever he appears on the scene, he is evidently the principal person, occupying a position above king or priest. Yet after this period Samuel made but comparatively few public appearances; of his own free will he seems to have retired into privacy, and only in emergencies to have left his retirement.

(26) A band of men.—Among these early friends, doubtless, were to be found the names of the distinguished men of whom we hear later surrounding Saul. Slow to take offense, Saul and his valiant adherents busied themselves in conciliating the disaffected, and in preparing for a decisive action against the enemies who were on all sides harrying the land.

(27) The children of Belial.—See note on 2:12.

And they despised him.—These malcontents were probably princes and leading men of the great tribes of Judah and Ephraim, displeased that the new king should be selected from the small unimportant tribe of Benjamin. "They despised him," because in no way had he made his mark, either in the arts of war or peace. From verses 11 and 12 it is evident that Saul was a man of no special culture; his early years had been spent in agriculture and work on his father's lands in the neighborhood of Gibeah.

11

(1) Nahash the Ammonite.—For his relation to David, see II Sam. 17:25; I Chron. 2:16, 17. The Ammonites were a kindred race to the Moabites, being descended from the same ancestor, the patriarch Lot. They asserted that a portion of their territory had been taken from them by Israel, and in the days of the judges sorely harassed the people. The judge Jephthah attacked and defeated them with great slaughter.

It was, no doubt, to avenge the disgrace they had suffered at the hands of Jephthah that their warlike monarch, Nahash—deeming the opportunity a favorable one, owing to the old age of the reigning judge, Samuel—invaded the Israelitic country bordering upon his kingdom, and besieged the city of Jabesh-gilead. Jabesh-gilead was situated in Northern Gilead, in the territory assigned to Manasseh.

(2) On this condition.—The object of Nahash's cruelty was to incapacitate the inhabitants of Jabesh from ever further assisting his enemies in war; they would henceforth be blinded in the right eye, while the left eye would be concealed by the shield which fighting men were in the habit of holding before them.

(4) Then came the messengers to Gibeah.— It was resolved by the beleaguered city to send messengers to all the coasts of Israel, but we only hear of the action taken by Saul in Gibeah. It may be assumed, therefore, that this was the first city they sent to, not only on account of their ancient friendship with Benjamin (see Judg. 21), but because Gibeah was the residence of the newly-elected sovereign, Saul.

(5) And, behold, Saul came after the herd out of the field.—Saul was still busied with his old pursuits. At first this would seem strange, but it must be remembered that the regal authority was something quite new in republican Israel, and that the new king's duties and privileges at first were vague, and but little understood.

(6) And the Spirit of God came upon Saul.—Nothing, perhaps, could have moved Saul so deeply as this news respecting the distress of Jabesh-gilead; he was affected not merely by the disgrace to Israel, but by the sore peril which menaced the ancient friend and ally of his tribe. On Saul's heart, thus prepared for action, the Holy Spirit fell, and endued him with extraordinary wisdom, valor, and power for the great and difficult work which lay before him.

(8) The children of Israel were three hundred thousand, and the men of Judah thirty thousand.—It has been suggested that this verse was the addition of some late reviser of the book, who lived in the northern kingdom after the final separation of Israel and Judah, but such a supposition is not necessary to account for the separate mention of Judah and Israel, or for the apparently great disproportion in the numbers supplied by the great southern tribe. The chronicler, with pardonable exultation, especially mentions the splendid result of the young hero's first summons to the tribes. It is to be remembered, too, that in the Old Testament books, owing to the mistakes of copyists, numbers are not always to be strictly relied upon.

(9) To morrow, by that time the sun be hot.—That is, about noon the army of

rescue will be at hand. The distance from Bezek (in the open plain of Jezreel, in Issachar) to Jabesh was not much more than twenty miles.

(11) The morning watch.—The morning watch was the last of the three watches, each lasting for four hours; this was the old Hebrew division of the night. Thus the first onslaught of the men of Israel under Saul would have taken place some time between two and six a.m. The battle, and subsequent rout of Ammon, continued evidently for many hours.

(15) And there they made Saul king before the Lord in Gilgal.—Gilgal was in the Jordan Valley, near Jericho, in the now royal tribe of Benjamin. The Gilgal convention was nothing more than a solemn national confirmation of the popular election at Mizpeh. The words "before the Lord" imply the presence of the Ark, or of the high priest with the mystic Urim and Thummim. After this, the people would not allow Saul any longer to lead a private life, but they made him to assume the royal state and authority to which he had been appointed by God.

12

This is doubtless a true and detailed account of all that took place on that day— the real inauguration of the earthly monarchy, that great change in the life of Israel which became of vast importance in the succeeding generations. In such a recital the words used by that grand old man Samuel, who belonged both to the old order of things and to the new, who was the link between the judges and the kings, would surely be treasured up with a jealous care. This gives a special and peculiar interest to the present chapter, which contains the summary of the proceedings of the Gilgal assembly.

The old judge Samuel, with the hero-king Saul standing by his side, presents the king to the people of the Lord under the title of the "Anointed of the Eternal," and then in a few pathetic words speaks first of his own pure and upright past. The elders reply to his moving words. Then he rehearses the glorious acts of the Eternal King, and repeats how He, over and over again, delivered the people from the miseries into which their own sins had plunged them; and yet, in full memory of all this, says the indignant old man, in the place of this invisible Ruler, so full of mercy and pity, they had asked for an earthly king. The Lord has granted your petition now.

At this juncture Samuel strengthens his argument by invoking a sign from heaven. Awe-stricken and appalled, the assembled elders, confessing their sin, ask for Samuel's prayers. The old prophet closes the solemn scene with a promise that his intercession for king and people shall never cease.

13

(1) Saul reigned one year.—The usually accepted meaning is that Saul had reigned one year when the events related in the last chapter took place, and after he had reigned two years he chose out the 3,000 men, and did what is related in this chapter.

(2) Saul chose him three thousand men of Israel.—This is a very important statement, as it tells us of the first beginning of a standing army in Israel. This was the first step toward the development of Israel into a great military power. It was Saul's military genius and foresight which enabled David and Solomon to make those great conquests which raised Israel for a time to the position of one of the greatest Eastern powers. But Israel was at this period by no means trained or armed to undertake a regular war with such an enemy as the Philistines. He therefore adopted the wise course here related.

Whereof two thousand were with Saul in Michmash.—Michmash was a position strongly situated at the head of a pass some nine miles northeast of Jerusalem. The "one thousand" he placed under the command of his son Jonathan, and stationed them in the neighborhood of his old home, where he would have the benefit of the aid of his family and kinsfolk. This is the first mention of the gallant and chivalrous prince, the story of whose unbroken and romantic friendship with David is one of the most touching episodes of these books. Personal beauty and swiftness of foot in attack or retreat gained for him among the troops the name of "gazelle." (The first lines of the song, II Samuel 1:19, can only be explained on the supposition that Jonathan was well-known by this name in the army.)

(5) And the Philistines gathered themselves together to fight with Israel.—The figures here of the numbers of this vast army are perfectly untrustworthy. (See note on 11:8.)

In the rolls of the most famous armies there never appear anything like this number. (Comp. Judg. 4:3; I Kings 10:26.) Here the more probable reading would be "300" not 30,000.

(8) The people were scattered from him.—This trial of the king's faith was doubtless a severe one. The panic which pervaded all Israel was every hour thinning the host Saul had gathered around him at Gilgal. The martial king longed for a chance of joining battle, and this he was forbidden to do until the seer had offered sacrifice and publicly inquired of the Lord; and the day passed by, and Samuel did not come (See note on 10:8, 9.) An attack on the part of the Philistine army, encamped at no great distance, seemed imminent, and Saul's forces were rapidly melting away.

(9) Bring hither a burnt offering to me.—It has been supposed by many that the greatness of the sin of Saul consisted in his offering sacrifice with his own hand, but not a hint of this is given us anywhere. It is more than probable that the sacrifice which was offered so prematurely in the absence of the seer of God was performed by the hand of Ahiah the priest, who no doubt was in attendance on the king. No unlawful assumption of priestly functions, as in the case of King Uzziah (II Chron. 26:18), is anywhere charged on Saul.

(14) Now thy kingdom shall not continue.—The twice-repeated assertion of Samuel, "Thou hast not kept the commandment of the Lord" (verses 13, 14)—an assertion uncontradicted by Saul—shows us that this whole transaction was an act of overt rebellion against the will of the Eternal. The succession was, therefore, formally transferred elsewhere; still, when the words of doom were spoken by the prophet, David could at that time have been but a mere child. Had King Saul repented what he had done, he might have been forgiven, for God's threatenings, like His promises, are conditional. There is no fatalism in the Bible, only a loving discipline for man's recovery. But behind it stands the divine foreknowledge and omnipotence, and so to the prophetic view Saul's refusal to repent, his repeated disobedience, and the succession of David were all revealed as accomplished facts.

(16) Gibeah of Benjamin.—Saul and his son, uniting their sadly diminished forces, entrench themselves at Geba, in a strong position at the end of a pass, from which they could watch the movements of the

239

Philistines. Their small numbers forbade any idea of an attack on the enemy.

(17) And the spoilers came out.—The compiler of these books of Samuel does not profess to give a detailed account of this or any of the wars of Saul. It would seem that the Philistines, with their great armed demonstration (verse 5), had completely frightened the Israelites, certainly in the southern part of Canaan. Probably the allied forces were now permitted to leave the Philistine host, and we next hear of the old raids beginning again. The three companies spoken of in this and the next verse were directed to ravage districts in the tribe of Benjamin, for in that locality are situated all the places mentioned. Unchecked, they seem to have carried out their plans.

(22) There was neither sword nor spear.—These words must not be pressed too literally. The general result of the raids alluded to in verses 16, 17 was that there was an absence of arms. Even the Israelites' implements of tillage were dull (verse 20). This fact is especially dwelt upon, for the Philistines appear to have armed their fighting men to the teeth. (Compare the description of their champion, Goliath, who is described as "clad in armour.")

(23) The garrison of the Philistines went out.—These words form an introduction to the recital of the heroic deed of Jonathan related in the following chapter. The Philistines are represented as sending forward an armed detachment, or outpost detachment, beyond the camp of Michmash, as a protection against a surprise on the part of the Israelitic force under the king and his son.

14

(1) Now it came to pass.—Jonathan was the typical warrior of that wild and adventurous age—recklessly brave, chivalrous, and generous, possessing evidently vast strength and unusual skill in all warlike exercises. He was animated with an intense faith in the willingness and power of the Eternal to help Israel. But King Saul utterly lacked it; hence his rejection.

The young prince's heart burned within him at the degradation which the Philistine occupation brought upon the people. Under any other circumstances—without the consciousness of supernatural help—to attempt such a feat of arms would have been

madness; but Jonathan had an inward conviction that an unseen Arm would hold a shield before him. It is noticeable that he never communicated his desperate purpose to his father, Saul.

(6) The term "uncircumcised" is commonly applied to the Philistines, and to other of the enemies of Israel. It is used as a special term of reproach. The enmity between Philistia and Israel lasted over a long period, and was very bitter.

(13) And they fell before Jonathan ..—The sign he prayed for was given him (verse 10). There were probably but few sentinels at their posts; the inaccessibility of the craggy fortress had lulled the garrison into security. The few watching him at first mocked, and then, as Jonathan advanced with strange rapidity, they seem to have been, as it were, paralyzed—the feat was hardly human—as the man, all armed sprang over the rocky parapet. In a moment a panic seized the garrison, and a hurried flight ensued, for they felt they had to deal with no mortal strength (see verse 15).

(16) And the watchmen of Saul in Gibeah of Benjamin looked ...—The distance between the outposts of the little Israelite army and the vast Philistine host was only about two miles, but a deep ravine or chasm lay between them. The watchmen of Saul were well able to see the scene of dire confusion in the outposts, a confusion which they could discern was rapidly spreading through the more distant camp of the main body.

(18) And Saul said unto Ahiah ...—The LXX renders here, "And Saul said to Ahijah, Bring higher the ephod; for he bore the ephod in those days before the children of Israel." But the Hebrew reads, "Bring hither the ark of God." What does this mean? Was the Ark, then, with that little band of Saul? We never before, or after find the slightest hint that the sacred coffer ever left Kiriath-yearim until David bore it to Zion. Then, again, no question or oracle could be asked of the Ark or by the Ark. The Urim and Thummim alone were used to give answers to questions solemnly asked by king and people, and were connected not with the Ark, but with the high-priestly ephod. On the whole, the reading of the LXX probably represents the original Hebrew. The present Hebrew text, with the word "ark," is, however, clearly of extreme antiquity; the second part of the verse is most likely an explanatory gloss of some ancient scribe. Josephus' account of this transaction shows us that he had before him a text corresponding to the LXX.

(23) So the Lord saved Israel ... —It was a decisive victory, crushing in its results to the Philistines, who were driven back so effectually as not to reappear until the close of Saul's reign. The king was now at liberty to develop the military character of the people; and until the disaster which closed his life and reign, his various campaigns against the idolatrous nations who surrounded Israel generally appear to have gone on from victory to victory.

(32) And the people flew upon the spoil ... —The battle and pursuit had then extended some twenty miles of country. No doubt, had the men of Israel not been so faint for want of food, and utterly weary, many more of the Philistine host would have fallen. As it was, vast spoil was left behind in the hurried flight; but it was the beasts that the conquerors greedily seized, their hunger was so great.

(33) Roll a great stone unto me this day. —The object of this was that the people should kill their beasts upon the stone and the blood run off upon the ground. It was a rough expedient, but it showed the wild soldiers that their king and general determined that the Law of Moses should be kept and honored, even under circumstances of the direct necessity. (See Lev. 17:10-14; 19:26.) This scrupulous care shows us what a strange complex character was Saul's: now superstitiously watchful lest the letter of the Law should be broken; now recklessly careless whether or not the most solemn commands of God were executed.

(36) Let us go down after the Philistines by night. —Only one man in that army flushed with victory dared, with the bravery which alone proceeds from righteousness, to withstand the imperious sovereign. The high priest, Ahiah, doubted whether such a wholesale bloodshed was in accordance with the will of God. No command to exterminate these Philistines had ever been given. Ahiah said, "Let us first inquire of the oracles of God"—alluding, of course, to the jewels of Urim and Thummim on his high-priestly ephod.

(37) But when the mysterious gems refused to shine, or in any way to signify the divine approbation or disapproval (verse 37), the high priest seems to have concluded that some public transgression had been committed, and that special atonement must be made before the desired answer could be expected. Then Saul would ask God's help in the casting of lots (verse 38), to discover who of these was the transgressor, whose sin made dumb the divine Oracle.

(41) Give a perfect lot. —The rendering "show the innocent" is a better and more accurate rendering of the Hebrew.

(43, 44) Lo, I must die. —These wild and thoughtless vows are peculiarly characteristic of this half-barbaric period. A similar terrible oath, equalling Saul's in its rashness, had been taken by Jephthah (Judg. 11:30, 31). It is noticeable that not only Saul, but also Jonathan was convinced that the vow, though perhaps hastily and rashly made, must be kept.

Over against Saul's oath the people set their own. Probably Saul was not unwilling in this awful question, when his son's life trembled in the balance, to submit his will for once to the people's.

(46) Then Saul went up from following the Philistines. —Saul recognized now that the fault was his, and not Jonathan's. He drew off his forces then from the direction of the enemy, and went up, no doubt, to Gibeah.

(47) So Saul took the kingdom over Israel. —The words are simply introductory to the list of wars waged from the very beginning of his government. This enumeration of the nations with whom he fought literally included the countries on every side of the Land of Promise: Moab and Ammon on the east; Edom on the south; the Philistines on the west, along the coast of the Mediterranean; and Zobah, a district of Syria, on the northeast.

(48) Smote the Amalekites. —Out of the many wars the king waged, this war with Amalek is singled out, for in the new development of Hebrew power by which Saul's reign was harked this campaign or series of campaigns was especially prominent. This war is related with some detail in the next chapter, but it is there introduced on account of other considerations. The English translators in their rendering, "he gathered an host," have followed the Syriac and Vulgate; the marginal translation, "he wrought mightily," is the more accurate.

(49) The sons of Saul. —See 31:2, 6; Abinadab is supposed to be the same as Ishui. For the daughters, see 18:17-21.

(50) Saul's wife. —We know nothing of Saul's queen besides her name. It has been surmised that she was of the family of Eli, the high priest. (Comp. II Sam. 21:8-12.)

The captain of his host was Abner. —This

"cousin"—or, as some have understood the sentence, the uncle—of King Saul was evidently a man of rare powers and ability. The brilliant campaigns of this reign were, no doubt, in no small measure owing to the military skill of this great commander. (See I Chron. 27:21.)

15

(1-3) Samuel also said unto Saul ... — The compiler of the history, selecting, no doubt, from ancient state records, chose to illustrate the story of the reign and rejection of Saul by certain memorable incidents as good examples of the king's general life and conduct. The incidents were also selected to show the rapid development of the power and resources of Israel at this period. The sacred war with Amalek is thus introduced without any "note of time."

(2) That which Amalek did to Israel.— The Amalekites were a fierce, untameable race of wanderers, who roamed at large through those deserts which lie between Southern Judea and the Egyptian frontier. They were descended from Esau's grandson, Amalek. Not long after the Exodus from Egypt, they attacked and cruelly harassed the almost defenseless rear-guard of Israel in the desert of Rephidim. They were then, at the prayer of Moses, defeated by Joshua; but, for this cowardly unprovoked attack, solemnly doomed to destruction.

(3) Smite Amalek, and utterly destroy ... —Amalek was to be looked upon as accursed; human beings and cattle must be killed; whatever was capable of being destroyed by fire must be burned. The cup of iniquity in this people was filled up. Its national existence, if prolonged, would simply have worked mischief to the commonwealth of nations. Israel here was simply the instrument of destruction used by the Almighty. It is vain to attempt in this and similar transactions to find materials for the blame or the praise of Israel. We must never forget that Israel stood in a peculiar relation to the unseen King, and that this nation was not unfrequently used as the visible scourge by which the All-Wise punished hopelessly hardened sinners, and deprived them of the power of working mischief.

(9) Agag, and the best of the sheep, and of the oxen.—Agag seems to have been the official title for the sovereigns of Amalek. It would seem that Saul carried out the awful curse to the letter (with the exception that he spared the king) in the case of the human beings and the less valuable of their beasts. But covetousness seems to have suggested the preservation of the choicest cattle, and pride probably induced the Hebrew king to save Agag alive, that he might show the people his royal captive.

(14) What meaneth then this bleating? ... —"Saul is convicted of falsehood by the voices of the animals which he has spared, contrary to God's command. Samuel's mode of citing them against him by the question, 'What meaneth these voices?' has an air of holy humor and cutting irony."—(Lange).

(15) The people spared the best of the sheep ... —At once the king understood the drift of his old friend's words; still more, perhaps, the stern, sorrowful look of reproach which accompanied them. There seems something strangely cowardly in this trying to transfer from himself to the people the blame of disobedience to the divine commands. It is unlike Saul's old character; but covetousness and vanity invariably lead to moral cowardice.

(17) When thou was little in thine own sight.—The prophet's words were simply to remind Saul that the Lord, whose clearly expressed will he had disregarded, had raised him in bygone days from a comparatively humble station to the proud position he was then occupying as chief of Israel. The old counsellor reminds the king that there had been a time when he judged himself unequal to this great work to which his God summoned him; but now, how strange the contrast! Flushed with success, he was trusting alone in his unaided strength, and openly disobeying the divine commands.

(19) Didst fly upon the spoil.—The expression used evidently includes the idea of greedy eagerness, as though Samuel detected a spirit of grasping covetousness at the bottom of this disobedient act of Saul's.

(22) Behold, to obey is better than sacrifice.—In this answer it would seem that the Spirit of the Lord descended upon Samuel, and that he here gave utterance to one of those rapt expressions which now and again in the course of each of these Hebrew prophets' lives these famous men were commissioned by the divine power to give out to their fellows. The words of Samuel here were reproduced, or at least referred to, by other prophets and teachers (see Pss. 50:8-14; 51:16, 17; Isaiah 1:11; Jer. 6:20; Hosea 6:6; Micah 6:6-8). Our Lord Himself,

in His words recorded in Matt. 9:13, if not actually referring to this passage, makes substantially the same declaration.

(23) For rebellion is as the sin of witchcraft.—Witchcraft, more literally "soothsaying" or "divination," was a sin constantly held up to reprobation in the Old Testament. It was the greatest of all the dangers to which Israel was exposed, and was in fact a tampering with the idol worship of the surrounding nations. Impurity, and an utter lack of all the loftier principles of morality which the one true God and His chosen servants would impress on the people of the East, characterized the various systems of idol worship then current in Syria and the adjacent countries. And Samuel here, in this solemn inspired saying, briefly gives the grounds of the Lord's rejection of His Anointed.

(24) Because I feared the people.—He, with stammering lips, while deprecating the divine sentence, still seeks to justify himself; but all that he could allege in excuse only more plainly marked out his unfitness for his high post. He could, after all, only plead that he loved the praise of men more than the approval of His God.

(26) I will not return with thee.—Samuel too clearly sees what are the true springs of Saul's repentance, and refuses at first to pardon his sin. It was only a fear on the part of the king of losing the kingdom and of incurring public disgrace. The prophet for reply again repeats the terrible divine sentence of rejection.

(28) The Lord hath rent the kingdom.—The prophet at once looks upon the garment (the hem or outer border of the tunic rather than the "mantle," verse 27) torn by the passionate vehemence of the king as an omen for the future, and uses the rent vesture as a symbol to show Saul that thus had the Lord on that day rent the kingdom from him.

A neighbor of thine.—It had not yet been revealed to the seer who was to replace the rebellious king, so he simply refers to the future anointed one quite indefinitely as "a neighbour."

(29) The Strength of Israel will not lie.—This title of the Eternal would better be rendered "the changeless One of Israel." The Hebrew word is first found in this passage. God, in the case of King Saul, was said to repent of His choice because, owing to Saul's deliberate choice of evil, the divine purposes could not in his case be carried out. Predictions and promises in the

Scriptures are never absolute, but are always conditional. Still, God is ever "the Changeless One of Israel." (See Ps. 33:11; Mal. 3:6.)

(31) So Samuel turned again after Saul.—The prophet, after the repeated and pressing request of the king, consents publicly to worship the Lord in his company. There is little doubt but that the principal motive which induced Samuel on this occasion not to withdraw himself from the public thanksgiving was a desire to prevent any disaffection toward the monarchy. His known disapproval of Saul's conduct, and his declining the king's earnest prayer to stay, would probably have been the signal to the discontented spirits in Israel to revolt, under the pretext that such a revolt would be pleasing to the great seer. Such a revolt in those critical times would have been disastrous to the growing prosperity of the chosen people.

It has been well suggested that many blessings came upon the unhappy Saul and the nation over which he ruled in answer to Samuel's intercession on this occasion for him. (See verse 35.)

(32) Bring ye hither to me Agag the king of the Amalekites.—There were, no doubt, amply sufficient reasons for the seemingly hard sentence on the people of Amalek, such as their past crimes, their evil example, the unhappy influence which they probably exercised on the surrounding nations. Weighed in the balance of the divine justice, Amalek had been found wanting, and perhaps this death, which was the doom of Amalek, was sent in mercy rather than in punishment. From Samuel's words in verse 33 he seems, even among a wicked race, to have been pre-eminent in wickedness.

16

(1) How long wilt thou mourn for Saul?—The constant references to the influence Saul acquired, and the love and admiration he attracted, is a striking feature in this most ancient Book of Samuel, where the fall and ruin of the first Hebrew king is so pathetically related. But for these touches of feeling, we would be tempted to condemn Saul with far too sweeping a condemnation.

(3) And thou shalt anoint.—From very early times the ceremony of anointing to important offices was customary among the Hebrews. In the first instance, all the priests were anointed (Exod. 40:15; Num. 3:3), but afterward anointing seems to have been reserved especially for the high priest (Exod. 29:29). Prophets also seem occasionally to have been anointed to their holy office. Anointing, however, was the principal ceremony in the inauguration of the Hebrew kings. It belonged in so special a manner to the royal functions that the favorite designation for the king in Israel was "the Lord's anointed." In the case of David, the ceremony of anointing was performed three times—(1) on this occasion by Samuel, when the boy was set apart for the service of the Lord; (2) when appointed king over Judah at Hebron (II Sam. 2:4); (3) when chosen as monarch over all Israel (II Sam. 5:3). All these official personages, the priest, the prophet, and peculiarly the king, were types of the great expected Deliverer, ever known as the "Messiah," "the Christ," "the Anointed One."

(5) Peaceably: I am come to sacrifice.— There was nothing unusual in his sanctifying Jesse, evidently a man of some wealth, and his sons. This was evidently the principal family in the place, and the village sheik and his sons would be the fittest persons to assist in preparing for, and then carrying out, the sacrificial rites.

(11) There remaineth yet the youngest.— As so often, God's thoughts are not our thoughts, and in a moment Samuel saw that in the ruddy shepherd boy—small of stature, and held of little account in his father's house—he beheld the future king of Israel.

(13) Anointed him in the midst of his brethren.—It would seem probable that Samuel kept silence for the present respecting the high destinies of the boy standing before him, and that he merely anointed him as one chosen to be his assistant in the sacrifice he was about to offer. From this time forward much of David's time was doubtless spent in Samuel's company. David was, before everything, Samuel's pupil, and the last years of that long and memorable career of the prophet were spent in molding the life of Israel's greatest king.

And the Spirit of the Lord came upon David ... (14) But the Spirit of the Lord departed from Saul.—The effect of this "descent" of the Spirit of the Lord upon David was that the shepherd boy grew up into a hero, a statesman, a scholar, and a wise, far-sighted king. The effect of the "departure" of the Spirit from Saul was that from that hour the once generous king

became a prey to a gloomy melancholy and a victim to a torturing jealousy of others which increased as time went on, and which goaded him now and again to madness ruining his life, and marring utterly the fair promise of his early years.

(15) An evil spirit from God.—(See note on 19:9.) The form in which the evil spirit manifested itself in Saul was apparently an incurable melancholy, which at times blazed forth in fits of uncontrollable jealous anger. When Saul's attendants, his officers, and those about his person perceived the mental malady under which their king was evidently suffering, they counseled that he should try whether the evil influence which troubled him could not be charmed away by music (see 18:10; 19:23, 24). There is no doubt but that King Saul's nervous, excitable temperament was peculiarly subject to such influences.

(18) And a mighty valiant man, and a man of war.—It has been suggested that, in addition to combat with wild beasts (17:34, 35), which we know in those days frequented the thickets of the Jordan and were a terror to the Israelitish shepherds, David had most likely been engaged in repelling one or more of the Philistine marauding expeditions so common in those wild days. Bethlehem, we know, was a strong place or garrison of these hereditary foes of Israel. (See II Sam. 23:14; I Chron. 11:16.)

(21) And he became his armour-bearer.— But probably only for a very short time David returned, we should conclude, to Samuel, whose pupil and friend we know he was. The seer was watching over the young man with a view to his lofty destiny. Saul apparently, from his question in 17:55, had forgotten all about him. There is no note of time, so we are not able to determine how long a period had elapsed between the events narrated in this chapter and the combat with the Philistines told in chap. 17. It is however, likely that the king's malady which was making rapid progress in this period of his reign, had already obscured his once powerful mind; his memory for the past was likely enough to have been treacherous.

17

(1) Pitched between Shochoh and Azekah. —The locality was some twelve or fifteen miles southwest of Jerusalem, and nine of en from Bethlehem. the home of the family of Jesse. The name Ephes-dammim. the "boundary of blood." is suggestive, and tells of the constant border warfare which took place in this neighborhood.

(4) Goliath, of Gath.—The Philistine champion belonged to a race or family of giants. the remnant of the sons of Anak (see Josh. 11: 22), who still dwelt in Gath. Gaza. and Ashdod. The height mentioned was about nine feet two inches. We have in history a few instances of similar giants.

(5) A coat of mail.—The Philistine armor was made of metal scales. like those of a fish, whose defensive coat was, no doubt, imitated at a very early date by this warlike race, who dwelt on the seashore. and whose life and worship were so closely connected with the great sea. This coat of mail, or corselet, was flexible, and covered the back and sides of the wearer. The weight of the different pieces of the giant's panoply largely exceeds the weight of medieval suits of armor.

(8) Am not I a Philistine?—The literal rendering is "the Philistine." The Targum of Jonathan adds here the proud boast of the giant warrior that it was he who had slain Hophni and Phinehas (the sons of Eli, the high priest), and had carried the Ark to the temple of Dagon. This Targum, although comparatively a late compilation, doubtless embodied many ancient national traditions.

And ye servants to Saul.—Must we not deem it probable that the fact of the separation of the prophet from the king had been made public in Philistia, and that the present daring challenge was owing to their knowledge that the Spirit of the Lord—whom we know these enemies of the Hebrews dreaded with so awful a dread—had departed from Saul and his armies?

(9) Then will we be your servants.—Each of the positions which the two opposing armies held was well-nigh impregnable; thus it seemed as though a single combat was the only way of deciding the present campaign. In those ancient times such single combats between renowned chieftains of the opposing armies were not by any means uncommon. (Comp. the speeches of Glaucus and Diomede in Book 6 of the **Iliad**.)

(12-14) It is better (with the Syriac Version) to place all the words after "Bethlehem-judah" down to the end of verse 14 in a parenthesis. These historical books of the Old Testament are, no doubt, made up from contemporaneous documents, stored

up most probably in one or other of the prophetic schools. It is. therefore. to be expected that certain facts will be found occasionally repeated.

(15-17) Augustine (on Ps. 143) comments on "Bethlehem." "forty days." and "thy brethren" in parallel to the experience of Christ.

(20) He came to the trench.—Literally. "to the wagon rampart"; a circle of wagons formed a rude fortification about the camp of Israel. There. within the fortified enclosure. he left his baggage ("carriage." verse 22). the ten cheeses. etc.. and hastened to the "front." where he knew his brethren and the men of Judah would be posted. (See Num. 10:14.)

(23) The Philistine of Gath.—There is a difficulty connected with the Philistine giant's name (see II Sam. 21:19). It is possible that Goliath was a general designation of these monstrous descendants of the ancient Anakim in Gath.

(25) And make his father's house free in Israel.—The exact signification here of the Hebrew word rendered "free" is disputed. The simple meaning would seem to be freedom from personal service in the army and elsewhere. It also probably includes a certain exemption from taxation or enforced contributions to war expenses.

(37) Go, and the Lord be with thee.—This permission and blessing of King Saul recalls the Saul of old days. before the covenant between him and the Mighty One of Israel was broken, before the Spirit of the Lord had departed from him. We must bear in mind that it was no mere duel between two fighting men, an Israelite and a Philistine, but the fortunes of the nation for an indefinite period were to be staked on this momentous single combat between a tried warrior of gigantic strength and a boy quite unaccustomed to martial exercises, and a stranger even to a soldier's dress and martial equipment.

(40) And he took his staff in his hand.—It was a true stroke of military genius in David, this determination of his to fight only with the weapons, weak and unimportant though they seemed, with which he was familiar, and in the use of which he was so skillful; nor was the issue of the combat, now he had resolved to use the sling, even doubtful. Augustine (sermon 32) calls these five smooth stones the five books of Moses taken from the flowing stream of Judaism, and recalls that Christ overcame His tempter by the precepts of the Law.

245

(43) By his gods.—This should be rendered "by his God." No doubt the idolator here made use of the sacred Name, so dear to every believing Israelite, thus defying the Eternal of Hosts.

(47) For the battle is the Lord's ... —Although we possess no special ode or psalm composed by David on the occasion of this mortal combat, in which, owing to his sure trust in Jehovah, he won his never-to-be-forgotten victory, yet in many of the compositions attributed to him in the Psalter we find memories of this, his first great triumph. (Comp. Pss. 33:16-20; 44:6-8.)

(49) And smote the Philistine in the forehead.—The headpieces of the armor then do not appear to have possessed "visors"; the face was covered with the heavy shield, which was borne before him (verse 7). No doubt the Philistine, utterly despising his youthful "unarmed" antagonist, advanced toward him without using, as was customary, the face protection of the shield. (See the "slingers" of Judg. 20:16.)

(54) The head of the Philistine.— Although the fortress of Jebus, on Mount Zion, was in the hands of the Jebusites, and continued to be so until David captured the stronghold many years later, the city of Jerusalem already belonged to the Israelites. (See Josh. 15:63; Judg. 1:21.) This "place of arms" was naturally selected for the home of the famous trophy, being the nearest stronghold to the scene of the victory.

But he put his armour in his tent. —In 21:9 we read of the "sword of Goliath wrapped in a cloth behind the ephod." The expression "in his tent" may mean the "tabernacle of Jehovah"—"**His** tabernacle," so termed pointedly by the compiler of the history, because David, in later days, with great ceremony, "pitched it" in his own city (II Sam. 6:17) comp. Acts 15:16).

(55) Whose son is this youth?—See notes on 16:21; 17:12-14.

18

(1) The soul of Jonathan was knit with the soul of David.—We have in this and the following chapters somewhat of a detailed account of David at the court of Saul. In 16:21-23 this court life of the future king has been already touched upon. But this

mention considerably anticipated the course of events. The writer of what we may term the episode, treating of the influence of music and poetry passed over, so to speak, the story of several years, in the course of which took place the single combat of David with the Philistine giant. The history here takes up the thread of the future king's life, after the campaigns which immediately followed the discomfiture of the Philistine champion.

Jonathan loved him as his own soul.— The long and steady friendship of Jonathan (see note on 14:1) no doubt had a powerful and enduring influence on the after life of the greatest of the Hebrew sovereigns. The words, the unselfish, beautiful love, and, above all, the splendid example of the ill-fated son of Saul, have no doubt given their coloring to many of the noblest utterances in David's psalms and to many of the most heroic deeds in David's life.

We read of this friendship as dating from the morrow of the first striking deed of arms performed by David when he slew the giant. It is clear, however, that it was not the personal bravery of the boy hero, or the rare skill he showed in the encounter, which so singularly attracted Prince Jonathan. What won Jonathan's heart was the shepherd boy's sublime faith, his perfect childlike trust in the Lord. Jonathan and David possessed one thing in common—an intense, unswerving belief in the power of Jehovah of Israel to keep and to save all who trusted in Him.

(6) When David was returned.—The triumphant return of the young and popular (verse 5) soldier does not refer to the homecoming after the death of the giant, but to the close of the campaign which followed that event. Evidently a series of victories after the fall of the dreaded champion—perhaps spread over a very considerable period—had for a time restored the supremacy of Israel in Canaan. In this war, David, on whom after his great feat of arms the eyes of all the soldiery were fixed, established his character for bravery and skill.

(7) Saul hath slain his thousands, and David his ten thousands.—These words, which sing of the early glory of David in battle, are quoted again in 29:5. They were, no doubt, the favorite refrain of an old national or folk song.

(8) What can he have more but the kingdom?—In this foreboding utterance of Saul there was involved not only a conjecture which the result confirmed, but a

deep inward truth. Some years had passed
since he first heard from the lips of his old
prophet-friend Samuel the divine sentence
of his rejection from the kingdom. In that
sad period he had doubtless been on the
lookout for the one destined by the
Invisible King to be his successor. This
dread expectation of ruin and dethronement
had been a powerful factor in the causes
which had led to the unhingement of Saul's
mind. Was not this gifted shepherd boy—
now the idol of the people—the future hope
of Israel?

(9) And Saul eyed David.—From the
hour on which the king listened to the
people's lilt in honor of the young hero, in
Saul's distempered mind hate alternated
with love. He still in his heart longed for
the presence of the only human being who
could charm away his ever-increasing
melancholia, but he dreaded with a fierce
jealousy the growing influence of the winning
and gifted man whom he had taken from
the sheepfolds; and now through the rest of
the records of this book we shall see how
the hate gradually obscured the old love.
All our memories of Saul seem bound up
with his lifelong murderous pursuit of David.

(10) The evil spirit.—The evil spirit comes
now over the unhappy king in quite a new
form. Heretofore, when the dark hour
came upon Saul, the madness showed itself
in the form of a hopeless melancholia. (This
earlier phase of the "soul's malady" has
been exquisitely pictured by Browning in
his poem of "Saul.") Now the madness
assumes a new phase, and the king is consumed with a murderous jealousy that fills
his whole soul and drives him now to open
deeds of violence.

And he prophesied.—The conjugation
employed in the original Hebrew of the
word rendered "prophesied" is the **Hithpa-
el**, which is never used by an Old Testament
writer of real true prophecy, this being
always expressed by the **Niphal** conjugation. This of Saul's was but an imitation.
Saul was in a state of frenzy, unable to
master himself, speaking words of which he
knew not the meaning, and acting like a
man possessed. In all this there was something akin to the powerful emotions which
agitated the true prophet, only it was not a
holy influence but one springing from violent passions.

(16) But all Israel and Judah.—See note
on 11:8. In David's case, although he was of

Judah, the future king was equally popular
with the northern tribes.

(19) She was given unto Adriel.—Saul's
capricious wavering nature, so painfully
prominent in the last part of his reign,
displayed itself in this sudden change of
purpose. It may have been brought about
owing to some great fit of jealousy of David; or possibly the large gifts in money or
valuables offered by the wealthy Adriel for
the princess's hand may have occasioned
this arbitrary act of Saul. Such gifts to the
father in return for the daughter's hand
were customary.

**(20) And Michal Saul's daughter loved
David.**—The love of the younger of the two
royal princesses for her father's brilliant
officer gave the unhappy king a fresh
excuse to expose David's life to peril, while
at the same time he appeared to be endeavoring to carry out an old formal promise
(see 17:25).

**(28) Saul saw ... that the Lord was with
David.**—The success of the last savage
enterprise, and the return of David with his
ghastly spoils, filled the unhappy king with
dismay. His daughter's love, too, for the
rising soldier contributed to his trouble.
Saul felt that all that David undertook
prospered—that surely another and a higher
Power was helping him. So his fear grew,
and jealous hatred deepened into lifelong
enmity.

19

(4) Jonathan spake good of David.—The
heir to the throne—the one above all men
likely to be injured by the growing
popularity of David—with great power and
intense earnestness, represented to his father
the king the great virtues, the unrivalled
gifts, and, above all, the splendid services of
the young soldier whose life Saul was so
anxious to cut short.

(6) And Saul hearkened.—The moving
eloquence of Jonathan touched Saul's heart,
and for a brief space something of the old
noble spirit influenced the king, and he
swore he would not attempt his life.

(7) As in times past.—The old life went
on as before, and David seemingly was
received on terms of intimacy and affection
by the king, but a new cause was soon
supplied which again lit up the slumbering
fires of jealousy in the king's heart.

**(9) And the evil spirit ... was upon
Saul.**—To the expression **Ruach Jehovah,**

"Spirit of Jehovah" (for "of" is more accurate than "from"), and the equivalent phrase, **Ruach Elohim**, "Spirit of God" (16:14, 15), the epithet "evil" is added. To suppose that these malignant or evil beings were part of the heavenly host employed by the Eternal is a supposition utterly at variance with our conception of the All-Father. We may, however, safely grant (1) the existence of evil spirits—probably beings fallen through sin and disobedience from their high estate; and (2) that these evil spirits receive occasional permission, for some wise—though to us unknown—reasons, to tempt and plague for a season the souls of certain men. (Comp. Job 1:6; 2:1-7; I Kings 22:19-22.)

(12) So Michal let David down.—Psalm 59 may allude, in part, to this occasion. With this desperate flight began those long weary wanderings, those perpetual risks of his life, which went on until the death of King Saul released David from his deadly enemy.

(13) An image.—See note on Gen. 31:19. An image in the Hebrew is **teraphim**—a plural form, but used as a singular. In this case, probably, it was a life-size figure or bust. In spite of the stern command to avoid idolatry, the children of Israel seemed to love to possess these lifeless images. The teraphim were probably a remnant of the idolatry originally brought by some of Abraham's family from their Chaldean home. These idols varied in size from the diminutive image to the life-size figure, which the Princess Michal here used to make her father's guards believe that her sick husband, David, was in bed.

(18) And came to Samuel.—The influence and authority which Samuel still preserved in the nation, even in the stormy close of Saul's career, must have been great for the frightened David to have sought a refuge in his quiet home of prayer and learning. The exile, fleeing before his sovereign, felt that in the residence of the old seer he would be safe from all pursuit, as in a sanctuary. He stood to the old seer in the relation of a loved pupil.

(19) Naioth.—Naioth was not a town, but, as the name denotes, "a cluster of dwellings." Samuel had his own house in Ramah, and these dwellings, where his prophetic schools were established, were in the immediate neighborhood. It was to this school he took David on this occasion.

(24) And he ... prophesied before Samuel in like manner.—This was certainly not the first time that Saul had experienced a similar influence of the Spirit of God (see 10:10). What was the meaning of the outpouring upon the faithless king now? Once more the pitiful Spirit pleaded with the man whom the Lord had chosen to be His anointed. But, when the moment of strange excitement was over, the blessed pleading was forgotten.

And lay down naked.—Not necessarily without any clothes, for under the tunic there was worn by men of the upper ranks certainly a fine-woven shirt of linen or cotton. The words "stripped off his clothes" simply denotes that he threw off his upper garment, his royal robe.

20

(5) The new moon.—On the religious ceremonies connected with the day of the new moon at the beginning of each month, see the Mosaic enactments in Num. 10:10; 28:11-15.

Jonathan persisted in looking upon his father's later designs against the life of David as simply frenzied acts, incident upon his distressing malady, and evidently believed that after his strange seizure at Ramah he would return and treat David with the confidence of old days when he met him at the feast of the new moon. David, however, believed otherwise, and was convinced, to use his own expressive words, that there was but a step between him and death. He would not trust himself, therefore, to Saul's hands until his friend had made the experiment he suggested. It is clear that David did not purpose being present at his tribal center for sacrifice, and therefore the excuse was a feigned one. The morality of this request of David is by no means sanctioned by the compiler of the history; he simply relates the story.

The question might be asked: Where did the compiler of the book derive his intimate acquaintance with what took place at these meetings, when David was **alone** with Jonathan? Ewald suggests that when in after years David drew to his Court the posterity of Jonathan, he often told them himself of these last events before their separation, events with which no one but the two friends could be acquainted.

(12) Behold, if there be good toward David.—In the event of the news being good—that is, if Saul, contrary to David's expectation, spoke kindly to him—then

Jonathan would send to him a special messenger. If, on the other hand, the king displayed enmity, in that case Jonathan would come himself and see David (for the last time). This sad message should be brought by no messenger.

(14) And thou shalt not only while yet I live shew me the kindness of the Lord, that I die not.—The last words tell us with striking clearness how thoroughly convinced was Jonathan that in the end David's cause, as the cause of their God, would surely triumph. Mournfully he looked ahead to his father's downfall and his own premature death; and in full view of this he bespoke the interest of his friend—though his friend would probably in a few hours become an exile and outlaw—on behalf of his own children, who would, he foresaw, before many years had expired, be landless, homeless orphans.

(20) I will shoot three arrows.—The two friends agree on a sign. It was a very simple one, and seems to speak of early primitive times. Jonathan slightly varies from his original purpose (verse 12). He evidently took these precautions not knowing whether or not he would be accompanied by friends of his father from the city, in which case the "sign" agreed upon would be sufficient to tell David what had happened at the feast. As it turned out, Jonathan was able to escape observation and to go alone with his servant to the place of meeting. He used the sign to attract his friend's attention, and then followed the last sorrowful parting, told in verses 41 and 42.

(30) Saul's anger was kindled.—As David expected, his absence kindled into a flame the anger of Saul. Probably he had determined at that very feast, surrounded by his own devoted friends and members of his family, to carry out his evil designs against David's life. But the absence of the intended victim marred the plot. His own son Jonathan, the heir of his kingdom, suspected him, and openly sympathized with his friend David, for whose pointed absence he thus publicly apologized.

Thou son of the perverse rebellious woman.—These words, spoken in public, in any sense were a bitter insult to the prince. Another and better rendering has, however, been suggested: "Thou son of perversity of rebellion," a common Hebraism for a man of perverse and refractory nature. (Lange) This avoids the extreme improbability that Saul insulted his own wife, Jonathan's mother, which, as has been observed, contradicts the Hebrew family spirit.

(31) Thou shalt not be established.—Here the king gives expression to the thought which was always torturing that poor diseased brain of his—David, his own kind physician, his faithful soldier, and his son's dearest friend and loved companion, was plotting basely against that master for whom he had done so much, and the son whom he loved so well.

(41) Until David exceeded.—The expression apparently signifies that while Jonathan wept bitterly at the parting, David wept still more.

(42) Go in peace.—The abruptness of the closing words is most natural and accords with the evident deep emotion of the speaker. David's heart was too full to reply to his friend's words; blinded with tears, he seems to have hurried away speechless.

21

(1) Then came David to Nob.—The town of Nob was situated between Anathoth and Jerusalem, about an hour's ride from the latter. Before leaving his native land, David determined once more to see, and if practicable to take counsel with, the old high priest of Israel. He hoped, too, in that friendly and powerful religious center to provide himself and his few companions with arms and other necessaries for his exile; nor is it improbable that he purposed to make some inquiry of the Urim and Thummim concerning his doubtful future. The unexpected presence of Doeg (see notes on verse 7 and 22:9, 10, 18), the powerful and unscrupulous servant of Saul, at the sanctuary, no doubt hurried him away in hot haste across the frontier.

(2) The king hath commanded me.—This is one of the sad episodes in a glorious life. Dismayed at his sudden fall and loss of home, wife, friends, and rank must plead as his excuse for his falsehood to Ahimelech and his flight to the hereditary enemies of his race, the Philistines. But here, as in so many places, the Holy Spirit who guided the pen of the compiler of this true history could not lie, but fearlessly tells the repulsive truth which must ever be deeply damaging to the favorite hero of Israel.

I have appointed my servants.—This portion of his words to Ahimelech was, no doubt, strictly true. Those alluded to here probably joined him soon after his parting with Jonathan. Our Lord, in Mark 2:25, 26, speaks of the priest giving the shewbread to David and to those who were with him, when both he and they who were with him were hungry.

(4) There is no common bread.—The condition of the priests in these days of Saul was evidently a pitiable one. Here the almost destitute condition of the ministers of the principal sanctuary of Israel appears from the quiet answer of the high priest to David, telling him they had positively no bread but the stale bread removed from before "the Presence" in the holy building. This "hallowed bread," or shewbread, five loaves of which David petitioned, consisted of twelve loaves, one for each tribe, which were placed in the Tabernacle fresh every Sabbath Day. The Law of Moses was that this bread, being most holy, could be eaten only by the priests in the holy place. Our Saviour, in Matt. 12:3, especially uses this example, drawn from the Tabernacle's honored customs, to justify a violation of the letter of the Law, when its strict observance would stand in the way of the fulfillment of man's sacred duty to his neighbor.

(5) And the bread is in a manner common.—The original is here very difficult, almost utterly obscure. Lange maintains that the words in question must contain a remark by which the priest is to be induced to give the bread, and would translate, "Though it is an unholy (ceremonially illegal) procedure (to take the shewbread), yet it is sanctified (today) through the instrument" (David, the appointed messenger of the Lord's anointed, or Ahimelech, the sacred person of the high priest).

(7) A certain man.—Doeg is the first instance of a foreigner employed in a high function in Israel, being an Edomite, or Syrian. According to Jewish tradition, he was the steward who accompanied Saul in his pursuit after the asses, who counseled him to send for David, and who ultimately slew him.

Detained before the Lord.—Several interpretations have been suggested for these words: (a) he was at the sanctuary of the Tabernacle as a proselyte; (b) he was there for his purification on account of supposed leprosy, or simply in fulfillment of a temporary Nazarite vow; (c) he had committed some trespass and had offered the appointed sacrifice. Any one of these reasons, all sufficiently probable in themselves, would have occasioned a residence long or short at the sanctuary at Nob.

250

(10) Achish the king of Gath.—Achish was one of the Philistine lords, perhaps the hereditary lord of Gath. He is called Abimelech in the title of Ps. 34, that apparently being the **nomen dignitatis** of the hereditary (or elected) chief among the Philistines, like Agag among the Amalekites. Gath was the nearest Philistine city to the sanctuary of Nob where David then was.

(11) Is not this David?—It is needless to suppose that the sword of Goliath betrayed the identity of the hero although David in his humility did not suspect how widely spread was his fame, he was evidently as well known in Philistia as in his own land. That popular lilt, the folk song of the Israelitish maidens, was no doubt current in frontier towns like Gath. We hear of no attempt made upon his life, or even against his liberty. The feeling among his generous foes was rather pitiful admiration mingled with wonder at seeing the doer of such splendid achievements in poverty and in exile. Here the title king is vaguely used.

(14) Then said Achish ... the man is mad.—See title and tenor of Ps. 34. The Philistine king would look with peculiar sorrow and repulsion on a madman if, as according to Jewish tradition, his own wife and daughter were insane. The device, however, succeeded, as David hoped it would, and he was allowed to depart in safety. In old times the insane were looked upon as persons in some peculiar way possessed by, and therefore under the more immediate protection of, Deity. The life then of the hunted fugitive was perfectly safe from the moment the Philistines considered him mad.

22

(1) The cave Adullam.—The great valley of Elah forms the highway from Philistia to Hebron. There are many natural caves, some of great extent, roomy and dry, which are still used by the shepherds as dwelling places, and as refuges for their flocks and herds. David chose one of these natural fastnesses as the temporary home for himself and his followers. The name Adullam was probably given to the largest of these great caverns from its proximity to the old royal Canaanitish city of Adullam (Josh. 15:35).

(2) Every one that was in distress.—These persons "in distress" were especially those who were persecuted by Saul and his men for their attachment to David. The several statements of the refugees who took shelter in David's armed camp cover a considerable time. They did not all flock to his standard at once. Some were "in debt." Throughout the whole long story of Israel this unhappy love of greed and gain has been a characteristic feature of the chosen race, ever a prominent and ugly sin. In the Mosaic Law, most stringent regulations were laid down to correct and mitigate this ruling passion of avarice among the Jews (See Exod. 22:25; Lev. 25:36; Deut. 23:19.) These 400 seem soon to have increased to 600 (see 25:13).

And he became a captain over them.—It was evidently no undisciplined band. David quickly organized the refugees, among whom, by degrees, many a man of mark and approved valor and ability were numbered. To complete the picture we must unite in one the scattered notices of this same period which occur in the Second Book of Samuel and in the Books of Kings and Chronicles.

(3) Mizpeh.—This particular Mizpeh is mentioned nowhere else. The word means "a watch tower"; it was probably some mountain fortress in Moab. David evidently sought hospitality among his kin in Moab. Jesse, his father, was the grandson of Ruth the Moabitess. The distance from the south of Judah where the fugitives were wandering was not great.

Till I know what God will do for me.—It is interesting to note that David, when addressing the Moabite sovereign, speaks of Elohim, not of Jehovah. This was probably out of deep reverence; an idolator had nothing to do with the awful name by which the Eternal was known to His covenant people. The "Name," however, was not unknown in Moab, for the mystic letters which compose it occur in the inscription of Mesha, dating about 150 years from the days of David's exile.

(5) The prophet Gad.—From this time onward throughout the life and reign of David, Gad the prophet occupied evidently a marked place. He is mentioned as the king's seer in II Sam. 24:11; and in I Chron. 29:29 he appears as the compiler of the acts of David, along with Samuel and Nathan. (See also II Sam. 24:11ff; II Chron. 29:25.) Gad appears to have been one of the rarely favored few brought up in the schools of the prophets, and the presence of such a person in this outlaw camp of David

must have been of great advantage to the captain.

(7, 8) We have here a fair specimen of Saul's manner of ruling in his later years. It is no wonder that the heart of the people gradually was estranged from one of whom in earlier years they had been so proud. The suspicious and gloomy king had evidently given all the posts of honor and dignity to men of his own tribe and family, or to strangers like Doeg. Such a sovereign had surely forfeited his kingdom. The consequences of such a weak and shortsighted policy were plainly visible in the thin array he was able in his hour of bitter need to muster together on the fatal field of Mount Gilboa against his sleepless Philistine enemies. (See chap. 31.)

(9) Then answered Doeg the Edomite.—It is strange that this renowned man, whom evidently David looked upon as the evil genius of Saul at the period when he wrote the sad, bitter words of Psalm 52, and spoke of the tongue of this Doeg as being like a sharp razor, and dwelt with singular persistence on the wickedness, falsehood, and slander of this relentless enemy, should have gone down among the noteworthy Talmudical traditions as the greatest Rabbinist (i.e., the most deeply learned in the Mosaic Law, and in its interpretation) of his time.

(15) Did I then begin to inquire?—An alternative rendering is: "That was the first day that I inquired of God for him, and I did not know that it was displeasing to thee." Ahimelech allowed the sacred Urim to be consulted because he supposed David had come (as he represented) on a direct mission from King Saul. Surely, thought the blameless high priest, I never supposed my king would have been wroth with me for that.

(18) And Doeg the Edomite ... —No doubt, assisted by his own attached servants, Doeg carried out this deed of unexampled barbarity. For this act the Edomite servant of Saul has been execrated in the most ancient Jewish writings perhaps above any other of the famous wicked men who meet us in the Holy Scriptures. (Comp. II Sam. 21:1.)

(20) Abiathar.—The exact period of his coming to the exiled band under David is uncertain; in many of the recitals in this book no note of time is given. (See 23:6.) From that time, nevertheless, Abiathar, who became high priest after his father's death, occupies an important place in the story of David's life. Throughout his reign he continued his faithful friend, and seems to have been a worthy holder of his important office. (See I Kings 2:26.) The close of his life, however, was a melancholy one.

23

(1) Then they told David . . . —Saul was becoming more and more neglectful of his higher duty to protect his people. As time went on and his malady increased, all his thoughts were concentrated on David's imaginary crimes, and the history of the latter part of his reign is little more than a recital of his sad, bewildered efforts to compass the young hero's destruction. The task of protecting the people from the constant marauding expeditions of the Philistines, and probably of the neighboring nations, then was entrusted to David. To point this out to the son of Jesse was evidently the first great mission of Gad the seer. Samuel's mind was, no doubt, busied in this matter. It is more than probable that Gad was first dispatched to join David at the instigation of the aged, but still mentally vigorous, prophet.

(2) David inquired of the Lord.—The inquiry was made, no doubt, through Gad, for Abiathar had not yet arrived with the ephod (see verse 6). Comp. verse 9. We know that such inquiries were made through prophets, for we possess a detailed account of such an inquiry being made by Jehoshaphat of the prophet Micaiah (I Kings 22:5, 7, 8), in which passage the same formula is used as in this case.

(3) Here in Judah.—This does not imply that Keilah was out of the territory of Judah, but simply that the district in the neighborhood around Keilah was at that time under Philistine domination. The open country in times of Philistine supremacy first fell under their control; their strong places, like Keilah, would resist for a much longer period.

(9) Bring hither the ephod.—In this ephod were set twelve precious stones, one for each of the twelve tribes. The names of the tribes were engraved on these gems, the Rabbis tell us, along with some other sacred words. On important solemn occasions these stones were allowed by the providence of God to be used as oracles. According to a most ancient tradition the use of the sacred gems was restricted to the high priest, who could only call out the supernatural power at the bidding of the king or

the head of the State for the time being. The divine response given by the sacred gems seems to have been the visible response to earnest, faithful prayer. The common belief is that the ephod stones gave their answer to the royal and high priestly questions by some peculiar shining.

(14) The wilderness of Ziph.—This wilderness probably lies between Hebron and En-gedi. Some of these "stations" in the wanderings of the future king are only doubtfully identified.

Saul sought him every day, but God delivered him.—This is merely a general remark, and intended to cover a long period of time, including the remaining portion of Saul's reign, during which David was perpetually exposed to Saul's attempts to destroy him. It quietly mentions also that though Saul was armed with all the power of the king in Israel, he was powerless, for the invisible King of Israel declined to give this hated David into his hand.

(17) And I shall be next unto thee.—This same generous, loving friend found a grave on Mount Gilboa instead of a home with David, whom he admired with so ungrudging an admiration. That brave, romantic career was nearly run when he met David for the last time in the woods of Ziph. As far as we can judge, if Jonathan had lived he would have certainly ceded any rights he had to the throne of his father Saul in favor of David, unlike that other comparatively unknown son of Saul, Ishbosheth, who set himself up as a rival claimant to the son of Jesse.

(19) On the south of Jeshimon.—Jeshimon is not the name of a place, but it signifies a "desert" or "solitude" (see Isa. 43:19). It is used here for the dreary desert which extends between the Dead Sea and the Hebron Mountains. This is the wilderness of Judea spoken of in Matt. 3:1. David was just then encamped with some of his followers in some thickets bordering on this trackless desert. The Ziphites kept their promise faithfully, and in the pursuit which followed the arrival of Saul and his forces, David was in extreme danger of capture. The news that the Philistines had invaded the territories of Saul in great force hastily summoned the king from the district, and David was thus spared a destruction which appeared to be imminent. This, as Lange well observes, was "God's plan to save David."

(24) The plain.—Literally, "the Arabah," the desert track which extends along the Jordan Valley from the Dead Sea to the

Lake of Gennesareth. The term is also
applied to the desolate valley which lies
between the Dead Sea and the Gulf of
Akaba.

24

(1) When Saul was returned.—How intent
Saul was on his bloody purpose with regard
to his supposed rival is clear, for no sooner
was the Philistine raid repulsed than with
sleepless animosity he at once set forth with
a force of considerable magnitude to hunt
down his foe. Saul was encouraged in this
fresh enterprise by the offer of the Ziphites
(see 23:19-23).
   En-gedi.—David and his band were now
wandering along a lofty plateau, upon the
tops of cliffs some 2,000 feet above the
Dead Sea. En-gedi is a beautiful oasis in the
barren wilderness to the south of Judah. Its
original name was Hazazon Tamar—"The
Palm Wood" (see II Chron. 20:2). It has in
all ages been a favorite spot with the posses-
ors of the land. The remains of ancient
gardens tell us that in the golden days of the
kings En-gedi was probably a favorite
resort of the wealthy citizens of Jerusalem.
See Song of Solomon 1:14.)
   (3) The sheepcotes.—"These sheepcotes
are generally made by piling up loose stones
in front of the cave's entrance in a circular
wall, which is covered with thorns as a
further protection against thieves and wild
animals who would prey on the sheep. During cold storms and in the night the flocks
retreat into the cave, but at other times they
remain in the enclosed cote. ... These
caverns are as dark as midnight, and the
keenest eye cannot see four paces inward;
but one who has been long within, and
looking outward toward the entrance, can
observe with perfect distinctness all that
takes place in that direction. David, therefore, could watch Saul as he came in ...
but Saul could see nothing but impenetrable
darkness." (Thomson)
   (5) David's heart smote him.—There is
no sign at all of David's regretting he had
cut off the fringe of the king's garment. It
was the far more terrible thought of slaying
the God-anointed king which troubled David. The words of the next verse show us
clearly what was passing in his mind. He
gravely rebuked his men, and evidently
restrained them, with some little trouble,
from rushing upon Saul, even after he had
left the sleeping form, with the piece of the

mantle in his hand. The Hebrew word
rendered "stayed" is a forcible one, and,
literally, would be "crushed down."
   (8) And cried after Saul.—The outlaw
allowed the king and his companion to
proceed some little way—possibly down the
deep ascent which led up to the cave's
mouth—and then called after Saul, but with
an address of the deepest reverence, accompanied too with an act of the profoundest homage which an inferior could pay
to a superior. He would show Saul at least
he was no rival king.
   One of the most beautiful characteristics
of David's many-sided nature was this enduring loyalty to Saul and to Saul's house. No
jealousy, or even bitter injuries done in
later years could affect the old love, the old
feeling of loyal reverence, the more than
filial affection; it was even proof against
time. Years after Saul was in his grave,
David gave the most conspicuous proof of
his faithful memory of his old, devoted
friendship for Saul and his house, when he
pardoned Mephibosheth, the grandson of
Saul, for his more than suspected treason in
the matter of the revolt of Absalom, and
restored to him a large portion of his
forfeited lands (II Sam. 19:24-30).
   **(16) And Saul lifted up his voice, and
wept.**—There is nothing strange in this sudden change of feeling in one so nervous
and excitable as was Saul. It is clear that for
the moment Saul meant to alter his conduct
to David, but the sad sequel shows that the
impression made was only transitory; and
David, by his conduct, clearly saw this, for
he made no effort to return to his old home
and position with Saul, but maintained his
independent, though precarious, position as
an outlaw.
   **(20) And now, behold, I know well that
thou shalt surely be king.**—Never had Saul
for one moment forgotten the words of
Samuel, that the Lord had rent the kingdom
from him, and had given it to a neighbor
that was better than he (15:28). Since that
awful denunciation, the unhappy Saul was
only too sensible in knowing that the blessing of Jehovah no longer rested on his head.
Strong, therefore, in this conviction, and for
the time humiliated and grieved at the sorry
part he had been playing in this restless
persecution of one destined to fill so great a
position, the king positively entreats the
outlaw to swear to him the strange promise
contained in verse 21.
   (21) Swear now therefore unto me.—So
strongly was Saul convinced at this moment

253

that David would at no distant period of time occupy the throne of Israel that he implored him, when that day should come, not to destroy all his (Saul's) children. This barbarous custom has been always too common a practice in the jealous East. (Comp. I Kings 15:29; 16:11; II Kings 10:11.) It seems to have been equally dreaded by Jonathan (see 20:15). It was no vain dread of what might happen in the future which made King Saul ask this of David. Doubtless the fear of some such awful catastrophe happening to his own loved children and friends was a large part of the punishment of Saul.

25

(1) And Samuel died.—Since Moses, none so great as Samuel had arisen. Before his time, the words and traditions which the great lawgiver had with some success impressed upon the great nomadic tribe of the Beni-Israel were almost forgotten; and the people soon would have been hardly distinguished from the warlike tribes of Canaan in the neighboring countries. But Samuel quickened into life again the dying traditions of the race, and taught them who they really were—**the chosen of God.** He restored the forgotten laws of Moses, by the keeping of which they once became great and powerful; and by the creation of an earthly monarchy he welded into one the separate interests of the twelve divisions of the race, so that from Dan to Beersheba there was but one chief, one standard. But his greatest work was the foundation of the prophetic schools, in which men were trained and educated carefully, with the view of the pupils becoming in their turn the teachers and guides of the people.

Note here that **all** the Israelites—not one portion or fragment only, as might have been expected in that time of division and confusion—lamented the father of all alike.

The wilderness of Paran.—Paran is properly the south of the Arabian peninsula, west of Sinai; but it seems to have given its name to a vast extent of pasture and barren land, of which the wilderness of Judah and Beersheba would virtually form part, without the borders being strictly defined.

(2) Maon.—Maon was in the hill country of Judah. The Carmel here mentioned is not the famous Mount Carmel in the north, but the small town near Maon, where Saul set up a monument after the war with Amalek (15:12).

And the man was very great.—The wealthy chief was a descendant of Caleb, who at the time of the conquest of Canaan obtained vast possessions in the valley of Hebron and in the south of Judah. The occasion of David's mission to Nabal was the annual sheepshearing of the rich sheepmaster—always a great occasion, and accompanied usually on large estates by festivities.

(3) Nabal.—The word "Nabal" means "fool," connected with **naval**, to fade away. The name was probably a nickname given him on account of his well-known stubborn folly.

Abigail.—This famous beautiful woman afterward became David's wife. Her name, which signifies "whose father is joy," was most likely given her by the villagers on her husband's estate, as expressive of her sunny, gladness-bringing presence. From early training she derived her wisdom and deep, far-sighted piety.

(4) And David heard in the wilderness.—There is no doubt that the presence of the armed band of David during the latter years of Saul afforded considerable protection to the border land. Nabal's conduct appears to have been more than rude and foolish, for David, according to the showing of Nabal's own shepherds, had on many occasions been of substantial service to them as they tended their flocks in exposed and dangerous localities. The testimony of these shepherd folk may be accepted generally as the popular estimate of David and his acts during this rough and sorely tried period of his life.

(7) Neither was there ought missing unto them.—The request was certainly a fair one, for, as Lang and Ewald remark, "David had a certain right to ask a gift from Nabal's wealth. He had indirectly no small share in the festal joy of Nabal and his house. Without some part of the superfluity of the inhabitants whom he protected, he could not have maintained himself and his army."

(13) Gird ye on every man his sword.—The formal preparation and the largeness of the force showed how terribly David was in earnest, and how bent he was on wiping out the insult of Nabal in blood. In Nabal, the rich sheep-master, the rude refuser of the fairly earned gift, David saw a deadly political adversary who would hunt him down like a wild beast. Without this explanation, David's wrath and determination to take such speedy and bloody vengeance on mere selfishness is inexplicable. David's anger is quite to be accounted for, though not to be excused.

(17) A son of Belial.—Belial was not a proper name, though it subsequently came to be considered one. It signifies simply worthlessness; here a "son of Belial" is an expression for a bad, worthless person.

(21, 22) These verses must be understood as a kind of parenthesis in the narrative. They express what David felt, and, as it were, his justification in his own mind for the violent and vengeful act he was about to carry out.

(26) Seeing the Lord hath withholden.— So confident is this pious and wise woman that she is doing the Lord's work, and that He is standing by her, that, in presence of the armed band and their angry leader, she speaks as though the danger to her husband's house was a thing of the past, and that David had real cause for thankfulness in that he had been prevented from doing a wanton, wicked act. (See verses 30, 31.)

(28) For the Lord will certainly make my lord a sure house.—The unconscious prophetess, we may be sure, never dreamed of that glorious and holy One in whose person, far down the stream of ages, the Eternal would make good her words, and indeed found for that outlawed chieftain, before whom she was then kneeling, a sure house.

The battles of the Lord.—Abigail, in common with the pious Israelites of her time, looked on the wars waged by the armies of Israel against the idolatrous tribes and nations around them as the wars of Jehovah. We hear of an ancient collection of ballads, now lost, entitled "The Book of the Wars of the Lord" (Num. 21:14). For several years now since his famous combat with Goliath, David had been the popular hero and the favorite subject of those folk songs.

(29) Shall be bound in the bundle of life.—This is one of the earliest and most definite expressions of a sure belief in an eternal future in the presence of God, and Hebrew tradition from the very earliest times has so regarded it. The image, as so often in Eastern teaching, is taken from the common everyday habit of packing up in a bundle articles of great value or of indispensable use, so that the owner may carry them about his person. Thus, a just judge is said to be bound up in the bundle of righteousness; a lover in the bundle of love. **And the souls of thine enemies, them shall he sling out, as out of the middle of a sling.**—The reference in the first instance was to the fate of the enemies of God in this life; but Hebrew theologians in all times have understood it in a deeper and more solemn sense, as a reference to the doom after death reserved for all unrighteous.

Men and women in the Canaan of Samuel and Saul believed in the glories of the life eternal with God, and looked on to a future state of rewards and punishments, instead of limiting their hopes and fears to the sitting in quiet peace under the vine and the fig tree of their own loved land of promise. The knowledge of a future state of existence was always the blessed heritage of the chosen race. But the spread of that knowledge and the reawakening of that belief we ascribe to the beneficial influence of Samuel, the founder of those great prophetic schools, where the lamp of the knowledge of God was kept burning with a steady flame.

(33) And blessed be thy advice.—It is noticeable how, in this age of deeper religion and of higher culture, the old superstitions reverence for vows, taken in moments of frenzy or of extreme excitement, had given place to a calmer and more reasonable spirit. Never had a more solemn vow been taken than David's that morning, when he took a solemn oath that he would murder the whole house of Nabal; and yet, before the sun set he is convinced of the wickedness of his purpose, and sooner than carry it out he deliberately breaks the oath. (Comp. Judg. 11:34, 40; I Sam. 14:24, 45.)

(37) His heart died within him.—These words are generally understood as signifying that an attack of apoplexy had seized the intemperate man. The immediate cause probably was fear, he hearing to what a terrible danger he had been exposed. In that drunken sleep, out of which he was then scarcely awakened, terror and horror seized him, and the "stroke" followed.

(43) David also took Ahinoam of Jezreel. —Jezreel is not the city in Issachar (Josh. 19:18), but a town in the southern part of Canaan, situated in the hill country of Judah, near Maon. The fatal results of this disastrous and unhappy Oriental custom of polygamy, as time went on, showed themselves in King David's household; a plentiful crop of intrigues, crimes, and murders in the royal palace were the sad fruits of his yielding to the practice.

(44) Michal his daughter.—See 18:20; II Sam. 3:13-16; 6:20-23.

26

The accounts contained in chaps. 23, 24, and 26 refer, in spite of obvious resemblances, to two distinct and separate events (so Keil, Lange). The object of one such recital in an account of the early life of the great founder of Israelitic greatness is clear, but why was a second narrative of an incident of like nature inserted in a book where conciseness is studied so carefully? We suggest that everything conducive to the glory of the favorite hero of Israel was of the deepest interest to the people, and the surpassing nobility and generosity of David to his deadly foe was considered worthy of these detailed accounts even in the necessarily brief compilation of the inspired writer of the history of this time.

(5) In the trench.—The LXX translates the Hebrew word by "covered chariots." The meaning is, no doubt, that the king lay down within the barricade or rampart formed by the baggage wagons.

(6) Abishai the son of Zeruiah.—Zeruiah was David's sister. Abishai, later one of the famous generals of David, was brother to Joab, afterward the captain of the royal host. There was a third younger brother, Asahel, also high in the favor of his kinsman David. Between these three sons of Zeruiah and Abner a blood feud seems to have existed. Abner, the near relative, and captain of the host of Saul throughout that monarch's reign, is closely associated with the fortunes of Saul. The bloody sequel to the feud is strictly in accordance with what we should expect in these fierce, wild days. Some time after Saul's death Abner slew the young Asahel, who seems to have been passionately loved by his elder brother. Abner became reconciled to David, but the reconciliation did not save the friend of Saul and the slayer of Asahel from the vengeance of Joab and Abishai, who murdered the illustrious Abner in cold blood.

(9, 10) David looked upon the person of Saul as made sacred and inviolable by the royal anointing. Through the anointing Saul had become the possession of Jehovah; only Jehovah, then, could lawfully take away that sacred life. David suggests three possible cases in which the divine arm might smite the "anointed of Jehovah": by some sudden death from disease (as in the recent death of Nabal); by what is termed "natural death"; by some blow received in battle.

(11) The spear ... and the cruse of water.—The spear was Saul's special sign of royalty. "A very ancient usage explains why the cruse of water is here brought into such special prominence. According to this custom, some high dignitary always had in keeping a costly ewer for the king's necessary ablutions, and it was especially his duty to take it with him, and present it to the king during campaigns or other journeys, so that its disappearance would involve almost as great a disgrace to the king as the loss of his sceptre." (Ewald) Comp. Ps. 60:8.

(15) Wherefore then hast thou not kept?—The whole of this bitter sarcastic address seems to imply that a deadly feud existed between David and Saul's captain and kinsman, Abner. If this be the case, the royal generosity and nobility of David's character was well shown in his subsequent friendship with this Abner, and in his deep sorrow for the great captain's untimely death. (See II Sam. 3.)

(19) Let him accept an offering.—In other words, "If you think or feel that **God** stirs you up to take this course against me, the innocent one, pray to God that He may take the temptation—if it be a temptation—from thee." This conception that the movement comes from God runs through the Old Testament. It is apparently expressed in such passages as "the Lord hardened Pharaoh's heart," and in such sayings as "an evil spirit from the Lord haunted Saul." Some have explained the conception by referring it to the intensity with which the Israelites had grasped the idea of the omnipresence of the Deity, and of His being the one power by whose energy all things exist and all acts are done; evil and good alike come from God, for He alone is the source of all.

(21) I have played the fool.—There seems something more in these words of Saul than sorrow for the past. He seems to blame himself here for putting himself again in David's power through overconfidence in his own strength. In all his words there is a ring of falseness; and this was evidently the impression made on the outlaw, for he almost immediately removed himself from the dominions of Saul altogether. Here the two whom Samuel had anointed as kings—the king who has forfeited his crown, and the king of the golden future—parted for ever. They never looked on each other's faces again.

27

(1) And David said in his heart.—David's position seems to have grown more and more untenable during the latter days of Saul's reign. The words and persuasions of such men as Cush (see Ps. 7), Doeg, probably Abner, the men of Ziph, and others, quickly erased from the memory of Saul such scenes as witnessed in the En-gedi cave, and, still more recently, in the hill of Hachilah, and more than counterbalanced the devotion and powerful friendship of true warriors like Jonathan. In David's words, after he had taken the spear and cruse from the side of the sleeping Saul, we see something of what was passing in his mind: his constant fear of a violent death; his knowledge that powerful and wicked men were constantly plotting against him; and his determination to seek a home in another land, where, however, he expected to find a grave far from the chosen race, among the idolators and enemies of Jehovah of Israel (26:19, 20). He now realizes a part of these sorrowful forebodings. But in this determination of the son of Jesse we never hear of prayer or of consultation with prophet or priest. A dull despair seems at this time to have deprived David at once of faith and hope.

Into the land of the Philistines.—David chose to seek a refuge among these warlike people, for he believed he would be in greater security there than among his friendly kinsfolk, the Moabites, where, in former days, he had found such a kindly welcome for his family in the first period of Saul's enmity. He probably doubted the power of Moab to protect him.

(2) Achish, the son of Maoch, king of Gath.—The whole of Philistia subsequently fell under King David's rule. It seems, however, that he permitted Achish, even after the conquest, to remain in his old city of Gath, most likely as his tributary, thus paying back the old debt of kindness to Achish.

Ewald considers that it was during the residence at Gath that David exercised himself as a musician in the Gittite—i.e., the Philistine—style, which he afterward transferred from there to Judah and Jerusalem. (See titles of Pss. 8, 81, and 84, "upon the Gittith.") Gittith is a feminine adjective derived from Gath.

(5) Why should thy servant dwell in the royal city with thee?—The real reason why David wished a separate residence was that he might conduct his forays and other affairs apart from the supervision of his Philistine friends. **They** had one purpose in welcoming him and his band (see I Chron. 12), **he** had quite another. Achish trusted that through David's assistance powerful military demonstrations in the southern districts of Saul's kingdom might be made. At this time the Philistine nation was preparing for that grand national effort against Saul which culminated in the battle of Mount Gilboa. David, on the other hand, intended, from a comparatively secure center of operations somewhere in Philistia, to harrass those nomad foes of Israel whose home was in the deserts to the south of Canaan.

(6) Wherefore Ziklag pertaineth unto the kings of Judah unto this day.—These words supply us with a double note of time in the question of the date of this first Book of Samuel. They tell us that it was cast in its present shape **after** the revolt of Jeroboam, and certainly **before** the days of the carrying away of Israel to Babylon.

(8) Went up.—The expression is accurate. The nomad tribes against whom his expeditions were directed dwelt on higher ground than David's home at Ziklag, apparently on the wide extent of the mountain plateau, that high tableland at the northeast of the desert of Paran. It is not easy to identify the first two of these nomads against whom David directed his operations. They were a widely scattered race of nomad Arabs (see Deut. 3:14; II Sam. 15:8). The third, the Amalekites, were the remnant of that once powerful tribe destroyed by Saul in his famous war, when his disobedience incurred the wrath of Samuel. David's raids extended as far as the desert frontier of Egypt.

(9) And left neither man nor woman alive.—David had no charge of extermination, thereby to be an instrument of God's wrath; therefore these acts of ferocious barbarity are simply without excuse. But his reason for them is told us in verse 11. No captive was to be left alive to tell the tale to King Achish, who was under the delusion that David's feats of arms were carried out at the expense of his own countrymen, whose lands he was harrassing. (See I Chron. 28:3.)

(10) And David said, Against the south of Judah.—The answer of David to his sovereign lord, the King of Gath—for he was now, to all intents and purposes, a vassal prince of Achish—was simply a falsehood. David represents that the cattle and apparel had been captured from his own countrymen, whose territory he was foraging.

28

(1) The Philistines gathered their armies together for warfare.—This was evidently, as Josephus remarks, a great effort on the part of the Philistines. It was no ordinary raid or border incursion, such as seems to have been so frequent all through the reign of Saul. The Philistines are now strong enough to strike a blow at the center of the kingdom, and to challenge a battle on the plain of Jezreel, or Esdraelon, north of Ephraim and Issachar. King Saul, quickly assembling the fighting men of Israel, marched in pursuit, and coming up with them in the Esdraelon plain, took up his position opposite the Philistines—only a few miles parting the two hosts—on the slopes of another group of mountains known as Mount Gilboa, lying to the south of the Philistine frontier.

And Achish said.—David soon found into what a grievous error he had fallen by taking refuge with the hereditary foes of his people. Want of faith and patience had urged him to take this unhappy step. The results of his course of action were soon manifest. His nation sustained a crushing and most humiliating defeat. His own general recognition as king was put off for nearly seven years, during which period a civil war hindered the development of national prosperity. During this time of internal divisions the seeds were too surely laid of the future disastrous separation of Judah and the south from the northern tribes, a division which eventually took place in his grandson's time, when his strong arm and Solomon's wisdom and power were things of the past.

The summons of Achish to his great military vassal was perfectly natural. The king of Gath and his colleagues in Philistia saw that, in the divided state of Israel, their chances of success were great, and it is highly probable that they looked forward to establishing their friend and follower David on the throne of Saul as a Philistine vassal king.

(3) The wizards.—Literally, "the wise people." These are always connected with those who had familiar spirits. The name seems to have been given in irony to these

dealers in occult and forbidden arts. The Mosaic command respecting these people was clear and decisive: "Thou shalt not suffer a witch (or wizard) to live" (Exod. 22:18; Lev. 20:27). Saul, in his early zeal, had actively put in force these edicts of Moses, which apparently, in the lax state of things which had long prevailed in Israel, had been permitted to lie in abeyance.

(6) And when Saul inquired of the Lord.—How was the inquiry made? It has been suggested by eminent Biblical scholars that after the murder of Ahimelech and the flight of Abiathar to David, Saul removed the national Sanctuary from desecrated Nob, and established it at Gibeon, where, during the first year of David's reign, we find the Tabernacle, with Zadok, son of Ahitub, of the house of Eleazar, acting as high priest, probably having been placed in that office by Saul. Zadok and Abiathar seemed to have divided the honors and responsibilities of the high priesthood. (See II Sam. 8:17; 15:24, 29, 35; I Chron. 15:11; 18:16.) This Zadok, we may assume, "inquired" for Saul: some suppose by means of an ephod made in imitation of the ancient breastplate with the Urim in possession of Abiathar; but, as may be readily imagined, no response was received.

(7) Behold, there is a woman that hath a familiar spirit at En-dor.—Jewish tradition speaks of the "two men" who accompanied Saul as Abner and Amasa, and further mentions that the witch of En-dor was the mother of the great Abner. If this is true, it would account for her having escaped the general pursuit after witches mentioned above in the early days of Saul.

(8) And Saul disguised himself.—The disguise and the time chosen for the expedition served a double purpose. The king would, he thought, be unknown in the darkness and disguise when he came to the witch's dwelling, and there was, too, a far greater probability of his escaping his Philistine foes, whose army lay between him and the village of En-dor.

Divine unto me by the familiar spirit.—The sorcerer or sorceress possessed, or was supposed to possess, a "familiar." Through the aid of this "familiar," the departed spirit was compelled or induced to revisit this world and to submit to certain questioning. This miserable power, if it did exist, was one of the things the Israelites learned from the original inhabitants of Canaan.

And bring me him up.—The popular idea has always been that Sheol, the place of departed spirits, is somewhere **beneath** the ground or earth on which we live, just as heaven, the abode of God and His holy angels, is in a region **above** the earth. "With our modes of thought, which are so bound up with time and space, it is impossible to represent to ourselves in any other way the difference and contrast between blessedness with God and shade-life in death." (Keil)

(11) Bring me up Samuel.—Saul's state of mind on the eve of his last fatal fight at Gilboa affords a curious study. He felt himself forsaken of God, and yet, in his deep despair, his mind turns to the friend and guide of his youth, from whom he had been so hopelessly estranged. There must have been a terrible struggle in the proud king's heart before he could have brought himself to stoop to ask for assistance from one of that loathed and proscribed class of women who professed to have dealings with familiar spirits and demons.

(12) And when the woman saw Samuel, she cried with a loud voice.—Nothing is more clear from the narration than that the woman of En-dor saw something she never dreamed of seeing. Whatever did appear that night was different from anything she had seen before. Whether or not she was an imposter matters little to us. From the severe enactments in the Mosaic code respecting these practices, it would seem as though in the background there was something dark and sinister. At all events, on this memorable occasion, the witch was evidently amazed and appalled at the success of her enchantments.

And the woman spake to Saul.—How did she come to recognize Saul in the unknown? Josephus (6:14, 2), no doubt writing from traditional sources, asserts that Samuel had most likely revealed the presence of Saul to the witch. It was some word—probably spoken by Samuel—not related here which betrayed the king's identity to the women.

(13) I saw gods ascending out of the earth.—"Gods" is the rendering of the Hebrew word **Elohim**. The best scholars, reasoning from Saul's words which immediately follow—"What is **his** form?"—suppose the **Elohim** to signify, not a plurality of appearances, but one God-like form: something majestic and august. The feeling, however, of antiquity seems to have been in favor of more than one supernatural form entering into the En-dor dwelling on that awful night.

(15) And Samuel said to Saul, Why hast thou disquieted me, to bring me up?— These words by themselves do not decide the question as to **what** power called up the "spirit." They simply assert that Samuel had been disturbed from his rest by Saul, and ask the reason why.

(17) And given it to thy neighbour ... David.—An evil spirit impersonating Samuel would not have spoken in this way; he would not have wished to help David to the throne of Israel; nor would an evil spirit have spoken in such solemn terms of the punishment due to rebellion against God.

(19) Moreover the Lord will also deliver Israel ... into the hands of the Philistines.—Three crushing judgments, which were to come directly upon Saul, are contained in the prophet's words: (a) the utter defeat of the army of Israel; (b) the violent death of Saul himself and his two sons in the course of the impending fight; (c) the sacking of the Israelitish camp, which was to follow the defeat, and which would terribly augment the horrors and disasters of the rout of the king's army.

To morrow shalt thou and thy sons be with me.—Samuel uses a mild and charitable expression, applicable to all, good and bad, "Thou shalt be as I am: no longer among the living." In the vision of the world of spirits, revealed to us by our blessed Lord, the souls of Dives and Lazarus may be said to be together in the abode of the departed spirits, for Dives saw Lazarus, and conversed with Abraham, though there was a gulf fixed between them. By using the gentler expression, Samuel mildly exhorted Saul to repentance.

(23) And sat upon the bed.—That is, upon the divan, or cushioned seat, which usually runs around the walls of rooms in Eastern dwellings. There is nothing in the narration to support the common idea, represented so often in painting, that the scene above related took place in a cave. The witch probably lived in a dwelling of her own at En-dor. There is nothing, either, in the narrative to indicate that she was living in a place of concealment.

29

(1) Aphek.—The name Aphek was a common one, and was given to several "places of arms" in Canaan. It signifies a fort or a strong place. This Aphek was most likely situated in the Plain of Jezreel. Eusebius places it in the neighborhood of En-dor.

(2) David and his men.—David, in return for the lands around Ziklag given him by the king of Gath, seems to have owed a kind of military service to his suzerain Achish. The difference in the arms and equipments of the Israelitish warriors in the division of David, which was marching under the standard of Gath, no doubt excited questions. The general appearance of the Hebrews was, of course, well known to their hereditary Philistine foes.

(8) And David said unto Achish, But what have I done?—David never contemplated fighting in the ranks against Israel, and yet he speaks thus. It has been suggested that these suspicions of his loyalty on the part of the Philistine leaders had been aroused by David deliberately, in order to bring about his dismissal from the army in the field. This is possible, for the situation in which David now finds himself was most embarrassing from every point of view.

(11) To return into the land of the Philistines.—No doubt David and his officers rejoiced at their escaping the terrible alternative of either turning traitors to the kindly man who had so hospitably received them in their distress, or of appearing in arms with the Philistines when they came into collision with the Israelites under Saul.

30

(1) The Amalekites had invaded the south.—This was partly in retaliation for the late raids of David in the Amalekite country, partly because Amalek had heard that, owing to the Philistine and Israelite armies having left the southern districts for the central part of Canaan, all the south country was left unguarded. "The south," that is, "the Negeb" or the dry land—all the southern part of Judea—included also a part of the Arab Desert.

And smitten Ziklag.—This was an act of vengeance, Ziklag being the city of that famous Israelite chieftain David, who had done so much damage to Amalek, and who had treated the captives with such cruelty. While other parts of the south were simply plundered, Ziklag, marked for utter destruction, was sacked and burned.

(2) They slew not any.—The women and children possessed a marketable value, and were carried off to be sold into slavery, probably in Egypt, with which country the Amalekites, as neighbors, had constant

dealings. Verse 13 tells of an Egyptian slave in the army.

(6) But David encouraged himself in the Lord his God.—He encouraged himself in prayer, thus casting himself and his fortunes on God. This perfect, childlike, implicit trust had been the source of the marvelous success of the chosen people. When they forgot the invisible King, who for His own great purposes had chosen them, their fortunes at once declined; they fell to the level, and often below the level, of the surrounding nations. But, when with weeping and mourning they returned to their allegiance, success and victory returned to them. This is what happened now to David at Ziklag, while about the same time Saul, alone and distrustful, fought and fell on the bloody day of Gilboa. David, with the help of his God, on whose mercy he had thrown himself, obtained his brilliant success over Amalek, and restored his prestige not only among his own immediate followers, but through all the cities and villages of southern Canaan.

(7) And Abiathar brought thither the ephod.—Many commentators prefer to disbelieve in any response coming through the medium of the Urim in the ephod. They either pass over the whole transaction in silence, or assume that some divine inspiration came to the high priest when vested with the sacred garment. The plain meaning, however, is that in some way or other the divine will was made known through the agency of the mysterious Urim and Thummim. This peculiar divine response is carefully distinguished from the manifestation of the will of God in a dream or a vision, or through the divine instrumentality of the prophet or seer (comp. 28:6). The ancient Hebrews had no hesitation in attributing to the sacred precious stones an occasional special power of declaring the oracles of God. And it seems in the highest degree arbitrary to reject the ancient traditional belief of the Hebrew race contained in the Talmud with respect to this most mysterious ephod and its sacred gems, and to adopt another interpretation, which fits in lamely with the plain text.

(11) An Egyptian.—The Amalekites' wanderings would have taken them to the frontiers of Egypt, therefore the probability of their having Egyptian slaves in their tribe. They seem to have been a ruthless, cruel race, the scourge of the desert, and of the people dwelling near its borders.

(12) Three days and three nights.—This

was a note of time as to the head start of the Amalekite leader with the plunder. It may well be conceived there was no time to lose. The cruelty of the Amalekites to their slaves was the cause of their ultimate discomfiture; for with the considerable start they already had, if David had not been quite certain of their route, the pursuit would have been utterly hopeless.

(20) The flocks and the herds, which they drave.—David's motive in choosing the sheep and oxen (for his warriors certainly the least desirable part of the Amalekite possession) is evident from verses 26-31.

(21-25) The scene here related chronicles an act of greed and heartless covetousness. The wise compiler of the book chose it as part of the memoirs of David, which were to be preserved in the sacred volume, because it was another authoritative declaration on the part of the beloved king respecting a question which would crop up again and again on the conclusion of a campaign. The Chronicler was justified in his selection, for this famous decision of David continued in force until the time of the Maccabees. (See II Macc. 8:28-30.) A somewhat similar law had been enacted by Moses. (See Num. 31:27.)

(26) He sent of the spoil.—To have made it worthwhile to have sent presents to all the places enumerated in verses 27-31, the spoil of the Amalekites captured on this occasion must have been enormous. They were probably the main division of the great tribe, and had with them the bulk of their flocks and herds, besides what they had just captured in their raid in southern Canaan. No doubt the cities to whom rich gifts of cattle were sent were those places where, during his long wanderings, he and his followers had been kindly received and helped.

31

(1) Now the Philistines fought against Israel.—The narrator here is very abrupt. No doubt a devoted patriot, he found it bitter to write the story of the fatal day of Gilboa. Curtly he picks up the dropped threads of 28:1-5, and 29:2. The locality of the fight is not mentioned, but it was most likely somewhere in that long vale which was spread out at the foot of the hills occupied by the hostile camps. Israel was defeated, and fled upward toward their old position on the slope of Gilboa.

(2) And the Philistines slew Jonathan, and Abinadab, and Melchishua, Saul's sons.—While in his own record of the national disaster, the compiler or historian, in his stern sorrow, expunges every detail, and represses every expression of feeling which he gives us in II Sam. 1:17-27, we see the stately elegy in the beautiful moving words which the successor to the throne wrote on the death of the first king and his heroic son. Without comment he copies into his record the hymn of David on Saul and Jonathan, just as he found it in the **Book of Jashar** (the collection of national odes celebrating the heroes of the Theocracy).

The hero Jonathan and his two brave brothers, as far as we can gather from the scanty details of the battle after the army was routed in the valley of Jezreel, retreated (fighting all the while) to the hill of Gilboa. There, it seems, they made the last stand with the **fideles** of the royal house of Saul (verse 6), and there, no doubt defending the king to the last, they fell.

(3) And he was sore wounded of the archers.—The more accurate translation is, "He was sore afraid" (or was greatly alarmed at them): so Gesenius, Keil, Lange. All seemed against him. Perhaps the words he had heard only a few hours before at Endor from the dead prophet were ringing in his ears, "To-morrow shalt thou and thy sons be with me."

(4) His armourbearer.—Jewish tradition tells us that this faithful armorbearer was Doeg, the Edomite, and that the sword which Saul took apparently from the hand of the armorbearer was the sword with which Doeg had massacred the priests at Gibeon and at Nob.

A sword.—In II Sam 1:6-10 we have another account of the death. Keil and Lange regard the Amalekite's story as an invention framed to extract a rich gift from David, who, the savage Arab thought, would rejoice to hear of his great enemy's fall. Ewald, however, sees no reason to doubt the trustworthiness of the Amalekite's story. (See notes on II Sam. 1:6, 10.)

(6) So Saul died.—This is one of the rare instances of self-destruction among the chosen people. It seems to have been almost unknown among the Israelites. Prior to Saul the only recorded example is that of Samson, and his death in the great Dagon temple at Gaza ranks with the heroism of one dying in battle rather than with cases of despairing suicide. There is another instance after the days of Saul, that of

Ahithophel, who hanged himself. There is also, of course, the case of Judas. Theologians are divided in their judgment on King Saul. The Bible closes the record of his life, and leaves the first great king, the first anointed of the Lord, in the hands of his God.

And all his men.—We must not interpret this statement quite literally; I Chron. 10:6 explains it by "all his house." Ishbosheth, his son, for instance, and Abner, the captain of the host, we know were not among the slain on that fatal day.

(8) They found Saul and his three sons fallen in mount Gilboa.—It is expressly stated that the Philistines found the royal corpses on the morrow of the great fight. So desperate had been the valor with which the king and his gallant sons had defended their last positions on the hill, that night had fallen before the din of battle ceased. In the meantime the Amalekite had found and carried off the crown and royal bracelet.

The historian with extreme brevity records the savage treatment of the royal remains, which, after all, was but a reprisal. The same generation had witnessed similar barbarous procedure in the case of Goliath, the great Philistine champion.

(9) And they cut off his head, and stripped off his armour.—On comparing verse 12, where the bodies of his sons are especially mentioned, it is clear that this act was not confined to the person of the king. The sense of the passage there is that the heads of the king and his three sons were cut off and their armor stripped from their bodies. The heads and armor were sent as trophies around the different towns and villages of Philistia, and the headless corpses were fastened to the wall of the city of Beth-shan.

(10) The house of Ashtaroth.—The pieces of armor belonging to the four men were placed together in the famous Astarte temple, at Askelon, which Herodotus (1:105) describes as the most ancient of the temples dedicated to the worship of the Syrian Venus.

The wall of Beth-shan.—Beth-shan was in the tribe of Manasseh, some four miles west of the Jordan, and twelve miles south of the Sea of Galilee. The Canaanitish element in the population was perhaps the reason why Beth-shan was chosen for the barbarous exhibition (see Judg. 1:27). The Canaanites would probably have welcomed the miserable spectacle which seemed to degrade their ancient enemies. The writer of the chronicle adds one more ghastly detail to this account: "They fastened the head (skull) of Saul in the Temple of Dagon" (I Chron. 10:10).

(11) The inhabitants of Jabesh-Gilead.—It was remarkable how the first deed of patriotism done in the early fervor of Saul's consecration bore fruit after so many long years. Jabesh-Gilead, a city of Manasseh, was on the further side of Jordan, perhaps about fourteen miles from Beth-shan (see Judg. 21:8).

(12) And burnt them there.—Burning the corpse was never the custom in Israel, and was restricted to criminals convicted of a crime of the deepest kind (Lev. 20:14). The Jews in all cases buried their dead. The reason for the action here is clear. The mutilated trunks had been exposed for some days to the air, and the flesh was no doubt in a state of putrefaction. The flesh only was burned. The bones were reverently and lovingly preserved, and laid to rest beneath the friendly shade of the great tamarisk tree of Jabesh. (See II Sam. 21:12, 14.)

SECOND SAMUEL

1

At the moment when this book opens, the events narrated in I Sam. 31 were not known to David. At the time of the fatal battle between Saul and the Philistines, David had been engaged in his successful attack upon the Amalekites who had spoiled Ziklag (I Sam. 30) and it was not until two days after his return (verse 2) that the news reached him. The two Books of Samuel really form one continuous narrative.

(1) Two days in Ziklag.—See Josh. 19:5 and Neh. 11:28. Its most probable locality is some ten or twelve miles south of Beersheba, and nearly equidistant from the Mediterranean and the Dead Sea. It was therefore almost four days' journey from Mount Gilboa, and the messenger who brought the news of the battle must have left the field before David's return to Ziklag.

(2) Did obeisance.—This was not merely an act of Oriental respect, but was intended as a recognition of David's rank as having now become king. The messenger, although an Amalekite (verses 8, 13), had earth upon his head and his clothes rent as marks of sorrow for the defeat of David's people and the death of their king.

(6) Upon mount Gilboa.—The battle appears to have been fought in the plain of Jezreel, but when the Israelites were routed they naturally fled up the mountain range of Gilboa, though apparently much scattered. It was in this straggling flight that the Amalekite happened upon that part of the mountain where Saul was. The true account of the death of Saul is given in I Sam. 31:3-6. (See note on verse 10.) It is uncertain whether the man saw Saul at all before his death, and it is extremely unlikely that he found him without warriors or armor-bearer, wounded and alone.

(8) An Amalekite.—The Amalekites were hereditary foes of Israel (see Exod. 17:8-13; Num. 14:45; Deut. 25:18; Judg. 3:13; 6:3). Some years before this they had been terribly defeated by Saul (I Sam. 15:4-9), and it is possible that the present messenger may either have attached himself to the army of the conqueror, or have been compelled, according to ancient custom, to serve in its ranks (see verse 3). One of their bands had also just received a severe blow at the hands of David, but the Amalekite could not have known of this last attack.

(10) Slew him.—This story is inconsistent with that given in I Sam. 31:4, 5, and was evidently invented by the Amalekite to gain favor with David. At the same time, he is careful not to carry the story too far, and asserts that Saul was only put to death at his own request, and after being mortally wounded. However, he must have been one of the first to find the body of Saul after his death, since he brought his crown and bracelet to David—a prima facie evidence of the truth of his whole story. The offering of these emblems of royalty shows that the Amalekite recognized David as the future king, a recognition which most of the tribes of Israel were unwilling to make for a long time.

(12) They mourned.—On hearing the tidings of the Amalekite, David and all his people showed the usual Oriental signs of sorrow by rending their clothes, weeping, and fasting. The whole narrative shows that David not only, as a patriotic Israelite, lamented the death of the king, but also felt a personal attachment to Saul, notwithstanding his long and unreasonable hostility. But Saul did not die alone; Jonathan, David's most cherished friend, fell with him, and large numbers of his countrymen also were slain.

(14) How wast thou not afraid?—It does not matter whether he fully believed his story or not; the man must be judged by his own account of himself. (See verse 16.) Regicide was not in David's eyes merely a political crime; he considered taking the life of "the Lord's anointed" as a religious offense of the greatest magnitude. It was an especially grievous thing for a foreigner and an Amalekite thus to smite him whom God had appointed as the monarch of Israel.

(15) Fall upon him.—All question of David's authority to pronounce a capital sentence is here quite out of place. The Amalekite had just recognized him as king. And by his own confession the Amalekite was guilty of high treason.

(17) Lamented with this lamentation.—This is the technical expression for a funeral dirge or elegy, such as David also composed on the death of Abner (3:33, 34), and Jeremiah on the death of Josiah (II Chron. 35:25). It is the only instance preserved to us (except the few lines on the death of Abner) of David's secular poetry.

(18) In the book of Jasher.—Note that the reference is to "the children of Judah" rather than to all Israel, because for the following seven and a half years, while the memory of Saul was fresh, David reigned only over Judah and Benjamin. This book is also referred to in Josh. 10:13, and nothing more is really known about it. It is supposed to have been a collection of songs relating to memorable events and men in the early history of Israel, and it appears that this elegy was included among them.

The song is in two parts, the first relating to both Saul and Jonathan (verses 19-24), the second to Jonathan alone (verses 25, 26).

(20) Lest the daughters of the Philistines.— As in Gath and Askelon, it was customary generally for women to celebrate national deliverances and victories (Exod. 15:21; I Sam. 18:6). The word "uncircumcised" might be applied to all the heathen, but it so happens that, with the exception of Gen. 34:14, it is used in the historical books only of the Philistines (Judg. 14:3; 15:18; I Sam. 14:6; 17:26, 36; 31:4; I Chron. 10:4).

(24) Clothed you in scarlet.—This refers to Saul's division among the people of the spoil of his conquered foes, and to the prosperity resulting from his many successful campaigns. Notwithstanding that his light at last went out under the cloud of a crushing defeat, he had been on the whole a successful warrior.

(26) Passing the love of women.—It was such an affection as could only exist between noble natures and those united in the fear of God. In these last verses of the elegy, which relate to Jonathan alone, David has given expression to his own personal sorrow.

2

(1) Inquired of the Lord.—At this important juncture of affairs, David's first concern is to know the divine will. He is concerned to secure the throne, in view of the opposition made to him by the adherents of the house of Saul. And as yet he has had no opportunity to put his Philistine experiences in their true light before his people. His inquiry was, doubtless, made through the high priest Abiathar, as in I Sam. 23:9, 10 (comp. 22:20; 23:1, 4). The answer definitely directed him to go up to Hebron.

Hebron is one of the most ancient cities of the world, built "seven years before Zoan in Egypt" (Num. 13:22). (See notes on Gen. 13:18; 23:2; see also Num. 13:22; Josh. 20:7; 21:11, 13.) It is situated in a valley among the hills of southern Judea, at a

height of nearly 3,000 feet above the Mediterranean. From Ziklag, where David had been living, it was a distance of about thirty-eight miles. Here was the home and the throne of David for the next seven and a half years (verse 11; 5:5). The larger part of the land, since the recent defeat, was in the power of the Philistines; and Hebron, on account of its situation at the far south, and its strategical strength as well as its sacred associations, was a peculiarly fitting place for the beginning of David's reign.

(2) His two wives.—See I Sam. 25:42 and 43.

(4) They anointed David.—The first private anointing of David (I Sam. 16) had been in token of his divine commission; this was a sign of his recognition as king by the tribe of Judah; and there was still a third subsequent anointing (5:4), when he was accepted by all Israel. The "men of Judah" had been on friendly terms with him during his long outlawry; they had also lately received presents from him in recognition of their kindness to him, one of their tribe (I Sam. 30:26-31).

(8) But Abner the son of Ner.—See I Chron. 9:36. Abner had been made by Saul the commander-in-chief of his army (I Sam. 14:50). He was, both by kindred and office, strongly attached to the house of Saul. He had been with Saul in his pursuit of David, and may have resented David's address to him on that occasion (I Sam. 26:14-16). There is no statement of the time that had elapsed after the death of Saul before Ishbosheth was set up as king by Abner, but it was probably four or five years.

Ish-bosheth.—Called in I Chron. 8:33 and 9:39, "Eshbaal" (the fire of Baal), just as his nephew, Mephibosheth (II Sam. 4:4), is called in the same places "Meribaal." These names compounded with Baal may have been originally given in consequence of the manful opposition to idolatry of those who bore them, and have been subsequently changed to a compound with "bosheth" (shame), in view of the sequel of their histories. (Comp. Gideon's name, Judg. 6:32; 8:35; II Sam. 11:21.)

Mahanaim, famous in the story of Jacob (Gen. 32:2), was on the east of the Jordan, and not far from the brook Jabbok. A Levitical city (Josh. 21:38), in comparative safety from the Philistines, it was well chosen by Abner for the coronation and residence of his new king. Mahanaim afterward became the place of refuge for David in his flight from Absalom (17:24)

The expression "brought him over" refers to the crossing of the Jordan.

(12) To Gibeon.—Gibeon was five and a half miles northwest from Jerusalem, and at a long distance both from Mahanaim and from Hebron. The pool (verse 13) was a reservoir, the ruins of which remain 120 feet long and 100 feet wide. Here the generals of the rival monarchs met, possibly by design, but more likely each engaged in the effort to extend his respective master's sway over the tribe of Benjamin.

(13) Joab the son of Zeruiah.—See note on I Sam. 26:6.

(14) Let the young men.—To avoid unnecessary bloodshed between the tribes of a common parentage, and also, perhaps, to prevent the weakening of the nation in the face of their common Philistine foe, Abner proposes that the struggle should be decided by a combat between a few champions chosen on either side, and Joab immediately accepts the proposal. But nothing was decided, and a large battle ensued.

(19) Asahel pursued after Abner.—The spears were sharpened at the "hinder end" for the purpose of sticking them into the ground (I Sam. 26:7). Abner's reluctance to kill Asahel may have been partly on account of his extreme youth, but was chiefly through dread of the vengeance of Joab (verse 22). "The fifth rib" here, and wherever else it occurs (3:27; 4:6; 20:10), should be translated "abdomen."

(27) Unless thou hadst spoken.—Joab's reply to Abner admits that he had intended to keep up the pursuit only until the following morning, but as Abner already pleaded for mercy, he was content and would stop now.

(28) Neither fought they any more.—i.e., in this present campaign (see 3:1).

3

(1) There was long war.—There was no actual fighting of pitched battles, but a state of hostility, in which Ishbosheth and David each claimed the allegiance of the whole nation, and this continued until the death of Ishbosheth. During this time Ishbosheth was too weak to carry on actual war, and David was content to abide the fulfillment of the promises of the Lord in His own good time. (See I Chron. 12:19-22.)

(2-5) It is quite in accordance with the habit of the sacred historians to insert at the beginning or at some turning point in each reign statistics about the house or family of the king. (See I Sam. 14:49-51; II Sam. 5:13; I Kings 3:1; 14:21: 15:2, 9; etc.)

Amnon.—In Hebrew written "Aminon" in 13:20. His great crime and miserable end are related in chap. 13.

Chileab.—Called "Daniel" in I Chron. 3:1. None of the attempts to explain these as two forms of the same name have been successful. As he does not appear in the subsequent troubles, it is supposed that he died early.

Absalom.—His history, rebellion, and death are narrated in chaps. 13-18.

Adonijah.—After the death of his three elder brothers, Adonijah considered himself the rightful heir to the throne, and embittered the last days of his father by a rebellion (I Kings 1). He was at last put to death by Solomon (I Kings 2:25).

Of the other two sons, Shephatiah and Ithream, and of the mothers of the last three, nothing is known.

(7) Wherefore hast thou gone in?—The harem of an Eastern monarch was considered as the property of his successor, and therefore the taking of a woman belonging to it as the assertion of a claim to the throne. (See 12:8; 16:21; I Kings 2:22.) It is this implied charge of treachery that so greatly rouses the anger of Abner.

(9) So do God to Abner.—The anger of Abner culminates in a solemn oath to transfer the kingdom to David. Abner does not propose to do this in order to fulfill the divine will, for his words show that he had been acting in conscious opposition to that will, but to revenge himself for the insult now offered him. He had doubtless also become convinced of his master's entire unfitness for the throne, and his power over Israel opened before him the prospect of high preferment from David.

(13) Except thou first bring Michal.—David consents to negotiate with Abner only on condition of the previous restoration of his lawful wife. Besides the justice of this demand, and besides all question of affection toward one who had loved him and saved his life (I Sam. 18:20; 19:11-17), there were obvious political reasons of importance for the demand.

(24) What hast thou done?—Joab's somewhat rough remonstrance with David may have been supported by an honest suspicion of Abner, for which there was some ground in Abner's long opposition to the known divine will and his present revolt from Ishbosheth; but there was also a

265

personal enmity, due partly to the fear of being himself supplanted by an older and famous warrior, and partly to the desire to revenge the death of his brother Asahel. Joab seeks to poison David's mind against Abner, that he may better carry out his revenge.

(28, 29) Joab's act was entirely without David's knowledge, and was not only against his will on moral grounds, but was in danger of proving disastrous to him politically. The strong curse here pronounced by David shows that Joab's act could not be justified as that of the "Goel," or lawful avenger of his brother's blood, for Abner had slain Asahel in battle, unwillingly and in self-defense. It is also to be remembered that Hebron was a city of refuge (Josh. 21:13), and that here not even the "Goel" might slay the murderer without a trial (Num. 35:22-25). The curse falls "on his father's house," since Abishai also (verse 30) had been connected with him in the murder.

David still remains at fault, however, for continuing Joab in his high and responsible position; but this seems to have been the result of inability to inflict proper punishment upon so powerful a subject, an inability which David on his deathbed sought to remedy by his charge to Solomon. (See verse 39 and I Kings 2:5.) On the violent end of Joab see I Kings 2:31-34.

(34) Thy hands were not bound.—The people were moved greatly by the sight of David's sorrow, but still more by this brief elegy over Abner. All the circumstances are summed up in a few pregnant words: Abner, so valiant in war, with his hands free for defense, with his feet unfettered, unsuspicious of evil, fell by the treacherous act of a wicked man.

4

(3) Fled to Gittaim.—Neither the cause of their flight, nor the place to which they fled, can be determined for certain. The Beerothites here appear as of the tribe of Benjamin (see Josh. 9:17; 18:25) and it is probable that they fled from the incursions of the Philistines, and that Gittaim is the place mentioned in Neh. 11:35 as occupied by the Benjamites returning from Babylon. The expression "until this day" makes it likely that the writer was not far removed from the events which he relates.

(4) A son that was lame.—The reason for

the introduction here of this account of Mephibosheth, Jonathan's son, is to show that he being physically incapacitated for the throne, the house of Saul became practically extinct with the death of Ishbosheth. There were other descendants, but they were either illegitimate or females, (21:8, 9), and therefore there was none other of his house to claim the throne.

(6, 7) Gathering wheat (probably for their soldiers) was a pretext to cover their purpose. On "the fifth rib," see note on 2:23. There is no difficulty with the repetition in verse 7 of what has been already mentioned in verse 6, for it is common in the Scripture narratives to repeat statements when any additional fact is to be mentioned. (See 3:22, 23; 5:1-3.)

(9) Who hath redeemed.—David's answer shows that he could trust in God to avenge him, and did not encourage or need the crimes of men to help him.

(10) Who thought that I would have given him.—The literal translation is better: "which was the reward I gave him." This shows plainly David's view of the motive which prompted the Amalekite to his lie recorded in 1:10.

(11) A righteous person—i.e., righteous, not at fault, as far as the matter in hand and his relation to the assassins is concerned.

5

(1) Thy bone and thy flesh.—It is probable that this gathering to David, already prepared by the negotiations of Abner, took place immediately after the death of Ishbosheth. They assign three reasons for their action: (1) that they were of such common descent that it was unfitting for them to constitute separate nations; (2) that David, even in Saul's reign, had been their military leader, and therefore they had confidence in his prowess and sagacity; (3) that the Lord had chosen him for their king. The exact language of the divine promise quoted is not found in the record, but is either a summary of the communications made to David, or else some unrecorded language of one of the prophets.

(3) Made a league with them.—It would be an anachronism to understand this of the establishment of a constitutional monarchy, but the "league" may have had reference to certain special matters, such as leading them against their enemies, not destroying the remnant of the house of Saul or its late adherents, and not showing partiality (as Saul had done) to the members of his own tribe.

(4) Thirty years old.—This statement of the age and the length of the reign of David (see I Chron. 29:26, 27) shows us approximately the length of time since the combat with Goliath as some ten or twelve years. It also proves that the greater part of Saul's reign is treated briefly in I Samuel, and that David was seventy years old at his death.

(5) Seven years and six months.—It was the habit of the sacred historians either to omit such fractions or else to count them as whole years (see verse 4; I Chron. 29:27), thus introducing a certain element of indefiniteness into the chronology, which is very marked in the parallel narratives of the kings of Israel and of Judah. (Comp. 2:11; I Chron. 3:4.)

(6) Went to Jerusalem.—See Josh. 10:23-26; 12:10; Judg. 1:7, 8, 21; 19:11, 12. That Jebus and Jerusalem were two names of the same city is stated in I Chron. 11:4. This expedition must have taken place immediately after the coronation, since the length of reign over all Israel and of the reign in Jerusalem are said in verse 5 to be the same. David doubtless saw the importance of at once uniting the tribes in common action as well as the advantages of Jerusalem for his capital (Hebron being much too far southward), and the necessity of dislodging this remnant of the old Canaanites from their strong position in the center of the land.

Except thou take away.—The Jebusites, confident in the natural strength of their fortress, boast that even the lame and the blind could defend it. Their citadel was upon Mount Zion, the highest of the hills of Jerusalem, southwest of the temple hill of Moriah, and surrounded on three sides by deep valleys.

(8) Getteth up to the gutter.—The most probable sense is "watercourses" (see Ps. 42:7), such as were connected with the precipices around Mount Zion. David applies to all the Jebusites the expression they had just used of those who would suffice to resist his attack. The clause "that are hated of David's soul" shows that in this siege no quarter was to be given; the Jebusites were under the old ban resting on all the Canaanites, and were to be destroyed. (See I Chron. 11:6.)

(9) Millo.—It is probably an old Canaanitish name for the fortification on the northern end of Mount Zion, "inward"

from which the palace was situated. (Comp. I Kings 11:27; II Chron. 32:5.)

(11) Hiram king of Tyre.—This is the same Hiram, variously spelled "Hirom" and "Huram," who was afterward the friend of Solomon (I Kings. 5:1; II Chron. 2:3). It is unlikely that several years may have elapsed between the two events, during which "David went on and grew great" (verse 10), thereby attracting the attention and regard of Hiram.

The Israelites evidently had little skill in architecture, since they relied on the Phoenicians for workmen both for this palace and for Solomon's, as well as for the Temple.

(13) More concubines and wives.—David certainly came perilously near a violation of the law of Deut. 17:17, although he did not, like his son Solomon, take wives and concubines in enormous number for the sake of having a great harem—an important element in the Oriental ideas of regal magnificence. Altogether, here and in Chronicles, the names of nineteen sons are mentioned; those of the daughters are not given, although one, Tamar, is mentioned in the story in chap. 13.

(14) These be the names.—The same list, with some variations, is given in I Chron. 3:5-8; 14:4-7. The first four were children of Bathsheba and were consequently not born until a later period of David's reign. Solomon and Nathan are the two sons through whom Matthew and Luke trace our Lord's genealogy. The variations in the names are chiefly mere difference of spelling. Eliphalet and Nogah, given in both lists in Chronicles, are omitted here, probably because they died young, the name of the former being given again to the last son in all the lists.

(18) Rephaim.—It was a fruitful valley, stretching some three miles south and southwest from Jerusalem, and only separated from the valley of Hinnom by a narrow ridge. It gave ample room for a large encampment. (See Josh. 15:8.)

(21) Their images.—The Philistines took their idols with them to battle, as the Israelites had formerly taken the Ark, and the suddenness and completeness of their defeat is shown by their leaving them on the field. The statement that David "burned" them is taken from I Chron. 14:12, the Hebrew here being simply "took them away."

(23) Shalt not go up.—The enemy, on the same battleground, would have prepared for attack from the same direction as before;

267

consequently David is directed to go around them and attack them unexpectedly from the opposite quarter.

(25) From Geba ... to Gazer.—The distance of the pursuit from Gibeon (not Geba, as I Chron. 14:16 apparently has the correct reading) was about twelve miles, and six miles more must already have been passed over before reaching Gibeon from the valley of Rephaim. In I Chron. 14:8-17 these battles are placed between the unsuccessful (13:5-14) and the successful (chap. 15) attempts to bring up the Ark to Jerusalem. It is impossible now to determine the exact details of the chronology.

6

This chapter contains a condensed narrative of the bringing up of the Ark to Jerusalem, of which a much fuller account is given in I Chron. 13-16. There is no sufficient reason to doubt that Ps. 68 was composed and chanted on this occasion, its martial tone being natural in connection with the recent victories over the Philistines. Pss. 15 and 101 were probably sung at the removal of the Ark from the house of Obed-edom (verses 12-16), while Ps. 24 was undoubtedly the triumphant chant with which the Ark entered the city. All these should be studied in connection with this narrative. Ps. 132 also, more doubtfully, referred to this period.

(2) From Baale of Judah.—In Josh. 15:9 and 1 Chron. 13:6, Baale is said to be another name for Kirjath-jearim. This was the place to which the Ark was carried after its removal from Bethshemesh (I Sam. 7:2), and it had remained here ever since. It was three or four hours march from the capital.

Whose name is called.—The Ark is described as being the visible symbol of God's presence and of His covenant with His people.

(3) Upon a new cart.—The "new" cart, one which had been used for no other purpose, was doubtless intended as a mark of respect (comp. I Sam. 6:7); yet it was a violation of the Law (Num. 7:9), requiring that the Ark be **borne** by the Levites. It is not necessary to suppose that David intended to violate the Law; but the Ark having been left neglected for more than two generations, the exact requirements in regard to it may easily have passed out of mind.

(6) Nachon's threshingfloor.—This place

is entirely unknown. The turning aside of the oxen to snatch the scattered grain of the threshingfloor may have caused the trouble.

(7) For his error.—Uzzah was probably a Levite, or, at any rate, had been in the house with the ark so long that he ought to have made himself familiar with the law in regard to it (see Num. 4:5, 15, 19, 20). What may seem, at first thought, an exceeding severe penalty for a well-meaning, though unlawful act, is seen on reflection to have been a necessary manifestation of the divine displeasure; for this act involved not only a violation of the letter of the law (of which David also was guilty), but a want of reverence for the majesty of God as symbolized by the Ark, and showed a disposition to profane familiarity with sacred things. Judgments of this kind were, however, temporal, and give in themselves no indication of the treatment of the offender beyond the grave.

(10) Obed-edom the Gittite.—He was a Levite, but whether of the family of Kohath (see I Chron. 26:1, 4, 8, 13-15), or Merari (see I Chron. 15:17, 18) is uncertain. The one here mentioned was a Gittite, i.e., born at, or belonging to, Gath-rimmon, a Levitical city on the confines of Dan and Manasseh (Josh. 21:24, 25). The Obed-edoms of David's time were porters of the Tabernacle, Levitical musicians, and took an active part in bringing the Ark to Jerusalem, and afterward in ministering before it (I Chron. 15:16, 18, 21, 24; 16:4, 5, 37, 38; 26:1, 4, 13-15). (Comp. II Chron. 25:24.)

(12) Went and brought up.—The immediate reason for David's action was the knowledge of the blessings which had come to Obed-edom through the presence of the Ark, in contrast to the punishment of Uzzah; yet this implies neither jealousy nor a wish to deprive his subject of a blessing. It had been his original purpose to carry the Ark to Jerusalem, and he had only desisted in fear. He now saw that such fear was groundless, and went on to the completion of his unfinished action. (See I Chron. 15; 16:1.)

(14) David danced.—The religious dances on occasions of great national blessing were usually performed by women only (Ex. 15:20, 21; Judg. 11:34; I Sam. 18:6). The king, by now taking part in them himself, marked his strong sense of the importance of the occasion, and his readiness to do his utmost in God's honor.

Girded with a linen ephod.—The ephod

of "bad" (as distinguished from the ephod of the high priest, which was made of "shesh") was simply a garment worn by any one engaged in a religious service. It was not, therefore, a peculiarly priestly dress, though naturally more worn by them than by any one else.

(16) She despised him.—The contrast is here strongly brought out between the spirit of Saul's house in which Michal had been brought up, and that of David. In Saul's time the Ark had been neglected, and true religion was uncared for. Michal, therefore, who had fallen in love with David as a brave hero, could not understand the religious enthusiasm which led him to rank himself among the common people before the Lord.

(17) The tabernacle.—Not the Tabernacle made for it in the wilderness, and which seems to have been now at Gibeon, but a special tent which David had prepared for it.

(22) Base in mine own sight.—While Michal had charged him with making himself base in the eyes of the maidservants (who were no fit judges of such matters), he was ready to abase himself in his own eyes, to do anything, however humbling it might seem even to himself, which should be for the honor and glory of God.

7

(1) Had given him rest.—This narrative is placed here (see I Chron. 17), not because it followed the last chapter chronologically, but because it is closely related in subject, and the historian, after telling of the removal of the Ark, wished to record in that connection David's further purposes in the same direction. It is likely to have been in a time of quiet prosperity, before the troubles of his latter years.

(2) Nathan.—This is the first mention of him, but he was already a confidential counselor of the king, and became prominent later in this reign and in the opening of that of Solomon (chap. 12; I Kings 1:10, 12, 34, 38). Nathan "the prophet" and Gad "the seer" wrote parts of the history of this and the succeeding reign (I Chron. 29:29; II Chron. 9:29).

Within curtains.—This the word used in Exod. 26 and 36 for the covering of the tabernacle. The Ark was not now within that, but in a similar temporary structure. David's heart is moved by a comparison of

his own royal residence with the inferior provision for the Ark. Compare the opposite state of things among the returned exiles in Haggai 1:10.

(5) Shalt thou build?—The question implies the negative, as it is expressed in I Chron. 17:4-5.

After David was told that he should not be allowed to build a Temple for God as he desired, he is promised that God will make for him a sure house, and will accept the building of the Temple from his son. David is called "my servant," an expression used only of those eminent and faithful in the service of God, as Moses and Joshua, thus showing—as in fact the whole message does—that the prohibition conveyed nothing of divine displeasure; but no reason for it is here expressed. Comp. I Chron. 22:8; 28:3.

(12) Which shall proceed.—The promise here given certainly has immediate reference to Solomon, and it is thought by many that the use of the future shows that he was not yet born. But the same expression might have been used after Solomon's birth, the future tense being merely an assimilation to the futures of the whole passage, and the point of the promise being that David's son **shall** succeed to his throne.

(14) If he commit iniquity.—The promise has plainly in view a human successor or successors of David upon his throne; and yet it also promises the establishment of David's kingdom forever by an emphatic threefold repetition (verses 13 and 16), which can only be fulfilled, and has always been understood as to be fulfilled, in the Messiah. (See Deut. 18:15-22; Luke 1:32, 33.)

(16) Before thee.—The thought is that David is now made the head of the line in which shall be fulfilled the primeval promise originally given simply to the human race (Gen. 3:15); then restricted to the nation descended from Abraham (Gen. 22:18, etc.); then limited to the tribe of Judah (Gen. 49:10; comp. Ezek. 21:27); and now to be fulfilled in the family of David.

(18) Then went king David in, and sat.—As always at every important point in his life, David's first care is to take that which he has in his mind before the Lord. The place to which he went must be the tent he had pitched for the Ark. Here he sat to meditate in God's presence upon the communication which had now been made to him, and then to offer his thanksgiving (verses 18-21), praise (verses 22-24), and prayer (verses 25-29). (Comp. Deut. 4:7, 32-34; Ps. 110.)

(The divine name is here printed with the word GOD in small capitals. This is always done in the King James Version wherever it stands for JEHOVAH in the original. The same custom is also followed with the word LORD. Out of reverence for the name, Jehovah never has its own vowels in Hebrew, but is printed with those belonging to Lord, or in case this word also is used, then with those belonging to God.)

8

(1) Subdued them.—In its connection this implies not merely the victory of a single battle, but the reversal of the former relation of the Philistines to Israel and their reduction to a condition of inferiority and tribute.

Took Metheg-ammah.—No place of this name is known. The translation should be, "took the bridle (i.e., the key) of the metropolis." This seems sustained by the parallel phrase in I Chron. 18:1, "took Gath and her towns."

(2) He smote Moab.—David's former friendly relations with Moab (probably connected with his own descent from Ruth), are mentioned in I Sam. 22:3, 4. The cause of his entire change of bearing toward them is not known for certain, but according to Jewish tradition the Moabites had proved false to their trust, and had put to death David's father and mother.

With two lines.—David measured off the bodies of his prostrate enemies with a line divided into three equal parts. When they had been made to lie down upon the ground, side by side, the line was stretched over them. Such as were found under the first two parts of it were put to death, those under the third part were spared; thus two-thirds of all the Moabite men perished.

(3) To recover his border.—What happened is more fully explained in 10:13-19: the Ammonites had obtained the help of the Syrians when their combined armies were defeated by David; Hadadezer then attempted to summon to his aid the tribes "beyond the river" (i.e., the Euphrates), but David cut short his plans by another crushing defeat, which reduced them all to subjection.

(4) A thousand chariots.—Seven hundred horsemen should be changed to 7,000, in accordance with I Chronicles, this being a

more fitting proportion to 20,000 infantry in the plains of Syria. The difference is only in two dots over the letter marking the numeral in Hebrew.

Houghed, i.e., hamstrung, to render them incapable of use in war. (Comp. Josh. 11:6, 9.) This act may have been the entering wedge for Solomon's direct violation of Deut. 17:16, by sending to Egypt to "multiply horses to himself."

(9) Toi king of Hamath.—Hamath, the capital of the kingdom of the same name, was situated on the Orontes. According to I Chron. 18:3, David's victory was on the borders of this kingdom.

(12) Of Syria.—I Chron. 18:11 reads Edom. The two names differing in the original only by one similar letter (the **d** and **r,** which are so often confused), it might be supposed that one was an error for the other, were it not that both were actually conquered and the spoils of both dedicated by David.

Amalek.—This is the only allusion to a war with Amalek after David came to the throne. They were a nation of many tribes, and Saul's victory (I Sam. 15) can relate to only one branch. (See I Sam. 30.)

(16) Was recorder.—This was a different office from that of "the scribe" (filled by Seraiah), and appears to have been one of considerable importance (comp. II Kings 18:18-37; II Chron. 34:8; Esther 6:1). He not only registered the king's decrees, but also was his adviser. The same person continued to fill the office in the early years of Solomon's reign (I Kings 4:3).

(17) Ahimelech, the son of Abiathar.—So Ahimelech is also described in I Chron. 18:16; 24:6; on the other hand, Abiathar is expressly said to be the son of Ahimelech in the narrative in I Sam. 22:20-23. The simple solution of the difficulty seems to be that **both** names were borne alike by father and by son, so that both of them are spoken of sometimes under one name, sometimes under the other.

(18) The Cherethites and the Pelethites.—These bodies of men, mentioned for the first time, afterward appear frequently, constituting the most trusted part of the king's army, and forming his special bodyguard (15:18; 20:7, 23; I Kings 1:38, 44; I Chron. 18:17). But the meaning of the words has been much disputed, and the question does not seem to admit of positive determination.

Chief rulers.—The word **cohen** is the one generally used for "priest," and there seems here to be a reminiscence in the word of that early time when the chief civil and ecclesiastical offices were united in the head of the family or tribe. Such use of the word had become now almost obsolete, and quite so in the time when the Chronicles were written.

9

(1) For Jonathan's sake.—There is no note of time to show when this occurred, but, as Mephibosheth was only five years old at the time of his father's death (4:4), and now had a young son (verse 12), it must have been several years after David began to reign in Jerusalem. (This account is omitted entirely from Chronicles.) His motive is sufficiently expressed—for the sake of his early and much-loved friend Jonathan.

(3) The kindness of God.—i.e., kindness such as God shows, very great, and in the fear of God. The crippled Mephibosheth, the only surviving descendant of Saul in the male line, disheartened by the misfortunes of his house, and probably fearing the usual Oriental custom of cutting off all the heirs of a monarch of another line, was living in such obscurity that he was only found through the information of his servant Ziba, a man of considerable substance, and perhaps known to some of the court.

(4) Machir, the son of Ammiel, in Lodebar.—From 17:27-29, the situation of Lodebar must have been east of the Jordan, and near Mahanaim, and Machir appears as a man of wealth and position. Up to this time he was probably secretly an adherent to the house of Saul; but David's kindness to his master's son won his heart, and afterward, in David's own great distress during his flight from Absalom, he proved a faithful friend.

(7) Fear not.—Mephibosheth could not have remembered the affection between David and his father Jonathan, and was naturally in fear. To eat bread at the king's table was a mark of great honor in Oriental lands.

(8) Such a dead dog.—The most contemptible thing possible. Mephibosheth's humility is more than Oriental; it is abject, arising no doubt in part from his infirmity.

(12) Had a young son.—As far as is recorded, this was his only child, but he had a numerous posterity (I Chron. 8:35-40; 9:40-44).

10

This same war (chaps. 10-12) has already been briefly mentioned in 8:3-8, 13, 14, in the general summary of David's reign, but is here given with more detail in connection with his sin. (Comp. I Chron. 19:1-20:3.) Up to this point the reign has been one of exemplary piety and great prosperity; from now on it is overclouded by sin and its consequent punishment. This turning point may be nearly fixed as about the middle of David's reign. (Comp. Pss. 60 and 68.)

(1) The king.—Nahash was probably a son or grandson of the Nahash whom Saul conquered (I Sam. 11), as more than fifty years must have passed since that event. The kindness he had shown to David is not recorded, but may have been some friendly help during his wanderings, or merely a congratulatory message on his accession.

(4) Shaved off the one half of their beards.—According to Oriental ideas, so to have been shaved was the most extreme insult which could have been inflicted.

(6) In I Chron. 19:7 the composition of the force is different. Here only infantry are mentioned, there only chariots and cavalry. It is plain from the result of the battle (verse 18 in both places) that all three arms of the service were employed; either, therefore, some words have been dropped from both texts, or else the writer in each case did not care to go into details.

(9) When Joab saw.—The keen eye of this experienced general at once took in both the advantages and the danger of the disposition of the enemy. He threw his whole force between their two divisions, organizing his own army in two parts, one facing the Ammonites and the other the Syrians, but each capable of supporting the other in case of need. The enemy was thus cut in two, while the Israelites formed one compact body.

(17) He gathered ... and passed.—David, hearing of the great Syrian rally, now took the field in person. Joab may have been with him, but more probably was employed at the south in holding the Ammonites in check and preventing their forming a junction with their confederates.

(18) Seven hundred chariots.—In this campaign David delivered a crushing blow upon his foes, from which they did not recover during the rest of his reign or that of his son. The number 700 here is evidently correct (comp. I Chron. 19:18; and see note on verse 6).

271

11

(2) In an eveningtide.—Late in the afternoon, when David had taken the siesta customary in Oriental countries, he arose from his couch and walked on the roof of his palace, which in the cool of the day was the most pleasant part of an eastern house. This palace was on the height of Mount Zion, and looked down upon the open courts of the houses in the lower city.

David's grievous fall was possibly a result of his long course of uninterrupted prosperity and power, which had somewhat intoxicated him and thrown him off his guard. It is no part of the plan of Scripture to cover up or excuse the sins of even its greatest heroes and saints. This sin was followed by the deepest repentance and by the divine forgiveness; nevertheless its punishment overclouded all the remaining years of David's life. His fall, as Augustine has said, should put upon their guard those who have not fallen, and save from despair those who have.

(3) Wife of Uriah the Hittite.—His name appears (23:39) in the list of David's thirty chief heroes, and the whole story represents him as a brave and noble-minded soldier.

(4) Sent messengers, and took her.—This does not imply the use of violence. Bathsheba, however beautiful, appears from the narrative of I Kings 2:13-22 to have been a woman of little discretion, and now yielded to David's will without resistance, perhaps flattered by the approach of the king.

For she was.—Under the Law she was unclean until the evening. She therefore remained in David's palace until that time, scrupulous in this detail while conscious of a capital crime and a high offense against God. David, nevertheless, was a far greater offender.

(5) Sent and told David.—Because her sin must now become known, and by the Law (Lev. 20:10) adulterers must both be punished with death.

(6) Send me Uriah.—David proposed this to cover up his crime. By calling for Uriah and treating him with marked consideration, he thought to establish a friendly feeling on his part, and then by sending him to his wife, to have it supposed that the child, begotten in adultery, was Uriah's own.

(13) He made him drunk.—This was the second attempt of David to conceal his crime by attempting to send Uriah to his house, but Uriah's resolve was so strong that it still governed his conduct.

(15) Retire ye from him.—This part of David's orders was not carried out. Perhaps Joab thought it would make the stratagem too evident, or perhaps it was not practicable. At all events, the consequence was that others were slain with Uriah, and thus a larger blood guiltiness fell upon David.

(27) Bare him a son.—During all this time David was not only the civil ruler of his people, but also the head of the theocracy. It may be asked why he should have been left so long without being brought to a conviction of his sin. One obvious reason is that this sin might be openly fastened upon him beyond all possibility of denial by the birth of the child. But besides this, however hardened David may appear to have been in passing from one crime to another in an effort to conceal his guilt, yet it is scarcely possible that his conscience should not have been at work and oppressing him with that sense of unconfessed and unforgiven sin which prepared him at last for the visit of Nathan.

12

(1) There were two men.—Beyond all question Ps. 51 is the expression of David's penitence after the visit of Nathan, and Ps. 32 the expression of his experience after the assurance of divine forgiveness, set forth for the warning, instruction and comfort of others. The parable is designed to bring out David's indignation against the offender without being so clear as to awaken at first any suspicion of a personal application. It does not allude to the special crimes of David, but to the meanness and selfishness of the transaction, qualities which David was still in a condition to appreciate. For a similar use of parables see 14:2-11; I Kings 20:35-41.

(7) Thou art the man.—The boldness and suddenness of this application brought a shock to David which at once aroused his slumbering conscience. This could not have been the case had David been essentially a bad man. He was a man whose main purpose in life was to do God's will, but he had yielded to temptation, had been entangled in further and greater guilt in the effort to conceal his sin, and all the while his conscience had been stupefied by the delirium of prosperity and power. Now what he had done is suddenly brought before him in its true light. For like prophetic rebukes of royal offenders see I Sam. 15:21-23; I Kings 21:21-24; Isa. 7:3-25; Matt. 14:3-5.

(9) Hast slain him.—This is a different and stronger word than "killed," in the first part of the verse, and might well be translated "murdered." It was murder in the eyes of the Lord, although accomplished indirectly by the sword of the Ammonites.

(10) Shall never depart.—Here it must mean "as long as David lives"; and the punishment denounced found its realization in a long succession of woes, from the murder of Amnon to the execution of Adonijah.

(13) Thou shalt not die.—David had committed two crimes for which the Law imposed the penalty of death—adultery (Lev. 20:10) and murder (Lev. 24:17). As an absolute monarch he had no reason to fear that the sentence would be put in force by any human authority; and the divine word is to him of far more importance as an assurance of forgiveness than as a warding off of any possible earthly danger.

(14) Thou hast given great occasion.— David was forgiven; yet since his sin brought great scandal on the church, it was necessary that he should suffer publicly the consequences of that sin. This was especially important in David's case, both for the vindication of God's justice, and to destroy the hope that other sins also might go unpunished. The effect of sin generally is similar. The far greater part of David's sufferings was from consequences which flowed from it under the immutable laws of the world's moral government.

(23) I shall go to him.—As far as the mere words themselves are concerned, this might be taken as the expression of a Stoic's comfort. But David, in his whole nature and belief, was as far as possible from being a Stoic, and these words in his mouth can scarcely be anything else than an expression of confidence in a life of consciousness beyond the grave, and of the future recognition of those loved on earth.

(24) Called his name Solomon.—The birth of Solomon could hardly have taken place until after the events mentioned in verses 26-31, since it is not likely that the siege of Rabbah would have occupied two years.

(25) Jedidiah.—It does not appear that this name "beloved of the Lord" was intended to do more than express the divine acceptance of Solomon; and it never came into use as a personal title.

(26) Took the royal city.—The parallel narrative is resumed at this point in I Chron. 20:2. Rabbah was situated in the narrow valley of the upper Jabbok, on both sides of the stream, but with its citadel on the cliff on the northern side.

(31) The brick-kiln.—The Hebrew margin has "through Malchan"; and therefore some have supposed that David made the Ammonites pass through the same fire by which they were accustomed to consecrate their children to Molech.

13

(1) It came to pass after this.—The series of narratives that follow, as far as chap. 22, are chiefly accounts of the misfortunes that befell David and his household after his great sin. These are entirely omitted from the Chronicles, which also omit the account of that sin.

Absalom and Tamar were children of Maachah, daughter of Talmai, king of Geshur, and the former, at least, had been born during David's reign at Hebron (3:3). It is probable that the events here narrated occurred soon after the war with the Ammonites and David's marriage with Bath-sheba.

Amnon was David's first-born son (3:2).

(3) Jonadab, the son of Shimeah.—See I Sam. 16:9.

(13) Speak unto the king.—The marriage of half brothers and sisters was strictly forbidden in the Law (Lev. 18:9, 11; 20:17), and it is not to be supposed that Tamar really thought David would violate its provisions for Amnon; but she made any and every suggestion (see verse 12) to gain time and escape the pressing danger. Amnon, however, knew the Law too well to have any hope of a legitimate marriage with Tamar, and, therefore, persisted in his violence.

(15) Hated her exceedingly.—"It is characteristic of human nature to hate one whom you have injured" (Tacitus). This result shows that Amnon was governed, not by love, but by mere animal passion.

(21) He was very wroth.—The remembrance of his own sin, and Amnon's being David's first-born, tended to withhold David's hand from the administration of justice. David's criminal weakness toward his children was the source of much trouble from this time to the end of his life.

(23) Absalom had sheepshearers.—

273

Absalom chose to give full opportunity for his father to punish Amnon's iniquity if he would; and by this long quiet waiting he so far disarmed suspicion that he was able to carry out his purpose. Sheepshearing always was, and still is, a time of feasting. (Comp. I Sam. 25:2.)

(29) As Absalom had commanded.—If Chileab (or Daniel) was already dead, as seems probable, Absalom stood next in the succession to Amnon, and, however it may have been with himself, his retainers may have looked upon this as a preparatory step toward the throne.

(34) Behind him.—i.e., from the west, the Oriental always being supposed to face the east in speaking of the points of the compass.

(37) Went to Talmai.—His maternal grandfather (See 3:2-5).

For his son every day.—Amnon is certainly the son here meant, for whom David continually mourned until his grief was gradually assuaged by the lapse of time.

(39) The soul of King David.—The verb is impersonal and gives the sense, "David desisted from going forth against Absalom." He ought to have arrested and punished him for a murder, which was at once fratricide and high treason, as being the assassination of the heir-apparent; but the flight to Geshur made this difficult, and as time went by David gradually gave up the thought of punishing Absalom.

14

(1) Was toward Absalom.—The Hebrew preposition unquestionably expresses hostility in the only other place (Dan. 11:28) in which this form of the phrase occurs. "Toward" should be translated "against." Therefore his stratagem to obtain his recall, which would otherwise have been quite unnecessary.

(2) Tekoah.—A village on a high hill five miles south of Bethlehem, the home of the prophet Amos. There is no ground whatever for suspecting this "wise woman" of being a "witch," or in any way disreputable.

(6) They two strove together.—The woman represents the fratricide as unpremeditated and without malice. This really made the case essentially different from that of Absalom; but at this point of the story the object is to dispose the king favorably toward the culprit, while by the time the

application is reached this point will have passed out of mind.

(7) We will destroy the heir also.—The woman puts this into the mouth of the family, because this would be the result of what they proposed. The effect of the parable is greatly heightened by this, and there is no doubt intended a covert allusion to Absalom as the heir of David.

(13) Against the people of God.—The woman finds that the time has come when she must show the king that he stands condemned for his conduct toward Absalom by his own decision. She does this cautiously; she rather hints at than plainly expresses what she wants to say. Her first point is that the king is in some way wronging the people, and then that he does this in opposition to the spirit of the decision he has just given, by leaving Absalom (whom she does not name) in banishment.

(14) We must needs die.—The woman now goes on to a further argument from the uncertainty of life. She craftily withdraws attention from the real point—the question of right and justice—and, assuming that the thing ought to be done, suggests that delay is unsafe since life is uncertain.

(21) I have done.—This is the Hebrew text; the margin has "thou hast done." The former is simply a form of granting Joab's request; the latter would convey an implied censure of Joab's stratagem, although in the next clause there is a compliance with his wish.

(24) Let him not see my face.—David allowed Absalom's return, but forbade him his presence. The former had been done in weakness, the latter through a sense of justice. The effect of this half measure was unfortunate; Absalom was irritated, and yet placed in a favorable position to carry out his plots.

(26) Two hundred shekels.—The value of the shekel "after the king's weight" is unknown. If it was the same with the shekel of the sanctuary, the weight mentioned would be about six pounds.

(27) Three sons.—Their names are not given, from which it might be supposed that they died in infancy; and this is made sure by 18:18.

(32) If there be any iniquity.—Absalom makes no acknowledgment of having done wrong, but simply says that this state of half-reconciliation is intolerable. He must either be punished or fully pardoned. Joab's intercession accomplishes its purpose.

15

(1) Prepared him chariots and horses.— As a preparation for his rebellion, it was necessary to impress the people with his wealth and splendor. (Comp. I Kings 1:5.) This was the first use in Israel of chariots and horses as a part of regal pomp.

(3) There is no man deputed of the king.— Absalom uses the same arts which have been used by the demagogue in all ages. He does not accuse the king himself of wrong, but insinuates that the system of government is defective and expresses his own earnest wish to set things right.

(7) After forty years.—Absalom was born after David began his reign in Hebron, and his whole reign was only forty years. Absalom therefore was not yet forty at his death. The reading found in the Syriac and most MSS of the Vulgate, and adopted by Josephus, "four" years, is probably correct.

Pay my vow . . . in Hebron.—We have no means of knowing whether this vow was real or fictitious; certainly Absalom now uses it as a pretext, and yet there is nothing improbable in his having actually made such a vow during his exile. As a holy city and place of Absalom's birth, Hebron was well adapted to be the starting place of Absalom's rebellion; and it is likely that the men of Hebron may have resented the transfer of the capital to Jerusalem, and therefore have lent a willing ear to Absalom. He veils his crime under the cloak of religion, pretending submission to his father and receiving his blessing at the very moment when he is striking at his crown and his life.

(12) Sent for Ahithophel.—It is more likely that Ahithophel and many others of the tribe of Judah were alienated because, in the rapidly growing empire of David, their relative importance was of necessity constantly diminishing. It is noteworthy that the rebellion was cradled in Judah, and seems to have found there its chief strength. Psalm 41 may have been written on this occasion. Its ninth verse certainly applies pointedly to Ahithophel; and his conduct, both in his treachery and his suicide, forms a striking parallel to that of Judas, to whom this verse is applied in John 13:18. Many writers also consider that Ps. 55 was composed with reference to Ahithophel.

(18) See I Sam. 22:1, 2; 27:2; 29:2; 30:1-9; II Sam. 2:3; 5:6; 10:7; and note on 8:18.

(19) Ittai the Gittite.—From the fact that David afterward entrusted Ittai with the command of a third of his forces, it is clear that he must have been an experienced general. It cannot be shown positively that he was a proselyte, although this is probable. Here David neither means to recognize Absalom as king, nor yet to speak of him ironically; he only means to tell Ittai that, as a foreigner, he need not concern himself in such a question, but is quite justified in serving the king **de facto**, whoever he may be. Ittai's answer may be compared with Ruth's (Ruth 1:16, 17).

(23) The brook Kidron.—A valley with a watercourse, filled in winter, lying immediately east of Jerusalem, between the city and the Mount of Olives.

(26) Let him do to me as seemeth good.— David recognizes that he is suffering under the punishment pronounced by Nathan for his sin, and he seeks to throw himself entirely into the hands of God, trusting in His mercy. (Comp. 24:14.) He is, therefore, unwilling to have the Ark carried with him lest he should seem to undertake to compel the divine presence and blessing. He feels sure that if God so wills, he shall be brought again in peace; but if not, yet he will perfectly submit himself to God's ordering.

(34) Say unto Absalom.—David here counsels fraud and treachery, and Hushai willingly accepts the part assigned to him in order to thwart Ahithophel's counsel and weaken Absalom's rebellion. The narrative simply states the facts without justifying them.

16

(1) Ziba . . . met him.—It is evident from the sequel of the story (19:24-30) that Ziba grossly slandered his master, doubtless for the purpose of personal gain (see verse 4). This story was, indeed, almost too improbable to be believed; yet David, apt to be hasty in his judgments, was in a state to believe in any story of ingratitude and to be deeply affected by Ziba's large contribution to his necessities. Ziba shows entire want of principle, and could, therefore, have adhered to David's cause only because he had the shrewdness to foresee its ultimate success.

(10) So let him curse.—David, throughout, recognizes that all his sufferings were from the Lord's hand, and he wishes to submit himself entirely to His will. He does not, of course, mean to justify Shimei's wrong, but only to say that, as far as his sin bears upon himself, it is of divine appointment and he cannot resent it.

(11) How much more now may this Benjamite.—The "Benjamite" is in contrast to his own son, because he represents the adherent of another and rival dynasty. It is noticeable that David accuses Absalom not only of seeking his throne, but also his life.

(16) God save the king.—Absalom is surprised at Hushai's coming to him, and inclined to distrust one who has deserted his former friend and master. But Hushai succeeds in explaining his conduct as based upon the principle of loyalty to the government **de facto**; he argues that this has the divine authority, and his faithfulness to the former king is a pledge of faithfulness to the present one.

(21) And Ahithophel said.—The counsel of Ahithophel was in effect that Absalom should make the breach between him and his father absolute and irreconcilable. His followers would thus be assured of the impossibility of his securing a pardon for himself while they were left to their fate. After adopting this course, he must necessarily persist to the end. The taking of the harem of his predecessor by the incoming monarch was an Oriental custom, to the enormity of which the mind was blunted by the practice of polygamy.

(22) A tent upon the top of the house.—Nathan had foretold that the nature of David's public punishment should correspond to the character of his secret crime. The fact that this punishment takes place on the very roof where David had first yielded to his guilty passion makes it particularly striking.

17

(1) Pursue after David this night.—Ahithophel saw clearly that Absalom's success depended on striking an immediate blow. He felt confident, and perhaps with reason, that David in his distress and weariness was in no condition to resist a sudden attack. That he was wise in his counsel is made plain by the opposition of Hushai and the anxiety to send tidings to David with all speed.

(5) Call now Hushai.—The good sense of Absalom and all the people at once approved the counsel of Ahithophel; but, at

a crisis so important, Absalom sought the advice also of the other famous counselor of his father.

(11) I counsel that all Israel.—Hushai emphasizes all the possible hazards and contingencies of the plan recommended by Ahithophel, and proposes, on the other hand, a plan attended with no risk, on the supposition that the great mass of Israel already were, and would continue to be, on Absalom's side, a supposition which, with delicate flattery, he assumes as true.

(16) Lodge not this night.—Hushai's advice, couched in hyperbole and promising certain success (verse 13), had been taken at the moment, but it might easily be exchanged for Ahithophel's. At all events there was instant danger for David, and Hushai urges him to place the Jordan without delay between himself and the rebels.

(17) En-rogel.—A fountain just outside the city, on the boundary between the tribes of Benjamin and Judah (Josh. 15:7; 18:16). The loyalty of the high priests to David must have been well known, and it would have been quite unsafe for their sons to start from the city itself as bearers of tidings to David; even with all their care they were pursued. Their hiding place, however, was well chosen, as women resorted to the fountains to draw water, so that communications could be had without attracting observation.

(23) And hanged himself.—Ahithophel was moved, not merely by distress at the rejection of his counsel, but was shrewd enough to see that, with this delay, Absalom's rebellion would inevitably fail, and he himself be likely to come to a traitor's death.

(24) Mahanaim.—See note on 2:8. The same reasons which made it a favorable place for the capital of Ishbosheth recommended it also as a place of refuge to David and a rallying point for his adherents.

(25) Amasa.—Joab having adhered to David and gone away with him, Absalom chose his cousin to succeed him as commander-in-chief.

(26) Pitched in the land of Gilead.—Gilead is the tract of country on the east of the Jordan, extending from the land of Moab on the south to Bashan on the north. The site of Mahanaim has not been identified, but it was almost certainly within the territory of Gilead. Absalom, however, did not actually reach Mahanaim before he met and was defeated by the forces of David.

(27) Shobi the son of Nahash.—See 10:2; 12:29-31. It is possible that after dismantling the royal city David had left a brother of the late king as governor over the conquered territory, and that he now came forward to show his gratitude and faithfulness.

Machir the son of Ammiel.—See note on 9:4. David now reaps a reward for his kindness to the crippled son of Jonathan.

18

(3) Now thou art worth ten thousand of us.—The people urge truly that David is the very center of their whole cause, and suggest that, even while avoiding unnecessary exposure, he may yet be equally helpful by keeping a reserve in the city to help them in case of need.

(4) What seemeth you best.—David was willing to avoid the personal encounter with his son, and readily yielded. However, he encouraged the troops by reviewing them as they passed out, and improved the opportunity to give his generals special and public charge concerning Absalom. He speaks of him tenderly as "the young man" (verse 5; comp. verses 29 and 32), to imply that his sin was a youthful indiscretion.

(8) The wood devoured more.—The battle and the pursuit covered a wide range of country; more were slain in the pursuit through the wood, both by accident and by the sword, than in the actual battle itself.

(9) His head caught hold of the oak.—Absalom in his flight found himself among his enemies, and sought to escape into the denser parts of the forest. As he did so his head caught between the branches of a tree, his mule went from under him, and he hung there helpless. There is nothing said to support the common idea (which seems to have originated with Josephus) that he hung by his long hair, though this may doubtless have helped to entangle his head.

(14) I may not tarry thus.—Joab evidently feels the weight of the man's argument, but, determined on his deed of violence, he sees that it is worse than useless to delay. His act was simply murder. In a lawless age it was defensible as the one act which terminated the rebellion and made a renewal of it impossible, and destroyed a traitor and potential patricide who was likely otherwise to escape punishment. But it was a distinct disobedience of express orders, and Joab's taking the execution into his own hands was willful and deliberate murder.

Three darts.—The word means a "rod" or "staff." Joab seized such sticks as were at hand in the wood and thrust them into Absalom, giving him most painful and probably mortal wounds, but not instantly killing him.

(21) Cushi.—Rather, the "Cushite," probably an Ethiopian slave in Joab's service, for whose falling under the king's displeasure he had little care.

(32) Absalom.—To the Cushite's tidings David replies with the same question as before; but this messenger does not appreciate the state of the king's feelings, and answers with sufficient plainness, though in courteous phrase, that Absalom is dead.

(33) Was much moved.—David's grief was not merely that of a father for his son, but for that son slain in the very act of outrageous sin. His sorrow, too, may have gained poignancy from the thought—which must often have come to him during the progress of this rebellion—that all this sin and wrong took its occasion from his own great sin. Yet David was criminally weak at this crisis in allowing the feelings of the father completely to outweigh the duties of the monarch.

19

(5) And Joab came.—Joab's whole character appears strikingly in his conduct on this occasion. With his hand red with the blood of the beloved son, he goes, in the hardest and most unfeeling terms, to reproach the father for giving way to his grief. He treats the king with thorough insolence, and with the air of a superior; yet he counsels David for his own welfare and for that of the kingdom as a wise and loyal statesman. It may be doubted whether David yet knew of Joab's part in the death of Absalom.

For the Oriental custom to which Joab alludes, see note on Judg. 9:5.

(7) I swear by the Lord.—The statement which Joab emphasizes with this solemn oath is not that he will lead the people into revolt; but it is simply an assurance of the extreme danger of the course David was pursuing, put in such a strong and startling way as to rouse him from the selfishness of his sorrow.

(9) The king saved us.—With the collapse of the rebellion the accompanying infatuation passed away, and the people began to remember how much they owed David. There seems to have been a general disposition among the people to return to their allegiance, yet the movement was without organization or leadership.

(11) The elders of Judah.—Judah was naturally particularly slow in returning to its allegiance. It had shown special ingratitude to David and had formed the cradle and center of the rebellion. Even now Jerusalem probably had a garrison of Absalom's soldiers. They might naturally doubt how they would be received, and their military organization in Absalom's interest threw special obstacles in their way.

(13) Say ye to Amasa.—Amasa, like Joab, was David's nephew. In this offer of the commander-in-chief to the rebel general, David adopted a bold but rash and unjust policy. Amasa should have been punished, not rewarded for his treason. He had given no evidence of loyalty, nor was there proof that he would be trustworthy. Moreover, this appointment would be sure to provoke the jealousy and hostility of Joab. But David had long been restless under the overbearing influence of Joab (see verse 22; 3:39; 16:10), and now since he had murdered Absalom, was determined to be rid of him. He therefore took advantage of the opportunity by this means to win over to himself what remained of the military organization of Absalom.

(15) Judah came to Gilgal.—The two parties met at the Jordan, David coming from Mahanaim to the eastern side of the ford, near Jericho, and the representatives of the tribe of Judah to Gilgal on the opposite bank.

(20) The house of Joseph.—Joseph, as the name of the most prominent member, stands for all the tribes outside of Judah. The expression was used at the earliest date when there began to be a certain separation and distinction between Judah and the other tribes, which was soon after the conquest of Canaan (see Judg. 1:35). See also I Kings 11:28; I Chron. 5:1, 2; Pss. 80:1, 2; 81:5; Amos 5:15.

(23) The king sware unto him.—This oath of David assuring immunity to Shimei is to be viewed from a political point. Shimei had been guilty of high treason in David's distress. From the character of the man, and from Solomon's address to him in I Kings 2:44, it is plain that he remained thoroughly disloyal. David saw this, and hindered by his oath from treating him as

278

he deserved, pointed out the case to Solomon (see I Kings 2:8, 9). Solomon settled the matter by a compact; after a few years he violated this condition and was executed.

(25) Wentest not thou with me?—David had heard and believed the story of Mephibosheth's ingratitude and treachery (16:3, 4). But his present remonstrance is so gentle and kind as to show that Mephibosheth's appearance at once produced an impression, and suggested in David's mind a doubt of the truth of what Ziba had told him.

(41) All the men of Israel.—Jealousies between the tribes, and especially between Judah on the one side and the ten tribes on the other, had existed all along, the tribe of Ephraim being particularly sensitive (Judg. 8:1; 12:1). By the successful wars of Saul these jealousies were held in check, but broke out in national separation on his death. After seven and a half years they were partially healed by David and were kept in abeyance by the wise administration of Solomon; but at his death they broke out with fresh power and dismembered the nation for ever.

20

(2) Men of Judah clave.—David's negotiations with Judah had now resulted in an entire reversal of the position of the tribes toward him; Judah, among whom the rebellion originated and who had been tardy in returning to its allegiance, was now fierce in its loyalty, while Israel, who had only joined the already organized rebellion, and afterward had first proposed the return of David, had become alienated and rebellious.

(6) David said to Abishai.—David is determined to pass over Joab, and, therefore, when Amasa fails in this crisis, requiring immediate action, he summons Abishai and puts him in command of such forces as were at hand in Jerusalem, giving him orders for the rapid pursuit of Sheba.

(7) Joab's men.—This was the body of men usually under Joab's immediate command, and who would readily follow his brother, whom they had been accustomed to see associated with him. On Cherethites and Pelethites, see note on 8:18. "The mighty men" (see 23:8) appear to have been a special body of heroes, probably made up chiefly of those who had been with David in his life as an outlaw.

(8) As he went forth it fell out.—The object of this verse is to explain how Joab, in consequence of the arrangement of his dress, was able to stab Amasa without his purpose being suspected. He had a girdle bound around his military coat, and in this he had stuck a dagger so arranged that it might fall out as he advanced. He then picked this up naturally in his left hand, and stretching out his right hand to greet Amasa, his movements gave rise to no suspicion.

(10) In the fifth rib—"Abdomen." (See note on 2:23.)

(11) One of Joab's men.—Joab must put down the rebellion of Sheba by rapid action, and thereby render himself impregnable in the high office which had been his, and which he had now again usurped. He left one of his trusty men, however, by the body of Amasa, with a battle cry which should suggest that he had rightly been put to death for his doubtful loyalty, and that all who were attached to Joab and loyal to David should follow Joab. Joab's real motive for murdering Amasa, as for murdering Abner (3:27), was personal jealousy and ambition.

(15) Stood in the trench.—The "trench" is the space between the wall of the city and the lower outer wall. When the besiegers had succeeded in planting the mounds for their battering engines in this space, they had already gained an important advantage.

(18-21) Abel, at the extreme north of the land, had become proverbial for its wisdom. Joab strongly disclaims the idea of any further harm to any one than the necessary destruction of the rebel Sheba.

(23-26) In the four closing verses of this chapter there is again given a short summary of the chief men of David's reign, as if to form the conclusion of this account of his life. A similar summary has already been given in 8:16-18, and the changes introduced here mark a later period of the reign.

21

(1) Then there was.—It is plain from verse 7 that the events here narrated occurred after David had come to know Mephibosheth; and if in 16:7 there is an allusion to the execution of Saul's sons, it must have happened before the rebellion of Absalom. The narrative is omitted from the Book of Chronicles.

Three years.—A famine in Palestine was always a consequence of deficient winter rains, and was not very uncommon; but a famine enduring for three successive years was alarming enough to awaken attention and to suggest some special cause.

Inquired of the Lord.—The phrase is a different one from that often used in Judges and Samuel, and agrees with other indications that this narrative may have been obtained by the compiler from some other records than those from which he drew the bulk of this book.

(2) Two questions are often asked in connection with this narrative (see Josh. 9): (1) Why the punishment of Saul's sin should have been so long delayed? and (2) why it should at last have fallen upon David and his people, who had no share in the commission of the sin? The answer to both questions is in the fact that Israel both sinned and was punished **as a nation**. The lesson of the continuity of the nation's life, and of its continued responsibility from age to age, was greatly enhanced by the delay. Besides this, there were so many other grievous sins for which Saul was to be punished, that it was hardly possible to bring out during his lifetime the special divine displeasure at this one.

(4) No silver nor gold.—Money compensations for sins of blood were extremely common among all ancient nations, but were expressly forbidden in the Law of Moses (Num. 35:31). In this respect the Gibeonites appear to have accepted the teaching of the Law of Israel.

(6) Let seven men of his sons.—The head of the house and his household were closely identified in all the ideas of antiquity. Saul being dead, his male descendants were considered as standing in his place, representing him, and responsible for his acts, just as is largely the case in legal affairs and matters of property at the present day. The method of execution for the seven (a number denoting completeness) is that of hanging or fastening to a stake, either by impaling or by crucifixion, the word being used for both methods of execution.

Unto the Lord—i.e., publicly. The sin had been outrageous; its punishment must be conspicuous. The place of execution is fitly chosen in the home of Saul. The expressions "the Lord's chosen" and "unto the Lord" go together; what Saul had done he had done as the head of the theocracy, as

279

God's chosen ruler, and now his family must be punished in the presence of Him against whom he had offended.

(8) Took the two sons of Rizpah.—David took no advantage of this opportunity to strengthen himself further against the house of Saul. His choice of victims was directly opposed to such a supposition. He spared, for Jonathan's sake, the only descendants of Saul in the male line who could have advanced any claim to the throne. The text has "Michal" instead of "Merab"; but this must be an error of the scribe, since it was Merab, not Michal, who was married to "Adriel the Meholathite," and Michal was childless (6:23).

(9) The beginning of barley harvest.—This was immediately after the Passover (Lev. 23:10, 11), and therefore about the middle of April. The rains of autumn began in October, so that Rizpah's watch must have been about six months. It was not until these rains began (which may probably have been somewhat earlier than usual) that the people were assured of the divine forgiveness, and therefore the bodies of the executed were left unburied until then.

(15) Had yet war again.—This, like the preceding narrative, bears no note of time except that it occurred after some other wars with the Philistines; but this is only to say that it was after David ascended the throne. From the latter part of verse 17 it is plain that it must have been after David had become king of all Israel, and probably after he had become somewhat advanced in years. (See I Chron. 20:4-8, where again chronology is not the design.)

In the verses that follow, the state of the text accounts for variations from Chronicles.

(17) Sware unto him.—This was a solemn transaction, by which David should hereafter be restrained from personal exposure in battle. That he should be spoken of as "the light of Israel" implies that his government over all Israel had continued long enough already to make its immense benefits sensible.

22

This chapter, with numerous slight variations, constitutes Ps. 18, the first verse here serving as the title there, with only such differences as the nature of the Book of Psalms required. With this title may be compared the inscriptions of other historical psalms, as Exod. 15:1; Deut. 31:30.

No more definite time can be assigned for the composition of this hymn of thanksgiving than that already given in its title. Verse 51 shows that it must have been after the visit of Nathan promising the perpetuity of David's kingdom. On the whole, the form given in the Psalms seems to be the later, and to have been in some points intentionally altered—probably by David himself—to adapt it to the exigencies of liturgical worship.

These two recensions of this magnificent hymn are instructive, as showing that Providence has dealt with the MSS of the Old Testament as with those of the New, securing them during the long succession of ages from all substantial error, and yet not so destroying ordinary human action but that mere slips of the pen should sometimes creep in, and care and diligence be required to ascertain precisely what was originally written, and sometimes, perhaps, in the merest minutiae, leaving the original form still uncertain.

23

(1) The son of Jesse said.—The word "said," used twice, is a peculiar form (used more than two hundred times) of direct divine utterances, and applied to human sayings only here, in Num. 24:3, 4, 15, 16, and in Prov. 30:1, in all of which special claim is made to inspiration. This prophecy has not been incorporated into the Book of Psalms, because it is not a hymn for public worship, although an unquestionable utterance of David, and laying special claim to divine inspiration.

(2) The Spirit of the Lord spake by me.—In accordance with verse 1, there is here, and also in the next clause, most explicit assertion that this was spoken under the prompting and guidance of the divine Spirit.

(5) Although my house.—The LXX, the Vulgate, and the Syriac interpret this to mean that David recognizes how far he and his house have failed to realize the ideal description set forth; yet since God's promise is sure, this must be realized in his posterity. (Comp. Nathan's promise in chap. 7.)

(6, 7) The figures used are to show that, although the wicked injure whatever touches them, means will yet be found by which they may safely be put out of the way.

The Chaldee Targum, giving the ancient Jewish interpretation of the prophecy, offers a Messianic application to the whole. (Comp. Ps. 72.)

(8) These be the names.—Here, in the summary at the close of David's reign, is naturally given a list of his chief heroes. A duplicate of this list, with several variations, and with sixteen more names, is given in I Chron. 11:10-47, which is useful in correcting such clerical errors as have arisen in both. The list in Chronicles is given in connection with David's becoming king over all Israel; but in both cases the list is not to be understood as belonging precisely to any definite time, but rather as a catalog of the chief heroes who distinguished themselves at any time in the life of David. Of but few of them is anything further known.

24

(1) Again.—The word clearly refers to chap. 21, and so places this after the three years' famine for the Gibeonites. The fact that Joab was engaged in the work nearly ten months (verse 8) shows that it must have been a time of profound peace. The story in Chronicles is immediately followed by the account of David's final preparations for the building of the Temple. All these considerations concur in placing it near the close of his reign.

Kindled against Israel.—This was not in consequence of the numbering of the people (see Exod. 30:12; Num. 1 and 26), but in consequence of that which ultimately led to that act. We are not told why the anger of the Lord was kindled, but doubtless because He saw both in king and people that rising spirit of earthly pride and reliance on earthly strength which led to the sin.

He moved.—The pronoun here stands for "the Lord," yet in I Chron. 21:1 the temptation is attributed to Satan, and Satan is clearly meant of the devil, and not simply of "an adversary." This is a striking instance of attributing directly to God whatever comes about under His permission. And yet it is more than that. God has established immutable spiritual as well as material laws, or rather those laws themselves are but the expression of His unchanging will. Whatever comes about under the operation of those laws is said to be His doing.

David's numbering the people was the natural consequence of the condition of worldliness and pride into which he had allowed himself to fall. God then moved him, because He had from the first so ordered the laws of the spirit that such a sinful act should be the natural outcome of such a sinful state.

The word "number" in this verse is a different one from that used in the rest of the chapter, and means simply to "count," while the other conveys the idea of a military roll or list.

(3) Why doth my lord?—Even in the eyes of the unscrupulous Joab David's act was abominable. Joab never gives evidence of being influenced by religious motives, but his natural shrewdness sufficed to show him that David's act was at variance with the fundamental principle of the national existence.

(5) Pitched in Aroer.—The census began on the east of Jordan, at the extreme south, from there passed northward through the eastern tribes, and crossing the Jordan, passed southward through the western tribes. Aroer is the city described in Deut. 2:36 and Josh. 13:16 as on the river Arnon, at the extreme southern border of the trans-Jordanic territory.

(9) In Israel eight hundred thousand.—Here Israel is said to be 800,000, in Chronicles, 1,100,000; but the latter probably includes an estimate of the omitted tribes of Benjamin and Levi, and perhaps of portions of other tribes. There is no reason to doubt the general reliability of the round numbers, which would give a probable total population of five or six million, or from 415 to 500 to a geographical square mile—a number not at all impossible in so fertile a country.

(11) For when David.—There is no suggestion in the original that David's repentance was in consequence of the visit of Gad; on the contrary, it was in consequence of his repentance and confession that the prophet was sent to him.

(13) Seven years.—In Chronicles "three years," and so the LXX reads here also. This would be more in accordance with the "three" months and "three days."

(14) Let us fall now into the hand of the Lord.—Here the spirit of David in his earlier years reappears; he chooses that form of punishment which seems to him most directly and immediately dependent upon God Himself. He places himself in His hands rather than suffer those other punishments in which the will of man seemed to have a greater share. And it may be noticed also that he chooses that form of punishment which from his own royal position would afford him no immunity.

(17) These sheep.—David seeks to take all blame to himself, and prays that punishment may fall only upon him and his father's house. But his prayer was impossible to be granted. Such was the divinely ordained federal relation between the ruler and his people that they were necessarily involved in the guilt of their head.

(18) Threshing-floor of Araunah.—This was on the lower hill of Mount Moriah, which afterward became the site of the Temple, and was included within Jerusalem. It was doubtless this event that determined the Temple site.

(24) Of that which cost me nothing.—The principle on which David acted is that which essentially underlies all true sacrifice and real giving to God.

For fifty shekels of silver.—In I Chron. 21:25 the reading is "six hundred shekels of gold by weight." In one of the places the statement of price must have been altered in transcription. In the entire uncertainty as to the extent of the purchase of Araunah (the whole hill of Moriah, or only a part), and of the value of land in the locality and at the time, it is impossible to decide between the two.

(25) Built there an altar.—Thus, with David's repentance and reconciliation to God after his second great sin this narrative and this book close. David's reign and life were now substantially ended, a witness to all time of the power of divine grace over human infirmity and sin, of God's faithfulness and mercy to those who trust in Him, and of the triumph of an earnest and humble faith notwithstanding some great and grievous falls.

FIRST KINGS

1

(1) Now king David.—"Now" is the simple illative conjunction "and." It marks the general conception of the unity of the whole history, but implies nothing of special connection of time or authorship with the books of Samuel. (See II Chron. 9:29; the Books of the Kings must be considered a compilation of royal annals, temple records, and biographies of the prophets.) In fact, although these books are in some sense the continuation of the former, yet the narrative is hardly continuous. The history passes at once to the closing scene of David's life, leaving a comparative blank in the period succeeding the restoration after the defeat of Absalom—a blank which is partly filled up in the later books (I Chron. 22-29).

Stricken in years—about seventy years old. Since "clothes" mean "bed-clothes," the meaning is that the king was now too feeble to rise from his bed.

(3) A Shunammite.—Shunem is in the territory of Issachar (Josh. 19:18), and in the plain of Jezreel (I Sam. 28:4), near Mount Gilboa. As Eusebius calls it "Sulem," it has been conjectured that Abishag is the "fair Shulamite" of the Song of Solomon (6:13). The conjecture certainly throws some light on the occurrences of 2:13-25. Probably the whole notice of Abishag is only introduced on account of her subsequent connection with the fate of Adonijah.

(5) Adonijah, David's fourth son, born in Hebron (II Sam. 3:4), at least thirty-three years before. From 2:22 we may gather that he claimed the throne since he was now the eldest son. Therefore it is probable that Chileab (see note on II Sam. 3:3), the second son, was dead, as well as Amnon and Absalom. The means which Adonijah employed are exactly imitated from the example of Absalom (II Sam. 15:1). But Adonijah hardly shows the craft and ruthless determination of the elder rebel. His attempt on the crown seems crude and ill-planned in conception, and wanting in promptness of action.

(7) Joab.—The Books of I and II Samuel have brought out clearly the career and character of Joab, as being (in some degree like Abner) a professed soldier, raised to a formidable and half-independent power by the incessant wars of Saul and David. He

stands out in consistent portraiture throughout, as a bold, hard, and unscrupulous man, yet not without some right instincts of policy and of duty to God.

Abiathar the priest.—Of Abiathar we also know that he had been the companion of all David's adversity, and his reign at Hebron; that he was installed (with Zadok) as high priest at Jerusalem; and that he remained faithful to David in the rebellion of Absalom.

The adhesion of these two faithful servants of David to the rash usurpation of Adonijah seems strange at first sight. The explanation would seem to be that the attempt of Adonijah was not viewed as an actual rebellion. Solomon was young; David's designation of him for the succession might be represented as the favoritism of dotage; and the assumption of the crown by the eldest son, a man in the prime of life and of popular qualities, might seem not only justifiable, but even right and expedient.

(8) Zadok the priest (son of Ahitub) was the representative of the family of Eleazar, elder son of Aaron, as Abiathar of the family of Ithamar, the younger son (I Chron. 24:3).

Benaiah, the son of Jehoiada, a chief priest and therefore of Levitical origin. His command of the bodyguard gave him special importance, second only to that of Joab (II Sam. 20:23), and perhaps of even greater importance for immediate action.

Nathan the prophet.—See II Sam. 7:2; 12:1, 25. In the whole chapter he appears as a chief officer and counsellor of David, rather than in the loftier aspect of the prophetic character. He was also the royal chronicler of the reigns of David and Solomon (I Chron. 29:29; II Chron. 9:29).

Shimei, and Rei.—Of Rei, we have no mention elsewhere; but there is a Shimei (in I Kings 4:18), a high officer of Solomon.

The mighty men.—It is commonly inferred that they were the successors of the six hundred men of David's band during his life of wandering and exile, and that "the three" and "the thirty" (II Sam. 23) were their officers.

(11) Wherefore Nathan.—The initiative taken by Nathan is especially natural, since he had been the medium both of the prophecy to David of the son who should build the Lord's house (II Sam. 7:12-15) and of the blessing on Solomon (II Sam. 12:25).

(13) Didst not thou ... swear.—Of this

oath we have no mention elsewhere. It may have belonged to the time of Solomon's birth (II Sam. 12:24, 25). In I Chron. 22:6-13, we find a designation of Solomon for succession, apparently earlier than this time, it being clearly understood (see verse 20); according to Oriental custom, that such designation, without strict regard to priority of birth, lay in the prerogative of the reigning king.

(21) Shall sleep with his fathers.— Without connecting with the use of this phrase anything like the fullness of meaning which the New Testament attaches to "the sleep" of the departed servants of God, it seems reasonable to recognize in it at least a rudimentary belief in death as rest and not extinction. The addition "with his fathers" has probably a reference to "the tombs of the kings."

(32) Call me Zadok.—This sudden flash of the old energy in David, and the clear, terse directions which he gives, are striking in contrast with the timidity and despondency with which he had received the news of Absalom's rebellion. Then he felt the coming of God's threatened chastisement; now he knows that God is on his side.

(33) Gihon ("breaking forth") is clearly a place in the valley, under the walls of Jerusalem (II Chron. 32:30).

(34) Anoint him ... king.—As in the appointment of Saul and David himself, the right to anoint was recognized as belonging to the prophetic order (see 19:16), inasmuch as it signified the outpouring of the Holy Spirit of the Lord. (Comp. Acts 10:38.) In the case of David, such anointing had marked (I Sam. 16:13) his first private designation for the kingdom by Samuel, and his public accession to royalty, first over Judah (II Sam. 2:4), then over all Israel (II Sam. 5:3).

(35) Over Israel and over Judah.—The phrase clearly refers to the distinction, already tending to become a division, between Israel and Judah in relation to the monarchy. In the case of David himself, it may be observed that the record of his accession to royalty over Israel contains the notice of "a league" made by him with the elders of Israel (II Sam. 5:3), to which there is nothing to correspond in the account of his becoming king over Judah (II Sam. 2:4). This perhaps indicates from the beginning a less absolute rule over the other tribes. Certainly the history of II Sam. 15:10, 13; 18:6, 7; 19:41-43; 20:1, 2, shows a looser

allegiance of Israel than of Judah to the house of David.

(38) The Cherethites, and the Pelethites.— See II Sam. 8:18; 15:18; 20:7, 23. The bodyguard—perhaps of foreign troops— "the executioners and runners" to carry out the king's commands.

(39) An horn of oil out of the tabernacle.— The Tabernacle proper was still at Gibeon (see II Chron. 1:3); but a tent or tabernacle had been set up in Zion over the Ark (II Chron. 1:4).

(49) And all the guests.—Nothing is more striking than the sudden and humiliating collapse of the attempt of Adonijah, strongly supported as it was by Joab and Abiathar, in contrast with the formidable character of the rebellion of Absalom. This is another indication that the royal power had been greatly consolidated during the last peaceful years of David's reign.

(50) The horns of the altar.—The horns were projections from the attar, to which (see Ps. 118:27) the victims were fastened, and on which the blood was sprinkled (Exod. 29:12). To take hold of them was, of course, to claim the right of sanctuary. Adonijah, by the acknowledgment of Solomon, seems to represent his usurpation as one of those acts of haste and inadvertency, to which alone sanctuary was conceded (see Exod. 21:14).

2

For the interval between the two chapters, see I Chron. 28 and 29.

(3) Keep the charge.—The main charge to Solomon is noble enough. He is to "show himself a man," in spite of his youth; he is to take heed in all things to follow the law of the Lord; he is to trust both in the general promise of God to obedience, and in the special promise made to the house of David (II Sam. 7:12-16). It is remarkably in harmony with the beautiful psalm, "the last words of David," preserved in II Sam. 23:3-5. Nor does it accord less with the equally beautiful prayer of I Chron. 29:18, 19, for Solomon and for the people.

(5-9) In the special charges that follow we see the worldly prudence of the old statesman, and in one case some trace of a long-remembered grudge, singularly true to imperfect human nature, although utterly unworthy of an ideal picture of a hero-king. (See II Sam. 3:27-29, 37-39; 16:5-8; 19:18-23, 37-40; comp. Ps. 69.)

(10) Buried in the city of David—that is, evidently in Mount Sion (see Neh. 3:16; II Sam. 5:7, 9). They became the regular tombs of the kings, with some exceptions. It was in token of special honor that the high priest Jehoiada, the preserver of the royal dynasty, was buried there (see II Chron. 24:16).

(12) His kingdom was established greatly.—From the events in verse 25 to the closing of the chapter it would seem that, under the smooth surface of apparent loyalty, there lurked some elements of disaffection and danger. And we may gather from 11:14-25 that the death of David was the signal for some attempts at rebellion in the conquered nations.

(13) And Adonijah ... came.—While the wives of the king, being many, are seldom held to be of any great political account, the mother of the reigning king is a person of great dignity and influence. We may notice how constantly the name of each king's mother is recorded in the history.

(15) Thou knowest.—The petition had a covert design, for, by universal Eastern custom, to take a king's wives was the known privilege or duty of his successor. If, therefore, Adonijah had publicly espoused Abishag, it might have seemed a virtual renewal of his claim to the crown. This Solomon sees at once, though Bath-sheba, strangely enough, does not see it.

(22) And why dost thou ask?—In Solomon's answer there is a certain bitterness, venting itself in irony. His passionate feeling certainly gives some probability to the conjecture (see note on 1:3) that Abishag was the "fair Shulamite" of the Song of Solomon, already loved by the youthful king. In his wrath he infers, rightly or wrongly, that the hand of the conspirators is seen in this petition, and executes vengeance accordingly, summarily and without giving them any trial or opportunity of excusing themselves.

(27) That he might fulfill.—The prophecy referred to is I Sam. 2:30-35; 3:11-14. While the Tabernacle remained at Gibeon under Zadok's charge, and the Ark was in Mount Zion under Abiathar, there might, indeed, be something like co-ordination between the two. This, in any case, must have disappeared at the building of the Temple; and the disgrace of Abiathar determined that the undivided dignity should pass to Zadok.

3

(1) Pharaoh king of Egypt.—It would appear, from the Egyptian records and traditions, that at this time Egypt was weak and divided, and that what is called the twenty-first dynasty of the Tanite kings was ruling in Lower Egypt. This, and a corresponding abeyance (judging from the monuments) of Assyrian power, gave scope for the rise to sudden greatness and wealth of the Israelite kingdom under Solomon. The sacred historian finds no fault with the alliance, for the Egyptians were never looked upon with the same aversion as the strange women of the Canaanite races.

(2) In high places.—The historian writes from the point of view of his own time, when, after the solemn consecration of the Temple, the worship at "the high places," which form natural sanctuaries, was forbidden. These high places were of two kinds: places of sacrifice to false gods; and unauthorized sanctuaries of the Lord, probably associating His worship with visible representations of deity. The former class were, of course, absolute abominations, like the high places of the Canaanite races, so sternly denounced in Deut. 12:2, 3. The prohibition of the other class of high places appears to have had three distinct objects: to guard against all local corruptions of God's service, and all idolatry, worshiping Him (as at Bethel) under visible forms; to prevent the breach of national unity, by the congregation of the separate tribes round local sanctuaries; and to serve as a remarkable spiritual education for the worship of the invisible God, without the aid of local and visible emblems of His presence, in accordance with the higher prophetic teaching, and preparatory for the perfect spirituality of the future. It is, indeed, hardly to be conceived that there should not have been before the Captivity some places of non-sacrificial worship, in some degree like the synagogues of the period after the exile, although not as yet developed into a fully organized system. These places of prayer and praise and instruction would be different in their whole idea from the "high places" rivaling the Temple. After the solemn consecration of the Temple, the circumstances and the character of such worship were altogether changed.

(4) Gibeon.—The name itself indicates its position on the central plateau of Israel, in the land of Benjamin, where rise several round hills, on one of which the town stood. There the Tabernacle was now reared.

(5) The Lord appeared.—This direct communication to Solomon by a dream is perhaps the first indication of some temporary abeyance of the prophetic office, and of a loss of leadership in the priesthood. At the same time it is to be noted that the vision of the Lord through dreams, being of a lower type than the waking vision, is mostly recorded as given to those outside the Covenant, as belonging to the early stages of revelation, and as marking the time of cessation of the regular succession of the prophets during the Captivity.

(6) And Solomon said.—On Solomon's "wisdom," see note on 4:29. Here it is clear that the wisdom which he asks is that involving elements both moral and intellectual. His age is variously estimated from twelve to twenty at this time. In the characteristic spirit of the true godliness of the Old Testament, he looks for wisdom, not as the mere result of human teaching and experience, but as an inspiration of God, and prays for it accordingly, in a prayer of singular beauty and humility, pleading simply God's promise to his father and its fulfillment in his own accession to the throne. (Comp. Matt. 6:33).

(14) I will lengthen.—In this promise only one point, "length of days," is conditional; and it was not fulfilled. Though Solomon's age at the time of death is not given, yet, as his reign is given as lasting forty years, it could hardly have exceeded sixty. The rest received an extraordinary fulfillment. Then, for the first and last time, did the monarchy assume something of the character of an empire, unequalled in peaceful prosperity of wealth and power, and in splendor of civilization.

(16) Then came there.—The celebrated "judgment of Solomon," given here as a specimen of his wisdom, is simply an instance of intuitive sagacity. It is in the knowledge how to risk failure rather than be reduced to impotence, and how to go straight to the heart of a difficulty when the slow, regular approaches are impossible, that we recognize what men call "a touch of genius," and what Scripture here calls the "wisdom of God."

4

(1) King over all Israel.—The emphasis

laid upon "all" is characteristic of the writer, who compiled the book after the disruption of the kingdom. This record is evidently drawn from the national archives.

(2) And these were.—The officers described are of two classes—those attached to Solomon's Court, and those invested with local authority.

The princes appear to be Solomon's high counselors and officers. It is significant that whereas in the lists of David's officers in II Sam. 8:16-18; 20:23-26, the captain of the host stands first, and is followed in one list by the captain of the bodyguard, both are here preceded by the peaceful offices of the priests, scribes, and the recorder.

Azariah the son of Zadok the priest.—In I Chron. 6:9, 10, we find Azariah described as the son of Ahimaaz, and so grandson of Zadok, and as high priest at the time the Temple was built.

(3) Sons of Shisha.—Comp. I Chron. 18:16; II Sam. 20:25. Probably these are variations of the same name, and the office may have become virtually hereditary. The "scribe," is constantly referred to as a high officer, issuing the king's edicts and letters, and acting in his name.

Jehoshaphat the son of Ahilud is named in II Sam. 8:16; 20:24 and I Chron. 18:15 as having been under David also the "recorder" or "remembrancer," probably the analyst who drew up and preserved the archives of the kingdom.

(4) Zadok and Abiathar ... the priests.—Abiathar, though disgraced and practically deposed, was still regarded theoretically as priest, for the priesthood was properly for life.

(5) Son of Nathan.—Probably Nathan, son of David, and brother of Solomon (I Chron. 3:5), is here intended (see II Sam. 8:18).

(6) Adoniram ... over the tribute, evidently the head of Solomon's great public works. It is to be noticed that in the enumeration of David's officers in the early part of the reign (II Sam. 8:16-18) no such officer is found. It has been thought that the numbering of the people recorded in II Sam. 24 and I Chron. 21 was in preparation for such forced work.

(7) Provided victuals for the king and his household.—This denotes the collection of revenue—mostly, no doubt, in kind—for the maintenance of the Court and household and guards of the king; and perhaps may have included also the management of the royal domain lands, such as is described under David's reign in I Chron. 26:25-31. The office must have been of high importance and dignity, for in two cases (verses 11 and 15) the holders of it were married into the royal house. The provinces over which they had authority—nine on the west and three on the east of Jordan—coincide only in a few cases with the lands assigned to the several tribes. It is likely that by this time much of the tribal division of territory had become obsolete, although we see from I Chron. 27:16-22, that for chieftainship over men, and for levy in war, it still remained in force.

(20) Were many.—The description of the condition of the people here and in verse 25 is evidently designed to specify not only their general prosperity and wealth, but also the fact (see 9:20-22) that at this time they were a dominant race, relieved from all burden of labor, and ruling over the subject races, now reduced to complete subjection and serfdom. (That it was otherwise hereafter is clear from the complaints to Rehoboam in 12:4.) Now, for the first time, did Israel enter on full possession of the territory promised in the days of the Conquest (Josh. 1:4), and so into the complete fulfillment of the promise to Abraham (Gen. 22:17).

(21) And Solomon reigned.—His dominion is described as extending on the south to the land of the Philistines and the border of Egypt, including what we call Arabia (see Ps. 72:10, and comp. 10:15); on the east to "the river" Euphrates, as far north as Tiphsah; on the west it would, of course, be bounded by the sea; and on the north it extended far beyond Damascus, probably up to the borders of the Assyrian Empire. As in all ancient Eastern empires, it represented, not an organized monarchy, but the supremacy of a dominant kingdom over tributaries gathered around. Such an empire would rise rapidly, and as rapidly fall to pieces; and in Solomon's case it was sustained less by military power than by the peaceful forces of wealth and policy, and was largely dependent on his own personal ascendancy.

(22) Measures.—The "measure" (**cor**) is variously estimated (from 42 to 86 gallons). In any case the quantity is large.

(24) On this side the river.—This translation, although it expresses the true reference, viz, to the country west of the Euphrates, is literally incorrect. The words mean "on the further side of the river," considered from the point of view of

Babylon (see the use in the later books, or in Ezra 4:6; 6:6; etc.), and accordingly indicate composition at the time of the Exile, or, at any rate, at a period when the Babylonish empire was so established in supreme sovereignty as to determine the geographical nomenclature of the East. (Azzah is the well-known Philistine city, Gaza.)

(26) Forty thousand.—It seems clear that "four thousand" should be read instead of "forty thousand." (Comp. 10:26 and II Chron. 9:25.) This multiplication of horses and horsemen had been forbidden to the future king (Deut. 17:16) but foretold by Samuel (I Sam. 8:11, 12). The Israelite armies, in frequent contradistinction from their enemies, had been thus far mainly of infantry (see Josh. 11:9). Such armies were powerful for defense, not for invasion.

(29) Wisdom and understanding . . . and largeness of heart.—In this passage, "understanding," which is high intellectual power, and "largeness of heart," which is clearly capacity of knowledge, are both distinguished from the higher gift of wisdom, to which they are but means; the one is the capacity of wisdom within, the other the education of that capacity from without. Wisdom, in the true sense in which it is used in Scripture, is properly the attribute of God, and then, by His gifts of revelation and inspiration, reflected in man.

(30) The wisdom of all the children of the east.—What their wisdom was, the utterances of Job and his friends may testify, showing as they do large knowledge of nature and of man, speculating on the deepest moral questions, and throughout resting upon the consciousness of the one God. The Egyptian wisdom (as the monuments show) was a part of a more advanced and elaborate civilization, enriched by learning and culture, and manifesting itself in art and science, but perhaps less free and vigorous than the simpler patriarchal wisdom of the children of the east.

(31) He was wiser.—The wisdom of "Heman, Ethan, Chalcol, and Darda," then rivals of Solomon's fame, is now only known to us from this passage. (Comp. I Chron. 6:33, 44; 25:5; Pss. 88, 89, titles.)

(32) Proverbs.—If the "three thousand" of the text be intended to be taken literally, it is obvious that only a small part of Solomon's proverbs has been preserved. His declension into idolatry might induce care in selection, by such prophetic compilers as "the men of Hezekiah" (Prov. 25).

His songs.—We have still ascribed to

Solomon the "Song of Songs" and two psalms (72 and 127); but nothing else is, even by tradition, preserved to us. This passage is singularly interesting for it shows that the Old Testament Canon is not a collection of chance fragments of a scanty literature, but that out of a literature, which at this time, at any rate, was large and copious, deliberate selections by prophetic authority were made.

(33) He spake of trees.—An examination of the Song of Songs, Proverbs, Ecclesiastes, several of the psalms, and Job, which has been thought by some to belong to the age of Solomon, shows in them repeated exemplifications of a deep sense of the wonder and the beauty of nature, and also a keen observation of natural history in detail. If in the works here referred to, and now lost to us, there were (as Ewald supposes) "the rudiments of a complete natural history," it would be an anachronism to doubt that they were marked by these leading characteristics.

5

(1) Hiram is first mentioned in II Sam. 5:11 and I Chron. 14:1 as having sent workmen and materials to David for the building of his house. (Comp. I Chron. 22:4.) The message here from Hiram is clearly one of congratulation, perhaps of renewal of loyalty.

(6) Cedar trees out of Lebanon.—In the lower ranges of Lebanon there was a rich abundance of timber, especially precious to the comparatively treeless country of Palestine (see Ps. 104:16). The forest of Lebanon was proverbial for its beauty and fragrance (Song of Solomon 4:11; Hosea 14:6, 7), watered by the streams from the snowy heights (Jer. 18:14), when all Palestine was parched. Solomon's request—couched almost in the language of command—is simply for cedar wood, or rather, for skilled labor in felling and working it, for which the Tyrians were proverbially famed in all ancient records.

(9) Shall bring them.—The timber was to be carried down, or, perhaps, let down on slides along the face of the mountain toward the sea, and brought around by rafts to Joppa (II Chron. 2:16), to save the enormous cost and difficulty of land carriage. The grant of food for Hiram's household in return brings out that which is recorded so many ages afterward in Acts 12:20—that

the country of the Tyrians was "nourished" by Palestine. All their energies were turned, not to agriculture, but to seamanship (see Ezek. 27).

(13) Levy out of all Israel.—Thus exceptionally introduced (see 9:22) at first for the special service of God, it may have been the beginning of what was hereafter an oppressive despotism over the Israelites themselves. But the whole description suggests to us—what the history of Exodus, the monuments of Egypt, and the description by Herodotus confirm—the vast sacrifice of human labor and life, at which, in the absence of machinery to spare labor, the great monuments of ancient splendor were reared (see II Chron. 2:17).

(16) The chief of Solomon's officers.—The passage in II Chron. 2:18—reckoning them at 3,600—seems to imply that they were, like the overseers of Israel in the Egyptian bondage (Exod. 5:14, 15), taken from the subject races.

(18) The stone-squarers.—Comp. Ps. 83:7; Ezek. 27:9. As they are distinguished from Hiram's builders, it is possible that they were serfs under them, like the Canaanites under Solomon's builders.

6

(1) The date, given with marked precision, forms a most important epoch in the history of Israel, on which, indeed, much of the received chronology is based. The period includes the conquest and rule of Joshua, the era of the Judges down to Samuel, the reigns of Saul and David, and the three years of Solomon's reign already elapsed. Of these divisions, only the last three can be ascertained with any definiteness, at about eighty-three years. The time occupied by the conquest and rule of Joshua cannot be gathered with any certainty from the Scripture. The same is the case with the duration of some of the subsequent judgeships. (Note that Paul uses a round number, Acts 13:19-21.) These vague chronological statistics cannot constitute a sufficient ground for setting aside a date so formally and unhesitatingly given at an important epoch of the history, corresponding to the equally formal determination of the date of the Exodus in Exod. 12:40, 41.

(2-22) According to Exod. 26:16-23 the Temple itself was in all its proportions an exact copy of the Tabernacle, each dimension being doubled, and the whole, therefore, in cubical contents, eight times the size. It was, whatever measure we take for the cubit, a small building. Taking the usual calculation of eighteen inches for the cubit, the whole would be ninety feet long, thirty feet wide, and forty-five feet high. This likeness is carried out in the existence of the porch (which is even represented in II Chron. 3:4 as rising into a lofty entrance tower), the division of the house into two parts, like a nave and chancel, the provision of something like aisles (through opening outwards) and of gallery windows, and the high pitch of the roof. The "Oracle," or Most Holy place, was lower than the rest, forming an exact cube of thirty feet; the height of the Holy place (sixty feet long and thirty feet wide) is not given, but was probably the same, so that there would be an upper chamber over the whole under the roof—which, like that of the Tabernacle, appears to have been a high-pitched roof—fifteen feet high along the central beam, with sloping sides. The Temple was, in fact, only a shrine for the ministering priests—the outer court, or courts, being the place for the great assembly of the congregation—and it relied for magnificence not on size, but on costliness of material and wealth of decoration.

(23-28) Cherubims.—These were copied from the Tabernacle, but apparently with some differences, over and above the necessary increase of size, and the change of material from solid gold to olive-wood overlaid with gold (see Exod. 25:18-20; 37:7-9). The cherubim over the Ark are described only in three places in the Old Testament: in the passages in Exodus, here (and in the parallel II Chron. 3:10-13), and in those great visions of Ezek. 1:4-25; 10:1-22, which have determined the imagery of the Apocalypse. In no case is their form distinctly mentioned. But, whatever the cherubim were, it is certain that they were in no sense representations or emblems of deity, like the winged figures of Assyria or Egypt, with which they have been often compared. They appear to symbolize the great physical forces of the universe, as guided by superhuman angelic intelligence to serve the supreme will of God. (See Gen. 4:24; Ps. 18:10; Ezek. 1:10; Rev. 4:6-8; 5:8, 9.) Possibly the change of attitude of the cherubim in the Temple denoted a change of idea, characteristic of Solomon and his age. The old attitude is clearly that of worship of God;

the new rather of manifestation of His glory to man. (Comp. Isa. 6:3.)

(36) The inner court (probably the "higher court" of Jer. 36:10) is described as built around the Temple proper, evidently corresponding to the outer court of the Tabernacle. As this was (see Exod. 27:9-13) 50 cubits by 100, it may be inferred, that by a duplication similar to that of all dimensions of the Temple itself, Solomon's Court was 100 cubits (or 150 feet) by 200 cubits (or 300 feet), covering a little more than an acre. In this court stood the altar of burnt offering and the laver, and here all sacrifices were made. It was what was called afterward the "Court of the Priests," and in it (see Ezek. 40:45) appear to have been chambers for the priests.

The mention of the "inner court" suggests that there was an outer court also. (See II Kings 21:5; 23:12; Ezek. 40:17; 42:1, 8; Josephus. **Antt.** 8.3, §3.)

(37, 38) Zif corresponds to about May, Bul to about November. The whole time occupied was, therefore, seven years and a half.

7

(1) Solomon's "house" must have constituted a large group of buildings enclosed in a great court, situated on the western hill, which is opposite the Temple on Mount Moriah, with a viaduct crossing the intervening valley by which the king went up to the House of the Lord (see 10:5; I Chron. 26:16; II Chron. 9:4).

(2-5) The house of the forest of Lebanon—evidently so-called from the forest of cedar pillars which supported it—was apparently a great hall of audience, 150 feet long, 75 feet wide, and 45 feet high; along it rows of pillars ran longitudinally, supporting cedar beams and walls over them, and cedar roofs. This was the hall of state.

(7) The porch of judgment was clearly a separate building, not described in the text, except as having been floored and ceiled with cedar. It has been compared with the remains of Assyrian and Persian examples, having been square, supported on four pillars in the center, between which the throne stood, and having openings on the four sides for the public, the king, and his officers.

(8-11) The residence of the king, and the separate palace for the queen, distinct from the apartments of the inferior wives and concubines, are not described, except that they lay "within the porch," that is, in the rear in another court, and were of "like work." (See Jer. 22:14.)

(12) The great court.—This resembled the "inner court" of the Temple, and seems evidently to have enclosed the whole palace. It may have contained quarters for the guards and the household.

(13-50) The exceedingly graphic and elaborate description of the work of Hiram on the vessels and furniture of the Temple bears the most evident marks of historical accuracy and of the use of contemporary documents. Looked at in itself, it shows that the Temple depended for its effect, not so much on size or proportion, as on rich material, elaborate decoration, and costly furniture, on which all the resources both of treasure and art were lavished. But besides this, the sense of the special sacredness attached to all the vessels of the Temple, which was hereafter to degenerate into a Pharisaic superstition (see Matt. 23:16-18), suggested the most careful record of every detail, and reverently traced to "the Spirit of God" the gifts of the workmen. As in Bezaleel and Aholiab for the Tabernacle (Exod. 35:31, 32), so also in Hiram for the Temple.

(23-26) A molten sea—a gigantic laver for the ablution of the priests—corresponding to the laver of brass in the Tabernacle (Exod. 30:18-21; 38:8). It had a diameter of 15 feet, and a height of 7½ feet; it held 2,000 baths, that is, 17,000 gallons. The sea stood on twelve oxen, corresponding perhaps to the twelve tribes of Israel—the ox being possibly the same emblem which was used in the form of the cherubim—until it was taken down and placed on the pavement by Ahaz (II Kings 16:17), and, like the great pillars, was broken up at last by the Chaldeans for the sake of the brass (II Kings 25:13).

(27-29) The smaller lavers of brass for washing the sacrifices, and the movable bases on which they rested, are described still more elaborately. Each laver was 6 feet in diameter, and held 40 baths, or about 360 gallons. The whole stood high, no doubt to bring it nearly on a level with the brazen altar, which was 15 feet high. In form, perhaps, each laver was a smaller copy of the molten sea.

(39) The sea.—This was placed on the southeastern side of the Temple, on one side of the great altar; the ten smaller lavers were ranged five on each side.

(40) The lavers.—In II Chron. 4:1, and in Josephus' account, it is expressly said that a brazen altar, 30 feet square and 15 feet high was made by Hiram. Probably the absence of all mention of it here is simply an omission in the record.

(48) The altar of gold.—The altar of gold (6:20, 22) is the altar of incense. (See Exod. 30:1-10; Lev. 4:7, 18; 16:18, 19; Ps. 141:2; Heb. 9:11, 12, 24; 10:19-22.)

For the table of shewbread, see Exod. 25:23-28; 37:10-15; for the shewbread itself, see Lev. 24:5-9.

(49, 50) The candlesticks of pure gold.—Whether these ten candlesticks were to supersede the one seven-lighted candlestick made for the Tabernacle (Exod. 25:31-40; 37:17-24), or were to be used in addition to it, we are not told. The latter supposition is, however, far more probable. The candlestick is elaborately described in the history of the construction of the Tabernacle, as of great costliness of material and workmanship. Placed in the Holy Place, opposite the table of shewbread, and fed carefully with the sacred oil, it appears to have symbolized the gift of light to the world, as the shewbread the gift of life and sustenance, flowing from the presence of God.

The various other articles here mentioned are also enumerated in the description of the furniture of the Tabernacle, Exod. 25:29, 38.

(51) The things which David his father had dedicated.—For the account of the dedication of various treasures, by David and by the princes of Israel, for the House of the Lord, see I Chron. 18:8, 10, 11; 22:3-5, 14-16; 28:14-18, 29:2-5, 12, 14. The accumulation was enormous. It had evidently been the work of years to gather it out of the spoils of many victories, offered in that spirit of thankful devotion.

8

The beauty and spiritual significance of this chapter, which from time immemorial has been made to yield teaching and encouragement for the consecration of Christian churches, stand in remarkable contrast with the mere technical detail of the preceding; yet each, in its own way, bears equally strong marks of historical accuracy. The compiler must have drawn his information from some contemporary record, probably from some official document preserved in the temple archives.

Throughout the whole history, the sole majesty of the king is conspicuous. Solomon, and he alone, is for the time king, priest, and prophet, in one—in this a type of the true "Son of David," the true "Prince of Peace." It is likely that from this unequaled concentration on his head of temporal and spiritual dignity came the temptation to self-idolatry, through which he fell; and that the comparative abeyance of the counterbalancing influences wielded by the prophet and (in less degree) by the priest gave occasion to the oppressive, though splendid, despotism under which Israel groaned in later days.

(2) The month Ethanim (called after the Captivity **Tisri**), corresponded with the end of September and beginning of October. The feast in this month was the Feast of Tabernacles—of all feasts of the year the most joyful—marking the gathering in of all the fruits of the land, commemorating the dwelling in tabernacles in the wilderness, and thanking God for settlement and blessing in the land (Lev. 23:33-44). It was, perhaps, the time when the Israelites could best be absent from their lands for a prolonged festival; but there was also a peculiar appropriateness in thus giving it a higher consecration, by celebrating on it the transference of the Ark from the movable tabernacle to a fixed and splendid habitation. In this instance the festival was doubled in duration, from seven to fourteen days. (See verse 65.)

(4) The tabernacle of the congregation was still at Gibeon; and the priests and Levites had until now been divided between it and the lesser tabernacle over the Ark on Mount Zion. Probably each section of the priests and Levites now brought up in solemn procession the sacred things entrusted to them. (See Num. 3:25-37 for the order.) What became of the Tabernacle and its furniture (as far as this was disused), we are not told; but all was probably deposited, as a sacred relic of antiquity, somewhere in the precincts of the Temple (see II Macc. 2:4-6).

(6-8) The detail is given here for a good reason. Up to this time it had been forbidden to withdraw the staves (Exod. 25:13-15), so that the Ark might always be ready for transference; now the withdrawal marked the entrance on a new period, during which it was to rest unmoved.

The phrase "there they are unto this day" is an interesting indication of quotation from older documents, for at the time of the compilation of the book the Temple and all that it contained had been destroyed or removed. It is remarkable that in the record of the successive spoilings of the Temple by the Chaldaeans (II Kings 24:13; 25:13-17), nothing is said of their carrying away the Ark, which would have been the choicest, as most sacred, of all the spoils. (See Jer. 3:16.)

(9) There was nothing.—The emphasis of this (repeated in II Chron. 5:10) is remarkable, and seems intended to make it clear that the various things laid up "before the testimony"—the pot of manna (Exod. 16:33, 34), the rod of Aaron (Num. 17:10), the copy of the Law (Deut. 31:24-26)—were not in the Ark, but at "the side of the ark." Unless any change afterward took place— which is highly improbable—this clear statement must determine the interpretation of Hebrews 9:4. (See Exod. 25:16; 40:20.)

There is something singularly impressive in the special hallowing of the granite tables of the Law of Righteousness as the most sacred of all the revelations of the nature of God, thus indissolubly binding together religion and morality. (Comp. Jer. 23:6 and 31:33.)

(10) The cloud.—The bright Shechinah of the divine presence, at once cloud and fire— which had been the sign of the presence of God on Sinai (Exod. 24:15-18), and had hallowed the consecration of the Tabernacle (Exod. 40:34, 35)—now similarly descended on the Temple, as a sign of its acceptance with God. (See Ezek. 10:4, 18; Haggai 2:7, 9; comp. II Chron. 5:11-13.)

(14) And the king.—We are told in II Chron. 6:13 that the king stood on a "brasen scaffold" three cubits high, in the midst of the court before the altar of sacrifice, so that he could alternately turn toward the Temple and toward the people in the outer court.

(15-21) His address to the people— apparently preceded by a silent blessing with the usual uplifting of the hands—is the counterpart and expansion of the few abrupt words which he had just uttered before God, calling them to bless God with him for the fulfillment of one part of His promise to David in the present acceptance of the Temple.

(23-53) The prayer of Solomon, uttered (see verse 54) on his knees with hands uplifted to heaven, long and detailed as it is, is yet of extreme simplicity of idea. Verses 23-25 are a thankful acknowledgment of the fulfillment of one part of the great promise to David, and a prayer for the like fulfillment of the other; verses 26-30, acknowledging that God's presence can be limited to no Temple, yet asks that His peculiar blessing may rest on prayer uttered toward the place which He has hallowed; and verses 31-53 apply that petition to various contingencies, and extend it not only to Israel but to the stranger who shall acknowledge and invoke the Lord Jehovah. (See Lev. 26; Deut. 28.)

(23) There is no God like thee.—These words, used in Pss. 71:19; 86:8, 89:6), and especially found in the thanksgiving of David (II Sam. 7:22), are evidently suggested by more ancient utterances of devotion, as for example, in the first recorded psalm at the Red Sea (Exod. 15:11). In them we trace the spiritual process by which the Israelites were trained from the polytheism of their forefathers to the knowledge of the one only God.

(27, 28) Will God indeed dwell.—The thought expressed here exemplifies a constant antithesis which runs through the Old Testament. On the one hand, there is the most profound conception of the Infinity of the Lord whom "the heaven of heavens cannot contain"; and the spirituality of this conception is guarded by the sternest prohibition of that idolatry which limited and degraded the idea of God, and by rebuke of the superstition which trusted in an intrinsic sacredness of the Ark or the Temple. On the other hand, there is an equally vivid conviction that the infinite Jehovah is yet pleased to enter into a special covenant with Israel. The two conceptions co-exist in complete harmony, both preparing for the perfect manifestation of a "God with us" in the kingdom of the Messiah (comp. Acts 7:48). The words of Solomon in spirit anticipate the utterance of the prophet (Isa. 66:1), and even the greater declaration of our Lord (John 4:21-24) as to the universal presence of God to all spiritual worship.

(51-53) For they be thy people.—This pleading with God implies the belief not only that the declared purpose of God cannot fail, but that, even for the manifestation of His glory to man, it must necessarily be visibly fulfilled before the eyes of the world. (Comp. Exod. 32:12, 13; Num. 14:13, 14; Ps. 79:9, 10.) Indeed, all that might seem to us strange or unworthy in such prayers vanishes at once, when we consider that the knowledge of God in His self-manifestation is the highest happiness of man. Therefore, in the Lord's Prayer, the

three petitions "for God's glory," preceding all special petitions for our own needs, are really prayers for the highest blessing of all mankind. God's care for His glory is not for His own sake, but for ours.

(63) And Solomon offered.—The idea that the king on this occasion, and on others, performed the priest's ministerial office is manifestly improbable. At all times he who brought the sacrifice was said to "offer" it. The priest accepted it in the name of the Lord, and poured the blood at the foot of the altar of sacrifice, or sprinkled it on the altar of incense.

The number here given, enormous as it is, can hardly be supposed due to any error in the text, for it is exactly reproduced in the Chronicles and by Josephus. It is comparatively easy to conceive how such a mass of victims could be brought as offerings or consumed, when we consider the vastness of the assembled multitude from the whole of the great dominions of Solomon. (Verse 65 notes from Lebanon to the border of Egypt; see Num. 34:5; Josh. 15:4.) Even at the Passovers of the last days of Jerusalem the multitude of worshipers seems to have been numbered by hundreds of thousands.

9

(1) And it came to pass.—The variation in II Chron. 7:11 suggests that the notice in this verse is merely a summary of the history of chaps. 6-8, which records the whole of the building works of Solomon, and is not intended to fix the date of the vision of verses 2-9.

(3-9) And the Lord said unto him.—This vision of the Lord presents a remarkable contrast with that recorded in 6:11-13, while the Temple was being built. Then all was promise and encouragement, now only warning mingled with promise. In its reference to the two parts of the promise to David, there is a subtle and instructive distinction. As for the Temple, now just built in fulfillment of that promise, it is declared without reserve that, in case of unfaithfulness in Israel, it shall be utterly destroyed, and become an astonishment and a proverb of reproach before the world. But in respect of the promise of the perpetuity of David's kingdom—the true Messianic prediction, which struck the keynote of all future prophecies—it is only said that Israel shall be "cut off from the land," and so "become a proverb and a byword" in captivity. Nothing is said to contradict the original declaration, that, even in case of sin, the mercy of God would chastise and not forsake the house of David (II Sam. 7:13, 14; Ps. 89:30-37). So again and again in prophecy captivity is denounced as a penalty of Israel's sin; but the hope of restoration is always held out, and thus the belief in God's unchanging promise remains unshaken.

(14) Hiram sent to the king sixscore talents of gold.—The payment, on any calculation, was a large one, though little more than a sixth of Solomon's yearly revenue. (See 10:14.) It may possibly be a note referring back to verse 11, and explaining the amount of gold which Hiram had sent. If this is not so, it would then seem to be a payment in acknowledgment of the cession of the cities, as being of greater value than the debt which it was meant to discharge.

(15-28) The rest of the chapter consists of brief historical notes, partly referring back to the previous records. Thus, verse 15 refers back to 5:13; verses 20-22 to 5:15; verse 24 to 7:8; verse 25 is a note connected with the history of the dedication of the Temple.

(15) Millo.—It is possible that "the Millo" of Jerusalem may have been the name of a quarter of the old Jebusite city. From the derivation of the word ("heaping up") it would seem that the work was the raising of a high fortification of earth crowned with a wall, where the hill of Zion slopes down toward the valley.

Hazor, and Megiddo, and Gezer.—These cities were all of important geographical positions, and all had belonged to the subject races. Hazor was in the north, on high ground near the waters of Merom. Megiddo lay in the great plain of Jezreel or Esdraelon, the battlefield of Northern Palestine. Gezer or Gazer, was near Bethlehem, close to the maritime plain.

(17, 18) The three, Gezer, Beth-horon, and Baalath, evidently form a group of fortified places commanding the passes from the seacoast. Tadmor, or Palmyra, is described by Josephus as "in the desert above Syria, a day's journey from the Euphrates, and six long days' journey from Babylon the Great."

(19) That which Solomon desired to build.—See, in Eccl. 2:4-10, the description of the vineyards, gardens, and orchards in Jerusalem, and in Song of Solomon 2:10-13;

4:8; 7:11-13 the vivid pictures of the pleasure gardens of Lebanon. The text seems evidently to refer to these, in contradistinction from the cities of commercial and military importance previously mentioned.

(26) Ezion-geber.—See Num. 33:35; Deut. 2:8. It lies at the head of the Gulf of Akabah, the nearest point of the Red Sea, on the edge of the mountain country of Edom. Its very name ("the giant's backbone") indicates the nature of the country around it. From II Chron. 8:18 it appears that the ships, or the materials from which they were built, were sent from Tyre.

(27) Shipmen that had knowledge of the sea.—The Tyrians were known far and wide as the great sailors both of the Mediterranean and the seas beyond it. (See Ezek. 26-28). The Israelites, on the contrary, had but little care for the sea, and little knowledge of seamanship. Even at the height of their power they were content to use the maritime skill of the Tyrians, without encroaching upon their commerce or attempting to seize their famous ports. The sea is mostly regarded in the Old Testament in its terrible power of wave and storm, restrained from destroying only by the Almighty hand of God; and even the one psalm (Ps. 107:23-31), which describes the seafarer's experience, dwells with awe on "God's wonders in the deep." In the description of the glory of "the new heaven and earth" of the hereafter, it is declared with emphasis that "there was no more sea" (Rev. 21:1).

(28) Ophir.—All that can be certainly gathered from the mention of Ophir in the Old Testament is, first, that it was situated to the east of Palestine and approached by the Red Sea; and next, that so famous was the gold imported from it, that the "gold of Ophir" became proverbial (I Chron. 29:4; Job 22:24; 28:16; Ps. 45:9; Isa. 13:12). All else is a matter of speculation and tradition. Tradition is in favor of India.

10

(1) The queen of Sheba.—The name "Sheba" is found in the ethnological lists of Gen. 10:7, among the descendants of Cush of the Hamite race, in Gen. 10:28, among the Semitic Joktanites, and in Gen. 25:3, among the Abrahamic children of Keturah. The kingdom of Sheba referred to in this passage must certainly be placed in Arabia Felix, the habitation of the Joktanite race in which the Keturahites appear to have been merged. The queen of Sheba would therefore be of Semitic race, not wholly an alien from the stock of Abraham. It is probably from confusion between Sheba and Saba that Josephus (**Ant.** 8:6, 5) represents the queen of Sheba as a "queen of Egypt and Ethiopia."

Hard questions.—The "hard questions," or riddles, (in which Solomon is said by Josephus to have had a contest with Hiram also) must surely have been rather those enigmatic and metaphorical sayings, so familiar to Eastern philosophy, in which the results of speculation, metaphysical or religious, are tersely embodied. The writings representing the age of Solomon—Job, Proverbs, and Ecclesiastes—are all concerned with these great problems, moral and speculative, which belong to humanity as such, especially in its relation to God.

(6-9) And she said.—These words, repeated almost word for word in II Chron. 9:5-8, are clearly from some contemporary document. They breathe at once the spirit of Oriental compliment, and a certain seriousness of tone, as of a mind stirred by unusual wonder and admiration. It is worth notice that they touch but lightly on external magnificence and prosperity, and go on to dwell emphatically on the wisdom of Solomon, as a wisdom enabling him to do judgment and justice, and as a gift from Jehovah, his God.

(13) All her desire.—The terms here employed indicate a position of inferiority, although well graced and honored, in the queen of Sheba. Her present is of the nature of tribute.

(14) Talents.—The word properly signifies a "circle," or "globe," and the talent (among the Hebrews and other Orientals, as among the Greeks) denoted properly a certain weight. Based on Josephus' calculations, 666 talents would give a weight of gold now worth $20,000,000. But based on computations from Exod. 30:13-15; 38:25-28, the figure would be about $10,-000,000. Considering that this is expressly stated to be independent of certain customs and tributes, the smaller sum seems more probable; in any case, the amount is surprisingly large. But it should be remembered that at certain times and places accumulations of gold have taken place, so great as practically to reduce its value, and lead to its employment, not as a currency, but as a precious ornament. It is not improbable that the same may have occurred in the time of Solomon.

(22) A navy of Tharshish.—There seems little doubt that the Tarshish of Scripture is properly Tartessus in Spain, which name, indeed, is drawn from an Aramaic form of Tarshish. (See Gen. 10:4; Jonah 1:3; 4:2.) But the phrase "ships of Tarshish" appears to have become a technical phrase for ships of large size (see Isa. 2:16; 60:9; Ps. 48:7); hence a "navy of Tarshish" would not necessarily mean a navy going to Tarshish. (See note on II Chron. 9:21.)

(23-29) All the kings.—These verses indicate the character of the empire of Solomon as a loosely-compacted group of tributary states around the dominant kingdom of Israel, kept to their allegiance mainly by the ascendency of his personal wisdom and ability, partly by the ties of commercial intercourse and the attractions of his wealth and splendor, and to some degree by an imposing military force. In the grand description of it in Ps. 72, we observe that while its wealth and prosperity are painted in bright colors, the chief stress is laid on its moral greatness, as a kingdom of righteousness and peace. In this higher character it was the type of the kingdom of the true Son of David.

11

(1-13) The defection of Solomon is distinctly traced to his polygamy, contracting numerous marriages with "strange women." It was carried out on a scale corresponding to the magnificence of his kingdom, and probably had the political object of alliance with neighboring or tributary kings. We find it inherited by Rehoboam (II Chron. 11:18-21), and it probably became in different degrees the practice of succeeding kings. While polygamy, as everywhere in the East, had to some degree existed in Israel from patriarchal times, yet it must have been checked before by the marriage regulations of the Law. (See Exod. 34:12-16; Deut. 7:3, 4.)

(1) Moabites, Ammonites, Edomites, Zidonians, Hittites.—The first three of these races were kindred to Israel and of the stock of Abraham, and were now among the subjects of Solomon; the last two were of the old Canaanitish stock, and were now inferior allies. The marriage with the daughter of Pharaoh is apparently distinguished from these connections, which are so greatly censured (see Ezra 9:2, 11, 12; Neh. 13:23-29), for there is no mention of the introduction of any Egyptian idolatry.

(4) When Solomon was old.—The evil influence belonged to the time of senile feebleness, possibly the premature result of a life of indulgence. It is not at all likely that Solomon forsook the worship of God (see verses 5, 6, and 9:25); it would seem, rather, that his idolatry was the inclination to an eclectic adoption of various forms of faith and worship, as simply various phases of reverence to the one supreme Power, each having its own peculiar significance and beauty. Or, it may have been thought good policy to conciliate the subject races by doing honor to their religions, much as the Roman Empire delighted to do, when faith in its own religion had died out.

(5) Ashtoreth (or **Astarte**) was the goddess of the Zidonians, and possibly the Hittites, corresponding to Baal, the great Tyrian god, and representing the receptive and productive, as Baal the active and originative, power in Nature. The name **Milcom** is probably only a variety of the well-known **Molech**, which is actually used for it in verse 7. The name "Molech" is a general title, signifying only "king" (as Baal signifies "lord"), and might be applied to the supreme god of any idolatrous system. Thus the worship of "Molech," with its horrible sacrifice of children "passing through the fire," is forbidden in Lev. 18:21; 20:2, evidently as prevailing among the Canaanite races (comp. Ps. 106:37, 38). As the worship of Ashtoreth was stained with impurity, so the Molech-worship was marked by the other foul pollution of the sacrifice of human blood. The name **Chemosh** probably means "the Conqueror" or "Subjugator," and indicates a god of battles. In the history, moreover, of the Moabite war against Jehoram (II Kings 3:26, 27) it seems that to Chemosh, as to Molech, human sacrifice was offered.

(12, 13) For David my servant's sake—that is, in order to fulfill the promise to David. By the postponement of the chastisement, the blessing promised to his son personally would be still preserved; by the retaining of the kingdom, though shorn of its splendor, and limited to Judah, the larger and more important promise, the continuance of the family of David until the coming of the Messiah, would be fulfilled. The "one tribe" is Judah, with which Benja-

min was indissolubly united by the position of the capital on its frontier.

(14) Hadad the Edomite.—According to ancient authorities Hadad is a Syriac title of the sun—in this respect like the more celebrated title **Pharaoh**—assumed by the king, either as indicating descent from the sun-god, or simply as an appellation of splendor and majesty. The war here described is briefly noted with some differences of detail in II Sam. 8:12-14; I Chron. 18:11-13, and Ps. 60 (title and verse 8). It is referred to here in connection with the prophecy just recorded.

(23) Rezon the son of Eliadah.—The name **Rezon** (see "Rezin," II Kings 16), appears to signify "prince," and might naturally mark the founder of a new power in Damascus (see "Hezion," I Kings 15:18). The account of this war is found in II Sam. 8:1-13.

(26) Jeroboam the son of Nebat.—As the great rebel against the House of David, the leader of the revolution which divided Israel and destroyed its greatness, the introducer of the idolatry of the temples of Dan and Bethel, and the corrupter of the worship of Jehovah in deference to an astute worldly policy, he stands out in a vividness of portraiture unapproached, until we come to the history of Ahab at the close of the book.

(29) Ahijah the Shilonite.—We find in Ahijah the first of the line of prophets, who resumed a paramount influence like that of Samuel or Nathan, protecting the spirituality of the land and the worship of God, and demanding both from king and people submission to the authority of the Lord Jehovah.

(30) Rent it in twelve pieces.—The use of symbolical acts is frequent in subsequent prophecy (especially see Jer. 13:1; 19:1; 27:2; Ezek. 4; 5; 12:1-7; 24:3, 15), often alternating with symbolical visions and symbolical parables or allegories. The object is, of course, to arrest attention. Ahijah's rending of his own new garment is used, like Saul's rending of Samuel's mantle (I Sam. 15:27, 28), to symbolize the rending away of the kingdom.

(31-39) The message delivered by Ahijah first repeats exactly the former warning to Solomon, marking, by the two reserved pieces of the garment, the duality of the "one tribe" reserved for the house of David (see note on verse 13); next, it conveys to Jeroboam a conditional promise like that

295

given to David; and lastly, it declares that sin in the house of David should bring with it severe chastisement, but not final rejection (see II Sam. 7:14-16).

(40) Solomon sought therefore to kill Jeroboam.—From verse 26 it may be inferred that Jeroboam, characteristically enough, had not patience to wait for the fulfillment of the promise, and that he sought in some way by overt act to clutch, or prepare to clutch, at royalty.

Shishak king of Egypt.—The Shishak of the Old Testament is certainly to be identified with the **Sheshenk** of the Egyptian monuments; and the identification is an important point in the Biblical chronology, for the accession of Sheshenk is fixed by the Egyptian traditions at about 980 B.C. He was, therefore, king for the last fifteen years of Solomon's reign; and his favorable reception of the rebel Jeroboam indicates a natural change of attitude toward the Israelite power.

(41) The book of the acts of Solomon.— Comp. II Chron. 9:29. The prophets appear here in the character of analysts. The narrative as given in the Book of Kings is evidently a compilation drawn from various sources, differing in various parts, both in style and in degree of detail.

12

(1) All Israel were come to Shechem to make him king.—Rehoboam seems to succeed without question to the throne of Judah, but to need to be "made king" by the rest of Israel, with apparently some right on their part to require conditions before acceptance. (Comp. II Sam. 5:3.) It is significant that this ceremonial is fixed, not at Jerusalem, but at Shechem, the chief city of Ephraim, which became the capital of the northern kingdom after the disruption. Perhaps, in this arrangement, which seems to have had no precedent, there was some omen of revolution.

(4) We will serve thee.—The imposition of the burdens of heavy taxation and forced labor on the people was against old traditions, and even against the practice of Solomon's earlier years. (See 4:20; 9:20-22.) To demand a removal, or alleviation of these, was perfectly compatible with a loyal willingness to serve the new king.

(6-11) Both the policies suggested show how corrupt and cynical the government of Israel had become. The advice of the old

counselors has no largeness of policy or depth of wisdom. It is simply the characteristic advice of experienced and crafty politicians. Whether it was in itself more than superficially prudent would depend on the seriousness of the grievances, and the social and political condition of the people. The advice of the young men—the spoiled children of a magnificent and luxurious despotism, of which alone they had experience—is the language of the arrogant self-confidence which mistakes obstinacy for vigor. It is couched in needlessly and absurdly offensive language.

(11) Scorpion is probably (like the Roman **flagellum**) a whip, the lash of which is loaded with weights and sharp points.

(15) For the cause was from the Lord.— Holy Scripture refers all to God's will, fulfilling or avenging itself in many ways, inspiring and guiding the good, and overruling the evil, in man. But it as invariably implies human freedom and responsibility. Rehoboam's folly and arrogance worked out the ordained judgment of God; but they were folly and arrogance still.

(20) Jeroboam was come again.—The assembly at Shechem probably broke up in disorder, carrying everywhere the news of the rebellion (verses 18, 19). It would be quite in harmony with Jeroboam's astuteness, if, after setting the revolution on foot, he himself stood aloof from leadership and waited until the duly summoned assembly sent for him and offered the crown. The title "king over all Israel" indicates a claim on the part of the ten tribes to be the true Israel, relying perhaps on the prophetic choice and blessing of Jeroboam, and professing to have risen in the name of the Lord against the idolatry of Solomon and his house. Perhaps it also indicated a desire for the subjugation of Judah, which Jeroboam, with the aid of Shishak, certainly seems to have subsequently attempted.

(25) Jeroboam built Shechem.—From its proximity to Shiloh, and to the inheritance of Joshua, Shechem assumed something of the character of a capital (Josh. 24:1, 32) before it was destroyed by Abimelech (Judg. 9). We then hear nothing more of it until this chapter. Jeroboam is said to have "built it" anew. This may be taken literally, or it may simply mean that he fortified and enlarged it as his capital. Subsequently it gave way to Tirzah and Samaria.

Penuel.—See Gen. 32:30, 31; Judg. 8:8, 17. Jeroboam rebuilt it—perhaps out of the ruin in which it had been left by Gideon—

as an outpost to his new capital, and a royal stronghold among the tribes on the east of Jordan.

(27, 28) Heretofore Jeroboam's new royalty had been inaugurated under a Divine sanction, both as receiving distinct promise of permanence and blessing (11:37, 38), and as protected by open prophetic interference (verses 22-24), at the critical moment when its ill-consolidated force might have been crushed. Nor is it unlikely that it may have been supported by a wholesome reaction against the idolatry, as well as against the despotism, of Solomon. Now, unsatisfied with these securities of his kingdom, and desirous to strengthen it by a bold stroke of policy, he takes the step which mars the bright promise of his accession.

Yet the policy was exceedingly natural. In Israel beyond all other nations, civil and religious allegiance were indissolubly united; it was almost impossible to see how separate national existence could have been sustained without the creation of local sanctuaries to rival the sacredness of Jerusalem.

Nor was the breach of divine law apparently a serious one. The worship at Dan and Bethel was not the bloody and sensual worship of false gods, but the worship of the Lord Jehovah under the form of a visible emblem, meant to be a substitute for the Ark and the overshadowing cherubim. (See Exod. 32:8.) It might have been plausibly urged that, to wean Israel from all temptation to the abominations which Solomon had introduced, it was necessary to give their faith the visible support of these great local sanctuaries. But the step, once taken, was never retraced. Eminently successful in its immediate object of making the separation irreparable, it purchased success at the price, first, of destruction of all religious unity in Israel, and next, of a natural corruption, opening the door at once to idolatry, and hereafter to the grosser apostasy, against which it professed to guard. (See Deut. 4:15-18; Ps. 106:20.)

(29) Bethel, and ... Dan, chosen as the frontier towns of the kingdom, had, however, associations of their own, which lent themselves naturally to Jeroboam's design. (See Gen. 28:19; 35:14, 15; Judg. 18:30.)

(32, 33) The fixing of Jeroboam's festival of dedication for the Temple of Bethel to this special day is characteristic. It at once challenged likeness to the Feast of Tabernacles, which was the occasion of Solomon's dedication at Jerusalem (8:2), and yet took liberty to alter the date, thus assuming the right to set aside the letter of the old law, while professing still to observe the worship of Jehovah. Jeroboam already had set aside the peculiar sanctity of the Levitical priesthood (verse 31), and so was naturally prepared to crown this process by acting as head of the unauthorized priesthood which he had created.

13

In II Chron. 9:29 we read of "the visions of Iddo the seer against Jeroboam the son of Nebat." It is natural to conjecture that from these this record is drawn.

(2) Thus saith the Lord.—This is one of those rather infrequent prophecies found in Holy Scripture, which, not content to foreshadow the future in general outline, descend to striking particularity of detail (comp. Isa. 44:28). (The name is significant, for Josiah means "one healed" or "helped by Jehovah.") It was the supernatural gift of a power to enter, in some measure, into "the mind of God," in whose foreknowledge all the future is already seen and ordained. On the fulfillment of this prediction, see II Kings 23:15-20.

(3, 4) The sign.—The sign, announced to secure credence to the prediction, is itself a visible type of what that prediction foretold, in the shattering of the altar and the scattering of the ashes of the burnt offering. The sign actually given includes, besides this, the sudden withering of the king's hand, stretched out in defiance of the prophet. It was an equally plain symbol of the miserable failure of his strength and policy, when opposed to the Law and the judgment of God. The withdrawal of this last sign of wrath, on the submission of the king and the prayer of the prophet, was apparently designed to give Jeroboam one more opportunity of repentance.

(7) Come home with me ... —The invitation savors of astute policy in Jeroboam: for the acceptance of hospitality and reward would in the eyes of the people imply a condonation of the idolatrous worship, which might well destroy or extenuate the impression made by the prophet's prediction. It was evidently to provide against this, as fatal to the effectiveness of the prophet's mission, that the prohibition of verse 9 was given. (Comp. Num. 22:18.)

(11) An old prophet in Beth-el.—This old

prophet was not a mere pretender to prophetic inspiration, nor an apostate from the worship of Jehovah. Like Balaam, he united true prophetic gifts with a low worldliness of temper, capable on occasion of base subterfuge and deceit. Such union of elements, which should be utterly discordant, is only too characteristic of man's self-contradictory nature.

(18) An angel spake unto me.—The lie was gross, and ought to have been obvious to one who had received a plain command. It was believed, no doubt, because it accorded with some secret reluctance to obey, and, by obedience, to give up all reward and hospitality. Therefore the belief was a self-deceit. The most terrible feature in the history is, probably, that the divine sentence is spoken (verses 20-22) through the lips which by falsehood had lured the prophet of Judah from the right path, and at the table of treacherous hospitality.

(33) Probably the death of the man of God had been used to discredit his warning. The result is seen in the significant notice: "After this thing, Jeroboam returned not from his evil way." Thus we see the seriousness of the disobedience, which played into the hands of wickedness, and the startling severity of the penalty.

14

(2) Shiloh, the regular habitation of Ahijah, is hardly mentioned in Scripture after the time of Eli. It is evident that the old blind prophet still remained there and exercised his prophetic office for the benefit of Israel, though he stood aloof from, and denounced, the new idolatry of Bethel. This idolatry is always described as pre-eminently the "sin of Jeroboam," who by it "made Israel to sin." The people no longer had the Temple and the consecrated royalty of David, therefore the prophetic ministrations were of pre-eminent importance. Accordingly, the wife of Jeroboam is bidden to approach the prophet disguised as a daughter of the people.

(7, 8) I exalted thee.—Comp. 11:31, 37, 38. The sin of Jeroboam lay in the fact that he had had a full probation, with unlimited opportunities, and had deliberately thrown it away in the vain hope of making surer the kingdom which God's promise had already made sure.

(9) But hast done evil above all that were before thee.—The guilt of Jeroboam's act

was enhanced by the presumptuous contempt of the special promise of God, given on the sole condition of obedience. The effect of the sin was unprecedented, coming at a critical point in the history of Israel, and from that time onward poisoning the springs of national faith and worship. Other idolatries came and passed away; this continued, and at all times "made Israel to sin."

Other gods, and molten images.—Ahijah holds these molten images, expressly forbidden in the Law, to be really objects of worship. Moreover, from verse 15 it appears that the foul worship of the **Asherah** ("groves") associated itself with the idolatry of Jeroboam. (See II Kings 23:15.)

(10) Him . . . and him.—The first phrase is used also in I Sam. 25:22; I Kings 21:21; II Kings 9:8, to signify "every male," implying (possibly with a touch of contempt) that even the lowest should be destroyed. The sense seems to be "the child" who keeps at home, "and the man" who goes abroad.

(11) Him that dieth.—In ancient times the natural horror of insult to the remains of the dead was often intensified by the idea that in some way the denial of the rites of burial would inflict suffering or privation on the departed soul. Whether such ideas may have lingered in the minds of the Israelites we have no means of knowing. But certainly their whole system of law and ritual was calculated to give due honor to the body in life, as consecrated to God; and this would naturally tend to teach them that the body was a part of the true man, and therefore to deepen the repugnance, with which all reverent feeling regards outrage on the dead.

(14) Shall raise him up a king.—Baasha. (See 15:27-30.) Like Jeroboam, he had (16:2-4) a probation before God, in which he failed, drawing down doom on his house.

(15) And he shall root up Israel.—The first prophecy of future captivity, and that beyond the Euphrates, is here pronounced against the kingdom of Israel, on account of their share in the idolatry of Jeroboam and in the worse abominations of the "groves." The prophecy uttered does not foreclose the probation of future ages. This is only one illustration of the great truth that, however impossible it is for us to comprehend the mystery, the foreknowledge of God does not preclude the freedom and responsibility of man. (See Jer. 18:7, 8.)

Their groves.—Properly **Asherah**, an

298

idol, apparently the straight stem of a tree, surmounted by an emblem of the goddess represented. It is thought to have been an image of some deity like Astarte, the goddess of good fortune. But the worship dates from a far earlier time, and the word itself is etymologically distinct from "Ashtoreth" or "Ashtaroth."

(17) Tirzah.—From this incidental notice it would seem that Jeroboam had moved his habitation to Tirzah, a place renowned for beauty (Song of Solomon 6:4), and further from the hostile frontier than Shecem. It seems to have continued as the capital until the foundation of Samaria.

(21) And Rehoboam.—Here begins the second series of the book—a series of brief annals, touching only the main points of the history of the kings of Israel and Judah, until the appearance of Elijah (17:1). Comp. II Chron. 11-17.

The city which the Lord did choose.—This emphatic notice is, no doubt, intended to place Jerusalem and its worship in marked contrast with the new capitals and unauthorized sanctuaries which had sprung up.

(22) Judah did evil.—This extraordinarily reckless plunge into abominations of the worst kind is ascribed not, as in the case of Solomon and most other kings, to the action of Rehoboam, but to that of the people at large. The king himself seems to have been weak, unfit for taking the initiative either in good or evil. The apostasy of Judah was evidently the harvest of the deadly seed sown by the commanding influence of Solomon, under whose idolatry the young men had grown up.

(23) High places, and images, and groves.—On the "high places," see note on 3:2. The "images" of this passage seem undoubtedly to have been stone pillars, as the "groves" (i.e., the asherahs) were wooden stumps of trees (possibly in both cases surmounted by some rude representation of the deity worshiped). See note on verse 15. The stone pillars appear to be associated with the worship of Baal, as the **Asherah** with that of Ashtoreth.

(24) Sodomites.—See 15:12 and II Kings 23:7. There is a horrible significance in the derivation of this word, which is properly "consecrated," or "devoted," for it indicates the license, and even the sanction, of unnatural lusts in those consecrated to the abominations of nature-worship. The appearance of such in the land, whether Canaanites or apostate Israelites, is evi-

dently noted as the climax of the infinite corruption which had set in, rivalling the abominations of the old inhabitants of the land.

(25) Shishak.—The Egyptian army, coming as allies of Jeroboam, took those cities which were hostile or disloyal to him. It is likely that the whole invasion was instigated by Jeroboam, in that desire to crush the kingdom of Judah which afterward suggested his war with Abijam. (See II Chron. 12 and 13.)

(26) He even took away all.—There is a touch of pathos in the description of the utter spoil of the treasures in which Solomon and Israel had gloried, and which now served only to buy off the victorious Egyptians. There is no notice of any sack of Jerusalem, nor, as in later cases, of any desecration of the Temple, or even of the plunder of its decorations. The record seems to imply surrender of the city and its treasures.

(29) The chronicles of the kings of Judah.—See II Chron. 12:15.

(30) There was war . . . —The meaning may simply be that there was continued enmity, breaking off all peaceful relations; but in the scantiness of the record we can have no certainty that actual war did not take place, though it has found no place in the history.

15

(1) Abijam.—The variation in spelling (comp. II Chron. 13, "Abijah"), if not a mere false reading, may have been made for the sake of distinction from the son of Jeroboam.

(2) Maachah, the daughter of Abishalom.—In all probability this is Absalom (see II Chron. 11:20), the rebel son of David, whose mother (II Sam. 3:3) was also named Maachah. Chronological considerations would suggest that she must have been the granddaughter of Absalom (see II Chron. 13:2). She is mentioned below (verse 13) as prominent in the evil propensity to idolatry.

(3) Walked in all the sins of his father.—It is a curious irony of circumstance that Abijam should be recorded as inveighing against the degradation of His worship in Israel, while he himself countenanced or connived at the worse sin of the worship of rival gods in Judah.

(4) Give him a lamp in Jerusalem.—

There is here a brief allusion to the victory recorded in the Chronicles, which obviously was the turning point in the struggle, saving the "lamp" of the house of David from extinction, and "establishing" Jerusalem in security. "For David's sake" is the fulfillment of the promise to David (II Sam. 7:12-16).

(6) And there was war.—The repetition of the notice of Rehoboam seems inexplicable. Probably there is error in the text.

(10) His mother's name was Maachah.—Maachah was (see verse 2) the wife of Rehoboam, and, therefore, grandmother of Asa. She appears, however, still to have retained the place of "queen mother," to the exclusion of the real mother of the king.

(11) Asa did that which was right.—This reign—happily, a long one—was a turning point in the history of Judah. Freed from immediate pressure by the victory of Abijah over Jeroboam, Asa resolved—perhaps under the guidance of the prophets Azariah and Hanani—to renew the true strength of his kingdom by restoring the worship and trusting in the blessings of the true God, extirpating by repeated efforts the false worships introduced by Rehoboam and continued by Abijah, and solemnly renewing the covenant with the Lord. Of all this the text here gives but brief notice; the record in II Chron. 14 and 15 contains a detailed account.

(16) There was war ... —According to verse 33, Baasha reigned from the third to the twenty-seventh year of Asa. The phrase, here repeated from 14:30 and 15:6, 7, appears simply to mean that the old hostile relations remained, combined with, perhaps, some border war (comp. II Chron. 12:15).

(17) Built Ramah.—Ramah—the word signifying only "elevation"—is mentioned in Josh. 18:25 as a city of Benjamin, situated (see Jos. **Ant.** 8:12, 3) about five miles north of Jerusalem. (See Judg. 4:5; 19:13; Isa. 10:29; Jer. 40:1.) This fortification of Ramah close to the hostile capital was a standing menace to Judah. Baasha, who was a military chief, seems to have been warned by the bad success of former attempts to invade and subjugate Judah, and to have used this easier means of keeping the enemy in check and provoking a conflict on his own ground.

(18) Sent them to Ben-hadad.—This shows that Syria, recovering its independence at the fall of Solomon's empire, was already attaining the formidable power, which so soon threatened to destroy Israel altogether. The Ben-hadad of the text is the grandson of Hezion, who must be the Rezon of 11:23. Already there had been leagues between Syria and Judah in the preceding reign (verse 19). It is clear that Baasha had attempted to supersede these by a closer league—possibly, like Pekah in later times (II Kings 16:5, 6), desiring to strengthen and secure himself against invasion by the subjugation of Judah. Asa naturally resolved to bribe Ben-hadad by presents to prefer the old tie to the new; but he went beyond this, and proposed a combined attack on Israel, for the first time calling in a heathen power against his "brethren, the children of Israel." For prophetic rebuke, see II Chron. 16:7-9 (comp. Isa. 30:1-17).

(20) Smote.—The portion smitten now, as hereafter in the Assyrian invasion (II Kings 15:29), is the mountain country near the source of the Jordan, which lay most exposed to the great approach to Israel from the north.

(27) Baasha, sprung from an obscure tribe, hardly at any time distinguished in the history, and himself, as it would seem (16:2), of low origin in it, is the first of the many military chiefs who by violence or assassination seized upon the throne of Israel. The constant succession of ephemeral dynasties stands in striking contrast with the unchanged royalty of the house of David, resting on the promise of God.

16

(1) Jehu the son of Hanani—probably of Hanani the seer of Judah in the reign of Asa (II Chron. 15:7). Jehu must now have been young, for we find him rebuking Jehoshaphat after the death of Ahab, and writing the annals of Jehoshaphat's reign (II Chron. 19:2; 20:34).

(2) Forasmuch as I exalted thee. ... —The prophecy—closely resembling that of Ahijah against Jeroboam—clearly shows that Baasha had a probation, which he neglected; and it seems to be implied in verse 7 that his guilt was enhanced by perseverance in the sins for which, by his hand, so terrible a vengeance had been inflicted. Sin which works out God's purpose is not the less truly sin; Baasha's act, though foretold, was not thereby justified.

(9) Drinking himself drunk.—There seems

an emphasis of half-contemptuous condemnation in the description of Elah's debauchery, evidently public, while war was raging at Gibbethon. Zimri's name passed into a proverb for unusual treachery. (See II Kings 9:31.) His desperate act (verse 18) seems to indicate that there was held to be something especially treasonable, and therefore unpardonable, in his assassination of Elah.

(16) Made Omri ... king.—This exaltation of Omri, as a matter of course, shows how entirely the kingdom of Israel had become the prize of the sword. By a curious coincidence (see 15:27) the dynasty of Baasha had been founded in the camp before the same city of Gibbethon. Zimri's conspiracy appears to have been hastily planned, with no provision of adequate means of support, for Tirzah is taken at once.

(21) Tibni.—Of him we know nothing. No doubt he also was a military chief—possibly Zimri's colleague, under the supreme command of Omri—and the LXX speaks of a brother, Joram, who fought and fell with him. By comparison of verse 23 with verse 15, it appears that the struggle had lasted four years.

(23) Began Omri to reign over Israel.—The accession of Omri after this long civil war opened a new epoch of more settled government and prosperity for about forty-eight years. Omri had (20:34) to purchase peace with Syria by some acknowledgment of sovereignty and cession of cities. He then allied himself with the royal house of Tyre, probably both for strength against Syria and for revival of the commercial prosperity of the days of Solomon, and proceeded to found a new capital in a strong position.

(24) Built on the hill.—Omri only followed the usual practice of a new dynasty in the East, but the site of Samaria must have been chosen by a soldier's eye. Its Hebrew name (**Shomerôn**) means a "watchtower." Its position was one of great beauty, and, in the warfare of those days, of singular strength, as is shown by the long sieges which it withstood (I Kings 20:1; II Kings 6:24; 17:5; 18:9, 10). It lay northwest of Shechem, on an isolated hill with precipitous sides, rising in the middle of a basin of the hills of Ephraim, not far from the edge of the maritime plain, and commanding a view of the sea.

(25) Did worse than all that were before him.—This phrase, used of Jeroboam in 14:9, may indicate, in addition to the acceptance and development of the old idolatry, some anticipation of the worse idolatry of Baal, formally introduced by Ahab. (See Micah 6:16.)

(31) Ethbaal king of the Zidonians.—He is said by Josephus to have assassinated Pheles, king of Tyre, within fifty years after the death of Hiram, and to have founded a new dynasty. His priestly origin, and possibly also this revival of the old ideas and spirit of the Phoenician race, may account for the fanatic devotion to Baal visible in Jezebel and Athaliah, which stands in marked contrast with the religious attitude of Hiram (I Kings 5:7; II Chron. 2:12). The marriage of Ahab with Jezebel was evidently the fatal turning point in the life of a man physically brave, and possibly able as a ruler, but morally weak, impressible in turn both by good and by evil. History shows again and again the contrast of character (compare the contrast between Shakespeare's Macbeth and Lady Macbeth), and the almost complete supremacy of the strong relentless nature of Jezebel.

(32) The Baal here referred to is the Zidonian god, worshiped as the productive principle in nature, in conjunction with Astarte, the female or receptive principle. The name itself only signifies "Lord," and is marked as being a mere title by the almost invariable prefix of the article. Being, therefore, in no sense distinctive, it may be, and is, applied to the supreme god of various mythologies. The worship of the Phoenician Baal was now introduced on a great scale, with profuse magnificence of worship, enforced by Jezebel with a high hand, not without persecution of the prophets of the Lord. The conflict between it and the spiritual worship of Jehovah became now a conflict of life and death.

17

With this chapter begins a section of the book marked by a complete change in the character of the history. The two great prophets, Elijah and Elisha, themselves stand out as two distinct types of the servants of God. Elijah's mission, one of narrow and striking intensity, is embodied in his name—"My God is Jehovah." Appearing at the great crisis of the conflict against the sensual and degrading Baal-worship, he is not a teacher or a lawgiver, or a herald of the Messiah, but simply a warrior of God, bearing witness for Him by word and by deed, living a recluse ascetic life, and suddenly emerging from it again to strike some special blow. The "spirit of Elias" has become proverbial for its stern and fiery impatience of evil. Elisha builds on the ground which Elijah had cleared, filling a place hardly equalled since the days of Samuel, as a teacher and guide both of king and people. His miracles, with one exception, are miracles of kindliness and mercy, helping the common life from which Elijah held aloof. It is impossible not to see in him a true, though imperfect type, of the greater than Elias, who was to come.

(1) Gilead—properly "the rocky region" that lay on the east of Jordan. Open to the desert on the east, and itself comparatively wild, with but few cities scattered through it, it suited well the recluse dweller in the wilderness. This inclusion distinguishes from the Tishbe in Naphtali.

The Lord God of Israel . . . before whom I stand.—This adjuration is characteristic. Elijah is the servant of God, standing to be sent where He wills. This is evidently not the first appearance of Elijah (see James 5:17). There had been a struggle against the Baal-worship of the time, and, no doubt, previous warnings from Elijah or from some one of the murdered prophets. This chapter introduces us suddenly to the catastrophe.

(4) The ravens.—It is futile to seek to explain away one wonder in a life and an epoch teeming with miracles. It is notable, indeed, that the critical period of the great Baal apostasy, and of the struggle of Elijah and Elisha against it, is the second great epoch of recorded miracle in the Old Testament, the still more critical epoch of Moses and Joshua being the first.

(9) Zarephath—the **Sarepta** of the LXX and of the New Testament (Luke 4:26). The words "which belongeth to Zidon" appear to be emphatic, marking the striking providence of God, which, when the land of Israel was apostate and unsafe, found for the prophet a refuge and a welcome in a heathen country, which was moreover the native place of his deadliest enemy.

(16) The barrel of meal wasted not.—The miracle is doubly remarkable. First, God's higher laws of miracle, like the ordinary laws of His providence, admit within their scope the supply of what we should consider as trivial needs. Next, it is a miracle of multiplication, which is virtual creation, doing rapidly and directly what, under ordinary laws, has to be done slowly and by indirect process.

(20) Hast thou also brought evil.— Elijah's complaint is characteristic of the half-presumptuous impatience seen more fully in chap. 19. He apparently implies that his own lot, as a hunted fugitive not protected by God's almighty power, is so hard that it must be his presence which has brought trouble even on the home that sheltered him.

(21) He stretched himself upon the child.— The idea in this passage (comp. II Kings 4:34; 13:21) clearly is of a certain healing "virtue," attaching in measure to the person of the prophets, as without measure it belonged to our Lord Himself (Luke 8:45, 46). But it is to be noted that in the case of the prophet the power to heal or raise up is made distinctly conditional on prayer.

(24) Now by this I know. . . . —In these words we trace the final victory of faith, brought out by the crowning mercy of the restoration of her son. First, the widow had spoken of Jehovah from without (verse 14); next, she had come to recognize Him as God (verse 18); now she not only believes, as she had never believed before, that His servant is "a man of God," but seems undoubtedly to express conversion to Him. (Compare the stages of faith in the nobleman at Capernaum, John 4:47, 50, 53.)

18

(3) Obadiah.—The name ("servant of Jehovah") here corresponds to the character of the man. It is curiously significant of the hesitating and temporizing attitude of Ahab, that, while Jezebel is allowed to persecute, a high officer in the court is able to profess openly the service of Jehovah and secretly to thwart the cruelty of the queen. In his heart Ahab always seems to acknowledge the true God, but is overborne by the commanding and ruthless nature of Jezebel.

(4) Jezebel cut off the prophets.—The persecution here referred to, in which for the first time the royal power was placed in distinct antagonism to the prophetic order, is known only by this allusion. It may probably have followed on the denunciation of judgment; and Elijah's retirement to Cherith and Zarephath may have been a means of escape from it.

(17) Art thou . . . —Probably (as in verse 7) the rendering should be, "Thou here, the troubler of Israel!"—defying vengeance in the land which you have troubled.

(19) Carmel.—Mount Carmel—rightly called "the park," well planted and watered, of central Palestine—is a limestone ridge, with deep ravines thickly wooded, running northwest for about twelve miles from the central hills of Manasseh, so as to form the south side of the bay of Ptolemais, and almost to reach the sea, leaving, however, a space around which the southern armies constantly poured into the plain of Jezreel. It varies from 600 feet to 1,700 feet in height. Near its higher eastern extremity, where there is a commanding view of the sea, is the traditional scene of Elijah's sacrifice. In the prophetic writings it is referred to as proverbial for its luxuriant pasturage and beauty. (See Isa. 33:9; Jer. 4:26; Amos 1:2; 9:3; Song of Solomon 7:6.) No more striking scene could well be found for the great drama of this chapter.

The prophets of the groves (Asherah) ... —These, being probably the devotees of the female deity Astarte, seem to have been especially favored by the queen. It is to be noted that, in spite of Elijah's challenge, they do not appear at all in the subsequent scene. (See verses 22 and 40.)

(21) How long halt ye between two opinions?—In this exclamation is expressed the very motto of Elijah's life. It is that of righteous impatience of the "halting (i.e., limping to and fro) between two opinions"— at all times more dangerous, because easier than apostasy—which was evidently characteristic of Ahab, and probably of the mass of the people. It might have suited well the accommodating genius of such polytheism as had been brought into Israel since the days of Solomon himself, but was utterly incompatible with the sole absolute claim of the worship of Jehovah. Perhaps Jezebel would have scorned it equally for Baal. Comp. Ezek. 20:31, 39.

(24) And call ye on the name of your gods.—This gift of a "sign from heaven"— not unfamiliar to Israelite experience (see Lev. 9:24; I Chron. 21:26; II Chron. 7:1)— which may not, as our Lord teaches us (Matt. 12:38, 39; 16:1-4), be craved for or demanded as a ground of faith, is, like all other miracles, granted unasked when it is seen by God's wisdom to be needed, in order to startle an ignorant and misguided people into serious attention to a message from heaven. In this instance the worship of Baal was a worship of the power of nature, impersonated perhaps in the sun; and the miracle therefore entered on the visible

sphere, especially usurped in his name, in order to claim it for the Lord Jehovah.

(27) Elijah mocked them.—The wild excited cry stands in an instructive contrast (which has been splendidly emphasized in Mendelssohn's music) with the simple, earnest solemnity of the prayer of Elijah. Comp. the righteous scorn of the psalmists or the prophets—Pss. 115:4-8; 135:15-18; Isa. 44:9-20; 46:1-7; Jer. 10:2-10, etc.—for the worship of "the vanities" of the heathen. There was no place for toleration of prejudice, or tender appreciation of a blind worship feeling after God, like that of Paul at Athens (Acts 17:22, 23). The conflict here was between spiritual worship and a foul, cruel idolatry; and the case was not of heathen ignorance, but of Israel's apostasy.

(31) Twelve stones.—The emphatic notice of these, as emblematic of the twelve tribes, is significant. In spite of political division, and even religious separation, the tribes were still united in the covenant of God.

(32) Measures.—The "measure," the third part of the ephah, was something less than three gallons.

(33) Fill four barrels—or pitchers. The filling of these at the time of drought has naturally excited speculation. But a perennial spring in the neighborhood of the traditional scene of the sacrifice has never been known to fail in the severest drought. From this, no doubt (as indeed Josephus expressly says), the water was drawn, with the object of precluding all idea of fraud or contrivance, and bringing out strikingly the consuming fierceness of the fire from heaven, so emphatically described in verse 38.

(36) Lord God of Abraham.—In this solemn and earnest invocation of God, as in Exod. 3:15; 6:2, 3, the name Jehovah, describing God as He is in Himself—the One eternal self-existent Being—is united with the name which shows His special covenant with "Abraham, and Isaac, and Israel." The prominence of the name "Jehovah," repeated three times in this short prayer of Elijah, is significant as of the special mission, symbolized in his name, so also of his immediate purpose. The God of Israel is to show Himself as the true worker, not only in the outer area by miracle, but in the inner area by that conversion of the hearts of the people, which to the prophet's eye is already effected.

(40) Slew them.—The law was adapted (as in the terrible crucial example of the slaughter of the Canaanites) to the "hardness of men's hearts." In the imperfect moral and religious education of those times, it did recognize the difference between moral and political offenses punishable by human law, and the religious sin or apostasy which we have been taught to leave to the judgment of God alone; and it enjoined an unrelenting severity in the execution of righteous vengeance, which would be morally impossible to us, who have been taught to hate the sin, and yet spare, as far as possible, the sinner. (See Luke 9:54.) In this particular case it is to be remembered that those slain were no doubt implicated in the persecution headed by Jezebel, and that the Baal-worship was a licentious and perhaps bloody system. Elijah felt himself the avenger of the slaughtered prophets, as well as the instrument of the judgment of God.

(43) Go again seven times.—From this delay of the answer to prayer Elijah's example became proverbial for intensity and perseverance in supplication (James 5:17). The contrast is remarkable between the immediate answer to his earlier prayer (see verses 36, 37) and the long delay here. The one was for the sake of the people; the other for some lesson—perhaps of humility and patience—to Elijah himself. When the answer does come, it fulfills itself speedily.

(45) Jezreel.—This is the first mention of the city Jezreel, a city of Issachar (Josh. 19:18), as a royal city. It was made a royal residence by Ahab, as Samaria by Omri. It stands in a position of some strength and great beauty, supplied by unfailing springs of water, visible from Carmel, and commanding views east and west far over the plain.

19

(1, 2) There is a certain grandeur of fearlessness and ruthlessness in the message of Jezebel, which marks her character throughout and places it in striking contrast with the vacillating impressibility of Ahab, whom she treats with natural scorn. (See 21:7.) Her message seems intended to give the opportunity for a fight, which might degrade Elijah in the eyes of the people.

(3) Beer-sheba.—(See Gen. 21:14, 33; 22:19; 28:10; 46:1.) This frontier town of Palestine to the south is seldom mentioned after the patriarchal time. The note that "it belonged to Judah" is, perhaps, significant. Judah was now in half-dependent alliance

with Israel; even under Jehoshaphat, Elijah might not be safe there, though his servant—traditionally the son of the widow of Zarephath—might stay without danger.

(4) Juniper tree.—A sort of broom, found abundantly in the desert. Its roots were much prized for charcoal, the "coal" of verse 6.

I am not better than my fathers.—Evidently he had hoped that he himself was "better than his fathers" as a servant of God, singled out beyond all those who went before him, to be the victorious champion of a great crisis. Now he thinks his hope vain, and sees no reason why he should succeed when all who went before have failed.

(5) An angel touched him.—It is notable that angels, whose appearances are so often recorded in earlier days, hardly appear during the prophetic period, as though the place of their spiritual ministry, as messengers of God, to the people had been supplied by the prophetic mission. Here, and in II Kings 6:17, the angel is but auxiliary to the prophet, simply ministering to him in time of danger and distress, as the angel of the agony to the Prophet of prophets.

(8) Forty days and forty nights.—This interval of retirement was for rest and solitary meditation, like the sojourn of Moses in Horeb, and the sojourn of our Lord in the wilderness (Exod. 24:18; Matt. 4:2), during which the spirit of the prophet might be calmed from the alternations of triumph and despondency, to receive the spiritual lesson which awaited him.

(9) The word of the Lord came to him.—The connection suggests that this message came to Elijah in vision or dream at night. What he replies in imagination in the vision, he repeats next day in actual words.

(10) And he said.—The reply to the implied reproof is one of impatient remonstrance. He himself (he says) had been very jealous for the Lord; yet the Lord had not been jealous for Himself, allowing this open rebellion of the people, the slaughter of His prophets, the persecution to death of the one solitary champion left. What use is there in further striving, if he is left unsupported and alone? (Comp. Isa. 64:1; Jonah 4:1-3.)

(11) And, behold.—The whole of the vision is best understood by comparison with two former manifestations at Horeb, to the people and to Moses (Exod. 19:16-18; 34:5-8). The vision of Elijah stands out in contrast with the one and in harmony with the other. It disclaims the visible manifestation in power and vengeance, for which he had by implication craved; it implies in "the still small voice" a manifestation of the higher power of the Spirit, penetrating to the inmost soul which the terrors of external power cannot reach. (See Zech. 4:6.)

(16) And Jehu.—Of this charge Elijah fulfilled in person but one part, in the call of Elisha (for the fulfillment of the other two parts see II Kings 8:8-13; 9:1-6). The history, indeed, records no actual anointing of Elisha; and it is remarkable that in no other place is any such anointing of a prophet referred to, unless Ps. 105:15 be an exception. The anointing, signifying the gift of grace, was first instituted for the priests (Exod. 40:15; Num. 3:3); next it was extended to the royal office, and became, in common parlance, especially attached to it.

(17) Him that escapeth the sword of Hazael.—Elisha's mission was obviously not one of such vengeance. He had to destroy enmity, but not to slay the enemies of God. Probably Elisha's mission is here described in the terms in which Elijah would best understand it. His spirit was for war; he could hardly have conceived how the completion of his mission was to be wrought out by the weapons of peace in the hand of his successor. (Comp. II Cor. 10:3-6.)

(19) Twelve yoke of oxen indicate some wealth in Elisha's family, which he has to leave to follow the wandering life of Elijah. The rough hair-mantle was characteristic of the ascetic recluse. The act is said to have been a part of the form of adoption of a child; thus its spiritual significance here, which, after a moment's bewilderment, Elisha seems to read.

(20) Let me, I pray thee.—Comp. Luke 9:61, 62. In both cases we have the stern but necessary rejection of half-hearted service, even if the heart is distracted by the most natural and sacred love. But Elijah sees that Elisha means simply farewell, and he apparently waits until it is over.

20

(1) Ben-hadad.—This is the inherited title of the Syrian kings. (See Amos 1:4; Jer. 49:27.) From the allusion in verse 34 it appears that this Ben-hadad was the son of a king who had been victorious against Omri—possibly pushing still further the advantage gained in the time of Baasha. It is evident that he assumed, perhaps by inheritance, a sovereignty over Israel.

Thirty and two kings.—All the notices of Syria show it as divided into small kingdoms, confederated from time to time under some leading power. Now Damascus, under the dynasty of Hadad, assumes a most formidable predominance. Ahab cannot stand before it, but shuts himself up, probably after defeat, within the strong walls of Samaria.

(6) Whatsoever is pleasant.—The demand, which is virtually for the plunder of Samaria, probably neither expects nor desires acceptance, and is therefore a refusal of all but unconditional surrender. It is notable that in the last extremity Ahab falls back on an exceptional appeal to the patriotism of the people.

(13) There came a prophet.—The appearance of this unknown prophet evidently shows that Ahab's enmity to the prophetic order was over since the great day at Carmel, and that the schools of the prophets were forming themselves again. It is notable that in all these political functions of prophecy Elijah does not appear, reserving himself for the higher moral and religious mission from God. Ahab receives the prophet's message with perfect confidence and reverence; he has returned in profession to the allegiance to Jehovah, which he had, perhaps, never wholly relinquished.

(20) And they slew ... —For the plan of attack, comp. Judg. 7:16-23; I Sam. 14.

(22) The return of the year.—The early part of the next year, after the winter was over, "when kings go out to battle" (II Sam. 11:1).

(23) Gods of the hills.—The idea of tutelary gods, whose strength was greatest on their own soil, is naturally common in polytheistic religions, which, by the very multiplication of gods, imply limitation of the power of each. The greater part of the territory where Jehovah was worshiped was hill country. Samaria in particular, the scene of recent defeat, lay in the mountain region of Ephraim.

(26) Aphek.—There are two places which suit well enough with the Aphek ("fortress") of this passage and II Kings 13:17, as being a battlefield in the plain country between Israel and Syria. One is the Aphek of I Sam. 29:1, evidently in the plain of Esdraelon; the other a place on the road to Damascus, about six miles east of the Sea of Galilee.

(27) Were all present.—The marginal reading "were supplied," with all things necessary for war, seems correct. The comparatively small number of the Israelite forces, even after the great victory of the year before, appears to show that, previous to the siege of Samaria, Ahab had suffered some great defeats, which had broken the strength of Israel.

(28) The vindication of the majesty of God before the Syrians is a foreshadowing of that view of all nations, as in some degree having knowledge of God and probation before Him, which is afterward worked out fully in the prophetic writings. The intense and powerful Monotheism of the religion of Israel, in spite of all its backslidings, could hardly have been without influence over the neighboring nations (see II Kings 5:15), especially at a time when the remembrance of Solomon's vast empire, and still wider influence, would yet linger through the tenacious traditions of the East.

(33) The whole description is graphic. The Syrians speak of "thy slave Benhadad." Ahab, in compassion or show of magnanimity, says "my brother." Eagerly the ambassadors catch the word, which, according to Eastern custom, implied a pledge of amity not to be recalled; and Ahab accepts their inference, and seals it publicly by taking the conquered king into his chariot. (Comp. II Kings 10:15, 16.)

(34) Make streets.—This concession implies a virtual acknowledgment of supremacy; for the right to have certain quarters of the city ("streets") for residence, for trade, perhaps even for garrison, in the capital of a king, belongs only to one who has sovereignty over him. Thus it goes beyond the significance of the restoration of the cities. The narrative seems to convey an idea that the covenant was made hastily, on insufficient security. The great point was that a war, victoriously conducted under prophetic guidance, should not have been concluded without prophetic sanction.

(35) A certain man—according to Josephus, Micaiah, the son of Imlah. This tradition, or conjecture, agrees well with the subsequent narrative in chap. 22.

The sons of the prophets.—This phrase, constantly recurring in the history of Elijah and Elisha, first appears here. (See I Sam. 10:5, 10; 19:20.) The prophetic office seems never to have been, like the priesthood or kingship, hereditary. "Sonship," therefore,

no doubt means simply discipleship; and it is likely enough that the schools of the sons of the prophets were places of higher religious education, including many who did not look for the prophetic vocation; although the well-known words of Amos 7:14 clearly indicate that from their ranks, generally though not invariably, the prophets were called. Probably the institution had fallen into disuse, and had been revived to seal and to secure the prophetic victory over Baal-worship.

(39-43) The parable is, of course, designed (like those of II Sam. 12:1-4; 14:5-11) to make Ahab condemn himself. In Ahab, however, it does not excite compunction, but characteristic sullenness of displeasure, like that of 21:4.

The rash action of Ahab, like the deliberate disobedience of Saul (I Sam. 15), may have been due partly to compassion, partly to weakness. In either case it had no right to stand unauthorized between God's judgment and him on whom it was pronounced, for even soft-heartedness, as in the case of Eli, may be treason to the cause of righteousness. (For the fulfillment of the prophet's words, see 22:34-36.)

21

(1) Which was in Jezreel.—Compare II Kings 9:25, 26. The question of the position of the vineyard, apparently the scene of Naboth's murder, is difficult. It may have been an outlying property near Samaria, which Ahab might suppose Naboth likely to sell. In favor of this probable supposition is the emphatic prediction of verse 19, which in 22:38 is declared to have been fulfilled at the pool of Samaria. Moreover, the whole action of the chapter, as far as Ahab is concerned, seems to have been at Samaria; and, indeed, if we take verse 18 literally, this is actually declared to be the case.

(2-4) And Ahab spake.—At first, as the desire of Ahab was natural, so his offer was courteous and liberal. The refusal of Naboth —evidently grounded on the illegality, as well as the natural dislike, of alienation of "the inheritance of his fathers" (see Lev. 25:13-28; Num. 36:7), and therefore not only allowable but right—has nevertheless about it a certain tone of harshness, perhaps of unnecessary discourtesy, implying condemnation, as well as rejection, of the offer of the king. It is characteristic of the weak and petulant nature of Ahab, that he neither recognizes the legality and justice of Naboth's action, nor dares to resent the curt defiance of his refusal. His temper of sullen, childish discontent is the natural seedplot of crime under the instigation of more determined wickedness.

(7) The scorn of Jezebel is, like the impatience of Lady Macbeth, expressed in a striking boldness of emphasis. First comes bitter irony; then half-contemptuous recognition of a self-indulgent weakness of nature.

(8) Sealed them with his seal—with the name, or token, of the king, engraved on stone, and impressed (see Job 38:14) on a lump of clay attached to the letter. The sealing (as the modern sense of "signature" implies) was the pledge of authenticity and authority. The use of the seal—ordinarily worn or carried on the person—implies Ahab's knowledge that something is being done in his name, into which he does not take care to inquire.

(9) Proclaim a fast.—This might be only to cover all that was to be so foully done with a cloak of religious observance, or, perhaps more probably, to imply that some secret sin had been committed, which would draw down vengeance on the whole city, and so to prepare for the false accusation by the "sons of worthlessness" (verse 10).

(15) Take possession.—Naboth's sons (see II Kings 9:26) were murdered with him, so that there was none to claim the inheritance. Even had this not been so, the property of executed traitors would naturally fall to the king, although no enactment to this effect is found in the Law.

(19) Hast thou killed, and also taken possession?—The stern, indignant brevity of Elijah's accusation, at once shaming the subterfuge by which Ahab shifts his guilt to Jezebel, and unmasking the real object of the whole crime, leaves the king speechless as to defense, unable to stay the sentence which at once follows.

(20) Hast thou found me, O mine enemy?—The cry is partly of dismay, partly of excuse. Ahab, having no word of defense to utter, endeavors to attribute Elijah's rebuke and condemnation to simple enmity. The crushing answer is that the prophet came not because he was an enemy, but because Ahab had "sold himself"—had become a slave instead of a king—under the lust of desire and the temptation of Jezebel.

(21-24) Behold, I will bring evil.—Distinct from that message of personal judgment is the doom of utter destruction

pronounced on the dynasty of Omri (comp. 14:10, 11; 16:3, 4). It is, indeed, called forth by the last sin of Ahab, but the ground assigned for it (verse 22) extends to the whole course of idolatry and apostasy. It is only this more general sentence which is postponed by the repentance of Ahab (verse 29).

(23) The dogs shall eat Jezebel.—Now, briefly and sternly, the prophet notices the bolder criminal pronouncing against her a doom of shame and horror, seldom falling upon a woman, but rightly visiting one who had forsworn the pity and modesty of her sex. In the ditch outside the walls, where the refuse of the city gathers the half-wild dogs, the scavengers of Eastern cities, her dead body is to be thrown as refuse, and to be torn and devoured.

(29) How Ahab humbleth himself.—As there is something entirely characteristic of Ahab's impressible nature in this burst of penitence, so in the acceptance of it there is a remarkable illustration of divine mercy. Ahab himself is still to suffer the predicted doom; but he is to die in honor, and the utter destruction waits, until Jehoram shall fill up the measure of iniquity.

22

Chapter 22 is the continuation of chap. 20 (which in the LXX immediately precedes it) in record of the Syrian war, but in tone far grander and spiritually instructive, a fit catastrophe of the tragedy of Ahab's reign. In it, for the first time since 15:24, the history of Judah is touched upon; and there is an almost verbal coincidence with II Chron. 18.

(2) Jehoshaphat the king of Judah came down.—The fuller account of II Chron. 17 notices that the early part of his reign had been marked by a continuance or increase of the prosperity of Asa; but 18:1 adds, in significant connection, that this prosperity was, in part, dependent on a change of policy from enmity to alliance, with apparently some measure of dependence, dangerous alike spiritually and politically, but probably thought to be a necessity. The visit of Jehoshaphat was one of festivity, of which Ahab took advantage.

(3) Ramoth in Gilead.—The city is first mentioned (Deut. 4:43; Josh. 20:8; 21:38) as a city of refuge in the territory of Gad. In the Syrian wars it appears as a frontier fortress, taken and retaken. It had fallen into the hands of the Syrians, and had not been restored according to promise. The defeat and death of Ahab were subsequently avenged by Jehoram, who took it, and held it against all the attacks of the enemy (II Kings 9:1-14).

(7) Is there not here a prophet of the Lord.—Jehoshaphat's discontent makes it clear that the four hundred were not in his view true prophets of Jehovah. (Probably they were devoted, like the old prophet of Bethel, to the service of the idolatry of Jeroboam.) The rendering of the great name "Jehovah" by "the Lord" obscures the sense of the passage. In the previous utterance of the prophets (verse 6) the word (**Adonai**) is merely "Lord" in the etymological sense, which might mean the Supreme God of any religion. Jehoshaphat, struck with their shrinking from the distinctive name Jehovah, asks, "Is there not a prophet of Jehovah?"—one who is not ashamed or afraid to speak in His awful name?

(8) Micaiah ("who is like Jehovah")—the name being the same as Micah. According to Josephus, he was the prophet of 20:35-43, who had "prophesied evil" of Ahab for his rash action toward Ben-hadad, and had already been imprisoned by him (see verse 26).

(10) Each on his throne.—The description evidently implies that, having reluctantly consented to send for Micaiah, Ahab seeks to overawe him by display not only of royal pomp, but of prophetic inspiration, professing to come, like his own, from the Lord Jehovah.

(15) Go, and prosper.—Micaiah is a true disciple of Elijah in the defiant irony of the tone in which he takes up and mocks the utterance of the false prophets, so bitterly as at once to show Ahab his scorn of them and him. But his message is couched in metaphor and symbolic vision, unlike the stern directness of the style of Elijah.

(19-22) The vision of Micaiah (comp. Job. 1:6-12) is to be taken as a symbol, and nothing more. The one idea to be conveyed is the delusion of the false prophets by a spirit of evil, as a judgment of God on Ahab's sin, and on their degradation of the prophetic office. The imagery is borrowed from the occasion.

(23) The Lord ... the Lord.—The emphatic repetition of the name Jehovah here is an implied answer to the insinuation of mere malice in verses 8 and 18.

(24) Smote Micaiah on the cheek.—The words accompanying evidently convey a

sarcastic reference to the knowledge of the secret dealings of God, implied in Micaiah's vision, with a view to turn it into ridicule. Micaiah's answer accordingly passes them by, and merely declares the shame and terror, with which Zedekiah shall find out hereafter the truth of the prophecy of evil.

(27) Bread of affliction ... —This is a command of severe treatment, as well as scanty fare. Of Micaiah's fate we know nothing; but it is hard to suppose that his bold and defiant testimony could escape the extreme penalty of death, when Ahab's fall gave opportunity of revival to the ruthlessness of Jezebel.

(28) Hearken, O people.—It is a curious coincidence that these are the opening words of the prophetic Book of Micah. They are not found in some MSS of the LXX, and are supposed by some to be an early interpolation in this passage from that book.

(29) So ... Jehoshaphat.—The continued adhesion of Jehoshaphat, against the voice of prophecy, which he had himself invoked (comp. II Chron. 18:31), and, indeed, the subservient part which he plays throughout, evidently indicate a position of virtual dependence of Judah on the stronger power of Israel, of which the alliance by marriage— destined to be all but fatal to the dynasty of David (II Kings 11:1, 2)—was at once the sign of the cause.

(34) A certain man.—Josephus says, "a young man named Naaman." (Compare II Kings 5:1: "because by him the Lord had given deliverance to Syria.")

This is the first place where the chariot, introduced by Solomon from Egypt (10:29), is mentioned as actually used in war. (See II Kings 9:16, 21; 23:30; and compare the proverbial expression of this period, II Kings 2:12; 13:14.)

(38) They washed his armour.—There seems little doubt that this is a mistranslation, and that the LXX rendering (supported also by Josephus) is correct: "And the harlots bathed in it," that is, in the blood-stained pool, the usual public bathing place of their shamelessness. The dog and the harlot are the animal and human types of uncleanness.

(41) Jehoshaphat.—The compiler contents himself with the insertion of a few brief analytic notices of the kingdom of Judah, taking up the thread of the narrative of 15:24, except where it becomes again connected with the history of Israel. (Comp. II Chron. 17:6; 20:33; II Kings 3:6-9; see notes on I Kings 10:22; I Chron. 9:21.) In the Chronicles, on the contrary, there is a full and interesting account of the reign of Jehoshaphat, and especially of his great religious revival (II Chron. 17-20).

(51) Ahaziah.—In this short reign the influence of Jezebel, evidently in abeyance in the last days of Ahab, revives; and the idolatry of Baal resumes its place side by side with the older idolatry of Jeroboam, and (see II Kings 1:2) with the worship of the Canaanitish Baalzebub.

SECOND KINGS

1

The division of the Book of Kings at this point is artificial and arbitrary. The present narrative obviously continues that of I Kings 22:51-53.

(1) Moab rebelled against Israel.—David reduced Moab to vassalage (II Sam. 8:2; comp. 23:20). After that event, Scripture is silent as to the fortunes of Moab. It probably took occasion of the troubles which ensued upon the death of Solomon to throw off the yoke of Israel. The famous Moabite stone supplements the sacred history by recording the war of liberation which Mesha, king of Moab, successfully waged against the successors of Ahab. The death of Ahab and the sickness of Ahaziah (verse 2) would be Moab's opportunity. The revolt of Moab is mentioned here parenthetically (see 3:4-27).

(2) Baal-zebub.—Here only in the Old Testament. Flies are an extraordinary pest in the East; and when we remember that divination by watching the movements of flies is an ancient Babylonian practice, we can hardly doubt that "Lord of Flies" is the true significance of the title "Baal-zebub."

Ekron.—**Akir** (Josh. 13:3). Of the five Philistine cities it lay farthest north, and so nearest to Samaria.

(3) King of Samaria.—Not "Israel," a mark of Judaean feeling.

A God in Israel.—Comp. Micah 4:5.

(4) Now therefore.—For this act of faithlessness, and to prove by the event that there is a God in Israel, whose oracle is unerring. (Comp. I Kings 18:24, seq.)

(5) Turned back unto him.—Unto Ahaziah, as the Syriac and Vulgate actually read. Although Elijah was unknown to the envoys, such a menacing interposition would certainly be regarded as a divine warning, which it was perilous to disregard.

(8) An hairy man.—This refers to a hairy cloak or mantle, a mark of the prophetic office from Elijah downward. (Comp. Zech. 13:4 and Matt. 3:4.)

Girt with a girdle of leather.—Such as only the poorest would wear. The girdle was ordinarily of linen or cotton, and often costly. The prophet's dress was a sign of contempt for earthly display, and of sorrow for the national sins and their consequences, which it was his function to proclaim. (Comp. Isa. 20:2.)

(9) Then the king sent.—With hostile intentions, as is proved by his sending soldiers, and by the words of the angel in verse 15. (Comp. I Kings 18:8 and 22:26, seq.)

A captain of fifty.—The army of Israel was organized by thousands, hundreds, and fifties, each of which had its "captain." (Comp. Num. 31:14, 48; I Sam. 8:12.)

(10) Let fire come down from heaven.—A phrase found only here and in II Chron. 7:1. The words "come down" are appropriate, as repeating the captain's bidding to the prophet.

Consume.—"Eat," or "devour." Here, as in I Kings 18:38, Jehovah is represented as vindicating His own cause by the means most adequate to the necessities of the time, viz., a manifest miracle.

(12) Consumed him and his fifty.—The destruction of the captains and their companies emphasizes the authority properly belonging to the prophet, and help and protection which Jehovah bestows on His prophets. The captains and their men are simply conceived as instruments of a will opposing itself to Jehovah, and are accordingly annihilated. These considerations render irrelevant all questions about the moral justice of their fate, and comparative degrees of guilt. (Comp. 2:23, seq., 6:17.)

(15) Be not afraid of him.—The former two captains, as being the willing tools of the king, might have shown their zeal by instantly slaying the prophet.

(16) Off.—"From," as in verses 4 and 6. The words of the oracle are repeated verbally three times. The peculiar form of the story suggests that it was derived in the first instance from oral tradition rather than from a written source. Comp. 2:2-6.

(17) In the second year of Jehoram.—Comp. I Kings 22:52. Either our present Heb. text is corrupt, or the compiler followed a different source in this place.

2

(1) And it came to pass ... whirlwind.—The compiler has prefixed this heading to the following narrative by way of connection with the general thread of the history. It seems to be indicated that the event happened in the beginning of the reign of Jehoram; but see note on II Chron. 21:12.

Gilgal.—This Gilgal was in Ephraim, on a hill southwest of Shiloh, near the road leading to Jericho. (See Deut. 11:30; Hosea 4:15; Amos 4:4.) Hosea and Amos connect

Gilgal with Bethel, as a sanctuary. It was probably marked by a ring of stones like those at Stonehenge. From this spot the mountain land of Gilead, the Great Sea, and the snowy heights of Hermon, were all visible, so that the prophet could take from there a last look at the whole country which had been the scene of his earthly activity.

(2) Tarry here, I pray thee.—This was said, not to test Elisha's affection, nor from a motive of humility, that Elisha might not witness his glorious ascension, but because Elijah was uncertain whether it was God's will that Elisha should go with him. (Comp. verse 10.) Elisha's threefold refusal to leave him settled the doubt.

The Lord hath sent me to Beth-el.— Why? His mission was to visit the prophetic schools, or guilds, established there, and at Gilgal and Jericho, and to confirm their fidelity to Jehovah. Gilgal and Beth-el, as ancient Canaanite sanctuaries, were centers of illegal worship of the God of Israel. The guilds of the prophets may have been intended to counteract this evil influence at its headquarters.

They went down.—From Gilgal. The phrase proves that the Gilgal between the Jordan and Jericho cannot be meant in verse 1. (See Josh. 4:19 and 5:10.)

(3) The sons of the prophets.—See note on I Kings 20:35.

Hold ye your peace.—Elisha says this, not to prevent the gathering of a crowd to witness the spectacle of Elijah's departure, nor yet to intimate that his master's modesty will be shocked by much talk of his approaching exaltation, but simply to suggest that the subject is painful both to him and to his beloved master. The Hebrew term, **heheshû,** imitates the sound, like our "hush"!

(7) Stood to view.—"Taken their stand opposite," i.e., directly opposite the place where the two were standing by the brink of the river, yet at some distance behind. They wished to see whether and how the companies would cross the stream at a point where there was no ford.

(8) Smote the waters.—A symbolical action like that of Moses smiting the rock, or stretching out his rod over the sea. (Comp. also the use of Elisha's staff, 4:29.) In all these cases the outward and visible sign is made the channel of the invisible and spiritual force of faith.

(9) A double portion.—The expression is used in Deut. 21:17 of the share of the first-born son, who by the Mosaic law inherited two parts of his father's property. Elisha asks to be treated as the first-born among "the sons of the prophets," and so to receive twice as great a share of "the spirit and power" of his master as any of the rest. "Make me thy true spiritual heir": not "Give me twice as great a share of the spirit of prophecy as thou possessest thyself," as many have wrongly interpreted.

(10) Thou hast asked a hard thing.—To grant such a petition was not in Elijah's own power, but in God's only. In the next words the prophet connects the fulfillment of his follower's wish with a condition depending entirely upon the divine will. Elijah thus disclaims power to fulfill the request. At the same time, it is implied that his departure will be something exalted above the perception of ordinary men.

(11) The Hebrew mind recognized the presence and working of Jehovah in the terrific phenomena of nature. (Comp. Pss. 18:6-15; 104:3.) We must therefore be cautious of taking the words before us in too literal a sense. The essential meaning of the passage is that God suddenly took Elijah to Himself, amid a grand display of His power in and through the forces of nature. (See verse 16.)

As regards the miraculous removal of Elijah and Enoch (Gen. 5:24), von Gerlach remarks: "All such questions as whither they were removed, and where they now are, and what changes they underwent in translation, are left unanswered by the Scriptures." It may be added that the ascension of Elijah into heaven is nowhere alluded to in the rest of the Bible.

(12) And Elisha ... cried.—Literally, "And Elisha was seeing, and he (emphatic) was shouting." (Comp. verse 10, "If thou see me taken from thee.")

My father, my father expresses what Elijah was to Elisha. (See note on verse 9.)

The chariot of Israel, and the horsemen thereof expresses what Elijah was to the nation. The personal work and influence of a prophet like Elijah was the truest safeguard of Israel. The force of the expression will be seen if it is remembered that chariots and horsemen constituted, in that age, the chief military arm, and were indispensable for the struggle against the Aramean states.

Rent them in two pieces.—From top to bottom in token of extreme sorrow (comp. I Kings 11:30.)

(13) The mantle of Elijah.—See verse 8 and note on 1:8, and comp. I Kings 19:19.

311

The badge of the prophet's office was naturally transferred to his successor.

(14) Where is the Lord God of Elijah?—Has He left the earth with His prophet? If not, let Him now show His power, and verify the granting of the request (verse 9). The words are a sort of irony of faith. Elisha "seeks" Jehovah as the only source of power.

(15) To view.—It is not clear whether these sons of the prophets are the fifty who "went, and stood to view afar off" (verse 7), or not. On the whole, it seems likely that **all** the guild residing at Jericho is meant. Awaiting Elisha's return, they had assembled at the river side, and witnessed the miracle, which was evidence to them that Elisha was to be their future head.

(18) Did I not say.—Or, "command." Elisha could now fairly remind them of his authority. So the phrase "Go not" is, in the Hebrew, imperative. (Comp. "Ye shall not send," verse 16.) With these words, the history of Elijah significantly closes.

(19) The men of the city.—Not "the sons of the prophets," but the citizens make this trial of the prophet's miraculous powers.

The situation of this city is pleasant.—Jericho, "the city of palms" (Deut. 34:3), had a fine position, rising like an oasis from a broad plain of sand.

The water is naught.—Heb., "bad."

And the ground barren.—Verse 21 ("from thence") shows that the waters, not the soil, were the cause of the evil complained of. "The ground," or rather, "the land" is here put for its inhabitants, including the lower animals; and what is said is either "the country bears dead births," or, "the country has many miscarriages." (Comp. Exod. 23:26; Mal. 3:11.) "The ground is barren," or unfruitful, is therefore an incorrect translation.

(20) A new cruse.—A new one, because the holy purpose demanded an instrument uncontaminated by use. (Comp. Num. 19:2; II Sam. 6:3.)

Salt.—As an antiseptic, an appropriate sacramental medium of the divine influence which was to expel the corruption of the spring.

(21) Thus saith the Lord.—Not the prophet's own power, nor the natural virtues of the salt, but the divine creative will was effectual to the healing of the spring.

(23) Mocked.—Elisha was probably going up the steep road slowly, and his prophet's mantle attracted attention. Baldness was a reproach (Isa. 3:17; 15:2), and suspicious as

one of the marks of leprosy (Lev. 13:43). Elisha, though still young—he lived fifty years after this (13:14)—may have become bald prematurely.

(24) Cursed them.—"To avenge the honor of Jehovah, violated in his person" (**Keil**). (Comp. Exod. 16:8; Acts 5:4.) The curse of a prophet was an inspired prediction of punitive disaster. Beth-el was a chief seat of idolatry (I Kings 12:29, seq.; Amos 4:4; 5:5; 7:10), and the mobbing of the new prophetic leader may have been premeditated. At all events, the narrative is too brief to enable us to judge of the merits of the case; and what is related belongs to that dispensation in which judgment was made more prominent than mercy, and directly fulfills the menace of Lev. 26:21, seq.

(25) To mount Carmel.—Elijah had often lived there (comp. I Kings 18), as its caves were well fitted for solitude and concealment. Elisha may have retired there to prepare himself for his public ministry by prayer and fasting. (Comp. Matt. 4:1, seq.)

To Samaria.—There he had his permanent abode. (Comp. 6:32.)

3

(1) The eighteenth year.—Comp. note on 1:17 and 8:16.

(2) Like his mother.—Jezebel lived throughout his reign (9:30), which explains why he did not eradicate the Baal-worship (10:18-28).

(3) He cleaved unto the sins of Jeroboam.—I Kings 12:28, seq., 16:2, 26.

(4) The revolt of Moab is continued from 1:1. Ahaziah did not reign two full years, and his accident seems to have prevented any attempt on his part to reduce the Moabites.

Rendered year by year. This tribute is referred to in Isa. 16:1.

(5) Rebelled—i.e., refused payment of the annual tribute.

(7) Wilt thou go.—So Ahab asks Jehoshaphat in I Kings 22:4. Jehoshaphat assented, in spite of the prophetic censures of his alliance with Ahab and Ahaziah (II Chron. 19:2; 20:37), perhaps because he was anxious to inflict further punishment on the Moabites for their inroad into Judah (II Chron. 20), and to prevent any recurrence of the same (**Keil**).

(8) Which way.—Moab's strongest defenses were on the north frontier, and the allies would be liable to attacks from the

Syrians in Ramoth-gilead (8:28). The longer and more difficult southern road, at the extremity of the Dead Sea, may have been chosen partly on these grounds, and partly because Jehoshaphat wished to march as far as possible within his own territory and to get a contingent from Edom, which was at this time subject to him (I Kings 22:48). Moreover, the Moabites were less likely to be on their guard on the southern border, which was more difficult of access.

(9) They fetched a compass.—The confederates appear to have lost their way among the mountains of Seir. They would, in any case, be greatly delayed by the cattle which it was necessary to take with them for subsistence. It is evident from the context that the distress began **after** the Edomite contingent had joined.

(11) But Jehoshaphat ... by him?—The same question is asked by Jehoshaphat in I Kings 22:7. He is for seeking Jehovah through a prophet, in contrast with Jehoram, who at once despairs.

Here is Elisha.—The prophet must have followed the army of his own accord, or rather, as Keil suggests, under a divine impulse, in order that, when the hour of trial came, he might point Jehoram to Jehovah as the only true God.

(12) The king of Israel and Jehoshaphat.—Jehoshaphat said what follows either on the ground of Elijah's reputation, or because the news of Elisha's succession had already reached Judah. They "went down to him" from the royal tents, which were probably pitched on an eminence, so as to overlook the camp. The three kings went to consult the prophet as persons of ordinary station might do. This shows the estimation in which he was held.

(13) The prophets of thy father—i.e., the Baal prophets (comp. I Kings 18:19) and false prophets of Jehovah (I Kings 22:6, 11). Elisha's sarcasm indicates that the former had not been wholly rooted out.

(14) Jehoshaphat is accepted because of his faithful dependence on Jehovah (verse 11). Jehoram still maintained or tolerated the cultus of Bethel and Dan. (See verse 3.)

(15) Bring me a minstrel—i.e., a player on a stringed instrument. Elisha called for music as a natural means of calming his perturbed spirit (verses 13, 14). Composure and serenity of soul were essential, if the prophet was to hear the voice of God within.

(19) And ye shall smite ... shall fell ...—These verbs are continuative of those in the last verse, i.e., they do not **command** a course of action, but **foretell** it. (Comp. 8:12, 13.) Taken as commands, they appear to conflict with Deut. 20:19. Keil, however, explains that the law relates to Canaanite territory which the Israelites were to occupy, whereas Moab's was an enemy's country, and therefore not to be spared.

(20) When the meat offering was offered.—The reckoning by hours was unknown before the captivity. According to the Talmud, the morning sacrifice was offered in the Temple the moment it became light. That help came to the distressed army just at the hour of morning worship was a striking coincidence.

There came water.—It would seem that a sudden storm of rain had fallen on the mountains of Seir, at some distance from the camp (Josephus says at a distance of three days' march); and the water found its natural outlet in the dry wady. There are different kinds of miracles, and, in the present instance, the miraculous element is visible in the prophet's prediction of the coming help, and in the coincidence of the natural phenomena with the needs of the Israelites. (Comp. 7:1, 2, seq.)

(22) And the sun shone upon the water.—The red sunrise tinged the water with the same color. The sun rose behind the Moabites, and, furthermore, the red earth of the locality (Edom) would further redden the water.

(23) The kings are surely slain.—The supposition was not improbable. Confederates of different races often had been known to fall out among themselves (comp. Judg. 7:22; II Chron. 20:23), and in this case the old enmity of Edom toward Israel, and the suppressed jealousies between Israel and Judah, made such a result likely. The Moabites would know also that the wady had been waterless, so that their mistake was natural.

(26) The battle was too sore for him.—The garrison was giving way under the destructive fire of the slingers.

To break through even unto the king of Edom.—The Edomite contingent seemed to be the most vulnerable point in the allied army, and he hoped that these unwilling allies of Israel would allow him to escape through their ranks.

(27) Offered him for a burnt offering.—To Chemosh, without doubt, by way of appeasing that wrath of the god which seemed bent on his destruction.

Upon the wall.—Of Kir-haraseth. This

was done that the besiegers might see, and dread the consequences, believing, as they would likely do, that the divine wrath was now appeased.

And there was great indignation against Israel.—The Moabite garrison was inspired with new courage, while the besiegers were proportionally disheartened. The result was that the allied forces raised the siege and returned to the land of Israel. Why did divine wrath fall upon Israel rather than upon Moab? The words of the text indicate that the object of the dreadful expiation was attained, and that **the wrath of Chemosh** fell upon the Hebrew alliance. It is certain that belief in the supremacy of Jehovah did not hinder ancient Israel from admitting the real existence and potency of foreign deities. (See note on I Chron. 16:25, 26; 17:21; and comp. Num. 21:29, Judg. 11:24.) This peculiar conception is a token of the antiquity of the record before us. In the second half of Isaiah the foreign gods are called nonentities.

4

(1) Thou knowest that thy servant did fear the Lord.—She makes this the ground of her claim on the prophet's assistance. The Targum and Josephus identify the dead man of this verse with Obadiah, who is supposed to have spent all his property in maintaining the prophets (I Kings 18:3, 4). Possibly the widow meant to say that her husband's debts were not due to profligate living.

The creditor is come to take unto him my two sons.—According to the law (Lev. 25:39), they would have to continue in servitude until the year of jubilee.

(2) A pot of oil.—Keil says that there was oil enough for an anointing. The Jews, like the Greeks and Romans, anointed themselves after the bath (II Sam. 12:20).

(4) And when ... thou shalt shut.—The object was to avoid disturbance from without; publicity was undesirable in the case of such a miracle. (Comp. Luke 8:51, 54.)

(5) Who brought ... poured out.—Literally, "They were bringing to her, and she was pouring continually." She did not leave her pouring. The story is evidently abridged in this verse.

(8) And it fell on a day.—Literally, "during that day," referring to the period of the miracle just related. Perhaps, too, the con-

trast of the poor and rich women is intentional.

Passed.—"Crossed over" the plain of Jezreel, which he would have to do, whether he went from Samaria, or from Carmel to Shunem, which lay on the slope of Little Hermon, about midway between the two.

A great woman—i.e., of high rank, or rich (I Sam. 25:2; II Sam. 19:32). Rabbinic tradition identifies her with Abishag the Shunammite of I Kings 1:3. But in that case she must have been at this time more than 200 years old.

(10) A little chamber ... on the wall.—Rather, "a little upper chamber with walls"—i.e., a chamber on the roof of the house, walled on each side as a protection against the weather. (Comp. I Kings 17:19.) Here the prophet would be secure from all interruption or intrusion on his privacy, and so would be likely to honor the house longer with his presence.

(13) Wouldest thou be spoken for to the king?—Dost thou stand in need of an advocate at court? Is there any favor thou desirest from the king? This shows what influence Elisha enjoyed at the time; but it does not prove that Jehu, whom he anointed, was already on the throne, for Jehoram respected and probably feared the prophet. (The commander-in-chief, or "captain of the host," was the most powerful person next to the king.)

(14) She hath no child.—That was at once a misfortune and a reproach. (Comp. Gen. 30:23; I Sam. 1:6, 7; Luke 1:25; Deut. 7:13, 14; Ps. 128:3, 4.)

(19) My head, my head.—The boy had a sunstroke. It was the hot season of harvest, and his head was probably uncovered.

(23) It shall be well.—Omit "it shall be." The expression may be equivalent to our common "all right," admitting the truth of what is said about the custom, yet persisting in one's purpose. She did not want to be delayed, nor to have her faith shaken by argument.

(25) To mount Carmel.—The distance was considerable. Elisha must have dwelt there at least occasionally. (Comp. verse 9.) Carmel probably served as a fixed center of prophetic teaching for the north, as Gilgal, Beth-el, and Jericho for the south.

(26) It is well.—She said this merely to avoid further explanation. She would open her grief to the prophet's own ear, and to none other.

(27) But Gehazi came near to thrust her away.—He thought her vehemence a trespass upon the dignity of his master. (Comp. Matt. 19:13; John 4:27.)

The Lord hath hid it from me.—Supernatural knowledge of every event was not a characteristic of the gift of prophecy. (Comp. II Sam. 7:3, seq.)

(29) If thou meet any man, salute him not.—An injunction of utmost haste. (Comp. Luke 10:4.) A short greeting might end in a long halt. "Orientals lost much time in tedious salutations" (**Keil**).

Lay my staff upon the face of the child.—It seems to be implied that if the mother had had faith this would have sufficed for raising the child. (Comp. 2:8; Acts 19:12.) Keil supposes that the prophet foresaw the failure of this expedient, and intended by it to lift the minds of his disciples to higher and more spiritual conceptions of the prophetic office.

(33-37) Compare the narrative of Elijah's raising the widow's son (I Kings 17:17-24), which is imitated in the present account.

(38) And Elisha came again.—This refers to the prophet's annual visit. (Comp. verse 25.) The story is not put in chronological sequence with the foregoing.

(39) Wild gourds.—Wild gourds, or cucumbers, are oval in shape and taste bitter. When ripe they are apt to burst upon being touched. If eaten they act as a violent purgative. They were mistaken on the present occasion for edible gourds, a favorite food of the people (Num. 11:5).

(40) There is death in the pot.—The bitter taste, and perhaps incipient effect of the pottage, made them think of poison.

(41) Then bring meal.—Reuss appears to be right in saying that "by mistake a poisonous (not merely a bitter) plant had been put into the pot, and the prophet neutralizes the poison by means of an antidote whose natural properties could never have had that effect." The "meal" here, therefore, corresponds to the "salt" in 2:21.

(42) Bread of the firstfruits.—Compare Num. 18:13; Deut. 18:4, according to which all firstfruits of grain were to be given to the priests and Levites. Such presents to prophets appear to have been usual in ordinary times. On the present occasion, which was "a time of dearth" (verse 42 is connected by the construction with the preceding narrative), **one** pious person brought his opportune gift to Elisha.

(44) And they did eat, and left thereof.—Compare our Lord's miracles. Keil rightly calls attention to the fact that Elisha does not **perform**, but only **predicts**, this miracle.

5

(1) Now.—The construction implies a break between this narrative and the preceding. Whether the events related belong to the time of Jehoram or of the dynasty of Jehu is not clear. Evidently it was a time of peace between Israel and Syria. (See note on verse 6.)

By him the Lord had given deliverance unto Syria.—Notice the high prophetic view that it is Jehovah, not Hadad or Rimmon, who gives victory to Syria as well as Israel. (Comp. Amos 9:7.) It is natural to think of the battle in which Ahab received his mortal wound (I Kings 22:30, seq.). The Midrash makes Naaman the man who "drew the bow at a venture" on that occasion. The "deliverance" was victory over Israel.

(3) For he would recover him.—"Then he would receive him back." (Comp. Num. 12:14, 15.) In Israel lepers were excluded from society. Restoration to society implied restoration to health. The same verb came to be used in the sense of healing as well as of receiving back the leper.

(5) Ten talents of silver.—About $20,000. **Six thousand pieces of gold**—i.e., six thousand gold shekels = two talents of gold, about $60,000. The total sum appears much too large, and the numbers are probably corrupt, as is so often the case.

(6) Now.—The message presupposes a not altogether hostile relation between the two kings; and the words of the next verse point to the time of comparative lull which ensued after the luckless expedition to Ramoth-gilead (I Kings 22) and the short reign of the invalid Ahaziah. It refers to the reign of Jehoram, **not** to that of Jehoahaz, in which Israel was wholly crushed by Syria (13:3-7).

(7) Am I God, to kill and to make alive?—See Deut. 32:39; I Sam 2:6. Leprosy was a kind of living death.

(8) When Elisha . . . had heard.—He was in Samaria at the time (verse 3), and would hear of the coming of the great Syrian captain and of the king's alarm. Why did not Jehoram think at once of Elisha? King and prophet were not on good terms with each other. (Comp. 3:14.) Besides, Elisha had not as yet done any miracle of this sort; and his apprehensions may have made the king unable, for the moment, to think at all.

(10) Elisha sent a messenger.—Thus he avoided personal contact with a leper. (Comp. verse 15, where Naaman, when restored, goes in and stands before the prophet.) Perhaps reverence held back those who consulted a great prophet from entering his presence (comp. 4:12). There is really no trace of pride about Naaman; in verse 11 he indicates the feeling of being mocked.

Wash in Jordan.—This command would make it clear that Naaman was not cured by any external means applied by the prophet. He was healed by the God of Israel, at His prophet's prayer. (Comp. verse 15.)

Thy flesh shall come again to thee, and thou shalt be clean.—Leprosy is characterized by raw flesh and running sores, which end in entire wasting away of the tissues.

(12) Both rivers have clear water, as being mountain streams, whereas the Jordan is turbid and discolored. If mere washing in a river be enough, it was easy to do that at home, and to much better advantage.

(14) Seven times.—"Because **seven** was significant of the divine covenant with Israel, and the cure depended on that covenant; or to stamp the cure as a divine work, for **seven** is the signature of the works of God" **(Keil)**. In the Assyrian monuments there is an almost exact parallel, from the age of Sargon of Accad (before 2200 B.C.), to this method of seeking a cure. It thus appears that in bidding Naaman bathe seven times, Elisha acted in accordance with ancient Semitic belief as to the healing virtue of running streams.

(15) I know that ... in Israel.—Naaman, like most of his contemporaries, believed in locally restricted deities. The powerlessness of the Syrian gods and the potency of Jehovah having been brought home to his mind by his marvelous recovery, he concludes that there is no god anywhere except in the land of Israel. His local conception of deity still clings to him. What a mark of historic truth appears in this representation!

(16) I will receive none.—Theodoret compares our Lord's "Freely ye have received, freely give" (Matt. 10:8). Such may have been Elisha's feeling. His refusal, strongly contrasting with the conduct of ordinary prophets, would make a deep impression upon Naaman and his retinue.

(17) Two mules' burden of earth?—It was natural for Naaman, with his local idea of divinity, to make this request. He would build his altar to Jehovah on a foundation

of earth from Jehovah's own land, or construct the altar itself with it.

(18) Leaneth on my hand.—A metaphor denoting the attendance on the king by his favorite grandee or principal adjutant. (Comp. 7:2, 17.)

The Lord pardon thy servant.—Naaman had solemnly promised to serve no god but Jehovah for the future. He now prays that an unavoidable exception—which will, indeed, be such only in appearance—may be excused by Jehovah. His request is not, of course, to be judged by a Christian standard. In his reply, the prophet, as spokesman of Jehovah, acceded to Naaman's prayer.

(26) Went not mine heart ... meet thee?—The prophet, in severe irony, adopts Gehazi's own phrase: "I was there in spirit, and witnessed everything." The sentence has given the commentators much trouble.

Is it a time to receive.—The prophet's question comes to this: The disciple is bound, like his master, to seek not worldly power but spiritual, for the time is one of ardent struggle against the encroachments of paganism.

(27) Unto thy seed for ever.—If it be thought that the sentence is too strong, it should be remembered that the prophet is really pronouncing inspired judgment upon the sin of Gehazi, and milder language might have produced erroneous impressions. Covetousness and lying are never spared in Scripture. (Comp. Acts 5.)

6

(1) The place where we dwell with thee.—The phrase occurred in 1 Kings 4:28. The common hall is meant; whether that at Gilgal or at Jericho is uncertain. The prophet's disciples did not live in a single building, like a community of monks. Their settlement is called "dwellings" in the plural (I Sam. 19:18); and they could be married (4:1).

Too strait.—Their numbers had increased. (Comp. 4:43.)

(6) The iron did swim.—The iron axhead rose to the surface. It had fallen in near the bank. Elisha's throwing in the stick was a symbolical act, intended to help the witnesses to realize that the coming up of the iron was not a natural, but a supernatural, event, brought about through the instrumentality of the prophet. The symbol was appropriate to the occasion. It indicated that iron could be made to float like wood by the sovereign power of Jehovah. The properties of material substances may be suspended or modified at His pleasure. The moral of this story is that God helps in small personal troubles as well as in great ones of larger scope. His providence cares for the individual as well as the race.

(8) Then the king of Syria warred.—The time intended cannot be the reign of Jehoahaz, for here the Syrians achieve nothing of importance. (Comp. verse 32.)

(10) Not once nor twice refers to the statement of the entire verse. On more than one occasion, and in regard to different inroads of the Syrians, Elisha gave the king forewarning.

(11) Which of us is for the king of Israel?—"Who betrays me to the king of Israel?" This would be the natural supposition of the Syrian king when he found himself unexpectedly confronting an armed Israelitish force.

(12) One of his servants.—The old interpreters thought of Naaman, but Elisha's fame may have been otherwise known at Damascus.

(13) Dothan.—It lay on a hill, twelve Roman miles northeast of Samaria, in a narrow pass on the caravan route from Gilead to Egypt (Gen. 37:17).

(15) The servant of the man of God.—Not Gehazi, who is never called Elisha's minister ("servant"), and is usually mentioned by name.

(17) Horses and chariots of fire.—Fire was the well-known symbol of Jehovah's visible presence and protective or destroying might, from the days of the patriarchs onward. "It is a fine thought," says Thenius, "that on this occasion the veil of earthly existence was lifted for a moment for one child of man, so as to allow him a clear glimpse of the sovereignty of Providence." The form of the supernatural appearance was, no doubt, conditioned by the circumstances of the time. Chariots and horses were the strength of the Aramean oppressors of Israel; therefore, Jehovah causes His earthly ministers to see that He also has at His command horses and chariots, and that **of fire.**

(18) And when they came down to him.—The reading of the Syriac and Josephus is, "And they (Elisha and his servant) went down to them"—i.e., to the Syrian force; and this is apparently right. The sight of the heavenly host guarding his master had inspired the prophet's follower with courage to face any danger in his master's company.

Blindness.—The term used in Gen. 19:11, and nowhere besides. It denotes not so much blindness as a dazing effect, accompanied by mental bewilderment and confusion.

(19) This is not the way, neither is this the city.—The "dazing" had caused the Syrians to go wandering about in the valley at the foot of the hill, vainly seeking to find the right way up to the city gate. If the prophet found them in this plight, his words would be literally true.

(22) Wouldest thou smite ... thy bow?—Elisha denies the king's right of disposal of these prisoners of Jehovah. The purpose of the miracle would have been frustrated by killing the Syrians. That purpose was to force their king and them to acknowledge the might of the true God.

(23) So the bands of Syria came no more.—The stress lies on the word "bands." The Syrians, dreading Elisha, did not make any further clandestine attempts to injure Israel. They now resolved to try the fortunes of regular war with the whole strength of their army (verse 24). We must not think of any gratitude on their part for the clemency of Jehoram.

(24) Ben-hadad.—Ben-hadad II, who besieged Samaria in the reign of Ahab (I Kings 20:1). He is mentioned on the monuments of Shalmaneser II.

(25) Fourscore pieces.—Eighty shekels—i.e., about $10.00. Ass's flesh would not ordinarily be eaten at all, and the head of any animal would be the cheapest part.

The fourth part of a cab of dove's dung.—The "cab" was the smallest Hebrew dry measure. It held a little over a quart. The term "dove's dung," in all probability, denotes some kind of common vegetable produce, perhaps a sort of pulse, which was ordinarily very cheap. Such a designation is not unparalleled.

Five pieces of silver.—"Five (shekels in) silver," about $3.00.

(27) Jehoram, in the irony of despair, reminds the woman of what she well knows—that the corn and wine, the staple foods of the time, are long exhausted. The character of Jehoram is consistently drawn. But perhaps the point is: "Jehovah alone is the giver of corn and wine" (Hosea 2:8, 9). "Appeal not to me for these." (Comp. 3:10.)

(28) With the hideous facts here recorded, comp. Deut. 28:56, seq. Similar things were done during the sieges of Jerusalem by Nebuchadnezzar (Lam. 4:10; Ezek. 5:10).

(31) If the head of Elisha ... this day.—The king's horror at the woman's dreadful story is succeeded by indignation against Elisha, who had probably counseled an unyielding resistance to the foe, in the steadfast faith that Jehovah would help His own, and who, prophet though he was, and endued with miraculous powers, had yet brought no help in this hour of urgent need. (Comp. I Kings 19:2.)

(32) But Elisha sat ... with him.—This shows the important position which the prophet occupied at the time. The elders, who were the nobles and chiefs of Samaria, were gathered around him in his house to learn the will of Jehovah, and to receive comfort and counsel from his lips. (Comp. Jer. 21:1, 2; 38:14, seq.)

This son of a murderer.—The reference is to Ahab's murder of Naboth (I Kings 21:19) and the prophets of Jehovah. At the same time, we must not forget the idiom by which a man is called a "son" of any quality or disposition which he evinces. (Comp. II Sam. 7:10; Job. 41:34.)

Is not the sound ... behind him?—Elisha's reason for bidding the elders hold the door was that he foresaw that Jehoram would hasten in person after his messenger to see that his savage order was carried out. (Keil thinks, with Josephus, that Jehoram repented, and hurried off to restrain the sword of his minister.)

(33) The messenger.—Ewald's correction, "the king" (**melek** for **mal'āk**), is certainly right. In the rapid progress of the story, the arrival and momentary exclusion of the messenger is understood.

7

(1) A measure.—See notes on I Kings 18:32; II Kings 6:25.

(2) On whose hand ... leaned.—See note on 5:18.

Behold, if the Lord ... this thing be?—Even granting the unlikely supposition that Jehovah is about to make windows in the sky to rain down supplies through them, the promised cheapness of provisions can hardly ensue so soon. The tone is that of scoffing unbelief.

(3) Why sit we?—No one brought these leprous men food any longer, owing to the pressure of the famine. It has been suggested that they were Gehazi and his sons.

(6) The kings of the Hittites.—Comp. I Kings 9:20; 10:29. The tract of north Syria between the Euphrates and the Orontes was the cradle of the Hittite race, and it was over this that these kings of the several tribes bore sway. In the thirteenth century B.C. their power extended over a great part of Asia Minor, as rock inscriptions prove. Carchemish, Kadesh, Hamath, and Helbon were their capitals. (See Gen. 23; 26:34; II Kings 17:24, 30; II Chron. 8:4; Amos 6:2.)

The kings of the Egyptians.—Little is known of the state of Egypt at this time (toward the close of the twenty-second dynasty). The Syrians were seized with panic, under the idea that they were about to be attacked on all sides at once. Some such wild rumor as that expressed by the words of the text must have been spread through the camp. It is evident from the style of the narrative in chapters 6 and 7 that it rests upon "oral tradition," so that it would be a mistake to press subordinate details.

(8) Went and hid it.—A common practice of Orientals, with whom holes in the ground or in the house wall supply the place of banks.

(9) Some mischief will come upon us.—Vulg., "we shall be accused of wrongdoing."

(13) Five.—Used as an indefinite small number, like our "half a dozen." (Comp. Lev. 26:8; Isa. 30:17.) The actual number taken was two pairs (verse 14).

The horses that remain, which are left in the city.—Literally, "the remaining horses that remain in it." The repetition dwells pathetically on the fewness of those that survive.

Behold, they are as all ... consumed.—The king's adviser supposes two contingencies: the horses (and their drivers) may return safe, in which case they share the fortune of "all the multitude of Israel that are left" (i.e., have survived the famine, but are likely to die of it); or they may be taken and slain by the enemy, in which case they will be "even as all the multitude that are consumed" (i.e., by the famine and fighting). The sense is thus the same as in verse 4.

(14) Two chariot horses—i.e., teams for two chariots, or two pairs of horses. The chariots and their drivers are implied, not mentioned. Two chariots were sent, so that if attacked they might make a better resistance; or perhaps in order that, if one were captured by the enemy, the other might escape with the news.

(17) Trode upon him.—"Trampled him down," as he was trying to discharge his duty. This probably happened, as Thenius suggests, when the crowd was returning from the Syrian camp, wild with excess of food and drink, after their long abstinence. Thus he "saw the plenty with his eyes, but did not eat thereof" (verse 2).

8

(1) Then spake Elisha.—The time is not defined by the phrase. It was **after** the raising of the Shunammite's son (verse 1), and **before** the healing of Naaman the Syrian, inasmuch as the king still talks with Gehazi (verse 5). Moreover, the famine here foretold appears to be that of 4:38, seq., so that the present section must in the original document have preceded chap. 5. Thenius thinks the compiler transferred the present account to this place, because he wished to proceed chronologically, and supposed that the seven years' famine came to an end with the raising of the siege of Samaria.

(2) In the land of the Philistines.—The lowlands of the coast were not so subject to droughts as the limestone highlands of Israel. (Comp. Gen. 12:10; 26:1.) The Philistines, besides, dealt with foreign traders who put in to their shores. (Comp. Joel 3:4-6.)

(3) For her house and for her land.—She found them in the possession of strangers. The state may have occupied the property as abandoned by its owner; or, as is more likely, some neighboring landowner may have encroached upon her rights. She therefore appealed to the king.

(4) Tell me, I pray thee, all the great things.—By many repetitions the history of the prophets took a fixed shape long before it was committed to writing, and the written record preserves all the essential features of the narratives that passed from mouth to mouth, and were handed down orally from father to child.

(7) And Elisha came to Damascus.—In the fragmentary condition of the narratives, **why** he came is not clear. Rashi suggests that it was to fetch back Gehazi who had fled to the Syrians (1 Kings 2:39, seq.). Keil and others think the prophet went with the intention of anointing Hazael, in accordance with a supposed charge of Elijah's

(1 Kings 19:15). Ewald believes that Elisha retreated to Damascene territory, in consequence of the strained relations existing between him and Jehoram, owing to the latter's toleration of idolatry. Obviously all this rests upon pure conjecture. It is clear from verse 7 that Elisha's visit was not expected in Damascus, and further, that there was peace at the time between Damascus and Samaria. We do not know how much of Elisha's history has been omitted between 7:20 and 8:7; but we may fairly assume that a divine impulse led the prophet to Damascus. The revelation, of which he speaks in verses 10 and 13, probably came to him at the time, and so was not the occasion of his journey.

(8) Hazael.—See I Kings 19:15, 17. Hazael appears to have been the highest officer in Ben-hadad's court; Josephus says, "the trustiest of his domestics."

(9) Thy son Ben-hadad.—Comp. 4:12; 5:13; 6:21; 13:14. "Father" was a respectful mode of addressing the prophet.

(10) Thou mayest certainly recover.—Elisha sees through Hazael's character and designs, and answers him in the tone of irony which he used to Gehazi in 5:26, "Go, tell thy lord—as thou, the supple and unscrupulous courtier wilt be sure to do—he will certainly recover. I know, however, that he will assuredly die, and by thy hand."

(11) Until he was ashamed.—Hazael, conscious that Elisha had read his thoughts aright, shrank from that piercing gaze. His tone of amazement and language of self-depreciation (verse 13) betray the hypocrite.

(12) The evil that thou wilt do unto the children of Israel.—Fulfilled in 10:32, 33; 13:3, 4. The cruelties enumerated here were the ordinary concomitants of warfare in that age. (Comp. Amos 1:3, 4, 13; Hosea 10:14; 13:16; II Kings 15:16.)

(15) A thick cloth.—The Hebrew term (makbēr) means, etymologically, something "plaited" or "interwoven." It is not found elsewhere, but a word of the same root occurs in I Sam. 19:13. It is clear from the context that the **makbēr** must have been something which when soaked in water, and laid on the face, would prevent respiration. Josephus says Hazael "strangled" his master with a mosquito net.

(16) In the fifth year of Joram the son of Ahab.—The name Joram is an easy contraction of Jehoram. In this verse and in verse 29 the king of Israel is called Joram, and the king of Judah Jehoram; in verses 21, 23, 24 Joram is the name of the king of Judah. In 1:17 and II Chron. 22:6, both kings are called Jehoram.

Jehoshaphat being then king of Judah.—Were the reading correct, it would be implied that Jehoram was for some reason or other made king or co-regent in the lifetime of his father, just as Esarhaddon united his heir Assurbanipal with himself in the government of Assyria. But the clause should be omitted as a spurious anticipation of the same words in the next line. The clause as it stands is an unparalleled insertion in a common formula of the compiler, and there is no trace elsewhere of a co-regency of Jehoram with his father.

(18) In the way of the kings of Israel.—Jehoram, as son-in-law of Ahab and Jezebel, lent his countenance to the **cultus** of the Tyrian Baal. Under the influence of his wife Athaliah, as it may be surmised, Jehoram slew his six brothers directly after his accession to the throne (II Chron. 21:4). The reason why the details added in Chronicles are here omitted is to be found in the studied brevity of the compiler in the case of less important characters.

(19) To give him alway a light.—Comp. I Kings 11:36; 15:4; and for the promise to David, II Sam. 7:12-16.

(20) In his days Edom revolted.—Although Jehovah was not willing to extirpate Judah, yet He allowed it to be seriously weakened by the defections recorded in verses 20-22. The point of the latter statement in verse 22 is that the success of Edom encouraged Libnah to throw off the Judaean supremacy. For the locality see Josh. 10:29 seq.; 15:42; 21:13.

(23) The rest of the acts.—See especially II Chron. 21:11-19.

(26) Ahaziah.—Called Jehoahaz (II Chron. 21:17). Ewald thinks he assumed the name of Ahaziah on his accession.

The daughter of Omri—i.e., granddaughter. Omri is mentioned rather than Ahab as the founder of the dynasty, and the notorious example of its wickedness. (Comp. Micah 6:16.)

(28) And he went with Joram.—He was persuaded by his mother and her family (II Chron. 22:4).

Against Hazael ... in Ramoth-gilead, which strong fortress Ahab had vainly tried to wrest from Ben-hadad (I Kings 22:6, seq.).

(29) Which the Syrians had given.—It is likely that the imperfect verb is here used in the sense of repetition, implying that Joram was wounded on more than one occasion.

And Ahaziah ... went down.—Ahaziah went down either from Ramoth or from Jerusalem; probably from the former, as no mention is made of his having left the seat of war and returned to Jerusalem.

9

(1) One of the children of the prophets.—Rashi says it was Jonah, who is mentioned in 14:25.

(2) And when thou comest thither.—This makes it clear that the Israelites had retaken Ramoth from the Syrians (comp. verses 3, 15), probably before Joram returned to Jezreel (verse 14). Josephus expressly asserts this.

Jehu.—Probably Jehu had been left in supreme command of the forces at Jehoram's departure, as being the ablest of the generals (so Josephus).

The son of Jehoshaphat.—Nothing is known of Jehu's origin. He is mentioned by Shalmaneser II, king of Assyria, in a fragment of his Annals relating to the campaign against Hazael, as one of his tributaries. On the Black Obelisk, also, there is a representation of Jehu's tribute-bearers, and, perhaps, of Jehu himself, kneeling before Shalmaneser.

(5) The captains of the host were sitting.—The council of war had convened with Jehu in the court.

(6) I have anointed thee.—The commission to Elijah (I Kings 19:16) was thus fulfilled by his successor.

Over the people of the Lord.—Israel being Jehovah's people, Jehovah was Israel's true king, and therefore it was within His sovereign right to appoint whom He would as His earthly representative.

(7) The blood of all the servants of the Lord.—See I Kings 18:4, 13. We are not told so elsewhere, but it is probable that Jezebel persecuted to the death those who clung to the exclusive worship of Jehovah.

(12) It is false.—This is too strong, and does not convey the exact force of the reply. The captains reply to Jehu's "Oh, you know all about it!" with "You are pretending!" They then assume a tone of persuasion: "Do tell us." Even if they had really guessed the import of the prophet's visit, their manner now convinced Jehu that he might safely trust them.

(13) Then they hasted.—The moment

320

they heard it, they hastily took up their outer garments, and laid them as a carpet for Jehu to walk upon. (Comp. Luke 19:36.) The instantaneous action of the generals shows that there must have existed in the army a strong feeling against Joram, and an enthusiasm for Jehu which required only a word from him to precipitate a revolution. The stairway on the outside of the house, leading to the roof, served as an extemporized throne, or rather platform, for the king. (Comp. 11:14.)

(16) Ahaziah king of Judah was come down.—See 8:29. After relating what had meanwhile occurred with the army at Ramoth, the narrative returns to the point.

(17) The company.—The word means literally "overflow," and so a "multitude" of waters (Job 22:11), of camels (Isa. 60:6), of horses (Ezek. 26:10). Jehu was accompanied, therefore, by a considerable force.

Is it peace?—This hardly represents the force of the original. Joram is not yet apprehensive. His question merely means, "What is the news?" He expects news from the army at Ramoth.

(18) What hast thou to do with peace?—Conscious of his strength, Jehu can despise the royal message, and the messenger dared not disobey the fierce general, when ordered summarily to the rear. Of course Jehu wished to prevent an alarm being raised in Jezreel.

(20) The son of Nimshi.—Jehu was "son of Jehoshaphat," son of Nimshi. The former phrase may have fallen out of the text here. (Yet comp. 8:26, "Athaliah daughter of Omri.")

He driveth furiously—i.e., the foremost charioteer so drives. The word rendered "furiously" is related to that rendered "mad fellow" in verse 11. Jehu's chariot swayed unsteadily as he drove madly on.

(21) Against Jehu.—Rather, "to meet Jehu." Joram was curious to know why his messengers had not returned, as well as why the commander-in-chief had left the seat of war. Had he suspected treachery, he would hardly have left the shelter of the walls of Jezreel and ventured forth without a guard.

In the portion of Naboth.—Comp. Naboth's vineyard, I Kings 21:16, 18, and see note on I Kings 21:1.

(22) Is it peace, Jehu?—Joram meant, "Is all well at the seat of war?" Jehu's reply left no doubt of his intentions. He assumes the part of champion of the legitimate worship against Jezebel and her foreign innovations,

and the lawless tyrannies by which she sought to enforce them. (Comp. verses 25, 26.)

Whoredoms.—In the spiritual sense, i.e., idolatries. (See note on I Chron. 5:25.)

Witchcrafts—i.e., sorceries, the use of spells and charms, common among Semitic idolaters. (Comp. the prohibitions in Exod. 22:18; Deut. 18:10, 11.)

(26) Yesterday.—Ahab seized the vineyard the day after the murder of Naboth, a detail not exactly specified in I Kings 21:16.

And the blood of his sons.—The murder of the sons of Naboth is neither stated nor implied in I Kings 21. It would be quite in accordance with ancient practice to slay the sons of one accused of blasphemy along with their father (comp. Josh. 7:24, 25). The present is the exact version of an eyewitness, viz., Jehu himself, while the former was probably derived from a less direct source.

I will requite thee in this plat.—Another important detail not given in the former account.

Plat.—"Portion," as in verse 25.

(27) The ascent of Gur is not mentioned elsewhere. Ibleam lay between Jezreel and Megiddo. (Comp. Judg. 1:27; Josh. 17:11.) See the note on II Chron. 22:9, where a different tradition respecting the end of Ahaziah is recorded. The definite assignment of localities in the present account is a mark of greater trustworthiness.

(29) In the eleventh year of Joram.—Comp. 8:25. Such a difference is not remarkable, inasmuch as the synchronisms between the reigns of the two kingdoms are not based upon exact records or identical computations. (The verse is a parenthesis, and perhaps spurious.)

(30) And she painted her face.—Rather, "and she set her eyes in paint"—i.e., according to the common practice of Oriental ladies, she painted her eyebrows and lashes with a pigment composed of antimony and zinc. The dark border throws the eye into relief, and makes it appear larger. (Comp. Jer. 4:30.)

Tired.—An old English word, meaning "adorned" with a "tire" or headdress. (Comp. Isa. 3:18.) Jezebel, like Cleopatra, put on her royal apparel in order to die as a queen. Ewald's notion that Jezebel thought to captivate the conqueror by her charms is negatived by the consideration that she was the grandmother of Ahaziah, who was twenty-two years old when Jehu slew him, and the fact that Oriental women faded early.

(31) Had Zimri ... master?—The phrase (literally, "Is it peace?") is vague enough to admit of many meanings, according to circumstances. Perhaps Jezebel, in her mood of desperate defiance, repeats the question which Jehoram three times had asked of Jehu, as a hint that **she** herself is now the sovereign to whom Jehu owes an account of his doings. She goes on to call him a second Zimri—i.e., a regicide like him who slew Baasha, and likely to enjoy as brief a reign as he. (See I Kings 16:15-18.)

(36) This is the word of the Lord.—See I Kings 21:23, where this oracle of Elijah is given.

(37) So that they shall not say.—The sense is, So that men will no longer be able to recognize her mangled remains. The continuation of the prophecy, although probably original, is not given in I Kings 21.

10

(1) Ahab had seventy sons.—His posterity in general are meant. Seventy is a favorite round number. Ahab had been dead about fourteen years (3:1; I Kings 22:51), and had had two successors on the throne.

Jehu wrote letters, and sent to Samaria.—Jehu was crafty as well as fierce. He could not venture to the capital without first sounding the inclination of the nobles of the city.

(3) His father's throne—i.e., "Ahab's" throne. (Comp. II Chron. 17:3; 21:12; 29:2; where David is called the father of Jehoshaphat, Jehoram, and Hezekiah in turn.)

Fight for your master's house.—Jehu thus declares his own warlike intentions, beyond the mocking yet perceptive irony of verse 2, leaving the nobles, whom his prompt and decisive action had taken by surprise, no choice between improvised resistance and instant submission. Knowing Jehu's character as a soldier, they chose the latter.

(6) To Jezreel.—A journey of more than twenty miles.

By to morrow this time.—Time is all-important. Jehu wishes to convince the people of Jezreel as soon as possible that none of the royal princes were left to claim the crown, and that the nobles of Samaria have joined his cause.

(9) And stood—i.e., "took his place." Jehu sat as judge in the palace gateway,

according to royal custom, and gave audience to the people. The citizens would naturally be struck with consternation at the sight of the two ghastly pyramids in front of the palace, and would crowd together in expectancy at the gates. Jehu goes forth to justify himself, and calm their fears.

But who slew all these?—Jehu hints that as Jehovah had foretold the destruction of the house of Ahab, He must have brought it to pass; and therefore no one is to blame (verse 10).

(13) The brethren of Ahaziah king of Judah—i.e., Ahaziah's "kinsmen." His brothers, in the strict sense of the word, were slain by a troop of Arabs, in the lifetime of his father Jehoram (II Chron. 21:17; 22:1). The news of the taking of Ramoth, and of Joram's convalescence, may have reached Jerusalem, and induced these princes to make a visit of pleasure to the court of Jezreel, not suspecting the events which had meanwhile happened with the headlong rapidity characteristic of Jehu's action. Jehu slew them (verse 14) because of their connection with the doomed house of Ahab. Keil thinks he dreaded their conspiring with the partisans of the fallen dynasty in Samaria.

(15) Jehonadab the son of Rechab.—Comp. Jer. 35:6-11; I Chron. 2:55. Ewald supposes that the Rechabites were one of the new societies, having retired to the desert, formed after the departure of Elijah for the active support of the true religion. Their founder in this sense was Jonadab.

And he saluted him.—It was important to Jehu to be seen acting in concert with a man revered for sanctity and powerful as a leader of the orthodox party.

(18) Ahab served Baal a little; but Jehu shall serve him much.—Ahab had, as the people well knew, served Baal more than a little; but the antithesis was not too strong for Jehu's hidden meaning. He was thinking of his intended holocaust of human victims (verse 25).

(23) That there be here with you none of the servants of the Lord.—This precaution of Jehu's suggests suspicion to a modern reader, but it would suggest the very contrary to the Baal-worshipers—viz., an extraordinary reverence for Baal; a dread lest some profane person should be present in his sanctuary.

(25) As soon as he had made an end.—The Syriac has, "when they (i.e., the Baal priests) had made an end." This is probably right. For the massacre Jehu chose the moment when all the assembly was absorbed in worship.

(27) The image of Baal.—The word is "pillar," which in this case is the conical pillar of stone representing the Baal himself. The wooden pillars ("images") of verse 26 probably symbolized companion deities of the principal idol.

(28) Thus Jehu destroyed Baal.—Objectively considered, the slaughter of the servants of Baal was in perfect harmony with the Law; but, subjectively, the motive which influenced Jehu was thoroughly selfish. The priests and prophets of Baal in Israel, as depending entirely on the dynasty of Ahab, the king who had originally introduced the Baal-worship, might prove dangerous to Jehu. By exterminating them he might hope to secure the whole-hearted allegiance of the party that stood by the legitimate worship. His maintenance of the **cultus** established by Jeroboam (verse 29) proves that he acted from policy rather than religious zeal. (Comp. I Kings 12:28, seq., 15:26, 30, 34.)

(30) Thy children of the fourth generation.—The fulfillment of this oracle is noticed in 15:12. (Comp. Exod. 20:5.)

(32) In those days.—As a vassal and ally of Assyria (see notes on 9:2), Jehu drew upon himself the active hostility of Hazael. From the point of view of the sacred writer, this verse states the consequence of Jehu's neglect of "walking in Jehovah's instruction with all his heart" (verse 31). Through Hazael and the Syrians God began to cut off part after part of Israelite territory. These conquests of Hazael were characterized by great barbarity. (Comp. Amos 1:3-5, and Elisha's prediction of the same, 8:12.)

(36) In Samaria.—The Hebrew puts this phrase last, perhaps to indicate by emphasis that Jehu made Samaria, and not Jezreel, the seat of his court.

11

(1) And when Athaliah ... saw.—As to Athaliah and her evil influence on her husband Jehoram, see 8:18, 26, 27. By her ambition and her cruelty she now shows herself a worthy daughter of Jezebel.

Her son.—Ahaziah (9:27). The history of the Judaean monarchy is resumed from that point.

Destroyed all the seed royal.—"The seed of the kingdom" means all who might set up claims to the succession. Ahaziah's brothers

had been slain by the Arabs (II Chron. 21:17), and his "kinsmen" by Jehu (10:14). Those whom Athaliah slew would be for the most part Ahaziah's own sons, though other relatives are not excluded by the term.

(3) And he was with her.—The words "in the house of the Lord" should immediately follow. The word "hid" is connected with "six years" in the Hebrew, and relates to the infant prince only. Joash was with his aunt in one of the chambers allotted to the priests, perhaps even in the high priest's (Jehoiada's) residence, which may have been within the sacred precincts.

(4) Made a covenant with them.—The chronicler's whole transaction, while generally coinciding with that given here, presents certain striking differences, of which the most salient is the prominence assigned to the priests and Levites in the matter. The compilers of the two canonical histories were determined in their choice of materials and manner of treatment by their individual aims and points of view, which differed considerably. The account before us is the older and more original, and therefore, the more valuable regarded as mere history.

(5) The watch of the king's house.—There were two places to be occupied for the success of the present movement—the royal palace and the Temple, "the king's house" and "the house of the Lord." In the former was Athaliah, the usurping queen, whose movements must be closely watched, and whose adherents must be prevented from occupying and defending the palace; in the latter, the young heir to the throne, who must be protected from attack. The "gates" mentioned in verse 6 were side and principal entrances to the palace (see verse 19).

(10) King David's spears and shields.—Comp. II Sam. 8:7; II Chron. 23:9. The arms which David had laid up in the Temple as spoils of war were now to be used, appropriately enough, for the restoration of David's heir to the throne.

(12) And gave him the testimony.—Some rabbis explain this to mean a royal robe; others think of a phylactery on the coronet. (See Deut. 6:8.) Thenius says it was the Law—i.e., a book in which were written Mosaic ordinances, and which was held in a symbolic manner over the king's head after he had been crowned.

(16) She went ... king's house.—Athaliah was conducted to the royal stables which adjoined the palace, and there put to death.

(17) A covenant.—Rather, "the covenant." The high priest solemnly renewed the original compact between Jehovah and the king and people—a compact which had been violated by the Baal-worship of recent reigns.

(18) All the people of the land went into the house of Baal.—In the fervor of their newly-awakened enthusiasm for Jehovah, the assembly may have hurried off at once to the work of demolition. It seems to be implied that the "house of Baal" stood on the Temple mount, in ostentatious rivalry with the sanctuary of Jehovah.

(19) And he took the rulers . . . the land.— Jehoiada now arranges a procession to escort the king in triumph from the Temple to the palace, concluding with the solemn enthronement in the palace of his fathers.

(20) The city was in quiet.—The citizens of Jerusalem accepted the revolution without attempting any counter movement. No doubt there was a strong element of Baal-worshipers and partisans of Athaliah in the capital. "The people of the land" are contrasted with the citizens of Jerusalem.

And they slew Athaliah.—Rather, "and Athaliah they had slain"; an emphatic recurrence to the real climax of the story (verse 16), by way of conclusion.

12

(1) Forty years.—A common round number. David and Solomon are each said to have reigned forty years.

Beer-sheba.—A famous Simeonite sanctuary and resort of pilgrims (Amos 5:5; 8:14).

(3) Sacrificed . . . burnt.—The worship of the high places continued even under the regime of Jehoiada.

(4) The money of the dedicated things.— Comp. I Kings 15:15.

Even the money of every one that passeth the account.—Rather, "current money" (Gen. 23:16). The currency at this period consisted of pieces of silver of a fixed weight. There was no such thing as a Hebrew coinage before the exile. The reason "current money" was wanted was that it might be paid out immediately to the workpeople employed in the repairs.

The money that every man is set at—i.e., every kind of redemption money, such as was paid in the case of the first-born (Num. 18:16) and of a vow (Lev. 27:2, seq.). In the latter case, the priest fixed the amount to be paid.

And all the money that cometh into any

man's heart to bring.—That is, all the free will offerings in money. It is noticeable that Jehoash and not Jehoiada took the initiative in the matter.

(5) The breaches of the house.—The dilapidations of the Temple were serious, not because of its age—it had only stood about 130 years—but owing to the wanton attacks of Athaliah and her sons (comp. II Chron. 24:7), who had, moreover, diverted the revenues of the sanctuary to the support of the Baal-worship.

(7) Now therefore receive no more money.—Commentators disagree upon the question of the degree of blame attaching to the priests for their neglect. Probably the revenues of the sanctuary had been in a languishing condition during the late reigns, and the priesthood had used whatever offerings they received for their own support. They would now naturally be unwilling to appropriate to the work of repair any part of the revenues which they had come to regard as their own. It is likely that the moral tone of the whole order had degenerated in the late period of apostasy.

(9) Jehoiada the priest took a chest.—By order of the king (II Chron. 24:8).

Put.—The chest was kept locked, and the Levitical doorkeepers received the money from those who offered it, and dropped it at once into the chest. This obviated all suspicion of a possible misapplication of the contributions.

(10) Put up in bags, and told.—The high priest and the royal secretary put the pieces of silver into bags of a certain size, and then counted the bags, weighed, and sealed them up. These would be paid out as money (verse 11) to the overseers, and then by them to the workmen (comp. verse 15).

(16) It was the priests'.—The priests were not deprived of their lawful revenues by the new arrangement. They received their ancient dues from the trespass and sin offerings. (See Lev. 5:15-18; 6:26-29; Num. 5:8.) The change initiated by Jehoash was that from now on gifts intended for the sanctuary itself were kept apart from the gifts intended for the priesthood.

(17) Then.—Hazael's invasion of the south followed upon his successes against Jehoahaz, who became king of the northern kingdom in the year when Jehoash took in hand the restoration of the Temple. (Comp. verse 6 with 13:1, 3.) It appears from II Chron. 24:23 that the high priest Jehoiada was dead, and Jehoash had already swerved from his counsels.

Fought against Gath.—At the time Gath either belonged to, or was in league with, Judah (see II Chron. 11:8). It was perhaps at this time the only important outpost of the capital on the western side. Ewald assumes that the petty Philistine states had invited the intervention of Hazael between themselves and their suzerain, the king of Judah. Gaza, Ashdod, Ascalon, and Ekron, but **not** Gath, appear as Philistine kingdoms in the annals of Sennacherib and Esarhaddon, a century later.

(18) The hallowed things that ... Jehoram, and Ahaziah ... had dedicated.—Although these kings had sought to naturalize the Baal-worship, they had not ventured to abolish that of Jehovah. On the contrary they even tried to conciliate the powerful priesthood and numerous adherents of the national religion by dedicating gifts to the sanctuary. The treasure in question, especially that of the Temple, appears to have been regarded as a reserve, only to be touched in case of grave national emergency like the present.

And he went away from Jerusalem.—The serious defeat of the army of Jehoash, related in Chronicles, accounts satisfactorily for the sacrifice of his treasures here specified, while the withdrawal of the Syrians after their victory, as told in Chronicles, is explained by the bribe which Jehoash is here said to have paid them. The two narratives thus supplement each other.

(20) In the house of Millo.—See notes on II Sam. 5:9; I Kings 9:15. The chronicler relates that Jehoash was murdered in his bed.

13

(3) He delivered them into the hand of Hazael.—The meaning is that Jehovah allowed Israel to be defeated in successive encounters with the Syrian forces, and to suffer loss of territory, but not total subjugation. Comp. 10:32, seq.

All their days.—The phrase is an indefinite designation of a long period of disaster.

(4) And the Lord hearkened unto him.—Not, however, immediately. (See verse 7.) The Syrian invasions, which began under Jehu, were renewed again and again throughout the reign of Jehoahaz (verse 22), until the tide of conquest began to turn in the time of Joash (verse 15), whose incomplete victories (verses 17, 19, 25) were followed

up by the permanent successes of his son Jeroboam II (14:25-28).

The parenthesis marked in verse 5 really begins, therefore, with the words, "And the Lord hearkened." The historian added it by way of pointing out that although the prayer of Jehoahaz did not meet with immediate response, it was not ultimately ineffectual.

(6) Nevertheless they departed not.—The restoration of divine favor did not issue in the abolition of the irregular worship introduced by Jeroboam I as the state religion of the northern kingdom. It does not appear from the history of Elijah and Elisha, incorporated in his work, that either of those great prophets ever protested against the worship established at Bethel and Dan.

And there remained the grove also in Samaria.—With the return of peace and the renewal of prosperity, luxury also soon reappeared, and the idolatry that especially countenanced it (the Asherah, the productive principle in nature) lifted up its head again.

(14) O my father, my father.—Comp. note on 2:12. Joash laments the approaching loss of his best counselor and helper. The prophet, by his teaching and his prayers, as well as by his sage counsel and wonder-working powers, had been more to Israel than chariots and horsemen.

(16) Elisha put his hands upon the king's hands.—This was to invest the act of shooting with a prophetic character, and, further perhaps, to signify the consecration of the king to the task that the shooting symbolized.

(17) Eastward.—In the direction of Gilead, which was occupied by the Syrians (10:33).

Shoot.—The old illustration of declaring war by shooting an arrow into the enemy's country is not without bearing on this case, although it obviously does not exhaust the meaning of the act.

In Aphek.—Josh. 13:4; I Kings 20:26. The scene of former defeats was to become that of triumph.

(19) The man of God was wroth with him.—In the second symbolic act, smiting the ground meant striking the enemy to the ground. His present want of zeal presaged a like deficiency in prosecuting the war hereafter. Soothsaying by means of arrows was a practice of unknown antiquity in the Semitic world. Shooting an arrow, and observing where and how it fell, was one method of trying to fathom the secrets of that Power which overrules events and foreknows the future. (Comp. I Sam. 20:36, seq.) In principle it is quite analogous to casting lots, a practice familiar to readers of the Bible. The second process (verse 18) seems equally to have depended upon chance, according to modern ideas. The prophet left it to the spontaneous impulse of the king to determine the number of strokes, because he believed that the result, whatever it was, would betoken the purpose of Jehovah (see Prov. 16:33). Elisha's anger was the natural anger of the man and the patriot, disappointed at the result of a divination from which he had hoped greater things.

(20) **And the bands of the Moabites invaded.**—They took advantage of the weakened condition of Israel to revenge the devastation of their country described in 3:25. "At the coming in of the year" means in the spring. (Comp. II Sam. 11:1.)

(21) **He revived.**—Thenius thinks that the sacred writer regarded this miracle as a pledge of the fulfillment of Elisha's promise to Joash. Bahr says: "Elisha died and was buried, like all other men, but even in death and in the grave he is avouched to be the prophet and servant of God."

(23) **And the Lord was gracious.**—The verse is a remark of the compiler's, as is evident from the style, the reference to the Covenant, and the expression "as yet," or rather, "until now"—i.e., the day when he was writing, and when the northern kingdom had finally perished.

(24) **Ben-hadad.**—The name Ben-hadad (here Ben-hadad III) does not, of course, signify any connection with the dynasty overthrown by Hazael. It was a divine title. (Comp. note on 6:24.) This Ben-hadad was probably a feebler sovereign than Hazael.

(25) **The cities, which he had taken**—i.e., which Hazael had taken. The cities referred to must have been cities on the west of Jordan (comp. verses 3 and 7), for the Trans-Jordan had been subdued by Hazael in the time of Jehu (10:32, seq.). Jeroboam II, the son of Joash, restored the ancient boundaries of Israel (14:25).

14

(5) **As soon as the kingdom was confirmed**—i.e., as soon as he was firmly established on the throne, as soon as he felt his power secure. (Comp. I Kings 2:46.)

(7) **The valley of salt.**—Comp. II Sam.

8:13. This was the salt plain of the Dead Sea, which Amaziah would traverse in marching against Edom.

Selah—i.e., the crag, the Hebrew name of the famous rock-hewn town of Petra.

Joktheel.—The name probably means "God's ward," referring to the wonderful strength of the natural position of the town. (Comp. Josh. 15:38.) The reduction of the capital implies that of the country. The defeat of Jehoram (8:20, seq.) was thus avenged. Chronicles gives a more detailed account of the re-conquest of Edom, and its consequences (II Chron. 25:5-16).

(8) **Come, let us look one another in the face.**—This was a challenge to battle. It appears likely that Amaziah, intoxicated by his recent success, aimed at nothing less than the recovery of the Ten Tribes for the house of David. Josephus (**Antt.** 9:9, §2 gives what is intended to be the letters which passed between the two kings on this occasion.

(9) **Give thy daughter to my son to wife.**—This perhaps hints at Amaziah's demand for the surrender of Israel (the "daughter" of Jehoash) to Judah (the "son" of Amaziah).

And there passed by a wild beast that was in Lebanon.—It is obvious to compare with this brief but most pithy parable that of Jotham (Judg. 9:8-15). The contrast between the northern and southern kingdoms in point of military strength and resources, and the disdainful tolerance with which the former regarded the latter, could hardly have found more forcible expression.

(10) **Thou hast indeed smitten**—i.e., thou hast "thoroughly" worsted; gained a "brilliant" victory over Edom. (The "indeed" qualifies "smitten.")

Glory of this, and tarry at home—i.e., be content with the glory thou hast achieved. Rest on thy laurels, and do not risk them by further enterprises which may not turn out so favorably.

(11) **Beth-shemesh.**—Jehoash proposed to attack Jerusalem from the west, as Hazael also had intended (12:17).

(13) **Came.**—The Hebrew text has, "brought him." So Chronicles and the Vulg. Jehoash brought Amaziah a prisoner to his own capital.

From the gate.—The gate of Ephraim lay on the north side of the city, and was also called the "Gate of Benjamin." The corner gate was at the northwest corner of the wall at the point where it turned southward. Four hundred cubits is about 222 yards.

(14) **That were found.**—This expression

seems to hint that there was not much treasure to carry off. (Comp. 13:18.)

Hostages.—Having humbled the pride of Amaziah, Jehoash left him in possession of his throne, taking hostages for his future good behavior. Similar acts of clemency are recorded of themselves by the Assyrian kings of the dynasty of Sargon.

(19) They made a conspiracy.—The fact that no individual conspirators are mentioned appears to indicate that Amaziah's death was the result of a general disaffection; and this inference is strengthened by the other details of the record. (See note on verse 22.)

Lachish.—Now "Um Lâkis." Of old it was a strong fortress. (Comp. II Kings 18:14; 19:8; II Chron. 11:9.) Amaziah's flight there seems to indicate either a popular rising in Jerusalem, or a military revolt.

(21) Took.—The expression seems to imply that Azariah was **not** the eldest son. As Amaziah was fifty-nine years old at his death, he probably had sons older than sixteen. Azariah was therefore chosen as a popular, or perhaps military, favorite.

Azariah.—See note on II Chron. 26:1.

(22) He built Elath.—Amaziah perhaps had not vigorously prosecuted the conquest of Edom, having been greatly weakened by his defeat in the struggle with Jehoash. He may even have suffered some further losses at the hands of the Edomites, and this may have led to the conspiracy which brought about his death and the accession of his son. The warlike youth Uzziah took the field at once, and pushed his victorious arms to the southern extremity of Edom, the port of Elath, and thus restored the state of things which had existed under Solomon and Jehoshaphat.

(23) Reigned forty and one years.—According to the statement of this verse, Jeroboam reigned fourteen years concurrently with Amaziah, who reigned altogether twenty-nine years (verse 2), and thirty-seven years concurrently with Azariah (15:8), so that he reigned altogether not forty-one but fifty-one years. (The discrepancy originated in a confusion of the Hebrew letters used as numerical equivalents.)

(25) He restored—i.e., he wrested out of the hands of the Syrians the territory they had taken from Israel.

From the entering of Hamath.—This was the originally determined boundary of Isra-

el on the north. (Comp. Num. 13:21; 34:8; Josh. 13:5.)

The sea of the plain—i.e., the Dead Sea (Josh. 3:16). The whole length of the Dead Sea and the country beyond Jordan are included.

Jonah, the son of Amittai, the prophet.—Comp. Jonah 1:1. The activity of this prophet must have occupied a very large field, as tradition connects him with Nineveh.

Gath-hepher.—See Josh. 19:13. This was not far north of Nazareth.

(27) Said not—i.e., by any prophet.

Blot out the name.—The figure is taken from blotting out writing. (Comp. Num. 5:23.) The Hebrews used inks that soon faded, and could easily be wiped off the parchment. (Hence the partial obliteration of words and letters which is one of the causes of textual corruption.)

(28) Damascus, and Hamath.—This refers not to the entire states so named, which were powerful independent communities, but to portions of their territory, which had belonged to Israel in the days of Solomon. The prostration of his enemy accounts for the permanent success of Jeroboam, who was himself a vassal of Assyria.

For Israel.—It may be that by an oversight the Judean editor wrote "to Judah," instead of "to Israel," and that some scribe added a marginal note "in Israel," which afterward crept into the text. It is curious to find certain districts of Hamath leagued with Azariah, king of Judah, against Tiglath-pileser. (See note on 15:1.)

15

(1) In the twenty and seventh year of Jeroboam.—An error of transcription for the "fifteenth year." Amaziah reigned twenty-nine years (14:2), fourteen concurrently with Joash, and fifteen with Jeroboam.

(5) And the Lord smote the king.—The chronicler relates the reason—viz., because of his usurpation of priestly functions in the sanctuary. This happened toward the end of the reign. Jotham, the regent, was only twenty-five when Azariah died (verse 33).

In a several house—i.e., a royal residence outside of Jerusalem (Lev. 13:46; II Kings 7:3) set apart for such cases. Lepers were "emancipated" from all social relations and duties.

Judging the people of the land—i.e., as

327

his father's representative. (Comp. I Sam. 8:6, 20; I Kings 3:9.) This passage is strong evidence against the assumption of joint sovereignties of princes with their fathers, so often made by way of escaping chronological difficulties in Hebrew history. Jotham is not co-regent but viceroy of Azariah until the latter dies.

(8) In the thirty and eighth year of Azariah.—This agrees with the assumption that Jeroboam reigned fifty-one years (14:23).

(9) As his fathers—i.e., the dynasty of Jehu, of which he was the last member. Like all his predecessors, he upheld the illicit worship established by Jeroboam I.

(10) Before the people.—The open assassination of the king, in contrast with the secrecy with which former conspiracies had been concerted, is a symptom of the rapidly increasing corruption of morals, which allowed people to look on with indifference while the king was being murdered.

(14) Went up from Tirzah.—Menahem was Zachariah's general, who at the time was quartered with the troops at Tirzah, near Samaria (I Kings 14:17). On the news of the murder of Zachariah, Menahem marched to the capital. The month of Shallum's reign was probably taken up with preparations for hostilities on both sides.

(16) Tiphsah.—The name means "ford," and elsewhere denotes the well-known Thapsacus on the Euphrates (I Kings 4:24). Here, however, an Israelite city in the neighborhood of Tirzah is obviously intended.

The coasts thereof.—Literally, "her borders" (or, "territories"). (Comp. Josh. 17:8.)

(18) He did that which was evil.—Ewald says that at the outset Menahem appeared to be guided by better principles, referring to Zech. 11:4-8.

All his days.—In the Hebrew these words occur at the end of the verse. They are not found in any other instance of the common formula which the verse repeats (comp. I Kings 15:26, 34; 16:26; 22:53; II Kings 3:2; 10:31; etc.), and almost certainly belong to the next verse.

(19) Pul.—For the identity of Pul, king of Assyria, with Tiglash-pileser II, see note on I Chron. 5:26.

A thousand talents of silver.—About $2,-000,000.

That his hand might be with him.—Pul (Tiglash-pileser) came at the invitation of Menahem to establish the latter in the

sovereignty against other pretenders as a vassal of Assyria. (Comp. Hosea 5:13; 7:11; 8:9.) Tiglath-pileser had first reduced Rezin, king of Syria-Damascus, which was probably much weakened by the victories of Jeroboam II.

(25) With Argob and Arieh.—Pekah slew these two persons, probably officers of the royal guard, who stood by their master, as well as the king himself. Josephus accounts for the short reign of Pekahiah by the statement that he imitated the cruelty of his father. (Comp. verse 33 and 17:1.) These data make the duration of Pekah's reign from twenty-eight to thirty years. We must, therefore, either assume, with Thenius, that the numeral sign for 30 has been corrupted into 20, or, with Ewald, that "and nine" has been accidentally omitted after "twenty."

(30) Hoshea . . . slew him, and reigned in his stead.—Hoshea secured his hold on the crown only by recognition of the suzerainty of Assyria. The brief record of Kings does not mention this; but 17:3 represents Hoshea as paying tribute to Shalmaneser IV, the successor of Tiglath-pileser.

In the twentieth year of Jotham.—This is a suspicious statement (comp. verse 33).

(37) In those days—i.e., in the last year of Jotham. The attacks of the allies at first took the form of isolated raids. In the next reign the country was invaded by them in full force. (See 16:5.)

16

(3) Made his son to pass through the fire.—The chronicler rightly explains this as a sacrifice by fire. That such an appalling rite is really intended may be seen by reference to 17:31; Jer. 19:5; Ezek. 16:20; 20:31; Jer. 32:35. The expression, "To make to pass through the fire to Moloch" (Lev. 18:21) may have originated in the idea that the burning was a kind of passage to union with the deity, after the dross of the flesh had been purged away. Ahaz appears to have been the first Israelite king who offered such a sacrifice. He regarded it, no doubt, as a last desperate resource against the oppression of his northern enemies.

(5) Then Rezin king of Syria . . . to war.—Comp. Isa. 7:1. The last of a series of strong and generally successful princes, Jotham had died at a critical moment, when Pekah and Rezin were maturing their plans against his kingdom. The opposing parties in northern Israel suspended their feuds to make common cause against Judah (Isa. 9:21), and the proud inhabitants of Samaria hoped by this policy to more than restore the prestige forfeited in previous years of calamity (Isa. 9:9, 10). At the same time the Syrians began to operate in the eastern dependencies of Judah, their aim being to possess the harbor of Elath on the Red Sea, while the Philistines attacked the Judaeans in the rear and ravaged the fertile lowlands. (See Isa. 9:12, 14.) Ahaz was no fit leader in so critical a time; his character was petulant and childish, his policy dictated in the harem (Isa. 3:12). Nor was the internal order of the state calculated to inspire confidence. The rich nobles were steeped in sensual luxury, the court was full of gallantry, and feminine extravagance and vanity gave the tone to aristocratic society (Isa. 3:16; 5:11; comp. 3:12; 4:4), while masses were ground down by oppression.

They besieged Ahaz.—The allies wanted to compel Judah to join them in their attempt to throw off the burdensome yoke of Assyria, imposed in 738 B.C. (15:19); they thought the best way to secure this was to dethrone the dynasty of David and set up a creature of their own (Isa. 7:6).

(8) Ahaz took the silver and gold.—The only conditions on which protection would be assured were acceptance of the Assyrian suzerainty with the payment of a huge tribute; thus an embassy was dispatched laden with all the treasures of the palace and the Temple. The ambassadors had no difficulty in attaining their object. The expedition in 734 B.C. was directed against Pekah, who probably saved himself by an instant submission. It was only after Tiglath-pileser had settled matters with the northern kingdom, and so isolated Damascus, that he turned his arms against Rezin. Two whole years were spent in reducing him (733-732 B.C.).

(10) Ahaz went to Damascus, to meet Tiglath-pileser.—The great king appears to have held his court there after the capture of the city, and to have summoned the vassal princes of Palestine to do him homage in person before his departure.

And saw an altar.—In a national crisis of the first magnitude Ahaz found no more pressing concern than the erection of a new altar in the Temple on a pattern brought from Damascus. (Comp. II Kings 18:16; 23:12.) He imagined that the introduction of a few foreign novelties gave lustre to a reign which had fooled away the independence of Judah, and sought a momentary

deliverance by accepting a service the burden of which was fast becoming intolerable.

(12) The king approached to the altar, and offered thereon.—Comp. I Kings 12:32, 33. It appears that Ahaz, like Uzziah, personally exercised the priestly function of sacrifice. From the present narrative it does not appear that he offered his thank-offering (for deliverance from deadly peril) to Jehovah. Like most of his contemporaries, Ahaz thought the traditional worship of Jehovah compatible with the **cultus** of foreign deities.

(14) And he brought also the brasen altar ... —Urijah had pushed it forward nearer to the sanctuary, and set the new Syrian altar in its place. Ahaz, not satisfied with this arrangement, which appeared to confer a kind of precedence on the old altar, drew it back again, and fixed it on the north side of his new altar. Ahaz orders that the daily national sacrifices, the royal offerings, and those of private individuals, shall all be offered at the new altar (verse 15).

(17, 18) Ahaz spoiled the Temple of its ornamental work, not out of wanton malice, but from dire necessity. He had to provide a present for the king of Assyria. Thus these verses are really a continuation of the first statement of verse 10. They inform us how Ahaz managed not to appear empty-handed at Damascus. The incidental mention of this fact in a fragment of the history of the Temple incorporated in the Book of Kings is sufficient evidence of the straits to which the kingdom of Judah was reduced.

17

(1) In the twelfth year of Ahaz.—If Pekah reigned thirty years, and Ahaz succeeded in Pekah's seventeenth year (16:1), Ahaz must have reigned thirteen years concurrently with Pekah. Hoshea, therefore, succeeded Pekah in the fourteenth year of Ahaz. On the news of the death of Tiglath-pileser, he probably refused further tribute.

(3) Against him came up Shalmaneser king of Assyria.—Shalmaneser V, the successor of Tiglath-pileser III, and predecessor of Sargon II, reigned 727-722 B.C. No annals of his reign have come down to us in the cuneiform inscriptions.

(4) Conspiracy—i.e., a conspiracy with the king of Egypt against his suzerain. Shalmaneser regarded Hoshea, and probably the king of Egypt also, as his "servant" (verse 3). (Comp. 12:20 and Jer. 11:9.) It appears that at this time Lower Egypt was divided among a number of petty principalities, whose recognition of any central authority was uncertain, a fact which rendered an Egyptian alliance of little value to Israel. (See Isa. 19 and 20.)

Therefore ... shut him up.—Comp. Jer. 32:2, 3; 33:1; 36:5. This statement seems to imply that Shalmaneser took Hoshea prisoner **before** the siege of Samaria, a supposition which finds support in the fact that Sargon, who ended the siege, makes no mention of the capture or death of the Israelite king.

(5) Then the king of Assyria came up ... and besieged it three years.—Sargon states that he took Samaria in his **first** year. Shalmaneser therefore had besieged the city some two years before his death. The brief narrative before us does not discriminate between the respective shares of two Assyrian sovereigns in the overthrow of the kingdom of Israel.

(6) Comp. Hosea 10:5 seq.; Micah 1:6; Isa. 28:1-4. These places, like Kir (16:9), probably were in Mesopotamia.

(23) So was Israel carried away.—That the land was not entirely depopulated appears from such passages as II Chron. 30:1; 34:9. But henceforth the distinctive character of the nation was lost; such Hebrews as remained in their old land became mixed with their heathen neighbors (see verse 24). It was only in much later times that the mixed population of Samaria came to possess the Pentateuch, and set up a worship on Mount Gerizim, in imitation of the ritual of the second Temple. We have no reason to think that the captive Ephraimites were more able to retain their distinctive character than their brethren who remained in Palestine. The problem of the lost tribes, which has so much attraction for some speculators, is a purely fanciful one. The people whom Hosea and Amos describe were not fitted to maintain themselves apart from the heathen among whom they dwelt.

(25) The Lord sent lions.—In the interval between the Assyrian depopulation and the re-peopling of the land, the lions indigenous to the country had multiplied naturally enough. Their ravages were understood by the colonists as a token of the wrath of the local deity on account of their neglect of his worship.

(29) Howbeit.—The colonists, under the instruction of the priest at Bethel, the center of calf worship, did not fear Jehovah in a monotheistic sense; they simply **added** his **cultus** to that of their ancestral deities.

The Samaritans—i.e., the people of northern Israel. (Comp. "Samaria" in verse 24.)

(32) Of the lowest of them.—Rather, "of all orders," or "promiscuously." (Comp. I Kings 12:31.) This is another indication that it was Jeroboam's mode of worship which was now restored.

(34) They fear not the Lord.—The mixed population fear Him not in the sense of a right fear; they do not honor Him in the way He has prescribed in the Torah.

After their statutes, or after their ordinances.—The writer here thinks of the remnant of the Ten Tribes who amalgamated with the new settlers (23:19; II Chron. 34:6, 9, 33; John 4:12).

(38) Neither shall ye fear other gods.—This formula is repeated three times (verses 35, 37, 38), as the main point of the covenant between Jehovah and Israel.

18

(1) Hezekiah.—See 16:20. The name in this form means "my strength is Jah" (Ps. 18:2), and its special appropriateness if exemplified by Hezekiah's history.

(4) He removed.—According to this statement, Hezekiah made the Temple of Jerusalem the only place where Jehovah might be publicly worshiped. (Comp. verse 22.)

Brake in pieces the brasen serpent that Moses had made.—It is clear that the compiler of Kings believed that the brasen serpent which Hezekiah destroyed was a relic of the Mosaic times. (See Num. 21:4-9; Deut. 8:15.) His authority may have been oral tradition or a written document. The great antiquity of this relic is tenable, for Egyptian and Babylonian remains which have come down to our time have lasted many centuries more than the interval between Moses and Hezekiah; and some of them were already ancient in the Mosaic age.

(5) He trusted ... Israel.—Hezekiah is thus contrasted with idolatrous kings, such as those who trusted in the Nehushtan, the "great serpent."

After him was none like him among all the kings of Judah.—This does not contradict what is said of Josiah (23:25). Hezekiah was pre-eminent for his "trust" in Jehovah (against polytheism), Josiah for "his strict adherence to the Mosaic Law."

(7) He rebelled against the king of Assyria —i.e., refused the tribute which Ahaz his father had paid. In this matter also it is implied that Hezekiah succeeded. The mention of Hezekiah's revolt here does not imply that it happened at the beginning of his reign, for verses 1-12 are a preliminary sketch of his entire history. The subject here mentioned briefly is continued in verses 13 ff.

(8) He smote.—The reduction of the Philistines was probably subsequent to the retreat of Sennacherib. (Comp. II Chron. 32:22; Isa. 11:14.) The entire land of Philistia was ravaged by the Judaean forces.

(9-12) (Comp. 17:3-6.) We see a contrast between the utter overthrow of the stronger kingdom and the deliverance of its smaller and weaker neighbor, because Hezekiah trusted in Jehovah (verse 5).

(13) In the fourteenth year of king Hezekiah.—The fall of Samaria is dated 722-721 B.C., both by the Bible and by the Assyrian inscriptions. That year was the sixth of Hezekiah, according to verse 10. His fourteenth year, therefore, would be 714-713 B.C. Sennacherib's own monuments, however, fix the date of the expedition against Judah and Egypt at 701 B.C. It must be borne in mind that the Assyrian documents are strictly contemporary, whereas the Books of Kings were compiled long after the events they record, and have only reached us after innumerable transcriptions; while the former, so far as they are unbroken, are in exactly the same state now as when they first left the hands of the Assyrian scribes. But see note on verse 34.

Sennacherib—i.e., "Sin (the moon-god) multiplied brothers." He was son and successor of Sargon II, and reigned from 705-681 B.C. He invaded Judah in his third campaign.

(14) Lachish.—This is in the southwest corner of Judah, close to the Philistine border and near the high road from Judaea and Philistia to Egypt. The fortress was important to Sennacherib, as it commanded this route. In fact, Sennacherib's chief aim was Egypt, as appears from 19:24, and Herodotus (2:141), and it was necessary for him to secure his rear by first making himself master of the fortresses of Judah, which were in league with Egypt.

Three hundred talents of silver, and thirty talents of gold.—The sum mentioned is about a seventh less than that exacted by Pul from Menahem (15:19).

(16) Cut off the gold from the doors.— Comp. I Kings 6:18, 32, 35.

(17) And they went up and came—i.e., the Assyrian army corps under the commander-in-chief (the "Tartan"), the courier (the "Rabsaris"), and the chief officer (the "Rab-shakeh").

(21) The staff of this bruised reed.—As to the Judaean expectations from Egypt, comp. Isa. 20:1-5; 30:1-8; 31:1-4; passages in which such expectations are denounced as implying want of faith in Jehovah.

(22) Ye shall worship . . . in Jerusalem?— The great altar of burnt offering was to be the one altar, and Jerusalem the one city, where Jehovah might be worshiped.

(23) Give pledges to.—The "rab-sak" sneers at Hezekiah's want of cavalry, an arm in which the Assyrians were preeminently strong, and further hints that even if horses were supplied him in numbers sufficient to constitute an ordinary troop, he would not be able to muster an equivalent number of trained riders. The "one captain of the least of my master's servants" is the "rab-sak" himself (verse 24).

(25) The Lord said to me.—Some have supposed that Sennacherib had consulted certain of the captive priests of the Northern Kingdom. Others think some report of the menaces of the Hebrew prophets may have reached Assyrian ears. It is possible that there was some renegade prophet of Jehovah in the Assyrian camp. At all events, the form of the oracle is thoroughly authentic. Isaiah 10:5 seq. shows how true was the boast of the arrogant invader, in a sense which lay far above his heathenish apprehension.

(26) Speak, I pray thee . . . in the Syrian language.—Hezekiah's ministers naturally dread the effect of Rab-shakeh's arguments and assertions upon the garrison of the city. The people, many of whom had always been accustomed to worship at the high places, might very well doubt whether there were not some truth in the allegation that Jehovah was incensed at their removal (verse 22).

(27) That they may eat . . . —These coarse words are meant to express the consequence of their resistance: it will bring them to such dire straits that they will have to appease the cravings of hunger and thirst with the vilest garbage. (Comp. 6:25 seq.)

(29) Let not Hezekiah deceive you.—

331

Rab-shakeh was quick-witted enough to take instant advantage of Eliakim's unwary remark, and to come forward in the character of a friend of the people.

(31) And then eat ye—i.e., If you surrender at once, no harm shall befall you; but you shall enjoy your own land, until I remove you to a better. (Comp. I Kings 5:5.)

(34) Out of mine hand?—Sennacherib speaks as if he were one with his father, a circumstance which lends some support to the suggestion that the successive Assyrian invasions were not kept quite distinct in the Hebrew tradition.

19

(1) Went into the house of the Lord.—He did so to humble himself before Jehovah and pray for help. (Comp. II Chron. 32:20.)

(3) The children are come ... —This proverb is expressive of the utter collapse of all human resources (comp. Hosea 13:13).

(7) Behold, I will send a blast upon him.—Rather, "Behold, I am about to put a spirit within him." The prophets believed that all acts and events—even the ruthless barbarities of Assyrian conquerors—were Jehovah's work. The lowly wisdom of the peasant, as well as the art of good government, was a divine inspiration (Isa. 11:2; 28:26, 29).

In consequence of the spirit of despondency or fear with which Jehovah would inspire him, Sennacherib would hastily retire upon hearing ill news.

(8) Libnah.—See note on 8:20.

(10-13) Sennacherib's second message repeats the arguments of 18:29-35. Verses 10-13 may be regarded as embodying the substance of the letter, which the envoys first delivered orally, and then presented the letter to authenticate it. But perhaps the contents of the letter were not preserved in the Hebrew annals.

(14) Spread it before the Lord.—One who could think of his God as having made heaven and earth, and as the **only** God, would not be likely to imagine Him ignorant of the contents of a letter until it had been laid before Him in His sanctuary. Hezekiah's act was a solemn and perfectly natural indication to his ministers and people that he had put the matter into the hands of Jehovah.

(15) Which dwellest between the cher- ubims.—Comp. Exod. 25:22; I Sam. 4:4; Ps. 18:10; Ezek. 1:26.

(16) Open, Lord, thine eyes, and see.—The figurative language in Hezekiah's mouth simply meant "Intervene actively between me and my enemy," although, no doubt, such expressions originally conveyed the actual thoughts of the Israelites about God.

(18) For they were no gods.—This idea is common in the latter half of the Book of Isaiah. The question has been raised whether the compiler of Kings has not made Hezekiah express a stricter monotheism than had been attained by the religious thought of his days. (But comp. Isa. 2:18-21; 8:10; 10:10 seq.; Amos 4:13; 5:8; 9:6, 7.) We do not think, however, that the utterance of Hezekiah on this occasion was necessarily recorded in writing at the time. The prayer may well be a free composition put into the king's mouth by the author of this narrative.

(21) The virgin the daughter of Zion.—A poetic personification of place. Zion here, as Jerusalem in the next line, is regarded as mother of the people dwelling there. (Comp. II Sam. 20:19.) The term "virgin" naturally denotes the inviolable security of the citadel of Jehovah.

Hath shaken her head at thee.—(Comp. Ps. 22:8.) The people of Jerusalem nod in scorn at the retiring envoys of Sennacherib.

(22) The Holy One of Israel.—This is a favorite expression of Isaiah's, in whose book it occurs twenty-seven times, and only five times elsewhere in the Old Testament (Pss. 71:22; 78:41; 89:19; Jer. 50:29; 51:5).

(23) To the sides of Lebanon—i.e., the strongholds of Judaea, which Sennacherib had already captured. Lebanon, as the northern bulwark of the land of Israel, is used as a representative or symbol for the whole country. (Comp. Isa. 14:13; Zech. 11:1.)

And will cut down ... —Cedars and firs in Isaiah's language symbolize kings, princes, and nobles, all that is highest and most stately. (See Isa. 2:13; 10:33, 34.)

(24) I have digged and drunk strange waters.—Scarcity of water has hitherto been no bar to my advance. In foreign and hostile lands, where the fountains and cisterns have been stopped and covered (II Chron. 32:3), I have digged new wells. And neither mountains nor rivers avail to stop my progress.

(25) Hast thou not heard ...?—The "it"

is the thing long since foreordained by Jehovah.

(27) But I know thy abode ... —(See Ps. 139:2.) The thought expressed is this: I know all thy plans and thy doings; I see also thy present rebellion against me. What thou hast hitherto done was done because I willed it: now I will check thee.

(28) I will put my hook ... lips.—Comp. note on II Chron. 33:11, where this threat is shown to be no mere figure of speech. The metaphor is taken from wild animals, which are thus held in check (Ps. 32:9; Isa. 30:28; Ezek. 19:4).

(29) And this shall be a sign unto thee.— The prophet now addresses Hezekiah.

A sign.—"The sign consists in the foretelling of natural and nearer events, which serve to accredit the proper prediction. The intention of it is that this and the next year the country will be still occupied by the enemy, so that men cannot sow and reap as usual, but must live on that which grows without sowing. In the third year, they will again be able to cultivate their fields and vineyards, and reap the fruits of them" (Keil). Comp. Isa. 6:13; 11:11-16; 27:6.

(34) For my servant David's sake.—See II Sam. 7; I Kings 11:12, 13.

(35) The angel of the Lord went out.— See Exod. 12:12, 13, 23; II Sam. 24:15-17. These passages undoubtedly favor the view that the Assyrian army was devastated by pestilence, as Josephus asserts. In any case, a supernatural causation is involved not only in the immense number slain, and that in one night (Ps. 91:6), but in the coincidence of the event with the predictions of Isaiah. An Egyptian account preserved in Herodotus 2:141 cites Egypt as the location of "the camp of the Assyrians."

(36) And dwelt at Nineveh, implying that he did not again invade the west. Sennacherib continued to reign twenty years. He records five subsequent expeditions to the east, north, and south of his dominions, but these obviously were nothing to the peoples of Palestine.

(37) Esar-haddon reigned 681-669 B.C.

20

Parallel accounts may be read in Isa. 38, 39; II Chron. 32:24-33.

(1) In those days—i.e., in the time of the Assyrian invasion. The illness may have been caused, or at least aggravated, by the intense anxiety which this grave peril created. See note on verse 7. That Hezekiah recovered before the catastrophe recorded at the end of the last chapter, is evident from the fact that no allusion to the destruction of his enemies is contained in his hymn of thanksgiving (Isa. 38:10-20). See verse 6.

(3) Remember now how I have walked ... —Hezekiah deprecates an untimely death—the punishment of the wicked (Prov. 10:27)—on account of his zeal for Jehovah and against the idols. There is nothing surprising in his apparent self-praise, if we remember such passages as Neh. 13:14; Pss. 7:8; 18:20.

(6) And I will deliver thee ... —Thus the Assyrians had not yet retired from the West. For the rest of the verse see 19:34.

(7) Take a lump of figs.—Many commentators suppose the figs to be mentioned as a remedy current at the time. But the plaster of figs is rather a sign or symbol of the cure, like the water of the Jordan in the narrative of Naaman (II Kings 5:10). That in antiquity figs were a usual remedy for boils of various kinds appears from the testimony of Pliny.

Laid it on the boil.—It is not to be supposed that Hezekiah was suffering from the very plague which destroyed the army of Sennacherib. The word "boil" denotes leprous and other similar ulcers (Exod. 9:9; Job 2:7), but not plague.

(9) It is obvious that a kind of sun-dial is meant, though what kind is not so clear. The word "degrees" means "steps" or "stairs" wherever it occurs. There is probability, therefore, in the conjecture that "the dial of Ahaz" consisted of a column rising from a circular flight of steps, so as to throw the shadow of its top on the top step at noon, and morning and evening on the bottom step. This, or some similar device, was set up in the palace court, and was probably visible to Hezekiah lying on his sick bed and facing the window.

(10) It is a light thing for the shadow to go down.—That was the ordinary course of things. As a natural phenomenon, of course, the sudden extension of the shadow would have been as wonderful as its retrogression; but what is in any way a familiar occurrence always seems easier than what has never fallen under observation.

(11) And Isaiah the prophet cried unto the Lord.—Thus the sign is evidently regarded by the historian as something directly involving the divine agency, i.e., as a miracle.

He brought ... Ahaz.—Ephrem Syrus, and other church fathers believed that the sun receded in its celestial path; but the text does not say that the sun went back, but the shadow. (Isa. 38:8 uses a perfectly natural **usus loquendi.**) Keil assumes "a wondrous refraction of the sun's rays effected by God at the prayer of Isaiah." Cheyne agrees with this, assuming, further, that the refraction was local only. (See II Chron. 32:31.)

(12) At that time Berodach-baladan.— "Berodach" is a transcriber's error for "Merodach" (Jer. 50:2). A king of this name occupied the throne of Chaldea at intervals, during the reigns of the four Assyrian sovereigns Tiglath-pileser, Shalmaneser, Sargon, and Sennacherib.

He had heard that Hezekiah had been sick.—The ostensible business of the embassy was to congratulate Hezekiah on his recovery, and to inquire about the sign that had been vouchsafed him; but the Assyrian records make it clear that the real object was to ascertain the extent of Hezekiah's resources, and to secure his alliance against the common enemy.

(13) The silver, and the gold.—This, as well as the phrase in verse 17, "that which thy fathers have laid up," appears to contradict 18:15, 16. Some commentators regard this as an indication that Hezekiah's illness and the embassy of Merodach-baladan belong to the time preceding Sennacherib's invasion, c. 704-703 B.C. But comp. II Chron. 32:23.

(17) Behold, the days come ... —Comp. II Chron. 32:25, 26, 31. It was not only the king's vanity which displeased a prophet who had always consistently denounced foreign alliances as betokening deviation from absolute trust in Jehovah; and a more terrible irony than that which animates the oracle before us can hardly be conceived. Thy friends, he cries, will prove robbers; thine allies will become thy conquerors. That Isaiah should have foreseen that Assyria, then at the zenith of its power, would one day be dethroned from the sovereignty of the world by that very Babylon which, at the time he spoke, was menaced with ruin by the Assyrian arms, can only be accepted as true by those who accept the reality of supernatural prediction. (Comp. Isa. 14:29; seq., 21:9.)

(18) Thy sons ... beget—i.e., thy descendants. Comp. Dan. 1:3; II Chron. 33:11.

(19) Is it not good, if peace ... —Severe as is the prophetic word of judgment, it contains an element of mercy, in that Hezekiah himself is spared.

(20) A pool ... a conduit ... water.—See notes on II Chron. 32:4, 30, and Isa. 7:3.

21

(1) Manasseh.—This king was a tributary to Esarhaddon and Assurbanipal successively. His name, like that of his successor Amon, suggests Egyptian influence. (We know that combinations with Egypt against Assyria were popular during this epoch.) This early accession to power may help to explain his deviation from the religious policy of his father. According to the datum of the text, he was born a year or two after the Assyrian invasion.

(2) And he did that which was evil.— Perhaps under the pernicious influence of his courtiers. (Comp. the case of Rehoboam.)

(3) Worshipped all the host of heaven.— See 17:16 and 23:12. The Babylonian star-worship and astrology, with concomitant superstitions, had been introduced under Ahaz.

(5) In the two courts.—Even in the inner and more sacred court, where the sacrifices were offered to Jehovah, Manasseh erected idolatrous altars.

(6) "In the time from Manasseh onwards, Moloch-worship and worship of the Queen of Heaven appear as prominent new features of Judah's idolatry. It is also probable that the local high places took on their restoration a more markedly heathenish character than before" (**Robertson Smith**). See note on II Chron. 33:6.

(7) In the house of which the Lord said ... —See I Kings 8:16 and 9:3. The Asherah was erected within the Temple itself, probably in the holy place—an act which was the climax of Manasseh's impiety. (See note on Jer. 7:30 seq.)

(8) Neither will I make the feet of Israel move ... —Comp. II Sam. 7:10. The reference is to the migration to Egypt, and the thought is that the permanent possession of the Promised Land depends on the permanent adherence of the nation to Jehovah only.

(9) To do more evil.—The idolatry of Judah was worse than that of the Canaanites, because they worshipped only their national gods, whereas Judah forsook its own God and was ready to adopt almost any foreign **cultus** with which it was brought into contact (Jer. 2:11).

(10) By his servants the prophets . . . —The protests in question probably were those of Isaiah's disciples. (The style is not Isaiah's.) It appears likely that the passage (verses 11-15) is a sort of résumé of the substance of many such prophetic addresses.

(13) And I will stretch over Jerusalem . . . —The sense is, I will deal with Jerusalem by the same rigorous rule of judgment as I have dealt already with Samaria. The figure of the measuring line and plummet suggests the idea that Jerusalem should be leveled with the ground.

As a man wipeth a (the) dish . . . —The wiping of the dish represents the destruction of the people; the turning it upside down, the overthrow of the city itself.

(16) Moreover Manasseh shed innocent blood . . . —"As the nation fell back into the grooves of its old existence, ancient customs began to reassert their sway. The worship which the prophets condemned, and which Hezekiah had proscribed, was too deeply interwoven with all parts of life to be uprooted by royal decree, and the old prejudice of the country folk against the capital, so clearly apparent in Micah, must have co-operated with superstition to bring about the strong revulsion against the new reforms which took place under Manasseh. A bloody struggle ensued . . ." (**Robertson Smith**). Talmudic tradition relates that Isaiah himself was sawn asunder in the trunk of a cedar tree in which he had taken refuge. (Comp. Heb. 11:37.)

(17) Now the rest of the acts of Manasseh . . . —See II Chron. 33:11-19 for the story of his captivity, repentance and restoration, which is now allowed by the best critics to be genuine history, though at one time it was the fashion to consider it an edifying fiction of the chronicler's.

(19) Amon.—The name is perhaps that of the Egyptian sun-god "Amen," as Amon's father was an idolater.

(22) And he forsook the Lord . . . —It is noteworthy that the long reign of Manasseh-Amon is described by the sacred historian simply on the side of its relation to the religion of Israel: astonishing corruption of worship; perverted yearning after foreign rites; bloody persecution of those who maintained the ancient faith; prophetic menaces of coming retribution. Such are the main points of the brief but impressive

story. As usual, moral and religious license went hand in hand. (See Zeph. 1:4, 5; 3:1, 4; Micah 6:10 seq., 7:2-6.)

22

(1) Josiah.—The name seems to mean "Jah healeth." (Comp. Exod. 15:26; Isa. 30:26.)

(2) And he did that which was right . . . —Josiah did not succeed, any more than Hezekiah, in rooting out the spirit of apostasy. (See Jer. 2:11; 4:2). The young king was, no doubt, influenced for good by the discourses of Jeremiah and Zephaniah; but it is not easy to account for his heeding the prophetic teachings, considering that, as the grandson of a Manasseh and the son of an Amon, he must have been brought up under precisely opposite influences (**Thenius**).

(4) Go up to Hilkiah the high priest. —The account of the repair of the Temple under Josiah naturally resembles that of the same proceeding under Joash (12:10, seq.). More than 200 years had since elapsed, so that the fabric might well stand in need of repair, apart from the defacements which it had undergone at the hands of heathenish princes (II Chron. 34:11).

Hilkiah.—See 1 Chron. 6:13. He is a different person from Hilkiah, the father of Jeremiah, who was a priest, but not high priest (Jer. 1:1).

(8) I have found.—The definite form of the expression proves that what the high priest found was something already known; it was not **a** book, but **the** book of the Torah. Critics disagree widely as to the precise character and contents of the book in question. But according to Thenius, what is meant is a collection of the statutes and ordinances of Moses, which has been worked up in the Pentateuch, and especially in Deuteronomy. This work is referred to by Jeremiah (Jer. 11:1-17), and was called "The Book of the Covenant" (Jer. 23:2). According to II Chron. 17:9 it already existed in the time of Jehoshaphat (comp. II Kings 11:12, "the Testimony"). It was probably preserved in the Ark (Deut. 31:26), along with which in the reign of Manasseh it was cast aside. When after half a century of disuse it was found again by the high priest in going through the chambers of the Temple with a view to the intended repairs, it appeared like something **new**, because it had been wholly forgotten for a time, so that Shaphan could say: "Hilkiah has given me **a book**" (verse 10). (See note on II Chron. 34:14.)

(13) Inquire of the Lord.—Josiah wished to know whether any hope remained for himself and his people, or whether the vengeance must fall speedily. He identifies the people and their fathers as one nation. (Comp. Exod. 20:5.)

(14) Went unto Huldah the prophetess.— Huldah "dwelt in Jerusalem"; Jeremiah and Zephaniah did not, at least at this time. Huldah, however, must have enjoyed a high reputation, as "prophets" are mentioned in 23:2.

In the college.—The word really means "the second part of the city"—i.e., the lower city. (See Neh. 11:9; Zeph. 1:10.)

(17) With all the works of their hands— i.e., With the idols they have made. (See I Kings 16:7.)

(20) In peace.—These words are limited by those which follow. Josiah was slain in battle (23:29); but he was spared the greater calamity of witnessing the ruin of his people.

23

(3) A covenant.—"The covenant," which had so often been broken. Josiah pledged himself "to walk after the Lord," and imposed a similar pledge on the people.

(4) In the fields of Kidron.—Northeast of the city, where the ravine expands considerably. (Comp. I Kings 15:13; Jer. 31:40.) They were burned outside Jerusalem as unclean, and according to the law of Deut. 7:25 and 12:3.

(5) The idolatrous priests.—Here, as in Hos. 10:5, it denotes the unlawful priests of Jehovah, as contrasted with those of the Baal, mentioned in the next place.

(6) And he brought out the grove ...— This was the Asherah set up by Manasseh (21:3, 7), and removed by him on his repentance (II Chron. 33:15), but restored (probably) by Amon (21:21).

The graves of the children of the people— i.e., the common graves (Jer. 26:23); it was a mark of utter contempt. Verse 7 shows that the last infamy of Canaanite nature-worship had been established in the very sanctuary of Jehovah. The revolt of Judah could go no farther.

(9) Nevertheless ...—These irregular priests were not permitted to approach the altar, being considered to be incapacitated

for that office by their former illegal ministrations. They might not even eat their share of the meat offerings in company with the legitimate priests, but had to take their meals apart. To "eat of the unleavened bread" is a technical phrase, meaning to live upon offerings. (See Lev. 2:1-11; 6:16-18; 10:12.) These priests were probably employed in the inferior duties of the Temple.

(10) Topheth—i.e., "the burning place." Molech is another form of melech, "king." In I Kings 11:7, the god of the Ammonites is called Molech, but elsewhere, as in verse 13, Milcom, another variation of the same word. Melech was a title of the sun-god in one of his aspects.

(11) The horses ... the sun.—These horses drew "the chariots of the sun" in solemn processions held in honor of that deity. (See Herod. 1.189; Xenoph. **Anab.** 4.5.34, seq.) Horses were also sacrificed to the sun. The sun's apparent course through the heavens, poetically conceived as the progress of a fiery chariot and steeds, explains these usages.

(12) And the altars that were on the top of the upper chamber of Ahaz.—The roof of an upper chamber in one of the Temple courts, perhaps built over one of the gateways (comp. Jer. 35:4), appears to be meant. The altars were for star-worship, which was especially practiced on housetops. (Comp. Jer. 19:13; 32:29; Zeph. 1:5.)

(13) The high places that were before Jerusalem ...—See I Kings 11:5-8. "Before" means "to the east of," because, to determine the cardinal points, one faced the sunrise. The right hand was then the south.

The mount of corruption.—The southern summit of the Mount of Olives was so-called because of the idolatry practiced there.

Did the king defile.—As it is not said that they were pulled down, these high places may have been merely sacred sites on the mountain, consisting of a leveled surface of rock, with holes scooped in them for receiving libations, etc. Such sites have been found in Palestine; and it is hardly conceivable that "chapels" erected by Solomon for the worship of Ashtoreth, Chemosh, and Milcom would have been spared by such a king as Hezekiah, who even did away with the high places dedicated to Jehovah (18:3). The "images" and "groves" (verse 14) may have been pillars and sacred trees set up in these "high places."

(15) It is noteworthy that the present passage indirectly agrees with Hos. 10:6, for no mention is made of what used to be the chief object of worship at Beth-el—the golden bullock. It had been carried away to Assyria, as the prophet foretold.

(18) With the bones of the prophet... —See I Kings 13:31, 32.

(19) Josiah took away.—Comp. II Chron. 34:6. How was it that Josiah was able to proceed thus beyond the limits of his own territory? It is possible that, as a vassal of Assyria, he enjoyed a certain amount of authority over the old domains of the ten tribes. His opposition to Necho favors the idea that he recognized the Assyrian sovereign as his suzerain. Moreover, it is in itself likely that the remnant of Israel would be drawn toward Judah and its king as the surviving representatives of the past glories of their race, and would sympathize in his reformation, just as the Samaritans, in the times of the return, were eager to participate in the rebuilding of the Temple. Another supposition is that, as the fall of the Assyrian empire was imminent, no notice was taken of Josiah's proceedings in the west.

(21) Keep the passover.—Comp. II Chron. 35:1-19 for a more detailed account of this unique celebration. Josiah had the precedent of Hezekiah for signalizing his religious revolution by a solemn passover (II Chron. 30:1).

In the book of this covenant.—The book was that which Hilkiah had found in the Temple, and which gave the impulse to the whole reforming movement.

(24) Moreover the workers ... —After abolishing public idolatry, Josiah attacked the various forms of private superstition. "That were spied" is a significant expression.

(25) With all his heart ... —See Deut. 6:5. That Josiah's merits did not consist merely in a strict observance of the legitimate worship and ritual is evident from Jer. 22:15, 16, where he is praised for his righteousness as a judge.

(26, 27) The historian naturally adds these remarks to prepare the way for what he has soon to relate—the final ruin of the kingdom; and probably also to suggest an explanation of what must have seemed to him and his contemporaries a mysterious stroke of providence—the untimely end of the good king Josiah.

(29) Pharaoh-nechoh.—Necho II, the successor of Psammetichus, and the sixth king of the 26th or Saite dynasty. (See Herod. 2:158, 159; 4:42.) He reigned c. 611-605 B.C.

The king of Assyria.—If, as the Chronology of Eusebius and Jerome represents, Cyaraxes the Mede took Nineveh in 609-608 B.C., then Necho's expedition (c. 609 B.C.) was really directed against a king of Assyria in the strict sense. After the death of Assurbanipal (626 B.C.), it appears that two or three kings reigned at Nineveh, including Esar-haddon II. Nineveh must have fallen before 606 B.C., as Assyria does not occur in the list of countries mentioned by Jeremiah (Jer. 25:19-26) in the fourth year of Jehoiakim, i.e., 606 B.C. A year or so later Necho made a second expedition, this time against the king of Babylon, but was utterly defeated at Carchemish. Josephus says that Necho went to wage war with the Medes and Babylonians, who had just put an end to the Assyrian empire, and that his object was to win the dominion of Asia.

King Josiah went against him.—This action was taken probably as a vassal of Assyria, and as resenting Necho's trespass on territory which he regarded as his own.

At Megiddo.—In the plain of Jezreel (I Kings 4:12). (Comp. Zech. 12:11.)

When he had seen him—i.e., at the outset of the encounter. Comp. II Chron. 35:22 seq. Thenius thinks that Jer. 15:7-9 was spoken on occasion of Josiah's departure with his army from the north, and that the prophet's metaphor, "her sun went down while it was yet day," refers to the eclipse of Thales, which had recently happened, 610 B.C. (Herod 1.74, 103).

(31) Jehoahaz.—Shallum (Jer. 22:11; I Chron. 3:15), which may have been his name before his accession. He is not to be confused with the Shallum in Samaria (15:13).

(32) And he did that which was evil... —Jehoahaz is called a young lion that "devoureth men," alluding to his oppressive rapacity and shameless abuse of power (Ezek. 19:1-4).

(33) Riblah lay in a strong position on the Orontes, commanding the caravan route from Palestine to the Euphrates. Necho had advanced so far, after the battle of Megiddo, and taken up his quarters there, as Nebuchadnezzar did afterward (25:6, 20, 21). Josephus relates that Necho summoned Jehoahaz to his camp at Riblah. Ezek. 19:4 suggests that he got the king of Judah into his power by fraud.

(34) Turned his name to Jehoiakim.—
Eliakim is "El setteth up"; Jehoiakim, "Jah
setteth up." Necho meant to signify that the
new king was his creature. Eliakim, the
elder son, may have paid court to Necho;
or the Egyptian may have deposed Jehoahaz, as elected without his consent, and
perhaps as likely to prove a stronger king
than his brother.

And he came to Egypt, and died there.—
Jeremiah had foretold the fact (Jer.
22:10-12).

(35) But he taxed . . .—The king kept his
pledge to Pharaoh, but not out of his own
means. He exacted the money from people
of all classes, levying a fixed contribution
even upon the poorest of his subjects.

(37) He did that which was evil . . .—See
Jer. 22:13 seq., 26:20 seq. Ewald thinks that
he introduced Egyptian animal-worship
(Ezek. 8:7 seq.), which is rendered highly
probable by his relation of dependence on
Necho. (Comp. the introduction of Assyrian
star-worship under Ahaz.)

24

(1) In his days.—In Jehoiakim's fourth
year Nebuchadnezzar defeated Necho at
Carchemish (Jer. 46:2). He succeeded his
father, Nabopolassar, on the throne of Babylon in the same year (Jer. 25:1). Toward
the end of Jehoiakim's fifth year the king of
Babylon was expected to invade the land
(Jer. 36:9). When this took place, Nebuchadnezzar humbled Jehoiakim, who had
probably made his submission, by putting
him in chains and carrying off some of the
Temple treasures (II Chron. 36:6, 7.) Left in
the possession of his throne as a vassal of
Babylon, Jehoiakim paid tribute three
years, and then tried to throw off the yoke.

**(2) And the Lord sent against him bands
of the Chaldees.**—Jehoiakim's revolt was no
doubt instigated by Egypt. While Nebuchadnezzar himself was engaged elsewhere in his great empire, predatory bands
of Chaldeans, and of the neighboring peoples the hereditary enemies of Judah, ravaged the Judaean territory (comp. Jer.
12:8-17).

According to the word of the Lord.—
Isaiah, Micah, Urijah, Huldah, Jeremiah,
Habakkuk, and doubtless others whose
names and writings have not been transmitted, had foretold the fate that was now
closing in upon Judah.

(4) Which the Lord would not pardon.—

The sins of Manasseh are regarded as a
climax in Judah's long course of provocation; the cup was full, and judgment ready
to fall. It was only suspended for a time, not
revoked in the reign of the good king
Josiah. The sufferings of the exile were
necessary for the purification of Israel from
its inveterate tendency to apostatize from
Jehovah.

**(5) Now the rest of the acts of Jehoiakim
. . .**—Comp. Hab. 2:9-14; Jer. 22:13-17.
This is the last reference to the authority of
Chronicles. Bähr concludes that the work
did not extend beyond the reign of
Jehoiakim.

(6) So Jehoiakim slept with his fathers.—
The usual notice of the king's burial is
omitted, and the omission is significant,
considered in the light of prophecy (Jer.
22:18, 19; comp. Jer. 36:30). Jehoiakim
appears to have been slain in an encounter
with the bands of freebooters mentioned in
verse 2, so that his body was left to decay
where it fell, all his followers having perished with him.

**(7) And the king of Egypt came not again
any more . . .**—The verse indicates the
posture of political affairs at the time when
Jehoiachin succeeded his father. Necho had
been deprived by Nebuchadnezzar of all his
conquests, and so crippled that he dared not
venture again beyond his own borders.
Thus Judah was left, denuded of all external
help, to face the consequences of its revolt
from Babylon, which speedily overtook it
(verse 10). It is clear, from the statement
before us, that before the battle of Carchemish Necho had made himself master of
the whole of Syria and the country east of
the Jordan.

**(12) And Jehoiachin the king of Judah
went out . . .**—Despairing of the defense,
he threw himself upon the clemency of
Nebuchadnezzar, probably hoping to be allowed to keep his throne as a vassal of
Babylon. (Comp. Jer. 25:1 and 46:2.)

(13) And he carried out thence . . .—It is
certainly surprising to find that anything
was left in the Temple treasury after the
repeated spoliations which it had undergone. The fact not only indicates the probable existence of secret (subterranean)
storechambers, but also lends some support
to the chronicler's representations of the
great wealth stored up in the sanctuary.

As the Lord had said—e.g., to Hezekiah
(20:17; comp. Jer. 15:13 and 17:3).

(15) He carried away Jehoiachin . . .—
This was the fulfillment of Jer. 22:24-27.

(17) Mattaniah his father's brother.—
Mattaniah was the third son of Josiah
(comp. Jer. 1:3' and 37:1), and full brother
of Jehoahaz-Shallum (23:31). Jehoiachin
was childless at the time (comp. verses 12
and 15 with 25:7 and Jer. 22:30). In the
exile he had offspring (I Chron. 3:17, 18).
His former name meant "gift of Jah"; his
new one, "Jah is righteousness." (See Jer.
23:1-9.)

(19) And he did that which was evil...
—See Jer. 24:8; 37:1, 2; 38:5; Ezek. 8-11;
17:11-21. That such a prince as Zedekiah
was raised to the throne was itself a token
of divine displeasure, for his character was
such as to hasten the final catastrophe.

(20) That Zedekiah rebelled.—Zedekiah
had high hopes inspired by negotiations
with other peoples: comp. Jer. 27:3 seq.,
37:5; 44:30; Ezek. 17:15. Jeremiah opposed
the project of revolt to the utmost of his
power; and the event proved that he was
right. In the early part of his reign
Zedekiah had tried to procure the return of
the exiles carried away in the last reign
(Jer. 29:3); and in his fourth year he visited
Babylon himself, perhaps with the same
object, and to satisfy Nebuchadnezzar of his
fidelity (Jer. 51:59). The date of his open
revolt cannot be fixed.

25

(1) And it came to pass.—With the account which follows, comp. Jer. 52:4 seq.,
39:1-10, chaps. 40-43.

(2) Unto the eleventh year.—The siege
lasted altogether one year, five months, and
twenty-seven days (comp. verses 1 and 8).
The Chaldaeans raised the siege for a time,
and marched against Pharaoh-Hophra, who
was coming to the help of the Jews (Jer.
37:5 seq., comp. Ezek. 17:17; 30:20 seq.).

(3) The famine prevailed.—The horrors
of the siege are referred to in Lam. 2:11
seq., 4:3-10; Ezek. 5:10; Baruch 2:3.

(4) Broken up.—Comp. II Chron. 32:1. A
breach was made in the wall with battering-
rams, such as are depicted in the Assyrian
sculptures. The Chaldaeans forced their entry on the north side of the city, i.e., they
took the Lower City (22:14; comp. Jer.
39:3).

**By the way of the gate between two walls
which is by the king's garden.—**This gate
lay at the south end of the glen between
Ophel and Zion, and is the same as "the
Gate of the Fountain" (Neh. 3:15). The two

walls were necessary for the protection of
the Pool of Siloam and the water supply,
and the point was naturally weak for purposes of defense.

Now the Chaldees ... round about.—
This indicates that even by this route the
king and his warriors had to break through
the enemy's lines, as the city was completely
invested. (Comp. Ezek. 12:12.)

(5) In the plains of Jericho.—In the
neighborhood of Jericho, the Arabah expands to the breadth of eleven or twelve
miles. The part west of Jordan was called
the plains of Jericho; and that which lay
east of the river was known as the plains of
Moab (Num. 22:1; Josh. 4:13).

(6) And they gave judgment upon him.—
Nebuchadnezzar, with the grandees of his
court, held a solemn trial of Zedekiah, as a
rebel against his liege lord, in which, no
doubt, his breach of oath was made prominent (II Chron. 36:13; Ezek. 17:15, 18).

(7) And they slew ... —The verbs are all
singular in Jer. 39:6, and 52:10, 11, so that
the acts in question are attributed directly
to Nebuchadnezzar, to whose orders they
were due. The blinding of Zedekiah need
not have been done by the conqueror himself, although in the Assyrian sculptures
kings are actually represented as blinding
and otherwise torturing their captives.

Put out the eyes.—This was a Babylonian
punishment (Herod. 7:18). This was the
meaning of Ezekiel's prediction (Ezek.
12:13).

(8) Nebuzaradan.—A month elapsed between the taking of the city (verse 4) and its
destruction (verses 9, 10). This factor, with
the implication of verses 18-21, has led
Thenius to suggest a staunch defense of the
city of David, the strategical center of
Jerusalem.

(15) Such things as were ... silver.—This
is an expression intended to include all
other objects of the same material as the
two kinds mentioned. The verse treats of
the utensils of the holy place. Many such
had doubtless been carefully concealed by
the priests on the occasion of the first
plundering of the Temple (24:13). (Comp.
Jer. 27:19 seq.)

(18, 19) This list of the chief personages
taken by Nebuzaradan in the Temple and
the city of David may be regarded as an
indirect proof that the upper city was not
captured before.

(21) So Judah was carried away ... —
This sentence evidently concludes the whole
account of the destruction of Jerusalem and

the deportation of the people (comp. 17:23; Jer. 52:27), and not merely that of the proceedings of Nebuzaradan. Comp. the prophecy of Obadiah; Ps. 137; Lam. 4:21, 22.

(22) Gedaliah the son of Ahikam.— Nebuzaradan committed the prophet Jeremiah to the care of Gedaliah, who probably, like his father (Jer. 26:24), sympathized with Jeremiah's views (Jer. 39:13, 14). After hesitating whether to accompany Nebuzaradan to Babylon or not, the prophet finally decided upon returning to Gedaliah at Mizpah (Jer. 40:1-6). Gedaliah's magnanimous behavior in regard to Ishmael (Jer. 40:16 seq.) shows that he was not a traitor and deserter as some have misnamed him. Rather he was a disciple of Jeremiah, and did his utmost to induce the remnant over which he was appointed governor to submit with patience to their divinely-ordered lot, as the prophet urged them to do.

(25) In the seventh month.—Only two months after the fall of Jerusalem (verse 8).

Of the seed royal.—Perhaps this reveals Ishmael's motive. He thought his claim to the government of the community was greater than Gedaliah's (see Jer. 41:1). Baal-is, king of the Ammonites, had incited him to the crime (Jer. 40:14).

(26) Arose, and came to Egypt.—They took Jeremiah with them (Jer. 43:6). This verse only gives the end of the story as it is told in Jeremiah.

(27) Evil-merodach.—He came to the throne 562 B.C., upon the death of Nebuchadnezzar, who had reigned forty-three years. According to the canon of Ptolemy, Evil-merodach reigned two years. He was murdered by his brother-in-law Neriglissar— i.e., Nergal-sharezer.

(30) All the days of his life.—Jehoiachin may have died before Evil-merodach was murdered. There would be nothing strange in this, considering his age and his thirty-seven years of imprisonment.

The writer evidently dwells with pleasure on this faint gleam of light amid the darkness of the exile. It was a kind of foreshadowing of the pity which afterward was to be extended to the captive people, when the divine purpose had been achieved, and the exile had done its work of chastisement and purification. (Comp. Ps. 106:46; Ezra 9:9; Neh. 2:2.)

I CHRONICLES

1

In the LXX, the title of the books known to us as I and II Chronicles is **Paralipomena**, referring to "things added." It was the opinion of the Greek translators that the work was intended to be a kind of supplement to the older historical books. The name "Chronicles," which fairly represents the Hebrew, is derived from Jerome. It is usually suggested that Chronicles, Ezra, and Nehemiah constituted a single great history.

The abrupt opening of the narrative with a series of proper names presupposes that the reader is already acquainted with their historic import. The chronicler intends to give a synopsis of the archaeology of man, as recorded in the Book of Genesis, by way of fixing the place of Israel in the great human family.

Chapter 1 falls naturally into three sections: (1) the ten generations of the first age of humanity, with a table of races and countries, given in genealogical form according to ancient conceptions (verses 1-23; see notes on Gen. 5 and 10); (2) the ten generations after the Flood, from Shem to Abraham, the second age of man, with a list of the races claiming descent from Abraham (verses 24-42; see notes on Gen. 11, 16, 17, 21, 25, 36); (3) a catalog of the kings of Edom anterior to the Israelite monarchy and of the tribal chieftains of that country (verses 43-54; see notes on Gen. 36).

2

Dismissing the sons of Esau-Edom, the narrative proceeds with the sons of Israel (see notes on Gen. 35:23-29), who are named in order, by way of introduction to their genealogies, which occupy chaps. 2-8.

The rest of chap. 2 treats of the leading tribe of Judah and its sub-divisions under the heads of Zerah and Perez (verses 3-41; see notes on Gen. 38), and Caleb (verses 42-55; see notes on Josh. 15), while chaps. 3 and 4 complete the account of this tribe, as far as the fragmentary materials at the writer's disposal permitted.

3

Chapter 3 resumes the genealogy of the Hezronite house of Ram, suspended at 2:17: (1) the nine sons of David (verses 1-9; see notes on II Sam. 3:2-5); (2) the Davidic dynasty from Solomon to Zedekiah (verses 10-16; see notes on I and II Kings); (3) the line of Jechoniah-Jehoiachin, continued apparently to the ninth generation (verses 17-24); this section is peculiar to the chronicle.

4

This chapter comprises a compilation of fragmentary notices relating to the clans of Judah, their settlements and handicrafts, at an epoch which is not determined. It serves at once as a supplement to the account of Judah already given in chaps. 2 and 3, and as a first installment of the similar survey of the other tribes which follows (verses 24-27). Similar notices relating to the tribe of Simeon are contained in verses 24-38. (See notes on Gen. 38, 46; Exod. 6; Num. 26; Josh. 14, 19.)

5

The tribes east of Jordan—Reuben (verses 1-10; see notes on Gen. 49), Gad (verses 11-17; see notes on Josh. 13), and half-Manasseh—are considered, with short notices of their conquest and their final captivity (verses 18-26; see notes on II Kings 15, 17).

(25) Went a whoring after the gods of the people (peoples).—Jehovah was the true Lord (**Ba'al**) and Husband (**Ish**) of Israel. Apostasy from Him is, in the prophetic language, whoredom. (See Hos. 1-3.) According to II Kings 17, the fatal sin of Israel evinced itself in the worship of the high places, in adoration of the heavenly bodies and the productive powers of nature, and in the practice of magic and divination.

(26) Pul king of Assyria, and ... Tilgath-pilneser king of Assyria.—No trace of Pul as distinct from Tiglath-pileser has been found in the Assyrian monuments, which, it must be remembered, are contemporary. (See II Kings 15.) Pul appears to have been the original name of Tiglath-pileser, which, upon his accession to the throne of Assyria (745 B.C.), he discarded for that of the great king who had ruled the country four centuries before his time. Perhaps the chronicler meant here to indicate the identity of Pul and Tiglath.

6

This chapter concerns: (1) the genealogy of Aaron, including his descent from Levi, and his successors in the line of Eleazar until the Babylonian exile (verses 1-15; see notes on Gen. 46; Exod. 6); (2) a double series of the three sons of Levi (verses 16-48; see notes on Exod. 6; Num. 3); and (3) a repetition of the line of Aaron, from Eleazar to the age of David and Solomon, as prelude to the account of the cities of the Levites (verses 49-81; see notes on Josh. 21).

7

Here are given the great clans of Issachar (verses 1-5), Benjamin (verses 6-12), Naphtali (verse 13), West Manasseh (verses 14-19), Ephraim (verses 20-29), and Asher (verses 30-40). (See notes on Gen. 46; Num. 26; Josh. 16 and 17.)

8

The narrative returns to the tribe of Benjamin. The present register is quite different from that preserved in 7:6-12, which is an extract from a document drawn up for military purposes. Apparently based on a topographical register, this new list agrees better than the other with the data of Gen. 46 and Num. 26, allowance being made for the mistakes of generations of copyists. The chronicler may well have thought the short section of chap. 7 too meager as an account of a tribe which had furnished the first royal house, and had afterward inseparably linked its fortunes with those of the legitimate dynasty. Here, therefore, he supplements his former notice. Perhaps, also, he returns to Benjamin by way of introduction to the royal genealogy with which the section concludes, i.e., having to tell of Saul, he starts from the tribal patriarch to whom the house of Saul traced back its long descent.

See notes on Gen. 46; Num. 26; I Sam. 9 and 14.

9

On these matters regarding resident priests and Levites in Jerusalem, see notes on Neh. 11.

342

Verses 35-44 are a duplicate of 8:29-38. The genealogy of Saul seems to be repeated, according to the chronicler's habit, as a transition or introduction to something else, in this case the account of that king's final ruin in chap. 10.

10

Chapters 10-29 record the history of King David, who made Jerusalem the political and religious center of Israel, organized the Levitical ministry in its permanent shape, and amassed great stores of wealth and material for the Temple, which his son and successor was to build.

Verses 1-12 here constitute a brief narrative of the overthrow and death of Saul, by way of prelude to the reign of David. (See notes on I Sam. 31.)

(13-14) These verses constitute a concluding selection from the mind of the chronicler himself. He sums up his extract concerning the ruin of Saul by assigning the moral ground of it—Saul's "unfaithfulness whereby he showed himself unfaithful to Jehovah." The same charge was made against the Transjordan tribes in 5:25, and against the people of Judah in 9:1.

11

The chapter contains the election of David in Hebron and his conquest of Jerusalem (verses 1-9), and a list of David's chief warriors, with short notices of their famous deeds (verses 10-47).

(10-44) On the former group of verses, see notes on II Sam. 5. The latter group answers to II Sam. 23:8-39 (see notes), which catalog, however, breaks off with Uriah the Hittite, whereas our text includes sixteen additional names. This fact proves that the chronicler had either a fuller source or a different recension of Samuel. The numerous variant spellings are in general mistakes of transcription.

12

Chapter 12 is a sort of supplement to chap. 11, and is throughout peculiar to the Chronicle. It contains registers of the warriors who successively went over to David during his outlaw career (verses 1-22; see notes on I Sam. 22 ff.), and of the tribal

representatives who crowned David at Hebron (verses 23-40).

13

Chapters 13-16 form a complete section
relating to the transfer of the Ark from
Kirjath-jearim to its new sanctuary at
Jerusalem. The continuity of the narrative
is suspended only by the short parenthetic
chap. 14. Chap. 13 is closely parallel to II
Sam. 6:1-11 (see notes). The introduction,
however (verses 1-5), is much fuller than
that of Samuel, which is condensed into one
brief sentence.

(6) From this point our narrative coincides with that of II Sam. 6:2-11 (see notes).
The original text was plainly the same,
whether the chronicler drew directly from
the Book of Samuel or from another
source. Such differences as appear consist of
abridgments, paraphrases, and corrections.

14

This section is a duplicate of II Sam.
5:11-25 (see notes). In the older work it
follows immediately upon the account of
the taking of Jebus (II Sam. 5:6-10; see
notes), and precedes that of the removal of
the Ark. Neither Samuel nor the chronicler
has observed the order of chronology. The
chronicler may have transposed the two
accounts, in order to represent the removal
of the Ark to the new capital in immediate
connection with the acquisition of the city.

The chapter treats David's palace building and family (verses 1-7), and his two
victories over the Philistines in the valley of
Rephaim (verses 8-17).

15

The thread of the narrative dropped at
13:14 is now resumed, and the subject of
this and the following chapter is the solemn
transfer of the Ark from the house of Obed-
edom by the lawful ministry of priests and
Levites. The elaborate account presented
here corresponds to a brief section of eight
verses in Samuel (II Sam. 6:12-20a; see
notes), which it incorporates, subject to certain variations (15:25-16:3, 43).

Chapter 15 relates David's preparation
for the ceremony of the transfer by erection
of a tent for the Ark (verse 1), by assem-

bling representatives of all Israel—
especially the priests and Levites, and consulting with the latter (verses 2-16), and by
choice of individuals to conduct the proceedings (verses 17-24). Verses 25-29 contain the incidents of the procession.

16

(4-42) This entire section, concerning the
institution of a ministry for the Ark, and
recording the ode sung on the day of institution, is peculiar to the Chronicle. Verse
43 is almost identical with II Sam. 6:19, 20.
Compared, then, with the older text, this
relation of the chronicler's looks like a
parenthesis interpolated from another
source into the history, as narrated in II
Sam. 6:12-20 (see notes).

(7) It may be that this composite hymn,
beginning here and continuing through
verse 36, was sung in the time of the
compiler, on the anniversary of the removal
of the Ark, which may in later times have
been commemorated by a special service.
Hence it was easy to infer that it was the
ode sung at the original service under David. It is probable that this ode does not
constitute an original part of the Chronicles, but has been inserted by a later hand.
The Psalm is a **cento** consisting of portions
of three others (Pss. 105, 96, 106) extant in
the Psalter, and so loosely patched together
that the seams are quite visible. The Psalter
itself does not refer the three psalms in
question to David; if, however, the editors
of the Psalter had read in the Chronicles a
clear assertion of Davidic authorship, they
would hardly have left them anonymous.
Critics generally agree that it is not here
expressly said that David composed this
ode, and, in fact, its ideas and language
betray a later origin than the Davidic age.
Nor does it contain specific allusion to the
occasion for which it purports to have been
written. If no record was preserved of the
psalms actually sung at the festival, it was
natural that some editor should attempt to
supply the apparent **lacuna** from the Psalter.

17

David, desiring to build a house for God,
receives from Nathan a divine promise of
perpetual dominion (verses 1-15). His prayer is recorded in verses 16-27. This section

343

is a duplicate of II Sam. 7 (see notes). The differences are mostly verbal rather than essential, and are due, as usual, to a natural tendency to interpret and simplify archaisms and obscurities in the original narrative.

18

Chapters 18-20 represent the warlike aspect of David's character, just as chaps. 15-17 portrayed him from the religious point of view as zealous for the due observance of the divine order in worship. The narratives are closely parallel to the corresponding ones in II Samuel, and are given in the same order. The variations may be accounted for by mistakes of copyists, and by the chronicler's habit of explaining difficult expressions, abridging what appeared needlessly prolix, and adding here and there small details from another source.

This chapter contains a summary account of David's wars of conquest (verses 1-13), and his internal administration (verses 14-17). See notes on II Sam. 8.

19

Here is reported the war with the sons of Ammon and their Aramaean allies. The chapter is a duplicate of II Sam. 10 (see notes). The story of David's kindness to Mephibosheth (II Sam. 9), creditable as it was to David, is omitted by the chronicler, as belonging rather to the private than the public history of the king.

20

Verses 1-3 report the completion of the Ammonite campaign. (See notes on II Sam. 11:1; 12:26, 30, 31.) The chronicler omits the long intervening account of David's guilt in relation to Uriah and Bathsheba, not because he had any thought of wiping out the memory of David's crimes (an object quite beyond his power to secure, even if he had desired it, unless he could first have destroyed every existing copy of Samuel), but because that story of shame and reproach did not harmonize with the plan and purpose of his work, which was to portray the bright side of the reign of

David, as founder of the legitimate dynasty and organizer of the legitimate worship.

Verses 4-8 constitute a fragment relating how three heroes of Israel slew three Philistine giants. This section corresponds to II Sam. 21:18-22 (see notes). The chronicler has omitted the history of Absalom's rebellion, with all the events which preceded and followed it, as recorded in II Sam. 13-20; and, further, he has excluded the touching story of the sacrifice of seven sons of Saul at the demand of the Gibeonites (II Sam. 21:1-14).

(5) The Hebrew text and LXX of Samuel have the very different statement: "And Elhanan son of Jaare-oregim the Bethlehemite slew Goliath the Gittite." There are good critics who maintain that we must recognize here a proof that popular traditions fluctuated between David and the less famous hero Elhanan as slayer of Goliath, an uncertainty supposed to be faithfully reflected in the two accounts preserved by the compiler of Samuel (I Sam. 17; II Sam. 21:19). Other scholars believe that the text of Samuel should be corrected from the Chronicles. But this must depend on the general view we take of the chronicler's relation to the Books of Samuel. It is easy, but hardly satisfactory, to allege that he felt the difficulty and altered the text accordingly. Now, it is fair to say that hitherto we have observed no signs of arbitrary alteration, but that we **have** had abundant proof that the chronicler actually possessed other sources beside Samuel. It is quite possible that Elhanan is another, and, in fact, the original name of **David**. The appellative David, "the beloved," may have gradually supplanted the old Elhanan in the popular memory. Solomon we know was at first named Jedidiah; and it is highly probable that the true designation of the first king of Israel has been lost, the name **Saul** ("the asked") having been given in allusion to the fact that the people had **asked** for a king. We may compare, besides, the double names Jehoahaz-Shallum, Mattaniah-Zedekiah, and perhaps Uzziah-Azariah. (The Targum on Samuel partly supports this suggestion.) And **Jaare** in Hebrew writing is an easy corruption of **Jesse**, so that the original reading of II Sam. 21:19 may have been, "And Elhanan the son of Jesse the Bethlehemite, slew Goliath," etc. In that case, the reading of Chronicles must be considered an unsuccessful emendation, due probably to the compiler whose work the chronicler followed.

21

Omitting the magnificent ode which David sang to his deliverer (II Sam. 22), and the last words of David (II Sam. 23:1-7), as well as the list of David's heroes (II Sam. 23:8-39), which has already been repeated in chap. 11, the chronicler resumes the ancient narrative at the point coincident with II Sam. 24 (see notes). Though the two accounts obviously had a common basis, the deviations of our text from that of Samuel are much more numerous and noteworthy than is usual. They are generally explicable by reference to the special purpose and tendency of the writer.

In Samuel the narrative of the census (verses 1-6) comes in as a kind of appendix to the history of David; here it serves to introduce the account of the preparations for building the Temple and the organization of its ministry. The plagues are discussed as consequent upon the census (verses 7-17) and prior to this hallowing of the Temple area (verses 18-30).

(25) So David gave to Ornan for the place six hundred shekels of gold by weight.—Samuel has, "And David purchased the threshingfloor and the oxen for silver, fifty shekels." The two estimates are obviously discordant. We have no means of calculating what would have been a fair price, for we know neither the extent of the purchase nor the value of the sums mentioned. But comparing Gen. 23:16, where four hundred shekels of silver are paid for the field and cave of Machpelah, fifty shekels of silver would seem to be too little. On the other hand, six hundred shekels of gold appears to be far too high a price for the threshingfloor. Perhaps for "gold" we should read "silver." It has, indeed, been suggested that the authors were writing of two different things—that Samuel assigns only the price of the threshingfloor and oxen, whereas the chronicler, when he speaks of "the price," means the entire Mount of the Temple (Moriah), on which the floor was situated. However this may be, the chronicler has doubtless preserved for us what he found in his original.

The concluding remarks in verse 28— 22:1 are not read in Samuel, but the writer, no doubt, found some basis for them in his special source. They tell us how it was that Ornan's threshingfloor became recognized as a permanent sanctuary and the site ordained for the future Temple. They thus form a transition to the account of David's preparations for the building (22:2-19).

22

(1) This is the house of the Lord God.— The verse resumes the narrative suspended at 21:28. Obviously, we have here the goal of the entire narrative of the census and the pestilence, which the chronicler would probably have omitted, as he has omitted that of the famine (II Sam. 21), were it not for the fact that it shows how the site of the Temple was determined.

On preparations for building the Temple, and David's charge to Solomon, see notes on II Sam. 7; I Kings 2 and 5.

23

After a brief notice of Solomon's coronation in David's old age, the chronicler passes to the main subject of chaps. 23-26— David's organization of the priests and Levites. The chapter before us presents a summary account of the number and several duties of the Levites (verses 2-5; comp. Num. 4), and the father-houses or clans of the Levites, with an appendix of remarks about their duties from this time forward (verses 6-32; comp. Exod. 6; Num. 10).

(1) He made Solomon his son king.—This short statement is all that the chronicler has chosen to repeat from I Kings 1 (see notes), a narrative intimately connected with David's family affairs, and with which he is not concerned to deal. (See introductory note to chap. 20.)

24

Chapter 24 contains an account of the organization of the priests in twenty-four classes (verses 1-19; comp. Exod. 6; Lev. 10; Josh. 7), and a recapitulation of the Levitical classes, as described in the last chapter (verses 20-31).

25

This chapter concerns the twenty-four classes of singers, or minstrels. (Comp. Ezra 3.)

26

Chapter 26 deals with the classes of the porters, or warders (verses 1-19), the keepers of the treasures of the sanctuary (verses 20-28), and the officials charged with external business, chiefly scribes and judges (verses 29-32). (Comp. Exod. 30; Neh. 3; I Kings 10.)

27

The account of the religious organization (chaps 23-26) is naturally followed here by a sort of outline of the military and civil administration, given in the form of a catalog of officers and ministers of the king. (See notes on II Sam. 15 and 23.)

28

Chapters 28 and 29 record David's last instructions and death. In this present chapter, verses 1-10 concern David's charge to Solomon before the National Assembly to build the Temple, and verses 11-21 regard David's delivering to him the plans and materials of the building and its furniture. (See notes on I Kings 2, 7, 8.)

29

This chapter is a continuation of proceedings in the Assembly. On the concluding remarks upon David's history (verses 26-30), see notes on II Sam. 5; I Kings 1 and 2.

II CHRONICLES

1

Chapters 1-9 treat the reign of Solomon. This chapter describes a national sacrifice at Gibeon, and in connection with it a dream in which God reveals His will to Solomon (verses 1-13; see notes on I Kings 3). A few details are added respecting Solomon's power, wealth, and commerce (verses 14-17; comp. I Kings 10.)

2

Chapters 2-7 are concerned with the writer's principal topic—the building and consecration of the Temple. Verses 1, 2, 17, 18 of chap. 2 have to do with securing of laborers; verses 3-16 deal with Solomon's treaty with Huram (Hiram) of Tyre. (See notes on I Kings 5.)

3

Chapter 3 speaks of building the Temple and making the sacred vessels: site and date (verses 1, 2); dimensions of porch and Holy place (verses 3-7); Holy of Holies, with cherubim and veil (verses 8-14); two bronze pillars in porch (verses 15-17). (See notes on I Kings 6 and 7.)

4

This is a continuation of the discussion regarding the sacred vessels of the Temple: brazen altar (verse 1); brazen sea (verses 2-5; ten lavers (verse 6); candlesticks, tables, bowls, courts, and further catalog (verses 7-22). Verses 7-9 are peculiar to the Chronicle. (See notes on I Kings 7.)

5

The chapter is an almost literal duplicate of the parallel text, I Kings 8:1-11 (see notes). The desire is to explain and abridge accounts for such variations as are not due to the transcribers. Here the topic is the national ceremony of the transfer of the Ark into the Temple at its dedication.

6

Verses 1-11 also are in verbal agreement with the parallel account, I Kings 8:12-21 (see notes), with a few slight exceptions. Solomon blesses his people and his God. Verses 12-42 are Solomon's prayer of consecration (See notes on I Kings 8:22-53).

(41, 42) The two verses are slightly altered from Ps. 132:8-10. It would seem that the chronicler selected them as forming a more natural and appropriate conclusion to the Prayer of Dedication than that which he found in the older account. The aptness of the quotation may be admitted without assuming that for lack of this summons to take possession of the sanctuary, the whole prayer is pointless in Kings. The peroration of I Kings 8:50-53 (see notes) is quite natural, though different, the closing thoughts being a return to those with which the prayer began. The prayer forms a well-rounded whole, and the suggestion of a lacuna is out of place. There is no difficulty in this view; the difficulty lies rather in maintaining the originality of these verses here. Comp. the free adaptation of several late Psalms in the Hymn of Praise in I Chron. 16:7ff. (see notes). The versification of the original psalm is neglected here, as there.

7

God's confirming the dedication of the Temple by fire from heaven (verses 1-3) is followed by sacrifice and festival (verses 4-11; see notes on I Kings 8:62-66). Further confirmation takes the form of God's revelation to Solomon (verses 12-22; see notes on I Kings 9:1-9). It should be noted that verses 1-3 do not appear in I Kings 8:54ff., where we read instead of it an address of Solomon to the people.

8

Chapters 8 and 9 provide further particulars of Solomon's public works, regulation of worship, foreign relations, revenues, wisdom, glory, authorities, and notice of death. For chap. 8 see notes on I Kings 9:10-28.

9

See notes on I Kings 10:1-29; 11:41-43.

(21) For the king's ships went to Tarshish.—Comp. I Kings 10:22; II Chron. 20:36. It is generally assumed that the words of the chronicler are an erroneous paraphrase of the expression, "Tarshish fleet," i.e., a fleet of ships fitted for long voyages. (Comp. Isa. 2:16.) Solomon may have had a fleet in the Mediterranean trading westward, as well as in the Red Sea, trading south and east.

10

Chapters 10-36 constitute a history of the kings who reigned in Jerusalem, from Rehoboam to the Exile.

Considered by itself, chap. 10 might be pronounced a transcript of I Kings 12:1-24 (see notes). Such differences as appear in the Hebrew text are mostly unimportant, consisting of merely verbal modifications and omissions not affecting the general sense.

11

The account of Rehoboam's strengthening the defenses of his kingdom (verses 5-12) is peculiar to the Chronicle. So also is the section reporting the desertion of the northern kingdom by all who would be faithful to the legitimate worship (verses 13-17), though it is indirectly confirmed by notices in I Kings 12:31; 13:33. The particulars regarding Rehoboam's family (verses 18-23), while lacking in the Book of Kings, appears to have been derived from the sources designated in 12:15.

12

Shishak's invasion of Judah and the preaching of Shemaiah are the subjects of this chapter (verses 1-12; see notes on the briefer parallel passage, I Kings 14:25-28). Verses 13-16 sum up the reign of Rehoboam (see notes on I Kings 14:21, 22, 29-31).

13

The reign of Abijah is reported here. (See notes on I Kings 15:1-8.)

14

Chapters 14-16 concern the reign of Asa. In this present chapter verses 1-8 deal with his efforts to root out illegitimate worship and to strengthen the system of national defenses (see notes on I Kings 15:9-15), while verses 9-15 treat the invasion of the Cushite Zerah and his overthrow. This latter section has no parallel in the Book of Kings.

15

This chapter treats Asa's reformation of religion, a matter peculiar to the Chronicle. Verses 1-7 give the address of the prophet Azariah ben Oded, and verses 8-15 speak of the reform of worship and renewal of the covenant.

(1) Azariah the son of Oded.—The prophet is unknown, except from this chapter. The name Oded comprises the same radical letters as Iddo (9:29; 12:15); but whether the same prophet or another is meant is beyond decision.

(7) Your work shall be rewarded.—See Jer. 31:16. We have here the moral of the prophet's address. The ruinous results of not "seeking," and "forsaking," Jehovah (verse 2) have been briefly but powerfully sketched from the past history of the nation. The conclusion is, Do not ye fall away like your forefathers; but let your allegiance to Jehovah be decided and sincere.

(8) And renewed the altar.—The context seems to imply that this "renewal" consisted in reconsecration, the altar having been defiled by an illegal **cultus**. The altar had now stood sixty years. (Comp. 24:4.)

(17) The heart of Asa was perfect.—The Book of Kings adds, "with Jehovah." The meaning is, that though he failed to get rid of the high places, Asa himself was always faithful to the lawful worship of the Temple. (Comp. I Chron. 28:9.)

(19) And there was no more war unto the five and thirtieth year of the reign of Asa.—In I Kings 15:16 we find a different statement: "And there was war between Asa and Baasha king of Israel all their days," a statement which is repeated in verse 32 of the same chapter. The chronicler has evidently modified the older text, in order to assign a precise date to the outbreak of active hostilities between the two monarchs. (Both I Kings 15:16 and the present verse

19 begin with the same two Hebrew words, meaning "and war was," but the chronicler inserts a **not**). The verse of Kings need not imply more than that no amicable relations were ever established between the two sovereigns. They had inherited a state of war, although neither was in a condition to make an open attack upon the other for some years.

For the dating, see note on 16:1.

16

(1) These statements of date are obviously irreconcilable with I Kings 15:33; 16:8. We suppose that the text here is unsound, and thirty-six has been substituted by an error of transcription for sixteen or twenty-six; and that in 15:19 by a similar mistake thirty-five has taken the place of fifteen or twenty-five.

(7) **Hanani the seer.**—See I Sam. 9:9. The use of this term seems to point to an ancient source of this narrative which is peculiar to the chronicler. Nothing beyond what is told here is known of Hanani. He was perhaps the father of the prophet Jehu the son of Hanani, who prophesied against Baasha (I Kings 16:1) and rebuked Jehoshaphat (II Chron. 19:2).

Therefore is the host of the king of Syria escaped out of thine hand.—Asa had doubtless been afraid that Benhadad would cooperate with Baasha his ally in hostilities against Judah, and therefore bribed the Syrian king at the expense of the Temple treasury (verse 3). This politic act secured its object, but from the prophetic point of view such success was no better than loss and failure, for it had deprived Asa of an assured triumph over the combined forces of Israel and Syria. Not only the defeat of Baasha's schemes, but victory over his formidable ally, would have been conceded to faith (comp. II Kings 13:14-19).

(8) **Were not the Ethiopians and the Lubims a huge host?**—An instance confirming what was said in verse 7. Cushites and Lybians were banded together in Zerah's great army, just as Syrians and Israelites might have united in assailing Judah, yet the victory had fallen to Asa (14:9-15). Neither the Libyan contingent nor the horsemen are mentioned in chap. 14. Apparently the writer is making extracts from fuller sources.

Verses 11-14 record the conclusion of Asa's reign. (Comp. I Kings 15:23, 24.

17

Chapters 17-20 concern the person and reign of Jehoshaphat. Chapter 17 in particular reports his labors to strengthen his realm internally and externally.

(9) **The book of the law of the Lord.**— The writer evidently means the Pentateuch; and if this notice were derived by him from a contemporary source, e.g., the "book of Jehu the son of Hanani," to which he refers as an authority for the reign (20:34), it would constitute an important testimony to the existence, if not of the five books, at least of an ancient collection of laws at this early date (circ. 850 B.C.).

(14-19) The army of Jehoshaphat was organized in five grand divisions, perhaps corresponding to five territorial divisions of the southern kingdom. The totals are the largest assigned to the two tribes anywhere in the Old Testament—Judah 780,000 and Benjamin 380,000: in all, 1,160,000. In the absence of adequate data for modifying these certainly startling figures, it is well to bear in mind that we need not understand by them an army which ever actually mustered in the field or on parade, but simply an estimate of the total male population liable to be called out for the national defense; yet even upon that understanding, the total appears to be at least three times too great, considering the small extent of the country.

18

Here Jehoshaphat makes affinity with Ahab and takes part in the Syrian war at Ramoth-Gilead (see notes on I Kings 22:2-35). Only the introduction of the narrative (verses 1, 2) differs from that of Kings—a change necessitated by the fact that the chronicler is writing the history, not of Ahab, but of Jehoshaphat.

19

The whole chapter is original, as far as regards the Book of Kings. Verses 1-3 speak of Jehu's denunciation of alliance with Ahab, and verses 4-11 report further proceedings in the reform of justice and religion.

(2) **Therefore is wrath upon thee.**—In the case of David, the divine wrath was embodied in pestilence; what form did it take

349

with Jehoshaphat? The following chapters seem to supply the answer. His land suffered invasion and his fleet shipwreck; his posterity was evil and came to an evil end (chaps. 20-22). There may be reference also to the failure of the campaign in which Jehoshaphat had engaged, and his inglorious return to his own land.

20

The chronicler only has preserved a historic account of this great deliverance from invasion (verses 1-30). But certain of the Psalms have been supposed with much probability to commemorate it. The contents of Pss. 46-48 harmonize well with this assumption; and they are referred by their titles to "the sons of Korah," a fact which corresponds with the statement of verse 19 that certain of the Korahite Levites sang praises to Jehovah on occasion of the prophecy of Jahaziel. Further, Jahaziel himself was an **Asaphite** Levite, and it is noteworthy that Ps. 83, which is a prayer against a hostile confederacy of Edom, Ammon, Moab, and other races, is headed "A Psalm of Asaph." It may have been composed by the prophet whose name is recorded only in this chapter.

Verses 31-37 constitute concluding notices to the reign of Jehoshaphat. Comp. I Kings 22:41-50, a brief section yet the whole account of the reign in the older narrative.

21

The reign of Jehoram is discussed here. Verses 2-4 concern his murdering his six brothers, verses 5-11 his idolatry and the revolt of Edom and Libnah (see notes on II Kings 8:17-22), verses 12-15 his letter from Elijah, and verses 16-20 his incurable disease.

(12) And there came a writing to him from Elijah the prophet.—This is the chronicler's only mention of the great prophet of the northern kingdom. Elijah, though a very old man, may have been still alive. His extreme old age would account for his sending a written prophecy, rather than going in person to warn Jehoram. If, however, it is supposed that the author of Kings has told the story of Elijah's translation in its right place chronologically, and that the campaign described in the following chap-

350

ter, in which Jehoshaphat took part, was really subsequent to that event, we may say that this "writing from Elijah the prophet," containing the substance of some last utterances of his directed against Jehoram and Athaliah, was now put into written shape and forwarded to Jehoram by one of the prophet's pupils, perhaps by his great successor Elisha. (See II Kings 2:15; 3:11.) Elisha's ministry probably began some time before his master's ascension, and the description of him in II Kings 3:11 need not mean more than the fact of his being a servant to Elijah.

22

This chapter deals with the short reign of Ahaziah (verses 1-9) and the governance of Athaliah (verses 10-12). See notes on II Kings 8:25-29 and 11:1-3, respectively.

(9) And he sought Ahaziah.—In II Kings 9:27, 28 we find a different, though not difficult, tradition concerning the death of Ahaziah. (Perhaps "and they smote him" has fallen out before the words "on the ascent of Gur.") Such divergences are valuable, because they help to establish the independence of the two accounts.

23

Here are discussed the fall of Athaliah and the succession of Joash. (See notes on II Kings 11:4-20.)

24

Here, and in the parallel passage II Kings 12 (see notes), stand the striking events of Joash's reign. Prominent are the repair of the Temple under Jehoiada (verses 1-14), national apostasy and the murder of Zechariah ben Jehoiada (verses 17-22), and the Syrian invasion of Judah (verses 23-27). It is interesting that the writer, in his own fashion, in verses 13, 14 freely modifies the older account to suit the needs of his contemporaries.

25

The subject of this chapter is the reign of Amaziah. (See notes on II Kings 14:1-20.) Verses 5-13, regarding Amaziah's military strength and the conquest of Edom, are the most peculiar to the Chronicle. In Kings the conquest of Edom is recorded in a single verse (II Kings 14:7). The character of his administration is confirmed by his refusing the prophetic warning regarding idolatry (verses 14-16) and his defeat in battle by Joash of Israel (verses 17-28).

26

(1) Uzziah is the prominent personality in this passage. (See notes on II Kings 14:21, 22; 15:2, 3.) So the chronicler always names him, except in I Chron. 3:12, where the name "Azariah" appears, as in II Kings 14:21; 15:1, 6; etc. In II Kings 15:13, 30, 32, 34, "Uzziah" occurs, as also in the headings of the prophecies of Hosea, Amos, and Isaiah. It is not, therefore, to be regarded either as a popular abbreviation or a transcriber's blunder. Clearly, he was known by both names, but to foreigners chiefly by the latter.

(6-15) This section is peculiar to the Chronicles. Although the Book of Kings passes over the facts recorded here, they are essential to forming a right conception of the strength and importance of the southern kingdom during the age of Uzziah and Jotham; and they are fully corroborated, not only by comparison with the date of Isaiah (Isa. 2-4) upon the same subject, but also by the independent testimony of the cuneiform inscriptions of the period. (See note on II Kings 14:28.) A telling proof for the accuracy of the Biblical account of Uzziah's well-founded power is the fact that the name of Uzziah is conspicuously absent from the list of western princes who, in 738 B.C., sent tribute to Tiglath-pileser II.

(16-23) This section also is mainly peculiar to the chronicler. II Kings 15:5-7 (see notes) correspond to verses 21-23 only.

27

The character of Jotham's reign is cited here. (See notes on II Kings 15:32-38.)

28

The major concerns here under the governance of Ahaz are the Syro-Ephraite War, in which Judah receives hurt rather than help from Assyria (verses 5-21) and the

Syrian idolatry and closing of the Temple (verses 22-27). (See notes on II Kings 16:5-20; Isa. 7.)

29

Chapters 29-32 record the reign of Hezekiah. (See notes on II Kings 18-20.) This present chapter concerns the length and spirit of the reign, and the solemn purgation and hallowing of the Temple.

30

The point of this chapter is to describe the Passover to which Hezekiah summoned all Israel from Dan to Beer-sheba. Verses 13-22 report the observance particularly at Jerusalem. (See Num. 9:10, 11.)

(26) For since the time of Solomon ... there was not the like.—The chronicler himself thus compares this great festival with the twofold Feast of the Dedication of the Temple (7:1-10). That festival, like this one, had been prolonged seven days because the Feast of Tabernacles immediately followed it; and there had been no other since the time of Solomon that could compare with this in respect of duration, abundance of sacrifices, number of participants, or the joy that distinguished it.

(27) And their voice was heard.—The priestly blessing was a prayer that Jehovah would bless. (See Num. 6:22-27.) That the prayer was heard on the present occasion the writer infers from the progress of reform among the people and the wonderful deliverance from Assyria, as related in the ensuing chapters.

31

Here is reported the progress of the religious reformation under Hezekiah. For the destruction of the images and high places, comp. II Kings 18:4; for the tithe, comp. the "heave offerings" in Num. 18:19.

32

The narrative here is parallel to II Kings 18:13-20:21, which is repeated in Isaiah 36-39. (See notes.) It concerns the invasion of Sennacherib, Hezekiah's recovery from deadly sickness, his pride and wealth, his reception of the embassy from Babylon, and the end of his reign.

It is noteworthy that verses 2-8, regarding preparations for the defense, are peculiar to the Chronicle yet "perfectly credible" (Thenius), and are borne out by Isa. 22:8-11; II Kings 20:20, and the inscription of Sennacherib.

33

The reigns of Manasseh and Amon are recorded in chap. 33. This section is closely parallel with II Kings 21 (see notes).

(6) **And dealt with a familiar spirit, and with wizards.**—The source of all these modes of soothsaying was Babylon. Like the first king of Israel, Manasseh appears to have despaired of help or counsel from Jehovah. (Comp. Jer. 44:17, 18.) The heavy yoke of Assyria again weighed the nation down, and the great deliverance under Hezekiah was almost forgotten. As life was embittered by foreign bondage, the darker aspects of heathenism became dominant in Manasseh's imitations of foreign religion.

(11) The **hooks** ("thorns") might be such as the Assyrian kings passed through the nostrils and lips of their more distinguished prisoners. (Comp. Job 41:2; Isa. 37:29; Amos 4:2.) Sennacherib relates: "Suzubu king of Babylon, in the battle alive their hands took him; in fetters of bronze they put him, and to my presence brought him. In the great gate in the midst of the city of Nineveh I bound him fast." This happened in 695 B.C., only a few years before the similar captivity of Manasseh.

(18) **The words of the seers that spake to him.**—These "words of the seers" were incorporated in the great history of the kings, which is mentioned at the end of the verse, and which was one of the chronicler's principal authorities.

(19) **Among the sayings of the seers.**—In the history of Hozai ("prophets" or "seers" as in verse 18), this work was, therefore, the source from which the chronicler derived his additional information about the reign of Manasseh.

34

The history of Josiah, as related in chaps. 34, 35, is in substantial agreement with the narrative of II Kings 22, 23 (see notes). The main difference lies in the fact that the

chronicler assigns the various reforms of this king to his eighth, twelfth, and eighteenth years, whereas the compiler of Kings groups them all together, in connection with the repair of the Temple and finding of the Book of the Law, in the eighteenth year of the reign. Our account, moreover, briefly describes the suppression of idolatry, and dwells at great length on the celebration of the Passover; in Kings the contrary is the case.

(14) This verse is not in II Kings 22. It supplements the older account by assigning the occasion of the discovery during the cleansing and repair of the Temple (verses 8-13).

Josephus makes Hilkiah find the book in the treasure-chamber of the Temple which he had entered to get gold and silver for making some sacred vessels. According to Rabbinical tradition it was found hidden under a heap of stones, where it had been placed to save it from being burned by King Ahaz.

35

Josiah's Passover receives brief but emphatic notice in the short section of Kings which records it (II Kings 23:21-23). The passage is freely copied in III Esdras 1:1-22. It is of peculiar importance, as giving a more complete representation of the Passover than the Pentateuchal data supply.

(3) **Put the holy ark in the house.**—This command implies that the Ark had been removed from its place in the inner sanctuary. The removal probably took place under Manasseh or his son, with the object of saving the sacred symbol from profanation. Or perhaps the repair of the Temple under Josiah had necessitated such a step.

(4) **According to the writing of David ... Solomon his son.**—Comp. I Chron. 28:19, where David refers to such a writing. The words seem to imply the existence of written memorials of the regulations of public worship, which David and Solomon instituted.

On the conflict between Josiah and Pharaoh-necho of Egypt, see notes on II Kings 23:29.

(25) **And Jeremiah lamented**—i.e., wrote a dirge. The special mourning of the land over Josiah is mentioned in Kings.

They are written in the lamentations.—The dirges alluding to Josiah's untimely end, and among them Jeremiah's, were preserved in a Book of Dirges, which may have been extant in the chronicler's day. (Comp. the allusions in Jer. 22:10, 18; Zech. 12:11.) This collection, however, was quite different from the canonical Book of Lamentations, the subject of which is the ruin of Judah and Jerusalem by the Chaldeans.

36

This last chapter of the Chronicle concerns the fortunes of Jehoahaz (verses 1-4; see notes on II Kings 23:30-35; comp. III Esdr. 1:32-36), Jehoiakim (verses 5-8; see notes on II Kings 23:36-24:7; comp. III Esdr. 1:37-41; Jer. 25 and 26), Jehoiachin (verses 9, 10; see notes on II Kings 24:8-17; comp. III Esdr. 1:41-44; Jer. 22:20-30; Ezek. 19:5-9), and Zedekiah (verses 11-21; see notes on II Kings 24:18-25:21; comp. III Esdr. 1:44-55; Jer. 39 and 52).

(20, 21) The seventy years are reckoned from the 4th of Jehoiakim, when the prophecy was uttered (Jer. 25:1, 12), to the first year of Cyrus and the return under Zerubbabel, 536 B.C.

On the edict of Cyrus authorizing the return of the captives (verses 22, 23), comp. Ezra 1:1-3; Isa. 44:28, and chaps. 45-47; III Esdr. 2:1-5.

EZRA

1

The First Return Under Zerubbabel

(1-4) The decree of Cyrus marks an epoch of great importance, and therefore is repeated almost word for word from the end of Chronicles.

(1) The first year.—Cyrus became king of Persia in B.C. 559. Twenty years later he took Babylon from Belshazzar; and this first year of his rule in Babylon was his beginning as an agent in Jewish affairs and for the Kingdom of God.

Stirred up.—By a direct influence, probably through the instrumentality of Daniel. This prophet we may suppose Cyrus to have found in Babylon, and to have had his mind directed to the express prediction of Isa. 44:28, where his name is mentioned. But the writer, who again and again records the prophetic intervention of Haggai and Zechariah (5:1; 6:14), makes no allusion to the part that Daniel the prophet had taken. He refers only to the divine prediction by Jeremiah, which must be fulfilled (Jer. 25:12; 29:10).

(2) Thus saith Cyrus king of Persia.—We may assume that **Ormazd** in the original was reproduced in the Hebrew version that accompanied it by its equivalent, "Jehovah." The decree runs much in the style of those found in the majority of Persian inscriptions, such as "By the grace of Ormazd is Darius king"; and the spirit of tolerance and piety in it is perfectly in harmony with all ancient testimonies to the character of Cyrus.

(4) Let the men of his place help him.—The heathen subjects of Cyrus are required to assist the departing sojourner, and expected also to send freewill offerings to the Temple. Note that in all these terms the spirit and phrase of the Hebrew people are used, and that there was more in the decree than is here given, as appears in the sequel. Cyrus was under strong influence, both human and divine.

(5) With all them whose spirit God had raised.—The same influence that prompted the decree of Cyrus was necessary to overcome the inertness of the captives; many preferred to remain in Babylon.

(7) His gods.—Merodach, whom he called "his lord" (Dan. 1:2). From II Kings 25:13-17 it appears that much had been taken away which Cyrus had not been able to find.

(8) Mithredath.—"Dedicated to Mithra," the sun-god of the Persians, whose worship among the Vedic Indians had reached Persia years earlier.

Sheshbazzar.—The Chaldee name of Zerubbabel, whose title, however, as Prince of Judah is given him from the Hebrew side. He was the legal heir of Jehoiachin, being the son of Pedaiah (I Chron. 3:19), who possibly married the widow of Salathiel or Shealtiel. And the title "Prince of Judah," or "Prince of the captivity," was especially given to him in common with a very few others.

(11) Bring up.—They were not, as sometimes said, the freewill offering of Cyrus. Sheshbazzar brought these rich vessels "with them of the captivity," and they were sent as already belonging to God, who vindicated by His judgment on Babylon their desecration at the feast of Belshazzar.

2

(1) The children of the province that went up out of the captivity.—They came from "the captivity," which was now as it were a generic name—"Children of the captivity" in Babylon (2:1), in Judah (4:1)—and became "children of the province," the Judaean province of Persia.

Every one unto his city.—So far, that is, as his city was known. The various cities, or villages, are more distinctly enumerated in Nehemiah.

(2) Which came with Zerubbabel: Jeshua . . . —The leaders of the people, perhaps the twelve tribes, are represented by twelve names, one of which, Nahamani, is missing here.

(43) The Nethinims.—By the etymology, "those given": known by this name only in the later books. (See I Chron. 9:2.) They were temple-bondsmen, the lowest order of the ministry, performing the more laborious duties of the sanctuary. Their history runs through a long period. Moses apportioned them first, from the Midianite captives (Num. 31:47); they were reinforced from the Gibeonites (Josh. 9:23), and probably later by David (8:20).

(55) The children of Solomon's servants.—These are mentioned in I Kings 9 as a servile class, formed of the residue of the Canaanites. They were probably inferior to the Nethinims, but are generally classed with them, as in the general enumeration here. Both these classes retained during their captivity their attachment to the service into which they had been received; and, the Levites being so few, their value in the reconstitution of the Temple gave them the special importance they assume in these books.

(63) With Urim and with Thummim.— See Exod. 28:30. Without Ark or Temple, the people had not as yet that special presence of Jehovah before which the high priest could "inquire of the Lord by Urim and Thummim." Zerubbabel might hope that this privilege would return, and thought the official purity of the priestly line of sufficient importance for such an inquiry. But the Holy of Holies in the new temple never had in it the ancient "tokens"; and by Urim and Thummim Jehovah was never again inquired of.

(64) This sum total is the same in Nehemiah; but the several sums in Ezra make 29,818, and in Nehemiah 31,089. The apocryphal Esdras agrees in the total, but makes in the particulars 33,950, adding that children below twelve were not reckoned. Many expedients of reconciliation have been adopted; but it is better to suppose that errors had crept into the original documents.

(69) The whole would be nearly $475,-000, not an exorbitant sum for a community far from poor. But Nehemiah's statement is smaller, and probably more correct.

(70) All Israel in their cities.—The emphasis lies in the fact that, though Judah and Benjamin contributed the largest part, it was a national revival; and the constant repetition of "in their cities" has in it the same note of triumph.

(4) According to the custom.—It is necessary here to read Deut. 16; Lev. 23; Num. 29. The intention obviously is to lay stress on the provision made for an entire renewal of the Mosaic economy of service, as appears in the next verse.

(7) The sea of Joppa.—The Jewish port to which the cedar trees were sent by sea, therefore thirty-five miles inland to Jerusalem.

The grant.—The authority of Cyrus over Phoenicia seems certain.

(8) In the second year.—The second year of Cyrus, 537 B.C., was their second year in the holy place.

In the second month.—Zif, chosen apparently because it was the same month in which Solomon laid the first foundation (I Kings 6).

(10) After the ordinance of David, king of Israel.—All goes back to earlier times. As the first offerings on the altar were according to what was "written in the law of Moses, the man of God," so the musical ceremonial of this foundation is according to the precedent of David (see I Chron. 6; 16:25).

(11) They sang together.—They answered each other in chorus, or antiphonally.

(12) But many of the priests and Levites ... wept with a loud voice.—This most affecting scene requires the comment of Hag. 2 and Zech. 4. The first house was destroyed in 588 B.C., fifty years before. The weeping was not occasioned by any comparison as to size and grandeur, unless indeed they marked the smallness of their foundation stones. They thought chiefly of the great desolation as measured by the past; the younger people thought of the new future.

3

(1) The seventh month was come.—Tisri, approximate to our September, was the most solemn month of the year, including the Day of Atonement and the Feast of Tabernacles, afterward distinguished as "the feast" pre-eminently.

(2) Builded the altar.—Only as the beginning of their work. The Temple was, as it were, built around the altar, as the center of all.

(3) Upon his bases.—Upon its old site, discovered among the ruins. Thus was it signified that all the new was to be only a restoration of the old.

4

(1) The adversaries.—The Samaritans, so termed by Nehemiah (4:10). These were a mixed race, the original Israelite element of which was nearly lost in the tribes imported into the northern part of the land by Sargon, Sennacherib, and Esar-haddon. (See II Kings 17:24-34.)

(2) As ye do.—"They feared the Lord, and worshiped their own gods" (II Kings 17:33); thus they came either in the spirit of hypocrites or with an intention to unite their own idolatries with the pure worship of Jehovah. In any case, they are counted enemies of the God of Israel.

We do sacrifice unto him since the days of Esar-haddon.—He ended his reign 668 B.C., and therefore the Samaritans speak from a tradition extending backward a century and a half.

(3) Ye have nothing to do with us.—The account in II Kings 17 carefully studied will show that the stern refusal of the leaders was precisely in harmony with the will of God; there was nothing in it of that intolerant spirit which is sometimes imagined. The whole design of the Great Restoration would have been defeated by a concession at this point. The reference to the command of Cyrus is another and really subordinate kind of justification, pleaded as subjects of the king of Persia, whose decree was absolute and exclusive.

(5) And hired counsellors against them.—They adopted a systematic course of employing paid agents at the court and continued for eight years, until 529 B.C. Cambyses, his son, succeeded Cyrus; he died in 522 B.C.; then followed the pseudo-Smerdis, a usurper, whose short reign Darius did not reckon, but dated his own reign from 522 B.C. A comparison of dates shows that this was the first Darius, the son of Hystaspes.

(6) In the beginning of his reign.—This Ahasuerus, another name for Cambyses, reigned seven years; and his accession to the throne was the time seized by the Samaritans for their "accusation," of which we hear nothing more. It suffices to say that the building languished.

(7) In the days of Artaxerxes.—This Artaxerxes has been thought by many commentators to be the Longimanus of the sequel of this book and of Nehemiah, and they have identified the Ahasuerus of Ezra and Esther with Xerxes. Persian princes had often more than one name. At the same time, there is nothing to make anticipatory and parenthetical insertion impossible (see verses 23, 24).

(12) Virulence, craft, and exaggeration are stamped on every sentence of the letter. It only says, however, that "they are preparing the walls thereof, and joining the foundations." Afterward, the charge is modified in verses 13 and 16.

(13) Toll, tribute, and custom.—Toll for the highways; custom, a provision in kind; tribute, the money tax.

(15) The book of the records of thy fathers.—i.e., the Chronicles (comp. Esther 6:1).

(24) The second year.—The record here

returns to verse 5, with more specific indication of time. The suspension of the general enterprise—called "the work of the house of God which is at Jerusalem"—lasted nearly two years. But it must be remembered that the altar was still the center of a certain amount of worship.

5

(1-2) Now occurs the intervention of the two prophets, Haggai and Zechariah, whose testimonies and predictions should at this point be read. They reveal a state of apathy to which Ezra does not allude, such a state of things, in fact, as would have thwarted the whole design of Providence had it not been changed. Hence the abrupt return of the spirit of prophecy, some of the last utterances of which provoked or "stirred up"—as Cyrus had been stirred up—the spirit of the two leaders and of the heads of the families.

(3) Tatnai, governor on this side the river.—Satrap, or Pechah, of the entire province of Syria and Phoenicia, and therefore with a jurisdiction over Judaea, and over Zerubbabel its Pechah or sub-Satrap. What Shimshai was to the Samaritan Pechah, Rehum, Shethar-boznai seems to be to Tatnai—his secretary. (See 4:8.)

Who hath commanded you?—It is obvious that the overthrow of Smerdis, the Magian hater of Zoroastrianism and destroyer of temples, had encouraged the builders to go on without fearing molestation from the Court of Darius. (See note on 4:5.) Moreover, the two prophets had made their duty too plain to be deferred. Still, the decree of the preceding chapter had never been expressly revoked.

(4) What are the names of the men? ...—It is clear that this graphic account is much compressed. We must understand (see verse 10) that the authorities demanded names of the chief promoters of the building in order to make them responsible.

(6) The copy of the letter.—This letter of Tatnai is introduced much in the same way as Rehum's; but its dispassionateness and good faith are in striking contrast with the latter.

(8) To the house of the great God.—A solemn tribute to the God of the Jews, which, however, the decree of Cyrus enables us to understand in this official document. Tatnai probably dwelt at Damascus, and when he went to Jerusalem was deeply impressed. But he only gives a statement of the progress which he observed in the Temple. "The walls" here are the walls within the Temple, not the city walls.

(11) And thus they returned us answer.— The elders of the Jews take the Syrian satrap into their confidence, and give in a few most pathetic words the record of their national honor, their national infidelity, and their national humiliation. Every word is true to the history, while the whole exhibits their deep humility and holy resolution.

(16) Since that time.—No account is taken of the long interruption. Whether these words are part of the answer given to Tatnai by the Jewish leaders, or his own statement to Darius, it is evident that the unfinished building of a house decreed to be built by Cyrus is regarded as demanding investigation as to the nature and validity of the decree itself.

6

(2) At Achmetha.—That is, Ecbatana, the Median capital of Cyrus. It is probable that the original roll of parchment had been destroyed at Babylon by Smerdis, but a copy of it was found here, probably in a Chaldean transcript.

(3) Strongly laid.—"Thy foundation shall be laid" (Isa. 44:28). The decree adds a word that signifies "with sufficient support."

(5) And also let the golden and silver vessels ... be restored.—The desecration of these vessels by Belshazzar (Dan. 5:2, 3) was thus to be expiated. Every word, including the twise repeated "house of God," is most emphatic.

(6) Now therefore, Tatnai.—Here there is an abrupt transition to the decree of Darius itself, the terms of which were either drawn up by Jewish help, or are freely rendered into the national phraseology by the historian.

(10) That they may offer sacrifices ... and pray for the life of the king.—Two ends are to be answered: the God of heaven is to be honored, and the dynasty of Darius interceded for by the Jews. (Comp. Jer. 31:7.)

(14) Cyrus, and Darius, and Artaxerxes king of Persia.—This verse includes all the agents in the great work with which the book deals: from Cyrus to Artaxerxes; the elders, that is, the heads of the Jews; the prophets (see 5:1); but all is from the God of Israel, whose commandment Cyrus and all others fulfilled.

Artaxerxes king of Persia.—Evidently the Artaxerxes Longimanus of the sequel, whose contributions and help did so much toward the perfecting of the general design, though the "finishing" here mentioned took place fifty years before his reign. Observe that he alone is called "king of Persia," which shows that Ezra is writing in his time, and adds his name to the original record. Just as the later Artaxerxes is introduced, so the earlier Cyrus is, in this comprehensive review.

(15) The third day of the month Adar, which was in the sixth year.—The event around which this part of the history revolves is dated with due care; it was on the third day of the last month of the ecclesiastical year, 516-515 B.C. Haggai (1:15) gives the exact date of the recommencement; the time therefore was four years five months and ten days. But, dating from the first foundation (3:10), no less than twenty-one years had elapsed.

(19) Upon the fourteenth day of the first month.—Recording the special celebration of the Passover at the dedication of the second temple—after the precedent of Hezekiah and Josiah—Ezra returns to the Hebrew language. The occasion was, as it were, a renewal of the redemption from Egypt, and another wilderness had been passed.

(22) And kept the feast.—The Mazzoth, or week of unleavened bread, was the symbol of entire separation from evil, to the service of that God whom on the Passover they accepted as their God. The special joy of this feast was the feeling that the Lord had "turned the heart of the king of Assyria." The king of Persia is so called as a remembrance of their oppression by his forerunners.

7

The Second Return Under Ezra

(1) After these things.—Fifty-seven years after. This special phrase is alone used here. During the interval we must place the events of the Book of Esther.

Ezra the son of Seraiah.—His lineage is given, as frequently in Scripture, compendiously, and according to the genealogical law which makes every ancestor a "father" and every descendant a "son." We do not know the reason why certain names supplied in I Chron. 6 are omitted here; but Seraiah is claimed as the father of Ezra because he was the eminent high priest who last ministered in Solomon's Temple and was slain at Riblah (II Kings 25:18-21).

(6) A ready scribe.—The "ready writer" of Ps. 45:1. Ezra was a priest, and this title is rightly placed before that of scribe in what follows; but here at the outset, when he first appears in history, the title is used which expressed his pre-eminent function, that of guarding and interpreting the law (verse 10).

According to the hand of the Lord his God upon him.—The full formula for that special providence over God's servants which both Ezra and Nehemiah recognized.

(8) In the seventh year.—The repeated notes of time must be marked. The journey itself comes afterward: it is here indicated as having occupied four months. Ezra's company also is summarized beforehand, according to the manner of this book.

(14) Seven counsellors.—These are mentioned in Esther 1:14, and were probably the heads of those families who aided Darius Hystaspes against the pseudo-Smerdis, as mentioned by Herodotus.

According to the law of thy God.—Ezra's commission was first to inquire into the condition of the city and province, with regard to the relation of both to the divine law.

(18) The rest ...—This clause of large latitude would be of great importance for the general beautifying of the Temple (verse 27).

(22) Unto an hundred talents of silver ...—A certain restriction is laid upon the amount, although the restriction seems almost indefinite. The silver might reach $200,000. As to the rest, Palestine abounded in these productions, which were regularly remitted to the kings's service.

(23) Whatsoever is commanded by the God of heaven.—The last is the strongest ground for such an ample authorization. In the solemn and devout commission the phrase "the God of heaven" occurs twice, and the Persian prince deprecates His wrath. In this seventh year of Artaxerxes, 458 B.C., the tide of success turned for Persia against the Athenians in Egypt.

(24) We certify you.—The exemption of so large a number as the entire ministry of the Temple from all kinds of taxation is emphatically introduced.

(25, 26) The kings's commission, return-ing directly to Ezra, makes him supreme in the province over the Jewish population in matters both civil and religious.

(27) Blessed be the Lord God.—This is the solitary expression of Ezra's private devotion; and it is incorporated with his record in so artless a manner as to confirm the impression that the whole narrative is from his hand. This sudden ejaculatory thanksgiving, in the midst of his narrative, reminds us of Nehemiah's habit.

8

(1) This is the genealogy.—The names of the heads of houses is followed generally by that of the wider families to which they belonged. With this list is to be compared the register of those who went up with Zerubbabel (2:2 seq.).

(15) None of the sons of Levi.—Only seventy-four had returned with Zerubbabel (2:40); and here we have evidence that the disinclination continued. The importance of Levitical service in the Temple accounts for the anxiety of Ezra.

(20) The Nethinims.—It is here alone recorded that David appointed these to aid the Levites. (See note on 2:43.)

(21) To seek of him a right way for us.—The wilderness was now before them, and an enemy, indefinitely referred to, was in the way: probably desert tribes, always lying in wait for unprotected caravans.

(31) The hand of our God was upon us.—This sums up the history of the journey. After three days of rest and devotion, the king's commission was delivered over to the proper military and civil authorities (verses 32-36).

9

(1) Now when these things were done.—The remainder of the book is occupied with the execution of Ezra's function as a moral reformer. One chief disorder is mentioned, that of the mixed marriages (verse 2), which the new lawgiver evidently regarded as fatal to the purity of the divine service and to the design of God in separating for a season these people.

The princes.—Heads of tribes, native rulers of Jerusalem, as distinguished from the satraps and governors. Zerubbabel's office had no successor; and the term princes expressed rather their eminence than their authority, which had been powerless to check the abuses of which they complain.

(3) I rent my garment and my mantle.— The actions of Ezra betoken his horror and grief. But both the rending of the outer and inner garment and the plucking the hair were symbolical acts, teaching their lesson to the people who witnessed, and, as we see, were deeply impressed.

(5) And at the evening sacrifice I arose up.—Until the afternoon Ezra had sat silent and in grief before the Temple, and in the presence of the people. Then, amidst the solemnities of the sacrifice, he uttered the prayer which he had been meditating.

(6) And said, O my God.—The confession begins with "O my God"; but Ezra is the representative of the people, and it proceeds "O our God" (verse 10), without once returning to the first person. In these common prayers of Ezra, Nehemiah, and Daniel, the race of Israel is regarded as one, and national sins as one great trespass.

(9) A wall.—Like "the nail" (verse 8), a figurative expression for security. The literal wall was not yet rebuilt. This completes the description of divine mercy: the people were a delivered remnant; the Temple was a sure nail for the future of religion; and their civil estate was made secure.

(10) After this.—But all was a mercy for which there had been no adequate return.

(11) Saying.—In the later Old Testament Scriptures the quotation of the earlier is often of this character, giving the substance of many passages. The same style is observable in the New Testament.

10

(2) Shechaniah.—The son of one of the transgressors (verse 26), whose action as the representative of the people gives him an honorable memorial in Scripture.

There is hope in Israel.—A noble sentiment for a reformer even at the worst of times.

(9) Within three days.—From the time of hearing the summons. No town was more than forty miles distant; and of course only those would come who were able, and who came within the scope of the proclamation, the precise terms of which are not given. They were not more than could assemble "in the street," or open court of the Temple. The minute specifications of date, and the two reasons for the trembling of the people, and the whole strain of the narrative, bear witness to the veracity of an eyewitness.

(10) Ezra the priest.—He stood up, not as the commissioner of Artaxerxes, not at this moment as the scribe, but as the representative of God.

(11) Do his pleasure.—This procedure, humanly severe, is connected with the divine will. The marriages were but a subordinate branch, though a very important one, of the wider sin: confederacy with idolators.

(17) And they made an end.—Though the number of transgressors was only one hundred thirteen, two months were occupied, which shows the care taken to do justice, especially to the claims of the women put away.

(22) Pashur.—Comparing 2:36-39, we find that all the priestly families that returned with Zerubbabel were implicated in the national offense.

(25) Of Israel.—Of the laity eighty-six are mentioned, belonging to ten races which returned with Zerubbabel.

That Ezra ends his history with a catalog of the delinquents is strong testimony to the importance he attached to the reformation. But the thoroughness of the excision did not continue long (see Neh. 13:23-29).

NEHEMIAH

1

(1) In the month Chisleu.—Chisleu, the ninth Jewish month, is approximate to our December.

In the twentieth year.—Of the reign of Artaxerxes Longimanus, which began 465 B.C. and ended 425 B.C.

In Shushan the palace.—Susa, where, after the capture of the Babylonian empire, a great palace was built by Darius Hystaspes. It was the principal and favorite residence of the Persian court, alternating with Persepolis, the older capital, and Babylon. Shushan was one of the most ancient cities in the world. It is associated with the feast of Ahasuerus (Dan. 8:2; Esther 1:3).

(2) He and certain men of Judah.—Hanani was Nehemiah's own brother (7:2).

(3) In great affliction and reproach.—In distress because of the contempt of the people around. All these expressions are familiar in the prophets; but they are united here in a peculiar and affecting combination. As to the city, the report is that the walls were still "broken down": lying prostrate, with partial exceptions, as Nebuchadnezzar left them a hundred and forty-two years before (II Kings 25:10), and, moreover, what had not been recorded, "the gates thereof burned with fire." Though the Temple had been rebuilt, there is no valid reason for supposing that the walls of the city had been in part restored and again demolished.

(4-11) Nehemiah's appeal to God. The prayer is a perfect example of the private and individual devotion with which the later Hebrew Scriptures abound. It begins with a formal and appropriate invocation (verses 5-8), flows into earnest confession (verses 6, 7), pleads the covenant promises (verses 8-10), and supplicates a present answer (verse 11). The extant Scriptures, freely used, are the foundation of all.

(11) For I was the king's cupbearer.—One of his cupbearers, therefore in high authority, having confidential access to him.

2

(1) Nisan.—The old Abib, the first month of the Jewish year, following the vernal equinox. As we are still in the twentieth year of the king, the beginning of his reign must be dated before Chisleu.

(2) Then I was very sore afraid.—Waiting on Providence, Nehemiah had discharged his duties for three months without being sad in the king's presence; but on this day his sorrow could not be repressed. A sad countenance was never tolerated in the royal presence; and, though Artaxerxes was of a milder character than any other Persian monarch, the tone of his question showed that in this respect he was not an exception.

(3) Nehemiah's family was of Jerusalem. He does not as yet betray to the king the deepest desire of his heart, but simply refers to the desecration of his father's sepulchres, an appeal which had great force with the Persians, who respected the tomb.

(6) I set him a time.—Whatever that was, circumstances afterward prolonged it.

(9-11) His journey to Jerusalem, occupying some three months, and safe under escort, is passed over in the narrative, as Ezra's had been. It is mentioned, however, that Sanballat, one of the "governors," was roused to hostility. Sanballat was from one of the Beth-horons, which had been in Ephraim, and were now in the kingdom of Samaria. His name is seemingly Babylonian, while that of Tobiah is Hebrew. The revival of Jerusalem would be a blow to the recent ascendency of Samaria.

(13) The gate of the valley, opening on Hinnom, to the south of the city. "The dragon well" is nowhere else mentioned and is not now to be traced.

(17) Then.—There is no note of time. When his plans were matured, Nehemiah made an earnest appeal to their patriotism.

(19) Geshem the Arabian.—This name completes the triumvirate of the leaders of the opposition to the mission of Nehemiah. They were not independent chieftains. Tobiah was Sanballat's servant and counsellor, while Geshem was probably the leader of an Arabian company mostly in his service. The account of their contemptuous opposition is given in a few touches, as is the contempt with which it was met. They charged Nehemiah with rebellion, as afterward, in 6:6.

(20) He will prosper us.—The reply is a defiance in the name of the God of heaven. The closing words imply that, as in the days of Zerubbabel, the Samaritan enemies desired really to have their share in the undertaking. Nehemiah makes Zerubbabel's answer, but strengthens it; they had nothing in common with Jerusalem, not even a place in its memorials, except one of shame.

3

Here is a memorial of the builders. To succeeding generations of dwellers in Jerusalem, this is a deeply interesting chapter. It contains also a very important topographical account of the ancient city, since repeatedly destroyed. But it must be remembered that the record does not so much describe the process as sum up the result. Much of the work of the gates must have required time, but all is described here as if everything were finished at once.

(1) Then Eliashib.—The account begins with due honor to the high priest and the priesthood.

The sheep gate was in the neighborhood of the priests' quarter. Through it the victims passed for sacrifice, first being washed in the neighboring pool of Bethesda. This being built, "they sanctified it" as an earnest of the subsequent consecration of the entire wall. Their work and the sanctification of it extended to two towns near each other at the northeast corner.

(3) The fish gate.—Through which fish entered from the Jordan and Galilee.

(5) The Tekoites.—This verse is remarkable (1) as introducing men of Tekoah, not mentioned among Zerubbabel's returned, who furnish the solitary instance of internal opposition to the building, and (2) as terming the common work "the work of the Lord." The ordinary people of the place, however, did double duty. (See verse 27.)

(7) Unto the throne.—"Unto the seat" of the pechah of the whole district this side the Euphrates: his residence when he came to Jerusalem.

(15) The pool of Siloah.—Called earlier "the king's pool," which received its water as "sent" through a long subterranean conduit, and supplied the king's gardens. (See 2:14.)

(16) The pool that was made.—This may have been the reservoir of Hezekiah (Isa. 22:11); and "the house of the mighty" may have been the barracks of David's elect troops (I Chron. 11:10).

(25) That was by the court of the prison.—The palace generally had its prison, and near this was the "prison gate" of 12:39.

(28) From above the horse gate.—This gate was between the Temple and the palace, and the space from the wall of Ophel seems not to have needed repair.

(31) And of the merchants.—Possibly there is some connection between the traders, who brought their doves and so forth for the worshipers, and the Nethinim to whose house or depot they brought them. Near the sheep gate was the "going up of the corner," or an ascent to the gate Miphkad, about which nothing is known.

4

(1) Mocked the Jews.—The mockery comes afterward. Here, as often in Nehemiah, a general statement is made which is later expanded.

(2) Will they sacrifice?—This is the provocation of God mentioned in verse 5.

(4) Hear, O our God.—The habit of Nehemiah is to turn everything to devotion as he goes on. This prayer is full of an angry jealousy for the honor of a jealous God.

(6) Unto the half.—Up to half the height the wall was now continuous.

(8) And conspired.—Not fearing the Persian authority, they resolved to attack the city; but they soon abandoned that project.

(9) Because of them.—Rather, "over against them": opposite to each point of their encampment. The setting watch was accompanied by solemn and united prayer.

(10) And Judah said.—As hereafter, in the case of the complaints of the people (chap. 5), the writer gives a summary of difficulties. The Jews, or "Judah"—a significant term—complained of their growing feebleness, especially as so many were diverted to the watches.

(11) They shall not know.—As to the adversaries, their plan was evidently to watch and surprise, instead of making the threatened attack.

(13) After their families.—In allusion to the ambushes of verse 11, Nehemiah set families together—besides the appointed guards—"in the lower places," where the wall was not raised to the due height, and where enemies might be better seen.

(15) We returned.—This verse remarkably condenses the frustration of the attempt and the cessation of the special guard.

(16) My servants.—The building was resumed with special precautions, very minutely described. Nehemiah's own servants

361

are distinguished from "all the house of Judah." The former were divided into two parties, one of which wrought on the work still unfinished and the other held their weapons.

Habergeons are coats of mail, thin plates of metal sewn upon leather.

(17) They which builded.—Divided into masons and their burden-bearers. The latter held in one hand a weapon; the former built with both hands, and had their weapons at their side.

(21) So we laboured.—This is a general recapitulation, with additional note of the length of the day's work during this pressing season.

5

(1) Their brethren the Jews.—Nehemiah's other troubles had come from the enemies without. He begins this account by laying emphasis on the hard treatment of Jews by Jews.

(2) We take up.—"Let us receive." This is a general appeal for the governor's help.

(6) And I was very angry.—Nehemiah, recently arrived, had not known this state of things. The common wailing and the three complaints in which it found expression are distinct. The matter was complicated as the transgressors had violated rather the spirit than the letter of the law. Hence the rebuke (verse 7), that they exacted usury each of his brother, failed in its object; and the governor called a general assembly, not "against them," but "concerning them."

(9) Because of the reproach.—The text of another strong argument used in the assembly. We learn in chap. 6 how watchful the heathen were. All matters were reported to them, and every act of oppression would become a reproach against the God of the Jews.

(12) We will restore.—The promise was given to restore the mortgaged property and to require no more interest. But Nehemiah required an oath to give legal validity to the procedure, and the priests' presence gave it the highest religious sanction.

(13) Shook my lap.—This symbolical act imprecated on every man who broke this covenant an appropriate penalty: that he be emptied of all his possessions, even as the fold of Nehemiah's garment was emptied. And it is observable that the iniquity thus stopped is not referred to in the subsequent

covenant (chap. 10), nor is it one of the offenses which the governor found on his second return (chap. 13).

(14) Twelve years.—The whole narrative, thus far, was written after his return from Jerusalem, and on a review of his governorship. Of his second appointment the same thing might have been said; but that, at the time of writing, was in the future.

I and my brethren have not eaten the bread of the governor.—At the close of the twelve years' term, Nehemiah could say that he and his official attendants had not drawn the customary allowances from the people.

(15) So did not I, because of the fear of God.—Nehemiah contrasts his forbearance with the conduct of former governors; we cannot suppose him to mean Zerubbabel, but some of his successors. The practice he condemns was common among the satraps of the Persian princes. Note that usury and severity were forbidden in Lev. 25:36, 43, with the express command, "Fear thy God."

(16) I continued.—That is, as superintendent. His servants and he himself did not take advantage of the people's poverty to acquire their land by mortgage; they were, on the contrary, absorbed in the common work.

(17) At my table.—The charge on the governor's free hospitality was heavy.

(19) Think upon me, my God.—Inserting the present prayer far from this people, Nehemiah humbly asks his recompense not from them, but from God. Nothing was more distant from his thoughts than the fame of his good deeds.

6

(5) The fifth time with an open letter in his hand.—Four times they strive to induce Nehemiah to meet them, under various pretexts, with the intention of doing him personal harm. Each time his reply was to the effect that he was finishing his own work, not without a touch of irony. (This answer has a universal application, which preachers have known how to use.) In the fifth letter the tactics are changed. The silken bag containing the missive was not sealed, and it was hoped that Nehemiah would be alarmed by the thought that its contents had been read by the people.

(6) It is reported among the heathen, and Gashmu saith it.—Nehemiah can quote the very letter, with its dialectical change of

Geshem into Gashmu. Sanballat sends To-biah in his own name, and represents Geshem as circulating a report which, reaching the distant king, would be inter-preted as rebellion. It is hinted that the heathen, or "the nations," would take the part of the king. And the words of the prophets concerning the future king are referred to as likely to be attributed to Nehemiah's ambition. Finally, the letter suggests the desirableness of friendly coun-sel to avert the danger.

(10) I came unto the house.—As a speci-men of another kind of attack, through false prophets, Shemaiah's plot is mentioned.

(13) An evil report.—Nehemiah per-ceived that not God, but Shemaiah himself, had uttered the prophecy "against me," and that he was hired to bring the governor into discredit as a violator of law.

(14) Think thou upon Tobiah.—This ap-peal to God is to be understood as an official prophetic prayer. Nehemiah puts God's own cause into God's own hands. The mention of the name of Noadiah, no-where else referred to, shows the circum-stantial nature of the narrative, and is an in-direct evidence of its truth.

(15) In fifty and two days.—The twenty-fifth day of Elul answers to about our September 15th; and, dating back, the wall began in the latter part of July, soon after Nehemiah's arrival. If we bear in mind that the wall was only partially overthrown, that the materials for restoration were at hand, and that the utmost skill had been shown in organizing the bands of workmen, the time will not appear too short.

(16) They perceived that this work was wrought of our God.—Not miraculously, but under the divine sanction and help. By this expression Nehemiah at once tri-umphed over his foes, and gives the glory where it was due. His own heroic part in the work is utterly forgotten.

(17-19) A supplementary account is here introduced, explaining the intrigues within Jerusalem to which reference has been made.

7

(1-4) Measures were taken for the securi-ty of the city, now made a complete for-tress. The comparative thinness of the popu-lation taxed the governor's resources, and the result appears at a later stage.

(5-37) The genealogical reckoning of the people, as the first step toward increasing the population of the metropolis, is deter-mined on, not without, express divine sug-gestion; the allusion to this inspiration from God is, as in 2:12, very emphatic. The original register of Zerubbabel is found and copied. The express language of both Ezra and Nehemiah makes it plain that this is no other than the list of those who came up with Zerubbabel and Joshua after the de-cree of Cyrus, in 538 B.C. Nehemiah's own census follows, in chap. 11.

(73) And when the seventh month came.—Here a new subject begins. As Ezra, whom he copies, Nehemiah adopts the last words of the Chronicles, and with similar slight changes.

8

(1) As one man.—The unanimity rather than the number is emphatic here.

And they spake unto Ezra.—He appears in this book for the first time, having prob-ably been at the court for twelve years.

(3) From the morning.—"From day-light." The Book of the Law must have been a comprehensive one. Out of it Ezra and his companions read hour after hour, selecting appropriate passages.

(6) And Ezra blessed the Lord.—The book was formally and solemnly opened in the sight of the people. At his request the multitude arose, and, after a doxology of-fered by Ezra, they all uttered a double Amen, "with lifting up of their hands," in token of their most fervent assent, and then "with faces bowed to the ground," in token of adoration.

(8) Gave the sense.—They expounded more obscure passages, and in doing so naturally translated into the vernacular Aramaic dialect.

(9) Mourn not, nor weep.—The days of high festival were unsuitable for public and, as it were, objective sorrow. The Day of Atonement was coming for that, as also the special day of fasting and covenant, which was already in the plan of Nehemiah and Ezra.

(13) Even to understand.—That is, to learn the full meaning of the almost forgot-ten festival (the Feast of Tabernacles). The dwelling in booths had fallen into disuse.

(17) Done so.—Though the feast had been kept (1 Kings 8; Ezra 3), it had never been kept with universal dwelling booths. (See Lev. 23:36.)

363

9

(2) The seed of Israel separated themselves from all strangers.—The change to "seed" has here a deep propriety. They carefully avoided the many aliens among them throughout this fast.

(3) One fourth part.—Both day and night were divided into four parts. All orders standing in their respective place, the reading occupied the morning and the worship the afternoon. It is the latter which is now made prominent, as the former had been prominent in the preceding chapter.

(4) Their God.—When the people are called upon (verse 5), it is "your God"; hence these eight Levites offered a prayer which is not inserted.

(6) The LXX inserts "and Ezra said" before verse 6. The psalm was perhaps composed by Ezra, but uttered by the Levites in the name of the congregation.

(14) Madest known unto them thy holy sabbath.—Every word here, as well as the other prominence given to this among the other "commandments," must be noted as illustrating the importance of this ordinance in the covenant of chapter 10 and throughout the book.

(20) Thy good spirit.—Probably a reference to Num. 11:17, 25. The epithet given to the Spirit is in Ps. 143:10. But His teaching function occurs here only, and is a remarkable anticipation of the New Testament.

(37) In great distress.—Not so much under the Persian yoke as in the remembrance of God's judgments. The pathetic comparison between the divine purpose in giving the land originally and their present bondage in it extends almost to every word.

(38) Because of all this.—On the ground of this confession, and to prove our sincerity.

Seal unto it.—Each party impressed his seal on moist clay, which was then hardened. Sometimes these seals were attached to the document by separate strings.

10

(2) Seraiah.—The family name of the high-priestly house to which Ezra and Eliashib belonged, one of whom—probably Ezra—affixed its seal.

(29) They clave to their brethren.—It was a union of the people as such, and sprang from a deep national conviction.

Entered into a curse, and into an oath.—The oath assumed the obligation; the curse imprecated the penalty of violation. (Comp. Deut. 29:12.)

(32) Also we made ordinances for us.—The covenant proceeds now to certain new regulations and resumption of neglected duties. Comp. verse 32 with Exod. 30:13 and Matt. 17:24; verse 34 with Lev. 6:12; verse 36 with Num. 16:15, 16; verse 37 with I Kings 6 and II Chron. 31:11; and verse 38 with Num. 18:22-26.

(39) We will not forsake the house of our God.—Both the pledge and the violation of it in the sequel are explained by 13:11-14.

11

(1) And the rulers.—The narrative joins on to 7:4. The festival month had prevented the immediate carrying out of the governor's purpose.

The rest of the people.—The rulers being already in the capital, Nehemiah ordered that one man in ten should be chosen by lot to transfer his family.

Jerusalem the holy city.—Remembering the "separation" that had taken place (chap. 9), and the recent covenant (chap. 10), we see the solemnity of this epithet, now first used, and repeated in verse 18.

(2) The people blessed all the men, that willingly offered themselves.—We are not told that any compensation was made to them; and these words seem to indicate that the chosen ones freely submitted, their patriotism being applauded by all. Jerusalem was the post of danger, and in any case it was a hardship to leave their country possessions (verse 3).

(3) Of the province.—This betrays the hand of Nehemiah, who was still a Persian official as well as a governor of Judah; and it shows that here we have a general heading for the rest of the chapter. Compared with I Chron. 9, the roster is by no means complete.

12

(1-9) The priests and Levites of the First Return are enumerated.

(10, 11) The six generations of this pedigree of certain high priests, with supplement from a later hand (as verses 22, 23), stretch over 200 years—from 536 B.C. to 332 B.C. Jaddua is most probably the high priest who confronted Alexander the Great.

(24) And the chief.—The account resumes with the Levites, and gives a list of the extant officers of the Temple, many names being the same as in earlier times.

(27) They sought the Levites.—The dedication of the wall was to be processional and musical, as well as sacrificial, after the pattern of Solomon's dedication of the Temple.

(32) After them.—These verses show that the clerical and the lay elements were mingled.

(36) Ezra the scribe before them.—Between the singers and the princes came he who was the greatest in dignity, though the second in office.

(40) In the house of God.—They first stood outside, but later entered to present their offerings. But the main interest of the day was the professional worship under the open heavens.

(44) For Judah rejoiced.—Not only was like the completeness of the Davidical period, but the people also everywhere took pleasure in the ministrations of the Temple and provided amply for them. Hence the need of men to take charge of the treasures of the firstfruits and tithes.

(46) Of old.—Always there is a reverence shown for the old precedents.

13

(1) On that day.—Probably the season of the Feast of Tabernacles, as before.

They read in the book of Moses.—That is, in the Pentateuch, and especially Deut. 23. This is introduced for the sake of the action taken, and the history is given in brief, with a striking and characteristic parenthesis of Nehemiah's own concerning the curse turned into a blessing.

(3) The mixed multitude.—See note on Exod. 12:38. The process here was that of shutting out heathen who were in the habit of mingling with the people in the services. In chap. 9 it was the people's separation from the practices and spirit of the heathen.

(4) Eliashib the priest, having the oversight.—Probably the high priest of 3:1, whose office alone would not have given him control over "the chamber," that is, the series of chambers running around three walls of the Temple. He "was allied unto Tobiah," but in what way is not stated. (See verse 28.)

Before this.—That is, before the return of Nehemiah; indeed, there is a suspicious absence of Eliashib's name throughout the high religious festivities of the preceding chapters.

(6) King of Babylon.—Probably it was at Babylon that Nehemiah found the court, and therefore he does not say "King of Persia."

After certain days.—The time is left indefinite. But the "two and thirtieth year" shows that he had been in Jerusalem twelve years before his return to the king.

(10) Fled every one to his field.—They who performed the work of the Temple were obliged to seek their sustenance by cultivating the fields apportioned to them in the Levitical cities (Num. 35:2). The rich men had taken advantage of Nehemiah's absence to indulge their covetousness.

(13) And I made.—The reform was made effectual by organization. Eliashib had failed in his duty (verse 4); and the appointment of treasurers (12:44) is now confirmed. One of the treasurers was a layman named Hanan (10:22); but they were all faithful men, and are mentioned in connection with the building of the wall. The majority being priests and Levites, they distributed "to their brethren." Zadok was probably the Zidkijah of 10:1, and the secretary of Nehemiah.

(15) Saw I in Judah.—In the country Nehemiah marked the most determined profanation of the Sabbath; and this extended to Jerusalem, into which all kinds of burdens were on that day, as on others, carried.

(17) That ye do.—The nobles, in the absence of Nehemiah, had been responsible, and the sin is charged upon them. The appeal supposes their familiarity with the express prediction of Jeremiah and its literal fulfillment (Jer. 17:27).

(20) Once or twice.—For a time they lodged outside. The unseemliness of this, and the evidence it gave that they were only waiting to evade the law, made Nehemiah testify in word, and threaten forcible action. This effectually removed the evil.

(23) Saw I Jews.—The punishment shows that these were exceptional cases; but the transgression was of the most flagrant kind (see verse 1).

(25) Cursed them.—Nehemiah simply echoed the covenant sanction on this point (10:29, 30).

(26) Did not Solomon ... —Here it is implied that the language of Scripture concerning Solomon was familiar both to Nehemiah and to these transgressors. It is a remarkable instance of the faithful application of their own chronicles.

(28) I chased him from me.—Eliashib himself was allied by marriage to Tobiah, and one of his grandsons was now brought into prominence as married to Sanballat. Him Nehemiah drove into exile.

(29) Remember them.—This priestly violation of Law is committed to God alone for punishment.

(31) Remember me, O my God, for good.—With these words Nehemiah leaves the scene, committing himself and his discharge of duty to the Righteous Judge. It may be added that with these words end the annals of Old Testament history.

ESTHER

1

(1) Ahasuerus.—Three persons are called by this name in the Old Testament—(1) the Ahasuerus (probably Cyaxares) of Dan. 9:1, the father of "Darius the Mede"; (2) the Ahasuerus of Ezra 4:6, doubtless the same with Cambyses, the son of Cyrus; and (3) the one now before us, almost certainly Xerxes. Xerxes succeeded his father, Darius Hystaspes, in the year 485 B.C., five years after the momentous battle of Marathon. Undeterred by his father's failure, he resolves upon a fresh attack on Greece and sets out in 481 B.C., from Susa for the West. All that we know of the further course of the reign of Xerxes, following defeats at Salamis, Plataea, and Mycale to 479 B.C., is but one unbroken tale of debauchery and bloodshed, which came to an end in 464 B.C., when he was murdered by two of his officers. Artaxerxes Longimanus, his son (see Exra 7; Neh. 2), reigned in his stead. Herodotus was a contemporary and important source for Xerxes' history.

(2) Shushan.—Susa. Mentioned also in Neh. 1:1. It was the general abode of the Persian kings.

(3) In the third year of his reign.—Assuming the identity of Ahasuerus and Xerxes, this will be 483 B.C., when Xerxes held a meeting at Susa of his princes to make arrangements for invading Greece. At so important a gathering, the feasting was a very obvious adjunct; and besides the coming campaign, a successful war had just been concluded in Egypt, and rejoicings for the past might have mingled with high hopes for the future.

(4) An hundred and fourscore days.—As a period of mere feasting, this long time (half a year) is simply incredible, but we must understand it as a time during which troops were collected and the plan of invasion settled.

(9) Vashti.—According to Gesenius, the name Vashti means "beautiful." Among the Persians it was customary that one wife of the sovereign should be supreme over the rest, and we sometimes find Vashti exercising an authority which contrasts strangely with the degraded position of women generally. We find, however, that the name given by the Greek writers to the queen of Xerxes was Amestris, of whose cruelty and dissolute life numerous details are given us by Herodotus and others. There seem good grounds for believing that she was the wife of Xerxes before he became king, which if established would of itself be sufficient to disprove the theory of some who would identify Esther and Amestris. We may assume that Vashti is Amestris, the two names being different reproductions of the Persian, or Vashti being a sort of title.

(14) The seven princes.—There were seven leading families in Persia, the heads of which were the king's chief advisers, the "seven counsellors" of Ezra 7:14. Herodotus (3:84) speaks of the seven nobles who rose against the Pseudo-Smerdis as chief in the nation.

(16) Answered before the king.—Memucan, like a true courtier, gives palatable advice to his master, by counsel which is the true echo of the king's angry question.

(22) He sent letters.—The Persian Empire was the first to possess a postal system (see Herod. 7:98). The Greek word for "compel," in Matt. 5:41; 27:32, is simply a corruption of the Persian word for the impressment of men and horses for the royal service.

2

(5) Mordecai.—It may be assumed that Mordecai was a eunuch, by the way in which he was allowed access to the royal harem (verses 11, 22). The name Mordecai occurs in Ezra 2:2; Neh. 7:7, as one of those who returned to Judaea with Zerubbabel. The character of Mordecai strikes us at the outset as that of an ambitious, worldly man who, though numbers of his tribe had returned to the land of their fathers, preferred to remain behind on alien soil. Why endure hardships, when there is a chance of his adopted daughter's beauty catching the eye of the sensual king, when through her he may vanquish his rival and become the king's chief minister?

(6) Jeconiah.—That is, Jehoiachin. (See II Kings 24:12-16.)

Nebuchadnezzar . . . had carried away.—This was in 598 B.C., 117 years before this time, so that the four generations are readily accounted for.

(7) Hadassah.—This is evidently formed from the Hebrew **hadas**, the myrtle; Esther is generally assumed to be a Persian name, meaning a star. Unless we assume that this latter name was given later, and is here used by anticipation, we have here an early case of the common Jewish practice of using two names, a Hebrew and a Gentile one.

(10) Esther had not shewed. ... —From the hope of Mordecai's part that she might pass for a native Persian, and that her Jewish birth should be no hindrance to her advancement. The king does not learn his wife's nation until some time later (7:4).

(11) Mordecai walked ... —Apparently he was one of the royal doorkeepers. (See 2:21; 5:13.)

(16) The month Tebeth.—The time referred to in the verse will be the January or February of the year 478 B.C., and must have been shortly after Xerxes' return to Susa from the West. The long delay in replacing Vashti is simply to be explained by the long absence of Xerxes in Greece.

(19) And when the virgins ... —Here begins a fresh incident in the history, the date of which we cannot fix precisely, except that it falls between the marriage of Esther and the twelfth year of Ahasuerus (3:7). How the word "love" is degraded in this connection is seen by the fact that after she had been his wife certainly less than five years, there takes place a second gathering of virgins like the one previously mentioned (2:2).

(20) Esther had not yet. ... —Perhaps this verse is added to meet the supposition that the king wished to replace Esther through finding out her nation.

(22) And Esther certified the king thereof.—Doubtless by this means an increased influence was gained over the capricious mind of the king, an influence which before long served Esther in good stead.

(23) Hanged on a tree.—Crucifixion was a common punishment among the Persians, especially on rebels (Herod. 3:120, 125, 159, etc.). The dead body of Leonidas was crucified by Xerxes' orders after the desperate stand at Thermopylae.

Book of the chronicles.—Herodotus often refers to these Persian Chronicles (7:100; 8:85, 90).

3

(1) Haman ... the Agagite.—Nothing appears to be known of Haman except from this book. His name, as well as that of his father and his sons, is Persian; and it is thus difficult to see the meaning of the name "Agagite," which has been assumed—but improbably—by some to imply descent

from Agag, king of the Amalekites, with whom the name Agag may have been dynastic (Num. 24:7; I Sam. 15:8).

(2) Bowed not.—The objection on Mordecai's part was evidently mainly on religious grounds, as giving to a man divine honors, for it elicits from him the fact that he was a Jew (verse 4), to whom such an act of obeisance would be abhorrent.

(7) In the first month ... Nisan, in the twelfth year.—In April of 474 B.C.

Pur.—This is evidently a Persian word for "lot," for both here and in 9:24 the usual Hebrew word is added. The people who cast Pur were seeking for a lucky day, as indicated by the lots, for the purpose in hand. A lot was cast for each day of the month, and for each month in the year, and in some way or other one day and one month were indicated as the most favorable.

The twelfth month ... Adar.—The lunar month ending at the new moon in March. Nearly a year intervened between the throwing of the lot and the carrying out of the scheme. Thus in God's providence ample time was allowed for redressing matters.

(8) Neither keep they ... —The charge of disloyalty has been a favorite weapon in the hands of persecutors. Haman was not the first who had brought this charge against the Jews (see Ezra 4:13, 16). Our Lord's accusers were those who knew no king but Caesar. The early Christians found to their cost how deadly was the accusation of disloyalty to the Empire.

(9) Ten thousand talents of silver.—This would be about two and a half million sterling, being indeed more than two-thirds of the whole annual revenue of the Empire (Herod. 3:95). Haman may have been a man of excessive wealth, or he probably may have hoped to draw the money from the spoils of the Jews.

(12) On the thirteenth day of the first month.—From the next verse we see that the thirteenth of Adar was to be the lucky day for Haman's purpose, which may have suggested the thirteenth of Nisan as a suitable day for this preliminary step. This day was the eve of the Passover, so that Haman's plot against the Jews strangely coincides in time with one five hundred years later, when the Jews themselves sought to vanquish the Saviour; and as the trembling Jews of Persia were delivered by God's goodness, so too by His goodness the Lamb that was slain did triumph.

(15) Perplexed.—The inhabitants of the

capital were puzzled and alarmed at so marvelously reckless an order. Their sympathies, too, were clearly with the Jews and against Haman. (See 8:15.)

4

(1) Mordecai rent his clothes.—This was a common sign of sorrow among Eastern nations generally. It will be noticed that the sorrow both of Mordecai and the Jews generally (verse 3) is described by external manifestations solely. There is rending of garments, putting on of sackcloth and ashes, fasting and weeping and wailing; there is nothing said of prayer and entreaty to the God of Israel, who is able to save. Daniel and Ezra and Nehemiah are all Jews, who, like Mordecai and Esther, have to submit to the rule of the alien, though, unlike them, they, when the danger threatened, besought, and not in vain, the help of their God. (See Dan. 6:10; Ezra 8:23; Neh. 1:4, etc.)

(11) There is one law of his. ... —There is one unvarying rule for such. No one who had not been summoned might enter the king's presence under pain of death.

(14) From another place.—We may suppose that Mordecai here refers to divine help, which he asserts will be vouchsafed in this extremity. It does not necessarily follow, however, that we are to see in this declaration a proof of the earnestness of Mordecai's faith. Probably had his faith been like that of many of his countrymen he would not have been in Persia at all, but with the struggling band in Judaea.

Thou and thy father's house shall be destroyed.—It is clear there is a good deal of force in these last words of Mordecai. Esther's rise had been so marvelous that one might well see in it the hand of God, and if so there was clearly a special object in view, which it must be her anxious care to realize. In the whole tone of the conversation, however, there seems a lack of higher and more noble feelings, an absence of any suggestion of turning for aid to God; and thus in return, when God carries out His purpose, and grants deliverance, it seems done indirectly, without the conferring of any special blessing on the human instruments.

5

(3) To the half of the kingdom.—This tremendous offer occurs in further promises of Ahasuerus (5:6; 7:2). The same reckless promise is made by Herod Antipas to the daughter of Herodias (Mark 6:23).

(4) Let the king and Haman come this day unto the banquet.—It was natural enough that, with so much depending on her request, the queen should show some hesitation. She gains time, securing an especially favorable opportunity for bringing forward the request; and the king clearly sees that she has kept her real petition in reserve, by himself again raising the question.

(9) He stood not up.—In 3:2 Mordecai refused to bow or prostrate himself to Haman. Here he refuses even the slightest sign of respect. The honorable independence of the former case here becomes indefensible rudeness.

(14) Gallows.—The Hebrew is **tree.** (See note on 2:23.) Doubtless the punishment intended for Mordecai was crucifixion, for hanging, in the common sense of the term, does not seem to have been in use among the Persians. The Greek word employed is the same as that used in the New Testament for our Saviour's cross (Acts. 5:30; 10:39; etc.).

Fifty cubits high.—That is, about seventy-five feet, the great height being to call as much attention as possible to the execution, that thereby Haman's glory might be proportionately increased.

6

(1) Could not the king sleep.—Here, in the most striking way in the whole book, the workings of God's providence on behalf of His people are shown. God Himself is here, although His name is absent. The king's sleepless night falls after the day when Haman has resolved to ask on the morrow for Mordecai's execution, a foretaste of the richer vengeance he hopes to wreak on the whole nation of the Jews.

(2) It was found written.—See 2:21-23.

(3) What honour and dignity hath been done.—The names of those who were thought worthy of being accounted "royal benefactors" were enrolled on a special list, and they were supposed to be suitably rewarded, though not necessarily at the time. The reward was, in theory at any rate, a thing to which the "benefactor" had a distinct claim and an almost legal right.

(8) Let the royal apparel be brought ...

369

—These exceedingly great distinctions Haman suggests, thinking with unaccountable vanity (for nothing is said or implied as to any service rendered by him to the king) that the king must necessarily have been referring to him, and in a moment he is irretrievably committed. He shows the lack of the most ordinary discretion; his vanity is so inordinate that he cannot see the possibility of any one's merits save his own.

(10) The Jew.—Mordecai's nationality would doubtless be given in the book of records. Thus Esther, in urging her subsequent petition, had already on her side the king's good will to one prominent member of the proscribed race.

7

(2) What is thy petition?—The king takes for granted that Esther's invitations to her banquets do not constitute her real request, but merely prepare the way for it.

(4) To be destroyed . . .—The identical words used in the king's proclamation for the destruction of the Jews. Herein Esther at once makes confession of her nationality, and relying on the king's still recent gratitude to one of the race, aided by his present cordiality to herself, she risks, as indeed she can no longer help doing, the fate of herself and her race on the momentary impulse of her fickle lord. Happily for her, God has willed that these, perhaps at any other time untrustworthy grounds of reliance, shall suffice.

Although the enemy . . .—This may mean that Haman, though willing to pay a large sum into the royal treasury, cannot thereby make up for the loss which the king must incur by wholesale massacre being carried on in his realm.

(8) The bed.—i.e., the couch on which she had been reclining at the banquet. This was the customary posture at meals, not only of the Persians, but also of the Greeks and Romans, and of the later Jews. The Last Supper was thus eaten. Haman had obviously thrown himself at the queen's feet to ask for mercy. The king on his return was evidently full of wrath against Haman, and though he was for the time God's instrument in averting Haman's wicked design, his own base and worthless character is none the less conspicuous.

(9) Hang him.—Not only does God promise to deliver Mordecai's people, but He brings on the enemy the very destruc-

tion he had devised for his adversary. Our Saviour has rescued us from our enemy who was too mighty for us, and has trodden down our foe, to be destroyed for ever in His own good time.

8

(2) Took off his ring . . . and gave it unto Mordecai.—Mordecai's position had now become what Daniel's had been to Darius, that nobler servant to a worthier lord (see Dan. 6:2, 28). He was the queen's cousin, and he had on one occasion been the means of saving the king's life. Therefore he starts under distinctly favorable auspices.

(3) Besought him . . . to put away the mischief.—Esther's work was as yet only half done. She had seen the condemnation of the foe of her race and the exaltation of her kinsman to his office. But the royal edict sent out against the Jews still remains valid, and being a written decree, sealed with the king's seal, is supposed to be beyond the possibility of alteration. It was not, therefore, a case where Mordecai's newly-acquired dignity would authorize him to interfere, and therefore Esther, who, now that the ice is once broken, becomes more courageous, and makes a fresh appeal to the king to do what theoretically was beyond the king's power.

(9) The month Sivan.—Sivan began with the new moon in May. More than two months had thus passed since the first edict had been sent out.

(11) To stand for their life.—As far as the edict authorizes, the Jews are not permitted to take the initiative, but merely to stand on the defensive. As it was, it was risking civil war in all the cities of the empire, though the results were considerably lessened by numbers of people taking the hint obviously presented by the second edict.

Take the spoil of them.—When the storm actually came, the Jews declined to take advantage of this part of the edict. (See 9:10, 16.)

(17) Became Jews.—That is, embraced their religion as proselytes.

9

(1) Drew near.—Arrived, came, as in 8:17.

(2) To lay hand on such as sought their hurt.—How far the Jews acted according to the strict letter of the edict, and "stood for their lives" only when attacked, is perhaps to be doubted. They had on their side all the executive of the empire (verse 3), and evidently to all intents and purposes the second edict was considered virtually to repeal the first. The Jews, therefore, being in favor at Court, and, as was not unnatural after their alarm, being now full of indignation and vengeance, were probably resolved to use their opportunities while they had the chance.

(13) Then said Esther ... —Before the slaughter of the 13th of Adar was actually over, it is obvious that the Jews were no longer in any danger. It was known that the sympathies of the Court were entirely with the Jews, and the officers of the king consequently took their part. After one day's slaughter, in which in the capital alone 500 men were killed, we may be quite certain that the Jews were masters of the situation, and therefore we do not hesitate to call Esther's fresh action needless butchery. Were anything needed to bring out the matter in its true light, it might be seen in the request that the sons of Haman might be hanged. They had already been killed (verse 10), doubtless among the first, and Esther, therefore, asks for the dead bodies to be crucified, a gratuitous outrage on the dead.

(16) Seventy and five thousand.—The whole history shows the recklessness of human life which then prevailed among the sovereigns of the most celebrated nations of the Eastern world. If Greece had not triumphed in her struggle with Asia, Oriental ruthlessness and Oriental polygamy might have become dominant in the West, and greater difficulties would have obstructed the progress of civilization and Christianity. The Book of Esther reveals to us that the hand of God wrought for the deliverance of mankind at Salamis and at Plataea, as well as for the preservation of the Jews in the provinces of Persia.

(26) Purim.—The festival of Purim is still observed by the Jews on the 14th and 15th of Adar, the day preceding being kept as a fast. At Purim, the whole Book of Esther is read through in the service in the synagogues, a custom that can be traced back to the Christian era (II Macc. 15:36; Josephus, **Ant.** 11:6,§13; Mishna, **Rosh-ha-Shanah**, 3:7).

(29) This second letter.—It seems that the first letter must be that extracted from the king by Esther (8:8), and consequently this "second letter" is Mordecai's (9:20), which is now confirmed in a more authoritative way.

(32) In the book.—It is doubtful what "the book" here means. The Vulgate explains it of the Book of Esther itself, and so many scholars. Still "the book" hardly seems a natural Hebrew way of referring to a work on the part of its author as he writes it, and no similar case is adducible. Others think it must have been a book written at the time on the subject of the festival which is, perhaps, possible. Rawlinson identifies it with "the Book of the Chronicles of the Kings of Media and Persia," because such is the use of the word "book" in 2:23.

10

(1) Laid a tribute.—The disastrous expedition to Greece must have taxed the resources of the empire to the utmost, and fresh tribute would therefore be required to fill the exhausted coffers. Besides this, a harassing war was still going on, even ten years after the battle of Salamis, on the coast of Asia Minor, and this would require fresh supplies.

The isles of the sea.—The chief island yet remaining to the Persian Empire was Cyprus. Those in the Aegean Sea were now free from Persian rule, but possibly, even after the loss, the old phrase may have been retained.

(3) Mordecai the Jew was next unto king Ahasuerus. The events recorded in this book carry us to the year 470 B.C., at which time Mordecai was at the zenith of his greatness. How long he kept it, whether death or disgrace brought it to a close, and if the latter, from what cause, we cannot say. All we know is that near the end of Xerxes' reign his favorite and chief adviser was Artabanus, the captain of the guard, by whom he was murdered in 464 B.C. The last we hear of Mordecai, whatever was his after-fate, is that he was loyal to his people, and approved himself their benefactor, "seeking the wealth (i.e., weal—literally, 'good'), and speaking peace to all his seed," all of the stock of Israel.

THE BOOK OF JOB

1

(1) There was a man in the land of Uz.—The first mention of this name is in Gen. 10:23, where Uz is said to have been one of the sons of Aram, who was one of the sons of Shem. (Comp. I Chron. 1:17; see also Gen. 22:21; 36:28.) From the mention of "the land of Uz" (Lam. 4:21) and "the kings of the land of Uz" (Jer. 25:20), where in each case the association seems to be with Edom, it is probable that the land of Job is to be identified with the district south and southeast of Palestine.

Whose name was Job.—The name is carefully to be distinguished from the Job who was the son of Issachar (Gen. 46:13), and from the Jobab who was one of the kings of Edom (Gen. 36:33). The form of the name may suggest the signification of "the assaulted one," as the root from which it appears to be derived means "was an enemy."

Perfect and upright . . .—The character here given to Job is that in which wisdom is declared to consist. (Comp. 28:28.) It has the twofold aspect of refusing the evil and choosing the good, of aiming at a lofty ideal of excellence and of shunning that which is fatal or opposed to it.

(3) The men of the east.—The Arabs still call the Hauran, or the district east of Jordan, the land of Job. It is said to be a lovely and fertile region, fulfilling the conditions of the poem.

(5) Job sent and sanctified them . . .—The earliest records of society exhibit the father of the family acting as the priest. This is one of the passages which shows that Job was outside the pale and influence of the Mosaic law, whether this was owing to his age or his country. His life in this respect corresponds with that of the patriarchs in Genesis more nearly than any other in Scripture.

(6) Sons of God.—Comp. 38:7; Gen. 6:2, 4; and for the sense comp. I Kings 22:19. The phrase probably means "the angels"; or at all events an incident in the unseen spiritual world is referred to simultaneous with a corresponding one on earth. (Comp. I Cor. 11:10.) In the latter sense, a solemn thought is suggested by it to those who join in the public worship of God.

Satan.—The word appears in the Old Testament as the name of a specific person only here and in Zech. 3:2, and possibly in I Chron. 21:1 and Ps. 109:6. If this psalm is David's, according to the inscription, no reliance can be placed on speculations as to the late introduction of a belief in Satan among the Jews, nor, therefore, on any as to the lateness of these early chapters of Job. Precisely the same word is used, apparently as a common name, in the history of Balaam (Num. 22:22, 32), also in I Sam. 29:4, and I Kings 5:4; 11:14, 23, 25, where it can hardly be otherwise. Here only and in Zechariah it is found with the definite article "the adversary." The theory of the personality of the evil one must largely depend upon the view we take of these and other passages of Scripture containing an authoritative revelation.

(7) From going to and fro . . .—Compare I Pet. 5:8.

(9) Doth Job fear God for nought?—Manifesting the worst kind of scepticism, a disbelief in human goodness. Satan knows that the motive of an action is its only value, and by incrimination calumniates the motives of Job. The object of the book is thus introduced, which is to exhibit the integrity of human conduct under the worst possible trial, and to show man a victor over Satan.

(12) All that he hath is in thy power . . .—Mighty as the principle of evil is in the world, it is nevertheless held in check by One who directs it to His own ends. Such is the uniform teaching of Scripture. We are not under the uncontrolled dominion of evil, strong as the temptation may be at times to think so. (See II Cor. 12:7, 9; I Thess. 2:18, etc.)

(15) The Sabeans.—Literally, "Sheba." It is probably the son of Jokshan and grandson of Abraham (Gen. 25:3) who is referred to here, whose descendants led a predatory and marauding kind of life in the country bordering on that of Job. (Comp. Ezek. 38:13.)

(16) The fire of God.—It is characteristic of the Old Testament poetry to see in the convulsions of nature the immediate action of the Most High; but perhaps it is intended throughout Job that we should see more than this, as the book undoubtedly assumes to be the record of a divine revelation.

(17) The Chaldeans.—Literally, "Chasdim," or descendants of Chesed (Gen. 22:22).

(18) Thy sons and thy daughters.—The marvelous accumulation of disasters points us to the conclusion that it was the distinct work of Satan, according to the permission given him (verse 12), and consequently supernatural.

(20) And worshipped.—Compare the conduct of David (II Sam. 12:20) and of Hezekiah (II Kings 19:1). Moments of intense sorrow or trial, like moments of intense joy, force us into the immediate presence of God.

(21) Thither.—If taken literally, can only refer to the womb, which in that case must here mean the earth, with a probable allusion to Gen. 3:19. (Comp. Job 17:14.)

Blessed be the name of the Lord.—The very word used in a contrary sense (verse 11). Thus was Satan foiled for the **first** time.

(Comp. Heb. 5:8.) This was the lesson Job was learning.

(11) Eliphaz the Temanite.—Teman was the son of Eliphaz, the son of Esau, to whose family this Eliphaz is probably to be referred (Gen. 36:4, 10, 11). If so, this may roughly indicate the date of the book. The inhabitants of Teman, which lay northeast of Edom, were famed for their wisdom (Jer. 49:7).

Bildad the Shuhite probably derived his origin from Shuah, the son of Abraham by Keturah (Gen. 25:2). Of the district from which Zophar the Naamathite came nothing is known.

2

(4) Skin for skin.—This is a more extreme form of the insinuation of 1:9. He means Job takes care to have his **quid pro quo**; and if the worst come to worst, a man will give up everything to save his life. If, therefore, Job can save his life at the price of subservience to God, he will willingly pay that price rather than die; but his service is worth no more than that selfish object implies.

(6) But save his life.—God's faithfulness cannot fail even if, as Satan hints, Job's should do so (II Tim. 2:13). There was One who cared for Job's life more than he cared for it himself.

(7) Sore boils.—Supposed to be Elephantiasis, in which the skin becomes clotted and hard like an elephant's, with painful cracks and sores underneath.

(9) Then said his wife.—Thus it is that a man's foes are they of his own household (Micah 7:6; Matt. 10:36; etc.). The worst trial of all is when those nearest to us, instead of strengthening our hand in God and confirming our faith, conspire to destroy it.

(10) Shall we receive good ...? —The words were fuller than even Job thought; for merely to receive evil as from God's hands is to transmute its character altogether, for then even calamities become blessings in disguise. What Job meant was that we are bound to expect evil as well as good from God's hands by a sort of compensation and even-handed justice, but what his words may mean is a far more blessed truth than this. There is a sublime contrast between the temptation of Job and the temptation of Christ (Matt. 26:39-42, etc.).

3

(5) Stain.—Literally, "redeem"—i.e., claim as their rightful inheritance.

Blackness of the day—i.e., preternatural darkness, inopportune and unexpected darkness, like that of eclipses.

(8) That curse the day—i.e., Let those who proclaim days unlucky or accursed curse that day as pre-eminently so; or let them recollect that day as a standard or sample of cursing. "Let it be as cursed as Job's birthday."

(12) Prevent—i.e., "Why was I nursed with care, instead of being allowed to fall to the ground and be killed?"

(14) Desolate places—i.e., gorgeous tombs and splendid sepulchres, which, being tenanted only by the dead, are desolate. It is possible that the Pyramids may here be hinted at.

(17) There—i.e., in the grave, the place indicated, but not distinctly expressed.

(18) The oppressor.—As this is the word rendered "taskmaster" in Exodus, some have thought there may be an allusion to that history here.

(25) For the thing which I greatly feared ... —Comp. Prov. 28:14. It means that he had always had in remembrance the uncertainty and instability of earthly things, and yet he had been overtaken by a calamity that mocked his carefulness and exceeded his apprehensions.

4

(2) If we assay.—Rather, perhaps, "Has one ever assayed?" or, "Has a word ever been tried?" It appears from 29:9, 10, that Job was held in great honour and reverence by all, and Eliphaz regarded him with awe such as would have constrained him to be silent, but he is so convinced that Job is wrong and deserves reproof, that he cannot refrain from speaking. He strikes a note, however, which the friends all sound, namely, that it is the wicked who suffer, and that all who suffer must be wicked. This, in a variety of forms, is the sum and substance of what they have to say.

(3) Behold, thou hast instructed many.—There is a conspicuous want of feeling in Eliphaz. He charges Job with inability to derive from his own principles that support which he had expected them to afford to others, and seems almost to rejoice malevolently that one who had been so great a help to others was now in need of help himself.

(6) Is not this thy fear, thy confidence . . . ?—The meaning seems to be, "Should not thy fear or piety be thy confidence, and the uprightness of thy ways thy hope? Should not the piety thou wast so ready to commend to others supply a sufficient ground of hope for thyself?"

(7) Remember, I pray thee, who ever perished, being innocent?—His object may be to prove to him that if he is what he was supposed to be, that itself is a ground of hope, inasmuch as no innocent person is allowed to perish. God will never fail, though He may try, those who trust in Him.

(8) They that plow iniquity.—Comp. Gal. 6:7, 8; and comp. also the strange expression of Isa. 5:18.

(11) The old lion perisheth . . . —This means that even though wickedness is joined with strength, it is equally unable to prosper. It is to be observed that no less than five different words are used here for lion, showing that these animals must have been common and of various kinds in Job's country.

(12) Now a thing.—He now proceeds to enforce and illustrate what he has said in highly poetical language, which has been versified in one of Byron's Hebrew Melodies.

(15) A spirit passed before my face.—The notion of **seeing** a spirit is absurd in itself, because it involves the idea of seeing the invisible; but it is conceivable that the perceptions of the inner spirit may be so vivid as to assume the character of outward manifestations.

(17) Shall mortal man be more just than God?—This is the burden, or refrain, upon which the friends of Job are always harping. It is perfectly orthodox, but at the

same time perfectly inadequate to deal with the necessities of Job's case. He is willing to admit that it is impossible for any man to be just with God; but then arises Job's dilemma—Where is God's justice if He punishes the innocent as the guilty? The word rendered "mortal" man is really "weak," "frail" man, involving, it may be, the idea of mortality, but not immediately suggesting it.

(20) From morning to evening.—The process is continual and unceasing, and when we consider the ravages of time on history, we may well say, as in verse 20, that "none regardeth it."

The next verse, however, may seem to imply that they themselves are unmindful of their decay, it is so insidious and so complete.

5

(1) Call now.—The speaker now becomes more personal and direct in his tone and bearing. He insinuates that Job is "unwise" and "silly," and promises swift destruction for all such.

(3) I cursed.—All these general results of experience have the sting of insinuations in them that they contain the key to Job's unfortunate condition. There is secret unsoundness there which is the cause of the manifest and open misery. It is impossible that a man so stricken should be otherwise than, for some unknown reason, the guilty victim of the righteous wrath of a just judge.

(4) They are crushed.—Rather, perhaps, "they crush one another." Their internal rivalries and dissensions bring them to ruin. They exemplify the house divided against itself.

(6, 7) Although affliction . . . —Eliphaz is comparing man's lot as prepared for him by God with his own pride and presumptuous ambition. Man is born to labor, but, like sparks of fire, he makes high his flight. Trouble and toil is no accidental growth, but a lot appointed by God, which would be beneficial if man did not thwart it by his own pride. They lift themselves up and soar on high like sparks of fire with daring and presumptuous conduct, and so bring on themselves deserved punishment. The same word means "trouble" and "toil," and it may be understood in the two consecutive verses in these cognate, but slightly different, senses.

(11) To set up on high those that be low.—Thus his doctrine is that man's exaltation must come from God, and not from his own vain strivings. (Comp. Ps. 75:4-10, and the prayer of Hannah, I Sam. 2:6-8; also Ps. 113:7; etc.)

(13) He taketh the wise.—The word rendered "froward" means "crooked," "perverse," or "tortuous." The name Naphtali is derived from the same root (Gen. 30:8).

(14) Darkness in the daytime.—This is possibly an allusion to the Egyptian plague of darkness "that may be felt" (Ex. 10:21), as the words are similar. This may be a note of probable date. This is one of the many passages of Job in which there seems to be an indication of some acquaintance with the events related in the Pentateuch, though the points of contact are too slight for us to be quite sure of it.

(15) From the sword, from their mouth.—It is worthy of special note that the Lord is thus conceived of and represented as the Saviour, and the Saviour of them who have no saviour. Is not this an idea confined to the circle of the sacred writings? At all events, it so abounds and predominates in them as to be pre-eminently, if not exclusively, characteristic of them.

(18) He maketh sore, and bindeth up.—The sentiment here expressed is one of those obvious ones which lose all their force from familiarity with them, but which come home sometimes in sorrow with a power that is boundless, because divine.

(19) In six troubles.—The special form of speech here used is characteristic mainly of the Proverbs (see 6:16; 30:15, 18, 21). Since evil was emphatically touching Job, the actual irony of these words must have been bitter indeed.

(20) He shall redeem thee.—It is rather, "he hath redeemed thee," as though the speaker could appeal to Job's own experience in the matter which itself became a ground of confident hope for the future.

(24) Sin.—The word rendered "sin" literally means also "to miss the mark," as in Judges 20:16, and that is probably its meaning here: "Thou shalt visit thy dwelling-place, and miss nothing," since one does not see clearly why the promise of not sinning is connected with visiting the habitation or fold.

(25) Great.—The word also means "numerous," which seems to suit the parallelism better here. The whole description is a beautiful and poetical one of the perfect security of faith, though it is to a certain extent vitiated by its want of strict correspondence with facts, of which the case of Job was a crucial instance. This was the special problem with which his friends had to deal, and which proved too hard for them. May we not learn that the problem is one that can only be solved in practice and not in theory?

(26) Thou shalt come to thy grave.—The grave in such a case is not the melancholy end of life, but rather the passage to a higher life for which one is already ripe. (Comp. II Tim. 4:8.)

(27) So it is.—It is the boastful confidence of Eliphaz which is so hard to bear. He speaks as though Job's experience were as nothing to his. "This is mine: take it to thyself, and make it thine."

6

(1) But Job answered and said.—Job replies to Eliphaz with the despair of a man who has been thwarted of sympathy when he hoped to find it. We cannot trace, nor must we expect to find, the formal reply of a logical argument. Eliphaz, he feels, has so misjudged his case that he is neither worthy of a direct reply nor susceptible of one. It is enough for him to reiterate his complaint, and long for one who can enter into it.

(3) Swallowed up.—That is, "words are useless and powerless to express it."

(8) Oh that I might have my request.—Baffled in the direction of his fellow creatures, he turns, like many others, to God as his only hope, although it is rather from God than in God that his hope lies. However exceptional Job's trials, yet his language is the common language of all sufferers who think that relief, if it comes, must come through change of circumstances rather than in themselves in relation to circumstances. Thus Job looks forward to death as his only hope; whereas with God and in God there were many years of life and prosperity in store for him. So strong is this feeling in him, that he calls death the thing that he longs for, his hope or expectation. (Comp. chap. 17, where even the hope that he had in death seems to have passed away and to have issued in blank hopelessness.)

(9) Even that it would please God ...—The sequence of thought in these verses is obscure and uncertain. The speaker may mean that, notwithstanding all that might befall him, his consolation would still be that he had never denied the words of the Holy One.

(14) But he forsaketh the fear of the Almighty.—It is difficult to determine the precise relation of dependent clauses in an archaic language like the Hebrew; but the King James Version is not correct here, the sense rather being, "Even to one that forsaketh the fear of the Almighty."

(15) Have dealt deceitfully as a brook.—This is one of the most celebrated poetical similes in the book, and carries us to life in the desert, where the wadies so mighty and torrent-like in the winter, are insignificant streams or fail altogether in summer.

(18) They go to nothing.—"The caravans that travel by the way of them turn aside, and go into the waste and perish." (See verse 19.)

(19) The troops of Tema.—Fürst says of Tema that it was a tract in the north of the Arabian Desert, on the borders of the Syrian one, where traffic was carried on from the Persian Gulf to the Mediterranean by caravans (Isa. 21:14; Jer. 25:23). Sheba, as understood here, was probably a district on the Arabian Gulf (see 1:15), where merchants trafficked with the distant cities of the East, as well as enriched themselves with the plunder of their neighbors, as in 1:15.

(22) Did I say, Bring unto me?—"It is not as though I had abused your former kindness. I never laid myself under obligations to you; I never asked for your help before. Had I done so, I might have wearied out your patience, and brought upon myself your present conduct justly; but you cannot convict me of this."

(25) How forcible are right words!—"How forcible are words of uprightness! But what doth your reproof reprove? Open rebuke is better than secret love; better to be honestly and openly rebuked by you than be subject to the secret insinuations which are intended to pass for friendship."

(30) Is there iniquity?—Or, "injustice in my tongue? Is my taste so perverted that it cannot perceive what is perverse?" "Ye appear to think that I am wholly incapable of judging my own cause because it is my own; but if ye will only condescend to return in due course, ye shall find that I know what is right as well as you, and that there is no more vicious reasoning in me than there is with you, and probably less."

7

In this chapter Job turns away from his friends to God, to whom he appeals for compassion (verses 1-11). He asks whether man does not have a campaign to serve upon earth. Job does not regret that man's time is short upon earth, for he says that he longs eagerly for his end, but he regrets that it is so full of misery. It is the character of the appointed time, and not the shortness of it, that he laments.

(5) With worms and clods of dust.—It is characteristic of elephantiasis that the skin becomes hard and ridged, and then cracks and becomes ulcerated.

(9) As the cloud is consumed.—It is a fine simile that man is as evanescent as a cloud; and apt is the figure, because, whether it vanishes on the surface of the sky or is distributed in rain, nothing more completely passes away than the summer cloud. It is an appearance only, which comes to nought.

(10) Neither shall his place ...—We need not force these words too much, as though they forbad our ascribing to Job any belief in a future life or in the resurrection, because, under any circumstances, they are evidently and accurately true of man as we know him here. Even though he may live again in another way, it is not in this world that he lives again, and it is of this world and of man in this world that Job is speaking. And man, in the aspect of his mortality, is truly a pitiable object, demanding our compassion and sympathy. Happily, the appeal to man's maker is not in vain, and He who has made him what he is has looked upon his misery.

(12) Am I a sea, or a whale ...?—This hard verse it seems most reasonable to explain, if we can, from Scripture itself: e.g. Jer. 5:22. The writer was probably familiar with Egypt when the Nile, which is still called the sea, was carefully watched and guarded by dykes that its overflow might not destroy the land. So Job exclaims, "Am I like the sea, or one of its monsters—like that Leviathan which Thou hast made to take his pastime therein, that Thou keepest guard over me and makest me thy prisoner continually, shutting me up on every side so fast in prison that I cannot go free?"

(17, 18) What is man ...?—Here is another point of contact with Ps. 8:4; but the spirit of the psalmist was one of devout adoration, whereas that of Job is one of agony and desperation.

(19) Till I swallow down my spittle.— This is doubtless a proverbial expression, like "the twinkling of an eye," or "while I fetch a breath."

(20) I have sinned—i.e., "Putting the case that I have sinned, yet what then can I do unto Thee, O thou keeper of men?" with a possible allusion to verse 12, though the verb is not the same.

(21) And why dost thou not pardon my transgression?—In Job's belief, sin was the origin of all disaster, and so he thinks that if he were but pardoned his sorrows would pass away.

8

The burden of Bildad's speech is much what that of Eliphaz was: the justice of God, and the impossibility of one who is not a wicked man being forsaken of God and punished. What is so conspicuous in the speeches of Job's friends is their total want of refinement and delicacy of feeling. They blurt out without the slightest compunction the most unscrupulous charges, and they cast the most reckless insinuations against him. Here, for instance, Bildad does not hesitate to say that Job's sons died for the transgressions because God is a righteous God, and He would not have been righteous had they, being innocent, perished. Thus, in order to save the credit of the righteous God facts must be distorted or misrepresented to any extent, as though God were not a God of truth as well as of righteousness.

(6) If thou wert pure and upright.—Of course, then, there is but one inference: thou art not pure and upright. Bildad brings to the maintenance of his point the experience of former generations. It appears that Bildad contemplates two representative characters, the two which are so prominent throughout this book—namely, the righteous and the wicked. He depicts the latter first, and describes him under the likeness of the paper-reed, or rush that grows in the mire of Egyptian swamps, which, though surrounded with moisture, yet as a matter of fact is liable soon to wither: so is the wicked man, according to this moralist and philosopher. He is surrounded by mercies and blessings, but they avail him nought; he withereth in the midst of abundance.

(11) The flag is the plant of Gen. 41:2, which the cattle feed upon. This figure is enforced by a second, that, namely, of the spider's web, the most fragile and transient of tenements.

(15) It shall not endure.—The description of the wicked man ends here.

(16) He is green.—Here begins another and an opposite picture, which fact is marked in the Hebrew by an emphatic pronoun. There is not the same promise of verdure, but a greater realization of it.

(17) His roots are wrapped about.—This is the cause of his continual luxuriance, that his roots receive moisture from below, where they are wrapped about the spring which fertilizes them underneath.

And seeth the place of stones.—He sees the permanent and durable edifice of stone which is the habitation of civilization and culture, and here his holding is so firm that, even if plucked up, his roots and suckers are so numerous that they leave behind them descendants and offshoots, so that out of his earth others grow.

(21) Till he fill thy mouth with laughing.— The attitude of Bildad is one of unsympathetic selfishness. He wishes to think well of his friend because he is **his** friend, but he cannot reconcile his afflicted condition with any theory or righteous government, and therefore is driven to suspect that all is not right with him, though he feels warranted in promising him that if he casts away that secret sin all shall yet be well with him.

9

(1) Then Job answered ... —Job's reply to Bildad differs from that to Eliphaz, inasmuch as he exposes the hollowness of Bildad's position by sapping his foundation. Admitting the general propriety of all he has said, he confronts him with the anterior question, "How can weak man be just with God?" and this is the question, if fairly dealt with, which must always confound shallow generalizers like Bildad.

(3) If he will contend with him.—If man choose to contend with God, he cannot answer Him one question of a thousand, once in a thousand times.

(8) Waves of the sea.—The various physical phenomena of earthquake, eclipse, and hurricane are here described as the field of divine action and the operations of His hands.

(9) Which maketh Arcturus ... —This shows us that in the time of this writer, whoever he was, his fellow-countrymen had attained to such knowledge of astronomy as is here implied in the specific names of definite constellations. The Great Bear is the glory of the northern hemisphere, Orion of the southern sky, and the Pleiades of the east; the chambers of the north are the unknown and unexplored regions, of which the speaker has no personal experience.

(11) He passeth on also.—This, again, is an expression Eliphaz had used in 4:15. Here in words of great sublimity Job depicts the unapproachable majesty of God omnipotent, but invisible, and shows the utter hopelessness of entering into judgment with Him. Unfortunately, though this is a proposition to which all must assent, yet none is virtually so much repudiated or practically so often contravened. Men still cast about to justify themselves before God, and will do so until the end of time; but it is in teaching such as this that the Book of Job has laid the foundation of the Gospel by preparing for its acceptance by overthrowing man's natural and habitual standing-ground in himself.

(12) What doest thou?—Putting the case even that God were, so to say, in the wrong, and the assailant, yet even then He would maintain His cause from sheer might, and crush His adversary.

(15) Though I were righteous.—He now puts the alternative case: that he were actually righteous; yet even then supplication, and not assertion, would best become him.

(18) Take my breath.—The action being that of breathing again after complete exhaustion—recovering breath and the power to breathe, etc. "If I say I am perfect, it also shall prove me perverse by the very act of saying so; because for man to maintain his righteousness before God is at once to proclaim his iniquity. The finite cannot come into competition with the Infinite, nor measure itself therewith."

(19) If I speak of strength.—All this is the most uncompromising acknowledgment of the absolute inability of man to stand in judgment before God. The whole of this is abrupt and enigmatical, though naturally the general drift of it is obvious enough.

(23) The scourge slay suddenly.— Probably meaning that in the case of hidden calamity overtaking an innocent man, He, God, will laugh at it: that is to say, take no more notice of it than if it furnished Him with sport. The fact of such calamity befalling, as it often does, the innocent is at all events, in one view, a proof of His indifference to it who, by the exercise of His providence, could easily interpose to prevent it, and so looks as if He winked at it. Job's argument is the argument of a man who wilfully shuts out faith in his estimate of God's dealings; not that Job is devoid of faith, but in the course of arguing with his friends, who maintain the strict, rigid justice of God, he confronts them with the severe logic of facts, which they can neither contradict nor explain. Of course, for the requirements of argument, he takes the pessimist view of the divine providence, and declares even that the earth is given over into the hands of the wicked man.

(25) Swifter than a post.—The runner, with his messages and dispatches. He now turns away from the contemplation of God and His dealings to that of his own misery.

(26) Swift ships.—Literally, "ships of Eveh," probably a proper name, and perhaps referring to a particular kind of boat in use on the Nile; if so, this is one instance out of many of Job's acquaintance with Egypt. Job is a problem to himself; he is confident of his innocence, and yet he is confident that very innocence will avail him nothing before God; he is sure that he must be condemned. Now, it is impossible to deny that this is the attitude of the Gospel; it is, therefore, if we bear in mind the vast antiquity of the confession, both a witness to the truth of the Gospel and an anticipation of it that God alone could give. Indeed, it is hopelessly impossible to enter into the position of Job unless we are ourselves enlightened with the teaching of the Gospel, and able to look at it from the Gospel standpoint. While, therefore, admitting this fact, we are the better able to appreciate the wonderful confession Job is about to make in verses 32, 33.

(32, 33) For he is not a man, as I am ... —Is not that confession, if we believe that such a daysman as Job longed for has been given, itself a witness that it came from God, and was given by God? The light that has shined upon us was shining then in the heart of Job, and shines forever in the pages of his book. Job felt, as he had been taught to feel, that in himself there not only was no hope, but no possibility of justification with God, unless there should be an umpire and impartial mediator, who could make the cause of both his own, and reconcile and unite the two in himself. It is useless to inquire what other particular form the aspiration of Job may have taken, or how far he understood and meant what he said; but here are his words, and this is what they must mean, and it is for us to adore the wisdom by which they were taught accurately to correspond with what we know has been given to us by God. We know that a daysman has laid his hand upon us both; and while we see that this is what Job wanted, we cannot but see more plainly that this is what we want. It is to be observed that this word daysman, or judge, is immediately connected with the Scripture phrase, "the **day** of the Lord," and Paul's words, "the **day** shall declare it" (I Cor. 3:13).

10

In this chapter Job reaches the climax of his complaint, which leaves him in the land of thick darkness, where the light is as darkness.

(2) I will say unto God ... —This is a model of prayer for all, combining the prayer of the publican (Luke 18:13), and a prayer for that light for which we long so earnestly in times of affliction and darkness.

(10) Poured me out as milk.—An allusion to the embryo. (See Ps. 139:13-16.)

(13) These things hast thou hid in thine heart.—Job implies that his sense of God's goodness is embittered by the thought that while showing him such kindness, He had in reserve for him the trials and sorrows under which he was then laboring: while showering good upon him, He intended eventually to overwhelm him with affliction. This was the purpose He had hidden in His heart.

(16) For it increaseth.—This verse is obscure. Some understand it thus: "But is it so glorious a thing that Thou shouldst hunt me like a fierce lion, and then again show Thyself mysterious and wonderful toward me? hunting me like a lion, and yet hiding alike Thy person and Thy motive from me?"

(17) Thou renewest thy witnesses against me.—Some understand this of the sores on Job's person, which his friends regarded as witnesses—proofs of his guilt; but it seems more probable that the figure is forensic. The sublimity of this indictment against God is only equalled by the sense of terrific awe with which one reads it. The language is Job's, and so far has the sanction of Holy

Writ; but we may surely learn from it the condescension as well as the loving-kindness of the Most High.

(20) Cease then, and let me alone.—In reading this reply of Job's, one cannot but feel that it moves upon the very verge of blasphemy, and is only redeemed from it by its pervading reverence and deep undertone of faith. Job never gives up his faith in God, though, like Jacob, he wrestles with Him in the dark, and the issue shows that God is not displeased with such an unburdening of the soul that keeps close to the straight line of truth, which is, after all, one of the many manifestations of God.

11

(1) Zophar, the third of Job's friends, has a clearly defined character, distinct from that of the others; he is the ordinary and commonplace moral man, who expresses the thoughts and instincts of the many. Eliphaz was the poet and spiritual man, who sees visions and dreams dreams; Bildad was the man who rested on authority and appealed to tradition; Zophar is the man of worldly wisdom and common sense. In some respects he is the most offensive of the three. He is astonished that Job has not been silenced by the replies of the other two, and thinks he can do no less than help to silence him. Thus he at once begins with "a multitude of words," and "full of talk," and "lies," and "mockery."

(4) Clean in thine eyes.—Zophar, who professes superior wisdom, desires that God would show Job how far short he falls of it; and were He to do this, Job would find to his dismay that God still credited him part of the penalty due to him.

(10) If he cut off.—"If, then," says Zophar, "God acteth thus, or if He delivers up a man into the hands of his enemies, or if He calls together a multitude against him— alluding apparently to 11:11, 12, and 10:17— then who can turn Him back from His intent?" adopting Job's own question at 11:10: "Who can hinder Him?" Some understand the three terms forensically: "if He arrest, and imprison, and hold assize"; but it is probable that Job's own statements are alluded to.

(12) For vain man would be wise, etc., is extremely difficult, because it is hard to distinguish subject and predicate. Whether it means that if God did not thus conceal His observation of human actions, the very fool and the most obstinate would become instructed and disciplined, whereas now they are allowed to go on in their folly and obstinacy; or whether, again, it is meant that by reason of the divine discipline the hollow-hearted man is disciplined, and the wild ass colt is born a man and humanized, it is hard to decide. The uncertainty in part arises from our not knowing the exact meaning of the first verb: whether it is to get understanding or to be deprived of it—for either is possible. One point is pretty clear, that by the wild ass's colt Zophar means Job. However, he suggests that if he will become something better and wiser, and will put away his secret sin, which he is convinced must cling to him, then he shall again know prosperity and be established in it.

(17) Thine age shall be clearer than the noonday.—Rather, "there shall arise for thee a lifetime brighter than the noonday; thou shalt soar on high; thou shalt be like the morning," which is conceived of as having wings (Ps. 139:9). (Comp. Mal. 4:2, of the "Sun of Righteousness.")

(18) Thou shalt dig about thee.—Rather, "thou shalt look around or search about thee, and see that thou canst lie down in safety." (Comp. Josh. 2:4, and Job 39:29.)

(20) As the giving up of the ghost.—Omit the "as" of comparison. Thus ends the first part of this mighty argument, the first division of this grand poem.

12

(1) And Job answered and said.—Each of the friends has now supplied his quota, and Job proceeds to reply to the third, showing that he is far more conversant with the wisdom and majesty of God than they are themselves, though in their own esteem they alone are wise.

(5) Is as a lamp despised in the thought of him that is at ease.—The meaning is that there is contempt for calamity in the thoughts of him that is at ease; it is ready at hand for them who are tottering with their feet.

(9) Who knoweth not in all these that the hand of the Lord hath wrought this?—This is the only place in the dialogue parts of Job in which the sacred name of Jehovah is found, and Job's use of the word in such a context is the clearest evidence of the super-

ior knowledge that he claims. No one of his friends makes use of the name; but Job uses it here, and shows thereby his knowledge of the covenant name.

(11) Doth not the ear try words?—Bildad had appealed to the wisdom of authority and tradition, but Job reminds him that it is given to the wise man not to accept everything he has received, but to discriminate. He allows that wisdom is the prerogative of age, but reminds him that the Ancient of Days must needs be wise indeed.

(14) Behold, he breaketh down ... —God has equal power over the moral and physical world.

(18) He looseth the bond of kings.—He looses the confederacy of kings, by which they bind themselves together, and girds them to fight against each other. Some understand it of the girdle of servitude in contrast to the girdle of state.

(19) He leadeth princes.—The latter part of this chapter seems to re-echo the sentiments of Eliphaz in 5:11-16. Eliphaz is quite sure he possesses the key to the interpretation of the ways of Providence. Job fears that his ignorance is so profound as to amount almost to sheer hopelessness. It is to be observed, however, that Job's breadth of view far exceeds that of Eliphaz, inasmuch as the latter generalizes vaguely, while Job declares that not men, but nations, are the subjects of God's guiding providence.

(23) He increaseth the nations, and destroyeth them.—Zophar was prepared, at all events, to imply that the dealings of God were intelligible, and approved themselves to the conceptions of human equity. Job, on the other hand, declared that they were inscrutable, and, consequently, from their very darkness, suggested the necessity for faith. His teaching here may seem to savour of fatalism, but that is simply because he deals only with one side of the problem. Had he found occasion, he would have stated with equal force the correlative truth of the absolute responsibility of man, even though but as clay in the hands of the potter; for, in fact, were it not so, how then should God judge the world? Into the mazes of this problem Job does not enter, being concerned with other questions and mysteries. Job's conception, therefore, of the righteous government of God as far transcended that of his friends as their estimate of his righteousness fell short of the truth. Justly, therefore, he exclaims, "I am not inferior unto you."

13

(2) I am not inferior unto you.—"I fall not short of you." But it is this sense of the inscrutableness of God's dealings that makes him long to come face to face with God, and to reason with Him on the first principles of His action.

(4) Ye are forgers of lies.—He now retorts upon his friends in terms not more deferential than their own. He feels that they have failed miserably and utterly to understand him.

(7) Will ye speak wickedly for God?—And now, in these verses, he gives utterance to a sublime truth, which shows how truly he had risen to the true conception of God, for he declares that He, who is no respecter of persons, desires to have no favor shown to Himself, and that in seeking to show favor they will greatly damage their own cause, for He is a God of truth, and by Him words as well as actions are weighed, and therefore nothing that is not true can stand any one in stead with Him.

(13) Hold your peace.—He now prepares to make a declaration like the memorable one in chap. 19. He resolves at all hazards to face God in judgment.

(15) Though he slay me, yet will I trust in him.—This rendering is almost proverbial; but, to say the least, its accuracy is very doubtful, for the better reading does not warrant it, but runs thus: "Behold He will slay me. I have no hope; yet will I maintain my ways before Him." It is true we thus lose a beautiful and familiar resolve; but the expression of living trust is not less vivid. For though there is, as there can be, no gleam of hope for victory in this conflict, yet, notwithstanding, Job will not forego his conviction of integrity; for the voice of conscience is the voice of God, and if he knows himself to be innocent, he would belie and dishonor God as well as himself in renouncing his innocence.

(16) He also shall be my salvation.—Comp. Ps. 27:1, etc. It is characteristic of Job that, living, as he probably did, outside the pale of Israel, he nevertheless shared the faith and knowledge of God's chosen people; and this cannot be said of any other nation, nor does any literature give evidence of it. Indeed, it is this which most markedly distinguishes Job from his friends, in that he can and does trust God unreservedly, in spite of all adverse circumstances, overwhelming as they were; while his friends are ignorant of the great central

fact that He is Himself the sinner's hope, and are content to rest only upon vague and bald generalities. It is because, therefore, he has said, and can say, "He is and will be my salvation," that he can also say, "I know that I shall be justified, that I am righteous, because I trust in Him" (Gen. 15:6). We do not, in thus speaking, import the Gospel into Job, but exhibit that in Job which had already been manifest in Abraham, and probably recorded of him.

(19) If I hold my tongue, I shall give up the ghost.—A marvelous confession, equivalent to, "If I give up my faith in Him who is my salvation, and my personal innocence, which goes hand-in-hand therewith, I shall perish. To give up my innocence is to give up Him in whom I hold my innocence, and in whom I live."

(21) Withdraw thine hand far from me.—That is, "Cease to torture me bodily, and to terrify me mentally; let me at least have freedom from physical pain and the undue apprehension of Thy terrors."

14

(1) Man that is born of a woman is of few days.—He now takes occasion to expand on the miserable estate of man generally, rising from the particular instance in himself to the common lot of the race. It is not improbable that these words should be connected with the last of the former chapter. After having resolved to come into judgment with God, he pictures to himself the miserable creature with whom God will have to contend if He contends with **him**.

(6) Accomplish.—Rather, "have pleasure in; rejoice at the day when his wages are paid him." Job had used the same image before (7:2). He now proceeds to enlarge on the mortality of man, comparing man, as is so often done in all literature, to the vegetation of the earth (Isa. 40:7; 65:22); with this difference, however—that a tree will sprout again when it is cut down, but even a strong man succumbs to death.

(11) As the waters fail from the sea.—The comparison that is implied, but not expressed, is one of contrariety. The waters will have failed from the sea, and the rivers will have wasted and become dry, and yet the man who hath lain down (in death) will not arise: i.e., before that will happen, the sea will fail and the great rivers become dry. There is no hope of any future life, still less of any resurrection here; but neither can we regard the language as involving an absolute denial of it. What Job says is equally true in full view of the life to come and of the resurrection; indeed, there seems to glimmer the hope of an ardent though unexpressed longing, through the very language that is used. At all events, the statement uttered so confidently is not proof against the inevitable doubt involved in verse 14.

(14) If a man die, shall he live again?—Why ask the question if it were absolutely certain that he would not? "All the days of my warfare—i.e., as long as I live—I will hope, till my change or transition from life to death comes, that Thou shalt call and I shall answer Thee, that Thou wilt long for the work of Thine hands."

(16) For now thou numberest my steps: dost thou not watch over my sin?—Persecution so persistent would wear out the strongest, even as the mountain and the rock are gradually worn away. How much more then must I be the subject of decay?

15

Eliphaz returns to the argument with the repetition of what he and his friends have said before. He reproaches Job, professes a high idea of the majesty and righteousness of God, and reiterates the assertion that the wicked man, by the sure retribution of the divine Providence, receives the reward of his iniquity in this world. In verse 16 he uses strong general language, which is probably meant to reflect on Job, and the inference is suggested that Job himself, because so sorely chastened, must be wicked.

(2) Should a wise man utter vain knowledge ... —Job, therefore, is not wise, and his words have been vain and windy.

(3) Should he reason with unprofitable talk?—Nay, his arguments, though pretentious and apparently obscure, are unprofitable, and can do no good.

(4) Yea, thou castest off fear.—The tendency also of Job has been to encourage a kind of fatalism (e.g., 12:16-25), and therefore to check the offering of prayer to God, besides setting an example which, if followed, as from Job's position it was likely to be, would lead to murmuring and blasphemy.

(14) What is man?—This is the ceaseless burden. (See 4:17; 9:2; 14:4; etc.)

(16) How much more abominable and filthy is man ... —This strong language,

thus couched in general terms, is doubtless intended to reflect on Job, otherwise it would not need to have been so strong.

(18) Which wise men have told from their fathers.—Here Eliphaz adopts the language of Bildad (8:8), appealing both to his own experience and that of universal tradition in an age prior to civil commotion and foreign disturbance.

(20) Travaileth with pain.—This and the following verses contain the result of this experience. A sound of terror is forever in his ears lest the spoiler should come upon him in his prosperity—he always seems to dread his war-swoop. And this condition of darkness within, which contrasts so painfully with his outward prosperity, he sees no escape from; he is always in fear of a sword hanging over him, like Damocles.

(28) Which are ready to become heaps.—This completes the description of the haughty tyrant. He dwelt in cities that are to be desolate, or that are desolate, which are ready to become heaps.

(30) He shall not depart out of darkness.—"When he expires it shall be the end of him; he shall leave nothing permanent that is destined to last."

(32) It shall be accomplished.—That is, paid in full before its time.

The remainder of this chapter calls for little explanation. In it the speaker only repeats the familiar proverb that the wicked are punished in life, and therefore, by implication, the good rewarded: a maxim which fails utterly in the face of afflictions like those of Job, unless, as his friends insinuated, he was one of the wicked. After stating the doom of the ungodly, Eliphaz, in the last verse, sums up the character of those he has been denouncing. Not only are they evil in themselves, but they hatch evil; but it is evil that recoils on themselves.

16

(1) Then Job answered.—Job, in replying, ceases to continue the argument, which he finds useless; but, after complaining of the way his friends have conducted it, and contrasting the way in which they have treated him with that in which he would treat them were they in his case, he proceeds again to enlarge upon his condition, and makes a touching appeal to heaven, which prepares us for the more complete confession in chap. 19. He ends by declaring that his case is desperate.

(7) But now he hath made me weary.—He turns again, in his passionate lament, to God, whom he alternately speaks of in the third person and addresses in the second. "Thou hast made desolate all my company," by destroying all his children and alienating the hearts of his friends.

(8) Witness against me.—As in 10:17. The wrinkles in his body, caused by the disease, were a witness against him; and certainly, in the eyes of his friends, they furnished unquestionable proof of his guilt.

(9) He teareth me in his wrath.—Terrible as the language is that Job has used against God, he seems here almost to exceed it, for he calls Him his adversary. It is hardly possible not to understand the expression of God, for though he immediately speaks of his friends, yet just afterward he openly mentions God.

(11) The ungodly and **the wicked** are the terms he retorts upon his friends, and they have certainly earned them.

(12) I was at ease.—A highly poetical passage, in which Job becomes, as it were, a St. Sebastian for the arrows of God. It is hardly possible to conceive a more vivid picture of his desolate condition under the persecuting hand of the Almighty.

(15) I have sewed sackcloth upon my skin.—Referring, probably, to the state of his skin, which had become hard and rugged as sackcloth. As the second half of the verse must be figurative, there seems to be no reason to understand the first half otherwise.

(19) My witness is in heaven.—It is very important to note passages such as these, because they help us to understand, and serve to illustrate, the famous confession in chap. 19. This is surely a wonderful declaration for a man in the position of Job. What can the believer, in the full light of the gospel revelation, say more, with the knowledge of One in heaven ever making intercession for him? And yet Job's faith had risen to such a height as this, and had grasped such a hope as this. In no other book of the Bible is there such a picture of faith clinging to the all-just God for justification as in the Book of Job.

(20) My friends scorn me.—Or, as an apostrophe, "Ye my scorners who profess and ought to be my friends: mine eye poureth out tears unto God that one might plead for man with God as the son of man pleadeth for his neighbor"—this is what he has already longed for in 9:33.

(22) When a few years are come.—It is strange to find Job speaking, in his condition, of **years**, but so, for that matter, is it to find a man so sorely tormented as he was indulging in so long an argument. Perhaps this shows us that the narrative of Job is intended to be an ideal only, setting forth the low estate of sin-stricken humanity: this is only a suggestion; no weight is assigned to it more than it may chance to claim. Perhaps, however, these words are spoken by Job in contemplation of his condition as a **dying** man, even had he not been so afflicted.

17

(3) Lay down now . . . —i.e., "Give now a pledge; be surety for me with Thyself." He has declared that he has a witness in the heavens, but he desires some present token of the vindication to come of which he is confident, and so he asks God to give him such a pledge. This is virtually the same prayer that we find Hezekiah using (Isa. 38:14). Job felt that his only hope of this fulfillment or expiation of non-fulfillment lay with God Himself: that same God who had put this sense of obligation within him; therefore he says, "Be surety for me with Thyself." He longed for the daysman who should lay his hand upon both him and God; he now longs for that surety with God that God alone can give. The surety must be divine if his witness is in the heavens; it must be the witness of God to God Himself. In this wonderful way does the language of Job fit in with all that we have since and elsewhere learned of the persons in the Godhead.

Who is he that will strike hands with me?—This was the method of becoming surety; but he knows that there is no one among his friends who will do this, or that could do it if he would (Comp. Ps. 49:7.)

(5) He that speaketh flattery to his friends.—Any one who would undertake to be surety for me would naturally expect my friends to share the responsibility; but so far from this, the eyes of his sons will fail in looking for it; they would never see it.

(6) He (i.e., God) **hath made me also a byword of the people; and aforetime I was as a tabret.**—Or, "I am become as a tabret, or drum openly," i.e., a signal of warning. "My case will be fraught with warning for others." But some render it, "I am become an open abhorrence, or one in whose face they spit." The general meaning is perfectly clear, though the way it may be expressed varies.

(10) But as for you all, do ye return.— This is probably said with irony. "Come again and renew the argument between us; but I shall not be able to find a wise man among you. I am willing to listen to your argument, but I am confident as to the result of it."

(12) They change the night into day.— Comp. 11:17. So little did his friends enter into his case that they wanted him to believe that his night of trial was the reverse of darkness, and that there was light at hand. This was to him only the more painful mockery, because of its contrast to his felt condition. He, on the contrary, says that his only hope is in the grave.

18

(1) How long?—Bildad begins very much as Job himself had done (chap. 16).

(3) Wherefore are we counted as beasts.— Referring to Job's words (13:4, etc.; 16:2, etc.). In this chapter there is a marked increase in his harshness and violence. It has, however, a certain resemblance to chap. 8, inasmuch as Bildad works out a simile here, as he did there; and in verse 16 the two similes touch.

(4) He teareth himself in his anger.—As Eliphaz had charged Job (15:4) with the evil tendencies of his speeches, so Bildad here compares him to a maniac, and assumes that the effect of his teaching will be to banish God from the earth, and remove the strength and hope of man. The last clause is a direct quotation from Job in 14:18; it looks, therefore, very much like a wilful perversion of Job's words, for it is clear that he used them differently.

(8) He is cast into a net.—Job had compared himself to one hunted by the Almighty (10:16), and Bildad here describes the evil man as snared in a net, but it is one for which he has no one to thank but himself. It is his own pit he falls into; the insinuation being that Job is likewise responsible for his calamities, which are the punishment of his sin. It is to be observed that in this and the following verses the speaker heaps together every word he can find descriptive of the art of snaring.

(13) The strength of his skin.—This verse should probably be rendered, "It shall devour the members of his body, even the

first-born of death shall devour his members"; and by the "first-born of death" is probably to be understood some wasting disease such as Job's, the phrase being so used as a euphemism.

(14) The king of terrors.—Perhaps the most remarkable personification of unseen forces to be found in the Bible.

(15) It shall dwell in his tabernacle.— "Which is none of his" may hint that it had been violently taken from some one else. "Brimstone shall be scattered on his dwelling" is probably an allusion to the cities of the plain (Gen. 19).

(16) His roots shall be dried up.—With tacit allusion to what he had said in 8:12, and also to the destruction of Job's own offspring, which had already been accomplished.

(17) His remembrance shall perish.—This is the doom which above all others is dreaded by the modern roamers of the desert. (Comp. also Jer. 35:19.)

(20) Shall be astonied at his day.—That is, his doom, or destiny. He shall stand forth as a warning and monument to all.

(21) Dwellings of the wicked.—That is to say, of the wicked man. As Bildad designedly uses the singular here, there can be little doubt that he as designedly intended this terrible and cruel picture to represent Job himself.

19

(2) How long?—Job begins as Bildad himself had begun in both cases. His last speech had been offensive and unfeeling. Moreover, Bildad had infused a kind of personal malice into his charges, which Job felt most keenly.

(6) Know now that God hath overthrown me.—Bildad had spoken a great deal about the wicked being snared by his own sin, and now Job, without actually quoting his words—for he uses a word for "net" that Bildad had not used—speaks to their substance. It is God who has taken him in His net and compassed him about with it. This is the assertion he has made before (16:7; 13:27; etc.).

(7) Behold, I cry out of wrong.—The description he now gives of himself as persecuted and forsaken by God is necessary to enhance the value of the confession he is about to make. Severely has God dealt with him, but that severity of dealing has only drawn him nearer to God and made him trust the more. He groups together a rich variety of figures to express his desolate condition. He is suffering assault, and can get no protection or redress; he is imprisoned on every side, his hope is torn up like the tree of which he had before spoken (14:7).

(13) He hath put my brethren far from me.—The psalmist has apparently copied this in Ps. 88:8. The sense of human desertion is hardly less terrible than that of being forsaken by God, and this has been added to him. It is not easy to read these sad complaints of Job without seeing how fitly they apply to the sorrows of the Man of sorrows. It shows how completely Christ entered into the heart of human suffering, in that the deepest expressions of suffering inevitably remind us of Him, whether those expressions are met with in the Book of Job, in the Psalms of David, or in the Lamentations of Jeremiah.

(20) My bone cleaveth to my skin and to my flesh in one indistinguishable mass, and I have escaped with the skin of my teeth, because the teeth have no skin, or, as others explain, because the teeth have fallen out. This expression, which is by no means clear in the context, has passed into a proverb expressive of a narrow escape—a meaning which can only by inference be obtained from this place in Job.

(23) Oh that my words were now written!—Since the three verses, 25-27, are manifestly more emphatic than any he has yet spoken, though they do not stand quite alone, there is no reason why it should not be especially these very words which he desires more than any others to have recorded.

Oh that they were printed.—This points us to primitive time, when writing materials and the use of writing involved more or less of engraving, as, for instance, in later times was the case with tablets of wax.

(25) For I know that my redeemer liveth.—We must carefully note all the passages which lead up to this one. First, we must bear in mind that Bildad (18:17-20) had threatened Job with the extinction of his name and memory, so he now appeals to the verdict of futurity, and with what success we ourselves who read and repeat and discuss his words are witnesses. Then in Job's own speeches we have, as early as 9:32-35, his longing for a daysman to come between himself and God. Then in 10:7 and 13:15-19, he emphatically declares his inno-

cence, and appeals to God as conscious of it. In 16:19 he affirms that his witness is in the high heavens; in verse 21 of the same chapter he longs for an advocate to plead his cause. In 17:3 he calls upon God to be surety for him. Therefore he has already recognized God as his judge, his umpire, his advocate, his witness, and surety, and in some cases by formal confession of the fact, in others by earnest longing after and aspirations for someone to act in that capacity. Here, then, he goes a step further in expression, if not by implication, and declares his knowledge that he has a Goel or Redeemer. This goel was the name given to the next of kin whose duty it was to redeem, ransom, or avenge one who had fallen into debt or bondage, or had been slain in a family feud. The various and conditional functions, then, of this Goel, Job is assured, God will take upon Himself for him; He will avenge his quarrel (comp. Ps. 35:1, 23), He will be surety for him. He will vindicate him before men and before God Himself; He will do for him what none of his professed friends would undertake to do. And as to this matter, he has not the slightest doubt: he states most emphatically that he himself **knows** that this Goel liveth. Now, this alone is assuredly a marvelous confession. It states the reality and eternity of God. It is faith in the I am.

(26) And though after my skin.—This is referring, probably, in the first instance, to his present personal faith, notwithstanding the corruption produced by his disease. "I can and do still see God, whom I know as my Redeemer"; but perhaps more probably put in contrast to this present knowledge as implying something yet to come, when the Redeemer stands at the last upon the earth, which also seems to be yet further expressed in the following verse.

(27) My reins be consumed within me.—i.e., with longing to see Him; literally, "my reins are consumed in my bosom." The words "in my flesh" may mean "from my flesh," or, "without my flesh." Taken in the former sense and applied to the future, it is hard not to recognize in them, at the least, some dim conception of a resurrection.

Whom I shall see for myself.—The words "see for myself" may mean "see on my side," i.e., as my Judge and Avenger; or they may be the personal intensifying of the conviction which seems confirmed by the words, "and not a stranger." Do Job's words then teach the doctrine of the resurrection? Possibly not directly, but they express the firm conviction of that faith of which the resurrection is the only natural justification; they express a living trust in a living personal God, who, if He is to come into contact with man, cannot suffer His Holy One to see corruption nor leave His soul in hell. How far Job believed in the resurrection of the flesh hereafter, he certainly believed there was life out of death and through death here; and no man can believe in a living God and not believe that He must and will triumph over death.

(28) Seeing the root of the matter.—It seems preferable to render, "For ye say, What is a persecuted man to Him (why should He persecute any man without cause?), and therefore the root of the matter (i.e., the cause of the afflictions) is, i.e., must be found in me."

(29) Be ye afraid ... —Job threatens his friends with that suitable punishment of which they regarded him as a conspicuous example.

20

(1) Then answered Zophar.—Zophar retorts with yet greater vehemence than before, and assumes a more ornate and elaborate style, still reiterating the former burden of the speedy doom of the wicked man.

(3) The spirit of my understanding causeth me to answer.—Or, more literally, "Out of my understanding my spirit answereth me," or, "causeth me to answer." He professes to be moved by an impulse within, which he cannot but obey.

(5) The triumphing of the wicked is short. —He affirms that the destruction of the wicked is not only certain, but speedy. (Comp. Ps. 103:16 and Job 7:8, 10.)

(12) Though wickedness be sweet in his mouth.—He draws a picture of the wicked man after the pattern of a gourmand or glutton, which, if it were intended to apply to Job, was a fresh instance of heartless cruelty, as well as of an entire want of discernment of character, and of unfitness for the office of judge he was so ready to assume. It is possible that the reproach here aimed at Job was that of inordinate love of riches, which Zophar extracts from the bare fact of his having been a wealthy man.

(17) The brooks of honey and butter.— He uses language which might lead one to suppose he was familiar with the promise of Canaan, except that, as the phrase is not precisely identical, it may perhaps rather

show a community of proverbial language, and that the "land flowing with milk and honey" may have been an expression in use, and not one original with the Pentateuch.

(19) Because he hath oppressed and hath forsaken ... —For these insinuations there was not a vestige of ground, but Job formally refutes them in chap. 31.

(25) Yea, ... terrors are upon him.—Even when he has escaped a second and a third calamity, terrors shall still be upon him. This was all perfectly true in a sense, yea, even a truism, but it was utterly false in its application to Job himself.

(27) The heaven shall reveal his iniquity.— All nature shall combine to bring about his ruin, which is, in fact, decreed by God. We here take leave of Zophar, who does not reply again; he has exhausted himself, notwithstanding verse 2.

21

(1) But Job answered.—Having, in chap. 19, declared his belief in a retribution to come, Job now proceeds to traverse more directly Zophar's last contention, and to show that even in this life there is not the retribution which he maintained there was.

(4) Is my complaint to man?—"It is not to man that I complain. I do not ask for your sympathy, and, therefore, why should ye resent an offense that is not given? If, however, I did ask it, might not my spirit with good reason be impatient? But, on the contrary, my complaint is to God; and, concerning the ways of God, I venture to ask why it is that His justice is so tardy; and this is a problem which when I remember it I am troubled, and horror taketh hold on my flesh, so difficult and arduous is it."

(8) Their seed is established in their sight.—Not only are they mighty in power themselves, but they leave their power to their children after them (comp. Ps. 17:14). This contradicts what Eliphaz had said (15:34), what Bildad had said (18:19), and what Zophar had said (20:10).

(13) In a moment.—They go down to death without being made to feel the lingering tortures that Job had to undergo.

(16) Lo, their good (i.e., their prosperity) **is not in their own hand.**—And that constitutes the mystery of it, for it is God who gives it to them.

(17) How oft is the candle of the wicked put out?—This and the following verse are either a concession on the part of Job, as much as to say, "I admit that it is as you say with the wicked"; or else they should be read interrogatively, "How often is it that we do see this?"

(23) One dieth.—Job enlarges on the inequality of human fate, showing that death is the only equalizer.

(26) They shall lie down alike in the dust.—Not only, therefore, is the inequality of their life a stumbling block, but so also is the equality which obliterates all distinction between them in death.

(28) Of the prince—i.e., of the generous, virtuous, princely man?—the antithesis of the wicked man.

(30-33) That the wicked ... —These verses contain the result of their experience.

(33) The clods of the valley shall be sweet unto him.—Death is robbed of its repulsiveness and horror, seeing that all will be glad to join in his funeral procession, and after him all men will draw (in endless procession), and before him they will be without number.

22

(1) Then Eliphaz ... answered—Eliphaz proceeds to reply in a far more exaggerated and offensive tone than he has yet adopted, accusing Job of definite and specific crimes. He begins by asserting that the judgment of God cannot be other than disinterested, that if, therefore, He rewards or punishes, there cannot be anything personal in it.

(5) Is not thy wickedness great?—This was mere conjecture and surmise, arising simply from a false assumption: namely, that a just God can only punish the wicked, and that therefore those must be wicked whom He punishes.

(6) Thou hast taken a pledge from thy brother.—These specific charges, false as they were, show the depth to which Eliphaz had sunk.

(8) But as for the mighty man.—By the "mighty and the honourable" man is probably meant Job.

(10, 11) Snares ... about thee.—"God is too great to take note of the affairs of men, their sin or their good deeds. He is so far off that He cannot see what goes on in the earth, for His dwelling-place is in heaven." Eliphaz attributes to Job the kind of sentiments that he had himself attributed to the wicked man in 21:14, etc.

(16) Which were cut down out of time.— It is generally supposed that there is an allusion here to the history of the Flood; if so, the reference is of course important in its bearing on the age of that record, since the book of Job can hardly fail to be very old itself.

(17) Which said unto God, Depart from us.—Here again he attributes to Job the thoughts he had ascribed to the wicked (20:14, 15).

(18) Yet he filled their houses.—The bitterness of his irony now reaches its climax in that he adopts the formula of repudiation Job had himself used (14:16).

(19) The righteous see it.—That is, "the destruction of the wicked, as in the days of Noah."

(20) Whereas our substance ... —These are probably the words of the righteous and the innocent: "Surely they that did rise up against us are cut off, and the remnant of them the fire hath consumed."

(22) The law from his mouth.—It would be highly interesting to know whether by this law (Torah), the Law, the Torah, was in any way alluded to. One is naturally disposed to think that since Job seems to be the one Gentile book of the Old Testament, the one book in which the literature of Israel touches the world at large, it must, therefore, be prior to the Law, or else have been written in independence and ignorance of it. The former seems by far the more reasonable supposition, and certainly the life depicted appears to be that of the patriarchal times before the giving of the Law. And yet, on the other hand, it is hard to know what could be meant by "His words" prior to the Mosaic Revelation, unless, indeed, the expression is a witness to the consciousness of that inner revelation of the voice of God in the conscience which the holy in all ages have never lacked.

(23) Thou shalt put away iniquity.—All this implies the imputation of apostasy and iniquity to Job.

(24) The gold of Ophir.—And, moreover, that the wealth for which he was so famous among the children of the East was the accumulation of iniquity and wrongdoing. The situation of Ophir has always been a matter of dispute. Josephus placed it in India (**Antt.** vii. 6, §4); others suppose it to have been an Indian colony in Southern Arabia, and others have placed it on the east coast of Africa.

(25) The Almighty shall be thy defence.— Rather, "And the Almighty shall be thy treasure, and precious silver unto thee."

(28) Thou shalt also decree a thing.—As,

387

for instance, in the memorable case of Abraham's intercession for Sodom, to which there is not improbably an allusion here.

(30) He shall deliver the island of the innocent is undoubtedly "He shall deliver him that is not innocent." It is remarkable that this, which is the last word of Eliphaz, has in it the significance of a prophecy, for it is exactly thus that the history of Job closes; and Eliphaz himself exemplified his own promise in being indebted to Job for the act of intercession by which he was pardoned, together with his friends (42:8, 9).

23

(1) Then Job answered.—Job replies to the insinuations of Eliphaz with the earnest longing after God and the assertion of his own innocence; while in the twenty-fourth chapter he laments that his own case is but one of many, and that multitudes suffer from the oppression of man unavenged, as he suffers from the stroke of God.

(3) Oh that I knew where I might find him.—The piteous complaint of a man who feels that God is with him for chastisement, but not for healing.

(7) There the righteous might dispute.— He has learned this marvelous truth, which the Gospel has so effectually brought to light, that it is God the Saviour who is Himself the refuge from God the Judge (John 12:47); and then, in the solemn conviction of His presence, he makes use of the most sublime language expressive of it, being assured, though He may hide Himself with the express purpose of not interfering in his cause, yet that all things work together for good to them that love Him (Rom. 8:28), and that when his time of trial is over, he himself will come forth like gold. Job's case teaches us that if an innocent man is falsely accused, God's honour is vindicated and maintained by his holding fast his conviction of innocence rather than by his yielding to the pressure of adversity and owning to sins he has not committed, or relaxing his hold on innocence by yielding to irritability.

(13) He is in one mind.—Job declares His unchangeable purpose.

(15) Therefore am I troubled at his presence.—The victim of an ever-present paradox and dilemma; afraid of God, yet longing to see Him; conscious of His presence, yet unable to find Him; assured of His absolute justice, and yet convinced of his own suffering innocence. His history, in fact, to the Old World was what the Gospel is to the New: the exhibition of a perfectly righteous man, yet made perfect through suffering. It was therefore an effort at the solution of the problem of the reconciliation of the inequality of life with the justice of God.

24

(1) Why, seeing times are not hidden.— Job, in this chapter, gives utterance to this perplexity, as it arises, not from his own case only, but from a survey of God's dealings with the world generally. Even those who love and serve God are as perplexed about His principles of government as those who know Him not.

(2) Some remove the landmarks.—Now follows a description of the wrongdoings of various classes of men.

(3) They drive away the ass.—He first describes the oppression of the country, and then that of the city (verse 12). The writer and the speaker seem to have been familiar with some such abject and servile race, who haunted the desert and suffered at the hands of the more powerful tribes.

(13) They are of those that rebel against the light.—A very remarkable expression, which seems to anticipate the teaching of John (1:9; etc.).

(14) With the light.—The mention of light as a moral essence suggests its physical analogue, so that by the contrast of the one with the violence done to the other, the moral turpitude of the wrongdoing is heightened. It seems impossible to interpret the light in the former case (verse 13) otherwise than morally, and if so, the mention of the "ways thereof" and the "paths thereof" is very remarkable. The order in which these crimes of murder, adultery, and theft are mentioned according, as it does, with that in the Decalogue, is, at all events, suggestive of acquaintance with it.

(18) He beholdeth not.—Rather, "he"— that is, each of them—"turneth not the way of the vineyards," which is frequented and cultivated, but chooseth rather lone, desolate, solitary, and rugged paths.

(19) So doth the grave those which have sinned.—Job had already spoken of the sudden death of the wicked as a blessing (9:23; 21:13), as compared with the lingering torture he himself was called upon to undergo.

(20) The womb shall forget him.—Some understand this verse as expressing what **ought** rather to be the doom of the wicked. "His own mother **should** forget him."

(22) He draweth also the mighty.—He now appears to revert to his former line, and describes another case—that, namely, of a great tyrant who draws others by his influence and example to the same courses.

(25) And if it be not so now.—Job also has his facts, as ready and as incontrovertible as those of his friends, and yet irreconcilable with theirs.

25

Bildad attempts no formal reply to Job's statements; he merely falls back upon the position twice assumed by Eliphaz before (4:17-21 and 5:14-16), and twice allowed also by Job (14:4)—the impossibility of man being just with God—and therefore implies the impiety of Job in maintaining his righteousness before God. God, he says, is almighty, infinite, and absolute. How can any man contend with Him, or claim to be pure in His sight? This is the final speech of the friends. Bildad no longer accuses Job; he practically owns himself and his companions worsted in argument, seeing that he attempts no reply, but reiterates truisms that are independent of the special matter in hand. Job, in 23:3-12, had spoken of his longing for the divine judgment; so Bildad labors to deprive him of that confidence, as though he would say, "I have nothing to do with your facts, nor can I explain them; but be that as it may, I am certain that you, or any mortal man, cannot be pure in the sight of God."

26

(1) Job answered.—Job himself has virtually said much the same as Bildad (9:2; 14:4), so he makes no further comment on his remarks here, but merely asks how he has helped him thereby, or others like him in a weak and helpless condition.

(4) To whom.—That is, "Is it not to one who had said the same thing himself? Was it not my own breath, my own teaching, that came forth from you?" He then proceeds to show that it is not only the starry heavens that declare the glory of God, but the underworld likewise, and the universe generally.

(7) He stretcheth out the north over the empty place, and hangeth the earth upon nothing.—If these words mean what they seem to—and it is hard to see how they can mean anything else—then they furnish a remarkable instance of anticipation of the discoveries of science. Here we find Job, more than three thousand years ago, describing in language of scientific accuracy the condition of our globe, and holding it forth as a proof of divine power. Some have attempted to explain the latter clause of the destitution caused by famine; but that is precluded by the terms of the first clause.

(10) He hath compassed the waters with bounds.—Rather, "He hath described a circle upon the face of the waters, unto the confines of light and darkness." The phenomenon described is that of the horizon at sea, which is a perfect circle, and which is the limit apparently of light, and beyond which is darkness, for all is invisible.

(11) The pillars of heaven tremble.—The phenomenon of storm and tempest is alluded to.

(12) He divideth the sea.—The word is taken in the two opposite senses of "stirring up" and "calming"; perhaps the latter is more appropriate to the context, which seems to speak of God's mastery over nature.

By his understanding he smiteth through the proud.—Literally, Rahab, which certainly is at times a name for Egypt (see Isa. 51:9, e.g.), and which, if used in that sense here, can only refer to the judgments on Egypt at the Exodus. According to our view of this matter will be the indication derived therefrom of the date of Job.

(13) The crooked serpent.—By this expression is doubtless meant the forked lightning-flash. Others understand by it the constellation of the Northern Dragon, to whose influence storms were ascribed.

(14) These are parts.—We can hear only the faintest whisper of His glory, and cannot understand or endure the full-toned thunder of His majesty. Here, then, is Job's final reply to the arguments of his friends. He shows himself even more conscious than they of the grandeur and holiness of God; but that has in no way rendered his position as a sufferer more intelligible—rather the reverse—nor theirs as defenders of the theory of exact retribution. He cannot understand and they cannot explain; but while he rejects their explanations, he rests secure in his own faith.

27

(1) Job continued his parable.—The remainder of Job's speech—now, for the first time, called his "parable"—consists of his determination not to renounce his righteousness (verses 2-6); his own estimate of the fate of the wicked (verses 7-23); his magnificent estimate of the nature of wisdom (chap. 28); his comparison of his former life (chap. 29) with that of his present experience (chap. 30); his final declaration of his innocent and irreproachable conduct (chap. 31).

(2) As God liveth, who hath taken away my judgment.—Job's faith leads him to see that, though there may be no explanation for his sufferings, yet they are laid upon him by God for purposes of His own, which are veiled from him.

(5) God forbid that I should justify you.—To admit the wickedness with which his friends charged him would have been to justify them—to say that they were right and he was wrong. This he resolves not to do.

(7) Let mine enemy be as the wicked.—While, however, he admits that the wicked is often a prosperous man, he declares that he has no envy for him, but would have only his adversaries to be like him.

(13) This is the portion of a wicked man.—Some have thought that the remainder of this chapter, if not chap. 28 also, constitutes the missing third speech of Zophar, and that the usual words, "Then answered Zophar the Naamathite, and said," have dropped out; but whatever may so be gained in symmetry seems to be lost in dramatic effect. We have seen that Bildad had but little to say, and that was only a few truisms; it is not surprising, therefore, that when it came to Zophar's turn he had nothing more to say, and Job was left virtually master of the field. Job is willing to show how completely he is prepared to accept the facts of his friends, although he will not admit their inferences. He, like them, is quite ready to allow that the prosperity of the wicked must be seeming rather than real, and that it must eventually come to nought.

(19) But he shall not be gathered.—The "gathering" may refer to his wealth. "He openeth his eyes, and it (i.e., his wealth) is not"; or it may mean that as soon as he opens his eyes, hoping to enjoy his riches, he shall be no more, but be suddenly cut off. This sense appears to accord with the following verses.

28

(1) Surely there is a vein for the silver.—In this chapter Job draws out a magnificent contrast between human skill and ingenuity and divine wisdom. The difficulty to the ordinary reader is in not perceiving that the person spoken of in verse 3 is man, and not God. Man possesses and exercises this mastery over nature, but yet is ignorant of wisdom unless God bestows it on him. That Job should say this is but natural, after his painful experience of the want of wisdom in his friends.

(4) The flood breaketh out ... —The very course of rivers is subject to the will and power of man. Those who walk over the place forget that it was once a river, so completely has man obliterated the marks of it.

(5) As for the earth ... —While the plowman and the reaper till and gather the fruits of the earth on its surface, the miner far below maintains perpetual fires, as also does the volcanic mountain, with its fields and vineyards luxuriant and fertile on its sides.

(9) He putteth forth his hand upon the rock.—The process described is that of tunneling and excavating, and that of making canals and lining them with stone; and in the course of such works many precious things would be discovered. The canals and cisterns were made so accurately that they retained the water, and did not even weep or trickle.

(12) But where shall wisdom be found?—With magnificent effect comes this question, after the gigantic achievements of man just recounted; notwithstanding his industry, science, and skill, he is altogether ignorant of true wisdom. Neither his knowledge nor his wealth can make him master of that; nor can he find it where he discovers so many other secret and precious things.

(17) The exchange of it.—Or, according to some, "the attraction of it." There is a general resemblance between this chapter and Prov. 8, and both seem to imply a knowledge of the Mosaic narrative of creation.

(23) God understandeth the way thereof.—

God is the author of wisdom, and His fear is the beginning thereof; so with His infinite knowledge of the universe He cannot but be cognizant of the place and way thereof. The two ideas which Job starts with are man's ignorance of the price and the place of wisdom. Neither he nor nature knows the place of it: neither all living, nor the deep, nor the sea; and as for its price, though man is prepared to give any high price for the costly stones and jewels of the earth, yet all that he has to give is not to be mentioned in comparison with the value of wisdom. Wisdom, however, is to be purchased by the poor, as we may infer from the language of the prophet Isaiah or, at all events, that which ranks with wisdom; and in like manner Christ represented the kingdom of heaven as a pearl of great price, which would demand all that a man had to buy it, and yet he represented the poor as those especially to whom it was preached.

(27) The terms employed with reference to the Lord's knowledge of wisdom are remarkable. They are: (1) seeing, or intuition; (2) declaring or numbering, ratiocination; (3) preparing or establishing, determination; (4) searching out, or investigation. Each of these actions implies the operation of mind, and is so far opposed to the fatality of an impersonal law or the fixed necessity of an inevitable nature.

(28) And unto man he said.—No one can for a moment suppose that this is an historical statement, or is to be treated as being one; but it is nevertheless profoundly and universally true. It is the wisdom of man as man to fear the Lord and to depart from evil; and this is God's primary revelation to man, which virtually underlies and is involved in all others. It is to be observed that the word rendered "the Lord" here is not the four-lettered name Jehovah which was used by Job in 12:9, but the other name for the divine Being (Adonai), which was in later times universally substituted for the name Jehovah by the Jews in reading.

29

(1) Job continued his parable.—In this chapter he recounts wistfully his past happiness. In his case it was indeed not without cause, though in point of fact he was **then** passing through a time of trial which was itself bringing fast on his time of deliverance, and which was to make his name famous throughout the world and in all

time. And in most similar cases we have need to bear in mind the words of Solomon (Eccl. 7:10): "Say not thou, What is the cause that the former days were better than these? for thou dost not enquire wisely concerning this."

(4) In the days of my youth.—Literally, "my autumn": i.e., in the ripeness, maturity of my days. He was then in the depth of winter. Some suppose, however, that as with the ancient and modern Jews the year began with the autumn, it is used much in the same way as we use spring.

The secret of God.—Or, "the counsel of God."

(7) To the gate.—There business was transacted.

(11) When the ear heard me, then it blessed me.—This is a direct negative to the charges of Eliphaz in 22:6; etc. He has felt them too deeply to pass them by in total silence.

(14) I put on righteousness.—Comp. Isa. 61:10; 28:5; 62:3; II Tim. 4:8; James 1:12; I Peter 5:4; I Thess. 2:19. His judgment, the result of his personal righteousness, was as a robe of honor and a crown of glory to him.

It clothed me.—Literally, "it clothed itself with me." First, righteousness is the garment, and then he is the garment to righteousness. (Compare the expressions "Put ye on the Lord Jesus Christ," Rom. 13:14 and II Cor. 5:2, 3, 4, and the Hebrew of Ps. 143:9, where "I flee unto thee to hide me" is, "I have covered myself with thee," or, "have hidden me with thee.") This is the truth of the interchange of sin and righteousness between Christ and the believer. He bears our sins; we are clothed with the robe of his righteousness.

(25) I . . . sat.—It is still the custom among the Jews for mourners to sit upon the ground and for one who wishes to console them to occupy a seat above them. Such is Job's pathetic lamentation over the days that were gone. He is the type and representative of suffering humanity, of man waiting for redemption, but as yet unredeemed. It is in this way that he points us on to Christ, who, Himself the Redeemer, went through all the sorrows of sinful and unredeemed humanity. He is able to describe his former state and all its glory and bliss, while his friends are constrained to listen in silence. They have said their worst, they have aspersed and maligned his character, but they have not silenced him; he is able to make the most complete vindication of all his past life.

30

(1) Whose fathers I would have disdained.—The complaint is that the children of those who were so inferior to him should treat him thus.

(2) Whereto might the strength of their hands profit me, is the description of the fathers; verse 3 seq. describes their children. The people here spoken of seem to have been somewhat similar to those known to the ancients as Troglodytes (Herod. iv. 183, etc.), the inhabitants of caves, who lived an outcast life and had manners and customs of their own. They are desolate with want and famine. They flee into the wilderness on the eve of wasteness and desolation, or when all is dark (yesternight), waste, and desolate. It is evident that Job must have been familiar with a people of this kind, an alien and proscribed race living in the way he mentions.

(7) Among the bushes they brayed.—Herodotus says their language was like the screeching of bats, others say it was like the whistling of birds. This whole description is of the mockers of Job.

(9) And now am I their song.—It is quite appropriate to give to the complaints of Job a Messianic interpretation.

(19) He hath cast me into the mire.—He now turns more directly to God, having in verse 19 turned from man to his own condition—dust and ashes.

(24) Though they cry in his destruction.—This is a very obscure verse. Some render it, "Howbeit, God will not put forth His hand to bring man to death and the grave when there is earnest prayer for them, nor even when in calamity proceeding from Him there is a loud cry for them." That Job should speak of himself as a "ruinous heap" seems strange; neither is it at all clear what "these things" are because of which a cry is uttered. "His destruction" must mean, at all events, "the destruction that cometh from Him."

(25) Did not I weep for him?—Job declares that he has not withheld that sympathy with sorrow and suffering for which he himself has asked in vain.

(26) When I looked for good.—Before, in 3:25, 26, he had spoken as one who did not wish to be the "fool" of prosperity, and so overtaken unawares by calamity, and who therefore looked at things on the darker side; now he speaks as one who hoped for the best, and yet, notwithstanding that hope, was disappointed and deceived.

31

(1) I made a covenant with mine eyes.—Job makes one grand profession of innocence, rehearsing his manner of life from the first; and here he does not content himself with traversing the accusations of his friends, but professes his innocence also of sins less manifest to the observance of others, and affecting the secret conduct and the heart—namely, sensual transgression and idolatry. His object, therefore, is to show his friends that he has really been more upright than their standard demanded or than they supposed him to be, till his affliction made them suspect him; and this uprightness was the consequence of rigid and inflexible adherence to principle, for he made a covenant with his eyes, as the avenues of sinful desires. (Comp. Matt. 5:28.)

(4) Doth not he.—The "He" is emphatic, obviously meaning God. His appeal is to the All-seeing knowledge of God, whom nothing escapes, and who is judge of the hearts and reins (Pss. 7:9; 44:21; Jer. 17:10; 20:12). (Comp. Acts 25:11.)

(7) If my step hath turned out of the way.—The form of the expression is emphatic: the narrow way of strict integrity and righteousness. (Compare the expression applied to the first believers, Acts 9:2— "men of the way.")

(10) Then let my wife grind.—i.e., perform all menial offices, like a slave.

(13) If I did despise.—In 22:8, Eliphaz had insinuated that Job had favored the rich and powerful, but had oppressed and ground down the weak. He now meets this accusation, and affirms that he had regarded his own servants even as brethren, because partakers of a common humanity.

(24) If I have made gold my hope.—He here refers to the admonition of Eliphaz (22:23, 24), and declares that such had not been his practice.

(26) If I beheld the sun.—It is remarkable that the kind of idolatry repudiated by Job is that only of sun and moon worship. He seems to have been ignorant of the more material and degraded kinds.

(29) If I rejoiced at the destruction.—He now proceeds to the realm of the wishes and thoughts, and is, therefore, far more thorough and searching with his own case than his friends had been.

(33) As Adam.—Or, "as man," i.e., commonly does. There may or may not be here some indication of acquaintance with the narrative of Genesis.

(35) Oh that one would hear me!—More correctly, perhaps, "That I had the book or indictment that my adversary hath written; would that I had it in black and white before me, that I might deal with it accordingly, and answer it point to point." Verses 35-37 ought to come after verses 38-40; but the writer's ideas of symmetry and order were not as ours, and this, in some respects, may be more natural, though, strictly speaking, less correct.

(38) Or that the furrows likewise thereof complain.—A strong impersonation to express the consequence of oppression and wrongdoing. It is to be observed that throughout this defense Job has far more than traversed the indictment of his friends. He has shown that he has not only not broken the moral law, as they insinuated, but, much more, has shown himself exemplary in all relations of life, so that, according to the narrator of the history, he was not only one that "feared God and eschewed evil" (1:1), but also was "perfect," i.e., of sincere and consistent conduct and "upright."

32

(1) So these three men ceased.—The next six chapters are taken up with the reply of a fourth person not before mentioned, but who appears to have been present during the discussion, and who is described as Elihu, the son of Barachel the Buzite, of the kindred of Ram. The name appears to mean, "He is my God." The person from whom he was descended seems to have been the son of Nahor, Abraham's brother (Gen. 22:21); and a city of the like name is mentioned in Jer. 25:23. This specification of Elihu serves to show that he was a real, and not an imaginary, personage. The Targum speaks of Elihu as a relative of Abraham. If we are right in putting the life of Elihu so far back, the whole position and surroundings of Job's history become the more probable, because what is told us of Abraham and the patriarchs corresponds with the description and character of Job; and then, also, the traditional Mosaic origin of the Book of Job becomes the more probable.

(4) Now Elihu had waited till Job had spoken.—The line taken by Elihu is an intermediate one, and is neither that of Job nor his friends. He admits the integrity of Job—or, at least, he does not deny it— although he uses very strong expressions as to the course which Job had adopted (34:7-9, 35-37); but he considers that the divine afflictions have a disciplinary object, and that they may be sent because God has discerned the seeds of unfaithfulness and defection in the sufferer; and this may serve to explain their purpose in the case of Job. He has lofty ideas of the righteousness of God (34:10, etc.), and of His power and majesty (37:23). He holds that with regard to the Almighty we cannot find Him out, but that we may safely trust His mercy and His justice. This is the position to which he leads Job when the Lord answers him out of the whirlwind.

(6) I am young.—The way in which Elihu comes forward is very interesting, and full of character. It gives us also a picture of the times and habits.

(8) And the inspiration of the Almighty. —Rather, "And the breath of the Almighty that giveth them understanding." It is the expression used in the Mosaic narrative of the origin of man, and may perhaps show acquaintance on the part of the writer with that narrative (Gen. 2:7). Elihu means to say that it is not years as much as the spirit and illumination of the Almighty that maketh a man pre-eminent in wisdom.

(12) There was none of you.—In Elihu's judgment there was no one who touched the main point of the argument with Job.

(22) In so doing my maker would soon take me away.—Or perhaps the meaning may be, "My Maker will almost have to forgive me": that is for being too candid, frank, and straightforward; for speaking too plainly. Some commentators regard Elihu's character with great disfavor, and consider him to be an empty and arrogant talker, mainly, perhaps, from verses 18, 19; others accept him as a wise and pious friend of Job, who not only gave him good advice, but perhaps more nearly than any other of the disputants hit the truth about Job's afflictions. We are probably more right in this latter view because at the climax of the poem we do not read that Elihu had any share in the condemnation which was passed by God on the three friends of Job. He is not noticed for either praise or blame.

It is to be observed that the last eight verses of this chapter are a kind of soliloquy, unlike the former part of it, which was addressed to the friends, or the next chapter, which is addressed to Job.

33

(1) Wherefore, Job, I pray thee.—He begins by professing his sincerity and integrity; and with reference to Job's expressed desire to find an umpire (9:33), and one who would maintain his right with God (16:21), he declares that he is ready to do so, and that he is, like Job, made out of the clay, and consequently disposed to deal favorably with him.

(9) I am clean without transgression.—Job has nowhere used this language; but many of his statements were capable of being so perverted and misrepresented (9:20, 21; 16:17; 23:10-12, 27:5, 6). This shows that Elihu even was incapable of entering fully into Job's position. He did not understand that a man could alone be righteous in proportion as he trusted God, but that, trusting God, he was righteous with His righteousness. This was the truth that Job dimly perceived and was faintly, though surely, striving after; and to his friends it was unintelligible, and not wholly apprehended by Elihu.

(13) Why dost thou strive against him?—Job had not striven against God; he had only expressed his longing to come into judgment with Him (23:3, etc.). Job was striving with and against the darkness that was round about His throne, not with the justice of God, which he entirely trusted.

(14) For God speaketh once, yea twice.—The two ways are dilated upon (verses 15-18 and 19-26).

(17) From his purpose.—Rather, "That He may withdraw man from carrying out his evil actions, and may remove that pride from man which he secretly cherishes." This is the main point of Elihu's teaching: that the purposes of God are disciplinary, to keep man from the sin which otherwise he would be prone to commit. In this way Job might have been a righteous man, and yet be justly chastened lest he should prove unrighteous.

(19) He is chastened.—This is the second manner in which God speaks—first by dreams, etc., then by afflictions.

(23) To show unto man his uprightness.—This angel, who is one among a thousand, and discharges the function of an interpreter, is a remarkable anticipation of the existence of that function with God which is

discharged by the Advocate with the Father (I John 2:1; Rom. 8:34; Heb. 7:25). It is impossible for us who believe that all Scripture is given by inspiration of God not to see in this an indication of what God intended afterward to teach us concerning the intercession and mediation of the Son and the intercession of the Holy Spirit on behalf of man (Rom. 8:26). (Comp. John 14:16.)

(24) Then he is gracious unto him—i.e., God is gracious; He accepts the mediation of the mediating angel. These words of Elihu's must have fallen on Job's ear with a grateful and refreshing sound, confirming to him his longing for the daysman (9:33).

And saith—i.e., to the destroying angels of verse 22. It is remarkable that it is God who finds the ransom, as it was by God's grace that the interpreting angel was forthcoming. It is not man's righteousness that has saved him, but the ransom that God has found, even though God, who judgeth the actions, may have justly recognized what of righteousness there was in man.

(26) He will be favourable unto him.—Very beautiful is this description of the restoration of the penitent sinner and his recovery from sickness. He shall thankfully resort unto the house of God with joy, for that He has rewarded him according to his righteousness, which was the fruit of faith (Gen. 15:6; Ps. 32:1, 2).

(30) To bring back his soul.—Here, again, is the very keynote of Elihu's doctrine. God's dealings are for the purpose of education and discipline, and this is what he wishes to impress upon Job.

(32) I desire to justify thee.—He wishes to justify Job before his friends, that is, to maintain that his afflictions are not on account of past sin, but as a preservative against possible future defection. This being so, he considers that Job's case may justly be defended, and Job himself vindicated against his friends.

34

(1) Furthermore Elihu.—Elihu here hardly makes good the profession with which he starts, for he begins immediately to accuse Job in no measured language. Elihu makes, indeed, a great profession of wisdom, and expressly addresses himself to the wise (verse 2), and insists upon the necessity of discrimination (verses 3, 4). It is to be observed that Job himself had given utterance to much the same sentiment in 12:11.

(9) It profiteth a man nothing.—Comp. what Job had said (9:20-22, 30, 31; 10:6, 7, 14, 15). Eliphaz had virtually said the same thing, though the form in which he cast it was the converse of this (see 22:3), for he had represented it as a matter of indifference to God whether man was righteous or not, which was, of course, to sap the foundations of all morality.

(10) Ye men of understanding.—Elihu now appeals to the men of understanding, by whom he can hardly mean the three friends of whom he has already spoken disparagingly, but seems rather to appeal to an audience, real or imagined, who are to decide on the merits of what he says. This is an incidental indication that we are scarcely intended to understand the long-continued argument as the record of an actual discussion. Elihu begins to take broader ground than the friends of Job, inasmuch as he concerns himself, not with the problems of God's government, but with the impossibility of His acting unjustly (Gen. 18:25), and the reason he gives is somewhat strange—it is the fact that God is irresponsible, He has not been put in charge over the earth; but His authority is ultimate and original, and being so, He can have no personal interests to secure at all risks; He can only have in view the ultimate good of all His creatures, for, on the other hand, if He really desired to slay them, their breath is in His hands, and He would only have to recall it. The argument is a somewhat strange one to us, but it is sound at bottom, for it recognizes God as the prime origin and final hope of all His creatures, and assumes that His will can only be good, and that it must be the best because it is His. (Comp. John 10:12, 13.)

(17) Shall even he ...—The argument is that one who holds such a position of absolute rule cannot be other than most just. He who is fit to rule must be just, and He who is the ultimate ruler must be fit to rule, and must, therefore, be just; but if He is absolutely just, how shall we condemn His government or Him on account of it, even though we cannot explain it all or reconcile it with our view of what is right?

(20) In a moment shall they die—i.e., "they all alike die, rich and poor together; the hour of death is not hastened for the poor nor delayed for the rich. They all alike die."

The people shall be troubled at midnight.

—It is hard to think that the writer did not know of Exodus 12:29. It is better to read these statements as habitual presents and not as futures.

(23) For he will not lay upon man more than right.—He hath no need to consider any man's case twice or to rectify His first decision. He is infallible, and cannot do otherwise than right, whatever He does.

(25) Therefore.—The writer, believing in God's justice, infers that since God acts in this manner He knows the works of man, and has grounds for acting as He acts.

(31, 32) I have borne chastisement ...
—These verses express the attitude that should be assumed toward God: one of submission and penitence.

(33) And not I.—"If thou art to influence and direct His dealing and government, why may not I? why may not any one? And if so, He is no longer supreme or absolute. What knowest thou, then? Speak, if thou hast anything to say to this reasoning."

(36) My desire is that Job may be tried.—There seems to be reason to consider the words as addressed to God: "Oh my Father, let Job be tried, etc." Elihu's words cannot have fallen upon Job with more acceptance or with lighter weight than those of his other friends. He must have felt, however, that his cause was safe with God, whatever the misunderstanding of men.

35

(2) My righteousness is more than God's.—Job had not in so many words said this, but what he had said was capable of being so represented, and perhaps seemed to involve it. (Comp. 9:22; 10:15.) Here, again, there was a misrepresentation of what Job had said. He certainly did not mean that he was none the better for being righteous; but it was perfectly true that he had said that his righteousness had not delivered him from suffering.

(4) And thy companions.—Elihu professes to answer Job's friends as well as himself. It is indeed true that God is too high to be affected by man's righteousness or unrighteousness, but it does not follow therefore that He is indifferent, for then He would not be a righteous judge. (See note on 34:9.)

(9) By reason of the multitude of oppressions.—The argument seems to be that among men there may be oppression, but not with an almighty and just Judge. The right course, therefore, is to wait.

(11) Who teacheth us.—Then the sense will be that the oppression is so severe that the victims of it forget that God can give songs in the night, and that He has favored men more than the beasts of the field, and that, as not one sparrow can fall to the ground without Him, so He has even numbered the hairs of those who are of more value to Him than many sparrows.

(15) But now, because it is not so.—The general bearing of the verse is that Job is encouraged in his murmurings, because God hath dealt too leniently with him. Elihu's reproaches must have been some of the heaviest that Job had to bear. Happily the judgment was not to be long deferred. (See 38:1.)

36

(1) Elihu also proceeded.—It is not easy to acquit Elihu of some of the "arrogance" he was so ready to ascribe to Job. He professes great zeal for God, but it is hard to see that some of his great professions are warranted.

(9) Then he sheweth them their work.—The true nature of their conduct and their transgressions, that they have behaved themselves proudly. This is Elihu's special doctrine, that God's chastisements are by way of discipline, to reform the future rather than to chastise the past.

(15) He delivereth the poor in his affliction.—The point of Elihu's discourse is rather that He delivers the afflicted by his affliction; He makes use of the very affliction to deliver him by it as a means.

(16) Even so would he have removed thee.—It is possible to understand this verse somewhat otherwise, and the sense may perhaps be improved. Elihu may be speaking, not of what God would have done, but of what He has actually done: "God in His mercy, saw that thou wast in danger, and He removed the cause of temptation, and thy chastisement would have been a short duration hadst thou been submissive and resigned; but thou hast been bold and daring, like the wicked, and hast reaped the judgment of the wicked."

(22) Behold, God exalteth by his power.—The rest of Elihu's speech is splendidly eloquent. He dilates on the power and majesty of God, and appears to be speaking in contemplation of some magnificent natural

phenomenon—as the tempest, or hurricane, or whirlwind—out of which the Lord ultimately spake (38:1). It is probable that this storm was beginning to gather, and that it suggested the glorious imagery of Elihu's speech. The points are that (1) God is the source of greatness; (2) that there is no teacher like Him (verse 22); (3) that He is absolute as well as almighty (verse 23); (4) that He is unsearchable and eternal (verse 26).

(31) For by them—i.e., these roots of the sea, these drops of water, these rain clouds. "He judgeth peoples" by withholding them, or "giveth meat in abundance" by sending rain on the earth; or He may use them in excess, to chastise nations by inundations and the like.

(32) With clouds.—The word here rendered "clouds" really means "hands." The figure is that of a man hurling a stone or bolt, and taking aim; and it is a fine image.

(33) The noise thereof sheweth concerning it.—There can be no doubt but that the general meaning is that all nature participates in the terror caused by the thunder, which is regarded as the audible voice of God; but what the exact expression of this general thought may be it is very hard to say.

There should be no break between this chapter and the next.

37

(1) At this also my heart trembleth.—Elihu is discoursing of the same matter. He says, "Not only are the cattle terrified, but at this also my heart trembleth and is moved out of its place. Hark! listen to the sound of His voice."

(4) And he will not stay them when his voice is heard.—"The thunder and lightning travel in paths which none can explore. Vivid as the lightning is, who shall pursue its course?"

(6) For he saith to the snow.—All the operations of nature obey the behest of God—the snow, the gentle showers, the drenching downpour. By means of these He sealeth up the hand of every man, obstructing and impeding their works and movements, so that all the men whom He has made may know it or know Him. Men may learn from these things that they and their works are under the control of God. They are not the entirely free agents they suppose.

(18) Spread out the sky.—Some understand this of the action of the sun in dispersing the clouds; but some say that it refers to God. "Hast thou spread out with Him the magnificent dome of heaven?"

(20) Be swallowed up.—Unquestionably the sense is clearer if we understand it of the sun: "Shall it be told of him? Shall I, indeed, speak it? or hath any man ever ventured to say, in such a case, that the sun is swallowed up, extinguished?"

(21) And now men see not the bright light—i.e., the sun. It is apparent that this rendering adds great sublimity, and points to the opening of the next chapter.

(23) Touching the Almighty, we cannot find him out.—He is excellent, or mighty, in power and justice, etc.

38

(1) Then the Lord answered Job.—This chapter brings the grand climax and catastrophe of the poem. Unless all was to remain hopelessly uncertain and dark, there could be no solution of the questions so fiercely and obstinately debated but by the intervention of Him whose government was the matter in dispute. And so the Lord answered Job out of the whirlwind, or tempest: that is to say, the tempest which had been long gathering, and which had been the subject of Elihu's remarks. The one argument which is developed in the remaining chapters is drawn from man's ignorance. There is so much in nature that man does not know and cannot understand, that it is absurd for him to suppose that he can judge aright in matters touching God's moral government of the world. Though Job is afterward (42:8) justified by God, yet the tone of all that God says to him is more or less mingled with reproach.

(2) Who is this?—The question may be answered by Job's own words (14:1). It is a man as so described, a dying and enfeebled man, like Job himself, not even a man in his best estate, but one so persecuted and exhausted as Job: one, therefore, altogether unequal to the task he has undertaken.

That darkeneth counsel.—That is, probably, "my counsel," which was the matter under debate. The words, however, are often used proverbially in a general sense. Such discussions, carried on, as they cannot but be, in entire ignorance by blind mortals, must to God's omniscience seem thus,

and cannot be otherwise than the darkening of counsel by words without knowledge.

(4) Where wast thou?—The comparison of the creation of the world to the building of an edifice is such a concession to the feebleness of man as serves of itself to heighten the effect of the inevitable answer to the question preferred.

(7) The morning stars.—The context seems to suggest that by the stars are meant the angels entrusted with their guardianship, from which Milton has borrowed his conceptions.

(14) As clay to the seal.—In the darkness every object is without form and void, just as clay or wax, which has no distinctness of shape until the seal is applied, and then the impression is clear and manifest. So with the coming of the daylight after darkness.

(18) The breadth of the earth.—The earth being conceived of as a vast plain (comp. verse 13). Unscientific as all this language is, it is not a little remarkable that the majestic sublimity of it is not affected by it at all.

(21) Knowest thou it?—It is better to read this verse without an interrogation, as sublime irony. "Doubtless thou knowest all this, for thou wast born then, and the number of thy days is so great!"

(26) To cause it to rain on the earth.—Because God is mindful of His creation, independently of the wants of man.

(31) The sweet influences.—With reference to their supposed effect on weather and the like, "Canst thou regulate the influences exerted by these several constellations in either direction of increase or diminution?"

(32) Mazzaroth is commonly understood to mean the signs of the Zodiac, and by the children of Arcturus the three stars in the tail of Ursa Major.

(33) The ordinances of heaven.—Comp. 28:26. That is, the recurring seasons and their power of influencing the earth.

(36) Wisdom in the inward parts.—The mention of the inward parts and the heart here, in the midst of natural phenomena, perplexes every one; but it is a natural solution to refer them to the lightnings personified: "Who hath put such understanding in their inward parts?"

(37) Who can stay the bottles of heaven?—This is understood in two opposite senses—of pouring out the bottles or of laying them up in store. It is not easy to decide which is most in accordance with the context, for the context also is somewhat uncertain, according as we interpret the solid mass of thick mud or of hard, dry soil. The survey of physical phenomena ends with this verse.

(39) Wilt thou hunt the prey?—The new chapter ought to begin here with this verse, inasmuch as the animal creation now passes under review.

39

(7) The crying of the driver.—Or, "the shouting of the taskmaster." The word is the same as is applied to the taskmasters of Egypt, and this suggests the question whether or not there may be a reminiscence of that bondage here.

(9) The unicorn.—It is a mistake to identify this animal with the rhinoceros, as was formerly done; it is more probably the same with the buffalo, or wild ox. The most glaring form of the mistake is in Ps. 22:21; "Thou hast heard me also from among the horns of the unicorns." The way in which the animal is here spoken of, as in analogous contrast to the domestic ox, suggests that it is not wholly dissimilar. It is familiar and homely toil that the wild ox is contemplated as being put to, in the place of tame cattle, whose work it is.

(13) Gavest thou the goodly wings unto the peacocks?—Rather, "The wing of the ostrich is superb, but are her pinions and her feathers like the storks?" Ostrich feathers beautiful and valuable as they are, are hardly like the plumage of a bird, and are not used for flight; on the contrary, the ostrich runs like a quadruped, it is stated at the rate sometimes of fifty or sixty miles an hour.

(18) She lifteth up herself.—The ostrich has a habit of running in a circle, which alone enables horsemen to overtake and kill or capture her. As in verse 13 a comparison seems to be drawn between the ostrich and the stork, so here, probably, the subject spoken of is the stork. Swift and powerful as the ostrich is, yet no sooner does the stork, on the contrary, rise on high into the air than she—as, indeed, any bird—can baffle the pursuit of horsemen.

(19) Thunder—i.e., with "terror," such as thunder causes. Some refer it to the moving or shaking of the mane.

(20) Canst thou make him afraid as a grasshopper?—Rather, "Hast thou made him to leap as a locust?"

(26) Doth the hawk fly?—The more symmetrical order of these descriptions would

be for the ostrich to have come after the war-horse and before the hawk; in that case there would have been a gradual transition from the fleetest of quadrupeds to the fleetest of birds by means of the ostrich, which, though winged like a bird, cannot use its wings as birds do, but only run on the ground like a quadruped.

(30) Where the slain are, there is she.—Comp. Matt. 24:28, and Luke 17:37.

40

(2) Shall he that contendeth with the Almighty instruct him?—It might, perhaps, tend to make these verses (verses 4, 5) more effective if we transposed them after 42:6, and regarded them as the climax of the poem, as some have done. But this is not necessary, and is an arrangement that has no support from external evidence. If, however, it were adopted, Job's resolution, "Once have I spoken; but I will speak no more: yea, twice; but I will not again" (verse 5), would not be literally inconsistent, as it now is, with what he says in 42:1-6.

(8) Wilt thou also disannul my judgment?—God is about to show Job his inability to govern the world and administer judgment among men, so as to rule them morally, from his acknowledged inability to govern the more formidable animals of the brute creation. If he cannot restrain them, how is it likely that he will be able to tread down the wicked in their place? And if he cannot hold the wicked in check and compel them to submission, how, any more, can he protect himself from their violence? how can he save himself from the outbursts of their fury? Or, if not save himself from them, how much less can he deliver himself from the hand of God? If he cannot hide them in the dust together, and bind them (i.e., restrain the threatenings of their rage in the hidden world) in the secret prison-house, how much less can he save himself, and be independent of the help of a saviour?

(15) Behemoth.—The identification of behemoth has always been a great difficulty with commentators. The word in Hebrew is really plural, "domestic cattle"; and this fact would suggest the idea that more than one animal may be meant in the description (verses 15-24), which scarcely seems to answer to one and the same. In this way the verses 15-20 would describe well the elephant, and verses 21-24 the hippopotamus. The objection to this is that the word is commonly used of domestic cattle in contrast to wild beasts, whereas neither the elephant nor the hippopotamus can come under the category of domestic animals.

Which I made with thee.—Fellow creatures of yours, to inhabit the world with you: thus skilfully reminding him that he had a common origin with the beasts.

41

(1) Leviathan.—There can be little doubt that by this is meant the crocodile or alligator, whatever may be the true meaning of behemoth.

(4) A servant for ever.—The crocodile being probably quite untameable.

(6) Shall the companions make a banquet of him?—Or, "Shall the bands of fishermen make traffic of him?"

(9) Behold, the hope of him is in vain—i.e., the hope of the rash man who would venture to attack him: **at the sight of him,** i.e., the infuriated crocodile.

(10) None is so fierce that dare stir him up.—"If, therefore, the creatures of My hand strike so much terror, how far more terrible must I be? If you cannot save yourself from them, how much less canst you be saved without Me?"

(33, 34) Upon earth there is not his like.—Some have proposed to take away the last two verses of chap. 41 from their connection with the crocodile, and to transpose them, referring them to man, so as to come before verse 8. It cannot be denied that this makes very good sense, but it seems to be too great a liberty to take with the text as we find it to adopt this as the true order of the verses; for in that case, what is there that we might not deal with in a like manner? Those who advocate this transposition in the order of the verses would also place 40:1-5 so as to follow 40:6. There is a certain amount of sharpness and point obtained in thus making this confession the climax of the poem, and a kind of formal consistency is secured in regarding this resolution as Job's last utterance instead of making him speak again, as he does, according to the present order, in 42:2. But this consistency is formal rather than real, inasmuch as there is no inconsistency in the tone of 42:2 seq., and the promise of 40:5. At all events, the climax of 42:6 as it stands

is a very noble one, and we may question whether we can heighten its grandeur.

42

(3) Who is he that hideth counsel?—It is quite obvious that the right way of understanding these verses is, as in Isa. 63:1-6, after the manner of a dialogue, in which Job and the Lord alternately reply. "Who is this that hideth counsel without knowledge?" were the words with which God Himself joined the debate in 38:2.

(4) Hear, I beseech thee.—This, as in 38:3 and 40:7, must be referred to God; then the confession of verses 5 and 6 comes in grandly. How much of our knowledge of God is merely hearsay? and it is not until the experimental teaching of the Holy Ghost has revealed God to our consciences that we really see Him with the inward eye. The confession of Job, therefore, is the confession of every converted man. Compare in a much later and very different, and yet analogous area, the confession of Paul (Gal. 1:16).

(7) And it was so.—The verdict that is spoken against the friends of Job is based rather on the tone and spirit of what they have said than on any of their actual words, for many of these are conspicuous for their wisdom, truth and beauty. But throughout they had been on the wrong side, and seemed to think that the cause of God had need to be upheld at all risks, and that it might even be required to tell lies for God (13:7); and it was this that provoked the divine indignation.

(8) Therefore take unto you now seven bullocks and seven rams.—It is remarkable that the sacrifices prescribed for Job's friends were similar to those which Balaam prescribed for Balak (Num. 23:2-29). This is probably one indication out of many that the age of Job was that of Moses, or before it. "My servant Job shall pray for you." This, strange to say, was the very promise with which Eliphaz himself had closed his third and last speech. His words therefore received a striking fulfillment in the case of himself and his friends. The intercession of Job seems to show us that his character is a typical one, representing to us the character of Christ as the sufferer and the mediator on behalf of man; and as in Job there is no trace of acquaintance with the divine covenant, the book shows us a sort of anticipation of the Gospel to the Gentile world, that the mercies of God are not limited, as some have thought, to the chosen race, but that the principles of God's action are the same universally. He deals with men upon a principle of mediation: whether the mediator be Moses, as the mediator of the first covenant; or Job, who was the accepted mediator for his friends beyond the pale of the covenant; or whether the mediator be Jesus Christ, as the one Mediator between God and man.

(10) When he prayed for his friends.— Job's personal discipline was not complete until he passed from the area of his own sorrows to the work of intercession for his friends, and it was through the act of this self-oblivion and self-sacrifice that his own deliverance was brought about. When he prayed for his friends, we are told, the Lord turned his own captivity: that is, restored and reinstated him in prosperity even greater than before.

This is the true moral of all human history, which is to be accomplished in the world of the regeneration, if not here. Had Job been able to look forward with confidence to his actual deliverance, he would have been able to bear his affliction; it was because he could not that all was dark. If Job's is a representative history, as we are bound to believe it must be, then the lesson of it must be that what is not explained or mended here will be explained and mended hereafter. It is God alone who can enlighten

the darkness which surrounds His counsels; but at the same time we must remember that with Him is the well of life, and in His light we shall see light.

(12) Fourteen thousand sheep.—The number of Job's cattle here is exactly the double of those in 1:3.

(16) An hundred and forty years.—The particularity of this detail forbids us to suppose that the character of Job was other than real; his great age also shows that he must be referred to the very early patriarchal times, probably anterior to Moses.

(17) So Job died, being old and full of days.—Such is the close of this mysterious book, which deals with the greatest problems that can engage the human mind, and shows us the way in which the ancients solved them, and the help which God promised them, apart from His covenant revelation and before the dawning of the gospel light. And the great lesson of the history is the way in which the malice of Satan is foiled. It is remarkable that Job is only twice mentioned in Scripture, once in the Old Testament and once in the New. Ezekiel was acquainted with Job's history (14:14, 20), and James (5:11) refers to him as a familiar standard of patience. It is evident, however, that the Book of Job was well known, from the many instances in the Psalms and elsewhere in which we find traces of the influence produced by familiarity with the language of the book.

PSALMS

Book I

1

Psalm 1 has generally been regarded as a kind of preface or introduction to the rest of the Psalter. The absence of an inscription favors this view, since this absence is rare in the first book. It is still further favored by the traditional arrangement which left the psalm without a number, combining it with Psalm 2. The two psalms seem to have been placed side by side by the compilers of the collection in order to form together such a general introduction. In the one we see the blessing attending the loyal fulfillment of the covenant of Jehovah in the case of the individual; in the other in the case of the nation at large, under its ideal prince. Just as the righteous man in Ps. 1 is contrasted with the wicked **individuals**, so in Ps. 2 the chosen Israel is contrasted with the surrounding nations who do not submit voluntarily to Jehovah; and, combined, the two strike the keynote of the whole Psalter, the faithfulness of God's dealings with men, whether in their individual or national relation to Him, and the indissoluble connection between righteousness and blessing.

For determining the date, there is not only the indication of a comparatively late composition afforded by the growing reverence for the written Law (tôrah), but also the extreme probability that Jeremiah 17:8 is founded on this psalm, which approximately fixes the furthest limit to which it may be brought down. It harmonizes also with the dominant feeling of the later period of the monarchy.

(1) Walketh ... standeth ... sitteth.—The good man is first described on the negative side. In the short summary of evil from which he has been saved, it is the custom of commentators to see an epitome of the whole history of sin. The three terms employed for evil have distinctive significations. (1) **The ungodly.** Properly, restless, wanting in self-control, victims of ungoverned passion, as defined in Isa. 57:20. (2) **Sinners.** General term for wrongdoers. (3) **Scornful.** A proverbial word, defined in Prov. 21:24; Aquila has "mockers"; Symmachus "imposters"; the LXX "pests." It has an official sound, and without unduly pressing the language, we think of the graduation in vice which sometimes ends in

deliberate preference for those who despise virtue. (Comp. Ps. 26:4, 5.)

(2) But.—The positive side of a good man's character is now described according to the standard which prevailed when the written law first came truly into force.

(3) And he.—The full moral bearing of the image appears in our Lord's parabolic saying, "A good tree cannot bring forth corrupt fruit, nor an evil tree good fruit." The physical growth of a tree has in all poetry served as a ready emblem of success, as its decay has of failure.

(4) But are like.—They shall be winnowed out of the society of the true Israel by the fan of God's judgment. The image is a striking one, although so frequent as almost to have become a poetical commonplace (Hab. 3:12; Joel 3:14; Jer. 51:33; Isa. 21:10).

(5) The congregation of the righteous.—A phrase repeating itself in different forms in the Psalms. It implies either Israel as opposed to the heathen, or faithful Israel as opposed to those who had proved disloyal to the covenant. In theory all the congregation was holy (Num. 16:3), but we meet in the Psalms with the feeling expressed in the Apostle's words, "They are not all Israel that are of Israel."

2

As Psalm 1 describes the results of fulfilling the covenant for the individual by contrasting the condition of those who fail in their allegiance, so Psalm 2 shows how the covenant relation exalts Israel over the heathen; but some particular political situation seems to be indicated. Jerusalem appears to be threatened by a confederacy of hostile and rebellious powers—a confederacy that took advantage of the succession of a young and inexperienced monarch to throw off the bonds of subjection and tribute. David, Solomon, Ahaz, and Uzziah, have each of them been regarded as the hero and theme of the poem, but in each case there is some lack of correspondence between the history and the psalm. The psalm must therefore be regarded as expressing an ideal view of the future. The poet shapes an ideal monarchy and an ideal king—one who, though encountered by the worst forms of opposition, would prove himself a true son of David, and by his fidelity to his God and nation, a true son of God. Such a view of the psalm alone explains its want of exact historic coincidence, and vindicates the claims universally made for it of Messianic prevision; for there is but a step between the ideal king and the Messianic king—a step which, though perhaps unconsciously, the poets and prophets of Israel were forever taking.

(1) Imagine.—Better, "meditate," or "plan." In old English "imagine" was used in a bad sense.

(2) Against the Lord.—The word Messiah is applicable in its first sense to anyone anointed for a holy office or with holy oil (Lev. 4:3, 5, 16). Its distinctive reference to an expected prince of the chosen people, who was to redeem them from their enemies, and fulfill completely all the divine promises for them, probably dates from this psalm, or more distinctly from this psalm than from any one passage. At least, that the traditional Jewish interpretation had fastened upon it as of this importance is shown by the frequent and emphatic quotation of this psalm in the New Testament. (See Acts 4:25).

(4) He that sitteth.—Here the psalm, with a sublimity truly Hebrew, turns from the wild confusion on earth to the spectacle of God looking down with mingled scorn and wrath on the fruitless attempts of the heathen against His chosen people.

(7) I will declare.—The anointed king now speaks himself, recalling the covenant made with him by Jehovah at his coronation.

The Lord hath.—The figure of an ideal prince who was always about to appear, but was never realized in any actual successor on the throne, may possibly, by the time of this psalm, have assumed its great place in the nation's prophetic hopes. Certainly the whole line of tradition claims the passage in a Messianic sense. (See note on verse 2; and Acts 13:33; Heb. 1:5; 5:5. For the king, spoken of as "God's son," see Ps. 89:26, 27, and comp. II Sam. 7:14.)

(12) Kiss the Son.—This familiar translation must be surrendered. It has against it the weight of all the ancient versions except the Syriac. It must be taken figuratively, with sense of doing homage, as in Gen. 41:40 (margin), or worshiping (I Kings 19:18; Hosea 13:2). The most consistent rendering is, therefore, "proffer pure homage (to Jehovah), lest he be angry." It may be added that the current of Rabbinical authority is against our King James version.

Put their trust.—Notice in the close of the psalm the settled and memorable belief that good must ultimately triumph over evil. The rebels against God's kingdom must be conquered in the noblest way, by being drawn into it.

3

With this psalm the hymnbook of Israel properly begins. The title indicates it as the first psalm of a Davidic collection formed at some time previous to the arrangement of the rest of the Psalter—a date, however, which we cannot recover. We also find ourselves on probable historical ground. There is a beautiful conjecture which connects the two psalms with the actual day of the flight from Jerusalem—the day of whose events we have a more detailed account than of any other in Jewish history. The close connection of the two psalms is seen by a comparison of Ps. 4:7 with Ps. 3:3, and Ps. 3:5 with Ps. 4:8, and of both with the narrative in II Sam. 15, 16, and 17. The rhythmical arrangement is so artistic that we must suppose the poem composed at leisure, after the excitement of the rout was over.

Title.—"Mizmor," which occurs only in the inscriptions to psalms, must be regarded as the technical term for a particular kind of lyric composition, and possibly originated with David. It means "a song composed for musical accompaniment."

(2) Selah.—This curious word must apparently remain forever what it has been ever since the first translation of the Bible was made—the puzzle of ordinary readers, and the despair of scholars. Selah occurs no less than seventy-one times in the compass of thirty-nine psalms, and three times in the ode of Habakkuk (Hab. 3:3, 9, 13). There is only one conclusion, now universally admitted, that selah is a musical term, but in the hopeless perplexity and darkness that besets the whole subject of Hebrew music, its precise intention must be left unexplained. The conjecture that has the most probability on its side makes it a direction to "play loud." The derivation from sâlah, "to raise," is in favor of this view.

(3) My glory, and the lifter up of mine head.—The significance of this sublime trust comes out as we read in II Sam. 15:30 how the humiliated monarch went barefoot over Olivet, with head bent down and muffled in his mantle; no glory of dignity left;

mute and humiliated under the insults and curses of Shimei.

(8) Thy blessing ... —Rather, "let thy blessing be upon thy people." It is not the statement of a fact, but an intercessory prayer. The true Shepherd of His people was a noble and generous man. This close, as Ewald says, "throws a bright light on the depth of his noble soul.

4

This psalm most probably belongs to the same occasion as that which produced Psalm 3 (see Introduction to that psalm), but was sung in an hour of still greater trial. Psalm 4 was one of those repeated by Augustine at his conversion.

Title—To the chief Musician.—The rendering of a word occurring fifty-five times in the inscriptions, and in Hab. 3:19. The form here employed must imply "one who has obtained the mastery," or "holds a superior post." Hence "master," "director," or "overseer" (II Chron. 2:18; 34:12). But from the description in I Chron. 15:16, et seq., we see that the musical directors had themselves cymbals, and took part in the performance, and hence the word would answer to a leader of the band; but as in the case of the Psalms there is vocal music as well, perhaps "precentor" is the best equivalent.

On Neginoth.—Another musical term occurring, with a slight variation in the preposition, in the titles of six psalms. Its derivation is from a root meaning "to touch the strings." It seems natural to join the two directions—"to the conductor of those playing on stringed instruments," or, "to the leader of the harps."

(1) Hear me.—The conception of God as supremely just, and the assertor of justice, is one of the noblest legacies from the Hebrew faith to the world. It is summed up in the question, "Shall not the judge of all the earth do right?" The strength of the innocent in the face of slander or oppression lies in the appeal to the eternal source of righteousness.

(2) Leasing.—i.e., "lying." (Comp. verse 6.)

(3) But know.—It is the privilege of true and heroic natures to rise to a consciousness of their strength and dignity in the hour of peril, and when the victims of unjust persecution. Besides his innate greatness, David has a grandeur and dignity,

derived from his deep sense of the covenant between God and His anointed, and his own imperfect but sincere endeavor to act worthily the part of God's vice-regent on earth. His selection by Jehovah is an unanswerable reply to his slanderers, and the surest proof of his own uprightness.

(6) Lift thou up ... —This is an echo of the priestly benediction (Num. 6:24, et seq.), which must so often have inspired the children of Israel with hope and cheerfulness during their desert wanderings—which has breathed peace over so many deathbeds in Christian times.

(8) Thou, Lord, only.—The authority of all the ancient versions, including the LXX and Vulgate, is for taking the adverb with the predicate, not with the subject as in the King James Version: "Thou, Jehovah, makest me to dwell alone in safety." We see from Jer. 49:31 and Micah 7:14 that isolation from other nations was, in the Hebrew view, a guarantee against danger. This certainly favors the view that the poem is national rather than individual.

For the concluding verses of the psalm Luther had a great affection, and desired Ludvig Teuffel to set them as the words of a requiem for him.

5

Verse 7 makes the inscription to this psalm suspicious. (See note.) The psalm is rightly assigned to the troublous times of the later monarchy, possibly the reign of Manasseh. The bitterness of possible estrangement from the Temple and its services makes itself visible enough here, in feelings natural to this period. It is plain that when Psalm 5 was composed the adherents of Jehovah's religion were the objects of dislike and slander.

Title.—(See note to inscription, Ps. 4.)

Nehiloth.—Properly, **nechilôth**: that is, "bored instruments." Of the use of flutes in the religious services of the Hebrews we have proof in I Sam. 10:5; I Kings 1:40; Isa. 30:29.

(3) The daily morning sacrifice sees the psalmist in the Temple. The word "direct," or, better, "prepare," is the same used in Lev. 1:8, 12; 6:12, of the priest laying out the wood for the sacrifice, or the parts of the offering itself, and suggest that the author may himself have been a priest. The word "offering" should be supplied, instead of "prayer."

Look up.—The Hebrew is from the root which forms "Mizpeh," or "watchtower." The psalmist looks up for the answer to his prayer as the seer on his tower (Hab. 2:1) looked up for his inspiration. The usual attitude of prayer in the East was then, as now, either standing or prostrate, the hands lifted up or spread out (Exod. 9:33; Pss. 28:2; 134:2; 141:2). To raise the eyes was not so usual.

(7) House . . . temple.—These words must certainly be taken literally. The reference to worship hardly allows the rendering "palace." No other explanation would have been suggested but for the title to the psalm; and it is clear that historical exactness was not regarded in affixing the psalm titles.

Worship.—Literally, "prostrate myself towards," as in I Kings 8:29; Ps. 28:2. (Comp. Daniel's attitude of prayer toward Jerusalem, and that of the Moslems now toward Mecca.)

(12) Shield.—Heb., **tsinnah.** The long large shield fit for a giant (I Sam. 17:7, 41), which could protect the whole body.

Luther, when asked at Augsburg where he should find shelter if his patron, the Elector of Saxony, should desert him, replied, "under the shield of heaven."

6

The end of this plaintive poem seems to belong to a different situation from the beginning. At first it sounds like a voice from a bed of sickness, of sickness likely to terminate fatally. But at verse 8 the tone changes. We hear no longer of sickness; but of enemies and wicked men, and prayer gives place to defiance and triumph. Can then the suffering described in the former part be of the soul instead of the body? In any other than Hebrew literature we should answer in the negative. But with such passages as Isa. 1:5, 6 before us we feel that no picture of physical pain and disease is too vivid or too personal to express moral evil. Rightly, therefore, has the Church made this the first of the penitential psalms. As the personality of the writer is thus merged we need not attempt to recover it. Perhaps he intended it not only to be merged, but lost in the collective application to the suffering faithful in Israel. The Exile period best suits this confession of national sin.

Title.—For "chief musician" and "Neginoth," see introduction to Ps. 4. "Upon Sheminith" has been variously understood, and still waits for a satisfactory explanation.

(5) For in death.—As in Ps. 30:9, the sufferer urges as a further reason for divine aid the loss Jehovah would suffer by the cessation of his praise. The Israelite's natural dread of death was intensified by the thought that the grave separated him from all the privileges of the covenant with God. (Comp. Isa. 38:18.) There can be neither remembrance of His past mercies there, nor confession of His greatness. The word translated "grave," in exact parallelism with death, is **shêol,** or "underworld," in the early conception merely a vast sepulchral cave, closed as rock-tombs usually were by gates of stone or iron (Isa. 38:10; Job 17:16). The derivation of the word is disputed, but the primary meaning appears to have been "hollowness." It occurs sixty-five times in the Bible, and is rendered in the King James Version three times as "pit," and then with curious impartiality thirty-one times as "grave," and as many "hell." When it ceased to be merely a synonym for "grave," and began to gather a new set of ideas we cannot ascertain. But it acquired these new ideas slowly.

7

In this psalm we seem to be once more on sure historical ground. It not only breathes the feeling when David and his outlawed band were daily evading the snares laid for them by the emissaries of Saul, but seems to refer pointedly to the two most romantic incidents in all the romantic period—the chance encounter of pursuer and pursued—(1) In the cave of En-gedi, and (2) (if the two are not the same under different versions) in the wilderness of Ziph (I Sam. 24 and 26).

Title.—Shiggaion either means generally "poem" or "psalm"; or it is derived from **shãgah,** "to wander," and denotes a wild passionate ode. The fact of the tribal relation with Saul is quite enough to allow us to conjecture that Cush was some person high in favor with that monarch, servilely eager to injure David.

(3) If there be iniquity.—A comparison with I Sam. 24:12, 13, and still more I Sam. 26:18, shows how closely this psalm is connected with the two notorious instances of David's magnanimous and generous conduct toward Saul.

(5) Selah.—See note on Ps. 3:2. This is one of the places which suggests its interpretation as a direction to the music, to strike up with passion and force.

(6) In the rapid succession of abrupt utterance of feeling in ejaculations, we see the excitement of the poet's mind.

(7) For their sakes.—The poet has a vision of judgment. Jehovah summons the nations, arranges them at His tribunal, and then returns to His high throne to preside. This picture of arraigned nations is certainly in favor of the view which makes the psalm the expression of the feelings of the community rather than of an individual.

(14) Behold, he travaileth.—The poet's thought recurs to the slanderer, whose sin has deserved all this divine wrath, and he sees the truth that God's judgments are not arbitrary, but follow naturally on sin as its consequence. The verb "travaileth" gives the general figure, which is elaborated in the two clauses which describe the stages of conception and pregnancy. (For the image, comp. Job 15:35.)

Verses 15 and 16 are quoted by Eusebius of the overthrow of Maxentius by Constantine, with special reference to the fact that in preparing a bridge of boats he had prepared the means for his own destruction.

8

This psalm has been aptly called a lyric echo of the first chapter of Genesis. There is no reason to doubt the traditional ascription to David. This exquisite little poem is a record of his shepherd's days, when, under the midnight sky of Palestine, brilliant with stars, he mused on things deep and high, on the mystery of the universe and man's place in it, his relation to the Creator on the one hand, to the rest of creation on the other.

Title.—Upon Gittith. (Comp. Pss. 81 and 84.) The most probable explanation connects it with Gath, the Philistine town. It was a Philistine lute, just as there was an Egyptian flute and a Doric lyre.

From a comparison of the three psalms so inscribed, it cannot be a title having any reference to the subject.

(1) O Lord our Lord.—"Jehovah our Lord." For the first time in the Book of Psalms the personal feeling is consciously lost sight of in a larger, a national, or possibly human feeling. The poet recognizes God's relation to the whole of mankind as to the whole material creation. Thus the hymn appropriately lent itself to the use of the congregation in public worship, though it does not follow that this was the object of its composition.

(2) Ordained strength ... —The context, speaking the language of war, seems to demand the primitive meaning, "stronghold" or "defense." The truth which the Bible proclaims of the innate divinity of man, his essential likeness to God, is the principal subject of the poet; and in the princely heart of innocence of an unspoiled child he sees, as Wordsworth saw, its confirmation: "Trailing clouds of glory do we come, From God who is our home." Such a proof is strong even against the noisy clamor of apostate men, who rebel against the divine government, and lay upon God the blame of their aberration from His order.

(4) Man ... son of man ... —The first, possibly, with suggestion of frailty; the second to his life derived from human ancestry. The answer to this question must always touch the two poles, of human frailty on the one hand, and the glory of human destiny on the other. "O the grandeur and the littleness, the excellence and the corruption, the majesty and the meanness, of man."—**Pascal.**

(5) The Hebrew poet dwells on neither of these aspects, but at once passes on to the essential greatness of man and his superiority in creation, by reason of his moral sense and his spiritual likeness to God.

For thou hast made him a little lower than the angels.—Literally, "thou makest him want but a little from God": i.e., hast made him little less than divine. We should read, however, instead of "for thou," "and thou hast made," etc. Undoubtedly the word Elohim, being used to express a class of supernatural beings, includes angels as well as the divine being (I Sam. 28:13; Zech. 12:8). But here there is nothing in the context to suggest limitation to one part of that class. (Comp. Heb. 2:6, 7.)

(6) The poet continues, in a rapturous strain, to complete the cycle of animated nature, and to describe man's kingship over all other created beings. For Paul's expansion of the thought, and elevation of it into yet a higher sphere, see I Cor. 15:27.

9

In the LXX and Vulgate, Psalms 9 and 10 are combined into one. This arrangement appears the more ancient of the two, and possibly is original. Psalms 10 and 33 are the only compositions of the original Davidic collection (Pss. 3-41) without a title. The Hebrew division, no doubt, is based on the fact, that while at first sight Psalm 9 seems to be a thanksgiving for victory, breathing only triumph and hope, Ps. 10 is a prayer against violence and blood.

The authorship and date of the combined psalms cannot be ascertained. Their redaction for congregational use must be referred to post-exile times. The whole piece was originally alphabetical.

Title.—For the "chief musician," see Introduction to Psalm 4.

Upon Muth-labben.—Of the perplexing titles, this is one of the most perplexing. No conjecture of the meaning of the Hebrew as it stands is satisfactory. The text must be emended.

(5) Put out.—Better, "blotted out." The family is extinct and its name erased from the civil register.

(6) Their memorial.—Better, "their very memory is perished." The LXX and Vulgate read, "with a sound," referring to the crash of falling cities. Some would substitute enemies for cities, but they lose the emphasis of the passage, which points to the utter evanishment from history of great cities as a consequence and sign of divine judgment. Probably the poet thinks of Sodom and Gomorrha, whose overthrow left such a mark on the thought of Israel. We think of the mounds of earth which alone represent Nineveh and Babylon.

(7) But the Lord shall endure.—Better, "but Jehovah sits enthroned for ever," being in close parallelism with the next clause, "For judgment has erected his throne."

(10) They that know.—They who know the name of Jehovah will trust Him, because they know it to be a watchword of strength and protection.

Seek.—From root meaning "to tread" or "frequent a place," possibly with allusion to frequenting the courts of the Temple.

(12) When.—Better, "for he maketh inquisition"; literally, "the seeker of bloods": i.e., "the avenger of blood." The allusion is to the **goel**, the nearest relative of the murdered man, who must, according to Oriental custom, avenge him.

(13) That lifteth me up from the gates of death.—For the gates of sheol, see note to Ps. 6:5. (Comp. Ps. 107:18, and the Homeric phrase "the gates of Hades.") We might perhaps paraphrase "from the verge of the

grave," if it were not for the evident antithesis to "gates of the daughter of Zion" in the next verse. We understand, therefore, "gates" in sense of "power," "rule," the gate being the seat of the judge or king, and so, like our "court," synonymous for his power.

(14) Daughter of Zion.—i.e., Zion itself (see Isa. 37:22): a common personification of cities and their inhabitants. So of Edom (Lam. 4:21); of Babylon (Ps. 137:8, etc.).

(16) Higgaion. Selah.—Higgaion occurs three times in the Psalms—here, Ps. 19:14, and Ps. 92:4 (Heb.). The word apparently indicates some change in the music, or possibly, as joined with **selah**, a direction to some particular part of the orchestra.

(17) The wicked.—This is a most unfortunate rendering. The true translation is, "the wicked shall return," as in LXX and Vulgate (not "be turned") "to the grave," i.e., "to dust," according to the doom in Gen. 3:19, or "to the unseen world" as in Job 30:23; Ps. 90:1-3. The verse is closely connected with the previous one. The wicked are bringing about their own destruction, and so witnessing to the righteous judgment of Jehovah.

10

See Introduction to Ps. 9

(16) The Lord is King.—If the psalm has to this point been personal, it here swells out into a larger strain of national hope and faith.

(18) Oppressed.—See Ps. 9:9. "God's choice acquaintances are humble men."— **Leighton.**

11

The tradition assigning this psalm to David is accepted by some of the greatest of modern scholars, but it is difficult to assign it to any known period of his history. Both in his troubles under Saul and in the rebellion of Absalom, he adopted the flight which this poet scorns as unworthy of one whose conscience is clear, and whose faith in Jehovah is sure; the tone of the psalm is too personal to allow it to be taken as merely representative of a type of character.

(3) The foundations.—By this word must be understood the principles of morality, which are the foundation of society. Symmachus and Jerome render "laws." But the rendering "What could the righteous do?" is doubtful. The image is of a house shattered by an earthquake (comp. Ps. 82:5); in such a case how find safety? A suggested emendation, involving but a slight change in the Hebrew letters, would produce, however, a far better sense: "If the foundations be destroyed, what will become of the tower, or superstructure?"

(4) Temple.—Here, plainly from the parallelism, not any earthly building, but "the heavenly palace of the divine King." One thought of God's supreme righteousness, high above earth's anarchy and sin, is enough to reassure the psalmist and make him strong. "God's in His heaven; all's right with the world."—Browning, **Pippa Passes.**

(6) Horrible tempest.—Literally, "wind of heats"; as in Latin, **aestus** combines the ideas of heat and violent motion; so the Hebrew word here.

May we see one more reminiscence of the fate of Sodom and Gomorrha stamped indelibly on the Hebrew mind?

(7) His countenance.—Better, "the upright shall behold His countenance." This beautiful religious hope finds its highest expression in the beatitude on the pure in heart. By the vision of God the Hebrew poet means triumph of right and the acknowledgment of his innocence—light and peace after darkness and trouble.

12

The tradition of the Davidic authorship must be discarded here. The psalm is an elegy, but not for personal suffering. It is a lament over the demoralization of men and the corruption of social life. But God has not left Himself without a witness. Prophetic voices have been raised—perhaps Isaiah's—in noble assertion of truth and justice, and the poet recalls one such voice, proclaiming the coming and the establishment of a righteous kingdom upon earth, the hope of which had already become the consolation and stay of the faithful.

For **Title**, see Introduction to Ps. 6.

(5) For the oppression.—i.e., on account of the oppression. Here, as in so many psalms and prophecies, we have an ancient oracle of God introduced. The poet first quotes it, and then in verse 6 contrasts its truth and genuineness with the false speeches of hypocrites.

(6) As silver.—This solemn promise of Jehovah may be relied on, for His words

are not like those of deceitful men—alloyed with self and falsehood—but are pure as silver seven times smelted.

13

In this short poem we see the power of lyric expression for rapid changes of emotion. In the compass of three short stanzas, decreasing in length as they proceed, we have an alternation from the deepest despair to the profoundest peace. Perhaps here is the record of an eventful period of David's life, when he had to make a hundred shifts to escape from Saul, and feared often to close his eyes lest he should never awake. But verse 3 sounds rather like the cry of one suffering from sickness. All we can be certain about is that the psalm is intense in its record of personal feeling.

(2) Take counsel.—The plans formed in the mind turn to sorrows as they are frustrated. The next verse confirms the suspicion that suicide had been in the psalmist's mind.

(5) But I.—Emphatic, "but as for me." The most complete peace has taken the place of the despair with which the psalm opens. The LXX and Vulgate have an additional clause not found in any MS., "Yea, I will praise the name of the Lord most high."

14

With some variations this psalm appears again as Ps. 53. The most striking variation consists in the change of **Jehovah** into **Elohim.**

In this poem the dramatic element blends with the lyric. In the great drama of the world, as unfolding before the psalmist's eyes, God is seen to look from the windows of His heaven down on the races of men, as He did before the Flood, and He finds no vestige of good left, except in the oppressed nation of Israel; all the rest are hopelessly corrupt. Then (verse 4) comes His voice in some ancient oracular saying that the foes of the chosen people are instantly cowed and thrown into panic. Possibly Babylon, the great representative of the giant powers of the heathen world, and the devourer of other nations, now itself already on the verge of ruin, was in the poet's thought.

(1) Fool.—Heb., **nabal**, from a root meaning "to wither"; hence flat, insipid

(insipiens). But this is not speculative atheism, but practical—a denial of the moral government of God—so that fool and wicked become almost synonymous.

They have done abominable works.—The LXX and Vulgate have caught the sense, "They have become abominable in their practices." Instead of works, Ps. 53 has "iniquity."

(2) Looked down.—Literally, "bent forward to look as from a window." (Comp. Song of Solomon 6:10.)

Did understand.—Better, "any man of understanding," in contrast with "fool," in verse 1, and certainly meaning one who regulates his conduct on the conviction of the existence of a holy and just God.

(5) There were they.—Ps. 53 adds, "which was no fear." The local "there" brings the scene before us as in a picture. We evidently have not here any indication by which to fasten on a particular event. Whether the addition in Ps. 53 gives any is discussed there.

(7) Oh that.—The thoughts of the exiles turn to the Holy City as the one source of deliverance, as if Jehovah's power would only manifest itself from His hallowed abode. So Daniel looked toward Jerusalem in his prayer. It appears, besides its literal reference to the exile, to have been applied proverbially to the removal of any misfortune (Job. 42:10).

15

This is the portrait of a perfect character after the ideal of Israel. We naturally compare with it, on the one hand, the heathen types of perfection as we see them in the ethical philosophy of Greece and Rome, and, on the other, the Christian standard as we see it in the New Testament. In heart and tongue, in deed and word, as a member of society and as an individual, the character of Ps. 15 is without reproach.

(3) He that backbiteth not.—Literally, "he has not footed it on his tongue." Very expressive of those who go about from house to house carrying gossip. (Comp. I Tim. 5:13.)

Reproach.—The Hebrew word has a striking derivation. Properly, "the stripping of the trees of autumn fruit"; so, "stripping honor and reputation from a person."

(5) Usury was not forbidden in the legitimate commercial dealings with foreigners (Deut. 23:20); and the laws against it seem to have had exclusive reference to dealings among Israelites themselves, and were evidently enacted more with a view to the protection of the poor than because the idea of usury in itself was considered wrong (Exod. 22:25; Lev. 25:36). So here the context plainly seems to limit the sin of usury to unjust application of the principle, being connected with bribery. The best illustrations of invectives of prophets and psalmists against extortionate usurers are supplied by Shakespeare's play, **The Merchant of Venice.**

16

Ewald's arguments for grouping this psalm with Psalms 17 and 49, as those of one time, and even one author, are almost irresistible; and this not merely from general similarity of language and sentiment, but especially from the feelings expressed about death. The vision of immortality wanting to the early Jews, to Moses, even to David, has at length, however, faintly and dimly dawned. It will be long before it becomes a world belief, or even a definite individual hope. But the germ of a truth so great must grow, as we see it growing in the Book of Job, till the time is ripe for apostles to quote the words of the ancient poets, as if they had not only felt for themselves the necessity of an immortal existence, but had seen prophetically how in Christ it would be assured to men.

Psalm 16 is decidedly individual in its experience, and the inscription to David as author receives a certain amount of probability from a comparison of verse 5 with I Sam. 26:19. But such slight indications give way before the reference to the bloody sacrifices in verse 4, which brings the date down to a time subsequent at least to Solomon.

Title.—Michtam occurs in five other psalms (56-60)—all, like Psalm 16, ascribed to David. The greatest uncertainty attaches to the word. Probably some musical direction, the key to which is lost, is conveyed by the word.

(4) Their sorrows.—From the evident allusion to the curse on Eve in Gen. 3:16, and the fact that the verb rendered "hasten" means to buy a wife, it seems that the psalmist had the common prophetical figure for idolatry, viz., adultery, in his mind; but as he is not speaking of the Church as a whole, he does not work it out as the prophets do, by representing the idolaters as adulteresses.

The "libations of blood" seem to refer to the ghastly rites of Moloch and Chemosh. For the last clause comp. Exod. 23:13. To the Hebrews the very name of a god included a predication of his power. Therefore the avoidance of even mentioning **baal**, but substituting **bosheth,** i.e., shameful thing, for it, even in proper names.

(5) The portion.—There is allusion here to the Levitical portion (Num. 18:20): "I am thy portion and thine inheritance." The poet, whom we must imagine exiled from his actual inheritance in Canaan, consoles, and more than consoles himself, with the sublime thought that this "better part" could not be taken away from him.

For the figure of the cup, see Ps. 11:6. It had already become a synonym for "condition in life."

(6) The lines are fallen unto me.—The allusion is to the "measuring cords" by which allotments of land were measured, and they are said to "fall" possibly because after the measurement the portions were distributed by "lot" (Josh. 17:5; Micah 2:5).

(7) My reins.—i.e., my heart.

Instruct me.—Better, "warn me." Conscience echoes the voice of God. The Hebrew word, from a root meaning "bind," includes the sense of obligation. Once heard, the divine monition becomes a law to the good man, and his own heart warns him of the slightest danger of deviation from it.

(9) Shall rest in hope.—"Shall rest in security." In "heart, soul, flesh," the poet comprises the whole living man. (Comp. I Thess. 5:23.) The psalmist feels that the body must share with the soul the immunity from evil which is insured by fellowship with God. Carried out to its full issue, the logical conclusion of this is the doctrine of immortality; but we must not see a conscious reference to it here.

(10) Leave.—Rather, "commit," or "give up."

In hell.—Better, "to the unseen world" (Sheol), as in Ps. 6:5, where see note.

Holy One.—Better, "thy chosen," or "favored," or "beloved One." Heb., **chasîd,** one standing in a state of covenant favor with Jehovah. The received Heb. text has the word in the plural, but with the marginal note that the sign of the plural is superfluous. The weight of MS. authority of all the ancient versions, and of the quotations Acts 2:27; 13:35, is for the singular.

Corruption.—Heb., **shachath,** a pit. The meaning of the passage is clearly that Jehovah will not abandon His beloved to death. "To be left to Sheol" and "to see the pit" are synonyms for "to die," just as "to see life" (Eccl. 9:9, King James Version, "live joyfully") is "to be alive"; or, as in the next clause, "to make to see the path of life." At the same time we discern here the first faint scintillation of that light of immortality which we see struggling to break through the darkness in all the later literature of Israel; the veil over the future of the individual, if not lifted, is stirred by the morning breath of a larger faith, and so the use is justified which is made of this passage in the New Testament (Acts 2:25).

17

For the general scope of this psalm, compare the Introduction to Ps. 16. It would be satisfactory if we could actually identify the author—doubtless the same man—of the two; but if we lose sight of him in thinking of the righteous part of Israel generally, suffering under the attacks of the ungodly or the heathen, and with only its faith to sustain it, the question of authorship loses its importance.

Title.—A prayer. From Ps. 72:20, "the prayers of David the son of Jesse are ended," we naturally regard **tephillah,** i.e., prayer as a name applicable to all the pieces of the collection, though it only actually occurs as an inscription five times, and only one—the present—belongs to the first two books.

(8) Apple of the eye.—Literally, "little man." The **mannikin** is the reflection seen in the pupil.

Hide me under the shadow of thy wings.— The figure of the sheltering wings of the parent bird, so common in Hebrew literature, generally refers to the eagle or vulture, as in Deut. 32:10, 11, the source of both the beautiful images of the text. Our Lord's use of the figure is made more tender by the English rendering, "hen" (Matt. 23:37).

(9) Deadly.—Literally, "with the soul," or "life," or better, as in the Syriac, "against the life," and so "deadly." Others take it adverbially with the verb, "eagerly compass."

(10) They are inclosed ... —Literally, "their fat have they shut up." The "proudly" of the next clause suggests that "fat" is only a figure for the conceit of prosperity.

(15) I—is emphatic. The satisfaction of worldly men is in their wealth and family honors, that of the poet in the sun of God's presence and the vision of His righteousness. (Comp. note on Ps. 11:7.)

Instead of "likeness," render "image," or "appearance." But what does the poet mean by the hope of seeking God when he wakes? Some think of rising to peace after a perplexing trouble; others of health after suffering; others of the sunlight of the divine grace breaking on the soul. But the literal reference to night in verse 3 seems to ask for the same reference here. Instead of waking to a worldling's hope of a day of feasting and pleasure, the psalmist wakes to the higher and nobler thought that God is a conscious presence to him, assuring him of justice and protection. But as in Ps. 16, so here, we feel that in spite of his subjection to the common notions about death the psalmist may have felt the stirrings of a better hope. Such "cries from the dark," even if they do not prove the possession of a belief in immortality, show how the human heart was already groping its way, however blindly, toward it.

18

This magnificent ode is David's, if anything at all of David's has come down to us. Its recurrence in II Sam. 22, the mention of the monarch by name in the last verse, and the general contents bear out the tradition of the title.

If no other literary legacy had been left by the Hebrew race, we should have from this psalm a clear conception of the character of its poetic genius. Above all, the bard of Israel wrote under the mighty conviction of the power and presence of Jehovah. The phenomena of the natural world appealed to his imagination as to that of poets generally, but with this addition, that they were all manifestations of a supreme glory and goodness behind them.

Title.—See II Sam. 22:1. The differences are such as might be expected between a piece in a collection of hymns and the same introduced into a historical book.

(1) My strength.—This strikes the keynote of the whole poem. The strong, mighty God is the object in David's thought throughout. It is a warrior's song, and his conception of Jehovah is a warrior's conception.

(2) Rock.—Better here, "cliff," keeping "rock" for the next clause. In the first figure

the ideas of height and shelter, in the second of broad-based and enduring strength, are predominant.

Horn of my salvation.—The allusion seems to be not to a means of attack, like the horn of an animal, but to a mountain peak (called "horn" in all languages), such as often afforded David a safe retreat. Render "my peak of safety."

(5) Hell.—Heb., sheôl. (See note on Ps. 6:5.)

(6) Out of his temple.—As in Pss. 11:4; 29:9, the heavenly abode of Jehovah.

(7) The earth shook.—The sudden burst of the storm is the divine answer to the sufferer's prayer. The whole realm of poetry cannot show a finer feeling for nature in her wrath.

(10) Cherub.—See Exod. 25:19. This passage alone would show how naturally the idea of winged attendants on the divine Being grew out of the phenomena of cloud and storm. No doubt many featues of the developed conception were derived from contact with Assyrian art, but for the poetry of this passage we have only to think of those giant pinions into which cloud so often shapes itself, this clause being in close parallelism with "wings of the wind."

(14) He sent out.—In the majesty of the storm we have almost forgotten its cause, the divine wrath against the enemies of the poet. They are abruptly recalled to our remembrance in the "them" in this verse.

(16) He drew me.—By an exquisite transition from the real to the figurative the poet conceives of these parted waters as the "floods of affliction" (verse 4), from which Jehovah has rescued him by means of the very storm which was sent, in answer to his prayer to overwhelm his enemies.

(19) A large place.—Comp. Ps. 4:1. But there is direct historical allusion to the settlement of Israel in Canaan.

(20-23) For this protestation of innocence comp. Pss. 7, 17 and Job, passim. Self-righteous pride and vindication of one's character under slander are different things. If taken of the nation at large, comp. Num. 23:21.

(25-27) The human heart makes its God like itself, and to the pure and just He will be a pure and just God, to the cruel and unjust, cruel and unjust. It is, in fact, nothing more than a re-statement of the truth of which the history of Pharaoh is the most signal historic declaration, and which we maintain whenever we speak of the natural consequences of sin as retributive justice, the truth which is summed up in the text, "Whatsoever a man soweth that shall he also reap." We must at the same time remember that the form of the statement in the psalm is due to the view current in Israel before the development of the conception of Satanic agency, that all suggestions, evil as well as good, came from the mind of the Supreme Disposer of events.

(29) A graphic reminiscence of warlike exploits.

(31) Comp. Deut. 32:31, where we see that "rock" was a common term among the tribes of Canaan for their divinities.

(32) **Girdeth.**—The importance of the girdle in a country where the dress was loose and flowing is shown by many passages of Scripture. It is essential to the warrior as here (comp. Eph. 6:14, and the Greek expression, "to be girt"=**to be armed**), but also for all active exertion.

(33) This verse is borrowed in Hab. 3:19. For "swiftness" as an essential of a warrior in Oriental esteem comp. II Sam. 1:23, and the invariable epithet in Homer's **Iliad**, "swift-footed Achilles." For "hind" comp. Gen. 49:21.

(37-40) Another retrospective glance of the poet over his past wars.

(43) **People.**—The parallelism favors the interpretation which takes "people" as equivalent to "peoples"—the Gentiles. But as in Samuel it is "my people," explaining the early political troubles of David.

(46-50) The psalm concludes with a burst of joyous praise, in which the previous figures are recalled in brief touches.

(49) In Rom. 15:9, Paul quotes this verse, together with Deut. 32:43 and Ps. 117:1, as proof that salvation was not in God's purpose confined to the Jews. It seems almost too magnificent a thought in David. Perhaps we are only to think of the nations as brought (see verse 44) an **unwilling** audience of the praises which the conqueror raises to his God for the strength that had subdued them.

19

The abrupt change in rhythm, and apparently in thought, at verse 7 of this poem suggests a compilation from two originally distinct pieces. This view, it is true, is not supported by any ancient texts or versions, and, among modern scholars, there are

some of eminence who still maintain the original unity. They urge that the psalm merely repeats what is the fundamental principle of the theocracy, which is expressly testified by the Old Testament from the earliest times—the identity of the God of revelation with the Creator of the universe. But this gives a very imperfect, and hardly a correct, explanation of the psalm. For the second part does not treat the moral law as a revelation of God to man, but as a revelation to man of his duties, and implies that man continually needs forgiveness for lapsing from the road of right. It would be truer to the spirit of the Old Testament to urge that a poet, thrown by the contemplation of the glory of the heavens into a state of religious emotion, naturally passes on to the Law where he has prepared for him a guide and help in his religion. The Davidic authorship of the first part of the psalm is hardly to be questioned.

(1) **The heavens declare.**—Better, "the heavens are telling." The poet is even now gazing at the sky, not philosophizing on a familiar natural phenomenon, nor is he merely enjoying beauty. Not only is his aesthetic faculty satisfied, but his spirit, his religious nature is moved. He has an immediate apprehension, an intuition of God. He is looking on the freshness of the morning, and all he sees is telling of God, bringing God before him. This constitutes the essence of the greater part of Hebrew poetry. This is the inspiration of the bard of Israel—a "religious" inspiration.

(4) **Their line.**—The use which Paul makes of these words (Rom. 10:18) is as natural as striking. The march of truth has always been compared to the spread of light.

(7) **The law.**—The ear catches even in the English the change of rhythm, which is as marked as the change of subject. In verses 7-9 in each clause the Law, under one or another of its many names and aspects, is praised, first for its essential character, then for its results.

(12) His eulogium on the Law was not Pharisaic or formal, for the poet instantly gives expression to his sense of his own inability to keep it. If before we were reminded of Paul's, "The law is holy, and the commandment holy, and just, and good" (Rom. 7:12), his own spiritual experience, contained in the same chapter, is here recalled: "For the good that I would I do not: but the evil that I would not, that I do."

20

This psalm is addressed to a king going to battle, and was plainly arranged for part-singing in the Temple. The congregation lead off with a prayer for the monarch's success (1-5). The priest, or the king himself, as priest, after watching the successful performance of the sacrificial rites, pronounces his confidence of the victory (6-8), upon which the shout "God save the king!" is raised by the whole host, which acclaim again sinks down into the calmer prayer, "May he hear us when we cry."

It is not necessary to discuss the authorship or the question of what particular king it was intended for. It may be taken as a type of sacrificial hymn. There is, however, a strong Jewish tradition which connects its use, if not its composition, with Hezekiah.

(6) Now know I.—Better, "now know I that Jehovah hath saved his anointed," i.e., the king who is the subject of the poem, it being out of keeping with the rest of the poem to understand "Israel" or the "ideal" king here. The **now** is emphatic. After seeing the sacrifice performed, and feeling sure of its acceptance, this confidence is expressed.

From his holy heaven.—The prayer in verse 2 had mentioned the sanctuary as the residence of the divine power, and its symbol, the Ark, being deposited there (I Sam. 4:4). The inspiration now expresses a yet higher conviction. The manifestation of succor will not be through any earthly symbol of God's might, but immediately from His dwelling-place on high.

(7) Trust.—The mention of horses and chariots suggests a Syrian war, since the armies of Syria were peculiarly strong in this arm.

21

The preceding psalm was a prayer for success; this is a thanksgiving after victory. Possibly, as many think, the two refer to the same event, and are by the same author. The composition is also similar, since here also the arrangement is for a part song. The people—probably a chorus of maidens, or of Levites—meet the returning hero with their shouts of praise to Jehovah (verses 1-7). The monarch himself is then addressed, perhaps by the leader of the procession (verses 8-12), and the whole concourse again unites in a burst of praise to God at the end.

(3) Thou preventest.—i.e., "comest to meet him." (Comp. Ps. 79:8; I Thess. 4:15.) The "crown" is by some identified with that won by David at Rabbah Moab. Others make it refer to a coronation. Probably no more is intended than a symbol of victory and rejoicing. Maidens were accustomed to meet a monarch returning in victory, and to offer a "crown," or "garland," which was a symbol of extraordinary rejoicing. (Comp. I Sam. 18:6; Ps. 68:11; Song of Solomon 3:11.)

22

The fact that Jesus uttered from His cross the words of bitter woe that begin this poem have given and must ever give it a special interest and importance. It was natural that Christian sentiment should fasten lovingly on it, and almost claim it, not only as a record of suffering typical of our Lord's suffering, but as actually in every detail prophetic of Him. But the signs of a true Messianic character of prophecy are to be looked for in moral likeness, not in accidental resemblances of situation, or co-incidences of language, and in this sense Ps. 22 must always be considered Messianic.

Nothing in David's recorded life bears out the title. The identification of the sufferer with Jeremiah, though much more probable, is excluded by the joyous and hopeful tone of the conclusion of the poem. But is it an individual sufferer at all, and not rather suffering Israel whose profound misery in the first part, and whose happy restoration in the second, the poet depicts?

Such a view certainly suits the conclusion of the psalm better than any other. The individual sufferer at all events there disappears, and his fortunes merge in those of the nation (notice the change to the plural in verses 26 and 29), and the brilliant prospect of a time when the tale of God's righteousness shall be handed down from generation to generation is that of the prophet who has mourned his country's woes rather than his own, and has seen in faith the prayers of Israel heard, and the promises made to her amply performed.

Still, the strong personal tone in the opening of the poem suggests that this prophet was himself closely identified with the sufferings he depicts, and shared them not only in sympathy but in reality, and the great consensus of opinion looks for the author among the sufferers in the exile, and probably among the Levites.

Upon Aijeleth Shahar.—i.e., a particular tune to which the psalm was to be sung.

(1) My God, my God.—For the despairing tone comp. Ps. 80:14. It suits the whole of pious Israel in her times of trouble even better than any individual. For its use by Christ, see Matt. 27:46.

(3) But.—In spite of his seeming desertion the poet still believes Jehovah is the God of the covenant—still the Holy One in whom His people could trust.

The phrase "inhabiting the praises of Israel," recalls the more usual "thou that dwellest between the cherubims" (I Sam. 4:4; II Sam. 6:2; Pss. 80:1, 99:1). But the idea here is more spiritual. The everascending praises of His people become a throne for the divine King, and take the place of the outstretched wings of the cherubim. Perhaps there is a reminiscence of Exod. 15:11, 12.

(21) Unicorns.—See Num. 23:22; either "buffaloes" or "antelopes." There is some uncertainty about the translation of the second clause of this verse. It may be "And from the horns of buffaloes hear me," i.e., hear me calling for help from the horns, etc.

(26) Your heart.—The feast that was made after a great sacrifice, such as II Chron. 7:5, not improbably suggested the figure of the banquet at which all the restored of Israel should meet; afterward elaborated in the prophets (comp. Isa. 25:6), and adopted in its refined spiritual sense by our Lord (Luke 14:16).

The prophetic glance reaches further than the immediate occasion, and in the sufferer's triumphant sense of vindication and restoration he embraces the whole world. (Comp. Jer. 16:19.) The interposition of divine judgment in favor of Israel will warn the nations into sudden recollection of Him, and bring them submissive to His throne.

(31) They shall come.—i.e., the generation just foretold: it shall announce His righteousness to a still younger generation (literally, "to a people born") that He wrought. The tale of Jehovah's goodness to Israel would be handed on from age to age.

23

Under two images equally familiar in Hebrew poetry—that of the shepherd watching over his flock, and of the banquet where Jehovah presides over the just—this psalm expresses the tranquility and happiness of those who are conscious of the divine protection. But, after the Hebrew lyric manner, direct allusions to circumstances mingle with the images. We think therefore of some real person and some actual experience, and not of an allegorical reference to the return of the people of Israel from exile, or of the guidance of the rescued nation from Egypt through the wilderness, which were favorite modes of explanation among the Rabbis. The mention of the house of Jehovah seems decisive against the Davidic authorship, which else it would be fascinating to accept, breathing, as the exquisite verse does, the freshness and beauty of the "sweet singer's" early shepherd days. The feast, too, under the enemies' eyes, might have been a reminiscence of Mahanaim; but if David's fortunes have thus colored the psalm, it must have been through the mind of some later writer.

(1) Shepherd.—This image, as applied to God, appears in Hebrew literature first (Gen. 48:15, 49:24) of his relation to the individual (comp. Ps. 119:176); as the shepherd of His people the image is much more frequent (Pss. 78:52, 80:1; Isa. 40:11, 63:11; Ezek. 34; Micah 7:14).

(2) "The psalmist describes himself as one of Jehovah's flock, safe under His care, absolved from all anxieties by the sense of this protection, and gaining from this confidence of safety the leisure to enjoy, without satiety, all the simple pleasures which make up life—the freshness of the meadow, the coolness of the stream. It is the most complete picture of happiness that ever was or can be drawn. It represents that state of mind for which all alike sigh, and the want of which makes life a failure to most; it represents that heaven which is everywhere if we could but enter it, and yet almost nowhere because so few of us can" **(Ecce Homo** 5, 6).

(4) The valley of the shadow of death . . .—This striking expression, to which the genius of Bunyan has given such reality, was probably on Hebrew lips nothing more than a forcible synonym for a dark, gloomy place. Comp. "darkness of a dungeon" (Ps. 107:10); "the pathless desert" (Jer. 2:6); and metaphorically of "affliction" (Isa. 9:2).

By "valley" we must understand a deep ravine. Palestine abounds in wild and gloomy valleys, and shepherd life experiences the actual peril of them.

Thy rod and thy staff.—Used both for guiding and defending the flock.

(5) Such a sudden transition from the figure of the flock to that of a banquet is characteristic of Hebrew poetry.

(6) The house of the Lord can hardly be anything but the Temple; though some commentators treat this even as figurative of membership in the divine family.

24

Here, as in Ps. 19, we come upon a poem made up of two separate pieces, united without due regard to the difference both of tone and rhythm. Notice that the didactic character of the first ode (verses 1-6) does not harmonize with the warlike march of the second. In the first it is the pious Israelite who is, by virtue of the correspondence of his character to the godlike, to ascend the Holy Mountain; in the second it is Jehovah Himself who comes to claim admission to the fortress by virtue of His prowess in battle, or, more exactly, it is the ark which represents Him, and which was understood by its presence to secure victory, which is brought in triumph to that hill where it was from then on to have its home. The fact that in the early part of the psalm Jehovah appears in full possession of His mountain, which is already a center for pious worshipers, seems to bring its composition down to a time following the removal of the Ark to Zion.

This hymn was naturally adopted by Christians as figurative of the Resurrection and Ascension.

(1) The Lord's.—The majesty of Jehovah as Lord of the universe is a reason to the psalmist for insisting on rectitude and sincerity in those who become His worshipers. Paul uses the same truth, referring to this place (I Cor. 10:26), to show that all things are innocent and pure to the pure; so that a Christian (apart from a charitable regard for the weak) may eat whatever is sold in the shambles, without troubling himself to inquire whether it has been offered to idols or not.

(5) Righteousness.—This is the real blessing that comes from God. That virtue is her own reward is the moral statement of the truth. The highest religious statement must be looked for in Christ's "beatitudes."

(7) Gates.—The poet deems the ancient gateways of the conquered castle far too low for the dignity of the approaching Monarch, and calls on them to open wide and high to give room for His passage.

Everlasting doors.—Better, "ancient doors," "gates of old"; an appropriate description of the gates of the grim old Jebusite fortress, "so venerable with unconquered age."

The King of glory shall come in.—This name, in which the claim for admission is made, connects this psalm immediately with the Ark; that glory, which had fled with the sad cry, Ichabod, has returned; the symbol of the divine presence and of victory comes to seek a lasting resting place.

(10) The Lord of hosts.—A second challenge from the reluctant gates serves as the inauguration of the great name by which the divine nature was especially known under the monarchy. (See note on I Sam. 1:3.)

25

This acrostic psalm offers nothing definite for ascertaining its date, but is usually referred to the exile times, when the faithful among the captive Israelites were "waiting" (verses 3, 5, 21) for the redemption of their race. It is full of plaintive appeal to God for help, and reflects that disposition to trust entirely to the divine pity, which is characteristic of the better minds of Israel under affliction. Indeed we may hear here the voice of the community acknowledging the sins of its younger days (verse 7) before trouble had come to teach the divine lesson of penitence and hope of forgiveness.

(10) Mercy and truth.—Or, "grace and truth"; recalling John 1:4-17, and showing how the conception of God and His ways was gradually passing over from the domain of the Law to that of the Gospel.

(14) Secret.—Rather, "familiar intercourse" (so Symmachus). The Hebrew word primarily means "couch," and then the confidential talk of those sitting on it. (Comp. Ps. 55:14, "sweet counsel.")

And he will shew them his covenant.—This is closely parallel with the preceding clause. The communion enjoyed by the pious is the highest covenant privilege.

26

A priestly or Levitical psalm (see verses 6-8), calm and regular, composed of twelve verses, each verse a distich. The writer has nothing to reproach himself with; he can appeal to the strict tribunal of God without fear. The protest against apostasy is evidently made not for himself alone, but for the pious part of the community.

(6) I will wash.—First a symbolical action (Deut. 21:6 seq.; Matt. 27:24), then a figure of speech (Job 9:30; Ezek. 36:25). The Levitical authorship or, at all events, the Levitical character of the psalm appears from comparison of this with Exod. 30:17 seq.

So will I.—Better, "that I may," etc. There is no other reference in Jewish literature to the custom of pacing round the altar. It is, however, implied from the Talmud that it was part of the ceremonial of the Feast of Tabernacles for people to march around the altar with palms.

27

The opening of this ode reads like the expression of a warrior's faith. On the other hand, verses 4 and 6 point to a Levitical origin. Probably a priest or Levite speaks here for the nation at large, deprived for the present by foreign persecution of the regular temple services. The tone is confident and even triumphant until we come to verse 7, when an abrupt change occurs both in feeling and rhythm. The situation which inspired these latter verses was plainly sad—quite changed from the confidence of the earlier part. The attitude of praise is changed for that of prayer. Many therefore regard the psalm as composite, the work of two different minds.

(1) The Lord is my light.—This noble thought appears nowhere else so grandly. To the ancient bard Jehovah was the guiding and cheering beacon-fire, proclaiming his victory and pointing him the happy homeward way. From this to the belief in God as the source both of moral and intellectual light is a long but glorious stage, along which the world has been guided by such words as Isa. 60:1, still more by the recognition of the incarnate Son as the Light of men (John 1:5; 3:19; 12:46; etc.).

(6) Sacrifices of joy.—Literally, "of shouting." The custom of blowing trumpets (Num. 10:10; comp. Ecclus. 50:16-18) at the time of the burnt offering illustrates this expression even if there is no direct allusion to it.

(7) The change of tone so marked here,

from the warlike to the plaintive, leads to the supposition that verses 7-12 are interpolated from another song of quite another kind in contents, art and period.

28

This psalm gives no distinct indication of its authorship or date of composition. The writer appears to be in a critical condition of health (verse 1), and fears death as a mark of divine punishment, involving him, though innocent, with the wicked. If the psalm is the product of one pen and time, and is really the expression of individual feeling, the writer was a king (verse 8). But the last two verses seem, both in rhythm and tone, to be from another hand, and to be the expression of national, not individual, confidence and hope.

(1) My rock.—Heb. **tsûr** from a root implying "bind together" (Deut. 14:25), not necessarily therefore with sense of height, but with that of strength and solidity. We see from Deut. 32:30, 31 and I Sam. 2:2, that "rock" was a common metaphor for a tutelary deity, and it is adopted frequently for Jehovah in the Psalms and poetical books.

Them that go down into the pit—i.e., "the dead," or "those just about to die" (Ps. 30:3). In Ps. 88:4 the expression is parallel to "My life draweth nigh unto the grave." This expression suggests that the psalmist was on a bed of sickness.

(2) Lift up my hands.—For interesting illustrations of this Oriental custom see Exod. 9:29; I Kings 8:22, etc.

Holy oracle.—Better, "the shrine of thy sanctuary" i.e., the holy of holies, the adytum, or inner recess of the Temple in which the Ark was placed, as we see from I Kings 6:19-22.

(3) Draw me not.—Better, "Drag me not." In Ezek. 32:18 seq. we have a magnificent vision of judgment, in which the wicked nations are represented as being dragged to death and destruction. In the person of the poet, Israel prays not to be involved in such a punishment.

(4) Give them according to their deeds.—The justice of the **lex talionis** was deeply impressed on the mind of Israel, and we need not wonder to find its enforcement made the subject of prayer. There is no indication of personal animosity or vindictiveness. The poet, even if expressing his own feelings, was identified with devout

Israel, to whom it was natural not only to expect from Jehovah the manifestation of judgment which could alone remove the conditions that were so unfavorable to the true religion, but also to pray that He would at the same time vindicate Himself and justify those faithful to Him.

(6) This burst of thanksgiving, breaking in on the poet's prayer, has led to the supposition that an interval elapsed between the composition of the former part of the psalm and this verse, and that the writer takes up his pen to record the answer his supplications have received. Others regard the psalm as composed by the union of two distinct pieces.

29

This is a piece of storm-music which the poetry of no country or age has surpassed. To the Hebrew a storm, at the same time terrible and magnificent, was the direct manifestation of the grandeur of God, and here the poet gives the liveliest expression to that feeling by representing all the phenomena as the immediate result of the divine utterance—consequent on, if not produced by, the thunder, the divine voice. Two scenes are presented—one on earth, where we see the storm sweeping majestically along from the north to the south over the length of Palestine; the other in heaven, where the "sons of God"—i.e., all the angelic intelligences and powers—stand as spectators of the grand drama below, and at the invocation of the poet raise the cry, "Glory," in praise of the divine greatness and power. The two concluding lines are evidently a liturgic addition, and did not form part of the original ode.

(1) Ye mighty.—If it is used in a general sense for beings of supernatural power, but inferior to God, the expression **benê-elîm** for angels would be intelligible, i.e., for angels (comp. Job 1:6; Isa. 6:3) in the widest sense as ministers of God, and so including the lightning and storm. (Comp. Ps. 104:4.) The poet calls on the grand forces of nature themselves to offer praise to their divine Master, for the glory which they have been commissioned to reveal. It is they who at the beginning and end alike of the psalm sing the praises of Him who summoned them to speak to men in His name, and make His voice to be heard.

(2) In the beauty of holiness.—Better, "in holy attire"; an image borrowed from the

416

splendid vestments of the priests and Levites (II Chron. 20:21; Ps. 110:3). So the presences that attend the courts of heaven are bidden to be robed in their most magnificent attire, as for a high and sacred ceremony.

(3) The voice.—The invocation to the angels over, the storm bursts, and seven successive peals of thunder mark its course of fury and destruction.

(9) In his temple.—The angelic spectators of the magnificent drama enacted below them cry, each one, "Glory," obeying the poet's invocation in the prelude.

Notice that the effect of the storm on men is supposed to be all summed up in the poet's own attitude of listening awe. There is no actual mention of this part of creation; but one feels from the poem that while inanimate nature trembles and suffers, and the godlike intelligences of heaven are engaged in praise, man listens and is mute.

(10) The Lord sitteth.—The word translated "flood" is exclusively, except in this place, applied to the Deluge (Gen. 6, 7). Perhaps the Deluge may have passed into a proverbial term for any great rain.

30

This psalm, which is plainly an expression of thankfulness for recovery from a dangerous, and nearly fatal, sickness, does not in a single line or word bear out the title, which suggests either the dedication of the site of the future temple (II Sam. 24; I Chron. 21) or of the citadel on Zion (II Sam. 5:11), or of the rededication of the palace profaned by Absalom. On the other hand, the fact that the psalm is, in the Jewish ritual, used at the Feast of Dedication, the origin of which is to be found in I Macc. 4:52 seq., suggests that the title may have been appended after the institution of that feast, in order to give an historical basis for the use of the psalm. The reason of its choice we must look for in the feelings produced by the first successes in the war of independence. After the sad period of humiliation and persecution, the nation felt as the writer of this psalm felt—as if saved from the brink of the grave. Thus the psalm is in application national, though in origin and form individual. Who the author was, it is vain to conjecture; the tone and even the language suggest Hezekiah or Jeremiah.

(3) Grave.—Sheol. (See note to 6:5.)

(5) For his anger.—It is thoroughly Oriental. Sorrow is the wayfarer who comes to the tent for a night's lodging, but the metaphor of his taking his leave in the morning is not carried on, and we have instead the sudden waking with a cry of joy, sudden as the Eastern dawn without twilight or preparation. Never was faith in the divine love more beautifully expressed. (Comp. Isa. 54:7, 8.)

31

This psalm is full of tantalizing expressions which raise the expectation of a satisfactory historical basis for its composition, only to disappoint by the obscurity of their allusion. Moreover, the psalm oscillates between plaintive prayer and assured trust in a way to indicate that we cannot here have the experience of one single event, but the gathered sentiments of a whole lifetime. Who appear here are those who hate the pious Israelite because they themselves adore other gods (verse 6)—they are the wicked—their arms are recrimination, slander, contempt, the insolence of the powerful against the humble and weak. The psalm seems, therefore, to reflect the later times of the monarchy, when the pure religion of Jehovah had to struggle against idolatrous tendencies favored in high places. The recurrence of phrases common in his writings show that if Jeremiah was not the author of the psalm, he was very familiar with it, or the writer of the psalm was imbued with his style.

(5) I commit.—Most memorable, even among expressions of the Psalms, as the dying words of our Lord Himself (Luke 23:46), and a long line of Christian saints. Polycarp, Bernard, Huss, Henry V, Jerome of Prague, Luther, Melanchthon, are some of the many who have passed away comforted and upheld by the psalmist's expression of trust. But death was not in his thought, it was in life, amid its troubles and dangers, that he trusted (Hebrew, "deposited as a trust") his spirit.

(8) Shut me up into the hand.—This is the exact phrase used by David (I Sam. 23:11, 12) in consulting the divine oracle by the ephod. But this does not prove the authorship, for it was evidently a common phrase. (See I Sam. 24:18; II Kings 17:4.)

(15) My times are in thy hand.—i.e., the vicissitudes of human life (LXX and Vulgate have "my destinies") are under divine control, so that the machinations of the foe

cannot prevail against one whom God intends to deliver. For the expression comp. I Chron. 29:30, "the times that went over him" (Isa. 33:6).

The sense of security in this trusting phrase may be contrasted with the feeling of danger in another Hebrew phrase, "my soul is continually in my hand" (Ps. 119:109).

(21) In a strong city.—Some see a reference to David's adventures at Ziklag or Keilah; others to Jeremiah's in Jerusalem (Jer. 38). It is, however, better to regard it merely as a general image of the divine protection.

32

No other Old Testament saint that we know of could have written this psalm except David. And yet at the outset we are met by the fact that the history makes David's repentance after each of his great sins turn on the reproof of a prophet. But even a prophetic glance from the outside cannot read the whole history of a soul, while one who can feel profoundly is not unlikely, when reviewing the past, to dwell exclusively on the intense sense of guiltiness before God, without referring to the outward circumstance which may have suddenly brought it home to him. And if we are not led away by the interest of a particular situation, but consider how David, wishing to express in song the happiness of penitence, might color his half-didactic purpose with the recollection of his own personal experience of sin and forgiveness, a recollection still vivid with him, we shall not wonder at the apparent contradiction between the beginning and end of the psalm, and may readily allow the correctness of the inscription.

"Augustine used often to read this psalm with weeping heart and eyes, and had it before his death written on the wall over his sickbed, that he might exercise himself therein, and find comfort therein in his sickness."

Title.—Maschil (**maskhil**), a title prefixed to thirteen psalms, and in several cases joined to musical directions. In Ps. 47:7 the word is joined to a term meaning to play or sing in such a way as to indicate a musical reference, a reference fully borne out by some of the titles, and also by the description of the Levitical musicians (II Chron. 30:22), by the participle of this verb, as "those who play skilfully with good taste." Therefore render "a skillful song."

(1, 2) Transgression—sin—iniquity.—The same terms used here to express the compass and heinousness of sin are found, though in different order, in Exod. 34:7. For Paul's reading of this passage see Rom. 4:6, 7.

(8) I will guide thee with mine eye.—The Hebrew may be rendered "I will fix mine eye upon thee." This verse changes so abruptly to the first person that it is better to suppose them the words of deliverance that sound so sweet in the psalmist's ears.

33

This is a hymn of praise to Jehovah, as at once Almighty Creator and Ruler of the universe, and the Protector of His chosen people. It was plainly for liturgical use, and beyond this, as even the compilers of the collection left it anonymous, it is useless to inquire into its authorship or date. All that we see clearly is that faith in the protection of Jehovah and not in material force, that which we regard as the traditional faith of Israel, had by this time been firmly implanted. In subject this psalm bears a close relation to Ps. 147.

(2) With the psaltery and an instrument of ten strings.—Properly, as LXX and Vulgate, "with the ten-stringed psaltery." (See I Sam. 10:5.) Evidently a more elaborate instrument than the **khinnôr,** ("harp") and with greater capacities. From the Greek psalterion comes the title "psalter" for the Book of Psalms. By its derivation it meant an instrument played with the fingers.

(3) A new song.—This expression occurs in Pss. 96:1; 98:1; 149:1; Isa. 42:10, and was adopted in Rev. 5:9 and 14:3. The term apparently marked the revival of national psalmody after the Captivity.

Play skilfully with a loud noise.—The latter words represent a Hebrew expression of common hymnic use, describing the full choral effect when instruments and voices were joined in the service of the sanctuary (Pss. 95:1; 100:1; etc.).

(4) Right.—The first inspiring cause of praise for a faithful Israelite is the righteousness of the God of the Covenant. But the pregnant expression, "word of Jehovah," naturally leads him on from the thought of its truth to the thought of its power, and in verses 6 and 7 we have praise of the creative act of the Almighty.

(10) The Lord bringeth.—The thought now passes on to the irresistible rule of Jehovah. His counsel stands for all generations, and being righteous as well as eternal frustrates the counsel and thoughts of the heathen, while His chosen people (verse 12) rest in stable peace under the Theocracy. (Comp. Acts 5:38.)

Verse 12 is the pivot, as it were, on which the whole psalm turns, and was doubtless sung in full chorus.

34

This psalm consists of a string of pious sayings of a proverbial kind, all beautiful in themselves, but combined with no art beyond the alphabetical arrangement, and even this, as in Ps. 25, not strictly carried out. Certainly the composition is of time far later than David, and the inscription (see note) is of no historic value. A late, even an Aramaic origin, is indicated. But beyond this there is nothing by which to appropriate the psalm to any particular period, still less to any particular event or individual. It reads more like a gnomic composition expressive of the faith of the pious community than as the outpouring of individual feeling.

Title.—An inscription so entirely foreign to the contents of the psalm, and containing besides an historical blunder in the king's name (I Sam. 21:13, 14).

(7) The angel of the Lord is an expression which has given rise to much discussion. From comparison with other passages it may be (1) any commissioned agent of God, as a prophet (Haggai 1:13); (2) one of the celestial court (Gen. 22:11); (3) any manifestation of the divine presence, as the flame in the bush (Exod. 3:2), the winds (Pss. 35:5, 6; 104:4); (4) Jehovah Himself, as in the phrase "the angel of his presence" (Isa. 63:9). It may very well be, therefore, that the psalmist uses it here in a general sense for the divine manifestation of protection.

(11) Come, ye children ... —A common proverbial style. See Prov. 1:8, and **passim.** (Comp. also I John 2:1, etc.)

(12) Desireth life.—Better, "the man delighting in life." These gnomic sayings are echoes from the Book of Proverbs. (See especially Prov. 4:23.)

(15) The eyes.—A verse quoted in I Pet. 3:12. This psalm had a deep hold on the national mind.

(16) To cut off.—Notice the fear, so intense and recurring to the Semitic mind, of the extinction of race. (Comp. Ps. 21:10; Job 18:17; etc.)

35

This psalm opens in a warlike tone, so as to suggest a soldier for its author, and for its occasion the eve of some battle. But we soon (verses 7, 8, 11, 12) perceive that these warlike expressions are only metaphors, and that the foes of the poet are malicious slanderers and scoffers of the pious Israelites—it may be the court party in the time of one of the later kings, or, more probably, the anti-national party (see note on verse 16) at a later time, the innovators affected by Persian or Grecian influence.

Few good critics, at all events, consider the psalm Davidic. Some ascribe it to Jeremiah. But whoever was its author, it expresses, not an individual feeling alone, but that of a community despised and maligned for its piety, and appealing to Jehovah against its oppressors, with that longing for retributive justice which in an individual becomes, in a Christian view, wickedly vindictive, but to the Old Testament Church was the vindication of the divine honor which was pledged to do justice to the chosen but afflicted people.

(5) As chaff.—Comp. Ps. 1:4, and see note. There can be little doubt that the "angel of Jehovah" in this and the following verse is (comp. Ps. 104:4) a personification of the "hurricane" itself, which drives before it all obstacles, and overwhelms even whole armies in dangerous places.

(13) And my prayer returned into mine own bosom.—This has been most variously explained. The context evidently implies something done for the benefit of the former friends for whom, in their sickness, the poet had worn sackcloth, and had fasted and adopted all the signs of mourning.

The probable meaning, "my prayer came back again and again to my bosom," i.e., was repeated over and over again; just as we say, "the thought recurred to my mind."

(15) The abjects ... —The Hebrew word occurs only here. It is derived from a root meaning to "smite," but its form is perplexing. The Chaldee, "the wicked who smite me with their words," probably is a correct paraphrase.

(16) With hypocritical mockers in feasts.— The word rendered "hypocritical" more properly means "profane" or "impious."

With these meanings we get a very good sense (with evident reference to the malicious attacks of foreigners, or of the anti-national party that affected foreign ways) "with profanity and barbarism."

(20) Quiet in the land.—They are evidently the pious Jews who wished to preserve their national life and religion against foreign influence and intervention, and certainly among them were Levites.

36

This psalm consists of three distinctly defined stanzas of nearly equal length. The first portrays the wicked man who has reached the lowest grade of impiety. The second exalts the goodness and justice of God. The third, which is, in a sort, a practical application of the others, expresses, under the form of a prayer, the right choice to make between the two tendencies, the pious and the impious.

Those who understand by "God's house," in verse 8, the Temple, reject the Davidic authorship. But understood of the world generally, or, better, of the heavenly abode of the divine, it does not serve as an indication of date, and there is nothing else in the poem to decide when it was written.

Title.—For "servant of the Lord," as applied to David, see Ps. 18 (title).

(3, 4) From the secret promptings of sin, the description of the ungodly passes on to its issues in words and deeds. It is an awful picture of wickedness of a man abandoning himself without check or remorse to the inspiration of his own evil heart. He goes from bad to worse. But this man "deviseth mischief upon his bed." When even the worst criminals shudder at their own deeds, whispering to their "deaf pillows" the agonies that creep over them with darkness and silence, this ungodly man of the Hebrew poet's picture is occupied rather in scheming fresh villainies.

(8) The **house** of God may either be the whole earth (Gesenius), or, more probably, heaven, just as the temple is used (Pss. 11:4; 18:6; 29:9).

(9) In thy light.—This wonderful verse contains the germ of that moral and spiritual teaching which had its highest development in the epistles of John. But the original intention of the words seems to be that the favor and bounty of God commend themselves as divine in origin, especially to those in the covenant relation.

37

This psalm is mainly composed of quotations and adaptations from older writings, especially the Book of Proverbs, which are strung together with no other art than that suggested by the alphabetical arrangement, all having one end, to comfort the pious Israelite under the spectacle of successful wickedness, confirming him in his trust in Jehovah, and warning him neither to envy the prospects of the impious, nor to despair of his own state. It is by no means a speculative poem. It does not treat the perplexing problems of life philosophically. The poet has one answer, and only one, for the questions handled so pathetically and profoundly in the Book of Job. The happiness of the wicked cannot endure, and the justice of Jehovah will assuredly re-establish the right, punishing the godless and recompensing the patience and fidelity of the godly. The time of the exile, when the hope of regaining the Promised Land was the consolation of the pious, probably produced the psalm.

(11) Shall inherit.—A repetition of verse 3. Better, "are heirs of the land, i.e., Canaan. Christ's Beatitude (see Matt. 5:3) widens the promise and lifts it to a higher level. The quiet, unpretending, contented servant of God gets more true blessedness out of the earth, and so more truly possesses it, than the ungodly, though they be lords of broad acres.

38

The complaint of bodily suffering (verses 1-11) gives way to a description of active and deadly enemies, who, in the figure so common in the Psalms, beset the pious with snares. We should think not of the individual but rather of the sufferings of the community of the faithful, who have learned to attribute their troubles to their own sins, here described, after the manner of the prophets (Isa. 1:6) but even more forcibly, under the figure of distressing forms of sickness.

Title.—Comp. title, Ps. 70. See also I Chron. 16:4, where in the words "thank" and "praise" it is natural to see allusion to the **Hodu** and **Hallelujah** psalms, so called because beginning with those words, and as "to record" is in Hebrew the word used in this title and that to Ps. 70, it brings these two psalms also in connection with the

420

Levitical duties. "The memorial" was a regular name for one part of the meat offering, and possibly the title is a direction to use these psalms at the moment it was made.

(7) Loathsome disease.—The Hebrew word is a passive participle of a verb meaning to "scorch," and here means "inflamed" or "inflammation." Ewald renders "ulcers."

(9) All my desire.—Notice the clutch at the thought of divine justice, as the clutch of a drowning man amid that sea of trouble.

(18) Sorry.—The note of true penitence is here. The sorrow is for the sin itself, not for its miserable results.

(19) But mine enemies are lively.—The parallelism and a comparison with Ps. 35:19 lead to the suspicion that the true reading is "without cause."

39

"Undoubtedly," says Ewald, "the finest elegy in the Psalter." The many points of similarity with the Book of Job must be taken to indicate the acquaintance of its author with this Psalm. Perhaps it is from this elegy that he takes up the problem offered by the contradictions of life which he carries so much farther.

Title.—Jeduthun is identified with Ethan (I Chron. 15:17) the Merarite, who with Heman the Korahite and Asaph the Gershonite were appointed musical directors (I Chron. 15:19) of the temple service. (Comp. titles of Ps. 62 and 77.)

(1) My tongue.—To enter into the feeling of the poet we must remember the unrestrained way in which Orientals give way to grief. He determines to endure in silence and mutely bear the worst, rather than speak what may in the eyes of the impious be construed into a murmur against divine Providence, into impatience under the divine decree. (Comp. Ps. 38:13, 14.)

(3) The fire burned.—The attempt at repression only makes the inward flame of feeling burn the more fiercely, till at last it is too much for the resolution that has been formed, and the passion of the heart breaks out in words. But thought is too much for him, and he breaks into speech, not, however, fretfully, still less with bitter invective against others. It is a dialogue with the ruler of destiny, in which frail man wants to face his condition, and know the worst.

(4) Rhythmically and from every other reason the psalm onward from this verse must be treated as the utterance to which the poet's feelings have at length driven him.

(7) And now, Lord ... —"If such is man's condition, what," says the psalmist, "is my expectation?" We seem to hear the deep sigh with which the words are uttered; and we must remember that the poet can turn for comfort to no hope of immortality. That had not yet dawned. The thought of God's mercy and the hope of his own moral deliverance form the ground of his noble elevation above the oppressive sense of human frailty.

(8) Here the psalmist recurs to his initial thought, but lets us see deeper into his heart. It was no mere fancy that if he gave vent to his feelings the wicked might find cause for reproach; the cause was there in his own consciousness of transgression.

(12) For I am a stranger.—A reminiscence of Gen. 23:4, and adopted I Peter 2:11 from the LXX (comp. Heb. 11:13). The psalmist, like the apostle, applies Abraham's words metaphorically to this earthly pilgrimage (comp. I Chron. 29:15), and pathetically asks why, when the tenure of life is so uncertain, God looks angrily on him? For the passionate appeal for a respite, comp. Job. 10:20, 21.

incorporated here; that we have at least the substance of it, if not the words. Possibly the very words are taken up in verse 4. And we are to find the "newness" in the magnificent vindication of spiritual above formal worship.

(6) Mine ears hast thou opened.— Literally, "Ears hast thou dug for me," which can hardly mean anything but "Thou hast given me the sense of hearing." The words are an echo of I Sam. 15:22. The attentive ear and obedient heart, not formal rites, constitute true worship. Comp. the words so frequent on the lips of Christ, "He that hath ears to hear let him hear." The fact that the plural **ears** is used instead of the singular excludes allusion to the symbolic act by which a slave was devoted to perpetual servitude (Ex. 21:6), because then only one ear was bored. For the well-known variation in the LXX see Heb. 10:5.

(7) Then said I.—This rendering, which follows the LXX and Vulgate, and is adopted in the epistle to the Hebrews, must be abandoned. The Hebrew means, "Lo! I come, bringing the book written for me," which no doubt refers to the Law, which in the person of the poet, Israel here produces as warrant for its conduct. Some see a particular allusion to the discovery of the Book of Deuteronomy in Josiah's reign.

40

The phenomenon presented in this psalm of a burst of praise (verses 1-10), followed by plaintive prayer (verse 11 onward), is so peculiar, and so contrary to the usual method of psalm composition, as to lead of itself to the conjecture of a composite poem. The fact that verses 13-17 appear again in Psalm 70 adds some force to this conjecture. We must in any case notice the prophetic power of the singer. In the true spirit of the Hebrew prophets he exalts spiritual above merely formal religion.

If we must fix on an author, the Deuteronomist suggests himself, or Jeremiah. That the psalm was written after the discovery of the Book of the Law, in Josiah's reign, there can be little doubt.

Title.—See Ps. 3 (title).

(2) Rock.—The common image of security (Pss. 18:2; 27:5), the occurence of which makes it probable that the "pit" and "clay" are also not realities, but emblems of confusion and danger.

(3) New song.—See Ps. 33:3. It seems natural to suppose that this new song is

41

Recalling the treachery of some pretended friends, the writer in this psalm pronounces, in contrast, a eulogy on those who know how to feel for and show compassion to the suffering. There is nothing, however, to indicate who the author was, or what particular incidents induced him to write. Possibly the sickness is entirely figurative, and the psalm is the expression of the feelings of the community of pious Israelites.

The doxology in verse 13 does not belong to the psalm, but closes the first book of the collection.

(1) Blessed is he.—This general statement of the great law of sympathy and benevolence—fine and noble however we take it— may be explained in different ways, according as we take the Hebrew word **dal** as "poor," with the LXX and Vulgate (comp. Exod. 30:15), or as "sick," "weak in body" (comp. Gen. 41:19), or give it an ethical sense, "sick at heart." (Comp. II Sam. 13:4.) Verse 3 strongly favors the view that the sickness is physical.

Considereth.—The Hebrew word implies wise as well as kindly consideration. So LXX and Vulgate, "he that understands."

(3) Wilt make.—Literally, "hast turned." To "turn" here is to "change," as in Pss. 66:6; 105:29, and what the poet says is that, as in past times, divine help has come to change his sickness into health, so he confidently expects it will be now.

(9) Hath lifted up his heel.—The meaning is, possibly, "kicked violently at me." (See John 13:18.) The rights of Oriental hospitality must be remembered to bring out all the blackness of the treachery here described.

(11) By this I know.—Better, "shall know." His restoration would be a sign of the divine favor, and a pledge of his victory over his enemies.

BOOK II

42

Psalms 42 and 43 form in reality one poem. In style, in subject, in tone, they have been recognized as from one time and pen. The poems thus united into one are seen to have three equal stanzas. All three stanzas express the complaint of a sufferer sinking under the weight of his misfortunes; the refrain in contrast expresses a sentiment of religious resignation, of unalterable confidence in divine protection and favor. We can even realize the situation of the sufferer. We find him not only far from Jerusalem, and longing anxiously for return there, but actually on the frontier, near the banks of the Jordan, not far from the sources of the river, on the great caravan route between Syria and the far east, on the slopes of Hermon. We seem to see him strain his eyes from these stranger heights to catch the last look of his own native hills, and from the tone of his regrets—regrets inspired not by worldly or even patriotic considerations, but by the forcible separation from the choral service of the Temple, we conjecture him to have been a priest or a Levite.

Title.—(See title, Pss. 4 and 32.) "For the sons of Korah." This is a title of Pss. 42, 44-49, 84, 85, 87, 88.

We see from I Chron. 6:16-33 that the Korahites were, when that history was written, professional musicians. In the older documents the singers and porters are mentioned separately from the Levites (Ezra 7:7, 24; 10:23, 24; Neh. 7:1), and it is only in those of a later date that we find them

included in that tribe. Therefore we regard these "sons of Korah" (in one passage a still more vague appellation, "children of the Korhites," II Chron. 20:19), not as lineally descendants from the Korah of Num. 16:1, but as one of the then divisions of the body of musicians who were treated as Levitical.

(2) Appear before God?—Exod. 23:17 shows that this was the usual phrase for frequenting the sanctuary (comp. Ps. 84:7), though poetic brevity here slightly altered its form and construction.

(4) For I had gone with the multitude.—The poet indulges in a grateful recollection of some great festival, probably the Feast of Tabernacles.

(5) Why art thou.—The refrain here breaks in on the song like a sigh, the spirit of dejection struggling against the spirit of faith.

(6) Cast down.—The poet, though faith condemns his dejection, still feels it, and cannot help expressing it. The heart will not be tranquil all at once, and the utterance of its trouble, so natural, so pathetic, long after served, in the very words of the LXX, to express a deeper grief, and mark a more tremendous crisis (John 12:27; Matt. 26:38).

From the land of Jordan.—i.e., the uplands of the northeast, where the river rises. The poet has not yet passed quite into the land of exile, the country beyond Jordan, but already he is on its borders, and as his sad eyes turn again and again toward the loved country he is leaving, its sacred summits begin to disappear, while ever nearer and higher rise the snow-clad peaks of Hermon.

Hermonites.—Either collectively for the whole range, or with reference to the appearance of the mountain as a ridge with a conspicuous peak at either end. In reality, however, the group known especially as Hermon has three summits, situated, like the angles of a triangle, a quarter of a mile from each other, and of almost equal elevation. Some lower ridge or pass, over which the exile may be supposed wending his sad way, was actually called "the little," or "the less."

(7) Deep calleth unto deep at the noise of thy waterspouts.—The exile is describing what was before his eyes and in his ears. There can, therefore, be little doubt that this image was furnished by the windings and rapids of the Jordan, each hurrying to dash itself with yet fiercer vehemence of sounding water over some opposing ledge of rocks "in cataract after cataract to the sea." Thus every step taken on that sorrowful journey offered an emblem of the grief's accumulating on the exiles's heart.

All thy waves and thy billows.—The poet passes on to the more general image of "sea of troubles," the waves of which break upon him or roll over his head. The image is common in all poetry.

(8) And in the night his song.—The parallelism of this verse seems to confirm the conclusion drawn from the sentence at the end of Book II, that the title "prayer," and "song" were used indiscriminately for any of the hymns in religious use.

(9) Apparently we have now the very words of the prayer just mentioned.

(10) As with a sword.—This, no doubt, refers to actual ill-treatment of the exile by his conductors, who heaped blows, as well as insults, on their captives. We may even suppose this violence especially directed at this particular sufferer, who could not refrain from lingering and looking back, and so irritating his escort, who would naturally be in a hurry to push forward. How vividly, too, does the picture of the insulting taunt, "Where is thy God?" (verse 3) rise before us, if we think of the soldiers overhearing the exile's exclamations of prayer.

43

(3) O send out thy light and thy truth: let them lead me.—Instead of the violent and contemptuous escort of Assyrian soldiers, leading the exile away from the "holy hill," the poet prays for God's light and truth to lead him, like two angel guides, back to it.

44

In spite of the singular used in verses 6 and 15, we recognize, in this psalm, a hymn expressive not of individual but of national feeling; a feeling, too, which certainly could not have received such expression before the exile, before the spell of the fascination of the Canaanitish idolatries had passed away. Nor can the psalm be assigned to the exile period itself, for it does not reflect the profound spiritual insight that characterizes the literature which undoubtedly belongs to that time. The majority of critics prefer the time of Antiochus Epiphanes. It might well have been inspired by one of those reverses, which so often came upon the struggling

community of Israel, in consequence of their scrupulous concern for the Sabbath day, which did not even allow them to defend themselves. (See verses 13 and 14.)

Title.—See title, Pss. 32, 42.

(1) We have heard.—The glorious traditions of ancient deliverances wrought by Jehovah for His people were a sacred heritage of every Hebrew. (See Exod. 10:2; 12:26, seq., Deut. 6:20; etc.) This, and all the historical psalms, show how closely interwoven for the Jew were patriotism and religion.

(3) The light of thy countenance.—Notice the contrast to this in verse 24; in times of distress God's face seemed hidden or averted.

(4) Thou art my King.—What God has done in the past may be expected again, and for a moment the poet forgets the weight of actual trouble in the faith that has sprung from the grateful retrospect over the past.

(5) Push down.—The image of the original is lost here, the LXX has retained it. It is that of a buffalo or other horned animal driving back and goring its enemies. Deut. 33:17 applies it as a special description of the tribe of Joseph. The figure is continued in the next clause; the infuriated animal tramples its victim under foot.

(13, 14) These verses become very suggestive, if we refer them to one of those periods under the Seleucidae, when the Jews were so frequently attacked on the Sabbath, and from their scrupulous regard to it would make no resistance.

(19) In the place of dragons.—This expression evidently means "a wild desert place," from comparison with Jer. 9:11; 10:22; 49:33. The jackal is the animal that best answers the requirements of Isa. 34:13; Jer. 14:6; and Job 30:29.

45

From Calvin to this day this psalm has been recognized as an ode celebrating the nuptials of some king. There is just enough of historical allusion in the psalm to invite conjecture as to the monarch who is its theme, and too little to permit of his identification. But, as in the case of the Song of Solomon, religious scruples soon rejected this secular interpretation, and sought by allegorical and mystical explanations to bring the poem more within the circle of recognized sacred literature. With glowing prophetic visions of a conquering Messiah

423

before them, it was most natural for the Jews to give the psalm a distinctive Messianic character. Equally natural was it for Christians to adopt the psalm as allegorical of the marriage of the Church with the divine Head.

Title.—"Upon Shoshannim," i.e., "upon lilies." The same inscription occurs again in Ps. 69 and in an altered form in Pss. 60 and 80. The most probable explanation makes it refer to the tune to which the hymn was to be sung. The expression, "a song of loves," means either a love song, or a "song of the beloved "

(1) Inditing.—From the meaning of its derivative (a "pot," or "cauldron"), this word must have something to do with a liquid, and means either to "boil over," or to "bubble up." The "spring," or "fountain," is a common emblem of inspired fancy.

(6) Thy throne, O God, is for ever and ever.—This is the rendering of the LXX, Vulgate, and of the versions generally. But whether they supposed the words to be addressed to the divine Being, or that the theocratic king is thus styled, is uncertain. The Christian use of the verse as applied to the Messiah (Heb. 1:8) does not help us to explain how the monarch, who is the poet's theme here, could be addressed as God. "Thy throne is of God for ever" is grammatically preferable.

(8) Out of the ivory palaces, whereby they have made thee glad.—It would have been strange if a nuptial ode, giving a picture of the splendor and pomp accompanying the marriage, had missed the mention of music, and at this verse we may imagine the doors of the palace thrown open for the issue of the bridal train (the procession immediately follows the bath, verse 7), not only allowing the strains of music to float out, but also giving a glimpse into the interior, where, surrounded by her train of ladies, the queen-bride stands.

(13) Her clothing.—Eastern tales speak of the custom of repeatedly changing the bride's dress during the marriage ceremonies, each time presenting her in greater magnificence than before.

(16) Whom thou mayest make princes.—Historical illustrations have been found in I Kings 22:26, where Joash, David's son, appears as a governor or a prince of a city (comp. Zeph. 1:8), and in the division of his realm into principalities by Solomon (I Kings 4:7).

46

This psalm reflects the feelings with which a people, secure in the sense of divine protection, looks on while surrounding nations are convulsed, and calmly awaits the issue. Such a situation was that of Israel in the seventh century B.C., while the giant powers of Egypt and Assyria were rending the East by their rivalries. The period suggests itself as the probable date of the psalm, from its resemblance to much of the language of Isaiah when dealing with events that culminated in the destruction of Sennacherib's army. Compare especially the recurrence of the expression, "God is with us," with the prophet's use of the name "Immanuel."

Title.—For the first part see titles to Pss. 4, 42. Since 'alāmôth means maidens, the most natural interpretation is "a song for sopranos." (Comp. title, Ps. 6.)

(2) Though the earth be removed.—The psalmist was thinking of the sudden convulsion of earthquake, and figures Israel fearless amid the tottering kingdoms and falling dynasties.

(5) Right early.—Literally, "at the turning of the morning." Evidently metaphorical of the dawn of a brighter day.

47

The story refuses to be satisfactorily identified. Some public rejoicing for victory evidently gave it birth, but whether it was that of Jehoshaphat (II Chron. 20), or of Hezekiah (II Kings 18:8), or of John Hyrcanus over the Idumaeans (Jos., **Ant.**, 13:9, 1), must remain in the region of conjecture. The occasion, whatever it was, seems to have led to a rededication of the Temple (verse 5), such as we read of I Macc. 4:54.

Title.—See titles, Pss. 42 and 44.

(5) Is gone up.—Not as in Gen. 17:22; Judg. 13:20, to heaven, but, as in Ps. 24, to the Temple, as is shown by the public acclaim accompanying the ark to its resting place after victory. (Comp. II Chron. 20:28; Ps. 68:17; Amos 2:2.)

48

Jerusalem has been in great peril from some coalition either of neighboring monarchs or of the tributary princes of one of the great world powers, and has been delivered through some unexplained sudden panic. With this event the poet of this psalm is contemporary (see verses 4-8); but on what precise event we are to fix is not so clear. There are resemblances to the deliverance of Jehoshaphat (II Chron. 20:25), to the fate of Sennacherib's host (II Kings 19), to the harassment of Ahaz by Pekah and Rezin (II Kings 15:37), and to other important changes of fortune in later times of Israel's history.

But if we can enter into the spirit of blended piety and patriotism which makes the poem so expressive of the whole better feeling of the best times of the nation, the recovery of the precise date of its production is immaterial.

Title.—See Ps. 41.

(2) Sides of the north.—A common phrase, generally taken to mean the quarter or region of the north, but which, from the various uses of two words making it up, might mean "northern recesses" or "secret recesses." With the former of the two meanings we should see a reference to the relative position of the Temple and its precincts to the rest of the city. If, on the other hand, we elect to render "secret," or "hidden," or "secure recesses," we have a figure quite intelligible of the security and peace to be found in God's holy city. And the thought is taken up in the word "refuge" in the next verse. (Comp. Ezek. 7:22, where the Temple is actually called "Jehovah's **secret** place.")

(4) The kings.—With the striking picture of the advance and sudden collapse of a hostile expedition that follows, comp. Isa. 10:28-34 as possibly of the same event.

(7) Breakest.—It is natural at first sight to connect this verse immediately with the disaster which happened to the fleet of Jehoshaphat (I Kings 22:48, 49; II Chron. 20:36).

Isaiah, in chap. 33, compares Assyria to a gallant ship. For the "east wind," proverbially destructive and injurious, and so a ready weapon of chastisement in the divine hand, see Job 21:18; Isa. 27:8; Ezek. 27:26, where its harm to shipping is especially mentioned.

(9) Thy temple.—This verse seems to indicate a liturgic origin for the psalm.

(12) Walk about Zion.—Notice here the strong patriotic feeling of Hebrew song. The inhabitants of the city are invited to make a tour of inspection of the defenses which, under God's providence, have protected them from their foes.

49

This psalm is didactic, not only cast in lyrical form, but rising into true poetry both of expression and feeling. Indeed, it is not as a philosophical speculation that the author propounds and discusses his theme, but as a problem of personal interest (verses 15, 16); therefore throughout the composition a strain of passion rather than a flow of thought.

Title.—See titles, Pss. 4 and 42.

(4) I will incline mine ear.—The psalmist first listens, that he may himself catch the inspiration which is to reach others through his song. It was an obvious metaphor in a nation to whom God's voice was audible.

(15) But God will.—Better, "But God shall redeem my life from the hand of sheol when it seizes me." Taken by itself, this statement might only imply that when just at the point of death, the divine favor would draw him back and rescue him. But taken with the previous verse, we must see here the dim foreshadowing of a better hope, that death did not altogether break the covenant bond between Jehovah and His people, a hope to which, through the later psalms and the book of Job, we see the Hebrew mind feeling its way. (Comp. Ps. 16:10; and see note to Ps. 6:5.)

(16, 17) After expressing his own hopes of escaping from death, or being rescued from corruption, the psalmist returns to the question of verse 5, and completes the answer to it. He need not fear, however prosperous and wealthy his adversaries become, for they will die, and, dying, can take none of their possessions with them.

(18) Though, while he lived . . . —This is abundantly illustrated by our Lord's parable of the rich fool (Luke 12:19; comp. Deut. 29:19).

(19) They shall never.—i.e., "never live again," implying, in contrast, a hope of a resurrection for the upright.

50

The one great corruption to which all religion is exposed is its separation from morality, and of all religions that of Israel was pre-eminently open to this danger. It was one of the main functions of the prophetical office to maintain the opposite truth —the inseparable union of morality with religion. This psalm takes rank with the prophets in such a proclamation. It makes it under a highly poetical form, a magnificent vision of judgment, in which, after summoning heaven and earth as His assessors, God arraigns before Him the whole nation, separated into two great groups; sincere but mistaken adherents to form; hypocrites, to whom religious profession is but a cloak for sin.

Title.—Asaph was a Levite, son of Berachiah, and one of the leaders of David's choir (I Chron. 6:39). He was also by tradition a psalm writer (II Chron. 29:30; Neh. 12:46). It is certain, however, that all the psalms ascribed to Asaph (73-83) were not by the same hand, or of the same time (see Introduction to Ps. 74); and, as in the case of the Korahite psalms, probably the inscription, "to Asaph," only implies the family of Asaph, or a guild of musicians bearing that name (I Chron. 25:1; II Chron. 20:14; Ezra 2:41).

(5) My saints.—This verse is of great importance, as containing a formal definition of the word **chasidim**, and so a direction as to its interpretation wherever it occurs in the Hebrew hymn book. The "saints" are those in the "covenant," and that covenant was ratified by sacrifices. As often, then, as a sacrifice was offered by an Israelite, it was a witness to the existence of the covenant, and we are not to gather, therefore, from this psalm that outward acts of sacrifice were annulled by the higher spirit taught in it (see verse 14); they were merely subordinated to their proper place, and those who thought more of the rites that bore testimony to the covenant than of the moral duties which the covenant required, are those censured in this part of the psalm.

(16) But.—The psalm here turns to address a worse class, those who, while undisguisedly wicked, shelter themselves under the name of the covenant.

51

This psalm traditionally has been identified with David. Yet we must either break this long cherished association, or admit the last two verses of the psalm to be a later addition for liturgical use.

But the question of authorship does not affect the estimation in which this psalm has always been held and always will be held, in the Church, as the noblest expression of penitence. Even if it was not originally, directly, and exclusively the expression of an individual's repentance, but rather the voice of the people of Israel deploring, during the exile, its ancient errors and sins, and praying for a new lease of covenant favor, yet the associations of the psalm with individual experience of sin and repentance from it are now far too close to be broken, and it must always remain in the truest sense one of the penitential psalms, suited for private use as well as for that of the Church.

Title.—See title, Ps. 4.

(3) For I.—The thought that he had been unfaithful to the covenant was an accusing conscience to him, keeping his sin always before his eyes, and until, according to his prayer in verses 1 and 2, he was received back into conscious relationship again, his offense must weigh upon his mind. This explanation holds, whether an individual or the community speaks.

(4) Against thee, thee only . . . —This can refer to nothing but a breach of the covenant-relation by the nation at large. An individual would have felt his guilt against the nation or other individuals, as well as against Jehovah. The fact that Paul quotes (from the LXX) part of the verse in Rom. 3:4 has naturally opened up an avenue for discussion on the bearing of the words on the doctrines of freewill and predestination. But the immediate object of his quotation appears to be to contrast the **faithfulness** of the God of the covenant with the **falsehood** of the covenant people. The honor of God, as God of the covenant, was at stake. It is this thought which appears in the last clauses of this verse.

(5) Behold, I was shapen . . .—The later rabbis, combining this verse with the mystery hanging over the origin and name of David's mother, represent him as born in adultery. The word rendered "conceived" is certainly one generally used of animal desire. But the verse is only a statement of the truth of experience so constantly affirmed in Scripture of hereditary corruption and the innate proneness to sin in every child of man. The argument for a personal origin to the psalm from this verse seems strong; but in Ps. 129:1, and frequently, the community is personified as an individual growing from youth to age, and so may here speak of its idolatrous ancestry as the mother who conceived it in sin.

(11) Cast me not away.—This phrase is used of the formal rejection of Israel by the God of the covenant (II Kings 13:23; 17:20; 24:20; Jer. 7:15). Its use here confirms the explanation in favor of understanding the whole psalm of the community.

Take not thy holy spirit.—As the parallelism shows, the petition is equivalent to a prayer against rejection from the divine favor, and is not to be pressed into any doctrinal discussion.

(12) Joy of thy salvation.—This again points to a sense of restoration of covenant privileges.

(16) Sacrifice.—The rabbinical commentators on this verse represent the penitence of David as having taken the place of the sin-offering prescribed by the Law. In the mouth of an individual, language with such an intention would not have been possible. To the nation exiled and deprived of the legal rites, and by the very deprivation compelled to look beyond their outward form to their inner spirit, the words are most appropriate. While vindicating spiritual religion, the psalmist no more abrogates ceremonies than the prophets do. As soon as their performance is possible they will be resumed.

52

In this psalm the voice of the community of pious Israel plainly speaks. The tyrant, or mighty man, who is addressed, is most probably one of those base time-servers who, against the national party, and against the religious sentiment, sold themselves to the foreign power that happened to be heading toward power; and who, by lending themselves as the instruments of tyranny, became the means of rousing the patriotic spirit which at length, under the hand of Maccabaeus, succeeded in shaking off the foreign yoke.

Title.—See title, Pss. 4 and 32. This is one of a series of three Elohistic psalms.

The historical reference in this inscription (I Sam. 22:17) serves to cast discredit on the inscriptions generally, as showing on what insufficient grounds they could be received.

(6) Fear ... laugh.—The mingled feelings of awe at the tyrant's terrible fall, and exultation at his overthrow, are finely caught and described.

(8) But I am like.—The flourishing olive alternates with the vine, in Hebrew poetry, as an emblem of prosperous Israel.

53

This psalm is a variation from Psalm 14. (See Introduction.)

Title.—See title, Ps. 4.

Upon Mahalath.—One of the most perplexing of the perplexing inscriptions. We have a choice of explanations from derivation between "upon a flute," and "after the manner of sickness." As in other cases (Ps. 88), we look for some musical direction here, and if we take the root, meaning "sick" or "sad," we must render "to a sad strain," or "to the tune of a song beginning with the word 'sadness.'"

(1) Iniquity.—Instead of the general term, "doings," in Ps. 14, as if the adapter of the psalm felt that a word applicable to good as well as evil was not strong enough to express the hideousness of the profanity.

(5) Where no fear was.—This—the most interesting variation from Ps. 14—appears plainly to have been inserted to bring the psalm into harmony with some circumstance belonging to the time for which it was adapted. Apparently, from the immediate context, this statement is made not of the enemies of Israel, but of Israel itself, and was so constantly applicable to a people supposed to be living under the immediate protection of God, and yet liable to sudden panics, that we need not try to recover the precise event referred to.

54

If this psalm is the outcome of individual feeling, the traditional title will suit it as well as any that conjecture can supply. But it reads more like the cry of a people in distress, an oppressed race, powerless except in its religious hope.

Title.—See notes to titles of Pss. 4 and 32; and comp. I Sam. 23:19 and 26:1.

(3) For strangers.—This verse, with some variations, occurs again (Ps. 86:14). With the received reading we must understand the word "strangers" as "foreign oppressors" —though, doubtless, the inscription of the psalm may be defended by taking the word in a derived sense of those Israelites who have degenerated, and so deserve the name "aliens."

55

This is one of the most passionate odes of

427

the whole collection—bursts of fiery invective alternating with the most plaintive and melancholy reflections: it has supplied to Christianity and the world at least two expressions of intense religious feeling, the one (verses 6, 7) breathing despair, the other (verse 22) the most restful hope.

Its date and authorship must be left in the region of mere conjecture. The traditional ascription to David cannot on any ground be maintained. That Ahithophel is the subject of verses 12-14, 20, 21 is contrary to all we know of the history of the rebellion of Absalom. And it must be noticed that the psalm does not represent the author as the victim of a revolution, but of oppression (verses 3, 4). The frightful picture of disorder arising from disorganization of the government, given in verses 9-11, is most inapplicable to the state of Jerusalem in David's reign.

The rest of the poem speaks of enemies in the plural, and the individual on whom the poet especially turns may only be the representative of a class—the class of perfidious Israelites who, forsaking national and religious traditions, sided with the foreign oppressors, and, as usual in such cases, carried their animosity to the party they had betrayed to the bitterest end.

Title.—See title, Ps. 4.

(9) Destroy.—This sudden change from plaintive sadness to violent invective is one of the marked features of this poem. Some think there has been a transposition of verses, but in lyric poetry these abrupt transitions of tone are not uncommon nor unpleasing.

(19) God shall hear.—(Comp. James 1:17.) The reason of the assertion that, in spite of his invariableness, the wicked do not fear God, appears in the next verse. Instead of respecting those in covenant with one who does not change, they have not feared to attack and oppress them.

(20) He hath.—As in verse 12, the individual especially prominent in the traitorous crew is here singled out, and his treachery exposed.

(22) Burden.—The LXX by rendering "care" have prepared the way for the Christian consolation in I Peter 5:7.

56

If the title referring to an imprisonment of David at Gath is to be defended, it must be from I Sam. 21:10-15, on the supposition

that the feigned madness did not succeed in its object, although the narrative gives reason to suppose that it did. The alternative of rejecting the inscription appears less objectionable. We have no clue, however, either to the person of the author or his time (beyond the general picture of danger and hostility), and the language rather gives the idea of large combined forces than of individual foes, especially in the prayer of verse 7. Probably the speaker is here again only the mouthpiece of oppressed and suffering Israel.

Title.—See Pss. 4 and 16, title.

Upon Jonath-elem-rechokim.—i.e., "upon a silent dove of distant (places)." These were perhaps the first words of some well-known song to the tune of which this psalm might be sung.

(4) In God.—This verse forms the refrain (verses 11 and 12 are wrongly separated). The obvious treatment is to take the construction as in Ps. 44:8, "I praise God with my word," i.e., in spite of all my enemies I find words to praise God.

57

This psalm offers a good example of the way in which hymns were sometimes composed for the congregation. It is the work of a man with a fine poetic sense. Yet it is plainly a composition from older hymns. (Comp. especially Pss. 7:15, 9:15, 36:5, 6; 56:2, 3.) The second part has itself in turn been used by another compiler. (See Ps. 108.)

Title.—See Pss. 4 and 16, title, and comp. titles of Pss. 58, 59 and 75.

Al-taschith.—i.e., "destroy not," the first words of some song to the tune of which this was to be sung.

(4) Them that are set on fire.—Rather, "greedy ones" (literally, "lickers") in apposition to "lions." The verse expresses the insecurity of the poet, who, his dwelling being in the midst of foes, must go to sleep every night with the sense of danger all around him. How grandly the refrain in verse 8 rises from such a situation.

58

After a challenge to certain corrupt magistrates, the poet in this psalm shows his detestation of the wicked, and anticipates their fate. There is nothing in the contents of the psalm to bear out the traditional title; but neither is there anything to help us to fix on any other author or date. The vivacity of the language and the originality of the imagery indicate the freshness and power of an early and vigorous age of literary activity.

Title.—See title to last psalm.

(3) The wicked.—The poet passes from his indignant challenge to the unjust judges to speak of the wicked generally. He finds that such maturity of vice points to early depravity. Such hardened sinners must have been cradled in wickedness.

(7, 8) After the types of obstinate and fierce malignity, come four striking images of the fatuity of the wicked man's projects, and his own imminent ruin.

59

The conjecture which connects this psalm with the Scythian irruption into Judaea in the reign of Josiah is not easily surrendered. Some wild nomad tribe supporting itself by pillage, terrifying the inhabitants of a beleaguered city with an outlandish gesture and speech, seems indicated by the recurring simile of the "dogs" (verse 6, 14, 15). And, again, the mode in which the heathen are spoken of in verse 8, and the effect to be produced far and wide by the evidence of Jehovah's power (verse 13), seems to point to a foreign invasion.

Title.—See titles, Pss. 4, 16, and 57 and see **Introduction.**

(11) Slay them not, lest my people forget ...—National feeling has often insisted on extreme modes of punishment, partly from vindictive feeling, partly for deterrent purposes. But where is the parallel to the feeling that seems uppermost in the psalmist's mind, viz., a wish for protracted retribution on the nations for the moral benefit of Israel?

(13) That they may not be.—Better, "That they may be no more." These words are to be taken closely together. The notable overthrow of the poet's foes is to be a proof to the ends of the world of the sovereign rule of the God of Jacob.

60

This psalm is composite; certainly two (verses 1-5, 6-12), probably three, independent pieces (verses 1-5, 6-8, 9-12) compose it. (See Ps. 108:6-13.)

Most scholars agree in thinking that the oracular verses (6-8) are Davidic, or belong to a period as old as David's; and the inscription no doubt refers us to the series of events which this part of the poem reflects. It evidently reflects a period of national depression, either from some crushing defeat by a foreign enemy, or from civil strife, in which the pious part of the community had suffered.

Title.—See title, Pss. 4 and 16.

Upon Shushan-eduth (comp. Ps. 80 and Ps. 45, title).—We take it as the beginning of some hymn, to the tune of which this psalm was to be sung.

To teach.—This psalm, like the elegy over Saul and Jonathan (II Sam. 1:18) was possibly used to kindle the martial ardor of youthful Israel.

When he strove with ...—The allusions are to be explained by the events narrated in II Sam. 8 and 10.

(1) Hast scattered us.—A word in II Sam. 5:20 applied to the rout of an army, an event which gave its name to the locality, "plain of breaches." On the other hand, the two succeeding verses seem to refer to a **political** convulsion rather than a **military** defeat, and it has been conjectured that the breach between the two kingdoms is here indicated.

(6, 7, 8) In these three verses, forming the center of the poem, the speaker is God Himself, who, according to a familiar prophetic figure, appears in the character of a warrior, the captain of Israel, proclaiming the triumphs won through His might by their arms. (Comp. Isa. 63:1-6.) Here, however, the picture is rather playful than terrible—rather ironic than majestic. Here the champion simply proclaims the result of his victory as he proceeds to disarm and prepare for the bath—figures expressing the utmost contempt for the foe so easily subdued.

(9) Who will ...—i.e., how can this ancient divine oracle be fulfilled now in present circumstances? This is the poet's question. He may be a king himself eager for triumph, or more probably Israel personified. Edom is the particular foe in view, and as the difficulties of the undertaking present themselves, misgivings arise and the assurance gained from the triumphs of olden time turns into prayer, half plaintive, half confident, that the divine favor and power may be once more on the side of the chosen people.

61

Here we have the prayer of an Israelite living at a distance from his country, and declaring in the simplest possible manner that in spite of this banishment he does not feel remote from God nor deprived of the divine protection. It is a forecast of the great principle of spiritual worship which Jesus Christ was to proclaim. Tradition assigns this exquisite little song, with its fine spiritual discernment, to David. But many critics think it breathes rather of the time of the captivity.

Title.—See title, Ps. 4.

Neginah, probably **neginoth,** as in Ps. 4; or it may be an anomalous form of **neginah,** which, in Job 30:9, means a satirical song.

(2) Lead me to the rock ... —The elevated rock is a symbol of security, which cannot be obtained without the divine help. Others take the expression as figurative for a difficulty which it needs God's help to surmount.

(4) Thy tabernacle ... —It is difficult to decide whether this indicates the Mosaic tabernacle, and so may be used as an index of the date of the poem; or whether the tent is a general figure for the protection of God, wherever it may be found. It certainly recalls Ps. 23:6.

(5) Heritage.—As the King James Version states, the "heritage" is length of days, one promised generally to those who fear Jehovah (Prov. 10:27; 19:23), and particularly to Israel (Deut. 6:2) and its kings (Deut. 17:19, 20, which passage may have been in the psalmist's mind). But the LXX and Vulgate read, "to them that fear thy name," meaning, of course, by the heritage, Canaan.

62

The many close resemblances between this psalm and Ps. 39 lead to the inference that it belongs to the same time, and is even from the same pen. The author and his age are, however, alike unknown; and there is no indication to guide to their discovery. The psalm records an experience common in every age, of the vanity of those objects on which man is apt to set his affections;

but an experience particularly likely to find expression in days such as so many of the psalms reflect, when there was open conflict between the national sentiment and the ruling classes. The poet's is a voice raised in behalf of pious Israel suffering under tyranny.

Title.—See titles, Pss. 4 and 39.

(5) As in verse 1. "Truly to God, be silence my soul." The state of resignation is one which can only be preserved by prayer. We may say, "I will," but can only "feel" it through prayer.

63

The figure of the first verse misunderstood led to the inscription referring this psalm to the wandering period of David's life, a reference entirely out of keeping with the contents of the poem, even if it were Davidic. The conjecture is far more probable which makes it the sigh of an exile for restoration to the sacred scenes and institutions of his country, now cherished in memory. The last verse seems to carry us back to the troubled times immediately before the destruction of Jerusalem, when the existence of monarchy was trembling in the balance, and when some of those already in exile might be supposed to be watching its fortunes with feelings in which hope contended with misgiving, and faith with fear.

(1) Early will I seek thee.—LXX and Vulgate, "to thee I wake early," i.e., my "waking" thoughts are toward thee, and this was certainly in the Hebrew, since the verb here used has for its cognate noun the "dawn." The "expectancy" which even in inanimate nature seems to await the first streak of morning is itself enough to show the connection of thought. (Comp. Song of Sol. 7:12 and Luke 21:28.)

(2) To see thy power.—The psalmist means that while he saw with his eyes the outward signs of divine glory, he had a spiritual vision (the Hebrew word is that generally used of prophetic vision) of God.

(3) Because.—Such a sense of the blessedness of divine favor—here in its peculiar sense of covenant favor—that it is better than life itself, calls for gratitude displayed all through life.

(11) Sweareth by him.—Those who are loyal to Jehovah, who appeal to Him in all troubles, will find this promise true, while the unfaithful and false, not daring to make the solemn appeal, will have their mouth stopped. (Comp. Rom. 3:19.)

64

The situation indicated in this psalm is one that frequently occurs in Israel's hymnbook. A prey to misrepresentation, the poet for himself, or, more probably, for the community, implores the protection of God, and then suddenly takes up the prophetic strain—persuaded, from the known order of Providence, that retribution must come—and foretells the sudden dissipation of the deeply-laid schemes of those who vex and oppress God's chosen people.

Title.—See title, Ps. 4.

(7, 8) In the moment of their imagined success, their deeply-laid schemes just on the point of ripening, a sudden divine retribution overtakes the wicked, and all their misrepresentations invented with such cunning, fall back on their own heads. The last clause seems to pronounce the law which prevails in divine judgment. While God orders the retribution, it is yet the recoil of their own evil on the guilty.

65

The feeling pervading this psalm is indicated by the initial words. The attitude of Israel toward God is one of silent expectation, or expressed thankfulness—it waits hopeful of blessing to be granted in history and nature, and then bursts forth, like the refreshed and renewed earth, into a loud song of praise. There is only one direct indication of the probable date of the poem—the mention of the Temple, which sets aside the traditional ascription to David. But we can afford to leave undiscovered the author and date of a poem which is perennially fresh and true—a harvest song for the whole world and for all time.

Title.—See titles to Pss. 4 and 45.

(2) Unto thee shall all flesh come.—This has usually, and most truly, been taken as prophetic of the extension of the true religion to the Gentiles. But we must not let what was, in the divine providence, a fulfillment of the psalmist's words, hide their intention as it was conscious to himself. The psalm shows us the exclusiveness of Hebrew belief, and, at the same time, the nobler and grander feelings which are from time to time found struggling against it. The peculiar privilege of Israel has been stated in the first verse. In this the other nations have no part; but all flesh may approach Jehovah in prayer. (Comp. verse 5.)

(3) Iniquities ... transgressions.—There appears in this verse an antithesis between **iniquity** and **transgression**. The latter certainly sometimes seems to be applied in distinction to the violation of the covenant, and possibly the distinction is present here. The frailty and sin common to all flesh has not exempted Israel; but the chosen people have to mourn besides transgressions of their own law. These, however, will be by sacrifice purged away, and then, brought back into full covenant privilege, the offenders will approach the earthly dwelling place of the divine, and dwell there.

66

The compilers of the Psalter found no tradition of authorship attached to this psalm, and did not themselves conjecture one, nor have we any guide toward the time of its composition beyond the tone of innocence assumed in the last part, which marks that part as belonging to a period subsequent to the captivity, when persecution and suffering were no longer regarded as punishment for national disloyalty to the covenant.

Title.—See titles to Pss. 4 and 48.

(15) I will offer.—Such a holocaust could hardly have been vowed by a single person. It is the community that speaks. Besides, the ram was not a sacrifice for any individual, but particularly enjoined for the high priest (Lev. 9:2), the head of a tribe (Num. 7), or a Nazarite (Num. 6:14). Incense is here the ascending smoke of the sacrifice.

67

This is a noble hymn of praise, which for its fine and free expression of grateful dependence on the divine grace was worthy to become, as it has become, a church hymn for all time. The last two verses connect the hymn immediately with harvest, and it would look as if this allusion had actually been added for some special occasion to what was a general song of praise, since the refrain in verse 5, besides marking its choral arrangement, indicates what appears to be the proper ending of the psalm.

Title.—See titles to Pss. 4 and 66.

(1) This verse is an adaptation of the priestly benediction (Num. 6:24-26).

431

68

Psalm 68 will no doubt remain what it has been called, "the cross of critics, the reproach of interpreters"; but it tells us some facts of its history and character that are beyond question: (1) The mention of the Temple in verse 29, in context, brings down the composition to a period certainly subsequent to Solomon. (2) The poet makes free use of older songs. Most prominent among these references are those to Deborah's magnificent ode (Judg. 5) which is with the writer throughout, inspiring some of his finest thoughts. (3) The poem appears to have been inspired by that general confidence in the protection of God which Israel's prophets and poets ever drew from the history of the past. These few features lend probability to the conjecture which sees in this psalm a processional hymn of the second Temple. That Temple needed gifts and offerings from the Persian monarchs, and was rising into completion at a time when Israel could boast of no military greatness, but found its strength only in religion.

Title.—See titles to Pss. 4 and 66.

(4) By his name JAH.—This abbreviated form of Jehovah is first found in Exod. 15:2. No doubt the verse is a fragment of a song as old as the Exodus. It may be noticed here that the dependence of this psalm on older songs is nowhere more conspicuous than in the various use of the divine names, **Elohim, Adonai, El, Shaddai, Jehovah, Jah.**

(7-10) We come now to the first of three unmistakable historic retrospects—the rescue from Egypt, the conquest of Canaan (11-14) and the establishment of Jerusalem as the political and religious capital (15-18). In these patriotic recollections the poet is naturally inspired by the strains of former odes of victory and freedom. The music especially of Deborah's mighty song (Judg. 5), which, directly or indirectly, colored so much of later Hebrew poetry (see Deut. 33:2; Hab. 3) is in his ears throughout.

(13, 14) The agreement of the ancient versions in rendering these difficult verses shows that their obscurity does not arise, as in the case of so many passages of the Psalms, from any corruptions in the text, but from the fact that they are an adaptation of some ancient war song to circumstances to which we have no clue.

(18) For Paul's citation of this verse, or its original, see Eph. 4:8.

(19-27) The abrupt transition from the scene of triumph just described to the actual reality of things which the psalmist now for the first time faces, really gives the key to the intention of the poem. It is by God's favor and might, and not by the sword, that deliverance from the enemies actually threatening the nation is to be expected. These hopes of national deliverance are kept alive in the worship of the sanctuary.

(29) Kings.—This verse is a strong argument for referring the psalm either to the time of the rebuilding of the Temple, or its rededication after the pollution by Antiochus Epiphanes.

69

If we cannot identify the author of this psalm with any other known individual, we must certainly set aside the traditional ascription to David. Verses 10, 11 and 12 cannot by any ingenuity be worked into his known history. The real author is lost in the general sufferings of these victims of religious persecution (verse 9), for whom he speaks (verse 6). The expression of this affliction is certainly figurative, and therefore we cannot fix the precise nature of the persecution. There appears to have been two parties in Israel itself, one zealous for the national religion, the other indifferent to it, or even scornful of it (verses 9-13). It is on the latter that the fierce torrent of invective that begins with verse 22 is poured.

Except for Ps. 22, no other hymn from ancient Israel supplied more for quotation and application to the young Christian community, when searching deep into the recognized sacred writings of their nation to prove that the despised and suffering one was the Christ. That in so doing they fastened on accidental coincidences, and altogether ignored the impassable distance between one who could be the mouthpiece of such terrible curses and Jesus Christ, need not blind us to the illustration which is thrown on Him and His life by the suffering and endurance of this, as of all martyrs in a right cause.

Title.—See title, Pss. 4 and 45.

(5) My foolishness.—This does not conflict with a true Messianic application of the psalm, but is fatal to that which would see in the author not an imperfect type, but a prophetic mouthpiece of Christ.

(6) Let not them.—We again meet the feeling so common in the Psalms (see especially 44:17-22), that the sufferings of any member of Israel must bring dishonor on the name of Jehovah and on His religion. Here, however, it seems to touch a higher chord of feeling and to approach the true churchmanship which attaches a greater heinousness to the sin because it may harm the brethren.

70

For this detached fragment, broken off even in the middle of a clause, see Ps. 40:13-17.

Title.—See titles, Pss. 4 and 38.

71

The Palestinian collectors of the sacred songs of Israel found no traditional inscription to this psalm, and left it without conjecture of its authorship. The resemblance between this psalm and Jeremiah's writings has led many critics to ascribe it to that prophet, a conjecture also borne out by the fact that it is, in great part, an adaptation of other psalms, chiefly 22, 31, 35 and 40, since such dependence on older writings is a prominent feature in Jeremiah. Still it is quite as likely that we have here another of those hymns composed, or, more properly speaking, in this case, arranged, to express not individual feeling and experience, but that of suffering Israel.

(6) Took me out.—This allusion to birth and retrospect of life, from the earliest infancy, is not unsuitable to Israel personified as an individual, or rather it suits both the individual and the community of which he is the mouthpiece. So it has often been in application treated as an epitome of the history of the Christian Church.

(11) The formal "saying," introducing a quotation, is an indication of a late date, the early literature employing no signs of quotation. (See, e.g. Ps. 68:12, 26).

72

Odes in honor of royalty generally tell their own tale, and here we certainly have a prayer for a king, the sons of a king, who is to be at once glorious and good, and whose empire is to be as wide abroad as the government is righteous and beneficent at home. But, making every allowance for poetical exaggeration, it is impossible to find any monarch of Israel whose reign the poem exactly describes. The name of Solomon is naturally the first to suggest itself, as it did to those who prefixed the inscription. Undoubtedly the memory of his imperial greatness inspired the song; Josiah has been suggested by Ewald. But the view which regards the psalm as Messianic, i.e., descriptive of the peace and plenty and power anticipated under a prince as yet unborn and unknown, who was to come of David's line to restore the ancient glory of the theocracy, best suits its general tone.

Title.—According to usage, this inscription can mean only "of Solomon," denoting authorship.

(1, 2) Whether Solomon is the intended subject of the poem or not, the prayer made in his dream at Gibeon (I Kings 3:9) is the best comment on these verses. (Comp. Isa. 11:4; 32:1.)

(8) He shall have ... —That the river in the next clause is the Euphrates there can be no question, but are we, therefore, to see precise geographical limits in the expression "from sea to sea" (from the Mediterranean to the Red Sea), as in Exod. 23:31, or is it merely poetical for a wide extent of empire? The vague and general expression, "ends of the earth," which takes the place of the definite "desert," in the passage of Exodus, makes us favor the latter view. So, too, do the hyperbolic expressions in verses 5, 11 and 17. On the other hand, verse 10 mentions particular places. The same phrase in Zech. 9:10 describes the Messianic kingdom, and is certainly poetical, but whether that or this passage is the original is doubtful.

BOOK III

73

The motive of this psalm shows itself clearly in verse 3—perplexity at the sight of the prosperity of the wicked. Two psalms have already dealt with the question at some length, viz., Pss. 37 and 49. The problem is stated here more fully, the poet trying to account not only for one, but for both sides of the paradox, the troubles that beset the righteous as well as the good fortune that befalls the ungodly. The solution, however, on the first side falls short of that reached in Ps. 49. The author contents himself with the thought that the wicked stand in slippery places, and may at any

433

moment come to ruin. On the other hand, he is beginning to feel the way toward a higher truth than was discerned before, the truth that while the success of evil is apparent and momentary, that of good is real and final; he even catches a glimpse of the still higher truth revealed in the pages of Job, that communion with God is itself a bliss above happiness, and that the consciousness of possessing this gives a joy with which the pleasures of mere temporary prosperity are not to be compared.

Title.—See title to Ps. 50.

(1) Truly.—The question arises whether the second clause of the verse limits, or only repeats the first. No doubt in theory God was understood to be good to Israel generally, but the subject of the psalm seems to require a limitation here. The poet sees that a moral correspondence with their profession is necessary, even in the chosen people—the truth which Paul stated with such insistence, "For they are not all Israel which are of Israel."

(17) Then understood I . . . —The Temple service, with its blessings on righteousness, and stern warnings against wickedness, as they were read from the Book of the Law or from one of the prophets, or were chanted from some ancient song, gave the needed turn to the psalmist's speculations. He began to think not of the present, but the future; not of the advantages of sin, but its consequences—but still consequences in this world, the thought of a hereafter not having established itself sufficiently to have an ethical force.

(24) To glory.—Better, "With honor," as LXX and Vulgate; or **achar** may be taken as a preposition: "Lead me after honor," i.e., in the way to get it. The thought is not of a reward after death, but of the true honor which would have been lost by adopting the views of the worldly, and is only to be gained by loyalty to God.

74

With a certainty allowed by no other of the psalms, this, with Ps. 79, can be referred to the year before the patriotic rise of the Asmoneans. Indeed, as Delitzsch remarks, their contents coincide with the prayer of Judas Maccabaeus preserved in II Macc. 8:1-4. The only argument of any weight against this conclusion is the expression in verse 3, "ruins," which appears at first sight too strong a term for the mischief wrought

by the Syrians at the command of Antiochus. But we must allow at such a crisis a little license to patriotism and poetry.

Title.—See titles, Pss. 1 and 32.

(7) They have cast fire into.—Literally, "They have cast into fire thy sanctuary." Probably a hyperbolic expression, and purporting to express the vastness of the conflagration. We learn from I Macc. 4:38, and Josephus, **Antt.** 12:7, 6, that Judas Maccabaeus, in coming to restore the Temple, found that the gates had been burned.

(8) All the synagogues of God in the land.—This expression excludes from **moed** either of the meanings possible for it in verse 4, "the Temple," or "the assembly." Thus we have a clear note of time, indicating a period not only later than the rise of the synagogue in Ezra's time, but **much** later, since it takes time for a new institution to spread over a country.

(9) There is no more any prophet.—This was the constant lament of the Maccabaean period (I Macc. 4:46; 9:27; 14:41), and suits no earlier time—at least none into which the rest of the psalm would fit. During the exile period Jeremiah and Ezekiel were prophesying, and the complaint took quite a different form then and probably for some time afterward (Lam. 2:9; Ezek. 7:26).

Neither is there among us any that knoweth how long.—This, too, carries us on past the time of Jeremiah, who had given an exact date for the termination of the exile.

(10-15) In the true prophetic spirit, as Moses brought the cries of distress "by reason of their bondage" from the oppressed Israelites to God (Exod. 5:22), so this poet carries to the same God the pathos of this later cry, "How long? how long?" In answer, the deliverances of old rush into his mind.

75

The note of despair in the last psalm is succeeded here by one of mingled expectancy and exultation. It is as if the pathetic question, "How long?" had suddenly and unexpectedly been answered by the appearance of a deliverer, sent, like one of the judges of old, exactly at the needful moment. No period in the history suits this attitude like the early days of the Asmonean successes. Mattathias and his sons are those whom God "setteth up." The "horn" that is to be cut off is Antiochus Epiphanes, who in the Book of Daniel is described as "a little horn, which waxed exceeding great, toward the south, and toward the east, and toward the pleasant land" (Dan. 8:9).

Title.—See titles, Pss. 4, 57 and 58.

(2) When I.—It is quite clear that the speaker of these words is God Himself, who suddenly, as in Ps. 46:10, breaks in with the announcement of judgment. But how far the divine utterance extends in the psalm is not quite clear. Some end it with verse 3; others with verse 5.

(8) A cup.—The figure of the cup of divine fury is developed, as Ps. 11:6 compared with Ps. 16:5 shows, from the more general one which represents life itself as a draught which must be drunk, bitter or sweet, according to the portion assigned. It appears again in Ps. 60:3, and is worked out in prophetic books (Isa. 51:17; Hab. 2:16; etc.; Ezek. 23:32-34, and frequently in Jeremiah).

76

At an early period this psalm was, as it is still by many scholars, connected with the overthrow of Sennacherib. Certainly the verses 5 and 6 are most suitable to that event. On the other hand, the phrase in verse 9, "all the meek of the earth," breathes of a time of national oppression, and suggests a later date. Verses 8 and 9 compared with verses 7 and 8 of Ps. 75 lead to the conclusion that both were inspired by the Song of Hannah and may both refer to the same circumstances. And some critics not only bring it into the Maccabaean age, but fix on the victory of Judas over Seron (I Macc. 3) as the actual event celebrated in this poem.

Title.—See titles, Pss. 4, 50 and 65.

(6) Are cast into a dead sleep.—The same Hebrew expression is used of Sisera's profound slumber (Judges 4:21). Deborah's Song and Exod. 15 are in the poet's mind, as they were to the author of Isa. 43:17, and as they have inspired the well-known lines of Byron's "Sennacherib."

77

The affliction out of which the mournful cry of this psalm rises is presented in such general terms that there is no single indication by which to refer it to one period more than another. As the consolation is sought entirely in the history of national deliverance, and not in any display of divine goodness toward the author individually, it is safe to conclude that the troubles described are also national rather than personal. At all events, for the time the poet's individuality is entirely merged in the sense of public calamity.

Title.—See title, Pss. 4 and 39.

(16-20) The prominence given to Joseph is a feature common to the Asaphic psalm. With this magnificent lyric of the passage of the Red Sea comp. Hab. 3:10, 11. The narrative in Exodus says nothing of a storm, but Josephus has preserved the tradition (**Ant.,** 2:16, 3). Philo also mentions the storm.

78

This is the first and the longest specimen in the Hebrew hymnbook of a species of composition peculiar to it, and indeed peculiar to the literature of the Jews, as combining narrative with instruction. It has been rightly called "epi-didactic." It does not tell the story of the past with any view of celebrating heroic ancestors, or exalting conspicuous national virtues. On the contrary, it is a long confession of national failings. It is impossible to resist the conclusion that the author is quite as much concerned to establish the divine purpose in rejecting Ephraim in favor of Judah, as in choosing Israel as a nation in distinction from the heathen. The psalm from verse 67 dwells with genuine satisfaction on the rejection of the northern tribes, and on the exclusive choice as the seat of the theocracy of the southern tribe, Judah. This prominence given to the disruption has led some critics to date the poem at the time of that event.

Title.—See Ps. 32:1.

(9) Armed, and carrying bows.—By understanding a comparison of the general character of Ephraim to a bow with a relaxed string that fails at the moment it is wanted (a figure made more expressive by the fact that archery was a practice in which Ephraim excelled), we are freed from the necessity of conjecturing a particular incident to account for this verse, which seems to break the sequence of thought. The whole historical retrospect is intended to lead up to the rejection of the northern kingdom (represented by Ephraim), but the

435

poet is unable to keep back his climax, and thrusts it in here almost parenthetically.

79

The relation of this psalm to Ps. 74 is so close, notwithstanding some points of difference, that commentators are almost unanimous in assigning them to the same period, if not the same author. Verse 1, indeed, by itself seems to point to a **profanation** of the Temple, such as that by Antiochus, and not a **destruction** like Nebuchadnezzar's. To one of these events the psalm must refer. The best commentary on the psalm is the first chapter of I Maccabees.

Title.—See title, Ps. 50.

(6, 7) The poet prays in prophetical strain, that the fire of indignation may be turned from Israel and directed against the heathen oppressors. (Comp. Jer. 10:25.)

80

This plaintive cry for restoration to a state which should be indicative of the divine favor arose from Israel when groaning under foreign oppression which it was powerless to resist. And if, with the almost unanimous consent of critics, we are right in rendering verse 6, "Thou makest us an object of strife to our neighbors," we should be able to approximate very nearly to the date of the poem. There are only two periods when Palestine became an object of dispute between rival powers: when Assyria and Egypt made it their battleground; and, at a much later date, when it was the apple of discord between the Ptolemies and the Seleucidae. But at the earlier of these two periods the language of the poet descriptive of utter prostration and ruin (verse 16) would hardly have been suitable. We hear, again, in verse 4, the pathetic "how long?" of the Maccabaean age. Comp. Pss. 74:10 and 79:5.

Title.—See Pss. 45, 60, and comp. title of Ps. 69.

(8) Thou hast brought.—The vine (or vineyard), as an emblem of Israel, is so natural and apt that we are not surprised to find it repeated again and again in the Old Testament, and adopted in the New. Probably Isa. 5:1-7 was the parent image, unless the patriarchal benediction on Joseph (Gen. 49:22) suggested that song.

(17) Man of thy right hand.—This verse

is a continuation of verse 15. It is a fine instance of the mode in which the thought can pass naturally from the figurative to the literal. In the words "son," "son of man," some see a reference to the Messiah. But the parallelism and context show that the poet is thinking of Israel as a community, of which the vine is the emblem.

81

This is plainly a festival song, but by no means one of that jubilant class of festival songs that conclude the Psalter. The poet is in the truest sense a prophet, and, while calling on all the nation to join in the music of the feast, he tries to convince them of the sad lapse in religion from the ideal which the appointed feasts were intended to support. But the psalm does not end with sadness. After the rebuke comes the promise of rich and abundant blessing, upon the condition of future obedience.

The particular festival for which the psalm was composed, or which it celebrates, has been a matter of controversy. Verse 3 favors the Feast of Tabernacles (see Num. 19:12; Lev. 23:24).

Title.—See titles, Pss. 4, 8 and 50.

(7) Thou calledst.—The recital of God's past dealings with the people usual at the Feast of the Tabernacles (Deut. 31:10-13; Neh. 8:18) appears to follow here as if the feast were actually in progress and the crowd were listening to the psalmist.

(10) Open ...—A condensed statement of God's gracious promise (Deut. 7:12, 13; 8:7, 9; 11:13, 16; etc.). It is said to have been a custom in Persia, that when the king wishes to do a visitor special honor he desires him to open his mouth wide, and the king then crams it full of sweetmeats, and sometimes even with jewels.

82

This psalm represents the conviction which was so profoundly fixed in the Hebrew mind, that justice is the fundamental virtue of society, and that its corruption implies total disorganization and ruin. The mode in which this conviction is presented is also distinctively Hebrew. We have here once more a vision of judgment. With a calm dignity the divine arbiter comes to take His place as presiding Judge among the magistrates themselves, and depose

them. Then the poet himself, with a wider
sweep of view, that takes in not only the
administrators of law, but the political situation of his nation, makes appeal to the
"judge of all the earth," who in the conviction of Israel must do right. The date of
such a poem, if it could be recovered,
would crown its interest.

Title.—See title, Ps. 50.

(1) He judgeth among the gods.—For
"gods," applied to men delegated with office
from God, see Exod. 21:6 and Ps. 8:5. The
custom of designating God's vicegerents by
the divine name was a very natural one.
The whole point of verse 6 lies in the
double meaning the word can bear.

(6) I have said.—It is interesting to notice
that verses 1 and 6 were quoted by Constantine at the opening of the Council of
Nicaea, to remind the bishops that their
high office should raise them above jealousy
and party feeling. (For the interest gained
by the passage from our Lord's use of it to
rebut the charge of blasphemy brought
against Him by the scribes, see John 10:34.)

(8) Arise.—The psalm would have been
incomplete had not the poet here resumed
in his own person, with an appeal to the
Supreme Judge to carry His decrees into
effect against the oppressors of Israel. Here,
at least, if not all through it, the affliction
of the community, and the perversion of
justice by foreign rulers, are the motives of
the song.

83

The array of proper names in this poem
seems, at first sight, to promise an easy
identification with some definite historical
event. But our records nowhere speak of a
confederation composed of all the tribes
enumerated here; so that if we are to be
governed by literal exactness, it is impossible to refer the psalm to any known period of Israelite history.

We must therefore, in any case, refer the
mention of so many hostile tribes as combined in one confederacy to poetical exaggeration, and look for other indications
which may guide us to the event most
probable as the origin of the poem. In the
fact that after his victorious progress Judas
Maccabaeus reviewed his troops in the
great plain which had witnessed the slaughter of Sisera's host, and in the comparison
drawn between the conduct of the city of
Ephron (I Macc. 5:46-49) with that of Suc-

coth and Penuel, toward Gideon (Judges
8:4-9), we have enough to account for the
selection of examples from the times of the
judges rather than from later history.

Title.—See titles, Pss. 48 and 50.

(3) Hidden ones.—i.e., those under God's
close protection, as in Pss. 17:8; 27:5;
31:20. God and His "hidden ones" are one,
a truth preparing the way for that grander
truth of the identification of the Son of man
with all needing help or pity in Matt. 25.

84

By an almost complete agreement of
commentators this psalm is descriptive of a
caravan of Israelites either returning from
exile to Jerusalem or on its way up to one
of the regular feasts. It has so many points
of resemblance to Pss. 42 and 43 that it has
been ascribed to the same author and
referred to the same events. The singer,
generally, is undoubtedly at present unable
(see verse 2) to share in the Temple services
which he so rapturously describes.

Title.—See titles, Pss. 4, 8 and 42.

(5-7) In these verses, as in the analogous
picture (Isa. 35:6-8; comp. Hosea 2:15, 16),
there is a blending of the real and the
figurative; the **actual** journey toward Zion is
represented as accompanied with ideal
blessings of peace and refreshment. It is
quite in the Hebrew manner to mix up the
ideal with the actual, and to present the
spiritual side by side with the literal. We
have, then, here recorded the actual experience of a pilgrim's route. But quite naturally and correctly has the world seen in it a
description of the pilgrimage of life, and
drawn from it many sweet and consoling
lessons.

85

There is more than the statement of its
first verse to connect this psalm with the
post-exile period. Its whole tone belongs to
that time. The attitude with regard to national sin explains itself only by this reference. The punishment had fallen, and in the
glad return Israel had seen a proof that God
had covered her guilt, and taken away her
sin. But the bright prospect had quickly
been overclouded. The troubles that succeeded the return perplexed those who had
come back, as they felt purified and forgiv-
en. Therefore many such pathetic cries as

those of this psalm. In this particular instance, the cry, as we gather from verse 12, arose from the dread of famine, which was always regarded as a judgment on national sin. But, even as he utters his lament, the prophet (for the psalm has a true prophetic ring, and is in the highest sense Messianic) sees the clouds break, and hails the promise of abundant harvest.

Title.—See title, Pss. 4 and 42.

(4) Turn us.—Here equivalent to "restore us once more." If, the poet felt, the captivity had taught its lesson, why, on the restoration, did not complete freedom from misfortune ensue? It is this which supplies the motive of his song.

(13) Righteousness shall ... —Nothing is more instructive than the blending in verses 12 and 13 of material and moral blessings. They do go together, as experience, especially national, testifies.

86

This psalm is mainly composed of a number of sentences and verses from older compositions, arranged not without art, and, where it suited the adapter, so altered as to present forms of words peculiar to himself. There is also evidence of design in the employment of the divine names, Adonai being repeatedly substituted for Jehovah.

Title.—See end of Ps. 42 and Introduction above.

(5) For thou.—Up to this time the psalmist has only put forward his needs in various aspects as a plea for God's compassion. Now he clenches his petition by an appeal to the nature itself of the divine Being. The originals of the expressions in this verse will be found in Exod. 20:6; 34:6-9; Num. 14:18, 19.

Ready to forgive.—The Hebrew word occurs nowhere else in the form found here. Etymologically it means "remitting." The LXX has a word for which perhaps our "considerate" is the nearest equivalent, implying that legal right is overlooked and suspended in consideration of human weakness.

(8) For the sources of this verse, see Exod. 15:11 and Deut. 3:24. After expressing his conviction of God's willingness to hear prayer, the psalmist goes on to his confidence in divine power to save.

(17) A token for good.—i.e., some sign of continued or renewed providential care and love, such, indeed, as an Israelite under the old covenant saw, and every pious heart under the new sees, in what to others is an everyday occurrence. The expression "for good" is a favorite one with Nehemiah (5:19; 13:31) and Jeremiah (24:5, 6, and comp. Rom. 8:28, etc.).

87

According to the common interpretation of this obscure psalm, it is unique not only in the Psalter but in Hebrew literature. Not even in Isaiah is Jewish exclusiveness so broken down. A nameless poet goes beyond the prophetic visions of the forceful submission of the Gentile world to anticipate the language of the gospels and the spirit of Paul. Zion becomes in his song the "mother of us all"—Gentiles as well as Jews. A first glance at the song sees in it little more than a grand eulogy on the Holy City as a birthplace, which is declared dear to Jehovah not only above heathen countries, but above any city of Jacob. But exclusiveness even more rigid than usual appears here, and we must see in the poem the exultation of a native of Jerusalem over all other Israelites, or of a Palestinian Hebrew over those who share the same blood but have the misfortune to date their birth from some Jewish colony rather than Jerusalem.

As to the time of composition the suggestion ventured on above would of itself bring it down to a very late date, a supposition supported in some degree by the fact that not Assyria but Babylon is mentioned in verse 4.

Title.—See title, Ps. 42.

(4) Rahab undoubtedly stands for "Egypt," but the exact origin of the term and of its connection with Egypt is much disputed. Most probably it is a term (possibly Coptic) for some large sea or river monster symbolic of Egypt. (Comp. the word "dragons," Ps. 74:13, and see Job 26:12.)

(6) The proud boast of the preceding verse is repeated here with allusion to the census or birth-register of citizens. (See Ezek. 13:9; Isa. 4:3; Ps. 69:28.) No doubt these lists were often produced or appealed to in triumph to mark the superiority of a native of Jerusalem over those born at a distance.

88

This psalm stands alone and peculiar for

the sadness of its tragic tone. From beginning to end—with the one exception of the word "salvation" in the first line—there is nothing to relieve its monotony of grief. If this wail of sorrow is the expression of individual suffering, there is no particular interest in ascertaining its date, unless we could also fix on its author. Indeed it is extremely doubtful whether the psalm is a picture of individual sorrow at all, and not rather a figurative description of national trouble.

Title.—See titles Pss. 32, 42, 48, 53; I Kings 4:31; I Chron. 2:6.

(10) Shall the dead arise? . . . —These words are not to be taken in the sense of a final resurrection as we understand it. The hope of this had hardly yet dawned on Israel. The underworld is imagined as a vast sepulchre in which the dead lie, each in his place, silent and motionless, and the poet asks how they can rise there to utter the praise of God who has forgotten them (verse 5). That this is meant, and not a coming forth again into a land of living interests, is shown in the next two verses.

All the passages cited confirm the impression from this psalm of the Hebrew conception of the state of the dead. They were languid, sickly shapes, lying supine, cut off from all the hopes and interests of the upper air, and even oblivious of them all, but retaining so much of sensation as to render them conscious of the gloomy monotony of death. (Comp. Isa. 38:18.)

(11, 12) In these verses appear three prominent features of the Hebrew conception of the underworld. It is a place of "destruction" (comp. Job. 26:6; 28:22), of "darkness" (comp. verse 6), and of "forgetfulness" (comp. Ps. 31:12.)

(13) But unto thee . . .—The pronoun is emphatic. The speaker has **not** gone down to the land where all is silent and forgotten, and can therefore still cry to God, and send his prayer to meet (prevent, i.e., go to meet; see Ps. 17:13) the divine Being who still has an interest in him. And this makes the expostulation of the next verses still stronger. Why, since the sufferer is still alive, is he forsaken, or seemingly forsaken by the God of that covenant in which he still abides?

89

This long psalm comes evidently from a time of great national depression and trouble. The idolatries that led to the Captivity, and the Captivity itself, are already in the past, and the poet can think only of the splendid promises of God to the race, and the paradox that while made by a God of truth and faithfulness, they have yet been broken; for Israel lies prostrate, a prey to cruel and rapacious foes, and the cry, "How long?" goes up in despair to heaven. In the "servant" and "anointed" (verses 38 and 39) the whole nation is individualized and presented in the person of one of the Davidic princes, as in that of David himself (Ps. 132:17). The time of the persecution of Antiochus Epiphanes suits best all the conditions presented by the psalm.

Title.—For "Maschil" see title, Ps. 32; I Kings 4:31.

(2) Mercy . . . faithfulness.—These words, so often combined, express here, as commonly in the psalms, the attitude of the covenant God toward His people. The art of the poet is shown in this exordium. He strikes so strongly this note of the inviolability of the divine promise only to make the deprecation of present neglect on God's part presently more striking.

(5-13) The heavens.—Having repeated the divine promise, the poet appeals to nature and history to confirm his conviction of the enduring character of the truth and grace of God.

(26) He shall cry.—This verse is interesting in view of the theological development in the psalter. We might think that the poet was referring to an actual psalm of David, with whom the expression, "My God, the rock of my salvation," was familiar (see Ps. 18:1, 2, etc.), were it not for the word "Father," a title for the divine Being which the national religion did not frame until the exile period (Jer. 3:4, 19; Isa. 63:16).

(27) Firstborn.—Jesse's youngest son became the first born, the favorite son of God. Here, of course, the epithet is extended to all the Davidic succession.

(30-33) An elaboration of II Sam. 7:14, 15, and evidently made with a purpose. The poet acknowledges the sin of Israel in past times, but also regards the sufferings of the exile as having been the punishment foretold by them. Therefore the sin has been expiated, and the perplexity arises why Israel is still afflicted.

(38) But thou.—The poem takes a new departure here. God is reproached for violating the covenant, and the contrast between the actual condition of things in

Israel at present, and the glorious destiny promised, is feelingly set forth.

The boldness of this expostulation has scandalized the Jewish expositors. But see exactly similar language in Ps. 44:9, 22. The point of the poem, indeed, is gone if we soften down these expressions. The stronger the conviction of the inviolability of God's promises, the more vehement becomes the sense of right to expostulate at their seeming violation, the delay of the fulfillment of the covenant.

(46) How long.—With this persistent cry of the Maccabaean age (see Ps. 74:10), the poet shows that faith is not extinct, though it has a sore struggle with despair.

BOOK IV

90

The subject of the brevity and vanity of life has occupied reflective minds in all periods and countries. Only a Hebrew could have handled it as it is handled here; but the contrast drawn between human frailty and divine immutability is more suited to a later age of Israel than an early one. The first verse seems to take a far more extended retrospect than was possible to Moses, while the pathetic cry, "How long?" in verse 13, suggests, as we have seen in the case of other psalms, even the Maccabaean age.

In one view it would be a misfortune to be able to fix on the precise moment when this poem was composed, and the voice that first spoke it. For it is what it has been well called, "the funeral hymn of the world," and it belongs not to one race or age, but to the sorrows and the hopes of all the successive generations, who at the open grave have derived, or shall derive, consolation and faith from its divine words.

Title.—See Deut. 33:1; Josh. 14:6; I Chron. 23:14; II Chron. 30:16; Ezra 3:2.

The Mosaic authorship is a question depending in a great measure on the view held as to the date of the latter part of Deuteronomy, to which there are resemblances in many points of style and some points of detail. Those who bring the composition of that work down to the eighth century before Christ will unhesitatingly refer this psalm to a date as late as, if not later.

(4) A thousand years.—This verse, which, when II Peter was written, had already begun to receive an arithmetical treatment, and to be made the basis for millennarian computations, merely contrasts the unchangeableness and eternity (verse 2) of the divine existence and purpose with the vicissitudes incident to the brief life of man (verse 1). To One who is from the infinite past to the infinite future, and whose purpose runs through the ages, a thousand years are no more than a yesterday to man.

(7) We.—The change to the first person plural shows that the poet was not merely moralizing on the brevity of human life, but uttering a dirge over the departed glory of Israel. Instead of proving superior to vicissitude the covenant race had shared it.

(10) For it is soon cut off.—This seems hardly to give, as it professes to do, a reason for the fact that the prolongation of life beyond its ordinary limit brings trouble and sorrow, and we are compelled to see if the words can convey a different meaning. Literally the clause means that even though we may have prayed for an extension of life, it brings with it such weariness that we long at last to escape—a fact sufficiently true to experience.

(13) How long?—See note on Ps. 74:9.

91

There is no data for ascertaining either the author or the date of this psalm. The variety of the figures employed seems to indicate a general view of life and its possible perils. It may have been a time when both war and pestilence were raging, but we cannot recover it. Whoever first breathed these words of trust, thousands have found them a source of strength and faith in the hour of trial and danger.

(1, 2) He ... I.—The different names for God employed here should be noticed. By their accumulation the poet makes the sum of assurance doubly sure.

(4) Feathers ... wings ... —For this beautiful figure, here elaborated, see Ps. 17:8, note.

(11) Angels.—The idea of a special guardian angel for each individual has possibly been favored by this verse, though it had its origin in heathen belief: "By every man, as he is born, there stands a spirit good, a holy guide of life." (Menander) Here, however, it is not one particular individual, but all who have fulfilled the conditions of verses 9 and 10 who are the objects of angelic charge. (Comp. Ps. 34:7.) (For the well-known quotation of this and verse 12 in the temptation of Jesus see Matt. 4:6; Luke 4:10, 11.)

92

In this psalm we seem to have the Sabbath musings of one who had met the doubt born of the sight of successful wickedness, and struggled through it to a firm faith in "the Rock in whom is no unrighteousness," though sometimes on earth iniquity seems to flourish and prevail. It is difficult to determine whether the psalm simply expresses the religious feelings of Israel generally after the restoration, or whether it owes its origin to any special event. In I Macc. 9:23 there is an evident echo of, or quotation from, the Greek version of verse 7.

Title.—Properly, "a lyric psalm," i.e., one especially intended for singing.

For the sabbath day.—The Talmud says that this psalm was sung on the morning of the Sabbath at the drink offering which followed the sacrifice of the first lamb (Num. 28:9).

(3) Ten strings.—See note on Ps. 33:2.

(4) The Vulgate rendering of this verse is quoted by Dante in a beautiful passage descriptive of the happiness which flows from delight in the beauty of the works of God in nature. But the reference is to the works in history, not in nature. The psalmist is really expressing his gladness at God's wonders wrought for Israel. (Comp. Ps. 90:15, 16.)

(7) This verse apparently introduces the statement of the truth which the sensualist does not understand, viz., that the prosperity of the wicked is only momentary, and will render their destruction all the more impressive. The prosperity of an evil class or community gives an impulse to evil, and apparently for a time iniquity seems to have the upper hand, but it is only that the inevitable destruction may be more signal.

93

There is a power in the very brevity of this song. God is King, and all the rage and unrest of the world are impotent before that fact. It may have been inspired by some particular event, which it is hopeless to seek to recover, but it expresses a general truth. The angry tumult of men beats as vainly against the granite firmness of His righteous will as the waves against the shore. The

tempests of history subside and pass as the tempest of the sea, but His laws remain for ever fixed and sure.

(5) Thy testimonies.—This statement must be taken in close connection with that of the preceding verse. The permanence of the covenant, and of the outward signs that attest it, is to the Israelite proof of the superiority of the divine power over the forces of nature. We may extend the thought, and say that the moral law is a truer evidence of the existence of God than the uniformity of natural laws.

94

Verses 5 and 14, and, by implication, verse 10, show that this psalm was the expression, not of individual, but of national, sense of wrong and injustice. Yet the poet must, in his own person, have experienced the bitterness of the trouble, from the reference he makes, toward the close, to his own experiences. Apostate Jews may have been joined with the heathen oppressors (verse 6). There is no indication on which to found a conjecture as to date or authorship.

(6) Stranger.—The mention of the stranger as one friendless and helpless (Exod. 22:21), under the tyranny of the great, seems to imply that domestic, and not foreign oppression, is the grievance. This carelessness of heaven to injustice and crime, which, in the mouth of the heathen (or, perhaps, of apostate Jews), appeared so monstrous to the Hebrews, was a doctrine of the philosophy of ancient times.

(8-10) The reality of a divine Providence is proved both from nature and history—from the physical constitution of man and the moral government of the world. The psalmist's question is as powerful against modern atheism, under whatever philosophy it shelters itself, as against that of his day. Whatever the source of physical life or moral sense, their existence proves the prior existence of an original mind and will.

(12, 13) Blessed.—A far higher note than one of mere complaint, or even of trust in God, is struck here. The beatitude of suffering could not be made altogether plain in the Old Testament, though in Job the spirit of it is nearly reached. Here the poet sees thus far, that he who is the victim of misfortunes may be congratulated if he may stand aside and calmly watch the course of divine Providence involving evil men in punishment. What he has himself endured has chastened him.

(15) But.—God's righteousness **will** triumph over the injustice under which Israel groans; His ways will be vindicated, so that all the upright in heart will acknowledge that "there is a reward for the righteous, a God who judges in the earth" (Ps. 58:11). Luther's fine paraphrase, "For Right must, whatever happens, remain Right," expresses the feeling; but, better still, the question, "Shall not the Lord of all the earth do right?"

95

The LXX prefixes a title ascribing this psalm to David, and in quoting it the epistle to the Hebrews (4:7) uses the expression "in David." This, however, is only a mode of saying "in the Psalms." We may conjecture, from the contents, that some danger to religion was observed by the author, since the disobedience and perversity of the early history of the race are recalled. Beyond this we only perceive that the psalm was composed for congregational use. (Psalms 93 and 95 through 100 appear to form a group of songs composed for the celebration of the return from Exile.) From earliest times it has played the part of an invitatory psalm in the Christian Church.

(1) O come.—The invitation is general, and may be contrasted with the heathen warning to the uninitiated **procul este profani**. This exhortation to worship God, not with penitence, but with loud thanksgiving, is the more remarkable considering the strain in which the latter part of the psalm is written.

Make a joyful noise.—There is no one English expression for the full burst of instrumental and vocal music which is meant by the Hebrew word here applied to the Temple service. Vulgate, **jubilemus**.

Rock of our salvation.—As in Ps. 89:26. (Comp. "rock of refuge," Ps. 94:22.)

(3) Above all gods.—Commentators vex themselves with the difficulty of the ascription of a real existence to these tribal deities in the expression, "King above all gods." But how else was Israel constantly falling into the sin of worshiping them? It was in the inspired rejection of them as possessing any sovereign power, and in the recognition of Jehovah's supremacy shown by the psalmists and prophets, that the preservation of Israel's religion consisted.

(8) Provocation . . . temptation.—It is better to keep here the proper names **Meribah** and **Massah** (Exod. 17:1-7; Num. 20:13 comp. Deut. 33:8).

(9) Proved me.—Properly, of trying metals. This term is used of man's attitude toward Providence, both in a good and bad sense (Mal. 3:10, 15).

(11) Rest.—This is, of course, the Promised Land, as the context unmistakably shows. The freedom taken with the passage by the author of the epistle to the Hebrews (chap. 3), in order to make the psalm point us to a "future" rest, was such as Jewish doctors ordinarily used, and of which other instances occur in the New Testament—notably Paul's argument in Gal. 3:16.

96

This "new song," breathing indeed aspirations and hopes which were not wholly new to Israel, but ideal, and still waiting for their complete fulfillment, most probably dates, according to the conjecture of the LXX, from the rebuilding of the Temple after the Captivity. No one can miss the points of resemblance with the literature of that period, especially the evidence of deeper sympathy with nature, and extended interest in mankind. The outward world has become instinct with emotion, while the barrier of faith and feeling between Israel and other races is gradually breaking down. The LXX inconsistently goes on to ascribe the psalm to David, probably because of its insertion in I Chron. 16.

(1) A new song.—See note on Ps. 33:3. It appears to have been a kind of national and religious "lyric cry" after the restoration (Comp. Isa. 42:10.)

(6) Honour . . . —The whole universe displays Jehovah's majesty, but chiefly his sanctuary in Israel, where it is typified by the costly splendor of the building and its rites. The chronicler having adopted this psalm as suitable for the occasion when the Ark was brought to Zion by David, has substituted "strength and gladness are in his **place**," possibly because the Temple was not built at that time.

(7-9) These verses are a relic of Ps. 29:1, 2, but instead of being addressed to the angels, it is, in accordance with the world of new ideas and feelings in which Israel lived after the Captivity, addressed to all the people of the world. A truly Messianic character is thus impressed on the psalm.

97

Though in a great measure a compilation from earlier writings, this psalm, by more than one fine touch, proves itself the product not only of a thoughtful, but also of a truly poetic mind. (Notice especially verses 2, 10, and 11.)

(1) Multitude of the isles.—This wide glance to the westward embracing the isles and coasts of the Mediterranean (Ps. 72:10), possibly even more distant ones still, is characteristic of the literature of post-exile times. (Comp. Isa. 42:10, 11; 51:15.)

(2) Clouds and darkness.—Comp. Ps. 18:10-12. The imagery in the first instance is borrowed from the Theophany at Sinai. (See Exod. 19:9, 16; 20:21; Deut. 4:11; 5:22, 23.) The immediate effect on the Hebrew mind of the awful manifestation of the divine power in nature is not fear, but a sublime sense of safety in the established right and truth of God.

(5) The Lord of the whole earth.—An expression first met with exactly in Josh. 3:11-13, though Abraham speaks of God as judge of the whole earth (Gen. 18:25). (Comp. Micah 4:13; Zech. 4:10; 6:5.) Though Jehovah was the tribal God, yet in marked distinction to surrounding tribes Israel regarded Him as having universal dominion.

98

This psalm plainly belongs to that cycle of literature produced by the joy of the Restoration, and is in fact little more than a compilation from Isa. 26, 40, and from other psalms, especially Ps. 96.

Title.—This is the only hymn of the whole collection with the bare inscription "a psalm."

(1) Victory.—The word is more commonly rendered "salvation," as in the next verse.

99

This psalm plainly belongs to a group (see Ps. 95, Introduction) to be referred to the post-exile times, when the renewed worship and nationality made it possible for the poet to compare his age with that of the greatest saints and heroes of old.

(3) Great and terrible name.—The rabbis see here the mystic tetragrammaton, whose pronunciation was kept so secret.

For it is holy.—This is grammatically possible, but as verses 5 and 9 repeat the expression, evidently as a refrain, and there it needs the masculine, it is better to read here, "Holy is He."

(5) Worship at his footstool.—The earth is called the "footstool" of God (Isa. 66:1; comp. Matt. 5:35); in other places the expression is used of the sanctuary (Ps. 132:7; comp. Isa. 60:13; Lam. 2:1). In I Chron. 28:2 it seems to refer to the Ark. No doubt here, after mentioning the throne above the cherubim, we must think of the ground on which the Ark stood, or of the Ark itself.

(8) Thou tookest vengeance of their inventions.—This does not refer to the personages just mentioned but to the people at large. The train of thought is as follows:— "There are great saints among us, as in olden time but, as then, their prayers, while often procuring forgiveness, could not altogether avert punishment for sin; so the present community must expect retribution when sinful, in spite of the mediation of the better part of the nation."

100

This liturgic psalm, which as a hymn is so universally known and loved, is composed of four verses of triplets. Even when performed in the Temple, amid the exclusive notes of Judaism, its opening words must have inspired something of that catholic sentiment which pervades a congregation when singing what we know as the "Old Hundredth."

Title.—Of praise.—Better, "for thanks," or, possibly "for the thankoffering," i.e., especially adapted for that particular ceremony. At all events it is a liturgical direction.

(3) And not we ourselves.—Most commentators prefer the reading "His we are," as keeping the parallelism better, besides having great MS. support. The concluding part of the verse is an echo of Ps. 95:7.

101

This psalm has been called a "mirror for princes," "a mirror for magistrates," and "the householders' psalm." It is full of stern exclusiveness, of a noble intolerance. It is not against theological error; not against uncourtly manners; not against political insubordination;—but against the proud

443

heart; the high look; the secret slanderer; the deceitful worker; the teller of lies. These are the outlaws from king David's court; they alone are the rebels and heretics whom he would not permit to dwell in his house or tarry in his sight. Tradition may, indeed, well have been right in ascribing such a noble vow to David. And possibly this connection led to the insertion of the first verse as suited to the "sweet singer," and also as giving the vow more the character of a hymn. It probably did not form part of the original composition.

Title.—See Introduction.

(1) Mercy and judgment—or, as some render, "grace and right"—are the especially requisite attributes of a good monarch, or of magistrates generally. (See Matt. 23:23, where the failure to practice them is charged on the ruling class in Judea at that time, though, of course, also required in the conduct of every man; Micah 6:8.) Here, no doubt, as almost all commentators have seen, they are first regarded ideally as attributes of the divine King.

(2) O when wilt thou come unto me?—This clause is so awkward, however translated, that some critics go the lengths of pronouncing it spurious. In the Old Testament, with the exception of Exod. 20:24, the coming of God to a person is associated with the idea of punishment or inquisition (Ps. 17:3); and to see a reminiscence of II Sam. 6:9 seems farfetched. It is better, therefore, to take the verb as the third person feminine instead of second masculine, with "perfect way" as its subject. The only difficulty in the way of this rendering is the interrogative; but, as in Prov. 23:22, it becomes a simple adverb of time, we may treat it so here: "I will give heed to a guileless way when it comes to me," i.e., whenever a course of action arises, presenting an alternative of a right and wrong, or a better and worse, I will choose the better.

I will walk within my house.—This vow of an Eastern monarch should be read with the thought of the palace of a caliph at Bagdad, or a sultan at Constantinople, before the mind. But it is a reflection of universal application, that piety should begin at home, and religion show itself in the household as much as at church.

102

This psalm is peculiar for its title, which stands quite alone among the inscriptions.

It is neither historical nor musical in its reference, but describes the character of the psalm, and the circumstances amid which it would be found useful. That it was, therefore, affixed at a late time, when the collection had come to be employed, not merely for liturgical purposes and in public worship, but in private devotion, there can be little doubt. But the composition of the psalm must be referred to national rather than individual feeling. It is natural, from verses 14 and 15, to refer the composition to the exile period. With this also agree the many points of coincidence with the prophecies of the second part of Isaiah. But it must be remarked that the causes which the prophets of the exile assign to the national captivity or catastrophe do not appear here. There is no expression of repentance or contrition, nor yet of the deeper insight which, toward the end of the exile, brought into prominence the doctrine of vicarious suffering. Those in whose name the psalmist writes are the servants of Jehovah, and have never been anything else. He does not distinguish them as an exception to the mass of the people, who are guilty and deserve the destruction in which the whole universe is to be involved. For this reason many critics bring the psalm down to the Antiochean period, when Jerusalem suffered so much, and at one time presented a desolation like that mourned in the psalm (I Macc. 1:38, 39).

Title.—See Introduction.

(12) For ever.—The eternity of God, which must survive the world itself, is a pledge of the truth of the national hopes, in spite of the vicissitudes of individuals, and the swift succession of generations. For the word "remembrance," see Ps. 30:4. It is explained by Exod. 3:15, "This is my name for ever, and this is my memorial unto all generations." The generations come and go, and the memory of man perishes, but the name "Jehovah" endures still, the object of adoration and praise.

(13-16) The prospect (Isa. 40:1-5) that the restoration of Jerusalem will take place simultaneously with the coming of Jehovah in glory, is here re-echoed from the prophet in a lyric form. "The set time" must not be rigidly explained by the "seventy years" of Jer. 25:11. The expression is general: "The hour is come." (Comp. Isa. 40:2.)

(14) Stones ... dust.—This touching description on the devotion of the Jews to their ruined city is best illustrated by the actual history in Neh. 3, 4, and by the scenes so often described by travelers at the "wailing place" in modern Jerusalem.

(15) Heathen.—The same result of the restoration of the Holy City, vis., the recognition of Jehovah's power and glory by the heathen, occupies the great prophecy (Isa. 40-46).

(18) Written.—This is interesting as being the only place in the Psalms where the memory of great events is said to be preserved in writing. Oral tradition is mentioned in Pss. 22:30; 44:1; 78:2.

(24) Take me not away.—The fear of not living to see the restoration of his race prompts the psalmist to this prayer to the God whose years are not, like man's, for one generation, but endure from age to age.

103

This psalm has been compared to a stream which, as it flows, gradually acquires strength and volume till its waves of praise swell like those of the sea. The poet begins by invoking his own soul to show its gratitude for the divine favor, and, by a highly artistic touch, makes the psalm, after rising to sublime heights, end with the same appeal to personal experience. But national mercies fill much the larger space in his thought, and he speaks throughout as much in the person of the community as his own. Beyond one probable Aramaism in verse 3, and a possible dependence in one passage on the Book of Job (comp. verse 16 with Job 7:10), there is nothing to indicate the time of the psalm's composition.

(3) Forgiveth.—The first "benefit" to one who aims at the higher life is the knowledge of the divine readiness to forgive and renew, and this, as Augustine remarks, implies a quick moral sense: "God's benefits will not be before our eyes unless our sins are also before our eyes."

Diseases.—Here chiefly in a moral sense, as the parallelism "iniquity" shows, even if the next verse, taken literally, implies an allusion to physical suffering as well.

(5) The eagle's.—The idea that the eagle renewed its youth formed the basis of a Rabbinical story, and no doubt appears also in the myth of the Phoenix. But the psalmist merely refers to the fresh and vigorous appearance of the bird with its new plumage.

(6) Oppressed.—From individual the poet passes to national mercies, and goes back to the memorable manifestations of divine fa-

vor vouchsafed to Moses. Comp. Exod. 33:13; 34:6.

(13) Father.—This anticipation of Christ's revelation of the paternal heart of God is found also in the prophets.

(20) Just as in the highest revelation made by Jesus Christ the angels in heaven rejoice over the repentant sinner, so in the psalmist's view the mercy of Jehovah to His faithful people is cause for high acclaim among the hosts around the throne.

104

This psalm touches the highest point of religious poetry. It is the most perfect hymn the world has ever produced. Even as a lyric it has scarcely been surpassed; while as a lyric inspired by religion, not only was all ancient literature, except that of the Hebrews, powerless to create anything like it, but even Christian poetry has never succeeded in approaching it.

At the very opening of the poem we feel the magic of a master inspiration. The world is not, as in Genesis, created by a divine decree. It springs into life and motion, into order and use, at the touch of the divine presence. Indeed, the pervading feeling of the hymn is the sense of God's close and abiding relation to all that He made; the conviction that He not only originated the universe, but dwells in it and sustains it. No other poet has displayed a finer feeling for nature, and that not in her tempestuous and wrathful moods—usually the source of Hebrew inspiration—but in her calm, everyday temper. He is the Wordsworth of the ancients, penetrated with a love for nature, and gifted with the insight that springs from love.

This majestic hymn is anonymous in the Hebrew. The LXX has ascribed it to David. Its close connection with Psalm 103, and an Aramaic word in verse 12, indicate a post-exile date for its composition.

(2) Curtain.—Especially of a "tent" (see Song of Sol. 1:5, etc.), the tremulous movement of its folds being expressed in the Hebrew word. Different explanations have been given of the figure. Some see an allusion to the curtains of the Tabernacle (Exod. 26, 27). The associations of this ritual were dear to a religious Hebrew, and he may well have had in his mind the rich folds of the curtain of the Holy of Holies.

Herder refers the image to the survival of the nomadic instinct. But there is no need to put a limit to a figure so natural and suggestive. Possibly images of palace, temple, and tent, all combined, rose to the poet's thought.

(4) Who maketh ... —Keeping the order of the Hebrew, "Who maketh His messengers of winds, and His ministers of flaming fire." This is plainly the meaning required by the context, which deals with the use made by the divine King of the various forms and forces of nature. Just as He makes the clouds serve as a chariot and the sky as a tent, so He employs the winds as messengers and the lightnings as servants.

Taken quite alone, the construction and arrangement of the verse favors the interpretation of the author of the epistle to the Hebrews (Heb. 1:7). This was the traditional Jewish interpretation, and on it were founded various theories of angelic agency. But not only do the exigencies of the context set aside this interpretation, but Hebrew literature offers enough instances to show that the order in which a poet arranged his words was comparatively immaterial.

(5) Who laid ... —(Comp. Job 38:4-6; Prov. 8:29.) The inconsistency of this with Job 26:7, "He laid the earth upon nothing," need not cause difficulty. Both treatments are poetical, not scientific. The word "foundations" implies stability and endurance (comp. Ps. 82:5.) The verse has a historical interest from having supplied the Inquisition with an argument against Galileo.

(9) A bound.—It is striking to observe what a deep impression their little line of coast, the barrier which beat off the waves of the Mediterranean, made on the Hebrew mind. The sea was an object of dread. Or if dread passes into reverent wonder, as in verses 25, 26, it ends there; the Jew never took delight in the sea. Hence, the coast has for him only one purpose and suggestion. It is not for enjoyment or recreation, or even for uses of commerce. It is simply the defense set by God against the hostile waters.

(16) The trees ... —The parallelism shows what are Jehovah's trees. The cedar of Lebanon (see I Kings 4:33) was the grandest and fairest tree known to the Hebrew, and like lightning and the tropical rain, is honored by the epithet most expressive of grandeur. Such trees the poet feels must have been planted by the divine hand itself—man could grow herbs, but not cedars—and here, as a proof of the lavish provision made by the Creator for the fertility of the earth, he states that even these monarchs of the wood have enough.

(26) Ships.—The poet writes like one who had been accustomed to see the navies of Phoenicia, one of the indications which leads to the hypothesis that he belonged to the northern part of Palestine. And here for once we seem to catch a breath of enthusiasm for the sea—so rare a feeling in a Jew.

Leviathan.—See Ps. 74:14. In Job 41 it is the crocodile, but here evidently an animal of the sea, and probably the whale. Several species of **cetacea** are still found in the Mediterranean, and that they were known to the Hebrews is clear from Lam. 4:3. Various passages from classic authors support this view. It is a rabbinical tradition that Leviathan is God's plaything (see Job 41:5).

(30) Spirit.—Rather, "breath," as in verse 29. We must not here think of the later theological doctrine of the Holy Spirit. The psalmist evidently regards the breath of God only as the vivifying power that gives matter a distinct and individual, but transient, existence. Even in the speculative Book of Ecclesiastes, the idea of a human soul having a permanent separate existence does not make its appearance. At death the dust, no longer animate, returns to the earth as it was, and the breath, which had given it life, returns to God who gave it—gave it as an emanation, to be resumed unto Himself when its work was done. Still less, then, must we look in poetry for any more developed doctrine.

(35) Sinners be consumed.—This imprecation, which comes in at the close of this otherwise uniformly glad hymn, has been variously excused. The truth seems to be that from a religious hymn of Israel, since religion and patriotism were one, the expression of the national feeling against heathen oppressors and apostates who sided with them could not well be absent, whatever its immediate subject and tone. But the poet touches even a more profound truth. The harmony of creation was soon broken by sin, and the harmony of the song of creation would hardly be complete, or rather, would be false and unreal, did not a discord make itself heard.

Bless thou the Lord.—This is the first "hallelujah" in the Psalter. Outside the Psalter it is never found, and was therefore a liturgical expression coined in a comparatively late age. It is variously written as one or two words.

105

The motive of this historical psalm is plainly declared in verses 44 and 45, and the scope which the author allowed himself in the survey of the past appears in verse 11. He wishes this generation to remember that the continued possession of the Promised Land is contingent on obedience to the covenant God. In fact, the psalm is an elaboration of the charge so often repeated in Deut. 15:4, 5. The psalm dates from a time prior to the composition of the first Book of Chronicles, for it forms part of the compilation of song in chap. 16; but there is no other indication by which to assign date or authorship. The conjecture is probable that it was compiled for liturgic use soon after the resettlement in the country after the Captivity.

(1) **Call upon his name.**—Literally, with idea of **proclamation** as well as **invocation**. This verse, which is found word for word in Isaiah 12:4, is apparently one of the recognized doxologies of the Hebrew Church.

(11) This verse marks the scope of the psalm, to show how the promise made to Abraham was fulfilled.

(15) **Anointed.**—In the plural, "my anointed ones." As referring to the patriarchs, the expression is not technical, since they were never, like priests, prophets, and kings in later times, actually anointed. But the terms being sometimes applied to the covenant people as a whole (see Ps. 89:38, 51), its application to the founders of the race, especially those to whom the "promises came," is very just. As to the term "prophet," the poet found it expressly conferred on Abraham in Gen. 20:7.

106

The motive of this historical psalm differs from that of the last as it does from that of Ps. 78. Its survey of the past is neither hymnic nor didactic, but penitential. Though the first of the series of "Hallelujah" psalms, it is closely related to these long liturgical confessions of national sins which are distinctly forbidden in Deut. 26, where the type form of them is given, and of which the completest specimen is retained in Neh. 9.

But this example sprang from particular circumstances. It evidently dates from the exile period, and may well, both from its spirit and from its actual correspondence of

thought and language in some of the verses, have been composed by Ezekiel, to encourage that feeling of penitence from which alone a real reformation and restoration of the nation could be expected.

(1-5) These verses form an introduction to the psalm, and make it evident that while the writer spoke as one of a community, and for the community, he still felt his **personal** relation to Jehovah.

(1) This formula of praise in the Jewish Church occupied, as a choral refrain, a similar position to the **Gloria Patri** in Christian worship. The precise date of its appearance cannot be ascertained. (See I Chron. 16:34; II Chron. 7:3; Ezra 3:11; Jer. 33:11.) Its use became more general after the Captivity; and it was in use in the Maccabaean period (I Macc. 4:24).

(2) **Praise.**—**Tehillah,** a term that has become technical for a liturgic hymn. (**Tehillim** is the general Hebrew word for the Psalter.) The psalmist asks in this verse who is worthy or privileged to sing a **tehillah**, and replies himself that loyalty to the covenant confers this privilege.

(5) The tone of this verse indicates a prospect of a speedy advent of good, and serves itself to give a probable date to the psalm.

(6) **We.**—Regard must be paid to the fact that the confession includes the speaker and his generation, as well as the ancestors of the race. The psalm proceeds from the period of the Captivity, when the national conscience, or at all events that of the nobler part of the nation, was thoroughly alive to the sinfulness of idolatry.

(17) The omission of Korah is in keeping with the historical accounts, which indicate a difference both in the attitude of Korah and his family from that of Dathan and Abiram, and also a difference of fate, (Comp. Num. 16:23, seq.; Deut. 11:6; Num. 26:10.)

(22) **Land of Ham.**—A synonym for Egypt, peculiar to the historic psalms (Pss. 78:51; 105:23, 27).

(28) **Ate the sacrifices of the dead.**—i.e., the sacrifices of a dead divinity. Num. 25:2 shows that here we must not see any allusion to necromantic rites, such as are referred to in Deut. 18:11; Isa. 8:19, and the parallelism shows that the "god" in question is Baal-peor.

(33) **Spake unadvisedly.**—Compare the same verb with the same addition, "with the lips," in Lev. 5:4. This interpretation of the fault of Moses is partial. A comparison of

all the historical narratives shows that it was rather for a momentary lapse into the despairing spirit of the people, than for addressing them as rebels, that Moses was excluded from the Promised Land.

(38) Innocent blood.—Human sacrifice, and especially that of children, was a Canaanite practice. It seems to have been inherent in Phoenician custom, for Carthage was, two centuries after Christ, notorious for it.

(40-43) Having made review of the sinful past, the poet briefly but impressively describes the punishment which once and again had fallen on the nation. But as his purpose is to make his generation look on the Captivity as a supreme instance of this punishment, and to seek for deliverance by repentance, he mentions only the judgments inflicted by foreign foes.

(48) Blessed . . . —The doxology, which is only slightly altered from that at the end of the second book, is quoted as part of the psalm in I Chron. 16:36—an indication that by that time this book was complete, if not the whole collection.

BOOK V

107

While this psalm may properly be regarded as a lyric embodiment of the lessons of the Captivity (verses 2, 3), it applies these lessons to the human lot generally, and travels over the whole experience of human life for the pictures under which it represents them. The fortunes of his own race were uppermost in the psalmist's mind, but the perils depicted are typical of the straits into which men of all lands and all times are driven; and he had learned that the goodness and wisdom which at the cry of prayer come to extricate and save are not confined to one race, but are universal and continuous.

Critics unite in assigning a late date for the composition of this poem, and no one doubts that it was intended for liturgic use. Of the unity of the poem there is considerable doubt (see note on verse 33.)

(1) For this doxology see note on Ps. 106:1.

(2) Redeemed of the Lord.—See for this grand expression, for which so high a destiny was prepared. Isa. 62:12; and comp. 63:4 and 35:9.

(3) Gathered them.—The usual prophetic

word for the Restoration (comp. Isa. 49:12.)

The poet speaks, successively, in terms of the wanderers (verses 4-9), the prisoners (verses 10-16), the sick (verses 17-22), and the storm-tossed mariners (verses 23-32).

(32) Let them exalt.—The addition of this to the refrain, as of 22 to that of the last stanza, clearly points to a liturgical use in this psalm.

(33) The change in character and style of the psalm at this point is so marked as to suggest an addition by another hand. It is not only that the artistic form is dropped, and the series of vivid pictures, each closed by a refrain, succeeded by changed aspects of thought, but the language becomes harsher, and the poet, if the same, suddenly proclaims that he has exhausted his imagination. Comp. Isa. 35:7; 41:18, 19; 42:15; Job 12:21, 24; 21:11; Hos. 14:9.

108

This psalm is taken with some variations from Pss. 57 and 60, verses 1-5 being from Ps. 57:7-11 and verses 6-13 being from Ps. 60:7-14. The principal variations are in verse 3, **Jehovah** for **Adonai.** For the authorship of the parts of which the psalm is composed, see their Introductions. The ascription of the composite production to David furnishes a strong presumption against the historical value of the inscriptions.

109

This psalm was, as the inscription shows, actually, if not primarily, intended for use in the public service of the sanctuary. This very use at once divests it of one of the greatest sources of difficulty, its personal character. Whatever its origin, whoever the original object of the imprecations, it is certain that they became public, ecclesiastical, national. It is quite possible that from the first the writer spoke in the name of the persecuted nation against some oppressive heathen prince, such as Antiochus Epiphanes. Certainly, when sung by the congregation it expressed not an individual longing for revenge, but all the pent-up feeling—religious abhorrence, patriotic hatred, moral detestation—of the suffering community.

Title.—"To the chief musician." (See note to title of Ps. 4.)

(6) Set thou a wicked man over him.—This rendering is abundantly confirmed by Lev. 26:16; Num. 4:27; 27:16; Jer. 15:3; 51:27. The wish expressed is that the persons indicated may fall into the hands of an unscrupulous judge. Here the imprecatory part of the psalm begins.

Satan.—By no means here a proper name, although the LXX and Vulgate have **diabolus.** The use of the same word in verses 4, 20, 29 is decisive on giving it the general meaning "adversary" here, even though without the article. (Satan is used for the tempting angel in I Chron. 21:1, and in Zech. 3:1 we find the same post, "at the right hand," assigned to the accuser.) An unscrupulous judge and an adversary as accuser are the substance of this imprecation.

(7) Let his prayer become sin.—The judgment just spoken of is that of an earthly tribunal. Therefore we must render here, "let his prayer be an offense," that is, instead of procuring him a mitigation of his sentence, let it rather provoke the unscrupulous judge to make it heavier. For sin in this sense of offense, see Eccl. 10:4, and comp. I Kings 1:21.

(13) Posterity.—The Hebrew theory of the divine government was, that if ruin did not overtake the sinner himself, it would fall on his posterity; his name would be forgotten, and his race extinct.

(14) Fathers.—The sweet of vengeance lies in its completeness. The curse must strike backward as well as forward, and the root as well as the branch be destroyed. Undoubtedly the Mosaic Law, which proclaimed that the "iniquity of the fathers should be visited on the children," suggested the form of the imprecation.

Sin of his mother.—Is the necessity of the parallelism sufficient to account for this mention of the mother, or is some definite circumstance in the poet's thought? The theory which makes this portion of the psalm (verses 6-20) a quotation of curses really uttered by Shimei against David, finds an allusion to the Moabitish descent on the mother's side. (Comp. the Rabbinical explanation of Ps. 51:5.)

110

At first sight the authorship and purpose of this psalm are, for a Christian expositor, not only placed beyond the necessity of conjecture, but even removed from the region of criticism, by the use made of its first verse by our Lord, and the emphatic manner in which He quotes it as the divinely inspired utterance of David (Matt. 22:41-45; Mark 12:35-37; Luke 20:41-44). But it is now generally admitted that, in matters of literature and criticism, our Lord did not withdraw Himself from the conditions of His time, and that the application He made of current opinions and beliefs does not necessarily stamp them with the seal of divine authorization. See Introduction to Ps. 95.

The prominent thought in the psalm is the formal union in one person of the royal dignity and the priesthood. Now all the kings of Israel and Judah at times assumed priestly functions, but only twice in their history can the offices be said to have been formally combined—in the person of Joshua son of Josedech (Zech. 11:12, 13) and in that of the Asmonean Jonathan and his successors (I Macc. 11:57). The latter reference is preferable. And the choice of Melchizedek, as type (verse 4), does not arise from any idea of contrasting his order with that of Aaron, but from the necessity of going back to him for an instance of actual and formal priesthood combined in the same person, with kingly rank.

The abrupt ending of this short psalm has led many critics to regard it as a fragment.

(1) My Lord.—Heb., **adonai,** an address of honor to those more noble than the speaker, or superior in rank: to a father (Gen. 31:35); to a brother (Num. 12:11); to a royal consort (I Kings 1:17, 18); to a prince (I Kings 3:17); with addition of the royal title, "my lord, O king" (II Sam. 14:19). The question of the person here intended is, of course, closely bound up with the general question of the authorship and meaning of the psalm. A Messianic application has been made by many, and if so, with a prophetic consciousness of His Divinity, or, at least, His superiority as a Prince over all other princes.

Nothing more can be assumed from the words themselves than an invitation to sit at Jehovah's right hand to watch the progress of the victorious struggle in which wide and sure dominion is to be won for this Prince. But even this is obscured by the concluding part of the psalm (see verse 5), where Jehovah is said to be at the right hand of the person addressed, and is beyond question represented as going out with him to battle. Therefore, we are led to the conclusion that the exact position ("at the right hand") is

449

not to be pressed in either case, and that no more is intended than that, with Jehovah's help, the monarch who is the hero of the poem will acquire and administer a vast and glorious realm.

Footstool.—The imagery of the footstool is no doubt taken from the custom mentioned in Josh. 10:24.

(5) The Lord at thy right hand.—We are naturally tempted to understand this as still of the king whom the first verse placed at Jehovah's right hand. But the word for Lord here is **Adonai**, which is nowhere else used except of God. Moreover, God throughout has as yet appeared as the active agent. It is He who stretched out the scepter and conferred the office of priest; and until now the king has been the person addressed. It is therefore necessary still to consider him as addressed, and suppose that the change of position of Jehovah from the king's right hand to his left is simply due to the usage of the language. "To "sit at the right hand" was an emblem of honor; to "stand at the right hand" was a figure of protecting might (Pss. 16:8; 109:31); and the imagery of a battle into which the song now plunges caused the change of expression.

111 and 112

Psalms 111 and 112 should be read closely together, the one being a pendent of the other. They are both acrostics of at once the simplest and most perfect construction, each clause (not, as usual, each verse of two or more clauses) exhibiting the alphabetical arrangement. There are therefore exactly twenty-two clauses, nearly three words each. In order to limit the number of verses to ten—considered a perfect number—the last two verses in each psalm are arranged as triplets.

The close relation of the two psalms is also exhibited in their subject. The first exhibits Jehovah in covenant with man; the second, man in covenant with Jehovah. The one sings the divine praise in view of the kindness God has shown to Israel; in the second, the feeling of the just man—i.e., the Israelite faithful to the covenant, is the subject. In both we discover the strength of these religious convictions, which, in spite of the contradictions experienced in actual life, persist in maintaining the grand principle of divine justice, and declaring that the cause of virtue will triumph, and success and wealth never fail the faithful.

The close relation of the two psalms is marked, again, by the echo in the second, of phrases applied in the first to Jehovah. (Comp. e.g., Pss. 111:3 with 112:3, 9; 111:4 with 112:4, 6.)

113

This psalm begins the "Hallel," or as is sometimes called, "the great Hallel"—though that name more properly is confined to Ps. 136—recited at the great Jewish feasts. It is partly modelled on Hannah's song. No doubt the joyful mother of verse 9 is emblematic of the nation itself restored to prosperity and joy.

114

This psalm is among the most artistic in the whole collection. Though ending so abruptly as to suggest that it may be a fragment (the LXX, Syriac, Arabic versions, and some MSS capriciously join it to the following psalm), it is perfect in form. But a higher art displays itself here. The reserve with which the divine name is withheld, until everything is prepared for its utterance, and the vivid manner in which each feature of the rapid scene is flashed upon us by a single word so that a whole history is accurately presented in a few graphic touches, achieve a dramatic and a lyric triumph of the most remarkable kind. The psalm is part of the Hallel, and the hymn sung with Christ before His passion.

115

That this is a late liturgical psalm all commentators agree, but the precise period of its composition cannot be ascertained. The belief that death cut the Hebrew off from all the privileges of the covenant seems to forbid so late a date as the Maccabaean age, though a psalm so priestly in its character, and which apparently celebrates some martial success, would otherwise be appropriately ascribed to the Asmonean period.

(2, 3) It is difficult for us to reproduce in imagination the apparent triumph, which the idolater, who could point to **his** deity, felt he had over the worshiper of the invisible God, when outward events seemed to be going against the latter. But we may estimate the strength of the conviction which, even under the apparent withdrawal of divine favor, could point to the heavens as the abode of the Invisible, and to misfortune itself as a proof of the existence and power of One who could in everything do what pleased him.

(9) O Israel.—There is consummate art in this sudden change of address. It is like the pointed application of some general truth in a sermon. It is possible that in the liturgic use a change in the music was made here.

(17, 18) The connection of these verses with the rest of the psalm is far from plain. Why the psalmist should suddenly be struck with the dreadful thought that death broke the covenant relationship, and silenced prayer and praise, is not easy to see. Was the psalm first chanted after some victory? and was this suggested by the sight of the slain, who, though they had helped to win the triumph, could yet have no share in the praises that were ascending to Jehovah?

116

The late date of composition of this psalm is shown both by the presence of Aramaic forms and the use made of earlier portions of the Psalter. It was plainly a song of thanksgiving, composed to accompany the offerings made after some victory. The most important question arising from it is whether it is personal or the voice of the community. As in other cases, a strong individual feeling does not exclude the adaptation of a psalm to express the feelings of the people of Israel as a whole.

(7) Return ... —In a very different spirit from the fool's address to his soul in the parable. The psalmist's repose is not the worldling's serenity nor the sensualist's security, but the repose of the quiet conscience and the trusting heart.

(13) Cup of salvation.—The "drink offering" or "oblation" which accompanied festival celebrations (Num. 29:19, etc.). Others think of the Passover cup mentioned in Matt. 26:27, when this psalm as part of the Hallel was sung. Others, again, take the figurative sense of cup—i.e., portion, lot, as in Ps. 16:5.

(15) Precious ... —This is only another form of the statement in Ps. 72:14. But again we have to ask why the thought of death should intrude upon the psalmist at this moment. (See note on Ps. 115:17.) The answer is that, as in verse 8, a recent

deliverance from death is spoken of. It is natural to take this psalm as a thanksgiving song for the safety, perhaps victory, of the survivors in some battle, but then the grateful community naturally and dutifully remember the dead.

117

This, shortest of all the psalms, might well be called **multum in parvo**, for in its few words it contains, as Paul felt (Rom. 15:11), the germ of the great doctrine of the universality of the Messianic kingdom. That it was intended for liturgical use there can be no doubt, and possibly it is only one of the many varieties of the Hebrew Doxology. What is also noticeable is the ground on which all the world is summoned to join in the praise of Jehovah—His covenant kindness and the fulfillment of His promises to Israel. The idea latent under this is shown in the second word rendered "praise"; properly, to "soothe." The nations are imagined coming to make their peace with Israel's God after seeing His display of power for their sakes; but a wider and nobler truth emerged out of this.

118

The character of this psalm as a Temple song of thanksgiving is stamped on every line of it. It is not, however, by any means certain to what particular event or time the psalm is to be assigned. Many incidents in connection with the rebuilding of the second Temple have been fixed upon in connection with verses 22, 23. Others have gone to the Maccabaean period for the occasion of the thanksgiving. Several expressions seem to allude to a particular feast, with its peculiar prayers and sacrifices (verses 24-27), and there can be little doubt that this was the Feast of Tabernacles. The words of verse 25 were, we know, sung on one of the days—called the Great Hosanna (**Save now**)—of the feast, a name given also to the boughs carried and waved in the sacred procession. If verses 19-23 imply the completion of the Temple, it is natural to fix on the first complete celebration of the Feast of Tabernacles after the Return (Neh. 8:14 seq.).

(17) I shall not die, but live.—It is Israel, and not an individual, who thus claims a continuance of life for the display of God's glory. But as we find so often, the hope is so expressed as to suit not only the community for whom the psalm was composed and sung, but also each member of it individually.

(19) The gates of righteousness.—This is explained by the next verse as the gate of the Temple, where the righteous, i.e., Israel alone, entered. There does not seem the least reason for taking the words here in any but this literal sense, though doubtless they are capable of endless spiritual applications. We must imagine a procession chanting the triumphal song as in Ps. 24, and summoning the gates to open on its approach.

(22) The stone.—There is no article. Israel is, of course, this stone, rejected as of no account in the political plans of those who were trying to shape the destinies of the Eastern nations at their own pleasure, but in the purpose of God destined to a chief place in the building up of history. The image is developed by Isa. 28:16, 17, and prepared, by the Messianic hope poured into it, for the use of Christ Himself and the repeated applications of it to Him by the apostles (Matt. 21:42-44; Acts 4:11; I Pet. 2:7; Eph. 2:20).

(26) Blessed ...—These words of welcome are probably spoken by the Levite in charge to the procession approaching the gates. According to Rabbinical writings, pilgrim caravans were thus welcomed on their arrival at Jerusalem.

119

An acrostic must wear an artificial form, and one carried out on the elaborate plan set himself by this author could not fail to sacrifice logical sequence to the prescribed form. Why the number eight was selected for each group of verses, or why, when the author succeeded in all but two of the 176 verses, in introducing some one synonym for the law, he failed in two, verses 122 and 132, we must leave to unguided conjecture. The repetition of the name Jehovah, occurring exactly twenty-two times, could hardly have been without intention, but in the change rung on the terms that denote the Law there is no evidence of design. That the aphorisms in which the praise of the Law is thus untiringly set forth were not collected and arranged as a mere mnemonic book of devotion appears from the undercurrent of feeling which runs through the psalm, binding the whole together. At the same time, it is quite inconsistent with the ordinary

history of literary work to suppose that such a mechanical composition could owe its origin to the excitement of any one prominent occurrence; rather it is the after reflection of one, or more likely of many, minds on a long course of events belonging to the past, but preserved in memory, reflections arranged in such a way as not only to recall experiences of past days, but to supply religious support under similar trials. And if there is a monotony and sameness in the ever-recurring phrases, which under slightly different expressions state the same fact, the importance of that fact, not only to a Jew, but to a Christian also, cannot be exaggerated.

ALEPH

(6) Have respect unto.—Literally, "look upon," or "into," as in a mirror. (Comp. James 1:23.) The divine Law is as a mirror, which shows man his defects; the faithful, in looking in it, have no cause to blush.

BETH

(9) Wherewithal.—We must not, from the mention of youth, conclude that this psalm was written in that period of life. Perhaps, on the contrary, it is one who, like Browning's Rabbi ben Ezra, while seeking how best to spend old age, looks back on youth, not with remonstrance at its follies, but with the satisfaction that even then he aimed at the best he knew.

GIMEL

(19) I am a stranger.—A comparison of verse 54 with Gen. 47:9 (comp. Ps. 39:12) shows that the general transitory condition of life, and not any particular circumstance of the psalmist's history, is in view. Human intelligence does not suffice to fathom the will of God. The mortal is a stranger on the earth; both time and strength are wanting to attain to knowledge which only divine wisdom can teach.

(23) Speak.—This verse reads as if Israel, and not a mere individual, were the subject of the psalms.

DALETH

(25) Quicken thou me according to thy word.—See verses 88, 107, 149, 154, 156. This reiterated prayer, with its varied ap-

452

peal to the divine truth, lovingkindness, constancy, must certainly be regarded as the petition of Israel for revived covenant glory, though, at the same time, it offers a wide and rich field of application to individual needs.

HE

(35) Path.—From root to "tread, the trodden way," plain with the track of all the pious pilgrims' feet of past times.

VAU

(46) The Vulgate (which in the tenses follows the LXX) of this verse was the motto of the Augsburg Confession, **Et loquebar in testimoniis tuis in conspectu regum, et non confundebar.**

ZAIN

(56) This I had, because ... —i.e., this consoling recollection of the mercies of God, of His covenant grace, came to him in consequence of his habitual obedience. Virtue is indeed then most of its own reward in times of quiet reflection, like the night, when to the guilty come remorse and apprehension, but to the good man calm thoughts.

CHETH

(59) I thought on.—The Hebrew implies repeated and frequent meditation.

TETH

(68) It is characteristic of this psalm that the higher the conception of the divine nature, the more earnest becomes the prayer for knowledge of His will in relation to conduct.

JOD

(74) They ... will be glad.—The great truth of spiritual communion, and the mutual help and consolation derived from it, is latent here. In its primary sense the verse teaches that the preservation and deliverance of the righteous, who are victims of persecution, afford comfort and joy to all truly good.

CAPH

(84) As in Ps. 89:47, 48, the psalmist here utters what was the dread of each generation of Israel, a dread lest it should have passed away before the day of deliverance should arrive.

LAMED

(96) I have seen.—The exact thought of the psalmist here is doubtful, and it offers such a wide application, embracing so many truths of experience, that possibly he had more than one meaning in his mind. Keeping as close to the context as possible, the meaning will be: "To all perfection (or apparent perfection) a limit is visible, but the divine Law is boundless alike in its scope and its requirements." This, translated into the language of modern ideas, merely says that the actual can never correspond with the ideal.

MEM

(98) Better, "Thy commandments make me wiser than my enemies." The same correspondence of wisdom with loyal obedience to the Law is found in the Book of Proverbs.

NUN

(108) Freewill offerings of my mouth.—i.e., thanks and praise.
(109) My soul.—For this figure of peril see Judges 12:3; I Sam. 19:5, etc.

SAMECH

(113) I hate vain thoughts.—Rather, "I hate men who halt between two opinions," following I Kings 18:21, where the cognate noun from the same root, "to divide," appears. Probably we are to think of those among the Jews who were for political reasons favorably inclined toward foreign customs and ideas, and who would not throw in their lot frankly and courageously with the national party.
(119) Thou puttest away.—For this common Scriptural figure comp. Jer. 6:28-30; Ezek. 22:18-20. This is indeed a process which is continually going on, and it is one test of the true religious character that it can discern it at work under the seeming contradictions of the world. Where apparently vice succeeds and prospers it is really marked out for expulsion.

AIN

(122) Be surety.—Just as Judah became surety for the safety of Benjamin (Gen. 43:9), so the psalmist asks God to be answerable for the servant who had been faithful to the covenant, and stand between him and the attacks of the proud. So Hezekiah (Isa. 38:14) asks God to "undertake" for him against the threat of death. There is also, no doubt, the further thought that the divine protection would vindicate the profession which the loyal servant makes of his obedience, as in Job 17:3, where God is summoned as the only possible guarantee of the sufferer's innocence.

PE

(132) As ... name.—Rather, "according to the right of." It was not only theirs by custom, but by right of the covenant.

TZADDI

(141) These words are hardly applicable to an individual, while to the struggling Israel, in relation to the great Eastern powers, they are peculiarly suitable.

KOPH

(147) Prevented.—See Pss. 18:5; 79:8. The King James Version gives the sense, "I was up before the morning."

(150, 151) Near.—Notice the antithesis. "They, the wicked," are near with their temptation to sin and their hindrances to virtue. **Thou** art near with the aid and support of Thy law.

RESH

(158) Transgressors.—Better, the "faithless" (or, "traitors").

Was grieved.—The Hebrew is a far stronger word, and the sense is intensified by the rare conjugation: "was filled with loathing at; sickened with disgust."

SCHIN

(161) Princes.—Here again we have an indication of the national character of the psalm. It was the whole community which suffered from the intrigues and violence of princes.

(164) Seven times.—Some commentators think the number is used here only in a general way for "often," "repeatedly"; but the number seven evidently had some sacred association for the Hebrews. (Comp. Lev. 26:18; Prov. 24:16; Matt. 18:21; etc.) No doubt the seven canonical hours were partly derived from this verse. Elsewhere we find three times as the stated occasions of prayer (Ps. 55:17).

TAU

(176) I have gone astray like a lost sheep.—It would be in accordance with a true religious character that even at the end of a long protestation of obedience to the divine Law the psalmist should confess his weakness and sin. More likely, however, there is a reference to the condition of the community, for the word rendered "lost" (literally, "perishing") is used in Isa. 27:13 of the exiled Hebrews, and is rendered "outcasts"; the emphatic "I do not forget Thy commandments," which is the real ending of the psalm, seems to make this view imperative.

120

This is the first of the fifteen "songs of degrees," as the title appears in our version ("of steps" in the LXX and Vulgate; literally, "of goings up"). The probable meaning is that they were chanted by the Levites at the Feast of Tabernacles as they stood during the waterdrawing on the steps leading from the court of the men to that of the women. The number of steps so occupied was in fact fifteen. If the poem is personal, it records an experience which every phase of life in all ages presents, the mischief arising from slander. If—the more probable conjecture—it is national, then we must look for its motive in the complications which would naturally arise when Israel had to struggle amid foreign powers and influences to maintain its religious and national existence.

Title.—"Song of degrees." Rather, "lyric song of goings up," or "ascents."

(2) Deliver ... —Of all the elements of bitterness which made up the lot of Israel under foreign dominion, taunts and slanders seem to have made the deepest wound, and left the most lasting scar. This was "the torture prolonged from age to age," under which we hear psalmist after psalmist raising his cry for deliverance.

(5-7) No doubt these verses are intended

to indicate the nature of the malicious speeches mentioned in verses 2 and 3. We imagine Israel in peculiarly difficult political relations under the Persians, possibly soon after the Return, trying to keep in favor and peace with the ruling powers, but continually drawn into trouble by the jealousy and bitterness of other subject tribes.

121

This simple but exquisite little hymn of four four-line verses dwells almost exclusively on the sleepless guardianship of His people by the God who made the world. The poet seems to want nothing to heighten his truthful confidence, neither vivid coloring nor elaborate imagery, except the repetition again and again of the one word "keep."

Title.—The Hebrew, in many editions, presents a variation from the usual "song of degrees." Here, "a song for the degrees" has been claimed in support of two rival theories, since it favors equally the view which makes these hymns pilgrim songs, and that which sees in them a reference to the actual "steps" leading up to the Temple.

(1) Whence.—The hills are those on which Jerusalem is built. This gaze of hope does not absolutely decide the standpoint of the poet. He might have been like Ezekiel (6:2) when bidden to turn "towards the mountains of Israel" in the distant plain of Mesopotamia; or he may have been close to the end of the pilgrim journey, and actually under the sacred hills. But wherever he stands, he knows that help will come from God's holy hill "out of Zion." The poet may in his mind have been contrasting the confidence with which a worshiper of Jehovah might look up to the sacred city on the crest of the holy hill with that superstition and idolatry which was associated with so many hills and high places in Canaan.

(2) My help cometh . . . —It is noticeable that the style, "maker of heaven and earth," is a peculiarity of psalms which are certainly post-exile, and show how strongly the contrast with heathenism impressed the creative power of God on the Hebrew mind. When the idolater, pointing to his visible god, taunted the Israelite with having no god, the reply, that He made the heavens, and the earth, and all things, and that these were the proofs of His being, was most natural. (See Jer. 10:11.)

122

It is on this psalm chiefly that the theory of the "pilgrim odes" is based. It tells its design in almost so many words, and actually refers to the ordinance which directed every male Israelite to visit the holy city three times a year. The poet stands in imagination or memory at the gates of Jerusalem. The journey is done, and at this moment the excitement and joy with which it was begun are lovingly recalled. Then follow the impressions produced in the caravan of country strangers by the aspect of the city, the throngs of pilgrims pouring in at the several gates, the royal residences and courts of justice. At this moment the feelings of patriotic admiration and reverence get the better of mere wonder, and a prayer for the city's welfare rises to the lips of the poet.

Title.—The addition of "David" is plainly a gratuitous conjecture. The LXX knew nothing of it.

(5) Thrones.—Jerusalem, at first a cause of wonder as a city, is now to the pilgrims a cause of admiration as the "capital." The mention of the "House of David" itself disposes of the title, but does not prove that the monarchy was still in existence, since even the Sanhedrin might be said to administer justice from the throne of the house or successors of David.

(9) Because . . . —Now for the first time the religious motive of the pilgrimage appears, rendered all the more emphatic by being kept for the concluding verse.

123

This psalm has been beautifully called **Oculus Sperans** (the Eye of Hope). That it reflects the feelings of Israel under foreign oppression there is no doubt, but there is no indication of precise time, unless we are to adopt the Hebrew margin, and see in the concluding word a reference to the **Ionians**, which would bring the psalm within the Macedonian period.

124

In this psalm we have a reminiscence of a catastrophe so tremendous that all the combined images under which the poets of past times had figured the many vicissitudes of Israel appear insufficient. Nothing but the total ruin of the city and Temple, and the captivity of the nation, could have left an impression so deep and lasting. It is the restored remnant that thus ascribe to Jehovah their escape—so marvelous, so miraculous, that the older deliverance from Egypt colors the language in which it is described. The Aramaisms of the poem leave no room for upholding the ascription to David.

Title.—"Of David." The LXX knows nothing of this addition. The imagery recalls Davidic poems, and possibly suggested the inscription.

(2) Men.—In this use of the general term, we must see an indication of the time of composition of the psalm. One who could so speak of the whole world as separated into two parts ("Jews" and "heathen") discloses a sense of isolation and exclusiveness which brings us far down from the time of the prophets. They, indeed, spoke of it as the ideal of the future. This psalmist regards it as an accomplished fact.

Captivity enables the psalmist to anticipate a similar change from gloom to gladness now.

(4) Captivity.—Here there is a change. The joy of the great Return was too great not to last on through many vicissitudes. But the poet now thinks of the many exiles still dispersed among the nations, and prays for another manifestation of divine favor and power.

(6) The form of the expression suggests the long patient labor of the sower and the reward which patience and perseverance always brings—a harvest in proportion to the toil and trouble of seedtime. The words of the prophet Haggai (1:10, 11: 2:19) contemporary with the Return, should be compared. The word rendered "precious" in the King James Version may be correctly represented by "handful" (comp. Amos 9:13). The contrast so beautifully painted in this verse was certainly realized in Ezra 6:16 (comp. 6:22; Neh. 12:42).

125

This psalm brings out prominently the danger to which Israel was subjected from heathen rule—a danger of being forced or seduced away from the political and religious principles of the restored nation. From this danger the poet believes those who keep faithful to the religion of Jehovah are secured, as Jerusalem itself is secured by the strength of its geographical situation.

(2) As the mountains.—In the first verse, the **stability** of the faithful is compared to that of Mount Zion; here their **security** to that of the city girt by its hills. The sacred city lies upon the broad and high mountain range, which is shut in by the two valleys, Jehoshaphat and Hinnom. All the surrounding hills are higher. In Zech. 2:4, 5, the protecting care of Jehovah is likened to a wall around the city, instead of to the rampart of the mountains, as here.

126

The two stanzas of this exquisite little poem, though telling with the distinctness of actual description the nature of the circumstances amid which it was written, give no indication of an exact date. All we can see with certainty is that the psalm is post-exile. The recollection of the exuberant burst of joy at the first news of the return from the

127

Man's toil, skill, and care all would be unavailing were there not a "divinity shaping our ends." This is the thought common in Hebrew literature, now so expressed as to include not only the greater purposes of human activity, but even the homeliest duty of everyday life. All fall under the same benign and watchful surveillance. If any particular set of circumstances must be sought for this expression of a truth so firmly planted in Israel, it is natural to look for them during the troubles and anxieties which accompanies the restoration and rebuilding of Jerusalem. Possibly the haste to rebuild the private houses before the public necessities were supplied (comp. Haggai 1:2, 4) may have given the motive of the poem, though it is but in the most delicate way, and under figures universally applicable, that the people are reminded that home, family, and property alike depend on God.

Title.—"For Solomon." The rendering is wrong even if the inscription is admitted. "Of Solomon" would be the usual form of ascribing authorship. It was natural to think of Solomon, the great builder, in connection with the opening of the psalm, and the resemblance to the Book of Proverbs, both in form and sentiment, is marked. See, for example, Prov. 10:22, which sums up the prevailing thought of the psalm.

(2) It ... sleep.—The Sermon on the Mount, by the contrast of man's restless ambition with the unconscious dependence on the divine bounty of birds and flowers, reflects the intention of this psalm. Labor is decried as unnecessary neither here nor in the Sermon on the Mount, but undue care is dismissed as unworthy, and those who, from past experience, ought to trust the goodness of the great Provider.

128

This psalm, while announcing the promises attached to fidelity to Jehovah, still confines itself to the domestic circle—with the implied truth that national prosperity is bound up closely with domestic happiness and depends on the cultivation of domestic virtues. And the idyllic picture here of peace and happiness is the natural effects of that spirit of simple piety which often preserves itself through many generations under a humble roof. But the happiness could not be real or sincere which did not look beyond the home circle to the prosperity of the larger circle of the nation of which it forms part; and to that end the psalmist ends with a patriotic prayer.

(2) For thou.—This picture of a successful and peaceful husbandry, which itself throws a whole flood of light on the condition of Palestine and of the people, now not nomadic but agricultural, is rendered still more emphatic by references to the numerous passages where it is foretold that enemies would devour the harvests (Deut. 28:30-33; Lev. 26:16).

129

Out of some deadly peril Israel looks for deliverance to the righteousness of Jehovah, which from the childhood of the race has repeatedly manifested itself in help and deliverance. As the cord of bondage was cut in Egypt so will it be cut again, and the same shame and confusion will overtake the present oppressors which fell upon the Pharaohs. But of the precise time and occasion there is no indication.

(3) Furrows.—The double image, suggesting the lash given to a slave, and at the same time the actual and terrible imprints of oppression left on the country as well as the race, is as striking as poetry ever produced. It, in fact, combines two separate prophetic figures (Isa. 50:6 and 51:23).

(8) This harvest scene is exactly like that painted in Ruth 2:4, and the last line should be printed as a return greeting from the reapers.

130

It is the soul of the people which here throws itself on the divine forgiveness, waiting for deliverance as one waiteth for the dawn. Verses 7 and 8, which are evidently taken up by the full choir, leave no doubt of the national character of the psalm. But the strong personal feeling breathed into it has made it even more the **de profundis** of individuals than of churches or nations. This psalm was prepared to be what it has become, one of the penitential psalms of the world. Luther's fondness for this psalm is well known.

(6) Watch for the morning.—Comp. Ps. 123:2 for another figure of the same earnest upward gaze. In the "watcher for the dawn" there may be an allusion to the Levite-sentinel whose duty it was to signal the first ray of dawn, and the moment for commencing the sacred rites of the Temple (Ps. 134:1), but the figure if general, as marking the impatience of a deeply agitated soul—a sufferer waiting for relief, a contrite sinner for forgiveness—is as striking as graceful. (See Deut. 28:67.)

131

The most perfect and sincere resignation breathes through this short poem. It is so plain from the last verse, that not an individual, but Israel, is here represented, that we need not discuss the addition to the inscription, which makes David its author (probably with recollection of II Sam. 6:22), or to conjecture whether Nehemiah or Simon Maccabaeus, or any other particular person, has left here an expression of his feelings.

132

This psalm, at first sight, seems from comparison with II Chron. 6 to be a hymn of Solomon's, or of his age, in commemoration of the completion and dedication of the Temple. But verse 6 clears up only as we take a more and more distant standpoint from the incidents it notes. A late poet might easily refer the Temple altogether to David, and see in the removal of the Ark a step in a prepared design. Other indications (verse 10) point to the Asmonean dynasty as that in those whose honor the poem was composed.

(3-5) It is vain to search the historical accounts for this vow. It may be implied from II Sam. 7:2, and from the persistent purpose which David certainly nourished.

(6) Lo, we heard.—This verse has been pronounced inexplicable, and yet the general intention is clear. The vow in which David declared his purpose has just been quoted, and that which is now said to have been heard and found can hardly be anything else than this purpose. We need not go from the plain direction of such places as Gen. 35:19; 48:7; Ruth 4:11; Micah 5:2, which pronounce the identity of Ephratah with Bethlehem, to seek any other locality which might possibly be so called. David's purpose would naturally be connected—especially after a long lapse of time—with the birthplace of his family. That "the fields of the wood" is one designation of Kirjath-jearim (city of Yaarim), which went by so many names: Jer. 26:20; Ezra 2:25; Josh. 15:10, 11, there can be little doubt. We must not, of course, think here of David's contemporaries, but of those of the psalmist, who poetically are represented as taking important part in the early plans for building the Temple.

(7) Tabernacles.—These words do not, as the last verse, recall an incident of the past, but express the determination of the present. The result of David's project is that the present generation has a place of worship. It does not detract from this explanation to refer the psalm to post-exile times, and to the second Temple, since the fact of the existence of a temple at any time could be poetically ascribed to David.

(8-10) These are the words which the chronicler (II Chron. 6:41, 42) puts into Solomon's mouth at the dedication of the Temple. The psalmist does not at his distance from the events distinguish between David and Solomon. He merges the executor of the work in the projector; and in honor of the second Temple it is as natural for him to take up words used at the actual dedication of the first as it was to refer to the original purpose in David's mind. All is blended together in the long perspective of poetry.

(10) The most obvious construction of this verse is that which makes it an intercession, on the ground of the divine partiality for David, in behalf of another prince—one of his successors—by the people at large. In the original (II Chron. 6:42) it is of course Solomon who prays for himself; here we must naturally think of one of the Asmonean princes.

(13) Zion.—The dynasty of David and the location of the sanctuary at Zion are intimately associated, as in Ps. 78:67, 68. (Comp. Ps. 122:4, 5.)

(17) Horn of David.—The sprouting or growing horn is an image of young, vigorous life. The Messianic application of the prediction comes out in Zachariah's song (Luke 1:69).

133

The unity eulogized in this poem is not mere brotherhood, not political or even religious union generally, but unity at Zion, as the last clause of the beautiful little poem convincingly proves. The "blessing" (see verse 3), the covenant blessing, which rested on Zion, where was the center both of the political and religious life of the nation, is the subject of this psalm. For determining the date of the poem, there is not the slightest indication. The inscription may be dismissed as a Rabbinical conjecture.

(2) It is like.—The italics of the King James Version are wrongly inserted. "Unity" could not be said to "flow down." The other term of the simile is implied in verse 3. The point of the comparison lies in the word three times repeated—"descending." Our version unfortunately obscures this point by rendering this recurrent participle each time by a different word. The oil descends from Aaron's head over his face and beard; the dew of Hermon descends on Zion—low in actual measurement, but exalted by the divine favor above the loftiest hills. It is not "unity," then, in itself which is the subject of the poem, but the unity of the covenant under which all blessings flowed down from above, rested on Mount Zion, and took outward shape and form there in the political and religious constitution.

134

This little song, with its appeal and its

response, fitly closes the Songs of the Steps. It is a challenge to the Levites going on duty for the night (comp. I Chron. 9:33) to praise Jehovah, as others have already done by day. The importance of this psalm in deciding the date of the close of the Psalter is seen in the Talmudic tradition assigning this night service to the time of Queen Alexandra, i.e., the middle of the first century before Christ.

135

This psalm is a mosaic from older writings, and was plainly put together for liturgic use. It pretends to no originality, and shows very little art or care in the composition. The date must be very late.

(1) The psalm opens with an adaptation and expansion (comp. Ps. 116:19) of Ps. 134:1. As there, the priestly class is addressed. Some, however, think that the addition "courts of the house of our God," as well as verse 19, make the application to all these standing in covenant relation to Jehovah.

(4) Peculiar treasure.—A special covenant-name for Israel (Exod. 19:5; Deut. 7:6, etc.) and of private property (I Chron. 29:3; Eccles. 2:8).

(8) Egypt.—This abrupt change from the miracles of nature to the marvels of history is apparently copied from the next psalm, verse 10.

136

The recurrence in this psalm of the ancient liturgic refrain (see Pss. 106:1; 118:1), not after every verse, but after every clause, marks clearly the peculiarity of its choral use, and shows that it was composed expressly for the Temple service. It is invariably allowed to be one of the latest hymns in the collection. It has generally been known among the Jews as the Great Hallel, a designation, however, at other times given to the series Pss. 120-136 (according to others Pss. 135:4-136).

(10) For his mercy.—Here the refrain, after the mention of the destruction of the Egyptian first-born, and subsequently after that of war and slaughter, sounds harsh to Christian ears. But the word mercy **(khesed)** in the Hebrew motto implies distinctly "covenant grace," that special favor of Jehovah in which the heathen did not share,

and which was often most signally shown in their destruction.

(25) All flesh.—Here apparently the word "mercy" takes a wider image and applies to all men. But only apparently so. Israel could think of Jehovah providing for the bodily wants of all as He was the creator of all, but the covenant grace was for them alone.

137

This fine song, blended as it is of tears and fire, with its plaintive opening and its vindictive close, it one of the clearest records left in Hebrew literature of the captivity, but whether it dates immediately from it, or looks back with a distant though keen and clear gaze, is difficult to decide. Babylon may only have been on the verge of its doom, or she may already have fallen (verse 8). It is possible that just as long afterward another great power was symbolized under the name, so here the ruin of the Persian or Grecian dominion may be covertly invoked under the symbol "daughter of Babylon."

(2) Willows.—It is perhaps not necessary to attempt to identify the trees mentioned in this verse, since the touching picture may only be a poetical way of expressing the silence during the exile of all the religious and festal songs.

(3) Songs of Zion—or, as in the next verse, "songs of Jehovah," were of course the liturgical hymns. Nothing is more characteristic than this of the Hebrew feelings. The captors asked for a national song, as the Philistines asked for sport from Samson, to amuse them. The Hebrew can think only of one kind of song, that to which the genius of the race was dedicated.

(5) Her cunning.—i.e., the skill of playing on the harp. If at such a moment the poet can so far forget the miserable bondage of Jerusalem as to strike the strings in joy, may his hand for ever lose the skill to touch them.

(7) Remember ... —The prophecy of Obadiah (verses 10-12) gives the best comment on this verse.

138

The suggestion contained in the last addition made to the Hebrew inscription by the LXX, "Of Haggai and Zechariah," brings this psalm within the post-exile period, the

459

most likely time of its composition. The tone and tenor are what we should look for if Zerubbabel or Nehemiah were its author. Some great success had evidently just been gained (verses 1-5); but trouble still pressed on the community for whom the poet speaks—some work of pressing need was impeded, and Jehovah's strong hand could alone bring it to completion. This would suit the times of Ezra and Nehemiah. On the other hand, the achievement already performed may have been of a military kind, and the psalm may breathe the hopes of the Maccabaean period.

(8) The special intention of the prayer depends on the origin of the psalm. If it arose out of the troubles of rebuilding Jerusalem and reconstituting the state, it is intelligible and expressive. Or the reference may be to all Jehovah's gracious intentions for Israel.

139

In its tone this psalm is personal and reflective rather than speculative, yet some of the profoundest metaphysical questions are touched, or at least suggested; and as we read we feel at every moment that we stand on the verge of the discovery of weighty truths concerning God's nature and his relation to man. But, suddenly, as only a Hebrew poet could do, the writer breaks away from the subject, to denounce ungodly men with a storm of indignation nowhere surpassed. For the explanation of this, see note to verse 19.

The superscription ascribing the psalm to David must be abandoned in the face not only of the strong Aramaic coloring of the psalm, but also of the development of its eschatology, which marks a late epoch. It is certainly as late as the latest in the collection.

Title.—See title to Ps. 4.

The Codex Alex. of the LXX adds, "of Zechariah," and a later hand, "on the dispersion."

(7) Spirit.—If this clause stood alone we should naturally understand by God's "Spirit" His creative and providential power, from which nothing can escape (comp. Ps. 104:30). But taken in parallelism with "presence" in the next clause the expression leads on to a thought toward which the theology of the Old Testament was dimly feeling, but which found its perfect expression in our Saviour's announcement to the woman of Samaria (John 4:24).

(8) If I make my bed in hell.—This conviction that the underworld (**Sheol**) was not exempt from the vigilance and even from the visitation on Jehovah makes an advance in thought from Ps. 6:5 (see note), where death is viewed as cutting off the Hebrew altogether from his relation to the Theocracy.

(10) Even there ... —The expressions "lead me," "hold me," are elsewhere used of the protecting and guiding providence of God (Pss. 5:8; 23:3; 27:11; 73:24). And yet the psalmist speaks here as if he were a guilty being trying to escape from the divine notice. The truth is a profound one. Even when God discovers and overtakes those who guiltily try to hide from Him, it is to take them under His loving care.

(13, 14) The prime thought is that every birth is a divine creation. Or if the reference is national rather than individual, it would imply, as so frequently, the choice of Israel by Jehovah in distinction to other races.

(15) In the lowest parts of the earth.—This figurative allusion to the womb is intended no doubt to heighten the feeling of mystery attaching to birth. There may also be a covert allusion to the creation from dust, as Ecclus. 40:1, "From the day that they go out of their mother's womb, till the day that they return to the mother of all things." This allusion falls in with the view which meets us in other parts of the Old Testament, that the creation of Adam is repeated at every birth (comp. Job 33:6).

(19-24) This abrupt transition from a theme so profound and fascinating to fierce indignation against the enemies of God would certainly be strange anywhere but in the Psalms. And yet, perhaps, philosophically regarded, the subject of God's omniscience must conduct the mind to the thought of the existence of evil and speculation on its origin and development. But the Hebrew never speculated for speculation's sake. The practical concerns of life engaged him too intensely. Where a modern would have branched off into the ever-recurring problem of the entrance of evil into the world, the Israelite turned with indignation on those who then and there proved the existence of sin in concrete act.

140

The date of its composition is in no way indicated in this psalm. Besides the conjecture of Davidic authorship by the Rabbins, further developed by the addition in the Syriac, "when Saul threw the spear," Manasseh's reign, the immediate post-exile times, and the Maccabaean age, have all been selected for the situations out of which the psalm sprang. It is most in harmony with its feeling to suppose Israel speaking as a community, or an individual who identifies his own fortunes entirely with that of the better part of the nation. Heathen oppressors and foreign influences are undoubtedly attacked in the poem, and the blessings attending a loyal adherence to the religious and national traditions supply the cheerful and confident tone in which it ends. Comp. Pss. 58 and 64.

Title.—See Ps. 4.

141

This is one of the most obscure psalms in the whole Psalter, hardly a clause of verses 5, 6, 7 offering anything more than a conjectural meaning. The author appears from verse 2 to be a priest or Levite, being so familiar with the rites of the sanctuary as to use them as metaphors. From verses 3 and 4 we gather that he (or as verse 7 indicates, the community for which he speaks) is under a temptation to betray the cause of Jehovah and true religion, either by pronouncing some blasphemy, or indulging in some license forbidden by a high covenant ideal. The reference to the unlawful "dainties" in verse 4 naturally suggests either idolatrous feasts (comp. Ps. 16:4) or banquets connected with the games and other foreign innovations against which, when introduced under Grecian influence, the stricter Jews so bitterly protested.

The Davidic inscription cannot be for a moment maintained. There is no period of David's life which the psalm could represent. The overthrow of some oppressive and persecuting court party, such as existed at Jerusalem either in the Persian or Grecian period, is surely indicated in verse 6.

142

This is one of the eight psalms assigned by their inscriptions to the time of David's persecution by Saul. There is nothing in the contents either to support or controvert the title, unless the recurrence of expressions found in Pss. 42, 61 and 77, marks dependence on them. But such dependence would not detract from the originality of the poem

before us, an originality shown rather in the passion and play of feeling than in the poetic figure and expression.

Title.—Maschil. (See title, Ps. 32.)

(7) Out of prison.—This expression, which must certainly be figurative of distress (comp. Ps. 143:11), probably led to the inscription.

143

This psalm is chiefly interesting as an instance of the way in which the deeper religious life of the post-exile times was upheld and cherished by the experience of past times and the faith of older generations as it had found expression in prophecy and song. There is hardly a phrase which is not derived from some older source—a fact which at once disposes of the inscription. Probably it is not an individual, but the community, which thus under affliction confesses its sin and comforts itself with reflections on the past.

(1) Faithfulness ... righteousness.—The first word recalls the covenant promise, the second the faith, expressed so frequently, on which the covenant rested, that the Judge of all the world must do right. John found the appeal for forgiveness on the same pair of divine qualities (I John 1:9; comp. Ps. 65:5).

(2) And enter not.—The divine justice has just been invoked, and now the appellant suddenly seems to deprecate it. These verses really sum up the apparent paradox of the Book of Job. as also the expressions recall that book. (See Job 4:17; 9:2, 32; 14:3, seq., 15:14; 22:4; etc.)

144

There is nothing more curious in the composition of the Psalter than the union of the two entirely dissimilar pieces which compose this psalm. Verses 1-11 are a mere cento from former psalms, the eighteenth furnishing the greater number of expressions and figures, and, must from this circumstance be regarded as one of the latest in the collection, whereas verses 12-15 are composed of a fragment of some ancient song, whose beginning is lost, and which has neither grammatical nor logical connection with the medley of quotations that precedes it. This interesting fragment gives, unfortunately, no indication of its date or authorship. We can imagine it, however, chanted at harvest, at festivals, or as "the help tune" of the reapers.

(5) Come down.—The theophany for which the psalmist prays is described in the classic language for such manifestations taken from Ps. 18:9, 13, 16, 17, 43, 45, with reminiscences of Ps. 104:32; Exod. 19:18. But there are touches of originality, as in the next clause.

(15) Happy.—It is only a narrow and one-sided religion that can see anything out of place in this beatitude of plenty and peace. If we could rejoice with the psalms, fully and without misgiving, in the temporal blessings bestowed by heaven, we should the more readily and sincerely enter into the depths of their spiritual experience. And the secret of this lies in the full comprehension and contemplation of the beautiful and pleasant as the gift of God.

145

This alphabetical psalm recalls in many expressions and phrases the thoughts and feelings of older songs. It has been identified with the "New Song" promised in Ps. 144:9. Possibly some thought of the kind may have led to its following it. The song, though abounding in familiar psalm expressions, deserves the claim of originality from the insistance of its conviction of the divine love and pity and care for all the world and all creatures.

The acrostic arrangement is incomplete (the **nun** stanza, which should come after verse 13, having been lost), thus supplying only twenty-one instead of twenty-two stanzas.

Title.—This is the only psalm inscribed **tehillah**, though the whole collection is, in Hebrew, called **Tehillîm**, or **Tillîm**. It is possibly from verse 21; or perhaps this distinction is due to the early rise of the custom of repeating it daily at the noonday repast. So it would be called "Praise," just as we speak of "the grace" before and after a meal.

(9, 10) All.—This wide outlook over the world as the object, with all that it contains, of the divine pity and love, is a noble anticipation of our Lord's teaching in the Sermon on the Mount and is introduced in a similar manner. Just as the subjects of the kingdom of heaven should exceed the heathen in kindness and goodness, because they know the universal and impartial grace of the Father, so here the "saints, the members of the covenant," are to "bless" Jehovah, who shows them peculiar favor, but also lets His tender mercies flow in an unchecked stream over all His works. All Jehovah's works confess Him, but His saints "bless" Him.

146

This liturgical hymn, beginning and ending with the familiar "Hallelujah," is the first of the series of five which are sometimes called the "Greek"—in distinction to the "Egyptian"—Hallel. It was evidently composed for a time of great national depression, when the community, sick of dependence on the favor of foreign princes, turned more and more to the thought of the eternal righteousness and faithfulness of Jehovah.

The recurrence in a slightly changed form of verse 4 in I Macc. 2:63 shows that the psalm was in existence when the book was written, and also serves to confirm the impression that it belongs to the Maccabaean age.

147

Composed of three pieces, without any regular rhythmical structure, and only loosely connected by the same general thought and method of expression, this psalm yet deserves to rank high in the poetry of the Bible. While freely using existing materials, especially Pss. 33; 104; Isa. 40; and the Book of Job, the author gives proof of his own powers in the keenness of his observation of nature, and in his sympathy with the life and movement of the world, as well as by the free play of his fancy around each phenomenon that attracts him.

The evident allusion to a rebuilding of Jerusalem has been referred both to the great restoration under Nehemiah and to the repairs and fortifications of Hyrcanus (I Macc. 16:23).

(4) Stars.—This proof of God's power to help, by reference to the stars of heaven, which are beyond man's power to count, much more to name, but which the Almighty both numbers and names, seems rather abruptly introduced, but the train of thought is clear. To assemble the dispersed of Israel, however numerous and scattered, was easy to the ruler of the hosts of heaven.

The original promise to Abraham was, of course, in the poet's mind, but still more Isa. 40:26-28, from which the expression may have been taken.

148

This glorious anthem has been the model of countless hymns of praise. The motive is quite different from the sympathetic feeling for nature which enters so largely and powerfully into modern poetry. Not that this feeling was entirely unknown to the Hebrew mind. It makes itself felt elsewhere; but here it is not because the poet wants nature to join him in praise that he summons the universe to his choir, but that he may, in the last verse, enhance the glory and privilege of Israel. All nature has reason to praise the Creator who called it into being, and gave it its order so fair and so established, and poetically the universe may be imagined full of adoring creatures, but in reality, praise as a privilege belongs only to Israel. It is not here a contrast between inanimate and animate, rational and irrational creation. On the contrary, it is the covenant people that alone possess the privilege. Expression is piled on expression to establish this fact: "His people," "His saints," "a people near unto Him."

The immediate occasion of the psalm may very probably have been some victory, but conjecture cannot recover it.

(14) The raising of the horn evidently implies some victory, or assurance of victory, which, no doubt, gave the first impulse for this song of praise. (For the figure see Ps. 75:4, 5.)

The verse is a repetition of a frequent statement of the Psalms. While poetically all the universe, inanimate as well as animate, all men, heathen as well as Hebrews, can be called to sing "hallelujah," it remains as it has ever been, the covenant privilege of Israel. This explanation disposes at once of the charge which has been brought against this verse of narrowing a grand universal anthem, and ending the psalm with an anticlimax.

149

The age when such a psalm of religious

and patriotic zeal was most likely to be produced was undoubtedly that of the Maccabees, and the coincidence between verse 6 of the psalm and II Macc. 15:27 may indicate the very series of events amid which, with hymns of praise in their throats, and a two-edged sword in their hand, the **chasidîm** in battle after battle claimed and won the honor of executing vengeance on Jehovah's foes.

(4) He will beautify the meek ... — Rather, "He adorns the oppressed with salvation." Not only is the victory which achieves the deliverence of the afflicted people a relief to them, but the honor won in the sight of the world is like a beautiful robe, a figure no doubt suggested by the actual triumphal dresses of the victors, or the spoils in which they appeared after the battle. (Comp. Isa. 55:5; 60:7; 61:3; Judges 5:30.)

150

In the place of the short doxology, such as concludes each of the former books of the Psalter, this psalm was fitly composed or selected to close the whole collection. It has been well called "the finale of the spiritual concert," and no doubt afforded a good musical display, music performed with full orchestra and choir, every kind of instrument known to the Hebrews, "wind," "string," and "percussion," being mentioned, and in the last verse all who had breath and voice being invited to join. The form of the invocation embracing heaven and earth, and putting forward as the object of praise both Jehovah's majesty and His great works wrought for Israel, is also exactly suited for a conclusion to the great collection of Israelite song.

(6) Every thing that hath breath.—We naturally wish to give these words their largest intent, and to hear the Psalter close with an invocation to the whole earth to praise God. But the psalm distinctly and positively brings us into the Temple (verse 1, "sanctuary") and places us among the covenant people engaged at their devotions. It is, therefore, not all breathing beings, but only all assembled in the sanctuary, that are here addressed; and the loud hallelujah with which the collection of psalms actually closes rises from Hebrew voices alone.

THE PROVERBS

1

1.—Introduction Describing the Purpose of the Book (verses 1-6)

(1) Solomon.—The absolute quiet and prosperity of the reign of Solomon (the man of peace) as described in I Kings 4:20, seq., would naturally be conducive to the growth of a sententious philosophy; whereas the constant wars and dangerous life of David had called forth the impassioned eloquence of the Psalms.

(2) To know.—That is, they are written that one may know. The writer in this and the following verses heaps up synonyms with which to bring out the wide purpose of the instructions he offers.

Wisdom.—The original meaning of this word is "firmness," "solidity," having an opinion based upon sound reasons; the opposite state of mind to being "carried about with every wind of doctrine" (Eph. 4:14).

Instruction.—Or rather, "discipline," the knowledge how to keep oneself under control. (Comp. II Pet. 1:6: "Add to your knowledge temperance," or self-control.)

To perceive the words of understanding.—Comp. Heb. 5:14; Phil. 1:10. The opposite condition to this is having the heart made "fat" (Isa. 6:10) by continuance in evil, so that it can no longer understand.

(3) Equity.—Literally, "what is straight," so true, honest.

(4) Subtilty.—For the meaning here, comp. Matt. 10:16: "Be ye wise as serpents."

Simple.—Literally, "those who are open" to good impressions and influences, but who also can be easily led astray. (Comp. 8:5 and 14:15.)

Discretion.—Or rather, "thoughtfulness."

(5) A wise man will hear.—That is, if he listens to these proverbs. (Comp. 9:9.) It is not the young only who will derive profit from them.

Wise counsels.—Literally, "arts of seamanship": i.e., guiding himself and others right through the "waves of this troublesome world."

2.—Fifteen Didactic Poems, or Discourses on Various Subjects (1:7-9:18)

(a) **First Discourse:—Against**

Companionship in Robbery
(1:7-19)

(7) The fear of the Lord is the beginning of knowledge.—The first discourse is prefaced by a couplet, which serves as a keynote to all the teaching of the book. This expression, "the fear of the Lord," occurs thirteen times in the Proverbs, and plays a prominent part throughout the Old Testament. That law which was given amid "blackness, and darkness, and tempest" was enforced by the threat, "Cursed is every one that continueth not in all things which are written in the book of the law to do them" (Gal. 3:10). Men had to be taught how hateful sin was to God, and the lesson was for the most part instilled into them by the fear of immediate punishment. (Comp. Deut. 28.) But when the lesson had been learned, and when mankind had found by experience that they were unable to keep the Law of God by their own strength, then the new covenant of mercy was revealed from Calvary, even free justification "by [God's] grace, through the redemption that is in Christ Jesus" (Rom. 3:24). And with this new message a new motive to obedience was preached. The "fear of the Lord" was now superseded by the higher duty of the "love of God," and of man, for His sake.

Fools.—Self-willed, headstrong persons, who will listen to no advice.

(10) If sinners entice thee.—A warning against taking part in plundering, a crime to which Palestine was at all times peculiarly exposed, from the wild character of its formation, and from its neighborhood to predatory tribes, who would invade the country whenever the weakness of the government gave them an opening. The insecurity of life and property thus occasioned would provide a tempting opportunity for the wilder spirits of the community to seek a livelihood by plunder.

(16) For their feet ... —The first reason against taking part with them: the horrible nature of the crime they are committing.

(17) Surely in vain ... —The second reason: their folly in so doing, for God will bring punishment upon them; in the same "net which they hid is their own foot taken" (Ps. 9:15). Even birds are wiser than they. It is useless to spread a net in the sight of any bird.

(18) And they lay wait.—Yet they cannot see that in truth they are laying wait, not for the innocent, but for themselves, as God will deliver him, and bring the mischief they designed for him upon their own head.

(b) Second Discourse:—Wisdom Addresses her Despisers (1:20-33)

(20) Wisdom.—It is in the plural, signifying the multiform excellences of wisdom. It is possible that Solomon may have originally meant in this passage only to describe, in highly poetic language, the influence and work in their generation of those in whom "the fear of the Lord" dwells. So, too, many of the psalms (Ps. 45, for example), in the first instance it would seem, are intended to describe the excellence of some earthly saint or king, yet they are completely fulfilled only in the Son of man, the ideal of all that is noblest and best in man. And thus the description of Wisdom in her manifold activity, as represented in chaps. 1, 8 and 9, so closely corresponds to the work of our Lord, as depicted in the New Testament, that from the earliest times of Christianity these passages have been held to be a prophecy of Him.

(21) Crieth.—She cannot bear to see sinners rushing madly on their doom.

(23) I will pour out my spirit unto you.—Comp. the prophecy of Joel 2:28, promised by our Lord (John 7:38, 39), and fulfilled at Pentecost (Acts 2:17).

I will make known my words unto you.—For a similar promise that God's will shall be revealed to those who fear and follow Him, comp. Ps. 25:14; John 7:17.

(24) Because I have called.—Wisdom's call having been rejected, she now changes her tone from "mercy" to "judgment" (Ps. 101:1).

(26) I also will laugh ... I will mock.—For expressions like this, comp. Pss. 2:4; 37:13; 59:8, where the same actions are attributed to God. They are not to be taken literally, of course, for the sight of human folly can give no pleasure to Him. They signify that He will act as if He mocked when He refuses to hear their cry.

(32) Prosperity of fools—i.e., the security, apathy of dull, stupid people, who cannot believe that God will fulfill His threatenings. (Comp. Ps. 73 throughout.)

(33) Shall dwell safely ... —Comp. Ps. 37 throughout for similar promises.

2

(c) Third Discourse:—An Exhortation to follow after Wisdom (chap. 2)

(4) If thou seekest her as silver.—That the process of mining was understood long before the time of Solomon, is proved by the remains of copper mines discovered in the peninsula of Sinai, and the gold mines in the Bishàree desert of Egypt. Rock inscriptions have been found near the former, dating from a great age, in the opinion of Lepsius from 4000 B.C. Comp. also the description in Job 28:1-11; and see II Chron. 9:14, 21.

Searchest for her as for hid treasures.—From the great insecurity of life and property in Eastern countries, the hiding of treasures in the earth has always been of frequent occurrence. It would often, no doubt, happen that the owner would die without disclosing the place of concealment to any one else, and the treasure thus be lost. Hunting after such hoards has in consequence been always of the keenest interest to Orientals, and as such furnishes the groundwork for one of our Lord's parables (Matt. 13:44).

(5) Find the knowledge of God.—It is the highest of all gifts, even eternal life itself, to know God, the Giver of all good things. It was to bestow this knowledge upon man that Christ came into the world (John 17:3). He promises the manifestation of Himself as the reward of obedience and love. (14:21).

(6) For the Lord giveth wisdom.—As James (1:5) expresses it, He gives it to every man "liberally, and upbraideth not": i.e., blames him not for asking it.

(8) His saints.—The word "saint" implies dedication to God, as Israel was a "holy nation" (Exod. 19:6) to God, and Christians (Phil. 1:1) are now in the same position.

(14) Delight in the frowardness of the wicked.—This positive taking pleasure in evil is mentioned by Paul (Rom. 1:32) as the last stage of degradation.

(16) To deliver thee from the strange woman.—Another work of wisdom, to save from profligacy. It would seem as if the evil example of Solomon (I Kings 11:1), in marrying foreign women, had become common in Israel, and that they, by their vicious lives, had become a deadly source of corruption. Brought up in the lax views of morality which prevailed among heathen nations at this time, they would not consider themselves bound by the highest standard of purity which was enjoined upon Hebrew women by the Law.

(16-19) Besides the literal sense of this passage, commentators have generally found in it a spiritual meaning, a warning against idolatry and apostasy. The union of Israel

465

to God is so frequently spoken of in the prophets under the figure of a marriage, and their rejection of Him for idols as adultery, that the passage well may bear this further sense, especially as Jeremiah (3:4) has borrowed this phrase, "guide of her youth," for a passage in which he is reproving the Jews for their faithlessness. The figure is also common in the New Testament, as descriptive of the union of Christ and the Church.

3

(d) **Fourth Discourse: Exhortation to Various Virtues** (3:1-18).

(3) **Mercy.**—Mercy and truth are often joined, as in this place. They are the two special attributes by which God is known in His dealings with men (Exod. 34:6, 7), and as such must be imitated by man (Matt. 5:48).

Bind them about thy neck . . . —These directions resemble the figurative orders with regard to the keeping of the Law in Exod. 13:9 and Deut. 6:8, the literal interpretation of which led to the use of prayer-fillets and phylacteries among the Jews. Certain texts of Scripture were copied out, enclosed in a leather case, and tied at the time of prayer on the left arm and forehead.

(7) **Fear the Lord, and depart from evil.**—The same result is reached by Job also (28:28) in his inquiry after wisdom.

(8) **Navel.**—As being the center, and so the most important part of the body. (Comp. the epithet applied to Delphi, "navel of the earth.")

(11) **Despise not the chastening of the Lord . . .** —Comp. Job 5:17. A wonderful advance beyond the teaching of the Pentateuch. When He sends trouble upon His children, He is no longer to be regarded as an offended father punishing their faults, but as one who in love is correcting them. Even the New Testament quotes these words with approval, and without adding anything to their teaching (Heb. 12:5-13). There it is shown how all God's children must, without exception, submit to this discipline.

(17) **Peace.**—The highest reward of the New Testament for the life of thankful dependence upon God (Phil. 4:6, 7).

(18) **A tree of life.**—Evidently an allusion to Gen. 2 and 3. No mention is made of it

except in Proverbs (11:30; 13:12; 15:4) and Revelation (2:7; 22:2).

(e) **Fifth Discourse:—Wisdom as Creator and Protector** (3:19-26)

(19) **The Lord by wisdom . . .** —A passage anticipatory of the doctrine of John 1:3. (Comp. Pss. 104:24 and 136:5.) A further advance toward the personality of the Creator is made in 8:27, sqq.

(20) **Are broken up.**—Or, "burst forth": the word used in Gen. 7:11 of the breaking forth of the waters from the interior of the earth at the flood. (Comp. Job 38:8.)

(f) **Sixth Discourse:—Exhortation to Charity, Peace, Contentment** (3:27-35)

(27) **Them to whom it is due**—i.e., the poor and needy. An exhortation to us to make to ourselves "friends of the mammon of unrighteousness" (uncertain riches, Luke 16:9), remembering that we are not absolute owners, but "stewards of the manifold grace of God" (I Pet. 4:10), so that when we "fail," i.e., die, "they," the friends we have made by our liberality, may welcome us to heaven.

(33) **He blesseth the habitation of the just.**—By some there is thought to be a distinction intended between the well-built "house" of the wicked and the slightly constructed cottage of the humble just man, no better than a shepherd's hut.

(34) **Surely he scorneth the scorners.**—Another form of the teaching of 1:24-33. If man rejects God's offers of mercy, they will in time be withdrawn from him. And so, as man deals with God, will God at last deal with him. The verse is quoted in Jas. 4:6 and I Pet. 5:5.

4

(g) **Seventh Discourse:—Recollections of his Father's Instructions** (4:1-5:6)

(3) **For I was . . . son . . .** —It is not only his own advice that he has to offer; he can tell disciples of the excellent discipline and teaching he received from his parents in his old home. It may be remarked that the notices of Solomon's early years which occur in this and the following verses harmonize well with what we know of him from the historical books of the Bible.

(18) **But the path of the just . . .** —The

just have the Lord for their light (Ps. 27:1), on them the "Sun of righteousness" has arisen (Mal. 4:2), and this light, that is, their knowledge of God, will become clearer and clearer until the "perfect day," when they shall see Him as He is (I John 3:2).

(19) The way of the wicked is as darkness.—By refusing to "walk in the light" of God's Word, and conscience (I John 1:7), the light that was in them has become darkness (Matt. 6:23); they know not where they are going (John 12:35), and stumble (11:10) over difficulties which in the light they might have avoided.

(23) Keep thy heart with all diligence.—Rather, "above all things that are to be guarded."

For out of it are the issues of life.—That is, from it comes life (and also death). From it proceed "all holy desires, all good counsels, and all just works," signs of the life with God within the soul; or, "evil thoughts, murders," (Matt. 15:19), "the end of which things is death" (Rom. 6:21).

(26) Let all thy ways be established.—Or, "directed aright"; see that they lead straight to the end (Ps. 119:5).

(27) Turn not . . . —Comp. the direction of Josh. 1:7, and the praise accorded to David (I Kings 15:5).

5

(5) Take hold on hell.—They lead straight to it.

(6) Lest thou shouldest ponder . . . —The meaning appears to be, "To prevent thy choosing the path of life, she leads thee by devious paths that thou knowest not where thou art." By these words is described the reckless career of a vicious woman, who at last dares not think where her steps are leading her, but as it were with eyes shut, totters on until she falls to rise no more.

(h) **Eighth Discourse:—Against Adultery, and in Praise of Marriage** (5:7-23)

(7) Hear me now therefore, O ye children.—In this verse Solomon apparently ceases to report the words of his father, and resumes his speech in his own person.

(8) Remove thy way . . . —The great safeguard in such temptations, as all moralists with one mouth advise, is flight.

(11) When thy flesh and thy body are consumed.—Ruin of health has followed ruin of property.

(12) How have I hated instruction.—The last stage of misery is the remorse which comes too late. (Comp. Matt. 25:30.)

(14) I was almost in all evil . . . —The offender's eyes are now opened, and he shudders at the thought of the still greater troubles into which he might, in his infatuation, have fallen.

(15-20) Drink waters out of thine own cistern . . . —In these verses Solomon urges his disciples to follow after purity in the married life; he pictures in vivid terms the delights which it affords as compared with the pleasures of sin.

Out of thine own cistern.—The "strange woman," on the other hand, says "Stolen waters are sweet" (9:17). The same figure is employed in Song of Solomon 4:15. In Jer. 2:13 God compares Himself to a "fountain of living waters," and complains that Israel had deserted Him, and hewed out for themselves "broken cisterns that can hold no water." This passage in Proverbs has in like manner often been interpreted as an exhortation to drink deeply from the living waters of the Holy Spirit given in the Word and Sacraments (John 7:37).

(17) Let them be only thine own.—The deepest joys and sorrows of each heart are sacred, and cannot be shared with others (14:10), and so it is with the various relations of family life also, strangers have no part in them.

(18) Let thy fountain . . . —As a reward for purity of life, the blessing of a numerous offspring is invoked. (Comp. Ps. 128:3, where the wife is a "fruitful vine," and the children numerous and flourishing like olive branches.)

(19) Loving hind and pleasant roe.—The deer and chamois, from their grace and speed and lustrous eyes, have always been chosen by the Oriental poets as figures of human strength and beauty. (Comp. Song of Solomon 2:9, 17; 7:3; 8:14; Ps. 18:33.) Both these animals are said to be remarkable for their affection to their young.

(21) For the ways of man . . . —Another reason for avoiding sin is the certainty of detection by the Judge, whose "eyes run to and fro through the whole earth" (II Chron. 16:9; comp. Ps. 11:4.

(22, 23) His own iniquities . . . —The final scene in the life of the profligate is here described. He has sinned so long that he is "tied and bound," hand and foot, with the "chain of his sins," and cannot get free even had he the wish to do so.

(23) He shall die without instruction.—

Rather, "for want of discipline," because he would not control himself.

6

(i) Ninth Discourse:—Against Suretyship (6:1-5)

(1) If thou be surety for thy friend.— When the Mosaic Law was instituted, commerce had not been taken up by the Israelites, and the lending of money on interest for its employment in trade was a thing unknown. But at the time of Solomon, when the commerce of the Israelites had enormously developed, and communications were opened with Spain and Egypt and (possibly) with India and Ceylon, while caravans penetrated beyond the Euphrates, then the lending of money on interest for employment in trade most probably became frequent, and suretyship also, the pledging of a man's own credit to enable his friend to procure a loan. And when the wealth that accompanied this development of the national resources had brought luxury in its train, borrowing and suretyship would be employed for less worthy purposes, to supply the young nobles of Jerusalem with money for their extravagance. Therefore possibly the emphatic language of the text and 20:16 and 27:13.

Stricken thy hand.—That is, as we should say, "shaken hands on the bargain."

With a stranger.—Or rather, "for another," i.e., thy friend.

(3) When thou art come . . . —Rather, "for thou hast come under the power of thy friend"; thou hast made thy freedom and property dependent on him for whom thou hast become surety.

Make sure.—Rather, "assail impetuously, importune."

(j) Tenth Discourse:—Against Sloth (6:6-11)

(11) As one that travelleth.—While the sluggard sleeps, poverty is coming on swiftly.

As an armed man.—Against whom the sleeper will be defenseless. Verses 10 and 11 are repeated in 24:33 and 34.

(k) Eleventh Discourse:—Against Deceit and Malice (6:12-19)

(13) He winketh with his eyes . . . —A picture, taken from the life of a malicious tattler and scandalmonger, who fills out his lying tale with winks and signs, whereby

even more is suggested than he says, to the blasting of his neighbor's character.

(15) Suddenly shall he be broken.—This character of a malicious mischief maker would seem to be especially hateful to God; it is described in like terms in Ps. 64 and a similar fate foretold of it; in verse 19 also it is held up as the worst of the seven detestable things mentioned there.

(16) These six things doth the Lord hate . . .—It is a sort of climax—He hates six things, but the seventh more than the others. This numerical form of proverb, to which the name of **middah** is given by later writers, is found also in 30:15, 16, 18, 19, 21-23, 29-31; Job 5:19; Amos 1:3-2:1; Ecclus. 23:16; 25:7; 26:5, 28; and in all these instances the number first named is increased afterward by one.

(17) A proud look.—Hateful to God, because it renders men unfit to receive grace. Until they acknowledge their weakness, they will not seek for His strength, and without it they can make no progress in holiness. (Comp. I Pet. 5:5, and Christ's commendation of the "poor in spirit," Matt. 5:3.)

(18) Feet that be swift in running to mischief.—Who do not yield to temptation after a struggle against it, but give themselves up as willing slaves to their lusts.

(l) Twelfth Discourse:—Against Adultery (6:20-35)

(21) Bind them continually upon thine heart.—See note on 3:3.

(23) For the commandment is a lamp . . . —Comp. Pss. 19:8 and 119:98-100, 104, 105. The servant of God may often feel much perplexity as to his duty, darkness may seem to have settled upon his path. But there is always some "commandment," or positive order, about which he can have no doubt, calling for his immediate obedience; there is always some "law," or rather "instruction" in God's Word offering itself as his guide; there are always some "reproofs of discipline," that is, he knows he has certain things to shun, others to follow, for the purpose of self-discipline.

(30) Men do not despise a thief . . . —A man who is driven to theft by poverty is more worthy of pity than disdain; not so the adulterer. Again, the thief can make retribution, while the adulterer can have none to offer.

(31) But if he be found, he shall restore sevenfold.—The law only required a two- or four- or fivefold compensation (Exod. 22);

he may do even more. "Sevenfold" signifies full restitution (Comp. Gen. 4:24; Lev. 26:28.)

7

(m) **Thirteenth Discourse:—Also Against Adultery** (chap. 7.)

(3) **Bind them upon thy fingers.**—See note on 3:3. The thong of the phylactery or fillet for the left arm was wound seven times round it, and as many times round the middle finger.

(8) **And he went the way ...** —The word is used of the slow step of a religious procession (II Sam. 6:13), here of the sauntering of the idle youth up and down the street within view of the temptress's house.

(9) **In the twilight ...** —He has no excuse of sudden temptation to offer; from twilight until dark night he had trifled with danger, and now at last his "calamity comes" (6:15).

(10) **Subtil of heart.**—Feigning love to her husband and devotion to her lovers, yet caring for none, only to satisfy her own passions.

(11) **Her feet abide not in her house.**—She is not a "keeper at home," as Paul (Titus 2:5) would have Christian matrons be.

(14) **I have peace offerings with me.**—The peace, or thank offering as it is also rendered, was purely voluntary, in token of thanksgiving for some mercy. (See Lev. 3 and 7.) Peace offerings were offered on occasions of national rejoicing, as we see in Exod. 24:5; I Sam. 11:15; II Sam. 6:17; etc. This turning of what should have been a religious festival for the family into an occasion for license, is paralleled by the desecration of the Agapae at Corinth (I Cor. 11:20 sqq.)

(19) **The goodman.**—Literally, "the man"; she does not even call him "my husband."

(23) **That it is for his life.**—i.e., at the cost of it, when "his flesh and body are consumed," and remorse has seized upon him (5:11).

8

(n) **Fourteenth Discourse:—The Praise of Wisdom** (chap. 8)

(1) **Doth not wisdom cry?**—In contrast with the secret allurements of vice under the cover of night, is here represented the open invitation of Wisdom.

(2) **She standeth in the top of high places.**—i.e., in the higher parts of the city, where her voice will best be heard.

By the way ... —She goes everywhere where she may find the greatest concourse of people, "God not being willing that any should perish, but that all should come to repentance" (II Pet. 3:9). So the apostles made large centers of population such as Antioch, Ephesus, or Corinth, the headquarters of their missionary enterprise.

(9) **They are all plain ...** —Because "the secret of the Lord is (only) with them that fear him" (Ps. 25:14), and God reveals such things unto them by His Spirit (I Cor. 2:10), while the "natural man receiveth not the things of the Spirit of God, for they are foolishness unto him" (ibid., verse 14).

(13) **The fear of the Lord is to hate evil.**—Because there can never be any truce between the kingdoms of light and darkness (Matt. 6:24), so if we are the friend of one, we must be the enemy of the other.

(16) **All the judges of the earth.**—By the aid of heavenly wisdom only can they give right and just judgments, and so fulfill the high office delegated to them by God Himself, from the possession of which they are themselves termed "gods" (Exod. 22:28; Ps. 82:1). For the same reason kings, as ruling by His authority, have the same title accorded to them (Ps. 45:6).

(18) **Riches and honour are with me.**—Doubtless the "true riches" (Luke 16:11) are here alluded to, the consciousness of possessing God's honor and favor, called in Eph. 3:8 the "unsearchable riches of Christ."

(20) **I lead in the way of righteousness.**—Comp. Ps. 37:23; also a prayer for such guidance (Ps. 119:33, 143:8); and a promise of it (Isa. 30:21).

(21) **That I may cause those that love me to inherit substance.**—The work which each one by my help shall do will be stored up for him in heaven (Matt. 6:20), it will be as "gold tried in the fire" (Rev. 3:18), which will abide the trial of "the day" (I Cor. 3:13).

(22) **The Lord possessed me in the beginning of his way.**—The Hebrew word translated "possessed" in this passage seems originally to have signified to "set up" or "establish," and is applied to the "forming" of the heavens (Gen. 14:19) and the "begetting" of a son (Deut. 32:6). The sense of the passage is that wisdom was "formed" or

469

"begotten" before the Creation (comp. Ps. 104:24). When in Christian times it was observed how well the description of Wisdom in Job and Proverbs harmonized with that of God the Son in the New Testament, such passages as this were universally applied to Him, and the present one was rightly interpreted as describing His eternal generation from the Father. Such was the view, for instance, of Justin Martyr, Irenaeus, and Tertullian.

In the beginning of his way.—It is probable that this verse should be translated, "He brought me forth as the beginning of His way, as the earliest of His works from of old," i.e., before the depths, and mountains, and hills.

(26) The highest part of the dust of the world.—Literally, "the head of the dusts of the fertile earth," i.e., the heaps of the clods and arable land, or better perhaps, "the sum of the atoms of dust." Some refer to Gen. 2:7, and interpret the words of man, as formed out of the dust.

(27) When he set a compass upon the face of the depth—i.e., when He stretched the vault of heaven over it: the same expression is used in Job 22:14. It is also interpreted of the circle of the horizon.

(30) I was daily his delight.—The pronoun "his" does not occur in the Hebrew, which is, literally, "I was delights," i.e., all joy, delight, as Ps. 109: 4: "I am prayer," i.e., give myself wholly to it. The words express the joy with which Wisdom carried out the work of God.

(31) My delights were with the sons of men.—Or rather, "in them." (Comp. Gen. 3:8, where it would seem that the "Lord God" had been in the habit of assuming human form, and admitting man to His presence.) Such appearances as this, and that to Abraham in Gen. 18, and to Joshua in Josh. 5, were supposed by the Fathers to have been anticipations of the Incarnation of God the Son, who is here described under the name of Wisdom.

(32) Now therefore hearken—i.e., now that ye know how great my power is, and what love I have to you, in that I rejoice in you, and call you my sons. (Comp. I John 3:1.)

(34) Watching daily at my gates.—A figure taken from an ardent scholar waiting until the doors of the school are opened, and he can begin his studies. Or it represents a courtier expecting the appearance of his sovereign, or a lover that of his mistress. (Comp. Wisd. 8:2.)

470

(35) Whoso findeth me findeth life.—Comp. I John 5:12; John 8:51; and above, 3:18, where Wisdom is described as a "tree of life."

(36) He that sinneth against me.—Rather, "He that misses me does not find me." So in Greek, sin is a "missing" of the true object of life.

9

(o) **Fifteenth Discourse:—the Invitation of Wisdom and Folly** (chap. 9)

(1) Wisdom hath builded her house—i.e., in preparation for the feast to which she is about to invite her guests. It is not an unusual custom in the Old Testament to describe intimate communion with God, and the refreshment which the soul of man thereby receives, under the figure of a festival. (See Exod. 24:11; Isa. 25:6, 65:13; Zeph. 1:7, 8.) The idea is brought out in the New Testament with great fullness in the parables of the great supper (Luke 14) and the marriage of the king's son (Matt. 22). Christ, the supreme Wisdom, has "builded His house" by taking man's flesh at His Incarnation, and thus rearing for Himself a "temple of the Holy Ghost" (John 2:19); and also by building for Himself a "spiritual house" (I Pet. 2:5), "the house of God, which is the church of the living God" (I Tim. 3:15). In the previous chapter Christ's work as Creator was described; now He is set forth as Regenerator of mankind.

She hath hewn out her seven pillars.—Suggestive of the sevenfold gifts of the Spirit (Isa. 11:2; Rev. 1:4), typified by the seven-branched candlestick of the Tabernacle (Exod. 25:37).

(3) She hath sent forth her maidens.—Wisdom being here described under the figure of a woman is properly represented as attended by her maidens, whom she sends forth to summon the guests. But the King (Matt. 22) dispatches His servants for the same work, viz., His prophets and wise men and scribes (Matt. 23:34), whom from age to age He sends forth as His messengers.

(4) Whoso is simple ... as for him that wanteth understanding.—So God does not call many "wise men after the flesh, not many mighty, not many noble" (I Cor. 1:26); but chooses the "foolish," "weak," and "base," whom man might overlook; not being willing that any should perish (II Pet. 3:9), especially His "little ones" (Matt.

18:14), who are liable to fall through their inexperience and want of judgment.

(6) Forsake the foolish.—Rather, "the simple"; be no longer counted among the weak, who can be "carried about with every wind of doctrine" (Eph. 4:14), but "stand fast in the faith, quit you like men, be strong" (I Cor. 16:13).

(7) He that reproveth a scorner . . . — Wisdom does not address the scoffer, nor the godless: this would be "giving that which is holy unto the dogs, and casting pearls before swine" (Matt. 7:6). Compare our Lord's own plan of teaching by parables, that His hearers might not understand (Luke 8:10).

(10) The fear of the Lord . . . —Comp. Isa. 11:2, where the "spirit of knowledge" and of the "fear of the Lord" is counted as the gift of God. (For the general sense of the passage, see note on 1:7.)

(13) A foolish woman.—Rather, "the Foolish woman"; Folly personified, in opposition to Wisdom described above.

(14) She sitteth at the door of her house.— She does not care, like Wisdom, to send forth her maidens "to seek and to save that which was lost" (Luke 19:10); she contents herself with sitting at ease, just outside her own door, and calling to the passers-by.

(16) Whoso is simple . . . —She imitates Wisdom closely in her address: Satan, too, transforms himself into an "angel of light" (II Cor. 11:14). Folly attracts those undecided characters who are in the right track, but have not the constancy to persevere in it; who, "in time of temptation, fall away."

(17) Stolen waters are sweet.—See note on 5:15.

Bread eaten in secret.—The same figure is used in 30:20.

(18) The dead are there.—Comp. 2:18.

10

3.—A Collection of 375 Separate Verses on Various Subjects, Marked by a New Heading (10:1-22:16)

(1) The proverbs of Solomon.—The new title and different style of composition mark a new collection of proverbs. Each verse is distinct and complete in itself; but the collector appears to have endeavored to throw together such as touched on the same subject. For instance, 10:4, 5, show why one man fails and another succeeds; verses 6 and 7, how blessings and curses follow different persons. But the connection is sometimes so slight as to be difficult to catch.

(2) Treasures of wickedness—i.e., gained by wrongdoing.

Righteousness delivereth from death.— The Hebrew word translated "righteousness" has a much wider meaning than its English equivalent, which generally bears the sense only of deciding fairly, being especially applied to judges. But a "righteous" man in Hebrew is one who "renders to all their due," whether to God or to man. In this passage it forms a contrast to riches gained by wrong, and therefore would seem particularly to signify "alms-giving," as its Greek equivalent does in II Cor. 9:10. It "delivers from death," as being a sign of the divine life within, which is "hid with Christ in God" (Col. 3:3).

(6) Violence covereth the mouth of the wicked.—Curses and deeds of violence have proceeded from his mouth, but God frustrates them, they "return unto him void" (Isa. 55:11), and, as it were, stop his mouth, reducing him to silence. Comp. verse 11, where it conceals under deceitful words the mischief intended for others.

(8) A prating fool.—See note on 1:7.

(9) Walketh surely.—He has no cause to fear lest anything to his discredit should come out, but can trust quietly in the Lord (Ps. 112:7); while he that goeth by crooked paths will be found out (Matt. 10:26), and the fear of this gives him perpetual uneasiness. Or the meaning may be that he will be "instructed," i.e., punished by misfortune, as Jer. 31:19.

(12) Hatred stirreth up strifes . . . — Hatred rakes up again old feuds which have slumbered, but love covers up and refuses to look at any wrong done to it. A similar expression occurs in I Peter 4:8 and James 5:20, though probably in a somewhat different sense.

(14) The mouth of the foolish is near destruction—i.e., is a near, ever-threatening calamity; one never knows what awkward or dangerous thing he will say next: whereas wise men store up knowledge, and bring it forth as it is wanted (Matt. 13:52).

(15) The rich man's wealth is his strong city—i.e., an actual protection to him against his enemies, for by it he can get aid; or (as 18:11) it gives him the consciousness of power, courage: whereas poverty drags a man down, and prevents his advance in life, or makes him timid, and unable to defend himself.

(16) The labour of the righteous tendeth

to life.—For the gains of his honest toil have the blessing of God upon them, and so bring him satisfaction of mind and the power of performing his duties in life; whereas all that the wicked man acquires only helps him to sin yet more, by enabling him to indulge his evil passions.

(19) In the multitude of words there wanteth not sin, for they are sure to fail in truthfulness, or charity, or opportuneness, and will come under the condemnation of Matt. 12:36, as being the outcome of a careless heart.

(21) The lips of the righteous feed many— i.e., sustain them by words of counsel, encouragement, and comfort, giving to each one his "meat in due season" (Matt. 24:45).

For want of wisdom.—Or it may be translated, "Through one who is destitute of wisdom." As one righteous man will guide many aright, so one unwise man will lead many fools to ruin.

(24) The fear of the wicked—i.e., that of which he is afraid. (Comp. Isa. 66:4; Heb. 10:27.)

The desire of the righteous shall be granted.—For they submit their will to the will of God, and pray for what He sees best for them, which accordingly He grants; moreover, the Holy Spirit also aids them, making intercession for them "according to the will of God" (Rom. 8:27).

(27) The fear of the Lord prolongeth days.—The special Old Testament blessing for obedience (comp. 9:11), often fulfilled now, too, in the case of those who live on to old age, in the quiet fulfillment of duty; while others are shortening their lives by excessive anxieties, or the pursuit of pleasure.

(29) The way of the Lord—i.e., in which He has directed men to walk. (Comp. Ps. 25:12; Matt. 22:16; Acts 9:2.) It is a strong protection to the righteous, for no harm can happen to them while they follow it (I Peter 3:13); "but it is destruction" (not, there is destruction) "to the workers of iniquity," because the fact of their having rejected the teaching of God will be their condemnation. (Comp. II Cor. 2:15, 16.)

(31) Bringeth forth wisdom.—As the fields their "increase" (Deut. 32:13); therefore words are termed the "fruit of the lips" (Isa. 57:19).

Shall be cut out.—Comp. Christ's warning (Matt. 12:36). Sins of the tongue will be severely judged, because, besides doing mischief to others, they are signs of an evil mind within (ibid. verse 34).

472

11

(1) A false balance is abomination to the Lord.—A similar proverb is found in 20:23, and praise of just weights, 16:11; 20:10. The repetition suggests that this form of cheating had become common in the time of Solomon, when the commerce of Israel began to develop. If so, there would be good reason for these frequent warnings, for it would have been useless to raise the superstructure of a religious life, as is the intention of this book, without first laying the foundation of common honesty between man and man.

A just weight.—Literally, "stone," stones having been used for weights from early times. (Comp. Lev. 19:36.) A standard weight, "the king's stone," seems to have been kept by David (II Sam. 14:26).

(5) Shall direct his way.—Or, "make smooth," as 3:6. The just man by his exact performance of all duty both toward God and man receives more and more light, and therefore continually sees more clearly how to avoid the difficulties that beset his path. The wicked darkens his conscience more and more by the commission of evil, until he stumbles as in the night (John 11:9), and at last falls, and does not rise again.

(6) In their own naughtiness.—Rather, "passionate desire," as at 10:3. Their own strong passions are their ruin.

His expectation.—What he hoped for, worldly prosperity. (Comp. Wisd. 5:14.)

(9) An hypocrite.—Rather, "the impure, profane."

Through knowledge.—The just, by the knowledge given them by God, shall see through the fraud.

(14) In the multitude of counsellors there is safety—i.e. where there are plenty to guide the state.

(15) He that is surety for a stranger.— Rather, "for another," as 6:1.

Is sure.—Rather, "is in quiet," undisturbed by the anxieties described in 6:3-5.

(21) Though hand join in hand.—For this sense comp. Isa. 28:15, sqq. The passage may also mean "hand to hand," i.e., from one generation to another; or, what is most probable, "the hand to it," i.e., assuredly. For the general sense of the verse, comp. Ps. 37.

(22) As a jewel of gold in a swine's snout.—Rather, "a nose ring" run through the right nostril and hanging down over the mouth; a female ornament used from earliest times (Gen. 24:47; Isa. 3:21; Ezek. 16:12), and still worn in the East.

(23) The desire of the righteous is only good, and therefore it, being in accordance with the will of God, is granted to them.

The expectation of the wicked is wrath.— Rather, "presumption"; they do not ask in the way or for the things which God wills they should (Jas. 4:3), and therefore it is mere presumption on their part to expect the fulfillment of their desires.

(24) There is that scattereth—i.e., with bounteous hand (comp. Ps. 112:9), "and yet increaseth" in wealth and blessings (comp. 19:17, and the old epitaph, "What we spent, we had; what we saved, we lost; what we gave, we have.")

(28) He that trusteth in his riches shall fall.—Because of their uncertainty, and because they prevent his trusting in the living God (I Tim. 6:17).

(29) He that troubleth his own house.— Possibly by his niggardliness and avarice, as 15:27.

Shall inherit the wind.—Will get nothing for his pains.

(30) The fruit of the righteous is a tree of life.—The righteous, by the performance of his duty to his neighbors, brings, as it were, life and healing (Rev. 22:2) to them, and "the wise man winneth souls," attracts them to himself, and induces them to follow his example.

(31) Behold the righteous shall be recompensed in the earth.—That is, even he shall be punished for his misdeeds, as were Jacob, Moses, David, how much more shall "the wicked and the sinner." The LXX translates freely, "If the righteous scarcely be saved, where shall the ungodly and the sinner appear?" a rendering adopted in I Peter 4:18.

12

(1) Whoso loveth instruction loveth knowledge.—Rather, "he that loveth knowledge loveth discipline," i.e., to put himself in the place of a learner; while "he that hateth reproof," who will not take advice, is "brutish," "nourishing a blind life within the brain," like the animals who are incapable of improvement.

(8) According to his wisdom—i.e., intelligent observance of the ends to be pursued in life, and the best means of attaining to them; in other words, finding out the will of God and how to fulfill it.

(9) He that is despised.—That is, lowly in his eyes and those of others, as David (I Sam. 18:23); if "he hath a servant," that is,

if he be in easy circumstances. It has been remarked that "the first necessity of an Oriental in only moderate circumstances is a slave."

He that honoureth himself.—Boasts of his pedigree, it may be, and is all the while starving.

(12) The wicked desireth the net of evil men—i.e., to enrich himself by prey as they do; but the "root of the righteous yieldeth fruit," by their own exertion they gain all they require without injuring others.

(13) The wicked is snared by the transgression of his lips.—For his words, the product of his evil heart, while designed to injure others, often bring the offender himself into trouble (Ps. 7:16), and moreover, as being the true index of the inner life of the soul, are being stored up as a witness against him at the "day of judgment" (Matt. 12:37). The "just man," on the contrary, avoids all this "trouble."

(14) A man shall be satisfied with good by the fruit of his mouth . . . —Even in this life the wise counsel and kindly deeds by which others are aided, the "bread cast upon the waters" (Eccl. 11:1), return to the giver in the shape of love and respect, and, it may be, of similar aid; while the full recompense, "good measure, pressed down, shaken together, and running over," will come later, at the great day of retribution.

(16) A fool's wrath is presently known.— He cannot contain himself if he thinks himself slighted or injured; the "prudent man," on the other hand, "covereth shame," not noticing an insult at the time, but waiting for a convenient opportunity of telling the offender of his fault and bringing him to a better mind (Matt. 18:15).

(18) There is that speaketh.—Rather, "that babbleth," like the piercing of a sword, that chatters on, not noticing or caring how he may wound the feelings of others by his inconsiderate remarks.

The tongue of the wise is health.—Or, "healing"; soothing the wounds made by the other's indiscriminate chatter.

(19) A lying tongue is but for a moment.— Being detected and silenced by the providence of God. (Comp. Ps. 64:7, 8.)

(21) There shall no evil happen to the just.—Comp. our Lord's promise as to temporal matters for those who "seek the kingdom of God" (Matt. 6:33) and for God's care in spiritual matters (I Cor. 10:13).

(23) A prudent man concealeth knowledge.—Until the right opportunity for bringing it forth presents itself; while "the heart of fools proclaimeth foolishness," cannot help blurting out and displaying its ignorance and folly, which it mistakes for wisdom.

(25) Heaviness in the heart of man maketh it stoop.—But, as this is not favorable to the spiritual life, we have warnings against excessive anxiety (Matt. 6:34), and exhortations to cast all our care upon God (I Pet. 5:7; Ps. 37:5) as a religious duty, that trusting in Him, and so having from Him the "peace which the world cannot give," our hearts may be "set to obey" His commandments.

(26) The righteous is more excellent than his neighbour.—Though, perhaps, inferior to him in worldly advantages. Or, it may signify, the just man is a guide to his neighbor, showing him "the way wherein he should walk"; the wicked, on the other hand, so far from guiding others, himself wanders helplessly.

13

(7) There is that maketh himself rich, yet hath nothing.—Comp. Luke 12:21, and the advice given in Rev. 3:17.

There is that maketh himself poor.—Comp. Luke 12:33.

(9) The light of the righteous rejoiceth—i.e., burns joyously, as the sun "rejoiceth as a giant to run his course" (Ps. 19:5). A distinction may be drawn between the "light" of the righteous and "lamp" of the wicked. The one walks in the "light" of God's truth, and so his path becomes continually more plain (see note on 6:23); the other walks by the glimmer of his own "lamp," the "fire" and "sparks" of his own kindling (Isa. 50:11), the fancies of his own devising, and so his end is darkness. But this distinction is not always observed. (Comp. Job 18:5, 6, where "light" and "lamp" are both applied to the wicked.)

(10) Only by pride cometh contention.—Rather, "by pride cometh nothing but contention." A man who is too proud to receive counsel is sure to fall out with others; they are wise who allow themselves to be advised.

(11) Wealth gotten by vanity.—As we should say, "in an unsatisfactory manner," that is to say, by dishonesty.

(21) Evil pursueth sinners.—The "snares, fire, and brimstone," of Ps. 11:6; while the "good measure, pressed down, shaken together, and running over" (Luke 6:38), awaits the righteous.

(23) Tillage.—Properly, "the newly-made field," on which much labor has been expended. The poor hard-working man, by God's blessing, gains an abundant living, while many (rich persons) are ruined for their neglect of what is right.

(24) Betimes.—While he may yet be influenced rightly, and before faults are rooted in him.

14

(1) Every wise woman buildeth her house.—This should be rendered, "Wisdom buildeth . . . , but folly plucketh it down. . . ."

(3) "In the mouth of the foolish (self-willed) **is a rod of pride."**—He has to smart for his ill-judged sayings; or, he punishes others with them. But this does not agree well with what follows.

But the lips of the wise shall preserve them (the wise) from the difficulties into which the foolish come by their rash talk.

(4) Where no oxen are, the crib is clean . . . —A proverb which may be taken in various ways. Some have seen in it an exhortation to kindness toward animals in consideration of their great usefulness. Others, that labor has its disagreeable aspect, but also brings its reward, whether material prosperity ("much increase") or a more enduring reward. (Comp. Gal. 6:9.)

(6) A scorner seeketh wisdom, and findeth it not.—Because "God resisteth the proud" (I Peter 5:5), and none can give wisdom but He who alone has it (I Cor. 2:11); but He teaches him that "feareth the Lord" (Ps. 25:12).

(7) Go from the presence of a foolish man—i.e., a dull, stupid one, when the time comes that you see you can do him no good; for "evil communications corrupt good manners."

(9) Fools make a mock at sin.—Rather, perhaps, "sin mocks fools" (they miss the gratification they expected from it); or, "the sin offering mocks them." God does not accept it, and so they have the trouble and cost of offering it for nothing; "but among the upright there is favor." God is well-pleased with them.

(11) The house of the wicked shall be overthrown.—Observe the contrast between the "house" and "tabernacle" (tent); the slighter one shall stand, while the more strongly built one shall perish. (Comp. 3:33.)

(12) There is a way which seemeth right unto a man, and yet he will be punished if he follows it, for his perverted conscience may arise from his desertion of God, and his refusal of the light He offered. (Comp. Rom. 1:28, sqq.)

(14) The backslider in heart—i.e., who turns away from God. (Ps. 44:19.)

Shall be filled with his own ways.—Comp. 1:31; Matt. 6:2; etc.: "They have their reward."

(18) The simple inherit folly.—As weeds spring up in unoccupied soil, so "simple" (1:22) persons, whose minds are unoccupied with good, often become self-willed; while the knowledge which the "prudent" gain by looking well to their steps (verse 15) adorns them as a crown.

(19) The evil bow before the good.—(Comp. 1 Sam. 2:36.) That this final retribution is certain is implied by the tense employed, though it may be long delayed until the "awakening" (Ps. 73:20) of God and man to judgment. (Comp. Wisd. 5:1, sqq.)

(24) The crown of the wise is their riches.—They adorn and set off the wisdom of the wise, and bring it more prominently into notice; but the "foolishness of fools" remains folly. The rich fool only displays his folly all the more from being set in a conspicuous position.

(26) His children.—Either, the children of the man who fears the Lord, as the blessing of Abraham (Gen. 17:7, 8) and David (Jer. 33:20, 21) descended to their children; or the pronoun may refer to God's children, i.e., those who look up to Him as a father, an expression which occurs in the Old Testament (e.g., Ps. 73:15), but is brought forward more prominently in the New Testament.

(28) In the multitude of people is the king's honour.—Not in ambitious wars. In these words speaks the "man of rest" (I Chron. 22:9). (Comp. the description of Solomon's kingdom in the days of his prosperity; I Kings 4:20.)

(30) A sound heart—i.e., one in healthy condition, of which the passions and emotions are under control.

(31) Reproacheth his Maker.—For having placed him in such a lowly condition. The equality of all men, as being all of them the work of God, is taught by Gen. 1:27; Job 31:15; Prov. 22:2. The duty of aiding the poor is in Matt. 25:40 based on the still higher ground of the union of Christ with His people, which makes Him regard good done to them as done to Himself.

15

(3) Beholding the evil and the good.—Waiting until the iniquity of the one is full (Gen. 15:16), watching to aid the other (Ps. 34:15, 17).

(4) A wholesome tongue.—One which heals and soothes by its gentleness and judicious words. (Comp. 12:18.)

A breach in the spirit—i.e., deeply wounds another's spirit.

(6) In the house of the righteous is much treasure.—For God's blessing (3:33) is upon it; while the wicked, from his recklessness in the pursuit of gain, brings trouble (verse 27) upon himself and his family.

(8) The sacrifice of the wicked is an abomination to the Lord.—And their prayers also (Isa. 1:11). The worthlessness of sacrifice without obedience (comp. 1 Sam. 15:22) may be here especially mentioned, because men are apt to think that what involves cost and trouble must be pleasing to God, even when not accompanied with what alone He cares for—a loving heart.

The prayer of the upright is his delight.—Even when offered by itself, without sacrifice.

(11) Hell and destruction.—"Hell" is here the general name for the unseen world (**Hades**) beyond the grave, so called, according to one derivation, from its always "asking" for more victims, and never being satisfied. (Comp. 27:20.) "Destruction" (**Abaddon**) is the lowest hell, corresponding to the "deep" of Luke 8:31 and Rev. 9:1, 11; the abode of evil spirits and the lost. (For the thought, comp. Job 26:6 and Ps. 139:8.)

(15) All the days of the afflicted are evil.—Another caution against over-anxiety. The "afflicted" here evidently means not one who has to bear great misfortunes, but one who makes the worst of everything, to whom the "clouds return after the rain" (Eccl. 12:2); while one who is "of a merry heart" does just the contrary.

(23) A man hath joy by the answer of his mouth.—So much mischief is done by the tongue, and its slips are so many, that when a man makes a suitable reply, he may well rejoice and look upon it as the gift of God (16:1).

(25) The proud—who trust in their own strength; while He will "establish the border," or landmark, of the helpless widow, who has none to cry to but Him. The frequently threatened punishment against one who removes his neighbor's landmark, shows the offense to have been a common form of oppression. (Comp. Deut. 19:14; 27:17; Prov. 22:28; Job 24:2; Hos. 5:10.)

(27) He that is greedy of gain.—Ill-gotten gain, especially bribes, as is seen in the next line.

(28) The heart of the righteous studieth to answer—i.e., aright, knowing how much good and evil is caused by words. (Comp. Jas. 3:5, sqq.)

16

(2) All the ways of a man are clean in his own eyes.—Yet that does not excuse his faults in God's sight. (Comp. I Cor. 4:4.) So much the more reason is there for anxious self-examination and testing the conduct by God's Word, and, when this has been done to the best of our power, still to pray for cleansing from faults which have escaped our notice. (Ps. 19:12.)

(3) Commit thy works unto the Lord.—Literally, "roll them upon Him," as a burden too heavy to be borne by thyself. "Thy works" signify all that you have to do. (Comp. Ps. 37:5.) God provides such works for us. (Comp. Eph. 2:10.)

And thy thoughts shall be established.—Thy plans shall prosper, for they will be undertaken according to the will of God, and carried out by His aid. (Comp. I Cor. 3:9; II Cor. 6:1.)

(4) The Lord hath made all things for himself—i.e., to serve His own purposes, that His wisdom, goodness, etc., may be thereby revealed. Or the passage may be translated, "hath made all for its own end or purpose." The assertion that "He has made the wicked for the day of evil," does not mean that He created any one for punishment—i.e., predestined him for destruction. It only teaches that even the wicked are subservient to God's eternal purposes. But God by His longsuffering shows that He is "not willing" that any should "perish," but rather "should come to repentance" (II Pet. 3:9). This appears to be also the teaching of Paul regarding Pharaoh in Rom. 9:17, sqq.

(5) Though hand join in hand.—See note on 11:21.

(10) His mouth transgresseth not in judgment.—Or, "should not transgress," as being the representative of God upon earth, and so distinguished by the title of "God" himself (Ps. 82:6). This verse recalls the days of Solomon's youth, when it was his highest

aspiration to judge his people righteously (I Kings 3:9). Comp. David's noble words (II Sam. 23:3).

(11) A just weight and balance are the Lord's.—See note on 11:1.

(12) It is an abomination to kings ...—This and the following verse are, like verse 10, descriptive of the ideal king who, above all things, loves truth and justice. Ps. 72 works out the thought more fully. How feebly the character was fulfilled by Solomon or the best of his successors the history of Israel shows. It was too high a conception for man to carry out, and was fulfilled only in the person of David's Son, who is "King of kings, and Lord of lords" (Rev. 19:16).

(15) A cloud of the latter rain.—This fell at the end of March, maturing the barley and wheat crops before the harvest in April. It was eagerly looked for as of great importance. (Comp. Ps. 72:6 for the same figure.)

(21) The sweetness of the lips increaseth learning.—Power to express the thoughts in graceful language adds greatly to the value of learning.

(22) The instruction of fools is folly.—It may mean, "the discipline which fools have to endure is folly." If they will not be taught by wisdom, their own folly will serve as a rod to correct them.

(23) Addeth learning to his lips.—His wisdom and learning do not remain hidden in his heart, but continually rise to his lips, like the waters of an ever-flowing fountain, for the instruction of others.

(27) Diggeth up evil.—Digs, as it were, a pit for others by his malicious plottings and slanders (Ps. 7:15).

In his lips there is as a burning fire.—"Set on fire of hell" (James 3:6).

(32) He that is slow to anger ...—For victory over self is the hardest of all victories. (Comp. I Cor. 9:27.)

(33) The lot is cast into the lap ...—In other words, much that we attribute to chance is due to the providence of God. (Comp. Matt. 10:29, 30.) This should be an encouragement to trust in Him.

17

(2) A wise servant shall have rule over a son that causeth shame ...—This was strikingly exhibited in the case of Ziba (II Sam. 16). Slaves, especially those "born in the house," often rose to a position of great trust. (Comp. Gen. 24:2; 39:4-6.) Eliezer would have been Abraham's heir had not Isaac been born (Gen. 15:3).

(3) The fining pot is for silver. See note on 2:4.

The Lord trieth the hearts.—By allowing sorrows and temptations to assail them, in order that they may come out of the trial as pure gold (Mal. 3:3; I Cor. 3:13; I Pet. 1:7; Rev. 3:18), purged of earthly infirmities.

(5) Whoso mocketh the poor reproacheth his Maker.—See above on 14:31.

He that is glad at calamities.—Of enemies. (Comp. 24:18; Job 31:29.)

(7) Much less do lying lips a prince.—Or, "liberal person" (Isa. 32:8): **noblesse oblige.**

(8) A gift is as a precious stone ... —A description of the influence of bribery. The constant warnings against this form of corruption, from the time of Moses (Exod. 23:8) to that of the prophets (Amos 5:12; Isa. 1:23; etc.), show the prevalence of the evil in Israel.

(9) He that covereth a transgression seeketh love—i.e., one who does not notice, but rather conceals and excuses, anything done against him; that man "follows after charity" (I Cor. 14:1). (Comp. 10:12.)

He that repeateth a matter, who is always returning to old grievances, "alienates (even his) chief friend."

(14) The beginning of strife is as when one letteth out water.—The drops which ooze through a tiny hole in the bank of a reservoir soon swell into an unmanageable torrent; so from insignificant beginnings arise feuds which cannot be appeased. Solomon constructed large pools (Eccl. 2:6) beyond Bethlehem, and is supposed to have brought water from these by an aqueduct into Jerusalem.

Before it be meddled with.—The same expression is used in 18:1 and 20:3. It probably means "before (men) show their teeth," a metaphor from an angry dog.

(15) He that justifieth the wicked—i.e., acquits. The perversion of justice was a fruitful source of evil in Israel, and a constant topic of reproach in the mouth of the prophets (I Sam. 8:3; Ps. 82:2; Isa. 5:7).

(16) Wherefore is there a price ... —He will still remain a fool, though he has paid high for instruction, if he has no capacity for taking it in.

(18) In the presence of his friend.—Or, "With his neighbor." (For the same warning, comp. 6:1, sqq.)

(19) He that exalteth his gate.—Builds himself a sumptuous house.

(22) A merry heart doeth good like a medicine.—Or rather, "Makes good a recovery." (For the duty of religious gladness, in gratitude for the love of God toward us, comp. Phil. 3:1; 4:4.)

(23) A wicked man taketh a gift out of the bosom.—Or rather, "receives it." "From the bosom" signifies the folds of the dress in which the bribe was concealed, ready to be slipped into the judge's hand whose favor was to be bought.

(24) Wisdom is before him that hath understanding—i.e., he can easily find her.

But the eyes of a fool are in the ends of the earth.—He is looking for her everywhere, while all the time she lies in front of him. (For the thought, comp. Deut. 30:11-14.)

18

(1) Through desire a man, having separated himself ... —This should probably be rendered, "The separatist seeketh after his own desire, against all improvement he shows his teeth." The man of small mind is described here, who will only follow his own narrow aims, who holds himself aloof from men of wider views than his own, and will not join with them in the furtherance of philanthropic or religious plans, but rather opposes them with all his power, as he can see nothing but mischief in them. (For his temper of mind, comp. John 7:47-49.)

Intermeddleth.—See note on 17:14.

(6) His mouth calleth for strokes, which he provokes by his insolence and quarrelsomeness.

(7) A fool's mouth is his destruction.—See note on 12:13.

(8) The words of a talebearer are as wounds.—Or, more probably, "as dainty morsels" that are eagerly swallowed, and "go down into the innermost parts of the belly," i.e., are treasured up in the deepest recesses of the heart, to be remembered and brought out again when an opportunity for employing them occurs.

(10) The name of the Lord is a strong tower.—The "name of the Lord" signifies the titles by which He has made Himself known, descriptive of His attributes, as "merciful, gracious, longsuffering, abundant in goodness and truth," (Exod. 34:5, 7); the righteous takes refuge in these, and finds himself in safety, lifted above the trouble which seemed ready to overwhelm him. The rich man's "strong city" and "high wall" are such only in "his own conceit," and fail him in the time of need. (Comp. 23:5.)

(16) A man's gift.—Judicious liberality "maketh room for him," helps him to make his way through life. (Comp. Luke 16:9, and the advice there given so to use temporal riches as to gain those of heaven.)

(19) Their contentions.—Of such as have once been friends, "are like the bars of a castle," or palace, forming an almost impassable barrier to reconciliation. The bitterness of quarrels between friends is proverbial.

(22) Whoso findeth a wife ...—One who deserves the name of wife, as the one described in 31:10, sqq.

(23) The rich answereth roughly.—A warning against the hardening effect of riches. (Comp. Mark 10:23.)

(24) A man that hath friends must shew himself friendly.—Rather, "a man of many friends will suffer loss," for he will impoverish himself by constant hospitality, and in trouble they will desert him (Ps. 41:9); but "there is a friend," one in a thousand, "that sticketh closer than a brother." (Comp. 17:17.)

19

(1) Perverse in his lips.—One who distorts the truth; translated "froward" in 4:24. That a rich man is here intended appears likely from the parallel passage in 28:6.

(2) Also, that the soul be without knowledge, it is not good.—Ignorance is bad, as well as folly.

He that hasteth with his feet sinneth.—Haste without knowledge misses the mark aimed at. (See note on 8:36.)

(4) The poor is separated from his neighbour.—Or, "but the feeble, his friend separates himself (from him)." It was just in order to counteract these selfish instincts of mankind that the merciful provisions of such passages as Deut. 15:7, sqq., and Luke 14:13 were laid upon God's people.

(8) He that getteth wisdom.—Literally, "heart." For that "wisdom," or "knowledge," that begins with the "fear of the Lord" (see note on 1:7), and ends with loving Him, is not a matter of intellect only, but of the heart also—i.e., the will and affections.

(10) Delight is not seemly for a fool.—He is ruined by prosperity and luxury: much more is a slave unfit to rule over princes. The writer has in mind the case of an

emancipated slave being raised to high place by court favor, and then insolently trampling on those who were once far above him. (Comp. 30:22; Eccl. 10:6, 7.)

(11) It is his glory to pass over a transgression.—In this he imitates a Greater. Comp. Mic. 7:18; Rom. 3:25; Matt. 5:45.)

(13) A continual dropping.—As of the rain leaking through the flat roof of an eastern house on a wet day. (Comp. 27:15.)

(17) Lendeth unto the Lord.—Who "for our sakes became poor, that we through his poverty might be rich" (II Cor. 8:9), and who regards all done to one of His poor brethren as done unto Himself (Matt. 25:40).

(18) And let not thy soul spare for his crying.—Or, "but set not thy soul on his destruction." Do not go so far as to kill him in thy zeal for his good, or despair of his amendment. (Comp. Eph. 6:4; Col. 3:21.) It may also signify "do not let him perish for want of chastisement," as 23:13 is also explained.

(23) The fear of the Lord tendeth to life.—To life in this world, the reward of uprightness promised to the Israelites of old (Isa. 37:29); and to life in the next (Mark 10:30).

He shall not be visited with evil.—(Comp. Lev. 26:6.) A higher blessing is promised in the New Testament; not immunity from trouble, for trouble may be needed for advance in holiness (Rom. 8:28), but protection in it (I Pet. 3:13; Rom. 8:35, sqq.).

(24) A slothful man hideth his hand in his bosom.—Better, in the "dish" that stood in the middle of the table at an Oriental dinner, into which the guests dipped their hands to take out the food for themselves (Matt. 26:23).

(25) Smite a scorner, and the simple will beware.—So God at first punishes sinners for their good (Amos 4:6ff.), afterwards, when they are obdurate, as a warning to others (ibid. 12; Deut. 29:21ff.).

20

(1) Wine is a mocker, strong drink is raging—i.e., producing these effects in those who subject themselves to their power.

(3) Will be meddling.—Or, rather, "showing his teeth": (Comp. 17:14) thinking that his own personal dignity is at stake.

(9) Who can say, I have made my heart clean?—Though we may have done our best by self-examination and confession, and repentance and trust in the atoning blood of Christ to obtain remission of sin, still the heart is so deceitful (Jer. 17:9), sins may so easily have escaped our notice (Ps. 19:12; I Cor. 4:4), that satisfaction with ourselves ought never to be allowed (Rom. 11:20).

(10) Divers weights and divers measures . . .—See note on 11:1.

(11) Even a child is known by his doings . . .—The disposition soon shows itself; all the more reason, therefore, to train it early (comp. 13:24).

(14) It is naught, saith the buyer.—He cries down the goods he wants to purchase.

Then he boasteth.—How he has outdone the seller, and got the goods below their value. For other notices of cheating in trade, see note on 11:1.

(16) Take his garment that is surety for a stranger.—Another warning against suretyship. (See note on 6:1.) If a man is rash enough to become surety for another, he must suffer for his imprudence, and learn wisdom by feeling the effects of his folly.

(22) Wait on the Lord, and he shall save thee.—Do not look for vengeance on enemies (for they are to be forgiven), but for deliverance from their attacks; forget their malice, remember only God's love for you, and trust in Him. (Comp. I Peter 3:13; Rom. 8:28.)

(26) And bringeth the wheel over them.—Comp. Isa. 28:27. A sort of sledge or cart was driven over the stalks of corn spread upon the threshing floor, by means of which the grain was separated from the husk. A wise king winnows out evil persons from among his people, thus putting an end to their corrupting influence. (Comp. Matt. 3:12.)

(27) The spirit of man is the candle of the Lord.—The spirit of man, breathed into him at first by the Creator (Gen. 2:7), and afterward quickened and illumined by the divine Spirit, is the "candle of the Lord," given to man as an inward light and guide.

Searching all the inward parts of the belly.—That is, of the inmost heart of man; testing all his thoughts, feelings, desires, by God's Law, approving some, condemning others, according as they agree with it or not. The word "belly" is equivalent to "heart" or "soul" in Job 15:2, 35; 32:19. (Comp. John 7: 38.)

(28) Mercy and truth preserve the king.—See note on 3:3. The love and faithfulness he shows to his subjects draw out the same qualities in them, and these are the safe-guard of his throne. So (Ps. 130:4) the mercy shown by God inspires man with a reverent fear of Him, while harshness might have made him a slave, or driven him through despair into rebellion. (Comp. Jer. 33:9.)

(29) The beauty of old men is the grey head.—As suggesting the possession of experience and wisdom. It is the fault of the aged, therefore, if they do not receive the honor due to them, and this arises from their not having so spent their youth and middle age as to make their old age venerable.

(30) The blueness of a wound.—Rather, "the stripes of a wound," or wounds which cut into the flesh, cleanse away evil.

So do stripes the inward parts of the belly.—Better, "and blows (which reach) the inward parts of the belly," i.e., which are felt in the inmost recesses of the heart (comp. verse 27). Kindness is thrown away upon some people: they can only be touched by punishment.

21

(1) As the rivers of water.—Channels for irrigation (comp. Ps. 1:3). He turns the heart of the king, whose favor is as the latter rain (16:15) and dew (19:12), now toward one suppliant and now toward another, as He thinks fit, for "the hearts of kings are in His rule and governance."

(4) The plowing of the wicked—i.e., their work, all they do; for it is not done to please God but themselves; nor carried on in His strength, but in reliance upon their own, and therefore it is "sin," not pleasing to Him. For the word here translated "plowing," see note on 13:23, where it is rendered "tillage." It may also signify "lamp" (see note on 13:9).

(9) It is better to dwell in a corner of the housetop.—Though there exposed to all the storms of heaven. The flat tops of houses were, in the East, used for exercise (II Sam. 11:2), sleeping (I Sam. 9:26), devotion (Acts 10:9), and various domestic purposes (Jos. 2:6).

(16) Shall remain in the congregation of the dead.—Described in Isa. 14:9; he shall not take part in the resurrection of Isa. 26:19. A prophecy of retribution after death.

(17) Wine and oil.—The accompaniments of a feast. The oil, or precious unguents, were poured over the head (comp. Ps. 23:5).

479

These perfumes were sometimes of great value, the "pound of ointment of spikenard" (John 12:3) was worth "more than three hundred pence," the wages of a day laborer (Matt. 20:2) for nearly a year.

(18) The wicked shall be a ransom for the righteous.—The righteous is "delivered out of trouble (11:8; comp. Isa. 57:1), and the wicked cometh in his stead" to receive upon his own head God's descending punishment. So it was with Mordecai and Haman.

(21) Righteousness and mercy.—He who endeavors to give God and man their due (see note on 10:2), and to show love to them (3:3), will gain for himself length of days (3:16), power to live more and more uprightly, and present honor from God and man for doing so. In a higher sense he will gain life eternal now and hereafter (John 17:3), righteousness, or the forgiveness of sins (Rom. 2:13), and honor (Rom. 8:30) at the last day, when he will be acknowledged as a true son of God (Rom. 8:19).

(23) Whoso keepeth his mouth and his tongue.—See note on 12:13.

(26) He coveteth greedily all the day long, that he may "consume it on his lusts" (Jas. 4:3), while the righteous (verse 21) gives to all who need, remembering that he is a steward (Luke 16:9), not an owner, and that blessing will attend upon him for so doing (Acts 20:35).

(27) How much more when he bringeth it with a wicked mind?—Plotting at the same time future wickedness, or thinking to make God, by the sacrifice, overlook his sin, and so become, as it were, his confederate.

(31) The horse is prepared against the day of battle.—These had been imported largely from Egypt in Solomon's time, though this was in direct contravention of the Law (I Kings 4:26 and Deut. 17:16).

22

(2) The rich and poor meet together.—Are thrown together in the world in order to aid each other in the path through life, remembering that they are brethren, sons of one Father. (Comp. I Cor. 12:27.)

(13) The slothful man saith, There is a lion without ... —No excuses are too absurd for him, he fears to meet a lion in the open country, or he might be murdered in the streets.

(14) Strange women.—See note on 2:16.

(15) Foolishness is bound in the heart of a child.—Self-will is meant. (See note on

1:7.) Children have to be taught to yield their wills to others.

4.— An Introduction, Containing an Exhortation to "Hear the Words of the Wise," Serving As a Heading to 22:22-24:22

(17) Hear the words of the wise.—Comp. 1:6. As "wise" is in the plural, it would seem as if the following section contained proverbs written by others than Solomon, although they may have been collected by him. (Comp. 24:23.)

(19) I have made known to thee this day, even to thee these counsels of the wise. The words, "this day," recall the warning of Heb. 3:13, and the emphatic "to thee, even to thee," imply that the message of God, though it may be general in its form, yet is addressed to each individual soul among His people (comp. Isa. 55:1); each being well-known, and an object of love on the part of his Redeemer.

(21) That thou mightest answer the words of truth to them that send unto thee?—This rendering is somewhat doubtful, but seems to give the best sense to the passage. The scholar is to be instructed not for his own profit alone, but in order that he may be able to teach others also. (Comp. I Pet. 3:15.)

5.—First Appendix to the "Proverbs of Solomon" (10:1-22:16), Containing Proverbs of Different Lengths, From the Distich to the Lengthened Didactic Poem (22:22-24:22).

(22) Neither oppress the afflicted in the gate.—The place of business (Gen. 34:20) and of judgment (Deut. 21:19; Amos 5:15).

(26) Be not thou one of them that strike hands.—Another warning against suretyship. (See note on 6:1.)

(27) Why should he take away thy bed from under thee?—If the mantle was taken in pledge, it had to be restored before sundown for the poor man to sleep in; but this merciful provision of the Law was evidently evaded. (Comp. Ezek. 18:12.)

(28) Remove not the ancient landmark.—The stones marking the boundaries of the fields: evidently a not uncommon crime, from the earnestness with which it is forbidden. (Comp. 23:10; Deut. 19:14; 27:17.)

23

(1) Consider diligently what is before

thee.—Rather, "Who is before thee"; that your host is not an equal, but one who, if offended, might do you deadly harm.

(2) And put a knife to thy throat.—Use the strongest methods to keep your appetite in check, if you are likely to give way to it, and then, overcome by meat and drink, to say or do anything to offend your host.

(3) Deceitful meat.—Not offered out of friendship and love to you; for an unguarded word spoken in the insecurity of the festive hour might bring ruin to you.

(6) Him that hath an evil eye.—A sordid, grudging temper.

(8) Shalt thou vomit up.—Shall be disgusted at having partaken of hospitality which was not freely offered to you.

And lose thy sweet words.—All thy civil speeches and thanks for the cold welcome thou hast had.

(10) Remove not the old landmark.—See note on 22:28.

(11) Their redeemer is mighty.—They may have no near kinsman (Lev. 25:25) to redeem their land, yet they have a mighty Deliverer (Exod. 6:6), who will redress their wrongs.

(13) He shall not die—i.e., a moderate correction, such as that advised in 19:18 (see note), will not injure him—quite the reverse.

(14) And shalt deliver his soul from hell—i.e., Hades, the abode of the dead (Isa. 14:9), death being the punishment of sin, and long life the reward of well-doing (3:2).

(16) My reins shall rejoice.—These being represented in Hebrew poetry as the seat of the deepest affections, answering to "heart" in verse 15. (Comp. Ps. 7:9; Jer. 12:2; Rev. 2:23.)

(18) An end, which shall be peace (Ps. 37:37), corresponding to the "manifestation of the sons of God" (Rom. 8:19), when we shall be "like" God (I John 3:2).

(23) Buy the truth, and sell it not.—The "truth" is here described under the three heads of wisdom, self-discipline, and understanding. (See note on 1:2.) All these are to be obtained from God (James 1:5), who gives to every man "liberally," "without money and without price" (Isa. 55:1). (Comp. Rev. 3:18, and the "treasure" and "pearl of great price" of Matt. 13:44-46.)

(26) My son, give me thine heart.—For that is the one gift alone worthy of acceptance which man can offer to God, and the only one which God will accept; an offering which man endeavors to keep for himself, substituting for it alms, unreal prayers, out-

ward observances of religion, and obedience in matters of little moment. (Comp. Matt. 22:37.)

(27) Strange woman.—See note on 2:16.

(30) They that go to seek mixed wine.—Or, "To test"; to see whether it is to their taste. The wines of the ancients were not generally drunk pure, but diluted with water or flavored with spices. (See 9:2.)

(33) Thine eyes shall behold strange women.—i.e., look out for them, impurity being the constant attendant of drunkenness. Or, the word may be translated "strange things," referring to the strange fancies of a drunkard, the horrible and fantastic visions present to his disordered brain.

Perverse things.—His notions of right and wrong being completely distorted.

(34) As he that lieth down in the midst of the sea.—And so would inevitably be drowned if he trusted to its smooth, glassy appearance.

As he that lieth upon the top of a mast.—Whom every roll of the ship might hurl into the waves. The absolute insensibility of the drunkard to danger is described here. Or it may mean that everything around the drunkard and the ground on which he lies, seem to rock like the waves of the sea, or the masthead of a ship.

24

(3) Through wisdom is an house builded.—See note on 14:1.

(7) Wisdom is too high for a fool.—For "wisdom" (literally, "wisdoms"), comp. note on 1:20. He has been too self-willed to learn; so while others express their opinions when the business or justice of his city is being transacted (see note on 22:22) he has to remain sheepishly silent.

(9) The thought of foolishness is sin.—Rather, "Sin is the contrivance (plotting) of self-will." Sin is the "transgression of the law" of God (I John 3:4), when we desert the plain rule of duty, and plot how we can indulge our own self-will.

(12) If thou sayest, Behold, we knew it not.—Man being too much inclined to answer after the manner of Cain (Gen. 4:9), "Am I my brother's keeper?" when he might give aid to those who need it.

(16) For a just man falleth seven times, and riseth up again.—That is, falls into trouble (not, "sin," as is often supposed). Therefore thy malice will be of no avail, for

God's protection is about him. (Comp. Job 5:19; Ps. 34:19, and 37:24.)

Seven times—i.e., frequently. (Comp. Matt. 18:21.)

(18) And he turn away his wrath from him.—Upon thee as having sinned more deeply than thine enemy in thus rejoicing at his misfortunes. (Comp. 17:5.)

(19) Fret not thyself because of evil men.—i.e., at the sight of their prosperity, the same difficulty which occurred to the psalmist (Ps. 37:1). (Comp. also Ps. 73:3 and Jer. 12:1.)

The candle of the wicked shall be put out.—See note on 13:9.

> 6.—Second Appendix to "The Proverbs of Solomon," Containing Proverbs of Various Lengths, resembling 1:7-9, and the Book of Ecclesiastes (24:23-34).

(23) These things also belong to the wise.—i.e., have the wise for their authors. (Comp. 1:6; 22:17.)

(26) Every man shall kiss his lips . . . Rather, "He kisseth the lips that giveth right answers." His words are as pleasant as if he had kissed the inquirer's lips.

(28) Without cause.—i.e., do not mention thy neighbor's faults unless for some good reason, not for malice or love of gossip.

(29) Say not, I will do so to him as he hath done to me.—This is a wonderful anticipation of New Testament teaching, different from the spirit of Lev. 24:19, 20. Comp. 20:22, and James 2:13.

(30) I went by the field of the slothful . . .—The parable of the vineyard let out to husbandmen for them to render the fruits in due season (Matt. 21:33), and of the thorns which choked the word (ibid., 13:7), suggest a spiritual meaning for this passage. It warns us not to allow the weeds of evil habits to spring up in the garden of the soul through sloth, nor to suffer God's protecting care (the wall) to be withdrawn from us because we have not sought it constantly in prayer.

25

> 7.—The Third Great Division of the Book; Another Collection of Solomonic Proverbs, Chiefly parabolic in Character (chaps. 25-29).

(1) These are also proverbs of Solomon,

which the men of Hezekiah . . . copied out.—To this time they had existed, it may be, partly by oral tradition, partly in writing; but now Hezekiah, in his anxiety to preserve these sacred memorials of the past had them copied out and formed into one collection. To his care we probably also owe the compilation of Books II (Ps. 42-72) and III. (73-89) of the Psalter, in the former of which are included several psalms of David's which had not found a place in Book I, though this last-named book consists almost, if not entirely, of psalms ascribed to him. In the same manner the present book (chaps. 25-29) contains proverbs of Solomon which apparently were not known to the compiler of the previous collection.

(2) It is the glory of God to conceal a thing.—For the more we search into the mysteries of nature or revelation, the more do we discover depths of which we had no idea before. God has so ordered things that man may not presume to measure himself with his Maker, but may recognize his own insignificance. (Comp. Rom. 11:33 ff.)

But the honour of kings is to search out a matter.—To see their way through political difficulties, and to unmask crime and fraud.

(7) In the presence of the prince whom thine eyes have seen, and whose place thou hast shamelessly taken. The same lesson was repeated by our Lord in Luke 14:10, sqq., and enforced on the ground of His own example. (Matt. 20:25, sqq.)

(9) Debate thy cause with thy neighbour.—As our Lord says, "If thy brother trespass against thee, go and tell him his fault between thee and him alone" (Matt. 18:15). Or it may mean, "If you must go to law with another, do not drag others into the matter by disclosing their secrets in order to help your cause."

(11) A word fitly spoken.—Or, it may be, "at the proper time." (Comp. 15:23.)

Apples of gold in pictures of silver.—Probably golden-colored apples are meant, or fruit of the same tint, such as pomegranates, citrons, or oranges. "Pictures" of silver probably mean "figures," i.e., baskets or dishes of ornamental work.

(13) As the cold of snow in the time of harvest.—Not a snowstorm, as this would be a calamity (26:1), but snow employed to cool drinks in the summer heat. The use of this was probably familiar to Solomon in his summer palace at Lebanon (I Kings 9:19).

(14) Whoso boasteth himself of a false

gift.—i.e., talks loudly of what he is going to do for another, and then does nothing.

(16) Hast thou found honey?—A common occurrence in Palestine, where swarms of wild bees abounded in the woods. (Comp. Judg. 14:8; I Sam. 14:27.) From this came the expression of a "land flowing with (milk and) honey."

(18) A maul.—i.e., "hammer." A false witness is as injurious as the most deadly weapons.

(20) As vinegar upon nitre, by which the nitre is rendered useless.

(22) Thou shalt heap coals of fire upon his head.—You shall make him burn with shame at the thought of the wrong he has done you. Thus, to bring a sinner to repentance is well-pleasing to the Lord, who shall reward you for it. This is far better than to indulge in resentment, which must bring sorrow to oneself, punishment from God—whose prerogative of vengeance (Rom. 12:19) has been usurped—and only serves to harden the offender in his hostility.

(24) It is better to dwell in the corner of the housetop.—See note on 21:9.

(25) Good news from a far country.—This is suggestive of the little communication which in old times took place between distant countries.

(26) A righteous man falling down before the wicked ... —The mouth of the righteous was described (10:11) as a "well of life," from the comfort and refreshment it brings to the weary through the just and kindly counsel it offers. But if the righteous man yields to the pressure put upon him by the wicked, and through fear or favor gives up his principles, then he can no longer give forth counsel out of a pure heart; he becomes like a fountain which has been fouled by the feet of cattle drinking at it (Ezek. 34:18), and like a corrupted spring.

(28) Like a city that is broken down, and without walls.—Exposed to the assault of every temptation.

26

(1) As rain in harvest.—This was unusual in Palestine (comp. I Sam. 12:17, sqq.), and of course unsuitable for carrying on the work of harvest.

So honour is not seemly for a fool.—i.e., for a dull person, confident in his own wisdom (1:22). It only confirms him in his good opinion of himself, making him less inclined than ever to learn.

(4) According to his folly.—Do not lower yourself by disputing or arguing with him; he will not take in your meaning, and will think he has got the better of you, perhaps will insult you. It is noticeable that our Lord never answered a question which should not have been asked Him, but always passed it up (e.g., Matt. 21:23, sqq.; Luke 13:23, 24; 23:9; John 21:21, 22; Acts 1:6, sqq.).

(5) Answer a fool according to his folly.—As his folly deserves, sharply and decisively, and in language suited to his comprehension.

(6) Cutteth off the feet.—He wants his business done, but if he sends a fool to do it, he might as well cut off his messenger's legs, for the business will not be transacted; nay, worse than this, he will "drink damage," i.e., suffer positive mischief from the blundering of his emisary.

(8) As he that bindeth a stone in a sling ... —i.e., the stone is soon gone from the sling and seen no more, so honor and a fool soon part company.

(11) So a fool returneth to his folly.—Though he knows it to be folly, and ruinous to him: but vice has become to him a second nature, and he cannot, even if he would, escape from it. This is especially true of those who have given way to drink or impurity of life.

(12) Seest thou a man wise in his own conceit.—Comp. the warnings of Rom. 12:16, and Rev. 3:17, 18.

(13) The slothful man saith, There is a lion in the way ... —See note on 22:13.

(15) The slothful hideth his hand in his bosom.—See note on 19:24.

(17) Meddleth with strife.—Rather, "that is excited with strife." If quarreling and taking revenge on our own account are forbidden (Rom. 12:18, 19), how much more is the mixing up of ourselves in the disputes of other persons.

Like one that taketh a dog by the ears.—Who deserves to be bitten for his pains, the usual result of interfering in quarrels.

(18) Firebrands.—Arrows to which some blazing material was attached, in order that they might set on fire whatever they touched.

(22) The words of a tale-bearer are as wounds.—See note on 18:8.

(23) Burning lips.—i.e., burning with love, while there is an evil heart within.

A potsherd covered with silver dross.—Pottery glazed with dross of silver, a well-known method of ornamentation. For similar proverbs, comp. Matt. 23:27; Luke 11:39.

(27) Whoso diggeth a pit shall fall therein.—A simile taken from hunters making pits as traps for wild animals. The same doctrine of retribution being brought upon the sinner's head by God the righteous Judge is taught in Ps. 7:11, sqq.

27

(1) Boast not thyself of to-morrow.—This is forbidden also in James 4:13, sqq; but there on the higher ground that it argues a want of submission to the will of Almighty God. This temper of mind, as well as the opposite one of too great anxiety for the morrow (Matt. 6:34), proceed from the same cause, too much dependence upon self, and are only to be met by learning to realize the love of God for His children (ibid., 26, 30, 33), and looking up to Him daily for protection, guidance, and support.

(4) But who is able to stand before envy?—Rather, "jealousy." (Comp. 6:34.) "Wrath" and "anger" rage for awhile like a storm, and then subside; but jealousy can never be completely set at rest.

(6) Faithful are the wounds of a friend.—i.e., the "open rebuke" of the previous verse, the "smiting" and "reproof" of Ps. 142:5.

(7) The full soul loatheth an honeycomb.—So the moderate use of the good things of this life increases our enjoyment of them. But in spiritual things, the less we content ourselves with, the less hunger we feel, and less enjoyment do we derive from them.

(10) Better is a neighbour that is near.—"Near" and "far off"—i.e., in feeling.

(11) My son.—The address of a father to his son, or master to pupil.

That I may answer him that reproacheth me for having brought you up badly when he sees you ignorant or ill-behaved. So Christians are exhorted to let their "light so shine before men" that their Father in heaven may be glorified by it (Matt. 5:16).

(14) He that blesseth his friend with a loud voice . . . —If gratitude is to be acceptable, the time, place, and manner of showing it must all be well chosen. A man who is so eager to express his thanks that he begins early in the morning, and in so loud a voice as to draw upon his patron the attention of all the bystanders, is looked upon as a nuisance; any one would as soon be cursed as blessed by him. So God loves

heartfelt gratitude offered in secret. (Comp. Matt. 6:5, 6.)

(15) A continual dropping in a very rainy day.—See note on 19:13.

(16) Whosoever hideth her hideth the wind.—i.e., you might as well try and stop the wind from blowing as seek to restrain her.

And the ointment of his right hand which bewrayeth itself.—i.e., if he puts out his hand to stop her she slips through it like oil.

(17) So a man sharpeneth the countenance of his friend.—i.e., the play of wit with wit sharpens and brightens up the face.

(19) So the heart of man (answereth) **to man.**—What is in our own hearts we find in others also. Whatever are the distinguishing features of our own characters we discover and elicit the same in others. The merciful, the generous, the devout, the pure, recognize the same qualities in others, and themselves feel and receive sympathy from such persons. So the evil, too, find themselves in harmony with those of like disposition.

(20) Hell and destruction.—See note on 15:11.

The eyes of man are never satisfied.—Comp. Eccl. 1:8 and 4:8. God would thus teach us that in Him only can man find complete satisfaction. (Comp. Ps. 36:8, 9 and I Cor. 2:9.)

(21) So is a man to his praise.—i.e., as the fining pot and furnace test the metals put into them, so does that on which a man prides or boasts himself. Observe what this is—e.g., wealth, or show, or popularity, or duty—and you will see what sort of man he is.

(22) Though thou shouldest bray (i.e., pound) **a fool** (a self-willed, headstrong person) **in a mortar among wheat with a pestle.**—This would separate completely the husks from the wheat; but obstinacy has become a part of such a man's nature, and cannot be got rid of even by such violent measures.

(23) Be thou diligent to know the state of thy flocks . .—In the last five verses of this chapter the peace and security of the pastoral life are described as being far superior to the uncertainty attending other sources of wealth and the regal power. For the spiritual sense of this passage comp. I Pet. 5:2-4.

28

(2) For the transgression of a land many

are the princes thereof.—Comp. I Kings 15:27, sqq.. and indeed the whole history of the kingdom of Israel as compared with the regular succession of the family of David in accordance with the promise of Ps. 89:33.

(3) A poor man that oppresseth the poor.—If the recollection of his own former troubles has not softened his heart toward his poor neighbors, he will become more callous to their sufferings.

Is like a sweeping rain which leaveth no food.—That sweeps away grain and soil, instead of bringing plenty with it.

(4) They that forsake the law praise the wicked.—The mark of extreme wickedness. (Comp. Rom. 1:32.)

But such as keep the law contend with them.—Just as the sight of ill-doing was the one thing which roused our Lord to wrath, while insults and wrong cast on Him were passed by unnoticed.

(8) He that by usury ... increaseth his substance.—See note on 6:1.

He shall gather it for him that will pity the poor.—The "pound" is taken from him who knows not how to use it (Luke 19:24), and given to one who does. (Comp. I Sam. 15:28.)

(13) Whoso confesseth and forsaketh them shall have mercy, and be at once completely forgiven; though he must still suffer the punishment due for his offenses (II Sam. 12:14, sqq.), and will, for having yielded to temptation, be the less able to resist it when next assailed by it.

(14) Happy is the man that feareth alway lest he should fall, and so, distrusting himself, seeks heavenly aid (Phil. 2:12).

(15) A ranging bear—i.e., wandering hungrily in great want of food.

Over the poor people—i.e., a people too weak to resist him, over whom he can tyrannize without fear.

(17) A man that doeth violence to the blood of any person.—Rather, "that is burdened with his blood," has willfully murdered any one.

Shall flee to the pit.—Fulfilling the curse of Gen. 9:6.

(21) For a piece of bread.—A thing proverbially of little value. (Comp. Ezek. 13:19.)

That man will transgress.—So degrading is the habit of servility.

(22) Hath an evil eye.—Envies others their prosperity, and keeps all he has for himself.

(23) He that rebuketh a man, afterwards shall find more favour ... —i.e., when the man reproved comes to his senses, and finds how true a friend the reprover has been to him.

(24) It is no transgression.—Because all would in time come to him.

The companion of a destroyer.—Comp. 18:9. Though the deed may be done secretly, yet he is no better than one who by open violence and wrong assails his neighbor.

(27) He that giveth unto the poor shall not lack.—See note on 11:24.

29

(1) Hardeneth his neck.—And will not bear the "easy yoke" of God. (Comp. Matt. 11:29, 30.)

Shall suddenly be destroyed.—Literally, "shattered," like a potter's vessel that cannot be mended (Jer. 19:11; Isa. 30:14).

And that without remedy.—For what more can be done for him, if he has despised God's warnings? (Comp. Heb. 6:4, sqq.)

(6) In the transgression of an evil man there is a snare.—For he knows not how by repentance to escape God's wrath.

But the righteous doth sing and rejoice.—Being assured of God's mercy to those who repent, he rejoices because his conscience is clear, and the "peace of God" (Phil. 4:7) keeps his heart.

(12) If a ruler hearken to lies, all his servants are wicked.—If a ruler shows that he likes adulation and falsehood rather than unpleasant truths, his attendants will provide him with what he wishes. (Comp. Ecclus. 10:2.) So Jeremiah complains (5:31) that prophets, priests, and people were all willfully deceiving each other.

(15) A child left to himself.—Allowed to wander unchecked as the wild ass (Job. 39:5).

Bringeth his mother to shame.—Whose foolish indulgence has ruined him.

(18) Where there is no vision.—No revelation of God's will (Isa. 1:1), when God teaches none by His Spirit that they may instruct others. So it was in the evil days of Eli (I Sam. 3:1) and Asa (II Chron. 15:3).

The people perish.—Or, "run wild." (Comp. Hosea 4:6.)

(19) A servant will not be corrected with words.—A slave must be corrected by sterner means; it is only fear of punishment which will move him. The willing obedience of a son, and the grudging obedience of a slave, are contrasted in Rom. 8:15.

(21) Shall have him become his son at the

485

length.—Confidential slaves sometimes rose to be the heirs of their master's property. (See note on 17:2.) But here the warning seems to be rather against spoiling a slave by overindulgence, lest he at the last forget his position.

(22) Aboundeth in transgression.—For what will he not say and do when overcome by anger?

(24) He heareth cursing.—Rather, the "oath" or adjuration of the judge that anyone cognizant of the theft shall give information with regard to it. He hears and remains silent, and thus, becoming the accomplice of the thief, he shares his punishment.

(25) The fear of man bringeth a snare.—Even, it may be, the loss of eternal life. (Comp. Matt. 10:28 and John 12:25.)

30

8.—The Proverbs of Solomon End Here. The Rest of the Book is Composed of Three Appendices: (a) The Words of Agur; (b) The Words of King Lemuel; and (c) The Praise of a Good Wife (chaps. 30 and 31).

Appendix (a)

(1) The words of Agur the son of Jakeh, even the prophecy.—Jewish interpreters have seen in these titles (but apparently without a shadow of reason) a designation of Solomon himself, the "convener" and instructor of assemblies (Eccl. 1:1; 12:11), son of the "obedient" man after God's own heart. But they in all probability belong to some otherwise unknown sage, whose utterances were thought not unworthy of being joined with those of the wise king of Israel himself. In support of this view I Kings 4:30 may be adduced as a proof of the estimation in which the wisdom of foreign nations was at this time held. Some light may be thrown upon the nationality of Agur by the words translated in the King James version "the prophecy" (**massa**). It has been proposed to translate the beginning of the verse thus: "The words of Agur the son of Jakeh the Massan," i.e., a descendant of the Massa mentioned in Gen. 25:14 as a son of Ishmael. This would place his home probably in North Arabia, and Lemuel would be a king of the same tribe.

Unto Ithiel, even unto Ithiel and Ucal.—These most probably were disciples of his.

Their names may mean "God with me," and "I am strong."

(4) Who hath ascended up into heaven ... —The reason of Agur's sadness is declared here. He feels himself far off from possessing anything that may be called knowledge of God or of His works. (Comp. Gal. 4:9 and I Cor. 13:12.) The questions in this verse are intended to bring out the nothingness of man as compared with the might of the Creator of the universe; they resemble Job 38-41 and Isa. 40:12, sqq.

Who hath bound the waters in a garment?—Stretching out the clouds as a "curtain" (Ps. 104:2; Isa. 40:22), to keep the rain from falling upon the earth. (Comp. Job 26:8.)

What is his name?—No words will describe Him adequately, for not until the next life shall we see Him as He is (I John 3:2), and He has been pleased to reveal Himself only partially to us. (See Exod. 34:5, sqq.)

What is his son's name?—See the description of wisdom in 8:22, sqq., and the notes there.

(5) Every word of God is pure.—Comp. Ps. 19. Every word of God is "pure," i.e., tested and proved in the furnace of experience; e.g., His promise to be a "shield" (Gen. 15:1) to those who trust in Him. (Comp. Ps. 18:30.)

(7) Two things have I required of thee.—The beginning of a series of numerical proverbs. (See note on 6:16.)

(8) Food convenient for me.—Literally, "bread of my portion," such as is apportioned to me as suitable by the care of the heavenly Father. Comp. "daily bread" (Matt. 6:11) in the sense of "proper for our sustenance."

(9) Lest I be full, and deny thee.—For "pride and fullness of bread" were among the sins which brought destruction on Sodom (Ezek. 16:49). (Comp. 21:14, 15.)

And take the name of my God in vain.—Literally, "handle it roughly, irreverently"; particularly in finding fault with His providence.

(11) There is a generation ... —The words "there is" are not in the Hebrew, so it is left in doubt what is the predicate of these four evil "generations," whether Agur means by them to describe the men of his own time, or to say that such are unbearable. (Comp. verse 21.) The same characters are to be found in the description of men of the "last days" (II Tim. 3:1, sqq.).

(15) The horseleach hath two daughters,

crying, Give, give.—The word "crying" is not in the Hebrew. The leech is here chosen as the emblem of insatiable greed; if it could speak, its "daughters," i.e., the words it would utter, would be "Give, give." So it forms an introduction to the quartette of "insatiable things" which follow.

(17) The ravens of the valley shall pick it out—i.e., the rebellious son shall die of a "grievous death" (Jer. 16:4). The inclination of ravens to attack the eyes is well known.

(18) Too wonderful for me.—The wonder in Agur's eyes seems to be that none of the four leave any trace behind them.

(23) For an odious woman when she is married.—She pays off, with interest, the slights which she had formerly to endure from her married friends.

An handmaid that is heir to her mistress, and who is nervously anxious to preserve her newly-acquired dignity.

(26) The conies are but a feeble folk, being only about as big as a rabbit, with nails instead of claws, and weak teeth. Its Hebrew name signifies a "hider," from its habit of living in clefts of the rocks. In general appearance it resembles a guinea pig or marmot.

(28) The spider taketh hold with her hands.—The lizard, rather than the spider, seems to be intended here. As each first line of these four verses is an expression of weakness, it has been proposed to translate them: "The lizard thou canst catch with the hands, and yet," etc. (Comp. for this praise of wisdom, Eccl. 9:14, sqq.)

(31) A greyhound.—It is doubtful what animal is meant here as being "girt [i.e., slender] in the loins."

(32) Lay thine hand upon thy mouth—i.e., be silent. Agur deprecates two things which may easily lead to a quarrel, arrogance and malice. He explains this in the next verse.

31

Appendix (b)

(1) The words of king Lemuel . . . —More probably this should be translated, "The words of Lemuel, king of Massa." (See note on 30:1.) "Lemuel," which most likely signifies (dedicated) "to God," has been, like Agur, supposed to be a designation of Solomon, but with no good reason.

The prophecy that his mother taught him.—Mothers were looked upon with great veneration in the East. (Comp. 1:8 and 6:20.) The mothers of kings especially were treated with marked respect, receiving the title of "queen-mother." (Comp. I Kings 2:19 and 15:13.) This seems to be the reason why the mothers of Jewish kings are so constantly mentioned, e.g., I Kings 14:31; 15:2; II Kings 21:1.

(2) What, my son?—i.e., what shall I say? The question, thrice repeated, shows her extreme anxiety to give good advice to this son, who was "tender, and only beloved in the sight of his mother."

(3) Nor thy ways to that which destroyeth kings.—A slight change in the punctuation will give a better sense, "to those who destroy kings," i.e., women. Do not give your life to dissipation at their bidding. (Comp. 6:24, sqq.; I Kings 11:1).

(4) It is not for kings to drink wine.—Another of the temptations of kings. (Comp. I Kings 16:9; 20:16; Eccl. 10:17.) Perversion of justice as the result of revelry is also noted by Isaiah (5:22, 23).

(6) Give strong drink unto him that is ready to perish.—Comp. Paul's advice (I Tim. 5:23). It was out of a merciful remembrance of this passage that the pious ladies of Jerusalem used to provide a medicated drink for criminals condemned to be crucified, in order to deaden their pain. This was offered to our Lord (Matt. 27:34), but He would not drink it, as He wished to keep His mind clear to the last, and was willing to drink to the dregs the "cup which his Father had given him."

Appendix (c):—The Praise of a Good Wife (31:10, sqq.)

This is written in the form of an acrostic, the twenty-two verses composing it each beginning with a letter of the Hebrew alphabet. This may have been done, as in the case of several of the psalms, which are of a didactic character (e.g., 25, 34, 37, 119), to render it more easy for committal to memory. By some writers the acrostic form has been supposed to argue a late date for the poem, but there is no evidence for this. One psalm, at all events, of which there seems no reason to doubt the Davidic authorship—the ninth—is cast in this form.

(10) Who can find a virtuous woman?—Various mystical interpretations of the person implied here have been held at different times. She has been supposed to signify the Law, the Church, or the Holy Spirit.

ECCLESIASTES

1

(2) **Vanity of vanities.**—This verse strikes the keynote of the whole book. The unity of the book is rather that of a musical composition than of a philosophical treatise. A leading theme is given out and followed for a time. Episodes are introduced, not perhaps logically connected with the original subject, but treated in harmony with it, and leading back to the original theme which is never lost sight of, and with which the composition comes to a close (12:8).

The word translated "vanity" (which occurs thirty-seven times in this book, and only thirty-three times in all the rest of the Old Testament) in its primary meaning denotes breath or vapor (comp. James 4:14). It is the same word as the proper name Abel, on which see note on Gen. 4:2. It is frequently applied in Scripture to the follies of heathenism (Jer. 14:22, etc.), and also to the whole estate of men (Pss. 39:5, 6; 62:9; 144:4). Comp. Rom. 8:20.

Saith the Preacher.—This formula is one which might conceivably be employed if the words of Kohéleth ("the Preacher," a proper name) were written down by himself; yet it certainly rather suggests that we have here these words as written down by another.

(3-11) Man is perpetually toiling, yet of all his toil there remains no abiding result. The natural world exhibits a spectacle of unceasing activity, with no real progress. The sun, the winds, the waters, are all in motion, yet they do but run around, and nothing comes of it.

(12-18) Having in the introductory verses stated the argument of the treatise, the writer proceeds to prove what he has asserted as to the vanity of earthly pursuits, by relating the failures of one who might be expected, if any one could, to bring such pursuits to a satisfactory result. Solomon, in this book called Kohéleth, pre-eminent among Jewish sovereigns as well for wisdom as for temporal prosperity, speaking in the first person, tells how, with all his advantages, he could secure in this life no lasting or satisfying happiness. He relates first how he found no satisfaction from an enlightened survey of human life. He found (verse 14) that it presented a scene of laborious exertion empty of profitable results. His researches (verse 15) only brought to light errors and defects which it was impossible to remedy, so that (verse 18) the more thought a man bestowed on the subject, the greater his grief.

(13) **Gave my heart.**—The phrase occurs again in this book (verse 17; 7:25; 8:9, 16) and often elsewhere. (See Dan. 10:12; II Chron. 11:16; etc.) The heart among the Hebrews is regarded as the seat, not merely of the feelings, but also of the intellectual faculties, and so the word is constantly used in what follows. "I gave my heart" is the same as "I applied my mind."

2

(1-8) Kohéleth, having tried wisdom and philosophic investigation, proceeded next to see what cheerful enjoyment could do for human happiness.

(9-11) Kohéleth carried out his plan of tempering his enjoyment with discretion, but while he took his fill of the pleasure that fell to his lot, he found in it no abiding profit. He goes on to complain that the wisdom and other advantages he possessed in his search for happiness render his failure the more disheartening.

(16) It might be urged on behalf of the Solomonic authorship that Solomon himself might imagine that in the days to come he and his wisdom would be forgotten, but that such a thought does not become a long subsequent writer who had been induced by Solomon's reputation for wisdom to make him the hero of his work. It would seem to follow that the writer is here only giving the history of Solomon's reflections, and not his ultimate conclusions.

(18) There seems to be no special reference to Rehoboam, but only the assertion of the general principle that the wisest of men must leave all that his labor has gained to be enjoyed by another who may be destitute of wisdom. The thought is not so much that it is a hardship for the wise man to leave what he has gained, as that it is that he should have no advantage over the fool who enjoys the same without any merit.

3

The thought expressed at the end of the last chapter is developed in this chapter, which treats of the supremacy of God. Man can have no enjoyment except as He is pleased to bestow it. He has pre-ordained the times and seasons of all human events, and success cannot be obtained except in conformity with His arrangement.

(11) The world.—The word here translated "world" has that meaning in post-Biblical Hebrew, but never elsewhere in the Old Testament, where it occurs over 300 times. Where the word occurs elsewhere it means "eternity," or "long duration," and is so used in this book (1:4, 10; 2:16; 3:14; 9:6; 12:5;. Taking this meaning of the word here, we may regard it as contrasted with that for "time," or season, immediately before. For each of these "times" God has appointed its time or season, and in its season each is good. But man does not recognize this; for God has put in his heart an expectation and longing for abiding continuance of the same, and so he fails to understand the work which God does in the world.

(17) A time there.—viz., with God. In this verse a judgment after this life is clearly spoken of, not yet asserted as a conclusion definitely adopted, but only as a belief of the writer's conflicting with the doubts expressed in the following verses.

(19) Breath.—The same word as "spirit" (verse 21; Gen. 7:15; Ps. 104:30).

(21) The LXX, followed by a great body of interpreters, ancient and modern, translate, "Who knoweth whether the spirit of man goeth upward?" etc., and this agrees better with the context of this paragraph. The sceptical thought is, "We see that death resolves into dust (Gen. 3:19; Eccl. 12:7; see also Ecclus. 41:10) the bodies of men and animals alike; and if it be alleged that there is a difference as to what becomes of their spirits, can this be asserted with the certainty of knowledge?" The writer here seems to have read both Ps. 49:14 and Prov. 15:24.

4

(1-6) Having dwelt on the instability of human happiness, the Preacher now turns to contemplate the actual misery of which the world is full.

(7) Then I returned.—The vanity of toil is especially apparent in the case of a solitary man. It is possible, as has been suggested (see 2:18), that this may have been the writer's own case. Verses 7-12, which speak of the advantages of friendship and unity, are of a more cheerful tone than the rest of the book.

(13) The section beginning here presents great difficulties of interpretation, in overcoming which we have little help from the context because of the abruptness with which, in this verse, a new subject is introduced.

(15) I considered.—The Preacher reverts to the general topic and considered all the living with the "second youth," i.e., the second generation which shall succeed them. He saw the old generation hardened in its ways and incapable of being admonished, and then displaced by a new generation, with which the next will feel equal dissatisfaction.

5

(1) In the Hebrew division this is the last verse of the preceding chapter; but clearly here a new section begins, containing proverbs in the second person singular, which has not heretofore been used. There is no obvious connection with what has gone before; possibly the precepts here introduced were traditionally known to have been part of Solomon's teaching.

(4) There is here a clear recognition of Deut. 23:21. Comp. Num. 30:2; Pss. 50:14; 66:13, 14; 76:11; Prov. 20:25; Acts 5:4.

(6) Error.—The word is that which describes sins of **ignorance** (Num. 15). The tacit assumption in this verse, that God interposes to punish when His name is taken in vain, clearly expresses the writer's real conviction, and shows that such a verse as 9:2 is only the statement of a speculative difficulty.

(9) Is served by.—This verse is to be connected with verses 10-12, constituting a consideration intended to mitigate the difficulty felt at the sight of riches acquired by oppression, namely, that riches add little to the real happiness of the possessors.

(15) There is a clear use of Job 1:21. (See also Ps. 139:15.) And this passage itself is used in Ecclus. 40:1.

(18) The Preacher is led back to the conclusion at which he had arrived (2:24; 3:12, 22).

6

In this section it is remarked how even when riches remain with a man to the end of his life they may fail to bring him any real happiness. That a man should be so occupied in the pursuit of riches as never to take any enjoyment from them is a common enough experience; but that the same man should have no sepulchre to preserve his name after him need not necessarily happen, so that one is tempted to think that the Preacher has some actual occurrence in his mind.

7

In the sections immediately following, the continuity of the history of the Preacher's mental struggles is broken by the introduction of a number of proverbs, some of which have so little apparent relation to the context that Renan even takes them to be intended as specimens of the "many words which increase vanity." But of any work, whether actually representing or intended to represent the teaching of Solomon, proverbs might be expected to form a necessary part. And though the ingenuity may not be successful which has been employed in trying to find a strict logical sequence in this part of the work, yet the thoughts are not unconnected with each other, nor out of harmony with the whole. The question with which the preceding chapter concludes, "Who knoweth what is good for a man?" is taken up in this, verses 1, 2, 3, 5, 8, 11, all beginning with the word "good." This characteristic would have been better kept up in translation if the first word of all these verses had been made "better."

(16) Righteous over-much.—The caution is against morbid scrupulosity and over-rigorism. We may illustrate by the case of the Jews, who refused to defend themselves against their enemies on the Sabbath day. The next verse is a necessary corrective to this: "Yet be cautious how thou disregardest the restraints of law."

(18) In the uncertainty of the issues of life, it is good for a man to make trial of opposite rules of conduct, provided he always restrains himself by the fear of God. (Comp. 11:6.)

(23) The confession of failure to attain speculative knowledge gives energy to the Preacher's next following enunciation of the practical lesson which he has learned from his experience.

8

(1) This verse in praise of wisdom can be

connected either with what precedes or what follows. (See Hos. 14:9.)

(2) The counsels given here and 10:4 are not what we should expect from Solomon, but rather from one who had himself lived under a despotism.

The oath of God.—Unsuccessful attempts have been made to find in those words a definite historic reference. But we need not look beyond the Bible for proof that an oath of vassalage was imposed on the Jews by their foreign masters, and that the breach of such an oath was regarded by the prophets as sin (II Chron. 36:13; Ezek. 17:13, 16, 18). And there is reason to think that similar pledges had been given to native kings (I Sam. 10:3; I Chron. 29:24; II Chron. 23:3).

(9, 10) The context speaks of the small gain from his oppressions to the tyrant himself. His prosperity is but temporary, for soon comes death, burial, and forgetfulness of his honor.

(15) The writer returns to the sentiment expressed already (2:24; 3:12, 22; 5:17).

Eat, and to drink, and to be merry.—The three words occur together in I Kings 4:20.

(16) It would have been better if the new chapter had been made to begin here. The sentiment is that already expressed in 3:11.

9

(3) We have again the sentiments expressed in 2:14-16; 3:19; 5:15; 6:12.

(4) The shepherd's dog is spoken of in Job 30:1, and watchdogs in Isa. 56:10. Elsewhere in the Old Testament the dog is an unclean animal living or dead.

(7) Accepteth.—The thought has been expressed before (2:24; 8:15), that earthly enjoyment is to be received as given by God's favor.

(14) Idle attempts have been made to find a historic reference in this passage. What is here told is so like the story (II Sam. 20) of the deliverence of Abel-beth-Maachah by a wise woman, whose name, nevertheless, has not been preserved, that we cannot even be sure that the writer had any other real history in his mind.

10

(1) The sense is that a little folly invalidates the effect of much wisdom. (Chapter

9 might better have been brought to a close at the end of verse 12.)

(2) At his right hand.—The thought is the same as 2:13, namely, that though the actual results of wisdom are often disappointing, the superiority of wisdom over folly is undeniable.

(7) Considering that the importation of horses was a new thing in the reign of Solomon, we look on it as a mark of later age that a noble should think himself dishonored by having to go on foot while his inferiors rode on horseback.

(8) The common theme of these proverbs is the advantage of wisdom, and here in particular of caution in great enterprises. It is forcing the connection to imagine that the enterprise from which the writer seeks to dissuade is that of rebellion against the ruler whose error is condemned (verse 5).

(10) The mention of cutting wood in the preceding verse suggests the illustration from the axe, exemplifying how wisdom will serve instead of strength.

(11) The mention of the serpent in verse 8 seems to have suggested another illustration of the advantage of wisdom, as used by the expert or the unskillful. The phrase, "master of the tongue," seems to have been chosen in order to lead on to the following verses, which speak of the different use of the tongue by the wise man and the fool.

11

(1) In this section the Preacher is drawing to a close, and he brings out practical lessons different from those which views of life like his have suggested to others. From the uncertainty of the results of human effort, he infers that we ought the more diligently to make trial of varied forms of exertion, in order that this or that may succeed. From the instability of human happiness, he draws the lesson that we ought to enjoy freely such happiness as life affords, yet with a temperate and chastened joy, and mindful of the account we shall have to render.

Verse 6, which speaks distinctly of the sowing of seed, is the best commentary on the present verse, which means, cast thy seed, even though you cannot see where it will fall. Possibly the application of the figure is not to be restricted to acts of beneficence; but the next verse may lead us to think that these are primarily intended,

and to these especially the encouragement at the end of the verse applies. In other cases this book gives a less cheerful view of the possible success of human plans.

(3) The world is ruled by fixed laws, the operation of which man has no power to suspend.

(4) But it is idle to try to guard against all possibilities of failure. To demand a certainty of success before acting would mean not to act at all.

(9) The beginning of the last chapter would more conveniently have been placed here than where the division is actually made. It is hard to interpret the judgment spoken of in this verse of anything but future judgment, when we bear in mind how much of the book is taken up with the complaint that retribution does not take place in this life.

12

(1) Creator.—This occurs as a divine name in Isa. 40:28; 43:15, and elsewhere. Here it is in the plural, like the divine name Elohim.

(2) Here the style rises, and we have a figurative description of the "evil days"; but, as sometimes happens in the case of highly wrought poetry, it is much easier to perceive the general effect intended than to account for all the words which produce it. English readers generally have been deeply impressed by verses 6, 7 (see Zech. 4:3), in a general way understanding them as speaking of the dissolution of the noble structure of the bodily frame.

(3) Expositors have generally understood the house here described as denoting the decaying body of the old man. But when it is attempted to carry out the figure, and to find anatomical explanations of all the other images employed, the interpretation becomes so forced that some have preferred to understand verse 3 as only a general description of the consternation produced by such a tempest as is spoken of in verse 2.

(7) The Preacher has risen above the doubts of 3:21. (See also Gen. 3:19.)

(9) The epilogue which follows is an integral part of the book. It seems clear that the writer, who has up to this recorded the words of Kohéleth, now speaks in his own name and informs his readers that the Preacher, whose teaching of the people he preserves, was also a writer, and the author of the well-known Proverbs.

(11) Words of the wise.—In this and the

next verse the weighty words of sages, such as was Kohéleth, are contrasted with the volubility of modern bookmakers. Though the general purpose of the verses is plain, the words used are enigmatical, and one cannot feel great confidence in assigning their precise meaning. With regard to the "nail," compare Ezra 9:8; Isa. 22:23. "Assemblies" is a word not coming from the same root as that from which Kohéleth is derived. It might mean collections of sayings as well as of people. It is difficult to affix any meaning to the last clause, except that the sages, of whom the verse speaks, have been given for the instruction of the people by Israel's great Shepherd (Ps. 80:1).

(13) Whole duty of man.—Rather, "the duty of every man." The sacred writer practically anticipates the teaching of Rom. 3:29.

(14) Considering that the book is filled with complaints of the imperfection of earthly retribution, this announcement of a tribunal cannot be reasonably understood of anything but a judgment after this life, so that this book, after all its sceptical debatings, ends by enunciating, more distinctly than is done elsewhere in the Old Testament, the New Testament doctrine of a day when God shall judge the secrets of men (Rom. 2:16), shall bring to light the hidden things of darkness, and make manifest the counsels of the hearts (I Cor. 4:5).

THE SONG OF SOLOMON

1

Verse 1 contains the title of the book. This has been understood as meaning "one of Solomon's songs," with allusion to the 1,005 songs (I Kings 4:32) which that monarch composed. It is not merely "a song of songs" (comp. holy of holies), i.e., "a very excellent song," but "**The** song of songs," i.e., the most excellent or surpassing song.

(3) **Virgins.**—Heb., **alamôth**; "young girls." Those who understand Solomon to be the object of the desire expressed in these verses understand by **alamôth** "the ladies of the harem."

(4) **The king hath brought me.**—The dramatic theory of the poem has been in a great measure built up on interpretations given to this verse. We understand it as a repetition, in another form, of the protestation of love made in verses 1-3.

(5) **As the tents of Kedar.**—See Gen. 25:13. As the poet puts this description of the lady's complexion into her own mouth, we must understand it as a little playful railery, which is immediately redeemed by a compliment. It also prepares the way for the reminiscence of an interesting passage in her early life. See next verse.

(6) **The sun** . . . —The "all-seeing sun" is a commonplace of poetry, but here with sense of scorching. The heroine goes on to explain the cause of her exposure to the sun. Her dark complexion ("blackish") is accidental, and cannot therefore be used as an argument that she was an Egyptian princess, whose nuptials with Solomon are celebrated in the poem.

Mine own vineyard . . . —The general sense is plain. While engaged in the duties imposed by her brothers, she had been compelled to neglect something—but what? The obvious interpretation connects the words immediately with the context. Her **personal appearance** had been sacrificed to her brothers' severity. While tending their vines she had neglected her own complexion.

(8) **If thou know not.**—With this verse one subsection of the poem plainly ends. Most of the supporters of the dramatic theory make verse 9 begin the second scene of Act I; and we understand this reply to the heroine's question as one of the many playful ways in which the poet either recalls

or arranges meetings with the object of his passion (comp. 2:10-14).

(12) **While the king sitteth.**—There is no need to imagine a scene where the monarch, having failed in his attempt to allure the shepherdess by fine offers, retires to his banquet, leaving her to console herself with the thoughts of her absent shepherd love. As in verse 2 the poet makes his mistress prefer his love to wine, so here she refers the thought of union with him to all the imagined pleasures of the royal table.

(14) For En-gedi, see Josh. 15:62. It is the only place in Southern Palestine mentioned in this poem, the other allusions (except Heshbon, 7:4, which is in Moab) being to the northern localities.

(15) **Behold, thou art fair.**—The song is now transferred to a male speaker—the advocates for the dramatic theory cannot agree whether Solomon or the shepherd; and the poem gives no indication.

(16) **Our bed is green.**—The heroine replies in similar terms of admiration, and recalls "the happy woodland places" in which they were accustomed to meet.

2

(1) **Of Sharon.**—Better, "of the plain," as in the LXX, but without definite local allusion to the district north of Philistia. The verse is taken by many as a snatch of a song into which the heroine breaks in answer to the eulogies on her beauty. It is certainly spoken with modest and lowly intention: "I am a mere flower of the plain, a lily of the valley."

(7) **My love.**—This verse (which is repeated in 3:5 and 8:4) marks natural breaks in the poem and adds to the dramatic effect. The "daughters of Jerusalem" are present only in the poet's imagination. It is his manner to fancy the presence of spectators of his happiness and to call on outsiders to share his bliss (comp. 3:11; 5:16; 6:13; etc.), and it is on this imaginary theater which his love conjures up that the curtain falls, here and in other places, on the union of the happy pair.

(8) **The voice of my beloved!**—So here there is no need of the clumsy device of supposing the heroine in a dream. This most exquisite morsel of the whole poem falls quite naturally into its place if we regard it as a sweet recollection of the poet's, put into the mouth of the object of his affections.

493

(14) O my dove . . . in the clefts of the rock.—The rock pigeon, the origin of the domestic races, invariably selects the lofty cliffs and deep ravines (comp. Jer. 48:28; Ezek. 7:16) for its roosting places, and avoids the neighborhood of men. The modesty and shyness of his beloved are thus indicated by the poet. See Obad. 3.

(15) Foxes.—Comp. Judg. 15:4. Whether the fox or the jackal (Heb., **shual**), it is known to be equally destructive to vineyards. In the allegorizing commentators they stand for heretics.

(16) He feedeth.—Heb., "he that is feeding his flock"—the pastor.

3

(4) I held him . . . —Bossuet, following Bede, regards this as prophetic of Mary Magdalene (type of the Church) on the morning of the Resurrection.

(6) Who is this that cometh.—The dramatic feeling is decidedly shown in the passage introduced by this verse, but we will regard it as a scene passing only in the theater of the fancy, introduced by the poet in his Epithalamium, partly from his sympathy with all newly-wedded people, partly (as 8:11) to contrast the simplicity of his own espousals, of which all the joy centered in true love, with pomp and magnificence of a royal marriage, which was a State ceremony.

4

(6) Until the day break.—We have come to another break in the poem, the end of another day, and, as before, though the metaphor is changed, the curtain falls on the complete union of the bridegroom with his bride.

(8) Come with me.—We have here another reminiscence of the obstacles which had attended the union of the pair under another figure. The course of true love is beset here by tremendous difficulties, symbolized by the rocks and snows of the range of Lebanon, which shut in the poet's northern home, and the wild beasts that haunted these regions. Like Tennyson's shepherd, he believes that "love is of the valleys," and calls to her to come down to him from her inaccessible heights. They are named as emblems of height and difficulty. Shenîr (Senir, I Chron. 5:23) is one of the peaks of

Hermon. **Amana** has been believed to be a name for the district of Anti-Libanus in which the Abana (**Barada**) has its source, but nothing is certain about it. The LXX translates **amana** by **pistis**, and this has been turned into an argument for the allegorical treatment of the book. But it is a common error of the LXX to translate proper names (Comp. 6:4.)

The appellative "spouse" (**khallah**) first occurs in this verse. Its use does not by itself prove that the pair were united in wedlock, but its presence strongly confirms the impression produced by the whole poem, that it describes over and over again the courtship and marriage of the same couple.

(12) A garden enclosed.—Comp. with this passage verses 12-15; Prov. 5:15, 21. The closed or walled garden and the sealed fountain appear to have been established metaphors for the pure and chaste wife.

(13) Thy plants.—Some have thought the offspring of the marriage intended here; but the poet is plainly, by a new adaptation of the language of flowers, describing the charms of the person of his beloved.

(16) Blow upon my garden.—After the description of his beloved's charms under these figures, the poet, under a companion figure, invokes the "airs of love" to blow upon the garden, that the object of his affections may no longer keep herself reserved and denied to him.

5

(1) I am come into my garden.—This continues the same figure, and under it describes once more the complete union of the wedded pair. Here, as throughout the poem, it is the "new strong wine of love," and not the fruit of the grape, which is desired and drunk.

(2) I sleep.—This begins the old story under an image already employed (3:1). Here it is greatly amplified and elaborated. The poet pictures his lady dreaming of him, and when he seems to visit her, anxious to admit him. But, as is so common in dreams, at first she cannot. The realities which had hindered their union reappear in the fancies of sleep. Then, when the seeming hindrance is withdrawn, she finds him gone, and, as before, searches for him in vain. This gives opportunity to introduce the description of the charms of the lost lover, and so the end of the piece, the union of the pair, is delayed to 6:3.

(9) What is thy beloved?—This question, introducing the description of the bridegroom's person, raises almost into certainty the conjecture that the poem was actually sung, or presented as an epithalamium, by alternate choirs (or single voices) of maidens and young men, vying the one in praise of the bridegroom, the other of the bride. Mere love-poems contain descriptions of the charms of the fair one to whom they are addressed, but not of the poem himself.

6

(1-3) Whither is thy beloved gone ... —By a playful turn the poet heightens the description of the lover's beauty by the impression supposed to be produced on the imaginary bystanders to whom the picture has been exhibited. They express a desire to share the pleasures of his company with the heroine, but she, under the figure before employed (4:12-16), declares that his affections are solely hers, and that, so far from being at their disposal, he is even now hastening to complete his and her happiness in their union.

(4) Beautiful ... as Tirzah.—There is no sufficient reason for the employment of Tirzah side by side with Jerusalem in this comparison, but the fact that they were both capitals, the one of the northern, and other of the southern kingdom. This fixes the date of the composition of the poem within certain limits. Jeroboam first selected the ancient sanctuary of Shechem for his capital; but, from some unexplained cause, he moved the seat of his government, first to Penuel, on the other side of Jordan, and then to Tirzah, formerly the seat of a petty Canaanite prince. (See I Kings 14:17; 15:21, 33; 16:6, 8, 15, 17, 23; Josh. 12:24.) Tirzah only remained the capital till the reign of Omri, but comes into notice again as the scene of the conspiracy of Menahem against Shallum (II Kings 15:14-16). The LXX translates Tirzah by **eudokia,** Vulgate **suavis;** and the ancient versions generally adopt this plan, to avoid the mention of the two capitals, because this went against the Solomonic authorship.

As Jerusalem.—See Lam. 2:15. As to the idea involved in a comparison so strange to us, we notice that this author is especially fond of finding a resemblance between his love and familiar localities (see 5:15 and

7:4, 5); nor was it strange in a language that delighted in personifying a nation or city under the character of a maiden (Isa. 47:1), and which, ten centuries later, could describe the new Jerusalem as a bride coming down from heaven adorned for her husband (Rev. 21:9, seqq.).

(8) There are threescore queens.— Presumably a description of Solomon's harem (comp. 8:11, 12), though the numbers are far more sober than in I Kings 11:3. Probably the latter marks a later form of the traditions of the grand scale on which everything at the court of the monarch was conducted, and this, though a poetic, is a truer version of the story of his loves.

(9) My dove ... is but one.—It is impossible not to see in this a eulogy on monogamy, which, in practice, seems always to have been the rule among the Jews, the exceptions lying only with kings and the very rich. The eulogy is made more pronounced by putting an unconscious testimony to the superiority of monogamy into the mouths of the "queens and concubines," who praise and bless this pattern of a perfect wife.

(13) O Shulamite.—The fact that Abishag was a Shunamite, and that Adonijah sought her in marriage (I Kings 1:3), has given rise to the conjecture that these two are the heroine and hero of this poem.

7

(1) O prince's daughter!—Nothing relating to the rank of the heroine can be deduced from the recurrence of **nadib** (noble) here. The reference may be to character rather than descent, just as in the opposite expression, "daughter of Belial" (I Sam. 1:16).

Joints.—This probably refers to the rapid movements in dancing, and the image is suggested by the graceful curves formed by a chain or pendulous ornament when in motion. Or the reference may be to the contour of the person.

(10, 11) I am my beloved's.—This verse ends a section, not, as in the King James Version, begins one. Comp. 2:10 and 6:11, for the same reminiscence of the sweet courtship in the happy "woodland places."

8

(1) O that thou wert as my brother.—The

poet makes his beloved recall the feelings she had for him before the obstacles to their union were removed. She dared not then avow her affection for him as a lover, and wished that their relationship had been such as to allow of their meeting and embracing without reproach.

(5) Who is this that cometh.—This begins a new section, which contains the most magnificent description of true love ever written by a poet. The dramatic theory encounters insuperable difficulties with this strophe. Again we presume that the theater and the spectators are imaginary. It is another sweet reminiscence, coming most naturally and beautifully after the last. The obstacles have been removed, the pair are united, and the poet recalls the delightful sensations with which he led his bride through the scenes where the youth of both had been spent, and then bursts out into the glorious panegyric of that pure and perfect passion which had united them.

There thy mother ... —The poet delights to recall these early associations, the feelings with which he had watched her home and waited her coming. So in later times the tree has been taken to stand for the cross, the individual excited to love under it the Gentiles redeemed at the foot of the cross, and the deflowered and corrupted mother the synagogue of the Jews (the mother of the Christian Church), which was corrupted by denying and crucifying the Saviour.

(6) A most vehement flame.—Literally, "a flame of Jah," the only place where a sacred name occurs in the book, and here, as in the King James Version, adverbially, to express something superlatively great and strong.

(7) It would utterly be contemned.—This fine passage, with its reference to the invincible might and untempted constancy of true love, hardly leaves a doubt that the poem, while an ideal picture of the passion, is also a reminiscence of an actual history of two hearts that had been tried and proved true both against difficulties and seductions.

(8) We have a little sister.—Commentators are almost all at one in the feeling that the poem properly ends with verse 7. Those who construct the poem on the plan of a drama can find no proper place for what follows (unless as a meaningless epilogue), and the want of cohesion with the main body of the work is so evident that many scholars have rejected it as a later addition. But the author had no regard to artistic form, or not the same conception of it as we have.

A little sister ... —The recollection is carried back to the childhood of the bride. Her brothers are supposed to be debating how to deal with her when an offer of marriage should be made for her.

(9) If she be a wall.—The "wall" and "door" are emblems of chastity and its opposite. If the maiden grows up virtuous and inaccessible to seduction, we will so provide for her in marriage that from her may spring an illustrious house; but if otherwise, the strongest precautions shall be taken to guard her honor. This passage is one of the strongest arguments for the theory that chaste wedded love is the theme of this book, the poet going on in verse 10 to put into the heroine's mouth a protestation of purity, and by which virtuous disposition, even more than by her beauty, she had won her husband's love.

(11, 12) Solomon had a vineyard ... — Here the poet repeats the sentiment of 6:8, 9 —the contrast of his love for one chosen bride with the state of feeling and morality fostered by polygamy. But while in the former passage the contrast lay in number only, here it lies also in the value which comes to be set on the possession. Any one member of the harem of Solomon is no dearer to him than one of his many vineyards, which has to be cultivated by hirelings, and is valued only for the return it yields. But the one wedded wife is a vineyard tended by the owner, loved for its own sake as well as valued.

Baal-hamon.—If the poet had any definite place in his mind he merely used it for the play on words (**Baal-hamon** = lord of multitude). The correct translation is "a vineyard was to Solomon **as** lord of a multitude." We further note that **Baal**, as "lord" with us, often means "husband," and **Baal-hamon** has a covert allusion to the polygamy of the king.

(14) Make haste, my beloved.—The poem ends with two short verses that compress into them all that has been over and over again related under different figures: the wooing and the wedding of two happy souls.

ISAIAH

1

(1) The vision of Isaiah the son of Amoz . . .—The term "vision," as descriptive of a prophet's work (I Sam. 3:1), is the correlative of the old term "seer," as applied to the prophet himself (I Sam. 9:9). To see visions was one of the highest forms of the gift of the spirit of Jehovah (Joel 2:28). It describes the state, more or less ecstatic, in which the prophet sees what others do not see, the things that are yet to come, the unseen working of the eternal laws of God. As compared with "the word of the Lord," it indicates a higher intensity of the ecstatic state; but the two terms were closely associated, and, as in 2:1, Judah and Jerusalem are named as the center, though not the limit, of the prophet's work.

(2) I have nourished and brought up children.—It is significant that the prophet starts from the thought of the fatherhood of God in His relation to Israel. The people might be unworthy of their election, but He had chosen them (Exod. 4:22; Deut. 14:1; Hos. 11:1).

(4) They have forsaken the Lord . . . — The three verbs paint the several stages of the growth in evil. Men first forsake, then spurn, then openly apostatize. (Comp. Luke 16:13). In the "Holy One of Israel" we have the divine name on which Isaiah most delights to dwell, and which had been impressed on his mind by the **Trisagion**, which accompanied his first call to the office of a prophet (6:3). The thought expressed by the name is that all ideas of consecration, purity, and holiness are gathered up in God. The term occurs fourteen times in the first part of Isaiah and sixteen times in the second. A corrupt people needed to be reminded more and more of the truth which the name asserted.

(5) The whole head is sick . . .—The sin of the people is painted as a deadly epidemic, spreading everywhere, affecting the noblest organs of the body (see Jer. 17:9) and defying all the resources of the healing art. The description may have connected itself with the prophet's personal experience or training in the medicine and surgery of his time (see 38:21; II Chron. 21:18; 26:20). It would seem, indeed, from II Chron. 16:12, that the prophets, as an order, practiced the art of healing, and so were rivals of the "physicians," who depended chiefly on idol-atrous charms and incantations. Every part of the body is tainted by the poison. We note a certain technical precision in the terms used. As the diagnosis is technical, so also are the therapeutic agencies. But no such remedies, the prophet says, had been applied to the spiritual disease of Israel.

(7) Your country is desolate . . . —It is natural to take the words as describing the actual state of things when the prophet wrote. There had been such invasions in the days of Ahaz, in which Israel and Syria (7:1), Edom and the Philistines, had been conspicuous (II Chron. 28:17, 18); and the reign of Hezekiah already had witnessed that of Sargon (20:1).

(8) As a besieged city.—The comparison of the besieged city to itself is at first startling. Rhetorically, however, it forms a climax. The city was not at this time actually besieged, but it was so hemmed in with perils, so isolated from all help, that this was what its condition practically came to.

(9) Except the Lord of hosts . . . —This name also had been stamped on the prophet's mind at the time of his call (6:3). The idea of the "remnant" left when the rest of the people perished is closely connected with the leading thought of 6:12, 13. It had, perhaps, been impressed on the prophet's mind by the "remnant" of Israel that had escaped from Tiglath-pileser or Sargon (II Chron. 30:6; comp. Mic. 5:7).

(10) Hear the word of the Lord, ye rulers of Sodom.—The rulers thus addressed were probably those who were outwardly active in Hezekiah's work of reformation, or had taken part in the older routine worship under Uzziah. For princes and people alike that reformation was but superficial. The priestly writer of the Book of Chronicles might dwell only on the apparent good in either reign (II Chron. 27:2, chaps. 29-31); but the eye of Isaiah saw below the surface. In "the word of the Lord," and "the law of our God," we have two different aspects of the revelation of the divine will, the first being the prophetic message of the prophet, the second pointing primarily, perhaps, to the law given by Moses, but including also all forms of direct ethical teaching.

(11) To what purpose is the multitude of your sacrifices? . . . —Comp. Hos. 6:6; Amos 5:21-24; Mic. 6:6-8, utterances of contemporary prophets, who may have exercised a direct influence on his teaching. The description points primarily, perhaps, to the reign of Uzziah, but may include that of Hezekiah. The account of the sacrifices agrees with II Chron. 29:21-29.

(16, 17) The words were probably as an echo of Ps. 51:7. Both psalmist and prophet had entered into the inner meaning of the outward ablutions of ritual. Such words the prophet might have heard in his youth from Amos (Amos 5:14, 15). What had then been spoken to the princes of the northern kingdom was now repeated to those of Judah.

(18) Come now, and let us reason together.—The King James Version suggests the thought of a discussion between equals. The Hebrew implies rather the tone of one who gives an authoritative **ultimatum**, as from a judge to the accused, who had no defense or only a sham defense, to offer (Mic. 6:2, 3).

Though your sins be as scarlet.—The two colors point to the dyes of Tyre, and the words probably received a fresh emphasis from the fact that robes of these colors were worn by the princes to whom Isaiah preached (II Sam. 1:24). To the prophet's eye that dark crimson was as the stain of blood. What Jehovah promises is that the guilt of the past, deep-dyed in grain as it might be, should be discharged, and leave the character with a restored purity. Men might dye their souls of this or that hue, but to bleach them was the work of God. Comp. the reproduction of the thought, with the added paradox that it was the crimson "blood of the lamb" that was to bleach and cleanse, in Rev. 3:4, 5; 7:14.

(21) How is the faithful city become an harlot! . . .—The opening word, as in Lam. 1:1, is the keynote of an elegiac wail, which opens a new section. The idea of prostitution as representing apostasy from Jehovah was involved in the thought that Israel was the bride whom He had wooed and won (Hos. 1-3; Jer. 2:2). The imagery was made more impressive by the fact that actual prostitution entered so largely into the ritual of many of the forms of idolatry to which the Israelites were tempted (Num. 25:1, 2; comp. Ezek. 16:1-59; Matt. 12:39). The fact that Hosea, an earlier contemporary, had been led to tell how he had been taught the truth thus set forth by a living personal experience, is not without significance in its bearing on the **genesis** of Isaiah's thoughts.

(26) I will restore thy judges as at the first.—The prophet looks back to the good old days, the time probably of David, or the early years of Solomon (I Kings 10:9), when judges were faithful, princes upright, and the people happy—to such an ideal polity as that of Pss. 15 and 24.

(27) Zion shall be redeemed with judgment . . .—The condition of the redemption which primarily proceeds from the compassion of Jehovah is found in the renewed righteousness of man to man described in the preceding verse. Without that no redemption was possible, for that was of its very essence.

2

(1) The word that Isaiah the son of Amoz saw.—The moral and social state described here points to an earlier date than the reformation of Hezekiah. The sins of the people are more flagrant; but there is not as yet with them the added guilt of a formal and ceremonial worship. Key considerations are the character of the king (3:12), the influence of the Philistines (verse 6), and the mention of "ships of Tarshish" (verse 16). We fix the date, therefore, as early years of the reign of Ahaz, with, perhaps, a backward glance at evils which belonged also to the reigns of Uzziah and Jotham.

The title of the superscription unites in an exceptional form the two ideas of the prophet and of the seer. What follows is "the **word**" of Isaiah, but it is a word that he has **seen**.

(2) It shall come to pass in the last days.—The three verses that follow are found in almost identical form in Mic. 4:1-3, with the addition of a verse (Mic. 4:4) which describes the prosperity of Judah. Micah prophesied, like Isaiah, under Ahaz, Jotham, and Hezekiah, and so either may have heard it from the other. But comp. Mic. 3:12 with Jer. 26:18.

For "in the last days" read **latter** or **after days**, the idea of the Hebrew words, as in Gen. 49:1; Num. 24:14, being that of remoteness rather than finality. For the most part (Deut. 4:30; 31:29) they point to the distant future of the true King, to the time of the Messiah.

All nations shall flow unto it.—Early in his work was Isaiah (half unconsciously as to the manner in which his vision was to be realized) the prophet of a universal religion, of which the truths of Judaism were the center, and of a catholic church. In the admission of proselytes, commemorated in Ps. 87 (probably written about this time), we may see what may either have suggested the prophecy, or have seemed as the first-fruits of its fulfillment. The language of

Paul suggests that there may be in the future a yet more glorious mission, of which Jerusalem shall once more be the center (Rom. 11:12-15).

(4) And they shall beat their swords into plowshares.—The words invert the picture of an earlier prophet, who spoke of a time of war (Joel 3:10). Isaiah must have known that prediction, and yet he proclaims (following Hos. 2:18) that peace, not war, is the ideal goal toward which the order of the divine government is tending. (Comp. Zech. 9:10; Luke 2:14.)

(5) O house of Jacob ...—The ideal of the future has been brought before Israel; but it is still far off, and the people must learn repentance, must themselves "walk in the light of the Lord," before they can be as light-bearers to other nations. (Comp. Rom. 11:11-15.)

(6) The disasters of the time are viewed as chastisements for sin, and the sin consisted in casting off their national allegiance to Jehovah, in a mania for divination, and in contracts with foreign nations.

(7, 8) The long and prosperous reign of Uzziah had reproduced the wealth of the days of Solomon (comp. I Kings 10); and the idolatry in the land recalled the reigns of Ahaz and Jotham (comp. II Chron. 27, 28).

(10) Enter into the rock.—See verses 19-21. The limestone caverns of Palestine were natural asylums in times of terror and dismay (Judg. 6:2; I Sam. 13:6; I Kings 18:4). Here, as in Mic. 1:4, we may probably trace the impression left by the earthquake under Uzziah (Amos 1:1), when the people fled in terror from the city (Zech. 14:5). Isaiah foresees the recurrence of a like panic in the future.

The descriptions which follow must have found a fulfillment in the ravages of Sargon's and Sennacherib's armies.

(15) Upon every high tower.—Generic as the words are, they have a special reference to the fortifications which were the glory of Uzziah's reign, and which were continued by his successors (II Chron. 26:9, 10; 27:3, 4; Hos. 8:14; Mic. 5:11; Ps. 48:13).

(16) And upon all the ships of Tarshish.—The words point to the commerce in the Red Sea carried on by the fleets of Uzziah and Jotham (I Kings 22:48), and perhaps also to that in the Mediterranean with Tarshish, or Tartessus (Spain), as in Jon. 1:3. The "ships of Tarshish" had come to be used generically for all ships of the class used in such commerce, whether crossing the Mediterranean to Spain or circumnavigating Africa, or passing over the Persian Gulf to Ophir.

3

(1) For, behold, the Lord, the Lord of hosts, doth take away from Jerusalem ...—From the general picture of the state of Judah as a whole, of the storm of divine wrath bursting over the whole land, Isaiah turns to the Holy City itself, and draws the picture of what he saw there of evil, of that which would be seen before long as the punishment of the evil.

The stay and the staff may be identified with the "pillars of the state," the great women and men who are named afterward. But verse 7 implies the pressure of famine, and the prophet may have intended to paint the complete failure of all resources, both material and political.

(4) I will give children to be their princes.—The words may point obliquely to Ahaz, who had ascended the throne at the age of twenty (II Chron. 28:1). Manasseh was but twelve when he became king; Josiah but eight (II Chron. 33:1; 34:1). In an Eastern monarchy the rule of a young king, rash and without experience, guided by counselors like himself, was naturally regarded as the greatest of evils (see verse 12), and the history of Rehoboam had impressed this truth on the mind of every Israelite. (Comp. Eccles. 10:16.)

(6, 7) Disorder (verse 5) was followed by destitution. The elder brother would gladly transfer to the younger the responsibilities of the first-born, though he has but a ruined tenement to give him. And instead of accepting what most men would have coveted (Gen. 25:31-33), the younger brother rejects it. He has enough bread and clothing for himself, and no more. It is not for him to bind up the wounds of others, or to try to introduce law where all is lawlessness. A supreme selfishness asserts itself in his answer.

(16-23) From the princes that worked evil (verses 12-15), Isaiah turns to their wives, sisters, concubines, who were showing themselves degenerate daughters of Sarah and Rebecca. Comp. 32:9-12, but this is without a parallel in the minuteness of its detail. It is as though the prophet had gone into the boudoir of one of the leaders of the fashions of Jerusalem and taken an inventory of what he found there. Twenty-one distinct articles are mentioned. Their names for the most part appear to have a foreign stamp on them. Then, as at other times, luxury imported its novelties, and the women of Judah took up the fashions of those of Tyre or Damascus or Philistia.

Verses 24-26 describe the terrible contrast of the day of destruction that is coming on all this refined luxury.

4

(1) And in that day seven women ...—The chapter division wrongly separates this verse from the foregoing. It comes as the climax of the chastisement of the daughters of Zion, as the companion picture to 3:6. As men sought eagerly, yet in vain, a protector, so women should seek for a husband. The picture is of a land depopulated by war, and so making polygamy natural.

To take away our reproach.—The reproach is that of being childless. From the Jewish standpoint that was not only the great sorrow, but also the great shame, of womanhood, implying, as men thought, a sin of which it was the chastisement (Gen. 30:23; I Sam. 1:6; Luke 1:25).

(2) In that day ...—The dark picture of punishment is relieved by a vision of Messianic glory, like that of 2:1-4. The "day" is, as in 3:18, the time of Jehovah's judgments.

The branch of the Lord ...—Here we have the first distinct prophecy in Isaiah of a personal Messiah (comp. 11:1). He is the "Branch of Jehovah," raised up by Him, accepted by Him. And the appearance of that Branch has as its accompaniment the restoration of outward fertility. That thought Isaiah had inherited from Ps. 72:17; Hos. 2:21, 22; Joel 3:18; Amos 9:13. He transmitted it to Ezek. 34:27; Zech. 9:16, 17. The prophecy of the Branch here comes after a picture of desolation. The thought seems applied by our Lord to Himself in John 12:24.

(3) He that is left in Zion ...—The prophet turns from the Jerusalem that then was, with the hypocrisies and crimes of the men and the harlot fashions of its women, to the vision of a new Jerusalem, which shall realize the ideal of Pss. 15 and 24.

(4) When the Lord shall have washed away the filth ...—This serves as the connecting link with 3:16-24. Jehovah will wash away, as with the baptism of repentance, the moral uncleanness that lay

beneath their outward show of beauty. The "blood of Jerusalem," in the next clause, has a wide range of meaning, from the "murders" of 1:15, 21 to the Moloch sacrifices in which the women had borne a conspicuous part (Ps. 106:38; Isa. 57:5; Ezek. 22:2, 3).

(5) See Exod. 13:21; Num. 9:15; 10:34; 14:14. In that Presence there would be safety and peace. The image is a favorite one with Isaiah, possibly as connected with the vision of 6:4, for God's protection of His people. On "tabernacle" in verse 6, comp. Pss. 27:5; 31:20.

5

(1) Now will I sing to my wellbeloved.—Literally, "Now let me sing." The chapter bears every mark of being a distinct composition, perhaps the most elaborately finished in the whole of Isaiah. The parable with which it opens has for us the interest of having obviously supplied a starting point for a later prophet (Jer. 2:21), and for our Lord's teaching in the like parable of Matt. 21:33-41. Here, however, there is the distinctive touch of the irony of the opening verse. The prophet presents himself, as it were, in the character of a minstrel, ready to sing to his hearers one of the love songs in which their culture delighted (Amos 6:5.) In its language and rhythm it reminds us of the Song of Solomon, and may suggest how early that poem lent itself to a mystical interpretation. One might almost conjecture that the prophet appeared with harp or pipe in hand. The frequency of such hymns (chaps. 12, 25; 26:1-6) shows, at any rate, that the prophet had received the training of a psalmist.

The "beloved" is purposely not named, but appears afterward as none other than Jehovah. The "fruitful hill" was Canaan as a whole, with a special reference to Judah and Jerusalem.

(2) In the "fence" we may recognize the law and institutions of Israel which kept it as a separate people (Eph. 2:14); in the "stones" that were gathered out, the removal of the old idolatries that would have hindered the development of the nation's life; in the "tower" of the vineyard, the monarchy and throne of David, or the watchtower from which the prophets looked forth (Hab. 2:1; Isa. 21:5-8); in the "winepress," the temple in which the fruits of righteousness were to issue in the wine of joy and adoration (Zech. 9:17; Eph. 5:18). In the last clause of the verse the pleasant song suddenly changes its tone, and the "wild grapes" (sour and hard) are types of deeds of harsh and cruel injustice on which the prophet proceeds to dwell.

(3) And now, O inhabitants of Jerusalem.—"The song of the vineyard" comes to an end and becomes the text of a discourse in which Jehovah, as the "Beloved" of the song, speaks through the prophet. Those to whom the parable applies are invited, as David was by Nathan, to pass an unconscious judgment on themselves. (Comp. Matt. 21:40, 41.)

(5) I will take away the hedge . . . —This involved the throwing open of the vineyard to be as grazing land which all the wild bulls of Bashan—**i.e.**, all the enemies of Zion—might trample. The interpretation of the parable implies that there was to be the obliteration, at least for some time and in some measure, of the distinctness and independence of the nation's life. (Comp. Hos. 3:4.)

(6) There shall come up briers and thorns. —The picture of desolation is still part of a parable. These are the base and unworthy who take the place of the true leaders of the people (Judg. 9:7-15). The absence of the pruning and the digging answers to the withdrawal of the means of moral and spiritual culture (John 15:2; Luke 13:8). The command given to the clouds (comp. II Sam. 1:21) implies the cessation of all gracious spiritual influences.

(8) Woe unto them that join house to house.—The series of "woes" which follows has no precedent in the teaching of earlier prophets. The form of Luke 6:24-26 seems based upon it. For the original ideas of order now sought to be violated, see Lev. 25:13; 27:24; Num. 27:1-11; 33:54; Deut. 19:14; 27:17; Neh. 5:5.

(9) The sentence by God that follows is one of righteous retribution: there shall be no profit or permanence in the property thus unjustly gained.

(13) My people are gone into captivity.— The great captivity of Judah lay as yet far off, but the prophet may be speaking of it as already present in his vision of the future. Probably, however, the disastrous wars of Ahaz had involved many captures of the kind referred to (II Chron. 28:5, 8, 17, 18).

(14) Therefore hell hath enlarged herself.— The Hebrew **Sheol**, or **Hades**, like "hell" itself in its original meaning, expressed not a place of torment, but the vast shadow-world of death, thought of as being below the earth (Pss. 16:10; 49:14). Here, as elsewhere (Jonah 2:2; Prov. 1:12; 30:16), it is half-personified, as Hades and Death are in Rev. 6:8; 20:13, 14. In that unseen world there were, in the later belief of Judaism, the two regions of Gehenna and of Eden or Paradise. What the prophet says is that all the pomp and glory of the rich oppressors are on their way to that inevitable doom.

(26) From the end of the earth.—The words point to the Assyrians, the Euphrates being the boundary of Isaiah's political geography.

(27-29) None shall be weary . . . —The three verses paint the progress of the invading army. Unresting, unhasting, in perfect order, they march onward. The light-armed troops are there, probably the Medes and Elamites in the Assyrian army (13:18). The chariots of the Assyrians themselves are there, sweeping onward like a tempest.

6

(1) In the year that king Uzziah died.— The chapter gives us the narrative of the solemn call of Isaiah to the office of a prophet. It does not follow that it was written at that time, and we may even believe that, if the prophet were the editor of his own discourses, he may have designedly placed the narrative in this position that men might see what he himself saw, that all that was found in the preceding chapters was but the development of what he had then heard, and yet, at the same time, a representation of the evils which made the judgments he was commissioned to declare necessary.

The date is obviously given as important, and we are led to connect it with the crisis in the prophet's life of which it tells. He had lived through the last twenty years or so of Uzziah's reign. There was the show of outward material prosperity; there was the reality of much inward corruption. The king who had profaned the holiness of the Temple had either just died or was dragging out the dregs of his leprous life in seclusion (II Chron. 26:21). The question as to what was to be the future of his people must have been much in the prophet's thoughts. The earthquake that had terrified Jerusalem had left on his mind a vague sense of impending judgment. It is significant that Isaiah's first work as a writer was to write the history of Uzziah's reign (II Chron. 26:22).

I saw also the Lord sitting upon a throne.—Isaiah had found himself in the court of the Temple, probably in that of the priests. Suddenly he passes into a state of ecstatic trance, and as though the veil of the Temple was withdrawn, he saw the vision of the glory of the Lord. The King of kings was seated on His throne, and on the right hand and on the left were the angel-armies of the host of heaven, chanting their hymns of praise. (Comp. Exod. 24:10; Amos 9:1.)

(2) Above it stood the seraphims . . . — Here only the seraphim are mentioned as part of the host of heaven. The "living creatures" of Rev. 4:7, 8, seem to unite the forms of the cherubim of Ezek. 1:5-11 with the six wings of the seraphim of this passage. Symbolically the seraphim would seem to be as transfigured cherubim, representing the "flaming fire" of the lightning, as the latter did the storm-winds and other elemental forces of nature (Ps. 104:4).

(3) The threefold repetition—the **Trisagion**—may represent either the mode of utterance, first antiphonal, and then in full chorus, or the Hebrew idiom of the emphasis of a threefold iteration (Jer. 7:4; 22:29). Viewed from the standpoint of a later revelation, many have naturally seen in it an allusive reference to the glory of Jehovah in the past, the present, and the future, or even a faint foreshadowing of the Trinity of Persons in the Unity of the Godhead. Historically we cannot separate it from the name of the Holy One of Israel, which with "the Lord of hosts" was afterward so prominent in Isaiah's teaching.

(5) Then said I, Woe is me!—The cry of the prophet expresses the normal result of man's consciousness of contact with God. (See Exod. 3:6; Job 42:5-6; Luke 5:8.) Man at such a time feels his nothingness in the presence of the Eternal, his guilt in the presence of the All-holy.

I am a man of unclean lips.—The dominant thought is that his lips have been defiled by past sins of speech. How can he join in the praises of the seraphim with those lips from which have so often come bitter and hasty words, formal and ceremonial prayers? (Comp. James 3:2, 9). He finds no comfort in the thought that others are as bad as he is, that he "dwells in the midst of a people of unclean lips." Were it otherwise, there might be some hope that influence from without might work his purification. As it is, he and his people seem certain to sink into the abyss. To

"have seen the King, the Lord of hosts," was in such a case simply overwhelming.

(6, 7) The symbolism is deep in meaning if we think of the seraph as descending from the height above the throne to the altar of incense, near which Isaiah actually stood. It was from that altar that the glowing charcoal was taken. What had seemed part of the material of a formal worship became quickened with a living power. The symbol became sacramental. (See Ps. 51:7.) Fire is throughout the Bible the symbol at once of the wrath and the love of God, destroying the evil and purifying the good. Pardon and purity are the conditions alike of the prophet's work and of the completeness of his own spiritual life.

(8) Whom shall I send, and who will go for us?—The union of the singular and plural in the same sentence is significant. The latter does not admit of being explained as a **pluralis majestatis**. Here, as elsewhere (e.g., Gen. 1:26; 11:7), Jehovah is represented as a king in council. Christian thought has scarcely erred in believing that the words were as a dim foreshadowing of the truth, afterward to be revealed, of a plurality within the Unity. The question reveals to the prophet that there is a work to be done for Jehovah, that He needs an instrument for that work. It is implied that no angel out of the whole host, no man out of the whole nation, offers to undertake it. The prophet, with the ardor for work which follows on the sense of pardon, volunteers for it before he knows what it is. He reaches in one moment the supreme height of faith (Heb. 11:8).

(11) Lord, how long?—The prophet asks the question which is ever on the lips of those who are brought face to face with the problems of the world, with the great mystery of evil, sin permitted to work out fresh evil as its punishment, and yet remaining evil (verses 9, 10). See Dan. 8:13; Rev. 6:10.

(12) And the Lord have removed men far away.—The words point to the policy of deportation adopted by the Assyrian kings. From the first hour of Isaiah's call the thought of an exile and a return from exile was the keynote of his teaching, and of that thought thus given in germ, his whole afterwork was but a development, the horizon of his vision expanding and taking in the form of another empire than the Assyrian as the instrument of punishment.

(13) But yet in it shall be a tenth . . . —What the prophet is led to expect is a series of successive chastisements sifting the people, till the remnant of the chosen ones alone is left. (Comp. Ezek. 5:12; Zech. 13:8, 9.) The "tenth" is taken (Lev. 27:30) for an ideally consecrated portion.

In the further illustration, the tree might be stripped of its leaves, its branches lopped off, and nothing but the stump left; but from that seemingly dead and decayed stock, pruned by the chastisements of God, a young shoot should spring, holy, as consecrated to Jehovah, and carry on the continuity of the nation's life. In 10:33-11:1 the same image is especially applied to the house of David, and becomes, therefore, essentially Messianic.

7

(1) It came to pass in the days of Ahaz.— The whole reign of Jotham comes between chaps. 6 and 7. The work of the prophet now carries him into the main current of history, as recorded in II Kings 15, 16; II Chron. 28, and in Assyrian inscriptions. The facts to be borne in mind are: (1) that the kingdom of Israel under Menaham had already become tributary to Assyria (II Kings 15:19, 20); (2) that the object of the alliance between Pekah, a bold and ambitious usurper, and Rezin, was to organize a resistance against Assyria, such as that in which Uzziah had taken part, that first Jotham (II Kings 15:37), and then Ahaz, apparently refused to join the confederacy, and that the object of the attack of the allied kings was either to force Ahaz to join, or else to depose him, bring the dynasty of David to a close, and set a follower of their own, probably a Syrian, on the throne of Judah.

But could not prevail against it.—The words obviously refer to a special stage in the campaign. The king of Syria seems to have been the leading spirit of the confederacy. II Chron. 28:5-15 represents Judah as having sustained a great and almost overwhelming defeat. Jerusalem, however, though besieged (II Kings 16:5), was not absolutely taken.

(3) Go forth now to meet Ahaz...—At this crisis the prophet finds the king halting between two opinions. He is making a show of resistance, but in reality he is not depending either on the protection of Jehovah or the courage of his people, but on a plan of his own. Why should he not continue to pay tribute to Assyria, as Uzziah and Menahem (II Kings 15:19) had done, and write to

Tiglath-pileser to attack the territories of the invading kings, as he actually did at a later stage in the war (II Kings 15:29)?

Thou and Shear-jashub thy son.— Assuming chap. 6 to give the first revelation of the idea of the "remnant," it would follow that the birth of the son whose name **(remnant returns**—i.e., "is converted") embodied a prophecy must have followed on that revelation, and he was probably, therefore, at the time a stripling of sixteen or eighteen. The mother of his children was herself a prophetess, sharing his hopes and fears (8:3, 18; comp. Hos. 1, 2).

(8) The prediction of the failure of the alliance is emphasized. Each city, Damascus and Samaria, should continue to be what it was, the head of a comparatively weak kingdom, and should not be aggrandized by the conquest of Judah and Jerusalem. There is an implied comparison of the two hostile cities and their kings with Jerusalem and its supreme King, Jehovah. We have here first direct chronological prediction in the prophet's utterances. Others follow in 16:14; 17:1; 21:6; 23:1. Reckoning from 736 B.C. as the probable date of the prophecy, the sixty-five years bring us to 671 B.C. At that date Assyrian inscriptions show that Assurbanipal, the "Asnapper" of Ezra 4:2-10, co-regent with his father Essarhaddon, had carried off the last remnant of the people of Samaria and peopled it with an alien race. This completed the work which had been begun by Shalmaneser and Sargon (II Kings 17:6). Ephraim then was no more a people.

(10) Ask thee a sign... —The method of giving a sign by predicting something in the near future as a pledge for predictions that belong to a more remote time is especially characteristic of Isaiah. (Comp. 37:30; 38:7.)

(12) I will not ask... —That which lay beneath this show of humble trust was simply self-will and utter lack of faith. Ahaz had already made up his mind to the Assyrian alliance, against which he knew Isaiah was certain to protest. The fact that the words that follow are spoken to the whole house of David may, perhaps, imply that the older members of the royal family were encouraging the king in his Assyrian projects, and had, perhaps, suggested his hypocritical answer.

(14) Behold, a virgin shall conceive, and bear a son... —Better, "behold, the young woman shall conceive." The noun has the definite article in the Hebrew, and the word, though commonly used of the unmarried, strictly speaking denotes rather one who has arrived at marriageable age. But Matt. 1:23 decides the entire meaning of the Immanuel prophecy (see also LXX). The prophet may have seen clearly, and with a full consciousness of its meaning, the history of the Incarnation and the marvel of the travail-pangs of the virgin mother. The vision of the future Christ thus presented to his mind colors all his afterthoughts and forms the basis of his whole work. The article emphasizes the definiteness of his visions. He sees "**the** virgin mother" of the far-off future. And the prophet learns to connect the vision with the history of his own time. The growth of that Christ-child in the far-off future serves as a measure of time for the events that were passing, or about to pass, within the horizon of his earthly vision. Before the end of an interval not longer than that which separates youth from manhood, the Syro-Ephraimitic confederacy should be broken up. No other such allusion is found in Isaiah, nor in the prophets that follow him; the Jewish interpreters never include this among their notes of the Christ. It is indeed one of the strongest arguments for the historical, non-mythical character of the series of events in Matt. 1 and Luke 1 and 2 that they were contrary to prevailing expectation.

See notes on 9:6; 11:1.

(**16**) **For before the child shall know...** —The words imply the age of approaching manhood and predict the downfall of Pekah and Rezin, as the longer period of verse 8 predicted the entire downfall and annihilation of one of the two kingdoms which they represented.

The land that thou abhorrest.—The prediction was fulfilled in the siege of Samaria by Shalmaneser and its capture by Sargon (II Kings 16:9; 17:6), a fulfillment all the more remarkable in that it was preceded by what seemed an almost decisive victory over Judah (II Chron. 28:5-15), of which the prophet makes no mention.

(**17**) **The Lord shall bring upon thee...** —The prophet's language shows that he reads the secret thoughts of the king's heart. He was bent on calling in the help of the king of Assyria. Isaiah warns him that by doing this he is bringing on himself a more formidable invasion than that of Syria and Ephraim, worse than any that had been known since the separation of the two kingdoms. (See II Chron. 28:19, 20.) This was but the precursor of the great invasions under Sargon and Sennacherib.

(**18**) See Exod. 8:24; Deut. 1:44; Ps. 118:12. The mention of Egypt indicates that some of the king's counselors were then, as afterward (18:2; 31:1), planning an Egyptian alliance, as others were relying on that with Assyria. The prophet tells them that each is fraught with danger. No help and much evil would come from such plans. Consistent in his policy from first to last, the one counsel he gives is that men should practice righteousness and wait upon the Lord.

(**20**) **Shall the Lord shave with a razor that is hired.**—The term "hired" applies to the tribute which Ahaz was about to pay to Tiglath-pileser. He thought that he was securing an ally; he was but hiring a razor that should sweep away all the signs of strength, and leave him an open shame and scorn to all who looked on him (II Sam. 10:4). From head to foot, not sparing even the beard, to maltreat which was the last extreme of Oriental outrage, he and his kingdom should be laid bare to his enemies.

8

(**1**) **Moreover the Lord said unto me...** —The prophecy that follows was clearly separated by an interval of some kind, probably about a year, from that in chap. 7. In the meantime much that had happened seemed to cast discredit on the prophet's words. The child that was the type of the greater Immanuel had been born, but there were no signs as yet of the downfall of the northern kingdom. The attack of Rezin and Pekah, though Jerusalem had not been taken, had inflicted an almost irreparable blow on the kingdom of Judah. (See II Kings 16:6; II Chron. 18:5, 15-17.) If such were the state of things when the word of the Lord came to Isaiah, was he to recant and confess that he had erred? Far different than that. He was to repeat all that he had said, more definitely, more demonstratively than ever.

Take thee a great roll...—The writings of the prophet were commonly written on papyrus and placed in the hands of his disciples to be read aloud. For private and less permanent messages men used small wooden tablets smeared with wax, on which they wrote with an iron stylus. (Comp. Job 19:24; Isa. 30:8.) Here the tablet was to be large, and the writing was to be with a pen such as the common workmen used for sign boards, that might fix the gaze of the careless passer-by (Hab. 2:2), and on that tablet,

as though it were the heading of a proclamation or dedication, he was to write TO
MAHER-SHALAL-HASH-BAZ. That mysterious name, which we may render "Speed-
plunder, haste-spoil," was, for at least nine
months, to be the enigma of Jerusalem.

(4) Here was another sign like that of
7:14-16. The two witnesses of verse 2 were
probably summoned to the circumcision
and naming of the child, and the mysterious
name at which all Jerusalem had gazed with
wonder was given to the newborn infant.
Within a year of its birth, the spoils of the
two capitals of the kings of the confederate
armies should be carried to the king of
Assyria. The conclusion of the period thus
defined would coincide more or less closely
with the longer period assigned at an earlier
date (7:16). Historically the trans-Jordanic
region and Damascus fell before Tiglath-
pileser, and Samaria, besieged by Shalmaneser, before his successor Sargon (II
Kings 15:29; 16:9; 17:6).

(6-8) What line was the prophet to take?
Was he to take the side of the king, or that
of his rebellious subjects who were ready to
sacrifice their independence? As it is, he
sides with neither, and has a warning for
each. Each is running blindly into destruction. The armies of Assyria are like a river
in flood; the outspread waters on either side
of the main stream are like the expanded
wings of a great bird sweeping down on its
prey. The prophet could hardly have
blamed the people of Syria and Israel for
following their own kings; but it was for
him a strange and monstrous thing that
Judah should follow their example. We
must remember, too, that in spite of the
weakness and wickedness of Ahaz, the
prophet's hopes rested on the house of David (11:1), and that Hezekiah was already
old enough to justify that hope.

(14) But for a stone of stumbling and for
a rock of offence... —See Matt. 21:44;
Rom. 9:33; I Pet. 2:8. To enter into fellowship with Jehovah is to enter into the sanctuary. He who stands on the stone which
forms the threshold of that sanctuary has
gained an asylum. But to do that requires
the clear vision of faith. He who walks
blindly, without faith, may stumble on that
very stone of the threshold, and what was
safety and life for others might for him
bring pain and shame. The expression "both
the houses of Israel" implies a hope of the
restored unity of the nation's life, in spite of
their self-chosen blindness.

(17) And I will wait upon the Lord, that

hideth his face... —The prophet enforces
precept by example. He has learned to
conquer the feverish desire to know the
future, which led men to trust in soothsay-
ers and diviners, and from which even his
own disciples were not altogether exempt.
He is content to "wait," even though Jehovah "hide his face," though predictions seem
to fail and all seems dark and hopeless.
Seeking God, the prophet says (verse 19), is
the only true pathway to such knowledge as
is good for man.

(18) Behold, I and the children whom the
Lord hath given me... —In the mystic
significance of his own name (Isaiah—
"Salvation of Jehovah") and of the names of
his sons ("Remnant shall return," and
"Speed-plunder, Haste-spoil"), possibly also
in that of Immanuel, the prophet finds a
sufficient revelation of the future. Each was
a nomen et omen. (See Heb. 2:13, where it
is noticeable how little the writer of that
epistle cared in this and other quotations
for the original meaning of the words as
determined by the context.)

(20) To the law and to the testimony.—
The words here mean, as in verse 16, the
"word of Jehovah," spoken to the prophet
himself, the revelation which had come to
him with such an intensity of power.

9

(1) Nevertheless the dimness... —It is
obvious that what follows forms part of the
same prophetic utterance as chap. 8. The
prophet had seen in the closing verses there
the extreme point of misery. But the future
should be in striking contrast with the past.
The lands of Zebulun and Naphtali, the
region afterward known as the Upper and
Lower Galilee, had been laid waste and
spoiled by Tiglath-pileser (II Kings 15:29).
That same region, described by the prophet
in different terms (the former representing
the tribal divisions, the latter the geographical) is hereafter to be the scene of a glory
greater than Israel had ever known before.

Beyond Jordan refers to the Perea of
later geography, which included the regions
of Gilead and Bashan, the old kingdoms of
Moab and Ammon, the tribes of Reuben,
Gad, and half the tribe of Manasseh. These
also had suffered from the ravages of the
Assyrian armies under Pul (I Chron. 5:26).

(2) The people that walked in
darkness... —See 8:21, 22. The prophet
sees in his vision a light shining on the

505

forlorn and weary wanderers. Now there breaks in the dawn of a glorious day. Historically the return of some of the inhabitants of that region to their allegiance to Jehovah and the house of David (II Chron. 30:11, 13) may have been the starting point of the prophet's hopes. The words are quoted in Matthew 4:15, 16 in connection with our Lord's ministry in Galilee, perhaps with His being "of Nazareth," which was in the tribe of Zebulun. The context shows that the prophet was thinking of Assyrian invasions, and the defeat of Assyrian armies, of a nation growing strong in numbers and prosperity. In this, as in other cases, the Evangelist adapts the words of prophecy to a further meaning than that which apparently was in the mind of the writer, and interprets them by his own experience.

(6) For unto us a child is born.—The picture of a kingdom of peace could not be complete without the manifestation of a king. In the description of that king Isaiah is led to use words which cannot find a complete fulfillment in any child of man. His condition was one more ecstatic and therefore more apocalyptic than before, and there flashes on him, as it were, the thought that the future deliverer of Israel must bear a name that should be above every name that men had before honored. And yet here also there was a law of continuity, and the form of the prediction was developed from the materials supplied by earlier prophets. In Ps. 110 he had found the thought of the king-priest after the order of Melchizedek, whom Jehovah addressed as Adonai. In Ps. 2, though it did not foretell an actual incarnation, the anointed King was addressed by Jehovah as His Son. The throne of that righteous king was a throne of God (Ps. 45:6). Nor had the prophet's personal experience been less fruitfully suggestive. He had given his own children mysterious names. That of the earthly Immanuel, as the prophet brooded over it, might well lead on to the thought of One who should, in a yet higher sense than as being the pledge of divine protection, be as "God with us."

That which follows is given not as many names, but one. We have four elements of the compound name: (1) Wonderful-Counsellor (2) God-the-Mighty-One (3) Father of Eternity (4) Prince of Peace. Each couplet of the name has its special significance: (1) The first embodies the thought of the wisdom of the future Messiah. (2) The word for "God" is not Elohim, but **El**, which is never used by Isaiah, or any other Old Testament writer, in any

506

lower sense than that of absolute deity, and which had been specially brought before the prophet's thoughts in the name Immanuel. (3) Isaiah uses the name of "Father" because none other expressed so well the true idea of loving and protecting government. And if the kingdom were to be "for ever and ever," then in some very real sense he would be, in that attribute of Fatherly government, a sharer in the eternity of Jehovah. (4) The prophet clings, as all prophets before him had done, to the thought that peace, and not war, belonged to the ideal Kingdom of the Messiah. (See Mic. 5:5.) It is remarkable, looking to the grandeur of the prophecy, and its apparently direct testimony to the true nature of the Christ, that it is nowhere cited in the New Testament as fulfilled in Him (comp. Luke 1:32, 33).

(8) The vision of the glory of the far-off king comes to an end, and the prophet returns to the more immediate surroundings of his time. The "word" which Jehovah sends is the prophetic message that follows. The terms "Jacob" and "Israel" stand practically for the Kingdom of Judah as the true representative of Israel, the apostate Kingdom of the Ten Tribes being no longer worthy of the name, and therefore described here, as in 7:5, 8, 17 simply as Ephraim. The occasion of the prophecy is given in verse 9. Pekah, the king of Ephraim, was still confident in his strength, and in spite of his partial failure, and the defeat of his ally (II Kings 16:9), derided the prophet's prediction.

(11) Syria, after the conquest by the Assyrian king (II Kings 16:9), apparently was compelled to take part in a campaign against Samaria. The Philistines were enemies to Judah (II Chron. 28:18), but their hostilities extended to the northern kingdom also.

(15) The ancient and honourable ... — These, the prophet seems to say, were the true leaders of the people. The ideal work of the prophet was, indeed, that of a teacher who was to lead even them; and to Isaiah, as to Jeremiah, there was no class so contemptible and base as that of spiritual guides whose policy was that of a time-serving selfishness.

(19, 20) Ephraim and Manasseh were devouring "the flesh of their own arm" when they allowed their old tribal jealousies (Judg. 8:1; 12:1-4; II Sam. 19:43) to break up the unity of the nation. The only power of union that showed itself in the northern kingdom was to perpetuate the great schism in which it had its origin. The idea that

Israel as such was a nation was forgotten. Ephraim and Manasseh could join in a common expedition against Judah when they could join in nothing else.

10

Verses 1-4 continue the discourse of chap. 9. With verse 5 a new section begins, and is carried on to 12:6, which deals, for the first time in the collection of Isaiah's writings, exclusively with Assyria, and is followed in its turn by utterances that deal with Babylon and other nations.

(5) **O Assyrian.**—Assyria had been named in connection with the Syro-Ephraim alliance against Judah (7:17-20, 8:7, 8). Some years had passed since the date of the alliance and invasion. Tiglath-pileser had taken Damascus and reduced Samaria to submission. Pekah and Ahaz had met at Damascus to do homage to their common suzerain. In 727 B.C. Shalmaneser succeeded to the throne of Assyria, and began the conquest of Samaria and the deportation of the Ten Tribes in 722 B.C. (II Kings 17:3-6). On his death in 721 B.C., the throne was seized by Sargon, who had been his commander-in-chief (20:1). It was probably to this king, exulting in his triumphs and threatening an attack on Judah, and not to his son Sennacherib, who succeeded him 704 B.C., that the prophet now addressed himself. The great king was but an instrument working out the divine intent. (Comp. Jer. 51:20.)

(10) **As my hand hath found the kingdoms of the idols.**—It is quite in character with the Assyrian inscriptions that Sargon should ascribe his victories (verses 8, 9) to Asshur as the Supreme God, before whose sovereignty all local deities were compelled to bow. To the Assyrian king the name of Jehovah would represent a deity whose power was to be measured by the greatness of the nation that worshiped Him, and inferior, therefore, to the gods of Carchemish or Hamath. The worship of Baal, Moloch, and other deities, in both Israel and Judah, had of course tended to strengthen this estimate. (Comp. 36:18, 19.)

(11) **Shall I not, as I have done . . .** —The verse (see also verses 12-15) gives the occasion of Isaiah's utterance. Sargon was threatening Jerusalem, probably in the early years of Hezekiah's reign. The inscriptions show, as does also 20:1, that he made war against Philistia and besieged Ashdod.

(16) The overthrow of the Assyrian is painted in the twofold imagery of famine and of fire. The fire that burns the glory of the king is explained in the next verse as the wrath of Jehovah. The divine glory, which is a consuming fire (27:4) to the enemies of Israel, is to Israel itself as the very light of life.

(21) **The remnant shall return . . .** —The form of the words "Shear-jashub") shows that the prophet had the "Immanuel" promise in his thoughts, just as "the mighty God" (the same word as in 9:6) must have reminded men of the Child who was to bear that name in the age to come. (Comp. II Chron. 30:6.)

(22) **Though thy people Israel be as the sand of the sea.**—The word "remnant" has, however, its aspect of severity as well as of promise. Men are not to expect that they, the hypocrites and evil-doers, shall escape their punishment. The promise of restoration is for the remnant only. (Comp. Rom. 9:27, 28).

(24) **O my people . . . be not afraid of the Assyrian.**—The practical conclusion of all that has been said is that the people should not give way to panic as they had done in the days of Ahaz (7:2), but should abide the march of Sargon, or his successor, with the tranquillity of faith.

(28) **He is come to Aiath . . .** —A new section begins here, connected with the former by unity of subject, both referring to Sargon's invasion of Judah. That such an invasion took place at or about the time of that King's attack on Ashdod (20:1) the inscriptions leave no doubt. There is nothing in the passage itself to determine whether verses 28-32 are predictive or historical, or when they were first uttered. Assuming that the Messianic prophecy of chap. 11 is in close connection with them, it seems most probable that now, as in the earlier attack of Pekah and Rezin (chap. 7), as in the later invasion of Sennacherib (chap. 37), the bright vision of the future came to sustain the people when they were at their lowest point of depression. This would obviously be when Sargon's armies were actually encamped around the city, when they had reached the last halting place of the itinerary which Isaiah traces out. Aiath is probably identical with the Ai of Josh. 7:2, the Aija of Neh. 11:31, in the tribe of Benjamin, not far from Bethel. Nob is memorable as having been one of the resting places of the Tabernacle in the time of Saul (I Sam. 21:1), obviously a position that

507

commanded Jerusalem. So far shalt thou go, the prophet says to Sargon (verses 33, 34), as he said afterward to Sennacherib (37:28-32), and no farther.

11

(1) There shall come forth a rod out of the stem of Jesse . . .—We enter on another great Messianic prophecy developing that of 9:6, 7. More specifically than before the true King is named as springing from the house of David, and His reign is painted as the return of a golden age. The figure with which the section opens is carried on from the close of chap. 10. The cedar of Lebanon, the symbol of the Assyrian power, was to be cut down, and its fall was irretrievable. But the oak, the symbol of Israel, and of the monarchy of the house of David (6:13), had a life remaining in it after it had been cut down, and the rod that was to spring from its roots should flourish once again in greater glory than before. (Comp. (Ezek. 17:22.) In the Branch (**netzer**) we have the word which suggested Matthew's generalization of the prophecies of this type in the words, "He shall be called a Nazarene" (see Matt. 2:23), and which corresponds, in idea though not in words, to the great prophecies which speak of the Messiah as the Branch (**Zemach**) in Jer. 23:5; Zech. 3:8. (Comp. Mic. 5:2.) It is obvious here, as in 9:6, 7, that Isaiah is not speaking of Hezekiah as the actual sovereign of Judah, or of any prince then within the horizon of his earthly vision, though we may legitimately think of the virtues of that king as having been welcomed by him as a pledge and earnest of the ideal future.

The copious use of the vocabulary of the Book of Proverbs in the verses that follow is interesting as showing the part which that book played in the prophet's education.

(6-8) It is significant of the prophet's sympathy with the animal world that he thinks of that also as sharing in the blessings of redemption. (Comp. Rom. 8:21.) The words may have a literal fulfillment. It may be, however, that each form of brute cruelty was to the prophet's mind the symbol of a human evil, and the imagery admits, therefore, of an allegorical rather than a literal interpretation.

(9) The earth shall be full of the knowledge of the Lord.—This was for the prophet the crown and consummation of the work

of redemption. More than all removal of physical evil, he thought of a victory over moral and spiritual darkness. As it is, in the existing order of the world, few fear God; still fewer know Him as He should be known. But not so in that new earth. Hence the transition was natural to the prophecies which speak at once of the restoration of Israel and the ingathering of the heathen. It should be remembered that in Hos. 3:5; Joel 2:28; 3:17, similar prophecies had preceded Isaiah's utterance. In Hab. 2:14 it is all but verbally reproduced.

(10) In that day there shall be a root of Jesse . . . —The "root," as in 53:2; Deut. 29:18, is the same as the "rod" and "branch" growing from the root in verse 1. The new shoot of the fallen tree of Jesse is to grow up like a stately palm, seen afar off upon the heights of the "holy mountain," a signal around which the distant nations might rally as their center. (See Rev. 5:5; 22:16.)

(11) The Lord shall set his hand again the second time . . . —The "first" time, implied in the "second," was obviously that of the Exodus. The list of countries that follows rests in part on the fact of a dispersion already begun, as in II Kings 15:29; 17:6; Isa. 43:5, 6, and partly on the prophet's prevision of the coming years.

(13) The envy also of Ephraim shall depart . . . —The prophet's vision of the future would not have been complete if national unity had not been included in it. In the times of the Christ the sense of unity should be stronger than the old hostilities. The prophet's hope connects itself with Hezekiah's efforts after a restored unity (II Chron. 30:1-12).

(14) The whole verse is singularly characteristic of knowledge. The seer has had revealed to him the glory of the Messianic kingdom as a restored Eden, full of knowledge of Jehovah, the Gentiles seeking light and salvation from it. Suddenly he blends this with anticipations that belong to the feelings and complications of his own time. He sees Philistines, Moabites, Ammonites, in that far future. They will be then, as they were in his own times, the persistent foes of Israel (comp. Zeph. 2:7-9), but will be, at last, subdued.

(16) And there shall be an highway for the remnant . . . —The "highway" is the raised embanked road made by Eastern kings for the march of their armies. Such a road the prophet sees in his vision (see 40:3), stretching across the great plains of

Mesopotamia for the return of Israel. It was to be for that "second time" of restoration what the passage of the Red Sea had been for the "first time" of the Exodus, for the exiles in Assyria what another passage of the Egyptian sea was to be for those in Egypt.

12

The prophet becomes the psalmist of the new Exodus, and the hymn that follows is based upon the type of that in Exod. 15. Confession must be blended with thanksgiving. The fact that the prophet appears as a psalmist was a natural result of the training of the schools of the prophets (see 1 Sam. 19:20), possibly also of his familiarity with the Temple service as a priest or Levite. The group of psalms ascribed to the sons of Korah presents so many parallelisms to the writings of Isaiah, and so obviously belongs to the same period, that we may reasonably think of him as having been associated with that goodly company.

(3) Therefore with joy shall ye draw water . . . —In the later ritual of the Feast of Tabernacles, the priests went in solemn procession to the Pool of Siloam, filled a golden vase with water, carried it to the Temple, and poured it out on the western side of the altar of burnt offering, while the people chanted the great Hallel (Hymn of Praise) of Pss. 113-118. (See note on John 7:37.) If we may assume that this represented the ritual of the monarchy, we may reasonably infer that the words of Isaiah pointed to it.

(6) Great is the Holy One of Israel . . . —The hymn ends with the divine name which is characteristic of Isaiah. The presence of the Holy One was to be a joy and blessing to the remnant who were worthy of their calling. With this hymn the whole of what has been called the Immanuel volume of Isaiah's prophecies comes to its close.

13

(1) The burden of Babylon . . . —The title "burden," which is repeated in 15:1; 17:1; 19:1; 21:1; 22:1; 23:1, indicates that we have in this division a collection of prophetic utterances bearing upon the future of the surrounding nations, among which Babylon was naturally pre-eminent. The

thought cf a Babylonian, as of an Egyptian, alliance had, no doubt, presented itself to the minds of the statesmen of Judah as a means of staying the progress of Assyrian conquests. But the chapters now before us do not seem written with reference to such an alliance, and in 14:25 Babylon seems contemplated chiefly as the representative of the power of Assyria. It seems probable, accordingly, that the king of Babylon in 14:4 is to be identified with Sargon, the Assyrian king, who, the records tell us, took the title of "Vicar of the Gods in Babylon."

(3) I have commanded my sanctified ones . . . —The word is applied even to the fierce tribes of the future destroyers, as being appointed, or **consecrated**, by Jehovah for that special work. (Comp. Jer. 6:4; 22:7; 51:27.) So in the later prophecies Cyrus appears as "the anointed" of the Lord (45:1).

(17) Behold, I will stir up the Medes.— Among the descendants of Japheth, Aryan conquerors having mingled with an earlier Turanian race and differing in this respect from the Persians, the Medes had been recently brought before the prophet's notice by Shalmaneser's deportation of the Ten Tribes to the cities of the Medes (II Kings 17:6). In naming the Medes and not the Persians as the conquerors of Babylon, Isaiah was probably influenced by the greater prominence of the former, just as the Greeks spoke of the Medo-Persian monarchy under Darius and Xerxes. It is noticeable that they were destined to be the destroyers both of Nineveh and Babylon: of the first under Cyaxares, in alliance with Nabopolassar, and of the second under Cyrus the Persian and Darius the Mede (Dan. 5:31). Isaiah thus looks at Babylon as the representative of Assyrian rather than Chaldaean power, giving to them as its destroyers.

14

(1) For the Lord will have mercy on Jacob . . . —The words imply a prevision of the return of the Israelites from exile, and therefore of the Exile itself. The downfall of Babylon was certain, because without it the mercy of the Lord to Israel could not be manifested. The whole section is an anticipation of the great argument of chaps. 40-46.

(4) See notes on 13:1, 17 for "king of Babylon."

(8) Assurbanipal and other Assyrian kings boasted that wherever they conquered they cut down forests and left the land bare. (Comp. 37:24.) As the fir tree, the cedar, and the oak were the natural symbols of kingly rule (Jer. 22:7; Ezek. 17:3; 31:3), this devastation represented the triumph of the Chaldaean king over other princes. On his downfall, the trees on the mountain, the kings and chieftains in their palaces, would alike rejoice.

(10) Art thou also become weak as we?— The king of Babylon, the report of whose coming had roused awe and wonder in "hell" (**Sheol**, verse 9), is found to be weak as any other. With these words the vision of the spectral world ends, and verse 11 takes up the taunting song of the liberated Israelites, the language of which is, however, influenced by the imagery of the vision.

(12) How art thou fallen from heaven, O Lucifer, son of the morning!—The word for Lucifer is, literally, "the shining one," the planet Venus, the morning star, as the symbol of the Babylonian power, which was so closely identified with astrolatry. The use of the word in medieval Latin as a name of Satan, whose fall was supposed to be shadowed forth in this and the following verse, makes its selection here singularly unfortunate. It is the king of Babylon, and not the devil, who is addressed as Lucifer.

(13) In contrast with the **Sheol** into which the Chaldaean king had sunk, the prophet paints the heaven to which he sought to rise. The "mountain of assembly" is neither Jerusalem nor the Temple, but where the great gods in whom the king of Babylon ("in the sides of the north") believed sat in council.

(16) The picture before the prophet's eye is no longer the shadow-world of Hades, but the field of battle. Men look at the corpse of the mighty conqueror as it lies dishonored, bloody, and unburied. To lie thus unburied, "a prey to dogs and vultures" (Homer, **Iliad**, 1:4), was, as with the Homeric heroes, the shame of all shames.

(21) Prepare slaughter for his children.— The judgment of God falls necessarily on the last members of an evil and cruel dynasty. In this sense the sins of the fathers are visited on the children, while, in the eternal judgment which lies behind the veil, each soul stands on its own personal responsibility and may win pardon for itself (see Ezek. 18:4).

(23) The force of the image is that Babylon is to be swept away as men sweep away some foul rubbish from their house. The world is cleaner for its destruction. The solemn doom closes the "burden" of Babylon.

(24-27) The long "oracle" of Babylon is followed by a fragmentary prophecy against Assyria, possibly misplaced, possibly added by way of proof, that the word of the Lord of Hosts would be fulfilled on Babylon, as it had been on Assyria, with which, indeed, Babylon was perhaps identified in his thoughts. The words found their fulfillment in the destruction of Sennacherib's army.

(28) In the year that king Ahaz died was this burden.—The prophecies against Babylon and Assyria are naturally followed by a series of like predictions, dealing with other nations which played their part in the great drama of the time. The date of that which comes next in order is obviously specified, either by Isaiah himself or by the compiler of his prophecies, that it might be seen that it did not come after the event. The death year of Ahaz was 727 B.C.

15

As the concluding verses of the preceding chapter convey the burden against Philistia ("Palestina"), so the oracle which fills the next two chapters deals with the coming history of Moab.

16

This chapter continues the burden against Moab. History is, indeed, silent as to the manner of its fulfillment. It was probable, however, that the armies of Shalmaneser or Sargon swept, as those of Pul and Tiglath-pileser had done (I Chron. 5:26), over the region east of the Jordan, and so invaded Moab. We note from verse 14 that there was to be a "remnant," but not like that of Israel, the germ of a renewed strength.

17

The burden against Damascus is cited here. Syria had been confederate with the kingdom of Israel against Judah in the reign of Ahaz, and the prophet had then foretold its overthrow by Assyria (7:1-16). In II Kings 16:9 we have a partial fulfillment of that prediction. Writing probably early in the reign of Hezekiah, Isaiah now looks forward to a further fulfillment in the future.

Verses 12-14 stand as an isolated fragment, probably placed here as beginning like 18:1. They may have been connected with the progress of Sennacherib's army. In the "rushing of mighty waters" to describe the march of an army we have a parallel to 8:7, 8.

18

A new kingdom, heretofore unnamed by Isaiah, comes now within his horizon. The movements of Tirhakah, king of Cush or Ethiopia, from the upper valley of the Nile, subduing Egypt, and prepared to enter into conflict with the great Assyrian king (37:9), had apparently excited the hopes of such of Hezekiah's counselors as put their trust in an arm of flesh. To these Isaiah now turns with words of warning.

The prophet foresees, as one result of the defeat of the Assyrian armies, that the nation, which he again describes instead of naming, will offer themselves to the service of Jehovah. (See Pss. 68:31; 87:3.) Messengers who may have justified Isaiah's words were probably found among the envoys mentioned in II Chron. 32:23. Here, again, the words have been referred, as before, to Israel.

19

In its political bearings, as Egypt and Ethiopia were at this time under the same ruler, Tirhakah, this prophecy presents nearly the same features as the preceding. Its chief characteristic is that it presents the condition of the conquered nation as distinct from that of the conqueror. The opening words declare that the long-delayed judgment is at last coming. The discord predicted was probably the natural consequence of the overthrow of the Ethiopian power by Sargon, the Assyrian king, in 720 B.C.

(18-21) The prophecy is parallel to that affecting Ethiopia in 18:7, and at least expresses the yearnings of the prophet's heart after the conversion of Egypt to the worship of Jehovah. Like the previous prediction, it connects itself with Ps. 87. The "language of Canaan" (verse 18) is Hebrew, and the prediction is that this will become the speech of the worshipers of Jehovah in the Egyptian cities. Substantially the prophet saw in the distant future a time in which the connection between Judah and Egypt should be one influencing the latter for good, and not the former for evil. The admission of Egyptian and Ethiopian proselytes was as the first fruits of such an influence. The pillar (verse 19) was the familiar obelisk of the Egyptians, commonly associated with the worship of the sun. The point of Isaiah's prediction was that the symbol should be rescued from its idolatrous uses, and stand on the borderland of Egypt and of Judah, as a witness that Jehovah, the Lord of hosts, was worshiped in both countries.

(23, 24) The nearest historical approximation to this prophecy is, perhaps, found in the Persian monarchy, including, as it did, the territory of Assyria, of Israel, and of Egypt, and acknowledging, through the proclamations of Cyrus, Jehovah as the God of heaven (Ezra 1:2).

20

(1) Sargon the king of Assyria.—Much light has been thrown by the Assyrian inscriptions on the events connected with this king. Prior to that discovery there was no trace of his name to be found elsewhere than in this passage, and his very existence had been called in question. As it is, he comes before us as one of the greatest of Assyrian monarchs. He succeeded Shalmaneser VI, the conqueror of Israel, in 721 B.C. His reign lasted until 704 B.C., when he was succeeded by Sennacherib.

(2) Go and loose the sackcloth from off thy loins.—Against any scheme of alliance Isaiah was prompted to prophesy in act as well as words. The "nakedness" was confined to laying aside the rough outer robe, and appearing in the short tunic worn near the body (I Sam. 19:24; II Sam. 6:14-20; John 21:7). Like instances of prophetic symbolism are I Kings 22:11; Jer. 27:2; Ezek. 4:4; and Acts 21:11.

(4) So shall the king of Assyria lead away the Egyptians ... —The prediction did not receive its fulfillment in the reign either of Sargon or Sennacherib, but Esarhaddon subdued the whole of Egypt, carried off its treasures, and appointed satraps over its provinces. (See Nah. 3:8.) And the whole seaboard population would find out too late that they could not resist Assyria even with the help of Egypt and Ethiopia (verse 6).

511

21

(1) The burden of the desert of the sea ...
—The title of the prophecy is obviously taken from the catchword of "the desert" that follows. The "sea" is best explained by Xenophon's description of the whole plain of the Euphrates, intersected by marshes and lakes, as looking like a sea.

As whirlwinds in the south ... —The "South" (or **Negeb**) is here, as elsewhere, the special name of the country lying south of Judah, principally the Arabian desert. The tempests of the region seem to have been proverbial (Jer. 4:11; 13:24; Hos. 13:15; Zech. 9:14).

(2) A grievous vision ... —The verse contains, as it were, the three tableaux that came in succession before the prophet's gaze: (1) the treacherous dealer, the Assyro-Chaldaean power, spoiling, oppressing, and breaking treaties; (2) the summons coming to Elam and Media to put an end to this tyranny; and (3) the oppressed peoples ceasing to sigh and rejoicing in their liberation.

(11) Dumah, i.e., "silence," is a modification of "Edom." In this case, as in the preceding, there is first the oppressive silence of expectancy, and then of desolation.

(17) And the residue ... —The Hebrew word is the same as the characteristic "remnant" of Isaiah's earlier prophecies. In Jer. 49:28, 29 we have an echo of the prediction, which pointed to the conquest by Nebuchadnezzar.

22

The "valley of vision" (verse 1), against which this word is directed, is Jerusalem, lying as it did (Jer. 21:13) in a valley, as compared with the hills round about it (Ps. 125:2). That valley would be to him, assuredly, a "valley of vision," where he saw things present and to come. Possibly the name became more characteristic from the impulse given to the prophetic dreams of all who claimed to be seers. The prophet looks out and sees the people in a state of excitement, caused probably by the near approach of the Assyrian armies.

(4) Therefore said I, Look away from me.—The tone is that of one who wishes to be alone in his sorrow. It is too deep for visits of consolation. He "refuses to be comforted." Isaiah bewails the destruction of "the daughter of his people" in much the same strain as that of Jeremiah over a later catastrophe (Lam. 3:48).

(6) Elam ... Kir ... —The two nations are named as the chief elements of the Assyrian army then invading Judaea. Elam, previously named as the destroyer of Babylon (21:2), was at this time, as the inscriptions of Sargon show, subject to Assyria. (See Jer. 49:35.) "Kir" (II Kings 16:9) was the region to which Tiglath-pileser carried off the people of Damascus.

(11-14) Material defenses, the prophet affirms, will avail but little if they forget Him who was the true "builder and maker" of the city, and who alone can secure its safety. National danger, Isaiah adds, should call to a national repentance in its outward manifestations, like the fast described in Joel 2. As things were, however, the danger, imminent as it was, led not to repentance but to recklessness and sensuality. The cry of the baser form of epicureanism in all ages (I Cor. 15:32) was acted upon, and the prophet echoes the words in tones of burning indignation.

(15) Go, get thee unto this treasurer, even unto Shebna.—The section that follows opens a chapter in the internal politics of the reign of Hezekiah. Shebna had supreme control over the treasury of the king and the internal affairs of his kingdom. It is obvious that his influence was exercised to thwart the prophet's counsels; and the probable sequence of thought connecting the two sections is that he was prominent as the representative of the false security and luxury which the prophet had condemned. He was probably also of the party which rested their hope on an alliance with Egypt.

(18) Not content with riding on an ass or mule, as even judges and counselors rode (Judg. 5:10; 10:4; 12:14; II Sam. 17:23), he had appeared in public in stately chariots, such as were used by kings (Song Sol. 1:9; 3:9). These were to accompany him in his exile (perhaps in the large plain of Mesopotamia), but it would be as the spoil of the conqueror. There are no records of the fulfillment of the prediction, and the judgment may have been averted by repentance; but when we next meet with the proud, ambitious Shebna (36:22) he is in the inferior position of a scribe.

(20) Eliakim the son of Hilkiah.—Nothing is known of Eliakim's previous history, but "my servant" bears witness to his faith and goodness; and we may well believe him to have been in heart, if not openly, one of Isaiah's disciples. He was

512

apparently, at the time, in some subordinate office.

(22) And the key of the house of David will I lay upon his shoulder... —The key of the king's treasure-chambers and of the gates of the palace was the natural symbol of the chamberlain's office, and (9:6) it was solemnly laid upon the shoulder of the new official, perhaps as representing the burden of the responsibilities of the duties of his office. In Matt. 16:19 and Rev. 3:7, as also in the custom of admitting a rabbi to his office by giving him a key, we have a reproduction of the same emblem.

(25) Shall the nail that is fastened in a sure place be removed... —There is, the prophet says, a judgment for the misuse of power portrayed in the previous verse. The "nail" that seems so firmly fixed should be removed, **i.e.,** Eliakim should cease to hold his high office, and with his fall should come that of all his kindred and dependents. Here, as in the case of Shebna, we have no record of the fulfillment of the prediction, but either it was fulfilled or the penalty was averted by a timely reformation.

23

The chapter calls us to inquire into the political relations of Tyre at the time of Isaiah. In the days of David and Solomon there had been an intimate alliance between Israel and Hiram, King of Tyre. Ps. 45:12 indicates at least the interchange of kingly gifts, if not the acknowledgment of sovereignty by payment of tribute. Ps. 83:7, which we have some reason to connect with the reign of Uzziah, shows that this alliance had passed into hostility. The position of Tyre naturally threw it into more intimate relations with the northern kingdom. Tyre was the most flourishing of the Phoenician cities, and had succeeded to the older fame of Zidon. The action of Ahaz in inviting the help of Tiglath-pileser against Israel and the Syrians had tended to make Tyre also an object of attack by the Assyrian armies. The prophecy now before us would seem to have been connected with that attack, and foretells the issue of the conflict on which Tyre had rashly entered. In anticipation of these events, the prophet utters his note of warning to the great merchant city.

(7) Her own feet shall carry her.—The context paints the past glory of Tyre in contrast with her coming calamities. So

taken, the words point to her numerous colonies, of which Carthage was the chief.

(9) The Lord of hosts hath purposed... —This is the prophet's answer. The kings of Assyria were but instruments in the hand of Jehovah Sabaoth, working out what He had planned.

(11) He shook the kingdoms.—The picture of the great convulsion of the time includes more than Tyre and its subject states. Egypt, Ethiopia, Babylon, Syria, Israel, and Judah were all affected, shaken as to their very foundations, by the rapid progress of the restored Assyrian empire under Tiglath-pileser and his successors.

(15) Tyre shall be forgotten seventy years. —This is a symbolic number for a long period of indefinite duration, reckoned from its conquest by the Assyrians.

According to the days of one king.—We look in vain for any ruler of Assyria or Babylon whose reign was of this length. Possibly the "one king" may stand for one dynasty.

(18) Her merchandise and her hire shall be holiness to the Lord.—The harlot city, penitent and converted, might be allowed, strange as it would seem, to bring the gains of her harlotry into the temple of the Lord. Interpreted religiously, the prophet sees the admission of proselytes to the worship of Israel in the future, as he had seen it probably in the days of Hezekiah (Ps. 87:4). Interpreted politically, the words point to a return to the old alliance between Judah and Tyre in the days of David and Solomon (I Kings 5:1-12), and to the gifts which that alliance involved (Ps. 45:12).

24

The chapters from 24-27, inclusive, are to be taken as a continuous prophecy of the overthrow of the great world powers which were arrayed against Jehovah and His people. Of these Assyria was then the most prominent within the horizon of the prophet's view; but Moab appears in 25:10, and the language, with that exception, seems deliberately generalized, as if to paint the general discomfiture in every age (and, above all, in the great age of the future Deliverer) of the enemies of Jehovah and His people.

(It is interesting for the history of Christian doctrine that verse 22 furnished to Origen and his followers an argument in

513

favor of the ultimate restitution of all created spirits.)

25

The burst of praise in verse 1 follows, like Paul's in Rom. 11:33-36, upon the contemplation of the glory of the heavenly city.

(2) Thou hast made of a city an heap.— The city is identified with the oppressors and destroyers of his people—**i.e.,** Nineveh or Babylon; but that city was also for him the representation of the world power which in every age opposes itself to the righteousness of God's kingdom. The Babylon of Isaiah becomes the type of the mystical Babylon of the Apocalypse.

(6) And in this mountain shall the Lord . . . —The mountain is, as in 2:2, the hill of Zion, the true representative type of the city of God. True to what we may call the catholicity of his character, Isaiah looks forward to a time when the outlying heathen nations shall no longer be excluded from fellowship with Israel, but shall share in its sacrificial feasts even as at the banquet of the great King.

(8) Comp. Hos. 13:14; 1 Cor. 15:54; Rev. 7:17; 21:4.

(10) Moab shall be trodden down . . . — The inscription of the Moabite stone, in connection with chap. 15, helps to explain the nature of the allusion. Moab had been prominent among the enemies of Israel; the claims of Chemosh, the god of Moab, had been set up against those of Jehovah, the God of Israel, and so the name had become representative of His enemies. There was a mystical Moab, as there was afterward a mystical Babylon, and in Rabbinic writings a mystical Edom (**i.e.,** Rome). The proud nation was to lie wallowing in the mire of shame, trampled by its conquerors.

26

The prophet appears once more, as in 5:1 and 12:4, in the character of a psalmist, and what he writes is destined for nothing less than the worship of the new city of the heavenly kingdom.

(3) Thou wilt keep him in perfect peace.— More literally, and more impressively, we read, "Thou establishest a purpose firm; peace, peace, for in Thee is his trust." Completeness is expressed, as elsewhere, in

the form of iteration. No adjectives can add to the fullness of the meaning of the noun.

(4) For in the Lord Jehovah.—The Hebrew presents, as in 12:2, the exceptional combination of the two names Jah (Ps. 68:4) and Jehovah. In the Hebrew for "everlasting strength" we have, literally, the "Rock of Ages" of the well-known hymn. We have the same name of Rock applied to express the unchangeableness of God, as in Deut. 32:4.

(15) Thou hast increased the nation . . . —The nation is Israel, whose prosperity the prophet contrasts with the downfall of its oppressors (comp. 9:3). Jehovah will restore it to its old remoter boundaries, as in the days of David and Solomon. This belongs, of course, to the ideal, and not the historical restoration.

(19) Thy dead men shall live.—The words, though they imply a belief more or less distinct in a resurrection, are primarily like the vision of dry bones in Ezek. 37:1-14, and like Paul's "life from the dead" in Rom. 11:15 (comp. Hos. 6:2), used of national and spiritual resurrection.

(20) Come, my people, enter thou into thy chambers.—The vision of the judgments and the glory of the future leads the prophet to his work as a preacher of repentance in the present. His people need also the preparation of silent and solitary prayer (Matt. 6:6; Pss. 27:5; 31:21). As men seek the innermost recesses of their homes while the thunderstorm sweeps over the city, so should they seek God in that solitude until the great tempest of His indignation has passed by.

27

(1) Leviathan the piercing serpent.—The verse paints in vivid symbolic language the judgment of Jehovah on the great world powers that had shed the blood of His people. "Leviathan" is used generically for a monster of the serpent type. (See Job 41:1; Ezek. 29:3; Dan. 7:3-7.)

(2) In that day sing ye . . . —The prophet appears once again, as in 26:1, as the hymn writer of the future day of the triumph of the redeemed. He had chanted a dirge over the vineyard that was unfruitful, and therefore given over to desolation. He now changes the wailing into a poem.

(6) He shall cause them that come of Jacob . . . —The figure of Israel as the vine of Jehovah's vineyard is carried to its close.

The true Israel of God shall go through its normal stages of growth, and its restoration shall be as "the riches of the Gentiles" (Rom. 11:12; Hos. 14:6). With this picture of blessedness the psalm of the church of the future comes to an end.

(13) **The great trumpet shall be blown...** —The symbolism had a probable origin in the silver trumpets, used for the purposes of Lev. 25:9; Num. 10:1-10. It reappears in the apocalyptic eschatology of Matt. 24:31; I Cor. 15:52; I Thess. 4:16, standing there, as here, for any great event that heralds the fulfillment of a divine purpose. That purpose, in this instance, is the proclamation of the Year of Redemption, the restoration of the dispersed of Israel from the countries of their exile, of which (11:11; 19:23) Assyria and Egypt are the two chief representatives.

28

The prophet's work was not limited to Judah and Jerusalem, but extended to the northern kingdom. The warning was clearly uttered before the capture of Samaria by Shalmaneser, or, more probably, by Sargon, and paints in vivid colors (Amos 6:4-6) the license into which the capital of the northern kingdom had fallen.

(2) **The Lord hath a mighty and strong one...** —This refers to the king of Assyria as the instrument of Jehovah's vengeance (8:7, 8; 25:4). Here the picture is that of the "destroying storm," the "pestilent" or "blasting" tempest withering, and the flood sweeping away, the beautiful "garland" of Samaria.

(11) **With stammering lips and another tongue...** —The "stammering lips" are those of the Assyrian conquerors, whose speech would seem to the men of Judah as a barbarous **patois**. They, with their sharp commands, would be the next utterers of Jehovah's will to the people who would not listen to the prophet's teaching. In I Cor. 14:21, the words are applied to the gift of "tongues," which, in its ecstatic utterances, was unintelligible to those who heard it, and was therefore, as the speech of the barbarian conquerors was in Isaiah's thoughts, the antithesis of true prophetic teaching.

(16) **Behold, I lay in Zion for a foundation...** —In the stone which was made "the head of the corner" (Ps. 118:22) we have a like thought. From the prophet's standpoint this was identical with the manifestation of

Jehovah's righteousness in and through the Temple in its higher spiritual aspect. The true fulfillment of the words is in the Person of the Christ (Eph. 2:20; I Peter 2:6, 7). The "cornerstone" is that upon which two walls at right angles to each other rest and are bonded together. The "tried stone" may be one which stands every test, or one which tries those who come in contact with it, becoming an asylum, or a "stone of stumbling," according to their character. (Comp. Luke 2:34, 35; 20:18.)

He that believeth shall not make haste.— The LXX gives "shall not be ashamed," which is a paraphrase rather than a translation. The English, following the Vulgate, represents the meaning of the Hebrew, haste and hurry being regarded in their contrast to the calm temper of a steadfast faith.

(20) **For the bed is shorter...** —The image represents vividly a policy that ended in failure. Hezekiah's counselors had "made their bed" and would have to lie on it—in their Egyptian alliance—but it would not meet their wants. Bed and blankets would be all too scanty, and leave them in a restless disquietude.

(23) **Give ye ear...** —The words remind us of the style of the "wisdom" books of the Old Testament (Prov. 2:1; 4:1; 5:1; Ps. 34:11) in which Isaiah had been trained. The idea that lies at the root of the parable is like that of Matt. 16:2-4, that men fail to apply in discerning the signs of the times the wisdom which they practice or recognize in the common phenomena of nature and the tillage of the soil. As that tillage presents widely varied processes, differing with each kind of grain, so the sowing and the threshing of God's spiritual husbandry presents a like diversity of operations.

29

(1) **Woe to Ariel, to Ariel.**—The name, a poetic synonym, probably was coined by Isaiah himself. It may have been part of the secret language of the prophetic schools, as Sheshach stood for Babel (Jer. 25:26), Rahab for Egypt (51:9), and in the language of later rabbis, Edom, and in that of the apocalypse, Babel for Rome (Rev. 17:5). "Ariel" has been interpreted as "the lion of God." (See II Sam. 23:20; Rev. 5:5.) In the words "the city where David dwelt," the prophet interprets the mystic name for the benefit of his readers.

(8) **It shall even be as when an hungry**

man ... eateth.—The foes of Jerusalem were greedy of their prey, eager to devour; they thought it was already theirs. The rude awakening found them still empty. The lion of Judah was not to be devoured even by the strong bull of Assyria.

(10) The Lord hath poured out upon you ... —The prophet sees in the stupor and panic of the chief of the people what we call a judicial blindness, the retribution of those who had willfully closed their eyes against the light. (Comp. Rom. 11:8.) Verse 16 indicates that some were acting practically as atheists.

(11) The vision of all ... —The words perhaps imply that the entire substance of Isaiah's teaching had been committed to writing, but that to the unbelievers they were as "the roll of a sealed book." (See Rev. 5:2.) The wise of this world treated its dark sayings as seals, which forbade their making any attempt to study it. The poorer unlearned class could plead a more genuine and less guilty ignorance, but the effect was the same with both.

(13) Their fear toward me ... —The words point to an anticipated Pharisaism. Side by side with the great commandments of the Law and with the incisive teaching of the prophets there was growing up even then a traditional system of ethics and religion, based upon wrong principles, ending in a dishonest casuistry and a formal devotion. Commentaries even then were darkening counsel by words without knowledge, as they did in the Mishna and the Gemara of the later days of Judaism (Matt. 15:3; Mark 7:6).

(15) Woe unto them ... —The sins of which he speaks here may have been either the dark sensualities which lay beneath the surface of religion, or, more probably, their clandestine intrigues with this or that foreign power—Egypt, Ethiopia, Babylon— against the Assyrian invader, instead of trusting in the Lord of hosts.

(21) That make a man an offender for a word ... —The words indicate that Isaiah had been accused, as Jeremiah was afterward (Jer. 37:13), of being unpatriotic, because he had rebuked the sins of Israel and its rulers. The "snare" was laid for the "righteous man," precisely because he "reproved in the gate"—i.e., preached in the open air in the places of public concourse, even in the presence of the rulers and judges as they sat there.

30

(1) Woe to the rebellious children.—The interjection perhaps expresses sorrow rather than indignation. The prophet hears that the intrigues of the palace have at last issued in favor of an alliance with Egypt, and that an embassy has been sent already. This was the course into which even Hezekiah had been led or driven, and it had been done without consulting Isaiah as the recognized prophet of Jehovah (verse 2).

(5-7) The prophet paints the dreary disappointment of the embassy. They found Egypt at once weak and false, without the will or power to help them.

(8) Now go, write it before them in a table. —Comp. 8:1 for this as one of Isaiah's methods for giving special emphasis to his teaching. The word, we may believe, passed into the act in the presence of his astonished hearers. In some way or other he feels sure that what he is about to utter goes beyond the immediate occasion, and as a lesson for all time which the world would not willingly let die.

(15) In returning and rest ...—The words describe a process of conversion, but the nature of that conversion is determined by the context. In this case it was the turning from the trust in man, with all its restless excitement, to a trust in God, full of calmness and of peace. Verse 18, furthermore, seems to embody the thought that "man's extremity is God's opportunity."

(20) The bread of adversity.—The words allude to the scant rations of a siege such as Jerusalem was to endure from the Assyrian armies. For this there should be the compensation that the true teachers of the people, Isaiah and his fellow-workers, should at least be recognized. The clearer vision of the truth was to be the outcome of the sharp teaching of chastisement. In the mission of 37:2 we have a virtual fulfillment of the prediction.

(23) Following in the steps of Joel (2:21-26), the prophet draws a picture of the outward plenty that should follow on the renewal of the nation's inner life.

(33) The king of Assyria, though he did not die at Jerusalem, is represented as burned with stately ceremonial in Tophet. Tophet was the Valley of Hinnom, outside Jerusalem, where Ahaz had made his sons pass through the fire to Molech (II Kings 16:3.) Probably it was the burial place of the corpses that were lying around the city after the pestilence had destroyed the Assyrian army, and they were literally burned there. For such a Moloch funeral, making the valley of Hinnom then, as it afterward became, a fit type of Gehenna, a trench deep and wide and a mighty pyre were needed. (Comp. Jer. 19:12.)

31

We hear again the Keynote of Isaiah's teaching. The true strength of a nation lay in its spiritual, not in its material, greatness: in seeking the Holy One of Israel by practicing holiness. Without that condition the alliance with Egypt would be fatal both to those that sought for help and those who gave it.

32

Verses 1-8 form a separate section, standing in the same relation to the foregoing chapter that the picture of the ideal king in chap. 11 does to the anti-Assyrian prophecy of chap. 10. "The king" is accordingly the true Anointed one of the future, not, of course, without a reference to the character of Hezekiah as the partial and present embodiment of the idea.

Verse 9 begins a new section, probably a distinct sermon or pamphlet, against the evils of which the prophet had spoken in 3:16-26, and which continued, it would seem, unabated, in spite of Hezekiah's reformation. It probably finds a place here as painting the harem influence, which lay behind the counsels of the king and his ministers. The whole tone is that of invective against the women of the pseudo-aristocracy that had been covertly attacked in the preceding verses.

33

No chapter in the prophet's writings presents so little traceable connection. A thought is expressed in one or two verses, and then another follows without anything with which to link it. This may be explained on the assumption that we have a series of rough notes, memoranda for a long discourse, which was afterward delivered in a more continuous form. The opening words are addressed to Sennacherib when he entered on his second campaign against Judah, as it seemed to Isaiah, without the slightest provocation. Hezekiah had submitted, and had paid an enormous indemnity for the costs of the war (II Kings 18:13-16) at the close of the first campaign, and had, in the meantime, taken no aggressive action. The invasion was one of undisguised spoliation and rapacity. Upon such aggressiveness there was sure to come a righteous retribution, and in that thought the prophet finds comfort.

(15, 16) He that walketh righteously . . . —The answer to the question shows that the words point not to endless punishments, but to the infinite holiness of God. The man who is true and just in all his dealings can dwell in closest fellowship with that holiness which is to others as a consuming fire. (Comp. Pss. 15 and 24.)

(17) Thine eyes shall see the king in his beauty . . . —Torn from their context, the words have been fitly used to describe the beatific vision of the saints of God in heaven. Their primary meaning is, however, obviously historical. The "king" is Hezekiah, who shall be seen in all the "beauty" of triumph and of majesty; and the "land that is very far off" is the whole land of Israel, all prosperous and peaceful.

(20) Look upon Zion . . . —See Pss. 46 and 48, which were written probably by the sons of Korah on the destruction of Sennacherib's army.

34

Chapters 34 and 35 have a distinct character of their own. They form, as it were, the closing epilogue of the first great collection of Isaiah's prophecies, the historical section that follows (chaps. 36-39) serving as a link between them and the great second volume, which comes as an independent whole. Here, accordingly, we have to deal with what belongs to a transition period, probably the closing years of the reign of Hezekiah. The Egyptian alliance and the attack of Sennacherib are now in the background, and the prophet's vision takes a wider range. In the destruction of the Assyrian army he sees the pledge and earnest of the fate of all who fight against God (comp. Ezek. 39:11-16), and, as a representative instance of such enemies, fixes upon Edom, then, as ever, foremost among the enemies of Judah. They had invaded that kingdom in the days of Ahaz (II Chron. 28:17). They probably played a part in Sennacherib's invasion of Judah, in his attack on Jerusalem, analogous to that which drew down the bitter curse of the Babylonian exiles (Ps. 137:7). The chapters are further noticeable as having served as a model both to Zephaniah throughout his prophecy, and to Jer. 25; 46:3-12; 50; 51.

(16) Seek ye out of the book of the Lord ... —The phrase is an exceptional one. Isaiah applies that title either to this particular section, or to the volume of his collected writings. When the time of the fulfillment comes, men are invited to compare what they shall then find with the picture which Isaiah had drawn. It has to be remembered, however, that the decay was gradual. The ruins of Petra and other Idumaean cities are of Roman origin, and indicate a period of culture and prosperity stretching far into the history of the empire.

35

The desolation of the chief enemy of Israel is contrasted with the renewed beauty of Israel's own inheritance.

(8) An highway shall be there.—We are still in the region of parables, but the thought has a special interest as a transition, at the close of the first volume of Isaiah's writings, to the opening of the second. The use of the road has been referred by some to the return of the exiles from Babylon. Rather, it is the road by which the pilgrims of all nations shall journey to the mountain of the Lord's house (2:2).

(10) With songs and everlasting joy ... —The first volume of Isaiah's prophecy closes fitly with this transcendent picture, carrying the thoughts of men beyond any possible earthly fulfillment. The outward imagery probably had its starting point in the processions of the pilgrims who came up to the Temple singing psalms, like those known as the "songs of degrees" at their successive halting places (Pss. 120-134).

Sorrow and sighing shall flee away.—The words have a special interest as being the closing utterance of Isaiah's political activity, written, therefore, probably in his old age and in the midst of much trouble, whether he wrote at the close of Hezekiah's reign or the beginning of Manasseh's, which must have been sufficiently dark and gloomy. (See II Chron. 32:26; 33:1-10.) The

518

hopes of the prophet were, however, inextinguishable, and they formed a natural starting point for the words "Comfort ye, comfort ye, my people," with which the second collection opens (40:1), the intermediate chapters being obviously of the nature of a historical appendix. (Comp. Rev. 7:17.)

36

(1) It came to pass in the fourteenth year of king Hezekiah ... —The inscriptions of Sennacherib fix the date of his campaign against Hezekiah in the third year of his reign (700 B.C.), and that coincides not with the fourteenth but with the twenty-seventh year of the king of Judah. The error arose perhaps from the editor of Isaiah's prophecies taking for granted that the illness of Hezekiah followed on the destruction of Sennacherib's army, or, at least, on his attack, and then reckoning back the fifteen years for which his life was prolonged from the date of his death. Many scholars have come to the conclusion that the illness preceded Sennacherib's campaign by ten or eleven years, and this, of course, involves referring the embassy from Babylon (chap. 39) back to about the same period.

Sennacherib king of Assyria.—According to the Assyrian inscriptions, the king succeeded Sargon, who was assassinated in his palace, 704 B.C., and after subduing the province of Babylon which had rebelled under Merodach-baladan, turned his course southward against Hezekiah with several distinct complaints (see II Kings 18:14, 24).

(2) The king of Assyria sent Rabshakeh.— The word is a title (**the** Rabshakeh), probably the chief officer or cupbearer. In II Kings 18; II Chron. 32, we have the previous history of the war. Hezekiah, on hearing Sennacherib's reproach, began to strengthen the fortifications of Jerusalem, called his officers and troops together, and made an appeal to their faith and courage. In chap. 22 we have the prophet's view of those preparations. Probably by Isaiah's advice, who put no confidence in this boastful and blustering courage, Hezekiah sent to Sennacherib, who was then besieging Lachish, to sue for peace, acknowledging that he had offended. A penalty of three hundred talents of silver and thirty talents of gold was imposed and paid, Hezekiah being reduced to empty his own treasury and that of the Temple, and even to strip the Temple doors and pillars of the plates of gold with which they were overlaid. Peace, however, was not to be had even at that price. Encouraged, perhaps, by this prompt submission, and tearing up the treaty (the breach of covenant of which Isaiah complains in 36:1), Sennacherib sent his officers, the Tartan, the Rabsaris, and the Rabshakeh (the names are all official titles) to demand an unconditional surrender.

(11) Speak, I pray thee, unto thy servants ... —The king's officers, knowing the "little faith" of their people (verse 7), are not, perhaps, without misgivings of their own. Might not the townsmen, listening eagerly on the wall, recognize in Rabshakeh's words an echo of Isaiah's, and lose courage, as feeling that they were fighting against the God who was chastising them (verse 10; 7:17, 18)?

In the Jews' language.—It is uncertain whether this means simply Hebrew, which Isaiah elsewhere calls the language of Canaan (19:18), or a special dialect of Judah. The Moabite stone, on the one hand, shows that Hebrew was the common speech of Palestine and the border countries. On the other hand, dialects spring up quickly. Neh. 13:24 is the only other passage (the parallels of II Kings 18:26 and II Chron. 32:18 excepted) in which the term meets us in the narrower sense, and that is after the Exile.

37

(2) Unto Isaiah the prophet.—At last, then, the people did "see their teacher" (30:20). In that supreme hour of calamity the prophet, who had been despised and derided, was their one resource.

(4) Lift up thy prayer for the remnant ... —Isaiah's characteristic word (1:9; 10:21) had impressed itself on the king's mind. Now that town after town of Judah had fallen into Sennacherib's hands (forty-six, according to his inscriptions), those who were gathered within the walls of Jerusalem were as a mere remnant of the people.

(7) The word "blast" stands for the strong impulse which overpowers previous resolves. By "rumour" is meant either a prediction rising out of a purely supernatural foresight, or some secret intelligence which Israel had received as to the movements of Tirhakah (verses 8, 9).

(10-13) The message is in substance a repetition of its predecessors, more defiant, perhaps, as if in answer to the threatened attack of Tirhakah's armies, which Sennacherib could scarcely fail to connect with Hezekiah's confident hope of deliverance.

(14) And spread it before the Lord.—The act was one of mute appeal to the Supreme Arbiter. The **corpus delicti** was, as it were, laid before the judge, and then the appellant offered up his prayer.

(16) Thou art the God, even thou alone.— The absolute monotheism of the faith of Israel is placed in strong antithesis to the polytheism of Rabshakeh (verse 12). (Comp. Jer. 10:11; Isa. 40-42.)

(21) Then Isaiah the son of Amoz ... —According to rectified chronology, the grand burst of prophecy which follows was the last of Isaiah's recorded utterances. It is interesting to note the points of contact that present themselves both with his earlier prophecies and with the great prophetic poem (chaps. 40-66; see note on 40:1) traditionally ascribed to him. The prayer of Hezekiah, if he were not present at its utterance, was reported to him, and in the name of Jehovah he was commissioned to reply to it.

(26) Hast thou not heard ... —The speech of Sennacherib (verses 24, 25) ends, and that of Jehovah begins. The events of history had all been foreseen and ordered, as in the remote past, by the counsels of Jehovah. Kings and armies were but as His puppets in the drama of the world's history.

(30) And this shall be a sign unto thee.— The prophet now turns to Hezekiah, and offers (7:11; 38:8) a sign within the horizon of the nearer future as the pledge of the fulfillment of a prediction which had a wider range. It was then autumn. The Assyrian invasion had stopped all tillage in the previous spring, and the people had to rely upon the spontaneous products of the fields. In the new year that was about to open they would be compelled still to draw from the same source; but in twelve months' time the land would be clear of the invaders, and agriculture would resume its normal course. The fulfillment of this prediction within the appointed limit of time would guarantee that of the wider promise that follows.

(33-35) Isaiah's prediction is not only that Jerusalem will not be taken, but that the enemy, though now encamped around it, will not even proceed to the usual operations of a siege. The two motives of Jehovah's action were "for His own sake," as asserting His majesty against the blasphemy

519

of the Assyrians, and for "David's sake," as
mindful of the promise made to him.

(36) Then the angel of the Lord.—
Interpreted by I Chron. 21:14, the words
imply the action of some form of epidemic
disease, spreading, it may be, for some
days, and then, aggravated by atmospheric
conditions, such as the thunderstorm implied in 29:6; 30:27-30, culminating in one
night of horror. To Isaiah, who had learned
to see in the winds the messengers of God
(Ps. 104:4), it was nothing else than the
"angel of the Lord." The narrative of Isaiah
leaves room for a considerable interval between his prophecy and the dread work of
the destroyer (II Kings 19:35). "In that
night" does not necessarily imply immediate sequence, the demonstrative adjective
being used for "that memorable night."

(37) So Sennacherib ... —The Assyrian
king had been engaged in the siege of
Libnah, probably also in an Egyptian expedition, which from some cause or other was
unsuccessful. The course of events was
probably this: that in Egypt he heard of the
ravages of the pestilence, returned to find
his army too weak to fight, and then, abandoning all further action in the south, withdrew to Nineveh.

(38) And it came to pass.—The Assyrian
inscriptions fill up the gap of twenty years
between the events which appear here, as if
in immediate sequence, with five campaigns
in the north and east of the Assyrian Empire, chiefly against the Babylonians, who
revolted again under the son of Merodach-
baladan.

38

(1) In those days.—The narrative of
Hezekiah's illness takes us back to a time
fifteen years before his death, and therefore
to an earlier date than the destruction of the
Assyrian army, which it here follows. (So in
verse 6, the deliverance of the city is spoken
of as still future.) We are carried to a time
ten or eleven years before the invasion,
which was probably in part caused by the
ambitious schemes indicated in chap. 39.
There is no ground for assuming that the
illness was an attack of the plague that
destroyed the Assyrian army, or that the
treasures which Hezekiah showed to the
Babylonian ambassadors were in part the
spoil of that army.

Set thine house in order.—The words are
a striking illustration, like Jonah's an-

nouncement that Nineveh should be destroyed in three days (Jonah 3:4), of the
conditional character of prophecy. It would
seem as if Isaiah had been consulted half as
prophet and half as physician as to the
nature of the disease. It seemed to him
fatal; it was necessary to prepare for death.
The words may possibly imply a certain
sense of disappointment at the result of
Hezekiah's reign. In the midst of the king's
magnificence and prosperity there was that
in the inner house of the soul, as well as in
that of the outer life, which required ordering.

(5) Fifteen years.—The words fix the date
of the illness as 713 B.C. Verse 6 shows that
there was danger at the time to be apprehended from Assyria, but does not necessarily refer to Sennacherib's invasion. Sargon's
attack (20:1) may have caused a general
alarm.

(7) This shall be a sign unto thee ...
—See notes on II Kings 20:8-11, where the
story is more fully told. The sun dial of
Ahaz, probably, like his altar (II Kings
16:10), copied from Syrian or Assyrian art,
would seem to have been of the form of an
obelisk standing on **steps** (the literal meaning of the Hebrew word for "dial"), and
casting its shadow so as to indicate the
time, each step representing an hour or
half-hour. The nature of the phenomenon
seems as curiously limited as that of the
darkness of the crucifixion. There was no
prolongation of the day in the rest of Palestine or Jerusalem, for the backward movement was limited to the step dial. At Babylon one such phenomenon had been observed, and one ostensible purpose of Merodach-baladan's embassy was to investigate
its nature (II Chron. 32:31). The most probable explanation of the fact recorded is that
it was the effect of a supernatural, but
exceedingly circumscribed, refraction. A
prolonged afterglow following on the sunset, and reviving for a time the brightness
of the day, might produce an effect such as
is described to one who gazed upon the step
dial.

(9) The writing of Hezekiah ... —Verses
21 and 22 would seem to have their right
place before the elegiac psalm that follows.
The hymn presents echoes of the Book of
Job as well as of the earlier Psalms.

(10) The residue ... —The words assume
a normal duration, perhaps of seventy
years, on which the sufferer, who had, as he
thought, done nothing to deserve punishment, might have legitimately counted. (See

520

Ps. 90:10.) Then Hezekiah was about forty years old.

(11) I shall not see the Lord . . . —The words are eminently characteristic of the cheerless dimness of the Hebrew's thoughts of death. To Hezekiah, it would seem, the outward worship of the Temple, or possibly, the consciousness of God's presence in the full activity of brain and heart, was a joy which he could not bear to lose. The spiritual perceptions of the life after death would be spectral and shadowy, like the dead themselves. Verse 18 says that in that region of dimness there are no psalms of thanksgiving, no loud hallelujahs. The thought of spiritual energies developed and intensified after death is essentially one which belongs to the "illuminated" immortality (II Tim. 1:10) of Christian thought.

(19) Hezekiah's son and successor, the wicked Mannasseh, who was only twelve years old at his father's death (II Kings 21:1), was not born until two or three years later. At the time of his illness the king may have been still childless, and the thought that there was no son to take his place may have added bitterness to his grief.

39

(1) Merodach-baladan.—The name is conspicuous in the Assyrian inscriptions of Sargon, as having rebelled against him and set up an independent monarchy. The mission had two ostensible objects (see II Chron. 32:31); but really, we may believe the object of Merodach-baladan was to open negotiations for an alliance with Judah.

(2) Shewed them the house of his precious things.—This fixes the date of the embassy at a time prior to the payment to Sennacherib (II Kings 18:15, 16). The display of the resources of the kingdom was intended to impress the Babylonian ambassadors with a sense of Hezekiah's importance as an ally.

(6, 7) Behold, the days come . . . —The words received a twofold fulfillment, under widely different conditions. Hezekiah's son Manasseh, unborn at the time when Isaiah spoke, was carried as a prisoner to Babylon by Esarhaddon, king of Assyria (II Chron. 33:11). The last lineal heir of the house of David, Jehoiachin, died there after long years of imprisonment (II Kings 25:27). (See also Dan. 1:3.) Sennacherib indeed boasts that he had carried off not only the king's treasures and his musicians to Nineveh, but his daughters also.

40

(1) Comfort ye . . . —The great prophetic poem that follows is the work of Isaiah himself. It has a link with the earlier collection of his writings in 35:9, 10. The prophet's mind is obviously projected at the outset into the future, which it had been given him to see, when the time of punishment and discipline was to be succeeded, having done its work, by blessedness and peace. The keynote is struck in the opening words, a distinct echo of Hos. 2:1.

Saith your God.—This formula is at once peculiar to Isaiah and common to both his volumes (1:11, 18; 33:10; 41:21; 66:9).

(2) Speak ye comfortably . . . —The command is addressed to the prophets whom Isaiah contemplates as working toward the close of the exile, and carrying on his work. In Hag. 1:13; 2:9; 3:19-23; and Zech. 1:13; 2:5-10; 9:9-12, we may rightly trace the influence of the words as working out their own fulfillment.

(3) The voice of him that crieth . . . — The passage is memorable as having been deliberately taken by John the Baptist as defining his own mission (John 1:23). As here the herald is not named, so he was content to efface himself—to be a **voice** or nothing. The image is drawn from the march of Eastern kings, who often boast, as in the Assyrian inscriptions of Sennacherib and Assurbanipal, of the roads they have made in trackless deserts. The wilderness is that which lay between the Euphrates and Judah, the journey of the exiles through it reminding the prophet of the older wanderings in the wilderness of Sin (Judg. 5:4; Ps. 68:7).

(5) All flesh.—The revelation is not for Israel only, but for all mankind. (See Luke 3:6.) The phrase occurs again in 49:26; 66:16, 23, 24, marking the growing catholicity of the prophet's thoughts.

(6, 7) The questioner is probably the prophet himself, asking what he is to proclaim. The truth which he is to enforce thus solemnly is the ever-recurring contrast between the transitoriness of man and the eternity of God and of His word, taking that term in its highest and widest sense. (See Ps. 119:41, 65, 89; John 1:1.)

(9) O Zion, that bringest good tidings.— A new section begins. We note the first occurrence of the word which, passing through the Greek of the LXX and the New Testament (**euangelidzesthai**) has had so fruitful a history, as embodying the message of the Gospel—glad tidings—to mankind. The primary meaning of the Hebrew word is "to make smooth," or bright, and so "to gladden."

(12) Who hath measured . . . ?—Another section opens, expanding the thought of the eternal majesty of Jehovah, as contrasted with the vanity of the idols, or "no-gods," of the heathen. The whole image is divinely anthropomorphic. Verse 15 moves the thought from the material world into human history.

(18) To whom then will ye liken God . . . —The thought of the infinity of God leads, as in Paul's reasoning (Acts 17:24-29), to the great primary argument against the folly of idolatry. It is characteristic, partly of the two men individually, partly of the systems under which they lived, that while the tone of Isaiah is sarcastic and declamatory, that of Paul is pitying, and as with indulgent allowance for the "times of ignorance." Of course, the apostle speaks to those who had known nothing better than the worship of their fathers, the prophet to those who were tempted to fall into the worship of the heathen from a purer faith.

(21) Have ye not known? . . . —The prophet appeals to the primary intuitions of mankind, or, at least, to a primitive revelation, rather than to the commandments of the Decalogue. (Comp. Rom. 1:20; Ps. 19:4.) Thus he returns in verse 28 to address Israel.

(27) Why sayest thou, O Jacob.—The eternity and infinity of God is presented not only as rebuking the folly of the idolater, but also as the ground of comfort to His people. His is no transient favor, no capricious will. (Comp. Rom. 11:29-36.)

(31) Shall mount up with wings.—Better, "shall put forth wings' feathers," like Ps. 103:5 implying the belief that the eagle renewed its plumage in extreme old age. For the faithful there is no failure, and faith knows no weariness.

41

(1-4) The prophet sees a vision of what shall come to pass in the "latter days" (see verses 21-24), and not only the forms of the old empires on their way to Hades (14:9-12)

but the appearance on the scene of the new conqueror. The man so raised up to rule over the "islands" and the "peoples" is none other than Koresh (Cyrus), the future restorer of Israel. The thought of Cyrus as working out the righteousness of God is dominant in these chapters (42:6; 45:13). In the rapidity of his conquest, the prophet bids men see the proof that he is doing God's work. So Jeremiah speaks of Nebuchadnezzar as the servant of Jehovah (Jer. 27:6).

(5-7) The words paint the terror caused by the rapid conquests of Cyrus, but the terror led to something different from the acknowledgment of the Eternal. The gods of each nation had to be propitiated by new statues, and a fresh impetus was given to the manufacture of idols, probably for the purpose of being carried forth to battle as a protection. (Comp. 1 Sam. 4:5-7; Herod. 1:26.)

(8) But thou, Israel, art my servant . . . —The verse is important as the first introduction of the servant of the Lord who is so conspicuous throughout the rest of the book. The idea embodied in the term is that of a calling and election, manifested now in Israel according to the flesh, now in the true Israel of God, realizing its ideal, now, as in the innermost of the three concentric circles, in a person who gathers up that ideal in all its intensity into himself. (See Rom. 9:7; Gal. 3:7, 16.)

(9) I have chosen . . . —Isaiah becomes the preacher of the divine election, and finds in it, as Paul found, the ground of an inextinguishable hope for the nation of which he was a member. Verse 14 reminds this people that they have no strength in themselves. It remained for them to "make their calling and election sure" (II Pet. 1:10), though God, in the unchangeableness of His nature, had chosen them before the foundation of the world.

(17) When the poor and needy . . . —The promise may perhaps take as its starting point the succor given to the return of the exiles, but it rises rapidly into the region of a higher poetry, in which earthly things are the parables of heavenly, and does not call for literal fulfillment.

(25) The north points to Media, the east to Persia, both of them under the rule of the great Deliverer. The words find a fulfillment in the proclamations of Cyrus cited in II Chron. 36:22, 23; Ezra 1:2-4.

42

43

(1) Behold my servant ... —Here the words point not, as before, to the visible, or even the ideal Israel, but to One who is the center of both, with attributes which are reproduced in His people in the measure of their fulfillment of the ideal. "Elect" meets us four times (45:4; 65:9, 22), and is echoed and interpreted in the voice from heaven of Matt. 3:17. The Son of Man was "the servant of the Lord," and throughout His life we trace an ever expanding and conscious reproduction of the chief features of Isaiah's picture (e.g., Matt. 12:17-21).

(2, 3) Isaiah's ideal of a teacher, but partly realized in himself, is that of one exempt from the violence of strong feelings, calm in the sereneness of authority, strong in his far-reaching and pitying sympathy.

(4) The isles shall wait for his law.—The relation of "the servant" to the far-off Gentile world is still dominant in the prophet's mind. The words describe the "earnest expectation," the unconscious longing of the heathen for One who shall be a true teacher (Rom. 8:22).

(6) A covenant of the people.—The context limits the "people" here to Israel. The words may well have furnished a starting-point for the "new covenant" of Jer. 31:31, and the whole series of thoughts that have grown out of it.

(8, 9) I am the Lord ... —God cannot look with indifference on the transfer to the "graven image" of the worship due to Him. With his vision of Cyrus still present to his thoughts, the prophet again presses the unique point of prediction as distinguishing the religion of Israel from that of the heathen.

(14) I have long time holden my peace... —What is actually meant is the period of the exile, during which, until the advent of the deliverer, there had been no interposition on behalf of Israel. To the exiles this had seemed endless in its weariness. Now there were the travail-pangs of a new birth for the nation. (Comp. Matt. 24:8.)

(20) With a clear vision into the future, the prophet sees that the future Israel will be as far from the ideal as his contemporaries had been. In the scribes and Pharisees in the time of **the** Servant we find we find the fulfillment of his vision.

(1) But now ... —The outpouring of love that follows is contrasted with the wrath of the preceding passage.

(3) I gave Egypt for thy ransom ... —Speaking after the manner of men, the prophet paints Jehovah as surrendering Egypt and other kingdoms to the arms of Cyrus, as if they were a price paid to him for liberating the Jews of Babylon. (See Prov. 11:8; 21:18.) Historically, the words find a fulfillment in the conquest of Egypt by Cambyses, who carried into effect his father's plans. As a man would sacrifice any number of slaves to ransom a son, so was it in Jehovah's dealings with His people (verse 4).

(5) From the east ... —Even from Isaiah's standpoint, the dispersion of Israel might well be contemplated in all this wide extent. The Ten Tribes were already carried off to the cities of the Medes (II Kings 17:6). The Babylonian exile had its beginning under Esarhaddon (II Chron. 33:11). For other prospects, see Joel 3:6; Zeph. 3:10.

(8) Bring forth the blind people... —In 42:18-20 Israel saw but did not observe, had eyes and yet was blind. Here the blind and deaf—**i.e.,** the heathen, or the Israel that had fallen into heathenism—are spoken of as having capacities for sight and hearing which will one day be developed.

(18, 19) Remember ye not ... —All the wonders of the great historic past of Israel were to be as nothing compared with the new manifestation of the power of Jehovah, which Isaiah sees as already dawning in the future.

(22) But thou hast not called upon me.— Isaiah's experience taught him that there would be in the future, as in the past, a dark as well as a bright side to the picture. The mercies shown to the exiles would not be according to their merits, but to God's great goodness. The worship of the restored exiles would be as that of the people had been in his own time, meager and unthankful. Visions of failure alternate with the glowing hope that the ideal will be realized, and this alternation constitutes the great problem of all apocalyptic intimations.

(23) I have not caused thee to serve... —The words practically imply the suspension of sacrifices during the exile. Jehovah had not imposed that bond-service on them— had not wearied them with demanding

523

incense when they were far away from the Temple to whose ritual it belonged.

44

(1) The thoughts of Israel are turned from their own sins to the unchanging love of God, and that is the ground of their hope.

(2) Jesurun is the ideal name of Israel as "the upright one." The name is substituted for the Israel of the preceding verse, as pointing to the purpose of God in their election.

(5) One shall say, I am the Lord's.—The words paint, like Ps. 87:4, 5, the eagerness of heathen proselytes to attach themselves to Israel.

(6) Thus saith the Lord ... —A new section opens, repeating the broad arguments of chaps. 41 and 43 against idolatry.

(24) Thus saith the Lord.—The section begun is carried on to the end of chap. 45. The contrast between the foreknowledge of Jehovah and the no-knowledge of the worshipers of idols culminates in the proclamation (verse 28) of the name of the deliverer and his restoration of the temple.

(28) That saith of Cyrus.—The prediction of the name of the future deliverer has its only parallel in that of Josiah (I Kings 13:2). Such a phenomenon admits of three possible explanations: (1) that it is a prophecy after the event—**i.e.,** that the whole of Isaiah, or this part of it, was written at the close of the exile; (2) that the name was revealed to the prophet in a way altogether supernatural; (3) that the name came within the horizon of the prophet's vision from his natural standpoint, the supernatural element being found in the facts which he is led to connect with it. Of these, the last seems to commend itself as most analogous with the methods of prophetic teaching. The grandfather of the great Cyrus is said to have borne the same name (Herod. 1:111). The name **Kur'us**, meaning "the sun," if not a titular epithet, like the Pharaoh of Egypt, may yet have had the prestige of antiquity and dignity, historical or mythical.

45

(1) To his anointed ... —The name is none other than the Messiah, the Christ, with which we are familiar, here and here only applied to a heathen king. But the

words had not yet received the special application given to it in Dan. 9:26, and had been used of the theocratic kings, of Saul (I Sam. 26:9, 11, 16), of the house of David (II Sam. 22:51; 23:1), and of the patriarch Abraham (Ps. 105:15). What is meant, therefore, is that Cyrus, the future deliverer, would be as truly a king "by the grace of God" as David had been, not only, like Nebuchadnezzar, "a servant of Jehovah" (Jer. 27:6; 43:10).

(13) I have raised him up in righteousness ... —This was the answer to the murmurers. It would be seen by the results—the city rebuilt, the exiles restored to their home—that the conquests of Cyrus had been ordered by the loving righteousness of Jehovah; and he would do this, not through the greed and ambition of other conquerors, but because the spirit of the Lord stirred him (II Chron. 36:22).

(14) Thus saith the Lord ... —Here the prophet goes a step farther than his description of the proselytes in 43:3. They come in voluntary surrender to Israel's God. A partial fulfillment may have been found in the command given by Cyrus, that these and other nations should assist in the work of rebuilding the Temple (Ezra 1:4).

(20) Ye that are escaped of the nations.— Primarily, the words point to the survivors of the conquests of Cyrus, who are contemplated as acknowledging the God of Israel. Ultimately the words find their fulfillment in the conversion of the heathen to the true anointed of Jehovah, of whom Cyrus was a type. They will bear witness from their experience to the vanity of idols.

(21) A just God and a Saviour.—Stress is laid on the union of the two attributes which in human actions are often thought incompatible. (Comp. Ps. 85:10.) In virtue of that union the invitation of verse 22 is addressed to all the ends of the world. The offer of salvation is universal. And we note the application of the words of verse 23 to the Christ in Phil. 2:10; Rom. 14:11.

46

(1) Bel boweth down, Nebo stoopeth.— Bel ("Lord") is perhaps identical with Marduk or Merodach. Nabu ("the Revealer") was a kind of Assyrian Hermes. Isaiah sees the idols carried off as spoil, at the command of Cyrus, a heavy burden for the beasts that drag them.

(3) Hearken unto me.—The prophet's

choice of words is singularly emphatic. The false gods are borne away as a burden. The true God bears, **i.e.**, supports, His people. He is able to bear that burden. Every "I" is emphasized in the Hebrew.

(5) To whom will ye liken me?—The argument against idolatry is renewed in nearly its old form (40:18-25; 44:9-17). The fate of Bel and Nebo is urged against those who thought that they might worship Jehovah as those deities had been worshiped.

(11) Calling a ravenous bird.—Cyrus is thus described as Nebuchadnezzar is in Jer. 49:22; Ezek. 17:3. The image derives a special significance from the fact that the standard borne by Cyrus and his successors was a golden eagle (Xen., **Cyrop.** 7:1, 4; **Anab.** 1:10, 12). (Comp. also Matt. 24:28; Luke 17:37.) The "sun-rising" is Persia; the "far country" probably represents Media.

47

Babylon itself, personified as until now unconquered, is called to leave her throne and serve as a menial slave. The luxury which had been identified with Babylon was now to cease.

(8) I am, and none else beside me... —The boasts of Babylon are purposely embodied by the prophet in praises that recall Jehovah's assertion of His own eternity. She practically deified herself. So a like boast is put into the mouth of Nineveh in Zeph. 2:15.

(10) For thou hast trusted in thy wickedness... —Babylon, like other nations that have followed in her steps, took for its law that "might was right," practically denied the existence of a Ruler who saw and judged, and boasted of its wisdom. The context implies that the special form of wisdom spoken of was that of astrology and magic. Verse 15 indicates, as well, a comfort in commerce.

48

(1-4) Jehovah foresees not only the conquests of Cyrus, but also the hypocrisy and obduracy of His own people. In Egypt (Jer. 44) and in Babylon, as of old, they were still a stiff-necked people, inclined (verse 5) to ascribe their deliverance to another god and to worship that god in the form of a graven image.

(7) They are created now... —The

things which had been from the beginning in the mind of God are now, for the first time, manifested, through the prophet, as about to pass into act. What these are the prophet develops in the following chapters, as including the spiritual redemption and restoration of Israel. They were kept in store, as it were, to make men wonder (Rom. 16:25, 26).

Even before the day when... —The reason given for what we might almost call this method of reserve and reticence was that the people had been until now unprepared to receive the truth, and in their state it would but have increased their condemnation (Mark 4:33; John 16:12).

(12) Hearken unto me, O Jacob.—The prophet asserts the oneness, the eternity, the omnipotence, the omniscience of Jehovah.

(20) Go ye forth of Babylon... —The sorrow and sighing are past, and the prophet speaks to the remnant that shall return. They are to act without fear on the promises of God, on the decree of Cyrus, and to start at once on their homeward journey. As they go, they are to proclaim what great things God hath done for them.

(22) There is no peace.—The warning was needed even for the liberated exiles. There was an implied condition as to all God's gifts. Even the highest blessings, freedom and home, were no real blessings to those who were unworthy of them.

49

(1) The argument against idolatry has been brought to its close, and a new section opens. With it there is a new speaker, the mysterious and predestined "Servant of the Lord" (42:1), at once identified with Israel (verse 3), in fulfilling its ideal, and yet distinguished from it, as its Restorer and Redeemer. The invitation is addressed to the heathen far and near.

(3) Thou art my servant, O Israel.—The "Servant" is not merely the nation, but fulfills its ideal. "Israel" had begun with being an individual name. It should be so once more in the person of Him who would be truly "a prince with God."

(6-8) The Servant is to be the bearer of a message of peace to the whole race of mankind, and has "other sheep not of this fold" (John 10:16). Yet the doer of the great work is to be despised by his own people, by proud rulers (comp. I Cor. 1:27). Still he, and no other, will accomplish a new covenant with the people, an idea afterward developed by Jeremiah (31:31), reaching its fulfillment in Matt. 26:28; Luke 22:20.

(12) From the land of Sinim.—Many scholars make this refer to the Chinese. Phoenician or Babylonian commerce may have made that people known, at least by name, to the prophet. Porcelain with Chinese characters has been found in the ruins of the Egyptian Thebes. Discoveries tend to the conclusion that the commerce of the great ancient monarchies was wider than scholars of the sixteenth century imagined. The actual immigration of Jews into China is believed to have taken place about 200 B.C. (Delitzsch).

(16) Behold, I have graven thee . . . —The words point to the almost universal practice of tattooing. A man thus "engraved" the name of his god, or the face of her whom he loved, upon his hands or arms. So, by a boldly anthropomorphic figure, Jehovah had "graven" Jerusalem on His hands. He could not act without being reminded of her.

(18) Lift up thine eyes.—The daughter of Zion is called on to gaze on the returning exiles. They shall be her gems and her girdle as the bride of her new espousals.

50

(1) Where is the bill . . . ?—Jehovah had not formally repudiated the wife (Judah) whom he had chosen (Deut. 24:1) as he had done her sister Israel (Jer. 3:8; Hos. 2:2). (On the law of debt which supplies the image, comp. Exod. 21:7; II Kings 4:1; Neh. 5:5.) The divorce, the sale, were her acts and not His.

(5, 6) The Lord God.—The Servant continues his soliloquy. What has come to him in the morning communings with God (verse 4) is that he too is to bear reproach and shame (verse 6), as other disciples had done before him. The writer of Ps. 22:7, Job (Job 3:10), and Jeremiah (Jer. 20:7) were but foreshadowings of the sufferings that should fall on him. And all this the true Servant-Scholar accepts willingly, because it is his Father's will. Here again we cannot fail to trace the influence of Isaiah's words in all our Lord's utterances as to His passion. (Comp. Matt. 16:21; Mark 10:34; Luke 18:32.)

51

(1, 2) The implied argument is that the

wonder involved in the origin of Israel is as a ground of faith in its restoration and perpetuity. If so great a nation had sprung from one man (Heb. 11:12), so would God out of the faithful remnant once more create a people. (Comp. Ezek 33:24, where the exiles are represented as boastfully inverting the argument.)

(7) Ye that know righteousness.—Jehovah, through His Servant, speaks to the Israel within Israel, the Church within the Church. They need support against the scorn and reproach of men, and are to find it in the thought that the revilers perish and that Jehovah is eternal.

(17) Awake . . . —The words present a strange parallelism to verse 9. There they were addressed to the arm of Jehovah, and were the prelude of a glorious promise. Here they are spoken to Jerusalem as a drunken and desperate castaway, and introduce a painfully vivid picture of her (not irretrievable) desolation.

52

(1) Awake, awake . . . —The repetition of the burden of 51:9, 17 indicates, by a subtle touch of art, the continuity of thought. The call is addressed as before to Zion, as a castaway. It summons her to the highest glory. She is to put on the "garments of beauty," which belong to her as the priestly queen of cities.

(7) How beautiful . . . —In 40:9 Zion herself was the herald proclaiming the glad tidings; here the heralds are seen coming to Zion to tell her that her God is reigning. Comp. Rom. 10:15.

(11) Depart ye . . . —The command is addressed to the exiles in Babylon. They are not to plunder or carry off spoil that would render them unclean. They are to bring only "the vessels of Jehovah," i.e., the gold and silver which had been taken from His temple, and which Cyrus restored by them (Ezra 1:7).

(13) Behold, my servant . . . —There is absolutely no connection between verses 12 and 13, and absolutely no break between the close of chap. 52 and the opening of chap. 53. The whole must be treated as an entirely distinct section, and finds its only adequate explanation in the thought of a new revelation made to the prophet's mind. The prophet had seen partially good kings, like Uzziah and Jotham, and one who almost realized his ideal of what a king should be, in Hezekiah. None of these had redeemed or regenerated the people. As far as that work had been done at all, it had been through prophets who spoke the word of the Lord and were mocked and persecuted because they spoke it. Something like a law was dawning upon his mind, and that law was the power of a vicarious suffering, the might of martyrdom in life and death. Did it not follow from this that that ideal must be wrought out on a yet wider scale in the great work of restoration to which he was looking forward? The Servant of the Lord, in all the concentric developments of the thought which the word implied, the nation, the prophetic kernel of the nation, the individual Servant identifying himself with both, must himself also be made perfect through suffering and conquer through apparent failure. Granting that such a law exists, it will be no wonder that we should find examples of its working both before and after the great fulfillment, in Isaiah himself, in Jeremiah, in the exiles of the captivity, in the heroes of the Maccabean struggle, in the saints and martyrs of the Church of Christ. It remains true that the Christ alone fulfills the idea of the perfect sufferer, as He alone fulfills that of the perfect King.

(14) His visage was so marred . . . — Christian art prior to the time of Constantine represented the Christ as worn, emaciated, with hardly any touch of earthly comeliness. It is possible that the beauty may have been of expression rather than of feature or complexion.

53

(1) Who hath believed our report? . . . —The question comes from the lips of the prophet. The unusual plural is explained by his mentally associating with himself the other prophets, probably his own disciples, who were delivering the same message. (See Rom. 10:16.)

(2) The Hebrew tenses are in the perfect, the future being contemplated as already accomplished. The words present at once a parallel and a contrast to those of 11:1. There the picture was that of a strong vigorous shoot coming out of the root of the house of David. Here the sapling is weak and frail, struggling out of the dry ground. Jehovah was watching this humble and lowly growth, as a mother watches over

her weakest and most sickly child. (See note on 52:14.)

(3) The words "sorrow" and "grief" in the Hebrew imply the thought of bodily pain or disease, an essential condition of His fellowship with humanity.

(4) Surely he hath borne our griefs . . . —The words are spoken as by those who had before despised the Servant of Jehovah, and have now learned the secret of His humiliation. "Grief" and "sorrow," as in verse 3, imply "disease" and "pain." (See Matt. 8:17.) The word for "borne," like the Greek in John 1:29, implies both the "taking upon himself," and the "taking away from others," **i.e.**, the true idea of vicarious and mediatorial atonement.

(5) He was wounded . . . bruised. Both words refer to the death which crowned the sufferings of the Servant. That also was vicarious.

The chastisement of our peace—i.e., the punishment which leads to peace, that word including, as elsewhere, every form of blessing. In Heb. 2:10; 5:8, 9 we have the thought which is the complement of this, that the chastisement was also an essential condition of the perfection of the sufferer.

With his stripes we are healed.—See I Peter 2:24.

(6) All we like sheep have gone astray . . . —The confession of repentant Israel (Ps. 119:176) is the confession of repentant humanity (I Peter 2:25).

Hath laid on him.—The words express the fact, but do not explain the mystery, of the substitutive satisfaction. The two sides of that mystery are stated in the form of a seeming paradox. God does not punish the righteous **with** the wicked (Gen. 18:25). He accepts the suffering of the righteous **for** the wicked (Mark 10:45).

(7) As a lamb to the slaughter.—Jeremiah (11:19) appropriates the description to himself. In our Lord's silence before the Sanhedrin and Pilate it is allowable to trace a conscious fulfillment of Isaiah's words (Matt. 26:62; 27:14). (Comp. I Peter 2:23.)

(8) Who shall declare his generation?— "As to his contemporaries who will consider rightly?" The words that follow point to the fact which ought to have been considered, and was not, that though the Servant of Jehovah was smitten, it was not for His own sins, but theirs.

(9) And he made his grave . . . —The words are often interpreted as fulfilled in our Lord's crucifixion between the two robbers and His burial in the tomb of Joseph of Arimathea. It has to be noted. however, that the laws of parallelism require us to take the "rich" of one clause as corresponding to the "wicked" of the other, i.e., as in the sense of the wrongfully rich, the oppressors. Men assigned to the Servant, not the burial of a saint. with reverence and honor, but that of an unjust oppressor, for whom no man lamented. It may be questioned whether Isaiah would have looked on such a burial as that recorded in the gospels, clandestine, and with no public lamentation, as an adequate recognition of the holiness of the victim.

(10) Yet it pleased the Lord ... —The sufferings of the Servant are referred not to chance or fate, or even the wickedness of his persecutors, but to the absolute "good pleasure" of the Father, manifesting itself in its fullest measure in the hour of apparent failure. (Comp. Ps. 22:15.)

When thou shalt make ... —The sacrificial character of the death of the Servant is distinctly defined. It is a "trespass offering" (Lev. 6:6, 17; 14:12), an expiation for the sins of the people. The distinctive element in the trespass offering was that the man who confessed his guilt, voluntary or involuntary, paid his shekels, according to the judgment of the priest, and offered a ram, the blood of which was sprinkled upon the altar. It involved the idea not of an atonement only, but of a satisfaction, according to the nature of the sin.

(11) For he shall bear.—The importance of the renewal of the assurance given in verse 4 lies in its declaring the perpetuity of the atoning work. The sacrifice of the Servant is "forever" (Heb. 10:12).

(12) Because he hath poured out ... —The absolutely voluntary character of the sacrifice is again emphasized. So it was that **he bare** (and took away) **the sin of many,** and gained the power for availing intercession, both in the hour of death (Luke 23:34) and in the eternal triumph (Heb. 7:25). The ideal Servant, condemned, is seen, at last, to be identical with the ideal King.

54

(1) Sing, O barren ... —The words seem to carry on the jubilant strain of chap. 51 and 52:1-12, leaving the section 52:13-53:12, as a mysterious episode, inserted, it may be, by the prophet to show how it was that the restoration of Israel and the

victory of righteousness had become possible.

(4) Thou shalt forget.—The "shame of thy youth," was the Egyptian bondage, from which Jehovah chose Israel to be His bride (Jer. 3:1-11; Ezek. 16:1-14). The "reproach of widowhood" was the captivity in Babylon.

(6) For the Lord hath called thee.—The words find their explanation, perhaps their starting point, in the history of Hosea and Gomer (Hos. 1-3). The husband has punished the faithless wife by what seemed a divorce, but his heart yearns after her and he takes her back again.

(7) For a small moment.—Historically the words point to the seventy years of exile, as being but a transient interruption of the manifestation of the everlasting mercies. Spiritually they have wider and manifold fulfillments in the history of individuals, of the Church, of mankind.

(10) The covenant of my peace.— "Peace," as elsewhere in the Old Testament, approximates "salvation" of the New.

(11) I will lay thy stones with fair colours. —This is the first germ of the idealizing symbolism of the new Jerusalem. The language of Tobit 13:16, 17 shows the impression which it made on the Jews of the captivity. It takes its highest form, excluding all thoughts of a literal fulfillment, in Rev. 21:19-21.

55

(1) Ho, every one that thirsteth ... —The whole context shows that the water, the wine, the milk are all symbols of spiritual blessings as distinctly as they are, e.g., in John 4:10; Matt. 26:29; 1 Pet. 2:2. The invitation is addressed, as in a tone of pity, to the bereaved and afflicted one of 54:6, 7.

(3) I will make an everlasting covenant ... —The words find their explanation in the "new covenant" of Jer. 31:31, Luke 22:20, but those which follow show that it is thought of as the expansion and completion of that which had been made with David (II Sam. 7:12-17; Ps. 89:34, 35), as the representative of the true King, whom Isaiah now contemplates as identical with the "servant of the Lord."

(5) Thou shalt call a nation.—The calling of the Gentiles and the consequent expansion of the true idea of Israel is again dominant. (See Ps. 18:43.)

(6, 7) The appeal shows that the promised

blessings are conditional. There may come a time (Matt. 25:11) when "too late" will be written on all efforts to gain the inheritance which has been forfeited by neglect (II Cor. 6:2). The assertion of verse 8 refers to both the promise and the warning.

(11) So shall my word be ... —The point of the comparison (verse 10) is that the predominance of fertility in the natural world, in spite of partial or apparent failures, is the pledge of a like triumph, in the long run, of the purposes of God for man's good over man's resistance.

56

(1) Thus saith the Lord.—Verses 1-8 form a distinct section, and had a historical starting point. Circumstances in the closing years of Isaiah's life may well have given occasion to his teaching here. It obviously does not stand in any close connection with the preceding chapter.

(2) That keepeth the sabbath from polluting it ... —It lies in the nature of the case that a devout king like Hezekiah would be an observer of the Sabbath. It is almost certain that the counselors of the young Manasseh, abandoning the religion of Israel in other things, would also disregard this. The prophet's teaching was, no doubt, directed against that evil.

(6) Also the sons of the stranger ... — Proselytes also were to share in the blessings of the wider covenant. The germ of Isaiah's thought appears in Solomon's dedication prayer (I Kings 8:41-43). It receives its highest development (in its entire separation from the building with which there and here it is associated) in John 4:23.

(7) Even them will I bring ... —The words foreshadow the breaking down of the "middle wall of partition" (Eph. 2:14). Every privilege of the Israelite worshiper is to belong also to the proselyte. The development of truth is in such cases gradual, and it was left for Paul to complete the work of Isaiah (Rom. 2:26-29; Gal. 6:15).

(9) All ye beasts of the field ... —The sudden change of tone indicates an entirely new section, which extends to the close of chap. 57. The contents of that section fit in with the assumption of its having been written early in the reign of Manasseh, better than with that of a date after the Exile. The opening words summon the enemies of Israel to do their work of punishment, and this is followed naturally by a denunciation of the sins which had made it necessary.

57

(1) The righteous perisheth ... —The words seem written as if in the anticipation or in the actual presence of Manasseh's persecution of the true prophets. Isaiah finds comfort in the thought that the death of the survivors of Hezekiah's regime was a deliverance from yet worse evils.

(2) He shall enter into peace ... —For the righteous there was peace in death as in life. For the wicked there was peace in neither (verse 21).

(5) Slaying the children in the valleys ... —This had been done by Ahaz (II Chron. 28:3). It was perfectly natural that it should be done by Manasseh. There is not the slightest trace of the revival of the practice among the exiles in Babylon or after their return. The scenery described belongs distinctively to Palestine.

(9) Thou wentest to the king ... —The great king of Assyria, whose religion Judah had basely and shamefully adopted, is meant. The sin of Ahaz (II Kings 16:11) had been reproduced by his grandson. The description that follows is that of a harlot adorning herself for her evil calling (comp. Prov. 7:14-17). The "ointment" and "perfumes" are symbols of the treasures which were lavished to secure the Assyrian alliance. The words help us to understand Isaiah's indignation at what must have seemed to him the initial step of a like policy on the part of Hezekiah (39:3-7).

(19) The fruit of the lips ... —The words point to the praise and thanksgiving of the pardoned penitent. All these alike have their origin in the creative fiat of Jehovah, which proclaims "peace" (**i.e.,** salvation) to all, whether near or far, Jews in Jerusalem, or Jews in exile, or the Gentiles whose distance was that of spiritual remoteness. The message of healing is for all, yet conditional (verses 20, 21).

58

(1-7) The work of the preacher of repentance is not to be done slightly or by speaking smooth things (comp. Ezek. 13:10-15). The words point generally to the incongruous union, possible in the reign of Manasseh, but hardly possible after the exile, of this formal recognition of Jehovah with an apostate life. Every phrase rings in the tone of an incisive irony, describing each element of a true devotion which the people did **not** possess.

(8) All these images are heaped together to paint the fulness of blessing that follows on that true renunciation of the old evil selfishness of which fasting is but a symbol and a part.

(14) I will cause thee to ride upon the high places of the earth, i.e., of Canaan, the idea being that of a victorious march to occupy all commanding positions, and thus connecting itself with the full enjoyment of the heritage of Israel in the next clause.

59

(1) Behold, the Lord's hand ... —The declaration is an implied answer to the complaint, like that of 58:3, that the glorious promises had not as yet been fulfilled. The murmurers are told that the hindrance is on their side.

(9) Therefore is judgment.—The pleading of the prophet is followed by the confession which he makes on their behalf. They admit that the delay in the manifestation of God's judgment against their enemies, and of His righteousness (**i.e.,** bounty) toward themselves, has been caused by their own sins.

(20) And the Redeemer shall come ... —The picture of the theophany is continued—Jehovah comes as a Redeemer (**Goel**) to the true Zion, to those who have turned from their transgression. (See Rom. 11:26.)

(21) As for me, this is my covenant ... —See Gen. 17:4; Jer. 31:31; Heb. 8:10; 10:16. The new covenant is to involve the gift of the spirit, that writes the law of God inwardly in the heart, as distinct from the Law, which is thought of as outside the conscience, doing its work as an accuser and a judge.

60

(1) Arise, shine ... —The description is of the redeemed Zion—i.e., the new Jerusalem—seen in the prophet's vision as under the forms of the old. She has been prostrate, as in the darkness of Sheol (51:23; 57:9). The word comes that bids her rise to a new life, radiant with the glory of the Lord. (See Eph. 5:14.)

(8) Who are these ... —The vision of the

prophet brings before him the cloud-like sails of the ships that are bringing back the exiles over the Mediterranean and the Red Seas, hastening to their home like doves to their dove cote. See verse 11, which thought John transfers to the heavenly Jerusalem (Rev. 21:25, 26).

(14) The sons also of them that afflicted thee ... —The words are an expression of the law of inherited retribution, which entered so largely into the Hebrew's thought of the moral government of the world. That law will show itself in the prostrate homage with which the descendants of the old oppressors will recognize that the restored city is indeed the Zion of the Holy One of Israel.

(17) For brass I will bring gold ... —The material wealth of the days of Solomon (I Kings 10:21-27) furnishes another element in the picture of the ideal city (see verse 13).

61

(1) The Spirit of the Lord God is upon me ... —Guided by 41:1; 50:4-9, we recognize here, as there, the utterance of the ideal Servant of Jehovah. Our Lord applies the passage to His own work in Luke 4:16-22 (see notes). The opening words repeat what had been said by Jehovah of the Servant in 42:1.

(6) But ye shall be named the Priests of the Lord ... —This had been the original ideal of the nation's life (Exod. 19:6), forfeited for a time through the sins of the people (Exod. 28:1), to be fulfilled at last in the citizens of the new Jerusalem. (Comp. I Pet. 2:9.) The thought implies, it may be noted, that as Israel has succeeded to the position of the sons of Aaron, so mankind at large is to occupy the position of Israel, as chosen and redeemed. (See Rom. 11:12.)

62

(1) For Zion's sake ... —The speaker is the Servant of Jehovah. The true Servant will carry on what in the language of later theology may be called his mediatorial intercessory work, that there may be no delay in the fulfillment of the glorious promises that have just been uttered.

(4) Thou shalt no more be termed Forsaken ... —The change of name (see verse 2) is here partially indicated, and probably finds its starting point in the marriage of Hezekiah with Hephzibah (II Kings 21:1), which, on the assumption of Isaiah's authorship of these chapters, would be fresh in the prophet's memory. It would be entirely after his manner to see in the bride's name, as in those of his own sons, an omen of the future. The Hebrew word for Forsaken (**Azubah**) had been born by a previous queen, the mother of Jehoshaphat (I Kings 22:42). "Hephzi-bah" means "my delight is in her," and "Beulah," "married."

(6) **I have set watchmen upon thy walls ...** —The "watchmen" are the prophets. The prophets of the return from exile, Zechariah, Haggai, Malachi, may be thought of as representative examples of such "watchmen."

(11) **The Lord hath proclaimed ...** —A partial fulfillment of the words is found in the decree of Cyrus (Ezra 1:1, 2); but they have also a wider range, and take in all the events by which history becomes as the voice of God, proclaiming His will.

63

(1) **Who is this that cometh from Edom? ...** —There is no apparent connection between verses 1-6 and what precedes and follows. They must be dealt with, accordingly, as a separate section, though not by a different writer. The Edomites had been persistently hostile toward Judah. (See Amos 1:9-11; Obad. 10, 11.) They had been allies of the Assyrian invaders (Ps. 83:6) and had smitten Judah in the days of Ahaz (II Chron. 28:17). And later they would exult at the capture of Jerusalem (Ps. 137:7; Lam. 4:21). The memory of these things sank deep into the nation, and the first words of the last of the prophets echo the old hatred (Mal. 1:2-4). In the later days of Judaism, when rabbis uttered their curses against their oppressors, Edom was substituted for Rome, as John substitutes Babylon (Rev. 18:2). Isaiah, possibly starting from the memory of some recent outrages in the reign of Hezekiah, and taking Edom as the representative of all the nearer hereditary enemies of Israel, passes into an ecstacy of jubilation and sees the conquering king returning from his work of vengeance. He is none other than the ideal Servant of the Lord of Hosts, sharing His attributes.

(6) **Make them drunk** implies a change of imagery from that of the battle ("wine-press," verse 3) to that of the cup of wrath. The true analogue in the New Testament is that of the victory of the triumphant Christ in Rev. 19:11-13; but the agony and the cross were themselves a conflict with the powers of evil, and as He came out of that conflict as a conqueror, the words in which Isaiah paints the victor over Edom may, though in a much remoter analogy, be applicable to Him in that conflict also.

(7) **I will mention ...** —The words begin a psalm of thanksgiving for redemption (verse 16). Possibly, in the arrangement of the book it was thought that such a psalm followed rightly on the great dramatic dialogue which represented the victory of the Redeemer. The psalm begins, according to the implied rule of Ps. 50:23, with praise, and passes afterward to narrative and supplication.

(10) **Vexed his holy Spirit ...** —Here, and in Ps. 51:11, as in the "Angel of the Presence" (verse 9), we may note a foreshadowing of the truth of the trinal personality of the unity of the Godhead, which was afterward to be revealed.

(16) **Doubtless thou art our father, though Abraham ...** —The passage is striking as being an anticipation of the New Testament thought, that the Fatherhood of God rests on something else than hereditary descent, and extends not to a single nation only but to all mankind. Abraham might disclaim his degenerate descendants, but Jehovah would still recognize them. The words may possibly imply the idea (II Macc. 15:13, 14; Jer. 31:15) that Abraham was thought of as watching over his posterity and interceding for them. So, eventually, Abraham appears in the popular belief of Israel as welcoming his children in the unseen world (Luke 16:22).

64

(1) This is really a continuation of the prayer of 63:15-19.

(4) **Neither hath the eye seen, O God, beside thee ...** —The sense is not that God alone knows what He has prepared, but that no man knows any god who does such great things as He does. Paul, in I Cor. 2:9, applies the words freely, after his manner, to the eternal blessings which God prepares for His people. (See Clement of Rome, I Cor. 34.)

(7) **Hast consumed us, because of our iniquities.** —The previous clause had point-

ed to the people's forgetfulness of God—their indifference—as the root-evil. This states that that sin led, in the righteous judgment of God, to open iniquities. (See Rom. 1:21-24.)

(11) Our holy and our beautiful house ... —The destruction of the Temple, which the prophet sees in vision, with all its historic memories, comes as the climax of suffering, and, therefore, of the appeal to the compassion of Jehovah.

(12) Wilt thou refrain ... ?—The final appeal to the fatherly compassion of Jehovah: Could the God of Israel look on the scene of desolation, and not be moved to pity?

65

(1) I am sought of them ... —This was written after a considerable interval, and the prophet utters what had been revealed to him as explaining why the plaintive appeal of 64:12 did not meet at once with the answer that might have been expected. Jehovah speaks to the same people in verses 1 and 2, and both alike speak of indifference and hardness. Such words were a true description of the state of Israel, and are in close agreement with what follows. (Comp. Hos. 1:10; 2:1; Rom. 9:25, 26; I Pet. 2:10.)

(8) As the new wine ... —The transition from the denunciations which precede is abrupt, and suggests the thought of an interval of time and absence of direct continuity. God chastens, but does not destroy.

Destroy it not ... —The thought is that as even one fruitful cluster of grapes will lead the vinedresser to spare an otherwise fruitless vine in the hope of a fuller blessing in the future, so Jehovah will spare a sinful nation for the few righteous (Gen. 18:23-33). The words "destroy it not" are those which stand at the head of Pss. 57-59, as indicating the tune to which they were to be sung; and it is a natural inference that it may have been a popular vintage song, and therefore doubly apt for the prophet's purpose.

(11) That forget my holy mountain ... —The words imply, like verses 3-5, the abandonment of the worship of the Temple for a heathen ritual, but those that follow point to Canaanite rather than Babylonian idolatry. (Comp. Ps. 137:5.)

(17) Behold, I create new heavens ... —See Acts 3:21; Rom. 8:19; Gal. 4:26; II Pet. 3:13; Rev. 21:1, 10.

(25) The wolf and the lamb ... —In Paul's language, the "whole creation groaneth and travaileth together" (Rom. 8:22). In the new heaven and the new earth of the prophet's vision there would be no such discords. The condition of the ideal Paradise should be restored. While we dare not press the **letter** of prophetic visions as demanding a fulfilment, yet the permanence of Israel as a people suggests the possibility of a restored Jerusalem.

66

(1) The heaven is my throne ... —We are left to conjecture the historical starting point of this word of divine truth. Isaiah 56:7; 60:7, and the writings of Ezekiel, Haggai, and Zechariah, all presuppose the existence of a new Temple. We see in the words the utterance, in its strongest form, of the truth that God dwells not in temples made with hands, that utterance being compatible, as in the case of Solomon himself (II Chron. 6:18), of our Lord (John 2:16, 17; 4:21-23), of Stephen (Acts 7:48-50), with the profoundest reverence for the visible sanctuary.

(2) All those things ... —God, the Maker of the universe, can need nothing that belongs to it. The most stately temple is to Him as the infinitely little. What He does delight in is something which is generically different, the spiritual life which answers to His own, the "contrite heart," which is the true correlative of His own holiness. He who offers that is a true worshiper, with or without the ritual of worship; in its absence, all worship is an abomination to the Eternal. (Comp. 1:11-18; 57:15.)

(3) He that killeth an ox ... —Now the prophet declares that there may be as real an apostasy beneath an orthodox creed and an irreproachable ritual. Each act of the hypocrite's worship is as an idolatrous abomination.

(7-9) The implied thought is that God will not leave His work of national restoration unfinished. There shall not be that frustration of hopes when they seem just on the point of being fulfilled which the history of the world so often records. (Comp. 37:3.)

(13) One whom his mother comforteth ... —The image of maternal love, with which the prophet's mind is full, is presented in yet another aspect. The love which Zion gives, the love which her children receive from the nations (verses

10-12), are both but shadows of the infinite tenderness of Jehovah.

(19) I will set a sign among them ... —The "sign" is one of supernatural deliverance. The thought of a "remnant" to be saved is still characteristically dominant, and that "remnant" is to act as heralds of Jehovah to the far-distant nations who had not been sharers in any open antagonism to Israel, and who were, therefore, not involved in the great judgment.

(22) As the new heavens and the new earth ... —The transformation of 65:17 is presupposed, but that future kingdom of God shall perpetuate the historical continuity of that which has preceded it. Israel (the prophet's range of vision seems limited to the outward Israel, while Paul extends it to the spiritual) shall still exist. The ideal represented by that name will have an indestructible vitality.

(24) And they shall go forth ... —The vision of restoration and blessedness is balanced by that of the righteous condemnation of the wicked. The words "the worm shall not die" and "the fire shall not be quenched" became the starting point of the thoughts of later Judaism as to Gehenna (Ecclus. 7:17; Judith 16:17, and the Targum), and of the words in which our Lord Himself gave (Mark 9:44-48) the dominant eschatology of Christendom.

There is a strange solemnity in this being the last word of the prophet's book of revelation (comp. Matt. 25:46, at all but the close of our Lord's public teaching). When this chapter, or Eccles. 12, or Mal. 3 was read in the synagogue, the next to the last verse would be repeated after the last, so that mercy might appear as in the end triumphant after and over judgment (Cheyne).

JEREMIAH

1

(1) The words of Jeremiah.—The Hebrew for "words" has a somewhat wider connotation than the English, and is translated "acts" in I Kings 11:41; II Chron. 33:18.

Hilkiah.—Possibly the high priest of that name (II Kings 22:4, 23:4).

Anathoth.—In the tribe of Benjamin, one of the cities assigned to the priests, apparently to the house of Ithamar, to which Abiathar belonged (I Kings 2:26; Josh. 21:18; I Chron. 6:60).

(2) In the thirteenth year of his reign.—Josiah was at that time in his twentieth or twenty-first year, having grown up under the training of Hilkiah (II Kings 22). His active work of reformation began five years later. The near coincidence of the commencement of Jeremiah's work as prophet with that of the king must not be forgotten. As Josiah reigned for thirty-one years, we have to place eighteen years of the prophet's ministry as under his rule.

(3) It came also . . .—The short reigns of Jehoahaz (three months) and Jehoiachin or Jeconiah (three months also) are passed over, and mention made of the more conspicuous reigns of Jehoiakim (eleven years) and Zedekiah (also eleven). Assuming Jeremiah to have been about twenty when the prophetic call came to him, he was sixty or sixty-one at the time of the captivity.

(4) The word of the Lord came unto me.—The words imply obviously a revelation, the introduction of a new element into the human consciousness. In many cases such a revelation implied also the spiritual tension of an ecstatic or trance-like state, a dream, or an open vision. It almost presupposed a previous training, outward or inward, a mind vexed by hot thoughts and mourning over the sins of the people. (See Isa. 49:1.)

(5) I knew thee.—This implies not foreknowledge only, but choice and approval (Pss. 1:6; 37:18; Amos 3:2).

Unto the nations.—This was the distinguishing characteristic of Jeremiah's work. Other prophets were sent to Israel and Judah, with occasional parentheses of prophecies that affected the Gentiles. The horizon of Jeremiah was to extend more widely. In part his work was to make them drink of the cup of the Lord's fury (25:15-17); but in part also he was a witness to them of a brighter future (48:47; 49:39). It is as though he had drunk in the Spirit of Isaiah, and thought of the true prophet as one who was to be a light of the Gentiles (Isa. 49:6).

(6) I am a child.—Later Jewish writers fix the age of fourteen as that up to which the term rendered "child" might be used. With Jeremiah it was probably more indefinite, and in the intense consciousness of his own weakness he would naturally use a word below the actual standard of his age. There is, accordingly, nothing against assuming any age up to twenty-one. The words are memorable as striking a note common to the lives of most men as they feel themselves called to any great work. (See Exod. 4:10; Isa. 6:5; Luke 5:8; I Tim. 4:12.) In tracing the whole course of Jeremiah's work, we must never forget the divine constraint by which he entered on them (see I Cor. 9:16).

(9) The Lord put forth his hand . . .—The "hand of the Lord," as in Ezek. 3:14; 8:1; etc., was the received symbol of the special influence of the Spirit of the Lord; and here, as in the case of Isaiah, the act implied the gift of new powers of thought and utterance.

(10) I have this day set thee . . .—The work at first seems one simply of destruction. But beyond that there is the hope of a work of construction. He is to "build up" the fallen ruins of Israel, to "plant" in the land that had been made desolate. The whole sequel of the book is a comment on these words. It passes through terror and darkness to the glory and the blessing of the New Covenant (31:31).

(11) In contrast to the words of terror, in harmony with the words of hope, he sees the almond-bough, with its bright pink blossoms and its pale green leaves, the token of an early spring rising out of the dreariness of winter. The name of the almond-tree made the symbol yet more expressive. It was the **watcher**, the tree that "hastens to awake" out of its wintry sleep, and thus expresses the divine haste which would not without cause delay the fulfillment of its gracious promise, but would, as it were, make it bud and blossom, and bear fruit.

(13) A seething pot; and the face thereof is toward the north.—More correctly, **from the north**. The next symbol was one that set forth the darker side of the prophet's work. It told too plainly the terrors which were to be expected from the regions that lay to the north of the land of Israel, Assyria and Chaldaea.

(16) I will utter my judgments against them.—See 39:5, Nebuchadnezzar's sentence on Zedekiah. And yet the invaders in their sentence are to be but the ministers of a higher judgment than their own. In the words "my judgments" He recognizes their work.

(17) Gird up thy loins.—Be as the messenger who prepares to be swift on his errand, and to go wherever he is sent. The vivid image of intense activity reappears in the New Testament, and has become proverbial in the speech of Christendom.

Be not dismayed.—The reign of Manasseh had shown that the work of the prophet might easily lead to the fate of the martyr (II Kings 21:16), thus the repeated calls to courage.

2

Chapters 2-6 constitute one continuous whole, and, looking to the fact that the original record of his prophetic work during the reign of Josiah (3:6) had been destroyed by Jehoiakim (36:23), and was afterward rewritten from memory, it is probable that we have a kind of **précis** of what was then destroyed, with some additions (36:32), and possibly some omissions.

(2) The scene of the call was in his home at Anathoth. Now the prophet is sent to begin his work in Jerusalem. Here the faithfulness of the past is contrasted with the unfaithfulness of the present.

(3) Holiness unto the Lord.—The thought was that expressed in the inscription on the gold plate worn on the high priest's forehead (Exod. 28:36). The prophet was taught that Israel, as a nation, had a priestly character, and was consecrated to the Lord as the "firstfruits" of the great harvest of the world. Comp. Jas. 1:18; Rom. 11:16.

(5) Vanity.—As in the character of a husband wronged by his wife's desertion, Jehovah pleads with His people and asks whether He has failed in anything.

(8) The priests said not ...—As throughout the work of Jeremiah and most of the prophets of the Old Testament, that which weighed most heavily on their souls was that those who were called to be guides of the people were themselves the chief agents in the evil. The rebuke, we must remember, came from the lips of one who was himself a priest.

(9, 10) Comp. Hos. 2:2. The injured lord and husband will appear as the accuser of the faithless bride, and set forth her guilt as in an indictment. The whole earth might be searched without finding a parallel to the guilt of Israel.

(16) Also the children of Noph ...—We pass from the language of poetry to that of history, and the actual enemies of Israel appear on the scene, not as the threatening danger in the north, but in the far south. The LXX translators, following an Egyptian tradition, identify the Hebrew Noph with Memphis in northern Egypt.

(18) In the way of Egypt ... ?—The words point to the tendency to court the alliance now of one, now of the other, of the great kingdoms of the world. The Egyptian party gained ground under Jehoiakim, while Jeremiah, opposing its strength, urged the wisdom of accepting the guidance of events and submitting to the Chaldaeans (so far continuing the line of action adopted by Hezekiah), and ultimately was accused of deserting his own people and "falling away" to their oppressors (37:13).

(20) The "high hill" and the "green tree" point to the localities of idol-worship—the "high places" (I and II Kings), the "tops of the mountains" and the "oaks and poplars and elms" (Hos. 4:13). Tree worship in Judaea appears to have exercised a wonderful power of fascination.

(23, 24) The words paint with vividness the eager, restless state of the daughter of Zion in its harlot-like lust for the false gods of the heathen. The female camel and the wild ass, at the season when the stimulus of animal desire is strongest, were now fit images for her who had once been the betrothed of Jehovah.

(30) Your own sword hath devoured your prophets.—In the long reign of Manasseh, for example, the prophets who rebuked him had to do so at the risk of their lives. Isaiah, according to tradition, had been foremost among the sufferers. Much innocent blood had been shed from one end to another of Jerusalem (II Kings 21:11-16).

(35) Yet thou sayest ...—Here, as in verse 33, there is an implied reference to the partial reformation under Josiah. The accuser retorts, and renews his pleadings against her. Confession might have led to forgiveness, but this denial of guilt excluded it and was the token of a fatal blindness.

(36) Why gaddest thou ... ?—Shame and confusion should follow from the alliance with Pharaoh-nechoh, as it had followed from that with Tiglath-pileser (II Kings 16:10; II Chron. 28:20).

3

(1) See Deut. 24:4, which forbade the return to the past husband as an abomination, a law which the recent discovery of the Book of the Law (II Kings 22:10, 11) had probably brought into prominence. But there is also an obvious allusion to the like imagery in Hosea. Jeremiah has to make the apostate adulteress at least feel that she had sinned too deeply to have any claims to forgiveness.

(2) **Lift up thine eyes.**—The consciousness of guilt was the only foundation of repentance, and the prophet's work, therefore, in tenderness, is to paint that guilt in the darkest colors possible. Still keeping to the parable of the faithless wife, he bids Israel to look to the "high places" that have witnessed her adulteries with those other lords for whom she had forsaken Jehovah.

As the Arabian in the wilderness.—The Arabian is chosen as the representative of the lawless predatory tribes of the desert. As they lay in ambush, waiting eagerly for their victims, so had the harlot Israel laid wait for her lovers, and so the land had been polluted.

(3) **Therefore the showers . . .** —Outward calamities were looked upon as chastisements for these sins. There had apparently been a severe drought in the reign of Josiah (9:12; 25:1-6). The influence of the newly-discovered book of Deuteronomy (II Chron. 34:14; II Kings 22:8) had doubtless given a fresh emphasis to this view of natural disasters.

(6) **The Lord said also unto me . . .** —The main point of the new prophecy, delivered, like the former, under Josiah, is the comparison of the guilt of the two kingdoms of Israel and Judah. The latter had been looking on the former with contemptuous scorn. She is now taught—the same imagery being continued that had begun in the first discourse—that her guilt is by far the greater of the two.

(10) **And yet for all this . . .** —Judah was so far worse than Israel that there had been a simulated repentance, as in the reformations under Hezekiah and Josiah, but it was not with the whole heart and soul. Thus the **renegade** was better than the **traitoress**; open rebellion was better than hypocrisy (verse 11).

(13) **Only acknowledge . . .** —This was the one sufficient, indispensable condition of pardon—the confession that kept nothing back, and made no vain excuses.

(14) **I am married unto you.**—The tender pity of Jehovah leads Him to offer pardon even to the adulterous wife. Jeremiah had learned, in all their fullness, the lessons of Hos. 1-3. The limitation to the "one" and the "two" is after the manner of Isaiah's reference (1:9) to the "remnant" that should be saved.

(16) **They shall say no more, The ark of the covenant of the Lord.**—This is noteworthy as containing the germ of the great thought of the New Covenant developed in 31:31. The Ark, the very center of the worship of Israel, the symbol of the divine presence, should pass away (see II Kings 18:4), and take its place as belonging only to the past. The words had, of course, a fulfillment in the ritual of the second Temple, where there was no ark in the Holy of Holies, and that loss was probably what Jeremiah foresaw most clearly, and for which he sought to prepare his people, as the writer of the Epistle to the Hebrews (8:13) did to prepare those of his time for the more entire destruction of the Temple and its worship.

(18) As with Isaiah (11:13), so with Jeremiah, the hope, however distant, of national reformation was bound up with that of a restoration of national unity. The healing of the long-standing breach between Israel and Judah, coeval almost with the commencement of Israel as a people, was to be the glory of the Messiah's kingdom. The thoughts of the prophet turn chiefly to the land of the exile of the ten tribes; but his words imply that he foresees a like exile also in the north for Judah. In that far-off land the house of Judah shall walk **to** the house of Israel, seeking its alliance, asking for reconciliation, and both should once again dwell in the land of their inheritance.

4

(3) **For thus saith the Lord. . .**—The words seem the close of one discourse, the opening of another. The parable of Israel is left behind, and the appeal to Judah and Jerusalem is more direct. (Comp. Hos. 10:12; Matt. 13:7.)

(4) **Circumcise yourselves to the Lord.**—The words show that the prophet had grasped the meaning of the symbol which to so many Jews was merely an outward sign. He saw the fleshly, unrenewed nature as contrasted with the "spirit," the "old man" which Paul contrasts with the new (Rom.

6:6; 8:7). The verbal coincidence with Deut. 10:16 and 30:6 shows the influence of that book, of which we find so many traces in Jeremiah's teaching.

(6) From the north.—The Chaldaean, and possibly the Scythian, invasion, as in 1:14.

(7) Without an inhabitant.—The language, like that of Isaiah (6:11), was probably in some measure hyperbolical, but the depopulation caused by the Chaldaean invasion (39:9) must have been extreme.

(8) Gird you with sackcloth.—From the earliest times this was the outward sign of mourning, and therefore of repentance (Joel 1:8; Isa. 22:12).

(9) The heart of the king shall perish.—The heart represents the mind generally. Judgment and wisdom were to give way to panic and fear.

(10) Ah, Lord God! surely thou hast greatly deceived this people.—The words are startling, but are eminently characteristic. Jeremiah had been led to utter words that told of desolation and destruction. But if these were true, what was he to think of the words of the other prophets, who, speaking in the name of the Lord, had promised peace through the reign of Josiah, and even under Jehoiakim? Had not Jehovah apparently sanctioned those prophets also?

(12) A full wind from those places—i.e., more tempestuous than those which serve for the work of the thresher, and blowing away both grain and chaff together. This wind was devastating, and a fit symbol of the terrible invader.

Give sentence against them—against the sinful people of Judah and Jerusalem.

(13) Swifter than eagles.—For the flight of the eagle as representing the swift march of the invader, comp. Lam. 4:19; Hos. 8:1; Hab. 1:8.

(14) O Jerusalem.—The prophet answers the cry that comes from the city. In that "washing of the heart" which had seemed impossible before (2:22), but is thought of now as "possible with God," is the one hope of salvation. (Comp. Isa. 1:16.)

(15) Dan ... mount Ephraim.—The two places are chosen, not like Dan and Beersheba, as extreme limits, but as stages in the march of the invader: first Dan (as in 8:16), the northernmost point (Deut. 34:1; Judg. 20:1) of the whole land of Israel, then Mount Ephraim, as the northern boundary of Judaea.

(17) Field.—The image is that of a nomadic tribe encamped in the open country,

or of men watching their flocks (Luke 2:8) or crops (Job. 27:18). So shall be the tents of the invaders around Jerusalem—keeping. or (II Sam. 11:16) "observing," i.e., "blockading" the city.

(19) My bowels, my bowels!—The cry of anguish is that of the despairing people with whom Jeremiah identifies himself. We thus have the utterances of three of the great actors in the tragedy: here of the people, in verse 22 of Jehovah, in verse 23 of the prophet. The "bowels" were with the Hebrews thought of as the seat of all the strongest emotions, whether of sorrow, fear, or sympathy (Job 30:27; Isa. 16:11).

(21) How long shall I see ...—The "standard," as in verse 6, is the alarm signal given to the fugitives. The "trumpet" sounds to give the alarm, and quicken their flight to the defensed city. The prophet sees no end to the miseries of the coming war.

(23) I beheld the earth.—In words of terrible grandeur the prophet speaks as if he had already seen the consummated destruction, and repeats the words "I beheld" as if he had passed through four distinct visions, describing its completeness.

Without form, and void.—An obvious quotation from the **tohu va-bohu** of Gen. 1:2. The goodly land of Israel was thrown back, as it were, into a formless chaos, before the words "Let there be light" had brought it into order.

(28) For this shall the earth mourn ...—As with all true poets, the face of nature seems to the prophet to sympathize with human suffering. (Comp. Amos 8:9; Matt. 24:29.)

(30, 31) The prophet draws his pictures with a terrible intensity. On the one side is Zion as the harlot, in her gold and crimson and cosmetics; on the other we see the forlorn and desperate castaway, in the hour of a woman's utter helplessness, outraged and abandoned, stretching out her hands to implore mercy from the assassins who attack her, and imploring it in vain.

5

(1) Run ye to and fro.—The dark shades of the picture seem at first hardly to belong to the reign of Josiah, which is brought before us in II Kings 22, 23; II Chron. 34, 35, as one of thorough reformation. It is, of course, possible that parts of the picture may have been worked up when the prophecies were rewritten under Jehoiakim

(36:32); but, on the other hand, it is equally possible that the prophet may have seen even at the time how hollow and incomplete that reformation was. The form in which he utters his conviction reminds one of the old story of the Greek sage, Diogenes, appearing in the streets of Athens with a lantern, searching for an honest man. (Comp. Gen. 18:25, 32.)

(2) The Lord liveth.—The guilt of the men of Jerusalem was that they took the most solemn formula of all, "Jehovah liveth," and yet were guilty of perjury. In verse 7 we find traces of the practice: of swearing by other gods, with which this "oath of Jehovah" is apparently contrasted.

(5) But these.—The great as well as the poor, the learned as well as the ignorant, are altogether evil, the former even more defiant in breaking through all conventional constraints than the latter.

(6) A lion out of the forest.—The imagery is vivid in itself. The three forms of animal ferocity—lion, wolf, leopard—represent, perhaps, the three phases of simple fierceness, ravenousness, and cunning; possibly even three oppressors in whom those attributes were to be impersonated are brought together to embody the cruelty of the invader.

(7) There is probably an implied reference to the covenant to which the people had sworn in the time of Josiah. The singular "house" is correct, perhaps used because the prophet thinks primarily of the idol's temple as the scene of the adulteress's guilt, which here, as elsewhere, is the symbol of national apostasy.

(12) It is not he—i.e., It is not Jehovah who speaks. They listened to the prophet's warnings as if they came from himself only, and brought with them no certainty of the "sword" or "famine" which they foretold. Perhaps, however, the words refer also to the denial that Jehovah was working in the sufferings that fell upon the people, or even to a more entire denial, like that of the fool in Ps. 14:1.

(15) Whose language thou knowest not.—To the Jew, as to the Greek, the thought of being subject to a people of alien speech, a "barbarian," added a new element of bitterness. Comp. Isa. 28:11; Deut. 28:49.

(18) I will not make a full end.—What seems the extremest sentence is tempered by the assurance that it is not absolutely final. It is intended to be reformatory, and not merely penal. (See verse 10; 4:27.)

(22) Which have placed the sand ... —

The greatness of Jehovah is shown by the majesty of His work in nature. (Comp. Job 38:8-11.) Here was the token that even the forces which seem wildest and least restrained are subject to an over-ruling law. Even the sand which seems so shifting keeps in the surging waters.

(23) But this people ... —The contrast seems to lie in the fact that the elements are subject to God's will, but that man's rebellious will, with its fatal gift of freedom, has the power to resist it.

(24) The Lord our God, that giveth rain ... —The "early" rains are those that come in autumn, the latter those which close the season in spring. The former argument in what we may call the prophet's natural theology had been drawn from the presence of law in the midst of what seemed the lawless elements of nature. Now he urges that drawn from regularity of succession. Comp. Deut. 11:14; Prov. 16:15; James 5:7.

The appointed weeks of the harvest—the seven weeks included between the beginning of the barley harvest at the Passover and the completion of the wheat harvest at Pentecost.

(25) These things—i.e., the rain and the harvest which, from the prophet's point of view, had been withheld in consequence of the sins of the people.

(27) A cage.—The large wicker basket (Amos 8:1, 2) in which the fowler kept the birds he had caught, or, possibly, used for decoy-birds.

(28) They overpass the deeds of the wicked.—The prophet dwells not only on the prosperity of the wicked, but on their callous indifference to the well-being of the poor.

(31) My people love to have it ... —The words imply more than an acquiescence in evil, and describe an ethical condition like that of Rom. 1:32. The final question implies that the people were running into a destruction which they would have no power to avert.

6

(1) O ye children of Benjamin.—The city, though claimed as belonging to Judah, was actually on the border of the two tribes. The boundary ran through the valley of Ben-Hinnom (Josh. 15:8; 18:16), and its northern walls were in that of Benjamin. It was natural that the prophet of Anathoth should think and speak of it as connected with his own people.

Blow the trumpet in Tekoa—i.e., "give the signal for the fugitives to halt, but not till they have reached the southernmost boundary of Judah." Tekoa was about twelve miles south of Jerusalem (II Chron. 11:6).

Beth-haccerem—i.e., **the house of the vineyard**, halfway on the road from Jerusalem to Tekoa. There, too, the smoke signal was to be raised that the fugitives might gather around it.

(3) This refers to the leaders and the armies of the invaders. The work of plunder was to go on everywhere. The imagery is drawn from the attack of a nomadic tribe on a richly-cultivated plain.

(4) Prepare ye war.—The opening of the battle was accompanied by sacrifices, divinations, and prayers. The cry thus given with dramatic force comes from the soldiers of the invading army impatient for the fight. They are so eager that, instead of resting at noon, as usual, for their midday meal, they would press on for the assault. Their orders are against this, and, as the shadows lengthen, they raise their cry of complaint.

(6) The words describe graphically the process of an Eastern siege. (See note on Ezek. 4:2.)

(9) Turn back thine hand.—The image of the grape-gatherer carrying on his work to the last grape or tendril was a natural parable of unsparing desolation. The command is addressed to the minister of destruction, Nebuchadnezzar, or, it may be, to the angel of death.

(11) I will pour it out.—The words that follow describe the several stages of man's life, upon all of which that torrent of wrath is to flow forth.

(13) Is given to covetousness.—The Hebrew word does not necessarily involve the idea of dishonest gain, though this is often implied. What the prophet condemns is the universal desire of gain, sure to lead to a gratification of it by fair means or foul.

From the prophet even unto the priest . . .—The two orders that ought to have checked the evil are noted as having been foremost in promoting it.

(14) Peace, peace.—The word is taken almost in the sense of "health." The false prophets were as physicians who told the man suffering from a fatal disease that he was in full health. As the previous words show, the prophet has in his mind the false

encouragements given by those who should have been the true guides of the people. Looking at Josiah's reformation as sufficient to win the favor of Jehovah, they met Jeremiah's warnings of coming evil by the assurance that all was well, and that invasion and conquest were far-off dangers.

(16) Stand ye in the ways.—In the prophet's mind the people were as a traveler who has taken a self-chosen path, and finds that it leads him to a place of peril. Is it not well that they should stop and ask where the old paths (literally, **the eternal paths**) were, on which their fathers had traveled safely? The call, however, was in vain. The people chose to travel still in the broad way that led them to destruction.

(17) Watchmen.—These are the prophets blowing the trumpet of alarm, proclaiming, as in verse 1, the nearness of the invader, and calling on them to flee from the wrath of Jehovah. They call, however, in vain. The people refuse to hearken.

(22) From the north country . . . —The words point, as in 1:13-15, to the Chaldaean, perhaps to the Scythian, invasion. So the "north quarters" are used in Ezek. 38:6, 15; 39:2 of the home of Gog as the representative of the Scythian tribes.

(23) Cruel.—The ferocity of the Chaldaeans seems to have been exceptional. Prisoners impaled, or flayed alive, or burned in the furnace (29:22; Dan. 3:11) were among the common incidents of their wars and sieges.

They ride upon horses.—This appears to have been a novelty to the Israelites, accustomed to the war chariots of Egypt and their own kings rather than to actual cavalry. (Comp. 8:16; Job 39:21-25; Hab. 1:8; Isa. 30:16; Ezek. 38:4; 39:3.)

(26) Wallow thyself in ashes.—The ordinary sign of mourning was to sprinkle dust or ashes on the head (II Sam. 1:2, 13:19; Josh. 7:6). This, as in 25:34; Micah 1:10; Job. 2:8, indicated more utter wretchedness and prostration.

(28) Brass and iron.—Base metals serving for vile uses, no gold or silver in them. The imagery carries on the thought of the previous verse. (Comp. Isa. 1:22, 25; Ezek. 22:18-22; Mal. 3:3.)

(29) The bellows are burned.—In the interpretation of the parable the "bellows" answer to the life of the prophet as filled with the breath or spirit of Jehovah. He is, as it were, consumed with that fiery blast, and yet his work is faulty.

(30) Reprobate silver.—Better, "refuse sil-

539

ver," the dross and not the metal: so worthless that even Jehovah, as the great refiner, rejects it utterly, as yielding nothing.

7

(1) This chapter and the three that follow form again another great prophetic sermon delivered to the crowds that flocked to the Temple. The description of idolatry as prevalent, and possibly the reference to the presence of the Chaldaean invader in 8:16 and 10:22, fit in by date with the reign of Jehoiakim; and from the special reference to Shiloh in 26:6, 9, as occurring in a prophecy delivered at the beginning of that reign, it was probably this discourse that drew down that king's displeasure (see verse 14).

(2) **The gate of the Lord's house.**—As a priest, Jeremiah would have access to all parts of the Temple. On some day when the courts were thronged with worshipers (verse 10), probably a fast-day especially appointed, he stands at the inner gate of one of the courts, and looking about on the multitudes that thronged it, speaks to them the message which he had been especially commissioned to deliver.

(4) **Trust ye not in lying words . . .** —The emphatic threefold repetition of the words thus condemned—"The temple of the Lord"—points to its having been the burden of the discourses of the false prophets, possibly to the solemn iteration of the words in the litanies of the supplicants. With no thought of the divine Presence of which it was the symbol, they were ever harping on its greatness, identifying themselves and the people with that greatness, and predicting its perpetuity. (Comp. Matt. 24:1.) The higher truth that the "congregation" of Israel was the living Temple (I Cor. 3:16; I Pet. 2:5) was not likely to be in the thoughts of those whom Jeremiah rebuked.

(6) **The stranger, the fatherless, and the widow**—the three great representatives of the poor and helpless, standing most in need, therefore, of man's justice and of the divine protection (Deut. 14:29; 24:19-21).

(10) The people tried to combine the worship of Baal and Jehovah, and passed from the one temple to the other. They went away from the fast or feast in the house of the Lord with the feeling that they were "saved," or "delivered." They had gone through their religious duties and

might claim their reward. The prophet seems to repeat their words in a tone of irony: they were "delivered," not **from** their abominations, but as if set free to do them.

(11) **A den of robbers.**—The words had a special force in a country like Palestine, where the limestone rocks presented many caves, which (I Sam. 22:1, 2) were the refuge of outlaws and robbers. Those who now flocked to the courts of the Temple were as such robbers, finding shelter there and soothing their consciences by their worship. The word for "robber" implies the more violent form of lawless plunder. (See Matt. 21:13; Mark 11:17; Luke 19:46.)

(12) **My place which was in Shiloh.**—The history of the past showed that a Temple dedicated to Jehovah could not be desecrated with impunity. Shiloh had been chosen for the center of the worship of Israel after the conquest of Canaan (Josh. 18:1), and was reverenced as such through the period of the Judges. It had not, however, been a center of light and purity (see Judg. 21:19-21; I Sam. 2:22; etc.). And so the judgment came. It is possible, as the words "temple" (I Sam. 1:9; 3:3) and "house" (Judg. 18:31; I Sam. 3:15) applied to it suggest, that substantial buildings may have gathered around the original tabernacle, and that those wasted ruins may have given a special force to Jeremiah's allusion. Yet these Jews presently were startled when they heard that as terrible a doom was impending over the Temple of which they boasted.

(13) **Rising up early and speaking.**—A characteristic phrase of Jeremiah's, and used (twelve times) by him only. In its bold anthropomorphism it takes the highest form of human activity, waking from sleep and beginning at the dawn of day, to represent the like activity in God.

(15) **The whole seed of Ephraim.**—The fate of the tribes of the Northern kingdom, among which Ephraim had always held the leading position, was already familiar to the people. They were dwelling far off by the cities of the Medes (II Kings 15:29; 17:6; 18:11). A like exile was, they were now told, to be their own portion.

(16) **Pray not thou.**—The words imply that a prayer of intercession was rising up in the heart of the prophet. He is told that he must check it. Judgment must have its way. The discipline must be left to do its work. A like impulse met by a like repression is found in 11:14 and 14:11.

(18) **The queen of heaven.**—The goddess

thus described was a kind of Assyrian Artemis, identified with the moon and connected with the symbolic worship of the reproductive powers of Nature.

(22) I spake not ... concerning burnt offerings or sacrifices.—What is meant is that they were not the end contemplated. The first promulgation of the Law, the basis of the covenant with Israel, contemplated a spiritual, ethical religion, of which the basis was found in the ten great commandments of Exod. 20. The ritual in connection with sacrifice was prescribed partly as a concession to the feeling which showed itself, in its evil form, in the worship of the golden calf, partly as an education. The book of Deuteronomy, representing the higher truth from which Moses started (Exod. 19:5), and upon which he at last fell back, bore its witness to the original purport of the Law (Deut. 6:3; 10:12). Its rediscovery under Josiah left, here as elsewhere, its impress on the mind of Jeremiah. But other prophets (I Sam. 15:22; Pss. 50, 51; Hos. 6:6; 8:11-13; Amos 5:21-27; Mic. 6:6-8) had all along borne a like witness, even while recognizing to the full the fact and the importance of a sacrificial ritual.

(25, 26) The general thought was that the whole history of Israel had been one of progressive deterioration, reaching its climax in the generation in which Jeremiah lived.

(30) In the house which is called by my name.—This had been done by Ahaz (II Chron. 28:2); and after the Temple had been cleansed by Hezekiah (II Chron. 29:5) it had been repeated by Manasseh (II Kings 21:4-7; II Chron. 33:3-7). Josiah's reformation again checked the tendency to idolatry (II Kings 23:4; II Chron. 34:3); but it is quite possible that the pendulum swung back again when his death left the idolatrous party in Judah free to act.

(31) Tophet.—See note on 19:12.

To burn their sons and their daughters.—Comp. 32:35. The children were, in some cases at least, actually burned, though often, perhaps (see Ezek. 16:21), slain first. Horrible as the practice seems to us, it was part of the Canaanite or Phoenician worship of Molech or Malcom (Lev. 18:21; 20:2-5), and had been practiced by Ahaz (II Kings 16:3; II Chron. 28:3) and Manasseh (II Kings 21:6; II Chron. 33:6).

8

(1) At that time.—The time is that of the destruction of Jerusalem by the Chaldaeans and of the burial of the slain. Not even the dead should sleep in peace. The motives of this desecration of the sepulchers might be either the wanton ferocity of barbarian conquerors, or the greed of gain and the expectation of finding concealed treasures. So Hyrcanus, to the great scandal of the Jews, broke open the sepulcher of David (Jos. **Ant.** 7:15).

(7) The eye of the prophet looked on nature at once with the quick observation of one who is alive to all her changes, and with the profound thought of a poet finding inner meanings in all phenomena. The birds of the air obey their instincts as the law of their nature. Israel, with its fatal gift of freedom, resists that which is its law of life.

(8) How do ye say ... ?—The question is put to priests and prophets, who were the expounders of the Law, but not to them only. The order of scribes, which became so dominant during the exile, was already rising into notice. The discovery of the Book of the Law (II Chron. 34:15) would naturally give a fresh impetus to their work. They were boasting of their position as the recognized instructors of the people.

Lo, certainly ... —The **pen** was the iron **stylus** made for engraving on stone or metal. The sophistry of men was turning the truth of God into a lie and emptying it of its noblest meaning. In his protest against the teaching of the scribes, with their traditional and misleading casuistry, Jeremiah appears as foreshadowing the prophet of Nazareth (Matt. 5:20-48; 23:2-26).

(9) They have rejected the word of the Lord.—The "wise men" are apparently distinguished from the scribes, probably as students of the ethical books of Israel, as distinct from the Law. The reign of Hezekiah had been memorable for such studies (Prov. 25:1). They, too, kept within the range of traditional maxims and precepts, perhaps with stress on ceremonial rather than moral obligations; and when the word of Jehovah came to them straight from the lips of the prophets, they refused to listen to it.

(16) Heard from Dan.—The invasion by an army of which cavalry and war chariots formed the most terrible contingent was a special terror to Israelites. Even at Dan, the northern boundary of Palestine, there was a sound of terror in the very snortings of the horses. (See 4:13, 15.)

(17) The image of terror is from the fiery serpents of Num. 21:6, or from the connection of Dan with the "serpent" and "adder" (Gen. 49:17). The symbolism which identified a hissing, venomous snake with the Assyrian or Chaldaean power had already appeared in Isa. 14:29. The "deaf adder" that "refuseth to hear the voice of the charmer" represents an implacable enemy waging a pitiless war.

(20) The harvest is past . . . —The question of Jehovah (verse 19), admitting of no answer but a confession of guilt, is met by another cry of despair from the sufferers of the future. They are as men in a year of famine—"The harvest is past," and there has been no crop for men to reap. It is well to remember that the barley harvest coincided with the Passover, the wheat harvest with Pentecost, the fruit gathering with the autumn Feast of Tabernacles.

(22) Is there no balm in Gilead . . . ?— The resinous gums of Gilead were prominent in the pharmacopoeia of Israel, and were exported to Egypt for the embalmment of the dead (Gen. 37:25; 43:11; Jer. 46:11; 51:8). A plaster of such gums was the received prescription for healing a wound. The question of the prophet is, therefore, a parable. Are there no means of healing, no healer to apply them, for the spiritual wounds of Israel? The prophets were her physicians, repentance and righteousness were her balm of Gilead.

9

(1) Oh, that my head were waters . . . !— Literally, **Who will give my head waters . . . ?** The form of a question was, in Hebrew idiom as in Latin, the natural utterance of desire.

(2) A lodging place of wayfaring men.— In shelter far from the cities of Judah, the prophet, with a feeling like that of the psalmist (Ps. 55:6-8) would find refuge from his treacherous enemies, "adulterers," alike spiritually and literally (5:8).

(4) Take ye heed . . . —The extreme bitterness of the prophet's words is explained in part by what we read afterward of his personal history (12:6; 18:18). Then, as at other times, a man's foes were those of his own household (Matt. 10:36).

(7) I will melt them and try them.—The prophet, speaking in the name of Jehovah reverts to the imagery of 6:28-30 and Isa. 48:10. Evil has progressed to the point that nothing is left but the melting of the fiery furnace of affliction.

(12) Who is the wise man . . . ?—Sage (comp. 8:9) and prophet are alike called on to state why the misery of which Jeremiah speaks is to come upon the people. But they are asked in vain, and Jehovah, through the prophet, makes answer to Himself.

(14) Baalim.—The generic name for false gods of all kinds, and therefore used in the plural. (Comp. 2:8, 23.)

(17) Mourning women . . . cunning women.—Eastern funerals were attended by mourners, chiefly women, hired for the purpose. Wailing was reduced to an art, and they who practiced it were cunning. (Comp. 22:18; Eccles. 12:5; Amos 5:16; Mark 5:38.) They are summoned as to the funeral, not of a friend or neighbor, but of the nation.

(20) Teach your daughters wailing.—The words rest upon the idea that wailing was an art, its cries and tones skillfully adapted to the special sorrows of which it was in theory the expression. They perhaps imply also that death would do its work so terribly that the demand for mourners would be greater than the supply. (Comp. Luke 23:27, 28.)

(22) As the handful.—The reaper gathered into small sheaves what he could hold in his left hand, as he went on cutting with his sickle. These he threw down as they became too big to hold, and they were left strewn on the field until he returned to gather them up into larger sheaves. So should the bodies of the dead be strewn, the prophet says, on the open field, but there should be none to take them up and bury them.

(23) Let not the wise man glory in his wisdom.—The long prophecy of judgment had reached its climax. Now there comes the conclusion of the whole matter—that the one way of salvation is to renounce all reliance on the wisdom, greatness, wealth of the world, and to glory only in knowing Jehovah. (Comp. John 17:3; I Cor. 1:31; II Cor. 10:17.)

(26) All the heathen are in God's sight as uncircumcised, whether they practice the outward rite or not—and the state of Israel was no better than theirs, for she too was uncircumcised in heart. Once again Jeremiah is the forerunner of Paul (Rom. 2:25-29).

10

(2) Be not dismayed at the signs of heaven.—The special sin of the heathen, which the "house of Israel" was disposed to follow, is set forth in words of scorn and indignation. The astrologers, the star-gazers, the monthly prognosticators of the Chaldaeans (Isa. 47:13), found portents either in the conjuncture of planets and constella-tions, or in eclipses, comets, and other like phenomena.

(5) Upright as the palm tree.—(On verses 3-5, comp. Isa. 41:7, 44:9-17, 46:5-7.) The Hebrew refers to the twisted palmlike columns of a temple, to which the stiff, formal figure of the idol, with arms pressed close to the side, and none of the action which we find in Greek statues, is compared. The thought is that the idol which the men of Judah were worshiping was like one of the "pillars" placed by Greeks and Romans in gardens and orchards as scarecrows. Like figures appear to have been used by the Phoeni-cians for the same purpose, and the prac-tice, like the kindred worship of the **Ash-erah,** would seem to have been gaining ground even in Judah.

(7) King of nations.—Emphatically, "King of the heathen," expressing the universal sovereignty of Jehovah in contrast with the thought that He was the God of the Jews only. (Comp. Rom. 3:29.)

(9) Tarshish.—As elsewhere in the Old Testament, Spain, the Tartessus of the Greeks (Gen. 10:4; Jon. 1:3; Ezek. 27:12) from whence Palestine, through the Phoenicians, was chiefly supplied with silver, tin, and other metals.

Uphaz.—Possibly an error of transcrip-tion or dialectical variation, for Ophir, giv-ing the meaning "gold-coast" (Dan. 10:5). Some interpreters connect it with one of the tributaries of the Indus. (See I Kings 9:28.)

Blue and purple.—Both were colors ob-tained from the **murex,** a Mediterranean shell-fish, and were used both for the cur-tains of the Tabernacle (Exod. 25:4) and for the gorgeous apparel of the idols of the heathen. "Purple" must be understood of a deep crimson or scarlet. (Comp. Matt. 27:28; Mark 15:17.)

(11) Thus shall ye say unto them.—The verse is not, like the rest of the book, in Hebrew, but in Chaldee or Aramaic, the language of the enemies of Israel. Probably the prophet, whose intercourse with the Chaldeans had made him familiar with their language, put into the mouths of his own countrymen the answer they were to give when they were invited to join in the worship of their conquerors. Little as they might know of the strange language, they might learn enough to give this answer. The

words in the original have the ring of a kind of popular proverb.

(16) The Lord of hosts is his name.—The time-honored and awful name is obviously brought in as in emphatic contrast to all the names of the gods of the heathen. Among them all there was no name like "Jehovah Sabaoth," the Lord of the armies of heaven, of the stars in their courses, of the angels in their ordered ranks, and of the armies of Israel upon earth.

(17) The section from verses 1-16 inclu-sive had been as a long parenthesis, reprov-ing Israel for the sin which placed it among the "uncircumcised in the heart" (9:26). Now the prophet returns to his main theme, the devastation of the land of Israel as the penalty of that sin.

(18) That they may find it so.—The He-brew verb stands by itself without an object. The ellipsis should be filled up by "me," i.e., Jehovah.

(19) Woe is me ... —From this verse to the end of the chapter we have, with the prophet's characteristic dramatic vividness, the lamentation of the daughter of Israel in her captivity, bewailing the transgressions that had led to it.

(23) O Lord, I know ...—The confession is made not by the prophet for himself, but as by and for Israel.

The way of man.—The path which a man takes for good or evil, for failure or success. His conduct in life depends, the prophet says, on something more than his own choice. (Comp. Prov. 16:9; 20:24.) Two Hebrew words for "man" are used in the two clauses, the first expressing the weak-ness, the latter the strength, of men. Even the strong man has to confess that he needs a hand other than his own to direct his steps.

(24) With judgment.—The discipline that comes from God as the righteous Judge, at once retributive and reformative, is con-trasted with the punishment which is simply vindictive.

11

(1) The word that came to Jeremiah.—We are entering on a distinct message or discourse, which goes on probably to the end of chap. 12. Internal evidence points to an early period of Jeremiah's work, proba-bly in the reign of Josiah. The invasion of the Chaldeans is not as near as in the preceding chapter. Jeremiah is still residing at Anathoth (11:21). By some critics, however, it is referred to the reign of Jehoiachin.

(2) The words of this covenant.—The phrase had obviously acquired a definite and special sense in consequence of the discovery of the lost book of the Law under Josiah, and the covenant into which the people had then entered (comp. II Kings 23:3).

(3) Cursed be the man ... —The "iron furnace" was Egypt, the "furnace of affliction" (Isa. 48:10), in which the people had endured sufferings of which that was the only adequate symbol. The word used denoted the "furnace" of the smelter, but the actual form of bondage through which the Israelites had passed, working in the brick-kiln furnaces (Exod. 1:14), had probably given a special force to the phrase.

(5) A land flowing with milk and honey.—The description appears for the first time in Exod. 3:8, 17. It rapidly became proverbial, and is prominent in Deut. 6:3 and Josh. 5:6. It points primarily to the plenty of a pastoral rather than an agricultural people, and so far to the earlier rather than the later stages of the life of Israel.

(9) A conspiracy.—The words explain the rapid apostasy that followed on the death of Josiah. There had been all along, even while he was urging his reforms, an organized though secret resistance to the policy of which he was the representative.

(13) The reference is probably made to the formal recognition of Baal-worship in the days of Manasseh (II Kings 21:3; II Chron. 33:3), but the sin may have been repeated as soon as the restraint of Josiah's reign had been removed.

(14) Therefore pray not.—See note on 7:16.

(16) A green olive tree.—The parable is essentially the same, though a different symbol is chosen, as that of the vine (Isa. 5:1; Jer. 2:21), or the fig tree (Luke 13:6). The olive also was naturally a symbol of fertility and goodness, as in Ps. 52:8; Hos. 14:6; Zech. 4:3, 11. In the words "the Lord called thy name" we have the expression of the divine purpose in the "calling and election" of Israel. This was what she was meant to be.

(18) And the Lord hath given me knowledge.—A new section opens abruptly. The prophet speaks no longer of the sins of Israel and Judah at large, but of the "doings" of his own townsmen, of their plots against his life. Unless this is altogether a distinct fragment, connected, possibly,

with 9:8, the abruptness suggests the inference that the plots of the men of Anathoth against him had suddenly been brought under his notice. On verse 19, comp. Isa. 53:7; Luke 4:29.

(20) Let me see thy vengeance on them.—The prayer, like that of the so-called vindictive Psalms (69, 109), belongs to the earlier stage of the religious life when righteous indignation against evil is not yet tempered by the higher law of forgiveness. As such it is not to be imitated by Christians, but neither is it to be hastily condemned. The appeal to a higher judge, the desire to leave vengeance in His hands, is in itself a victory over the impulse to take vengeance into our own hands.

(23) There shall be no remnant of them.—In Ezra 2:23; Neh. 7:27, we find that 128 of Anathoth returned from exile. The words must therefore be limited either to the men who had conspired against the prophet, or to the complete deportation of its inhabitants. The situation of Anathoth, about three or four miles northeast of Jerusalem, would expose it to the full fury of the invasion.

12

The sequence of the several sections is not very clear, and possibly we have a series of detailed prophecies put together without system. Verses 1-3 continue the address to the men of Anathoth; verse 4 points to a drought, verse 12 to the invasion of the Chaldeans, and verse 14 to the "evil neighbours" who exulted in the fall of Judah.

(1) Yet let me talk with thee.—The soul of the prophet is vexed, as had been the soul of Job (21:7), by the apparent anomalies of the divine government. He owns as a general truth that God is righteous, yet he will question the divine Judge until his doubt is removed.

(2) Thou hast planted them.—The wicked flourish, so that one would think God had indeed planted them. Yet all the while they were mocking Him with hypocritical worship, uttering His name with their lips while He was far from that innermost being which the Hebrew symbolized by the "reins."

**(6) The proverb which our Lord more than once quotes—"A prophet is not without honour save in his own country and in his own house" (Matt. 13:57; Luke 4:24;

John 4:44)—probably had its origin in the sad experience of Jeremiah.

(9) Mine heritage is unto me as a speckled bird.—As in verses 7 and 8, the speaker is clearly Jehovah. The image was probably suggested by something the prophet had observed, birds of prey of one species collecting and attacking a solitary stranger of another, joined by the beasts of the field, who scent their prey. The word "speckled" perhaps points to the bird attacked as being of more goodly plumage than the others, and therefore treated as a stranger and an enemy.

(10) Many pastors have destroyed my vineyard.—Here the image (as in 6:3) is that of the **shepherds** of a wild, nomadic tribe (who represent the Chaldean and other invaders), breaking down the fence of the vineyard, and taking in their flocks to browse upon the tender shoots of the vine.

(12) The sword of the Lord.—War is thought of as instrumental in working out a Will mightier than man's own. The sword of the Chaldean invader was, after all, His sword. The thought was more or less the common inheritance of Israel, but it had recently received a special prominence from Deut. 32:41.

(14) Mine evil neighbours.—These were those who rejoiced in the fall of Judah, and attacked her in her weakness (II Kings 24:2; Pss. 83:6-9; 137:7). In the midst of his burning indignation against the sins of his own people the prophet is still a patriot, and is yet more indignant at those who attack her. For them, too, there shall be a like chastisement (comp. 25:18-26), but not for them so signal a deliverance as that in store for Judah. They should be "plucked out" from their own land, but Judah from the land of its exile.

13

The prophecies of Jeremiah are arranged in an order which is not chronological, and that which we have now reached belongs to a later date than many that follow. Comparing the notes of time in writings of the prophet with those in the history, we get the following probable sequence of events. In the early years of Jehoiakim the prophet's preaching so provoked the priests and nobles that they sought his life (26:15). Then came the burning of the roll (36:23), which Jeremiah had not ventured to read in person. This was in the fourth year of that

king's reign (36:1). During the seven years that followed we hear little or nothing of the prophet's work. Then came the short three months' reign of Jehoiachin, and he reappears on the scene with the prophecy in this chapter. The date is fixed by the reference, in verse 18, to the queen (the queen-mother) Nehushta (II Kings 24:8), who seems to have exercised sovereign power in conjunction with her son. During this interval, probably toward its close, we must place the journey to the Euphrates now recorded. It may be added that the special command given by Nebuchadnezzar in Jeremiah's favor (39:11) implies some previous knowledge which may reasonably be connected with this visit.

(1) A linen girdle.—The linen girdle was part of Jeremiah's priestly dress (Exod. 28:40; Lev. 16:4), and this also was significant in the interpretation of the symbolic act. Israel, represented as the girdle of Jehovah, had been chosen for consecrated uses. The word "get" implies the act of purchasing, and this too was not without its symbolic significance.

Put it not in water.—The work of the priest as a rule necessarily involved frequent washings both of flesh and garments. The command in this case was therefore exceptional. The unwashed girdle was to represent the guilt of the people unpurified by any real contact with the "clean water" of repentance (Ezek. 36:25).

(6) After many days.—The interval is undefined, but it must have been long enough (seventy days?) to be an adequate symbol of the seventy years' exile which the act of placing the girdle by Euphrates represented. (Comp. Hos. 3:3.)

(7) The girdle was marred.—The symbolism is explained in verse 9. The girdle stained, decayed, worthless, was a parable of the state of Judah after the exile, stripped of all its outward greatness, losing the place which it had once occupied among the nations of the earth.

(9) The pride of Judah.—As the girdle was the part of the dress on which most ornamental work was commonly lavished, so that it was a common gift among princes and men of wealth, it was the natural symbol of the outward glory of a kingdom. (See Exod. 28:40.)

(11) The whole house of Israel.—The sense of national unity is still strong in the prophet's mind. Not Judah only, but the whole collective Israel had been as the girdle of Jehovah, consecrated to His service, designed to be, as the girdle was to man, a praise and glory (Deut. 26:19).

(12) Every bottle shall be filled with wine.—Another parable follows on that of the girdle. The thought is that the effect of the wrath of Jehovah is to cause an impotence and confusion like that of drunkenness (Ps. 60:3; Isa. 51:17). The "bottle" in this case is not the "skin" commonly used for that purpose, but the earthen jar or flagon (Isa. 30:14; Lam. 4:2).

(13) The kings that sit upon David's throne.—The plural is probably used in pointing to the four—Jehoahaz, Jehoiakim, Jehoiachin, and Zedekiah—who were all involved in the sufferings that fell on Judah.

(17) My soul shall weep in secret places for your pride.—The words deserve to be noted in their exquisite tenderness as characteristic of the prophet's temperament (comp. Lam. 1:16), reminding us of Luke 19:41. Nothing remained for one who found his labors fruitless but silent sorrow and intercession.

(18) The queen.—The title of a queen-mother, probably Nehushta, the mother of Jehoiachin (II Kings 24:8), who shared the throne during her son's minority.

(19) The cities of the south.—The strategy of Nebuchadnezzar's attack (as it had been of Sennacherib's, II Kings 18:13) was to blockade the cities of the Negeb, and then, when they were cut off from sending assistance, to attack Jerusalem.

(20) Lift up your eyes.—Jerusalem was the natural protectress of the other cities. The "beautiful flock" of those cities had been committed to her care, and she is now called to give an account of her stewardship.

Them that come from the north.—These are, as in 1:14 and elsewhere, the invading army of the Chaldeans, and probably also their Scythian allies.

(22) Are thy skirts discovered.—The flowing train worn by women of rank, the removal of which was the sign of extremest degradation.

Thy heels made bare.—Made to walk barefoot, like menial slaves or, possibly, like the outcast harlot.

(23) Can the Ethiopian . . . ?—The evil of Judah was too deeply ingrained to be capable of spontaneous reformation. There remained nothing but the sharp discipline of the exile. Possibly the use of leopard skins by Ethiopian princes and warriors, as seen on Egyptian monuments and described by

Herodotus (7:69), had associated the two thoughts together in the prophet's mind.

(24) Stubble.—The Hebrew word is applied to the broken straw left on the threshing floor after the oxen had been driven over the corn, which was liable to be carried away by the first gale from the Arabian desert.

(27) Thine adulteries.—The words refer primarily to the spiritual adultery of the idolatries of Judah. The "neighings" (2:24; 5:8) express the unbridled eagerness of animal passion transferred in this passage to the spiritual sin. The "abominations on the hills" are the orgiastic rites of the worship of the high places, which are further described as "in the field" to emphasize their publicity.

14

(1) Concerning the dearth.—This discourse continues to 17:18. As 15:15 implies that Jeremiah had already suffered scorn or persecution for his prophetic work, we may reasonably assume the date here to be not earlier than the reign of Jehoiakim.

(4) As the "gates" in verse 2 stood for the people of the city, so the "ground" stands here as in visible sympathy with the tillers of the soil. Cities and country alike are plunged into the utter blackness of despair.

(5) Each region has its representative instance of misery. The hind of the field (the female of the common stag), noted for its tenderness to its young, abandons it and turns away to seek pasture for itself, but fails to find any.

(7) O Lord . . . —From the picture of suffering the prophet turns to a prayer for pardon and a confession of sins. He is sure that the drought has not come without cause, and that it calls men to repentance.

Do thou it.—**Act thou**, not according to the rigor of inexorable justice, but according to the Name which witnesses of mercy and long-suffering (Exod. 34:6).

(9) Thou, O Lord, art in the midst of us.—After all, then, so the prophet's reviving faith tells him, Jehovah is more than the passing guest. He abides still among His people. He is as a mighty man, strong to save, though as yet He refrains from action.

(11) Pray not . . . —As in 7:16 and 11:14, the saddest, sternest part of the prophet's work is to feel that even prayer—the prayer that punishment may be averted—is unavailing and unaccepted.

(13) Ah, Lord God!—We have had in 5:31 a glimpse of the evil influence of the great body of the prophetic order; and now the true prophet feels more bitterly than ever the misery of having to contend against it. The schools of the prophets had rapidly degenerated from their first ideal, and had become corrupt, ambitious, seekers after popularity. (Comp. Ezek. 13; Mic. 3:8-11.) For them there was the righteous retribution that they should perish in the very calamities which they had asserted would never come (verse 15).

(19) Hast thou utterly rejected Judah?— The heart of the patriot overpowers even the conviction of the prophet, and, though bidden not to pray, he bursts forth, in spite of the command, with a prayer of passionate intercession.

(21) The prophet can make no plea of extenuation, but he can appeal to the character of God and urge, with a bold anthropomorphism, that mercy is truer to that character than rigorous justice, and that His covenant with Israel pledges Him to that mercy. The "throne of thy glory" is the temple.

15

(1) Then said the Lord unto me.—With a bold and terrible anthropomorphism, the prophet again speaks as if he heard the voice of Jehovah rejecting all intercession for the apostate people. Here Moses (Exod. 32:11; Num. 14:13-20) and Samuel (I Sam. 7:9; 12:23) are named as having been conspicuous examples of the power of the prayer of intercession. Comp. the mention of Noah, Daniel, and Job in Ezek. 14:14.

(4) Manasseh the son of Hezekiah.—The horror of that long and evil reign still lingered in the minds of men, and the prophet saw in it the beginning of the evils from which his people were now suffering. The name of Hezekiah may have been inserted as an aggravation of the guilt of his successor.

(6) I am weary with repenting.—The long-suffering of God is described, as before, in anthropomorphic language. He had "repented," i.e., changed His purpose of punishing, but patience was now exhausted; justice was weary of the delay and must take its course.

(9) Her sun is gone down while it was yet day.—The image of this eclipse of all joy and brightness may possibly have been suggested by the actual eclipse of the sun in 610 B.C., the year of the battle of Megiddo, just as the earthquake in the reign of Uzziah suggested much of the imagery of Isa. 2:19; Amos 1:1, 2; 4:11; Zech. 14:5).

(12) Assuming this verse to carry on the thought of verses 1-9, after the interruption, possibly the interpolation, of verses 10 and 11, we note that the prayer of the prophet, strong though it may be, cannot change the inflexible purpose of Jehovah to chastise His people's sins. For "steel" we should read **bronze**. The word is commonly translated "brass," but that compound was unknown to the metallurgy of Israel.

(13) Without price.—As in Ps. 44:12; Isa. 52:3, this implies the extremist abandonment. The enemies of Israel were to have an easy victory, for which they would not have to pay the usual price of blood; nor did God, on His side, demand from them any payment for the victory He bestowed. He gave away His people as men give that which they count worthless. (Comp. verses 5, 6.)

(19) Therefore thus saith the Lord... —The Divine voice within makes answer to the passionate complaint of verses 17 and 18. The prophet also needs, not less than the people, to "return" to his true mind (verse 16), to repent of his murmurings and distrust. Upon that condition only can he again "stand before" the Lord in the full sense of that word, and minister to Him as a prophet-priest. Above all he must beware of being tempted by his sense of failure, to **return** to the people in the temper of one who tunes his voice according to the time.

(20) I will make thee unto this people... —It is significant that the promise reproduced the very words which the prophet had heard when he was first summoned to his work (1:18, 19). Jehovah had not been unfaithful to His word, but, like all promises, it depended on implied conditions, and these the fainthearted, desponding prophet had but imperfectly fulfilled.

16

(1) The word of the Lord came also unto me.—The formula introduces a new and distinct message, extending to 17:18. It is even more terrible in its threatenings than any that have preceded it. We may think of it as dating probably from the close of the reign of Jehoiakim, when that king was trusting in an alliance with Egypt (17:13), and the people taunted the prophet with the non-fulfillment of his predictions (17:15).

(2) Thou shalt not take thee a wife... —To an Israelite and to a priest marriage, and the hopes which it involved, was not only a happiness but a duty; and to be cut off from it was to renounce both, because the evil that was coming in the nation was such as to turn both into a curse.

(5) My peace.—It is Jehovah's peace: that which He once had given, but which He now withholds. Men were to accept that withdrawal in silent awe, not with the conventional routine of customary sorrow. (See Ezek. 7:18; Amos 8:10; Prov. 31:6; Hos. 9:4.)

(14, 15) Behold, the days come... — Judgment and mercy are tempered in the promise. Here the former is predominant. Afterward (23:5-8) it is connected with the hope of a personal Deliverer. The main thought is that which the people will endure in the land of the Chaldaeans, so that, when they return, their minds will turn to their deliverance from it, rather than to the Exodus from Egypt, as an example of the mercy and might of Jehovah. Then once again, and in a yet higher degree, it should be seen that man's extremity is God's opportunity.

(16) I will send for many fishers... —The "fishers" (Amos 4:2) are the invading nations, surrounding Judah and Jerusalem as with a drag-net and allowing none to escape. The process is described under this very name of "drag-netting" the country by Herodotus (3:149; 6:31), as applied by the army of Xerxes to Samos and other islands.

(18) I will recompense their iniquity and their sin double.—A restitution, or fine, to double the amount of the wrong done was almost the normal standard of punishment under the Law of Moses (Exod. 22:4, 7). The words threaten accordingly a full punishment according to the utmost rigor.

(19) The Gentiles shall come unto thee.— The sin and folly of Israel are painted in contrast with the prophet's vision of the future. Then, in that far-off time of which other prophets had spoken (Mic. 4:1; Isa. 2:2), the Gentiles should come to Jerusalem, turning from the "vanities" they had inherited; and yet Israel, who had in-herited a truer faith, was now abasing herself even to their level or below it.

17

(1) A pen or iron—i.e., a stylus or graving tool (Job 19:24), chiefly used for engraving in stone or metal. In Ps. 45:1 it seems to have been used of the instrument with which the scribe wrote on his tablets.

With the point of a diamond.—The word expresses the idea of the hardness rather than the brilliancy of the diamond, and is rendered "adamant" in Ezek. 3:9 and Zech. 7:12. Strictly speaking, it was applied only to the diamond-point set in iron used by engravers. Such instruments were known to the Romans (Pliny, **Hist. Nat.** 37:15), and may have been in use in Phoenicia or Palestine. The words describe a note of infamy that could not be erased.

(3) My mountain in the field.—This is a poetic phrase for Jerusalem or Zion. "My mountain" is the mountain of Jehovah. The words predict the plunder of the city, perhaps especially the plunder of the Temple.

(5) Cursed be the man... —The words are vehement and abrupt, but they burst from the prophet's lips as proclaiming the root evil that had eaten into the life of his people. Their trust in an arm of flesh had led them to Egyptian and Assyrian alliances, and these to "departing from the Lord." The anathema has its counterpart in the beatitude of verse 7.

(9) The heart is deceitful... —If the blessing and the curse are thus so plainly marked, how is it that man chooses the curse and not the blessing, the portion of the shrub ("heath," verse 6) in the desert rather than that of the tree planted by the waters (verses 7, 8; comp. Ps. 1:3, which surely suggested these words)? The answer is found in the inscrutable self-deceit of his nature blinding his perceptions of good and evil.

(11) As the partridge sitteth on eggs... —The words point to a popular belief among the Jews that the partridge steals the eggs of other birds and adds them to her own, with the result that when the eggs are hatched the broods desert her. It thus became a parable of the covetous man, whose avarice leads him to pile up riches which are not rightly his, and which after a while "make to themselves wings" and are seen no more. As covetousness was the besetting sin of Jehoiakim (22:17), the prediction may have pointed especially to him.

(13) Written in the earth.—In implied contrast with the name graven on the rock forever (Job 19:24) are those written on the dust or sand. The Eastern habit of writing on the ground, which was the common practice in Jewish schools, gave a vividness to the similitude which we have almost lost. (See John 8:6.)

(15) Behold, they say unto me.—The speakers are clearly the mockers who questioned Jeremiah's prophetic character on the ground (comp. Deut. 18:22) that his threats had received no fulfillment. Presumably, therefore, the words were written before the death of Jehoiakim and the capture of Jerusalem.

(19) Thus said the Lord unto me ...—Here begins an entirely fresh series of messages, arranged probably in chronological order, but having no immediate connection with what precedes, and narrated with a much fuller account of the circumstances connected with them. This series was delivered before the sins of the people had assumed the hopeless, irremediable character which is implied in the two previous chapters. The first part may probably be referred, therefore, to the early years of the reign of Jehoiakim.

The gate of the children of the people ...—No gate so described is mentioned in Neh. 3 or elsewhere. The context shows that it was a place of concourse, a gate of the Temple rather than of the city. The name may indicate, as in 26:23, that it was that "of the common people," or "laity" (see II Chron. 35:5) as distinguished from that used by the priests and Levites; and it would appear, from the nature of the warning proclaimed there, to have been the scene of some open desecration of the Sabbath. (See Neh. 13:15-22; Isa. 56:2-6; 58:13.)

18

(1) The word which came to Jeremiah.—This message comes in close sequence upon that of the preceding chapter, probably before the fourth year of the reign of Jehoiakim. It has the character of a last warning to king and people, and its rejection is followed in its turn by the more decisive use of the same symbol in chap. 19.

(2) The potter's house.—The place was probably identical with the "potter's field," the well-known spot on the southern face of the valley of Hinnom, south of Jerusalem, where the workers in that art carried on their business (see Matt. 27:7). The purchase of the field to "bury strangers in" implies, however, that it was looked upon as a piece of waste ground, and that its use had been exhausted.

(3) He wrought a work on the wheels.—See Ecclus. 38:29, 30. The potter sat moving one horizontal wheel with his feet, while a smaller one was used, as it revolved, to fashion the shape of the vessel he was making with his hands. The image had been used already of God's creative work in Isa. 29:16; 45:9; 64:8.

(6) Cannot I do with you as this potter?—The clay can resist the potter, or can yield itself willingly to his hands to be shaped as he wills. Its being "marred" is through no fault of the potter, but—in the framework of the parable—through the resistance of the human agents whom God is fashioning. And when it is so marred one of two courses is open to the potter. He can again remold and fashion it to his purpose, or, if it be hopelessly marred, can break it and cast it away, and with fresh clay mold a fresh vessel.

(7-10) He is now taught that his work (1:10) was throughout conditional. In bold anthropomorphic speech Jehovah represents Himself as changing His purpose, even suddenly, if the nation that is affected by it passes from evil to good or from good to evil. The apparent change is but the expression of an eternal law of righteousness, dealing with men according to their works. This, and not the assertion of an arbitrary, irresistibly predestinating will, was the lesson the prophet had been taught by the parable of the potter's wheel.

(11) I frame evil.—The verb chosen is that which especially describes the potter's work, and from which the Hebrew word for potter is itself derived. This, so to speak, is the shape of the vessel actually in hand, determining its use, but its form is not unalterably fixed. It is shown **in terrorem**, and the people are invited to accept the warning by repentance.

(12) And they said.—This was the ever-recurring answer (see 2:25) which they made to the prophet's pleas. It was the answer of defiance rather than of despair.

(13) Ask ye now among the heathen.—The appeal of 2:10, 11 is renewed. Judah had not been true, even as heathen nations were true, to its inherited faith and worship. The virgin daughter of Israel—the epithet is emphasized, as contrasted with the shame that follows—had fallen from a greater height to a profounder depth of debasement.

(16) A perpetual hissing.—The Hebrew word is onomatopoetic, and expresses the inarticulate sounds which we utter on seeing anything that makes us shudder, rather than "hissing" in its use as an expression of contempt or disapproval.

(18) Come, and let us devise devices.— The priests and people thus far appear to have listened to the prophet, but at the threatening words of the preceding verse their anger becomes hatred, and their hatred seeks to kill (verse 23).

For the law shall not perish . . . —The words meant apparently that they had enough guidance in the Law, in the priests, and in the prophets who met their wishes, and that they might trust in the continuance of that guidance in spite of the threatenings of destruction that the prophet had just spoken. We probably find the result of the conspiracy in the measures taken by Pashur in 20:1-3.

(20) Remember that I stood before thee.— The phrase is used frequently, though not uniformly, of the act of worship. The prophet refers to his repeated though fruitless entreaties for the people in chaps. 14 and 15. (See II Macc. 15:14.) Men had come to recognize that the spirit of intercession had been the prophet's dominant characteristic.

(21-23) The prayer was the utterance of an indignation, not unrighteous in itself, yet showing all too plainly, like the language of the so-called imprecatory Psalms (35, 69, 109), the contrast between the Jewish and the Christian way of meeting wrong and hatred. (See Acts 7:60.) The New Testament utterances of Peter (Acts 8:20) and of Paul (Acts 23:3; Gal. 1:9; and II Tim. 4:14) present an apparent parallelism; but the words spoken in these cases have more the character of an authoritative judicial sentence.

19

(1) And get a potter's earthen bottle.— The parable dramatized represents the darker side of the imagery of 18:3, 4. There the vessel was still on the potter's wheel, capa-

ble of being reshaped. Now we have the vessel which has been baked and hardened. No change is possible. If it is unfit for the uses for which it was designed, there is nothing left but to break it. As such it became now the fit symbol of the obdurate people of Israel. Their polity, their nationality, their religious system, had to be broken up. Representatives of the civil and ecclesiastical rulers were to be the witnesses of this acted prophecy of the destruction of all that they held most precious. A summary reference to his discourse to all the people is given in verse 15.

(2) Unto the valley of the son of Hinnom.—The site was chosen as having been the scene of the most hateful form of idolatry to which the people had addicted themselves, perhaps also as connected locally with the potter's field. (See note on 7:31 and Matt. 27:7.) The "east gate" was a small gate leading into the valley just at the point where it was filled with rubbish, possibly with broken fragments like those which were now to be added to it. The connection both of the name of the gate and its use with the symbolism of the prophet's act may have determined the command which was thus given him.

(3) O kings of Judah.—The plural seems to include both the reigning king, Jehoiakim, and his heir-apparent or presumptive.

His ears shall tingle.—The phrase, occurring (I Sam. 3:11) in the prophecy of the doom of the earlier sanctuary, seems intentionally used to remind those who heard it of the fate that had fallen on Shiloh. The destruction of the first sanctuary of Israel was to be the type of that of the second (Ps. 78:60; Jer. 7:14). The following words refer especially to the guilt of Manasseh (II Chron. 33:4).

(7) I will make void.—The Hebrew verb is onomatopoetic, as representing the gurgling sound of water flowing from the mouth of a jar. It contains (verse 1) the root of the word rendered "bottle," and was obviously chosen with an allusive reference to it. The primary meaning is "to pour out, to spill," and so "to waste, to bring to nought." (Comp. Isa. 19:3.) Some interpreters have supposed that the words were accompanied by corresponding symbolic acts, and that the earthen bottle, which the prophet had brought filled with water, was now emptied in the sight of the people.

(9) I will cause them to eat . . . —See Deut. 28:53. The woes of that memorable chapter had obviously furnished the prophet both with imagery and language. In Lam. 2:20 and 4:10 we find proof of the fulfillment of the prediction. Thus, by the dread law of retribution, were the people to pay the penalty of their sin in the Molech sacrifices, in which they, sinning at once against natural affection and against the faith of their fathers, had slain their sons and daughters.

(10) Then shalt thou break the bottle ... —See Ps. 2:9. Happily for Israel, there was a depth of divine compassion which the parable failed to represent. Subsequent history showed that, though as far as that generation went, the punishment was final, and their existing polity could never be made whole again, there was yet hope for the nation. The fragments of the broken vessel might be gathered from the heap of rubbish on which the prophet had flung them and brought into a new shape for uses less glorious indeed than that for which it had been originally designed, but far other than those of a mere vessel of dishonor.

(12) And even make this city as Tophet.— This is an allusive reference partly to the state of the valley of Hinnom as a heap of ruins and rubbish, partly to the meaning of the name Tophet, as a place spat upon and scorned.

(13) Upon whose roofs they have burned incense.—The flat roofs of Eastern houses were used for exercise (II Sam. 11:2), for prayer and meditation (Acts 10:9), for worship addressed to the host of heaven (Zeph. 1:5). Comp. Strabo, 16.

20

(1) Pashur the son of Immer.—The description distinguishes him from the person of the same name in 21:1. We may probably identify him with the father of the Gedaliah named in 38:1 as among the "princes" (I Chron. 24:14) that at a later date opposed the prophet's work. The name of Pashur appears again, after the Captivity, in Ezra 2:37, 38.

(2) Then Pashur smote Jeremiah the prophet.—It is the first time that he has been so described, the office to which he was called being apparently named to emphasize the outrage which had been inflicted on him. The word "smote" implies a blow struck with the priest's own hands rather than the infliction of the legal punishment of forty stripes save one (Deut. 25:3). The English word "stocks" expresses adequately enough the instrument of torture which, like the **nervus** of Roman punishment, kept the body (Acts 16:24) in a crooked and painful position. In that humiliating position the prophet was left for the whole night in one of the most conspicuous places of the city.

(3) Magor-missabib.—The words are a quotation from Ps. 31:13, "Fear is round about" (see 6:25). We may venture to think that the Psalm had been his comfort in those night-watches of suffering, and that he now uttered the words which described the bitterness of the Psalmist's sorrow, as at last feeling sure that they belonged to his persecutor rather than to himself. Pashur should be an object of self-loathing, outer fears intensifying his inward terror and acting through him on others. He is the center from which terrors radiate as well as that to which they converge (verses 4-6).

(6) To whom thou hast prophesied lies.— We may infer that Pashur was one of those who encouraged the people to fight against the Chaldaeans, and to despise Jeremiah's warnings by holding out the hope that an alliance with Egypt would avert the threatened danger (14:13 and 23:17).

(7) The narrative ends, and a psalm of passionate complaint begins. Jehovah now appears to the prophet as a hard taskmaster who had forced him, **against his will** (17:16), to enter on a work from which he shrank, and who gave him scorn and derision as his only wage. (Comp. Isa. 8:11 and I Cor. 9:16.)

(9) The sense of a hopeless work, destined to fail, weighed on the prophet's soul, and he would have withdrawn from it; but it would not be restrained. Like so much of Jeremiah's language this also came from the hymns of Israel (Ps. 39:3).

(14) Cursed be the day wherein I was born ... —This is a strange relapse from the confidence of the two previous verses into a despair yet deeper than before. It is best explained by the supposition that it is in no sense part of the same poem or meditation, but a distinct fragment belonging to the same period and placed in its present position by Jeremiah himself or by the first editor of his prophecies. Thought, structure, even grammar are, in their abruptness and irregularities, alike significant of intense emotion.

21

(1) The word which came unto Jeremiah

... —There is obviously a great gap at this point in the collection of the prophet's utterances, and we enter on a new group of prophecies which extends to the close of chap. 33. Thus far we have had his ministry under Jehoiakim and the roll which was read before that king, forming the first part of his work. Now we pass to the later stage, which forms what has been called the roll of Zedekiah. The judgment predicted in the previous roll had come nearer. The armies of Nebuchadnezzar were gathering around the city. The prophet was now honored and consulted, and the king sent his chief minister, Pashur (**not** the priest who had been the prophet's persecutor), and Zephaniah, the deputy of 52:24, to ask his intercession. We learn from their later history that they were in their hearts inclined to the policy of resistance and ready to accuse Jeremiah of being a traitor (38:1-4).

(2) Nebuchadrezzar.—This form of the name is more correct than that of Ne-buchadnezzar, which we find elsewhere, and even in Jeremiah's own writings (34:1 and 39:5). The name has been interpreted as "Nebo protects against misfortune."

If so be that the Lord will deal with us ... —The messengers come to inquire of the prophet, and yet suggest the answer which he is expected to give. Jehovah is to show His wondrous works in the deliverance of the city. The history of Sennacherib's army (II Kings 19; Isa. 37) was probably present to their minds. It was apparently an attempt on the part of the king and his counselors, under the show of a devout reverence, to entice Jeremiah to change his tone and side with the policy of resistance to the Chaldaeans. Jeremiah's answer, however, is far from what they had even ventured to suggest. Judgment could no longer be averted. For the literal fulfillment of verses 7 and 10, see 52:10, 13, 24-27.

(8, 9) There is something like a solemn irony here. The "way of life" is no longer that way of righteousness which the men of Judah had forsaken, leading to the life of eternal blessedness, but simply submission to the Chaldaeans, and the life so gained was one of exile and poverty if not of bondage also. The words must have seemed to the messengers to counsel treachery and desertion, and were remembered against the prophet in the taunt of 37:13. They were, however, acted on by many (39:9 and 52:15).

(12) Execute judgment in the morning.—The words point to one of the chief duties of the ideal Eastern king. To rise at dawn of day, to sit in the gate and listen to the complaints of those who had been wronged, was the surest way to gain the affection of his people. (See I Kings 3:28.) The words may have the character of a last promise, and therefore a last warning.

(13) The king and his people trusted, as the Jebusites of old had done (II Sam. 5:8), in what seemed to them the impregnable strength of their natural position.

(14) I will kindle a fire in the forest thereof.—The desolation wrought by an invading army such as that of Nebuchadnezzar (II Kings 19:23) showed itself in this destruction of forests in its most conspicuous form, and explains the comparative scarcity of trees in Palestine.

22

(1) Thus saith the Lord ... —The message reviews the history of the three preceding reigns, and apparently reproduces the very words of the warnings which he had uttered in each to the king who then ruled, and which had been terribly fulfilled. It was delivered to the king as he sat in the gate in the presence of his people (verse 2).

(10) Weep ye not for the dead.—The "dead" for whom men are not to weep is Josiah, for whom Jeremiah himself had composed a solemn dirge, which seems from II Chron. 35:25 to have been repeated on the anniversary of his death.

For him that goeth away.—This is obviously Jehoahaz (the same as Shallum in verse 11), the son and successor of Josiah, who was deposed by Pharaoh-nechoh and carried into Egypt (II Kings 23:31-34; II Chron. 36:2-4). The doom of the exile who was to return no more was a fitter subject for lamentation than the death of the righteous king who died a warrior's death (II Kings 23:29).

(11) Shallum.—This was probably the name assumed on Jehoahaz's succession to the throne. Such changes were common at the time. The short and disastrous reign of Shallum, and the meaning of the word ("retribution") probably account for the prophet's using the private rather than the kingly name. The fact that the name had been borne by one of the later kings of Israel whose reign lasted but for a single month (II Kings 15:13) may have given a further point to its use, as being full of disastrous memories that made it ominous of evil.

(12) Shall see this land no more.—There is no record of the duration of the life of Shallum in his Egyptian exile, but the total absence of his name in the history that follows is presumptive evidence of the fulfillment of the prediction. There is no trace of his being alive when the prophet is dragged by his countrymen to Egypt (43:6, 7).

(13) Woe unto him that buildeth . . . — The prophet now turns to Jehoiakim, and apparently reproduces what he had before uttered in denouncing the selfish bearing of that king. Jehoiakim had continued building palaces when his kingdom was on the verge of ruin, and his subjects were groaning under their burdens. He was probably impelled by a vainglorious desire to imitate the magnificence of the Egyptian king (Pharaoh-necho) who had placed him on the throne.

(15) The words are obviously those of praise. Josiah was not an ascetic, devotee king, but lived his life happily and did well his true kingly work of judgment and justice. There was a truer greatness in that than in the stateliness of Jehoiakim's palaces.

(19) He shall be buried with the burial of an ass.—See the same prediction in another form in 36:30. We have no direct record of its fulfillment, but its reproduction shows that the prophet's word had not failed. The king was dragged in chains with the other captives who were being carried off to Babylon (II Chron. 36:6), and probably died on the journey, his corpse left behind unburied as the army marched.

(20) All thy lovers.—The word points (comp. Ezek. 23:5, 9) to the Egyptians and other nations with whom Judah had made alliances. The destruction reached its climax in the overthrow of Pharaoh-necho's army by Nebuchadnezzar at Carchemish (46:2).

(24) Coniah the son of Jehoiakim.—Coniah was king for a short three months' reign. The name appears also as Jeconiah and Jehoiachin, probably the regal title assumed on his accession (52:31; Ezek. 1:2). The meaning of the name "Jehovah establishes" is constant in all the forms. There is probably a touch of scorn, as in the case of Shallum, in the prophet's use of the earlier name instead of that which he had assumed as king.

The signet upon my right hand.—The seal-ring was (as in Hag. 2:23 and Esth. 3:10) the symbol of kingly power, authenti-

cating every edict. It was, therefore, the type of all that was most precious.

(26) Thy mother that bare thee.—The youth of Coniah (see II Kings 24:8, and the erroneous transcription of II Chron. 36:9) probably led to his mother assuming the authority of a queen-regent. She directed the policy of his brief reign and shared in his downfall.

(30) Write ye this man childless.—The scribes who kept the register of the royal genealogies (Ezek. 13:9; Ps. 69:27, 28) were told how, without waiting for his death, they were to enter Coniah's name in that register. The prediction was fulfilled in Jeconiah's being the last kingly representative of the house of David, his uncle Zedekiah, who succeeded him, perishing before him (52:31). In him the sceptre departed, and not even Zerubbabel sat upon the throne of Judah.

23

(1) Woe be unto the pastors . . . —Verses 1-8 come as a natural sequel to chap. 22. The unfaithful shepherds who had been there denounced are contrasted with those, more faithful to their trust, whom Jehovah will raise up. The "pastors" are the civil rulers, not the prophets or the priests, of Israel (see 2:8). The parallelism with Ezek. 34, delivered about the same time in the land of exile, is suggestive either of direct communication between the two writers, or of traditional lines of thought common to the two priest-prophets.

(2) Ye have scattered my flock.—The charge was true literally as well as spiritually. The dispersion of the people in Egypt, Assyria, and Chaldaea was the result of the neglect, the tyranny, the feebleness of their rulers.

(3) To their folds.—There was hope (Isa. 1:9 and 6:13) for the "remnant" of the people, though the sentence on their rulers was final and irreversible.

(4) I will set up shepherds . . . —The words imply a return to the theocracy, the breaking off of the hereditary succession of the house of David, and the giving of power to those who, like Ezra and Nehemiah, and, later on in history, the Maccabees, were called to rule because they had the capacity for ruling well.

(5) Behold, the days come.—The words point to an undefined distant future, following on the provisional order implied in verse 4, when the kingdom should once more rest in one of the house of David.

A righteous Branch.—See Isa. 11:1. In both cases the word means "sprout" or "scion," springing up from the root even after the tree had been cut down, and not a branch growing from the trunk. (Comp. Zech. 3:8 and 6:12.) Here the propet speaks of the one great Shepherd.

A King shall reign.—As with all the Messianic prophecies of this class, the thoughts of the prophet dwell on the acts and attributes of a sovereignty exercised personally on earth. Such a sovereignty (Matt. 28:18) was indeed given to the Christ, but not after the fashion that men expected.

(6) The Lord our Righteousness.—The King, the righteous Branch, will look to Jehovah as giving and working righteousness. We cannot forget that, at the very time when Jeremiah uttered this prophecy, a king was on the throne whose name (Zedekiah: "righteous is Jehovah") implied the same thought. His reign had been a miserable failure, and the prophet looks forward to a time when the ideal, which was then far off, should at last be realized. The Christ answered to the name, not as being Himself one with Jehovah, though He was that, but as doing the Father's will, and so fulfilling all righteousness (comp. Matt. 3:15).

(7) The days come, saith the Lord.—See note on 16:14, 15.

(9) Mine heart within me is broken . . .—The abrupt transition shows that we are entering an entirely new section. The Hebrew order and punctuation of the words is—"Concerning the prophets: My heart is broken within me," the first words being the superscription and title of what follows. The four clauses describe the varied phenomena of horror and amazement, and then comes the cause of the horror—the contrast between the words of Jehovah and His holiness on the one side, and the wickedness of priests and prophets on the other. The whole section is the complement of that which denounced the wickedness of the civil rulers in verses 1-4.

(23) Am I a God at hand . . . ?—The false prophets acted as if God were far away out of their sight (Pss. 10:11; 73:11; 94:7), not knowing or caring what men did, as if their affairs came under a "colonial department." The true prophet feels that He is equally near, equally God, in all places alike. (See Ps. 139:7-12.)

(27) As their fathers have forgotten . . .

—The two evils of open idolatry and of false claims to prophecy stood (see verse 25) on the same footing. The misuse of the name of Jehovah by the false prophets was as bad as the older worship of Baal and the prophesying in his name. (Comp. verses 13 and 14.)

(29) Is not my word like as a fire? . . .—The prophet speaks out of the depths of his own experience. The true prophetic word burns in the heart and will not be restrained, and when uttered it consumes the evil and purifies the good. It will burn up the chaff of the dreams and utterances of the false prophets. What these words paint in the language of poetry, Paul describes without imagery in I Cor. 14:24, 25. (Comp. also Heb. 4:12.)

(31) That use their tongues, and say, He saith.—The scornful phrase indicates the absence of a true inspiration. These plagiarists (verse 30) plan their schemes and take their tongue as an instrument for carrying them into effect.

(36) The burden of the Lord shall ye mention no more . . . —The term misused by the false prophets was no longer to be applied to the messages of Jehovah. If men continued to apply it to the words of their own heart, they would find it a "burden" in another sense too heavy to be borne. This would be the righteous punishment of the reckless levity with which they had treated the sacred Name which Jeremiah reproduces in all the amplitude of its grandeur.

24

(1) The Lord shewed me . . . —The chapter, as the two preceding, belongs to the reign of Zedekiah, i.e., after the first capture of Jerusalem and the captivity of the chief inhabitants. The opening words indicate that the symbols on which the prophet looked were seen in vision. The figs were as a votive offering, first-fruits (Exod. 23:19; Deut. 26:2) or tithes brought to the Lord of Israel. (Comp. Amos 8:1, 2.)

The carpenters and smiths.—See II Kings 24:14. The word for "carpenters" includes **craftsmen** of all kinds. The deportation of these classes was partly a matter of policy, making the city more helpless by removing those who might have forged weapons or strengthened its defenses, and partly of ostentation, that they might help in the construction of the buildings with which Nebuchadnezzar was increasing the splendor of his city. (Comp. 1 Sam. 13:19.)

(5) So will I acknowledge.—The expected revelation came. The two baskets represented the two sections of the people. The captives who had been carried to Babylon were, for the most part, of higher rank than those who were left behind. There are many indications that under the teaching of Daniel and his companions, and of Ezekiel, they were improving morally under their discipline of suffering. Their very contact with the monstrous idolatry of Babylon made them more conscious than they had ever been before of the greatness of their own faith. The process which, at the end of the seventy years of exile, made them once more and forever a purely monotheistic people had already begun.

(6) I will set mine eyes upon them for good.—The state of the Jews at Babylon at the time of the return from exile was obviously far above that of slaves or prisoners. They had money (Ezra 2:69), they cultivated land, they built houses (29:4, 28). Many were reluctant to leave their new home for the land of their fathers.

(8) And them that dwell in the land of Egypt.—These had been carried into captivity with Jehoahaz by Pharaoh-nechoh, or had fled there in order to avoid submission to Nebuchadnezzar. We meet with them later on in chap. 44. For these there was to be no return, no share in the work of restoration. They formed the nucleus of the Jewish population of Egypt, and in time (150 B.C.) set up a rival temple at Leontopolis. (See Isa. 19:19.)

25

(1) In the fourth year of Jehoiakim the son of Josiah.—We are carried back in the present arrangement of Jeremiah's prophecies to a much earlier period than that of the preceding chapter. It is the fourth (in Dan. 1:1, the third) year of the reign of Jehoiakim, who had been made king by Pharaoh-nechoh after his defeat of Josiah and capture of Jerusalem. Nebuchadnezzar was now the master of the East, and it was given to Jeremiah to discern the bearings of the new situation on the future destinies of Judah. He saw that the wisdom of its rulers would be to accept the position of tributary rulers under the great conqueror instead of rashly seeking either to assert their independence or to trust to the support of Egypt,

crushed as she was by the defeat at Carchemish. The clear vision of the prophet saw in the Chaldaean king the servant of Jehovah—the instrument of the designs of the Providence which orders the events of history—and he became, from that moment, the unwelcome preacher of the truth that the independence of Judah had passed away, and that nothing but evil could follow from fanatical attempts or secret intrigues and alliances aiming at resistance.

(3) The three and twentieth year (603-4 B.C.).—Thus there had been nineteen years of prophetic work under Josiah, and between three and four under Jehoiakim (1:2). Of the former period we have but scanty record. The year is noticeable as that which apparently witnessed the first collection of Jeremiah's prophetic utterances (36:5-8).

(9) Nebuchadrezzar ... my servant.—The use of the word which is applied by psalmists and prophets to David (II Sam. 7:8; Ps. 78:70) and to the future Christ (Isa. 42:1; 52:13) is every way remarkable. It has its parallel, and, in fact, its explanation, in the language in which Isaiah speaks of Cyrus as the shepherd, the anointed, of Jehovah (Isa. 44:28; 45:1.) Each ruler of the great empires of the world was, in ways he knew not, working out the purposes of God.

(11) Shall serve the king of Babylon seventy years.—This is the first mention of the duration of the captivity. The seventy years are commonly reckoned from 606 B.C., the date of the deportation of Jehoiakim and his princes, to 536 B.C., when the decree for the return of the exiles was issued by Cyrus. In II Chron. 36:21 the number is connected with the land "enjoying her Sabbaths," as though the long desolation came as a retribution for the people's neglect of the law of the Sabbatical year, and, perhaps, also for their non-observance of the weekly Sabbaths.

(12) I will punish the king of Babylon ... —The words are omitted in the LXX, and there are some internal grounds for suspecting it to be a later addition, probably from Baruch as collecting and editing Jeremiah's writings (and so verses 13 and 18). It is not easy, furthermore, to see why the same prophetic discourse should contain both (verse 26) veiled and open prediction.

(17) Then took I the cup ... —The words describe the act of the prophet as in the ecstasy of vision. One by one the nations are made to drink of that cup of the wrath of Jehovah of which His own country was to have the first and fullest draught.

(19) Pharaoh king of Egypt ... —The list of the nations begins from the south and proceeds northward, those that lay on the east and west being named, as it were, literally, according to their position. The Pharaoh of the time was Nechoh, who had been defeated at Carchemish.

(26) The kingdoms of the world.—The words are limited by the horizon of the prophet's vision. As the "world" of the New Testament writers was the Roman Empire, so in the life of Jeremiah it was identical with that of Babylon.

The king of Sheshach.—The traditional Rabbinic explanation is that we have here the earliest known example of the use of a cypher-writing to disguise the meaning of what was written from all but the initiated. The cypher consisted in the use of the Hebrew alphabet in an inverted order, thus giving SHeSHaCH as an equivalent for Ba-BeL. This, then, was the crowning mystery reserved to the last. The Chaldaean kingdom was to do its work as the scourge of God upon the nations; but it was simply an instrument in His hand, as the Assyrians had been in their day (Isa. 10:15); and when the work was done, the law of a righteous retribution would be felt by it and by its rulers. Thus the Chaldaeans, if they came across it, would not be likely to understand its meaning of the way in which the captivity would at last be brought to its close.

26

(1) In the beginning of the reign of Jehoiakim.—The section which follows is among the earlier fragments of the book, some three years before that of the preceding chapter. There is no mention of the Chaldaeans, and Jehoiakim is on friendly terms with Egypt (verse 22). This points to the very earliest period of his reign. The chapter that follows, though referred to the same period in the present Hebrew text, really belongs to the reign of Zedekiah. (See note on 27:1.) The common element that led the compiler of the book to bring the narratives together is the conflict of Jeremiah with the false prophets.

(7) The priests and the prophets.—The mention of the latter is significant. Jeremiah had to separate himself from both the orders to which he belonged, in the one case by birth, in the other by a special vocation.

His bitterest foes were found among those who claimed to speak as he did, in the name of the Lord, but who tuned their voice according to the time, and prophesied deceits.

(8) Thou shalt surely die.—The threat of the men of Anathoth (11:21) is repeated by the priests and prophets of Jerusalem. They look on Jeremiah as one who has incurred the condemnation of Deut. 18:20.

(16) This man is not worthy to die.—The lay-rulers are in favor of the true prophet, whom the priests and false prophets would have condemned. The whole history reminds us of the condemnation of the One greater than Jeremiah (Luke 23:4). Here, however, as yet the people are with the true prophet, and against the priests, as they were when they shouted their Hosannas to the prophet's great Antitype.

(17, 18) The elders speaking in the time of Jehoiakim (ca. 608 B.C.) remembered the tradition of what had passed, a century or so before, in the reign of Hezekiah (726-698 B.C.), and could appeal to it as a precedent in favor of the prophet. (See Mic. 3:12; 4:1, 2.) Here was a case, is the implied argument of the elders, in which a threat did its work, and therefore was not fulfilled. It did good, and not evil (II Chron. 29:6-10; 32:26).

(19) Did Hezekiah ... put him at all to death?—The result of the counsel thus given is left to be inferred. It obviously left the prophet free to continue his work as a preacher, though probably under a kind of police surveillance, like that implied in 36:1-5. The favorable result is attributed in verse 24 to the influence of Ahikam.

(20) And there was also a man that prophesied ... Urijah.—The verses that follow, seeing that they state a fact which tends in the opposite direction, cannot be regarded as part of the argument of the "elders" of verse 17. Verse 24 shows that Jeremiah, or the compiler of the book, wished to record the fact that he did not stand absolutely alone, but that another took up the strain of Jeremiah and reproduced it. Of this Urijah we know nothing beyond what is here recorded.

(24) Nevertheless the hand of Ahikam ... —The family to whom the prophet's protector belonged played a conspicuous part in the history of this period, and may be said to have furnished examples of three generations of Jewish patriotism. (See II Kings 22:12; II Chron. 34:8, 20.) Here stress is laid on the fact of Ahikam's protection, as showing how it was that Jeremiah escaped the fate which fell on Urijah.

27

(1) In the beginning of the reign of Jehoiakim.—The mention of the name of Zedekiah as king of Judah in verse 3 shows that the Hebrew text has here in verse 1 perpetuated an error, due probably to the transcriber or first editor of the collected prophecies. (See 28:1.) The tone of the prophecy seems to indicate a time about the middle of Zedekiah's reign. His position was that of a tributary sovereign, subject to Nebuchadnezzar. He and the neighboring kings, who were in a like position, had not quite renounced the hope of throwing off the yoke and asserting their independence.

(2) Make thee bonds and yokes.—This method of vivid symbolic prediction had a precedent in the conduct of Isaiah (Isa. 20:2). We have to realize the infinitely more vivid impression which the appearance of the prophet in this strange guise, as though he were at once a captive slave and a beast of burden, would make on the minds of men, as compared with simply warning them of a coming subjugation. (Comp. Ezek. 12:5, 7.)

(4) Thus saith the Lord of hosts, the God of Israel.—As addressed to the outlying heathen nations, who were not His worshipers, the proclamation of the message as coming from Jehovah Sabaoth, the God of Israel, had a special force. They, with their hosts of earth, were setting themselves against the Lord of the hosts alike of heaven and of earth.

(6) Nebuchadnezzar . . . my servant.—See note on 25:9.

(7) And his son, and his son's son.—The words point to an undefined prolongation, subject only to the fact that there was an appointed limit. Historically we may note the fact that Nebuchadnezzar was succeeded by his son, Evil-merodach (52:31), he by his brother-in-law, Neriglissar, and he by Nabouahid and his son Belshazzar.

Shall serve themselves of him.—The confederacy of nations which shall overthrow the Babylonian monarchy, Medes and others, is described more fully in 51:11, 27, 28. The words were clearly meant to point two ways. They warn the nations not to resist the Chaldaean king then; they warn the king not to think that he is founding a dynasty of long duration.

(11) But the nations that bring their neck under the yoke . . . —The advice given to the five nations that were seeking an alliance with Judah before the actual invasion is specifically addressed to Judah in the next verse and is repeated more fully after the population of Judaea had been carried into captivity (chap. 29). The first warning had been despised, and the exiles were then reaping the fruit of their selfwill; but the principle that obedience was better than resistance remained the same.

(17) Hearken not unto them.—The prophecy of the restoration of the vessels of the Temple (II Kings 24:13; II Chron. 36:7) was clearly not a mere prediction. It had been used as an incentive to rebellion. The prophet saw that such an effort would but hasten the utter destruction of the Temple and the city.

(19) See I Kings 7:21-37.

(22) The fulfillment of the prediction is recorded in II Kings 25:13-17. The date is not given definitely, but seventy years had been already named as the period between the plunder and the restoration (25:12). Here the undefined vagueness of "the day that I will visit them" is contrasted with the equally indefinite but more exciting "shortly" of the false prophets (verse 16).

28

(1) And it came to pass the same year . . . —Of the Hananiah who appears as the most prominent of the prophet's adversaries, we know nothing beyond what is here recorded. He was clearly one of the leaders of the party of resistance at work trying to form an alliance with the neighboring nations, whose hopes had been revived by the accession of Pharaoh-Hophra (Apries) to the throne of Egypt in 595 B.C.

(3) Within two full years.—The conspiracy of Judah and the neighboring states against Nebuchadnezzar was clearly ripening, and he looked on its success as certain. Prediction stood against prediction, and, as there were no signs or wonders wrought, men had to judge from what they knew of the lives of the men who uttered them who was more worthy of credit.

(4) We get here a new glimpse into the nature of the anti-Chaldaean confederacy. Zedekiah was to be deposed as too submissive to Nebuchadnezzar, and the young Jeconiah was to be brought back from his prison at Babylon and re-established in the kingdom as the representative of the policy of resistance, resting on the support of Pharaoh-Hophra.

(12) Then the word of the Lord . . . —The word declared, keeping to the same symbolism as before, that all attempts at resistance to the power which was for the time the scourge, and therefore the servant, of Jehovah, would only end in a more bitter and aggravated bondage.

29

(1) These are the words.—The prophecy in this chapter was addressed to those whom we may describe as the first of the Babylonian exiles who had been carried into captivity with Jeconiah (see 35:2). Among these also, probably in connection with the projects traced in the preceding chapter, there was a restless disquietude fostered by false prophets, who urged the people to rebel against their conquerors. Against that policy Jeremiah, in accordance with the convictions on which he had all along acted, enters an earnest protest. The letter was sent by special messengers (verse 3), and shows that Jeremiah had been kept well informed of all that passed at Babylon. The date of the letter was probably early in the reign of Zedekiah, before the incidents of the previous chapter. It is brought before us as following in almost immediate sequel on the deportation mentioned in verse 2. Ezekiel himself may be thought of as among the priests and prophets.

(2) The carpenters, and the smiths.—(See note on 24:1.) Among the princes were, doubtlessly, Shadrach, Meshach, and Abednego (Dan. 1:6, 7).

(3) By the hand of Elasah . . . —Elasah was the brother of Jeremiah's protector, Ahikam (26:24). Gemariah (not the same as in 36:12) was probably the son of Hilkiah, the high priest under Josiah who found the lost Book of the Law (II Kings 22:4) and took a prominent part in the work of reformation. Each would therefore naturally take his place among the prophet's friends and supporters. That they had been sent as envoys by Zedekiah indicates that the policy of the weak and vacillating king had been to some extent affected by the counsels of Jeremiah.

(4) Thus saith the Lord of hosts . . . —Here is the nearest parallel in the Old Testament to the Epistles of the New, the very text of a written letter sent to those

with whom the teacher was no longer able to hold personal communication.

(5) Build ye houses, and dwell in them.— The command counseled a patient acceptance of the present state of things, and announced that their exile would last for at least two generations. It indicates, also, the comparative leniency with which the exiles were treated.

(14) I will turn away your captivity . . . —On the substance and fulfillment of the prediction, see notes on 23:3-8.

(15) Because ye have said . . . —The words point to the boast of some of the exiles that they, too, had the guidance of prophets whom (verses 20, 24) they were inclined to follow in preference to Jeremiah. In answer to that boast, he emphasizes the contrast between the exiles in whom the prophet sees the future hope of his nation and the worthless king (Zedekiah) and people who had been left in Jerusalem, and for whom he foretells yet sharper sufferings.

(24) Thus shalt thou also speak to Shemaiah . . . —This section is of the nature of a fragment attached to the Epistle to Babylon on account of its associations with it, but not forming part of it. Jeremiah's letter had naturally roused the indignation of the rival prophets at Babylon, and they organized a movement, of which Shemaiah was the chief instigator, for his destruction.

(29) And Zephaniah the priest . . . — Zephaniah does not act as Shemaiah wished him. At the most he only uses the letters as a threat, possibly to put the prophet on his guard against the machinations of his enemies, possibly also to induce him to moderate his tone.

30

(2) Write thee all the words . . . —The general character of chaps. 30 and 31, probably in part consequent on the acceptance of the prophet's teaching by the exiles of Babylon, is one of blessing and restoration, and he is thus led on to the great utterance which, from one point of view, makes him more the prophet of the Gospel even than Isaiah.

(3) I will bring again the captivity of my people Israel and Judah . . . —There is no narrow provincialism in the prophet's heart. He yearns for the exiles of Judah who are far off on the Euphrates; he yearns also for those of Israel who are yet farther in

Assyria and the cities of the Medes (II Kings 17:6).

(9) David their king ... —The name of the old hero-king appears as that of the new representative of the house who is to restore the kingdom. There is to be a second David for Israel, a true king answering to the ideal which he imperfectly represented. Zerubbabel was, in his measure, another partial representative of such a king (Hag. 2:21-23).

(11) Though I make a full end of all nations.—While the destruction of the national life of the heathen nations on whom judgment was to fall should be complete and irreversible, the punishment of Israel should be remedial as well as retributive, working out, in due time, a complete restitution. (See Ps. 6:1.) That thought sustains the prophet in his contemplation of the captivity and apparent ruin of his people. (Comp. Hos. 4:7.)

(17) I will restore health unto thee ... —That extremest misery (verses 12-16) had touched the heart of Jehovah with pity, even for the adulteress who had forsaken Him. The promise of restoration takes naturally then a material form.

(21) Who is this that engaged his heart to approach unto me?—The question points to the ruler of the house of David whom the prophet sees in visions—in other words, to the far-off Messiah. The dominant thought is that of one who will not be treacherous or faithless, like the degenerate heirs of the house of David whom Jeremiah had known, but one who would "engage" (or pledge) his heart and soul to the service of Jehovah. In the advent of such a king the true relation between God and His people should yet be re-established.

31

(1) The God of all the families of Israel.— The union of the ten tribes of Israel and the two of Judah is again prominent in the prophet's mind. He cannot bear to think of that division, with its deep lines of cleavage in the religious and social life of the people, being perpetuated. Israel should be Israel. This is the crown and consummation of the promise of 30:24.

(2) The people which were left of the sword ... —The past experience of God's love is a pledge or earnest for the future. The prophet thinks of the captives that had escaped the sword of the Chaldaeans and of

their finding grace in the wilderness that lies between Palestine and the Euphrates. The verses that follow show, however, that the prophet is thinking also of the more distant exiles, the ten tribes in the cities of the Medes beyond the Tigris (II Kings 17:6).

(6) The watchmen upon the mount Ephraim shall cry ... —The special fact is given as the ground of the previous prediction. The rival worship in Bethel and in Dan, which had so long kept the ten tribes of Israel from the Temple at Jerusalem, should cease, and from the mountains of Ephraim there should be heard the cry which, with a solitary exception in the reign of Hezekiah (II Chron. 30:11, 18), had not been heard for centuries—"Let us go up to Zion." The long schism, which had caused the ruin of the nation would at last be healed. Unity of worship, at once the ground and symbol of national unity, should be restored.

(15) A voice was heard in Ramah.—The sharp contrast between this and the exulting joy of the previous verse shows that we are entering on a new section. It repeats in altered form the substance of the foregoing, presenting in succession the same pictures of present woe and future gladness. The prophet sees first the desolation of the captivity. Rachel, as the mother of Joseph, and therefore of Ephraim, becomes the ideal representative of the northern kingdom. (See Matt. 2:18.)

(17) And there is hope in thine end ... —The hope here is defined as that of the return of Rachel's children to their own border—the return, that is, of the Ten Tribes from their captivity. They have been longer under the sharp discipline of suffering. By this time, the prophet thinks, they must have learned repentance.

(21) Set thee up way marks ...—The figure is changed from "Ephraim, the dear son," to Israel, the "back-sliding daughter." The first group of those who came back is called on to set up "heaps of stones" to mark the way for those who followed. She was to pass in her joy through the same cities that had then seen her in her shame.

(22) In the normal order of man's life, the bridegroom woos the bride. In the spiritual relationship which the prophet has in view, this shall be inverted, and Israel, the erring but repentant wife, shall woo her Divine husband. (Comp. Hos. 2:14-20.)

(23) As yet they shall use this speech in the land of Judah ... —The prophet turns from the northern kingdom to that of Judah, and sees it also as a sharer in the restoration. Jerusalem should be blessed, and be worthy of blessing. The "holy mountain" is used with a special reference to Moriah and the Temple. And the prophet's ideal of the restored life of Israel is that it should combine the best features of the patriarchal and the kingly life.

(29, 30) The fathers have eaten a sour grape . . . —Men found in this proverb an explanation of their sufferings which relieved their consciences. They were suffering, they said, for the sins of their fathers, not for their own. Both Ezekiel and Jeremiah felt now that the time had come when the other aspect of God's government had to be asserted in all its fullness; therefore they lay stress on the truth that each man is responsible for his own acts, and for those alone, and that the law of the inheritance of evil leaves untouched the freedom of man's will.

(31) I will make a new covenant . . . —The common proverb about the sour grapes had set the prophet thinking on the laws of God's dealings with men. He felt that something more was needed to restrain men from evil than the thought that they might be transmitting evil to their children's children—something more even than the thought of direct personal responsibility, and of a perfectly righteous retribution. And that something was to be found in the idea of a law—not written on tablets of stone, not threatening and condemning from without, and denouncing punishment on the transgressors and their descendants, but written on heart and spirit (II Cor. 3:3-6). In Ezekiel also the promise of a "new heart and new spirit" comes in close sequence upon the protest against the adage about the "children's teeth being set on edge" (Ezek. 18:2, 31).

(33) This shall be the covenant . . . —The experiment, so to speak, of a law requiring righteousness had been tried and had failed. There remained the hope—now, by the divine word that came to him, turned into an assurance—of a Power importing righteousness, writing the "law in the inward parts," the center of consciousness and will.

(34) They shall teach no more every man his neighbour . . . —We trace in that hope for the future the profound sense of failure which oppressed the mind of the prophet. What good had come of all the machinery of ritual and of teaching which the Law of Israel had provided so abundantly? To

know Him as He is required nothing less than a special revelation of His presence to each man's heart and spirit. That revelation was now promised for all who were willing to receive it as the special gift which opened to his view a restored Israel. (See Isa. 54:13; John 6:45.)

I will forgive their iniquity . . . —The second clause repeats the promise of the first. Our thoughts of God as the All-knowing preclude the idea of any limitation of His knowledge, such as the words "I will remember no more" imply. What is meant is that He will treat the past offenses, even though their inevitable consequences may continue, as though they had never been, so far as they affect the communion of the soul with God.

(35, 36) Which giveth the sun for a light by day . . . —The leading thought in the lofty language of this passage is that the reign of law which we recognize in God's creative work has its counterpart in His spiritual kingdom. The stability and permanence of natural order is a pledge and earnest of the fulfillment of His promises to Israel as a people.

32

(1) In the tenth year of Zedekiah . . . —We are carried over a period of six years from the prophecy of 28:1 to 589 B.C., when the treacherous and intriguing policy of Zedekiah had provoked Nebuchadnezzar to besiege Jerusalem in the ninth year of the king of Judah's reign. The king, irritated by Jeremiah's continued predictions of defeat, had imprisoned him in the dungeon for state-prisoners attached to the palace (Neh. 3:25). He was not allowed to leave his prison, but friends were permitted to have access to him.

(3, 4) Behold, I will give this city into the hand of the king of Babylon . . . —To see the king of Babylon face to face, to stand before him in shame and confusion, was to be the end of the king's frantic resistance to the divine purpose. The prophecy of Ezekiel (12:13), and the fact that Nebuchadnezzar put out the eyes of the captive king (39:7), give a special force to Jeremiah's word (see II Kings 25:6, 7; Jer. 39:6; 52:10, 11). Of Zedekiah's fate after he arrived in Babylon we know nothing, but the absence of his name when Jehoiachin was released from his imprisonment (52:31) by Evil-merodach suggests the conclusion that he was then dead.

(7) Behold, Hanameel the son of Shallum . . . —The teaching of the narrative that follows is brought out distinctly in verse 44. With all the certainty of desolation, misery, exile in the immediate future, the prophet was to give a practical proof that he was as certain of the ultimate restoration. It was worthwhile to buy a field even for what might seem the contingency of that remote reversion. Note in Lev. 25:24, 32 and Ruth 3:12; 4:4 the option of purchase offered in the first instance to the next of kin (the **Goël**, or "redeemer," of the family), so that it might still be kept in the line of succession.

(12) Baruch the son of Neriah, the son of Maaseiah.—This is the first mention of a man who played a more or less prominent part in connection with Jeremiah's later work. He belonged to the nobler families of Judah (see 51:59). In relation to the prophet, he appears in 36:4 as acting as his secretary, as accused of instigating Jeremiah to preach submission to the Chaldaeans (43:3), as sharing his sufferings and dangers (36:26), and, according to Josephus (**Ant.** 10:6, § 12) as thrown into prison with him. He was probably an influential member of the Chaldaean party in the court of Judah, protesting against the policy which courted an alliance with Egypt and entered into intrigues and schemes of rebellion against the power of Babylon. The book that bears his name is probably pseudonymous, but it bears witness to the importance of the position which he occupied in the politics of the time.

(14) Put them in an earthen vessel . . . —Such a vessel was obviously a better protection against damp or decay than one of wood, and was, as it were, the "safe" of a Jewish household. In the "many days" we have an implied warning to the listeners that they were not to expect a speedy deliverance or restoration, however certain might be their assurance that it would come at last.

(16) I prayed unto the Lord.—The prophet, it is obvious, records his own prayer. Nowhere, perhaps, do the writings of the Old Testament present us with so striking an example of the manner in which a devout Israelite poured out his heart to God, dwelling on the greatness of His attributes—praying for himself, interceding for his people. (But comp. Ezra 9:5-15; Isa. 37:16-20; Dan. 9:4-19.)

(27) Is there any thing too hard for me?—The answer to the prayer is an echo of the prayer itself (verse 17). The prophet is assured that he was not wrong when he cast himself, in the full confidence of faith, on the loving omnipotence of God.

(31) From the day that they built it . . . —The thoughts of the prophet turn to the time when Israel was yet one people under David and Solomon. Even then, he seems to say, the city had fallen far short of the holiness which it ought to have attained, and which David sought for it (Pss. 15-24.) Jerusalem had been a Jebusite city before David took possession (II Sam. 5:6-10), but it was so much enlarged and altered after this capture that the words which so describe it may have been not only practically, but almost literally, true.

(40) I will make an everlasting covenant . . . —The "covenant" thus promised is identical with that of 31:31. The curse of Israel had been that they had been without that fear to restrain them from evil, and that the mere dread of punishment had proved powerless to supply its place.

33

(1-3) The second time, while he was yet shut up.—This discourse belongs to the same period as the preceding chapter and presents the same general characteristics. Its connection with the operations of the siege to which Jerusalem was exposed will be traced in verse 4. As with other prophecies, its starting point is found in the thought of the majesty of the attributes of God.

(7, 8) I . . . will build . . . I will cleanse . . . I will pardon . . . —The vision of the return of the exiles and of a restored city, prominent in 31:38-40, is not allowed to overshadow the yet more glorious vision of spiritual blessings of purity and pardon.

(11) Praise the Lord of hosts . . . —The words were used as the recurring doxology of the Temple services (Ezra 3:11; II Chron. 7:6; 20:21; Ps. 136:2, 3; I Macc. 4:24). The Courts of the Temple, now hushed in silence, should once again re-echo with the Hallelujahs of the Priests and Levites.

(14-16) See notes on 23:5, 6. In the passages there is a remarkable difference. There the title "The Lord our Righteousness" is given to the future King, and the passage has accordingly been used as a proof of the deity of the Christ, who is that King. Here it is given to the city, and can

561

only mean that that name will be the watchword of her being. She will be a city marked by a righteousness which will be the gift of Jehovah.

(17) David shall never want a man... —Comp. the promises of II Sam. 7:16; I Kings 2:4; Ps. 89:29, 36. Here it is repeated under very different circumstances. Then it had been given when the line of David was in all the freshness of its strength; now it is uttered when that line seemed on the very point of dying out. The hope of the prophet is, however, inextinguishable. He is certain that the true King will always be of the house of David; and, while he pictured to himself an unbroken succession of sovereigns of David's line, there was in fact a higher fulfillment in the continuous sovereignty of the Christ as the true Son of David.

(18) Neither shall the priests the Levites want a man... —The Levitical priesthood passed away (Heb. 7:11), but Christ was made a Priest after the order of Melchizedek. And by virtue of their union with Him, His people became a holy priesthood (Heb. 10:19-22), offering, not the burnt-offerings and meat-offerings which were figures of the true, but the spiritual sacrifices of praise and thanksgiving (I Pet. 2:5), the sacrifice of body, soul, and spirit, which alone was acceptable to God (Rom. 12:1).

(19-22) And the word of the Lord came unto Jeremiah, saying... —The new repeats, in substance, the promise of verses 17, 18, but it reproduces them with yet greater solemnity.

(24-26) The prophet's declaration of the steadfastness of God's covenant was made in answer, not to the taunts of the heathen, but to the despair of Israel (see verse 10; 32:43). In contrast with this despondency, the prophet renews his assurance of the permanence of the kingly and priestly lines, and strengthens it by reference to the three great patriarchs of the race.

34

(1) When Nebuchadnezzar king of Babylon... —The prophecy that follows is probably a fuller statement of that in 32:3, 4, and delivered shortly before it, being referred to there as the cause of his imprisonment.

(5) And with the burnings of thy fathers... —Spices and perfumes were burned as a mark of honor at the burial of

kings and persons of high rank. The Hebrews never adopted the practice of burial by cremation, and for the most part embalmed their dead after the manner of Egypt (comp. Gen. 50:2; John 19:39, 40).

(8) After that the king Zedekiah had made a covenant... —The remainder of the chapter brings before us an historical episode of considerable interest. The law of Moses did not allow in the case of a free-born Hebrew more than a temporary bondage of seven years (Exod. 21:2; Deut. 15:12-18), extended in the later regulations of Lev. 25:39, 40 to the time that might intervene between the date of purchase and the commencement of the next year of jubilee. In II Kings 4:1 we have an instance of the working of the law as bringing even the sons of a prophet into this modified slavery. Only if the man preferred his state as a slave to the risks of freedom could his master retain him after the appointed limit (Exod. 21:5, 6). The law had apparently fallen into disuse, and the nobles of Judah had used the law of debt to bring a large number of their fellow citizens into slavery, just as their successors did after the return from Babylon (Neh. 5:5). Zedekiah had been led to promise freedom to all the slave population of this class that were within the walls of Jerusalem. When the Chaldaean danger was past, temporarily, however, the princes who had agreed to the emancipation returned to their old policy of oppression, and those who had been liberated were brought under a bondage all the more bitter for the temporary taste of freedom. Against this perfidious tyranny the prophet bears his protests. His sympathies, like those of true prophets at all times, were with the poor and the oppressed.

(18) When they cut the calf in twain... —The passage is interesting as showing the survival of one of the oldest rites of Patriarchal times. (See notes on Gen. 15:10-17.)

35

(1) In the days of Jehoiakim.—The prophecy that follows carries us back over a period of about seventeen years to the earlier period of the prophet's life and work. Jerusalem was not yet besieged. Jehoiakim had not filled up the measure of his iniquities. The armies of the Chaldaeans and Syrians were, however, in the meantime moving on the outskirts of the kingdom of Judah (verse 11) or were driving the nomad inhabitants, who had heretofore dwelt in tents, to take refuge in the cities (comp. 4:6 and 8:14). The first capture of the city by Nebuchadnezzar was 607 B.C.

(2) Go unto the house of the Rechabites ... —The word "house" is used throughout the chapter in the sense of "family." The founder of this tribe or sect was the Jonadab, or Jehonadab, who appears as the ally of Jehu in the overthrow of the house of Ahab (II Kings 10:15). He is described as the "son of Rechab," which means "son of the chariot." The life which Jonadab enforced on his followers presented all the characteristic features of that of Elijah. Note in verses 6-10 that they were nomads and Nazarites.

(3) Then I took Jaazaniah the son of Jeremiah ... —The names (Jaazaniah—Jehovah hears; Jeremiah—Jehovah exalts; Habaziniah—Jehovah gathers) show that the Rechabites were conspicuous witnesses for the faith of Israel. The name Jeremiah may possibly indicate that there was some previous connection between the Rechabites and the prophet's family.

(4) I brought them into the house of the Lord ... —The Temple of Solomon appears from I Kings 6:5 to have had apartments constructed in its precincts which were assigned, by special favor, for the residence of conspicuous priests or prophets. Hanan is described as "a man of God," and therefore sympathetic with Jeremiah. It would seem, from the narrative, that Jeremiah had no chamber of his own. The stress laid on details was probably intended to show that the memorable dramatic scene that followed, daring as it seemed, was acted in the presence of representatives of the priestly, prophetic, and official orders.

(13) Will ye not receive instruction ... —The argument of the prophet is naturally an **à fortiori** one. The words of Jonadab had been kept faithfully as a rule of life for 300 years by his descendants or his order. The people generally, too, had the same promise that by obeying they should dwell in the land which He had given them, but they had turned a deaf ear both to the promise and the warning which it implied.

(18) Because ye have obeyed the commandment of Jonadab your father.—The law which Jeremiah received as given by God laid down no such rule of life. A righteous life was possible without it. What he was taught to praise was the steadfastness and loyalty with which they adhered to a merely human precept, not at variance with

the letter of any divine law, and designed to carry the spirit of that law to its highest point.

(19) Jonadah the son of Rechab shall not want a man to stand before me for ever.— The words "stand before" are definitely liturgical, expressing the ministrations of the Levites who were chosen to "stand before" the Lord (Deut. 10:8; 18:5, 7). The natural inference would be that the Rechabites were by these words admitted, in virtue of their Nazarite character, to serve as Levites in the Temple—to be, in fact, a higher class of Nethinim (see I Chron. 9:2; Ezra 2:43).

36

(1) The fourth year of Jehoiakim ... — Considering the date, it is a reasonable inference that we have in chap. 25 the substance of part, at least, of what was written by Baruch from the prophet's dictation in verse 4. The contents exactly agree with the description of the prophecy given here in verse 2.

(2) Take thee a roll of a book ... —The same phrase is used in Ps. 40:7, but does not occur in any earlier prophet or historical book. It is found in later prophets (Ezek. 2:9; 3:1; Zech. 5:1, 2). It probably followed the introduction of parchment as a writing material, and the consequent substitution of the roll for the papyrus books, for which, from their fragile fabric, a different form was necessary. It is interesting to note the parallelism between Jeremiah's **modus operandi** (see verse 18) and Paul's (Rom. 16:22; Gal. 6:11; II Thess. 3:17). From time to time the prophet collects, repeats, revises, and edits what he has uttered. We have here accordingly what may be described as the history of the first volume of his discourses—a volume which perished, as the chapter records, but of which the earlier chapters of the present book are substantially a reproduction.

(4) Then Jeremiah called Baruch the son of Neriah.—(See note on 32:12.) Baruch had to act not only as the prophet's amanuensis, but as the preacher of his sermon (verses 6-8). Note that an interval of some months elapsed between the dictation and public utterance (verse 9).

(6) In the Lord's house upon the fasting day.—Probably the king had proclaimed the fast by the advice of the priests and false prophets to arouse the people to the "holy war" of an enthusiastic religious resistance to the Chaldeans. This may account for the eagerness of Jeremiah to counteract the scheme by the unexpected sermon.

(10) In the chamber of Gemariah the son of Shaphan.—The man thus named belonged to a family which, through three successive generations, presented conspicuous examples of devout patriotism. (See 26:24; II Kings 22:3; 23:12.) Here Gemariah places his chamber in the Temple court at the service of the prophet's delegate.

(11) When Michaiah the son of Gemariah ... —It seems that Michaiah's reporting Baruch's discourse was probably part of a preconcerted plan, arranged between the prophet and his friends, so as to give an opening for bringing Baruch into the presence of the king and his counselors as they sat in their council-chamber.

(20) They laid up the roll in the chamber of Elishama ... —The step was a material one, from the official standpoint. If either the prophet or the disciple were to be prosecuted for what had been spoken, it was important that the corpus delicti should itself be ready for reference, whether on behalf of the accusers or accused. The precaution taken indicates an apprehension that the king, in his passionate waywardness, might act as he actually did.

(23) Three or four leaves.—The English suggests the idea of a papyrus book rather than a parchment roll (see note on verse 4), but the Hebrew may indicate the column of writing on such a roll, as well as a leaf. The act, in its childish impatience, betrayed the anger of the king. He could not bear to hear of the seventy years of exile which were in store for his people, and which, if we assume the roll to have included the substance of chap. 25, would have come into one of the earlier columns. The "pen-knife" here is the knife which was used to shape the reed, or **calamus**, used in writing.

(27) Then the word of the Lord came to Jeremiah.—This was probably during the concealment of the two friends, and to the command thus given we probably owe the present form of chap. 25—perhaps, also, of the earlier chapters of the book. But, in addition to the reproduction of the judgment denounced upon the nation at large, there was now a special prediction as to Jehoiakim himself.

(32) And there were added besides unto them many like words.—The passage is interesting as showing the **genesis** of the present volume of the prophet's writings. The discourse delivered in the Temple court

was revised and enlarged, dictated to Baruch as before, and in this shape handed down to us in chap. 25.

37

(1) And king Zedekiah the son of Josiah ... —The eight chapters that follow form a continuous narrative of the later work and fortunes of the prophet. They open with recording the accession of Zedekiah, following on the disposition of Coniah (or Jeconiah). The relative pronoun "whom" refers to Zedekiah.

(2) But neither he, nor his servants ... —The verse gives a general survey of the character of Zedekiah's reign preparatory to the actual history that follows, which falls toward its close, probably in the seventh or eighth year of his reign.

(3) And Zedekiah the king sent Jehucal ... —The time and occasion of the mission are given in verse 5. The Chaldaeans had raised the siege of Jerusalem on hearing of the approach of the Egyptian army under Pharaoh-Hophra, the Apries of Herodotus (Herod. 2:161-169; Ezek. 17:15-17; 29:1-16; 30:1-32:32), and the king seems to have thought that an opportunity presented itself for asserting his independence. He wished to gain the sanction and the prayers of the prophet for this policy.

(9, 10) Deceive not yourselves ...—The king and his counselors had buoyed themselves up with expectations of deliverance. The prophet tells them, in the language of a bold hyperbole (comp. Isa. 30:17), that even the wounded remnant of the Chaldaean army should be strong enough to accomplish the purpose of Jehovah in the destruction of Jerusalem.

(12) Then Jeremiah went forth out of Jerusalem ... —The prophet's motive in leaving the city may well have been his apprehension that the answer he had sent would move the king's anger, and lead, as it actually led, to an order for his arrest. The fact that the Chaldaeans had raised the siege gave him free egress. As a priest belonging to Anathoth, he had property in the land of Benjamin, and he now went to look after it. But he was charged with treachery—with "falling away to the Chaldaeans" (verse 13). It was assumed that, though the Chaldaeans had gone, the prophet was about to make his way to their encampment to incite them to return, and so work out the fulfillment of his own prediction.

(15) The princes ... put him in prison in the house of Jonathan the scribe.—The house was probably chosen as being under the direct control of one who, as scribe, exercised functions like those of a minister of police. It had not only the subterranean dungeon and pit common to all Eastern prisons, but separate cells for the confinement of individual prisoners (verse 16). Of the severity with which the prophet was treated there, we may judge from his entreaty not to be taken back there after his release (verse 20; 38:26). The "many days" of his imprisonment began before the second siege of Jerusalem, which lasted for nearly two years (II Kings 25:1-3); and when the city was taken he was still in the court of the prison. The incidents of chaps. 32-34 belong to this period.

(18, 19) The cruelty of his treatment draws from the prophet an indignant protest. Then the failure of the past predictions of the false prophets is urged on the king as a reason why he should not trust them in the present crisis. (See 28:3.)

(21) Into the court of the prison ... — This was obviously a concession to Jeremiah's request (verse 20), and here he remained, with one brief exception (38:6), until the capture of the city. It was above ground, with free access for light and air. The prophet was treated with respect, and not left to starve.

38

(4) Let this man be put to death.—The words of verses 2 and 3 carry us back to 21:9, and in any chronological arrangement of the book the one chapter would follow the other. It is obvious that to all who did not recognize the divine mission of the prophet, words like those which he had then spoken would seem to come from the lips of a traitor. The hatred of the princes of Judah becomes more bitter than ever, and they seek to overcome the king's lingering reverence for the prophet. Even in the reign of Jehoiakim they had said that he was worthy of death (26:11).

(6) The dungeon.—In Lam. 3:53-55 we have probably a reminiscence of these days of horrible suffering. The cistern had been partly dried up (possibly through the supply of water having been cut off during the protracted siege), but there remained a thick deposit, three or four feet deep, of black fetid mud; there (verse 9) his enemies

meant to leave him to die of hunger. They probably shrank from the odium of a public execution, or thought that in this way they could escape the guilt of shedding the prophet's blood.

(7) Ebed-melech the Ethiopian.—The name signifies "servant of the king." The use of Ethiopian or Cushite slaves in the king's household, probably as keeping guard over the harem, had been of long standing. The law of Moses, it may be noted, forbade such mutilation in the case of Israelites (Deut. 23:1). The Ethiopian descent of Jehudi (36:21) may probably have brought him into contact with an officer of the king's household of the same race, and Ebed-melech's feelings may have been drawn to the prophet by what he thus heard.

In the gate of Benjamin.—This was on the northern wall of the city, the most exposed to the attack of the invading army. The king apparently had gone there either to direct the operations of the defense, or, perhaps, to prevent others from following, as they might think, Jeremiah's example, and either deserting to the enemy or abandoning the defense of the city.

(11-13) Nothing could show the acuteness of the prophet's sufferings more vividly than the precautions which the thoughtful kindness of the eunuch thus suggested. The pit was so deep that ropes were needed to draw him up, as they had been to let him down; and lest they should cut into the flesh of Jeremiah's emaciated form, improvised cushions had to be fastened to the ropes that he might rest his armpits on them.

(16) As the Lord liveth, that made us this soul.—The formula of the oath was obviously intended to be one of unusual solemnity. The king swears by Jehovah as the living God, author and giver of his own life. The twofold promise shows that the king felt the implied reproof of Jeremiah's question (verse 16). It is characteristic of Zedekiah's weakness that even now the oath is given secretly.

(17, 18) The prophet places before the king the alternative of surrender and safety—resistance and destruction—and leaves him to make his choice.

(24-26) Let no man know ... —The weak king vacillated to the last moment. He feared the prophet, but he feared the princes yet more. The nature of the interview was concealed, and events took their course. Jeremiah remained in the court of the prison until the city was taken.

39

(1) In the ninth year of Zedekiah ...
—The great crisis came at last, as Jeremiah
had long ago predicted. A fuller narrative
of the siege and capture is given in chap.
52. The two verses which open the chapter
seem to have been inserted here by the
editor of the prophecies in their present
form, as explaining the fact with which
chap. 38 had closed. The siege had lasted
eighteen months, beginning in 590 B.C. and
ending 588 B.C. It came to an end, as we
learn from 52:6, through the pressure of the
famine, of which we have seen traces in
37:21.

(5) In the plains of Jericho.—The **Ara-
both** of the Jordan was the enlargement of
the Jordan Valley, three miles wide, near
Jericho. The intention of the king was apparently to make his way to the ford near
Jericho, cross the river, and escape to the
open country of Gilead.

Riblah in the land of Hamath.—Riblah,
on the Orontes near its source, was a center
from which great lines of traffic projected
in every direction. It was, therefore, a natural post of observation for the Chaldaean
king while his generals were carrying on the
siege of Tyre and Jerusalem. (See II Kings
23:33.)

(7) Moreover he put out Zedekiah's eyes.—
The special form of punishment is noticeable as fulfilling two prophecies: that
Zedekiah should see the king of Babylon
and be taken to that city (32:4); and that
though he was to die in Babylon, he should
never see it (Ezek. 12:13). Beyond this, the
fate of the last king of Judah is unknown.
His brother Jehoiachin was already a
prisoner in Babylon (II Kings 24:15), but
we do not know whether the two were
allowed to meet. Twenty-six years later Jehoiachin was released by Evil-merodach (II
Kings 25:27); but there is no mention of
Zedekiah, and it is a natural inference that
his sufferings had ended previously.

**(8) And the Chaldeans burned the king's
house.**—This was the work of Nebuzar-adan
(52:12, 13), who had been sent by Nebuchadnezzar, on hearing of the capture of the
city. It included the destruction of the Temple as well as the palace.

(9) The defenders and deserters were involved in the same doom of exile. As in the
case of the conquests of Tiglath-pileser (II
Kings 15:29), Shalmaneser (II Kings 17:6),
Esar-haddon (II Kings 17:24), and Sennacherib (II Kings 18:32), this wholesale depor-

tation was part of the systematic policy of
the great Assyrian and Babylonian monarchs. To distribute the lands of the exiles
thus dispossessed among "the poor of the
people" (verse 10), was, it was thought,
likely to enlist their interests on the side of
the conqueror; and, by keeping up the cultivation of the soil secured the payment of
tribute.

(11, 12) It is clear that Nebuchadrezzar
had been well informed of the part which
Jeremiah had taken from first to last in
counseling submission. From the time of
Nebuzar-adan's arrival, the position of Jeremiah was obviously changed for the better,
and he became an honored and trusted
counselor.

(14) According to 40:1 the prophet was
set free at Ramah. It seems likely that, at
first, he was sent back to the prison where
he had been found, until he could be placed
under the protection of Gedaliah. Gedaliah
was the representative of a house which for
three generations had been true to the
prophets who spoke in the name of the
Lord. We hear nothing more of Ebed-
melech, the faithful Ethiopian, but we may
believe that he was spared by the Chaldaeans, probably at the prophet's intercession
(verse 16).

40

**(1) The word that came to Jeremiah from
the Lord.**—This introduction is not followed by any specific utterance of prophecy. It stands as a kind of heading to the
section of the collected prophecies subsequent to the capture of the city.

(2-4) The Lord thy God ... —Such a
recognition did not imply more than the
belief of the polytheist that each nation had
its own guardian deity. As a prophet, however, Jeremiah is treated with marked respect—in part, perhaps, due to the policy he
had advocated, and in part, possibly, to the
influence of men like Daniel and his friends
at Babylon—and offered the option of
going to that city or remaining in Judaea.
The prophet obviously chooses the second
alternative.

(5) Governor over the cities of Judah.—
The official title is significant. Jerusalem is
treated as if it had been blotted from the
face of the earth and required no superintendence. Gedaliah, the prophet's friend,
had obviously acted on his counsels and
accepted the sovereignty of Nebuchadnez-

zar as being for the time the ordinance of God. A true patriot might well hold it to be his duty at such a time to accept office under the conqueror, in the hope of being able to do something for the remnant of the nation that was left under his charge.

(7) Now when all the captains of the forces.—A new section of the history begins, ending with the murder of Gedaliah and its sequel (41:18). The king of Babylon had, by appointing Gedaliah, himself a prince of Judah, shown a disposition to treat the conquered people leniently.

(11) When all the Jews that were in Moab . . .—Many of the dwellers in Judaea had fled before the march of the Chaldaean armies, taking refuge in the neighboring regions. These, on hearing of the generous policy adopted by Gedaliah, took courage and returned in time to profit by his permission to gather the produce which otherwise would have been left to perish on the soil.

(14) Ishmael, belonging to the royal house of Judah, seems to have been still plotting with the king of the Ammonites against the authority of the Chaldaeans. Open resistance being now impossible, they have recourse to assassination. The plot becomes known; Gedaliah refused to believe, and will not sanction another crime by way of precaution.

41

(1) It came to pass in the seventh month.—As the seventh month included the Feast of Tabernacles, it is likely that the murderers came as if to share in its festivities. Three months had passed since the capture of the city (39:2).

(5) There came certain . . .—The eighty travelers were coming apparently on a pilgrimage of mourning to the ruins of the Temple, perhaps to keep the Feast of Tabernacles, in the hope of finding at least an altar there on which they might present their oblations.

(7) Ishmael the son of Nethaniah slew them.—The purpose of the new murder does not appear at first sight. The very presence of the devout mourners may have aroused him to bitterness; their recognition of Gedaliah may have seemed the act of traitors to their country; the act may have been one of vindictive retaliation for the murder of his kinsmen (52:10); or it may

have been perpetrated for the sake of plunder.

(9) Which Asa the king had made for fear of Baasha . . . —See I Kings 15:22; II Chron. 16:6.

(13) They were glad.—The words are significant as implying the popularity of Gedaliah, and the joy of those who had been under him at seeing the prospect of his murder being avenged. They at once took refuge with the leader of the avenging party.

(17) The plan of the fugitives under Johanan took them to Bethlehem, as lying on the road to Egypt, where they hoped to find a refuge both from the anarchy in which the land had been left by the death of Gedaliah, and from the severe punishment which the Chaldaeans were likely to inflict.

42

(2) Pray for us unto the Lord thy God.—Jeremiah had gone to Gedaliah at Mizpah (40:6) and would seem to have been among the captives whom Ishmael was carrying off when they were rescued by Johanan at Gibeon (41:13, 14). The people now turn to him, acknowledging him as a true prophet, and, trusting his patriotism, ask for his guidance. Their position was difficult and dangerous.

(7-12) The interval of ten days is significant—the prophet would not give an answer of his own on the spur of the moment. The prophet's counsel is, as it had been all along, that the people should accept the punishment which God had inflicted on them, that they should stay where they were and as they were, and not in terror or suspicion seek safety in plans of their own devising. They should at once be allowed to return each man to his own field and vineyard.

(14) No; but we will go into the land of Egypt.—As of old, it was still the granary of the East, and its plenteous harvests formed a bright contrast to the famine which they had experienced during the invasion of the Chaldaeans. Jeremiah, however, has simply to reject the plan, as from first to last he had resisted altogether the thought of an Egyptian alliance (2:36; 37:7). Comp. Ezek. 17:11-18; 29:1-32:32.

(20) For ye dissembled in your hearts . . .—Looks and whispers betrayed the secret counsels of their hearts. They had made a false profession of their readiness to obey, and really meant all along to act as they liked, with the prophet's approval, if they could get it—if not, without. Hypocrisy such as this could not fail to draw down a righteous punishment.

43

(3) Baruch the son of Neriah setteth thee on against us.—This was the solution which presented itself to the suspicions of the murmurers. The prophet's amanuensis had become his leader, making use of him as a tool for the furtherance of his own designs, and those designs were to court the favor of the conqueror by delivering the remnant of the people into his hands. (The warning of 45:5 may perhaps be taken as an indication that there was a certain ambition and love of eminence in Baruch's character which gave a color to the suspicion.) The apocryphal Book of Baruch represents him as being actually at Babylon at the time of the capture of Jerusalem. This was probable enough, for he has not appeared here since the days of Jehoiakim (36:32). On this assumption Jeremiah was perhaps suspected of actually receiving instructions from the Babylonian Court through Baruch, who in verse 6 suddenly reappears as the prophet's companion. Prophet and scribe were apparently seized and carried off by force to prevent their carrying out the schemes of which they were suspected. As the emigration (verses 5, 6) included all who had gathered together under the protection of Gedaliah, it must have left the lands of Judah almost entirely depopulated, and the fear of this result may well have been among the reasons that determined Jeremiah's counsels.

(7) Thus came they even to Tahpanhes.—The town was obviously on the northeastern frontier of Egypt. In Judith 1:9 it appears between the Rhinocolura, which river divided Egypt from Palestine, and all the land of Goshen. In Ezek. 30:16-18 it is named, in conjunction with No (Thebes) and Noph (Memphis) among the chief cities of Egypt. Here apparently the emigrants determined to settle and found a new home for themselves.

(9) The brickkiln.—It seems better, with Hitzig, Furst, and others, to take the Hebrew word as meaning a structure of brick, a raised **pavement**, like the Gabbatha or Pavement on which Pilate sat (John 19:13), in front of the entrance of the palace, on which the king naturally placed his throne when he sat in judgment or received petitions. Assyrian and Babylonian monuments present many instances of kings thus seated. The symbolic act was of the same type as the breaking of the potter's vessel (19:10), the yoke worn on the prophet's shoulders (27:2), and Ezekiel's digging through the wall (Ezek. 12:7).

(10) His royal pavilion.—Here, again, the meaning of the Hebrew word is doubtful. Hitzig and others find in it, not a canopy, but the leather covering which was placed over the pavement on which the throne was set, upon which the criminal knelt as on a scaffold to receive the death stroke of the executioner. So taken, the prediction assumes a more definite and terrible aspect.

(12) As a shepherd putteth on his garment.—To take possession of the whole country will be as quick and light a matter as when the shepherd takes up his garment at night and wraps it around him. Hitzig suggests there may be a reference to the fact that when the shepherd so wraps himself, he turns the fleecy coat which he wears inside out. So, the prophet may suggest, shall the conqueror turn the whole land upside down. (Comp. II Kings 21:13). The fulfillment of the prediction, as far as it referred to the defeat and death of Pharaoh-hophra (verse 13), is related by Josephus (**Ant.** 10:9 §7). (See 44:30.)

44

(1) There is no certain note of the interval between the arrival of the Jews in Egypt and the delivery of the discourse, but it would appear that there had been time for the Jews to disperse and settle in the three or four cities here named and to adopt the worship of the Egyptians. It is, however, implied throughout that the prophet is speaking to the emigrants themselves, and not to their descendants (verses 17, 21).

(13) I will punish them that dwell in the land of Egypt.—The words point, like those of 43:11, to a punishment which should fall on the whole of Egypt, and from which the Jews who dwelt in it should find no exemption.

(14) To the which they have a desire to return.—The words are significant as showing that the exiles still cherished the hope of getting back to the land of their fathers. But escape would be difficult.

(15) All the men which knew that their

wives had burned incense.—The fact thus mentioned incidentally shows that the prophet's words in verse 9 had not missed their mark. As of old, the women practiced a **cultus** in which their husbands acquiesced, even though they did not join in it. On the "queen of heaven" in verses 18, 19, see note on 7:18.

(20-23) Then Jeremiah said ... —The prophet makes an effective rejoinder to the assertion that the prosperity of past years had coincided with the idolatrous worship which he condemned. The tenor of his argument was that which Augustine adopts in his treatise **De Civitate Dei.**

(24-28) Hear the word of the Lord ... —The appeal to the experience of the past is followed by a prediction of the future. That "great name" (Gen. 22:16) of the Lord God **(Jehovah Adonai)** shall be profaned no more by the Egyptian exiles, not because they, of their own accord, would cease to use it, but because none of them should be left there. The small remnant that survived the sword and the famine should return to Judah as a witness of the judgment that had fallen on them, and of the truth of the prophet's warning.

(30) Behold, I will give Pharaoh-hophra ... —The fate of the Egyptian king is announced as a "sign" that the prediction of the fugitives' doom also would in due course be accomplished. The king thus named (the Apries of Herod. 2:161-169) reigned for twenty-five years—from 594 B.C. to 569. Jeremiah probably delivered his prediction ca. 580 B.C., and it is the last recorded event in his life. A late Christian tradition, resting probably on a Jewish one, states that then, or shortly afterward, the Egyptian Jews, irritated by his reproaches, rose up against him and stoned him to death (Tertull. **Adv. Gnost.**, 8; Hieron. **Adv. Jovin.**, 2:37.) See Heb. 11:37.

45

The chapter is obviously misplaced as far as chronological order is concerned, and ought to follow chaps. 35 and 36. It gives us a glimpse of singular interest into the character of Jeremiah's helper. Baruch was discouraged and desponding, and yet the very despondency was that of an ambitious temperament eager to take the lead. His master was in prison. Neither king nor nobles listened to him. The scribe must accept the doom that fell on him as on others. He must not hope to pass unscathed, still less to attain the "great things" which he had imagined for himself.

What his future was to be was not revealed unto him, but the closing words pointed to a life of wandering and exile. Baruch was among those who went down to Egypt (43:6), and had probably been for some years at Babylon (Bar. 1:1). According to one tradition he died in Egypt (Jerome, **Comm. in Isa.** 30); another represents him as having returned to Babylon after his master's death, and ending his life there. The apocryphal book that bears his name testifies to the reverence felt for him by a later generation. (Comp. II Kings 5:26; Matt. 20:20-23.)

46

(1) The word of the Lord ... —We come here upon something like the traces of a plan in the arrangement of Jeremiah's prophecies. Those that were concerned exclusively with the outside nations of the heathen were collected together, and attached as an appendix to those which were addressed directly to his own people. Most of those that follow were connected historically with 25:15-26, and may be regarded as the development of what is there given in outline, and belong accordingly to the reign of Jehoiakim (ca. 607 B.C.).

(2) Against Egypt, against the army of Pharaoh-necho.—The last of Egypt's great native sovereigns, he was the sixth king of the twenty-sixth dynasty of Manetho. He succeeded his father Psammetichus in 610 B.C., and reigned for sixteen years. Herodotus (2:158, 159) relates as his chief achievements that he anticipated the Suez Canal by endeavoring to connect the Nile with the Red Sea, but was stopped by an oracle, and sent a fleet of Phoenician ships to circumnavigate Africa. One hundred twenty thousand lives were said to have been sacrificed in the former enterprise. On desisting from it, he turned his attention to other plans of conquest. In the course of invasion against the Babylonian Empire, then ruled by Nabopolassar, the father of Nebuchadnezzar, he defeated and slew Josiah at Megiddo (II Chron. 35:20-24), deposed Jehoahaz, and appointed Jehoiakim (II Chron. 36:4). After the capture of Carchemish, Necho appears to have returned to Egypt. Three years later (606 B.C.) Carchemish was taken by Nebuchadnezzar with

569

the almost total defeat of Necho's army. It is of this defeat which Jeremiah now proceeds to speak as in a song of anticipated triumph at the downfall of the Egyptian oppressor.

(26) Afterward it shall be inhabited, as in the days... —As in the earlier utterance of Isaiah (19:21-25) and the contemporary prophecies of Ezekiel (29:11-16), there is a gleam of hope at the end of the vision of judgment. Egypt was to revive, though not again to take its place among the conquerors and tyrants of the world. (Comp. 48:47 and 49:39.)

(27, 28) Fear not thou, O my servant Jacob... —See 30:10, 11. These words were inserted here either by the prophet himself or by some later editor of his writings as an appropriate conclusion, contrasting the care of Jehovah for His people with the sentence upon the power in which they were trusting for protection.

47

(1) Against the Philistines. —Here also we have, as in the preceding chapter, a message connected with 25:20. This attack may have been on Necho's return from his victory at Carchemish, but verse 2 seems better to indicate that Nebuchadnezzar is meant. Comp. Ezek. 25:15 as a contemporary and parallel prediction.

48

(1) Against Moab... —In this long prophecy Jeremiah in part follows in the wake of "the burden of Moab" in Isa. 15, 16, entering even more fully into geographical details. The relations between Moab and Israel had for a long period been more or less uneasy (see II Kings 3, 13). The self-glorifying boasts of Moab seem to have been almost proverbial (verse 29; Isa. 16:6).

49

(1) Concerning the Ammonites. —The history of this people was, to a great extent, parallel with that of the Moabites. Their king Baalis appears as prompting the conspiracy of Ishmael, the son of Nethaniah (40:14). The prophecy here was probably delivered before that time, in or about the fourth year of Jehoiakim (25:21). Its open-

ing words recall long-standing territorial controversy.

(7) Concerning Edom. —The Edomites allied themselves with the Chaldaeans and were conspicuous for their triumphant exultation in the destruction of Jerusalem (Ps. 137:7; Lam. 4:21; Ezek. 35:15; 36:5). Obadiah had prophesied against them before Jeremiah's utterance, and what we find here stands in the same relation to his language as the prophecy against Moab in chap. 48 does to Isa. 15 and 16.

(23) Concerning Damascus. —Damascus is named as the capital of Aram (Syria). In the history of I and II Kings we find it engaged in constant wars against Israel and Judah or in alliance with Israel against Judah. The Syrians continued subject to Assyria until the downfall of that empire, when they naturally fell before the power of Nebuchadnezzar. The language of the prophet is vague, but probably points to his attack.

(28) Concerning Kedar... —The name belonged to a tribe of the Bedouin type, descended from Ishmael (Gen. 25:13). In Ps. 120:5 it appears as the representative of the fierce nomadic life of the Arabians.

(34) Against Elam. —This is the only prophecy in chaps. 48 and 49 with a date attached to it. It indicates a time later than that of those that precede it, which belong probably to the group of predictions connected with chap. 25. The tone of the prophecy seems to imply that Elam had been prominent among the enemies of the people of Jehovah (Isa. 22:6), and this has led to the inference that they had taken part in the attack on Judah as auxiliaries in the army of Nebuchadnezzar. The thought that Elam is to be the instrument of Jehovah for the destruction of Babylon (Isa. 21:2), and that out of it was to come the appointed deliverer of Israel, does not seem to have been present to the prophet's mind. His horizon is, as it were, bounded for the time by the more immediate future.

50

A continuous prophecy occupies the place of a great finale in the collection of Jeremiah's writings (chaps. 50 and 51). We may well believe that when the great catastrophe had come upon Jerusalem, and the people were in exile by the waters of Babylon, he desired to comfort them with the thought that the righteous law of retribution under which they were suffering would in due time bring down the pride of their oppressor. (See Isa. 13, 14, 46, 47.) When he had told them that their captivity would last for seventy years (29:10), that lands should once again be bought and sold, and plowed and planted in Judah (32:15), there was an implied foreknowledge of the doom of the golden city. The authenticity of the chapter has been questioned by some critics. Many are hostile to the concept of prediction, while others pose stylistic differences; but such judgments are always more or less precarious.

(3) Out of the north there cometh up a nation.—The very phrase which had described the danger that threatened Judah from Babylon (1:14) is now used for the danger that threatened Babylon itself from Media. It is as though the prophet watched that northern quarter of the heavens, and saw storm after storm, torrent after torrent, bursting out upon the south.

(4) The children of Israel shall come ... —The union of the divided sections of the people is significant as being that for which the prophet all along had hoped (3:14-16). And the united people are to return with tears of mingled joy and penitence (comp. Ezra 3:13; 8:21-23).

(9) An assembly of great nations from the north country.—Like all the great monarchies of the East, the Medo-Persian kingdom, which was to be the destroyer of Babylon, was made up of a congeries of many different races. Herodotus (7:61-69), in his account of the army of Xerxes, names twenty-two, from the Medes and Persians at the head of the list to the Arabians and Ethiopians at its close.

(17) Israel is a scattered sheep ... —The words paint vividly the two blows that had fallen on Israel, as a sheep driven from the fold: first from the Assyrian conquest of the northern kingdom by Shalmaneser, and then, when, as it were, the carcass was half devoured and only the bones left, from that of Judah by Nebuchadnezzar. The "lion" appears here, as in Dan. 7:4, as the symbol of the great Eastern monarchies. The sculptured winged lion appears constantly in the remains both of Assyria and Babylon.

(18) As I have punished the king of Assyria.—Nineveh had fallen before Cyaxares and Nabopolassar, and Babylon was in like manner to fall before Cyrus. The one judgment was the pledge and earnest of the other.

(19) I will bring Israel again to his habitation.—The "scattered sheep" was to be brought back and to find pasture. The regions named are the representatives of the most fertile districts of Palestine, Carmel and Mount Ephraim on the west, Bashan and Gilead on the east, of Jordan.

(20) The prophetic language points to the far-off times of the Christ. Their restoration to their earthly homes was but a small thing. That which was to the prophet the great blessing of the future was that it would bring with it the New Covenant of 31:31; "the remnant," the reserved ones, would be pardoned.

(24) I have laid a snare for thee.—The two captures of Babylon, "the hammer of the whole earth" (verse 23), by Cyrus and Darius both answered to this description. (See 51:20.) Cyrus turned aside the waters of the Euphrates into another channel and entered by the river bed, so that the city was taken before those who lived in the middle of the city knew that it was attacked (Herod. 1:191). In the latter case the gates were opened to Darius by the treachery of the Babylonian general Zophyrus (Herod. 3:158). (Comp. Dan. 5:30; Isa. 45:1) In 52:31, 32 we have the same fact more vividly described.

(40-46) Comp. 6:22-24 and 49:19-21. The reproduction in identical terms is probably connected with the thoughts of the retribution, on which the prophet dwells in verse 15. All that she had done Babylon was now to suffer.

51

(6, 7) Comp. the mystical Babylon, Rev. 14:8; 17:4, 5; 18:4.

(10) The Lord hath brought forth our righteousness ... —Comp. Isa. 62:1. The exile in Babylon had been a time of reformation and growth in righteousness. The day of vengeance on the oppressing city was also a day of acquittal for Israel. It was seemly that she had not forfeited the favor of Jehovah.

(41) How is Sheshach taken!—See note on 25:26.

(44) And I will punish Bel in Babylon.— See 50:2. The god whom Babylon worshiped is thought of as sharing her downfall. He is made to disgorge his spoil, the vessels of the Temple of Jehovah that had been placed in his temple (Dan. 5:2 and Ezra 1:7).

(53, 58) See note on Dan. 4:30.

(59) Seraiah the son of Neriah.—The great prophecy has reached its close, and the remainder of the chapter is of the nature of an historical appendix. Seraiah was the brother of Jeremiah's friend and secretary, Baruch (32:13). It was natural that the prophet should select him as the depository of the great prediction. He would seem to have been attendant on Zedekiah, probably appointed by Nebuchadnezzar to regulate the details of the journey to Babylon. The prediction would seem to have been of the nature of a parting gift to him. It lies in the nature of the case that a duplicate copy was kept by Baruch or Jeremiah, of which the present text of chaps. 50 and 51 is a transcript.

In the fourth year of his reign.—The date is significant as giving a missing link in the history.

(63) Thou shalt bind a stone to it.—The meaning of the symbolic act is explained in the following verse. The parchment roll by itself might have floated, and been picked up and read by the Babylonians, and so the stone was tied to it that it might sink at once, thus prefiguring the destruction of the city. (Comp. Rev. 18:21, the destruction of the mystical Babylon.)

(64) Thus far are the words of Jeremiah.— The words are clearly of the nature of an editorial note by the compiler of Jeremiah's prophecies, Baruch or another. He is careful to inform his readers that the narrative that follows in chap. 52 was not written by Jeremiah.

52

This historical appendix is, to a great extent, identical with II Kings 24:18-25:30. For the most part, accordingly, the reader is referred to the notes on those chapters.

Whether the compiler of II Kings copied from the editor of Jeremiah, or conversely; whether the prophet was his own editor, or whether that office was undertaken by a contemporary, Baruch or another, or at a much later date; whether it was written at Babylon or Jerusalem, are questions which must remain unsettled. The last fact mentioned in each case, the release of Jehoiachin by Evil-Merodach, indicates a date ca. 562 B.C. It may be noted that the copyist, in any case, exercised an independent judgment, for while II Kings 25 presents the form Nebuchadnezzar, Jer. 52 had Nebuchadrezzar, the latter being the more accurate form.

The variations between the two chapters are important, though insignificant in themselves, implying that a consistent belief in the substantial truthfulness of the historical records of the Old Testament is independent of mere verbal accordance in matters of minute detail.

(11) And put him in prison till the day of his death.—This also is an additional detail not mentioned in II Kings 25, and its absence is probably due to the fact that that was the earlier narrative of the two. The LXX renders "prison" by "house of the mill," as though Zedekiah, after he had been blinded, had been made to do slave-work like that of Samson. Possibly this was merely an inference from Lam. 5:13. Such treatment of captive kings was, however, quite in keeping with the character of Assyrian and Chaldaean rulers.

(28) This is the people ... —Here the parallelism with II Kings 25, which goes on to give a brief summary of the history of Gedaliah and Ishmael, as narrated in chaps. 40-43, ceases, and the writer of the appendix goes on to give particulars as to the various stages of the deportation of the captives.

LAMENTATIONS

1

This book as it stands in the Hebrew text, is absolutely anonymous. But the LXX prefixed a short note by way of introduction: "And it came to pass after Israel had been led into captivity and Jerusalem had been laid waste, Jeremiah sat weeping, and he lamented with this lamentation over Jerusalem, and said—How doth the city," etc.

(1) How doth the city . . . —The poem of twenty-two verses divides itself into two symmetrical halves: (1) verses 1-11, in which the prophet laments over Jerusalem; and (2) verses 12-22, more dramatic in its form, in which the daughter of Zion bewails her own miseries.

Provinces.—The word here indicates the neighboring countries that had once, as in the reign of Hezekiah, been subject to Judah. "Tributary," as used here, implies (Josh. 16:10) personal servitude, rather than the money payment, for which, at a later period, it was commuted (see Esther 10:1).

(2) She weepeth sore in the night.—The intensity of the sorrow is emphasized by the fact that the tears do not cease even in the time which commonly brings rest and repose to mourners. The "lovers" and the "friends" are the nations, Egypt, Edomites, Moabites, and others, with which Judah had been in alliance, and which now turned against her. (Comp. 4:21; Ps. 137:7; Jer. 2:36; 40:14; Ezek. 25:3-6.)

(3) Because of affliction.—The Hebrew admits of the rendering "from affliction," speaking of the forcible deportation of the people from misery at home to a yet worse misery in Babylon as the land of their exile (Deut. 28:65).

(4) The ways of Zion do mourn.—The words paint what we may call the religious desolation of Jerusalem. The roads leading to it, the "gates" by which it was entered, were no longer thronged with pilgrims and worshipers.

(6) Her princes are become like harts . . . —Probably a reference to the flight and capture of Zedekiah (II Kings 25:5; Jer. 39:5), who, with his sons and princes, fell into the hands of the Chaldaeans, like fainting and stricken deer.

(8) Therefore she is removed.—The verb is used technically for the separation of a woman under ceremonial defilement; and

the daughter of Zion in her sin and shame is compared (verse 17) to such a woman. The figure is continued with a startling boldness.

(9) O Lord, behold my affliction.—The words are not those of the prophet, but of Zion, anticipating the dramatic personation which begins systematically at verse 12.

(10) Whom thou didst command.—Stress is laid on the profanation rather than the plunder of the sanctuary. Ammonites and Moabites were excluded from the congregation (Deut. 23:3), and yet they and other heathen nations now rushed even into the Holy of Holies, which none but the High Priest might enter.

(11) All her people sigh . . . —The words which describe the famine at Jerusalem are in the present tense, either as painting the sufferings of the past with the vividness of the historic present, or because the sufferings still continued even after the capture of the city. The remnant that was left had to bring out their treasures, jewels, and the like, and offer them for bread.

(12) Is it nothing to you . . . —What the mourning city felt most keenly was that her unparalleled sufferings were met with an unparalleled indifference.

(14) The Lord.—It is noticeable that here, and in thirteen other passages in this book, the word **Adonai** is used instead of the more usual Jehovah, as though the latter, the covenant name of the God of Israel, was less appropriate on the lips of one who was under His condemnation.

(15) The winepress is the symbol of judgment and slaughter; see Isa. 63:2; Rev. 14:19; 19:15.

(16, 17) The unparalleled misery finds vent in a flood of bitterest tears and in a posture of lamentation and despair.

(18) The Lord is righteous . . . —Misery does its work, and issues in repentance. The suffering comes from the all-righteous Judge. (Comp. II Chron. 12:6; Jer. 12:1.) It is significant that with this beginning of conversion the name "Jehovah" reappears.

(19) I called for.—The "lovers," as in verse 2, are the former allies of Judah.

My priests and mine elders.—The pressure of the famine of the besieged city is emphasized by the fact that even these, the honored guides of the people, had died of hunger.

(20) Behold, O Lord . . . —Deserted by men, the mourner appeals to Jehovah. "Bowels" and "heart" are used almost as synonymous for the deepest emotions of the soul.

(22) Let all their wickedness . . . —The prayer for a righteous retribution, the first natural prayer of the outraged, reminds us of Pss. 69; 109; 137; yet more strongly of the language of the prophet in Jer. 18:21-23. It is something more than a prayer for revenge, and rests on the underlying thought that righteousness requires the punishment.

2

(1) How hath the Lord . . . —The second dirge follows the pattern of the first, opening with a description of the sufferings of Jerusalem (verses 1-10), and closing with a dramatic soliloquy spoken as by the daughter of Zion (verses 11-22).

The image that floats before the poet's mind is that of a dark thundercloud breaking into a tempest, which overthrows the "beauty of Israel," the Temple (Isa. 64:11), or, as in II Sam. 1:19, the heroes who defended it. The footstool is the Ark of the covenant (I Chron. 28:2; Ps. 99:5). The "Lord" is, as before, **Adonai**, not Jehovah.

(3) All the horn of Israel . . . —The horn (I Sam. 2:1; Pss. 92:10; 112:9) is the symbol of strength, aggressive or defensive, and may therefore stand here for every element of strength—warriors, rulers, fortresses.

(4) He stood with his right hand . . . —The point of the phrase is that the "right hand," the natural symbol of divine power, which had been of old stretched forth to protect, was now seen shooting the arrows and wielding the sword of vengeance.

The tabernacle . . . —Not here the Temple, but the city itself as the habitation of the people, who are collectively represented as "the daughter of Zion."

(7) His sanctuary.—The word points to the Holy of Holies, and "the walls of her palaces" are therefore those of the Temple rather than of the city.

They have made a noise.—The shouts of the enemies in their triumph, perhaps even the shouts of their worship, had taken the place of the hallelujahs of the "solemn feast."

(8) He hath stretched out a line.—The phrase implies the systematic thoroughness of the work of destruction. (See II Kings 21:13; Isa. 34:11; Amos 7:7.)

(9) Her gates . . . —The picture of ruin is completed. Outward desolation was but the

shadow of that of the nation's spiritual life. The despondency of the people is indicated by the outward signs of woe (verse 10).

(11) My liver is poured upon the earth . . . —The "liver," like the "heart" and the "bowels," is thought of as the center of all intense emotions (Prov. 7:23). As such it is represented as giving way without restraint (comp. verse 19) under the pressure of the horror caused by the calamities which the next words paint. The present sufferings of Zion had no parallel in history (verse 13).

(14) Thy prophets have seen vain and foolish things.—The words are eminently characteristic of Jeremiah, whose whole life had been spent in conflict with the false prophets (Jer. 2:8; 5:13; 6:13; 8:10; 14:14; 28:9).

(17) The Lord hath done . . . —The writer points, in opposition to the boasts of the enemies, to the true author of the misery of the people. In that thought, terrible as it might at first seem, there was an element of hope. It was better to fall into the hands of God than into those of men (II Sam. 24:14). The suffering came as a chastisement for past transgressions, and might therefore be mitigated by repentance. The Destroyer was also the Healer, and would answer the prayers of those who called on Him.

(18) The apple of thine eye—i.e., the "pupil" of the eye.

(20) To whom thou hast done this—i.e., not to a heathen nation, but to the people whom Jehovah Himself had chosen. There follow accounts of cannibalism and murder, both within and without the sanctuary. (Comp. Deut. 28:57; II Kings 6:28; Jer. 19:9; Ezek. 4:16, 17; 5:16.)

3

(1) I am the man.—The elegy is one of more intense personality. For that very reason it has been the true inheritance of all mourners, however widely different in time, country, circumstance, whose sorrows have approximated to that intensity.

(2) Into darkness.—The moral darkness of perplexity as well as misery. The cry of the mourner was like that of Ajax (Hom. **Il.** 17. 647), "Slay me if thou wilt, but slay me in the light."

(4) Hath he made old.—Better, "He hath wasted," the verb describing the wear and tear of life rather than the effects of age. "Flesh," "skin," "bones," are grouped together as representing the whole being of the mourner.

(5) He hath builded.—The attack of sorrow is presented under the figure of a siege. "Gall" stands (Jer. 8:14) for bitterest sorrow; "travel" means "travail."

(7) He hath hedged.—From the darkness of Hades we pass to that of the prison-house, in which the mourner is bound with a heavy chain.

(9) He hath inclosed.—Yet another figure of resourceless misery follows. A massive wall of stone runs across the mourner's way. When he turns aside into bypaths, they are turned and twisted in labyrinthine confusion, and lead nowhere.

(10) As a bear . . . as a lion.—The figure found in Hos. 13:8; Amos 5:19, is especially characteristic of Jeremiah (Jer. 4:7; 5:6; 49:19; 50:44). Comp. Dante (**Inferno,** 1:31-51).

(11) He hath made me desolate.—Better, "astonished." The verb (which occurs forty times in Jeremiah's prophecies and three times in Lam.) paints the stupefaction of terror.

(12) He hath bent his bow.—(Comp. Job 16:12.) The figure is changed, but there is a natural sequence of thought. The lion suggests the huntsman, but he appears on the scene not to save the victim, but to complete the work of destruction.

(14) I was a derision.—The personal experience of the prophet breaks through the succession of imagery. The arrows that pierced to the quick were the taunts of the mockers who derided him. (Comp. Job 30:9; Jer. 20:7.) Such are continued in the metaphor of food and drink.

(18) I said, My strength.—The sorrow of the mourner comes to the verge of despair. But, as the sequel shows, this despair was the beginning of a reaction. The name of Jehovah (no longer Adonai) reminded him of the everlasting mercies.

(21) This I recall to my mind.—The first gleam of hope breaks through the darkness. The sorrow has not been in vain; it has brought humility, and out of humility springs hope.

(22) It is of the Lord's mercies.—It is part of the elaborate art of this poem that verses 22-42, which form its center, and that of the whole book, represent the highest point of trust to which the mourner attains, being both preceded and followed by words of lamentation.

(25) The Lord is good.—The adjective is predicated, first of the essential character of

Jehovah, and then of the conditions in man on which the manifestation of that character depends.

(27) Bear the yoke in his youth.—The tone of the maxim is that of one who looks back from the experience of age on the passionate complaints of his earlier years (Jer. 15:10; 20:7-18).

(29) He putteth his mouth in the dust . . . —The image is that of the prostration of an Eastern subject before a king, his face laid in the dust, so that he cannot speak.

(30) He giveth his cheek . . . —The submission enjoined reaches its highest point— a patience like that of Job 16:10 and Matt. 5:39. It was harder to accept the divine chastisement when it came through human agents. Not so had Jeremiah once taught and acted (Jer. 20:1-6; 28:15). (Comp. Isa. 50:6.)

(31-33) The counsels of submission are followed by the grounds of hope. The first is a quotation from Ps. 77:7 (comp. Jer. 3:5, 12); the second rests on the fact that compassion underlies chastisement (Ps. 30:5; Job 5:18; Isa. 54:8); the third depends on the truth that the primary eternal will of God is on the side of love, and that punishment is, as it were, against that will.

(34-36) The fact that the righteous judgment of God is against those who, unlike Him, cause willful and needless suffering is another ground of hope to the sufferer. The three forms of evil specified are (1) the cruel treatment of prisoners of war (such as Jeremiah had witnessed daily at the hands of the Chaldeans); (2) the perversion of justice in a public tribunal acting in the name of God (Exod. 23:6); and (3) every form even of private injustice.

(37-39) New grounds of patient faith are given: the evil which He permits is under the control of this loving purpose. See Ps. 33:9, affirming the sovereignty of God.

(40) Let us search . . . —Warnings against murmurs are followed by counsels which point to a more excellent way. Suffering calls a man to self-scrutiny. We should seek to know the sins which it is meant to punish and correct.

(42) We have transgressed . . . —Both pronouns are emphatic. The suppliant has sinned and God has not yet pardoned, in the sense of ceasing to punish. The verses that follow give the prayer which answers to the call of verse 41.

(52) Without cause . . . —It has been suggested by some that Jeremiah speaks not of the Chaldeans as enemies of his nation, but of those who were individually his persecutors (see Jer. 26:8-17; 37:14; 38:7). But, on the other hand, those expressions may be figurative here, as in Pss. 42:7; 88:7; 124:4.

(56) Thou hast heard ... hide not thine ...—There is something eminently suggestive in the sequence of the two clauses. The recollection that prayer was answered in the past prompts its utterance in the present. (See Jer. 38:7.)

(64) Render unto them ... —Comp. Ps. 28:4; II Tim. 4:14.

(65, 66) The imperatives of recompense are better rendered as futures.

4

(1) How is the gold ... —The chapter, considered as a distinct poem, traces more fully the connection between the sufferings and the sins of Judah. The "gold" and the "stones of holiness" are none other than the material treasures of palace or temple.

(2) The precious sons of Zion ... The adjective is applied not to a special class, but to all the "sons of Zion" in their ideal character as a "kingdom of priests" (Exod. 19:6). They had been equal to their weight in fine gold, the work of God.

(3, 4) The comparison was obviously suggested by facts like those referred to in 2:20.

(6) The punishment of the iniquity.—The words point to guilt rather than its penalty, though the greatness of the former is inferred from that of the latter. The point of comparison was that Sodom was not doomed to a protracted misery, like that which had been the lot of Jerusalem.

No hands stayed on her ... —i.e., her destruction was the direct work of God, and not of human agents, with their more merciless tortures.

(7) Her Nazarites ... —Amos 2:11, 12 shows that they were prominent as a body during the history of the monarchy, and the drift of Jeremiah's mind, as seen in his admiration of the Rechabites (chap. 35), shows that he was likely to think of them with reverence. The temperance, purity, cleanliness of such a body seem to have made them conspicuous among their fellows for an almost angelic beauty. They had the red and white complexion which was in the East the ideal of comeliness (I Sam. 17:42; Song of Sol. 5:10).

(8) Their visage is blacker ... —We look, as it were, on the two pictures: the bloom and beauty of health, and the wan, worn, spectral looks of starvation.

(10) The hands of the pitiful women.—See note on 2:20.

(11) And hath kindled a fire ... —The phrase is partly literal (II Chron. 36:19), partly figurative, for the complete destruction of Jerusalem by the wrath of Jehovah.

(12) Would not have believed.—The city had been strongly fortified by Uzziah, Hezekiah, and Manasseh, and the failure of Sennacherib's attempt had probably led to the impression that it was impregnable.

(13) That have shed the blood of the just ... —The words point to incidents like those recorded in II Kings 21:16; II Chron. 24:21; Jer. 26:7; and possibly to some unrecorded atrocities during the siege on the part of the priests and false prophets, who looked on the true prophets as traitors (Jer. 26:23). The murderers were abhorred among their countrymen and the heathen alike (verses 14, 15).

(17) In our watching.—Better, "upon our watch tower." (Comp. Hab. 2:1.) The people of Judah are represented as looking out for the approach of an ally, probably Egypt (Jer. 37:7), and looking in vain.

(20) The breath of our nostrils.—The "breath of life" of Gen. 2:7. The phrase emphasizes the ideal character of the king as the center of the nation's life. So Seneca (**Clement** 1:4) speaks of a ruler as the **spiritus vitalis** of his people.

Of whom we said.—The words that follow point to the scheme which was rendered abortive by Zedekiah's capture (Jer. 39:5). Those who followed him had hoped to find a refuge among some friendly neighboring nation, where they might at least have maintained the continuity of their national existence, and waited for better days.

(21) O daughter of Edom.—The triumph of Edom in the downfall of Zion was the crowning sorrow of the mourner (see Ps. 137). But with this sorrow there is a vision of judgment, which is also a vision of hope.

(22) Is accomplished.—The mourner shares in the Messianic hopes of Isa. 40:2, and expresses it nearly in the same words.

He will no more carry thee away.—Interpreted by later history, the words, like all promises, were dependent upon implied conditions. For five centuries, however, the prophet's words held good, and there was no thorough dispersion of the Jews until that Roman conquest subsequent to their rejection of the Christ.

5

(1) Remember, O Lord.—The fact that the number of verses is, as in chaps. 1, 2 and 4, the same as that of the Hebrew alphabet suggests that this chapter also, though not actually alphabetic, was intended to have been so, and that we have the last of the five elegies in a half-finished state. It would seem as if Jeremiah first wrote freely what was in his mind, and then set to work as an artist to bring it under the alphabetic scheme. This chapter has more the character of a prayer than any other, and the prayer begins with recapitulating the woes of those left in Judah as a ground for the compassion of Jehovah.

(6) We have given the hand.—The recognized phrase for submission (Jer. 50:15). "Assyria," as in Jer. 2:18; Ezra 6:22, stands for "Babylon." The people had been forced by sheer pressure of hunger to submit to one or other of these princes. "Egypt" refers, probably, to the fugitives who had sought a home in that country (Jer. 42:14).

(7) We have borne their iniquities.—The words seem at first parallel to the proverb of the "sour grapes" (Jer. 31:29; Ezek. 18:2). Here, however, it is followed (verse 16) by a confession of personal guilt, and the complaint is simply that the former generation of offenders had passed away without the punishment which now fell upon their descendants, who thus had to bear, as it were, a double penalty.

(8) Servants have ruled over us.—The Chaldaeans added insult to injury, sending as rulers those who had filled menial offices in the courts of their kings. (Comp. Jer. 39:3.)

(9) The sword of the wilderness.—Those who were left in the land were attacked, as they gathered in their scanty harvest, by the nomad tribes of the wilderness. (Comp. Jer. 40:14.)

(13) They took . . . —Better, "Young men bear the mill": i.e., were set not only to grind the handmill, which was itself the work of a menial slave, commonly of women, but were made to carry the mill itself, probably as they marched along with the Chaldaean armies on their way to Babylon. (Comp. Isa. 47:2.)

(14) Have ceased from the gate.—The gate in an Eastern city was the natural place of meeting for the elder citizens as for counsel and judgment (Josh. 20:4; Ruth 4:1), and also for social exchange (Job 29:7; Prov. 31:23). There was a like interruption of the social joys of the young.

(16) The crown is fallen.—The phrase is naturally symbolic of degradation, and need not be restricted to the destruction of the Temple or the devastation of Jerusalem.

(17) For this . . . for these things.—The first clause refers to the loss of national honor indicated in verse 16; the latter, to all the horrors named in verses 8-15.

(19) Thou, O Lord, remainest.—The lamentation is drawing to its close, and the mourner finds comfort in the thought of the eternity of God (Ps. 102:12), and therefore the unchangeableness of His purpose of love toward His people.

(20) Wherefore dost thou forget . . . — This was the problem of the mystery of suffering then, as it has been at all times. Jehovah had seemed forgetful of His people, indifferent to their miseries.

(21) Turn thou us . . . O Lord . . . —The answer to the problem was found in man's submission and in prayer. He could not turn himself, and so re-establish the old filial relation. He could ask God to turn him, and he felt that the prayer would not be asked in vain.

In synagogue use, and in many manuscripts, verse 21 is repeated after verse 22, so that the book may not end with words of so terrible a significance. The same practice was used in the case of the last verse of Isaiah, Ecclesiastes, and Malachi.

EZEKIEL

1

(1) The thirtieth year.—This was probably the age of Ezekiel himself, particularly impressive to him because it was the age at which the Levites by the law (Num. 4:23, 30, 39, 43) entered upon their duties. It coincided with the fifth year of Jehoiachin's captivity (verse 2).

Among the captives—i.e., in the midst of the region where they were settled. The vision which follows was seen by Ezekiel only, and was probably vouchsafed to him in solitude. "The captives" is the same word as is used of Jehoiachin, and yet must be somewhat differently understood in the two cases. Jehoiachin was actually in prison for many years; his people, within certain limits, were free. They were more than **exiles**, but less than prisoners.

(3) The hand of the Lord was there upon him.—This is a form of expression to indicate that special power and influence which the Spirit exercised over the prophets at times when they were called to become the means of the divine communications. (Comp. I Kings 18:46, and Ezek. 3:22; 37:1.) It is noticeable that Ezekiel here speaks of himself in the third person, while in verse 1, and always after this, he uses the first person. It has been suggested that this, together with the mention of his own name (only here and in 24:24), may indicate the insertion of these two verses on a revision of his work by the prophet.

(4) A whirlwind came out of the north.—It was common with the prophets to represent the divine judgments upon Judaea as coming from the north (see Jer. 1:14, 15; 4:6; 6:1), and it was from that direction that the Assyrian and the Chaldaean conquerors were accustomed to descend upon the Holy Land. The vision is actually seen in Chaldaea, but it has reference to Jerusalem, and is described as if viewed from that standpoint.

A great cloud.—See Exod. 19:9-16. The cloud serves at once as the groundwork for all the other details of the manifestation. The transposition of a single letter from the end of one word in the Hebrew to the beginning of the next will change the reading to "a whirlwind out of the north brought up a great cloud."

A fire infolding itself—literally, **catching itself.** The idea is that of flames around the cloud, the flashes succeeding one another so

rapidly that each seemed to lay hold on the one that had gone before; there were tongues of flame, where each one reached to another. The vision thus far seems molded on the natural appearance of a terrific thunderstorm seen at a distance, in which the great black cloud appears illuminated by the unceasing and coalescing flashes of lightning.

(5) The likeness of four living creatues.—The prophet makes it plain that this was a vision, that these were symbolic, not actually existing creatures. Their prominent characteristic is that they were "living." This word is used over and over again in connection with them; and in Ezekiel and Revelation (4:6, etc., where it is mistranslated **beasts**) it occurs nearly thirty times. Their life is represented as most closely connected with the source of all life, the "living God" (verse 26).

Ezekiel does not here say what these living creatures were, but in a subsequent vision, when he saw them again in connection with the Temple, he recognized them as the cherubim (10:15, 20), always indicative of the immediate presence of the God of holiness. (See 41:18-20.) The Greeks tried to delineate the divine attributes with the utmost beauty of form and harmony of detail under some human figure in which those attributes were conspicuous. In consequence, the mind of the worshiper lost sight of the ideal, and became absorbed in the sensuous imagery by which it was represented, while here, by the very strangeness, and sometimes grotesqueness, of the imagery, its purely symbolic character was kept constantly in view.

They had the likeness of a man.—With all the strange variety of details to be described immediately, they had yet a general human form, and are to be understood as like man in whatever is not specified. There is much emphatic repetition throughout the description. (Both cherubim and seraphim, being merely symbolical figures, are variously represented. See 10:21; 41:18, 19; I Kings 6:27; Isa. 6:2; Rev. 4:7, 8.)

(9) Their wings were joined one to another—i.e., the outstretched right wing of one cherub was joined at its tip to the left wing of another, so that although four, they yet constituted in some sense but one creature, all moving in harmony and by a common impulse. This applies to the cherubim only when in motion; when they stood, the wings were let down (verse 24).

They turned not when they went.—They

could still go in the direction toward which they looked, since they looked in all directions, and the round soles of their feet made it equally easy to move in any way.

(12) Whither the spirit was to go.—One informing spirit animated all the living creatures alike, in accordance with which all their movements were ordered.

(15) Behold one wheel upon the earth by the living creatures.—The vision up to this point seems designed to show forth the power and activity, the irresistible energy and brilliance, of the agencies employed for the fulfillment of the divine purposes, and at the same time their perfectly harmonious action, controlled by one supreme will.

We now enter upon a fresh phase of the vision, in which the same things are represented still further by an additional and peculiar symbolism. The wheel was **one** in the same sense in which the living creatures were one, yet actually four, as appears from the following verse and the whole subsequent description (but comp. 10:9). The cherubim had been seen in the cloud (verses 4, 5); now they need to be connected below with the earth, and presently (verse 26) above, with the throne of God. Therefore the wheel is "upon the earth," but of a great height (verse 18). There was a wheel in front of each of the cherubim, again forming a square, yet so that they might in a sense be all considered as one wheel. (Comp. I Kings 7:32, 33.)

(16) Their work was like unto the colour of a beryl.—"Work" is used in the sense of workmanship or construction; and "beryl" here is rather topaz, having the luster of gold, and in harmony with the frequent mention throughout the vision of fire and brilliant light.

A wheel in the middle of a wheel.—We are to conceive of the wheels as double, and one part at right angles to the other, like the equator and a meridian circle upon the globe, so that they could go, without being turned, equally well in any direction.

(17) Upon their four sides—i.e., forward or backward upon the one wheel, and to the right or the left upon the other. **Four** directions are considered throughout the vision as representing all directions, just as elsewhere the four winds represent all winds, and the four corners of the earth the whole earth.

(18) Full of eyes.—Comp. 10:12, 20-22; Rev. 4:8. The symbolism sets forth God's perfect knowledge of all His works: here as showing the absolute wisdom of all His

doings (comp. II Chron. 16:9), there as resulting in perfect and harmonious praise from all His works. The Hebrew seers always looked through all secondary causes directly to the ultimate force which originates and controls all nature, and which they represent as intelligent and self-conscious. To do this the more effectively, they often use in their visions such concrete imagery as this before us.

(19-21) The object of these verses is by every repetition and variety of expression to represent "the living creatures" and "the wheels" as one, animated by one spirit, and moved by one impulse. All formed together one strange, symbolic whole. The mention of the wheels being "lifted up from the earth" simultaneously with the living creatures was to show that God's purposes are carried out as He wills in this world. This brings out, in addition, the perfect harmony of these purposes, whether relating to earth or to heaven.

(25) A voice from the firmament.—This is a new feature in the vision: the voice is quite different from the sounds mentioned before, and although not here expressly said to have been articulate, yet it is probably to be identified with the divine voice spoken of in verse 28; 3:12; etc. When the voice was heard the cherubim stood still, the mighty sounds of their going were hushed, and their wings fell motionless, all in the attitude of reverential attention to the majesty above.

(26) The vision now advances to another and final stage; we come to the throne itself, and to Him that sat upon it. The constant repetition of the words "likeness" and "appearance" is very striking throughout this vision. The prophet thus labors to make it plain that what he saw was not the realities of existing things, but certain symbolic representations given for the purpose of producing their fitting impression upon the mind. It was not the divine Being Himself whom Ezekiel saw, but certain appearances to impress upon him the character and attributes of Him whom "no man hath seen, nor can see."

The appearance of a man.—As in the case of the cherubim the form of a man, as the highest known in nature, was made the groundwork to which all their peculiarities were attached, so here, in rising to something still higher, the same basis must be retained in the impossibility of anything better. But that which is added is more vague, as being incapable of any definite

579

description. Possibly there may be even here a hint at the great truth of the incarnation. (Comp. Dan. 7:13; Rev. 1:13.)

(27) The verse is simply an attempt, by various repetitions, to convey an idea of the exceeding brightness and glory of the vision, yet also with the notions of purity and holiness, of power and activity always associated with fire. (Comp. Exod. 24:17; Dan. 7:9; Rev. 1:14, 15; 4:5.)

(28) As the appearance of the bow that is in the cloud.—The addition, "in the day of rain," is not merely a reference to the ordinary natural phenomenon, but distinctly connects this vision with the gracious promise in Genesis, and shows that God, who has in this vision presented His attributes of terrible majesty, will add to them also those of mercy and loving-kindness. It was in both alike that He was to be made known to His people through the prophet who is now receiving his commission.

I fell upon my face.—The immediate manifestation of the divine has always proved overpowering to man. (Comp. 3:23; Isa. 6:5; Dan. 8:17; Acts 9:4; Rev. 1:17. Comp. also Luke 5:8; 8:37.)

In considering the general significance of this vision, it is to be remembered that it was seen four times by Ezekiel in various connections in his life-work. First, at this time, when he is called to the exercise of the prophetic office; a second time when, shortly afterward, he is sent to denounce judgments upon the sinful people, and to foretell the destruction of Jerusalem and the Temple (3:23, etc.); again, a year and a half later (8:4; 10:15), while he is made to understand the evils and abominations wrought in the Temple (which is still standing), until the "glory of the Lord" forsakes His house and departs from the city (11:23), in token that God had given them over to punishment; finally, in the prophecy of future restoration and blessing, when he again sees the presence of the Lord re-enter and fill the house (43:3-5). Its meaning, therefore, clearly relates to the whole prophecies of Ezekiel, whether of judgment or mercy; it represents the resistless divine activity, controlling alike the agencies of judgment and of mercy, directed to every corner of the earth, and requiring of all profoundest homage and veneration. The perfect unity of purpose in all God's doings is made especially prominent, while over all seems to be written, "Holiness unto the Lord."

2

Chaps. 2 and 3 record the call of the prophet to his office and the instructions given him for his work. As far as 3:13, this seems to have been still in the presence of the vision of chap. 1; then he was directed otherwise. The full time occupied by these things is not expressly mentioned, but it was apparently just eight days from the first to the second appearance of the vision—from the beginning to the completion of his prophetic consecration. This period, corresponding to the period of the consecration of Aaron and his sons (Lev. 8:33-9:4), must have been peculiarly impressive to the priestly Ezekiel, and have added its own power of association to the other solemnities of his call. Since the time of Moses there had been no other prophet whose call had been accompanied by such manifestations of the divine glory, and perhaps no time in which the condition of the Church had made them so important.

(1) Son of man.—The voice that now came to Ezekiel was articulate. The "He" in connection with the vision before him could be none other than the Most High, whose glory that vision was given to reveal. The phrase "son of man" is common enough throughout the Scriptures, as meaning simply **man**, but is never used in an address to a prophet, except to Ezekiel and Daniel. To Daniel it is used only once (8:17), while to Ezekiel it is used more than ninety times. The address to Ezekiel here is doubtless in compassion to his weakness. The strengthening command "Stand upon thy feet" was given that he might be able to receive the communication God is about to make to him.

(2) And the spirit entered into me.—There can be no doubt that **the spirit** is here the Spirit of God, and not merely the prophet's own human vigor and courage (see 3:24). We are not to think of any physical force exerted upon the prophet, but of all these things as still taking place in vision.

(3) I send thee to the children of Israel.—Here properly begins the distinct commission of the prophet. After the captivity of the ten tribes, the two forming the kingdom of Judah, with such remnants of the others as had been induced by Hezekiah and others to cast in their lot with them, are constantly spoken of as "Israel." (See Ezra 2:2.) The continuity of the whole nation was considered as preserved in the remnant, and hence this same mode of expression passed into the New Testament. (See Acts 26:7.) It is only when there is special occasion to distinguish between the two parts of the nation, as in 4:5, 6, that the name of Israel is used in contrast with that of Judah.

The following verses enlarge, with a variety of epithets and repetitions, upon the hardheartedness and perverseness of the people. (See Hos. 1:9; John 8:39.)

(5) Whether they will hear, or whether they will forbear.—Comp. 3:11. God's Word remains the same whatever reception man may accord to it. But while the mighty power of the divine Word must thus produce its effect (Isa. 55:11; II Cor. 2:15, 16), the character of the effect depends upon those to whom it comes. So it would be among the captives by the Chebar: some would be brought back to their allegiance to their God, and would constitute the remnant through whom He would bless His people and the world; and some, resisting the offered grace, would be thus made more obdurate than ever. In either case, they could not remain as before.

(8) Eat that I give thee.—This is to be understood like all that has gone before, as done in vision, as in the case of the book eaten by John in Rev. 10:9, 10. The figure of eating for receiving into the heart, so as to be thoroughly possessed by what is communicated, is not an uncommon one. (Comp. Jer. 15:16; John 6:53-58.)

(9) A roll of a book.—Books were anciently written upon skins sewed together, or upon papyrus in long strips, which were rolled up. One hand unrolling and the other rolling up from the other end as the contents were read. These were ordinarily written on one side only, as it would have been inconvenient to read the other; but in this case it was written on both sides, "within and without," to denote the fullness of the message.

3

(3) It was in my mouth as honey for sweetness.—The first impression made upon him by his prophetic call was one of delight. But see verse 14 (and comp. Rev. 10:10) for his experience when he went with his heavy message to a people indisposed to give ear.

(5) To a people of a strange speech.—In verses 4-7 it is emphasized that Ezekiel's immediate mission is to be, like that of his great Antitype, to "the lost sheep of the house of Israel," and yet that they would not give the heed to him which men far below them in spiritual privilege would have gladly yielded. Why then should so much of the divine compassion be expended upon a nation which so generally refused to avail itself of its blessings? Only thus could even a few be raised at all above the very lowest spiritual plane, and the raising of these few leads ultimately to the elevation of many.

(7) All the house of Israel means the people generally, as the word **all** is often used in Scripture and elsewhere. There were even then among them such saints as Jeremiah and Daniel.

(8) Thy face strong against their faces.—The main thought is taken from the figure of horned animals in their contests, and God promises Ezekiel to make him in the struggle stronger than those who oppose him. The same thing is expressed by another figure in verse 9, where **adamant** is the diamond (Jer. 17:1). The people were as hard as flint, but as the diamond cuts flint, so Ezekiel's words should be made by the divine power to cut through all their resistance. Armed with this strength, he need not fear their obduracy, however great.

(11) Get thee to them of the captivity.—His immediate mission to the house of Israel is limited to that part of it which, like himself, was already in captivity. At this time, and for several years to come, this was a comparatively small part of the whole nation; but before Ezekiel's ministrations were finished, it embraced the mass of them. God directs him to go, not to **My**, but to **thy** people; He refuses to recognize them in their present state as really His own. At the same time, there is thus indirectly suggested to the prophet a reminder that he is himself one of the same people, and needs therefore to be on his guard against the sin and obduracy which characterize them.

(14) I went in bitterness, in the heat of my spirit.—The prophet now begins to realize the sorrow of the trial of the task laid upon him. The command of the Lord was sweet (verse 3), its performance bitter. Comp. Jer. 20:8, 9 and Amos 3:8.

(15) I came to them of the captivity at Tel-abib.—Tel-abib, described as still by the same "river of Chebar," signifies the "mound of ears (of grain)," and was probably a place of special fruitfulness. It appears to have been the central place of the captivity.

Remained there astonished among them

581

seven days.—**To be silent** was the characteristic of mourners (Lam. 3:28); **to sit,** their proper attitude (Isa. 3:26; Lam. 1:1); **seven days,** the set time for mourning (Job 2:13). By this act the prophet shows his deep sympathy with his people in their affliction. This week of silent meditation corresponds to the week of the consecration of his fathers to their priestly office (Lev. 8).

(16) At the end of seven days.—A fresh divine communication comes to the prophet, designed especially to impress upon him the responsibility of his office (verses 16-21). In 33:1-20 the same charge is repeated with some amplification. What is said there is expressly required to be spoken to the people (verse 1), while this seems to have been immediately for the prophet's own ear.

(20) When a righteous man doth turn from his righteousness.—The Scripture here, as often elsewhere, represents the upright man as exposed to temptation and in danger of falling into sin. The duty of the prophet, therefore, is not only to seek to turn the wicked from his evil way, but also to warn the righteous against falling into the same path. Both terms must necessarily be taken as comparative; but they show that there was even now a considerable difference in character among the captives. In Ezekiel's office of "watchman," there is even an approach to the pastoral "cure of souls" under the Christian dispensation. Such an office had almost no place under the Old Testament, and Ezekiel is the only one of the prophets who is charged to exercise this office distinctly toward individuals.

(25) They shall put bands upon thee.—There is no trace of ill treatment throughout the book, nor is it likely that it would have been permitted by Nebuchadnezzar among his captives, or possible under the administration of Daniel. "Bands" must be understood figuratively (comp. 4:8). The compulsion described in this and the following verse was a moral one. Ezekiel's countrymen, especially during the period of his warnings until the destruction of Jerusalem, should so absolutely refuse to hear him that it would become practically impossible for him to declare his prophecies; he would be as if he were bound.

(26, 27) Until the destruction of Jerusalem (24:27, 33:22) he should be greatly restrained in his ordinary utterances by the opposition of the people; yet there would be times when God would give him a message with such power that he would be constrained to declare it, whether the people would hear or whether they would forbear. Such messages are those contained in this book, which at this point begin to be recorded. By all this the difficulties and trials under which the prophet must exercise his office are clearly and strongly set before him.

4

(1) Take thee a tile.—When intended for preservation, writing or drawing was made upon soft and plastic clay, which was afterward baked. It is from the remains of great libraries prepared in this way that most of our knowledge of Nineveh and Babylon has been derived. It is likely that Ezekiel simply described, rather than actually performed, these symbolical acts.

(2) Lay siege against it.—It must have seemed at this time unlikely that Jerusalem would soon become the subject of another siege. The only power by whom such a siege could be undertaken was Babylonia, Egypt having been so thoroughly defeated as to be out of the question for a long time; and Nebuchadnezzar had now, within a few years, thrice completely conquered Judaea, had carried two of its kings, one after the other, captive in chains, and had also taken into captivity 10,000 of the chief of the people, setting up as king over the remnant a creature of his own, who was yet of the royal house of Judah. A fresh siege could only be the result of a fresh rebellion, an act, under the circumstances, of simple infatuation. (See Zedekiah, II Kings 24:20.) The prophecy itself is undated, but must have been between the call of Ezekiel in the fifth month of the fifth year (1:2) and the next date given (8:1), the sixth month of the sixth year. The siege began, according to Jer. 52:4, in the tenth month of the ninth year, so that the prophecy preceded its fulfillment by only about four years.

Build a fort against it.—A tower was built, as was customary, of sufficient height to overlook the walls and thus obtain information of the doings of the besieged. Instruments for throwing stones or darts were also sometimes placed in such towers; next, a sort of artificial hill was built to give the besiegers an advantage; then camps were set around the city to prevent all traffic; and finally "the battering rams" are brought against the walls. These last were heavy beams, headed with iron, and slung in towers, so that they could be swung against the walls with great force. The practice of forming the end of the beam like a ram's head belongs to the Greeks and Romans; but the instrument itself was much older.

(3) An iron pan, more accurately, a flat plate. This was to set for a wall of iron between the prophet (representing the besiegers) and the city, doubtless as symbolical of the strength of the besiegers' lines, and of the impossibility there would be of an escape from the city.

(4) Ezekiel is here, in a fresh feature of the symbolical prophecy, to represent the people as enduring the divine judgment upon their sins. "The house of Israel" is here expressly distinguished from "the house of Judah," and means the ten tribes. They are symbolized by the prophet's lying on his **left** side, because it was the Oriental habit to look to the east when describing the points of the compass, and the northern kingdom was therefore on the left.

(6) The iniquity of the house of Judah forty days.—This forty days is clearly subsequent and additional to the 390 days (verse 5), making in all a period of 430 days. The great disproportion between the two is in accordance with the difference in the two parts of the nation and the consequent divine dealings with them. Judah had remained faithful to its appointed rulers of the house of David, several of whose kings had been eminently devout men; through whatever mixture with idolatry it had yet always retained the worship of Jehovah, and had kept up the Aaronic priesthood, and preserved with more or less respect the law of Moses. It was now entering upon the period of the Babylonish captivity, from which, after seventy years, a remnant was again to be restored to keep up the people of the Messiah. Israel, on the other hand, had set up a succession of dynasties, and not one of all their kings had been a God-fearing man; they had made Baal their national god, and had made priests at their pleasure of the lowest of the people, and in consequence of their sins had been carried into a captivity from which they never returned.

(8) I will lay bands upon thee.—See note on 3:25.

(9) Take thou also unto thee wheat.—The grains enumerated are of all kinds from the best to the worst, indicating that every sort of food would be sought after in the critical calness of the siege. See Lev. 19:19; Deut. 22:9, thus again indicating the stern necessity which should be laid upon the people.

(10) By weight, twenty shekels a day.—The allowance of twenty shekels equals something less than eleven ounces, scarcely enough to sustain life. "Meat" is used here, as often in Scripture, of any kind of food. The extreme scarcity of food is also denoted by its being weighed rather than measured.

(11) The sixth part of an hin.—Authorities make the sixth part of an hin from six-tenths to nine-tenths of a pint.

(12) As barley cakes.—These were commonly cooked in the hot ashes, hence the special defilement caused by the fuel required to be used. Not merely revolting in itself, it was ceremonially polluting (verse 14; see Lev. 5:3; 7:21). A mitigation of the requirement is granted to him (verse 15).

(15) Cow's dung.—In the scarcity of fuel in the East, cow's dung, and especially camel's dung, is dried, and becomes the common fuel.

5

(1) Upon thine head, and upon thy beard.—The cutting off the hair was a common mark of mourning (see Job 1:20; Isa. 22:12; Jer. 7:29); but the allusion here seems to be rather to Isa. 7:20, in which God describes his coming judgments upon Israel. The symbolism was the more marked because Ezekiel was a priest, and the priests were expressly forbidden in the law to shave either the head or the beard (Lev. 21:5). The shaving, therefore, of a priest's head and beard with a sword presaged a most desolating judgment.

(2) The meaning of this verse is explained beginning in verse 12. The third, which is scattered, plainly signifies the small part of the people who, escaping destruction, shall be scattered among the heathen. A similar prophecy, referring however to a later time, may be found in Zech. 13:8, 9. (See Lev. 26:33.) Plain prophecy is here mixed with the symbolism.

(3) A few in number, and bind them in thy skirts.—A small remnant of the people was still left in the land after the great captivity (II Kings 25:22); but even of these some were to perish by violence in the disorders which arose. (See Jer. 40; 41.) The ultimate result was the expatriation of all that remained in Judaea and the entire emptying of the land of the chosen people.

At this point the use of symbolism ceases for a while, and the prophet now, for the first time, begins to utter his prophecies in plain language. Accordingly, he changes his style from prose to the more ordinary form of prophetic utterance in parallelisms, which constitute the distinctive feature of Hebrew poetry, and this continues until another vision begins with chap. 8.

(5) I have set it in the midst of the nations.—This was eminently true of Israel, as represented by Jerusalem, in all ages of its history. It constituted one of the great opportunities of Israel had they been faithful to their calling, while it became a chief source of their disasters when they went astray from God. Centrally situated among the chief kingdoms of antiquity, Israel had the opportunity of presenting to the world the spectacle of a people strong and prosperous in the worship, and under the guardianship, of the one true God, and of becoming the great missionary of monotheism in the ancient world. At the same time they were separated from most of these nations by natural barriers, isolating them and allowing their free development, without interference, as a God-fearing people. But when, by the unfaithfulness of the Israelites to their religion, the one bond of national unity was weakened, they became a ready prey to the nations around them. In the divine ordering of the world, responsibility must always be proportioned to privilege; and the failure to fulfill the responsibility leads, as in this case, not only to a withdrawal of the privilege, but to corresponding condemnation.

(6) God's judgments are always relative and proportioned to the opportunities He has granted to men. The point is that the Israelites had **resisted His judgments** more than the heathen; they had sinned against greater light.

(9) The prophet here intends a comparison between different judgments upon the Jews and upon others. As they had received at His hand higher opportunities and privileges than He had before given or would afterward give to any other nation, so must the punishment for their sin be more severe and more conspicuous than He had inflicted or would inflict on any other. All the divine judgments upon them through all time may therefore be considered as here coming into view. And they would not end with the destruction of Jerusalem.

(13) I will be comforted.—The word employed here is used of consoling oneself by

taking vengeance. The divine honor, wounded by the sins of the chosen people and dishonored before the heathen, should be vindicated by their punishment in the sight of all the world.

6

(2) Toward the mountains of Israel.—It is not uncommon to address prophetic utterances to inanimate objects as a poetic way of representing the people. The mountains are especially mentioned as being the chosen places of idolatrous worship. (See Deut. 12:2; II Kings 17:10, 11; Jer. 2:20; 3:6; Hos. 4:13.) Baal, the sun-god, was the idol especially worshiped upon the hills.

(3) To the rivers, and to the valleys.— These words are specifications of the same general character. Such places were also favorite places for idolatrous rites (see II Kings 23:10; Isa. 57:5, 6; Jer. 7:31; 32:35), especially for the worship of the Phoenician Astaroth, the female divinity worshiped in conjunction with Baal. By the expression, "I, even I," strong emphasis is placed on the fact that these judgments are from God. Inasmuch as they were to be wrought by human instrumentality, the attention might easily be taken up with the secondary causes; but by thus declaring them beforehand, and claiming them as His own work, God would make it evident that all was from Him.

(4) Your images.—The original word indicates that these were images used in connection with the worship of the sun. The whole verse is taken from Lev. 26:30. The same woes were there foretold by Moses in the contingency of the people's disobedience.

Your slain men before your idols.— There was nothing so utterly defiling under the Mosaic law as the touch of a dead body. (See Num. 9:6-10; II Kings 23:14, 16.) The Israelites had defiled the land with idols, now the idols themselves should be defiled with their dead bodies.

(6) May be abolished.—The word **abolished** is a strong one, meaning utterly obliterated. This was what Israel should have done to the nations who inhabited Canaan before them; they and their works should have been so utterly blotted out that no temptations from them should have remained. But Israel had failed to observe the divine command, and now in turn their works, done in imitation of the guilty nations they had supplanted, must be blotted out.

(8) Yet will I leave a remnant.—This divine plan pursued from the beginning, as is shown by Paul in Rom. 9:1-13, of purifying the people by setting aside the mass, and showing mercy to a remnant, looks far beyond the Babylonish captivity. (See Zech. 10:9.) Beyond this brief glimpse at the remnant, however, the cloud settles down again upon the prophecy, for the period until the destruction of Jerusalem must be almost exclusively a period of the denunciation of judgment.

(9) Because I am broken.—The translation should be, "Because I have broken their whorish heart . . . and their eyes," the eyes being mentioned as the means by which their hearts had been enticed to evil. Here, as constantly in all parts of Scripture, apostasy from God is described under the figure of unfaithfulness in the marriage relation. "They shall loathe themselves" indicates a true repentance; they shall loathe the sin and themselves for having committed it.

(11) Smite with thine hand, and stamp with thy foot.—To clap the hands and stamp the feet, either singly (Num. 24:10; Ezek. 21:14, 17; 22:13) or together (25:6), is a gesture of strong emotion or earnestness of purpose. The prophet is here directed to use it as indicating God's unchangeable determination united to a sense of grievous wrong.

7

(2) The four corners.—A frequent Scriptural phrase for every part. (Comp. Isa. 11:12; Rev. 7:1.) The origin of the expression is to be sought, not in any supposed popular belief that the earth was square, but in the fact that so many common things had just four sides or four corners (see Exod. 25:12; 27:2; Job 1:19; Acts 10:11, etc.) that the phrase came naturally to be a common expression of universality.

Verses 3 and 4 are repeated almost exactly in verses 8 and 9. The frequent repetitions of this chapter are designed and give great force to the denunciation of woe.

(5) An only evil, that is, an evil so all-embracing as to be complete in itself, needing no repetition. Comp. the same thought in Nahum 1:9.

(7) The morning is come unto thee.—The most probable sense is "the circuit of thy

sins is finished, and the end is come upon thee."

The sounding again of the mountains.—Comp. Isa. 16:10; Jer. 25:10, denoting the joyous sounds of the people, especially at harvest-time, filling the land and echoing back from the mountains. Instead of this shall be the tumult of the day of war.

(10) See note on verse 7. In Num. 17:8 the rod of Aaron was made to bud and blossom by divine power in evidence of his having been chosen of God; here the rod representing the tribe at Jerusalem in its self-will and pride has budded and blossomed to its destruction.

(13) The seller shall not return.—The previous verse described the general cessation of all the business of life in the utter desolation of the land. Among the Israelites the most important buying and selling was that of land, and it was provided in the law (Lev. 25:14-16) that this should in no case extend beyond the year of jubilee, when all land must revert to its possessor by inheritance. The seller in that year should return to his possession. Now it is foretold that the desolation shall continue so long that, even if the seller lived, he should be unable to avail himself of the jubilee year.

(14) None goeth to the battle.—The people are so enfeebled by their sins as to have no power against the enemy. Consequently (verse 15) they shall all perish, directly or indirectly, at the hands of their foes.

(16) Like doves of the valleys.—To this general destruction there will be exceptions, as generally in war there are fugitives and captives; but these, like doves whose home is in the valleys driven by fear of the mountains, shall mourn in their exile.

(19) Cast their silver in the streets.—As in the rout of an army the soldier throws away everything, even his most valuable things, as impediments to his flight and temptations to the pursuing enemy, so the Israelites in their terror should abandon everything. Their riches will be utterly unavailing. The expression in the original is even stronger; their gold shall be to them "an unclean thing," "filth," because they shall perceive that it has been to them an occasion of sin.

(22) My secret place.—The holy of holies, sacredly guarded from all intrusion, and representing the very culmination both of the religion and of the national life of Israel, shall be polluted. The agents in this pollution are immediately mentioned as "the robbers," i.e., the Chaldaean armies.

And the trouble which they would effect would touch all classes (verses 26, 27).

8

Here begins a fresh series of prophecies, extending through chap. 19. This is introduced, as before, by a remarkable vision which, with its accompanying messages, occupies chaps. 8-11. The date (8:1) shows that this series began just a year and two months after Ezekiel's call to the prophetic office (1:1, 2), while the next date (20:1) allows eleven months and five days for its completion. The vision of chaps. 8-11, and the following prophecies of chap. 12, are directed to Jerusalem exclusively, rather than to the nation generally, because of the extreme sinfulness of the people remaining there. Afterward they again become more general, and there are some especially relating to the exiles; but still this whole section, to chap. 19 inclusive, is mainly occupied with the people still remaining in their own land.

(1) **The elders of Judah sat before me.**—It is plain that Ezekiel was held in consideration among the captives. Judah is not used in contradistinction to Israel; but as the captives were chiefly of the tribe of Judah, so their elders were known as "the elders of Judah."

(2) **A likeness as the appearance of fire.** — This is not a reappearance of the vision of chap. 1. That vision bursts again on the prophet after he has been carried in the spirit to the Temple at Jerusalem (verse 4). Ezekiel, in this present experience, takes pains to show that it was only a vision, not an outward reality. The elders saw nothing themselves, but must have witnessed his ecstasy, and thus have been prepared for his telling them at its close (11:25) "all the things that the Lord had showed" him.

(3) **The image of jealousy** is explained as a descriptive name which aroused the divine indignation. There actually were heathen idols set up in the temple, and nothing could give a more vivid picture of the corruption of priests and people alike than the mention of their presence. Idolatry had been growing more general and more bold from the time of Solomon. All the subsequent kings of Judah, except Josiah, were wicked men; and although this particular sin is not distinctly recorded of Zedekiah, yet it seems altogether likely that he too made use of the temple for idolatrous worship, and that Ezekiel in vision now saw his idols standing in the court.

(5) **The way toward the north.**—Ezekiel in his vision was within the court of the priests, otherwise he could not have looked **toward** the north to see the idol in the north gate.

(6) **That I should go far off from my sanctuary.**—There was a strong feeling among the people that they were safe at Jerusalem; God, whom they still regarded, notwithstanding their idolatries, as a powerful national God, would certainly protect His temple. It is the office of the prophet to show that the transgressions of the people led, as their natural consequence, to his giving over the city to desolation. The people's own acts make necessary the judgments impending over them.

(7) **To the door of the court.**—This is clearly a different place from that in which the prophet had hitherto been in his vision, and yet is not so described that its locality can be certainly fixed. He had been inside the inner court near its north gate; in verse 14 he is taken to the north gate of the outer enclosure of the temple precincts. It is probable, therefore, that this was between them. Here he finds a hole, or window, too small for entrance, and is directed to enlarge it that he may go in. The object of this part of the vision is to show the extreme secrecy of what he is now to see, a secrecy made necessary by the connection of this idolatry with Egypt, the foe of Chaldaea. It was during this period that Jeremiah was obliged to contend strenuously against the desire of a considerable part of the court to enter into an alliance with Egypt against Chaldaea. The party among the Jews who sought an Egyptian alliance was also the party most unwilling to submit to the divine commandments. They were the persons who engaged in this creature-worship (verse 10); and they are here represented as constituting the leaders of the nation.

(11) The seventy elders were not the Sanhedrin, which was not constituted until after the return from Babylon; but the number has probable reference to Exod. 24:9, 10, and Num. 11:16. In contrast with those selected for special nearness to God, these seventy are engaged in abominations most abhorrent to Him. For Jaazaniah, perhaps here the **grandson** of Shaphan, see 11:1; II Kings 22:3, 14; Jer. 29:3; 36:10, 11, 12; 39:14; 40:5, 11.

With every man his censer in his hand.—The burning of incense was the exclusive function of the priesthood (Num. 16; II Chron. 26:16-18); and it was alike the necessity and the choice of the idolaters of Israel to devolve this office upon those who were not of the Aaronic family. (Comp. I Kings 12:31.) When the seventy elders offered incense to their idols, they claimed thereby to be the priests of those idols.

(14) Women weeping for Tammuz.— Tammuz is nowhere else mentioned in Scripture, but is identified by ancient tradition (incorporated into the Vulg.) with the Greek Adonis, the beloved of Venus. His worship is first heard of in Phoenicia, and was widespread throughout Syria and the adjacent countries. As the creature worship before mentioned was undoubtedly connected with political reasons, while aid was being sought from Egypt, so the worship of Adonis may have been affected by the league which Zedekiah attempted to form (Jer. 27:1-11) with the Edomites, Moabites, Ammonites, and Philistines against Nebuchadnezzar. The annual feast of Adonis consisted of a mourning by the women for his death, followed by a rejoicing over his return to life, and was accompanied by great abominations and licentiousness.

(16) Between the porch and the altar.— These are probably the high priest and the heads of the twenty-four courses, representing the whole body of the priests, as the elders represented the whole body of the people. The adoration of the sun, probably the earliest form of false religion, was the special worship of Persia, but had been long since practiced by the kings and people of Judah (II Kings 23:5, 11). Thus all classes of the nation are seen to be involved in common sin; and the priests particularly, the special guardians of true religion, are found practicing this sin under circumstances of peculiar insult to God. (See II Chron. 36:14.)

(17) For they have filled the land with violence.—Corruption in religion here, as always, bore its proper fruit in moral deterioration. Within the memory of those still living, the good King Josiah, supported by the prophet Jeremiah and many others, had made great effort at reformation and had purged the Temple of its abominations; hence God says the people "have **returned** to provoke me to anger."

Put the branch to their nose.—This is an obscure expression, perhaps a reference to the habit of the Parsees (mentioned by Strabo) in their worship to hold twigs of tamarisk, palm, and pomegranate before their mouths.

9

(1) He cried also ... with a loud voice.— The pronoun refers to the same Being as throughout the previous chapter. His nature is sufficiently shown by the prophet's address to Him in verse 8. The "loud voice" was to give emphasis to what is said; it is the natural expression of the fierceness of the divine indignation and wrath.

(2) One man among them was clothed with linen.—He was **among** them, but not of them. He carried in his girdle the "inkhorn," i.e., the little case, containing pens, knife, and ink, commonly worn by the Oriental scribe. There is no occasion to understand this person as our Lord. There is nothing mentioned which can give him any special identification. He is simply a necessity of the vision, an angelic messenger, to mark out those whose faithfulness to God amid the surrounding evil exempts them from the common doom (comp. Rev. 7:3). The courts of the Temple were built in stages, the innermost the highest. This "way of the higher gate," then, was the gate of the inner court, and was on the north, both as the place where the prophet had been shown the idolatries, and as the quarter from which the Chaldaean destruction was poured out upon the nation.

(4) Set a mark upon the foreheads.—The word for mark is literally a **tau**, the last letter of the Hebrew alphabet. This, in many of the ancient alphabets, and especially in that in use among the Hebrews up to this time, and long retained upon their coins, was in the form of a cross. The symbolism is taken from such passages as Gen. 4:15; Exod. 12:7, 13; 28:36; and it is used in Rev. 7:3; 9:4; 14:1. Such marks may be necessary for the guidance of the angelic executors of God's commands, and at all events, the symbolism is of value to the human mind. It is with reference to such Scriptural instances of marking, doubtless, that the Church has provided for the signing of the baptized with the sign of the cross. It is to be observed here that the distinction of the marking has reference wholly and only to character.

(7) Defile the house.—The utmost possible pollution under the Mosaic economy was the touch of a dead body. (See Num. 19:11; I Kings 13:2; II Kings 23:16.) It

587

might be thought that the Temple would be spared this defilement; but not only must the execution of justice override all technicalities (see I Kings 2:28-31), but in this case the very defilement itself was a part of the judgment, since God was about to forsake His sanctuary (10:4, 18, 19).

(8) I was left.—No mention is made here of those who were to be saved; they were so few among the mass as to have no effect upon the general impression of the vision. Yet they are not forgotten.

10

This chapter is chiefly occupied with a fresh description of the vision of chap. 1, but includes two new points: the giving up of the city to fire (verse 2), and the abandonment of the Temple (verse 18, 19).

11

This chapter continues and concludes the vision; yet its scenes are not to be considered as consecutive with those which have gone before. In chap. 9 all who had not the divine mark upon their foreheads were slain by the destroying angels; in chap. 10 the city itself was given up to fire; but here the evildoers are seen again, and again made the subject of the prophetic denunciation. It is, therefore, rather a looking at the same things from another point of view than an account of them in historical sequence.

The latter part of the chapter foretells the divine blessing upon the repentant and restored remnant of the exiles. Then the glory of the Lord departs altogether, and the prophet is restored to Chaldaea to communicate the vision to the captives.

(3) The princes of the people now appear in Ezekiel's vision as taking up the prophecy of Jer. 29 and contradicting it. The princes further confirmed the people in their fancied security.

(10) In the border of Israel.—To be arraigned and punished "in the border," i.e., at the extremity or outside of the land of Israel, was most terrible to a Jew. (See II Kings 25:20, 21; Jer. 52:9-11; and note on 12:6.)

(14) Again the word.—This does not mark the beginning of a separate prophecy, but only the divine answer to the prophet's intercession. This answer differs entirely from the denunciations that have gone before.

588

fore, because it turns to the exiles and foretells God's mercy and blessing upon them.

(15) Thy brethren—i.e., those who were with Ezekiel in the Captivity. The prophet is taught that these despised exiles, deprived of so many privileges, are yet his true brethren, and that he is to regard these as his true kindred rather than the corrupt priests at Jerusalem. In this word there is an allusion to the office of **Goel**, the next of kin, whose duty it was in every way to assist his impoverished or unfortunate kinsman.

(16) As a little sanctuary, rather for a little while, during the term of their captivity, God's presence with them would be spiritually instead of the outward symbolical presence in His Temple. The contrast is striking. God has already said that He would abandon the Temple, give up Jerusalem to destruction, and cast out its people; but now to the exiles, scattered among the heathen, He would Himself be for a sanctuary.

(17) I will give you the land of Israel.—The people of Jerusalem, who claimed the land as their own exclusive possession, shall be cast out; the exiles whom they despised shall be gathered again and possess the land.

(19, 20) Here follows one of those germinant and ever developing prophetic promises which in fuller and fuller degree have formed from the very first the hope of the future. True religion and a service acceptable to God must spring from a subjection of the affections of the heart to His will. Ezekiel here, and with more fullness in 36:26, 27), speaks of it as a part of the blessing of the restoration. A marked progress was then made toward it in the hearty abandonment of idolatry, and the better appreciation of religion as a matter of internal heart service; but the prophecy of Jer. 31:33, given about the same time, shows that it looked forward to the Messianic days for a more complete realization.

(19) One heart.—Unity of purpose among the restored exiles was to be at once a consequence and a condition of their improved moral condition. The opposite evil is cited as one of the sins of the people in Isa. 53:6. Self-will, which leads to division, and submission to God's will are necessarily contradictory terms.

Stony heart ... heart of flesh.—A stony heart is unnatural and incongruous. "An heart of flesh" is one that can be moved by the divine appeals and is suitable to the whole being and condition of the people. The effect of this change will be obedience to the divine will, and consequently a realization of the covenant relation in a fellowship with God.

(23) Stood upon the mountain.—This mountain was afterward known as the Mount of Olives. It is considerably higher than the city, and commands a view over its entire extent. Here the divine glory rested after taking its departure from the Temple and the city in the vision of the prophet. (See Zech. 14:4; Luke 21:20; 24:50, 51.)

The vision is now closed, and the prophet is transported in spirit back into Chaldaea to declare what he had seen to his fellow-captives and show them the vanity of their trust in the preservation of the guilty city.

12

(3) Prepare thee stuff for removing.— Stuff includes all that an emigrant would require; "removing" is the same word as is translated **captivity** in verse 4. The symbolical action was that of one preparing to leave his home to go into captivity.

(5, 6) The wall was probably of adobe, sun-dried brick, the common building material of the country, and there was, therefore, no great difficulty in digging through it; but this way of entering the house indicates something of stealth and secrecy. This covering of the face might primarily be a token of grief; but as the whole action is distinctly prophetic, so especially was this sign. See II Kings 25:4-7; Jer. 39:4-7; 52:7-11, where Zedekiah, with his men of war, escaped from the city secretly by night, was pursued and captured, and carried to Riblah, where his eyes were put out. He was then taken in chains to Babylon.

(14) I will scatter toward every wind.— The people of Judah were not carried captive to Babylon only, but many of them were scattered wherever they could find refuge; and, finally, the remnant left in the land by Nebuchadnezzar, after the murder of his governor Gedaliah, escaped into Egypt (Jer. 41-43).

(16) May declare all their abominations.— This they were to do, that the false impression that God was unable to protect His people might be removed from the minds of the heathen, and the truth that He was punishing them for their sins be made known.

(18) Eat thy bread with quaking.—In another symbolical action the prophet is to eat and drink as men in the terror and distress of a siege.

(19) Unto the people of the land, i.e., of the land of Chaldaea: Ezekiel's fellow-captives. All these prophecies, though concerning Jerusalem and its people, were immediately addressed to the exiles, and their teaching was primarily for them. It is not unlikely, however, as Jerome says, that all these prophecies of Ezekiel were sent to Jerusalem, and the corresponding utterances of Jeremiah, made in Jerusalem, were sent to Chaldaea.

(21-28) These verses contain two distinct messages from the Lord, both designed to meet the objection that warning prophecies had been uttered now for a long time, and as they had not come to pass there was no reason to expect their fulfillment, at least until some far distant future. It is always the tendency of sinful man to take this ground while experiencing the long-suffering and forbearance of God (see Matt. 24:43; II Pet. 3:4). In this case, the objection was evidently encouraged by false prophets (verse 24), and accordingly the following chapter is devoted to them.

13

(5) Ye have not gone up into the gaps.— The **gaps** refer to the breaches in the wall made by the enemy, which became the rallying point of every brave leader (see 22:30). The word "hedge" should rather be translated **wall**. The false prophets, like the hireling shepherds of John 10:12, were only selfish, and had no care for the flock. The whole language is figurative, the breaches in the material walls representing the moral decay of the people.

(10) One built up a wall.—One of the false prophets would build a wall, set up of his own device—some vision as a defense against the warnings of calamity; and his fellow prophets would join in his deceit by covering this wall "with untempered mortar." Calvin understands it of mortar mixed with sand and water only, the lime being left out. It is a common practice in the East to cover over their walls with stucco. In this case the other false prophets are represented as joining with the one who built the wall by covering over its weaknesses and defects with a fair-seeming plaster. (Comp. Matt. 23:27; Acts 23:3.) They helped on the delusion by giving it the weight of their influence and persuading the people to believe a lie.

(17-23) This passage deals with a class of people, the false prophetesses, who are not mentioned elsewhere in the Old Testament. True prophetesses, as in the case of Miriam (Exod. 15:20), Deborah (Judg. 4:4), and, at this very time, Huldah (II Kings 22:14; II Chron. 34:22), and somewhat later, Noadiah (Neh. 6:14), are frequently spoken of, and continued to exist in New Testament times, as in the case of Anna (Luke 2:36). Their course in deceiving the people was essentially the same as that of the false prophets, but they are described as doing this in ways suited to their sex.

(19) Handfuls of barley.—It was an ancient custom to bring presents to a prophet on consulting him (I Sam. 9:7, 8; I Kings 14:3); but as barley was a cheap grain, and handfuls a very small quantity, these words show the exceedingly small gains for which these false prophetesses were willing to pervert the truth and lead the people to destruction. God was "polluted" by attaching His name and authority to that which was not true.

14

(3) Have set up their idols in their heart.— It was not the open idolatry of Judaea which is reproved among these elders of the captivity; that had already passed away, but still their heart was not right. Like Lot's wife, they longed for that which they dared not do. With such a disposition, they were in the greatest danger, putting the temptation to sin directly before them. And they kept themselves in a state of alienation from God, so that it was idle to imagine He would allow Himself to be inquired of by them. The question implies the negative answer which is fully expressed in the following verses.

(6) Repent and turn.—The announcements of self-deception and illusion form the basis for the earnest call to a true repentance. There can be no hope for Israel in any merely outward reformation. The only repentance acceptable to Him is that which has its seat in the affections of the heart.

(7) Or of the stranger.—Under the Mosaic legislation, "the stranger" living among the Israelites was bound to observe a certain outward deference to the law of the land. Israel being a theocracy, its fundamental law against idol-worship could not be violated with impunity by those who sought the protection of its government (Lev. 17:10; 20:1, 2, etc.). The point insisted upon here is not so much the idol-worship in itself, as the hypocrisy of attempting to join with this the inquiring of the Lord. God declares that He will answer such hypocrisy, in whomsoever it may be found, interposing to punish the inquirer and to make him an example to deter others from a like course.

(9) And if the prophet be deceived.—In verses 3, 4, 7, the Lord has refused to allow an answer through the prophet to the hypocritical inquirer; but if the prophet, by giving the desired answer, allows himself to become a partaker of the sin which God abhors, then God will treat him according to that general method of dealing with sin which is here described. False prophets were especially abundant toward the close of the kingdom of Judah and form a marked characteristic in the New Testament prophecies of "the last days." No more terrible judgment can be imagined than that of thus giving up the sinner to the consequences of his own sin.

(14) Noah, Daniel, and Job.—These three are selected, doubtlessly, not only as examples of eminent holiness themselves, but as men who had been allowed to be the means of saving others (see Gen. 6:18; Dan. 2:17, 18; Job. 42:7, 8). Moses and Samuel might seem still more remarkable instances of the value of intercessory prayer; but these had already been cited by Jeremiah (15:1). The mention of Daniel, a contemporary of Ezekiel, with the ancient patriarchs, Noah and Job, need occasion no surprise. Were there in Jerusalem the most holy men of either past or present times, it would avail nothing. (The Jews might well have thought that Daniel's influence in the royal court would avail to avert the threatened calamity.)

(22) Ye shall be comforted concerning the evil.—In this and the following verse it is promised that a remnant shall be brought from Jerusalem; and it is clearly implied that they shall come to Babylonia. There the present exiles shall see them, and thus be comforted. But in what sense comforted? When they should see the wickedness of this remnant, they will cease to mourn over the judgment, for they cannot but perceive that it was a righteous act of God.

15

This chapter contains a single simile and its application, designed to show that Israel, having failed to fulfill the purpose for which they had been chosen, were worthless and could have no other end than destruction.

The comparison of Israel to a vine or to a vineyard is common in Scripture (Ps. 80:8-13; Isa. 5:1-7; Jer. 2:21; Hos. 10:1; Matt. 21:33-41, etc.) and is very apt, for the vine, bringing forth its appointed fruit, was among the most precious of the earth's productions; but failing this, it was utterly worthless for anything but fuel. The fact that Israel did not yield the fruit required is not especially mentioned, being taken for granted here, and abundantly expressed in the connected prophecies. The fruit of righteousness, as our Lord has shown in John 15:1-8, under the same figure of the vine, is only possible by a steadfast clinging to the Source of righteousness, and this was the point in which the Jews of this time had signally failed.

16

In magnificent allegory the sin and consequent rejection of Israel is set forth here in still stronger terms than in anything which has gone before. There are three main parts of the chapter: the sin (verses 3-34), the punishment (verses 35-52), and the final restoration of Israel (verses 53-63). The extreme aggravation of the sin is shown from the fact that Israel had no original claim upon God's favor, nor anything to make her attractive—she was merely an exposed and repulsive foundling (verses 3-5)—when God took pity upon, and saved, and cared for her (verses 6, 7). Then when she had come of age, He entered into covenant with her and greatly blessed her (8-14); but she proved utterly unfaithful to her covenant and wanton beyond all precedent (15-34). Hence her punishment.

(4) The rubbing of the body of the newborn infant with salt, a custom still prevailing in some parts of the east, probably had a symbolical as well as a supposed physical effect. The wrapping the body tightly in swaddling-bands (comp. Luke 2:7) is still common. The time here referred to in the life of Israel is that in which it passed from its embryonic state in the family of the patriarchs to a nation in the bondage of

Egypt. Despised, oppressed, and enslaved, no other people ever became a nation under such circumstances.

(6) Live.—While they were in this condition, God took pity on them. He delivered them from their oppressors; He raised up a leader for them; He gave them a law and a Church, with its priesthood and its sacraments; He led them into the land of promise, delivered them from their enemies, and constituted them a nation under the most favorable circumstances for their growth and development in all righteousness.

(15) Didst trust in thine own beauty.—There can scarcely be a more striking instance of the working of the hand of Providence in history than the story of the kingdom of Israel during and after the reign of Solomon. Raised as a theocracy to great power and wealth by the divine blessing, it began to trust in its own beauty. Solomon's policy was to make it a great and powerful empire among the nations of the earth, losing sight of its true character as the kingdom of God. Consequently the very means he took to aggrandize it became the instruments of its fall. His vast Oriental harem, gathered from all surrounding nations, introduced idolatry into the palace and fostered it throughout the land. This apostasy from God is represented as harlotry, and not only so, but as indiscriminate harlotry, for Israel never adopted any one false God, but worshiped the abominations of every nation which prevailed over her.

(62) Establish my covenant with thee.—The old covenant, having failed, is merged in the new and better covenant promised in 11:19; 18:31; Jer. 31:31-34. This new covenant, established through a perfect Mediator, can alone perfectly fulfill God's gracious designs for man, although the way for it must necessarily have been prepared by the less perfect covenant of old. The remembrance of God's covenants is the basis of His mercy toward the penitent.

17

This chapter contains a "riddle" or "parable" (verses 3-10), with its explanation (verses 11-21), closing with a clear Messianic prophecy couched in language taken from the parable (verses 22-24). The meaning of the parable is explained: the first eagle (verses 3-6) is Nebuchadnezzar; "the top of his young twigs" is Jehoiachin, carried to

591

Babylon; the "vine of low stature" is Zedekiah; the second eagle is Pharaoh (verse 7). The historical facts on which the parable is based are recorded in II Kings 24:8-20; II Chron. 36:9-13; Jer. 37 and 52:1-7.

(22) I will also take.—In what has passed, all has been done according to God's will, but yet through human instrumentality: Israel has been punished; Jehoiachin has been, and Zedekiah is about to be, carried into captivity, as God designed. Yet Nebuchadnezzar has done it all for his own purposes. Now God Himself directly interposes, and takes a scion of the same "high cedar," the royal house of David. In accordance with the allegory, this can be only a historical personage, and from the description which follows this person can only be the Messiah. So it has been understood by nearly all interpreters, Jewish and Christian. (See Isa. 11:1; 53:2.)

18

The certainty of the divine judgments had now been repeatedly and most emphatically foretold; but that this might have the effect of leading the people to true repentance, it was still necessary that the sense of sin should be brought home to them individually. The people were by no means inclined to acknowledge their own personal guilt, but were rather disposed to look upon their sufferings as the consequence of the sins of others who had gone before. This disposition is here met by the most full and emphatic assurance that God deals with each man in view of his own acts.

Beginning with verse 5, four cases are discussed separately: (1) That of the righteous man who honestly seeks to follow the ways of the Lord (verses 5-9); (2) that of his wicked son (verses 10-13); (3) that of the righteous son of the wicked father (verses 14-20); (4) that of a change of character in the individual, whether from sin to righteousness or the reverse (verses 21-29).

The three last verses of the chapter contain an earnest exhortation to the Israelites, based on the principles of God's dealings with man just now declared, to repent and receive His mercy and blessing. The question of salvation is still one which each man must decide for himself before God. The whole point of the chapter is that God's dealing with man is determined by man's own attitude toward Him.

19

This chapter forms the close of this long series of prophecies, and consists of a lament over the fall of the royal family of Israel and over the utter desolation of the nation itself. It fitly closes the series of warnings, and takes away any lingering hope of escape from the divine judgments.

(3) It became a young lion.—There can be no doubt (see verse 4) of the reference of this to Jehoahaz (II Kings 23:30-33). In verse 6 Jehoiachin is also spoken of particularly (II Kings 24:9). These two are mentioned as examples of all the other kings after Josiah. Jehoiakim and Zedekiah are simply passed over, although it may be that the prophet looked upon them as creatures of Pharaoh and Nebuchadnezzar rather than as legitimate kings of Israel. Jehoiakim, moreover, died in Jerusalem, and Zedekiah was at this moment still upon the throne.

(9) Brought him to the king of Babylon.—II Kings 24:8-17. Jehoiachin reigned only three months when Jerusalem was conquered by Nebuchadnezzar. He was carried to Babylon and put in prison, where he was still living at the time of this prophecy. It was not until many years later that he was released (Jer. 52:31, 32).

(10) A vine in thy blood.—The figure here changes to the more common one of a vine, yet by no means the "vine of low stature" of 17:6; it is rather a **strong and goodly vine.** The general sense is that Israel was planted a strong and fruitful vine, with every advantage for growth and full development.

(12) She was plucked up.—With the captivity of Jehoiachin and a part of the people, the desolation had begun. Much still remained to be accomplished, but it was now close at hand; and the prophet speaks of it in the past tense, as if he saw it already fulfilled.

(13) In a dry and thirsty ground.—Such was Babylon to Israel in its national relations, and even after the return from the exile the Jews never rose again to much importance among the nations of the earth. But in the meantime they were being disciplined, that at least a few of them might be prepared for the planting among them of that kingdom not of this world, spoken of at the close of chap. 16, which should fill the whole earth.

(14) Fire is gone out of a rod of her branches.—Many of the kings did their full share of the evil work; but a "rod" is here spoken of in the singular, with special reference to the last king, Zedekiah, who finally brought on the utter ruin of both himself and his people.

20

Here begins a new series of prophecies, extending to the close of chap. 23. It begins two years, one month, and five days after Ezekiel's call to the prophetic office (1:2), or eleven months and five days (comp. verse 1 with 8:1) after the beginning of the former series; and it is just two years and five months (24:1) before another series begins. It is simultaneous in date with the beginning of the final siege of Jerusalem.

(4) Wilt thou judge them?—The form of the repeated question is equivalent to an imperative. Instead of allowing the elders' inquiry and entreaty for the averting of judgment, the prophet is directed to set before them their long series of apostasies and provocations.

(5) When I chose Israel.—In verses 5-9 the Lord takes up the first, or Egyptian, period of the history of Israel. The record of that period, as it has come to us in the Pentateuch, does not contain either any commands against idolatry, or any notice of the rebellion of the people against such command; but both are clearly implied. (See Exod. 6:2-4; 32:12; Lev. 17:7.)

(10) Brought them into the wilderness.— Here begins the second period of the history under review—the earlier part of the life in the wilderness (verses 10-17). It includes the Exodus, the giving of the law, the setting up of the Tabernacle, the establishment of the priesthood, and the march to Kadesh. By all this the nation was constituted most distinctly the people of God and brought into the closest covenant relation with Him.

(18) Unto their children.—The third part of the historical retrospect (verses 18-26) concerns the generation which grew up in the free air of the wilderness and under the influence of the legislation and institutions given at Sinai. But it would be a mistake to confine what he says exclusively to that generation, for he regards Israel as a whole and treats of national characteristics which may have come to their most marked development only at a later time. The whole Book of Deuteronomy is the comment on verses 18-20.

(27) Your fathers have blasphemed me.— The fourth period of Israelitish history, though actually far the longest, is briefly passed over (verses 27-29). It includes the whole period of the settlement in Canaan, from the conquest to the prophet's own time, and was marked by the same characteristics as before. The particular way here specified by which they blasphemed was by the erection of idolatrous altars on every high place.

The second part of this prophecy extends from verse 33 to verse 44 (where the chapter closes in the Hebrew). The object of this concluding part of the prophecy is to declare the mingled severity and goodness with which God is about to deal with His people to wean them from their sins and prepare them to receive His abundant blessing.

21

(3, 4) The righteous and the wicked.— This explains **the green tree** and **the dry** of 20:47; and "all flesh" of verses 4, 5, corresponds to "all faces" of the same. These expressions are meant to show the universality of the approaching desolation. But the general terms of this prophecy are to be limited by what is elsewhere said of the mercy which shall be shown to a remnant.

(5) It shall not return any more—i.e., until it has fully accomplished its purpose. Other judgments upon Israel had been arrested in mercy—the sword had been returned to the scabbard while its work was still incomplete. This will go on to the end.

(10) Contemneth the rod of my son.— This refers to Gen. 49:9, 10, in which Jacob addresses Judah as "my son," and foretells that "the sceptre shall not depart from" him until Shiloh come. There is another allusion to the same passage in verse 27. Comp. also note on 17:22.

(18) Heretofore it has only been foretold that Judah shall be desolated; now it is added that this shall be effected by the king of Babylon, and that he shall also extend his conquests to the Ammonites.

(19) Appoint thee two ways.—The prophet is directed to represent Nebuchadnezzar as about to go forth with his armies, and hesitating whether he should take first the road to Jerusalem or to the capital of the Ammonites. His choice of the former is determined, as he supposes, by his divinations, but really by the overruling hand of the Lord, who thus shows beforehand what it shall be. The whole is set forth in the vivid and concrete imagery so characteristic of Ezekiel; but it is impossible that the scene in real life was to be thus determined by the prophet's open interference. The whole is a vision, in which life and action is conveyed by this manner of describing the course of future events as actually taking place before the eyes of his hearers.

(21) Made his arrows bright.—Rather, **shook his arrows**. This was a mode of divination in use among the ancients (see **II., 3:316; Koran 3:39; 5:4, 94**). Several arrows, properly marked, were shaken together in a quiver or other vessel, and one drawn out. The mark upon the one drawn was supposed to indicate the will of the gods. It was thus simply one form of casting lots.

Consulted with images.—The particular images mentioned here were "teraphim," small idols, which are often spoken of in Scripture as used in divination by the Israelites themselves, and common also among the heathen. (See I Sam. 15:23, where the word "idolatry" is in the original "teraphim.") Nothing is known of the way in which these were used in divination.

Looked in the liver.—The inspection of the entrails of sacrificial victims as a means of ascertaining the will of the gods is frequent in classical literature. There is evidence that the same custom prevailed also in Babylonia.

(26) Remove the diadem.—The word translated "diadem" is rendered in every other place in which it occurs **the mitre** (of the high priest), and undoubtedly has the same sense here. Not only was the royal but also the high-priestly office to be overthrown in the approaching desolation. Neither of them was ever recovered in their full power after the captivity.

(27) Until he come whose right it is.— Comp. Gen. 49:10. The promise made here refers plainly both to the priestly and to the royal prerogatives, and a still more distinct foretelling of the union of both in the Messiah may be found in Zech. 6:12, 13. In Him, and in Him alone, will all this confusion and uncertainty come to an end. See Dan. 7:14.

(28) Concerning the Ammonites.—This prophecy is added to show that His judgments shall certainly fall on them also, and in this case the ruin foretold is final and hopeless, without the promise given to Israel in verse 27. (See 25:1-7.) As a matter of

history, the Ammonites were conquered, and their country desolated, by Nebuchadnezzar a few years after the destruction of Jerusalem, and they gradually dwindled away until their name and place among the nations finally disappeared.

22

In verses 2-16 the sins of Jerusalem are recounted, with evident reference to chap. 18; in verses 17-22 the punishment and purification of Israel is represented under the figure of melting mixed metals in the furnace; in verses 23-31 there is a return to the recounting of other sins than those mentioned in the first, showing that the corruption pervades all classes, and warning of certain punishment. This chapter, like chap. 20, is a justification of the divine judgment.

(4) A mocking to all countries.—This is frequently cited in Ezekiel, and is the necessary result in all ages of the contrast between high professions and inconsistent performance. Israel's law stood far above the legislation of any other nation of the period, but the habitual conduct of her people was in utter disregard of that law. (Comp. Rom. 2:24.)

(6) Were in thee to their power.—The rulers, who should have preserved order and administered justice, were foremost in deeds of violence. (See II Kings 21:16; 24:4.)

(16) Shalt take thine inheritance.—The meaning is that through their own misconduct they forfeit the privileges of a holy nation and become profaned or dishonored in the sight of the heathen. The terrible warning of verses 14-16 has shown the extreme suffering necessary for the purification of Israel.

(18) Become dross.—The figure taken from the refining of silver is a favorite one with the prophets (see Isa. 1:25; Jer. 6:29; Zech. 13:9; Mal. 3:3). The peculiar appropriateness of this figure has been often noted in the fact that the completion of the process of refining silver in the furnace was determined by the parting of the floating dross and the reflection of the image of the refiner from its molten surface. This figure, while setting forth the punishment of Israel, shows clearly that this punishment was for the purpose of purification.

(25) A conspiracy of her prophets.—The opposition of false prophets to the divine measures for the reformation of the people is continually spoken of (comp. chap. 13; Zeph. 3:4) as among the most serious obstacles to the work of the true prophets. There is also frequent mention of them in history (I Kings 22, etc.), as they had been foretold from of old in prophecy (Deut. 18:20-22).

(30) Make up the hedge is only another form of "stand in the gap," added for the sake of emphasis. Both refer to intercession for the people (see Ps. 106:23). It is not meant that there was not a single godly man, but not one of such a pure, strong, and commanding character that his intercessions might avert the threatened doom.

23

This chapter consists of an extended allegory in connection with the sinfulness of Judah. The allegory is much like that of chap. 16, but differs from it by omitting the historical features so prominent there. It is almost entirely concerned with the southern kingdom, enough only being added in reference to the northern, which had long since passed away, to bring out the comparison.

(4) Samaria is Aholah, and Jerusalem Aholibah.—Samaria, as the capital, is put for the northern kingdom, and is called Aholah (**her own tabernacle**) because she set up her own worship instead of resorting to the Temple. The southern kingdom, represented by Jerusalem, is called Aholibah (**my tabernacle is in her**) because she still contained the sanctuary of the Lord.

(10) She became famous.—A better word would be **notorious**. The conquest of Samaria and the captivity of the northern tribes had now been accomplished more than 130 years, and had made them a byword among the nations.

(11) She was more corrupt.—The idolatries of Judah not only comparatively but actually exceeded those of her sister kingdom. (See II Kings 21:1-16; II Chron. 33:1-9.) Verses 45-49 speak again of common punishment because of common sin.

24

(1) In the tenth day of the month.—Jehoiachin's captivity (by which all these prophecies are dated) coincided with Zedekiah's reign. The date given here is therefore the same as in Jer. 39; 50; 52:4; II Kings 25:1, and was afterward observed by

the Jews as a fast (Zech. 8:19). It was doubtless the day on which the siege of the city was completed. On the exact day on which Nebuchadnezzar besieged Jerusalem the fact was revealed to the prophet in Chaldaea, and he was commanded to declare the fate of the city by a parable (verses 3-14).

(6) Scum, that is, **rust.** The thought is that not only the inhabitants of the city are wicked, but that this wickedness is so great that the city itself (represented by the cauldron) is, as it were, corroded with rust. It is therefore to be utterly destroyed; no discrimination is to be made, so great and public had been her crimes.

(10) Spice it well.—The sense of the word translated "spice" is doubtful. It is always used in connection with the preparation of compound incense or spices, and seems therefore to refer to the thoroughness of the work: Boil thoroughly. The process is to be continued until the water in the cauldron is all evaporated, the flesh consumed, and even the bones burned.

(15) Also the word.—Ezekiel is told on the same day (verse 18) of the sudden death of his wife, who is described as deeply beloved, and yet he is forbidden to make any sign of mourning for her. On the following morning the strange conduct which had been commanded him was observed by the people; their curiosity is awakened, and they come to inquire the meaning of his actions. In reply (verses 20-24), he announces again the destruction of the Temple, and that in the depth of sorrow and trouble at its fall there shall be no outward show of mourning.

25

Here another great division of the prophecies of Ezekiel begins. Chapters 25-32 are directed entirely against foreign nations. This collection is not arranged chronologically like the rest of the book, but on the plan of putting together the prophecies against each nation. Chap. 29:17-21 is dated more than sixteen years after the fall of Jerusalem, and chap. 32 about two months after the tidings of that event; all the others which are dated are before, but only a little before, the capture of Jerusalem. Most of those undated seem to be in their chronological place, except that the first of them (chap. 25) was evidently after the fall of Jerusalem. After that

595

great judgment was made known to the prophet, there is a marked change in his utterances, and from that time his general tone is far more cheering and consolatory.

The reasons for general prophecies against the heathen, as different from the specific and more detailed ones of some of the other prophets, must be sought in the special circumstances of each case in which they were uttered. In the present instance, both the nations mentioned and the one omitted (Babylon) suggest a common purpose in the prophecy. Those mentioned are seven in number—Ammon, Moab, Edom, Philistia, Tyre, Sidon, and Egypt. All these were so far allies of Judah that they were in common hostility to Babylon; and it appears from Jer. 27:1-3 that an attempt had been made in the reign of Jehoiakim to unite five of them in a league against Babylon, while Egypt was continually looked to by the disobedient Jews for aid against their common enemy. It was, therefore, necessary for Israel to know that there was no help to be found against Babylon in any earthly power; all the enemies of Chaldaea were to fall alike. Moreover, it was important to show by these prophecies that the judgment about to come upon the surrounding heathen was from God Himself. Besides these general reasons, there were other special ones in the case of each nation.

(2) Set thy face against the Ammonites.—The Ammonites, descended from Lot's incest with his younger daughter, had been for centuries persistent enemies of Israel (Judg. 3; 11; I Sam. 11; II Sam. 10; I Kings 11; II Chron. 20). From verse 3 it appears that their hostility arose not only from national jealousy, but from a special hatred against the Jewish religion (comp. also Ps. 83:7). They are the frequent subject of prophetic denunciation (Isa. 11:14; Jer. 49:1-6; Amos 1:13-15; Zeph. 2:8-11).

(8) Moab and Seir.—The two nations, here mentioned together, are afterward treated separately—Moab, verses 8-11, and Edom, verses 12-14. Moab, springing from the same source with Ammon, was closely associated with it in its history and fortune, and is denounced in nearly the same prophecies. Additional prophecies in regard to it may be found in Num. 24:17 and Isa. 15; 16. The Moabites, as far as they were separated from the Ammonites, lay immediately to the south of them.

(12) Edom hath dealt against the house of Judah.—The reason of Edom's hostility to Israel is expressly said to be revenge. De-

scended from the elder son, they had never looked complacently on the spiritual superiority given to the descendants of the younger. (See Num. 20:18-21; II Sam. 8; I Kings 9.) At this time they not only joined the armies of Nebuchadnezzar, but appear to have urged on the conqueror to greater cruelty, and themselves to have waylaid the fugitives to cut them off (35:5). Other prophecies against Edom may be found in Num. 24:18, 19; Isa. 11:14; Jer. 49:7-12; Joel 3:19.

(15) The Philistines.—The historical books of the Old Testament are almost a continuous record of the hostility of the Philistines. Although belonging to another branch of the Hamitic family, their land was included with that of the Canaanites in the territory to be given to the Israelites (Josh. 13:2, 3). The land lay along the coast of the Mediterranean, on the highway between Egypt, Assyria, and Chaldaea, and consequently, in the struggles of those nations with each other the Philistines were gradually more and more reduced, until they disappeared entirely. The many prophecies against them include Isa. 14:29-32; Jer. 47; Amos 1:6-8; Zeph. 2:4-7.

26

Ezekiel's denunciation of Tyre occupies nearly three chapters, and each of these forms a distinct prophecy, the last verses of chap. 28 constituting a separate prophecy against the associated Phoenician city of Sidon. The first of these here consists of four sections: verses 3-6 describe the ultimate desolation of Tyre by "many nations"; verses 7-14 describe circumstantially its more immediate conquest by Nebuchadnezzar; verses 15-18 show the effect upon the islands and coasts, doubtless with reference to her colonies and those with whom she was commercially connected; verses 19-21 are an energetic repetition and summary of her doom. (See Isa. 23.)

The prediction of verses 20, 21 is that when Tyre, who is now rejoicing in the calamity of Judah, shall be past and forgotten, numbered with the dead, then God will establish His people as a living Church to Himself. A ray of Messianic promise shines through the prediction, although, for the time, it might seem nothing more than a foretelling of the restoration from the Captivity.

27

This chapter has been well called "The Dirge of Tyre." It is a lamentation over its fall, not because the prophet could wish it to be otherwise, but simply because of the terror and sorrowfulness of the event itself. The greatness of Tyre is described in full detail under the figure of a well-built ship, thoroughly manned and equipped, sailing everywhere, engaged in lucrative commerce in the central and eastern Mediterranean world; but at last, brought into rough seas and storm, she is wrecked and sinks.

28

This chapter consists of prophecies against the prince of Tyre (verses 1-19) and against Zidon (verses 20-26). In the former of these the pride of the prince is described, and he is warned of his approaching death (verses 1-10); then follows a lamentation (verses 11-19).

(2) I am a God.—The arraignment of the prince occupies verses 2-5, his consequent doom verses 6-10. The point of the charge is inordinate pride, begotten of great prosperity; this prosperity, being attributed to his own powers instead of to its true source, led him to imagine himself almost more than mortal.

The seat of God.—This expression is chosen not merely with reference to the great natural beauty and apparently impregnable position of Tyre, but also to the fact that it was called "the holy island," and looked up to by all its colonies as the central sanctuary of their worship. The Temple of Melkarth was said by the priests to have been founded as far back as 2750 B.C., and Arrian speaks of it as the oldest sanctuary in the annals of mankind.

(3) Wiser than Daniel.—This is ironically spoken. Daniel was so famed for his wisdom in the great Chaldaean Empire (Dan. 1:20; 2:48; 4:18; 5:11, 12; 6:3; etc.) that the report must have already reached Tyre. He had been in Nebuchadnezzar's court twenty years when Jerusalem fell, and the siege of Tyre was five years later.

Verses 11-19 contain the doom upon the prince of Tyre. He is represented as like the first man, perfect, and placed in Eden, until, upon his fall (verses 15, 16), he is ignominiously driven forth. The passage is strongly ironical.

(14) Upon the holy mountain of God.—

See Exod. 18:5. The prophet still has his mind upon Mount Zion, but yet the words are ironically spoken of Tyre as a venerated sanctuary, rising up from the sea.

Stones of fire.—We understand the imagery as similar to that in Rev. 2:1, and suppose the prophet to have had in mind such a passage as Exod. 24:10. This would then be one of the ways in which the king of Tyre is ironically represented as assuming to himself God-like attributes.

(15) Till iniquity was found in thee.—This and the following verse renew still more clearly the comparison with Adam. The king was altogether prosperous until his sin became manifest; then, when his heart was corrupted by his prosperity (verse 16), he was cast out for ever, like Adam from his paradise.

There are several reasons why at least a word of prophecy should have been directed especially against Zidon. In the first place, Zidon was the more ancient city from which Tyre had sprung, and always maintained her independence. Hence she might seem not to be exposed to the judgment of God upon Tyre, unless especially mentioned. Then also Zidon had been peculiarly the source of corrupting idolatrous influences upon Israel. (See Judg. 10:6; I Kings 11:33.) Idolatry reached its consummation under the reign of Ahab, who married Jezebel, the daughter of the king of Zidon and high priest of Baal (I Kings 16:31), and who set up the worship of Baal as the state religion of Israel.

(25) Sanctified in them in the sight of the heathen.—The course of God's providence is distinctly marked out in these verses of promise. Judgment upon Judah, the fall of the holy city, and the captivity of the people lead them to repentance, and thus His holiness and justice are exhibited to the world. Then comes the promise of the return, and the judgment of the ungodly enemies who have despised Judah (verse 26). This, too, shall be accomplished in its time, and then peace and prosperity shall return to Israel.

29

The series of prophecies beginning here is arranged substantially on the same plan as that against Tyre: first, a prophecy against Egypt (chaps. 29; 30); then a picture of her greatness and fall (chap. 31); and finally a dirge over her (chap. 32).

597

(1) In the tenth year, in the tenth month.—This was exactly a year and two days after the siege of Jerusalem by Nebuchadnezzar (24:1, 2; II Kings 25:1), and about six months before its fall, or seven before its destruction (II Kings 25:3-8). It must have been, therefore, after the time when the siege was temporarily raised by the approach of the Egyptians under Pharaoh-Hophra (Jer. 37:5, 11).

(4) Hooks in thy jaws.—An allusion to the ancient way of taking and destroying the crocodile ("dragon," verse 3), otherwise invulnerable to their arms.

Fish of thy rivers shall stick unto thy scales.—As the crocodile, the lord of the Nile, represents the royal power of Egypt, so the fish represent the people dependent upon him. Pharaoh is not to fall alone, but shall drag his people with him into a common ruin.

(6) A staff of reed.—See Isa. 36:6. The figure is taken from the reeds, which grew abundantly on the banks of the Nile, and the statement is historically amplified in the following verse, where the reference is to be understood not of any single fact so much as of a continual, often repeated result.

(12) Scatter the Egyptians among the nations.—The people are to pass into a condition like that of the Israelites in the wilderness, in which they were to endure the judgment of God upon their sins. This is expressed, after the manner of Ezekiel, in strong concrete terms (verses 9-11), the literal fulfillment of which was neither intended nor expected. Nebuchadnezzar, on his conquest of Egypt, sent great numbers of the people captive to Babylon; others doubtless, as in similar cases, took refuge in Ethiopia, Libya, and other neighboring lands.

(17) In the seven and twentieth year.—This is the latest date among all Ezekiel's prophecies, and is more than sixteen years after the prophecy of the former part of the chapter. This date coincides with the thirty-fifth year of Nebuchadnezzar's reign (see II Kings 25:2, 8), and, from verse 18, was evidently uttered after the close of the siege of Tyre. As that siege lasted thirteen years, it must have been begun at least as early as Nebuchadnezzar's twenty-second year, or within three years after the destruction of Jerusalem. (See note on 30:20.)

(18) Yet had he no wages.—The siege of Tyre is here represented as a service to God, for which Nebuchadnezzar had not yet received his reward. This is quite in accordance with the whole Scriptural representation of that monarch as a man raised up to execute God's judgments. He was himself unconscious of this, and yet did that which had been foretold.

(21) In that day.—These consequences were primarily the conviction of the futility of trust in any earthly aid, and hence a turning to their neglected God, and, as a result of this, the giving up of their long cherished idolatries. Israel's reviving prosperity should date from the destruction of its trust in earthly aid.

30

(3) The time of the heathen.—The judgment upon Egypt is but an individual instance, and is symbolic of general judgment upon all merely worldly power. Her fall is one step in the general overthrow of whatever exalts and opposes itself to God.

(5) Men of the land that is in league.—Jerome and Theodoret understood this expression of the Jews who had sought refuge from Nebuchadnezzar in Egypt after the murder of Gedaliah (Jer. 42; 43; 44), to whom Jeremiah had expressly prophesied that the sword and famine of which they were afraid should overtake them there (Jer. 42:16-18).

(20) The eleventh year.—See note at beginning of chap. 29. Chronologically, this passage apparently follows 29:1-16. This was the year of the fall of Jerusalem.

(21) I have broken.—This refers to the breaking of the power of Egypt by the former conquests of Assyria, and perhaps especially to the great battle of Carchemish (about twenty years before), in which Egypt received a blow from which she never recovered.

31

This chapter consists of a further prophecy against Egypt, but so couched in the form of a parable that it all relates to Assyria, except the opening (verses 1 and 2) and close (verse 18), which bring it to bear upon Egypt. Assyria had conquered and held Egypt in vassalage, and had then herself been conquered and annihilated only thirty-seven years before the date of this prophecy, and that by the same Chaldaean power now foretold as about to execute judgment upon Egypt. Egypt could not hope to resist the conqueror of her conqueror. There is this great difference between the fate of the two empires: Assyria was to be utterly supplanted by Babylonia, and its nationality blotted out, but Egypt, as the prophet had already foretold (29:14, 15), should continue, though as "a base kingdom," stripped of its supremacy.

(3) A cedar in Lebanon.—Lebanon is mentioned only because it was the place where the most famous cedars grew in their greatest perfection. Assyria did, indeed, at one time possess Lebanon, but this was never its home or seat of empire. The word "shroud" in the description refers to the thickness of the shade of the branches.

(8) The garden of God.—This is not a representation of Assyria as being in the garden of God, as in the case of Tyre in 28:13, but only a further expression of its greatness by a comparison of the tree representing it with the trees of Paradise. Yet this comparison may have been suggested by the fact that the traditional site of Eden was within the bounds of the Assyrian Empire.

(10) Among the thick boughs.—As verses 3-9 have described Assyria's greatness, so verses 10-14 speak of her fall. This was now a past event, yet is in part poetically spoken of in the future (verses 11, 13), making the whole more graphic and effective. The future may also have been used because the object of this parable is not Assyria, but Egypt, whose fall was still to come. The ground of the judgment upon Assyria is its pride (see II Kings 18:32-35).

(11) The mighty one of the heathen—the Chaldaean monarch. At the time of the fall of Assyria this was Nabopolassar, Nebuchadnezzar's father. In this verse, and partially in the next, the prophet drops his figure to make clear literal statements.

(15) I covered the deep for him.—Verses 15-17 describe the effect of Assyria's fall. Verse 15 speaks of the mourning of the nations and of the drying up of the streams, or sources of Assyria's prosperity (verse 4).

(18) To whom art thou thus like.—In this closing verse the whole chapter is brought to a point. Egypt, like Assyria in glory, shall be like her in experience of the judgments of God.

32

This chapter, which consists of two distinct prophecies (verses 1-16, 17-32), with the interval of only a fortnight between

them, closes the series at once against Egypt and against foreign nations. The former of these prophecies is a further declaration of the approaching conquest of Egypt by "the king of Babylon," while the latter is a dirge over its fall, like the dirge over Tyre in chap. 28.

(1) In the twelfth year.—This was one year and between six and seven months after the destruction of Jerusalem, and when, therefore, one great hindrance to Nebuchadnezzar's march upon Egypt had been removed. It is also nearly two months (33:21) since Ezekiel had heard of this calamity through a fugitive. It could not have been very long before the arrival of the fugitive Jews in Egypt, after the murder of Gedaliah; yet that it was somewhat earlier is plain from 33:24. (Comp. Jer. 43; 44.)

(3) Spread out my net over thee.—The figure (verses 4-6) of drawing the crocodile ("whale") to land and casting him upon the desert for food to the birds and beasts of prey is the same as in 29:4, 5. Verse 6 may be taken either of the land on which his blood is poured out, or, more probably, the land of the inundations of the Nile, now to be watered with blood.

(7) Make the stars thereof dark.—This verse follows closely Isa. 13:10, spoken of Babylon. In this and the following verse the judgments of God are described in the common prophetic figure of changes in the heavenly bodies.

(13) Will destroy also all the beasts thereof from beside the great waters.—The figurative description of this and the following verses is taken from the vast herds of cattle in Egypt going to the river to drink, and trampling the banks and disturbing the water with their feet. These represent the restless activity and stir of Egyptian life, and its constant disturbance of surrounding nations. With its conquest all this ceases, and, restrained within its own boundaries, Egypt shall no longer be a disturber.

In verses 22-30 there follows an enumeration of the most prominent of the fallen nations, with a few words about each. Some of them were not yet fallen; but in this prophetic view it is their ultimate condition which rises to the prophet's mind. All worldly power that opposes itself to God must go down and share the judgment soon to fall on Egypt.

33

At the close of his prophecies toward

foreigners, and with the renewal of his instructions to Israel, a fresh charge is given to Ezekiel as a sort of fresh induction to his prophetic office. Ezekiel uttered the prophecy of verses 1-20 on the evening before that recorded in the latter part of the chapter. This prophecy of the evening before he received the official tidings of the fall of Jerusalem is placed, like all his other prophecies (except those against foreign nations), in its proper chronological order. The prophecy itself is an amplification of the charge given in 3:16-21, but also with constant reference to chap. 18.

(21) In the twelfth year.—Comp. II Kings 25:8; Jer. 52:12. It was now a year and five months since the final destruction of Jerusalem and the Temple. This seems to be a long time to be occupied in carrying the news to Chaldea. The news itself must have reached Babylon long since, but Ezekiel was to receive the tidings, doubtless with full and circumstantial details, from the mouth of a fugitive, and there are reasons why this could not well have occurred earlier. After the capture of the city, the general, Nebuzaradan, took the mass of the people and the abundant spoil to carry them to Babylon. He first took them to Nebuchadnezzar at Riblah, where a few were executed, and some time must have been occupied in settling the affairs of the desolated land. After this, the journey of the captives, carrying along with them the weighty spoil, was a slow one, and perhaps with frequent halts. We know from Ezra 7:9 that the returning captives, not thus hindered, occupied exactly four months in the journey from Babylon to Jerusalem. This prophecy was nearly two months before that recorded in chap. 32.

(24) Inhabit those wastes.—The poor of the people were left in the land for vinedressers and for husbandmen, and these were joined by fugitive Jews from Moab and Ammon and other places. It is to these that the present part of this prophecy (verses 23-29) is addressed, and it is plain that the murder of Gedaliah, and consequent flight into Egypt, had not yet taken place.

Abraham was one . . . we are many.—The argument used by these people was a simple one: the land was promised to Abraham and his seed in perpetuity. He was but one, and the promise is fulfilled; we, his seed, are many, and it cannot fail us. These Jews, to avoid the force of the prophet's reproofs, passed from one subterfuge to another. First

600

it was that God would not abandon His holy city and Temple; then that the judgments were so far in the future that they need cause no present alarm; now, when these warnings had all been fulfilled, they clung to the fact that the land was theirs by promise, forgetting the conditions which had been attached from the first to its enjoyment. (Comp. John 8:33-39.)

(28) Most desolate.—When the people of the northern kingdom had been carried into captivity, the land had been repopulated by colonies brought from various quarters by the king of Assyria, for the ten tribes were not to return. But now the land of Judah was to be left utterly desolate and uninhabited, that it might yet be reoccupied by the returning exiles. The complete dispersion of the people, not to be effected even by war and conquest, was finally accomplished by the flight of the remnant into Egypt (Jer. 43:5-7) in consequence of their fears.

(30) The children of thy people.—The few remaining verses of this chapter are concerned with those in exile—perhaps not so much those who had been with Ezekiel all along as fresh captives of a worse moral character now just brought from Jerusalem. Yet of them all alike it was still true that they were much more ready to listen with deferential air to the words of the prophet than to take them to their hearts and act upon them in their life.

34

The latter part of the Book of Ezekiel, after the fulfillment of the great judgment in the destruction of Jerusalem, is consolatory in its character and full of rich promises to the afflicted people of God. But this necessarily involves denunciations of the oppressors and enemies of the people. Chap. 34 may be looked upon as an amplification of the short prophecy in Jer. 23:1-8.

(2) Shepherds of Israel.—This is a common Scriptural expression for rulers, and the whole context shows that these are the persons intended here. The name itself is a peculiarly appropriate one and seems to have been in use throughout the East, but expecially in Israel from the time when David was taken from the care of the flocks to feed the Lord's people.

That do feed themselves.—This selfishness is characteristic of the unfaithful shepherd (comp. John 10:1-17) and is enlarged in verses 3, 4. The history shows that for a long time it had been eminently true of the rulers, and especially of the kings of Israel. The calamities of the people are attributed to the idolatries, the oppressions, and the disobedience of their rulers (verse 5). In such a state of things, plainly the first act of mercy to the flock must be the removal of the unfaithful shepherds (verses 7-10).

(11) Behold, I, even I.—The rich promises of the following verses are all essentially contained in Jehovah Himself being the Shepherd of His flock. It is the same assurance as that given by the Saviour in John 10, and here, as there, must necessarily be understood spiritually. In the following verses many promises are given of an earthly and temporary character; these were fulfilled partly in the restoration from exile, and partly in the glorious deliverance of the Church from its foes under the Maccabees. But these deliverances themselves were types of the more glorious Messianic deliverance of the future and the necessary means whereby it was secured.

(23) My servant David.—The name of David is put here simply, as in verse 24; 37:24, 25; Jer. 30:9; Hos. 3:5, instead of the more usual designations of the Messiah as the Son, the Branch, the Offspring of David. David, as the head of the theocracy and the ancestor of our Lord after the flesh, constantly appears in the Scriptures as the type of the Messiah, and there can be no reasonable doubt that this prophecy must have been so understood, even at the time when it was uttered.

(26) Round about my hill.—"My hill" is Zion. (Comp. Isa. 31:4.) The center of the old theocracy is always spoken of in Scripture as also the center from which the new covenant of salvation goes forth. This was historically fulfilled in the coming of Christ.

(31) The flock of my pasture.—The chapter closes with the strongest and tenderest assurance that the object of its figurative language is to point out the renewed and close communion which is to come about between God and His people. They are to be His flock, and He is to be their God. Yet the vast and infinite distance between them is brought prominently forward—they are men, He is God. They were not yet prepared to understand **how** this infinite chasm could be bridged, except that it should be by their shepherd David. His Antitype was the Mediator, both God and man, thus uniting both in one.

35

Chapters 35-36:15 form one continuous prophecy, while 36:16-38 is another and distinct one. Ezekiel had already foretold the desolation of Edom (Mount Seir, 25:12-17); but in the present prophecy this becomes a foil to set off the prosperity of Israel, and in fact, under the circumstances, a necessary element of that prosperity. Moreover, as in the last chapter Israel stood as the representative of the Church of God, so here Edom and Israel, while they stand in the foreground as actually existing nations, are yet evidently regarded in the Word as representing, the one the kingdom of God, and the other all hostile powers of the world. This typical and symbolical way of looking at present things becomes increasingly prominent in all the latter part of Ezekiel.

(5) Perpetual hatred.—Enmity toward Israel is also imputed to the Ammonites, Moabites, and Philistines in chap. 25; but that of Edom was deeper and coeval with its first ancestor (see Gen. 25:22, etc., 27:41); its peculiar malignity is noticed by Amos 1:11. (Comp. also Obad. 10-15.)

(10) These two countries shall be mine.—In verses 3-9 the sin charged upon Edom is its hatred of Israel, in verses 10-15 its desire to possess itself of Israel's inheritance. The **two** nations and countries are, of course, the two kingdoms of Israel and Judah.

Whereas the Lord was there.—This fact brings out the real sin. Edom desired Israel's possessions, not as it might have desired those of other nations, but knowing that this was the peculiar inheritance given by God to His people, and which it thought ought to have been given to itself as the elder branch, thus arraying itself in direct opposition to God.

(14, 15) When all the earth shall rejoice in the salvation of God, and "the earth shall be full of the knowledge of the Lord," then Edom, the hostile power of the world, shall be desolate. The desolation of Edom, though ultimately perpetual as far as its nationality is concerned, is not inconsistent with the fact foretold by Amos (9:12), that a remnant even of Edom should at last be received into the Church. (Idumea is essentially the same country, but is a more recent name, and when it came into use the boundaries had somewhat changed.)

36

(3) In the lips of talkers, and are an infamy—a phrase equivalent to **a by-word and a reproach**. (Comp. Deut. 28:37; I Kings 9:7, etc.) "Have swallowed you up" should rather be "pant for you," the word being taken from the snuffing and panting of wild beasts. It was after this fashion that "the residue of the heathen," all those whom the conquests of Nebuchadnezzar had yet left, panted for the possession of the lands of Israel.

(8) Shoot forth your branches.—The land of Israel, represented by its mountains, is now to put forth its fruit, for the time is at hand when the people will return—a strong and vivid way of setting forth at once the certainty and the nearness of the return. Yet one cannot but feel that the language of promise goes beyond the historic fulfillment.

Verses 16-38 declare that Israel has been scattered among the heathen because they had defiled the land by their sin. Although they had yet further profaned God's name among the heathen, He had pity for that name's sake, and, accordingly, He will gather and restore Israel. The great point of the prophecy is the moral change foretold in verses 25-27, 31.

(26) A new heart.—See note on 11:19. With this prophetic preaching of the Gospel, comp. Jer. 31:31-34, and particularly the connection of that passage with the temporal promises in its continuation (verses 35-40).

37

In verses 1-14 the prophet sees a vision and is directed in consequence to utter a prophecy; in verses 15-28 he is told to perform a symbolical act and explain its meaning to the people. There is a close connection between the two, and also between the latter and the two following chapters.

(1) Which was full of bones.—The bones were not heaped together, but thickly strewn upon the face of the plain. After the prophet's mind had so long dwelt upon the desolating campaigns of Nebuchadnezzar, these ghastly reminders of the loss of human life might naturally enter into his thoughts.

(2) Very dry—as showing that it was a long time since life had left them, and that the possibility of their living again was far removed.

(3) Can these bones live?—The question is put to the prophet in order to emphasize the human impossibility of that which is immediately brought about by the divine omnipotence. It was precisely this teaching which the people needed. As they had formerly refused to believe his announcements of impending judgment, so now that this had come they were utterly incredulous in regard to his declarations of future blessing.

(5) Breath.—"Breath," "wind," and "spirit" are represented in the Hebrew by the same word, and the context must determine which sense is intended. Similarly in Greek there is the same word for the last two of these. (Comp. John 3:5-8.)

(8) No breath in them.—The restoration of the dry bones to life is described as taking place in two stages, with evident reference to the record of the creation of man in Gen. 2:7. In the first, they are restored to perfect form, but yet without life; in the second, they receive breath and become "living creatures."

(9) Upon these slain.—The bones were those not merely of dead but of slain men. In this was their likeness to Israel: as desolated, and their nationality for the time destroyed by their enemies.

(14) Put my spirit in you.—Here, as throughout this series of prophecies, the moral resurrection of the people and their restoration to their own land are intimately associated. The former was at once the necessary condition of the latter, and would also be its consequence in a still higher development. Comp. John 5:21-29.

Verses 15-28 predict that the two long-severed nations of Israel shall be reunited and prosperous under the rule of the future David, while He Himself will dwell among them, and they shall be obedient to Him. These promises prepare the way for the prophecy of the great and final attack of the enemies of the Church (chaps. 38, 39) and their overthrow by the power of God.

(16) One stick ... another stick.—The object is to represent by the two pieces of wood the two kingdoms. It would be insufficient, therefore, to mention Judah only, for with him Benjamin had been always associated, and also considerable fragments of the other tribes (II Chron. 11:16; 15:9). Joseph, as including the two great tribes of Ephraim and Manasseh, is put for the whole of the ten tribes, and Ephraim is specified as being the leading tribe.

(21) Will gather them.—The restoration of Israel from their captivity among the heathen here is the first step in the fulfillment of the divine promises. This, however, like the other promises, was fulfilled only to a "remnant," a course which (Rom. 9) had been forseen and foretold from the first. A fulfillment on a larger scale was perpetually prevented by the sins of the people; God did for them all that their obdurate disobedience would allow Him to do. Yet He did not wholly reject them, but allowed a remnant to keep alive His Church, and become the channel of those richer blessings of the new covenant, in which all who will accept His salvation are united in a holier bond and led to a land of higher promise than Israel after the flesh could ever know.

(24) David my servant.—See note on 34:23.

(27) My tabernacle also.—Comp. II Cor. 6:16. This promise was in type and shadow set before the eyes of the people with the restoration of the Temple of Zerubbabel, but in its reality began to be fulfilled at the Incarnation of the Son of God (John 1:14). It is continued by the indwelling of the Holy Spirit in the hearts of believers (I Cor. 3:16; 6:19), while it is to receive its final consummation in that future when the tabernacle of God shall be with men (Rev. 21:3-22).

38

Chapters 38 and 39 form one continuous prophecy, divided into four main parts by the renewed command to the prophet, "Son of man" (38:1, 14; 39:1, 17), and these again into smaller divisions by the repetition of the form, "Thus saith the Lord" (38:3, 10, 14, 17; 39:1, 5, 8, 10, 13, 17, 20, 25). The whole passage is to be considered as one sustained prophetic parable, in which vividness and force are given to the truth the prophet would set forth by the introduction of so many concrete details that one would be tempted to understand them literally, were it not that they carry within themselves the evidence that they were not so intended. It is to be remembered that this prophecy immediately follows chap. 37, in which God's people are represented as united in one fold, purified from their sins, and dwelling in perpetual covenant with

Him, under the care of His "servant David." (See Rev. 20:7-10, where Gog and Magog are both symbolic names of nations.)

(2) Gog, the land of Magog.—"Magog" is mentioned in Gen. 10:2 (I Chron. 1:5) in connection with Gomer (the Cimmerians) and Madai (the Medes), as the name of a people descended from Japheth. Early Jewish tradition, adopted by Josephus and Jerome, identifies them with the Scythians. But the name of Scythians must be understood in a geographical, rather than in a strictly ethnological, sense of the tribes living north of the Caucasus. Driven from their original home by the Massagetae, they had poured down upon Asia Minor and Syria shortly before the time of Ezekiel, and had advanced even as far as Egypt. Their name was a terror to the whole eastern world for their fierce skill in war, their cruelty, and their rapacity. It was probably the memory of their recent disastrous inroads that led Ezekiel to the selection of their name as the representative of the powers hostile to the Church of God.

The chief prince of Meshech and Tubal.—Rather, **the prince of Rosh, Meshech, and Tubal.** Rosh refers to a Scythian tribe dwelling in the Taurus, although the attempt to derive from it the name of **Russian** cannot be considered as sufficiently supported. Meshech and Tubal are Moschi and Tibareni, between the Black and Caspian Seas, famous for dealing in slaves and copper.

(4) I will turn thee back.—The meaning is not the turning back from the holy land. It is to be taken in the sense in which it is used in Isa. 47:10 and Jer. 8:5: "I will lead thee astray." In Rev. 20:8, this leading astray of the nations is ascribed to Satan, just as in II Sam. 24:1, God, and in I Chron. 21:1, Satan, are said to move David to number the people; in either case God is said to do that which He allows to be done by Satan. (See Joel 3:2; Zech. 14:2, 3.)

(5) Persia, Ethiopia, and Libya.—Having summoned the nations from the extreme north, the prophet now turns first to the east, and then to the south and west. No neighboring nations are mentioned at all, but only those living on the confines of the known world are summoned to this symbolic contest. The supposition of a literal alliance of nations so situated is out of the question.

(6) Gomer ... Togarmah.—Again the address turns to the extreme north. Gomer, like Magog, is a people descended from Japheth and identified with the Cimmerians; the house of Togarmah refers to the Armenians. This was to be a general gathering of the strength of the world against the Church of God.

(7) Be thou a guard unto them.—Every preparation is to be made on the part of Gog and the nations, and then Gog himself is to be their guard, or to control and guide the assault.

(8) After many days thou shalt be visited.—The words are the usual form of expressing a coming judgment. The whole course of God is viewed here together as a single transaction. It is not merely his ultimate destruction, but the steps which led to it, his hostile attacks upon the Church, which are represented as brought about under God's providence and forming a part of the visitation upon him. It is as if one spoke now of a man's whole career of sin as a divine visitation upon the sinner in consequence of his neglect of proffered grace, instead of speaking only of his ultimate punishment.

(10) Think an evil thought.—In verses 10-14 the motives of Gog in his attack upon Israel are fully exposed. It is to be remembered that in verse 4, and again in verse 16, the leading of this foe against the Church is represented as God's own act; here it is explained that God did this by allowing him to follow out the devices of his own heart.

(12) In the midst of the land.—Literally, **in the navel of the earth**. (See note on 5:5.)

(13) Sheba, and Dedan ... Tarshish.—The first two are districts of Arabia, and the last is probably the Tartessus in Spain. These names seem to be added to those of verses 5, 6, to show that all the nations of the world sympathize in this attack upon the Church.

(14) Shalt thou not know it?—The second part of this prophecy (verses 14-23), describing the doom of God, is introduced (verses 14-16) with a repetition of the peaceful security of Israel, and of God's leading against her this great foe in whose destruction He shall be magnified before all people.

(17) Of whom I have spoken in old time. But the name of Gog is not mentioned in any earlier prophecy now extant. This concurs with many other indications in the prophecy to show that it does not relate to any particular event, but that Gog and

his allies represent the enemies of the Church in general, and that the prophet is here depicting the same great and prolonged struggle between evil and good, between the powers of the world and the kingdom of God, which has formed the burden of so much of both earlier and later prophecy.

39

(6) A fire on Magog.—Magog is the country of Gog (38:2), and the divine judgment is to fall therefore not only upon the army in the land of Israel, but also upon the far-distant country of Gog. In Rev. 20:9 this fire is represented as coming "down from God out of heaven."

In the isles.—This common Scriptural expression for the remoter parts of the earth is added here to show the universality of the judgment upon all that is hostile to the kingdom of God.

Verses 11-16 again present the magnitude of the attack upon the Church by describing the burial of the host after it is slain. The language, if it could be supposed it was meant to be literally understood, would be even more extravagant than that of verses 9, 10.

(11) The valley of the passengers.—This denotes some (probably imaginary) thoroughfare, which is to be blocked by the buried bodies of the slain. No definite locality is assigned to it, except that it is on the east of the Dead Sea. It was to be, therefore, on the extreme southeastern outskirts of the land.

The valley of Hamon-gog—The valley of the multitude of Gog. (See verses 15, 16.)

(16) Thus shall they cleanse the land.—The extremest defilement, according to the Mosaic law, was caused by a dead body or by human bones. From this the land could be purified only by the burial of the last vestige of the host of Gog. In the spiritual contest which this prophecy is designed to set forth under these material figures, this cleansing looks to the purification of the Church from everything "that defileth and is unclean." (Comp. Eph. 5:26, 27; Rev. 21:27.)

With verse 17 the last part of this remarkable prophecy is introduced. Its representations are not to be considered as subsequent to those of the former part of the chapter, but as depicting the same thing under another figure.

40

These closing chapters of Ezekiel form one continuous prophecy of a distinctly marked character. They present a vision of the Temple in minute detail, with careful measurements of its parts; various ordinances for the Temple, for the Levites and the priests, and for the prince; A new and remarkable division of the land; and the vision of the life-giving waters issuing from the sanctuary. The whole passage differs too much from anything in the past to allow for a moment the supposition that it is historical in character; and uttered, as it was, at a time when the Temple lay in ashes, and the land desolate, it is equally clear that it cannot describe the present. It must, therefore, have been prophetic, a symbolic representation rather than an actual image of things. If the literal sanctuary and state of restoration had been meant, it is inconceivable that there should be no allusion to the language of Ezekiel in the historical books of Ezra and Nehemiah, and in the prophecies of Haggai, which all relate to this period and describe the return and settlement in the land and the rebuilding of the Temple.

(1) In the five and twentieth year.—This was fourteen years after the destruction of Jerusalem. A substantial period had, therefore, elapsed in which this great judgment would have produced its effect upon the minds of the exiles. There was thus now occasion for bringing before them the brighter hopes of the future.

(2) In the visions of God.—This expression presupposes that what follows is not to an actual image of existing things, but a symbolic representation of their substance.

Upon a very high mountain.—Comp. Isa. 2:2; Mic. 4:1. This cannot apply literally to the hill of Moriah, surrounded by greater heights, but is frequently used to mark the spiritual importance of the Temple site.

(5) By the cubit and an hand breadth.—It is difficult to fix with precision the length of the cubit of Scripture, especially as the value of the measure appears to have changed in the course of ages. Ezekiel adds "an hand breadth" to the common cubit. Different writers vary in their estimate of the length of the measure thus obtained from eighteen to twenty-four inches. Considering it twenty inches provides a convenient number for use and cannot be far wrong. The "reed of six cubits" was therefore about ten feet long.

41

This chapter gives the measurements and describes the ornaments of the Temple itself and its various appurtenances. It is noticeable how very little is said of its interior furniture and arrangements. There is no mention at all of that profuse overlaying with gold so characteristic of Solomon's Temple; nothing is said of the candlestick, or the table of showbread; even the Ark itself, that 'climax of Israel's symbolic worship, is not mentioned. The prophet seems to be looking forward to the time described by his contemporary, Jeremiah, when these outward symbols should be forgotten in the higher spiritual presence of the Lord (Jer. 3:16, 17).

42

This chapter describes what is not only new in this vision, but also unknown in either the former or the later Temple—certain chambers for the priests, together with explanations of their purposes.

43

The new Temple had now been shown to the prophet with all its arrangements and measurements; it remained that the structure should be divinely accepted by the manifestation of the glory of the Lord, as in the case of the Tabernacle (Exod. 40:34, 35) and of the former Temple (I Kings 8:10, 11; II Chron. 5:13, 14; 7:1-3). The description of this and the accompanying message occupy verses 1-12. With verse 13 begins the account of the ordinances of divine worship to be celebrated in the Temple, the altar for the sacrifices, the central act of the ancient worship, being the focal point. This matter is continued to the close of chap. 46.

44

The altar being consecrated, the next thing is to provide for the purity of the worship of which it is the center. The pollutions of former times had been largely introduced by the princes, and by the Levites and priests; these classes are therefore treated in this chapter.

45

This chapter describes the setting apart of a large portion of the whole land for the sanctuary, the priests, the prince, and the city, in a way and in a geographical position entirely unknown either in the past or in the subsequent history of the people. Directions are given concerning the daily sacrifices and the feasts, these feasts being in part unknown to the law, while some feasts that were prominent in the law are entirely omitted, with the ritual of nearly all greatly changed. The whole is so different from the arrangements of the Mosaic economy, and so foreign to the restoration of that economy on the return from the exile, that it can be explained only of an ideal picture which both prophet and people understood was not to receive a literal realization.

46

The first fifteen verses of this chapter, concerning the prince and his role in the matter of sacrifice, belong to chap. 40. The prophet then goes on to provide for the sacrifices for the Sabbaths and new moons, for free-will offerings, and for the daily sacrifices.

47

The ideal character of this "vision of the living waters" (verses 1-12) is immediately clear. Passages in which water is used as the symbol of the influence of the Spirit are numerous and familiar. (Comp. Isa. 44:3; Ezek. 36:25-27; Zech. 13:1, etc.) Ezekiel, having in the previous chapters described the dwelling of the Lord among His people with characteristic minuteness of detail, now proceeds to set forth the blessing that flow from this presence. Verses 13-23 properly belong to chap. 48, and give the boundaries of the land to be divided among the tribes, together with provision for the inheritance of strangers living among them.

48

The closing chapter of Ezekiel is occupied mainly with the distribution of the land in detail. Beginning at the north, a portion is assigned to each of seven tribes (verses 1-7); then the "oblation" is described, with its parts for the Levites, the priests and Temple, the city and those that serve it, and the prince (verses 8-22); and lastly portions are assigned for the remaining five tribes. The chapter and the book close with an account of the size and the twelve gates of the city, the whole ending with its name, "The Lord is there."

The distribution of the land is entirely different from that made under Joshua, nor is it easy to trace any historical reasons for it, except that the central portion, containing the Temple, the land of the priests and the prince, is flanked by the two tribes of the southern kingdom, Judah and Benjamin. The tribes are not arranged either according to their seniority or their maternity. The territory falling to each tribe was much smaller than of old, partly because of the large space occupied by the "oblation" (fully one-fifth of the whole), and partly because the remainder was to be divided among the whole twelve tribes instead of among only nine and a half. The portion thus given to each tribe was less than two-thirds that assigned, on the average, by Joshua.

DANIEL

1

Of the personal history of this great seer nothing is known beyond what is recorded of him in the Book of Daniel. Being apparently of royal descent (1:3), and when still a youth, he was taken to Babylon captive by Nebuchadnezzar in the fourth year of Jehoiakim. As history does not state that he ever revisited his native land, it is highly probable that he continued in the East from the year of his exile until the third year of Cyrus, which is the last date mentioned in the book. Here his position and his well-known character, no doubt, enabled him to render much aid to his fellow countrymen, whether at home or in exile.

The Book of Daniel is anonymous. No title is prefixed to it such as appears in the case of the books of Isaiah or Jeremiah. But chaps. 7-12 present Daniel speaking in the first person; and although in chaps. 1-6 he is presented in the third person, the language and uniformity of style throughout attest a single authorship from the Babylonian-Persian period.

(1) In the third year.—The word "came" means "went," as Gen. 45:17; II Kings 5:5, and it is the natural word for a Hebrew to use who wrote from Babylon, and may be translated "marched." It is therefore implied in this verse that Nebuchadnezzar started from Babylon in the third year of Jehoiakim. The rest of the history is easily supplied from other portions of Scripture. In the fourth year of Jehoiakim he conquered Pharaoh at Carchemish (Jer. 46:2), and then advanced upon Jerusalem.

(2) His god—i.e., Bel-Merodach, who was originally an Accadian deity, the significance of the second part of the name being "he that measures the path of the sun." The planet Jupiter was worshiped under this name. He was the tutelary god of Babylon, and to his honor Nebuchadnezzar dedicated a temple. (See Baruch 6:14, 15. On Shinar, see note on Gen. 10:10.)

(3) The king's seed.—According to the story of Josephus (*Ant.* X 10, 1), Daniel and the three holy children were all connected with Zedekiah. The context makes this opinion perfectly admissible.

(4) It appears, from comparing this with verse 19, that some form of examination was held by the king before he admitted the courtiers into his immediate service. The language of Chaldaea at this time was Sem-

itic; but there was a sacred language in use besides, which probably belonged to the Turanian family. In both these languages Daniel was educated.

(5) Three years.—The king appears to have had sufficient insight into the extraordinary character of these youths to enable him to prescribe not only the subjects of their studies, but also the length of their course of instruction. It appears that Nebuchadnezzar was a man of far higher character than many Assyrian and Babylonian kings. We shall see that his heart was fitted for the reception of divine truth, and that in the end he was brought to know the true God.

(6) Now among these . . . —The narrative of the book is concerned with only four people. Daniel calls our attention to the fact that the four whom Providence had endowed with the greatest natural gifts were those by whose example the king was converted. The names of these four were subsequently changed, with the view of showing that they had become nationalized Chaldee subjects. (Comp. II Kings 23:34, 24:17.) The name Belteshazzar is said to mean "protect his life." Abed-nego is apparently "Servant of Nebo." Shadrach and Meshach have not been explained.

(8) Daniel purposed in his heart.—He was cautious from the first. He feared that he might eat something that had been consecrated to idols. (See I Cor. 8.)

(9) Into favour.—The similarities between Daniel and Joseph are many. Each finds favor with his master, and afterward with a foreign monarch. The grace of God enables each to overcome the temptations into which his circumstances lead him; the acute natural faculties of each are miraculously increased by God; and each is sent into a foreign land to comfort exiled Israel. (See Gen. 39:21; I Kings 8:50; Neh. 1:11; Ps. 106:46.)

(15) Appeared fairer.—Thus was God beginning to assert His power among the Babylonians. This change in the appearance of Daniel was the effect of his free grace, not of the meat that came from the king's palace.

(17) Learning and wisdom.—These appear to be contrasted in this verse. The former refers to literature, and implies the knowledge of secular subjects; the latter implies philosophy and theology, and perhaps, also, an acquaintance with the meaning of portents.

(18) At the end of the days, i.e., the three

years specified in verse 5. Before the conclusion of this time, it appears (2:1), Daniel was enabled to give a proof of his wisdom. (See 2:28.)

(21) Continued.—The phrase does not mean that "he prophesied," but that he lived until the time specified; by no means implying that he died in the first year of Cyrus. This year is specified on account of its importance to the Jewish people as the year of their deliverance. We are led to think of Daniel during this period holding high positions in the courts of Nebuchadnezzar, Belshazzar, and Darius, yet so using the things of this world that at the close of his life (10:11) he became the man greatly beloved by God.

2

(1) The second year.—Nebuchadnezzar was proleptically spoken of as "king of Babylon" in 1:1, for his father did not die until after the battle of Carchemish. (On the reign of Nebuchadnezzar, see note on II Kings 24:1.)

Dreams.—The one dream (verse 3) consisted of several parts. For the effects of the dream upon the king's mind, comp. Gen. 41:8.

His sleep brake.—The anxiety which the vision caused him prevented him from sleeping again. And no wonder. The battle of Carchemish, which forced Egypt to retire within her ancient frontiers, had indeed made Nebuchadnezzar master of all the district east of the Euphrates; but there was a growing Median power north of him, which he may have dreaded.

(2) Probably the Chaldaeans spoken of in this verse did not form a separate class of magicians, but denoted the priests, and was contained in the first class of magicians mentioned in the verse. It appears that Daniel excelled (1:17) in all classes of magic learning.

(3) I have dreamed.—It has been questioned whether the king had really forgotten his dream, or whether he only pretended to have done so in order that he might prove the skill of his wise men (comp. verse 10). It is more in accordance with what is stated about the anxious condition of the king's mind to assume that he remembered a portion of the dream, but that he had lost the general outline of it.

(4) In Syriack.—Probably a fresh title, indicating to the copyist that the Chaldee

portion of the book begins here. It has been conjectured that 2:4-7:28 is a Chaldee translation of an original Hebrew work, but there is no authority for the conjecture. God is about to reveal facts connected with the Gentile world, and therefore a Gentile language is used as the vehicle of the revelation. (See Matt. 2:1, 2; I Tim. 2:3, 4).

Live for ever.—For this common form of salutation, comp. 3:9, 5:10, etc.

(9) There is but one decree.—He refers to the decree (verse 5) that both the dream and the interpretation must be told.

Ye have prepared ... be changed—i.e., "you have made an agreement among yourselves to postpone the matter until a more lucky time for explaining the dream shall come." On Eastern notions about fortunate days, comp. Esther 3:7.

(11) A rare thing—i.e., a difficult matter. Here the reference is to a doctrine of Babylonian theology, according to which every man from his birth onward had a special deity attached to him as his protector. The deity, being united to the man, became a partaker of human infirmities. Even these deities, the wise men urge, cannot do what the king requires. Such wisdom belongs only to the gods whose dwelling is apart from man.

(16) Daniel went in.—We are not told in so many words that this extension of time was granted, or that Daniel undertook to show more than the interpretation of the dream. A true account of what happened can be gathered only by reading verses 18 and 28 by the side of this verse. Many narratives of Scripture are related in a condensed form, fuller details being added afterward.

(18) The God of heaven.—We meet with this title of Almighty God for the first time in Gen. 24:7. After the Captivity, it frequently designates the true God as contrasted with the heathen gods. (See Ezra 1:2; Neh. 1:5; Ps. 136:26.) It is used by Daniel in this sense in this verse.

(20) Blessed be the name.—Daniel's prayer is for the most part framed upon the model of Scriptural language, while on the other hand it appears to have been adapted to their own special needs by later pious servants of God. The Doxology, with which it begins, is founded upon the liturgical formula concluding Ps. 41, the substance of it being repeated by Nehemiah (Neh. 9:5).

(24) Therefore—i.e., now that he knows the dream and the interpretation. Daniel approached the king through Arioch (as we must suppose in verses 15 and 16), for it is probable that the Babylonian custom, like the Persian (Esther 5:1) or Median (Herod. 1.99), did not permit any persons except the principal officers of state to have direct access to the royal presence.

Destroy not.—Observe Daniel's humanity toward his heathen teachers. It was owing to his intercession only that the king's decree was not carried out. (See Ezek. 14:14.)

(26) Art thou able.—What surprises him is, that after the wise and experienced had failed to tell him his dream, one so young and a mere novice should succeed.

(27) The secret ... —In this and the next verse Daniel justifies the astonishment of the king, and explains to him that what the wise men had stated was perfectly true. Daniel here teaches us what Scripture lays down elsewhere (Gen. 20:3; 41:16, 25, 28; Num. 22:35), that all power of prediction is to be excluded from heathen gods, and is possessed by wise men only so far as they acquire it through the God of heaven.

(29) Hereafter—i.e., in the course of history, not only in the Messianic days.

(31) A great image.—Properly, "one great image." This is one important feature in the vision. The image, though representing many things, was itself only "one." That the image was of human form is evident from the further descriptions of the various parts of the body given in verses 32, 33, 42. The "greatness" of the image implies the magnificence and size of it. Throughout the various parts it represented the many complex phases of the one history of the world.

(32) Breast ... —It should be remarked that though many different parts of the body of the image are mentioned, Daniel regards the whole thing as made up of only four parts, each corresponding to one of the four metals. Similarly he shows the history of the world in its relation to God's people, complicated though it may be and varied in its aspect, consists of no more than four principal parts. It will be noticed that by the additional matter mentioned in verses 41, 42, certain minor complications of history are intended, which, however, do not interfere with the fourfold division of which the outline is here given.

(35) Like the chaff.—This language recalls Ps. 1:4. It is emblematic of divine judgments (Isa. 41:15, 16; Jer. 51:33, etc.). Comp. the description of the Judgment (7:9-14). Observe, however, that the stone did not crush the head, breast, or loins of the body.

These became fragments by falling when the feet were broken.

(36) We—i.e., Daniel and his three friends, for to their intercession (verses 17, 18) the revelation was due.

(37, 38) Interpretation of the vision. Nebuchadnezzar, who reigned forty-three years, is the head; or, in other words, he is the first of the four kingdoms which are denoted by the image. His kingdom was the largest that the world until then had known.

(39) Another kingdom.—The second kingdom is the Medo-Persian. The inferiority is to be found in the divided character of that empire, as compared with the massive solidity of its predecessor. This is signified in the image, partly by the inferiority of the metal, silver instead of gold, and partly of the symbol of division, the **two** breasts opposed to the **one** head. It must not be forgotten that in other respects, such as extent of territory and duration of empire, the Medo-Persian far exceeded the Babylonian kingdom.

Another third.—The metal implies a certain inferiority, but the phrase "shall bear rule over the whole earth" speaks of an empire that extended further than the preceding. This is the Graeco-Macedonian Empire (comp. 7:6; 8:5-7).

(40) And the fourth.—The description of this kingdom is much fuller than those of the preceding empires. The same fact holds for the later visions (7:7, 8, 19, 20).

Breaketh all these.—Remembering that the comparison is between iron and the fourth empire, this portion of the vision implies that the Roman empire will crush out all traces that remain of preceding empires, just as iron is capable of breaking gold, silver, or copper. Of the second and third empires, each borrowed something from that which preceded it. The fourth empire introduces a new system, and a new civilization.

(42) So the kingdom.—This strength, however, is only apparent. There are certain discordant elements in the fourth empire. These are here represented by the iron and clay, which cannot be made to cohere.

(43) Seed of men.—Daniel appears to be contrasting what man is endeavoring to accomplish by his own efforts with that which the God of heaven (verse 44) will carry out. (Comp. Jer. 31:27). Man will form his plans for uniting the discordant parts of this empire by encouraging marriages between the royal families that rule the various component kingdoms.

(44) In the days of these kings.—Yet no kings have been mentioned heretofore. They must therefore correspond to the toes of the image. It appears that while this fourth kingdom still schemes to exist in some modified form, while its component parts are in a state of war and turmoil, the kingdom of God shall come. (Comp. 7:24-27.)

(45) The stone was cut out of the mountain. —The mountain was not mentioned in verse 34. In the language of prophecy, it must mean Mount Zion, which appears in other passages to be closely connected with the Messiah and His kingdom, e.g., Isa. 2:2; Ps. 50:2. The stone is set free from this mountain; and as it rolls on in its destructive course, it overthrows all the kingdoms of the world, becoming a mountain which fills the whole earth. (The Messiah is elsewhere spoken of under the figure of a stone: Isa. 28:16; Matt. 21:42). The phrase "cut without hands" refers to the supernatural agency by which the stone accomplishes its work. As empire after empire passes away, while the history of the world remains continuous, such is not the case with the stone. The work that it does is instantaneous. The moment it falls on the feet of the image the whole collapses, or, in other words, the history of the world comes to an end. Such is the relation in which the kingdom of God stands to the kingdoms of this world. They are all transient, in spite of their apparent strength, and their history will cease, as soon as the "stone shall fall and grind them to powder" (Matt. 21:44).

(46) Worshipped.—The Hebrew word employed here is always used of paying adoration to an idol. Probably the king imagined that the gods were dwelling in Daniel in a higher sense from that in which they dwelt with his other wise men, and worshipped them on account of the marvellous revelation which they had granted to him through the means of Daniel.

(47) God of gods.—He does not acknowledge Jehovah as the true God, but deems Him worthy of a place in the Babylonian Pantheon.

(49) Over the affairs.—Comp. Neh. 2:16; Esther 3:9. These holy children, it appears from this verse, were satraps under Daniel's supervision.

Gate of the king.—Comp. Esther 3:2. Daniel was of higher rank than his three friends, and was therefore admitted into the inner part of the palace.

3

(1) An image.—If this image were made after the manner described (Isa. 44:9-20), the body was formed of wood, and the whole, when properly shaped, was covered with thin plates of gold. As the height of the whole is disproportionate to the width, it is probable that the height of the pedestal on which the image stood is included under the sixty cubits. This was probably an image of Bel Merodach, and the occasion its dedication.

(6) Shall . . . be cast . . .—This punishment was not uncommon among the Babylonians. One instance of it is mentioned in Jer. 29:22. The occasion being a national festival, any refusal to worship the national gods would be regarded as high treason. Any foreign subjects would be expected to take part in the ceremony, their gods being supposed to have been conquered, and being regarded as demons. (Comp. II Kings 19:12; II Chron. 28:23.)

(8) Wherefore i.e., because certain Jews were noticed to be absent at the time. It is natural to suppose that the promotion of three men of Jewish extraction would have been viewed with the greatest jealousy by the Babylonian officers, who, no doubt, had been carefully watching their opportunity of revenge. (Comp. 5:11.)

(12) Whom thou hast set.—The high position of these men is mentioned partly to explain the king's anger on account of his supposed ingratitude, and partly to account for the malice and jealousy of their accusers. But why was Daniel absent from the ceremony? His behavior some years later (6:10) leaves it beyond question that he would not have taken part in any idolatrous rites. Possibly his position as "chief of the wise men" (2:48) made his presence unnecessary.

(16, 17) They mention the king by name, so as to make their address correspond with his (verse 14). His attention would in this way be directed to the strong antithesis between his statement (verse 15) and theirs. Great though the distinction was between king and subject in such a country as Babylon, yet that distinction was lost when any collision occurred between duty to Jehovah and obedience to a royal edict. The three holy children are quite content to leave the whole matter in the hands of Providence. They know that the law of obedience is the first law of all, and this they are resolved to keep. There is not the slightest ground for supposing that they expected a miraculous deliverance. Their language implies no more than faithful obedience. (See Isa. 43:2.)

(22) Urgent.—The king's command had been uttered while he was in a furious rage, and in consequence of this, the furnace was raised to so high a temperature that the executioners were slain. The death of the executioners forms an evident contrast with the deliverance of those who had been sentenced to die.

(25) The Son of God.—These words, let us remember, are uttered by a heathen king, who calls this same Person, in verse 28, "an angel" of the God whom the three children worshiped. Probably Nebuchadnezzar thought that He stood to Jehovah in the same relation that he himself did to Merodach. His conceptions of the power of Jehovah were evidently raised by what he had witnessed, though as yet he does not recognize Him as being more than a chief among gods. He has not risen to that conception of the unity of God which is essential to His absolute supremacy. But still the question has to be answered, What did the king see? The early patristic interpretation was that it was none other than Christ Himself. We have no means of ascertaining anything further, and must be content with knowing that the same "Angel of God's presence" who was with Israel in the wilderness watched over the people in Babylon.

4

(1) Peace ...—The date of the matter recorded in this chapter cannot be ascertained, as a blank falls upon the last eighteen years of Nebuchadnezzar's reign. By this time, however, the king has become so powerful that he regards himself as universal monarch, so that some time must have elapsed since the events mentioned in the last chapter.

(2) Signs and wonders.—Comp. Isa. 8:18. The appearance of various Scriptural phrases in this letter leads us to believe that Daniel must have written it at the king's request.

(10) A tree.—For this symbol of majesty, comp. Ezek. 31:3, etc. (The dream of Cambyses [Herod. 1.108] was of a similar nature.) The tree could be seen from the most distant parts of the known world (verse 11.)

(15) A band.—As the vision continues, the typical language is gradually laid aside, and it begins to appear that by the tree a man is intended. We must not understand by "the band" the chains by which the unfortunate king would be confined, but metaphorically trouble and affliction, as Pss. 107:10; 149:8. The inscriptions of Nebuchadnezzar, and accounts of his reign written by historians, being all composed with the view of glorifying the monarch, naturally suppress all mention of his madness.

(16) Seven times.—The period intended is very uncertain. It is probable that the expression is used to signify some definite period of time, which, as appears from the words "over him," was in some way marked out by the heavenly bodies.

(17) Ruleth ...—i.e., Almighty God disposes of human empires as He pleases. (Comp. 5:21.)

(22) This gives us to understand that Nebuchadnezzar had arrived at the zenith of his power. The extent of his dominions may be estimated with tolerable accuracy as follows: Northward he possessed Armenia, and a considerable portion of Asia Minor; in the west, Syria, and at one time Egypt; southward, his power reached the Persian Gulf; while in the east, the Medes and Elamites were subject to him. Possessing, as he did, the Mediterranean and the Persian Gulf, all the treasures of the known world were at his command. In his first vision he was represented as the golden head of the image. In his pride he desired the whole image to be of gold, and himself to be the image—but this was the sin for which he was to suffer.

(26) They commanded.—In verse 13 the command is only ascribed to one of the watchers. This makes it appear that they form a council in which one acts in behalf of all.

Shall be sure.—No successor shall be appointed during his life. The "stump" remained, anticipating that green branches might shoot forth again (verse 15).

Do rule—i.e., the heavens, or One in heaven ruleth the kingdoms of men.

(27) Break off.—The metaphor is taken from a refractory beast casting off the yoke. Daniel therefore counsels the king to rebel against his sins, such as pride, harshness, and cruelty toward his captives, and to put all these sins aside. And how can he do this in a better manner than by practicing the contrary virtues?

(30) Great Babylon.—The area of Babylon is said to have been 200 square miles. It was surrounded by walls 85 feet in width, 335 feet high. In these were brazen gates leading to various terraces which faced the river Euphrates. Within the walls the city was laid out in smaller towns, separated from each other by parks, plantations, and gardens; in fact, it is stated that corn sufficient for the whole population could be grown within the walls. There were also magnificent public buildings. Nebuchadnezzar mentions no less than eight temples which he completed, besides the huge temple of Merodach immediately across the Euphrates facing the royal palace. Walking on the flat roof of this palace, and with this grand spectacle before him, the king uttered these words. True, indeed, they were, but they show that during the twelve months which had been allotted to the king for repentance his pride remained unabated; he had not repented as Daniel had counselled him.

(33) The thing fulfilled.—The malady of Nebuchadnezzar was a form of mania known as lycanthropy. The peculiar features of it mentioned in this verse are partially connected with the life which the sufferer's delusion forced him to lead. It appears, however, that he retained his consciousness, as "he lifted up his eyes to heaven" (verse 34) before "his understanding" returned to him. It is remarkable to observe that an interval is mentioned in his inscription during which he executed no great public works.

(34) Whose dominion . . . —It is hard to suppose that the king was so thoroughly versed in the Hebrew Scriptures that he should be able to make use of them as doxologies. This gives support to the conjecture that the letter was composed by Daniel and not by the king.

(37) The King of heaven.—How far the king arrived at a belief in one God is not clear. There was, however, a progress in his spiritual character, effected by the grace of God, after each of the interviews which he held with the prophet. (Comp. 2:26, 47; 3:15.) This thanksgiving here makes it possible to suppose that he had relinquished much of his belief in his former superstitions, and that he was advancing toward, if not actually in possession of, the truth.

5

(1) Belshazzar.—As he was the son of Nabonidus, a space of about thirty years must have elapsed since the event recorded in the last chapter. The Babylonian empire survived the death of Nebuchadnezzar only twenty-five years.

(2) The sacred vessels were brought out of the temple of Merodach, and profaned in this manner for the purpose of defying Jehovah. But what led him to think of Jehovah in the midst of the revelry? It may have been that some drunken fancy seized him. It may have been that he had been warned that the prophets of Jehovah had foretold the overthrow of Babylon by Cyrus, whose armies were now in the neighborhood. Whatever the true explanation may be, there can be no doubt that the whole act was one of defiance of Jehovah (verses 4, 23).

(5) In the same hour—i.e., suddenly and unexpectedly. Observe that it was only a portion of the hand that the king saw (comp. verse 24), and that we are not told whether the guests saw the hand or not. That the writing was visible to all is plain from verse 8. As in other supernatural manifestations recorded in Scripture, a portion only has been witnessed by many, while the whole has been seen only by one or by a few. (Comp. John 12:28, 29; Acts 9:7.)

Candlestick.—This, of course, would make both the hand and the writing more distinctly visible to the king.

(8) Then—i.e., after the king had addressed the wise men whom he had summoned. But why could they not read an inscription which Daniel deciphered at first sight? The only true explanation is to be found in the supernatural character of the inscription, and in the inspiration of Daniel. In this way God asserts Himself against the false wisdom of the heathen.

(9) The terror of Belshazzar and his lords is caused by the impression that the inability of the wise men to read the inscription is the portent of some terrible calamity.

(11) Thy father.—No blood relationship is necessarily implied by this word. It means no more than "predecessor." (See note on verse 1.)

(13) And the king spake.—The words of the queen mother, especially her mention of the circumstance that Daniel's name had been changed to Belteshazzar, at once recalls the whole of the circumstances to the king's mind. That Belshazzar knew him by reputation is plain from the description given of him at the end of the verse. He calls him by his Hebrew name, so as to avoid one which sounded so much like his own. Daniel was now nearly ninety years of age.

(21) His dwelling ... —This is a fact supplementary to what is stated in chap. 4.

(22) Though thou knewest.—The whole history of Nebuchadnezzar was known to Belshazzar. He had not, however, learned the moral lesson conveyed by it. He was therefore doubly guilty in the sight of God, because his blasphemy was willful.

(25) Mene ... —The word **Mene**, "numbered," is repeated twice for the sake of emphasis. The days of Babylon are numbered; it is God Himself who has numbered them. "Mene" is used in the double sense of "numbering" and "bringing to an end." Similarly, **Tekel** implies both the act of "weighing" and the fact of "being light." It appears from verse 28 that the divided empire of Babylon and the Medo-Persian empire are signified.

6

(2) Three presidents.—See 5:7. If there had been a triumvirate in Babylon, Darius continued the form of government which he found already existing, and retained Daniel in the official post to which he had been promoted by Belshazzar.

(4) Concerning the kingdom—i.e., "in his official capacity." The plan of the conspirators was to place Daniel, who "was preferred" (literally, "he outshone," verse 3) above the others, in such a situation that his civil and religious duties might be forced to clash with each other. This conspiracy was evidently the result of jealousy on the part of the other officers at the advancement of Daniel.

(7) All the presidents.—The spokesman represents all these officers to have come to a fixed determination after due deliberation. This was false, as it is plain from verse 24 that all were not involved in the conspiracy. The object of the decree was political, as well as hostile toward Daniel. By consenting to the plan proposed, Darius would acknowledge the Babylonian system of theology, according to which the king was "the living manifestation of all the gods," while, at the same time, his subjects would have an opportunity of doing him religious homage. Probably this prevented the king from perceiving any plot against Daniel.

(10) Toward Jerusalem.—On the custom of praying thus, see I Kings 8:33, 35; Pss. 5:7; 28:2; and on prayer at the intervals mentioned here, see Ps. 55:17. There is nothing ostentatious in Daniel's prayer. He removed the lattices (see Ezek. 40:16) from his window, that he might see as far as possible in the direction of Jerusalem, and then continued his devotions just as though the king's decree had not been recorded. The prophet must by this time have been near ninety years of age, but still his faith is as firm and unwavering as was that of his three companions many years before.

(16) They brought Daniel.—By adding that he was a foreigner (verse 13), Daniel's antagonists expected further to incense the king. According to Eastern custom, the sentence was generally executed on the day when it was pronounced. This explains why the king's efforts to commute the sentence were prolonged until sunset (verse 14). The lions were probably kept here for sporting purposes. The form of the den is unknown, but the etymology suggests a vaulted chamber.

(20) Is thy God ... able?—The faith of this king is very weak. In verse 16 he expressed a vague hope that God would protect His servant. That hope seems now to have died out, though afterward (verse 26) it appears stronger than that of Nebuchadnezzar (comp. 4:37). The phrase "living God" is remarkable, coming as it does from a heathen king. (See I Sam. 17:36.)

(28) So this Daniel.—The first part of the book, which terminates here, concludes with a notice similar to that in 2:48 and 3:30. The history of Daniel and of the three holy children has thus far been traced in its relation to their work among the people in the midst of whom they were living as exiles. The purpose of the miracles which God wrought in behalf of His servants all tended to exalt Him in the eyes of the Gentiles. The second part of the book speaks of the future destinies of the kingdoms of the world in relation to the kingdom of God. The whole of this remaining section (chaps. 7-12) presents a series of revelations supplementary to that which was recorded in chap. 2.

7

The date of this and of the following chapter comes in chronological order after the fourth chapter.

(2) The great sea.—The meaning here cannot be the Mediterranean, for, according to verse 17, we are justified in explaining the "sea" to mean the nations of the world (Ps. 46:3; Isa. 27:1). The raging of the winds from the four quarters of the sky points to the various political and social agitations which disturb the world's history, and lead to the changes and revolutions which mark its progress as it tends toward the end.

(3) Four great beasts.—The monstrous forms of the beasts are implied, rather than the hugeness of their size. (Other instances of beasts being taken as emblems of kingdoms may be found in Isa. 27:1; Ezek. 29:3; 32:2.) The beasts do not rise up simultaneously, but in succession to each other. In this way, and in the difference of their character, they form a parallel to the subject matter of the vision recorded in chap. 2.

(4) The first was like a lion.—The lion and the eagle are chosen as being emblems of strength and swiftness respectively. They characterize the empire of Nebuchadnezzar, and correspond to the golden head of the Colossus (chap. 2).
The wings ... plucked.—The eagle, deprived of its wings, loses its power of swiftness and unrestrained motion.
From the earth.—The beast was raised from being on its four feet into the position of a man, as is indicated by the words "a man's heart." We have not sufficient historical details respecting the last years of Nebuchadnezzar's reign to enable us to point to the reference.

(5) And behold another beast.—We are not told what became of the first beast. (Comp. verse 12.) The second beast corresponds to the silver portion of the Colossus (chap. 2).
One side.—The two sides of the bear are parallel in meaning to the two breasts and two arms of the Colossus. It is implied, therefore, that the second kingdom consists of two parts, and the raising up of one side implies that one part of the kingdom would come into greater prominence than the other. Such was the case with the Medo-Persian Empire (comp. 8:3), in which the Persian element surpassed the Median.
Three ribs.—These signify kingdoms which had already been subdued; and by the command, "Arise and devour," the second empire is permitted to make further conquests before its disappearance. The three ribs have been understood from the

time of Hippolytus to mean the Babylonians, the Lydians, and the Egyptians.
(6) A leopard.—More correctly, "a panther." The third beast corresponds to the copper belly and thighs of the image (chap. 2). As unity characterizes the first beast, and duality the second, so quadruplicity marks the third. It has four wings—wings as of a bird, not of an eagle—by which a degree of swiftness is implied inferior to that of the first beast. It has four heads, indicating four kingdoms, into which the third kingdom should develop itself.
(7) A fourth beast.—This is so different from the preceding three, and so terrible in appearance, that Daniel can hardly find words to describe it. The distinguishing feature of it is the power which it possesses of breaking and stamping out all that it meets. In this way it corresponds to iron in 2:40. The description of the destructive might of this beast is heightened by the mention of "iron teeth" and "brazen claws." Horns imply strength, while the ten horns correspond to the ten toes of the image.
(8) I considered.—Here, for the first time in the course of the vision, there appears a change taking place in the object itself. Among the ten horns of the fourth beast there was seen to grow up a "little horn," which destroyed three of the other horns. That a man, and not a kingdom, is intended, though the man may be the representative of a kingdom, appears from the mention of the eyes, indicating craft and cunning, and the mouth, speaking vanity and blasphemy.
(9) Ancient of days.—The attribute of age expresses the majesty of the judge. Notwithstanding the title "Ancient" is applied to the "Anou," yet his titles "generator and father of the gods" are so completely at variance with Old Testament doctrines that it is inconceivable that Daniel should have incorporated in his vision any portions of Babylonian mythology. Similar remarks apply to the Son of man in verse 13.
White as snow.—Indicating, like the "pure wool," the purity and justice of the Judge.
Fiery flame.—Fire appears in Scripture as a metaphor for affliction or punishment, as a symbol of the chastening and punitive righteousness of God, and as the setting forth of the fiery indignation which devours the enemies of God. The figure of speech is here used in each of these senses. The "wheels" represent the omnipresence of Almighty God.

(10) The books—i.e., the unerring record of man's thoughts, words, and deeds, which is written in the unfailing memory of God. (Comp. Exod. 32:32; Pss. 56:8, 69:28; Isa. 4:3; Mal. 3:16.)

(11) Burning flame.—Such is the doctrine of final retribution as revealed to Daniel. (Comp. Isa. 66:24; Rev. 19:20; 20:10.)

(13) The Son of man.—The title implies one descended from man; but as this Person is spoken of as being "like" one of human descent, it follows that He was not merely a man. The early Jewish and Christian interpretations that this is the Messiah are confirmed by our Saviour's solemn appropriation of the title to Himself (Matt. 24:30). In this verse the judgment is supposed to have taken place upon earth already and the Son of man comes in the clouds to claim His kingdom.

(14) Serve him.—In Biblical Chaldee this word is used only of rendering divine service or worship. The "Son of man" is therefore here spoken of as God.

(16) That stood by—i.e., one out of the multitudes mentioned (verse 10).

(23) The fourth kingdom.—The ten horns (verse 24) are spoken of as existing simultaneously. Various attempts have been made to account for them, but the marks by which the little horn may be identified have been graciously revealed to us by God Himself.

(25) And he shall speak.—The marks of identification of the little horn are: (1) blasphemy of God; (2) persecution and affliction of the saints; (3) attempts, apparently ineffectual, against all institutions, whether of divine or human authority; in short, a general spirit of lawlessness and unbelief. It appears that the little horn, the Antichrist of the last days, or the beast, will be successful for a time in his blasphemies and persecutions, but in the end he will be destroyed. (See II Thess. 2:8.)

Time and times and the dividing of time.—This is frequently explained to mean three years and a half. Those who adopt this explanation assume that by "times" a dual is implied, which in Chaldee is represented by the plural. They next assume that by "a time" is meant one year, resting their assumption partly on 4:16, and partly on a comparison of 12:7 with Rev. 13:5; 11:2, 3. This gives a sum of three years and a half, which is interpreted either literally, or explained to mean half a sabbatical period, or half some divinely-appointed period symbolized by the number "seven." A more correct view of the prediction is that the reign of Antichrist will be divided into three periods—the first long, the second longer, the third shortest of all. It also appears that the last is to be the severest time of trial. In chap. 9 the seventy weeks are divided into three periods, forming a similar series, $7 + 62 + 1 = 70$.

(26) The judgment.—The language is similar to that in verse 10. The destruction of the beast recorded in verse 11 is here omitted.

8

(1) The Hebrew language is resumed here. The visions recorded in the remaining portion of the book having no connection with Babylon, the Chaldee dialect is dropped.

Third year.—Most probably, not long before the end of his reign. This vision is supplementary to the one recorded in the preceding chapter, giving various details respecting the second and third empires omitted there, showing also how a "little horn" is to grow out of the third as well as out of the fourth empire.

(3) A ram—i.e., a single ram. The ram was standing before the river, or eastward of it, and represented the Medo-Persian empire (verse 20). The two horns, like the two breasts and arms of the image, or two sides of the bear, symbolize the twofold character of this empire. The higher horn denotes the Persians, the dominant race.

(4) I saw the ram pushing.—The ram pushes in three different directions. This corresponds to the three ribs in the mouth of the bear. The animal does not push toward the east, as it is presumed that he has already made conquests in those quarters.

(5) An he goat.—This, according to verse 21, means the Greek empire, the large horn being the first king, or Alexander the Great. The goat and the ram form the same contrast as the panther and the bear. Matchless activity is contrasted with physical strength and brutal fierceness.

Touched not the ground.—An exact prediction of the early conquests of Alexander, all whose movements were characterized by marvelous rapidity. This is expressed by "the wings of a fowl" (7:6).

A notable horn.—This is explained (verse 21) to be Alexander himself.

(8) Was broken.—This points to the sudden and unexpected end of Alexander (323 B.C.). The "four horns," which take the place of the "notable horn," may mean either that this empire was dispersed to the four winds of heaven on the death of its founder, or it may hint at the ultimate division of the empire into four parts—Thrace, Macedonia, Syria, Egypt, under Symmachus, Cassander, Seleucus, and Ptolemy respectively.

(9) Little.—Literally, "out of littleness." This is explained more fully in verse 23. See the campaigns of Antiochus Epiphanes (1 Macc. 1:16; 3:31-37; 6:1-4).

The pleasant land—i.e., Palestine, which here, as in Isa. 19:23, 24, is spoken of as a third land, between south and east. The phrase was suggested to Daniel by the language of Jer. 3:19; Ezek. 20:6, 15.

(10) The host of heaven.—Probably in a metaphorical sense indicating the people of Israel. (Comp. Exod. 7:4; Num. 24:17.) The actions of Antiochus, predicted here, are related (1 Macc. 1:24, 30, 37; 2:38; II Macc. 9:10).

(11) Prince of the host—i.e., Jehovah Himself. (Comp. verse 25 and 11:36.)

The daily—i.e., everything permanent in the worship of God, such as sacrifices, etc. On this conduct of Antiochus relating to the Temple see I Macc. 1:39, 45; 3:45.

(12) An host ... —The host is apparently the same as that which is mentioned in verse 10, and means some of the Jewish people. It is known that some of them lapsed under the persecution of Antiochus, and joined in his idolatrous rites.

The truth—i.e., the word of God, as appears from I Macc. 1:43-52, 56, 60.

(13) One saint—i.e., an angel, who, however, has not been mentioned before. This part of the vision recalls 7:16. It is implied that the angels were conversing upon the subject of this awful revelation concerning the future of God's people. Only a portion of what they said is here recorded.

(14) Unto two thousand and three hundred days.—Judas Maccabeus took Jerusalem in the year 165 B.C., and kept the Feast of Dedication the same year, Antiochus being at the time in Armenia. The period apparently begins with the events mentioned in II Macc. 4:32-39, which occurred about 171 B.C. The dates, however, not being recorded precisely, it is impossible to figure with certainty where the starting point is to be dated. The 2,300 complete days of twenty-four hours make a period of six years 140 days. This period

616

falls short of seven years (a week of years) by about two-thirds of a year. If, then, seven years is the number of years symbolical of divine chastisements, the prophecy implies that the people shall not suffer persecution according to their full deserts, but "for the elect's sake those days shall be shortened." (See note on 7:25.)

(17) The time of the end—i.e., either at the final period of earthly history, or at the time which lies at the limit of the prophetic horizon. Jerome observes that what happened in the times of Antiochus was typical of what shall be fulfilled hereafter in Antichrist.

(23) Transgressors ... —When transgressors have filled up the measure of their guilt so as to exceed the limits of God's mercy, then this event shall take place. The transgressors are the apostate Jews. The king is shameless; he has no reluctance in pursuing the cruelties which he has designed. He uses falsehood and dissimulation to carry out his purposes.

(24) Not by his own power.—Not might, but cunning, will cause his success. (Comp. I Macc. 1:10, etc.) Thus his destructive powers become astonishing.

(26) The concluding words of the angel are intended to comfort the Jewish church in the days of her persecution. They teach her that God has foreseen her future affliction, that it comes from Him in His love, and that it shall last only for a short while. This promise accounts for the firmness which was exhibited by the saints of the Maccabees. (See Heb. 11:34-38.)

9

(2) Understood.—He gave special attention to Jeremiah's prophecy of the seventy years of the Captivity (see Jer. 25:11 and 29:10; comp. verses 9, 11, 12). There existed at this time a collection of sacred books, consisting of what already had been admitted into the Canon.

Seventy years.—It appears from Hag. 1:2; Zech. 1:12, that considerable uncertainty prevailed as to the time when the seventy years were to be estimated. Three periods of seventy years occur in connection with the Captivity (1) from 606 B.C., the date of Jeremiah's prophecy, to 536 B.C., the edict of Cyrus; (2) from 598 B.C., Jehoiachin's captivity, to 528 B.C., the period of Ezra 4:6; (3) from 588 B.C., the destruction of the Temple, to 518 B.C., the edict of Darius

(Ezra 6:1). In the first year of Cyrus, seventy years had elapsed since the captivity of Daniel, but to him it was a question of melancholy importance whether his computation had begun at the right date.

(5) Four stages of sin are pointed out by the prophet, corresponding to the four different words which he uses: "sin" refers especially to sins of deed; "committing iniquity" to sins of word; "done wickedly" to sins of thought; "rebelled" implies the person against whom the sin has been committed. The whole result of sin under these several aspects is expressed by "departing from thy precepts."

(13) Made we not our prayer.—The reference is, as in verse 6, to the conduct of the nation from the first. There had been plenty of external show of praying, as appears from Isa. 1 and elsewhere, but these prayers were of no effect on account of their formalism. The conditions of acceptable prayer are implied in the closing words of the verse regarding the revelation of God.

(14) Watched.—By the use of this word it seems that Daniel is again referring to the prophecies of Jeremiah. (See Jer. 1:12; etc.) He prays that as all the curses foretold by that prophet have been poured upon the nation, so also the release from the Captivity, which was also promised by him, may be accomplished.

(15) That hast brought.—The mention of past mercies moves Daniel to pray that future mercies may be granted. His language is founded partly upon Jer. 32:17-23, and partly upon Isa. 63:11-16. The Babylonian exile is frequently compared by Isaiah (e.g., Isa. 51:9, 10) to Egyptian bondage. Daniel reproduces the thought in this verse.

(20) Whiles I was speaking.—Daniel had not even finished his prayer when the answer came. The angel Gabriel, whom he had seen (8:16), comes to him, and reveals to him the mystery of the seventy weeks, yet future, rather than seventy years which were already passed. The time of the evening sacrifice (verse 21) is 3 p.m., being the hour of evening prayer. (See Exod. 29:39; Num. 28:4.)

(24) Seventy weeks.—Great difficulty is experienced in discovering what sort of weeks is intended. Verses 25-27 are sufficient to show that ordinary weeks cannot be meant. It is generally assumed that we must understand the weeks to consist of years and not of days, the principle of year-weeks depending upon Num. 14:34; Lev. 26:34; Ezek. 4:6. The word "week" in itself furnishes a clue to the meaning. It implies a "Heptad," and is not necessarily more definite than the "time" mentioned in 7:25.

To make reconciliation—i.e., atonement. The two former clauses show that during the seventy weeks sin will cease. The prophet now brings out another side of the subject. There will be abundance of forgiveness in store for those who are willing to receive it. He proceeds to combine the notions of "righteousness" and "eternity," which elsewhere are characteristics of Messianic prophecy. (See Ps. 89:36; Isa. 46:13; 51:5-8; Dan. 2:44, 7:18, 27.) It appears, too, that the prophet is speaking of the absolute cessation of all prophecy.

To anoint the most Holy.—From the careful manner in which this and the following verse are connected by the words "Know therefore," it appears that the words "most Holy" are parallel to "Messiah the Prince" (verse 25), and that they indicate a person. (See Lev. 6:18; I Chron. 23:13.) This was the opinion of the Syriac translator, and of the LXX. Any reference to Zerubbabel's temple, or to the dedication of the temple by Judas Maccabeus, is opposed to the context.

(25) The punctuation in the Hebrew text is misleading, for verse 26 connects the sixty-two weeks with the Anointed, and not with the building of the city. That the command to build was the edict of Cyrus (Isa. 44:28; Ezra 6:14) is not explicit here.

Messiah the Prince.—He is to be "anointed," that is, King and Priest at once (see I Sam. 10:1; 13:14; 25:30); in fact, He is to possess those attributes which in other passages are ascribed to the Messiah. By no calculation can Cyrus (Isa. 45:1) be said to have come either seven weeks or sixty-nine weeks from the time of the beginning of the Captivity.

In troublous times.—The whole history of the rebuilding of Jerusalem tells us one long tale of protracted opposition. See Ezra 4:1-6, 12; 5:6; Neh. 1:3.

(26) After threescore and two weeks.—These words can only mean that in the seventieth week the Anointed one shall be cut off. Observe the care with which the seventy weeks are arranged in a series of the form $7 + 62 + 1$. During the period of seven weeks Jerusalem is to be rebuilt. The "troublous times" are not to be restricted to this period, but may apply to the sixty-two weeks which follow. After the end of the sixty-nine weeks Messiah is to be cut off. By "Messiah" we must understand the same person who is spoken of in verse 25. It should also be observed that the word "prince," which is applied to Messiah in verse 25, is here used of another person—some secular prince, who stands in opposition to the Messiah.

But not for himself.—Taking the sense according to the context, the meaning is either that He has no more a people, or that His office of Messiah among His people ceases.

That shall come.—Two such hostile princes already have been mentioned (7:23; etc.; 8:23; etc.), Antiochus and his great antitype, namely, Antichrist. We are not to identify this "prince" with either of these. Another typical prince is introduced here, who shall destroy the city and the sanctuary after the rejection of the Messiah. But it must be noticed that the work of destruction is attributed here to the "people" and not to the "prince."

The end thereof.—It is not clear grammatically what end or whose end is signified. But upon comparing this clause with the following, it appears that by "the end" is meant the whole issue of the invasion. This is stated to be desolation, such as is caused by a deluge.

(27) And he shall confirm.—It is appropriate to take Messiah as the subject. During the last closing week of the long period mentioned, Messiah, though cut off, shall confirm God's covenant (comp. 11:22, 28, 30, 32) with many, that is, with those who receive Him.

Until the consummation.—These words refer back to verse 26. That which is foretold by Daniel is the complete and final destruction of the same city and temple which evoked the prophet's prayer. There is no prophecy that the desolater himself is destined to destruction.

10

The vision comprising this final section of Daniel occurred two years after the departure of the exiles from Babylon, and at a time when those who were rebuilding the city were beginning to experience the "troublous" times spoken of in 9:25. This section is partly supplemental to chaps. 8 and 9, and introduces details with regard to the fourth Empire (chap. 7).

(1) A thing.—The contents of the revelation are specified in truth and long tribulation. "Time appointed" is translated "warfare" in Isa. 40:2, meaning "hardship" or "tribulation." This revelation, however, speaks of the "warfare" which not Israel only, but all God's people must undergo before the coming of the Messiah in His kingdom.

And he understood.—The duration of the tribulation was not clearly revealed to the prophet, though he received enigmatic declarations respecting it (12:10, etc.). Comp. 8:27 and 12:8.

(2) I . . . was mourning.—Daniel's fast was not in consequence of some breaches of the passover ritual, although his people had been guilty. But there was in Israel the sin of faithlessness to God's promises, which grieved the aged seer's heart. The number of those who had obeyed the prophet's command (Isa. 48:20) was comparatively insignificant, and those who should have been foremost in leading their fellow countrymen—namely, the Levites—had preferred the life in Babylon to the trials and hardships of rebuilding their own city (Ezra 2:40; comp. Ezra 8:15).

(4) The four and twentieth day.—After the end of his three weeks' fast the prophet was upon the bank of the Tigris, where he saw the following vision. Hiddekel is the Accadian name of the river. (Comp. Gen. 2:14.)

(5) A certain man.—The dress especially recalls the clothing of the high priest. (See Exod. 39:27-29; comp. Rev. 1:13.) The person himself is carefully distinguished from Michael (10:21) and Gabriel (9:21). He is the same man who stood before Daniel (8:15), and must be regarded as "the Angel of God" (Exod. 32:34) or "God's Presence" (Exod. 33:14)—in fact, the One who was the Logos.

(8) This great vision.—Daniel again distinguishes this from former visions. The glory of the man who appeared to him was far in excess of what he had witnessed previously (8:17). The effects of the vision upon him are also mentioned: he grew pale with terror at what he saw, and fainted.

(13) The prince of the kingdom.—Perhaps no single verse in the whole of the Scriptures speaks more clearly than this upon the invisible powers which rule and influence nations. As spiritual beings carry out God's purpose in the natural world (Exod. 12:23; II Sam. 24:16) and in the moral world (Luke 15:10), so also they do in the political world. But not only Israel had a spiritual champion (verse 21) to protect her in her national life; the powers opposed to Israel also had their saviours which were antagonists of those who watched over Israel. The "princes" of the heathen powers are devils, according to 1 Cor. 10:20.

Withstood me.—The verse implies that the spiritual powers attached to Persia were influencing Cyrus in a manner that was prejudicial to the interests of God's people. It must be borne in mind that the vision occurred at the time of the Samaritan intrigues with the Persian Court in opposition to Zerubbabel.

Michael.—See Jude 9 and Rev. 12:7.

I remained there.—The person is explaining to Daniel how it had happened that he had received no visible answer to a prayer that had been offered with success three weeks previously. There had been a conflict between the powers of light and darkness, in which the former had gained the victory, which had been decisive. By the kings of Persia are meant all the successors of Cyrus. From this time onward the Persian kings were generally favorable to the interests of Israel.

(14) The latter days.—Comp. 2:28 and 8:17. The time is here more narrowly defined as the period when the vision of chap. 11 shall receive its complete fulfillment. The "vision" is identical with "the thing" (10:1), or "the vision" (verse 16). It must be carefully borne in mind that there is no reference to preceding visions, except so far as the revelation contained in chap. 11 develops certain details of other visions.

(15) I set my face.—The conduct of Daniel described in this verse is not to be ascribed to his fear, for that had been driven away already (verse 12), but to his reverence for the majestic person who was before him (comp. verse 17), and to the gratitude that he felt for the answer to his prayer.

(20) Before he proceeds to make this revelation, he prepares Daniel's mind for a portion of what is about to be revealed, by mentioning the spiritual powers which ruled over Greece. Providence had watched over Israel during the Persian sovereignty; "but while I am gone forth the prince of Javan will come." The prophet is in this manner prepared for troublous times, which will occur under the Macedonian supremacy.

(21) And there is none . . .—A ground of encouragement is that Michael, who stood up as Israel's champion under the Persian troubles, will prove himself strong against the evil powers which lead Javan.

11

(1) In the first year of Darius.—These words must be closely connected with the last verse of chap. 10. The allusion is, most probably, to the fall of Babylon and the return from the Exile, at which time, as at the Exodus, the angel of the Lord went before His people.

(2) The truth.—This is the beginning of the revelation promised in 10:14; and from this point until the end of the book the difficulties that have to be encountered in attempting an exposition are almost insuperable. It has been customary from the time of Jerome, if not from an earlier epoch, to explain most of what follows as referring to the Ptolemies and Seleucidae. But the mere similarity which exists between certain things predicted here and what actually occurred in the times of the Ptolemies is not sufficient to limit the fulfillment of the prophecy to those times, still less to justify the assumption that the section before us is a history of what occurred from the disruption of the Greek Empire to the death of Antiochus. Just as Antiochus (8:23-25) is a type of Antichrist (7:21), so the events and political combinations which preceded Antiochus may be regarded as typical of what will occur before the coming of the Messiah and the general resurrection, with a prediction of which (12:2, 3) this revelation concludes.

Three kings.—Cyrus being on the throne already, it is most probable that his three successors are intended—Cambyses, Darius, and Xerxes. Those four kings appear to have been selected whose influence was most prominent in its bearings upon Israel. (The short reign of the Pseudo Smerdis is not taken into account.) It should be noticed that at the time of the invasion of Europe by Xerxes, Greece was in no sense a kingdom (realm). Such language is incompatible with an authorship during the Maccabean period.

(3) A mighty king.—No clue is given to show over what nation this king reigns. Those who explain what follows to refer to the Ptolemies and Seleucidae identify him with Alexander the Great (comp. 7:6; 8:5-8, 21, 22). But there was nothing in the context which makes it necessary to limit the passage to him.

(4) Broken.—The shortness of the king's reign is implied; the moment that he has arisen he will come to nothing. This has been explained to mean the sudden collapse and dismemberment of the Greek empire after the death of Alexander.

Not to his posterity.—This is explained of the partition of Alexander's empire among his generals, and of the murder of his two sons, Hercules and Alexander, but the language is too indefinite to make any such identification certain. The revelation directs our attention to a self-willed king, whose large empire is to come to a sudden and unexpected end; the ruins of it are not to benefit his posterity, but apparently two strangers, who are designated king of the north and king of the south respectively.

(5) The king.—The vagueness of the language prevents us from asserting that the reference is to Ptolemy Soter, who assumed the title of king about 304 B.C. Equally obscure is the phrase "one of his princes." But we know that Ptolemy took Jerusalem 320 B.C., and that these times must have been very critical to the Jews.

(6) In the end.—It appears from 10:14 that this revelation bears upon the future of Israel, and it does not appear that this marriage affected the Jewish people more than any other marriage. The traditional interpretation—that reference is made to the marriage between Antiochus II with Berenice, daughter of Ptolemy Philadelphus —is unsatisfactory. The language refers to what is mentioned as one of the characteristics of the last empire (2:43), that of various attempts to consolidate earthly powers by political marriages. These do not characterize the era of the Seleucidae any more than they do many other periods of history.

Shall not retain.—The meaning appears to be that the marriage will not accomplish its intended purpose. The king of the south, instead of becoming independent of his northern rival, will only become more subjected to him than he was previously. This does not appear to have happened with regard to Ptolemy Philadelphus and Antiochus Theos.

(7) Ptolemy Philadelphus and Antiochus Theos were at war for ten years or more. In this and the following verses there is a description of a severe war, in which the southern king is victorious. This is explained as the conflict between Ptolemy Evergetes and Seleucus Callinicus (246-243 B.C.). The coincidence between history and prophecy is far from establishing the truth of the explanation; but the mention of Egypt in verse 8 directs our attention to a country which will hereafter become the scene of the fulfilment of the prophecy.

Out of a branch of her roots.—Comp. Isa. 11:1. The meaning is, "a branch growing from her roots shall stand up in the place of the person last mentioned."

With an army.—The person spoken of comes to attack the army, and the fortress has been supposed to be Seleucia. However, the use of the plural "them" in the latter part of the verse makes it more probable that the word "fortress" is used collectively for fortified cities.

(8) He shall continue.—The meaning is that he shall stand as an ally of the northern king several years. The reference is said to be to the cessation of hostilities between Ptolemy and Seleucus, but there is nothing in these verses which leads us to infer what history states as a fact, that the northern king was completely crippled by a serious defeat, and that his fleet was dispersed by a storm.

(9) The king of the south.—The LXX supports this reading, but according to the Hebrew text, the meaning is, "The king of the **north** shall come into the kingdom of the southern king," and then shall return to his own land—i.e., the north—apparently without gaining any advantage.

(10) His sons.—If the king of the north last mentioned is Seleucus Callinicus, his sons must be Seleucus Ceraunus, a man of no importance, and Antiochus the Great. It is here stated of the sons that they are stirred up; that they collect a vast army, which advances steadily, overflowing like a torrent, while its masses pass through the land; that they shall return and carry on the war up to the frontier of the southern king. Considering the uncertainty of the readings in the Hebrew text, and the ambiguity of the language, this is anything but a definite statement. However, it has been explained to refer to the wars of Antiochus and Ptolemy Philopator, in course of which they took Seleucia. Tyre, and Ptolemais, besieged the Egyptians in Sidon, and actually took possession of Gaza.

(11) And the king.—The ambiguity of this verse is great. But it is most probable that "he" refers to the northern king, "his hand" to the hand of the southern king. This is supported by verse 12, where we read of the arrogant conduct of the southern king after his victory. Therefore, this has been suggested to be the successes of Ptolemy against the "multitude" of Antiochus at Raphia (217 B.C.).

(12) But he shall not be strengthened— i.e., he does not prove as successful as he had hoped. His aim was to gain complete supremacy over his rival, but he was unable to gain his object. Those interpreters who see a distinct reference to the wars of Ptolemy and Antiochus point out that though the loss of the Syrians was great, yet Ptolemy did not follow up his success as he should have done. Instead of striking a decisive blow, he was content with regaining the towns which Antiochus had taken from him.

(13) Much riches.—This has been explained of the invasion of Egypt by Antiochus and Philip of Macedon, some thirteen or fourteen years after the battle of Raphis, when Ptolemy Epiphanes, a mere child, had succeeded his father, Philopator. Ptolemy Philopater, after his victory at Raphia, had attempted to enter the Holy Place, as is mentioned in the Third Book of Maccabees. It should be remembered that the Jews suffered considerably from both parties during the whole of this period; but though the prophecy is supposed to have been written for their comfort and encouragement at this very juncture, yet not a word is said which bears allusion to them.

(14) In those times.—At this verse—the earliest in which there is any reference to Daniel's people and to the vision (10:1, 7, 8)—we appear to be approaching the great crisis. We appear to be within "a very few days" (see verse 20) of the vile person who corresponds to the little horn of the fourth beast. At this period the king of the south suffers from many hostile opponents, while certain others, more closely connected with the Jews, become prominent for a while, but then fail. Historical allusions are uncertain, but some commentators refer to insurrections during the early years of Ptolemy Epiphanes, and a league which some of the Jews made with Antiochus the Great against Ptolemy.

To establish the vision.—The meaning is that the result of their acts is to bring about the accomplishment of the vision (10:14). The significant part of the verse is the "falling" of the robbers (see Ps. 17:4; Isa. 35:9; Jer. 7:11; Ezek. 7:22, 18:10). It seems to mean that the conduct of these men shall bring them just the reverse of what they had expected.

(16) But he that cometh.—The northern king follows up the vision mentioned in the last verse, enters the glorious land i.e., Palestine, and commits great ravages in it. This has been applied to the conduct of Antiochus the Great, but history does not speak of any acts of destruction committed by him in Palestine.

(17) He shall also.—He has further plans for subduing the dominions of the southern king. He brings together all the forces he can amass, and then attempts by means of a political marriage to establish peace; but this also proves a failure.

(18) Shall he turn.—This has been explained of the victories gained by Antiochus the Great in Asia Minor. He thus came into contact with the Romans, and was defeated by L. Scipio, who is identified with "the prince" mentioned in this verse. But some take "prince" collectively to mean the rulers of the "isles."

(20) A raiser of taxes.—The effect of this policy by the new king of the north was that he fell victim to a conspiracy in a few days. According to Jerome, the person alluded to was Seleucus Philopator.

With this verse the first part of the prophecy concludes. It is to be observed that thus far the whole prophecy is eschatological, and refers to a series of wars and political intrigues of two opposing earthly powers which will affect the destiny of God's people in the last times. Verse 21 introduces the most prominent object of the prophecy—a person who remains before the reader until the end of the chapter, while the southern king gradually disappears (verses 25, 27, 40), and what is apparently his country is mentioned without its sovereign (verse 43).

(21) A vile person.—See Ps. 119:141; Jer. 22:28. The moral character of the man is especially described. The words that follow explain more fully that he was not worthy of receiving royal majesty. Just as his predecessors resembled in various points the kings spoken of in verses 1-20, so Antiochus Epiphanes resembles the person described here.

(22) The overwhelming forces of invading armies are swept away by the troops of this terrible king. But besides the enemy, the "prince of the covenant" is to be destroyed also. This expression means "those who were at peace with him," "prince" being used as a collective noun (see verse 18). But this has been supposed by some to refer to the murder of Onias III (II Macc. 4:1; etc.; 33; etc.)

(23, 24) These verses suggest the perfidious conduct of Antiochus Epiphanes (I Macc. 3:27-30) after the defeat of the Syrian army by Judas Maccabeus.

(25-27) This account is supposed to describe the war of Antiochus with Ptolemy Philometor (see I Macc. 1:16-19), or his war with Physcon (see Livy, 44.19).

(28) The prophecy points distinctly to Antiochus after his return from Egypt. (See I Macc. 1:19-28; II Macc. 5:11-17.) This was the occasion of his first attack upon the theocracy.

(29) At the time appointed—i.e., in God's own time. According to I Macc. 1:29, it was after two years had fully passed since his return to Syria that Antiochus made another attack upon Jerusalem. This attack was made after his return from Egypt. But no such success attended him at the latter as at the former invasion.

(30) Ships of Chittim.—On Chittim, see Gen. 10:4; comp. Num. 24:24. The LXX explains this of the Romans, referring to the story in Livy, 45.11.

Return.—That is, to Palestine, where he will indulge his anger.

Have intelligence—i.e., pay attention to them. These persons are such as those who are mentioned in I Macc. 1:11-16, who were anxious to Hellenize all their institutions, not only forsaking the outward sign of the covenant, but actually taking Greek names. (On the manner in which Antiochus treated the apostates, see II Macc. 4:14; etc.; and comp. verse 39.)

(31) Here is a further statement of the assistance (arms) which the king obtains in his attacks upon all sacred institutions. "Sanctuary of strength" was apparently a name for the Temple, so called because it was the spiritual support of God's people, as well as a very powerful fortress. (See I Macc. 1:44; 6:7; II Macc. 6:4, which speak of the various deeds of Antiochus upon this occasion.)

(32) Such as do wickedly.—In these verses are traced the effects of the apostasy upon the people of God (see verse 30). They had begun with indifference to true religion; they have now become intolerant of it.

But the people . . .—While the large mass of people becomes obedient to the persecutor, there is a party of true believers remaining, who confirm the covenant. That such a party existed in the time of Antiochus Epiphanes appears from I Macc. 1:62; etc.; 2:3; etc. Similarly in all times of persecution there will be a remnant, though it may be very small, which will remain firm to their covenant with God. (Comp. I Kings 19:18.)

(33) They that understand.—This is the

name by which those are called who were spoken of in the last verse as "knowing their God." Their example shall give instruction to "the many" who yield to the flatteries mentioned in the last verse. They show them where they are drifting. (See I Macc. 2:1; etc.; II Macc. 6:18.) The prophecy of the last clause obviously refers to martyrdom. The deaths mentioned in I Macc. 1:57; etc.; 3:41; 5:13, may be taken as typical of the sufferings of the Church in the last times.

(34) Now when they shall fall.—This refers to all those who suffer during this persecution. In the Maccabean persecutions help was given to the sufferers by Judas and his brethren (I Macc. 3:11; etc.; 4:14; etc.). This prevented the faithful from disappearing entirely.

(35) Some of them.—The reason of this persecution is revealed: they would themselves profit by their sufferings. Gradations are mentioned to cause them to become completely purified. (Comp. Ps. 51:7; Isa. 1:18). In this way the dissemblers are made known. The patient example of the sufferers is followed by others who are faithful, while the "flatterers" become open apostates.

(36) The king raises himself by his thoughts and deeds, not only above the heathen deities, but also above the true God. The northern king is still spoken of, but the features of Antiochus are gradually fading away from the portrait. In no sense can Antiochus be called an atheist. According to Polybius 26:10, sec. 11, Antiochus exceeded all kings in the sacrifices which he offered at the gates, and in the honors which he paid to the gods. Nor does the language of II Macc. 9:12 correspond with the words of this verse. Antiochus' main object was to Hellenize the Jewish religion, and to force the Greek gods upon the Jews. The character of the northern king, on the contrary, finds a parallel in Paul's description of Antichrist (II Thess. 2:4).

Marvellous things.—That is, his utterances and blasphemies against the true God will be astounding. (Comp. 7:8, 11, 20.) This will continue until God's indignation against His people is accomplished.

(37) Neither shall they.—A further description is now given of the godlessness of this king, but the people of Israel are no longer mentioned in their relation to him. The northern king appears twice again in Palestine (verses 41, 45), and apparently dies there. He discards his hereditary religion, he has no regard to that natural affection which women look upon as most desirable, but exalts himself over all.

(38) In his estate—i.e., in the place of the God whom he has rejected, he will worship the "god of forces." The whole religion of the king is the taking of fortresses. To him war is everything, and to war everything else must give way. To war, as if it were a god, he does honor with all his wealth.

(39) A strange god.—By this help he carries out his schemes, and all who acknowledge him are rewarded. (Comp. Rev. 13:4, 16, 17.) Dividing the land is evidently a reward offered to those who join his ranks.

(40-45) These verses speak of the last expedition of the northern king, and of the disappearance of the king of the south. The portrait of Antiochus (see note on verse 36) now has completely faded away. No such invasion of Egypt as that mentioned here is recorded in history. (But for the remainder of the story of Antiochus Epiphanes, see I Macc. 3:27-37; etc.; 6:8.)

(40) Time of the end.—Comp. 8:17. The words mean the end of the world, with which (verse 45) the end of this king coincides. The word "push" (see 8:4) from the context infers that the southern king begins the last conflict, in the course of which both kings come to an end.

(41) The glorious land.—On the occasion of his hasty march against Egypt, while passing through Palestine, the king takes the shortest route, avoiding the three tribes which had been distinguished by their hostility toward the people of Israel. It is remarkable that these nations (two of which appear as figures of Antichrist, Isa. 25:10; 63:1) should escape, while other nations fell before Antichrist. It is also noteworthy that these three tribes are called nations, for after the return from the exile it appears that they ceased to have any distinct national existence. As tribes they had some considerable power, taking the part of Antiochus in the Maccabean wars. (See I Macc. 3:10; 5:1-8.)

(44) He shall go forth.—While in Egypt the northern king has bad news brought to him from the north and from the east, which stirs up feelings of revenge. Once again he halts in Palestine, where he comes to an end. That this cannot apply to Antiochus is evident from the following facts: (1) Antiochus was in Persia when the news of

the defeat of Lysias reached him (see note on verse 40); (2) Judaea and Jerusalem cannot in any sense be regarded as either east or north of Persia; (3) Antiochus died in Persia, and not near Jerusalem.

(45) The king is here represented as halting between the Mediterranean and the Dead Sea, while a palatial tent is being erected for him.

The glorious holy mountain is generally explained to be Mount Zion. (Comp. Ps. 48:2.) This he threatens, as once did the Assyrian (comp. Isa. 10:32-34), but without success.

He shall come to his end.—The end of this king is placed in the same locality which is elsewhere predicted by the prophets as the scene of the overthrow of Antichrist (Ezek. 39:4; Joel 3:2, 12; Zech. 14:2).

12

(1) The times spoken of in 11:45, previous to the overthrow of the king, is the tribulation mentioned in Matt. 24:21, 22. It should be observed that the mere presence of Michael does not avert the times of trouble.

(2) Many ... that sleep in the dust.—The word "sleep" is applied to death (Jer. 51:39; comp. I Thess. 4:14), while "dust" is used for the grave (Ps. 22:29). Note the use of the word "many" where "all" would have been expected. We may suppose that by the word "many" some contrast is implied, which is apparently between the many who sleep in the dust and the comparatively small number of those who are alive. (See John 5:28; etc.) This passage teaches not only the doctrine of a general resurrection, which had already been incidentally revealed by Daniel's contemporary, Ezekiel (37:1-4), but also the facts of eternal life, and a resurrection of the unjust as well as of the just.

(3) They that be wise.—"The wise" are the same as "those that understand" (11:33), meaning those who by faithfulness to their covenant with God had set a bright example to the others. Such is the consolation held out for the support of those who shall witness the tribulation of the last days. (See Matt. 24.)

(4) Now the prophet is told that the book in which this revelation is written must be placed in a safe and sure place, for the need of it will be felt in "the time of the end," that is, in the time when the fulfillment

623

makes the meaning of the prophecy clear and unambiguous. Many will anxiously search in this book for knowledge of the manner of God's dealings with His people, and will derive comfort and understanding from it.

(6) And one said.—The speaker is evidently one of the persons just mentioned, but the LXX and Jerome suppose Daniel to address the man clothed in white linen, who is the same person who has already spoken (10:5; etc.). The position which he occupies is striking. If, as is frequently the case in the symbolical language of Scripture (see Ps. 93:4; Isa. 8:6, 7), waters or streams are the emblems of nationalities, the Hiddekel will represent the Persian Empire, in the third year of which Daniel had this vision, and the position of the person implies his power to protect his people from all the assaults of the Persians. But at the same time, the remarkable word used for "river" recalls the Nile, and seems to be employed for the purpose of assuring the readers of the book that He who smote the waters of the Nile will restrain all earthly powers which war against His people.

How long ... end.—The end is that which has been frequently spoken of (11:40-12:3). The end appears always to be at hand, yet it never comes. How long will this continue?

**(7) A time, times ... **—See note on 7:25; and observe that any reference to the period of the persecution under Antiochus is impossible, because of the difference between the measures of time. (See 7:14.)

To scatter.—The ancient versions (except the LXX) appear to have regarded it as a prediction of the regathering of Israel, which would immediately precede the coming of Elias. But by the "holy people" are meant, more probably, those who shall suffer in the last days (comp. 7:25, "the saints"). The words imply that the end will not come until persecution appears to have stamped out all that remains of godliness.

(9) Go thy way.—That is, be at peace. The matter is not explained to Daniel any further. His is assured that the end will most certainly come. Compare another gentle rebuke that was addressed to one who wished to see further than was fitting into the future (John 21:21, 22).

Closed up and sealed.—See note on verse 4.

(10) Many shall be purified.—See Rev. 22:11, and comp. 11:35.

(11) From the time.—It appears as if at this verse the prophecy recurs to the more immediate future, and that these words point to the same subject as 11:31. The language used respecting the "abomination" is almost verbally the same as that in 8:3, 11; 9:27, and prevents us from arriving at any other conclusion. The great and apparently insoluble difficulty is the relation which the 1,290 or the 1,335 days occupy with regard to the 2,300 days, or the time, times, and the dividing of a time. It is obvious that the two periods mentioned in this and the following verse cannot be made to agree with three years and a half without setting the rules of arithmetic at defiance. Also the obscurity which rests over the greater portion of the history of Israel should guard us against assuming that we can explain all the contents of the last three chapters by means of what occurred in those times, and also against assuming our historical facts from Daniel and then making use of them to illustrate his prophecies.

(13) In thy lot.—The reference is to the partition of Palestine by lot in the time of Joshua. Even so shall one greater than Joshua divide the heavenly Canaan among His saints who follow Daniel in faith, firmness, and consistency. (See Col. 1:12.)

HOSEA

1

(1) In the days of Uzziah.—This superscription furnishes a rough conception of the period over which Hosea's prophetic activity extended. It may be affirmed that no cogent argument has yet been adduced impugning its historic accuracy. Indications are that approximately 726 B.C. may be assumed as the **terminus ad quem** of the prophet's career. The references to Judah in chaps. 4-14 are such as point to the national degradation brought about by the reign of Ahaz (4:6, 13; 6:11). Moreover, Samaria was not yet destroyed, but there are evidences in the closing chapters that the impending shadows of that terrible catastrophe darkened his soul (9:13; 10:3-8, 14, 15; 13:7-11, 15, 16) and added pathos to his last appeal (chap. 14).

(2) Go, take unto thee a wife of whoredoms.—How are we to interpret the prophet's marriage to the licentious Gomer? Is it an historic occurrence, the only too real tragedy of the author's personal experience, employed for the purpose of illustration? (Comp. Isa. 8:1-4.) Or is this opening chapter a merely allegorical representation, designed to exhibit in vivid colors the terrible moral condition of Israel? (Comp. Isa. 20:1-3; Jer. 25:15-29; Ezek. 4:4-6.) Able writers have advocated each of these opposed theories; but the balance of evidence seems to incline to the former view. The further question arises, Was Gomer guilty before or after the marriage? The former supposition involves the harshness of conceiving such a marriage as the result of a divine command; but the latter supposition admits of a satisfactory interpretation. The wickedness which after marriage revealed itself to the prophet's agonized heart was transfigured to the inspired seer into an emblem of his nation's wrong to Jehovah.

Children of whoredoms.—These are children of Hosea's marriage. The whole result of his family history was included in this divinely ordered plan.

(3) Gomer the daughter of Diblaim.— Gomer means complete, or perfect, but whether in external beauty or in wickedness of character is not easy to determine.

(4) Jezreel means "God shall sow." The prophet had already discovered the faithlessness of his spouse, and that his married life was symbolic of his nation's history.

Jezreel was the name of a very fertile plain in the tribe of Issachar, which was often the scene of terrible struggles (Judg. 6:33; I Sam. 29:1). It was also the name of a town associated with the guilt of Ahab and Jezebel (I Kings 21; II Kings 9:21; 10:11).

(5) I will break the bow of Israel in the valley of Jezreel.—Jehu was to be punished for the assassination of Ahab's descendants. Though the destruction of the house of Ahab was divinely appointed, its value was neutralized by Jehu's tolerance of the calf-worship.

(6) Lo-ruhamah.—"Unloved," or, perhaps "unpitied." The prophet's growing despondency about his country's future is revealed in her name.

(7) Will save them ... —We may consider this verse to have been literally fulfilled in the destruction of Sennacherib's army. The prophetic outlook anticipates the fact that when Judah is captive and exiled, her restoration by the divine hand would take the form of mercy and forgiveness. (Comp. Ps. 76; Isa. 40:1, 2.)

(10) Here is an abrupt transition from dark forboding to bright anticipation. The covenant blessings promised to Abraham shall yet be realized.

(11) Shall come up out of the land.—The envy of Israel and Judah shall cease (Isa. 11:12, 13; Ezek. 34:24; 37:24). A worldwide dominion shall be established under the restored theocracy. Under the word "land" Palestine is evidently meant. Then the true Israel, having chosen their true king, shall demonstrate the greatness of the day of Jezreel. The brothers and sisters will then drop the curse involved in their names, and recognize the divine proprietorship of Jehovah and the abundance of His pity.

2

(2) Plead with your mother ... —By "mother" we are to understand the nation Israel, viewed as a collective abstract; and by the "children" (verse 4), the inhabitants who are units in the total aggregate. **Ammi** and **Ruhamah** without the negative prefix show that this awakening of conscience has given them back their privileges.

"Her whoredoms" are her meretricious guiles, her unblushing idolatry, her voluptuous service of gods that are no Gods. This strong image was constantly on the lips of the prophets, and had been burned by cruel sorrow into the very heart of Hosea. It

625

acquired ominous meaning in the hideous impurities of the worship of Baalpeor and Ashtoreth, against which the Jehovah worship was a tremendous protest.

(3) Set her ... —i.e., reduce Israel to the destitute exposed condition in which she struggled into being in Egyptian bondage, and endured the wanderings and terrors of the wilderness. Probably we have here an allusion to the custom of female infanticide, the child being simply abandoned to death on the day that she was born. (Comp. Ezek. 16:4.)

(4) Her children.—The children are like their mother: not only are they born of doubtful parentage, but are personally defiled. Not only is idolatry enshrined in the national sanctuary and the royal palace, but the people love to have it so. They endorse the degradation of their mother, whose shame is that she seeks them, and not they her. She attributes to these idol-gods all those temporal benefits which theocratic history shows to have been Jehovah's gift, and the consequence of loyalty to Him (verse 5).

(6, 7) She may anticipate in her exile closer proximity to her idol-lovers, but in respect of national prosperity or religious satisfaction she will make a complete blunder.

(9) Therefore will I return, and take ... —The king of Assyria (Tiglath-pileser, 734 B.C.) was the agency by which this was to be accomplished. (Comp. Isa. 10:5.) Jehovah will retrieve from Israel His gifts, and the idol-gods whom she has courted shall see her prostration, and their own helplessness to deliver or relieve.

(12) Destroy.—The vine and fig tree are employed as the symbol of possession and peace (I Kings 4:25; Isa. 36:16; etc.).

(14) Therefore.—Grace transforms her suffering into discipline. The exile in Babylon shall be a repetition of the experiences of the wilderness in which she was first espoused to Jehovah.

(15) The valley of Achor (or trouble), associated with the disgrace and punishment which befell Israel on her first entrance into Palestine (Josh. 7:25, 26), would in later days be regarded as the threshold of a blessed life. The sorrowful associations of the past were to be illuminated with happy anticipation.

(16) Baali.—The husband of the bride was frequently called her "lord" (Isa. 54:5; Exod. 21:22). But such a name, as applied to Jehovah, was after this to be strictly avoided on account of its idolatrous associations.

(18) Make a covenant ... —There shall be harmony without, corresponding to the moral harmony within. The brute creation shall change from hostility to man. (Comp. Isa. 11:6-9.) Wars with foreign foes shall not desolate Israel's borders.

(19, 20) Jehovah turns again to the wife of His youth. "Righteousness" and "judgment" indicate the equitable terms on which God would accept the penitent; and lest this thought should crush her with fear, "loving-kindness" and "tender mercies" follow; and lest this should seem too good. He adds "with faithfulness" (to Myself).

(23) Paul considers this great prediction to be truly fulfilled when, by the acceptance of the divine hope of Israel, both Jews and Gentiles shall be called the children of the living God (Rom. 9:25, 26).

3

Some interval apparently elapsed since the events of Hosea's domestic life, detailed in chap. 1. Meanwhile, the immoralities of Gomer have continued. She at length abandons the home of her lawful husband, and cohabits with one of her lovers. At this point comes the divine injunction to the prophet.

(2) So I bought her.—Gomer was treated as no longer a wife, but requiring to be restored to such a position. The price paid by Hosea was "fifteen pieces of silver." According to Exod. 21:32, this was the compensation enacted for a slave gored to death by a bull, and is a hint of the degradation to which Gomer had sunk.

(3) Will I also be for thee—i.e., I will have no intercourse with thee. This was only to be a temporary discipline.

(4) The prophet suddenly passes from his personal history to that of Israel, which it symbolized. The isolation of Gomer's position prefigured that of Israel in the exile. Her bitter experience was a parable of Israel's utter deprivation of all civil and religious privilege. There was to be no king, or prince, or sacred ritual of any kind. (See Exod. 24:4; Judg. 18:14, 17-20; I Sam. 19:13-16.)

(5) David their king.—This means the predicted representative of the Davidic dynasty. The phrase "latter days" is used indefinitely of the distant future, the horizon of the seer's gaze. We can only see the fulfillment of this anticipation in the Messianic reign. (Comp. Ezek. 34:23; 37:24.)

4

Here begins a new part in the collection of Hosea's prophecies. The entire chapter is one terrible series of accusations, supporting the severe character of the imagery already employed. It may have been composed during the years that immediately succeeded the reign of Jeroboam II.

(1) Controversy—i.e., a judicial suit, in which Jehovah is plaintiff as well as judge (Isa. 1:23; 41:21). By the "children of Israel" we are to understand the northern kingdom of the ten tribes, as distinguished from Judah.

(2) Blood toucheth blood—i.e., murder is added to murder with ghastly prevalence. References to false swearing and lying are repeated in terrible terms by Amos 2:6-8 and Micah 7:2-8; and the form of the charge suggests the Decalogue and pre-existing legislation (Exod. 20:13-15).

(4, 5) The voices of wise counsel will be silenced. Ephraim will in his obstinate wrongdoing be left alone, and the nation will be destroyed.

(6) For lack of knowledge, which you, O priest, should have kept alive in their hearts. The Lord's "controversy" repudiates the entire priesthood, as they had rejected the true knowledge of God. They had inclined to calf-worship, had been vacillating respecting Baal, and had connived at moral offenses.

(7-10) The increase in numbers and prosperity probably refers to the priesthood, who, as they grew in numbers, became more alienated from the true God. These eat up, or fatten on, the very sins they ought to rebuke. As the people will be punished, so will the priest.

(15) Israel ... Judah.—The prophet warns Judah of Israel's peril, and perhaps hints at the apostasy of some of her kings, as Ahaziah, Joram, and Ahaz. He returns to the symbolic use of the word "whoredom," and Judah is exhorted not to participate in the idolatries of Gilgal or the calves of Bethel.

(16) Will feed them as a lamb in a large place.—Most commentators understand it in an unfavorable sense, i.e., will lead them forth into the desolate wilderness, a prey to wild beasts, or into the loneliness that a lamb would feel in a boundless pasture.

(17) Ephraim ... idols.—The prophet calls on Judah to leave Ephraim to himself. Some Jewish interpreters understand this as the appeal of Jehovah to the prophet to leave Israel to her fate, that so perhaps her eyes might be opened to discern her doom.

5

(1) House of the king refers to his following on both sides of the Jordan—Mizpah on the east side, in Gilead, and Tabor on the west. They are singled out as being military strongholds, where the princes of the royal house, with the apostate priests, exercised their deadly hold upon the people, waylaying them, as birds and beasts are snared in the mountains of prey. (Comp. 6:8, 9.) The time is the commencement of the reign of Pekah.

(5) The pride of Israel is the false object of pride to which they had yielded (comp. Amos 6:8). Arrogance led Ephraim, on numerous occasions in earlier sacred history, to resent the supremacy of Judah. This jealousy culminated in the rebellion of Jeroboam I, and characterized their history until the reign of Ahab. Arrogance will be their ruin now; and in this Judah is represented as likewise involved. This last feature is a new note in prophetic utterance. (Comp. 4:15.)

(6) This refers to the vain effort to repent when it is too late. The spirit with which sacrifices of flocks and herds were offered is of more consequence than the multitude of such oblations (Ps. 40:6; Isa. 1:11; Mic. 3:4).

(7) Strange children refers to offspring that followed in the ways of their mother. (Comp. chap. 1.) Some reference is inferred to the consequences of intermarriage with heathen. The "month" may be a personification of the period of a month, during which takes place the now closely impending invasion by Tiglath-pileser (II Kings 15:29; I Chron. 5:26). This invasion was due in part to Ahaz having sought the aid of Assyria against Pekah and Rezin.

(8) Hosea does not mention the metropolis, but he reveals the imminent peril of Jerusalem if these high towers, within sight of her defenders, were giving the alarm at the approach of the Assyrian king.

(10) Like them that remove the bound.—See Deut. 19:14; 27:17.

(12) Both images express concealed

causes of irreparable destruction which come suddenly to view when it is too late.

6

(2, 3) These words represent the haste of the seeming penitents for the fulfillment of their hope. They expect the rapid restoration of the national prosperity, prompted by the abundance of the divine love, and His response to the first touch of penitence (signified in 5:15). (To bring in the resurrection of Christ with no authority from the New Testament is farfetched over-refinement, and breaks the consistency of the passage.)

(6) Mercy.—Better rendered, "love." This passage is richly sustained by our Lord's adoption of its teaching (Matt. 9:13; 12:7). Mark 12:33 shows that according to even Old Testament teaching, the moral ranks above the ceremonial, that ritual is valueless apart from spiritual conformity with divine will.

(7) God made a covenant with Adam, and promised him the blessings of Paradise on condition of obedience. He broke the condition, transgressed the covenant, and was driven from his divine home. So Israel had violated all the terms on which the goodly land of conditional promise had been bestowed (see Ps. 82:7; Job. 31:33).

(11) An harvest.—The harvest is not of joy, but of sorrow and affliction, befalling Judah, like Israel, for her sins—a contrast to the usual accompaniments of the season when the Feast of Tabernacles was celebrated (Deut. 12:13-16; Lev. 23:40; Ps. 126:5, 6).

7

(3) Glad.—The evil awakens no alarm, but rather sympathy and gladness, in the breasts of their kings and rulers, who are ready to follow suit in all deeds of violence. This oracle is probably in the beginning of Hoshea's reign.

(4) The baker is unremitting in his exertions to keep up the heat of the oven, the smoldering fire being fed on camel's dung and the like fuel, except when he is obliged to occupy himself with preparing the dough for baking—an apt image of the incessant burning rage of lust and violence.

(6) The metaphor of verse 4 is resumed. The baker, having left his dough to become

leavened and his fire to smolder, can afford to sleep. The baker may mean the evil passion which has been raging. After the murderous plots and carousal (verse 5), the conspiracy ripens with the day; then will come the outburst of violence.

(8) Cake not turned.—Ephraim was consumed by the unhallowed fire of Baal-worship, with all its passion and sensualism—a cake burned on one side to a cinder, and on the other left in a condition utterly unfit for food. So the activity of foreign idolatries and foreign alliances, and the consequent unfaithfulness to Israel's God, are the nation's ruin.

(11) Silly dove.—No creature is less able to defend itself than the dove, which flies from the bird of prey to the net of the fowler. In this powerful metaphor we have a political allusion. While Hosea was sending tribute to Assyria, he was secretly negotiating with Egypt. The alliance between Egypt and the king of Israel (II Kings 17:4) took place later, after Tiglath-pileser's death, and led to Israel's ruin.

(12) When they shall go.—This refers to the ultimate ruin produced by this policy of dependence on foreign states and of double-dealing intrigue, even at this early stage foreseen by the prophet, and portrayed under the simile of Jehovah's net snaring the unwary bird.

(14) Cried ... —God discriminates between a heart-cry to Him, and a howl of despair, resembling the yell of a wild beast. A howl upon their bed is not a sob of true repentance. All their simulated penitence, furthermore, is to secure physical comforts, not to show conformity with the divine will.

(16) Like a deceitful bow.—Religious observance has the appearance of a bow with the arrow on the string, apparently aimed at some object, but the string being slack, the aim is diverted. In the land of Egypt they would thus become objects of derision. (Comp. Isa. 30:1-8.)

8

(1) Eagle.—The image of swiftness (Jer. 4:13; 48:40). So Assyria shall come swooping down on Samaria, to which Hosea, though with some irony, gives the name "House of Jehovah," recognizing that the calf was meant to be symbolic in some sense of Israel's God.

(4) Set up kings.—The passage refers to

the short reigns of usurpers and to the foul murders which disgraced the annals of the northern kingdom since the death of Jeroboam II. Jehovah repudiates all participation in their anarchy.

(7) Wind ... whirlwind.—The great law of divine retribution, the punishment for sin being often a greater facility in sinning—indifference to God becoming enmity, forgetfulness of duty or truth becoming violent recoil from both.

(9) Wild ass is the image of untamed waywardness (Job 39:5 seq., Jer. 2:24). Israel, like a solitary wild ass, seeks strange loves, courts strange alliances. (See Ezek. 16:32-34.) Ephraim pays abnormally for her own shame.

(11) Many altars.—Multiplication of altars was condemned in the law (Deut. 12:5 seq.). Josh. 22 shows that unity of altar and sanctuary was essential to the unity of the nation. In the first clause sin equals transgression; in the last, transgression **plus** guilt and peril.

(12, 13) The tense "I write" is imperfect, and represents the continuous process—the prophetic teaching as well as the ancient Mosaic law. In the wild lust for a foreign religion, the pure and spiritual Mosaic worship and the religious influence of prophecy had been forgotten.

9

(1) For joy.—The bounteous yield of the harvest is called the "harlot's hire," which lures Jehovah's faithless bride to worship the false deity from whose hands these gifts were supposed to come. The people's momentary prosperity is attributed to their idols.

(6) Hosea prophesies an exile to Egypt after the anticipated invasion. That many exiles took refuge in Egypt in 721 B.C., after the great overthrow of the northern kingdom (as in the case of Judah in the days of Jeremiah), cannot be doubted. (Comp. 8:13 and verse 3 above; see 11:5.)

(7) The latter part of the verse should be translated "Crazed is the prophet, mad the inspired one, because of the multitude of thy iniquity, while persecution is increased." The prophet is crazed either in the depraved public opinion that Hosea scornfully describes, or, he is driven mad by the persecutions to which he is subjected. The latter is more probable. (Comp. the

following verse, where there is reference to persecution in the house of God itself.)

(10) Baal-peor was the place where Moabitic idolatry was practiced. This great disgrace had burned itself into their national traditions and literature (Num. 25; Deut. 4:3; Ps. 106:28-31).

(11) From the birth ... —An ascending climax. Progeny was the glory of ancient Israel (Gen. 22:17; Deut. 7:13, 14; Ps. 127:5; Prov. 17:6).

(13) The impregnable fortress of Tyre was a conspicuous object in the days of Hosea. Similarly Samaria was a stronghold which was able to resist prolonged sieges. (Comp. Isa. 28:1-4; Amos 6:1.) Yet there is impending overthrow and massacre (721 B.C.). Better universal childlessness than that the offspring should be exposed to so terrible a fate (verse 14).

(15) Gilgal.—Gilgal was a seat of idolatrous worship (see 4:15). "My house" here, and in 8:1 ("Jehovah's house"), is interpreted to mean the "holy land," Canaan. The term seems to have blended the conception of a people and the territory they occupied. Similarly, Egypt is called (Exod. 20:2) "the house of slaves." The word "house" reminds us of the domestic episode (chaps. 1-3): Ephraim, like an adulterous wife, is turned out of house and home (comp. 3:4), and is no longer Jehovah's people (1:9).

(17) Wanderers.—This is strangely confirmed from Assyrian monuments and the entire subsequent history of the bulk of Israel.

10

(1) The metaphors of the vintage are still prevalent in the mind of the prophet. Israel experienced a wild strong growth, as compared with Judah. Misapprehending the cause of their temporal prosperity, and wilfully ignoring Jehovah's forbearance and love, they attributed their mercies to the grace of Baal, and multiplied idolatrous shrines.

(3) To us.—The prophet, having witnessed a succession of Israelite kings overthrown, and anarchy as its consequence, predicts yet another time of confusion and helplessness, a full vindication of the threatenings of the prophet Samuel. (Comp. 1 Sam. 8:19.)

(5) It is hard to express the sarcastic force and concentrated scoff of the original:

629

"calves," literally, "she calves," the feminine form to express contempt, the plural in allusion to the scattered worship in numerous shrines throughout Israel (or, perhaps, a **pluralis majestatis** of mockery).

(6) See 5:13.

(7) **Foam ... water.**—Here is one of the most striking images in the prophecy. Translate: "Like a chip on the waters' surface." The king is tossed on the raging seas of political life like a helpless fragment. Such was the instability of the throne of Israel at this period. (Comp. 13:11.)

(8) The prophet not only predicts utter ruin for king and calf, temple and shrine, but the future desolation which should conceal all. Meanwhile, the people shall desire death rather than life. (Comp. Luke 23:30; Rev. 6:16; 9:6.)

(9) **O Israel ... Gibeah.**—You began your obscene transgressions long before the disruption of the kingdom of Rehoboam, even at Gibeah. Gibeah is emblematic of gross and cruel sensuality, in allusion to Judg. 19:20, just as Sodom is used for unnatural vice.

(11) Here the idea seems to be that Ephraim loves the easy and free work of treading out the corn, and so becomes fat and sleek. But I will cause a rider, Assyria, to take possession of her, and she shall be bound in unwelcome toil to do the bidding of another.

(12) In their despair come some characteristic gleams of hope on the desolation; the eternal law which makes reaping a consequence of sowing will still apply. The mercy of God will be the harvest of a sowing to the Spirit. (Comp. Micah 6:8; Rom. 8:7-13; Gal. 6:8.) The soil of the soul is fallow and unbroken. Seek Jehovah, and He will come as never before.

(14) **Shalman.**—The allusion is obscure. Some have suggested that it refers to an episode in the campaign of Shalmaneser III to the "cedar country" (Lebanon) in 775 B.C., or to Damascus in 773. He might then have penetrated into the Transjordanic country and destroyed Arbela, near Pella. The kind of barbarity here referred to is illustrated by II Kings 8:12; Ps. 137:8, 9.

(15) **King ... cut off.**—The close of the kingdom (721 B.C.), already more than once referred to (comp. verse 7), is here prophesied. Hoshea was early and utterly cut off, leaving neither root nor branch.

11

(1) Comp. 9:10 and Exod. 4:22, 23. In this context there cannot be a prophecy of the Christ, for obstinate conduct and rebellion would thus be involved in the prediction. It is true that Matt. 2:15 quotes the passage in illustration of the fact that the true Son of God was also submitted in His youth to the hard schooling of a cruel exile. The calling out of Egypt of the Messiah gave a new indication of the cyclical character of Hebrew history. The passage helps us to understand what is meant by the formula, "that it might be fulfilled," etc.

(2) **As they called them, so they went from them.**—Israel sought to avoid the voice and presence of the prophets.

(4) **Cords of a man.**—In contrast with the compulsive cords with which unmanageable beasts are held in check, Israel is led with "bands of love." The last clause expresses the tenderness, delicacy, and condescension of personal regard.

(5) **Return**—i.e., to God.

(7) The people were called by sufficient means to the highest worship, but they were bent on the lowest.

(8) In the depth of despair the prophet delivers himself of one of the most pathetic passages in Hebrew prophecy. A nation so much beloved as Israel cannot be destroyed by Him who has fostered it so tenderly. As the prophet loved his faithless bride, so Jehovah continued to love His people. The "how" of this verse expresses the most extreme reluctance. Admah and Zeboim were cities of the plain destroyed with Sodom and Gomorrah, which are often referred to as the type of irremediable catastrophe.

Mine heart is turned within me.—Better, "against me"—a violent revulsion of feeling. Divine compassion pleads with divine justice.

(11) **Will place them.**—The prophetic word looks beyond the restoration of the sixth century B.C. to the gathering together of some from east and west, from all the places where they are hidden in exile under the lion of the tribe of Judah; the broader and grander accomplishment will satisfy and more than fulfill the yearnings of the spiritual Israel.

12

(1) **East wind.**—Comp. Isa. 27:8 and Job 27:21. That which is unpleasant and revolt-

ing in life is compared by Orientals to the east wind, which parches the vegetation and precedes famine. The idea expressed here is the same as in Job 15:2, combining the notions of destructiveness and emptiness. The covenant with Assyria refers to the events of the reign of Hoshea. Covenants with Assyria and presents to Egypt were to Hosea curses in disguise.

(2) Jacob refers to the northern kingdom.

(5) Lord God of hosts.—Probably the hosts were the stars, conceived of as celestial spirits (1 Kings 22:19). These are to be identified, in all probability, with the sons of God (Gen. 6:2), described in Job 1:6. (Comp. Pss. 103:21; 104:4; Heb. 1:7.)

His memorial—i.e., his name: the self-existent One who nevertheless came into personal relations with Israel. (See Exod. 3:14, 15.)

(6) Therefore . . . —There is an implied contrast between the patriarch and his degenerate descendants in the days of Hosea.

(7) He is a merchant.—The rendering "he is a merchant" originates from the fact that Canaan (rendered "merchant") is often used predominantly of Phoenicia, and Canaanites of Phoenicians, the great trading race (Isa. 23:11). The descendants of Canaan (the son of Ham, the abhorred son of Noah) became in their whole career a curse and a byword in every religious and ethical sense. The princes of Tyre, the merchandise of Phoenicia, were, perhaps, then in the prophet's mind. (Comp. Ezek. 27.)

Moreover, the prophet hints that Ephraim had imbibed Phoenicia's love of gain and habits of unscrupulous trade. The literature of this period contains frequent references to these tendencies in Israel (Amos 2:6; 8:5; Micah 6:10).

(9) Tabernacles.—The prophet here speaks of Israel's moral restoration under the form of a return to the old ideal of simple agricultural life, in which every good gift is received directly from Jehovah's hand. To the true theocratic spirit the condition here spoken of is one of real blessedness, but to the worldly, grasping Canaan or Ephraim it would come as a threat of expulsion, desolation, and despair. (Comp. 2:14; 3:3.)

(11) Whether referring to a past event—i.e., to the desolating invasion of Gilead by Tiglath-pileser in 734 B.C.—, or to a future calamity, from this time forth we hear no more of Gilgal as a religious center.

(13) A prophet.—The reference is to Moses, and there is, perhaps, a hint that the Lord would yet again save Israel from worse than Egyptian bondage by the words and warnings of a prophet.

13

(1) This points to the revolt of the Ten Tribes, and the consequent abandonment of the pure traditions of Jehovah worship for those of Baal. This idea and that of 12:14 may have been brought into prominence by the recent untoward antagonism aroused by the Syro-Ephraimitish war against Judah.

(7) I will be . . . —The idea of this and the following verses is that of a divine judgment suspended over Israel, destined soon to fall with overwhelming ruin (721 B.C.).

(10) The original demand for a king who should be a visible token to Israel of protection against their surrounding foes was adverse to the true spirit of the kingdom of God upon earth, and, though granted, proved to the united kingdom, and afterward to the kingdom of Israel, an age-long curse. Probably the special reference here is to the latter—the erection of the Ten Tribes into a separate monarchy.

(11) Gave . . . took.—The past tenses should be present. The whole succession of Israelite kings, who generation after generation had been taken away, some by violent death, would close with Hoshea, who was to disappear as "a fragment on a stormy sea" (10:7).

(13) Travailing woman.—Ephraim is first addressed as a travailing woman; but the imagery passes to the condition of the unborn child, which tarries just where it should issue into the light of the world. Lack of seasonable repentance increases the danger at this critical stage of Israel's destiny.

(14) O death . . . O grave.—The rendering should be as the LXX has it, and as it is quoted in 1 Cor. 15:55. Many Christian interpreters regard this as the sudden outburst of a gracious promise, as Paul takes it. The last clause then signifies that the gift and calling of God are without repentance. There is no room for any further merciful change of purpose. But it should be remembered that Paul quoted from Isaiah, "Death shall be swallowed up in victory," and then, as here, calls in derisive irony upon death and Sheol to do their worst at the moment when they are about to be cast into the lake of fire.

631

(15) Wind of the Lord.—The armies of Assyria are referred to.

14

In this last chapter, uttered in gentlest mood, he shows a bow of promise painted on the darkness of the storm cloud.

(2) Say unto him.—This putting of words into the lips of penitents and others is found in Ps. 66:3; Isa. 48:20; Jer. 31:7. The words of true repentance which we take with us shall be our offerings in place of calves. (Comp. Ps. 51:17.)

(3) The three crying sins of Israel are here recounted: (1) Expected salvation from Assyria; (2) dependence on the world power of Egypt, famed for war-horses and chariots; (3) ascription of divine names and homage to wrought images of the divine glory.

(5, 6) As the dew.—For this imagery see Ps. 130:3. The lily. which carpets the fields of Palestine (Matt. 6:29). has slender roots. which might easily be uptorn. but under God's protection. even these are to strike downward like the roots of the cedars.

(7) The form of these promises is derived from the external signs of national prosperity. (Comp. 12:10.) But corn and wine are throughout the Scriptures the great symbols of spiritual refreshment. and are still the memorials of the supreme love of Him whose body was broken and whose blood was shed for us.

(10) "Wisdom" and "wise men" take in the later Hebrew literature the place of "prophecy" and "prophets." Wisdom interprets both the word and its fulfillment.

JOEL

1

(1) Joel.—The name is compounded of Jehovah—El, the composite title of God of revelation and of nature, which is the subject of Psalm 19. There is nothing known of the personal history of Joel the prophet, except the name of his father, Pethuel.

(2, 3) Hath this been in your days.—The introduction points to the startling nature of the portent: it was unexampled; it was a cause of consternation to all who beheld it; it would be recollected as a subject of wondering comment among succeeding generations. The hand of God was evident, recalling the marvelous things he did in the land of Egypt, in the field of Zoan.

(4) That which the palmerworm hath left.—The picture is introduced suddenly and graphically. The earth is bared by locusts beyond all previous experience. There were different sorts of locusts; as many as ninety have been reckoned. The four names, palmerworm, locust, cankerworm, caterpiller, indicate different swarms of the insect. The first points to its voracity; the second, its multitude; the third, its manner of "licking up" the grass like cattle; the fourth, its destructive effect. The number "four" draws attention to the "four sore judgments" with which Ezekiel was instructed to threaten Jerusalem, and to the four foreign invasions by the Assyrians, Chaldaeans, Macedonians and Romans.

(8) For the husband of her youth.—The land is addressed as a virgin betrothed, but not yet married, and forfeiting her marriage by unworthy conduct. Such was the relation of Israel to the Lord: He was faithful, but Israel unfaithful. Now let her mourn the penalty, as all the outward and visible signs of communion with God are cut off (verse 9).

(13) Gird yourselves, and lament.—The priests are exhorted to begin preparations for a national humiliation, beginning with themselves. The visitation touches them in a vital point: they have no sacrifices to offer to the Lord.

(15) Almighty—Shaddai, a title signifying the omnipotence of God, especially with reference, as here, to His power to destroy. See note on Gen. 17:1.

(17) The corn is withered.—The results of the terrible drought, coincident with the ravages of the locusts, are now described.

(19) The fire hath devoured.—This may be explained as produced by the scorching heat bringing about spontaneous combustion, or by the efforts of the people to exterminate the locusts by burning the trees, or by the mark, as of fire, left upon all vegetation after the locusts had finished their work of devastation.

(20) The beasts of the field cry also unto thee.—As yet, man seems dumb.

2

(1) Blow ye the trumpet.—The preaching of the prophet increases in its intensity. Behind the locusts, exemplified by them, there is a still more terrible visitation. He sees on the horizon a mustering of the nations hostile to his people, bent on destroying them. Let the priests stir up the people for a fast, and for the defense of their land, by the trumpet. The locusts have done their symbolical work; they have left their mark on the country. Now the day of Jehovah, the manifestation of His power, is imminent.

(3) Before them ... behind them.—As with the locusts, so with the invading hosts of enemies: the country is found a paradise, and left a desert.

(4) As the appearance of horses.—Comp. Rev. 9:7, 9.

(6) All faces shall gather blackness.—The comparison is in this case between the faces growing black under the influence of fear, and of pots under the action of fire. Comp. Nahum 2:10.

(7-9) They shall run like mighty men.—The onward irresistible march of the invaders is graphically described by the illustration of the advance of locusts. They appear on the mountains which environ the city, they mount the walls, they rush through the streets, they enter the houses, they are in possession of Jerusalem.

(10) The earth shall quake before them.—Some commentators call this description "a specimen of the highly-wrought hyperbolical features of Hebrew poetry," but it is the presence and judgment, the voice of the Lord in the thunder, which causes this trepidation. The signs in the heavens will be manifested at the judgment day.

(12) Saith the Lord.—The word "saith" is here no common word in the Hebrew. It implies an authoritative and most weighty utterance, used in almost every instance of the immediate utterance of God Himself.

Turn ye even to me.—The question,

"Who can abide it?" (verse 11) is left unanswered. But the only possible reply is inferred in the touching appeal which the prophet is inspired by Jehovah to make, that His righteous anger may be averted.

(13) Repenteth him of the evil.—The judgments of God, like His mercies, are conditional. As the "Lord repented (i.e., grieved) that He had made Saul king over Israel," and revoked the appointment, so now He repenteth Him of the evil which will fall on His people if impenitent.

(14) Even a meat offering.—The returning favor of the Lord will enable the daily sacrifices to be restored, which had failed through the visitation (1:9).

(20) The northern army.—This is an exception to the usual direction of the flight of locusts, but it may be literally applied to the Assyrian hordes, of whom the Jews generally spoke as dwelling in the north. (In Jeremiah 1:13 the symbolical caldron is represented as pouring its contents—the Chaldaean army—southward from the face of the north.) Under the image of the destruction of the locusts, the prophet points to the deliverance from the northern invaders. The east sea is the Dead Sea; the utmost or hinder sea is the Mediterranean; the desolate land is the southern desert. The northern invader shall be expelled all along the coasts of Palestine. (Comp. the eighth plague, Exod. 10.)

(23) The former rain moderately.—The gift of rain is a witness to the people of the existence and beneficence of God. (Comp. Acts 14:17.) The possibility of the interpretation of "the former rain moderately" out of the Hebrew words by a "teacher of righteousness," as in the Vulg., has led to the connection of this passage with a prophetic intimation of the advent of the Messiah.

(25) I will restore to you the years—i.e., the years which would have been necessary in the ordinary course of nature for the land to recover from the ravages of the "great army."

(27) I am in the midst of Israel.—This divine assurance, similar to that with which the book ends, prepares the way for the spiritual blessings about to be announced.

(28) I will pour out my spirit upon all flesh.—Holy Scripture is itself the interpreter of this most weighty promise. Peter's quotation and application of it in the Acts is its commentary. "Afterward"—"in the last days,"—i.e., in the Christian dispensation, when, after the punishment of the Jews

by the heathen, their king came—"my Spirit" (Peter renders "of my spirit," after the LXX, indicating the gifts and influences of the Holy Ghost) will be poured out "upon all flesh," i.e., without distinction of race or person. The outward manifestation of these gifts, as on the Day of Pentecost, was in accordance with this prediction.

(30, 31) The sun ... and the moon.—These words, recalling some of the portents in the ancient history of the Jews (especially as instanced in some of the plagues of Egypt) are taken up by our Lord Himself, as ushering in the great day of judgment. The sun and moon, etc., may include the luminaries in heaven and the potentates on earth.

(32) Deliverance.—Paul quotes from this verse (Rom. 10:13), transferring the reference to the Messianic advent, to prove the universality of the deliverance effected by our Lord, who abolished the difference between Jew and Greek.

3

(1) That time.—The whole course of the events of the world is shown to lead up by divine providence to the Great Day of the Lord. Then will the people of God be brought out of captivity, and vengeance executed upon their enemies. This progress, with its final consummation, is the subject of the concluding lines of Joel's prophecy.

(2) The valley of Jehoshaphat.—See II Chron. 20. The victory there was an occasion of immense exultation, and seems to supply the imagery with which Joel describes the day of the Lord. The name of Jehoshaphat was at some period given to the Kedron Valley, but it is here used rather in its grammatical meaning as the scene of the divine judgment, the words signifying "the valley where Jehovah judgeth."

(4) What have ye to do with me?—God, identifying Himself with His people, threatens retaliation upon their enemies for the wrongs they had inflicted upon them (see verses 3, 5, 6). Comp. II Chron. 21:17; Ezek. 27:13.

(8) I will sell your sons ...—The Philistines came under the power of Uzziah and Hezekiah, who may have sold them to the Sabeans on the Persian Gulf, by whom they would have been passed on to India. The Philistines were also sold in great numbers by the Grecian conquerors in the time of the Maccabees.

(10) Beat your plowshares ... —When the contest between Jehovah and the nations was over, and His victory achieved, Micah (4:3) foresaw the reversal of this order: the weapons of offense were once more to resume their peaceful character.

(13) Put ye in the sickle.—In the enthusiasm of his vision the prophet crowds together metaphors to intensify the description of the coming encounter between Jehovah and the enemies of His people. It is represented by the judgment seat, the harvest, and the vintage.

(14) Multitudes.—The command has gone forth; it is obeyed; and the prophet stands aghast at the vast multitudes assembling in the valley of decision, the place of judgment.

(16) The Lord also shall roar ... —This is the keynote of the prophecy of Amos, who opens his appeal with these words. The majestic roar of the lion is transferred to express victorious utterance of the Lord's judgment: it is irresistible. The temporal success of the Jews in their future conflict with their enemies is blended with the final triumph of the Lord in the judgment day.

(18) The valley of Shittim.—Shittim, in the land of Moab, is symbolical of the barrenness and sterility of land where there is no water. The heathen, to whom God is not known, shall yet become covered with the knowledge of the Lord.

(19) Egypt shall be a desolation.—Egypt and Edom always excited feelings of abhorrence in the hearts of the Jews. The memory of the exile in Egypt was always fresh and sharp; no retrospect of their past history could leave it out of account. And the national detestation of the false and cruelhearted Idumaean kinsmen is recalled by Obadiah in his prophecy and touching record (comp. Ps. 137).

(21) The Lord dwelleth in Zion.—Over a raging and swelling world, probably unconscious of Him, the Lord nevertheless reigns in the heavenly Jerusalem, and all His redeemed shall dwell securely under His eternal rule (see Ezek. 48:35).

AMOS

1

The prologue to the prophecies of Amos consists of a series of denunciations of the surrounding peoples. The ground of the awful threatenings is the word of Jehovah made known to the prophet. The reason for the doom predicted on such high authority is the resistance and cruelty that were offered by these nations to the theocratic people, and, still more, their own moral offenses, condemned by universal conscience. The denunciations begin with a judgment upon Syria (1:3-5), the age-long enemy of Judah, sometimes confederate with Israel. Then he passes to Philistia (1:6-8), which had been a thorn in the side of Israel and Judah from the days of the Judges until his own. Then he directs his gaze upon Phoenician cities (1:9, 10), the emporium of the most extensive commerce in the world. Next he passes in review three other nations (Edom, 1:11, 12; Ammon, 1:13-15; Moab, 2:1-3), more closely related to Israel in blood, language, and proximity, and which, nevertheless, had often manifested an undying hatred of the covenanted people. After this Judah (2:3-5), his own tribe, does not escape. Lastly, the prophet gathers up all his strength to denounce Israel, then at the height of prosperity and splendor.

(1) The early life of the prophet Amos was spent at Tekoa, an elevated spot between four and five miles due south of Bethlehem. Amos was by birth not a prophet, but a herdsman, and likewise a dresser of sycamore fruit. Respecting his prophetic work, we know that it was directed almost entirely to the northern kingdom, and was likewise exercised there. It is difficult to assign a probable date for the entire collection of oracles. We know from the superscription that they were delivered two years before "the earthquake," an event so terrible and marked in its character that it is referred to again by Zechariah (Zech. 14:5), and that he prophesied during the reigns of Jeroboam and Uzziah. But we do not know the date of the earthquake, nor whether the prophetic ministry of Amos continued after the death of Jeroboam II. We suggest, nevertheless, that the prophetic career of Amos was probably subsequent to 780 B.C. The fact that the prophet never makes mention of the name of Assyria, although he refers

expressly to the destinies of surrounding nations, seems to imply that Assyria was at that period not as disturbing a force in Syro-Palestinian politics as it had been in a former generation, and as it was destined to become during the ministry of the prophet Hosea.

(3) Three transgressions . . . —This form of transgression, which occurs eight times in the prologue, is not an arithmetical, but a strongly idiomatic phrase, signifying "multiplied or repeated delinquencies."

(4) I will send a fire . . . —Comp. Jer. 49:27, where this language is repeated at a time when punishment had fallen for a while on Damascus, and she had become, as Isaiah predicted, "a ruinous heap" (Isa. 17:1).

(6) The proceedings of Philistia, here represented by Gaza as the principal city, imply a veritable sack of Jerusalem (comp. II Chron. 21:16, 17). The extreme barbarity from which Judah suffered was that her children were delivered up to the implacable enemy Edom. (Comp. the language of Joel 3:4-6.) The utter fall of Philistian independence is depicted (comp. 6:2).

(9) The brotherly covenant.—This was the league made between Hiram and David, and afterward between Hiram and Solomon (II Sam. 5:11; I Kings 5:1, 12). This ancient covenant was forgotten in Phoenicia's mercantile avarice, and Tyre was tempted to sell Hebrew captives to Greeks and Idumeans. (Comp. Isa. 23; Ezek. 26.)

(12) Teman.—According to Gen. 36:11, a name for a grandson of Esau. The district and chief town of this name are often referred to in the prophets (Jer. 49:7; Ezek. 25:13; Hab. 3:3). See note on Obad. 8, 9.

(13) The precise event of atrocious cruelty is not mentioned in the historical books; but the barbarous modes of warfare which prevailed in those days are mentioned in I Sam. 11:2; II Kings 15:16; Hos. 13:16; and in Assyrian inscriptions.

(14) Jeremiah gives a vivid account of the impending doom of Ammon, quoting and expanding this very passage (49:1-3).

2

(1) Comp. Isa. 15, 16; 25:1-12; Jer. 48. The historical reference is obscure. (See II Kings 3:26, 27.)

(4) Their lies—i.e., their false deities, which they have treated as divine. "The lies after which the fathers walked deceived the children. The children canonise the errors of their fathers. Human opinion is as dogmatic as revelation" (Pusey). High privilege does not involve immunity from punishment. Judah shall be chastized with the same penalty as Edom, Philistia, Ammon and Moab.

(6) Transgressions of Israel.—The storm of divine threatening which had swept over the whole political horizon gathers, at last, over Israel. The sin consists in the perverse straining of the law, which allowed an insolvent debtor to sell himself into bondage to redeem a debt (comp. II Kings 4:1; Lev. 25:39). In this case the debtor was a righteous man in sore straits for no fault of his own. A paltry debt, equivalent, in worth, to a pair of sandals, would not save him from bondage at the hands of an oppressive ruler.

(7) Dust of the earth on the head of the poor.—They long to see the poor reduced to such distress that dust is thrown on their heads in token of grief. The meek are defrauded as being too weak to claim their own. The latter part of the verse points to the sensuality of the popular worship, the "maid" being really a prostitute.

(8) Rapacity and cruelty follow on pride, selfishness and lust. The money that had been wrung from those who could not pay, or, who had been sold into slavery, is spent in rioting and feasting.
In the house of their god.—Probably here, as in the previous verse, we are to understand the high places of syncretic, or heathenish, Jehovah worship.

(11, 12) God added to the mercies of His providence (verse 9, 10) the transcendent blessings of special revelation. The Nazarite was a link between the prophet and the priest, upon whom, without hereditary rank or sacerdotal rite, great privileges were bestowed. The assault upon both is highly characteristic of the disloyalty of Israel.

(13) I am pressed.—Better, "I am pressing." Jehovah, in the awful judgment which He inflicts, is symbolized by the heavily-laden wagon. Israel, the nation weighted with the doom of past iniquities, bequeathes a yet more crushing load to future generations.

(14) This doom Amos darkly foreshadows to be invasion and military overthrow, with all its attendant calamities.

3

Chaps. 3-6 form a connected series, standing, however, as a natural sequence upon the previous section. With searching minuteness the whole of Israel's sin and doom are laid bare by the prophet; the blindness to the warnings of prophecy, the pride and luxury of the powerful, and the misery of the oppressed, as well as the prevailing idolatrous corruption. A solemn dirge over Israel and Judah (chaps. 5, 6) closes the first part of these prophetic addresses.

(1) Children of Israel rather than "house of Israel" is a phrase not so usual in Amos. There is significance in the former, as Amos addresses himself to both kingdoms in the phrase "the whole family." Yet the kingdom of the Ten Tribes seems to be chiefly in the mind of the prophet.

(2) Known.—The knowledge of God is love. There was special knowledge and intimacy between God and Israel. Upon such knowledge followed innumerable advantages and privileges. This intimacy of knowledge is the ground of gracious chastizement. For nation or man to be allowed to go on in sin without rebuke is the greatest curse that can befall it or him.

(3) Two.—The two here represented are God and Israel, the expression denoting not merely God's knowledge of a man, but also man's response to God. Will God walk with man, guiding, shielding, strengthening him, if man is not in harmony with Him? This is the first of a series of parabolic apothegms, all of which require a negative answer. Each states an event, closely and indissolubly related to another in the bond of cause and effect. All these symbolic utterances point on to the climax in verses 7, 8.

(8) Roared.—Comp. the imagery of 1:2, and that of verse 4. The voice of the Lord is so audible, so clearly portending the coming judgment, that universal terror inevitably follows.

(10) Know not to do right.—Not merely have they lost the perception of what is and what is not right, but they are indifferent to such distinctions. They know not and care not—the awful state of utter moral impotence, wherein not only the intellectual consciousness, but also the impulses to action are languid or even paralyzed.

(11) Thy strength points mainly to the stronghold of Samaria, which the "adversary" (Assyria) was to bring down or reduce to ruins, but it may likewise include the chief warriors who were to be led away captive.

(12) Taketh out ... taken out.—The agricultural image, used by Amos, is very impressive. The shanks and pieces of the ear, worthless portions, saved from the lion's jaws, represent the remnants of Samaria's population that shall escape.

In Damascus in a couch.—The relations between Syria and Israel at this moment were intimate. The meaning is that even the noblest and wealthiest will be regarded, if saved, as worthless salvage.

4

(1) Bashan.—This contained the rich pasture-lands east of the Jordan, between Hermon and the mountains of Gilead, where cattle flourished. The "strong bulls of Bashan" (Ps. 22:12) were descriptive of the malignant enemies of the ideal sufferer. The feminine "kine" refers to the luxurious self-indulgent women of fashion in Samaria.

(2) Fishhooks.—This is descriptive of the suddenness and irresistible character of the seizure, whereby, as a punishment for their wanton selfishness, the nobles were to be carried away as captives from their condition of fancied security.

(3) Every cow ... —Render "each one (ref. to the women, verse 1) straight before her." The enemy shall have broken down the city's defenses, and the women shall tamely go forth through the breaches into captivity. The next clause is very obscure. It is best to take the verb as passive, and to treat the obscure word as a proper name: "Ye shall be cast out to the mountains of Armenia" (their place of banishment).

(4) Bethel ... Gilgal.—In bitterly ironical words the prophet summons Israel to the calf-worship of Bethel, and to similar rites at Gilgal. These spots were full of sacred associations. The sarcastic force of the passage is lost unless "three years" be read "every three days." The law only required a tithe every third year (Deut. 26:12); but here the prophet is lashing the people with hyperbolical irony for their excessive generosity to the base priests and spurious sanctuaries. Also in verse 5 Amos ironically calls upon them to break the Levitical law (Lev. 7:13; 23:17), as he knew they were in the habit of doing.

(6) Cleanness of teeth is, by the poetic parallelism, identified with the want of bread, the former phrase being a graphic

representation of one of the ghastly aspects of famine—clean, sharp, prominent teeth projecting from the thin lips. Jehovah is here introduced as grieving over the failure of His disciplinary treatment of Israel. So also in drought, famine, plague, earthquake, and volcanic eruption (verses 7-11).

(12) Thus will I do.—What He is about to do is left in awful uncertainty, but the doom is wrapped up in the boundless possibilities of the divine judgment involved in the drawing very near of the Lord Himself, to execute what He has said and sworn by His Holiness in verses 2 and 3. All that had previously been done was not final, and had failed in its effect. The summons to meet God in some other unknown form than these is solemn.

(13) God of hosts.—The Lord whom they have to meet is no mere national deity, but the supreme Creator.

5

(2) "Virgin" is a feminine designation of Israel poetically expressive of grace and beauty. Comp. the epithet "daughter of Zion," nations and cities being represented by a feminine personification. She is not annihilated, but obliterated as a nation.

(5) Seek.—The same word is used for the searching, or inquiring at idol shrines, which is here fervently condemned. (Respecting Beersheba, see note on 8:14.)

(8) We prefer to render, "As for him who made the Pleiades ... Jehovah is his name," i.e., The God of the Hebrews is the supreme universal Lord (comp. 4:13). This is profoundly impressive, since the prophets were surrounded by the pompous nature-worship of the East. The Heb. word for the Pleiades (seven stars) means properly "heap" or "cluster," and that for Orion signifies "stout, strong one." The appearance of the Pleiades indicated the "sweet influences" of spring, that of Orion the winter solstice. The death-shadow suggests the darkest experiences of human life. Jehovah pours His light upon the deepest gloom of our lot. He, too, can make the day dark with night, covering the noonday sky with funereal pall, as at the Crucifixion. God is made also the perennial source of the rain, that always rises at His command from the great sea.

(12) I know.—The "I" is likely to be the prophet himself. The idea involved in the word rendered "bribe" is the ransom which the poor and defenseless were obliged to pay to a tyrannical judge, in order to escape a harsh sentence. The "gate" is the place where judgment is passed by the chief men.

(14, 15) These verses break in like a beam of sunshine in the darkness. The fearful doom, already spoken of, is after all conditional. Let a moral change be wrought in them, and even now Jehovah may be with them.

(17) Pass through thee.—Whenever Jehovah is said to pass through a land or a city, heavy punishment is intended. (Comp. Exod. 12:12.)

(18) Desire the day of the Lord—i.e., expect that day to bring you deliverance and judgments upon your enemies. It shall bring the reverse!

(19) Your escape will be impossible. You will avoid one calamity, only to fall into a worse.

(21-23) These verses closely resemble the condemnation which Isaiah pronounces (1:10-15) upon mere ritual, however punctilious, mere profession of orthodoxy, however exacting, which was not accompanied by righteousness and mercy, and was not the expression of inward penitence and purity.

(25-27) Nearly all exegetes follow the LXX., Vulg., Targ., in taking verse 25 as interrogative. The expected answer is negative. The words apply to the nation as a whole, or to the great mass of the people, individual exceptions being passed by. The following verse then expresses opposition between the Jehovah-worship, which they suspended, and the idol-worship which they carried on. This is a possible interpretation, but some suggest that it is more in harmony with grammatical usage to translate verse 26 by a future. To his thought verse 27 forms a natural development. Moreover, in the light of this interpretation the logical connection of verses 21-27 becomes much simpler. On the difficult clause, **Chiun,** etc., in verse 26, see Acts 7:42, 43.

at this period the Assyrian power had destroyed the importance of these places, though the prophet may have regarded that issue as imminent. (See Gen. 10:10; II Kings 14:28; Isa. 10:9.) Were Calno, Hamath, Gath, more important than Zion or Samaria? Then, says the prophet, do not expect in your opulence and self-satisfaction immunity from a worse doom.

(3) Far away.—They choose to think that the day of reckoning is far off, and cling yet closer to their habits of self-indulgence and of defrauding the poor at the seat of judgment.

(9, 10) This and one other passage (I Sam. 31:12) imply that under special circumstances the Hebrews burned their dead. In this case pestilence made cremation a necessity. The references in II Chron. 16:14; 21:19; Jer. 34:5, are to honorific burning of spices in memory of the dead.

(12) The questions require a negative answer, and show that the conduct of Israel is as inconsistent and senseless as the supposition involved in the interrogation. The conception of oppression, luxury, and pride being the forerunners of prosperity and peace is anomalous. The idea is that that which should have insured the stability of the state, the embodiment of its conscience, had been turned into narcotic poison—the self-satisfaction of personal greed.

(13) A thing of nought refers to the calf-worship, the idol in which Israel is glorying and trusting, the idolatrous travesty of the Eternal that they call "the excellency of Jacob." (Comp. verse 8 and 8:7.)

(14) From . . . unto.—The entire limits of the kingdom of Israel after the victories of Jeroboam II were, according to II Kings 14:25, identical with the region which is here threatened with invasion, i.e., extending from the mouth of the Orontes valley (comp. Num. 34:8; Josh. 13:5) to the Wady el Ahsa, the southern boundary of Moab. (Comp. Isa. 15:7.)

7

Here begins the third portion of the prophecy. It is of a different class from that which has preceded, and may have formed the main heads of the parabolic ministry of the prophet in the earlier stages of his career. These fiats of destruction, contained in the visions and dreams of coming doom, had been arrested by the intercession of the prophet himself. But the time was ap-

6

(1) The upper luxurious classes, the rulers to whom Israel, the supreme and highly-favored nation, comes up for judgment and for guidance in all civil affairs, are now summoned to listen to the rebuke of the divine Judge.

(2) We have no reason for believing that

proaching when prayer would be of no avail, and the desolation of the kingdom would be complete.

(2) The grass of the land.—For "grasshoppers" in verse 1, read "locusts." Amos saw the first wave of disaster in the destruction of the food of the people, and he interceded for respite and forgiveness.

(3) The Lord repented.—The judgment is withheld. On the anthropomorphism of Jehovah repenting, see note on Gen. 6:5.

(4) Fire.—The poetical description of a yet more terrible calamity: God announces His intention of judging, i.e., punishing by fire. The image is that of a prairie fire that should eat up the later grass spared by the locusts. The consuming of the "great deep" is a strong hyperbole, the meaning of which appears to be that not only the solitary remnant of pasture, but the deepest springs of moisture, will be scorched up in the blaze.

(5, 6) Instead of "forgive," the prophet now only ventures to say "cease," a cry for arrest of judgment. Yet the same plea for pity is urged as before. Jeroboam II and his house are spared for awhile. But another awful vision comes to the prophet.

(7) Wall made by a plumbline—i.e., a perpendicular wall, the stability of the kingdom being represented by the closely-fitting, well-jointed stones of a lofty wall. Right in the heart of this strong-built city, the Lord Himself marks the extent of the desolation, the plumbline being used in dismantling buildings, as well as erecting them (II Kings 21:13; Isa. 34:11).

(8) Pass by them.—In the sense of sparing. There will come a time when prayer will be of no avail. All intercessions, however passionate or eager, will be too late. The door of mercy is shut.

(9) High places of Isaac.—The residents in the neighborhood of Beersheba may have boasted of the favor or honor belonging to them, as occupying the home of Isaac and the birthplace of Jacob.

Will rise against.—This dreadful doom fell on the house of Jeroboam, and was the prelude of the final destruction of the nations by Shalmaneser IV, in 721 (II Kings 15:10).

(10) There follows a brief historical interlude of much interest. It shows that the effect of the preaching of the Judaean prophet had been felt in the sanctuary at Bethel and the palaces at Samaria. The chief priest of the Temple, with the characteristic exaggeration of fear and anger, accuses Amos of treason against the house of Jeroboam.

(12, 13) Jeroboam treated the charge made by Amaziah with indifference, or perhaps with awe—at least with silence. And so the priest of Bethel takes upon himself to dismiss the prophet from the kingdom: "there live on your profession as a prophet," not here. To this Amos replies that that was not his profession (verse 14). Men blinded by prejudice, and bewildered by the light of our Lord's holy presence, besought him to depart from them. The awful peril of imploring God's messenger to withdraw is frequently referred to in Scripture. (Comp. Luke 10:10-12.)

(15) Followed the flock.—There is no hint of any lack of education or refinement through the exclusion of any special aid derived from the training of earlier prophets. In this case God's inward call had been more than sufficient.

(17) Harlot.—This doom on Amaziah's wife is to be regarded as the hideous consequence of war. She shall be ravished. By the polluted land we are to understand Assyria, or the land of exile, for food eaten in any other land than Canaan, the land of Jehovah, was regarded as unclean. We hear no more of Amaziah, nor do we know how or where he met his doom.

8

(1, 2) The visions are resumed as though the priest at Bethel had trembled at the presence of Amos, and had ceased to persecute him. It is harvest time, the end of the agricultural year. Israel is ripe for his final doom, that shall sweep down like a scythe. For "pass by," see note on 7:8.

(5) When ... gone.—They desired that the festivals of the New Moon and Sabbath should be over, when they might not only return to their secular employments, but pursue their search for ill-gotten gains—a proof that these festivals were observed in the northern nation, even if they were disliked. (See Lev. 19:35, 36; Deut. 25:15; Prov. 11:1; Micah 6:11.)

(6) On this perverse straining of the Law, comp. 2:6. Their money-making propensity was carried to such unscrupulous lengths, that they even sold the refuse of corn, little better than mere chaff.

(7) Excellency of Jacob.—The "excellency" which He abhorred (6:8) was the miserable substitute which they had made for His great name. Here He gives it the value which, in itself, it ought to possess.

(9) Darken the earth.—The darkening of the sun at noonday gives an image of confusion and terror (comp. 5:20). The eclipse of the sun, like the earthquake in the preceding verse, is employed as a powerful image of national calamity, the extinction of the royal house, and perhaps the final overthrow of Israel. (Comp. Jer. 15:9; Ezek. 32:7-10.)

(10-13) The imagery is very vivid. The prophet threatens a famine of the word of Jehovah, and a parching thirst for the Water of Life, now no longer attainable. Such terrible destitution often ensues on the neglect of the Word of God, the power to discern the ever-present Word being exhausted. Then comes the withdrawal of revelation, the silence of seers. From various districts the distracted superstitious Hebrew would seek in vain help in idolatrous forms of divination.

(14) Thy God, O Dan, liveth.—The "way of Beersheba" was the ritual practiced at Beersheba, another mode of designating the deity himself (probably Baal). Similarly the "sin of Samaria" means the golden calf that was worshiped there (Hos. 8:5).

9

(1) The last vision is transferred to the shrine at Bethel, the seat of the calf-worship. The prophet sees Jehovah Himself standing in pomp by the altar of burnt offering, and by His side the angel of His presence, to whom now, as on many other occasions, the mission of destruction has been entrusted. To him the words of Jehovah are addressed. With a blow that shakes the very threshold, the ornamented altar horns are broken to fragments, which are hurled down upon the panic-stricken multitude of eager devotees below. Escape from the universal Lord is impossible (verses 2-4).

(5, 6) In grand imagery accumulate the majesty, power, and irresistible resources of the Lord, who has at length become their enemy.

(7) Israel had presumed on the special favor of Jehovah. The prophet asks them whether, after all, they are better or safer than the Ethiopians, whom they despised. He who led Israel from Egypt also brought the Philistines from Caphtor (probably Crete; see Gen. 10:14) and the Syrians from Kir (probably east of the Euphrates; see 1:5).

(8) Sinful kingdom—i.e., the kingdom of the ten tribes, which had so utterly revolted from the true center and spiritual ideas of the worship of Jehovah.

(9, 10) Sift.—That which is not chaff shall be preserved and dispersed as seed. The race shall live, though the kingdom be destroyed. (See Lev. 26:33; Deut. 28:64; Hos. 9:17.) The prediction is remarkable, as pointing to the indestructible vitality of the race, and its wide diffusion among all nations.

(11, 12) These verses present some difficulties, as the quotation of the passage in Acts 15:15-17 is a free reproduction by James of the rendering of the LXX. The apostle uses it to show that there was a prophetic promise that after the dispersion of Israel the power and throne of David should be so re-established that it might be a rallying-place of the rest of the nations, "that the residue of men should seek after the Lord" (LXX "me"). The clause which is quoted shows that the LXX made its translation from a different Hebrew text from ours, and probably an inferior one. But our criticism will best display itself in judging his words according to his standard, and not according to one which, it is plain, he did not follow.

(13) Shall overtake the reaper.—So rapidly will the harvest follow the plowing. These closing verses foreshadow the glories of the restored kingdom of David (comp. Hos. 3:5), wherein we see the germ of the great Messianic prophecies of Isaiah.

OBADIAH

(1) The vision of Obadiah.—There are three recognized headings to prophetical books—"word," "burden" (i.e., oracle), and "vision"—and all are used without the article, and in a general way, for the contents of the books, without any intention to distinguish between different kinds or modes of prophecy. The word "vision" appears, from I Sam. 3:1; 9:9, to have acquired this general sense at an early time. It is not necessary from the use of the word to suppose that the future was unfolded to Obadiah in the form of sights spread out before his mind.

Thus saith the Lord God concerning Edom.—After these words we should expect the words of the message, not the statement that a message had come. Among the attempts at explanation, the two most plausible are: (1) The twofold heading is due to a later hand than Obadiah, who only prefixed the first part, "vision," etc., to his work; (2) These words are merely a mode of stating generally that the seer of the vision was divinely inspired. The view taken of the authorship and composition must decide between these two. (Comp. Jer. 49:7.)

Arise ye . . . —Long ago, in the mysterious oracle of Dumah (Isa. 21:11), the foreboding of a pending chastisement of Seir found a voice, and now, as in consequence of a signal from heaven, or as if brought by an angel, goes forth the summons to the nations to begin the movement against Edom. The cup of iniquity was full. There is a suggestiveness even in the vagueness of the summons. The nations, without distinction of good or bad, must become the instruments of the divine chastisement of arrogant pride. For the full picture, here suggested only in a word, see Isa. 13:1-17, and comp. Jer. 51:11; Joel 2:11.

(2) Small among the heathen.—In comparison with the giant empires of Egypt and Assyria, Edom was a mere speck on the map. (Edom proper is not to be confused with the later kingdom of Idumaea.) The original Mount Seir (Gen. 32:3), or, as our prophet calls it, Mount Esau, was a narrow tract of country on the east of Wady Arabah, extending from Elath to the brook Zered, about 100 miles in length and nowhere more than twenty miles broad. The contrast is between the size of the nation

and its overbearing pride created by the consciousness of the natural strength of its position (verses 3, 4). Petra, whose rugged cliffs are renowned, was its capital.

(4) And though thou set thy nest among the stars . . . —The image of the eagle nesting among the stars is among the most forcible even in Hebrew poetry. With a range of mountain rocks framed into a city, whose streets were ravines and whose houses were caverns, the Edomites felt secure in their lofty fastness.

Thence will I bring thee down, saith the Lord.—In man's sight Edom's boast was well founded; but what before God? This sentence against pride, not only national but individual too, is indeed the divine declaration, uttered in warning voice throughout Scripture. The doom pronounced against Edom is but one special instance of the universal truth told so powerfully by Isaiah 2:11 seq. And it was the more than once repeated declaration of the Son of God: "He that exalteth himself shall be abased, and he that humbleth himself shall be exalted."

(5, 6) The overthrow awaiting Edom is no mere inroad of a marauding tribe. Notice how the sad, almost pathetic, conviction of this breaks out—as if rather from a friend than an enemy—in the parenthetical "how art thou cut off!" in the very middle of the sentence. Every one must perceive, the prophet seems to say, a higher hand at work here.

(7) All the men of thy confederacy . . . —This desertion by allies is doubtless put prominently forward as the due retribution on Edom for his treachery and cruelty to his natural ally, his brother Jacob. The members of the confederacy are not specified. Comp. Ps. 60:8; Jer. 27:3; Ezek. 25:8. Fugitives from the ruin of Edom, flying into the territory of neighboring and allied tribes for help, are basely driven back to their own frontier and left to their fate. From Ps. 41:9, we are led to the conjecture that the expression "they that eat thy bread" (literally, "men of thy bread") forms part of a proverb for one bound by the closest ties of fellowship and hospitality.

(8) Shall I not . . . —The tradition of a peculiar sagacity in Edom, and especially in Teman (see Jer. 49:7), lingered long. (Job's sage friend Eliphaz was a Temanite.) See Baruch 3:22, 23; Job 2:11. So the utter want of perception and foresight in Edom seems unaccountable, until we think of the divine purpose and end in it all. The wise were destroyed, and the mighty men dismayed, "to the end that every one of the mount of Esau may be cut off by slaughter." It is the prophetic statement of the truth of the old heathen proverb: "Whom God wishes to destroy He first dements."

(10) For thy violence... —The crime was the more heinous because against the brother tribe. Probably the birth-name, Jacob, of the twin brother of Esau is used purposely to bring out the full wickedness of the descendants of Esau. In spite of all provocations, Israel long maintained the duty of a friendly feeling for the kindred race (Deut. 2:5; 23:7). On the other hand, Edom from the first assumed a jealous and hostile attitude (Num. 20:14, seqq.), never imitating the generous disposition of their great ancestor (Gen. 33:4).

(11) The three clauses in this verse form a climax: (1) plunder of the open country; (2) entry into the gates of the cities; (3) casting lots for the spoil in the very capital itself. It is natural to regard this latter event as identical with that in Joel 3:3, the final destruction of Jerusalem and disperson of its inhabitants into captivity.

(12) Thou shouldest not... —The warning against these particular offenses undoubtedly springs from the reminiscence of such conduct in former times. The passage is neither definitely historical nor definitely prophetic. What has happened in the past becomes a type of what will happen in the future.

(13) The day of their calamity.—This is three times repeated to bring into prominence the malignity of Edom's conduct. The same connection is used by Ezekiel (35:5), in the same connection, probably with reference to the same occasion. For the open violence assumed by the Edomites when they saw their chance had come, comp. Ps. 137:7; Joel 3:19; Amos 1:11.

(15) The day of the Lord.—Whether this phrase first makes its appearance in written prophecy in Joel or Obadiah depends on the question of the relative date of the two. Probably it had become a recognized prophetic expression long before it was committed to writing. The primary meaning is not the day of judgment, but the day on which Jehovah reveals His majesty and omnipotence in a glorious manner, to overthrow all ungodly powers and complete His kingdom. As the misfortunes of Israel increased, and the hostility of surrounding nations gathered to a successful head, it was natural that the idea of retribution upon

them for their violence to the chosen race should usurp the prominent place in prophecy. (Comp. Isa. 34:8; Zeph. 1:18.) The fading of the temporal hopes implied in the expression naturally led to its higher religious use; and the various phrases for the same idea—"the day," "the great day," "the day of judgment," "the last day"—passed first into Jewish, and later into Christian, eschatology, taking with them all the prophetic imagery which painted the expectancy of Israel.

(16) As ye have drunk... —For the figure, so common in prophecy and so expressive, comp. Jer. 25:27, 28; Ps. 75:8; Isa. 51:17; Rev. 18:3-6. If taken in a literal sense, the drinking on Mount Zion would refer to the carousing and revelry which always followed heathen victory, and sometimes with terrible aggravation (Joel 3:3). Taking the passage in this sense, we must understand the prophet to take Edom as a type of all heathen in their attitude toward Israel, so that what he says of one nation applies to all. But it is quite possible that our text embodies an old oracular saying addressed to Israel. (This is Ewald's view.)

(17) Deliverance.—While the judgment is falling upon all the heathen nations, Mount Zion will be an asylum for all the Israelites who had fled for safety, and been scattered and dispersed.

Their possessions.—The parallelism is undoubtedly in favor of the view that the remnant of Israel would be saved and regain their old possessions. Having stated this, the prophet goes on to describe what would happen to Edom and its possessions.

(19) After the destruction of the heathen the new kingdom of Zion will be restored, at least as far as the ancient territories which are at present held by the Idumaeans, to the north and west of the original Edom, are concerned. Three divisions are enumerated of the house of Jacob (i.e., Judah, the "house of Joseph"; see verse 18), and separate mention made of Benjamin (see Gen. 49:27).

(20) But there are still others of the restored Israel, besides those comprised within the ancient territory of Judah. The prophetic survey proceeds northward, and we get a general idea from this verse that there were exiles, who had found refuge on the northwestern and northern boundaries of ancient Palestine, who would settle themselves partly on the seacoast of Tyre and Sidon, partly in the south country, whose habitants had pushed downward into Edom.

But while this is plainly its general drift, the text is full of difficulties.

(21) Saviours.—Comp. Judg. 3:9, 15; Neh. 9:27. The Jewish interpreters understood men like the judges of old, Gideon, Barak, etc.

And the kingdom shall be the Lord's.—Zechariah gives this anticipation of the pure form of the theocracy in its wider extent. But here, too, the prophetic look over the world seems to extend far beyond Judah and the fortunes of the Jewish race, and as the vision widens Zion and Edom both retire from sight; both are comprehended in the one divine kingdom, and God is all in all.

JONAH

1

(1) Jonah the son of Amittai.—The prophet is identical with the Jonah of II Kings 14:25. A native of Gath-hepher, of the tribe of Zebulun, Jonah the son of Amittai prophesied at the beginning of the reign of Jeroboam II, i.e., in the latter part of the ninth century B.C. Beyond this we know nothing of him until he abruptly bursts forth as the prophet commissioned to announce the destruction of Nineveh.

(2) Nineveh, that great city.—The size of Nineveh is throughout the book brought into prominent notice. (See 3:2, 3; 4:11.) The traditions preserved in Greek and Roman writers dwell on the same feature; and modern researches among the huge mounds scattered along the left bank of the Tigris more than confirm the impression produced on the ancient world by the city, or rather group of cities, buried beneath them. (Comp. Gen. 10:11.)

For their wickedness is come up before me.—As Pusey remarks, the Hebrew implies especially evil-doing against others, that "violence" which in 3:8 is recognized by the Ninevites themselves as their characteristic sin.

(3) But Jonah rose up to flee.—The motive of the prophet's flight is given by himself (4:2). He foresaw the repentance of the city, and the mercy which would be displayed toward it, and was either jealous of his prophetic reputation, or had a patriotic dislike of becoming a messenger of good to a heathen foe so formidable to his own country.

Tarshish.—This can hardly be any other than Tartessus, an ancient Phoenician colony on the river Guadalquivir, in the southwest of Spain. (See Gen. 10:4; I Chron. 1:7.) A profound moral lesson lies in the choice of this remote refuge by Jonah.

From the presence of the Lord.—The words may imply (1) the belief in a possibility of hiding from the sight of God (as in Gen. 3:8), a belief which, as we gather from the insistence on its opposite in Ps. 139, lingered late in the popular conception; (2) a renunciation of the prophetic office. (Comp. Deut. 10:8; I Kings 17:1); (3) flight from the Holy Land, where the divine presence was understood to be especially manifested.

Joppa—now "Jaffa," the port of Jerusalem. (See Josh. 19:46; II Chron. 2:16.)

He found a ship.—Probably a Phoenician vessel trading between Egypt and Spain, and accustomed to touch at Joppa.

(5) And was fast asleep.—The fatigue of the hasty flight to the seashore accounts for this deep slumber. The same expression is used of Sisera (Judg. 4:21). Besides, when a resolution is once irrevocably taken, conscience ceases to disturb with its wakeful warning, and the restlessness of remorse has not yet arrived. There is a brief time during which "the exile from himself can flee."

(6) What meanest . . . —i.e., How canst thou sleep so soundly? The motive of the question was no doubt partly the need of sympathy, (see Mark 4:38), and partly a belief in the efficacy of the prophet's prayer. This belief seems to have sprung not solely from superstitious fear lest any deity should be overlooked, but from a vague sense that the God of Israel was preeminently great and good. The term used is **Elohim,** "the God."

(7) Come, and let us cast lots.—We are to suppose that Jonah, coming on deck in compliance with the captain's request, adds his prayers to those of the crew. Finding all unavailing, the sailors propose recourse to the ancient custom of casting lots to discover the guilty person against whom the deities are so enraged. Classical authors as well as the Bible afford many illustrations of the belief that the presence of an impious man would involve all who shared his company in indiscriminate ruin.

(9) Which hath made . . . —These words mark the great change that has already come upon the prophet. He feels now how futile it was to try to hide or fly from the Creator of all the universe. But he speaks also for the sake of the crew, who, though recognizing the existence of Jehovah as the tribal God of Israel, had never realized His relation to themselves as Creator of the world in which they lived, and of the sea on which they sailed. The storm preached the omnipotence of God.

(10) For the men knew that.—Jonah's answer in verse 9 is evidently intended only as an abbreviation of what he actually replied.

(12) Cast me forth into the sea.—There was no need of prophetic inspiration to enable Jonah to pass this sentence upon himself. He is too manly not to prefer to perish without involving others in his ruin. And it is a fine trait in these sailors that they will not obey the prophet's request to throw him overboard until all efforts to save the ship have been tried (verse 13).

(14) Wherefore they cried unto the Lord.—There is presented here, as throughout the book, a strong contrast between the readiness of the heathen to receive religious impressions, and the stubbornness and obstinacy of Israel.

The "law of retaliation" was as familiar to them as to the Hebrews (Deut. 19:21). The storm, the lot, the request of the prophet himself, all showed that the sailors were but instruments in carrying out the divine purpose.

(17) Had prepared.—Render "appointed"; comp. 4:6, 7, 8, where the same word is used of the gourd, the worm, and the east wind. Previous special preparation is not implied, still less creation for the particular purpose. God employs existing agents to do His bidding.

A great fish.—The Hebrew **dag** is derived from the prolific character of fish, and a great fish might stand for any one of the sea monsters. The notion that it was a whale rests on the LXX and Matt. 12:40. The event has been regarded by some as literal history, and by others as parabolic teaching. Explanations given by commentators divide themselves into those of a strictly preternatural kind, as that a fish was created for the occasion, or into the natural or semi-natural, as that it was a ship, or an inn bearing the sign of the whale.

2

(1) Then Jonah prayed.—This introduction, to what is in reality a psalm of thanksgiving, has its parallel in Hannah's song (I Sam. 2:1-10), which is introduced in the same way. Comp. also the note appended by the psalm collector at the end of Ps. 72.

(2) Out of the belly of hell.—This remarkable expression—a forcible figure for imminent death—has its nearest parallel in Isa. 5:14, where **sheôl** (see Ps. 6:5) is represented as opening a huge mouth to swallow the princes of the world and their pomp. The "underworld" represents the Hebrew word sheol more nearly than "hell" or the "grave." (Comp. Pss. 18:5; 30:3.)

(4) Yet I will look again.—The Hebrew is impressive, and reads like one of those exile hopes so common in the Psalms. (Comp. Ps. 28:2.)

(5) The weeds were wrapped about my

head.—This graphic touch is quite original. The figure of overwhelming waters is a common one in Hebrew song to represent some crushing sorrow, but nowhere is the picture as vivid as here.

(6) Bottoms of the mountains.—Mountains were in the Hebrew conception the pillars of the world (see Job 9:6; 26:11), having their foundations firmly planted in the sea. These hidden bases of the hills were therefore the verge of the earth itself, and one lost among them would be close on the underworld of death.

(9) But I will.—The prophet is not among those who forfeit their own share of the covenant of grace (verse 8). He has sinned, but is still a member of the covenant people, and by sacrifice can be formally restored to that favor which repentance has regained.

3

(2) Preach.—In 1:2 the word is rendered "cry."

(3) Of three days' journey.—The circuit or circumference of the walls was the most obvious measurement to give of an ancient city. Herodotus variously reckons a day's journey at about eighteen or twenty-three miles (4:101; 5:53); and the circuit of the irregular quadrangle composed of the mounds now generally allowed to represent ancient Nineveh is about sixty miles. This agrees sufficiently with the obviously vague and general statement of the text.

(4) And Jonah began to enter into the city a day's journey.—Whether his course was straight or circuitous is immaterial. The writer has no thought of furnishing data for ascertaining the exact dimensions of Nineveh, but only of producing a general sense of its vast size.

(5) Believed God.—Notice again an implied contrast to the dullness of the Jews, who were slow to believe the prophetic warnings addressed to themselves.

(6) For word came.—The writer intended to describe the effect produced on each district of the vast city in succession, and on all grades of people. The piercing cry uttered from street to street, from square to square, reaches at last the king on his throne of state.

(7) Beast.—Herodotus (9:24) and Plutarch (Alexander) have both preserved instances in which horses and mules were associated with human beings in the signs of public mourning. The instinct which underlies the custom is a true one. Not only are the destinies of the animals which minister to man's wants often identical with his own, but there is a bond of sympathy between them and man; and one remarkable feature of this book is the prominence given to this truth. (See 4:11.)

(8) Let them turn.—Notice the insistence on a moral change, and the implied contrast, again showing itself, with the formality of Judaism. Even in this repentance the edict does not stop to distinguish beast from man, but includes all, as all were involved in the threatened destruction.

Violence.—This is the characteristic of Assyrian manners most frequently noticed in the prophets. (See Nahum 2:11, 12; 3:1; Isa. 10:13, 14.) The cuneiform inscriptions abundantly illustrate this point.

(9) Who can tell . . . ?—This sudden recognition of one God by a king of Nineveh appears far more striking if contrasted with the long lists of deities usually mentioned in the Assyrian inscriptions.

(10) And God repented.—See note, Gen. 6:6.

And he did it not.—As we are entirely ignorant of the nature of the threatened destruction, so are we also of the mode in which it was averted. Possibly some inscription throwing light on the book of Jonah may yet be discovered.

4

(1) He was very angry.—Selfish jealousy for his own reputation, jealousy for the honor of the prophetic office, a mistaken patriotism disappointed that the great enemy of his country should go unpunished, Jewish exclusiveness which could not endure to see the divine clemency extended to the heathen, have each been adduced as the motive of Jonah's anger. Possibly something of all these blended in his mind. David's feeling at the death of Uzziah (II Sam. 6:8; I Chron. 13:11) is described in the same terms.

(4) Doest thou well? . . . —Jonah apparently gave his own interpretation to the question, one that suited his mood, "Is thine anger just?" Such a question might imply that the doom of the city was only deferred, and that he had been too hasty in giving up the fulfillment of his prediction. Accordingly he went outside the walls, and sat down to watch what the issue would be. On the other hand, the rendering "Art thou so very angry?" suits best the reply in verse 9.

(6) A gourd.—"The bottle gourd is very commonly employed in Palestine for the purpose of shading arbors. Its rapid growth and large leaves render it admirably adapted for training on trelliswork. . . . But the plant withers as rapidly as it shoots, and after a storm or any injury to its stem, its fruit may be seen hanging from the leafless tendrils, which so lately concealed it, a type of melancholy desolation" (Tristram).

(7) A worm.—Possibly to be taken collectively, as in Isa. 14:11, for a swarm of caterpillars.

(8) Vehement east wind.—The derivation from a root meaning "silent" points to what travelers describe as the "quiet kind of sirocco," which is often more overpowering than the more boisterous kind. Ewald, however, thinks differently, and makes it a rough, scrapy, stingy wind.

It is better.—Physical suffering was now added to the prophet's chagrin, and, as usual, added to the moral depression. It seemed much worse that the logical consistency of Jonah's teaching should go for nothing now that he was so uncomfortable. (Comp. Num. 11:15; I Kings 19:4.)

(9) Doest thou well . . . ?—See note on verse 4. Jonah was really hurt at the loss of his shade, not sorry for the destruction of the gourd. But it is very true to nature that the moment a worthier excuse is suggested, he accepts it, without perceiving that by so doing he prepared the way for his own condemnation. The lesson is to all who would sacrifice the cause of humanity to some professional or theological difficulty.

(11) More than . . . —This number of infants, 120,000, according to the usual reckoning, gives a population of 600,000.

MICAH

1

(1) Micah the Morasthite.—Micah introduces his personality with reference to his native village, Moresheth-gath, which was situated in the lowland district of Judah. The name—a shortened form of Micaiah, meaning "Who is like Jehovah"—was chiefly famous in times prior to the prophet, through Micaiah, the son of Imlah, who, about 150 years previously, had withstood Ahab and his false prophets.

Samaria and Jerusalem.—The younger capital is placed first because it was the first to fall through the greater sinfulness of the northern kingdom. The chief cities are mentioned as representatives of the wickedness of the respective nations.

(2) Hear, all ye people.—The threefold repetition of the appeal, "Hear ye," seems to mark three divisions in the book: 1:2; 3:1; 6:1. Micaiah, the son of Imlah, ended his appeal to Ahab and Jehoshaphat with the words with which Micah opens his prophecy (I Kings 22:28).

(4) The mountains shall be molten.—The manifestations of the presence of God are taken from the description of the giving of the Law. (See Ps. 97:5.)

(5) The transgression of Jacob ... the sins of the house of Israel.—The corruption of the country came from the capital cities. Samaria set an example of idolatry, drunkenness, and all the evils of a most profligate society; and even Jerusalem gave a home in the Temple of Jehovah to heathen deities.

(7) And all the hires thereof.—The falling away of Israel from her loyalty to God is compared generally by the prophets to a wife deserting her husband; and these "hires" are the offerings made to the shrines of the idols to which the Israelites forsaking Jehovah had transferred their worship. All these treasures shall be destroyed; the Assyrians shall carry them off for the adornment of their temples.

(8) Dragons ... owls.—Literally, "jackals" and "ostriches." They are selected by reason of the dismal howls and screeches they make during the night.

(13) Bind the chariot to the swift beast—i.e., make haste to escape with thy goods. Lachish was the most important of the cities enumerated. It was fortified by Rehoboam, and was sought as a refuge by Amaziah from the conspiracy formed against him in

Jerusalem. After the capture of the Holy City by Nebuchadnezzar, Lachish and Azekah alone remained of the defensed cities of Judah. It appears, from its position as a border city, to have been the channel for introducing into the kingdom of Judah the idolatry set up by Jeroboam in Israel.

(14) Achzib was a town on the seacoast between Accho and Tyre. Its name means false, deceptive; it is used of a river drying up, and disappointing the traveler. In like manner Achzib shall fulfill the import of its name, and prove a lie, a broken reed, to the kings of Israel.

(15) Yet will I bring an heir.—Rather, "the possessor," one who shall take it by force—i.e., Sennacherib.

Adullam the glory of Israel.—Adullam, in the neighborhood of Mareshah, was situated at the base of the hills, and gave its name to the famous cave in which David took refuge. This, now the last refuge of the glory of Israel, shall be seized by the invader.

(16) Make thee bald.—The shaving of the head as a token of grief was common among Eastern nations, and is distinct from the idolatrous custom of cutting the hair in a peculiar shape denounced by Jeremiah (7.29), and forbidden by the Jewish Law (Lev. 19:27, 28).

The terms in which Joel speaks of the entire desolation of the cities of Judah must refer to a more complete calamity than that inflicted by Sennacherib; they rather suit the period of the Babylonian captivity.

2

(1) Woe to them that devise.—The prophet proceeds to denounce the sins for which the country was to receive appropriate punishment at the hands of God. There is a gradation in the terms employed. They mark the deliberate character of the acts; there were no extenuating circumstances. In the night they **formed** the plan, they **thought it out** upon their beds, and **carried it out** into execution in the morning. (Comp. Ps. 1.)

(2) And they covet fields.—The desire to accumulate property in land, in contravention of the Mosaic Law, was denounced by Micah's contemporary, Isaiah (Isa. 5:8).

(3) I devise an evil.—As they devise evil against their brethren, so am I devising an evil against them: they shall bow their necks under a hostile yoke.

(4) Shall one take up a parable against you—i.e., the enemies shall repeat in mockery the doleful lamentations with which they bewail their pitiable state. The land they were taking from others God would give into the hands of an idolatrous king. They would have no part or inheritance in the congregation of the Lord (verse 5)—apparently referring to the ancient division of the land by lot.

(6) Prophesy ye not.—This verse contains the address of the oppressors to the true prophets, and their reply. The oppressors desire the prophets to cease prophesying; nevertheless, the prophecies shall be continued, but without benefit to those who will not put away their shame.

(7) Is the spirit of the Lord straitened?—In this verse the prophet expostulates with the people who are the people of the Lord, the house of Jacob, in name only. The Spirit of the Lord, who changeth not, is still the same toward them. They brought their sufferings on themselves; those who put away their shame, and walk uprightly, shall receive benefit from the prophet's words.

(8) Ye pull off the robe.—Micah dwells upon the continued greed of the people. They robbed the quiet inoffensive traveler of both outer and inner garment; they took away both "cloak" and "coat." (Comp. Matt. 5:40; Luke 6:29.) They did not even spare the widows and fatherless, the objects of God's tender care (verse 9). They are attracted, furthermore, by a lying spirit (verse 11).

(10) This is not your rest.—The Lord, repaying them for their cruelty to the poor and defenseless, declares that their own time of trouble was imminent. They should be thrust forth from the land which they polluted. It was no place of rest for them.

(12, 13) I will surely assemble . . .—With a characteristic abruptness Micah turns from the height of sin and punishment to the height of the deliverance. Israel and the remnant shall be gathered together as a goodly flock in the luxuriant pastures of Idumaean Bozrah. The return from captivity symbolized the eventual restoration of the people of God into His everlasting kingdom. The Breaker is, by the confession of the Jews, the title of the Messiah.

3

(1) Hear, I pray you.—In the second division of his prophecy Micah protests against the evil influences exercised upon the people by those in high places. The princes, the prophets, and the priests, to whom their interests were confined, were guilty of wrong, oppression and robbery.

(2, 3) Who hate the good . . . —The judges, instead of fulfilling the obligations of their office, whereby they should be for interests of the people God-ward, perpetrated the most flagrant cruelty upon them. Micah compares it to the process of preparing food, in which every part of the animal, even to the bones, is utilized. So the judges robbed the people until there was nothing left to them.

(5) That bite with their teeth.—The concluding statement that the false prophets declare war against those who do not put into their mouth indicates the meaning of the former expression, namely, "they say peace to those who feed and bribe them." The Hebrew word, **nashak**, which is rendered "bite," is strictly applied to serpents, and is therefore especially appropriate to the false and lying nature of the prophets.

(8) I am full of power.—Micah reverts to his denunciation of sin in high places with the fearlessness of his namesake. He contrasts himself with the prophets of the "lying spirit," and declares his own commission from the Spirit of the Lord, and the ample equipment with which he was endowed.

(10) They build up Zion with blood—i.e., they acquire money for the erection of splendid buildings by robbery, not stopping short of murder, yet they claim the protection of Jehovah (verse 11). (So also Habakkuk—2:12—denounces the king of Babylon for the bloody wars with which he obtained wealth for the enlargement of the city.) Isaiah contrasts in scathing terms the profession of holiness with the vicious life as seen in Jerusalem, and likens the city, with its rulers, to Sodom (1:10-15).

(12) Therefore shall Zion . . . —See Jer. 26:17-19.

4

(1) But in the last days.—There is again a sudden transition. As the third chapter began with a startling denunciation, following immediately upon the predicted blessings of the restored kingdom, so upon that chapter, closed in deepest gloom, there now rises a vision of glorious light. The first three verses are almost identical with Isa. 2:2-4. The preponderance of opinion is in favor of Micah being regarded as the original writer.

(2) Many nations shall come.—This prepares the way to the more definitive prophecies. Even to this day the hearts of Jews and Christians alike yearn toward Jerusalem—a physical representative of the love which turns spontaneously to the Messiah.

(3) They shall beat their swords . . . —See note on Joel 3:10.

(4) They shall sit . . . —This was a proverbial expression for the feeling of security brought about by a peace which no foreign power was strong enough to disturb. The vine and the fig tree are the representative trees of Palestine.

(5) For all people will walk.—The comparatively near future to Micah, and the still distant future to us, are blended in the prophet's vision, just as in the prophecies of our Lord the destruction of Jerusalem is described in terms which have their final accomplishment in the day of judgment. Micah's description of the universal rule of Messiah is primarily applicable to the antecedent prosperity, after the return of the Jews from the Captivity. The zeal of the Jews for Jehovah was stirred up after witnessing the example of "the children of this world" in Babylon. The zealous society for a national return to the strictness of the Law of Moses at first distinguished and honored by the name of Pharisees took its rise after the return from the Captivity.

(6, 7) The promise immediately refers to the return when God would re-establish the Jews, and eventually come Himself to the restored Temple.

(10) Thou shalt go even to Babylon.—It was a century after Micah's time (when Assyria was in the ascendancy) before Babylon recovered its ancient dignity. The fact, however, remains that Micah prophesied, "Thou shalt go to Babel"; and there is the other fact, that the people of Judah (not Israel) did go. Micah also declared "There shalt thou be delivered": and in the time of Cyrus the Jews were delivered there.

(13) Arise and thresh.—Micah, having likened Israel to the sheaves safely gathered, pursues the metaphor by calling upon the daughter of Zion to thresh her enemies after the manner of oxen treading out the corn; and under the symbolism of the horn—the weapon of strength—he promises that God will strengthen her for the work.

5

(1) O daughter of troops.—This verse coheres better with the former chapter, to which it is attached in the Hebrew Version. Micah again inserts a prediction of trouble and dismay between the sentences describing triumph and glory. The sentence of smiting the judge has its historical fulfillment in the indignities which happened to King Zedekiah.

(2) But thou, Beth-lehem Ephratah.—This is a passage of immense significance, through the interpretation given to it by the chief priests and scribes in the gospel according to Matthew. The two names, modern and ancient, are united, each of them having reference to the fertility of the country. In the gospel the scribes quote, evidently from memory, the passage from Micah, in reply to Herod's question; and their first variation is in the title of the town—"Thou, Beth-lehem (not Ephratah, but), land of Judah." (Comp. John 7:42.)

Yet out of thee.—Matthew helps to show that the quotation is really a paraphrase, conveying the ultimate intention of the prophet's words, which contrasts the smallness of the chiliad with the greatness of its destiny.

(3) Therefore will he give them up.—There is a suggestion here of a parable, setting forth the smallness of Bethlehem, which gave birth to the mighty Ruler that was to come from it. So the nation was to be brought very low before the nativity of the Virgin-born.

(4) He shall stand and feed—i.e., He shall stand with the majesty of an assured sovereignty, uniting the dignity of king with the tenderness of a shepherd's care—a thought which, underlying the notion of a Jewish monarch (see Ps. 78:70-72), becomes a distinguishing attribute of the King Messiah (see Isa. 40:2; Ezek. 34:2).

His God.—The Messiah, of eternal nativity (verse 2), was to be subordinate to the Father in heaven. It is impossible to conceive this prophecy as satisfied by any event short of that which is the foundation of the Christian faith.

(5) When the Assyrian shall come into our land.—This may refer to the imminent apprehension of the invasion of Sennacherib, but the actual event does not correspond to it. The land of Nimrod (verse 6) represents the opposing world power.

(7) As a dew from the Lord.—The Jews should, on their return from captivity, pour down their influence upon the nations, as God-sent showers upon the grass. So, through the dispersion of Jewish Christians, on the death of Stephen, the Lord caused the knowledge of the truth with which the Jews were charged to descend upon many people. (See Ps. 72:6). But there is righteous wrath as well as all-embracing mercy with God (verse 8).

(10) It shall come to pass in that day.— The prophet now passes on to the purification of the Church from the defilements mentioned in Isa. 2:6-10, with reference to the ultimate holiness which shall be established "in that day." (See the prohibition of Deut. 17:16; and comp. Ps. 20:7.)

(14) I will pluck up thy groves—i.e., either the statues, pillars, or trees connected with the worship of Baal and Astarte. (See II Kings 23:6.)

(15) Such as they have not heard.— Rather, "which have not been obedient"— i.e., which had not availed themselves of the opportunities of learning the true religion.

6

(1) Hear ye now what the Lord saith.— The third portion of Micah's prophecy opens with a solemn appeal to nature to hear the Lord pleading with His people. (Comp. Deut. 32:1.)

(4) For I brought thee up.—Moses, Aaron, and Miriam are mentioned as the three great members of the family to whom it was committed to carry out the divine decree.

(5) What Balaam the son of Beor answered.—There is no more conclusive instance extant of the will of man controlled to do the exact opposite of his intended action in the history of mankind. It is better to put a period after "answered him." The next sentence records an independent instance of the interposition of God on behalf of Israel. Shittim was the name of a valley in the plains of Moab, from which place Joshua sent two spies to view Jericho immediately before the passage of the Jordan to Gilgal was effected.

(16) Wherewith shall I come . . . ?—This has been taken by some commentators as Balak's question to Balaam, who gives his reply in verse 8. But it is rather in harmony with the context to understand it as the alarmed and conscience-stricken reply of the Jewish people impersonated in some earnest speaker to the pleading brought

before them by the prophet in the Lord's name.

(7) The fruit of my body.—There may possibly be an allusion to human sacrifices, such as Ahaz offered to Molech, or to the act of Mesha, King of Moab.

(10) The scant measure.—The Jews were much addicted to the falsification of weights and measures. See Lev. 19:35, 36; Deut. 25:13, 14; Amos 8:5.) The sins of spoliation and fraud were practiced by men who had not even the pitiable excuse of poverty and distress (verse 12). And insensitivity to hunger, together with desire for material preservation, characterized them (verse 14).

(16) The statutes of Omri.—The people of Judah, instead of keeping the commandments of the Lord diligently, adopted the statutes of the house of Omri, the founder of the idolatrous dynasty of Ahab. They reproduced the sins of the northern kingdom, and their conduct was aggravated by the advantages vouchsafed to them. The greatness of their reproach should therefore be in proportion to the greatness of the glory which properly belonged to them as the people of God.

7

(1) Woe is me!—Micah gives here a fearful picture of the demoralized state of society in Judah which had called down the vengeance of God. As the early fig gathered in June is eagerly sought for by the traveler, so the prophet sought anxiously for a good man.

(4) The day of thy watchmen—i.e., the time which thy prophets have foreseen, about which they have continually warned thee (see Jer. 6:17).

(5, 6) Trust ye not . . . —All is now distrust and suspicion. The households are divided each against itself, and the relationships which should mean mutual confidence and support have become the occasion of the most bitter hostility. (Comp. Matt. 10:35; Mark 13:12; Luke 12:53.)

(9) I will bear.—Micah places himself and his people with confidence in the hands of God. (Comp. II Sam. 24:14). This is the temper of all penitents when stricken by God, or under chastisement from Him.

(11) In that day shall the decree be far removed.—Some interpret this prophecy to mean that the decree of God concerned not the Jews only, but distant nations who should press into the kingdom of God. This explanation coincides with the effect of the decree, which was to bring to Jerusalem people from "the ends of the world."

(12) In that day also he shall come.—The prophet beholds people coming from all parts of the earth to Jerusalem. Isaiah foresaw the like future, and spoke of Assyria, Egypt, and Israel being assembled together (see Isa. 19:25). The Christian reader can hardly refrain from discerning on the horizon of Micah's vision that marvelous assembly of the representatives of the nations in Jerusalem on the Day of Pentecost.

(13) Notwithstanding the land shall be desolate.—There is still bitterness in the cup. In the midst of the triumphant expectation of the glory to come, there rises up the vision of the desolation of the land in the near future, by reason of the sins of the people.

(14) Feed thy people with thy rod.—The prophet lifts up his prayer for the people, either dwelling "alone" among the idolaters

of Babylon, or living a nation, mysteriously apart from other nations, returned from Babylon, and settled on the fruitful mountain range of Carmel or in the rich pasture land on the east of Jordan.

(15) According to the days of thy coming out.—The promise of Jehovah, in reply to the prophet's supplication, graciously recalls His interposition in the land of Egypt. This interposition shall be repeated.

(18) Who is a God like unto thee?— Micah, with an allusion to the significance of his own name, concludes his book with a burst of enthusiastic homage to the God of gods. The gracious character here ascribed to Jehovah is unparalleled in the Bible in human utterances; it is the response of the prophet to the glorious words spoken by Jehovah of Himself (Exod. 34:6, 7). The promise there made to Moses is here extended by the inspiration of the prophet to the Gentiles. The "remnant" refers to the returned from the Captivity.

NAHUM

1

(1) The burden of Nineveh—i.e., the "sentence" against Nineveh (see Isa. 13:1). "Nahum" means "comforter." His date can be conjectured only from his allusions to political events. Elkosh remains to be discovered. The place doubtless lay within the borders of the Holy Land, but it is impossible to determine its situation precisely.

(2) God . . . furious.—This verse lays the groundwork for the declaration of God's sentence against the offending city. There are, of course, several passages in the Law which attribute the same character to Jehovah, e.g., Exod. 20:5; Deut. 4:24. Nahum's model, however, is a passage of opposite purport, the well-known proclamation of Jehovah's attribute of mercy (Exod. 34:6, 7).

(3) And great in power.—Jehovah's forbearance is not attributable to weakness. To vindicate His power, Nahum, after the manner of other Hebrew poets and prophets, reverts to the wonders of the Exodus (verses 4, 5). (Comp. Hab. 3:6-10.)

(8) But.—Jehovah protects His afflicted servants, and therefore He exterminates their oppressor.

(9) Affliction—i.e., Nineveh's affliction of Israel, whereas "the place thereof" (verse 8) is Nineveh itself. The same Hebrew word is used in verse 7 to denote Israel's "trouble" or "affliction" proceeding from Nineveh. (See also verse 12.) Nineveh shall not afflict Israel a second time. The whole passage refers to the destruction of Sennacherib's host.

(10) For while.—The verse compares the victims of Jehovah's wrath, first, to a compact bundle of thorn fagots used for fuel; secondly, to a material equally combustible, the dry straw and stubble of the threshing-floor. In the final siege of Nineveh a great defeat of its forces was effected by a surprise while the king and his captains were sunk in revelry (Diod. Sic. 2:26). Ben-hadad, king of Syria, and Belshazzar, king of Babylon, were overcome under similar circumstances (I Kings 20:16; Dan. 5:1-30). The introduction of this detail adds to the metaphor a certain grim humor. Soaked in wine though the enemy be, he shall surely burn like driest fuel in the day of Jehovah's fiery wrath.

(11) Come out of thee.—The verse is addressed to Nineveh. The reference in the verses following is sufficiently plain for us to identify this enemy of God with Sennacherib. (Comp. the language used by his envoy Rab-shakeh in II Kings 18 and 19.)

(13) Now will I break.—Comp. Isa. 14:25; Jer. 30:8.

(14) And the Lord hath given.—The denunciation of the Assyrian here passes from the third to the second person. Sennacherib is told that the royal line of Nineveh is to be suddenly exterminated—a prediction accomplished when his great-grandson Saracus, the last king of Nineveh, destroyed himself in despair. He is also told that the Assyrian idols are destined to destruction, and that their very temple is to witness his own death (comp. Isa. 37:38; Dan. 5:27).

(15) Behold upon the mountains.—It is not plain why this verse has been made the first of chap. 3 in the Hebrew. It is evidently the finale of the proclamation against the Assyrian invader, and rightly stands in the LXX as the last verse of chap. 2. It portrays the announcement of Sennacherib's fate to the towns and villages of Judah. (Comp. Isa. 52:7.)

2

The siege and sack of Nineveh is described here. From the destruction of Sennacherib's host in 699 B.C., and his death in the temple of Nisroch in 680, the prophet suddenly passes to the extermination of the Assyrian Empire, cir. 625. Here then, strictly speaking, is the beginning of Nahum's "vision," 1:9-15 being limited to the great blow sustained by Assyria in the preceding generation.

(1) Keep the munition . . . —These four sententious directions to Nineveh are, of course, ironical like Elijah's instructions to the priests of Baal in I Kings 18:27.

(2) The sacred nation is Jehovah's vine, destined to send out its tendrils all over the earth. But Jehovah has allowed its hedge to be broken down (see Ps. 80:12, 13). In the punishment of one notoriously oppressive world power the prophet sees a pledge that the branch of Jehovah shall be again "beautiful and glorious" (Isa. 4:2). It appears best to attach a special emphasis to the names "Jacob" and "Israel" in connection with their original signification. "Jacob" is the birth name—the nation regarded apart from its religious privileges; "Israel" is the chosen of God. The name given by Jehovah is from now on to have its full significance, as in the days of old. "Jacob," the name which is so often used after the deportation of the ten tribes, is again to be indicated as "Israel," the favored people of God.

(3) His mighty men.—That is, those of the besieger of verse 1. (Both Medes and Babylonians were engaged in the present siege.) The "flashing steel" (flaming torches) refers to scythes or sharp instruments fastened to the wheels. Some form of this weapon may well have been in use long before the present date. Xenophon relates that Cyrus was the first to introduce the scythe-chariots. Ctesias, however, speaks of it as of much earlier origin. The swiftly-moving war chariots are likened to flashing torches, as they are in the next verse, which, with verse 5, describes the state of the city while sustaining this siege.

(5) And the defence shall be prepared.—Here the surprise and disorder of Nineveh is even more plainly portrayed than in the chariots of the besieged city, darting to and fro in wild undisciplined attempts to resist the invader's onset. The Assyrian king considers his stoutest warriors, but they stumble in their paths in nervous perplexity. Men hasten to the city wall, but against it the besiegers have already erected their storming-shed—a proceeding which ought to have been prevented by the discharge of stones and other missiles from the walls. The storming-shed protected the battering-rams. Representations of these are preserved in the monuments of Nineveh.

(6) The gates of the rivers.—This verse is one of great importance. The account of Ctesias, preserved by Diodorus Siculus, tells us that for over two years the immense thickness of the walls of Nineveh baffled the engineering skill of the besiegers. The walls are reported to have been a hundred feet high, so that three chariots could drive upon them abreast. Against ramparts such as these the most elaborate testudo of ancient times may well have been comparatively powerless. On the other hand, the force of a swollen river has often proved suddenly fatal to the strongest masonry. It would be especially destructive where, as in the case of Nineveh, the walls inundated were of sun-dried brick. Thus the fate of the city may well have been precipitated in accordance with the terse prediction of this verse. The "gates of the rivers" were the dams fencing the Khausser, which ran

through Nineveh, and the Tigris, which was outside it.

(7) And Huzzab shall be led away captive ... —"Laid bare," the common figure of the virgin city put to certain ("Huzzab") shame by capture (comp. Isa. 47:1-5). The "maidens" are probably Nineveh's dependent cities, represented as standing gazing on the awful catastrophe, groaning aloud and beating the breast in a horror of despair.

(10) And the faces of them all gather blackness.—See note on Joel 2:6.

(11-13) The figure of the lion appears so frequently on the Assyrian monuments that we may perhaps suppose it to have been a national shield.

3

(2, 3) The entry of the victorious besiegers is described here.

(4-6) Because of the multitude.—In the idolatry and superstition of Nineveh the prophet finds the cause of her destruction. Perversion of religious instinct is frequently denounced under the same figure in Scripture. Here, however, a more literal interpretation is possible, since there is reason to believe the religious rites of Assyria were characterized, like those of Babylon, by gross sensuality. (Comp. Herod. 1:199; Baruch 6:43.)

(8) Populous No.—Thebes, the capital of Upper Egypt, was known to the Hebrews as "No Amon" (perhaps, "house of the god Amon"). Assyria herself, under Sargon in 716 B.C., Esar-haddon in 670 B.C., and Asshur-banipal in 668 and 665 B.C., had reduced the power of Thebes. The present passage may refer either to this last event or to Esar-haddon's previous capture of Thebes. The fall of the city was certainly a thing of the past when Nahum wrote. The allusion, therefore, helps us to assign the date of the composition. To mere human reasoning the downfall of Thebes testified to the power of Assyria, its conqueror. But to the inspired vision of Nahum, the ruin of the one world-power is an earnest of the ruin of the other. Both had been full of luxury and oppression, both were hated of mankind and opposed to God.

(13) Thy people ... are women, not in their notoriously effeminate and luxurious habits, but with reference to their panic-stricken condition at the time of the catastrophe. They are fearful as women (comp.

Jer. 50:37; 51:30), because they find avenues laid open to the enemy, and the remaining defenses consuming in the flames.

(14) Draw thee waters.—In this desperate
plight Nineveh is scoffingly advised to pro-
tract her resistance. What shall it avail her?
In the midst of her preparations, fire and
sword shall again surprise her. As in Isa.
44:12 seq., so here the irony gains force by
a minute and elaborate description of operations destined to be futile.

(15, 16) Nineveh is compared in its numbers, destructive influence, and sudden disappearance to the locust. The comparison
suggests that Nineveh herself has been a
locust-pest to the world.

(17) Thy crowned.—The subordinate
kings who represent the Assyrian empire in
her tributary provinces.

Captains.—An Assyrian term denoting

some high military office. The sudden dis-
pearance of the Assyrian locust-pest is enlarged upon here. The insect designations—
"cankerworm," "locust," "great grasshopper"
—all represent varieties of the locust species.

(18) Shepherds—i.e., chief officers, as in
Micah 5:2 and passim. (Comp. I Kings
22:17.)

(19) Clap the hands over thee.—All that
hear the "bruit" or report of the fall of
Nineveh clap their hands with joy (Ps.
47:1), for where has not her oppressive rule
been felt? The verse is addressed to the king
as the representative of the empire, perhaps
also in view of his terrible end. The cruelty
of the Ninevite régime is illustrated in the
sculptures by the rows of the impaled, the
prisoners through whose lips rings were
fastened, whose eyes were put out, who
were flayed alive.

HABAKKUK

1

(1) The prophet.—This title is applied only to Habakkuk, Haggai, and Zechariah. In the later historical books it is used to designate the members of those prophetical colleges which were founded by Samuel, and kept up until the time of Elisha. It is uncertain whether in these three minor prophets it has a similar force, or merely, as in the Pentateuch, indicates a chosen minister whom God inspires to reveal His will.

(4) The law—the Mosaic **tôrâh**—which ought to be a bond of security and social welfare is "slacked" or "paralyzed"; it is unable to do its work. "Judgment" (i.e., "redress of evils") "doth never go forth," for the wicked have hemmed the righteous in; and, therefore, there are no judicial sentences, except such as favor the wicked.

(5) Among the heathen.—Here begins Jehovah's answer (verses 5-11) to Habakkuk's complaint (verses 1-4) of the apparent triumph of wickedness among his countrymen. These words imply that Jehovah will no longer manifest Himself among His chosen people, but among the Gentiles. Let them look abroad, and they shall see Him using the Chaldaeans as His instrument for their own chastisement. They are to "wonder," not at God's choice of an agent, but at the consequences of the visitation, which resulted in the sack of the Temple, and the deportation of 10,000 captives. The words "among the heathen" were misread by the LXX translators "ye despisers." In Acts 13:41 Paul is represented as citing the verse in its LXX form, as a warning to his Jewish hearers at Antioch. This citation, of course, gives no authority whatever to the variant.

(6) I raise up the Chaldeans—i.e., I am bringing up the Chaldaean or Babylonian armies into Judaea. The phrase implies that the Chaldaeans were not yet in Judaea, but there is no occasion to find an allusion to the recent rise of the Chaldaean nation. Certainly, the rapidity with which Babylon rose from the position of an Assyrian colony to that of ruler of Asia was marvelous. But the work which is to make the Jews wonder is not God's choice of an agent, but that agent's proceeding; not the elevation of one Gentile power in the place of another, but the attack which that new power is to make upon the sacred city.

With respect to the whole passage 6-11,

Kleinert well remarks, "The present passage is the **locus classicus** for the characteristics of this warlike people, just as Isa. 5:26 seq. is for the characteristics of the Assyrians."

(7) Their judgment . . . —Their "judgment" means their claim to adjudge the affairs of mankind. It proceeds from "themselves," as irresponsible, recognizing no Supreme Being as the source of justice.

Their dignity, in like manner, proceeds from "themselves," because self-sustained, unsanctioned by the King of kings and Lord of lords.

(8) The ideas intended are those of activity and ferocity, both prompted by hunger. The evening wolf coming out of his lair to find prey is elsewhere an illustration of ravenous greediness. (See Zeph. 3:3; Ps. 59:7; and comp. II Sam. 1:23; Jer. 4:13; 5:6).

(10) Kings, and princes are deposed or enthroned at the invader's pleasure. Thus Nebuchadnezzar set Jehoiakim as a tributary sovereign on the throne of Jerusalem, and three years later deposed his son and successor Jehoiachin and made Zedekiah king.

For they shall heap dust, and take it.— Mounds of earth were employed either to place the besieger on a level with the besieged, and so facilitate the operations of siege engines, or to form an inclined plane, up which the besieger might march his men, and so take the place by escalade. They were used by the Egyptians (Ezek. 17:17) and the Assyrians (II Kings 19:32), as well as by the Babylonians (Jer. 6:6, and **passim**). (Comp. Thucydides, lib. 2). In the present passage the term "dust" is used to indicate these mounds of earth, as expressing the contemptuous ease with which the invader effects his capture of strongholds.

(11) Then shall his mind change . . . —By an abrupt transition the latter half of the verse diverts our attention from the human view of the world-conqueror to his appearance in God's sight. Men see only an irresistible force sweeping over the face of the earth like a whirlwind. But, even as Daniel at Belshazzar's feast, Habakkuk pronounces the oppressor's doom in the very hour of triumph. His guilt consists just in what men deem so glorious, in his self-reliant irresponsible pursuit of grandeur. God shall bring on him ruin and ignominy, and the very nations which have marveled at his prowess shall taunt and despise him (2:6). Here, then, is the keynote of so much of the second canto (1:12 to 2:20) as relates to the downfall of the invader.

(12) We shall not die—i.e., God's people may suffer, but shall not be obliterated.

(13) The prophet's confidence is tempered, however, with anxious fear. Why does not God show plainly that He authorizes this visitation? The triumph of this godless invader appears to impugn God's majesty.

(16) The prophet has already stated that the Chaldaean deifies his own military prowess. Of this statement the present verse is an expansion. Weapons of war may have been literally worshiped by the Babylonians. But probably the language is metaphorical.

2

(1) The tower.—The practice of ascending a high place to secure an extensive view suggests the figure here. (See II Kings 9:17; II Sam. 18:24.) We need not suppose that Habakkuk himself literally went to a solitary height to wait for a revelation.

(2) Upon tables.—The definite article probably indicates certain well-known tables on which the prophets customarily inscribed their utterances for public edification. These tables may have been hung up in the Temple (Calvin) or market place (Luther and Ewald).

That he may run that readeth it—i.e., the prophecy is to be inscribed plainly and legibly, so that the reader may "run his eye" quickly through it.

(3) It will not tarry.—This translation is unfortunate. The prophet has just said that it **will** tarry. Nevertheless, he adds, men are to wait for it, because it will surely come on its appointed day. This and verse 4 are welded into the apostle's exhortation in Heb. 10:37 (LXX).

(4) Behold, his soul ... —The soul of the Chaldaean invader is inflated with pride, self-dependence ousting from his mind all thoughts of God. (Verse 5 adds drunkenness and insatiable covetousness.) It is therefore unsound and distorted. Habakkuk leaves the inference that it shall die, and hastens to the antithesis. The word "live" is emphatic. The reward promised to patient waiting on God is "life"—deliverance from destruction. How far the promise extends, and whether it includes that aspiration after future life which is plainly expressed by many Hebrew poets and prophets, we cannot determine. The student must be cautioned against renderings suggested by the Pauline quotations

Rom. 1:17 and Gal. 3:11. Whatever force we assign to Paul's citation, here, at least, the words have no doctrinal significance. Their ethical importance is, however, undeniable.

(6) How long?—i.e., how long shall this continual annexation be witnessed?

That ladeth himself with thick clay!—Better, "That accumulates to himself usury." This is the Targum translation.

(7) Bite.—This verb in the original also means "to oppress with usury," and this is its force here. Thy turn shall come, and men shall exact usury from thee. Similarly, the verb translated "vex" is, literally, "to shake violently," in allusion to a creditor's forcible seizure of his debtor. (Comp. Matt. 18:28.) The prediction of Habakkuk in these verses was fulfilled by the rise of the Medo-Persian power and the capture of Babylon by the forces of Cyrus, ca. 538 B.C.

(9) Woe to him that coveteth ... —i.e., who gathers spoil from the nations, and stows it away in an impregnable treasure house. The expression "sets his nest on high" finds more than sufficient illustration in the exaggerated accounts of Babylon given by Herodotus and Ctesias. The former gives 337 1/2 feet, the latter 300 feet, as the height of its walls. The height of the towers was according to Ctesias, 420 feet. There were 250 of these towers, irregularly disposed, to guard the weaker parts of the wall. The space included by these colossal outworks was, according to Herodotus, about 200 square miles.

The language of this verse recalls Jeremiah's rebuke of Jehoiakim (Jer. 22:13 seq.). There, however, the sentence is on individual sin; here it is on that of a nation personified.

(14) With the knowledge.—See the same promise in Isa. 11:9. It is here introduced in contrast to the short-lived glory of Babylon. The enslaved nations raised the Babylonian palaces only for the fire to destroy them (comp. Jer. 51:58). But Jehovah's glory shall be made known all the world over, and shall not be effaced.

(15, 16) Woe unto him.—It is possible that wanton outrages committed by the debauched Babylonian soldiery in the hour of triumph are meant here. And this is in accordance with the mention in verse 5 of drunkenness as their special sin. But we much prefer to treat the language as figurative. The invader has made his neighbors drink the cup of his cruel anger until they

657

have reached the depths of shameful degradation.

Puttest thy bottle.—It is possible to render, "pourest out thy wrath," and this makes the metaphor less obscure.

(17) For the violence of Lebanon ... — The rest of the verse is a refrain taken from the first woe (verse 8). Habakkuk probably foresees how the invader will cut down the cedar forests in Lebanon to adorn the palaces of Babylon. (Comp. Isa. 14:7, 8.) All these outrages shall in due time be avenged on himself. Some commentators, however, take Lebanon to represent the Holy Land (of which it was the beauty), or even the Temple, both of which Nebuchadnezzar laid waste.

(20) But the Lord.—While all this false worship prevails, the true World-ruler abides, and His presence is in His temple at Jerusalem. To Him the prophet's eyes are now turned. He ceases his denunciations of the invader, and finds solace in the glorious anticipations of the lyrical ode (3:1-15) which follows.

3

(1) Upon Shigionoth.—This term points, not to the contents of the composition, but either to its metrical structure or its musical setting. See note on the Inscription of Psalm 7. Inasmuch as this ode is throughout an account of the deliverance anticipated by prayerful faith, it is called not a Psalm, but a prayer.

(2) Thy speech.—Better, "thy report." The tone is that of Ps. 44:1. Jehovah's doings at the **beginning** of the years are well known; the prophet seeks that they may be manifested again, now in the midst of the years. The petition "in wrath remember mercy" implies—though Thy visitation be well deserved, yet mercifully limit its duration, as on former occasions.

(3-15) Habakkuk describes the "Theophany," or self-manifestation of Jehovah, which is to introduce the desired deliverance. All the verbs in this section refer, in the Hebrew, to a scene really future, but brought by the grasp of faith into the immediate present. While, however, his eyes are fixed on a future deliverance, the basis of all Habakkuk's anticipations is God's doings in time past; the chief features in the

portraiture are, in fact, borrowed from the books of Exodus and Judges.

(3) God came.—Jehovah reveals Himself from the south: i.e., from Mount Sinai, as in Deut. 32; Judg. 5; Ps. 68. The southern country is here designated as "Teman," i.e., Edom to the southeast, and "Paran," the mountainous region to the southwest, between Edom and Egypt.

(8) Of salvation.—The allusion is obviously to Israel's miraculous passages through the Red Sea and the Jordan.

(9) Thy bow was made quite naked.—God's chastisements, which are compared in Ps. 21:12 to arrows fitted to the string, are here represented as a bow taken out of the case. On the term "Selah," see note on Ps. 3:4.

(11) The sun and moon stood still in their habitation.—Here, of course, Habakkuk has in mind Josh. 10:12, 13. Apparently, the conception is that the surpassing brightness of the theophany shames the heavenly bodies, which accordingly cease to pursue their journey.

(13) Even for salvation ... —In the last half of the verse two figures are blended—those of a house and a human body. (Comp. Ps. 110:6.) The obvious meaning is that the house or race of the Chaldaeans is to be destroyed, "root and branch."

(15) Thou didst walk.—With this glance at the miraculous passage of the Red Sea (see verse 8), this prophetic poem comes to a sudden termination.

(18) Yet—i.e., in spite of all the afflictions predicted in verse 17. We are reminded of Paul's expression of confidence in Rom. 8:37.

(19) The Lord God.—This is an adaptation from Ps. 18:33. The "hinds' feet" indicate the strength and elasticity of the prophet's confidence; the "high places are the heights of salvation which stand at the end of the way of tribulation, and which only the righteous man can climb by the confidence of faith" (Kleinert).

To the chief singer—i.e., to the precentor, or presiding singer. The rubric may be interpreted "To him who presides over my stringed instruments." The same direction occurs with the words in the same order in six psalms. (On the terms used, see Ps. 4:1.) It has been inferred—though it is unlikely—from the use of the possessive pronoun, "**my** stringed instruments," that Habakkuk was a Levite, and therefore himself entitled to accompany the temple music.

ZEPHANIAH

1

(1) Hizkiah.—Or, "Hezekiah." It is quite possible that Zephaniah lays claim to descent from the royal family of Judah. Of the prophet's life nothing is known. The name "Zephaniah" means "Jehovah hides" or "protects."

(3) The stumblingblocks with the wicked—i.e., the enticements to sin together with the sinners. The prophecy in Manasseh's reign (II Kings 21:13) should be compared.

(4) The remnant of Baal—i.e., Baal worship shall be completely and utterly abolished. Not even a remnant of it shall be left. The term "remnant" need not imply that a large part of the Baal-worship had been already overthrown by Josiah's reformation.

The Chemarims.—In II Kings 23:5, this is the designation of the "idolatrous priests whom the kings of Judah had ordained to burn incense in the high places." The term is used again in Hos. 10:5.

The priests are probably a certain section of the Jewish priesthood who had winked at this establishment of false worship.

(5) The worship "on the housetops" is mentioned elsewhere as the cult of a certain class of apostates (see Jer. 19:13; 32:29) who ascended roofs and other high places to adore the hosts of heaven. (See Josiah's reformatory procedure, II Kings 23:12.) The last half of the verse refers to those who divide their allegiance between the true God and the false. The name Malcham occurs elsewhere as the name of an Ammonite deity, probably identical with Moloch. (See I Kings 11:5; Jer. 49:1-3.) The allusion to the adoration of the "host of heaven upon the housetops" gains additional force if this deity is identical with the planet Saturn, as some have supposed.

(7) A sacrifice.—The word includes the idea of the feast in which it was customary to consume the remains of the sacrifice. (See Ps. 22:26, 29.) God's guests are here those foreign nations whom He has selected to be His ministers of chastisement. They are invited, as it were, to banquet upon God's apostate people. (Comp. Isa. 34:6.)

(8) The king's children.—The misfortunes which were to befall Josiah's children, Jehoahaz and Jehoiakim (see II Kings 23 and 24), are perhaps in the prophet's eye. But if the date of writing is 641 B.C.-630 B.C.,

these princes must have been as yet mere children. It therefore appears better to suppose that the king's brothers or uncles are meant.

Clothed with strange apparel.—Zephaniah means those who have imitated the luxurious dress of foreign nations: e.g., perhaps the gorgeous apparel of Assyria and Babylonia (Ezek. 23:12-15). This desire for strange clothing is especially noticed as a mark of apostasy, because the national dress was appointed for a reason (see Num. 15:38, 39).

(9) Their masters' houses.—The idolaters had adopted a usage prevalent in the Philistine temples of Dagon—that of leaping over the threshold on entering the idol's temple. (See I Sam. 5:5.) When they entered it they filled it with "violence and deceit" by bringing offerings acquired by fraud and oppression.

(10) From the hills.—The "hills" are probably Mount Zion and Mount Moriah, the sites of the old Davidic city and the Temple. Thus all parts of the city are to be included in this destruction.

(11) Maktesh.—Better, "the mortar," a term indicating probably some part of the city lying in a hollow, perhaps that part which was in the valley of Tyropoeon. Thus some detect in the name "mortar" an allusion to the noisy din of the commerce conducted here.

(12) The men that are settled on their lees.—The figure is taken from wine which has become harsh from being allowed to stand too long on the lees. The persons intended are selfish, whose souls have stagnated in undisturbed prosperity, and whose inexperience of affliction has led them to deny the agency of God in the world. (Comp. Luke 12:16-20.)

(13) Comp. the curse on apostasy, Deut. 28.

2

(1) Gather yourselves together.—Rather, "Bend yourselves, yea bend." The disobedient nation is exhorted to "bend" in submission to Jehovah before His judgment is revealed.

(2) Before the decree bring forth—i.e., before God's ordinance, against which they have offended, brings forth the curse foretold in chap. 1.

Before the day pass as the chaff.—The

time for repentance is speeding by like chaff whirled before the wind.

(4-15) Jehovah's chastisement of foreign powers. These divine visitations are intended to lead God's people to repent and put their faith in Him who orders the destinies of all mankind. Also, as being inflicted on hostile peoples, they are in Israel's favor, and ought therefore to elicit gratitude. But more especially are they all steps toward the establishment of Jehovah's supremacy, and the inclusion of the Gentiles in His kingdom upon earth. This part of the divine sentence is presented in three strophes of four verses each—the chastisement of Philistia (verses 4-7); of Moab and Ammon (verses 8-11); of Ethiopia and Assyria (verses 12-15).

(4) It is noticeable that it is these four of the five Philistine cities which are denounced by Amos (1:6-8) and Jeremiah (25:20). See also Zech. 9:5. The prophecy appears only to indicate broadly that the Philistines as a nation should be obliterated, and the remnant of Judah be exalted. This effacement of the Philistine race had probably occurred before the Christian era. The last mention of the Philistines as a nation is in II Macc. 3:5.

(5) The Cherethites!—Perhaps Cretans. See I Sam. 30:14; Ezek. 25:16, where the same term is applied to the Philistines.

Canaan originally means "low-lying ground." It indicates here the low maritime plain inhabited by the Philistines, which is to be ravaged and depopulated (verse 6).

(7) The allusion to the captivity of Judah and its termination is remarkable. "Who save He in whose hand are human wills could now foresee that Judah should, like the ten tribes, rebel, be carried captive, and yet, though like and worse than Israel in its sin, should, unlike Israel, be restored" (Pusey).

(8) Reproach—i.e., abusive speech, or offensive design expressed in words. The conspiracy described in Ps. 83 illustrates this combination of Moab and Ammon for hostile purposes.

(9) The breeding of nettles.—The propriety of illustrating the fate of Moab and Ammon by that of the cities of the plain is the greater in that Lot, the ancestor of these nationalities, was an inhabitant of Sodom and narrowly escaped sharing its destruction. Ravages in Moab and Ammon were effected by Nebuchadnezzar in 582 B.C., probably in revenge for the murder of Gedaliah, the ruler of his appointment (Jos.,

Ant. 10.9, §7). But the allusion here is to some later and more permanent work of destruction. The national existence of both Moab and Ammon appears to have ceased long before the Christian era.

(11) Every one from his place.—This passage is one of the few which foretell that the worship of Jehovah shall find centers outside the Holy Land. The usual prediction represents the converted nations as "flowing" to Jerusalem.

(12) Ethiopia is to suffer by the sword in the execution of God's purpose of magnifying His people. The conjunction of Ethiopia and Assyria is probably suggested by the earlier passage in Nahum 3:8 seq. In addition to its earlier vicissitudes at the hands of Assyrian invaders, Ethiopia perhaps suffered as an ally of Egypt after the battle of Carchemish. It was probably invaded by Nebuchadnezzar; see Ezek. 30:4. With the Median ascendancy came a fresh series of calamities.

(13-15) The sentence against Assyria in the north was fulfilled as early as 625 B.C., when Nineveh was taken and destroyed by the Medes and Babylonians. (Comp. Isa. 23:7; 47:8; Jer. 50:23; Nahum 3:19.)

3

(2) Obeyed not the voice—i.e., of Jehovah, when He addresses her, as in 2:1-3. She does not trust in Jehovah, but in her own wealth (1:12); she does not draw nigh to her God, but to Baal and Moloch (1:4-6).

(5-7) In contradistinction to universal corruption, Jehovah daily exemplifies the law of righteousness, yet sinners are not moved to repentance (verse 5). He sets forth the great judgments He has executed on other sinful nations, but the warning is not heeded (verses 6, 7).

(10) The daughter of my dispersed.—Even from the southern limit of the known world shall the new church draw adherents. The "dispersed people" are not Jewish exiles, but the Gentile tribes of the dispersion (Gen. 11:8) which have been until now alienated from their Creator by ignorance and vice. (Comp. John 11:51, 52.)

(11) No more be haughty ... —His privileges—the adoption and the Shechinah, and the covenants, and the giving of the law, and the Temple service—had to this time been used by the Jew as a pretext for obduracy. The reinstated nation shall be purged of this spiritual pride.

(15) Taken away thy judgments—i.e., removed what He had "appointed concerning them" (verse 7) in the way of punishments.

The king of Israel.—The recognition of Jehovah as "king" is elsewhere a prominent feature in the portraiture of the extended dispensation. (Comp. Pss. 93:1; 96:1; 97:1; 99:1; Obad. 21.)

(18) The festival of the accomplishment of salvation is represented under the figure of the joyous Feast of Tabernacles, as in Zech. 14:16. None shall be impeded from attending on this joyous occasion, for the oppressors shall be overthrown (verses 19 and 20).

To whom the reproach of it was a burden—i.e., on whom their exile, and consequent inability to attend at Jerusalem, had brought derision.

HAGGAI

1

The First Utterance

(1-11)—The neglect of God's house is denounced, and is declared to be the cause of the prevalent dearth.

(1) Darius the king.—Darius I, son of Hystaspes, who became king of Persia in 521 B.C. There were still men living who had seen the first Temple (2:3), which fell in 586 B.C. Prophecy is now dated by the years of a foreign ruler, for Zerubbabel, though a lineal descendant of David, was only a **pechâh,** or viceroy of Persian appointment, not a king in his own right.

The sixth month.—Elul, corresponding nearly with our September.

In the first day.—See Ezek. 46:3; Isa. 66:23. This was an appropriate occasion for Haggai to begin a series of exhortations so intimately connected with the Temple. It appears to have been an ancient custom that the people should resort to the prophets for religious instruction on new moons and Sabbaths. (See II Kings 4:23.)

Came the word ... —This expression, which occurs repeatedly in this book, indicates that Jehovah was the direct source of these announcements, and Haggai only their vehicle.

The prophet.—See note on Hab. 1:1. Haggai is in point of time the first of the prophets of the Post-Captivity period. Of his tribe and parentage nothing is recorded in Scripture.

Governor.—"Satrap," or "viceroy," a term applied in the Old Testament to the provincial prefects of the Assyrian, Babylonian and Persian empires. Haggai addresses Zerubbabel as the civil, Joshua (a prominent character in the prophecy of Zechariah) as the ecclesiastical head of the restored exiles.

(2) The time is not come—i.e., it is not yet time to assemble and begin preparations for building. It is not stated on what grounds the people based this assumption; but probably they excused their indifference to religion by a pretended dread of Persian hostility. Darius, however, unlike his predecessor Artaxerxes, gave the enemies of the Jews no favor when a report was actually made to him on the subject. (See Ezra 5 and 6.)

(4) Is it time for you ... —If the adverse decree of Artaxerxes, which disallowed the building of Jerusalem (Ezra 4:21), had not hindered them from erecting magnificent residences for themselves, how could it reasonably excuse an utter neglect of God's house?

(5) Consider your ways.—A common expression in this prophet. The results of their conduct are set forth in verse 6: they are left to infer from these what its nature has been. The last clause of verse 6 expresses in a bold metaphor the general prevalence of poverty.

(9) I did blow upon it for the purpose of dispersing it. Even the little that was brought into the garner was decimated by God's continued disfavor.

The Second Utterance

(12-15)—The people turn a willing ear to Haggai's exhortation, and the prophet is now charged to inform them of the return of God's favor.

(12) With all the remnant of.—The word may mean either "the remnant" restored from Babylon, or merely "the remainder" of the people. Similarly in verse 14 and 2:2.

(15) It must be supposed that the intervening three weeks had been spent in collecting timber in the upland region, as was ordered in verse 8, and resuming the "work of the house of God."

2

The Third Utterance

(1-9)—This utterance treats of the glory which, in a later time, is to attach itself to the sacred spot whereon the return exiles are laboring. It was intended more especially as a message of consolation to those who remembered Solomon's magnificent structure, and who now gazed sadly on the humble proportions of its successor.

(1) In the one and twentieth day.—Here, again, the day selected is significant. The twenty-first day of the seventh month (Tisri) was the seventh and last day of the Feast of Tabernacles. This was the festival of harvest thanksgiving, and its occurrence had always been marked by observances of a peculiarly joyous character. Moreover, the sacrifices on this occasion were numerous. Thus the scanty harvest and the small beginnings of the Lord's house would both be brought into prominence.

(5) According to the word.—The clause is connected with the closing words of verse 4. Jehovah is present with them, and so is His promise made by solemn covenant in the days of old.

So my spirit.—Besides such promises of God's abiding favor as Exod. 29:45, 46, they have among them the abiding presence of His Holy Spirit. Having these, let them not be afraid. The evidence of the divine presence was the mission of inspired prophets, such as Haggai and Zechariah, and the Targum and the rabbis are perhaps right in referring the words "and my spirit" exclusively to the "spirit of prophecy."

(6) Yet once, it is a little while.—The meaning of these clauses is that given by Keil: "that the period between the present and the predicted great change of the world will be but one period—i.e., one uniform epoch—and that this epoch will be a brief one." (See Heb. 12:27.) The original passage here, as in other cases, must be treated without deference to its meaning when interwoven in New Testament argument. There is yet to be an interval of time, of limited duration, and then shall come a new era, when the glory of God's presence shall be manifested more fully and extensively. Notwithstanding its intimate connection with the Jewish Temple (verses 7 and 9), this new dispensation may well be regarded as that of the Messiah, for Malachi in like manner connects His self-manifestation with the Temple. If the words are to be pressed, their fulfillment at Christ's coming must be searched rather in the moral than the physical sphere, in changes effected in the human heart (comp. Luke 3:5) rather than on the face of nature.

(7) And the desire of all nations shall come.—The rendering of the King James Version, based on Jerome, is grammatically impossible with the present text. Its retention in some of the modern commentaries is mainly attributable to a natural unwillingness to give up a direct Messianic prophecy. Also, it must be remarked that the Messiah was not longed for by all nations; and that if He had been, there would be no point in mentioning the fact in the present connection. The significance of the utterance is that by agencies not specified, the Gentile world is to be converted and induced to offer worship and homage to Jehovah.

The Fourth Utterance

(10-19)—The recent season of scarcity is again accounted for and immediate blessings are announced. This address dates about two months later than its predecessor—viz., from the ninth month (Chisleu, or November—December), when the early rain would be looked for to water the newly-sown crops.

(12) Holy flesh.—Even in the light of

Lev. 6:27, according to Haggai, the guilt of impiety incurred by the Jews in neglecting the Temple had tainted the labor of their hands, and caused famine. And what merit they might claim for restoring the altar-worship and keeping the prescribed feasts (Ezra 3:2-6) was not conveyed further. It was cancelled by their neglect of an equally important duty.

(13) Unclean.—The defilement incurred by contact with a dead body was one of the deepest (See Num. 19:11-16.)

(15) Before a stone was laid... — Alluding to the recent resumption of building, not to the laying of the foundations fifteen years previously.

(16) Since those days were—i.e., throughout that whole period of neglect up to the date when they resumed the work of restoration. Throughout that period the harvests had grievously disappointed expectation.

(18) Even from the day.—The rendering of the King James Version makes the passage quite unintelligible. The Temple had been founded fifteen years before, in the second month of the second year of Cyrus (Ezra 3:10). The work of building had been carried on intermittently until within two years of the present time. It had then been entirely suspended, and had only been actively taken in hand after Haggai's address in the sixth month of this year. The force of the passage is sufficiently plain if we render as "even to the day."

(19) Is the seed yet in the barn?—The prospect was one of deepest gloom. But human helplessness is God's opportunity. He pledges His word even at this crisis by the mouth of Haggai, "From this day I will bless."

The Fifth Utterance

(20-23)—The heathen powers shall be consumed one of another, but the line of Zerubbabel shall stand secure, and be a witness to Jehovah's faithfulness. Here, as in verses 6-9, the only satisfactory interpretation is that Haggai was charged with a prediction—purposely vague and indistinct in character—of the extension of God's kingdom by the Christian dispensation. "Zerubbabel," the descendant of David, includes in himself Him who was according to the flesh his lineal descendant. Just in the same way in older prophecy "David" is himself identified with that Messiah in whom the glories of the Davidic house were to culminate. It is unnecessary to find a literal fulfillment of the prediction of the overthrow of the world-powers.

ZECHARIAH

1

(1-6) On the twenty-fourth day of the sixth month of the second year (520 B.C.) of Darius Hystaspis, the rebuilding of the Temple had been resumed (Hag. 1:15); and on the twenty-first day of the seventh month, the prophet Haggai had foretold "the latter glory of this house be greater than its former" (Hag. 2:9); and now, but a few weeks later, Zechariah receives his mission. He is commanded to exhort the people to avoid such punishments as fell on their fathers, and to make themselves worthy of the glory which should be revealed, by turning unto the Lord with sincere repentance.

(1) The prophet is, no doubt, to be referred to Zechariah. Zechariah is spoken of as the lineal representative of Iddo, and one of the heads of the priestly houses in the days of Joiakim, the successor of Jeshua (Neh. 12:12-16). Comp. Ezra 5:1; 6:14. The name Zechariah probably means "Yah remembers."

(3) Unto them—i.e., to the prophet's contemporaries, whose fathers are spoken of in the preceding verse, where the ground is given whereon the exhortation to repentance is founded. Zechariah warns the people by the history of their fathers that no spiritual privileges will profit them without holiness, but rather will aggravate their guilt, and increase their condemnation if they disobey God. Observe in this and the next verse the emphatic threefold "saith the Lord of hosts."

(4) The former prophets—viz., those who prophesied when Jerusalem was inhabited and in prosperity (7:7), before the captivity.

(5) Fathers ... prophets.—To show the evil result of the obstinate disobedience of their fathers, the prophet asks, "Your fathers, where are they?"—i.e., they are perished through their iniquity. To this the people answer, "But the prophets, did they go on living for ever?"—i.e., the prophets, who did not sin, they are dead too; so what is your argument worth?

(6) My words.—True, says the prophet, both your fathers and the former prophets are dead; "but" for all that, the words of the prophets were actually fulfilled in your fathers, as they themselves confessed. (Comp. Lam. 2:17.)

A Series of Seven Visions

Zech. 1:7-6:15. Between the beginning of Zechariah's prophetic labors and the incidents recorded in Zech. 1:7-6:15, the prophet Haggai received the revelation contained in Hag. 2:10-23. Just five months after the rebuilding of the Temple was resumed, Zechariah sees a succession of seven visions in one night, followed by a symbolic action (6:9-15).

First Vision—The Horseman Among the Myrtles

(8) I saw.—Not in a dream, but apparently, from 4:1, awake, in an ecstatic vision.

Red horse, and ... the bottom.—The construction of the Hebrew shows that "the man that stood among the myrtles" and "the angel of the Lord" (verse 11) are identical. (See notes on Gen. 16:7; 18:2.) Commentators endeavor to attach special significance to the expression, "the myrtles which were in the hollow," and similarly respecting the color of the horses. But in a vision or a parable we must not expect to find something in the interpretation to correspond with each detail of the figurative representation: the setting must not be confounded with the gem. So, in this case, the fact that the horsemen were standing among the myrtles in a certain hollow is mentioned merely as a natural incident. The writer of Revelation has (Rev. 6) adopted the colors mentioned in Zech. 6, and himself given to them a special significance in his own writings. But to interpret Zechariah in this case by the light of the Book of Revelation would be most uncritical.

(9) O my lord.—This is the angel-interpreter, whose office it was to interpret the visions (1:9; 2:3; 4:1, 4, 5; 5:5-10; 6:4), and who is often referred to simply as "he."

(11) The angel of the Lord.—The horsemen had been sent forth to act as scouts, and to bring back on account of the state of the world, that at the intercession of the angel of the Lord comforting words might be announced to Zechariah, and by him to the people. They reported the world to be dwelling in self-confident security. The overthrow of the kingdoms foretold by Haggai (2:20-23) had not yet begun, and so, although the building of the Temple was being carried on (Ezra 5:6), Judah was still insecure as long as the heathen nations flourished. Consequently, the angel of the

Lord intercedes for Jerusalem and the cities of Judah.

(12) These threescore and ten years.— From the taking of Jerusalem by Nebuchadnezzar (605-606 B.C.) to the date of the decree of Cyrus for the return of the Jews (538 B.C.) is sixty-eight years. These are the seventy years of captivity foretold by Jeremiah (25:11; 29:10). But eighteen years had now elapsed since that decree of Cyrus.

(13) Angel.—The Lord does not reply directly to the intercessor, but addresses the angel-interpreter, who at once, in the words of verses 14-17, delivers the message of comfort to the prophet.

(14) I am jealous.—The verb is in the perfect, like "I am returned" (verse 16), denoting that the Lord **had already** shown His jealous love for Israel in bringing them out of captivity, and that He **would continue to do so** in completing the restoration of Jerusalem.

(16) A line.—To measure, and mark out its confines. (Comp. 2:1, 2.)

Second Vision—The Four Horns and the Four Smiths

(18) Horns.—The horn is a symbol of power and hostility. The "four horns" denote the heathen nations which had oppressed them.

(19) Judah, Israel, and Jerusalem.—The expression "Israel and Jerusalem" is a closer definition of Judah, as in Mal. 2:11. (For undoubted instances of the name Israel being used in reference to Judah after the separation of the kingdoms, see II Chron. 12:1; 15:17, seqq.)

(21) The word "scattered" might, if standing alone, be taken as discharging the duties of historic and, at the same time, of prophetic perfect. But since the dependent clause reads "so that no man **did lift up** his head"— in the perfect—the word "have scattered" can refer only to the actual past. We must, therefore, reject all reference to the four monarchies—Assyrian, Babylonian, Medo-Persian, and Graeco-Macedonian—, because the Graeco-Macedonian had not yet come into existence. If, then, the "four horns" do symbolize four monarchies, they can be only the Assyrian, Egyptian, Babylonian, and Medo-Persian. Here, as in verse 8, we must not draw too close a comparison between the symbol and the thing symbolized, and should understand the "four work-men" ("carpenters," verse 20) not as specific kings, but merely as ones figuring the destruction of these nations for the good of the Jewish nation, without the manner of its accomplishment being accurately defined.

The vision, a natural consequent of the preceding, is one of comfort, its object being to assure the people that as the former nations which had been hostile to Israel and Judah had been destroyed, so the present Medo-Persian monarchy, which also had at times oppressed them, should have the horn of its hostility utterly cast out, and should protect them and encourage the rebuilding of Jerusalem.

2

Third Vision—The Man With the Measuring Line

(1-5) This vision is a prophetic realization of the fulfillment of the promise that "a line shall be stretched forth upon Jerusalem" (1:16).

(1) A man does not seem to mean "an angel," as in 1:8, for he has no message to deliver or mission to perform; but he is to be considered rather as a mere figure in the vision, performing an action for which, indeed, he is implicitly rebuked. The whole vision is prophetic of the state of Jerusalem from its restoration to the time when God's protection should be eventually removed from it. To this latter event, however, no reference is as yet made.

(4) This young man is by some supposed to be Zechariah; but it gives a much more definite turn to the meaning of the vision to understand the expression as referring to "the man with the measuring line."

Towns without walls.—The "other angel," for the instruction of Zechariah, directs the angel-interpreter to inform the man who was measuring that there could be no object in taking an exact measure of Jerusalem, since it would soon exceed its original limits. Josephus (**Bell. Jud.** 5:4, 92) says that in the time of Herod Agrippa Jerusalem had, "by reason of the multitude" of its inhabitants, gradually "extended beyond its original limits," so that another hill had to be taken in, which was fortified, and called "Bezethá."

(5) A wall of fire.—This verse is not intended to disfavor the building of walls to Jerusalem, a thing which was actually done under Nehemiah (445 B.C.), but is simply a solemn promise of God's protection. Many indeed were the troubles which fell on the city in the times which intervened between the days of Zechariah and those of our Lord; but still, abundant proof was given that God had not forgotten His promise to shield it.

(6-13) This address to Zion, whether taken as the words of the prophet himself, or of the angel who had been speaking before, was intended to be communicated to the people by the prophet, whose mind had been prepared by the foregoing vision for the reception of such a revelation.

(6) The land of the north—i.e., Babylonia, as in Jer. 1:14; 6:22; 10:22.

For I have spread you abroad.—The tense may be regarded as the prophetic perfect, meaning "for it is my fixed intention to spread you abroad." Thus they are encouraged to flee from Babylon by being warned of the judgments which were to come upon her (verses 8, 9), and because God was determined so to bless them, that they should spread out to all quarters of the globe.

(8) After the glory—i.e., in search of God's glory upon the heathen in judgment and mercy, by first breaking their power (verse 9), and afterward attaching them to His service (verse 11).

(10-13) The prophecy contained in these verses is admitted by most Jewish as well as Christian commentators to be of a Messianic character; but opinion is not as unanimous with regard to the nature of its fulfillment. A reasonable view of the nature of prophecy would seem to be that in the fulfillment, while all that is essential to the grand idea of God's purpose, as revealed to and by the prophet, actually comes to pass, the historical details which surround its accomplishment are not often such as the prophet himself seems to have expected. Upon the supposition, then, that Zechariah had no certain knowledge of the time and actual manner of the fulfillment of God's purpose, of the essential points of which he had, however, a grand and faithful prophetic preception, there is no difficulty in interpreting this passage, and others like it, of the coming of Christ in the flesh, and the establishment of the Christian Church.

(10) I will dwell in the midst of thee.— These words (comp. 8:3) were, no doubt, meant by the prophet to refer, in the first place, to God's indwelling in the second Temple (see Hag. 2:9), although the visible

manifestation of His presence (the **Shekinah**) was not again given. This prophecy received a glorious fulfillment in the great event chronicled in John 1:14.

(11) Many nations.—Comp. 8:20-22. This prophecy, which is clothed in Old Testament imagery, was spiritually fulfilled by the gathering in of the Gentiles to the Church of Christ.

And thou ... unto thee.—The pronouns are in the feminine, and refer to the "daughter of Zion" (verse 10).

Sent me.—The person changes (comp. verse 8). These words seem to imply an expectation of a near fulfillment of the prophecy, such as would prove to the people the truth of the prophet's (or angel's) mission. (Comp. 4:9; 6:15.) But when the promise was fulfilled in Christ, it was just "the city" that failed to perceive its fulfillment (Luke 19:44).

(12) The holy land.—This is the only passage in which this term is used. So far from God's then inheriting Judah or the Holy Land, and choosing again Jerusalem, the coming of Christ was but the beginning of the rejection of His people, and the destruction of Jerusalem. But we may believe, on the authority of Paul, that God has not cast off His own people, and that a time will come when all Israel shall be saved (Rom. 11).

(13) Raised.—Better, "roused." The figure is that of a lion roused up from its lair. (Comp. the still bolder metaphor of Ps. 78:65.)

3

Fourth Vision—Joshua Before the Angel of the Lord

(1-7) The accusation against Joshua was not that of neglecting the building of the Temple (for the rebuilding had been resumed five months before), nor was it that he had allowed his sons to marry foreign wives (for that took place some sixty years later), but, rather, as high priest he was the representative of the priestly nation, and so was looked on as laden, not only with his own, but also with the sins of the whole people. Moreover, the priesthood itself had fallen under the severest condemnation (Ezek. 22:26).

(1) And he.—Probably, the angel-interpreter.

Standing before.—There is a great variety

of opinion among commentators with respect to the capacity in which Joshua is represented as standing before the angel of the Lord. Theodoret and Hengstenberg maintain that Joshua is seen in the sanctuary engaged in the work of his priestly office **before** the angel of the Lord. Ewald imagines that at this time the high priest was accused at the Persian court, and that a defamation and persecution of this kind may be discerned as underlying this vision. Koehler regards Joshua as standing before the judgment seat of the angel, while Satan stands at his right hand (Ps. 109:6) to accuse him. But, while this interpretation is in the main correct, it must be remembered that no formal judicial process is described in the vision.

Satan.—Literally, "the adversary." A belief in a personal devil was current among the Jews from, at any rate, the time of the composition of the Book of Job to Talmudic times. (See Job 1; 2; I Chron. 21:1.)

(2) The fire was that of penal suffering in the captivity in Babylon. (Comp. Amos 4:11.) As with the guilt, so with the pardon and promise; in both, Joshua was the representative of the people.

(3) Filthy garments.—Such as would render him unfit to appear before God as priest. They are a symbol of the guilt and defilement of sin. (See Isa. 64:6.)

(4) Those that stood before him is an expression meaning courtiers and counselors (I Kings 13:6-8); and here, probably, it means angels of inferior grade to the "angel of the Lord."

(5) Fair—i.e., clean. The prophet seems to have felt constrained to make the request contained in this verse from an idea that the changing of Joshua's raiment might be only a sign of the removal of the high priest's own guilt. That the prophet was justified in making the request is shown by the fact that it was granted, and that even before the "garments" were put on. (Comp. Exod. 28:38.) The figure throughout seems to be borrowed from Isa. 61:10.

(6-10) The angel of the Lord now proclaims to Joshua a fourfold promise: (1) the confirmation of his official authority, and the elevation of his own spiritual nature; (2) the mission of the Saviour; (3) God's providential care for the House, which was being rebuilt; and, (4) the peace and prosperity of the nation.

(7) My house.—The expression "my house" is probably to be understood in a metaphorical sense for "my people" (comp.

Num. 12:7; Hos. 8:1; 9:15; Heb. 3:6; I Tim. 3:15). The sense then is that the high priest was to direct the people in all things respecting the law of God, and especially to judge those who ministered in the sanctuary. But some think that the Temple then in course of construction is referred to. In the latter case the meaning is not very different: the high priest was to rule and direct the services of the sanctuary and Holy of Holies, and to keep away every kind of idolatry and ungodliness from its outer courts. Thus Joshua is confirmed in his office of high priest, which had been called in question by the accusation of Satan.

Among these that stand by.—He is promised free spiritual access to God among the holy angels.

(8) I will bring.—Literally, "I (am) bringing," a somewhat indefinite tense, the exact meaning of which can be decided only by the context. (Comp. Hag. 2:6.) Thus in Isa. 7:14 the context (verse 16) shows that what the prophet looked on as a fulfillment could not be far off; in Ezek. 24:17 this tense is shown by the next verse to be the imminent future; while in Zech. 12:2 a similar form of construction seems to refer to a distant future.

My servant ... —Better, "my servant Branch." Comp. Isa. 11:1; 53:2. These passages Jeremiah had, doubtless, in mind when he uttered the prophecies of 23:5; 33:15. From these passages Zechariah adopts "Branch" as the proper name of the Saviour. He may have expected that this promised Saviour would be found in Sheshbazzar (i.e., Zerubbabel) (Ezra 1:8), who should build the House (Hag. 2:23; Zech. 4:9). But the expression "my servant" (Hag. 2:23) is also a recognized title of the Messiah in Ezek. 34:23 and Isa. 53:11. (This last passage is probably the foundation of the expression in Acts 4:27.) A glimpse of Messianic times is here, indeed, revealed to the prophet, but the clearness of his view is obscured by the medium through which he views them.

(9) The stone.—"The stone" means "the stones," the singular noun being used as a noun of multitude (comp. Gen. 11:3; Exod. 39:10). "The stones" are the material stones with which the House was to be built; the laying them before Joshua is used as figuring the whole command to build the House.

Upon one stone.—Better, "upon one particular stone," i.e., either the foundation stone laid in the time of Cyrus, or chief cornerstone; or, possibly, "upon each stone," i.e., upon the whole scheme and process of rebuilding.

Seven eyes.—They represent the all-embracing, and here special, providence of God (4:10). The expression "to put the eyes upon" is used in Jer. 39:12; 40:4, in the sense "to protect," "take care of." The completion of this material building was an important era in the train of events, which, under divine providence, was preparing the way for the coming of the Messiah.

In one day.—The day when the Temple should be completed and consecrated. The successful completion—the finishing, or "graving thereof"—of this great work would be a sign and seal of the forgiveness of the past "iniquity of the land."

(10) Comp. I Kings 4:25; Micah 4:4, etc. It is an announcement of the approaching fulfillment of the promise of Jer. 33:16. Such prophecies were partially fulfilled in the restoration of the Jews after the Captivity; but perhaps their complete fulfillment is to be expected in the future (Rom. 11:26).

4

Fifth Vision—The Golden Candlestick.

(1) Came again, and waked.—The angel may have gone forth, as before (2:3), to receive some fresh instruction from a higher angel, or from God, and now come back again. From this verse it would appear that between some of the visions the prophet fell in to a state of lethargy, and that the angel roused him.

(2) This visionary candlestick differed in four points from the original of the Tabernacle and Solomon's Temple—viz., in having "a bowl," "pipes," and "olive trees" each side of it, and "two golden spouts."

Seven pipes.—Better, "seven pipes apiece." There were, then, forty-nine pipes, but as the candlestick is only visionary, we need not trouble ourselves about the difficulties of its construction. The number seven in the original candlestick was, perhaps, mystical, in which case the forty-nine pipes in the vision would be so too. At any rate, it would seem that a great number of pipes is mentioned to indicate the unlimited nature of the supply of oil.

(6) This . . . word.—The vision is called "the word," as being a symbolical prophecy. (Comp. 1:7.) As the golden candlestick was placed in the holy place of the Tabernacle (and the Temple) for a purpose

(Exod. 27:21), so did the congregation on whose behalf was the candlestick, require a sanctuary. This sanctuary Zerubbabel was to complete (verse 9)—not by any merit or strength of his own or of Israel, but simply by the Spirit of the Lord of Hosts (Ezek. 37:11-14).

(7) O great mountain?—This is figurative of the colossal difficulties which the neighboring powers put in the way of completing the Temple. (Comp. Matt. 21:21.)

Grace, grace unto it.—The head stone is used to represent the whole Temple. The words are a prayer, which takes the form of a shout of triumph (like **Hosanna!**), and mean, "May God's grace or favor rest on the house for ever!"

(8) Me.—The word of the Lord now comes directly to the prophet, as, possibly, in 2:6-13.

(9) Thou . . . unto you.—Such a change in number is common in Hebrew, especially when addressing a nation, which at one time is viewed as a corporate unity, at another as a collection of individuals.

(10) For they shall rejoice . . . whole earth.—If you do not despise this day of small things, when you see but the foundation of the Temple laid, the providential care of the Lord (comp. 3:9) shall rejoice to see Zerubbabel taking the last perpendicular of the completed work; but if you doubt the possibility of this, know that God's providence extends over the whole earth, and that, therefore, He can make all things and all nations work together for the good of His chosen, Israel.

(12) Which through . . . themselves.—The meaning appears to be that on each side of the golden bowl at the top of the candlestick was a golden spout turned upward, into which the two clusters of olives poured their oil spontaneously, and from which the oil flowed into the bowl, and from it through the forty-nine pipes to the seven lamps. "The gold" stands for pure bright oil.

(14) The . . . anointed ones.—Literally, "two sons of oil": Joshua, the high priest, and Zerubbabel, the Prince of Judah, appointed instruments through whom He causes His Spirit to flow to His congregation. Thus, as by the preceding vision it was signified that the religious head of the nation was accepted by God and purified, so in this vision the civil head receives the assurance of God's assistance in his work. The anointed priest and the anointed prince are mentioned together in the last verse to show that it is by their joint efforts that the prosperity of the nation is to be brought about.

5

Sixth Vision—The Flying Scroll,
the Woman in the Ephah, and
the Two Women With Storks' Wings

This is to be regarded as essentially one vision in three dissolving views (verses 1-4, 5-8, 9-11).

(1) Flying roll.—A scroll floating in the air. (Comp. Ezek. 2:9, 10.)

(2) He.—The angel-interpreter.

The length ... and the breadth ... — These were the dimensions of the holy place of the Mosaic Tabernacle, also of the porch of Solomon's Temple. If, then, we are to consider the measurement of the scroll as symbolical, we may regard it as indicating that the measure of the sanctuary is the measure of sin; that is, the sinner must not say, "I am not worse than my neighbor," but should measure his conduct by the standard of Lev. 11:44; Matt. 5:48.

(3) For every one ... on this side ... on that side according to it.—Thieves are mentioned on one side of the scroll as a specimen of sinners against the second table of the Decalogue, as false to man; and false swearers on the other side as sinners against the first table, as false to God.

(6) This is an ephah ... all the earth.—As in an ephah the separate grains are all collected together, so will the individual sinners over the whole length and breadth of the land be brought into one confused heap. (Comp. Matt. 13:30.) It is not mentioned until later that they are to be carried away.

(7, 8) Talent.—These verses should be taken as the words of the angel-interpreter. First, representatives of the two classes of sinners are mentioned; then they are heaped into an undistinguishable mass, and afterward spoken of as **one** woman, who impersonates wickedness.

(9) Behold ... —We need not enter into the minute details of the verse (comp. note on 1:8). The wings of the woman do seem, however, to be represented as filled with the wind to enable them to carry their burden with greater ease and velocity through the air. The prophet, perhaps, borrowed his imagery from some of the grotesque figures he had seen in Babylon.

(11) Land of Shinar.—Where mankind had first organized a rebellion against God (Gen. 11:2); it was also the land of the Captivity of the Jews (Babylonia).

This vision is a circumstantial symbolization of the promise given in 3:9. While it is a promise of the remission of the punishment of their iniquity, it serves also as an exhortation to the returned exiles to leave in Babylon the iniquity which had been the cause of their being transported there.

6

Seventh Vision—The Four Chariots

(1) There came.—The prototypes of these two mountains were, no doubt, the Mount of Olives (14:4) and Mount Zion, between which lies the Valley of Jehoshaphat, where the Lord judges the nations (Joel 3:2, sqq.). But the mountains themselves were visionary, and are represented as of brass, to denote, according to some, the immovable firmness of the place where the Lord dwells, and where he has founded His kingdom.

(5) "Winds" ("spirits") out of which He makes His messages (Ps. 104:4) are most appropriately used here, as symbolical of the working of God's Spirit. (Comp. Jer. 49:36; Dan. 7:21; John 3:8.) Here the words of the angel-interpreter pass imperceptibly into the prophet's own description of the scene.

(6) The black ... therein go.—It would seem that two chariots go into the "north country," because there were there two powers to be overcome: the remnant of the old Asshur-Babylonian and the Medo-Persian.

The south country is Egypt. After the battle of Marathon (490 B.C.), Egypt revolted from Darius, was conquered by Xerxes (485 B.C.), and finally wrested from the hands of Persia by Alexander (332 B.C.).

(7) Bay.—Better, "powerful"; but in the Hebrew the word which the English renders "red" must be substituted here, and rendered "bay." Then the destinations of all the four-colored horses—bay, black, white, gray ("grisled," verse 3)—will be accounted for.

(8) Have quieted my spirit.—"Spirit" is used, as in Judg. 8:3, in the sense of "wrath" (comp. Ezek. 5:12; 16:42; 24:13). Many commentators have, without any warrant, drawn their interpretation of the colors of the horses in this vision from the Book of Revelation. But it is better to consider the horses as representing different colors merely in order to give greater distinctness to the vision. (Comp. 1:8; 5:9.) The commentators fail to discover any ethical or historical reason for famine (black) and victory (white) being especially sent to the north, and various chastisements (gray) to the south, or why the "red," i.e., "bay horses" (war), should not have been sent out at all.

(10) Of them of the captivity.—Even those who had returned from the Captivity were so called (Ezra 4:1; 6:19). These were probably, however, Jews who intended to remain in the land of their exile, but who had come on a visit to Jerusalem, bringing offerings of silver and gold, to show their sympathy with their brethren who were carrying on the work of the rebuilding of the Temple.

Heldai is called "Helem" in verse 14, and Josiah seems to be called "Hen." It is common for a person to be called by several different names in the Bible.

(11) Crowns.—Better, "a composite crown." No crown was placed on Zerubbabel, for such an act would have been a seeming restoration of the kingdom, when it was not to be restored. The crown had been definitely taken away in the time of Zedekiah, until the Branch should come (see Isa. 32:1; Jer. 22:30; 23:5; Ezek. 21:27). But the high priest in his person symbolized the twofold office of the Messiah, who, like Melchizedek, was to be a priest and king (Ps. 110). That the high priests during a succeeding period were practically the rulers of the nation is not sufficient to account for the terms of this prophecy, especially for the emphatic personality of the royal priest mentioned in the next verse.

(12) BRANCH.—See note on 3:8.

Shall build.—Since Zerubbabel is not even mentioned in this passage, Zechariah's hearers could not possibly have thought that this symbolical action was merely a repetition of the promise of 4:9, but must have perceived that the building of the Temple here spoken of referred to something of a higher nature than the material building then in progress.

(13) Even he ... and he.—The pronoun is most emphatic in both cases. It implies that "He" shall be the true builder, "He" the true ruler.

Shall be between them both.—The interpretations of this verse are various. But the expression can only mean between two **persons**, not between the two abstract ideas of royalty and priesthood. Nor can it mean between the king and the priest, for one person only is mentioned, who is himself a priest on a royal throne. The only two persons mentioned are "Branch" (the Prince of Peace: Isa. 9:6) and the Lord Himself. It can, then, mean only between them. When, in the light of later revelation, we consider the divine nature of "Branch," we can understand the fitness of the expression "between them both," though to the prophet's original hearers it must have sounded enigmatical.

(15) And they that are far off.—Hardly the Jews of the Dispersion only, but non-Jews also. (Comp. Hab. 2:14; Zech. 2:11.)

7

(1) Fourth year ... This was in 518 B.C., the second year after the beginning of the rebuilding of the Temple, and about two years before its completion.

(3) In the fifth month.—On the tenth of the fifth month (Ab), Nebuzar-adan burned the Temple and Jerusalem with fire (Jer. 52:12, 13), but in II Kings 25:8-10, the seventh day of the fifth month is given as the date; perhaps it was in flames for three days. Now that the rebuilding was well in progress, they naturally desired to know whether the fast which had been kept in commemoration of the past calamity should be still held.

Chaps. 7:4-8:23. The prophet's answer is contained in four sections (7:4-7, 8-14; 8:1-17, 18-23), each of which is introduced by the words, "The word of the Lord of hosts came," etc., as a testimony that he spoke not of himself.

(4-7) The people (as in Isa. 58:3-8) are rebuked for the hypocritical, or merely formal, nature of their fasts. The prophet does not, even further on, give any direct answer to their inquiry.

(5) All the people.—No question was asked about the fast of the tenth month, because the fast in Ab being in connection with their mourning for the destruction of the Temple, it was natural that, now the rebuilding of it had progressed so far, they should inquire whether that particular fast should be kept. The fast of the third of the seventh month (Tishri), which was kept in memory of the assassination of Gedaliah, took place soon after the destruction of the Temple. The seventy years to which he refers are those between the seventh month 587 B.C. (the date of the assassination of Gedaliah) and the ninth month 518 B.C. (the date of the Bethel—"house of God," verse 2—mission).

(8-14) The prophet implies that true fasting is to loose the bands of wickedness and leave off oppression. But Israel had adopted quite the opposite course, and therefore God, in accordance with Deut. 4:27, had scattered them among the nations.

8

The third section of the prophet's answer is divided into seven separate sayings (verses 2; 3; 4, 5; 6, 7; 8; 9-13, 14-17), and the fourth into three (verses 19, 20-22, and 23), each of which begins with "Thus saith the Lord of hosts." These are not merely the words of man; they are an express revelation from God.

(4-5) This promise may well be regarded as having been fulfilled to the letter in the days of Simon the Maccabee (I Macc. 14:4-15).

(7) From the east . . . and from the west.— There were Jews in exile in the west as well as in the east (Joel 3:6); and, indeed, a general dispersion may be almost implied from Isa. 43:5, 6.

(9) Prophets.—It would almost seem that there were other prophets who spoke at the time besides Haggai and Zechariah.

That the temple might be built.—These words seem to be used in reference to the resumption of the building (Hag. 1:14), when the people set themselves to work with a will, as contrasted with the first laying of the foundation in the second year of Cyrus, king of Persia, 537 B.C. (Ezra 3:10; comp. 1:1), after which the work of building was suspended for about sixteen years.

(10) The expedition of Cambyses against Egypt, when the Persian hosts marched southward through Palestine, must have caused much distress to the Jews in their already narrow circumstances because of the unproductiveness of the land.

(14-17) As the Captivity had been brought about by God's decree, so, too, the Restoration. The people, therefore, need not fear, if only they do that which is righteous in His sight.

(18-23) This fourth section gives at last all that the prophet intends to answer concerning the fast of the fifth month (7:3), and

also concerning the other fasts. (See Nebuchadnezzar's siege and capture of Jerusalem, II Kings 25:1; Jer. 39:2; 52:4; 52:6, 7.) As, on account of their sins, their feasts had been changed into fasts, and their days of rejoicing into mourning (Amos 8:10), so now the prophet promises that if only they will keep the required conditions their fasts should be transformed into feasts.

(20-23) Comp. Micah 4:2; Isa. 2:2, 3; 45:14-17. According to the figurative language of the Old Testament, the nations are represented as coming up to Jerusalem with the object, doubtless, of keeping there the festivals. (Comp. 2:10-13, 14:16-19.) However, we must not look for a literal fulfillment of such prophecies. The one before us seems virtually to be fulfilled in the fact that through Jesus Christ (who was a Jew according to the flesh) the knowledge of the true God has been spread among most nations of the world. But see Rom. 11, yet future in fulfillment.

9

We maintain, against theories to the contrary, the unity and post-exilic authorship of Zechariah. Both "sections," chaps. 1-8 and 9-14, evince an extensive acquaintance with the later prophets, and differences of style may reasonably be attributed to differences of circumstances and application. (See notes, below.)

(1-4) The terms of the denunciation of Syria (verse 1) are so general, that if they stood alone we should be at a loss to fix the era of their fulfillment. But the case is different with Phoenicia (verses 2-4); for, though Tyre was besieged by Shalmanezer, and perhaps even taken by Nebuchadnezzar, it was certainly never "devoured with fire" until Alexander (333 B.C.). To this date we consider this prophecy to refer.

(6) A bastard—i.e., a mixed race. It was a special point in Alexander's policy, as here in Philistia, to break up nationalities and to fuse different peoples.

(7) Blood . . . abominations.—viz., their "idolatrous sacrifices."

Jebusite.—Since the "Jebusite" seems to be parallel with the "governor," rather than contrasted with it, it seems probable that it refers to the Jebusite people, who "dwelt with the children of Judah in Jerusalem" as equals, and not as a conquered race (Josh. 15:63). Nothing is known of any great conversion of Philistines to Judaism at this

671

time; indeed, in later times we still hear of them as hostile to the Jews (I Macc. 3:41; 10:83). But after this last reference they disappear from history as a separate nation, probably because they were no longer distinguishable from the Jews or the Greek settlers of those regions.

(8) Amid all these dangers, Israel is promised, under divine protection, a certain immunity.

Him that passeth ... returneth.—The promise was undoubtedly fulfilled when Alexander entered Jerusalem, prostrated himself before the high priest, and treated the Jews with peculiar favor.

(9-17) The advent of the king. It has been urged as an objection against the post-exilic authorship of this passage that "Ephraim" and "Jerusalem" are mentioned, as though Israel were still separated from Judah. But, on the contrary, Ephraim and Jerusalem are here strictly parallel terms, as are also "Judah" and "Ephraim" (ver. 13). The nation was now one (Ezek. 37:22). This passage is generally admitted to be Messianic. But the prophecy was not immediately to be fulfilled. The nation had yet severe sufferings to endure and triumphs to achieve in those struggles which render the Maccabean period (167-130 B.C.) one of the most noble pages in Jewish history.

(9) **Of an ass.**—Riding on an ass indicates an absence of pomp and worldly display. This prophecy was literally fulfilled by our Lord's entry into Jerusalem on Palm Sunday (Matt. 21:5-11). He deliberately, in view of this prophecy, performed that act, not merely in order to fulfill the prophecy, but rather as a symbolical act, by which He intended to correct the false notions concerning the mission of the Messiah entertained by His friends, as well as by His enemies. The wording of this verse is borrowed from Isa. 17:25, and seems to indicate that when their King should come, the nation would be enjoying a certain political independence, but that their military power would have come to an end.

(12) **Strong hold.**—Those who still remained in Babylon are exhorted to come forth. Comp. 8:8 (which is on all sides admitted to be written after the return from the Captivity). They are "prisoners" still in Babylon, but "of hope," because, if they chose to accept them, they are the subjects of glorious hopes and promises.

(13-17) These verses are prophetic of the military prowess of Israel, through the aid of the Lord God, and were signally fulfilled

in the triumphs of the Maccabees over the Grecian rulers of Syria (167-130 B.C.), even though the prophet may not have had any distinct notion of such distant events.

(16) **Flock.**—Observe here the first introduction of the word and idea of "flock," which plays such a prominent part in the following chapters.

10

(2) **Idols.**—Better, "teraphim" (Judg. 17:5). Against the postexilic origin of this passage, and of 13:2, it has been objected that idols and false prophets harmonize only with a time prior to the exile. But it must be remembered that the marriage with heathen women, which is so often spoken of after the Captivity, must have been, as was the case with Solomon, a continual source of danger in that respect. Moreover, idolatry, soothsaying, etc., were actually practiced up to the time of the destruction of Jerusalem by Titus. (See Neh. 6:10-14; Mal. 3:5; II Macc. 12:40.)

(3) **The goats** are, probably, to be identified with "the shepherds" (Ezek. 34), and both to be referred to foreign rulers and leaders, since the latter part of the verse seems to denote that the whole people is to be changed from a timid flock into a nation of warriors (see verses 6, 7; comp. 9:13).

(4) It is much disputed whether "him" means "the Lord of Hosts" or "Judah." It appears best to take it as referring to "Judah" —i.e., to the whole Jewish nation.

Corner, or **cornerstone**, denotes a chieftain, on whom the whole national fabric is put together (I Sam. 14:38; Isa. 28:16). So also **Nail**, etc. The meaning of the passage is that when the Lord of hosts visits His flock, He will cause to arise from them such rulers and leaders as may be necessary to enable them successfully to resist their enemies. (See verses 5-7; comp. Ezek. 37:16, 17, 22; I Macc. 3:39; 4:7, 31; 6:30, 35, etc.)

(8) A yet further redemption of Israel was to take place before the consummation of these victorious promises. Some critics have considered this passage as conclusive against the assumption of a post-exilic origin of these latter chapters. But 8:8 speaks in similar terms, and yet the genuineness of that passage has never been called in question. The fact is that the restoration under Zerubbabel was most incomplete; only some 42,-360 returned from exile under him. There

was a further return of exiles under Ezra, in 458 B.C., some twenty years after the probable date of the prophecies contained in these last chapters, and numbers, no doubt, returned at various other times.

(9) Sow is never used in a bad sense, i.e., "to scatter," but rather means to "spread" and "multiply" (Hos. 2:23; Jer. 31:27). There is, therefore, no word here of a new dispersion of the people, but rather of an increasing and ingathering. They will "turn again," because they "remember" God in the land of their captivity, and feel a yearning for the place where He has set His name again.

(10, 11) Egypt is, no doubt, mentioned here as the typical oppressor of Israel (Hos. 8:13; 9:3), as the Exodus is the typical deliverance (Isa. 11:16). "Out of Egypt and Assyria" may be looked upon as a stereotyped expression for deliverance.

Gilead and Lebanon represent the old territory of the ten tribes on both sides of Jordan.

11

(1-3) Here, as in 9:1-8, we have intimation of an invasion of the land of Israel from the north, only, whereas in the former case Philistia, as well as Syria and Phoenicia, was to be the sufferer, here it is "the pride of Jordan that is to be spoiled." Some have considered the first three verses of this chapter to be a distinct prophecy by themselves. To this supposition no valid objection can be made. But the terms of the prophecy are so vague that it is impossible to decide with any degree of satisfaction to what particular invasion it refers.

(4-17) The great difficulty of this passage, which is metaphorical and symbolical throughout, consists in the fact that hardly any clue to the interpretation is given to us. Thus commentators are quite unable to agree as to whether the shepherds spoken of are heathen or native rulers. And on this point the whole nature of the interpretation turns. Guided by the language of verses 6 and 10, we conclude that the shepherds represent foreign oppressors. (Comp. Ezek. 34:11, 12, 15, 16; 37:16-22.)

(7) Will feed.—The prophet, acting as God's representative (see verse 13), performs a symbolical action, figuring thereby God's treatment of His people.

Beauty.—Or, "favor."

Bands.—Or, "binders." The first staff

denotes the return of God's favor to His people; the second the binding together of Judah and Ephraim in "brotherhood," which latter took place, for the first time since the separation, on the return from Babylon.

(8) The effect of the prophet's (i.e., God's) feeding the flock is that He "cut off three shepherds in one month." As in Ezek. 4:4-6; Dan. 9:24-27, the space of time mentioned here seems to be symbolical; and taking a day for a year, one month will mean about thirty years. Some take "one month" to mean "a short time." This interpretation will also agree with our view of the case. "The three shepherds" may be, then, the Syro-Grecian kings (172-141 B.C.)—Antiochus Epiphanes, Antiochus Eupator, and Demetrius I.

(10) The people ("them," verse 8) rejected Him; therefore He broke His staff "Favor," and so annulled the covenant He had made with the nations in behalf of His people. This was fulfilled at the close of the glorious Maccabean period, when the nation became corrupted, and as a consequence was harassed by the nations on every side.

(12) My price.—The shepherd demands a requital for his toil, as a test of the gratitude of the sheep.

And if not, forbear.—Comp. Ezek. 3:27, etc. God does not force our will, which is free. He places life and death before us; by His grace alone we can choose Him, but we can refuse His grace and Himself.

Thirty pieces of silver.—The price set on a foreign slave (Exod. 21:32).

(13) Potter.—The price was so contemptible that it is flung to the meanest of craftsmen. It seems probable that "to the potter with it!" was a proverbial expression, used of throwing away anything that was utterly worthless.

A goodly price ... of them.—That is to say, "What a price!" ironically. The prophet—in imagination, no doubt—goes into the Temple, and there before God and Israel, in the place where the covenant had been so often ratified by sacrifice, he meets a potter, and there flings to him the "goodly price," and so pronounces the divorce between God and the congregation of Israel. The prophet, in his symbolical act, represented God (Ezek. 34:5), but at the same time he must have represented "the Good Shepherd," in whose rejection the ingratitude of the chosen nation culminated. (See Matt. 27:10.)

(14) That I might break the brotherhood.—

673

This was the result of their rejection of the Good Shepherd, and of their consequent rejection by Him. It began with the civil discords which followed the victorious days of the Maccabees, and reached its worst in the horrible scenes which took place during the siege of Jerusalem by the Romans.

(15, 16) The foolish shepherd we understand to mean all the misrulers of Israel from the time of the decline of the glories of the Maccabean period to the day when they rejected the Christ. (Comp. Dan. 7:7, 19, 23.)

(17) Though the wicked useless shepherd is allowed for a time to illtreat and neglect the flock, in the end the judgment of God will fall upon him. The reader is urged to read 13:7-9 in close connection with 11:15-17.

12

(1-9) This prophecy seems to recur to the same events as were foretold in chaps. 9, 10: viz., the successful contests of the Maccabean period.

(1) "Israel," "Judah," "Ephraim," and "Joseph" were terms interchangeable after the captivity, and refer, with a few exceptions, to the nation of the Jews in general. (Comp. 9:1, 10, 13; 10:3, 6, 7; 11:14; Isa. 42:5; Ezek. 37:15-28; Amos 4:12; Mal. 1:5.)

(2) This verse seems to imply that all who should attack Jerusalem would do so to their injury, and that Judah should suffer as well as Jerusalem, though, as is promised before and after, they should both come out victorious.

(5) The strength of the fortress of Jerusalem should be the saving of Judah, but that strength would depend on the protection of "the Lord of hosts, their God."

(7) The deliverance of Judah is made to take precedence ("first," i.e., "as in former times") of that of Jerusalem. "Judah" seems here to denote the rest of the people, in contradistinction to the inhabitants of Jerusalem and the princes of the house of David. The Maccabees were deliverers raised up from the people (see I Macc. 2:1), not from the royal house.

(9) He would have utterly destroyed the nations, that is, have given the Jews complete victory over them, but for Israel's sin. (Comp. Exod. 4:24; Josh. 23:5, 12, 13.)

(10-14) These are verses of almost unprecedented difficulty. Verse 10 cannot be taken in a figurative sense, as denoting that

they shall respond to the Lord whom they had so grievously mistreated. Neither can we understand the words as referring to some unknown martyr, or to the Messiah directly, since such a reference would be so abrupt as to have presented no meaning to the prophet's original hearers. We are compelled, therefore, to propound a theory which will obviate most of the difficulties of the passage. We consider these verses to be misplaced, and propose to place them after 13:3 (see note).

(11) Hadad-rimmon.—The fact that a place in the tribe of Issachar was, in the prophet's time, known by an Assyrian name seems a proof that the date of this prophecy is post-exilic.

13

(1-3) We suggest that these verses should be placed between 12:9 and 10.

(1) The meaning of this verse seems to be that the people would keep the law with more heartfelt earnestness, and consequently acceptably. (Comp. Num. 8:7; 19:9.)

(2) Unclean spirit.—This is the only passage in the Old Testament where may be found the expression "unclean spirit," which is of such frequent occurrence in the New.

(3) The reaction from superstition would be scepticism. The people would no longer believe in prophecy at all, and even the parents of a prophet would slay him as an imposter, even though he was not legally convicted of falsehood (Deut. 18:19-22).

But God would have pity, and "pour out ... the Spirit ... so that they should look on him whom they pierced," etc. The word "pierced" in 12:10 is the same as is better rendered here "thrust through." The Hebrew has "shall look upon me," but by the addition of a small letter it would mean "upon him," which suits better the succeeding clauses, and has the support of Aquila, Theodotion, and Symmachus, is defended by Ewald, and is quoted in John 19:37. We, accordingly, adopt this rendering. If our conjecture concerning the original position of 12:10 in the text is correct, the whole passage will mean that when scepticism should have reached such a pitch that parents would without hesitation slay their son if he should pretend to prophetic powers, then God would smite the people with prickings of the heart, and they would look on such a case with the utmost remorse, making lamentation for the victim. As with

11:12, so this prophecy must not be regarded as being fulfilled in one single event only. But, certainly, in the case of Christ it received its most signal fulfillment.

(4) Now he reverts to those who are **really** false prophets.

(6) In.—His interrogator accuses him of having cut himself in idolatrous worship (I Kings 18:28). In reply he states that they are the stripes he has received in loving chastisement in the house of his parents or relatives. He is anxious to disavow any pretense to prophecy.

Throughout these passages "that day" extends over a considerable period, the limits of which are hidden even from the prophet himself.

(7-9) The **house** of David had not ceased with the Captivity; on the contrary, Zerubbabel was its representative on the return. Moreover, the thought expressed by the prophet in 12:7, that the glory of the house of David, and that of the inhabitants of Jerusalem, should not magnify itself over Judah, is one which could never have entered into the conceptions of a prophet writing before the exile.

(7) Fellow.—Perhaps the "foolish shepherd" (11:15) could hardly be called by the Lord "the man of my fellowship." If so, this argument is conclusive for the retention of this passage in its present position. The smiting of the shepherd was on account of the sin of the flock. The shepherd, then, must be understood to be He whom they are before represented as having insulted and rejected (11:12). Part of this verse is quoted by our Lord (Matt. 26:31).

(9) The third part.—The humble and patient—the "third part" (verse 8). Amidst all the calamities which should overtake the land, a remnant should be saved and purified. In the light of the Gospel we may understand these words as fulfilled in those who embraced Christianity.

14

The Day of the Lord

The eleventh book of the minor prophets is acknowledged on all sides to be the most difficult of all the prophets. Jews and Christians are all loud in their complaints with regard to the difficulties of interpreting this book. But, difficult as are all the preceding chapters, this chapter surpasses them all in obscurity. It is a chapter which seems to defy all historical explanation. We decide, then, to interpret it entirely in a figurative and Messianic sense. The prophet, amid the corruptions of his age, perceives that it is only by passing through the furnace of affliction that his nation can become sufficiently purified to be fit recipients of the spiritual blessings which the whole prophetic school, in one stream of unbroken continuity, had foretold should be the portion of Israel in the days of the Messiah. He foresaw the glorious Messianic "day," but what he sees, he sees from the Old Testament point of view. The greatest affliction that had as yet visited the nation was the destruction of Jerusalem by Nebuchadnezzar, and accordingly, after the analogy of this catastrophe, the prophet draws the picture of the troubles which should precede the advent of the Messiah. The two ideas—that of the reign of God Himself, and that of the reign of His anointed—run in parallel, and sometimes even in converging lines, but they never actually meet in the Old Testament. (Comp. Pss. 96-99.) It remained for the gospel revelation to show how the reign of Jehovah and that of the ideal David were to be combined in one Person.

(1) The day of the Lord cometh—viz., on which He will signally manifest His glory. One stroke of the pen renders the most vivid description of the first feature of this "day"—judgment upon Jerusalem. (Some suggest interpreting this of the taking of Jerusalem by Titus.)

(4) Shall cleave.—Earthquake is commonly represented as an accompaniment of the Lord's appearing (Exod. 19:18; Isa. 29:6; Ezek. 38:19, 20). The Mount of Olives shall be divided eastward to westward, and its two halves will be removed northward and southward respectively, so that a valley will be formed between them.

(5) The earthquake in the days of Uzziah is not mentioned in the sacred history, but it was an event that left such an impression on the popular mind that it became an era from which to date (Amos 1:1). The second person, "ye fled," need not be taken as referring directly to the persons addressed, but, considering the fact of the continuity of the national existence. may be understood as denoting the same nation at an earlier period (see Josh. 24:5). The addition of the words "king of Judah" to the name of Uzziah might be taken to imply that the prophecy was delivered so long after the time of Uzziah that it was necessary for the prophet to remind his hearers who this Uzziah was.

(7) It shall be.—As the darkest hour precedes the dawn, so the climax of man's direst need is the precursor of the dayspring of God's saving power. And so now, when "at evening time" they shall be expecting the gross darkness of night to set in, suddenly they shall be flooded with the light of God's salvation.

(8) Living waters.—The symbol of divine knowledge and spiritual vitality (Joel 3:18; Ezek. 47).

Former—or "front," i.e., eastern, meaning the Dead Sea.

Hinder—i.e., western, meaning the Mediterranean. These boundaries denote the whole of the Holy Land.

(9) And his name one—i.e., and He alone shall be worshiped as God.

(10) Shall be turned as a plain.—It extends with some interruptions from the slopes of Hermon to the Elamitic gulf of the Red Sea.

And it.—The idea of the lifting up of Jerusalem is suggested by its geographical position, situated, as it is, in a nest of mountains (Ps. 125:2). The language is figurative, and denotes the religious prominence of Jerusalem.

The place of the first gate was, perhaps, at the northeastern corner, and "the corner gate" at the northwestern corner (II Kings 14:13; Jer. 31:38). Thus this description denotes the whole breadth of the city from east to west.

The tower of Hananeel (Jer. 31:38; Neh. 3:1; 12:39) was at the north corner of the city, and "the king's wine-presses," no doubt, in the king's gardens at the south end of the city (Neh. 3:15); thus these latter are the northern and southern boundaries.

(14) Judah.—Taking courage from the panic which had struck their adversaries, the whole people of Judah—not merely those who had escaped out of the city, but also those outside the walls—fight once more "at Jerusalem," or in its streets, against the terror-driven, plague-stricken foe.

(16) Go up ... to worship.—The judgment on the nation is to be remedial. The result of it is to be that they will earnestly embrace the worship of the one only true God. The chief object of the Feast of Tabernacles is, from a material point of view, the thanksgiving for the ingathering of the harvest and vintage. It is most appropriate, then, that the prophet should represent the nations of the earth as joining the Jews in keeping their festival, which is that on which the Lord is especially praised as the beneficent God of nature. This prophecy is, of course, not to be taken literally. The prophet is merely foretelling in Old Testament language the future ingathering of the nations. (See John 4:35.)

(17) No Rain.—Though the worship of the Lord is to become universal, apostasy is not regarded as impossible. The punishment for defection is spoken of in such figurative language as suits the symbolic description of the nations' conversion.

(20) In that day there will be a general elevation of everything in sanctity. Even the bridles upon the horses will, like the plate of gold on the miter of the high priest, have inscribed on them "Holiness to the Lord" (Exod. 28:36, etc.). The pots of the sanctuary will be raised to the grade of sanctity of the bowls in which the blood was caught; and ordinary pots will be raised to the grade of sanctuary pots.

(21) Canaanite, in reference to the early days of Israel's existence, denotes "alien, unbeliever."

MALACHI

1

(1) Malachi.—Absolutely nothing is known historically of the life of the prophet Malachi. By some the word Malachi, which might be taken to mean "my messenger," has been regarded as the prophet's official title, not as his personal name. But, in default of any positive evidence to the contrary, it is only reasonable to suppose that Malachi is the personal name of the prophet, and that it is a form meaning "Messenger of Yah," or "of God."

(2) I have loved—i.e., shown abundant proof of my love. The prophet goes on to show how God has shown so great proofs of His love.

I loved Jacob (3) and I hated Esau . . . —The ethical reason for God's love of Jacob and hatred of Esau is not touched upon here, nor is it necessary to the argument. It is God's love for Israel that the prophet wishes to dwell on, and he mentions the hatred toward Esau merely for the sake of a strong contrast. The nations, Israel and Edom, are here referred to, not the individuals, Jacob and Esau. (See Ps. 137:7; Rom. 9:13.)

Laid his mountains . . . waste . . . —It is a somewhat disputed point to what historical fact this refers. But, on the whole, we may reasonably infer from Jer. 49:7, 17-21, compared with Jer. 25:9, 21, that the subjugation of the Edomites by Nebuchadnezzar is here referred to. And Edom's ineffectual attempts to restore itself will be looked on as proofs of God's wrath against the nation on account of its wickedness (verse 4).

(5) From the border.—The meaning seems to be that the Lord, whose protecting presence hovers especially over the border of Israel, is now great, in that He has restored Israel, but has destroyed the nationality of the wicked descendants of the godless Esau. "Border of Israel" is purposely used in contrast to "border of wickedness" (verse 4.)

(6) A father.—God is distinctly called the Father of Israel in Deut. 32:6, 18. (Comp. Exod. 4:22: "My son, my firstborn, is Israel.")

My fear.—The fear and love required by God of His children are that reverence which loves to serve Him, and that love which dreads to offend Him.

(7) Polluted bread.—The context shows that the words "polluted bread" mean "food unfit to be offered." (Comp. Lev. 3:11, 16; 21:6, 8, 17, 21, 22; 22:25.) This, then, is not the shewbread, which was not offered upon the altar. "Polluted me" is the same as "profaned [my name]" verse 12), for in the Hebrew Scriptures "God" and "God's name" are often equivalent expressions. (Comp. 2:5.)

(8) Blind . . . lame . . . sick.—This was contrary to Lev. 22:22, etc. And now, to show them the heinous nature of their offense against the majesty of God, the prophet asks them whether they could offer such unsound animals to their civil ruler with any chance of acceptance.

(9) This verse is severely ironical. The word "God" is expressly used, rather than "the Lord," as a contrast to the human "governor" mentioned above.

This hath been by your means.—The meaning is: "By means of **you** (priests), who ought to have directed the people aright, has this disgraceful conduct been occasioned."

Will he regard your persons?—That is, can you be deemed worthy intercessors, when these are the actions you perform? The question is, of course, a practical negation. (Comp. Zech. 4:10.)

(10) The prophet is now supposed by many commentators to say that the Temple might as well be closed, as far as concerns any pleasure the Lord takes in their offerings.

(11) This verse contains no verb, and, as far as the rules of grammar are concerned, its participles may be rendered either by presents or futures. If we take the words as referring to the present, we are met by the insurmountable difficulty that in no sense, at the time of Malachi, could the Lord's name be said to be great over all the earth, or pure sacrifices to be offered to Him in every place. We are compelled, therefore, to take the words as a prophetic announcement of the future rejection of Israel and calling of the Gentiles.

In every place.—In contradistinction to the **one** place (Deut. 12:5-7). (Comp. John 4:21-24.)

Incense shall be offered . . . —We prefer to take the words thus: "an oblation shall be burnt to my name, even a pure offering." In any case, unless we are to expect some future establishment of a universal offering of material sacrifices, we must understand both expressions in a spiritual sense, which is, in truth, the only reasonable way of interpreting such passages. (See Zech. 2:6-13; 3:8-10; 6:9-15; 14:16-21.)

(12) But ye have.—The word "it" (for "my name," verse 11) is said by Jewish tradition to be an euphemism for "me." The present contemptuous conduct of God's priests, who do not take the trouble to offer such things as are prescribed by the Law (verses 13, 14), is contrasted with the prophesied reverence of heathen nations.

2

(2) Your blessings.—Some take this as meaning the priests' tithes, atonement money, and their portions of the sacrifices, in accordance with a common usage of the word in the sense of "gift"—e.g., Gen. 33:11. Others refer the words to the blessing which the priests pronounce on the people (Num. 6:23-27).

(3) I will corrupt your seed.—Because the people neglected to pay the tithes, the Levites were obliged to go and till the fields (Neh. 13:10).

Dung of your solemn feasts.—The dung of the sacrificial animals was to be carried to an unclean place outside the camp, and burned there. The priests, because they had profaned God's name by offering unfit animals in sacrifice, were to be treated in the most ignominious manner.

(4) That my covenant might be—i.e., so that this new decree, which I have been compelled to make against the house of Levi (see note on 3:3), may be my covenant with him instead of the old one, of which the prophet goes on to speak.

(9) In the law—i.e., in the administration of justice. The authority of the priests, Levites, and of the judges of the day, in all matters ceremonial and civil, is expressly inculcated by Deut. 17:8-13. (See Matt. 23:2.)

(10-17) The prophet now rebukes the two great sins of the nation at this time: marriage with idolatresses; and divorce of the first (Israelitish) wife.

(10) One father—i.e., not Adam, Abraham, or Jacob, but God Himself (1:6; Deut. 32:6, 18), who is the spiritual Father of the nation, and in whom they are all brothers and sisters; so that when an Israelite married a heathen woman, or divorced an Israelitish wife, it was an offense against God, a "profaning the covenant of the fathers," and a violation of the fraternal relation. Moreover, "one God created" them for His glory

(Isa. 43:7), for the special purpose of being a witness to His unity. The admission of idolatresses into their families would be fatal to this object.

(12) The master and the scholar.—It is better to render "watchman and answerer": i.e., the watchman who cried in the city, "Who comes there?" and him who answers, "Friend," which is an exhaustive expression for all living persons, and so, in this context, "all posterity." This is the interpretation of Gesenius.

And him that offereth an offering... —Since the highest privilege of the Jew was to bring offerings to the sanctuary, the words may be merely a repetition of the former expression in different terms, and mean "a descendant enjoying religious privileges." The intermarriage with heathens referred to here is that mentioned in Neh. 13:23-28, not the earlier case recorded in Ezra 9:1, 2.

(13) The prophet now rebukes the people for their frivolous divorces of their first wives, which was a natural result of their marriage with heathen women.

Covering the altar ... with tears ... and with crying out—i.e., with the plaints of the Israelitish women who were divorced against their will.

(15, 16) These are two very difficult verses, which should perhaps be rendered as follows:—For did He not make [man and his wife, Gen. 2:24] one? and has he [the husband] any superiority of spirit [that he should divorce at will]? And what is this [pair which become] one? [Answer.] It seeketh a godly seed. Therefore take heed to yourselves [literally, your spirit] and with respect to the wife of thy youth—Let none be faithless.

For [I] hate divorce [of the first wife], saith the God of Israel, and he [the divorcer of his first wife] covers his garment with injury saith the Lord of hosts: therefore take ye heed to your spirit, and do not be faithless.

The whole must be taken as the words of the prophet. (Comp. Matt. 19:3 seq.)

(17) A new section of the prophecy begins with this verse. The prophet now directs his reproofs against the people for their discontent and their want of faith in the promises of God, because the expected manifestation of God's glory did not take place immediately. (Comp. Ps. 73, etc.)

3

(1) I will send.—Or, "I send." It is the participle used as the prophetic present. (Comp. note on 1:11.)

My messenger.—Heb., "Malachi, my angel," or "my messenger," with a play on the name of the prophet. In 2:7, he calls the priest the "angel" or "messenger" of the Lord. There can be little doubt that he is influenced in his choice of the term by his own personal name. Moreover, from the nature of his mission, he is proved to be identical with the "Elijah" of 4:5. These words had their first, if not their perfect fulfillment in John the Baptist (Matt. 17:12). Comp. Isa. 40:3.

The messenger (or angel) **of the covenant.**—This expression occurs only in this passage. Identified as He is here with "the Lord," He can be no other than the Son of God, who was manifested in the flesh as the Messiah, In the word "covenant" there is, perhaps, some reference to the "new covenant" (Jer. 31:31), but the meaning of the word must not be limited to this.

(2) This coming of the Lord to His Temple acts as a crucial test (comp. Luke 2:35); the people ought, therefore, seriously to have considered how far they were prepared for that advent before they desired it so eagerly and impatiently.

(3) Sons of Levi.—Meaning especially the priests, the sons of Aaron, son of Amram, son of Kohath, son of Levi (Exod. 6:16-20); judgment must begin at the house of God. (Comp. Jer. 25:29; Ezek. 9:6; I Pet. 4:17.)

In righteousness refers rather to the moral character of the offerer than to the nature of the sacrifices, as being such as were prescribed by the Law. This and the following verse do not, of course, imply that there are to be material sacrifices in Messianic times. The prophet speaks in such language as was suitable to the age in which he lived. (See note on 1:11.)

(5) All these crimes were explicitly forbidden by the Law: sorcery (Exod. 22:18), adultery (Exod. 20:14; Lev. 20:10; Deut. 22:22), false-swearing (Lev. 19:12), defrauding, or withholding of wages (Lev. 19:13; Deut. 24:14, 15), oppressing the widow and orphan (Exod. 22:22-24), doing injustice to a stranger (Deut. 24:17; 27:19). (Comp. also Zech. 7:9, 10; 8:16, 17.)

(6) For I am the Lord, I change not.—See Ezra 9:14, 15. Because it is the Eternal's unchangeable will that the sons of Jacob,

His chosen people, should not perish as a nation, He will purify them by the eradication of the wicked among them, that the remnant may return to their allegiance. (Comp. Rom. 11.)

(8) Robbed me.—The tithes are said to be offered to Jehovah, and then He gives them to the Levites in place of an inheritance. (See Exod. 23:19; Lev. 27:30-33; Num. 18:12, 21-24; Deut. 18:4.)

(10) The emphasis is on the word "all."

Storehouse.—From the time of Hezekiah (II Chron. 31:11) there were at the sanctuary special storehouses built for this purpose; so, too, in the second Temple (Neh. 10:38, 39; 12:44; 13:12, 13).

Meat—i.e., food for the priests and Levites.

Open you ... —According to the promise of Deut. 11:13-15. (Comp. II Chron. 31:10.)

(11) For your sakes.—The same word as in 2:3: here in a good sense, there in a bad.

The devourer—i.e., the locust, etc.

(14) Mournfully—i.e., with all outward signs of fasting. (Comp. Matt. 6:16.) The fasting referred to is not that of the Day of Atonement, but of voluntary fasts. We see here, in already a somewhat developed form, that disposition to attribute merit to observances of outward forms of religion for their own sake, without regard to the secret attitude of the heart, which reached such a pitch among the majority of the Jews in the time of our Lord, and especially among the Pharisees.

(15) And now.—The prophet gives the words of the murmurers. The statements of verse 13 show that they were of a different character from such faithful servants on Jehovah as were at times sorely tempted against their will to waver in their faith. We may observe here the seeds of sceptical Sadduceeism, as in verse 14 of hypocritical Phariseeism. (Comp. Pss. 37; 73, and the Books of Job and Eccl.)

Tempt.—The same word is used which in verse 10 is translated "prove." The difference in the two cases consists in the different nature of the actions. In verse 10 the Jews are exhorted to obey the Law faithfully, and experience that God certainly would perform His part in the covenant. In verse 15 the heathen, by their pride and wickedness, tempt God to judgment.

(16) Then.—As the godless in Israel conversed together, so did the godly; but the talk of the one was the opposite of the talk of the other. (Comp. Ezra 9:4.)

Book of remembrance.—Men's actions are said figuratively to be recorded in it (Ps. 56:8; Dan. 7:10). Compare the custom of the Persian kings (Esther 6:1).

(17) And they shall be ... my jewels.—"Special possession" (Exod. 19:5). Comp. Ps. 115:11.

4

(1) Comp. Isa. 5:24; Obad. 18; Zeph. 1:18.

(2) As the rising sun diffuses light and heat, so that all that is healthy in nature revives and lifts up its head, while plants that have no depth of root are scorched up and wither away, so the advent of the reign of righteousness, which will reward the good and the wicked, each according to his deserts, will dissipate all darkness of doubt, and heal all the wounds which the apparent injustice of the conduct of affairs has inflicted on the hearts of the righteous.

Wings.—Figurative for "rays." The fathers and early commentators have understood Christ by the Sun of Righteousness. They are right in that it is the period of His advent to which reference is made; but there can be no personal reference to Him in the expression, since "sun" is feminine in Hebrew; and the literal rendering of the word translated "in his wings" is "in **her** wings."

(4) See Deut. 4:1; 8:14; Josh. 1:2, 8. The best preparation for the reception of the New Covenant (Jer. 31:32) must necessarily be the hearty observance of the spirit of the Old.

(5) Elijah.—There is no more reason to suppose that this refers actually to "Elijah" the prophet, and that he is to appear upon earth, than to imagine from Hos. 3:5; Ezek. 34:23; 37:24; Jer. 30:9, that David himself is to come again in the flesh. That John the Baptist is the "messenger" of 3:1 and the "Elijah" of this verse is shown conclusively by Matt. 3:1-12; Mark 1:2-8; Luke 1:16, 17; 3:2-18. Comp. Matt. 11:10 seq.; Luke 7:27 seq. It is a significant fact that these two greatest of Old Testament prophets, Moses and Elias, who are mentioned together in this last prophetic exhortation, are the two who appeared with Christ on the Mount of Transfiguration, when all that which is contained in the Law and the prophets was about to be fulfilled.

(6) And he shall turn ... to their fathers.—This does not refer to the settlement of family disputes, such as might have arisen from marriage with foreign wives. "The fathers are rather the ancestors of the Israelitish nation, the patriarchs, and generally the pious forefathers ... The sons, or children, are the degenerate descendants of Malachi's own time and the succeeding ages" (Keil). (Comp. Isa. 29:22-24.)

Curse.—Better, "ban." (Comp. Zech 14:11.) As with the conclusion of Isaiah, Lamentations, and Ecclesiastes, so here the Jew in the synagogue reads verse 5 over again after the last verse, to avoid concluding with words of ill omen.

MATTHEW

1

(1) The book of the generation.—The opening words of the gospel show that it is written by a Jew for Jewish readers. They are an essentially Hebrew formula (as in Gen. 5:1), and were applied chiefly, though not exclusively (Gen. 37:2), to genealogies such as that which follows here.

Jesus Christ.—When Matthew wrote, there were many who bore the name of Jesus (see 27:17; Col. 4:11). It was necessary to state that the genealogy that followed was that of Jesus the Messiah, the true "anointed" of the Lord.

The son of David.—This was added as the most popular of all the names of the expected Christ, owned alike by scribes and rabbis (Matt. 22:42), by children (Matt. 21:9), and by the poor (Matt. 15:22; 20:30).

The son of Abraham.—There is no reason to think that this was ever a Messianic title. If there is any special significance in its occurrence here, it is as emphasizing that which the Messiah had in common with other Israelites. (Comp. Heb. 2:16.)

(3) The occurrence of the names of women in genealogies was the exception rather than the rule among the Jews. It was enough that the women were historically notable. In the case of Thamar there were precedents sufficient for such an honorable mention. It would appear from the language of the Talmud as if the Jews looked on her strange (and to us revolting) history with quite other feelings. To them she was as one who, at the risk of shame, and, it might be, death, had preserved the line of Judah from destruction, and "therefore was counted worthy to be the mother of kings and prophets." (See Ruth 4:12; I Chron. 2:4.)

(5) It has been conjectured that Salmon may have been one of the two unnamed spies whose lives were saved by Rahab, the harlot of Jericho. The mention of Rahab in Jas. 2:25; Heb. 11:31, shows that her fame had risen at the time when Matthew wrote. (The Talmud legends, curiously enough, reckon eight prophets among her descendants, including Jeremiah and Baruch, but not any of the line of David.) The succession is the same as in Ruth 4:21. The new fact of Salmon's marriage explains the readiness with which the sons of Naomi marry two women of the Moabites, and the ab-

sence of any repugnance to such a union on the part of Boaz.

(6) Once again we have the mention of a woman who at least played a memorable part in the history of Israel. It is at least suggestive that all the names are those of women who, either as of heathen origin (Bathsheba, like her husband, was probably a Hittite) or by personal guilt, were as those whom the strict judgment of the Pharisee excluded from his fellowship. Matthew may have meant men to draw the inference that, as these women were not excluded from the honor of being in the Messiah's line of ancestry, so others like them would not be shut out from fellowship with His kingdom.

(9) Ozias is the Uzziah of the Old Testament. Three names are omitted between Joram and this king—Ahaziah, Joash, Amaziah. Apparently the motive for the omission was simply the desire of bringing the names in each period into which the genealogy is divided to the arbitrary standard of fourteen. We learn from this fact that the words "A begat B" are not to be taken literally, but are simply an expression of the fact of succession with or without intermediate links.

(11) Jechonias and his brethren.—Here again there is a missing link, for Jeconiah was the grandson of Josiah (II Kings 23:34).

(12) The most probable solution through a cluster of genealogical difficulties beginning here is that Assir was the only son of Jeconiah, and died childless before his father; that the line of Solomon thus came to an end; and that the descendants of Nathan, another son of David, took their place in the succession and were reckoned by adoption as the sons of the last survivor of the other line.

(17) The arrangement into three triads of fourteen generations each was obviously in the nature of a **memoria technica**. The periods embraced by the three groups were of unequal length; and the actual omission of names in one of them makes it possible that the others may have been treated in the same way. The difference between the rosters of Matthew and Luke (Luke 3:23-38) is strong presumptive evidence that neither of the two evangelists had seen the record of the other. It is otherwise hardly conceivable that the element of difficulty which these differences involve should have been introduced by one or the other without a word of explanation. Each, it may be presumed, copied a document which he found, and the two documents were drawn up on a different plan as to the ideas of succession recognized in each of them.

(18) Matthew, for some reason or other, omits all mention of what Luke relates fully as to the events that preceded the birth of Jesus and brought about the birth at Bethlehem. Either he had no access to any document full and trustworthy like that of which Luke made use, or, as every writer of history must fix a beginning more or less arbitrary, he found his starting point in those facts which took a foremost place in what bore upon the fulfillment of Messianic prophecy.

The omission of any mention of Mary's parents suggests the idea of orphanhood, possibly under the same lineage and guardianship of Joseph. The absence of Joseph in the records of our Lord's ministry makes it probable that he died in the interval between the visit to the Temple (Luke 2:42) and the preaching of the Baptist, and that he was older than Mary. Both were poor: Joseph worked as a carpenter (Matt. 13:55); Mary offered the cheaper sacrifice of "two young pigeons" (Luke 2:24). They had no house at Bethlehem (Luke 2:7). Mary was related to Elizabeth, the wife of Zechariah the priest (Luke 1:36). Both were within the circle of those who cherished Messianic expectations, and to whom, therefore, the announcement that these expectations were to be fulfilled would come as the answer to their hopes and prayers.

Was espoused to Joseph.—Betrothal among the Jews was a formal ceremony, the usual symbolic act being, from patriarchal times, the gift of a ring and other jewels (Gen. 24:53). The interval between betrothal and marriage was of uncertain length, but among the Jews of our Lord's time was commonly for a whole year in the case of maidens. During that time all communications were conducted through "the friend of the bridegroom" (John 3:29).

Of the Holy Ghost.—To Joseph and those who heard the new report from him, prior to the more precise truths revealed by our Lord's teaching, the words would at least suggest a divine creative energy, quickening supernaturally the germ of life (Gen. 1:2; Ps. 104:30).

(19) Joseph her husband.—The word was applied with strict accuracy from the moment of betrothal. Comp. "wife" in verse 20.

Being a just man . . .—Joseph dared not take to himself one who seemed thus to have sinned. But love and pity alike hindered him from pressing the law, which made death by stoning the punishment of such a sin (Deut. 22:21), or even from publicly breaking off the marriage on the ground of the apparent guilt. There remained the alternative, which the growing frequency of divorce made easy, of availing himself of a "writ of divorcement," which did not necessarily specify the ground of repudiation, except in vague language implying disagreement (Matt. 19:3). Thus the matter would be settled quietly without exposure. The "bill of divorcement" was as necessary for the betrothed as for those who were fully man and wife.

(20) In a dream.—From the Jewish point of view, dreams were the received channels of divine communications to the aged, open visions in the state of ecstasy to the young (Joel 2:28). This coincides with what has been inferred as to Joseph's age.

Joseph, thou son of David.—The latter words were, in the highest degree, significant. His character as the heir of Messianic hopes, which was indeed at the root of his fears, was fully recognized. That which he was bidden to do would not be inconsistent with that character, and would bring about the fulfillment of those hopes.

(21) Thou shalt call his name Jesus.—The name Jesus was one full of meaning, but it was not as yet an especially sacred name. In its Old Testament form of Jehoshua (Num. 13:16), Joshua or Jeshua (Num. 14:6; Neh. 8:17), it meant "Jehovah is salvation." The change of the name of the captain of Israel from Hoshea, which did not include the divine name, to the form which gave this full significance (Num. 13:16) had made it the expression of the deepest faith of the people. After the return from Babylon it received a new prominence in connection with the high priest Joshua, the son of Josedech (Hag. 1:1; Zech. 3:1), and appears in its Greek form in Jesus the father, and again in the son, of Sirach. In the New Testament itself we find it borne by others (see note on verse 1). It had not been directly associated, however, with Messianic hopes, and the intimation that it was to be the name of the Christ gave a new character to men's thoughts of the kingdom: not conquest, but "salvation"—deliverance, not from human enemies only, nor from the penalties of sin, but from the sins themselves. As recorded by the evangelist it was a witness that he had been taught the true nature of the kingdom of the Christ.

(22) All this was done.—The evangelist

pauses in his narrative to introduce his own comment. He could not possibly regard the agreement of prophecy and event as a chance coincidence; there was no alternative but purpose.

(23) Behold, a virgin shall be with child.— This child was associated by Isaiah with no common hopes. (See notes on Isa. 7:14; 9:6; 11:1.) Those Messianic expectations were not then fulfilled, but remained for a later generation to feed on with yearning desire. But they did not suggest to any Jewish interpreter the thought of a birth altogether supernatural; and thus is rendered invalid the objection that the narrative was a mythical outgrowth of the prophecy as popularly received. Matthew, however, having to record the facts of our Lord's birth, and reading Isaiah with a mind full of the new truths which rested on the Incarnation, could not fail to be struck with the correspondance between the facts and the words which he here quotes, and which in the Greek translation were even more emphatic than in the Hebrew, and saw in them a prophecy that had at last been fulfilled.

2

(1) In the days of Herod the king.—The death of Herod took place in the year of Rome A.U.C. 750, just before the Passover. This year coincided with what in our chronology would be 4 B.C. Our common reckoning is erroneous, but we fix 5 B.C. or 4 as the date of the Nativity.

No facts recorded either in Matthew or Luke throw much light on the season of the birth of Christ. The flocks and shepherds in the open field indicate spring rather than winter. The day, December 25, was not kept as a festival in the East until the time of Chrysostom, and was then received as resting on the tradition of the Roman Church. It has been conjectured that the time was chosen in order to substitute the purified joy of a Christian festival for the license of the Saturnalia which were kept at that season.

The time of the arrival of the wise men was after the Presentation in the Temple (Luke 2:22). The appearance of the star coincided with the birth. The journey from that region vaguely called the East would occupy at least several months.

Wise men from the east.—The Greek word is Magi. That name appears in Jer. 39:3, 13; and Herodotus speaks of them as a priestly caste of the Medes, known as interpreters of dreams (I:101, 120). With Mat-

thew, as with Plato, the Magi were thought of as observers of the heavens, students of the secrets of nature. Where they came from we cannot tell. The name was spread too widely at this time to lead us to look with certainty to its original home in Persia. The popular legends that they were three in number, that they were kings, and that the represented the three great races of the sons of Noah, being named Gaspar, Melchior, and Balthasar, are simply apocryphal additions, originating probably in dramatic representations, and perpetuated by Christian art.

(2) We have seen his star in the east.— We know too little of the astrology of that period to determine what star might or might not seem to those who watched the heavens as the precursor of a great king. Stories of the appearances of such stars gathered around the births of Alexander the Great, Mithridates, and Caesar. (Comp. Num. 24:17.) The most we can say is that the "wise men" were Gentiles. They do not ask for **our** king, but for the king of the Jews; and yet, though Gentiles, they were sharers in the Messianic hopes of the Jews. They came to do homage, as subjects of the newborn King. When they saw what they interpreted as the sign that the King had come, they undertook a four months' journey (if they came from Babylon, Ezra 7:9; more, if they came from Persia), naturally making their way to Jerusalem as certain to hear there some tidings of the Jewish King.

(3) Herod the king.—When the Magi reached Jerusalem, the air was thick with fears and rumors. The old king was drawing to the close of his long and blood-stained reign. Two years before he had put to death, on a charge of treason, his two sons by Mariamne, his best-loved wife, through sheer jealousy of the favor with which the people looked on them. At the time when this history opens, the eldest son, Antipater, was under condemnation. The knowledge that priests and people were alike looking for the "consolation of Israel" (Luke 2:25, 38), the whispers that told that such a consolation had come, the uneasiness excited in the people by the "taxing" in which he had been forced to acquiesce—all these were elements of disquietude prior to the arrival of the Magi.

(4) For the "chief priests" see II Chron. 23:8; Luke 1:5. The "scribes" were the interpreters of the Law, casuists and collectors of the traditions of the elders, for the most part Pharisees. The meeting thus convened was not necessarily a formal meeting of the Sanhedrin or Great Council.

(5) In Bethlehem of Judaea.—The words of the people in John 7:42 show the same belief thirty years later. The Targum of Micah 5:2 (see note) inserts the words, "Out of thee the Messiah shall come." The evangelist is not quoting (in verse 6) the prophecy of Micah himself, but recording it as it was quoted by the scribes.

(9) We need not suppose that they found the child whom they sought in the "manger" described by Luke. There had been time for the crowds that had been gathered by the census to disperse, and Joseph and Mary may have found a house in which they could lodge. The expectations that connected Bethlehem with the coming of the Christ might naturally lead them to remain there at least for a season.

(11) Gold, and frankincense, and myrrh.—These were natural enough as the traditional gifts of homage to a ruler. Comp. Pss. 45:8; 72:15; Isa. 60:6. The patristic interpretation of the gifts is interesting: the gold, of kingly power; the incense, of divinity; the myrrh, of death and embalment.

(12) So ends all that we know of the visit of the Magi. Matthew, writing for Hebrews, recorded it apparently as testifying to the kingly character of Jesus. Christendom, however, has seen in it a yet deeper significance, and the "wise men" have been regarded as the first fruits of the outlying heathen world, the earnest of the future ingathering.

(13) Flee into Egypt.—The nearness of Egypt had always made it a natural asylum for refugees from Palestine. The number of Jews who were settled in Alexandria and other cities of Egypt had probably made the step still more common during the tyranny of Herod's later years.

(15) Out of Egypt have I called my son.—The words in Hos. 11:1 refer to the history of Israel as being in a special sense, among all the nations of the world, the chosen son of Jehovah (Exod. 4:22, 23). But a coincidence in what seems a mere circumstance of the story carries Matthew's mind on to some deeper analogies. In the days of the Exodus, Israel was the one representative instance of the Fatherhood of God manifested in protecting and delivering His people. Now there was a higher representative in the person of the only begotten Son.

(16) The fact of the slaughter of the infants of Bethlehem is not mentioned by Josephus or by any other writer. It was an act, however, every way in harmony with Herod's character. Tormented with incurable disease, and yet more incurable suspicion, he might well have given such a command as this among the cruel and reckless acts of the last months of his life.

(18) In Rama was there a voice heard.—Here again Matthew applies a passage that had a direct bearing upon the events of the time when it was delivered to those which his narrative had brought before him. The tomb of Rachel (Gen. 35:19) had been one of the sacred places of the land. In Jeremiah's picture of the sufferings and slaughter of the captives of Judah, the image which best embodied his feelings of sorrow for his people was that of Rachel, as the great "mother in Israel," seeing, as from the "high place" of her sepulchre, the shame and death of her children and weeping for her bereavement. (See Jer. 31:15.) Historically (Jer. 40:1) this was the place to which the prisoners were dragged, that Nebuzaradan might assign some to death, others to exile, and others again to remain as bondsmen in the land. That picture, Matthew felt, had been reproduced once again. The tomb of Rachel was familiar to the people of Bethlehem, standing but one mile to the north of the town.

(22) Archelaus.—Strictly speaking, this prince was never recognized as a king by the Roman emperor, but received the inferior title of Ethnarch. The character of Archelaus was as cruel and treacherous as that of his father. Nine years later the oppression of Archelaus became so intolerable that both Jews and Samaritans complained of him to the emperor, and he was deposed and banished to Gaul.

(23) He shall be called a Nazarene.—Matthew does not cite the words of any one prophet by name, but says generally that what he quotes had been spoken by or through the prophets. No such words are to be found in the Old Testament. He speaks simply from the impression made on his mind by the verbal coincidence of fact with prediction. He had heard men speak with scorn of "the Nazarene," and yet the syllables of that word had also fallen on his ears in one of the most glorious of the prophecies admitted to be Messianic—"There shall come forth a rod out of the stem of Jesse, and a **Netzer** (Branch) shall grow out of his roots" (Isa. 11:1). So he found in the word of scorn the **nomen et omen** of glory.

3

(1) John the Baptist.—For the birth and early life of the forerunner of the Christ, see notes on Luke 1. The manner in which he is mentioned here shows that his name was already well-known to all readers of the gospel. (See Josephus, **Ant.** 18:5, §2.) The symbolism of ablution as the outward sign of inward purification was derived from the Mosaic ritual. (See Exod. 29:4; Lev. 14:8.) It had received a fresh prominence from its being used on the admission of proselytes from heathenism. The question asked by the priests and Levites in John 1:25 implies that it was expected as one of the signs of the coming of the Messiah, probably as the result of such prophecies as Isa. 1:16; Zech. 13:1. That which distinguished the baptism of John from all previous forms of the same symbolism was that it was not for those only who were affected by a special uncleanness, nor for the heathen only, but for all. All were alike unclean, and needed purification, and their coming to the baptism was in itself a confession that they were so. The baptism was, as the name implied, an immersion, and commonly, though not necessarily, in running water.

The abrupt way in which the narrative is introduced "in those days," after an interval of thirty years from the close of chap. 2, may be explained as referring to the well-known period of the commencement of John's ministry; or it may loosely refer to 1:23, and imply that time had gone on with no change in the general circumstances.

In the wilderness of Judaea.—The name was commonly applied to the sparsely populated region in the southern valley of the Jordan (Luke 3:3), including even part of the district east of the river. In this region John had grown up (Luke 1:80).

(2) Repent.—The Greek word implies change of mind and purpose. It connotes pity and regret, and includes the sorrow out of which the change comes.

The kingdom of heaven.—The phrase is used by Matthew about thirty times, and by him only among the New Testament writers. The name, as descriptive of the kingdom of the Messiah, had its origin in the vision of Dan. 7:13. To Gentile readers—to whom the term would convey the thought of the visible firmament, not of the invisible dwelling-place of God—the term might have been misleading, and therefore in the gospels intended for them "the kingdom of God" (which occurs also in Matt. 6:13;

12:28) is used instead of it. It is probable that both terms were used interchangeably by the Baptist and our Lord.

(3) This is he.—The words show how strongly the great second part of Isaiah had impressed itself on the minds of men. Historically, the connection of those opening chapters with the protests against idolatry (Isa. 40:18-24; 41:7; 44:9-20), and with the name Cyrus (Isa. 44:28; 45:1), shows that the prophet blended his glorious visions of the ideal polity of the future with the return of the exiles from Babylon. The return came, and the ideal was not realized. The kingdom of heaven seemed still far off. Now, the Baptist came to proclaim its nearness.

Prepare ye the way of the Lord.—The imagery is drawn from the great strategical works of the conquerors of the East. They sent a herald before them to call the people of the countries through which they marched to prepare for their approach. A "king's highway" had to be carried through the open land of the wilderness, valleys filled up, hills levelled, winding bypaths straightened, for the march of the great army. Interpreted in its spiritual application, the wilderness was the world lying in evil, and the making low the mountains and hills was the bringing down of spiritual pride. When the poor in spirit were received into the kingdom of heaven, the valleys were exalted; when soldier and publican renounced their special sins, the rough places were made plain and the crooked straight.

It is probable that the stress thus laid upon "the way of the Lord," in the first stage of the gospel, led to the peculiar use of the term "the way" by Luke to denote what we should call the "religion" of the Apostolic Church (Acts 9:2; 18:25, 26; 19:9, 23; 22:4; 24:14, 22).

(4) His raiment of camel's hair.—The dress was probably deliberately adopted by the Baptist as reviving the outward appearance of Elijah (II Kings 1:8; Zech. 13:4; comp. Mark 12:38; Luke 7:25). The Nazarite vow of Luke 1:15 probably involved long and shaggy hair as well.

Locusts and wild honey.—Locusts were among the articles of food permitted by the Law (Lev. 11:21), and were used by the poor in Palestine and Syria. The "wild honey" was that found in the hollows of trees (I Sam. 14:25) or in the "rocks" (Deut. 32:13; Ps. 81:16). Stress is laid on the simplicity of the Baptist's fare, requiring no skill or appliances, the food of the poorest wanderer in the wilderness, presenting a marked contrast to the luxury of the dwellers in towns.

(6) Were baptized.—The Greek tense implies continual succession. Crowd after crowd passed on, and still they came "confessing their sins"—i.e., as the position of the word implies, in close connection with the act of immersion. The Greek word for "confessing" always implies public utterance, and included a specific mention of the more grievous individual sins.

(7) Parisees and Sadducees.—The name "Pharisees" appears for the first time in the gospel history. (Comp. Josephus, **Ant.** 13:5.) The meaning of the name is the "separated" ones, and may help us to trace the history. The attempt of Antiochus Epiphanes to blot out the distinctness of Jewish life by introducing Greek worship and Greek customs was met with an heroic resistance by priests and people. (See I Macc. 2:42; 7:13, 17, II Macc. 14:6.) They looked to Judas Maccabeus as their leader. Later on, as the holding aloof from the heathen became more and more characteristic of them, they took the name of Pharisees, and under John Hyrcanus became a powerful and organized body. They maintained the ethical side of the Law as against the sacrificial. They insisted on alms, fasting, and prayer as the three great elements of the religious life, and on the Sabbath as its great safeguard. They did much to promote education and synagogue building. In gathering the traditions of older rabbis, they held themselves to be "setting a fence round the Law" to maintain its sacredness, and were eager in the mission work of Judaism (Matt. 23:15). They revived the doctrine of the resurrection of the dead, and of the rewards and punishments that were to follow. On the other side, their "separation" developed almost into the exclusiveness of a caste. Their casuistry inverted the right relation of moral and ceremonial duties. They despised the mass of their own countrymen as the "brute people of the earth." Within the sect there were two schools, represented at this time by the followers of Shammai and of Hillel: the former Sabbatarian, hard and bitter in its spirit; the latter of wider culture, gentler temper, easier casuistry. Both schools were emphatically lay religionists, unconnected with the priesthood, and often in opposition to it.

Etymologically, the name "Sadducees," though connected with the Hebrew word for "righteous," must be derived from the proper name "Zadok," found in the Old Testament as belonging to the high priest in the time of Solomon. For the most part, they were of the higher priestly order, as contrasted with the lay scribes of the Pharisees. They admit the authority of the written Law, not of traditions. They deny the existence of angels and spirits, as well as the Resurrection and the immortality of the soul, making up for the absence of the fears of the future by greater rigor in punishments on earth. They courted the favor of their Roman rulers, and to some extent even of the Herods.

(8) Fruits meet for repentance.—The thought is that by coming to the baptism you profess repentance; bring forth, therefore, "fruit worthy of repentance"—i.e., of a changed heart and will.

(9) We have Abraham to our father.—The boast seems to have been common (John 8:33-39), and was connected with the belief that this alone, or taken together with the confession of the creed of Israel "the Lord our God is one Lord" (Deut. 6:4), would be enough to insure for every Jew an admission into Paradise. "We have Abraham as our father" was to the Jew all that **civis Romanus sum** was to the Romans.

Of these stones.—The words were obviously dramatized by gesture, pointing to the pebbles on the banks of the Jordan. In their spiritual application, they contain the germs of all the teaching of our Lord, of Paul, and of John, as to the calling of the Gentiles and the universality of God's kingdom.

(11) With water unto repentance.—The result of John's baptism, even for those who received it faithfully, did not go beyond the change of character and life implied in "repentance." The higher powers of the unseen world were to be manifested afterward.

Whose shoes I am not worthy to bear.—Comp. Luke 3:16. Among Jews, Greeks and Romans alike this office of untying and carrying the shoes of the master of the house or of a guest was the well-known function of the lowest slave of the household. When our Lord washed the disciples' feet (John 13:4, 5), He was taking upon Himself a like menial task which, of course, actually involved the other. The remembrance of the Baptist's words may in part account for Peter's indignant refusal to accept such services.

He shall baptize you with the Holy Ghost, and with fire.—As heard and understood at the time, the baptism with the Holy Ghost would imply that the souls thus baptized would be plunged, as it were, in that creative and informing Spirit which was the source of life, holiness, and wisdom. The baptism "with fire" would convey, in its turn, the thought of a power at once destroying evil and purifying good. The appearance of the "tongues like as of fire" that accompanied the gift of the Spirit on the day of Pentecost was an outward visible sign, an extension of the symbolism.

(12) The scene brought before us is that of the large hardened surface which was the "threshing floor" of the East, the sheaves of corn thrown over it, the oxen treading on them, and the large winnowing fan driving on them the full force of the strong current of air, leaving the wheat in the middle, while the chaff is driven to the outskirts of the field to be afterward swept up and burned. The interpretation of the parable lies on the surface. The chaff are the ungodly and evildoers; and the unquenched fire is the wrath of God against evil, which is, in its very nature, eternal, and can only cease with the cessation or transformation of the evil.

(13) Then cometh Jesus.—Why did the Lord Jesus come to be baptized of John? The Sinless One had no sin to confess, no need of repentance. We must believe, however, that His righteousness was essentially human, and therefore capable of increase, even as He increased in wisdom and stature. Holy as He was at every stage of life in proportion to its capacities, there yet rose before Him height upon height of holiness as yet unattained, and after which we may say with reverence He "hungered and thirsted." It was fitting that He should fill up the full measure of righteousness in all its forms by accepting a divine ordinance, even, perhaps, **because** it seemed to place Him in fellowship with sinners.

(14, 15) The "now" of verse 15 is emphatic, in contrast with what was to follow. Hereafter, John should be the receiver and not the giver, but as yet it was appropriate that each retain his position (Heb. 2:10). Even He had to pass through the normal stages of growth, and so an outward ordinance was even for Him the appointed way to the fullness of spiritual power. He was in His place receiving that rite; John was doing his proper work in administering it.

(16) The Baptist bears record that he, too, beheld the Spirit descending (John 1:33, 34), but there is no ground for supposing that there was any manifestation to others. That which they did see served, as did the tongues of fire on the day of Pentecost, as an attestation to the consciousness of each of the reality of the gift imparted and of its essential character. That descent of the Spirit, "as it were a dove" (Luke 3:22 adds "in bodily form") taught the Baptist that the gift of supernatural power and wisdom brought with it also the perfection of the tenderness, the purity, the gentleness of which the dove was the acknowledged symbol.

(17) The precise force of the latter clause points to a definite divine act or thought rather than to a continued everpresent acceptance. This was none other than the King to whom had been spoken the words, "Thou art my Son" (Ps. 2:7), who was to the Eternal Father what Isaac was to Abraham (Gen. 22:2), upon whom the mind of the Father rested with infinite content.

What change was actually wrought in our Lord's human nature by this descent of the Spirit? The words of John 3:34 imply the bestowal of a real gift. The words that follow here, "He was led by the Spirit" (4:1), "The Spirit driveth him" (Mark 1:12), show, in part, the nature of the change. We may venture to think even there of new gifts, new powers, a new intuition (comp. John 3:11), a new constraint, as it were, bringing the human will that was before in harmony with the divine into a fuller consciousness of that harmony, and into more intense activity—above all, a new intensity of prayer.

4

(1) The narrative here is the record of an actual experience. To assume that this record was miraculously revealed to Matthew and Luke is, however, to introduce a hypothesis which cannot be proved, and which is, at least, not in harmony with their general character as writers. They are, one by his own statement, the other by inference from the structure and contents of his gospel, distinctly compilers from many different sources, with all the incidental variations to which such a process is liable. There is no reason to look on this narrative as an exception to the general rule. The difference in the order of the temptations is, as far as it goes, against the idea of a supernatural revelation. We have here, then, that which originated in some communication from our Lord's own lips to one of His disciples,

His own record of the experience of those forty days. So taken, all is coherent, and in some sense natural, throwing light on our Lord's past life and explaining much that followed in His teaching.

Led up of the spirit.—Comp. Mark 1:12; Luke 4:1. What is meant by such language? The state so described is one more or less of the nature of ecstasy, in which the ordinary phenomena of consciousness were in great measure suspended. That gift of the Spirit had on the human nature of the Son of man something of the same overpowering mastery that it has had over others of the sons of men (comp. Ezek. 8:3; Rev. 1:10). A power mightier than His own human will was urging Him on, bringing Him into conflict "not with flesh and blood," but with "principalities and powers in heavenly places."

To be tempted of the devil.—At the outset of the narrative, the existence and personality of the power of evil are placed before us in the most distinct language. The name of devil (**diabolos**, accuser or slanderer) appears in the LXX version of I Chron. 21:1; Job 1:6; 2:1, as the equivalent for the Hebrew, Satan (the adversary; comp. Zech. 3:1). He appears there as a spiritual being of superhuman but limited power, tempting men to evil, and accusing them before the throne of God when they have yielded to the temptation. In Wisd. 2:24, the name is identified with the tempter of Gen. 3; and as that book belongs to the half-century after our Lord's birth, it may fairly be taken as representing the received belief of the Jews in His time.

Into conflict with such a being our Lord was now brought. If His life had passed on to the end without it, the holiness which was inseparable from it would have been imperfect at least in one respect: it would not have earned the power to understand and sympathize with sinners. There was a divine fitness that He too should suffer and be tempted even as we are (Heb. 2:18). The scene of the Temptation was not far from that of the Baptism, probably on the eastern rather than the western side of the Jordan. The traditional Desert of Quarantania (the name referring to the forty days' fast) is in the neighborhood of Jericho.

(2) Forty days and forty nights.—Comp. Exod. 34:28; I Kings 19:8. The effect of such a fast on any human organism, and therefore on our Lord's real humanity, would be to interrupt the ordinary continuity of life and quicken all perceptions of the

spiritual world into a new intensity. Luke describes the Temptation as continuing through the whole conflict, gathering into one the struggles by which it had been preluded.

(3) Nothing in the narrative suggests the idea of a bodily presence visible to the eye of sense; but it is no less real and true because it lies altogether in the spiritual region of man's life.

If thou be the Son of God, command that these stones be made bread.—"These stones," as if in union with glance and gesture, point to the loaf-like flints of the Jordan desert. If He were the Son of God, did not that name involve a lordship over nature? Could He not satisfy His hunger and sustain His life? Would He not in so exercising that power be establishing his **status** as the Christ in the eyes of others? That thought presented itself to His mind, but it was rejected as coming from the enemy. It would have been as an act of self-assertion and distrust, and therefore would have involved not the affirmation but the denial of the Sonship which so recently had been attested.

(4) It is written.—The words of all the three answers to the tempter come from two chapters of Deuteronomy, one of which supplied one of the passages (Deut. 6:4-9) for the phylacteries or frontlets worn by devout Jews. A prominence was thus given to that portion of the book, which made it an essential part of the education of every Israelite. If His Father has given Him a work to do, He will enable Him to fulfill it. As this act of faith reflects, as the others, the training of the childhood, so we trace its echoes in the subsequent teaching of the Sermon on the Mount (Matt. 6:25-32), of Matt. 10:39, yet more of John 6.

(5) The order of the last two temptations is different in Luke. The impressions left on the minds of those to whom the mystery had been communicated were slightly different. Especially was this likely to be the case, if the trial had been (as the narrative of Mark and Luke show) protracted and the temptations therefore recurring. Matthew's order seems better, the "Get thee behind me, Satan" fitting in better with the close of the conflict.

A pinnacle of the temple.—The Greek word "pinnacle" is the diminutive of "wing," and seems to have been applied to any pointed roof or gable. In this case, looking to the position and structure of the Temple, we may think of the parapet of the portico of Herod overlooking the Valley of Jehoshaphat, rising to a dizzy height of 400 cubits above it (Jos., **Ant.** 15:11, 5). Now a new thought is brought before Him. Shall He test the attestation that He was the beloved Son by throwing Himself headlong down? Had not the psalmist declared of the chosen One of God that His angels should bear Him up? (See Ps. 91:11.) The answer to the tempter (verse 7; see Deut. 6:16) shows that the suggestion tended, not to vainglory, but to distrust simulating reliance.

(8) An exceeding high mountain.—Here we have evidence that all that passed in the Temptation was in the region of which the spirit, and not the senses, takes cognizance. Luke's addition "in a moment of time," in one of those flashes of intuition which concentrate into a single act of consciousness the work of years, adds to the certainty of this view.

(9) All these things will I give thee.—Luke's addition indicates that the offer made by the tempter rested on the apparent evidence of the world's history. Its Herods and its Caesars seemed to have attained their eminence by trampling the laws of God under foot, and accepting evil as the lord and master of the world. In part, the claim is allowed by our Lord's language and that of His apostles (John 12:31; 14:30; Eph. 6:12). In this case the temptation is no longer addressed to the sense of Sonship, but to the love of power.

(10) Get thee hence, Satan.—(See Deut. 6:13; 10:20; comp. Matt. 16:23.) The use of the formula here, for the first time in the conflict, is significant as implying that in the previous temptations evil had presented itself in disguise, making sins of distrust appear as acts of faith, while now it showed itself in its naked and absolute antagonism to the divine will.

(11) Angels came and ministered unto him.—Here also we are in the region of the spiritual rather than the sensuous life. The fact recorded by Matthew explains the words recorded by John (1:51) as uttered but a few days later, and Luke's end to his record of the Temptation may well be noticed here. The conflict was not yet ended, but was from time to time renewed.

(12) For events transpiring between verses 11 and 12, see John 1:29-3:36. At this stage comes in the imprisonment of John (mentioned here, but not narrated until 14:3-5) and the consequent journey through Samaria to Galilee (John 4:1-42). This present verse implies a ministry in Judea, which for some reason the writer does not narrate.

(13) Leaving Nazareth.—The fact (Luke 4:16-30) connects with His rejection by the men of the place where He had been brought up, and their attempt upon His life. Capernaum's position on the shore of the lake, as a town with a garrison and a custom-house, made it the natural center of the fishing trade of the Lake of Galilee. The four first-called disciples, though two of them were of Bethsaida, were already partly domiciled there. An easy day's journey from Nazareth, and a half-Romanized city, it offered our Lord a certain degree of protection and of influence (see Luke 7:5; John 4:46-54).

The chronology of John 5:1 is uncertain (see notes), but at some time before, or shortly after, this migration to Capernaum we must place the visit to Jerusalem and the miracle at Bethesda which John there records.

(17) From that time Jesus began to preach.—We have in these words Matthew's record of the beginning of our Lord's Galilean ministry. It is important to remember that it had been preceded by a ministry of some months in Judaea; that that ministry had been outwardly like that of the Baptist (John 4:1); and that He had withdrawn from it upon John's imprisonment because He knew that His own growing fame had attracted the notice of the Pharisees. Taking the data given by John 2:13, 23; 5:1; and 6:4, we are able to fix the time of His first appearance as a prophet in His own country in the autumn or winter of the interval between the Passover of A.D. 26 and that of A.D. 27.

Of the usual method of our Lord's synagogue-preaching, Luke 4:17-21 gives us a representative example.

(18) And Jesus, walking by the sea of Galilee.—Those who were now called had some months before accepted Him as the Christ (see notes on John 1:35-43), and had been with Him during His visit to Jerusalem. The sons of Jona and the sons of Zebedee had grown up in Bethsaida (probably on the northwest shore of the Lake of Galilee), and were partners in their work as fishermen. For a short time they were His companions in His journeyings. When He began the first circuit of His Galilean ministry, He was alone, and left them to return to their old calling. They could not tell whether He would ever care to use their services again, and it was under these circumstances that the new call came.

(19) Follow me.—The command came as, in some sense, the first parable in our Lord's teaching (comp. Matt. 13:47). The sea is the troubled and evil world (Isa. 57:20), the souls of men are the fish that have to be caught and taken from it, and the net is the Church of Christ. (Comp. Jer. 16:16.)

(23) Healing all manner of sickness.—Sickness implies a less serious form of suffering than "disease," as the "torments" of the next verse imply something more acute. Matthew mentions our Lord's miracles, not directly as evidence of a supernatural mission, but almost as the natural accompaniments of His work; they were signs not of power only, but of the love, tenderness, pity, which were the true marks of the kingdom of heaven.

(24) Possessed with devils ... lunatic.—The word rendered "devil" is not the same as that used for the tempter in 4:1, but "demon" in the sense of an evil spirit. The possessed with demons are at once grouped with the "lunatics," both exhibiting forms of mental disease, and distinguished from them. The latter term implies "moonstruck madness"—the belief that the moon exercised a disturbing influence on the brain, and that the intensity of the disturbance varied, when the disease had once set in, with the moon's changes.

(25) Decapolis.—The district so named was formed by the Romans on their first conquest of Syria, 65 B.C., and included a tract of country east and southeast of the Sea of Galilee. The ten cities from which the region took its name are given by Pliny (5:18) as Scythopolis, Hippos, Gadara, Pella, Philadelphia, Gerasa, Dion, Canatha, Damascus, and Raphana.

5

(1) What is known as the Sermon on the Mount is obviously placed by Matthew (who appears in the earliest traditions connected with his name as a collector of our Lord's "oracles" or discourses) in the forefront of his record of His work as a great pattern-discourse, which more than any other represented the teaching with which He began His work. More than any other part of that record did it impress itself on the minds of men in the first age of the Church, and more often is it quoted by the writers of

that period—James, Barnabas, Clement of Rome, Ignatius, and Polycarp. This discourse and the Sermon on the Plain (Luke 6:20-49) are quite distinct, and each has traceably a purpose and method of its own.

The Sermon, as it stands here, might have been spoken in thirty or forty minutes. There is no reason to think that this was the necessary or even customary limit of our Lord's discourses. Assume a single discourse somewhat longer than this, heard by a multitude, with no one taking notes at the time, but many trying, it may be some years afterward, to put on record what they remembered; and then think of the writer of a gospel coming to collect, with the aid of the Spirit (John 14:26), the **disjecta membra** which all held so precious. He compares, if he himself had heard it, what others had written or could tell him with what he recalled—and we have a process of which the natural outcome is what we find here.

(3) Blessed.—The word differs from that used in Matt. 23:39; 25:34, as expressing a permanent state of felicity rather than the passive reception of a blessing bestowed by another.

The poor in spirit.—In Luke 6:20 there is no qualifying phrase, and there the words speak of outward poverty as in itself a less perilous and therefore happier state than that of riches. Here the blessedness is that of those who, whatever their outward state may be, are in their inward life as those who feel that they have nothing of their own, must be receivers before they give, must be dependent on another's bounty. To that temper of mind belongs the "kingdom of heaven," the eternal realities, in this life and the life to come, of that society of which Christ is the Head.

(4) They that mourn.—Here, as before, there is an implied, though not an expressed, limitation. The "mourning" is not the sorrow for failure, suffering, and the consequences of sin, but the sorrow over sin itself and the stain which it has left upon the soul.

They shall be comforted.—The promise implies the special comfort (including counsel) which the mourner needs; "comforted" he shall be with the sense of pardon and peace, of restored purity and freedom.

(5) The meek.—It may be worthwhile to recall Aristotle's account of meekness (**Eth. Nicom.** 5:5) as the character of one who has the passion of resentment under control, and who is therefore tranquil and untroubled, as in part determining the popular use of the word and in part also explaining the beatitude.

They shall inherit the earth.—See Dan. 7:27, which had done so much to fashion the Messianic expectations of the time. The words have, however, a wider and continuous fulfillment. The influence of the meek and self-controlled is in the long run greater than that of the impulsive and passionate. Their serenity helps them to find the maximum of true joy in all conditions of life, for to them the earth is not a stage for self-assertion and the graspings of desire, but as "inheritance" which they have received from their Father.

(6) Which do hunger and thirst.—We seem in this to hear the lesson which our Lord had learned from the recent experience of the wilderness. The craving of bodily hunger has become a parable of that higher yearning after righteousness, that thirsting after God which is certain, in the end, to gain its full fruition.

(7) The merciful.—The thought is the same as that afterward embodied in the Lord's Prayer. They who are pitiful toward men their brethren are **ipso facto** the objects of the divine pity. (Comp. Jas. 2:13.) No motive to mercy is so constraining as the feeling that we ourselves needed it and have found it.

(8) Pure in heart.—Here, as with the poor in spirit, the noun determines the region in which the purity is to be found—the "heart," as representing desires and affections, as the "spirit" represents the will and higher personality.

Shall see God.—The promise finds its fulfillment in the beatific vision of the saints in glory, seeing God as He is (I John 3:2). But "purity of heart" also brings with it the power of seeing more than others see in all through which God reveals Himself— the beauty of nature, the inward light, the moral order of the world, the written Word, the life and teaching of Christ.

(9) The peacemakers.—Rightly does this beatitude follow on that of the "pure in heart," for it is the absence of all baseness and impurity that gives the power to make peace.

(10) Persecuted for righteousness' sake.— Here again there is a profound significance in the order. The work of the peacemakers is not a light and easy work. There is something suggestive in the fact that this last promise is the same as the first. We end, as we began, with "the kingdom of heaven"; but the path by which we have been led brings us to see that that includes all the intermediate blessings, of which at first it seemed but the prelude and beginning.

(11) Blessed are ye.—The words contain three forms of suffering: (1) vague contempt, showing itself in gibes and nicknames; (2) persecution generally; (3) deliberate slanders, such as those of the foul orgies and Thyesteian banquets, which were spread against the believers in Christ in the first two centuries.

Falsely.—The word is absent from the best MSS, and was probably added as a safeguard against the thought that a man might claim the reward of the persecuted, even if really guilty of the crimes laid against him.

(12) Your reward.—The temper to which the "reward" is promised practically excludes the possibility of such claim as of right. The reward is for those only who suffer "for righteousness, for Christ," not for those who are calculating on a future compensation.

So persecuted they the prophets.—See I Kings 18:4; II Chron. 24:21; Jer. 11:21; 20:2. Isaiah may be added from tradition. But the words were true of the prophetic order as a whole. In the words "the prophets which were before you" there is a tacit assumption that the disciples also to whom He spoke were called to a prophetic work.

(13) Ye are the salt of the earth.—The words are spoken to the disciples in their ideal character as the germ of a new Israel, called to a prophetic work, preserving the earth from moral putrescence and decay. The general reference to this antiseptic action of salt is (as in Col. 4:6) enough to give an adequate meaning to the words, but the special reference to the sacrificial use of salt in Mark 9:49 makes it probable enough that there was some allusion to that thought also here.

Wherewith shall it be salted?—The words imply a relative if not an absolute impossibility. If gifts, graces, blessings, a high calling, and a high work fail, what remains? The parable finds its interpretation in Heb. 6:1-6.

To be trodden under foot of men.—The Talmud shows that the salt which had become unfit for sacrificial use in the storehouse was sprinkled in wet weather upon the slopes and steps of the Temple to prevent the feet of the priests from slipping. We may accordingly see in our Lord's words a possible reference to this practice.

(14) The light of the world.—In its highest or truest sense the word belongs to Christ, and to Him only (John 1:9; 8:12). The comparison to the "candle" or "lamp" in verse 15 shows, indeed, that even here the disciples are spoken of as shining in the world with a derived brightness flowing to them from the Fount of light.

A city that is set on an hill.—Assuming the Sermon on the Mount to have been preached from one of the hills of Galilee near the "horns of Hattin," our Lord may have looked or pointed at Safed, 2,650 feet above the sea, commanding one of the grandest panoramic views in Palestine. The imagery might, however, come from the prophetic visions of the Zion of the future, idealizing the position of the actual Zion (Isa. 2:2; Mic. 4:1). No image could so vividly set forth the calling of the Church of Christ as a visible society.

(15, 16) The motive to publicity is the direct opposite of the temper which led the Pharisee to his ostentatious prayers and almsgiving: not "to be seen of men" and win their praise, but to win men, through our use of the light which we know to be not our own, to glorify the Giver of the light.

(17) Here a new section of the discourse begins, and is carried on to the end of the chapter. From the ideal picture of the life of the society which He came to found, our Lord passes to a protest against the current teaching of the scribes, sometimes adhering to the letter and neglecting the spirit, sometimes overriding even the letter by unauthorized traditions—lowering the standard of righteousness to the level of men's practices, instead of raising their practices to the standard which God had fixed.

"The Law and the prophets" were popularly equivalent to the whole of the Old Testament, though a strict classification required the addition of the **Hagiographa,** or "holy writings," i.e., the poetical and miscellaneous books. Explained by the immediate context, the words "not ... to destroy, but to fulfil" would seem to point chiefly to our Lord's work as a teacher. He came to fill up what was lacking, to develop hints and germs of truth, to turn rules into principles. Interpreted on a wider scale, He came "to fulfil the law and prophets" as He came "to fulfil all righteousness" (3:15) by a perfect obedience to its precepts.

(18) Verily.—This is the familiar "Amen" of the Church's worship. Coming from the Hebrew root for "fixed, steadfast, true," it

was used for solemn affirmation or solemn prayer: "so be it." From the worship of the synagogue it passed into that of the Christian Church.

One jot or one tittle.—The "jot" is the Greek **iota,** the Hebrew **yod,** the smallest of all the letters of the alphabet. The "tittle" was one of the smaller strokes or protrusions of other letters. The meaning is obvious enough: Nothing truly belonging to the Law, however seemingly trivial, shall fade and be forgotten until it has done all that it was meant to do.

(19) Shall break one of these least commandments.—The context proceeds at once to deal with moral laws and does not touch on ceremonial. The "least commandments" are those which seemed trivial, yet were really great—the control of thoughts, desires, words, as compared with the apparently greater commands that dealt with acts. The obvious import of His words is that the disciples were to raise, not lower, the standard of righteousness which had been recognized previously.

(20) Scribes and Pharisees.—Here, for the first time, the scribes are mentioned in our Lord's teaching. The frequent combination of the two words implies that, for the most part, they were of the school of the Pharisees, just as the "chief priests" were, for the most part, of that of the Sadducees. See note on 3:7; comp. Ezra 7:6, 12.

The "kingdom of heaven" is here the ideal and invisible Church on earth—that which answers to its name, that to which belong the blessings and the promises. Into that Church none enter who are content with an outward conventional standard of righteousness.

(21) Whosoever shall kill shall be in danger of the judgment.—The fact that these words are not found in the Old Testament confirms the view that our Lord is speaking of the traditional comments on the Law, and not of the Law itself. The "judgment" spoken of was that of the local courts of Deut. 16:18. They had the power of capital punishment, but the special form of death by stoning was reserved for the Sanhedrin, or Council.

(22) Raca was in common use as expressing not anger only but insolent contempt. The temper condemned is that in which anger has so far gained the mastery that we no longer recognize a "brother" in the man who has offended us, but look on him with malignant scorn.

The council.—Offenses of this kind are

placed by our Lord on the same level as those which came before the great court of the Sanhedrin. (That word, though it looks like Hebrew, is really only a transliterated form of the Greek word for council.) The court consisted of seventy or seventy-two members, with a president and vice-president, and was made up of the heads of the twenty-four courses of the priests, with forty-six or forty-eight from the "elders" and "scribes." It took cognizance (26:65; Acts 6:13) of blasphemy and other like offenses, and its peculiar prerogative was that it could order death by stoning. The point of our Lord's teaching was, therefore, that to scorn God's image in man is to do dishonor to God Himself.

Thou fool.—The Greek is a translation of some word which, like the "fool" of the Old Testament, implied (Ps. 14:1) utter godlessness as well as lack of intellectual wisdom. With that meaning it embodied the temper of fixed and settled hatred. That it was the temper and not the utterance of the mere syllables which our Lord condemned is seen in that He Himself used the word of the scribes and Pharisees (Matt. 23:17, 19), and Paul of the sceptical Greek materialist (I Cor. 15:36).

Of hell fire.—Confusion has arisen here and elsewhere from the use of the same English word for two Greek words of very different meanings: (1) **Hades**, answering to the **Sheol** of the Old Testament, the unseen world, the region or state of the dead, without any reverence to their blessedness or misery; (2) **Gehenna**, which had come to represent among the later Jews the place of future punishment. Originally, it was the Greek form of **Ge-hinnom** (the Valley of Hinnom) and was applied to a narrow gorge on the south of Jerusalem (Josh. 15:8). There Solomon erected a high place for Molech (I Kings 11:7). There the fires of that god had received their bloody offerings of infant sacrifice under Ahaz and Manasseh (II Kings 16:3; II Chron. 28:3; 33:6). Josiah, in his great work of reformation, defiled it (II Kings 23:10-14); and the Jews on their return from captivity showed their abhorrence of the idolatry of their fathers by making it, as it were, the place where they cast out all the refuse of the city. Outwardly, it must have been foul to sight and smell, and thus it became, before our Lord's time, a parable of the final state of those in whom all has become vile and refuse. It is often said that fires which were kept burning to consume the solid refuse

added to the horror of the scene, and that the bodies of great criminals were sometimes deprived of burial rites and cast out into the Valley of Hinnom.

Thus, the meaning of the clause is obvious. Our passing words, expressing states of feeling, and not the overt act of murder only, are subject to the judgment of the Eternal Judge and may bring us into a guilt and a penalty like that of the vilest criminals. Such also is the spirit of verses 23-26.

(28) To lust after her.—The intent is strongly marked in the Greek. It is not the passing glance, not even the momentary impulse of desire, but the continued gaze by which the impulse is deliberately cherished until it becomes a passion. Our Lord's words speak primarily of "adultery," but are applicable to every form of sensual impurity.

(29) The Greek verb "offend" means, strictly, to cause another to stumble or fall into a snare. The bold severity of the phrase "pluck it out" excludes a literal interpretation. The seat of the evil lies in the will, not in the organ of sense or action, and the removal of the instrument might leave the inward taint unpurified. What is meant is that any sense, when it ministers to sin, is an evil and not a good, the loss of which would be the truest gain.

(31) Whosoever shall put away . . .—The quotation is given as the popular rabbinic explanation of Deut. 24:1, which, as our Lord teaches in Matt. 19:8, was given, on account of the hardness of men's hearts, to prevent yet greater evils.

(32) Saving for the cause of fornication.—The most generic term seems intentionally used to include ante-nuptial as well as postnuptial sin, possibly, indeed, with reference to the former only, seeing that the strict letter of the Law of Moses made death the punishment of the latter, and so excluded the possibility of the adultery of a second marriage. The words "causeth her to commit adultery" imply that the "putting away" was legally a divorce **a vinculo**, leaving the wife (and **a fortiori** the husband) at liberty to marry again, for otherwise she could not have incurred the guilt of adultery by a second marriage; but they assert that in such a case, when divorce was obtained on any other ground than the specific sin which violated the essence of the marriage contract, man's law (even that of Moses) was at variance with the true eternal law of God.

Whosoever shall marry her that is di-

vorced.—The words "put away" would necessarily convey to His Jewish hearers the idea of an entire dissolution of the marriage union, leaving both parties free to contract a fresh marriage; and if it were not so, then the case in which He specially permits that dissolution would stand on the same level as the others. The injured husband would still be bound to the wife who had broken the vow which was of the essence of the marriage contract. But if he were free to marry again, then the guilt of adultery could not possibly attach to her subsequent marriage with another. The context, therefore, requires us to restrict that guilt to the case of a wife divorced for other reasons, such as Jewish casuistry looked on as adequate.

(34) Swear not at all.—The context shows that the sin which our Lord condemned was the light use of oaths in common speech, and with no real thought as to their meaning. Such oaths practically involved irreverence and therefore were inconsistent with the fear of God. The real purpose of an oath is to intensify that fear by bringing the thought of God's presence home to men at the very time they take them, and they are therefore rightly used when they attain that end. (See 26:63, 64; Rom. 1:9; II Cor. 1:23.)

(34, 35) When men swear by God, there is an implied appeal to the Supreme Ruler. We invoke Him to assist and bless us according to the measure of our truthfulness, or to punish us if we speak falsely. If such formulae as these here have any force at all, it is because they imply a reference to the Eternal. Heaven is His throne, earth is His footstool, and Jerusalem is the city of the great King. To use them lightly is to profane the holy name which they imply. Men do not guard themselves either against irreverence or perjury by such expedients.

(38) An eye for an eye.—As originally given (see Exod. 21:24), this was a check on the "wild justice" of revenge. Where the equilibrium of right had been disturbed by outrage, the work of the judge was not to do more than restore the equilibrium: not less than the "eye for an eye," for that might lead to connivance in guilt; not more, for that would open a fresh score of wrong. The scribes in their popular casuistry made the rule one not of judicial action only, but of private retaliation; and it was thus made the sanction of the vindicative temper that forgives nothing.

(39) Turn to him the other also.—Comp. John 18:22, 23; Acts 23:3. The principle in

this matter is clearly and simply that the disciple of Christ, when he has suffered wrong, is to eliminate altogether from his motives the natural desire to retaliate or accuse. (The same forbearing and gracious temper is encouraged in verses 40-42.) But he has other duties which he cannot rightly ignore. The law of the Eternal has to be asserted, society to be protected, the offender to be reclaimed, and these may well justify—though personal animosity does not—protest, prosecution, punishment.

(43) Thou shalt love thy neighbour, and hate thine enemy.—In form the latter clause was a rabbinic addition to the former; and this is important as showing that our Lord deals throughout not with the Law as such, but with the scribes' exposition of it. But it can hardly be said these words, as far as national enemies were concerned, were foreign to the spirit of the Law. The fault of the scribes was that they stereotyped the Law, which was in its nature transitory, and extended it in a wrong direction by making it the plea for indulgence in private enmities.

(44) Bless them that curse you . . .—The extension of the command to love our neighbor (Lev. 19:18) is such that it includes even those whom natural impulse prompts us to hate. The stress is laid on prayer as the highest utterance of that love.

(46) The publicans.—See Matt. 9:9. Here our Lord puts Himself, as it were, on the level of those to whom He speaks. They despised the publicans as below them, and He speaks as if He were using their own familiar language, yet with a widely different application. Were they after all above the publicans, if they confined their love to a reciprocity of good offices?

(48) Be ye therefore perfect.—Literally, "Ye therefore shall be perfect"—the ideal future that implies an imperative. The idea of perfection implied here is that of the attainment of the end or ideal completeness of our being. In us that attainment implies growth, and the word is used (I Cor. 2:6; Heb. 5:14) of men of full age as contrasted with infants. In God the perfection is not something attained, but exists eternally; we draw near to it and become partakers of the divine nature when we love as He loves.

6

From the protest against the casuistry which tampered with and distorted the great primary commandments, the Sermon on the Mount passes to the defects of character and action which vitiated the religion of Pharisaism even where it was at its best. Its excellence had been that it laid stress on the three great duties of the religious life—almsgiving, fasting, and prayer—rather than on sacrifices and offerings. Verbally, Pharisaism accepted on this point the widest and most spiritual teaching of the prophets, and it gained a hold on the minds of the people which the priests never gained. But a subtle evil found its way even here. Love of praise and power rather than spontaneous love, and self-denial and adoration, was the mainspring of their action; and so that which is the essence of all religion was absent even from the acts in which the purest and highest form of religion naturally shows itself.

(2) Alms.—In the original meaning of the Greek it was the quality of mercy, or rather of "mercifulness," as something more complete. The practice of the Hellenistic Jews limited the word (**eleemosyna**) to money gifts. It passed with this meaning into the language of Christendom.

Hypocrites.—Derived from a Greek verb which signifies answering, taking part in a dialogue, acting a part in a play, the noun in classical Greek was used simply for an actor, a man who plays a part. In one passage only in the LXX (Job 36:13) it appears in the figurative sense of one who pretends a virtue which he does not have. It thus lay ready for the wider use which the evangelists have given it. It is not used by any writer of the New Testament except Matthew, Mark, and Luke.

(3) Let not thy left hand know.—The phrase was probably proverbial, and indicates, in the form of free hyperbole, extremest secrecy. The "right hand," used to offer gifts at the altar, is the higher spiritual element in us that leads to acts of true charity; the "left" is the baser, self-seeking nature. We ought to set a barrier between the two, as far as possible, i.e., to exclude that mingling of motives, which is at least the beginning of evil.

(5) Standing in the synagogues.—The Jewish custom was to pray standing, with outstretched, uplifted hands, and there was nothing in the attitude as such that made it an act of ostentatious devotion. Our Lord's words point to the custom of going into the synagogue to offer private devotion, and of doing this so as to attract notice, the worshiper standing apart as if absorbed in prayer, while secretly glancing around to watch the impression which he might be making on others who were looking on.

(6) Enter into thy closet.—Neither in synagogue nor street, neither in courtyard nor on housetop, where men were likely to pray—these might present the temptations of publicity—but in the steward's closet, the place which seemed to men least likely, which they would count it irreverent to connect with the idea of prayer. The principle is, of course, that personal prayer should be strictly personal and private.

(7) Use not vain repetitions.—The Greek is formed from a word which reproduces the repeated attempts of the stammerer to clothe his thoughts in words. It might be rendered, "Do not stutter out your prayers, do not babble them over." The words describe only too clearly the act of prayer when it becomes mechanical. On the other hand, it is clear that the law of Christ does not exclude the iteration of intense emotion, for in the great crisis of His human life our Lord Himself prayed three times "using the same words" (Matt. 26:44). For the "heathen" practices, comp. I Kings 18:26; Acts 19:34.

(9) Our Father.—The very word "Abba" (**father**) uttered by our Lord here (Mark 14:36) so impressed itself on the minds of men that, like "Amen," "Hallelujah" and "Hosanna," it was used in the prayers even of converts from heathenism and Hellenistic Judaism. (See its special association with the work of the Spirit in Rom. 8:15; Gal. 4:6.) The thought of the Fatherhood of God was not altogether new. As the disciples heard it, it would not at first convey to their minds thoughts beyond those with which they were familiar. (See Exod. 4:22; Isa. 64:8; Jer. 31:9; Hos. 11:1.) But time and the teaching of the Spirit were to develop what was now in germ. That it had its ground in the union with the Eternal Son, which makes us also sons of God; that it was a name that might be used, not by Israelites only, but by every child of man; that of all the names of God that express His being and character, it was the fullest and the truest—this was to be learned as men were guided into all the truth.

Which art in heaven.—The earlier books of the Old Testament express His universal presence (Gen. 14:22; Deut. 4:39; Josh. 2:11). Later on, men began to be more conscious of the infinite distance between themselves and God, and represented the contrast by the thought that He was in heaven and they on earth (Eccles. 5:2). This thought became a liturgical formula in the great dedication prayer of Solomon (I Kings 8:32, 34; II Chron. 6:21). The phrase became current as symbolizing the world visible and invisible, which is alike the dwelling place of God, uttering in the language of poetry that which we vainly attempt to express in the language of metaphysics by such terms as the Infinite and the Absolute.

Hallowed be thy name.—The first expression of thought in the pattern prayer is not the utterance of **our** wants and wishes, but that the Name of God should be to all men a consecrated name. The words "Jehovah, hallowed be His name," were familiar enough to all Israelites and are found in many of their prayers; but here the position of the petition gives a new meaning to it and makes it the key to all that follows.

(10) Thy kingdom come.—Historically, the prayer had its origin in the Messianic expectations embodied in the picture of the ideal king (Isa. 11:1-6; 42:1-7; Dan. 7:14). It had long been familiar to all who looked for the consolation of Israel. Now the kingdom of God, that in which He manifests His sovereignty more than in the material world or in the common course of history, had been proclaimed as near at hand. And insofar as the kingdom, though in one sense it has come, and is in the midst of us, and within us, is yet far from the goal toward which it moves, ever coming and yet to come, the prayer is one that never becomes obsolete, and may be the utterance of the saints in glory no less than of toilers and sufferers upon earth.

(11) Give us this day our daily bread.— The word translated "daily" is found nowhere else, with the one exception of the parallel passage in Luke 11:3. As far as we can judge, it must have been coined for the purpose as the best equivalent for the unknown Aramaic word which our Lord actually used. The form of the word admits of the following meanings: (1) sufficient for the day now coming; (2) sufficient for the morrow; (3) sufficient for existence; (4) over and above material substance. Perhaps the warnings in verses 25-31—not only against anxiety about what we shall eat and drink, but against **seeking** these things instead of seeking simply the kingdom of God and His righteousness—help us to see that He meant His disciples, in this pattern prayer, should seek for the nourishment of the higher and not the lower life. So taken, the peti-

tion, instead of being a contrast to the rest of the prayer, is in perfect harmony with it, and the whole raises us to the region of thought in which we leave all that concerns our earthly life in the hands of our Father, without asking Him even for the supply of its simplest wants, seeking only that He would sustain and perfect the higher life of our spirit. So when we ask for "daily bread," we mean not common food but the "Bread from heaven, which giveth life unto the world."

(12) Forgive us our debts.—"Duty" and "debts" are, it may be noted, only different forms of the same word. A duty unfulfilled is a debt unpaid. Primarily, therefore, the words, "our debts," represent sins of omission, and "trespasses" sins of commission. Confession of the debt was enough to insure its remission, and then there was to come the willing service of a grateful love instead of the vain attempt, which Pharisaism encouraged, to score up an account of good works as part payment.

As we forgive our debtors.—The better reading gives, "We have forgiven," as a completed act before we begin to pray. In the act of prayer we are taught to remind ourselves of the conditions of forgiveness. Even here, in the region of the free grace of God, there is a law of retribution. The temper that does not forgive cannot be forgiven, because it is **ipso facto** a proof that we do not realize the amount of the debt we ourselves owe.

(13) Lead us not into temptation.—The thought is of sufferings which test or try. We are taught not to think of the temptation in which lust meets opportunity as that into which God leads us (Jas. 1:13, 14). But trials of another kind—persecution, spiritual conflicts, agony of body or of spirit— these may come to us as a test or as a discipline. (See I Cor. 10:13.) It is hardly possible to read the prayer without thinking of the recent experience of "temptation" through which our Lord had passed.

Deliver us from evil.—The Greek may, grammatically, be "evil one," as equivalent to the "devil." (See 13:19, 38; Eph. 6:16; II Thess. 3:3; I John 2:13, 14; 3:12; 5:18, 19.) Again we connect our Lord's words with His own experience. The prayer against temptation would not have been complete without reference to the tempter whose presence was felt in it.

For thine is the kingdom . . .—The whole clause is wanting in the best MSS and in the earlier versions, and is left unnoticed by the early Fathers, who comment on the rest of the prayer.

(16) When ye fast.—Under the Law there had been but the one great fast of the Day of Atonement (Lev. 23:27; Num. 29:7). Other fasts were occasional, in times either of distress or penitence (Joel 1:14; 2:15) or of religious zeal (I Kings 21:9, 12). The tradition of the Pharisees, starting from the true principle that fasting was one way of attaining self-control, and that as a discipline it was effectual in proportion as it was systematic, fixed on the fasts "twice in the week" (Luke 18:12). The second and fifth days of the week were fixed, and connected with some vague idea that Moses went up Mount Sinai on the one and descended on the other. Our Lord recognizes fasting, as He recognizes alms-giving and prayer, and warns His disciples against the ostentation that vitiates all three.

(22) The light of the body.—See Prov. 20:27. The spirit of man, under the name of "conscience," discerns spiritual realities, distinguishes right from wrong, gives the light by which we see our way. If this discerns clearly, all is well. The "whole body," the life of the man in all its complex variety, will be illumined by that light. Singleness of intention will preserve us from the snare of having a double treasure, and therefore a divided heart.

(24) No man can serve two masters.—The clauses that follow describe two distinct results of the attempt to combine the two forms of service which are really incompatible. In most cases, there will be love for the one, and a real hatred for the other. "Mammon" means in Syriac "money" or "riches." There is no ground for believing that it ever became the name of any deity, who, like the Plutos of the Greeks, was worshipped as the god of wealth. Here, there is obviously an approach to a personification for the sake of contrasting the service or worship of money with that which is due to God. (Comp. **Par. Lost**, 1:678).

(25) Take no thought.—The Greek word expresses anxiety, literally the care which "distracts" us. The temper against which our Lord warns His disciples is not that of foresight, which merely provides for the future, but the allowing ourselves to be harassed and vexed with its uncertainties. The teaching of the whole passage that follows is that, assuming a personal will, the will of a Father, as that which governs the order of the universe, we may trust to its wisdom and love to order all things well for

the highest as for the meanest of its creatures.

(27) One cubit unto his stature.—The Greek for the last word admits either this meaning (as in Luke 19:3) or that of age (as in John 9:21, 23). Either gives an adequate sense to the passage. The latter, however, better satisfies the teaching of the context. Men are not anxious about adding to their stature, but they are often anxious about prolonging their life. Admit the thought that our days are but "as a span long" (Ps. 39:5), and then the addition of a cubit becomes a natural metaphor. (Comp. Luke 12:26.)

(30) The grass of the field.—The term is used generically to include the meadow flowers which were cut down with the grass and used as fodder or as fuel. The scarcity of wood in Palestine made the latter use very common. The "oven" in this passage was the portable earthen vessel used by the poor for baking their bread. The coarse ligneous hay was placed below it and around it; and short-lived as the flame was, so that "the crackling of the thorns" (Ps. 118:12; Eccles. 7:6) became proverbial, it had time to do its work.

(32) After all these things do the Gentiles seek.—The tone is one of pity rather than of censure, though it appeals, not without a touch of gentle rebuke (as in verse 5), to the national pride of Israelites: "You look down upon the heathen **nations**, and think of yourselves as God's **people**; yet in what do you excel them, if you seek only what they are seeking?"

(33) Seek ye first the kingdom of God.—The context shows that the words point to the "seeking" of prayer. What is thus to be sought is "the kingdom of God" (the change from the less personal "kingdom of heaven" is significant), the higher spiritual life in its completeness, for ourselves and for others; and with it we are to seek "His righteousness," that which, being perfect beyond the righteousness of the scribes and Pharisees, must be His gift to us, and therefore to be sought in prayer. One who seeks for this may well be content to leave all else in his Father's hands.

(34) Take therefore no thought for the morrow.—That which was really new in our Lord's teaching was the ground on which the precept rested. It was not simply the search after a maximum of enjoyment, nor the acceptance by man's will of an inevitable destiny, nor the vain struggle to rise above that inevitable fate. Men were to look forward to the future calmly, because they had a Father in heaven who cared for each one of them with a personal and individualizing love.

Sufficient unto the day is the evil thereof.—"Evil" is too strong here; but it reminds us that our Lord is speaking not of what we call the simple accidents or misfortunes of life, but of the troubling elements which each day brings with it and against which we have to contend, lest it should lead us into sin. That conflict is more than enough for the day, without anticipating further trouble.

7

While chap. 5 is mainly a protest against the teaching of the scribes, and chap. 6 mainly a protest against their corruption of the three great elements of the religious life (almsgiving, prayer, and fasting) and the worldliness out of which that corruption grew, this deals chiefly with the temptations incident to the more advanced stages of that life when lower forms of evil have been overcome—with the temper that judges others, the self-deceit of unconscious hypocrisy, the danger of unreality.

(1) Judge not, that ye be not judged.— The words point to a tendency inherent in human nature, and are therefore universally applicable; but they had a special bearing on the Jews. They, being in the vanguard of the religious progress of mankind, took on themselves to judge other nations.

How far can **we** obey the precept? Must we not, even as a matter of duty, be judging others every day of our lives? The answer is not found in the distinctions of a formal casuistry. Our Lord here gives principles rather than rules, and embodies the principle in a rule which, because it cannot be kept in the letter, forces us back upon the spirit. What is forbidden is the censorious judging temper, eager to find faults and condemn men for them. Briefly, we may say: judge no man unless it be a duty to do so; as far as may be, judge the offense and not the offender; confine judgment to the earthly side of faults, and leave their relation to God, to Him who sees the heart; never judge at all without remembering one's own sinfulness, and the ignorance and infirmities which may extenuate the sinfulness of others.

(3) Why beholdest thou the mote ...?— The Greek noun so translated means a

"stalk" or "twig" rather than one of the fine particles of dust floating in the sun to which we attach the word "mote." The illustration seems to have been a familiar one among the Jews. It teaches that men are keen sighted as to the faults of others, blind as to their own.

(5) Thou hypocrite.—The man deserves this name; he acts the part of a teacher and reformer, when he himself needs repentance and reform the most. The hypocrisy is all the greater because it does not know itself to be hypocritical.

(6) That which is holy.—The words point to the flesh which has been offered for sacrifice (Lev. 22:6, 7, 10, 16). To give that holy flesh to dogs would have seemed to the devout Israelite the greatest of all profanations. Our Lord teaches us that there is a like risk of desecration in dealing with the yet holier treasure of divine truth. Another aspect of the same warning is brought out in the second clause. The fashion of the time had made pearls the costliest of all jewels (13:45), and so they too became symbols of the preciousness of truth. The "dogs" and the "swine," in their turn, represent distinct forms of evil, the former being (Phil. 3:2; Rev. 22:15) the type of impurity, the latter (Ps. 80:13) of ferocity.

(7) Ask, and it shall be given.—Where shall we find the courage and the wisdom which we need in this work of reforming ourselves and others? The answer is in prayer for those gifts. The three imperatives imply distinct degrees of intensity.

(11) The words at once recognize the fact of man's depravity. Yet in the midst of all our evil there is still that element of natural and pure affection which makes the fatherhood of men a fit parable of the Fatherhood of God. The context shows that the "good things" are spiritual and not temporal gifts. The wisdom and insight which we all need (Luke 11:13) are included in the diversity of the one gift of the Holy Spirit.

(12) There is, of necessity, an implied limitation. The rule is safe only when our own will has been first purified, so that we wish only from others that which is really good. Reciprocity in evil or in folly is obviously altogether alien from the mind of Christ.

(13) Enter ye in at the strait gate.—The figure was suggested possibly by some town actually in sight—e.g., Safed, the "city set on a hill" (5:14), or some other, with the narrow pathway leading to the yet narrower gate, the "needle's eye" of the city, through which the traveler entered. The meaning of the parable here lies on the surface. The way and the gate are alike the way of obedience and holiness, and the gate is to be reached not without pain and effort; but only through it can we enter into the city of God, the heavenly Jerusalem. A deeper significance is, however, suggested even by our Lord's own teaching. (See John 10:7; 14:6.)

That leadeth to destruction.—The word implies not annihilation, but the loss of all that makes existence precious. It means, in relation to material things, the breaking up of outward form and beauty; and in spiritual things, the wretchedness of a wasted life.

(15) Beware of false prophets.—How was the narrow way to be found? Who would act as guide? Many would offer their help who would simply lead men to the destruction which they sought to escape. Such teachers had been prevalent in the days of Isaiah and Jeremiah, and would be again. The true gift of prophecy is followed always by its conterfeit. (See Acts 5:37.) The illustration implies something like the conception of the wolf disguising himself as a sheep in order to gain entrance into the fold. (Comp. John 10:12; Acts 20:29.)

(16) Ye shall know them by their fruits.— This refers to the practical outcome of doctrine in life, character, and deeds. We are to judge the teaching of those who claim authority by the test of the measure in which, in the long run, it promotes purity, peace, and holiness.

(21) A further development of the same thought is found in John 7:17. We are taught that it is by doing the will of God ourselves, or rather by **willing** to do it, that we gain the power to distinguish truth from error. The disciples had already begun to use the title Lord (**Kurios**) in speaking to their Master (comp. Luke 5:8), but as that word was at the time in common use as one of courtesy (Matt. 8:2, 6; John 20:2), it would not necessarily follow that they had used it in all the later fullness of its meaning.

(22) Many will say to me in that day.— No part of the Sermon on the Mount is more incomprehensible to those who see in Christ only a human Teacher with a higher morality than Hillel or Seneca. In "that day" of judgment (Mal. 4:5) the words "Lord, Lord" would mean more than the expression of human courtesy.

(24) These sayings of mine.—The reference to what has gone before tends to the conclusion that we have in these chapters a continuous discourse, and not a compilation of fragments (see verse 28). On the assumption that the Sermon on the Plain was different from that on the Mount, the recurrence of the same image there makes it probable that this or some similar parable was not an uncommon close to our Lord's discourses.

I will liken him unto a wise man.—As in all hilly countries, the streams of Galilee rush down the torrent beds during the winter and early spring, sweep all before them, overflow their banks, and leave beds of alluvial deposit on either side. When summer comes, their waters fail (comp. Job 6:15; Jer. 15:18); and what had seemed a goodly river is then a tract covered with debris of stones and sand. A stranger coming to build might be attracted by the ready-prepared level surface of the sand. It would be easier to build there instead of working up the hard and rugged rock. But the people of the land would know and mock the folly of such a builder, and he would pass into a by-word of reproach. The house stands for the general fabric of an outwardly religious life. "The rock" is the firm foundation of repentance and obedience. The "sand" answers to the shifting, uncertain feelings which are with some men the only ground on which they act—love of praise, respect for custom, and the like. The "wind," the "rain," the "floods" represent collectively the violence of persecution, of suffering, of temptations from without, beneath which all but the life which rests on the true foundation necessarily gives way.

(29) The "I say unto you" had been contrasted with what had been said "to them of old time"; the assumption had been made that He was the Head of the divine kingdom and the Judge of the living and dead. More striking still is the entire absence of any reference by name to the teaching of other interpreters of the Law. As a rule, the scribe hardly ever gave his exposition without at least beginning by what had been said by Hillel or by Shammai. In contrast with all this, our Lord fills the people with amazement by speaking to them as One who has a direct message from God. It is the prophet—perhaps the king— who speaks, and not the scribe.

8

(1) We enter on a series of events common to Mark and Luke, but not narrated here in the same order. While there is difficulty in harmonizing the gospel narrative with any certainty, three conclusions may fairly be received: (1) The independence of each record. (It is scarcely conceivable that Mark or Luke would have departed so widely from Matthew's order had they had his gospel before them.) (2) The derivation of all three from earlier records, written or oral, each embracing some few acts or discourses of our Lord. (3) The absence of any direct evidence as to the order of these events, so that each writer was often left to his own discretion or to some internal principle of grouping.

(2) A leper.—The probable origin of leprosy was in the squalor and wretchedness of the Egyptian bondage (Deut. 28:27). In the Egyptian legends of the Exodus, indeed, the Israelites were said to have been expelled because they were lepers. Its main features were the appearance of a bright spot on the flesh, whiter than the rest, spreading, inflaming, cracking, oozing, becoming hard and scaly. One so affected was regarded as unclean (Lev. 13:3, 11, 15), and was looked upon as smitten with a divine plague. He had to live apart from his fellows, to wear on his brow the outward sign of separation, to cry out the words of warning, "Unclean, unclean" (Lev. 13:45). The idea seems to have been one of abhorrence rather than precaution. The disease was loathsome, but there is no evidence that it was contagious.

If thou wilt, thou canst make me clean.— Comp. Mark 1:40; Luke 5:12. The words of the man involve a singular mingling of faith and distrust. He believes in the power; he does not as yet believe in the will. Can it stoop to one as foul as he? If he shared the common feeling that leprosy was the punishment of sin, he might ask himself, Will He pity and relieve one so sinful?

(4) The offering of the gift was an act of obedience to the Law (Lev. 14:10, 21, 22), and was therefore the right thing for the man to do. In this way also our Lord showed that He had not come to destroy the Law, but to fulfill it. It was, too, the appointed test of the reality and completeness of the cleansing work. Better for the man's own spiritual life was it to cherish his gratitude than to waste it in many words.

The treatment of leprosy in the Mosaic code was clearly symbolical rather than sanitary, and dealt with the disease as the special type of sin in its most malignant form. So in the healing of the leper we may fairly see the symbol of our Lord's power to purify and save from sin, and in His touching the leper, the close fellowship into which He entered with our unclean nature, that through His touch it might be made clean.

(5) Matthew records the miracle more with reference to the associated teaching, Luke (Luke 7:1) after closer inquiry into the details and circumstances. Here the centurion is said to have come to our Lord himself; but from Luke's report we learn that he never came at all in person, but sent first the elders of the Jews, and then his friends.

A centurion.—The presence of a centurion (a word originally meaning the commander of a hundred soldiers) implied that of a garrison stationed at Capernaum to preserve order. Here, as in the case of Cornelius (Acts 10), the faith and the life of Judaism had made a deep impression on the soldier's mind. He found a purity, reverence, simplicity, and nobleness of life which he had not found elsewhere; and he built anew the synagogue of the town.

(6) He is described as paralyzed, and the words "grievously tormented" point to acute suffering. The fact that this suffering touched his master's heart with pity was itself a sign of something exceptionally good in the centurion's character. It was not thus, for the most part, that the wealthy Romans dealt with their slaves when they were sick. It is probable that the centurion had heard specifically of the healing of the "nobleman's son" at Capernaum (John 4:46-54). There he had found a precedent which now determined his own line of action, showing that a word from those lips might be enough to heal without touch or even presence.

(8) Lord, I am not worthy.—The sense of unworthiness implied at once the consciousness of his own sins, and the recognition of the surpassing holiness and majesty of the Teacher he addressed.

Speak the word only.—This was the special proof of the speaker's faith. He had risen above the thought of a magic influence, operating by touch or charm, to that of a delegated power (see verse 9) depending only on the will of Him who possessed it. His faith was so unlike Israel's, who sought a material sign (verse 10).

(11) Many shall come from the east and west.—Our Lord saw in the centurion the firstfruits of the wide harvest of the future. Like the words of the Baptist in Matt. 3:9, what He now said contained, by implication, the whole Gospel which Paul preached to the Gentiles. "East and west" were used as limits that included all the nations of the earth.

Shall sit down.—Literally, "shall recline," as at the table of a feast. As in the phrase of Abraham's bosom, this was the received parable of the blessedness of the kingdom.

(12) The children of the kingdom—i.e., as in "the children of the bride chamber," those who belonged to the kingdom: the Israelites, to whom the kingdom of heaven had, in the first instance, been promised, the natural heirs who had forfeited their inheritance.

Into outer darkness.—The words continue the imagery of the previous clause, the darkness outside the king's palace being contrasted with the interior, blazing with lamps and torches.

There shall be weeping and gnashing of teeth.—In their literal meaning the words express that intensest form of human anguish in which it ceases to be articulate. Their spiritual meaning we naturally connect with the misery of those who are excluded from the joy and blessedness of the completed kingdom.

(17) Himself took our infirmities.—We see in Isa. 53 a picture of our Lord's spiritual work of redemption; and the words quoted are almost the cardinal text for the special view of the Atonement, which sees in the sufferings of Christ the freely accepted penalty that was due for the transgressions of mankind. The evangelist, with the memory of that evening (verse 16) present to his mind, saw them fulfilled in this removal of the "infirmities" and "sicknesses" that oppressed the bodies of men. Our Lord Himself "took" and "bore" the sufferings which He removed. He suffered with those He saw suffer. The power to heal was intimately connected with the intensity of His sympathy, and so was followed by weariness and physical exhaustion. (Comp. Mark 1:35; Luke 4:42.)

(19) A certain scribe came.—Jesus was now on the eastern shore of the Sea of Galilee. The fact that it was a scribe that came is striking, as showing that the impression made by our Lord's teaching was not confined to the "common people" that "heard him gladly." As Nicodemus had already come confessing that He was a "Teacher come from God," so in Galilee there was one whom the Sermon on the Mount, or some like discourse, had led to volunteer at least the show of discipleship.

(20) The foxes have holes.—Our Lord's answer does seem to indicate that it was hardly more than the show. The scribe had not counted the cost, and, like the young ruler that had great possessions, needed to be taught. To follow the Son of Man was not to be the adherent of a new sect or party, or the servant of a king marching onward to an earthly throne, but to share in poverty, privation, homelessness.

The Son of man.—The passage is the first in this gospel in which occurs the name afterward so prominent in our Lord's teaching. As found in the Old Testament, the term is the literal translation of the Hebrew **ben-adam**, the latter word expressing the generic weakness and frailty of man's nature, as the Hebrew **ish** expresses its greatness and its strength. It stands, therefore, as representing man idealized under the one aspect of his being. (Comp. Ps. 8:4.) The title received a new prominence about the time of the Captivity from its use in Ezekiel's prophecies. There it appears no fewer than eighty-seven times as the title with which the prophet is addressed by the voice of Jehovah, meaning that the prophet was still subject to all the weakness and temptations of man's nature, and ought therefore to have compassion on their infirmities. Yet a fresh aspect of the name was presented in the mysterious vision of Dan. 7:13 (**bar-enosh**, not **ben-adam**—but there is no traceable distinction of meaning between the two). Here the thought was that One who shared man's weakness also should be a sharer of God's glory and the Head of the divine kingdom. The prominence which the Maccabean struggles gave to the predictions of Daniel drew attention to the name as it had thus been used. The "Son of Man" became one of the titles of the expected Christ. It was, accordingly, with these ideas attached to it—involving at once fellowship with the lowest of the heirs of our humanity, and yet also participation in the eternal glory of the Highest—that our Lord claimed the title and used it with such marvellous frequency. We might almost say that it serves as the chief connecting link between the teaching of the first three gospels and the fourth. Outside the gospels it is found in the New Testament only in Acts 7:56 and possibly in Rev. 1:13; 14:14.

(21) The form of the petition probably means that he asked to remain with his father until his death. The request was a plea for indefinite postponement. This fits

701

in with the apparent severity of our Lord's answer.

(22) Let the dead bury their dead.—"Let those who have no spiritual life linger in the circle of outward routine duties, and sacrifice the highest spiritual possibilities of their nature to their fulfillment. Those who are really living will do the work to which their Master calls them, and leave the lower conventional duties to be done or left undone as the events of their life shall order."

(26) Why are ye fearful, O ye of little faith?—Storms such as that described in verse 24 are of common occurrence in all inland seas. The word "of little faith" was singularly appropriate. They had not altogether lost their trust in Him; but they had not learned the lesson of the centurion's faith, and were only at ease when they heard His voice and saw that He was watching over them.

Rebuked the winds and the sea.—This seems to have been almost our Lord's formula in working miracles. The fever (Luke 4:39), the frenzy of the demoniac (Mark 9:25), the tempest, are all treated as if they were hostile and rebel forces that needed to be restrained.

(28) The country of the Gergesenes.—The exact determination of the locality presents difficulties. In all the three gospels we find various readings, of which the best supported are Gadarenes in Matthew, and Gerasenes in Mark and Luke. Gadara was a city east of the Sea of Galilee, about sixteen miles from Tiberias, at the northwest extremity of the mountains of Gilead. The tombs of the city, chambers in the limestone rock often more than twenty feet square, are its most conspicuous feature. Gerasa was a city in the Gilead district, twenty miles east of the Jordan. It is likely that "Gerasenes" was used vaguely for the whole Gilead district. On the more remote and improbable Gergesa, comp. Gen. 10:16; Josh. 3:10.

Two possessed with devils.—Mark and Luke speak of "one" only. A like difference meets us in Matthew's "two blind men" at Jericho (Matt. 20:30) as compared with the "one" of the two other gospels. The natural explanation is that, in each case, one was more prominent than the other in speech or act, and so was remembered and specified, while the other was either forgotten or left unnoticed. To dwell in such tombs was, to the ordinary Jew, a thing from which he shrank with abhorrence, as bringing pollution, and to choose such an abode was therefore a sign of insanity. According to

Mark, whose account is the fullest of the three, the insanity was so homicidal that "none could pass by that way," so suicidal that he was ever cutting himself with stones, howling day and night in the wildness of his seizures. Luke adds that he wore no clothes (i.e., strictly, no outer garment; the word does not imply actual nakedness).

(29) The man identifies himself with the demons; looks forward, when the hour of judgment shall come, to condemnation; and claims, in the meantime, to be let alone. The command given to the "unclean spirit" to "come out of the man" had, we find from Mark and Luke, been given previously, as the man drew near, and was the occasion of this frenzied cry. At this stage, too, they add, our Lord asked the question, "What is thy name?" The most terrible phenomenon of possession was the divided consciousness which appears in this case. Now the demon speaks, and now the man. The question would recall to the man's mind that he once had a human name, with all its memories of human fellowship. It was a stage, in spite of the seizure that followed, in the process of recovery, insofar as it helped to disentangle him from the confusion between himself and the demons which caused his misery. The irresistible might, the full array of the Roman "legion," with its six thousand soldiers, seemed to the demoniac the one adequate symbol of the wild, uncontrollable impulses of passion and of dread that were sweeping through his soul.

(31, 32) "If thou cast us out, send us into the herd of swine. If the power to terrify and disturb men is taken from us, let us, at least, retain the power to destroy brutes." Only in some such way could the man be delivered from the inextricable confusion between himself and the unclean spirits in which he had been involved. Not until he saw the demoniac forces that had oppressed him transferred to the bodies of other creatures, and working on them the effects which they had wrought on him, could he believe in his own deliverance.

(34) Comp. Mark 5:18-20. The man formerly possessed went his way proclaiming what Jesus had done for him—a true evangelist to a people whose panic terror showed that they were as yet in darkness and the shadow of death.

9

(1) Matthew makes the return to Capernaum follow the healing of the Gadarene demoniacs. Mark and Luke place it after that of the leper; but as if uncertain as to its exact position, they note "after certain days," or "on one of the days." Mark states definitely that Capernaum had become Jesus' "own city" since His departure from Nazareth (Matt. 4:13).

(2) Luke (Luke 5:21) states that among the hearers were Pharisees and Doctors of the Law, who had come from Jerusalem. This fact is important as one of the few traces in the first three gospels of an unrecorded ministry in Jerusalem, and throws light on much that follows. They had apparently come to see how the new Teacher, who had so startled them at Jerusalem, was carrying on His work in Galilee, and, as far as they could, to hinder it. Persistency on behalf of the paralytic (Mark 2:3, 4) implied faith in Jesus' power to heal. The words of forgiveness were addressed to the secret yearnings of the sufferer. Sickness had made him conscious of the burden of his sins. The Healer saw that the disease of the soul must first be removed, and that then would come the time for restoring strength to the body.

(3) **This man blasphemeth.**—For the grounds of their accusation, see Mark 2:7; Luke 5:21; comp. John 5:18. All sins are offenses against God, and therefore the ultimate act of forgiveness belongs to God only; for a mere man to claim the right of forgiving thus absolutely was to claim a divine attribute, and therefore to utter words as disparaging as open profaneness to the majesty of God.

(5) The words, "Thy sins are forgiven thee," could not be put to any outward test, and only the consciousness of the sinner could attest their power. It was a bolder and a harder thing to risk the utterance of words which challenged an immediate and visible fulfillment; and yet He was content to utter such words, without fear of the result. Ultimately, however (verse 6), our Lord's answer rests on the higher, and not the lower, of the two grounds on which the objectors might have been met.

(9) **A man, named Matthew.**—The sympathy and power shown in healing the paralytic impressed itself on the mind of one who, as a publican, felt that he too had sins that needed to be forgiven. Mark and Luke give the name as Levi; the former adds that he was the "son of Alphaeus." A new name was offered here that practically superseded the old (comp. 10:2). Matthew means "the

gift of God," or, more strictly, "the gift of Jehovah."

Sitting at the receipt of custom.—The customs levied there were probably of the nature of an **octroi** on the fish, fruit, and other produce that made up the exports and imports of Capernaum.

He arose, and followed him.—Luke adds, "he left all." There was not much to leave— his desk at the custom, his stipend or his percentage; but it was his all, and no man can leave more than that.

(10) The insertion of the name Jesus injures the sense. What seems to have been meant is, that while Matthew reclined (after Roman fashion), many publicans and sinners came and reclined with Jesus and His disciples. There is a noticeable humility in omission of the fact that he had made "a great feast" (Luke 5:29). It was apparently a farewell feast to old friends and neighbors before he entered on his new calling. They were naturally mostly of his own class, or on a yet lower level. The publican was the pariah of Palestine, and no decent person would associate with him.

(12, 13) Those of whom He speaks were suffering from the worst form of spiritual disease, but in their own estimation they were without spot or taint. (Comp. Luke 4:23.) The words of Hos. 6:6, furthermore, asserted the superiority of ethical to ceremonial law. To have withdrawn from contact with sinners would have been a formal "sacrifice," such as Pharisees delighted to offer, and from which they took their very name; but the claims of "mercy" were higher, and bade Him mingle with them.

(14) **The disciples of John.**—The followers of the Baptist continued during our Lord's ministry to form a separate body. They obeyed rules which he had given them, more or less after the pattern of those of the Pharisees. Acting with the Pharisees, and perhaps influenced by them, they were perplexed at conduct so unlike that of the master they revered, and came therefore with their question. But they were, at least, not hypocrites, and they are answered without the sternness which had marked the reply to their companions.

(15) **The days will come, when the bridegroom shall be taken from them.**—This is noteworthy as the first recorded intimation in our Lord's public teaching (that in John 3:14 was less clear until interpreted by the event, and was addressed to Nicodemus alone) of His coming death. The joy of the guests ("children of the bridechamber") at

the wedding feast would cease, and then would come the long night of expectation. The time that was to follow the departure of the Bridegroom would be one of sorrow, conflict, discipline, and at such a time the self-conquest implied in abstinence was the natural and true expression of the feelings that belonged to it.

(16) No man putteth a piece of new cloth.—Such a patch sewn upon a weak part of the old cloak would, on the first strain, tear the cloth near it. The meaning of the parable in its direct application lies near the surface. The "garment" is that which is outward, the life and conversation of the man, which show his character. The old garment is the common life of sinful men, such as Matthew and his guests; the new garment is the life of holiness, the religious life in its completeness; fasting, as one element of that life, is the patch of new cloth which agrees not with the old, and leads to a greater evil, a "worse rent" in the life than before.

(17) Neither do men put new wine into old bottles.—The bottles are those made of hides partly tanned, and retaining, to a great extent, the form of the living animals. These, as they grew dry with age, became liable to crack, and were unable to resist the pressure of the fermenting liquor. The "new wine" represents the inner, as the garment did the outer, aspect of Christian life, the new energies and gifts of the Spirit, which, as on the day of Pentecost, were likened to new wine (Acts 2:13).

(18) A certain ruler.—As an elder of the synagogue, Jairus would probably have been among the elders of the Jews who came as a deputation to our Lord, and would thus have been impressed with His power to heal in cases which seemed hopeless. Luke adds that the ruler's only child was twelve years old, and that she "lay dying."

(20) Behold, a woman . . .—The "issue of blood" was probably of the kind that brought with it ceremonial uncleanness (Lev. 15:26). This accounts for the sense of shame which made her shrink from applying to the Healer openly, and from confessing afterward what she had done.

Touched the hem of his garment.—Comp. Matt. 14:36; John 19:23. Our Lord's outward garb included first, nearest the body, the coat or tunic without seam, woven from the top throughout; then, over that, the garment or cloak, flowing loosely after the manner of the East; and this had

its "border or fringe," probably of a bright blue mingled with white, that on which the scribes and Pharisees laid stress as being in accordance with the Law (Num. 15:38), and which they wore, therefore, of an ostentatious width (Matt. 23:5). (Later tradition defined the number of the threads or tassels of the fringe, so that they might represent the 613 precepts of the Law.)

(22) Thy faith hath made thee whole.—There may be imperfect knowledge, false shame, imperfect trust, and yet if the germ of faith is there, Christ, the Healer both of the souls and bodies of men, answers the longing desire of the soul to be freed from its uncleanness. Weak as the faith was, it was accepted, and outward things were endowed with a "virtue" which was not their own. (Comp. Acts 19:12.)

(23-26) The other gospels fill in the details. Now Peter, James, and John for the first time are chosen from among the chosen for the special blessedness of being with Jesus in the greater and more solemn moments of His ministry. The restored life of the child was dependent, after the supernatural work had been completed, upon natural laws, and there was the risk of renewed exhaustion. As in other cases, He charged the parents that they should not make it known. It was not good for the girl spiritually or physically that she should be the object of the visits of an idle curiosity.

(27) Two blind men.—The two narratives that follow are peculiar to Matthew. The title "Son of David" was that which expressed the popular belief that He was the expected Christ.

(28) Into the house.—The article indicates the house in which He sojourned at Capernaum, probably that of Peter.

(29) Then touched he their eyes.—This is the first recorded instance of the method which our Lord seems always to have adopted in the case of the blind. They were shut out from His look of sympathy, and for them its absence was supplied by acts which they naturally would connect with the purpose to heal them.

(32) A dumb man possessed with a devil.—The phenomena presented in this case were those of insanity showing itself in obstinate and sullen silence. The dumbness was a spiritual disease, not the result of congenital malformation. The work of healing restored the man to sanity rather than removed a bodily imperfection.

(34) Through the prince of the devils.—See notes on 12:24-30.

(35, 36) Comp. 4:23. This may be described as recording our Lord's second mission circuit in Galilee, and was intended to lead up to the great discourse of chap. 10.

(37, 38) Nowhere in the whole gospel record is there a more vivid or more touching instance of the reality of our Lord's human emotions. It is not enough for Him to feel compassion Himself. He craves the sympathy of His companions and disciples, and needs even their fellowship in prayer. A great want lies before Him, and He sees that they are the right agents to meet it, if only they will pray to be made so.

10

(1-4) What is described here is not the choice but the mission of the Twelve. That selection had been made before (Luke 6:13). The number at once suggested the thought that they represented the twelve tribes of Israel (Matt. 19:28), and were as such to be His messengers to the whole people of the dispersion. The name apostle signified literally "one who is sent." According to our Lord's teaching they were sent by Him, even as He had been sent by the Father (John 20:21).

A comparison of the four lists of the apostles (Mark 3:16-19; Luke 6:13-16; Acts 1:13) brings out some interesting observations: (1) The name of Peter is always first, that of Judas always last. In the former case we recognize acknowledged pre-eminence, in the latter infamy. (2) All the lists divide themselves into three groups of four, the persons in each group being always the same (assuming that the three names, Judas **the brother** [see Jude 1] of James, Thaddaeus, and Lebbaeus, belong to the same person), though the order in each group varies. (3) The first group includes the two sons of Jona and the two sons of Zebedee, whose twofold call is related in 4:18-21; John 1:40. Like these men, Philip also came from Bethsaida. (4) The absence of any mention of Bartholomew in John's gospel, or of Nathanael (John 1:45) in the other three, has led many commentators to the conclusion that they were two names for the same person; and the juxtaposition of the two names in their lists agrees with the fact that it was Philip who brought him to Jesus as the Christ (John 1:45). (5) As the name of Thomas, or Didymus, means "twin," there seems some ground for believing, from the way in which his name and Matthew's are grouped together, that here too we have another pair of brothers called to the service of their Master. (6) "James the son of Alphaeus" has been conjectured, too, to be a brother of Matthew (there are no grounds for assuming two persons of the name of Alphaeus; see note on 9:9), and probably, therefore, of Thomas also. If the Clopas (not Cleopas) of John 19:25 was only the less Graecized form of the name Alphaeus, then his mother Mary may have been the sister of Mary the mother of the Lord. (7) Lebbaeus suggests a derivation from the Hebrew **leb** (heart), and points to warmth and earnestness of character; **thad** meant the female breast, and may have indicated a feminine devotedness. The names together suggest that he was one of the youngest of the Twelve, and was looked upon by the others with an affection which showed itself in the name thus given to him. (8) Simon, like Judas the brother of James (i.e., Thaddaeus), needed a distinguishing epithet. It was found in the two forms of Zelotes and Cananite (not Canaanite), pointing (**kana**, "to be hot") to zeal as his chief characteristic. (9) The term "Iscariot" is local, the Graecized form of Ish-Kerioth (a man of Kerioth), a town in Judah (Josh. 15:25). Thus we have in Judas the only one among the Twelve of whom it is probable that he was of Judah, and not of Galilee.

(5) Go not into the way of the Gentiles.— The limitation was confined to the mission on which they were now sent, and did but recognize a divine order: the priority of Israel in God's dealing with mankind, "to the Jew first, and also to the Gentile." It was necessary that the Twelve should learn to share their Master's pity for the lost sheep of the house of Israel before they could enter into His yearnings after the sheep that were "not of this fold" (John 10:16).

(8) Raise the dead.—The words are omitted by the best MSS, and their absence is more in accordance with the facts of the gospel history, which records no instance of that highest form of miracle as wrought by the disciples during our Lord's ministry. That was reserved for His own immediate act. The insertion of the words was due probably to a wish to make the command cover such instances of power as that shown in regard to Dorcas (Acts 9:40) and Eutychus (Acts 20:9-12).

Freely ye have received.—They were not in this their first mission to require payment from others. When the kingdom had been established, the necessities of the case might require the application of the principle that "the labourer is worthy of his hire" (see Paul's application of verse 10 in I Tim. 5:18); but the principle of "giving freely" in this sense is always applicable in proportion as the work of the ministers of Christ has the character of a mission. They must proclaim the kingdom until the sense of the blessing it has brought shows itself in the thank offerings of gratitude.

(10) Scrip.—The "scrip" or wallet was a small basket carried on the back, or by a strap hanging from one shoulder, containing the food of the traveler. (See I Sam. 17:40.)

(14) Shake off the dust of your feet.—The act was a familiar symbol of the sense of indignation (Acts 13:51). The Jewish maxim, that even the dust of a heathen land brought defilement with it, added to its significance. It was a protest in act, declaring (as our Lord declares in words) that the city or house which did not receive the messengers of the Christ was below the level even of the Gentiles.

(16) Harmless as doves.—The Greek indicates more than simple harmlessness—a character in which there is no alloy of baser motives. Once again truth appears in the form of paradox. The disciples of Christ are to be at once supremely guileful ("wise as serpents") and absolutely guileless. Our Lord's reference to this symbolism gains a fresh significance in the light of Matt. 3:16. In and by that Spirit the two qualities that seem so contradictory are reconciled.

(17) They will scourge you in their synagogues.—The words imply the actual infliction of the punishment within the walls of the building. Paul's language in Acts 22:19; 26:11 seems to place the fact beyond the shadow of a doubt. The stripes of which the apostle speaks in II Cor. 11:24 were probably so inflicted.

(19) Take no thought.—In the same sense as in Matt. 6:25: "Do not at that moment be over-anxious." The words indicate an almost tender sympathy with the feelings of Galilean disciples, "unlearned and ignorant men," standing before those who were counted so much their superiors in power and knowledge. The courage of Peter and John before the Sanhedrin is at once the earliest and the most striking instance of the fulfillment of this promise regarding both content and form of speech (Acts 4:13).

(22) He that endureth to the end—i.e., endures, as the context shows, in the confes-

sion of the name of Christ as long as the trial lasts, or to the end of his own life.

(23) When they persecute you.—The counsel is noteworthy as suggesting at least one form of the wisdom of the serpent. Men were not to imagine that they were "enduring to the end" when, in the eagerness of their zeal, they courted martyrdom; but they were rather to avoid danger instead of courting it, and to utilize all opportunities for the continuance of their work. (Comp. Polycarp and Cyprian.)

Till the Son of man be come.—The thought of another Coming than that of the days of His humiliation and of His work as a Prophet and a Healer, which had been implied before (Matt. 7:21-23), is now explicitly unfolded. The Son of Man should come (Dan. 7:13) in the clouds of heaven, with power and great glory, to complete the triumph of His kingdom. For the difficult connection of the words with the preceding limit of time, see notes on chap. 24.

(25) Beelzebub.—The Greek gives the form **Beel-zebul**. It appears in the form **Baal-zebub**, the "Lord of flies" (probably as sending or averting the swarms of flies or locusts that are one of the plagues of the East), as the name of a god worshiped by the Philistines at Ekron, and consulted as an oracle (II Kings 1:2) in cases of disease. Later Jews, identifying all heathen deities with evil spirits, saw in the god of their nearest and most hated neighbors the chief or prince of those "demons," and in their scorn transformed the name into **Baal-zebel**, "Lord of dung," or **Baal-zebul**, "Lord of the dwelling"—i.e., of the house of the evil spirits who are the enemies of God. Our Lord's connection of the name with "the master of the house" seems to point to the latter meaning as that present to our Lord's thoughts. The reference is clearly made to the charge that had already been implied in Matt. 9:34.

(27) What I tell you in darkness.—The words point to our Lord's method of teaching, as well as to the fact of its being esoteric, and disclosed only to the chosen few, and to them only as they were "able to bear it" (John 16:12). To "proclaim on the housetops"—the flat roofs of which were often actually used by criers and heralds for their announcements—is a natural figure for the fullest boldness and freedom in their preaching.

(28) Fear him which is able . . .—The meaning is not: "Fear not men; but fear the Spirit of Evil, the great Adversary . . ."; we are nowhere taught in Scripture to fear the devil, but rather to resist and defy him (Eph. 6:11; Jas. 4:7). The reference is, rather, to God, who is in no case willing to destroy, but who has the power to inflict that destruction where all offers of mercy and all calls to righteousness have been rejected.

(29) The coin mentioned here is the tenth part of the **denarius**. The fact that the **denarius** was the average day's wages of a soldier or a laborer gives a fair approximation to its value. The primary thought is obviously that the providence of God extends to the meanest of His creatures. Even the incidents of life, furthermore (verse 30), that seem most trivial are working together for good to those who love God. They are not at any moment of their lives to think that they are uncared for by their Father.

(34-37) Comp. Luke 14:26, 27. Our Lord speaks here of conditions of discipleship. Where two affections come into collision, the weaker must give way; and though a man ought not to cease to love, yet he must act as if he hated—disobey, and, it may be desert—those to whom he is bound by natural ties, that he may obey the higher supernatural calling.

(38) He that taketh not his cross.—The words were hardly a specific announcement of the manner of our Lord's death, though they imply, interpreted by events, a distinct prevision of it (comp. John 3:14). To the disciples they would recall the sad scene which Roman rule had made familiar to them, the procession of robbers or rebels, each carrying the cross on which he was to suffer. They would learn that they were called to a like endurance of ignominy and suffering.

(42) One of these little ones.—The term was familiarly used of the scholars of a rabbi, and in this sense our Lord, as the great Master, sending forth His disciples, now employs it. He would not disregard even the cup of cold water given to the humblest disciple as such and for the sake of Christ. The language of Matt. 25:40 justifies the extension of these words to every act of kindness done to any man in the name of that humanity which He shares with those whom He is not ashamed to call His brethren (Heb. 2:11).

11

(2) When John had heard in the prison.—

The position of the Baptist was so far that of a prisoner treated with respect. In the prison of Machaerus, he was languishing with the sickness of hope deferred for the Messianic kingdom, which he had proclaimed. His disciples brought back word of what they had seen and heard (Luke 7:18), and yet there was no deliverance either for himself or Israel. Under the influence of this disappointment, he sent his two disciples with the question of verse 3.

(5) The blind receive their sight.—At least one instance of each class of miracle has already been recorded (see 8:2; 9:6, 25, 27; Luke 7:14, 15). What the Baptist needed was not the knowledge of fresh facts, but a different way of looking at those he already knew. Where these works were done, there were tokens that the coming One had indeed come. But above all signs and wonders, there was another spiritual note of the kingdom, which our Lord reserves as the last and greatest: **Poor men have the good news proclaimed to them**. It is as though our Lord knew that the Baptist, whose heart was with the poor, would feel that One who thus united power and tenderness could be none other than the expected King.

(7-10) There was an obvious risk that those who heard the question of the Baptist, and our Lord's answer, might be led to think with undue harshness, perhaps even with contempt, of one who had so far failed in steadfastness. As if to meet that risk, Jesus turns, before the messengers were out of hearing, to bear His testimony to the work and character of John. The imagery first was drawn from the rushes that grew upon the banks of the Jordan. Had they gone out to see one who was swayed this way and that by every blast of popular feeling? No, not that. Had they seen, then, one who shared in the luxury, and courted the favor, of princes? No, not so, again. These words had a more pointed reference than at first sight appears. Jewish historians record how in the early days of Herod the Great a section of the scribes (the Herodians) had attached themselves to his policy and party, and in doing so had laid aside the somber garments of their order and had appeared in the gorgeous raiment worn by Herod's other courtiers. (We may trace a vindictive retaliation for these words in the "gorgeous robe" with which Herod arrayed Him in mockery when the tetrarch and the Christ stood for one brief hour face to face with each other. See Luke 23:11.) They had gone out to see a prophet, and they were not disappointed. Nothing that they had seen or heard since was to lead them to think less worthily of him now. See Mal. 3:1; Luke 1:76.

(11) He that is least in the kingdom of heaven.—The Greek gives the comparative, not the superlative—he whose relative position in the kingdom of heaven is less than that of John. That one of His disciples, rejoicing in His presence, in communion with Him, in His revelation of the Father, though less than John in fame, work, the rigor of ascetic holiness, was yet above him in the knowledge of the truth, and therefore in blessedness and joy.

(12) The words describe the eager rush of the crowds of Galilee and Judaea, first to the preaching of the Baptist, and then to that of Jesus. The "violent" are men of impetuous zeal, who grasp the kingdom of heaven—i.e., its peace, pardon, and blessedness—with as much eagerness as men would snatch and carry off as their own the spoil of a conquered city. There is no thought of hostile purpose in the words.

(13) All the prophets and the law.—The usual order is inverted, because stress is laid on the prophetic rather than the legislative aspect of previous revelation. They did their work pointing to the kingdom of heaven in the far-off future of the latter days, but John saw it close at hand, and proclaimed its actual appearance.

(14) This is Elias.—The words of Mal. 4:5 had led men to expect the reappearance of the great Tishbite in person as the immediate precursor of the Christ. It was the teaching of the scribes then (Matt. 17:10; John 1:21). The true meaning of the words of Malachi had, however, been suggested by the angel in Luke 1:17: "He shall go before him in the spirit and power of Elias."

(15) He that hath ears to hear.—The formula is one which our Lord seems to have used habitually after any teaching, in parable or otherwise (13:9; Mark 4:9), which required more than ordinary powers of thought to comprehend. To take in the new aspect of the coming of Elijah required an insight of that nature.

(16) It is like unto children sitting in the markets.—The comparison is drawn from one of the common amusements of the children of an Eastern city. They form themselves into companies, and get up a dramatic representation of wedding festivities and funeral pomp. They play their pipes, and expect others to dance; they beat their breasts in lamentation, and expect others to weep. They complain if others do not comply with their demands. To such a company our Lord likens the evil generation in which He and the Baptist lived. They were loud in their complaints of the Baptist because he would not share their self-indulgent mirth; they were bitter against Jesus because He would not live according to the rules of their hypocritical austerity. The verses that follow give the language in which the same generation vented its anger and scorn against the two forms of holiness. But while the evil world rejects all who seek to overcome its evil, true seekers after wisdom will welcome holiness in whatever form it may appear.

(21) Woe unto thee, Chorazin! woe unto thee, Bethsaida!—No miracles are recorded in the gospels as wrought at either of these cities. The latter was near the scene of the feeding of the five thousand, but that comes later on in the gospel narrative. The former is known to us only through this passage and the parallel words of Luke 10:12-16. The position of Chorazin is described by Jerome as being on the shore of the lake, about two miles from Capernaum. The Bethsaida here spoken of was probably that on the western shore of the Sea of Galilee. The name in Aramaic signifies "House of Fish."

Tyre and Sidon.—The two cities are chosen as being, next to Sodom and Gomorrah (10:15), the great representative instances of the evil of the heathen world, and of the utter overthrow to which that evil was destined (Ezek. 27, 28). Over and above their immediate import the words are full of meaning as throwing light on the ultimate law of God's dealings with the heathen world. Men are judged not only according to what they have done, but according to what they might or would have done under other circumstances and conditions of life.

(23) And thou, Capernaum.—This city had already witnessed more of our Lord's recorded wonders than any other. In this sense, and not in any outward prosperity, had Capernaum been "exalted unto heaven." All this, however, had been in vain, and therefore the sentence was passed on it that it should be "brought down to hell," i.e., to **Hades**, the grave, not **Gehenna**. The words have had an almost literal fulfillment. A few ruins conjecturally identified mark the site of Capernaum; not one stone is left upon the other in Chorazin and Bethsaida.

(25) Answered and said.—Luke 10:17-24 connects the words with the return of the

Seventy; but as their mission is not recorded by Matthew, it seems reasonable to connect them, as here recorded, with the return of the Twelve, and their report of their work (Mark 6:30; Luke 9:10). Their presence is implied in the narrative with which the next chapter opens.

The "wise and prudent" (comp. I Cor. 1:19) were the scribes and Pharisees, wise in their conceit, seeking men's praise rather than truth as truth, and therefore shut out from the knowledge that requires above all things sincerity of purpose. The "babes" were the disciples who had received the kingdom in the spirit of a little child, childlike in their thoughts of it, but who, being in earnest and simple-hearted, were brought under the training which was to make them as true scribes for the kingdom of heaven.

(27) All things are delivered.—The "all things" are shown by the context to refer especially to the mysteries of the kingdom implied in the word "reveal." The wider meaning of the words appears more clearly in 28:18.

Neither knoweth any man the Father.—The Greek implies full and complete knowledge. In that sense it was true that no one knew the Son as such in all the ineffable mystery of His being and His work but the Father, that no one fully entered into the Fatherhood of God but He whose relation to Him had been from eternity one of Sonship.

(28) Labour and are heavy laden.—The words are wide enough to cover every form of human sin and sorrow, but the thought that was most prominent in them at the time was that of the burdens grievous to be borne, the yoke of traditions and ordinances which the Pharisees and scribes had imposed on the consciences of men.

I will give you rest.—The "I" is emphasized in the Greek. He gives what no one else can give—rest from the burden of sin, from the weariness of fruitless toil.

(29) Take my yoke upon you.—As the teaching of the Pharisees was a yoke too grievous to be borne, so the yoke of Christ is His teaching, His rule of life.

(30) My burden is light.—The "burden" of Christ was the commandment that most characterized His teaching—the new commandment that men should love one another; and those who obeyed that commandment would find all to which it bound them light and easy.

12

(1) At that time.—See Luke 6:1. The event is clearly between the Passover and the Feast of Pentecost, between the beginning of the barley and the end of the wheat harvest. But we can only regard the words "at that time" as belonging to the separate history in some other position than that in which Matthew has placed it.

Began to pluck the ears of corn.—The act was permitted by the Law as far as the rights of property were concerned (Deut. 23:25), but it was against the Pharisees' interpretation of the law of the Sabbath. To pluck the ears was to reap, to rub the husks from the grain was to thresh; and the new Teacher was therefore, they thought, tacitly sanctioning a distinct breach of the holiness of the day of rest.

(3) Have ye not read . . . ?—See I Sam. 21:6. Would they accuse David of sacrilege and Sabbath breaking because he, in a case of urgent need, set at nought the twofold law of ordinances? If they shrank from that, was it not inconsistent to condemn the disciples of Jesus for a far lighter transgression?

(4) How he entered into the house of God.—The shewbread, or "bread of oblation," consisted of twelve loaves, in two rows of six each, which were offered every Sabbath day (Exod. 25:30; 40:23; Lev. 24:5-9), the loaves of the previous week being then removed and reserved for the exclusive use of the priests. The necessity of the case, however, was in this instance allowed to override the ceremonial ordinance, and our Lord teaches men through that single instance to see the general principle that when positive commands and necessities involving the good of man come into collision, the latter, not the former must prevail.

(5) The priests in the temple profane the sabbath.—The work of the priests (Num. 28:9) involved an amount of labor which, in work of any other kind, would have broken the Sabbath rest; yet no one blamed the priests, for they were serving in the Temple of Jehovah.

(6) In this place is one greater than the temple.—The body of the Son of Man was the truest, highest temple of God, and the disciples who ministered to Him were entitled to at least the same privilege as the priests in the Temple at Jerusalem. The range of the words is, however, wider than this, their first and highest application. All works of love done for the bodies or the souls of men as little interfere with the holiness of a day of rest as did the ministrations of the priests as they labored to weariness in the ritual of the Temple. (Comp. I Cor. 6:19.)

(7) **I will have mercy, and not sacrifice.**— Moral and not positive duties made up the true life of religion, and were alone acceptable to God. It was because they had inverted the right relation of the two that they had, in this instance, condemned those whom our Lord now declares to have been in this respect absolutely guiltless. (Comp. Hos. 6:6.)

(11, 12) The casuistry of the rabbis allowed the healing art to be practiced on the Sabbath in cases of life and death, but the "withered hand," a permanent infirmity, obviously did not come under that category. The Talmud discusses the former question, but does not decide it. Some casuists solved the problem by a compromise. The sheep was not to be pulled out of the pit until the Sabbath was over, but in the meantime it was lawful to supply it with fodder. The alternative thus presented as a dilemma was a practical answer to their casuistry, for not to do good when it lies in our power is practically to do evil.

(13) **It was restored whole**—i.e., as the tense implies, in the act of stretching the hand forth. The man's ready obedience to the command, which if he had not believed in the power of Jesus would have seemed an idle mockery, was, **ipso facto**, a proof that he had "faith to be healed."

(17) **That it might be fulfilled.**—The quotation of Isa. 42:1 in reference to this reserve and reticence (verse 16) shows how deep an impression it had made on the mind of the evangelist in connection with our Lord's conduct. One who united thus the attributes of divine power with such entire freedom from the ostentation of ambition could be none other than the true ideal King.

(18) See Isa. 42:1. The work of preaching the Gospel to the Gentiles had not yet begun, but Matthew notes, as it were, by anticipation, the spirit of love and gentleness which would bring them also within the range of the life-giving truths of the righteous Judge. It is one of the many instances in which his record, though obviously written for Jews, is yet emphatically a Gospel for the Gentiles. (See verse 21.)

(20) The prophet's words described a character of extremest gentleness. The "bruised reed" is the type of one broken by the weight of sorrow, care, or sin. Such a one men in general disregard or trample on. The Christ did not so act, but sought rather to bind up and strengthen. The "smoking flax" is the wick of the lamp which has ceased to burn clearly, and the clouded flame of which seems to call for prompt extinction. Here we read a parable of the souls in which the light that should shine before men has grown dim. For such the self-righteous Pharisee had no pity; he simply gave thanks that his own lamp was burning. But the Christ in His tenderness sought, if it were possible, to trim the lamp and to pour in the oil until the flame was bright again. This tender compassion was to characterize the whole work of the Christ until the time of final judgment should arrive, and truth should at last prevail.

(24) **Beelzebub the prince of the devils.**— (See note on 10:25.) The words appear to have been whispered by the Pharisees among the people. They were not addressed to Jesus. The charge is significant as showing that the Pharisees admitted the reality of the work of healing which they had witnessed, and were driven to explain it by assuming demoniacal agency. Of all the accusations brought against Him this was the one that caused the greatest pain and drew forth the most indignant answer.

(26) **If Satan cast out Satan.**—Satan, on the assumption of the Pharisees, casts out himself. Satan is not personally identified with the demon, the deaf or dumb spirit, that had possessed the man, but the language implies that where evil enters into the soul, Satan enters also. (Comp. John 13:27.) There is, as it were, a seeming ubiquity in the power of evil, as there is admittedly in the sovereign power of good.

(28) The work was confessedly superhuman, either from the power of Satan (the "strong man," verse 29) or that God, but the former hypothesis was excluded by the reasoning of verses 25-27; the latter was therefore the only explanation. If Jesus gave proof that He was thus filled with the power of the Spirit to heal and save, then He was what He claimed to be, the Head of the divine kingdom. That kingdom had burst upon men unawares.

(31) **The blasphemy against the Holy Ghost.**—Better, "against the Spirit." See note on Mark 3:30. The word "Holy" is not found in any MS of authority. What is this blasphemy against the Holy Ghost? The context helps us to understand something of

its nature. The Pharisees were warned against a sin to which they were drawing perilously near. To condemn the Christ as a gluttonous man and a wine-bibber, as breaking the Sabbath, or as blaspheming was to speak a word against the Son of Man. These offenses might be sins of ignorance, implying no more than narrowness and prejudice. But to see a man delivered from the power of Satan to God, to watch the work of the Spirit of God, and then to ascribe that work to the power of evil, was to be out of sympathy with goodness and mercy altogether. In such a character there was no opening for repentance, and therefore none for forgiveness. The capacity for goodness in any form was destroyed by this kind of antagonism.

(33) Either make the tree good.—The men to whom our Lord spoke were in direct hostility to Him, and here, therefore, He presses on them logic rather than practical consistency: reckon the tree and the fruit as having the same character. If to cast out demons was a good work, then the power from which it flows must be good also. Works of that kind do not come from a corrupt source. Such is the burden also of verses 34-37.

(39) An evil and adulterous generation.—The true relation between Israel and Jehovah had been represented by the prophets as that of the wife to her husband (Jer. 3, Ezek. 16; 28; Hos. 1; 2). The adulterous generation was therefore one that was unfaithful to its Lord—demanding a sign, instead of finding sufficient proofs of faithfulness and love in what He had already done.

(40) "The sign of the prophet Jonas" was fulfilled, in part, by Jesus' preaching repentance to the wicked and adulterous generation as Jonah had done to the Ninevites. But if we believe that our Lord had a distinct prevision of His Resurrection, and foretold it, sometimes plainly and sometimes in dark sayings (comp. 16:21; 26:32; John 2:19), then the history of Jonah presented a further analogy which it was natural that He should notice. The purely chronological difficulty is explained by the common mode of speech among the Jews, according to which any part of a day, though it were but a single hour, was for legal purposes considered as a whole. Comp. I Sam. 30:12, 13; it is possible that in the history of Jonah itself the measurement of time is to be taken with the same laxity.

Some incidental facts are worth noticing:

(1) that the word translated "whale" may stand vaguely for any kind of sea monster; (2) that "the heart of the earth" means more than the rock-hewn sepulcher, and implies the descent into Hades, the world of the dead, which was popularly believed to be far below the surface of the earth; and (3) that the parable has left its mark on Christian art.

(41) A greater than Jonas.—No chapter contains more marvelous assertions of our Lord's superhuman majesty: greater than the Temple (verse 6), greater than Jonas, greater than Solomon (verse 42). Could this be rightly claimed by any man for himself who was not more than man?

(43) When the unclean spirit is gone out of a man.—How was it that Israel had sunk to such a depth of evil? The answer was found in the similitude here. As far as possession was identical in its phenomena with insanity, there might be sudden and violent relapses after intervals of apparent cure. The spirit of the man, under the influence of exorcisms, prayers, or the sympathy of friends, might assert its freedom for a time, and then yield again to the oppressor. In the history of such a demoniac, which our Lord narrates in the language of the popular belief, He sees a parable of the history of the Jewish people. (Comp. Tobit 8:3.)

(44) Empty, swept, and garnished.—The words symbolize the state of the nation of which the demoniac is made the type. They portray the state of the man who has been delivered from the wilderness of frenzy, but has been left to the routine of common life and conventional morality, with no higher spiritual influence to protect and guard him.

(45) Seven other spirits more wicked than himself.—The number seven (Mark 16:9; Luke 8:2) represent a greater intensity of possession, showing itself in more violent seizures of frenzy and with less hope of restoration. Israel's first "possession" was her idolatry between the Exodus and the Captivity. When idolatry seemed to be banished forever, the "house" was thus "empty, swept, and garnished." But there was no indwelling presence of the enthusiasm of a higher life—only an outward ceremonial religion and rigid precepts, and the show of piety. Then the old evil ("seven other spirits") came back in the form of Mammon-worship, bitterness and hate, the license of divorce, self-righteousness, want of sympathy, and that antagonism to good which had

711

come so terribly near to "the sin against the Holy Ghost." And our Lord's words point to a future that should be yet worse: the destruction of Jerusalem, an adequate measure of the "last state" of that "wicked generation."

(46) His mother and his brethren.—Who were these "brethren of the Lord"? The facts in the gospel records are scanty: (1) The Greek word translated "brother" has the same latitude as the term in English. Like that, it might be applied to half-brothers, brothers by adoption, or national or religious brotherhood. (2) The names of four brethren (and reference to sisters) are given in Mark 6:3. But we are unable to decide whether the brothers and sisters were older children of Mary and Joseph, or children of Joseph by a former marriage—either an actual marriage on his own account, or what was known as a Levirate marriage (Deut. 25:5), for the sake of raising up seed to a deceased brother—or the children of Mary's sister, Mary the wife of Clopas (John 19:25). (3) Up to the time of the Feast of Tabernacles that preceded the Crucifixion, within six months of the close of our Lord's ministry, His brethren did not believe in His claims to be the Christ (John 7:3-5).

The motive which led the mother and the brethren to seek to speak to our Lord on this occasion was protest and attempt to control and check His work. Note the tone of disclaimer, as it were, in which He now speaks.

(50) Whosoever shall do the will.—This is what Christ recognizes as the ground of a spiritual relationship (verse 49): not outward, but inward fellowship; not the mere fact of baptism, but that which baptism signifies; that doing the will of God, which is the essence of holiness. This is that which makes the disciple as dear to the heart of Christ as was the mother whom He loved so truly.

13

(3) He spake many things unto them in parables.—This is the first occurrence of the word in Matthew's gospel, and it is clear from the question of the disciples in verse 10 that it was in some sense a new form of teaching to them. The word had been employed by the Greek translators of the Old Testament for the Hebrew word **mashal,** which we commonly render by "proverb,"

and which, like the Greek **parabole,** has the sense of similitude. In the later and New Testament use of the word, however, the parable takes the fuller form of a narrative embracing facts natural and probable in themselves. (See verse 52.) The mode of teaching by parables was familiar enough in the schools of the rabbis, and the Talmud contains many of great beauty and interest (Ecclus. 38:33). With what purpose our Lord now used this mode of instruction will appear in His answer to the question of the disciples. The prominence given in the first three gospels to the parable that follows shows how deep an impression it made on the minds of men, and so far justified the choice of this method of teaching by the divine Master.

A sower.—Literally, "the sower"—the man whose form and work were so familiar, in the seedtime of the year, to the peasants of Galilee. The outward framework of the parable requires us to remember the features in which Eastern tillage differs from our own: the ground less perfectly cleared—the road passing across the field—the rock often cropping out, or lying under an inch or two of soil—the patch of good ground rewarding, by what might be called a lucky chance rather than skill of husbandry, the labor of the husbandman.

(11) To know the mysteries.—The Greek word does not mean a truth which none can understand, but one which, kept a secret from others, has been revealed to the initiated. Interpreted by our Lord's teaching up to this time, the mysteries of the kingdom may be referred to new birth (John 3:5), judgment (John 5:25), power to forgive sins (Matt. 9:6), new ideas proclaimed as to the Sabbath (Matt. 12:8), and fasting, prayer, and alms (Matt. 6:1-18). Those ideas had been proved occasions of offense, and therefore, for the present, the Teacher falls back upon a method of more exoteric instruction.

(12) Our Lord tells His disciples that they had some elements of that wisdom, and therefore, using their knowledge rightly, could pass on to more. The people, including even scribes and Pharisees, were as those that had few or none, and not using even the little that they had, were in danger of losing even that. The lesson is the same as that afterward developed in the parables of the Talents and the Pounds.

(14) In them is fulfilled.—The prominence given to these words of Isa. 6:9 in the New Testament is noticeable. (See John

12:40; Acts 28:26.) It is as though the words, which sounded at the opening of Isaiah's prophecy as the knell of the nation's life, dwelt on the minds of the Master and His disciples and prepared them for the seeming fruitlessness and hopelessness of their work (verses 13, 15).

(17) Many prophets and righteous men.— The prophets of Israel saw afar off the glory of the kingdom of the latter days. Comp. Heb. 11:16; I Pet. 1:10.

(19) When any one heareth the word.— The classes of hearers who had gathered around our Lord were represented, generally, by the four issues of the seed scattered by the sower. The first man hears a discourse on the kingdom, but does not understand it (the fault being moral rather than intellectual). The "wicked one" snatches it away even from his memory; "the birds of the air," in their rapid flight and their gathering flocks, may well represent the light and foolish thoughts that are as the tempter's instruments. The "wayside" thus answers to the character, which is hardened by the wear and tear of daily life, so that the words of Truth make hardly the most transient impression on it.

(20, 21) The second type of character stands in marked contrast with the first: rapid change, strong emotion, a quicker show of conversion than in the case where it is real. The "root" is obviously the conviction which ripens into a purpose and strikes its fibers deep down into reason, conscience, and will. "Anon" and "by and by" mean "immediately."

(22) The third character is not one that wastes its strength in vague emotions, but has the capacity for sustained effort. The evil here is that while there is strength of purpose, there is not unity of spirit. The man is double-minded, and would serve two masters.

(23) The fourth man discerns the meaning of the message. Here there are different degrees of the holiness which is symbolized by "bearing fruit," varying according to men's capacities and opportunities.

(25) His enemy came and sowed tares.— The act described was then a common form of Eastern malice or revenge. It easily escaped detection; it inflicted both loss and trouble. The tares, or darnel, grew up at first with stalk and blade like the wheat; and it was not until fructification began that the difference was easily detected. The seeds of the tares were not merely useless as food, but were positively noxious.

(31) The kingdom of heaven is like to a grain of mustard seed.—What we call mustard does not grow in the East into anything that can be called a tree. Probably, however, the name was used widely for any plant that had the pungent flavor of mustard. Here again the sower is the Son of Man; but the seed in this case is not so much the "word" as the Christian society, the Church, which forms the firstfruits of the word. It was sown in God's field of the world, and it was to grow until it became greater than any sect or school, a tree among the trees of the forest, a kingdom among other kingdoms. The "birds of the air" (no longer, as before, the emblems of evil)—i.e., the systems of thought, institutions, and the like, of other races—were to find refuge under its protection.

(33) The kingdom of heaven is like unto leaven.—The parable sets forth the working of the Church of Christ on the world, but not in the same way as that of the mustard seed. There the growth was outward, measured by the extension of the Church, dependent on its missionary efforts; here the working is from within. The "leaven"— commonly, as in the Passover ritual, the symbol of malice and wickedness (I Cor. 5:8)—causing an action in the flour with which it is mingled that is of the nature of decay and tends to actual putrescence, here becomes the type of influence for good as well as evil. It can permeate the manners, feelings, and opinions of societies until they become blessings and not curses to mankind. The **three** measures of meal admit of several references. The descendants of the three sons of Noah, as representing the whole of mankind, or body, soul, and spirit as the three parts of man's nature which the new truth is to permeate and purify, are equally legitimate applications.

(34) Without a parable spake he not unto them.—See Ps. 78:2. From this time forward parables are the dominant element in His teaching to the multitude, whereas the mysteries of the kingdom are reserved for the more esoteric instruction of the disciples.

(36) Declare unto us the parable of the tares of the field.—The question was asked privately, probably in the house of Peter, to which our Lord had retired with the disciples after the listening crowd upon the beach had been dismissed. It implies that the disciples had thought over the parable, and had found it harder to understand than those of the mustard seed and the leaven.

Primarily, the parable refers to the kingdom of heaven—i.e., to that new order of things which the Christ came to establish, and which is conveniently described as the Church which owns Him as its Lord. It offers, accordingly, an explanation of the presence of evil in that Church. There is the most distinct recognition of a personal power of evil, the enemy of God thwarting His work, who sowed the tares "while men slept." The time of danger for the Church is one of apparent security. Errors grow up and develop into heresies, carelessness passes into license, and offenses abound. The first impulse of zealous pastors of the Church is to clear the kingdom from evil by extirpating the doers of the evil. But to seek for the ideal of a perfect Church in that way may lead to worse evils than those it attempts to remedy. True wisdom is found, for the most part, in what might seem the policy of indifference: "Let both grow together until the harvest." That is the broad, salient lesson of the parable. (See Dan. 12:1-3, and notes on Matt. 8:12.)

(44) The kingdom of heaven is like unto treasure hid in a field.—Comp. Prov. 2:4. The salient points are the eagerness of the man to obtain the treasure and the sacrifice he is ready to make for it. The case described is that of a man who, not having started in the pursuit of holiness or truth, is brought by the seeming accidents of life—a chance meeting, a word spoken in season, the example of a living holiness—to the knowledge of the truth as it is in Jesus. Such, we may well believe, had been the history of the publicans and the fishermen who made up the company of the Twelve.

(45) Like unto a merchant man, seeking goodly pearls.—The caprices of luxury in the Roman empire had given a prominence to pearls as an article of commerce which they had never had before (comp. 7:6; I Tim. 2:9). Such a merchant seeking them, either on the shores of the Mediterranean, or as brought by caravans to other traders from the Persian Gulf or the Indian Ocean, must have been a familiar presence to the fishermen of Capernaum. The parable in its spiritual bearing has much that is common with the preceding, but there is this marked and suggestive difference: the "search" is presupposed. The man has been seeking the "goodly pearls" of wisdom, holiness, and truth, and has found them in the higher knowledge of communion with the life of Christ. For that he is content to resign all that he had before prized most highly.

(47) The kingdom of heaven is like unto a net.—The net in this case is not the hand net of 4:18, but the great dragnet, which drew in a larger haul of fishes. The day's teaching in the method of parables ends in an easy lesson, which the former experience of the disciples would enable them to understand. As in the parable of the tares, the main thoughts are the mingling of the evil with the good in the visible kingdom of Christ on earth, and the ultimate separation of the two, that each may receive according to the divine law of retribution.

(52) Therefore every scribe which is instructed unto the kingdom of heaven.—The verse is interesting as one of the few passages in which our Lord compares His own work and that of the apostles after Him to that of the scribes of the Jewish schools. That He was so regarded during His ministry is seen from the fact that men thought of Him as a rabbi no less than as a Prophet or as the Christ. But His method of training was altogether of another kind than that of the masters of the schools.

Things new and old.—Our Lord's own teaching was, of course, the highest example of this union. There were the old eternal laws of righteousness, the proclamation of the true meaning of all that every true teacher had included in the idea of duty and religion, but there were also new truths, such as His own mission as the Head of the divine kingdom and the future Judge of all men, and the work of the Spirit as regenerating and sanctifying. As the years passed, and new facts, such as the Crucifixion, Resurrection, and Ascension, supplied the groundwork for new doctrines, these also took their place in the storehouse of the well-instructed scribe. And the words applied also to the manner no less than to the substance of the teaching.

(54) When he was come into his own country.—We are compelled to admit the almost entire absence of any trustworthy notes of chronological sequence beyond the grouping, in some cases, of a few conspicuous facts. In comparing, however, this passage and Mark 6:1-6 with Luke 4:16-31, there seems no sufficient ground for hastily assuming identity. The circumstances of the case in Matthew's record suggests a different motive for this visit to Nazareth. He had recently, as in 12:48, when His mother and His brethren had come in their eager anxiety to interrupt His work, spoken in words that seemed to repel them to a distance from Him. This visit may have been meant to show that, though as a Prophet He could not tolerate that interruption, His heart still yearned over His brethren and His townsmen, and that He sought to raise them to a higher life.

(55) Is not this the carpenter's son?—In Mark the question appears as, "Is not this the carpenter?" It is probable that He both helped in the workshop during Joseph's life and assisted the "brethren" to carry on the work after his death. Justin Martyr (**Dial. c. Tryph.**, c. 88) relates that in his time articles said to have been made by Him, such as rakes and harrows, were in demand as relics. (Comp. apocryphal **Gospel of the Infancy**.)

(57) Comp. 11:6. They could not reconcile the new wisdom and the claim which the teaching implied with the obscurity and commonness of the earlier life, and so they did not believe. The proverb seems to have been one often on our Lord's lips, and obviously tells of a prolonged experience of indifference and unbelief in all their many forms.

14

(1) Herod the tetrarch was the son of Herod the Great by Malthace. Under his father's will he succeeded to the government of Galilee and Peraea, and as ruler of a fourth part of the Roman province of Syria. Herodias, the wife of his half-brother Philip (not the Tetrarch of Trachonitis, Luke 3:1, but son of Herod the Great by Mariamne), was daughter of Aristobulus, the son whom Herod put to death. Prompted partly by passion, partly by ambition, she left Philip and became the wife of Antipas (Jos. **Ant.** 18:5, §4). The marriage, at once adulterous and by the Mosaic law doubly incestuous, shocked the conscience of the stricter Jews. It involved Antipas in a war with the father of the wife whom he had divorced and dismissed, and it was probably in connection with this war that we read of soldiers on actual duty as coming under the teaching of the Baptist in Luke 3:14. The prophetic spirit of the Baptist, the very spirit of Elijah in his dealings with Ahab and Jezebel, made him the spokesman of the general feeling, and so brought him within the range of the vindictive bitterness of the guilty queen.

(2) This is John the Baptist.—The policy of the tetrarch connected him with the Sadducean priestly party rather than with the more popular and rigid Pharisees. His acceptance of the rumor is, then, every way remarkable. The superstitious terror of a conscience stained with guilt is stronger than his scepticism as a Sadducee, even though there mingled with it the wider unbelief of Roman epicureanism. To him the new Prophet, working signs and wonders which John had never worked, was but the reappearance of the man whom he had murdered.

(5) He feared the multitude.—Mark adds that Herod himself "feared John," knowing "him to be a just man and a holy," and was extremely perplexed. There was yet a struggle of conscience against passion in the weak and wicked tetrarch, as there was in Ahab in his relations with Elijah. In Herodias, as in Jezebel, there was no halting between two opinions, and she, in the bitterness of her hate, thirsted for the blood of the prophet who had dared to rebuke her guilt.

(7) He promised with an oath.—The scandalous chronicles of the time were not without stories of extravagant rewards paid to dancers, and Herod might fancy that in this also he was reproducing the magnificence of the imperial court at Rome. Her name is given by Josephus (**Ant.** 18:5, §4) as Salome.

(9) The king was sorry.—It was the last struggle of conscience. Had there been only the personal influence of Herodias, his conscience might have prevailed; but, like most weak men, Herod feared to be thought weak. (See note on 17:12.)

The accomplices of this deed of blood had a dismal future. When her brother, the young Agrippa, had obtained the title of king, through the favor of Caligula, Herodias, consistent in her ambition, stirred up her husband to seek the same honor. With this view she accompanied him to Rome; but they were followed by complaints from the oppressed Galileans, and the result was that he was deposed from his tetrarchy and banished to Gaul. She accompanied him there, faithful to his fallen fortunes, in spite of overtures from her brother to return to Judaea, and there they died (Jos. **Ant.** 18:7, §2). A tradition or legend relates that Salome's death was retributive in its outward form. She fell upon the ice, and in the fall her head was severed from the body.

(13) When Jesus heard of it.—The motives of this withdrawal were the strong personal emotion which the death of one whom Jesus had known and loved could not

715

fail to cause, the wish to avoid being the center of the popular excitement which the death of John was likely to cause, the return of the Twelve from their missionary circuit (Mark 6:30, 31; Luke 9:10) and their need for an interval of repose, and the Passover (John 6:4), for which feast all the roads of Galilee were thronged with companies of pilgrims hastening to Jerusalem.

Into a desert place.—In Mark's account the disciples sail after the feeding of the five thousand, to the other Bethsaida; and as this appears in John 6:17 to have been in the direction of Capernaum, the scene of the miracle must have been Bethsaida-Julias, on the northeast shore of the lake.

(15) The narrative that follows is, in many ways, one of the most important in the gospel narratives: (1) It is the only miracle recorded by all four evangelists. (2) It was the fullest manifestation of the sovereignty of the Son of man over the world of nature, i.e., it was an act of creative power. (3) No narrative of any other miracle offers so many marks of naturalness, both in the vividness of coloring with which it is told and the coincidences, clearly without design, which it presents to us. (4) The miracle was appropriate symbolically to the text of the dialogue at Capernaum (John 6), in which communion with the life of Christ was represented by the figure of eating the flesh of Him who is the true Bread from heaven.

(20) Twelve baskets full.—The basket here is the **cophinus**, a small basket carried in the hand, and often used by travelers to hold their food. (Comp. Juvenal, **Sat.** 3:14.) John, who gives the fullest account (see notes on John 6), records that the gathering was made by our Lord's express commands "that nothing be lost." The marvelous display of creative power was not to supersede forethought, thrift, economy in the use of the gifts it had bestowed. It is probable (Mark 6:37; John 13:29) that they were in the habit of distributing food to the poor in the villages and towns in which they preached, and the fragments were, we may believe, reserved for that use.

(21) Beside women and children.— Matthew is the only evangelist who mentions their presence, but all four use the word which emphasizes the fact that all five thousand were **men**. As the crowd had come in many cases from considerable distances, the women and children were probably few in number, were grouped together by themselves, and were not counted, so that the round number remained in men's minds without reference to them.

(22) Straightway Jesus constrained his disciples.—The people sought to seize Him and make Him a king against His will (John 6:14, 15), and He, shrinking from that form of sovereignty, withdrew from His disciples, dismissed the multitude, and on the mountain height passed the night in prayer. The disciples at His bidding were crossing to Bethsaida (Mark 6:45) on the western shore of the lake near Capernaum (John 6:17). It was as if in this stir of popular excitement—not against Him, but in His favor—this nearness to a path of earthly greatness instead of that which led onward to the cross, He saw something like a renewal of the temptation in the wilderness, needing special communion with His Father that He might once again resist and overcome it.

(25) In the fourth watch of the night.— The Jews, since their conquest by Pompeius, had adopted the Roman division of the night into four watches; and this was, accordingly, between 3 a.m. and 6 a.m., in the dimness of the early dawn. John adds, as if guarding against explanations that would minimize the miracle, that they were about twenty-five or thirty furlongs from the point from which they had started—i.e., as the lake was five miles wide, nearly three-fourths of the way across.

(28) The incident that follows is narrated by Matthew only. It may have been one which the apostle did not willingly recall, and which was therefore omitted by his disciple Mark and by his friend John, while Luke, writing as a compiler, came into the circle of those among whom it was seldom, if ever, mentioned. It is, however, eminently characteristic.

(32) Mark records, and gives a significant reason for, their astonishment: "For they reflected not on the loaves, for their heart was hardened." This was the later analysis which the disciples made of their feelings on that night. Had they understood all the divine creative energy which the miracle of the loaves involved, nothing afterward, not even the walking on the waves or the lulling of the storm, would have seemed startling to them.

(34) They came into the land of Gennesaret.—The name belonged to the western shore of the lake to which it gave one of its titles, and included Capernaum, to which (John 6:17, 24) the disciples were steering. The region was one of singular fertility (the name has been explained as meaning the

"Garden of Sharon"), and was then one of the most populous districts of Palestine.

(36) That they might only touch the hem of his garment.—See notes on 9:20-22.

15

(2) They wash not their hands when they eat bread.—Mark (7:3, 4), writing for Gentiles, explains the nature of the tradition more fully. What the Pharisees insisted on was not cleanliness as such, but the avoidance of ceremonial pollution. They shrank not from dirt, but from defilement. The pride which led them to stand aloof from the rest of mankind showed itself in this, as in all their other traditions. Indifference to their rules in peasants and fishermen, as such—as belonging to the crowd whom they scorned as the brute "people of the earth"—they could afford to tolerate. What shocked them was to see the disciples of One who claimed to be a prophet or a rabbi indulging in that indifference. According to their traditions, the act of which they complained stood on the same level as sexual impurity, and exposed those who were guilty of it to the excommunication of the Sanhedrin.

(3) By your tradition.—Our Lord's answer is an indirect one. He shows that their traditional casuistry was in direct opposition to the "commandment" of God, and the natural inference from that antagonism was that in itself, apart from the commandment, it had no binding authority as a rule of life.

(4) In our Lord's teaching, a lower, natural duty was to give way exceptionally to a higher and supernatural one (see note on 10:37); otherwise it remained in full force. In that of the Pharisees the natural duty, enforced by a direct divine commandment (see Exod. 20:12; 21:17), was made to give way to one which was purely human, arbitrary, and conventional. The two cases were not only not analogous, but stood on an entirely different footing.

(5) It is a gift.—Mark (7:11) gives the Hebrew term, Corban, which was literally applied to that which had been consecrated—theoretically to God, practically to the service or ornamentation of the Temple. The train of thought which led them to so startling a conclusion would seem to have been this: To divert to lower human uses that which has been consecrated to God is sacrilege, and therefore a man who turned

all his property into a Corban was bound not to expend it on the support even of his nearest relations. But the time of fulfilling the vow of consecration was left to his own discretion, and no one had a right to call him to account for delay. With this loophole, the Corban practice became an easy method of evading natural obligations.

(11) Not that which goeth into the mouth.—Up to this time the question had been debated indirectly. The scribes had been convicted of unfitness to speak with authority on moral questions. Now a great broad principle is asserted, which not only cut at the root of Pharisaism, but, in its ultimate tendency, swept away the whole Levitical system of ceremonial purity—the distinction between clean and unclean meats and the like. It went, as the amazement of the disciples showed (verses 12, 15, 16), far beyond their grasp as yet. Even those who sat at the feet of Jesus were slow to take in the thought that purity was inward and not outward, a spiritual and not a physical quality. (Comp. Acts 10:14.)

(13) Every plant, which my heavenly Father hath not planted.—The disciples could hardly fail to connect the words with the parable which they had heard so lately. The system and the men that they had been taught to regard as pre-eminently religious were, after all, in their Master's judgment, as the tares and not as the wheat (13:37, 38). As far as they were a sect or party, His Father had not planted them. They, too, were left, according to the teaching of that parable, to grow until the harvest, but their end was sure—they should be "rooted out." For the proverb of verse 14, comp. Luke 6:39; Rom. 2:19.

(15) Declare unto us this parable.—The answer shows that Peter's question referred to what seemed to him the strange, startling utterance of verse 11. It was significant that he could not as yet take in the thought that it was a truth to be received literally.

(21) Into the coasts of Tyre and Sidon.—Comp. Mark 7:31. Here we have the one recorded exception to the self-imposed law of His ministry which kept our Lord within the limits of the land of Israel. We may see a relation like that which afterward connected the vision of Peter at Joppa with his entry into the house of Cornelius at Caesarea. He was showing in act, as before in word (11:21), that He regarded Tyre and Sidon as standing on the same level as Chorazin and Bethsaida. The dust of the heathen cities was no more defiling than that of Capernaum. The journey from Capernaum to Tyre was one which might be made in one long day of active walking.

(22) A woman of Canaan.—The terms Canaanite and Canaan, which in the earlier books of the Old Testament were often applied in a wider sense to all the original inhabitants of what was afterward the land of Israel (Gen. 10:18; Judg. 1:10), were used more specifically of Phoenicia and its inhabitants (Exod. 3:8, 17; Ezra 9:1), and are employed here with that meaning.

O Lord, thou son of David.—The words show that the fame of the Prophet of Nazareth had traveled beyond the limits of Galilee (see Mark 7:24), and that He was known to the people of the Tyre and Sidon district by the most popular of the Messianic names. Luke 6:17 suggests a direct source of knowledge.

(24) I am not sent but unto the lost sheep of the house of Israel.—This was what had restrained Him. Those wandering sheep, without a shepherd, were the appointed objects of His care. Were He to go beyond that limit in a single case, it might be followed by a thousand, and then, becoming, as it were, before the time, the Apostle of the Gentiles, He would cease to draw to Himself the hearts of Israel as their Redeemer. (The centurion in 8:10 had built a synagogue and was practically, if not formally, a proselyte of the gate.)

(26) To cast it to dogs.—The word used was diminutive in its form, and as such pointed not to the wild, unclean beasts that haunt the streets of an Eastern city (Ps. 59:6), but to the tamer animals that were bred in the house and kept as pets. (Comp. Tobit 5:16.) The answer did not go beyond the language with which the woman must have been familiar, and indicated the line of demarcation which gave a priority to the claims of the family of Israel to those of strangers. We may well believe that there was no intentional scorn in it, though it emphasized an actual distinction.

(27) Truth, Lord: yet the dogs eat of the crumbs.—The woman catches at the form which had softened the usual word of scorn and presses the privilege which it implied. She did not ask that the "children" might be deprived of any fragment of their portion; but taking her place, contentedly, among the "dogs," she could still claim Him as her Master and ask for the "crumbs" of His mercy.

(28) O woman, great is thy faith.—The answer of the woman changed the conditions of the problem. Here again, as in the case of the centurion, our Lord found a faith greater than He had met with in Israel. The woman was a child of the faith, though not of the flesh, of Abraham (Rom. 4:16), and as such was entitled to its privileges.

(32) I have compassion on the multitude.—The obvious resemblance between the details of the narrative and that of the feeding of the five thousand has led some critics, who do not regard either as the record of a fact, to treat this as only another version of the same legend. The notes of distinctness are, however, too numerous to admit of that explanation: the number of the people fed, their three days' waiting until their food was exhausted, the number of the loaves at hand, and the baskets in which the fragments were collected after the meal. (The words rendered in both narratives by "basket" are not the same in the Greek. Here the word is **spuris**, the hamper in which provisions were packed as for a party traveling together, large enough—Acts 9:25—to hold a man; in the other it was the **cophinus**, or smaller basket, which a man carried in his hand.) Our Lord's words in 16:9, 10 distinctly recognize the two miracles, and connect the close of each with the word which was thus especially appropriate to it. It is significant that here, as so often before, the display of miraculous power in its highest form originates not in answer to a challenge, or as being offered as a proof of a divine mission, but simply from compassion.

(39) Into the coasts of Magdala.—The better MSS give the reading Magadan. The narrative implies that it was on the western shore of the lake. Mark gives Dalmanutha as the place where our Lord disembarked. This has been identified with a glen which opens upon the lake about a mile from Magdala.

16

(1) The Pharisees also with Sadducees.—The members of the latter sect do not elsewhere appear in our Lord's Galilean ministry. (Magdala, 15:39, was on the western shore of the lake.) The Herodians (Mark 8:15) were the Galilean Sadducees, and the union of the two hostile parties was the continuation of the alliance which had begun after our Lord's protest against the false reverence for the Sabbath, which was common to both parties (Mark 3:6).

That he would shew them a sign from heaven.—The signs and wonders that had been wrought on earth were not enough for the questioners. What they asked was a sign like Samuel's thunder from the clear blue sky (I Sam. 12:18), or Elijah's fire from heaven (I Kings 18:38).

(4) The sign of the prophet Jonas.—See notes on 12:39, 40.

(12) The doctrine of the Pharisees and of the Sadducees.—The leaven (verse 6) was "hypocrisy" (Luke 12:1), the unreality of a life respectable, rigid, outwardly religious, even earnest in its zeal, and yet wanting in the humility and love which are of the essence of true holiness. That of the Sadducees and of Herod, was, we may believe, the more open form of worldliness and self-indulgence which allied themselves with their denial of the Resurrection and therefore of eternal life.

(13) Caesarea Philippi.—Again crossing the lake (Mark 8:13), Jesus and the disciples came to the eastern Bethsaida (Mark 8:22), and from there to Caesarea Philippi. There is in all these movements an obvious withdrawal from the populous cities which had been the scene of His earlier labors, and which had practically rejected Him and cast in their lot with His enemies. This last journey took them to a district which He had apparently never before visited, and to which He now came, it would seem, not as a preacher of the kingdom, but simply for retirement and perhaps for safety.

Caesarea Philippi (so called to distinguish it from the town of the same name on the seacoast) does not appear in the history of the Old Testament. It lay at the foot of Hermon, near the chief source of the Jordan. (An old name of the city, Paneas, indicates its former dedication—under the Syrians—to the Greek god Pan.) Herod the Great built a temple there in honor of Augustus (Jos. *Ant.* 15:10, §3), and his son Philip the tetrarch (to whose province it belonged) enlarged and embellished the city, renaming it in honor of the emperor and to perpetuate his own memory. With the one exception of the journey through Sidon (Mark 7:31), it was the northern limit of our Lord's wanderings.

Whom do men say that I the Son of man am?—The question occupied a fitting place in the spiritual education through which our Lord was leading His disciples. It was a time of seeming failure and partial deser-

tion (John 6:66). And even the Twelve had shown signs of wavering (verse 8). It was time that they should be put to a crucial test, and the alternative of faith or want of faith pressed home upon their consciences.

(14) See 14:2; Luke 9:7; Mal. 4:5. The name of Jeremiah introduces a new train of legendary thought. It was said that the spirit of Jeremiah had passed into Zechariah (see Matt. 27:9), and on that assumption another reappearance might well seem probable. He, it was believed, had hidden the Ark, the Tabernacle, and the altar of incense, and was expected to come and guide the people to the place of concealment (II Macc. 2:1-7). He had appeared to Judas Maccabeus in a vision as guardian prophet of the people (II Macc. 15:13-16). As the prophet who had foretold the new covenant and the coming of the Lord our Righteousness (Jer. 23:6; 31:31) he was identified, as thoroughly as Isaiah, with the Messianic expectations of the people (See Dan. 7:13.)

(16) Thou art the Christ, the Son of the living God.—The confession was made by Peter, partly as the representative of the others, partly from the personal fervor of his character. His words recognized to the full our Lord's character as the Christ; they identified Him with the Son of man in Daniel's vision, and, more than this, they recognized in that Son of man one who was also not "a son" only, but, in some high incommunicable sense, "**the** Son of the living God."

(17) Blessed art thou, Simon Bar-jona.—We recognize in these words something like a tone of exalted joy. It is the first direct personal beatitude pronounced by Him; and, as such, it presents a marked contrast to the rebukes which had been addressed to Peter, as to the others, as being "without understanding," "of little faith," with "their heart yet hardened." Here He had found at last the clear, unshaken, unwavering faith which was the indispensable condition for the manifestation of His kingdom as a visible society upon earth. The beatitude is solemnized by His distinguishing between the old natural and the new supernatural life. (Comp. John 1:42; 21:15.)

Flesh and blood hath not revealed it unto thee.—The disciple had received the faith which he now professed, not through popular rumors, not through the teaching of scribes, but by a revelation from the Father. He was led, in the strictest sense of the words, through the veil of our Lord's human nature to recognize the divine.

(18) Thou art Peter, and upon this rock . . .—It seems clear that the connection between Peter and the rock (the words in the Greek differ in gender, **petros** and **petra,** but were identical in the Aramaic, which our Lord probably used) was meant to be brought into special prominence. **Petros** is a "stone" or fragment of rock, while **petra** is the rock itself. The Aramaic **Cepha,** it may be noted, has the former rather than the latter meaning. On the assumption of a distinction there follows the question, what is the rock? Was it Peter's faith (subjective), or the truth (objective) which he confessed, or Christ Himself? The facts of the case seem to favor the last view. Christ and not Peter is the Rock in I Cor. 10:4, the Foundation in I Cor. 3:11. The poetry of the Old Testament associated the idea of the Rock with the greatness and steadfastness of God, not with that of a man (Deut. 32:4, 18; Ps. 18:2, 31, 46; Isa. 17:10). Thus the Rock on which the Church was to be built was Himself, in the mystery of that union of the divine and the human which had been the subject of Peter's confession.

I will build my church.—This is the first occurrence of the word church (**ecclesia**) in the New Testament, and the only passage but one (18:17) in which it is found in the whole cycle of our Lord's recorded teaching. Its use was every way significant. It came, partly, with the associations which it had in the Greek of the Old Testament, as used for the "assembly" or "congregation" of the Lord (Deut. 18:16; 23:1; Ps. 26:12); and, partly, it brought with it the associations of politics. The **ecclesia** was the assembly of free citizens, to which belonged judicial and legislative power and from which aliens and slaves were alike excluded. The mere use of the term was, accordingly, a momentous step in the education of the disciples. They had been looking for a kingdom with the King as its visible Head, sitting on an earthly throne. They were told that it was to be realized in a society, a democratic assembly. Christ claims the work of building as His own. Whatever others may do, He is the supreme Master-builder. As in His sacerdotal character He is at once Priest and Victim, so under the aspect now presented He is at once the Founder and the Foundation of the new society.

The gates of hell shall not prevail against it.—The gates of **Hades,** not of Gehenna, the place of torment. Hades, as the shadow-world of the dead, the unseen counterpart of the visible grave, into whose gates all things human pass, and from which issue all forces that destroy is half-idealized, half-personified, as a power of death. (Comp. Isa. 38:10; Rev. 6:8.) And as the gates of the Eastern city were the scene at once of kingly judgment (II Sam. 15:2) and of the council of the elders (Prov. 31:23), they became the natural symbol of the polity which ruled there. Nothing in our Lord's teaching is more wonderful than the utterance of such a prophecy at such a time. It was a time of seeming failure; He was about to announce, with a clearness unknown before, His coming death as a malefactor; and yet it was at this moment that He proclaimed the perpetuity and triumph of the society which as yet existed only in the germs of a half-realized conception.

(19) I will give unto thee the keys of the kingdom of heaven.—The palace of a great king implied the presence of a chief officer as treasurer or chamberlain. Of this the key of office, the key of the gates and of the treasure, was the recognized symbol. In the highest sense that key of the house of David belonged to Christ Himself as the King. That power was now delegated to the servant whose very name, as an apostle, marked him out as his Lord's representative; and the subsequent history of Peter's work, when through him God "opened the door of faith unto the Gentiles" (Acts 14:27; 15:7), was the proof of his faithful discharge of the office assigned to him.

With this thought there was another, which in the latter clause of the verse becomes the dominant one. The scribes of Israel were thought of as stewards of the treasures of divine wisdom. When they were admitted to their office they received, as its symbol, the "key of knowledge" (Luke 11:52), which was to admit them to the treasure-chambers of the house of the interpreter, the **Beth-Midrash** of the rabbis. For this work the Christ had been training His disciples, and Peter now was qualified to be a "scribe instructed unto the kingdom of heaven . . ." (13:52). The "key" made him not a priest, but a teacher and interpreter. The words that follow as to "binding" and "loosing" were the formal confirmation in words of that symbolic act. They point primarily to legislative or interpretative functions, not to the judicial treatment of individual men. Here, too, the subsequent work of Peter was an illustration of the meaning of the words. When he resisted the attempt of the Judaizers to "put a yoke upon the neck of the disciples" (Acts 15:10), he was **loosing** what was also loosed in heaven. When he proclaimed, as in his epistle, the eternal laws of righteousness, holiness, and love, he was **binding** those laws on the conscience of Christendom. And the power was not given to Peter alone, but equally to all the apostles (see 18:18).

(20) Then charged he his disciples that they should tell no man.—Had the disciples gone about, not only as proclaiming the kingdom and as preachers of repentance, but sounding the watchword that the Christ had come, it might not have been difficult for them to gather around Him the homage of excited crowds. It was not such homage, however, that He sought, but that which had its root in a deeper faith.

(22) Peter took him, and began to rebuke him.—It is obvious that the mind of the disciple dwelt on the former, not the latter, part of the prediction (verse 21). The death was plain and terrible to him, for he failed to grasp the idea of the Resurrection. Personal love for his Lord, his own desire to share in the glory which that promise had implied, were united in his refusal to accept this as the issue toward which they were tending. The words of remonstrance were more than a prayer, as though his power to bind and to loose extended even to the region of his master's work and the means by which it was to be accomplished.

(23) Get thee behind me, Satan.—The sharpness of the words indicates a strong and intense emotion. The chief of the apostles was addressed in the same terms as those which had been spoken to the tempter (see note on 4:10). It was, indeed, nothing less than a renewal of the same temptation to gain the crown without the cross, and attain a kingdom of this world as the princes of the world obtain their kingdoms.

Thou savourest not the things that be of God.—Our savor and the French savoir are both forms derived from the Latin sapere, describing a mental state. The word is rendered "mind" in Rom. 8:5, and "set affection on" in Col. 3:2. Peter's sin lay in the fact that his mind was set on the things of earth, its outward pomp and pageantry, measuring the future by a human and not a divine standard.

(24) Let him deny himself, and take up his cross.—The man is to deny his whole self, all his natural motives and impulses, as far as they come into conflict with the claims of Christ. If he does not so deny

himself, he is in danger. The self-denial here commanded has, accordingly, its highest type and pattern in the Son of God (see Phil. 2:7). The words "take up his cross," which the disciples had heard before (see note on 10:38), were now clothed with a new and more distinct meaning by the words that spoke so clearly of the death of which the cross was to be the instrument.

(27) For the Son of man shall come.—The fact stands in a logical relation to verse 26. The fact that the Son of man is about to come to execute judgment clothes its abstract statement with an awful certainty. No bribe can be offered to the Eternal Judge to change the sentence of forfeiture if that forfeiture has been rightfully incurred. From first to last in our Lord's teaching this claim to be the future Judge of all men is never absent. It is asserted in every great discourse, implied in almost every parable.

(28) There be some standing here, which shall not taste of death . . .—The immediate sequence of the vision of the Son of man transfigured from the low estate in which He then lived and moved, into the "excellent glory" which met the gaze of the three disciples (17:2-8), is not the fulfillment of this prediction. The solution of the problem is to be found in the great prophecy of chap. 24. In a sense which was real, though partial, the judgment which fell upon the Jewish Church, the destruction of the Holy City and the Temple, the onward march of the Church of Christ, was the coming of the Son of man in His kingdom. His people felt that He was not far off from every one of them. He had come to them in "spirit and in power," and that advent was at once the earnest and the foreshadowing of the "great far-off event," the day and hour of which were hidden from the angels of God, and even from the Son of man Himself (Mark 13:32).

17

(1) After six days.—Luke's "about eight days" (Luke 9:28) may be noted as an example of the mode of reckoning which spoke of the interval between our Lord's death and Resurrection, about thirty-six hours, as three days. (See note on 12:39, 40.)

Peter, James, and John.—See notes on 9:23-26; II Pet. 1:13-16.

Into an high mountain.—The gospel narratives leave the locality altogether uncertain; but as Caesarea Philippi was the last place mentioned, and a journey through Galilee follows (Mark 9:30), it is probable that the scene is to be found on one of the heights of Hermon.

(2) And was transfigured before them.— Elsewhere the word is used in its spiritual sense and rendered "transformed." Luke adds the profoundly significant fact that this was while He was in the act of prayer. It was in that act of communion with His Father that the divine glory flowed out into visible brightness. Transcendent as the manifestation was, it has its lower analogies in Exod. 34:29; Acts 6:15. The Transfiguration was a stage in the training of the disciples. They had risen to the highest faith; they had been offended by the announcement of our Lord's rejection, His sufferings, His death. Something was needed which might sustain their faith, on which they might look back as the earnest of a future glory. For Him, too, this might have been a time of strength in preparation for the cross and passion. His form and features shine with a new glory, bright as the sun, as though the Shechinah cloud had wrapped around Him.

(3) Moses and Elias.—The identification of the forms which the disciples saw was, we may well believe, intuitive. In the state of consciousness to which they had been raised, they were capable of a spiritual illumination which would reveal to them who they were who were thus recognizing their Master's work and doing homage to His majesty. There was a singular fitness in each case. One was the great representative of the Law, the other of the whole goodly fellowship of the prophets. (See Deut. 18:18; Mal. 4:5; Gal. 3:24.) The close of the ministry of each was not after the "common death of all men" (Deut. 34:6; II Kings 2:11). Both were associated in men's minds with the glory of the kingdom of the Christ; and their presence now was an attestation that their work was over, and that the Christ had come.

(4) The words seem to imply an abounding joy at being thus brought into a glory which fulfilled the apostle's brightest hopes. His thoughts traveled back to the records of the Exodus, when the Lord talked with Moses in the Tabernacle (Exod. 33:7-10). Would not this be a better consummation than the shame and death at Jerusalem?

(5) A bright cloud overshadowed them.— See Exod. 33:9; I Kings 8:10. It was, in later Jewish language, the Shechinah, or

abiding presence of Jehovah. The form of the word connects it with both the Hebrew and the Greek words for tabernacle—the symbol that He was with His people. Its appearance at this moment, followed by the voice out of the cloud (comp. 3:17), was a witness that no tabernacle made with hands was now needed, that the humanity of Christ was the true tabernacle of God (John 1:14; Rev. 21:3).

(12) Elias is come already.—See verse 13. These words, the emphatic repetition of what had been said before in 11:14 (see note), is decisive as to the issue raised in verse 11. As far as the prophecy of Malachi required the coming of Elijah, that prophecy had been fulfilled in the Baptist. The disciples need not look for any other personal appearance. The use of the future tense in verse 11 points to a deeper truth, which they were to learn afterward. The Elijah ministry, the work of the preacher of repentance, is not a transient phenomenon belonging to one stage only of the Church's history, but was to be, throughout the ages and on to the end of all things, the indispensable preparation for the coming of the Lord.

But have done unto him whatsoever they listed.—It is significant that our Lord charges the guilt of the rejection and death of John upon the scribes and the people at large, with no special reference to the Tetrarch Antipas. The passions and intrigues of the palace were but instruments working out the intent of the Pharisees and Sadducees.

Likewise shall also the Son of man suffer of them.—This is another instance of what may be called the new color which from the time of the Transfiguration spreads over our Lord's teaching. All is darker, sadder, more somber. He is drawing nearer to the cross, and He brings the thought of the cross closer to the minds of the disciples.

(15) Lunatic.—See note on 4:24. The boy had a "dumb spirit" (Mark 9:17). Slowly, and as with difficulty, the seizure passed off, and the sufferer was wasting away under the violence of the attacks. The phenomena described are those of epilepsy complicated with insanity.

(17) O faithless and perverse generation.— The words were obviously addressed both to the scribes (Mark 9:14-16) and the disciples. Both had shown their want of the faith which utters itself in prayer to the Father; both were alike "perverse" in finding in the misery brought before them only an occasion of wrangling and debate. This was not the way to obtain the power to heal, and the formulae of exorcism were but as idle charms, without the faith of which they were meant to be the expression.

(20) If ye have faith as a grain of mustard seed.—The hyperbolical form of our Lord's words are repeated in 21:21. The "grain of mustard seed" was (13:31) the proverbial type of the infinitely little. To "remove mountains" was the proverbial type of overcoming difficulties that seemed insurmountable (see I Cor. 13:2).

Nothing shall be impossible unto you.—The words, absolute as they sound, are yet conditional. Nothing that comes within the range of faith in the wisdom and love of God, and therefore of submission to His will, is beyond the range of prayer.

(21) This kind goeth not out but by prayer and fasting.—The words imply degrees in the intensity of the forms of evil ascribed to demons amounting to a generic difference. The disciples did not as yet fast (9:14, 15), and the facts imply that they had been weak and remiss in prayer. The words are noticeable as testifying to the real ground and motive for "fasting," and to the gain for the higher life to be obtained, when it was accompanied by true prayer, by this act of conquest over the lower nature.

(24) They that received tribute money.—The word for tribute here is **didrachma**, and differs from that of verse 25 and 22:17. The latter is the **census**, or Roman poll tax (see Luke 2:2; Acts 5:37); the former was the Temple rate, paid by every male Israelite above the age of twenty (Exod. 30:13-16; II Chron. 24:9). It was fixed at a half-shekel a head. It was collected even from the Jews in foreign countries, was paid into the Corban, or treasury of the Temple, and was used to defray the expenses of its services. The three great festivals of the Jewish year were recognized as proper times for payment; and the relation of this narrative to John 7 makes it probable that the collectors were now calling in for the Feast of Tabernacles the payments that had not been made at the Passover or Pentecost previous. Their question implies that they thought the Prophet of Nazareth had evaded or would disclaim payment. They tracked Him, probably to Peter's house, and put the question to His disciple.

(26) Then are the children free.—The point which our Lord decides had been debated between the Pharisees and Sadducees. After a struggle of seven days in the Sanhedrin, the Pharisees carried their point regarding the Temple rate, made it (what it had not been before) a compulsory payment, and kept an annual festival in commemoration of their victory. Our Lord, placing the question on its true ground, pronounces judgment against the Pharisees on this as on other points. They were (like the state) placing the Israelites on the level of a "stranger," not of a "son." (The true law for "the children of the kingdom" was that which Paul afterward proclaimed in II Cor. 9:7.)

(27) Lest we should offend them.—Our Lord includes Himself and Peter among those who, as "children of the kingdom," might have claimed exemption. But those who had not learned the higher law of the free gift of love would be tempted to make their freedom an excuse for giving nothing. Devout and generous minds would be shocked at what would seem to them to cut off the chief support of the outward glory of the House of God. (Comp. Rom. 14:21.)

A piece of money.—The **stater** was reckoned as equal to four **drachmae**, and would therefore pay the **didrachma** both for Peter and his Master. We note, incidentally, the light which this throws on the poverty of our Lord and His disciples. They had returned from their wanderings in the north of Palestine, occupying some three or four weeks, and they were now absolutely penniless.

18

(1) Who is the greatest in the kingdom of heaven?—We may well believe that the promise made to Peter, and the special choice of the three for closer conversation, as in the recent Transfiguration, had given occasion for the rival claims which thus asserted themselves. Those who were less distinguished looked on this preference, it may be, with jealousy, while, within the narrower circle, the ambition of the two sons of Zebedee to sit on their Lord's right hand and on His left in His kingdom (Matt. 20:23) was ill-disposed to concede the primacy of Peter.

(2) Jesus called a little child unto him.—As the conversation was "in the house" (Mark 9:33), and the house probably was Peter's, the child may have been one of his. As in other like incidents (Matt. 19:13; 21:15, 16), we may discern in our Lord's act a recognition of the special beauty of childhood. A late tradition of the Eastern Church identified the child with Ignatius, Bishop of Antioch.

(3) Except ye be converted.—"Conversion" was not used in the definite sense of later religious experiences. What was needed was that they should "turn" from their self-seeking ambition, and regain, in this respect, the relative blamelessness of children.

Ye shall not enter into the kingdom of heaven.—The Twelve were disputing about precedence in the kingdom, and in that dispute they were showing that they were not truly in it. It was essentially spiritual, and its first condition was abnegation of self (verse 4). Even the chief of the apostles was self-excluded when he gloried in primacy.

(6) That a millstone were hanged about his neck.—Jerome states (in a note on this passage) that such was practiced in Galilee, and it is not improbable that the Romans had inflicted it upon some of the ringleaders of the insurrection headed by Judas of Galilee. Our Lord's words, on this assumption, would come home with a special vividness to the minds of those who heard them. The infamy of offending one of the "little ones" was as great as that of those whose crimes brought upon them this exceptional punishment. It was obviously a form of death less cruel in itself than many others, and its chief horror, both for Jews and heathen, was, probably, that it deprived the dead of all rites of burial.

(8, 9) See notes on 5:29, 30.

(10) In heaven their angels.—The words distinctly recognize the belief in guardian angels, entrusted each with a definite and special work. That guardianship is asserted in general terms in Pss. 34:7; 91:11; Heb. 1:14. Those who have the guardianship of the little ones assigned to them are among the most noble of the heavenly host. The work of the Son of man in saving that which was lost is given as the ground of the assertion of the special glory of the angels of the little ones. They are, in their ministry, sharers in His work, and that work is the highest expression of the will of the Eternal Father (verse 11).

(12) If a man have an hundred sheep.—The parable is repeated more fully in Luke 15:4-6. The fact that it reappears there is significant as to the prominence, in our Lord's thoughts and teaching, of the whole cycle of imagery on which it rests. The parable involves the claim on our Lord's part to be the true Shepherd, and suggests the thought that the "ninety and nine" are, strictly, the unfallen creatures of God's spiritual universe and, relatively, those among men who are comparatively free from gross offenses. On verse 14, comp. I Tim. 2:4.

(15) The dispute in which the teaching recorded in this chapter had originated implied that the unity of the society which was then represented by the Twelve had for the time been broken. Each of the disciples thought himself, in some sense, aggrieved by others. It is significant that the substance of the precept is taken from the passage in Leviticus (19:17, 18), which ends with "Thou shalt love thy neighbour as thyself." In the more excellent way which our Lord points out, a man would, by sacrificing the lower gain through going to law, attain the higher, and win for God and for himself the brother with whom he had been at variance.

(16) The principle of action is the same as before. The first point attempted is to be the reformation of the offender without the scandal of publicity. If personal expostulation failed, then the "one or two" were to be called in. (Comp. I Cor. 6:5.) If the end is attained through them, well; if not, then they are in reserve for the final stage as witnesses that every effort has been made in the spirit of a righteous friendship. See Deut. 19:15.

(17) Tell it unto the church.—The words point to the final measures for the reformation of the offender and the vindication of the divine law of righteousness. When the two forms of private remonstrance have failed, the case is to be brought before the society at large. The appeal is to be made not to the rulers of the congregation, but to the congregation itself, and the public opinion of the **ecclesia** is to be brought to bear upon the offender. Should he defy that opinion and persist in his evil-doing, he practically excommunicates himself. Comp. I Cor. 5:1-5; II Cor. 2:6, 7.

(18) Whatsoever ye shall bind on earth.—(See note on 16:19.) The promise before made to Peter is now extended not only to the other apostles, but to the whole society of which they were the representatives, and is to be understood as dependent on the same implied condition. As far as the **ecclesia** was true to its Lord, and guided by His Spirit, it was not to think that its decisions depended on any temporal power. They were clothed, as truth and righteousness are ever clothed, with a divine authority.

(19) Shall agree on earth.—The promise, as before, is dependent on implied conditions. Those who pray must be gathered together in the name of Christ (verse 20), i.e., as trusting to His intercession, asking a prayer which is not the utterance of the natural but the spiritual man, asking it in entire submission to the will of their Father in heaven.

(20) Where two or three . . .—The true meaning of the words is embodied in the well-known patristic axiom, **Ubi tres, ibi Ecclesia** ("Where three are, there is a church"). The strength of the Christian society was not to be measured by a numerical standard, but by its fulfillment of the true conditions of its life. The presence of Christ was as true and mighty, His communion with His Church as real, when His followers were but as a remnant, as when they were gathered in the great congregation.

(22) Seventy times seven.—The use of the symbolic numbers that indicated completeness was obviously designed to lead the mind of the questioner altogether away from any specially numerical standard. As there was no such limit to the forgiveness of God, so there should be none to that of man.

(24) Ten thousand talents.—The sum is evidently named in its vague vastness to indicate the immensity of the debt which man owes to God, the absolute impossibility of his ever clearing off the aggregate, ever-accumulating, of sins of omission and commission which are brought home to his conscience when God "takes account" with him.

(27) Was moved with compassion.—The teaching of the parable deals tenderly even with that impotent effort at justification by works ("I will pay thee all"—verse 26). The sinner is absolved, and the vast debt which he could never pay is forgiven freely. As far as he believes his Lord's assurance, he is now justified by faith.

(28) Which owed him an hundred pence.—The "hundred pence" are a hundred Roman **denarii**, a hundred days' wages of the laborer and soldier, enough to provide a meal for 2,500 men (John 6:7). But out Lord here is seeking more than simply a rhetorical antithesis between the infinitely great and the infinitely little. To the fishermen of Galilee the "hundred pence" would appear a considerable sum, and when they came to interpret the parable they would thus be led to feel that it recognized that the offenses which men commit against their brothers

may, in themselves, be many and grievous enough. It is only when compared with their sins against God that they sink into absolute insignificance.

(30) The debtor now appears as creditor. But the course he takes is as unwise as it is ungenerous. He, as a slave, cannot command his fellow slave to be sold. He can cast him into prison; but in so doing he cuts the debtor off from all opportunities of gaining the money by which he might pay his debt. The interpretation of the parable here is that whatever be the nature of the offense, patience and forbearance at once encourage and enable the offender to make restitution.

(31) They were very sorry.—The fellow servants are, in the inner meaning of the parable, those who are members of the same spiritual society. Our Lord appeals as by anticipation to the judgment which Christians in general would pass upon such conduct. He describes them not as being angry or indignant, but as "exceeding sorry." Sorrow, rather than anger, is the mood of the true disciple of Christ as he witnesses the sins against love which are the scandals of the Christian society. Anger, the righteous wrath against evil, belongs (verse 32) to the Lord and Judge.

(34) Delivered him to the tormentors.—The words seem deliberately vague. We may see in them the symbols of whatever agencies God employs in the work of righteous retribution: the stings of remorse, the scourge of conscience, the scorn and reproach of men, whatever elements of suffering lie in the life beyond the grave.

(35) Do also unto you.—The parable teaches that the debt may come back. If faith does not work by love, it ceases to justify.

From your hearts.—A verbal, formal forgiveness does not satisfy the demands of the divine righteousness. God does not so forgive; neither should man.

19

(1) He departed from Galilee.—The verse covers a considerable interval of time. From Luke 9:51-18:30 we get the outlines of what has been called our Lord's Peraean ministry; from John 7:2 and 10:22, His visit to Jerusalem at the Feast of Tabernacles and again at that of Dedication. The journey from Galilee to Peraea appears (Luke

17:11) to have led our Lord through Samaria.

(3) Is it lawful for a man to put away his wife for every cause?—See note on 5:32. As far as the teaching of the Sermon on the Mount had become known, it gave a sufficiently clear answer to the inquiry of the Pharisees. It is, however, quite conceivable that it had not reached the ears of those who now put the question, or, that if it had, they wished to test His consistency, and to see whether on this point He still held with the stricter rule of Shammai, and not with the laxer rule of Hillel. If the narrative of the woman taken in adultery in John 8:1-11 is rightly placed (see notes), that might have given rise to doubts and rumors. In any case, they might hope to bring Him into conflict either with the stricter or the more popular school of casuists. The Jewish historian Josephus records how he had divorced two wives on grounds comparatively trivial (**Life,** c. 75, 76), and speaks incidentally in his history of "many causes of all kinds" as justifying separation (**Ant.** 4:8, § 23). Here in Peraea, the Herodian party might count either on the Teacher shrinking from expressing His convictions, or so uttering them as to provoke the Tetrarch Antipas' wrath, as the Baptist had done. In either case, a point would have been gained against Him.

(6) What therefore God hath joined.— Strictly interpreted, the words go further than those of 5:32, and appear to forbid divorce under all circumstances. They are, however, rather the expression of the principle that should underlie laws, than the formulated law itself, and, as such, they assert the true ideal of marriage without making provision (such as was made before) for that which violates and annuls the ideal. (See Gen. 1:27; 2:24; Eph. 5:31.) The essence of the marriage is made to depend not on laws, contracts, or religious ceremonies, but on the natural fact of union. Strictly speaking, that constitutes, or should constitute, marriage. The sin of all illicit intercourse is that it separates that union from the relations and duties which the divine order has attached to it, and makes it simply minister to the lusts of man's lower nature. The evil of every system that multiplies facilities for divorce is that it treats as temporary what was designed to be permanent. This may, in some stages of social progress, as the next verses indicate (see Deut. 24:1), be the least of two evils; but it does not cease to be an evil.

(8) Moses because of the hardness of your hearts.—The force of the answer lies in emphasized substitution of "suffered" ("permitted") for "commanded." Our Lord agreed with the ideal of marriage maintained by the followers of Shammai. He accepted as a legitimate interpretation of the Law that of the followers of Hillel. But He proclaimed, with an authority greater than that of Moses, that his legislation on this point was a step backward when compared with the primary law of nature, which had been "from the beginning," and only so far a step forward because the people had fallen into a yet lower state, in which the observance of the higher law was practically impossible. But for the possibility of divorce the wife would have been the victim of the husband's tyranny; and law, which has to deal with facts, was compelled to choose the least of two evils.

(9) Whosoever shall put away his wife.— Unlike in 5:32, here we have a statement bearing on the position of the husband in such a case: he by contracting another marriage "commits adultery." The legislation which permits the complete divorce on other grounds, such as cruelty or desertion on either side, is justified, as far as it is justifiable at all, on the ground of the "hardness of heart" which makes such a concession necessary. Comp. Paul's treatment of cases which the letter of this command did not cover (I Cor. 7:10-15).

(11) All men cannot receive this saying.— Reference is to the comment of the disciples in verse 10. Looking at marriage from a simply selfish point of view, and therefore with an entirely inadequate estimate of its duties on the one hand, and on the other of the temptations incident to the unmarried life when chosen on such grounds, they had come rashly to the conclusion that, if our Lord's rule held good, it was not expedient to marry. He declares that judgment to be false. There were but few (verse 12) who were capable of acting safely on that conclusion. The motives which Paul states as determining his own choice of the celibate life (I Cor. 7:7), or the counsel which he gave to others (I Cor. 7:32-34), are identical with this teaching in their principle.

(13) Then were there brought unto him little children.—Luke (18:15) uses a word which implies infancy. The fact that they were "brought" indicates that there was something in our Lord's look and manner that attracted children, and impressed their parents with the feeling that He loved them.

The motives of the disciples in rebuking those who brought them may be connected with what they had just heard from their Master's lips. What interest, they might have thought, could He have in these infants, when He had in those words appeared to claim a special dignity and honor for those "eunuchs" for the kingdom's sake?

(15) He laid his hands on them.—Mark records an act of caressing tenderness. Our Lord's words and action justify the Church of Christ at large in commending infants to the blessing of their Father.

(16) Behold, one came and said . . .—The man was, like Nicodemus, "a ruler of the Jews" (Luke 18:18), i.e., probably, a member of the Sanhedrin, like Joseph of Arimathaea. He was, beside this, conspicuously rich, and of high and ardent character. There is one other case in the first two gospels which presents similar phenomena leading some commentators to suggest that the man was Lazarus. (Comp. Mark 14:3; Luke 10:42; John 11:19, 24, 12:3.)

That I may have eternal life.—The question exhibits the highest and noblest phase of Pharisaism. The seeker has a firm belief in something that he knows as "eternal life." He thirsts for it eagerly. He believes that it is to be won, as a perpetual inheritance (Luke 18:18), by some one good deed of exceptional and heroic goodness. The Teacher has left on him the impression of a goodness such as he had seldom, if ever, seen before, and as being therefore able to guide him to the Supreme Good.

(17) Why callest thou me good?—The questioner had lightly applied the word "good" to One whom he has yet regarded only as a human teacher, to an act which, it seemed to him, was in his own power to perform. What he needed, therefore, was to be taught to deepen and widen his thoughts of goodness until they rose to Him in whom alone it was absolute and infinite, through fellowship with whom only could any teacher rightly be called good, and from whom alone could come the power to do any good thing.

Keep the commandments.—The questioner is answered as from his own point of view. If eternal life was to be won by doing, there was no need to come to a new Teacher for a new precept. It was enough to keep the commandments, the great moral laws of God, as distinct from ordinances and traditions (15:3), with which every Israelite was familiar.

(21) Jesus said unto him . . .—Mark (10:21) adds the striking words, "Jesus . . . loved him." There was something in the young seeker after holiness which drew to him, in a measure altogether exceptional, the affection of the Great Teacher. The same word is used in regard to him which is used in relation to the "disciple whom Jesus loved," and to Lazarus, Martha, and Mary (John 11:5).

Go and sell that thou hast.—It would be altogether a mistake to see in this an obligation binding on all seekers after eternal life. It was strictly a remedy for the special evil which hindered the young ruler's progress to perfection, applicable to others as far only as their cases are analogous.

(22) He went away sorrowful.—He shrank from the one test which would really have led him to the heights of holiness at which he aimed. Yet the sorrow, though it was a sign of the weakness of one whose heart was not yet whole with God, was not without an element of hope. A mere worldling would have smiled with cynical contempt, as the Pharisees did when they heard words of a like tendency (Luke 16:14). Here there was at least a conflict.

(23) Shall hardly enter.—Literally, "shall not easily enter." The words imply not so much the mere difficulty as the painfulness of the process. Here, as elsewhere, the "kingdom of heaven" is not the state of happiness after death, but the spiritual life and the society of those in whom it is realized even upon earth.

(24) It is easier for a camel to go through the eye of a needle.—The fact that in some Syrian cities the narrow gate for foot passengers, at the side of the larger gate, by which wagons, camels, and other beasts of burden enter the city, is known as the "needle's eye" has been assumed to have come down from a remote antiquity, and our Lord's words are explained by some as alluding to it. But the Talmud gives the parallel phrase of an **elephant** passing through a needle's eye, and the Koran reproduces the very words of the gospel. There is no reason to think that the comparison, even if it were not already proverbial, would present the slightest difficulty to the minds of the disciples. Like all such comparisons, it states a general fact— the hindrance which wealth presents to the higher growths of holiness—in the boldest possible form.

(26) With men this is impossible.— General as the words are in their form, we cannot help feeling that they must have seemed to the disciples to have rebuked their hasty judgment, not only as to the conditions of salvation generally, but as to the individual case before them. Their wider teaching is that wealth, though bringing with it many temptations, may be so used, through God's grace, as to be a help, not a hindrance, in that deliverance from evil which is implied in the word "salvation" (verse 25).

(27) Behold, we have forsaken.—The question betrayed the thoughts that had been working in the minds of the disciples. They had complied with their Master's commands; what were they to have as the special reward to which they were thus entitled? It is obvious that in asking for that reward they showed that they had complied with the letter only, not with the spirit, of the command. They had not, in the true sense of the word, denied themselves, though they had forsaken the earthly calling and the comforts of their home; and they were dwelling on what they had done, as in itself giving them a right to compensation.

(28) In the regneration.—There is to be a "new birth" for mankind as well as for the individual (Tit. 3:5). The sorrows through which the world was to pass were to be as the travail pangs of that passage into a higher life. (See 24:8.) Beyond them there lay the times of the "restitution of all things" (Acts 3:21), the coming of the victorious Christ in the glory of His kingdom. In that triumph the Twelve were to be sharers. Comp. the apocalyptic imagery of Dan. 7:14, 27; Rev. 4:4; 7:4. What approximations to a literal fulfillment there may be in the future lies behind the veil. They receive at least an adequate fulfillment if we see in them the promise that, in the last triumphant stage of the redeeming work, the apostles should still be recognized and honored as guiding the faith and conduct of their countrymen (see Rev. 21:14). The thought on which Paul dwells, that the "saints shall judge the world" (I Cor. 6:2), in like manner refers not only to any share which the disciples of Christ shall have in the actual work of the final judgment, but to the assured triumph of the faith, the laws, the principles of action of which they were then the persecuted witnesses.

(29) The disciples' claim to a special privilege and reward was at least indirectly rebuked. Not for them only, but for all who had done or should hereafter do as they did, should there be a manifold reward. But the act of forsaking home and wealth must

not originate in a far-sighted calculation of reward; it must proceed from devotion to a Person and a cause, must tend to the furtherance of the Gospel and the establishment of the divine kingdom. This spirit of insight and self-sacrifice for the sake of God's kingdom multiplies and intensifies even the common joys of life.

20

(1) The division of the chapter is here singularly unfortunate. We can scarcely understand it at all unless we connect it with the history of the young ruler who had great possessions, and the claims which the disciples had made for themselves when they contrasted their readiness with his reluctance.

Interpreting the parable, we may see in the householder our Lord Himself (comp. 10:25; 13:27, 52). And the "vineyard" is primarily the house of Israel, which the Anointed of the Lord had come to claim as His kingdom (comp. Isa. 5:1). The "early morning" answered accordingly to the beginning of our Lord's ministry; the "labourers" He then called were the disciples whom, at the outset of His ministry, He had summoned to follow Him. He had promised them a reward. Though at best they were unprofitable servants, He yet offered them wages, and the wages were the kingdom of heaven itself (5:3, 10).

(2) A penny a day.—The "penny"—i.e., the Roman **denarius**—was then the common standard of value in Palestine. It represented in its purchasing power, the average price of the unskilled labor of the tiller of the soil.

(3, 4) The Jewish day began at 6 a.m. The "market place" of a town was the natural place in which the seekers for casual labor were to be found waiting for employment. The absence of a definite contract in hiring the laborers who did less than the day's work obviously involved an implicit trust in the equity of the householder.

(6) About the eleventh hour.—The working day, which did not commonly extend beyond twelve hours (John 11:9), was all but over, and yet there was still work to be done in the vineyard, all the more urgent because of the lateness of the hour. The laborers who had been first hired were not enough. Is there not an implied suggestion that they were not laboring as zealously as they might have done? They were working on their contract for the day's wages.

(8) See 19:30; Deut. 24:15.

(9) Every man a penny.—The standard of payment was qualitative, not quantitative. In the interpretation of the parable, the "penny" represents the eternal life of the kingdom of heaven. No true laborer could receive less; the longest life of labor could claim no more.

(10) But when the first came, they supposed that they should have received more.—The disciples must have seen their own thoughts reflected in the parable. They too had been expecting to receive more. Eternal life was not enough for them, without some special prerogative and precedence over others.

(13) I do thee no wrong.—The answer of the householder is that of one who is just where claims are urged on the ground of justice, generous where he sees that generosity is right. Had the first-called laborers shared this generosity, they would not have grudged the others the wages that they themselves received, and would have found their own reward in sympathy with their joy. This is true when we pass to the spiritual interpretation of the parable. No disciple who had entered into his Master's spirit would grudge the repentant thief his rest in Paradise (Luke 23:43).

(16) So the last shall be first.—This, then, is the great lesson of the parable, and it answers at once the question whether we are to see in it an absolute equality in the blessedness of the life to come. There also there will be some first, some last, but the difference of degree will depend not on the duration of service, nor even on the amount of work done, but on the temper and character of the worker.

For many be called, but few chosen.—See note on 22:14. The better MSS omit it here.

(17) And Jesus going up to Jerusalem.—The narrative is not continuous, and in the interval between verses 16 and 17 we may probably place the events of John 10:40-11:54. These would seem to have been followed by a return to Peraea, and then the journey to Jerusalem begins. "Jesus went before them." It was as though the burden of the work on which He was entering pressed heavily on His soul, and therefore He needed solitude that He might prepare Himself for the sacrifice by communing with His Father. Instead of journeying with the disciples, He went on silently in advance.

(20) Then came to him the mother of Zebedee's children.—The mother of James and John was among those who "thought that the kingdom of God should immediately appear" (Luke 19:11); and probably the promise that the Twelve should sit on thrones judging the twelve tribes of Israel (19:28) had fastened on her thoughts, to the exclusion of those words which spoke of suffering and death. And so, little mindful of the teaching of the parable they had just heard, they too expected that they should receive more than others, and sought that they might be nearest to their Lord in that "regeneration" which seemed to them so near.

(21) The one on thy right hand.—The favor which had already been bestowed might, in some degree, seem to warrant the petition. (Comp. 16:23; 17:1; Mark 3:17; John 13:23; 19:26; 20:2.) The mother might well think that she was but asking for her sons a continuance of what they had heretofore enjoyed.

(22) To drink of the cup that I shall drink of.—That nearness to Him in His glory could be obtained only by an equal nearness in suffering. There can be little doubt that any reader of the Old Testament would at once recognize "the cup" as the symbol of a good or evil fortune. (Comp. Ps. 23:5; Jer. 25:15; Ezek. 23:33.) The meaning of the "baptism" was, perhaps, less obvious, but our Lord Himself had already used it in dim mysterious reference to His coming passion (Luke 12:50). There was enough, then, to lead them to see in their Master's words an intimation of some great suffering about to fall on Him, and this, indeed, implied in the form of their answer. That their insight into the great mystery of the passion went but a little way as compared with their Master's, lies, of course, in the nature of the case.

(23) Is not mine to give.—Our Lord does not say that it does not belong to Him to give what the disciples asked, but that He could give it only according to His Father's will and the laws which He had fixed. Considered as a prediction, there was a singular contrast in the forms of its fulfillment in the future of the two brothers. James was the first of the whole company of the Twelve to pass through the baptism of blood (Acts 12:2). For John was reserved the weariness and loneliness of an old age surviving the great storm of persecution which raged throughout the empire under Nero and Domitian.

729

To them for whom it is prepared of my Father.—See 25:34. The highest places in the kingdom must be reserved for those who do Christlike deeds of love.

(24-27) This was an indignation worthy of true followers of Jesus. The popular Jewish expectations, shared by the disciples, were really heathen in their character, substituting might for right, and ambition for the true greatness of service.

(28) Not to be ministered unto.—The words found a symbolic illustration when our Lord, a few days afterward, washed the feet of the disciples who were still contending about their claims to greatness (John 13:3, 4).

To give his life a ransom for many.—The word rendered "ransom" is primarily "a price made for deliverance," and in this sense it is found in the LXX for "the ransom" which is accepted instead of a man's life (Exod. 21:30; Prov. 13:8.) Those who heard could attach no other meaning to it than that He who spake to them was about to offer up His life that others might be delivered. It is the first distinct utterance of the plan and method of His work. He had spoken before of "saving" the lost (18:11); now He declares that the work of "salvation" was to be also one of "redemption." It could be accomplished only by the payment of a price, and that price was His own life. (Comp. Rom. 3:24; I Cor. 6:20; I Tim. 2:6; I Pet. 1:19.) The preposition "for" means "instead of," "in the place of," implying that our Lord's death was, in some way, representative and vicarious.

(30) Behold, two blind men sitting.—Mark agrees with Matthew as to time and place, but speaks of **one** blind man only, and gives his name as "Bartimaeus, the son of Timaeus." Luke speaks of one only, and fixes the time of the miracle at our Lord's entry into Jericho. The probable explanation is that of the two men, the one whom Mark names was the more conspicuous and better known, and that Luke, visiting the scene and having the spot pointed out to him outside the gates of the city, was left to conjecture. But it is possible, again, that Luke's local inquiries may have made his narrative more accurate than the recollection on which Matthew's and Mark's rested.

21

(1) And when they drew nigh unto Jerusalem.—Crowds of pilgrims were drawn to the Holy City either by the coming Passover or by wonder and curiosity to see what part the Prophet of Nazareth would take. Throughout the multitude there was a feverish expectation that He would at last announce Himself as the Christ and claim His kingdom (Luke 19:11).They reach Bethany "six days before the Pessover," probably on the Friday afternoon (John 12:1). They remain there for the Sabbath, probably in the house of Lazarus or Simon the leper (John 12:2; there we have the history of the anointing, which Matthew relates out of its chronological order—26:6-13). The narrative opens at the dawn of the first day of the week, the daybreak of Palm Sunday.

Bethphage.—The name signified "the house of unripe figs," as Bethany did "the house of dates," and Gethsemane "the oil-press," the three obviously indicating local features giving distinctness to the three sites. All three were on the Mount of Olives.

Two disciples.—The messengers are not named in any of the gospels. The fact that Peter and John were sent on a like errand in Luke 22:8 makes it probable that they were employed in this instance.

(2) An ass tied, and a colt with her.—Mark and Luke name the "colt" only. The command clearly implies a deliberate fulfillment of the prophecy cited in verses 4 and 5. They were to claim the right to use the beasts as for the service of a king, not to hire or ask permission.

(5) Tell ye the daughter of Sion.—See Zech. 9:9, 10. The words paint the ideal King coming not with "chariot" and "horse" and "battle bow," like the conquerors of earthly kingdoms, but as a prince of peace, reviving the lowlier pageantry of the days of the Judges (Judg. 5:10; 10:4; 12:14), and yet exercising a wider dominion than David or Solomon had done. That ideal our Lord claimed to fulfill. Thus interpreted, His act was in part an apparent concession to the fevered expectations of His disciples and the multitude, in part also a protest against the character of those expectations and the self-seeking spirit which mingled with them.

(8) And a very great multitude.—Part of the crowd had come with Him from Gaililee; part streamed from Bethany, excited by the recent resurrection of Lazarus (John 12:17). As they advanced they were met by a fresh crowd pouring forth from Jerusalem. Of the latter, John records that they came out with palm branches in their hands, as if to salute a king with the symbols of his triumph. (Comp. Rev. 7:9.)

Spread their garments in the way.—This, again, was a recognized act of homage to a king. (Comp. II Kings 9:13; AEschylus, **Agamemnon**, 891.)

(9) Hosanna.—The word was a Hebrew imperative, "save us, we beseech thee," and had come into liturgical use from Ps. 118. That Psalm belonged especially to the Feast of Tabernacles, and as such was naturally associated with the palm branches; the verses from it now chanted by the people are said to have been those with which the inhabitants of Jerusalem welcomed the pilgrims who came up to keep the feast. The addition of "Hosanna to the Son of David" made it a direct recognition of the claims of Jesus to be the Christ; that of "Hosanna in the highest" (comp. Luke 2:14) claimed heaven as in accord with earth in this recognition.

(12) And Jesus went into the temple.—John 2:13-25 records an act of like nature as occurring at the beginning of our Lord's ministry on the first visit to Jerusalem after His baptism. Both narratives are true. If Jesus of Nazareth had been only a patriot Jew, filled with an intense enthusiasm for the holiness of the Temple, what was more likely than that He should begin His work with a protest against its desecration? If the evils against which He thus protested, after being suppressed for a time, reappeared in all their enormity, what was more probable than that He should renew the protest at this stage of His work, backed as He now was by the equal enthusiasm of the people? There is, admittedly, a real difficulty in the omission of the earlier cleansing by the three, and in the absence of any reference to the later cleansing by the fourth; but the fact in either case is only one of many like facts incident to the structure of the gospels.

Cast out all them that sold and bought in the temple.—Pilgrims came from all parts of the world to keep the Passover, to offer their sacrifices, sin-offerings, or thank-offerings, according to the circumstances of each case. They did not bring the victims with them. What plan could be more convenient than that they should find a market (i.e., one of the courts of the Temple) where they could buy them as near as possible to the place where the sacrifice was to be offered? The pilgrims brought with them the coinage of their own countries, and their money was either not current in Palestine, or, as being

stamped with the symbols of heathen worship, could not be received into the Corban, or treasury of the Temple. For their convenience, therefore, moneychangers were wanted, who, of course, made the usual profit on each transaction.

(13) It is written.—See Isa. 56:7; Jer. 7:11. Palestine was then swarming with bands of outlaw brigands, who, as David of old in Adullam (I Sam. 22:1), haunted the limestone caverns of Judaea. The wranglings of such a company over the booty they had carried off were reproduced in the Temple, and mingled with the Hallelujahs of the Levites and the Hosannas of the crowds.

(15) The chief priests.—These, as commonly in the gospels, were the heads of the twenty-four courses of the priesthood, as well as Annas and Caiaphas, who were designated by the title in its higher sense, the one as actually high priest, the other as president of the Sanhedrin. (See note on Luke 3:2.)

(16) Have ye never read?—In this instance He cites the words of Ps. 8:2, the primary meaning of which appears to be that the child's wonder at the marvels of creation is the truest worship. As applied by our Lord their lesson was the same. The cries of the children were the utterance of a truth which the priests and scribes rejected.

(18) In the morning.—The word implies "daybreak," probably about 5 a.m. This was the usual Jewish time for the first food of the day. The greater part of the night had been spent either in solitary prayer or in converse with the disciples (Luke 21:37; John 18:1).

(19) He came to it.—Commonly at the beginning of April the trees that still grow out of the rocks between Bethany and Jerusalem are bare both of leaves and fruit, and so probably it was now with all but the single tree which attracted our Lord's notice. It was in full foliage, and being so far in advance of the others it might naturally have been expected to have had, in the first week of April, the "first ripe fruit" (Hos. 9:10), which usually was gathered in May. Luke 21:29, 30 suggests that the season was a somewhat forward one. (See note on Mark 11:13.)

Let no fruit grow on thee henceforward forever.—The words assume the character of a solemn judgment passed not so much on the tree as on that of which it became the representative. The Jews, in their show of the "leaves" of outward devotion, in the absence of the "fruits" of righteousness, were as that barren tree. The sentence which He now passed on the tree, and its immediate fulfillment, were symbols of the sentence and the doom which were about to fall on the unrepentant and unbelieving people. (Comp. the parable of Luke 13:6-9, and note the sentence then deferred as if in the hope of possible amendment.)

(21) If ye have faith, and doubt not.—The phrase to "remove mountains" (as in I Cor. 13:2) was a natural hyperbole for overcoming difficulties, and our Lord in pointing to "this mountain"—as He had done before to Hermon (17:20)—did but give greater vividness to an illustration which the disciples would readily understand. The hyperbole is used here, as elsewhere, to impress on men's mind the truth which lies beneath it.

(22) All things, whatsoever ye shall ask in prayer.—Here again there is the implied condition (7:7) that what is asked is in harmony with the laws and will of God. If it were not so it would not be asked in faith, and every true prayer involves the submission of what it asks to the divine judgment. The words suggest the thought (see John 11:42) that our Lord's miracles were less frequently wrought by an inherent supernatural "virtue" than by power received from the Father, and in answer to His own prayers.

(23) By what authority . . . ?—The right to take the place of an instructor was, as a rule, conferred by the scribes on one who had studied "at the feet" of some great teacher and been solemnly admitted (the delivery of a key, as the symbol of the right to interpret, being the outward token) to that office. The questions implied that those who asked it knew that the Prophet of Nazareth had not been so admitted.

(24-27) He challenges their right to interrogate Him on the ground of precedent. Had they exercised that right in the case of the Baptist, and if so, with what result? If they had left his claim unquestioned, or if they had shrunk from confessing the result of their inquiry, they had virtually abdicated their office and had no right, in logical consistency, to exercise it in the case of another teacher. Before such a tribunal the Prophet whom they called in question might well refuse to plead.

(28) Go work to day in my vineyard.—Both of those who are called to work are "sons," and not hired laborers—i.e., there is a recognition of both Pharisees and publicans, the outwardly religious and the conspicuously irreligious, as being alike, in a sense children of God.

(29) I will not.—The bold defiance of the answer answers to the rough recklessness of the classes (publicans and harlots) who were represented by the "first" of the two sons. Their whole life, up to the time of their conversion, had been an open refusal to keep God's laws, and so to work in His vineyard.

(30) I go, sir.—The tone of outward respect, as contrasted with the rude refusal of the elder son, is eminently characteristic as representing the surface religion of the Pharisees.

(31) They say unto him, The first.—The answer came apparently from the lips of the persons who were self-condemned by it, and so implied something like an unconsciousness that they were described in the person of the second son.

(32) Repented not afterward.—The words are repeated from the parable (verse 29) and sharpen its application. In relation to the preaching of the Baptist, the scribes and Pharisees were like the first of the two sons in his defiant refusal; they were not like him in his subsequent repentance.

(33) Which planted a vineyard.—The frequent recurrence of this imagery at this period of our Lord's ministry is significant. (Comp. 20:1, 21:28; Luke 13:6.) The parable points in the very form of its opening to the great example of the use of that image in Isa. 5:1. Taking the thought there suggested as the key to the parable, the vineyard is "the house of Israel"; the "fence" finds its counterpart in the institutions which made Israel a separate and peculiar people; the "wine press," in the Temple, is that into which the "wine" of devotion, thanksgiving, and charity was to flow; the "tower" (a place of observation and defense against the attacks of plunderers; comp. Isa. 1:8) represents Jerusalem and the outward polity connected with it. So, in like manner, the letting out to husbandmen and the going "into a far country" answer historically to the conquest by which the Israelites became possessors of Canaan, and were left, as it were, to themselves to make what use they could of their opportunities.

(34) When the time of the fruit drew near.—We see here the expectation that the developed life of Israel should be worthy of its calling, and the mission of the prophets who, as the servants of Jehovah, were sent from time to time to call the people to bring forth the fruits of righteousness.

(35, 36) The language paints the general treatment of the prophets, Isaiah, Jeremiah, Zechariah the son of Jehoiada being the most conspicuous instances. The language of our Lord in 23:30, 34, no less than that of Heb. 11:37, implies that the prophets, as a class, had no light or easy task, and were called upon, one by one, to suffer persecution for the faithful exercise of their office.

(37) Comp. Mark 12:6; Luke 20:13. Deliberation and doubt are evidently inapplicable, except by a bold anthropomorphism, to divine acts, but they set forth (1) the gradually ascending scale of those who were sent, culminating in a difference not of degree only, but of kind, like the contrast between the prophets and the Son in Heb. 1:1, 2, and (2) the employment by God, in His long-suffering pity, of all possible means to lead His people to repentance.

(41) They say unto him . . .—We see in the answer either a real unconsciousness that they were as the men on whom the punishment was to fall (see note on verse 31), or, more probably, an affected horror, by which they sought to disguise the conviction that the parable was meant for them. Their answer (comp. John 11:49-51) was an unconscious prophecy of the destruction of the Holy City and the transfer of the privileges that had belonged to Israel to the Gentile Church. The Lord of the vineyard would not be robbed of its fruits, and sooner or later would find faithful and true laborers.

(42) Did ye never read . . . ?—The quotation is remarkable as being found (Ps. 118:22) in the immediate context of the verse which had supplied the "hosanna" shouts of the multitude on the preceding day. In the primary meaning of the Psalm, the illustration seems drawn from one of the stones, quarried, hewn, and marked, away from the site of the Temple, which the builders, ignorant of the head architect's plans, had put on one side as having no place in the building, but which was found afterward to be that on which the completeness of the structure depended. As the mind of the psalmist included both David and Israel under the same symbolism, so here the Christ identifies Himself, more or less completely, with the Church which is His body. (Comp. Eph. 1:22, 23; 2:20.)

(44) Whosoever shall fall on this stone.—See Isa. 8:14, 15. In the immediate application of the words, those who "fell" were those who were "offended" at the outward lowliness of Him who came as the carpenter's Son and died a malefactor's death. But there the fall was not irretrievable. The bruise might be healed; it was the work of the Christ to heal it. But when Christ, or that Church which He identifies with Himself, shall come into collision with the powers that oppose Him, then it shall "grind them to powder." In its wider meaning it includes the destruction of all that resists Christ's kingdom, and so represents the truth of 16:18. (Comp. Dan. 2:35, 44.)

22

(2) Which made a marriage for his son.—The thought itself rested, in part at least, on the language of the older prophets, who spoke of God as the Bridegroom and Israel as His bride (Isa. 62:5), and who thought of the idolatries of Israel as the adultery of the faithless wife (Jer. 3:1-4) who had abandoned the love of her espousals (Jer. 2:2). In the interpretation of the parable, the king is none other than God; the wedding is that between Christ and His Church, the redeemed and purified Israel (Rev. 19:7-9); and the guests themselves, as far as they obey the call and are clothed in the wedding garment, are, in their collective unity, the Church which is the bride. (Comp. Eph. 5:23-27.)

(3-10) The circumstances are similar to those in the parable of the vineyard (21:33-46). In the interpretation of the parable we see again a prophecy of the calling of the Gentiles (comp. Acts 13:46). The assembly of the guests so gathered answers to the visible Church of Christ in which the evil are mingled with the good, waiting for the coming of the King "to see the guests."

(11) To see the guests.—The verb conveys the idea of inspecting. The king came to see whether all the guests had fulfilled the implied condition of coming in suitable apparel. The framework of the parable probably presupposes the Oriental custom of providing garments for the guests who were invited to a royal feast. Wardrobes filled with many thousand garments formed part of the wealth of every Eastern prince (6:19; Jas. 5:2), and it was part of his glory (II Kings 10:22), to bring them out for use on state occasions. On this assumption, the act of the man who was found "not having a wedding garment" was one of willful insult. The "wedding garment" is nothing less than

733

the "holiness, without which no man shall see the Lord" (Heb. 12:14), and that holiness, as in the framework of the parable and in the realities of the spiritual life, Christ is ever ready to impart to him who truly believes.

(13) Into outer darkness.—See note on 8:12.

(14) Many are called.—The "calling" answers to the "binding" or invitation of the parable; the "chosen" are those who both accept the invitation and comply with its condition. The "choice," as far as the parable is concerned, appears as dependent upon the answer given to the calling. The further truth of an election "according to the foreknowledge of God the Father" (I Pet. 1:2) is not here within view, but it follows necessarily on the assumption of that foreknowledge. The "choice," which in the parable comes as the close of all, must be thought of as having been present to the mind of the All-knowing from all eternity.

(16) With the Herodians.—The party's precise relation to the other sects or schools among the Jews is a matter of conjecture. The Herodians were known, first to the Romans and then to the people, as adherents of the house of the Herods. Why they now joined with the Pharisees is not clear; but two distinct theories have been maintained: (1) That, as it was the general policy of all the princes of the Herodian family to court the favor of Rome, their partisans were those who held that it was lawful to "give tribute to Caesar." On this supposition the narrative brings before us the coalition of two parties usually opposed to each other, but united against a common foe. (2) That they were partisans of the Herods in the sense of looking to them to restore the independence of the nation, and were therefore of one mind with the Pharisees on the tribute question, though they differed from them on most other points. (See notes on 11:7-10.)

Master, we know that thou art true.—Insidious as the praise was—intended, as it were, to goad Him who was thus addressed into showing, by some rash utterance, that He deserved it—it may be noted as an admission from the lips of adversaries of the supreme truthfulness and fearlessness of our Lord's teaching.

(17) Is it lawful to give tribute. . . ?—The question was framed obviously as a dilemma. If answered in the affirmative, the Pharisees would be able to denounce Him to the people as a traitor to His country,

courting the favor of their heathen oppressors. If in the negative, the Herodians could accuse Him, as He was eventually accused, of "perverting the nation, and forbidding to give tribute to Caesar" (Luke 23:2).

Tribute—i.e., the poll tax of a denarius per head, assessed on the whole population, the publicans being bound to transmit the sum so collected to the Roman treasury. As being a direct personal tax it was looked on by the more zealous Jews as carrying with it great humiliation, and was consequently resisted (see Acts 5:37).

(21) Render therefore unto Caesar.—As far as the immediate question was concerned, this was an answer in the affirmative. It recognized the principle that acceptance of the emperor's coinage was an admission of his *de facto* sovereignty. But the words that followed raised the discussion into a higher region, and asserted implicitly that that admission did not interfere with the true spiritual freedom of the people or with their religious duties. In all questions of real or seeming collision between secular authority and spiritual freedom, the former claims obedience as a *de facto* ordinance of God up to the limit where it encroaches on the rights of conscience and prevents men from worshiping and serving Him. (See notes on Rom. 13:1-7.)

(22) They marvelled.—We can picture to ourselves the surprise which the conspirators felt at thus finding themselves baffled where they thought success so certain. The Herodians could not charge the Teacher with forbidding to give tribute to Caesar. The Pharisees found the duty of giving to God what belonged to Him pressed as strongly as they had ever pressed it. They had to change their tactics, and to fall back upon another plan of attack.

(23-28) The Sadducees.—(See note on 3:7.) The form of their attack implies that they looked on our Lord as teaching the doctrine of the resurrection. They rested their denial on the ground that they found no mention of it in the Law, which they recognized as the only rule of faith. The case which they put, as far as the principle involved was concerned, need not have gone beyond any case of remarriage without children, but the questioners pushed it to its extreme as what seemed to them a **reductio ad absurdum.** Stress is laid on the childlessness of the woman in all seven marriages in order to guard against the possible answer that she would be counted in the resurrection as the wife of him to whom she had borne children.

(29) Ye do err.—This is the one occasion in the gospel history in which our Lord comes into direct collision with the Sadducees. On the whole, while distinctly condemning and refuting their characteristic error, the tone in which He speaks is less stern than that in which He addresses the Pharisees. They were less characterized by hypocrisy, and that was what called down His sternest reproof. The causes of their error were, He told them, twofold: (1) imperfect knowledge even of the Scriptures which they recognized; (2) imperfect conceptions of the divine attributes, and therefore an **a priori** limitation of the divine power. They could not conceive of any human fellowship in the life of the resurrection except such as reproduced the relations and conditions of this earthly life.

(30) They neither marry, nor are given in marriage.—His words teach absolutely the absence from the resurrection life of the definite relations on which marriage rests in this. The answer to all questionings is found in dwelling on the "power of God." Old relations may subsist under new conditions. The saintly wife of two saintly husbands may love both with an angelic and therefore a pure and unimpaired affection.

(31) That which was spoken unto you by God.—There are many passages scattered throughout the Old Testament in which the hope of immortality, and even of a resurrection, is expressed with greater clearness; but our Lord meets the Sadducees on their own ground, quoting from the Law which they recognized as of supreme authority. (See Exod. 3:6.) The principle implied in the reasoning is that the union of the divine name with that of a man involved a relation existing, not in the past only, but when the words were uttered. And if the relation was a permanent one, then it followed that those whose names were thus joined with the name of God were living and not dead.

(35) A lawyer.—The word suggests the thought of a section of the scribes who confined their attention to the Law while the others included in their studies the writings of the prophets also. In Luke 7:30; 11:45 they appear as distinct from the Pharisees.

Tempting him.—Better, "examining." There does not appear to have been in this instance any hostile purpose in the mind of the questioner (see Mark 12:34). It would

seem, indeed, as if our Lord's refutation of the Sadducees had drawn out a certain measure of sympathy and reverence from those whose minds were not hardened in hypocrisy. They came now to test His teaching on other points. The fact that they thus examined Him as if they were His judges showed an utterly imperfect recognition of His claims as a Prophet and as the Christ.

(40) All the law and the prophets.—The words are coupled, as in 5:17; 7:12, to indicate the whole of the revelation of the divine will in the Old Testament. The two great commandments (verses 37, 39; see Deut. 6:4, 5; Lev. 19:18) lay at the root of all. The rest did but expand and apply them; or, as in the ceremonial, set them forth symbolically; or, as in the law of slavery and divorce, confined their application within limits, which the hardness of men's hearts made necessary.

(43) Doth David in spirit call him Lord?—The words assume (1) that David was the writer of Psalm 110; (2) that in writing it, he was guided by a Spirit higher than his own; (3) that the subject of it was no earthly king of the house of David, but the far-off Christ. On this point there was an undisturbed consensus among the schools of Judaism, as represented by the Targums and the Talmud. It was a received tradition that the Christ should sit on the right hand of Jehovah and Abraham on His left. Its application to the Christ is emphatically recognized by Peter (Acts 2:34), and by Paul, though indirectly (Col. 3:1). In the argument of the Epistle to the Hebrews, it occupies nearly the chief place of all (Heb. 1:3; 5:6).

23

(1) To the multitude.—Now our Lord warns the multitude against the Pharisees. He appeals, as it were, to the unperverted conscience of the people, as against the perversions of their guides, closing His public teaching, as He began, by a protest against that false casuistry which had substituted the traditions of men for the commandments of God.

(2) The scribes and the Pharisees sit in Moses' seat.—The words were probably spoken of their collective action as represented in the Sanhedrin, rather than of their individual work as interpreters of the Law. As such, they claimed to be the authoritative exponents of the Law, and our Lord apparently recognizes their official claim to reverence.

(4) The rigorous precepts were for others, not themselves. Professing to guide, they neither helped nor sympathized with the troubles of those they taught. (Comp. Rom. 2:17-23.)

(5) Phylacteries.—The Greek word signifies "safeguard" or "preservative," and was probably applied under the idea that the phylacteries were charms or amulets against the evil eye or the power of evil spirits. The Hebrew word in common use from our Lord's time onward has been **tephillin**, or prayers. The things so named were worn by nearly all Jews as soon as they became children of the Law, i.e., at thirteen. They consisted of a small box containing the four passages in which frontlets are mentioned (Exod. 13:2-10, 11-16; Deut. 6:4-9; 11:13-22), written on four slips of vellum for the phylactery of the head, and on one for that of the arm. This is fastened by a loop to thin leather straps, which are twisted in the one case around the arm with the box on the heart, in the other around the head with the box on the brow. They were worn commonly during the act of prayer, and by those who made a show of perpetual devotion and study of the Law during the whole day. The Pharisees, in their ostentatious show of piety, made either the box or the straps wider than the common size and wore them as they walked to and fro in the streets or prayed standing (6:5), that men might see and admire them.

The borders of their garments.—See note on 9:20.

(6) The uppermost rooms.—Strictly speaking, they would be the "first places," nearest to the host, on the couches on which the guests reclined, these being assigned (John 13:23) to the most favored guests.

The chief seats in the synagogues.—These were at the upper or Jerusalem end of the synagogue, where was the Ark (or chest) that contained the Law. These were given, either by common consent or by the elders of the synagogue, to those who were most conspicuous for their devotion to the Law, and as such were coveted as a mark of religious reputation.

(7) Greetings in the markets.—The greetings referred to were more than the familiar "Peace with thee," and involved the language of formal reverence (comp. Luke 10:4) paid to those whom men delighted to honor.

Rabbi, Rabbi.—The title, which properly meant a "great" or "chief" one (II Kings 18:17), had come to be applied, in the day of Hillel and Shammai, to the teachers or "masters" of the Law, and as such was given to the scribes who devoted themselves to that work.

(9) Call no man your father.—This also, under its Hebrew form of **Abba**, was one of the titles in which the scribes delighted. In its true use it embodied the thought that the relation of scholars and teachers was filial on the one side, paternal on the other; but precisely because it expressed so noble an idea was its merely conventional use full of danger.

(12) Whosoever shall exalt himself.—The precept seems to have been one which our Lord desired especially to imprint on the hearts of the disciples. It had been spoken at least twice before (Luke 14:11; 18:14). The echoes of it in Jas. 4:10; I Pet. 5:6, show that the impression had been made.

(13) Woe unto you.—We enter in these verses on the sternest words of condemnation that ever came from our Lord's lips; but the element of sorrow, as well as indignation, is intended in Greek interjection. **Woe for you** is, perhaps, a better rendering.

Hypocrites.—See note on 6:2.

Ye shut up the kingdom . . .—"The key of knowledge" (Luke 11:52) was the symbol which was given to each scribe on his admission to his office. Our Lord's charge against them is that the only use they made of the key was to lock the door. They did not enter into the inner meaning of Law or prophets; they excluded (John 9:22; 12:42) those who were so entering into the higher life and the higher teaching of the kingdom.

(14) Ye devour widows' houses.—The avarice thus described may have attained its end either by using their advantages as the jurist and notaries of the time to press unjust claims against wealthy widows, or by leading devout women, under the show of piety, to bestow on them their estates or houses. To minister to the maintenance of a scribe was, they taught, the best use of wealth. The "long prayer" refers probably to the well-known Eighteen Prayers, which formed the standard of the Pharisee's devotion.

(15) To make one proselyte.—The zeal of the earlier Pharisees had showed itself in propagandism. They resorted to all the arts of persuasion, and exulted when they succeeded in enrolling a heathen convert as a member of their party. But the proselytes thus made were too often a scandal and proverb of reproach. There was no real conversion, and those who were most active in the work of proselytizing were, for the most part, blind leaders of the blind. The vices of the Jew were ingrafted on the vices of the heathen. Proselytes were regarded as the leprosy of Israel, hindering the coming of the Messiah. It became a proverb that no one should trust a proselyte, even to the twenty-fourth generation. Our Lord was, in part at least, expressing the judgment of the better Jews when He taught that the proselyte thus made was "two-fold more the child of hell"—i.e., of Gehenna—than his masters.

(16) Whosoever shall swear by the temple.—See notes on 5:34, 35. The "gold of the Temple"—not the gold used in its structural ornamentation, but that which in coin or bullion was part of the Corban, or sacred treasure (15:5)—had received a more special consecration than the fabric, and involved, therefore, a higher obligation, when used as a **formula jurandi**, than the Temple or the altar.

(23) Ye pay tithe of mint and anise and cummin.—Comp. Lev. 27:30; Deut. 12:17. The Pharisee, in his minute scrupulosity, made a point of gathering the tenth sprig of every garden herb and presenting it to the priest. As far as this was done at the bidding of an imperfectly illumined conscience our Lord does not blame it. It was not, like the teaching as to oaths and the Corban, a direct perversion of the Law. What He did censure was the substitution of the lower for the higher. With the three examples of the "infinitely little" He contrasts the three ethical obligations that were infinitely great—"judgment, mercy, and faith."

(24) Strain at a gnat.—In the Greek both nouns have the emphasis of the article, "**the** gnat—**the** camel." The scrupulous care described in the first clause of the proverbial saying was literally practiced by devout Jews in accordance with Lev. 11:23, 42. In the second clause, the camel appears not only (19:24) as the type of vastness, but as being among the unclean beasts of which the Israelites might not eat (Lev. 11:4).

(27) Ye are like unto whited sepulchres.—Contact with a sepulcher brought with it ceremonial uncleanness, and all burial-places were accordingly whitewashed once a year (on the fifteenth day of the month Adar—i.e., about the beginning of March) that passers-by might be warned by them, as

they were of the approach of a leper by his cry, "Unclean, unclean!" (Lev. 13:45).

(30) If we had been in the days . . .—There is no necessity for assuming that the Pharisees did not mean what they said. It was simply an instance of the unconscious hypocrisy of which every generation has more or less been guilty, when it has condemned the wrongdoing of the past—its bigotry, or luxury, or greed—and then has yielded to the same sins itself.

(34) Behold, I send unto you prophets.—The words are remarkable as including "scribes" no less than "prophets" among the ministers of the New Covenant. (See note on 13:52.)

(35) The blood of Zacharias son of Barachias.—See II Chron. 24:20-22. That Zacharias was, however, the son of Jehoiada; and the only "Zechariah the son of Barachias" in the Old Testament is the minor prophet whose writings occupy the next to the last place among the prophetic books of the Old Testament. Of his death we know nothing, and it is not probable, had he been slain in the manner here described, that it would have passed unrecorded. The death of the son of Jehoiada, on the other hand, is not only recorded in II Chron. 24 but had become the subject of popular legends, showing the impression which that death had made on the minds of men and explaining why it was chosen by our Lord as a representative example. The substitution of Barachias for Jehoiada may be accounted for as the mistake of a transcriber, led by the association of the two names, like that of Jeremy for Zechariah in 27:9. (Comp. Josephus, **Wars,** 4.5, §6; **Protoevangelion of James,** chap. 16.)

(36) All these things shall come upon this generation.—The words carry on the thought of the measure that is gradually being filled up. Men make the guilt of past ages their own, reproduce its atrocities, identify themselves with it; and so, what seems at first an arbitrary decree, visiting on the children the sins of the fathers, becomes in such cases a righteous judgment. If they repent, they cut off the terrible sequence of sin and punishment; but if they harden themselves in their evil, they inherit the delayed punishment of their fathers' sins as well as of their own.

(37) Thou that killest the prophets.—The words are in the present tense, as embracing the past and even the future. As with a sad prescience our Lord speaks of the sufferings which were in store for His messengers, and of which the deaths of Stephen (Acts 7:60) and of James (Acts 12:2) were representative instances. (See also Acts 8:1; 12:1; I Thess. 2:14, 15; Jas. 5:10.)

(38) **Your house.**—The words "your house" may refer either generally to the whole polity of Israel, or more specifically to the "house" in which they gloried, the Temple, which was the joy of their hearts.

(39) **Till ye shall say.**—See Ps. 118:26. There can be little doubt that our Lord points to the second Advent, and to the welcome that will then be given Him by all the true Israel of God. For that generation, and for the outward Israel as such, the abandonment was final.

24

(2) **There shall not be left here one stone upon another.**—So Josephus relates that Titus ordered the whole city and the Temple to be dug up, leaving only two or three of the chief towers, so that those who visited it could hardly believe that it had ever been inhabited (**Wars**, 7:1).

(3) **The sign of thy coming.**—Literally, "of thy presence." The passage is memorable as the first occurrence of the word **parousia**, which was so prominent in the teaching of the epistles (I Thess. 2:19; 3:13; Jas. 5:7; I John 2:28, **et al.**). Peter, James, John, and Andrew (Mark 13:3) had brought themselves to accept the thought of His departure and return, though time and manner were as yet hidden from them.

The end of the world.—Literally, "the end of the age." In the common language of the day, which had passed from the schools of the rabbis into popular use, "this age" or "this world" meant the time up to the coming of the Messiah; the "age or world to come" (13:40; 19:28; Heb. 2:5; 6:5) meant the glorious time which He was to inaugurate. The disciples had heard their Lord speak in parables of such a coming, and they naturally connected it in their thoughts with the close of the period in which they lived.

(4) **Jesus answered and said unto them . . .**—The great discourse which follows is given with substantial agreement by Mark and Luke, the variations being such as were naturally incident to reports made from memory, and probably after an interval of many years. In all probability, the written record came, in the first instance, from the lips of Peter, and it will according-

ly be instructive to compare its eschatology with that which we find in his discourses and epistles. Paul's reference in I Thess. 5:2 suggests that its substance had become known at a comparatively early date; but it was probably not published among Christian Jews until the time was near when its warnings would be needed.

(5) **Many shall come in my name, saying, I am Christ.**—Better, "the Christ." In the excited fanaticism of the time it was likely enough that pretenders should arise and disappear, after each had lived out his little day, and fill no place in history. The "many antichrists" of I John 2:18 may point to such phenomena; possibly, also, the prophecy of II Thess. 2:4.

(6) **Wars and rumours.**—The forty years that intervened before the destruction of Jerusalem were full of these in all directions; but we may probably think of the words as referring especially to wars, actual or threatened, that affected the Jews, such, e.g., as those of which we read under Caligula, Claudius, and Nero (Jos., **Ant.** 20:1, 6). The title which the historian gave to his second book, "The Wars of the Jews," is sufficiently suggestive. But the believers in Christ were not to think that the end was to follow at once upon the wars which were preparing the way for it.

(7) Such occurrences are noted, **inter alia**, in Acts 11:28; Josephus, **Ant.** 18:9, §§8, 9, 20:2, and **Wars**, 2:18, 4:4 §5; Suetonius, **Claud.** c.18, and **Nero**, 39; Seneca, **Ep.** 91; Tacitus, **Ann.**, 12:58, 14:27, 15:22, 16:13.

(8) **The beginning of sorrows.**—The words mean strictly, "the beginning of travail pangs." The troubles through which the world passes are thought of as issuing in a "new birth"—the "regeneration" of 19:28. (Comp. Isa. 37:3; Rom. 8:22.)

(9, 10) See Acts 13:50; 14:19, 23:12, 28:22; I Pet. 2:12; II Pet. 3:4; Josephus, **Wars**, 4.3; Tacitus, **Ann.**, 15:44.

(11) **Many false prophets shall rise.**—The later writings of the New Testament bear repeated testimony to this feature of the ten years that preceded the destruction of Jerusalem. (See I Tim. 4:1; II Pet. 2:1; I John 2:18; 4:1.) These show the extent of the evil which was the natural outcome of the feverish excitement of the people. In Josephus (**Wars**, 6:5, §2) we have the record of this working of false prophecy in more immediate connection with Judaea and Jerusalem. Up to the last moment of the capture of the city by Titus, men were buoyed up with false hopes of deliverance,

based on the predictions of fanatics and impostors.

(12) Because iniquity shall abound...—Better, "lawlessness." No word could more fitly represent the condition of Judaea in the time just referred to; brigandage, massacres, extortion, and assassination came to be common things. In the tendency to "forsake the assembling of themselves together" among the Hebrew Christians, we have, perhaps, one instance of the love growing cold (Heb. 10:25).

(13) He that shall endure unto the end...—The words have at once a higher and lower sense. Endurance to the end of life is in every case the condition of salvation, in the full meaning of the word. But the context rather leads us to see in the "end" the close of the period of which our Lord speaks, i.e., the destruction of Jerusalem.

(14) Shall be preached in all the world.—The words must not be strained beyond the meaning which they would have for those who heard them. They were certain to see in "all the world" (literally, "the inhabited earth" as in Luke 2:1; Acts 11:28) neither more nor less than the Roman empire. As a matter of fact, there was hardly a province of the empire in which the faith of Christ had not been preached before the destruction of Jerusalem. The word "nations," i.e., Gentiles, gives implicit sanction to the work of which Paul was afterward the great representative. So taken, the words prepare the way for the great mission of 28:19.

(15) The abomination of desolation.—The words, as they stand in Dan. 12:11, seem to refer to the desecration of the sanctuary by the mad attempt of Antiochus Epiphanes to stop the "daily sacrifice" and to substitute an idolatrous worship in its place (II Macc. 6:1-9). What analogous desecration do our Lord's words indicate? It is before the destruction of the Temple, and therefore cannot be the presence of the plundering troops; and since the "abomination" stands in the "Holy Place," it cannot be identified with the appearance of the Roman eagles in the lines of the besieging legions under Cestius, A.D. 68. The answer is probably to be found in the faction fights, the murders and outrages, the profane consecration of usurping priests, which the Jewish historian describes so fully (Josephus, **Wars** 4:6, §§6-8). The Zealots had gotten possession of the Temple at an early stage in the siege, and profaned it by these and other like outrages.

(16) See Eusebius, **Hist. Eccl.**, 3:5; Josephus, **Wars** 4:9, §1, 5:10, §1. The "mountains" may be named generally as a place of refuge, or may point, as interpreted by the event, to the Gilead range of hills on the east of Jordan.

(17) Let him which is on the housetop.—The houses in the streets of Jerusalem were built in a continuous line and with flat roofs, so that a man might pass from house to house without descending into the street until he came to some point near the wall or gate of the city and so make his escape. At a moment of danger (in this case that arising from the factions within the city, rather than the invaders without), any delay might prove fatal.

(19) Woe unto them.—Better, "woe for them." The tone is that of pity rather than denunciation. The hardships of a hurried flight would press most heavily on those who were encumbered with infant children, or were expecting childbirth. Perhaps the words point to the darker horrors of the siege, when mothers were driven, in the frenzy of starvation, to feed on their infants' flesh (Josephus, **Wars**, 6:3, §4).

(20) It is characteristic of Matthew, as writing for Jews, that he alone records the words "nor on the Sabbath day." Living as the Christians of Judaea did in the strict observance of the Law, they would either be hindered by their own scruples from going beyond a Sabbath day's journey (about one mile), which would be insufficient to place them out of the reach of danger, or would find impediments—gates shut, and the like—from the Sabbath observance of others.

(21) Such as was not since the beginning...—See Dan. 12:1. Josephus notes "that all miseries that had been known from the beginning of the world fell short" of those of the siege of the Holy City (**Wars**, 5:13, §§4, 5). Other sieges may have witnessed, before and since, scenes of physical wretchedness equally appalling, but nothing that history records offers anything parallel to the alternations of fanatic hope and frenzied despair that attended the breaking up of the faith and polity of Israel.

(22) The elect were those who, as believers in Jesus, were the "remnant" of the visible Israel and therefore the true Israel of God. It was for the sake of the Christians of Judaea, not for that of the rebellious Jews, that the war was not protracted, and that Titus, under the outward influences of Josephus and Bernice, tempered his conquests with compassion (**Ant.** 12:3, §2; **Wars,** 6:9, §2). See note on 22:14.

(24-26) See Acts 8:9-11; 13:6. So "signs and lying wonders" are the notes of the coming of the Wicked One, in whom the mystery of iniquity shall receive its full development (II Thess. 2:9). But for the warning thus given, even the Christians of Judaea and Jerusalem might have been carried away by the current of popular delusions. The pretenders there shunned the publicity which would test their claims.

(27) As the lightning cometh out of the east.—In this and the three preceding verses we are, as it were, on the dim borderland of the primary and the ultimate fulfillments of the words. In whatever way He came, whether in the final destruction of the Temple and polity of Israel, or at the end of the world's great drama, the advent would be sudden and unexpected as the lightning flash.

(28) The enigmatic proverb means that wherever life is gone, wherever a church or nation is decaying and putrescent, there to the end of time will God's ministers of vengeance, the vultures that do their work of destruction and so leave room for new forms of life, assuredly be found. What the disciples should witness in the fall of Jerusalem would repeat itself scores of times in the world's history, and be fulfilled on the largest scale at the end of all things. (See Isa. 46:11; Ezek. 39:4.)

(29) Immediately after the tribulation of those days.—From this point forward the prophecy takes a wider range, passing beyond the narrow limits of the destruction of Jerusalem to the final coming of the Son of Man. The one is represented as following "immediately" on the other. No other meaning could have been found in the words when they were first heard or read. The "days" of this verse are those which were shortened "for the elect's sake" (verse 22); the "tribulation" can be none other than that of verse 21, which was emphatically connected with the flight of men from the beleaguered city. How are we to explain the fact that already more than eighteen centuries have passed, and "the promise of his coming" still tarries? A partial answer to the question is that God's measurements of time are not as man's, and that with Him "a thousand years are as one day" (II Pet. 3:8). But the bolder and better answer follows: Of that "day and hour" knew no man, "not even the Son" (Mark 13:32), "but the Father only" (verse 36); and therefore He,

as truly man, and having, therefore, committed to accept the limitations of knowledge incident to man's nature, speaks of the two events as poets and prophets speak of the distant future. As men gazing from a distance see the glittering heights of two snow-crowned mountains apparently in close proximity, and take no account of the vast tract, it may be of many miles, which lies between them, so it was that those whose thoughts must have been mainly molded on this prediction, the apostles and their immediate disciples, though they were too conscious of their ignorance of "the times and the seasons" to fix the day or year, lived and died in the expectation that it was not far off, and that they might, by prayer and acts, hasten its coming (II Pet. 3:12). (See note on verse 36.)

Shall the sun be darkened.—The words reproduce the imagery in which Isaiah had described the day of the Lord's judgment upon Babylon (Isa. 13:10), and may naturally receive the same symbolic interpretation. Our Lord speaks here in language as essentially apocalyptic as that of the Revelation of John (Rev. 8:12), and it lies in the nature of such language that it precludes a literal interpretation.

(30) The sign of the Son of man is none other than the presence of the Son of man Himself, coming in the clouds of heaven, in the ineffable glory of His majesty. The "tribes" are any who have done evil, and who therefore dread the coming of the Judge. (See Heb. 6:6; Rev. 1:7.)

(31) With a great sound of a trumpet.—We know not what reality will answer to this symbol, but it is interesting to note how deeply it impressed itself on the minds not only of the disciples who heard it, but of those who learned it from them. (Comp. I Cor. 15:52; I Thess. 4:16.)

They shall gather together his elect.—The elect are those who are living on the earth at the time of the Second Advent. In these chapters there is, indeed, no distinct mention of the resurrection of the dead, though they, as well as the living, are implied in the parable of judgment with which the discourse ends.

(32) Now learn a parable of the fig tree.—As in so many other instances, we may think of the words as illustrated by a living example. Both time and place make this probable, for it was spring and on the Mount of Olives. What our Lord teaches is that as surely as the fresh green foliage of the fig tree is a sign of summer, so shall the

740

signs of which He speaks portend the coming of the Son of man.

(33) **So likewise ye.**—The pronoun is emphatic: Ye whom I have chosen, who are therefore among the elect that shall be thus gathered. The words are spoken to the four apostles as the representatives of the whole body of believers who should be living—first, at the destruction on Jerusalem, and afterward at the end of the world. Of the four, John alone, as far as we know, survived the destruction of Jerusalem.

(34) **This generation shall not pass . . .**—The natural meaning of the words is that which takes "generation" in the ordinary sense for those who are living at any given period. So it was on "this generation" (23:36; see note) that the accumulated judgments were to fall. The desire to bring the words into more apparent harmony with history has led some interpreters to take "generation" in the sense of "race" or "people," and so to see in the words a prophecy of the perpetuity of the existence of the Jews as a distinct people until the end of the world. But there is no authority for this meaning. The words of 16:28 (see note) state the same fact in language which does not admit of any such explanation.

Till all these things be fulfilled.—The words do not necessarily imply more than the commencement of a process, the first unrolling of the scroll of the coming ages.

(35) **Heaven and earth.**—The tone is that of One who speaks with supreme authority, foreseeing, on the one hand, death and seeming failure, but on the other, the ultimate victory, not of truth only in the abstract, but of His own word as the truth. (See Ps. 102:26; Isa. 40:8.) The Son of man claims for His own words the eternity which belongs to the words of Jehovah. (Comp. I Pet. 1:24, 25.)

(36) **No, not the angels of heaven.**—Mark 13:32 adds, "neither the Son." Assuming the close connection of that gospel with Peter, it is as if the apostle who heard the discourse desired, for some special reason, to place on record the **ipsissima verba** of his Master. And that reason may be found in his own teaching (see II Pet. 3:3-8). It is obviously doing violence to the plain meaning of the words to dilute them into the statement that the Son of man did not communicate the knowledge which He possessed as the Son of God. If we are perplexed at the mystery of this confession in One in whom we recognize the presence of "the fulness of the Godhead bodily" (Col. 1:19;

2:9), we may find that which may help us at least to wait patiently for the full understanding of the mystery in Paul's teaching that the eternal Word, in becoming flesh, "emptied himself" (see Phil. 2:7) of the infinity which belongs to the divine attributes and took upon Him the limitations necessarily incidental to man's nature, even when untainted by evil and in fullest fellowship, through the Eternal Spirit, with the Father.

(37) **As the days of Noe were.**—Comp. I Pet. 3:20; II Pet. 2:5; 3:6. Possibly the two evangelists who were writing for the Gentile Christians were led to omit the allusion to a history which was not as familiar to those whom they had in view as it was to the Hebrew readers of Matthew's gospel.

(40, 41) The one who is "taken" is received into fellowship with Christ, while the other is abandoned. What is taught is that the day of judgment will be, as by an inevitable law, a day of separation, according to the diversity of character which may exist in the midst of the closest fellowship in outward life.

(44) **In such an hour as ye think not.**—The words are important as showing that even the signs which were to be as the budding of the fig tree at the approach of summer were intended only to rouse the faithful to watchfulness, not to enable men to fix the times and the seasons which the Father hath set in His own power. All attempts to go beyond this in the interpretation of the apocalyptic eschatology of Scripture are destined to failure.

(45, 46) One function of the minister of Christ is to supply men with the spiritual food which they need for the sustenance of their higher life. There is an art, as it were, of spiritual dietetics, which requires tact and discernment as well as faithfulness. The wise servant will seek to discover not only the right kind of food, but the right season for giving it. (Comp. II Tim. 2:15.)

(47) **He shall make him ruler.**—The work of the faithful servant does not cease, either after his own removal from his earthly labor, or even after the final consummation of the kingdom. Over and above the joy of the beatific vision there will still be a work to be done analogous to that which has been the man's training here, and in it there will be scope for all the faculties and energies that have been thus disciplined and developed.

(48) **My lord delayeth his coming.**—See II Pet. 3:3, 4. Those who looked on that

delay as Peter looked on it would continue watchful, but the selfish and ungodly would be tempted by it to forget that Christ comes to men in more senses and more ways than one. Though the final coming may be delayed, moreover, the Judge is ever near, even at the doors (Jas. 5:9).

(51) And shall cut him asunder.—Here also, as in the case of the faithful servant, the words have more than one fulfillment. The form of punishment would seem here to have been chosen for its figurative fitness. The man had been a hypocrite, double-minded, trying to serve two masters, and his Lord, with the sharp sword of judgment, smites through the false, apparent unity of his life and reveals its duplicity.

25

The three parables of this chapter appear here as in closest sequence to the great discourse of chap. 24, and are as its natural conclusion. Yet no trace of such parables being then spoken appears either in Mark or Luke. It seems most probable that the strictly apocalyptic part of the discourse was frequently impressed by oral teaching and then reproduced in writing, while it was reserved for Matthew—here as elsewhere, eager in collecting parables—to add the teaching that actually followed it. The parables have a common aim, as impressing on the disciples the necessity at once of watchfulness and of activity in good.

(1) Be likened unto ten virgins.—See note on 22:2. While the bride is the Church in her collective unity, the contrasted characters of the members of the Church are represented here by the virgins, probably, the bride herself is not introduced as part of the imagery of the parable. The stage in the marriage rites which is brought before us is the return of the bridegroom to his own abode, bringing the bride with him. Jewish custom required the bridesmaids to wait at the bridegroom's house, to receive him and the bride, and as this was commonly after sunset, they were provided with lamps or torches.

(3) Took no oil with them.—In the interpretation of the parable, the lamp or torch is obviously the outward life of holiness by which the disciple of Christ lets his light shine before men (5:16), and the "oil" is the gift of the Holy Spirit, without which the torch first burns dimly and then expires.

The foolish virgins neglected to seek that supply.

(5) While the bridegroom tarried.—The time thus described includes the whole interval between our Lord's Ascension and His final advent.

(9) Go ye rather to them that sell.—The "exchangers" ("them that sell") are the pastors and teachers of the Church—the stewards of the mysteries of God. Through them, whether as preaching the divine Word or as administering the sacraments which are signs and means of grace, men may, by God's appointment, obtain the gift and grace they need. The "buying" and "selling" belong, of course, in their literal sense, to the parable only (See Acts 8:20).

(10) While they went to buy.—The words imply that had they gone earlier, as the wise virgins had done, all would have been well. It is too late, in other words, to have recourse to the ordinary means of grace at the moment of the crisis in personal or national life, which answers to the coming of the bridegroom. The door is then shut, and is no longer opened even to those who knock.

(14) The outward framework of this parable lies in the Eastern way of dealing with property in the absence of the owner. Two courses were open as an approximation to what we call investment. The more primitive and patriarchal way was for the absentee to make his slaves his agents. They were to till his land and sell the produce, or to use the money which he left with them as capital in trading. The other course was to take advantage of the banking, money-changing, money-lending system which at the time was in full operation throughout the Roman empire. The bankers received money on deposit and paid interest on it, and then lent it at a higher percentage or employed it in trade or in farming the revenues of a province. This was therefore the natural resource for those who had not energy to engage in business.

(15) Unto one he gave five talents.—See note on 18:24. A man's energies, gifts, capacities are called "talents," for the use of which he will have to render an account. But here an "ability" is presupposed in each case prior to the distribution of the talents, and we are led accordingly to the conclusion that the latter stand here less for natural gifts than for external opportunities. So taken, the parable does not repeat the lesson of that which precedes it, but is addressed specifically to those who hold any vocation or ministry in the Church of Christ, or have in their hands outward resources for working in it.

(18) He that had received one . . .—The presence of the opportunities brings with it a sense of responsibility. So faithfulness in a little receives its full reward, but the consciousness of having but a little, when men do not believe in their Master's wisdom and love in giving them but a little, tempts to discontent and so to sloth on the one hand, and on the other, as with Judas, to hasty and unscrupulous greed of immediate gain.

(19) After a long time.—Here, as in the previous parable ("midnight," verse 6), there is a faint suggestion of a longer delay than men looked for in the Coming which is the counterpart to this.

(21) I will make thee ruler over many things.—Here again, as in 24:47, we have the idea that in either the final judgment or that which follows upon each man's death, the reward of faithful work lies not in rest only but in enlarged activity.

(24, 25) The words are those of simulated rather than real fear. The excuse did but cover the implied taunt that he dared not venture anything in the service of a master who would make no allowance for intentions where the result was failure. So, in the life of the soul, a man wanting in the spirit of loyalty and trust contents himself with making no use of opportunities, and therefore they are to him as though they were not, except that they increase his guilt and his condemnation.

(27) Thus, if the servant had been honestly conscious of his own want of power, there would have been at least some interest allowed on the deposit. "The exchangers" in the interpretation of the parable are analogous to "them that sell" in verse 9 (see note).

(28, 29) Abilities themselves cannot be thus transferred; opportunities can, and often are, even in the approximate working out of the law of retribution which we observe on earth. One form of the penalty of the slothful will be to see work which might have been theirs done by those who have been faithful while on earth.

(31) We commonly speak of the concluding portion of this chapter as the parable of the Sheep and the Goats; but it is obvious from its beginning that it passes beyond the region of parable into that of divine realities, and that the sheep and goats form only

a subordinate and parenthetic illustration. See the vision of Dan. 7:13.

(32) Before him shall be gathered all nations.—Better, "all the Gentiles." We have had in this chapter (1) in the Wise and Foolish Virgins, the law of judgment for all members of the Church of Christ, and (2) in the Talents, that for all who hold any office or ministry in the Church; now we have (3) the law by which those shall be judged who have lived and died as heathen, not knowing the name of Christ, and knowing God only as revealed in nature or in the law written in their hearts.

As a shepherd divideth his sheep from the goats.—Elsewhere the shepherd's work is the symbol of protective, self-sacrificing love. Here we are reminded that even the shepherd has at times to execute the sentence of judgment which involves separation. The "right" hand and the "left" are used, according to the laws of what we might almost call a natural symbolism, as indicating respectively good and evil, acceptance and rejection.

(34) Inherit the kingdom prepared for you.—Not for Israel only, or those among the brethren who should in this life believe in Christ, had the kingdom been prepared, but for these also (see note on 8:11). That kingdom had been prepared from everlasting, though it was only through the work of Christ, and ultimate union with Him, that it could be realized and enjoyed.

(40) Inasmuch as ye have done it unto one of the least of these my brethren.—The heathen have acted from what seemed merely human affection toward merely human objects, yet they have, in their ministrations to the sons of men, been ministering to the Son of man. (See Heb. 2:11.)

(41) Ye cursed.—Note the omission of the words "of my Father" (verse 34). He is not the author of the curse. Those who have brought themselves under the curse by their own evil deeds He no longer acknowledges as His.

(44) When saw we thee . . . ?—The sins here are all sins of omission. As in the case of the parable of the Talents, the opportunities (here those that are common to all men, as there those that attached to some office or ministry in the Church) have simply not been used.

(46) Everlasting punishment . . . life eternal.—The two adjectives represent the same Greek word. Strictly speaking, the word, apart from its association with any qualifying substantive, implies a vast undefined duration, rather than one in the full sense of "infinite." The solemnity of the words at the close of the great prophecy of judgment tends obviously to the conclusion that our Lord meant His disciples, and through them His people in all ages, to dwell upon the division which was involved in the very idea of judgment as one which was not to be changed. Men must reap as they have sown, and the consequences of evil deeds, or of failure to perform good deeds, must in the nature of the case, work out their retribution, as far as we can see, with no assignable limit.

26

The portion of the gospel narrative on which we now enter is common, as far as the main facts are concerned, to all the four gospels. The first three gospels are in substantial agreement as to the order of the facts and the time at which they occurred; but the fourth, in some respects the fullest and most striking, differs from the three: (1) in omitting all mention that the Last Supper of our Lord with His disciples was also the Paschal Supper, and at least appearing to imply (John 13:1; 18:28) that it was before it; (2) in omitting all record of the institution of the Lord's Supper as the sign of the New Covenant, and of the agony in Gethsemane; (3) in recording much, both as to our Lord's acts and words, which the three do not record. The variations in the first three gospels are sufficiently explained by the hypothesis that they had a common origin in a history at first delivered orally, and reduced afterward to writing, with the diversities which are, in the nature of the case, incident to such a process.

(1) **All these sayings.**—The words clearly point to the great discourse of chaps. 24 and 25. The "disciples" to whom our Lord now speaks of His betrayal and death may have been either the four who are named in Mark 13:3, or the whole company of the Twelve.

(2) **After two days is the feast of the passover.**—The point at which the words were spoken would either be some time on Tuesday evening of Passion Week, or, following the Jewish mode of speech which found three days in the interval between our Lord's entombment and Resurrection, on the morning or afternoon of Wednesday.

(3) **Then assembled together.**—We learn from John 11:49, 50 that the plan, as far as Caiaphas was concerned, had been formed immediately after the raising of Lazarus. The meeting now assembled was probably a formal session of the Sanhedrin. The chief priests were the heads of the twenty-four courses; the elders of the people were the representatives of the citizens of Jerusalem; the scribes of the Council represented the whole class of interpreters of the Law, who bore that name in its wider sense.

The high priest, who was called Caiaphas.—Of his previous history we know that he had married the daughter of Annas, who had filled the office of high priest before him (John 18:13), and who still occupied, possibly as **Nasi** or President, an influential position in the Council and retained his titular pre-eminence. (See Luke 3:2.) He had been high priest from the beginning of our Lord's ministry, and had, therefore, watched His ministry in Jerusalem with a jealous fear. (See Mark 3:22; Luke 5:17.) The meeting in his house implied a coalition of parties commonly opposed, for Caiaphas and his personal adherents were Sadducees (Acts 5:17), and as such courted the favor of their Roman rulers (John 11:48), while the scribes were, for the most part, Pharisees and assertors of national independence.

(6) **Now when Jesus was in Bethany.**—The narrative is given out of its proper order on account of its connection (as indicated in John's record) with the act of the Traitor. Comp. John 12:1.

In the house of Simon the leper.—Of the man so described we know nothing beyond the fact thus mentioned. It is natural to infer that our Lord had healed him, but that the name still adhered to him to distinguish him from other Simons.

(7) Comp. the similar incident in Luke 7:37-40. We learn from John 12:3 that this was Mary the sister of Lazarus. The box was probably a vase of the material described as alabaster, with the lid cemented down so as not to admit of extraction like a cork or stopper. The value of the ointment is roughly estimated at three hundred denarii (John 12:5), a laborer's wages for nearly a whole year (20:2). Such preparations, consisting, as they did mainly, in the essential oils of carefully cultivated flowers, often brought an almost fabulous price. The fact that Mary had such an unguent by her indicates that the household of Bethany belonged to the comparatively wealthy class. It is probable that a like costly un-

guent had been used in embalming the body of the brother who had so recently been raised from the dead (John 11), and that this gave a special point to our Lord's comment on the act. Mark adds that she broke or crushed the vessel in order to pour out the ointment; John notes that she annointed His feet and wiped them with her hair.

(8, 9) John (12:4), as knowing who had whispered the first word of blame, fixes the uncharitable judgment on Judas Iscariot. The pretended zeal for the poor was the cloak for the irritation of disappointed greed. Judas was the treasurer of the traveling company, received the offerings of the wealthier disciples, and disbursed them either on their necessary expenditure or in alms to the poor (see John 12:6; 13:29). This was the "one talent" given to him "according to his ability," and in dealing with it he proved fraudulent and faithless.

(11) Ye have the poor always with you.— Our Lord dealt with the objection of the murmurers on their own ground as if it were genuine, and does not openly rebuke the dishonesty of the chief objector. But look and tone, and the solemn pathos of the words "Me ye have not always," must have made the traitor feel that he was in the presence of One who read the secrets of his heart.

(14) Then one of the twelve, called Judas Iscariot.—There was the shame, and therefore the anger, of detected guilt; there was the greed of gain that had been robbed of its expected spoil and thirsted for compensation. The purpose that had been formed by the priests and scribes after the resurrection of Lazarus (John 11:47) may well have become known and suggested the hope of a reward. All these feelings were gathering strength through the three days that followed. Possibly there mingled with them a sense of disappointment that the kingly entry into Jerusalem was not followed up by immediate victory. Luke's words that "Satan entered into Judas" (22:3) are remarkable as implying the personal influence of the tempter (comp. John 6:70).

(15) They covenanted with him for thirty pieces of silver.—The reward was relatively a small one, apparently about the market price of a common slave (Zech. 11:12); but the chief priests saw through the sordid baseness of the man, and, as if scorning both his Master and himself, gauged their reward accordingly.

(17) The first day of the feast of unleav-ened bread.—Mark and Luke, as writing for Gentile readers, explain that it was then that the Passover was to be slain. The precision with which all the first three gospels emphasize the fact leaves no room for doubt that they looked on the Last Supper as the celebration of the actual Paschal Feast.

Where wilt thou that we prepare for thee to eat the passover?—The Paschal lamb was to be slain and eaten in Jerusalem, and therefore special preparations were needed. Only once before (John 2:13) had the disciples kept that feast with Him in the Holy City. Were they expecting that this feast was to be the chosen time for the victorious manifestation of the Kingdom? We learn from Luke (22:8) that the two who were sent were Peter and John.

(18) To such a man.—The Greek word is that used when the writer knows, but does not care to mention, the name of the man referred to. The master of the house was probably a disciple, but secretly, like many others, "for fear of the Jews" (John 12:42), and this may explain the suppression of his name. He was, at any rate, one who would acknowledge the authority of the Master in whose name the disciples spoke.

(19) They made ready the passover.—The two disciples, after seeing that the tables were arranged and the benches covered with cushions, would have to purchase the lamb, the unleavened bread, and the bitter herbs, together with the wine and the conserve of sweet fruits which later practice had added to the older ritual. The Paschal victim would have to be slain in the courts of the Temple by one of the officiating priests. The lamb so slain would be roasted, the bitter herbs prepared, and the table set out.

(20) He sat down with the twelve.—We may think of our Lord as reclining in the center of the middle table, John next to Him and leaning on His bosom (John 13:23), Peter probably on the other side, and the others sitting in an order corresponding closely with the threefold division of the Twelve into groups of four. Upon the washing of the feet followed the teaching of John 13:12-20, and then came the "blessing" or "thanksgiving" which opened the meal. This went on in silence, until that silence was broken by the awful words which follow.

(21) One of you shall betray me.—The words would seem to have been intentionally vague, as if to arouse some of those who heard them to self-questioning. They had not, it is true, shared in the guilt of the Traitor, but they had yielded to tendencies which they had in common with him, and which were dragging them down to his level. They had joined him in his murmuring (verse 8); they had been quarreling, and were about to renew their quarrel, about precedence (Mark 9:34; Luke 22:24).

(24) The Son of man goeth as it is written.—The words are the first direct reference of the coming passion and death to the Scriptures which prophesied of the Messiah. It was appointed that the Christ should suffer, but that appointment did not make men less free agents, nor diminish the guilt of treachery or injustice. (See Acts 1:16-18; 4:27, 28.)

(25) Then Judas, which betrayed him . . .—The words appear to have been spoken in the spirit of reckless defiance (John 13:27). Did his Master indeed know his guilt? It would appear from John's narrative (13:29) that the dread answer, "Thou hast said," was not heard by all. All that they did hear was the command, "What thou doest, do quickly"; and they probably thought that that command referred to some matter connected with his customary work as the bursar of the company. Judas, however, understood the meaning of the words, and immediately went out (John 13:27-30).

(26) The words could scarcely fail to recall what had once seemed a "hard saying which they could not hear" (John 6:60). They had been told that they could enter into eternal life only by eating His flesh and drinking His blood—i.e., by sharing His life and the spirit of sacrifice which led Him to offer it up for the life of the world. Now they were taught that what had appeared impossible was to become possible through the outward symbol of the bread thus broken. They were to "do this" as a memorial of Him, and so to keep fresh in their remembrance that sacrifice which He had offered.

(28) For this is my blood of the new testament.—Better, "this is my blood of the covenant." (See note on Heb. 9:16.) The best MSS omit the word "new" both here and in Mark. The great prophecy of Jer. 31:31-34 was certain to have a prominent place in the minds of those who had come into contact, as Luke must have done, with the line of thought indicated in the Epistle to the Hebrews (chaps. 8, 9), and therefore we cannot wonder that we find the word "new" in the report of the words given by him (Luke 22:20) and by Paul (I Cor.

11:25). The "blood of the covenant" is obviously a reference to the history of Exod. 24:4-8). The blood which the Son of man was about to shed was to be to the true Israel of God what the blood which Moses had sprinkled on the people had been to the outward Israel. (See Gal. 3:19; Heb. 12:24.) The essence of that covenant was to be the inward working of the divine law, which had before been brought before the conscience as an external standard of duty—a truer knowledge of God, and through that knowledge the forgiveness of iniquity. All this, they were told, was to be brought about through the sacrifice of the death of Christ. As in 20:28, our Lord uses the indefinite "for many" as equivalent to the universal "for all." Comp. I Tim. 2:6.

(30) And when they had sung an hymn.—Comp. John 14:31. This was probably the received Paschal series of Psalms (115 to 118, inclusive), and the word implies a chant or musical recitative. Psalms 113 and 114 were sung commonly during the meal.

They went out into the mount of Olives.—The discourses reported in John 15; 16; 17, which must be assigned to this period in the evening, seem to imply a halt from time to time, during which the Master poured forth His heart to His disciples, or uttered intercessions for them (comp. verses 33-35 with Luke 22:32). John, who had "lain in his bosom" at the supper, would naturally be nearest to Him now, and this may, in part at least, explain how it was that so full a report of all that was thus spoken appears only in his gospel.

(31) The citation of this prophecy (Zech. 13:7) is every way suggestive as showing that our Lord's thoughts had dwelt, and that He led the disciples to dwell, on that chapter as applicable to Himself.

(35) Though I should die with thee.—Though foremost in announcing the resolve, Peter was not alone in it. Thomas had spoken like words before (John 11:16), and all felt as if they were prepared to face death for their Master's sake.

(36) A place called Gethsemane.—The word means "oil press," and was obviously connected with the culture of the trees from which the Mount took its name. John's description implies that it was but a little way beyond the brook Kidron (18:1), on the lower western slope of the mount. There was a garden (or rather, "orchard") there which was a frequent resort of our Lord and the disciples when they sought retirement.

(37) See notes on 9:23-26; 17:1. There is a mysterious contrast between the calm, triumphant serenity which had shone in the look and tone of the Son of man up to this time, and had reached its highest point in the prayer of John 17, and the anguish and distress that were now apparent. And in His sufferings we must remember there was an element absolutely unique. It was His to "tread the wine-press" alone (Isa. 63:3). It was not only, as it might be with other martyrs, the natural shrinking of man's nature from pain and death, nor yet the pain of finding treachery and want of true devotion where there had been the promise of faithfulness. The intensity of His sympathy at that moment made the sufferings and sins of mankind His own, and the burden of those sins weighed upon His soul as greater than He could bear (Isa. 53:4-6).

(39) If it be possible, let this cup pass from me.—He had spoken before to the disciples who were now near Him of the "cup" which His Father had given Him to drink (see 20:23). Now the "cup" is brought to His lips, and His human will at once shrinks from it and accepts it. The prayer which He had taught His disciples to use, "Lead us not into temptation," is now His prayer, but it is subordinated to that other prayer, which is higher even than it, "Thy will be done." In the prayer "If it be possible" we recognize (Mark 13:32) the natural, necessary limits of our Lord's humanity. The divine Omnipotence works through self-imposed laws; spiritual ends cannot be obtained except through their appointed and therefore necessary means. God might have redeemed mankind, men have rashly said, without the sufferings and death of the Son of man, but the higher laws of the divine government made such a course morally impossible.

(40) Mark (14:37) individualizes the words —"Simon, sleepest thou?" He had boasted of his readiness to do great things; he could not so much as rouse himself to watch for one hour. The last word may be fairly taken as partly measuring the time that had passed since their Master had left them.

(42) If this cup may not pass away from me.—There is a slight change of tone perceptible in this prayer as compared with the first. It is as though the conviction that it was not possible that the cup could pass away from Him had come with fuller clearness before His mind, and He was learning to accept it. He finds the answer to the former prayer in the continuance, not the removal, of the bitter agony that preyed on His spirit. (See Luke 22:43, 44.)

(44) Saying the same words.—The fact suggests that there is a repetition in prayer which indicates not formalism but intensity of feeling. Lower forms of sorrow may, as it were, play with grief and vary the forms of its expression, but the deepest and sharpest agony is content to fall back upon the iteration of the same words.

(47) A great multitude with swords and staves.—John's account (18:3) is fuller. The multitude included the cohort (Acts 10:1) of Roman soldiers sent by Pilate to prevent a tumult, armed with swords, and the officers of the chief priests, probably the Levites or Nethinim, who were the guards of the Temple, armed with "clubs."

(48) Whomsoever I shall kiss.—It is probable, from the known customs of the Jews and of the early Christians (Rom. 16:16; I Thess. 5:26), that this was the usual salutation of the disciples to their Master. John makes no mention of the sign, probably because here, as elsewhere, he seeks to give touches that others had passed over, rather than to repeat what the oral or written teaching of the Church already had made familiar.

(50) Friend, wherefore art thou come?—In classical Greek the word rendered "friend" was used by fellow soldiers or sailors of each other. Socrates used it in conversing with his scholars (Plato, **Repub.** 1, 334). It is probably immediately after the kiss had thus been given that we must insert the short dialogue between our Lord and the officers recorded in John 18:2-8.

(51) One of them which were with Jesus.—Though all four gospels record the fact, John alone (18:10, 11) records the names both of the disciple who struck the blow and of the servant whom he attacked (comp. Luke 23:33). The reticence of the first three gospels in this instance, as in that of the woman with the box of ointment, must have been intentional. Luke the physician (22:51) alone records the fact that our Lord touched and healed the wound thus made.

(52) The words which Matthew gives are not a general rule declaring the unlawfulness of all warfare, but are limited in their range by the occasion. Resistance at that time would have involved certain destruction. More than that, it would have been fighting not for God, but against Him, because it would have been against the fulfillment of His purpose. (See verse 54.)

(53) Could He have brought Himself to utter that prayer, it would have been answered; but He could not so pray unless He knew it to be in harmony with His Father's will. He had been taught, in that hour of agony, that it was not in harmony, and therefore He would not utter it. The number is probably suggested by that of the apostles: not twelve weak men, one a traitor and the others timorous, but twelve legions of the armies of the Lord of hosts. Note the Roman word appearing here (comp. Mark 5:9, 15), as the representative of warlike might.

(56) But all this was done.—We see from Mark 14:49 that this was not a comment of the evangelist's, but our Lord's own witness to the disciples and the multitude that the treachery and violence of which He was the victim were all working out a divine purpose and fulfilling the Scriptures in which that purpose had been shadowed forth. (See Isa. 53:10.)

(57) To Caiaphas the high priest.—John alone, probably from the special facilities which he possessed as known to the high priest (18:15, 16), records the preliminary examination before Annas (18:13, 19-24). It was obviously intended to draw from our Lord's lips something that might serve as the basis of an accusation. Caiaphas, we must remember, had already committed himself to the policy of condemnation (John 11:49, 50). The whole history that follows leaves the impression that the plans of the priests had been hastened by the treachery of Judas.

Where the scribes and the elders were assembled.—It was against the rules of Jewish law to hold a session of the Sanhedrin or Council for the trial of capital offenses by night. Such an assembly on the night of the Paschal Supper would have been still more at variance with usage. The present gathering was, therefore, an informal one—probably a packed meeting of those who were parties to the plot, Nicodemus and Joseph of Arimathaea (and probably others, like the young "ruler" of Luke 18:18) not being summoned. When they had gone through their mock trial, and day was dawning (Luke 22:66), they transformed themselves into a formal court, and proceeded to pass judgment.

(58) To see the end.—There is something singularly suggestive in this account of Peter's motive. It was more than a vague

curiosity. There was something of sorrowful anxiety, of reverential sorrow, but there was no fervent devotion, no prayer for himself or his Master, only the fevered restlessness of uncertain expectation, and so all the natural instability of his character had free play, with nothing to control it.

(59) Sought false witness.—The attempt to draw the materials for condemnation from the lips of the accused had failed. The law of Moses required at least two witnesses (Deut. 17:6; 19:15), and these were examined independently of each other. The haste which marked all the proceedings of the trial had probably prevented previous concert, and the judges could not convict in the face of a glaring discrepancy.

(61) This fellow said, I am able to destroy the temple of God.—Apparently, the second cleansing of the Temple (21:12) had revived the memory of the first, and brought back to men's minds the words that had then been spoken (John 2:19). What was now reported was a sufficiently natural distortion of what had then been said. Mark adds that even then the witnesses did not fully agree.

(63) I adjure thee by the living God . . .—See Exod. 22:11; Num. 5:19-22. The appeal was one of unusual solemnity. All else had failed to break through the silence, but this would surely rouse Him. The oath was skilfully worded so as to force upon our Lord the alternative either of denying what indeed He was, or of making a confession which would be treated as blasphemy.

(64) Thou hast said.—He was indeed what the words they had uttered implied. More than this, He was also the Son of man of Daniel's vision (Dan. 7:13), the Head of an everlasting kingdom. At the crisis of His history, when denial would have saved His life, He asserts His claim to be much more than a moral teacher.

(65) Then the high priest rent his clothes.—The act was a formal sign of condemnation. The judges in a Jewish trial for blasphemy were bound to tear their clothes when the blasphemous words were uttered, and the clothes so torn were never afterward to be mended.

(66) He is guilty of death.—The decision, as far as the meeting went, was unanimous. Sentence was passed. It remained, however, to carry the sentence into effect, and this, while the Roman governor was at Jerusalem, presented a difficulty which had to be met by proceedings of another kind. The Jews, or at least their rulers, who courted the favor of Rome, ostentatiously disclaimed the power of punishing capital offenses (John 18:31).

(67) Then did they spit in his face.—We learn from Mark 14:65 and Luke 22:63 that these acts of outrage were perpetrated not by the members of the Sanhedrin but by the officers who had the accused in their custody. Here, also, they were unconsciously working out a complete correspondence with Isaiah's picture of the righteous sufferer (Isa. 50:6). The word "buffeted" describes a blow with the clenched fist, as contrasted with one with the open palm.

(68) Prophesy unto us, thou Christ.—The words derived their point from the fact recorded by Mark 14:65, that the officers had blindfolded their prisoner. Was He able, through His supernatural power, to identify those who smote Him?

(70) But he denied.—This is the order of the apostle's denials: (1) On his entry into the courtyard of the palace, in answer to the female slave who kept the door (John 18:17); (2) As he sat by the fire warming himself, in answer to another damsel (Matt. 26:69) and other by-standers (John 18:25; Luke 22:58), including the kinsman of Malchus (John 18:26); (3) About an hour later (Luke 22:59), after he had gone into the gateway leading out of the courtyard, in answer to one of the damsels who had spoken before (Mark 14:69; Matt. 26:71) and to other by-standers (Luke 22:59; Matt. 26:74; Mark 14:20). There were thus three distinct occasions; but as the hasty words of denial rose to his lips, it is probable that they were repeated more than once on each occasion, and that several persons heard them.

The impulse which led to the denial was probably shame no less than fear. The feeling which had shown itself when he first heard of his Master's coming passion (Matt. 16:22) came back upon him, and he shrank from the taunts and ridicule which were sure to fall upon the followers of One whom they had acknowledged as the Christ, and whose career was ending in apparent failure. It was against that feeling of shame that our Lord on that occasion had specially warned him (Mark 8:38). The element of fear also was probably strong in Peter's nature. (Comp. Gal. 2:12.)

(72) With an oath.—The downward step once taken, the disciple's fall was fatally rapid. Forgetful of his Lord's command forbidding any use of oaths in common speech (Matt. 5:34), he did not shrink from invoking the divine name, directly or indirectly, to attest his falsehood. (See verse 74.)

(73) Thy speech bewrayeth thee.—The Galilean **patois** was probably stronger when he spoke under the influence of strong excitement. It was said to have, as its chief feature, a confused thick utterance of the guttural letters of the Hebrew alphabet, so that they could not be distinguished from each other, and the change of **Sh** into **Th**. The half-detection which the remark implied, and some sense of shame at the provincialism attracting notice, led to the more vehement denial that followed.

(75) Peter remembered the word of Jesus.—The Lord's look (Luke 22:61), full of tenderest pity and deepest sadness, recalled him to his better self, and the floodgates of penitence were opened. We may infer from his next appearance in company with John on the morning of the Resurrection (John 20:3) that he turned in his contrition to the friend and companion of his early years, who had probably witnessed his denials, and was not repulsed. The fact that the record of his fall appears in every gospel may indicate that in later years he did not shrink from letting men know of his guilt, but sought rather that men might find in him (as Paul afterward in his experience, I Tim. 1:12-16) a proof of the mercy and tender pity of his Lord.

27

(1) Took counsel.—Another formal meeting was held (according to the Jewish rule that the sentence of the judges was to be given at the same sitting as the trial) to confirm the previous decision, and probably to determine on the next step to be taken. It ended (verse 2) in sending our Lord to Pilate, and leaving to him the responsibility of punishing. They entered, as the sequel shows, on a kind of diplomatic struggle as to the limits of the ecclesiastical and imperial powers, the former seeking to make the latter its tool, the latter to avoid the responsibility of seeming to act in that character.

(2) Pontius Pilate.—The governor, or more accurately, the procurator, of Judaea is conspicuous as occupying a solitary prominence in the creeds of Christendom. He must have belonged, by birth or adoption, to the **gens** of the Pontii; the **cognomen** Pilatus means "armed with the **pilum** or javelin," and may have had its origin in some early military achievement. When Judaea became formally subject to the empire, on the deposition of Archelaus, a **procurator**, or collector of revenue, invested with judicial power, was appointed to govern it, subject to the governor of Syria (Luke 2:2). Pontius Pilate, of whose previous career we know nothing, was appointed, A.D. 25-26, as the sixth holder of that office. His administration had already, prior to our Lord's trial, been marked by a series of outrages on Jewish feelings. (See Josephus, **Ant.** 17:3, §§ 1, 2 and **Wars,** 2.9, §§ 2-4; Philo, **Leg. ad Caium,** c. 38; Luke 13:1, 12.) All attested his vacillating character.

(3) Then Judas, which had betrayed him.— Had he hoped that his Lord, when forced to a decision, would assert His claim as the Christ, put forth His power, and triumph over His enemies, and that so he would gain at once the reward of treachery and the credit of having contributed to establish the kingdom? Or did the mere remorse of one who, after acting in the frenzy of criminal passion, see the consequences of his deeds in all their horror, furnish adequate explanation of what follows?

Repented himself.—The Greek word is not that commonly used for "repentance," as involving a change of mind and heart, but is rather "regret," a simple change of feeling. The coins on which he had once gazed and clutched at eagerly were now hateful in his sight, and their touch like that of molten metal from the furnace. He must get rid of them somehow. There is something terribly suggesting in the fact that here there were no tears as there had been in Peter's repentance.

(5) He cast down the pieces of silver in the temple.—The Greek word for "temple" is that which especially denotes the "sanctuary," which only the priests could enter. They had stood, it would seem, talking with Judas before the veil or curtain which screened it from the outer court, and he hurled or flung it into the Holy Place.

Hanged himself.—Comp. Acts 1:18. The horrors there recorded may have been caused by the self-murderer's want of skill, or the trembling agony that could not tie the noose firmly enough.

(6) It is not lawful for to put them into the treasury.—The Corban was the sacred treasure chest of the Temple, into which no foreign coins were admitted, and from which the Law (Deut. 23:18) excluded the unclean offerings of the price of shame. By parity of reasoning, the priests seem to have

thought that the blood money which was thus returned was excluded also.

(7) The potter's field, in the Valley of Hinnom **(Gehenna)** on the south side of Jerusalem (Jer. 18:2; 19:2), was now in the state of a disused quarry. It was necessary, since Roman soldiers were often stationed in the city, and men of all nations came to it, to provide some burial place for them; but no Jew would admit their bones into the sepulcher of his fathers. On the other hand, every devout Jew would shrink from the thought of burying his dead in the foul and hateful spot which had become the type of the unseen Gehenna. (See notes on 5:22.) There was, therefore, a subtle fitness of association in the policy which the priests adopted. The place was itself accursed; it was bought with accursed money; it was to be used for the burial of the accursed strangers.

(9, 10) The words cited are found in our present Old Testament, not in Jeremiah, but in Zech. 11:13, and there is no trace of their ever having occupied any other place in the Hebrew Canon. How is this discrepancy to be explained? We remember the Jewish notion that the spirit of Jeremiah had passed into Zechariah; and that Jeremiah, having at one time stood first in the Jewish order of the prophets, was taken as representing the whole volume, as David was of the whole Book of Psalms. Or we may believe that the writer quoted from memory, and that recollecting the two conspicuous chapters (18 and 19) in which Jeremiah had spoken of the potter and his work, he was led to think that this also belonged to the same group of prophecies. The words given by Matthew represent neither the Greek version of Zech. 11:13 nor the original Hebrew, but have the look of being a free quotation adapted to the facts. As they stand in Zechariah, the words have an adequate historical meaning entirely independent of Matthew's application of them. This (comp. 1:23; 2:15-18; 4:15; 8:17; 12:18) was entirely compatible with the evangelist's manner of dealing with prophecy.

(11) And Jesus stood before the governor.—In his first conversation with the accusers, Pilate endeavored to throw the **onus** of judging upon them, and was met by the ostentatious disavowal of any power to execute judgment (John 18:28-32). The single question which Matthew records was followed by a conversation in which our Lord declared that, though He were a King, it was not after the manner of the kingdoms of the world (John 18:33-38). The impression thus made on the mind of the governor explains the desire which he felt to effect, in some way or other, the release of the accused. (See verse 18.)

(15) **The governor was wont to release.**— It is not known when the practice began, nor whether it was primarily a Jewish or a Roman one. If introduced by Pilate, it was, we may believe, a concession intended to conciliate those whom his previous severities had alienated (see note on verse 2). Before this stage of the proceedings we have to place the occurrences of Luke 23:4-12.

(16) **A notable prisoner, called Barabbas.**— There is considerable evidence in favor of the reading which gives "Jesus Barabbas" as the name of the prisoner. The commonness of the name "Jesus" might lead to his being known to his comrades and to the multitude chiefly as Barabbas ("son of a father"). John (18:40) tells us that he was a robber; Luke (23:19) and Mark (15:7) note that he had taken a prominent part with some insurgents in the city, and that he, with them, had committed murder in the insurrection. (This may have been the popular reaction to Pilate's using the Corban money to build an aqueduct—Josephus, *Wars*, 2.9 §4— which would explain his popularity with both priests and people.) As the term Abba (father) was a customary term of honor, as applied to a rabbi (Matt. 23:9), it is possible that the name by which he was popularly known commemorated a fact in his family history of which he might naturally be proud. "Jesus, the rabbi's son" was a cry that found more favor than "Jesus the Nazarene."

(19) **The judgment seat.**—The chair of judgment was placed upon a Mosaic pavement, and was indispensable to the official action of any provincial ruler. (Comp. John 19:13.)

His wife sent unto him.—See Tacitus, **Ann.** 3.33, 34. The apocryphal **Gospel of Nicodemus** (2:1) gives her name as Procula, and states that she was a proselyte to Judaism. About this time, both at Rome and in other cities (Acts 17:4, 12), Jews had gained considerable influence over women of the higher classes and carried on an active work of proselytism.

(22) **Let him be crucified.**—This was the first direct intimation of the mode of death to which the priests destined their prisoner. It was implied in their fixed resolve to make the Roman governor the executioner of their sentence (John 18:31); but now the

cry came from the multitude, as the result, we may believe, of the promptings described in verse 20, "Crucify him!"—punish Him as the robber and the rebel are punished.

(23) **Why, what evil hath he done?**—The question attested the judge's discernment of the innocence of the accused, but it attested also the cowardice of the judge. He was startled at the passionate malignity of the cry of the multitude and the priests, but had not the courage to resist it (see Luke 23:22).

(24) **He took water, and washed his hands.** —The act belonged to an obvious and almost universal symbolism. (Comp. Deut. 21:6; Ps. 26:6.) Pilate probably chose it partly as a relief to his own conscience, partly to appease his wife's scruples, partly as a last appeal of the most vivid and dramatic kind to the feelings of the priests and people.

(25) **His blood be on us, and on our children.**—The passionate hate of the people leads them, as if remembering the words of their own Law, to invert the prayer— which Pilate's act had, it may be, brought to their remembrance—"Lay not innocent blood unto thy people of Israel's charge" (Deut. 21:8), into a defiant imprecation. No more fearful prayer is recorded in the history of mankind. We have to remember, however, that but a fractional part of the people were present, and that some at least of the rulers, such as Joseph of Arimathaea, Nicodemus, and probably Gamaliel, had not consented to the deed of blood (Luke 23:51).

(26) **When he had scourged Jesus.**—The word used by Matthew, derived from the Latin **flagellum**, shows that it was the Roman punishment with knotted thongs of leather, not the Jewish beating with rods (II Cor. 11:24, 25). The prisoner was stripped sometimes entirely, sometimes to the waist, and tied by the hands to a pillar, with his back bent, so as to receive the full force of the blows. The scourge was of stout leather weighted with lead or bones. Jewish law limited its penalty to forty stripes, reduced in practice to "forty stripes save one" (II Cor. 11:24; Deut. 25:3), but Roman practice knew no limit but that of the cruelty of the executioner or the physical endurance of the sufferer.

(27) **The common hall.**—Literally, the **Praetorium,** a word which applied originally to the tent of the praetor, or general, and so to the headquarters of the camp, had come to be used for the residence of a

prince or governor (comp. Acts 23:35). Pilate's dialogue with the priests and people probably had been held from the portico of the Tower of Antony, which rose opposite the Temple Court and served partly as a fortress, partly as an official residence.

(28) **A scarlet robe.**—Here again we have a technical word, the **paludamentum**, used for the military cloak worn by emperors in their character as generals and by other officers of high rank (Pliny, 22:2, 3). Mark and John call it purple (Mark 15:17; John 19:2); but the "purple" of the ancients was "crimson," and the same color might easily be called by either name. It was a common practice to subject condemned prisoners before execution to this kind of outrage. Here the point of the mockery lay in the fact that their Victim had been condemned as claiming the title of a King. They had probably seen or heard of the insults of like kind offered by Herod and his soldiers (Luke 23:21), and now reproduced them with aggravated cruelty.

(29) The likeness of the crown or garland thus made to that worn by conquering kings and emperors fitted it admirably for the purpose. The reed or stalk represented the scepter which had been wielded by generals in their triumphs and had become the received symbol of sovereignty. Mark 15:19 implies a continued, not a momentary, act of mock homage, the whole band filing by and each kneeling as he passed.

(30) **They spit upon him.**—See note on 26:67.

(31) **They took the robe off from him.**—At this point we insert the account which John gives (19:4, 5) of Pilate's last attempt to rescue the "just man" whom he had unjustly condemned. The "raiment" which they put on Him again included both the tunic and the cloak, or overgarment. In this case, the former was made without seam or opening (John 19:23), and the mere act of drawing it roughly over the lacerated flesh must have inflicted acute agony.

(32) **They found a man of Cyrene, Simon by name.**—There seems at that time to have been a flourishing settlement of Jews in Cyrene, and members of that community appear as prominent in the crowd of the day of Pentecost (Acts 2:10; see also Acts 6:9; 11:20). Mark's mention of him as the father of Alexander and Rufus suggests the thought that his sons were afterward prominent as members of the Christian community. May we not infer that he was suspected even then of being a secret disciple, and

that this led the people to seize on him and make him a sharer in the humiliation of his Master? The act implied that our Lord was sinking beneath the burden, and that the soldiers began to fear that He might die before they reached the place of execution.

(33) **A place called Golgotha.**—The other gospels give the name with the definite article, as though it were a well-known locality. It is not mentioned, however, by any Jewish writer, and its position is matter of conjecture. It was outside the walls of the city (John 19:20; Heb. 13:12). There was a garden in it (John 19:41), and in the garden a tomb, which was the property of Joseph of Arimathaea (verse 60). The name has been supposed by some to point to its being a common place of execution; but it is improbable that the skulls of criminals would have been left unburied, and that a wealthy Jew should have chosen such a spot for a garden and a burial place. The facts lead rather to the conclusion that the name indicated the round, bare, skull-like character of the eminence which was so called. The more familiar name of Calvary (Luke 23:33) has its origin in the Vulgate rendering (**Calvarium**—a skull) of the Greek word **Kranion**, or **Cranium**, which the evangelist actually uses.

(34) **Vinegar to drink mingled with gall.**—Comp. Mark 15:23. Gall was clearly something at once nauseous and narcotic, given by the merciful to dull the pain of execution, and mixed with the sour wine of the country and with myrrh to make it drinkable. It is probable that the offer came from the more pitiful of the women mentioned by Luke (23:27) as following our Lord and lamenting. Such acts were among the received "works of mercy" of the time and place. The "tasting" implied a recognition of the kindly purpose of the act, but a recognition only. In the refusal to do more than taste we trace the resolute purpose to drink the cup which His Father had given Him to the last drop, and not to dull either the sense of suffering nor the clearness of His communion with His Father with the slumberous potion.

(35) **They crucified him.**—The cross employed in capital punishment varied in its form, being sometimes simply a stake on which the sufferer was impaled, sometimes consisting of two pieces of timber put together in the form of an "x" (as in what we know as the St. Andrew's cross), sometimes in the form of a "t," familiar to us in Christian art as the Latin cross. In this

instance, the fact that the title or superscription was placed over our Lord's head implies that the last was the kind of cross employed. In carrying the sentence of crucifixion into effect, the cross was laid on the ground, and the condemned man stripped and laid upon it. Sometimes he was simply tied; sometimes, as here, nails were driven through the hands and feet; sometimes a projecting ledge was put for the feet to rest on; sometimes the whole weight of the body hung upon the limbs that were thus secured. The clothes of the criminal were the usual perquisites of the executioners, and in this case included (John 19:23) the tunic worn next to the body as well as the outer garment. It was as the soldiers were thus nailing Him to the cross that He prayed, "Father, forgive them" (Luke 23:34). See Ps. 22:18.

(37) THIS IS JESUS THE KING OF THE JEWS.—This was what was technically known as the **titulus**—the placard showing who the condemned person was and why he was punished. Each gospel gives it in a highly different form, the variations explicable on the assumption of corresponding differences in the Hebrew, Greek, and Latin forms of the inscription, which reproduced themselves in the reports upon which the gospel narratives were based. On grounds of ordinary likelihood John's record, as that of the only disciple whom we know to have been present at the crucifixion (John 19:25), may claim to be the most accurate. The priests obviously felt the superscription to be a declaration to the people that One who had a right to be their King, who was the only kind of King they were ever likely to have, had died the death of a malefactor, and therefore they clamored for a change, which Pilate refused to make (John 19:20).

(38) Then were there two thieves crucified with him.—Better, "robbers," the word being the same as that used of Barabbas (John 18:40). It would seem that they were members of the same band, and had been sharers in the same insurrection. The legends of the apocryphal **Gospel of Nicodemus** (1:10) give their names as Dysmas and Gysmas.

(40) Thou that destroyest the temple.—See notes on 26:61, 64, 65. To accept the challenge to come down from the cross would have been to show that He did not trust the Father, just as it would have been not faith, but want of faith, to have cast Himself from the pinnacle of the Temple,

and therefore to disown His Sonship in the very act of claiming it.

(44) The thieves also ... cast the same in his teeth.—Literally, "reviled him." On the change which afterward came over one of them, see note on Luke 23:40.

(45) From the sixth hour.—The first three gospels agree as to time and fact. Assuming them to follow the usual Jewish reckoning, we make this noon, the fixing to the cross having been at the third hour 9 a.m. (Mark 15:25), and the darkness lasting until 3 p.m. (John names the "sixth hour" as the time of our Lord's final condemnation by Pilate, following apparently the Roman mode of reckoning from midnight to noon.) It is probable that our Lord had been taken to the high priest's palace about 3 a.m. (the "cock-crow" of Mark 13:35).

Darkness over all the land.—The narrative does not necessarily involve more than the indescribable yet most oppressive gloom which seems to shroud the whole sky as in mourning (comp. Amos 8:9, 10), and which, being a common phenomenon of earthquakes, may have been connected with that described in verse 51. It is an indirect confirmation of the statement that about this time there is an obvious change in the conduct of the crowd.

(46) Eli, Eli, lama sabachthani.—The cry is recorded only by Matthew and Mark, and is the only record in them of words from the cross. Its absence from John's narrative was due probably to the fact that he had before this taken Mary from the scene of the crucifixion as from that which was more than she could bear (John 19:27). To the Roman soldiers, and to many of the bystanders, Greeks or Hellenistic Jews, the words would be, as the sequel shows, unintelligible. Both the spoken words of our Lord's enemies (verse 43) and the acts of the soldiers (verse 35) must have recalled the words of Psalm 22:1. Our Lord as man was to taste death in all its bitterness for every man (Heb. 2:9), and He could not so have tasted it had His soul been throughout in full undisturbed enjoyment of the presence of the Father. Here He exhibited a strange union, or rather instantaneous succession, of the sense of abandonment and of intensest faith.

(47) This man calleth for Elias.—There is no ground for looking on this as a willful, derisive misinterpretation. The dominant expectation of the coming of Elijah (see notes on 16:14; 17:10) would predispose men to fasten on the similarity of sound, and the strange unearthly darkness would intensify the feeling that looked for a supernatural manifestation of His presence. See note on 17:12.

(50) When he had cried again with a loud voice.—This was the "It is finished" of John 19:30, and the "Father, into thy hands I commend my spirit" of Luke 23:46, expressing the fullness of peace and trust, and the sense of a completed work.

It was seldom that crucifixion as a punishment ended so rapidly as it did here. (See Mark 15:44.) The physical causes of our Lord's death may be ascribed, especially in connection with the fact recorded in John 19:34, and with the "loud cry," indicating the pangs of an intolerable anguish, to a rupture of the vessels of the heart.

(51) The veil of the temple was rent in twain.—It is the veil that divided the Holy Place from the Holy of Holies that is meant here. This, like other incidents, may have been reported by the "great multitude of the priests" who "became obedient to the faith" (Acts 6:7). The priests had, as far as they had power, destroyed the true Temple (comp. John 2:19); but in doing so they had robbed their own sanctuary of all that made it holy. The true veil, as that which shrouded the divine glory from the eyes of men, was His own flesh, and through that He had passed, as the Forerunner of all who trusted in Him, into the sanctuary not made with hands, eternal in the heavens (Heb. 10:20, 21).

(52) Many bodies of the saints which slept arose.—Those who believe that when our Lord passed into Hades, the unseen world, it was to complete there what had been begun on earth, i.e., to proclaim there His victory over death and sin, will hardly think it impossible that there should have been outward tokens and witnesses of such a work. And the fact which Matthew records supplies, it may be, the most natural explanation of language hardly less startling, which meets us in I Pet. 3:19; 4:6. Who they were that thus appeared we are not told. The term "saints" was applied almost from the first to the collective body of disciples (Acts 9:13, 32, 41); it seems natural, therefore, to see in them those who, believing in Jesus, had passed to their rest before His crucifixion. On this supposition, their appearance met the feeling, sure to arise among those who were looking for an immediate manifestation of the kingdom (comp. I Thess. 4:13), that such as had so died were shut out from their share in that

kingdom; and we have thus an adequate reason for their appearance, so that friends and kindred might not sorrow for them, as others who had no hope. The statement that they did not appear until after our Lord's Resurrection is significant. The disciples were thus taught to look on that Resurrection not as an isolated phenomenon, but as the "firstfruits" of the victory over death. See I Cor. 15:20.

(54) Truly this was the Son of God.—We must interpret this from the standpoint of the centurion's knowledge. To him the words "Son of God" would convey the idea of one who was Godlike in those elements of character which are most divine—righteousness, holiness, and love. The centurion felt that the words, as he understood them, were true, and not false, of the Sufferer whose death he had witnessed.

(56) Mary Magdalene.—She came from the town of Magdala, not far from Tiberias, on the western side of the Sea of Galilee. The two prominent facts in her history prior to her connection with the Resurrection are that our Lord had cast "seven devils out of her" (Mark 16:9; Luke 8:2)—i.e., had freed her from some especially aggravated form of demoniacal possession—and that she followed Him and ministered to Him of her substance.

Mary the mother of James and Joses.—In Mark 15:40 she is described as the mother of "James the less and Joses," the epithet distinguishing the former from James the son of Zebedee, and possibly also from James the son of Alphaeus. She may have been identical with the wife of Clopas (possibly another form of Alphaeus) mentioned in John 19:25 as standing near the cross with the mother of the Lord, and, according to a natural construction of the words, described as her sister. Whether the two names, which occur also in the list of the "brethren of the Lord" (Mark 6:3), indicate that she was the mother of those brethren, is a point which we have no evidence to settle. The presumption seems against it, as on this supposition the "brethren" would be identical with the three sons in the list of the Twelve, a view which may better be rejected. (See notes on 10:1-4; 12:46.)

The mother of Zebedee's children.—Mark 15:40 gives her name as Salome. She, and not the wife of Clopas, may, on a perfectly tenable construction of John 19:25, have been identical with the sister of our Lord's mother mentioned there.

(57) A rich man of Arimathaea.—The

place so named was probably identical with the Ramah of I Sam. 1:19, the birthplace of the prophet. The site is more or less conjectural, but it may be located about four miles northwest of Jerusalem. Of Joseph we are told by Mark (15:43) that he was "an honourable counsellor," i.e., a member of the Sanhedrin, and that he was looking for the kingdom of God; by Luke (23:50, 51), that he was "a good man, and a just"; by John (19:38), that he was "a disciple, but secretly for fear of the Jews." He was apparently a man of the same class and type of character as Nicodemus, respecting our Lord as a man, admiring Him as a teacher, half-believing in Him as the Christ, and yet, until now, shrinking from confessing Him before men.

(60) Laid it in his own new tomb.—See note on verse 33. Like most Eastern graves, it was an opening cut in the vertical face of the rock. John (19:39) notes the singularly interesting fact that Nicodemus shared with Joseph in these reverential offices. Luke and John give the reason for the speed with which the entombment was hurried on: it was now near sunset. The Sabbath was near to beginning, and there was no alternative but that of leaving the body on the cross for another twenty-four hours. This, though common enough as a Roman practice (which commonly, indeed, left the corpse for birds of prey to feed on), would have shocked Jewish feelings, especially at the Paschal season, as a violation of their law (Deut. 21:23).

(62) See note on verse 51; comp. Mark 15:42. There is something strange in the way in which Matthew describes the day as coming "after the preparation," instead of saying simply "the Sabbath." A possible solution of the difficulty is, on the assumption that the Last Supper was a true Passover, that the day of the Crucifixion as being on the Passover was itself technically a Sabbath (Lev. 23:7, 24). Two Sabbaths therefore came together, and this may have led the evangelist to avoid the more common phrase, describing the second as being "the day that followed the praparation," i.e., the ordinary weekly Sabbath. The fact that the Lord's body was under the care of one who was secretly a disciple aroused their suspicions, and they would naturally take the first opportunity, even at the risk of infringing on the Sabbath rest, of guarding against the fraud which they suspected.

(63) We remember that the deceiver said . . .—It appears that while they had deliberately stirred up the passions of the people by representing the mysterious words of John 2:19 as threatening a literal destruction of the Temple (26:61; 27:40), they themselves had understood, wholly or in part, their true meaning.

(65) Ye have a watch.—Better, "take ye a guard." The "watch," or "guard," was a body of Roman soldiers who could not be set to such a task without Pilate's permission.

(66) Sealing the stone.—The opening of the tomb had been already closed by the stone which had been rolled so as nearly to fill it. The sealing was probably effected by drawing one or more ropes across the stone and fastening either end to the rock with wax or cement of some kind.

And setting a watch.—Better, "with the guard." The priests were not content to leave the work to the soldiers, but actually took part in it themselves.

28

The recorded appearances of our Lord Jesus after His Resurrection follow this order: (1) To Mary Magdalene (John 20:14; Mark 16:9); (2) To Mary Magdalene and the other Mary (Matt. 28:9); (3) To Peter (Luke 24:34; I Cor. 15:5); (4) To Cleopas and another disciple at Emmaus (Luke 24:13-35); (5) To the ten apostles at Jerusalem (Mark 16:14; Luke 24:36; John 20:19); (6) To the eleven apostles at Jerusalem (John 20:26); (7) To the disciples—five named, and others—by the Sea of Galilee (John 21:1-24); (8) To the eleven on a mountain in Galilee (Matt. 28:16; Mark 16:14); (9) To the five hundred brethren, possibly identical with the preceding (I Cor. 15:6); (10) To James the brother of the Lord (I Cor. 15:7); (11) To the eleven at Jerusalem before the Ascension (Mark 16:19, 20; Luke 24:50; Acts 1:3-12).

(1) In the end of the sabbath.—The order of facts appears to have been as follows: (1) Mary Magdalene and the other Mary, the mother of James the Less, watched the burial just before the Sabbath began on the evening of the day of the crucifixion; (2) They stayed at home during the twenty-four hours of the Sabbath; (3) On the evening of that day (the Sabbath-rest being over) they bought spices for the embalmment. (4) At the earliest dawn, about 4 a.m., they set out to the sepulcher, reaching it when the sun had risen (Mark 16:2).

(2) There was a great earthquake.—The form of the angel is described in Mark 16:5 and Luke 24:4. This was the answer to the question they had been asking as they came, "Who shall roll away the stone for us?" (Mark 16:3). That would have been beyond their strength.

(5, 6) See Luke 24:5-7 for a more detailed reference to our Lord's prophecies of His Resurrection.

(8) The best solution of the questions presented by a comparison of the gospel narrative at this stage is that Mary Magdalene ran eagerly to tell Peter and John, leaving the other Mary and Joanna (Luke 24:10), and then followed the two disciples (John 20:2). Then when they had left, the Lord showed Himself first to her (John 20:14), and then to the others (Matt. 28:9), whom she had by that time joined, and then they all hastened together to tell the rest of the disciples.

(9) Held him by the feet.—Better, "clasped His feet." Mary Magdalene had already heard the words "Touch me not" (John 20:17); but, if we suppose her to have rejoined the other women, passionate and rejoicing love carried her as it carried the others, beyond the limits of reverential obedience.

(11) Some of the watch.—This incident, like that of the appointment of the guard, is reported by Matthew only. As writing primarily for the Jews of Palestine, it was natural that he should take special notice of the rumor which hindered many of them from accepting the fact of the Resurrection, and trace it to its corrupt source. The object of the soldiers was, of course, to escape the penalty which they were likely to incur for seeming negligence, but their statement to the priests was at first a truthful one.

(12) And had taken counsel.—It was a formal, though probably a packed, meeting of the Sanhedrin. They decided on the ready expedients of bribery and falsehood. The fact that the chief priests were Sadducees, and therefore specially interested in guarding against what would appear as a contradiction of their main dogma, must not be forgotten as in part determining their action. (Comp. Acts 4:2.)

(15) Justin Martyr mentions the report as current among the Jews of his time, the Jews having sent "chosen men" into all parts of the world to propagate it (**Dial c. Tryph.** c. 108).

(16) The writer passes over, for some reason, all the intermediate appearances, and passes on at once to that which connected itself with the mission and work of the apostles, and through them of the universal Church. The words imply some more definite announcement than that of verses 7 and 10.

(18) All power is given unto me.—Literally, "all authority was given," the tense in the Greek being that by which men speak of something that occurred at a given point of time. (Comp. Phil. 2:8.) The exaltation came, the authority was given, at the moment of the Resurrection, and as the crown of His obedience unto death.

(19) Teach all nations.—Better, "make disciples of all the heathen." The disciples, having learned fully what their Master, their Rabbi, had to teach them, were now to become in their turn, as scribes of the kingdom of heaven, the teachers of others. It is interesting that in this solemn commission stress should be laid on the teaching, rather than on the sacerdotal element, of the Christian ministry; but that element is not altogether excluded (see note on John 20:23). It is every way interesting, again, that this full declaration of the universality of the Gospel should be especially recorded in the gospel written especially for Jews.

Baptizing them in the name of the Father . . .—Converts from the house of Israel, already of the family of God, needed to be baptized into the name of Jesus as the Messiah as the condition of their admission into the Church which He had founded. (See Acts 2:38; 10:48; 19:5; Rom. 6:3; Gal. 3:27.) By that confession they gave a fresh life to doctrines which they had partially received before, and belief in the Father and the Spirit was virtually implied in their belief in Jesus as the incarnate Son. For the heathen, however, the case stood otherwise. They had worshiped "gods many and lords many" (I Cor. 8:5), had been "without God in the world" (Eph. 2:12), and so they had not known the Father.

There remains the question as to what is meant by being baptized "into a name." The answer is to be found in the fact so prominent in the Old Testament (e.g. Exod. 3:14, 15), that the name of God is a revelation of what He is. Baptism was to be no longer, as it had been in the hands of John as the forerunner, merely a symbol of repentance, but was the token that those who received it were brought into an altogether new relation to Him who was thus revealed to them. The union of the three names in one formula (comp. II Cor. 13:14) is, furthermore, in itself a proof at once of the distinctness and equality of the three divine Persons. We cannot conceive of a command given to, and adopted by, the universal Church to baptize all its members in the name (not "the names") of God, and a merely human prophet, and an impersonal influence.

(20) Even unto the end of the world.— Literally, "of the age." Here the context determines the significance of the phrase, as stretching forward to the end of the age, or aeon, which began with the first Advent of the Christ and shall last until the second.

MARK

1

(1) The beginning of the gospel.—The opening words are interesting as presenting a transition stage in the history of the word "gospel," i.e., between its earlier sense as meaning generally the "good news" of the kingdom of God, and the later sense as a book recording the main facts in our Lord's life and work. (Comp. I Cor. 15:1; II Tim. 2:8.)

The Son of God.—This also is significant as to the Church's faith at the time when Mark wrote. If we think of Mark as reproducing Peter's teaching, we cannot fail to connect the words, placed in the title of his gospel, with the apostle's confession in Matt. 16:16.

(2) In the prophets.—With one exception, and that doubtful as to its genuineness (see note on 15:28), this is the only quotation from a prophet made by the evangelist himself in this gospel. The fact that Mark wrote for Gentiles furnishes a partial explanation of his silence in this respect, as compared with the other gospels. See Mal. 3:1.

(3) The voice of one crying in the wilderness.—See note on Matt. 3:3.

(4) John did baptize.—No other gospel passes so abruptly into the actual work of the Forerunner. There is no account of the birth or infancy of our Lord, as in Matthew and Luke; none of the pre-existence of the Son of man, as in John. Mark is here, as elsewhere, emphatically the evangelist of action. The special phrase "baptism of repentance"—i.e., the sign of repentance, that which was connected with it and presupposed it—occurs in Luke 3:3 and Acts 19:4. Repentance was followed, even then, by forgiveness, although the blood which availed for that forgiveness (Matt. 26:28) had not as yet been shed.

(5, 6) See notes on Matt. 3:4-6.

(7) There cometh one mightier than I.—See note on Matt. 3:11. To stoop down and loosen the sandals was commonly the act of the servant who afterward carried them; thus Mark expresses more vividly what we should call the menial character of the office.

(8) I indeed have baptized you with water.—See note on Matt. 3:11. Mark omits the "fire" which Matthew joins with the

Holy Ghost, possibly as less intelligible to his Gentile readers.

(9-11) See notes on Matt. 3:13-17.

(12) Immediately the Spirit driveth him.—See note on Matt. 4:1; but observe Mark's characteristic "immediately" and the stronger word "driveth him."

(13) And he was there in the wilderness.—See notes on Matt. 4:2-5, 8-11. Mark compresses the history by omitting the several forms of the Temptation. Peculiar to him are the use of "Satan" instead of "the devil" and the statement that Jesus was "with the wild beasts." The implied thought is partly that their presence added to the terrors of the Temptation, partly that in His being protected from them there was the fulfillment of the promise in the Psalm (91:13) which furnished the tempter with his chief weapon.

(14) Now after that John was put in prison.—Mark agrees with Matthew in omitting all our Lord's early ministry in Galilee and Jerusalem, and takes the imprisonment of the Baptist as his starting point. That imprisonment is assumed here to be known; but the facts connected with it are not related until 6:17-20.

(15) The time is fulfilled.—The words are not found in the parallel passages of the other gospels, and are interesting as embodying the same thought as Paul's "in the fulness of time" (Gal. 4:4; Eph. 1:10). So, too, Mark adds "believe the gospel" to the simple "repent" of Matthew, and gives "the kingdom of God" instead of "the kingdom of heaven."

(16) As he walked by the sea of Galilee.—See notes on Matt. 4:18-22.

(20) With the hired servants.—This is peculiar to Mark's gospel, and of some interest as throwing light on the relative social position of the sons of Zebedee.

(21) And they went into Capernaum.—Here Mark's narrative ceases to run parallel with that of Matthew, and agrees almost verbally with Luke 4:31-37.

Straightway.—The frequent recurrence of this adverb is often disguised in the English as "immediately," "forthwith," "anon," "by-and-by." It occurs forty-one times in the gospel, nine times in this first chapter.

(23) An unclean spirit.—The phrase occurs in all the first three gospels (not in John's), but with special frequency in this. As in most Eastern cities, madness had an immunity from restraint, and the demoniacs seem to have mingled, if they chose, with the crowd of worshipers in the synagogue.

(24) The Holy One of God.—The name occurs, as applied to Christ, only here, in the parallel passage of Luke 4:34, and in the better MSS of John 6:69. It probably had its origin in the Messianic application of "Thy Holy One" in Ps. 16:10. Its strict meaning is "the Holy One whom God owns as such," who has attained, i.e., the highest form of holiness. (See note on 3:11.)

(32) And at even.—See note on Matt. 8:17.

(35) A great while before day.—Literally, "very early, while it was yet night." The note of time is peculiar to Mark. Prayer seems to have been sought now, as at other times, after a day of extraordinary and exhausting labor.

(38) For therefore came I forth.—In this form the words might refer simply to His leaving Capernaum; but the report in Luke, "for therefore am I sent" (Luke 4:43), connects them with His mission as a whole. In any case, however, the disciples, in this stage of their progress, would hardly enter into the full meaning of that mission. To them His "coming forth," even as being "sent," would be as from His home at Nazareth, not as from the bosom of the Father.

(40-43) And there came a leper.—See notes on Matt. 8:1-4. The miracle appears in Matthew as following closely on the Sermon on the Mount.

2

(1) And again he entered into Capernaum.—See notes on Matt. 9:1-8. The house may have been Peter's, as before in 1:29.

(3, 4) The number of the bearers is given by Mark only, as also strong expressions of the injury done to the roof.

(14-17) See notes on Matt. 9:9-13.

(17) I came not to call the righteous.—Closely as the three accounts agree, it is noticeable that here also Mark and Luke, as writing for Gentile readers, omit the reference (Matt. 9:13) to the words cited by our Lord from the Old Testament.

(18-22) See notes on Matt. 9:14-17.

(23-28) See notes on Matt. 12:1-8.

(26) In the days of Abiathar the high priest.—Mark's is the only record that gives the name of the high priest, and in so doing it creates a historical difficulty. (See I Sam. 21:1; 22:20; I Kings 2:26.) A probable conjecture is that our Lord gave the name of the more famous priest of the two, who acted then as a coadjutor to his father (comp. I Sam. 4:4), and who, as of David's party, was the chief agent in allowing him to take the shewbread.

3

(1-6) A man there which had a withered hand.—Mark alone names (verse 6) the Herodians as joining with the Pharisees in their plot for His destruction. On the Herodians, see notes on Matt. 11:8; 22:16.

(7, 8) The fact recorded here is interesting as in some degree implying the ministry in Jerusalem and its neighborhood, which the first three gospels, for some reason, pass over.

(8) From Idumaea.—This is the only passage in the New Testament in which this country is named. It had acquired a considerably wider range than the Edom of Old Testament, and included the whole country between the Arabah and the Mediterranean. It was at this time under the government of Aretas (II Cor. 11:32), the father of the wife whom Herod Antipas had divorced, and this had probably brought about a more frequent exchange between its inhabitants and those of Galilee and Peraea.

They about Tyre and Sidon.—The fact is interesting in its connection with the history of the Syro-Phoenician woman (Matt. 15:21; Mark 7:24), as showing how our Lord's appearance in that region was welcomed as that of one whose fame had traveled there before Him.

(11) And unclean spirits.—The testimony which had been given in a single instance (1:24; see note) now became more or less general. But it came in a form which our Lord could not receive. The wild cry of the frenzied demoniac had no place in the evidence to which He appealed (John 5:31-37), and tended, as far as it impressed men at all, to set them against the Teacher who was thus acknowledged.

(13) And he goeth up into a mountain.—What follows is, like the parallel narrative of Luke 6:12, 13, the selection rather than the mission of the Twelve, the latter appearing in Matt. 10. In Luke we notice that the night had been spent in prayer, apparently, as usual, alone, and that when it was day He called the company of the disciples, who had waited below, and made choice of the Twelve.

759

(16-19) On the list of the apostles, see notes on Matt. 10:2-4.

(17) Boanerges.—The word is an Aramaic compound, meaning "sons of thunder." We see in the name a witness to the fiery zeal of the sons of Zebedee (comp. Matt. 20:21; Luke 9:49, 54).

(21) And when his friends . . .—As the "mother and the brethren" are mentioned later on in the chapter as coming to check His teaching, we must see in these some whom they had sent with the same objective. To them the new course of action on which our Lord had entered seemed a sign of overexcitement, recklessly rushing into danger. Perhaps the random word thus uttered gave occasion to the more malignant taunt of the scribes in the next verse (comp. John 10:20).

(23-30) He hath Beelzebub.—See notes on Matt. 12:24-32.

(23) Said unto them in parables.—The word is used in its wider sense, as including any form of argument from analogy more or less figurative. As in most reports of discourses as distinct from facts, Mark is somewhat briefer than Matthew.

(30) Because they said.—This is peculiar to Mark. It is as though he would explain to his readers what had called forth so awful a warning. He does not absolutely identify what had been said with the sin against the Holy Ghost, but it tended to that sin, and therefore made the warning necessary.

(31-35) There came then his brethren and his mother.—See notes on Matt. 12:46-50.

4

(1-20) See notes on Matt. 13:1-23.

(8) Some thirty . . .—Here there is a difference from Matthew sufficient to establish a certain measure of independence: an ascending instead of a descending scale.

(10) They that were about him.—In Matthew, only the disciples are mentioned. Here the presence of others besides the Twelve is directly asserted.

(12) That seeing they may see . . .—Mark characteristically gives the words of Isa. 6:9, but not as a quotation. The form in this instance, at first sight, suggests the thought that our Lord's purpose was to produce the blindness and deafness of which He speaks. The real meaning of the words is, however, that such was to be the result of the willful blindness of those who rejected Him; and the acceptance of a foreseen result was, in Hebrew forms of thought, expressed as the working out of an intention. (See notes on Matt. 13:14.)

(21) Is a candle brought to be put under a bushel?—See Matt. 5:15. Mark omits all the other parables that follow in Matthew, and connects with that of the Sower sayings more or less proverbial, which in Matthew appear in a different context. Looking at our Lord's method of teaching by the repetition of proverbs under different aspects and on different occasions, it is likely that this of the "candle" was actually spoken in the connection in which we find it here.

(22) For there is nothing hid.—See Matt. 10:26. The Greek word here for "secret" is interesting as being the same as that which we find in our word "Apocrypha." The term was, in the first instance, applied to books that were surrounded with the secrecy of a spurious sacredness, but were not publicly recognized in the Church as being of divine authority, and was then transferred to all books which, whether "spurious" or "secret," wanted that recognition.

(24) With what measure ye mete.—See note on Matt. 7:12. In the Sermon on the Mount it appears as the law of retribution, which brings pardon to those who pardon, judgment without mercy to those who show no mercy. Here the law works in another region. With the measure with which we dispense our knowledge, God will, in His bounty, bestow more knowledge upon us.

(26) As if a man should cast seed into the ground.—What follows has the special interest of being the only parable peculiar to Mark, one therefore which had escaped the obvious eagerness of Matthew and Luke to gather up all that they could find of this form of our Lord's teaching. It runs to some extent parallel with the parable of the Sower, as though it had been given as another and easier lesson in the art of understanding parables; and if we assume a connection between Mark and Peter, it may be regarded as having in this way made a special impression on the mind of the apostle. Like many other parables, it finds an interpretation in the analogous phenomena of the growth of the kingdom both in the world at large and in the heart of each individual.

(28) The earth bringeth forth fruit of herself.—Stress is laid on the spontaneity of growth; and the lesson drawn from it is obviously one of patience and faith. In spiritual husbandry you do not take up the seeds to see whether they are growing. It is wiser to sow the seed, and to believe that sun and rain will quicken it. (See Eccles. 11:6.)

(29) He putteth in the sickle.—From one point of view, the harvest is the end of the world (Matt. 13:39), and the putting in the sickle is the coming of Christ to judge. (Comp. Rev. 14:14-18.) From the other, the harvest is the end of each man's life, and the sickle is in the hands of the angel of death.

(31, 32) It is like a grain of mustard seed.—See note on Matt. 13:31.

(33, 34) See note on Matt. 13:34.

(34) He expounded.—The word is the verb from which is formed the noun "interpretation" in II Pet. 1:20, and so takes its place in the coincidences of phraseology which connect that epistle with this gospel.

(35-41) See notes on Matt. 8:23-27.

5

(1-20) See notes on Matt. 8:28-34.

(7) Thou Son of the most high God.—This is the first occurrence of the name in the New Testament. As a divine name "the most high God" belonged to the earliest stage of the patriarchal worship of the one Supreme Deity (see Gen. 14:18; Num. 24:16; Deut. 32:8). In the prophets and the Psalms it mingles with the other names of God (see Isa. 14:14; Lam. 3:35; Dan. 4:17, 24, 32, 34; 7:18, 22, 25; Pss. 7:17; 9:2; 18:13; 46:4). In many of these passages it was used where there was some point of contact in fact or feeling with nations which, though acknowledging one Supreme God, were not of the stock of Abraham. The old Hebrew word **Elion** found a ready equivalent in the Greek **hypsistos**, which had already been used by Pindar as a divine name. That word accordingly appeared frequently in the LXX, and came into frequent use among Hellenistic Jews. It was one of the words which, in later as in earlier times, helped to place the Gentile and the Jew on a common ground. It seems to have been used frequently as a formula of exorcism; and this, perhaps, accounts for its coming from the lips of demoniacs (Luke 8:28; Acts 16:17). It was the name of God which had most often been sounded in their ears.

I adjure thee.—The phrase is peculiar to Mark, and confirms the notion that the demoniac repeated language which he had often heard. He, too, seeks in some sense to "exorcize," though it is in the language not of command but entreaty.

(19) The Lord hath done for thee.—Coming from our Lord's lips, and having "God" as its equivalent in Luke 8:39, the word "Lord" must be taken in its Old Testament sense as referring, not to the Lord Jesus, but to the Father.

(20) Decapolis.—See note on Matt. 4:25.

(22-43) And, behold, there cometh one of the rulers.—See notes on Matt. 9:18-25, where the narrative is found in a different connection as coming immediately after the feast in Matthew's house, which Mark has given in 2:14-18.

Jairus.—The name is given by Mark and Luke only. It was a Graecized form of the Jair of Judg. 10:3; Num. 32:41. It meets us in the apocryphal portion of Esther (11:2) as the name of the father of Mordecai.

(30) That virtue had gone out of him.—The word "virtue" is used in the old medical sense of the force which brings about a certain definite result (comp. Luke 5:17). The term is used here for the supernatural power that, as it were, flowed out at the touch of faith.

(38) Wailed greatly.—The word used is the same as that in I Cor. 13:1, in connection with the "tinkling" (or better, "clanging") sound of a cymbal.

(41) Talitha cumi.—Here, as in the "Ephphatha" of 7:34, the evangelist gives the same syllables which had fallen from the lips of the Healer and been proven to be words of power. It would probably be too wide an inference to assume from this that our Lord commonly spoke to His disciples and others in Greek; but we know that that language was then current throughout Palestine, and the stress laid on the Aramaic words in these instances, as in the "Eli, Eli, lama sabachthani" on the cross, shows that they attracted a special notice.

6

(1-6) See notes on Matt. 13:54-58.

(2) Such mighty works.—As the evangelist notes in verse 5 that no mighty work had been done in Nazareth, these must refer to what had been reported there.

(3) Is not this the carpenter?—Mark's is the only gospel which gives this name as applied to our Lord Himself.

(7) He called unto him the twelve.—See notes on Matt. 10:1-15. The omission by Mark of the greater part of the discourse connected with the mission of the Twelve in Matt. 10 is characteristic of the writer, whose main work it was to trace the ministry of action rather than of speech.

(12) And preached that men should repent.—The work of the apostles appears from this to have been a continuation of that of the Baptist. They announced the nearness of the kingdom of God—and repentance as the one adequate preparation for it—and baptized as the outward token of that repentance and the new life in which it was to issue (John 3:5; 4:2). But they did not as yet proclaim their Master as being Himself the Christ, and therefore the Head of that kingdom.

(13) Anointed with oil.—Mark is the only evangelist who mentions this as the common practice of the disciples. We learn from Jas. 5:14 that it was afterward in use, at least in the churches of Jerusalem and other Jewish communities. It was partly analogous to our Lord's treatment of the blind and deaf (7:33; 8:23; John 9:6), i.e., it was an outward sign showing the wish to heal, and therefore a help to faith; but as the use of oil was more distinctly that of an agent recognized as remedial in the popular therapeutics of the time, it had also the character of uniting the use of natural outward means of healing with prayer for the divine blessing.

(14) That John the Baptist was risen from the dead.—See notes on Matt. 14:1-12.

(31-44) See notes on Matt. 14:13-21.

(39) The "green grass" may be noted as an example of Mark's vividness, and serves as an indirect note of time pointing to the same season as that specified by John, i.e., a little before the Passover. (Comp. John 6:10.)

(44) Five thousand men.—Mark uses the word which excludes women and children.

(45) Unto Bethsaida.—There were two Bethsaidas, thus there is no real difficulty presented from the statement in Luke that the five thousand were fed at or near Bethsaida.

(46-52) See notes on Matt. 14:22-33.

(52) For they considered not.—This is peculiar to Mark, and may fairly be received as representing Peter's recollection of what had been the mental state of the disciples at the time. They had not drawn from the miracle of the loaves the conclusion which they might have drawn, that all natural forces were subject to their Master's sovereignty. The personal connection of the evangelist with the apostle may, perhaps, also account for his omission of the narra-

tive which Matthew gives of his rashness and failing faith.

(53-56) See notes on Matt. 14:34-36.

(56) The border of his garment.—Better, the "hem" or "fringe." See note on Matt. 9:20.

7

(1-23) See notes on Matt. 15:1-20.

(2) With defiled, that is to say, with unwashen, hands.—"Defiled" means literally "common." This came to be associated (Acts 10:14) with what was "unclean," and so, for Jews at all events, the word acquired a new meaning. Mark's Gentile readers, however, were not likely to understand what was meant by "common hands," and therefore he adds his explanation of "unwashed."

(3) For the Pharisees, and all the Jews.—For the sake of the same class of readers, Mark adds another explanatory note. The custom of which he speaks was not, he says, peculiar to the Pharisees as a sect; it had passed, through their influence, to the whole body of the people.

(4) Except they wash.—The Greek verb differs from that in verse 3, and implies the washing or immersion (the verb is that from which our word "baptize" comes) of the whole body, as the former does of part. The idea on which the practice rested was not one of cleanliness or health, but of arrogant exclusiveness, fastening on the thought of ceremonial purity. They might have come, in the crowd of the market, into passing contact with a Gentile, and his touch was as defiling as if it had been that of a corpse. So, too, the washing of cups and the like was because they might have been touched by heathen, and therefore impure, lips.

Tables.—Better, "couches"—i.e., the low, wide benches which were placed near the tables, and on which the guests reclined instead of sitting. These also had to be scrupulously washed, because it was possible that a heathen might have lain on them.

(9) Full well ye reject.—The adverb is peculiar to Mark, and has in it the ring of a scathing and indignant irony. The word "reject" is hardly formal enough, the Greek conveying the idea (Gal. 3:15; Heb. 7:18) of "rescinding" or "repealing." This the Pharisees practically did when they added traditions which pretended to be interpretations, but were in reality at variance with it.

(11) It is Corban.—The Hebrew word is peculiar to Mark. It occurs frequently in Leviticus and Numbers, but elsewhere in the Old Testament it appears only in Ezek. 20:28; 40:43. It had come to be applied specifically (as in the Greek of Matt. 27:6; Josephus, **Wars**, 2:9, §4) to the sacred treasure of the Temple.

(19) It entereth not into his heart.—The "heart" is, after the common Hebrew idiom, the symbol of the mind as well as the affections. (Comp. Prov. 7:7; 9:4, 16; 10:13.)

(22) An evil eye.—The "evil eye" (Matt. 20:15) is that which looks askance on the good of others—i.e., envy in its most malignant form.

Foolishness.—This is a rare word in the New Testament, occurring only in II Cor. 11:1, 17, 21. As interpreted by Prov. 14:18; 15:21, it is the folly which consists in the absence of the fear of God, the infatuation of impiety.

(24-30) See notes on Matt. 15:21-28.

(26) A Greek—i.e., in the sense which the word had gained in Palestine, a Gentile (Rom. 1:16; 2:9, 10).

Syrophenician.—The word (Juvenal, **Sat.** 8:159) is an instance of Mark's tendency to use Latin forms. The Emperor Hadrian divided the province of Syria into three parts—Syria proper, Syro-Phoenicia, and Syria-Palaestina—and we may well believe that this official distinction rested on a pre-existing nomenclature.

(31) Departing from the coasts of Tyre and Sidon.—The latter city lay about twenty miles to the north. It marks the extreme limit of our Lord's journeyings—we can hardly say of His ministry, for there is no indication that He went there as a preacher of the kingdom. We may, however, perhaps trace the feeling which prompted the visit in the words "It shall be more tolerable for Tyre and Sidon" in Luke 10:14, and in the "Other sheep, not of this fold" in John 10:16.

Decapolis.—See note on Matt. 4:25.

(32) They bring unto him one that was deaf.—The narrative that follows is peculiar to Mark. The locality is not named, but was probably somewhere near the eastern shore of the Sea of Galilee.

(33) He took him aside from the multitude.—We trace in this, and in the manual acts that followed, the same tender considerateness for the infirmities of the sufferer as in our Lord's treatment of the blind. (See note on Matt. 9:29.)

(34) Ephphatha.—See note on 5:41.

(37) And the dumb to speak.—Note the distinction between Mark's accurate description in verse 32, and the less precise language of popular amazement.

8

(1-9) See notes on Matt. 15:32-38.

(10) Dalmanutha.—Mark's use of the word, instead of the Magdala of Matthew, may be noted as an instance of his independence. It is mentioned by no other writer.

(11, 12) See note on Matt. 16:1-4.

(13-21) See notes on Matt. 16:5-12.

(22) And he cometh to Bethsaida.—This miracle also is recorded by Mark only. Judging by the localities named previously—Dalmanutha (verse 10), the passage across the lake (verse 13), and afterward "the villages of Caesarea Philippi" (verse 27)—it is probable that this was the Bethsaida on the northeastern shore of the Sea of Galilee.

(23) He took the blind man by the hand.—We note in the act the same considerate adaptation of the method of healing to the man's infirmities as in the case of the deaf man in 7:33. As far as the first three gospels are concerned, these are the two instances of the "spitting" here recorded, but it is one of the links that connect Mark with the fourth gospel (John 9:6).

(24) I see men as trees, walking.—His sight was not yet clear, but he interpreted what it told him rightly. Note the naturalness of this description of the first impression of the restored sense.

(26) Neither go into the town.—Our Lord seems to have prescribed quietude after the miracle as a spiritual discipline—partly because the work that had been done called for prayer for the right use of the new, or the restored, power, and partly because He would not seem Himself to court the fame of publicity. Both here and in verse 24, we may extend the application symbolically to stages in the work of spiritual illumination.

(27-29) See notes on Matt. 16:13-16.

(27) He asked his disciples.—The tense of the Greek verb implies that it was not a single question only, but a continued and, as it were, searching inquiry. The time was come to test the faith of the disciples thoroughly.

(30) And he charged them.—On the assumption of a connection between the writer of this gospel and Peter, the omission of the promise to the latter, recorded so fully by Matthew, may be regarded fairly as an evidence of the humility of the apostle, who shrank from what might seem to savor of self-assertion.

(31-33) See notes on Matt. 16:21-23.

(34-38) See notes on Matt. 12:39; 16:24-28.

(35) And the gospel's.—The addition is significant, as showing that though our Lord demanded in the first instance entire personal devotion, it was for Himself as identified with the cause of the good news from God of which He had borne witness, and of which He was to be the martyr (John 18:37).

9

(1) The division of the chapters is obviously wrong. The verse ought to come, as in Matthew and Luke, in immediate connection with the foregoing discourse. The present arrangement may have been made with a view of connecting it with the Transfiguration, as that which was the fulfillment of the promise; but if so, it was based on what is at least a doubtful interpretation. (See note on Matt. 16:28.)

(2-8) See notes on Matt. 17:1-8.

(7) This is my beloved Son.—Note that Mark omits the words "in whom I am well pleased."

(9-13) And as they came down from the mountain.—See notes on Matt. 17:9-13.

(13) As it is written of him.—The words are peculiar to Mark, and probably point to the special prediction of the coming of Elijah in Mal. 4, and to the parallelism between the career of the Baptist and that of the Tishbite prophet. What had been written of the one, the record of bold rebuke and consequent suffering for the truth, had received its fulfillment in the other.

(14-29) And when he came to his disciples.—See notes on Matt. 17:14-21. The narrative of Mark here becomes much the fullest of the three. He alone mentions, e.g., in this verse, the presence of the scribes disputing with the disciples; in the next, the "running" and the "greeting" with which the multitude received our Lord as He came down from the mountain; and in verse 16 the question as to the cause of the dispute.

(15) Were greatly amazed.—This fact is noted by Mark only. We are not told what caused it. Was there some lingering radiance, or some expression of divine joy hardly less radiant, that struck the disciples and the people as strangely unlike the sadness that had been shown in recent words and looks (8:30-33)?

(23) If thou canst believe.—Was this the way in which a man should speak who came to Him as a healer? Such a one had to learn the great primary lesson that "all things were possible to him that believeth," that the secret of previous failure lay, in part at least, in his own want of faith, as well as in that of the scribes and disciples who had tried their arts of exorcism in vain.

(29) But by prayer and fasting.—The better MSS omit the last two words. It is possible that they may have been added (like the "tears" of verse 24) to strengthen the words actually spoken, bringing in what had been found to offer a new intensity of spiritual volition and power over the unclean spirits that possessed them.

(33-37) And he came to Capernaum.—See notes on Matt. 18:1-5. The arrival at Capernaum is given by Matthew in connection with the narrative of the tribute money, which in his gospel immediately precedes that now before us. Mark alone records the previous dispute of the disciples, and the question which brought that dispute as into the light of day.

(36) When he had taken him in his arms.—The act is expressed in the Greek by a single participle which occurs only here and in 10:16 (see note). It may mean either that the child was taken up in our Lord's arms, or that the arms were folded around him. The latter is somewhat the more probable.

(37) Whosoever shall receive.—When we love a little child in the name of Christ, i.e., for His sake, and after His manner, we are sharers in His spirit; and when we love or receive Him who was One with the Father, we enter into fellowship with Him who is the Supreme and Eternal Love. (Comp. John 14:10, 23.)

(38) And John answered him.—The incident indicates the same zeal as Luke 9:52. The disciple desired to show, as in self-vindication, that he not only "received" his Master, but that he was unwilling to "receive" any who did not openly follow Him as a disciple. The fact of which he speaks is significant historically as indicating that one of the effects of our Lord's work had been to stir up and quicken the spiritual powers of men outside the range of the company of disciples that gathered around Him. True disciples of Christ are to hinder no one who is really doing His work. The fact that they do it will bring with it reverence and sympathy. They will not quickly be found among those who speak evil of the Son of man. (Comp. Num. 11:29; Phil. 1:18.)

(42-48) Whosoever shall offend.—See notes on Matt. 18:6-9. In verses 43 and 45 the words "into the fire that never shall be quenched" are omitted in some of the best MSS; and the same MSS, and others, omit both verses 44 and 46, leaving verse 48 to stand as the only description of Gehenna.

(43) Into hell.—Better, "Gehenna." See notes on Matt. 5:22.

(44) Where their worm dieth not.—The words are taken almost **literatim** from Isa. 66:24, where they appear as part of the description of the triumph of Jehovah. The scenery (comp. Isa. 63:1-6) is drawn from the slaughter of earthly battles. The prophet exults in vision over the putrid carcases and the blazing fires that consume them, and thinks of that scene as perpetuated throughout eternity. The imagery, thus already familiar, coalesced naturally with the ideas of Gehenna. Possibly the valley of Hinnom, receiving the solid as well as fluid sewage of Jerusalem, with putrid offal and blazing fires consuming them, had become in this way a visible type of the unseen Gehenna. Most commentators have seen in the gnawing worm the anguish of an endless remorse, the memory of past sins. Fire retains its force as the expression of the righteousness of God (Heb. 12:29) manifesting itself to the consciousness of the sinner in all its awfulness, never altering its essential character. The words declare distinctly the law of righteous retribution.

(49) "Fire" again represents the discipline of suffering. The "sacrifice" refers to the ritual of Lev. 2:13, which prescribed that salt should be added, as the natural symbol of incorruption, to every sacrifice. Here our Lord speaks of the spiritual sacrifice which each man offers of his body, soul, and spirit (Rom. 12:1), and declares that "salt," the purifying grace of the Eternal Spirit, is needed that it may be acceptable.

(50) Salt is good.—Comp. note on Matt. 5:13. Here the words speak primarily of inward grace, which alone makes the Church what it ought to be, "the salt of the earth."

10

The best harmonists place Matt. 18:15-35; Luke 10:1-17:10 (with the exception of 15:3-7); and John 7:1-11:54 between chapters 9 and 10 of this gospel. The "farther side of Jordan" implies what is known as the Peraean ministry of our Lord, related only by Luke.

(2-12) And the Pharisees came to him.—See notes on Matt. 19:3-12.

(12) And if a woman shall put away.—This is peculiar to Mark. It is noticeable as being the only passage in our Lord's teaching which distinctly states the case referred to, passing sentence on the wife who divorces her husband and marries again, as well as on the husband who divorces his wife and the wife who is so divorced. All three cases are dealt with on the same grounds: (1) that the marriage relationship ought to be indissoluble, and that one cause only justifies or permits its dissolution; and (2) that any further permission of divorce is but a concession to the hardness of men's hearts for the avoidance of greater evils.

(13-15) See notes on Matt. 19:13-15. To receive the kingdom of God "as a little child" is to receive it after the manner of a child—with simplicity and faith, humility and love. Unless these conditions were fulfilled, those who were disputing who was the greatest in it were as if they had not even entered it.

(17-27) See notes on Matt. 19:16-26.

(19) Defraud not.—This is peculiar to Mark. It seems as if intended to be a special application of the tenth commandment. One who had great possessions, gathered in the usual ways by which men gain wealth, needed to examine himself especially by that text. Were there no ill-gotten gains in his treasure?

(21) Then Jesus beholding him loved him.—The fact is narrated by Mark only, and implies that the love showed itself in the steadfast look, perhaps also in the kiss upon the brow with which the rabbis of the time showed their approval of their more promising disciples.

(28-31) See notes on Matt. 19:27-30; 20:16. Comp. I Pet. 4:12, 13.

(32-34) See notes on Matt. 20:17-19.

(35-45) And James and John.—See notes on Matt. 20:20-28.

(40) But it shall be given to them.—Our Lord disclaims, not the power to give, but

765

that of giving arbitrarily, otherwise that His Father willed.

(46-52) And they came to Jericho.—See notes on Matt. 20:29-34.

Blind Bartimaeus.—The later MSS have the definite article before "blind," as though he were well-known and conspicuous. It is noticeable that the name was Greek with the Aramaic prefix Bar (son), a combination not found elsewhere.

(51) Lord.—Better "Rabboni," the word being the same as in John 20:16, and occurring in these two passages only. It was an augmentative form of rabbi, and as such expressed greater reverence.

(52) Followed Jesus in the way.—In the apocryphal **Gospel of Nicodemus** he appears as one of the witnesses for the defense at our Lord's trail.

11

(1-11) See notes on Matt. 21:1-11.

(12-14) See notes on Matt. 21:18, 19.

(13) The precocious foliage had suggested the thought that some of the early ripe figs might be already formed; but it was no exception, as far as fruit was concerned, to others of its kind. The season, even of the earliest fruit, had not come. The seeing the fig tree "afar off" is a touch peculiar to Mark, and adds force to the narrative, as implying a keener pressure of hunger than Matthew's description.

(15-19) And Jesus went into the temple.—See notes on Matt. 21:12-17.

(16) And would not suffer that any man.—This is peculiar to Mark. The vessels referred to included, probably, the baskets and other common implements of traffic. Men were using the courts of the Temple as a short cut from one part of the city to another.

(20-24) See notes on Matt. 21:20-22. Mark alone names Peter as the speaker. The form of our Lord's answer, "Have faith in God," also is peculiar to him.

(24) Believe that ye receive them.—The better MSS give the latter verb in the past tense, "Believe that ye received them." As a rule, such words imply prayer for spiritual rather than temporal blessings. In that region the subjective faith becomes an objective reality. We are to believe, not that we shall one day have what we pray for in a future more or less distant, but that we actually receive it as we pray.

(25, 26) See Matt. 6:14. The reproduction of the words which are recorded as having been spoken in the Sermon on the Mount is significant. The prayer even of intensest faith is not perfect unless the temper of the worshiper is also that of the love which forgives offenses.

(27-33) And they come again to Jerusalem.—See notes on Matt. 21:23-27.

12

(1-12) And he began to speak unto them by parables.—See notes on Matt. 21:33-36.

(13-17) See notes on Matt. 22:15-22.

(18-27) Then come unto him the Sadducees.—See notes on Matt. 22:23-33.

(26) How in the bush God spake unto him.—The order of the words in the Greek shows that they point to "the bush," not as the place in which God spoke, but as the title or heading by which the section Exod. 3 was commonly described.

(28-34) And one of the scribes came.—See notes on Matt. 22:34-40.

(29) Hear, O Israel; The Lord our God is one Lord.—The opening words (from Deut. 6:4) were in common use under the name of the **Shema** (the Hebrew for "Hear"), and formed the popular expression of the faith of Israel. To say the **Shema** was a passport into Paradise for any child of Abraham.

(32) Well, Master, thou hast said the truth.—The words seem intentionally repeated from verse 14, but are uttered now, not with the covert sneer of the hypocrite, but in the sincerity of admiration. Note also the real reverence shown in the form of address, "Master," i.e., "Teacher, Rabbi." He recognizes the speaker as one of his own order. This, and all that follows, is peculiar to Mark. It is an addition of singular interest as showing the existence among the scribes of some who accepted our Lord's teaching as to the spiritual meaning of the Law, and were able to distinguish between its essence and its accidents (verse 33; comp. I Sam. 15:22; Ps. 50:8-14; Mic. 6:6).

(34) Thou art not far from the kingdom of God.—The words are significant as showing the unity of our Lord's teaching. Now, as when He spoke the Sermon on the Mount, the righteousness which fulfills the law is the condition of the entrance into the kingdom of God (Matt. 5:19, 20). It is instructive to compare our Lord's different method of dealing (Luke 10:25-37) with one who had the same theoretical knowledge, but who obviously, consciously or unconsciously, minimized the force of the commandments by his narrowing definitions.

(36) David himself said by the Holy Ghost.—Mark is more emphatic in ascribing the words of David to the influence of the Holy Spirit than either Matthew or Luke. (Comp. II Pet. 1:21.)

(38-40) In his doctrine.—See notes on Matt. 23:1-7, 14.

(41) And Jesus sat over against the treasury.—The narrative that follows is found in Luke also, but not in Matthew. The word used is not the "Corban" of Matt. 27:6, and is, perhaps, more definitely local. The treasure chamber of the Temple would receive the alms which were dropped into the trumpet-shaped vessels that stood near the entrance for the purpose of receiving them, but they probably contained also the cups and other implements of gold and silver that were used in the Temple ritual.

(42) And there came a certain poor widow.—Among the "many" who cast in much must have been some at least of the Pharisees who devoured widows' houses (verse 40). Here was a widow whose house had been devoured, and who yet showed by her act that she kept the two great commandments, which the scribes themselves declared to be above all burnt offerings and sacrifices.

Two mites, which make a farthing.—The "farthing" is one of the Latin words which characterize this gospel. The primary meaning of the word rendered "mite" is "thin" or "tiny."

(43) And he called unto him his disciples.—The act was significant. He sought to teach them to judge of acts by other than a quantitative standard. For him the widow's mites and the ointment that might have been sold for 300 pence stood on the same level, as far as each was the expression of a generous and self-sacrificing love.

13

(1) Here, again, the juxtaposition of narratives in Mark gives them a special point. The "stones" of Herod's Temple (for it was to him chiefly that it owed its magnificence) were of sculptured marble. The "buildings," or structures included columns, chambers, porticoes that were, as Luke tells us (21:5), the votive offerings of the faithful. The disciples gazed on these with the natural admiration of Galilean peasants. In spite of the lesson they had just received—a lesson

meant, it may be, to correct the tendency which our Lord discerned—they were still measuring things by their quantity and size. They admired the "goodly stones" more than the "widow's mite." They were now to be taught that, while the one should be spoken of throughout the whole world, the other should be destroyed, so that not a vestige should remain.

(4) When shall these things be?—Note, as characteristic of a gospel written for Gentiles, the use of the more vague words for the more definite "sign of thy coming, and of the end of the world" (Matt. 24:3).

(5) And Jesus answering them began to say.—The report which follows, common as it is to the first three gospels, serves as an admirable example of the extent of variation compatible with substantial accuracy, and with the recognition of an inspired guidance as insuring that accuracy. The discourse obviously made a deep impression on those who heard it, as afterward on those to whom they repeated it, and so it passed from mouth to mouth; but probably it was not committed to writing until the events which it foretold came within the horizon.

On all points common to the three records, see notes on Matt. 24.

(18) Pray ye that your flight be not in the winter.—Note Mark's omission of "nor on the Sabbath day," which is prominent in Matthew's report, as characteristic of a gospel for Gentile readers.

(32) Neither the Son.—The addition to Matthew's report indicates the self-imposed limitation of the divine attributes which had belonged to our Lord as the eternal Son, and the acquiescence in a power and knowledge which, like that of the human nature which He assumed, were derived and therefore finite. (Comp. Phil. 2:6, 7.) We therefore reject all interpretations which explain away the force of the words as meaning only that the Son did not declare His knowledge of the time of the far-off event.

(33) Take ye heed.—It would almost seem, from the different conclusions of the discourse in the three gospels, as if they had been based up to this point on a common document which then stopped and left them to a greater divergency of memory or tradition. The omission of Matthew's reference to the history of Noah is, perhaps, characteristic of Mark's as a Gentile gospel.

(34) And commanded the porter to watch.—Comp. Matt. 25:14-30. This feature is unique in our Lord's parables. The "servants" we accept at once as the disciples, and we understand generally what was the authority and the work assigned to them. But who was specifically the "gate keeper" or "porter"? (See John 10:3.) The answer may be found in the promise of the keys of the kingdom that had been made to Peter (Matt. 16:19). It was his work to open the door of that kingdom wide, to be ready for his Lord's coming in any of those manifold senses which experience would unfold to him. We may accordingly venture to trace in Mark's record, here as elsewhere, the influence of the apostle.

(35) At even, or at midnight.—The four times correspond roughly to the four (quarter) watches of the night, beginning at 9 p.m. The words may have been intended to leave on Peter's mind the impression that the promise of the coming of his Lord was undefined as to times or seasons (see II Pet. 3).

14

(1) After two days was the feast of the passover.—See notes on Matt. 26:1-5. Better, "was the passover, and the feast of unleavened bread." The latter designation is common to Mark and Luke, as an explanation intended for Gentile readers. The same fact accounts, perhaps, for the omission by both of the name of Caiaphas as the chief mover in the scheme.

(3-9) See notes on Matt. 26:6-13.

(3) Ointment of spikenard.—The Greek word so translated is of doubtful import. It is used by John 12:3 in his account of the same facts.

She brake the box.—As in the "breaking through" the roof in 2:4, the vivid touch that brings the manner of the act distinctly before our eyes is found in Mark only. The Greek word implies not so much the breaking of the neck of the costly jar or flask, but the crushing it in its entirety with both her hands.

(4) There were some that had indignation.—Note Mark's limitation of the murmurers to "some," as an intermediate stage between Matthew's "the disciples" and John's naming "Judas."

(10, 11) And Judas Iscariot.—See notes on Matt. 26:14, 15.

(12-21) See notes on Matt. 26:20-25.

(12) When they killed the passover.—Better, "when they used to sacrifice," the Greek tense implying a custom. Here, again, both Mark and Luke write as ex-

plaining the custom for their Gentile readers.

(22-25) See notes on Matt. 26:26-29.

(26-42) See notes on Matt. 26:30-46.

(36) And he said, Abba, Father.—The record of the word "Abba" as actually uttered is peculiar to Mark. We perhaps find traces of the impression it made on the minds of men in the "Abba, Father" of Rom. 8:15 and Gal. 4:6.

(43-50) See notes on Matt. 26:47-56.

(51) And there followed him a certain young man.—The remarkable incident that follows is narrated by Mark only. It had clearly made a deep impression on the minds of some of the disciples (probably on Peter), from whom, directly or indirectly, the report came. Some have supposed that the person here was Mark himself, but for this there is obviously no ground but the fact that this evangelist alone records it. A careful examination of the facts, however, suggests that he well might have been Lazarus. The man was "young," and the same term is applied to the ruler who had great possessions (Matt. 19:20). That he had apparently been sleeping not far from Gethsemane, with the linen sheet wrapped around him, suggests one who lived somewhere on the Mount of Olives. The officers were eager to seize him, when they allowed all the disciples to go their way (see John 12:10). As the "linen sheet" or *sindon* was especially used for the burial of the dead, it is conceivable that what had been the winding sheet of the dead Lazarus had been kept and used by him in memory of his resurrection. On the hypothesis thus suggested, the suppression of the name compares with the sister of Lazarus, who poured the precious ointment on our Lord's head at Bethany (Matt. 26:7; Mark 14:3), whom the evangelists must have known, but whom they mention simply as a "woman." Their lips were sealed as to the family of Bethany until the circumstances, whatever they may have been, that called for silence had passed away. He who had gone away sorrowful because he had great possessions had proved more faithful than the Twelve, and so the last had become the first (see note on Matt. 20:16).

(53-72) And they led Jesus away.—See notes on Matt. 26:57-75.

15

(1-14) See notes on Matt. 27:1, 2, 11-23.

(1) And the whole council.—The words in the Greek are in apposition with "the chief priests." We do not know of any other elements in the Council or Sanhedrin than the priests, scribes, and elders, and it is possible that the writer may have added the words in the sense of "even the whole Council," as giving the collective word for the body of which the three constituent parts already had been named.

(9) Will ye that I release unto you . . . ?— The form of the question in the Greek implies (like John 18:39) a half hope of an affirmative answer.

(16) Into the hall, called Praetorium.— See note on Matt. 27:27.

(21) The father of Alexander and Rufus.— The fact recorded here, and not elsewhere, is one of the most striking instances of the independent character of Mark's gospel. It is clear that it had a special interest for himself and the readers for whom he wrote; what that interest was we can only conjecture. The two names were so common that we cannot arrive at more than a probable identification, but the mention of a "Rufus chosen in the Lord" as prominent among the Christians of Rome (Rom. 16:13), taken together with the linguistic and other evidence which connects Mark's gospel with that Church, tends to the conclusion that he was one of the two brothers thus mentioned. Paul speaks of the mother of Rufus as being endeared to him by many proofs of material kindness, and so we are led to the belief that the wife of Simon of Cyrene must, at some time or other, at Antioch or Corinth, and afterward at Rome, have come within the inner circle of Paul's friends. This, in its turn, connects itself with the prominence given to "men of Cyrene" in Luke's account of the foundation of the Gentile Church of Antioch (Acts 11:20). (See note on Matt. 27:32.)

(21-38) See notes on Matt. 27:32-51.

(28) And the scripture was fulfilled.—The verse, if genuine, would be noticeable as one of the few instances in which Mark dwells on the fulfillment of prophecy; but it is omitted by nearly all the better MSS, and probably originated in a marginal note, calling attention to the fulfillment of the prophecy which we find quoted by our Lord as about to be fulfilled in Luke 22:37.

(32) Let Christ.—Better, "the Christ." The article is emphatic, and the word had not yet come to be used only as a name.

(34) Eloi, Eloi.—The form which Mark gives is a closer reproduction of the sounds of the Aramaic word than that in Matthew, who gives the Hebrew as it stands in Ps. 22:1.

(39-47) See notes on Matt. 27:54-61.

16

(1-8) See notes on Matt. 28:1-8.

(9-20) See notes on Matt. 28:16-20. The verses that follow are not found in two of the oldest MSS (the Sinaitic and the Vatican), are marked as doubtful in many others, and are wanting in some versions. In some of these (e.g., in the Vatican MS) there is a blank space left between verse 8 and the beginning of Luke, as though the writer had suspended his work and waited for materials. The absence was noticed by Jerome, who says that "nearly all the Greek texts omit them." Eusebius states the same fact as true of "the correct MSS"; and no reference is made to them in the tables of parallel passages which were constructed for reference by Eusebius and Ammonius. On the other hand, they are **referred to** by Irenaeus (about A.D. 170), and are found in the Alexandrian and Cambridge MSS and in twelve other uncials which are nearly as old as the two which omit them. The narrative, which up to this point had followed closely in the footsteps of Matthew, now becomes a condensed epitome of John's record of our Lord's appearance to Mary Magdalene (20:11-18), of Luke's account of the journey to Emmaus (24:13-35), of the appearance to the ten disciples in John 20:19-25 and Luke 24:36-43, of the mission of the eleven reported in Matt. 28:16-20, of the Ascension as given by Luke 24:50-53. Two explanations of these facts are possible: (1) That the writer of the gospel wrote two copies of it, leaving one unfinished, ending at verse 8; that this passed into the hands of persons by whom it was copied as complete; and that this became the archtype of the MSS in which the verses are wanting, while those that contain the subsequent verses were made from a more perfect text, written by Mark himself. (2) That the gospel, originally having been completed by the writer, was in some way, by accident or design, mutilated; and that as such it was reproduced faithfully by some transcribers, while others thought it better to give it a completion of some kind by condensing what they found in the other gospels. Of the two hypotheses the latter seems the more probable.

769

(9-11) See notes on John 20:11-18, but observe that Mark's account of Mary Magdalene as one from whom Jesus "had cast out seven devils" is not from John, but from Luke 8:2.

(12, 13) See notes on Luke 24:13-35.

(14) See notes on Luke 24:36-43.

(15) And he said unto them.—See notes on Matt. 28:16-20. There is much, however, that is so distinct in Mark's report as to suggest that it may have referred to a different occasion.

(17) They shall speak with new tongues.— This is noticeable as being the only distinct reference in the gospels to the form of the Pentecostal gift. The promise of the Spirit itself had been prominent, however, throughout our Lord's teaching (Luke 11:13; John 14:17, 26), and appears from Acts 1:8 to have been especially renewed between the Resurrection and Ascension.

On the nature of the gift itself, see Acts 2:4; 10:46, 19:6; I Cor. 12:10; 14:4-26.

(18) They shall take up serpents.—The instance of Paul at Melita is the only recorded example of the kind (Acts 28:1-6). Comp. Luke 10:19.

If they drink any deadly thing . . .—Of this there is no recorded instance in the New Testament, but it finds an illustration in the tradition of the poisoned cup which was offered to John.

(19, 20) See note on Luke 24:53. Matthew gives no account of the Ascension. (See Matt. 28:20.) Mark and Luke record it briefly; John implies it in his report of our Lord's words (John 6:62; 20:17). In Acts 1:3-11 it is narrated with greater fullness.

The form of the last two verses—the use of the "Lord" instead of Jesus—suggests their being a later addition to the original records of our Lord's life and teaching. (See note on Luke 7:13.)

LUKE

1

(1) Forasmuch as many have taken in hand.—Verses 1-4 are conspicuous in the Greek for their finished structure as compared with the simpler openings of the other gospels. This verse suggests the existence of many written documents professing to give an account of the Gospel history at the time when Luke wrote—i.e., probably before Paul's death in A.D. 65. The "many" **may** have included Matthew and Mark, but we cannot say. There is no tone of disparagement in the way in which the writer speaks of his predecessors. He simply feels that they have not exhausted the subject, and that his inquiries have enabled him to add something.

(3) Having had perfect understanding of all things.—Better, "having investigated all things from their source." The verb is one which implies following the course of events step by step. "In order," furthermore, implies a distinct aim at chronological arrangement.

Most excellent Theophilus.—The adjective implies at least high social position, if not official rank. The name, which means "Friend of God," might well be taken by a Christian convert at his baptism. Nothing more can be known of the person so addressed beyond the fact that he was probably a Gentile convert who had already been partially instructed in the facts of the gospel history.

(4) Wherein thou hast been instructed.—The verb used is "catechize," and implies oral teaching—in its later sense, teaching preparatory to baptism.

(5) There was in the days of Herod.—The two chapters that follow have every appearance of having been based originally on an independent document, probably a Hebrew one. On Herod and this period of his reign, see notes on Matt. 2:1.

Zacharias.—The name ("he who remembers Jehovah") had been borne by the son of Jehoiada (II Chron. 24:20), and by the prophet of the return from the Babylonian Captivity.

Of the course of Abia.—The Greek implies a system of rotation, each "set" or "course" of the priests serving from Sabbath to Sabbath. (See I Chron. 24:10; Ezra 2:36-39; Neh. 10:7, 12:4, 17.)

His wife was of the daughters of Aaron.—

The priests were free to marry outside their own caste under certain limitations as to the character of their wives (Lev. 21:7). The fact of a priestly descent on both sides was therefore worth noticing. The name "Elisabeth," in its Hebrew form of Elisheba had belonged to the wife of Aaron who was of the tribe of Judah (Exod. 6:23), and was naturally an honored name among the daughters of the priestly line.

(9) His lot was to burn incense.—The distribution of functions during the week was determined by lot. That of offering incense, symbolizing, as it did, the priestly work of presenting the prayers of the people, and joining his own with them (Ps. 141:2; Rev. 5:8), was of all priestly acts most distinctive (II Chron. 26:18).

(11) The altar of incense.—The altar stood just in front of the veil that divided the outer sanctuary from the Holy of Holies (See Exod. 30:1-7; 40:5, 26; Heb. 9:4.) It symbolized the closest approach to God which was then possible for any but the high priest, when, in his typical character, he entered the Holy of Holies on the day of Atonement.

(13) The words imply a prayer on the part of Zacharias that the kingdom of God might come. Praying for this he receives more than he asks. The name "John" means "Jehovah is gracious," a pledge of the outpouring of the grace of God.

(15) And shall drink neither wine nor strong drink.—The child now promised was to grow up as a Nazarite (Num. 6:4), and to keep that vow all his life, as the representative of the "separated" form of a consecrated life. (Comp. Samson, Judg. 13:4.) The close connection between the Nazarite and the prophetic life is seen in Amos 2:11, 12.

He shall be filled with the Holy Ghost.—The words would be understood by Zacharias from the Hebrew point of view, not as seen in the fuller light of Christian theology. As such they would convey the thought of the highest prophetic inspiration, as in Isa. 11:2; 61:1; Joel 2:28. The further thought of a life from first to last in harmony with itself and consecrated to the prophet's work had its prototype in Jeremiah (Jer. 1:5).

(16) The opening words of the message of the New Covenant spring out of the closing words of the last of the prophets (Mal. 4:6), and point to the revival of the Elijah ministry, more definitely announced in verse 17.

(19) Gabriel means "the strong one of God" (Dan. 8:16). As having appeared in the prophecies which, more than any others, were the germ of the Messianic expectations which the people cherished, there was a fitness in the mission now given to Gabriel to prepare the way for the Messiah's coming. The imagery was drawn from the customs of an Eastern Court, in which those stood who were the most honored ministers of the king, while others fell prostrate in silent homage.

(25) To take away my reproach among men.—The words express in strongest form the Jewish feeling as to maternity. To have no children was more than a misfortune. It seemed to imply some secret sin which God was punishing with barrenness. Comp. Gen. 30:1; I Sam. 1:6-10.

(26) A city of Galilee, named Nazareth.—The town was situated in a valley among the hills that rise to a height of about 500 feet on the north of the richly cultivated Plain of Esdraelon. It is a three days' journey from Jerusalem, about eighteen miles from the Sea of Galilee, and six from Mount Tabor. (See note on Matt. 2:23.)

(27) See notes on Matt. 1:18-20; 13:55.

(31) Behold, thou shalt conceive.—Luke does not refer to the prophecy of Isa. 7:14, but it is clear from Mary's answer that she understood the words of the angel in the sense which Matthew gives to those of the prophet. What perplexed her was the reference to the conception and the birth in a prediction which made no mention of her approaching marriage.

Shalt call his name JESUS.—See note on Matt. 1:21.

(32) Shall be called the Son of the Highest.—See note on Mark 5:7.

The throne of his father David.—The genealogies both in Matthew and Luke appear to give the lineage of Joseph only, and therefore, if this were the evangelist's point of view, our Lord, notwithstanding the supernatural birth, was thought of as inheriting from him rather than from Mary. The evangelist held that the "kingdom" was fulfilled in the spiritual sovereignty of the Christ.

(34) How shall this be?—The question is not altogether of the same nature as that of Zacharias (verse 18). He asks by what sign he shall know that the words were true; Mary accepts the words to her in faith, reverently seeking to know the manner of their accomplishment.

(35) The Holy Ghost shall come upon thee.—The context would suggest the aspect of the Spirit's work as quickening the dead

chaos into life (Gen. 1:2), as being the source of life to all creation (Ps. 104:30).

Therefore also . . . shall be called the Son of God.—The words appear to rest the title "Son of God" on the supernatural birth rather than on the eternal pre-existence of the Son (John 1:1). The message of the angel was a partial revelation of the mystery of the Incarnation.

(46) My soul doth magnify the Lord.—This is the first of the great canticles recorded by Luke, and forming part of the hymnal treasures of Western Christendom. We may think of the Virgin as having committed to writing at the time, or having remembered afterward, possibly with some natural modifications, what she then spoke. Here the song of praise—the **Magnificat**—is clearly based upon that of Hannah (I Sam. 2:1-10), both in its opening words and in much of its substance.

(54) Up to this point the hymn has been one of personal thanksgiving. Now her joy in the "great things" which God has done for her rests on the fact that they are "great things" for Israel also. One may see in the utterance of this hope already taken as realized an indication of the early date of the hymn. At the time when Luke wrote, the rejection, not the restoration of Israel, was the dominant thought in men's minds.

(59) They came to circumcise the child.—The day of circumcision, as the admission of the child into God's covenant with His people, was one on which relatives were invited to be present as witnesses, and commonly was followed by a feast. It was also the time on which the child received the name which was to bear its witness of the prayers of his parents for him, and of his personal relation to the God of his fathers.

(60) Not so; but he shall be called John.—It is obvious from what follows that the writing-tablet had been in frequent use, and in this way the husband must have told the wife of the name which had been given by the angel. It seems that Zacharias was deprived of the power of hearing as well as speech (see verse 62).

(68) Blessed be the Lord God of Israel.—The whole hymn that follows is, like the **Magnificat**, pre-eminently Hebrew in character, almost every phrase having its counterpart in Psalm or Prophet.

Redeemed his people.—Better, "wrought redemption for His people." The noun is formed from that which is translated "ransom" (see note on Matt. 20:28). Its occurrence here is noticeable as showing how large an element the thought of deliverance through a ransom was in all the Messianic expectations of the time. Verse 69 shows that he looked for this redemption as coming not through the child that had been born to him, but through the Son, as yet unborn, of Mary.

(69, 70) See Ps. 132:17; Gen. 3:15; 20:7.

(72) His holy covenant.—See Gen. 15:18; comp. Gal. 3:15-19.

(74) Might serve him without fear.—Here again the form of the hope points to its early date. What prospect was there, when Luke wrote his gospel, of any deliverance of the Jews from their earthly enemies? By that time, what was transitory in the hymn had vanished, and the words had gained the higher permanent sense which they have had for centuries in the worship of the Church of Christ.

(76) See Isa. 40:3; Mal. 3:1.

(78) The dayspring from on high.—Here the thought of the sunrise is prominent, connecting itself with such predictions (Isa. 60:1; Mal. 4:2). What has become a Messianic name is taken in its primary sense and turned into a parable.

(80) And the child grew.—We have no materials for filling in this brief outline of the thirty years that followed in the Baptist's life. The usual Jewish education, the observance of the Nazarite vow, study and meditation given to the law and the prophets, possible association with the Essenes who lived in that region, or with hermit-teachers—all this we may surmise as highly probable.

2

(1) The word "taxed" is used in the sense of simple "registration." The "world" is taken, as throughout the New Testament, for the Roman empire. Thus Augustus is said to have decreed a general census. Although no Roman or Jewish historian speaks distinctly of such a general census as made at this time, the collection of statistical returns of this nature was an ever-recurring feature of the policy of Augustus. We read of such returns at intervals of about ten years during the whole period of his government. (See Josephus, **Wars**, 1:27, §2; 29:2.) It may be noted that none of the early opponents of Christianity—such as Celsus and Porphyry—call the accuracy of the statement into question. Luke, as an inquirer, writing for men of education,

would not have been likely to expose himself to the risk of detection by asserting that there had been such a census in the face of facts to the contrary.

(2) And this taxing was first made when Cyrenius was governor of Syria.—Publicius Sulpicius Quirinus ("Cyrenius" is the Greek form) was Consul 12 B.C., and named as Governor of Syria after the deposition of Archelaus, A.D. 6. The true meaning is found by emphasizing the adjective: "This enrollment was the first under Quirinus' government of Syria." Luke expressly distinguishes it from other "taxings," e.g., the more memorable "taxing" of which Gamaliel speaks (Acts 5:37). Luke, it may be noted, is the only New Testament writer who uses the word. Justin Martyr confidently appeals to Roman registers as confirming Luke's statement that our Lord was born under Quirinus.

(4) Of the house and lineage of David.—Hillel, the great scribe, also boasted of such a descent. The special prerogative of Joseph was that the two lines of natural descent and inheritance—that through Nathan and that through Solomon—met in him.

(7) A tradition found in the apocryphal **Gospel of the Infancy** fixes a cave near Bethlehem as the scene of the Nativity, and Justin Martyr finds in this a fulfillment of the LXX version of Isa. 33:16. Caves in the limestone rocks of Judaea were so often used as stables that there is nothing improbable in the tradition. The traditional ox and ass which appear in pictures of the Nativity are probably traceable to a fanciful interpretation of Isa. 1:3, cited in the apocryphal gospel.

(8) Shepherds abiding in the field.—See notes on Matt. 2:1. The traditional season does not appear as such until the fourth century. The statement in the Mishna that the sheep intended for sacrifice in the Temple were pastured in the fields of Bethlehem gives a special interest to the fact thus narrated, and may, perhaps, in part, explain the faith and devotion of the shepherds. They had been rejoicing, at the Paschal season, over the lambs of their flocks; they now heard of the birth of "the Lamb of God, which taketh away the sin of the world" (John 1:29).

(14) On earth peace, good will toward men.—The better MSS give "on earth peace among men of good will"—i.e., among men who are the objects of the good will, the approval and love of God. The words stand in the Greek, as in the English, without a verb, and may therefore be understood either as a proclamation or a prayer. The "peace on earth" frequently has been connected (comp. Milton's **Ode on the Nativity**) with the fact that the Roman Empire was then at peace, and the gates of the Temple of Janus closed because there was no need for the power of the god to go forth in defense of its armies. We may see a reference to the thought of the angelic song in Paul's way of speaking of Christ as being Himself "our peace" (Eph. 2:14).

(17) They made known abroad . . .—The fact must be borne in mind, as tending to the agitation which reached its height on the arrival of the Magi in Jerusalem. (See note on Matt. 2:3.)

(19) Mary kept all these things.—On the assumption that the whole narrative is traceable to the Virgin herself as its first author, these brief and simple touches as to her own feelings are of singular interest. She could not as yet understand all that had been said and done, but she received it in faith and waited until it should be made clear. It was enough for her to know that her Child was, in some sense, the Son of God and the hope of Israel.

(21) See note on Matt. 1:21. In Gal. 4:4 we may, perhaps, see a reference to a narrative with which Paul's friendship with Luke must almost of necessity have made him familiar.

(22) When the days of her purification . . .—The primary idea of the law of Lev. 12:1-6 would seem to have been that of witnessing to the taint of imperfection and sin attaching to every child of man, just as that of circumcision (its merely physical aspects not considered) was that of the repression or control of one chief element of that sinfulness. Here neither was necessary; but the whole mystery of the birth was not as yet revealed to Mary, and therefore her act was simply one of devout obedience to the law under which she lived. The purification lasted for forty days from the birth.

To present him to the Lord.—This, as the next verse shows, was done only according to the law of Exod. 13:2, when the first-born child was a son. It obviously was a witness of the idea of the priesthood of the first-born—a survival of the idea in practice, even after the functions of that priesthood had been superseded by the priesthood of the sons of Aaron. The first-born of every house had still a dedicated life, and was to think of himself as consecrated to

special duties. (Comp. Heb. 12:23 as giving the expansion of the thought to the whole company of those who are the "first-born.")

(24) The law of Lev. 12:8 allowed these to be substituted for the normal sacrifices of a lamb. We see, therefore, another indication of the poverty of Joseph and his espoused wife. The offering had, like all other sacrifices, to be made in the Temple. It seems certain that this visit to Jerusalem must have preceded the visit of the Magi. After that, it would have been perilous in the extreme, and the narrative of Matt. 2 implies an immediate departure for Egypt after they had left.

(25) Whose name was Simeon.—Some writers have identified the man with the son of Hillel and father of Gamaliel, who became president of the Sanhedrin, A.D. 13. But Luke's way of speaking leaves the impression that the Simeon here was of a very advanced age, waiting for his departure; and, furthermore, he who names Gamaliel's position (Acts 5:34) would hardly have passed over Simeon's.

(29) The central idea is that of the manumission of a slave. The word for the Lord is not the usual **Kyrios**, but **Despotes**—a word seldom used of God, and then almost always of the relation of a master and the slave who is such by inheritance of purchase (comp. Acts 4:24; II Pet. 2:1; Jude 4; Rev. 6:10).

(30) Mine eyes have seen thy salvation.—The Greek word is not the usual feminine noun expressing the abstract idea of salvation, but the neuter of the adjective—that which brings or works out salvation. He saw in that infant child the means of deliverance for the world.

(31) Before the face of all people.—Literally, "of all peoples." The word expresses the universality of the salvation which verse 32 contemplates in its application to the two great divisions of the human family.

(34) The words start from the thought of Isa. 8:14, 15. The Christ is seen by Simeon as the stone on which some fall and are bruised (20:18), while others plant their feet upon it and rise to a higher life.

(35) A sword shall pierce through they own soul also.—The announcement of the special sorrow that was to be the Virgin Mother's portion comes as the sequel to "the sign that is spoken against," the antagonism with which her Son would meet. We may find fulfillment of it in 4:29; Matt. 12:46; John 19:26.

(36) One Anna, a prophetess.—It is remarkable that we find a woman recognized as a prophetess at a time when no man is recognized as a prophet. Eighty-four years (verse 37) was the duration of her widowhood. Assuming her to have been married at fifteen, this places her actual age at 106. She had lived through the whole century that preceded the birth of Christ, from the death of John Hyrcanus, and had witnessed, therefore, the conquest of Judaea by Pompeius and the rise of the Herodian house. Probably some chamber within the precincts was assigned to her (comp. II Chron. 34:22).

(39) They returned into Galilee.—Filling up the narrative from Matthew, we have to insert after the Presentation, the visit of the Magi, the massacre of the infants, and the flight into Egypt. It seems probable that Luke was not acquainted with Matthew's narrative, nor Matthew with Luke's. Each wrote from what he heard, or found in previous existing narratives, more or less incomplete, and thus cannot readily be brought into harmony with the other. In Matthew the return to Nazareth appears to be determined by their fears of Archelaus.

(40) The soul of Jesus was human, i.e., subject to the conditions and limitations of human knowledge, and learned as others learn. The heresy of Apollinarius is thus, as it were, anticipated and condemned. The latter words express more than guidance, more than strength, but a manifest outflowing of the divine favor in the moral beauty of a perfectly holy childhood.

(42) When he was twelve years old.—At age five the Jewish boy was to learn the Law, at first by extracts written on scrolls of the more important passages, the Shema of Deut. 6:4, the Hallel or Festival Psalms (Pss. 114-118, 136), and by catechetical teaching in school. At twelve he became more directly responsible for his obedience to the Law, and on the day when he attained the age of thirteen, put on for the first time the phylacteries which were worn at the recital of his daily prayer. (See note on Matt. 23:5.) It was, therefore, in strict accordance with usage, with perhaps a slight anticipation of the actual day, that the "child Jesus" should, at the age of twelve, have gone up with His parents to Jerusalem. In the later Maxims of the Fathers, two other stages of education were marked out. At ten, a boy was to enter on the study of the **Mischna** ("comments"), or body of traditional interpretations of the

Law; at eighteen, on that of the **Gemara** ("completeness"), or wider collection of sayings or legends, which, with the **Mischna**, made up what is known as the **Talmud** ("learning," or "doctrine").

(46) Sitting in the midst of the doctors.— A chamber of the Temple was set apart as a kind of open free school. The "doctors" or teachers (Acts 5:34) sat "in Moses' seat"; the older students on a low bench; the younger on the ground, literally "at the feet" of their instructor. The relation between master and scholar often was one of affectionate reverence and sympathy. It is interesting to think that among the doctors then present may have been the venerable Hillel; his grandson, the then youthful Gamaliel; Jonathan, the writer of the Chaldee Targum; and Shammai, the rival of Hillel, who "bound" where the latter "loosed."

(49) About my Father's business.—The words are the first recorded utterance of the Son of man, and they are a prophecy of that consciousness of direct Sonship, closer and more ineffable than that of any other of the sons of men, which is afterward the dominant idea of which His whole life is a manifestation. The words obviously are emphasized as an answer to Mary's words, "thy father."

(51) Was subject unto them.—There was no premature assumption of authority. In such a household as that of the carpenter of Nazareth, this subjection must, in the nature of things, have involved much manual and menial work—a share in the toil alike of the workshop and the house.

His mother kept all these sayings.—See note on verse 19.

(52) Here again (see note on verse 40) we have nothing but a normal orderly development. In striking contrast with the true record of the growth of the Son of Man is that which grew out of the fantastic imaginations of the writers of the apocryphal gospels.

3

(1) Tiberius Caesar had succeeded Augustus A.D. 14, so that we get the date A.D. 29 for the commencement of the Baptist's ministry. The rise of the city Tiberias, and the new name—the Sea of Tiberias—given to the Lake of Galilee, attest the desire of the Tetrarch Antipas to court his favor.

Pontius Pilate.—See note on Matt. 27:2.

He had entered on his office of Procurator in A.D. 26.

Herod being tetrarch of Galilee.—The tetrarch commonly was known as Antipas (a shortened form of Antipater) to distinguish him from his brothers. He had succeeded his father in his death, 4 or 3 B.C. He was deposed A.D. 39.

Philip tetrarch of Ituraea.—This was not the Philip whose wife Antipas had married (see note on Matt. 14:1), and who was the son of Mariamne, but his half-brother, the son of a Cleopatra of Jerusalem. The city of Caesarea Philippi was built by him (see note on Matt. 16:13). Our Lord's ministry brought Him into the region under Philip's rule just before the Transfiguration (see note on Matt. 17:1).

Lysanias the tetrarch of Abilene.—The district lay on the eastern slope of the range of the Anti-Libanus, and was watered by the Barada. The name of Lysanias appears as its ruler from the time of Antony and Cleopatra to that of Claudius, and passed probably through two or three generations.

(2) Annas and Caiaphas being the high priests.—Strictly speaking, there could be only one high priest and the office was filled at this time by Caiaphas. Annas had been appointed by the Roman Procurator Quirinus, A.D. 7, serving until A.D. 14. Joseph Caiaphas had married the daughter of Annas, and it was natural that this relationship should involve the restoration, as far as possible, of his old dignity. (See John 18:13; Acts 4:6.) Matthew and Mark do not name him.

(3-9) See notes on Matt. 3:1-11; Mark 1:4-6.

(10) And the people asked him ...—The questions that follow are peculiar to Luke. They are interesting as showing that the work of the Baptist was not that of a mere preacher of repentance, but that of a counselor, as well.

(13) Exact no more.—Under the "farming" system of taxation adopted by the Roman empire, this was the besetting temptation of all collectors employed in it, and it led naturally to the evil repute which attached, not in Judaea only, to the name of publican.

(14) The words are directed against a violent extortion of money or provisions by irregular troops. "Wages" means primarily the "rations" of a soldier, and then the money received in lieu of rations. (Comp. Rom. 6:23; I Cor. 9:7.)

(15-17) See notes on Matt. 3:11, 12.

(19-20) See notes on Matt. 14:3-5. Luke's account coincides in part with John's arrangement (John 3:24).

(21-22) See notes on Matt. 3:13-17. Luke's account is the shortest of the three first gospels, but it adds here, as afterward in his report of the Transfiguration, the fact that our Lord was "praying" at the time of the divine attestation to His Sonship. The words "bodily shape" are peculiar to Luke, and tend to confirm the traditional symbolism which finds in the dove the emblem of the Holy Spirit.

(23) Began to be about thirty years of age.—At this age the Levites entered on their full work (Num. 4:23, 30, 35), a kind of probationary period beginning at twenty-five (Num. 8:24) or even at twenty (I Chron. 23:27). No age was fixed for the beginning of the priesthood, nor of the prophet's work; but it may be inferred that thirty was looked upon as the time when manhood reached its completeness.

On the genealogy, see notes on Matt. 1:17, 18. It would seem that we have here the genealogy, not of Joseph, but of Mary, the words "being (as was supposed) the son of Joseph" being a parenthesis, and the first link being Jesus (the heir, and in that sense, son, of Heli. On this hypothesis, the Virgin, as well as Joseph, was of the house and lineage of David; and our Lord was literally, as well as by adoption, "of the seed of David according to the flesh" (Rom. 1:3), on the mother's side through the line of Nathan, on the reputed father's through that of Solomon. The fact that the genealogy goes back to Adam confirms the whole character of Luke's gospel as intended to set forth the universality of the Gospel, to prepare the way for the truth of the brotherhood of mankind in Christ. It represented Christ as the second Adam, as Matthew's genealogy represented Him as the heir of Abraham.

4

(1-13) See notes on Matt. 4:1-11.

(14) Returned in the power of the Spirit.— The phrase indicates a new phase of the life of the Son of man, a change from its former tenor as striking as that which passed over the apostles on the day of Pentecost, when new powers of thought and utterance were developed which had before been latent. The narrative of John 2-5 comes in between the Temptation and the beginning of the Galilean ministry.

(16) And he came to Nazareth.—The narrative that follows has the special interest of being peculiar to Luke. Luke may have journeyed from Caesarea to Nazareth during Paul's imprisonment in the former city and obtained his information on the spot, perhaps from the same informants from whom he obtained information of the Infancy. It is clear that our Lord did not begin His ministry at Nazareth. He came there when His fame was, in some measure, at least, already established.

As his custom was.—Children were admitted to the synagogue at the age of five. At thirteen attendance was obligatory. It was open to any man of reputed knowledge and piety, with the sanction of the ruler of the synagogue, to read the lessons (one from the Law and one from the Prophets), and our Lord's previous life doubtless had gained the respect of that officer. The work of preaching also was open to any qualified layman of adequate culture, who had a "word of exhortation" to address to the worshipers. (Comp. Acts 13:15.)

(17) The book of the prophet Esaias.—The Law commonly was written on one long roll. The other books in like manner—singly or combined, according to their length—were written on rolls of parchment, and were unrolled from the cylinder to which they were fastened. Here, it is clear, Isaiah formed a roll by itself, and contained the prophetic lesson for the day. The chapter which He read stands as the second lesson for the day of Atonement.

(18) The Spirit of the Lord is upon me.—The passage that follows reproduces, with a few unimportant variations, the LXX version of Isa. 61:1, 2 (see notes). The passage which Jesus read was one in which He wished men to see the leading idea of His ministry.

(19) The acceptable year of the Lord.—The primary reference was to the year of Jubilee, when land that had been mortgaged returned to its owner, debts were forgiven, and Israelite slaves released (Lev. 25:9, 10). It was to our Lord, as it had been to Isaiah, the type of the "year" of the divine kingdom.

(20) And sat down.—The chair near the place from which the lesson was read was the pulpit of the rabbi, and to sit down in that chair (Matt. 5:1; 23:2) was an assumption by our Lord, apparently for the first time in that synagogue, of the preacher's

function. This led to the eager, fixed gaze of wonder.

(21) This day is this scripture fulfilled.—This was what startled them: He had left them as the son of the carpenter—mother, brethren, sisters still were among them—and now He came back claiming to be the Christ, and to make words that had seemed to speak of a far-off glorious dream as a living and present reality.

(23) Physician, heal thyself.—There is something interesting in our finding this proverb in the gospel of the beloved physician. It was a common Jewish proverb; but there is no trace of it in Greek writers, and it therefore was likely to attract his notice.

(24) No prophet is accepted.—See Matt. 13:57; Mark 6:4; John 4:44.

(26) Sarepta, the Zarephath of I Kings 17:9, was a Phoenician city lying between Tyre and Sidon. The reference to this incident at the beginning of our Lord's ministry is a striking instance of His method of reading the underlying lessons of the narratives of the Old Testament. In what seemed a mere episode in the life of Elijah He finds a truth which implies the future calling of the Gentiles. When He complied with the prayer of the Syro-Phoenician woman, He was doing as Elijah had done.

(31) And came down to Capernaum.—See note on Matt. 4:13.

(33-37) See note on Mark 1:23-27. The narrative, as being common to these two gospels, and not found in Matthew, may be looked upon as having probably been communicated by one evangelist to the other when they met at Rome (Col. 4:10, 14).

(38, 39) See Matt. 8:14.

(40, 41) See notes on Matt. 8:16, 17.

5

(1-11) See notes on Matt. 4:18-22; Mark 1:16-20, although this is a different incident. On the assumption of difference we infer that while our Lord went by Himself to preach the Gospel of the kingdom to "the other cities," the disciples returned, as they did after the Resurrection, to their old manner of life, and were now called again to their higher work.

(12-16) See notes on Matt. 8:2-4.

(16) The addition that he "was praying" there is peculiar to Luke, who, throughout his gospel, lays stress on this feature in our Lord's life.

(17-26) See notes on Matt. 9:1-8.

(17) Pharisees and doctors of the law.—
The description of the crowd of listeners is
peculiar to Luke. The fact that many of the
doctors of the law had come from
Jerusalem obviously is important in its connection with John's account (chaps. 2; 5) of
our Lord's previous work in that city, and
as explaining the part now taken by them.

(27-32) See notes on Matt. 9:9-13.

(29) Of publicans and of others.—It is
characteristic of Luke as a Gentile that he
will not use the word "sinners" as Matthew
and Mark appear to have used it, as popularly including heathen as such, and substitutes the more vague word "others." He
will, however, in reporting what was said by
others, naturally give the word "sinners" as
it actually was spoken (see verse 30).

(33-39) See notes on Matt. 9:14-17.

**(39) No man also having drunk old
wine.**—This addition is peculiar to Luke.
The old wine represented the motive-power
of the Law in its rigid and Pharisaic form.
The new wine is the freer, nobler, life-
power of the Gospel. The words are spoken
in a tone of something like a tolerant pity
for the prejudices of age and custom.

6

(1-12) See notes on Matt. 12:1-14; Mark
2:23-28; 3:1-6.

(1) On the second sabbath after the first.—
Among those whom Luke seems to have
known at Antioch we find the name of
Manaen, or Menahem, the foster-brother of
Herod the Tetrarch (Acts 13:1), presumably
the son or grandson of Menahem, an Essene
prophet, who had predicted the future sovereignty of Herod the Great. Manaen may
have been among those drawn to the Baptist, supplying Luke with the technical term
that fixed the day of the journey through
the cornfields. If this were a new-moon
Sabbath, it must have been the beginning of
the moon of Nisan, possibly coinciding with
an actual Sabbath; and thus we have the
interesting fact that the lesson for the first
Sabbath in that month is from I Sam. 21,
which contains the history of the shewbread
to which our Lord refers.

(13-16) See notes on Matt. 10:1-4. In the
place which he assigns to the choice of the
Twelve, Luke agrees more closely with
Mark than with Matthew, who makes it
precede the narratives of the disciples

plucking the ears of corn and the healing of
the withered hand. But a precisely-
harmonized arrangement is unimportant.
The point to which Luke's record obviously
was intended to give prominence is that the
choice of the Twelve came as the result of
the night of prayer (verse 12), just as the
prominent thought in Matthew (9:36) is that
it grew out of our Lord's compassion for
the multitude that were as sheep without a
shepherd.

**(17) And he came down with them, and
stood in the plain.**—In Matthew (chap. 10)
the mission of the Twelve is followed by a
full discourse on their apostolic work and
its perils. Here it is followed by a discourse
which has many points of resemblance with
the Sermon on the Mount in Matt. 5-7.
Mark and Luke distinguish the choice of
the Twelve from their mission, the latter
meeting us in 9:1; Mark 6:7, and that in a
form which implies the previous existence
of the Twelve as a distinct body.

Comp. Matt. 4:24; Mark 3:7-12. It is
probable that each separate report of any of
our Lord's great discourses dwelt upon the
multitudes who were present to hear them.

(20-26) See notes on Matt. 5:1-12.

(24) We enter here on what is a distinct
feature of the Sermon on the Plain—the
woes that, as it were, balance the beatitudes.

(27-28) See notes on Matt. 5:44.

(29, 30) See notes on Matt. 5:39-42.

**(31) As ye would that men should do to
you . . .**—See note on Matt. 7:12.

(32) See notes on 5:29; Matt. 5:46.

(36) Be ye therefore merciful.—The form
of the sentence is the same as that of Matt.
5:48 (see note), but "merciful" takes the
place of "perfect" as being the noblest of the
divine attributes, in which all others reach
their completeness. (Comp. Shakespeare,
Merchant of Venice, 4:1.)

(37, 38) See notes on Matt. 7:1, 2; Mark
4:24.

(38) Into your bosom.—The large fold of
an Eastern dress over the chest, often used
as a pocket.

(39, 40) The verses are noticeable as
causing a break in the discourse which has
no parallel in the Sermon on the Mount,
and as giving an example of the wider sense
of the word "parable," as applicable to any
proverbial saying that involved a similitude. The disciples are warned against taking on themselves the office of a judge.
They were in this to follow the example of
their Master.

(41, 42) See notes on Matt. 7:3-5.

(43-36) See notes on Matt. 7:16-21.

(47-49) See notes on Matt. 7:24-27.

7

(2-10) See notes on Matt. 8:5-13.

(11) He went into a city called Nain.— The narrative that follows is peculiar to Luke. Nain lies on the northwestern edge of the "Little Hermon" in Galilee, as the ground descends into the plain of Esdraelon. It is approached by a steep ascent, and on either side of the road the rock is full of sepulchral caves. It was on the way to one of these that the funeral procession was met by our Lord.

(13) And when the Lord saw her.—The words are noticeable as being one of the comparatively few instances in which the term "the Lord" is used absolutely instead of Jesus. This use of "the Lord" occurs more frequently in Luke and John than in the other gospels. After the Resurrection it rose to still higher meaning, as in the exclamations of Thomas (John 20:28; comp. John 20:25) and of John (John 21:7).

(14) He came and touched the bier.— Here the facts make it clear that it was after the Jewish manner of burial. It was not a closed coffin, like the mummy-cases of Egypt, but an open bier on which the corpse lay wrapped up in its winding-sheet and swathing bands, as in the description of the entombment of Lazarus (John 11:44) and of our Lord (John 20:6, 7), with the **sudarium**, the napkin or handkerchief, laid lightly over the face. They who bore the bier "stood **still**," marveling that One who was known as a Teacher should touch that which most rabbis would have avoided as bringing pollution.

(16) A great prophet.—This was the first instance of our Lord's power as put forth to raise the dead, that of Jairus' daughter following in 8:40-56. In the history of the Old Testament there were examples of such wonders having been wrought by Elijah (I Kings 17:22) and Elisha (II Kings 4:34), and the people drew the natural inference that here there was at least a prophet of the same order.

(18-23) See notes on 6:1; Matt. 11:2-6.

(24-35) See notes on Matt. 11:7-19.

(36) One of the Pharisees . . .—We may reasonably infer that this was one of the better class of Pharisees who had a certain measure of respect for our Lord's teaching, and was half-inclined (comp. verse 39) to acknowledge Him as a prophet. Of such John tells us (12:42) there were many among the chief rulers. We find another example of the same kind in 11:37. Our Lord did not seek such feasts, but neither would He refuse them, for there too there might be an opening for doing His Father's work.

(37) A woman in the city, which was a sinner.—The word is used clearly as pointing to the special sin of unchastity. The question who she was must be left unanswered. The widespread belief that she was Mary Magdalene has absolutely no evidence in Scripture; nor can there be said to be anything like even a tradition in its favor, although it first gained general acceptance through the authority of Gregory the Great. That she was Mary of Bethany likewise is without support.

Brought an alabaster box of ointment.— See note on Matt. 26:7.

(40) The answer was, as the context shows, to the unspoken thoughts of the Pharisee. The name of the Pharisee is thus given to us, but it was too common to suggest any identification.

(41, 42) There was a certain creditor . . .— The parable has some points of resemblance to that of Matt. 18:23. The application of the parable treats the woman as a greater debtor than the Pharisee. She had committed greater sins. Each was equally powerless to pay the debt—i.e., to make atonement for his or her sins. Whatever hope either had lay in the fact that pardon was offered to both as a matter of free gift and bounty.

(44-46) The Pharisee's invitation was, in the end, hardly more than an act of ostentatious patronage. The acts of courtesy which were due to every guest (comp. Matt. 3:11; John 13:5; I Tim. 5:10), and which a rabbi might expect as a thing of course, were, in his judgment, superfluous for the carpenter's son. And if the new Teacher cared little about ablutions (Mark 7:8), why take the trouble to provide them for Him? (See note on Matt. 26:48.)

(47) Her sins, which are many, are forgiven.—Love is the natural consequence of the sense of being forgiven, and its manifestations are therefore evidence of a real and completed forgiveness. The antecedent conditions of forgiveness, repentance, and faith must be presupposed in her case as in others.

8

(2) The words bring before us a feature in this period of our Lord's ministry not elsewhere recorded, though implied in 23:49. The Master and the disciples formed at this period one traveling company. When they arrived at town or village, they held a mission, the Twelve heralding His approach and inviting men to listen to Him as He taught in synagogue, market-place, or open plain. Another company, consisting of devout women, mostly of the wealthier class, traveled separately, journeying in advance and arranging for the reception and the food of the Prophet and His followers. (Comp. II Kings 4:10.) It is said to have been a common practice in Judaea in our Lord's time for women of independent means to support a rabbi in his work as a teacher.

Mary called Magdalene.—See notes on Matt. 15:39; 27:56. The "seven devils" or "demons" point, as in the parable of Matt. 12:45 (see notes), to a specially aggravated form of possession. Her presence with the mother of our Lord and John at the Crucifixion (John 19:25) seems to imply some special tie either of sympathy or of earlier connection with them. She appears, from the names with which she is associated, and from the fact that she too "ministered of her substance," to have belonged to the more wealthy section of Galilean society.

(3) Joanna, the wife of Chuza.—Here again we have a convert of the upper class. Nothing further is known of Chuza—but the "steward" of the Tetrarch, the manager of his income and expenditure, must have been a man of some mark. We may think of him and his wife probably as having come under the influence of the Baptist or of Manaen. (See note on 6:1.) Joanna appears again in the history of the Resurrection (24:10).

Susanna.—The name, which meant a "lily," occurs in the apocryphal addition to the Book of Daniel known as **Susanna and the Elders.** Nothing further is known of the person thus named.

(5-15) See notes on Matt. 13:3-23; Mark 4:3-13.

(16-18) See Matt. 5:15, 16; 10:26, 13:12.

(19-21) See notes on Matt. 12:46-50.

(22-25) See notes on Matt. 8:18, 23-27.

(24) Master, master.—The Greek word **epistates**, which only Luke uses in the New Testament, is his equivalent (comp., e.g., 5:5) for the "Rabbi" or "Master" (**didaskalos**), in the sense of "teacher," which we find in the other gospels. It was the more classical word of the two.

(26-39) See notes on Matt. 8:28-34.

(41-56) See notes on Matt. 9:18-26; Mark 5:21-43.

9

(1-6) See notes on Matt. 10:5-15; Mark 6:7-13.

(7-9) See notes on Matt 14:1-12.

(10-17) See notes on Matt. 14:13-21; Mark 6:30-44.

(18-27) Luke omits the narrative of our Lord's walking on the water, of the feeding of the four thousand, of the Syro-Phoenician woman, and of the teaching as to the leaven of the Pharisees and Sadducees. We cannot get beyond a conjectural explanation of these phenomena, but it is possible that he simply did not learn these facts in the course of his inquiries and therefore did not insert them. This infers that he had not seen the gospels of Matthew and Mark in the form in which we now have them.

On this narrative see notes on Matt. 16:13-28; Mark 8:27, 34; 9:1.

(28-36) See notes on Matt. 17:1-13; Mark 9:2-13.

(29) And as he prayed.—We again note, as characteristic of Luke, the stress laid upon our Lord's prayers here, as before in 3:21; 5:16; 6:12.

(31) Spake of his decease.—Luke's is the only narrative that names the subject of the words that passed between our Lord and Moses and Elias. The use of the word "decease" (**exodos**) instead of "death" is remarkable: (1) because it had not been commonly so used by Greek authors; (2) because in its wider range of meaning it covered all the special phenomena connected with the close of the ministry of the Lawgiver and the Tishbite (comp. Deut. 34:5, 6; II Kings 2:11), and no less so, the Resurrection and Ascension of our Lord, as well as the Crucifixion; (3) because it meets us in close connection with a reference to the Transfiguration in II Pet. 1:15.

(37-43) See notes on Matt. 17:14-21; Mark 9:14-29. Luke's omission of the question and the teaching as to the coming of

Elijah given by the other two gospels is noticeable. There was no expectation of that coming among the Gentiles for whom he wrote. It was not necessary to correct that impression, or even to bring the difficulties which it suggested before their minds.

(46-50) See notes on Matt. 18:1-5; Mark 9:33-41.

(51) When the time was come that he should be received up.—Literally, "When the days of His assumption were being fulfilled." The noun is peculiar to Luke, and is derived from the verb used of the Ascension in Mark 16:19; I Tim. 3:16. It is as though Luke looked on all that follows as seen in the light of the Ascension. Every word and act was consciously a step forward to that great consummation.

(52) And sent messengers before his face.— The words "Samaria" and "Samaritan" do not occur at all in Mark, and in Matthew in one passage only (Matt. 10:5), and then in the command given to the Twelve that they were not to enter into any city of the Samaritans. Luke, on the other hand, seems to have carried his inquiries into that country, and to have treasured up whatever he could find of our Lord's acts and words in relation to it.

The city of Samaria first comes into notice as built by Omri to be the capital of the kingdom of Israel (I Kings 16:23, 24). It continued to occupy that position until its capture by Shalmaneser, 721 B.C. After the deportation of the ten tribes, Esar-haddon (Ezra 4:2, 10), after the manner of the great monarchs of the East, brought a mingled race from Babylon and other Eastern points to occupy the district thus left depopulated, and from these the Samaritans of later history were descended. They were accordingly of alien races, and their neighbors of Judaea kept up the memory of their foreign origin. Under the influence of a priest of Israel sent by the king of Assyria, they became worshipers of Jehovah (II Kings 17:41), and on the return to Judah and Benjamin from the Captivity, they sought to be admitted as co-religionists, to share with them in the work of rebuilding the Temple, and therefore to obtain like privileges as worshipers in its courts. That claim was, however, refused, and they in return, 409 B.C., guided by Manasseh, a priest who had been expelled from Jerusalem by Nehemiah (Neh. 13:28), obtained permission from the Persian king, Darius Nothus, to erect a temple on Mount Gerizim. The new wor-

ship thus started placed them at once in the position of a rival and schismatical sect, and their subsequent history presented the usual features of such antagonism. See John 4:9; Josephus, *Ant.*, 18:2, §2, 20:6, §1. In this present narrative we find our Lord apparently endeavoring to continue a work which had been successfully begun. (See notes on John 4.)

(54) When his disciples James and John saw this.—See Mark 3:17. Did not such a people deserve a punishment like Elijah had inflicted on the messengers of Ahaziah (II Kings 1:10, 12, 14)? Reference to "Elias," however, as well as the direct discourse in verses 55, 56 is absent from the best MSS.

(57-60) See notes on Matt. 8:19-22.

(61, 62) This example of our Lord's method of dealing with half-hearted disciples is peculiar to Luke. This man apparently was free from the closer and more binding ties of relationship, and the plea urged was therefore hollow and unreal. The image which our Lord used was, as usual, one that went home to the personal experience of His hearers. They were of the peasant class, and they knew that the eye of the plowman, if he is to do his work well, must look straight before him at the line of the furrow which he is making. To look back, while working, is to mar the work entirely. The man who so looks is disqualified for the work of God's kingdom.

10

(1) After these things the Lord appointed other seventy also.—The number had a threefold significance. (1) Seventy elders had been appointed by Moses to help him in his work of teaching and judging the people (Num. 11:16), and to these the spirit of prophecy had been given that they might bear the burden with him. In appointing the Seventy our Lord revived, as it were, the order or "school" of prophets which had been so long extinct. And the existence of such men in every church is implied in nearly every epistle (e.g., Acts 13:1; 15:32; I Cor. 12:28, 14:29; I Thess. 5:20). The Seventy, thought not sharers in the special authority and functions of the Twelve, were yet endowed with like prophetic powers, and the mysteries of the kingdom were revealed to them (verse 21). (2) As the Sanhedrin or great Council of scribes, priests and elders consisted of seventy members besides the president, the number having been fixed on the assumption that they were the successors of those whom Moses had chosen, our Lord's choice of the number could hardly fail to suggest the thought that the seventy disciples were placed by Him in a position of direct contrast with the existing Council, as an assembly guided, not by the traditions of men, but by direct inspiration. (3) Partly by a rough reckoning of the names of the nations in Gen. 10, partly on account of the mystical completeness of the number itself, seventy had come to be the representative number of all the nations of the world. Thus, what is here recorded is a step full of meaning, a distinct and formal witness of the future universality of the Church of Christ. This was a mission in which, from the nature of the case, the Twelve were not sharers (comp. Matt. 10:5), and which, therefore, naturally came to occupy a less prominent place in the recollections of those from whom the narratives of the first two gospels were primarily derived.

(2-16) See notes on Matt. 9:37-10:15, 11:21. The verses contain much in common with those spoken on the mission of the Twelve. We have here, as in the sermons on the Mount and on the Plain, an example of our Lord's repeating the expression of the same thoughts in nearly the same language.

(5-7) The labourer is worthy of his hire.— See I Tim. 5:18. Paul scarcely could have failed to have become acquainted, during his long companionship with Luke, with the materials which the evangelist was collecting for his great work. We can hardly doubt, accordingly, that he quotes this as one of the sayings of the Lord Jesus, as he quotes another in Acts 20:35, and clothes it with the same authority as the older Scripture. On this assumption, the gospel according to Luke must have been, in part, at least, written and recognized at the time when the Pastoral Epistles were written.

(17) And the seventy returned again with joy.—It is obvious from the immediate sequence of the two facts that the mission of the Seventy was confined within narrow limits of space and time.

(18) I beheld Satan as lightning fall from heaven.—While they were working, their Master had been following them in spirit, gazing, as it were, on each stage of their victorious conflict. Their triumph over the demons was the beginning and the earnest of a final conquest over Satan as "the prince of the demons." There may, possibly, be a

reference to the belief then beginning to be current among the Jews as to the fall of Satan after his creation; but the primary meaning of our Lord's words is that he was now dethroned from his usurped dominion in the "high places" (comp. Eph. 6:12), which symbolized the spiritual region of the soul and mind of man. The imagery reappears in a developed form in Rev. 12:9.

(19) Of a literal fulfillment of the words, Paul's escape from the viper at Melita (Acts 28:3) is the only recorded instance; but the parallelism between this promise and that of Ps. 91:13 shows that the literal meaning falls into the background, that the serpent and the scorpion are symbols of spiritual powers of evil.

(21, 22) In that hour Jesus rejoiced in spirit.—See notes on Matt. 11:25-27. This is the one instance where the word "rejoiced" is used of our Lord's human feeling of exultation. It indicates the enthusiasm of spiritual joy and conveys the impression that the disciples must have noticed something exceptional in their Lord's look and manner. The verbal agreement with Matthew indicates that both the evangelists must have drawn from a common source, documentary or oral.

(25) The question, though the same as that of the young man in Matt. 19:16 (see notes), is not asked in the same tone. There it was asked by one anxiously seeking to inherit eternal life; here there is a certain tone of self-conscious superiority, which required a different treatment. As the method of Socrates was to make men conscious of their ignorance of the true meaning of words which they repeated glibly, so here our Lord parries the question by another, makes him repeat his own formulated answer, and then teaches him how little he had realized its depth and fullness.

(30) A certain man went down.—We enter here upon the first of a series of parables, which differ from those in Matthew in having more the character of actual human histories, illustrating a truth, rather than mere similitudes composed for the purpose of illustration. There is obviously no reason why we should not believe them to have been statements of facts that actually had happened, and which had come under our Lord's observation as He traveled on His work of preaching the Gospel of the kingdom.

From Jerusalem to Jericho.—The journey was one of about twenty-one miles, for the most part through a rocky and desert country, with caves that were haunted by bands of robbers. In Jerome's time it was known as the "red" or the "bloody" way, in consequence of the frequency of such crimes.

(31) Passed by on the other side.—The priest shrank from the trouble and peril of meddling with a man whom robbers had just attacked, and from the fear of incurring a ceremonial defilement by coming into contact with what possibly might be a corpse before he reached it.

(32) Likewise a Levite.—The passage is memorable as the only mention of a Levite in the gospels. He is represented as at once better and worse than the priest—better in that he does not altogether turn aside, but "comes" and looks; worse in that his second thoughts are at variance with his first and prevail against them. If he has more light, he also sins more against it.

(33) A certain Samaritan.—See note on 9:52. Here there is a true human feeling in one who outwardly was involved in heresy and schism, and our Lord singles that out as infinitely preferable to the form of godliness without its power.

(34) The "oil and wine," which had been provided for personal refreshment, are freely given to be used, according to the primitive surgery of the time, the latter for cleansing the wounds, the former for soothing inflammation.

(35) Two pence—i.e., "two denarii," according to Matt. 20:2 the average wages of a laborer for two days; or, taking the estimate of Mark 6:37, enough for a meal of twenty-five men. It was therefore a sufficient and liberal provision for all probable contingencies.

(36) There is a certain subtle discernment in the form of the question. It is answered indirectly by the narrative, which showed who had proved himself a neighbor to the Jew. The Samaritan had shown himself a better interpreter of the commandment than the orthodox scribe. From the human point of view there is something noble in the manner in which our Lord thus singles out the Samaritan as a type of excellence, after His own recent repulse (9:53) by men of the same race; and something also courageous in His doing so after He recently had been reproached as being Himself a Samaritan (John 8:48.)

(37) Go, and do thou likewise.— Fellowship in the same human nature, and any kind of even passing contact, were enough to constitute a ground for neighborly kindness.

(38) "Martha" (Aramaic) means "Lord," and is therefore equivalent to the Greek **Kyria**, suggesting the possible identity of the sister of Lazarus with the elect Kyria (or elect Lady), to whom John addressed his second epistle. We can scarcely fail to notice the identity of character here (verse 39) and in the entirely independent narratives of John 11; 12. There also Martha is active and conspicuous in serving, Mary meditative and emotional, pouring her whole soul into one act of love.

11

(1) The facts of the case as here narrated, the common practice of the Jews, and the analogy of the prayers in John 11:41 and Matt. 26:39 (comp. 10:21; Matt. 11:25) all lead to the conclusion that our Lord prayed aloud. The disciples heard Him, and, unable to follow or to record what they had heard, wished to be able to enter into His spirit and pray as He prayed. The prayers of John's disciples were probably, like those of the Pharisees, offered three times a day, at the third, the sixth, and the ninth hours, and after the pattern of the well-known "Eighteen Prayers," which made up the Jewish manual of private devotion.

(2-4) See notes on Matt. 6:9-11. Luke uses the word "sin" instead of "debts," as being, perhaps, more adapted to the minds of his Gentile readers, while he retains the primary idea of Matthew's term in the words "every one that is indebted to us." Luke omits the final doxology found in some, but not in the best, MSS of Matthew.

(5-8) The man who prays must know that God will care for those for whom he pleads, and will give them also their "daily bread" in both the higher and the lower senses of the word. If prayer prevails over apathy and impatience, how much more will it prevail when we pray to One who knows our necessities before we ask Him? "Importunity" (verse 8) expresses a shameless persistence that knows no restraint.

(9-13) See notes on Matt. 7:7-11. But observe that here the one highest gift of the "Holy Spirit" takes the place of the wider and less definite "good things" in Matt. 7:11. The variation is significant, as belonging to a later stage of our Lord's teaching, and especially as spoken probably to some of the Seventy, who were thus taught to ask boldly for the Spirit that was to make them in very deed a company of prophets. (See note on 10:1.)

(14-23) Luke seems here to bring together into one narrative two incidents which in Matt. (9:32-34; 12:22-30; see notes) appear as separated.

(20) If I with the finger of God . . .— Comp. Exod. 8:19; 31:18. As "the hand" (Ezek. 1:3; 37:1) denotes power generally, so the "finger" symbolizes power in its concentrated and specially-directed energy.

(24-26) See notes on Matt. 12:43-45.

(27) A certain woman of the company.— The incident is peculiar to Luke, and, like many other of the facts recorded by him, seems to have been derived from the company of devout women (8:1) with whom he came into contact. It is interesting as being the first direct fulfillment of the words of the **Magnificat** (1:48), and as showing how the Son of Mary in this instance (comp. Matt. 12:46-50) extended the beatitude.

(29-32) See notes on Matt. 12:38-42.

(33-36) See notes on Matt. 5:15; 6:22, 23.

(37-44) See notes on Matt. 15:2; 23:6, 7, 23-27; Mark 7:3, 4.

(40-41) This is peculiar to Luke. The underlying principle of the teaching sweeps away the whole fabric of the law of ceremonial purity, as the words of Matt. 15:10-20 had, on different grounds, done before. The distinction between the two phases of the truth is that here greater stress is laid on the active purifying power of the love of which alms, if not given for the sake of man's praise, is the natural expression. That which defiles is selfishness; that which purifies is the unselfishness of love.

(45-48) See notes on Matt. 22:35; 23:4, 29, 30.

(49-51) See notes on Matt. 23:34-36.

(51) We note the absence here of the description "Zacharias, son of Barachias," which causes so much perplexity in Matthew's report. The omission favors the view that the additional words were inserted by the reporter of our Lord's discourse there, or by some early transcriber.

(52) Woe unto you, lawyers!—See notes on Matt. 23:13. This is the third occurrence of the word for "entering in" in Luke's gospel. (See notes on 8:16; 11:33.) The passage throws light on the promise of the "keys" of the kingdom made to Peter. (See note on Matt. 16:19.)

(54) Laying wait for him.—The words throw light on the subsequent question about paying tribute to Caesar (Matt. 22:15-22; Mark 12:13-17), and show it to

have been the acting out of a preconcerted policy.

12

(1-3) Comp. Matt. 6:2; 16:6. See note on Matt. 10:27.

(4-10) See notes on Matt. 10:28-32.

(11, 12) See notes on Matt. 10:18, 19. What had been a special promise to the Twelve is now extended to all whom the Lord calls His friends (verse 4; comp. John 15:14, 15).

(13) And one of the company.—The request implied a recognition of our Lord's character as a scribe or rabbi, but it was for the purpose of asking Him to assume that office in its purely secular aspect. As interpreters of the Law, the scribes were appealed to as advocates and arbitrators in questions of property or marriage. The words of the petitioner suggest that he was a younger son, who, on his father's death, claimed from his elder brother more than the share which, according to the usual practice of a double portion for the first-born (II Kings 2:9), of right belonged to him.

(14) Man, who made me a judge . . . ?— The address was one which expressed grave censure and indignation. Was it for this that men came to Him instead of seeking for the kingdom of God? He accordingly distinctly repudiates any but the purely spiritual aspect of a scribe's work, and will neither act publicly as judge nor privately as arbitrator. (Comp. John 8:11.)

(15) Take heed, and beware of covetousness.—Our Lord's words show that He had read the secret of the man's heart. Greed was there, with all its subtle temptations, leading the man to think that "life" was not worth living unless he had a superfluity of goods. The general truth is illustrated by a parable (verses 16-21), obviously selected by Luke, as especially enforcing the truth which he held to be of primary importance.

(19) Eat, drink, and be merry.—Comp. I Cor. 15:32; Jas. 4:13; Horace, **Odes,** 1:11.8. Extremes meet, and the life of self-indulgence may either spring from an undue expectation of a lengthened life, or from unduly dwelling on the fact of its shortness, without taking into account the judgment that comes after it. Any Jew, thus believing, sank to the level of the dissolute heathen, who was content to live in and for the present only.

(21) So is he that layeth up treasure for himself.—See Matt. 6:19; I Tim. 6:19.

(22-31) The previous words had been spoken generally to all who needed their warning against greed. These are addressed to those who already had been called to the consciousness of a higher life. See notes on Matt. 6:25-33.

(32) Fear not, little flock.—There is an implied recognition of the fact that "**the little flock**" (the Greek has the article) had passed beyond the stage of seeking for the kingdom. In its essence it was theirs already.

(33) Sell that ye have.—In its generalized form the precept is peculiar to Luke, but it has its parallel in the command given to the young ruler (see note on Matt. 19:21). Comp. Acts 2:45.

(34) For where your treasure is.—Comp. Matt. 6:20, 21.

(35) Let your loins be girded . . .—To "gird up the loins" was, in Eastern habits and with Eastern garments, the received symbol of readiness for active service (I Kings 18:46; II Kings 1:8; John 13:4; I Pet. 1:13). The "lights" are the lamps (Matt. 5:15) which the watchful hold in their hands. What follows has the interest of presenting the germ of the thought which was afterward developed into the parable of the wise and foolish virgins. (See notes on Matt. 25:1-13).

(38) And if he shall come in the second watch.—See Mark 13:35 for the Roman fourfold division of the night. Here we find the older Jewish division into three watches (Judg. 7:19; I Sam. 11:11).

(39, 40) See notes on Matt. 24:43, 44.

(42-46) See notes on Matt. 24:45-51. Here the words come as an answer to Peter's question (comp. Matt. 19:27). The promise was spoken, not for the Twelve only, but for every faithful and wise steward.

(47-48) These verses are peculiar to Luke. Those who, with their eyes open, sin against light and knowledge can expect in this world or in the world to come a penalty proportionably severe. Man's knowledge is the measure of his responsibilities; and in the absence of knowledge, more or less complete, though stripes may be inflicted as the only effective discipline for teaching men what things are or are not worthy of stripes, yet they shall be "few." We may well be content to leave questions of suffering more or less acute to Him who spake

the words, and in so doing gave the most convincing proof that the Judge of all the earth assuredly will do right (Gen. 18:25).

(49, 50) These words also are peculiar to Luke. See notes on Matt. 3:12; 20:22.

(51-53) Comp. Matt. 10:34, 35.

(54-57) See notes on Matt. 16:1, 2.

(58, 59) Comp. Matt. 5:25, 26. The "adversary" is the Law that accuses them (John 5:45); the judge is none other than the Judge of all the earth.

13

(1) The Galilaeans, whose blood Pilate had mingled with their sacrifices.—The incident is not related by Josephus or any other historian, but it was quite in harmony with Pilate's character. (See note on Matt. 27:2.) It may have originated in some outburst of zealous fanaticism (comp. Acts 5:37), while the pilgrims from Galilee were offering their sacrifices in the courts of the Temple, and have been repressed with the same ruthless severity as he had shown in other tumults. It was probably one, at least, of the causes of the enmity between Herod and Pilate of which we read in 23:12.

(2) Suppose ye that these Galilaeans . . . ?—The tale probably had been told with a conviction that the massacre had been a special judgment for some special and exceptional guilt. Our Lord at once (comp. John 9:7) sweeps away all their rash interpretations of the divine government, and declares that all, unless they repented, were under the sentence of a like destruction.

(4) Upon whom the tower in Siloam fell.—Here again we have a reference to an incident not recorded elsewhere. It was clearly one that had impressed the minds of men with horror, as a special judgment. The pool of Siloam (John 9:7), at the valley of the Kedron, was supplied through artificial conduits. It is likely that the tower in question was part of the works which Pilate had planned for the construction of an aqueduct, and for which he appropriated part of the Corban or sacred treasure of the Temple. If so, the popular excitement which this measure caused (see note on Matt. 27:2) might well lead men to look on its fall as an instance of a divine judgment on what they regarded as an act of sacrilege.

(6) A certain man had a fig tree.—The parable stands obviously in close connection with the foregoing teaching. The people had been warned of the danger of perishing, unless they repented. The barren fig tree is the symbol of a fruitless profession of godliness, while the delay represents the forbearance of God in allowing yet a time for repentance. More specifically, the vineyard is Israel (see note on Matt. 21:33); the owner of the vineyard is the great King, the Lord of Hosts (Isa. 5:7); the fig tree is the individual soul, which, inheriting its place in a divine order, is as a tree planted in the garden of the Lord (comp. Ps. 1:3; Jer. 18:8); the "three years" represent, as the symbol of completeness, the full opportunities given to men, the calls to repentance and conversion which come to them in the several stages of their lives; the dresser of the vineyard is the Lord Jesus Himself, who intercedes as for the nation as a whole, so for each individual member of the nation.

(11) Behold, there was a woman . . .—The narrative that follows is peculiar to Luke. The indefiniteness as to time and place indicate that it was probably one of the previously unrecorded traditions which he met when he entered on his personal search for materials. The description indicates the accuracy of the trained observer. The presence of such a sufferer in the synagogue may, perhaps, imply habitual devotion, and therefore the faith that made her receptive of the healing power.

(12) Woman, thou art loosed from thine infirmity.—The words were obviously a test of the woman's faith. The verb is in the perfect tense—the work of healing already was completed.

(13) And he laid his hands on her.—See note on Matt. 9:29.

(14) The traditional law for the work of the Jewish physician was that he might act in his calling in cases of emergency, life and death cases, but not in chronic diseases, such as this. This law the ruler of the synagogue wished to impose as a check upon the work of the Healer here.

(15, 16) See notes on Matt. 12:11, 12, where the principle is the same.

(18, 21) See notes on Matt. 13:31-33. The parables that follow may well be regarded as samples of the teaching which those who were in the synagogue had treasured up in their memories. They were fit and edifying parables at any time, not least so, assuredly, at this. When proof had been given that the kingdom of God had indeed come near to men, it was well to set before them something as to its nature, its extent, and its mode of working inwardly and outwardly; and the fact that the similitudes which did

this had been used before, did not necessarily make them inapplicable or unprofitable when used again.

(22) This is apparently the continuation of the same journey as that of which 9:51 recorded the beginning. There seems reason to believe that it lay chiefly through the cities and villages of Peraea, on the east side of the Jordan. Such a journey, though with comparatively little record of what happened on it, is implied in Matt. 19:1; Mark 10:1; John 10:40 (see notes).

(24) Strive to enter in at the strait gate.—See notes on Matt. 7:13, 14. Here, however, the variation "strive to enter in"—i.e., struggle as the wrestler struggles (comp. I Cor. 9:25; I Tim. 6:12) is conspicuously offered for the simple "enter ye in."

(25) The passage contains elements common to Matt. 7:22, 23, 25:10-12 (see notes).

(28, 29) See notes on Matt. 8:11, 12.

(30) And, behold, there are last . . .—Comp. Matt. 19:30; see note on Matt. 22:14. In point of time, this is the first utterance of the great law that God's judgment reverses man's. Here the application is primarily national, but the individual application of the words grows naturally out of the national.

(31) Herod will kill thee.—Our Lord's Peraean journeys apparently had brought Him near Machaerus (a place of hot medicinal springs), where John had been imprisoned, and in which was one of Herod's most stately palaces (Jos., **Wars**, 7:6). The Pharisees may have come with a threat (comp. 23:8), in which we may possibly trace the hand of Herodias.

(32) Go ye, and tell that fox . . .—The word was eminently descriptive of the character both of the Tetrarch individually, and of the whole Herodian house. The fact that the Greek word for "fox" is always used as a feminine, gives, perhaps, a special touch of indignant force to the original. He had so identified himself with Herodias that he had lost his manliness, and the proverbial type of the worst form of woman's craft was typical of him.

(33) The literal meaning in time here is altogether out of place. The same formula is used in the preceding verse, with the same meaning—i.e., as conveying the thought of a short, undefined interval. The word used for "it cannot be" occurs only here in the New Testament, and has a peculiar half-ironical force. Jerusalem had made the slaughter of the prophets a special prerogative, a monopoly, of which none might rob her.

(34, 35) See notes on Matt. 23:37-39.

14

(1) Into the house of one of the chief Pharisees.—The man was either a "ruler" in the same sense as Nicodemus (John 3:1) or the rich young man in 18:18—i.e., a member of the Sanhedrin (which seems most likely)—or else occupied a high position in the lay-hierarchy which had developed itself in the organization of Pharisaiam.

(2) A certain man before him which had the dropsy.—This is the only miracle of the kind recorded in the gospels. The term which Luke uses is strictly technical (**hydropikos**), and we see in the narrative another illustration of his professional character. He, more than others, had been lead to specific inquiries as to the nature of the diseases which our Lord had healed.

(3-6) The teaching of our Lord is identical in substance, and nearly so in form, with that in 6:6-11; Matt. 12:9-14; Mark 3:1-6 (see notes). Here, however, our Lord takes the initiative in the controversy, whereas before the scribes and Pharisees had asked Him the question.

(7-11) The passage has the interest of being, in conjunction with 11:43, the germ of the great invective of Matt. 23:6-12 (see notes).

(12, 13) Our Lord saw in that Sabbath feast nothing but an ostentatious hospitality, calculating on a return in kind. It might not be wrong in itself, but it could take no place, as the Pharisee clearly thought it would do, in the list of good works by which he sought to win God's favor. The fact that it met with its reward on earth excluded it from the reward of the resurrection of the just.

(14) At the resurrection of the just.—The passage is interesting as the first occurrence of the word "resurrection" in our Lord's teaching. On this point our Lord, while rebuking the pride and hypocrisy of the Pharisees, accepted the fundamental doctrine of their system, and so furnished a precedent for Paul's conduct in Acts 23:6.

(16-24) See notes on Matt. 22:1-13, where this parable is reproduced in an altered and expanded form.

(20) I have married a wife.—The Law of Moses allowed men to plead this, and the building of a house or planting of a vineyard, as ground for exemption from military service (Deut. 20:5-7). The sin of the invited guests was that they treated the invitation to the feast as though it were as burdensome as a military conscription.

(21) The repetition of the same four adjectives as had been used in verse 13 is singularly suggestive. Our Lord was following, in the spiritual feast of His kingdom, the rule which He had given for those who made great feasts on earth. Each class may possibly represent some spiritual fact which would seem to men a disqualification, but which was, for the pitying love of Christ, the ground of invitation and acceptance.

(24) None of those men which were bidden . . .—The absolute exclusion of the whole company of the first-invited guests has its anti-type in the general rejection of Israel from fellowship with the Church of Christ. It lies in the nature of a parable that it deals roughly with general facts, and so it passes over in this instance what would have answered to the admission of a chosen few, "the remnant according to the election of grace" (Rom. 11:5.)

(26, 27) See notes on Matt. 10:37-39. Here the words are spoken, not to the Twelve only, but to the whole multitude of eager would-be followers. Self-renunciation, pushed, if necessary, to the extremest issues, is with Jesus the one indispensable condition of discipleship.

(28-33) In the interpretation of the two parables, the tower reminds us of the house in Matt. 7:24-27, and so stands for the structure of a holy life reared on the one Foundation; the warfare brings to our remembrance the conflict described in Matt. 12:29, standing here for the conflict which every Christian carries on against sin, the world, and the devil, and of which we should take a clear estimate before we enter on it.

(34, 35) See notes on Matt. 5:13; Mark 9:50. The common element in all three instances is that salt represents the purifying element in life, the principle of unselfish devotion. Here, the special aspect of that element is self-renunciation. In proportion as that is incomplete, the salt loses its savor. A new and humbler use of salt, distinct from that of preserving food, or its symbolic meaning in sacrifice, is brought before us, and becomes the groundwork of a new parable. The salt serves, mingling with the dunghill, to manure and prepare the ground for the reception of the seed. The church and the individual man are alike fit only to

787

be "cast out" when they cease to influence the world.

15

(4-7) The parable gains fresh force and interest if we remember that it followed on the great parable of the Good Shepherd in John 10:1-16, and on the compassion for the lost sheep of which we read in Matt. 9:36. The primary application clearly is to be found in the immediate occasion of the parable, in the love which bids the Son of man to concentrate His thoughts, energy and prayers on some one soul among those publicans and sinners who were thus gathered together.

(8-11) The main lesson of the parable is identical with that of the Lost Sheep. The silver coin (the **drachma**) is a symbol of the human soul. The coin is what it is because it has on it the king's image and superscription; man is precious because he too has the image and superscription of the great King, the spiritual attributes of thought and will, by which he resembles God, stamped upon him. There is a special significance in the fact that the coin is lost **in** the house, while the sheep strays **from** the fold. What seems implied here is the possibility that a soul that is precious in the sight of God may be lost even within the society, Israel or the Church of Christ, which is for the time being the visible house of God. A woman seeks, not a man, the change being made to interest a different class of hearers—the women who were listening, who had no experience in going after the sheep that was lost. To "light the candle" can be nothing else than to put forth the full power of truth and holiness; to "sweep the house" can be nothing else than to use all available means for discovering the possible good that lies hidden or seemingly lost.

(11-32) This parable is not only peculiar to Luke's gospel, but has something of a different character, as giving more than those we find in the other gospels the incidents of a story of common daily life. As with the Good Samaritan, it seems to have rested on a substratum of facts that actually had occurred. It is obvious that in the social state of Palestine, brought into contact as the Jews were with the great cities of the Roman empire, such a history as that here recorded must have been but too painfully familiar.

In the immediate application of the para-ble, the father is the great Father of the souls of men; the elder son represents the respectably religious Pharisees; the younger stands for the class of publicans and sinners. On a wider scale, the elder son may stand for Israel according to the flesh; the younger for the whole heathen world.

(12) In its bearing on the individual life, the younger son represents the temper that is eager for independence, self-asserting, energetic; the elder that which is contemplative, devout, ceremonial quiescent. In the normal scale of distribution, the elder son would have as his portion two-thirds of the personal, and possibly also of the real, property, and the younger the remainder. In the framework of the story, the father and the elder son become, as it were, tenants in common (verse 31), the former still retaining the general direction of affairs. The state of things so described represents roughly the life of Israel under its theocracy, acknowledging God as its true King and Father.

(13) The "far country" is the state of the human spirit, of the Gentile world, in their wanderings far off from God. The "riotous living" is the reckless waste of noble gifts and highest energies on unbridled sensuality of life or sensuous, i.e., idolatrous, forms of worship. (See Rom. 1:19-32.)

(15) To a citizen.—The "citizen" represents the wisdom and knowledge, maxims of worldly prudence or principles of ethics without religion, which for a time sustain the soul, while yet they leave it in its wretchedness and do not satisfy its cravings.

To feed swine.—We feel at once the shudder that would pass through the hearers of the parable as they listened to these words. Could there be for an Israelite a greater depth of debasement? This perhaps implies a state in which the man's will and energies have but the one work of ministering to his baser appetites.

(16) The husks that the swine did eat.—These are commonly identified with the long bean-like pods of the carob tree, which some have identified with the "locusts" of Matt. 3:4, and which are used as food for swine in Syria and Egypt. Spiritually, they answer to the sensual pleasures in which brute appetites find adequate sustenance.

(18) The first impulse of the penitent, contrite heart is to take the lowest place.

(21) Father, I have sinned against heaven.—The iteration of the same words comes to us with a wonderful power and pathos. The contrite soul does not play with its contrition, or seek to vary its expression.

But the change is as suggestive as the repetition. Now that he has seen his father, he cannot bring himself to say again, "Make me as one of thy hired servants." That had been a natural and right wish before; it would savor of unreality and hypocrisy now.

(22) The "best robe" is the vesture of righteousness (Isa. 61:3), the new life and immortality with which it is the desire of the penitent to be clothed; the ring, as the signet upon the right hand (Jer. 22:24), is the token of the special favor of the Giver, the seal of his "calling and election"; the shoes answer to that "preparation" or "readiness" which comes from the gospel of peace (Eph. 6:15), and which makes him eager to do his work as a messenger who proclaims that Gospel to others.

(23) Bring hither the fatted calf.— Irenaeus saw in this an illustration of what seemed to him the special characteristic of Luke's gospel—the stress which it lays on the priestly aspect of our Lord's work and ministry.

(24) This my son was dead.—Absence, alienation, and self-chosen shame had made the father think of the son as "dead." Death would indeed have been far easier to bear. Spiritually, repentance is nothing less than the passing from the death of sin to the life of righteousness. The "lost" and "found" appear as furnishing the link that connects this with the preceding parables, and makes the trilogy, as it were, complete.

(29) Lo, these many years do I serve thee.—The obedience had all along been servile, prompted by fear and hope, even as the slave's obedience is. The language put into the mouth of the elder son clearly is meant to represent the habitual thoughts of the Pharisees. They are conscious of no transgressions; but in that very unconsciousness lies the secret of the absence of any sense of joy in being forgiven, of any power to sympathize with the joy of others, even of any satisfaction in the service in which they pride themselves. They are scandalized at the gladness which others feel when a penitent returns to God. It seems like an insult and wrong to themselves.

(31) Son, thou art ever with me.—All outward gifts that God could bestow—the covenants, the law, the promises, outward ordinances of worship, and the instruction of wise men and scribes—had been given to Israel, as like blessings are offered now to all members of the visible Church of Christ, the great family of God.

16

(1-12) The Unjust Steward represents primarily the Pharisees and scribes in their teaching and ministerial functions. But though spoken in the hearing of the Pharisees, the parable was addressed, not to them, but "to the disciples." (See notes on 12:42; comp. I Cor. 4:1, 2.) They, too, were called to be "stewards"; they, too, collectively and individually, would have to give an account of their stewardship. The rich man, like the "householder" in other parables, can be none else than God, who both appoints the stewards and calls them to account. In the further extension of the parable it is, of course, applicable to all who have any "goods" entrusted to them, any gifts and opportunities, any vocation and ministry in the great kingdom of God.

(1) The same was accused unto him that he had wasted his goods.—The Greek word for "was accused" commonly carries with it the idea of false, slanderous accusation. Probably, however, the idea connected with it, as seen in the word **diabolos**, or **devil**, which is derived from it, is that of malignant accusation, whether the charge were true or false. The Pharisees had heard the parable of the Prodigal Son. They had not "wasted their substance in riotous living," but now they were taught that the "goods" committed to them might be wasted in other ways than by being "devoured" in company with "harlots." They were guilty of that sin in proportion as they had failed to use what they had been entrusted with for the good of men and for God's glory.

(6) Take thy bill, and sit down quickly.— The steward by thus tempting the debtors with an immediate gain, and making them sharers in his frauds, took the readiest and most direct means of securing at once their favor and their silence. That which answered to this in the first application of the parable was the conduct of the Pharisees, just in proportion as they lost the moral force which they had once exercised, in accommodating their casuistry to the selfishness of their followers. (See notes on Matt. 15:4, 5; 23:16-23.)

(8) And the lord commended . . .—The "lord" is the rich man of the parable, the steward's master. He, too, in the outer framework of the story, is one of the children of this world, and he admires the sharpness and quickness of the steward's action. If this world were all, there would be a wisdom worthy of praise when a

Church or its teachers adapted themselves to men's passions or interests at the expense of truth. That which makes such action hateful is that by so doing the children of light transform themselves into the children of this world. "Children of light" are those in whom light is the prevailing element of their life, and they necessarily are also children of God (I John 1:5).

(9) Make to yourselves friends of the mammon of unrighteousness.—See note on Matt. 6:24. The right use of wealth in helping the poor, leading them to repentance and to God, will gain for us friends, perhaps the persons whom we have helped, perhaps even Christ and the Father, who will receive us into "everlasting habitations."

(10) He that is faithful in that which is least . . .—The context shows that by "that which is least" is meant what men call wealth, and which to most of them seems as the greatest, highest good. To be faithful in that is to acknowledge that we have it as stewards, not as possessors, and shall have to give an account of our stewardship. The word of warning was meant, we may believe, especially for the disciples. They, coming, for the most part, from the poorer classes, thought that they were in no danger of worshiping mammon.

(11, 12) Here the "true riches" stand in contrast with the vain, deceitful, unrighteous mammon, and answer to the true spiritual wealth of peace, pardon, and wisdom. Our Lord teaches His disciples that honesty, integrity, and benevolence in the use of this world's goods, be our portion small or great, is an indispensable condition of all spiritual advancement.

(13) No servant can serve two masters.—See notes on Matt. 6:24. Here it obviously comes in close connection with the previous teaching.

(14) The word for "covetous" is literally "lovers of money." "Derided" is a word that forcibly expresses the physiognomy of contempt (see Gal. 6:7). (Here again we have a word common to Luke and Paul.) That the teachers of Israel should be told that they were like the Unjust Steward, that they were wasting their Lord's goods, that they must make friends with the unrighteous mammon of quite another kind than those whom they were accustomed to court, was more than they could stand.

(15) The Pharisees forgot, in their self-righteousness and self-vindication, that they stood before God as the Searcher of all hearts.

(16) The law and the prophets were until John.—See notes on Matt. 11:11-15. What then had been said to the disciples of the Baptist is now reproduced to our Lord's own disciples and to the Pharisees. The latter had closed their eyes to the fact that all previous revelations led up to the work of John, as that in its turn was preparatory for the work of Christ.

(17) It is easier for heaven and earth to pass.—See notes on Matt. 5:18. The scribes and Pharisees had been tampering with the sacredness of laws which were everlasting, and they are told that their casuistry cannot set aside the claims of those laws in any single instance, such, e.g., as that which immediately follows.

(18) Whosoever putteth away his wife.—See notes on Matt. 5:31, 32; 19:3-9. The doctrine and discipline of divorce which the Pharisees taught, lowering the sacredness of the life of home, and ministering to the growing laxity of men's morals, was precisely what was meant by the Unjust Steward's practices (verses 6, 7).

(19) There was a certain rich man . . .—It is clear that the section of Pharisees for whom the parable was especially designed were the scribes who had attached themselves to the court of Herod Antipas, the Herodians (see notes on Matt. 22:16), and reproduced their mode of life. In the rich man himself we find features which must at least have reminded those who heard the parable of the luxurious self-indulgence of the tetrarch himself. It was fitting that they should learn what was the outcome of such a life when it passed "behind the veil."

(20) And there was a certain beggar named Lazarus.—This is the one instance of a personal name in our Lord's parables. The name may have been intended as a warning to Lazarus of Bethany, who may be identified with the young ruler that had great possessions. (See note on Matt. 19:16.) It may be noted that nearly every harmonized arrangement of the gospel history places the parable almost immediately before the death and raising of Lazarus.

Laid at his gate, full of sores . . .—The Greek word for "full of sores" is, literally, **ulcerated,** one which a medical writer like Luke would use to express a generally ulcerous state of the whole body. The description led, later, to the application of the leper's name to those who suffered from leprosy (e.g., **lazar, lazar-house**).

(21) And desiring to be fed with the crumbs.—Comp. Mark 7:28. Eastern feelings see in the dog an unclean beast, the scavenger of the streets. No doubt the beggar would have shrunk from their licking, even assuming, which is doubtful, that it brought with it some relief from merely physical pain.

(22) Was carried by the angels into Abraham's bosom.—Of the three terms in common use among the Jews to express the future state of blessedness—the Garden of Eden, or Paradise; the Throne of Glory; the bosom of Abraham—this was the most popular. It rested on the idea of a great feast, in which Abraham was the host. To lie in his bosom, as John in that of our Lord's (John 13:23), was to be there as the most favored guest. The being "carried by angels" was literally in accord with the popular Jewish belief.

(23) And in hell.—The Greek word is Hades, not Gehenna—the unseen world of the dead, not the final prison of the souls of the lost. (See note on Matt. 5:22.) The parable describes an earlier stage of the life after death than that in Matt. 25:31-46 (see notes).

In torments.—The Greek word was applied originally to the test of metals, then to the torture of which men had recourse as the one sure test of the veracity of witnesses, then to torments generally. The nature of the "torments" here is suggested by the "flame" of verse 24; but that word has to be taken with all its symbolic associations, and does not necessarily imply the material element of fire. (See notes on Mark 9:43-49.) What is meant is that there shall be for the soul of the evildoer, when brought face to face with that holiness of God which is as a consuming fire (Heb. 12:29), an anguish as intolerable as the touch of earthly flame is to the nerves of the mortal body.

(25) Remember.—The word has a terrible force in its bearing upon the question of the future life. Memory intensified, reproducing the past visions, pleasures, and base joys, and subject to the action of a conscience no longer narcotized into slumber, makes the sharpest pang of the deserved anguish.

(26) There is a great gulf fixed.—The scene brought before us is like one of the pictures of Dante's **Commedia**—steep rocks and a deep gorge, and on one side the flames that burn and do not consume, while on the other, the fair garden of Paradise, the kingly palace, and the banquet at which

Abraham presides. It is obvious that no single detail of such a description can be pressed as a literal representation of the unseen world. What was wanted for the purpose of the parable was the dramatic and pictorial vividness which impresses itself on the minds and hearts of men, and this could not otherwise be gained.

(28) For I have five brethren.—There is a special motive for the rich man's wishing Lazarus to be sent. The brothers had seen the beggar lying at his gate. If they were to see him now, as risen from the dead, they would learn how far more blessed his state had been than the luxurious ease in which they had passed, and were still passing, their lives.

(29) They have Moses and the prophets.—It was because the scribes and their followers were unfaithful in a little that more was denied them. "Moses and the Prophets" were enough to teach them that a life of self-indulgent luxury was evil in itself, and therefore must bring with it, in the end, shame and condemnation. (Comp. John 5:45, 46.)

(31) In a few weeks, or even days, according to the best harmonists, tidings came that Lazarus of Bethany (John 11) did "rise from the dead." And yet that wonder brought about no repentance. Scribes and Pharisees, and Sadducees and priests, simply took counsel together that they might put Lazarus also to death (John 12:10).

17

(1, 2) See notes on Matt. 18:2-6.

(3) Take heed to yourselves.—The position of the words is remarkable, and they have nothing corresponding to them in the parallel passage in Matt. 18:21. It is as though our Lord saw in the disciples the tendency to sit in judgment on the sins of others, on such sins especially as He had just condemned, and checked it by these words. They were in danger of faults hardly less fatal to the spiritual life than selfish luxury, and one of those faults was the temper of hard and unforgiving judgment.

(4) If he trespass against thee.—See note on Matt. 18:22.

(6) If ye had faith as a grain of mustard seed.—The words must have reminded the disciples of those of Matt. 17:20 (see note), which were called forth by the failure of the disciples to heal the demoniac boy after the Transfiguration. The "sycamine tree" is identified with the mulberry tree, still cultivated on the slopes of the Lebanon and in the neighborhood of Jerusalem.

(7-10) The words contained an answer to their question implicit in verse 5. They had been asking for faith, not only in a measure sufficient for obedience, but as excluding all uncertainty and doubt. They were looking for the crown of labor before their work was done, for the wreath of the conqueror before they had fought the battle. He presses home upon them the analogies of common human experience. In the life of the disciples, outward ministerial labor was to be followed by personal devotion: the "increase of faith" for which the apostles prayed was to come through outward and inward obedience to their Master's will.

(11) And it came to pass, as he went to Jerusalem.—This is the first distinct note of time in Luke's narrative since 9:51. It appears to coincide with the journey of which we read in Matt. 19:1; Mark 10:1, and is the beginning of the last progress through the regions in which our Lord had already carried on His ministry. The fact that it led Him through Samaria is peculiar to Luke.

(12) Ten men that were lepers.—See notes on Matt. 8:2-4. In this case there was no running and falling at the feet of Jesus. They kept, it would seem probable, to the legal limit of one hundred paces.

(16) And he was a Samaritan.—As in the parable of the Good Samaritan, Luke's purpose in the selection of the incident enhances the catholicity of his gospel. It is significant, in this case, that the barrier already had been broken down for a time by the common pressure of calamity, but no enduring sense of fellowship had as yet taken its place. The nine would seem to have separated themselves from the Samaritan as soon as they were cleansed.

(20) There were some who were really looking for the coming of the Messianic kingdom; there were some who altogether rejected the claim of Jesus of Nazareth to be the Christ. In the lips of the one set, the question implied a taunt; in those of the other, something like impatience. The terms of the answer contain that which met both cases.

(21) The kingdom of God is within you.—It was in that region, in the life which must be born again (John 3:3), that men were to look for the kingdom; and there, whether they accepted it or rejected it, they would find sufficient tokens of its power.

(22) When ye shall desire to see one of

the days of the Son of man.—The words express both the backward glance of regret and the forward look of yearning expectation. (Comp. Matt. 9:15; II Pet. 3:12.)

(23, 24) See notes on Matt. 24:23-27.

(25) But first must he suffer many things.—Comp. Matt. 16:21; 17:22. The interposition of this prophecy of the Passion in a discourse which bears primarily on the Second Advent is an individualizing feature of this record of Luke's.

(26, 27) See notes on Matt. 24:36-39. As in verse 24, the "days" of the Son of man take the place of the **parousia.**

(28) Likewise also as it was in the days of Lot.—The illustration does not occur in the otherwise parallel passage of Matt. 24:26, 27, but was naturally suggested by our Lord's frequent reference to the Cities of the Plain (10:12; Matt. 10:15; 11:23). Comp. II Pet. 2:7.

(31) See notes on Matt. 24:17, 18.

(32) Remember Lot's wife.—The reference to this, as to the history of Lot generally, is peculiar to Luke, and speaks strongly for the independence of his gospel. She had looked back, as the disciples were told not to look, and the glance had been fatal (Gen. 19:26; comp. Wisd. 10:7).

(33) Whosoever shall seek to save his life.—The better MSS give a word which is rendered elsewhere by "purchase" (Acts 20:28; I Tim. 3:13), and perhaps always suggests, as the other word for "save" does not, the idea of some transaction of the kind. So here, the man must purchase, as it were, his lower life at the price of the higher, and he will be a loser by the bargain. But it follows that the man who is content to risk his natural life shall gain a life of a higher spiritual order.

(34, 35) See notes on Matt. 24:40, 41.

(37) See note on Matt. 24:28.

18

(1) That men ought always to pray, and not to faint.—The whole verse is remarkable as being one of the few instances (verse 9 being another) in which a parable is introduced by a distinct statement as to its drift and aim.

(3) There was a widow in that city.—The neglect of the cause of the widow always had been noted by lawgiver and prophet as the extremest form of oppressive tyranny (Exod. 22:22; Deut. 10:18; 27:19; Isa. 1:17, 23; Ezek. 22:7).

Avenge me of mine adversary.—The term is used in its legal sense. She was plaintiff, and he defendant, or, it may be, **vice versa.** The judge put off his decision, and the delay was worse to her than the original wrong had been.

(4) He would not for a while.—The judge was callous and dead to pity (comp. verse 2), even for that extremest wretchedness. The pleadings of the widow were simply an annoyance, which at first he bore with indifference.

Though I fear not God, nor regard man.— Here, also, there is a graphic touch of intensity. The man had passed beyond the stage of hypocrisy, conscious or unconscious, and saw himself even as others— even as God—saw him.

(5) Lest by her continual coming she weary me.—In I Cor. 9:27 the word "weary" is rendered "**I keep under** my body." Literally it expresses the act of the pugilist when he strikes a blow which leaves a livid bruise on his opponent's face, and it would seem to have been transferred from the arena to common life.

(7) If reiterated entreaties prevail with men, whose character and wills are set against the disciples, how much more with God, in whom character and will anticipate the prayer? Here there is an intentional assumption by our Lord of a stand-point which was not His own, but that of those whom He sought to teach. Prayer has a marvelous self-purifying power, and the imperfect thoughts of God in which it may have had its beginning become clearer as it continues. It is one of the ever-recurring paradoxes of the spiritual life, that when we are most importunate we feel most strongly how little importunity is needed.

The "vengeance" is not that of retaliation such as human passions seek, but primarily the "vindication" of God's elect, the assertion of their rights, and includes retribution upon others only so far as it is involved in this. This is the first occurrence of the word "elect" in Luke's gospel, but it begins to be prominent about this time in our Lord's teaching. (See notes on Matt. 20:16; 24:22.)

(8) When the Son of man cometh, shall he find faith?—The question implies an answer in the negative. When Luke wrote his gospel, men were witnessing a primary, though partial, fulfillment of the prophecy. Iniquity was abounding, and the love of many was growing cold. And yet in one sense He was near, even at the doors (Jas. 5:8, 9).

(10) The one a Pharisee, and the other a publican.—The disciples would visualize the Pharisee with his broad blue **zizith,** or fringe, and the **Tephillin** (prayers), or phylacteries, fastened conspicuously on brow or shoulder; the publican would be in his common working dress, with no outward badge to testify that he was a child of the Covenant.

(11) The Pharisee stood and prayed thus with himself.—A false stress often has been laid on the Pharisee's attitude. Standing was, indeed, with the Jews, the customary attitude of prayer, although the Pharisee's standing "by himself," shrinking from contact with others, was an indication of self-righteous pride. Silent prayer, never customary among the Jews at any time, would have been at variance with every tradition of the Pharisees. (Comp. notes on Matt. 6:5, 7). As far as the phrase has any special point, it indicates that he was not praying to God at all; he was practically praying to himself, congratulating himself, half-consciously, that he had no need to pray, in the sense of asking for pardon, peace, or righteousness, though it might be right, by way of example, to perform his acts of devotion and to thank God for what he had received. The verb for "prayed" is in the tense which implies continuance. He was making a long address, of which this was a sample (20:47).

That I am not as other men.—This was the first false step. He did not compare his own imperfections with the infinite perfections of the Eternal, but with the imagined greater imperfections of his fellow-men.

Extortioners . . .—The word was chosen aptly, and obviously was suggested by the presence of the other supplicant. "Six publicans and half-a-dozen extortioners" had become a proverb; and the offensive epithet, if not meant to be heard by the publican, was, at any rate, mentally directed at him. In actual life, as our Lord teaches, there was a far worse sin, because a more hypocritical, "extortion" practiced generally by the Pharisees themselves (Matt. 23:25; Luke 11:39).

Or even as this publican.—This was the climax of all. He saw the penitent man smiting on his breast in anguish, and no touch of pity, no desire to say a word of comfort, rises in his soul.

(12) See note on Matt. 6:16. For the Pharisee, fasting and tithes have come to supersede the "weightier matter of the law" (Matt. 23:23).

(13) The publican, standing afar off.—

The words point to a sense of shame which kept the publican away from the crowd of worshipers who pressed forward to the ark end of the outer court of the Temple. He, too, stood, for that was the received attitude of prayer, and kneeling, at such a time and in that place, would have been ostentatious.

But smote upon his breast.—The same act was the expression of extremest sorrow in those who stood by the cross (23:48). As being spontaneous and involuntary, it attested the reality of emotion, and contrasted with the calm, fixed attitude of the Pharisee.

God be merciful to me a sinner.—Literally, "to me the sinner," as though, like Paul, he singled out his own guilt as exceptional (I Tim. 1:15).

(15-17) And they brought unto him also infants.—See notes on Matt. 19:13-15; Mark 10:13-16. Luke, possibly because he had recorded similar teaching in 16:18, omits the previous word as to divorce.

(16, 17) The close agreement with Mark in these verses makes it probable that this is one of the passages which Luke derived from personal communication with him.

(18-23) See notes on Matt. 19:16-25.

(24-27) See notes on Matt. 19:23-26.

(25) Through a needle's eye.—The Greek word for "needle" in the better MSS differs from that in Matthew and Mark, and is a more classical word. That which the others use was unknown to Attic writers. The fact, small as it is, takes its place among the signs of Luke's culture.

(28-30) See notes on Matt. 19:27-30.

(31-34) See notes on Matt. 20:17-19. Luke, like Mark, passes over the parable of the Laborers in the Vineyard. The insertion of the reference to the prophecies of the Passion is, on the other hand, peculiar to him, and is, perhaps, connected with the prominence given to those prophecies in 24:27, 44, 45.

(35-43) See notes on Matt. 20:29-34; Mark 10:46-52. Luke passes over the ambitious request of the sons of Zebedee.

19

(2) There was a man named Zacchaeus . . .—The narrative is peculiar to this gospel. The name "Zacchaeus" (Ezra 2:9; Neh. 7:14) meant "pure" or "innocent." Rabbinic writers mention a Zacchaeus, the

father of a famous rabbi, Jochanan or John, as living at Jericho about this time.

The chief among the publicans.—The position of Jericho near the fords of the Jordan made it a natural trade center for the imports from the Gilead country—myrrh and balsam. The "farming" system adopted in the Roman revenue probably gave Zacchaeus the status of a middle-man or sub-contractor between the great capitalists of Rome, the real **publicani**, and the "publicans" commonly so called, who were the actual collectors. As such he had abundant opportunities for enriching himself, and, as we may infer from his own words, had probably not altogether escaped the temptations of his calling.

(3) He sought.—Better, "was seeking." The motive is left to be inferred. It was not mere curiosity, for that would not have met with the Lord's warm approval. Had he heard that there was a publican like himself among the chosen disciples of the Teacher whom the people were receiving as the Son of David? Had someone told him of the parable of the Pharisee and the Publican? Had the fame of the miracle wrought on the entrance into Jericho made him eager to see the Worker?

(4) And climbed up into a sycamore tree.—The fig mulberry is the tree here meant. It grew to a considerable height in the Jordan valley, and was much used by builders and carpenters (I Kings 10:27). The care taken by Luke to distinguish between the "sycamine" of 17:6 (see note), and the "sycomore" here, may be noted as an instance of botanical accuracy, such as was likely to be found in a physician.

(5) To-day I must abide at thy house.—Jericho was at this time one of the chosen cities of the priests. Our Lord passed over their houses, and those of the Pharisees, in order to pass the night in the house of the publican. There, we may believe, He saw an opening for a spiritual work which He did not find elsewhere.

(7) With a man that is a sinner.—The term obviously was used from the popular Pharisaic standpoint, as attaching necessarily to the calling of Zacchaeus. He had placed Himself on a level with the heathen or the vilest Jew, and ought to be treated accordingly.

(8) The half of my goods I give . . .—It seems more natural to see in this the statement of a new purpose than that of an habitual practice. In the absence of any words implying a command of this nature, we must assume either that it was a spontaneous impulse of large-hearted devotion, or, possibly, that Zacchaeus had heard of the command given but a few days before to the young ruler (18:22). The promise implies immediate distribution. The compensation for wrongs that men might have suffered at his hands was to come out of the remaining half.

I restore him fourfold.—Here, also, are the words of a new purpose. He is ready to compensate now for whatever wrong had been done before. The Law required in cases of voluntary restitution the addition of one-fifth of the value of the thing restored (Lev. 6:5; Num. 5:6, 7).

(9) This day is salvation come to this house.—In one sense salvation had come in the personal presence of the Saviour, but we must remember all that the word implied—deliverance, not from the penalty only, but from the habit and the power of sin. This had come, and the words and acts of Zacchaeus showed the fruits. A son of Abraham, like him in his noble generosity (comp. Gen. 13:9; 14:23), was found where, to the common observer, it would have seemed hopeless to look for one.

(10) The Son of man is come to seek and to save that which was lost.—Similar words had been spoken once before. Then the loving purpose of the Christ had for its object the "little child," as yet untouched by the world's offenses (Matt. 18:2, 11); now it rested on the publican, whose manhood had been marred by them.

(11) He added and spake a parable.—As in 18:1, 9, so here, it is characteristic of Luke that he states, more fully than is common in the other gospels, the occasion and the purpose of the parable which follows. The verse throws light upon all the history that follows. In all previous visits to Jerusalem our Lord had gone up either alone or accompanied only by His chosen disciples. Now He was followed by a crowd.

Should immediately appear.—It is clear, from the tenor of the parable, that disciples and multitude alike were dwelling on the greatness to which they were to attain, on the high places in store for them on the right hand and on the left, rather than on their work and their duties in relation to that kingdom of God.

(12) A certain nobleman went into a far country.—See notes on Matt. 25:14-30, with which this parable has many obvious points of resemblance.

(13) And delivered them ten pounds.—Here we begin with equality; in Matt. 25:15 the servants start with unequal amounts, "according to their several ability." (Comp. also the larger increase, verse 16, with Matt. 25.) The difference implies that the trust in this case is that which all disciples of Christ have in common—their knowledge of the truth and their membership in the kingdom, and not the offices and positions that vary in degree. According to one estimate, a pound was equal to twenty-five shekels, or 100 **drachmae** or **denarii**. The word occurs in the New Testament in this parable only.

Occupy till I come.—The Greek verb occurs only here in the New Testament. A compound form of it is rendered, in verse 15, by "gained in trading."

(15) It came to pass, that when he was returned.—The absence of the words "after a long time" is noticeable. It suggests the thought that our Lord may have added them in the later form of the parable as a further safeguard against the prevalent expectations of the immediate coming of the kingdom, and against the thought which arose afterward in men's minds, that there was no kingdom to be received, and that the King would never return. (Comp. II Pet. 3:4.)

(17) The truth implied in Matt. 25:21, that the reward of faithfulness in this life, and probably in the life to come, will be found in yet wider opportunities for work in God's service, is stated here with greater distinctness.

(26) Unto every one which hath shall be given.—This takes its place among the oft-repeated axioms of our Lord's teaching. It meets us after the parable of the Sower (8:18; Matt. 13:12; Mark 4:25), in that of the Talents (Matt. 25:29), and here. (See notes on the several passages.)

(27) But those mine enemies.—This feature of the parable is peculiar to Luke's report. It represents, in bold figures drawn from the acts of tyrant kings, the ultimate victory of the Christ over the unbelieving and rebellious. (Comp. I Cor. 15:25.)

(28) He went before, ascending up to Jerusalem.—See note on Matt. 20:17. The journey from Jericho to Jerusalem was literally an ascent all the way (see 10:30), and in this sense, as well as following the language common to most nations, in speaking of their capitals, the verb might well be used.

(29-38) See notes on Matt. 21:1-11.

(37) The descent of the mount of Olives.—The Greek word for "descent" is not used by any other New Testament writer. As being a technical geographical word, it was one that naturally might be used by a pupil of Strabo or a student of his works.

All the mighty works . . .—The words probably refer to the recent miracle at Jericho (18:35-43), and, as interpreted by John's gospel, the recent raising of Lazarus.

(38) Peace in heaven, and glory in the highest.—Comp. 2:14. The substitution of "glory" for the "Hosanna" of Matthew and Mark is characteristic of the Gentile evangelist.

(39, 40) The section of the Pharisees that spoke was probably that which had all along more or less acknowledged our Lord as a "Master" (i.e., Teacher or Rabbi), and were willing to give Him what they thought a fair share of respect as such. To go beyond that, to receive Him as the promised "He that cometh," as "the king of Israel, the Christ," seemed to them but the wild frenzy of the disciples, which the Master ought to check. Comp. Hab. 2:11.

(41) He beheld the city, and wept over it.—This, and the tears over the grave of Lazarus (John 11:35), are the only recorded instances of our Lord's tears.

(42) The "at least in this thy day," the day that was still its own, was that in which it was called to repentance and action. The words were the utterance of the deepest human sorrow that the Son of man had known.

(43, 44) See note on Matt. 24:2. What is there said of the Temple is here repeated of the city as a whole, and describes a general demolition of everything that could be demolished. See Josephus, *Wars*, 8:1, § 1.

The time of thy visitation.—The phrase is not found in any other gospel. The idea of "visitation" presents two aspects—one of pardon (1:68, 78; 7:16), the other of chastisement (I Pet. 2:12). The Christ had visited it first with a message of peace; then came the discipline of suffering. But Jerusalem did not know how to make a right use of either.

(45-48) See notes on Matt. 21:12-17.

20

(1-8) See notes on Matt. 21:23-27.

(1) And preached the gospel.—The Greek verb (**to evangelize**) is one especially characteristic of Luke. He uses it ten times in the gospel, fifteen times in the Acts. Paul employs it twenty times. It was clearly one of the words which the two friends and fellow-workers had in common.

(9-19) See notes on Matt. 21:33-46.

(20-26) See notes on Matt. 22:15-22.

(27-39) See notes on Matt. 22:23-33.

(36) Neither can they die any more.—The record of this teaching is peculiar to Luke. The implied thought is that death and marriage are correlative facts in God's government of the world, the one filling up the gaps which are caused by the other. In the life eternal there is no need for an addition in this way to the number of the elect, and therefore there is no provision for it.

(38) For all live unto him.—Luke alone adds the words. They are of value as developing the meaning of those that precede them. All life, in the truest, highest sense of that term, depends upon our relation to God. When He reveals Himself as the God of those who have passed from earth, He witnesses that that relation continues still. They are not dead, but are still living unto Him. (See Acts 17:28.)

(39) The words came, it is obvious, from the better section of the Pharisees, who welcomed this new defense of the doctrine on which their faith rested.

(40) The singular omission by Luke of the question recorded by Matthew (22:34-40) and Mark (12:28-34) is one of the many proofs of his entire independence as a narrator.

(41, 42) See notes on Matt. 22:41-46; Mark 12:35-37.

(45-47) See notes on Matt. 23:6, 7.

21

(1-4) See notes on Mark 12:41-44. This may be one of the incidents which Luke derived from verbal communication with his fellow-evangelist.

(5, 6) See notes on Mark 13:1.

(5) Gifts.—Luke uses the more strictly classical word for "offerings," according to some of the best MSS, in the same form as the **Anathema** (I Cor. 12:3; 16:12), which elsewhere in the New Testament is confined to the idea of that which is set apart, not for a blessing, but a curse. The fact that he is the only writer to use it in its good sense is characteristic of his Gentile and classical training.

(7-19) See notes on Matt. 24:3-14; Mark 13:3-13. The variations in the report throughout imply an independent source of information, probably oral, as distinct from transcription either from one of the gospels or from a document common to both of them.

(20-24) See notes on Matt. 24:15-21. This is is Luke's equivalent, possibly chosen as more intelligible for his Gentile readers, for "the abomination of desolation," which we find in Matthew and Mark.

(22) These be the days of vengeance.— The words answer to the "great tribulation" of Matthew and Mark, and seem, as indeed does Luke's report of the discourse throughout, to be of the nature of a paraphrase. The word "vengeance" may have been chosen in allusive reference to the teaching of 18:7, 8.

(24) Until the times of the Gentiles be fulfilled.—The thought expressed in this clause, that the punishment of Israel and the desolation of Jerusalem were to have a limit, that there was one day to be a restoration of both, is noticeable as agreeing with the whole line of Paul's thoughts in Rom. 9-11, and being in all probability the germ of which those thoughts are the development.

(25-33) See notes on Matt. 24:29-35.

(28) Redemption.—The word is characteristic of Paul's phraseology (Rom. 3:24, 8:23; I Cor. 1:30; Eph. 1:7, etc.; comp. Heb. 9:15; 11:35). In its primary meaning here it points to the complete deliverance of the disciples from Jewish persecutions in Palestine that followed on the destruction of Jerusalem. The Church of Christ was then delivered from what had been its most formidable danger.

(34) Take heed to yourselves, lest at any time . . .—Comp. I Thess. 5:3. The whole passage, peculiar to Luke, agrees with his characteristic tendency to record all portions of our Lord's teaching that warned men against sensuality and worldliness.

(37, 38) The general statements include the fourth and fifth days of the week of the Passion, but it is remarkable that all three gospels are silent as to anything that happened on those days until the Paschal Supper. We may, perhaps, conjecture that they were spent by our Lord, in part at least, in Gethsemane (John 18:2), in prayer and meditation, in preparing Himself and the disciples for the coming trials of the Passion. Possibly, also, the narrative of the woman taken in adultery, which occupies so strangely doubtful a position in John's gospel, may find its true place here. (See John 8:1.)

22

(1, 2) See notes on Matt. 26:1-5; Mark 14:1, 2.

(3-6) See notes on Matt. 26:14-16. Comp. John 13:27; Acts 5:3.

(7-13) Then came the day of unleavened bread.—See notes on Matt. 26:17-19; Mark 14:12-16. Comp. I Cor. 5:7.

(14) See notes on Matt. 26:20. It is characteristic of the comparatively late date of Luke's narrative that he speaks of "the twelve **apostles**," while the other two reports speak of "the **disciples**." (Comp. 9:10; 17:5; 24:10.)

(15) With desire I have desired.—The peculiar mode of expressing intensity by the use of a cognate noun with the verb of action is an idiom characteristically Hebrew. Its use here suggests that Luke heard what he reports from some one who repeated the words which our Lord had spoken in Aramaic. The whole passage is peculiar to him, and implies that he had sought to fill up the gaps in the current oral teaching which is reproduced in Matthew and Mark.

(16) Until it be fulfilled in the kingdom of God.—Comp. verse 18; Matt. 26:29. The "Passover" was fulfilled in the kingdom of God (1) in the sacrifice on the cross and (2) in every commemoration of that sacrifice by the acts which He appointed. (Comp. verses 29, 30.)

(17) Take this, and divide it among yourselves.—The cup was probably the first of the three cups of wine mingled with water which Jewish custom had added to the ritual of the Passover. As being a distinct act from that of verse 20, it had a distinct symbolic meaning. Looking to the fact that wine is partly the symbol, partly the antithesis, of spiritual energy in its highest form (comp. Zech. 9:17; Acts 2:13; Eph. 5:18), and to the re-appearance of the same somewhat exceptional word for "divide," in the tongues "distributed" ("cloven" is a mistranslation) in Acts 2:3, we may see in this cup the symbol of the bestowal of the spiritual powers which each of the disciples was to receive, according to the gift of the same

Spirit, who **divideth** "to every man severally as he will" (I Cor. 12:11), just as the second was the pledge of a yet closer fellowship with His own divine life.

(19, 20) See notes on Matt. 26:26-28.

(19) This do in remembrance of me.— Literally, "as My memorial." The words are common to Luke and Paul, but are not found in the other two reports.

(21-23) See notes on Matt. 26:21, 25. Comp. Mark 14:18, 21; John 13:21, 35. The order of the first two gospels seems here the most probable, and agrees better with the fourth. The data do not enable us to say with certainty whether Judas partook of the memorial; but, if we follow the first two gospels, it would seem probable that he did not.

(24) And there was also a strife among them.—The incident that follows is peculiar to Luke. The dispute was apparently the sequel of many previous debates of the same kind, e.g., 9:46; Matt. 18:1; 20:23; Mark 9:34; 10:37. What had just passed probably led to its revival. Who was greatest? Even the disciples who were in the second group of the Twelve might have cherished the hope that those who had been thus rebuked for their ambition or their want of faith had left a place vacant to which they might now hopefully aspire.

(25) In Christ's kingdom true greatness was to be attained by benefiting others in the humblest services.

(31) And the Lord said, Simon, Simon.— The first three gospels agree in placing the warning to Peter after the institution of the Lord's Supper. The twofold utterance of the name, as in the case of Martha (10:41), is significant of the emphasis of sadness.

That he may sift you as wheat.—The word and the figure are peculiar to Luke's record. The main idea is, however, the same as that of the winnowing fan in Matt. 3:12. The word for "you" is plural. The fiery trial was to embrace the whole company of the disciples as a body. There is a latent encouragement in the word chosen. They were "to be sifted as **wheat**." The good grain was there; they were not altogether as the chaff.

(32) I have prayed for thee.—The individualizing pronoun is significant as indicating to the apostle, who was most confident of his claim to greatness, that he, of the whole company of the Twelve, was in the greatest danger.

(33) Lord, I am ready to go with thee.—

There is something like a latent tone of indignation as well as devotion. The disciple half-resented the thought that a special prayer should be necessary for him.

(34) I tell thee, Peter.—See notes on Matt. 26:34, 35.

(35) When I sent you without purse, and scrip.—The words refer especially to the command given to the disciples in 10:4; Matt. 10:9, 10. The whole incident is peculiar to Luke. The appeal to their past experience is interesting as showing that on their first mission they were welcomed by those who heard them, and received food and shelter that met all their wants.

(36) The mention of the "sword" introduces a new element of thought. Our Lord's words to Peter (Matt. 26:52) show that the disciples were not meant to use it in His defense. It is not likely that He would teach them to use it in their own, as they preached the gospel of the Kingdom. The Master knew that two of the disciples (Peter and another) had brought swords with them, and He sadly, and yet with the gentle sympathy with which a man speaks to those who are children in age or character, conveyed His warnings in the form which met their fears and hopes. If they meant to trust in swords, a time was coming then they would sorely need them.

(37) And he was reckoned among the transgressors.—The distinct reference to Isa. 53:12 was a hint given to the disciples before the Passion that they might learn, when it came, that it was part of the divine purpose that the Christ should so suffer.

(38) It is enough.—Here again there is a touch of grave irony. The "two swords" were enough, and more than enough, for Him who did not mean to use them to the swords at all.

(39) And went, as he was wont, to the mount of Olives.—Here, as in the parallel passage of Matt. 26:30 (see note), we have to insert the discourses of John 14-17.

(40-46) When he was at the place.—See notes on Matt. 26:36-46. Verses 43-45 are omitted by some of the best MSS, but the balance of evidence is in their favor. The Greek noun "agony" in verse 44 primarily describes a "conflict" or "struggle," rather than mere physical pain. The phenomenon described is obviously one which would have a special interest for one of Luke's calling, and the four words which he uses for "agony," "drops," "sweat," "more earnestly," though not exclusively technical, are yet such as a medical writer would naturally use.

They do not occur elsewhere in the New Testament. Who were Luke's informants? That "bloody sweat" must have left its traces upon the tunic that our Lord wore, and when the soldiers cast lots for it (Matt. 27:35; John 19:24), Mary Magdalene, who stood by the cross, may have seen and noticed the fact (John 19:25), nor could it well have escaped the notice of Nicodemus and Joseph when they embalmed the body (John 19:40).

(45) He found them sleeping for sorrow.—It is again characteristic of Luke that, while the other gospels state simply the fact that the disciples slept, he assigns it psychologically and physiologically to its cause. (Comp. 24:41.)

(47-49) See notes on Matt. 26:47-50.

(50-53) See notes on Matt. 26:52-56.

(50) It is possibly characteristic of Luke's technical accuracy that he uses the diminutive form of "ear," as if part only were cut off. In Deut. 15:17 it seems to be applied especially to the fleshly lobe of the ear.

(54-62) See notes on Matt. 26:57, 58, 69-75.

(63-65) See notes on Matt. 26:59-68.

(66-71) See notes on Matt. 27:11-14; Mark 15:1. Luke passes over the earlier stages of the trial: the false witnesses that did not agree, the charge of threatening to destroy the Temple, and the silence of Jesus until solemnly adjured.

(70) The question, as asked by the whole company of priests and elders, is given only by Luke. It apparently followed, as a spontaneous cry of indignant horror, on the answer which had been made to the adjuration of the high priest. The answer implies the confession that He actually was what they had asked Him.

23

(1-5) See notes on Matt. 27:11-14; Mark 15:1.

(2) The question asked in 20:20-26 obviously was intended to lead up to this.

(3) Thou sayest it.—Here, as in verse 70 and Matt. 26:64, the formula is one of confession.

(6) When Pilate heard of Galilee.—The incident that follows is peculiar to Luke, and may have been obtained by Him from Manaen or other persons connected with the Herodian household with whom he appears to have come into contact. It is obvious that Pilate catches at the word in the hope of shifting on another the responsibility of condemning One whom he believed to be innocent and had learned to respect, while yet he did not have the courage to acquit Him.

(9) He answered him nothing.—What were likely to have been among Herod's questions? The unbroken silence of the Accused must have been strangely impressive at the time, and is singularly suggestive when we remember how He had answered Caiaphas when He had been adjured in the name of the living God. He had spoken to Pilate in the tones of a sad gentleness (John 18:33-37). To Herod alone, the incestuous adulterer, the murderer of the forerunner, He does not condescend, from first to last, to utter a single syllable.

(12) Before they were at enmity between themselves.—The special cause of enmity is not known. (See 13:1.) The union of the two in their enmity against Jesus, though not mentioned in the gospels, is referred to in the first recorded hymn of the Church of Christ (Acts 4:27). Herod, however, passes no formal sentence. He is satisfied with Pilate's mark of respect for his jurisdiction.

(13-23) See notes on Matt. 27:15-23; Mark 15:6-14. The first summons to the members of the Council, and the reference to Herod's examination of the Prisoner, are, as the sequel of the previous incident, peculiar to Luke.

(24-28) See notes on Matt. 27:24-30.

(31) If they do these things in a green tree.—The "green tree" is that which is yet living, capable of bearing fruit; the "dry," that which is barren, fruitless, withered, fit only for the axe (Matt. 3:10; Luke 13:7). The words have the character of a proverb. If Pilate could thus sentence to death One in whom he acknowledged that he could find no fault, what might be expected from his successors when they had to deal with a people rebellious and in arms? (Comp. I Pet. 4:17.)

(33) The place, which is called Calvary.—See note on Matt. 27:33.

(34) Father, forgive them; for they know not what they do.—Again, the silence is broken, not by the cry of anguish or sigh of passionate complaint, but by words of tenderest pity and intercession. It is well that we should remember who were the primary direct objects of that prayer. Not Pilate, for he knew that he had condemned the innocent; not the chief priests and scribes, for their sin, too, was against light and knowledge. Those for whom our Lord then prayed were clearly the soldiers who nailed Him to the cross, to whom the work was but that which they were, as they deemed, bound to do as part of their duty.

(38) And a superscription.—See note on Matt. 27:37.

(39) And one of the malefactors.—The incident that follows is singularly characteristic of Luke. His probable informants were the devout women who followed Jesus to the place of Crucifixion, and who stood near enough to the cross to hear what was then spoken. The word for "hanged" is used by Luke (Acts 5:30; 10:39) and Paul (Gal. 3:13) as applied to crucifixion.

(40) But the other answering rebuked him.—We may think of him as impressed by the holiness and patience of Him upon whom he looked. What such a One claimed to be, that He must have a right to claim, and so the words uttered in mockery, "Christ, the King of Israel," became an element in his conversion. He accepted his punishment as just, and in so doing made it reformatory and not simply penal.

(43) To-day shalt thou be with me in paradise.—In the figurative language in which the current Jewish belief clothed its thoughts of the unseen world, the Garden of Eden took its place side by side with "Abraham's bosom," as a synonym for the eternal blessedness of the righteous, presenting a vivid contrast to the foul horrors of Gehenna. It is remarkable that this is the one occasion on which the word appears as part of our Lord's teaching. What He said in answer to the penitent's prayer was, in part, a contrast to it, in part, its most complete fulfillment. Not in the far-off "Coming," but that very day; not "remembered" only, but in closest companionship. The promise implied that the penitent should enter at once into the highest joy of the kingdom. The penitent thief is naturally prominent in the apocryphal legends of our Lord's descent into Hades, seen by His side as He enters Paradise (**Gosp. of Nicodemus**, 2:10).

(44-46) See notes on Matt. 27:45-50; Mark 15:33-37.

(47-49) See notes on Matt. 27:54, 55.

(50-56) See notes on Matt. 27:57-62.

24

(1-8) See notes on Matt. 28:1-4.

(9-11) See note on Matt. 28:8.

(12) See notes on John 20:3-10. The fact of Peter's visit to the sepulchre is common to Luke and John, but the former does not mention the companionship of the beloved disciple. On the assumption of Joanna being Luke's informant, we can understand that she told what she remembered—Peter's impetuous rush to the sepulcher—and did not notice that he was followed by his friend.

(13) And, behold, two of them.—The long and singularly interesting narrative that follows is peculiar to Luke. The Emmaus near Jerusalem (Josephus, **Wars**, 7:6, §6) was sixty **stadia** (eight miles) from Jerusalem. The name was connected with a "bath," indicating the presence of medicinal warm springs. We can hardly doubt, from the prominence given to the name of Cleopas, that he was Luke's informant.

(15) Jesus himself drew near, and went with them.—Neither of the two travelers belonged to the Twelve. They may possibly have been of the number of the Seventy. May we think that it was in tender sympathy with the trials to which their thoughtful and yearning temper specially exposed them, that their Master thus drew near to them? They had cherished the hope that the kingdom of God would immediately appear (19:11), and now it seemed further off than ever.

(18) One of them, whose name was Cleopas.—The name is to be distinguished from the Clopas of John 19:25, which was probably a Graecized form of the Aramaic name of a Galilean disciple. Here the name is a Greek contraction of Cleopatros (so Antipas, from Antipatros), and so far, as connected with Cleopatra, indicates Hellenistic and probably Alexandrian antecedents. This may in part, perhaps, account for his imparting to Luke what had not found its way into the current oral teaching of the Hebrew Church at Jerusalem, as embodied in the narratives of Matthew and Mark.

(19) Concerning Jesus of Nazareth, which was a prophet.—The words indicate the precise stage of faith which the two disciples had reached. They believed in Jesus as a prophet; they hoped that He would redeem Israel. They had not risen to the belief that He was the Christ, the Son of God. And now even that faith was tottering. The whole narrative suggests that our Lord was choosing this exceptional method of dealing with them as a step in the spiritual education which was to lead them on to the higher truth.

(25) O fools, and slow of heart to believe.—The word for "fools" (more literally, "silly, senseless") is not that which is used in Matt. 5:22; 23:17, but one belonging to a somewhat higher style of language. It is used by Paul of the "foolish Galatians" (Gal. 3:1), and elsewhere, and by no other New Testament writer. The word of reproof sounds strong, but we must remember that our Lord already had given hints as to the true interpretation of Messianic prophecies (9:22, 44; Mark 14:21), which might have led thoughtful men to see that they pointed to suffering and death, as well as to sovereignty and triumph.

(26) **Ought not Christ to have suffered?**— Better, "the Christ." The thought that the sufferings were a necessary condition of the glory that followed became from this time forth almost as an axiom of Christian thought. (See I Pet. 1:11.)

(27) **Beginning at Moses and all the prophets.**—From the great first gospel of Gen. 3:15, to the last utterance of the last of the prophets announcing the coming of Elijah (Mal. 4:5), with special stress, doubtless, on prophecies such as Pss. 16, 22; Isa. 53, that spoke of sufferings and of death as belonging to the perfect picture of the Servant of the Lord, and the ideal King, the unfolding of the divine purpose now was made clear to those who before had been "slow of heart to believe."

(30) **He took bread, and blessed it.**—This was meant to teach them, and, through them, others, the same lesson that had then been taught to the Twelve, that it would be in the "breaking of bread" that they would hereafter come to recognize their Master's presence. This meal became so full of spiritual significance that we may well anticipate the technical language of theology and say that it was to them "sacramental."

(31) **And he vanished out of their sight.**— In the order of time this is the first example of the new conditions of our Lord's risen life. It was not that He rose and left the room in which they sat. In a moment they knew Him with all the fullness of recognition; and then they saw Him no more. Now they were to be taught that that communion was no longer to depend, as before, on a visible and localized presence. (Comp. verse 36; John 20:19, 26.)

(33) On the narrative beginning here, see notes on John 20:19-23; I Cor. 15:5.

(36) **Jesus himself stood in the midst of them.**—The doors of the room had been closed for fear of the Jews (John 20:19). The mode of appearance in both gospels suggests the idea, as in verse 31, of new conditions of existence, exempted from the physical limitations of the natural body, and shadowing forth the "spiritual body" of I Cor. 15:44.

(39) **Behold my hands and my feet.**—The test thus offered to the disciples, like that afterward given to Thomas, was to be to them a proof that they were not looking on a specter from the shadow-world of the dead. The Resurrection was a reality. (Comp. I John 1:1.) The conditions must remain, however, transcendental and mysterious. There is a real corporeity, and yet there is a manifest exemption from the common conditions of corporal existence.

(41) **While they yet believed not for joy.**— We again note Luke's characteristic tendency to psychological analysis. As men sleep for sorrow (22:45), so they disbelieve for joy. What is brought before their eyes is too good to be true.

Have ye here any meat?—Comp. John 21:5. The resurrection body could be no shadow or specter that thus asked for food. What seems suggested is a spiritual existence capable, by an act of volition, on assuming, in greater or less measure, the conditions of corporeal.

(44) Our Lord leads His disciples to the true method of interpreting the prophecies which foretold the Christ. The threefold division of the Law, the Prophets (including most of the historic books), and the Psalms (the whole of the **Kethubim**, the **Hagiographa** or "holy writings," of which the Psalms were the most conspicuous portion) corresponded to that which was in common use among the Jews.

(45) **Then opened he their understanding.**—Assuming that this was the same meeting of the Lord with His disciples as that reported in John 20:22, we have here that which corresponds with the gift of the Holy Spirit He then imparted to them. They were conscious of a new spiritual power of insight and knowledge which they had not possessed before.

(47) There is clearly a break and condensation of the narrative at this point. Luke has no personal reminiscences. The second appearance, when Thomas was present, those on the mountain or by the lake in Galilee, are unrecorded by him, and probably were not known. He has before him the plan of his second book, and he is content to end his first with what will serve as a link leading on to it. In Acts 1:8 words that closely resemble these are placed at the end

of the forty days, which are there distinctly recognized.

(49) Until ye be endued with power from on high.—According to the Greek, the disciples were to be invested—i.e., clothed upon—with a new power, which was to be as the new garb in which their old nature and its gifts were to manifest themselves, purified and strengthened, but not losing their identity.

(50) The coincidences between the close of Luke's first book and the beginning of his second show that he already was looking forward to resuming his work, and that the interval of forty days is distinctly recognized in Acts 1:3, though there also, as here, there is no mention of any return to Galilee in the interval. On the brief narrative that follows, see notes on Acts 1:9-11.

(51, 52) The words "and was carried up into heaven" and "they worshipped him" are omitted from the best MSS.

(53) And were continually in the temple.— Comp. Acts 1:13. Their days were spent, not in the routine of common life, but in the prayer of fervent expectation; and for this no place was so fitting as the Temple, which their Master had taught them to regard as His "Father's house," the "house of prayer" (19:46; John 2:16). There all the memories of the precious days that had preceded the Passion would be with them in their fullest intensity.

Amen.—The word is wanting in the best MSS, as it is also in many in Matt. 28:20; Mark 16:20, and John 20:31. In each case it probably was added by the transcriber in devout thankfulness at the completion of his task.

JOHN

1

(1) In the beginning.—The reference to the opening words of the Old Testament is obvious. It is quite in harmony with the Hebrew tone of this gospel so to refer, and it can hardly be that John wrote his **Bere-shith** without having that of Moses present to his mind, and without being guided by its meaning. We exclude from **these** words the idea of "anteriority to time," which is expressed, not in them, but in the substantive verb which immediately follows. The Mosaic conception of "beginning" is marked by the first creative act. John places himself at the same starting point of time, but before he speaks of any creation he asserts the pre-existence of the Creator. In this "beginning" there already "was" the word.

With God.—These words express the co-existence, but at the same time the distinction, of person. The "with" represents "motion toward." The Being whose existence is asserted in the "was" is regarded as distinct, but not alone, as ever going forth in communion with God.

Was God.—This is the completion of the graduated statement. It maintains the distinction of person, but at the same time asserts the oneness of essence.

(2) The same was.—This is a summary in one clause of the three assertions made in the first verse; but yet it is more. The Word was one in nature with God. From this higher point of view, the steps to follow are seen more clearly. The Word was God; the eternal pre-existence and personality are included in the thought.

(3) From the person of the Word we are guided to think of His creative work. All things came into existence by means of the pre-existent Word; and of all the things that now exist, none came into being apart from Him. (Comp. Col. 1:15, 16.)

(4) In him was life.—The Word was ever life, and from the first existence of any creature became a source of life to others. Creation is not merely a definite act. There is a constant development of the germs implanted in all the varied forms of being, and these find their sustaining power in the one central source of life. (Comp. verse 17; Heb. 1:3.)

And the life was the light of men.—We are led from the relation of the Word to the universe to His relation to mankind. In every man there are rays of light, stronger or feebler, in greater or lesser darkness. In every man there is a power to see the light, and open his soul to it, and the more he has it still to crave for more. This going forth of the soul to God is the seeking for life. The Word is the going forth of God to the soul. He is life.

(5) And the light shineth in darkness.—The vision of brightness is present but for a moment, and passes away before the black reality of the history of mankind. The description of Paradise occupies but a few verses of the Old Testament. The outer darkness casts its gloom on every page. But in the moral chaos, too, God said, "Let there be light; and there was light." The emphatic present declares that the light still, always, "shineth in darkness."

Comprehended it not.—The meaning of this word differs from that rendered "knew not" in verse 10. The thought here is that the darkness did not lay hold of, did not appropriate, the light, so as itself to become light; the thought there is that individuals did not recognize it. Comp. Rom. 9:30; I Cor. 9:24; Phil. 3:12, 13, where the same Greek word occurs.

(6) On the mission of John, see notes on Matt. 3. For the first time in 400 years a great teacher had appeared in Israel.

(7) For a witness.—Compare with this purpose of the Baptist's work the purpose of the apostle's writing, as he himself expresses it in chap. 20. The word "witness," with its cognat forms, is one of the key notes of the Johannine writings recurring alike in the gospel, the epistles, and the Apocalypse. This is partly concealed from the general reader by the various renderings "record," "testimony," "witness," for the one Greek root.

(9) The true Light was not "true" as opposed to "false," but "true" as answering to the perfect ideal, and as opposed to all more or less imperfect representations. As ideally true, the Light was not subject to the changing conditions of time and space, but was and is true for all humanity, and "lighteth every man."

(10) In the world.—This manifestation in the flesh recalls the preincarnate existence during the whole history of the world, and the creative act itself (see notes on verses 2, 3). The world, then, in its highest creature man, with spiritual power for seeing the true Light, ought to have recognized Him. Spirit ought to have felt and known His presence. In this would have been the exercise of its true power and its highest good. But the word was sense-bound, and lost its spiritual perception.

(11) He came, as distinct from the "was" of the previous verse, passes on to the historic advent; but as that was but the more distinct act of which there had been foreshadowings in every appearance and revelation of God, these advents of the Old Testament are not excluded.

His own is neuter, and distinguished from the "world" of verse 10. It refers to the Jewish land, the city, the Temple bound up with every Messianic hope.

His own in the second clause is masculine. His own people, the special objects of His love and care. We turn from the coldness of a strange world to the warmth and welcome of a loving home. The world knew Him not, and He came to His own, and they despised him!

(12) As many as received him.—The nation as such rejected Him; individuals in it accepted Him; but not individuals of that nation only. All who according to their light and means accept Him receive from Him an authority and in Him a moral power, which constitutes them members of the true home to which He came, and the true children of God. They receive in acceptance the right which others lost in rejection.

To them that believe on his name repeats the width of the condition, and at the same time explains what receiving Him means. It seems natural to understand the "name" of the only name which meets us in this context, that is, of the **Logos** or Word, the representation of the will, character, and nature of God. To "believe on" is one of John's characteristic words of fuller meaning. To believe is to accept as true, to trust in, to confide in; to "believe on" has the idea of motion toward and rest upon.

(13) Which were born.—How could they become "sons of God"? The word which has been used (verse 12) excludes the idea of adoption, and asserts the natural relation of child to father. The nation claimed this through its descent from Abraham. But they are Abraham's children who are of Abraham's faith. There is a higher generation which is spiritual, while they thought only of the lower, which is physical. The condition is the submissive receptivity of the human spirit.

(14) And the Word was made flesh, and dwelt.—Man came to be a son of God,

because the Son of God became man. They were not, as the Docetae of that time said, believers in an appearance. The term "flesh" expresses human nature as opposed to the divine, material nature as opposed to the spiritual, and is for this reason used rather than "body," for there may be a purely spiritual body (see notes on I Cor. 15:40-44).

Dwelt among us.—The Greek word means "tabernacled," "sojourned" among us. It probably was suggested by the similarity of sound with "Shekhinah," a term frequently applied in the Targums or Chaldee Paraphrases to the visible symbol of the divine Presence which appeared in the Tabernacle and the Temple. The thought, then, of this Presence brings back to the writer's mind the months they had spent with the Word who had pitched His tent among them. He had been among the first to follow Him, and of the last with Him. (See notes on I John 1.)

The glory.—Comp. 2:11; 11:4. See notes on Matt. 17:2; II Pet. 1:17.

As of the only begotten.—The term as applied to the person of our Lord is found only in John: verse 18; 3:16, 18; I John 4:9. It is used four times elsewhere in the New Testament, and always of the only child. (See Luke 7:12; 8:42; 9:38; Heb. 11:17.) The close connection here with the word Father, and the contrast with the sonship by moral generation in verse 12, fixes the sense as the eternal generation of the Word.

Full of grace and truth.—These words refer to "the Word." The structure of the English sentence is ambiguous, but the meaning of the Greek words is quite clear. They represent a Hebrew formula expressing a divine attribute (comp. Exod. 34:6; Ps. 25:10).

(15) Comp. verses 27, 30. The words are quoted here as closely bound up with the personal reminiscence of verse 14, and with the thought of verses 6, 7 (see notes).

(16) And of his fulness.—This is not a continuance of the witness of John the Baptist, but the words of John the evangelist, and closely connected with verse 14. "Fulness" is a technical theological term, meaning the plenitude of divine attributes.

Have all we received.—The point of time is the same as in verse 12, and the "we all" is co-extensive with "as many as."

And grace for grace.—The original faculty of reception was itself a free gift, and in the use of this grace there was given the greater power. The words mean "grace in exchange for grace." The fullness of the supply is constant; the power to receive increases with the use, or diminishes with the neglect, of that which we already have.

(17) This is the essence of Christianity as distinct from Judaism. The Law was given (from without) by the human agency of Moses; the true grace and truth came into being by means of Jesus Christ. There is in Him an ever constant fullness of grace, and for the man who uses the grace thus given an ever constant realization of deeper truth.

(18) No man hath seen God at any time.— The full knowledge of truth is one with the revelation of God, but no man has ever had this full knowledge. The primary reference is still to Moses (comp. Exod. 33:20, 23).

The only begotten Son, which is in the bosom of the Father.—The oneness of essence and of existence is made prominent by a natural figure, as necessary in Him who is to reveal the nature of God. The "is in" is probably to be explained by the return to, and presence with, the Father after the Ascension. Some of the oldest MSS and other authorities read here, "Only begotten God, which is in the bosom of the Father."

He hath declared him.—The verb was used technically of the interpretation of sacred rites and laws handed down by tradition. Thus, no man has ever so known God as to be His interpreter; this Son is the only true Word uttering to man the will and character and being of God.

(19) The Jews.—This term, originally applied to the members of the tribe of Judah, was extended after the Captivity to the whole nation of which that tribe was the chief part. Used by John more than seventy times, it is to be understood generally of the representatives of the nation and of the inhabitants of Judaea, and of these as opposed to the teaching and work of Christ.

Priests and Levites.—The word "Levite" occurs only twice elsewhere in the New Testament—Luke 10:32 and Acts 4:36. It is clear from II Chron. 17:7-9; 35:3; Neh. 8:7, that part of the function of the Levites was to give instruction in the Law, and it is probable that the "scribes" often were identical with them. We have, then, here two divisions of the Sanhedrin, as we have two in the frequent phrase of the other evangelists, "scribes" and "elders," the scribes (Levites) being common to both, and the three divisions being priests, Levites (scribes), and elders (notables).

(21) The Lord declared "Elias is come already"; and yet the Forerunner can assert

that, in the literal sense in which they ask the question and would understand the answer, he is not Elias, still less "the prophet," by which, whether thinking of the words of Moses or the fuller vision of Isaiah from which he immediately quotes, he would understand the Messiah himself.

(23) See notes on Matt. 3:3.

(25) Why baptizest thou then?—Baptism, which was certainly one of the initiatory rites of proselytes in the second or third century A.D., was probably so before the work of the Baptist. It is not baptism, therefore, which is strange to the questioners, but the fact that he places Jews and even Pharisees (Matt. 3:7) in an analogous position to that of proselytes, and makes them to pass through a rite which marks them as impure and needing to be cleansed before they enter "the kingdom of heaven."

(27) He it is . . . is preferred before me.— This is the authority for baptism, the outer sign of the Messiah's Advent, for He is already standing in their midst. Here is the answer to their question. John's work is simply ministerial.

(28) Bethabara beyond Jordan should be, "Bethany beyond Jordan." Origen found "Bethany" in "almost all the copies"; but not being able to find the place, he came to the conclusion that it must be Bethabara which he knew, with a local tradition that John had baptized there. And in this he is followed by the Fathers generally. This inquiry of legates from Jerusalem was after the baptism of our Lord (verses 31, 33), and if so, after the Temptation also. (See note on Matt. 4:1.)

(29) Forty days had passed since they met before, and since John knew at the baptism that Jesus was the Messiah. The Messiah was the servant of Jehovah, the true Paschal Lamb of Isaiah's thought (Isa. 52:13; 53:12). He bears indeed no halo of glory, but the marks of the agonizing contest and yet the calm of accomplished victory. An alternative reading for "taketh away" is "beareth" (comp. Isa. 53:4; I Pet. 2:24).

(30) See notes on verses 15, 27.

(32) See note on Matt. 3:16.

(38) They address Him as "Rabbi," placing themselves in the position of His scholars; but they have not yet learned all that John had taught them of His office. The title is natural from them, for it was the current title of a revered teacher, and one that John's disciples applied to him (3:26); but the writer remembers it was a modern word (comp. Matt. 23:7, 8), known to Jews only since the days of Hillel (president of the Sanhedrin about 30 B.C.), not likely to be known to Greeks at all, and he therefore translates it, as he does Messias and Cephas in this same section.

(39) The tenth hour.—It was four o'clock in the afternoon.

(40) One of the two.—The evangelist here draws the veil over his own identity. The one is Andrew, even now marked out as brother of the better-known Simon Peter. (See notes on Matt. 10:2-4.)

(41) He first findeth his own brother.— Each of the two disciples in the fullness of his fresh joy went to seek his own brother. Andrew found Peter first. John records this, and by the form in which he does so implies that he himself found James. (Comp. Matt. 4:18-21; Mark 1:16-19; Luke 5:1-10.)

Messias.—The Hebrew form of the name occurs in the New Testament only here and in 4:25. Elsewhere John, as the other sacred writers, uses the LXX translation "Christ," and even here he adds it. Both words mean "anointed" (comp. Ps. 45:7).

(42) Cephas.—The word occurs only in this place in the gospels, elsewhere in the New Testament only in Paul (I Cor. and Gal.) The name seems meant to characterize the man.

(43) The day following, that is, the fourth day from the inquiry by the Sanhedrin (see verses 29, 35, 43).

(44) Of Bethsaida.—Philip was going home, and Bethsaida was on the way which Jesus would naturally take from Bethania to Cana (2:1, 2). It explains, too, the process by which Philip passed from Messianic hope to a full belief in the Christ. He was a fellow townsman of Andrew and Peter. This "Bethsaida of Galilee" is distinguished from the Bethsaida Julias, which was on the eastern side of the lake.

(45) Philip findeth Nathanael.— Nathanael is the Hebrew of the Greek word Theodorus, God's gift. He belonged to the town to which Jesus was going (Cana of Galilee, 21:2). Philip then probably went with Jesus and found Nathanael at or near Cana (verse 48). He is, perhaps, the same person as Bartholomew (see note on Matt. 10:3).

(46) The question is asked by an inhabitant of a neighboring village who looks upon the familiar town with something of local jealousy and scorn; but the form of the question would seem to point to an ill repute in reference to its people. The place

is unknown to earlier history, and is not mentioned even in Josephus. (Comp. Mark 6:6; Luke 4:29; see note on Luke 1:26.)

(47) Jesus saw Nathanael coming.— Nathanael is at once willing that his prejudice should give way before the force of truth. The word for "guile" is the same word as the LXX word for "subtlety" (Gen. 27:35). The thought then is, "Behold one who is true to the name of Israel, and in whom there is nothing of the Jacob" (Gen. 27:36). There is something in the words which comes as a revelation to Nathanael. Were they a proof that the Presence before whom he stood read to the very depths of his own thought? Under the shade of a tree, where Jews were accustomed to retire for meditation and prayer, had the Old Testament history of Jacob been present to his mind? Was he too "left alone," and did he "prevail with God"?

(51) Verily, verily.—This is the first use of this formula of doubled words, which is not found in the New Testament outside John's gospel. They are always spoken by our Lord, and connected with some deeper truth to which they direct attention. They represent, in a reduplicated form, the Hebrew "Amen," which is common in the Old Testament as an adverb, and twice occurs doubled (Num. 5:22; Neh. 8:6).

I say unto you ... ye shall see.—The earlier words have been addressed to Nathanael. The truth expressed in these holds for all disciples, and is spoken to all who were then present—to Andrew, John, Peter, James (verse 41), and Philip, as well as to Nathanael.

The angels of God ascending and descending.—This refers again to the history of Jacob (Gen. 28:12, 13).

The Son of man.—This is probably the first time that this phrase, which became the ordinary title used by our Lord of Himself, fell from His lips; but it meets us more than seventy times in the earlier gospels. (See note on Matt. 8:20.) The ladder from earth to heaven is in the truth "the Word was made flesh." In that great truth heaven was, and has remained, opened. From that time on, messengers were ever going backward and forward between humanity and its God.

2

(1) The third day—i.e., from the last note of time in 1:43, giving one clear day between the call of Philip and the day of the marriage.

Cana of Galilee is a little more than six miles to the northeast of Nazareth. It is some fifteen or sixteen miles from Tiberias and Capernaum. The mother of Jesus already was there, as a relation or friend, assisting in the preparations. Nathanael would have known of the wedding, and was perhaps also connected with one of the families.

(3) They have no wine.—The mother's implied hopes and musings were based on no previous miracle from Him (verse 11). But for many long years she had kept in her heart the Son's words and deeds (Luke 2:51). To cause the increase of meal, and prevent the failure of the cruse of oil (I Kings 17:14), was within the power of the prophet whom they expected as herald of the Messiah. Can He not supply this present need, and prove Himself indeed the Christ?

(4) Nothing but thoughts of reverence and honor is to be connected with the title "Woman," least of all in the words of One who claimed as His own highest dignity Sonship of, identity with, humanity. His hour for being openly manifested as the Messiah had not come. Mother and brethren alike regarded life in its events; for Him it is an unchanging principle. For them, action is determined by the outer stimulus; for Him, by the eternal will of the Father. Their hour is always ready; His is the development of a law. (Comp. 7:6.)

(6) Waterpots, or "pitchers," but larger than the vessels used for carrying water (4:28). These were placed in the outer court, away from the guest-chamber, for the governor of the feast is ignorant of the circumstances (verse 9). There were six of them, containing about twenty gallons apiece. (The "firkin" measured nearly nine gallons.)

(8) Draw out now, and bear unto the governor of the feast.—A vessel was let down into the pitcher, and was then carried to the ruler of the feast, who would distribute the wine in it to the guests. What exact office is denoted by "governor" is uncertain. The person intended is probably what we call the "head waiter," whose duty it was to taste the food and wines, to arrange the tables and couches, and to be generally responsible for the feast.

(9) Water that was made wine.—As the English poet has said, "The conscious water saw its God, and blushed." The simple meaning is that the change took place dur-

ing or after the drawing from the pitchers, and that that portion only was changed which was carried to the ruler and actually needed to supply the guests. The other pitchers would be in any case refilled for ablutions after the feast. They were at hand, meeting the eye. All possibility of collusion is thus excluded. They had been used not long before; they would soon be used again. The filling of all leaves to the servants the choice of one or more from which to draw. There is an unfailing potential supply; it becomes an actual supply only when needed and appropriated by human want. Here, as everywhere in divine action, there is an economy in the use of power.

(10) When men have well drunk.—The Greek word is invariably used in the New Testament (Matt. 24:49; Acts 2:15; I Cor. 11:21; Eph. 5:18; I Thess. 5:7; Rev. 17:6) to express the state of drunkenness. The physical meaning of the word is to saturate with moisture, to be "drenched," which is the same word as "drunk." There is clearly no reference to the present feast. It is a coarse jest of the ruler's, the sort of remark that forms part of the stock in trade of a hired manager of banquets.

(11) This beginning of miracles did Jesus in Cana of Galilee.—The form of the sentence makes it certain that it is the absolutely first, and not the first in Cana, which is meant. It is important to note here that John uses only once, and that in our Lord's test of the courtier, and connected with "sign" (4:48), the word which represents "miracle." He nowhere uses the word which represents "powers" or "mighty works." This gives the key, then, to the selection of "miracles" by John, and to their interpretation. He gives those which mark stages of fuller teaching. They are "signs" of a new revelation, and lead to a higher faith.

The other signs recorded in this gospel are the healing of the ruler's son (4:46-54); the healing of the impotent man at Bethesda (5:1-9); the feeding of the five thousand (6:5-59); the walking on the sea (6:15-21); the giving of sight to the man born blind (9:1-7); the raising of Lazarus (chap. 11); the draught of fishes (21:1-8). See notes on these passages, and on 20:30.

(12) After this he went down to Capernaum.—It was on the shore of the lake of Tiberias, and He must have gone "down" to it from any locality among the hills of Galilee. The words do not imply that they went to Capernaum direct from Cana. The "after this" allows of a return to Nazareth, and the mention of the "brethren" makes such a return probable. (See notes on Matt. 4:13; 9:1; 13:55; Mark 3:21-31; 6:3; Luke 4:16-30.)

(13) And the Jews' passover was at hand.— The earlier gospels place a cleansing of the Temple at the close of our Lord's ministry at the only Passover which comes within the scope of their narrative (see notes on Matt. 21:12). On the eve of the Passover the head of every family carefully collected all the leaven in the house, and there was a general cleansing. He was doing in His Father's house what was then being done in every house in Jerusalem.

(15) And the sheep, and the oxen.—For this read, "both the sheep and the oxen." The driving out with the scourge was not of "all (men) and sheep and oxen," but of "all," i.e., both sheep and oxen.

(16) My Father's house.—Some among those present now (verse 18) may have been present in that same house when He, a lad of twelve years (Luke 2:49), was there at the Passover. He has before claimed to be Son of Man. The Son was now claiming the sanctity and reverence due to His Father's house. The Messianic title is publicly claimed before the official representatives of the people at the great national festival, in the Temple, at Jerusalem.

(17) The child was taught to say by heart large portions of the Law, Psalms, and Prophets, and they formed the texture of the mind, ready to pass into conscious thought whenever occasion suggested. With the exception of the 22nd Psalm, no part of the Old Testament is so frequently referred to in the New as the psalm from which these words are taken (69:9), and yet that psalm could not have been in its historic meaning Messianic (see, e.g., verses 5, 22-26). This reference to it gives us, then, their method of interpretation.

(18) Then answered the Jews.—See note on Matt. 21:23. The Mosaic legislation contained a warning against the efficiency of the test by signs (Deut. 13:1-3), but it was of the essence of Pharisaism to cling to it (Matt. 12:38; I Cor. 1:22). It supplied an easy means of rejecting the moral conviction.

(19) Here a sign is given referring to His Resurrection. The enigma turns in the present case upon the double sense of the word "temple." It meant the sacred shrine of the Deity, the Holy and most Holy place, as distinct from the wider Temple area. But the true shrine of the Deity was the body of the Incarnate Word (see verse 21). The Temple of wood and stone was but the representative of the divine Presence. That Presence was then actually in their midst. We have an example of the use of "tabernacle" in a parallel sense in 1:14 (comp. II Pet. 1:13, 14), and the full idea of a spiritual worship and presence in 4:21-24.

(20) Forty and six years was this temple in building.—It is implied that it was not then finished. The date of the completion is given by Josephus (*Ant.* 20:9, §7) as A.D. 64. The same author gives the eighteenth year of the reign of Herod the Great (Nisan 734 - Nisan 735, A.U.C.) as the beginning of the renewal of the Temple of Zerubbabel (*Ant.* 15:11, §1). This would give A.U.C. 781-782, i.e., A.D. 28-29, as the date of the cleansing. Luke furnishes us with an independent date for the beginning of the ministry of John the Baptist. If we count the "fifteenth year of the reign of Tiberius" (comp. note on Luke 3:1) from the beginning of his first reign with Augustus (A.U.C. 765, i.e., A.D. 12), this date will be A.U.C. 780, i.e., A.D. 27. The present Passover was in the following year, i.e., A.D. 28.

(22) These passages of those familiar Old Testament writings later came to men who had been slow of heart to see them, with the quickening power of a new life. They saw that Christ ought to have suffered these things, and to enter into His glory. They saw in Moses and the Prophets the things concerning Him, and they believed in a new and higher sense the written and the spoken word. (Comp. Luke 24:26.)

(23) When they saw the miracles.—See note on verse 11. The original words imply that their faith was dependent upon the signs on which they gazed, without entering into their deeper meaning. It was the impulsive response of the moment, not based upon a previous preparation, nor resulting in a present deep conviction (verse 24). It came far short of the faith of the disciples, who passed from a true knowledge of Moses and the Prophets to a true knowledge of Christ without a sign; but it came far above the disbelief of scribes and Pharisees, who after a sign rejected Him.

3

(1) The visit of Nicodemus issues from the event of 2:23. The name Nicodemus was common among the Jews, and like Stephen,

Philip, Jason, etc., was derived from their intercourse with the Greeks. (Comp., e.g., Demosth. 549, 23, and Jos. **Ant.** 14:3, §2.) Of this particular Nicodemus, we know with certainty nothing more than is told us in this gospel (7:50; 19:39). The Talmud mentions Nakedimon (Bonai) as one of the disciples of Jesus and as one of the three richest Jews when Titus besieged Jerusalem. His family was reduced to the most abject poverty, the inference being that this change of fortune is connected with his becoming a Christian and with the persecution which followed. He has been identified by some with the Nicodemus of the Gospel. (See note on 1:19.)

(2) By night.—The Sanhedrin had officially taken a hostile position, and an individual member of it dare not openly take any other. His own conviction is expressed by his coming to Jesus at all; his fear of public opinion and of the possible exclusion from the synagogue by his coming at night. (Comp. 12:42, 43.)

Rabbi.—The customary title of reverence for a teacher (comp. note on 1:38), but given here by a technically trained rabbi to One who had no formal title to it (7:15).

We know that thou art a teacher come from God.—This explains the title he used. He does not go beyond this. The plural pronoun expresses nothing more than the general conviction that the power to work miracles was a divine attestation of the teaching (9:16, 33). The "we" occurs again in our Lord's reply in verse 11, and it may be that both find their true explanation in the fact that this interview took place in the house, and in the presence of John, who had led Nicodemus to come.

(3) Jesus answered and said unto him.—The words of Nicodemus are clearly only a preface to further questions: the coming of the Messiah, the divine Glory, God's kingdom.

Verily, verily, I say unto thee.—See note on 1:51. The words are in the decisive tone of authority and certainty.

Except a man be born again, he cannot see the kingdom of God.—The Greek permits the alternative renderings "born again" and "born from above," although the former is more in keeping with the context. On "the kingdom of God," which is of frequent occurrence in the earlier gospels, but in John is found only here and in verse 5, see note on Matt. 3:2. To "see" the kingdom is, in New Testament usage, equivalent to "enter into the kingdom." The

condition of the spiritual vision which can see this kingdom is spiritual life, and this life is dependent on being born anew.

(4) How can a man be born . . . ?—The thought is not wholly strange to him. The rabbis were accustomed to speak of proselytes as children, and the term "new creature" (comp. II Cor. 5:17) was in frequent use to express the call of Abraham. But he is himself a child of Abraham, a member of the theocratic kingdom. He does not wilfully misinterpret, for this is opposed to the whole character of the man, nor does he really suppose the physical meaning is intended; but after the method of rabbinic dialogue, he presses the impossible meaning of the words in order to exclude it, and to draw forth the true meaning.

(5) Of water and of the Spirit.—The subject is closely connected with that of the discourse in Capernaum (chap. 6). The baptism of proselytes already was present to the thought; the baptism of John had excited the attention of all Jerusalem, and the Sanhedrin had officially inquired into it. The message was baptism with water, by which the Gentile had been admitted as a newborn babe to Judaism, the rite representing the cleansing of the life from heathen pollutions and devotion to the service of the true God. John had declared (comp. Matt. 3:7) a like cleansing as needed for Jew and Gentile, Pharisee and publican, as the gate to the kingdom of heaven, which was at hand. There is no further explanation of the "outward and visible sign," but the teaching passes on to the "inward and spiritual grace," the birth of the Spirit, which was the work of the Messiah Himself. Of this, indeed, there were foreshadowings and promises in the Old Testament Scriptures (comp. Jer. 31:33; Ezek. 36:25); but the deeper meaning of such passages was buried beneath the ruins of the schools of prophets, and few among later teachers had penetrated to it. It is hard for this rabbi to see it, even when it is brought home to him.

(6) That which is born of the flesh is flesh.—The first step is to remind him of the law of likeness in natural generation. "Flesh," as distinct from "spirit," is human nature, consisting of the bodily frame and its animal life, feelings, and passions. "Flesh," as opposed to "spirit," is this nature as not under the guidance of the human spirit, which is itself the shrine of divine Spirit. It is this nature in its material constitution, and subject to sin, which is transmitted from father to son.

There is an analogous law of spiritual generation. Spirit as opposed to flesh is the **differentia** of man as distinct from all other creatures. It is the image of God in him, the seat of the capacity for the communion with God, which is the true principle of life. In the natural man this is crushed and dormant; in the spiritual man it has been quickened by the influence of the Holy Ghost. This is a new life in him, and the spiritual life, like the physical, is dependent upon birth.

(7) Ye must be born again.—Insofar as they were children of Abraham according to the flesh, they were children of Abraham's physical and sinful nature. The law of the regenerate nature was that the spirit, born by the influence of the divine Spirit, rose to a new life of communion with God, controlled the lower life, with its affections, feelings, and desires, and that these thus controlled became the motive power of the body; the whole man thus became spiritual, bringing forth the fruits of the Spirit.

(8) The wind bloweth where it listeth, and thou hearest the sound thereof.—These words are an explanation of the spiritual birth, the necessity of which has been asserted. And yet the new spiritual birth, like the physical, cannot really be explained. We can observe the phenomena, but we cannot trace the principle of life. He breathes where He wills, in the wide world of man, free as the wind of heaven, bound by no limits of country or of race. It is the beginning of a life which is a constant growth, and the highest development here is but the germ of that which shall be hereafter (I John 3:2).

The word **pneuma** occurs some 370 times in the Greek New Testament, and of these, twenty-three times in this gospel. It is nowhere rendered "wind" by our translators, except in this instance, and they have rendered the same word by "Spirit" in the same verse, and twice besides in the same context (verses 5, 6). There is another word for "wind" (**anemos**), which occurs thirty-one times in the New Testament, and which John himself uses in 6:18. **Pneuma** may mean "wind," "the breath of wind," but not where the word is restricted to its special meaning, as here. Thus, a better rendering would be, "The Spirit breatheth where He willeth." .. (Comp. Origen, Augustine, Bengel.)

(9) How can these things be?—The answer to the previous question has spoken of a spiritual birth, a spiritual life, and a

spiritual kingdom, but all this is in a region of which the rabbinic schools knew nothing. They were the authorized exponents of Law and Prophets; they knew the precise number of words, the shape of letters, the form of a phylactery, the width of a fringe, the tithing of garden herbs, and the manner of washing the hands. But how can a man's soul be born again?

(10) Art thou a master of Israel?—Better, "Art thou the teacher of Israel?" The article is emphatic, and points to the position of Nicodemus as a teacher of repute—"the well-known teacher"; or possibly it is to be understood of the Sanhedrin as represented by him—"Is this the teaching of Israel?" There is something of just indignation here, as everywhere when the words of Jesus Christ are addressed to the hypocrisy of the Pharisees. "You who teach others, have you need to learn the very first lessons of true religion?"

(11) The plural is not usual in the language of Christ. He apparently joins others with Himself—those who have spoken and known and testified, and whose testimony has been rejected by the Jews. In their measure and degree, as He in fullness, spoke what they knew and testified what they had seen. (Comp. 15:27.)

(13) And no man hath ascended up.—Comp. Prov. 30:4. No man had so passed to heaven and returned again to earth; but there was One then speaking with him who had been in heaven with God, and could tell him its eternal truths.

Which is in heaven.—These words are omitted in some MSS, including the Sinaitic and the Vatican. It is hard to account for the insertion by a copyist, but the omission is likely, owing to their seeming difficulty.

(14) And as Moses lifted up.—See Num. 21:9. This verse is closely connected by the conjunction "and" with what has gone before. Again the Old Testament Scriptures form the basis of the teaching to their expounder. The serpent of brass lifted up by Moses, in which the sufferer saw the means of recovery determined by God, and was healed by faith in Him, was symbolic of the means of salvation determined by God for the world. (Comp. 8:28; 12:32, 34.) Nicodemus must have understood that the healing power of the serpent of brass was in the fact that it led men to trust in Jehovah, who had appointed it. This was the current Jewish interpretation. In the divine counsels it was willed, and must be, that the Son of man should be the witness to the world of the eternal power and love which saves every man who grasps it.

(15) Not perish, but . . .—These words have been added here from the following verse. The sentence should be rendered, "that every one who believeth may have in Him eternal life." The thought of this verse is that as every Israelite, believing in God, had in the brazen serpent a message from God, so every man who believes in God ever has this message from God in the crucified Son of man. The object of faith is not expressed here. The words speak only of the man who believes, whose heart is open to spiritual truth. It should be remembered that the lifting up the serpent of brass followed the confession of the people.

(16) The last verse has spoken of "every one who believeth." This thought is now repeated and strengthened by the "might not perish," and the love of God is made the foundation on which it rests.

God so loved the world.—Familiar as the words are to us, they were uttered to Nicodemus for the first time. They are the revelation of the nature of God, and the ground of our love to God and man. (See notes on I John 4:7-11.)

His only begotten Son.—Here again the Old Testament Scriptures suggest and explain the words used. (See Gen. 22.) God wills not that Abraham should give his son, be He gave His only begotten Son. All that human thought has ever gathered of tenderness, forgiveness, and love in the relation of father to only child is an approach to the true idea of God. Yet the true idea is infinitely beyond all this; for the love for the world gives in sacrifice the love for the only begotten Son.

Believeth in.—The thought is of the Son of God given for the world, and every one who casts his whole being upon Him, and, like Abraham, rests all upon God, finds that God has provided Himself a lamb for a burnt offering instead of human sacrifice or death.

Everlasting life.—See note on Matt. 25:46.

(17) To condemn the world gives a stronger impression than that of the original Greek. Our word "judge" is probably the best rendering of **krino** in this context. Part of the current belief about the Messiah's advent was that He would destroy the Gentile world. God's love for, and gift to, the world has just been declared. This truth runs counter to their belief, and is not stated as an express denial of it. The purpose of the Messiah's mission is not to judge, but to save.

(19) And this is the condemnation.—Better, "judgment." The object is salvation, not judgment (verse 17); but the separation of the good involves the judgment of the evil. That men chose darkness rather than light was the act of their own will. The words must have had a special force to Nicodemus, who had come to Jesus in secrecy "by night."

(20) Here we have the explanation of the choice of the darkness and rejection of the light. Its presence makes manifest and reproves his works, which he would hide even from himself. It illumines the dark and secret chambers of the heart, and reveals thoughts and deeds which conscience would hide. Verse 21 contrasts the man in pursuit of truth in light.

(22) This verse points to a work in Judaea of which we know nothing more. It probably was not confined to one place. We have to think of Christ as continuing His teaching, of large numbers influenced by it (verse 26), and of these as being baptized by the disciples (4:2). His converts were the country people, and it is the action of the Pharisees which caused Him to retire to Samaria.

(23) AEnon near to Salim.—Jerome and Eusebius fix the place in the valley of the Jordan, eight miles south from Bethshan, or Scythopolis. The objection to this is that the text seems to limit us to Judaea (comp. 4:3, 4), whereas this Salim is more than thirty miles from it. The word AEnon means "springs," and probably belonged to more than one place where "there was much water." The mention of this is opposed to the locality of the Jordan valley, where it would not be necessary to choose a place for this reason. A more likely identification is **Wady Farah**, about five miles from Jerusalem.

(24) Was not yet cast into prison.—This Judaean ministry, then, preceded the Galilean ministry of the earlier gospels (See 4:3; note on Matt. 4:12.)

(25-28) John's disciples, with a natural attachment to their master, and without the knowledge of what that master's work really was, are jealous of what seems to them the rival work of Jesus. John had from the first known his own work, and the greater work. Some of his disciples had known it also, and had gone from him to Jesus. This which they see was the necessary result of the truth he had ever declared.

811

(29) He that hath the bride is the bridegroom.—This is the only instance in this gospel of the familiar imagery of an eastern marriage. (See note on Matt. 9:15.) The "friend of the bridegroom" was charged with the preliminaries of the marriage. He arranged the contract, acted for the bridegroom during the betrothal, and arranged for, and presided at, the festivities of the wedding day itself. It was a position of honor, in proportion to the position of the bridegroom himself, and was given to his chief friend. This in John's thought is an illustration of his own position (verse 30). The bridegroom is the Messiah; the bride is the Church.

(31) See note on verse 13. John's nature is, in accord with this origin, human and limited in faculty, as opposed to that of Him who is above all. His teaching, too, is from the standpoint of human nature and limited faculty, although embracing divine subjects and receiving divine revelation (1:33). This is the answer to the jealousy of John's disciples (verse 26), who wished to place him in a position of rivalry with Jesus.

(33) Earlier disciples, as Andrew and John (1:40), had passed from the Forerunner to the Great Teacher. Just as a man sets his private seal—here, probably, the common Eastern stamp that affixed the name—and by it attests the truth of a document, so they attested, in the power which that witness had over their lives, their recognition of it as truth.

(34) For God giveth not the Spirit by measure unto him.—See note on Matt. 3:16; comp. Luke 11:13; John 14:16; 15:26. The words "by measure," in the sense of limitation, are frequent in the classical and rabbinical writings. The rabbis seem to have applied the phrase to prophets and teachers. Thus God gives in this case not as in others. The Son who comes from above is above all. There is no gift of prophet, or of teacher, which is not given to Him. He has the fullness of the spiritual gifts which in part are given to men, and He speaks the very words of God.

(36) He that believeth not the Son.—Better, "he that obeyeth not the Son." The word, which occurs only here in the gospels, is not the same as that at the beginning of the verse, and shows that the faith there intended is the subjection of the will to the Son, to whom the Father hath given all things (verse 35). (Comp. Rom. 1:5.)

The wrath of God abideth on him.—This

wrath (comp. Rom. 2:8; Eph. 4:31; Col. 3:8; Rev. 19:15) is not the fierceness of passion, nor is it the expression of fixed hatred. It is the necessary aspect of love and holiness toward those who reject love and wilfully sin. The wrath of love must abide on hatred; the wrath of holiness must abide on sin.

4

(1) The report which reached John (3:26) had come to the Pharisees also, and the inference from Jesus' retirement is that it had excited their hostility. The hour to meet this has not yet come, and He withdraws to make, in a wider circle, the announcement which He has made in the Temple, in Jerusalem, in Judaea, and is about to make in Samaria and in Galilee.

(2) Though Jesus himself baptized not.—This is a correction, not of the writer's statement, but of the report carried to the Pharisees. There was a reason which they did not know for the fact that Jesus did not baptize with water, for it was He "which baptizeth with the Holy Ghost" (1:33), and this power His disciples had not yet received (7:39).

(3) Again.—This second return is the starting point of the history of our Lord's work in Galilee as told by the earlier gospels.

(4) He must needs go through Samaria—i.e., following the shortest and most usual road, and the one we find Him taking from Galilee to Jerusalem (see note on Luke 9:52). Josephus spoke of this as the customary way of the Galileans going up during the feasts at Jerusalem (**Ant.** 20:6, § 1). The Pharisees, indeed, took the longer road through Peraea, to avoid contact with the country and people of Samaria. But it is within the purpose of His life and work to teach in Samaria, as in Judaea, the principles of true religion and worship, which would cut away the foundations of all local jealousies and feuds, and establish for all nations the spiritual service of the universal Father (verses 21-24).

(5) The "Samaria" of this chapter is the province into which the older kingdom had degenerated, and which took its name from the capital city. (See Omri's purchase, I Kings 16:23, 24.) The city was given by Augustus to Herod the Great, who rebuilt it, and called it after the Emperor, Sebaste. As early as the fourth century, Sychar was distinguished from Shechem by Eusebius and Jerome. It was about half a mile north from Jacob's well. (See Gen. 33:19; 48:22; Josh. 24:32.)

(6) Jacob's well.—Jesus, passing from south to west, would enter the valley of Sichem between Ebal and Gerizim. Here is Jacob's field, and in the field is Jacob's well. Dug in the rock, it is about 9 feet in diameter and more than 100 feet deep.

About the sixth hour—i.e., as elsewhere in John, following the ordinary mode of counting, about 12 o'clock. (See note on 1:39.) It would seem that this was not the usual time for women to resort to the wells to draw water, as the narrative speaks of only one woman there.

(7) Of Samaria—i.e., of the country (verse 1), not of the city, which was nine miles farther north. She was of the people inhabiting the valley between Ebal and Gerizim, not, like Himself, a chance passenger by the well.

(9) Woman of Samaria.—Better, "Samaritan woman." In both cases the Greek has the adjective. It is the religious and national position as a Samaritan which is prominent in this verse.

Being a Jew.—This she would know from dress and language. See note on Judg. 12:5, 6, for the peculiarities of the Ephraimite pronunciation.

For the Jews have no dealings with the Samaritans.—This is a remark made by the writer to explain the point of the woman's question. She wondered that a Jew, weary and thirsty though he might be, should speak to her. (See notes on II Kings 17:24-41; Luke 9:52.) The later Jewish authors abound in terms of reproach for them. Jesus Himself speaks of a Samaritan as an alien (Luke 17:16, 18; comp. Luke 10:33), and is called a Samaritan and possessed of a devil (comp. 8:48). But at no time probably did the Galileans follow the practice of the Judaeans in this matter.

(10) We observe the turn given to her question by the emphatic pronouns, "**Thou** wouldest have asked of **Him**." There is a deep well of spiritual truth in communion with God, as necessary for man's true life as water is for the natural life. "If you knew this gift of God, and knew who it is that is now here to reveal it to you, you would have asked, and He would have given you that Spirit, which would have been in you as a fountain of living water" (verses 13, 14).

(20) Our fathers worshipped.—She gives

a sudden turn to the conversation. It is not that the question of worship is the all-engrossing problem of her mind, for which she seeks solution at this prophet's hands. But she will speak of anything rather than of self (verses 17, 18).

(21) Sychar was between Ebal and Gerizim, and she would point out the holy mountain with the ruins of the temple then in sight. It had been destroyed by John Hyrcanus, about 129 B.C. (Jos., *Ant.* 13:9, §1), but the mountain on which it stood continued to be the holy place of the Samaritans. They claimed that this mountain, and not Jerusalem, was the true scene of the sacrifice of Isaac, and Gentile tradition marked it out as the meeting place with Melchizedek. Jerusalem had never once been named in the Pentateuch, which was the only part of the Jewish canon which they accepted. It was but a modern city in comparison with the claim that Gerizim was a holy place from the time of Abraham forward.

(22) For salvation is of the Jews.—The contrast between the Samaritan and the Jewish worship lay in its history, its state at the time, and its rejection of the fuller teaching of the prophetical books of the Old Testament. Little as they knew the treasure they possessed, the Jews were the guardians of spiritual truth for the world. (Comp. Rom. 3:2; 9:4, 5.)

(23) In spirit and in truth.—The link between human nature and the divine is in the human spirit, which is the shrine of the Holy Spirit (I Cor. 6:19). All true approach to God must therefore be in spirit. (Comp. Rom. 1:9; Eph. 6:18.) Worship which is "in truth" is in harmony with the nature of the God whom we worship.

For the Father seeketh such to worship him.—The word "Father" came to her, it may be, now for the first time. He is not Vengeance to be appeased, nor Power to be dreaded, but Love to be received. (Comp. note on 3:16.) It is when men learn to think of God as Father that merely local and material worship must cease. The universal desire and practice of worship is the witness to a universal object of worship.

(24) God is a Spirit.—Better, "God is spirit." His will has been expressed in the seeking. But His very nature and essence is spirit, and it follows from this that all true worship must be spiritual. The appeal is made here to a doctrine of special prominence in the Samaritan theology. They had altered a number of passages in the Pentateuch, which seemed to them to speak of God in language properly applicable to man, and to ascribe to Him human form and feelings. But to believe in the spiritual essence of God contained its own answer both as to place and mode of worship.

(26) I that speak unto thee.—The announcement is being made. The solution of some of the problems which she connects with the Messianic advent is contained in the words she has heard.

(27) With the woman.—They are surprised, not at His talking with a Samaritan, but at His talking in public with a woman, which was directly contrary to the rabbinic precepts. A man should not speak in public to his own wife.

(35) Say not ye, There are yet four months.—Looking on the fields of springing corn, they would say that in four months there would be harvest. He sees signs of life springing up from seed sown in receptive hearts; and eyes lifted up and directed to the wide fields of the world's nations would see that the fullness of time was come, and that the fields were even now white to harvest. The Samaritans coming to Him are as the firstfruits, the earnest of the abundant sheaves which shall follow.

The legal beginning of harvest was fixed (Lev. 23:10; Deut. 16:9) for the 16th of Nisan (April). This would give us about the middle of the month Tebeth (January) as the date of this conversation. (Comp. 5:1.) For the idea of the harvest, comp. Matt. 9:36-38; 13:3.

(36-38) The sower is Christ Himself, whose words have been the seed in the woman's heart, already bringing forth a harvest in those who are coming to Him. The reapers are the disciples. In this harvest day they would learn, from sympathy with the souls of others, the joy of the reaper, and in that joy it was ordained that sower and reaper should rejoice together.

(39) Many of the Samaritans of that city believed.—The willingness to receive the truth on the part of the Samaritans is contrasted with the rejection of it on the part of the Jews. They refused the witness of a great prophet; these accept the witness of a woman. Their minds were prepared by the general expectation of the Messiah; and this woman witnesses that Jesus had revealed to her the whole past of her life.

(44) The narrative of the earlier gospels places the beginning of the ministry in Galilee. John has in these opening chapters told of an earlier ministry in Judaea and

Samaria. He now records the reception in Galilee to which this earlier ministry had been the real introduction.

(46) And there was a certain nobleman.—Perhaps "king's officer" represents the vagueness of the original better than any other English term. It is probable that the person was Chuza, and that his wife's presence in the band of women who followed Christ (Luke 8:3) is to be traced to the restoration of her child. (See note on Matt. 4:13.) The distance of Capernaum from Cana was from twenty to twenty-five miles. The report of Christ's return to Galilee had spread, then, over this wide area.

(48) Signs and wonders.—See note on 2:11. (The words are here addressed to Jews, for there is no reason to think that the nobleman himself was not one.) It had been so with the Jews in Jerusalem (2:18, 23), and it was so with the Jews in Galilee. (Comp. I Cor. 1:22.) See note on verse 39.

(50) His faith is to be strengthened, and is to pass beyond a trust in aid through bodily presence. Jesus will not go down, but he is himself to go with assurance. Up to this point he had believed on the testimony of others, but he, too, now believes on account of the word of Christ Himself.

(52) Yesterday at the seventh hour.—The Jews meant by the "seventh hour" the seventh from sunrise. After sunset the same evening they would have begun a new day, and this seventh hour would be to them as one o'clock the day before. We have thus an interval of five or six hours between the words spoken by our Lord and their confirmation by the servants.

(54) This is again the second.—John traces here, as before, in the case of the Samaritans (verses 41, 42), and of the disciples themselves (2:11), the successive development of faith. (See notes on Matt. 8:5-13, a separate but analogous incident.)

5

(1) A feast of the Jews.—The writer does not tell us what feast this was, and we must be content to remain without certain knowledge. The time limits are 4:35, which was in Tebeth (January), and 6:4, which bring us to the next Passover in Nisan (April), i.e., an interval of four months. The only feast which falls in this interval is the Feast of Purim, and it is with this that the best opinion identifies the feast of our text. It was kept on the 14th of Adar (March), in commemoration of the deliverance of the Jews from the plots of Haman, and took its name from the lots cast by him (Esth. 3:7; 9:24). It was one of the most popular feasts (Jos. **Ant.** 11:6, §13), and was characterized by festive rejoicings, presents, and gifts to the poor. At the same time it was not one of the great feasts, and while the writer names the Passover (2:13; 6:4; 13:1), the Feast of Tabernacles (7:2), and even that of Dedication (10:22), this has no further importance in the narrative than to account for the fact of Jesus being again in Jerusalem.

(2) **Bethesda** means "house of mercy." The "Hebrew tongue" was the current Hebrew, what we ordinarily call Aramaic, or Syro-Chaldaic. The pool of Siloam itself, near the "sheep-gate," was probably the pool of Bethesda. The remains of four columns in the east wall of the pool, with four others in the center, show that there was a structure half covering it, which resting upon four columns would give five spaces or porches. The fact that this pool is called Siloam in 9:7 does not oppose this view.

(3) The latter clause of the verse, "waiting for the moving of the water," and the whole of verse 4, is omitted by most of the oldest MSS, including the Sinaitic and the Vatican. The gloss explains the man's own view in verse 7, and the fact of the multitude assembled around the pool (verse 3).

(5) **Thirty and eight years.**—The period expresses the time during which he had suffered from the infirmity. The infirmity was in some way connected with youthful sin (verse 14), and the sufferer and his history would be well-known to those at Jerusalem. The exact knowledge of the writer tells us that for thirty-eight years he had paid sin's penalty.

(8) **Jesus saith unto him.**—There is no formal demand, or formal statement of faith as preceding the healing. If faith is an expression in words or anything outside man, then there is room for wonder; but if it be a living principle, then surely we may seek in vain for a more striking instance of its power than in this man, who in all, through all, and in spite of all, trusted in the mercy of God, and had faith to be healed. Jesus sees in him this receptive power, which in his helplessness is strength, and calls it forth.

(10) **The Jews therefore said unto him.**— Formalism had bound the letter around

men until it had nearly crushed all heart out of them. This is not the only place in this gospel where the words and works of Christ clashed with the current views of the sanctity of the Sabbath day. (Comp. 7:23; 9:14; see notes on Matt. 12:10-12.) Here the bearing of burdens was especially forbidden in the prophecy of Jer. 17:21 (comp. Neh. 13:15), and the rabbis pressed this to include a burden of any kind.

(12) The fact that this man was breaking their tradition is actually secondary. The real motive is a charge against Him whose power the body of the Jewish people was feeling as a life-current, quickening deadened energies, and rousing men to a sense of God's presence in their midst.

(14) **Sin no more.**—These words connect his past sufferings with individual sin. He has been freed from the effects, but if they have been truly remedial he has been freed from the cause too. He is in God's house. Let him accept restored powers as God's gift, and let their devotion be the true thank offering. The imperative is present, and points to a permanent condition of life.

A worse thing.—There is, then, something worse than a life of unmoving helplessness. There are limbs that had better never have moved. The power of existence is of infinite grandeur, but it is also of infinite responsibility. It has within its reach the highest good for self and for mankind; but if the God-given power is sacrificed to sin, there is within its reach an unutterable depth of woe.

(15) **The man departed, and told the Jews.**—The narrative does not suggest that he did this in a tone of defiance, still less that he used his new strength immediately to bring a charge against the Giver of it. The impression is rather that he felt that this power came from a prophet sent by God, and that he told this to those who were God's representatives to the nation, supposing that they would recognize Him too.

(16) The words express continuance or custom. It is either that from this one instance they generalize a law of practice to justify their persecution, or that some of the earlier unrecorded miracles also were performed on the Sabbath. (Comp. Luke 6:1-11.)

(17, 18) They charge Him with breaking the Law of God. His answer to this charge is that His action was the result of His Sonship and unity with that God. It was a claim which none other had ever made, that

God was in a peculiar sense His own Father. They feel it is a claim to divinity, a "making himself equal with God."

(19, 20) The works which He had done could be explained only by the unity of His work with that of the Father; but in the development of His own human nature and His mediatorial work, there will be shown to Him, and He will show to man by doing them in their midst, works of which these are but as the first signs.

Verses 21-29 show what the "greater works" of verse 20 are. They are the Resurrection and the Judgment; but these are regarded as spiritual as well as physical, as present as well as future. Once again the background of the thought is found in verse 17.

(21, 22) There is in His word, for the man who hears it and believes it, a moral change which is nothing other than an actual passing out of death into life (verse 24). The spiritual life given to some is a judgment of others. The reason why judgment is committed to the Son is given in verse 27 as resulting from His humanity. It is stated here as resulting from His deity. This power should lead all to give to the Son honor equal to that which they render to the Father. To reject Him was to reject the Father who sent Him. (Comp. verses 24, 30, 36, 37.)

(24) See note on 1:51. This truth explains the "whom he will" of verse 21 to have no limit but that of human receptivity. It again brings out the unity of Father and Son. It asserts that eternal life is not of the future only, but is already in germ possessed by the man who is thus brought into communion with the source of life. (Comp. I John 1:2.) This man comes not into judgment. He already has passed from the state of death to that of life. What remains for him is the development of life.

(25) The hour is coming.—The same solemn words repeat in another form the same great truth. The reference here, again, is to the spiritually dead. The "now is" cannot be applied to the physical resurrection (comp. verse 28), and cannot be explained by the instances of physical restoration to life during the earthly ministry of our Lord. In the last clause, also, "live" must mean the higher spiritual life, as it does in the whole context.

(26) Life in himself.—This giving of life to others can be only by one who has in himself an original source of life. To the Son in His pre-existent state it was natural, as being equal with the Father. To the Son who had emptied Himself of the exercise of the attributes which constituted the glory of the state (comp. Phil. 2:6), it was part of the Father's gift by which He exalted Him exceedingly, and gave Him the name which is above every name. It was, then, a gift in time to One who had possessed it before all time, and for the purposes of the mediatorial work had relinquished it. It was a gift, not to the Eternal Son, but to the Incarnate Word.

(27) The Son of man.—Render, "a son of man." The term differs by the striking omission of articles from the usual term for the Messiah (comp. Rev. 1:13; 14:14). It is here in contrast to the "Son of God" in verse 25. The explanation is to be found, again, in the thought of the Incarnation as an emptying Himself of the attributes which are the glories of the divine nature. It is not because He is Messiah (**the** Son of Man), but human (**a** son of man), that the Father gave Him the power to have life in Himself, and the authority to execute judgment.

(31) This verse is the link between the thoughts of Christ's person (verses 17-30) and the witness to Him (verses 32-40).

(33) They sought human witness (John 1:7, 19). He had witness which was divine (the Father, verse 32). Our Lord does not refer to John's witness for His own sake, but in order that they might be saved. He had a greater witness than that of John, but this they were not yet prepared to receive (verses 34-38). He refers to him now that that light may lead them to the true Source of Light.

(37) The Father . . . hath borne witness of me.—Reference to the revelation of the Old Testament Scriptures is demanded by the immediate context, while the voice at the Baptism and the Transfiguration are not only absent from the present circle of thoughts, but also from John's gospel. Jesus is answering a charge of breaking God's law, and of making Himself equal with God because He has claimed God's fatherhood in word for Himself, and has manifested it in life-power for man. Through the whole history of the nation, He had been revealing Himself to them. That charge was but an example of their unreceptive spirit.

(38) Abiding in you.—This striking thought of the word taking up its abode in the mind, and forming the mind in which it dwells, meets us only in John. (Comp. 3:36; 15:7; I John 2:14, 24; 3:9, 17.) They had, indeed, the word of God, but they had it not as a power ever living in them. They locked it up with sacred care in ark and synagogue, but it found no home in their innermost life, and had no real power on their practice. It was something outside themselves. Had it been in them it would have produced in them a moral consciousness, which would have accepted, as of the same nature with itself, every fuller revelation from God.

(39) Search the scriptures.—Better, "Ye search the Scriptures." We have here a reference to their habit of examining the Old Testament writings, rather than a command to do so. (Comp. the indicative verbs in verses 37-40.)

It may be that the true meaning of these words is to be found in their bearing upon the rabbinic lives and works. As early as the Book of Chronicles we find mention of the **Midrashim**, or **Commentaries** (see II Chron. 13:22; 24:27). These Midrashim sprang up after the Captivity, when the people had lost the older language of the Law and the Prophets. Hillel the First succeeded to the presidency of the Sanhedrin, 30 B.C.; Akiba was his successor in the compilation of the Mishna. The influence of the former was all-powerful among those who now accused Jesus of breaking what the Law did not contain but the Midrash did. Those who now listened to Christ were disciples or assistants of the great rabbi whose school of a thousand pupils left eighty names of note.

(43) I am come in my Father's name.— So far from self-assertion of honor-seeking, He came in the name of, and as representing, the Father—guided only by His will, doing only His work (4:34). Had they loved the Father, they must have received and reverenced His Son (8:42; Matt. 21:37). The absence of love is at the root of the rejection.

If another shall come in his own name.— This is to be understood of a false Messianic claim in opposition to the true. Sixty-four false Christs have been enumerated as appearing after the true Christ, and these words often are taken as a prophecy of one of the most famous of these, as Bar-Kochba. Some of the Fathers have understood the words of Antichrist. Perhaps the only definite reference is to the mental condition of the Jews. They would receive any other who came in his own authority, and seeking his own glory.

(46) For had ye believed Moses.—The present incredulity springs from that of the past. If they had really believed Moses, they would have seen in the whole spirit of the Pentateuch a manifestation of God, which would have led them to the fuller manifestation in Christ. Worship, sacrifice, offering, and priesthood were all meant to teach.

6

The feeding of the Five Thousand is the one miracle related in every gospel. (See notes on Matt. 14:13-21; Mark 6:30-44; Luke 9:10-17.)

The fact that this miracle of the Galilean ministry finds a place also in the record of the Judaean ministry is to be explained by the discourse which follows. Here, as elsewhere, the principle which has guided the writer's choice is that the sign is a teaching by work (comp. note on 2:11), and that those signs produce the fullest faith and life (20:31) which led up to the fullest teaching by word. According to verse 41, the discourse is addressed to Jews of Jerusalem among others, so that the chapter, though belonging locally to Galilee, is really within the sphere of John's narrative.

(1) Sea of Tiberias.—Comp. 21:1; but the phrases are not precisely the same. There it is simply "sea of Tiberias." Here it is "sea of Galilee, of Tiberias," the latter term being either an alternative rendering for Greek readers, or a limitation to that part of the lake which was opposite to the town of Tiberias (verse 23, and so named only here in the New Testament). The last chapter of the gospel should perhaps be regarded as an appendix; the present passage may mark the transition between the older names for the lake which meet us in the other gospels, and the later name, which meets us for the first time in John, but was afterward common in Greek writers.

(4) A feast.—See note on 5:1. This, added by John only, is not simply a note of time, but gives a key of interpretation to the sign itself, and to the discourse which followed.

(5) The converse with Philip is also peculiar to this gospel, and gives us a glimpse into the educational method of the great Teacher. The impression of the immediate antecedents of the miracle is different from, but not opposed to, that of the other narratives. They all represent the request coming from the disciples as the first step.

(7) Philip answered him.—The answer proves that Philip has not really learned the lessons of earlier teaching (e.g., the miracle at Cana, chap. 2). The question does not suggest to him the true answer of divine sufficiency, but leads him to think of the human difficulty. He looks on the vast throng of people. At the lowest estimate, it would take the value of 200 denarii to feed them—in actual labor—value nearly a workman's yearly wage. The denarius is the value of a day's work in the parable (Matt. 20:2). In A.D. 14, on the accession of Tiberius, one of the causes of revolt in the Pannonian legions is the smallness of their pay, and one of their demands (Tacit. **Ann.** 1:26) is a penny a day.

(8) One of his disciples.—Andrew, a member of the "inner circle" of Jesus, was one of the two disciples of the Baptist who first followed Him, and John's own companion (1:40). He is always named as one of the first group of the Twelve (see note on Matt. 10:2), and in some way was connected especially with Philip (1:44).

(9) The bread is barley loaves—the ordinary black bread of the Galilean peasant. Bread and fish formed the staple food of the people. The whole force of Andrew's remark, with its diminutive words in the original, rests upon the smallness of their power to help, while Philip had dwelt on the greatness of the need.

(14) Miracle.—See note on 2:11.

(15) When Jesus therefore perceived . . .—John has told us of the effect of the sign on the multitude (verse 14). He knows also the reason of Christ's retirement, while Matthew and Mark only state the fact that He retired to pray. They did not know that He wished to avoid that throng of people who thought of the Messiah as a temporal king, and would have carried Him with them to the great feast at the royal city.

(16-21) See notes on Matt. 14:22-33.

(21) The miracle is followed in the other accounts by the healings in the land of Genesareth. (See notes on Matt. 14:34-36; Mark 6:53-56.) For John the whole leads up to the discourse at Capernaum. He has told how our Lord and the disciples have crossed again to the west of the lake, but the narrative at once returns to the multitude who have seen the sign, and for whom there remains the interpretation.

(25) Rabbi, when camest thou hither?—This discourse took place in the synagogue at Capernaum (verse 59). They are amazed to find Him here. When and how could He have come? He had not gone in the boat with the disciples, and no other boats had

crossed but those in which they themselves came (verse 22).

(27) See note on 3:33.

(29) They speak of "works," regarding life as an aggregate of individual deeds. He speaks of "work," regarding separate acts as the outcome of principle. They had one great work to do, which indeed seemed not a work, but which when realized would be the living principle of every work, and would be as food abiding unto eternal life. To believe on Him whom God has sent is already to have the spiritual life which is eternal.

(30) What dost thou work?—They feel that His words are an assertion that He is the Messiah, and they demand of Him Messianic signs and works.

(32) Moses gave you not that bread.—They had implied a contrast between their fathers and themselves, between Moses and Jesus (verse 31). They expressed the glory of the Mosaic sign in the language of Ps. 78:25; but there the gift is ascribed to God, and it is named to mark the darkness of their unbelief. The gift of God was ever the same. He it was who gave then; He it is who ever gives.

(35) I am the bread of life.—Here they have asked for "this bread," the bread which giveth life, as distinct from that which perishes. It is now present with them. He is that bread, whose characteristic is life. He is the Word of God, revealing God to man, teaching the eternal truths which are the life of the spirit just as bread is of the body.

He that cometh to me . . . he that believeth on me.—The natural bread satisfied no need unless it was appropriated and eaten. The same law holds for the spiritual bread. It is taken by him who comes to Christ; it is eaten by him who believes on Him, and it satisfies every need.

(37) All that the Father giveth me.—There is something startling in this power of the human will to reject the fullest evidence, and to remain unbelieving, after the proof which it has itself demanded as a foundation for its belief. For the varying effects of His works upon men there is a cause (verses 38-40). He finds the reason (!) in the eternal will of God, of whose gift it is that man wills, and (2) in the determination of the will of man, of whose acceptance it is that God gives.

And him that cometh to me I will in no wise cast out.—The context points out the fulfillment of the Messianic kingdom as the Father's gift, and the individual difficulties of, and individual help given to, those who strive to enter it, and shall in no wise be cast out. There were men among those who heard Him who in darkness and difficulty were feeling their way; these men were guided and strengthened by an unseen hand until they found it. There were others then who were being cast out, but not by Him.

(42) Is not this Jesus?—"Jesus Bar-Joseph" would be the name by which He was commonly called; Joseph and Mary had been known, probably, to many in the crowd. All these indications point to an ordinary life in a Galilean village. It is human, and therefore they think it cannot be divine.

(44) No man can come to me.—The subject is still the mystery of the varying effects of His revelation on the minds of men. The word "draw" occurs in only one other passage in the New Testament—in the moral sense in the declaration of 12:32.

(45) It is written in the prophets . . .—i.e., in the Book of the Prophets. (Comp. Matt. 2:23; Mark 1:2; Acts 7:42; 13:40.) The immediate reference is to the LXX translation of Isa. 54:13 (comp. Jer. 31:34; Joel 3:1). The words bring out the meaning of the Father's drawing referred to in verse 44. The teaching is universal, but it may not be heard, and when heard may not be learned.

(46) See note on 1:18.

(47) He that believeth.—In verse 40 He declared the Father's will, that every one seeing the Son and believing on Him may have eternal life. No man had ever seen the Father; but the Son was then standing in human form before them. This will was being accomplished, and for the believer eternal life was not only of the future but of the actual present. (Comp. 3:15; 5:24.)

(48) I am that bread of life.—The essence of life is unseen; bread is the visible form which contains and imparts it. The invisible God is the source of eternal life; the human nature of the Son of God is the visible form which contains and imparts this to the souls of men.

(51) And the bread that I will give is my flesh.—This form of human flesh is, as bread, the means by which life is conveyed; it is the word by which the Eternal Spirit speaks to the spirit of man. (1:14 is the only other passage in this gospel where the word "flesh" is used of the person of Christ. Comp. Luke 24:39, of the resurrection

body, the only other passage in the New Testament.)

(53) In no less than seven passages of the Pentateuch had the eating of blood been forbidden (Gen. 9:4; Lev. 3:17; 7:26, 27; 17:10-14; 19:26; Deut. 12:16, 23, 24; 15:23). See also I Sam. 14:32; Ezek. 33:25; Acts 15:29. The prohibition is grounded upon the facts that the blood is the physical seat of animal life, and that the blood makes atonement for the soul. It was the life element poured out before God instead of the life of the soul that sinned. Such would be the thoughts of those who strove among themselves as to what His words could mean.

(54) Whoso eateth my flesh, and drinketh my blood.—The thought advances from the negative to the positive. The thought advances, too, from the "ye" of those immediately addressed to the "whoso," which has no limit but the fulfillment of the condition.

And I will raise him up at the last day.—The thought of the eternal life, which is the present possession of the spirit in communion with God, leads on once again to the fuller expansion of that life in the final victory over death. (Comp. verses 40, 44.)

(56) Dwelleth in me, and in him.—Comp. 14:2-23; 15:4; 17:23; I John 3:24; 4:16. It is one of those deeper thoughts which meet us only in the words of the beloved disciple. The union which results from the communication of life is not temporary, but is one that remains. By virture of it we abide in Christ, and He in us.

(59) As he taught in Capernaum.—The synagogue in this discourse was a gift to the Jews by a devout Gentile (Luke 7:5), and as such, of greater architectural beauty than was common among Galilean synagogues.

(60) Many therefore of his disciples—i.e., of the disciples in the wider sense. From verse 64, the apostles would seem to be included in the more general designation. In verse 67 they are separately addressed.

This is an hard saying; who can hear it?—i.e., not hard to be understood, but hard to hear, a stumblingblock in the way of their faith. For the word itself, comp. Matt. 25:24.

(62) John, in his own narrative, nowhere mentions the fact of the Ascension, nor does he in any way refer to it. That he could write these words without doing so is an assurance of his own knowledge of the glorious sequel of the Resurrection, and of its unquestioned acceptance in the Church.

(63) It is the spirit that quickeneth.— These words are immediately connected with the thought of the Ascension, which was to precede the gift of the Spirit. (Comp. 7:39; 16:7). We find in them, therefore, a deeper meaning than the ordinary one that His teaching is to be not carnally but spiritually understood. They think of a physical eating of His flesh, and this offends them; but what if they, who have thought of bread descending from heaven, see His body ascending into heaven? They will know then that He cannot have meant this. And the Descent of the Spirit will follow the Ascension of the Son, and men full of the Holy Spirit will have brought to their remembrance all these words (14:26), and they will then know what is the true feeding on Him.

(65) No man can come unto me.—This defection did not surprise Him. He already had used words which anticipated it. (Comp. notes on verses 37, 44.)

(69) The faith which first burned in the hearts of the Twelve has passed into the calm certainty of settled knowledge. The almost certain reading here is, "Thou art the Holy One of God." Like Messiah, or Christ, the title marks out the consecration to His work. (Comp. John 10:30; Eph. 2:20; Rev. 3:7.) This is the second confession of Peter, coming between those of Matt. 14:33 and 16:16 (see notes).

(70) One of you is a devil.—There was the same choice for all, made from their fitness and promise for the work for which all were chosen. There may be mystery connected with this life of Judas which none of us can understand; there are certainly warnings connected with it which none of us can refuse to heed. (See notes on Acts 1:16-25.)

(71) Judas Iscariot the son of Simon.— See notes on Matt. 10:4.

7

(1) After these things . . .—It would have been natural for Him to have gone up to the Passover of that year (6:4), but He did not do so because of the open hostility of the Jews. He continued his sojourn in Galilee. (See notes on Matt. 15-18.)

(2) The Jews' feast of tabernacles.—This began on "the fifteenth day of the seventh month" (Lev. 23:34), i.e., the 15th of Tishri (September). The interval from Passover to Tabernacles is about five months. The feast continued for seven days, during which all true Israelites dwelt in booths, in remembrance of their dwelling in tabernacles when they came out of the land of Egypt. Like the Feast of Unleavened Bread (Passover) and the Feast of Harvest (Pentecost), this Feast of In-gathering was one of the "three times in the year" when every male Jew was required to appear before the Lord God (Exod. 23:14). Josephus speaks of it as the holiest and greatest of the feasts. It was at once a thankful memorial of the national deliverance, and a yearly rejoicing at the close of each succeeding harvest (Deut. 16:13-16).

(3) His brethren . . .—See note on Matt. 13:55. They are excluded here by their own words from the band of disciples, as they are by John's from the believers (verse 5), and inferentially (verse 7) by the words of Christ Himself from the Twelve. His brethren, who have seen these works and do not believe, challenge Him to an open demonstration of them. There is another great feast at hand, and His disciples from parts will be at Jerusalem, where the rulers will test His claims. If He is the Messiah, no conspiracy to kill Him can prevail; and if these works are really divine, let the great body of disciples see them, and amid the joyous feast, and in the royal city, proclaim Him king.

(5) For neither did his brethren believe.— Even His brethren did not at this time believe Him to be the Messiah. That they are found in the Upper Room in Acts 1 is one of the striking instances of the hardened ground of human hearts passing into the fruitful ground receptive of the seed, as the case of Judas at the close of chap. 6 is an instance of the opposite.

(6) My time is not yet come.—See note on 2:4.

(8) I go not up yet unto this feast.—He is not going up unto the feast in the sense in which they intended—openly, with the usual caravan from Galilee. Another going up publicly, as they intended, and with an issue the dark presages of which now crowd upon Him, is present to His mind. The time is coming, but it has not yet full come. (See note on Luke 9:51.)

(9) He abode still in Galilee.—We find Him in Jerusalem between the 16th and 20th of Tishri (verse 14); He could not therefore have remained behind them more than three or four days. We have no record of any companion with Him until 9:2. If

John returned to Jerusalem after the discourse at Capernaum, we have an explanation of the brevity with which he treats the period between Passover and Tabernacles.

(10) Not openly, but as it were in secret— i.e., not with the usual company. Judging from His practice at another time (4:4), He would go through Samaria, while the caravan would go on the eastern side of the Jordan.

(15) How knoweth this man letters?— Their hostile spirit is seen in that at which they marvel. It is not the substance of His teaching that excites their attention, but the fact that He who never has been technically trained as a rabbi is acquainted with the literature of the schools.

(17) If any man will do his will, he shall know of the doctrine.—The teaching which is His in relation to them is not His of original source (verse 16). This human will to do the divine will is the condition of knowing it. Those who heard these words would naturally understand them of the divine will expressed in the Law and the Prophets (verse 19), but they include the will of God revealed to all men and in all times. The "any man" of Christ's own words excludes none from its reach.

(19) Did not Moses ... ?—They had the Law, which they all professed to accept, and yet no one kept it (5:45-47). Moses had commanded that the Law should be read in every Sabbatical year at this festival (Deut. 31:10); and there is good reason for believing that the current year was a Sabbatical year. The first portion of the Law which it was customary to read was Deut. 1:1-6:3. Within this section (5:17) came the command, "Thou shalt not kill." They were, then, in their persecution of Him (5:18), breaking the Law, of which their presence at the feast was a professed obedience.

(21) I have done one work—i.e., the one conspicuous work of healing the infirm man on the Sabbath day, which He did at His last visit to Jerusalem. There are references to other works in 2:23; 10:32.

(22-24) If circumcision be lawful on the Sabbath, much more is it lawful to restore the whole man.

(24) There was yet another precept of Moses which these judges were forgetting, though it, too, formed part of the first section of the Law read at Tabernacles (Deut. 1:16, 17). Let them who profess to judge Him by the Law obey it, and form a just and honest opinion, and not be biased by the appearance of a mere technicality.

(27) Howbeit we know this man.—They at once supply a corrective answer to their own question. They know this Man: He is the carpenter's Son. God's Anointed living among them as a man, with mother, and brothers, and sisters? This cannot be!

(28) Then cried Jesus in the temple as he taught.—The word rendered "cried" implies always an elevation of voice answering to the intensity of the speaker's feeling. (Comp. 1:15; 7:37; 12:44.) Here this feeling has been roused by another instance of their misapprehension because they think of the outward appearance only, and therefore do not grasp the inner truth of His having been sent from God (verse 29).

(30) The persons who sought to take Him are the members of the Sanhedrin. The people are mentioned in contrast in verse 31. For the present their efforts are confined to plots. That the hour was not yet come was not the immediate cause which influenced those who desired, but dared not, to lay hands upon Him. Verse 31 points out that there was a division in the multitude (comp. verses 43 and 44), and in the uncertainty of what the consequences may be, no one was bold enough to take the decisive step. But if not the immediate cause, the writer regards it as the primary cause. (See note on 2:4.)

(32, 33) The Pharisees see that faith in Him is spreading among the multitude, and that there is no time to be lost. They hastily call together the Sanhedrin, and the chief priests, who were for the most part Sadducees, join with them in an official resolve to take Him by force. Their action is the first attempt so to take Him. It brings to His mind the thought that the end is at hand. But a little while more, and the hour will have come. The manifestation of God's love to man then will be completed in its crowning sacrifice, and when the work of His mission is completed, He will return to Him who sent Him. Their questions (verses 35, 36) are but another instance of their total want of power to read any meaning which does not lie upon the surface.

(35) The abstract word "dispersion" is used like "the circumcision" as a comprehensive title for the individuals included in it. These were the Jews who did not dwell within the limits of the Holy Land, but spreading from the three chief centers of Babylonia, Egypt, and Syria, were found in every part of the civilized world. The Babylonian Diaspora owed its origin to the vast number of exiles who preferred to remain in the positions they had acquired for themselves in their new homes, and did not return to Palestine after the Captivity. They were by far the greater part of the nation, and were scattered through the whole extent of the Persian empire. The Egyptian Diaspora was greatly increased in number under Alexander the Great and his successors (Jos. **Ant.** 16:7, §2). Yet much less numerous than their brethren of Babylonia, they have, through their contact with Western thought and the Greek language, left a deeper and wider influence on subsequent ages. To them we owe the LXX translation of the Old Testament Scriptures and the Alexandrian school of Jewish philosophers, two of the most important influences which first prepared the way for, and afterward molded the forms of, Christianity. The Syrian Diaspora is traced by Josephus (**Ant.** 7:3, §1) to the conquests of Seleucus Nicator (300 B.C.). Under the presecution of Antiochus Epiphanes, they spread over a wider area, including the whole of Asia Minor, and then to the islands and mainland of Greece. It was less numerous than either that of Babylonia or Egypt, but the synagogues of this Diaspora formed the connecting links between the older and the newer revelation, and were the first buildings in which Jesus was preached as the Messiah.

But though thus scattered abroad, the Jews of the Diaspora regarded Jerusalem as the common religious center and maintained a close communion with the spiritual authorities who dwelt there. They sent liberal offerings to the Temple, were represented by numerous synagogues in the city, and flocked in large numbers to the chief festivals. (Comp. notes on Acts 2:9-11.) The Diaspora, then, was a network of Judaism, spreading to every place of intellectual or commercial importance, and linking it to Jerusalem, and a means by which the teaching of the Old Testament was made familiarly known, even in the cities of the Gentiles (Acts 15:21).

(37) In the last day, that great day of the feast.—The words commanding the observance in Deut. 16:13; Num. 29:12, mention only seven days; but this latter passage is followed in verse 35 by a reference to the solemn assembly on the eighth day (comp. Lev. 23:35, 36, 39; Neh. 8:18). Later the eight days of the festival are certainly spoken of as in the Talmud, II Macc. 10:6, and Jos. **Ant.** 3:10, §4. The best authorities are for the most part agreed that it was the

eighth day, i.e., the 22nd of Tishri, to which reference here is made.

Jesus stood and cried.—See note on verse 28.

If any man thirst, let him come unto me, and drink.—These words were almost certainly suggested by part of the ritual of the festival, which consisted in a solemn procession with music, and headed by a priest, which went on each morning from the Temple to the pool of Siloam, where the priest filled a golden vase (in size about one quart) with water and carried it to the Temple amid the joyful cries of the people. He then poured it out on the western side of the altar of burnt-offering, while another priest poured a drink-offering of wine, at the same time, on the eastern side of the altar, and the people during this act chanted the words of "the Hallel," Pss. 113-118. The current rabbinical interpretation of the symbolism connected it with the gift of the latter rain, which was at this season, and also with the gift of the Holy Spirit.

(38) He that believeth on me . . .—This is an advance on the thought of verse 37. That represented the satisfaction of the individual mind; this teaches the fuller truth that every one in living communion with Christ becomes himself the center of spiritual influence. No spirit grasps a great truth which satisfies its own yearnings, as the waters of the fountain quench physical thirst, without longing to send it forth to others who are seeking what he himself had sought. There is in him a river whose waters no barrier can confine. It is the link which binds men together and makes the life of every Christian approach the life of Christ, for he lives not for himself but for the world.

The exact words, "Out of his belly shall flow rivers of living water," are not found in any part of the canonical Scriptures of the Old Testament, and yet Christ Himself utters them with the formula of quotation. It may be that the words which our Lord actually uttered in the current language of Jerusalem were nearer to the words of some passage in the Old Testament than they seem to be in the Greek form in which John has preserved them to us.

(39) The word "given" is omitted in nearly all MSS except the Vatican. "Holy" before Ghost also is probably an insertion. These are additions of copyists who were anxious to preserve from all possibility of misinterpretation the doctrine concerning the Holy Spirit. This doctrine is more full expounded in chaps. 14-16 (see notes).

(40) Of a truth this is the prophet—i.e., the Prophet foretold by Moses in Deut. 18:15.

(42) Hath not the scripture said . . .—Comp. the prophecies in Mic. 5:1, 2; Isa. 11:1; Jer. 23:5, and the history in I Sam. 16.

(48) The rulers were the Sanhedrin, among whose official duties it was to prevent the introduction of false doctrines. (Comp. verses 32, 45; see note on 1:19.) "The Pharisees" were the orthodox party of the day, and they are the persons who ask the question. The matter was to be decided by authority, and not by truth. The pride of certainty that no one in a position of power or authority had believed on Jesus prompted the inquiry.

(50) He that came to Jesus by night.—See note on 3:2.

Being one of them contains the answer to their question, "Hath any of the rulers or of the Pharisees believed on him?" (verse 48).

(52) Art thou also of Galilee?—They imply that Nicodemus could not have asked a question which claimed for Jesus the simple justice of the Law itself, without being, like Him, a Galilean.

Search, and look: for out of Galilee ariseth no prophet.—The Sanhedrin, in their zeal to press their foregone conclusion that Jesus is not a prophet, are not bound by strict accuracy (comp. II Kings 14:25); and it is not unlikely that, in the general contempt of Judeans for Galilee, this assertion had become a by-word, especially with men with so little of the historical sense as the later rabbis. As compared with Judaea, it was true that Galilee was not a country of prophets.

(53) The section which follows (7:53-8:11) is one of the most striking instances of an undoubted addition to the original text of the gospel narratives. We believe that it belongs to the apostolic age, and preserves to us the record of an incident in the life of our Lord, but that it has not come to us from the pen of John.

8

(1) It is an instructive example of the way in which the artificial division into chapters often mars the sense, that one verse of this section is found at the close of the last chapter, and the remainder in this.

Jesus went unto the mount of Olives.—The Mount of Olives is nowhere mentioned by John. In 18:1 he describes the locality, but without this name (see note).

(5) Now Moses in the law commanded us, that such should be stoned.—Comp. Deut. 22:23, 24, which was the only case for which stoning was specified as a punishment. It would be a case of rare occurrence, and perhaps for this reason one on which the opinions of later rabbis were divided. Strangulation was regarded as the punishment intended when no other was specified.

But what sayest thou?—The question is, like that about the tribute money (see note on Matt. 22:17), a snare in which they hope to take Him, whatever answer He gives.

(6) The original has the imperfect of the continued action, pointing to the narrator's vivid remembrance of the scene. What precise meaning we are to attach to this action is uncertain. Any inquiry as to what He wrote is excluded by the fact that the narrative would certainly have recorded it had it been known, and though writing on sand was practiced in the rabbinic schools, this writing was on the pavement of the Temple (verse 2). We have to seek the meaning, then, in the symbolism of the action, remembering that the teaching by action and gesture, common everywhere, always has been especially common in the East. It seems that He deprecated the office of judge which they wished to impose on Him, and chose this method of intimating that He took no interest in what they were saying. Such was a common method of signifying intentional disregard.

(7) He that is without sin among you.—The word rendered "without sin," frequent in the classical writers but found in this place only in the New Testament, takes here a special meaning from the context, and is to be understood of the class of sins of which her sin was an instance. They who ask this question about the seventh commandment were themselves breaking the sixth and the ninth. Our Lord does not lay down sinlessness as the necessary condition of fitness for taking part in the punishment of guilt. This would be to nullify law, for there could be then no human executive power. He is not speaking in a case brought before the appointed tribunal, but in a case where men assume to themselves the position of judges of another's guilt.

Let him first cast a stone at her.—This was the duty of the witnesses. We must not take the words to express permission only; it is an imperative, expressing command.

(8) And wrote on the ground.—The repeated action repeats His determination to avoid the office of judge. He has answered them, and He leaves His answer to do its work. There is a law written in their hearts, and this, while He now writes on the ground, is convicting them.

There is a strange addition at the end of the verse in one of the older MSS of this section, showing how men have tried to give a definite meaning to the action of writing. It reads, "and wrote on the ground the sin of each one of them."

(11) Neither do I condemn thee: go, and sin no more.—His words must have come to her as words of mercy in contrast to the angry words of those who dragged her before Him. He does not condemn her, and yet by these words she must have been condemned more truly than by any words of accuser. He does not condemn her; and yet the very words which bid her go are the condemnation of her sin. It is a mark of truthfulness that the narrative tells us no more. It has not the completeness of an apocryphal story. She passed from His presence as her accusers had before. What came afterward to her and to them we cannot know. But the lessons are patent, and remain to condemn every human judgment of another's sin; to condemn every sin in our own lives; to declare to every sinner the forgiveness which does not condemn.

(12) I am the light of the world.— Omitting the inserted section, this verse immediately follows 7:52, but the words mark an interval of several hours. Once again we find this mold in which the truth shapes itself, in the ritual of the Feast of Tabernacles. On each of five nights there was an illumination in the court of the Temple to celebrate the "Rejoicing of the Water-Drawing." Four large golden candelabra shed their light through the whole city. Then there was dancing, singing, and music, which was continued through the night, until at daybreak the procession to the Pool of Siloam was formed. Once again, too, the ritual of the Feast of Tabernacles is a memorial of the wilderness life. As the water-drawing was bound up with thoughts of the water given in abundance to those dying of thirst, so this illumination was bound up with thoughts of the pillar of fire which was the guide of those who walked in darkness.

But shall have the light of life.—He who follows Christ not only has a light which guides his feet, but through participation in the Messianic life he actually possesses that light in himself. He is no more dead, but has eternal life.

(15) Ye judge after the flesh; I judge no man.—The origin of this thought of judgment arises from verse 13. The statement of the Pharisees was a condemnatory judgment based upon appearances. (Comp. note on 7:24.) They looked at the form of human flesh, and declared His witness false. Had they listened to the words He spoke, and judged according to their spiritual meaning, they would have heard the voice of the Messiah and have seen the Light of the world.

(16) I and the Father that sent me.— Comp. 5:30. Here, as there, He identifies every act of judgment with the eternal and unchangeable truth of the Father.

(17) It is also written in your law.—He now proceeds to show again that the technical requirement of the Law was satisfied by His witness. (Comp. the parallel reference to the Law in 10:34; 15:25.)

That the testimony of two men is true.— See Deut. 17:6; 19:15; comp. note on Matt. 18:16. The requirement of the Law would be satisfied with the evidence of two men; He has the witness of two Persons, but each is divine.

(20) These words spake Jesus in the treasury.—See note on Mark 12:41. This notice of place is interesting in many ways. The court of the women was one of the most public places in the Temple area. He taught, then, openly and fearlessly. The chamber in which the Sanhedrin held their session was between the court of the women and that of the men. The court of the women, moreover, was the spot where the great candelabra stood. (See note on verse 12.)

(21) The whole of the teaching and work which is included between 7:37 and 10:21 probably is to be placed on the last and great day of the feast (see 9:14). The persons addressed are the people assembled around Him in the Temple. Some of the officials take part in the discussion, for it is "the Jews" who reply in the next verse. There are thus two currents of thought and feeling. One is found in the honest hearts of the untutored multitude; the other is found in the priests and rulers, to whom the people are in intellectual and moral bondage.

It was the last day of the feast, and now its closing hours have come. That thronging multitude would be, before the close of another day, leaving Jerusalem to spread itself through all the extent of Palestine and the Dispersion. Before another Feast of Tabernacles He will, in a deeper sense, be going away. The result of the seeking and not finding is declared in the sadness of its fatal issue. (Comp. verse 24.)

(22) Comp. note on 7:35. Then they had asked in scorn if He would go to the Dispersion and teach the heathen? If so, they certainly could not follow Him. Here there is the same scorn. If He intends to go to Hades, He indeed will be beyond their reach. They expect to go to Abraham's bosom; between Him and them there will be the great gulf which no one can pass. (Comp. notes on Luke 16:22-26.)

(23) There is indeed a gulf which they cannot pass, but it is not that between souls in Abraham's bosom and souls in Hades. It is the gulf between heaven and earth. This He brings out in two pairs of antithetic clauses.

(25) Then said they unto him, Who art thou?—He had said, "I am" (verse 24); but they do not understand the words to be a divine name. Long before this time the name formed from these words, and which is now usually, but wrongly, read "Jehovah," had been regarded as too sacred to be uttered. They appear to take the sentence as though it were incomplete. As in verse 19 they attempt to draw from Him some statement which may be made the ground of a technical charge; but this He again avoids.

(26) And I speak to the world those things which I have heard of him.—It is the truth brought into and announced in the world, and which was heard during the pre-incarnate life with the Father. (Comp. verses 28, 38.)

(27) These men did not perceive that the Sender and the Father are one. Because of this Jesus proceeded to declare more fully that every act He did was done in the Father, that every word He spoke was taught by the Father, and that in every event of His life the Father was present.

(28) When ye have lifted up the Son of man.—See notes on 3:14; 6:62; 12:32, 34.) Both the Crucifixion and Ascension are implied here. Now, for the first time, they are marked out as the instruments of the Crucifixion (comp. Acts 3:15), and therefore the means by which He will return to His Father's throne.

(30) Many believed on him.—Those who believe are of the rulers ("those Jews," verse 31). They are convinced by the power of His words that He is divine. Where was

priest or rabbi who could appeal to the spotless purity of a life?

(31) Then are ye my disciples indeed.— He who reads the heart has no confidence in a momentary conviction which will not stand the test of true discipleship and all that this includes. (Comp. 2:23-25; 6:66.)

(32) And ye shall know the truth.—These Jews professed to know the truth, and to be the official expounders of it. They had yet to learn that truth was not only a system, but also a power; not only something to be written or spoken, but also something to be felt and lived. If they abide in His word, they will indeed be His disciples; living the life of truth, they will gain perception of truth.

And the truth shall make you free.— Here, as in 17:17, truth and holiness are spoken of as correlative. Sin is the bondage of the powers of the soul, and this bondage is willed because the soul does not see its fearful evil. When it perceives the truth, there comes to it a tower which rouses it and strengthens it to break the fetters by which it had been bound. Freedom from the Roman rule was one of the national hopes bound up with Messiah's Advent. There is indeed a freedom from a more crushing foe than the legions of Rome.

(33) They answered him—i.e., the Jews who had believed in Him. Note our Lord's own warning words in verse 31. He has tested their faith, and they fail in the first steps of discipleship. Their pride misinterprets His words, and expresses itself in a boast which passes the limits of historical truth.

(34) Committeth sin.—The Greek word is a present participle, expressing the continuance of the deeds of sin. It means, not simply the committing individual sins, from which no man is free, but the state of life which is sinful—the state which is opposed to doing the will of the Father. The truth is taught in the generality of a well-known maxim, but it has for them a special application. They claimed to be Abraham's seed, and therefore free; let their lives decide the question of their freedom. (Comp. Rom. 6:20; II Pet. 2:19.)

(35) The Son abideth ever.—The use of the capital in this verse is misleading. The clause is the expression of a legal maxim holding good for all servants and for all sons, but here specially applied to the sonship in Abraham's household. Here the thought is that if they were really the children of Abraham, they would be of Abra-

825

ham's spiritual nature, abiding in his home, and inheriting the promises made to him. They had not continued in the spiritual freedom of sons, but had departed from the house and had become, spiritually, bondmen.

(36) If the Son therefore shall make you free.—If they will enter into spiritual union with Him, and **abide** in this new spiritual relation, it will make them new creatures, freed from sin by the power of truth. The Son of the divine household will make them free, and in Him they will become members of the great family of God Himself.

Ye shall be free indeed.—Or, "ye shall be free in reality." They claimed political freedom, but they were in reality the subjects of Rome; they claimed religious freedom, but they were in reality the slaves to the letter; they claimed moral freedom, but they were in reality the bondmen of sin. The freedom which the Son proclaimed was in reality freedom, for it was the freedom of their true life delivered from the thraldom of sin and brought into union with God. All through this context the thoughts pass unbidden to the teaching of Paul, the great apostle of freedom.

(39) If ye were Abraham's children, ye would do the works of Abraham.—They are the physical seed of the patriarch, but they are not the ethical children, for the true child would bear the moral impress of the father which would be seen in his works. The distinction between "seed" and "children" is another instance of an idea which meets us in this section and was developed in the writings of Paul.

(40) The crime of seeking to kill Him is aggravated by the fact that He was One who came to tell them truth, and that from God. They seek to destroy the human life which for the sake of humanity He has assumed. The whole course of patriarchal life was directly opposed to the spirit of those who claim to be his children.

(41) Ye do the deeds of your father.—They did the works of that father who is now more clearly pointed out but still not named (see verse 44). Before, when he was referred to (verse 38), they could answer that Abraham was their father; but their works prove that they are not the true children of Abraham (verses 39, 40). They see that a spiritual father is intended, and they will claim God as their Father.

(44) Ye are of your father the devil.—The father who has been referred to in verses 38 and 41 is now definitely named. The refer-

ence to the murderer is suggested here by the fact that the Jews had been seeking to kill our Lord (verse 40). They are true to the nature which their father the devil had from the beginning. (See Rom. 5:12.)

(46) Which of you convinceth me of sin?—He appeals to their knowledge of His sinless life, as in verse 29 He asserted His own knowledge of entire conformity to His Father's will. It is an appeal that spotless purity alone could make, and is His own testimony uttered in the dignity of certain knowledge.

(48) Say we not well that thou art a Samaritan, and hast a devil?—There is no instance given of the term "Samaritan" being applied to our Lord, but the term itself is frequently used by the rabbis as one of opprobrium. The charge of being a Samaritan He passes over. His words soon after taught that a Samaritan may be more truly the child of God than priest or Levite is. (Comp. Luke 10:25-37; 17:16.) The statement that He is possessed by an evil power from the spirit world He denies.

(53) Whom makest thou thyself?—"If Abraham, who received God's covenant, himself died, and if the prophets, who uttered the oracles of God, themselves died, what kind of person dost Thou assert Thyself to be that Thy word shall deliver men from death?"

(56) Your father Abraham rejoiced to see my day.—He now contrasts the exultation of him whom they claimed as father, when he saw from afar the Messianic advent, with their rejection of the Messiah who is actually among them. Abraham realized the fullness of the promises made to him, and believed in the Lord that the blessing should be fulfilled to his seed. He, too, had kept God's word, and in the true sense had not seen death (see Gen. 15:1-6; 22:18).

(57) Thou art not yet fifty years old.—"Fifty years" was the period of full manhood (Num. 4:3, 39; 8:24.) This is expressed in round numbers, and there is no care to be more exact in comparison with the two thousand years which had passed since the close of Abraham's earthly life. The thought is, "Thou art still a young man, and hast thou seen Abraham who died twenty centuries ago?"

(58) Before Abraham was, I am.—Here they ask in wonder, mixed with scorn, if He was coeval with Abraham. The answer is that Abraham, like all men, came into being. There was a time when he was not. But there was never a time when the Son of

God was not. In the time before Abraham, in the eternity before time (1:1), He still was. No word which expresses becoming can be used of His existence. He is the I AM, present equally in the human "was," "is," and "is to come."

(59) **Then took they up stones to cast at him.**—At last the meaning of His words flashes upon them. They had heard this I AM before (verse 24) without perceiving that in it He applied to Himself the name Jehovah. Now there is no room for doubt. They will not acknowledge the claim, but they feel that He has made it. They have heard the fearful words which seemed to them as blasphemy, and they take up the stones which are at hand for the rebuilding of the Temple, in which they are, to cast at the Lord of the Temple.

9

(1) **And as Jesus passed by.**—As He was leaving the Temple to escape the fury of His enemies who had taken up stones to cast at Him, and was passing by the place where the blind man was, His eye fell upon him. The day was the Sabbath of the preceding discourse, now drawing to its close. The place was probably some spot near the Temple, perhaps one of its gates. Beggars were placed near these gates to ask alms (Acts 3:2), and this man was well known as one who sat and begged (verse 8).

A man which was blind from his birth.—The fact was well known, and probably was publicly proclaimed by the man himself or his parents (verse 20) as an aggravation of his misery and as a plea for the alms of passers-by. Of the six miracles connected with blindness which are recorded in the gospels, this is the only case described as blindness from birth.

(3) **Jesus answered, Neither hath this man sinned, nor his parents.**—The disciples' question (verse 2) sought to establish a connection between the suffering and some definite act of sin. The answer asserts that no such connection exists, and our Lord's words remain a warning against the spirit of judging other men's lives, and tracing in the misfortunes and sorrows which they have to bear the results of individual sin or the proof of divine displeasure. There is a chain connecting the sin of humanity and its woe, but the links are not traceable by the human eye. In the Providence of God vicarious suffering is often the noble lot of

the noblest members of our race. No burden of human sorrow was ever so great as that borne by Him who knew no human sin.

But that the works of God should be made manifest in him.—They had sought to trace back the result of sin which they saw before them to a definite cause. He will trace it back to the region of the divine counsel, where purpose and result are one. Evil is the result of the choice exercised by freedom, and without freedom goodness could not be virtue. Permitted by God, it is yet overruled by Him. It has borne its fearful fruit in the death and curse of humanity, but its works have led to the manifestation of the works of God in the divine plan of redemption.

(4) **I must work the works of him that sent me, while it is day.**—If we are right in placing the whole section from 7:37-10:21 on the same great day of the Feast, then this work must have come near the close of the day. The sun sinking to the west may have reminded them that the day was passing away, and that the night was approaching. He was reminded of the day of life, and the night of death.

(6) **And he anointed the eyes of the blind man with the clay.**—Our Lord here made use of means which, in part at least, were natural, and found their place in the ordinary prescriptions of the day. (Comp. Pliny, Tacitus, and Suetonius.) Physicians had applied such means commonly to cases of post-natal blindness, but congenital blindness always had been regarded as incurable, and no instance to the contrary ever had been heard of (verse 32). The Great Physician, then, by using the ordinary means, will teach men that the healing powers of nature are His gracious gift, and that they are increased at the Giver's will.

Another interpretation sees in the use of clay a symbolism which is to be traced to the first Creation, when man was formed from the dust of the earth. We find this as early as Irenaeus, and it may well, therefore, represent an oral explanation, going back to the days of the evangelist himself. The thought would be that our Lord will here exercise the same creative power as that which made man, and will complete, by the gift of sight, this man, who had heretofore been maimed and without the chief organ of sense.

See notes on Matt. 9:29; Mark 7:33; 8:23. In each case the loss of a channel of communication between the individual man and the outer world is compensated by some special means which may help to assure him of the presence of the true Healer, and may furnish a foundation for his faith and hope. The means is always chiefly moral, preparing the sufferer a mental condition which can receive the gift of healing. The physical gift is itself regarded as a stage in the spiritual education.

(7) Go, wash in the pool of Siloam.—See notes on 5:2; Luke 13:4. The attempt to show in the waters of Siloam an ordinary remedial agent must be abandoned, at least as far as regards blindness. It is a further stage in his spiritual education. It is a demand on the faith which realizes the presence of the Power to heal. The place is chosen, perhaps, as a well-known spot, or as one at some little distance, so as to afford time for reflection and a test for obedience. The pool of Siloam was, too, bound up with all the religious feelings of the Feast of Tabernacles. (See notes on 7:37-39.)

(13) They brought to the Pharisees.— Their question in the previous verse, and the fact stated in the following verse, seem to indicate that they did this in the spirit of opposition to our Lord. They may have been influenced also, as the parents were, by the agreement of the Jews to excommunicate any who should confess Christ (verse 22). By the term "Pharisees" we are not to understand the Sanhedrin, but a body of the leading Pharisees who were the most bitter foes of Christ, and who seem at this time to have formed practically a permanent committee of the Sanhedrin, always ready to take counsel or action against Him.

(14) And it was the sabbath day—i.e., most probably, the last day, that great day of the feast of 7:37. This is mentioned as a servile work which contravened the Sabbath law. The anointing the eyes with spittle on the Sabbath especially was forbidden by the decrees of the rabbis. They held that no work of healing might be performed on the Sabbath except in cases of immediate danger.

(16) This man is not of God, because he keepeth not the sabbath day.—Here the truth of the miracle is granted, but it is urged that the power by which it is wrought cannot be of God, because it was exercised on the Sabbath day. The inference is that it was done by the influence of the power of evil.

Others said, How can a man that is a sinner do such miracles?—This question is asked by the better party among the Phar-

isees, represented by Nicodemus and Joseph of Arimathaea, and perhaps by Gamaliel. They see the inference implied in the earlier question, and appeal to the nature of the miracles wrought.

(17) He is a prophet.—The education of the man has been doing its work. He is convinced that the power which has healed him is direct from God, and that the person who has exercised it is a messenger from God. His words, uttered in the brevity and calmness of clear conviction, are the direct negative to the statement of the Pharisees. Even in the language of the ordinary people, the word "prophet" did not mean simply a predictor of events in the future, but one who was as the representative of God— not only a "fore-teller" but also a "forth-teller," declaring God's truth.

(18) Until they called the parents.—After the Jews have done so, they can doubt the fact no longer (verse 26). But they hoped that the parents would from fear (verse 22) have given an answer which would have enabled them to deny the identity of person or the fact of congenital blindness.

(22) For the Jews had agreed already.— The word rendered "agreed" occurs again in the New Testament only twice. It expresses the covenant made with Judas (Luke 22:5) and the agreement of the Jews to kill Paul (Acts 23:20).

(29) We know that God spake unto Moses.—They would press here the authority of the great Lawgiver, which to every Israelite was final. They will not, therefore, accept this Man as a prophet. Their words have tacit reference also to the fact that His works were in their eyes a transgression of the Mosaic law. He, it is implied, by confessing Jesus to be a prophet, was practically denying the authority of Moses.

(31) Now we know that God heareth not sinners.—What they should have known, but asserted that they did not, he proceeds to declare. The argument of this and the two following verses may be stated in syllogistic form: (1) God does not hear sinners, but only those who worship Him and do His will. (2) That God hears this Man is certain, for such a miracle could be performed only by divine power. (3) This Man, therefore is not a sinner, but is from God.

(32) The eyes of one that was born blind.— The man expresses what was simply true, that no science or skill had at that time been equal to the removal of blindness which had accompanied birth.

**(34) Their reproach now takes the most

malignant form, and shrinks not from pressing the calamity of his birth as the mark of special sin. "Thou didst come into the world bearing the curse of God upon thy face. Dost thou, marked more than is the common lot of man by sin, teach **us**, who are the authorized teachers and expositors of the truth?"

(35) The man had been cast out. Our Lord hears of this, and knows it is because of his bold confession that He was a prophet. He will lead him from that confession to a higher one. He marks him out as distinct from others, and asks a question which is meant by its form to lead him to an affirmative answer. Although our Lord does not usually apply the title "Son of God" to Himself, He constantly asserts the truth which it expresses. (Comp. e.g., in this gospel, chaps. 5, 7, and 8.)

(38) And he said, Lord, I believe.—The title is repeated from verse 36 (where it should be rendered "Sir"), but now with the deeper meaning. The spiritual education has led him step by step from "the Man that is called Jesus" (verse 11) to the confession that He is "a prophet" (verse 17), and that He is "of God" (verse 33), to the belief that He is the Messiah.

And he worshipped him.—The act of adoration is the necessary expression of his faith in the Son of God, although we may not think that he has yet earned all that this term includes. John uses the word here rendered "worshipped" only when speaking of the worship of God (Comp. 4:20-24; 12:20.)

(39) For judgment I am come into this world.—See notes on 3:17-19; 12:37-50.

(41) Their true place is among those who were spiritually blind and were unconscious of it. As long as they think that they see, there is no ground for hope. (Comp. Matt. 9:12, 13.) The assertion of spiritual knowledge and independence was the original cause of sin (Gen. 3:4); and while spiritual pride exists, sin cannot cease.

10

(1) Verily, verily, I say unto you.—This formula is not used at the beginning of a fresh discourse, but is, in every case, the solemn introduction of some development of our Lord's deeper teaching. (Comp. note on 1:51.) This chapter, then, is part of the teaching begun in 9:35, and arising out of the sign of healing the blind man. This sign is present to their thoughts at the close of the discourse (verse 21).

He that entereth not by the door into the sheepfold.—The special form which the discourse here takes probably was due to the actual presence of sheepfold with the shepherds and their flocks. (See 5:2.) Bethesda was near the "sheepgate," and probably to be identified with a covered portion of the Pool of Siloam. We think of an open fold surrounded by a wall or railing, into which at eventide the shepherds lead their flocks, committing them during the night to the care of an undershepherd, who guards the door. In the morning they knock and the porter opens the door, which has securely been fastened during the night, and each shepherd calls his own sheep, who know his voice and follow him to the pasturage. This truth was bound up with their whole history. The greatest heroes of Israel— Abraham, Jacob, Moses, David—had all been shepherds, and no imagery is more frequent in prophecy or psalm than that drawn from the shepherd's work. (See Ps. 23; Isa. 40:11; Jer. 23:1-4; Ezek. 34; Zech. 11:4-17.)

The same is a thief and a robber.—The former is the petty thief; the latter is the brigand or highwaymen, e.g., Barabbas and the two crucified with our Lord.

(3) To him the porter openeth.—"Doorkeeper" is meant here. There is no necessity to further interpretation of what, in the spiritual fold, corresponds to the office of the porter, whereas the door and the shepherd are successively made the texts of fuller expositions of Christ's own work. But some have interpreted it here, however, of the Holy Spirit, whose special work it is to determine who are shepherds and who sheep, and to call each to the work and position given to him by God.

And he calleth his own sheep by name, and leadeth them out.—Now the sheep of the shepherd's own flock are singled out from the rest, each one by its own name. A mountain shepherd will know a single sheep among hundreds from other flocks, and there is nothing more strange in the sheep being trained to know its own name and its shepherd's voice. We have to think, also, of a close relationship between the owner and his sheep, which were almost part of his family.

(5) And a stranger will they not follow.— The "stranger" is any one other than their own shepherd. The thought is of the flock following the shepherd to the pasture. On the road they would meet other persons whom they would not follow. Some would, as thieves and robbers, seek to lead them away, calling them by their names and imitating their shepherd's cry; but they have, by long usage, gotten to know his voice, and will not follow a stranger.

But will flee from him.—A strange word is a source of alarm to them. With the known tone of the shepherd's voice they have learned to associate protection, guidance, food. His voice recalls these associations, whereas a stranger's voice is something unknown and therefore feared.

(6) This parable spake Jesus unto them.—Better, "this allegory (paroimia)." John nowhere uses the word "parable." The true parable is a story in which the outer facts are kept wholly distinct from the ideal truths that are to be taught, whereas here the form and the idea interpenetrate each other at every point. It is so in the other so-called "parable" in this gospel (chap. 15). Strictly speaking, neither the "Good Shepherd" nor the "True Vine" is a parable. It follows from this, therefore, that the interpretation of every point in the history of the material facts is not always to be pressed.

(7) Then said Jesus unto them again.—They did not understand what Jesus had said before. It is not that a new allegory begins at this place. He spoke in the beginning of the door and of the shepherd (verses 1, 2); He now proceeds to unfold the meaning of both.

(8) All that ever came before me are thieves and robbers.—The Old Testament teachers cannot be meant, because they witnessed to the true door. But there had been growing up since the return from the Captivity, and the close of the Old Testament canon, a priestly caste in the place of the prophetic schools, and these men had been in practice, if not in word, claiming for themselves the position of door to the kingdom of God. There were Hillels and Shammais, heads of parties and of factions, whose word was to their followers as the word of God; there were Pharisees then standing around Him who had solemnly decreed that any one who should confess Him to be the Messiah should be shut out from Temple and from synagogue, and that they themselves would in God's name pronounce a curse upon his head (9:22).

But the sheep did not hear them.—See verses 3-5. What is true of the sheep and the voice of the stranger is true also of man and of every voice which is not of God.

(9) By me if any man enter in.—The thought is parallel to that of the "strait gate" and "narrow way" in Matt. 7:13, 14, and with Paul's thought in Rom. 5:2 and Eph. 2:18. No one can really enter the fold and become a shepherd of the flock who does not seek to devote himself in entire self-sacrifice to the sheep whom he seeks to lead, and to live in unfailing communion with God, whose the sheep are.

He shall be saved.—The words refer primarily to the dangers without the fold from which he will be delivered. But in the wider thought they include the salvation from sin which is in this life to be realized, and is a necessary qualification for the pastor's work.

And shall go in and out, and find pasture.—In the devotion of his service, and in communion with God, he will daily have an increasing knowledge of truths new and old, and the truths which he learns he will give as food for the souls of men.

(10) The thief cometh not, but for to steal.—The description of the thief is opposed to that of the shepherd, who constantly goes in and out and finds pasture. His visits are but rare, and when he comes it is but for his own selfish purposes, and for the ruin of the flock. Each detail of his cruel work is dwelt upon, bringing out in all the baseness of its extent the corresponding spiritual truth.

And that they might have it more abundantly.—The word "more" is an insertion without any authority. It is not that a greater is compared with a less abundance, but that the abundance of life which results through Christ's coming is contrasted with the spiritual wants and death which He came to remove.

(11) I am the good shepherd.—He is the Shepherd who is ideally good, fulfilling every thought of guidance, support, self-sacrifice that had ever gathered around the shepherd's name. No image of Christ has so deeply impressed itself upon the mind of the Church as this. We find it in the earliest Christian literature and in the earliest efforts of Christian art. It comes to us naturally in our hymns and prayers. The pastoral staff is the fit emblem of the bishop's work, and the pastor is the name by which the humble wayside flock thinks of him who in Christ's name is appointed to be their guide.

Giveth his life for the sheep.—This was true of the actual shepherds. (Comp. I Sam. 17:34-37.) That self-sacrifice that would lead the shepherd to risk his own life for that of his flock has its ideal fulfilment in Him who is the Good Shepherd, and will give His life for mankind.

(12) But he that is an hireling.—The Greek word implies a lower position than the household servant. The thought follows from that of the good shepherd who in the time of danger will give his own life for the sheep. The hireling has no interest in the sheep, and cares for them only as far as to secure his own hire. We think here of all persons who from any other motive than love for humanity, and by any other way than the door which is Christ, or by any other call than that of the Holy Spirit, take upon themselves the office of shepherds of the flock. The hour of danger will distinguish between the shepherd and the hireling.

And the wolf catcheth them, and scattereth the sheep.—Under the general image we understand all the spiritual foes which destroy individual souls and rend the Church of Christ. The wolf is the natural enemy of the sheep, and the fit emblem of all evil persons, who are the natural enemies of the sheep of Christ's fold. (Comp. Matt. 7:15; 10:16 Luke 10:3; Acts 20:29.) While "wolves" represent all false teachers and foes to truth, "the wolf" represents him who is the source from which they come. As all shepherds are related to the Good Shepherd, so are all wolves to **the** wolf whose work they do.

(15) This deeper sense of union between the human spirit and Himself, and the wondrous likening of it to the union of Himself and the Father, is present to His mind as the close of His work on earth draws near. Comp. 14:20; 15:10; 17:8, 21. It is bound up with the thought of the love which lays down His own life for them (verses 17, 18).

(16) And other sheep I have, which are not of this fold.—He asserts that among the Gentiles—who are not of the Jewish fold— He already possesses sheep. The Old Testament prophets had foretold this coming of the Gentiles, e.g. Isa. 52:13; 53:10; Mic. 4:2; and it is present to our Lord's mind here as the result of His laying down His life for the sheep. (Comp. 11:52; 12:32.)

And there shall be one fold, and one shepherd.—Better, "There shall become one flock, and one shepherd." It is not uniformity which is promised, but unity. The distinction is not merely one of words, but upon it depends a wide and important truth. It is not unity of fold which is regarded as the future of the Church, but unity of flock. There will be many folds, in many nations, in many ages. But for all Christians there will be one true Shepherd who lays down His life for the sheep.

(17) Therefore doth my Father love me . . .—The Father loves the Son who of His own will gives Himself to die. It is as though the salvation of mankind had called forth a new relation of love between the Father and the Son.

That I might take it again.—This is given as part of the reason of the Father's love. In acts of sacrifice, the fact that that which is lost certainly will be regained seems to us to take away all value from the act; but for Christ the taking again of human life is itself a further sacrifice, and this is necessary for the completion of the Great Shepherd's work. The scattered sheep during the whole of the world's existence are to be gathered in by Him whose continued union with human nature makes Him at once the Shepherd who gives His life for the sheep, and the Door by whom we ever have access to the Father.

(18) No man taketh it from me.—The laying down of the life is absolutely self-determined, and therefore it is the reason of the Father's love. Up to the last moments of life He lays stress on the perfectly voluntary nature of His death.

I have power to lay it down, and I have power to take it again.—It is of His own will that He lays down His life and takes it again; but this, as the whole of the life of the Son, is in moral subordination to the Father. The taking again was under the Father's authority, and was therefore itself the Father's gift.

This commandment have I received of my Father.—He has asserted in fullest terms the entirely voluntary nature of His own sacrifice. He repeats in fullest terms the voluntary subordination of Son to Father, which is based upon equality of nature. Not only was the authority by which He would die and rise again derived from the Father, but both these acts were included in the decree which gave to Him the Messianic work.

(21) Others said, These are not the words of him that hath a devil.—We trace here again the presence of the better party among the Sanhedrin (comp. 9:16). "His words," they would say, "are words of calm teaching. The possession by a demon disorders, frenzies, makes the slave of madness. It is inconsistent with words like these. And surely a devil cannot open the eyes of the blind."

(22) Between the last verse and this there is an interval of time which may be taken roughly as two months. In this interval we may with great probability place the events and teaching contained in Luke 10:1-13:21, with parallels in Matthew.

Although John gives no hint that our Lord had left the neighborhood of Jerusalem, the specific mention of the city implies a return from a distance. "The Feast of the Dedication" was not here a feast in honor of the dedication of Solomon's or Zerubbabel's temple. We know of no annual festival connected with these dedications, and the statement that this feast was "in the winter" makes it almost certain that it was the feast instituted, 164 B.C., by Judas Maccabaeus, in commemoration of the cleansing of the Temple after its profanation by Antiochus Epiphanes (I Macc. 4:52-59). It is called "Chanuca," the Dedication. In this, as in other rejoicings, illumination was a prominent feature, and it was sometimes called the "Feast of Lights." (See **Talmud**, Shabbath 21 b.)

(23) In Solomon's porch.—See notes on Acts 3:11; 5:12.

(25) I told you, and ye believed not.—To have said He was the Messiah would have been to sanction their thought of Him as a temporal prince; to have said that He was not would have been to contradict the essential truth. He refers them, then, to His earlier words and deeds in proof of what He was. (See 5:36.)

(28) Eternal life.—Our Lord's thoughts of "eternal life" are never of the future only. They are a development rather than a simply future existence. We shall live eternally, because we now live spiritually in communion with the Spirit who is Eternal.

And they shall never perish.—The negative is in the strongest form—"They shall by no means perish forever."

Neither shall any man pluck them out of my hand.—Better, "and none shall pluck them . . ." The words should not be limited by the insertion of the word "man." They are to be taken as including every spiritual foe. (Comp. Rom. 8:38, 39.) The words "out of my hand" express alike the strength which protects, guidance which leads, and

comfort which cherishes. Out of this hand none shall pluck; yet we are to bear in mind that the sheep itself may wander from the shepherd's care, and that all the fullness of these promises depends upon the human will, which is included in the first clause, "My sheep hear my voice . . . and they follow me."

(30) I and my Father are one.—These words assert the oneness in power and nature of the Father and the Son. Yet they do more than this, for the Greek word for "one" is neuter, and the thought is not, therefore, of unity of person, but is of unity of essence. "The Son is of one substance with the Father." In the plural "are" there is the assertion of distinctness as against Sabellianism, and in the "one" there is the assertion of co-ordination as against Arianism. The best answer to all attempts to attach any meaning lower than that of the deity of our Lord to these His words is found in the conduct of the Jews themselves (comp. 8:58, 59): they sought to punish by stoning what seemed to them to be blasphemy (verse 33).

(34) Is it not written in your law?—Comp. Ps. 82:6, but the term "Law" is used here in a wide sense for the whole of the Old Testament. The words "ye are gods" are probably to be understood in the Psalm as spoken by God, who sits in judgment on the judges whom He had appointed, and gives the name of "gods" (**Elohim**) as representing Himself.

(36) Whom the Father hath sanctified, and sent into the world.—The tense in the Greek refers to the time of His consecration to His messianic work, and to the Incarnation, which was the beginning of it.

Because I said, I am the Son of God.—The law (Psalm) applied the term "Elohim" (gods) to men representing God. No word of that Scripture could fail to hold good. How much more, therefore, could the term Son of God be applied to Him who was not a man consecrated to any earthly office, but consecrated by God, and sent into the world to represent God to man.

(37) If I do not the works of my Father.—He has met the charge of blasphemy on technical grounds. In this and in verse 38 He advances from that defense to the ultimate test. Whether he is a blasphemer or not depends upon whether He represents God or not, and to prove this He appeals again to the works.

(40) Comp. Matt. 19:1. We think probably of Bethania, to the north of the Sea of

Galilee, on the eastern side of the Jordan, as the place of our Lord's retirement. He sees in all the preceding events the darkness which foreshadows the night, and He retires from the city to visit it no more until the final Passover. The time from Dedication to Passover (December to April) is divided, by the visit to Bethany near Jerusalem, and the raising of Lazarus, into two parts of uncertain duration, one of which is spent in Gaulonitis and the other in Ephraim (11:54).

(41) Although he worked no miracle, John the Baptist's spiritual intuition, in advance of the generation in which he lived, was itself a sign, and all things which he had said about the Messiah had, in the events which had taken place since they had seen Him in that place before, been proved to be true. The witness of the past is linked to that of the present. The enthusiasm which John had kindled still burns.

11

(1) Now a certain man was sick.—This is connected with the preceding narrative to introduce the reason for our Lord's leaving His retirement to go again into the neighborhood of Jerusalem.

Named Lazarus, of Bethany.—See note on Luke 16:20, the solitary instance of a name in our Lord's parables. It is probable that the form in which the truths of the world beyond the grave there took shape was suggested by the incidents which are recorded here. See also note on Matt. 19:16 for the suggestion that this Lazarus may have been identical with the young man who had great possessions. The induction rests upon an enumeration of instances which makes it at least probable in a high degree.

Bethany is a poor village on the eastern slope of the Mount of Olives, about two miles from Jerusalem (verse 18).

The town of Mary and her sister Martha.—See notes on Luke 10:38-42. The younger sister is mentioned here first as the better known from the events related in verse 2. Lazarus was probably younger than his sisters (12:2). The village was known, then, in the circles of the first disciples, as the village of Mary and Martha, by way of distinction from the "Bethany beyond Jordan."

(2) It was that Mary which anointed the Lord.—See notes on Matt. 26:7; Mark 14:3.

John himself relates the anointing in 12:3. There is no sufficient reason for identifying Mary of Bethany with the "woman which was a sinner" (see note on Luke 7:37), or for identifying either with Mary Magdalene.

(4) That the Son of God might be glorified thereby.—The sickness of Lazarus would not indeed issue in death, though it would end in what men call death, and would be the immediate cause leading to the death of the Son of man. The one would be as a sleep from which he would awake; the other should be the glorifying the Son of God, which would issue in the life of the world.

(5) The fact of His abiding two days where He was (verse 6) seems indeed opposed to the thought of His special love for the family. The most probable explanation is that which connects verses 5, 6, and 7 together, and makes the love the motive for going into Judaea again. The word "loved" means the love of chosen friendship. (Comp. 20:2; 21:15.)

(6) The hours of His work were marked out by signs that He alone could read (2:4), but every hour had its work, and every work its hour. It is certain that Lazarus was dead before they set out for Judaea (verse 11), but he was living when the words of verse 4 were spoken. The fact of death may have determined the hour of their departure.

(9) Are there not twelve hours in the day?—They had expressed their fears that danger and death would be the result of going into Judaea. His answer would say that the darkness of the night which they dreaded could not come yet. The natural night would come not until its appointed hour, until the twelve hours of the day had run their course. The day of His life is marked out by limits no less sure.

(11) Our friend Lazarus sleepeth.—They had probably understood the words of verse 4 to express that the illness was not mortal, and that Lazarus would recover. They had seen, therefore, no reason for facing the danger of Judaea (verse 7, 8). His words "our friend" gently remind them that Lazarus was their friend as well as His, for they as well as He probably had been welcome guests in the well-known house.

For the idea of sleep as the image of death, comp. 8:51; Matt. 9:24; I Thess. 4:14.

(15) And I am glad for your sakes that I was not there.—The utterance is not of sorrow, but of joy; the joy is not at the fact of death, but at the fact that He was not there. There is the assured consciousness of power over death itself, which sees as present all that is to follow, and sees in the strengthening of their faith ground for joy.

(16) Thomas, which is called Didymus.— The second of these names is the Greek translation of the first, which is Hebrew. Both mean "twin." See note on Matt. 10:3, in which he is coupled with Matthew, whose twin brother he possibly was. We have before us here a man looking at events from a mind full of the darkest apprehension. He is without hope that a return to Judaea can have any but one issue for his Master. But with all this there is the full love of a devoted disciple, who will follow his Master even unto death. (Comp. 20:24; 21:2.)

(17) He found that he had lain in the grave four days already.—The Jewish custom was to bury on the day of death. (Comp. Acts 5:6-10.) The whole tone of the narrative places the time of death at the point indicated by the summons to go into Judaea (verse 7). Counting the parts of the days on which they set out and on which they arrived as included in the four days, in accordance with the Jewish method, we have two whole days and parts of two other days spent upon the journey. Four days is perfectly natural for a journey from north of the Sea of Galilee (see note on 10:40).

(18) About fifteen furlongs off.—The distance was not much short of two miles. This is mentioned to account for the fact stated in the following verse, that many of the Jews came to comfort Martha and Mary.

(19) See note on 1:19. The family at Bethany was one of position and substance (see notes on Matt. 26:6-13), and they would naturally have had many friends among the higher rank of the Jews. The mourning usually lasted thirty days, which were divided into three days of weeping, seven days of lamentation, twenty days of sorrow. This fourth day after the death was the first of the seven days of lamentation.

(20) Martha goes forth to meet Jesus in a place where she can speak her heart's thoughts, apart from the oppressive ceremonial of the formal lamentation, and where He would not be exposed to a renewal of the attempts against His life.

(21) Lord, if thou hadst been here, my brother had not died.—The same words are spoken by Mary (verse 32). These sisters are among the many who had received our Lord in the fullness of a true faith, of whom

the gospel narrative gives us but a passing glimpse. Their belief is stated in the definiteness of full conviction; but they, like the courtier, connect the power to save with the bodily presence of our Lord. (Comp. 4:49.)

(22) But I know, that even now, whatsoever thou wilt ask of God . . .—The words express a half-formed hope, which she dare not utter, perhaps dare not even think, that her brother may be restored to life again. She probably had heard of the miracles of Luke 7:11; 8:41, 42.

(23) Thy brother shall rise again.—These words cannot be taken to exclude the restoration of Lazarus to physical life. At the same time, they are chosen to lead her from the passionate longing for her brother's restoration, and from a vague thought of the Lord's power and will to restore him, to a wider and truer conception of what life really is, and to a realization of the truth that for a true believer in Him there can be no such thing as death. This "sign," like every other, is to be no mere wonder, but is to lead to the spiritual truth which is signified.

(25) I am the resurrection, and the life.— Martha (verse 24) has spoken of the Resurrection as a truth which she believes, and as an event in the far-off future, so remote from the present life indeed, as to be powerless to comfort her now. The two first words of His answer, expressed in the fullness of emphasis, teach her that the Resurrection is to be thought of as His person, and that it is to be thought of as actually present.

(26) Shall never die.—The fact of what we call physical death is not denied, but in the fullness of the thought of life it is regarded as the passage to a new and higher life.

(28) And called Mary her sister secretly.— It was done secretly to avoid attracting the notice of the Jews who were with her (verses 19, 31). This accounts for the fact that our Lord did not Himself go to the house (see note on verse 20). That the care was necessary is seen from verse 46.

(33) He groaned in the spirit, and was troubled.—The word rendered "groaned" expresses disturbance of the mind— vehement agitation. This may express itself in sharp admonition in words of anger against a person, or in a physical shudder, answering to the intensity of the emotion. Here it is "in the spirit" (comp. 13:21); in verse 38 it is "in himself." Both mean the same thing, and point to the inner moral depth of His righteous indignation. The object of it, however, is not expressed. "Was troubled" points to the physical movement which accompanied the emotion, and made known to others the indignation which was excited in His own spirit. These Jews who came with Mary are those who had sought to stone their Teacher, and had resolved to cut off from all religious and social intercourse every one who acknowledged Him as the Messiah. With hearts full of hatred they can profess to be comforters, and can mingle their tears with hers. It is this hypocrisy which now stirs in His spirit an anger so intense that it causes nerve and muscle and limb to tremble beneath its force.

(35) Jesus wept.—The word means the calm shedding of tears. The central thought of John's gospel is "the Word was made flesh," and He is for us the Resurrection and the Life, because He has been manifested to us, not as an abstraction which the intellect only could receive, but as a person, living a human life and knowing its sorrows, whom the heart can grasp and love.

(37) What this group thinks of here is not raising the dead, but the possibility of preventing death; and the question is meant to imply that He could not have prevented this death. The inference they would draw is that, after all, the present failure is a proof that He did not open the eyes of the blind. Their evil thoughts are the cause of a new emotion of anger (verse 38).

(38) It was a cave, and a stone lay upon it.—Sepulchers were dug in the rock, either vertically, with an entrance from above (comp. Luke 11:44), or horizontally, with an entrance from the side, and were frequently adaptations of natural caves (comp. Matt. 27:60).

(39) For he hath been dead four days.—See note on verse 17. The body had been embalmed (verse 44); but the manner of the Jews was to embalm only with spice, and to wrap in linen clothes (19:40-42). There is no evidence that they at any time followed the Egyptian method of embalming. The only instance of Jewish embalming mentioned in the Old Testament is that of Asa (II Chron. 16:14).

(41) A rough slab had been placed at the entrance of the cave to prevent the approach of jackals or other beasts of prey. Jesus' attitude, as well as His words, is meant to express that the work which He is

about to do is one of the works from His Father.

(43) Lazarus, come forth.—He addresses him as we should address a friend whom we wished to arouse from sleep—by his name, the most familiar of all sounds, marking his personality. Literally, the Greek means, "Lazarus, Hither, out!" and contains no verb. There is a fitness in them as addressed to one already lying in the sepulcher.

(44) And he that was dead came forth.—The body may have been wrapped in a linen cloth, which encompassed the whole, except the head (Matt. 27:59), but still left motion possible. The word rendered "graveclothes" means properly the bands or straps by which the linen sheet was fastened to the body, and which kept the spice from falling out. (Comp. 19:40.)

And his face was bound about with a napkin.—It means the cloth placed around the forehead and under the chin, but probably not covering the face.

(46) But some of them went their ways to the Pharisees.—It is contrary to their position as believers to think that they did this as informers against Jesus. What they have seen carried conviction to their own minds, and they report it to the Pharisees, either as a proof that He really was the Messiah, or in any case to demand from them judgment on the facts which they report.

(47) Matters have reached too serious a stage for them to allow further delay. The Pharisees go in their difficulty to the chief priests, who were for the most part Sadducees, and they together summon a meeting of the Sanhedrin. The form of their question is a strange contradiction: they cannot but admit that He does many signs, and yet their pride will call Him by no name but the contemptuous "this Man!"

(48) Their existence as rulers depended upon the Mosaic law and upon the services of the Temple. Around these centers they had gathered human tradition and ordinance, to which they clung because they only could interpret them, and they only could use the vast powers which were thus exercised over men. With this the Roman empire, following its usual policy, had not interfered. But in direct opposition to both of them had been the work and teaching of Christ. His spiritual teaching was a cutting to the very root of their whole being. If all the people believed on Him, their **raison d'etre** would be gone, and the Romans would no longer allow an **imperium in**

835

imperio, which they now allowed because it swayed the masses of the people.

(49) And one of them, named Caiaphas.— See notes on Matt. 26:3; Luke 3:2.

(50) This remarkable counsel has linked itself in John's thoughts with the name of Caiaphas. He quotes it again in 18:14. There is a moral beauty in the words, in spite of the diabolical intent with which they are uttered; and John adds (verse 51) the explanation that they had an origin higher than the one who spoke them. Writing after the events, he has seen them fulfilled, and regards them as an unconscious prophecy. Like another Balaam, Caiaphas was the oracle of God in spite of himself, and there is in his words a meaning far beyond any that he had intended.

(52) And not for that nation only.— Caiaphas had said "die for the people," using the word which meant the people of the Jews. John said "die for that nation," using the wider word which meant the nation as one of the nations of the earth. He now passses to a wider meaning still. He has lived to see a partial fulfillment of the ingathering of the "other sheep" (10:16), and he thinks of that death as for God's children in all nations, who shall be one flock under one shepherd.

(53) Then from that day forth they took counsel . . .—On that day, then, the Sanhedrin officially decreed His death. The remaining question was how they could carry out this decree without exciting a popular tumult or bringing themselves into collision with the Romans. (Comp. Matt. 26:3-5.)

(54) Jesus therefore walked no more openly among the Jews.—He had heard of the decree of the Sanhedrin which had been made known publicly (verse 57), and therefore avoided persons who would have carried it into effect. The position of this "city" is not known with certainty. Jerome assumed it to be the same place as Ephron (the Ophrah of Josh. 18:23; I Sam. 13:17), some sixteen miles northeast of Jerusalem.

(55) And the Jews' passover was nigh at hand.—See notes on 2:13; 6:4.

12

(2) There they made him a supper.—See notes on Matt. 26:6; Mark 14:3, which are accounts of the same supper.

Lazarus was one of them that sat at the table with him.—The meal is in this case, as

afterward, in that of our Lord Himself (Luke 24:41-43), a physical proof of the Resurrection; and his presence by the side of our Lord calls forth from Mary the anointing, which testifies to her gratitude and love.

(3) Then took Mary a pound of ointment of spikenard.—Here John alone gives the name of her whom Matthew and Mark call "a woman." (Comp. Luke 10:40, 42.) This pound was the Greek **litra,** the Latin "libra," the pound of twelve ounces. Matthew and Mark both state that she anointed His head. This was the usual custom (comp. Luke 7:46; Ps. 23:5); but John remembers that the act of love went beyond common esteem in the depth of its gratitude and reverence.

(6) This verse which follows from the reference to Judas is, like it, peculiar to John. We think of Judas as treasurer of the common fund which supplied the wants of the little band, and from which gifts to the poor were made. The original expresses continuance of the act, and may refer to the recurring opportunities of fraud.

(7) Against the day of my burying hath she kept this.—Comp. Matt. 26:12; Mark 14:8. Her act is significant of the future which is approaching. Before the week ends His body will be carried to the sepulcher. The preparations for the grave already have been begun.

(10) But the chief priests consulted.— While no charge is brought against Lazarus, his life is a witness to the deity of Him whom they have condemned to death, and a denial of their own doctrine that there is no resurrection (Acts 23:8).

(12-19) See notes on Matt. 21:1-11.

(19) Perceive ye how ye prevail nothing?— They blame each other for the failure of all their plans (comp. 11:47), and prepare themselves to accept the counsel of Caiaphas (11:50).

(20) They were not **Hellenists,** i.e., Greek Jews, but **Hellenes,** i.e., Gentiles. The words imply that they were in the habit of going up to Jerusalem at the feasts, i.e., that though Greeks by birth, they had been admitted to the privileges of Judaism. They belonged to the class known as "Proselytes of the Gate." (Comp. Matt. 23:15; Acts 8:27.)

(21) The same came therefore to Philip.— John alone gives us this incident only of all that occurred, as we know from the earlier gospels, between the entry into Jerusalem and the Last Supper; and he relates this coming of the Greeks not for the sake of the fact itself, but for that of the discourse which followed upon it. They would be among the last words spoken in the Temple before the retirement to Bethany, on Wednesday evening. (Comp. Luke 21:37.) They were uttered, probably, in the Court of the Gentiles, as He passed from the Court of the Women, which, as the most public place for Jewish assemblies, was the frequent scene of His teaching. On the previous day, the Court of the Gentiles had been cleansed from the traffic and merchandise which had been customary in it. The court of the Gentiles was divided from the inner square of the Temple by a stone fence, bearing upon pillars, placed at regular distances, the following words in Greek and Latin:—"No alien must pass within the fence round the Temple and the court. If any one be caught doing so, he must blame himself for the death that will follow" (Josephus, **Ant.** 15:11, §5.)

(23) The hour is come.—This approach of men from outside the limits of Judaism brings back again the thought of the scattered sheep, for whose gathering the Shepherd's life must be laid down (10:16-19). They are the first-fruits of the great flocks of humanity, and their presence is as the first stroke of the bell which sounds the fatal but glorious hour.

(24) Except a corn of wheat fall into the ground and die.—He prepares them for it by what we call the analogy of a physical law, but what is really an instance of the working of the great law of life, which God has given to the moral and physical worlds alike. A grain of wheat, though containing in itself the germs of life, remains alone, and does not really live unless it falls to the earth. Then the life germs burst forth, and the single grain, in its own death, gives life to blade, stalk, and ear of corn. Its death then was the true life, for it released the inner life power which the husk before held captive; and this life power multiplying itself in successive grains clothes the whole field with a harvest of much fruit.

(25, 26) Comp. Matt. 10:39; 16:25; Mark 8:35; Luke 9:24; 17:33. The disciples had heard these words laid down as the law of their own life and work. They now hear them again, asserted as the law to which even His life is submitted. In self-sacrifice and death is His own glory and the life of the world. The point of the whole teaching is missed unless we think of the Greeks as present. They had come as volunteer disciples. Did they know what the discipleship was? The condition of discipleship is laid down for the new disciples, but in the presence of the older ones who in the dark days that have now come were to learn what sacrifice meant.

(27) As the fatal hour approaches, our Lord is shrinking from the darkness of the death which is at hand. The conflict exists but for a moment, but in all its fearfulness is real, and then the cup of the world's woe is seized and drunk to its bitter dregs. The agony of Gethsemane is here, and the words of Matt. 26:39 are echoed. "For this cause" may be understood as referring to the words which follow: ". . . for this cause came I unto this hour, that thy name be glorified . . ."

(28) I have both glorified it, and will glorify it again.—These words are without limit, extending to the whole past and to the whole future of God's revelation of Himself to man. The only limit in the context is that revelation is thought of as in the person and work of Christ.

(29) The fact that John clearly means us to understand (verse 28) that a distinct voice spoke from heaven does not forbid our understanding also that this voice was heard more or less distinctly, or was as a voice not heard at all, in proportion as the hearts of the hearers were or were not receptive of the voice of God.

(31) The title "prince of this world" was the regular rabbinic title for Satan, whom they regarded as the ruler of the Gentiles, the Jews not being included in his kingdom. The reign of the true Messiah is over the Gentile and Jewish world alike. The world itself, as opposed to Christ, is condemned, for its unbelief crucifies Jesus Christ; but the Resurrection and Ascension are heaven's witness that He is the Son of God. The world's condemnation is followed by the casting out of its ruler.

(32) And I, if I be lifted up from the earth.—The pronoun is strongly emphatic: "And I," in opposition to the prince of this world; the conqueror in opposition to the vanquished foe. The words "lifted up" have occurred before in 3:14 and 8:28; but the context here shows that they include the thought of the Ascension into heaven. It is from the heavenly throne that the Messiah will rule over His spiritual kingdom.

Will draw all men unto me.—The drawing unto Himself is the assertion of His reign over the world, from which the prince of evil shall be cast out. He will Himself be

837

the center of the new kingdom, from which none shall be shut out. These Greeks who are drawn to Him now are the first-fruits of the harvest of which the whole world is the field, and of which the last day is to be the great ingathering. The "drawing" is accomplished in the work of the Holy Spirit, whose mission to the Church was dependent on the Ascension of our Lord (7:39; 16:7).

(33) What death he should die.—The words are the apostle's interpetation of the saying of our Lord. (Comp. 3:14 and 8:28.) The words bear a double sense. Looking back upon the fact of the crucifixion he sees in that a lifting up which was part of the great moral victory over the world, and in the cross of shame he sees the throne of glory.

(34) See Pss. 89:36; 110:4; Isa. 9:6; Dan. 7:13, 14. This remark is an instance of the knowledge of rabbinic theology which interpreted such passages of a temporal Messianic reign. They expected Him to free them from Roman bondage, and to rule over them in an earthly paradise to which there should be no end. The Christ they thought was to abide forever. Anything else contradicts all their visions of a Messianic reign.

(35) See notes on 9:4; 11:9.

(37) But though he had done so many miracles before them.—"Before them" means "in their presence." John's narrative implies that the "signs" of the earlier gospels were well-known. He has himself recorded but six miracles, and all these, with the exception of the feeding the five thousand, belong to the Judaean ministry. (See note on 2:11.)

(38) See note on Matt. 1:22. Matthew and John both regard the events of our Lord's life as fulfilling the prophecies of the Old Testament Scriptures. The prophecies here are from Isa. 51:9; 52:10; 53:1. The latter refers especially to the power of the Lord manifested in the whole life of Christ.

(39, 40) See note on Matt. 13:14.

(42) Comp. 9:22. This submission to the Pharisees' yoke which kept them from Christ was itself blinding their eyes and hardening their hearts.

(44-50) Whereas verses 37-43 have given us the thoughts of John as he looked back on the unbelief of Judaism, he now gives other words of our Lord condemning the unbelief of which he had been speaking. They are a summary of words previously uttered by our Lord, but grouped together here as specially bearing upon the subject of

which he is writing. Comp. 1:14; 3:16-19; 7:16, 17, 28, 29; 8:12-15, 26, 28, 38; 9:5, 39; 12:35, 36.

13

(1) See notes on 2:4; 7:6; 11:9. By "his own" are here meant those who by believing on Him had received power to become the sons of God, those who by walking according as they had light were becoming sons of light. They are the true members of the family of God. (See notes on 1:11, 12.) Jesus' thoughts are for them and not for Himself. For Him there would be the return to the glory of His Father's throne; but His mind dwells on the bereavement of those He leaves behind, and this moves Him to a special manifestation of His love.

(2) The devil having now put into the heart of Judas Iscariot.—See notes on Matt. 10:4; 26:14. The fact is recorded here to explain the references to Judas which follow in our Lord's words (verses 10, 18, 21, 26, 27, 30).

(3) Jesus knowing that the Father had given all things into his hands...—This explains the act of humility which follows. With the full consciousness of His supreme power and divine origin, and of the divine glory to which He was about to return, He left the disciples an example of the self-denial which is the necessary outcome of love. (Comp. Phil. 2:6.)

(4) He riseth from supper, and laid aside his garments.—See notes on Luke 22:24-30. This parabolic act apparently was provoked by some self-assertion, which He thereby rebukes; or it may be that no one had offered the customary refreshment of water for the feet, before reclining at the table (Luke 7:44). The garment laid aside would be the outer garment, which would impede His action, leaving the tunic, which was the ordinary dress of a servant.

And took a towel, and girded himself.—This was itself a mark of the servant's position, and was meant to signify His assumption of the servant's work.

(5) After that he poureth water into a basin.—The basin and water being ready suggested that one of the disciples might have performed this act which the Lord now performs. That it was commonly regarded as an act of reverence from an inferior to a superior is made clear by rabbinical passages.

(6) Then cometh he to Simon Peter.—

The act was only begun, when it was interrupted by the objection of Peter. The natural impression is that Peter's turn came after that of at least one other, John himself, being nearest to his Master, being perhaps that other one (verses 24, 25).

(7) What I do thou knowest not now.— Here both pronouns are emphatic, and convey a rebuke to Peter. His word had almost implied that the Lord's act was wholly out of place, as of one who knew not what he was doing. The opposite was really the case.

But thou shalt know hereafter—i.e., in the teaching which is to follow (verses 13-17).

(8) Thou shalt never wash my feet.—It is the loving, impulsive, but self-confident Peter of the earlier gospels who is speaking here. He does not wait for that afterknowledge which our Lord promises him. He sees no ground on which our Lord's act can possibly be one which he can permit. The emphasis is on the negative.

If I wash thee not, thou hast no part with me.—By the act of washing their feet, He, their Lord, taught the spirit of self-sacrifice and love in opposition to the spirit of self-seeking and pride which ruled even in the apostles' hearts. That lesson every servant and apostle of Jesus Christ must learn, for the servant is not greater than the Lord, nor the apostle than the Sender. The sacrifice of will may be harder than that of life.

(10) He that is washed needeth not save to wash his feet.—Peter's words (verse 9) have implied that he was wholly unclean, and needed for feet, head, and hands—for the whole man—a moral cleansing. Christ answers that this was not so. The man who has been bathed is clean, but his feet coming in contact with the dust of the road need to be washed. It was so morally. They had been cleansed; their whole moral life had been changed, but they were liable to the corruption of everyday life through which they walked and needed to be cleansed from the pollution of it. The lesson is that all, from apostles forward, need the daily renewing of the grace of God; and that none should find in failure, or even in the evil which clings to his daily path, reason for questioning the reality of the moral change which has made him the child of God.

And ye are clean, but not all.—This is the moral application, accompanied by the mournful thought that it was not true of all. One there was among those who had been bathed who had allowed evil to enter into

his heart and pollute it. For him—Judas—cleansing had been neglected.

(13) Ye call me Master and Lord.—The word in the original is not "rabbi." (Comp. note on 11:28.) The Jewish pupils called their teachers "rabbi" and "mar" (teacher), and it was not permitted to any pupil to call his teacher by his proper name (**Sanhedr.**, 100, §1). The word "Master" here refers to His position as their teacher, the word "Lord" to the reverence which they paid to Him. These were the common titles of everyday life which He here asserts for Himself.

(14, 15) The example is in the principle, not in the specific act; it is not "that which I have done to you," but "according as I have done to you." The imitation is to be worked out in applying the same principle of love and self-sacrifice in all the varying circumstances of life in which we are placed.

(17) If ye know these things, happy are ye if ye do them.—The first clause of this verse assumes their knowledge of the things which He had been teaching them (verse 13-17). The second makes their blessedness depend upon their combining action with knowledge.

(18) He that eateth bread with me hath lifted up his heel against me.—See Ps. 41:9. Our Lord's quotation omits the earlier part of the verse, "Mine own familiar friend whom I trusted." He knew whom He had chosen. It could be that here, as in Ps. 69, we have the words of Jeremiah, and the special reference to the friend is unknown. If the Psalm were by David, then, as the king was the type of Christ, Ahithophel is doubtless the type of Judas. In any case the baseness of the treachery lay in the fact that the betrayer was one who did eat bread with the psalmist.

(21) He was troubled in spirit.—See note on 11:33. He has spoken of the future of those who are true to their commission as apostles (verse 20). He now turns in deep emotion to him of whom those words cannot be spoken.

(23) Now there was leaning on Jesus' bosom.—Leonardo da Vinci's famous masterpiece is in one respect misleading. (See note on Matt. 26:20.) The Jews followed the Persian method of reclining on couches at meals from the time of the Captivity. This method of eating the Passover had the special significance of security and possession of the Promised Land, as opposed to the attitude of one undertaking a journey, which was part of the original institution (Exod. 12:11).

One of his disciples, whom Jesus loved—i.e., John himself. (Comp. 21:2, 7, 20-23; 19:26.

(26) Our Lord would preside at the meal, and distribute to each guest his portion. When John asked the question (verse 25), He was about to give the morsel to Judas. He avoids the name, and makes the act which He is about to perform convey the answer to the question. That act is the token of friendship and love which even now would redeem the heart full of treachery, if that heart would but receive it.

(27) The Greek expresses vividly the very moment when the mind finally cast out love, and left itself as a possession for Satan. At that moment, when the last effort had been tried, the heart hardened itself against receiving from Jesus the sacred pledge of love. Jesus' charge was made only after Judas was wholly given up to evil.

(29) Because Judas had the bag.—See notes on 12:6.

(30) And it was night.—These words doubtless state the physical fact that at the time when Judas left the room, the darkness of night had already come on. Yet we feel that there is in them a fullness of meaning that cannot have been unintentional. It was night; and he stepped forth from light into darkness, from the presence and guidance of the Light of the World, to be possessed by and guided by the prince of darkness.

(31, 32) See notes on 11:4; 12:28.

(34) A new commandment I give unto you, That ye love one another.—We are not to seek the meaning of the "new commandment" in any contrast with the Decalogue. Love to one another, and therefore sacrifice of self for another's good, would be, in the truest sense, a realization of His presence in their midst. (Comp. I John 2:8.)

As I have loved you.—The earlier clause gives the principle of the new commandment; the latter repeats this, and prefaces the repetition by words referring to the fact of His own acts of love, which should be an example for them.

(35) By this shall all men know that ye are my disciples.—The thought of their state of orphanage (verse 33) when He should depart from them is still present. He gives them a bond of union, by which they always should be linked to Him and to each other in the principle of love. The followers of great teachers and rabbis had their distinctive marks. Here was the distinctive Christian mark, which all men should be able to read. The apologists of the first centuries delighted in appealing to the striking fact of the common love of Christians, which was a new thing in the history of mankind; and while the Church has sometimes forgotten the characteristic, the world never has.

(38) Wilt thou lay down thy life for my sake?—Peter had been using words of which he knew not the full meaning. He spoke of laying down his life for his Lord. He would hereafter be able to follow, because his Lord would lay down His own life for him. (See notes on Matt. 26:34.)

14

(1) Let not your heart be troubled.—The division of chapters is unfortunate, as it breaks the close connection between these words and those which have gone immediately before. The prophecy of Peter's denial had followed upon the indication of Judas as the traitor, and upon the announcement of the Lord's departure. These thoughts may well have brought troubled hearts.

Ye believe in God, believe also in me.—It is more natural to take both these clauses as imperative—"Believe in God, believe also in Me." The present trouble of the hearts of the disciples arose from a want of a true belief in God; and the command is to exercise a true belief, and to realize the presence of the Father, as manifested in the person of the Son. This faith is the simplest article of the Christian's creed.

(2) In my Father's house are many mansions.—The Jews were accustomed to the thought of heaven as the habitation of God; and the disciples had been taught to pray, "Our Father, which art in heaven." The Greek word for "mansion" occurs again in the New Testament only in verse 23, where it is rendered "abode." "Many" is not to be understood simply or chiefly of different degrees of happiness in heaven. Happiness depends upon the mind which receives it. The words refer, then, to the extent of the Father's house, in which there should be abiding places for all. Our Lord Himself is going away to prepare a place for them. There is to be then no separation.

(3) I will come again, and receive you unto myself.—This clause has been variously explained of the Resurrection, of the death of individual disciples, of the spiritual presence of our Lord in the Church, of the coming again of the Lord in the **Parousia** of the last day. The words refer, rather, as the same words in verse 18, to His constant spiritual presence in their midst, whereas the reception of them to Himself is to be understood of the complete union which will accompany that spiritual presence. That union will be begun in this life, advanced by the death of individuals, and completed in the final coming again. (Comp. 17:24.)

(4) And whither I go ye know, and the way ye know.—His words now are meant to contrast what they ought to have known with what they really did know, in order that He may more fully instruct them. To know our ignorance is the first step to its removal.

(5) Thomas saith unto him.—See note on 11:16. In all that Thomas has heard of the Father's house of many mansions, of being with the Lord, there is much that he cannot understand. The Messiah, they thought, was to reign upon earth. Where was this vast royal home, with dwelling places for all, to which Christ was going first, and to which they were to follow? They know not where, and without that knowledge they cannot even think of the way.

(6) I am the way.—The pronoun is emphatic: "I, and none besides Me." "The way" is again made prominent, reversing the order which Thomas had used.

No man cometh unto the Father, but by me.—This was the answer to the doubt of Thomas. This was the true "whither" which they knew not. The thought of heaven is not of a place far above, or of a time far before, but of a state now and hereafter. To receive the Truth and the Life revealed in the presence of the Son is to come to the Father by the only Way.

(8) Lord, shew us the Father, and it sufficeth us.—Comp. 1:44; 6:5; 12:21. Philip thinks of some revelation of the glory of God as that vouchsafed to Moses, or to those on the Mount of Transfiguration. One such vision of the Father, he thinks, would remove all their doubts, and would satisfy the deepest longings of their hearts.

(9, 10) The Father has been manifested in the person of the Son. In the Life and Truth revealed in Him is the full revelation of God. Comp. 8:38; 10:38; 12:44, 45.

(11) Jesus passes now from Philip, and addresses Himself to the whole body of the apostles. He claims from them a personal trust in Himself, which should accept His statement that He and the Father were immanent in each other. If they cannot receive the truth on the testimony of His word, He will take lower ground with them, placing before them the evidence He had placed before the Jews. Let them, if they will not hear Him, believe on account of the works which He had done.

(12) And greater works than these shall he do.—This explanation of these greater works is not to be sought in the individual instances of miraculous power exercised by the apostles, but in the whole work of the Church. The Day of Pentecost witnessed the first fulfillment of this prophecy. In the world-wide extent of Christianity there is a work greater even than any which He Himself did in the flesh.

Because I go unto my Father.—The words are the reason why the believer shall do the works that Christ does, as well as the reason why he shall do greater works: because He will be at the Father's right hand, and will do whatsoever they shall ask in His name.

(13) And whatsoever ye shall ask in my name, that will I do.—Comp. 15:16 and 16:23. The width and limitation of the promise are both to be noted. Personal petitions are not contemplated here, except as far as they are for the glory of God; and petitions asked in ignorance may be most truly answered when they are not granted. We commonly attach to our prayers, "through Jesus Christ our Lord." This implies an absolute self-sacrifice, and is a prayer that our prayers may not be answered except insofar as they are in accordance with the divine will.

(15) If ye love me, keep my commandments.—The connection here is through the condition "in My name," which includes willing obedience to His commands. The word "My" is emphatic.

(16) And I will pray the Father.—The word used for "pray" is one which implies more of nearness of approach and of familiarity than that which is rendered "ask" in verse 14.

And he shall give you another Comforter.—Better, "another Advocate." The word is used of the third Person in the Holy Trinity here and in verse 26, and in 15:26; 16:7. In each of these instances it is used by our Lord. It is found once again in the New Testament, and is there applied by John to our Lord Himself (I John 2:1).

That he may abide with you for ever.—The thought of the permanent abiding is opposed to the separation which is about to take place between them and the person of our Lord. He would come again to them in the person of the Paraclete, whom He would send to them (verse 18), and this spiritual presence should remain with them forever. (Comp. note on Matt. 28:20.)

(17) Even the Spirit of truth.—Comp. 15:26, 16:13; I John 5:6. He is called the Spirit of Truth, because part of His special office is to bring truth home to the hearts of men.

Whom the world cannot receive.—The Holy Spirit can be received only by those who have the spiritual faculty. The unbelieving world, caring only for things of the senses, has lost its spiritual perception. (Comp. I Cor. 2:14.)

But ye know him; for he dwelleth with you, and shall be in you.—The words describe the receptivity of the disciples as opposed to the moral blindness of the world. They had in part received the Spirit, and by that reception were prepared for the fuller gift.

(18) I will not leave you comfortless.— Better, "I will not leave you orphans." It is rendered "fatherless" in Jas. 1:27, which is the only other passage where it occurs in the New Testament.

I will come to you.—This coming is the spiritual presence in the person of the Paraclete.

(19) But ye see me—i.e., in the spiritual presence of the Paraclete. The world thought of Him as dead. To the believers, however, who had the power to see Him He appeared as living, and in very deed was more truly with them and in them than He had been before.

Because I live, ye shall live also.—Our Lord speaks of the essential life of which He is Himself the Source, and which is not affected by the physical death through which He is about to pass. They also who believe in Him shall have even here this principle of life, which shall develop into the fullness of the life hereafter.

(20) At that day ye shall know—i.e., the day of the gift of the Comforter, in whom Christ shall come to them. In the first reference the Day of Pentecost is meant, but the words hold good of every spiritual quickening, and will hold good of the final coming in the last day.

That I am in my Father, and ye in me, and I in you.—The Spirit should so bring the life of Christ to their hearts that they would read in it the manifestation of the Father, and feel that in and through that life

their own spirit has communion with God. The Spirit would witness with their spirit that they were the children of God. They would seek no longer for a Theophany from without, but in the depth of their innermost lives would cry, "Abba, Father."

(22) See note on Matt. 10:3.

(23) If a man love me, he will keep my words.—Our Lord repeats the condition necessary on the part of man (verse 21) in order that the manifestation of God to him may be possible.

We will come unto him, and make our abode with him.—For the plural, see note on 10:30. The thought of God as dwelling in the sanctuary and among the people was familiar to the disciples from the Old Testament Scriptures (Exod. 25:8; 29:45; Lev. 26:11, 12; Ezek. 37:26), and the thought of the spiritual temple in the heart of man was known to contemporary writers (Philo, **De Cherubim**, 124).

(26) But the Comforter, which is the Holy Ghost.—Better, "the Advocate." See notes on 7:39, 20:22, the only passages where the words "Holy Ghost" appear in this gospel. In four passages in the New Testament (Luke 11:13; Eph. 1:13, 4:30; I Thess. 4:8) our translators have preferred the rendering "Holy Spirit." The identification here with the Advocate brings out the contrast between the practical obedience and holiness (verse 23) of those to whom the Holy Spirit should be sent, and the disobedience (verse 24) of those who rejected the revelation by the Son.

Whom the Father will send in my name— i.e., as My representative. (See note on verse 13 and 16:13.) Their Master will depart from them, but the Father will send them another Teacher who will make clear to them the lessons they have heard already, and teach them things which they cannot bear now.

(27) Peace I leave with you, my peace I give unto you.—Men said to each other when they met and parted, "Shalom! Shalom!" (Peace! Peace!). He will leave them as a legacy the gift of "peace." And this peace is more than a meaningless sound or even than a true wish. He repeats it with the emphatic "My," and speaks of it as an actual possession which He imparts to them.

Not as the world giveth, give I unto you.—The contrast is not between the emptiness of the world's salutations and the reality of His own gift, but between His legacy to them and the legacies ordinarily left by the world. He gives them not land or houses or possessions, but "peace."

(28) For my Father is greater than I.—In the divine nature there is a subordination of the Son to the Father. (See verse 16, 17:5; I Cor. 3:23; 11:3; 15:27, 28; Phil. 2:9, 11.) The words could only have been uttered by one who meant in them to assert His own divine essence.

(30) For the prince of this world cometh.— See note on 12:31. The prince of evil is regarded here as working in and by Judas, who is carrying out his plans and doing his work. (See notes on 6:70; 13:2, 27.)

And hath nothing in me.—The words assert that the prince of this world possesses nothing in the Person of Christ. In Him he has never for a moment ruled. For this appeal to perfect sinlessness, comp. 8:29. It follows from this that His surrender of Himself is entirely voluntary. (See note on 10:18.) The world over which "the prince" has ruled will see in the self-sacrifice of Jesus the love of the Father (verse 31). That love will reclaim them from the bondage of the oppressor and restore them to the freedom of children.

15

(1) I am the true vine.—The thought is introduced suddenly, the natural explanation being that it was suggested by some external object which met the eye. If we suppose (comp. 14:31) that they were crossing the valley on the way to Gethsemane, there is reason to suppose that they passed a vineyard. The vineyard seen in the distance by moonlight suggested "the fruit of the vine" of which they had drunk. But comp. note on 17:1.

And my Father is the husbandman.—The thought here is of the owner of the vine, who himself cultivates and trains it.

(2) And every branch that beareth fruit, he purgeth it.—This means in the natural vine the cutting off of shoots which run to waste, and the removal of every appendage which hinders the growth of the branch. It means in the spiritual training the checking of natural impulses and affections, and the removal of everything, even though it be by a pang sharp as the edge of the pruner's knife, which can misdirect or weaken the energy of the spiritual life, and thus diminish its fruitfulness.

(3) The word was the revelation of God to them, and by reason of its moral power they had been cleansed.

(4) Abide in me, and I in you.—The union, and all that follows from it, is placed within the power of the human will. He who obeys this command has Christ abiding in him, and is a fruitful branch of the true vine.

As the branch cannot bear fruit of itself.— The branch regarded of itself has no original source of life, fulfilling its functions only when it is connected with the vine. So in the spiritual life, men apart from Christ have no original source of life and fruitfulness. The true life flows from Him to every branch that abides in Him, quickening by its power the whole man, and making him fruitful in good.

(5) For without me ye can do nothing.— The words bring out the fullness of the meaning of the fruitfulness of the man who abides in Christ. It is he, and he only, who brings forth fruit, for the man who is separate from Christ can bear no fruit.

(6) The thought passes from the fruitful to the sterile branch, from the man who abides to the man who will not abide in Christ. In the natural vineyard such a branch was cast forth, and then withered, and was gathered with others into bundles, and burned.

(7) The promise in all its width is the same as that in 14:13, 14 (see notes), and it is attended by the same condition, for they who abide in Christ, and in whom Christ's words abide, cannot pray otherwise than in His name.

(10) If he keep my commandments, ye shall abide in my love.—Comp. 14:21, 24. Keeping His commandments is the outward proof of love toward Him, so that the love of the human heart toward Christ, which itself flows from Christ's love to us (verse 9), becomes the condition of abiding in that love.

Even as I have kept my Father's commandments . . .—This is an appeal to His perfect sinlessness and willing subordination as Son to the Father. Keeping the commandments is not an arbitrary condition imposed upon human love, but a necessary result of love itself, and therefore as true in the relation of the Son to the Father as it is in our relation to Him.

(13) Greater love hath no man than this.— Nothing greater is conceivable in the thought of love. He has spoken of His own love for them as the measure of their love for each other. The thought of this verse dwells upon what His love really was and what theirs also should be. The point dwelt upon is the greatness of the love, and the

843

highest reach of love is the self-sacrifice which spares not life itself.

(16) Ye have not chosen me, but I have chosen you.—The thought of His love for them, which had exalted them from the position of slaves to friends (verses 14, 15), from fishermen to apostles, is made to remind them again (verse 17) of the duty of love to each other.

That whatsoever ye shall ask of the Father.—See notes on verse 7.

(18) If the world hate you.—He has spoken of their close union with Himself, and of their love to each other. He proceeds in the remainder of the chapter to speak of their relation to the world. There was the more need for them to be closely bound to each other, and to their Lord, because of the hatred which awaited them in the world.

(22-25) In these verses our Lord shows the sinfulness of the world's hatred, because it was in spite of His revelation to them by both word (verse 22) and work (verse 24). It was not now the negative evil of men who know not (Acts 17:30, 31), but the positive evil of men who, knowing the truth, wilfully reject it.

(25) That is written in their law.—See note on 10:34; comp. Pss. 35:19; 69:4.

(26) Whom I will send unto you from the Father.—See notes on 14:16, 17.

Which proceedeth from the Father.—The force of these words is to give weight to the witness which the Spirit shall bear of the Son. He is the Advocate whom the Son will send from the Father, but He is also and emphatically the Spirit of Truth proceeding from the Father, and His witness therefore will be that of the Father Himself.

16

(3) Because they have not known the Father, nor me.—Comp. 15:21. Ignorance of God is the cause of the world's hatred and persecution. Men think (verse 2) that in exclusion, anathemas, persecutions, and deaths of men made like themselves in the image of God, they are offering to God an acceptable sacrifice. They know nothing of the long-suffering and compassion of the Son of man, who pleaded even for His murderers.

(6) Sorrow hath filled your heart.—The thought of their own separation from Him, and of the dark future which lay before them, so filled their hearts that it left room

for no thoughts of Him and the brightness of the glory to which He was returning.

(7) For if I go not away, the Comforter will not come unto you.—Better, ... "the Advocate will not come unto you." For the connection between the departure of Christ and the coming of the Advocate, see notes on 7:39; Acts 2:33. The order fixed in the divine counsels was that the Son of man should complete His work on earth, offer the sacrifice of Himself for sin, rise from the dead, and ascend to the Father's throne, before the Advocate should come. The Son of man was to be glorified before the Spirit was to be given. Humanity was to ascend to heaven before the Spirit could be sent to humanity on earth. The conviction of sin, righteousness, and judgment could only follow the finished work of Christ.

But if I depart, I will send him unto you.—See notes on 14:16; 15:25.

(8) And when he is come, he will reprove the world.—This conviction of the world is by witness concerning Christ (15:26). It is the revelation to the hearts of men of the character and work of Christ, and, therefore, a refutation of the evil in their hearts. The result of this conviction is twofold: men embrace it and are saved by it, or reject it and are condemned by it. (Comp. II Cor. 2:15, 16.) The effect of Peter's sermon on the Day of Pentecost is the first great historical comment on this verse; but the comment is continued in the whole history of the Church's work. The remainder of the verse enumerates the three steps in this conviction, which are more fully defined in verses 9-11.

(9) Of sin, because they believe not on me.—Unbelief in Christ is stated as the cause of sin. Sin is missing the aim of life, the disordered action of powers that have lost their controlling principle. Christ is the revelation to the world of the Father's love. In union with God through Him the soul finds the center of its being and the true purpose of its life.

(10) Of righteousness, because I go to my Father.—The Spirit's representation of Christ brings also the conviction of righteousness, but this is the righteousness of Christ, not that of the world. The special reason of the conviction of righteousness is the Resurrection and Ascension of our Lord. His return to the Father was heaven's witness to His righteousness.

(11) Of judgment, because the prince of this world is judged.—See notes on 3:17, 18; 12:30, 31. The tense here is perfect, marking the completion of the condemnation. The conviction is regarded from the point of view of the coming of the Advocate when Christ's work shall have been completed. That work is the redemption of the world, and is, therefore, the condemnation of the prince of this world.

(12) The "many things" are defined by verse 13 to be things with regard to which the Spirit of Truth shall be their guide— i.e., they are parts of the revelation which the minds of the disciples are not yet fitted to receive.

(13) Howbeit when he, the Spirit of truth, is come.—See note on 14:17.

For he shall not speak of himself.— Comp. 5:19; 7:17, 18. The Holy Spirit, too, is subordinated to the Father, and His work is to seek the glory of Him that sent Him.

And he will shew you things to come.— These words, too, have their fulfillment in the Spirit's illumination in all time, but they find their first meaning in the Revelation to John.

(14) For he shall receive of mine, and shall shew it unto you.—See notes on I John 4:1, 2. The revelation of Christ is not an imperfect revelation which the Holy Spirit is to supplement. It is a full revelation imperfectly received, and His office is to illumine the heart, and bring home to it the things of Christ. Verses 14 and 15 imply the following doctrinal truths: the deity of the Son; the personality of the Holy Ghost. The Greek expresses this in the most emphatic way.

(16) A little while, and ye shall not see me.—The time here referred to is that between the moment of His speaking to them and His death.

And again, a little while, and ye shall see me.—The time here referred to is the interval between His death and the Day of Pentecost. That the vision is to be understood of our Lord's presence in the person of the Paraclete (14:18, 19) is confirmed by verse 23.

(20) See note on 1:51. The tears and the scoffs at the cross were the accomplishment of the first prophecy. In the second, they will rejoice in the presence of the Lord, when after a little while they will see Him and will feel that the separation necessarily went before the union, and that the sorrow was itself a matter of joy because it was the necessary cause of the joy (see verse 7; 20:20).

(23) Comp. Acts 1:6. The time referred to here is when the Paraclete shall fully illumine them so that they shall not need to ask the meaning of new thoughts and words as they have done heretofore. The thought is that the prayer is offered in Christ's name (comp. verse 24; 14:13), and that the answer to every such prayer is in virtue of His name.

(25) For "proverbs," read "parables." Comp. verses 16, 23. In that time He will be present with them in the Advocate and will no longer need parables or words, but will, to the depth of their spirit, communicate to them in all fullness and plainness the eternal truth of the Father (verse 13).

(28) I came forth from the Father.— Comp. verse 19. He repeats with emphasis that which in verse 27 He stated as believed by them. They had accepted the truth of the Incarnation; but in this there already was implied the truth of the Ascension, and in the truth of the Ascension there was implied the gift of the Paraclete, and the spiritual return and constant presence of Christ in the Church (see verse 7; 14:14-18).

(31) Our Lord did not doubt their present faith (17:8); but He knew that the hour of their full illumination had not yet come, firmly as they believed it had (verse 30). Their present light was momentary. The clear and continuing light was in the future, of which He has spoken to them.

(32) See notes on Matt. 26:31, 56.

(33) See notes on verse 11; 12:31; 14:27; 15:7.

17

(1) These words spake Jesus, and lifted up his eyes to heaven.—It has been suggested that the prayer of this chapter, as well as the discourses which preceded it, was uttered as they were preparing to leave the chamber after supper. But comp. note on 15:1. The upward look naturally is expressive of feeling, irrespective of place. This chapter is often spoken of as the High Priest's Prayer (comp. verse 19). Bengel speaks of this chapter as the simplest in word, and profoundest in thought, in the whole Bible. The key to the thought is in the presence of the Spirit, who shall guide into all truth (16:26).

Glorify thy Son, that thy Son also may glorify thee.—Glorifying the Son (comp. verse 5) implies the dark path of death, which has to be trodden before that glory will be attained. The glorifying of the Father by the Son is the manifestation of

God's glory in the completion of the Messianic work by the mission of the Advocate and the future victories of the Church.

(2) The glory for which He asks is in accordance with the decree which appointed His Messianic work. "All flesh" represents a Greek translation of a Hebrew phrase. Its special signification is humanity as such, considered in its weakness and imperfection. The Messianic work of Christ is to give eternal life to those whom God has given Him.

(3, 4) The accomplishment of the Messianic work consists in revealing to men the only true God through Jesus Christ.

(5) With the glory which I had with thee before the world was.—Jesus claimed for Himself the possession of the divine glory in His pre-existent state before the world was. He claimed this in personality distinct from, but in essence one with, God. (Comp. 1:1, 18; Phil. 2:4-9.) The thought here is uttered in the words of Christ Himself, and these words are a prayer to the Father. There can be no explanation of verses 1-5 of this chapter which denies that our Lord Jesus Christ claimed for Himself that He was divine and co-eternal with the Father.

(6) He thinks of the disciples as a body separated from the world and as given to Him by the Father. They were morally prepared by the earlier manifestation of God for the fuller manifestation in Christ. They were God's in more than name; and therefore when Christ was revealed to them, they recognized Him of whom Moses and the prophets did speak. The Son was only the completion of the revelation of the Father to them. Christ's word was that of the Father who sent Him.

(8) Our Lord explains here how the disciples attained to the knowledge of which He had spoken in verse 7, and lays stress on His own work in teaching them and on the matter taught as that which the Father had committed unto Him (12:49).

(9) The present prayer was like that which pious rabbis were accustomed to offer for their pupils. It is from its very nature applicable only to disciples. He is leaving them, and commends them to His Father's care. They were the Father's before they were given to the Son. By that gift they have become the Father's more fully (verses 6-8).

(10) The words are all-inclusive, asserting absolute community in all things between the Father and Son. The fact that Christ is glorified in them forms another reason for

His special prayer for them. Its accomplishment is more fully to be realized in that future of the Spirit's work which all through this chapter is regarded as present. (Comp. 16:14.)

(11) And now I am no more in the world.—The words have a special reference to the interval between His death and the day of Pentecost, which would be for the disciples a time of darkness and danger, when they would have special need of the Father's care.

Holy Father.—Comp. verses 1, 24, 25. There is a special fitness in the word "Holy" here, as in opposition to the world. The disciples were left in the world, but they were not of the world (verse 14). These were spiritually God's children, separated from the world (verse 6), and He commits them to the Holy Father, that they may be kept from the evil of the world and become themselves one with the Father.

(12) And none of them is lost, but the son of perdition.—The "son of perdition" was included in "them which thou gavest me." For him there was the same preservation and the same guardianship as for those who remained in the fold. The sheep wandered from the flock and was lost by his own act. (See notes on 6:37-39, 71.)

The term "son of perdition" is a well-known Hebrew idiom. A "son of perdition" is one in whose nature there is the quality expressed by "perdition." In the original, the phrase is used in Isa. 57:4 to express the apostasy of the Israelites, and occurs once again in II Thess. 2:3 of the "man of sin." It is used in the Gospel of Nicodemus of the devil.

That the scripture might be fulfilled.—See notes on 13:18; Acts 1:20.

(15) I pray not that thou shouldest take them out of the world.—There is a work for them to glorify Him (verse 10), and He prays not that they should be taken out of the world before their work is done. The Christian ideal is not freedom from work, but strength to do it; not freedom from temptation, but power to overcome it; not freedom from suffering, but joy in an abiding sense of the Father's love; not absence from the world, but grace to make the world better for our presence; not holy lives driven from the world, and living apart from it, but holy lives spent in the world and leavening it.

But that thou shouldest keep them from the evil.—Comp. note on Matt. 6:13. The usage of John is, beyond question, in favor of the masculine: "that thou shouldest keep them from the evil one."

(17) Sanctify them through thy truth.—They had through Christ received the Father's word, which was truth, and had passed into a new region of life, separate from the world (verses 6-8, 14-16). He has prayed that the Father would preserve them in this, and now He prays further that the Father would in this new region of life set them apart for the work to which He had sent them (verse 18.)

The idea at the root of the word rendered "sanctify" is not holiness, but separation. It is opposed not to what is impure, but to what is common, and is constantly used in the Greek of the Old Testament for the consecration of persons and things to the service of God. Therefore our Lord can use it of Himself in 10:36, and in this context (verse 19). He was Himself "set apart and sent into the world." He has to send them into the world in the same way (verse 18), and prays that they may be in the same way consecrated for their work.

(19) And for their sakes I sanctify myself.—See note on verse 17. The consecration here is that to the work which was immediately before Him—the offering Himself as a sacrifice. By this consecration of Himself He will, as both Priest and Sacrifice, enter into the Holy of Holies of the heavenly temple, and will send the Holy Ghost, who will consecrate them.

(20) Neither pray I for these alone.—The thought of the work to which the apostles are to be consecrated and sent leads on to a wider thought. The future of the Church is so immediately in our Lord's mind that it is spoken of as actually present. The prayer is enlarged to include them.

(21) That they all may be one—i.e., both "these" (the apostles) and "them also which shall believe on me through their word" (the whole body of believers in all times and places). He expresses in this grand thought of the unity of the whole Church the fullness of the purpose of His prayer. The result of the union of believers with God, and therefore with each other, will be that the world will see in it a proof of the divine origin of Christianity.

(22) And the glory which thou gavest me I have given them.—The fullness of the glory which awaits Him at His Father's right hand is thought of as already given to Him; and the believers who have become, and will become, one with Him, to whom

He has given eternal life (verse 2), are thought of as sharers in it.

(23) That they may be made perfect in one.—The unity is the result of their being made perfect. (Comp. notes on Heb. 10:14; I John 2:5; 4:12, 17, 18.)

(24) See note on verse 22. The preincarnate glory of the Son was of His divine nature only. That with which the Father has glorified Him is "the glory which He had with the Father before the world was" (verse 5), but it is the Son of man who is glorified with it, and therefore it is that human nature is made capable of receiving it.

For thou lovedst me before the foundation of the world.—See note on verse 5.

(26) In part this had been received, but in part only. The first steps in the spiritual lessons had been taken, but in His Presence in the Paraclete He will guide them into all truth, and make known to hearts quickened to receive it, the love of God which passes knowledge. The thought of Christ's prayer in this verse is expanded in Paul's prayer in Eph. 3:17-19.

18

(1) He went forth with his disciples—i.e., He went forth from the city. See notes on 15:1; 17:1.

The brook Cedron.—The name is formed from a Hebrew word which means "black," and was so called from the color of its turbid waters, or from darkness of the chasm through which they flowed. The name seems to have been properly applied not so much to the torrent itself as to the ravine through which it flowed, on the east of Jerusalem, between the city and the Mount of Olives. Its sides are for the most part precipitous, but here and there paths cross it, and at the bottom are cultivated strips of land. Its depth varies, but in some places it is not less than 100 feet.

Where was a garden.—See note on Matt. 26:36. John does not record the passion of Gethsemane, but this verse indicates its place in the narrative.

(3) John uses the technical word for the Roman cohort. It was the garrison band from Fort Antonia, at the northeast corner of the Temple. These were sent by the chief priests and Pharisees, with Judas for their guide (comp. Matt. 26:47), and their authority was supported by the civil power.

(4) The kiss of Judas, mentioned in all

the earlier gospels, must be placed here between "went forth" and "said unto them."

(6) They went backward, and fell to the ground.—There is nothing in the narrative to suggest that our Lord put forth miraculous power to cause this terror. The impression is rather that it was produced by the majesty of His person, and by the answer which to Jewish ears conveyed the unutterable name, "Jehovah" (I AM). (See notes on 8:24, 25.)

(9) See notes on 17:12. The quotation is not verbally accurate, i.e., John, quoting the words of Christ, is satisfied in giving the substance of it. His quoting with an application to temporal persecution that which had been spoken of spiritual persecution illustrates the way in which words are said to be "fulfilled" in more than one sense. And the quotation shows that in the thought of John himself, the prayer recorded in chap. 17 is no resume of the words of our Lord, but an actual record of His prayer; he quotes the "saying" as fulfilled, just as he would have quoted a passage from the Old Testament Scriptures.

(10) Then Simon Peter having a sword drew it . . .—See notes on Matt. 26:51.

(11) The cup which my Father hath given me, shall I not drink it?—See notes on Matt. 20:22; 26:39.

(13, 14) See notes on Matt. 26:3, 57; Luke 3:2; John 11:49-52. After this doctrinal investigation (verse 19), it was necessary that He should be sent to the legal high priest for official trial in the presence of the Sanhedrin (verse 24), before being handed over to the civil power (verse 28). This present investigation was altogether of an informal character.

(15) Another disciple.—It is usually understood that John himself is intended by this designation. How he was known to the high priest we have no means of judging. We may, however, note that the name "John" occurs among the names of the kindred of the high priest in Acts 4:6.

(17) On Peter's denials, see notes on Matt. 26:69-75.

(19) He asked, we may think, about the number of Christ's followers, the aim they had in view, and the principles which He had taught them. The object of the questions was apparently to find some technical evidence in Christ's own words on which they may support the charges they are about to bring against Him in the legal trial before Caiaphas.

(22) Comp. Acts 23:2. A blow on the face

was a customary punishment for a supposed offense against the dignity of the high priest; but in that case it was ordered by the high priest himself, and the fact that it was done here without authority by one of the attendants confirms the opinion that this was not a legal trial before the judicial authority.

(25) And Simon Peter stood and warmed himself.—Comp. verse 18. The words are repeated to draw attention to the fact that he was standing in the court at the time when Jesus was sent from Annas unto Caiaphas, that is, from one wing of the quadrangular building across the court to the other. In Luke 22:61 it is said that "the Lord turned, and looked upon Peter."

(27) And immediately the cock crew.—See note on Matt. 26:75.

(28) On the accusation before Pilate, see notes on Matt. 27:11-14.

The hall of judgment.—Literally, the **Praetorium.** Comp. note on Matt. 27:27.

And it was early.—The Greek word occurs in the division of the night in Mark 13:35 for the time between cock-crowing and sunrise, i.e., from three to six o'clock; but comp. Matt. 27:1; Luke 22:66.

(29) Pilate then went out unto them—i.e., because of their religious scruples they would not enter into the palace.

What accusation bring ye against this man?—He asks for the formal charge which they bring against Him. He knew by hearsay what this was, but demands the legal accusation without which the trial could not proceed. As the Roman procurator, he demands what crime Jesus has committed against the Roman law.

(31) Their law gave them power to punish, but not the right of capital punishment. If they claim that the matter is wholly within their own power of judgment, then the sentence must also be limited to their own power. The Jews had lost this power since the time that Archelaus was deposed, and Judaea became a Roman province (A.D. 6 or 7). The Talmud speaks of the loss of this power forty years or more before the destruction of Jerusalem.

On the stoning of Stephen, which was an illegal act, comp. Acts 7.

(32) Signifying what death he should die.—See notes on 3:14; 12:33; comp. Matt. 20:19. If the Jews had possessed the power to put Him to death, they would have condemned Him on the technical charge of blasphemy, for which the punishment was stoning. (Comp. 8:59, 10:31; Acts 7:51.)

Crucifixion was not a Jewish punishment, and it was in the fact that He was executed, not by Jewish authority and on the charge of blasphemy, but by Roman authority and on a charge of Majestas (high treason), that His own prophecy of the manner of His death was fulfilled.

(33, 34) In the political sense in which Pilate would use the title, and in this sense only the claim could be brought against Him in Roman law, He was not King of the Jews. In the theocratic sense in which a Jew would use that title, He was King of the Jews.

(36) Jesus answered, My kingdom is not of this world.—The answer of Jesus is twofold, declaring that He is not a King in the political sense, and that He is a King in the moral sense. By "of this world" we are to understand that the nature and origin of His kingdom are not of this world, not that His kingdom will not extend in this world.

(37) He has indeed a kingdom, and He came into the world to be a king; but His rule is that of the majesty of truth, and His kingdom is to be established by His witness of the eternal truth which He had known with His Father, and which He alone could declare to man.

(38) Pilate saith unto him, What is truth?—Pilate seems to have been irritated by the refusal of the Jews to furnish a formal accusation (verse 31), and more so at the question of Jesus in verse 34 and the subtleties, as he thinks them, of verse 36.

I find in him no fault at all.—Better, "I find no crime in Him." "I find no ground for the legal charge (verse 33). Whatever He may be, there is no proof of treason against the majesty of Caesar."

On the attempt of Pilate to release Jesus (verses 39, 40), see notes of Matt. 27:15-23; Luke 23:13-23. It is preceded in Luke by the trial before Herod (Luke 23:6-12).

19

For the scourging of Jesus and the delivery to be crucified (verses 1-16), see notes on Matt. 27:24-30.

(5) Behold the man!—Pilate's "Ecce homo!" is an appeal to the multitude. That picture of suffering—is it not enough? Will none in that throng lift up a cry for mercy, and save Him from the death for which the Sanhedrin are calling?

(7) We have a law, and by our law he ought to die.—They feel the bitter sarcasm of Pilate's taunt and appeal to their own law, which, in accordance with the general Roman policy, was in force in all questions which did not directly affect the government. They change the accusation then from one of treason against Caesar (verse 12), of which Pilate claimed to be judge, and assert that Jesus is by that law guilty of a capital offense, for which He ought to die.

(8) When Pilate therefore heard that saying, he was the more afraid.—He was afraid because of his wonder who Jesus really was. His wife's dream (Matt. 27:19) had furnished an evil omen which the superstititon of the most educated classes of the Roman empire would interpret as a message from the gods; and now the Jews speak of Him as one who claimed to be the Son of God.

(9) But Jesus gave him no answer.—Pilate's question was one which to him could not be answered in reality, and therefore was not answered in appearance. The answer had, indeed, already been given (18:37), but he had treated it with the impatience which showed he could not receive it now. Not of the truth, he could not hear the voice of the Son of God, and therefore that voice did not speak.

(11) Thou couldest have no power at all against me, except it were given thee from above.—By this is meant the power which was given to him by God, and the form in which it is expressed ("from above") has a special force in connection with the question of verse 9, "Whence comest Thou?" That power of which he boasted existed only because He against whom he boasts submitted to it of His own will. But that power was given to him of God for the carrying out of the Messianic purposes which rendered the death of Jesus necessary.

He that delivered me unto thee hath the greater sin.—Judas delivered our Lord to the Jews. But it was the Sanhedrin, and especially Caiaphas, the high priest, who, professing to represent God on earth, had delivered up the Son of God to Pilate, and had declared that by the law He ought to die. (Comp. 11:49; 18:14-28.)

(12) If thou let this man go, thou art not Caesar's friend . . .—They knew, indeed, that it was a claim to be "king" in a sense widely different from any which would have affected the empire of Caesar; but Pilate has refused to condemn Him on the political charge without formal trial, and he has refused to accept their own condemnation of Jesus on the charge of blasphemy. He dare not refuse the force of an appeal which says that he is not Caesar's friend, and suggests an accusation against himself at Rome. The pages of Tacitus and Suetonius abound with examples of ruin wreaked on families in the name of the "law of treason."

(13) The Pavement, but in the Hebrew, Gabbatha.—Both these words occur here only, and are instances of the writer's minute knowledge of the localities in Jerusalem. The word literally means "stoned-paved," and was the Greek name for the tesselated "pavement" of marble and colored stones with which from the time of Sylla the Romans delighted to adorn the Praetorium. The Chaldee word means "an elevated place," so that the one name was given to it from its form, and the other from the material of which it was made. Suetonius (**Life,** 46) tells us that Julius Caesar carried about with him such pieces of marble and stone, but the mention of the "place" bears the impression that it was a fixture in front of the Praetorium at Jerusalem, in which the Bema (judgment seat) was placed. (See note on Matt. 27:27.) Josephus mentions that the whole of the Temple mountain was paved with this kind of Mosaic work (**Ant.** 5:5, §2).

(14) And it was the preparation of the passover.—See note on Matt. 26:17.

And about the sixth hour.—See notes on Matt. 27:45. John is not careful to give the time more than roughly "about the sixth hour," where as Mark (15:25) states that the crucifixion took place at "the third hour" (nine o'clock). Their sorrow would have made minutes seem as hours, and the sun, which on other days marked the hours, was on that day itself darkened. Matthew is equally uncertain at what exact time there was the cry with a loud voice (27:46), and Luke does not give the exact time when the darkness began (23:44).

It must also be borne in mind that the third, sixth, and ninth hours (comp. Matt. 20:3, 5) seem to have been, in common life, rough divisions of the day, corresponding to the watches of the night. An event occurring at ten o'clock might have been spoken of roughly as about the third hour, while it might, on the other hand, be thought of as within the division called the sixth hour.

Behold your King!—The words are spoken in bitter irony toward the Jews, as those in verse 15 and those written over the cross (verse 19).

(15) We have no king but Caesar.—They

are driven by Pilate's taunt, and by their hatred of Jesus, to a denial of their own highest hopes. They who gloried in the Theocracy, and hoped for a temporal Messianic reign, which should free them from Roman bondage, confess that Caesar is their only king. The words were doubtless meant, as those in verse 12, to drive Pilate to comply with their wishes, under the dread of an accusation at Rome. They had this effect.

(16) Then delivered he him therefore unto them—i.e., to the chief priests. The Crucifixion was actually carried out by the Roman soldiers, acting under the direction of the chief priests.

(17, 18) For the way of the cross, see notes on Matt. 27:31-34; Mark 15:20-23, 27; Luke 23:26-33.

(19) See note on Matt. 27:37.

(20-22) These verses are peculiar to John, and furnish another instance of his exact knowledge of what took place at Jerusalem.

(20) Hebrew, and Greek, and Latin.— "Hebrew," i.e., the current Syro-Chaldaic, was the language of the people generally. "Greek" was the most widely-known language of the time. "Latin" was the official language of the Roman Empire.

(21) The inscription could be read by all comers, and the Messianic title "King of the Jews" would be exposed to scorn. Yet these are the men who said, in order to accomplish the death of Jesus, "We have no king but Caesar."

The expression "chief priests of the Jews" occurs only here in the New Testament, perhaps in contrast to the title "King of the Jews," to indicate that their anxiety about the title came from them as representatives of the national honor.

(23, 24) See notes on Matt. 27:35, 36; Luke 23:34.

(25-27) These verses relate an incident which is found in John only.

(25) See notes on Matt. 10:3; 27:56.

(26, 27) See note on 2:4. He now sees standing by the cross her who, by His death, will be left without son as well as without husband, for the silence of the history can be accounted for only on the supposition that Joseph already was dead; and in the tenderness of His love He commits her to the care of him whom He Himself had loved beyond others (see note on 13:23), because beyond others he could receive His love. The solemn committal is a double one.

(28-30) For accounts of the darkness and

death, see notes on Matt. 27:45-50; Mark 15:33-39.

(28) There seems to be good reason for understanding the words "that the Scripture might be completed" of the events of the whole life, and not of the words which immediately follow.

(29) And put it upon hyssop.—This detail is peculiar to John. The stalks, from a foot to a foot and a half high, would be sufficient to reach to the cross. The plant is named in one other passage in the New Testament (Heb. 9:19), and is frequent in the Greek of the Old Testament.

(30) It is finished.—The order of the seven words of the cross will be: (1) "Father, forgive them, for they know not what they do" (Luke 23:34); (2) "Verily I say unto thee, To-day shalt thou be with me in Paradise" (Luke 23:43); (3) "Woman, behold thy son," "Behold thy mother" (John 19:26, 27); (4) "Eli, Eli, lama sabachthani?" (Matt. 27:46; Mark 15:34); (5) "I thirst" (verse 28); (6) "It is finished" (verse 29); (7) "Into thy hands I commend my spirit" (Luke 23:46).

(31-37) The account of the piercing of the side is peculiar to John.

(31) The preparation, . . . an high day.— The Roman custom was to allow the bodies to remain on the cross. To the Jews this was defilement (Deut. 21:22, 23), against which they were the more anxious to take precaution because of the approaching Sabbath.

That their legs might be broken.—The breaking of the legs by means of clubs was a Roman punishment, known by the name of **crurifragium**, which sometimes accompanied crucifixion, and appears also to have been used as a separate punishment. That its purpose was, or that its effect would be, to cause death is the impression we derive from the present context (verse 33).

(34) But one of the soldiers with a spear pierced his side.—They had seen that He was dead, and therefore did not break the legs. To cause death was not, then, the object in piercing the side; and yet it may have seemed to make death doubly sure. It is certain (20:27) that the act caused a deep wound, and that the point of the lance therefore penetrated to the interior organs of the body.

And forthwith came there out blood and water.—It has been suggested that the physical death of Christ resulted from rupture of the heart, and that the cavities of the heart and the surrounding vessels contained a watery fluid.

(36) A bone of him shall not be broken.— See Exod. 12:46; Num. 9:12; Ps. 34:20. The reference is to the Paschal Lamb, in which John the Baptist had already seen a type of Christ (see note on 1:29), and which Paul afterward more definitely identifies with Him (I Cor. 5:7).

(37) They shall look on him whom they pierced.—See Zech. 12:10; comp. Rev. 1:7. John thinks of the prophecy which spoke of Jehovah as pierced by His people, and sees it fulfilled in the Messiah pierced on the cross. For at least partial fulfillment of the prophecy, see notes on 8:28; 12:32.

(38-42) For the burial, see notes on Matt. 27:57-61.

(39) Nicodemus, which at the first came to Jesus by night.—He is mentioned only by John. (See notes on 3:1, 2; 7:50.)

A mixture of myrrh and aloes.—See note on Matt. 2:11; comp. Ps. 45:8. The aloe is an Eastern odoriferous wood. Myrrh and aloes were probably pulverized and mixed together, and then placed in the linen in which the body was wrapped.

About an hundred pound weight.— Comp. 12:3. The quantity is clearly much more than could have been placed in the linen which surrounded the body; but the offering was one of love, and part of it may have been placed in the sepulcher. (See II Chron. 16:14.)

(40) And wound it in linen clothes with the spices.—See notes on 11:44.

20

(1, 2) For the visit of the women to the sepulcher and their announcement to the disciples, see notes on Matt. 28:1-4, 8.

(3-10) The details of the visit of Peter and John are peculiar to this gospel. Here we have the whole scene pictured with all the vividness and exactness of one who stated what he himself saw and experienced.

(9) For as yet they knew not the scripture.—This explains in what sense John now believed (verse 8). Up to this time they did not know the meaning of the Scripture which foretold the Resurrection; but from that moment at least they recognized in the fact of the absent body of Christ the truth that He must rise again. (See notes on 2:21, 22.)

That he must rise again from the dead.— See notes on Luke 24:26, 44.

(12) And seeth two angels in white sitting.—Comp. Matt. 28:5-7; Mark 16:5-7;

Luke 24:4-8. This is to be regarded as a distinct vision to Mary, which, from the fullness with which it is recorded, we must suppose that she herself related to the evangelist.

(15) Sir, if thou have borne him hence . . —The word rendered "Sir" is generally a mark of respect, used to a stranger and even to an inferior. The "gardener" would have been a servant of Joseph of Arimathaea, and as such may have become known to Mary at the time of embalming.

(16) Rabboni; which is to say, Master.— See notes on Mark 10:51, which is the only other passage in the New Testament where "Rabboni" occurs. She had heard in the well-known voice her own name, and it brought back to her all the old associations. It is the "Master," or, as the Hebrew word means, "My Master," and she falls at His feet to embrace Him.

(17) Touch me not; for I am not yet ascended to my Father.—The probable explanation of these words is to be found in the fact that she had cast herself at His feet with the customary reverential embrace of the knees, perhaps to make sure that it was the Lord's body, and that His words are meant to prevent this. "Touch" represents a Greek word which means to "cling to," to "fasten on," to "grasp" an object. The tense is present, and the prohibition is, therefore, not of an individual act but of the habit: "Do not continue clinging to Me." Her act supposed a condition which had not yet been accomplished. He had not returned to earth to abide permanently with His disciples in the presence of the Paraclete (comp. 14:18), for He had not yet ascended to the Father. There should come a permanent closeness of union in His presence in the soul; but then the spirit which her act was manifesting was one which would prevent this presence. The coming of the Paraclete depended upon His going to the Father (comp. 16:7), but she would cling to a visible presence, and has not learned the truth so hard to learn, "It is expedient for you that I go away" (16:7.)

But go to my brethren.—Comp. Matt. 28:10. There is a special force in the word "brethren" as spoken by the risen Lord, in that it declares the continuance of His human nature. (See Heb. 2:11.)

I ascend unto my Father, and your Father.—The present is used of the future, which He regards as immediately at hand. The message to the brethren is an assurance that the going to the Father, of which He

had so often spoken to them, was about to be realized. The victory over death has been accomplished. This appearance on earth is an earnest of the return to heaven.

(19-25) For this appearance to the disciples, see notes on Luke 24:36-43. Between the last verse and this we must suppose to occur the bribing of the guard (Matt. 28:11-15) and the conversation on the way to Emmaus (Luke 24:13-35; see also Mark 16:12, 13).

When the doors were shut where the disciples were assembled . . .—The body of the risen Lord was indeed the body of His human life, but it was not subject to the ordinary conditions of human life. The power that had upheld it as He walked upon the Sea of Galilee (6:16-21) made it during those forty days independent of laws of gravitation and of material resistance. (See notes on Luke 24:15, 31, 39.)

The "fear of the Jews" naturally followed the Crucifixion. The Shepherd was struck, and the flock was scattered. They would remember, too, His own words, which foretold persecution for them (15:18), and there may have been definite charges against some of them. Peter, e.g., had drawn upon himself the hostility of the high priest's household, and John was known to be among the disciples. (Comp. 18:8, 25.)

(20) He shewed unto them his hands and his side.—In Luke's account (24:39) we have "hands and feet." The piercing of the side is related by John only. (Comp. verses 25-27.)

(21) Then said Jesus to them again, Peace be unto you.—These words may be here a solemn repetition of the greeting in verse 19, by which our Lord's own message of peace is immediately connected with that which the apostles were to deliver to the world. He reminds them of the apostleship to which He has called them, gives them an earnest of the Presence which will never leave them, but always qualify them for it (verse 22), and places before them the greatness of the work to which He sends them (verse 23).

As my Father hath sent me, even so send I you.—Comp. 17:18, where the words occur in prayer to the Father. As spoken here to the disciples they are the indentification of them with Himself in His mediatorial work. He is the great Apostle (Heb. 3:1); they are ambassadors for Christ, to whom He commits the ministry of reconciliation (II Cor. 5:18). He stands in the same relation to the Father as that in which they stand to Him. He and they stand also in the same relation to the world.

(22) And when he had said this, he breathed on them.—The word rendered "breathed" occurs nowhere else in the New Testament, but was familiar from its use in the Greek (LXX) of Gen. 2:7. John writes of the first step in that great moral change which passed over the disciples after the crucifixion, and of which the day of Pentecost witnessed the accomplishment.

And saith unto them, Receive ye the Holy Ghost.—He then gave to them a sign, which was itself to faithful hearts as the first-fruits of that which was to come. His act was sacramental, and with the outer and visible sign there was the inward and spiritual grace. The word used was that used when He said to them, "Take (**receive ye**), eat; this is my body" (Matt. 26:26; Mark 14:22). It would come to them now with a fullness of sacred meaning. The risen body is present with them. The constant spiritual presence in the person of the Paraclete is promised to them.

(23) Whose soever sins ye remit, they are remitted unto them . . .—See notes on Matt. 16:19; 18:18. This power is here immediately connected with the representative character of the disciples as apostles sent by Christ, as He was Himself sent by the Father (verse 21), and its validity is dependent upon their reception of the Holy Ghost (verse 22), by whom Christ Himself is present in them (14:18; 16:7-11).

(24) But Thomas, one of the twelve, called Didymus . . .—See notes on 11:16; 14:5. His determination—"I will not believe" (verse 25)—is expressed in its strongest form by the double Greek negative: "I will by no means believe."

(26) And after eight days again his disciples were within.—That is, as we should now say, on the first Sunday after Easter. This appearance on the recurrence of the first day of the week takes its place among the steps by which the disciples passed from the observance of the Jewish Sabbath to that of the Christian Sunday.

(27) Then saith he to Thomas . . .—This implies a knowledge of the words of verse 25, which in itself would carry conviction to the mind of Thomas. This repetition must have carried with this conviction a sense of shame at his unbelief.

And be not faithless, but believing.—The words do not apply to the fact of the Resurrection only, but to the general spiritual condition of the apostle. His demand for

the evidence of the senses was a step backward, a resting on the less, not on the more, certain. His Master would have him retrace that step, and become one who rests upon the intuition of the Spirit.

(28) Thomas answered and said unto him.—It is implied that he did not make use of the tests which his Master offered him, but that he at once expressed the fullness of his conviction. This is confirmed by the words of verse 29, "Because thou hast seen me."

(29) The command of verse 27 had done its work, and the words are words of approval; but yet they are not wholly so. He had arrived at conviction by means of the senses, but the higher blessedness was that of those who see by the eye of the spirit and not by that of the body, who base their confidence on the conviction of the faith-faculty and are independent of the changing phenomena of the senses.

(30) And many other signs truly did Jesus in the presence of his disciples.—See note on 2:11. We must understand the "signs" not of the proofs of the Resurrection only, but of the works wrought during the whole life. The writer's narrative is drawing to a close, and he explains the fact that he has recorded so little of a life which contained so much. There were, indeed, many other signs which he, as an eyewitness, remembered, but which it was not within his purpose to relate.

It would seem to follow that verses 30 and 31 are the conclusion of the original gospel, and that chap. 21 is to be regarded as a postscript or appendix, yet proceeding from the hand of the apostle himself.

(31) But these are written, that ye might believe that Jesus is the Christ, the Son of God.—We have here the writer's own statement of his object in writing his narrative, and also the explanation of what seems an abrupt end. His object is that those for whom he writes may become believers and read in these signs the spiritual truths which lay behind them. The development of faith in the apostles themselves has reached its highest stage in the confession of Thomas. He has recorded the blessedness of those who shall believe without sight, uttered in his Master's words. In the confession of Thomas, and in the comment of our Lord, the object of the author finds its full expression, and with their words the gospel finds its fitting close.

21

(1) At the sea of Tiberias.—See note on 6:1. The name is found only in John.

(2) See notes on Matt. 10:1-4. It is most probable that we have here the names of all in the group of seven who were apostles, and that the two unnamed persons were disciples in the wider sense in which the word is often used by John (6:60, 66; 7:3; 8:31; 18:19). If they were Andrew and Philip, which has been supposed from 1:40, 43, it is not easy to understand their position in the list, or the absence of their names.

(3) Simon Peter saith unto them, I go a fishing.—Comp. Luke 5:5, 6. They returned to their ordinary work during the interval between the Passover and Pentecost. It does not express either an abandonment of their higher vocation, or an expectation of the presence of the Lord.

(7) Therefore that disciple whom Jesus loved saith unto Peter.—John, true to the life of contemplation, is first to trace in the present draught of fishes an analogy with the earlier one, and to discern that the Master who spoke then is present now. Peter, true to the life of action, is first to rush into that Master's presence when he is told that it is the Lord.

He girt his fisher's coat unto him (for he was naked).—That is, as the words in the original clearly imply, he put on the garment which workmen customarily used. This seems to have been a kind of linen frock worn over the shirt. The word "naked" makes it probable that Peter was wearing some under-garment, and that reverence for the Lord, into whose presence he is about to go, led him to add to this the outer frock. (Comp. Acts 19:12.)

(8) Two hundred cubits.—That is, about 100 yards. The shortness of the distance explains how they were able to drag the net in tow.

(11) The event of Luke 5:1-11 represents the visible Church, containing good and bad; the net is cast without special direction as to side; the net was broken and many escaped. This represents God's elect, foreknown by Him; all are good; the net is brought to shore, and none are lost. (See notes on the parable of the drawnet in Matt. 13:47-50.)

(14) This is now the third time that Jesus shewed himself to his disciples.—The writer is giving his own witness. He passes over, therefore, the appearances to Mary Magdalene and others, and counting only those "to the disciples"—to the Ten on the first Easter day, and to the Eleven on its octave—gives this appearance as the third. (See note on I Cor. 15:5-7.)

(15) Jesus saith to Simon Peter, Simon, son of Jonas.—The contrast of the name by which the evangelist denotes, and with that by which the Lord addresses Peter, at once strikes us as significant, and the more so because it comes in a context containing several significant verbal contrasts. Our Lord's words would seem to address him as one who had fallen from the steadfastness of the Rock-man and had been true rather to his natural than to his apostolic name. (See notes on 1:42; Matt. 16:17.)

Lovest thou me more that these?—i.e., than these disciples who are present here with you. The obvious reference is to Peter's own comparison of himself with others in the confidence of love which he thought could never fail. (Comp. Matt. 26:33; Mark 14:29.) The three questions have been generally understood to have special force in the restoration of him who had three times denied his Lord, now three times declares his love for Him, and is three times entrusted with a work for Him. And there may have been some significant recollections from the external circumstances of the event: the lake, the nets, (Matt. 4:19), the "fire of coals" (18:18).

Yea, Lord; thou knowest that I love thee.—Peter uses a less strong expression for love than that which had been used by our Lord.

(16) He saith to him again the second time.—Our Lord does not continue the comparison "more than these." He uses the same word for the higher, more intellectual love, and Peter replies by the same declaration of personal attachment, and the same appeal to his Master's knowledge of him.

(17) He saith unto him the third time.—This time the Lord uses Peter's own word, and His question seems to say, "Dost thou, in personal affection and devotion, really love Me?" This time the love which Peter knows has ever filled his soul seems to be doubted. **Feed my sheep.**—The order is "lambs" (verse 15), "sheep" (verse 16), "sheep" (verse 17). He who loved Christ is to be like Christ, a good shepherd, giving his life for the sheep who are Christ's. He who had been loved and forgiven, held up that he might not fall, restored after he had fallen, is to be to others what Christ had been to him—feeding men with spiritual truths as they can bear them, gently guiding and caring for those who are as the weak ones of the flock through ignorance, prejudice, waywardness. As a remarkable instance of how the Great Shepherd's words impressed themselves upon the apostle's mind, comp. I Pet. 2:25.

(18) Thou wast young.—Literally, "thou wast younger" (than thou art now). Peter must have been at this time (comp. Matt. 8:14) in middle age.

Thou shalt stretch forth thy hands, and another shall gird thee.—Tradition, from Tertullian forward (**Scorp.** 15; **De Praescr.** 35), states that Peter was crucified, so interpreting this prophecy by the event. It seems impossible, however, to adopt the traditional reference. We take the words "stretch forth thy hands" as expressing symbolically the personal surrender previous to being girded by another. To what exact form of death the context does not specify.

(19) This spake he, signifying by what death he should glorify God.—These words are a comment by the writer, and quite in John's style. (Comp. 2:21; 6:6; 7:39; 12:33.) "By what death" (comp. 12:33; 18:32) indicates generally the martyrdom of Peter as distinct from a natural death, without special reference to the crucifixion.

Follow me.—Now the familiar command has come again with the prophecy of martyrdom, and it must have carried to his mind the thought that he was to follow the Lord in suffering and death itself, and through the dark path which He had trodden was to follow Him to the Father's home.

(21) Lord, and what shall this man do?—The motive prompting this question was probably that of loving interest in the future of his friend John.

(22) If I will that he tarry till I come, what is that to thee?—The answer must be taken as reproving the spirit which would inquire into another's life and work, with the effect of weakening the force of its own. He is told to follow, but is ready to lead; he would know and guide his friend's life rather than his own. To him, and to all, there comes the truth that the Father is the Husbandman, and it is He who trains every branch of the vine.

The word rendered "tarry" is that which before has been rendered "abide" (see 12:34). It is here opposed to "Follow me" (in the martyrdom), and means to abide in life.

(23) Jesus said not unto him, He shall not die; but, If . . .—The mistake of the brethren arose from their not attending to the force of the conditional particle. They took as a statement what had been said as a supposition, and understood it in the current belief that the Second Advent would come in their own generation. (Comp. I Cor. 15:51, 52; I Thess. 4:17.) This idea ceased with the first generation of Christians, and the mistake therefore would point to the close of the first century as a limit beyond which the date of the Gospel cannot be placed.

(24) This is the disciple which testifieth of these things, and wrote these things.—Comp. 20:30, 31. As we have there the formal close of what seems to have been the original gospel, we have here the formal close of the epilogue. The words are, however, too wide to be limited to the epilogue, and clearly refer to all that has preceded.

And we know that his testimony is true.—Though the words are an addition, they are a contemporaneous addition present in every important MS and version, and an undoubted part of the original text. We cannot tell who are the persons whose words we here read—Andrew it may be, or Philip, or some of the seventy disciples who had been witnesses of the work of Christ, or some of the Ephesian Church, as Aristion or John the Presbyter, who felt that the apostle's personal character gave the stamp of truth to all he said, and add here the conviction that all these words were true.

(25) And there are also many other things which Jesus did.—The MS evidence for this verse also is so conclusive that almost every competent editor inserts it in his text, but it is not found in the Sinaitic Codex. The transference from the plural (verse 24) to the singular has led to the supposition that it is the individual testimony of an amanuensis who, from personal knowledge of the life of Christ, or from knowledge derived from the Apostle John or from others, feels that full beyond all human thought as this gospel is, it is but a part of the greater fullness. No book could record, no words could tell, what that life was, or what things Jesus did. The disciples saw and believed, and wrote these things that we may believe, and in believing may have life in His name.

The word "Amen" is not found in the better MSS, and in no part of the written text. It is the natural prayer of some copyist, as it is the natural prayer of every devout reader that the writer's purpose may be fulfilled.

855

ACTS

1

(1) The former treatise.—Literally, "word" or "discourse." The Greek term had been used by Xenophon (**Anab.** 2:1; **Cyrop.** 8:1, 2), as Luke uses it, of what we should call the several "Books" or portions of his "histories."

O Theophilus.—See note on Luke 1:3. It has been thought that the absence of the words "most excellent" implies that the writer's friendship with Theophilus was now of a more intimate and familiar nature.

That Jesus began both to do and teach.—The verb "begin" is especially characteristic of Luke's gospel, in which it occurs no less than thirty-one times. Its occurrence at the beginning of the Acts is, accordingly, an indication of identity of authorship. He sought his materials from those who had been "from the beginning" eyewitnesses and ministers of the word (Luke 1:2).

(2) Until the day in which he was taken up.—As a matter of style, the same periodic structure is found in the opening of the gospel, made more conspicuous in the Greek by an arrangement of the words which places "he was taken up" at the close of the sentence.

That he through the Holy Ghost had given commandments.—In His human nature the Lord Jesus, after (as before) His passion, spoke as one who was "filled with the Holy Ghost" (Luke 4:1), to whom the Father had given the Spirit not by measure (John 3:34). The apostles were still waiting for the promised gift.

(3) By many infallible proofs.—There is no adjective in the Greek answering to "infallible"; but the noun is one which was used by writers on rhetoric (e.g., Aristotle, **Rhet.** 1:2) for proofs that carried certainty of conviction with them, as contrasted with those that were only probable or circumstantial. No other New Testament writer uses it.

Being seen of them forty days.—Luke uses an unusual word for "being seen," perhaps implying that the presence was not continuous, and that our Lord was seen only at intervals. This is the only passage which gives the time between the Resurrection and the Ascension. It had its counterpart in the forty days of the temptation in the wilderness (Luke 4:2), as that had had in the earlier histories of Moses (Exod. 24:18; Deut. 9:9, 18) and Elijah (I Kings 19:8).

There was a certain symbolic fitness in the time of triumph on earth coinciding with that of special conflict. The character of our Lord's risen life between His manifestations to the disciples is suggested in the history of the earlier forty days. The life was one of solitude and communion with His Father—a life of intercession, such as that which uttered itself in the great prayer of John 17.

The things pertaining to the kingdom of God.—This implies much unrecorded teaching. What is recorded points (1) to the true interpretation of the prophecies of the Messiah (Luke 24:27, 44, 45); (2) to the extension of the mission of the disciples to the whole Gentile world, and their admission to the kingdom by baptism (Matt. 28:19); (3) to the promises of supernatural powers and divine protection (Mark 16:15-18); (4) to that of His own perpetual presence with His Church (Matt. 28:20).

(5) John truly baptized with water.—See notes on Matt. 3:11 and John 3:3-5. Now they were told that their spirits were to be as fully plunged into the power of the divine Spirit as their bodies had then been in the waters of the Jordan. The time was left undefined, as a discipline to their faith and patience.

(6) Lord, wilt thou at this time restore again the kingdom?—Comp. Luke 19:11; 24:21. Hopes again were revived by the Resurrection, but still were predominantly national. Even the Twelve were thinking, not of a kingdom of God, embracing all mankind, but of a sovereignty restored to Israel.

(8) But ye shall receive power.—The use of the same English noun for two different Greek words is misleading; but if "authority" is used in verse 7, then "power" is an adequate rendering here. The consciousness of a new faculty of thought and speech would be to them a proof that the promise of the kingdom had not failed.

Ye shall be witnesses unto me.—The words (comp. Luke 24:48) strike the key-note of the whole book. Those which follow correspond to the great divisions of the Acts—Jerusalem, chaps. 1, 7; Judaea, 9:32; 12:19; Samaria, chap. 8; and the rest of the book as opening the wider record of the witness borne "to the uttermost parts of the earth." This witness was twofold: (1) of the works, the teachings, and, above all, of the Resurrection of Jesus; (2) of the purpose of the Father as revealed in the Son. The witness was to be at once historical and dogmatic.

(9) He was taken up; and a cloud received him...—It is remarkable how little stress is laid in the gospels on the fact which always has been so prominent in the creeds of Christendom. (See John 6:62; Acts 2:33; 3:21; Eph. 1:20; 1 Tim. 3:16.) But there was something like a moral necessity, following upon the fact of resurrection, for such a conclusion to our Lord's work on earth. With our thoughts of the relations of the earth to space and the surrounding orbs, we find it hard to follow that upward motion, and to ask what was its direction and where it terminated. We cannot get beyond the cloud; but that cloud was the token of the glory of the eternal Presence, as the Shechinah that of old filled the Temple (1 Kings 8:10, 11; Isa. 6:1-4), and it is enough for us to know that where God is there also is Christ, in the glory of the Father, retaining still, though under new conditions and laws, the human nature which made Him like unto His brethren.

(11) See Matt. 26:64; comp. Dan. 7:13.

(12) From the mount called Olivet.—See Luke 19:29. Symbolically, there seems a fitness in our Lord's entering into His rest on the great day of rest, if such is the intention of the writer's method of stating the distance here. It is after Luke's manner, as in the case of Emmaus (Luke 24:13), to give distances. The "Sabbath day's journey" was figured at 2,000 paces, or about six furlongs (three-fourths of a mile).

(13) They went up into an upper room, where abode...—Better, "into the upper room, where they were abiding." The house may have been the same as that in which the Paschal Supper had been eaten (Mark 14:15). The room of the Paschal Supper probably was on the first floor, the guest chamber used for meals; that in which the disciples now met, on the second floor, or loft, was used for retirement and prayer. It would seem from Luke 24:53 that they spent the greater part of each day in the Temple, and met together in the evening.

Peter, and James.—On the lists of the twelve apostles, see notes on Matt. 10:2-4.

(14) With the women.—The mention of "the devout women" as a definite body is characteristic of Luke as the only evangelist who names them. (See Luke 8:1-3; 23:49.) They probably were among his chief informants. We may reasonably think of the company as including Mary Magdalene, Salome, Susanna, Joanna, Mary and Martha of Bethany, possibly also the woman that had been a sinner (Luke 7:37).

Mary the mother of Jesus.—Brief as the record is, it has the interest of giving the last known fact, as distinct from legend or tradition, in the life of the mother of our Lord. Some apocryphal books represent her as staying at Jerusalem with John until her death, twenty-two years after the Ascension; others represent her as going with him to Ephesus and dying there.

With his brethren.—The last mention of the "brethren" had shown them as still unbelieving (John 7:5). Various explanations of their change may be given. They may have been drawn to believe before the Crucifixion by the great miracle of the resurrection of Lazarus. And if the mother of Jesus were with John, the brethren also were likely to come, in greater or less measure, under the influence of their cousin. Note that the brethren are here emphatically distinguished from the apostles, and therefore that James the son of Alphaeus cannot rightly be identified with James the Lord's brother. (See note on Matt. 12:46.)

(15) The number of names together were about an hundred and twenty.—The number probably included the Seventy of Luke 10:1, perhaps also Joseph of Arimathaea and Nicodemus, and some of the "five hundred" who had seen their risen Lord in Galilee or elsewhere (1 Cor. 15:6). The use of "names" may be merely as a synonym for "persons," but it suggests the idea of there having been a list from which Luke extracted those that seemed most conspicuous.

(16) Men and brethren.—The tone of Peter's speech is that of one who felt that his offense had been forgiven fully, and that now he was restored by the charge given him (John 21:15-17) to his former position as guide and leader of the other disciples.

Which the Holy Ghost by the mouth of David spake...—We have here, obviously, the first fruits of the new method of interpretation in which the apostles had been instructed (Luke 24:27, 45). They already had been taught that the Holy Spirit which their Lord had promised to them had before spoken by the prophets. Comp. II Pet. 1:21, the correspondence being an evidence for the genuineness of that epistle.

(18, 19) See notes on Matt. 27:5-8. The whole passage must be regarded as a note of the historian, not as part of the speech of Peter. It was not likely that he, speaking to disciples, all of whom knew the Aramaic, or popular Hebrew of Palestine, should stop to explain that Aceldama meant "in their proper tongue, The field of blood."

(20) For it is written in the book of Psalms.—Peter's purpose in making the quotation is to show that the disciples should not be 'taggered by the treachery of Judas and the seeming failure of their hopes. The Psalms had represented the righteous sufferer as the victim of treachery.

(21) Wherefore of these men which have companied with us.—The apostles must present themselves to the people in their symbolic completeness, as sent to the twelve tribes of Israel, and the gap left by the traitor must be filled by one qualified, as they were, to bear witness of what had been said or done by their Lord during His ministry, and, above all, of His Resurrection from the dead. That would seem, even in Paul's estimate, to have been a condition of apostleship (I Cor. 9:1).

(23) They appointed.—It is uncertain whether this was the act of the apostles, presenting the two men to the choice of the whole body of disciples, or of the community choosing them for ultimate decision by lot.

Joseph called Barsabas, who was surnamed Justus.—Eusebius (Hist. 1:12) states that he was one of the Seventy. The name Barsabas (son of the oath, or of wisdom) may have been a patronymic, like Bar-jona, or may have been given, like Barnabas, as denoting character. (It appears again in Judas Barsabas of 15:22, and on the former assumption the two disciples may have been brothers.) The epithet Justus, the just one, is significant as possibly indicating, as in the case of James the Just, an especially high standard of ascetic holiness.

Matthias.—The name, like Matthew (see Matt. 9:9), signified "given by Jehovah," and had become popular in various forms, from the fame of Mattathias, the great head of the Maccabean family.

(25) That he might go to his own place.—We find in the words the kind of reserve natural in one that could neither bring himself to cherish hope nor venture to pronounce the condemnation which belonged to the Searcher of hearts. All that had been revealed to him was that "it had been good for that man if he had not been born" (Mark 14:21).

(26) And they gave forth their lots.—The most usual way of casting lots in such cases was to write each name on a tablet, place them in an urn, and then shake the urn until one came out. A like custom prevailed among the Greeks (Sophocles, **Aias.** 1285;

comp. Prov. 16:33). The practice was recognized, it may be noted, in the Law (Lev. 16:8).

He was numbered with the eleven apostles.—The suffrage of the Church unanimously confirmed the indication of the divine will which had been given by the lot. It may be that the new apostle took the place which Judas had left vacant, and was the last of the Twelve.

2

(1) The day of Pentecost.—The divine choice of the day on which the disciples were to receive the promise of the Father may have been determined either in view of the circumstances of the feast or of its history and symbolic fitness. Of all the feasts of the Jewish year, Pentecost was that which attracted the largest number of pilgrims from distant lands. (See 18:21; 20:16.) There was no other time on which the gift of the Spirit was likely to produce such direct and immediate results. Each aspect of the old Feast of Weeks, or "Fiftieth-day" Feast, as it was sometimes called, presented a symbolic meaning which made it, in greater or less measure, typical of the work now about to be accomplished. It was the "feast of harvest," "the feast of the first-fruits"; and so it was fitting that it should witness the first great gathering of the fields that were white to harvest (Exod. 23:16). It was one on which, more than on any other, the Israelite was to remember that he had been a bondsman in the land of Egypt, and had been led forth to freedom (Deut. 16:12); on it, accordingly, they were to do no servile work (Lev. 23:31). A day on which sacrifices of every kind were offered— burnt offerings, sin offerings, meat offerings, peace offerings—it so represented the consecration of body, soul, and spirit as a spiritual sacrifice (Lev. 23:17-20). The wave loaves of fine flour were to be offered, the type, it may be, in the light of retrospect, of the Jewish and the Gentile churches. And these loaves were to be leavened, as a witness that the process of the contact of mind with mind, which is naturally so fruitful in evil, might yet, under a higher influence, become one of unspeakable good: the new life working through the three measures of meal until the whole was leavened. (See Matt. 13:33.)

Was fully come.—Literally, "was being accomplished." The meeting of the disciples was either on the vigil of the feast day or in the early dawn. Assuming the Passover to have occurred on the night of the Last Supper, the Day of Pentecost would fall on the first day of the week, beginning at the sunset of the Sabbath.

With one accord in one place.—The scene is probably the same large upper room as in 1:13. We may reasonably think of the same persons as being present. The hour (verse 15) was early in the morning, and probably followed on a night of prayer. It is said, indeed, that devout Jews used to solemnize the vigil of Pentecost by a special thanksgiving to God for giving His Law to Israel; and this may well have been the occasion that brought the disciples together. The frequent occurrence of the Greek word for "with one accord" (1:14; 2:46; 4:24; 5:12) is significant as showing the impression made on the writer by the exceptional unity of the new society. Outside the Acts it is found only in Phil. 2:2.

(2) The description reminds us of the "sound of a trumpet" (Exod. 19:19; Heb. 12:19) on Sinai, of the "great and strong wind" that rent the mountains on Horeb (I Kings 19:11). (Comp. Gen. 1:2.) The Greek word for "wind" is not that commonly so translated (**anemos**), but one from the same root as the Greek for "Spirit" (**Pnoe** and **Pneuma**—both from **Pneo**, "I breathe"), and rendered "breath" in 17:25. It is obviously chosen here as being better fitted than the more common word for the supernatural inbreathing of which they were conscious (see John 20:22). It filled "the whole house," as if in token of the wide range over which the new spiritual power was to extend its working, even to the whole Church, which is the house of God (I Tim. 3:15), and to the uttermost parts of the earth.

(3) The word translated "cloven" cannot possible have that meaning. It is common (e.g., verse 45; Matt. 27:35; Luke 22:17; John 19:24), and is used always in the sense of dividing or distributing. What the disciples saw would, perhaps, be best described as a shower of fiery tongues, lighting for a moment on each head and then vanishing. The verb "sat upon" is in the tense which expresses momentary, not continuous, action.

(4) And they were all filled with the Holy Ghost.—The outward portent was but the sign of a greater spiritual wonder. As yet, though they had been taught to pray for the gift of the Holy Spirit (Luke 11:13), and

had found the answer to their prayer in sacred influences and gradual growth in wisdom, they never had been conscious of its power as "filling" them—pervading the inner depths of personality, stimulating every faculty and feeling to a new intensity of life. Now they felt as "borne onward" (II Pet. 1:21), thinking thoughts and speaking words which were not their own, and which they could hardly even control. They had passed into a state of rapturous ecstasy and joy. We must not think of the gift as confined to the apostles. The context shows that the writer speaks of all who were assembled, including the women, as sharers in it. (Comp. verses 17, 18.)

And began to speak with other tongues.—Two facts must be remembered as we enter upon the discussion here: (1) If we receive Mark 16:9-20 as a true record of our Lord's words, the disciples had, a few days or weeks before the Day of Pentecost, heard the promise that they that believed should "speak with new tongues" (see note on Mark 16:17), i.e., with new powers of utterance. (2) When Luke wrote his account of the Day of Pentecost, he must have had—partly through his companionship with Paul, partly from personal observation—a wide knowledge of the phenomena described as connected with the "tongues" in I Cor. 14. He uses the term in the sense in which Paul had used it. We have to read the narrative of the Acts in the light thrown upon it by the treatment in that chapter of the phenomena described by the same words as the Pentecost wonder. What, then, are those phenomena? Does the narrative of I Cor. 14 (see notes) bring before us any in addition?

We observe from that chapter: (1) That the utterance of the "tongue" is entirely unconnected with the work of instruction; it does not edify any beyond the man who speaks (I Cor. 14:2, 4). Paul desires to subject the exercise of the gift to the condition of the presence of an interpreter (I Cor. 14:5, 27). (2) That the free use of the gift makes him who uses it almost as a barbarian or foreigner to those who listen to him. What he speaks is as the sound of a trumpet blown uncertainly, of flute or lyre played with unskilled hand (I Cor. 14:7-9). (3) That those who speak with tongues do well, for the most part, to confine their utterance to the solitude of their own chamber or to the presence of friends who can share their rapture. If it was not right or expedient to check the utterance of the tongues altogether. Paul at least thought it necessary to prescribe rules for its public exercise which naturally tended to relegate it to the background as compared with prophecy (I Cor. 14:27, 28). The conclusion from the whole chapter is, accordingly, that the "tongues" were not the power of speaking in a language which had not been learned, but the ecstatic utterance of rapturous devotion.

As regards the terms which are used to describe the gift, the English reader must be reminded that the word "unknown" is an interpolation which appears for the first time in the version of 1611. It may be noted further that the Greek word for "tongue" had come to be used by Greek writers on rhetoric for bold, poetic, unusual terms, such as belonged to epic poetry (Aristot. **Rhet.** 3:3), not for those which belonged to a foreign language. If they were, as Aristotle calls them, "unknown," it was because they were used in a startlingly figurative sense, so that men were sometimes puzzled by them (Aristot. **Rhet.** 3:10). We have this sense of the old word (**glossa**) surviving in our **glossary**, a collection of such terms. It is clear that such use of the word would be natural in writers trained as Paul and Luke had been in the language of Greek schools.

In this chapter we find almost identical phenomena: (1) The work of teaching is done not by the gift of tongues, but by the speech of Peter, delivered either in the Aramaic of Palestine or, more probably, in the Greek, which was the common medium of verbal exchange for all the Eastern subjects of the Roman empire. In that speech we find the exercise of the higher gift of prophecy, with precisely the same results as those described by Paul as following on the use of that gift. (Comp. verse 37 with I Cor. 14:24, 25.) (2) The utterances of the disciples are described in words which convey the idea of rapturous praise. Doxologies, benedictions, adoration, in forms that transcended the common level of speech, rose, like the Magnificat, into the region of poetry. (3) There is a parallelism in verse 13 and I Cor. 14:23. In both cases there is an intensity of stimulated life. It is significant that Paul elsewhere contrasts the "being drunk with wine" with "being filled with the Spirit" (Eph. 5:18).

In the present case, however, there are exceptional phenomena. We cannot honestly interpret Luke's record without assuming either that the disciples spoke in the languages which are named in verses 9-11,

or that, speaking in their own Galilean tongue, their words came to the ears of those who listened as spoken in the language with which each was familiar. The first is at once the more natural interpretation of the language used by the historian. And it is clear that there was an end to be attained by such an extension of the gift in this case which could not be attained otherwise. The disciples had been present in Jerusalem at many feasts before, at which they had found themselves, as now, surrounded by pilgrims from many distant lands. Then they had worshiped apart by themselves, with no outward means of fellowship with these strangers, and had poured out their praises and blessings in their own Galilean speech, as each group of those pilgrims had done in theirs. Now they found themselves able to burst through the bounds that had thus divided them, and to claim a fellowship with all true worshipers from whatever lands they came.

(6) In his own language.—The word is peculiar to the Acts. (See note on 1:19.) It stands as an equivalent for the "tongue" in verse 11, but was used for "dialect," in the modern sense of the term, as well as for a distinct language.

(7) They were all amazed and marvelled.—This is precisely in accordance with what Paul describes as the effect of the gift of tongues. They were a "sign" to those who did not believe, filling them with wonder, but the work of convincing and converting was left for the gift of prophecy (I Cor. 14:22).

Are not all these which speak Galileans?—This is the first assertion of the fact as regards the whole company. The traitor apparently had been the only exception (see note on Matt. 10:4), and he had gone to his own place.

(9-11) The list is characteristic of the trained historian, one who would inquire carefully what nations were represented at that great Pentecost. There is a kind of order, as of one taking a mental bird's-eye view of the Roman empire, going generally from east to west. The absence of some countries that we should have expected to find in the list—Syria, Cilicia, Cyprus, Bithynia, Macedonia, Achaia, Spain—indicates that what we have is not an artificial list made up at a later date, but an actual record of those whose presence at the Feast had been ascertained by the historian. Possibly they may have been omitted because Jews and converts coming from them naturally would speak Greek, and there would be no marvel to them in hearing Galileans speaking in that language. The presence of Judaea in the list is almost as unexpected as the absence of the others. That might have been taken for granted; but perhaps the men of Judaea are named as sharing in the wonder that the Galileans no longer were distinguished by their provincial **patois**. (Comp. note on Matt. 26:73.) Note the special emphasis on the prominence of the Roman proselytes in that mixed multitude of worshipers.

(13) These men are full of new wine.—Literally, of "sweet drink" (the word "wine" not being used), stronger and more intoxicating than the lighter and thinner wines that ordinarily were drunk. The Greek word sometimes was used for unfermented grape juice. Here, however, the context shows that wine, in the strict sense of the word, was intended. (Comp. Job 32:19, LXX.) The word for "new wine" in Matt. 9:17; Mark 2:22 is different, but there also fermentation is implied. The words (see note on verse 4) point to a certain appearance of excitement in tone, manner, and words.

(14) But Peter, standing up with the eleven . . .—We are struck at once with the marvelous change that has come over the character of the apostle. Timidity has become boldness; for the few hasty words recorded in the gospels we have elaborate discourses. There is a method and insight in the way he deals with the prophecies of the Christ altogether unlike anything that we have seen in him before. The facts which Luke narrates are an adequate explanation of the phenomena. In the interval that had passed, Peter's mind had been opened by his Lord's teaching to understand the Scriptures (Luke 24:45), and then he had been endued, by the gift of the Holy Spirit, with power from on high. That which he now speaks is the first utterance of the new gift of prophecy, and followed properly on the portent of the "tongues" to bring about the work of conversion which they had no power to accomplish. The speech which follows was spoken either in the Aramaic of Palestine, or, more probably, in the Greek, which was common in Galilee, and which would be intelligible to nearly all of the pilgrims from distant countries.

And said unto them.—The verb is not the word commonly so rendered, but that which is translated "utterance" in verse 4. The unusual word probably was repeated here to indicate that what follows was just

as much an "utterance" of the Holy Spirit, working on and through the spiritual powers of man, as the marvel of the "tongues" had been.

(15) Seeing it is but the third hour of the day.—Were the disciples likely to be drunk at 9 a.m., and that on the morning of the Day of Pentecost, after a night spent in devotion, and when all decent Jews were fasting? (See Isa. 5:11; Eccles. 10:16; 1 Thess. 5:7.)

(17) It shall come to pass in the last days.—The prophecy of Joel (see notes on Joel 2) takes its place, with the exception, perhaps, of Hosea, as the oldest of the prophetic books of the Old Testament. The people were suffering from one of the locust plagues of the East and its consequent famine. The prophet calls them to repentance, and promises this gift of the Spirit as the great blessing of the distant future. He had been taught that no true knowledge of God comes but through that Spirit.

(19-21) Peter quotes the words of terror that follow, apparently, for the sake of the promise with which they end in verse 21. It may well have been that he looked for the "great and notable day" as about to come in his own time. (The imagery is drawn as from one of the great thunderstorms of Palestine.) As seen by the prophet, the day was terrible to the enemies of God, blessed to "the remnant whom the Lord shall call" (Joel 2:32). The Greek word for "notable" **(epiphanes)** lent itself readily to the thought of the great Epiphany or manifestation of Christ as the Judge of all. The invoking (verse 21) has the force of an appeal from a lower to a higher tribunal. (Comp. 25:11, 21, 25.) Here the thought is that that name of the Eternal, called upon in the prayer of faith, was the one sufficient condition of deliverance in the midst of all the terrors of the coming day of the Lord.

(22) Miracles and wonders and signs.—The words are three synonyms, expressing different aspects of the same facts, rather than a classification of phenomena. The leading thought in the first word is the power displayed in the act; in the second, the marvel of it as a portent; in the third, its character as a token or note of something beyond itself.

(23) By the determinate counsel and foreknowledge of God.—Comp. 10:42; 1 Pet. 1:2. It now has become the habit of the apostle's mind to trace the working of a divine purpose, which men, even when they are most bent on thwarting it, are unconsciously fulfilling. In 1:16 he had seen that purpose in the treachery of Judas; he sees it now in the malignant injustice of priests and people.

(24) Whom God hath raised up.—It is probable that rumors of the Resurrection had found their way among the people, and had been met by the counterstatement of which we read in Matt. 28:11-15; But this was the first public witness, borne by one who was ready to seal his testimony with his blood, to the stupendous fact.

Having loosed the pains of death.—Literally, "travail pangs." If we take the Greek word in its full meaning, the Resurrection is thought of as a new birth as from the womb of the grave.

Because it was not possible . . .—The moral impossibility was twofold: the work of the Son of man could not have ended in a failure and death which would have given the lie to all that He had asserted of Himself; and its issue could not run counter to the prophecies which had implied with more or less clearness a victory over death.

(25) For David speaketh concerning him.—Ps. 16 seems to speak of the confidence of the writer that he would be himself delivered from the grave and death. Some interpreters confine that confidence to a temporal deliverance; others extend it to the thought of immortality, or even of a resurrection. Peter teaches that the ideal of victory after suffering, no less than that of the righteous sufferer, was realized in Christ. The fact of the Resurrection had given a new meaning to prophecies which would not of themselves have suggested it, but which were incomplete without it.

He is on my right hand.—The psalmist thought of the Eternal as the warrior thinks of him who, in the conflict of battle, extends his shield over the comrade who is on the left hand, and so guards him from attack. When the Son of man is said to sit on the right hand of God (Ps. 110:1; Matt. 26:64) the imagery is different, and brings before us the picture of a king seated on his throne with his heir sitting in the place of honor by his side.

(27) Thou wilt not leave my soul in hell.—Literally, "in Hades." See note on Matt. 5:22. The death of Christ was an actual death; and while the body was laid in the grave, the soul passed into the world of the dead—the **Sheol** of the Hebrews, the **Hades** of the Greeks—to carry on there the redemptive work which had been begun in

earth. (Comp. 13:34-37; Eph. 4:9; I Pet. 3:19.)

Neither wilt thou suffer thine Holy One to see corruption.—The psalmist was expressing the confidence that he himself, as loving, and beloved of, God, would be delivered from destruction, both now and hereafter. Peter interprets the words as having received a higher fulfillment: Christ was "the Holy One" of God (Mark 1:24; Luke 4:34; comp. Heb. 7:26; Rev. 15:4; 16:5).

(29) His sepulchre is with us unto this day.—King David was buried in the city which bore his name (I Kings 2:10). Josephus relates that vast treasures were buried with him (**Ant.** 7:15, §4), and that John Hyrcanus opened one of the chambers of the tomb, taking out three thousand talents to pay the tribute demanded by Antiochus the Pious (**Ant.** 13:8, §4). Herod the Great also opened it, and found gold and silver vessels in abundance (**Ant.** 16:7, §1). It is difficult to understand how such a treasure could have escaped the plunderer in all the sieges and sacks to which Jerusalem had been exposed; but it is possible that its fame as a holy place may have made it a kind of bank of deposit, in which large treasures in coin or plate were left for safety.

(30, 31) In the vision of the future which Peter ascribes to David, the king had been led, as he interprets the words, not only to speak out his own hopes, but also to utter that which received its fulfillment in the fact of the Resurrection. What was conspicuously not true of the historical David was found to be true of the Son of David according to the flesh. (See Pss. 132:11; 16:10.)

(32) This Jesus hath God raised up . . .—From the first the apostles take up the position which their Lord had assigned them. They are witnesses, and before and above all else, witnesses of the Resurrection.

(33) Therefore being by the right hand of God.—The Greek has a dative of instrument, the image that underlies the phrase being that the eternal King stretches forth His hand to raise Him who was in form His Servant to a place beside Him on His right hand.

Having received of the Father.—The words of Peter, obviously independent as they are of the gospel of John, present a striking agreement with our Lord's language as recorded by him (John 14:26; 15:26). Comp. 1:4.

(34, 35) See notes on Matt. 22:43-45. Those who were then silenced are now taught how it was that David's Son was also David's Lord. (Comp. Ps. 110:1.)

(36) Both Lord and Christ.—The word "Lord" is used with special reference to the prophetic utterance of Psalm 110. The verse emphasizes the contrast between the way in which the Jews of Jerusalem had dealt with Jesus and the recognition which He had received from the Father. The utterance of the word "crucified" at the close, pressing home the guilt of the people on their consciences, worked the result described in verse 37.

(38) Repent, and be baptized every one of you in the name of Jesus Christ.—The work of the apostles is both a continuation and a development of that of the Baptist. There is the same indispensable condition of repentance, the same outward rite as the symbol of purification, and the same promise of forgiveness which that change involves. But the baptism is now, as it had not been before, in the name of Jesus Christ, and it is connected more directly with the gift of the Holy Spirit. Why is the baptism here (and in 10:48; 19:5) "in the name of Jesus Christ," while in Matt. 28:19 the apostles are commanded to baptize in the name of the Father, the Son, and the Holy Spirit? The most satisfactory solution is found in seeing the words of Matt. 28:19 (see note) the formula for the baptism of those who, as Gentiles, had been "without God in the world, not knowing the Father," while for converts from Judaism, or those who had before been proselytes to Judaism, it was enough that there should be the distinctive profession of their faith in Jesus as the Christ, the Son of God, added on to their previous belief in the Father and the Holy Spirit. In proportion as the main work of the Church of Christ lay among the Gentiles, it was natural that the fuller form should become dominant, and finally be used exclusively.

Ye shall receive the gift of the Holy Ghost.—The word for "gift" (**dorea**) is generic, and differs from the more specific "gift" (**charisma**) of 1 Cor. 12:4, 9, 28. The apostle does not necessarily promise startling and marvelous powers, but in some way they all should feel that a new Spirit was working in them, and that that Spirit was from God. The essence of Peter's appeal is that all to whom he speaks can claim the promise as fully as himself (verse 39).

(40) From this untoward generation.—Literally, "from this crooked generation" (comp. Luke 3:5; Phil. 2:15).

(41) Immersion had clearly been practiced by John, and was involved in the original meaning of baptism. (See Rom. 6:4; 1 Pet. 3:21.) The large number of people mentioned here in no way precludes that mode. The swimming-baths of Bethesda and Siloam (see John 5:7; 9:7), or the so-called Fountain of the Virgin, near the Temple enclosure, or the bathing places within the Tower of Antony (Jos. **Wars**, 5:5, §8), may well have helped to make the process easy. The sequel shows that many converts were made from the Hellenistic Jews who were present at the Feast (6:1), and that few, if any, of the converts were of the ruling class (4:1). Some of these converts may have gone back to the cities from which they came, and have been the unknown founders of the Church at Damascus, or Alexandria, or Rome itself.

(42) Four elements of the life of the new society are pointed out: (1) They grew in knowledge of the truth by attending to the teaching of the apostles. (2) They joined in outward acts of fellowship with each other—acts of common worship, acts of mutual kindness and benevolence. (The one Greek word diverges afterward into the sense of what we technically call "communion," as in 1 Cor. 10:16, and that of a "collection" or contribution for the poor, as in Rom. 15:26; 11 Cor. 9:13. (3) Luke uses the phrase "breaking of bread" in the same solemn commemorative sense as 1 Cor. 10:16. From the first what was afterward known as the Lord's Supper (see note on 1 Cor. 11:20) took its place with baptism as a permanent universal element in the Church's life. (4) Prayer included private as well as public devotions. The use of the plural seems to indicate recurring times of prayer at fixed hours.

(44) All that believed were together...—They had all things in common, not by a compulsory abolition of the rights of property (see 5:4), but by the spontaneous energy of love. But the experience taught the Church in course of time that this generous and general distribution was not the wisest method of accomplishing permanent good, and that here also a discriminate economy, such as Paul taught (II Thess. 3:10; 1 Tim. 3:8), was necessary as a safeguard against abuse. It was, perhaps, partly in consequence of the rapid exhaustion of its resources thus brought about that the Church at Jerusalem became dependent for many years upon the bounty of the churches of the Gentiles. (See note on 11:29.)

(46) Continuing daily with one accord in the temple.—The apparent strangeness of their being allowed to meet in the Temple is explained partly by the fact that its courts were open to all Israelites who did not disturb its peace, partly by the existence of a moderate, half-believing party in the Sanhedrin itself, including Nicodemus, Joseph of Arimathaea, and Gamaliel (5:35), and partly by the popularity gained for a time (verse 47) by the holiness and liberal almsgiving of the new community.

Did eat their meat...—As yet the solemn breaking of bread was closely connected with their daily life. Anticipating the language of a few years later, the Agape (or Love feast) was united with the Communion. The higher sanctified the lower. It was not until love and faith were colder that men were forced to separate them, lest (see notes on I Cor. 11:20, 21) the lower should desecrate the higher.

(47) The verb "added" is in the tense which, like the adverb "daily," implies a continually recurring act.

3

(1) No account is given as to the interval that had passed since the Day of Pentecost. Presumably the brief notice at the end of chap. 2 was meant to summarize a gradual progress, marked by no striking incidents, which may have gone on for several months.

At the hour of prayer, being the ninth hour—i.e., 3 p.m., the hour of the evening sacrifice (Jos., **Ant.** 14:4, §3). The traditions of later Judaism had fixed the third, the sixth, and the ninth hours of each day as times for private prayer. Daniel's practice of praying three times a day seems to imply a rule of the same kind, and Ps. 55:17 carries the practice up to the time of David. "Seven times a day" was, perhaps, the rule of those who aimed at a life of higher devotion (Ps. 119:164).

(2) The gate of the temple which is called Beautiful.—No gate of this name is mentioned by other writers, but it probably was identical with the Susa gate, on the eastern side, and named in memory of the old historical connection between Judah and Persia, leading into the outer court of the women. It was of fine Corinthian brass, a

door so massive that twenty men were required to open or shut it (Jos., **Wars,** 5:5 §3).

To ask alms of them that entered into the temple.—The approaches of the Temple commonly were thronged with the blind, lame, and other mendicants. (Comp. John 9:8.)

(6) In the name of Jesus Christ of Nazareth...—The full trust with which the words were spoken was in part a simple act of faith in their Master's promise (Mark 16:18), in part the result of a past experience in the exercise of like powers (Mark 6:13). And the name in which they spoke could hardly have been a new name to the cripple at the Temple gate (comp. John 5:2, 14; 9:7, 8). What made the call to rise and walk a test of faith was that, but a few weeks before, that name had been seen on the superscription over the cross on which He who bore it had been condemned to die as one who deceived the people (John 7:12).

(7) The precision with which the process of healing is described is characteristic of the medical historian.

(11) In the porch that is called Solomon's. —The "portico" or "cloister" was outside the Temple, on the eastern side. It consisted, in the Herodian Temple, of a double row of Corinthian columns, about thirty-seven feet high, and received its name as having been in part constructed, when the Temple was rebuilt by Zerubbabel, with the fragments of the older edifice. The people tried to persuade Herod Agrippa I to pull it down and rebuild it, but he shrank from the risk and cost of such an undertaking (Jos., **Ant.** 20:9 §7). It was, like the porticos in all Greek cities, a favorite place of resort, especially as facing the morning sun in winter.

(13) The God of Abraham, and of Isaac, and of Jacob.—Here we have an echo of our Lord's teaching. That name had been uttered in the precincts of the Temple, probably in the same portico, as part of our Lord's constructive proof of the resurrection of the dead (Matt. 22:32). Now it was heard again in connection with the witness borne by the apostles that He Himself had risen.

Hath glorified his Son Jesus.—Better, "Servant." The word is that used throughout the later chapters of Isaiah for "the servant of Jehovah" (Isa. 42:1; 48:20; 52:13; 53:11). It recurs in verse 26; 4:27, 30, and as applied to Christ is peculiar to the Acts, with the exception of the citation from Isaiah in Matt. 12:18. It is, therefore, more distinctive than "Son" would have been, and implies the general Messianic interpretation of the prophetic language in which it is so prominent.

(14) The Holy One and the Just.—The language, though startlingly new to the hearers, had been partially anticipated. It had been used of the Christ by the demoniacs (Mark 1:24). The best MSS give Peter's confession in John 6:69 in the form, "Thou art the Holy One of God." Pilate's wife, and Pilate himself, had borne witness to Jesus as emphatically "Just" (Matt. 27:19, 24). See I Pet. 3:18; I John 2:1.

(15) The Prince of life.—The word translated "Prince" is applied to Christ here and in 5:31. In Heb. 2:10 it is rendered "the **captain** of their salvation"; in Heb. 12:2, "the **author** and finisher of our faith." Its primary meaning (**princeps**) is one who takes the lead—who is the originator of that to which the title is attached. The "Prince of life," the "captain of salvation," is accordingly He who is the source from which life and salvation flow. (Comp. Num. 13:3; 24:17, LXX.)

(16) His name through faith in his name.—We have here the efficient cause distinguished from the indispensable condition of its action. The name did not work as a formula of incantation; it required, on the part both of the worker and the receiver, faith in that which the name represented, the manifestation of the Father through the Son.

(17) Peter's treatment of the relation of "ignorance" to "guilt" is in exact agreement with Paul's, both in his judgment of his own past offenses (I Tim. 6:13) and in that which he passed on the Gentile world (17:30). Men were ignorant where they might have known, if they had not allowed prejudice and passion to overpower the witness borne by reason and conscience. But because it was ignorance, repentance was not impossible. Even the people and rulers of Israel, though their sin was greater, came within the range of the prayer of Luke 23:34.

(19) That your sins may be blotted out.—This is the only passage in which the verb is directly connected with sins. The image that underlies the words (as in Col. 2:14) is that of an indictment which catalogs the sins of the penitent, and which the pardoning love of the Father cancels. (See Ps. 51:10; Isa. 43:25.)

When the times of refreshing shall come.—The thought is that again expressed both by Peter (II Pet. 3:12) and by Paul (Rom. 11:25-27): that the conversion of sinners, especially the conversion of Israel, will have a power to accelerate the fulfillment of God's purposes, and, therefore, the coming of His kingdom in its completeness. The "times of refreshing" are distinguished from the "restitution of all things" of verse 21, and would seem to be, as it were, the gracious preludes of that great consummation.

(21) Until the times of restitution of all things.—This is the only passage in which the word translated "restitution" is found in the New Testament, nor is it found in the LXX. Etymologically, it conveys the thought of restoration to an earlier and better state, rather than that of simple consummation or completion (Comp. II Pet. 3:13.) It does not necessarily involve the final salvation of all men, but it does express the idea of a state in which "righteousness," and not "sin," shall have dominion over a redeemed world.

(22) For Moses truly said unto the fathers.—The appeal is made to Moses in his twofold character as lawgiver and prophet. The words point to the appearance of a succession of true prophets as contrasted with the diviners of Deut. 18:14; and, even with Peter's interpretation before us, we may well admit those prophets as primary and partial fulfillments of them. But the words had naturally fixed the minds of men on the coming of some one great Prophet who should excel all others. None that come between Moses and Jesus had been "like unto the former," as marking a new epoch, the channel of a new revelation, the giver of a new law. (Comp. II Sam. 7:13, 14; Heb. 1:5.)

(25) And of the covenant . . .—This is a significant indication of the unity of apostolic teaching. Peter thus refers chiefly to the covenant made with Abraham (Gen. 12:3), with as full an emphasis as Paul does when he had learned to see that it implicitly involved the calling of the Gentiles into the kingdom of Christ (Gal. 3:8).

(26) Unto you first . . .—Note the agreement with Paul's formula of the purpose of God (13:46; Rom. 1:16; 2:9, 10). Peter does not as yet know the conditions under which the Gospel will be preached to the heathen; but his words imply a distinct perception that there was a call to preach to them.

His Son Jesus.—See note on verse 13.

4

(1) The captain of the temple.—The "captain of the temple" (see Luke 22:4) was the head of the band of Levite sentinels whose function it was to keep guard over the sacred precincts. He, as an inspector, made his round by night, visited all the gates, and roused the slumberers. His presence implied that the quiet order of the Temple was supposed to be endangered.

The Sadducees.—The higher members of the priesthood, Annas and Caiaphas, were themselves of this sect (5:17). They had already been foremost in urging the condemnation of Christ in the meetings of the Sanhedrin. The shame of having been put to silence by Him (Matt. 22:34) added vindictiveness to the counsels of a calculating policy. Now they found His disciples preaching the truth which they denied.

(3) It was now eventide.—The narrative started from 3 p.m. (3:1). The "eventide" began at 6 p.m.

(4) The number of the men was about five thousand.—It may be that Luke meant this as a statement of the aggregate number of disciples, not of those who were converted on that day. (As in the narrative of the feeding of the five thousand, women and children were not included.) The connection in which the number is given makes it probable that it represents those who, under the influence of the impression made by the healing of the cripple and by Peter's speech, attended the meetings of the Church that evening.

(6) And Annas the high priest . . .—These are mentioned by themselves as representing the section that had probably convened the meeting, and came in as if to dominate its proceedings. Annas had been made high priest by Quirinius, the governor of Syria, filled the office A.D. 7-15, and lived to see five of his sons occupy it after him. At this time, Joseph Caiaphas was the actual high priest (see John 11:49), having been appointed in A.D. 17. He was deposed A.D. 37. He had married the daughter of Annas; and the latter seems to have exercised a dominant influence.

John.—This may have been the Johanan ben Zaccai, who is reported by Jewish writers to have been at the height of his fame forty years before the destruction of the Temple, and to have been president of the Great Synagogue after its removal to Jamnia.

Alexander.—This name has been identified by some with Alexander, the brother of Philo, the **Alabarch** or magistrate of Alexandria (Jos., **Ant.** 18:8 § 1, 19:5, § 1).

(7) The Sanhedrin sat in a semicircle, the president being in the middle of the arc, the accused standing in the center. They put the question repeatedly, in many varying forms. They admit the fact that the lame man had been made to walk as too patent to be denied. (Comp. verse 16.) The question implied a suspicion that it was the effect of magic, or by the power of Beelzebub (Luke 11:15; John 8:48). There is a touch of scorn in the way in which they speak of the thing itself.

(8) See Matt. 10:19, 20; Luke 21:14, 15.

(9) If we this day be examined.—The word is employed in its technical sense of a judicial interrogation. It is used by Luke (Luke 23:14) and Paul (12:19; 24:8; I Cor. 2:14, 15; 4:3, 4), and by them only, in the New Testament.

(10) By the name of Jesus Christ of Nazareth, whom ye crucified.—Peter does not shrink now from confessing the Nazarene as the Messiah. He presses home the fact that, though Pilate had given the formal sentence, it was they who had crucified their King. Jesus has been raised from the dead, and is still as a Power working to heal as when on earth.

(11) This is the stone which was set at nought of you builders.—See notes on Matt. 21:42-44.

(12) Neither is there salvation in any other.—Here the full force of "hath been made whole" (verse 9) comes out; and Peter rises to its highest meaning, proclaiming a salvation, not from disease and infirmity of body, but from the great disease of sin. The Greek has the article before "salvation." That of which Peter spoke was **the** salvation for which the rulers professed to be looking.

Given among men.—To those to whom it had been made known, and who had taken in all that it embodied, the name of Jesus Christ of Nazareth was the one true source of deliverance and salvation. Where it is not so known, it rises to its higher significance as the symbol of a divine energy; and so we may rightly say that the heathen who obtain salvation are saved by the name of the Lord of whom they have never heard. (Comp. I Tim. 4:13.)

(13) Unlearned and ignorant.—The first

of the two words means, literally, "unlettered." Looking to the special meaning of the "letters" or "Scriptures" of the Jews, from which the scribes took their name (**grammateis**, from **grammata**), it would convey here the sense of "not having been educated as a scribe, not having studied the Law and other sacred writings." The second word means, literally, "a private person," one without special office or calling, or the culture which they imply—what might be called a "common man." (Comp. I Cor. 14:16, 23, 24.)

They took knowledge of them, that they had been with Jesus.—Better, "they began to recognize." The tense is in the imperfect, implying that one after another of the rulers began to remember the persons of the two apostles as they had seen them with their Master in the Temple.

(19, 20) The words assert the right of conscience, recognizing a divine authority, to resist a human authority which opposes it. The question at issue was one of bearing witness, and that witness they had received a special command to bear (1:8).

(24) They lifted up their voice to God with one accord.—The phrase seems to imply an intonation, or chant, different from that of common speech (14:11; 22:22). The joint utterance described may be conceived as the result of the people following Peter, clause by clause.

Lord.—The Greek word is not the common one for Lord (**Kyrios**), but **Despotes**, the absolute Master of the universe. (Comp. II Pet. 2:1; Rev. 6:10.) The hymn has the special interest of being the earliest recorded utterance of the praises of the Christian Church. As such, it is significant that it begins, as so many of the Psalms begin, with setting forth the glory of God as the Creator, and rises from that to the higher redemptive work.

(26) And against his Christ.—To maintain the connection with Psalm 2 and with the verb in verse 27, it would be better to say, "against his anointed."

(28) To do whatsoever thy hand . . .—The great problem of the relation of the divine purpose to man's free agency is stated (see 1:16; 2:23) without any attempt at a philosophical solution. In every fact of history, no less than in the great fact of which Peter speaks, the will of each agent is free, and he stands or falls by the part he has taken in it; and yet the outcome of the whole works out some law of evolution, some "increasing

purpose," which we recognize as we look back on the course of the events.

(30) There seems something like an intentional assonance in the Greek words which Luke uses—**iasis** (healing) and **Iesus** (Jesus)—as though he would indicate that the very name of Jesus witnessed to His being the great Healer. Comp. **Christos** and **Chrestos** (good, gracious) in Tertullian, **Apol.**, c. 3.

Thy holy child Jesus.—See note on 3:13.

(31) The place was shaken . . .—The impression on the senses was so far a renewal of the wonder of the Day of Pentecost, but in this instance without the sign of the tongues of fire, which were the symbols of a gift imparted once for all, and, perhaps also, without the special marvel of the utterance of the tongues. The disciples felt the power of the Spirit, the evidence of sense confirming that of inward, spiritual consciousness, and it came in the form for which they had made a special supplication, the power to speak with boldness the word which they were commissioned to speak.

(32) The description stands parallel with that of 2:42-47, as though the historian delighted to dwell on the continuance of a common life of equality and fraternity, in which the rights of property, though not abolished, were, by the spontaneous action of its owners, made subservient to the law of love, and benevolence was free and full. The form of expression implies that the community of goods was not compulsory. The goods still belonged to men, but they did not speak of them as their own. They had learned, as from our Lord's teaching (Luke 16:10-14), to think of themselves, not as possessors, but as stewards.

(34) It is possible that besides the strong impulse of love, they were impressed, by their Lord's warnings of wars and coming troubles, with the instability of earthly possessions. Property in Palestine was likely to be a source of anxiety rather than profit.

(36) Barnabas.—The later friendship between Paul and him makes it probable that there had been some previous companionship (see 9:27; 11:25), and it may well have been that he was sent from Cyprus to receive his education in the famous schools of Tarsus, or practiced with Saul in early life the craft of tent-making, for which Tarsus was famous, and in which they were afterward fellow-laborers (I Cor. 9:6). As a Levite he probably had taken his place in the ministries of the Temple, and may, therefore, have been among our Lord's actual hearers. His relative Mary, the mother of

John Mark, was living at Jerusalem. (See 12:12; Col. 4:10.) A tradition, as early as Clement of Alexandria (**Strom.** 2:116), makes him one of the Seventy and this **agrees with the prophetic character** which we have seen reason to attach to that body. (See Luke 10:1.) The new name which the apostles gave him, literally, by its Hebrew etymology "the son of prophecy," implies the possession of a special gift of persuasive utterance, in which the apostles recognized the work of the Spirit. An epistle bearing his name, and recognized as his by Clement of Alexandria and Origen, is still extant, but its authenticity is questionable. It consists mainly of allegorical interpretations of Old Testament narratives. Some critics have assigned the Epistle to the Hebrews to his authorship, as the expounder of Paul's thoughts.

5

(1, 2) The name "Ananias" had the same significance as "John," "the Lord be gracious." "Sapphira" is either connected with a precious stone, or from a Hebrew word signifying "beautiful" or "pleasant." The whole history must be read in connection with the act of Barnabas. He, it seemed, had **gained praise and power by his self-sacrifice;** Ananias thought that he could get at the same result more cheaply. The mere act of keeping back part of the price would not in itself have been sinful. The money was his own, to give the whole or part (verse 4). But the formal act, apparently reproducing that of Barnabas, was an acted lie. The part was offered as if it were the whole.

(3) To lie to the Holy Ghost.—Ananias may be said to "have lied unto the Holy Ghost" either (1) as lying against Him who dwelt in the apostles whom he was seeking to deceive, or (2) as against Him who was the Searcher of the secrets of all hearts, his own included, and who was "grieved" (Eph. 4:31) by this resistance in one who had been called to a higher life. Verse 4 teaches that while the apostles thought of the Spirit as sent by the Father, and therefore distinct in His personality, they yet did not shrink from speaking of Him as God, and so identifying Him with the divine essential Being.

(5) Peter's words, while they press home the intensity of the guilt, do not contain any formal sentence. In such a case, "the visitation of God" was the cause of death. The dominant apostolic idea of such punishments was that men were delivered to Satan for the destruction of the flesh, that the spirit might be saved in the day of the Lord Jesus. (See I Cor. 5:5; I Pet. 4:6.)

(11) For Ecclesia, see notes on Matt. 16:18; 18:17. Its frequent use in the LXX version for the "assembly" or "congregation" of Israel (Deut. 18:16; 23:1; Ps. 26:12; 68:26), and its associations with the political life of Greece as applied to the assemblies, every member of which was a full citizen, made it a natural and fitting word for the new society; and the use by our Lord either of the actual Greek word or of the corresponding Aramaic term stamped it with His sanction. The sudden startling death of Ananias and his wife naturally tended to give a new prominence to the society, the rulers of which were seen to be clothed with supernatural powers.

(12) Many signs and wonders . . .—See note on 2:22.

They were all with one accord in Solomon's porch.—See notes on 3:2, 4:24; John 10:23. It was at all times a favorite place of resort for teachers. Assuming some months to have passed since the Day of Pentecost, what is now related would be in the winter, when that portico, as facing the east and catching the morning sunlight, was more than usually frequented.

(13) Of the rest.—This does not mean that the apostles stood aloof in an isolated majesty, so that none of the other disciples dared associate themselves with them. But it was Luke's way of speaking of the Pharisees and other teachers, who also resorted to the portico, yet had not the courage to attach themselves to those with whom they really sympathized.

(14) The mention of women is characteristic of Luke as a writer who had seen and known the effect of the new religion in raising women to a higher life, and whose knowledge of its history was in great measure derived from them. So in 8:3 women are named as prominent among the sufferers in the first general persecution.

(15) That at the least the shadow of Peter . . .—Christ had healed sometimes without contact of any kind (Matt. 8:13; John 4:52); all that was wanted was the expectation of an intense faith as the subjective condition on the one side, the presence of an objective supernatural power on the other. Any medium upon which the imagination might happen to fix itself was a help to faith (comp. 19:12).

(17) Resurrection was a doctrine diametrically opposed to the stance of the Sadducees (see Matt. 22:23-33; John 5:25-29; 11:49, 50). The prominence of the Resurrection of Jesus in the teaching of the apostles now made the Sadducean high priests their most determined opponents.

(19) But the angel of the Lord.—The fact is obviously recorded by Luke as supernatural. Acts 12:7 may be noted as another instance of a like interposition. The marvelous deliverance was a sign, influencing the subsequent decision of the Council and encouraging the two apostles. It was no small boon, moreover, for them to be delivered even for a few hours from the vile companionship to which they had been condemned.

(21) All the senate . . .—The assembly, here distinguished from the Sanhedrin, was probably a body of assessors especially qualified by age and expression, and called in on special occasions. They may have been identical with "all the estate of the elders" of 22:5.

(24) The captain of the temple.—See notes on 4:1.

(29) The whole company of the Twelve was now the object of attack, and they all accept Peter as their spokesman. The words are an assertion of the same general law of duty as that of 4:19, 20, but the command of the angel in verse 20 had given them a new significance.

(30) See Deut. 21:23 (LXX); Acts 10:39; comp. Gal. 3:13.

(31) Him hath God exalted.—It is significant that Peter should use a word which, while it does not occur as applied to our Lord in the first three gospels, meets us as so applied in John (3:14; 12:32: "lifted up"). It was afterward used of the ascended and glorified Christ by Paul in Phil. 2:9. (Comp. Isa. 52:13, LXX.)

A Prince.—See note on 3:15.

To give repentance.—See note on 2:38.

(34) A Pharisee named Gamaliel.—We are brought into contact here with one of the heroes of rabbinic history. The instructor of Paul, he was the grandson of the great Hillel, the representative of the best school of Pharisaism and the tolerant and large-hearted rival of the narrow and fanatic Shammai, whose precepts remind us of the Sermon on the Mount. The fame of Hillel won for him the highest honor of Judaism—the title of Rabban (the **Rabboni** of Mark 10:51; John 20:16) and the office of President of the Council. Gamaliel rose now, with all the weight of years and au-

thority, to counsel moderation. One who was so prominent as a teacher could not fail to be acquainted with a fellow-teacher like Nicodemus, and may well have been influenced by the example of his gradual conversion and the counsels of caution which he had given (John 7:50, 51). The tone in which he speaks now might almost lead us to class him with the "many" of the chief rulers who secretly believed in Christ, but shrank from confessing Him (John 12:42, 43). Gamaliel, who is not mentioned by Josephus, continued to preside over the Sanhedrin under Caligula and Claudius, and is said to have died eighteen years before the destruction of Jerusalem. Christian traditions present him as having been secretly a disciple of Christ (Pseudo-Clement, **Recogn.** 1:65), and to have been baptized by Peter and Paul, with Nicodemus, who is represented as his nephew, and his son Abibas (**Photius Cod.** 171, 199). He appears as having buried Stephen and other Christians, and to have been buried himself in the same sepulcher with the Proto-martyr and Nicodemus (Augustine, **de Civ. Dei** 17:8; Serm. 318). Later rabbis looked on him as the last of the great teachers or rabbans, and noted that until his time men had taught the Law standing, while afterward they sat. The glory of the Law, they said, had departed with Gamaliel.

Commanded to put the apostles forth a little space.—The practice of thus deliberating in the absence of the accused seems to have been common. (Comp. 4:15.) The report of the speech that follows may have come to Luke from some member of the Council, or, probably, from Paul himself. The occasional coincidences of language with the writings of that apostle tend to confirm the antecedent likelihood of the conjecture.

(36) Theudas.—Josephus mentions no less than three insurrections of this type as occurring shortly after the death of Herod the Great (**Ant.** 17:10). One was headed by Judas (a name which appears from Matt. 10:3; Luke 6:16 to have been interchangeable with Thaddaeus or Theudas), the head of a band of robbers who seized upon the fortress of Sephoris.

(37) Judas of Galilee.—The insurrection of Judas was by far the most important of the attempts to throw off the yoke of Rome. He was assisted by a Pharisee named Sadduk, and the absolute independence of Israel was the watchword of his followers. One of the apostles probably derived his name of **Zelotes**, or **Cananite** (see notes on Matt. 10:4), from having been among the followers of Judas, who were known by that name. (See Luke 2:1, 2; Josephus, **Ant.**, 20:5, §2; **Wars**, 2.8, §1.)

(38) As a prudential dilemma, the argument was forcible enough. Resistance was either needless or it was hopeless. If needless, it was a waste of energy; if hopeless, it involved a fatal risk besides that of mere failure.

(41) Rejoicing that they were counted worthy.—The Twelve could not fail to remember their Lord's beatitudes (Matt. 5:11, 12). We may note, too, in the whole history, the fulfillment of the prediction and the promise of Matt. 10:17-20.

6

(1) Because their widows were neglected.— The words imply an organized administration of the common fund, widows and their children being the chief objects of relief. The rules of I Tim. 5:3-16 were probably the growth of a more mature experience; and here we have to think of a clamorous crowd of applicants besieging the house at which the apostles held their meeting at the times appointed for giving relief in money or in kind. Under the circumstances, jealousies and complaints were all but inevitable. The Twelve were all Galileans, and were suspected of favoring the widows of Palestine rather than those of the Dispersion. It was the first sign that the new society was outgrowing its primitive organization.

(3) Full of the Holy Ghost and wisdom.— The apostles did not limit their thoughts of the Spirit's working to prophecy and the gift of tongues. Wherever wisdom, charity, and kindness were requisite, there was need of a supernatural grace, raising men above prejudice and passion. Of these qualities, no less than of the good report, the whole body of believers were to be, in the first instance, the judges, the apostles reserving to themselves the right of final appointment. The number may have had its origin in the general reverence for the number seven among the Jews.

It is to be noted that the men thus appointed are never called "deacons" in the New Testament. When they are referred to again it is as "the seven" (21:8), as though they were a distinct and peculiar body.

Their functions were analogous to those of the "deacons" of the Pastoral Epistles and the later organization of the Church; but these had their prototypes in the "young men," as contrasted with "elders," in 5:6, 10; and the seven were probably appointed as "arch-deacons" to superintend and guide them. In some church, as at Rome, the number of deacons was fixed at seven, in conformity with this precedent, and they were considered, when the bishop came to be distinguished from the elders, as acting more immediately under the direction of the former, helping him in the details of his office.

(4) We will give ourselves continually to prayer, and to the ministry of the word.— Literally, "We will persevere in...." These formed the true work of the apostles, as afterward of the bishops or elders of the Church. "Prayer" includes the public worship of the Church in all its various developments, as well as private prayer and intercession; the "ministry of the word," all forms of teaching.

(5) And they chose Stephen ... and Philip.—The seven who were chosen all bear Greek names. It is a natural, though not a necessary, inference that they were all of the Hellenistic section of the Church, either because that section had a majority, or because the Hebrews generously voted for giving them special representatives of their own. The order of names may represent the actual order of election. There seems sufficient ground to believe that in Stephen, the proto-martyr of the Church, whose teaching and whose prayers exercised so marvelous an influence in the history of the Church of Christ, we have one of the earliest representatives of Roman Christianity. (See note on verse 9.) A tradition accepted by Epiphanius in the fourth century, however, leads to the conclusion that both Stephen and Philip were of the Seventy who were sent shortly after the last Feast of Tabernacles in our Lord's ministry into every city and village where He Himself would come (see note on Luke 10:1). Admitting the comparative lateness of the tradition mentioned by Epiphanius, it was still antecedently probable that men, who had been brought into prominence by their Lord's special choice, would not be passed over in such an election as that now before us. Philip's long-continued residence at Caesarea suggests the probability of an earlier connection with that city. The fact that he had four adult daughters when Paul came to Caesarea makes it probable that he was married at the time of his appointment.

Nicolas a proselyte of Antioch.—This is the first appearance in the history of the Christian Church of the city which was afterward to be the mother church of the Gentiles (see note on 11:19). Nicolas is memorable as the first person not of the race of Abraham named as admitted to full membership in the Church. The word "proselyte" is taken in its full sense, as including the acceptance of circumcision and the ceremonial law. The name of Nicolas has been identified by an early tradition (Clem. Alex. **Strom.** 3:4, 187; Euseb. **Hist.** 3:29) as the founder of the sect of the Nicolaitans condemned in Rev. 2:6.

Of the other four men we know nothing, nor are there materials even for probable conjecture.

(6) When they had prayed, they laid their hands on them.—This is the first mention of the act in the New Testament. It had an analogous meaning in the ritual of Israel (Num. 27:23) in acts of blessing (Gen. 48:13, 14) and the transmission of functions. Its primary symbolism would seem to be that of the concentration for the moment of all the spiritual energy of prayer upon him on whom men lay their hands, and so of the bestowal of any office for which spiritual gifts are required.

(7) The word of God increased. The tense indicates gradual and continuous growth. The "word of God" is here the whole doctrine of Christ as preached by the apostles and by the seven. The language acknowledges an expansion and development of doctrine.

A great company of the priests were obedient to the faith.—The fact is every way significant. No priest is named as a follower of our Lord's. None, up to this time, had been converted by the apostles. The new fact may be connected with the new teaching of Stephen. And the main feature of that teaching was an anticipation of what was afterward proclaimed more clearly by Paul: that the time for sacrifices had passed away, and that the Law and the ritual of the Temple were decaying.

(9) The structure of the sentence makes it probable that the Libertines, the Cyrenians, and the Alexandrians attended one synagogue, those of Cilicia and Asia another. The **Libertini** were emancipated Roman Jews, with probably some proselytes, descendants of those whom Pompeius had led captive, and who were settled in the transTiberine district of Rome in large numbers, with oratories and synagogues of their own. (See Tacitus, **Ann.** 2:85.) Andronicus and Junias probably were members of this synagogue. (See Rom. 16:7.) At Cyrene, also, on the north coast of Africa, lying between Egypt and Carthage, there was a large Jewish population (see Jos., **Ant.** 14:7, § 2), conspicuous for the offerings they sent to the Temple. Simon (Matt. 27:32) and his two sons Alexander and Rufus (Mark 15:21) probably were members of this society.

Next to Jerusalem and Rome, there was perhaps no city in which the Jewish population was so numerous and influential as at Alexandria. Here, too, they had their own quarter, assigned to them by Ptolemy Philadelphus; they were recognized as citizens by their Roman rulers (Jos., **Ant.,** 14.7, § 2, 10, § 1). From Alexandria had come the Greek version of the Old Testament—the Septuagint, or LXX—which was then in use among all the Hellenistic Jews throughout the empire, and largely read even in Palestine itself. There, at this time, living in fame and honor, was the great teacher Philo, the probable master of Apollos, training him, all unconsciously, to be the preacher of a wisdom higher than his own.

The word "Asia" is taken throughout the New Testament in its more restricted sense as denoting the pro-consular province including the old Lydia and Ionia, and having Ephesus as its capital. Jews of Asia were prominent in their zeal for the sacredness of the Temple (21:27). Paul, no doubt, was a leading member of this section of the second synagogue (Cilicia).

(11) Blasphemous words against Moses, and against God.—The words indicate with sufficient clearness the nature of Stephen's teaching. The charge was a false one, but its falsehood was a distortion of the truth, as that against our Lord had been. Stephen had taught that the days of the Temple were numbered; that with its fall the form of worship of which it was the representative would pass away; that the Law given by Moses was to make way for the higher revelation in Christ, and the privileges of the elect nation to be merged in the blessings of the universal Church. Pharisees and Sadducees, Hebrews and Hellenists, are once more brought into coalition against the new truth.

(15) Saw his face as it had been the face of an angel.—We scarcely can be wrong in tracing this description to the impression made at the time on Paul and reported by

871

him to Luke. Comp. Mark 16:5 for a possible indication of Stephen's young age.

7

(2) Men, brethren, and fathers.—The discourse which follows is clearly an unfinished fragment, interrupted by the clamors of the bystanders (verse 51). It is a true, though not necessarily a verbatim, report. Looking to the relation between Luke and Paul, and to the prominence of the latter among the accusers of Stephen, there is a strong probability that the report was derived from him. This is confirmed by some instances of remarkable parallelism between the speech and his later teaching. (Comp. verses 48, 53; 17:24; Gal. 3:19.) The speech is the first great survey of the history of Israel as a process of divine education. As Stephen was a Hellenistic or Greek-speaking Jew, it is probable that the speech was delivered in Greek, confirming the inference which has been drawn from the Aramaic words specially recorded in our Lord's teaching (See note on Mark 5:41.)

Before he dwelt in Charran.—Here the call of Abraham is spoken of as **before** he sojourned in Haran, or Charran, west of the Euphrates. In Gen. 12:1 it is first mentioned **after** Abraham's removal from that place. On the other hand, Gen. 15:7 speaks of God as bringing him "out of Ur of the Chaldees" —i.e., from Mesopotamia, or the east of the Euphrates (comp. Josh. 24:3; Neh. 9:7). The language of writers contemporary with Stephen (Philo. **De Abrah;** Jos., **Ant.** 1.7, §1) lays stress, as he does, on the first call as well as the second. Here, accordingly, it cannot be said that the statement is at variance with the Old Testament narrative.

(4) See notes on Gen. 11:26, 32; 12:4. The memory of Stephen or of his reporter concerned the broad outlines of the history, and was indifferent to chronological details. It is remarkable that like difficulties present themselves in Paul's own survey of the history of Israel. (See 13:20; Gal. 3:17.) A man speaking for his life, and pleading for the truth with a passionate eagerness, does not commonly carry with him a **memoria technica** of chronological **minutiae**.

(6) And that they should bring them into bondage ...—Taking the common computation, the interval between the covenant with Abraham and that with Moses was 430 years (Gal. 3:17), of which only 215 are

reckoned as spent in Egypt. (Comp. Exod. 12:40, LXX.) The chronological difficulty, however, lies in reconciling Paul's statement with the language of Gen. 15:13, which gives 400 years as the sojourning in Egypt, and with which Stephen is in substantial agreement. Even Josephus varies in given passages (Ant., 2.15; **Wars,** 5.9). All that can be said is that chronological accuracy did not affect the argument. Round numbers were enough for Stephen and Paul to mark the successive stages of God's dealings with His people.

(14) Threescore and fifteen souls.— Seventy is given as the number in Gen. 46:27; Exod. 1:5; Deut. 10:22. Here, however, Stephen had the authority of the LXX of Gen. 46:27, which makes up the number by inserting the son and grandson of Manasseh, and two sons and a grandson of Ephraim. With them it was probably an editorial correction based upon Num. 26:26-37. Stephen, as a Hellenistic Jew, naturally accepted, without caring to investigate, the number which he found in the Greek version.

(16) That Abraham bought for a sum of money.—The only recorded transaction in which Abraham appears as a buyer was his purchase of the cave of Machpelah from Ephron the Hittite (Gen. 23:16). The only recorded transaction in which the sons of Emmor, or Hamor, appear as sellers, was in Jacob's purchase of the field at Shechem (Gen. 33:19; Josh. 24:32). What we have here, apparently, is a Samaritan tradition carrying the associations of Shechem to a remoter past.

With the exception of verse 43, we have now come to the last of the difficulties, chronological, historical, or numerical, presented by Stephen's speech. Should there be errors of transcription, of report, or even of memory, they need not shake the faith of those who have learned to take a higher view of inspiration than that which depends upon the registers of genealogies or chronological tables. And it may be urged that the appearance of seeming inaccuracies, which a moment's reference to the Book of Genesis would have enabled the writer to correct, is evidence of faithfulness in his report of the speech which he thus reproduces.

(22) Moses was learned in all the wisdom of the Egyptians.—There is no direct statement to this effect in the history of the Pentateuch, but it was implied in Moses' being brought up as the son of Pharaoh's daughter, and was in harmony with later paraphrases and expansions of the earlier history. (Comp. Jos., **Ant.,** 1.9, §6; II Tim. 3:8; Jude 9.) The passage is instructive as an indirect plea on the part of Stephen, like that afterward made by Clement of Alexandria (**Strom.** 1:5, §28, 6:5, §42) and Justin (**Dial. c. Tryph.** c. 1-4), for the recognition of heathen wisdom as an element in the divine education of mankind; as having contributed to fix the attention of the more cultivated and scholarly of other early Christian critics, such as Origen, Jerome, and Augustine, on the teaching of Greek poets and philosophers, and having furnished them with a sanction for such studies.

For the tradition of Moses' military and romantic involvements, see Jos., **Ant.,** 2.10.

(36) **In the Red sea.**—The familiar name comes to us, not from the Hebrew word, which means, literally, "the Weed Sea," but from the LXX version, which gave the word **Erythraean**, or red, used by Greek travelers from Herodotus onward. Some have referred it to the color of the coast; some to the color of the seaweed; some to an attempt to give an etymological translation of its name as the Sea of Edom (Gen. 25:25; 36:1); some to a supposed connection with an early settlement of Phoenicians, whose name had, with the Greeks, the same significance.

(37) **A prophet shall the Lord your God raise up.**—The parallelism previously suggested is now distinctly proclaimed, and shown to be a fulfillment of the prediction of Deut. 18:18. (See note on 3:22.) The definite application of the words by Peter determined their bearing here. At this point we may reasonably think of the members of the Sanhedrin as catching the drift of his discourse, and showing signs of excitement, the effect of which is, perhaps, traceable in the greater compression of the narrative that follows.

(38) **That was in the church in the wilderness.**—The word **ecclesia** is used, as it had been in the LXX (Deut. 18:16; 23:1; Ps. 26:12), for the "congregation" of Israel. Stephen's thought is that the society of believers in Christ was like, in character and in its relation to God, to that of Israel. The new **ecclesia** was the development of the old. (See note on Matt. 16:18.)

(43) **I will carry you away beyond Babylon.**—Both the Hebrew and the LXX give "Damascus." The variation is perhaps intentional, emphasizing the actual fulfillment of the words as surpassing what the prophet had foretold. One section of the speech, that which accumulates proof that Israel had been all along a rebellious people, seems to end here. The next deals with the charge that Stephen had spoken blasphemous words against the Temple.

(44) **As he had appointed, speaking unto Moses.**—The answer to the charge lay in these words. Stephen admitted and asserted the divine sanction that had been given to Tabernacle and Temple. What he denied was that that sanction involved perpetuity.

(45) **Brought in with Jesus.**—This is the "Joshua" of the Old Testament (see note on Heb. 4:8). It would, perhaps, have been better to have reproduced the Hebrew rather than the Greek form of the Old Testament name; yet there is, in this instance, something gained in our attention being called to the identity of the two names. It is noticeable that though Stephen was on his trial as a disciple of Jesus of Nazareth, the name does not pass his lips as he speaks in his defense, except in this reference to the great captain of Israel.

(48) **Howbeit the most High dwelleth not in temples.**—The sequel shows the impression which these words made on the hearers. Stephen had risen to the truth which, though it had been proclaimed before, had been practically dormant. It broke down the thought of any exclusive holiness in the Temple, and therefore placed its downfall among the chances and changes which might be involved in God's chastisement of the people and His education of mankind. (Comp. John 4:21-23; Acts 17:24.)

(51) **Ye stiffnecked and uncircumcised . . .**—The sudden change of tone from calm argument to vehement indignation cannot be thought of as spontaneous. The excitement of the Sanhedrin, perhaps of the listening crowd also, at this point would seem to have become uncontrollable. Both the adjectives had been applied to the sins of the older Israel (Exod. 33:3, 5; 34:9; Jer. 6:10). They were now applied to those who boasted of their exclusive privileges as Israelites, and it is scarcely possible for us to estimate the sharp incisiveness with which they must have fallen on the ears of the Sanhedrin. It was to them all, and more than all, that "heretic" and "infidel" have been in the controversies of Christians.

(52) The verse emphasizes the act of the Sanhedrin and the people, and the persistence with which they urged on Pilate the

sentence of death, making them not merely accessories but principles in the deed of blood. For "the Just One," see Isa. 11:4, 5; Matt. 27:19; I John 2:1.

(54) They gnashed on him with their teeth.—This is the only example of the literal use of a phrase with which we are so familiar in its figurative application (Matt. 8:12; 13:42, et al.). Here it clearly expresses brute passion rather than despair. At this point rage and fury—the fury caused by the consciousness that the stern words were true—had become altogether beyond control.

(56) It is clear that the vision was given to the inward spiritual eye, and not to that of sense. The words "Son of man" call for notice as the only certain instance outside the gospels (except, perhaps, Rev. 1:13) of the use of the name which they record to have been constantly used by our Lord in speaking of Himself. (See note on Matt. 8:20.) And it is not without significance that He was manifested to Stephen's gaze as "standing" in the attitude of one who rises to help and welcome a follower who had shown himself faithful even unto death.

(58) The witnesses laid down their clothes.—The Law required, as if to impress on witnesses their solemn responsibility, that they should be the first, if the accused were condemned to death, to take part in his execution (Deut. 17:7; comp. John 8:7). The loose, flowing cloak, which was worn as an outer garment, would have impeded the free action of their arms, and had therefore to be laid on one side. (See 8:1.)

A young man's feet, whose name was Saul.—As defined by Philo, on the authority of medical writers, the term thus used extended from twenty-one to twenty-eight years of age. Looking to the prominent position taken by Saul in this matter, and to his description of himself as "Paul the aged," A.D. 64 (Philem. 9), it will be safe to assume that he had nearly attained the later limit. He was of the tribe of Benjamin (Phil. 3:5); the absence of any reference to the apostle's father and mother makes it probable that they both were dead before he appears on the scene. The son of a married sister is found, apparently residing in Jerusalem, in 23:16. At Tarsus the boy probably would receive instruction in the Holy Scriptures daily at home, and in Greek literature and philosophy in the schools for which the city was famous. Traces of the knowledge thus acquired are found in his quotations from the Cilician poet Aratus (17:28), Menander (I Cor.

15:33), Epimenides (Tit. 1:12), and the Festival Hymn quoted by him at Lystra (14:17). At twelve he no doubt became a child of the Law (see note on Luke 2:42); and showing great devotion to the studies thus opened to him, he probably was dedicated by his parents to the calling of a scribe. This, however, did not involve the abandonment of secular occupation; and after some years spent in Jerusalem, studying under Gamaliel (almost certainly before the beginning of our Lord's ministry), he returned to his native city and became a **"tent maker"** (18:3)—a manufacturer, i.e., of the coarse goats' hair sailcloth, for which Cilicia was famous. In the interval between the Ascension and the appointment of the seven deacons, he came up to Jerusalem, finding the new sect of the Nazarenes. How should he relate to it? Gamaliel, his master, counseled caution and a policy of expectation (5:35-39); Barnabas, his early friend, had joined the new society (4:36); Andronicus and Junia, his kinsmen, had followed the example (Rom. 16:7). But Saul had a zeal which was more fiery than theirs. The teaching of Stephen was a protest against Pharisaism, and told of its coming downfall. He, therefore, a strict Pharisee, could make no truce with that teaching.

(59) Lord Jesus, receive my spirit.—The words are memorable as an instance of direct prayer addressed, to use the words of Pliny in reporting what he had learned of the worship of Christians, "to Christ as God" (**Epist.** 10:97).

(60) Lord, lay not this sin to their charge.—The resemblance to the prayer of Christ (Luke 23:34) could hardly have been accidental. We may well think of the prayer as having for its chief object him who was the foremost of the accusers. The old words of Augustine (**Serm.** 314-318), that we owe the conversion of Saul to the prayers of Stephen, may be accepted as the expression of a great spiritual fact. (The death of Stephen is fixed by most writers at A.D. 38.)

8

(1) There was a great persecution against the church.—It is clear that this involved much suffering. From Jas. 2:6, 7 we see at once the measure of the violence of the persecution, and the prominence in it of the priesthood and the rich Saducean aristocracy.

Throughout the regions of Judaea and Samaria.—What seemed the pressure of circumstances was leading indirectly to the fulfillment of our Lord's commands that the disciples should be witnesses in Samaria as well as in Judaea (1:8). It is possible (see note on 6:5) that there was some point of contact between the seven, of whom Stephen was the chief, and that region.

Except the apostles.—The sequel of the history suggests two reasons for their remaining. (1) The Twelve had learned the lesson which their Master had taught them, "that the hireling fleeth, because he is an hireling" (John 10:13), and would not desert their post. A tradition is recorded by Clement of Alexandria (**Strom.** 6:5, §43) and Eusebius (**Hist.** 5:13) that the Lord had commanded the apostles to remain for twelve years in Jerusalem lest any should say "We have not heard," and after that date to go forth into the world. (2) The persecution which was now raging seems to have been directed especially against those who taught with Stephen that the "customs" on which the Pharisees laid so much stress should pass away. The apostles had not as yet proclaimed that truth, because, perhaps, they had not as yet been led to it. They may well have been protected by the favor and reverence with which the great body of the people still looked on them (see 10:14, 28), and so have been less exposed than the seven had been to the violence of the storm.

(2) In the legend or tradition as to the death of Stephen, reported and accepted by Augustine (**De Civ. Dei.** 17:8; **Serm.** 318, 319; **Tract. in Joann**, 120), Gamaliel and Nicodemus are named as actually taking part in the entombment. Commonly, one who had been stoned to death on the charge of blasphemy would have had no funeral honors (Jer. 22:19). The public lamentation on the part of men conspicuous for their devout zeal for the Law was therefore of the nature of a protest.

(3) As for Saul, he made havoc of the church.—The tense in the Greek implies continuous action, and so indicates the severity of the persecution. Further details are given by Paul himself. See 22:4; 26:11; I Tim. 1:13. There was a kind of insane ferocity in his violence. Even the word "haling" here implies a brutality which might well have been spared.

(4) As in later ages, the axiom that "the blood of martyrs is the seed of the Church" held true from the beginning. The attempt to stamp out the new faith did but give it a wider scope of action, and urged it on beyond the limits within which it might otherwise have been confined for a much longer period.

(5) Then Philip went down to the city of Samaria.—More accurately, "a city." The sequence of events implies that it was not the apostle, but his namesake who had been chosen as one of the seven—Philip the evangelist (21:8). The "city of Samaria" is described in precisely the same terms as in John 4:5, where it is identified with Sychar, the Sichem of the Old Testament. "Samaria," throughout the New Testament, is used for the province, and not for the city to which it had been attached in earlier times. This had been newly named **Sebaste** (the Greek equivalent of Augusta) by Herod the Great in honor of the emperor, and this had more or less superseded the old name (Jos., **Ant.** 15.8, §5).

Preached Christ.—The tense implies continued action, extending, it may be, over weeks or months. The expectation of the Messiah was as strong among the Samaritans as among the Jews (see John 4:25). Philip's work therefore was to proclaim that the long-expected One had come, and that the Resurrection was the crowning proof that He was the Christ the Son of God.

(9) But there was a certain man, called Simon.—The name indicates Jewish or Samaritan origin. He appears as the type of a class common at the time, that of Jews trading on the mysterious **prestige** of their race and the credulity of the heathen, claiming supernatural power exercised through charms and incantations. Such afterward were Elymas at Cyprus (13:8) and the vagabond exorcists at Ephesus (19:13).

Giving out that himself was some great one.—Verse 10 defines the nature of the claim more clearly: he purported to be an incarnation of divine power. Simon the Sorcerer appears as the earliest type of those who were to come with lying signs and wonders so as to deceive, if it were possible, even the elect (Matt. 24:24; II Thess. 2:9).

(13) What was the nature of his faith and the effect of his baptism? The verb "wondered" is the same as that rendered "bewitched" in verses 9 and 11. The tables were turned; the magician yielded to a spell mightier than his own, and was, in his turn, as one beside himself with amazement. The difference between Simon and the believing Samaritans is suggestive. His faith rested on outward miracles; with them the miracles did but serve to confirm a faith which rested on the "prophetic word" as spoken by the Son of Man (John 4:42).

(14) When the apostles which were at Jerusalem . . .—The tidings came to the Twelve as a proof that the limitation which had at first excluded Samaria from the range of their work as preachers of the kingdom had now passed away (Matt. 10:5), and that the time had now come when they were to be "witnesses" to Christ in Samaria as well as in Judaea (1:8). Old antipathies of race and worship (see John 4:9) disappeared, and without hesitation they sent the two who were, in many respects, the chief of the apostles to sanction the admission of the new converts. The apostle who in his zeal had once sought to call down the fire of the wrath of God on the village of the Samaritans (Luke 9:54) was now to bring to them that baptism of the Holy Ghost and of fire (Matt. 3:11) which spoke not of wrath but of love.

(15) Prayed for them, that they might receive the Holy Ghost.—The prayer clearly pointed to such a gift of the power of the Spirit as had been bestowed on the Day of Pentecost. It assumed that such gifts had been received by the disciples generally at Jerusalem, and that they were distinct from the new birth of water and the Spirit (John 3:5). The apostles looked on the Samaritans as qualified for that higher gift as well as for admission into the kingdom, and it was given to them, and not to Philip in his subordinate position as an evangelist, to be the channels of communicating it.

(17) Then laid they their hands on them.—See note on 6:6.

(18, 19) The words imply that the result was something visible and conspicuous. A change was wrought; and men spoke with tongues and prophesied. He who had purchased many secrets, after the manner of the time (comp. 19:19), from previous masters in the magic art thought that this might be obtained in the same way. The act thus recorded has given its name to a large class of offenses in ecclesiastical jurisprudence, and the sin of simony in all its forms, the act of purchasing spiritual powers and functions, perpetuates the infamy of the magician of Samaria.

(22, 23) Did the apostle think that the sin of Simon came near that "sin against the Holy Ghost which hath never forgiveness" (Matt. 12:31)? ("Bitterness" occurs for extreme moral depravity in Rom. 3:14; Eph. 4:31; Heb. 12:15.) The use of such words by

the chief of the apostles, after the apparent concession of a plenary power in John 20:23, are suggestive. He neither forgives nor condemns, but bids the offender turn to the Searcher of hearts and pray for forgiveness.

(24) Pray ye to the Lord for me.—He prays not for deliverance from "the bond of iniquity," but only from the vague terror of a future penalty. At this point Simon disappears from the history of the Acts, occupying a far more prominent place in numerous fantastic fables than in Luke's narrative. These have been preserved by Justin (**Apol.**; **Hom.**; **Recogn.**), Irenaeus (**Adv. Haer.**), and Eusebius (**Hist. Eccl.**), and in the **Constt. Apost.**

(26) Gaza was the southernmost or border city of the early Canaanites (Gen. 10:19). The tribe of Judah held it for a short time (Judg. 1:18), but it soon fell into the hands of the Philistines (Judg. 3:3; 13:1) and was held by them during the times of Samuel, Saul, and David (I Sam. 6:17; 14:52; II Sam. 21:15). Solomon (I Kings 4:24), and later on Hezekiah (II Kings 18:8), attacked it. It resisted Alexander the Great during a siege of five months, and was an important military position, the key of the country, during the struggles between the Ptolemies and the Seleucidae, and in the wars of the Maccabees (I Macc. 11:61). Its name meant the "strong." Philip was to go in faith to the less frequented, less promising route—through the **Negeb**—from Jerusalem to Gaza, apparently without passing himself through the Holy City, and so to intercept the traveler whose history was to become so memorable.

(27) A man of Ethiopia, an eunuch of great authority.—Ethiopia from which the traveler came was the region so named by the geographers of Luke's time in the upper valley of the Nile. There seems reason to believe that in the time of Manasseh, who (according to the statement in the narrative of Aristeas as to the LXX translation) formed an alliance with Psammetichus, king of Egypt, a considerable body of Jews were sent off to protect the outposts of his kingdom (comp. Zeph. 3:10). Jewish influences had accordingly been at work there for some centuries. (See Pss. 68:31; 87:4; Jer. 38:7-13; 39:16-18.) The fact that the traveler had come as a pilgrim or a proselyte shows that he was a circumcised "proselyte of righteousness." His baptism was not, like that of Cornelius, the admission of a Gentile as such. The strict letter of Deut. 23:1, forbidding the admission of eunuchs into the congregation of the Lord, already had been modified (probably on the assumption that the state was not one which they had brought about by their own act) by Isaiah (56:4); and we may well think of Luke as glad to record a proof that the discipline of the Church of Christ was as liberal on the point as the teaching of the evangelical prophet.

Under Candace queen of the Ethiopians.— The knowledge of the student of Strabo (Strabo, 17.) may, perhaps, be traced in the description. The occurrence of the name again in Plin. 4:35, Dion.-Cass. 54:5, indicates that it was, like Pharaoh, a dynastic name or title. Eusebius (**Hist.** 2.1) states that in his time (**circ.** A.D. 430) the region still was under the rule of a queen, according to the custom of the country.

(28) Sitting in his chariot read Esaias the prophet.—After the manner of most Eastern nations, to whom silent reading is almost unknown, the eunuch was reading aloud. Philip heard him, and so gained an opening for conversation. The whole narrative implies that he was reading the LXX version.

(32-34) In I Pet. 2:23 we find the outlines of a method of "preaching unto him Jesus" (see verse 35): the story of the Passion would be told; the silent patience of the Sufferer; His previous life and work; the proofs which both had given that He was none other than that which He claimed to be—the Christ, the Son of God. (See notes on Isa. 53.)

(36) They came unto a certain water.— Jerome and Eusebius fix the locality at Bethsura (II Chron. 11:7), about twenty miles from Jerusalem and two from Hebron. More recent scholarship suggests the Wady-el-Hasey, between Eleutheropolis and Gaza, not far from the old sites of Lachish and Egln. This agrees better with the mention of Gaza and with the epithet "desert" as attached to the "way."

(37) And Philip said . . .—The verse existed in the time of Irenaeus, who quotes it (3:12), but is wanting in all the best MSS and many versions. The motive for the interpolation lies in the absence of the confession of faith which was required in the Church's practice on the baptism of every convert. Even with the insertion, the shortness of the confession points to a very early stage of liturgical development, as does also the reference to it in Irenaeus.

(38) They went down both into the water.—The Greek preposition might mean simply "**unto** the water"; but the practice of immersion in the early Church suggests that the eunuch laid aside his garments, descended chest deep into the water, and was plunged under it "in the name of the Lord Jesus," the only formula recognized in the Acts. (See note on 2:38.)

(39) Philip was literally snatched away— abruptly and immediately—from his companion. (Comp. Elijah, I Kings 18:12.) The use of the same verb in II Cor. 12:2, 4 suggests that here also there was a suspension of the normal activity of consciousness. Philip rushed away, as drawn on he knew not where, as in a state of ecstasy.

Eusebius (**Hist.** 2.1) speaks of the eunuch as returning to his native country, and there preaching in fulfillment of Ps. 68:31. It is significant in connection with this history that the Ethiopian Church has been throughout its history the most strongly Jewish in its worship and tone of thought of all Christian communities.

(40) Azotus, the Ashdod of the Old Testament, was, like Gaza, one of the cities of the Philistines, about three miles from the sea and halfway between Gaza and Joppa. Like Gaza its history was marked chiefly by successive sieges. In more remote times it had been one of the headquarters of the worship of Dagon (I Sam. 5:5). The route which Philip would naturally take on this journey led through Lydda and Joppa, and we may probably trace the effect of his labors in the appearance in 9:32, 36 of organized and apparently flourishing Christian societies in both these towns.

The historical importance of Caesarea, lying on the great road from Tyre to Egypt, dates, as its name shows, from the Roman period. As described by Strabo, it was known only as Strato's Tower, with a landing place for ships. It rose to magnificence, however, under Herod the Great, who built theaters, amphitheaters, temples, and a harbor. In honor of his imperial patron he named it **Caesarea Sebaste** (the latter word meaning **Augusta**) (Jos., **Ant.** 16.5, §1). Philip took up his abode there and made it the headquarters of his work as an evangelist (21:8). In ecclesiastical history it became famous as the scene for a time of the labors of the great Origen, and as the home of the historian-bishop Eusebius.

9

(1) The "yet" implies a considerable interval since the death of Stephen, probably coinciding with the time occupied by the mission work of Philip in the previous chapter. During this interval the persecution probably had been continuing. If, as is probable, the admission of the Samaritans to the new community had become known to Jerusalem, it naturally would tend to intensify their hatred. It would seem to them as if the accursed people now were allied with the Galileans against the Holy Place and those who were zealous for its honor.

(2) And desired of him letters to Damascus.—Damascus was at this time under the government of Aretas, the king of Arabia Petraea (see II Cor. 11:32, 33). In the abeyance of control of the Roman power, Aretas may have desired to conciliate the priestly party at Jerusalem by giving facilities to their action against the sect which they would naturally represent as identified with the Galileans against whom he had been waging war. The Jewish population at Damascus was, at this time, very numerous.

If he found any of this way.—Literally, "of the way." We have here the first occurrence of a term which seems to have been used familiarly as a synonym for the disciples of Christ (19:9, 23; 22:4, 24:14, 22). It may have originated in the words of Christ Himself (see Matt. 7:13; John 14:6), or, perhaps, in the prophecy of Isaiah (40:3) cited by the Baptist (Matt. 3:3; Mark 1:3). Prior to the general acceptance of the term "Christian" (11:26) it served as a convenient designation by which the disciples could be identified.

(3) And as he journeyed.—The route by which the persecutor and his companions traveled probably was that taken by the Roman road, which extended from Jerusalem to Neapolis (Sychar, or Shechem), from there to Scythopolis, and so by the shores of the Sea of Galilee and Caesarea Philippi, and then under the slopes of Hermon, to Damascus. On this supposition Saul would traverse the chief scenes of our Lord's ministry, and be stirred to madness by the progress which the new sect had made in the cities of Samaria.

He came near Damascus.—This beautiful city has the interest of being one of the oldest in the world. It appears in the history of Abraham (Gen. 14:15; 15:2), and was, traditionally, the scene of the murder of Abel. It was the center of the Syrian kingdom in its alliances and wars with those of Israel and Judah (II Kings 14:28; 16:9, 10;

Amos 1:3, 5). At a later period it was the residence of the Ommiyad caliphs and the center of the world of Islam. Assuming the journey to have been continuous, the approach to Damascus would come on the seventh or eighth day after leaving Jerusalem.

There shined round about him a light from heaven.—Three accounts of the event that turned the current of the life of Saul of Tarsus meet us in the Acts: (1) this, which gives the writer's report of what he hardly could have heard from any lips but Paul's; (2) Paul's narrative before the Sanhedrin (22:6-11); (3) that which he gives before Agrippa (26:13-18). They present considerable variations (see notes), such as were natural in the records of a manifestation which was partial to some, and complete to one only. It is not possible in such a history to draw a hard and fast line between the objective and the subjective. It is enough for him that he sees what others do not see, and hears what they do not hear, while they too hear and see enough to prove both to themselves and to him that something has occurred beyond the range of ordinary phenomena.

(4) The narrative implies that the persecutor saw the form of the Son of man as well as heard His voice, and to that visible presence the apostle afterward refers as a witness to him of the Resurrection (I Cor. 9:1; 15:8). It is natural to think of the manner of appearance as being such as had met the gaze of Stephen.

(5) Who art thou, Lord?—The word "Lord" could not as yet have been used in all the fullness of its meaning. As in many cases in the gospels, it was the natural utterance of respect and awe (John 5:7; 9:36; 20:15), such as would be roused by what the prosecutor saw and heard.

I am Jesus whom thou persecutest.—The pronouns are both emphatic, "**I,** in my love and might and glory, I am the Jesus whom **thou,** now prostrate and full of dread, hast been bold enough to persecute." It was not the disciples and brethren alone whom Saul was persecuting. What was done to them the Lord counted as done unto Himself (Matt. 10:40).

It is hard for thee to kick against the pricks.—There is a decisive preponderance of MS authority against the appearance of these words here, and the conclusion of many critics is that they have been inserted in the later MSS from 26:14. In their outward form they were among the oldest and most familiar of Greek proverbs. The Jew who had been educated in the schools of Tarsus might have read them in Greek poets (Aeschylus, **Agam.** 1633; Pindar, **Pyth.** 2.173; Eurip. **Bacch.** 791). What they taught was that to resist a power altogether superior to our own is a profitless and perilous experiment. The goad did but prick more sharply the more the ox struggled against it. The "pricks" against which he had been "kicking" were the promptings, misgivings, warnings, which he had resisted and defied (see 4:36; 5:34-39; 6:15; 7:60). In his later retrospect of this stage of his life he was able, as by a subtle process of self-analysis, to distinguish between the element of ignorance, which made forgiveness possible, and that of a wilfull resistance to light and knowledge which made that forgiveness an act of free and undeserved compassion (I Tim. 1:12, 13).

(6) The word "Lord" now, we must believe, took on a new meaning, as applied to the Nazarene whom he had before despised. The entire surrender of his own will was made to that of Him whom he thus recognized as commanding his allegiance. At that moment Christ was formed in him (Gal. 1:16).

(7) Comp. 22:9. What is meant is clearly that they did not hear the words—could attach no meaning to the sounds which for Saul himself had so profound a significance. So, in like manner, they saw the light, but did not see the form.

(8) He saw no man.—The blindness was that of one who has been dazzled with excess of light (comp. 22:11), the natural result of the vision of the supernatural glory, a witness to the man himself that the vision was not a mere play of imagination. Traces of its permanent effect on his powers of sight have been found in 23:2-5; II Cor. 12:7; Gal. 4:15; 6:11; II Thess. 3:17 (see notes).

(9) He was three days without sight.—It is natural to think of this period of seclusion from the visible world as one of spiritual communion with the invisible. (See notes on II Cor. 12:1-4.)

(10) A certain disciple at Damascus, named Ananias.—In 22:12 Paul speaks of him as a "devout man according to the law," well reported of by all the Jews who dwelt at Damascus. The name was so common that any identification must be in some measure uncertain; but see Josephus (**Ant.** 20.2, §4), where the thought is that he too

was a preacher of the Gospel of Christ as Paul preached it.

(13) Lord, I have heard by many of this man.—The words are of interest as showing both the duration and the character of the persecution in which Saul had been the leader. The report of it had spread far and wide. The refugees at Damascus told of the sufferings of the brethren at Jerusalem.

Thy saints at Jerusalem.—This is noticeable as the first application of the term "saints" to the disciples. The primary idea of the word was that of men who consecrated themselves, and led, in the strictest sense of the word, a devout life. A term of like import—the **Chasidim**—had been taken by the more religious Jews in the time of the Maccabeans, who banded themselves together to resist the inroads of heathenism under Antiochus Epiphanes. The more distinctive name of Pharisees (Separatists), which came to be attached to the more zealous Chasidim, practically superseded this. Ananias may well have been among the Chasidim even prior to his conversion to the faith of Christ.

(15) The mission of the apostle was thus revealed to Ananias in the first instance. He welcomes that expansion of the kingdom, and is taught to see in the man of whom he had only heard as the persecutor one who had been trained and chosen as more fit than all others for the work of that expansion.

(17) The narrative clearly implies that here, as in 8:17, the being "filled with the Holy Ghost" was connected with the laying on of hands as a condition, and it is so far a proof that that gift was not one which attached exclusively to the apostles. It was, we may well believe, manifested in this instance, as in others, by the ecstatic utterance of "the tongues" (comp. 19:6; I Cor. 14:18) and by the gift of prophetic insight.

(18) There fell from his eyes as it had been scales.—The description suggests that the blindness was acute inflammation caused by an incrustation covering the pupil of the eye (comp. Tob. 11:13). Like phenomena are mentioned by Hippocrates, and the care with which Luke records the fact is another example of the technical precision of his calling as a physician.

Arose, and was baptized.—It is clear that both Saul and Ananias looked on this as the indispensable condition for admission into the visible society of the kingdom of God. The baptism almost certainly was administered by Ananias in the Abana or Pharpar River (II Kings 5:12).

(20) And straightway he preached Christ in the synagogues.—The "straightway" must be taken to refer to the apostle's first public appearance in the synagogues of Damascus after his return from Arabia. (See note on Gal. 1:17.) The tense of the verb implies that the work was continued for some length of time. The Samaritans had a synagogue of their own at Damascus, and he may thus have preached to them, so following in the footprints of Philip and taking his first step in the great work of breaking down the barriers that divided Israel from the world.

(23) Verse 23 connects with the more definite statement in Gal. 1:18 (see note), covering a period of otherwise unrecorded work. That period must have witnessed the growth of a Christian society at Damascus, with an order of discipline and worship based on the outlines of that at Jerusalem.

(24) They watched the gates day and night to kill him.—Comp. II Cor. 11:32. The governor, literally **ethnarch**, under Aretas, king of Arabia Petraea, the father of the wife whom Herod Antipas divorced in order that he might marry Herodias, took an active part in the plot against Paul. The ethnarch apparently wished to court the favor of the large Jewish population, and, looking on Paul as a disturber of the public peace, took measures for his arrest and condemnation.

(25) Let him down by the wall in a basket.—The basket was a wicker or ropework hamper. It seemed to follow, from the tone in which the apostle speaks of this adventure in II Cor. 11:33, that it had been made matter of ridicule. It is connected in his thoughts with the "infirmities" (probably with his smallness of stature) of which he was content to boast.

(27, 28) See notes on Gal. 1:18, 19.

(29) Disputed against the Grecians.—It was as the leader of the Hellenistic Jews of the synagogue named in 6:9 (see note) that Saul had first appeared in the history of the Church. Now, it would seem, he sought to undo the evil that he had then wrought by preaching to them the faith which he had then opposed.

(30) At Caesarea (not Caesarea Philippi) he would probably, as afterward in 21:8, find Philip, and the friend and the accuser of the proto-martyr met face to face as brethren. In returning to his home at Tarsus, from which he had been absent at the least for four years, and possibly for a much

longer period, it would be natural for him to resume his old employment as a tent maker. (See 18:3.) From there, as from a center, he did his work as an evangelist in the regions of Cilicia (Gal. 1:21), where in 15:41 we find churches already organized which had not been founded in what we call the first mission journey of Paul and Barnabas, and must therefore have been planted by the former at an earlier period. Here, for the present, we lose sight of him.

(32) As Peter passed throughout all quarters.—The plan of the writer, arranging his materials, leads him from this point to 12:18 to dwell entirely on the personal work of Peter. So far this section of the book may be described as the Acts of Peter. He gives only those acts as part of his general plan not caring to follow the apostle's course, as in a biography, but confining himself to tracing the steps by which he had been led to the part he played in the great work of the conversion of the Gentiles.

He came down also to the saints which dwelt at Lydda.—On the term "saints," see note on verse 13. Lydda, the Lod of the Old Testament (I Chron. 8:12; Ezra 2:33; Neh 7:37; 11:35), was a town in the rich plain of Sharon, between the central mountains of Palestine and the Mediterranean, one day's journey from Jerusalem. It was, at the time when Peter came to it, the seat of a rabbinic school. Gamaliel, son of the great rabbi who was Paul's master, presided over it. Philip apparently planted the faith of Christ there.

(33) A certain man named AEneas.—The Greek name (comp. Virgil's Trojan hero) perhaps implies that he belonged to the Hellenistic section of the Church. The word for "bed," used commonly of the couches of the lower class (see Matt. 2:4), suggests the thought that poverty also was added to his sufferings.

(34) See note on 4:30.

(36) There was at Joppa . . .—Joppa was famous in Greek legends as the spot where Andromeda had been bound when she was delivered by Perseus (Strabo, 16. 759; Jos., **Wars,** 1.6, §2). It was the nearest port to Jerusalem, and though the harbor was difficult and dangerous of access, was used for the timber that, first under Solomon, and afterward under Zerubbabel, was brought from Lebanon for the construction of the Temple (I Kings 5:9; II Chron. 2:16; Ezra 3:7). In the history of Jonah it appears as a port from which ships sail to Tarshish and Spain (Jonah 1:3). It was, at this time of

Roman domination, notorious as a nest of pirates. Here also we may see the work of Philip as the probable founder of the Church.

Tabitha, which by interpretation is called Dorcas.—Both the Hebrew and Greek names mean "antelope" or "gazelle." We may trace in the position which she occupied, in relation to the "widows" of the Church, something of the same prudential wisdom as had been shown in the appointment of the seven (6:3-5).

(37) They laid her in an upper chamber.—This implies some little delay in the usual rapidity of Eastern funerals. As Lydda was only nine miles from Joppa, the report of AEneas' recovery might well have travelled from the one city to the other, and led to the hope that the power which Peter had thus put forth might extend even to the farther work of raising from the dead.

(40) Peter put them all forth.—Comp. Matt. 9:23, 24, at which occasion he had been present. This work called for the silence and solitude of communion with God. Even the words which were uttered, if he spoke in Aramaic, must have been, with the change of a single letter, the same as the "Talitha cumi" of Mark 5:41.

(43) Many days in Joppa with one Simon a tanner.—Either as bringing with it, through contact with the carcases and hides of dead beasts, the risks of ceremonial defilement, or being generally a repulsive and noisome business, the occupation was one from which the stricter Jews generally would shrink. In taking up his abode with one of this calling, Peter must accordingly have been taking one step in advance toward greater freedom.

10

(1) Cornelius, a centurion of the band called the Italian band.—Cornelius' admission into the Church, even if it were not the first instance of the reception of a Gentile convert as such, became, through its super-natural accompaniments and its "prerogative" character, the ruling case on the subject. The office was a comparatively subordinate one, the centurion commanding the sixth part of a cohort, the sixtieth part of a legion. This cohort was distinguished from the others as Italian, i.e., as being at least commanded by Roman officers. Comp. the Augustan band, 27:1.

(2) A devout man, and one that feared God with all his house.—The word for "devout" is used by Luke for the special type of devotion that belonged to Gentile converts to Judaism. The phrase "those that feared God" is employed distinctly for this class in verses 22 and 35, and again in 13:16, 26. The centurion was not satisfied with having found a higher truth for himself, but sought to impart it to the soldiers and slaves who came under his influence. (Comp. verse 7.)

And prayed to God alway.—It is natural to infer that Cornelius was seeking for guidance as to the new faith which Philip had brought to Caesarea, and of which he scarcely could fail to have heard. Could he be admitted to the fellowship of the society which confessed Jesus as the Christ without accepting the yoke of circumcision and the ceremonial law from which, as a "proselyte of the gate," he had heretofore kept back?

(9) As they went on their journey ...—The distance from Caesarea to Joppa was about thirty Roman miles.

To pray about the sixth hour.—As in 3:1, Peter was observing (like Cornelius, verse 3) the Jewish hours of prayer. Probably it was one of the days, the second and fifth in the week, which the Pharisees and other devout Jews observed as fasts. The flat housetop of an Eastern house commonly was used for prayer and meditation (comp. Matt. 10:27; 24:17; Luke 17:31).

(13) Rise, Peter; kill, and eat.—In the symbolism of the vision the natural promptings of appetite were confirmed by the divine voice. That which resisted both was the scruple of a hesitating conscience, not yet emancipated from its bondage to a ceremonial and therefore transitory law.

(14) Not so, Lord ...—The emphatic resistance even to a voice from heaven is strikingly in harmony with the features of Peter's character, as portrayed in the gospels. (Comp. Luke 16:30; John 13:8.)

(15) What God hath cleansed, that call not thou common.—In the framework of the vision, the clean and the unclean beasts alike were let down from heaven in the same sheet. That had purified them from whatever taint had adhered to them under the precepts of the Law. In the interpretation of the vision, all that belongs to humanity had been taken up into heaven when man's nature was assumed by the eternal Word in the Incarnation (John 1:14) and then raised in the Ascension to the heaven of heavens (7:56; Mark 16:19; see note on verse 28).

881

(23) As it was about noon when Peter went up to the housetop to pray, the arrival of the messengers, allowing an adequate interval for the trance and the vision, may be placed at some time in the afternoon. We learn from 11:12 that there were six "brethren." (See Deut. 17:6; 19:15.)

(28) Ye know how that it is an unlawful thing.—Peter speaks from the standpoint of traditional Pharisaism rather than from that of the Law itself; but the feeling was widely diffused, and showed itself in forms more or less rigorous wherever Jews and heathen came in contact with each other.

God hath shewed me that I should not call any man common or unclean.—The apostle had at last learned the lesson which the vision had taught him, in all the fullness of its meaning. Humanity as such had been redeemed by the Incarnation and Ascension, and was no longer common or unclean, even in the most outcast heathen. God was willing to receive all men. Sin alone was that which separated men from Him. Impurity was thought of as a moral, not a physical, taint, and men were taught to see even in the sinner the potentialities of a higher life.

(34) Of a truth I perceive that God is no respecter of persons.—In regard to all distinctions of social rank, or wealth, or knowledge, Peter had seen in his Master that absence of "respect of persons" which even His enemies acknowledged (Matt. 22:16; Luke 20:21; comp. Jas. 2:1-7). The privileges and prerogatives of Israel, whatever blessings they might confer, were not to be set up as a barrier against the admission of other races to an equal fellowship in Christ. God had accepted the centurion. It remained for His servants to accept him also. (Comp. Rom. 2:11).

(35) In every nation he that feareth him.—The great truth which Peter thus proclaimed applies, not to those only who know the name of Christ and believe on Him when He is preached to them, but to all who in all ages and countries "fear God" according to the measure of their knowledge and "work righteousness" according to their belief and opportunities. The good works in such a case are fruits of faith, justification having been objectively bestowed for the merits of Christ and subjectively appropriated by faith which, in the providence of God, was possible under the conditions of the case. What such men gain by conversion is a fuller knowledge of the Truth, and therefore a clearer faith, a fuller

justification, and a higher blessedness; but as this history distinctly teaches, they already are accepted with God. They are saved even though they know not the name whereby they must be saved (4:12), by Christ, who is the Saviour of all. (See Rom. 10:9-14.)

(39) Both in the land of the Jews.—The words have the interest of implying the ministry in Judaea, of which the first three gospels record so little, but which comes out into full prominence in the fourth.

Whom they slew and hanged on a tree.—As in 2:23, Peter represents the crucifixion as virtually the act of the rulers and people of Jerusalem and not of the Roman governor. (See Deut. 27:26; Gal. 3:10.)

(41) Who did eat and drink with him.—See Luke 24:30, 42; John 21:13. This was the crucial test which showed that the form on which the disciples had looked was no phantom of the imagination.

(42, 43) These verses trace the result of our Lord's teaching between Resurrection and Ascension, demonstrating the method of prophetic interpretation regarding the kingdom of which Christ is Head. Assurance is given of His role as Judge. Not by submitting themselves to the bondage of the Law, not by circumcision and all that it implied, but by the simple act of faith in Christ, and in the power of His name, i.e., of all the attributes and energies of which the name was the symbol, they, Gentiles as they were, might receive that remission of sins which conscience, now roused to its full activity, taught them was the indispensable condition of acceptance and of peace.

(44) The Holy Ghost fell on all them which heard the word.—The words imply a sudden thrill of spiritual joy and elevation which showed itself, as it had done on the Day of Pentecost (see note on 2:4), in a burst of unpremeditated praise. Now, as then, the "tongues" (verse 46) manifested themselves, not as instruments of teaching, but in "magnifying God."

(47) Can any man forbid water . . .—Could the outward sign be refused, when thus the inward and spiritual grace had been so manifestly bestowed? All that remained was the outward act of incorporation with the society which owned Christ as its Head.

(48) Then prayed they him to tarry certain days.—Peter must have mingled freely with the new converts, eating and drinking with them (11:2), without any fear of being thereby defiled. Luke dwells on that visit to aesarea as one of the great turning points ｊn the apostle's life, attesting his essential greement with Paul. But Comp. notes on ｊal. 2:11, 12.

11

(2) The conversion of the Gentiles at ｊaesarea had given a new significance to ｊhe name of "those of the circumcision." ｊrom this time forth they are a distinct ｊarty in the Church, and here we have the ｊrst symptom of the line which they were ｊbout to take.

(15) As on us at the beginning.—The ｊords are spoken, it will be remembered, to ｊpostles and disciples who had been sharers ｊn the Pentecostal gift. Peter bears his testiｊnony that what he witnessed at Caesarea ｊvas no less manifestly the Spirit's work than ｊvhat they had then experienced.

(16) Then remembered I the word of the ｊord.—See note on 1:5. Then it had seemed ｊo refer only to the disciples, and the Day ｊof Pentecost had appeared to bring a comｊplete fulfillment of it. Now Peter had ｊearned to see that it had a wider range— ｊhat the gift might be bestowed on those ｊvho were not of Israel, and who were not ｊalled to come outwardly within the ｊovenant of Israel. If the baptism of the ｊloly Ghost had been thus given to them it ｊmplied, as the greater includes the less, that ｊhey were admissible to the baptism of ｊvater.

(18) They held their peace, and glorified ｊod.—The difference of tenses in the two ｊreek verbs implies that they first held ｊheir peace, and then began a continuous ｊtterance of praise. The fact was obviously ｊne of immense importance in its bearing ｊon the question at issue between Paul and ｊhe Judaizers, of which Luke had seen so ｊnuch and which he sought, by his narraｊive, to settle. The Judaizers, in opposing ｊaul, were acting against the Church from ｊvhich they pretended to derive their auｊhority.

(19) We are carried back to the date of ｊhe persecution of which Stephen was the ｊhief victim. It was probably, in the nature ｊf the case, that the Hellenistic Jews who ｊhad been associated with Stephen would be ｊhe chief sufferers. Philip we have traced in ｊamaria and Caesarea; others went to Phoeｊice, and were probably the founders of the ｊhurches which we find there in 21:4-7; ｊ7:3. In Cyprus (see note on 13:4) they

prepared the way for the work of Barnabas and Paul.

And Antioch.—We have here the first direct point of contact between the Church of Christ and the great Syrian capital which was for so many years one of its chief centers. (See note on 6:5.) It was situated on the Orontes, about fifteen miles from the port of Seleucia. It had a large colony of Jews, and Herod the Great had courted the favor of its inhabitants by building a marble colonnade which ran the whole length of the city. It became the headquarters of the Prefect of Syria, and the new faith was thus brought into more direct contact with the higher forms of Roman life than it had been at Jerusalem or Caesarea. There also it came into more direct conflict with heathenism in its most debasing forms. (See Juvenal, **Sat.** 3:62-64.)

(20) It seems that the word went on at Antioch for many months among the Hellenistic and other Jews (verse 19), and that the men of Cyprus and Cyrene arrived after the case of Cornelius had removed the scruples which had restrained them from giving full scope to the longings of their heart. Paul's action must have been parallel and independent, and may have been known to, and followed by, other missionaries.

(22-25) Barnabas, the friend of Paul (9:27), must have known his hopes and convictions of this matter (verse 25; see note on 9:30). The fact that he was himself of the same country also would qualify him for cooperating with the men of Cyprus, who were carrying on that work in Antioch. Words of praise are comparatively rare in this history, and we may think of them here as expressing Luke's personal estimate of the character of the preacher, which he was all the more anxious to place on record because he had to narrate before long the sad contention which separated him from his friend and fellow worker (15:39). Barnabas appeared to him to reproduce the mind and character of the martyr Stephen.

(26) The disciples were called Christians first in Antioch.—In its form the name was essentially Latin. It would seem to have grown out of the contact of the new society with the Romans stationed at Antioch, who, learning that its members acknowledged the **Christos** as their head, gave them the name of **Christiani.** As used in the New Testament, we note: (1) That the disciples never use it of themselves. (They keep to such terms as the "brethren," the "saints," and "those of the way.") (2) That the hostile Jews use the more scornful term of "Nazarenes." (3) That the term **Christianus** is used as a neutral and sufficiently respectful word by Agrippa (26:23), and at a somewhat later date, when it obviously had gained a wider currency, as that which brought with it the danger of suffering and persecution (I Pet. 4:16). It was natural that a name first given by outsiders should soon be accepted by believers as a title in which to glory.

Tradition ascribes its origin to Euodius, the first bishop of Antioch. Ignatius, his successor, uses it frequently, and forms from it the hardly less important word of **Christianismos**, as opposed to **Judaismos** (**Philadelph.** c. 6), and as expressing the whole system of faith and life which we know as "Christianity." And we may trace to Antioch, as well, the name of "Catholic" as well as "Christian" (Ignatius, **Smyrn.** c. 8). We learn from Tertullian (**Apol.** c. 3) that the name **Christianus** often was wrongly pronounced as **Chrestiani**, and its meaning not understood. Even the name of **Christos** was pronounced and explained as **Chrestos** (good). The Christians, on their side, accepted the mistake as a **nomen et omen**, an unconscious witness on the part of the heathen that they were good and worthy in their lives, that their Lord was "good and gracious" (I Pet. 2:3).

(28) **There stood up one of them named Agabus.**—The same prophet appears again in 21:10 as coming down from Jerusalem to Caesarea.

Which came to pass in the days of Claudius Caesar.—The reign of Caligula lasted from A.D. 37-41, that of Claudius from A.D. 41-54. The whole reign of the latter emperor was memorable for frequent famines (Suetonius, **Claud.** 28; Tacitus, **Ann.** 12:43; Josephus, **Ant.** 20.5).

(29) This was the beginning of that collection for the "poor saints at Jerusalem" which was afterward so prominent in the apostle's labors (24:17; Rom. 15:25, 26; I Cor. 16:1; II Cor. 9:1-15; Gal. 2:10), and which he regarded as a bond of union between the Jewish and Gentile sections of the Church.

(30) The elders of the Church are named here for the first time, and appear hereafter as a permanent element of its organization, which in this respect followed the arrangements of the synagogue. Officers filling like functions were known in the Gentile churches as Episcopi, or Bishops, and where

Jews and Gentiles were mingled, the two names were interchangeable (20:17, 18; Tit. 1:5, 7). Comp. Jas. 5:14, written probably about this time. It is likely that Luke here speaks of the journey narrated in chap. 15.

12

(1) **Herod the king.**—Herod Agrippa was the son of Aristobulus and Bernice, grandson of Herod the Great, and brother of Herodias. He had grown up in Rome on terms of intimacy with Caligula, the prince who afterward bestowed upon him several tetrarchies. At the time when Caligula's insanity took the form of a resolve to place his statue in the Temple at Jerusalem, Agrippa rendered an essential service to his people by using all his influence to deter the emperor from carrying out his purpose. Confirmed in his kingdom by Claudius, he found in Judaea a strong popular excitement against the believers in Christ, caused probably by the new step which recently had been taken in the admission of the Gentiles, and fomented by the Sadducean priesthood; and it seemed to him diplomatic to gain the favor of both priests and people by making himself the instrument of their jealousy.

(2) **He killed James the brother of John with the sword.**—Had the apostle been tried by the Sanhedrin on a charge of blasphemy and heresy, the sentence would have been death by stoning. Decapitation showed, as in the case of John the Baptist, that the sentence was pronounced by a civil ruler adopting Roman modes of punishment. The fulfillment of Matt. 20:23 was found for one brother in his being the proto-martyr of the apostolic company, as it was found for the other in his being the last survivor of it. What led to his being selected as the first victim we can only conjecture; but the natural vehemence indicated in the name of Son of Thunder may have marked him out as among the foremost teachers of the Church.

(3) **Because he saw it pleased the Jews.**— This was throughout the ruling policy of the Herodian house. The persecution did not spring from any fanatic political expediency. A tradition recorded by Jerome states that James was beheaded on the 15th of Nisan, i.e., on the same day as that of the Crucifixion. Peter was arrested probably at the same time; but the trial and execution were deferred until the seven days of the

east (Easter, i.e., Passover, verse 4) were over.

(12) Mary the mother of John, whose surname was Mark.—Mentioned by Peter as his "son" (I Pet. 5:13) Mark probably was converted by him. He was cousin to Barnabas and therefore connected with the tribe of Levi (4:36). The fact that Mary's house was the meeting place of the Church indicates comparative wealth, as did Barnabas' sale of his estate. The Latin name of Marcus indicates some point of contact with Romans or Roman Jews.

(15) It is his angel.—The language expresses the common belief of the Jews that every true Israelite had a guardian angel especially assigned to him, who, when he appeared in human form, assumed the likeness of the man whom he protected.

(17) Go shew these things unto James, and to the brethren.—At about this time, probably in consequence of the death of his namesake, the son of Zebedee, James the brother of the Lord comes into a fresh prominence. He is named as receiving Paul in Gal. 1:19, and as being, with Peter and John, one of the pillars of the Church (Gal. 2:9). Probably about this time he addressed the letter that bears his name to the twelve tribes that were scattered abroad. He presides at the Council of Jerusalem in 15:13, and acted as bishop of the Church at Jerusalem. According to a tradition preserved by Eusebius (**Hist.** 2:23), he was thrown from the pinnacle of the Temple upon proclaiming his faith in Christ.

(19) Commanded that they should be put to death.—Capital punishment was, according to Roman usage, the almost inevitable penalty for allowing a prisoner to escape (comp. 16:28).

(20) The two Phoenician cities were not subject to Agrippa, but were under the control of Rome with a nominal independence. They apparently feared that Herod would show his displeasure by prohibiting the export of corn, oil, and wine, on which the Phoenician cities, with their large population and narrow strips of territory, were dependent for subsistence. (Comp. I Kings 5:11; Ezek. 27:17.)

(21-23) According to Josephus (**Ant.** 19.8, §2), the scene was the theater at Caesarea, which had been built by Herod the Great. Agrippa was celebrating games in honor of the Emperor Claudius, who had succeeded Caligula in A.D. 41, possibly in honor of his return from Britain in A.D. 44. The king did not repress the flattery, which fell on the ears of all Jewish bystanders as a fearful blasphemy. He looked up, and seeing an owl perched on a rope behind him, recognized in it an omen of evil (Jos., **Ant.** 18:8). Sharp pain fell on him, and in five days he died. The intervention of the angel obviously is regarded by Luke as the only adequate explanation at once of the death of the persecutor and of the escape of his victim. It was a direct chastisement for an act of impiety. The specific form of the disease is not named by Josephus, but comp. the more memorable instances of it recorded in the histories of Antiochus the Great (II Macc. 9:2) and Herod the Great (Jos., **Ant.** 17:8).

(24) But the word of God grew and multiplied.—The words describe a continuous expansion. The death of the chief persecutor left free scope for the activity of the preachers of the Gospel, of which they were not slow to avail themselves.

(25) See note on verse 12.

13

(1) Of Simeon we suppose African origin; of Lucius, we conjecture that he was among the first evangelists at Antioch (see 11:20); of Manaen's early connection with Herod, see Josephus, **Ant.** 15.10, §5.

(2) Separate me Barnabas and Saul.—The Greek seems to indicate that the command given was in answer to a prayer, and that it was to be acted upon at once. The verb implies that they were to be set apart for a new work—the work of the apostleship to the Gentiles.

(3) And laid their hands on them.—See note on 6:6.

(4) Seleucia was situated at the mouth of the Orontes, about sixteen miles from Antioch, and served as the port for that city. It had been built by, and named after, Seleucus Nicator. The population of the island of Cyprus was largely Greek. The copper mines and its nearness to Syria probably had attracted a considerable Jewish population, among whom the Gospel had been preached by the evangelists of 11:19.

(5) Salamis was at the east end of Cyprus. It is probable that Mark was employed in baptizing converts, and, where a church was founded, in preparing for the Supper of the Lord. Looking to his later work, it would hardly be too much to say that he was, more than any other disciple, the courier of the Apostolic Church.

(6) When they had gone through the isle.—Paphos lay at its western extremity, and appears to have been the headquarters of the Roman governor. A local tradition points out a marble column to which Paul was bound and scourged by the citizens of Paphos, who are represented as having been among the most wicked of mankind.

They found a certain sorcerer.—See note on 8:9. The man bore two names: one, Bar-jesus, in its form a patronymic; the other, Elymas, an Aramaic title describing his claims to wisdom and supernatural powers. The lower class of Jews here, as in 19:13, seem to have been especially addicted to such practices.

(10) Thou child of the devil.—There is, perhaps, an intentional contrast between the meaning of the name Bar-jesus (son of the Lord who saves) and the character of the man, which led him to oppose righteousness in every form (see verses 7, 8).

(11) The form of the punishment suggests that Paul had looked back on his own blindness as being that which had been to him the process by which he was led to the light. (See notes on 9:8, 9.) That the blindness was to be "for a season" implies that it was designed to be remedial and not retributive.

(13) Perga was at this time the capital of Pamphylia, situated on the river Cestrus, about seven miles from its mouth. We are left to conjecture the motives of Mark's departure. He may have shrunk from the perils and hardships of the journey into the interior of the country. He may have been drawn by affection for his mother, who lived at Jerusalem. It is clear, in any case, from Paul's subsequent conduct (15:38) that he looked on the reason as insufficient, while Barnabas saw enough to admit the plea of extenuating circumstances.

(14) They came to Antioch in Pisidia.—The town was one of the many cities built by Seleucus Nicator and named after his father, Antiochus. It lay on the slopes of Mount Taurus, at the extreme limit of Pisidia, with Phrygia on the west and Lycaonia on the east.

(15) The rulers of the synagogue sent unto them . . .—The elders apparently saw strangers taking the position of teachers, probably in the garb of rabbis, and it belonged to their office to offer such persons an opportunity of addressing the people.

(17) Paul, as far as the plan of his discourse is concerned, follows in the footsteps of Stephen. Recapitulation of the main facts

of the history of Israel was a theme which Israelites were never tired of hearing. It showed that the apostles recognized it as the history of God's chosen people.

(20) The statement in the text assigning 450 years to the period of the judges, and apparently reckoning that period from the distribution of the conquered territory, is at variance with that in 1 Kings 6:1, which gives 480 years as the period intervening between the Exodus and the building of the Temple. The better MSS, however, give "about 450 years." The general tendency furthermore, in a discourse of this kind is to rest in round numbers. (See note on 7:6.)

(27) For they that dwell at Jerusalem.—The implied reason of the mission to the Gentiles and more distant Jews is that the offer of salvation had been rejected by those who naturally would have been its first recipients, and who, had they received it, would have been, in turn, witnesses to those who were "far off."

The voices of the prophets which are read every sabbath day.—The apostle appeals to the synagogue ritual from which the discourse started as in itself bearing witness, not to the popular notions of a conquering Messiah, but to the true ideal of the chief of sufferers, which had been realized in Jesus. (See verse 29.)

(33) The variant reading, "in the first Psalm," given by some MSS is interesting as showing that in some copies of the Old Testament, what is now the first Psalm was treated as a kind of prelude to the whole book, the numeration beginning with what is now the second.

Historically, Psalm 2 appears as a triumph song, written to celebrate the victory of a king of Israel or Judah over his enemies. The king had been shown by that day of victory to have been the chosen son of God—the day itself was a new begetting, manifesting the sonship. So, in the higher fulfillment which Paul finds in Christ, he refers the words, not primarily to the Eternal Generation of the Son of God, nor to the Incarnation, but to the Resurrection, the day of victory over death and Hades. Christ was to them the "firstborn of every creature," because He was also "the firstborn from the dead." (See Col. 1:15, 18.)

(35) See notes on the prophecy so cited in 2:25-31.

(38, 39) It is interesting to note in this first recorded example of Paul's teaching the occurrence of the word which came to be identified with him and his work. "Justified" is clearly used, as interpreted by the "forgiveness of sins" in the context, in its forensic sense, as meaning "acquitted," "declared not guilty." The Law, with its high standard of righteousness, its demand of entire obedience, its sacrifices which bore witness to the burden of sin yet had no power to liberate, had taught him that its function in the spiritual life of man was to work out the knowledge of sin, not to emancipate men from it. True life was to be found through faith in Christ.

(46) See Rom. 2:9, 10. The Jews were offered, as the fulfillment of the promise made to Abraham, the high privilege of being the channel through which "all families of the earth should be blessed" by the knowledge of Christ (Gen. 22:18). When they rejected that offer, it was made, without their intervention, to the Gentiles.

(47) I have set thee to be a light of the Gentiles.—The context of the quotation shows that Paul identified the "Servant of the Lord" in Isa. 49:6 with the person of the Christ. The citation is interesting as the first example of the train of thought which led the apostle to see in the language of the prophets, where others had found only the exaltation of Israel, the divine purpose of love toward the whole heathen world. (See Rom. 9:25; 10:12.)

(48) As many as were ordained to eternal life believed.—The Greek implies no more than that they fit in with the divine order which the Jews rejected. They were as soldiers who take the place assigned to them in God's great army. The **quasi**-middle force of the passive form of the verb is seen in the Greek of 20:13, where a compound form of it is rightly rendered "for so he had appointed," and might have been translated "for so he was disposed."

(49) Throughout all the region.—This clearly involves a considerable period of active working. It was not in Antioch only, but in the "region" round about, the border district of the three provinces of Phrygia, Lycaonia, and Galatia, that the new faith was planted.

(50) Raised persecution against Paul and Barnabas.—The memory of these sufferings came back upon Paul's mind, even in the last months of his life, as something never to be forgotten (II Tim. 3:11).

(51) They shook off the dust of their feet against them.—See Matt. 10:14. The act was the language of a natural symbolism which every Jew would understand, a declaration that not the heathen, but the unbelieving and malignant Jews, were those who made the dust on which they trod common and unclean.

And came unto Iconium.—The journey to Iconium is passed over rapidly, and we may infer that it presented no opportunities for mission work. That city lay on the road between Antioch and Derbe at a distance of ninety miles southeast from the former city, and forty northwest from the latter. The city, which from its size and stateliness has been called the Damascus of Lycaonia, was famous in the early apocryphal Christian writings as the scene of the exchange between Paul and his convert Thekla.

14

(2) The unbelieving Jews stirred up the Gentiles . . .—It is the distinguishing feature of nearly all the persecutions in the Acts that they originated in the hostility of the Jews. The case of Demetrius furnishes almost the only exception (19:24), and even there the Jews apparently fomented the enmity of the Greek craftsmen.

(3) Long time therefore abode they.—This can hardly be understood as involving a stay of less than several months, during which Paul and Barnabas, as before, were working for their livelihood.

Granted signs and wonders to be done by their hands.—Here, as so often elsewhere, the miracles that were wrought came as the confirmation of faith, not as its foundation.

(5) To use them despitefully.—The verb expresses wanton insult and outrage. Paul uses the noun derived from it to express the character of his own conduct as a persecutor (I Tim. 1:13), and must have felt, as afterward in the actual stoning of verse 19, that he was receiving the just reward of his own deeds

(6) And fled unto Lystra and Derbe, cities of Lycaonia.—See Matt. 10:23. The direction of the apostles' journey now took them into a wilder and less civilized region. The range of the Taurus cut it off from the more cultivated country of Cilicia and Pisidia. It is described as a dreary plain, bare of trees, destitute of fresh water, and with several salt lakes (Ovid, **Metaph.** 8:621). So wild a country was hardly likely to attract Jewish settlers; and there is no trace in Luke's narrative of the existence of a synagogue in either of the two cities. For the first time, as far as we know, Paul had to begin his work by preaching to the heathen. Lystra was about forty miles to the southeast of Iconium, Derbe about twenty miles further to the east. Among the converts of this region, and probably of this time, were Timotheus of Lystra (16:1) and Gaius of Derbe (20:4).

(9, 10) Here, as if it were the general law of miraculous working (see Mark 10:23), faith is presupposed as the condition. It follows from this, no less than from the tense of the verb "**used to listen** to Paul as he spoke," that he had for some days been among Paul's hearers, had heard the Gospel of the death and resurrection of Jesus, and had found that such a Saviour met his every need. The command, which would have seemed a mockery to one who did not rise beyond the limits of experience, is obeyed by the will that had been inspired by the new power of faith. (Comp. 3:6; Matt. 9:6; John 5:11.)

(11) Saying in the speech of Lycaonia.— This serves as a crucial instance showing that the "gift of tongues," which Paul possessed so largely (I Cor. 14:18), did not consist in a supernatural knowledge of every provincial **patois** with which he came in contact. (See note on 2:4.) The diglottic character of the people, here and in other Asiatic provinces of the empire, would make it perfectly natural that they should speak to one another in their own dialect, while Greek served for their communication with strangers. The "speech of Lycaonia" is said to have had affinities with Assyrian.

The gods are come down to us in the likeness of men.—The belief which the words expressed was characteristic of the rude simplicity of the Lycaonians. In accordance with the old legends of the district, which Ovid had recently revived and adorned (**Metam.** 8:625-724), Zeus and Hermes (Jupiter and Mercury) had come in human guise.

(12) They called Barnabas, Jupiter; and Paul Mercurius.—Luke gives, as was natural, the Greek forms—Zeus and Hermes. The main reason for the assignment of the two names was that the listeners recognized in Paul the gift of eloquence, which was the special attribute of Hermes. There may have been something in the taller stature and more stately presence of Barnabas which impressed them with the sense of a dignity like that of Jupiter.

(14) The act of rending the clothes (see Matt. 26:65) was the extremest expression of horror, hardly ever used except in deprecation of spoken or acted blasphemy. How far it would be fully understood by the heathen population of Lystra may be a question, but its very strangeness would startle and arrest them. It shows also that Paul and Barnabas solicited no such honors. (Comp. 10:26.)

(16) Who in times past suffered all nations.—We have here the first germ of what may be described as Paul's philosophy of history. The times of ignorance had been permitted by God; those who had lived in them would be dealt with equitably and judged according to their knowledge (comp. 17:30). In Rom. 1; 2; 11, we meet with it in an expanded form, as a more complete vindication of the righteousness of God. The ignorance and the sins of the Gentile world had been allowed to run their course, as the Law had been allowed to do its partial and imperfect work among the Jews. Both demonstrated the need of redemption and prepared for its reception. All were included in unbelief that God might have mercy upon all (Rom. 11:32).

(19) There came thither certain Jews from Antioch.—The context shows that the Pisidian Antioch is meant. The Jews of the former city had traveled no less than one hundred and thirty miles to hinder the apostle's work.

Having stoned Paul.—The mode of punishment shows that it was planned and executed by Jews. They were eager to satisfy themselves that they were inflicting punishment on a blasphemer: stoning him to death, and casting him out to be buried with the burial of an ass. The blinding, stunning blows fell on him as they had fallen on Stephen. It was the one instance in Paul's life of this form of suffering (II Cor. 11:25). The sufferings endured at Lystra stand out, at the close of his life, in the vista of past years with a marvelous distinctness (II Tim. 3:11).

(20) He departed with Barnabas to Derbe.—See note on verse 6. The journey was one that must have occupied several hours, and, in the light of the suffering of the previous day, it must have been one of peculiar hardship and fatigue. The whole region was infamous for its brigandage, and there may be a reference to this in the "perils of robbers" of II Cor. 11:26. The work done at Derbe (verse 21) implies a stay of some months' duration.

(23) On the institution of elders, see note on 11:30. It is interesting here to note that Paul and Barnabas plant among the churches of the Gentiles the organization which we have found in that of Jerusalem, and which was itself based on that of the synagogue.

(27) And when they were come.—More than two years (A.D. 45-48) had passed since their mission. During that interval little probably had been heard of them, and we can picture the eagerness with which the **Christiani** of Antioch would gather to listen to their report.

(28) There they abode long time.—The words probably cover an interval of more than a year, during which it is reasonable to suppose that the preaching of the two apostles drew together a large number of Gentile converts.

15

(1) We enter on the history of the first great controversy in the records of the Christian Church. It would seem that those who had raised objections to Peter's conduct in the case of Cornelius were not content to accept the conclusion which he drew from it. To them it may have seemed the exception that proved the rule. Where signs and wonders came in, they may have been content to accept an uncircumcised convert as a member of the Church, simply on the ground that God had dispensed in such cases with His own law. Yet circumcision had been given as an "everlasting covenant" (Gen. 17:13), and never had been formally abrogated. Who were the new teachers, that they should change what God had thus established? It is clear that they came claiming to speak in the name of James, the Bishop of Jerusalem. He distinctly repudiates having authorized them (verse 24); yet if we suppose, as is probable, that his epistle was written shortly before the Council, we can easily understand that they might rest their case on the words which he had used in Jas. 2:10. They were not prepared to draw distinctions between the positive and the moral, the transient and the permanent, obligations of that law.

(2) The two apostles obviously must have agreed in feeling that the teaching of the Judaizers involved a direct condemnation of all the work in which they saw the triumph of God's grace. The journey is almost certainly that to which allusion is made in Gal. 2:1.

(3) Wherever they went the tidings of the conversion of the Gentiles were received by the disciples at large with a gladness which presented the strongest possible contrast to the narrowness and bitterness of the Pharisee section of the Church of Jerusalem.

(5) It appears from Gal. 2:1 that here, as in so many later controversies, the general issue was debated on an individual case. Was Titus—a Greek, i.e., a Gentile, whom Paul had brought up with him—to be circumcised, or not? But circumcision did not stand alone. It carried with it every jot and tittle of the Law, the Sabbaths and the feasts, the distinction between clean and unclean meats. (See Tit. 1:10, 14, 15.)

(6) And the apostles and elders came together.—The meeting rightly takes its place as the first in the long series of councils which mark the course of the Church's history. It bore its witness that the government of the Christian society was not to rest in the autocracy of a single will, but in the deliberative decision of those who, directly or indirectly, having been appointed by the choice, or with the approval, of the people, represented the whole community. Presbyters had an equal voice with the apostles, whose position was analogous to that of the later bishops. The laity also were present at the deliberations and gave their vote. (Comp. note on verse 23.)

(7) When there had been much disputing.—This implies a full discussion, in which the Judaizing teachers on the one side, and the advocates of freedom on the other, took part. (Comp. Gal. 2:2-10.) Paul shrank from startling and offending the prejudices of his countrymen, and was content to argue that circumcision and the Law were not binding upon the Gentiles to press the precedent of the case of Cornelius and the analogy of the proselytes of the gate. Privately, in interviews with Peter, James, and John, he had gone further, and had declared his convictions that for Jew and Gentile alike circumcision and the Law were hindrances, and not helps, to the spiritual life, and that faith working by love was everything. And they, as the history of the Council and yet more their epistles show, accepted his teaching.

Ye know how that a good while ago . . .—Ten or twelve years had passed since the conversion of Cornelius. The apostle speaks of this as having been the first admission of the Gentiles. (See 11:20.)

(9-11) It is obvious that this implies the most entire acceptance of the teaching which Paul privately had communicated to the three who were as the pillars of the Church (Gal. 2:9). (Comp. Rom. 10:12.) No words of Paul's, in relation to the Law, could be stronger or clearer than these. They reproduced our Lord's own language in Matt. 11:30; 23:4. They were echoed by Paul in Gal. 5:1. This is the last appearance of Peter in the Acts, which from this period turns exclusively upon the work of Paul.

(13) James answered.—James, the brother of the Lord (see note on 12:17), occupies a pre-eminent place (comp. verse 19, "my sentence") in the Council, justifying the title of Bishop of Jerusalem, which later writers give him. No one speaks after him; he sums up the whole debate; he proposes the decree which is to be submitted to the Council for approval.

(16) After this I will return.—These words are taken from Amos 9:11, 12, LXX, already quoted by Stephen (7:42). The quotation suggests a fuller interpretation than is given in the summary of James' speech. It assumes that the "tabernacle of David," which to human eyes had been lying as in ruins, was being rebuilt by Christ, the Son of David, that He was doing the work which, in the prophecy, Jehovah claimed as His.

(17) That the residue of men . . .—The Hebrew gives, "That they may possess the remnant of Edom and of all the heathen which are called by my name." The LXX translators either paraphrased the passage, so as to give a wider and more general view of its teaching, or followed a reading in which the Hebrew for "man" (**Adam**) took the place of Edom. The argument of James turns upon the Greek rendering. So understood, the words became a prediction of the conversion of the Gentiles.

(20) But that we write unto them.—The ground on which the measure was proposed was of the nature of a compromise. The Gentiles could not complain that the burden imposed on them was anything very grievous. The Pharisee section of the Church could not refuse admission to those who fulfilled these conditions, when they had admitted the proselytes of the gate on like conditions to their synagogues, and had so treated them as no longer unclean. The rules on which stress was now laid found a place among the seven precepts traditionally ascribed to Noah, and based upon the commands recorded in Gen. 9:5. These were held to be binding upon all mankind.

From pollutions of idols.—As distinguished from the acts that follow, it indicates any participation, publicly or privately, in idolatrous rites. (See verse 29.) Under

the religion of Greece and Rome, sacrifices were so common that it might fairly be taken for granted that the flesh at any festive meal had been so offered. But a small portion of the flesh was burned upon the altar, and the rest was cooked for the household meal or sent to the market for sale. Such meat was, in the eyes of the strict Jews, polluted. (Comp. Dan. 1:8.) On this ground the Jew never bought meat in the market, nor of other than a Jewish butcher. It is natural that this restriction, which did not rest directly on a moral ground, should give rise to some resistance, and the controversy connected with it assumed many different phases. (Comp. Rom. 2:22; I Cor. 8-10; Rev. 2:14, 20.)

And from fornication.—The sin named was the widespread evil of the ancient world, against which Israel had from the first been called to bear its witness (Gen. 34:31; Lev. 19:29; Deut. 23:17; Prov. 7:6-27). The increasing laxity of morals throughout the Roman empire had led men to think of it as natural and permissible, bringing with it no sense of wrong or shame (comp. Horace, **Sat.** 1:2, 119), and it might well be that the ethical standard of the Gentile converts was not all at once raised to a true ideal of purity. This would legitimately be a grave stumblingblock in the admission of Gentile converts. Prostitution was in close alliance with idolatry, and so a reason for the prohibition; but the sin was forbidden on account of its own intrinsic evil.

Things strangled.—The prohibition rested on Gen. 9:4, and was connected with the symbolic meaning of the blood as representing life and therefore consecrated to Jehovah. It was repeated in the Law (Lev. 3:17; 7:26; Deut. 12:16; I Sam. 14:33). Here the moral element falls entirely into the background, and the prohibition has simply the character of a **concordat** to avoid offense. Paul and Peter were alike persuaded that "there is nothing unclean of itself" (10:15; Rom. 14:14).

From blood.—As distinguished from the preceding rule, this forbade the separate use of blood as an article of food. Dishes so prepared were common in the cuisine both of Greeks and Romans, and here also, therefore, the restriction would have involved a frequent and conspicuous withdrawal from social life.

(21) The Jews, who heard the Law in their synagogues every Sabbath, did not need instruction. It might be taken for granted that they would adhere to the rules now specified. So, in verse 23, the encyclical letter is addressed exclusively to "the brethren of the Gentiles."

(22) The apostles and elders, with the whole church.—The latter words are important as showing the position occupied by the laity. If they concurred in the letter, it must have been submitted to their approval; and the right to approve involves the power to reject and, probably, to modify.

Judas surnamed Barsabas.—See note on 1:23. The fact that he is spoken of in verse 32 as a prophet makes it probable that he was of the number of the Seventy (See Luke 10:1.)

Silas.—This may have been either a contracted form of Silvanus, or an Aramaic name for which Silvanus was adopted as the nearest Greek equivalent. It is probable that he, too, fulfilled the same conditons as his companion. Both he and Judas were sent with Paul and Barnabas to guard against suspicion.

(23) And they wrote letters by them.—What follows is clearly the transcript of a document—the first in the long list of decrees, canons and encyclical letters which mark the Church's history.

(24) The reference is obviously to the teachers (their names are wisely and charitably suppressed) who had appeared at Antioch, as in verse 1. The Gentiles had been "unsettled" by the teaching of the Judaizers. James declares that the teachers had had no commission of any kind from him. (See Gal. 2:12; Jas. 2:10.)

(28) These necessary things.—The letter does not say why these things were necessary, and the term probably was chosen as covering alike the views of those who held, like the Pharisee Christians, that they were binding on the Church forever, and those who, like Paul, held that they were necessary only for the time, and as a measure of wise expediency.

(35) With many others.—Among these we reckon the prophets of 13:1. Looking to the later history of the Church of Antioch, it is not improbable that we may think also of the martyr Ignatius, and Euodius, afterward Bishop of Antioch, as among those who were thus active, though they were not prominent enough, when Luke wrote, to be especially named.

(36) And some days after.—The commonly received chronology of the Acts makes the interval between the Council of

Jerusalem and Paul's second missionary journey somewhat more than a year.

(37-39) See note on 13:13. At this stage, both Barnabas and Mark disappear from the history of the Acts. Barnabas and Paul probably met again in the visit of 18:22 (see Gal. 2:11-13). For Paul's subsequent commendation of both Barnabas and Mark, see I Cor. 9:6; Col. 4:10; Philem. 24; II Tim. 4:11.

(40) See notes on verse 22. Here is obviously implied a full gathering of the Church and a special service of prayer on the departure of the two apostles. Silas, as thus sent forth by the Church, might now claim that title no less than Barnabas.

16

(1) A certain disciple was there, named Timotheus.—This is the first mention of the name of one who was afterward so dear to the apostle, his "own son in the faith" (I Tim. 1:2). On his probable conversion on Paul's first mission in Lystra, see note on 14:6. We have to think of him as still young, probably, as his youth is spoken of some twelve years later (I Tim. 4:12), not more than eighteen or twenty. In the six years that had passed since Paul's departure he had been conspicuous for his devotion and faith. On his person and training, see I Cor. 16:10; II Tim. 1:5; 3:15. The name Timotheus means "one who honors God."

(3) The act seems at first inconsistent with Paul's conduct as to Titus (Gal. 2:3), and with his general teaching as to circumcision (Gal. 5:2-6). The circumstances of the two cases were, however, different. Titus was a Greek; but the mixed parentage of Timotheus, according to the received canons of Jewish law, made him inherit from the nobler side, and he was therefore by birth in the same position as an Israelite. By not urging circumcision prior to baptism, or to his admission to that "breaking of bread" which was then, as afterward, the witness of a full communion with Christ, the apostle had shown that he did not look on it as essential to admission into the Christian Church. He now simply acted on his avowed principle of becoming to the Jews as a Jew (see 18:18; I Cor. 9:20), guarding against the difficulties which he would have encountered from those whom he sought to win to Christ had they seen, as one of the traveling company, an Israelite who was ashamed of the seal of the covenant of Abraham. It seems probable, from the youth of Timotheus, that at this period he took the place which had been before filled by Mark and acted chiefly as an attendant, the "work of an evangelist" coming later (II Tim. 4:5).

(6) When they had gone throughout Phrygia and the region of Galatia.—In the previous journey Paul, when he was at Antioch in Pisidia, was just on the border of the two provinces, but had not traveled through them, Phrygia lying to the west, and Galatia to the northeast. The former name was ethnological rather than political. It does not possess any special points of interest in connection with Paul's work, except as including the churches of the Lycus valley—Colossae, Laodicea, and Thyatira. Galatia was the scene of some of his most important labors. The province, named after the Gauls, had been conquered by the Romans in 189 B.C., and under Augustus it had been constituted as a Roman province. The inhabitants spoke a Keltic dialect and had adopted the religion of the Phrygians, consisting mainly in a wild orgiastic worship of the great Earth-goddess Cybele. (See note on Gal. 5:12.) The incidental reference to this journey in Gal. 4:13-15 (see notes) enables us to fill up Luke's outline.

Were forbidden of the Holy Ghost to preach the word in Asia.—The proconsular province of Asia, with its teeming cities like Ephesus, Smyrna, and Sardis, its large Jewish population, its great centers of idolatrous worship, was naturally attractive to one who was seeking with all his energy a rapid expansion of the kingdom of his Lord. But in ways which we are not told, they were led on, step by step, toward the northwestern coast, not seeing their way clearly as yet to the next stage of their labors.

(7) They assayed to go into Bithynia.—The verse describes very vividly the uncertainty produced day by day by this conflict between human plans and divine direction. Bithynia, lying to the north, had, like Pontus, a considerable Jewish population scattered along its shores, and they were inclined to take that as their next field of labor. They were led on, however, as before, westward and not northward. ("Assayed" is an archaic form for "attempted.")

The Spirit suffered them not.—The better MSS and versions give the reading, "the Spirit of Jesus," confirming the doctrine that the Spirit stands in the same relation to the Son as to the Father, and may therefore

be spoken of either as the Spirit of God, or of Christ (Rom. 8:9), or of Jesus.

(8) Came down to Troas.—Troas, on the coast of the Aegean, was at this time a Roman colony and a free city. It recalls to our memories the older Troy, and the great poem which tells us the tale of Ilium.

(9) There stood a man of Macedonia.—The term is applied to the Roman province, which included Macedonia, properly so-called, Illyricum, Epirus, and Thessaly, the province of Achaia including, in like manner, the whole of Southern Greece. The vision explained to Paul all the varied promptings and drawings-back of his journey. This was the door that was to be opened to him; the faith of Christ was to pass from Asia to Europe.

(10) Immediately we endeavoured . . .—The natural inference from the sudden appearance of the first person in a narrative previously in the third is that the author became at this point an actor in the events which he records. It seems to follow, as there is no mention of the conversion of the evangelist, that Paul and Luke must already have been known to each other, probably either at Tarsus or Antioch, the fullness with which the history of the latter church is given pointing to it as the scene of their previous intimacy. On this assumption, the narrator must have left Antioch after the Council of Jerusalem, probably after the dispute between Paul and Barnabas, and traveled through the interior of Asia Minor, in part, perhaps, in the track of Paul's earlier journey, and so gathered materials for his history until he came to Troas, and there carried on his work as an evangelist.

(12, 13) Their course lay to the northwest, and probably, after the manner of the navigation of the time, they put into harbor each night. The "straight course" implies that they had the wind in their favor. The current, which sets to the south after leaving the Hellespont, and to the east between Samothrace and the mainland, would, of course, be against them. In 20:6, the voyage from Philippi to Troas takes five days. This Neapolis ("new town") was in Thrace, about twelve miles from Philippi, which was the frontier town ("chief city") of Macedonia. Philippi had been rebuilt by the father of Alexander the Great.

(13) Where they had no synagogue, and in a military station ("a colony," verse 12) like Philippi there was not likely to be one, the Jews frequented the riverbanks, which made ablutions easy, and often succeeded in getting a piece of ground assigned for that purpose outside the walls of the city. (See Juvenal, **Sat.** 3:11-13, 296.)

(14) Lydia, a seller of purple, of the city of Thyatira.—It is probable that, like so many slaves and women of the **libertinae** class, Lydia took her name from her country. Thyatira, one of the cities in the Lycus Valley, was famous for its dyeing works. In Rev. 1:11; 2:18, it appears as one of the seven churches to which special epistles were to be sent from their divine Head.

(16) A certain damsel possessed with a spirit of divination.—Literally, "a spirit of Python." The Python was the serpent worshiped at Delphi, as the symbol of wisdom. After the manner of sibyls and sorceresses, the girl was looked upon as having power to divine and predict, her wild cries caught up and received as oracles. Plutarch (**de Defect. Orac.**, 737) speaks of the name Python as being applied commonly, in his time, to "ventriloquists" of this type. As she was a slave, her masters traded on her supposed inspiration, and made the girl, whom prayer and quiet might have restored to sanity, give answers to those who sought for oracular guidance in the perplexities of their lives.

(17) The same followed Paul and us, and cried, saying.—Note the symptom of a divided consciousness. That continual cry spoke of the girl's mind as longing for deliverance, peace, and calm. And yet the thraldom in which she found herself led her to cries that simply impeded their work. (See note on Mark 5:7.)

(19) Men could tolerate varieties of worship or the speculations of philosophers, but they were roused to madness by that which threatened their business. The market place, or **agora**, was, in all Greek cities, the center of social life.

(20) These men, being Jews.—The decree of Claudius (see 18:2), banishing the Jews from Rome on account of their disturbing that city, would give a special force to the accusation.

(21) Being Romans.—The people of Philippi, as a **colonia**, had a right to claim the title of Roman citizens, which could not have been claimed by those who merely were inhabitants of a Greek city, such as Thessalonica or Corinth. (See note on verses 12, 13.)

(22) Commanded to beat them.—The Greek verb gives the special Roman form of punishment—being beaten with the rods of the lictors. This, therefore, takes its place

as one of the three instances to which Paul refers in II Cor. 11:25. (See I Thess. 2:2.) As a Roman citizen, Paul was not supposed to suffer in this way, but he would not assert in this instance a right which would only have secured exemption for himself and left his companion to suffer the ignominious penalty of the law. (Comp. 22:25; see note on verse 37.)

(24) The den into which Paul and his friend were now thrust was a dark cavern-like cell, below the ground, with damp and reeking walls, and the companionship of the vilest outcasts. And, as if this were not enough, they were fastened in the "stocks"— a wooden frame with five holes, into which head, feet and arms were thrust, the prisoner left in an uncomfortable posture, of "little ease." Here, however, it would seem the feet only were fastened, the rest of the body being left lying on the ground. If Job 13:27; 33:11 in the LXX and the Vulgate are correct, the punishment was common at a very early period in the East. (Comp. Jer. 29:26.)

(25) And at midnight Paul and Silas prayed, and sang praises.—The act was, we may believe, habitual, and they would not intermit it even in the dungeon, and fastened as they were, so that they could not kneel. The hymn may have been one of the prayer-psalms of David, or possibly one of those of which Pliny speaks in his letters, and which may well have been in use half a century earlier, in which men offered adoration to Christ as God (**Epist.** 10:96).

(26) Every one's bands were loosed.—The chains of the prisoners were fastened to rings or staples in the wall, and the effect of a great shock would be to loosen the stones and so make it easy to escape.

(27) He drew out his sword, and would have killed himself.—See 12:19; 27:42. Here the man sought to anticipate his fate. Suicide was a natural recourse under such conditions everywhere.

(30) Sirs, what must I do to be saved?— Was he thinking of temporal safety from the earthquake, or from punishment? Or had there come upon him, in that suicidal agony, the sense of an inward misery and shame? The latter seems most probable. The circumstances which had brought Paul to the prison had pointed him out as "proclaiming the way of salvation" (verse 17). The witness of the demoniac girl was thus not altogether fruitless.

(32) And they spake unto him the word of the Lord.—It is clear that belief in the

Lord Jesus Christ, unless it were to be a mere formula, repeated as a charm, required an explanation. Even the Philippian jailer had to be a catechumen before he was baptized.

(33) He ... washed their stripes; and was baptized ...—The twofold washings, that which testified of the repentance of the jailer and his kindly reverence for his prisoners, and that which they administered to him as the washing of regeneration, are placed in suggestive juxtaposition. He, too, was cleansed from wounds which were worse than those inflicted by the rods of the Roman lictors. A public prison was likely enough to contain a bath or pool of some kind, where baptism by immersion would be feasible.

(37) They have beaten us openly uncondemned, being Romans.—By the Lex Porcia (247 B.C.), Roman citizens were exempted from degrading punishment, such as that of scourging. It was the heaviest of all the charges brought by Cicero against Verres, the governor of Sicily, that he had broken this law (Cic. **in Verr.** 5:57). The words **civis Romanus sum** acted almost like a charm in stopping the violence of provincial magistrates. Paul was a citizen by birth (see Acts 22:28), his father having probably been wealthy enough to buy the **jus civitatis**, which brought with it commercial as well as personal privileges. It did not necessarily involve residence at Rome, but makes it probable that there were some points of contact with the imperial city.

There is something like a tone of irony in the "being Romans," echoing, as it did, the very words of his accusers (verse 21). He, too, could stand in his rights as a citizen.

(40) They comforted them, and departed.—As the third person is now resumed, we may infer that Luke remained at Philippi, Timothy accompanied the other two. It would seem from 20:2 that the evangelist made Philippi the center of his evangelizing work for many years. Under the care of the beloved physician, the good work went on, and we probably may trace to his influence, and to Lydia's kindness, the generous help which was sent to Paul once and again when he was at Thessalonica (Phil. 4:15, 16), and at Corinth also (II Cor. 11:9). Long years afterward he cherished a grateful memory of the men and women who had labored with him at Philippi. Among these we may think of the Clement, of whom he thus speaks, possibly identical with the Flavius Clemens who occupies a prominent

position among the apostolic fathers and was traditionally the third Bishop of Rome. (See, however, note on Phil. 4:3.)

17

(1) Now when they had passed through Amphipolis and Apollonia.—Amphipolis was famous in the Peloponnesian War, and had been made under the Romans the capital of **Macedonia prima**. It was thirty-three Roman miles from Philippi and thirty from Apollonia, the latter being thirty-seven from Thessalonica. It seems clear that the names indicated the stages at which the travelers rested. Apparently there was no Jewish population to present an opening for the Gospel at either of these cities, and Paul, therefore, passed on to Thessalonica.

Thessalonica, where was a synagogue of the Jews.—The city (formerly Therma) had been enlarged by Philip of Macedon and named after his daughter. It was situated on the Thermaic Gulf, and had grown into a commercial port of considerable importance. As such, it had attracted Jews in large numbers.

(2) Paul, as his manner was ...—What we read of as occurring in the Pisidian Antioch (13:14, 15) was now reproduced. That he was allowed to preach for three Sabbaths in succession shows the respect commanded by his character as a rabbi, and, it may be, by his earnest eloquence. Comp. I Thess. 1:5, 9; 2:7. The Thessalonian Church was predominantly Gentile (verse 4).

(3) Opening and alleging.—The latter word is used in the sense of bringing forward proofs, and the two words imply an argument from the prophecies of the Messiah. In the intervals between the Sabbaths the apostle worked, as usual, for his livelihood, probably as a tent maker (II Thess. 3:8).

(5) Certain lewd fellows of the baser sort.—The word "lewd" is used in its older sense, as meaning worthless. The "baser sort" answers to a Greek word describing the loungers in the **agora**, or market place, ever ready for the excitement of a tumult.

Assaulted the house of Jason.—The ground of the attack was that he had received the preachers as his guests. The name was locally conspicuous as having belonged to the old hero of the Argonautic expedition, and to the tyrant of Pherae. It is probable, however, that Paul would, in the first instance, take up his abode with a Jew, and that Jason was the Greek equivalent of Joshua or Jesus (comp. II Macc. 4:7).

(7) These all do contrary to the decrees of Caesar.—The preachers not only were bringing in a **relligio illicita**, but also were guilty of treason against the majesty of the empire. It is clear from the epistle to the Thessalonians that the kingdom of Christ, especially His Second Coming as King, had been prominent in the apostle's teaching (I Thess. 4:14; 5:2, 23; II Thess. 1:7, 8; 2:1-12), and this may have furnished materials for the accusation.

(10) Sent away Paul and Silas by night unto Berea.—Timotheus apparently remained behind, partly to help the Thessalonian converts under their present trials, partly to be able to bring word to Paul as to their condition. Berea lay to the south of Thessalonica, not far from Pella. Here also there was a Jewish population, but the city was a far less important place commercially than Thessalonica.

(11) These were more noble than those in Thessalonica.—The word for "noble" is, literally, "well-born" (I Cor. 1:26). Here it stands for the generous, loyal temper which ideally was supposed to characterize those of noble origin. This was the quality which the apostle and the historian admired in the Bereans. They were not the slaves of prejudice. They were ready to believe in the Gospel which Paul preached as meeting their spiritual wants; on the other hand, with a quick and clear intelligence they searched the Scriptures daily to see whether Paul and Silas really did speak of a Christ who should suffer and rise again.

(14) To go as it were to the sea.—Many of the better MSS give "as far as the sea." The absence of any mention of places between Berea and Athens is presumptive evidence that Paul actually traveled by sea, and rounding the promontory of Sunium, entered Athens by the Piraeus. For the first time since the beginning of his missionary labors, Paul was absolutely alone.

(17) And in the market daily.—To teach in the synagogue, or to gather devout persons, was the usual pattern of Paul's work. Disputing in the market place, which in every Greek city was the center of its life, was a new experiment. He saw others so disputing, teachers of this or that school of philosophy. Why should he not take part in the discussion, and lead those who were apparently in earnest in their inquiries to the truth which they were vainly seeking?

(18) Certain philosophers of the Epicureans, and of the Stoics.—The two schools were at this time the great representatives of Greek thought. The former took its name from its founder, Epicurus (342-270 B.C.). His speculations embraced at once a physical and an ethical solution of the problems of the universe. The superstition which enslaved the minds of most men was the great evil of the world, the source of its crimes and miseries. The last enemy to be destroyed was the belief in an immortality of retribution. A man's first step toward happiness and wisdom was to emancipate himself from its thraldom; the next was to recognize that happiness consisted in the greatest aggregate of pleasurable emotions. But as no law was recognized as written in the heart, and human laws were looked on as mere conventional arrangements, each man was left to form his own estimate of what would give him most pleasure, and most men decided for a life of ease and self-indulgence. The poetry of Horace presents, perhaps, the most attractive phase of popular Epicureanism. In the world of physics, ideas of creation and control were alike excluded. Matter had existed from eternity, and the infinite atoms of which it was composed had, under the action of attractive and repelling forces as yet unknown, entered into manifold combinations, out of which had issued, as the last stage of the evolution, the world of nature as it now lies before us. (Comp. Lucretius, **De Rerum Natura**.)

We can understand how Paul would assert, as against this school of thought, the personality of the living God, as Creator, Ruler, Father; the binding force of the law written in the heart; intuitive morality as against mere utilitarianism; the nobleness of a hero-soul raised above pleasure and living not for itself, but for others and for God; and the assignment of glory and immortality to the patient worker of righteousness. (Comp. Rom. 2:7-9.)

The Stoics—who took their name, not from their founder (Zeno of Cyprus), but from the **Stoa poekile**, the painted porch, at Athens—presented a higher phase of thought. Josephus (**Vit.** c. 2) compares them with the Pharisees. They taught that true wisdom consisted in being the master, and not the slave, of circumstances. The things which are not in our power are not things to seek after, nor shrink from, but to be accepted with a calm equanimity. The seeker after wisdom learned, therefore, to be indifferent alike to pleasure or pain, and aimed at an absolute apathy. They spoke of a divine Mind pervading the universe and ordering all things by its Providence. In Epictetus, Marcus Aurelius, and Seneca we see how often the Stoics spoke in the accents of Christian ethics.

It is evident that there would be many points of sympathy between the better representatives of this school and Paul, but for them also the message that spoke of Jesus and the Resurrection—of God sending His Son into the world to be first crucified and then raised from the dead—would seem an idle dream. They would shrink from the thought that they needed pardon and redemption, and could do nothing true and good in their own strength without the grace of God.

What will this babbler say?—The Greek noun, literally "seed-picker," was primarily applied to a small bird of the finch family. The idle gossips of the agora picking up news, and, eager to retell it, the chattering parasites of feasts, were likened by the quick wit of Athenian humorists to such a bird as it hopped and chirped. (Comp. Diog. Laert. **Zeno** c. 19.) The philosophers, in their scorn of the stranger who was so ready to discuss great questions with any whom he met, applied the derisive epithet to him.

He seemeth to be a setter forth of strange gods.—This was the precise charge on which Socrates had been condemned (Xenoph. **Memor.** 1.1, §1).

Because he preached unto them Jesus, and the resurrection.—The verb implies continuous action; this was the ever-recurring theme of his discourses. It is possible that with the strong tendency of the Greek mind to personify all attributes and abstract thoughts, Paul's hearers saw in the word **anastasis** (resurrection) the name of a new goddess, representing the idea of immortality, to be worshiped in conjunction with Jesus, and therefore they used the plural and spoke of his bringing in "strange gods." What startled them in the apostle was that he taught not only the immortality of the soul—that had entered into the popular mystical belief, and had been enforced with philosophical arguments by Socrates and Plato—but also the resurrection of the body. Comp. I Cor. 15:35.

(19) They took him, and brought him unto Areopagus.—The name may stand either for the Hill of Mars (verse 22), simply as a locality, or for the Court which sat

there, the oldest and most revered tribunal in Athens.

(21) The restless inquisitiveness of the Athenian character had been all along proverbial. See Demosthenes (**Philipp.** 1, 43); Theophrastus (c. 8).

(22) Paul stood in the midst of Mars' hill.—The court sat in the open air on benches forming three sides of a quadrangle. A short flight of sixteen steps, cut in the rock, led from the agora to the plateau where the Court held its sittings. The temptation to have recourse to it, if only to cause a sensation and terrify the strange disputant, may well have been irresistible. As the apostle stood there, he looked from the slight elevation on the temple of the Eumenides below him, that of Theseus to the east, and facing him on the Acropolis, the Parthenon. On the height of that hill stood the colossal bronze statue of Athena as the tutelary goddess of her beloved Athens; below and all around him were statues and altars. The city was "very full of idols" (verse 16).

I perceive that in all things ye are too superstitious.—"Superstitious" is, perhaps, too strong on the side of blame; "devout," on the side of praise. Paul uses a word which, like our "devotee," though not offensive, was neutral with a slight touch of disparagement. The opening words would gain, and were perhaps meant to gain, the ears of the philosophers. Here, they would say, is one who rises, as we do, above the religion of the multitude.

(23) TO THE UNKNOWN GOD.—The adjective means something more than "Unknown." It adds the fact that the Unknown is also the Unknowable. It is the ultimate confession of man's impotence to solve the problems of the universe. It does not affirm atheism; but it does not know what the Power is, which yet it feels must be. Striking, indeed, is the parallelism presented by an altar found at Ostia. It represents what is known as a Mithraic sacrificial group, connected, i.e., with the worship of Mithras, the Sun god of later Persian mythology. It seems probable that the altar which Paul saw was an earlier example of the feeling represented by the Ostian inscription, and may well have found its expression, with a like characteristic formula, among the many forms of the confluent polytheism of Athens. Plutarch (**Pompeious**) speaks of the worship of Mithras as having been brought into Europe by the Cilician pirates whom

Pompeius defeated, and as continuing in his own time.

(25) The previous words had struck at a false theory of temples; this strikes at a false theory of worship.

(26) And hath made of one blood all nations of men.—The previous verses had given Paul's philosophy of religion; this gives his philosophy of history. And the position was one which no Greek, above all, no Athenian, was likely to accept. For him the distinction between the Greek and the barbarian was radical and essential. The one was by nature meant to be the slave of the other (Aristot. **Pol.** 1:2, 6). In rising above his own prejudices of fancied superiority of race, the apostle felt that he could attack, as from a vantage ground, the prejudices of others.

Hath determined the times before appointed.—The special gifts of character of each race have all their work to do. All local circumstances of soil and climate that influence character come under the head of the "bounds of men's habitation"; all conditions of time come under the head of the "appointed seasons."

(27) Should seek the Lord, if haply they might feel after him, and find him.—The word for "feel after" expresses strictly the act of groping in the dark. From the apostle's point of view, the whole order of the world's history was planned as part of the education of mankind, waking longings which it could not satisfy, leading men at once to a consciousness of the holiness of God and of their own sinfulness. The "if haply" expresses doubt whether the end had been attained in its completeness. The altar to the Unknown and Unknowable was a witness that they had not been found.

Though he be not far from every one of us.—The speaker appeals (Rom. 2:15) to the witness borne by man's consciousness and conscience. There, in the depths of each man's being, not in temples made with hands, men might find God and hold communion with Him. (See Deut. 30:11-14; John 1:9.) At this point the Stoics would recognize the affinities which Paul's thoughts presented to their own teaching. The Epicureans would be more and more repelled by this attack on the central position of their system.

(28) For in him we live, and move, and have our being.—Each of the verbs used has a definite philosophical significance. The first points to our animal life; the second, to our emotional nature; the third, to that which constitutes our true essential being, the intellect and will of man. In the teaching of Paul, the personality of God is not merged, as in that of the pantheist, in the thought of the great Soul of the World, but stands forth with distinctness in the character of King and Judge. (Comp. I Cor. 15:28.)

As certain also of your own poets have said.—A poet who was a countryman of Paul's—Aratus, probably of Tarsus (**circ.** 272 B.C.)—had written a didactic poem under the title of **Phoenomena,** comprising the main facts of astronomical and meteorological science as then known. It opens with an invocation to Zeus, which contains the words that Paul quotes. Similar words are found in a hymn to Zeus by Cleanthes (300 B.C.). The quotation would at once quicken the attention of the hearers. They would feel that they had not to deal with an illiterate Jew, like the traders and exorcists who were so common in Greek cities, but with a man of culture like their own, acquainted with the thoughts of at least some of their great poets.

(30) And the times of this ignorance God winked at.—Paul sees in that ignorance a mitigation of the guilt, and therefore of the punishment, due to the heathen world. The past history of the world had shown a praetermission of the sins, for which, on the condition of repentance, men now were offered a full remission. (See note on Rom. 3:25.) In thus teaching he was reproducing what our Lord had taught in Luke 12:48.

And now commandeth all men every where to repent.—At this point the feelings of both Stoics and Epicureans would almost inevitably undergo a change. A change such as the Greek for "repentance" implied—new aims and purposes, loathing of the past and efforts for the future—was altogether alien to their thoughts.

(31) The thought of a day of judgment as the consummation of history, which was so prominent in Paul's teaching, was altogether strange to them. Who the man was, and what proof there was that he had been raised from the dead, were questions either reserved for a later stage of teaching or interrupted by the derision of the hearers. Up to this point they had listened attentively, but that the dead should be raised again seemed to them—as to the Sadducean, to the Greeks generally—absolutely incredible (26:8; I Cor. 15:35).

(34) Dionysius the Areopagite.—As the constitution of the Court of the Areopagus required its members to have filled a high magisterial function and to be above sixty, the convert must have been a man of some note. According to Eusebius (**Hist.** 3:4, 4:23) he became Bishop of Athens.

Damaris.—Chrysostom says that she was the wife of Dionysius, but this obviously is only a conjecture.

And others with them.—The contrast between this and the "great multitude," the "many" at Thessalonica and Berea, is significant. No less striking is the absence of any reference to Athens in Paul's epistles. Of all the cities which he visited, it was that with which he had least sympathy. All that can be said is that he may have included them among "the saints which are in all Achaia" (II Cor. 1:1) in his prayers and hopes.

18

(1) And came to Corinth.—The position of Corinth on the Isthmus, with a harbor on either shore—Cenchreae on the east, Lechaeum on the west—had naturally made it a place of commercial importance at a very early stage of Greek history. With commerce had come luxury and vice, and the verb **Corinthiazein**—to live as the Corinthians—had become proverbial for a course of profligacy. The harlot priestesses of the Temple of Aphrodite gave a kind of consecration to the deep-dyed impurity of Greek social life, of which we find traces in I Cor. 5:1; 6:9-19. The Isthmian games, which were celebrated every fourth year, drew crowds of competitors and spectators from all parts of Greece, and obviously furnished the apostle with the agonistic imagery of I Cor. 9:24-27. Less distinguished for higher culture than Athens, it was yet able to boast of its artists, rhetoricians and philosophers. On its conquest by the Roman general Mummius (146 B.C.), many of its buildings had been destroyed and its finest statues had been carried off to Rome. A century later, Julius Caesar determined to restore it to its former splendor.

(2) And found a certain Jew named Aquila, born in Pontus.—His birth in Pontus indicates that he belonged to the dispersion of the Jews of that province (I Pet. 1:1), which, as the northeastern region of Asia Minor, lay between Bithynia and Armenia. Some from that province had been present at Jerusalem on the Day of Pente-

cost (2:9). As the Jews at Rome consisted largely of freed-men (see note on 6:9), it is probable that Aquila belonged to that class.

With his wife Priscilla.—The diminutive form is Prisca. The marriage probably was an example of the influence gained by educated Jews over the higher class of women at Rome. It was, perhaps, a natural consequence of her higher social position that her name is sometimes placed before Aquila's (verse 18; Rom. 16:3; II Tim. 4:19). The fact that she took part in the instruction of Apollos (verse 26) indicates that she was a woman of more than ordinary culture, a student and interpreter of the Old Testament Scriptures.

Because that Claudius had commanded all Jews to depart from Rome.—The account of the expulsion is given by Seutonius (**Claudius,** c. 25). The Jews, at this period, were settled mainly in the Trans-tiberine region of Rome, at the base of the Janiculum. They exercised considerable influence over the upper classes, had synagogues and oratories of their own, were tolerated as possessing a **relligio licita**, and had their own cemeteries on the Appian Way. Suddenly there is a change in their relations to the civil power, and the name of Chrestus is connected with it (see note on 11:26). The probable explanation of Claudius' decree is that men had come to Rome after the Day of Pentecost proclaiming Jesus as the Christ, that this had been followed by tumults like those of which we read in the Pisidian Antioch (13:50), Lystra (14:19), Thessalonica (17:5), and Berea (17:13), and that they understood this Christus to claim the title of king after the manner of the pretenders to an earthly throne. The first preachers of the new faith were those from Rome who were present at Pentecost (2:10). (See 6:5, 9; and the long list of names in Rom. 16:3-15.) To those and not to Peter, we probably may look as among the real founders of the Church of Rome.

(3) Because he was of the same craft.—See note on 9:43. The fact that Paul had learned this trade is not inconsistent with the comparative opulence suggested by his education both in boyhood at Tarsus and at the feet of Gamaliel in Jerusalem. The rabbinic proverb that "He who does not teach his son a trade, teaches him to be a thief" made such instruction almost universal. So the great Hillel was a carpenter. (Comp. I Cor. 9:15-19; II Cor. 11:7-13.)

(5) See I Thess. 2:18; 3:6. The First Epistle to the Thessalonians probably was sent back by the brethren who had accompanied Silas and Timothy on their journey to Corinth. Whether there was any connection between the arrival of Silas and Timothy and this strong feeling is a question which there are no sufficient data for answering. It is hardly satisfactory to say that they probably brought pecuniary supplies from Macedonia (II Cor. 11:9), and that he was therefore relieved from the obligation of working for his livelihood and able to give himself more entirely to the work of preaching. (See I Cor. 9:1.) A more probable explanation may be found in the strong desire (Rom. 15:23) that he had cherished for many years to see Rome and preach the Gospel there. Now he found himself brought into contact with those who had come from Rome, who formed, in fact, part of its population, and the old feeling was stirred to a new intensity.

(6) He shook his raiment.—On the symbolic significance of the act, see note on Matt. 10:14. As done by a Jew to Jews no words and no act could so well express the apostle's indignant protest. It was the last resource of one who found appeals to reason and conscience powerless, and was met by brute violence and clamor.

From henceforth I will go unto the Gentiles.—See 13:46. It is obvious in each case that the words have a limited and local application. The apostle did not renounce all future work among the Jews, but gave up preaching to those at Corinth.

(7) Justus was an uncircumcised Gentile, attending the synagogue as a proselyte of the gate. Up to this time, apparently, Paul had been lodging in the house of a Jew in the hope of conciliating his brethren according to the flesh. Now, in sight of the wild frenzied fanatics, he goes into a house which they would have shrunk from entering, even though it was next door to the synagogue, and though the man who lived in it was a devout worshiper.

(8) And Crispus, the chief ruler of the synagogue, believed on the Lord.—The office was one which gave Crispus an honorable position. In favor of so conspicuous a convert, Paul deviated from his usual practice and baptized Crispus with his own hands (I Cor. 1:14).

Many of the Corinthians hearing believed, and were baptized.—The tense of the two verbs implies a process going on daily for an undefined period. Among the converts we may note Gaius (Rom. 16:23) and the household of Stephanas (I Cor.

16:15), whom also Paul baptized himself (I Cor. 1:14, 15), Fortunatus and Achaicus, Chloe (I Cor. 1:11), Quartus, Erastus (Rom. 16:23), and Epaenetus (Rom. 16:5).

(11) And he continued there a year and six months.—This obviously gave time not only for founding and organizing a church at Corinth itself, but for work in the neighboring districts. (See Rom. 16:1; II Cor. 1:1.) The unimpeded progress of this period came to him as an abundant fulfillment of the Lord's promise (verses 9, 10), and prepared him for the next persecution when it came.

(12) And when Gallio was the deputy of Achaia.—Better, "proconsul," as also in 13:7. Achaia, which included the whole of Greece south of the province of Macedonia, had been an imperial province under Tiberius (Tacitus, **Ann.** 1:76), but recently had been restored to the senate by Claudius, as no longer needing direct military control (Suetonius, **Claud** c. 25). Gallio, or to give his full name, M. Annaeus Novatus, who had taken the **agnomen** of Gallio on his adoption by the rhetorician of that name, was the brother of L. Annaeus Seneca, the tutor of Nero. He was priased by his brother for calmness of temper, as one "who was loved much, even by those who had but little capacity for loving" (Seneca, **Ep.** 104).

And brought him to the judgment seat.—The habit of the Roman governors of provinces commonly was to hold their court in the **agora**, or marketplace, on certain fixed days (see 19:38), so that anyone might appeal to have his grievance heard.

(13) This fellow persuadeth men to worship God contrary to the law.—It is obvious that in this appeal to the proconsul the Jews must have meant, not the Law of Moses, but that of Rome. Their contention was that though Jews had been banished from Rome as a measure of policy, Judaism as such was still a **relligio licita**, tolerated and recognized by the State. Their charge against the apostle was that he was preaching a new religion, which was not so recognized. The words "this fellow," though the substantive is an interpolation, fairly expresses the contempt implied in the use of the Greek pronoun.

(15) In the emphasis laid on "your law" the judge intimates that he sees through their appeal to law. It is Jewish and not Roman law which they are seeking to vindicate, and he will not make himself as Pilate (John 18:3) had done, the executioner of an alien code.

(17) It would seem that Sosthenes (see I Cor. 1:1) became a convert to the new faith. If so, it is probable that he was already suspected of tendencies in that direction; and when the Jews at Corinth found their plans frustrated, it was natural that they should impute their failure to the treachery of the men who ought to have carried them to a successful issue. They did not shrink from giving vent to their rage even before the tribunal. The proconsul was clear-sighted enough to pay no regard to the clamors of Paul's accusers. If they chose, after failing in their attack on Paul, to quarrel among themselves, what was that to him?

(18) The time (after the passing of several months) of the apostle's voyage was probably, as in the second journey from Corinth to Jerusalem, after the Passover and before Pentecost. (See notes on 2:1.) It was the most favorable time of the year for traveling, and it brought the apostle into contact with a larger number both of Hellenistic Jews and Hebrews than were found at other times. The "vow" was that of the temporary Nazarite, as described in Num. 6:1-21. We cannot exclude from the probable motives the strong feeling of thankfulness for deliverance from danger; and we may add to this motive the principle on which Paul acted of being "all things to all men"—here a Jew to Jews (I Cor. 9:20). A Nazarite vow would testify to all his brethren by blood that he did not despise the Law himself nor teach other Jews to despise it. (See notes on 21:21-24.)

(19) Ephesus had been one of the early Greek colonies on the western coast of Asia Minor. It had from the first been celebrated for the worship of Artemis (see note on 19:24); and her Temple was visited by pilgrims of all nations. It was one of the cities in which East and West came into close contact with each other, and the religion of Greece assumed there a more Oriental character, being fruitful in magic, mysteries, and charms. The Jewish population was sufficiently numerous to have a synagogue; and Paul, as usual, appeared in it as a teacher, independent of Aquila and Priscilla, who pursued their craft.

(21) See note on verse 18. If he missed Pentecost, there would be no other feast until that of Tabernacles; and then, in October, traveling, whether by sea or land, became dangerous and difficult. (See 27:9.)

(22) And when he had landed at Caesarea.—It is obvious that a great deal is covered by the short record of this verse. We possibly may refer to some casualty in this voyage—one of the three shipwrecks of II Cor. 11:25. At Caesarea he probably would renew his association with Philip the evangelist. At Jerusalem there would be the usual gathering of the Church, the completion of his Nazarite vow in the Temple, and a friendly welcome on the part of James and the elders of the Church. To this visit to Antioch we probably may refer the scene which Paul narrates in Gal. 2:11-14.

(23) Went over all the country of Galatia and Phrygia in order.—It is clear from the Epistle to the Galatians that on this visit he found few traces of the work of the Judaizers. The change came afterward. (See Gal. 5:21.) What churches in Phrygia were visited we are unable to say. A possible construction of Col. 2:1 might lead us to think of those of the valley of the Lycus—Colossae, Hierapolis, Laodicea—as having been founded by him, but the more probable interpretation of that passage is that he included them in the list of those who had not seen his face in the flesh.

(24) And a certain Jew named Apollos, born at Alexandria.—Apollos occupied a prominent position in the history of the apostolic Church. Luther, looking to the Alexandrian character of the Epistle to the Hebrews and to the mystery which shrouds its authorship, and which led Origen to the conclusion that God alone knew who wrote it, hazarded the thought that Apollos was the writer. Later critics have adopted the hypothesis and have brought it to a closer approximation to certainty by an induction from numerous parallelisms in thought and language between the epistle and the writings of Philo, who lived between 20 B.C. and A.D. 40 or 50. It is yet obvious that a Jew coming from Alexandria at this time hardly could fail to have come under Philo's influence, and that his mode of interpreting the Scriptures naturally would present many analogies to that of the Alexandrian thinker. Jews of Alexandria were among those who disputed with Stephen (6:9). Some of these may have been more or less persuaded by his preaching, and have carried back to their native city some knowledge of the new faith.

An eloquent man.—The Greek adjective implies learning as well as eloquence. It was applied pre-eminently to those who wrote history with fullness and insight (Herod. 1:1, 2:3, 77). Comp. Heb. 11.

(25) The position of Apollos at this stage

was that of one who knew the facts of our Lord's life, death, and Resurrection, and had learned, comparing these with Messianic prophecies, to accept Him as the Christ. But his teacher had been one who had not gone beyond the standpoint of the followers of the Baptist, who accepted Jesus as the Christ during His ministry on earth. The Christ was for him the head of a glorified Judaism, retaining all its distinctive features.

(26) And expounded unto him the way of God more perfectly.—See notes on verse 2. "The way of God" which they expounded more accurately to him was the Gospel as they had learned it from Paul. It would include the doctrines of salvation by grace, justification by faith, the gift of the Spirit, union with Christ through baptism, and the Supper of the Lord.

(27) See notes on II Cor. 3:1-3; I Cor. 3:6, 10.

(28) He mightily convinced the Jews.—Apollos led men on, after the manner of Philo, into the deeper meanings that lay beneath the letter of Scripture, dealing with them as those who were pressing forward to the perfection of maturity in spiritual growth (Heb. 5:11-14), instead of treating them as children who must be fed with milk and not with solid food, as Paul had done (I Cor. 1:2). It was natural that this should attract followers to the new preacher, and give him a larger measure of real or apparent success in dealing with the Jews than had attended the labors of Paul. Apollos does not appear again in the Acts. Not a word escapes from Paul that indicates any doctrinal difference between himself and Apollos. Paul's feeling toward him continued one of affectionate interest. (See notes on I Cor. 16:12; Tit. 3:13.)

19

(2) Have ye received the Holy Ghost since ye believed?—Paul apparently noticed in them, as they attended the meetings of the Church, a lack of spiritual gifts.

We have not so much as heard whether there be any Holy Ghost.—The standpoint of the disciples so corresponds to that of Apollos when he arrived at Ephesus that we may reasonably think of them as having been converted by his preaching. They must, of course, have known the Holy Spirit as a name meeting them in the Sacred Books; they had been baptized with the

baptism of repentance, and were leading a life of fasting, prayers, and alms, but they had not experienced the pervading presence of the Spirit. It appears that they were Jewish, not Gentile, disciples.

(4) The baptism of John was, by his own declaration, simply provisional and preparatory. He taught his disciples to believe in Jesus; belief implied obedience, and obedience baptism in His name.

(5) They were baptized in the name of the Lord Jesus.—On the use of this formula in connection with the baptism of Jewish converts, see notes on 2:38; Matt. 28:19.

(6) They spake with tongues, and prophesied.—The verbs imply continuous action. (See notes on 2:4; 10:46.) The mere power of speaking foreign languages without learning them, as other men learn, seems a much less adequate result of the new gift than that which we find in the new enthusiasm and intensity of spiritual joy, of which the gift of tongues was the natural expression. It is interesting that the discussion of the two gifts in I Cor. 14 (see notes), in which the connection of the "tongues" with jubilant and ecstatic praise is unmistakable, was written not very long after this incident, and while the facts must yet have been fresh in Paul's memory. On the laying on of hands, which was the outward and visible sign of the inward and spiritual grace, see notes on 8:14-18.

(9) Disputing daily in the school of one Tyrannus.—The name is found in the **Columbarium** of the household of Livia on the Appian Way, as belonging to one who is described as a **Medicus**. Both names and professions in this class were commonly hereditary; and the hypothesis that this Tyrannus was also a physician, and that, as such, he may have known Luke, or, possibly, may have been among the Jews whom the decree of Claudius (18:2) had driven from Rome, and so shared the faith in Aquila and Priscilla, fits in with and explains the facts recorded. An unconverted teacher of philosophy or rhetoric was not likely to have lent his classroom to a preacher of the new faith.

(10) Ephesus probably came to be the center of Paul's activity, from which journeys were made to neighboring cities; thus we may legitimately think of the other six churches of Rev. 2 and 3 as owing their origin to him. The growth of the new community among both sections of the population became a conspicuous fact, and began to tell upon the number of pilgrims who brought their offerings to the shrine of Artemis or carried away memorials from it.

(12) Such a report of special and extraordinary phenomena was likely enough to be made by a physician like Tyrannus to one of the same calling, and probably of the same faith. The picture suggested is that of devout persons coming to the apostle as he labored at his craft, and carrying away with them the very handkerchiefs and aprons that he used, as precious relics that conveyed the supernatural gift of healing which he exercised. The efficacy of such media stands obviously on the same ground as that of the hem of our Lord's garment (see notes on Matt. 9:20, 21) and the shadow of Peter (see note on 5:15). The two conditions of the supernatural work of healing were a divine power on the one hand, and faith on the other, and any external medium might serve to strengthen the latter and bring it into contact with the former. It is not unreasonable to see in the works of healing so wrought a special adaptation to the antecedent habits of mind (i.e., amulets and charms) of a population like that of Ephesus (see note on verse 19).

(13) Certain of the vagabond Jews, exorcists.—See notes on 8:9; 13:6. To them "the name of the Lord Jesus," which was so often on Paul's lips, was just another formula.

(14) Seven sons of one Sceva, a Jew, and chief of the priests.—It seems that the title was part of the imposture. Sceva called himself a chief priest, and as such Luke, or Tyrannus, described him. The scene is brought before us vividly. The seven exorcists, relying partly in the mystical virtue of their number, stand face to face with a demoniac, frenzied and strong like the Gadarene of Matt. 8:28; Mark 5:3, 4. The possessed man (verse 15), identifying himself (as the Gadarene did) with the demon, stood in awe of the name of Jesus, when uttered by a man like Paul; but who were these seven pretenders, that they should usurp authority over them?

(17) The fact thus narrated had shown that the sacred name stood on quite a different level from that of the other names which exorcists had employed. It was a perilous thing for men to use it rashly, without inward faith in all that the name implied. Men thought more of it than they had done before, because they saw the punishment that fell on those who had profaned it.

(19) Many of them also which used curious arts . . .—These superstitious arts were almost the specialite of Ephesus. Magicians and astrologers swarmed in her streets (comp. II Tim. 3:8), and there was a brisk trade in the charms, incantations, books of divination, rules for interpreting dreams, etc.

And burned them before all men.—In this complete renunciation of the old evil past we probably may see the secret of the capacity for a higher knowledge which Paul recognizes as belonging to Ephesus more than to most other churches. (See note on 20:27.)

(21) Grave disorders at Corinth constituted an antecedent to this purpose. It had been necessary for him to send a letter, not extant, to warn the Corinthians (I Cor. 5:9); but these called for the apostle's presence. He also wished to revisit Jerusalem, and to appear there as the bearer of a munificent contribution from the Gentile churches to the suffering church of the Hebrews. (See notes on I Cor. 16:1; II Cor. 8:1.)

I must also see Rome.—This is the first recorded expression of a desire which (Rom. 1:13; 15:23) had been cherished for many years, possibly from the time when he first was told that he was to be sent far off to the Gentiles (22:21). It doubtless was strengthened by personal contact with the numerous disciples from that city whom he met at Corinth, some of them dating their conversion from a time anterior to his own (Rom. 16:7), and by the report which he heard from them of the faith and constancy of their brethren (Rom. 1:8). His work would not seem to him complete until he had borne his witness in the great capital of the empire.

(22) Timotheus and Erastus.—See I Cor. 4:17, 16:10; Rom. 16:23. Timothy was to return to Paul, and was accordingly with him when he wrote Second Corinthians (II Cor. 1:1). Sosthenes, who was with Paul when he wrote First Corinthians (I Cor. 1:1), probably had been staying some time at Ephesus, having been ruler of the synagogue.

(23) About that way.—Better, "the way." See note on 9:2.

(24) Demetrius, a silversmith, which made silver shrines for Diana.—The worship of Artemis (the Greek name of the goddess whom the Romans identified with their Diana) had from a very early period been connected with the city of Ephesus. The first temple, burned in 335 B.C. by Herostratus, was rebuilt with more state-

liness by Alexander the Great, and was looked upon as one of the seven wonders of the world. Large gifts and bequests were made for the maintenance of its fabric and ritual, and the city conferred its highest honors upon those who thus enrolled themselves among its illustrious benefactors. Pilgrims came from all parts of the world to worship or to gaze, and carried away with them memorials in silver or bronze, generally models of the sanctuary, in which the image of the goddess stood, and of the image itself. That image, however, was unlike the sculptured beauty with which Green and Roman art represented the form of Artemis, and would seem to have been the survival of an older **cultus** of the powers of nature, like the Phrygian worship of Cybele. A fourfold many-breasted female figure, ending, below the breasts, in a square column, with mysterious symbolic ornamentation, in which bees, ears of corn, and flowers were strangely mingled, carved in wood, black with age, and with no form or beauty, was the center of the adoration of that never-ceasing stream of worshipers.

The first real blow to the worship which had lasted for so many ages was given by the two years of Paul's work of which we read here. As by the strange irony of history, the next stroke aimed at its magnificence came from the hand of Nero, who robbed it, as he robbed the temples of Delphi, Pergamus, and Athens, of many of its art-treasures for the adornment of his Golden House at Rome (Tacit. **Ann.** 15:45). Trajan sent its richly-sculptured gates as an offering to a temple at Byzantium. When the empire became Christian, the temple of Ephesus, in common with that of Delphi, supplied materials for the Church of St. Sophia, erected by Justinian. Goths and Turks successively plundered it with reckless hand.

(25) Sirs, ye know that by this craft we have our wealth.—The opening words of Demetrius bring before us, with an almost naive simplicity, the element of vested interests which has at all times played so prominent a part in the resistance to religious and political reforms, and entered largely into the persecutions against which the early preachers of the Gospel had to contend.

(26) Not alone at Ephesus, but almost throughout all Asia.—The language of Demetrius, though perhaps betraying the exaggeration of alarm, confirms the statement of verse 10 as to the extent of Paul's labors.

"Asia" is used for the proconsular province, as "world" (verse 27) refers to the Roman empire (comp. Luke 2:1).

(29) Gaius and Aristarchus.—The former name represents the Roman "Caius," here a Macedonian. The latter appears as companion to Paul on the journey to Jerusalem (20:4), probably as a delegate from the Macedonian churches. He seems to have been a Jewish convert, and to have shared the apostle's imprisonment at Rome, that he might minister to his necessities (28:30; Col. 4:10).

(30) Paul probably refers to this when he speaks of having "fought with beasts at Ephesus" (I Cor. 15:32); not that there was any actual danger of martyrdom in that form, but that the multitude in their fanatic rage presented as formidable an ordeal. (Comp. Ignatius, **Ep. ad Rom.,** c. 3.)

(31) If First Corinthians were written about the time of the Passover (see I Cor. 5:6-8), we may place the tumult at some period in the spring, when the people were expecting the great festival in honor of Artemis, and were therefore more than usually open to excited appeals like that of Demetrius. This would also account for the presence of the Asiarchs at Ephesus.

There is something significant in the fact that the Asiarchs were Paul's friends. The manliness, tact, and courtesy which tempered his zeal and boldness, seem always to have gained for him the respect of men in authority (see 13:7; 18:14-17; 25:9, 26:28, 32; 27:3, 43). The Asiarchs, too, from different motives, took the same course as the disciples. They knew that his appearance would only excite the passions of the crowd, be perilous to himself, and increase the disturbance in the city.

(33) And they drew Alexander out of the multitude . . .—The fact that he was put forward by the Jews probably indicates that they were anxious to guard against the suspicion that they were at all identified with Paul or his companions. If we identify this Alexander with the "coppersmith" of II Tim. 4:14, who wrought so much evil against the apostle on his third and last visit to Ephesus, we may assume some trade connection with Demetrius which would give him influence with the crowd of artisans.

(35) And when the townclerk had appeased the people . . .—The Greek word is the same as the "scribe" of the gospels. He was the keeper of the records and archives of the city. If, as is probable, his office was a permanent one, he was likely to have more

903

weight with the people than the Asiarchs, who were elected only for a year, and who were not all of Ephesus. The language of the public officer is as characteristic in its grave caution as that of Demetrius had been in its brutal frankness. He, like the Asiarchs, obviously looks on Paul and his companions with respect.

The image which fell down from Jupiter.— The name often was given to old prehistoric images. It may have been merely a legendary way of stating that no one knew what artist had sculptured the image, or when it first had been worshiped.

(38, 39) The argument is that, should the alleged grievance be one that called for legislative rather than judicial action, the matter would have to be referred to the regular meeting of the **ecclesia**, which the town clerk probably had the right to summon.

(40) We are in danger to be called in question.—There was the risk that Demetrius and his party might find themselves defendants, and not plaintiffs, in a suit. A riotous "concourse" ("this **mob meeting**") taking the law into its own hands was not an offense which the proconsuls were likely to pass over lightly.

20

(1) Departed for to go into Macedonia.— When Paul wrote First Corinthians (see I Cor. 16:17), he intended to press on quickly and complete in person the work which it was to begin. (See 19:17; I Cor. 4:17-19.) He was led, however, to change his purpose, and to take the land journey through Macedonia instead of going by sea to Corinth (II Cor. 1:16, 17), and so from Corinth to Macedonia, as he had at first intended (see verse 3). Titus joined him perhaps at Philippi, and brought tidings that partly cheered him and partly roused his indignation. (See II Cor. 3:1; 6:6-12; 10:10.) The result was that Titus was sent back with the Second Epistle to the Corinthians (II Cor. 8:18, 19). About this time also, to judge from the numerous parallelisms of thought and language between it and the epistles to the Corinthians and the Romans, we place the date of the Epistle to the Galatians.

(2) He came into Greece.—Hellas seems to be used as synonymous with Achaia, the southern province. This may have led to an unrecorded visit to Athens. It certainly brought him to Corinth and Cenchreae. His

work in Greece done, he felt an impulse, not merely human, drawing him to the further west. A rapid journey to Jerusalem, a short visit there, and then the desire of his life might be gratified. To preach the Gospel in Rome—to pass on from Rome to the Jews at Cordova and other cities in Spain (Rom. 15:24-28)—was what he now proposed to himself.

(4) And there accompanied him into Asia . . .—The occurrence of the names Timotheus and Sosipater (Sopater) in Rom. 16:21 makes it probable that all of those here named were with Paul at Corinth. Of Secundus nothing is known, but the name may be compared with Tertius in Rom. 16:22 and Quartus in Rom. 16:23, as suggesting the probability that all three were sons of a disciple who had adopted this plan of naming his children. Tychicus (Roman inscriptions connect the name with an architect) would seem to have been a disciple from Ephesus, where freedmen of that calling naturally would find an opening. That they were seven in number suggests the idea of a reproduction either of the idea of the seven (deacons, chap. 6), or of the Roman institution upon which that probably was based.

The sudden change to the first person plural in the next verse reminds us that the name of Luke has to be added to the list of Paul's companions. We may, perhaps, assume that he went less as an official delegate from the church of Philippi than as a friend, and, probably, Paul's health needing his services, as physician.

(5, 6) The delay at Philippi enabled Paul to keep the Passover with the church there; the delay at Troas enabled him to observe the Lord's Day and the Lord's Supper.

(7) Upon the first day of the week . . .— This and the counsel given in I Cor. 16:2 are distinct proofs that the Church already had begun to observe the weekly festival of the Resurrection in place of, or, where the disciples were Jews, in addition to, the weekly Sabbath. That this was so in the regions of Troas and Asia we see from Pliny's letter to Trajan (**Epp.** 10:96), in which he describes the Christians as meeting on "a fixed day" for what he calls a **sacramentum** at break of day, and again in the evening to partake of a simple and innocent repast (**agape**).

Paul preached unto them.—The fact has a liturgical interest as showing that then, as in the more developed services of the second and third centuries, the sermon, and the lessons from Scripture which it implied, preceded what we now know as the Celebration.

(9) The name Eutychus was sufficiently common, especially among the freedman class. What follows obviously is related as a miraculous resuscitation. (Comp. I Kings 17:21; II Kings 4:34.)

(13) And sailed unto Assos.—The port of Assos lay about twenty-four miles to the south of Troas. We can only conjecture Paul's motive for going there himself by land while his companions went by sea. In 16:8 he had avoided Mysia to press on to Troas; but he may well have extended his labors there during his two years' sojourn in Asia, and have wished, before he started for Jerusalem, in the full belief that he was never to return to those regions (verse 25), to say a few words of parting counsel.

(14, 15) After the usual manner of the Mediterranean navigation of the time, the ship put into harbor, where it was possible, every evening. Each of the stations named—Mitylene (the capital of Lesbos), Chios, Samos—has legendary and historical associations of its own, full of interest for the classical student. (See Thuc. Book 3; Herod. 3:39-56, 5:28-36.)

(16) See notes on 19:21.

(17) And from Miletus he sent to Ephesus, and called the elders of the church.—They were known also (verse 28) as **episcopi** ("bishops" or "overseers"), the two names being interchangeable at this period. The many presbyters represented distinct churches or congregations. Most, if not all, of these must have been ordained by the apostle himself.

(19) Serving the Lord with all humility of mind.—The participle answers to the epithet of the "servant" or "slave" of Christ which Paul so often uses of himself (Rom. 1:1; Gal. 1:10; Phil. 1:1; Tit. 1:1). The "tears," too, are characteristic of the apostle, whose intense sensitiveness and sympathy had not been hardened into a Stoic apathy, and therefore found vent in a form which the Stoic would have scorned as unmanly. (Comp. Epictetus, **Enchirid.** c. 2.)

Temptations.—Better, "trials"—the word retaining its dominant meaning of troubles coming from without, rather than allurements to evil from within. The reference to the "lying in wait of the Jews" refers to something altogether distinct from the Demetrian tumult, and implies unrecorded sufferings.

(20) How I kept back nothing that was profitable.—The verb is one which belongs to the vocabulary of sailors, and was used for taking in or reefing sails. Paul had used no such reticence or reserve, but had gone on his course, as it were, before the wind, with all his canvas spread. In every case he considered what was required by the capacity of his disciples. That of Ephesus was wider than that of Corinth (see I Cor. 3:1, 2), and there, accordingly, he was able to set forth "the whole counsel of God" (verse 27).

(22) And now, behold, I go bound in the spirit.—See 19:21. The words refer to the higher element of Paul's own nature. (Comp. I Cor. 5:3; II Cor. 2:13.) "Spirit" is used because it points to that part of his being which was most in communion with the divine Spirit. (Comp. Rom. 8:16.) He was going to Jerusalem regardless of results, under a constraint which virtually limited the freedom of his human will.

(23) The Holy Ghost witnesseth in every city.—In every city—Corinth, Berea, Thessalonica, Philippi, Troas—there had been like utterances, of which, though they are implied here, we have no separate record. There was a general dread as to the results of his journey, which led the disciples who loved him to dissuade him from attempting it. The prophets of whom Paul speaks had genuine prevision of the future, and yet that gift did not make them infallible advisers.

(25) I know that ye all . . . shall see my face no more.—It is clear from these words (comp. Rom. 15:23, 24) that at this time Paul did not contemplate any further work in the Roman province of Asia or in Greece. But he did revisit Asia (II Tim. 1:15), and that visit included Troas (II Tim. 4:13), Miletus (II Tim. 4:20), and, in all probability, Ephesus also (I Tim. 1:3). The apostle expressly disclaims foresight of his own future. (See II Tim. 1:15.)

(26) Comp. Ezek. 3:18, 20.

(27) I have not shunned to declare unto you all the counsel of God.—The words point to a greater degree of receptivity for divine truth than had been found elsewhere. See Eph. 3:4, which, even on the assumption that it was an encyclical letter, was addressed to them principally. In "I have not shunned" we have the same word and image as in the "kept back" of verse 20.

(28) Over the which the Holy Ghost hath made you overseers.—See note on verse 31. The word used is the same as that commonly translated "bishops," but, as used here in

905

connection with the idea of the flock, it requires a word less technically ecclesiastical. It is commonly used in the New Testament as associated with this imagery. (See I Pet. 2:25; 5:2.)

To feed the church of God, which he hath purchased with his own blood.—It is clear that the words as they stand in the text are of immense importance as witnessing to the belief of the Apostolic Church at once in the absolute deity of Christ and in the nature of His redemptive work. The MSS, however, vary in their readings. Some of the best uncials and versions give "God"; others, of almost equal authority, give "Lord"; others, again combine the two "Lord and God." Internal evidence, however (e.g., I Cor. 1:2; II Cor. 1:1; Gal. 1:13; I Thess. 2:14, et al.), favors "Church of God." In the word "purchased" (or, more literally, "acquired for himself"), we recognize the idea of redemption. (Comp. I Cor. 6:20; Eph. 1:14; I Tim. 3:13.) The same idea is expressed in the "peculiar people" of I Pet. 2:9—literally, "a people for a purchased possession," and so, as it were, the **peculius** or personal property of Him who had paid the purchase money.

(29, 30) See I Tim. 1:20; II Tim. 2:17; 3:8, 13; II Pet. 2:1. Comp. Matt. 7:15; John 10:12. The note of heresy was that it was essentially self-asserting and schismatical.

(31) Therefore watch . . .—The word was an echo from our Lord's teaching (Matt. 24:42; 25:13, et al.). Here, however, it receives a fresh significance from its connection with the term **episcopi**. They who were the overseers, the "watchers" of the flock, ought, above all others, to set an example of vigilance.

By the space of three years.—Strictly speaking, the narrative of the Acts accounts for three months' preaching in the synagogue (19:8), two years in the school of Tyrannus (19:10), and an undefined period embracing the time immediately before and after the tumult of Demetrius. This would be enough to warrant his describing the time of his ministry, speaking roughly, as extending over three years.

(32) An inheritance among all them which are sanctified.—Comp. Eph. 1:14; 18; 5:5. The participle is in the perfect tense: "those that have been sanctified." That term was equivalent to, and co-extensive with, "the saints," as applied to the whole body of believers.

(33, 34) Among the many slanders against Paul, one was that he used his apostolic

ministry "as a cloke of covetousness." (Comp. II Cor. 7:2; 12:17, 18; I Thess. 2:5.) But the partnership with Aquila and Priscilla (18:3) continued; Philemon was probably a sharer in it (Philem. 17). See note on I Cor. 4:12.

(35) The words of the Lord Jesus.—The words that follow are not found in any of the four canonical gospels, nor indeed in any of the apocryphal. They furnish an example of the wide diffusion of an oral teaching, embodying both the acts and the words of Christ, of which the four gospels, especially the first three, are but partial representatives. The injunction to "remember" the words implies that they often had been prominent in the apostle's teaching.

21

(1) See note on 20:14, 15. Coos was famous both for its wines and its fine silk fabrics; Rhodes, then famous for its Colossus, was one of the largest and most flourishing islands of the Archipelago; Patara was a harbor on the coast of Lycia.

(3, 4) As soon as they sighted Cyprus, they stood to the southeast, and so had it on their left as they continued their voyage to Syria. At Tyre (in "Phenicia") they had to change their ship again. (It will be remembered that Paul had passed through that region at least once before. See 15:3. The church probably had been planted by the labors of Philip, as the evangelist of Caesarea.) See notes on 20:5-7. The repeated warnings are an indication of the exceeding bitterness of feeling with which the Judaizers and unbelieving Jews were known to be animated against him.

(7) Ptolemais.—This city, as Accho, appears in Judg. 1:31 as one of the old cities of the Canaanites which the Israelites of the tribe of Asher failed to conquer. It was conquered, rebuilt, and renamed by Ptolemy Soter, king of Egypt.

(8) Caesarea.—Comp. 8:40; 10:1. Paul's third visit there (9:30; 18:22), and we may well believe that he was simply renewing a previous friendship with Philip.

Philip the evangelist.—The title given to him is interesting as showing that the work of "serving tables" (6:3), i.e., of superintending the distribution of alms, had been merged in the higher work of a missionary preacher. (Comp. Eph. 4:11; II Tim. 4:5.) As far as we know, Philip and Luke had not met before. We can imagine that the latter, already contemplating his work as an historian, would welcome the acquaintance of the former, asking many questions as to the early history of the Church, and learning from him nearly all that we find in the first eleven chapters of this book.

(9) The same man had four daughters, virgins, which did prophesy.—Both elements of the description throw light on the life of the Apostolic Church. In the organization of women's work in the Church, the "virgins" formed apparently a distinct class, the complement of that of the widows of I Tim. 5:10. Paul had distinctly sanctioned such a life (see notes on I Cor. 7:8, 25, 26, 34). So Pliny, in his letter to Trajan (**Ep.** 10, §6), speaks of the women who were then called **ministrae** among the Christians, the latter term probably being used as the equivalent for "deaconesses." These virgins "prophesied," or preached. It follows that Paul's rules of discipline as yet had not obtained in all the churches. (See I Cor. 11:5, 14:34; I Tim. 2:12.) It is perfectly possible, however, that they may have confined their ministrations to those of their own sex, acting as deaconesses as a matter of decorum.

(11) He took Paul's girdle, and bound his own hands and feet.—It is interesting to note the revival of the old prophetic manner of predicting by symbolic acts (comp. Isa. 20:3, 4; Jer. 13:1-11; 27:2; Ezek. 4:1-3; 5:1-4). See note on 11:28.

(12) Both we, and they of that place . . .—For the first time the courage even of the apostle's companions began to fail, and Luke admits that he himself had joined in the entreaty. "They of that place" would include Philip and his daughters, and possibly, if he were still there, Cornelius and his friends.

(13) See note on 20:19.

(15) After those days we took up our carriages . . .—Better, "we took up our baggage." Comp. I Sam. 17:22.

(16) One Mnason of Cyprus, an old disciple, with whom we should lodge.—Better, "an early disciple." The word for "old" refers less to personal age than to his having been a disciple from the beginning of the Church's history. He may accordingly have been among those "men of Cyprus" who came to Antioch, and were among the first to preach the Gospel to the Gentiles. (See 11:20.) We may infer fairly that he was one of those who had been "from the beginning" among the eyewitnesses and ministers

of the word to whom Luke refers as his informants (Luke 1:2).

(18) The day following Paul went in with us unto James . . .—See 20:16. It seems natural to infer that this was on or near the day of Pentecost. The city would be crowded with pilgrims. The church would be holding its solemn festival, not without memories of the great gifts of the Spirit and prayers for their renewal.

(19) He declared particularly . . .—Better, "one by one, or in detail." This must have implied a narrative of considerable length, including an outline of all that had passed since the visit of 18:22, and ending with an account of the contribution which he and his companions had brought with them from nearly all the churches of the Gentiles.

(22) The report of Paul's arrival was sure to spread, and those who heard of it would be eager to see how he acted. Would he ostentatiously reproduce in Jerusalem that living as a Greek with Greeks (I Cor. 9:22) of which they heard as his manner at Corinth and Ephesus? The advice which followed was intended to allay the suspicion of the timid, and to disappoint the expectations of more determined adversaries. By connecting himself with such a vow Paul would show that he was content in these matters to follow in the footsteps of James, and that he looked upon the observance of the Nazarite vow, if not as binding, at any rate as right and praiseworthy.

(24) Be at charges with them . . .—Literally, "spend money on them." This involved payment for the act of shaving the head, for which probably there was a fixed fee to priest or Levite, and for the sacrifices which each Nazarite had to offer (Num. 6:9-12).

(25) As touching the Gentiles which believe.—See notes on 15:20. James adheres still to the terms of the **concordat** sanctioned at the council of Jerusalem. He thinks it fair to call on Paul to show that he too adheres to the compact, and has no wish to disparage the "customs" of the Law (Exod. 29:37; Lev. 12:2; Num. 12:14). Paul readily acts upon the suggestion. All promised well; but an interruption came from an unexpected quarter and overturned what seemed so wisely planned in the interests of peace.

(28, 29) The general charge was backed up by a more specific indictment that he had brought Greeks—uncircumcised Gentiles—into the Holy Place, i.e., beyond the middle wall of partition (Eph. 2:14) which divided the court that was open to strangers from which none but Jews might enter (Jos., **Ant.** 15.11, §5).

(31) The chief captain of the band.—See notes on 10:1. They were stationed in the tower ("castle," verse 34) known as Antonia, built by Herod the Great and named in honor of the Triumvir. Once again the apostle owed his safety from violence to the interposition of the civil power. (See 18:14-17.) The "beating" would seem to have been rough treatment with the fists rather than any regular punishment.

(38) Art not thou that Egyptian?—This was the inference drawn by the chief captain from the fact that his prisoner spoke in Greek. (See Jos., **Ant.** 20.8, §6; **Wars,** 2:13, §5.) The chief captain infers from the tumult raised by a Greek-speaking Jew that the Egyptian must have reappeared.

(40) Paul stood on the stairs.—He spoke, not as they expected in the Greek, which belonged to one who fraternized with Gentiles, but in the Hebrew or Aramaic, which he had studied at the feet of Gamaliel. It was a strange scene for that Feast of Pentecost. Twenty-five years before he had kept the garments of those who were stoning Stephen. And now he was there, accused of the same crimes, making his defense before a crowd as wild and frenzied as that of which he had then been the leader.

22

(2) They kept the more silence.—The opening words (verse 1) had done the work they were meant to do. One who spoke in Hebrew was not likely to blaspheme the sacred Hebrew books. What follows was conceived in the same spirit of conciliation.

(3) Brought up in this city at the feet of Gamaliel.—The rabbis sat in a high chair, and their scholars on the ground, literally at their master's feet.

Was zealous toward God.—The apostle claims their sympathy as having at one time shared all their dearest convictions. There is, perhaps, a touch of higher enthusiasm in the apostle's language. He was a zealot for God; they were zealots for the Law.

On the general history of Paul's conversion, see notes on 9:1-16.

(5) Annas is named as high priest at the time of Paul's conversion, acting probably with his son-in-law, Caiaphas, as his coadjutor. (See Luke 3:2; John 18:13.) Now the office was filled by Ananias, son of

Nebedaeus, who owed his appointment to Herod Agrippa II, then king of Chalcis, to whom Claudius had conceded the privilege of nominating the high priests (Jos., **Ant.** 20:5, §2). The official acts of his predecessors would be known to the high priest and to the Sanhedrin for the time being, and Paul therefore can appeal to his knowledge as confirming his own statements.

(6) About noon.—The special note of the hour may be taken as characteristic of a personal recollection of the circumstances of the great event, and so also the cause ("glory") of the light in verse 11.

(9) They heard not the voice ...—i.e., they did not hear it as a voice uttering articulate words. It was for them as though it thundered.

(14) And see that Just One.—See note on 7:52.

(15) Thou shalt be his witness.—This mission, identical with that which had been assigned to the Twelve (1:8), virtually placed the persecutor on a level with them, and was equivalent to his appointment as an apostle.

(16) Arise, and be baptized, and wash away thy sins.—Here, again, we have words which are not in the narrative of chap. 9. They show that for the apostle baptism was no formal or ceremonial act, but was joined with repentance, faith bringing with it assurance of a real forgiveness. In Paul's language as to the "washing" of regeneration (Tit. 3:5) we may trace his continued adherence to the idea which he had thus been taught to embrace on his first admission to the Church of Christ.

(17) When I was come again to Jerusalem.—This probably refers to the visit of 9:26 and Gal. 1:17, 18. The vision indicated that he was to have another field of work than Jerusalem and the Church of the Circumcision. (See II Cor. 12:1.)

(20) When the blood of thy martyr Stephen ...—The same Greek word is used in verse 15 (**martus,** "witness") as expressing the office to which Paul himself was called.

(23) Cast off their clothes, and threw dust into the air.—The gestures would seem to constitute a natural relief to the violence of uncontrolled passion. It may be, however, that the handfuls of dust were aimed at the apostle as a sign of loathing. (Comp. notes on 18:6; Matt. 10:14.)

(25) According to Roman custom, Paul was stripped to the waist and tied with leathern thongs, as our Lord had been, to the column or whipping post which was used within the fortress for this mode of torture. On the question of the rights of Roman citizens, and Paul's claim to those rights, see note on 16:37.

(28) With a great sum obtained I this freedom.—Better, "this citizenship," the word expressing, not the transition from bondage to freedom, but from the position of an alien to that of a citizen. The chiliarch was himself, apparently, an alien by birth, and, as was customary at the time, had obtained the citizenship by the payment of a large bribe.

I was free born.—The Greek is somewhat more emphatic: "I am one even from birth." This implies that Paul's father or grandfather had received the citizenship; how, we cannot tell. Many of the Jews who were taken to Rome by Pompeius as slaves first obtained their freedom and became **libertini**, and afterward were admitted on the register as citizens. (See notes on 6:9; 16:37.) The mention of kinsmen or friends at Rome (Rom. 16:7, 11) makes it probable that the apostle's father may have been among them.

(30) Failing to get the information by the process of torturing the prisoner, the chiliarch now has recourse to the other alternative of getting a formal declaration from the Sanhedrin, as the chief representative body of the Jews.

23

(2) The high priest Ananias.—See note on 22:5. The son of Nebedaeus was conspicuous for his cruelty and injustice, and had been sent to Rome as a prisoner to take his trial before Claudius (A.D. 52). He had been acquitted, or at least released, and had returned to Judaea. To him this assertion of a life so utterly unlike his own seemed almost like a personal insult.

(3) God shall smite thee, thou whited wall.—See note on Matt. 23:27. The whole utterance must be regarded by Paul's own confession as the expression of a hasty indignation, recalled after a moment's reflection; but the words so spoken were actually a prophecy, fulfilled some years later by the death of Ananias by the hands of the **sicarii** (Jos., **Wars**, 2:17, §§2-9).

(5) I wist not, brethren, that he was the high priest.—Paul, either from defective sight (see notes on 9:18), or because the high priest was not sitting as president of the Sanhedrin, did not know who it was

that had given the order, and thought it came from one of the subordinate members of the council.

Thou shalt not speak evil of the ruler of thy people.—See Exod. 22:28. To act on that law toward rulers; to see below all the corruptions of human society and the vices of princes the scheme of a divine order; to recognize that "the powers that be are ordained of God"—such were throughout the ruling principles of the apostle's conduct (Rom. 13:1-6; 1 Pet. 2:13-17).

(6) Paul seems to be acting, consciously or unconsciously, on the principle **divide et impera** to win over to his side a party who otherwise would have been his enemies. The true leaders of the Pharisees had given a prominence to the doctrine of the Resurrection which it had never had before. They taught an ethical rather than a sacrificial religion. Many of them had been, like Nicodemus and Joseph of Arimathaea, secret disciples of our Lord. At this time there were many avowed Pharisees among the members of the Christian Church (15:5). Paul, therefore, could not be charged with any **suppressio veri** in calling himself a Pharisee. It did not involve even a tacit disclaimer of his faith in Christ.

(7) There arose a dissension between the Pharisees and the Sadducees.—As a strategic act Paul's words immediately had the effect which he desired. They prevented the hasty unanimous vote which otherwise might have united the two parties, as they had been united in the case of Stephen, in the condemnation of the blasphemer. What follows shows that it was not without results as regards the higher aim.

(8) The Sadducees say that there is no resurrection.—On the general teaching of the Sadducees, see notes on 5:17; Matt. 22:23.

(10) The fear of the chiliarch naturally was heightened by his knowledge that he was responsible for the life of a Roman citizen. In the barracks of the fortress, as before probably in the same guard-room as that which had witnessed our Lord's sufferings at the hands of Pilate's soldiers, the prisoner would at least be in safety. (See 24:7.)

(11) These were words full of comfort and of hope. There might be delay and suffering, and a long trial of patience, but the end was certain: he was to reach the goal of Rome.

(12) Certain of the Jews banded together . . .—The casuistry of the more fanatic

Jews led them to the conclusion that a blasphemer or apostate was an outlaw, and that, in the absence of any judicial condemnation, private persons might take on themselves the execution of the divine sentence. (Comp. I Macc. 2:24; Jos., **Ant.**, 12:6, § 2, 15:8, §3.) Those who now thus acted probably were of the number of the Zealots, or Sicarii.

(15) Now therefore ye with the council . . .—The plot was necessary either because the Sanhedrin had lost, under Roman rule, its power to inflict capital punishment (see John 18:31); or because, even if they possessed that power, the chiliarch was not likely to allow its exercise in the case of a Roman citizen; or because the experience of the previous day had shown that the violent party was not likely to obtain a majority in the Council.

(16) Paul's sister's son.—The passage is noteworthy as being the only reference to any of Paul's relatives in the Acts. The fact that Paul lodged with Mnason suggests the probability that neither the sister nor the nephew resided permanently in Jerusalem. This nephew may have been one of them from Rome (Rom. 16:7, 11) who had come to Jerusalem to keep the feast. We see from the fact thus stated that Paul, though in custody, was allowed to hold free communication with his friends.

(23) At the third hour of the night.—Assuming that Luke uses the Jewish reckoning, this would be about 9 or 10 p.m. It was evidently the object of the chiliarch to place the prisoner beyond the reach of an attack before daybreak.

(24) Felix the governor.—Felix had obtained the procuratorship of Judaea through his brother Pallas' influence with Emperor Claudius. In the terse epigrammatic language of Tacitus, he governed as one who thought, in his reliance on his brother's power, that he could commit any crime with impunity, and wielded "the power of a tyrant in the temper of a slave" (Tacit. **Ann.** 12:54; **Hist.** 5:9). His career was infamous alike for lust and cruelty. Comp. Jos., **Ant.**, 20:7, §§1, 2; Suetonius, **Claud.** c. 28.

(27) The chief captain ingeniously colors his statement so as to claim credit for having rescued a Roman citizen, though, as a matter of fact, he did not discover that he was a citizen until he was on the point of scourging him without a trial.

(31) Antipatris.—The town was built by Herod the Great and named after his father. It was about forty-two miles from Jerusalem

and twenty-six from Caesarea. Having started probably about midnight, they would reach this town about six or seven a.m.

(34) He asked of what province he was.—The question was a natural one for a procurator of Judaea to ask as to any prisoner brought before him. (Comp. Luke 23:6.) Felix was ready to take cognizance of a matter which apparently, to judge by the precedent set by Pilate, belonged to the jurisdiction of another. Perhaps he had no motive for conciliating the favor of the governor of Cilcia, or thought that the nature of the accusation overruled the nationality of the accused.

24

(1) After five days.—The five days probably start from Paul's departure from Jerusalem. This agrees favorably with the reckoning of the twelve days from the apostle's arrival there (verse 11).

A certain orator named Tertullus.—Men of this class were to be found in most of the provincial towns of the Roman empire, ready to hold a brief for plaintiff or defendant, and bringing to bear the power of their glib eloquence, as well as their knowledge of Roman laws, on the mind of the judge.

(2) Seeing that by thee we enjoy great quietness.—The orator had learned the trick of his trade, and begins with propitiating the judge by flattery. Tertullus shows his skill in the emphasis which he lays on "quietness," practically the only distinguishing feature of Felix's administration (comp. Jos., **Ant.**, 20:8, §5; **Wars**, 2:13, §2; Tac., **Ann.**, 12:54).

By thy providence . . .—The tendency to clothe the emperors with quasi-divine attributes led to the appearance of the expression "the providence of Caesar" on their coins and on medals struck in their honor. Tertullus, after his manner, goes one step further and extends the term to the procurator of Judaea.

(5) We have found this man a pestilent fellow.—The advocate passes from flattering the judge to invective against the defendant, and lays stress on the fact that he is charged with the very crimes which Felix prided himself on repressing.

A mover of sedition among all the Jews throughout the world.—The language may simply be that of vague invective, but we may perhaps read between the lines some statements gathered from the Jews of Thessalonica (17:6) and Ephesus (21:28) who had come to keep the Feast of Pentecost at Jerusalem.

A ringleader of the sect of the Nazarenes.—This is the first appearance of the term of reproach as transferred from the Master to the disciples. (Comp. John 1:46.)

(6) Who also hath gone about to profane the temple.—See 21:28.

(10) We note at once the difference between Paul's frank manliness and the servile flattery of the advocate. The "many years" were actually six in number. Felix, after having ruled for a short time with a divided authority had superseded Cumanus in A.D. 52 or 53.

(15, 16) Paul's faith in all the authoritative standards of Judaism was as firm and full as that of any Pharisee. The question whether that belief did or did not lead to the conviction that Jesus of Nazareth was the Christ was one of interpretation, with which Felix had nothing to do, and which Paul, when making a formal **apologia** before a Roman ruler, declines to answer. Aligning with the great bulk of the Jewish people, he held that doctrine of a resurrection as a stern and solemn reality.

(17) Four years passed since the previous visit of 18:22. The "alms" were the large sums of money which Paul had been collecting since his last visit for the disciples at Jerusalem. This is the only mention in the Acts of that which occupies so prominent a place in the epistles of this period. (See Rom. 15:25; I Cor. 16:1-4; II Cor. 8:1-4.) The "offerings" were the sacrifices which the apostle was about to offer on the completion of the Nazarite vow with which he had associated himself.

(21) This, from Paul's point of view, was the one instance in which any words of his had been even the occasion of an uproar, and in them he had but proclaimed a belief which he held in common with their best and wisest teachers. As far as the proceedings before the Council were concerned, he had not even entered on the question of the Messiahship or the Resurrection of the Lord Jesus.

(22) Felix was too well-informed—perhaps through Philip, Cornelius, or even his wife Drusilla—to yield any answer to the declamatory statements of Tertullus. He saw, too, that the prisoner was no common **Sicarius**, or leader of sedition. Leaving the general attack on the "way" of the Christians, Felix proposes to inquire into the actual circumstances of the case brought before him. It is remarkable that this adjournment leads to an indefinite postponement. Possibly the accusers felt that the judge had made up his mind against them, and so withdrew from the prosecution. The favorable impression made on Felix is shown by the unusual leniency with which the prisoner was treated (verse 23).

(24) Felix came with his wife Drusilla.—She was the daughter of the first Herod Agrippa and the sister of the second. Felix employed the services of a Jewish magician named Simon, whom some writers have identified with the sorcerer of Samaria (see 8:9), to seduce her from her husband Azizus. By her marriage with Felix she had a son named Agrippa, who perished in an eruption of Vesuvius in A.D. 79 (Jos., **Ant.** 19:7, 20:5, 7). It would seem, from her being with her husband at these interviews, that she was eager to learn more of "the faith in Christ." Felix, too, seems to have been willing at first to listen. The procurator and his wife apparently were in the first stage of an earnest inquiry which might have led to a conversion.

(25) Righteousness, temperance, and judgment.—"Righteousness" includes in Greek ethics the duties which man owes to man. "Temperance" implies the state in which a man exercises control over all the passions that minister to sensuality. Felix's character was faulty in both respects. Paul sought to make the guilty pair before whom he stood feel that the warnings of conscience were but the presage of a divine judgment which should render to every man according to his deeds. There is no mention here of the forgiveness of sins, nor of the life of fellowship with Christ. Those truths would have come, in due course, afterward. As yet they would have been altogether premature.

Felix trembled, and answered . . .—Felix treats Paul as Antipas had treated the Baptist (Mark 6:20). He does not resent his plainness of speech; he shows a certain measure of respect for him; but he postpones acting and so becomes the type of the millions whose spiritual life is ruined by procrastination. Nothing that we know of him gives us any ground for thinking that the "convenient season" ever came.

(26) He hoped also that money should have been given him of Paul.—This greed of gain in the act of administering justice was the root evil of the weak and wicked character. He had caught at the word "alms" (verse 17); Paul, then, was not without resources.

He sent for him the oftener, and communed with him.—It is not difficult to surmise the character of these interviews: the suggestive hints—half-promises and half-threats—of the procurator; the steadfast refusal of the prisoner to purchase the freedom which he claimed as a right, and his fruitless attempts to bring a change for the better in his judge's character.

(27) The change of administration was caused by the complaints which the Jews brought against Felix, leading Nero to recall him. His successor, Festus, who came to the province A.D. 60, died in his second year of office (See Josephus, **Wars,** 2:14, §1.) Luke probably made use of opportunities during these two years to collect materials for his two histories.

<h2 style="text-align:center">25</h2>

(2) The Jews hoped to take advantage of the newness of Festus to his office. He was likely enough, they thought, to accept their statements and to yield to the pressure of those who had shown themselves powerful enough to bring about his predecessor's recall. Possibly Festus had heard from Felix or Lysias of the former plot, and took care to be on his guard against this. And so the conspirators again were baffled.

(5) Festus demanded that the charges against Paul should be supported by the leaders and representatives of the people, and not by a hired rhetorician like Tertullus.

(9-11) Festus offered the prisoner a trial before his own national tribunal, with the presence of the procurator as a check upon violence and injustice. It is clear from Paul's answer that the proposed trial would not be before Caesar's judgment seat, and he, for his part (and in keeping with his rights of Roman citizenship), preferred the secular to the ecclesiastical tribunal. By this appeal he would deliver himself from the injustice of a weak and temporizing judge, and make his long-delayed journey to Rome a matter of moral certainty.

(13) King Agrippa and Bernice.—Agrippa closes the line of the Herodian house. He was the son of the Agrippa whose tragic end in A.D. 44 is related in 12:20-23. On the death of his uncle Herod, the king of Chalcis, in A.D. 48 he received the sovereignty of that region from Claudius,

and with it the superintendence of the Temple and the nomination of the high priests. Four years later he received the tetrarchies that had been governed by his great-uncles Philip and Lysanias (Luke 3:1), with the title of king. In A.D. 55 Nero increased his kingdom by adding some of the cities of Galilee (Jos., **Ant.,** 19:9, §1, 20:1, §3, 8, §5). He lived to see the destruction of Jerusalem and died under Trajan (A.D. 100) at the age of seventy-three.

The history of Bernice reads like a page from the chronicles of the Borgias. She was the eldest daughter of Herod Agrippa I, and was married at an early age to her uncle the king of Chalcis. Incestuous and adulterous alliances were common in the Herodian house (see note on Matt. 14:1). Herod Agrippa II, whom she "married" after her uncle's death, was her own brother. The queen's unbridled passions gained the mastery, and she went from there to one illicit relationship after another. (See Sueton., **Calig.,** c. 24.) Vespasian was attracted by her queenly dignity, and yet more by the magnificence of her queenly gifts. His son Titus took his place in her long list of lovers, but he was compelled by the pressure of the senate and of public opinion to dismiss her. (See Jos., **Ant.,** 20:7, §3; Juv., **Sat.,** 6:155-9.)

(14) Festus probably thought that Agrippa, who knew all about the Jews and their religion, could throw some light on the peculiar position of his prisoner, who, though a Jew, and professing the utmost reverence for the Law and the Temple, was yet accused and denounced by his compatriots.

(19) What follows shows that Festus looked on Paul as not merely affirming, with other Pharisees, the general doctrine of a resurrection, but as connecting it with the specific witness that Jesus had risen from the dead.

(21) Unto the hearing of Augustus.—The title had first been given by the Senate to Octavianus (Sueton. **Aug.** c. 7), and was adopted by his successors. The month of August, dedicated to the first emperor as July had been dedicated to Julius, is interesting as perpetuating its memory.

(23) The fact was the first fulfillment of the promise that the apostle was to bear His witness before "kings" as well as rulers (9:15).

(25-27) The words constitute an emphatic declaration on the part of Festus that the accusers had failed to sustain their indictment. But a procurator transmitting a case to the supreme court of the emperor was bound to send a formal report as to the matter out of which the appeal arose, and it was on this point that the "perplexed" ruler desired the advice and co-operation of Agrippa.

(26) To write unto my lord.—The Greek corresponds to the title of "Dominus," which, though declined by Augustus and Tiberius (Sueton. **Octav.** c. 53; **Tiber.** c. 27), had been assumed by Caligula and Nero.

26

(1) Then Paul stretched forth the hand.—Paul now stood before the court as a prisoner, with one arm chained to the soldier who kept guard over him. (Comp. verse 29.)

(7) Our twelve tribes.—Paul, like James (Jas. 1:1), assumes the twelve tribes to be all alike sharers in the same hope of Israel and ignores the legend, so often repeated and revived, that the ten tribes of the northern kingdom of Israel, after they had been carried away by Shalmaneser, had wandered far away and were to be found, under some strange disguise, in far-off regions of the world. The earliest appearance of the fable is in the apocryphal II Esdras 13:40-46.

(8) The appeal is made to Agrippa as accepting the sacred books of Israel, in which instances of resurrection were recorded (I Kings 17:17-23; II Kings 4:18-37), and which ought to have hindered him from postulating the incredibility of the truth which Paul preached: the doctrine of a general resurrection, and the fact that Christ had risen. Agrippa, as probably allied, as the fact of his kindred had been, with the Sadducean high priests, some of whom he had himself nominated, was likely to reject both.

(9) Paul himself had been led from unbelief to faith; he will not despair of a like transition for others, even for Agrippa. (Comp. I Tim. 1:12-17.) On the relation of this account of the apostle's conversion to previous narratives, see notes on 9:1-20.

(10) I gave my voice against them.—Better, "gave my vote." The words show that Paul, though a "young man" (see note on 7:58), must have been a member either of the Sanhedrin itself or of some tribunal with delegated authority.

(11) Being exceedingly mad against them.—The words express vividly Paul's retrospective analysis of his former state. It was not only that he acted in ignorance (I Tim. 1:13); he also might plead the temporary insanity of fanaticism.

Even unto strange cities.—See note on 9:3.

(17) From the Gentiles, unto whom now I send thee.—The distinct mission to the Gentiles appears in 22:21 to be connected with the trance in the Temple, three years after the conversion. But Gal. 1:15, 16 agrees with what we find here in connecting it with the time when the Son of God was first "revealed in him." In the Greek word for "send" (**apostello**) we find the warrant for Paul's claim to be considered an apostle, "not of men, neither by man," but by the direct personal call of the Lord Jesus (Gal. 1:1). The word that had been used of the Twelve (Matt. 10:16) was used also of him; and the pronoun "I" is especially emphasized.

(21) For these causes . . .—With this brief touch, avoiding any elaborate vindication of his own character, Paul indicates the real cause of the hostility of the Jews. The one unpardonable sin, in their eyes, was that he taught the Gentiles that they might claim every gift and grace which once had been looked upon as the privilege and prerogative of Israel. The historical precedence of the Jew remained (see notes on 13:46; Rom. 3:1, 2), but in all essential points they were placed on a footing of equality.

(22) The prophets and Moses.—The order of the words in the Greek, "which the prophets said should come, and Moses," suggests the thought that the sentence would have stopped naturally at "come," and that the name of Moses was added in after thought to meet the case of those among the hearers who, like the Sadducees, placed the Pentateuch on a higher level of authority than the Prophets.

(23) That Christ should suffer.—The great body of the Jews had fixed their thoughts only on the prophetic visions of the glories of the Messiah's kingdom. Even the disciples of Jesus were slow to receive any other thought than that of conquest and triumph. So it was that a "Christ crucified" was still "to the Jews a stumbling-block" (I Cor. 1:23). The speech at Antioch in Pisidia (13:27-35) showed the emphasis which Paul laid on this point. And it was through the Resurrection only that the light shone in on those who had been sitting as in the shadow of death.

(24) The Roman governor forgot the usual dignity of his office, and burst, apparently, into a loud laugh of scorn. That one who had been crucified should rise from the dead and give light to the Gentiles seemed to him the very hallucination of insanity.

(27) Believest thou the prophets?—The appeal to Agrippa's knowledge was followed by the assumption of his accepting the ground on which Paul invited discussion. He might, of course, dispute Paul's interpretation of prophecy, but he could not, as a Jew, in the presence of other Jews, speak of the Law and the Prophets as Festus had spoken of Paul's "learning." And so the way might have been opened to that argument from prophecy which, when the apostle was reasoning with his own countrymen, was (see 13:16-41; 18:2, 3) his favorite method of producing conviction.

(28) Almost thou persuadest me to be a Christian.—The words run literally, "In," or "with, a little thou persuadest me"; and this may be completed by "with little **speech**," "with little **labour**," or "little **evidence**." So in Eph. 3:3 we have precisely the same phrase rendered "in few **words**." Agrippa's words, accordingly, are the expression, not of a half-belief, but of a cynical sneer. "Thou art trying to make a Christian of me with very few words, on very slender grounds," would be the nearest paraphrase of his derisive answer to Paul's appeal. It was, of course, evasive as well as derisive. On the word "Christian," see note on 11:26.

(29) "Almost" and "altogether" are better rendered "in a little or in a great (measure)," or, "with little labor and with great," corresponding with what Agrippa had just said. For the purpose of emphasizing the strong desire of his heart, Paul may have caught up the half-sarcastic phrase and used it as with a new meaning.

Except these bonds.—See note on verse 1.

(32) This man might have been set at liberty . . .—The decision to which Agrippa came showed the wisdom of the line which Paul had taken. The authorities could not now free themselves from responsibility for the safe custody of the prisoner. Thus the apostle at last gained that safe journey to the imperial city which had for many years been the great desire of his heart.

In subsequent years Festus and Agrippa continued the same **entente cordiale** as that which we have seen in this chapter. Agrippa took up his abode at Jerusalem in the old palace of the Asmonean, or Maccabean,

princes. It commanded a view of the city, and from a banquet hall which he had erected, he could look down upon the courts of the Temple and see the priests sacrificing even as he sat at meat. The Jews looked on this as a profanation, and built a wall which blocked up the view both from the king's palace and from the portico where the Roman soldiers used to stand on guard during the festivals. This was regarded by Festus as an insult, and he ordered the wall to be pulled down. The people of Jerusalem, however, obtained leave to send an embassy to Rome. They secured the support of Poppaea, already half a proselyte, after the fashion of the time among the women of the higher class at Rome, and, by the strange irony of history, the Temple of Jehovah was rescued from profanation by the concubine of Nero (Jos. **Ant.** 20:8, §7).

27

(1) A centurion of Augustus' band.—Literally, "of the Sebaste." See note on 10:1. Nero about this time had formed a kind of bodyguard, consisting of some 3,000 young men. To these he gave the name of **Augustani** (Tac. **Ann.** 14:15; Sueton. **Nero.** c. 25), a term of which Sebastene would be the natural Greek equivalent. As it is not said that the cohort itself was at Caesarea, it is possible that Julius may have accompanied Festus as an escort to his province and was now returning to Rome. (Comp. Tac., **Hist.**, 2:92.)

(2) Entering into a ship of Adramyttium.—Adramyttium was a town on the coast of Mysia, opposite Lesbos. It lay on the Roman road from Troas to Ephesus and Miletus, and was a port of considerable importance. There would seem to have been but little direct traffic by sea between Caesarea and Rome, and the voyage had therefore to be made first in one ship, then another. Possibly it was at first intended that the prisoners should go to Adramyttium, cross to Greece, and then proceed by land. Looking to the fact that the "fast," i.e., the Day of Atonement, was over when Paul reached Crete (see note on verse 9), the date of embarkation may be fixed, with much probability, toward the end of August.

One Aristarchus, a Macedonian of Thessalonica.—It is reasonable to infer that Aristarchus, who had come with Paul to Jerusalem (20:4), had remained in Palestine during the two years of the apostle's imprisonment and was now intending to return to his native city. The subsequent alteration of plan (verse 6), however, led to his accompanying him to Rome, and we find him there with Paul (Col. 4:10), sharing his imprisonment.

(4) We sailed under Cyprus . . .—Had the wind been favorable, the ship naturally would have taken the direct course from Sidon to Mysia, leaving Cyprus on the right, as in his previous voyage Paul had sailed from Patara to Tyre (21:1). As it was, the wind probably being from the northwest, they made for the channel between Cyprus and Cilicia, and, sailing close under the lee of the long, projecting east coast of the island from Salamis to the promontory of Dinaretium, were thus sheltered.

(6) A ship of Alexandria sailing into Italy.—Myra (verse 5) lay about two and a half miles from the mouth of the river Andriacus. The presence of this merchant-ship, probably engaged in the corn trade between Egypt and Rome, but driven off course, led to a change of plan. It seemed an easier and more expeditious route to go straight to Rome, instead of landing at Mysia, and then taking another ship to Macedonia in order to journey by land to the coast of the Adriatic.

(7) When we had sailed slowly many days.—The Etesian gales from the northwest, which prevail in the Archipelago during the latter part of July and the whole of August, were still blowing strongly. During the "many days" (probably three weeks) the ship had not been able to traverse more than 120 miles that lay between Myra and Cnidus. To reach the latter place they probably had coasted along Lycia, and gone through the straits between Rhodes and the mainland.

And scarce were come over against Cnidus.—Better, with "difficulty." Cnidus was situated on a neck of land with a harbor on either side, and was apparently a naval station for the ships that were engaged in the corn trade between Egypt and Greece (Thucyd. 8:35). Here, as the coast trends away to the north, and they had no longer the shelter of the land, they were exposed to the full force of the Etesian winds. It was useless to attempt to steer against these, and their only alternative was to steer southward, so as to get, if possible, under the lee of the coast of Crete.

(8) A place which is called The fair havens.—The ship would have been ex-

posed again, after passing Crete, or even its central promontory, to the full force of the northwest gales. About two miles to the east of the promontory, however, and therefore sheltered by it, there was good anchorage in a harbor known as the Fair Havens.

(9) Because the fast was now already past.—The Fast was the Jewish Day of Atonement, which fell on the tenth of Tisri (in that year, September 24), the seventh month of the Jewish ecclesiastical year. The manner in which Luke names the Fast, and not the Feast of Tabernacles five days later, makes it probable that the time now was between September 24 and October 1, when the Etesian winds, which are always of the nature of equinoctial gales, naturally would be most violent.

(10) Sirs, I perceive that this voyage will be with hurt.—Paul speaks more from the foresight gained by observation than from a direct supernatural prediction. He had had the experience of three shipwrecks (II Cor. 11:25), and the Epistle to Titus, though probably written later, shows an acquaintance with Crete which suggests that he may have had some knowledge even of the harbor in which they had found refuge. His advice, accordingly, was to remain where they were, in comparative safety, in spite of the drawbacks referred to in verse 12.

(12) The harbor of Phenice faced the northeast and southeast, the words being the names of the winds which blew from them, not of points on the compass. (See Ptolemy, 3:17.)

(13) There was a change at once in the force and the direction of the wind. The Fair Havens was across the bay, some thirty-four miles from Phenice. They still, however, hugged the coast, as afraid to venture too far into the open sea. The tense of the Greek verb for "they sailed close" implies that they were in the act of doing this when the storm burst upon them (verse 14).

(14) There arose against it . . .—The Greek pronoun is in the feminine; and as the noun used for ship is, throughout the narrative, in the neuter, the difference of gender presents a difficulty. Some translators refer the pronoun to Crete, others (e.g., Luther) to "purpose" (verse 13).

A tempestuous wind, called Euroclydon.—The Greek adjective **typhonic** is perpetuated in the word "typhoon," as applied to whirlwinds like that now described. The name **Euroclydon** means "wide wave" or "broad billow." A sudden change from south to north, with a great increase of violence, is a common phenomenon in the autumnal storms of the Mediterranean, and in this instance the blast would seem to have rushed down on the ship from the hills of Crete.

(15) And could not bear up into the wind.—The Greek verb is literally "to look into the wind's eye," to **face** the wind. The figure is a sufficiently natural one in all languages; but it perhaps received additional vividness from the fact that a large eye commonly was painted on the prow of Greek vessels. The ship now was driven in a southwest direction, scudding before the wind.

(16) And running under a certain island which is called Clauda.—The island lay about twenty-three miles to the southwest of Crete. Here they got under the lee of the shore, and availed themselves of the temporary shelter to prepare the ship more thoroughly than had been possible before to encounter the fury of the storm.

(17) They used helps, undergirding the ship.—The word "helps" answers to what we should call "precautions," or "remedial measures." The process described, technically known as "frapping," consisted in carrying a strong cable several times around the ship from stem to stern, so as to keep the planks secure and guard against the consequent leakage. The practice always has been a common one. (Comp. Thuc., 1:29; Horace, **Od.**, 1:14.)

Fearing lest they should fall into the quicksands.—The Greater Syrtis lay just to the west of Cyrene on the north coast of Africa. Quicksands were the terror of all Mediterranean sailors (Jos., **Wars**, 2:16, §4). The voyagers knew that the gale was bearing them in that direction, and did not dare to let the ship sail on full before the wind any longer. (See Lucan, **Pharsalia**, 9:303-10; Milton, **Paradise Lost**, 2:939.)

Strake sail.—They "lowered the ship's gear," the spars and rigging, and especially the heavy yard and ropes which the ancient ships carried, and which would, in such a gale, make the ship topheavy.

(18) The next day they lightened the ship.—The act shows that, in spite of the undergirding, leakage was still going on. The cargo, as coming from Alexandria, probably consisted largely of corn.

(19) We cast out with our own hands the tackling of the ship.—The fact that the passengers as well as the crew were pressed into service indicates the urgency of the peril. The Greek word for "tackling" (bet-

ter, "furniture") is wider in its range than the English, and includes beds, personal luggage and movables of all kinds. (Comp. Jon. 1.)

(20) When neither sun nor stars in many days appeared.—Before the invention of the compass, the sun and stars were the only guides of sailors who were out of sight of land. Now the sky was overcast, and this guidance failed.

(24) Fear not, Paul.—The words obviously came as an answer to the prayer, prompted by the fear, not of death or danger in itself, but lest the cherished purpose of his heart should be frustrated when it seemed on the verge of attainment. The words that follow imply that his prayer had not been bounded by his own interests, but had included those who were sharing the danger with him. We are reminded, as by the parallelism of contrast, of the words in which Caesar bade the pilot of his ship not to fear, but to commit himself to the wind, seeing that he carried "Caesar and the fortune of Caesar" (**Plutarch, de Fortun. Rom.,** 518).

(26) We must be cast upon a certain island.—This had clearly formed part of the special revelation that had been granted to the apostle. It was more than a conjecture, and the "must" was emphasized as by a prophetic insight into the future.

(27) When the fourteenth night was come. —The time is apparently reckoned from their leaving the Fair Havens. (Comp. verses 18, 19, 33.)

As we were driven up and down in Adria.—The name was used as including more than the Gulf of Venice. So Ptolemy (3:16) speaks of the Adria as washing the south coast of the Peloponnesus and the east coast of Sicily (3:4). (Comp. Jos., **Life**, c. 3.)

The shipmen deemed that they drew near to some country.—The sound of breakers, probably the white lines of foam seen through the darkness, gave rise to this impression. The country which they were nearing could hardly be any other than the eastern extremity of St. Paul's Bay in Malta.

(28) Twenty fathoms.—The Greek noun so rendered was defined as the length of the outstretched arms, from hand to hand, including the chest. It was reckoned as equal to four cubits, i.e., to about six feet.

(29) They cast four anchors out of the stern.—In ancient navigation the anchors commonly were cast from the bow. (In the

916

battle of the Nile, however, Lord Nelson had his ships anchored at the stern, and the fact derives a peculiar interest from the statement that he had been reading Acts 27 on the morning of the engagement.) The result of this operation was that the ship was no longer in motion, and would be found, when the morning came, with her head to the shore.

(30) And as the shipmen were about to flee . . .—The hour of danger called out the natural instinct of self-preservation. It was easy for the sailors to urge that the ship needed anchors fore as well as aft, and, while pretending to be occupied about this, to lower the boat which they had before hoisted on deck (verse 16) and so effect their escape.

(31) Except these abide in the ship . . .—It was obvious that landsmen like the soldiers and the prisoners would be quite unequal to the task of handling a large ship under such critical conditions, and the presence of the sailors was, therefore, from a human point of view, essential to the safety of the others. The action of verse 32 had to be the work of an instant. The boat already was lowered; the sailors were on the point of leaping into it.

(39) A certain creek with a shore.—In Homer and other Greek writers the word rendered here "shore" commonly is used for a flat, sandy beach.

To thrust in the ship.—The word was a quasi-technical one, answering to our "to run the ship aground."

(40) Loosed the rudder bands.—This was the necessary sequel to the previous operation. While the ship was anchored the two large paddle-like rudders with which ancient ships were furnished were lifted up out of the water and lashed with ropes to the ship's side. When the ship was under way again, and the rudders were wanted, the bands were loosed, and the rudders fell into the water.

(41) And falling into a place where two seas met.—At the west end of St. Paul's Bay lies the island of Salmonetta. From their place of anchorage the crew could not have seen that it was an island, and in trying to run the ship on the beach they grounded on a mud-bank between the small island and the coast. The waves swept around the island and met on the bank, and the position of the ship was accordingly one of extreme danger, the prow imbedded in the mud, the stern exposed to the billows.

(42) And the soldiers' counsel was to kill the prisoners.—The vigor of Roman law, which inflicted capital punishment on those who were in charge of prisoners and allowed them to escape (see notes on 12:19; 16:27), explains the apparently wanton cruelty of the proposal. In putting the prisoners to death the soldiers saw the only chance of escaping death themselves.

(43) The swimmers were commanded to plunge in first so as to get to the beach and be in readiness to help their comrades. Paul probably was among the former group (see II Cor. 11:25), and the order itself may well have been suggested by him.

28

(1) Then they knew that the island was called Melita.—The modern Malta was the only island known as Melita by the Greeks and Romans. The gale, which had been blowing for fourteen days since the ship left Crete, would drive her in that direction. The island of Malta was originally a Phoenician colony. It came under the power of Carthage in 402 B.C., and was ceded to Rome in 242 B.C.

(2) The barbarous people . . .—Luke uses the term, as Paul does (Rom. 1:14; I Cor. 14:11), as applicable to all races that did not speak Greek. For him "barbarian" was like the term "native."

(3) And when Paul had gathered a bundle of sticks . . .—The Greek is applied to the dry stalks of herbaceous plants rather than to the branches of trees, and, as such, exactly describes the stout, thorny heather that grows near St. Paul's Bay.

(4) No doubt this man is a murderer.—The natives of Melita, seeing the guards and Paul's chains, and ignorant of the prisoner's crime, and with their rough notions of the divine government of the world, rushed to the conclusion that they were looking on an example of God's vengeance against murder.

(6) The verb for "swollen" implies literally "inflammation." The miraculous escape naturally made an even stronger impression on the minds of the Melitese than what had seemed a supernatural judgment. Their thoughts may have traveled quickly to the attributes of the deities who, like Apollo or AEsculapius, were depicted as subduing serpents. The sudden change of belief may be noted as presenting a kind of inverted parallelism with that which had come over the people of Lystra. (See notes on 14:11, 19.)

(7) The chief man of the island.—The term probably designated the prefect or governor of the island. In the time of Cicero (**In Verr.** 4:18) Melita was included in the "province" of Sicily, and if that arrangement continued, Publius would be the "legate" of the Sicilian proconsul.

Lodged us three days courteously.—Reference here is probably to a chosen few, among whom Paul, Luke, and, most likely, the centurion Julius, were included.

(8) Lay sick of a fever and a bloody flux.—Literally, "with fevers and dysentery," both words being used by Luke with professional precision. The plural, "fevers," probably indicates the attacks of a recurrent fever, and its combination with dysentery would, according to Hippocrates, who also uses the plural form (**Aph.** 6:3), make the case more than usually critical.

Prayed, and laid his hands on him.—The close sequence of the work of the healing upon the escape from the serpent's bite reminds us of the juxtaposition of the two promises of Mark 16:18.

(10) Who also honoured us with many honours.—The word was especially applied, both in Greek and Latin, to the honorarium paid to the physician, and its use here is accordingly characteristic of Luke's calling. (Comp. Ecclus. 38:1.) In addition to these gifts of courtesy, the things that were wanted for their voyage—clothing, provisions, and the like—were supplied freely at their departure.

(11) After three months.—See notes on 27:2, 9, 27. The Fast, falling on the 10th of Tisri, which has been calculated as falling in that year on September 24, was passed, we are not told how long, when the ship left the Fair Havens (27:9). Then came the "fourteen days" of 27:27, bringing us to the end of October. Three months from the event of shipwreck carries us to the beginning of February. The crew of the Alexandrian ship naturally was anxious to take the earliest opportunity for pressing on to the destination. The fact of wintering in the island was normal to Malta, which lay on the usual line of the voyage from Alexandria to Italy.

Whose sign was Castor and Pollux.—The two sons of Zeus and Loda were regarded as the guardian deities of sailors. (See Horace, **Od.**, 1:3.2, 1:12, 25.) In Greek mythology, Zeus had rewarded their brotherly devotion by placing them among the stars as the **Gemini**, which were connected with the month of May in the signs of the

Zodiac, and Poseidon (Neptune) had given them power over the winds and waves that they might assist the shipwrecked. The figureheads of the Greek and Roman ships commonly were placed both at the prow and the stern.

(12) And landing at Syracuse . . .—The city, famous for the memorable siege during the Peloponnesian war, and at all times taking its place among the most flourishing towns of Sicily, was about eighty miles from Malta, and might be reached, accordingly, in from twenty-four to thirty-six hours. Ships bound from Alexandria to Italy commonly put in there.

(13) Came to Rhegium.—This town was in Italy, on the southern opening of the Straits of Messina. Ships from Alexandria to Italy commonly touched there, and Suetonius (**Tit.** c. 5) relates that the Emperor Titus, taking the same course as Paul, put in there on his way from Judaea to Puteoli, and then to Rome. Caligula began the construction of a harbor at Rhegium for the corn ships of Egypt; but this work, which the Jewish historian notes as the one "great and kingly undertaking" of his reign, was left unfinished (**Ant.** 19:2, § 5).

The south wind blew.—The south wind was directly in their favor, and they sailed without danger between the famous rocks of Scylla and the whirlpool of Charybdis.

We came the next day to Puteoli.—As the distance was about one hundred eighty miles, the ship clearly was making good way before the wind. Puteoli lies in a sheltered recess, forming the northern part of the Bay of Naples. It was at this time the chief port of Rome, and, in particular, the great emporium for the corn ships of Alexandria, upon which the people of Rome largely depended for their food. A pier on twenty-five arches was thrown into the sea for the protection of the harbor. But a few months prior to Paul's arrival it had been raised to the dignity of a **colonia** (Tac. **Ann.** 14:27).

(14) Where we found brethren.—The fact is significant as showing, in the absence of any distinct record, the extent to which the new society had been spreading silently. Who had been the agents in preaching the Gospel there we only can conjecture, but a city which was **en rapport**, like Puteoli, with both Alexandria and Rome, may have received it from either. See 18:24; Heb. 13:24. According to Josephus (**Ant.** 17:12, § 1), there was a considerable Jewish element in the population of Puteoli.

Were desired to tarry with them seven days.—See notes on 20:6; 21:4. The kindness of the centurion is seen once more in the permission which made compliance with the request possible.

And so we went toward Rome.—A journey of thirty-three miles from Puteoli would bring them to Sinuessa, where they would join the great Appian Road, running from Rome to Bundusium. From Sinuessa to Terracina they traveled fifty-seven miles, at which point they would have to choose between two modes of travel—the circuitous road around the Pontine Marshes, or the more direct line of the canal. Both routes met at Appii Forum, eighteen miles from Terracina. Nearly every stage of the journey is connected with some historical or legendary fact in classical antiquity.

(15) And from thence, when the brethren heard of us . . .—The seven days at Puteoli had given ample time for the news of the apostle's arrival to reach the disciples at Rome. All had probably read or heard the epistle to the Romans. It is clear from the salutations in Rom. 16 that the decree of Claudius banishing the Jews from Rome had been rescinded or allowed to lapse. The Jews had settled in their old quarters in the trans-Tiberine region and, perhaps, on the island of the Tiber. The influence of Poppaea was probably in their favor (see note on 26:32).

Appii forum, and The three taverns.—The latter town was ten miles from the former, and therefore thirty-three from Rome. It is mentioned often by Cicero in his letters, and appears to have been on the Via Appia, at a point where a road from Antium joined it (**Ad Att.** 2:10). It was, accordingly, a town of considerable importance.

He thanked God, and took courage.—The words imply a previous tendency to anxiety and fear. Were those Roman disciples to whom he had written so warmly still safe and well, and sound in the faith? Had persecution driven them from their homes, or had the Judaizers perverted their belief? The language of Rom. 1:10-12 shows how prominent they were in his thoughts and prayers. To these questions the arrival of the disciples was a full and satisfying answer, and the apostle resumed his journey with an eager and buoyant hope.

(16) And when we came to Rome.—Approaching the city, Paul would pass the cemetery of the Jews of Rome, lying on the east of the Appian Way. He would see,

perhaps, even then, the beginning of the Catacombs, where the Christians, who would not burn their dead like the heathen, and who were excluded from the cemetery of the Jews, laid their dead to sleep in peace. Continuing his journey, the apostle and his companions would pass under the Arch of Drusus, and enter the city by the Porta Capena, proceeding from there to the Palace of the Caesars, which stood on the Palatine Hill, and looked down, on one side upon the Forum, on the other upon the Circus Maximus.

Paul was suffered to dwell by himself.—The favor shown to Paul may have been due to the influence of the centurion Julius, from whom he had, from the first, received so many marks of courtesy. The manner in which Luke speaks of his "dwelling by himself" implies that he went at once, instead of accepting the hospitality of any friends, into a hired apartment.

With a soldier that kept him.—The prisoner was fastened by a chain to the soldier who kept guard over him, and so the apostle speaks of his "chain" (verse 20), of being a "prisoner" (Eph. 3:1; 4:1), an ambassador in **chains** (Eph. 6:20), of his "bonds" (Phil. 1:7, 13, 16; Col. 4, 18).

(20) The hope for which Paul suffered was twofold: (1) the expectation of the Messiah as bringing in a kingdom of heaven which was cherished by every Israelite; (2) the hope of a resurrection from the dead, which he proclaimed as attested by the Resurrection which proved (Rom. 1:3, 4) that Jesus was the Christ, the Son of God.

(22) We desire . . . as concerning this sect . . .—The speakers clearly had heard enough of the prisoner to identify him with the sect of the Nazarene, but they treat him personally with respect, probably due in part to the favor which the authorities had shown him, and wish for an authoritative exposition of his views. The Christians of Rome had obviously, even if they were Jews, withdrawn from the Jewish quarter, and the residents in that quarter knew of them only by reports. What was the nature of those reports we only can conjecture. They were, as the speakers say, "everywhere spoken against." The darker slanders included stories of Thyestean (i.e., cannibal) banquets and licentious orgies; "atrocious and shameful crimes, convicted by the hatred of mankind" (Tacitus, **Ann.** 15:44); new and criminal superstition (Suetonius, **Nero,** c. 16). Even then there may have been caricatures like that which was found among the **graffiti** of the Palace of the Caesars, representing Alexamenos, a Christian convert, worshiping his god, in the form of a crucified human figure with an ass's head. (Comp. Tertillian, **Apol.,** c. 16; Jos., **Cont. Apion** 2:7; **Tac., Hist.** 5:4.)

(23) There came many to him into his lodging.—The "lodging" was probably the "hired house," or apartment, of verse 30. (Comp. Philem. 22.) The discussion which followed obviously could only be given in outline. The address at Antioch in Pisidia (13:16-42), and the arguments of the epistles to the Galatians and the Romans, enable us to form a general estimate of its probable contents.

(25-27) The words (Isa. 6:9) had been cited by our Lord as describing the spiritual state of the Jews of Palestine (see Matt. 13:13; Mark 4:12; Luke 8:10). John (12:40) reproduces them as embodying the solution of the apparent failure of our Lord's personal ministry. What was true of the Jews of Jerusalem was true also of those of Rome. In both there was a willful blindness and deafness to that which ought to have produced conviction and conversion. (Comp. Rom. 11:25.)

(30) And Paul dwelt two whole years . . .— The word translated "hired house" means rather a "lodging" (as in verse 23) or "apartment," and does not imply that he occupied a whole house. He was a prisoner and therefore not allowed to go out to preach, but his friends were allowed free access to him. In this way there was probably a wider and more effectual opening for his personal influence than if he had spoken publicly, and so exposed himself to the risk of an organized antagonism. What seemed at first a hindrance to his work was so ordered, as he afterward acknowledged, that it worked "rather unto the furtherance of the gospel" (Phil. 1:12).

(31) No man forbidding him.—The fact is interesting as showing the attitude of the Roman empire to the new faith. The rulers were not as yet alarmed at the thought of the widespread secret organization of the Christian Society, and the influence of Seneca and Burrus may have contributed to this policy of toleration. The history closes somewhat abruptly. It may have been the intention of the writer to continue his narrative so as to include Paul's release and subsequent journey eastward, but he was in some way hindered. It is possible, on the other hand, that Theophilus, as an Italian convert (see note on 1:1) may have known what had passed in Rome during the apostle's first sojourn there, or subsequently, and that Luke did not aim at more than setting before his friend the stages by which Paul had been brought to the imperial city.

ROMANS

1

(1-7) In writing to the Romans, a church to which he was personally unknown, and which might be supposed, as far as it was Jewish, to be prejudiced against him, the apostle delivers with somewhat more than usual solemnity his credentials and commission. A divinely appointed minister of a system of things predicted by the prophets, and culminating in the revelation—divinely ordained and attested—of Jesus Christ, he greets the Roman Christians, themselves also divinely called. The repetition of terms signifying calling conveys the idea: "I and you alike are all members of one grand scheme, which is not of human invention, but determined and ordained of God—the divine clue, as it were, running through the history of the world."

(1) **Servant.**—More strictly, here as else-where in the New Testament, **slave**; and yet it is not wrongly translated "servant," because the compulsory and degrading side of service is not put forward.

Separated.—Comp. especially Acts 13:2, where human instruments are employed to carry out the divine will. The reference here is to the historical fact of the selection of Paul to be an apostle; Gal. 1:15 refers rather to the more distant act of divine predestination.

Unto the gospel of God.—The ambiguous genitive seems to mean "the gospel which proceeds from God," of which God is the **author**, not of which God is the **object**.

(2) **Which he had promised in the holy scriptures.**—There is a nicety of meaning expressed by the absence of the article before this last phrase. A slight stress is thus thrown upon "holy." The Scriptures are "holy" as containing the promises referred to in the text, and others like them. The writings in which the promises are contained, like the promises themselves, their fulfillment, and the consequences which follow from them, all are part of the same exceptional divine scheme.

Prophets.—The wider sense of the word is used, including not only Samuel (Acts 3:24), but also Moses and David, and all who are regarded as having prophesied the Messiah.

(4) **According to the spirit of holiness.**— In antithesis to "according to the flesh," and therefore coming where we should expect "in His divine nature." And yet there is a difference. The spirit of Christ is human, for Christ took upon Him our nature in all its parts. It is human; and yet it is in it more especially that the divinity resides. It is in it that the "Godhead dwells bodily," and the presence of the Godhead is seen in the peculiar and exceptional "holiness" by which it is characterized. The "spirit," therefore, or that portion of His being to which Paul gives the name, in Christ is the connecting link between the human and the divine, and shares alike in both. It is the divine "enshrined" in the human, or the human penetrated and energized by the divine. The junction of the human and divine must necessarily evade exact definition, and to carry such definition too far would be to misrepresent the meaning of the apostle. (Comp. I Tim. 3:16; I Pet. 3:18.)

It should be observed that this antithesis between the human and divine nature in Christ is not intended here to carry with it any disparagement of the former. Rather the apostle wishes to bring out the completeness and fullness of the dignity of Christ, as exhibited on both its sides. He is at once the Jewish Messiah (and with the Jewish section of the church at Rome this fact would carry great weight) and the Son of God.

By the resurrection from the dead.—The particular act in which the Sonship of Christ was most conspicuously ratified and confirmed was His resurrection from the dead, a manifestation of transcendent and divine power.

(5) **Grace and apostleship.**—Grace is here divine favor manifested in various ways, but especially in his conversion. Apostleship includes all those privileges which Paul possessed as an apostle; grace is all those privileges that he possessed as a Christian. The meaning tends in the direction of that particular object which is expressed in the next clause. The light in which the apostle valued most the gifts that had been bestowed upon him was in that they enabled him to preach the Gospel to the Gentiles.

Faith.—Faith is not here equivalent to "the faith"—a positive body of doctrine received and believed—but, in its strict sense, that active habit and attitude of mind by which the Christian shows his devotion and loyalty to Christ, and his total dependence on Him (Gal. 2:19).

921

(7) In Rome.—See verse 15, and the various notes on chaps. 15 and 16.

(8) I thank my God through Jesus Christ.—Christ is, as it were, the medium through whom God has been brought into close relation to man. Hence all intercourse between God and man is represented as passing through Him. He is not only the divine **Logos** by whom God is revealed to man, but He is also the Head of humanity by whom the tribute of thanks and praise is offered to God.

Throughout the whole world.—A hyperbole is the more natural as the apostle is speaking of Rome, the center and metropolis of the world as he knew it.

(9) With my spirit.—"Spirit" is with Paul the highest part or faculty in the nature of man. It is the seat of his higher consciousness—that by which he communicates with God. The "spirit" of man, when brought into contact with the Spirit of God, is capable of a truly religious life; but apart from this influence, it is apt to fall under the dominion of the "flesh"—i.e., of those evil appetites and desires to which man is exposed by his physical organization.

(11) That I may impart unto you some spiritual gift.—These are such gifts as would naturally flow to one Christian (or to many collectively) from the personal presence and warm sympathy of another, and in Paul's case heightened in proportion to the wealth and elevation of his own spiritual consciousness and life. His head and his heart alike are full to overflowing, and he longs to impart some of these riches to the Romans. Inasmuch as he regards all his own religious advancement and experience as the result of the Spirit working within him, he calls the fruits of that advancement and experience "spiritual gifts." All the apostolic gifts—miraculous as well as nonmiraculous—would be included in this expression. Indeed, we may believe that the apostle would hardly draw the distinction that we do between the two kinds. Both alike were in his eyes the direct gift of the Spirit.

To the end ye may be established—i.e., that they may grow and be confirmed and strengthened in the faith. As a rule the great outpouring of spiritual gifts was at the first foundation of a church. Paul was not the founder of the church at Rome, but he hoped to be able to contribute to its advance and consolidation.

(12) That is, that I may be comforted.— He does not wish it to be implied that it is for him only to impart, and for them only

to receive. He will not assume any such air of superiority. In the impulse of the moment, and in the expansiveness of his own heart, he had seemed to put it so; but his real meaning was that they should receive mutual comfort and edification.

Comforted together with you.—The Greek word has rather the sense of "encouraged," though the idea of "comfort" is also contained in it. The apostle looks to obtain benefit from his intercourse with the Roman Christians. He expects that their faith will help to increase his own. There is a truth underlying the apostle's courtesy which is not mere compliment. The most advanced Christian will receive something from the humblest.

(13) Let.—This is an archaism for "hindered," "prevented." It is hardly worthwhile to speculate on the causes that may have hindered the apostle from going to Rome. In a life like his there may have been many.

(14) To the Greeks, and to the Barbarians. —The apostle does not intend to place the Romans any more in the one class than in the other. He merely means all mankind, no matter what their nationality or culture. The classification is exhaustive. It may be remembered that the Greeks called all who did not speak their own language "Barbarians," and the apostle, writing from Greece, adopts their point of view.

Wise and foolish.—(Comp. 1 Cor. 1:20, 26-28.) The Gospel was at first most readily received by the poor and unlearned, but it did not therefore follow that culture and education were by any means excluded. Paul himself was a conspicuous instance to the contrary. And so, in the next century, the church which began with such leaders as Ignatius and Polycarp could number among its members before the century was out Irenaeus, Tertullian, Clement of Alexandria, Hippolytus, and Origen—the last, the most learned man of his time.

(16) The apostle will not be ashamed of his mission, even in the metropolis of the world. He cannot be ashamed of a scheme so beneficent and so grand. The preaching of the cross is the cardinal point of the whole Gospel.

Of Christ.—These words are missing in the oldest MSS.

Power of God.—A powerful agency put forth by God Himself—the lever, as it were, by which He would move the world.

Unto salvation.—The object of this Gospel is salvation—to open the blessings of the Messianic kingdom to mankind.

To the Jew first.—Here again we have another exhaustive division of mankind. "Greek" is intended to cover all who are not "Jews." Before the apostle was making what may be called the secular classification of men; here he makes the religious classification. From his exceptional privileges the Jew was literally placed in a class alone. They have an "advantage" (Rom. 3:1, 2). To them belong the special privileges of the first dispensation (9:4,5). They are the original stock of the olive tree, in comparison with which the Gentiles are only as wild branches grafted in (11:17). It was only right that the salvation promised to their forefathers should be offered first to them, as it is also said expressly in the fourth gospel that "salvation is of the Jews" (John 4:22).

(17) The righteousness of God.—By this is not meant an attribute of the divine nature, as if the essential righteousness of God were first made known through the Gospel. Paul goes on to show in verses 19 and 20 that so much at least of the nature of God might be known without any supernatural revelation. "Of God" means "which proceeds from God." And the "righteousness" which thus "proceeds from God" is that condition of righteousness in man into which he enters by his participation in the Messianic kingdom. The whole object of the coming of the Messiah was to make men "righteous" before God. This was done more by the death of Christ upon the cross, which, as we learn from 3:24-26, had the effect of making God "propitious" toward men. The benefit of this act is secured to all who make good their claim to be considered members of the Messianic kingdom by a loyal adhesion to the Messiah. Such persons are treated as if they were "righteous," though the righteousness that is thus attributed to them is not any actual merit of their own, but an ideal condition in which they are placed by God. This is the doctrine of justification by faith.

Revealed.—God's purpose of thus justifying men is in process of being revealed or declared in the Gospel. It is revealed theoretically in the express statements of the way in which man may be justified; it is revealed practically in the heartfelt acceptance of those statements and the change of life which they involved. To the Romans the moment of revelation was that in which they first heard the Gospel. Paul wishes them to know the full significance—the philosophy, as it might be called—of that which they had heard.

From faith to faith.—It is by faith that man first lays hold on the Gospel, and its latest product is a heightened and intensified faith. Apart from faith, the Gospel remains null and void for the individual. But when it has been once realized and taken home to the man's self, its tendency is to confirm and strengthen that faculty by which it was apprehended. (See Luke 17:5.)

The just shall live by faith.—The words are part of the consolatory answer which the prophet Habakkuk receives in the stress of the Chaldean invasion. Though his irresistible hosts sweep over the land, the righteous man who puts his trust in God shall live. Perhaps Paul intended the words "by faith" to be taken with "the just" rather than as they stand in the English—"The just by faith shall live."

The apostle uses the word "faith" in his own peculiar and pregnant sense. But this is natural from the way in which it was used by Habakkuk. The intense personal trust and reliance which the Jew felt in the God of his fathers is directed by the Christian to Christ, and is further developed into an active energy of devotion.

Faith, as understood by Paul, is not a purely intellectual process; neither is it merely a passive dependence upon an Unseen Power. But it is a further stage of feeling developed out of these—a current of emotion setting strongly in the direction of its object, an ardent and vital apprehension of that object, and a firm and loyal attachment to it.

(18) As a preliminary stage to this revelation of justification and of faith, there is another, which is its opposite—a revelation and disclosure of divine wrath. The proof is seen in the present condition both of the Gentile (verses 18-32) and Jewish (2:1-3:20) worlds.

Revealed.—The revelation of righteousness is, while the apostle writes, being made in the Person of Christ and in the salvation offered by Him. The revelation of wrath is to be inferred from the actual condition of degradation in which sin leaves its votaries.

Ungodliness and unrighteousness.—These two words stand respectively for offenses against religion and offenses against morality.

Who hold the truth in unrighteousness.—Conscience tells them what is right, but the will, actuated by wicked motives, prevents them from obeying its dictates. "The truth" is their knowledge of right, from whatever source it is derived, which finds expression in conscience. "Hold" (see "hinder" in II Thess. 2:6, 7) has the force of **to hold down,** or **suppress.**

(19) The apostle goes on to show how the Gentiles came to have such a knowledge of right, and how they repressed and contravened it. They had it, because all the knowledge ("natural religion") that mankind generally possessed of God they also possessed. So much as could be known without special revelation they had imprinted upon their consciences.

(20) Even his eternal power and Godhead.—This is a summary expression of those attributes which, apart from revelation, were embodied in the ideal of God. Of these, "power" is the most obvious. Paul does not go into the questions as to the other qualities which are to be inferred as existing in the Author of nature; but he sums them up under a name that might be used as well by a pagan philosopher as by a Christian—the attributes included in the one term "Godhead." What is meant is "divine nature."

(21) They knew enough of God to know that thanks and praise were due to Him; but neither of these did they offer. They put aside the natural instinct of adoration, and fell to speculations. Starting with two things —a portion of enlightenment on the one hand, and the natural tendency of the human mind to error on the other—the latter prevailed, and the former became eclipsed.

(22, 23) Relying upon their own wisdom, they wandered further and further from true wisdom, falling into the contradiction of supposing that the eternal and immutable Essence of God could be represented by the perishable figures of man, bird, quadruped, or insect. They **were made fools.** It is not merely that they expose their real folly, but that folly is itself judicially inflicted by God as a punishment for the first step of declension from Him.

(24-32) Hence they fell into a still lower depth, for in anger at their perversion of the truth God refrained from checking their downward course. He left them to follow their own evil bent. Their idolatry developed into shameless immorality and unnatural crimes. At last the extreme limit was reached. As they voluntarily forsook God, so He forsook them. They ran through the whole catalog of sins, and the cup of their iniquity was full.

The introduction of the doxology in verse 25 is due to an impulse of reverential feeling. Shocked at the language which he finds himself using, and at the connection in which the most holy name has been mentioned, the apostle turns aside for a moment to testify to his own humble adoration.

(28) To retain God in their knowledge.—The word for "knowledge" here means exact, advanced, thorough knowledge. They refused to hold the true idea of God so as to grow and increase in the knowledge of it.

Those things which are not convenient.—That which is unbecoming, disgraceful.

Fornication.—This word is wanting in the best MSS, as also the word "implacable" in verse 31.

Wickedness ... maliciousness.—These two words appear to be related together, so that the latter expresses the vicious disposition to do hurt to others, the former rather the active exercise of it. Similar catalogs of sin are given in other of Paul's epistles, e.g., II Cor. 12:20; Gal. 5:19; Eph. 5:3, 4; I Tim. 1:9, 10; II Tim. 3:2.

Murder, debate.—The apostle means "full of murderous thoughts." Debate is the spirit of strife and contention generally.

(30) Despiteful, proud, boasters.—The three words correspond to the distinction between act, thought, and word. The first implies distinctly insolence in outward bearing; the second is a strong self-esteem mixed with contempt for others; the third is used especially of braggadocio in language.

(31) Without understanding—i.e., without moral or spiritual understanding; incapable of discriminating between right and wrong, expedient and inexpedient.

Without natural affection.—The affection founded upon natural relationship—e.g., between parent and child, husband and wife, brother and sister. In illustration of this particular expression, we may remember that infanticide and divorce were very common at this period.

(32) Knowing.—The word again connotes full or thorough knowledge. They show that it is no mere momentary yielding to the force of temptation or of passion, but a radical perversion of conscience and reason, by the fact that they not only practice such things themselves but commend and applaud those who practice them.

2

The judgment of God will be according to the strictest laws of justice. It will reward the good and punish the wicked. Neither Jew nor Gentile will have any advantage. The Gentile cannot plead his freedom from law, for he has a law written in his conscience; the Jew cannot plead his enjoyment of the Law, for he has broken all its provisions. These old ethnological distinctions are quite confused. The real distinction between men is purely spiritual.

(1) The proposition with which the chapter begins, though general in form, is particular in substance. When the apostle says, "Whosoever thou art that judgest," he really means the Jews. This special application is suggested rather than expressed. This is eminently characteristic of the apostle's large and comprehensive way of handling history and the phenomena of humanity.

(2) We are sure.—There is still a strong allusion to the way in which the Jew was apt to fall back upon his privileges. The Jews, it seems, had an idea that the Gentiles only would be judged, while they would be able to claim admission into the Messianic kingdom as theirs by right of birth.

According to truth.—The principle on which God's judgment will proceed will be that of truth or reality, as opposed to appearance, worldly status, formal precedence, etc. It will ask what a man is, not to what race he belongs.

(4, 5) Comp. Exod. 34:6, 7. The moral character and relation to His people thus attributed to the Deity was a feature which especially distinguished the religion of the Old Testament from that of the surrounding heathen nations.

The one condition upon which the goodness of God will come into operation they directly contravene. Instead of being penitent, they are impenitent, and therefore the wrath which they have been accumulating against themselves remains unremoved. It is only waiting for the day of judgment to discharge itself upon them.

(6) The apostle here lays down with unmistakable definiteness and precision the doctrine that **works**, what a man has **done**, the moral tenor of his life, will be the standard by which he will be judged at the last day. How is this to be reconciled with the main theme of the epistle, the doctrine of justification by **faith**? In the doctrine of final retribution there is no opposition between faith and works; in the doctrine of justification there is no opposition between works and faith. In the former, works may be regarded as the evidence of faith; in the latter, they may be regarded as its natural and necessary outcome. Works may be sincere, or they may be hypocritical. They may have an inward foundation in the heart, or they may not. And the apostle looks at them in both lights, according as the course of his argument requires it.

(7) Before the words "eternal life," at the end of the verse, we must supply "He will render." The stress is upon the words "by patient continuance in well doing."

(8) But unto them . . . —In the original Greek the construction is changed. At the end of verse 7 is an accusative "(he will render) eternal life"; here we have the nominative: "(there shall be) tribulation and anguish" (verse 9).

Indignation and wrath.—The Greek equivalents for these two words are distinguished as the settled angry feeling from the passionate outbreak of anger.

(11) Respect of persons means regard for the external circumstances of a man as opposed to his internal condition, and here, especially, regard for the circumstances of birth and race. The essential equality of Jew and Gentile before God is not affected by the precedence of the former in point of time or order, whether as regards punishment or reward.

(12) Jew and Gentile alike will be judged, each by the method proper to his case: the Jew by the written Law against which he has sinned, the Gentile by the unwritten law of conscience against which he too has sinned. Here, as in the phrases which follow—"by law," "the hearers of law," "the doers of law," "the Gentiles which have not law," etc.—the article is wrongly inserted. Its absence shows that the apostle had in mind, not the particular Mosaic law, but the abstraction of law. "Behind the concrete representation—the Mosaic law itself—Paul sees an imperious principle, an overwhelming presence, antagonistic to grace, to liberty, to spirit, and (in some aspects) even to life—abstract law, which, though the Mosaic ordinances are its most signal and complete embodiment, nevertheless is not exhausted therein, but exerts its crushing power over the conscience in diverse manifestations" (Lightfoot).

(13) The present verse is explanatory of that which precedes. And the argument follows—the apostle digressing for a moment to pursue this point to its conclusion—that this exemption may apply quite as much to Gentile as to Jew.

(14) A parenthesis begins here. Verse 16 refers back to the main subject of the paragraph, and not to the particular point on which the apostle digresses in verses 14 and 15, the virtual operation of law among the Gentiles as well as Jews.

By nature means spontaneously, not acting under the coercion of any external rule, but simply by the promptings of their own conscience left to itself.

The things contained in the law.—In this one instance the article is used, meaning, however, not the Law of Moses, but "of this law," or "of such law"—i.e., the ideal law spoken of just before.

(15) The work of the law.—The practical effect or realization of the law—written in their hearts as the original Law was written upon the tables of stone. (Comp. Jer. 31:33; II Cor. 3:3.)

Also bearing witness.—There is a double witness; their actions speak for them externally, and conscience speaks for them internally.

The mean while.—Literally, **between themselves**—i.e., with mutual interchange, the thoughts of the heart or different motions of conscience sometimes taking the part of advocate, sometimes of accuser.

(16) This verse cannot refer to what immediately precedes. There the apostle is referring to the daily process that goes on whenever doubtful actions are submitted to the law of conscience; here he is speaking expressly of the final judgment held by God and not by man.

According to my gospel.—To what is it that the Gospel, as preached by Paul, testifies? It may be either to the simple fact that God will judge the secrets of men, or to the particular law or standard by which He will judge them. Probably the former is the preferable explanation.

(17) For "behold," a decisive consensus of the best MSS has "but if." Adopting "but if," the answering clause of the sentence is to be found in the question, "Teachest thou not thyself?" in verse 21. (The connecting particle "therefore" at the beginning of the same verse is merely resumptive.) Turning to the Jew, the apostle breaks out into indignant and vehement exclamation. The different features of the picture crowd into his mind to point the contrast between what the Jew claimed to be and what he was.

(24) As it is written—from the LXX version of Isa. 52:5. The sense of the original is that the name of God is dishonored by the enslavement and oppression of His people. (Comp. II Sam. 12:14; Ezek. 36:22, 23.) The apostle is not careful as to the

particular context from which he draws. He knew that he was giving the substance of Scripture, and he takes the aptest words that occur to him at the moment. The formula amounts to little more than "in the language of Scripture." The intention, as so frequently with Paul, seems to be divided between proof and illustration.

(25-29) This section forms a connecting link with the opening of the next chapter. The characteristic mark of the Jew has two sides—the one outward and formal, the other inward and real. Its essence consists in the latter, and without this inward circumcision the outward profits nothing. It is not necessary to be born a Jew to possess it.

3

(1, 2) The apostle asks what is the real value of these apparent advantages. He is about to answer the question fully, as he does later in 9:4, 5; but after stating the first point, he goes off upon a difficulty raised by this (verse 3), and does not return to complete what he had begun. One real and solid advantage on the part of the Jew was that he was made the direct recipient of the divine revelation. This privilege of his is not annulled by the defection of a part of the people. It rests not upon the precarious fidelity of men, but upon the infallible promise of God. Yet is not the ultimate triumph of that promise any excuse for those who have set it at nought. They will be punished just the same, and rightly.

(4) Good is, in some way inscrutable to us, educed out of evil. This is clearly foreseen by God and forms part of His design, though so as not to interfere with the free will of man. Psalm 51, in which the quotation occurs, is commonly (in accordance with the heading), though perhaps wrongly, ascribed to David after his sin with Bathsheba. The effect of this sin is to throw out into the strongest relief the justice of the sentence by which it is followed and punished. Paul adopts the rendering of the LXX, who make the last word passive instead of active (as the original), thus making it apply, not to the sentence given by God, but to the imaginary trial to which by a figure of speech that sentence itself is supposed to be submitted.

(5) But if our unrighteousness.—If the sin (here the unbelief) of man tends only to vindicate (commends or establishes) the righteousness of God, why should that sin be punished? The mere raising of such a question requires an apology; it is only as a man might speak about man that he dares to utter such a thought. That, too, is an impossible objection, for if it held good there could not be any judgment. All sin would thus cease to be sinful, and there would be nothing to hinder us from adopting the principle that is so slanderously attributed to us—that it is lawful to do evil that good may come. (See verses 6-8.)

(9) Once more the argument returns to the main emphasis of verses 1 and 2, and at last the apostle asserts distinctly and categorically what he had already proved indirectly—that the Jew is wholly as bad as the Gentile.

(10-18) The verses are a striking instance of the way in which the apostle weaves together passages taken from different sources. It also affords an example of the corruptions in the text of the Old Testament to which this practice gave rise. The quotations have different degrees of appositeness, as far as they may be considered probative rather than illustrative. The first, from Psalm 14, is couched in such general terms as to be directly in point. The second and third, from Psalms 5 and 140, are aimed specially against the oppressors of the psalmist; and so, too, the fourth, from Psalm 10, but in a more general and abstract form. The fifth indicates the moral degradation among Isaiah's contemporaries that had led to the Captivity, while the last, from Psalm 36, is an expression applied particularly to the wicked.

(19) In order to bring home this testimony of Scripture more directly to the Jews, and to prevent any subterfuge by which they might attempt to shift the reference from themselves on to the Gentiles, the apostle calls attention to the fact that the Law—i.e., the Old Testament, from which he has been quoting—speaks especially to those to whom it was given.

(20) All mankind alike owe the penalty for their sins, **because** not even the Law can protect its votaries. It has no power to justify. All it can do is to expose in its true colors the sinfulness of sin.

Knowledge of sin.—In the state anterior to law, man is not supposed to know what is sinful and what is not. Conscience, gradually developed, comes in to give him some insight into the distinction, but the full knowledge of right and wrong, in all its details, is reserved for the introduction of positive law. Law has, however, only this

enlightening faculty; it holds the mirror up to guilt, but it cannot remove it.

(21, 22) This then introduces the solemn enunciation, repeated more fully from 1:16, 17, of the great subject of the epistle—the declaration of that new scheme by which, through Christ, God had removed the guilt which the Law (whether Jewish or any other) could not remove.

(21) The righteousness of God—i.e., "bestowed by God," "wrought by Him," as 1:17. The reference is again, here as there, to the root-conception and condition of the Messianic kingdom.

Without the law.—In complete independence of any law, though borne witness to by the Law of Moses. The new system is one into which the idea of law does not enter.

Is manifested.—It has been, and continues to be, manifested. The initial moment is that of the appearance of Christ upon earth. The scheme which then began is still evolving itself.

Being witnessed.—The apostle does not lose sight of the preparatory function of the older dispensation, and of its radical affinity to the new. (See notes on 1:16, 17.)

(23) All have sinned, and come short.—Strictly, **all sinned.** The apostle looks back upon an act done in past time under the old legal dispensation, without immediate reference to the present. He then goes on to say that the result of that act—as distinct from the act itself—continues on into the present. The result is that mankind, in a body, as he now sees them, and before they come within the range of the new Christian system, fall short of, miss, or fail to obtain, the glory of God.

Glory of God.—What is this glory? It is probably something which is capable of being conferred in the present, such as the glory which comes from the favor and approval of God. This favor and approval Jew and Gentile alike before had failed to obtain, but it was now opened to all who became members of the Messianic kingdom.

(24) By his grace.—The **means** by which justification is wrought is the death and atonement of Christ; its **ulterior** cause is the grace of God, or free readmission into His favor, which He accords to man.

Redemption.—Literally, **ransoming.** The notion of ransom contains in itself the ideas of a bondage, a deliverance, and the payment of an equivalent as the means of that deliverance. The bondage is the state of sin and of guilt, with the expectation of punishment; the deliverance is the removal of this state, and the opening, in its stead, of a prospect of eternal happiness and glory; the equivalent paid by Christ is the shedding of His own blood. This last is the pivot upon which the whole idea of redemption turned. It is, therefore, clear that the redemption of the sinner is an act wrought objectively, and, in the first instance, independently of any change of condition in him, though such a change is involved in the appropriation of the efficacy of that act to himself. It cannot be explained as a purely subjective process wrought in the sinner through the influence of Christ's death. There is, if it may be so said, in the death of Christ something which determines the will of God, as well as something which determines the will of man.

The doctrine of the atonement thus stated is not peculiar to Paul, and did not originate with him. (See Matt. 20:28; Mark 10:45; Heb. 9:15; I Pet. 1:18, 19, 2:24; I John 2:2.)

(25, 26) The death of Christ had a twofold object or final cause: it was to be, like the sacrifices of the old covenant, an offering propitiatory to God and actualized in the believer through faith; it was to demonstrate the righteousness of God by showing that sin would entail punishment, though it might not be punished in the person of the sinner. His death served for the vindication of the retributive justice of God, at the same time that a way to escape from its consequences was opened through the justification of the believer.

(25) A propitiation.—There is a remarkable use of the same Greek word in the LXX to express the **mercy-seat,** i.e., the lid or covering of the Ark which was sprinkled by the high priest with the blood of the victim on the Day of Atonement. Some have thought that there is a reference to this here. Christ is the **mercy-seat** of the New Covenant. It is upon Him, as it were, that the divine grace, drawn forth by His own atoning blood, resides. (Comp. Heb. 9:11, 12.) There seem to be, however, on the whole, reasons for supplying rather the idea of "sacrifice," which is more entirely in keeping with the context, and is especially supported by the two phrases "whom God hath set forth" (i.e., exhibited **publicly,** whereas the Ark was confined to the secrecy of the Holy of Holies), and "in his blood." We should translate, therefore, **a propitiatory** or **expiatory (sacrifice).**

In his blood.—It seems best not to join these words with "through faith," but to refer them to the main word of the sentence: "Whom God set forth by the shedding of His blood to be a propitiatory offering through faith." It was in the shedding of the blood that the essence of the atonement exhibited upon the cross consisted.

(26) To declare.—Sins in times anterior to the Christian revelation were not wiped away and dismissed altogether, but rather "passed over" or "overlooked." This was due to the forbearance of God, who, as it were, **suspended** the execution of His vengeance. Now the apostle shows by the death of Christ that justice that had apparently slept was vindicated. Thus God appeared at once as just or righteous Himself, and as producing a state of righteousness in the believer. He had no such double character under the Old Testament.

(27-31) Here is a review of the consequences of this process of justification. It shuts the Jew out by laying stress no longer on works, which were the proper fulfillment of the first law as it stood, but upon faith. Faith is the true medium of justification, and belongs as much to Gentile as to Jew. Faith is the appointed means by which all mankind will be justified, and all before the same tribunal. Still this involves no abrogation of the Law, but rather a confirmation of it.

4

The subject of the chapter is an application of the foregoing to the special (and crucial) case of Abraham, with particular reference to two ideas that are continually recurring throughout the last chapter: the supposed superiority of Jew to Gentile, and the idea of boasting or glorying based upon this superiority. The apostle shows how even Abraham's case tells for, not against, the doctrine of justification by faith. It is entirely a mistake to suppose that they of the circumcision only are Abraham's seed, for the true seed of Abraham are those who follow his example of faith. He put faith in the promise; they must put faith in the fulfillment of the promise.

(3) The apostle gives proof of his assertion in verse 2. Abraham was not justified by works, and therefore had nothing to boast of in God's sight. He was justified by faith; His righteousness was not real, but imputed. Faith carries with it no such idea of merit or debt as works. It is met by a pure act of grace on the part of God.

Abraham believed God.—The quotation is taken from Gen. 15:6, where it appears as a comment upon Abraham's belief in the promise that he should have a numerous posterity. The same passage is elaborately commented upon by Philo and others, so that it would seem to have been a common topic in the Jewish schools. The word "faith" is not used in quite the same sense in the original and in the application. In Abraham's case it was trust in the fulfillment of the divine promise; in Paul's sense it is rather enthusiastic adhesion to a person. This is part of the general enlargement and deepening of the Old Testament terminology by Paul. He quotes the same passage in the same sense here as in Gal. 3:6.

It was counted unto him.—It should be observed that the same words are translated here **counted**, in verse 9 **reckoned**, in verse 22 **imputed**, in Gal. 3:6 **accounted**, in Jas. 2:23 **imputed**. Imputation is distinctly a forensic act. The righteousness attributed to Abraham is not an actual righteousness, but something else that is considered and treated as if it were equivalent to such righteousness. It is so treated by God acting as the judge of men.

(4) The proposition is put in a general form. Those who base their claim on works have a right to their reward. But those who rely only upon faith, even though ungodly themselves, have righteousness imputed to them (verse 5). This latter was Abraham's case.

(6-8) A further instance of the nature of the justification which proceeds from faith is supplied by David. From his evidence it will appear that such justification implies not the absence of sin but its forgiveness, not its real obliteration but the forebearance of God to impute it. It is an **amnesty**, not an **acquittal**. (See Ps. 32:1, 2.)

(9) The act of faith was the cause of Abraham's justification. But both the act of faith and the justification consequent upon it were prior to the institution of the rite of circumcision. (See Gen. 15 and 17.)

(11) The sign of circumcision—i.e., circumcision **as a** sign. The expression is an instance of the genitive of apposition.

A seal of the righteousness . . . —The apostle here puts forth his view of the real import of circumcision. It was not, as so many of his contemporaries supposed, the cause or condition of Israel's privileges as

much as the sign or ratification of them. It ratified a state of things already existing when it was instituted. Thus, to those who inherited that state of things—justification by faith—the want of circumcision was no bar.

(12) And on the other hand, the mere performance of the rite was no guarantee for justification, unless it was attended with a faith like Abraham's. Of the two things— faith itself and circumcision the sign of faith—the first only was essential, and the second was useless without it.

(13) Abraham was the father of **all** who walk in his steps. This **all** is not limited by the Law any more than it is limited by circumcision. The promise of that worldwide inheritance (explained by the Jews of the universal sovereignty of the Messiah) was not given through the agency of the Law, which at that time did not exist, but as an effect of the righteousness which proceeds from faith.

(14-17) This Messianic kingdom cannot have anything to do with law, for if it had, faith and the promise would cease to have any office. Faith and law cannot co-exist. The proper effect of law is punishment, for law only exposes sin. Faith, on the other hand, is the real key to the inheritance. It sets in motion grace; and grace, unlike law, excludes no one. It is open alike to the legal and to the spiritual descendants of Abraham.

(17) Who quickeneth . . . —"Who gives life to that which is dead, and issues His fiat to that which is not as though it were." The words have reference, in the first instance, to the dealings of God with Abraham, described in the verses that follow—to the overruling of the laws of nature indicated in verse 19, and to the declaration, "So shall thy seed be" (verse 18). There is, however, also an undercurrent of reference to the calling of the Gentiles.

(18) Who.—It must be noticed that the relative here refers to Abraham, whereas in the previous verse it referred to God.

Believed in hope.—The force of the preposition gives rather to the sentence the meaning of "grounded his faith upon hope"— that strong internal, subjective hope, though there were no objective grounds for hoping.

(20) Giving glory to God.—This phrase does not necessarily refer to a verbal ascription of praise, but may be used of anything which tends to God's glory, whether in thought, word, or deed. Here it seems to be applied to the frank recognition of God's omnipotence involved in Abraham's faith.

(24) That raised up.—It is an association of ideas which leads the apostle to this point. The birth of Isaac resembles the resurrection of Christ in that it involved the exercise of Omnipotence; in that Omnipotence Abraham believed, and we are to believe. The apostle is led further to allude to the Resurrection because of the place which it held in his theory of the Gospel.

(25) The death of Christ is the proper cause of justification, or means of atonement, according to Paul. The atoning efficacy lay in His death, but the proof of that efficacy—the proof that it was really the Messiah who died—was to be seen in the Resurrection. The Resurrection, therefore, gave the greatest impulse to faith in the atoning efficacy of the death upon the cross, and in this way helped to bring about justification. (Comp. I Cor. 15:17.) If the death of Christ had not been followed by His Resurrection, the inference would have followed that it was merely the death of an ordinary man, and without any special saving efficacy.

5

(1) Being justified.—This opening has a wonderful beauty which centers in the Christian idea of peace. After all the gloomy retrospect which fills the preceding chapters, the clouds break, and light steals gently over the scene. Nor is it merely the subsidence of storm, but an ardent and eager hope that now awakens and looks forward to a glorious future.

We have.—Some MSS read here, "Let us have," though the older reading would seem to make the better sense. A hortatory element is introduced into the passage, which does not seem quite properly or naturally to belong to it. It is possible that there may have been an early error of the copyist, afterward rightly corrected (in the two oldest MSS, Vaticanus and Sinaiticus, the reading of the Authorized Version appears as a correction) by conjecture.

Peace.—The state of reconciliation with God, with all that blissful sense of composure and harmony which flows from such a condition. "Peace" is the special legacy bequeathed by Jesus to His disciples (John 14:27; 16:33).

(2) By whom.—More accurately translated, "through whom also we have had

our access." "Have had" means when we first became Christians, and now while we are such.

Into this grace.—This is the state of acceptance and favor with God, the fruit of justification.

Rejoice.—The word is used elsewhere for "boasting." The Christian **has** his boasting, but it is not based upon his own merits. It is a joyful and triumphant confidence in the future, not only felt, but expressed.

The glory of God is that glory which the "children of the kingdom" shall share with the Messiah Himself when His eternal reign begins.

(3, 4) Here is a climax in which are put forward higher and higher grades of fortitude and constancy. "Experience" is "approvedness," the quality of being tried and approved. The result of patient endurance is to test, confirm, and refine the better elements of faith. Out of this, in its turn, grows hope. Hope is the knowledge of what is in store for him that, in the first instance, nerves the Christian to endure; and that endurance, being prolonged, gives him the steady, calm assurance no longer of the novice but of the veteran. This Christian hope does not disappoint or deceive. It is quite certain of its object, and the issue will prove it to be well-founded. This hope derives its certainty from the consciousness of justifying love.

(6) Without strength means powerless to work out our own salvation.

In due time.—Just at the moment when the forbearance of God (3:25) had come to an end, His love interposed, through the death of Christ, to save sinners from their merited destruction.

For the ungodly.—The force of the preposition here is "for the benefit of," not "instead of." Paul holds the doctrine of the vicarious sacrifice of Christ, but this is expressed by such terms as "propitiation" (3:25), "offering, and sacrifice for us" (Eph. 5:2), and "ransom for all" (I Tim. 2:6), not by the use of the preposition.

(7-8) The sacrifice of Christ is so paradoxical because it was for **sinners.** Even for a righteous man it is rare enough to find another who will be ready to lay down his life. Yet there are some such persons. The one thing which is most extraordinary in the death of Christ, and which most tends to throw into relief the love of God as displayed in it, is that He died for men as sinners, and at the moment when they were sinning all around Him.

(10) The interval that separates the state of enmity from the state of reconciliation is a large one, that which separates the state of reconciliation from the state of salvation a small one. And yet there is a difference. Reconciliation is the initial act—the removal of the load of guilt, or justification; salvation is the end of the Christian career, and of the process of sanctification. Justification is regarded as being especially due to the death of Christ; sanctification is brought about by His continued agency as the risen and exalted Saviour. The relation in which the risen Saviour still stands to the individual Christian is more fully worked out in 6:4; 8:34; I Cor. 15:22; II Cor. 4:10, 11; Phil. 3:10. But note that it is "now" (verse 11), in this present time, in our present condition. Reconciliation in the present is a foretaste of glory in the future.

(12) Wherefore, as by one man ...—We see here another instance of the apostle's fondness for transcendental theology, and for the development of the deeper mysteries of God's dealings with man. The rapidity with which ideas of this kind throng into his brain is such as to break the even flow and structure of his sentence. This clause ought to have been answered by "so by one Man grace and life entered." But how can it really be said that sin and death entered by Adam? Sin does not exist without law, and the law did not come until Moses. And yet we have proof that sin must have been there, for death, its consequence, prevailed all through this period in which law was still wanting. The fact was that the sin which then prevailed, and had such wide and disastrous effects, was Adam's, so that it is strictly legitimate to compare his fall with the act of redemption. By one man sin and death entered into the world, as life and grace entered by another. In either case the consequence was that of one man's act. (See note on verse 14.)

For that all have sinned.—Rather "because all sinned"—i.e., not by their own individual act, but implicitly in Adam's transgression. They were included in him as the head and representative of the race.

(13) Sin was in the world from Adam downward, but why guilt and death? The pre-Mosaic man sinned indeed, but could not rightly be condemned for his sin until there was a law to tell him plainly the distinction between right and wrong.

(14) After the similitude of Adam's transgression—i.e., in direct defiance of divine command. They had not incurred just punishment as Adam had, and yet they died. Why? Because of Adam's sin, the effects of which extended to them all, just in the same way as the effects of the death of Christ extend to all.

Who is the figure.—Better, **type.** There is thus intimated the parallelism which was omitted in verse 12. Adam was the type of Christ, his sin and its effects the type of Christ's death and its effects.

(15) The statement of the contrast extends over the next five verses.

One ... many.—Read throughout this passage, "the one," "the many." **The many,** in an antithesis to **the one,** are equivalent to **all** in verse 12, and comprehend the whole multitude, the entire species of mankind, exclusive only of **the one.** "In other words, the benefits of Christ's obedience extend to all men potentially. It is only human self-will which places limits to its operation" (Lightfoot).

The gift by grace.—The grace of God is the moving cause, and its result the gift (of righteousness, verse 17) imputed by His gracious act to the many.

(16) The judgment was by one.—The judgment, verdict, or sentence from a single case takes the form of condemnation, whereas the free gift, prompted by many sins, takes the form of justification. In the former of these cases the verdict is "Guilty," while in the other case the free act of grace which takes its place is a verdict of acquittal.

(17) Here is further confirmation of the contrast between the effect of Adam's sin and the atonement of Christ. The one produced a reign of death; the other shall produce a reign of life.

(19) Many were made sinners.—The **many,** or mankind collectively, were placed in the position of sinners.

Obedience.—This term is chosen in contradistinction to the disobedience of Adam. The obedience of Christ was an element in the atonement. (Comp. Phil. 2:8; Heb. 10:7.) But if we interpret Paul by himself, we must not see in it the sole element to the exclusion of the "propitiatory sacrifice" (3:25; Eph. 1:7; 5:2; I Tim. 2:6).

(20, 21) The apostle had already (verses 13, 14) alluded to the intervention of the Law. Now he returns to the topic. In order to complete his historical view of the origin of sin through Adam and its atonement through Christ, he considers what was its effect upon the former, and how that effect was met and neutralized by the latter. Mankind had already been led into sin by Adam. The Law came in to make matters still worse. It substituted conscious sin for unconscious, and so heightened its guilt. But all this is more than retrieved by grace.

In this last section we seem still to trace the influence of the school of Gamaliel. It appears that the Jewish doctors also attributed universal mortality to the fall of Adam, and regarded his sin as including that of the rest of mankind.

6

(1) Shall we continue in sin?—Again the apostle is drawn into one of those subtle casuistical questions that had such a great attraction for him. In previous chapters he had dealt with one of the two great root-ideas, justification by faith; he now passes to the second, union with Christ. The one might be described as the **juridical**, the other as the **mystical**, theory of salvation. The connecting link which unites them is faith. Faith in Christ, and especially in the death of Christ, is the instrument of justification.

(2) That are dead.—Rather, "that died." Lightfoot reminds us of the importance of keeping the strict aorist sense as opposed to that of the perfect (i.e., the single past action as opposed to the prolonged or continued action) in passages such as this. Paul regards this change from sin to righteousness, from bondage to freedom, from death to life, as summed up in one definite act of the past—potentially to all men in our Lord's passion and resurrection, actually to each individual man when he accepts Christ and is baptized. Then he is made righteous by being incorporated into Christ's righteousness, he dies once for all to sin, and he lives henceforth forever to God. This is his **ideal**. Practically, we know that the death to sin and the life to righteousness are inchoate, imperfect, gradual; but Paul sets the matter in this ideal light to force upon the consciences of his hearers the fact that an entire change came over them when they became Christians, that the knowledge and the grace then vouchsafed to them did not leave them where they were, that they are not and cannot be their former selves, and that it is a contradiction of their very being to sin any more. It is the definiteness and absoluteness of this change, considered as an historical crisis, which forms the central idea of Paul's teaching, and which the aorist

marks. Render also in verse 4, "we **were** buried" for "we are buried"; in verse 6, "the old man **was** crucified" for "is crucified"; in verse 8, "if we **died**" for "if we be dead."

(3) Were baptized into Jesus Christ—i.e., into communion with Him and incorporation in His mystical body. Baptism signified an intimately close and indissoluble attachment to Christ.

Were baptized into his death.—This attachment had a special relation to His death. It involved a communion or fellowship with His death. This fellowship is ethical, i.e., it implies a moral conduct corresponding to that relation to Christ which it assumes.

Why has baptism this special connection with the **death** of Christ? First, the death of Christ is the central and cardinal fact of the Christian scheme. It is especially related to justification, and justification proceeds from faith, which is ratified in baptism. Second, the symbolism of baptism was such as naturally to harmonize with the symbolism of death. It was the final close of one period, and the beginning of another—the complete stripping off of the past and putting on of the "new man."

(4) Burial is the consequence of death. It is the seal set upon it, as it were, which shows that no revival is possible. It is, besides, the one step which separates it from resurrection. The idea of "buried with Christ" is therefore introduced, on the one hand, to show that the ethical death with Him was final and decisive, and on the other, to prepare the way for an ethical (as well as physical) resurrection with Him.

(5) If we have been planted together.—Rather, if we have "grown into"—become "conjoined with." The metaphor is taken from the parasitic growth of a plant, but applies to **natural** growth, not "planted together with." The idea would correspond to the growth of a bud or graft regarded as part of that of the stock in which it is inserted, but without reference to the operation of budding or grafting. It is used here to express the closest intimacy and union.

This conformity means, of course, dying **to** trespasses and sins, being completely removed from the sphere of their influence, and entering a new sphere corresponding to the glorified life of the Redeemer. The ethical resurrection of the Christian ideally continues through life, and is completed with his physical resurrection.

(6) Our old man.—See Eph. 4:22, 24; Col. 3:9, 10. The old self was, ideally if not actually. mortified in our baptism. This change was wrought by a power brought to bear upon the will through the contemplation of the crucifixion of Christ. Thus. instead of saying simply "mortified." the apostle writes rather "crucified." i.e., put to death. not in any way. but especially **through the cross.**

That the body of sin might be destroyed.— The "body of sin" is the body subject to sin. or that supplies sin with the material on which it works. This substratum of carnal and fleshly desire, the apostle tells us. is to be ascetically chastened and disciplined until it ceases to be a source of sin.

(7) Is freed.—"Absolved," the same word that is used elsewhere for "justified." The dead man is no longer liable to have the charge of sin brought against him.

(9) Dieth no more.—The eternal subsistence of the life of Christ is a guarantee for the permanence and reality of our own life, as far as it is dependent on His. If it were possible that the life of Christ should fail, the whole fabric that the believer's faith builds upon it would fall to the ground. But it is not possible that the life of Christ should fail (verse 10). Death has lost all its power over Him.

(11) Theoretical application to the readers. They are to regard themselves as dead, i.e., insensible and inaccessible to sin, but living in close allegiance and devotion to God through union with Christ.

(12-14) Practical and hortatory consequence. Therefore expel sin, and refuse to obey its evil promptings. Let your bodies no longer be weapons in the hands of wickedness; let them rather be weapons with which to fight the battle of righteousness and of God. The same military metaphor (verse 13) is kept up in verse 23, "the wages of sin (your pay as soldiers of sin) is death."

(15) The apostle returns to a difficulty similar to that which presented itself at the beginning of the chapter. The answer is couched under a slightly different metaphor. It is no longer death to the one, life to the other, but freedom from the one, service to the other. These are correlative terms. Freedom from sin implies service to God, just as freedom from God means service to sin. (Comp. John 8:32-34, 36; Gal. 5:1.)

(19) I speak after the manner of men.—I am using a merely human figure of speech, a figure taken from common human relations, and not a high mystical phrase such as you might not be able to comprehend.

Your flesh.—This corresponds nearly to what is elsewhere called "the carnal mind." a mind alive only to material and sensible things.

(22) Ye have your fruit.—You are no longer without fruit. Your fruit is the new Christian life which leads on to sanctification and finally to eternal life.

(23) The gift of God.—The natural antithesis would be "wages"; but this would here be inappropriate, and therefore the apostle substitutes "the free gift." In spite of your sanctification as Christians, still you will not have **earned** eternal life; it is the gift of God's grace.

7

(1-6) The apostle takes up an idea to which he had alluded in 6:14, 15, "Ye are not under the law, but under grace"; and as he had worked out the conclusion of the death of the Christian to sin, so now he works out that of his death to the Law. This he does by an illustration borrowed from the marriage bond. That bond is dissolved by the death of one of the parties to it. In like manner the death of the Christian with Christ releases him from his obligation to the Law, and opens to him a new and spiritual service in place of his old subjection to a written code.

(1) To them that know the law.—The Roman Church was composed in about equal proportions of Jewish and of Gentile Christians. The Jews would naturally know the provisions of their own law, while the Gentile Christians would know them sufficiently from hearing the Old Testament read in the synagogues, where their public worship was still conducted.

(2) For the woman which hath an husband.—The proposition must be understood to be stated in a somewhat abstract form. Relations of the kind indicated are terminated **by death** (not necessarily the death of one party to them more than another). The relation of wife and husband ceases absolutely and entirely on both sides, and not merely so much of it as affects the person who dies.

(4) By the body of Christ—i.e., by the death of the human body of Christ upon the cross. The Christian is so united to Christ that whatever has happened to his Master has happened also to him. Christ was put to death upon the cross; **he** therefore has also been put to death with Him. But why put to death **to the Law?** Probably all that is meant is simply that the Christian died, and therefore all the relations contracted before that death came to an end. At the same time he entered upon new relations corresponding to his new and risen state. This mystical and ethical union with Christ will not be unproductive; it will have for its fruit a life consecrated to God.

(5) The "body" is regarded by Paul as a neutral principle, which is not in itself either good or bad. It is simply the material frame of men, which though itself "of the earth earthy" is capable of becoming a dwelling place for the Spirit, and being put to holy uses. The "flesh" is the same material frame regarded as the seat of sinful appetites, and with a tendency to obey the lower rather than the higher self. The proper way to overcome this lower self is by that spiritual asceticism which the believer goes through by his appropriation of the death of Christ.

Motions of sins.—The same word (Gal. 5:24) is translated "affections"—those emotions or passions which lead to sin.

Unto death.—Death is here personified as the king of that region which sin serves to enrich.

(6) **That we should serve.**—Rather, "so that we serve"—result, not purpose. Release from one master implied an engagement to another. Our new state is one in which we serve an active living Spirit; our old state was a bondage to the dead and formal letter. The "Spirit" is here the Holy Spirit, as the animating principle of the new life, and as opposed to a system which proceeds merely by external precepts and requirements.

(7) **What shall we say then?**—The apostle had spoken in a manner disparaging to the Law, and which might well give offense to some of his readers. It was necessary to correct this. Now he proceeds to lay down more precisely in what it was that the Law was defective, and what was its true function and relation to the history and struggles of humanity.

In what follows the apostle speaks throughout in the first person. He is really making a general statement which applies to all mankind; but this statement is based upon his own personal experience. The apostle goes back in thought to the time before he had embraced Christianity, and treats his own case as typical. The description which follows to the end of verse 24 is a description of the **unregenerate** state of man. It is one prolonged crisis and conflict, which at last finds its solution in Christ.

Is the law sin?—The Law is not actually immoral, but it is near being made so. It is not itself sin (sinful), but it reveals, and so in a manner incites to, sin.

I had not known.—Before the introduction of law, acts that are sinful in themselves, objectively viewed, may be done, but they are not sinful with reference to the person who does them. He has no knowledge or consciousness of what sin is until it is revealed to him by law.

I had not known lust.—The apostle introduces an illustration from a special law—the Tenth Commandment. The apostle did not know covetousness **as a sin** until he was confronted with the law against it.

(8) **Taking occasion.**—The word in the Greek implies originally a military metaphor: taking as a "base of operations," i.e., an advanced post occupied as the starting point and rendezvous for further advances. Sin (here a quasi-personification) is unable to act upon man without the cooperation of law, without being able to hold up law before him, and so show itself in its true colors.

Concupiscence.—Rather, "coveting"—the same word which had been used in verse 7. Sin, the evil principle in men, acting as the primary cause, and the Commandment as the secondary cause, led their unfortunate victim into all kinds of violation of the Law. This is done in two ways: the perverseness of human nature is such that the mere prohibition of an act suggests the desire to do that which is prohibited; the act, when done, is invested with the character of sin, which heretofore it did not possess. It becomes a distinct breach of law where previously there had been no law to break. Until there was a written prohibition, Sin (the evil principle) was powerless to produce sinful actions.

(9) **I was alive.**—The state of unconscious morality, uninstructed but as yet uncondemned, may, compared with that state of condemnation, be regarded as a state of "life."

Revived.—The original is that it "came to life **again**." Sin is lurking in the heart from the first, but it is dormant until the commandment comes.

(13) Was it possible that the Law, holy and good as it was, could simply lead miserable men to death and ruin? No, it was not possible. It was not the Law that did

this but sin—acting through the instrumentality of the Law. All this, however, only had for its end to show up Sin for the monster that it really is.

(14-25) Further and detailed proof why it was that though the Law appealed to all that was best in man, still he could not obey it.

(14) The Law is divinely given. But man, though capable of communion with God, is dominated by that part of his nature which is entirely earthly. This sensual part of his nature is the slave—and just as much the slave as if he had been sold in the auction mart—of sin.

(15) That which I do I allow not.—I act blindly, and without any conscious direction of the will. That higher part of me which should preside over and direct my actions is kept down by the lower physical nature. Paul uses three words for "to do" in this passage, the distinction between which is hard to represent in English. That which is employed here and in verses 17 and 20 is the strongest—**perform**—deliberate action, thoroughly carried out. The other two words differ, as "do" and "practice," the one referring to single, the other to habitual and repeated, actions.

(16-23) But the fact that I desire to do what is right is itself a witness to the excellence of the Law, which commands that which I desire. This, then, appears to be the true explanation of the difficulty. There is really a dualism in the soul. I am not to be identified with that lower self which is enthralled by sin. "The mind" (verse 23) is the moral and rational faculties considered as moral and rational. "The inward man" (verse 22) is the higher part of man's nature considered as capable of receiving the divine grace.

(24) So this intense struggle goes on unceasingly and reaches no decision, until at last the unhappy man cries out, almost in despair, Who will help me to overcome these fleshly desires, gendered by a corrupt human nature, which are dragging me down to imminent destruction? The body is the cause of sin, and therefore of death. If only it could be released from that, the distracted soul would be at rest and free.

The body of this death—i.e., "this body (the slave of sin and therefore the abode) of death." The words are a cry for deliverance from the whole of this mortal nature, in which carnal appetite, sin, and death are inextricably mingled. To complete this deliverance the triple resurrection—ethical, spiritual, and physical—is needed.

(25) It **has** been released. It is Jesus our Lord to whom the thanks and praise are due. Without His intervention there can be only a divided service. The mere human self serves with the mind the law of God, with the flesh the law of sin.

The deliverance wrought by Christ is apparently here that of sanctification rather than of justification. It is from the domination of the body, from the impulses of sense, that the Christian is freed, and that is done when he is crucified to them with Christ.

8

The apostle has now again reached a climax in his argument similar to that in the opening of chap. 5. His subject is once more the blissful condition of the Christian who has made full use of the means of grace offered to him. This is now worked out in detail. The eighth chapter may, in fact, be described as not only the climax of a particular argument, but also as the broad extended summit of the epistle. It differs from the first section of chap. 5 in this: while both describe the condition of the regenerate Christian, and both cover the whole range of time from the first admission to the Christian communion down to the ultimate and assured enjoyment of Christian immortality, chap. 5 lays stress chiefly on the initial and final moments of this period, whereas chap. 8 emphasizes rather the whole intermediate process. In technical language the one turns chiefly upon justification, the other upon sanctification. Hope and faith are connecting links between the two. A further link is suggested in the words of 5:5. There it is the consciousness of justifying love which is so diffused, but the doctrine of the special agency exercised by the Holy Ghost is largely expanded in chap. 8.

This chapter carries us into the inmost circle and heart of Christianity; it treats of that peculiar state of beatitude, of refined and chastened joy, for which no form of secularism is able to provide even the remotest equivalent.

(1) Therefore.—The apostle had already, at the end of the last chapter, touched the confines of that state of deliverance and of liberty which he is now going on to describe. The opening of this chapter is, therefore, connected in form with the close of the last. The intervention of Christ puts an end to the struggle waged within the soul.

Condemnation.—The condemnation which in the present and final judgment of God impends over the sinner is removed by the intervention of Christ and by the union of the believer with Him. By that union the power and empire of sin are thrown off and destroyed. (Comp. verse 3.) There is a certain play on the word "condemn." By "condemning" the law of sin, Christ **removed** "condemnation" from the sinner. He removed it objectively, or in the nature of things, and this removal is completed subjectively in the individual through that bond of mystical and moral attachment which makes what Christ has done His own act and deed.

To them which are in Christ Jesus.—To "have the Spirit of Christ" is a converse expression for the same idea. In the one case the believer is regarded as reaching upward, as it were, through faith, and so incorporating and uniting himself with the Spirit of Christ; in the other case, the Spirit of Christ reaches downward and infuses itself into the believer. This is the peculiar mysticism of the apostle.

Who walk not after the flesh, but after the Spirit.—These words are wanting in the foremost representatives of every group of authorities (except, perhaps, those MSS which belong to the region of Syria), and must certainly be omitted. They have been brought in here from verse 4.

(2) The law of the Spirit of life.—This is a phrase defining more fully the mode in which the union with Christ becomes operative in the believer. It begins by imparting to him the Spirit of Christ; this Spirit creates within him a law; and the result of that law is life—that perfect spiritual vitality which includes within itself the pledge of immortality.

From the law of sin and death.—The direct antithesis of the foregoing—not here the law of Moses, but the power of sin, the corrupt element in our nature, acting upon the soul, and itself erecting a kind of law. The effect of this reign of sin is death—spiritual death—bearing in itself the pledge of eternal death.

(3) In that it was weak through the flesh.—There was one constant impediment in the way of the success of the Law—it had to be carried out by human agents, beset by human frailty. Temptation and sin have their

roots in the physical part of human nature, and they were too strong for the purely moral influence of the Law. The Law was limited in its operations by them and failed to overcome them.

In the likeness of sinful flesh—i.e., in the flesh, but not in **sinful** flesh: with a human body which was so far like the physical organization of the rest of mankind, but yet which was not in Him, as in other men, the seat of sin.

And for sin.—This is the phrase which is used constantly in the LXX for the "sin offering." The essence of the original sin offering was that it was accepted by an act of grace on the part of God, instead of the personal punishment of the offender. Paul uses, in regard to the sacrifice of Christ, similar language to that which is used in the Old Testament of this particular class of sacrifice.

Condemned sin.—This expression refers to that which the Law was hindered from doing by the hold which sin had upon the flesh. That hold is made to cease through the participation of the believer in the death of Christ. Sin is, as it were, **dispossessed** as one who in court is dispossessed of a property.

In the flesh.—In that same area, the flesh, in which sin had hitherto had the mastery, it now stood condemned. It was unable to exercise its old sway any longer.

(5) Their whole mental and moral activity is set upon nothing else but the gratification of these cravings of sense. The phrase "who mind" (see verses 6-8) is not confined to the exercise of the intellect, but includes the affections; in fact it includes all those lesser motives, thoughts, and desires which are involved in carrying out any great principle of action—whether it be selfish and "carnal" or spiritual.

(9) The Spirit of God ... the Spirit of Christ.—It is to be observed that these two terms are used interchangeably. The Spirit of Christ is indeed the presence of Christ Himself in the soul.

Dwell in you.—This expression is the complement of the other "to be **in** the Spirit," "to be **in** Christ." It denotes the closest possible contact and influence of spirit upon spirit. No mysticism, however vivid and intense, can really go beyond this without infringing the bounds of personality, and contradicting the direct testimony of consciousness.

(10) Here the word "dead" is evidently used of physical death. The doom entailed by sin still, indeed, attaches to the body—but only to the body. But another side of human nature—the spirit—is full of vitality because it is full of righteousness, first imputed and then real. Life and righteousness are correlative terms.

(11) And this vitality extends beyond the grave. It will even react upon that material body which had just been spoken of as given over to death. Die it must; but the same Spirit to which the soul owes its life will also reinfuse life into the dead body, just as the body of Christ of Himself was raised from the dead.

By his Spirit . . . —The balance of authority is in favor of the reading, "because of His Spirit"; the other is an Alexandrian correction.

(14-17) This idea of "sonship" is the Christian transformation of the old theocratic idea. (Comp. Gal. 3:25; 4:1-7.) The Israelite, **qua** Israelite, had stood in this special relation to God; now it is open to the **spiritual** Israel, of whatever race they may be. The idea itself, too, is largely widened and deepened by the additional doctrines of the continued agency of the Spirit and of the Messiahship of Jesus. The sense of sonship is awakened and kept alive by the Spirit; and of all those in whom it is found, the Messiah Himself stands at the head, insuring for them a share in His own glory.

(15) **Spirit of bondage.**—The word "spirit" varies much in meaning in these verses. Here it is the "dominant habit or frame of mind"; in the next verse it is used both for the Spirit of God and the spirit of man.

Again to fear—i.e., so as to take you back under the old terrorism of the Law. The Law, if it contained promises, was still more essentially a system of threats; the threats took effect, while the promises remained ineffectual, because the Law could not be fulfilled.

Whereby we cry.—The intensity of the apostle's feeling comes out in this simple definition. Instead of any more formal elaboration of his meaning, he says the Spirit of adoption is that which prompts the impassioned cry, "Abba, Father."

Abba, Father.—"Abba" is the Aramaic equivalent for "father." The repetition is one of endearment and entreaty, taken from the natural impulse of children to repeat a beloved name in different forms.

(16) **The Spirit itself beareth witness.**—What is the nature of this concurrent testimony? The self-consciousness of the believer assures him of his sonship; the relation in which he feels that he stands to God he knows to be that of a son. But, besides this, he is aware of an eternal objective cause for this feeling. The cause is the influence of the Holy Spirit. This passage makes it clear that the apostle, in spite of the strongly mystic tone of his language elsewhere, never confuses the human and the divine.

(17) One characteristic of the son is that he is his father's heir. So it is with the Christian. He, too, has an inheritance—an inheritance of glory which he will share with Christ. But he must not be surprised if, before sharing the glory, he also shares the sufferings.

(18-25) The mention of "suffering" and of "glory" recalls the apostle to a sense of his own position. (See Acts 19:23-41; II Cor. 6:4, 5; 11:23-28; Phil. 3:8.) Here there follows a statement of the nature of the Christian's hope viewed, not only as it affects the individual, but also in its cosmical aspect.

(19) **Earnest expectation.**—A single word in the Greek, and a very striking one. It means, literally, a straining forward with outstretched head, just as we might imagine the crowds outside a race track straining over the ropes to catch a sight of the runners; it is an eager, intent expectation. The same word is used once again in the New Testament (Phil. 1:20).

Creature.—Rather "creation," the whole world of nature, animate and inanimate.

Waiteth for.—This is another strong word, "waits with concentrated longing and expectancy."

Manifestation.—Translate rather by the ordinary word, "revelation," as "glory which shall be **revealed**" in verse 18. The coming of Christ is to be accompanied by an appearance of the redeemed in glorified form.

(20) **For the creature.**—The apostle gives the reason for this earnest expectation in the present state of nature, pointing out what creation **is.** If creation were perfect, and were fulfilling the noblest possible purpose, there would be no cause for looking forward hopefully to the future.

Was made subject to vanity.—"Vanity" means "emptiness" or "nothingness." Creation is fulfilling an unworthy instead of a noble end. (Comp. Gen. 3:17, 18.) It was made subject to this not by its own act or with its own concurrence, but in pursuance of the sovereign purpose and counsel of God. The one thing which takes out the sting from this impoverished and degraded condition is hope of what creation **is to be** (verse 21).

(21) Delivered from the bondage of corruption.—The state of decay and ruin into which the world by nature has fallen is regarded as a servitude opposed to the state of liberty into which it will be ushered at the coming of Christ.

(22) Groaneth and travaileth.—In view of the physical evil and misery prevalent in the world, the apostle attributes a human consciousness of pain to the rest of creation. It groans and travails **together**, i.e., every member of it in common with its kind. The idea of travailing, as in childbirth, has reference to the future prospect of joyful delivery. (Comp. John 16:21.)

(23) Which have the firstfruits of the Spirit.—We have received only the first partial outpouring of the Spirit, as opposed to the plenitude of glory in store for us.

The adoption.—The Christian who has received the gift of the Spirit is **already** an adopted child of God. (See verses 15 and 16.) But this adoption still has to be ratified and perfected, which will not be until the coming of Christ.

The redemption of our body.—One sign of the imperfect sonship of the Christian is that mortal and corruptible body in which the better and heavenly part of him is imprisoned. That, too, shall be transformed and glorified, and cleared from all the defect of its earthly condition. (Comp. I Cor. 15:49-53; Phil. 3:21.)

(24) By hope.—It is usually faith rather than hope that is represented as the means or instrument of salvation. Nor can it quite rightly be said that hope is **an aspect** of faith, because faith and hope are expressly distinguished and placed as coordinate with each other in I Cor. 13:13. Hope is rather a secondary cause of salvation, because it sets salvation vividly before the believer, and so makes him strive to obtain it.

But it must not be overlooked that the phrase translated "by hope" may be taken rather to mean "**with**" or "**in** hope." It will then serve to limit the idea of salvation. We were saved, indeed, in an inchoate and imperfect manner; but our full salvation is still a subject for hope, and therefore it is not past but still in the future.

(26) Likewise.—While on the one hand the prospect of salvation sustains him, so on the other hand the divine Spirit interposes to aid him. The one source of encouragement is human (his own human consciousness of the certainty of salvation), the other divine.

With groanings which cannot be uttered.—When the Christian's prayers are too deep and too intense for words, when they are rather a sigh heaved from the heart than any formal utterance, then we may know that they are prompted by the Spirit Himself. It is He who is praying to God for us.

(27) God recognizes the voice of His own Spirit, because the prayers that the Spirit prompts are in strict accordance with His will.

(28) All things.—Here is the third reason for the Christian's patience in the midst of trial (see verses 21-25, 26-27). There is rather remarkable reading here, found in the Vatican and Alexandrian MSS, and in Origen, inserting "God" as the subject of the verb, and making "all things" the object. "God works all things with," or "cooperates in all things." This reading is very early, if not original.

To them who are the called.—Further description of those "who love God." They have also, as in His eternal counsels He had designed it should be, obeyed the call given to them in the preaching of the Gospel, and definitely enrolled themselves in the kingdom of the Messiah.

(29, 30) For whom he did foreknow, he also did predestinate.—The process already summed up under these two phrases is now resolved more fully and exactly into its parts, with the inference that to those who are under the divine guidance at every step in their career nothing can act but for good. The two phrases indicate two distinct steps. God, in His infinite foreknowledge, knew that certain persons would submit to be conformed to the image of His Son, and He predestined them for this. These, thus, are constituted "God's elect" (verse 33).

To be conformed . . . —The final cause of the whole of this divine process is that the Christian may be conformed to the image of Christ—that he may be like Him not merely in spirit, but also in that glorified body, which is to be the copy of the Redeemer's (Phil. 3:21), and so be a fit attendant upon Him in His Messianic kingdom.

Firstborn among many brethren.—The Messianic kingdom is conceived here of rather as a family. In this family Christ has the rights of primogeniture, but all Christians are His brethren (comp. Heb. 2:11); and the object of His mission and of the great scheme of salvation in all its stages is to make men **sufficiently like Him to be** His brethren, and so to fill up the number of the Christian family. The word "firstborn" occurs in Col. 1:15 and Heb. 1:6. It implies two things: (1) priority in point of time, or in other words the pre-existence of the Son as the divine Word; and (2) supremacy or sovereignty as the Messiah. The Messianic use of the word is based upon Ps. 89:27.

(30) Predestinate.—This is the term which seems most to interfere with human free will. Foreknowledge does not interfere with free will because the foreknowledge, though prior in point of time, is posterior in the order of causation to the act of choice. A man does not choose a certain action because it is foreknown, but it is foreknown because he will choose it. Predestination appears to involve a more rigorous necessity, but it must not be interpreted in any sense that excludes free will. Free will is a postulate on which all the superstructure of morals and religion must rest. The religious mind, looking back over the course by which it has been brought, sees the hand of God predominating in it; but however large the divine element in salvation may be, it must in the end be apprehended by faith, which is an act of free will. And the subsequent actions of which faith is the moving cause, though done under a co-operating divine influence, yet belong to the sphere of human freedom. (See note on 2:6.) It should be remembered that Paul is not now writing in the calm temper of philosophical analysis, but in an intense access of religious emotion, and therefore he does not stay to put in all the qualifying clauses that philosophy might require. It is well for mankind that he has done so. In all great and creative religious minds the consciousness of free will has retired into the background.

Called.—By presenting to them the Gospel, directly or indirectly, through the preaching of Christ and His apostles.

Justified.—In the Pauline sense, as in 3:24-31.

Glorified.—Strictly, the glorifying of the Christian awaits him in the future, but the apostle regards all these different acts as focussed together as it were on a single point in the past. Glorification is involved in justification.

(31-39) Now follows the sublime and triumphant conclusion from the foregoing—expressed with passionate energy and with the most intense consciousness of the reality of a Christian belief in penetrating and sustaining the mind in all outward trials, however severe. The whole passage forms a continuous proof of the certainty that all things shall be freely given to the Christian (verse 32). Nothing can frustrate this—either on the side of **God,** for when He justifies none can condemn (verse 33), or on the side of **Christ,** whose death, Resurrection, Ascension, and intercession are pledges that nothing can separate us from His love (verse 34).

(36) For thy sake we are killed.—Comp. II Cor. 6:4; 11:23, for the apostle's own actual experience. The quotation is taken from Ps. 44:22, which was apparently written at some period of great national distress; at what precise period the **data** does not enable us to say, but it was probably not earlier than Josiah. The sufferings of God's people at all times are typical of each other. There is the further reason for the application in the text that the Psalm does not lay stress upon the guilt of the people, but regards their sufferings as undergone in the cause of the theocracy. At the same time, the tone of the psalmist lacks the exulting and triumphant confidence of the apostle.

(38) Neither death, nor life . . . —The enumeration that follows is intended to include (poetically rather than logically) every possible category of being—agencies of every kind, personal or impersonal—especially those unseen powers of evil against which the warfare of the Christian was more particularly directed. (Comp. Ps. 139; Eph. 6:12.)

(39) The love of God.—It is to be observed that for the shorter phrase, "the love of Christ," the apostle now substitutes the fuller but, as it would seem, equivalent phrase, "the love of God **in** Christ."

9

There is a distinct break in the epistle at this point. The subject of the preceding chapters, the development of the Gospel scheme, has been worked up to a climax. We might imagine that at the end of chap. 8 the epistle was laid aside, and the apostle now begins upon a new topic, in the discussion of which, however, he still retains the same vein of deep emotion that had characterized his latest utterances. This new topic is the relation of the Christian system just expounded to the chosen people. The section including chaps. 9-11 is complete and rounded in itself.

(3) The wish, of course, related to what was really impossible. Still it is a nobly generous impulse that Paul would be separated from Christ and devoted to destruction. Does not the intensity of this expression help us to realize one aspect of the atonement—"being made a curse for us" (Gal. 3:13)?

(4) The adoption.—They are the theocratic people, the people whom God had, as it were, adopted to Himself, and taken into the special filial relation. (Comp. Exod. 4:22; Hos. 11:1.)

The glory.—The Shechinah, or visible symbol of God's presence. (Comp. Exod. 16:10; 24:16; I Kings 8:10, 11; Heb. 9:5.)

The covenants.—Not the two tables of stone, but the several compacts made by God with Abraham and his descendants (Gen. 12:1-3, 7; 13:14-17; 15:1-21; 17:1-22; 22:15-18; etc.)

The service of God.—The temple service and ritual.

The promises.—Especially the Messianic promises, a term correlative to the "covenants" above.

(5) The fathers.—The patriarchs—Abraham, Isaac, and Jacob.

Who is over all, God blessed for ever.—Trinitarian interpreters, as a rule, take these words with the punctuation of the Authorized Version, as referring to Christ. Socinian interpreters put a full stop after "came," and make the remainder of the verse a doxology addressed to God. Both ways are possible. The question is, Which is the most natural and probable? The balance of the argument stands thus: The order of the words, as well as the context, is somewhat in favor of the application to Christ. But, on the other hand, Pauline ascriptions of blessing in all other places where they occur (except II Tim. 4:18) are referred not to Christ, but to God. The title "God" does not appear to be elsewhere applied to our Lord by Paul, though all the attributes of Godhead are ascribed to Him, e.g., Phil. 2:6; Col. 1:15. (In I Tim. 3:16 the true reading is, "Who was manifested," and not "God was manifested.") John, however, certainly makes use of this title, not only in John 1:1 and 20:28, but also in the reading, adopted by many, of John 1:18, "God only begotten" for "Only begotten Son." Weighing the whole of the arguments, the applica-

tion to our Lord appears perhaps a little the more probable of the two. More than this cannot be said; nor is a stronger affirmation warranted by any considerations resting on the division of authorities.

(6) Now follows a vindication of the dealings of God in rejecting Israel.

Of Israel—i.e., descended from Jacob. (Comp. Gen. 32:28.) The promise of God was indeed given to Israel, but that did not mean inclusively all who could claim descent from Jacob without further limitation. Neither are all the bodily descendants (verses 7-9). It was expressly stated from the first that the promise was confined to a particular branch of his posterity derived miraculously through Isaac.

(10, 11) The restriction and special selection also appeared when Rebecca bore sons to Isaac. The children themselves had done nothing to make a preference be given to one over the other. The object of the declaration was to ratify the divine electing purpose which had already chosen Jacob to be the inheritor of the Messianic blessings. Here we have the doctrine of election and predestination stated in a very uncompromising form. Of the two elements which go to determine action—outward circumstances and inward disposition—neither can be said strictly to be made by the man himself. There is an opposition between sovereignty and free will irreconcilable to us with our present means of judging. We can take only the one proposition as qualified by the other.

(14-18) These verses contain the second part of the vindication. This power of choosing one and refusing another has always been reserved to Himself by God, as is seen by the examples of Moses and Pharaoh.

(15) For he saith to Moses.—In the most characteristic period of the Old Testament the divine favor was promised in this way to Moses and denied to Pharaoh. The original of the first quotation has reference to the special revelation vouchsafed to Moses on Sinai, "I will show grace to whom I will show grace."

(16) Of him that runneth.—A metaphor taken from the footraces as Paul may possibly have seen them practiced at Corinth. (Comp. Gal. 2:2; 5:7; Phil. 2:16.) The meaning is that the prize does not depend on human will or human effort, but on the grace of God.

(17) God also uses the wickedness of men as a means of exhibiting His power and justice. e.g., by the plagues of Egypt and by the overthrow of Pharaoh and his host in the Red Sea.

(18) **He hardeneth.**—The doctrine of the divine sovereignty is expressed here in its most trenchant and logical form. In Exod. 8:32; 9:34; 13:15; etc., the hardening of Pharaoh's heart is attributed to his own act. That act may, however, be regarded as a part of the design of Providence. God's decrees include human free will, without destroying it.

(19-21) These verses contain the third part of the vindication, which is based upon a possible extension of the objection. Not only might it seem as if this absolute choice and rejection were unjust in itself, but also unjust in its consequences. How can a man be blamed or punished, when his actions are determined for him? The apostle meets this by a simple but emphatic assertion of the absolute and unquestionable prerogative of God over His creatures.

(22) Here begins the concluding section of the vindication. All this scheme of God's dealings, apparently so severe, is really most merciful.

Willing.—While His will was ultimately to execute His wrath and display His sovereign judicial power, nevertheless He bore with evildoers and gave them time for repentance.

(24) **Even us.**—Now the apostle explains who are meant by his abstract terms. The "vessels of glory" are those who were intended to accept the Christian teaching, whether Jews or Gentiles. The "vessels of wrath" are the unbelieving mass of the people of Israel.

(25) **As he saith also in Osee.**—The original of the prophecy in Hosea relates to the pardon and reconciliation promised to the apostate and idolatrous people of the northern kingdom. It is here typically and prophetically applied to the Gentiles. Those who had ceased to belong to the chosen people, and those who had never belonged to it, were to all intents and purposes in the same position.

(26) **And it shall come to pass.**—This, too, was originally spoken of the restoration of the northern exiles to the land of Palestine. As applied to the conversion of the Gentiles, it would mean that the lands which had previously been heathen should become Christian.

(29) **Said before**—i.e., in an earlier part of his book. The Book of Isaiah was at this time collected in the form in which we have

it. In Acts 13:33 we find an express reference to the present numbering of the Psalms.

A seed.—Equivalent to the "remnant" of verse 27. The point of the quotation is that but for this remnant the rejection of Israel would have been utter and complete.

(30-33) The apostle now takes up a point of view which is the direct opposite of determinism, and in explaining the **causes** which led to the rejection of Israel, those which he puts forward are all such as depend for their validity on the freedom of the will. This is abundantly recognized in other parts of Paul's writings, especially in the earnest practical exhortations which he addresses to his readers. This, then, must be taken to qualify the argument that has preceded. The freedom of the will and the absolute sovereignty of God are two propositions which are reconciled in some way inscrutable to us.

(30) **Which followed not after righteousness**—i.e., not having a special revelation, and being inattentive to the law of conscience.

(31) Israel, on the other hand, though ostensibly pursuing a law the object of which was righteousness, did not reach such a law. They tried to keep the Law, but failed to keep it, and to bring themselves under its protection. "That stumblingstone" (verse 32) was Christ. When Christianity, with the justification by faith which goes with it, was offered to them, they "were offended" and refused it.

(33) See Isa. 28:16 and 8:14. In the first of these passages the prophet refers to the foundation stone of the Temple as a symbol of the divine faithfulness; in the second to God Himself. Paul, like the Jewish rabbis, applied both passages to the Messiah. The same two quotations appear in I Pet. 2:6, 7, and with similar variation from the LXX.

10

(1) **For Israel.**—The true text is, "for them." What made the rejection of Israel so peculiarly pathetic was that they were not a mere godless and irreligious people. On the contrary, they had a sincere zeal for religion, but it was a misdirected and ill-judged zeal.

(2) **A zeal of God, but not according to knowledge.**—It would be difficult to find a better description of the state of the Jews at this period. Their religion was legal and

formal to the last degree. Under an outward show of punctilious obedience, it concealed all the inward corruption described by the apostle in 2:17-29, the full extent of which was seen in the horrors of the great insurrection and the siege of Jerusalem.

(3) God's righteousness.—See 1:17 and 3:21.

(4) The end of the law.—"End" is used in the proper sense of termination or conclusion. Christ is that which brings the functions of the Law to an end by superseding it.

(6-8) In opposition to this righteousness of works, so laborious and so impracticable (verse 5), the apostle adduces another quotation to show that the righteousness which depends on faith is much simpler. The original of the quotation has, indeed, a quite different application. It referred to that law which the apostle is depreciating. Moses had described the Law as something quite easy and accessible; but history had shown that, especially in the development in which the Law was known to the apostle, the words were really much more applicable to his doctrine of a righteousness which was based upon faith. He therefore regards them as spoken allegorically and typically with reference to this. He repudiates the idea that the Christian is compelled to join Christ anywhere in literal bodily presence. A far easier thing is the faith of the Gospel. All the Christian has to do is to listen to it when it is preached, and then to confess his own adhesion to it.

(9) If thou shalt confess with thy mouth.—This is interesting as containing the earliest formal confession of faith; that in Acts 8:37 (see note) is not genuine.

There is no opposition between the outward confession and the inward act of faith. The one is regarded as the necessary consequence and expression of the other. In verse 10 this takes the form of Hebrew parallelism, in which the balanced clauses are regarded as equivalent to each other.

The Lord Jesus.—Jesus as Lord.

Hath raised him from the dead.—Comp. 4:25. Though the death of Christ apprehended by faith is more the cause of the Christian's salvation, still the apostle regards the Resurrection as the cardinal point, for without the Resurrection the proof of the Messiahship of Jesus would have been incomplete, and His death would not have had its saving efficacy.

(14-21) Thus there is a distinct order—belief, confession, invocation. But before

either the last or the first of these steps is taken the Gospel must be preached. The Jew, however, cannot plead that the Gospel has not been preached to him. It **has** been preached both to Jew and Gentile. Both Moses and Isaiah had foretold the conversion of the Gentiles, and Isaiah had also foretold the unbelief of the Jews.

(15) Preach the gospel of peace.—These words are omitted in the group of oldest MSS, and should be left out in the text. The whole of the quotation is not given by Paul.

(17) So then faith cometh.—This is the inference from the prophecy just quoted. Before men can believe, there must be something for them to believe. That something is the Word of God. The word for "report" in verse 16, and for "hearing" in verse 17, is the same, but with a slight difference of meaning. In the first place, both the act of hearer and preacher are involved; in the second place, only the act of the hearer.

By the word of God.—We should read here "by the word of **Christ**"—i.e., by the Gospel first delivered by Christ and propagated by His ministers.

(19) I will provoke you.—In requital for the idolatries of the Jews, Moses prophesied that God would bestow His favor on a Gentile nation, and so provoke their jealousy; and the apostle sees the fulfillment of this in his own day.

No people ... a foolish nation.—These terms were used by the Jews of their Gentile neighbors. They were "no people," because they did not stand in the same recognized relation to God. They were "a foolish nation," because they had not received the same special revelation, but, on the contrary, worshiped stocks and stones.

11

(1) I say then.—Are we to infer from the language of Isaiah just quoted (10:21; see Isa. 65:2) that God has cast away His people? Far be the thought. The apostle is himself too closely identified with his countrymen to look upon it with anything but horror.

I also.—This appeal to his own descent from Abraham seems to be called forth by the apostle's patriotic sympathy with his people, and not merely by the thought that he would be included in their rejection.

Of the tribe of Benjamin.—Of the purest blood, because the tribes of Judah and

Benjamin alone kept up the theocratic continuity of the race after the Exile. (Comp. Phil. 3:5.)

(2) Which he foreknew.—This must not be pressed too far. as implying absolute indefectibility of the divine favor. God. having in His eternal counsels set His choice upon Israel as His peculiar people. will not readily disown them. Nor is their case really as bad as it may seem. Now. as in the days of Elijah. there are a select few who have not shared in the general depravity.

(4) To the image of Baal.—The name "Baal" is here. as frequently in the LXX. in the feminine gender. Some have thought that the deity was androgynous; others have conjectured that the feminine is used contemptuously. Baal was originally the sungod.

(5, 6) As there was a remnant in Elijah's time. so also is there a remnant now. That there should be so is due not to any human merit on the part of those exempted from the fate of their nation. but to the spontaneous act of the divine grace selecting them from the rest. These two things. "grace" and "works." really exclude each other. The apostle reverts somewhat parenthetically to his idea of 9:11-16.

(7) What is the result? Not only did Israel fail to obtain the salvation which it sought. and which the select few succeeded in obtaining. but it was consigned to a state of complete spiritual apathy. and its blessings became a curse and a snare. "Were blinded" is an erroneous translation. The correct rendering is "were hardened." So. too, verse 25; II Cor. 3:14; Eph. 4:18. The term is one used in medicine for the forming of chalkstone.

(8) The spirit of slumber.—Etymologically. the word translated "slumber" would seem to be better rendered "remorse." It comes from a root meaning to "prick or cut with a sharp instrument." It appears, however. from the LXX usage. that the sense of "slumber" had certainly come to attach to the word used here by Paul. From the notion of a sharp wound or blow came to be derived that of the bewilderment or stupefaction consequent upon such a blow. and hence it came to signify stupor in general.

The quotation is a free combination of two passages of the LXX (Isa. 29:10; Deut. 29:4). no doubt put together by the apostle from memory.

(9) And David saith.—It appears highly improbable that Psalm 69 was really written by David. "David" merely seems to stand for the Book of Psalms. with which his name was traditionally connected. Paul is quoting freely from the LXX. In the original of Ps. 69 these verses refer to the fate invoked by the psalmist upon his persecutors; here they are applied by Paul to the fiat of the Almighty which had been pronounced against the unbelieving people of Israel.

And a recompence unto them.—The apostle means. Let their prosperity bring upon them retaliation for what they have done—namely. for their rejection of Christ.

(10) The Hebrew is. "Let their eyes be darkened. that they see not. and make their loins continually shake." "The darkening of the eyes denotes weakness and perplexity. as the enlightening of the eyes denotes renewed vigor and strength. Similarly. the shaking of the loins is expressive of terror and dismay and feebleness" (Perowne).

(11) The apostle goes on to consider further the bearings of the rejection in its more hopeful side. The Jews were. indeed (9:32-33). offended at Christ. But did their stumbling involve their utter and final ruin? It had a far more beneficent purpose than that. It brought salvation to the Gentiles. and it did this only to react as an incentive upon the Jews.

(12) Diminishing ... fulness.—If the fall of the Jews had such good results. much more might be expected from their reinstatement. The apostle seems to have in view not only the supersession of the Jews by the Gentiles. but also. under the figure of a defeat in battle. the reduction of their numbers to a small remnant. And. on the other hand. he looks forward to their full and complete restoration in the Messianic kingdom. The full "complement." as it were. of the nation is meant by "fulness"; its temporary reduction and degradation is expressed by "diminishing."

(13, 14) "Inasmuch. then. as I am the apostle of the Gentiles. I seek to do honor to my office. But not without an **arrière-pensée.** My motive is at least partly to win over my own countrymen."

(15) Reconciling of the world.—The Gospel could not be preached to the Gentiles until it had first been offered to. and rejected by. the Jews. Hence the casting away of the Jews might be said to have caused the reconciling of the rest of the world.

Life from the dead.—The reconversion of the Jews will be a signal to inaugurate that reign of eternal life which will be ushered in by the resurrection from the dead.

(16) And we have the strongest reason for believing in this reconversion of the Jews. Their forefathers were the first recipients of the promise, and what they were it is only natural to hope that their descendants will be. So we may believe that the latter end of Israel will be like its beginning, even though it is for a time interrupted. (See Num. 15:19-21.)

(17-24) The admission of the Gentile to the privileges of the Jew is no ground for boasting on his part. It is merely an **admission**. The Gentile is, as it were, a branch grafted into a stem that was none of his planting. His privileges are derived, not original. Nor is his position absolutely secured to him. It is held conditionally on the tenure of faith. He ought, therefore, anxiously to guard against any failure in faith. For the moment God has turned toward him the gracious side of His providence, as toward the Jew He has turned the severe side. But this relation may easily be reversed, and the Jew received back into the favor which he once enjoyed.

(25) Mystery.—The word always means throughout Paul's writings something which, though not to be known or fully comprehended by unassisted human reason, has been made known by direct divine revelation. It is thus applied to the whole or any part of the Christian system. Here the reference is to the whole of the divine purpose as shown in the dealings with Jew and Gentile, and especially in the present and future readmission of the former. This last point the apostle goes on to prove.

In part.—These words qualify "Israel." The hardness ("blindness"; see note on verse 7) extends over some, but not over all. There were Jewish as well as Gentile converts in Rome itself.

(26) When this ingathering of the Gentiles is complete (verse 25), then the turn of Israel will come again, and the prophecies of their conversion will be fulfilled.

There shall come ... —This prophecy is peculiarly appropriate as it refers to the exiles who had apostatized in Babylon. Then, as now, a part of the nation had remained true, and those who had not would come back to their obedience.

(28) The Jews have been allowed to fall into a state of estrangement in order to make room for the Gentiles. But this does not abrogate God's original choice of them. They are still His beloved people, for the sake of their forefathers, the patriarchs, if not for their own.

(29) Without repentance.—Not to be revoked or withdrawn, not even to be regretted.

(30, 31) The sight of the admission of the Gentiles is to act as a stimulus upon the Jews, and so lead to a renewal of their faith and obedience.

(32) For God hath concluded them all in unbelief.—This is a weighty sentence embracing the whole course of human history and summing up the divine philosophy of the whole matter. This grand and comprehensive view of the divine purposes makes so deep an impression upon the apostle that he breaks out into an impassioned ascription of praise (verses 33-36), with which the doctrinal portion of the epistle is brought to a close.

(33) Riches.—"Riches" means "inexhaustible resources," implying either that the wisdom and knowledge of God are inexhaustible, or that the materials at their command are inexhaustible. By means of these infinite resources God is able to bring good even out of evil.

Judgments.—"Decisions," such as that by which Israel was excluded and the Gentiles admitted.

(36) Of him, and through him, and to him.—All things proceed from God, all things are made or wrought by Him, and all things exist for His glory and to carry out His ends. The prominent idea is the unity of creation corresponding to the unity of the Godhead. The whole system of things issues from and returns to Him, accomplishing in its course His beneficent designs.

12

(1) At this point the apostle turns from the doctrinal portion of his epistle and begins a series of practical exhortations to his readers as to their lives as Christians. In the first two verses of the chapter he speaks of this in general terms, but then goes on to give a number of special precepts in no distinct order.

We may well believe that the apostle, having brought his argument to a climax at the close of the last chapter, would make a pause in his dictation and perhaps not resume it until another sitting. The one prevailing impression left on his mind, both by the argument just ended and by the whole previous portion of the epistle, is a profound sense of the merciful and benevolent purposes of God who, out of seeming evil, only educes the highest good. This sense he makes the link of transition by which the earnest practical exhortations which follow are bound to what precedes.

Your bodies.—This is not merely a periphrasis for "yourselves," but in the strict sense "your bodies," i.e., the very part of you which is apt to be "an occasion of falling." The apostle takes the two main parts of human nature separately. In this verse he deals with the bodies of men, in the next verse with the "mind," or intellectual and spiritual faculties.

A living sacrifice.—The idea contained in sacrifice is that of dedication. We are to **dedicate** our bodies to God. But there is to be this distinction between the old Jewish sacrifices and the Christian sacrifice: the one was of dead animals, the other of the living man. The worshiper must offer, or present, before God, **himself**, with all his living energies and powers directed consciously to God's service.

Holy, acceptable unto God.—The qualification sought in the Jewish sacrifices was that they were to be unblemished, without spot. In like manner the Christian's sacrifice must be holy and pure in God's sight, otherwise it cannot be acceptable to Him.

Reasonable service.—The sense of the Greek is "a service of the reason," i.e., a service **rendered** by the reason. Just as under the old dispensation the mind expressed its devotion through the ritual of sacrifice, so now under the new dispensation its worship takes the form of a self-dedication; its service consists in holiness of life, temperance, soberness, and chastity.

(2) Be not conformed ... but be ye transformed.—The two different words employed express the difference between an outward conformity or disguise and a thorough inward assimilation. The Christian is not to copy the fleeting fashions of the present time, but to be wholly transfigured in view of that higher mode of existence, in strict accordance with God's will, that he has chosen.

This world.—This is not here the same word as that used in I John 2:15-17, but another, which signifies rather the state of the world as it existed at the coming of Christ, as opposed to the newly-inaugurated Messianic reign. To be "conformed to this world" is to act as other men do—heathen who know not God; in opposition to this

the apostle exhorts his readers to undergo that total change which will bring them more into accordance with the will of God.

By the renewing of your mind.—The understanding, when informed by an evil principle, becomes an instrument of evil; when informed by the Spirit, it is an instrument of good. "The mind" here is not strictly identical with "conscience"; it is, as it were, the rational part of conscience, to which the moral quality needs to be superadded.

Prove.—As elsewhere, "discriminate, and so approve." The double process is included: first, of deciding what the will of God is; and, secondly, of choosing and acting upon it.

What is that good, and acceptable, and perfect, will of God.—The "will of God" is here, not the divine attribute of will, but the thing willed by God, the right course of action. We take the adjectives "good, and acceptable, and perfect" to be in apposition to the phrase: "that we may prove the will of God, that which is good, and acceptable, and perfect."

(3) Having thus stated the broad principle which is to govern the conduct of the Christian, the apostle now goes on to apply it to certain details. His first object is to secure that temper in the members of the Roman Church which will best enable them to act with union and efficiency.

Not to think of himself ... —The sense of the Greek is to have the thoughts and feelings habitually turned in a certain direction. Sobriety of mind must constantly be kept in view as the object or ideal toward which all the thoughts and feelings converge.

According as God hath dealt to every man.—The standard of action which each Christian ought to propose to himself should be in proportion to the amount of his faith as given to him by God. He who has the strongest faith may assume the highest standard, and offer himself for the highest offices, and so on down the scale. It is, however, essential that the estimate which each man puts upon the strength of his own faith should be thoroughly sincere, not biased by self love.

(4, 5) In the church there must be a hierarchy, a division of labor, every one doing that for which he is best fitted. All Christians, viewed collectively, make up one body, the unity of which is supplied by their relation to Christ. Viewed individually, they stand to each other in the same sort of relation as the different limbs and organs

945

of the natural body. This figure of the body and the members is worked out more fully in I Cor. 12:12-27.

(6) Gifts differing according to the grace.— The word translated "gifts" means "gifts of grace," grace standing here for the operation of the Spirit. Different kinds of grace, with different forms of expression, are given to different individuals, and they are to be cherished and used accordingly.

Prophecy.—The gift of prophecy is treated at length in I Cor. 14. It was a kind of powerful and anointed preaching which, unlike the gift of tongues, was strictly within the control of the person who possessed it.

According to the proportion of faith.— This refers to the active faculty of faith present in him who prophesies. It would then be nearly equivalent to the condition of verse 3. The prophet is to let his utterances be regulated strictly by the degree of faith of which he is conscious in himself.

(7) Ministry.—The word used is the technical term for the discharge of the office of deacon. The institution of this office is described in Acts 6:1-5. Its object was to provide for the practical business as opposed to the spiritual ministrations of the Church.

He that teacheth.—Comp. I Cor. 12:28; Eph. 4:11; I Tim. 5:17. Teaching was considered as a special office, though not, perhaps, confined to special persons.

(8) He that exhorteth.—In the apostolic writings, the one idea of "preaching" is divided into its several branches. Exhortation, corresponding perhaps to our word "encouragement," would be especially needed in the troubled circumstances of the early Church.

He that giveth.—In this and the following phrases the apostle passes on from considering the definite functions of the ministry to those which were common to all members of the church. "Giveth" is therefore here to be taken in a wide sense.

(9) Without dissimulation.—The same Greek word is translated "unfeigned" in II Cor. 6:6; I Tim. 1:5; II Tim. 1:5, and "without hypocrisy" in Jas. 3:17.

(10) With brotherly love.—The word for "kindly affectioned" is especially used of the family relation, and is, therefore, appropriately applied to the brotherhood of the Christian family.

Preferring one another.—The Christian is to take the initiative and show honor or respect to others without waiting for them to show it to him.

(11) In business.—Rather, "in zeal"; the reference is to the spiritual and not to the practical life.

Fervent.—In the literal and etymological sense, "boiling" or "seething." The temperament of the Christian is compared to water bubbling over the flame.

In spirit—i.e., not "in the Holy Spirit," but "in that part of you which is spirit."

(12) Patient in tribulation.—This virtue was especially needed in the troublous times through which the church was passing. So, again, in verse 13 the "hospitality" of which the apostle speaks is something more than the ordinary entertainment of friends. The reference is to a state of things in which the Christian was liable to be persecuted and driven from city to city, and often compelled to seek shelter with those who held the same faith as himself.

(13) Distributing to the necessity of saints.—By "saints" is meant simply "Christians." The reference is to the well-known poverty of the early Christian communities.

(14) Bless them which persecute you.— Comp. Matt. 5:44. It was probably just about the time that Paul was writing this epistle, or at most a year or two later, that the series of compositions which ultimately took the shape of our present gospels began. It is not, however, necessary to suppose that Paul had actually seen one of these. The record of our Lord's teaching was no doubt at first preserved and circulated in the church orally, and it would be in this form that Paul first became acquainted with the precept to which he here seems to allude. There is, perhaps, another reference to the Sermon on the Mount in I Cor. 7:10. Such references occur, as we should expect, more frequently in the Epistle of James.

(16) In every Christian community there should be that harmony which proceeds from a common object, common hopes, common desires. And humility is necessary to the Christian not only in his dealings with others, but also to keep his mind open and teachable. He sees his errors and learns from them.

(17) Provide things honest . . .—Let your purposes be such that all men shall recognize their complete integrity. Do not engage in enterprises of a doubtful character, that might bring not only yourselves but the Christian body into ill repute. (Comp. Matt. 5:14-16; II Cor. 8:21.)

(18) The Christian can be responsible

only for himself. As far as he is concerned, he is to do his best to maintain peace. The history of Paul himself, which is one of almost constant conflict, shows that this would not always be possible.

(19) Give place unto wrath.—It seems best to understand this of "the wrath of God" (indicated in the Greek by the use of the article). Stand aside yourself, and let the wrath of God have free course to accomplish itself as He shall think well. But another plausible interpretation would be, "Resist not evil" (Matt. 5:39). The sense, "Allow time for your own anger to cool," cannot be gotten out of the Greek. (Comp. Heb. 10:30.)

(20) Thou shalt heap coals of fire.—In Ps. 18:12, 13, 14, "coals of fire" is used of the divine vengeance. So here, but in a strictly metaphorical sense. There may be the underlying idea of awakening in the adversary the pangs of shame and remorse.

(21) Be not overcome of evil, but . . . —The infliction of vengeance is not a sign of strength, but of weakness. To repress the desire for revenge is to gain a victory over self, which is not only nobler in itself, but will also be much more effectual. It will disarm the enemy, and turn him into a friend.

13

(1-7) The duty of obedience is grounded upon the fact that the power wielded by the magistrate is derived from God, and that duty itself is stated without qualification. Although the duty of obedience is stated here without qualification, still the existence of qualifications to it is not therefore denied or excluded. Tribute is to be paid to whom tribute is due. This still leaves the question open, however, whether in any particular case tribute is rightfully due or not. There may possibly be a conflict of rights and duties, and the lower may have to yield to the higher. All that is alleged is that, **primâ-facie**, the magistrate can claim the obedience of the subject. There will always be a certain debatable ground within which opposite duties will seem to clash, and where general principles are no longer of any avail. Here the individual conscience must assume the responsibility of deciding which to obey.

But the question of political obedience cannot be rightly considered without taking into account the relation of Christianity to political life generally; neither can this isolated passage in an epistle of Paul's be considered apart from other teaching upon the same subjects in the rest of the New Testament. (Comp. I Pet. 2:13-17.) And going back to the fountainhead of Christian doctrine, we find, indeed, no express statements, but several significant facts and some important intimations. When He was arrested by the civil power, and unjustly tried and condemned, our Lord made no resistance; when the didrachma was demanded of Him, He supplied the sum required by a miracle; when a question was asked as to the legitimacy of the Roman tribute, He replied, "Render to Caesar the things which are Caesar's, and to God the things which are God's"; when appeal was made to Him to settle a disputed inheritance, He refused, saying to His petitioner, "Man, who made me a judge or a divider over you?" Here we have really the key to the whole question. As far as His practice was concerned, our Lord pursued a course of simple obedience; into the theory of political or civil obligation He absolutely refused to enter. What was Caesar's, and what was not? The ambiguity of the reply was intended. It was practically a refusal to reply at all.

The significance of this comes out strikingly when it is contrasted with the state of feeling and opinion current among the Jews at the same time. With them politics and religion were ultimately blended. They carried into the former sphere the fanaticism natural to the latter. Their religious hopes took a political form. The dominion of the Messiah was to be not a spiritual but a literal dominion, in which they, as a people, were to share. Clearly, the relations which our Lord assumed toward politics had special reference to this attitude of the Jews. He wished to disabuse His disciples once and for all of this fatal confusion of two spheres in themselves so distinct.

It is an expression of this deliberate policy which we find in these first seven verses of chap. 13. At the same time, the apostle may well have had a special as well as a general object. The church at Rome was composed largely of Jews, and these would naturally be imbued with the fanatical spirit of their countrymen. The mention of the Messiah would tend to fan their smoldering passions into flame. The apostle would be aware of this. His informants at Rome may have told him of excitement prevailing among the Jewish portion of the community. His experience in Palestine would tell

947

him to what unscrupulous acts of violence this might lead. And he forestalls the danger by an authoritative and reasoned description of the attitude which the Christian ought to assume.

It does not necessarily follow that precisely the same attitude is incumbent upon the Christian now. In this section of Christian teaching there was something that was temporary and local, and that had reference to conditions that have now passed away. And yet as a **general** principle, the injunctions of the apostle entirely hold good. The exceptions to this principle are few and far between. And he who would assert the existence of such an exception must count the cost well beforehand.

(1) There is no power.—The apostle seems to go almost out of his way to include even usurped and tyrannical power. He is, however, evidently speaking of the magistracy in its abstract or ideal form. It is the magistrate **quâ** magistrate, not **quâ** just or unjust magistrate. In this sense, not only is the human system of society a part of the divinely-appointed order of things, but it partakes more especially in the divine attributes, inasmuch as its object is to reward virtue and punish vice. It discharges the same functions that God Himself discharges, though in a lower scale and degree. In other words, the machinery of civil society is one of the chief and most conspicuous instruments by which God carries out His own moral government of mankind in this present existence. It may be said to be more distinctly and peculiarly derived from Him than other parts of the order of nature, inasmuch as it is the channel used to convey His moral approbation, or the reverse.

(3-5) It is clear from this passage that capital punishment is sanctioned by Scripture. At the same time its abolition is not excluded, as the abolition of slavery was not excluded, if the gradual development of Christian principle should seem to demand it. It follows, from this divine authority and title enjoyed by the magistrate, that he ought to be obeyed, not only from fear of the punishment that he is empowered to inflict, but also from the respect due to legitimate power. Of this respect conscience is the natural guardian.

(6) Ministers.—The words thus translated here and in verse 4 are not the same, but both are words commonly used in the New Testament of a sacred office; that in verse 4 is the original of our word "deacon," and that used in this verse is the original of our

word "liturgy." The choice of such terms harmonizes with the concept of the divine origin and character of the state system.

(8) Owe no man any thing.—The word for "owe" in this verse corresponds to that for "dues" in the last. The transition of the thought seems to be that, when you have paid all your other debts—taxes, customs, reverence, and whatever else you may owe—there will still be one debt unpaid—the universal debt of love. Love must still remain the root and spring of all actions. No other law is needed besides.

Another.—Literally, "the other"—i.e., his neighbor, the person with whom in any given instance he has to deal. (Comp. Matt. 22:39, 40; Gal. 5:14; Jas. 2:8.) It shows how thoroughly the spirit of the Founder of Christianity descended upon His followers, that the same teaching should appear with equal prominence in such opposite quarters. In Christianity, love is the lever which is to move the world; nor is it possible to find for human life, amid all the intricate mazes of conduct, any other principle that should be at once as simple, as powerful, and as profound. (See verse 10; comp. I Cor. 13:4-7.)

(11) The apostle now gives a reason for enforcing this and other duties upon his readers. The end of the world itself is near. And this law of love is the more incumbent on them to practice, because they know what a critical moment it is in which they are living.

(12) The night.—The time during which the Messiah is absent from His people is compared to night. He is the sun, whose coming converts it to day. (Comp. I Thess. 5:8.)

(13, 14) These verses, happening to catch the eye of Augustine, had a great effect in leading to his baptism and changed life.

14

There appears to have been a party in the church at Rome which had adopted certain ascetic practices over and above the common rule of Christianity. We gather that they abstained altogether from flesh and wine, and that they also made a point of observing certain days with peculiar sanctity. The origin and affinities of this party are difficult to ascertain. It seems best to regard the practices referred to as a natural development of purist elements within the church itself. These would be supplied by

hose who had come over to Christianity
rom the Essenes, with the tenets of which
ect the allusions in this chapter would
quite sufficiently agree. It would appear to
have been a further development of the
same doctrines which, at a later date, vexed
the church at Colossae. (See Col. 2:16-23.)

The whole of this chapter affords a most
striking instance of the practical wisdom of
Paul. It is a **locus classicus** on the subjects
of toleration and asceticism.

(1) Weak in the faith . . . —There may be
a sincere desire to lead a religious life, and
yet the mind is taken up with petty details,
each of which is painfully judged by itself
and not by reference to a central principle.

Doubtful disputations—judgment of his
doubtful thoughts. The strong are to deal
tenderly with the weak, and not engage
them in casuistical discussions.

(3) Let not him that eateth.—The two
classes of men are exposed to two opposite
faults. The strong **despise** the weak; the
weak **judge** the strong. In the one case there
is contempt for what is thought to be narrowness and pedantry. In the other case
censorious judgments are passed on what is
regarded as levity and irreligion.

(4) Who art thou?—This is addressed to
the weak. The apostle indignantly challenges his right to judge. That right belongs
to another tribunal, before which the conduct of the stronger Christian will not be
condemned but approved and upheld.
"Make him stand" is judicial—"secure his
acquittal."

(5) Comp. Gal. 4:10; Col. 2:16. It is clear
that the observance of special days has no
absolute sanction, but is purely a question
of religious expediency.

(6) For he giveth God thanks.—By the
saying of grace at meat, the meal, whatever
it may be, is consecrated to God, and he
who partakes of it shows that he does so in
no irreverent spirit.

(7-9) The larger principle holds good, and
therefore much more the smaller. It is not
only his food that the Christian consecrates
to God, but his whole life, to its very last
moments.

(10-12) Such being our relationships to
Christ, and such the judgment to which we
look forward, there is no room for any
human judgment. Censoriousness is thus
condemned. The true reading in verse 10 is
"judgment seat **of God.**"

(13) The word "judge" forms the connecting link between what follows and what
has gone before. If any judgment is to be

formed at all, let it be rather as a principle
to guide our own action, and not in the
shape of a criticism upon others. This principle, in the case of those who are themselves liberal and large-minded, should be
not to put temptation in the way of their
weaker brethren. The word translated "occasion to fall" is the origin of our word
"scandal." It is properly a trap or snare.
One of the special characteristics of Christianity is its tenderness for the weak.

(14) I know, and am persuaded.—The
apostle clearly identifies himself with the
less scrupulous party. For one of his intense
penetration and grasp on the realities of
things, any other position was impossible.
But while these essential features in the
apostle's character find the noblest expression, we cannot but note his attitude of
gentle forbearance toward those whose faith
is less deep and less robust than his own.

By the Lord Jesus.—The apostle is speaking from the depths of his Christian consciousness as one who knows that he has
himself put on the Spirit of Christ.

To him that esteemeth.—The quality of
uncleanness was not an objective property
in the thing itself, but a subjective quality in
the mind of the person regarding it as such.
Still, this subjective quality is for the individual a real one, and should be treated as
real.

(15) Two stages are noted in the words
"grieved" and "destroy." When one man
sees another do that which his own conscience condemns, it causes him pain, but
when he is further led on from this to do
himself what his conscience condemns, he is
in danger of a worse fate. The work of
redemption that Christ has wrought for him
is cancelled, and all that great and beneficent scheme is hindered of its operation
by an act of thoughtlessness or want of
consideration on the part of a fellow Christian.

(18) Serveth Christ.—Here the principle
of unity which holds together different sides
and manifestations of the Christian character is indicated.

(19) Edify.—It is the "upbuilding," or
mutual help and assistance in the spiritual
life which Christians receive from their
fellowship with each other.

(20) The work of God is the fabric which
the grace of God has begun, and which the
edification of Christians by each other may
help to raise in the soul; it is the gradual
formation of a truly Christian character,
both spiritual and moral.

For that man who eateth with offence.—
It seems best to refer the "eating" here to
the strong in faith, and the "offence" to that
which his eating causes to the weaker brethren. The force of the preposition is that
his eating is **attended** with offense.

(22) Reserve the exhibition of your faith
to the privacy of your direct communion
with God, and do not display it ostentatiously in public where it may do harm. It
is indeed a happy thing to have no self-
condemnatory scruples of conscience; but,
on the other hand, it is fatal to have scruples and to disregard them.

(23) But where faith is not strong enough
for this, and where the conscience deliberately approves one course, and the other
course is chosen, this alone stamps the act
as wrong.

15

Chapter 16 ends, according to the Received Text, with a twofold benediction and
a doxology, one at the end of verse 20,
another in verse 24, and the third covering
verses 25-27. Of these, the two benedictions
in verses 20 and 24 are alternatives. They
are not found in the same group of MSS at
both places, but the MSS which insert them
in the first place omit them at the second,
and **vice versâ**. Weighing the authorities on
both sides together, there can be little doubt
that the earlier position is the right one—
that the doxology ought to stand at 16:20
and to be erased in 16:24.

The longer, concluding doxology, furthermore, is also placed where it is by a number
of authorities. At the same time it is also
found at the end of chapter 14 in a number
of others, while some few have it in both
places. Marcion, the Gnostic writer, who
lived about A.D. 140, had a copy of the
epistle in which these last two chapters were
omitted altogether.

How is this series of facts to be accounted
for? The proof of the genuineness of the
chapters is overwhelming. Lightfoot suggests that the epistle was originally written
and sent to the Romans in the form in
which we have it now, except that it ended
at 16:23. The portion which was dictated by
Paul himself really concluded with the
benediction given in 16:20, but a brief and
informal postscript was added by Tertius
and his companions.

At some later period of his life, probably
during one or another of his two imprison-

ments, finding the epistle current in Rome,
it occurred to the apostle that it might with
advantage be circulated more widely. Accordingly he struck out the whole of the
more personal matter, i.e., chaps. 15 and
16. And, in order to give somewhat more
finish to the composition, he added the
elaborate doxology, which now concludes
the whole, at the end of chap. 14. At the
same time, at the beginning of the epistle,
he erased the express mention of Rome
(1:7), and left merely the general phrase "To
them that are beloved of God"—a change
of which some traces are still to be found
remaining in the MSS.

There was thus a shorter and a longer
recension of the epistle—the shorter with a
formal ending, the longer without. It was
the shorter form which happened to fall
into the hands of Marcion, who, for reasons
of his own, cut off the doxology. Later
copyists, observing the ragged edge which
was caused by the postscript of Tertius,
sought to remedy this by transferring the
benediction of verse 20 to verse 24; and
others, with more success, by adding to the
original epistle the doxology composed for
the shorter recension. The general tendency
in the scribes being to add and accumulate
rather than to subtract, all three forms have
come down to us.

It will be remembered that the Epistle to
the Ephesians seems to have gone through a
somewhat similar process, being circulated
in two forms—as a circular or general epistle, and also as one addressed to a particular church. Some conclude that the gospel
according to Luke, too, received additions,
and was issued in an enlarged form during
the lifetime of the evangelist himself.

(1) We then that are strong.—The opening verses of the chapter are intimately
connected with the close of the last. This
unbroken continuity in the two chapters
would be enough to show that the epistle
cannot originally have ended with chap. 14,
as some have supposed.

Bear the infirmities.—The object of this
tender dealing with others is to be their
benefit and growth in spiritual perfection
(verse 2). It is grounded on the example of
Christ Himself (verse 3; comp. Ps. 69:9).

(4) The promises and consolations of
Scripture support the Christian under his
trials, and enable him to endure them not
only patiently but cheerfully. These promises center in the hope of the future
Messianic glory.

(7-12) The duty of Christians to show

cordiality to each other is now based upon the comprehensiveness of the love of Christ, whose mission was directed with the same impartiality toward Jews and Gentiles. To the Jews He came to confirm and fulfill His promises; to the Gentiles He came mercifully, without benefit of covenant, to bring joys and hopes from which they had been heretofore excluded (See Deut. 32:43; Ps. 18:49; 117:1; Isa. 11:10.)

(14) And I myself also.—From this point onward the apostle gives a personal turn to his letter. The greetings at the end are naturally introduced by a few words of explanation as to the way in which the more general exhortations that preceded are to be received by the Roman Christians, and a somewhat longer statement on the part of the apostle of his own relations to the church at Rome. This might seem to be the more necessary as the church was not one of his own founding, and he might seem to be both going out of his way and acting in contradiction to his own principles in writing to them at all.

Knowledge—i.e., of the doctrinal aspects of Christianity as they had been set forth in the earlier portion of the epistle. No doubt the apostle had really much to teach his readers—he does not say that he had not—but he courteously gives them credit for all they knew.

(15) In some sort.—The apostle had taken a liberty, but not too great a liberty. He had spoken to them rather pointedly at times, but he had been careful not to go too far. The reference may be to exhortations such as those in chaps. 13 and 14, and in other parts of the epistle.

As putting you in mind.—Paul claims the right to do this because of the special grace given to him as an apostle. The Judaizing section in the church at Rome did not go as far as that in Galatia. It recognized the apostleship of Paul, and he knew that he could safely appeal to this recognition (see verse 17).

(16) Ministering the gospel of God.— Serving the Gospel of God as a priest stands at the altar in the service of the tabernacle. The offering which the priest is thus to present is the Gentile Church.

(19) Through mighty signs and wonders— i.e., through those extraordinary powers which found their expression in signs and wonders. "Signs and wonders" is the phrase regularly used throughout the New Testament for the Christian miracles. The two words are similar in meaning. They denote

the same acts, but they **connote** different aspects in which those acts may be regarded. The word "signs" tends to bring out the symbolical character of the miracle, the spiritual truth of which it was, as it were, the physical expression. In the word "wonders" stress is laid rather upon its character as a portent, a manifestation of supernatural, divine power. That Paul himself claimed miraculous powers is a fact that cannot be doubted.

And round about—i.e., in a sort of rough curve from Jerusalem (the extreme point eastward and southward of his own **public** ministry—not regarding the **private** retreat into Arabia). embracing a large portion of Asia Minor and finally turning toward the starting point again in Illyricum. Illyricum was a Roman province, stretching along the eastern coast of the Adriatic and forming the northwestern boundary of Macedonia. (See Acts 20:2.)

Fully preached.—Literally, "fulfilled." It seems probable that what is intended is the publication of the Gospel to its full geographical extent, and not the subjective sense in the apostle of his own fulfillment of the duty of preaching the Gospel laid upon him.

(20) The apostle set it before him as a point of honor, not merely to carry forward a work that others had begun, but to build up the whole edifice from the foundation himself.

(21) See Isa. 52:15 (LXX). The original has reference to the servant of Jehovah, first suffering and then glorified, so that **kings** should be dumb with astonishment at the change. Here it is applied to the evangelization of distant heathen nations.

(22) For which cause also.—And just because I was so anxious to preach the Gospel in new regions, and to finish what I had begun there, I have been prevented from coming to you sooner.

(23) But now having no more place.— The work had been finished, as far as the apostle was concerned, in Asia Minor, Macedonia, and Greece. The churches had been founded, and were making progress; and now he felt it his duty to go on to new fields, his duty in this respect also falling in with his wishes, as it would bring him to Rome.

(24) Into Spain.—In his eagerness to seek out entirely new regions, and to avoid any possibility of crossing the lines of his fellow apostles, desiring also himself to gather in the "fulness of the Gentiles" as far as lay in his power, he had determined to push on even to Spain. Whether he ever succeeded in carrying out his purpose we cannot say positively, but it is, perhaps, rather more probable than not. A tradition which dates back to the Epistle of Clement of Rome (**circ.** A.D. 95) says that he visited "the extreme limit of the West," a phrase which seems hardly satisfied by being interpreted simply of Rome. The author of the Muratorian Fragment (**circ.** A.D. 170) speaks expressly of a journey to Spain, though his language looks as if it might be an inference from this epistle. The Acts, it is true, do not carry the apostle beyond Rome, but the phenomena of the Pastoral Epistles and tradition together seem to justify our assuming the probability of a later journey or journeys not recorded in that volume; the argument from silence, as the book in any case stops short of the death of the apostle, counts for but little.

(25) In reference to this contribution, comp. Acts 24:17; I Cor. 16:1; II Cor. 8:1, 2; 9:1.

(26) The poor saints.—Literally, "for the poor among the saints." It cannot, therefore, be inferred from this that the church at Jerusalem consisted entirely of poor. Still from the first it would seem as if persons like Joseph of Arimathaea, and Nicodemus, and Mary the mother of Mark, were exceptions, and we know that the church at Jerusalem suffered severely during the famine in the reign of Claudius. Wealthier churches, such as those of Macedonia and Greece, would naturally be glad to have the opportunity of sending relief to the mother church, from which they might be said to be derived themselves. Paul himself proceeds to urge this argument.

(28) Sealed to them this fruit—i.e., placed in their hands the sum raised by the collection. Paul seems to regard this journey to Jerusalem as the close of his own apostolic labors in those parts, the dropping of the curtain, as it were, before a new act in his career.

(31) From them that do not believe.— This prayer of the apostle was partially granted. He escaped with his life from his unbelieving countrymen (Acts 23:27), but only to be delivered to the Romans. He was naturally in fear of the party to which he had himself once belonged, and who would regard him as one of the worst of apostates. But he expresses no apprehension of the Judaizing **Christians**, as might have been

expected if their antagonism had really been as violent as some would make out.

(32) The way in which he was received at Jerusalem would make a great difference to the feelings with which the apostle would arrive in Rome. A favorable reception in Jerusalem would add much to his enjoyment and benefit from fellowship with the Roman Christians.

(33) Amen.—The benediction was not intended, as some have thought, to close the epistle. Interrelated benedictions and doxologies are frequent in the writings of Paul. (Comp. 9:5; 11:36; Gal. 1:5; Eph. 3:20, 21, etc.)

16

Of all the epistles of Paul, Romans and Colossians contain the greatest number of personal salutations, though these were precisely the two churches that he had never seen up to the date of his writing. The apostle might think it invidious to single out individuals for special mention in the churches where he was known, while he would have no hesitation in naming those with whom he happened to be personally acquainted in churches where he was not known. The Christians at Rome, furthermore, had been recently in a state of dispersion. All Jews by birth had been expelled from Rome by Claudius. It was this fact which had brought Aquila and Priscilla to Corinth and Ephesus, where Paul joined them, and he would naturally meet with other members of the dispersed church in the same way.

We are apt to underrate the amount of rapid circulation which went on in these early Christian communities. We know from pagan writers that there was a great tendency all along the shores of the Mediterranean to gravitate toward Rome, and the population thus formed would naturally be a shifting and changing one, loosely attached to their temporary dwelling place, and with many ties elsewhere.

Analyzing these lists of names, we reach two general conclusions: (1) The church at Rome did not consist to any great extent of native Romans. From the first there seems to have been a large Greek element in the church at Rome, so much so that out of the twelve first bishops, only three seem to have borne Roman names, while the literature of the church, until the third century, was Greek. (2) The names seem to belong in the main to the middle and lower classes of society. Many are such as are usually assigned to slaves or freed-men. The inference is that Christianity had at this early date established itself in the palace of the emperor, though only among the lower order of servants (see Phil. 4:22).

(1) Phebe.—As the Roman church is especially exhorted to receive Phebe, it has been inferred that she was one of the party to which Paul entrusted his epistle, if not the actual bearer of it herself.

Our sister—i.e., in a spiritual sense—a fellow Christian.

Servant.—Rather, "a deaconess." Deacons were originally appointed to attend to the wants of the poorer members of the church. This is the first mention of women deacons (see I Tim. 3:11). The necessity for an order of deaconesses would gradually make itself felt where women were kept in a stricter seclusion, as in Greece and some parts of the East.

Cenchrea.—The port of Corinth, about nine miles from the city.

(3) Priscilla.—Prisca, of which form Priscilla is the diminutive. It is rather remarkable that the wife should be mentioned first. Perhaps it may be inferred that she was the more active and conspicuous of the two.

Aquila was a Jew of Pontus, whom Paul had found with his wife at Corinth (Acts 18:1). They had there been converted by him, and afterward appear in his company at Ephesus (Acts 18:18, 26; I Cor. 16:19). On verse 4, comp. I Cor. 15:32.

(5) The church that is in their house.—A party of Christians seems to have been in the habit of meeting in the house of Aquila and Priscilla for purposes of worship at Rome, as previously at Ephesus (I Cor. 16:19). Similar instances may be found in Acts 12:12; Col. 4:15; Philem. 2.

Firstfruits of Achaia.—For "Achaia" we ought certainly to read "Asia"—i.e., the Roman province including the whole western end of the peninsula of Asia Minor. Ephesus was the capital. By "firstfruits of Asia" is meant one of the first converts won over to Christianity in Asia.

(7) My kinsmen.—From the number and places of persons so designated, it would seem as if the word "kinsmen" was to be taken in a wider sense than that which it usually bears. It probably means members of the same nation—Jew like myself.

Fellow-prisoners.—The only imprisonment of Paul recorded in the Acts after this

date would be that at Philippi; but see II Cor. 6:5 and 11:23.

Of note among the apostles—i.e., "highly esteemed by the apostolic circle."

(8-10) Amplias, Apelles, and Urbane are common names, in several instances found in connection with the imperial household. Stachys, a rarer name, appears as that of a court physician in the inscriptions of about the date of this epistle. Aristobulus was a grandson of Herod the Great. By a somewhat common custom, his household may have been transferred to the emperor at his death. In that case, his slaves would be designated by a term such as we find in the Greek.

(11) Them that be of the household of Narcissus.—There had been a famous Narcissus, a freed-man and favorite of Claudius, who had been put to death three or four hears before this epistle was written. His household would naturally pass into the hands of the emperor, though still keeping his name. In the case of Aristobulus, the transference would be effected by bequest; in that of Narcissus by confiscation.

(12) Tryphena and Tryphosa were probably sisters or near relatives attached to the court.

(13) Rufus.—Simon of Cyrene is described in Mark 15:21 as "the father of Alexander and Rufus"; and as there is a substantial tradition favored by some internal indications that this gospel was written at Rome, it is likely that the same Rufus may be meant.

His mother and mine.—His mother, who has also been like a mother to me.

(14, 15) Taking the list of names as a whole, and comparing them with the inscriptions, we note the general coincidence with the mention of "Caesar's household" in Phil. 4:22.

(16) Salute one another.—As a mark of brotherly feeling among themselves, Paul desires those who are assembled at the reading of his epistle to greet each other in a Christian way. It is to be their own act and not a salutation coming from him.

With an holy kiss.—A common Eastern and Jewish custom especially consecrated in Christianity. (Comp. I Cor. 16:20; II Cor. 13:12; I Thess. 5:26; I Pet. 5:14.)

The churches of Christ.—The word "all" should be inserted. As being the apostle of the Gentiles, and knowing as he did the interest which all would take in the church of the great metropolis, Paul feels himself fully justified in speaking for all the churches of his foundation.

(17-20) Here the epistle would naturally end, but an afterthought occurs to the apostle. His experience of other churches, especially those at Corinth and in Galatia, suggests to him that he should warn his readers against false teachers, though such had not as yet obtained any great hold among them.

(18) Their own belly.—Comp. Phil. 3:18, 19. There the apostle is condemning Antinomian extravagances which professed to be based on his own teaching; here he would seem to have in view some more radical divergence of doctrine, "contrary to" that which they had learned.

(19) Simple concerning evil.—This is not at all the same word as that which is translated "simple" in verse 18. The first is that freedom from dishonest motives which makes a man an unsuspecting prey for designing persons; the second refers rather to the confirmed habit of one who has come in contact with evil and is still uncontaminated by it.

(20) The God of peace.—The reference seems to be to his near expectation of the Messiah's return, and with it the final victory of the faith. The Romans have not begun to feel the bitterness of divisions as yet; he foresees a time when they will do so, but beyond that he foresees a further time when all will be quelled and the Great Adversary himself forever overthrown. (See Gen. 3:15.)

(21) Timotheus.—Timothy had been sent in advance from Ephesus (Acts 19:22). He would seem to have gone on into Greece and to Corinth itself (I Cor. 4:17; 16:10). He had after that rejoined Paul on his way through Macedonia (II Cor. 1:1), and he was now with him again in Greece. Why his name does not appear in the heading of the present letter, as normally, we do not know. For Lucius, Jason, and Sosipater, see Acts 13:1; 17:5-9; 20:4, respectively.

(22) Tertius was the apostle's amanuensis. It was the custom of Paul to add a few words of parting benedictory encouragement or admonition in his own handwriting, partly as a mark of his own personal interest in his readers, and partly as a precaution against forgery. (See Gal. 6:11;

II Thess. 3:17.) Involved and broken style is to be accounted for by this habit of dictation, and, as it would seem, not very punctilious revision. We have the thoughts and words of the apostle as they came warm from his own mind.

(23) Gaius.—The Gaius of the epistle would probably be identical with Gaius of Corinth (I Cor. 1:14). The name was a common one.

Mine host, and of the whole church.—Paul was now lodging in the house of Gaius. It would seem that Gaius lent his house for the meetings of the church, or it is possible that Paul may be alluding, with graceful hyperbole, to the hospitality which he was always ready to exercise.

Erastus.—It is not easy to identify this Erastus with the one mentioned in Acts 19:22 and II Tim. 4:20, who there appears as a traveling companion of the apostle. The office of treasurer ("chamberlain") to an important city like Corinth would naturally, we should suppose, involve a fixed residence.

(24) The grace of our Lord Jesus Christ.—See notes at the beginning of chap. 15.

(25) The confirming and strengthening in all elements of Christian character was to take place through those appointed ways and means that are laid down in the Gospel and form the main topic of Christian preaching. The two clauses which begin with "according to" are co-ordinate, and are both dependent upon the word "stablish."

Of the mystery.—The word "mystery" is used in the sense of something which up to the time of the apostles had remained secret, but had then been made known by divine intervention. All through the Old Testament dispensation, the Christian scheme, which was then future, had remained hidden; now, with Christ's coming, the veil has been taken away.

Since the world began.—Literally, "in eternal times"—i.e., from this present moment, stretching backward throughout eternity—an emphatic way of saying, "never before."

The subscription in its present form hardly dates back beyond the ninth century. The earliest form of subscription up to the sixth century was simply "To the Romans."

I CORINTHIANS

1

(1) Paul, called to be an apostle.—Better, "a called Apostle of Jesus Christ." His apostolic authority, which was questioned by some in Corinth, is thus set out at the beginning of the epistle.

And Sosthenes our brother.—See note on verse 16; Acts 18:17. From his name being thus joined with that of the apostle, we may conjecture that he was his amanuensis in writing this epistle, the salutation only (16:21) having been written by Paul's hand.

(2) Church of God.—Chrysostom remarks how these opening words are a protest against the party-spirit prevailing at Corinth: "The Church of God—not of this or that man."

Them that are sanctified in Christ Jesus.—This is not another class of persons, but a description of those who compose "the Church." The term "saints" is never used by Paul with its restricted modern meaning. The English word which most nearly expresses the apostolic idea is "Christians"—used in its most comprehensive sense.

With all that in every place.—The Church at large is composed of all who call upon the Lord Jesus. This idea of the Church, put forward in the opening of the epistle, at once directs the reader's mind from the narrow spirit of faction which was exhibiting itself at Corinth.

(4-9) Expressions of thankfulness serve to secure at the very outset the attention of those to whom the apostle is writing. He thus shows that he is not blind to, or forgetful of, their good qualities, although this epistle is written especially to rebuke their present sins, and also that he is not about to utter words of hopeless condemnation, but of wholesome warning. (Comp. Phil. 1:6; I Thess. 5:24.)

(10) Now I beseech you, brethren.—With these words the apostle introduces the topic which is one of the chief reasons of his writing this epistle: the party-spirit existing in the Corinthian church. The treatment of this subject continues to 4:20. It is important to remember that the factions rebuked by Paul were not sects who separated themselves from the Church, but those who

within the Church divided themselves into parties, each calling itself by the name of some apostle whose teaching and practice were most highly esteemed. The nature and cause of these divisions we understand from the apostle's exhortation to unity, and his rebuke of the spirit which gave rise to them.

By the name of our Lord Jesus Christ.—That name adds strength to his exhortation to "speak the same thing"—i.e., to call themselves by this one name, and not each (as in verse 12) by a different designation, and that there should be no "schisms" among them. The word translated "divisions" signifies literally a "rent" (Mark 2:21); and the idea is carried on in the words "be perfectly joined together," which in the original signifies the repair of something which was torn (Matt. 4:21). The church at Corinth presents to the apostle's mind the idea of a seamless robe torn into pieces, and he desires its complete and entire restoration by their returning to a united temper of mind and judgment as to word and deed.

(11) The house of Chloe.—Who Chloe was we cannot tell. Slaves of her household, probably traveling on her business between Ephesus and Corinth, had brought to Paul the account of the distracted state of the church in their city.

Contentions among you.—Verse 12 goes on to point out the distinctive factions which called themselves respectively the party of Paul, of Cephas, of Apollos, and of Christ.

Paul places first that section of the Church which called themselves by his name —thus at the outset showing that it is not for the sole purpose of silencing opponents, or from a jealousy of the influence of other teachers, that he writes so strenuously against the disturbances in the Corinthian community. The Pauline party would no doubt have consisted chiefly of those who were the personal converts of the apostle. They allowed Paul's teaching (of the liberty wherewith Christ made them free) to develop in them an unchristian license and an uncharitable treatment of those who still clung to some of the outward forms of Judaism.

Apollos (see Acts 18:24-28) brought with him to Corinth the arts of the rhetorician and the culture of a Greek philosopher; and while preaching Christ crucified, these gifts and knowledge rendered him more acceptable than Paul had been, with his studied simplicity of style, to a certain class of intellectual and rationalizing hearers in Corinth. It ought to be remembered that Apollos was in no sense the founder of a party. It was the exaggeration and perversion of Apollos' teaching, by some of the converts, that really founded the party. (See detail in 1:18-2:16.) To the end he and Paul remained friends (see Tit. 3:13). He was probably with the apostle while the epistle was being written, and (16:12) refused, even when Paul suggested it, to go so soon again to Corinth, lest his presence should in the least tend to keep that party-spirit alive.

Cephas' (Peter) name was attached to the faction of the Corinthian church which still clung to many Jewish ceremonial ideas from which Paul was entirely free. (See detail in 7:1-11:1.) They exalted Peter as more worthy of honor than Paul because he had personally been with Christ, and been called "Cephas" (**rock**) by Him. They insinuated that Paul's supporting himself was not as dignified as the maintenance of Peter and others by the church, in accordance with their Lord's command (9:4-6; II Cor. 11:9, 10); and they unfavorably contrasted Paul's celibacy with the married state of Peter, and of "the brethren of the Lord" (9:5). It is probable that their animosity toward Paul was increased by the knowledge that there were certain matters in which he considered Peter to be in error, and "withstood him to the face" (Gal. 2:11).

There was still one other faction which dared to attribute to themselves the name of Christ Himself. These overestimated the importance of having seen Christ in the flesh, and despised Paul as one who had subsequently joined the apostolate. Contempt for all human teachers was by them exalted into a virtue. Their greatest sin was that the name which should have been the common bond of union (verse 13), the name by the thought and memory of which the apostle would plead for a restoration of unity, was degraded by them into the exclusive party-badge of a narrow section. (See allusion in II Cor. 10:7.)

(14) For Crispus, see Acts 18:8; for Gaius, see Rom. 16:23. The evident importance and position of these two, and that they were the first converts, may account for the apostle's having departed from his usual practice in baptizing them.

(16) Stephanas.—The mention of Stephanas and his household was, from the words preceding, evidently a subsequent correction by the apostle. He was reminded

of it possibly by Sosthenes, who was writing from his dictation, and would naturally have known the fact (see 16:15, 17; Acts 18:17).

(19) This is a further explanation of why the word of the Gospel, and not the word of merely human wisdom, is "the power of God" (verse 18). Words which originally applied to those who assumed to be the guides of the Jewish race (Isa. 29:14, LXX) apply with greater force to those who would presume to be Christian leaders.

(20) The second quotation (Isa. 33:18) was originally a song of triumph over the enemies of Israel. The apostle's general reference here is to those who would exalt human knowledge, while "the scribe" indicates the Jew, and the "disputer" the Greek, who discussed philosophy (Acts 6:9; 9:29).

(21) In the wisdom of God.—These words refer not to revelation, but to God's wisdom evidenced in nature and in the teachings of lawgivers and prophets. The world by its wisdom did not attain to a knowledge of God in His wisdom displayed in creation (Acts 17:26; Rom. 1:19).

It pleased God.—The world having thus failed to gain a true knowledge of God in His wisdom, He gave them that knowledge through that very proclamation of "the cross" which those "that perish" call foolishness (verse 18; see Rom. 1:16).

(25) Because.—This introduces the reason why Christ, as being crucified, is the power and wisdom of God: God's folly (as they call it) is wiser not "than the wisdom of men," but than men themselves—embracing in that word all that men can know or hope ever to know; and the weakness of God (as they regard it) is stronger than men.

(26) For ye see your calling.—The apostle directs them to look at the facts regarding their own calling to Christianity as an illustration of the truth of what he has just written. "The ancient Christians were, for the greater part, slaves and persons of humble rank; the whole history of the progress of the Church is in fact a gradual triumph of the unlearned over the learned, of the lowly over the great, until the emperor himself cast his crown at the foot of Christ's cross" (Olshausen).

(30) "Who *was* (not "is") made wisdom unto us *from* God." The past tense here refers us back to the fact of the Incarnation; in it Christ became to us God's revelation of Himself, thus giving us a wisdom from the source of all wisdom which surpasses utterly any wisdom we could have derived from nature or from man. Not only is Christ the source of whatever true wisdom we have, but also of whatever righteousness and holiness we have.

2

(1) And I.—The apostle now proceeds to show how he personally, in both the matter and manner of his teaching at Corinth, had acted in accordance with those great principles which he has already explained as God's method.

(2) I determined not to know.—We have here a statement of what was ever the subject matter of apostolic teaching. Paul did not dwell on the miraculous in the life of Christ, which would have catered to the Jewish longing for a "sign"; nor did he put forward elaborate "theories" of the Gospel, which would have been a concession to the Greek's longing after "wisdom"; but he preached a personal, crucified Christ (1:17, 23; Gal. 6:14; Phil. 2:8). We can scarcely realize now the stumblingblock which the preaching of a crucified Christ must have been to Jews and Greeks, and the enormous temptation to keep the cross in the background which the early teachers would naturally have felt.

(3) And I was with you.—The "weakness and fear and trembling" of which Paul speaks here had in it probably a large element of that self-distrust which so noble and sensitive a nature would feel in the fulfillment of such an exalted mission as the preaching of the cross. Yet there is reference also to physical apprehension of danger. The bravest are not those who do not experience any sensation of fear, but rather those who keenly appreciate danger, who have an instinctive shrinking from it, and yet eventually by their moral might conquer this dread.

(6) Howbeit we speak wisdom.—Nevertheless, there is a wisdom in the Gospel. The assertion is in the Greek a striking contrast to verse 4. In the original (verse 4) the word is "wisdom," and not **man's** wisdom." Thus the statement here is a verbal contradiction of that in verse 4.

Them that are perfect.—The "wisdom" of the Gospel is that deep spiritual truth which only those whose spiritual natures have been trained and cultivated were capable of understanding. This "wisdom," however the apostle had not taught the Corinthians; he

had taught them only the alphabet of Christianity, for they were still but "babes" (3:3).

(7) The writer explains his speaking of certain truths only to the initiated, and not to all (4:1; Col. 1:26). Comp. Rom. 16:25; Eph. 3:10.

(8) Lord of glory.—This is in striking contrast to the ignominy of the crucifixion.

(9) As it is written.—Although the words given here are not to be found in the same sequence in any passage in the Old Testament, still there are phrases scattered through the writings of Isaiah (see Isa. 64:4; 65:17; 66:15; LXX), which would easily be joined together in memory and resemble even verbally the passage as written here. Paul is not basing any argument upon a particular sentence, but merely availing himself of some thoughts or words in the Old Testament as an illustration of the truth which he is enforcing.

(11) Paul urges that man, as man, cannot know the things of God, but that his knowledge of these things is in virtue of his having the Spirit of God dwelling in him.

(12) We.—This must not be confined to the apostles exclusively. Though referring primarily to them, it includes all the members of the Christian Church as one with its teachers and rulers.

(13) Comparing spiritual things with spiritual.—The word translated "comparing" is used in the LXX in the sense of expounding or teaching, and especially of dreams, where the dream is, so to speak, "compared" with the interpretation. So here, the spiritual things are "compared" with the spiritual language in which they are stated.

(14) Paul speaks of man as consisting of body (**soma**), soul (**psyche**), and spirit (**pneuma**). The **soma** is our physical nature; the **psyche** is our intellectual nature, embracing also our desires and human affections; the **pneuma** is our spiritual nature. Thus in each of us there is a somatical man, a physical man, and a pneumatical man; and according as any one of those parts of the nature dominates over the other, so is the character of the individual person. One in whom the **soma** is strongest is a "carnal" man; one in whom the intellect or affections predominate is a "natural" man; and one in whom the spirit rules (which it can do only when enlightened and guided by the Spirit of God, which acts on it) is a "spiritual" man. (See I Thess. 5:23.)

(16) This is the proof that the enlightened spiritual man cannot be judged by any one who is not thus enlightened (verse 15). Paul does not mean to assert that the apostles knew all that the mind of Christ knew, but that all things which they did know were from Him and spiritual (John 15:15).

3

(1) Again, as in 2:6, the apostle shows how general principles which he has just explained were exemplified in his own conduct. And he proceeds to point out to them that their own character, as being wanting in spirituality, was the real hindrance to his teaching them the higher spiritual truth which may be called "the wisdom" of the Gospel. "Carnal" is here the opposite of "spiritual," and does not involve any reference to what we would commonly speak of as carnal sin.

(2, 3) Up to this point the apostle has been speaking of the condition in which he found the Corinthians when he came first to Corinth, and he proceeds from this to rebuke them for continuing in this condition. He does not blame them for having been "babes" at the outset, but he does blame them for not having yet grown up out of infancy.

(4) One saith, I am of Paul.—These and the following words explain exactly what the apostle means by their being "carnal," and walking after a merely human manner. Only two of the factions are mentioned as types of the rest. The factious spirit was in each and all the "parties" the same, but the particular difference between the teaching of the higher wisdom and the simpler truths of the Gospel was best illustrated by these two.

(5) The apostle now proceeds to explain (verses 5-9) what is the true position and work of Christian ministers. He asserts that all alike—both those who teach the simpler truths, and those who build up upon that primary knowledge—are only instruments in God's hand.

(6) I have planted, Apollos watered.—By an image borrowed from the processes of agriculture the apostle explains the relation in which his teaching stood to that of Apollos—and how all the results were from God. This indication of Paul's having been the founder, and Apollos the subsequent instructor, of the Corinthian Church is in complete harmony with Acts 18:27; 19:1.

(9) Three times in this verse the apostle repeats the name of God with emphasis to explain and to impress the assertion of the

previous verse, that men are to recognize the unity, and God alone the diversity, in the ministerial work and office. The image is thus suddenly altered from agriculture to architecture, as the latter can be more amplified and will better illustrate the great variety of work of which the apostle proceeds subsequently to speak. This sudden change of metaphor is a characteristic of Paul's style. (See 9:7; II Cor. 10:4-8; Eph. 3:17; Col. 2:6, 7.)

(10, 11) The argument in this and the following verse is that there can be only one foundation in the spiritual building—namely, the personal Jesus Christ. That foundation the apostle has laid. None can alter it or add to it as a foundation; but there may be an immense variety in the materials with which those who come after the laying of the foundation may build up the superstructure. Therefore their own work and how they build, and not the one foundation once for all and unalterably laid, should be the subject of their thought and care.

(12) "Precious stones" are not gems, but grand and costly stones, such as marble. "Hay" is dried grass used to fill up chinks in the walls; "stubble," stalks with the ears of corn cut off, was used for making a roof of thatch. The truth brought forward is primarily, if not exclusively, for teachers. The image of dwellings is taken from what would have met the eye of a traveler in Ephesus where Paul now was, or in Corinth where his letter was to be read. Then arose before the apostle's vision the thought of a city being visited by a mighty conflagration, such as desolated Corinth itself in the time of Mummius. The mean structures of perishable wood and straw would be utterly consumed, while the mighty palaces and temples would stand after the fire had exhausted itself. Thus, says Paul, it will be with the work of Christian teachers when the fire of the "day of the Lord" will prove and test the quality of each work.

(15) So as.—These words remind us that the whole passage is to be regarded as metaphorical. Forgetting this, Roman divines have evolved from these words the doctrine of purgatory.

(16) The temple of God.—From the thought of grand edifices in general the apostle goes on to the particular case of a building which is not only splendid but "holy." Thus the rich and valuable metals and stones spoken of previously represent spiritual attainments. He introduces the passage with words implying that their conduct was such as could be pursued only by those who were either ignorant or forgetful of the truth of which he now reminds them.

(17) Which temple ye are.—As God commanded the punishment of death to be inflicted on whoever defiled the actual Temple (see Exod. 28:43; Lev. 16:2), because it was holy unto the Lord, and His presence dwelt there, so they, having the same Spirit in them, were a temple also holy unto the Lord, and God would not leave him unpunished who destroyed or marred this spiritual temple.

(18) Merely human wisdom is in itself worthless for spiritual purposes, and, therefore, the possession of it alone is no reason for the exaltation of the teacher who is endowed with it.

(19) For it is written.—See Job 5:13; Ps. 94:8. Except for Jas. 5:11, this is the only allusion to the book of Job or to Job in the New Testament.

(21) Therefore.—Not because of what has been mentioned, but introducing what he is about to mention. Let party spirit cease. Do not degrade yourselves by calling yourselves after the names of any man, for everything is yours—then teachers only exist for you.

4

(1-5) Here is a further argument against party spirit as it existed in the Corinthian church: God alone can judge of any man's work whether it be worthy, and God, unlike man, who selects only some **one** for praise, will give to **every** worker his own proper share of approval.

(1) As of the ministers of Christ.—The word used for "ministers" here expresses more strongly the idea of subordination than the word which occurs in 3:5. It implies not only those who are under one superior, but also those who are in a still inferior position (as the officer who has to obey orders, Matt. 5:25). Even the steward in a Greek household was generally a slave.

(2) The argument here is that, as in the case of an earthly steward, inquiry is made into his character as to whether he be trustworthy, so it will be with them who are stewards of the mysteries of God. That inquiry is, of course, made in regard to an earthly steward by his master in which service he is; and so the Lord alone, whose stewards the apostles were, shall be the inquirer into **their** faithfulness.

(3) No earthly judgment is of any concern to him. The literal translation of "man's judgment" is **man's day.** Probably Paul lived with the idea of the day of the Lord as the judgment day so constantly before him, that he uses the words as synonymous. (Comp. 3:13.)

(6) These things—i.e., all that he has written about the factions. All that was said in condemnation of the spirit which exalted the apostle and Apollos into party leaders would apply with equal or greater force to all others. By their examples the Corinthians should learn not to go beyond what is written in the Scriptures—not to be found in any one particular passage, but in the general tone and scope of the Old Testament writings, which ever ascribe glory to God alone.

(7) For ... —This is the explanation of why such "puffing up" is absurd. Even if one possess some gift or power, he has not attained it by his own excellence or power; it is the free gift of God.

(9) For ... —This introduces the reason why he may well express the devout wish which he has just uttered (verse 8) for the coming of the kingdom of his Lord. The imagery of this passage would be easily understood by the Corinthians, familiar as they were with the arena. There is, perhaps, a slight contrast intended here between the Corinthians sitting by criticizing, and the apostles engaging actually in the struggle against evil—a contrast which is brought out more strikingly in the irony of verse 10.

(11) We both hunger.—From strong irony the apostle here passes, in the pathetic and sad description which occupies verses 11-13, to show how intensely true that last word "despised" was, as expressing his own position, not only in time past, but also at the hour of his writing. Here still there is an implied contrast between their condition ("full," "rich," "kings," of verse 8) and that of Paul himself.

(12) And labour.—While at Ephesus, where this letter was written, the apostle supported himself by working with Aquila and Priscilla at tent-making. This labor was hard and earnest work. (See I Thess. 2:8, 9; II Thess. 3:8.) And it was rendered more excessive from the apostle's characteristic generosity to others (Acts 20:17-38).

(14) I write not these things to shame you.—The mingled irony and reproach of the preceding verses here ceases, and from indignant expostulation the writer now turns to make a tender and touching appeal to their better nature and their sympathy. The following verses to the end of this chapter soften the severity of this early part of the epistle by explaining in what spirit he has written, and the right which he has as their "father in the faith" so to address them.

(17) For this cause.—When Paul contemplated a visit to the churches in Macedonia and Achaia, he sent Timothy and Erastus in advance (Acts 19:21, 22). It is to this fact that allusion is made here, and from 16:10 we see that the apostle did not calculate on Timothy's arrival in Corinth until after this letter had reached them. The rumors of the existence of factions in Corinth had reached Paul before Timothy had departed, and were the cause of his desire that before he himself visited Corinth Timothy should do so, and bring the Corinthians to a better frame of mind before the apostle's arrival. But after Timothy's departure from Ephesus the apostle heard from the household of Chloe how much worse than he had imagined from the previous rumors was the state of affairs at Corinth. It would not do to let such a condition of things continue to grow and intensify until Timothy should arrive there, delayed as he would be in visiting other places in Macedonia and Achaia **en route**. Thus was Paul influenced to send this letter to Corinth at once so as to anticipate the arrival of Timothy there. Paul had converted Timothy ("my beloved son") to the faith (Acts 16:1). Again Paul speaks of Timothy as his "brother" (II Cor. 1:1).

(21) This verse at once concludes this first part of the epistle, in which the party spirit and the evils resulting from it in Corinth are treated. The second topic to be discussed is the case of incest which had occurred, one of those things which would compel the apostle to visit Corinth, not "in love and in the spirit of meekness," but "with a rod."

5

A member of the Corinthian church has caused grave scandal by marrying his stepmother. (Paul uses the Hebrew phrase of Lev. 18:8.) This was aggravated by the fact that her husband, his father, was yet alive (II Cor. 7:12). Throughout the Roman empire such a union was regarded with abhorrence, and the toleration of it by the Christian community was calculated seriously to imperil the character of the early

church. Such a state of morals would be promptly seized upon by opponents, as an example of what must result from the "freedom of the gospel."

(3) For I verily.—The apostle had fully made up his mind that this offender must be removed, and insists on the Corinthians' doing it. Until now the factionalism had hindered them from uniting in common cause (verse 2).

(4, 5) These two verses contain the apostolic sentence on the offender. We recognize not merely a formal excommunication from church fellowship, but a more severe punishment, which could be inflicted only by apostolic authority and power—the actual infliction of some bodily suffering such as would destroy the flesh (not the body, but the flesh, the source and origin of the evil). (See Matt. 16:19; 18:18, 20; 28:20.) Explicit directions for the excommunication by the Church of an offender are given in chap. 7, but there is no direct instruction to inflict the further punishment spoken of here. It is, indeed, probable that the lesser punishment had the desired effect (see II Cor. 2:6), and we subsequently find Paul pleading for the loving readmission of the offender into all the privileges of Christian communion.

(6-8) There is possibly a reference to some boasting regarding their spiritual state contained in the letter which had reached Paul from Corinth, and to which part of this epistle is a reply. (See 7:1.) As long as there is that one bad person among them, it gives a bad character to the whole community. This epistle being written shortly before Pentecost (16:8), the leaven and the Paschal Feast naturally suggested themselves as illustrations. As with the most scrupulous care the Jew would remove every atom of leaven when the Paschal lamb was to be eaten, so our Paschal Lamb having been slain, we must take care that no moral leaven remains in the sacred household of the Church while she keeps her perpetual feast of prayer and thanksgiving.

(9) I wrote unto you in an epistle.—These words refer to some former epistle addressed to the Corinthian church, and which has not been preserved. It is natural to suppose that it was written probably from Ephesus, after a visit paid to Corinth of which we have no record, for in II Cor. 12:14; 13:1 we read of a third visit being contemplated, whereas only one is recorded. The condition of the church which caused the apostle that "heaviness," which he connects with this visit in II Cor. 2:1, would naturally have given rise to an epistle containing the kind of direction urged here.

(10) There are so many fornicators, and covetous, and idolaters in this world that men **must** meet with them. But the Christian must tolerate no such sins among themselves; they must exclude from the social circle any brother who, bearing the name of Christ, indulges in the vices of the heathen world. The Church is to be the light of the world, and not the recipient of the world's darkness.

6

(1) Having rebuked the Corinthian Christians for any attempt to judge those who are outside the Church—i.e., the heathen (5:12, 13)—Paul now insists, on the other hand, of the importance of their not submitting their affairs for decision to the heathen tribunals. Jewish converts would have more easily understood that they should settle disputes among themselves, as the Roman power (Acts 18:14, 15) had given this liberty to the Jews. The Gentile converts, however, would have been naturally inclined to continue to bring disputes before the tribunals with which they had been so familiar in a proverbially litigious condition of society before their conversion. We can well imagine how detrimental to the best interests of Christianity it would be for the Christian communion, founded as it was on principles of unity and love, to be perpetually, through the hasty temper and weakness of individual members, held up to the scorn of the heathen as a scene of internal strife. The words "unjust" and "saints" convey here no essentially moral ideas. They merely signify respectively "heathen" and "members of the Christian Church" (see verse 4).

(3) We shall judge angels.—The passage is a climax arising out of the apostle's intense realization of the unity of Christ and His Church triumphant—a point which seems ever present to the mind of Paul when he speaks of the dignity of Christianity. In this sense, redeemed humanity will be superior to, and judges of, the spiritual world. That the words have some such large significance, and are not the expression of a hard and literal fact regarding some members of the angelic host, is borne out by the subsequent words, where the contrast to "angels" is not "men," but "things" relating to this life.

(5) I speak to your shame.—In the whole Christian community at Corinth, which boasted of superior wisdom, is there not to be found even one man sufficiently esteemed for his wisdom to be trusted by the brethren with the settlement of their disputes?

(7) A fault.—Better, "a falling short" of your privilege and dignity as Christians. The apostle goes one step farther and condemns the Corinthians, not only on the ground of the tribunals to which they resorted being heathen, but for the spirit of litigation itself. He reminds them of how such a temper of mind is the opposite of that which the Lord Himself had commended to His followers (Matt. 5:40).

(11) Ye are washed.—The words "sanctified" and "justified" as used here (out of actual sequence) do not point to those definite stages in the Christian courses to which they generally refer in theological language. What the apostle urges is that, by the power of Christ's name and the Holy Spirit, they became holy and righteous, thus putting aside that impurity and that unrighteousness which once were theirs, and with which they could not enter into the kingdom.

(12) All things are lawful unto me.—This was probably a statement which the apostle had made himself; at all events, the freedom which it expresses was dear to him, and it may have been misused by some as an argument for universal license. Paul, therefore, boldly repeats it and proceeds to show that it is a maxim of Christian liberty, which does not refer to matters which are absolutely wrong, and that even in its application to indifferent matters it must be limited and guarded by other Christian principles. We must not regard the use of the singular "me" as being in any sense a limitation of the principle to the apostle personally. The words refer to all Christians.

But I will not be brought under the power of any.—There is such a thing as becoming the slave of liberty itself. If we sacrifice the power of choice which is implied in the thought of liberty, we cease to be free; we are brought **under** the power of that which should be **in** our power.

(13) Meats for the belly.—The apostle proceeds now to show that the question of eating meats offered to idols comes into that catalog of indifferent things on which an exercise of Christian freedom is permissible, and that the question of fornication does not. (See 8:4.) Lawful matters are to be decided upon the highest principle of expediency; but fornication is an unlawful matter, and therefore the question of its expediency does not arise at all. The use of the stomach is to receive and digest food, and only the animal organization is affected by that. It cannot be said that the man is made for fornication. The **person** of each is made for the Lord.

(14) Will also raise up us.—This phrase is remarkable as one of the few which show that the apostle, while he in common with the early church expected the early advent of Christ, did not think that it would necessarily occur in his own lifetime. Here, as ever, the resurrection of the dead is joined with the fact of the Resurrection of Christ the firstfruits.

(15, 16) Paul has shown the great dignity which attaches to our bodies, as immortal members of Christ. Genesis 2:24 originally applied to marriage, as showing the intimacy of that sacred union, but here Paul applies it to one aspect of a union which, in one respect, was identical with marriage.

(17) One spirit.—The union between Christ and each member of His Church is a spiritual one. This explains the sense in which we are the Lord's body, and intensifies the argument against any degradation of one who shares so holy and intimate a union.

(18) Without the body.—The word "body" is to be understood as used of the whole "human nature," which is spoken of in verse 19 as the temple of the Holy Ghost. Other sins may profane only outer courts of the temple; this sin penetrates with its deadly foulness into the very holy of holies.

(19, 20) What? know ye not . . . ?—Our bodies not being our own to do with as we like, we have no right to give them over unto sin. The last words of the verse are not a cold logical deduction from the previous argument, but rather an earnest exhortation suggested by the solemn thought of our oneness with Christ, and the price paid by Him to make us His.

7

(1) Concerning the things whereof ye wrote unto me.—Some members of the church having written to Paul to ask his counsel on matters concerning which there existed a difference of opinion at Corinth, the apostle now proceeds to answer these inquiries, and his reply occupies the remainder of the epistle (to 16:4). In the consideration of each of these subjects various collateral matters are introduced, and the great principles which guided the apostle, and which ever should guide the Church and individuals, are set forth. Many of the subjects were of purely local and temporary interest. The particular combination of circumstances which for the moment rendered them important has ceased to exist, and can never arise again; but the principles on which the apostle based his arguments, and which he enunciates as the ground of his decisions, are eternal.

The first subject concerning which the Corinthians sought advice was marriage. From the opening words of Paul's reply it would seem that those who wrote for the apostle's advice were inclined to regard celibacy as preferable to the married state, so much so, indeed, that they had scruples as to whether even those who had been married should not separate (verses 3-5). It would be natural for the Pauline party unduly to exaggerate the importance of celibacy and to undervalue matrimony. Paul's own example, and his strong preference for the unmarried state, would easily have come to be regarded by his followers as matters of moral import, and not of merely temporary advantage and personal predilection.

(2) To avoid fornication.—It may at first sight appear as if the apostle thus put marriage upon very low and merely utilitarian ground: but we must remember that he is here writing with a definite and limited aim, and does not enter into a general discussion of the subject. Paul's view of the higher aspects of matrimony are fully set forth when he treats of that subject generally (Rom. 7:4; II Cor. 11:2; Eph. 5:25-32).

(5) Any separation should be temporary, and with consent of both parties. Even then it must not be from mere caprice, but for some religious purpose, such as a special season of prayer. Again the reference is, as verse 2, to the moral condition surrounding them, and to the influence to which a man thus separated would be subject. The Corinthian Christians are here solemnly reminded that this sin, as all sin, is from Satan—because the Corinthians at large did not regard it as sin at all, but even mingled sensuality with worship.

(6) But I speak this by permission.—The apostle means that the foregoing instructions are not to be considered as absolute commands from him, but as general permissive instruction, to be applied by each individual according to circumstances.

(7) These words do not mean that the apostle wished that every one was unmarried, but that every one had the same gift of continence with which he himself was endowed, so that they might without risk of sin remain unmarried (see verse 26).

(8) It has been curiously conjectured (by Luther among others) from the passage where Paul recommends widows to "abide even as I," that the apostle was himself a widower. This, however, requires the word "unmarried" to be restricted to widowers, which is quite inadmissible; and even if such were admissible, it would contradict the almost universal tradition of the early church that Paul was never married.

(9) It is better . . .—Because to be influenced with unlawful desire is a sin, and to marry is no sin.

(10) And unto the married . . . —The apostle now gives his advice to those married persons who had been troubled with doubts as to whether they ought (if marriage were undesirable) to continue in that state.

I command, yet not I, but the Lord.—Comp. 14:37; I Thess. 4:15. Paul must not be regarded as here claiming for some of his instructions apostolic authority, and not claiming it for others. The real point of the contrast is between a subject on which our Lord Himself while on earth gave direct verbal instruction, and another subject on which He now gives His commands through His Apostle Paul. Christ had given directions regarding divorce, and the apostle here has only to reiterate what the Lord had already commanded.

Let not the wife depart from her husband.—The reason for the differences here from Matt. 5:32; 19:9 is found in the particular circumstances to which the apostle was applying the teaching of Christ; and this verbal difference is an instructive indication to us of how the apostles understood that even in the case of the Lord Himself it was the living spirit of His teaching, and not its merely verbal form, which was of abiding and universal obligation. There was no necessity here to introduce the one exceptional cause of divorce which Christ had allowed, for the subject under consideration is a separation voluntarily made, and not as the result of sin on the part of either husband or wife. And the mention here of the woman more prominently as separating from the husband does not in any way

affect the principle of the teaching; indeed our Lord probably did put the case in both ways. (See Mark 10:12.)

(11) But and if she depart.—The apostle, in case such a separation should already have taken place, anticipates the difficult question which might then arise by parenthetically remarking that in such a case the woman must not marry again, but ought to be reunited to her former husband.

(12) But to the rest.—Up to this point the writer has alluded only to Christians; he has spoken of the duties of unmarried persons, of widows, and of those already married. There still remains one class of marriages concerning which differences of opinion existed—mixed marriages. In a church like Corinth there would have been, no doubt, many cases where one of the partners was a heathen and the other a Christian, arising from the subsequent conversion of only one of the married couple. The case of a Christian marrying a heathen is not alluded to. In II Cor. 6:14 the marriage of a Christian to a heathen is forbidden.

A wife that believeth not.—Both here and in verse 13 the being "pleased to dwell" is put only in reference to the partner who is a heathen, for the apostle takes for granted that after the instructions he here gives to the Christian partner, no such desire for separation will arise on the part of a Christian.

(14) The unbelieving husband is sanctified by the wife.—In contrast to that other union in which the connection is defiling (6:16), the purity of the believing partner in this union, being a lawful one, as it were, entirely overweighs the impurity of the unbeliever, it being not a moral but a kind of ceremonial purity. The children of such marriages were considered to be Christian children; and the "sanctification" and "holiness" here spoken of is that consecration which arises from being in the body of Christ (Rom. 11:16).

(15) But if the unbelieving depart.—Supposing, however, the desire for separation arises from the unbelieving partner, how is the Christian partner to act? If the married life, for example, be made intolerable by the unbeliever urging the believer to join in such religious acts as conscience cannot approve, the apostle's previous commands for continued union do not hold good. This permission is in no way contrary to our Lord's permission of divorce on only one ground, for the apostle has carefully reminded his readers that our Lord's command does not apply to the case of a marriage between a believer and a heathen. In such cases we have no command from Him.

(16) The apostle declares that the remote contingency of the unbeliever's conversion is too vague a matter for which to risk the peace which is so essential an element in the Christian life. If the unbelieving partner will depart, do not let any thought as to the possible influence you may exercise over his religious convictions—about which you cannot **know** anything, but only at most vaguely speculate—cause you to insist upon his remaining.

(17) But as God hath distributed ... —These words limit in practice the broad liberty which the apostle has given regarding separation in cases of mixed marriages. In verse 15 the unbelieving partner is the only one who is spoken of as taking an active part in the separation. The believer is, merely for the sake of peace, to acquiesce in it; he is never to cause or promote a separation, for he is to be guided by the great principle that we are to continue to walk in those social and political relations by which we were bound when God called us. According as the Lord has divided to each man his portion in life, and as God has called each man, so in that condition let him continue to walk as a Christian. Let him not try to change it for another.

(18) Is any man called being circumcised?—The previous general rule is now illustrated by, and applied to, two conditions of life—circumcision (verses 18-20) and slavery (verses 20-24). If any man was converted after having been circumcised, he was not, as some over-zealous Christians might have been anxious to do, to remove every trace of his external connection with Judaism (Gal. 5:2).

(19) The circumcision of Timothy, and the refusal to circumcise Titus by Paul himself, are illustrations at once of the application of the truth enforced here, and of the apostle's scrupulous adherence to the principles of his own teaching. To have refused to circumcise Timothy would have attached some value to non-circumcision; to have circumcised Titus would have attached some value to circumcision. (See Acts 16:3; Gal. 2:3.)

(21) Art thou called being a servant?— The fact of your being in slavery does not affect the reality of completeness of your conversion; and so you need have no anxiety to try and escape from servitude.

But if thou mayest be made free, use it rather.—The apostle says that (so far from letting the servitude be a cause of distress to you) if you can even be free, prefer to use it, i.e., your condition as a converted slave. It, as well as any other position in life, can be used to God's glory.

How are we to account for Paul's never having condemned this servile system? One point certainly was his own belief in the near approach of the end of the age. If all existing relations would be overthrown in a few years, even such a relation as was involved in slavery would not be of so great importance as if it had been regarded as a permanent institution. But there were other grave considerations of a more positive and imperative nature. If one single word from Christian teaching could have been quoted at Rome as tending to excite the slaves to revolt, it would have set the Roman power in direct and active hostility to the new faith. And, in addition, there would be danger to the purity of the Church itself. Many might have been led, from wrong motives, to join a communion which would have aided them in securing their social and political freedom.

The object of Christianity—and this Paul over and over again insisted on—was not to overturn and destroy existing political and social institutions, but to leaven them with new principles. He did not propose to abolish slavery, but to Christianize it; and when slavery is Christianized, it must cease to exist. Christianized slavery is liberty.

(25) Now concerning virgins ... —A new subject is introduced here—the duty of parents regarding their young unmarried daughters. Ought they to give them in marriage? On this subject the apostle states that he has no actual command from Christ; it was a point to which our Lord had not directly alluded in His teaching. (See note on verse 10.)

(26) From this verse to the end of verse 35 the apostle deals again with the general question of marriage, introducing a new element of consideration—"the impending distress"; and at verse 36 he returns to the immediate subject with which he had started in verse 25—duty of parents regarding their young unmarried daughters. The "impending distress" is that foretold by Christ in Matt. 24:8. The apostle regarded the coming of Christ as no distant event, and in the calamities already threatening the

Church, such as the famine in the time of Claudius (Acts 11:28), and in the gathering persecutions, he heard the first mutterings of the storm which should burst upon the world before the sign of the Son of Man should appear in the heavens.

(28) The question is not one of sin, but merely of desirability. Matrimony, he says, will involve you in earthly troubles when the expected distress comes; therefore, in advising you to remain unmarried, my desire is to spare you them.

(29-31) Because the time of life is short, each must keep himself from being the slave of external conditions and relationships of life, though good and proper in themselves.

(32-35) These words take up again the form of expression in verse 28. The whole force of the passage is that married persons have, in the fulfillment of their obligations to each other, an additional interest and concern from which the unmarried are free. It must ever be distinctly borne in mind that this advice was given solely under the impression that the end of all earthly things was impending, and that the great trial and desolation was beginning to darken over the world. The apostle who wrote these words of warning himself expressly condemns those who applied them as involving general moral obligations, and not as suited merely to temporary requirements (1 Tim. 4:1, 3).

(36) Here the writer turns to the duty of parents, and there is a further explanation to such that the previous expressions are not binding commandments, but apostolic advice. If the case arises that a parent thinks he would be acting unfairly toward his unmarried daughter (i.e., exposing her to temptation) by withholding permission for her marriage, he ought to do as he feels inclined—i.e., let the lover and his daughter marry.

(37, 38) The previous verse must not be understood as applying to any other cases than those where positive harm is likely to result from the parent withholding his consent. Where no such necessity arises (i.e., where the parent's will is not under the control of the external necessity of the case), and where the parent has made this resolution in his heart, the result of which is to keep his daughter with him unmarried, he will do well.

This passage clearly shows how Paul has not been contrasting right and wrong, but comparative degrees of what is expedient. Throughout, the apostle takes for granted

the absolute control of the parent over the child, in accordance with the principles of both Greek and Jewish jurisprudence. Therefore, no advice is given to the young maiden herself, but only to her father.

(39, 40) The wife.—The question of the remarriage of widows is considered here. The widow may be married again if she desires, but "only in the Lord"—i.e., not to a heathen. She, being a Christian, should marry a Christian. But, Paul explains, she is happier to continue a widow (her case coming under the same considerations as referred to the unmarried in the previous verses).

I think also that I have the Spirit of God.—This is no expression of doubt as to whether he had the Spirit of God, but an assurance of his confidence that he, as well as other teachers (who, perhaps, boast more about it), had the Spirit of God to guide him in cases where no direct command has been given by Christ.

8

(1) Now as touching things offered unto idols.—In Corinth and other cities meat was offered for sale which had been used for sacrificial purposes in the heathen temples, having been sold to the dealers by the priests, who received a large share of the sacrifices for themselves, or by the individuals who offered them and had more remaining of their own share than they could use themselves. Thus, a Christian might unconsciously eat of meat which had been previously brought in contact by sacrificial usage with an idol. There were some in Corinth who felt no scruple on the subject, so completely and effectively had their Christianity dispelled all their previous heathen superstition. There were others at Corinth, however, who felt some scruples upon the subject. There were heathen converts who had not completely gotten rid of every vestige of the old superstition, or whose conscience would accuse them of not having wholly given up idolatry if they took any part even in its social aspect. And there were Jews, the intensity of whose traditional hatred of idolatry could not allow them to regard as "nothing" that against which Jehovah had uttered His most terrible denunciations, and against which He had preserved their race as a living witness. To both these latter sections of the Church the conduct of the more liberal party would prove a serious stumblingblock.

Knowledge puffeth up, but charity edifieth.—Those who grounded everything on knowledge are reminded parenthetically that knowledge by itself may have a bad effect, and also (verses 2, 3) that there is an element in the consciousness of our knowledge which destroys the truth and purity of that knowledge itself. Knowledge puffs up the man himself. Love builds up the whole Church.

(4-6) An idol is nothing in itself but a piece of wood or metal, and it really represents nothing, for we know that there is "no God but one." But even assuming that there do exist those beings which are called "gods," the difference between the heathen "gods many" and the "lords and gods" of whom the Old Testament speaks (see Deut. 10:17; Ps. 105:2, 3), is that the former are deities, and the latter only a casual way of speaking of angels and other spiritual subjects and servants of the one God.

(8) But meat ... —By showing that the eating is a matter of indifference, the apostle introduces his reason for yielding to the weakness of another, e.g., the heathen convert of verse 7, to whom the idol represents a reality. If the weakness involved a matter of our vital relation to God, then to yield would be wrong. But meat will not affect our relationship to God.

(9) But take heed.—In things which are not indifferent, right or wrong is the sole test of action. In things indifferent you must look for some other guide, and you must regulate your conduct by the effect it may have on others. Your liberty, which arises from the bare fact of the indifferent nature of the thing, may become a stumblingblock to others.

(10-12) The fact of your being avowedly advanced in the knowledge of the faith will make your example the more dangerous, because more effective. (Some went so far as not only to eat, but to eat in the precincts of the heathen temple. The apostle being concerned now only with the point of the eating, does not rebuke this practice here, but he does so fully in 10:14-22.) The people addressed had probably argued that the force of their example would build up others. Yes, says Paul, with irony, it will build him up—to do what, being weak, he cannot do without sin.

(13) Wherefore.—He states his own solemn determination, arising from the considerations which have just been urged. If a

matter of food cause a brother to fall in his Christian course, he would certainly never again eat any kind of flesh, lest he should be the cause of so making him to fall.

It is noticeable that Paul in discussing this question makes no reference whatever to the decision of the Council at Jerusalem (see Acts 15:29). Probably, the apostle felt the importance of maintaining his own apostolic authority in a church where it was questioned by some, and he felt that to base his instruction upon the decision of the church at Jerusalem might have seemed to imply that he had obtained authority from them, and not directly from the Lord. It was also more in accordance with Paul's usual style of instruction to base the smallest details of conduct upon the highest of all principles—our union as Christians with Christ.

9

The apostle remembered that another act of self-sacrifice on his part had not only been unappreciated, but made the grounds of an unworthy attempt on the part of some (probably the Jewish Christians of the Cephas faction; see note on 1:11) to depreciate and even call in question his apostolic dignity and authority. At Corinth (Acts 18:3), and elsewhere (Acts 20:34; I Thess. 3:7, 9), the apostle, instead of depending upon the church for support, had labored as a tent-maker. (**Cilicium,** a kind of cloth used for tent coverings, took its name from Cilicia, where the goats out of whose hair it was made were found in abundance; and the manufacture of it was naturally the handicraft which a native of Tarsus in Cilicia would, according to general custom, have learned in his boyhood.) The chapter is occupied with Paul's reply to their insinuations. If we remember that so long an epistle could not have been written at a single sitting, but probably occupied many days in its composition, such change in subject and style as we have in 8:13 and 9:1 will not seem so abrupt.

(1) Am I not an apostle?—To have seen Christ was a necessary qualification for the apostolate (Acts 1:21). The fact was generally admitted and universally known that Paul did actually see the Lord at the time of his conversion (Acts 9:4), and on other occasions (Acts 18:9; 22:17). And that they were his "work in the Lord" is a further proof of his apostleship, and therefore of his right or freedom to have demanded support from the church. (See 4:15.)

(2) If I be not an apostle unto others.— The allusion here is probably to some who may have arrived at Corinth subsequent to Paul's departure, and who, not recognizing his apostleship in relation to themselves, stirred up some of the Corinthians to repudiate it also.

(4) Have we not power . . . ?—Having established his right to be called an apostle by the fact that he had seen the Lord, and had been instrumental in their conversion, he now in the same interrogative style asserts his rights as an apostle. The use of the plural "we" carries on the thought that he is claiming this right as being one of the apostles—all of whom have, as apostles, such a right.

(5) To lead about a sister, a wife—i.e., to take with us on our journeys a Christian woman as a wife. Paul, in this verse, carries his statement of apostolic right to support one step further. Not only had he a right to be supported himself, but the support of the married apostles and their wives by the church implied the same right on the part of all.

(7) Who goeth a warfare any time at his own charges?—Three illustrations from human life and business show that the principle which has been adopted in the Christian Church is not exceptional. A soldier receives his pay; the planter of a vineyard eats the fruit of it; and the owner of a flock is supported by selling the milk. It has been observed that Paul's vindication falls naturally into three divisions: the argument (1) from induction, verses 1-6; (2) from analogy, verse 7; (3) from authority, verse 8.

(9, 10) The pointed and emphatic mention of the Law of Moses would give the words great weight with Jewish opponents. (See Deut. 25:4.) The good which such a provision as the Law achieved for the oxen was nothing compared to the good which it accomplished for man. God did not do this simply as a provision for the ox, but to teach us men humanitarianism—to teach us that it is a divine principle that the laborer should have his reward.

(11) The spiritual things are the things of the Spirit of God, by which their spiritual natures are sustained; the carnal things are those which the teachers might expect in return, the ordinary support of their physical nature.

(13, 14) The apostle now turns to appeal to an argument which would have weight with them as Christians. The rights of the ministry to be supported by the Church have already been established by an appeal to ordinary life and to the Jewish law; but the apostle, having that right, did not, for wise reasons, use it (verse 12). There is one higher step in the argument. It was not only a principle of Jewish law which Christ might have abrogated, but it was also a provision of the Jewish economy which Christ Himself formally perpetuated. (Comp. Lev. 6:16, 26; 7:6; Num. 5 and 18; Deut. 10 and 18.) The preaching of the Gospel is in the Christian ministry the function which corresponds to the offering of sacrifice in the Jewish priesthood.

(16) For though I preach the gospel, I have nothing to glory of.—Paul proceeds now to show how his maintenance by the Church would deprive him of his right to boast or glory in his work (verse 15). The mere preaching of the Gospel supplies no ground of boasting; a man can have none in doing that which he **must** do.

(19) Paul's reward was to gain the greatest number of converts—Jews (verse 20), Gentiles (verse 21), weak ones (verse 22). The only reward he sought in adopting that course of conduct, for pursuing which they taunted him with selfishness, was, after all, their good.

(22) I am made all things to all . . . — Although he had thus accommodated himself, as far as was consistent with Christian duty, to the weaknesses of all, he could only hope to win some of them. The word "save" means "win over to Christianity," as in 7:16. His subject was not, as enemies might suggest, to win them to himself—but to Christ.

(24) Know ye not . . . —The illustration which follows refers to these Isthmian games (so called from their taking place in the isthmus where Corinth stood) with which his readers would be familiar. These included every form of athletic exercise. For the Greek, these contests were great national and religious festivals.

So run—i.e., run in the way referred to, so that you may gain a prize.

(25) Every man that striveth for the mastery.—The Greek word **agonidzomenos** is identical with the English "agonize." Thus the use in devotional works of the phrase "to agonize in prayer," etc.

Is temperate in all things.—He fulfills not only some, but all of the necessary preliminary conditions. He indulges self in no way.

They do it to obtain a corruptible

crown.—There are two striking points of contrast between the earthly race and the spiritual course. There is but one who obtains a reward in the earthly contest; none need fail of it in the heavenly race. That reward in the one case is perishable; in the other it is imperishable.

(26) So fight I.—The illustration is changed from running to boxing, both being included in the word "contending" (verse 25). He has an adversary to contend against, and he strikes him, but not wildly and impotently so as only to beat the air.

(27) But I keep under my body.—The word is very strong, and implies to beat the flesh until it becomes black and blue. (See Luke 18:5.) The body is spoken of as his adversary, or the seat of those lusts and appetites which "war against the mind" (Rom. 7:23; Gal. 5:17).

Bring it into subjection.—The idea is carried on that the body is not only conquered, but led captive. The statement here refers to the subduing of the appetites and passions which are located in it. They should be entirely our servants, and not our masters.

Lest that by any means.—The apostle says that he has a further motive to live a life of self-denial—that he having acted as a herald, proclaiming the conditions of the contest and the requisite preliminaries for it, should not himself be found to have fulfilled them. (The apostle was himself **both** a runner in the Christian course, and a herald of the conditions of that race to others.) The word "cast away" conveys a wrong impression. The Greek word signifies one who had not behaved according to the prescribed regulations.

10

(1) Moreover, brethren ... —From the strong statement of personal self-distrust with which the previous chapter concludes, the apostle now passes on to show that Jewish history contains solemn examples of the falling away of those who seemed to stand strong in divine favor and privilege. The same kind of dangers still beset God's people, but they will never be greater than the strength which God will give to bear them. These thoughts are then applied to the immediate subject in hand: the partaking of meat which had been used in the heathen temples.

That ye should be ignorant.—The

thought here is not that his readers were at all likely to be ignorant of the mere historical fact which he now recalls, but that they were probably unmindful of the spiritual lessons which are to be learned from such a grouping of the facts as the apostle now gives, and of the striking contrast between the enjoyment of great privileges by **all** (literally, only two—Joshua and Caleb) and the apostasy of the greater part of them.

(2) Were all baptized unto Moses.—Moses was God's representative under the Law; and so they were baptized unto him in their voluntarily joining with that "Church" of God, as Christians are baptized unto Jesus Christ, God's representative in the New Dispensation. The "cloud" and the "sea" refer to the cloud that overshadowed the Israelites (Exod. 13:21; see Num. 14:14), and the passage through the Red Sea (Exod. 14:22; Num. 35:8).

(3) Spiritual meat.—The manna (Exod. 16:15) was not natural food, for it was not produced in the natural way. It was supplied by the Spirit and power of God. Bread from earth would be natural bread, but this was bread from heaven (John 6:31).

(4) That spiritual Rock that followed them.—There was a Jewish tradition that the Rock—i.e., a fragment broken off from the rock smitten by Moses—followed the Israelites through their journey, and Paul, for the purpose of illustration, adopts that account instead of the statement in Num. 20:11.

And that Rock was Christ.—As Christ was "God manifest in the flesh" in the New Dispensation, so God manifest in the Rock (the source of sustaining life) was the Christ of the Old. The Jews had become familiar with the thought of God as a Rock. (See I Sam. 2:2; Ps. 91:12; Isa. 32:2.) Though the Jews may have recognized the Rock poetically as God, they did not know that it was, as a manifestation of God's presence, typical of **the** manifestation which was yet to be given in the Incarnation.

(6) Paul regards everything that has happened in history as having a divine purpose of blessing for others (see verse 11). All this material suffering on their part will not be in vain if it teaches us the spiritual lesson which God would have us learn from it. The apostle proceeds to set forth the causes with which the majority of the Israelites neutralized the great advantages in which all had shared.

(8) And fell in one day three and twenty thousand.—In Num. 25:9 the statement is that twenty-four thousand perished. Either the apostle quoted from memory a fact of no great importance, or else he referred for his figures to some copy of the LXX in which the numbers might be specified as here.

(9) Neither let us tempt Christ.—The Israelites had, by their longing after the things left behind in Egypt, tried God, so that God had asserted Himself in visiting them with punishment; so Christians must be on their guard, with such a warning before them, not to tempt their Lord by yearning after those worldly and physical pleasures from which He by His death has delivered them. (See Num. 21:4-6.) Some of the Corinthian Christians seem by their conduct, as regards eating, drinking and indulging in sensuality, to long for that liberty in reference to things which they had enjoyed before conversion, instead of enjoying these spiritual blessings and feeding on the spiritual sustenance which Christ had provided for them.

(10) Neither murmur ye.—The historical event (Num. 16:41-47)—the murmuring of the Israelites against their God-given leaders, Moses and Aaron—is analogous to the murmuring of the Corinthians against their apostle, Paul.

(12) Wherefore.—This is the practical conclusion of the whole matter. We are to look back on that strange record of splendid privilege and of terrible fall and learn from it the solemn lesson of self-distrust. Christians, called forth from a more deadly bondage into a more glorious liberty than Israel, are in like peril.

(13) There hath no temptation taken you.—From the warning and exhortation of the previous verse the apostle passes on to words of encouragement. God permits the temptation by allowing the circumstances which create temptation to arise, but He takes care that no Fate bars the path of retreat. We have in this verse, perhaps, the most practical and therefore the clearest exposition to be found of the doctrine of free will in relation to God's overruling power. God makes an open road, but then man himself must **walk** in it. God controls circumstances, but man uses them. That is where **his** responsibility lies.

(15-17) Having warned them (verse 14) against any participation in idolatry, even such as would be involved in joining in the sacrificial feasts, as dangerous to themselves, he now proceeds to show that such a participation would be derogatory to, and

incompatible with, their union with Christ. The identity and intimacy of that union is first established by a reference to the Holy Communion, in partaking of which both the unity of the Church and its union with Christ are vividly expressed.

(20-22) The heathen world is regarded by the Christian Church as under the dominion of the evil spirit and his emissaries (Eph. 2:2; 6:12). In reminding the Corinthians that in Israel an eater of the sacrificial meat became a partaker with the altar of God, the apostle meant to warn them that they would, if they partook of sacrificial meats offered on an altar of devils, become a sharer with that altar and the beings to whom the altar appertained.

(23) All things are lawful for me.—The apostle now concludes, with some practical direction and advice, the question of the eating of meat offered to idols (see 8:13). He repeats the great principle of Christian liberty, "All things are lawful for me" (see 6:12), but insists, as before, that its application must be limited by a regard to the effect which each action has upon ourselves and its influence on the Church at large.

(24) But every man another's wealth.—The English word "wealth" has come to bear a limited significance, such as did not originally belong to it. Here it means "good," including more especially "moral welfare."

(25) Whatsoever is sold in the shambles.—Here is the practical application of the principle laid down. When a Christian sees meat exposed for sale in the public market, let him buy it and eat it; he need not ask any question to satisfy his conscience on the subject. Some of the meat which had been used for sacrificial purposes was afterward sold in the markets. The weaker Christians feared lest, if they unconsciously bought and ate some of that meat, they would become thereby defiled. The apostle's view is that when once sent into the public market, it becomes simply meat, and its previous use gives it no significance.

(28) But if any man ... —If, unlike the circumstance in verse 27, some weak brother points out that it is sacrificial meat, do not eat for his sake and for conscience sake (see verse 29). Here your personal liberty is to be modified by the principle mentioned in verse 24. If the weak brother see you eat the flesh which he has just informed you was used as a sacrifice, he may be led by your example to eat it himself. The fact of his having called your attention to it showed that he thinks it wrong, and so his conscience is defiled.

(31) Whatsoever ye do.—No act of life is in itself either religious or secular. The quality of each act depends on the spirit which guides it and the motive from which it springs. The commonest thing may be done in a high Christian spirit. The greatest deed may spring from a low and selfish motive. A religious act done in a secular spirit is secular. A secular thing done in a religious spirit is religious.

11

(1) Be ye followers of me.—"Become imitators of me, even as I am of Christ." This is the completion of the exhortation of 10:33. The apostle refers to His own example, but only to lead his readers up to Christ as the great example of One "who pleased not himself" (Rom. 15:3).

(3) But I would have you know.—After the general commendation in the previous verse, the reproof for neglecting, or desiring to neglect, his precepts in one particular case is thus introduced. The subject treated— the uncovering of their heads by women in assemblies for worship—is now of trivial importance. Every circumstance, however, which could in the least degree cause the principles of Christianity to be perverted or misunderstood by the heathen world was of vital importance in those early days of the Church. Here we find the apostle, who most fearlessly taught the principles of Christian liberty, condemning most earnestly every application of those principles which might be detrimental to the best interests of the Christian faith. To feel bound to assert your liberty in every detail of social and political life is to cease to be free—the very liberty becomes a bondage.

The head of every man is Christ.—There is a Head to the Church; therefore it is not a machine composed of various parts, but a body consisting of various members. As there is a subordination of the whole body to Christ, so there is in that body a subordination of woman to man. And, to give completeness to the thought, Paul adds that Christ is subordinate to the Father. Indeed, perhaps the idea is carried farther into the mystery of the divine nature itself, as consisting of three Persons co-eternal and co-equal, yet being designated with an unvarying sequence as "first," "second," and "third."

(4) Every man praying or prophesying.— The reference here is to public prayer and teaching, the word "prophesying" being used in its less restricted sense. The Greek practice was for men to have their heads uncovered when joining in religious ceremonies. To this practice Paul would incline, as being the national custom of the country, and as also being typical of the distinction between the sexes which he has just laid down. The apostle's teaching on this subject is a remarkable illustration of how completely he had overcome his old Jewish prejudice, for it was the custom among the Jews for the man to pray with covered head and veiled face. The apostle realized how an external symbol would infallibly tend to modify doctrine, and how thus the perpetuating of such a custom in the Christian Church might have hindered the full recognition of the great truth of the personal and direct communication of every individual soul with the Father.

(5) But every woman that prayeth . . . —In the public meeting of the whole Church women were to be silent (14:34; 1 Tim. 2:12), but the meetings spoken of here, though public as distinguished from the private devotions of individuals, were probably only smaller gatherings such as are indicated in Rom. 16:5; Col. 4:15; Philem. 2.

Dishonoureth her head.—Both among Jews and Greeks the long tresses of a woman were her glory. Only in times of mourning (Deut. 21:12), or when convicted of shameful sin, was a woman to have her hair cut short. The word "head" must be taken in its double significance. A woman with uncovered head dishonors the head itself by making it thus in the sight of others the type of a shame which is really not hers; and as her head typically is her husband, so she dishonors him also.

(6) Let her also be shorn.—The force of this argument depends on the fact that a woman's head being uncovered would be regarded by others as implying the same shame as was indicated by a woman's hair being cut short (i.e., shorn), or altogether removed (i.e., shaven). It is as if the apostle said, "If a woman insists on her right to pray and speak in an assembly with uncovered head, let her carry out this principle to its logical result; let her insist on her right to have her hair cut short, so as to show her equality with man—and what would be thought of her then! No woman with a spark of shame in her would think of doing that."

(7) For a man indeed.—In verses 4-7 the argument against the woman's head being uncovered was based upon the woman's relation to man and the man's relation to Christ in the Church. In verses 7, 8, and 9 the ground of the argument is changed, and the same conclusion is reached from a review of the woman's relation to man and man's relation to God in the physical creation. The external form of this argument is the same as that adopted previously. It is to be remembered all through this passage that Paul is speaking only of married women. It is most unlikely that any case had occurred of an unmarried woman attempting such an outrage upon social feeling and national custom. The Greek women when in public (except those of avowedly bad character) either wore a veil or drew the shawl over their heads.

(10) For this cause ought the woman to have power on her head.—If we bear in mind the apostle's constant use of words with a double significance, and if we also recall the reference made to a woman's abundance of hair in verses 5, 6 (see verses 14, 15), we may conclude that the "power" here spoken of is that long hair which is called in verse 15 her "glory." To the Jews the recollection of Samson's history would have given the word "power," when applied to hair, a remarkable significance. In the apostle's writings the thought of inferiority and superiority are frequently and almost paradoxically regarded and enforced as identical—you serve because you rule; you are weak because you are strong. Here, that very thing which is the symbol of your subjection to man is the sign of your beauty and "power" as a woman.

Because of the angels.—That the angels were present in assemblies for worship was an idea prevalent among the Jews (Ps. 138:1, LXX); and regarded as they were by the Christian as "ministering spirits" (Heb. 1:14), no doubt their presence would be realized in the meetings of Christians.

The apostle, in his argument upon the relation of the sexes to each other (verses 7-9), refers to the first three chapters of Genesis as illustrating and enforcing that relationship. It would be natural that his thoughts should have gone on to chap. 6 of the same book, where is the record of the angels' (in the LXX the word translated "sons of God" is "the angels"—**angeloi**) having been enamored by the beauty of women, and so having fallen from their high estate. (See Jude 1; II Pet. 2:4.)

Through rabbinical interpretations also this account would have been familiar to Paul's converts. Without at all necessarily expressing his belief in the historic accuracy of this legendary view of the fall of the angels, Paul might use it as an argument with those who did believe it (as in the case of the Rock—see note on 10:4). That thought ought to make Christian women feel that it is not seemly for them to be without a veil (of which their "power," i.e., their hair, is the type) in those assemblies where the angels are present as God's ministering spirits.

(12) For as the woman is of the man.—An appeal to the original act of creation proves the truth of the previous statement of the interdependence of the sexes. The first woman was made out of man; therefore woman is dependent on man. Every man has been born of a woman; therefore man is not independent of woman.

(14) Nature itself.—This means "the native inborn sense of what is seemly," as contrasted with revelation. The heathen who had no direct revelation did (by regarding long hair as a woman's glory) "by nature" the things contained in the Law (Rom. 11:14).

(16) But if any man seem to be contentious.—The apostle now adds that if, after all appeal to good sense, someone continues to argue the matter critically, and is not satisfied with the reason given, neither the apostles nor the churches of God have any such custom as that women should pray and teach with uncovered head. It is noticeable that the appeal is made to the practice of the churches (plural), not the Church. Thus it is not the authority of the Church as such that is quoted, but it is the uniformity of practice in the several Christian churches to which appeal is made. The church in Corinth has no right to become exceptional.

(18) The "first point" is the abuse regarding the Lord's Supper, which is more immediately treated; and the "second point," the abuse of spiritual gifts, beginning with 12:1. They are two branches of the one general subject: "irregularities in religious assemblies."

(20) When ye come together therefore into one place, this is not to eat the Lord's supper.—Verse 19 is a parenthesis. There being divisions among you, it is not possible for you, when you assemble as a church body, to partake of that supper which is dedicated to the Lord. The whole meal, the **agape** or "charity feast" (Jude 12), was distinguished from other meals by being united with the Lord's Supper. To these charity feasts the Christians brought contributions of food—the rich of their abundance, the poor whatever they could afford—and the food thus provided was partaken of in common by all. The Greek words in this verse for "Lord's Supper" are more general (**kuriakon deipnon**) than those used in verse 27 and in 10:16, 21 (**kuriou**). The whole meal was dedicated to the Lord by virtue of its union with the sacramental Supper of the Lord.

(21) Here follows a description of the conduct and mode of proceeding at this feast, which renders it impossible (verse 20) for it to be a Lord's Supper. Those assemblies will, through the misconduct of the wealthier Christians, have precisely the opposite result from that which they were intended to accomplish.

(23) For I have received of the Lord.— The whole structure of the passage seems to imply that what follows had been received by Paul directly from Christ, and that he is not appealing to a well-known tradition. The method of communication does not appear to cause either doubt or difficulty to those to whom the apostle conveyed the information thus miraculously bestowed upon him.

That which also I delivered unto you.— The apostle was not now for the first time communicating these solemn facts to the Corinthians. He had told them all this before, and therefore they were sinning against knowledge when they degraded a feast which they knew to be so solemn to a purpose so unworthy.

There now follows an account of the institution of the Lord's Supper. (Comp. Matt. 26:26-29; Mark 14:22-25; Luke 22:19, 20.) The evangelists wrote their accounts many years after the occurrence, and recorded what they remembered to have observed and heard. Paul writes here, within a few years at all events of his having received it, an account of what had been directly communicated by the Lord. This was also most probably the first written record of what occurred on that solemn night.

Luke's narrative agrees most closely with Paul's. In all the narratives, however, the outlines of the scene are the same. There can be no mistake as to their all being truthful and honestly independent records of an actual historical scene.

(24) The insertion of the words "take,

eat" and "broken" is not supported by MS evidence. The former were probably inserted so as to produce a verbal identity with Matthew's account, and the word "broken" possibly as explanatory. At the institution the act of breaking the bread explained sufficiently what was meant. "This do in remembrance of me" means all that was done then. Bless the bread, break it, distribute it, eat it.

(25) This cup is the new testament.— Better, "This cup is the new covenant." The word "new" is peculiar to this and Luke's narrative; it does not occur in the best MSS of Matthew and Mark. The new covenant of grace between God and humanity was ratified in the blood of Christ. The cup containing the symbol of that blood is therefore the pledge and witness of that covenant. This was a new covenant in blood (Rom. 3:25) as contrasted with the old covenant in blood (Exod. 24:8).

(26) For as often as ye . . . —The previous verse concluded the account of the institution as conveyed by Christ to Paul, and the apostle himself now again speaks. The Greek word for "ye show" is that used for making a public oral proclamation. In the pathetic words "until he come" we may find an expression of the belief, perhaps largely due to the hope, that the Second Advent was not far distant.

(27) Sin was the cause of that body being broken and that blood shed, and therefore the one who unworthily uses the symbols of them becomes a participator in the guilt of those who crucified that body and shed that blood.

(28) So let him eat.—This implies that a man should partake of this sacred feast only after he has carefully examined himself as to the spirit in which he was approaching such holy bread and wine.

(29) Damnation to himself.—The Greek word here does not imply final condemnation. On the contrary, it means only such temporal judgments as the sickness and weakness subsequently mentioned, and which are to save the man from sharing the final damnation of the heathen. (See verse 32.)

Not discerning the Lord's body.—The words "the Lord's" are to be omitted, the weight of MS evidence being altogether against their authenticity. The force of the passage is: "He who eats and drinks without discerning the Body (i.e., the Church) in that assembly, eats and drinks a judgment to himself, for if we would discern ourselves we should not be judged." The fault which Paul was condemning was the practice which the Corinthians had fallen into of regarding these gatherings as opportunities for individual indulgence, and not as Church assemblies.

(33, 34) Wherefore, my brethren.—To correct the abuses of which he has spoken, and to enable them to escape the judgments of sickness and death (verse 30) which were falling upon them, the apostle gives them this practical advice. When you come together to this eucharistic feast, do not eagerly eat what you have brought; wait until all have arrived, and then partake in common of this Christian meal. If, however, any man is really hungry, then let him satisfy his hunger at home, and come to this Supper so that he may partake of it not to his judgment.

12

(1) Now concerning spiritual gifts.—Again the sequence of the topics treated is probably decided by the subjects contained in the letter from Corinth (se 7:1; 8:1), and the apostle replies to inquiries regarding the comparative value and importance of certain spiritual gifts. The party spirit with which the Corinthian church seems to have been saturated naturally led to diverse views—some gifts were unduly exalted, some unduly depreciated. The truth that these gifts are valuable as evidence of the indwelling Spirit, and as far as they could be useful for the Church, was forgotten.

(2, 3) Here the apostle reminds his readers that so far from regarding the marvelous manifestations of the Spirit, such as speaking with tongues and prophesying, as the most wonderful miracles, the greatest miracle of all was their conversion. That blind followers of dumb idols should be transformed into intelligent believers in the living Word was the most striking work of the Spirit. (The contrast of the present state of Christians with their former state as heathens is a topic of frequent occurrence in Paul's writings—Rom. 11:30; Col. 1:21; 3:7; etc.) If any man say "Jesus is anathema," that is a proof that he has not the Spirit; if any man say "Jesus is Lord," that is a proof that he has that Spirit.

(4-6) Now there are diversities of gifts.—Although conversion is identical in every case, yet afterwards there are spiritual gifts which vary according to individual capacity

and character, but they all come from the one Spirit. There are varieties of ministration in which those spiritual gifts are employed, and the same Lord is served by these varied ministries; there are varieties of operations resulting from these gifts and ministrations, but it is the same God who works them all in all cases. We have here a clear indication of the doctrine of the Holy Trinity—the Holy Spirit, the direct source of spiritual gifts; the Son, the one in whose service these gifts are to be used as ministers; the Father, the one supreme origin of all powers thus bestowed in diverse manners by the one Spirit, and for diverse purposes in the ministering to the One Son.

(7) But the manifestation of the Spirit.—These gifts which flow from one source are intended to flow toward one object—the benefit of the whole Church.

Verses 8-10 illustrate the varities of endowments for the object of the manifestation of the Spirit, still, however, emphasizing the unity of their origin—the Holy Spirit. In the Greek the genera (so to speak) are divided by the word **hetero**, the species by **allo**, both words being rendered in the English by the one word "another."

(8) The "wisdom" and the "knowledge" differ, in that the former expresses the deep spiritual insight into spiritual truth which some possess, the latter the intellectual appreciation of Christian doctrine, which is not so profound as the former, and which as the man passes into the spiritual state will vanish away (13:8).

(9) Faith.—This cannot mean the faith which is necessary to salvation, for that belongs to all Christians; but it is such faith as is mentioned in Matt. 17:20; Luke 17:6. In the Greek "the word of wisdom" is said to be given **by** the Spirit; "the word of knowledge" **according** to ṭhe Spirit; and "the faith and gift of healing" **in** the Spirit. By the use of this variety of expression the apostle probably means to indicate the variety of methods of operation of the Spirit, as well as the diversity of the gifts which He lavishes.

(10) Prophecy.—This is to be taken not in its limited sense of foretelling the future, but forthtelling truth generally.

Discerning of spirits—i.e., the power to distinguish between the workings of the Holy Spirit and of evil and misleading spirits (see I Tim. 4:1; I John 4:1). On the gifts of tongues and interpretations of tongues, see notes on chap. 14.

(11) But all these.—Again, in striking

contrast to the great varieties of gifts, the common source of them all is emphatically repeated. The Corinthians estimated those gifts variously, according to their variety in operation. The apostle estimates their common value as proceeding from the One Spirit, distributed according to His will. Those who valued men more or less according to the kind of gift they possessed were really, if unconsciously, criticizing the giver.

(13) Here follows an illustrative proof of the former statement. The human body is composed of many members, and so also is the spiritual body of Christ, which is His Church. "To drink into one Spirit" is better translated (in accordance with the best MSS), **to drink one Spirit.**

(20) But now are they.—From the **reductio ad absurdum** of the previous verses the apostle turns to the fact as it is, and proceeds to state that there is a mutual interdependence in the members of the body. Here, no doubt, the illustration is drawn out in this particular direction to rebuke those who being themselves possessed of what were considered important spiritual gifts despised the gifts which the Spirit had bestowed on others.

(22) The weakest parts of the body are as necessary to the body as the strongest; and those parts which are considered less seemly are more abundantly cared for (by being carefully covered with clothes, as distinguished from the face and hands which are uncovered).

(27) Now.—We have here in general terms the application of the foregoing illustration, the detailed application of which follows in verse 28. The apostles were those selected by our Lord Himself, or afterward elected by them to join that body. On prophets and teachers, see verse 10. The teachers were probably a junior order of instructors (see Acts 13:1; Eph. 4:11). The enumeration of the gifts here corresponds with that previously given in verses 9 and 10, with the exception of the mention here of "helps" and "governments," and the omission of "interpretation of tongues" and "discernment of spirit." Possibly, therefore, the words inserted here are only another designation of the same thing, the "helps" being the aid required for those who heard tongues in order to understand them, and the "governments" being the due regulation of the acceptance of certain spiritual powers and rejection of others.

(31) All this argument is not meant to check ardor and to dampen enthusiasm. The Spirit divides to every man as He wills, but He wills to give to each the best gift that each desires and is capable of receiving. The receptivity which comes with earnest and practical desire is in the case of each individual the determining cause as to what gift the Spirit will give.

The last sentence, "And yet show I unto you a more excellent way," ought to form the opening clause of the next chapter. The "more excellent way" is not some gift to be desired to the exclusion of the other gifts, but a more excellent way of striving for those gifts. You are not to strive for any one gift because it is more highly esteemed, or because it is more apparently useful, or because it is more easily attained. That which will consecrate every struggle for attainment and every gift when attained is **love.**

13

(1) Though I speak . . . —The more excellent way is "love." Without it all moral and intellectual gifts are valueless. If there be love—the love of God, and the love of our brethren—in our hearts, all will be well. (That this passage should be found in the middle of a protracted argument suggests the idea that we have here the result of a sudden and direct inspiration.) The word **(agape)** which is used here for love is peculiar to the New Testament (and a few passage in the LXX). It is not to be found in any heathen writer. The word "charity," which signifies either tolerance or almsgiving, is an insufficient rendering of the original, and destroys the force. The rare purity of the surrounding atmosphere of this love will completely deprive it of any earthly or sensual taint.

Tongues of men and of angels.—The gift of tongues (see notes on chap. 14) is placed first as that most overestimated at Corinth. It is useless without love. The best conception of what Paul means by love can be found from the description which he subsequently gives of it.

As sounding brass.—Not a brass trumpet, or instrument of any kind, but simply a piece of metal, which when struck will merely produce noise.

A tinkling cymbal.—Better, "a clanging cymbal." This instrument can produce by itself no intelligible tune. (See Ps. 40:5.)

(2) Prophecy.—The apostle valued the

gift of prophecy—i.e., preaching—more highly than the gift of tongues, which stood first in Corinthian estimation. He therefore naturally selects it as coming into the same condemnation, if unaccompanied by love. All the secrets of God's providence and complete knowledge (see 12:8), even such a transcendent faith as Christ had spoken of as capable of moving mountains (Matt. 17:20), may belong to a man, and without love he is nothing.

(3) Bestow all my goods.—The Greek word has the thought of a charity extensive in its diffusion, as well as complete in its self-sacrifice—the whole of the bestower's property given in charity, and so divided as to reach the largest number.

I give my body to be burned.—A still greater proof of devotion to some person or cause is the sacrifice of life; yet even that may be without love. Although burning was not a form of martyrdom at this time, yet such histories as Dan. 3:19 would make the expression intelligible and forcible.

(4) Descriptions of positive characteristics and negations of evil qualities are now employed by the apostle in what he would have us believe to be his impossible task of adequately describing true love.

(8) The apostle now turns to contrast the imperishable character of love and other graces with the ephemeral nature of gifts. The Corinthians held an exaggerated estimate of the value of gifts such as tongues and prophecy, and under-valued the graces of faith and love. Now the apostle shows that they were thereby preferring the things which are for a time to the graces which are forever. One faction, indeed, exalted to the highest place the gift of tongues, which was the most ephemeral of all Christian gifts. (See note on 14:2.) "Prophecies" intimates the varied gradations of power possessed by the preachers, in some cases including that deep spiritual insight into the realities of the present which enabled the preacher to foretell distant events.

(9) We know in part.—Knowledge and preaching are incomplete; therefore, when this dispensation ends, and the complete dispensation is brought in, these imperfect gifts shall cease. Gifts are but the implements of the divine husbandry; graces are the seeds themselves. When the great harvest-time comes, the instruments, however useful, will be cast aside altogether; the seeds will, by the very process of death, be transformed into blossoms and fruits, and in that perfected form remain forever.

(10) That which is perfect.—This verse shows, by the emphatic "then," that the time when the gifts shall cease is the end of this dispensation. The imperfect shall not cease until the perfect is brought in. (See Eph. 4:11-13.)

(11) The natural childhood and manhood of this life are analogous to the spiritual childhood of this life and the spiritual manhood of the life to come.

(12) For now—i.e., in this earthly life.

Through a glass, darkly.—Comp. Jas. 1:23. If we remember the imperfect metal surfaces which formed the mirrors of those days, we can imagine how imperfect and enigmatical (the Greek word is "in an **enigma**") would the image appear. So the apostle says, "Like that image which you see when you look at an object in a mirror far off, with blurred and undefined outline, such is our knowledge here and now; but **then** (i.e., when this dispensation is at an end) we shall see as you see a man when you stand before him face to face.

(13) And now abideth . . . —The "now" is not here temporal, but logical. It is not "now" (i.e., the present life) contrasted with the future, but it is the conclusion of the whole argument. From all that has been urged in the previous verses it follows that these three graces—faith, hope, love— remain imperishable and immortal. Gifts such as the Corinthian Church rejoiced in shall pass away when the perfect succeeds the imperfect; the graces of faith, hope, and love shall remain in the next life, exalted and purified.

14

(1) Follow after charity.—The preceding chapter is parenthetical, and the apostle here returns to the subject with which he had been occupied before he branched off into that great Psalm of Love. He has spoken enthusiastically in praise of the superiority of love as the greatest among the graces, and of all graces as superior to all gifts; but still, spiritual gifts are to be "earnestly striven for." As there was a priority in graces, so there is in gifts. To prophesy is the greatest gift, because it makes us useful to our brethren.

(2) For he that speaketh in an unknown tongue.—The word "unknown" is not in the original, but it has been inserted in connection with the word "tongue" all through this chapter, so as to make the various passages seem to be consistent with the theory that the gift of tongues was a gift of languages. The gift of tongues here spoken of is identical with the gift of tongues which was first bestowed at Pentecost (Acts 2:1-13), and the phenomena described as occurring then must be explained by the fuller and more elaborate account of the nature of the gift which is given to us here.

Against the theory that the gift was one of a capacity to speak various languages we have three considerations: (1) The word **dialectos**, which is repeatedly used to express languages (Acts 1:19; 2:6, 8; 21:40; 22:2; 26:14), is never used by Paul or by the author of the Acts in reference to the utterances of those who possessed the gift of tongues, but the other word, **glossa**, which is, literally, the physical organ of speech—as if the utterances were simply sounds that proceeded from it. (2) There is no trace whatever of this knowledge of languages ever having been used for the purpose of preaching to those who spoke foreign languages. (That the hearers at Pentecost said they heard those who were filled with the Spirit "speak in our own language" would imply only that the outpouring on Pentecost had for the moment a miraculous effect.) (3) The description of the gift in this chapter is utterly inconsistent with its being a gift of languages. The gift was the result of a quickened spiritual power by the action of the Holy Ghost (see Acts 2:4; 10:44-46; 19:6); it poured itself forth in wild, impassioned utterances, which were sometimes mistaken for delirium (verse 23); and these were the expressions not of thoughts but of feelings, unintelligible always, if uninterpreted, to the listener and sometimes to the utterer himself.

(2, 3) They communed with God by the speaking with tongues; they communed with the brethren by prophecy—building up, stirring up, cheering up, as each required.

(4) He that speaketh in an unknown tongue.—The introduction of the word "unknown" destroys the whole force of the passage. All tongues—as distinct from languages—were unknown, i.e., unintelligible. The gift of prophecy is superior in usefulness to that of tongues, and therefore to be preferred. The use of the word "edify," as applied to an individual solely, as distinct from the individual as a part of the whole Church, is unusual with Paul, but is introduced so as to make the antithesis verbally as well as logically more striking.

(5) I would that ye all spake with

tongues.—To avoid danger of misunderstanding or misrepresentation the apostle emphatically asserts here that the error which he is combating is the undue exaltation of the gift of tongues to the depreciation of other gifts. The teacher of religious truth to others, who thereby builds up the whole edifice of the body of Christ, is a greater one than he who is himself benefited by being possessed of profound but uncommunicable emotion.

Except he interpret.—The gift of interpreting might therefore belong to the same person who had the gift of tongues; and if he had this power of articulating for the benefit of others the emotion which he incoherently expresses in reverie, then the gift of tongues was useful to the Church at large, and so was as valuable as prophecy.

(7-11) The truth that sounds of tongues are useless unless they convey definite ideas to the hearers is illustrated (1) by different instruments of music, (2) by different sounds of an instrument, and (3) by different words and languages of living men—in all of which cases the conveyance of distinct ideas is the sign and test of their utility.

(12) Even so ye.—Here follows the practical application of the previous teaching and illustration. The apostle passes now from the contrast between prophecy and tongues to give practical instruction (verses 12-19) as to how they should seek to use the gift of tongues.

(13) In an unknown tongue.—The gift of interpretation would make the gift of tongues useful for the edifying of the Church. This would be an object of unselfish prayer, which God would indeed answer. In the Greek it is suggested that the gift of interpretation is to be not only the object of his prayer, but that it will be the result.

(14) For if I pray in an unknown tongue.—Verses 14-19 are expressed in the first person (except verses 16, 17, which are a parenthesis), as enforcing the apostle's own example. A man praying in a tongue needed the gift of interpretation. The emotions of his spirit, kindled by the Spirit of God, found utterance in a "tongue," the gift of the Spirit of God; but his intellectual faculty grasped no definite idea, and could not, therefore, formulate it into human language. Thus the prayer which is offered merely in a tongue, from the spirit and not from the understanding, is useless as regards others. The apostle is here speaking of public worship (see verse 16), and not of private devotion; and the word "fruitless" implies the result, or rather the absence of result, as regards others.

(15) What is it then?—The apostle in answering this question—What, then, is the practical conclusion of the whole matter?—still speaks in the first person, quoting his own conduct and resolution. He will not let his public ministrations as regards prayer and praise evaporate into mere enthusiasm; nor will he, on the other hand, allow a cold intellectual creed to chill the warm emotions of the spirit.

(16) Here the apostle speaks in the second person, referring not to his practice, but to that of some in Corinth. How can the one who comes as a private person to the assembly, and does not lead the prayer and thanksgiving, say "Amen" when he does not know what is being said? He cannot know if you speak in a tongue, without interpreting. It would seem from this verse that from the earliest apostolic times the practice has been for the congregation to join in the thanksgiving by uttering "Amen" (the Hebrew "So be it") at the conclusion.

(17) For thou verily givest thanks well.— It is here implied that speaking in a tongue was, as regards an individual, an acceptable mode of worship, and it is the public use of it that all throughout this passage the apostle is dealing with.

(18, 19) I thank my God.—Here the apostle resumes in the first person, continuing his own desire and example. He does not undervalue that gift the misuse and exaggeration of which he is censuring; he possesses it himself in a remarkable degree. Yet in the Church he would prefer to speak five words with his mind rather than ten thousand with a tongue only, for the object of such assemblies is not private prayer or private ecstatic communion with God but the edification of others. The word used for "teach" in this verse is literally our word **catechize**.

(20) Howbeit in malice be ye children.— Their conduct in exalting these "tongues," against which he has been warning them, is a proof that they are yet children in knowledge. They ought to be full-grown. The only thing in which they ought to be children is evil, and in that they should be merely "infants."

(21, 22) In the law it is written.—The preceding teaching is illustrated and enforced by an appeal to Jewish history. The Old Testament as a whole was frequently thus designated "the Law." (See John 10:34;

12:34; 15:25.) The words are taken from Isa. 28:9-12. The passage there refers to the refusal of Israel to hearken to Jehovah when He spoke to them with clearness and simplicity, and His judgment of them taking the form of declaring that He would make a foreign people—the Assyrians—be His mouthpiece to them in the future in a language which they did not know. It is as if the apostle said: Remember there was a time in Jewish history when an unintelligible language was a sign sent by God, and proved unavailing as regards the conversion of Israel. The gift which you so exalt now is equally useless by itself for that same purpose.

Thus tongues should not be exalted in estimation above prophecy—inasmuch as the function of the latter is really grander than that of the former. Tongues were useful to arrest the attention of unbelievers, and, if rightly used, to arouse their convictions; but prophecy is in the highest sense useful for believers.

(23) Intended, as tongues were, for a "sign," they cease to be thus useful if not properly employed. The report of the strange utterances which take place in the assembled Church may lead some unbeliever to come there; but if there be tongues alone, and they uninterpreted, the stranger will simply think those present are mad. (See Acts 2:13.)

(24) But if all prophesy.—There is no danger of exaggeration regarding this gift. Each one uttering prophecy, telling forth the gospel truth, and revealing the mind of God, will have a message that will be useful to the unbeliever. As one after another they utter the words of divine truth, they each send something that pierces into his soul. By all of them he is convicted in his own conscience of some sin.

(25) And thus are the secrets of his heart made manifest.—His complete conversion is evidenced by his worshiping God and recognizing the presence of God in that assembly of Christians. It is to be noticed that though the apostle speaks in this passage of an "unlearned" person (i.e., a private person, one who has no gift of prophecy or tongues), or an "unbeliever," it is the latter that is most prominently before his mind, and the former only so far as he shared in common with the latter his ignorance and inability to understand.

(26) From a discussion as to the relative value of the gift of tongues and that of prophecy, the apostle now turns to practical

977

instructions as to the method of their employment in public church assemblies. The uppermost thought in each mind as they assembled for public worship was the individual gift which he possessed. If these varied gifts were employed by each for his own gratification, or even for his own spiritual advancement, they would not be used worthily of the occasion. In public these gifts were to be exercised not by each one for himself, but for the building up of the whole Church.

(27) If any man speak in an unknown tongue.—Here is the practical application of the general rule just laid down to the exercise of the gift of tongues. Those who had the gift of tongues were not all to speak together, and so cause confusion; only two, or at the most three, were to speak in each assembly, and each of such group was to speak one at a time. There was to be with each group one who had the gift of interpretation, and he was to interpret to the listeners.

(28) But if there be no interpreter.—But if there be no one with the gift of interpreting, then the speaker with tongues was not to exercise his gift publicly at all. He may only exercise his gift in private with himself and God.

(29) Let the prophets speak.—Here follows the application to those who had the gift of prophecy. Only two or three prophets are to speak in each assembly on each occasion; the others (not "other") who had the gift are to sit by silently, determining whether the utterances were from the Spirit of God. (See 12:3; I John 4:1-3.) If, however, while one prophet was standing speaking there came a sudden revelation of truth to some other prophet who was sitting by, the speaker would pause and the other prophet give utterance to the inspiration which had come to him. The suddenness of the revelation would show that it was a truth needed there and then, and so should find utterance without delay. This orderly prophesying (verse 31) will accomplish the instruction and comforting of all.

(32) The spirits of the prophets . . . — They might have said it was impossible to carry out Paul's instructions—that the rushing Spirit of God overcame them, so that they could not control themselves. To this Paul replies that it is not so; they **can** prophesy one by one, for the spirits of the prophets are under the control of the prophets.

(33-35) At Corinth one evil of neglecting

the principles of order just laid down was that women spoke in the public assemblies. This was not the custom in any other churches, therefore the example of other churches was against such a practice. They are not even to ask questions in public assemblies. They are to ask their husbands at home on every point on which they desire special instruction. (See chap. 7.)

(36-38) The church at Corinth had on some of these points acted at variance with the practice of the other churches, and in a manner which assumed an independence of Paul's apostolic authority. He therefore asks them, with something of sarcastic indignation, whether they are the source from whence the word of God has come, or whether they think themselves its sole recipients, that they should set themselves above the other churches and above him.

(40) Let all things be done decently.— Verse 39 reiterates in a condensed sentence the principles laid down regarding the gifts in the first part of the chapter (verses 1-25) This verse similarly deals with the general principle laid down in the latter part of the chapter regarding the style and order of public worship. The object of all church assemblies is to be the building up of the body of Christ, which is His Church, and ordered regularity is absolutely necessary to this end.

15

(1) This chapter is throughout occupied with the doctrine of the resurrection of the dead. The occasion which caused the apostle to dwell at such length and with such emphasis on this subject was not merely the perversion but also the denial of the Resurrection by some members of the Corinthian church. There were many elements in such a mixed body which would have contributed to the growth of this error. Among the Jewish converts would be some traces of the Sadducean (Matt. 22:23) denial of the Resurrection; in the Gentile section of the Church there would linger the spirit of the Athenians who "mocked when they heard of the resurrection of the dead" (Acts 17:32), and of the Epicurean philosophers who said, "Let us eat and drink, for tomorrow we die." The apostle, furthermore, probably intended this chapter not only as a reply to these corruptors of the faith, but as supplying those who remained faithful with a confirmation of their own faith and arguments with which they might meet their opponents.

(2) If ye keep in memory what I preached unto you.—The idea here is not that they were converted, and yet that heretofore no results have followed from their belief; it is the same thought which comes out more fully in verse 17. They are saved by their faith in the Gospel as preached by Paul, unless (which is impossible) the whole Gospel be false, and so their faith in it be vain.

(3) For I delivered . . . —We see here what was the subject of apostolic teaching—not indeed all the Gospel that the apostle taught, but what he considered of the first importance, and therefore put in the fore-front of his teaching—the historical fact of Christ's death for our sins, His burial, His Resurrection. This was the first creed of Christendom.

(4) According to the scriptures.—The re-iteration with each statement that it was "according to the scriptures," i.e., according to the Old Testament Scriptures, the gospel narratives not being in existence—shows how strongly the apostle dwelt on the unity of the facts of Christ's life and the predictive utterances of the prophets. The death, burial, and Resurrection of our Lord were all parts of that providential plan which the deep spiritual insight of God's servants of old illumined by the Holy Spirit had enabled them to foresee. The Resurrection was no subsequent invention to try and explain away or mitigate the terrible shock which Christ's death had given to His followers. (See Pss. 2:7; 16:10; Isa. 53:9, 10; 55:13; Hos. 6:2.)

(5) From the indications of sequence given here we may conclude that the appearances grouped together are arranged in chronological order. We have these appearances: (1) To Cephas (see Luke 24:34). (2) To the Twelve, the phrase "the Twelve" being used to indicate, not the number of those present, but the group to which they belonged (see Luke 24:36; John 20:19). (3) To above five hundred brethren at once, probably in Galilee, for at a later date the church at Jerusalem consisted of only one hundred and twenty disciples (see Matt. 28:16, 17; Acts 1:15.) (4) To James, this appearance being recorded only here and in the Gospel of the Hebrews, which is quoted by Jerome. (5) To all the apostles, Thomas being present (John 20:26). (6) To Paul himself (Acts 9:5). To these facts Paul appeals, Most of those who saw Him were alive. Their enemies were alive to dispute it

if they could. The witnesses had nothing to gain, everything to lose by telling the truth. The evidence was set forth some twenty-five or thirty years after the occurrence of the alleged facts. The apostle here maintains the truth of an historical fact. He appeals solely to historical proof, and accumulates a mass of historical testimony, such as in any matter of history, if produced so shortly after the occurrence, would be deemed overwhelming.

(8) Was seen of me also, as of one born out of due time.—The apostle here distinctly states that he saw the Lord at the time of his conversion as really as Peter and others had seen Him, though with touching pathos and strongly marked emphasis he adds that it was not at the same time as the "firstborn" had seen Him, but only as an "untimely born" one.

(9) For I am the least of the apostles.—Here the mention of his conversion—the thought of what he had been before, what he had become since—leads the apostle into a digression, occupying this and the next two verses. The two thoughts of his own inherent nothingness and of his greatness by the grace of God are mingled together here in expressions of intense personal feeling.

(12) If Christ be preached that he rose from the dead.—It has been proved as a matter of historical fact that a man has risen from the dead; it is therefore illogical to say that there is no ressurection of the dead.

(16) For if the dead rise not.—The apostle has completed the argument as to the historical fact of Christ's Resurrection, which proves that the denial of the doctrine of the Resurrection cannot be maintained unless it can be shown that the apostles are willfully bearing false testimony and that their preaching, and the faith of those who accepted it, is vain. He now maintains the doctrine of the Resurrection by showing the incredible absurdities to which a belief in the contrary must lead.

(20) The apostle turns to the hopeful faith to which a belief in the Resurrection leads. As the firstfruits were typical of the whole harvest (Lev. 23:10, 11), so is Christ. He rose not to the exclusion but to the inclusion of all humanity. If Paul wrote this epistle about the time of Passover (see 5:7; 16:8), the fact that the Paschal Sabbath was immediately followed by the day of offering of firstfruits may have suggested this thought.

(21) For since by man ...—The image of the firstfruits is followed by an explanation of the unity of Christ and humanity. The firstfruit must be a sample of the same kind as that which it represents. That condition is fulfilled in the case of the firstfruits of the Resurrection.

(22) As in Adam ..—The first Adam and the Second Adam stand here as the heads of humanity. All that is fleshly in our nature is inherited from the Adam; in every true son of God it is dying daily, and will ultimately die altogether. All that is spiritual in our nature we inherit from the Christ; it is immortal, rising daily, and will ultimately be raised with a spiritual and immortal body. The relationship of Christ to humanity is not to be dated only from the Incarnation. Christ stood in the same federal relation to all who went before as He does to all who have come since. (See 10:4.) The results of Christ's death are co-extensive with the results of Adam's fall—they extend to all men; but the individual responsibility rests with each man as to which he will cherish—the "offense" of Adam or the "grace" of Christ. There seems to be this moral significance in these words of Paul, as well as the obvious argument that, as all men die physically, so all shall be raised from the dead.

(23) But every man in his own order.—There is to be a sequence in the resurrection of the dead, and Paul explains this by the three groups: (1) Christ Himself, the firstfruits; (2) the faithful in Christ at His coming; (3) all the rest of mankind at the end, when the final judgment takes place. The interval between these latter two, as to its duration, or where or how it will be spent, is not spoken of here.

(24-28) The apostle carries on the thought of a triumph which the previous verse had suggested. There rises before the prophetic vision of Paul the final triumph of Christ over all evil, over all power, and the Son giving up to the Father the kingdom of this world, which in His humanity He conquered for the Father as well as for Himself. Christ, laying the spoils of a conquered world at the foot of the throne of the Father, shows, by that supreme act of self-sacrifice, that in His office as Redeemer He came not to do His own will but the will of the Father.

(29) Else—i.e., if there be no resurrection, etc. This is an **argumentum ad hominem.** The practice known as baptism for the dead was absurd if there be no resurrection. To practice it and to deny the doctrine of the Resurrection was illogical. There existed among some of the Christians at Corinth practice of baptizing a living person in the stead of some convert who had died before that sacrament had been administered to him. Such a practice existed among the Marcionites in the second century, and still earlier among a sect called the Cerinthians The idea evidently was that whatever benefit flowed from baptism might be thus vicariously secured for the deceased Christian. This custom possibly sprang up among the Jewish converts, who had been accustomed to something similar in their own faith. If a Jew died without having been purified from some ceremonial uncleanness some living person had the necessary ablution performed on him, and the dead were so accounted clean. Does Paul then, by what he here says, sanction the superstitious practice? Certainly not. He carefully separates himself and the Corinthians, no longer using the first or second person; it is "they" throughout this passage.

(30, 31) This is the same kind of argument now applied to the apostles themselves. Their conduct also would be illogical if they did not believe in a resurrection Such a life as Paul's, both as regards the spiritual battles in his own soul and the ceaseless conflict with enemies around him was indeed a daily dying (II Cor. 11:23-28)

(32) If after the manner of men ...—These words imply "merely from a human point of view." What is the advantage or necessity of my incurring daily risks, if I am merely a human being, with a life limited by what I see, and no immortality and resurrection awaiting me?

I have fought with beasts at Ephesus.—There is no mention in the Acts of any contest in the arena, and, moreover, Paul's Roman citizenship would have legally protected him against such treatment. The Ephesians themselves, therefore, must be spoken of as "beasts." Both Hebrew and Greek literature would have made such a form of expression familiar to the apostle and to his readers. (Comp. Ps. 22:12, 13, 20, 21.) The Cretians are called "evil beasts" by the poet Epimenides, whom Paul quotes in Tit. 1:12. Heraclitus calls the Ephesians "beasts"—the same word as Paul uses here; and Ignatius (**Epis. ad Rom.**) speaks of "fighting with beasts by land and sea," and having been "bound to 'ten leopards,' that is a band of soldiers." But we must not take this as indicating the scene described in Acts 19:23-34, which had probably not taken place when this was written; but no doubt the "many adversaries" (16:9) at Ephesus had already availed themselves of some opportunity of venting their rage on the apostle after the manner of wild beasts.

If the dead rise not?—If the dead be not raised, our conduct is illogical. Consistency then belongs to those who disregard God's call to repentance, and of whom we read in Isa. 22:13. The reference is directly to this passage in the prophet describing the conduct of abandoned Jews during the siege of Jerusalem; but the words indicate with equal accuracy that school of Epicurean philosophy of which, no doubt, there were many representatives at Corinth.

(35) The proof of the truth of the doctrine of the Resurrection is concluded in the last verse. The truth of the Resurrection is, in the early part of this chapter, maintained (1) by the historical fact of Christ's resurrection, (2) by a **reductio ad absurdum**, showing the consequences logically involved in a denial of it, and (3) by an **argumentum ad hominem**. The former two arguments are still those on which we must rest our belief in the doctrine; the latter is, like every argument of that nature, only of force to those to whom it was actually addressed. There still remain, however, two difficulties: in what manner are the dead raised? and what is the nature of that body?

(36-41) The apostle now proceeds to show, by the analogies in nature, how a resurrection of a body is possible, how substantial identity may be preserved under variation of form. Analogy cannot ever be regarded as logically conclusive of an argument, but it does show that the same difficulty exists in theory in other directions where we actually see it surmounted in fact. We have, in these verses, three illustrations of the preservation of identity of matter under change of form: (1) seeds growing into flowers and fruit; (2) flesh in the variety of men, beasts, fishes, and birds; (3) heavenly and earthly bodies in infinite variety of form and of glory. The God who is thus not limited to a monotonous form for the substance of which physical nature consists, need not be in any difficulty as to some other variety of form for human nature beyond that to which we see it confined during its earthly life.

(42) So also is the resurrection of the dead.—Here follows the application of these analogies to the subject in hand. As there is in the vegetable growth, in the varieties of animal life, and in the diversities of form assumed by inorganic matter, an identity preserved amid variety of "body," so a change in the form or glory of our organism which we call our "body" is compatible with the preservation of personal identity. The "it," the personality, remains the same— now in corruption, then in incorruption; now in dishonor, then in glory; now in weakness, then in power.

(44) Here is a further and different application of the three analogies. It is not only that there is a variety of body in these illustrations, but there is also an adaptability. The "body" which a plant has when it is in the form of seed is suited to the condition in which seed is placed, while the "body" which it has when grown into a plant is suited to the changed conditions in which a plant exists; the "flesh" in the "body" form of a bird is suited to its sphere of life; and so on. It is not all accidental but a purposely adapted variety. So it will be in the variety of "bodies" for humanity. A man's organism is sown (i.e., is born into this world) a natural body; it is raised (through and by death) a spiritual body. The body which we have here on earth is suited with a marvelous detail of adaptability to the life, physical and intellectual, amid which we are placed, and of which we form a part. It is, however, a hindrance to the spiritual man in each of us. (See II Cor. 5.) There will be a time for each when the body will become as perfectly adapted to the spiritual man in each as the human body here is to the natural man—no longer its hindrance, but its help. The "willing spirit" will then never be hampered and thwarted by a "weak flesh"; the body having become spiritual itself, will be spiritually strong.

(45) And so it is written.—See Gen. 2:7. Here Paul contrasts the two Adams—the first man and Christ—from whom we derive our natural and our spiritual natures, and our natural and spiritual bodies. The first Adam became, by his disobedience, a mere living soul, and from him we inherit that nature; the Second Adam, by His obedience, became a life-giving spirit, and from Him we inherit the spiritual nature in us. (Comp. Rom. 5:19.)

(49) We shall also bear the image of the heavenly.—Better, "let us bear also the image of the heavenly." Such is the reading in the best MSS. The words transport the thoughts of the reader to the future glory, and, at the same moment, show a light on present duty. The resurrection life is to be begun in us even now (II Cor. 3:18; Phil. 3:21).

(50) Flesh and blood, being corruption, cannot enter into the heavenly state, which is incorruption. This is still part of the answer to the question, "With what bodies do they come?" but the reply is no longer based upon any analogy. It comes now as a revelation of what Paul had been taught by the Spirit of God. Blood is everywhere the type of this lower animal life. (See Gen. 9:4). All offerings which typified the offering up and sacrifice of "self"—the lower sinful self—were sacrifices by shedding of blood, without which was no remission (Heb. 9:22). When the supreme Sacrifice was made on Calvary, the blood was shed—once for all. So when Christ showed His resurrection body to His disciples, He said, "A spirit hath not flesh and bones [not blood], as ye see me have." The blood of Christ is never spoken of as existing after His crucifixion. That was the supreme sacrifice of Self to God. The blood—the type of the human self—was poured out forever.

(51) Behold, I shew you a mystery.—A mystery means something which up to this time has been kept concealed, but is now made manifest (Rom. 11:25; Eph. 3:3-5).

We shall not all sleep, but we shall all be changed.—The apostle believed that the end of the world might come in the lifetime of some then living. We shall not all, he says, necessarily sleep, but we shall all be changed. The change from the earthly to the spiritual body is absolutely necessary. To some it will come through the ordinary process of death; to those who are alive at Christ's advent, it will come suddenly, and in a moment. The dead shall be raised, but we (the living) shall be changed.

(52) The last trump.—The trumpet was used to summon an assembly (Exod. 20:18; Ps. 81:3. Isa. 18:3; 27:13) or to sound a warning. This verse states with reiterated emphasis that this change shall not be a protracted process, but a sudden and momentary alteration in the condition of our bodies.

**(53) For this corruptible must ... **—Not only must the resurrection body be suited to the condition but also to the duration of the new life. As a spiritual body, it will be adapted to the needs of a spiritual state (verse 50); and as an immortal and incorruptible body, it will be adapted to a life which is everlasting.

(54) Death is swallowed up in victory.— These words, originally referring to the

Jewish people (Isa. 25:8), are naturally applied here to the human race, of which they were the chosen type.

(55) O death, where is thy sting?—Comp. Hos. 13:14. These words originally occur as, "Where is thy victory, O death? Where is thy sting, O hell?"—the word "hell" referring, not to the place of torment, but to the Hades of departed spirits.

(56) The sting of death is sin.—Death is pictured as a monster, and it is armed with a sting. Its sting is sin. If there were no sin, death would not be capable of inflicting pain, and the strength of sin springs from the fact that it is the violation of God's law. (See Rom. 5:12; 7:7.)

(57) But thanks be to God.—The future is so certain that the apostle speaks of it as a subject for present thanksgiving; the victory is one which God gives now through Jesus Christ. His Resurrection is the pledge of our resurrection. His death is the power by which we are enabled to conquer that lower self, from whose crucifixion and death we shall rise to the higher incorruptible life of the resurrection day.

(58) Therefore.—Because all this is so— because there is a life hereafter—let this life here be worthy of it. You might grow weak and fainthearted if you could think that all your work for God and truth here might be wasted; but it is not so. It cannot be "in vain" if it be "in the Lord."

16

(1) Now concerning the collection for the saints.—From the fact of a necessity existing for a collection for the poor Christians at Jerusalem, it is clear that the community of goods (see Acts 2:44) which had at the beginning been established in that church had not proved successful. Christianity was largely recruited from the lower classes, especially in Jerusalem (Jas. 2:5), and a common fund would not long have flourished with so few contributors and such a multitude of sharers. Moreover, the many who were shut up in prison had perhaps by this time been released in abject poverty, and would naturally be the subject of anxious solicitation to one who was identical with "persecuting Saul." (See Acts 26:10.) The apostle does not speak of them as "the poor," but as "saints." That was the true ground of their claim upon their brethren.

On the order to the Galatians, see Acts 26:10.

(2) Upon the first day of the week.—Already the day of the week on which Christ had risen had become noted as a suitable day for distinctively Christian work and Christian worship. It does not yet seem to have been designated by the phrase by which it became subsequently universally known in Christendom—"the Lord's Day"; that name occurs first in Rev. 1:10. This would be a convenient as well as a suitable day for each one to set aside something, as he had proposed, storing it up until the apostle's arrival, for this was already the usual day of Christians assembling themselves together (Acts 20:7).

As God hath prospered him.—These words do not imply that only in cases of exceptional prosperity was a man to contribute, but every man was to give out of whatever fruits he had from his labor.

(3) Whomsoever ye shall approve by your letters.—The apostle had not made up his mind finally whether he would take the gift himself or send it by messengers, whom he would accredit with letters, to the church at Jerusalem. The course finally adopted was that the apostle went himself, and the selected brethren with him (Acts 21:15).

(5) For I do pass through Macedonia.—A misrepresentation of these words gives rise to the incorrect statement that this epistle was written at Philippi, which is to be found in the subscription at the end of this chapter in our English Bible. The apostle does not here refer to where he is at the moment of writing, but to his intention regarding his journey. He had intended to go first to Corinth (see II Cor. 1:15, 16), but he has altered that plan, and says that his intention now is to pass through Macedonia first, and then visit Corinth.

(6) And it may be that I will abide ... —His former plan had involved but a brief visit to the church at Corinth, but the arrangement which he now contemplated would permit a longer stay. Where he would go from Corinth he had not yet determined; and, indeed, it was subsequently determined for him by a conspiracy against him, which was fortunately discovered in time (Acts 20:3, 6, 13, 17). He remained three months at Corinth, during winter.

(8) But I will tarry at Ephesus.—In this and in verse 9 the apostle returns to his immediate plans at Ephesus. It was probably now about Easter-time (see verse 7), and the hostility of enemies increases. (See Acts 19:9-23.) That must be subdued. A door has been opened wide for the effectual spread of the gospel (Acts 19:20). Of that the apostle must avail himself. Therefore he will remain where he is until Pentecost.

(10) Now if Timotheus come ... —See note on 4:17.

(11) For I look for him with the brethren.—Now that Paul knows how bad is the condition of the Corinthian church, and what need it has of vigorous treatment, he sends not only his epistle, but with it Titus and two other brethren. (See II Cor. 8:18, 22, 23.) In energy and firmness of character Titus was a striking contrast to Timothy, while he equally shared the spirit and confidence of Paul. (See II Cor. 7.) Titus was fully competent and willing to deal energetically with the recalcitrant spirit of some sections of the Corinthian church.

(12) As touching our brother Apollos.—Paul, free from the smallest spark of personal jealousy, had wished that Apollos, whose name had been used as the designation of a faction in opposition to the apostle himself, should go with this letter to Corinth. In the absence of Paul himself, Apollos would have been the most likely person to exercise authority there. The unselfish consideration of Paul is equaled by the thoughtful reluctance of Apollos, who fears that his presence might encourage the one faction and perhaps embitter the other.

(13, 14) Watch ye, stand fast.—The apostle's mind is full of the hope of beneficial results following from this letter and from the exertions of Titus; yet, after all, everything depends upon the Corinthians themselves.

(15) The apostle here reminds the Corinthians that the devotion of teachers, and all who serve in the gospel ministry, ought to be rewarded with a return of sympathy and devotion on the part of those whom they serve. Stephanas (verse 15), Fortunatus, and Achaicus had come from Corinth to Ephesus probably with the letter from the Corinthians (8:1), and their presence had cheered the apostle. They had made up for the want of zeal and love on the part of so many of the Corinthians. They had come on behalf of the whole church there, not enemies to bear tales, but well-wishing friends to obtain apostolic help and counsel for all.

(19) Aquila and Priscilla had been the apostle's friends at Corinth (Acts 18:1-3), and he now was with them at Ephesus. (See Rom. 16:3-5; II Tim. 4:19.)

(20) An holy kiss.—The kiss was the ordinary form of affectionate greeting in the

East. The Church adopted it; and when thus interchanged between those whose bond of friendship was not earthly, but spiritual, it was designated "the holy kiss." (See Rom. 16:16; I Thess. 5:26.)

(21) The salutation of me Paul with mine own hand.—It was the apostle's habit to dictate his epistles, but to add a few words at the end in his own handwriting. (See II Thess. 3:17.) The concluding verses here are, accordingly, Paul's autograph. The earlier portions had been written by Sosthenes. (See 1:1)

(22) If any man love not the Lord Jesus.— From all the argument and controversy which form the main portion of the epistle, the apostle with his own hand brings back the thoughts of the Corinthians to the true test of their Christianity. Do they love the Lord Jesus? The word used here for love signifies not merely affectionate regard, but personal devotion.

Let him be Anathema Maran-atha.— Better, "Let him be Anathema. Maranatha." There is no connection between these two words. **Anathema** signifies "accursed." The absence of love to Christ is condemnation. The word **Maranatha** is a Syriac expression— "the Lord is at hand." The uncertainty of the moment when the Lord may come is the most solemn thought with which to remind them of the importance of being one with Christ.

In reference to the erroneous subscription which follows this epistle in our English version, see notes on verses 5, 8, and 10.

II CORINTHIANS

1

(1) Timothy our brother.—The opening words of the epistle are nearly identical with those of I Cor. 1:1. Timotheus, however, takes the place of Sosthenes, having apparently left Corinth before the arrival of the first epistle, or, possibly not having reached it. It is natural to think of him as acting in this instance, as in others where the apostle joins his name with his own (Phil. 1:1; Col. 1:1), as Paul's amanuensis.

(4) Who comforteth us.—For the writer, the name "God of all comfort" (verse 3) was the outcome of a living personal experience. He had felt that ever-continuing comfort flowing into his soul, and he knew that it had not been given to him for his own profit only, but that it might flow forth to others (verse 5). The power to comfort varies with the measure in which we have been comforted ourselves. The words imply that Paul had passed through a time of tribulation himself. They imply also that he knew of their troubles. (Comp. 7:7-11.)

(6) Each state of the apostle's experience—that of affliction no less than that of consolation—tended to make others sharers in the latter and not in the former. The word "consolation" is added as presenting the objective side of the result of which Paul speaks, while "salvation" gives prominence to the subjective. But this deliverance is seen, not in a mere escape from, or avoidance of, sufferings, but in a patient, steadfast endurance of them.

(8) From the generalized language of the previous verses he passes to something more specific. The words "in Asia" suggest a wider range of suffering than that alluded to in Acts 19:24-31 or I Cor. 15:32, such as we find referred to in the speech to the elders at Miletus (Acts 20:19); and the context leads us to think of bodily illness as well as of perils and anxieties.

(9) We had the sentence of death in ourselves.—The word translated "sentence" was a term used in medical practice, which Paul may have adopted from Luke, expressing the "opinion" which a physician formed on his diagnosis of a case submitted to him. The apostle had found himself in a state in which, as far as he could judge for himself, that opinion would have been against the prospect of recovery. He ceased to trust in himself, i.e., in any remedial measures that

he could take for himself. He could trust only in God. Recovery in such a case was a veritable resurrection.

(10) The words imply that he was not yet altogether free, as man would judge, from the danger of a relapse. Life was for him, in relation both to bodily infirmities and perils of other kinds, a perpetual series of deliverances.

(11) That for the gift bestowed upon us by the means of many persons.—The Greek word for "person" **(prosopon)** is elsewhere throughout the New Testament translated "face" or "countenance," or "person" in the sense of "outward appearance." The use of the word **prosopon**, however, for the characters in a drama indicates that the noun was beginning to be used in a different sense, and this must clearly have been well established when it came to be used in theological language for the three "persons" of the Godhead. If this is its meaning here, it is probably one of the earliest extant instances of its being so used.

The "gift," in this instance, is the deliverance from danger and suffering spoken of in the previous verse. Safety and health deserved the name no less truly than prophecy and the gift of tongues. He assumes that they will be as ready to give thanks for his recovery or deliverance as they were to pray for it.

(12) With the feeling of jubilant thankfulness which has heretofore characterized his language there mingles another of a different character. It had, perhaps, been in the background of his thoughts all along. He had seemed, in I Cor. 4:21, to imply that he was coming to take strong measures against evil-doers; in I Cor. 16:2-8 he had spoken yet more definitely; and yet he had not come. Titus would seem to have told him what was said of this: "He was fickle, and changeable; perhaps he was afraid to come." He is eager to refute the charge without a formal pleading as in answer to it, and seems to cast about for an opening. He finds it in the words which he had just dictated. He has a right to assume that the Corinthians will pray and give thanks for him, for he can boast that he has never failed, conscience bearing him witness (comp. Acts 23:1; 24:16; Rom. 9:1), in transparent sincerity to them. (See I Cor. 2:1-6.)

In its fullest sense, the apostle can say that he had striven to **live** everywhere so as to avoid giving grounds for suspicion. Nowhere had he been more careful so to live than at Corinth, where men were suspicious in proportion to their own viciousness. (Comp. notes on 7:1, 2.)

(14) As also ye have acknowledged.—The parenthetical clause qualifies the fear which had been partly veiled by the hope. They had done him some, though not adequate, justice.

That we are your rejoicing . . .—The words must be connected with the future rather than the past. "I trust that you will one day recognize that you have as much reason to be proud of me as I have to be proud of you." The "day of the Lord Jesus," of His great advent to judge the world (comp. Rom. 2:16), defines the "end" to which the previous verse had pointed.

(15) His plan had been at first to go straight by sea from Ephesus to Corinth, then to pass on to Macedonia, then to return to Corinth, and from there to set sail for Jerusalem. When he wrote I Cor. 16:5, 6 (see notes), he had already modified his plan by deciding to go to Macedonia first. His original scheme had shown his wish to see as much of the Corinthians as possible. They were to have two visits ("a second **favour**"), and not one only. Had he shown less regard, he asks, in the change with which he had been taunted?

(16) To be brought on my way.—The change of word is significant. He did not intend merely to go from Corinth to Judaea, but expected the Corinthians to further his intentions, to help him on, to escort him solemnly to the ship in which he was to sail, perhaps to accompany him to Asia. The wish had been stated in I Cor. 16:6, but without more than a hint (I Cor. 16:4), that his destination might be Jerusalem.

(17) Did I use lightness?—This, then, was the charge which he is anxious to refute. But when had the Corinthians heard of the plan thus detailed? It had been already abandoned before the first epistle was dispatched. Had it been communicated in a lost letter (see note on I Cor. 5:9)? or was this what Timotheus, who started before the first letter was written (I Cor. 4:17), had been authorized to announce? Either alternative is possible.

Do I purpose according to the flesh . . . ?— "Am I weak and worldly in my purpose, changing my plans, and saying 'Yes' and 'No' in almost the same breath?" It is obvious that the words on which he dwells had been used of him by others. Some teacher of the party of the circumcision had, apparently, quoted the rule of the

Sermon on the Mount (Matt. 5:37) and of James (Jas. 5:12), and had asked, with a sneer, when the first epistle came and showed that the original plan had been abandoned, whether this was the way in which Paul acted on it. The passage has, accordingly, the interest of being indirectly a reference to our Lord's teaching, showing, like Acts 20:35, that "the words of the Lord Jesus" were habitually cited as rules of life.

(20) All the promises of God . . . —The promises of God have been fulfilled and ratified in Christ. He was, as it were, a living incarnate "Amen" to those promises. Comp. John's use of the word Amen as a name of Christ, the "faithful and true witness" (Rev. 3:14). The words "by us" are determined by the context as referring to the preacher rather than to the hearers of the Word.

(21) He which stablisheth us with you . . . —For a moment the thought of an apology for his own conduct is merged in the higher thought of the greatness of his mission. The word "stablisheth," or "confirmeth" (I Cor. 1:8) is connected with the previous "Amen" as the emphatic formula of ratification.

And hath anointed us.—This refers to a definite moment in the life of the disciples. (See Acts 2:38; 8:17; 10:44; 19:6.) The verb follows naturally on the mention of Christ the Anointed One.

(22) Who hath also sealed us.—The thought thus expressed is that the gift of the Spirit, following on baptism or the laying on of hands, is as the seal of the covenant which God makes with His people, attesting its validity. (Comp. Eph. 1:13; 4:30.)

And given the earnest of the Spirit.—The Greek word for "earnest" (**arrhabon**), which occurs here for the first time, is used only by Paul in the New Testament (5:5; Eph. 1:14). It was originally a Hebrew word, from a verb meaning "to mix," "to change," "to pledge." The full form came to be considered somehow as pedantic or vulgar, and was superseded in Roman law by the shortened "arrha," the payment of a small sum given on the completion of a bargain as a pledge that the prayer would fulfill the contract. As applied by Paul, it had the force of a condensed parable, such as the people of commercial cities like Corinth and Ephesus would readily understand. They were not to think that their past spiritual experience had any character of finality. It was rather but the pledge of yet greater gifts to come, even of that knowledge of God which is eternal life (John 17:3). The same thought is expressed, under a more Hebrew image in the "**firstfruits** of the Spirit" (Rom. 8:23). Grammatically, the "earnest of the Spirit" is the genitive of apposition, "the earnest which **is** the Spirit."

(23) I call God for a record.—The thought seems to come across Paul's mind that the Corinthians will require a more specific explanation of his change of plan (see I Cor. 4:21). Had he carried out his first purpose, he would have come to punish or chastise. He had been, on this account, reluctant to come. His not coming was an act of leniency.

(24) Not for that we have dominion over your faith.—He has scarcely written the words which imply authority, when the thought comes to him that he may seem to claim too much. He puts forward, therefore, the other side of his work. He was really seeking, not to domineer, or cause pain, but to be a fellow worker with their "joy and peace in believing" (Rom. 15:13). He knows that they have a standing-ground, independently of him, in their faith in Christ, and he seeks to confirm that faith.

2

(1, 2) The chapter division interrupts the sequence of thought. He did not wish to make his second visit to Corinth in grief; and if he had carried out his first plan, that would have been the almost inevitable result.

(3) And I wrote this same unto you.—We see here with what definiteness certain passages in his first letter were stamped upon his memory. His motive in so writing as to give pain had been to avoid giving and receiving pain when he came in person. He wanted his visit to be one of unmixed joy for himself, and if so, it could not fail, looking to their mutual sympathy, to give his disciples joy also.

(4) Out of much affliction and anguish.—Men might think that it had cost him little to write sharp words like those which he has in his mind. He remembers well what he felt as he dictated them—the intensity of his feelings, pain that such words should be needed, anxiety as to their issue, the tears which then, as at other times (Acts 20:19, 31; II Tim. 1:4), were the outflow of strong emotion. Those who were indignant at his stern words should remember, or at least

learn to believe this, and so to see in them the strongest proof of his abounding love for them. The word for "anguish" is used only by Luke and Paul in the New Testament and is, perhaps, another example of medical terminology. The anguish was like that of a tight pressure or constriction of the heart.

(5) But if any have caused grief.—The man who had been the chief cause of his sorrow is now prominent in his thoughts. (Comp. I Cor. 5:1-5.) The members of the Corinthian church were really the greatest sufferers from the scandal which brought shame upon it.

(6) Sufficient to such a man is this punishment.—This was somewhat after the course marked out in I Cor. 5:3-5. A meeting of the church had been held, and the man delivered to Satan. Possibly this was followed by some suffering of body, supernaturally inflicted, or coming as the natural consequence (not less divine because natural) of remorse and shame. It was almost certainly followed by excommunication and exclusion from religious and social fellowship. Paul had clearly heard what it had been, thought that it had been enough, and urged the offender's forgiveness and public reinstatement to the fellowship of the church (verses 7, 8).

Which was inflicted of many.—Actually, "by the majority." The decision, then, had not been unanimous. The minority may have been members either of the Judaizing "Cephas" party or the party of license.

(10) To whom ye forgive any thing, I forgive also.—The procedure of I Cor. 5:3-7 is again, obviously, in his mind. Though absent in body, he had made himself a sharer spiritually in that censure. He now, anticipating their compliance with his request, makes himself a sharer in the sentence of absolution. He forgives as though Christ were acting in or by him. The forgiveness is as authoritative as the censure.

(11) The language comes from a wide and varied experience. Paul had been buffeted by a messenger of Satan (12:7), had once and again been hindered by him in his work (I Thess. 2:18), was ever wrestling with principalities and powers (Eph. 6:12), and so knew how the tempter could turn even the rules of an ascetic rigor, or the remorse of a sin-burdened conscience, into an occasion of yet further and more irremediable sin.

(12) Furthermore, when I came to Troas.—The case of the offender had come in as a parenthesis in verses 5-8. He returns to the train of thought which it had interrupted, and continues his narrative of what had passed after he had written the first epistle. A church had probably been founded in Troas by Luke; but Paul's first visit to it had been limited to a few days, and there are no traces of his preaching there. Now he comes "for the gospel's sake." That there was a flourishing Christian community some months later we find from Acts 20:6.

(13) I had no rest in my spirit.—Instead of coming himself straight from Ephesus, as he had at first intended, and had intimated probably in the lost letter of I Cor. 5:9, or by Timotheus (I Cor. 4:17), or pressing on through Macedonia, as he purposed when he wrote the first epistle (I Cor. 16:5), he had sent on Titus to ascertain what had been the effects of that epistle on the Corinthian church. Titus was to return to him at Troas. Not meeting him there, Paul, in his eager anxiety to hear something more than Timotheus had been able to tell him, left Troas, in spite of the opening which it presented for his work as a preacher of the Gospel, and hastened on into Macedonia. Taking the route that he had taken before, he would probably go to Philippi, where he would find Luke; and we may conjecture, without much risk of error, that it was there that he and Titus met.

(14) Now thanks be unto God.—This burst of thanksgiving finds its source, not in what the apostle had written or spoken, but in what was passing through his memory. He had met Titus, and that disciple had been as a courier bringing tidings of a victory. The love of God had won another triumph.

The imagery that follows (verses 15, 16) is clearly that of the solemn triumphal procession of a Roman emperor or general. The conqueror would ride in his chariot, followed by his troops and prisoners, captive kings and princes, and trophies of victory. Fragrant clouds of incense accompanied his march, rising from fixed altars or wafted from censers. At the foot of the Capitoline hill some of the prisoners were led off to execution, while others were pardoned and set free.

So Paul claims to be an incense-bearer in the procession of the Conqueror. Words, whether of prayer or praise, thanksgiving or preaching, what were they but as incense clouds bearing to all around, as they were wafted in the air, the tidings that the Conqueror had come? In his belief in the

righteousness and mercy of Christ, he is content to leave the souls of all men to His judgment.

(17) For we are not as many, which corrupt the word of God.—The word for "corrupt," formed from a word which signifies "huckster" or "tavern keeper," implies an adulteration like that which such people commonly practiced. We, says Paul, play no such tricks of trade with what we preach; we do not meet the tastes of our hearers by prophesying deceits. The fact that we know the tremendous issues of our work would hinder that. And such works our sufficiency for these things (verse 16; comp. 3:5).

3

(1) Do we begin again to commend ourselves?—Titus has told Paul what has been said of him at Corinth. Referring, probably, to what he had said in his first epistle as to the "wisdom" which he preached (2:6), his having "laid the foundation" (3:10), his dwelling on his sufferings (4:11), his preaching without payment (9:15) as a thing he gloried in, they had sneered at him as always "commending himself." They had added that it was no wonder that he did so when he had no authoritative letters of commendation from other churches, such as were brought by other teachers.

Need we, as some others, epistles of commendation to you?—Possibly some of the Apollos party had contrasted the letters which he had brought from Ephesus (Acts 18:27) with Paul's want of them. Possibly the Judaizing teachers (11:13) had come with credentials of this nature from the church of Jerusalem. "Letters of commendation" deserve notice as an important element in the organization of the early church. A Christian traveling with such a letter from any church was certain to find a welcome in any other. They guaranteed at once his soundness in the faith and his personal character.

(2) Ye are our epistle written in our hearts.—This is an answer. They, the Corinthian converts, are written on his heart. In his thoughts and prayers for them he finds his true commendatory letter, and this is a letter which is patent to the eyes of all men.

(3) Forasmuch as ye are manifestly declared.—The metaphor appears to shift its ground from the subjective to the objective. It is not only as written in his heart, but as seen and known by others, that the Corinthians are as a letter of commendation. He had been as the **amanuensis** of that letter, but Christ was the real writer.

Written not with ink.—Letters were usually written on papyrus, with a reed pen and with a black pigment (**atramentum**) used as ink. (Comp. II John 12.) In contrast with this process, he speaks of the Epistle of Christ as written with the "Spirit of the living God." It is noteworthy that the Spirit takes here the place of the older "finger of God" in the history of the two tables of stone in Exod. 31:18.

(5) Not that we are sufficient ... —See note on 2:17.

(6) Able ministers of the new testament.— In the "new covenant"—new, as implying **freshness** of life and energy—we have a direct reference, both to our Lord's words, as cited in I Cor. 11:25, and given in the gospel narrative of the Last Supper (see notes on Matt. 26:28), and to Jer. 31:31. The idea of "spirit" comes from Ezek. 11:19; 36:26, 27.

For the letter killeth, but the spirit giveth life.—The word "letter" (**gramma**) stands not for what we call the literal meaning of Scripture as contrasted with one which is allegorical or spiritual, but for the whole written code or law of Judaism. Paul does not contrast the literal meaning of that code with the so-called mystical exposition of it (a view which has often led to wild interpretations), but speaks of the written code as such. Of this written code Paul says that it "killeth." What he means is stated with sufficient fullness in the three epistles written about this time (I Cor. 15:56; Gal. 3:10, 21; Rom. 7:9-11; 8:2, 3). The work of the Law, from Paul's view, is to make men conscious of sin. No outward command, even though it come from God, and is "holy, and just, and good" (Rom. 7:12), can do more than that. What was wanting was the life-giving power of the Spirit. The word here appears to hover between the sense of "spirit" as representing any manifestation of the divine Life that gives life (John 6:63), and the more distinctly personal sense in which Paul speaks of "the Spirit," the Holy Spirit. Of that Spirit, Paul says that "it quickens": it can rouse into life not only the slumbering conscience, as the Law had done, but the higher spiritual element in man.

(7-10) See Exod. 34:29-35. The ministration of the spirit—that which has spirit for its characteristic attribute, and proceeds

from **the** Spirit and imparts it to others—is that which Paul claims as his ministry. The glory of the new covenant must be as much above the glory of the old as the living, life-giving Spirit is above the dead and death-bringing code which he speaks of as the "letter." The imagery seems to bring before us the symbolic meaning of the Transfiguration. Moses and Elijah appear in glory, but the glory of the Son of Man surpasses that of either. (Comp. Matt. 16:1-4.)

(11) For if that which is done away ... —Comp. Heb. 8:13. The contrast between the transient and the permanent is expressed by the same Greek words as in I Cor. 13:8-11.

(13, 14) What was the object of this putting on of the veil? The English of Exod. 34:33 suggests that it was to hide the brightness from which they shrank. But the interpretation which Paul follows presents a different view. Moses put the veil over his face that **they might not see the end, the fading away** of that transitory glory. For them it was as though it were permanent and unfading. They did not see that the whole system of the Law, as symbolized by the brightness, had but a temporary being. And what was true of those older Israelites was true also of their descendants. They could not see the true end of the perishing system of the Law, its aim, purport, consummation. (Comp. Rom. 10:4.) But the apostle had no need to veil his face or his meaning, for he had no fear lest the glory of the Gospel of which he was a minister should fade away.

(15) Even unto this day, when Moses is read ... —The mention of Moses is decisive as to the meaning of the "Old Testament," or **covenant**, in the previous verse. When he, as being read, speaks to the people now, Paul reasons, there is still a veil between him and them; but it is subjective and not objective—on their heart, and not over his face.

(16) Nevertheless when it shall turn to the Lord.—The allegorizing process is still carried on. Moses removed the veil when he went into the Tabernacle to commune with the Lord (Exod. 34:35); so, in the interpretation of the parable, the veil shall be taken away when the heart of Israel shall turn, in the might of a real conversion, to the Lord of Israel.

(17) The verse explains that the "turning to the Lord" (verse 16) coincides with the "ministration of the Spirit." To turn to the

Lord is to turn to **the** Spirit which is His, which dwelt in Him, and which He gives. And he assumes, almost as an axiom of the spiritual life, that the presence of that Spirit gives freedom, as contrasted with the bondage of the letter. Compare the Spirit bearing witness with our spirit that we are the children of God, those children being partakers of a glorious liberty (Rom. 8:16-21), and the connection between walking in the Spirit and being called to liberty (Gal. 5:13-16).

(18) There is no veil over our hearts, and therefore none over the eyes with which we exercise our faculty of spiritual vision. We are as Moses was when he stood before the Lord with the veil withdrawn. We see God mirrored in Christ, who is "the image of the invisible God" (Col. 1:15), and as we gaze with our face unveiled, on that mirror, a change comes over us. The image of the old evil Adam-nature (I Cor. 15:49) becomes less distinct, and the image of the new man, after the likeness of Christ, takes its place. (Comp. Rom. 8:29.) It is through the Holy Spirit that the Lord, the Christ, makes His presence manifest to our human spirit.

4

(1) Therefore seeing we have this ministry.—The ministry referred to is that of which such great things have just been said: the ministry of the new covenant, of the Spirit, of righteousness, of glory (3:6, 8, 9). Two thoughts rise up in the apostle's mind in immediate association with this: (1) his own utter unworthiness of it, which finds expression in "as we have received mercy" (comp. I Tim. 1:12); and (2) the manifold trials and difficulties in the midst of which it had to be accomplished. The fact that he has been called to such a work is, however, a source of strength. He cannot faint or show cowardice in discharging it.

(2) He has defended himself against the charge of "fickleness" (1:17), but another charge, more disturbing still, had also been brought against him. Men had talked, so he had been told, of his "craftiness" (comp. 12:16), and to that imputation he now addresses himself. He appealed not to men's tastes, or prejudices, or humors, but to that in them which was highest—their conscience, their sense of right and wrong; and in doing this he felt that he was speaking and acting in the presence of the great Judge.

(3) But if our gospel be hid, it is hid to them that are lost.—He cannot close his eyes to the fact that the glorious words of 3:18 are only partially realized. There are some to whom even the Gospel of Christ appears as shrouded by a veil. And these are not Judaizing teachers only or chiefly, but the whole class of those who are at present **on the way to perish**, not knowing God.

(4) In whom the god of this world ...—Comp. John 14:30; Eph. 2:2. The work of the devil is directly in antagonism to that of God. He seeks to lead men back from light to darkness. Their spiritual state was, Paul seems to say, lower than that of Israel. The veil was over the heart of the one; the very organs of spiritual perception were blinded in the other.

(5) For we preach not ourselves.—The words, like those about "commending ourselves," imply a reference to something that had been said. He was charged with being egotistic in his preaching, perhaps with special reference to passages like I Cor. 2:1-4; 3:1-10; 4:11-13. He indignantly repudiates that charge. "Christ Jesus" had been all along the subject of his preaching. (Comp. I Cor. 2:2.) As far as he had spoken of himself at all, it had been as a minister and servant for their sake (I Cor. 3:22, 23; 9:19).

(7) But we have this treasure in earthen vessels.—The treasure is "the knowledge of the glory of God" (verse 6) as possessed by the apostle. It was the practice of Eastern kings, who stored up their treasures of gold and silver, to fill jars of earthenware with coin or bullion (Herod 3:103; comp. Jer. 32:14). "So," Paul says, in a tone of profound humility, "it is with us. In these frail bodies of ours—'earthen vessels'—we have that priceless treasure." The words have probably a side glance at the taunts that had been thrown out as to his bodily infirmities. "And it is that men may see that the excellence of the power which we exercise comes from God, and not from ourselves." The words that follow, contrasting sufferings and infirmities in their manifold variety with the way in which they were borne through God's strengthening grace, show this to be the true underlying sequence of thought.

(10) Always bearing about in the body the dying of the Lord Jesus.—The word for "dying" (again, probably, a distinctly medical term) is literally "**deadness**," "**the state of a corpse**." Comp. Rom. 4:19 for the word itself, and Rom. 4:19; Col. 3:5; Heb. 11:12

for the cognate verb. He was, as it were, dragging about with him what it was scarcely an exaggeration to call a "living corpse"; and this he describes as "the dying" (or **death-state**) "of the Lord Jesus." What seems implied is that it brought him nearer to the likeness of the Crucified; he was thus made a sharer in the sufferings of Christ, filling up what was lacking in the measure of those sufferings (Col. 1:24), dying as He died, crucified with Him (Gal. 2:20).

That the life also of Jesus . . . —The life of Jesus is the life of the new man, "created in righteousness and true holiness" (Eph. 4:24). It is not that the apostle is merely looking forward to the resurrection life, when we shall bear the image of the heavenly; he feels that the purpose of his sufferings now is that the higher life may, even in this present state, be manifested in and through them.

(12) So then death worketh in us, but life in you.—Comp. I Cor. 4:8-13. "You," he seems to say, "reap the fruit of my sufferings. The 'dying' is all my own; you know nothing of that conflict with pain and weakness; but the 'life' which is the result of that experience works in you as well as in me, and finds in you the chief sphere of its operation." On verse 13, comp. Ps. 116:10.

(14) Knowing that he which raised up the Lord Jesus . . . —From his present experience of the triumph of life over death he passes to the future victory of which that triumph was the earnest. It is clear that he speaks here not of any deliverance from danger or disease, but of the Resurrection of which he had spoken so fully in I Cor. 15. Paul's thoughts, however, dwell so continually on his fellowship with Christ that he thinks of the future resurrection of the body, no less than of the spiritual resurrection which he has already experienced (Eph. 2:6), as not only wrought **by** Him but also associated **with** Him; and in this hope of his he includes the Corinthians to whom he writes.

(16) For which cause we faint not.—He returns, after a long digression, to the assertion with which chap. 4 had opened. The "outward man," the material framework of the body, is undergoing a gradual process of decay, but the "inward man," the higher spiritual life, is "day by day" passing through successive stages of renewal, gaining fresh energies.

(17, 18) The immeasurable glory which he had in view includes the objects of faith: immortality, eternal life, the crown of righteousness, the beatific vision. These things are subject to no time limits, and endure through all the ages of God's purposes. Other things are but for a brief season, and then are as though they had not been.

5

(1) For we know that if our earthly house of this tabernacle were dissolved.—The words that follow give the secret of his calmness and courage in the midst of sufferings. He looks beyond them. A new train of imagery begins to rise in his mind, linked, perhaps, to that of the preceding chapter by the idea of the Tabernacle. It was in part, perhaps, suggested by his own occupation as a tent maker. The comparison of the body to the house or dwelling place of the Spirit was natural and common enough. The modification introduced by the idea of the "tent" emphasizes the transitory character of the habitation. What follows shows that he is thinking of that spiritual body of which he had said such glorious things in I Cor. 15:42-49.

(2) For in this we groan.—The "groaning" here, and in verse 4, may be a strong way of expressing the burden and the weariness of life but taken in connection with the epistle elsewhere, as pointing to the pressure of disease, we can scarcely fail to find in it the utterance of a personal or special suffering. (See notes on 1:8, 9.)

(3, 4) The confident expectation thus expressed is that in the resurrection state the spirit will not be "naked," will have, i.e., its appropriate garment, a body—clothing it with the attributes of distinct individuality. The conviction is identical with that expressed in I Cor. 15:35-49, against those who, admitting the immortality of the spirit, denied the resurrection of the body.

(5) He that hath wrought us for the selfsame thing.—The "very thing" is the consummation, by whatever stages it may be reached, in which mortality is swallowed up of life. The whole work of God in the past—redemption, the new birth, the gifts and graces of the Spirit—was looking to this as its result. He had given the "earnest of the Spirit" (see note on 1:22) as a pledge of the future victory of the higher life over the lower. Every gift of spiritual energy not dependent upon the material organism was an assurance that that organism was an impediment to the free action of the Spirit, which would one day be overcome.

(6) Therefore we are always confident.—The two verbs for being "at home" and "absent" are not found elsewhere in the New Testament. The latter conveys the special idea of being absent from a man's own home or country. The knowledge of the fact that follows is given as the ground of the apostle's confidence. It makes him long for the change, not wishing for death, but content to accept it, as it will bring him nearer to his Lord.

The sentence begun here is resumed in verse 8. If there seems to be some shadow of inconsistency with the expression of verse 4, we may look upon it as the all but inevitable outcome of the state which he describes in Phil. 1:21-25, as "in a strait between two," and of the form of life in which he now finds himself. The whole passage presents a striking parallelism, and should be compared with this.

(10) Before the judgment seat of Christ.—Here the judgment seat, or **bema**, is the tribunal of the Roman magistrate, raised high above the level of the **basilica**, or hall, at the end of which it stood. (Comp. Matt. 27:19; Acts 12:21; 18:12.)

That every one may receive the things done in his body.—It is impossible to evade the force of this unqualified assertion of the working of the universal law of retribution. No formula of justification by faith, or imputed righteousness, or pardon sealed in the blood of Christ, or priestly absolution, is permitted by Paul to mingle with his expectations of that great day, as revealing the secrets of men's hearts, awarding to each man according to his works. (Comp. Gal. 6:7.) The revelation of all that had been secret, for good or evil; the perfectly equitable measurement of each element of good or evil; the apportionment to each one as he deserves: that is the sum and substance of Paul's eschatology here. (Comp. I Cor. 4:5.)

(11) The English word "terror" is unduly strong, and hinders the reader from seeing that what Paul speaks of is identical with "the fear of the Lord"—the temper not of slavish dread, but reverential awe. (See Ps. 111:10.) Thus, "**We go on our way of winning men** to Christ."

(12) For we commend not ourselves again unto you.—He has scarcely uttered the words that precede this sentence when the poison of the barbed arrow of the sneer to which he had referred in 3:1 again stings

him. These words are the answer to that taunt. "In appealing to the witness of the work done in your consciences we give you an 'occasion' (or **starting point**) of a boast which we take for granted that you, the great body of the church of Corinth, will be ready to make for us."

(13) For whether we be beside ourselves.—The recollection of one sneer leads to another. There were some at Corinth who spoke of his visions and revelations, his speaking with tongues as in ecstasy, his prophecies of future judgment, as so many signs of madness. Others pointed to his tact, becoming all things to all men, perhaps even insinuated that he was making money by his work (9:12; 12:10). He answers accordingly both the taunts. What people called his "madness" lay between himself and God; what people called his "sobermindedness" he practiced not for himself but for his disciples, to win them to Christ, remove difficulties, strengthen them in the faith.

(14) For the love of Christ constraineth us.—Comp. Rom. 5:5; 8:35; I Cor. 16:24; II Cor. 13:14. It was the apostle's sense of the love that Christ had shown to him and to all men that was acting as a constraining power, directing every act of every spiritual state to the good of others, restraining him from every self-seeking purpose.

Because we thus judge, that if one died for all.—The thought is the same as in the nearly contemporary passage of Rom. 5:15-19, and takes its place among Paul's most unqualified assertions of the universality of the atonement effected by Christ's death. The Greek preposition does not in itself imply more than the fact that the death was **on behalf of all**; but this leads (comp. Matt. 20:28; Mark 10:45 with Mark 14:24; John 15:13) into the thought that the death was, in some real sense, vicarious—**in the place of** the death of all men.

Then were all dead.—Comp. Rom. 5:17-19; I Cor. 11:3; 15:22. Christ died for all as the head and representative of the race. But if so, the race, in its collective unity, died, as He died, to sin, and should live, as He lives, to God. Each member of the race is then only in a true and normal state when he ceases to live for himself and actually lives for Christ (verse 15). That is the mystic ideal which Paul placed before himself and others, and every advance in holiness is, in its measure, an approximation to it.

(16) Wherefore henceforth know we no

man after the flesh.—The logical dependence of this sentence on the foregoing lies in the suppressed premise. In living not to ourselves, but to Christ, we gain new standards of judgment, new ways of looking at things. To know a man "after the flesh" is to know him by the outward accidents and circumstances of his life: his wealth, rank, culture, knowledge. Paul had ceased to judge of men by those standards. With him the one question was whether the man was, by his own act and choice, claiming the place which the death of Christ had secured for him and living in Him as a new creature.

Yea, though we have known Christ after the flesh.—There was a party at Corinth claiming a special relation to Christ (I Cor. 1:12). They probably did so as having been personal disciples. If they were like those who elsewhere claimed to speak in the name of James (Acts 15:24; Gal. 2:12), they were likely to urge his claims as the brother of the Lord. To Paul such a way of judging would be to know Christ after the flesh—to judge of Him, as of others, by the lower standard of the world. Once Paul's own Messianic expectations had been those of an earthly kingdom restored to Israel. Jesus of Nazareth did not fulfill those expectations, and therefore he had opposed His claim to be the Messiah. Now he had come to take a different view of the work and office of the Christ. He speaks of the period that preceded his conversion, not of an imperfect state of knowledge after it, out of which he had risen by progressive stages of illumination and clearer vision of the truth. Now and from henceforth, he seems to say, we think of Christ not as the King of Israel, but as the Saviour of mankind.

(17) Therefore if any man be in Christ.—To be in Christ, in Paul's language, is for a man to be united with him by faith, to claim personally what had been secured to him as a member of the race for whom Christ died. In such a case the man is born again (Tit. 3:5)—there is a new creation. The old things of his life—Jewish expectations of a Jewish kingdom, heathen philosophies, lower aims, earthly standards—these things, in idea at least, passed away from him at the time when he was united with Christ. (Comp. Isa. 43:18, 19.)

(18) Who hath reconciled us to himself . . . —This is the first occurrence, in order of time, in Paul's epistles of this word "reconcile" as describing God's work in Christ, and so applied it occurs only in this epistle and in Rom. 5:10, written shortly afterward. The idea involved is that man had been at enmity and was now atoned and brought into concord with God. The work is described as originating with the Father and accomplished by the mediation of the Son.

(20) Now then we are ambassadors for Christ.—See Eph. 6:20. The preposition "for" implies the same representative character as in verses 14, 15. The preachers of the Word were acting **on behalf of** Christ; they were acting also **in His stead.**

We pray you in Christ's stead, be ye reconciled to God.—Paul recognizes the representative and vicarious character of the redeeming work of Christ. The whole work, from his point of view, originates in the love of the Father, sending His Son to manifest that love in its highest and noblest form. He does not need to be reconciled to man. He sends His Son, and His Son sends His ministers to entreat them to be reconciled to Him, to accept the pardon which is freely offered. In the background there lies the thought that the death of Christ was in some way, as the highest act of divine love, connected with the work of reconciliation; but the mode in which it was effective is left, in part at least, unrevealed.

(21) For he hath made him to be sin for us, who knew no sin.—The words are, in the first instance, an assertion of the absolute sinlessness of Christ. And then there comes what we may call the paradox of redemption. He, God, made the sinless One to be "sin." The train of thought is that God dealt with Christ, not as though He were a sinner, like other men, but as though He were sin itself, absolutely identified with it. (See Rom. 8:3; Eph. 3:13.) As Christ identified with man's sin, so mankind identified with Christ's righteousness—that is the truth, simple and yet unfathomable, in which he is content to rest.

That we might be made the righteousness of God in him.—The "righteousness of God" (Rom. 3:21, 22) expresses not simply the righteousness which He gives, nor that which He requires, though neither of these meanings is excluded, but rather that which belongs to Him as His essential attribute. The thought of Paul is that, by our identification with Christ—first ideally and objectively, as far as God's action is concerned, and then actually and subjectively, by that act of will which he calls faith—we are made sharers in the divine righteousness. (See II Pet. 1:4.) The importance of the passage lies in its presenting the truth that the purpose of God in the death of Christ was not only or chiefly that men might escape punishment, but that they might become righteous.

6

(1) We then, as workers together with him, beseech you ... —The thought of the marvel of the atoning love fills the heart of Paul with an almost passionate desire to see its purpose realized in those whom he has taught; and so, "as a fellow-worker with Him" (i.e., God), he renews his entreaty. The language in which he does so is significant. Those to whom he wrote had believed and been baptized, and so they had "received the grace"; but the freedom of the will to choose good or evil remained, and if they chose evil they would frustrate the end which the grace was intended to work out. (Comp. I Cor. 9:27; 15:10.)

(2) Behold, now is the accepted time ... —The word for "accepted" is much stronger than in the previous clause. "Entirely acceptable" is, perhaps, its best equivalent. The solemnity of the words was intensified in Paul's thoughts by what seemed to him the nearness of the impending judgment. Opportunities were offered which might never again recur. But the prolonged experience of the longsuffering of God has given to the words a yet more profound significance. There is, so to speak, a "now" running through the ages. (See Isa. 49:8.)

(4) But in all things approving ourselves as the ministers of God.—He does commend himself; but how? He looks back on his life of labor and sufferings and challenges comparison. Can others, with their letters of commendation, point to anything like this? What he means is that he, as the minister of God should do, commends himself by acts and not by words. It is obvious that what follows was likely to expose him to a repetition of the cynical sneer, but of this his generous indignation makes him nobly regardless.

It is not easy to specify what he refers to under each head. Possibly he used such words, as we habitually use them, without a formal classification. The root-idea of the first word of the triad ("afflictions") is that of being pressed upon; of the second ("necessities"), that of a constraint that leaves no choice of action; of the third

("distresses"), that of being so hemmed in that there is no room to move.

(5) In stripes ... —The list becomes more specific. "Stripes" we have seen at Philippi (Acts 16:23), and 11:23, 24 show that there were other instances. Of "imprisonments" that at Philippi is, so far, the only recorded instance (Acts 16:24); but there may well have been others, as in 11:23. "Tumults" (the same word as in Luke 21:9) point to Antioch in Pisidia (Acts 13:50), Lystra (Acts 14:5-19), Thessalonica (Acts 17:5), Corinth itself (Acts 18:12), and Ephesus (Acts 19:23-41). "Labours" describe the usual tenor of his life, the daily work of his calling as a tent maker, as well as that connected with his ministry. "Watchings" and "fastings" are (comp. 11:27) to be referred to voluntary acts—nights of vigil and self-imposed abstinence—rather than to privations incidental to his work.

(6) By pureness ... —The word refers to personal chastity. In the general state of morals throughout the empire, and especially in writing to such a city as Corinth, it was natural to dwell on this aspect of the Christian character. (Comp. I Cor. 7:7.) The "knowledge" is that of the mysteries of God (Eph. 3:4). In "kindness" we trace the consciousness of an effort to reproduce the graciousness which he looked on as a characteristic attribute of God and Christ (Eph. 2:7; Tit. 3:4). In the "Holy Ghost" we may see a reference both to spiritual gifts (I Cor. 14:18, 19) and to the impulses and promptings in which he traced the general guidance of the Spirit (Acts 16:6, 7). "Love unfeigned" (i.e., without hypocrisy) presents the same combination as in Rom. 12:9 ("without dissimulation").

(7) By the word of truth.—With the article, the same combination occurs in Eph. 1:13; II Tim. 2:15; and there can be no doubt that there the sense is objective—"the word which conveys the truth of God to men." (Comp. Jas. 1:18.)

By the power of God.—It seems natural to refer here chiefly, though, perhaps, not exclusively, to the supernatural power given by God for working miracles. (Comp. 12:12; I Cor. 2:5; 12:10, 28, 29.)

By the armour of righteousness ...—Comp. 10:4; Eph. 6:11-17; I Thess. 5:8. The weapon of the right hand is "the sword of the Spirit," aggressive in the conflict with evil. The armor for the left hand is defensive, the "shield of faith," which is our defense against the fiery darts of the wicked.

(8-10) The enumeration of the elements in and by which his ministry is carried on begins to take a more personal character. We trace once more in the words that follow the sensitiveness of a recent experience. He has to do his work, at one time, as through a **glory** which he has not sought; at another time, under an ignominy which he has not deserved.

(11) O ye Corinthians.—There was clearly a pause here as the letter was dictated. The rush of thoughts had reached its highest point. Nowhere else in the whole range of his epistles do we find any parallel to this form of speech—this "O ye Corinthians." He has to tell them that he speaks out of the fulness of his heart, that if his mouth has been opened with an unusual freedom it is because his heart has felt a more than common expansion.

(12) Ye are not straightened in us.—The word presents a natural contrast to the expansion, the dilation, of heart of the previous verse. There was no narrowness in him. But narrowness was found in their own "bowels"—i.e., in their own affections. They would not make room for him in those hearts that were so "straitened" by passions, prejudices, and antipathies. Therefore he urged an expansiveness of affection on their part (verse 13).

(14) Be ye not unequally yoked together with unbelievers.—The current of thought is not difficult to trace. There was a false latitude as well as a true. The baser party at Corinth might think it a matter of indifference whether they married a heathen or a Christian, whether they chose their intimate friends among the worshipers of Aphrodite or of Christ. Against that "enlargement" the apostle feels bound to protest. The Greek word for "unequally yoked together" is not found elsewhere, and was probably coined by Paul to give expression to his thoughts. Its meaning is, however, determined by the use of the cognate noun in Lev. 19:19. Cattle were unequally yoked together when ox and ass were drawing the same plow (Deut. 22:10). Men and women are so when they have no common bond of faith in God.

(15) What concord hath Christ with Belial?—This is the only occurrence of the name in the New Testament, nor does it appear in the Greek version of the Old. The Hebrew word signifies "vileness, worthlessness." (Comp. Deut. 13:13; I Sam. 2:12; 25:17.) The English version, following the Vulgate, translates the phrase as though

Belial were a proper name. Paul himself seems to use it as representing, or, as it were, personifying, the whole system of impure **cultus** that prevailed in the worship of Aphrodite at Corinth.

An infidel is not one who has rejected the faith, but simply one who has not as yet received it.

(16) And what agreement hath the temple of God with idols?—The apostle's thoughts travel back to the controversy about things sacrificed to idols. Was there not a risk that what he had said about "width" and "expansion" of feeling would be perverted by those who claimed the right to sit at an idol's feast even in the precincts of the idol's temple (I Cor. 8:10)? Against that perversion he thinks it necessary to enter his protest. And the ground of that protest is that they, collectively and individually (I Cor. 3:16; 6:19), are the temples of God, and that there can be no "agreement" between that temple and one dedicated to an idol. (Comp. Exod. 29:45; Lev. 26:12.)

(17) Wherefore come out from among them.—Another composite quotation follows, beginning with Isa. 52:11. In their primary historical sense, the words were addressed as to the priests and Levites who were to return from Babylon. They were not to bring back with them any symbol of that "unclean" ritual which they had witnessed there. The local and historical meaning has for the apostle passed away, and the "unclean thing" is identified with the whole system of heathenism. Note the close connection of this verse with the great prophecy of the atoning work of Christ (Isa. 53).

7

(1) Having therefore these promises ... let us cleanse ourselves from all filthiness.—The thought is identical with that of I John 3:3. The two thoughts—idolatry and impurity—were inextricably blended in his mind. He had been warning men against the feasts that were held in the idol's temple. He cannot close his eyes to the "hidden things of shame" that were their constant and inevitable accompaniments. But that contagion of impurity might spread to the inward parts. Mind and conscience might be defiled (Tit. 1:15). The element in man by which he is raised above the brute creatures sinks him to an infinite depth below them.

Perfecting holiness in the fear of God.—

The word for "holiness" involves the idea of consecration, and grows out of the thought that the "saints" of God make up collectively (6:16) the Temple in which He dwells. The former clause of the verse presents the negative aspect of purity, abstinence from all that desecrates; this presents the positive, perfect consecration in reverential awe.

(2) Here we find reference to charges of greed of gain and self-interested motives that had been whispered against him, and to which he refers again in 8:20 and 12:18. "Corrupted" and "defrauded" were used of those who sought gain by ministering to the vice of others—who became, as it were, purveyors of impurity. The words leave no room for doubt that, in the infinite pruriency of such a city as Corinth, even such things as these had been said of the apostle in the cynical jests of the paganizing party of license. They tolerated such things themselves (I Cor. 5:11).

(4) Great is my boldness of speech.—The context shows that he is not apologizing for bold and plain speaking, but uses the word as implying confidence (I Tim. 3:13; Philem. 8). He can speak without reticence now, because he is going to express his comfort and joy at what had been reported to him.

(5) His body was still suffering from want of rest, even though his spirit had found relief in the thought that the coming of Titus could not now be far off. We have no knowledge to what the "fightings" refers. It is natural to think either of dangers and persecutions from the heathen, or, probably, of conflicts with the party of the circumcision. The "fears" clearly refer to his alarm and anxiety about the effect produced by his first epistle.

(7) And not by his coming only.—There was joy, doubtless, in seeing his true son in the faith (Tit. 1:1) once again, but the great comfort was found in the news which he brought with him. On the part of the majority, at least, of those who had been present when the epistle was read, there had been all the feelings which he most desired to arouse.

(8) For though I made you sorry with a letter.—This Titus had told him; and commonly to have caused pain to others would have been a source of grief to him, but he cannot bring himself now to say, "I regret." He admits, however, that there had been a moment, either on first hearing of their grief or in his previous anxiety, when he

had half regretted that he had written so strongly. Now he sees that that grief was but transient, and he trusts that the good (repentance, verse 9) wrought by it will be abiding.

(11) That ye sorrowed after a godly sort.— The series of emotional words that follow represent the apostle's estimate of what he had heard from Titus. There was **earnestness** where there had been indifference to evil, or even approval of it (I Cor. 5:2). This was shown in the **vindication** of their conduct which they had sent through Titus; in their stern "indignation" against the offender; in their "fear," partly of the supernatural chastisement which Paul had threatened, partly of the judgment of God, which was against such things; in the **longing** to have him once more among them which mingled with their fear; in their new "zeal" for the law of purity; and in their actual **vengeance**, i.e., their sentence of condemnation passed upon the offender.

(12) Wherefore, though I wrote unto you.—The reference to the man that had suffered wrong implies that the offender in I Cor. 5:1 had married his step-mother during his father's life. There is an obvious tone of impatience, almost of annoyance, in the way in which Paul speaks of the whole business. It was one of those scandals in which, though it had been necessary to assert the law of purity and enforce the discipline of the Church, he could not bring himself at the time to feel any special interest in either of the parties. Afterward, when the sinner was repentant, there came, it is true, a new feeling of pity for him (2:6-8). But when he wrote, it was with a larger aim—to show them how much he cared for his disciples at Corinth, how jealous he was to clear away any stains that affected their reputation as a church.

The facts of the case suggest that both husband and wife were heathens, and that the son was the only convert of the family. In this case we may fairly assume that the wife had played the part of temptress, and that the husband's conscience, though weak, had been the more sensitive of the two. Here the exhortations against being "unequally yoked together" with unbelievers gains a fresh significance. Possibly some idolatrous festival had furnished the first opportunity of sin, and so the fact gave special protest against any attempt to combine the worship of Christ with that of Belial.

(14, 15) He had encouraged Titus, when

he sent him, with the assurance that he would find many elements of good mingled with the evil which he was sent to correct. And what he said of them to Titus turned out to be true. Now the recollection of what had passed at Corinth had bound Titus by ties of closest sympathy with the disciples there.

8

(1) Moreover, brethren, we do you to wit ... —The topic on which the epistle now touches, and which is carried on through this and the following chapter, was one dear to the apostle's heart. (See note on I Cor. 16:1.) When he wrote before he had simply given directions as to what the Corinthians were to do. Now he has something to tell them. The churches of Macedonia— Philippi, we must believe, prominent among them—had been true to their old generosity (11:8, 9; Phil. 4:15), and were now showing it, not, as before, in personal kindness to their teacher, but in the truer way of acting as he wished them to act. He sees in this a means of stirring up his friends at Corinth to an honorable emulation.

(2) In a great trial of affliction.—We do not know what is especially referred to, but a community of Christians in a heathen city was always exposed to trials of this kind, and the temper shown before by the rulers at Philippi and the Jews of Thessalonica (Acts 16:19, 20; 17:5, 6; I Thess. 2:14) makes it almost certain that they would carry on at least a petty persecution with more or less persistency. Consider also that the "poverty" at Philippi may have been due to the preponderance of women in the congregation; and that, furthermore, Macedonia and Achaia never recovered from the three wars between Caesar and Pompeius, between the Triumvirs and Brutus and Cassius, and between Augustus and Antonius.

(3) They were willing of themselves.— Literally, "spontaneously." This was the point of excellence which he wished to indicate as an example to the Corinthians. Those of Macedonia needed no appeal or counsel such as he had given to the Corinthians and to others.

(5) Not as we hoped ... —This means that they had done what was far beyond his hopes; and here the point lies in the fact that they gave, not their money only, but themselves—their time, thought, energy—

primarily to Christ as their Lord and then to the apostle as His minister. This they had done because they allowed the will of God to work upon their will.

(6) Insomuch that we desired Titus ... —When Titus came to Corinth, he, among other things, after seeing the satisfactory results of the first epistle in other respects, had begun to take measures for this connection for the poor of Jerusalem. He had been, to a certain extent, successful. Encouraged by the report of that success, Paul had now entreated Titus to return to Corinth, and to bring the good work to its completion. "This grace **also**" (see also verse 7) means this work of liberality, as well as that of repentance and loyal obedience already spoken of in chap. 7.

(8) I speak not by commandment.—He gives no commands in this matter to others because he has received no commandment from the Lord Himself. (Comp. I Cor. 7:6, 12, 25.)

(9) Grace as an act of liberality becomes prominent. The thought is the same as that expressed in Phil. 2:6, 7, especially in the words which ought to be translated **He emptied Himself.** He was rich in the ineffable glory of the divine attributes, and these He renounced for a time in the mystery of the Incarnation, taking our nature in all its poverty. This is the chief thought expressed, but we can scarcely doubt that the words refer also to the outward aspect of our Lord's life. He chose the lot of the poor, almost of the beggar. (See Matt. 10:10; Luke 8:1-3; John 12:6.) And this he did that men might by that spectacle of a life of self-surrender be sharers with Him in the eternal wealth of the Spirit, and find their treasure not in earth but heaven.

(10) And herein I give my advice.—Note the same careful distinction between command and counsel as in I Cor. 7:25.

Who have begun before ... —The Corinthians had formed the purpose of giving and had begun to lay by and to collect before their rivals had started. Yet it was "profitable for them" that he, as a bystander, should give them a hint. It is not easy to fix the exact limits of time indicated in the "year ago." The first epistle was written about Easter. Then, after remaining at Ephesus for a while, there came the journey to Troas; then that to Macedonia; then the coming of Titus, bringing word that the Corinthians had acted on the command of I Cor. 16:1. This would bring us to the autumn months; and Paul, reckoning, as a Jew would, the year as beginning with Tisri (September or October), might speak of what had taken place in April or May as done "last year," though there had not been an interval of twelve months.

(14) But by an equality.—The church of Jerusalem was at this time suffering from poverty, and, therefore, Paul exhorts the Corinthians to come to its assistance. A time might come in which their relative position would be inverted, and then he would plead no less earnestly that Jerusalem should assist Corinth. (See verses 12, 13.)

(15) Comp. Exod. 16:18 (LXX). The work of love was, in the apostle's thoughts, like the manna in the wilderness. In the long run all would be filled, each according to his several necessities.

(17) For indeed he accepted the exhortation . . .—The words show that Titus was authorized by the apostle and acting at his request, and yet that he was so eager to go that he did not even need to be requested. The tense "he went" is the epistolary aorist. Titus was to start, probably, as the bearer of this letter.

(18) The brother, whose praise is in the gospel.—We cannot get beyond probable conjecture in determining who this was. The general current of patristic interpretation favored Luke; but this rested on the assumption, against which there are strong probabilities, that he was already well known as the writer of a gospel. Even so, there is more evidence for Luke than for any other. If the words are interpreted as pointing to a preacher of the Gospel, we have indications of Luke's having done this at Antioch, at Troas, and at Philippi. None of the other companions of Paul was likely to be with him at the time at Philippi. And it may be noted further that there was no man so fitted to stir up the Corinthians, by his personal character, to a worthy completion of the good work they had begun. In his gospel he dwells emphatically on all parts of our Lord's teaching that point out the danger of riches and the blessedness of a generous almsgiving; and at Philippi, furthermore, his influence was traceable in the liberal supplies sent to Paul at Thessalonica (see Acts 16:40; Phil. 4:15) and at Corinth (see 11:9). The tense "we have sent" is, as in verse 17, the epistolary aorist, used of the time at which the letter was being written.

(19) Who was also chosen of the churches.—See verse 23. The word (Acts 14:23) implies a definite appointment, in this case, obviously, by popular election on the part

of the Macedonian churches. This coincides with the facts of the case as indicated by the use of the first person plural in Acts 20:5, and through the rest of the book.

(20) Avoiding this, that no man should blame us.—He gives this as the reason why he wished men thus appointed to travel with him. He desired to guard against the suspicion of those who were too ready to suspect. His companions were to bear witness that the sums which he took up with him from the several churches were what had actually been collected. They were to be, practically, auditors of his accounts. (See 12:18, 19; Acts 20:4.)

(22) And we have sent with them our brother.—Who this second unnamed brother was is again simply a matter of conjecture. Of the names connected with Paul at this period, that of Tychicus seems to have the greatest balance of probabilities in its favor. (Comp. Acts 20:4; Eph. 6:21; Col. 4:7; II Tim. 4:12; Tit. 3:12.) The name of Clement of Rome also has some claim to consideration (Phil. 4:3). This gives Clement a point of contact with the church of Corinth, to which he addressed his epistle. On the other hand, the distinction drawn in 9:4 between these brethren and the Macedonians may seem to exclude Clement, as it has been thought to exclude Aristarchus, Sopater and Secundus.

(24) Paul appeals, as he has done throughout the chapter, to that natural love of praise which takes its place as a legitimate, though subordinate, motive for the activity of Christian benevolence. They were not to consider only what he and Titus and the two brethren would think of them. The eyes of the churches were upon them. They have to compete with Macedonia; they have to show their love for their teacher; they have to sustain their own reputation.

9

(1-3) In reality there is no new topic, and all flows on with unbroken continuity. This was the boast to which he had referred in 8:24. Achaia (i.e., Corinth, and perhaps Cenchrea also) had been ready **last year.** The urgency of his present appeal indicates a latent misgiving whether he had not unconsciously overstated the fact, and had mistaken the "will" that had shown itself for an actual readiness to send off the money whenever it was called for. His purpose in the new mission was that the performance not fall short of the promise. They must be found ready, their money collected. (Comp. I Cor. 16:2.)

(4) Lest haply if they of Macedonia ... —"Surely you Achaians won't allow Macedonians to come and see that you fall short of what I told them about!" It is a probable but unnecessary inference that neither of the two unnamed brethren of 8:18, 22, were of that province. What he now indicates is that in all probability when he comes to pay his deferred visit he will be accompanied by Macedonians.

(5) Therefore I thought it necessary ... —The brethren were to go before Paul, so as to get all things ready for his arrival. There were to be no hurried and unsatisfactory collections then.

As a matter of bounty, and not as of covetousness.—Probably what is meant is this: "Let your gift be worthy of what you call it, a 'blessing' expressed in act, not the grudging gift of one who, as he gives, is intent on gaining some advantage through his seeming generosity." It is possible, however, that the word "covetousness" had been applied tauntingly to Paul himself, as always "asking for more," always "having his hand in people's pockets," and that this is his answer to that taunt. The use of the corresponding verb in 7:2; 12:17, 18, is strongly in favor of this view.

(6) Comp. Gal. 6:7, 8. The obvious meaning of the passage is that a man "reaps," i.e., gains, the reward of God's favor and inward satisfaction, not according to the quantitative value of the thing given, except as far as that is an indication of character, but according to the spirit and temper in which he has given it.

(7) Every man according as he purposeth.—The verb indicates, not a passing impulse nor a vague wish, but a deliberate resolve, deciding both on the end and on the means for its attainment. Such, Paul teaches, should be the purpose of the giver— not the outcome of a spent emotion, or a promise half-regretted, but formed with a clear well-defined perception of all attendant circumstances, and therefore neither "grudgingly," as regards amount, nor with reluctance, as giving under pressure.

God loveth a cheerful giver.—Here we have a distinct echo from the Book of Proverbs (22:8) as it stands in the Greek version. Coming so soon after the quotation from Prov. 3:4 in 8:21, it seems to suggest that the apostle had recently been studying

that book, and that his mind was full of its teaching. As a law of action, it may be noted that the principle has a far wider range of application than that of simple alms-giving. Cheerfulness in visits of sympathy, in the daily offices of kindness, in the life of home, in giving instruction or advice—all come under the head of that which God approves and loves. So the greatest of Greek ethical teachers had refused the title of "liberal" to the man who gave without pleasure in the act of giving. The pain he feels proves that if he could he would rather have the money than do the noble action (Aristotle, **Eth. Nicom.** 4:1).

(8, 9) God will bless the increase of those who give cheerfully, that they may have, not indeed the superfluity which ministers to selfish luxury, but the sufficiency with which all true disciples ought to be content. (Comp. **Meditations,** Marcus Aurelius 3:11.) See Ps. 112:9.

(11) Being enriched in every thing.—The context points primarily to temporal abundance, but we can scarcely think that the other thought of the spiritual riches that are found in Christ (8:9) was absent from the apostle's mind.

Which causeth through us thanksgiving to God.—His thoughts obviously extend to the time of his arrival at Jerusalem, to the announcement of the collected gifts of the Gentile churches at a solemn gathering of the church there, to the thanksgiving which would be offered.

(12) For the administration of this service.—Here the thought is implied that a large and liberal gift to Christ's poor, and for His sake, is the most acceptable of all forms of "service" in the liturgical sense of that word. Comp. Jas. 1:27.

Not only supplieth the want of the saints. —The wants of the "saints," i.e., the disciples of Jerusalem, were urgent. They had never quite recovered from the pressure of the famine foretold by Agabus (Acts 11:28), and the lavish generosity of the first days of the church (Acts 2:44, 45; 4:32) had naturally exhausted its resources.

(14) And by their prayer for you, which long after you.—He seems half lost in his anticipations of what will follow when he hands over the contributions of the Gentiles to the "saints" at Jerusalem. Their utterance of praise and thanksgiving will, he is sure, be followed by a yearning prayer of intercession for their benefactors.

(15) Thanks be unto God for his unspeakable gift.—We are left to conjecture to what gift the apostle refers: whether to the love of God as manifested in Christ, or to the spirit of love poured into men's hearts. The use of the word in the Acts (2:38; 8:20; 10:45; 11:17) is in favor of referring it to the gift of the Holy Ghost; that of Rom. 5:15, 17, to the gift of pardon or righteousness. Probably it did not enter into his thoughts to subject the jubilant utterance of praise to a minute analysis.

10

(1) Now I Paul myself beseech you.—His thoughts have traveled back to Corinth. The stinging words which Titus had reported to him (see verse 10) vex his soul. He speaks in the tone of the suppressed indignation which shows itself in a keen incisive irony. The opening formula is one which he reserves as emphasizing an exceptionally strong emotion (Gal. 5:2; Eph. 3:1; Philem. 19).

By the meekness and gentleness of Christ.—The temper described is that of one who does not press his rights, but acts in the spirit of equitable concession. The use of the formula of adjuration implies that he felt how the opponents of whom he is about to speak were lacking in those two excellencies, and he could appeal to what they knew of the personal character of Jesus as possessing them. This knowledge must have rested on a general acquaintance with the facts of the gospel history, like that implied in his treatment of the Lord's Supper in I Cor. 11:23-25, of the Resurrection in I Cor. 15:1-7, and in his reference to our Lord's teaching in Acts 20:35.

But being absent am bold toward you.—This also was one of the taunts. "It was easy to be bold at a distance; but would he have the courage to face them? Was not his delay in coming a proof that he was shirking that encounter?"

(2) He would be spared the necessity for boldness when he and those of whom he speaks meet face to face; but if the necessity comes it will be the worse for them. He "reckons" that he has daring enough to confront those who take that estimate of him.

(4) For the weapons of our warfare...—We learn from the earlier words of I Thess. 5:8, yet more from the later ones of Eph. 6:11-16, what these were—the energies

of spiritual powers given by the Eternal Spirit.

To the pulling down of strong holds.—The phrase is essentially military, used in the LXX for the capture and destruction of fortresses. He speaks as if leading an attack on the strong defenses of the powers of evil, possibly thinking of the great system of idolatry and impurity enthroned at Corinth and throughout the empire, possibly of those of pride and obstinate rebellion in the hearts of his individual opponents.

(6) And having in a readiness to revenge all disobedience.—He was not thinking of those to whom he writes, and whose repentance and obedience had filled him with so much joy (7:6-13), but only of the rebellious remnant. He would wait until all had obeyed who were willing to obey. He does not indicate what form of vengeance he thought of taking, but we may conjecture some such severe discipline as that indicated by "delivering to Satan" (I Cor. 5:5; I Tim. 1:20), with a view, if it were possible, to their ultimate restoration. (Comp. 13:3-10.)

(7) He has the party of resistance in his thoughts, but he writes to the whole community, as influenced—some more and some less—by the tendency to attach undue weight to the outward accidents of those who claimed their allegiance rather than to that which was of the essence of all true apostolic ministry. There can be no doubt that the words refer to those whose watchword was "I am of Christ" (see note on I Cor. 1:12), who laid claim to some special connection with Him, either as having been His personal disciples, or, at least, as having seen and known Him. In answer to that claim, he asserts that he is as truly chosen by Him as they were.

(8) For though I should boast somewhat more of our authority.—He claims (I Cor. 5:5; I Tim. 1:20) the power to enforce his authority by a supernatural chastisement, as, e.g., in the case of Elymas. He is anxious, however, to qualify his threat by the assertion that the power had been given him with a view, not "for destruction," but "for edification."

I should not be ashamed.—He was quite sure, without any shadow of misgiving, that if he proceeded to the extreme step of delivering his opponents to Satan, the result which he contemplates will follow.

(10) For his letters, say they, are weighty and powerful.—Allusive references to what had been said of him at Corinth have already appeared frequently. Here, for the first time, we have the words quoted. The scorn conveyed in them had wounded the apostle's sensitive nature; and we have here the nearest approach which the New Testament presents to the passionate complaints poured forth by some of the psalmists of the Old (Pss. 69, 109). Paul has in his thoughts here, and through the rest of the chapter, one conspicuous antagonist—the head of a clique and cabal of opponents.

(See note on I Cor. 5:9 for the hypothesis of a lost letter.)

His bodily presence is weak, and his speech contemptible.—The former words point to physical infirmities. The "contemptible speech" may refer either to a weak or unmusical voice, or to the absence of those oratorical methods in which Greek audiences delighted. These words give a fresh significance to a remarkable passage in an epistle written, in the judgment of many critics, within a few weeks of this. "You," he says to the Galatians (Gal. 4:13, 14), "though I came to you with that infirmity of the flesh which others sneer at, the chronic trial of my life, you did not contemn (the same verb as that used here) nor loathe me." There is clearly a contrast present to his thoughts between the mean insults of his rivals at Corinth and the affection which the Galatians had once manifested, and which made their subsequent alienation all the more painful to him.

(12) In the very act of saying, with a touch of irony, that he will not compare himself with the rival teachers, the apostle virtually does compare himself. And the point he makes is that they instituted no such comparison. They were their own standards of excellence. Collectively, they formed a "mutual admiration society." They who practice such self-admiration "are not wise." They lose, as the Greek verb more definitely expresses it, all power of discernment.

(13) But we will not boast of things without our measure.—The words imply that his opponents were doing this. He refers in it to the **concordat** established between himself and Barnabas, on the one hand, and Peter, James, and John on the other (Gal. 2:9). He had not transgressed the terms of that **concordat** by thrusting himself upon a church which had been founded by one of the apostles of the circumcision. He had gone, step by step, seeking fresh fields, until he had reached Corinth, at present the farthest limit of his work. In that apportionment of work, though it was a compact with human teachers, he saw the guidance of God.

(15) Not boasting of things without our measure ... —This was a charge that had been brought against him. They had spoken of him as pushing on from point to point, as with a measureless ambition. Perhaps the fact that he had worked at Antioch, where the Gospel had been preached by men of Cyprus and Cyrene (Acts 11:20), at Troas, where it had been preached by Luke (2:12; Acts 16:8), to the Romans whom he found at Corinth, and who, like Aquila and Priscilla, had been already converted (Acts 18:2), were thought to give a color to the charge that he was boasting in other men's labors.

Having hope, when your faith is increased.—The words are spoken in the spirit of one who seeks for fresh provinces to annex to the territory of his king. The growth of their faith will give him fresh courage, perhaps also fresh resources. The words seem further to imply something more than a mere extension of labors, and suggest the probability that in his journey to Jerusalem, with the large and liberal gifts of the Gentile churches, he had an intention to endeavor to modify the terms of the **concordat** referred to in Gal. 2:9, and to get the sanction of the church of Jerusalem for his mission work at Rome—though there the Gospel had been preached by others, and it was, primarily, at least, one of the churches of the circumcision. This supposition explains better than any other the apologetic tone of Rom. 15:20-29. It was his reluctance even to appear to build on another man's foundation that had heretofore kept him from them. He does not intend to appear, when he comes, in the character of the founder of this church, or even as building the superstructure, but only as a friend, seeking mutual help and counsel. Spain is his goal. He takes Rome as a parenthesis. But he is going to Jerusalem, and he hopes that the difficulty which has heretofore hindered him will be removed.

(16) To preach the gospel in the regions beyond you.—It is clear, from Rom. 15:19-24, that he is thinking of Western Greece, of Rome, and chiefly of Spain. There, apparently, he could hope to preach the Gospel without even the risk of its being said that he was building on another man's foundation.

11

(1) Ye could bear with me a little in my folly.—The inference here is that Titus had reported to him something as said by his opponents at Corinth. Their words had taken some such form as this: "We really can bear with him no longer; his folly is becoming altogether intolerable."

(2) For I have espoused you . . . —The underlying idea of the comparison is that the Church at large, and every separate portion of it, is as the bride of Christ. What the apostle now urges is that it is as natural for him to be jealous for the purity of the Church which owes its birth to him, as it is for a father to be jealous over the chastity of the daughter whom he has betrothed as to a kingly bridegroom.

(3) But I fear, lest by any means, as the serpent . . . —See Gen. 3; 1 Tim. 2:13-15. Paul either takes for granted that the disciples at Corinth will recognize the "serpent" as the symbol of the great tempter (Rev. 12:9), or, without laying stress on that identification, simply compares the work of the rival teachers to that of the serpent. "Subtilty" expresses the mischievous activity of a man who is **capable de tout**—ready, as we say, for anything.

(4) For if he that cometh preacheth another Jesus.—The words throw light on Gal. 1:7, 8. The false teachers in Galatia and those at Corinth were doing the same thing. In the absence of fuller knowledge of what they taught, it is difficult to define accurately to what precise form of error allusion is made. One thing, at least, is clear—that their Jesus was not his Jesus—not the Friend and Brother of mankind who had died for all men, that He might reconcile them to God. Reasoning from probabilities, we may infer that they spoke of Him as the head of a Jewish kingdom, requiring circumcision and all the ordinances of the Law as a condition of admission to it.

If ye receive another spirit.—Such as these were the "false prophets" of II Pet. 2:1; 1 John 4:3, simulating the phenomena of inspiration, perhaps thought of by the apostles as really acting under the inspiration of an evil spirit.

Another gospel, which ye have not accepted—i.e., different from that which you did accept from me. His Gospel was one of

pardon through faith working by love: theirs was based on the old Pharisaic lines of works, ritual, ceremonial and moral precepts, standing in their teaching on the same footing.

(5) For I suppose I was not a whit behind the very chiefest apostles.—The whole tone of the passage eliminates any possible reference to Peter, James and John as the pillars of the church of Jerusalem (Gal. 2:9). Those whom he holds up to scorn with an almost withering irony as "apostles-extraordinary" are the false teachers, claiming to stand in a special relation to Christ.

(6) But though I be rude in speech.—The word for "rude" is the same as that translated as "unlearned" in 1 Cor. 14:23, 24. This, then, had also been said of him by some at Corinth. It might seem at first as if the contemptuous criticism was likely to have come from the Hellenic or paganizing party of culture, who despised the apostle because he was without the polish and eloquence of the rhetoric in which they delighted. The context, however, makes it clear that the opponents now under the lash are the Judaizing teachers, the "apostles-extraordinary." They apparently despised him because he had abandoned, or had never mastered, the subtleties of rabbinic casuistry, the wild allegories of rabbinic interpretation. Side by side with the recognition of the dignity of labor in some Jewish proverbs (such, e.g., as that the father who did not teach his son to work taught him to be a thief), there was among the later rabbis something like the feeling of an aristocracy of scholarship. The word for "rude" was probably used as the equivalent for the Hebrew term by which the Pharisees held up the working classes to contempt as "the people of the earth."

(7) Have I committed an offence in abasing myself . . . ?—His enemies had detected what they considered a grave inconsistency. He had accepted help from the churches of Macedonia (verse 9); and in this they found ground for a charge that while he wasn't above taking money from other churches, he was too proud to take it from that of Corinth. This was made matter of personal offense. To take money at all was mean; not to take it from them was contemptuous.

(8) I robbed other churches, taking wages of them.—The word for wages is strictly rations, or wages in kind rather than in money. Its use in 1 Cor. 9:7 had, perhaps, given occasion for a sneer. From Paul's point of view, if what he had received had been wages at all, he had been guilty of an act of spoliation. He had received wages from one employer while he was acting in the services of another.

(9) I was chargeable to no man.—Paul means, in using the word "chargeable," to say, "I didn't drain you of your resources—did not live upon you." Our phrase which speaks of one man as "sponging" on another implies a like metaphor. In the word "parasitic" as applied to plants and animals, we have an inverted transfer of the same idea from the incidents of man's social life to that of lower organisms.

The brethren which came from Macedonia supplied.—The Acts of the Apostles present no record of any such supply, but Phil. 4:15 presents an interesting and confirmatory coincidence. The Philippians had sent supplies to him twice at Thessalonica, and it was a natural sequel to this that they should send to him also at Corinth. The apostle may well have accepted what they thus sent, and yet have thought his acceptance perfectly compatible with his boast that he was not preaching at Corinth for the sake of gain (I Cor. 9:16-18). He was not to be robbed of whatever credit attached to his working for his own livelihood at Corinth and elsewhere by any sneers which had that acceptance for their starting point. (See verse 10.)

And so will I keep myself.—Paul had acted on this principle both at Ephesus, which he had just left (Acts 20:34), and in the Macedonian churches which he was now visiting (II Thess. 3:8). The future tense obviously points to his resolution to continue to act on the same lines during his promised visit to Corinth.

(13) For such are false apostles . . . — Paul's estimate of the character of his rivals is now given in unsparing language as the reason why he desires to deprive them of any claim which may give them an adventitious superiority to him. In the term "false apostles" we have the explanation of the "apostles-extraordinary" of verse 5. These "**crafty** workers" were carrying on a system of imposture, trying to assume the character of being, in a higher sense than he was, "apostles of Christ."

(14) For Satan himself is transformed into an angel of light.—The present tense of the original excludes the thought that reference is made to any special incident (such as the appearance of Satan among "the sons

of God"—Job 1:6) recorded in the Old Testament or in tradition. The thought is rather that Satan is ever so transforming himself. (Comp. Gal. 1:8.) Paul may mean to imply that they were mistaking a satanic for an angelic apparition.

(15) If his ministers also be transformed as the ministers of righteousness.—The words seem to point to one of the special characteristics of the apostle's rivals. They represented themselves as the preachers of a righteousness which was, they asserted, neglected in Paul's teaching. They claimed the authority of one who was known as James the Just, or Righteous, and who had insisted emphatically on the necessity of a righteousness showing itself in act. They presented themselves as a kind of revival of the Chasidim, or righteous ones.

Whose end shall be according to their works.—Here he is content to rest on the eternal law of God's government, that what a man sows that shall he also reap. He felt that he must once for all remind the Corinthians of what he had done and suffered, and then leave them to judge between the rival claims.

(17) I speak it not after the Lord, but as it were foolishly.—In I Cor. 7:6, 10, 12 he distinguishes a private opinion from a principle or rule which he feels to be divine; here he draws the line of demarcation between human feelings and a divine inspiration. We take Paul's words in their plain and natural sense, believing that his words have just the authority which he claims for them, and no more. Speaking apart from these questions, there is something almost pathetic in the consciousness which he feels that self-vindication can never, as such, come from the Spirit of God, and that it is, at the best, a pardonable human weakness. It is not wrong, or else his conscience would have forbidden it. It is not the note of the highest or noblest temper, or else he would have felt the Spirit's guidance in it.

(18) Seeing that many glory after the flesh.—To boast after the flesh, as interpreted by 5:16 (see note), is to lay stress on things which are the accidents of the spiritual life, not of its true essence—on descent, prerogatives, rank, reputation, etc. There is a touch half of irony, half of impatience, in the way in which the apostle says that he too will for once descend to their level and do as they do. He falls back into the strain of irony of I Cor. 4:8-10, to which indeed, the whole passage presents a striking parallelism.

(20) Every word in the sentence clearly points to something that Titus had told him of the action of these rival teachers. They reproduced, in their worst form, the vices of the Pharisaism of Palestine (Matt. 23:4, 14, 25). They enslaved the consciences of men (see Gal. 2:4) by pressing on them an iron code of rules which left no room for the free play of conscience and of reason in those over whom they claimed to act as directors. This last form of outrage was, as Paul was soon to experience (Acts 23:2), not unfamiliar to Jewish priests and scribes as the most effective way of silencing an opponent. (See I Kings 22:24; I Tim. 3:3; Tit. 1:7.) It is obvious that he had heard of an instance in which this had actually been done at Corinth, and he taunts them with the tameness of their submission. (Comp. Matt. 5:39.)

(21) I speak as concerning reproach, as though we had been weak.—The taunt flung at his bodily infirmities is still present to his thoughts, and he assumes, in the bitterness of his irony, that it was through them he had been kept from like acts of self-asserting authority.

(22) Are they Hebrews?—This was one of their boasts. They were Jews of Palestine, speaking Aramaic, reading the Law and Prophets in the original. He, they implied, was a Hellenistic Jew (his birth at Tarsus naturally suggesting that thought), content to use the Greek version of the LXX, over which many of the more exclusive Hebrews mourned on an annual fast-day as a national degradation. Paul's answer is that he too was a Hebrew (Phil. 3:5). His parents were Jews of Palestine, and his birth in Tarsus had not annulled his claim to that nationality.

Are they Israelites? . . .—See Acts 22:3. The words imply another insinuation. They whispered doubts whether he had any right to call himself an Israelite at all. Had he a drop of Abraham's blood flowing in his veins? Might he not, after all, be but the grandson of a proselyte, upon whom there rested the stigma which, according to a Jewish proverb, was not effaced until the twenty-fourth generation? Did not this account for his heathen sympathies? Strange as the thought may seem to us, the slander survived, and the later Ebionites asserted (Epiphanius, **Haer.** 30:16) that he was a Gentile by birth, who had accepted circumcision only that he might marry the high priest's daughter.

(23) All that follows up to verse 28,

inclusive, is a proof of his claim to call himself a minister of Christ. The word "labours" is, of course, too vague to admit of more than a general comparison with the picture of his life presented in the Acts of the Apostles. The more specific statements show us that the writer of that book tends to understate rather than exaggerate the labors and sufferings of the apostle. It tells, up to this time, only of one imprisonment, at Philippi (Acts 16:23). The "deaths oft" (see 1:9; 4:10) probably includes dangers to life of other kinds as well as those arising from bodily disease.

(24) Of the Jews five times received I forty stripes save one.—None of these is recorded in the Acts. It is probable that the words refer to the early period of his work in Cilicia, which is implied though not recorded in that book. (See Acts 15:41.) The number of the stripes in Jewish punishments of this kind rested on the rule of Deut. 25:3, which fixed forty as the **maximum.** In practice it was thought desirable to stop short of the full number in order to avoid exceeding it. The punishment was inflicted with a leather scourge of three knotted thongs, and with a curiously elaborate distribution: thirteen strokes were given on the breast, thirteen on the right shoulder, and thirteen on the left.

(25) Thrice was I beaten with rods.—This (Acts 16:22, 23) was distinctively a Roman punishment. The instance at Philippi is the only one recorded in the Acts. As a Roman citizen he could claim exemption from a punishment which was essentially servile (Acts 16:37), and at Jerusalem (Acts 22:25) he asserted this claim.

Once was I stoned.—Here the Acts (14:19) give us the solitary instance at Lystra.

Thrice I suffered shipwreck.—Again we have a picture of unrecorded sufferings, which we must refer either to the period of his life between his departure from Jerusalem (Acts 9:30) and his arrival at Antioch (Acts 11:26), or to voyages among the islands of the Aegean Sea during his stay at Corinth or at Ephesus, or to that from Ephesus to Caesarea in Acts 18:22.

A night and a day I have been in the deep.—The words probably point to one of the shipwrecks just mentioned, in which, either swimming or with the help of a plank (Acts 27:44), he had kept himself floating for nearly a whole day, beginning with the night. They have, however, been referred by some writers to a dungeon-pit, like that into which Jeremiah was cast (Jer. 38:6), in which the apostle was either thrown or hid himself after the stoning at Lystra.

(26) In journeyings often.—Here we enter on a general list of activities and sufferings of which this is the only, or nearly the only, record. Some of them may be referred to journeys before his arrival at Antioch; some, probably to that from Antioch to Ephesus through the interior of Asia Minor (Acts 18:23; 19:1); some to excursions from Ephesus. As if with something like a climax he reserves the word "false brethren," such as those of Gal. 2:4, as the last and worst of his trials.

(27) From the use of the phrase in II Thess. 3:8, "weariness and painfulness" probably refers chiefly to Paul's daily labor as a tent maker. Other items are named as privations incident to his journeys or his labors. "Fastings," as distinguished from these, can hardly mean anything but times of self-chosen abstinence (Acts 13:2, 3), which would be natural in Paul both as a Pharisee and as a disciple of Christ.

(28) That which cometh upon me daily . . .—The word so translated primarily signifies a "rush" or "tumult" (Acts 24:12). Visitation, counseling, diplomacy—this is what we envision as present to Paul's thoughts as the daily routine of his life; and the absence of any conjunction between the two clauses clearly points to the fact that, in his mind, "the care (or anxiety) of all the churches" was all but identical with the "rush" of which he had just spoken.

(29) Who is weak and I am not weak . . .?—The words obviously spring from a recollection of all that was involved in that "rush" of which he had just spoken. If any come to him with his tale of body-sickness or soul-sickness, he, in his infinite sympathy, felt as if he shared in it. He claimed no exemption from their infirmities, but was reminded by every such tale of his own liability to them.

(31) Which is blessed for evermore.—The Greek participle is not a single predicate of blessedness, such as the English expresses, but is that constantly used in the LXX version as the equivalent of the Hebrew name for Jehovah: "He that is," the "I AM" of Exod. 3:13, 14; Jer. 14:13. So Philo, in like manner, speaks of "He that is" as a received name of God. (See John 8:58, 59; Rom. 9:5.)

(32, 33) The fact that follows is connected in some special manner with his "infirmities." There was, we can well imagine, an

element of the ludicrous—something that gave occasion to jests and sneers—in the way in which the apostle's escape had been effected. There was, so to speak, something undignified in it. Those who mocked at the stunted growth and weakness of his bodily presence would find good matter for their mirth of this. See Acts 9:24, 25.

12

(1) It is not expedient for me doubtless to glory. I will come . . .—The sequence of thought would seem to be that the apostle felt constrained by the taunts of his opponents to indulge in what looked like self-assertion in vindication of his own character; that he was conscious, as he did so, that it was not, in the highest sense of the word, expedient for him; and that, under the influence of these mingled feelings, he passed over other topics on which he might have dwelt, and came at once to that which had been made a matter of reproach against him.

Visions and revelations of the Lord.—The history of the Acts is full of such visions (Acts 9:4-6; 16:9; 18:9; 22:18; 23:11; 27:23). One other instance is referred to in Gal. 2:2. There is scarcely any room for doubt that this also had been made a matter of reproach against him, and perhaps urged as a proof of the charge of madness.

(2) I knew a man in Christ above fourteen years ago.—It is all but impossible to connect the facts that follow with any definite point of time in the apostle's life as recorded in the Acts. The date of the epistle may be fixed, without much risk of error, in A.D. 57. Reckoning fourteen years back, we come to A.D. 43, which coincides with the period of unrecorded activity between Paul's departure from Jerusalem (Acts 9:30) and his arrival at Antioch (Acts 11:26). We refer the visions to the beginning of his work at Antioch, when they would have been unspeakably precious, as an encouragement in his arduous work; and since Gal. 2:2 specifically refers to one revelation at Antioch, it may well have been preceded by others. The term "a man in Christ," as a way of speaking of himself, is probably connected with the thought that "if any man be in Christ he is a new creature" (5:17; Gal. 6:15).

Such an one caught up to the third heaven.—Paul, clearly dwelling on the surpassing excellency of his visions, thinks of himself as passing beyond the lower sky, beyond the firmament of heaven, into the third or yet higher heaven, where the presence of God was manifested. One rabbinic tradition, as well as the Koran, speaks of seven heavens.

(4) That he was caught up into paradise.— The stress laid on this second vision hinders us from thinking of it as identical with the former, either in time or in object matter. Paradise was emphatically the dwelling place of the souls of the righteous, the reproduction in the unseen world of the lost beauty of the Garden of Eden. The former vision revealed to his gaze the glory of the throne of God, with the heavenly hosts around it (comp. Exod. 24:10; Isa. 6:1-3; Ezek. 1:4-28; Rev. 4:2-11), while the latter brought before his spirit the peace and rest ineffable, even in their intermediate and therefore imperfect state, of the souls who had fallen asleep in Christ and were waiting for their resurrection.

Unspeakable words, which it is not lawful for a man to utter.—The hymns which John records in Rev. 4:8, 9; 5:12-14; 7:12, and 15:3 may give us some faint approach to what dwelt in Paul's memory and yet could not be reproduced: sounds of ineffable sweetness, bursts of praise and adoration, hallelujahs like the sound of many waters. In the mystic ecstatic utterances of the tongues we may, perhaps, trace some earthly echoes of that heavenly music. (See Acts 2:4; I Cor. 14:2.)

(7) There was given to me a thorn in the flesh.—He had said in verse 5 that he will glory only in his infirmities. Now he lays bare to their gaze the greatest of all those infirmities. The Greek word for "thorn" might better be translated **stake**. It is used, e.g., of stakes thrust into the ground to form a palisade around a grave (Homer, **Iliad,** 7:441). A sharp-pointed stake of this kind was used often as a means of torture in the punishment known as impaling, and the two Greek words for "impaling" and "crucifying" were indeed almost interchangeable (Herod. 1:128, 9:18). Celsus and Lucian, writing against the faith of Christians, used the term "stake" instead of "cross," as more ignominious, and spoke of Jesus as having been "impaled" instead of "crucified." So Chrysostom used the word "impaled" of Peter's crucifixion. On the other hand, medical writers, such as Dioscorides and Artemidorus, by whose use of the word, as possibly coming to him through Luke, Paul was likely to be influenced, apply the term

to what we call a "splinter" getting into the flesh and causing acute inflammation. The word used figuratively, therefore, brings with it the sense of some acute form of suffering, something **excruciating** in its character. So used, it might, as far as the word itself is concerned, be applied to any sharp agony, either of mind or body.

Some of the interpretations given to the "thorn in the flesh" have been that it was the remembrance of Paul's own guilt in persecuting the disciples of Christ; that it was some doubt as to the certainty of his own salvation, or of his being included in God's pardoning love; that it was his struggle with heathen enemies, like Demetrius, or Judaizing rivals. These may be disregarded as lacking support; but two hypotheses remain: (1) that he speaks of the conflict with sensual passion; and (2) that he refers to some chronic infirmity of body that brought with it constantly recurring attacks of acute pain. For the former, comp. Rom. 7:23; I Cor. 9:27; Eph. 6:16. But there is no trace of any sins of this nature in any of Paul's retrospects (as in Acts 22:3; 23:1; 26:4; Phil. 3:4, 6) of his state before his conversion. And it may be added, as almost decisive, that Paul, in writing to the Corinthians, would use language that they could understand, but there is no evidence that the word for "thorn" was ever used by any Greek writer of the sting of sensuous impulse. It was not likely, indeed, that they, accustomed to a licentious indulgence in this matter, would see in such an impulse any cause of pain and anguish.

Respecting the latter view, there is abundant evidence that Paul did suffer from some acute form of bodily disease. The word "stake," or "thorn," or "splinter" would suggest to the Corinthian readers of the epistle the idea of corporeal rather than mental suffering. (Comp. Acts 13:9; Gal. 4:15, 6:11.) Nor need we be surprised that this infirmity—neuralgia of the head and face, or inflammation of the eyes, perhaps, in some measure, the after consequences of the blindness at Damascus—should be described as "a messenger of Satan." That was, in fact, the dominant Jewish thought as to the causation of disease. What more effective check could there be than the sharp pain of body, crucifying the flesh with the affections and lusts (Gal. 5:24)? One who thus lived as in "the body of this death" could thank God who, even in this way, gave him the victory over the law of sin (Rom. 7:24).

(9) And he said unto me, My grace is sufficient for thee.—It seems infinitely more in harmony with our thoughts of God that the prayer to be relieved from pain should be refused, because it was working out a higher perfection than was attainable without it, than that a deaf ear should have been turned to a prayer to be relieved from the temptation to impurity. Such a prayer seems to us to carry with it something like an assurance of its own prevailing power.

Most gladly therefore will I rather glory in my infirmities.—The word is the same as the "weakness" in the answer to his prayer. He finds not comfort only, but actual delight (verse 10), in his consciousness of weakness, because it is balanced by the sense that the might of Christ **dwells in him and around him.** The word for "rest" is literally, as a similar word in John 1:14, **to dwell as in a tent,** and suggests the thought that the might of Christ was to him as the Shechinah cloud of glory encompassing him and protecting him.

(11, 12) The passage beginning here is remarkable for the reproduction in a compressed form of most of the topics, each with its characteristic phrase, on which he had dwelt before. Verse 12 is noticeable as being one of those in which Paul distinctly claims a supernatural power for himself, and appeals to its exercise. (Comp. Rom. 15:19—written shortly after this—and I Cor. 2:4.)

(13) What is it wherein ye were inferior to other churches?—His mind travels back to the insinuation that he cared less for them than he did for the churches of Macedonia, because he had maintained his independence and had received no gifts from them. If they complained of this, they should, at least, remember that this was the only point of inferiority. They had experienced fully all the advantages that flowed from his special power as an apostle. For that wrong, as far as it was a wrong, he asks their forgiveness.

(14) Behold, the third time I am ready to come to you.—The visit to Corinth of Acts 18:1, followed by a long sojourn, may perhaps be reckoned as the first occasion; then came the projected journey from Ephesus to Corinth and thence to Macedonia (1:16); now he was preparing for the third journey, announced in I Cor. 16:5-7, from Macedonia to Corinth. (See note on 13:1.)

I seek not yours, but you.—The words point to the secret motive of the conduct (i.e., working for his own maintenance) which had annoyed some of the Corinthians. He loved them, as all true friends love, for their own sake, not for anything he might hope to gain from them. He must be sure that he had gained their hearts before he could receive their gifts as poor substitutes for their affections. (Comp. Rom. 16:23.)

For the children ought not to lay up for the parents.—There is a touch of exquisite delicacy and tenderness, reminding us of like characteristics in the epistle to Philemon, in this apology for the seeming wrong of which men had complained. He could claim the rights of a father (I Cor. 4:15); might he not be allowed to fulfill a father's obligations, and to give to his children rather than receive from them?

(15) And I will very gladly spend and be spent.—The latter verb implies spending to the last farthing. As he sought not **theirs,** but **them,** so he is ready to spend for them not only all that he has, but even, as if to the verge of exhaustion, all that he is. And yet with all this there was the painful consciousness of toiling without adequate return. It seemed to him, in his intense craving for affection, as if their love varied inversely with his own.

(17) By any of them whom I sent unto you?—He has in his mind, as far as we know, Timotheus, who had been sent before the first epistle (I Cor. 4:17); Stephanas, Fortunatus and Achaicus, who were the bearers of that epistle (I Cor. 16:15); and Titus, who was sent to learn what its effect had been. None of these had asked for money on his account.

(18) I desired Titus, and with him I sent a brother.—Comp. 8:18-22. It is a natural inference from this that Titus also had worked for his own maintenance and lived in his own lodging. If we may assume the identity of Titus with the Justus into whose house Paul went when he left the synagogue at Corinth (see Acts 18:7), the appeal to the knowledge which the Corinthians had of him gains a new significance.

(20) For I fear, lest, when I come...—Something of the old anxiety which had led him to postpone his visit (1:23; I Cor. 4:21) comes back upon his spirit. He and some of those Corinthians are likely to meet under very unfavorable conditions, neither of them acceptable to the other, severity meeting with open or masked resistance.

The list that follows forms a suggestive parallelism of contrast to that in 7:11, the ethical imagination of the apostle, with its keen perception of the shades of human character, dwelling now on the manifold forms of opposition, as before it had dwelt on the manifold fruits of repentance.

(21) There is something almost plaintive in the tone in which the apostle speaks of the sin of his disciples as the only real "humiliation" which he has to fear. He has in his thoughts such persons as those described in I Cor. 6:9, and suspects that some of them have not really renounced the sins which he names there.

13

(1) This is the third time I am coming to you.—See note on 12:14. On the Old Testament quotation, see Num. 35:30; Deut. 17:6; 19:15; Matt. 18:16.

(2) I told you before, and foretell you... —He is referring, probably, to the threat of I Cor. 4:13-19, and implied in 1:23. The chief objects of this rigor were to be those whom he had described previously as "having sinned beforehand" (see 12:21); but he adds that his work as judge will extend to **all the rest** of the offenders. What he has in view is obviously passing a sentence of excommunication (I Cor. 5:5; I Tim. 1:20), with the assured confidence that that sentence would be followed by some sharp bodily suffering. In that case men would have, as he says in verse 3, a crucial **test** whether Christ was speaking in him, and learn that he whom they despised as **infirm** had a reserve-force of spiritual power, showing itself in supernatural effects even in the regions of man's natural life.

(9) For we are glad, when we are weak... —The last word covers the weakness of his bodily presence, of his physical infirmities, of the apparent failure of his supernatural powers because of the condition of the Corinthian church. He can find cause for joy in all these, if only the disciples whom he loves are strong with the strength of God.

This also we wish, even your perfection.—Better, "your restoration." This is the only passage in the New Testament in which the noun form of the word occurs; but comp. the verbals in Matt. 4:21; Mark 1:19; Gal. 6:1. Its proper meaning is to bring back to completeness. This, then, was what the apostle had been aiming at all along. In his seeming harshness and self-assertion, as in his overflowing tenderness, he was looking

forward to their restoration to their first love and their first purity. He would rather threaten than act, even at the cost of the threat appearing an empty vaunt, if only he might be spared the necessity for acting.

(11) Be perfect.—Better, "restore yourselves to completeness; amend yourselves." **Paraclesis,** "comfort," is the keynote of the whole epistle. Taking the verb and the noun together, the word occurs twenty-eight times in it.

Be of one mind.—His thoughts are apparently traveling back to the schisms over which he had grieved in I Cor. 1-3, and to which he had referred in 12:20. What he seeks is the restoration of unity of purpose, and with that of inward and outward peace.

(12) Greet one another with an holy kiss.—The tense of the Greek verb indicates that the apostle is giving directions, not for a normal and, as it were, liturgical usage, but for a single act. See note on I Cor. 16:20; comp. Rom. 16:16; I Thess. 5:26. What he meant was that, as the public reading of the epistle came to a close, the men who listened should embrace each other and kiss each other's cheeks, in token that all offenses were forgotten and forgiven and that there was nothing but peace and goodwill between them.

(13) All the saints salute you.—The salutation in the first epistle came from the "brethren" of the church of Asia. This comes from the "saints" of Philippi. The phrase shows that Paul, wherever he might be, informed the church of one locality when he was writing to another, and so made them feel that they were all members of the great family of God.

(14) The grace of the Lord Jesus Christ... —It is not without a special significance that the epistle which has been, almost to the close, the most agitated and stormy of all that came from Paul's pen, should end with a benediction fuller than any other found in the New Testament. The order of the names of the three divine Persons is significant. Commonly, the name of the Father precedes that of the Son (1:2; Rom. 1:7; I Cor. 1:3); here the order is inverted. But out of consideration of 8:9; 12:9, what would be more natural than that the first wish of his heart for those who were dear to him should be that that grace might be with them, working on them and assimilating them to itself? But the grace which thus flowed through Christ was derived from a yet higher source. It was the love of God in Christ reconciling the world unto Himself (5:18-20). And was it not through their participation, their fellowship in that Spirit (Phil 2:1) shedding down the love of God in their hearts (Rom. 5:5), that the grace of Christ and the love of the Father were translated from the region of abstract thoughts into the realities of a living experience?

The subscript, added by some unknown transcriber, though having no shadow of authority, is probably in this instance, as has been shown in 8:16-22, a legitimate inference from the **data** furnished by the epistle.

GALATIANS

1

(1-5) Paul had a twofold object in writing to the Galatians. They had disparaged his authority, and they had fallen back from the true spiritual view of Christianity—in which all was due to the divine grace and love manifested in the death of Christ—to a system of Jewish ceremonialism. And at the outset of his epistle, in the salutation itself, the apostle meets them on both these points. On the one hand, he asserts the divine basis of the authority which he himself claimed; and on the other, he takes occasion to state emphatically the redeeming work of Christ, and its object to free mankind from those evil surroundings into the grasp of which the Galatians seemed again to be falling.

(1) An apostle.—This title is evidently to be taken here in its strictest sense, as Paul is insisting upon his equality in every respect with the Twelve. The word was also capable of a less exclusive use, in which the apostle would seem to be distinguished from the Twelve (I Cor. 15:5, 7). In this sense Barnabas and James the Lord's brother, possibly also Andronicus and Junias in Rom. 16:7, were called "apostles."

Not of men, neither by man.—The kind of honor which Paul held as apostle was such as could be derived only from God; nor did human instrumentality confer it upon him. His appointment to the apostolate is connected by Paul directly with the supernatural appearance which met him upon the way to Damascus.

By Jesus Christ.—The preposition here, as in the last clause, is that which is usually taken to express the idea of mediate agency. It represents the channel down which the stream flows, not the fountainhead from which it springs. Thus it is applied appropriately to Christ as the **Logos**, or Word, through whom God the Father communicates with men as the divine agent in the work of creation, redemption and revelation. It is also applied to men as the instruments for carrying out the divine purposes.

The Father.—This is to be taken in the sense in which our Lord Himself spoke of God as "**My** Father," with reference to the peculiar and unique character of His own sonship—the Father, i.e., of Christ, not of all Christians, and still less, as the phrase is sometimes used, of all men. This appears from the context. The title is evidently given for the sake of contradistinction.

Who raised him from the dead.—Comp. Rom. 1:4. The resurrection is the act which the apostle regards as completing the divine exaltation of Christ. It is this exaltation, therefore, which seems to be in his mind. He had derived his own authority directly from God and Christ as sharers of the same divine majesty. It was not the man Jesus by whom it had been conferred on him, but the risen and ascended Saviour. The commission of the apostle was, in all respects, divine and not human.

(2) All the brethren which are with me—i.e., all his traveling companions. We are unable to say exactly who these were, especially since we do not know with any certainty the place from which Paul was writing. He may have had in his company most of those who are mentioned in Acts 20:4 as accompanying him back into Asia; in any case, probably Timothy, and perhaps Titus.

It was usual with Paul to join with his own name that of one or other of his companions in the address of his epistles. In writing to the Galatians, he includes all his companions in his greeting, hardly with the view of fortifying himself with their authority, but, perhaps, not altogether without the idea that he is possessed of their sympathy.

The churches of Galatia.—This opening salutation is intentionally abrupt and bare. Usually it was the apostle's custom to begin with words of commendation. He praises all that he can find to praise even in a church that had offended as seriously as the Corinthians. (See I Cor. 1:2, 4-7.) But the errors of the Galatians, he feels, go more to the root of things. The Corinthians had failed in the practical application of Christian principles; the Galatians (as far as they listened to their Judaizing teachers) could hardly be said to have Christian principles at all. The apostle is angry with them with a righteous indignation, and his anger is seen in the naked severity of this address. Galatia here refers to that narrow non-provincial (Roman) region of Asia Minor constituting the home of the descendants of the Gallic invaders.

(3) God the Father.—We may see by this verse how the title "Father," originally used in the present formula to distinguish between the divine Persons, came gradually to include more. God is, through Christ, the Father of all who by their relation to Christ are admitted into the position of "sons" (Rom. 8:14-17; Gal. 4:5-7). Therefore, where no special limitation is imposed by the context, this secondary sense may be taken as included.

And from our Lord Jesus Christ.— Strictly, it would be more in accordance with the theology of Paul to say that grace and peace were given **from** the Father, **by** or **through** the Son. Here the one preposition "from" is used to cover both cases, just as "by" had been used in verse 1. It is equally correct to use the word "from" with reference to a mediate and to the ultimate stage in the act of procession.

(4) For our sins.—In the Greek there are three prepositions which can be translated only by the single word "for" in English. The death of Christ was a sacrifice "for **(peri)** sins," i.e., the sins of mankind stood in a distinct relation to it, which was really that of cause. The sins of mankind set the whole scheme of redemption in motion, and to take away those sins was its main object. The death of Christ was a sacrifice "for **(huper)** sinners." It was a sacrifice wrought in their behalf, for their benefit. It was also a sacrifice wrought "in their stead **(anti)**." Christ suffered in order that they might not suffer. It is somewhat doubtful which of the first two prepositions is to be read here. In either case, the sins of me and the sacrifice of Christ have a relation to each other.

Deliver us.—The deliverance present to the mind of the apostle appears to be that of sanctification rather than justification. The object of redemption is regarded for the moment as being to deliver men from sin, and not so much to deliver them from guilt, the consequence of sin. The atonement has really both objects, but it is the first that the apostle has in view in this passage.

This present evil world is strictly "this present age." The Jews divided the history of the world into two great periods—the times antecedent to the coming of the Messiah, and the period of the Messianic reign. The end of the first and the beginning of the second were to be especially attended with troubles; and it was just in this transition period—the close of the older dispensation of things—in which the apostles regarded themselves as living. The iniquities of the pagan society around them would naturally give them an intense longing for release; but the release which they seek is moral and spiritual. The atonement frees men from guilt, but its efficacy does not cease there; it compels the Christian to use his best endeavors after a holy life. The

Galatians had lost sight of the power of the atonement to do this, and had fallen back upon the notion of a legal righteousness.

(6-10) The apostle is surprised at their rapid defection. The doctrine to which they had at first given in their adhesion was a doctrine of salvation by grace; they now imagined that they were only hearing a different version of the same truths. Now he plunges abruptly, and without more preface, into the midst of his charges against them. He cannot understand their sudden apostasy.

(6) Removed.—The Greek word is one regularly used for a "deserter," "turncoat," or "apostate," either in war, politics, or religion. The tense is strictly present: "You are now, at this moment, in the act of falling away."

(6, 7) Unto another gospel: which is not another.—The Greek has two words for "another," one (the first of those which is used here) implying a difference in kind, the other implying mere numerical addition. The inference to be drawn is that it is not a gospel in any sense of the word. This, then, may be dismissed.

(7) That trouble you.—The Judaizing party, with its restless factiousness and bigotry, causing schisms and divisions in the church. They "pervert" by substituting a doctrine of righteousness by works—self-justification before God by performing the precepts of the Mosaic law—for the doctrine of reconciliation with God through the free forgiveness which He has promised to faith in Christ.

The gospel of Christ.—We must not narrow too much the apostle's use of language. A somewhat vague and ambiguous term sometimes best expresses the fullness of his meaning. We might use the phrase "the gospel of Christ" to include at once "the gospel which **proceeds from** Christ" (subjective genitive), and "the gospel which **relates to** Christ" (objective genitive), all, in fact, which makes it in any sense **belong to** Him and bear His name.

(8) Than that.—The sense "contrary to," not "besides," seems better, because the gospel taught by the Judaizing teachers was "another," in the sense of being **different from** that of Paul. It was a fundamental opposition of principles, not merely the addition of certain new doctrines to the old.

Accursed.—See I Cor. 16:22. The original Greek word is retained in the translation, "Let him be Anathema." Attempts have been made to weaken its significance in this passage by restricting it to excommunication by the church; but this, though a later ecclesiastical use of the word, was not current at such an early date. In considering the dogmatic application, it is right to bear in mind the nature of the heretical doctrines which it was the apostle's object to denounce. They made no profession to be deduced from his own, but were in radical and avowed opposition to them.

(9) As we said before.—Probably upon his last (i.e., his second) visit, at the beginning of this, his third great missionary journey (Acts 18:23). The germs of the apostasy in the Galatian church would be already visible.

(10) Paul naturally laid himself open to the charge of men-pleasing by the flexibility and largeness of his character. The trifles about which others quarreled he could look upon with indifference, and his ready power of sympathy led him to enter as much as possible into the point of view of others. But where a question of principle was at stake, he knew how to take his stand, and he let the Galatians see it in the unequivocal language he is now using.

(11) The apostle now enters at length upon his personal defense against his opponents. He does this by means of an historical retrospect of his career, proving by an exhaustive process the thesis with which he starts, that the doctrine taught by him comes from a divine source and possesses the divine sanction. The thought continues through 2:21.

(12) By the revelation. There is an antithesis between "revelation" here and "taught" in the preceding clause. What was this revelation, and when was it given? The context shows that it must have been at some time either at or near the apostle's conversion. This would be sufficient to exclude the later revelation of II Cor. 12:1. But can it be the vision on the way to Damascus itself alone? At first sight it would seem as if this were too brief, and its object too special, to include the kind of sum of Christian doctrine of which the apostle is speaking. But this at least contained the two main points—the Messiahship of Jesus, and faith in Jesus, from which all the rest of the apostle's teaching flowed naturally and logically. Paul himself, by laying stress upon his retreat to the deserts of Arabia, evidently implies that the Gospel, as taught by him in its complete form, was the result of gradual development and prolonged reflection; but whether this is to be regarded as implicitly contained in the first revelation, or whether we are to suppose that there were successive revelations, of which there is no record in the Acts, cannot be positively determined.

(14) Profited.—Made progress. The kind of progress would correspond to the width of the term "Judaism," with which it is connected, and would imply, not merely proficiency in theological knowledge, but also increase in zeal and strictness of ritualistic observance.

My equals.—Strictly, "my equals in age." Paul is thinking of his contemporaries among the young men who came up, ardent like himself, to study the Law at the feet of Gamaliel or some other eminent rabbi.

Traditions.—The "traditions of the elders" (Matt. 15:2; Mark 7:3), the oral or unwritten law, which had gradually grown up by the side of the Pentateuch and was afterward embodied in the Mishnah. Paul's antecedents and education all told **against**, rather than **for**, a Christian belief of any kind.

(15) Pleased.—The word especially used of the free will and pleasure of God, determined absolutely by itself, and by no external cause.

From my mother's womb.—A comparison of other passages where this phrase is used seems to make it clear that the sense is rather "from the moment of my birth" than "from before my birth." (See Ps. 22:10; Isa. 49:1, 5; Matt. 19:12; Acts 3:2; 14:8.) From the moment that he became a living and conscious human being he was "marked out" ("separated") in the purpose of God for his future mission.

Called me.—The call is identical with the conversion of the apostle through the vision which appeared to him on the way to Damascus. As the apostle was conscious of having done nothing to deserve so great a mark of the divine favor, it is set down entirely to an act of grace.

(16) To reveal his Son in me.—Before the apostle could preach Christ to the Gentiles he needed to have first that intense inward conviction which was wrought in him during that sustained mental struggle which followed upon his conversion. It is possible that "in me" might be equivalent to "through me," but the other sense seems more likely.

That I might preach him.—The one process was preparatory to the other. But that firm inward apprehension was not to be attained all at once. First comes the instantaneous flash of the idea upon his soul; then the prolonged conflict and meditation, in which it gets thoroughly consolidated into his being (during the retirement into Arabia); lastly, the public appearance as a preacher to the heathen upon the return to Damascus.

With flesh and blood—i.e., with man, with special reference to human frailty and fallibility. (Comp. Matt. 16:17.)

(17) Unto Arabia.—The Boundary of Arabia at this period was not exactly defined. By some writers it was made to include Damascus itself. It is therefore possible that by "Arabia" may have been meant the desert in the neighborhood of the city. This would be the most obvious supposition. But, on the other hand, there would be a certain appropriateness if the scene of his sojourn were the region of Mount Sinai itself. The place where the Law was first given may have seen its renewal in his mind—not destroyed, but fulfilled in the new law of love. And if this were the case, we can the more readily understand the typical allusion to Mount Sinai later in the epistle. But the real locality must remain uncertain.

As to the time of the apostle's withdrawal, and its duration, little can be said beyond the fact that it must have come within the three years that intervened between his conversion and the first visit to Jerusalem. When we compare this account with the narrative of Acts 9:19, 20, 23, it is not clear how they are to be reconciled. But the discrepancy is only such as we might expect to find between two perfectly independent narratives, one of which was compiled from secondary sources, and is, besides, brief and summary in its form. We are obliged, by the apostle's own words, to believe that his withdrawal into Arabia took place "immediately" after his conversion; and as it would not take a long time to attract the attention or excite the animosity of the Jews at Damascus, it seems natural to suppose that this period of silent seclusion occupied the larger half of the whole period of three years.

Damascus.—We gather from II Cor. 11:32 that Damascus was at this time in the possession, or in some manner, at least, under the rule, of Aretas, the Arabian king. How this could have been is an obscure and difficult question. In any case, the most probable date of these events would be soon after the death of Tiberius in A.D. 37.

(18) After three years.—This date is probably to be reckoned from the great turning point in the apostle's career—his conversion. It need not necessarily mean three full years, just as the three days during which our Lord lay in the grave were not three full days. It may have been only one whole year and parts of two others; but the phrase may equally well cover three whole years. This ambiguity shows the difficulty of constructing any precise system of chronology.

To see.—The word used is a somewhat peculiar one, and is applied especially to sight-seeing—in the first instance of things and places, but secondarily also of persons. It would be used only of something notable. Paul's object was to make the personal acquaintance of Peter as the head of the Christian community, not to seek instruction from him.

Peter.—The true reading here is undoubtedly "Cephas." Paul seems to have used the two names indifferently. Roman Catholic commentators argue from this passage, not without reason that Peter must at this time have taken the lead in the church. (See Acts 9:28, 29.)

(19) Other of the apostles.—From the form of this phrase it would appear that James, the Lord's brother, was considered to be an apostle. If he were a cousin of our Lord, and identical with James the son of Alphaeus, then he was one of the original Twelve. If he were either the son of Joseph alone or of Joseph and Mary, then the title must be given to him in the wider sense in which it is applied to Paul and Barnabas.

The Lord's brother.—See Matt. 12:46; 13:55; John 7:3, 5. We maintain the firm conviction that the theory which identifies the "brethren of the Lord" with His cousins is untenable.

(21) Afterwards I came into the regions of Syria and Cilicia.—See Acts 9:30; 11:25, 26. The apostle was conveyed secretly by the disciples to the seaport Caesarea Stratonis; there he took ship and sailed for Tarsus. Here he was found, somewhat later, by Barnabas, and taken to Antioch, where he remained a year. It would thus appear that the order in which the two names, Syria and Cilicia, occur does not represent the order in which the two provinces were visited. The apostle, reviewing his past career at a distance of time, and with a certain special object in view, which is not affected by the geographical direction of his movements, speaks in this general way.

(22) Was unknown by face.—The Greek

is a shade stronger: "I continued unknown." If in Jerusalem itself the apostle had not had time to receive instruction from anyone, still less was this the case with the other Christian communities of Judaea. At the same time, so far were they from manifesting any opposition to his teaching that their one thought was joy to hear of his conversion (verse 24).

The churches of Judaea.—Judaea is here distinguished from Jerusalem. The phrase is noticeable as pointing to the spread and early organization of the church at a date removed by not more than ten years from our Lord's ascension.

Which were in Christ.—This is added in order to distinguish the Christian from the Jewish communities. It means, however, something more than merely "Christian." The various sections of the Christian Church not only professed a common creed, and were called by a common name, but they stood in the same direct and personal relation to Christ as their Head. It was His presence diffused among them which gave them unity.

(23) The faith.—The body of Christian doctrine was in process of forming rather than already formed. As yet, the one cardinal doctrine was faith in Christ.

2

(1-10) As the argument proceeds, thoughts crowd in upon the apostle with great vehemence. His amanuensis cannot take them down fast enough. Sentences are begun and not rightly ended, and much of the sense if left to be supplied by conjecture. The general drift of the passage is sufficiently plain, but there is much uncertainty about the details.

(1) Fourteen years after.—From what date is this fourteen years to be reckoned? The phrase "I went up **again**" seems to be decisive in favor of reckoning it from the visit to Jerusalem just mentioned. We should therefore have to add the three years of 1:18 in order to reach the date of the apostle's conversion. There appear to be sufficient reasons for identifying the visit to Jerusalem here described with that recorded in Acts 15, commonly known as the Council of Jerusalem, which is placed by the best chronologists about A.D. 50 or 51. (For another visit to Jerusalem, between this one and the one referred to in 1:18, see Acts 11:29, 30; 12:25.)

(2) By revelation.—It would seem that this inward spiritual guidance granted privately to the apostle coincided with a formal commission from the church at Antioch (Acts 15:2), which, as the external and apparent side of the transaction, is naturally related by the historian, while it is just as naturally omitted by the apostle, whose thoughts are directed rather to his own personal conduct and motives.

Communicated unto them—i.e., the church at Jerusalem. A distinction appears to be drawn between what the apostle said in his public intercourse with the church and the more detailed conferences into which he entered privately with the apostles.

Which I preach.—The present tense is noticeable. The Gospel which the apostle had been preaching up to the time of the Council of Jerusalem was the same as that which he still preached at the time of his writing to the Galatians. It had undergone no change in its essential features, especially in the one doctrine which he was most anxious to impress upon the Galatians—the doctrine of justification by faith.

Lest by any means.—The apostle did not really lack confidence in his own teaching. And yet he was aware that it rested solely upon his own individual conviction, and upon the interpretation that he had put upon the intimation to him of the divine will. There was, therefore, still a certain element of uncertainty and room for confirmation, which the apostle desired to receive.

I should run, or had run.—Paul here introduces his favorite metaphor from the foot races, such as he might see in the Isthmian games at Corinth. (Comp. Phil. 2:16; II Tim. 4:7.)

(3) But neither Titus . . . —This and the two following verses are parenthetical. The result of the private conference with the Judaic apostles is not given until verse 7. In addition to its bearing upon the main argument, there is probably a special reason for this mention of the case of Titus. At the beginning of his second missionary journey, on taking with him his youthful convert Timothy, Paul made so much of a concession to Jewish prejudices as to have him circumcised (Acts 16:3). This gave rise to a charge of inconsistency, which the Judaizing party in Galatia was not slow to use. (See 5:11.) But the meeting at Jerusalem was a crisis in the history of the church. The question of principle was at stake.

Concession in this would have been ruinous and fatal, and the apostle stood firm. On the other hand, the circumcision of Timothy was merely a practical compromise to smooth the way for the preaching of the Gospel in new regions. The apostle was too wise to incur needless opposition, which would bar the way to essential truths on a point which, though in some of its aspects involving principle, was yet in others of quite minor importance. Besides, it is to be noticed that whereas Titus was by descent wholly a Gentile, Timothy was, on his mother's side, a Jew.

(4) **Bring us into bondage.**—The reason why Titus was not circumcised was the evidently interested and treacherous motives of the Judaizing partisans who clamored for it. The "bondage" is, in the first instance, that of the Mosaic law, and through it the personal domination of those Jewish partisans.

(5) **The truth of the gospel.**—The Gospel in its true form, with all the liberty which its essential doctrine of justification by faith involves, not mutilated or restricted by any false conditions.

(6) **But of these who seemed to be somewhat.**—The phrase corresponds to "them which were of reputation" in verse 2; and here, as there, it is important to keep the present tense.

God accepteth no man's person.—"To accept the face" (or **person**)—originally a Hebrew analogy—in the New Testament always carries with it the idea of partiality. The meaning here is that even if the elder apostles had known Christ after the flesh (I John 1:1), God would not regard the advantages implied in this more than any other external advantage of birth, position, natural gifts, etc.

(7) **Gospel of the uncircumcision.**—The elder apostles recognized Paul because they saw that his teaching was fundamentally the same as their own. At the same time, the success of Paul among the Gentiles proved that his mission to them had the divine sanction, just as the success of Peter among the Jews especially marked him out as the "apostle of the circumcision."

(9) **James, Cephas, and John.**—These are, by name, ones of "reputation" in verse 1 and ones who "seemed to be somewhat" in verse 6. The way in which Paul speaks respectively of Peter and James is in strict accordance with the historical situation. When he is speaking of the general work of the church (as in the last two verses), Peter is mentioned prominently; when the reference is to a public act of the Church of Jerusalem, the precedence is given to James.

Right hands of fellowship.—The giving of the right hand is a symbol of friendship. Instances occur, both in the East and West (comp. Xen. **Anab.** 2.4, 1; Tac. **Hist.** 1.54, 2.8), in which images of clasped right hands were sent in suing for alliance.

(10) **The poor.**—Paul had already been the means of bringing contributions from the wealthier churches of Antioch to Jerusalem (Acts 11:29, 30). This seems to have been gracefully received, not only as an act of charity, but as a recognition of the claims of the mother church. The apostles expressed a hope that the same good feeling might continue, to which Paul willingly assented. That he did not forget his promise appears from Acts 24:17; Rom. 15:26, 27; I Cor. 16:3; II Cor. 8:1, 2; 9:1.

(11) **When Peter ...** —The visit alluded to probably took place soon after the return of Paul and Barnabas, in the interval described in Acts 15:35, shortly before the separation of these two apostles and the departure of Paul on his second missionary journey.

Because he was to be blamed.—The blame imputed to Peter was a subject of much controversy in antiquity. It was made a ground of accusation against both apostles (comp. the Ebionites, Marcion, Porphyry, **et al.**). The unfortunate result of these criticisms was that they led to attempts, on the part of the orthodox writers, to explain away the simple meaning of the narrative (comp. Clement of Alexandria, Origen, Chrysostom, Jerome, **et al.**). The true explanation of the incident is to be found in the character of Peter—at once generously impulsive and timidly sensitive to the opinion of others. Inconsistencies similar to this appear in Matt. 14:28-33; Mark 14:29, 66, and are, indeed, features in his character most conspicuous in the gospels. A little more attention to this would have saved many doctrinaire objections to the narrative of the Acts, where inconsistency of character is treated as if it stood in the way of the objective truth of the events.

(12) **Certain came from James.**—The expression used leaves it an open question whether the persons intended brought, or claimed to bring, any sort of official authorization from James (comp. Acts 15:24), or whether they merely belonged to the church of Jerusalem, in which, if James was not

actually bishop, he at least exercised a sort of presidential jurisdiction.

He did eat with the Gentiles.—By eating with Gentiles a Jew contracted Levitical defilement. Peter had been accused of this before (comp. Acts 11:3). He had not, however, stability and firmness enough to treat the question of principle as settled for him then once for all, and he yielded to a repetition of the old remonstrances. Our Lord Himself had braved Jewish opinion on this point (comp. Luke 15:2).

Withdrew and separated himself.—The Greek expression brings out the timid and gradual withdrawal, ending in complete separation.

(13) The other Jews ... —i.e., converts from Judaism, as distinct from Gentile converts, in the church at Antioch.

Dissembled.—The "dissimulation" or "hypocrisy" consisted in suppressing their real convictions, and acting as if from a set of convictions different from their real ones.

Barnabas also.—Rather, "even Barnabas," my own familiar friend, and so recently my ally in pleading the cause of the Gentiles. The beginning of the breach which soon afterward led to the definite separation of the two apostles would seem to be traceable here.

(14) Unto Peter before them all.—The apostle lays stress upon the publicity of his remonstrance, as showing that in his controversy with the apostles of the circumcision he did something more than hold his own.

Being a Jew means "with all the antecedents of a Jew." It is implied that a different rule must be applied to the Gentiles, with totally different antecedents.

Livest after the manner of Gentiles—i.e., in the matter of eating promiscuously with those with whom the Law (or rather, the Pharisaic tradition) forbids you to eat.

(15-21) We are led, without any real break, from the historical and personal to the doctrinal portion of the epistle. It is impossible to say exactly where the speech at Antioch ends and where the comment upon it begins; the apostle glides from one to the other without any conscious division in his own mind. (A similar mingling of narrative and comment is found in John's gospel: comp. e.g. John 3:14-21, 31-36, the first of which sections formally belongs to the discourse with Nicodemus, and the second to the reply of John the Baptist, though it is clear that much after comment of the evangelist's is interwoven with them.) If we are to draw a dividing line at all in the section before us, it might be said that verses 15 and 16 were still most nearly a paraphrase of the words actually addressed to Peter; while from verse 17 on the apostle is giving the rein more freely to his own reflections.

(15) The first clause is concessive: "We grant you that we were born Jews, and not Gentiles: members of the chosen race, and not sinners." The next clause explains why it was that, with all these privileges, the Christian, though thus born a Jew, transferred his allegiance from the Law to Christ. The reason was that the Law failed in the one great object—to justify us or obtain our acquittal in the sight of God.

(16) Is not justified.—Here the apostle introduces, for the first time in the epistle the word which plays so prominent a part in the Epistle to the Romans—"pronounced just or righteous"—free from guilt, and therefore from punishment—in the sight of God. This condition could not be produced by works done in obedience to the Law.

By the faith of Jesus Christ.—The preposition "by" occurs five times in this verse. In every case except the present it is represented by the same word in Greek. There is, however, no substantial difference of meaning; the only difference is that in the other cases stress is laid upon the **cause,** here rather upon the **means.** "Faith of Jesus Christ" means "faith **in** Jesus Christ."

By the words of the law shall no flesh be justified.—Comp. Ps. 143:2; Rom. 3:20. The inability of the Law to justify is exhibited in two ways: (1) It is impossible to render a "complete" obedience to it; and to offend in one point was "to be guilty of all"; and (2) It did not "help" men to justify themselves, for the Law was something dead and lifeless—a mere written letter, possessing none of those means of grace which are offered by Christianity.

(17) By Christ.—Strictly, "in Christ"—i.e., by the relation into which we are brought with Him. The reference is here, however, not exactly to the mystical union with Christ, which is regarded by the apostle in connection with sanctification (the actual growth in holiness) rather than with justification (the judicial absolution from guilt). In the present instance the apostle is speaking of justification, practically through faith in Him, or through the circle of forces within which we are brought by faith.

Is therefore Christ the minister of sin?—The question is put ironically, and as a sort of **reductio ad absurdum** of the Judaizing position. The Judaizers maintained the necessity of a strict fulfillment of the Mosaic law. However, they still called themselves Christians; and here Paul had a hold on them. No doubt he used some such argument as this in his controversy with Peter at Antioch, but it would probably be stated in a simpler and less speculative form. Here, in writing to the Galatians, the apostle paraphrases what he had said in language more suited to a theological treatise and to the natural speculative bias of his own mind.

God forbid.—The Judaizing theory was quite sufficiently condemned by showing the consequences to which it would lead. It makes Christ Himself a minister of sin—a suggestion which the apostle puts away with pious horror.

(18) For.—The connection is with the words immediately preceding. The idea is absurd as well as profane. "For," instead of the Pauline Christian (who follows Christianity to its logical results) being the sinner, it is really the Judaizing Christian who stands self-condemned—i.e., in returning to what he has forsaken. Paul is fond of metaphors taken from building. (Comp. Rom. 15:20; I Cor. 3:10-14; II Cor. 5:1; 10:4; Eph. 2:20-22.)

The things which I destroyed—i.e., the Mosaic law, the binding obligation of which had been done away in Christ.

A transgressor.—To this point the apostle had kept up a sort of studied ambiguity in his use of the words "sin," "sinner." The Jews called the Gentiles "sinners," simply from the fact of their being Gentiles. The Pauline Christian placed himself on the same footing with the Gentiles, as far as the Law was concerned, and therefore he, too, in the same phraseology, was a sinner. But now the apostle uses a word that could not be mistaken. The Christian might be a sinner, in the Judaizing sense of the word, but the Judaizer himself was the real sinner, for it was he who offended against the immutable principles of right and wrong.

(19) Through the law am dead to the law.—In what sense can this be said? The apostle himself had gotten rid of his obligations to the Law—not, however, by simply evading them from the first, but by passing through a period of subjection to them. The road to freedom from the Law lay through the Law. The Law, on its prophetic side, pointed to Christ. The Law, on its moral side, held up an ideal to which its votaries

could not attain. Paul would not have become a Christian if he had not first sat at the feet of Gamaliel. If we could trace the whole undercurrent of silent, and perhaps only half-conscious, preparation, which led to the apostle's conversion, we should see how large a part was played in it by the sense, gradually wrought in him, of the Law's insufficiency. Thus the negative side was given by his own private meditation; the positive side, faith in Christ, was given by the vision on the road to Damascus.

(20) By a natural transition, the apostle's thought passed from what the Law could not do to what Christianity could do. Here we come upon the same vein of mysticism that is developed in Rom. 6. One main way of conceiving of the Christian life is through the idea of union with Christ. This idea, when ultimately pressed to precise logical definition, must necessarily contain a certain element of metaphor. But, at the same time, there is possible to man an influence from above so penetrating and so powerful that it would seem as if the figure of union could alone adequately express it.

I am crucified...—The idea is something more than that of merely "dying with Christ"—i.e., imitating the death of Christ after a spiritual manner. It involves, besides, a special reference to the cross. It is through the power of the cross, through contemplating the cross and all that is associated with it, that the Christian is enabled to mortify the promptings of sin within him, and reduce them to a state of passiveness like that of death.

Nevertheless I live...—This death to sin, death unto one side of my nature, does not hinder me from having life upon another side. The fact is that I live in a truer sense than ever before. It is, however, no longer the old natural man in me that lives: it is not that part of the human personality which has its root in matter, but that part which is reformed by the Spirit of Christ.

Of the Son of God—i.e., faith of which the Son of God is the object, faith in the Son of God.

Who loved me.—Christ died for the whole world, but each individual Christian has a right to appropriate His death to himself. The death of Christ was prompted by love, not for the abstraction humanity, but for men as individuals.

(21) Frustrate.—The Greek word means "to render ineffectual." The grace of God goes forth with a certain mission to perform; but the Judaizing party, by still clinging to the Law, made it return void to its Giver.

Then Christ is dead in vain.—If the Law had been enough to give actual righteousness to its votaries, and with righteousness the judicial declaration of freedom from guilt, then there would have been nothing for which Christ should die. His death would have had no object and been of no benefit to mankind.

3

(1) Foolish.—"Foolish" refers to the absence or undisciplined condition of the reasoning faculty. The Gauls of Galatia were a people intellectually shallow and frivolous. A little reason and reflection would have kept them from so gross an inconsistency.

Bewitched you.—The Greek word for this is probably connected in origin with the Latin word from which is derived our own "fascinate," and the idea prominent in both is that which is embodied in the popular superstition of the "evil eye." The metaphor here is strikingly in harmony with that which follows. The cross of Christ has been "evidently set forth" (i.e., posted publicly in large and bold characters) before the Galatians, but some evil fascination (that of their Judaizing teachers) has drawn away their eyes from looking on it, and held them fixed upon another object (legal observances), as baneful as the cross was salutary.

(2) Received ye the Spirit.—The reference is to those spiritual gifts described more fully in I Cor. 12 and 14. The Galatians, it seems, had had a share in this outpouring, like the other churches, though their fickleness prevented them from reaping the full benefit from it. But a spiritual effect, such as this outpouring was, could only have a spiritual cause; it could not come from a mechanical performance of legal obligations.

By the hearing of faith—i.e., by that hearing (or preaching) which has for its subject faith. What the apostle had taught the Galatians on his first coming among them was not any system of laborious observances, but the duty of faith. They at first responded to his teaching; and in answer to their enthusiastic impulse of adhesion to Christ the gifts of the Spirit were abundantly shed upon them. Now all this had ceased.

(3) Made perfect by the flesh.—Do you

wish to finish and complete the career, thus auspiciously begun, under a system of things entirely different—a system carnal and material, narrow, slavish, and literal—the Law in place of the Gospel? By "the flesh" is here meant the Law, though the Law is described as spiritual in the context of Rom. 7:14. "The flesh" in 2:20 was simply this bodily human frame.

(4) Suffered so many things.—The Galatians, like other churches, were subjected to much persecution when they first embraced Christianity. The persecutors were probably their own Jewish countrymen, whose jealousy and rage they had braved in the name of the Gospel as preached by Paul. Now they were abandoning that very Gospel for the principles of those by whom they had been persecuted.

If it be yet in vain.—The apostle cannot quite bring himself to believe that it is, and he puts in this delicate qualification parenthetically to show the Galatians that, much as appearances may be against them, he will not give up that hope that a lingering spark or their first joyous conviction, in the strength of which they had undergone persecution, yet remained.

(5) Ministereth.—The notion contained in this word is not only that of "supply," but of "**liberal** supply." At Athens it was the custom for wealthy citizens to bear the cost of bringing out the chorus—which was practically equivalent to putting a play upon the stage—at the great public feasts. The word translated "ministereth" was the technical term for this. The same word is used in II Cor. 9:10; Col. 2:19; II Pet. 1:5 ("add"), 11.

Worketh miracles among you.—The Greek means not so much "causes miracles to be wrought in your midst" as "implants in you miraculous powers." The power to work miracles is regarded as a special faculty bestowed by God upon individual Christians. The means by which they become receptive of it is that enthusiastic condition aroused in them by faith. Mere formal obedience to a written law had no such efficacy.

(6) Even as.—The argument is here condensed. Ideas lie close together in the apostle's mind which are some distance apart in ours. He asks whether, in bestowing the gifts of the Spirit upon the Christian Church, God made use of the medium of the Law or of faith. The answer he assumes to be faith; and his thoughts fly at once to that crucial instance of faith—the faith of

Abraham. (Comp. Gen. 15:6; Rom. 4:3.)

(7-9) Unlike the Law, faith is open to all Gentiles as well as Jews. The promise, therefore, being annexed to faith, contained the death blow of all those exclusive privileges which the Judaizing party in Galatia claimed for themselves, and of all those burdensome regulations which they were for imposing upon the Galatian Christians. The universalism of the promise is accounted for by the fact that it is rested upon faith and not on works—thus showing a distinct prevision of a time when the whole world should be invited to claim a share in it by the exercise of faith. (Comp. Gen. 12:3; 18:18; Rom. 4:11, 12, 16; 9:6-8.)

(8) The scripture.—Here, with a more decided personification than usual, the Scripture is said to foresee what God, by whom Scripture is inspired, foresaw.

Would justify.—The use of the present tense in the original implies that the justification of the Gentiles is regarded as forming part of the eternal purpose of God, to whom the future and the present are one.

The heathen.—It is to be noticed that the same word is translated indifferently by "heathen," "nations," and "Gentiles."

In thee.—The righteousness which was imputed to Abraham his spiritual descendants also could claim by virtue of their descent from him. What applied to him applied (potentially and prophetically) to them. (Comp. Heb. 7:9.)

(10) For it is written.—The quotation is from Deut. 27:26, where it forms the conclusion of the series of curses to be pronounced from Mount Ebal. The absolute and sweeping nature of the condemnation would seem to be much less marked in the Hebrew. It is not, however, clear that this character was first given to it by Paul.

(11) The just shall live by faith.—The stress is on the word "faith." It is **faith** (not law) which gives life. A man is not just **before** the exercise of faith, but he **becomes** just **by** the exercise of it; and, in another aspect, the state of righteousness upon which he then enters is also a state of life. Strictly speaking, the order is—faith, justification, life.

The quotation is from Hab. 2:4, where it refers to the preservation of the righteous Israelite amid the general ruin caused by the Chaldean invasion. Though the wicked and proud shall be destroyed, the righteous man shall live "by his faith." There is some division of opinion among commentators as to whether the word translated "faith"

means, in the original, faith in the active sense or faith in the passive sense—"fidelity," "faithfulness," or "trust in God." The sense in which the word is used by Paul is most nearly related to the latter. It has the full-developed Christian meaning, which begins in belief, includes trust, and passes on to become an active energy of devotion. (See note on Rom. 1:17.)

(12) Shall live.—The idea of life receives an enlargement, corresponding to the fuller revelation of immortality in the New Testament as compared with the Old. In the Old Testament, "life is an existence upon earth, shortened by no judgment, reposing upon God, and delighting itself in God." On the other hand, "death is the sudden and dreadful end, the destruction of this existence through a judgment of some special kind" (Schultz). Such a judgment would be the Chaldean invasion; and when the prophet Habakkuk says that the "just shall live," he means that he should be saved from this calamity, and still continue to enjoy the divine favor and protection. The promise in Lev. 18:5 declares that he who keeps the Law shall be preserved from all judgments of this kind. With Paul, as in the Old Testament, the root idea is that of drawing support and sustenance from God. But with him this is not confined to the present life, or extended beyond the grave only in some dim and shadowy way: it begins in time and stretches on into eternity.

(13) Christ hath redeemed us.—This deliverance is represented under the form of a ransom. Christ "bought off" the human race from the penalty of its sins, the price paid being His death. (Comp. I Cor. 6:20; 7:23; II Pet. 2:1; Rev. 5:9; 14:4.) The word used in these passages, as well as in that before us, is the general word for "buying." But that the "buying" intended is that more definitely conveyed by the idea of "ransom" appears from the use of the special word for ransom in Matt. 20:28; Mark 10:45; I Tim. 2:6. The word commonly translated "redemption" (Rom. 3:24; I Cor. 1:30; Eph. 1:7, 14; 4:30; Col. 1:14; Heb. 9:15) also contains the same special idea of "a ransoming."

Us.—In the first instance, "the Jews," but not to be confined too strictly to them. The apostle is writing to a Gentile (though Judaizing) church, and he does not wish to exclude any of his readers. Though the Gentiles do not come directly under "the curse of the Law," they came under God's condemnation. From this they were released, and the blessings of the theocracy up to this time annexed to the Law were thrown open to them by the death of Christ.

Being made a curse.—Being treated as if He were accursed. (Comp. II Cor. 5:21.) The idea is somewhat strengthened by the use of the substantive for the adjective. The curse identifies itself with its object: seizes, as it were, upon the person of its victim.

For us—i.e., "on our behalf," "for our sakes." It is impossible to escape the conclusion that Paul, like the rest of the apostles, regarded the sufferings of Christ as undergone "in our stead." The idea is, indeed, distinctly expressed in this passage; but it must be gathered from the context, not from the use of the preposition. (See note on 1:4.)

As it is written.—The way in which the curse of the Law fell upon Christ was through His death. The ignominious death by which He died was one to which the curse of God especially attached. The Law expressly declared that that criminal who died upon the cross was an object of the divine wrath. Christ died as such a criminal, and so came under the curse. (See Deut. 21:23.)

It is to be observed, in considering the doctrinal bearings of this passage, that the curse which fell upon Christ was **not** the same curse as that described as the consequence of human guilt in failing to keep the requirements of the Law. It is not the accumulated penalty for the whole mass of human disobedience, but rather an incidental defilement, contracted by an involuntary breach of a particular ceremonial precept. The death of Christ involved a curse because the manner of it was by suspension from a cross. Christ, the sinless One, died. But it is not said that the actual load of human guilt was laid on Him. It is not said that His death was the actual punishment of that guilt. The death of Christ removed the necessity for the punishment of men, but it could not be regarded as a punishment in relation to Christ Himself. In this respect it would seem as if the symbolism of the scapegoat (which is sometimes adduced in explanation of the present passage) was imperfectly applicable (Lev. 16:21, 22). No such process as this really took place in the case of our Lord; nor is it applied to Him in I Pet. 2:24, otherwise than in vague and general metaphor. The curse which fell upon Christ must be distinguished from the curse which was due to the sins of men, though the incurrence of the one led to the abrogation of the other.

(14) Receive the promise of the Spirit.— A special outpouring of the Spirit was to be one of the characteristics of the great Messianic manifestation. (Comp. Joel 2:28, 29; Acts 2:16-21.) The promise is said to be "received" by the generation on which it is fulfilled, not by that to which it is given. (Comp. Acts 2:33; Heb. 9:15.)

(15) Though it be but a man's covenant.— A covenant, even though it is only between two men—though it is regulated by the provisions only of human law—does not admit of alteration or addition after it has once been signed and sealed; much more a covenant which depends on God.

Covenant.—The word thus translated is that which gave its name to the Old and New "testaments." The word may have two senses. It meant originally a "disposition" or "settlement," and came, on the one hand, to be confined to a "testamentary disposition," while, on the other hand, it was taken to mean a settlement arrived at by agreement between two parties. The first sense is that most commonly found in classical writers; the second is used almost entirely in the LXX and New Testament. The one exception is in Heb. 9:15-17, where the idea of "covenant" glides into that of "testament," the argument rather turning upon the double meaning of the word. (See notes on 3:18-20.)

Addeth thereto.—New clauses could be added only by a second covenant. The reason why the apostle introduces this point is that the Law might be supposed to restrict the bearings of the promise. It might be thought to add certain new and limiting conditions, without compliance with which the blessings of the promise could not be obtained. This was the position of the Judaizing party against which Paul is arguing.

(16) The object of this parenthesis is to prove a point which the Judaizing opponents of the apostle would not contest— viz., that the fulfillment of the promise to Abraham was reserved for the Messianic dispensation to which they themselves belonged. The Law therefore intervened between the promise and its fulfillment, but, inasmuch as it was itself later than the promise, could not alter the terms of its fulfillment.

To Abraham and his seed were the promises made.—The quotation appears to be made from Gen. 13:15 or 17:8. The word "promise" is put in the plural because the promise to Abraham was repeated several times—to Abraham first, and, after him, to the other patriarchs. The object of the promise was, in the first instance, the possession of the land of Canaan; but Paul here, as elsewhere, gives it a spiritual application.

And to seeds, as of many; but as of one.—The argument of the apostle turns upon the use, both in the Hebrew and in the LXX, of a singular instead of a plural noun. In both cases, however, the noun, though singular, is collective. It meant, in the first instance at least, not any one individual, but the posterity of Abraham as a whole. The apostle refers it to Christ and the "spiritual Israel" (i.e., the Church, of which He is the Head), on the same principle on which, throughout the New Testament, the history of the chosen people under the old covenant is taken as a type of the Christian dispensation. Comp. Matt. 2:15, where an allusion to the Exodus of Israel from Egypt is treated as a type of the return of the Holy Family from their flight into Egypt. Such passages are marked illustrations of the organic unity which the apostolic writers recognized in the pre-Christian and Christian dispensations. Not only had both the same Author, and formed part of the same scheme, but they were actually the counterparts one of the other.

(17) The fulfillment of the promise is thus to be seen in the Messianic dispensation now begun. The Law, which was given four hundred thirty years after the promise, had no power to cancel it.

This verse contains the direct inference from the argument stated in verse 15. When a document has been sealed, no subsequent addition can affect it. The Law was subsequent to the promise; therefore the Law cannot affect it.

In Christ.—These words, on MSS evidence, should certainly be omitted. If retained, the translation should be "unto Christ"—i.e., "with a view to Christ," to find its fulfillment in Christ.

Four hundred and thirty years after.— The giving of the Law from Mount Sinai is thus placed four hundred and thirty years after the giving of the promise to Abraham. This would include the two periods of the sojourn of the patriarchs in Canaan and the sojourn in Egypt. (Comp. Ex. 12:40, where the LXX and Samaritan Pentateuch add "and in the land of Canaan.") According to another system of chronology, the sojourn in Egypt alone occupied four hundred and thirty—cr, in round numbers, four hundred —years (Gen. 15:13; Acts 7:6). It is possible that the shorter reckoning may have arisen from difficulties observed in the longer, though it may be questioned whether it does not raise greater difficulties itself.

(18) The inheritance.—In the first instance, the temporal inheritance of the land of Canaan, but here understood of the spiritual blessings of the Messianic kingdom.

Gave it.—In the original a strong word: "God hath freely given it." There is an antithesis to the idea of "covenant" or "contract," in which both parties have to perform a part. The promise was given by God to Abraham gratuitously, unfettered by any engagement on his side by the non-fulfillment of which it might be made void.

(19, 20) If such was **not** the function of the Law—if it had **no** power to modify the promise—what was its true function? It was a temporary measure respecting transgressions, of force only until it should be superseded by the coming of the Messiah. Unlike the promise, too, it was a contract. It was given by a person acting between two parties, with rigid conditions binding them. On the other hand, the promise was given unconditionally by the sole act of God.

In stating the true function of the Law, the apostle brings out its inferiority to the promise in four respects: (1) it dealt with sins, not with holiness; (2) it was temporary and transitory; (3) it was given, not directly, but indirectly, through the double mediation of the angels and of Moses; (4) it was conditional, and not like the promise, unconditional. It depended upon the fallible action of man, and not only upon the infallible word of God.

(19) It was added.—The Law was a parenthesis in the design of Providence. The direct line of God's dealings with man ran through the promise and its fulfillment.

Because of transgressions.—It has been usual to give to this one of two opposite interpretations: (1) to check or put down transgressions; (2) to multiply and increase transgressions (Rom. 5:20). The expression seems wide enough to cover both ideas. Its original purpose was to make them known, and by imposing a penalty to check them; its real effect was to provoke and enhance them.

(20) This passage is said to have received as many as 250 or 300 interpretations. The following view appears most satisfactory: The very idea of a mediator involves two parties at least. The Law had a mediator, therefore the Law involves two parties. In other words, it is a contract. On the other hand, God, the giver of the promise, stands alone: therefore the promise is **not** a contract; and, resting on God, it is indefeasible.

(21-24) If the Law was thus inferior to the promise, does it therefore follow that it is contrary to it? By no means. The Law could not indeed give life; it could not justify, or place in a state of righteousness. Its real result was rather to place all men in a state of sin. But by so doing it prepared the way for the fulfillment of the promise in all who put faith in Christ. The Law was a close and strict, yet salutary, discipline to make us fit for faith in Christ.

(22) Hath concluded.—The word means to "shut up," "hem in," "prevent from straying either to the right hand or to the left," as a shepherd shuts up his flock in the fold. (Comp. Rom. 11:32.)

(23) We were kept.—Better, "we were kept in ward," so as to bring out more clearly the force of the metaphor which runs through the verse. The Law was a kind of prison house in which we were kept shut up. It was a custody from which we were not permitted to escape—a stern guardian that we were made to obey.

(24) The Law was our schoolmaster.—Not quite a satisfactory translation, yet it is difficult to suggest a better. The Greek word is that from which is derived the English "pedagogue." Originally it meant the slave who was placed in charge of a child, and whose duty it was to conduct it to school. The idea is that of moral rather than of intellectual discipline. The care of the "pedagogue" ceased where that of the schoolmaster began, but it was he who had more to form the character of the child.

To bring us unto Christ.—The words "to bring us" are supplied. The metaphor is not to be pressed to the extent of supposing that Christ represents the schoolmaster proper to whom the child is led by the pedagogue slave. The work of Christ as a **Teacher** is not what the apostle has in mind. It is rather a higher kind of guardianship, which is to succeed that of the Law, and to which the Law **hands over** its pupil. Once brought within the guardianship of Christ, and so made a member of the Messianic kingdom, the Christian is justified by faith, receives an amnesty for his past sins, and is accounted righteous before God.

(26) Children of God.—The translation "children" here is unfortunate, as the point to be brought out is that Christians are no longer in the condition of "children," but in that of grown-up "son." The pre-Messianic period bears to the Messianic period the same relation that a childhood or minority bears to full age. The Christian, as such, has the privileges of an adult son in his Father's house. He is released from pupilage, and has received his freedom.

(27) Baptized into Christ.—To be baptised **"into"** Christ is something more than merely "to be baptised **in the name of** Christ." It implies the contracting of a close and intimate relation. To "put on Christ" is a metaphor commonly used in the LXX, where it means "to adopt" or "take to oneself."

(28) Greek.—The spread of the Greek race through the conquests of Alexander, their ubiquitous presence, and the use of the Greek language as a universal medium of communication, led to the name "Greek" being applied to all who were not Jews. "Jew and Greek" is intended to be an exhaustive division of the human race, just as "bond or free," "male and female."

This verse marks the immense stride made by Christianity in sweeping away the artificial distinctions which had been the bane of the ancient world, and prevented any true feeling of brotherhood springing up in it. Christianity, at one stroke, established the brotherhood and abolished the distinctions.

4

The idea of constraint and freedom is treated directly in the first seven and last eleven verses, and forms the link of transition to the next chapter, the opening keynote of which is "freedom." The middle portion of chap. 4 is somewhat of a personal digression, the object of which, however, is really to support this view of the opposition between the apostle and the Judaizing party as one between liberty on the one hand and slavery on the other.

(1) Differeth nothing from a servant.—Both the child and the slave were incapable of any valid act in a legal sense; the guardian was as entirely the representative of the one as the master of the other. Both the child and the slave were subject to the same restraint, discipline, correction.

(2) Under tutors and governors.—The distinction between these two terms is that between guardians of the person and stewards of the property.

(3) We.—That is, in the first instance, the Jews; but the Gentiles are also included. Before the coming of Christ both Jews and Gentiles had been subject to law; and what the apostle says of the Law of Moses applies more faintly to the law of conscience and of nature.

Elements of the world.—The word translated is derived from a simpler word which means "a row." The derivative is applied to the letters of the alphabet, because they were arranged in rows. Thus it came to mean the "elements" or "rudiments" of learning, and then "elements" of any kind. These are called "the elements of **the world**" because they were mundane and material; they included no clear recognition of spiritual things. The earlier forms of Gentile and even of Jewish religion were much bound up with **the senses**; the most important element in them was that of ritual. (Comp. Col. 2:8, 20.)

(4) The fulness of the time.—That which was predetermined in the counsels of God as the right and proper time when the whole course of previous preparation both for Jew and Gentile was complete. Here we have a clear expression of the conception of religion as progressive, finding its culmination in Christianity.

Sent forth—i.e., from Himself (John 1:1). The pre-existence of the Son is distinctly recognized by Paul.

Made of a woman.—Perhaps better translated, "born of a woman." There is no allusion here to the miraculous conception. The phrase was of common use (comp. Matt. 11:11). Here the expression is intended to bring out, not the divinity, but the true humanity of Christ.

Made under the law.—"Born under law"—i.e., born into a state of things where the whole world was subject to law—born under the legal dispensation, though Himself destined to put an end to that dispensation.

(5) That we might receive the adoption of sons.—Redemption is followed by adoption. The admission of the believer into the Messianic kingdom, with its immunities from sin and from law, implies an admission into the Messianic family, of which God is the Father and Christ the eldest Son, "first born among many brethren."

(6) Abba, Father.—A reduplication of loving entreaty. (See note on Rom. 8:15.) For similar instances of a Greek word being repeated in Aramaic, or an Aramaic word in Greek, comp. Rev. 9:11; 12:9. The Aramaic "Abba" appears in our word "abbot."

(7) If a son, then an heir . . . —The Roman law (which the apostle seems to be following) treated **all** the sons as heirs, and provided for an equal division of the property between them.

Of God through Christ.—The true reading here appears to be, **through God**—a somewhat unusual expression. The Christian is admitted as an heir, not through any merits of his own, but through the process of redemption and adoption wrought for him by God.

(8) Them which by nature are no gods.—The gods of the heathen are called by Paul "devils." (See I Cor. 10:20.)

(9) Again.—In the Greek a double phrase, for the sake of emphasis, "over again from the very beginning," as a child might be said to go back to his alphabet.

Weak and beggarly elements.—"Elements" is used here, as in verse 3, of that elementary religious knowledge afforded in different degrees to Jew and Gentile before the coming of Christ. These are called "weak" because they were insufficient to enable man to work out his own salvation. They are called "beggarly," or "poor," because, unlike the Gospel, they were accompanied by no outpouring of spiritual gifts and graces.

(10) The description mounts in an ascending scale—days (Sabbaths, fasts), months (the "new moon"), seasons (Passover, Pentecost, etc.), years (sabbatical, Jubilee). It is quite clear that Paul places all such matters under the head of "elements" or "rudiments." They belong to the lowest section of Christian practice, and the more advanced a Christian is the less he needs to be bound by them. This, again, is qualified by the consideration that it is dangerous for any one individual to assume his own advanced condition, and to think himself able to dispense with the safeguards which his brother-Christians require. It is safest to follow the general rule of the Church, as long as it is done intelligently—i.e., with a consciousness of the reason and expediency of what is done, and not in a spirit of mere mechanical routine.

(12) Be as I am.—Use the same Christian freedom that I use.

For I am as ye are.—I lay no stress on my pure Jewish descent. I stripped myself of all this, and became a Gentile among Gentiles.

Ye have not injured me at all.—The apostle goes back in thought to his first visit to Galatia. They did him no injury, showed him no unkindness, but, on the contrary, received him gladly.

(13) Through infirmity of the flesh—i.e., some bodily weakness or ill health. We should gather from this that Paul was detained in Galatia accidentally by illness, and that this led to his preaching the Gospel there at an earlier time (Acts 16:6, as distinguished from Acts 18:23).

(14) My temptation which was in my flesh.—The true reading is "your temptation in my flesh"—i.e., my bodily infirmities, which might have been a temptation to you to reject me. Paul seems to have suffered from grievous bodily infirmity, which he elsewhere (II Cor. 12:7) describes as a "thorn in the flesh." The effects of this were seen in his personal appearance, which his enemies described as "mean" (II Cor. 10:10); and he himself felt it as a corrective against any tendency to spiritual pride (II Cor. 12:7). An attack of this malady came upon him during his visit to Galatia, and it was with health shattered by this that he first preached the Gospel to the Galatians. Still, to their credit, they took no notice of it, and gave him the warmest possible reception.

(15) Ye would have plucked out your own eyes.—The word "own" should be struck out, and the emphasis laid on "eyes." The inference which has been drawn from this passage, that Paul suffered from an affection of the eyes, hardly seems to hold good. The "eyes" may be mentioned only as something peculiarly dear and precious. (Comp. Deut. 32:10; Ps. 17:8; Prov. 7:2.)

(16) Because I tell you the truth.—It would seem that something had happened upon Paul's second visit to Galatia (Acts 18:23) which had caused a change in their feelings toward him. His plain speaking had given offense.

(17) They would exclude you.—The Judaizers desire to win your favor, then separate you from the rest of the Gentile churches, making a sect by itself, in which they themselves may bear rule. All the other Gentile churches had accepted the freer teaching of Paul; the Judaizing party wished to make of Galatia an isolated center of Judaism. They did this with personal motives, not from honest and honorable motives, with a view to secure their own ascendancy.

(19) My little children.—This is used to heighten the tenderness of the appeal. The simple form "my children," however, rather than the diminutive, is found in some of the best MSS and perhaps should be adopted. Paul regards as his spiritual children all who first received the Gospel from him.

Of whom I travail in birth again.—The struggle which ends in the definite winning over of his converts to Christ, the apostle compares to the process of birth. In the case of the Galatians, after their relapse, this struggle has all to be gone through again.

Until Christ be formed in you.—Just as the formless embryo by degrees takes the shape of man, so the unformed Christian by degrees takes the likeness of Christ. As he grows in grace that likeness becomes more and more defined, till at last the Christian reaches the "stature of the fulness of Christ" (Eph. 4:13).

(20) I stand in doubt of you—i.e., I do not know what to say to you—how I ought to deal with you so as to win you back from this defection. If the apostle had been present, so as to see what effect his words were having, he would know what line to take. As it is, in writing to them he is at a loss, and fears to make matters worse instead of better.

(22) For.—This particle expresses a reason for the question which had been asked just before: "For the Law **does** supply a case in point."

(23) Both were alike in being children of Abraham; they were unlike in that one was born naturally, the other by divine instrumentality. The promise itself, in the case of Isaac, is conceived of as possessing a creative power. (See Gen. 18:10.)

(21-31) Paul applies the history of the natural Israel allegorically to the spiritual Israel; and not only does he do this with reference to the history of the formed theocracy, but he goes back to its origin in the time of the patriarchs, and traces there the first beginnings of the separation between the Law and the promise. The same history had been already allegorically treated, though quite differently, by Philo.

(24) Which things are an allegory.—The allegorical sense does not exclude the literal sense, but is added to it. Paul speaks in like manner in I Cor. 10:11, though elsewhere a distinction is drawn between "type" and "allegory," the first implying that the narrative on which it is based is true, the second that it is fictitious. Paul does not use the word here in this strict sense. The argumentative force of the passage evidently rests on the apostolic assertion of Christian liberty, not upon the logical cogency of the inference from the details of the type to the thing typified.

(25) For this Agar is mount Sinai in Arabia.—There appears to be sufficient evidence to show that Hagar may be regarded as the Arabic name for Sinai, so that there would be a special reason for identifying Hagar allegorically with the old covenant.

Answereth to Jerusalem which now is.— The word for "answereth" is a technical term in philosophy, applied to the parallel columns containing such antithetical pairs as good—evil; one—many; finite—infinite, etc. Here it will be illustrated by the parallel arrangement of the different points of the allegory given above. "Answereth to" will thus mean "stands in the same column with." Hagar, Sinai, the old covenant, the Jewish nation, or the earthly Jerusalem, all stand on the same side of the antithesis.

Jerusalem which now is—i.e., the Jewish people still subject to the Law. It is opposed to "Jerusalem which is above," as the pre-Messianic to the Messianic system.

And is in bondage with her children.— Jerusalem is, as it were, personified, so that "with her children" means "all who are dependent upon her"—the Jewish system and all who belong to it.

(26) Jerusalem which is above.—Comp. Heb. 12:22; Rev. 21:2. This "new" or "heavenly" Jerusalem is the seat or center of the glorified Messianic kingdom, just as the old Jerusalem had been the center of the earthly theocracy. The conception of the "heavenly Jerusalem" among the Jews, like the rest of their Messianic beliefs, took a materialistic form. (Comp. Rev. 21:16.) No such materialistic notions attach to the idea as presented by Paul. "Jerusalem which is above" is to him a spiritual city, of which the Christian is a member here and now. It is part of the Messianic kingdom, to the whole of which the apostle gave an ideal character. (See Phil. 3:20.)

(27) Rejoice, thou barren.—See Isa. 54:1. The quotation has reference, in the first instance, to the restoration of the exiled Jews to Jerusalem and to the coming greatness of the newly-settled city. Though at present it is desolate and in ruins, it shall become greater and more populous than ever it had been in its best days before. The revived theocracy under Zerubbabel is

naturally taken as a type of the final theocratic reign of the Messiah. The representation of the theocracy under the figure of marriage is common, both in the prophetic writings and in Paul.

The desolate ... she which hath an husband.—In the original, Jerusalem after the exile, opposed to Jerusalem in the time of its prosperity under David and Solomon; in the typical application, Sarah, who had long been barren, as opposed to Hagar, whose marriage had been fruitful; in the antitypical application, the new dispensation, Christianity, with its small beginnings and persecutions, as opposed to the old dispensation, with its material possessions and privileges.

(29) Persecuted.—See Gen. 21:9. The Jewish traditions added that Ishmael took out the child Isaac and "shot at him with arrows under pretence of sport." The Arab tribes, Ishmael's descendants, had always been a thorn in the side of their Israelite neighbors.

Him that was born after the Spirit.—A miraculous agency intervened in the birth of Isaac, and the Christian Church was inaugurated by the same agency—that of the Spirit. The Messianic reign was realized through the Spirit; and their participation in this reign made all Christians true and spiritual descendants of Abraham.

(30) The son of the bondwoman shall not be heir.—A bold declaration of the incompatibility of Judaism with Christianity: the essential character of the Christian Church is freedom. The practical conclusion is given in the opening verse of the next chapter, which should be taken in close connection with the end of this.

5

(1) The yoke of bondage—i.e., the Judaizing restraints and restrictions.

(2) Behold, I Paul.—The strong personality of the apostle asserts itself; instead of going into an elaborate proof, he speaks with dogmatic authority, as though his bare word were enough.

Shall profit you nothing—i.e., in the way of justification, as producing that state of righteousness in the sight of God by virtue of which the believer is released from wrath and received into the divine favor. The apostle says that if this state of justification is sought through circumcision, it cannot be sought through Christ at the same time.

(3) For I testify again.—The act of circumcision placed a man under the legal system, just as the act of baptism placed him under the Christian system. From that time forward he could not choose one part and refuse another, but was bound alike by all.

(4) Are justified.—Strictly, "seek to be justified."

Ye are fallen from grace.—The Christian is justified by an act of grace, or free, unearned favor, on the part of God. He who seeks for justification in any other way loses this grace.

(5) Through the Spirit.—It is the Spirit which makes faith effectual and righteousness real. The righteousness which comes by the Law is entirely human or "carnal," the product of a man's own efforts. The righteousness which is by faith is the gift of God, and that gift is communicated through the Spirit.

(6) Faith which worketh by love.—Devoted attachment to Christ is the great motive power, the source or mainspring of action; and the law by which that action is regulated is the law of love. (Comp. verses 13, 14; Rom. 13:8-10.) It is clear that the faith thus described by Paul does not stop short in a mere head notion, and so is in no conflict with the teaching of James. (See Jas. 2:14-26.)

(7) Ye did run well.—Again, as in 2:2, a metaphor from foot racing. The Galatians had made a good start, but suddenly changed their course.

Who did hinder you?—The original meaning of the word translated "hinder" is to "break up a road," as an army before the advance of hostile forces.

The truth—i.e., the doctrine taught by Paul in opposition to the Judaizing tenets which had been introduced into the Galatian Church.

(8) This persuasion ... —He who "calls" the Galatians is here, as elsewhere, God; and certainly, the apostle says, it can have been by no intimation or guidance from Him that they were led to accept such perverted teaching.

(9) A little leaven ... —The proverb is true which says that "a little leaven leavens the whole mass of dough." And so, in your case, the malcontents may be few, but they will soon ruin the whole Church.

(10) I have confidence in you through the Lord.—This has reference to the main body of the Church; an exception is immediately made as to the disaffected party, and especially their leader.

Whosoever he be.—The apostle does not fix upon any one particular person as the cause of the troubles in the Galatian Church, but he says that, whoever he may be, God will judge him.

(11) And I, brethren.—Paul had at one time seemed to preach, or at least to permit, circumcision. Thus, in Acts 15, we should gather from the account of the conference at Jerusalem that he did not insist strongly upon this point, and on taking Timothy with him upon his second missionary journey—the very journey in which he first visited Galatia—his first step was to have him circumcised. It was only natural that the progress of time and of events should deepen the apostle's conviction of the radical antagonism between the ceremonial Judaism and Christianity. This he is now stating in the most emphatic manner, and he feels that he is open to a charge of something like inconsistency. The Galatians might say that he preached circumcision himself. His answer is, that if he really preached circumcision he would not be so persecuted by the Judaizing party. Circumcision is taken as occupying, in the Judaizing system, the same place that the cross of Christ occupied in that of Paul. The two things are alternatives. If one is taught, there is no need for the other.

(12) I would they were even cut off.—The words may mean "cut themselves off," i.e., from your communion, but it seems far better, and more in keeping with the historic consensus, to take the words as referring to an extension of the rite of circumcision, such as the Galatians might see frequently practiced by the priests of Cybele, whose worship had one of its most important centers in their country—"I would they would even make themselves eunuchs." Let them carry their self-mutilation still further, and not stop at circumcision.

(13) An occasion to the flesh.—Sensual excess was the special danger of the Gentile churches, such as Corinth, from which the apostle may have been writing. Galatia, too, was a Gentile church; and though it was for the present subject rather to Judaizing influences, the character of the people was fickle, and Paul may have thought it well to hint a caution in this direction.

Serve.—There is a stress upon this word. The apostle had been dissuading the Galatians from submitting to other forms of servitude. This one will permit them. The theme of love to one's neighbor (verse 14) is worked out at length in Rom. 13: 8-10.

(17) For the flesh . . . —Here is brought out most distinctly the antithesis between the flesh and the Spirit, which is one of the root ideas in the psychology of Paul. It does not amount to dualism, for the body, as such, is not regarded as evil. There is nothing to show that Paul considered matter **in itself** evil. But the body becomes the seat of evil; from it arise those carnal impulses which are the origin of sin. And it is the body, looked at in this light, which is designated as "the flesh." The flesh is the body, as animated by an evil principle. It thus becomes opposed to the good principle, whether the good principle in itself—the Spirit of God, or that organ in which the good principle resides—the spirit in man.

So that ye cannot do the things that ye would.—The opposition between the flesh and the Spirit, each pulling a different way, prevents the will from acting freely. (See Rom. 7:15-23, 25.)

(18) Ye are not under the law.—The flesh and law are correlative terms; to be free from the one is to be free from the other. The flesh represents unaided human nature, and law is the standard which this unaided human nature strives, but strives in vain, to fulfill. By the intervention of the Spirit, the law is fulfilled at the same time that its domination is abolished and human nature ceases to be unaided. In its highest part it is brought into direct contact with the divine nature, and the whole tenor of its actions changes accordingly.

(19) Now the works of the flesh are manifest.—The effects which the flesh produces are plain and obvious enough. The catalogue which follows divides itself roughly under four heads: (1) sins of sensuality; (2) sins of superstition; (3) sins of temper; (4) excesses.

Adultery.—This word is omitted in the best MSS.

Uncleanness, lasciviousness.—The first of these words signifies any kind of impurity, secret or open; the second, flagrant breaches of public decency.

(20) Idolatry.—When the Christian is warned against idolatry, it is not, of course, systematic idolatry that is meant, but that occasional compliance with idolatrous customs into which he might easily be led by his intercourse with his heathen neighbors.

Witchcraft.—"Sorcery," or "magic." It would seem that practices of this kind were

especially common in Asia Minor. (See Acts 19:19.)

Variance.—"Strife," or "contention."

Emulations.—Singular and plural are somewhat strangely mixed throughout the list. There is a division of authorities as to the reading in the case of this word. It seems probable that the singular is right— "jealousy." "Wrath," on the other hand, should be "wraths"—i.e., outbreaks of wrath.

Strife.—The true derivation of this word is to be sought in a word meaning "a day-laborer." Therefore we get the senses (1) labor for hire; (2) interested canvassing for office; (3) a spirit of factious partisanship. (This word, too, is really in the plural.)

Seditions, heresies.—These renderings sound as if the first is related to factions in the State, and the second in the Church. This is not really so. The two words are distinguished from each other, as the lighter and more aggravated forms of division: the first, divisions; the second, divisions organized into parties.

(21) Murders.—There is considerable doubt as to whether this word ought to stand in the text. It is wanting in the two oldest MSS and in some other good authorities. Internal considerations may be made to tell either for its omission or for its retention.

I tell you before.—I tell you before the event proves my words to be true—i.e., before the day of judgment.

As I have also told you in time past.— The occasion appears to have been on Paul's last or second visit to Galatia.

(22) The fruit of the Spirit.—There does not seem to be any essential difference between this term and that used above: the **works** of the flesh." The fruit of the Spirit is that which naturally grows out of the operation of the Spirit, in which it naturally results.

The list which follows brings out in a striking manner the peculiar finish and perfection which belongs to the Christian morality. It differs at once from any form of pagan or philosophic ethics. At the head of the list is "love," which Christianity takes as its moving principle—not being, perhaps, alone in this, but alone in the systematic consistency with which it is carried out. Next comes "joy," a peculiarly Christian grace, which has a much deeper root than mere natural cheerfulness of temper, and is rather the unfailing brightness and equanimity which proceeds from calm and settled principles animated by the Spirit Himself. It may be questioned whether "peace" is here the tranquillity which is shed abroad in the heart by the sense of reconciliation with God, or rather, from the context that follows, peaceableness toward men. The remainder of the list is made up of those delicate and fragile forms of virtue which the ordinary course of society is least likely to foster. Patriotism, courage, generosity, prudence, fortitude, are virtues that would be produced by the regular action of natural selection left to itself. "Long-suffering," "gentleness," "goodness," "faith," "meekness," "temperance," need a more spiritual process for their development.

Gentleness, goodness.—Rather, "kindness, goodness." The second word would represent a more positive tendency of disposition than the first.

Faith.—Rather, "faithfulness"; not here in the sense peculiar to Paul, in which faith is the primary Christian virtue, but rather (as the context shows) "trustworthiness" in dealing with men, along with, perhaps, that frank and unsuspicious temper which Paul ascribes especially to charity (I Cor. 13:7).

(23) Meekness, temperance.—"Meekness" is a gentle submissiveness to the divine will. By "temperance" is meant, in a general sense, "self-control"—a firm control over the passions.

There is no law.—For such things law has no condemnation, and therefore they are removed beyond the sphere of law. This is the first and obvious meaning; it may be noticed, however, that these delicate Christian graces are above law as well as beyond. The ruder legal system of commands, sanctioned by punishment, would have no power to produce them; they can grow only in a more genial and softer soil, under the direct influence of the Spirit.

(24) Have crucified the flesh.—See Rom. 6:2-14. The relation into which the Christian is brought with Christ is such as to neutralize and deaden all the sensual impulses within him; and inasmuch as the central point in that relation is the crucifixion, the Christian is said not merely to "kill" but to "crucify" the flesh, with its evil appetites and passions.

Affections and lusts.—"Affections" are passive—susceptibility to evil impressions; "lusts" active—desire for that which is forbidden.

(25) Let us also walk in the Spirit—i.e., "by the rule" of the Spirit, as the Spirit dictates (comp. verse 16). The life which the Spirit quickens needs human cooperation, an active effort on the part of the Christian, to realize it completely in practice. Paul first sets before his readers what God has done for them, and then uses this as an argument and stimulus to renewed efforts on their own part.

(26) Let us not be.—When he left the Galatian Church, Paul was satisfied with their condition, but he fears that they will change. The warning that he addresses to them exactly hits the weak points in the national character—fickleness, vanity, and a quarrelsome disposition.

6

(1) Brethren.—The conventional use of this word tends to weaken our sense of the delicacy and earnestness of this appeal. It has been suggested that the apostle's tone in this passage has been affected by the recent occurrence at Corinth, where he had to warn the Corinthians against over-severity (see II Cor. 2:6-8).

If a man be overtaken.—"If a man be caught red-handed," in the very act, before he can escape. A special expression is used in order to aggravate the circumstances of the detection. No matter what these circumstances may be, one who is truly spiritual will still deal gently with the offender.

Ye which are spiritual.—Paul assumes that all Christians are animated by the Spirit of God. If, while claiming to be better than others, and to condescend toward them, they were not so animated, their presumption would be seen in all the more glaring light.

Restore.—The idea is that of correcting with no feeling of resentment or thought of punishment, but with a single eye to the amendment of the offender. The same word is used for "**mending** their nets" in Matt. 4:21; Mark 1:19. It is also found as a medical term for setting dislocated limbs.

(2) So fulfil.—By showing sympathy to others in their distress, of whatever kind that distress may be—whether physical, mental, or moral—the Christian will best fulfill that "new commandment" bequeathed to him by his Master, the "law of love." (See John 13:34; I John 3:23.)

(3) He deceiveth himself.—A peculiar word, perhaps coined by Paul: "puts himself under an hallucination"; persuades himself of the existence of that which has no reality.

(4) Prove.—"Test," or "examine," by reference to an objective standard. The word is used especially of the assaying of metals.

Rejoicing in himself alone, and not in another.—Rather, "he shall have his ground of boasting with reference to himself alone, and not with reference to his neighbor." He will judge his own actions by the standard properly applicable to them. His standard will be absolute and not relative, and the amount of his boasting will be proportioned accordingly. He will not seek to excuse himself by dwelling on his neighbor's weaknesses.

(5) Every man shall bear his own burden.—In verse 2 the Christian is bidden to "bear the burdens" of others, in the sense of sympathizing with them in their troubles. Here he is told that he must "bear his own load," in the sense that he must answer directly to God for his own actions. His responsibility cannot be shifted on to others. It will make him no better that there are others worse than himself. (Comp. II Cor. 10:12-14.)

(6) Communicate . . . in all good things.—Let the learner impart or share with his teacher in all those temporal goods with which God has blessed him. Even at this early date there seems to have been a more or less organized system of instruction in the church. The teacher would not receive any settled and regular payment, but the scholar would make him presents—many of them, probably, in kind—so as to relieve him from the care of providing for his own livelihood, and so give him more leisure for his work of teaching.

(7) Whatsoever a man soweth that shall he also reap.—Comp. II Cor. 9:6, where the same metaphor is used in reference to the same thing—liberality in almsgiving.

(8) He that soweth to his flesh.—The seed sown is a man's actions here on earth. If the object of those actions is merely self-indulgence, they are, as it were, sown in a field the owner of which is the flesh (i.e., the lower, carnal self). The flesh alone benefits by them, and for it alone are they garnered up.

He that soweth to the Spirit . . .—On the other hand, where all the actions are like seed deposited in the field of which the owner and lord is the Spirit, the same Spirit will reward them in the world to come with the gift of everlasting life.

(10) Them who are of the household of faith.—The Church is represented as a household in I Tim. 3:15; Heb. 3:6; I Pet. 2:5; 4:17.

(11) How large a letter.—Rather, "in what large letters." The exact significance of these words is somewhat enigmatic, and can only be matter of conjecture. Two points, however, are clear: (1) The latter part of the Greek phrase means "in" or "with" letters—i.e., characters of handwriting—and not "a letter," "an epistle"; (2) The former half of the phrase means "how large," strictly in respect of size. The apostle, for some reason or other, points out that the characters in which he is writing are larger than usual. What is his reason? It is hard to say. Some have thought that the reference was to the "shapelessness" of the letters, whether as due to the fact that the apostle himself was not accustomed to the manual work of writing, or possibly to physical weakness from the hardships that he had undergone. It seems, on the whole, most probable that the size of the characters expresses the emphasis and authority with which the apostle is writing. He adds to the epistle—which had so far been written by an amanuensis—a few bold incisive strokes in his own hand, trenchantly exposing the motives of the Judaizing faction, and reasserting his own position.

I have written.—Does this refer to the whole previous portion of the epistle, or only to these concluding paragraphs? The Greek may, quite fairly and tenably, be translated "I write"; and that being so, considerations of exegesis would seem to tell somewhat decidedly in the same direction. The whole character of this concluding section is much what we should expect if Paul followed his usual custom of taking the pen from the amanuensis to write it, and its brief weighty summarizing style would correspond well with the "large letters" in which he says it was written.

With mine own hand.—It was the apostle's custom to make use of an amanuensis, and only to add a few final words in proof of the genuineness of the writing. (See II Thess. 3:17; and comp. Rom. 16:22; I Cor. 16:21; Col. 4:18.)

(12) To make a fair shew in the flesh.—To obtain a reputation for religiousness in externals, thereby gaining favor among their countrymen, the Jews, by seeming to win over proselytes to the Mosaic law.

Only lest they should suffer persecution for the cross of Christ.—What aroused the antagonism of the Jews against the Christians was evidently not so much the confession of the Messiahship of Jesus as the declared abolition of the Law of Moses. By suppressing this side of Christian teaching, the Judaizers could easily obtain toleration for their other tenets. If, on the other hand, they were to emphasize it, the full weight of persecution would fall upon them, its ostensible ground being the doctrine of a crucified Messiah. Accordingly, they persuaded as many of the Galatians as they could to accept circumcision, and made the most of this propagandist zeal to their Jewish neighbors.

(14) God forbid that I should glory.— There is a stress upon the pronoun "I," in emphatic contrast to the party who had been the subjects of the last verse. They make their boast in a mere external; but for me—far be it from me to make my boast in anything but the cross of Christ.

The cross of our Lord Jesus Christ.—The apostle is aware that in this he is putting forward a startling paradox. The cross of Christ was to the Jews a stumbling block. They attached to it only ideas of ignominy and shame, and yet it is precisely this of which the apostle is most proud.

By whom.—The antecedent is thus not Christ, but more especially the **cross** of Christ. It is the intense contemplation of a **crucified** Saviour through which the Christian dies to the world.

The world.—By this is meant here the world of sense, the sphere of outward and sensible things, at once with its many temptations to sin and with its inadequate methods of escaping from them—mere external rites, such as circumcision.

(16) According to this rule.—The word for "rule" is the same that afterward received a special application in the phrase "Canon of Scripture." It meant originally a carpenter's rule, hence a standard; and, from that, the list of books coming up to a certain standard, not (as might be thought) which themselves supplied a standard.

The apostle confines his benediction to those who hold the fundamental truths of Christianity—i.e., here more especially, the doctrine of justification by faith and the spiritual view of Christianity connected with it, as opposed to the merely external and mechanical system of the Judaizers.

And upon the Israel of God.—"And" is equivalent to "namely." By the "Israel of God" is here meant "spiritual Israel," all who prove their real affinity to Abraham by a faith like Abraham's. (Comp. 3:7-9, 14, 29; Rom. 4:11, 12; 9:6-8.)

(17) The marks.—The "stigmata," or marks inflicted with branding irons, such as those which show that a slave is attached to a particular temple or to the service of some particular deity. Those slaves with which the Galatians were most familiar would be engaged in the worship of Cybele.

(18) With your spirit.—The grace of God works especially on the "spirit," or highest part, of man.

(The subscription appears for the first time in MSS dating from about the beginning of the ninth century, though before this the epistle had been described as written from Rome by Theodoret, Euthalius, and Jerome. Corinth is the much more probable source.)

EPHESIANS

1

(1) By the will of God.—This phrase, used in I Cor. 1:1; II Cor. 1:1; Col. 1:1; II Tim. 1:1 (comp. the equivalent expression of I Tim. 1:1), appears to be Paul's ordinary designation of the source of his apostolic mission and authority. It was used whenever there was nothing peculiar in the occasion of the epistle or the circumstances of the Church to which it was addressed.

To the saints ... and to the faithful in Christ Jesus.—The two epithets are correlative. Without the call and the grace of God, men cannot believe; without energy of faith they cannot be, in effect as well as in opportunity, "saints." Both epithets belong in capacity and profession to all members of the Church militant; and Paul applies them accordingly to the whole body of any church which he addresses, without hesitation or distinction.

Which are at Ephesus.—These words are omitted in the oldest MSS. (See note on 3:2.)

(2) Grace be to you, and peace.—Paul's all but invariable salutation in every epistle is found also in the epistles of Peter, II John, and the Apocalypse.

(3) With the single exception of the Second Epistle to the Corinthians, all Paul's epistles addressed to particular churches pass at once from the salutation to refer to the particular circumstances, gifts, and needs of the Church, generally in the form of thanksgiving and prayer, sometimes (as in Gal. 1:6) in rebuke. (Comp. I Pet. 1:3.)

Who hath blessed us ... in heavenly places.—It should be, **who blessed us** (once for all), in the election and predestination spoken of in the next verse. The sense of the phrase "in heavenly places" thus becomes far clearer. The local sense agrees best with the context here, for the apostle is speaking of the election "before the foundation of the world" as made by the foreknowledge of God in heaven, where Christ is "in the beginning with God."

(4) According as he hath chosen us in him before the foundation of the world.—It should be, **He chose us for Himself.** The eternal election of God is inseparably connected with the blessing of the Spirit. This passage stands alone in Paul's epistles in its use of this word "chosen" in connection with God's eternal purpose. See I Pet. 1:20,

where it is applied to the foreordaining of His sacrifice in the divine counsels. The word is used by our Lord of His choice of the apostles (John 6:70; 13:18; 15:16-19); of Acts 1:2, 24; 6:5; 15:7, 22, 25 of His choice or the choice of the apostles; and in Acts 13:7 of the national election of Israel. Clearly in all these cases it is applied to the election of men to privilege by an act of God's mercy here. In this passage, on the contrary, the whole reference is to the election "in Christ," by the foreknowledge of God, of those who should hereafter be made His members. From this examination of Scriptural usage it is clear that the visible election to privilege is constantly and invariably urged upon men, and that even here it clearly refers to all members of the Church, without distinction.

That we should be holy and without blame before him.—In these words we have the object of the divine election declared, and the co-operation of the elect implied, by the inseparable connection of holiness with election. It seems clear that the words refer not to justification in Christ, but to sanctification in Him. They express the positive and negative aspects of holiness; the positive in the spirit of purity, the negative in the absence of spot or blemish. The key to their interpretation is to be found in the idea of Rom. 8:29, "Whom he did foreknow, he did predestinate to be **conformed to the image of his Son.**"

In love.—It is best to connect these words with the verse following, "Having predestinated us in love."

(5) The idea of election depends on the union of the sense of actual difference between men, as to privilege and spiritual life, with the conviction of God's universal sovereignty. In all cases, therefore, it leads back to the conception of the divine purpose in the mind of God before its realization in actual fact. On the doctrine of predestination note that here (1) its source is placed in God's love; (2) its meritorious cause is the mediation of the Lord Jesus Christ; (3) its result is adoption; (4) it is in itself the expression of "the good pleasure of His will" on which all ultimately depends; and (5) its final purpose is to show forth God's glory in the gift of His grace.

(6) To the praise of the glory of his grace.—That is, He is pleased to consider His glory best realized in the spectacle of souls redeemed and regenerate by His grace, and to decree that it should be thus realized for our sakes.

Wherein he hath made us accepted in the beloved.—This special title is given to our Lord to mark a connection with the "love" declared in the last verse to be the source of God's predestination. It is a love to all mankind, as in God's foreknowledge already made one with His beloved Son. (See John 17:23, 25.)

(7) In whom we have redemption through his blood, the forgiveness of sins.—The primary idea in "redemption" is deliverance from a bondage, mostly the bondage of sin itself (see Rom. 8:23; Tit. 2:14; Heb. 9:15; I Pet. 1:18-21), but occasionally (and in this sense with a different Greek word) the bondage under sentence of punishment for sin (Gal. 3:13; 4:5). The primary idea in "the forgiveness of sins through his blood" is propitiation, that is, the offering to God a full, perfect, and sufficient sacrifice for sin, by One who is the Head and Representative of the human race (Rom. 3:25; I John 2:2; 4:10). Thus the former phrase looks at the Atonement from the side of God, the latter from the side of man, both being wrought by Him who is Son of God and Son of Man at once. Together they represent the whole truth.

(9) Having made known unto us the mystery of his will.—(See 3:5; I Cor. 2:7; Col. 1:27.) The ordinary sense of the word "mystery"—a thing of which we know that it is, though how it is we know not—is not implied in the original meaning of the word; but it is a natural derivative from it. Reason can apprehend, when revealed, that which it cannot discover; but seldom or never can it comprehend it perfectly.

(10) That ... he might gather together in one all things in Christ.—In these words Paul strikes the great keynote of the whole epistle, the unity of all in Christ. The full meaning of this expression is "to gather again under one head" things which had been originally one, but had since been separated. (See Col. 1:16-20.) In Christ, as the Word of God in the beginning, all created things are considered as gathered up, through Him actually made, and in Him continuing to exist. This unity, broken by sin, under the effect of which "all creation groans" (Rom. 8:22), is restored in the Incarnation and Atonement of the Son of God. By this, therefore, all things are again summed up in Him, and again made one in Him with the Father. In both passages Paul uses expressions which extend beyond humanity itself (Comp. John 1:3, 4, 12.)

(10, 11) Even in him: in whom also we have obtained an inheritance.—The word "we," in the light of succeeding verses, seems to limit the thought to the original Jewish believers—the true Israel, who (like the whole of Israel in ancient days) have become "a people of inheritance" (Deut. 4:20; 9:29; 32:9), so succeeding to the privileges (Rom. 11:7) which their brethren in blindness rejected.

(12) That we ... who first trusted in Christ.—The interpretation seems to be, "who have hoped in the Christ before He came"—that is, who, taught by prophecy, entering into that vision of a great future which pervades the older Covenant, looked forward "to the hope of Israel," and who accordingly in due time became, on the Day of Pentecost, the firstfruits of His salvation.

(13) In whom ye also trusted ... in whom also after that ye believed, ye were sealed.—The insertion of the word "trusted" (suggested by the word "trusted" in the previous verse) is probably erroneous. The irregularity of construction will surprise no one who studies Paul's epistles, and especially these epistles of his Captivity, remembering that they were dictated, and in all probability read over again to the apostle for addition or correction.

Ye were sealed with that holy Spirit of promise.—The original idea of this sealing is best seen in Rev. 7:3-8—an outward badge, to be at once a pledge and means of safety amid the destruction coming on the earth. In like sense, circumcision appears to be called "a seal" of previously existing righteousness of faith (Rom. 4:11; I Cor. 9:2). But the word is used in a deeper sense whenever it is connected with the gift of the Holy Spirit. Then it has the character of a sacrament, and is not a mere badge, but a true means of grace. The "promise" is clearly the promise in the Old Testament (as in Jer. 31:31-34; Joel 2:28-32) of the outpouring of the Spirit on all God's people in "the latter days." (Comp. baptism as the seal of conversion, Acts 2:38.)

(14) Which is the earnest of our inheritance.—On the word "earnest," a precious gift, as surety for a fuller gift hereafter, see II Cor. 1:22. The word "inheritance" has a correspondent meaning. It is a present possession (as in Acts 7:5), which shall be developed into a more precious future.

Until the redemption of the purchased possession.—The "redemption" here is the complete and final salvation from sin and death (as in Rom. 8:23). The original word here rendered "purchased possession" properly means "the act of purchase or acquisition," and is so used in I Thess. 5:9; II Thess. 2:14; Heb. 10:39.

(16) Cease not to give thanks for you, making mention of you in my prayers.— Almost all Paul's epistles are introduced by this union of thanksgiving and prayer, which is, indeed, characteristic of the right harmony of all Christian worship. (See Rom. 1:8, 9; Phil. 1:3, 4; Col. 1:3, 4; I Thess. 1:2, 3; II Tim. 1:3; Philem. 4.) But the proportion of the two elements varies.

(17) The God of our Lord Jesus Christ.— (See John 20:17.) The phrase refers entirely to our Lord's nature as the true Son of Man. In that respect God is in the full sense (which in us is interrupted by sin) His God, in whom He lived and had His being. In proportion as we are conformed to His likeness, "God is our God for ever and ever."

The Father of glory.—Better, **of the glory**. This phrase is unique. God is here called "the Father of the glory" of the incarnate Deity in Jesus Christ (see John 1:14), called in II Cor. 4:6, "the glory of God in the face (or **person**) of Jesus Christ." The prayer which follows connects the knowledge (which comes from revelation) of the glory of our inheritance with the exaltation of our Lord in glory.

(18) The eyes of your understanding.— The true reading is **of your heart**, for which the words "of your understanding" have been substituted, so as to yield a simpler and easier expression. The heart is similarly spoken of in relation to spiritual perception in Rom. 1:21; I Cor. 2:9; 4:5. It signifies the inner man in his entirety; and the phrase here used seems to convey the all-important truth, that for the knowledge of God all the faculties of understanding, conscience, and affection must be called into energy by the gift of the light of God.

That ye may know.—The knowledge which Paul here desires for the Ephesians, in accordance with the whole tone of this epistle, is a knowledge of heavenly things, experienced only in part upon earth—with an experience, however, sufficient to be an earnest of the hereafter. To each idea the conception of looking onward is attached; to the "calling" "hope," to the "inheritance" "glory," to "power" the exaltation of Christ (and of us with Him; see 2:6) to the right hand of God.

(20) Which he wrought in Christ.—The reality of the work of God upon us is insured by the reality of that work upon the true son of Man, whose members we are, in His Resurrection, His Ascension, His exaltation over all things at the right hand of God, and His headship of the Church. It is notable that, while it is on the spiritual meaning of the resurrection of Christ that the chief stress is laid in the earlier epistles (as in Rom. 6:4-11; I Cor. 15:12-22, 50-57), in these later epistles the apostle passes on beyond this, as taken for granted (see Col. 3:1), and dwells on Christ in heaven, exalted far above all created things, but yet vouchsafing to be in a peculiar sense the head and life of the Church on earth. (See Phil. 2:9-11; Col. 1:14-19.) In this advance of thought he approaches to the idea of our Lord's own great intercession (John 17:5, 24), constantly connecting the unity of His Church in Him with the glory which was His from all eternity, and to which He was to return.

(21) Far above all principality, and power, and might, and dominion.—The words used here are intended to include all possible forms of power, corresponding to the exhaustive enumeration in Phil. 2:10. The words rendered "principality and power" more properly signify "government and the authority committed to it." Paul mostly employs this whole group of words, especially in the epistles of the Captivity, with a manifest reference to angelic, not earthly, powers of good or evil. It is likely that he was induced so to do by the half-gnostic speculation on the nature and worship of angels, prevalent in the later Judaism, of which we have a specimen at Colossae (Col. 2:18)—in the same spirit which leads the author of the Epistle to the Hebrews to dwell so emphatically (in chaps. 1 and 2) on the infinite superiority of the Son of God to all angels. In this passage the names point to different aspects, rather than to different orders, of superhuman power. The first two words signify appointed government and the authority which is committed to it, the last two the actual force and the moral force of dignity or lordship in which it is clothed.

(22) And hath put all things under his feet.—See I Cor. 15:25-28, where Paul deals with the quotation from Ps. 8:6, in application to our Lord's mediatorial kingdom. In this passage these words fill up the picture of our Lord's transcendent dignity, by the declaration of the actual subjugation of all the powers of sin and death, rising up against Him, in the spiritual war which is to go on until the appointed end.

And gave him to be the head over all things to the church, (23) which is his body. —This is the first time that this celebrated phrase is used. Here, in accordance with the great doctrine of this epistle—the unity of the whole of humanity and of the whole Church, ideally co-extensive with that humanity, with Christ—the body is looked upon as a whole, Christ as its Head (see 4:15, 16; 5:28; Col. 1:18; 2:19). With some variation it is expressed also in other metaphors—the building and the cornerstone, the bride and the bridegroom. But under the title of the "Head" Christ is looked upon especially in His ruling, guiding, originating power over the Church. Probably the idea of His being the seat of its life, though not excluded, is secondary; whereas in His own figure of the vine and the branches (John 15:6) it is primary.

The fulness of him that filleth all in all. —The word **pleroma,** "fulness," is used in a definite and almost technical sense in the epistles of the Captivity, and especially in the Epistle to the Colossians, having clear reference to the speculations as to the divine nature and the emanations from it, already anticipating the future Gnosticism. The word itself is derived from a verb signifying, first, to "fill," next (more frequently in the New Testament), to "fulfill" or **complete.** In these epistles it is applied, almost technically, to the fullness of the divine nature (see Col. 1:19; 2:9). As the individual, so the Church, by the presence "of Him who filleth up all things for Himself in all," comes to be "His fulness," the complete image of Him in all His glorified humanity. Thus by a daring expression, Paul describes our Lord as conceiving His glorified humanity incomplete without His Church; and then, lest this should seem to derogate even for a moment from His dignity, he adds the strongest declaration of His transcendent power, "to fill up for Himself all things in all," in order to show that we are infinitely more incomplete without Him than He without us.

2

(1) And you hath he quickened.—Paul here begins the particular application to the Ephesians, which is the main subject of this chapter, broken off in verses 3-10, and resumed in verse 11.

Trespasses and sins.—These two words, more often used separately, are here

brought together to form a climax. The word rendered "trespass" signifies a "swerving aside and falling"; the word rendered "sins" is generally used by Paul in the singular to denote "sin" in the abstract, and signifies an entire "missing of the mark" of life. Hence, even in the plural, it denotes universal and positive principles of evil doing, while "trespass" rather points to failure in visible and special acts of those not necessarily out of the right way.

(2) The course of this world.—Here again are united the two words often rendered by "world," the former signifying simply "the age," or appointed period of this visible universe, the latter its material and sensuous character. We are warned against the one in Rom. 12:2: the "vanity," that is, the transitoriness and unreality, of the present life; and against the other in Gal. 4:3; 6:14: its "pomp," its carnal, material unspiritual splendor. Here the former life of the Ephesians is described as at once transitory and carnal.

The prince of the power of the air.—The connection of the "world" with the Evil One as its "prince" is not uncommon in Holy Scripture (see John 12:31; 14:30; 16:11); and the "power" of this passage is exactly that which Satan claims as "committed" to him in Luke 4:33. The word "power" (see note on 1:21), both in the singular and the plural, is used in this epistle, almost technically, of superhuman power. Here, therefore, the Evil One is described as "the prince," or **ruler,** of such superhuman power—considered here collectively as a single power, prevailing over the world, and working in the children of disobedience—in the same sense in which he is called the "prince of the devils," the individual spirits of wickedness (Matt. 9:34; 12:24). The "air" is here meant simply to describe a sphere, and therefore a power, below the heaven and yet above the earth. The word and its derivatives carry with them the ideas of cloudiness, mist, and even darkness. Hence it is naturally used to suggest the conception of the evil power, as allowed invisibly to encompass and move above this world, yet overruled by the power of the true heaven, which it vainly strives to overcloud and hide from earth.

The spirit that now worketh in the children of disobedience.—The Greek here shows that the word "spirit" must be taken in apposition, not to "prince," but to "power." As the individual demons when considered as working on the human spirit are called spirits (Acts 19:12; I Tim. 4:1), so here the collective power of evil, considered as working in "the children of disobedience," is called "a spirit," like the "spirit of the world" (I Cor. 2:12), but here even more distinctly opposed to the "Spirit of God." (See Acts 10:28; 26:18; II Thess. 2:9.)

(3) Among whom also we all . . . —Up to this point Paul had addressed himself especially to the Ephesians as Gentiles; now he extends the description of alienation to "all," Jews and Gentiles alike, as formerly reckoned among the children of disobedience. It is indeed the great object of this chapter to bring out the equality and unity of both Jews and Gentiles in the Church of Christ; and this truth is naturally introduced by a statement of their former equality in alienation and sin.

And were by nature the children of wrath, even as others.—From this passage the phrase "children of wrath" has passed into Christian theology as an almost technical description of the unregenerate state. It is notable that the word for "children" here used is a term expressing endearment and love, and is accordingly properly, and almost invariably, applied to our relation to God. When, therefore, it is used as in this passage (comp. I John 3:10), there is clearly an intention to arrest the attention by a startling and paradoxical expression. The word "nature," applied to humanity, indicates what is common to all, as opposed to what is individual, or what is inborn, as opposed to what is acquired. But whether it refers to humanity as it was created by God, or to humanity as it has become by "fault and corruption of nature," must always be determined by the context. Here the reference is clearly to the latter. What is really original, however, in any case, is not sin, but righteousness.

(5, 6) The thought in these verses follows exactly the same course as in 1:19, 20. The type and earnest of the working of God's mighty power are placed in the Resurrection, the Ascension, the glorification of Christ Himself in His human nature. All Christians are declared to be quickened (or, **risen again**) to spiritual life with Christ, according to His promise (John 14:19). This partaking of the life of Christ is brought out as a partaking, not only of His resurrection (as in Rom. 6:5; I Cor. 15:20-22; Phil. 3:11), but also (in a phrase of thought peculiar to these epistles) of His Ascension "to the heavenly places." This is "in Christ Jesus," in virtue of a personal and individu-

al union with Christ. It implies blessings, both present and future, or rather one blessing, of which we have the earnest now and the fullness hereafter, for the Resurrection and Ascension of Christ are even now the perfection and glorification of humanity in Him. The one thing which Paul does not attribute to us is that which is His alone— the place "at the right hand of the Father."

(7) In his kindness.—The word "kindness" (properly, **facility,** or **readiness to serve another**) is applied to that phase of God's mercy in which it shows Him as ready to receive, and most willing to pardon. The repetition of the name of our Lord "through Christ Jesus" is appropriate, for this gentle patience and readiness to receive sinners was so marked a feature of His ministry that to the Pharisees it seemed an over-facility, weakly condoning sin. "Through Him," therefore, the kindness of God was both shown and given.

Verses 8-10 (taking up and working out the parenthetical "by grace ye are saved" of verse 5) form an instructive link of connection between these epistles and those of the earlier group, especially the Epistles to the Galatians and Romans. (Comp. Phil. 3:9.) In both there is the same doctrine of justification by faith, the same denial of the merit of good works, the same connection of good works with the grace of God in us. But what is there anxiously and passionately contended for, is here briefly summarized, and calmly assumed as a thing known and allowed.

(8) By grace are ye saved through faith.— Properly, **ye have been saved**; ye were saved at first, and continue in a state of salvation. In verse 5 this thought is introduced parenthetically, naturally and irresistibly suggested by the declaration of the various steps of regeneration in Christ. Paul now returns to it and works it out, before passing on, in verse 11, to draw out by "wherefore" the conclusion from verses 1-7. Remembering how the epistles were written from dictation, we may be inclined to see in this passage, among others, an insertion made by the apostle, on a revision of that already written.

The two phrases "justification by faith" and "salvation by grace" are popularly identified, and, indeed, are substantially identical in meaning. But the latter properly lays stress on a more advanced stage of the process of redemption in Christ. Thus, in Rom. 5:9, 10, salvation is spoken of as following on the completed act of justification; and it is described here and elsewhere as a continuous process, a state continuing till the final judgment. Hence to lay special stress on salvation accords better with the whole idea of this epistle—the continuous indwelling in Christ—than to bring out, as in the Epistle to the Romans, the one complete act of justification for His sake. It is to be noted that the use of the name "Saviour," applied both to God and to Christ, belongs entirely to the later epistles. It is used once in this epistle (5:23) and in Phil. 3:20, but no less than ten times in the Pastoral Epistles of Paul, and five times in Second Peter. The phrase in the text is, as always in this epistle, theologically exact. Grace is the moving cause of salvation, faith only the instrument by which it is laid hold of.

And that not of yourselves: it is the gift of God.—This attribution of all to the gift of God seems to cover the whole idea—both the gift of salvation and the gift of faith to accept it. The former part is enforced by the words "not of works" (verse 9), the latter by the declaration "we are his workmanship" (verse 10).

(9) Not of works, lest any man should boast.—In this verse we have the echo of the past Judaizing controversy; it sums up briefly the whole argument of Rom. 3:27-4:25. There is a similar reminiscence, but more distinct and detached, in Phil. 3:2-9.

(10) We are his workmanship.—This verse, on the contrary, is unique and remarkable, characteristic of the idea with which this epistle starts—the election and predestination of God, making us what we are—and applying it very strikingly, not only to the first regeneration, but even to the good works which follow it. The word rendered "workmanship" is only used elsewhere in Rom. 1:20, where it is applied to the "works" of God in creation. Probably here also it does not exclude our first creation. We are His wholly and absolutely. But the next clause shows that Paul refers especially to the "new creation" in Christ Jesus (comp. II Cor. 5:17; Gal. 6:15).

Unto good works.—Properly, **on the basis** (or, **condition**) **of good works** (as in Gal. 5:13; I Thess. 4:17; II Tim. 2:14). The good works, in themselves future, are contemplated as already existent in God's foreknowledge, and as an inseparable characteristic of the regenerate life.

There is, perhaps, in all Scripture, no stronger expression of the great mystery of God's predestination than the clause that follows, for it is here declared in reference, not only to the original call and justification and regeneration of the soul, but also to the actual good works, in which the free-will and energy of man are most plainly exercised. Comp. much the same sense in Phil. 3:12, 13.

(11) Gentiles in the flesh—i.e., not having the bodily impress of circumcision, sealing the Jewish covenant.

Who are called Uncircumcision by that which is called the Circumcision.—The use of the phrase "called"—with a touch of the contempt implied in our phrase "the so-called"—simply implies that now Circumcision and Uncircumcision were mere names, virtually "nothing." The declaration of the nullity of circumcision as a religious distinction is often repeated, yet takes various forms. See I Cor. 7:19; Gal. 5:6; 6:15; Col. 3:11. (Comp. also the whole argument of Rom. 2:25-4:12.)

In the flesh made by hands.—Paul, however, not content with this, suggests by the addition of these last words a contrast between the false or carnal, and the true or spiritual circumcision, attributing the former to the unbelieving Jews, the latter to all Christians. This contrast is expressly announced in the other epistles of this period. (See Phil. 3:2, 3; Col. 2:11.)

(12) This verse gives a dark and terrible picture of the former heathen condition of the Ephesians, intentionally contrasted in every point with the description of Christian privilege in verses 19, 20. That condition is first summed up in one expression. They were "separate from Christ." Then from this are drawn two gloomy consequences: first, that they had no part in God's special covenant; next, that they had "no hope" of spiritual life and immortality, and were "godless" in thought and act. On the first it is to be noted that the covenant with Israel, as it was held in trust for the blessing of "all families of the earth," so also was simply the true birthright of humanity, from which mankind had fallen. The first "covenant" in Scripture (Gen. 9:8-17) is with the whole of the post-diluvian race, and is expressly connected with the reality of "the image of God" in man (Gen. 9:6). The succeeding covenants (as with Abraham, Moses, and David) all contain a promise concerning the whole race of man. Hence the Gentiles were exiles from what should have been their home; and their call into the Church of Christ was a restoration of God's wandering children. In relation to the next, we observe that Paul's description ought to be applied strictly, not to heathen life in its nobler and purer forms, but to the heathen life of Asia Minor in his days. What that was in moral degradation and in loss of all spiritual religion, ill compensated by the inevitable proneness to various superstitions, all contemporary literature testifies. From it came, as the Romans declared, the corruption which overspread the whole empire, and which Paul describes so terribly in Rom. 1:18-32.

(13) This verse speaks of the restoration of the heathen as taking place, first, in virtue of union with Christ through all the acts of His mediation; and next, through that special act of mediation, which is emphatically an atonement for sin—such sin as Paul had been declaring above to be the cause of spiritual deadness. They had power now "to enter into the holiest by the blood of Jesus" (Heb. 10:19).

(14) He is our peace.—Here only is our Lord called not the giver of peace, but the peace itself—His own nature being the actual tie of unity between God and mankind, and between man and man. Through the whole passage thus introduced there runs a double meaning, a declaration of peace in Christ between Jew and Gentile, and between both and God.

Who hath made both one, and hath broken down the middle wall of partition between us.—The reunion of Jew and Gentile is thus described. "The middle wall of the hedge" refers, perhaps, to the wall separating the court of the Gentiles from the Temple proper (Jos. **Ant.** 15 §5), and by an inscription denouncing death to any alien who passed it. It may be noted that the charge of bringing Trophimus, an Ephesian, beyond that Temple wall had been the cause of Paul's apprehension at Jerusalem (Acts 21:29), and nearly of his death. Hence the Asiatic churches might well be familiar with its existence. This Temple-partition suits perfectly the double sense of this passage, for, while it was primarily a separation between Jew and Gentile, it was also the first of many partitions—of which the "veil of the Temple" was the last—cutting all men off from the immediate presence of God. At our Lord's death the last of these partitions was rent in two. How much more may that death be described as breaking down the first!

(15) Having abolished in his flesh the

enmity, **even the law of commandments contained in ordinances.**—Comp. Col. 2:14. The word rendered "to abolish" is the word used by Paul for "to supersede by something better than itself"—translated "to make void" in Rom. 3:31, and to "bring to nought" in I Cor. 1:28. The Law, therefore, is abolished as a law "in ordinances"—that is, "in the letter"—and is established in the spirit. Christ, "the end of the law," has superseded by the free covenant of the Spirit the formal commandments enforced by penalties on disobedience, and He has done this for us "in His flesh," especially by His death and resurrection. But in what sense is this Law called "the enmity," which (see verse 16) was "slain" on the cross? Probably first, as a cause of separation and hostility between the Gentiles and those Jews whom they called "the enemies of the human race," and next, as a cause of alienation and condemnation between man and God through the rebellion and sin of man. (Comp. Heb. 10:19.)

For to make in himself of twain one new man, so making peace.—In this clause and the following verse the two senses, hitherto united are now distinguished from each other. This phrase, "the new man" (see 4:24; Col. 3:10), is peculiar to these epistles, corresponding, however, to the "new creature" of II Cor. 5:17; Gal. 6:15, and the "newness of life" and "spirit" of Rom. 6:4; 7:6. Christ Himself is the "second man, the Lord from heaven" (I Cor. 15:47).

(16) On the reconciliation of man to God, see the great passage II Cor. 5:18-21. But it should be noted that in the original the word used here and in Col. 1:20, 21 (and nowhere else) is a compound signifying not simply "conciliate," but properly to "reconcile"—that is to reunite those who were originally united, but afterward separated by the sin of man. This brings out the profound idea, which so especially characterizes these epistles, of a primeval unity of all created being in Christ, marred and broken by sin, and restored by His manifestation in human flesh. On the other hand, this passage characteristically still lays stress on the idea "in one body"—that is, as throughout, His mystical body, the Church—although probably the phrase is suggested here by the thought of the natural body of the Lord offered on the cross, which is clearly referred to in Col. 1:21.

(18) For through him we both have access by one Spirit unto the Father.—In this verse the two meanings again unite. The greater idea of access to God is still prominent; but the lesser idea of union with each other in that access is still traceable as an undertone. "Access" is properly "the introduction," a technical word of presentation to a royal presence. So says Chrysostom, "We came not of ourselves, but He brought us in." (Comp. I Pet. 3:18.) We have here one of the implicit declarations of the doctrine of the Holy Trinity, so frequent in this epistle. The unity of the whole Church, as united "to the Father," "through the Son," and "in the Spirit," is here summed up in one sentence, but with as much perfection and clearness as even when it is unfolded in the great passage, 4:4-6.

(19) Strangers and foreigners.—Here the word rendered "stranger" means properly **an alien**, or foreigner, and is opposed to "fellow-citizen"; while the word translated "foreigners," opposed to members of the "household of God," signifies the resident aliens of an ancient city, who were but **half-aliens**, having free intercourse with the citizens, although no rights of citizenship. As to the metaphor, the unit in ancient law was always the family, and not the individual. The Gentiles were now brought into a "household," and that household the household of God Himself.

(20-22) In these verses there is a sudden change from a political to a physical metaphor, possibly suggested by the word "household." The metaphor of the Church as "a building of God" reaches its full perfection in this passage. This conception of unity is less absolute than that conveyed by the metaphor of the body. It differs from it in three respects: first, it carries with it the notion of a more distinct individuality in each stone; next, it conveys (as in the "graffing in" of Rom. 11:17) the idea of continual growth by accretion of individual souls drawn to Christ; lastly, it depicts the Church as having more completely a distinct, though not a separate, existence from Him who dwells in it.

(20) Built upon the foundation of the apostles and prophets.—In spite of much ancient and valuable authority, it seems impossible to take "the prophets" of this verse to be the prophets of the Old Testament (comp. 3:5; 4:11). Emphasis on the present runs through the whole chapter. The most natural interpretation, furthermore, makes the apostles and prophets to be themselves "the foundation." It is clear that in this passage Paul deliberately varies the metaphor in relation to our Lord, making

Him not the foundation, or both foundation and cornerstone, but simply the cornerstone, "binding together," according to Chrysostom's instructive remark, "both the walls and the foundations." The genius therefore of this passage itself, supported by the other cognate passages, leads us to what may be granted to be an unexpected but a perfectly intelligible expression.

Jesus Christ himself being the chief corner stone.—Comp. Ps. 118:22; Matt. 21:42; Mark 12:10; Luke 20:17; Acts 4:11. In Isa. 28:16; I Pet. 2:6, 7, it may be noted that both the metaphors are united, and "the tried cornerstone" is also "the sure foundation." It appears to mean a massive cornerstone, in which the two lines of the wall at their foundation met, by which they were bonded together, and on the perfect squareness of which the true direction of the whole walls depended, since the slightest imperfection in the cornerstone would be indefinitely multiplied along the course of the walls. The doctrine which, if taken alone, it would convey is simply the acceptance of our Lord's perfect teaching and life, as the one determining influence both of the teaching and institutions which are the basis of the Church and of the superstructure in the actual life of the members of the Church itself. That this is not the whole truth seems to be implied by the variation from the metaphor in the next verse, for the cornerstone is only a part, though a dominant part, of the building (Comp. 4:16.)

3

(1) The prisoner of Jesus Christ.—The phrase is repeated in 4:1; Phlm. 9; II Tim. 1:8. In this passage Paul seems to speak of his captivity as a special proof of the reality of his mission and a new step in its progress (comp. 6:20; Phil. 1:13, 14; Phlm. 13); and he appeals to it, accordingly, just as in the final salutation of the Colossian epistle, "Remember my bonds."

For you Gentiles.—This was literally true of the origin of his captivity, proceeding as it did from the jealousy of the Jews, excited by the free admission of the Gentiles to the Church; but the reference is not to be limited to this. Paul regards the captivity as only one incident in a mission sending him entirely to the Gentiles (Acts 21:21; Rom. 11:13; Gal. 2:9). From these words the digression of verses 2-13 starts, bringing out the reality and greatness of that mission.

(2) If ye have heard.—The passage bears on the question whether the epistle was an encyclical letter or one addressed to the Ephesian Church. The argument which has been drawn from it in the former direction is not as strong as appears in the English, for the original implies no doubt that the readers of the epistle had heard, and the hearing might have been not about Paul, but from Paul himself. Still, there is a vague generality about the expression which suits well an address to the Asiatic churches generally, but could hardly have been used to a church so well known and beloved as Ephesus, where "the signs of an apostle" had been wrought abundantly.

The dispensation of the grace of God which is given me to you-ward.—The grace of God is spoken of as given to Paul, not so much for his own sake, as for ministration to them of the dispensation," that is (comp. 1:10), the peculiar office in the ministration of the grace of God to the world, assigned to Paul by His wisdom.

(3) How that by revelation he made known unto me the mystery.—The words "by revelation" are doubly emphatic. This revelation we may refer especially to Acts 22:17-21.

(As I wrote afore in few words.)—The reference is to 1:10-14 and 2:11-22. It is one of those parenthetical remarks, which, remembering how Paul's epistles were dictated, almost irresistibly suggest insertion on the reading over the epistle.

(5) Although it is probably wrong to restrict to the children of Israel, or to the prophets, words which by their very nature apply to all mankind, yet the phrase "sons of men" seems to be used with a suggestion of the contrast between the old dispensation and the new. The application of the epithet "holy" to the apostle has been thought strange as coming from one of their number; and it is worth notice that this exceptional application is certainly more appropriate to the comparatively impersonal style of an encyclical epistle. But the epithet (applied to the Old Testament prophets in Luke 1:70; Acts 3:21; II Pet. 3:2), like the frequent use of it as the substantive "saints," in application to all Christians, refers not to personal character but to official call and privilege.

(6) In Christ by the gospel.—These words should be joined with all the three preceding. Of all the privileges of the new life— acceptance by God, incorporation into the mystical Body, and enjoyment of spiritual blessings—the being "in Christ" is the substance, the reception of the Gospel in faith the instrument.

(8) Less than the least of all saints.— Comp. I Cor. 15:9, 10; II Cor. 11:30; 12:9-11; I Tim. 1:12-16. It may be noted that in each case his deep sense of unworthiness is brought out by the thought of God's special grace and favor to him.

The unsearchable riches of Christ.—The word "unsearchable" properly carries with it the metaphor (latent in our word "investigate") of tracking the footsteps, but not tracking them completely to their source or issue—thus gaining an evidence of a living power, but of no other particulars. Here it is applied to that "wealth" or fullness of Christ on which this epistle lays such special stress, as a wealth of truth which we can see in part but cannot wholly measure, and a wealth of grace which we can enjoy but cannot exhaust.

(9, 10) The New Testament constantly dwells on the mediation of Christ as belonging in some form to the relation of humanity to God in itself, and not merely to that relation as affected by the Fall. Paul then passes on to consider the manifestation of God in Christ as brought home not only to the race of man but to the angels, who are described (I Pet. 1:12) as "desiring to look into" the consummation of the gospel mystery. (Comp. I Cor. 4:9; Heb. 12:22.) Angels are represented to us as not only ministering in the Church of Christ, but learning from its existence and fortunes to know more and more of the wisdom of God. The world, itself a speck in the universe, may be—perhaps as a scene of exceptional rebellion against God, certainly as a scene of God's infinite goodness—a lesson to other spheres of being, far beyond our conception.

(13) There is a peculiar beauty in the thought suggested by the words "which is your glory." Here Paul pursues the same line of thought as in I Cor. 4:10—there half ironically, here seriously—that, while the suffering falls on himself, the glory passes to the Church, for which he suffers, and in which he is content to sink himself. Hence he bids the Ephesians find encouragement and glory for themselves, instead of a cause for "fainting," in the afflictions endured on their behalf and overcome in Christ. As he identifies himself with them, so he would have them take what might be his glory to be their own.

(15) Of whom the whole family in heaven

and earth is named, that is, every body of rational beings in earth or heaven united under one common fatherhood, and bearing the name (as in a family or clan) of the common ancestor. The apostle looks upon the fathers whose names they delight to bear as the imperfect representatives of God, and upon the family itself, with its head, as the type in miniature of the whole society of spiritual beings united in sonship to the Father in heaven.

(16) To be strengthened with might by his Spirit in the inner man.—From the Father, as the source of all life and being, Paul passes on to the Spirit, "proceeding from the Father," as the giver of life to men. The inner man is represented here (as in Rom. 7:22; II Cor. 4:16) in his entirety, including all faculties—intellectual, emotional, moral—which make up his spiritual nature. And Paul emphasizes this prayer strikingly by asking that the gift may be unlimited as the illimitable glory of the divine Nature itself. Moreover, a closeness of communion is clearly indicated here, for strength comes from an indwelling power, making itself perfect in weakness, and continually growing from grace to grace.

(17) That Christ may dwell in your hearts by faith.—What that indwelling power is he now indicates, so passing to another Person of the Holy Trinity. It is (see Col. 1:27) "Christ in you, the hope of glory." The indwelling of Christ (as here the construction of the original plainly shows) is not a consequence of the gift of the Spirit; it is identical with it, for the office of the Holy Spirit is to implant and work out in us the likeness of Christ. (See John 14:16-20; Gal. 2:20.) Faith is simply the condition of that indwelling of Christ (comp. 2:8), the opening of the door to Him that He may enter in.

The prayer is here complete, all that follows being but consequent from it. In accordance with the universal law of revelation, all is from the Father, all is through the Son vouchsafing to tabernacle in our humanity, all is by the Spirit effecting that indwelling of Christ in each individual soul.

That ye, being rooted and grounded in love.—The idea implied in "rooted" is of the striking down deeper and spreading wider into the soil; in "grounded" ("founded") of the firm basis on which ultimately we rest. Love is not itself the root or foundation (for this is Jesus Christ Himself), but the condition under which growth takes place. Here that growth is downward,

deeper and deeper into the communio with God in Christ. As in relation to mar so also to God, love is at once the recogn tion of an existing unity between spirit an spirit, and probably the only means of mak ing that unity energetic and deepening continually. Hence love is the first conse quence of the indwelling of Christ in th soul; and by it the soul becomes rooted an grounded in the unity, given by that indwel ling, with man and God.

(18) May be able to comprehend with al saints what is the breadth, and length, an depth, and height.—Of what? Paul has ob viously of set purpose omitted all defini tion. If anything is to be supplied, it shoul probably be "of the mystery"—i.e., of th whole mystery on which Paul had bee dwelling, including the predestination, th redemption, the call and union of Jews an Gentiles. The prayer is that we may know i every way, in every direction in which th soul can go forth toward God.

It may be noted that comprehension i placed after love, just as in Phil. 1:9. Th spiritual order of revelation differs fron that of the "wisdom of the world." It ha first faith, next love, and finally knowledge because its object is a person, not an ab stract principle.

(19) To know the love of Christ, whicl passeth knowledge.—In the original, th word "to know" is in a tense which ex presses cognition in a particular case; henc the meaning of Paul's prayer seems to b that they may know from time to time, a each opportunity offers, what must in it entirety pass all human knowledge, either tc discover or fully to understand, even wher revealing itself; so that they may always gc on from faith to faith, from knowledge tc knowledge, and yet find new depths still tc be fathomed. The "love of Christ" is the love which He bears to us, and which is the motive of His sacrifice for our redemption.

That ye might be filled with all the ful ness of God.—This clause must be taken as dependent on the whole sentence. It de scribes the final and glorious consequence of the indwelling of Christ in the heart. The meaning is more clearly seen in 4:13. The process of conformation is described in II Cor. 3:18, its consummation in I John 3:2.

(21) In the parallelism of these clauses is implied the great idea of the epistle—the unity of the Church in Christ. Hence all that is "in the Church" is "in Christ Jesus." The visible unity of the Church represents, as it depends on, the invisible unity with

God in Him. And each generation adds its own peculiar thanksgiving to the great chorus of praise which fills eternity.

4

(1) Worthy of the vocation wherewith ye are called.—This "being worthy of the Christian calling" may obviously show itself in any of the graces of regenerate humanity, all being features of the image of Christ. (Comp. I Pet. 1:15; Phil. 1:27-30.) In this passage the special point which has been dwelt upon in their calling is the fact that they were aliens, helpless and miserable, and that they are now united in one body with the ancient people of God. Hence, naturally, the graces declared to correspond with their calling, so viewed, are the graces of humility and gentleness, teaching them to sink all thought of self in "the unity of the Spirit."

(2) With all lowliness and meekness, with longsuffering.—See Col. 3:12, and the first, third, and fifth beatitudes of the Sermon on the Mount. The word "lowliness of mind" is a word newly coined in Christian terminology, and even the root from which it comes is used mostly by the heathen moralists in a bad sense of meanness and slavishness. "Meekness" is mostly "gentleness," the natural, though not the invariable, fruit of humility, winning souls by its very absence of bitter self-assertion, and so "inheriting the earth." "Longsuffering" is the manifestation of such meekness, with something of special effort and struggle in the bearing of injury.

(2, 3) The word rendered "endeavouring" is, in the original, a word expressing "earnestness" of thought and exertion to secure a thing not lightly obtained. Paul here passes from the negative aspects of love, summed up in forbearance, to the more positive and energetic enthusiasm for unity and peace. Love is in both aspects the "uniting bond" of peace (comp. Col. 3:14). But, if love be real, it must necessarily pass into active energy (comp. I Cor. 13:4-7); if it is to win the final beatitude of "blessing to the peacemakers," it must labor for peace.

(3) The unity of the Spirit is certainly the unity given by the indwelling of the Holy Ghost. This we cannot create, for it is the gift of God; but we can "keep" it, that is, cherish it, guard it, and make it effectual by love. And all experience proves that, if we would so keep it, we need the positive

earnestness of exertion against evils without and within.

(5) One Lord, one faith.—From the idea of "the calling," uniting in spite of inequalities and strifes, the apostle passes naturally to Him who calls and to the method of His calling to Himself. It is on the indwelling of Christ in each heart by faith that the spiritual unity of all Christians—primarily with Him, secondarily with one another—depends; and that spiritual unity is "put on" in baptism (Gal. 3:27).

(6) One God and Father of all.—We cannot limit this universal. Fatherhood, although, undoubtedly, the context shows that the immediate reference is to those who are His children by adoption in Jesus Christ. The Church is essentially catholic, inheriting by special gift what is the birthright of all humanity.

Verses 7-11 pass from the unity of the Church to the diversity of graces and offices in its members, all being gifts of the ascended Lord, and results of that universal mediation which fills all things.

(8) Wherefore he saith.—The reference is to Ps. 68, a psalm which (as the quotation from Num. 10:35, in the first verse, shows) is a psalm celebrating some moving of the Ark, traditionally connected with David's bringing up of the Ark (II Sam. 6) to Mount Zion. The text of the original runs, **Thou receivedst gifts in man**—a clause which (from verses 29-31) we may suppose to refer to the homage of the heathen to the Lord Jehovah. The psalm was recognized as a Messianic psalm, foreshadowing the dwelling of "God with us" in the universal kingdom of the true Mediator. Paul accordingly uses it with a bold variation suiting his context.

He led captivity captive.—In the original it is simply "a body of captives." Paul's use here is probably best interpreted by Col. 2:15.

(9) The lower parts of the earth.—This may mean either **the regions of the earth**, as "lower" than heaven, or the **regions beneath the earth**. The reasoning of the text in itself would be satisfied by the former. But form and usage of the phrase itself seem to point to the other meaning, which is held by almost all ancient interpreters. It agrees with the strong expression of "filling all things" in verse 10, and it may be thought to correspond by antithesis to the "far above all heavens" of the next verse.

(10) That he might fill all things.—Comp. 1:23. In both cases the reference is to the gift of the fullness of His grace, flowing from His glorified humanity to all His members. But the words here are too wide for any spatial limitation.

(11) He gave.—In the original, "He" is emphatic—He and He alone, as the ascended Head of humanity. The word "gave," instead of the more obvious word **set**, or **appointed**, is suggested by verse 8. They who are ministers of His gifts are themselves gifts from Him to the Church.

Some, apostles; and some, prophets ...—Comp. Rom. 12:6-8; I Cor. 12:28. In all three cases there is the same general idea, first of the one body, and then of the one Spirit, guiding and animating it through various ministries.

Some, apostles.—The name "apostles" is certainly used here in its technical and restricted sense, as applying to the Twelve, with whom Paul claims equality. It is, indeed, used in a wider sense, with words distinctly implying a derivation and human mission, as in II Cor. 8:23 and Phil. 2:25. But such use is rare and cannot be applied to a passage like this, which is distinctive of a special and primary class. The apostles, properly so called, stood out in office absolutely unique and supreme.

Some, prophets.—For the nature and function of prophecy in the Church, see the detailed treatment in I Cor. 14. From very early times the "prophets" are mentioned as a separate class, distinguished from teachers, and in this epistle especially they are spoken of, in connection with the apostles, as being the foundation of the Church. Their office, like the Apostolate, is clearly extraordinary, distinct from the ordinary and permanent teaching of the evangelists and pastors.

Some, evangelists; and some, pastors and teachers.—Here is the twofold office of the regular ministry of the Church—first, to preach the Gospel to the heathen or the unconverted, and next, to fulfill our Lord's pastoral charge (John 21:15-17) of feeding and shepherding those who are already His sheep. It is clear that the same person may be invested with the two offices (as Timothy), and that in some degree the two offices must always be united. But the two elements of duty will co-exist in different proportions in different persons.

(12) The perfecting of the saints.—The word rendered "perfecting" is derived from a root which signifies either to "mend" what is broken (as in Matt. 4:21), or to "complete" what is unfinished (as in Luke

6:40; Rom. 9:22); hence it is used spiritual for to "restore" the fallen (Gal. 6:1), or t "perfect" the imperfect Christian (I Thess 3:10; Heb. 13:21). Both processes are neces sarily implied. Some ministries are mor blessed to the individual perfecting of th saints, others to the building up of th whole Church.

(13) Till we all come.—The full grasp o that faith is the first object of all the minis tries of the Church, since by it both th individual perfection and the corporate uni ty begin to be secured. Such faith alway goes on to knowledge.

Of the Son of God.—These words shoul be connected with the word "faith" (as ir Gal. 2:20) as well as "knowledge." They ar probably to be considered as a distinctive phrase, designating our Lord especially a glorified and exalted to the right hand o the Father. (See Rom. 1:4; Heb. 4:14.) Not in John's First Epistle the constant refer ence to the belief in and confession of Jesu as "the Son of God" as the one thing needful (4:15; 5:5, 10-12, 20), for on th belief not only of what He was on earth, bu of what He is in heaven, all distinctive Christianity depends.

Unto a perfect man, unto the measure of the stature of the fulness of Christ.—Ir these words are described the second grea object of the ministries of the Church. Thi image of Christ in "fulness" is the absolute ly perfect humanity, showing forth the image of God. Each can partake of it only up to "the measure" which God gives him (See verse 7.) When he so partakes of it to the utmost, he is "full-grown" (relatively not absolutely, perfect) up to the spiritual "stature" assigned to him. On the word "fulness," see note on 1:23.

(14) That we ... be no more children.—Here the process of growth is described negatively, in the next verse positively. The word "children" used here is a word almost always applied in a bad sense, like our word "childish"—not to the guilelessness, the trustfulness, or the humility of children, which our Lord emphatically blessed (Matt. 18:2-4), but to their unforeseeing and unthinking impulsiveness. (Comp. I Cor. 3:1; Gal. 4:1.) The description is of liability to disturbance and change by every external impression from without.

Tossed to and fro, and carried about with every wind of doctrine.—The metaphor is of a ship drifting at the mercy of a storm. Then the evil influences to which childish instability is a prey are described—first, as

e sleight of hand of the dice-thrower,
escribing quick, sudden deceit of detail;
ext, as a craftiness devoted to the systemat-
: plan of deceit, thus referring to deeper
nd subtler forms of delusion. This refer-
nce is so definite in the original that we
re tempted to believe Paul to have had in
iew some particular scheme of erroneous
:aching (perhaps Gnosticism), which had
lready struck root in the soil of Asia
1inor. The Epistle to the Colossians shows
1at such false teaching had appeared at
'olossae.

(15) But speaking the truth in love.—The
orrect rendering is, **being true in love,**
1cluding in this the "being true" to others,
y speaking truly and acting honestly
>ward them (as in Gal. 4:16), but including
lso the "being true" absolutely—that is, the
oving the truth and clinging to it at all
osts. The latter element, indeed, is the one
vhich stands here more properly in antithe-
is to the childish instability described in
he preceding verse, as it is in itself the
nore important, and is, in fact, the only
>asis for the other. This "being true" is
xpressed in many forms. (See John 3:21;
':44; 18:37; I John 1:8; 2:21; II John 4.)

The head, even Christ.—In this name of
ur Lord we have the link of connection
>etween the individual perfection and cor-
>orate unity. He is (as in I Cor. 11:3) the
lead of each man. He is also the Head of
he whole Church.

(16) By that which every joint supplieth.—
The word employed has commonly the
neaning of "joint," and is so used by Greek
>hysiologists; but its original sense is ab-
tract—the "joining" or "touching"—and
ippears the simplest here. The supply
comp. Phil. 1:19) is again almost a techni-
:al word for the abundant outflow of
trength and nervous energy from the head.
-Hence the phrase seems to stand in closer
:onnection with the "maketh increase" be-
ow than the "compacted together" above.
The body grows, in every part of its com-
>lex unity, through contact with the divine
supply of grace through the head.

(17) This I say therefore.—Here the prac-
:ical section of the epistle begins. The
>hrase seems to be used by Paul in return-
ing from some lofty aspiration or profound
reasoning, in which some might not be able
to follow him, to a solid, practical ground,
which all may tread.

The vanity of their mind.—In these
words Paul describes the fundamental condition of heathenism. The "mind," that is,

the "inner man"—the spiritual intuition of
invisible principles of truth and right, which
is the true humanity—has become "subject
to vanity—the vanity of which the Book of
Ecclesiastes so often speaks. In losing the
living conception of a living God, it has lost
also the conception of the true object and
perfection of human life. With what absolute fidelity Paul describes the heathen
world of his day, its history and its literature alike testify. (Comp. Rom. 1:21-32.) In
that passage the prominent idea is mainly of
"judicial blindness," sent by God as a penalty on willful apostasy from Him; here Paul
rather dwells on self-chosen blindness (intellectual) and hardness of heart (moral).

(19) Paul continues the metaphor of cal-
lousness: **they have lost the capacity of
pain**—the moral pain which is the natural
and healthful consequence of sin against our
true natures. Consequently, losing in this
their true humanity, they give themselves
over to "lasciviousness." The word used
here signifies a lust devoid of all sense of
decency, recklessly and grossly animal.
Hence its result is not only to work out
uncleanness of every kind, but to do so
"with greediness," with a reckless delight in
foulness for its own sake. The union of this
brutality of sensual sin with intellectual
acuteness and aesthetic culture was the most
horrible feature of that corrupt Greek civilization, tainted with Oriental grossness, of
which he was especially writing.

(20) Ye have not so learned Christ.—The
name "the Christ" is here used emphatically, in distinction from the "Jesus" of the
next verse. "To learn the Christ" is to enter
into the true meaning of His office as
Mediator, in whom we escape from the
guilt and bondage of the sins described
above.

(21) As the truth is in Jesus.—The use of
the simple name Jesus, so common in the
gospels, is rare indeed in the epistles, where
we constantly find the fuller description
"Jesus Christ," "the Lord Jesus," "Jesus the
Son of God." Wherever it occurs, it will be
found to be distinctive or emphatic. This
distinctiveness is most strikingly evident in
Rom. 8:11: the "raising up of Jesus" is the
historical resurrection of Jesus of Nazareth;
the "raising up the Christ" points to the
mysterious effect of that resurrection on
those for whom He is the Mediator. Other
passages in which the simple name occurs
are usually either mere reiterations with the
due title of honor or of a creed declaring
the historic Jesus. In the Epistle to the

1043

Hebrews, where, in accordance with one main purpose of the epistle, this usage is least rare, in all cases either special stress is laid on the lowly and suffering humanity of the Lord, or the historic facts of His ministry on earth are in reference. The familiar use of the simple name "Jesus" has little authority in apostolic usage.

(22) Concerning the former conversation—that is, as concerns the mode of life described in verses 17-19 as the moral condition of heathenism. It is in relation to this, the corruption of the true humanity, and not in relation to the true humanity itself, that the "old man" is put off. The word rendered "corrupt" expresses not so much pollution as disintegration and decay. The unregenerate nature, subject to the lusts of the spirit of delusion, is gradually sinking into the spiritual decay which must become spiritual death, unless by the effort of faith, entering into the communion with Christ, it be once for all "put off." The qualities of the nature thus stripped off are variously described in Rom. 13:12; Heb. 12:1; Jas. 1:21; I Pet. 2:1.

(24) And that ye put on . . . —The effect of "the putting off of the old man" is at once absorbed in the stronger idea of "putting on the new man." Here is implied not merely youthfulness, but the freshness of a higher nature. To "put on the new man" is, therefore, to "put on the Lord Jesus Christ" by that divine process of which we have the beginning in Gal. 3:27, the continuation in Rom. 13:14, and the completion in I Cor. 15:53, 54; II Cor. 5:3.

Holiness.—The last part of this verse should read "holiness of truth." (The word is used elsewhere only in Luke 1:75.) It describes the "purity of heart" of which our Lord Himself speaks as a still higher grace, gifted with a higher reward, than even "hunger and thirst after righteousness" (Matt. 5:6, 8). "Righteousness" is goodness shown to others, to man and to God; "holiness" is goodness in itself. Stress is laid upon it here in contrast with the lusts and uncleanness described above. "Truth" is similarly opposed to the "deceit" of verse 22. Christ is Himself "the Truth." And Truth is the first condition of the mutual confidence which is the basis of all unity (verse 25).

(26) Be ye angry, and sin not.—A quotation from the LXX version of Ps. 4:4. Anger itself is not sin, for our Lord Himself felt it (Mark 3:5) at the "hardness of men's hearts." It is frequently attributed to God Himself, in language no doubt of human accommodation. In the form of resentment it performs a stimulating function in the strife against evil. But it is a dangerous and exceptional weapon, and hence the exhortation "sin not" and its practical enforcement.

Let not the sun go down upon your wrath.—In this command (for which a Pythagorean parallel may be found) Paul gives a twofold safeguard against abuse of even righteous anger. It is not to be prolonged beyond the sleep which ends the old day and leads in the freshness of the new, and for which any godly man must prepare in commendation of himself to God and in prayer for His forgiveness. It is not to be brooded over and stimulated. The word "wrath" is properly **self-exasperation**, that "nursing of wrath to keep it warm," which can be checked even by those who cannot control the first outburst, and which constantly corrupts righteous indignation into selfish personal anger, if not into malignity.

(27) Neither give place to the devil.—The name "Satan" simply describes him as "the enemy"; "devil" describes one method of his enmity (as "the Tempter" another), for it signifies "one who sets at variance," makes with God, and man with man. Since this fiendish work is mostly contemplated as wrought by slander, "devil" is commonly taken to mean "the slanderer." Excess of wrath is forbidden as giving opportunity to the enemy, who desires to break up unity and "set at variance" those who should be one in Jesus Christ.

(28) Let him that stole steal no more . . —In this verse Paul is not content with forbidding dishonesty, but he directs that it be superseded by the opposite spirit of self-sacrifice, working in order to give to others what is honestly our own. The sense of unity will always exhibit itself in working, what is "good" (verse 29) for the sake of others.

(30) And grieve not the holy Spirit.—This verse refers to all practical commands given above. The four cardinal sins forbidden—falsehood, anger, theft, and corrupt speech—are regarded as "grieving the Holy Spirit of God." In that expression, even more than in the cognate expressions of Thess. 5:19 and Acts 7:51, there is implied a personal relation to a divine Person, capable of being "grieved" by our transgressions, partly as sins against His perfect holiness, partly as suicidal rejections of His unfailing love. This sin effects the marring of the Body.

Whereby ye are sealed.—See notes on :13, 14. The "sealing unto the day of redemption" reminds us of the glorious consummation to which we are destined, and from which every sin is a falling off. The very thought of this perfection, with all its associations of purity and love, should shame us from sin.

(31) Let all bitterness.—There is a similar numeration in the parallel passage, Col. :8. Here the first symptom of the temper forbidden is "bitterness," or **sharpness**—that is, an acerbity of temper, ready to take offense and break out in anger. The next stage is passionate outburst and the deeper anger of which it is at once effect and cause. In these the smoldering bitterness kindles into flame. The last stage is "clamour," being the loud fury of the first burst of wrath, passing into the more deliberate "evil speaking," as the temper cools down without losing its settled anger ("malice").

(32) Kind ... tenderhearted.—"Kindness" is gentleness in bearing with wrong. "Tenderheartedness" is more positive warmth of sympathy and love. Both issue in free "forgiveness," after the model of the universal and unfailing forgiveness "of God in Christ" to us. (See Luke 6:36.)

5

(1) Followers of God, literally, **imitators of God.** The word "therefore" implies that his imitation of God must be chiefly in His essential attribute of love. (Comp. Matt. 5:48.)

As dear children.—As His "beloved children" we imitate Him most naturally in love, and especially in that form of love which we call "mercy." (Comp. I John 4:11, 19.)

(2) As Christ also hath loved us.—To this idea of the "imitation of God," essential to all true religion, Paul now adds an exhortation to follow the example of our Lord Jesus Christ in that special exhibition of love by suffering and self-sacrifice, which was the ultimate purpose of His Incarnation. (See John 15:12, 13.)

An offering and a sacrifice to God.—Comp. Heb. 10:5, which is a quotation from Ps. 40:6.) The word "offering" signifies simply a gift offered to God, and is applied especially to unbloody sacrifices, while "sacrifice" distinctly implies the shedding of blood. Each word, when used alone, has constantly a more general sense. But when placed in juxtaposition they must be held distinctive; and hence we may conclude that our Lord made Himself "an offering" in the perfect obedience of His great humility, and gave Himself a "sacrifice," when He completed that offering by shedding His blood on the cross. Both are said to be offered "for us," i.e., on our behalf. We have, therefore, here a complete summary of the doctrine of the Atonement.

(3) See Col. 3:5. "Fornication" is closely joined with "uncleanness," of which general sin it is a flagrant species. "Uncleanness" is a sin against our own body and soul; covetousness" (literally, the **insatiable desire for more**) is a sin against our neighbor.

(4) Neither filthiness, nor foolish talking, nor jesting.—Paul here is passing from impurity of the inward soul to impurity in outward expression. Of such foul speaking he appears to distinguish two forms. There is, first of all, the talk of "the fool," in the worst sense in which that word is used in Scripture. There is then "jesting," which will find occasion for wit or levity in anything, however sacred, fearing nothing so much as to be dull, and mistaking all seriousness and reserve for dullness. The former kind of foul talking is coarse and brutal, the latter refined and deadly.

Which are not convenient, that is, "which are out of character" in a Christian. They pollute the Christian mind and tongue even in condemning them.

(5) Covetous man, who is an idolater.—Whatever becomes the chief object of our desire, so as to claim our chief fear and love, is an idol. There are two distinct stages, passing, however, by invisible gradations into each other—first, the resting on some visible blessing of God, as the one thing in which and for which we serve Him, and so by degrees losing Him in His own gifts, and next, the absolute forgetfulness of Him, and the setting up, as is inevitable, of some other object of worship to fill the vacant throne.

(6) Let no man deceive you with vain words.—It seems likely that Paul has in view, not mere worldly condonation of evil or low heathen morality, but some anticipation of that Antinomian form of Gnosticism which held that the things done in the body, being evil only by the irresistible, inevitable gravitation of matter to evil, could not touch the soul. We know that in the Colossian Church there was an anticipation of the more ascetic Gnosticism (Col. 2:21; comp. also I Tim. 4:1-5). As the earlier

Judaistic rigor had assumed this later form, so the earlier Antinomianism (of Rom. 6:1) may probably have passed into the more systematic and speculative Antinomianism of the gnostic type. (Comp. Phil. 3:18, 19.)

(9) For the fruit . . . —The true reading is **of the Light,** for which the easier phrase, "the fruit of the Spirit," has been substituted, to the great detriment of the force and coherency of the whole passage. Light has its fruits; darkness (see verse 11) is "unfruitful."

(10) Proving what is acceptable unto the Lord.—(Comp. Rom. 12:2.) "To prove" is to try in each case, by the full light of God, what is accordant to His will. It is a work partly of thought, partly of practical experience; and it always implies a searching examination of heart and action by the touchstone of God's Word.

(11) Have no fellowship with the unfruitful works of darkness.—This is not to refuse to take part in them (for this surely might be taken for granted), but to keep no terms with them, to have no sympathy or indulgence or excuse for them. It is through such weak or cowardly indulgence, more than the actual love of evil, that sin is allowed to prevail.

Rather reprove them.—In the word "reprove" there is described a double function—to "convince," if it may be, the sinner in himself; to "convict" him, if the other function fails, before men and angels. Both these functions Paul urges here.

(13) For whatsoever doth make manifest is light.—It should be, **for everything which is illuminated is light.** Paul here explains what he means by illumination. It implies the catching the light and reflecting it, so as to become a new source of light. The subject of the sentence is not "the works of darkness," but "all things" in general. Hence the whole process is described as threefold: first, the things, or persons, are dragged out of darkness into light; then they are illuminated; lastly, they become light in themselves and to others. The whole metaphor is more striking to us as science enlarges our knowledge of the manifold effects of light, not only to illuminate but to change and to vivify.

(14) No Scriptural passage can be adduced which, with the fullest allowance for the apostolic freedom of quotation, comes near enough to be a satisfactory original of this passage. Hence we are driven to conclude that the quotation is not from Holy Scripture. Yet the very form shows that it is

1046

from something well known. An apocryphal quotation is imagined by some; others have supposed it a traditional saying of our Lord. On the whole, it seems most likely that it is from some well-known Christian hymn. The growth of defined and formal expressions is notable in the later epistles and especially in the "faithful sayings" of the Pastoral Epistles. The use of some liturgical forms is traced with high probability to a very early date. The embodiment of popular faith in hymns was peculiarly natural and adapted to the imperfect education of many early converts, and to the practice of trusting so much to memory and so comparatively little to writing. Some such usage certainly appears to be referred to in the celebrated letter of Pliny to Trajan, the first heathen description of Christian worship.

For the substance of the message, comp. II Pet. 1:19; Rev. 22:16.

(15) See then that ye walk circumspectly.—The word rendered "circumspectly" is properly **strictly,** or **accurately**—generally used of intellectual accuracy or thoroughness. The idea is not of looking around watchfully against dangers, but of finding out the clear line of right and then keeping to it strictly.

(16) Redeeming the time, rather, **the opportunity,** whenever it arises. To "redeem" is "to buy up for oneself"—not having essentially the idea of ransom or redemption, which attaches to the use of the word in Gal. 3:13; 4:5, only from the nature of the context. As applied to opportunity, it carries with it the idea, first of making sacrifice for it, then quickness in seizing it and sagacity in using it to the utmost. The reason given that "the days are evil" must be taken in the widest sense of all that induces temptation to swerve out of the "strictness" of the right way.

(18) Be not drunk with wine, wherein is excess.—From the general idea of reckless levity, Paul passes on to the special sin of drunkenness, as not (like gluttony) primarily a gratification of the appetite, but as a reckless pursuit of excitement at all costs. Contemporary writers, e.g., Horace, glorified drunkenness; and some, as in the Dionysiac or Bacchanalian frenzy, actually confused it with a divine inspiration. How necessary the admonition was we see by the directions as to the choice of clergy in the Pastoral Epistles (I Tim. 3:8; Tit. 1:7; 2:3), the more necessary because the right use of wine was recognized. Hence Paul emphatically brands drunkenness as "excess," a word properly signifying "recklessness," and naturally passing through this want of self-restraint into profligacy.

But be filled with the Spirit.—The antithesis is startling, but profoundly instructive. To the artificial and degrading excitement of drunkenness Paul boldly opposes the divine enthusiasm of the Spirit, one form of which was scoffingly compared to it on the Day of Pentecost (Acts 2:13). He is not content with warning us of its ruinous excess, or urging the strictness of stern self-restraint. Drunkenness comes from an unnatural craving for excitement, stimulated by unwholesome conditions of life, physical and mental. He would satisfy the craving, as far as it is natural, by a divine enthusiasm, brighter and stronger than even duty to God and man, breaking out in thanksgiving, adoration, and love.

(19) Speaking to yourselves in psalms and hymns and spiritual songs.—(Comp. Col. 3:16.) There the idea is of teaching, here simply of a natural vent for emotion, especially of thanksgiving, and referring, perhaps, chiefly to public worship (antiphonal singing). The "psalm" is music with instrumental accompaniment, and can hardly fail to refer to the Old Testament psalms, familiar in Jewish worship, and as we know, used in the first instance we have of apostolic worship (Acts 4:24; see I Cor. 14:26; Jas. 5:13). The "hymn" is purely vocal music, apparently of the whole company (see Matt. 26:30; Acts 16:25), more especially directed to praise of God, and probably designating the new utterances of the Christian Church itself. From the use of the word "song," or "ode," as applied to lyric poetry, it may perhaps be conjectured that it describes more varied and elaborate music, sung by one person only—a spiritual utterance of one for the whole congregation.

(21) The strong and frequent emphasis laid in the New Testament on subjection, whether (Rom. 13:1-7; I Pet. 2:13-17) to the civil powers, or (Col. 3:18-4:1) to domestic authority, or (I Thess. 5:12, 13; II Thess. 3:6, 14, 15) to ecclesiastical authority, probably indicates some tendency, in the first exuberance of Christian liberty and enthusiasm, to disregard the wholesome restraints, laws, and conventions of outward life. Hence Paul's general caution here, prefatory to the more detailed teaching of subjection which follows.

(22) Wives, submit yourselves unto your own husbands.—Probably the sense of the fundamental equality in Christ (see Col. 3:18), while it was rightly accepted as showing that there is no spiritual inferiority in woman—such as Oriental theory asserted, and even Greek and corrupt Roman practice implied—was perverted to the denial of the greater natural weakness of woman, from which subordination comes, and to the foolish and reckless disregard of all social conventions. Paul, as usual, brings out the simple truth of principle, sanctioning whatever is fundamental and natural in woman's subordination, and leaving the artificial enactments of law or custom to grow by degrees into accordance with it. The principle of subordination is permanent; the special regulations of it in the world or in the Church must vary as circumstances change.

(23, 24) Comp. I Cor. 11:3. Here we note, first, that in accordance with the general idea of the epistle, the headship of Christ over the Church at large takes the place of His headship over the individual; next, that from the idea of His headship so conceived is derived the further idea of a spiritual unity, involving self-sacrifice in the head, as well as obedience to the head; and, lastly, that the very idea of unity in Christ is unity with God.

The subjection of the Church of Christ is a free subjection, arising out of faith in His unspeakable wisdom and goodness, and of love for His unspeakable love. The subordination of the wife is not that of the slave, by compulsion and fear, but one which arises from and preserves freedom. It can endure only on condition of superior wisdom and goodness and love in the husband. And while it is like the higher subordination in kind, it cannot be equally perfect in degree, for the antitype is, as usual, greater than the type.

(25) The love of Christ for His Church is such that He counts Himself incomplete without her (1:23), and raises her to be one with Himself; that He bears with her weakness and frailty; that He draws her on by the cords of love; and that He gives up Himself for her. Only so far as the husband shows the like love in perfect sympathy, in chivalrous forbearance, in abhorrence of tyranny, in willingness to self-sacrifice, has he any right to claim lordship.

(26) That he might sanctify and cleanse it ... —(See note on Tit. 3:5.) To "sanctify" is here to consecrate to Himself after purification. (Comp. John 17:17, 19; I Cor. 6:11.) In virtue of such consecration the Church visible is "holy" in idea and in capacity, the

1047

Church invisible here (which will be the Church triumphant hereafter) holy in the actual purity which becomes a consecrated nature.

(27) A glorious church, not having spot, or wrinkle... —(See note on 1:4, and comp. II Cor. 11:2.) Here the customary sacrificial terms (Col. 1:22) are applied in nuptial metaphor.

(29) His own flesh.—There are two parts of the natural care for our own bodies: first, "to nourish" (properly, **to rear them up from childhood**), and then "to cherish" (literally, **to keep them warm**), to provide all they need for health, comfort, and life. In all that corresponds to both, the husband is to show love to the wife, not only as a self, but as a weaker self, for whom he is bound to think and to act. The very comparison accords with the Christian idea of the body as a part of the true self redeemed to be a temple of God, and is utterly incongruous with the gnostic conceptions of all matter as the source of evil.

(31) Shall a man leave his father... — The relation of parentage is one of common flesh and blood, and stands at the head of those natural relations which we do not make, but into which we are born. The relation of marriage, however, itself originally voluntary, supersedes all natural ties. (See Matt. 19:6.) It strikingly represents that unity with Christ—voluntarily initiated by Him, voluntarily accepted by us—which yet so supersedes all natural ties that it is said to oblige a man to "hate his father and mother ... and his own life also" (Luke 14:26).

6

(1) In the Lord.—The phrase itself is a brief indication of the great subject—unity with and in Christ. Here to "obey in the Lord" is to obey under the light and grace of that unity, as already belonging both to parents and children, and transfiguring all natural relations to a diviner glory.

This is right, i.e., by fundamental laws of humanity, recognized in all races and all ages, declared and sanctioned in God's commandments (verses 2, 3), which are at once both old and new "in the Lord."

(3) That it may be well with thee... —(See Exod. 20:12; Deut. 5:16.) By the omission of the limiting words, "which the Lord thy God hath given thee," Paul at once generalizes the application and deter-

mines it to the earth, and not to "the good land" of heaven. The words so interpreted are, therefore, a promise that obedience "in the Lord" to the great natural law on which society rests shall bring with it reward on earth.

(4) Provoke not your children to wrath.—The word is the same as in 4:26. It denotes the exasperation produced by arbitrary and unsympathetic rule.

Nurture and admonition of the Lord.—"Nurture" is a word signifying generally "the treatment due to a child," but by usage appropriated to practical training, or teaching by discipline; "admonition" is the "putting children in mind" by word of instruction. In accordance with the characteristic sternness of ancient education, both words have a tinge of severity in them. The "nurture" of this passage is the same as the "chastening" of Heb. 12:4-11. The "admonition" is used in Tit. 3:10 for rebuke. In this, as in other cases, Christianity gradually softened this stern authority of the father— so strikingly exemplified in the addition of the phrase "of the Lord."

(5) Your masters according to the flesh.—This phrase (see Col. 3:12) at once implies the necessary limitation of all human slavery. It can subjugate and even kill the body, but it cannot touch the spirit; and it belongs only to the visible life of this world, not to the world to come. The slave is a man in spiritual and immortal being, not a "living tool" or "chattel," as even philosophy called him.

Singleness of your heart, as unto Christ.—"Singleness of heart" means having but one aim, and that the one which we profess to have, with no duplicity of reservation or hypocrisy. Such singleness of heart cannot be given perfectly to any merely human service, because no such service has a right to our whole heart; hence Paul adds, "as unto Christ," bidding them look on their service as a part of the service to Him who can claim absolute devotion. Verses 6 and 7 merely expand the idea of "singleness of heart."

(8) The same shall he receive of the Lord.—This verse clenches the previous exhortations by the inculcation of a sense of responsibility and hope. A slave in the eye of the law had no rights. Paul therefore bids him, as a Christian, lift his thoughts to a region in which all, bond and free alike, may hear the blessing, "Well done, good and faithful servant."

(9) Do the same things unto them—i.e.,

treat them as flesh and blood like yourselves, having, as men, the same claims on you as you on them. Col. 4:1 is the best comment on this: "Give unto your servants what is just and equal." "To forbear threatening," which is so common, is one example of this sense of sympathy. Threatening implies at every moment compulsion and coercion from a position of tyrannical superiority, dealing with the slave as one who has in him no free energy and no sense of duty, and who must be driven like a brute-beast, not led or guided as a man.

Your Master also.—Paul's general attitude toward slavery will be best considered in the Epistle to Philemon. Here, while the institution, unnatural as it is, is left untouched, the declaration of a common fellowship in Christ enunciates a principle absolutely incompatible with slavery and destined to destroy it.

(10) Here Paul begins to sum up his practical exhortation in that magnificent description which has ever since laid hold of Christian imagination, both in metaphor and in allegory. He paints the Christian life as a battle against spiritual powers of evil, waged in the strength of the Lord, and in the panoply of God.

(11) Put on the whole armour.—The special emphasis in this verse is not mainly on its strength or its brightness, but on its completeness, leaving no one point unguarded by a carelessness which may be fatal on all. To put on the "armour of God" is declared to be to "put on the Lord Jesus Christ." Hence its completeness corresponds to the divine perfection of His true humanity.

The wiles of the devil.—The word "wiles" (used only here and in 4:14) is an almost technical word for the stratagems of a skillful leader. These "wiles" are ascribed to the devil, the "prince of the evil spirits" directing his hosts against the army of Christ; the actual "wrestling" (verse 12) of hand-to-hand struggle is with these evil spirits themselves. The word "wrestling" is, of course, not used technically, otherwise the counsel must have been (as in Heb. 12:1) to divest oneself of all encumbrance.

(12) Flesh and blood, literally **blood and flesh.** The sense is clearly "mere human power." Possibly the word "blood" is here put first to prevent even a moment's confusion with the idea of wrestling against "the flesh" as an evil power within ourselves. In many passages of this epistle Paul had dwelt on the opposition of the Christian to the heathen life, and the duty of rebuking and putting to shame the works of darkness; but here he warns us that the struggle is not with wicked men, but a truceless war with the spiritual powers of evil themselves.

Against principalities, against powers.—See note on 1:21.

The rulers of the darkness.—This phrase is a poetical expression of the idea conveyed by the title "the prince of this world," applied to Satan in John 12:31; 14:30; 16:11. This "darkness" is "the darkness of this present world," as a world overshadowed by sin and so kept, wholly or partially, from the light of God. The title "the prince of this world" was applied by the Jews to Satan, especially in reference to his power over the heathen, as lying outside the safety of the covenant. Paul applies it in a corresponding sense here to those outside the wider covenant of the Gospel, just as in I Cor. 5:5; I Tim. 1:20, he speaks of excommunication from the Church as a "delivery to Satan."

Spiritual wickedness in high places.—The spiritual hosts of evil are described as fighting in the region above the earth. But the meaning underlying this figure surely points to the power of evil as directly spiritual, not acting through physical and human agency, but attacking the spirit in that higher aspect, in which it contemplates heavenly things and ascends to the communion with God.

(14) Your loins girt about with truth, and having on the breastplate of righteousness.—The order in which the armor is enumerated is clearly the order in which the armor of the Roman soldier was actually put on. It nearly corresponds with the invariable order in which Homer describes over and over again the arming of his heroes. It is curious to note that Paul omits the spear (the **pilum** of the Roman soldier)—exactly that part of his equipment which, when on guard within, the soldier would not be likely to assume. Truth and righteousness are virtually identical, or, at least, inseparable. Hence they are compared to the strong belt, and to the breastplate continuous with it, forming together the armor of the body. Perhaps "truth" is taken as the belt because it is the one bond both of society and of individual character. (Comp. Isa. 11:5; 59:17; I Thess. 5:8.)

(15) Shod with the preparation of the gospel of peace.—Each piece of armor is a quality, not a function. The context suggests that we should explain the word "preparation" here by its Hellenistic use, as signifying simply the "footing" or "basis." The **caligae**, or sandals, of the Roman soldiers were heavy sandals studded with hobnails to give a secure foothold to those who would stand firm. Paul identifies these with the firm "footing of the gospel of peace."

(16) Above all.—The shield here is the large heavy shield covering the whole body, in which the arrows, with the points made red hot, or wrapped in with burning tow (comp. Ps. 7:13; 120:4), may fix and burn themselves out without harm. Paul likens it to the faith of patience and endurance, the almost passive faith, trusting in God's protection and submissive to His will, on which the darts of temptation, whether from fear, or from lust, or from doubt, fall harmless. The best commentary on the words is found in Christian's conflict with Apollyon in **Pilgrim's Progress.**

(17) The helmet of salvation.—The word here rendered "salvation" is a general expression for "that which tends to salvation." The helmet guarding the head, the most noble and vital part, is "salvation" concrete, not abstract—all that is of the Saviour, all that makes up our "state of salvation" by His atonement and grace—received in earnest now, hoped for in perfection hereafter.

The sword of the Spirit, which is the word of God.—In this we pass to the one offensive weapon of the Christian, which, like the helmet, but unlike the rest of the defensive armor, does not become a part of himself, but is absolutely of God. Comp. Heb. 4:12, where the original word is the larger and deeper word (**Logos**), signifying the truth of God in itself, and gradually leading up to the ultimate sense in which our Lord Himself is the "Word of God," revealing the godhead to man. Here we have another expression (**Rhema**), signifying the Word as spoken. We cannot limit it to Holy Scripture, though we naturally remember that our Lord used the Scriptures as His only weapon in the Temptation. It is the Gospel of Christ, however and wherever spoken, able to put to shame and to flight the powers of evil.

(18) Praying always with all prayer and supplication.—In this verse the metaphor gives place to direct exhortation, unless in the word "watch" there still lingers some reference to the soldier on guard. "Prayer"

is the general word for "worship," appropriated to God alone; "supplication," used also toward man, is one element of such worship—the asking what we need from God. In Phil 4:6 we have first the general word "prayer," and then the two chief elements of worship, "supplication with thanksgiving." It is by prayer that all the heavenly armor is put on.

And watching thereunto with all perseverance.—"Perseverance" implies exertion, holding out against fatigue and difficulty. The corresponding verb is used in relation to all kinds of spiritual labor, but especially in connection with prayer. Perhaps from this frequent connection Paul is induced to add to it "supplication," being willing to sacrifice some part of the perfect appropriateness of idea since the whole picture hitherto has been of the fight, waged by each for himself, in the combined power of watchfulness and prayer for God's help.

(20) In bonds.—The allusion is undoubtedly to the custom of chaining the prisoner by the hand to the soldier who kept him. (See Acts 12:6; 21:33.) Here the singular number is probably to be understood literally. Paul was free except for the one chain, which the soldier was responsible for holding, and perhaps did not always think it needful to hold. That chain he seems to speak of as the badge of his ambassadorial dignity. To ambassadors, indeed, it belongs to be safe from imprisonment; but it was his greater glory to wear the chain for Christ.

(21) Tychicus is first mentioned with Trophimus in Acts 20:4, as being "of Asia" and accompanying Paul on his last journey from Corinth to Asia. It is highly probable that he was one of the "messengers of the churches" (II Cor. 8:18-23) sent to bear the alms to Jerusalem. He was made by Paul the bearer of this epistle and the Epistle to the Colossians. He is alluded to as still Paul's companion in the interval between the first and second captivity (Tit. 3:12), and in the second captivity is dispatched once more to Ephesus (II Tim. 4:12).

(23, 24) It is impossible not to notice the difference between the generality of the terms used here and the personal "you" of all the other epistles, a difference which would be inexplicable if this epistle were addressed to the well-known and loved Church of Ephesus alone.

PHILIPPIANS

1

(1) Paul and Timotheus, the servants of Jesus Christ.—To the Philippian, as to the Thessalonian Church, Paul does not think it needful to assert his apostleship; but he writes, in a tone of affectionate and confident familiarity, as to those whom he could thoroughly trust. Here he and Timotheus are simply "servants"—a title of humility assumed by James and Jude, but nowhere else by Paul without the addition of some title of apostolic authority. (Comp. Rom. 1:1; Tit. 1:1.) It is to be noted also that here, as again (with Silas) in the Thessalonian epistles, Timotheus is joined with Paul almost on a footing of equality, whereas, in other epistles (see II Cor. 1:1; Col. 1:1; Philem. 1) he is separated from the apostle and distinguished as "Timotheus the brother." This is probably to be accounted for partly by the absence of all necessity for assertion of his own apostleship, partly also by the fact that (with Silas) Timotheus was Paul's fellow-worker in the conversion of the Macedonian churches, and accordingly his chosen messenger to them from time to time (Acts 19:22; 20:5).

With the bishops and deacons.—In this passage the word "bishop" is, for the first time, used as a title, although in Acts 20:28 it is employed as a description of duty, with a distinct reference to its etymological meaning and origin. In the Pastoral Epistles we find it similarly used (as I Tim. 3:2; Tit. 1:7). The two titles of "bishop" and "presbyter" are applied in the Scriptures (comp. I Clement 19) to the same persons—the latter, however, being in Paul's epistles the more frequent and conventional term, while the former seems almost always used with reference to its actual meaning. The two titles are of diverse origin. The "presbyter," or "elder," is a Jewish title directly descended from the synagogue. The title of "bishop," or "overseer," is of heathen origin, used in classical Greek for a commissioner from headquarters, and applied in the LXX to various secular offices. The former is simply a title of dignity; the latter is a title of official duty. Like the words "pastor" and "apostle," it belongs properly only to the Lord Jesus Christ (Heb. 3:1; I Pet. 2:25), but derivatively to His ministers, as having the oversight of His Church. The

indifferent use of the two names is made absolutely clear in Tit. 1:5-7.

The name "deacon" is also used for the first time, unless, indeed, as is probable, it is applied officially to Phoebe in Rom. 16:1. Although the office of the Seven (Acts 6:1-7) is undoubtedly the germ of the diaconate, and although the cognate words ("ministration" and "serve") are used in connection with them (see verses 1, 2), yet the actual title of deacons is nowhere given to them. This mention of the ministers as distinct from the Church in salutation is unique.

(3-8) Here Paul strikes that keynote of joy and confidence which is dominant throughout the whole epistle, and which is singularly remarkable when we remember that it was written in captivity. The words "joy" and "rejoice" occur no less than thirteen times in this short epistle; they express what his own feeling is, and what he desires that theirs should be.

(5) For your fellowship in the gospel.—See the more limited use of the same Greek word (Rom. 15:26; II Cor. 9:13) in the sense of "contribution," in which case the word "towards" ("in") introduces the objects of almsgiving there specified. Accordingly, Paul must be taken here to mean the fellow-working of the Philippians in the ministry of the Gospel, of which he speaks still more distinctly in verse 7. That fellow-working had been shown (see 4:15) even in the beginning by a contribution to Paul's needs—not perhaps his personal needs only—which from them, and from them only, he consented to accept.

(6) That he which hath begun . . .—The ground of Paul's confidence in their perseverance is the belief that it was God's grace which began the good work in them, and that, not being resisted, He would complete what He had begun.

The day of Jesus Christ.—As is usual in the epistles, the day of the Lord is spoken of as if it were near at hand. But it is, of course, clear that, in respect of the confidence here expressed, it makes no difference whether it be near or far away. The reality of the judgment as final and complete is the one important point.

(7) Both in my bonds, and in the defence and confirmation of the gospel.—Paul unites his bonds with his pleading for the Gospel against objections and establishment of it by positive teaching (see verses 12, 13). He accepts the help sent him by the Philippians, in which they had (see 4:14) "communicated with his affliction" as a means of fellowship with him in the whole of this work of evangelization.

Ye all are partakers of my grace—i.e., of the privilege described in Eph. 3:8.

(8) God is my record.—We have a similar adjuration in Rom. 1:9; II Cor. 1:23; I Thess. 2:5, 10. These instances show in what sense Paul interpreted such commands as Matt. 5:34.

In the bowels of Jesus Christ.—This corresponds to our use of "heart" as the seat of affection, the word "heart" itself in the New Testament being employed, in a wider sense, to signify the whole inner man. (See note on Eph. 1:18.) But the phrase is striking and even startling. The deep yearning of love which Paul feels for them he knows to be an emanation, faint indeed, but true, from the "heart of Jesus Christ" dwelling in him.

(9, 10) Paul always thanks God for what is strong in the church to which he writes, and prays God for the supply of that in which it is weak. Now he thanks God for the characteristic enthusiasm and largeheartedness of the Philippians; he prays for their advance in knowledge, perception, judgment—the more intellectual and thoughtful side of the Christian character—in which they, and perhaps the Macedonian churches generally, were less conspicuous.

Here Paul singles out the way of love—the enthusiasm of love to God and man which he knew the Philippians had—and prays that it may overflow from the emotional to the intellectual element of their nature and become a means of spiritual insight. He connects with it, as a direct consequence, the power of testing the things that are excellent. The word here translated "excellent" carries with it the idea of distinctive and relative excellence, conspicuous amid what is either evil or defective.

(12) The things which happened unto me—since he parted from them (see Acts 20:6)—his arrest at Jerusalem, and the long captivity of years, first at Caesarea, then at Rome. Nothing could have appeared to be a more fatal blow to the progress of the Gospel; but Paul assures them that, on the contrary, all these things tended to its furtherance. His acquaintance with the Roman soldiers at Caesarea probably prepared for him an opening at Rome, which he could not otherwise have found, even into Caesar's household.

(13) My bonds in Christ are manifest.—i.e., my captivity is understood as being a

part of my Christian life and work, and so becomes a starting point for the preaching of the Gospel. (Comp. Acts 28:20; Eph. 6:20.)

In all the palace, and in all other places.—The word "palace" is **praetorium**. (It may be noted that coincidence with Acts 23:35 is the chief, and almost the sole, argument for the untenable idea that this epistle belongs to the Caesarean and not the Roman captivity.) Its sense here has been disputed. It has been variously interpreted as the emperor's palace, or the praetorian barrack attached to it, or the praetorian camp outside the walls. But the difficulty is that, although the word might be applied to any of these places, yet, as a matter of fact, it is not found to be so applied. Moreover, we notice here that the words "in all other places" are an inaccurate rendering of a phrase really meaning "to all the rest." The connection therefore seems even in itself to suggest that the "praetorium" may more properly refer to a body of men than to a place. According to Lightfoot the word "praetorium" is undoubtedly used for the "praetorium guard." "My bonds," says the apostle, "are known in all the praetorian regiments and to all the rest of the world, whether of soldiers or of citizens." This would leave it an open question where Paul was imprisoned, only telling us that it was under praetorian surveillance.

(14) Waxing confident by my bonds.—There is a twofold sense here, corresponding to the twofold division of preachers made in verses 15-17. Those who preached Christ "of contention" trusted in Paul's captivity as giving them scope; those who preached "of good will" found in it a striking example of evil overruled to good, and so gained from it fresh encouragement.

(15) Of envy and strife.—Doubtlessly, this refers to the Judaizing party, Paul's old antagonists. The whole tenor of the Epistle to the Romans shows how strong a Judaic element there was in Roman Christianity. Even in approaching Rome, the apostle had felt doubtful of his reception there by the Church (Acts 28:15).

(16) Not sincerely.—The original is "not purely," i.e., not with unmixed and singleminded enthusiasm for Christ. Paul does not impute to them hypocrisy, but an admixture of partisanship, and therefore of a narrow-minded hostility to him.

To add affliction.—The uneasiness of the government in relation to the Jewish population at Rome is well known. The growth of a secret society (for such Christianity was held to be) among them might easily induce greater severity toward a leader of the sect. (Comp. verses 19, 20, in which Paul states his confidence that this malignant policy would be disappointed.)

(18) The contrast of this verse with such passages as II Cor. 12:4; Gal. 1:6; and Phil. 3:2-16, is singularly instructive. Paul, in the words "in pretence" and "in truth," is speaking of the motives of the preachers, not of the substance of their preaching. For the latter he cares much; for the former nothing. When (as at Corinth) the rejection of his personal authority was bound up with rejection of his apostolic doctrine, he rebukes it vehemently; when (as here) there was no such connection, it is to him a very small thing. But we may also gather from this that, whatever might be the case at Philippi, at Rome Paul's epistle had done its work, and the battle of principle was won. (Comp. Col. 2:16-23.) The differences between the parties at Rome were no longer fundamental, although, as so often is the case, the bitterness of division might remain.

(19) Shall turn to my salvation.—The word "salvation" is used in the sense of "safety." The enemies of the apostle thought to stir up fresh danger and difficulty for Paul; but the attempt will only turn out to a safety which he believes (see verses 25, 26) will be shown "in life," by his actual release and return to his beloved churches, but which, if God so wills it, will be at least equally manifested in the "death," which would bring him safe home to Christ. In either case he will be safe from all the enmity both of open sin and of malignant jealousy.

The Spirit of Jesus Christ.—Of the application of this name to the Holy Ghost we have instances in Rom. 8:9; II Cor. 3:17; Gal. 4:6; I Pet. 1:11. The name has always some special emphasis. Here, the whole conception of the passage is of Christ—"to me to live is Christ"; hence the use of this special and comparatively rare name of the Holy Ghost.

(20) My earnest expectation.—The word is found only here and in Rom. 8:19. It implies an intense and almost painful longing for some crisis. The phrase is one of the many indications that the joyful and confident tone so often noticed in this epistle did not come from the absence of yearning for the freedom and activity of apostolic life,

but from the victory over such longings through faith.

In nothing I shall be ashamed.—The phrase is elsewhere used by Paul with special reference to the shame which comes from hopes disappointed and professions unfulfilled. (See II Cor. 7:14; 9:4; 10:8.) He trusts that in the hour of trial the confidence which he has felt and professed may not come to shameful failure. There is a subtle touch of true Christian feeling in the fact that, when he speaks of the chance of failure, he uses the first person: "I shall be ashamed"; but when of triumph, it is "Christ shall be magnified" in me.

(21) To live is Christ.—This means "Christ is my life" in the sense that the whole concrete state of life is so lived in Him that it becomes a simple manifestation of His presence. The opposition in the passage is between the states of living and dying, not between the principles of life and death.

To die is gain.—This follows from the other. Death is a new stage in the progress of union with Christ. (Comp. II Cor. 5:6, 7.) "To depart" (see verse 23) is, in a higher sense than can be realized here, "to be with Christ."

(23) I am in a strait betwixt two.—The word here used signifies "to be hemmed in," or "confined," and is generally associated with some idea of distress. Our Lord uses it of mental distress in Himself (Luke 12:50). Paul's mind is "hemmed in" between two opposing considerations, till it knows not which way to move, even in desire.

Having a desire . . . —The metaphor for "depart" is drawn from striking tents and breaking up a camp. The body (as in II Cor. 5:1) is looked upon as a mere tabernacle. Each day is a march nearer home, and death is the last striking of the tent on arrival. The original at the end of the verse is an emphatic double comparative, "far, far better."

(26) By my coming to you again.—See in I Tim. 1:3 the evidence of the fulfillment of this confident expectation.

(27-30) In these verses Paul exhorts the Philippians to unanimous boldness and steadfastness, under some conflict of antagonism or persecution which threatened them at this time. Of the history of the church at Philippi we have no historical record after the notice of Paul's first visit, and of the violence which he then had to endure (Acts 16:12-40). But comp. II Cor. 7:5 and 8:2, written certainly from Macedonia, probably from Philippi, toward the close of the third missionary journey. It would seem that the subsequent history of the Philippian Church corresponded only too well to the circumstances under which its Christianity first began.

(27) Let your conversation ... —The original is "Use your citizenship (that is, of the kingdom of heaven) worthily of the Gospel of Christ" (comp. 3:20). The same word is employed by Paul in Acts 23:1, with an obvious reference to his citizenship in the chosen nation of Israel. Its use in this epistle is suggestive—both as natural to one contemplating the great imperial city, and writing to the people of a Roman colony proud of their full citizenship, and also as leading on to that great conception of the unity of the Church in earth and in heaven.

Striving together for the faith.—The faith of the Gospel—the power of Christianity— is personified. The Philippians are to be combatants on the same side against the same foes (comp. 4:3). The metaphor seems drawn from the games, as is seen by the use of the simple verb in II Tim. 2:8. In the exhortation to stand fast (Eph. 6:13, 14) we have the element of passive endurance, here of active and aggressive energy.

(28) Which—i.e., your fearlessness, in the absence of all earthly means of protection or victory. The effect which it had on the heathen themselves is shown even by the affected contempt with which the Stoics spoke of it, as a kind of "madness," a morbid "habit," a sheer "obstinacy." (See Epictetus, 4:7; Marc. Aurelius, *Med.* 11.3.)

(30) Having the same conflict which ye saw in me.—The allusion is, of course, to the lawless scourging and imprisonment of Acts 16:22-24. How deeply this outrage impressed itself on the apostle's own mind we see, both by his conduct to the magistrates at the moment, and also by the allusion in I Thess. 2:2. Here he uses the remembrance to suggest to the Philippians that their struggle was only the same which he had borne, and borne successfully. (Comp. II Tim. 3:10.)

2

(1) If there be therefore any consolation ... —"Consolation" is properly "encouragement"—the stirring up of spiritual activity—ascribed in Acts 9:31 to the action of the Holy Spirit, but here viewed as a practical manifestation of the life flowing

from union with Christ. Out of it comes naturally the deep and thankful sense of comfort in His love, lovingly given to our brethren. (See II Cor. 1:3-7). "Communion of the Spirit" refers to our being brought into that unity with Christ; and of this, still keeping to the main idea of love, he makes the manifestation to be both in strong affection and in compassion or pity.

(4) Look not every man on his own things.—This verse continues to describe the positive effect of "being of one mind" as consisting in power of understanding and sympathy toward "the things of others"— not merely the interests, but also the ideas and feelings of others. To "look upon" expresses that insight into the thoughts, hopes, aspirations of others, which only a self-forgetting love can give, as well as the care to consider their welfare and happiness. Yet by the word "also" we see that Paul does not, in the spirit of some forms of transcendentalism, denounce all self-consciousness as in a bad sense "selfish."

(5-8) From a practical introduction, in the familiar exhortation to follow the example of our Lord, Paul passes on to what is, perhaps, the most complete and formal statement in all his epistles of the doctrine of His "great humility." In this he marks out, first, the Incarnation, and next, the Passion. Inseparable in themselves, these two great acts of His self-sacrificing love must be distinguished. As "the Word of God" manifested in the Incarnation, our Lord is the treasure of all humanity as such; as the Saviour through death, He is the special treasure of us as sinners.

(6) In this passage the "being in the form of God" describes our Lord's essential, and therefore eternal, being in the true nature of God, while the "taking on Him the form of a servant" refers to His voluntary assumption of the true nature of man. It should be noticed that, whereas in Paul's earlier epistles the main idea is always of our Lord as the mediator between man and God, yet in the later epistles (as here) stress is laid on His gathering all things in heaven and earth unto Himself, and, even more explicitly, on His partaking of the divine nature and possessing the divine attribute of creation. All this naturally leads up to the great declaration of His true and perfect Godhead in John 1:1-13.

Thought it not robbery to be equal with God—i.e., "thought it not a prize to be grasped at to be equal with God," which begins in it the statement of our Lord's voluntary self-humiliation, to be completed in the words "but emptied Himself of glory." The sense is that, being in the form of God, and therefore having equality with God, He set no store on that equality, as a glory to Himself, compared with the power of giving salvation to all men, which He is pleased to consider a new joy and glory.

(7) But made himself . . . —This verse needs more exact translation: "But emptied Himself of His glory by having taken on Him the form of a slave and having been made in likeness of men." The "glory" is the "glory which he had with the Father before the world was" (John 17:5; comp. 1:14), clearly corresponding to the **Shechi-nah** of the divine presence. Of this He stripped Himself in the Incarnation. He resumed it for a moment in the Transfiguration; He was crowned with it anew at the Ascension.

Made in the likeness of men.—The key to the meaning is to be found in such passages as Rom. 8:3; Heb. 2:17; 4:15. It would have been an infinite humiliation to have assumed humanity, even in unique and visible glory; but our Lord went beyond this, by condescending to seem like other men in all things, one only of the multitude, and that, too, in a station which confused Him with the commoner types of mankind.

(8) And being found . . . —Paul proceeds to the last act of His self-humiliation. His death is not here regarded as an atonement, for in that light it could be no pattern to us, but as the completion of the obedience of His life. (See Rom. 5:19.) In this light His death is the perfection of the suffering which, in consequence of the power of sin in the world, must be faced in doing the will of God (see II Tim. 3:12); in this light we can follow it, and even "fill up what is lacking of the sufferings of Christ" (Col. 1:24).

(9) Wherefore God also hath highly exalted him.—The exaltation, like the humiliation, belongs to Him as Son of Man; He was "lifted up," as on the cross, so in the Ascension. It raises Him to the throne of mediation.

Given him a name.—See Rev. 19:12, 13, where "the name which no man knew but himself" is the "Word of God." The adoration described in verse 10 is in the original passage (Isa. 45:23; comp. Rom. 14:11) claimed as the sole due of God Himself.

(10) At the name of Jesus every knee should bow.—"In the name" is the phrase constantly used in the Old Testament for worship of God (comp. Ps. 63:4). It denotes worship to Christ, not through Him.

Of things . . . —For "things" we may better substitute "beings," for the reference is properly to personal beings. (See Eph. 1:20, 21; Rev. 5:13.)

(11) That Jesus Christ is Lord.—The word "Lord" is the word constantly used in the LXX to translate, though inadequately, the name Jehovah. The context would suggest that meaning here, for the worship paid is obviously the worship done to God. (On this confession of Jesus as Lord, see Acts 2:36; Rom. 10:9.)

To the glory of God the Father.—The acknowledgment of the glory of Christ is the acknowledgment of the glory of the Father, as the Source of Deity, manifested perfectly in Him. (See John 1:18; 14:9).

(12) As ye have always obeyed.—By the word "wherefore" Paul connects this exhortation with the great passage above. It is notable that this epistle is the only one which contains no direct rebuke. This "obedience" was to the will of God as set forth by Paul. In referring to it, there is an allusion to the "obedience" of Christ (verse 8); hence their obedience includes also that willingness to suffer which He Himself has shown. (See 1:29, 30.) To this, perhaps, there is a further allusion in the "fear and trembling." (See II Cor. 7:15; Eph. 6:5.)

Work out your own salvation.—To "work out" is (as in Eph. 6:13) to carry out to completion what is begun. This is the function of man, as fellow-worker with God, first in his own soul, and then among his brethren. God is the "beginner and perfecter" of every "good work" (see 1:6); man's co-operation is secondary and intermediate.

(13) For it is God which worketh in you both to will and to do.—In this famous paradox Paul calls on men to work by their own will, just because only God can grant them power both to will and to do. The origination of all in God, and the free action of man, are both truths recognized by our deepest consciousness, but to our logic irreconcilable. (Comp. Rom. 9:14-24.) The only encouragement to work, in a being weak and finite like man, is the conviction that the Almighty power is working in him, both as to will and deed. The word "worketh in you" is constantly applied to the divine operation in the soul (see I Cor. 12:6, 11; Gal. 2:8; Eph. 1:11, 20; 2:2), but rarely, as here, to the action of

men. It must necessarily extend to the will as well as the action; otherwise God would not be sovereign in the inner realm of mind.

(14) Without murmurings and disputings. —Paul seems purposely to leave this precept in perfect generality. The word "disputings" seems mainly to indicate intellectual questionings. "Murmuring" is used of outward wranglings of discontent proceeding not so much from the mind as from the heart. The primary reference would seem to be to their relation toward men, in spite of the close connection with the preceding verse. It is on unity among themselves that the main stress of the exhortation of this chapter turns.

(16) The phrase "the word of life" signifies the Gospel of Christ. Paul's usual metaphor includes the "race" and the "struggle" of wrestling or boxing (comp. I Cor. 9:24-26; Gal. 2:2; II Tim. 4:7). Here the more general word "labour" (see Col. 1:29) may be taken to express that element of endurance and watchfulness which the struggle in the arena represents.

(17) If I be offered upon the sacrifice and service of your faith.—The striking metaphor of "If I am being poured out"—if my life-blood is poured out—"over the sacrifice and religious ministration of your faith." The same word is used in II Tim. 4:6. The allusion is to the practice of pouring out libations or drink-offerings over sacrifices, both Jewish and heathen. Such libation was held to be a subsidiary or preparatory element of the sacrifice. In that light Paul regards his own possible martyrdom, not so much as having a purpose and values in itself, but rather as conducing to the self-sacrifice of the Philippians by faith, a sacrifice apparently contemplated as likely to be offered in life rather than by death.

(18) Do ye joy ... —The epistle lays great stress on joy, not only as a privilege, but as a duty, following from Christian faith and proving its reality. A Christianity which has no power to rejoice, either in flashes of joy amid tribulation, or, better still, in the calm steady light of cheerfulness, may be true, but it is imperfect.

(19) That I also may be of good comfort.— The words express some anxiety, but greater confidence, as to the news which Timothy on returning was likely to bring. We have instances of a similar but far stronger anxiety of affection in II Cor. 2:13; 7:6, 7; I Thess. 3:1-9. In regard to the Philippians it might exist in detail, but was

swallowed up in confidence on all main points.

(20) For I have no man likeminded.—See 1 Tim. 1:2. The word "naturally" should be translated "genuinely," without either counterfeit or duplicity of aim; and the word "care" implies something of the same absorbing anxiety which is expressed on Paul's part in this passage.

(21) For all seek their own, not the things which are Jesus Christ's.—Paul had certainly some "brethren" with him (4:21). But the scanty notice of them in the close of this epistle contrasts strongly with the detailed and affectionate mention of his companions by name in Col. 4:7-14; Philem. 23, 24. It would seem as if at this time he was either separated accidentally from his most trusty disciples, or that there had been a temporary falling away from him (comp. II Tim. 4:9, 10, 16). His words need not be taken as accusing all of absolute selfishness and unfaithfulness, but they are nevertheless startling enough.

(22) The proof of him.—The allusion is justified by their intimate personal knowledge. Timothy was at Philippi with Paul on his first visit (Acts 16:12-40); we find him sent to Thessalonica shortly after (I Thess. 3:2), and he probably then paid a second visit to Philippi; from Ephesus (Acts 19:22) he is sent again to Macedonia; and with Paul on the way to Jerusalem he was at Philippi once more (Acts 20:4-6).

(23) How it will go with me.—Probably some crisis in the imprisonment was at hand, with which the expectation of release implied in verse 24 was connected.

(24) But I trust ... —Compare Philem. 22, where the expectation seems even more immediate. The interval between the letters is unknown. The received belief of Paul's release, and subsequent re-imprisonment (resting on unvarying tradition, and on the evidence of the Pastoral Epistles), supposes this expectation to have been fulfilled in due time.

(25) Epaphroditus.—The name was often shortened into Epaphras. It was a common name; thus any identification with the Epaphras of Col. 1:7; 4:12; Philem. 23, is extremely precarious. It is unlikely that one who was a native Colossian would be a resident and chosen messenger of Philippi. The three titles here given him are closely joined together in the original, and form a kind of climax.

Your messenger.—The original word is "apostle." "Messenger" is a correct rendering, however, just as in II Cor. 8:23, where there is a similar reference to the transmission of alms.

(26) For he longed after you all ... —For two clauses of the verse are distinct from each other. Paul's first reason for sending Epaphroditus was in itself a sufficient one, that in his convalescence he yearned for home, and needed a change there. But besides this he was "distressed and uneasy," because of the effect which the news of his apparently fatal illness might cause at home.

(27) God had mercy on him ... and on me also.—The apostle's power of miracle, great as it was, was not his own to use at his own will. When it was needed to be "the sign of an apostle" (II Cor. 12:12) it was given; and at times it was given in special fullness (Acts 19:11). It would seem there were special occasions on which miracles came out prominently in the apostle's preaching. We may infer from certain points in the descriptions of Acts 3:4 and 14:8 that some spiritual intimation warned them when the hour of miracle was come. But an apostle could not, as our Lord would not, work miracles for his own needs. Thus in this case, deeply as he sorrowed for Epaphroditus, there is no hint of his exercising that power on his behalf. He could only pray that God would have mercy on him, and thank God when that prayer was heard.

(30) To supply your lack of service.—There is, in the original, no touch of reproach. Epaphroditus' presence and activity are said to have "filled up the one thing wanting" to make the service of the Philippians effective for its purpose.

3

(1) Finally.—The same word is used in 4:8 to usher in the conclusion. Here it stands nearly in the middle of the epistle. Moreover, the commendation above of Timothy and Epaphroditus is exactly that which, according to Paul's custom, would mark the final sentences of the whole. The resumption of the words "rejoice in the Lord" in 4:4, where the actual conclusion begins, is striking. It seems, therefore, highly probable that in this place the letter was originally drawing to an end, and that some news was at that moment brought which induced the apostle to add a second part, couched in language of equal affection, but

of greater anxiety and more emphatic warning. Of such a break, and resumption with a far more complete change of style, there is notable instance at the beginning of II Cor. 10, as also of the addition of postscript after postscript in Rom. 16.

To write the same things to you.—These words refer to the abrupt and incisive warnings that follow. They are a repetition of Paul's previous teaching, by word or by letter. For the use here of the word "to write," though it suits better the idea of former communication by writing, cannot exclude oral teaching. That there was more than one Pauline epistle to Philippi has been inferred in Polycarp's letter to the Philippians (sect. 3). It seems natural, however, to refer to Paul's former teaching as a whole. (See Acts 15:41; 17:5.) What, then, would be more natural than to introduce a new warning on the subject—shown to be necessary by news received—with a courteous half-apology, making assurance doubly sure?

(2) Beware of dogs.—The context appropriates the word to the Judaizing party, who claimed special purity, ceremonial and moral, and who probably were not characterized by peculiar impurity—such as, indeed (verses 17-21), would seem rather to attach to the Antinomian party, probably the extreme on the other side. There may be some allusion to the dogs, not as unclean, but as, especially in their half-wild state in the East, snarling and savage, driving off as interlopers all who approach what they consider their ground. Nothing could better describe the narrow Judaizing spirit.

The concision.—By an ironical play upon words Paul declares his refusal to call the circumcision, on which the Judaizers prided themselves, by that time-honored name. In Eph. 2:11 he had denoted it as the "so-called circumcision in the flesh made by hands." Here he speaks more strongly, and calls it a mere outward mutilation, no longer, as it had been, a "seal" of the covenant (Rom. 4:11). There is a still more startling attack on the advocates of circumcision in Gal. 5:12.

(5) An Hebrew of the Hebrews.—See Rom. 11:1; II Cor. 11:18-23. The Hebrew Jew, who retained, wherever born, the old tongue, education, and customs of his fathers, held himself superior to the Grecian or Hellenist, who had to assimilate himself to the heathen world around him. Paul united the advantages both of the true Hebrew, brought up at the feet of Gamaliel, and of the Hellenist of Tarsus, familiar with Greek language, literature, and thought. (See Acts 22:3, 4; 23:6; 26:5.)

(6) Concerning zeal, persecuting the church. —The word "zeal" is probably used almost technically to describe his adhesion to the principles of the Zealots, who, following the example of Phinehas, were for "executing judgment" at once on all the heathen as traitors, ready alike to slay or to be slain for the Law. He shows how in this he departed from the teaching of Gamaliel when he fanatically persecuted the Christians.

Touching the righteousness which is in the law, blameless.— The "righteousness in law," which our Lord called "the righteousness of the scribes and Pharisees" (Matt. 5:20), is the righteousness according to rule, not the righteousness according to principle. While Paul confined himself to the lower form of righteousness, he could feel himself "blameless"; but when he began to discern this higher righteousness in the Law, then he felt the terrible condemnation of the Law (comp. Rom. 7:7-12).

(7) I counted loss . . . —Not merely worthless, but worse than worthless, because preventing the sense of spiritual need and helplessness which should bring to Christ. Paul first applies this declaration to the Jewish privilege and dignity of which he had spoken. Then, not content with this, he extends it to "all things" which were his to sacrifice for Christ.

(8) Dung.—The word appears to mean "refuse" of any kind. Lightfoot quotes instances of its use for the fragments from a feast, and remarks on the old derivation of the word from that which is "thrown to dogs." This use would suit well enough with the ideas suggested by the retort of the name "dogs" on the Judaizers.

(9) Not having mine own righteousness, which is of the law.—This is a righteousness resulting from the works of the Law (Gal. 2:16), earned by an obedience to the Law, which Paul declares (Rom. 10:3-6) to have been blindly sought by Israel. There is here a remarkable link of connection with the earlier epistles of the Judaizing controversy, corresponding to Eph. 2:8-10, but cast more nearly in the ancient mold. Yet it is, after all, only the last echo of the old controversy, which we trace so clearly in the Galatian and Roman epistles. The battle is now virtually won.

But . . . the righteousness which is of God by faith.—This verse is notable, as de-

scribing the true righteousness as "a righteousness coming from God on the sole condition of faith"—faith being here viewed not as the means, but as the condition, of receiving the divine gift (as in Acts 3:16). In the Epistle to the Romans we have righteousness "through faith," "from faith," "of faith," for there it was needful to bring out in various forms the importance of faith. Here, now that the urgent necessity has passed, we have the stress laid simply on the opposition of the gift of God through Christ to the merit of the works of the Law.

(10, 11) The order of these verses is notable and instructive. (1) First comes the knowledge of the power of the Resurrection. Historically this was the main subject of the first apostolic preaching. The power, or **efficacy**, of His resurrection is the justification, and regeneration inseparable from it, which lie at the entrance of Christian life. (2) Next comes the partaking of His sufferings and conformity to His death, which are the taking up the cross, and following Him, in the obedience even unto death. (3) Lastly comes the attainment to the resurrection (properly) **from** the dead, which is the resurrection unto life and the glorification in Him. Of our resurrection (see I Cor. 15:12-23) His resurrection is not only the pledge, but the earnest. Comp. the resurrection to life (I Cor. 15:51-57) with the first resurrection (Rev. 20:6). This is the completion of all; Paul dared not as yet anticipate it with the confidence which hereafter soothed his dying hour (II Tim. 4:7, 8).

(12) Not as though . . . —To "attain" (probably the prize, see verse 14) is a single act; "to be perfected" a continuous process. Clearly Paul has no belief either in any indefectible grasp of salvation or in any attainment of full spiritual perfection on this side of the grave. We may note our Lord's use of the word "to be perfected" to signify His death (Luke 13:32), and a similar application of the word to Him in Heb. 2:10, 5:9; also the use of the words "made perfect" to signify the condition of the glorified (Heb. 11:40; 12:23).

If that I may apprehend . . . —The metaphor throughout is of the race, in which he, like an eager runner, stretches out continually to "grasp" the prize. But, following out the same line of thought as in verses 7, 8, he is unwilling to lay too much stress on his own exertions. The hope to apprehend rests on the knowledge that he had been apprehended by One out of whose hand no man could pluck him.

(13) I count not myself ... —Not only does Paul refuse to count that he has ever yet "attained"; he will not allow that he is yet in a position even to grasp at the prize. (Comp. I Cor. 9:27.)

Forgetting those things which are behind ... —The precept is absolutely general, applying to past blessings, past achievements, even past sins. The ineradicable instinct of hope, which the wisdom of the world holds to be a delusion, or at best a condescension to weakness, is sanctioned in the gospel as an anticipation of immortality. Accordingly hope is made a rational principle, and is always declared to be not only a privilege but a high Christian duty, co-ordinate with faith and love (I Cor. 13:13; Eph. 4:4). Past blessing is but an earnest of the future; past achievements of good are steppingstones to greater things; past sins are viewed in that true repentance which differs from remorse in having a sure and certain hope of the final conquest of all sin. Eternal life in Christ is a present gift, but one test of its reality in the present is its possession of the promise of the future.

(14) The high calling of God. —Properly, "the calling which is above." (See Rom. 8:30; Col. 3:12.)

(15) Perfect. —The word is apparently used with a touch of irony (comp. "spiritual" in Gal. 6:1) in reference to those who hold themselves "to have already attained, to be already perfect." It is, indeed, mostly used of such maturity in faith and grace as may be, and ought to be, attained here (Matt. 5:48; I Cor. 2:6; 14:20; Eph. 4:13; Col. 1:28; 4:12; Heb. 5:14). The prospect of being "perfect" in indefectible faith or grace is the Christian's hope. Paul, by a striking paradox, bids those who hold themselves perfect to prove that they are so by a consciousness of imperfection.

(16) Let us walk ... —The word "walk" is always used of pursuing a course deliberately chosen. (See Acts 21:24; Rom. 4:12; Gal. 5:25; 6:16). In this passage Paul will have the "perfect" understand that they have attained only one thing—to be in the right path, and that it is for them to continue in it; he also bids them refrain from setting themselves up above "the imperfect," for the very fact of division would mark them as still "carnal," mere "babes in Christ" (I Cor. 3:1-4).

(17) Followers together of me. —In accordance with the genius of the whole epistle, Paul offers his example as a help not only to rectitude but also to unity. (See I Cor. 11:1.) In that consciousness, knowing the peculiar power of example, Paul will not allow even humility to prevent his bringing it to bear upon them. Yet even then we note how gladly he escapes from "followers **of** me" to the "having **us** for an example."

(18) The enemies of the cross of Christ. — The doctrine of the cross has two parts, distinct, yet inseparable. There is the cross which He alone bore for us, which we cannot share. There is also the cross which we are "to take up and follow him" (Matt. 10:38; 16:24). Under cover, perhaps, of absolute acceptance of the one form of this great doctrine, the Antinomian party, "continuing in sin that grace might abound," were, in respect of the other, "enemies of the cross of Christ."

(19) Who mind earthly things. —This last phrase, which in itself might seem hardly strong enough for a climax to a passage so terribly emphatic, may perhaps be designed to bring out by contrast the glorious passage which follows. But it clearly marks the opposition between the high pretension to enlightened spirituality and the gross carnal temper which it covers, grovelling on earth, incapable of rising to heaven.

(20) Our conversation. —The original may signify either "our city" or "our citizenship" is in heaven. The kingdom is real, because there is a real King, who has given us a place there, who will one day be manifested to take us home. The city is spoken of as ours already. As all the citizens of Philippi, the Roman colony, were citizens of the far distant imperial city, so the Philippian Christians even now were citizens of the better country in heaven.

(21) Who shall change ... —The contrast here signifies that humiliation is but the outward fashion or vesture of the body; the likeness to Christ is, and will be seen to be, its essential and characteristic nature. What is here briefly described as change to conformity with that glorified humanity is worked out in I Cor. 15:42-44, 53, 54. John describes that glorification with brief emphatic solemnity, and draws out explicitly the moral which Paul here implies (I John 3:2, 3).

According to the working ... —See I Cor. 15:24-28. Of that power the primary exhibition in which He is pleased to delight is salvation, gradually preparing His own for heaven; the secondary exhibition, undertaken under a moral necessity, is in retributive judgment. It is of the former only that Paul speaks here, as it shall be made perfect in the resurrection unto eternal life.

4

(1) Dearly beloved and longed for ... —The peculiar affectionateness of this verse is notable. (Comp. I Thess. 2:19.) But it has just the addition natural to the yearnings of captivity. The "crown" is here the garland, the sign of victory in the apostolic race and struggle of which he had spoken above (3:12-14).

(2) Euodias.—The name should be "Euodia." Of Euodia and Syntyche nothing is known. Evidently they were women of note, leaders at Philippi, where the Gospel was first preached to women (Acts 16:13), and the church first formed in a woman's house (Acts 16:14, 40). We may note the many female names in the long list of greetings to the church of Rome (Rom. 16).

(3) True yokefellow.—Perhaps the most likely supposition is that it may refer to Epaphroditus the bearer, perhaps the amanuensis, of the epistle, who had certainly come to help Paul bear his yoke of suffering, and in whose case the sudden address in the second person would cause no ambiguity.

Clement.—From the time of Origen downward this Clement has been identified with the famous Clement, bishop of Rome, and author of the well-known "Epistle to the Church at Corinth," of whom Irenaeus expressly says that he had seen and been in company with "the blessed apostles." In his own epistle he refers emphatically to the examples both of Peter and Paul, as belonging to the times "very near at hand" (see his "Epistle," chap. 5). The fact that he was at this time working at Philippi—considering that Philippi, as a Roman colony, was virtually a part of Rome—is no objection to this identification; nor is the chronology decisive against it, though it would make Clement an old man when he wrote his epistle. The identification may stand as probable, while the commonness of the name Clemens makes it far from certain.

(4) Rejoice in the Lord ... —The original word is the word always used in classical Greek for "farewell" (i.e., "Joy be with you!"), and this verse is obviously a resumption of 3:1, after the digression of warning.

1060

(5) The Lord is at hand.—A translation of the Syriac "Maranatha" of I Cor. 16:22—obviously a Christian watchword, probably referring to the Second Advent as near at hand.

(6) Be careful for nothing.—An exact repetition of our Lord's command, "Take no thought" (Matt. 6:25, 34). The prohibition is of that painful anxiety which is inevitable in all who feel themselves alone in mere self-dependence amid the difficulties and dangers of life. Therefore the apostle passes on at once to speak of the trustfulness of prayer. (See I Pet. 5:7; II Cor. 6:1.)

Prayer and supplication with thanksgiving.—By "prayer" is meant worship generally, so called because in this state of imperfection prayer must be its leading element, as praise will be in the perfection of the future. To this general word is subjoined the distinction of the two great elements of worship, "supplication with thanksgiving." Both words "prayer" and "supplication" have the article in the original, and may probably refer to the recognized worship of the Church. (See Acts 2:42.)

(7) The peace of God—i.e., the peace which God gives to every soul which rests on Him in prayer. It includes peace with God, peace with men, peace with self. It keeps or guards our whole spiritual action, both in its source and its developments. It is "through Christ Jesus," for "He is our peace" (Eph. 2:14. Comp. John 14:27.)

(8, 9) The apostle again draws to a conclusion, in a comprehensive exhortation to stand fast in all that is good on the foundation which he had laid in the name of Christ. The exhortation is marked by the reiteration of affectionate earnestness, in which we may trace an underlying method. In each pair of epithets there seems to be reference both to an inner reality and to the outward development, by which it is at once manifested and perfected. In both Paul would have them grow up to perfection.

(8) If there be any virtue, and ... praise.—Still there is the same antithesis—"virtue" is the inherent quality; "praise" is virtue's due. But the word "virtue," so frequent in human morality, is hardly ever used in Scripture. The only other application to man is in II Pet. 1:5, where it seems especially to signify the energy of practice by which faith grows into knowledge. The reason of this is clear. To the very name of "virtue" clings the idea of self-reliance—such self-reliance as the Stoic philosophy (then the only dominant system of Roman opinion which had any nobleness in it) made its essential characteristic; and the idea is, of course, foreign to the whole conception of Christian morality. The occurrence, therefore, here of an appeal to "virtue" and to "praise" seems strange. Probably it is an appeal to the lower conceptions of the society, so characteristically Roman, around them: "Even if there be any truth in the virtue and praise of mere human morality," etc.

(9) Ye have both learned, and received.— The reference is here to Paul's teaching which he "delivered" to them (see I Cor. 15:1-3; Gal. 1:12) as a message, "received" by revelation of God, and which they "received" accordingly. His example was subsidiary to his teaching and confirmatory of its truth.

(10) Now at the last.—There is in these words an expression of some heretofore disappointed expectation, not wholly unlike the stronger expression of wounded feeling in II Tim. 4:9, 10, 16. At Caesarea Paul would have been necessarily cut off from the European churches; at Rome, the metropolis of universal concourse, he may have expected some earlier communication. But he feared wounding the Philippians by even the semblance of reproof, in their case undeserved. Epaphroditus would seem to have arrived early, almost as soon as Paul's arrival at Rome gave them the opportunity which they previously lacked.

(11) I have learned.—The "I" is here emphatic. There is evident reference to the habit peculiar to Paul of refusing that maintenance from the churches which was his of right. (Comp. Acts 20:33, 34; I Cor. 9:14.)

Content.—Such self-sufficiency was the special characteristic claimed by the Stoics for the ideal wise man of their philosophy— a characteristic full of nobleness, as far as it involved independence from all the things of the world. It is difficult not to suppose that Paul makes his claim with some reference to a philosophy so essentially Roman in practical development.

(13) I can do all things.—Properly, "I have strength in all things," rather (according to the context) to bear than to do. But the universal extension of the maxim beyond the immediate occasion and context is admissible. It represents the ultimate and ideal consciousness of the Christian: to throw off mere self-sufficiency, to know our weakness and sin, to accept the salvation of God's free grace in Christ.

Through Christ which strengtheneth me.— The word "Christ" is not found in the best MSS; it is a gloss, perhaps suggested by I Tim. 1:12. (Comp. Eph. 6:10.) In this sentence we have the world-wide distinction between the Stoic and the Christian. Each teaches respect for the higher humanity in the soul; but to the one that humanity is our own, while to the other it is "the Christ within," dwelling in the heart, regenerating and conforming it to Himself. The words of Paul are but a practical corollary to the higher truth (comp. 1:21).

(14) Ye have well done in sending the offerings. In this, says Paul, they made his affliction their own, helping him to bear it by sympathy and sacrifice for his sake. The whole is an illustration of his own words (Acts 20:35). He had the lower blessedness, they the higher; and he rejoiced that it was so.

(15) In the beginning of the gospel.—The time referred to is his leaving Macedonia for Athens and Corinth (Acts 17:14). At Corinth we know that he received offerings from Macedonia (II Cor. 11:9). His language to the Thessalonian Church (I Thess. 2:9; II Thess. 3:8) precludes all idea that any part of this contribution was from Thessalonica; we learn here that it was from no other church than Philippi.

(16) Even in Thessalonica.—At Thessalonica, as at Corinth, he refused maintenance and lived mainly by the labor of his own hands (I Thess. 2:9; II Thess. 3:8). But it appears from this passage that even then he received occasionally some aid from Philippi.

(17) Fruit that may abound to your account.—Their gift is a token of love and gratitude to him; but, as Christian almsgiving, it is something more, and what that something more is will be seen hereafter, when all accounts shall be finally taken. (Comp. Prov. 19:17.)

(19) My God.—The expression is emphatic. Paul had accepted the offerings as made, not to himself, but to the God whose minister he was. Hence he adds, "my God"— the God whom ye serve in serving me.

In glory.—There is constant reference to "glory" in the epistles of the captivity. Where the word relates to God in Himself, His "glory" is His true nature as manifested to His creatures; where it refers to man, "glory" is the perfection of man's nature in the communion with God in heaven. Here the latter sense is to be taken.

(20) Now unto God and our Father . . . —The doxology seems suggested by the use

1061

of "glory" in the previous verse. "Glory" may be derivatively the privilege of man; but "the glory" (the original has the article—the essential and incommunicable glory—must be ascribed to God alone. Such doxologies are common with Paul (See Rom. 16:27; Gal. 1:5; Eph. 3:21; I Tim. 1:17; II Tim. 4:18).

(21) The brethren, which are with me.— The list of those who were with Paul at one time or another during his imprisonment may be gathered from Col. 4:10-15 and Philem. 23, 24. How many of these were with him at this particular time we cannot tell. They are distinguished from "all the saints"—the body of the Church in general.

(22) Of Caesar's household.—This included a multitude of persons of all ages, rank, and occupations. Lightfoot, remarking that these Christians of Caesar's household are alluded to as if well known to the Philippians, has examined the various names mentioned in Rom. 16 (three years before this time), and finds many of them identical with names actually found in sepulchral inscriptions, as belonging to members of the imperial household. These were earlier converts; but, wherever Paul's prison was, he can hardly have failed to gain through the praetorians some communication with the household of the emperor, whose bodyguard they were; and the allusion here seems to show that for some reason these Christians of Caesar's household were in special familiarity with him. Probably, therefore, he had added from that household new converts to Christ; and he mentions this here (comp. 1:13) in order to show the Philippians that his very imprisonment had given special opportunity for the spread of the Gospel.

COLOSSIANS

1

(1) Timotheus our brother.—Except in the mention of Timotheus (as in the other epistles of the captivity), the salutation is almost verbally coincident with the opening of the Epistle to the Ephesians. In a special epistle like this Timotheus would be joined with Paul as usual. In a general epistle to the churches of Asia, the apostle alone could rightly speak.

(2) From God our Father and the Lord Jesus Christ.—The best MSS show the salutation simply "from God the Father," thus varying from Paul's otherwise universal phraseology. Such variation can hardly be accidental. It could have been suggested to Paul's mind, in connection with his special desire to emphasize the true Godhead of Christ, by an instinctive reluctance to use any phrase which might even seem to distinguish His nature from the Godhead.

(3, 4) Comp. Eph. 1:15, 16, where there is an almost exact verbal coincidence. The Colossian Church, though well-known to Paul, was not known by personal knowledge.

(5) For the hope which is laid up for you in heaven.—The prominence given to the thought of "the heavenly places" in the epistles of the captivity, and therefore to Christ in heaven, even more than to Christ risen, is evident to the careful reader. Accordingly, the hope, which is the instinct of perfection in man, and which becomes realization of heaven in the Christian, naturally comes out with corresponding emphasis.

Ye heard before.—That is, at their first conversion. There is an implied warning against the new doctrines, which are more fully noticed in the next chapter.

(6) Which is come unto you ... —There are two lessons implied. First, the universality of the Gospel, in which it stands contrasted, as with all local and national religions, so also with the secret doctrines of Gnostic speculation, intelligible only to the initiated few. Next, the test of its reality both by practical fruit of action and by the spiritual growth connected with it. Both these lessons were evidently needed, in consequence of the appearance at Colossae of the occult mysticism and the unpractical speculation noted in 2:8, 10, 18. But the Church itself was still faithful. Hence, the implied warning is by no means a condemnation.

(7) Ye also learned of Epaphras.—Of Epaphras we know nothing, except what we gather from this passage and from 4:12; Philem. 23. The name is a shortened form of Epaphroditus, but it is most unlikely that he is the same as the Epaphroditus of Phil. 2:25 and 4:18. Being, it seems, a native of Colossae itself, he was apparently its first evangelist, and is afterward described as feeling some responsibility for it and its neighboring cities, Laodicea and Hierapolis (4:13). That he was Bishop of Colossae is probably a mere guess of tradition. But he may have had some such charge as that which was afterward more formally committed to Timothy at Ephesus and to Titus in Crete. At this time, however, he remained with Paul and apparently shared his captivity.

Who is for you a faithful minister of Christ.—There is considerable MS authority for the reading "on our behalf," that is, "in our stead." This makes Epaphras a representative, perhaps an actual messenger, of Paul for the conversion of the church at Colossae, sent probably at the time when the apostle had his headquarters at Ephesus, and when "all that dwelt in Asia heard the word of the Lord Jesus" (Acts 19:10). This interpretation explains the attitude of authority here assumed by Paul toward a church which he had not seen, differing so markedly from the tone of his epistle to the Romans in a like case.

(8) Who also declared unto us.—This refers to news recently brought by Epaphras to Paul at Rome. He had been a minister in Paul's stead; he now, like Timothy afterward, visited him to give account of his deputed work.

(9) The knowledge of his will.—The "knowledge" here spoken of is the full knowledge to be attained in measure here, to be made perfect in heaven. (See I Cor. 13:12.) It is not speculation as to the nature of God, or as to emanations from Deity, or even as to the reasons of God's mysterious counsels, but knowledge of what actually is His will. This knowledge of God's will is man's "wisdom."

(10) Here Paul begins to dwell on the practical life, much in the same spirit of Eph. 4:1. To walk worthy of Christ is to have His life reproduced in us, to follow His example, to have His mind. The word "pleasing" used here is not found elsewhere in the New Testament, but is employed in classic and Hellenistic Greek to mean "a general disposition to please"—a constant preference of the will of others before our own. The path toward the knowledge of God indicated here is not the path of thoughtful speculation, or of meditative devotion, but the path coordinate with these— the path of earnest practice.

(11) On the use of "the glory" of God, frequent in these epistles, see Eph. 1:6, 12, 14. The prayer, however, in the Ephesian epistle looks to "knowledge of the love of Christ" as its object, the prayer here to power of endurance of trial and suffering.

"Patience" is here "endurance," rather than what we usually call patience. It is spoken of by James (1:3) as the result of the bracing effect of trial, and is illustrated by the typical example of Job (Jas. 5:11). To this "patience," here as elsewhere (II Tim. 3:10), Paul adds "longsuffering"—a word generally connected (I Cor. 13:4) with the temper of gentleness and love, which hardly feels to the utmost such spiritual trials as vexed the righteous soul of Job. Of such longsuffering our Lord's bearing of the insults and the cruelties of the Passion is the perfect type. Yet even then Paul is not content without "joyfulness." The ground of such joy, so often shown in Christian martyrdom, is given by I Pet. 4:13. Of that joy Paul himself was a bright example in his present captivity. (See Phil. 1:18, 19; 2:17, 18.)

(12) In light.—See Eph. 4:8-14, a passage dwelling on the idea of the kingdom of light almost as strongly and exhaustively as John himself (I John 1:5-7, etc.). "In the light" (opposed to "the power of darkness" of the next verse) is in the light of God's countenance, revealed in the face of Jesus Christ.

(13-23) Here we have the great characteristic section of this epistle, distinguished from corresponding parts of the Epistle to the Ephesians by the explicit and emphatic stress laid upon the divine majesty of Christ. It corresponds closely with the remarkable passage opening the Epistle to the Hebrews. In the epistles of the preceding group—Corinthians, Galatians, and Romans —prominence is given to the universal mediation of Christ; in these epistles we pass on to that which such universal mediation necessitates—the conception of Christ as the Head of all created being and as the perfect manifestation of the Godhead. Paul's emphatic assertion of the great truth here comes naturally in the order of revelation, leading up to the full doctrine of "the

1064

Word" in John. As the spiritual meaning of the Resurrection, the great subject of the first preaching, had to be sought in the Atonement, so the inquiry into the possibility of a universal atonement led back to the Incarnation, and to Christ as pre-existent.

(13) Who hath delivered us from the power of darkness.—"Delivered" is "rescued," properly applied to dragging a person out of battle or the jaws of danger. "The power of darkness" (Luke 22:53) is the power of evil, permitted (Luke 4:6) to exist but in itself a usurped tyranny (as Chrysostom expresses it), not a true "kingdom."

And hath translated us . . . —The word "translated" is a word properly applied to the transplanting of races and the settlement of them in a new home. Salvation, begun by rescue, is completed by the settlement of the rescued captives in the new kingdom of Christ.

His dear Son.—The original is far more striking and beautiful. It is "the Son of His love," corresponding to "the beloved" of Eph. 1:6, but perhaps going beyond it.

In whom we have . . . —From the love of the Father, the first cause of salvation, we pass to the efficient cause in the redemption and propitiation of the Son.

Verses 15-17 pass from Christ as our Mediator to Christ as He is in Himself from all eternity, "the image of the invisible God," and as He is from the beginning of time, the creator and sustainer of all things in heaven and earth. What was before implied is now explicitly asserted; what was before emphatically asserted is now taken for granted, and made the steppingstone to yet higher and more mysterious truth.

(15) The image of the invisible God.— The word "image" (like the word "form," Phil. 2:6, 7) is used in the New Testament for the real and essential embodiment, as distinguished from mere likeness. (Comp. Rom. 1:23; I Cor. 11:7; 15:49; II Cor. 3:18; Heb. 1:3; 10:1.) It is not to be forgotten that at this time in the Platonizing Judaism of Philo, "the Word" was called the eternal "image of God." This expression (not peculiar to him) seems to have represented in the Jewish schools the idea complementary to the ordinary idea of the Messiah in the Jewish world. Just as John took up the vague idea of "the Word," and gave it a clear divine personality in Christ, so Paul seems to act here in relation to the other phrase, used as a description of the Word. In Christ he fixes in solid reality the floating vision of the "image of God."

There is an emphasis here on the words "of the invisible God." Now, since the whole context shows that the reference is to the eternal pre-existence of Christ, ancient interpreters (of whom Chrysostom may be taken as the type) argued that the image of the invisible must be also invisible. But this seems opposed to the whole idea of the word "image" and to its use in the New Testament and elsewhere. The true key to this passage is in our Lord's own words in John 1:18 (here is the remarkable reading, "the only begotten God"). In anticipation of the future revelation of Godhead, Christ, even as pre-existent, is called "the image of the invisible God."

The firstborn of every creature.—Better, "begotten before all creation," thus the "begotten before all worlds" of the Nicene Creed. In Himself He is "the image of God" from all eternity. From this essential conception, by a natural contrast, the thought immediately passes on to distinction from, and priority to, all created being. Exactly in this same order of idea we have Heb. 1:2, 3 and John 1:3. The word "firstborn" is used of the Messiah as an almost technical name (derived from Pss. 2:7; 89:28), as is shown in Heb. 1:6. Hence the idea contained in the word is sovereignty (Ps. 89:28; comp. Dan. 8:13, 14), as well as likeness to God and priority to all created being. In the first clause, then, we have the declaration of His eternal unity with God; in the second we trace the distinctness of His Person and the subordination of the co-eternal Son to the Father. The union of the two marks the assertion of Christian mystery, as against rationalizing systems of the type of Arianism on one side, of Sabellianism on the other.

(16) For by him ... were all things created ... by him, and for him.—Carrying out the idea of the preceding clause with accumulated emphasis, Paul speaks of all creation as having taken place "by him," "through him," and "for him." (Comp. Rom. 11:36; Heb. 2:10.) Here we observe that the apostle takes up a phrase belonging only to Godhead and usually applied to the Father, and distinctly applies it to Christ, but with the significant change of "from whom" into "in whom," indirectly condemning by anticipation the fancy of incipient Gnosticism, that He was but an inferior emanation or agent of the supreme God.

Thrones, or dominions ... —Comp. Eph. 1:21. The word peculiar to this passage is "thrones," which in all the various specula-

tions as to the hierarchy of heaven, naturally represents the first place of dignity and nearness to the throne of God. But it seems difficult to attach distinctive meanings to those titles and to trace out their order. If Paul alludes at all to the rabbinical hierarchies, he takes their titles without attending to their fanciful orders and meanings. Whatever they mean, all are infinitely below the glory of Christ.

(17) He is before all things.—The words "He is" are both emphatic. Hence "before" should be taken, not of supreme dignity, but of pre-existence. (Comp. John 1:15; 8:58.)

By him all things consist.—That is, "hold together in unity," obeying the primaeval law of their being. In this clause is attributed to our Lord, not only the creative act, but also the constant sustaining power, which, even less than the creative agency, can be supposed to be a derivative and finite power, such as that of the Demiurgus of Gnostic speculation.

(18-20) In these verses Paul returns from dwelling on the eternal nature of the Son of God to describe Him in His mediatorial office as Son of Man, becoming the "Head" of all humanity, as called into "his body, the church." (See Eph. 1:10, 20, 22; 2:19, 21; 4:15, 16.) There is in this epistle more stress on the supreme dignity of the Head, as in the other more on the unity, blessing, and glory of the body. In this mediatorial office, there is throughout a mysterious analogy to His eternal sonship.

(18) The firstborn from the dead.—In his sermon at Antioch in Pisidia (Acts 13:33), Paul quotes the passage, "Thou art my Son; this day have I begotten thee," as fulfilled in that "He raised up Jesus again." (Comp. Rom. 1:3; Heb. 5:5; Rev. 1:5.) The Resurrection is the beginning of exaltation, contrasted with His birth on earth in great humility, and of His entrance on the glory of His mediatorial kingdom. (See Eph. 1:20-23.)

(19) For it pleased the Father.—There is nothing corresponding to "the Father" in the original. The simplest grammatical construction would be to take "the fulness" as nominative. But the personification of "the fulness," common in Gnostic speculation, is hardly after the manner of Paul. Perhaps, on the whole, the rendering of our version is to be preferred, especially as it suits better with the following verse. The sense is, however, quite clear, and is enforced by 2:9. On the word "fulness" (**pleroma**), see note on Eph. 1:23. The "fulness of the

1065

Godhead" is the essential nature, comprising all the attributes, of Godhead. The indwelling of such Deity in the humanity of Christ is the ground of all His exaltation as the "Head," "the beginning," the "firstborn from the dead," and the triumphant King, on which Paul had already dwelt. By it alone can He be the true Mediator between God and man.

(20) Having made peace through the blood of his cross.—Comp. Eph. 2:13-18. This present passage includes in the reconciliation by the blood of Christ, not merely all humanity, but "all things, whether things on earth or things in heaven." This is, indeed, only a fuller exposition of the truth of Rom. 8:19-21 and II Cor. 5:19. As there is a physical unity in the universe, so there is a moral and spiritual unity also in Jesus Christ.

(22) In the body of his flesh.—We may naturally suppose that there was present to Paul's mind the thought of the Gnosticism which depreciated the body as evil and which must have always inclined to the idea that "Jesus Christ had not come in the flesh" (I John 4:2, 3), and that the presence of this thought induced some special emphasis in his language.

(23) The hope.—See note on verse 5. Here, as there, great emphasis is laid on "hope." But here there may possibly be reference to some ideas (comp. II Tim. 2:18) that "the resurrection was past already," and that the hope of a true resurrection and a real heaven was either a delusion or a metaphor.

(24-29) Paul dwells on his own mission to set forth the universal Gospel to the Gentiles. In the Ephesian epistle this declaration is made a direct introduction to practical exhortation (comp. chaps. 4, 5, 6); here it leads up to the earnest remonstrance against speculative errors in chap. 2, which precedes a similar practical exhortation.

(24) Who now rejoice.—The rejoicing is in suffering, not in itself, not solely because it is borne with and for Christ, but also because it is for the sake of the Church.

Fill up that which is behind of the afflictions of Christ.—This is a clearer and more striking expression of the truth conveyed in II Cor. 1:5: the sufferings of Christ overflow to us, so that we bear our part in addition to the full measure which He bore. (Comp. Matt. 20:22, 23; Phil. 3:10; I Pet. 4:13.) But, looking to the meaning and use of the word "affliction," we note that "the afflictions of Christ" must be His sufferings

on earth considered simply as a part—though immeasurably the chief part—of the burden of humanity in a sinful world. They represent, not the cross of atonement, on which He alone could suffer, but the cross of struggle against sin even to death, which He expressly bade us take up if we would follow Him. This He has still left "behind"; this in His strength every one of His servants bears, partly for himself, partly also for others.

(25) The dispensation of God.—See notes on Eph. 3:2-9.

(26) The mystery.—See note on Eph. 1:9. In this passage, perhaps, it is defined with perfect clearness as a secret long hidden and now revealed.

(27) The riches of the glory.—See Eph. 1:18; 3:16.

Which is Christ in you.—Here the mystery itself is boldly defined as "Christ in you." (Comp. Eph. 3:6.) On the great idea in the purely individual relation, see Phil. 1:21; Gal. 2:20; and in the more general form, see Rom. 8:10; II Cor. 13:5; Gal. 4:19.

The hope of glory.—As in verses 5 and 23, the special emphasis laid on the hope of heaven. Christ is "our hope," as He is "our life," i.e., the ground of our certainty of the future, as of our spiritual life in the present.

(28) Perfect.—See Eph. 4:13; Phil. 3:15. Here, as in I Cor. 2:6, 7, the reference may be to "initiated in mystery." Paul, in opposition to the exclusive claim of "perfection" by the speculators in mystic knowledge, would present every man, learned or ignorant, perfect before God. In this universality of privilege lies the glorious distinction between the Gospel and all schools of philosophy.

(29) Whereunto I also labour.—In this verse Paul passes from the plural to the singular, evidently in preparation for the strong personal remonstrance of 2:1-7.

His working . . .—See Gal. 2:8; Eph. 1:12. There is special allusion to the grace given to him for his apostleship of the Gentiles.

2

(1) What great conflict.—This describes the intense earnestness of the whole struggle against evil which Paul was undergoing for them; but perhaps we may refer it especially to "striving in prayer" for them (see 4:12). It is probably dwelt upon here to show why, although unknown to them personally, he yet writes so urgently to them.

And for them at Laodicea.—Comp. 4:13. The three cities lay near together in the valley of the Lycus, a tributary of the Maeander; probably they were converted at one time, and are evidently regarded as forming one Christian community, for which Epaphras, the evangelist of Colossae, felt himself responsible. Colossae and Laodicea are actually directed to exchange the apostolic Letters sent to them (see 4:16) and to read both alike in the churches. Of Laodicea, the greatest and richest of the three cities, we have no further notice in Scripture, except that stern apocalyptic letter (Rev. 3:14-22), which has made its name proverbial for spiritual lukewarmness and presumptuous self-reliance. Of Colossae and Hierapolis we read only in this epistle. Lightfoot points out that, while Hierapolis and Laodicea play a prominent part in the subsequent history of Christianity in Asia Minor, Colossae never attains importance.

As many as have not seen my face.—See note on 1:7. Epaphras apparently had been commissioned by Paul, and thus, indirectly, the apostle might be held to be the founder of Colossae. Accordingly, this Letter stands midway between the unreserved familiarity of the epistles to Corinth or Philippi, and the more formal reserve of the Epistle to the Romans.

(2) The acknowledgement . . . —This clause explains what the "fullness of intelligence" is. Christ, as indwelling man, is the mystery which alone solves the problem of humanity—what it is, and where it tends. Here Christ is the "mystery of God"—i.e., He in whom the inscrutable nature of God is revealed to us. The name again leads up to the doctrine of "the Word of God."

(3) In whom are hid all the treasures.— The word "hidden" (**apocryphi**) is an almost technical word for secret teaching given only to the initiated; used originally as a term of honor, afterward, from the character of these "apocryphal" books, it came to signify spurious and heretical. Paul evidently takes up here a word, used by the pretenders to a special and abstruse knowledge, and applies it to "heavenly things." From our full comprehension they are hidden; but we can have full practical apprehension of them by our knowledge of Christ, who knows them—a knowledge begun in faith and perfected chiefly in love.

Wisdom and knowledge.—The word "knowledge" (**gnosis**) was the word which,

certainly afterward, probably even then, was the watchword of "Gnosticism"—the unbridled and fantastic spirit of metaphysical and religious speculation then beginning to infest all Christian thought. It can hardly be accidental that Paul here, as elsewhere, subordinates it to the higher gift of wisdom.

(4) Beguile you.—"To beguile" here is "to reason into error"; and "enticing words" are words of "persuasion" rather than of reason or revelation. Both words are used by Paul only in this passage. It would be difficult to describe more accurately the marvelous fabrics of gnostic speculation, each step claiming to be based on some fancied probability or metaphysical propriety. We know these in all the elaborate monstrosity of full growth; Paul doubtless saw them as yet only in embryo.

(5) Your order, and the stedfastness.— From the days of the ancient Greek interpreters downward, it has been noted that both words have military associations—the one being used for discipline generally, and the other for the firm compact solidity of the phalanx, and (as in Eph. 6:11-17) that the use of them may have been suggested by Paul's captivity under military guard. If both words be referred to their "faith," the apostle obviously characterizes it as having "order" in its various parts and "solidity" against all trials.

(7) Rooted and built up in him.—Paul bids them seek not only the first basis of their faith, but their continual growth, in Christ alone, by continual "strengthening in the faith" which rests in Him. In the gnostic teaching faith was held good for the beginner or the common herd; knowledge was the bright particular jewel of those who went on to perfection.

(8) Spoil you.—Properly, "lead you away as a spoil," triumph over you as a captive, and make you a slave.

Philosophy and vain deceit—i.e., a philosophy which is inseparably connected with vain deceit. (See I Cor. 8:1; I Tim. 6:20.) The warning implied here seems to be twofold. It is, first, against considering Christianity primarily as a "philosophy," i.e., a search for and knowledge of speculative truth, even the highest. Christianity is not a philosophy, but a life—not a knowledge of abstract principles, but a personal knowledge of faith and love of God in Christ. It is, next, against accepting in philosophy the "vain deceit" of mere speculation and imagination instead of the modest, laborious investigation of facts.

After the tradition of men.—This is the keynote of our Lord's condemnation of the old Pharisaic exclusiveness and formalism (Matt. 15:2, 3, 6; Mark 7:8, 9); it is equally the condemnation of the later half-Jewish mysticism which Paul attacks here. The apostle often claims reverence for "traditions" (I Cor. 11:2; II Thess. 2:15; 3:6), but they are traditions having their starting point in direct revelation of God (Gal. 1:12), and, moreover, traditions freely given to all, as being His. The "tradition of men" here condemned had their origin in human speculation, and were secretly transmitted to the initiated only.

The rudiments of the world.—See note on Gal. 4:2. These are matters of ritual, law, ascetic observance, and the like. They belong to the visible sphere, fit only for the elementary education and intended simply as preparation for a higher teaching.

(9) In him dwelleth all the fulness of the Godhead bodily.—Here almost every word is emphatic. Christ is not a mere emanation from the Supreme Being. It "dwells" and remains forever, not descending on Him for a time and leaving Him again. "Bodily" means incarnate in His humanity. The whole is an extension and enforcement of 1:19. The horror of all that was material, as having in it the seed of evil, induced denial either of the reality of our Lord's body, or of its inseparable connection with the Godhead in Him. Thus the emphasis of John 1:14; I John 4:3.

As in the later Gnosticism, so probably in its earlier forms, the word "fulness" (**pleroma**) was used for the infinite nature of the Supreme Deity, out of which all the emanations (afterward called **Æons**) received in various degrees of imperfection, according to their capacity. Probably for that reason Paul uses it so emphatically here. In the same spirit, John declares (John 1:16), "Out of his (Christ's) fulness have all we received." It is not finite, but infinitely perfect; hence we all can draw from it, yet leave it unimpaired.

(10) Ye are complete.—Comp. Eph. 3:19; 4:13. To partake of the divine **pleroma** is not the special privilege of the initiated; it belongs to all who are united to the Lord Jesus Christ.

Principality and power.—See note on 1:16.

(11) The circumcision made without hands.—The enforcement of Jewish observance was strangely mixed with "philosophy" at Colossae. (Comp. Eph. 2:11.) The phrase "made without hands" is so constantly used of heavenly realities (as in Mark 14:58; II Cor. 5:1; Heb. 9:11, 24) as opposed to earthly symbols that it comes to have the positive sense of "spiritual."

(12) Buried with him in baptism . . .—Comp. Rom. 6:4. What in Romans is the "likeness of his resurrection" is here the participation of it. Here, as in Eph. 1:19-23, 2:5-7, the operation of the mighty power of God is conceived as actually working both in the Head and in the body, so that we through it partake of the Resurrection, the Ascension, and the glorified majesty of Christ. The comparison shows an instructive development in this epistle of the consequences of the unity with Christ.

(13) And you . . .—Here, exactly as in Eph. 2:1-18, there is a remarkable intermixture of the word "we" and the word "you," the former conveying the universal statement of the gospel message of mercy, the other applying it emphatically to the Gentiles as Gentiles. There is, as always, strong similarity, yet complete independence.

(14) Blotting out the handwriting.—The "handwriting" is the bond, exacting payment or penalty in default. (Comp. Eph. 2:15.) The metaphor, however, here is different, and especially notable as the first anticipation of those many metaphors of later theology, from Tertullian downward, in which the idea of a debt to God, paid for us by the blood of Christ as "a satisfaction," is brought out. It is misleading only when we hold it to be not only the truth, but the whole truth, forgetting that legal and forensic metaphors can but imperfectly represent inner spiritual realities.

Nailing it to his cross.—Comp. Gal. 3:13. Paul boldly speaks of that curse as a penalty standing against us, and as nailed to the cross with Himself, so to be forever cancelled in the great declaration, "It is finished." If any be inclined to refer to the "title" on the cross, it was probably nailed to it. Such title declared the explanation of the sufferer's death. The cancelled curse of the Law was just such an explanation of the great atoning death, and the title, declaring His mediatorial kingdom, showed the curse cancelled thereby.

(15) Having spoiled principalities and powers.—Taking (as in II Cor. 2:14-16) his metaphor from a Roman triumph, Paul represents Him as passing in triumphal majesty up the sacred way to the eternal gates, with all the powers of evil bound as captives behind His chariot before the eyes of men and angels. The word here translated "having spoiled" means "having stripped himself," in 3:9. Perhaps Paul purposely omitted the object after the verb, in order to show that it was by "stripping Himself of all" that He conquered by becoming a show in absolute humiliation, making the powers of evil a show in His triumph.

(16) In meat, or in drink.—According to the context, the immediate reference is to the distinctions of meats under the Jewish law, now done away, because the distinction of those within and without the covenant was also done away (Acts 10:11). But a study of Rom. 14:2, 20, 21, written before this epistle, and I Tim. 4:3, written after it—to say nothing of the tone of this passage itself, or of the known characteristics of the later Gnosticism of the ascetic type— show that these laws about eating and drinking were not mere matters of law, but formed significant parts of a rigid mystic asceticism.

An holyday, or of the new moon, or of the sabbath.—Comp. Isa. 1:13, 14; Ezek. 45:17; Hos. 2:13; Gal. 4:10. The "feast" would seem to be one of the great festivals; the "new moon" the monthly, and the sabbath the weekly solemnity. But the passage has a wider meaning (like Rom. 14:6), showing the different position which even Christian festivals held in apostolic days. It is obvious that Paul gives no hint of any succession of the Lord's Day to be, in any strict sense, a "Christian Sabbath." We know, indeed, that the Jewish Sabbath itself lingered in the church, as having a kind of sacredness, kept sometimes as a fast, sometimes as a festival. But its observance was not of obligation. (With verse 17, comp. Heb. 10:1.)

(18) Beguile you of your reward.—The original is a word used, almost technically, for an unfair judgment in the stadium, robbing the victor of his prize. The prize here (as in I Cor. 9:24; Phil. 3:14) is the heavenly reward of the Christian course.

In a voluntary humility.—In this passage alone in the New Testament "humility" is spoken of with something of the condemnation accorded to it in heathen morality. The reason of this is obvious and instructive. Humility is a grace of which the essence is unconsciousness, and which, being itself negative, cannot live, except by resting on some more positive quality, such as faith or love. Whenever it is consciously cultivated and "delighted in," it loses all its

grace; it becomes either unreal, or it turns to abject slavishness and meanness.

Worshipping of angels.—It might seem strange that on the rigid monotheism of Judaism this incongruous creature-worship should have been engrafted. But the worship of the angels, of which the Essenic system bore traces, was excused on the ground that the Law had been given through the "ministration of angels" (see Acts 7:53; Gal. 3:19), and that the tutelary guardianship of angels had been revealed in the later prophecy. (See Dan. 10:10-21.) The "angels" in this half-Jewish system held the same intermediate position between the divine and the human which in the ordinary gnostic theories was held by the less personal ÆEons, or supposed emanations from the Godhead. They provoke pretensions to supernatural knowledge by which (as in I Cor. 8:1) the mind is said to be "puffed up."

(19) Not holding the Head.—In this lay the fatal error. All these speculations and superstitions interfered with the direct hold of the soul on the mediation of Christ, as the Head, from whom alone come all spiritual life and growth. Therefore they had a practical and spiritual importance.

(20) If ye be dead with Christ.—The death with Christ is a death unto "the life of the flesh." This may be (as in Rom. 6:1, 2, 6, 7, 11) "the life of sin"; or it may be the outward and visible life "of the world." The latter is the sense to be taken here (see verses 1 and 8). Comp. Gal. 2:19 and 4:9.

(21) Touch not; taste not; handle not.— The first and last of these renderings should be inverted. There is in the commands a climax of strictness. These commands are marked by the ordinary ascetic preference of spiritual restraint to spiritual energy.

(23) See note on verse 18.

3

(1) If ye then be risen with Christ.—As the partaking of the death of Christ taught the negative lesson of death to the Law, so the partaking of His resurrection teaches the positive lesson of the spiritual life.

Seek those things ... (2) set your affection on things above.—The spiritual life in its continuance is described first as looking, and so growing, to perfection (Phil. 3:12-16), and next anticipating heaven, not only in hope, but also in tone and temper. These two graces must be united. In the one is the secret of growth, in the other the present earnest of perfection. (See Eph. 2:6.)

(3) Ye are dead.—Properly, "ye died." (See note on 2:20.)

Your life is hid with Christ in God (4) ... Christ, who is our life.—Our Lord's ascent to His glory in heaven is at once the pledge and the means of our spiritual communion with God. "Christ is our life" now as well as hereafter. This is simply a summary of two truths: "Christ liveth in me" (Gal. 2:20) as the source of life; and "To me to live (the actual condition of life) is Christ" (Phil. 1:21).

(4) When Christ ... shall appear, then shall ye also appear with him in glory.—This describes the last stage of the spiritual life—the glorification with Christ in heaven, manifesting what now is hidden, and perfecting what exists only in germ.. (Comp. I John 3:1, 2; Phil. 3:21.)

(5) Mortify therefore your members which are upon the earth.—As a rule, Scripture more clearly marks the distinction between the members and "the law of sin in the members" (Rom. 7:5, 23); and we are usually bidden not to "kill our members," but to turn them from "instruments of unrighteousness" to be "instruments of righteousness unto God" (Rom. 6:13). This passage contains only half the truth, corresponding to the death with Christ, and not the whole truth, including also the resurrection to the new life. Accordingly, as the next verse shows, the members to be mortified are actually identified with the vices of the old man residing in them.

Fornication, uncleanness ... covetousness, which is idolatry.—See note on Eph. 5:3.

Inordinate affection, evil concupiscence.—This is the condition of unrestrained passion and desire, the former word implying a passive receptiveness of impression from without, the other the positive energy of desire to seek gratification.

(8) Anger, wrath, malice, blasphemy, filthy communication.—See note on Eph. 4:31.

(9, 10) Comp. Eph. 4:22-25.

(11) Where there is neither ... —Comp. Gal. 3:28. The insertion of "barbarian, Scythian" is clearly intended to rebuke that pride of intellect, contemptuous of the unlearned, which lay at the root of Gnosticism. The "barbarian" was simply the foreigner (comp. I Cor. 14:11); the "Scythian" was the savage toward whom the contempt implied for the "barbarian" assumed explic-

itness, and reached its climax. The omission of "male nor female" is noteworthy. In the Oriental society, as in Galatia, the dignity of women needed to be asserted against supposed inferiority. In Graecized society, as at Corinth, Ephesus, and Colossae, the new "freedom" of the Gospel was apt to be abused to license; hence it was rather the "subjection" of women which needed to be suggested. (Comp. I Cor. 11:3-16; 14:34, 35; Eph. 5:22-24; and I Tim. 2:11-15.) Under aspects both of Colossians and Galatians the catholicity of the Gospel is equally brought out, here by the direct union of all alike with Christ, there by the resulting unity of all with one another.

(12) Holy and beloved.—There are here two signs of election. The elect are "holy," consecrated to God in thought and life, and "beloved," accepted and sustained in their consecration by His love. They are "beloved," therefore they should love one another (verses 12-15); they are holy, therefore they should thank God and live to His glory (verses 16, 17). Comp. Eph. 4:2, 31; 5:1, 2. The word "tenderhearted" in those passages corresponds to the "bowels (or, **heart**) of mercies" here.

(13) Even as Christ forgave you.—In Eph. 4:31 we have "God in Christ forgave you," because there the example of Christ, as Son of Man, is afterward to be set forth emphatically as an example of self-sacrifice (verse 2). Here, in accordance with the emphatic exaltation of Christ, as all in all, the simpler phrase "Christ (or, **the Lord**) forgave you" is employed.

(14) The bond of perfectness.—The phrase is apparently suggested by the claim to perfection set up by the Gnostic teachers. They sought such perfection in knowledge peculiar to the few; Paul in the love which is possible to all.

(16) The word of Christ.—It will be observed how all such phrases prepare for the full conception of Him as Himself "the Word of God." The indwelling Word of God is described as manifesting itself, first, in the wisdom of mutual teaching, next, in the grace of hearty thanksgiving. Comp. Eph. 5:19, 20, where the whole is described as a consequence of "being filled with the Spirit."

(17) All in the name of the Lord Jesus.—Comp. I Cor. 10:31. This is the first principle of all godly life. The main object of all life, speculative or practical, is declared to be, not our own happiness or perfection, not the good of our fellow men, but the "glory of God"—the carrying out of His will, and so manifesting His moral attributes.

Chap. 3:18-4:1 deals with the three great relations of life—between wives and husbands, children and parents, servants and masters. In this section we have the closest parallelism with the Epistle to the Ephesians (5:22-6:9). But the treatment of the first relation is far briefer, having nothing to correspond to the grand and characteristic comparison of marriage to the union between Christ and the Church. Even in the second there is somewhat greater brevity and simplicity. The third is dwelt upon with marked coincidence of language and at least equal emphasis. We can hardly doubt that the presence of Onesimus, the runaway slave, suggested this peculiar emphasis on the right relation between the slave and his master.

4

(3) A door of utterance.—Comp. I Cor. 16:9; II Cor. 2:12. There the opened door is the door of external opportunity; here the "door of utterance" is the removal of all internal impediments to preaching.

(5) Walk in wisdom ... redeeming the time.—Comp. Eph. 5:15. There the "strictness" and "wisdom" are to guard against excess or recklessness within; here the "wisdom" is to watch against external dangers and make full use of external opportunities.

(6) Seasoned with salt.—It seems impossible not to trace here a reference to our Lord's words in Mark 9:50. There the salt is spoken of as the preservative from corruption, and the warning against "corrupt" words in Eph. 4:29 has been thought to point in the same direction. But the context appears certainly to suggest that the use of salt is to teach "how to answer every man," and that this answer (comp. I Pet. 3:15) is to be given to "those without." Probably, therefore, the "seasoning with salt" is to provide against insipidity. Their speech is to be primarily kindled by the true life of Christian grace in it; secondarily, it is to have good sense and point, so as to be effective for the inquirer or against the scoffer.

(7, 8) These verses present an almost exact verbal coincidence with Eph. 6:21, 22. In the verses, however, which follow, the particularity and detail of this epistle

stand in marked contrast with the brief generality of Eph. 6:23, 24. Remembering that the two epistles were sent at the same time, and that Ephesus was a church far better known than Colossae, we cannot but regard this as supporting the idea of an encyclical character in our Epistle to the Ephesians.

(9) Onesimus.—See Philem. 10-17. The emphatic reference to him as being "faithful and beloved" like Tychicus, and "one of you" like Epaphras, is a remarkable commentary on Paul's exhortation as to slaves and masters in the preceding chapter.

(10) Aristarchus my fellowprisoner.— Apparently a Jew, one "of Thessalonica" and first named (in Acts 19:29) as dragged with Gaius into the theater in the tumult at Ephesus; from there he accompanied Paul (Acts 20:4), at any rate as far as Asia, on his journey to Jerusalem. When, after two years' captivity, the apostle starts from Caesarea on his voyage to Rome, Aristarchus is again named by Luke as "being with us" (Acts 27:2). From this fact, and from his being called here "my fellow-prisoner" (a name which there seems no adequate reason to consider as metaphorical), it would appear that, whether voluntarily or involuntarily, Aristarchus really shared his captivity.

Marcus, sister's son to Barnabas.—This is the first notice of John Mark since the day when Paul rejected him (Acts 15:38). Then he had gone with Barnabas to Cyprus to take part in an easier work. Now the formal charge to the Colossian Church to "receive him"—a kind of "letter of commendation" (II Cor. 3:1)—evidently shows that they had known of him as under Paul's displeasure, and were now to learn that he had seen reason to restore him to his confidence. In Philemon 24 Mark is named among his "fellow-labourers." In Paul's last epistle, written almost with a dying hand (II Tim. 4:11), there is a touch of peculiar pathos in the charge which he, left alone in prison with his old companion Luke, gives to Timothy to bring Mark, as now being right serviceable for the "ministration" from which he had once rejected him. Evidently Paul's old rebuke had done its work, and, if Mark did join him in his last hours, he probably thanked him for nothing so much as for the loving sternness of days gone by. Before this, he was with Peter (I Pet. 5:13), and must be identified with Mark the evangelist, subsequently, as tradition has it, bishop and martyr at Alexandria.

(11) Jesus, which is called Justus.—The surname "Justus" is found in Acts 1:23; 18:7. We learn from tradition that by it James, "the Lord's brother," was known. (See Acts 22:14; comp. Luke 23:47.) Of this Justus there is no other notice, not even in the Epistle to Philemon, in which all the other names recur.

(12) Epaphras.—See note on 1:7.

Perfect and complete.—In the two epithets—perfect and fully established in conviction—we may again trace reference to the pretensions of the gnostic teachers to exclusive perfection in wisdom. Paul's true fellow-worker, like himself, prays that this perfection may belong to all, and that it may have its basis not in the secrets of heavenly knowledge, but in the revealed "will of God."

(13) On the natural union of Laodicea and Hierapolis with Colossae, see note on 2:1.

(14) Luke, the beloved physician, and Demas.—Comp. Philem. 24. The original is even more emphatic, "Luke the physician, the beloved one." Demas, on the contrary, is barely named. It is impossible not to pass on in thought to the last notice of the two by Paul (II Tim. 4:10). On the relation of Luke to Paul, we need only remark that the mention of him suggests the idea that it was both as physician and as friend that Luke, now, as in the last captivity, was with the apostle. Though the captivity was not, according to ancient ideas, severe, it must have told upon his weak and shattered health.

(15) And Nymphas.—Of Nymphas we know nothing, except from this passage. He is obviously a man of importance, a center of church life, in the Christian community at Laodicea.

The church which is in his house.—This phrase is found elsewhere only as applied to Aquila and Priscilla (Rom. 16:5; I Cor. 16:19), and to Philemon (Philem. 2). Thus this "church in the house" is seen to have gathered only around persons of some mark and leadership. The houses sanctified by such gatherings were the parents of the material churches of the future.

(16) When this epistle.—In the implied direction to read this epistle in the church (comp. I Thess. 5:27) we discern the method of first publication of the apostolic epistles; in the direction to interchange epistles with the Laodicean church we trace the way in which these epistles became more widely diffused and recognized as authoritative in the church at large. Thus it was that they were "canonized," i.e., accepted as a part of the "canon" or rule of divine truth.

The epistle from Laodicea.—It seems perfectly clear, from the obvious parallelism of this epistle from Laodicea with the Epistle to the Colossians itself, that it was a letter not from the Laodicean church, not from any other apostle, or apostolic writer, but from Paul himself, written either at Laodicea, or (as is more likely) written to the Laodicean church, and to be sent "from Laodicea" to Colossae. The most probable supposition identifies it with our Epistle to the Ephesians, an encyclical letter. In particular it should not be forgotten that Marcion expressly calls it an "Epistle to the Laodiceans." Laodicea lay lower down the valley, and was the larger town; an encyclical letter might well be left there to be sent on to Colossae. The two epistles have strong likeness and marked distinction. Nothing could be more natural than that they should be interchanged, according to the direction of the text.

(17) Say to Archippus.—See note on Philem. 2. The whole tone of the passage here suggests that his was a ministry of some prominence in the church. (Tradition makes him afterward a bishop of Laodicea.) Whether this was at Colossae or Laodicea cannot be gathered with any certainty from the context. The exhortation comes in close connection with Laodicea; yet, on the other hand, it seems strange to send through one church a message to a chief pastor of another. In any case this indirect transmission of a charge is curious, standing in marked contrast with the direct personal addresses of Phil. 4:2, 3.

(18) The salutation by the hand of me Paul.—This invariable autograph salutation was "Grace be with you" in various forms, from the brevity of the text here to the fullness of II Cor. 13:14, which has become the universal Christian blessing. In different epistles it is associated with different phrases of blessing or charge.

Remember my bonds.—In what spirit they were to be remembered we may gather from Eph. 3:13; 6:20; Phil. 1:13; 2:17. Paul evidently does not desire to use his captivity as an appeal for sympathy (see Philem. 9); but mainly he dwells on it as a "glory" both to himself and to his converts.

FIRST THESSALONIANS

1

(1) Paul, and Silvanua, and Timotheus.—There was no need to add "apostle" to the name of Paul in writing to a church with which his relations were so familiar and so cordial. It is probably omitted for the same reason in the Epistle to the Philippians and in that to Philemon.

(2) We.—All three are regarded as the writers, and no doubt the sentiments of all are expressed, though the letter is Paul's own composition. In 2:18 he corrects himself for using "we" where it was only true of himself. It may be noticed that Paul never speaks of himself alone in the plural in any of the other epistles.

(3) Faith . . . love . . . hope.—In this first of his writings, Paul has already fixed upon the three great **abiding** principles (I Cor. 13:13) of the Christian life, and the forms in which they mainly exhibit themselves. The genitive in such phrases is almost equivalent to a very emphatic adjective.

In our Lord.—The words in the Greek go with all three clauses. He is the object of the faithful work and loving labor, as well as of the hopeful patience. This latter includes, but is not limited to, the hope of His second Advent.

(4) Election, in the language of Paul and Peter, seems primarily to refer to a gracious admission into religious privileges in **this** life. The word implies nothing as to the final condition of the persons thus elected (see II Pet. 1:10; and comp. Eph. 1:4 with Eph. 5:5, 6, 7). They may, according as they please, unsettle their election, or make it sure. Of course, however, this does not much affect the doctrine of predestination. The question must still remain why God brings some in this life to the knowledge of His truth, and others not; but the observation, at any rate, destroys the notion of an arbitrary damnation and salvation.

(5) In the Holy Ghost.—The Greek here omits the definite article. In such cases attention is not so much called to the Person Himself, as to the exalted, inspired enthusiasm with which He fills us. The union of the divine and human spirit is so close (see I Cor. 6:17) that it is often hard in the New Testament to distinguish which is meant.

(6) Followers.—Not "disciples," but "imitators."

In much affliction.—For examples of troubles in the early days of the Thessalonian Church, see Acts 17:5, 8.

(7) To all that believe—i.e., **now**, not to those that **then** believed; Philippi was the only such church.

Macedonia and Achaia.—These two provinces comprised all Roman Greece. The influence of the Thessalonians spreads far beyond their own country.

(8) Your faith does not mean "your creed," but "the report of your extraordinary faith."

(9) Shew.—Rather, "announce." Both sides of the story are told: (1) of **us**—what kind of entry we made among you (2:1-12); (2) of **you**—how truly converted you were (2:13-3:13).

Living and true God.—In contrast to the lifeless and false idols. The Thessalonians had been Gentiles. Perhaps Paul was thinking of his own speech on Mars Hill, which recently had been uttered.

(10) And to wait.—The idea of the Advent is that which both here and throughout the epistle occupies the foreground in the minds of Paul and his friends.

Whom he raised not only proves His Sonship (Rom. 1:4), but also gives a kind of explanation of the "awaiting Him **from heaven.**"

2

(1) For yourselves, brethren, know.—The writers' purpose is practical, not didactic; they therefore animate their converts with the stirring memories of their conversion.

Not in vain draws a little too much attention to the **result** of their coming. It should be, "not vain," i.e., not purposeless and idle. This may be seen from the contrast drawn in the following verses.

(2) The marks of their ill-treatment at Philippi were fresh on them at Thessalonica. (See Acts 16; 17:1.)

(3) In guile.—The preposition is changed: "nor yet by the use of tricks." Not only were their motives sincere and pure, but their manner of dealing straightforward.

(4) Were allowed.—The word implies examining and approving, and is repeated emphatically ("trieth"): "being examined and approved by God, we study to please Him who constantly examines and approves us, not to court those to whom we are sent." Paul expresses here, as elsewhere, a

1073

total disregard of men's opinions about him (I Cor. 4:3; Gal. 1:10).

(5) Cloak of covetousness—i.e., some specious pretext, under cover of which we might gain a worldly advantage; so (though the Greek word is different) I Pet. 2:16, "a cloke of maliciousness." The absence of flattering words was a thing of which human witnesses could judge; the freedom from covetous designs was known to God alone.

(6) Been burdensome.—The original is, "might have been in weight"—i.e., "have dealt heavily with you," in all the pomp of apostolic dignity, making people acknowledge our "glory." Although, no doubt, one means of asserting their authority would have been to claim their maintenance from the Church (comp. I Cor. 9:1-6), more is meant than the mere obtaining of money.

Apostles of Christ.—The title seems here to be bestowed on Silas and Timothy just as in Acts 14:14 upon Barnabas. As official dignity is here the point, it cannot simply (according to etymology) mean "Christ's missionaries." The episcopal office (which Timothy, at any rate, held somewhat later) may perhaps be here ranked with the apostolate. Thus, in Gal. 1:19, James, the Bishop of Jerusalem, wears the title, though it is scarcely probable that he was one of the Twelve. Andronicus and Junias (Rom. 16:7) and Epaphroditus (Phil. 2:25, "messenger") also are called apostles. The definite article in the present verse should be struck out.

(9) For.—As in verse 1, the general principles of the foregoing verses are supported by facts which the Thessalonians will remember. If the word attaches itself to any particular phrase, it is to "impart our own souls," "we were ready to die for you; indeed, you remember how we worked ourselves almost to death."

Labour and travail—not mere synonyms here: the first describes the kind of work; the second, the intensity of it.

(10) Ye are witnesses.—As in verse 5, God is appealed to, because the readers could only judge of the outward propriety of their teachers' conduct; and it is a moral law that (as Aristotle says) "the righteous man is not he that does acts which in themselves are righteous, but he that does those acts in **such a mind** as befits righteous men."

(11) Every one.—Now they appeal to the individual recollection of the Thessalonians. It gives us an incidental glimpse of the apostolic method—dealing with individual

souls. (Comp. Acts 20:20, 31; Col. 1:21.) Chrysostom exclaims: "Fancy! not one in all that multitude passed over!" The image is changed from that of motherly tenderness to that of fatherly direction.

(13) The first part of this chapter draws attention to the apostles' part in the conversion of Thessalonica. From this point generally to the end of chap. 3, the action of the converts is the chief subject.

(14) For ye.—The effectual power of this word upon them is shown in their joining the church in spite of such difficulties.

Followers.—Better, "imitators." The churches of Judaea are probably selected for example, not only as being the oldest and best-organized churches, but the most afflicted, both by want (Acts 11:29; 24:17; Rom. 15:26), and (chiefly) by persecution from the Jews.

Your own countrymen.—See Acts 17:8, 9. It was always the Jewish policy to persecute by means of others. Evidently the Thessalonian Church is almost entirely Gentile.

(15) Who both killed.—A tremendous invective against the Jews, the purpose of which is to show the deep sympathy of Paul with the persecuted Thessalonians, to register his indignation against the persecutors, and to make them see still more deeply the value of their faith by the efforts made to keep it from them. The memories of Stephen's speech (Acts 7:52) seem to be waking in the mind of him who was once a persecuting Jew himself.

They please not God, though to serve and please Him was the special purpose for which the nation was set apart, "and are at cross purposes with all mankind." The historian Tacitus gives, as a characteristic of the race, "an attitude of hostility and hatred towards all others." Juvenal makes the same accusation.

(16) The apostle indicates the special way in which their opposition showed itself. Paul seems to mean that there may be a certain sum of wickedness which God will allow a nation, a church, a person, to complete, before cutting them off from all spiritual help; the Jews were industriously laboring to complete the sum. "The wrath" is the wrath from which Jesus is delivering us (1:10), and it had already come upon the Jews, though its outward manifestation in the destruction of Jerusalem was yet to come. The particular moment at which Paul means that the wrath "came" must have been the moment of their final rejection of the Messiah.

(18) Even I Paul—showing that Silas and Timothy had not shared his intention. Why had they not? The answer shows the minute truthfulness of the Acts. Both were left at Berea (Acts 17:14). It was during this period that Paul felt so eager a desire to return to his persecuted children. His longing may have been stimulated by seeing his messengers start for the north, first when he sent for his two companions (Acts 17:15), and secondly when he dispatched Timothy himself to Thessalonica (3:2).

But Satan hindered.—Paul has no doubt that his disappointment was a direct manifestation of the work of evil. Elsewhere he is quite as clear that the obstruction of his own plans is owing to God. (See Acts 16:6, 7; I Cor. 16:12.) The difficulty is to tell in each case whether God is directly saving us from a worse course, in spite of ourselves, or permitting a momentary, and yet if rightly used a disciplinary, triumph of evil.

Satan.—The Thessalonians, though originally Gentiles, had doubtless been taught enough at their conversion to recognize the word. Though it is quite clear from other passages (e.g., I Cor. 7:5; II Thess. 2:9; I Tim. 3:7) that Paul believed in the existence of personal fallen spirits, it cannot be positively affirmed that he here means anything more than a personification of all that is opposed to God—the hostility of wicked men, etc.

3

(1) We could no longer forbear.—The Greek word contains the metaphor of a vessel too full and bursting with its contents. "We" must be understood here by the limitation of 2:18, and by the direct singular of verse 5, to mean Paul alone, not him and Silas.

To be left at Athens alone.—See Acts 17:15, 16; 18:5. It seems reasonable to suppose that Silas and Timothy joined Paul at Athens, and were almost as soon sent back into Macedonia—Silas to Berea or Philippi, and Timothy to Thessalonica. This would explain Paul's being left alone, and also how in Acts 18:5 both Timothy and Silas come from Macedonia to Corinth. The dispatching of Silas from Athens is not mentioned here, simply because it had no particular interest for the Thessalonians. If

the two men did not reach Paul at all during the time he was at Athens, after receiving so imperative a message, they must have been very slow, for a week would have allowed ample time for their journey from Berea, and Acts 17:17; 18:1 certainly imply a much longer period of residence there. "To be left alone" was a great trial to Paul's affectionate nature; such a sacrifice may well impress the Thessalonians with the strength of his love for them.

(2) And minister . . . —Timothy being a person so well-known at Thessalonica, it is difficult to see why he should be thus particularized, unless he were the bearer of the letter, and Paul wished to insist upon their paying him due deference in spite of his youth.

(3) We are appointed thereunto.—The "we" means all Christian people; their election into the Church must needs be an election to suffering.

(5) The tempter.—See Matt. 4:3. The word and the tense in the Greek imply not only that it is his character to tempt, but also that it is his constant occupation.

Have tempted you . . . —The original implies no doubt on the writer's part that the Thessalonians had been tempted; the only doubt was, how they had borne it.

(6) Timotheus came.—See notes on verses 1 and 2. Timothy had already returned from his mission to Thessalonica (Acts 18:5), and the occasion of this present letter will be Paul's relief at the news brought by him.

Good remembrance.—If the Thessalonians had been beginning to fall away, they would not have cared to see their teachers.

(7) In all our affliction and distress.—The words give no decisive indication whether such came from within or without, and it is impossible to specify in what it consisted; but either way it suits very well with Acts 18:5-17 and I Cor. 2:3.

(10) See your face.—Seeing them by proxy might satisfy for the while, but not for long. This exceeding importunate prayer is caused by the feeling that it was Satan's hindrance (2:18), not God's will, which forbad the meeting.

That which is lacking in your faith.— What the deficiencies were is unknown, but they certainly include want of knowledge of the state of the dead and concerning the Advent.

(11) And our Lord . . . —An important theological point may be noted from the use of the singular in the verb "direct." The prayer implies the equality of the two Persons. (See II Thess. 2:17.)

(13) To the end.—Perfect and settled sanctification in the eyes of God is the object in view, and the means by which it is to be attained is growing and overflowing love toward mankind. (See Col. 3:14.) Paul is already thinking, probably, how he will treat the subject of chastity in the next chapter.

4

(1) The first point in this practical portion of the epistle on which the Thessalonians need instruction is in the matter of social purity (verses 1-8).

Exhort is correct, though "encourage" suits the context a little better, as assuming that they are already so acting, but not with enough heart.

How ye ought to walk.—Literally, "the how." It indicates that part of the apostolic tradition was a systematic moral code, almost as if it were the title of a well-known book. "We gave you the 'How ye ought to walk, so as to please God.'" The best texts add immediately after, "even as also ye walk."

(2) By the Lord Jesus.—Not as if the Lord were the person who took the commandments from Paul to the Thessalonians, but the person by means of whose inspiration Paul was enabled to give such commandments.

(3) Your sanctification.—In opposition to the word "this." Our conversion, justification, salvation are not the only aim of God; He would have us holy. The general idea of sanctification passes here, as the following clauses show, into the more limited sense of purification.

Fornication.—The word is used often in late Greek for any kind of impurity, but here it must be understood in its strict sense. To the Gentile mind, while the wickedness of adultery or incest was fully recognized, it was a novelty to be told that fornication was a "deadly sin" (comp. the strange connection in which it stands in the Synodal letter to the Gentile churches [Acts 15:20, 29; 21:25]). This consideration makes it easier to understand how Paul can praise these Gentile Thessalonians so heartily, although they need earnest correction on this vital point.

(4) To possess his vessel.—The word "vessel" here has been interpreted in two ways: "his

wife"; "his body." The latter better suits the context here. The body is not dissociated from the man's personality, as in the fanciful Platonism of Philo, but almost identified with it; the Incarnation has taught us the true dignity of the body. Thus it becomes easy to understand what is meant by "knowing how to gain possession of" such an instrument as the body with its many faculties, rescuing it from its vile prostitution, and wielding it wisely for its proper uses.

(5) Not in the lust of concupiscence.—The word here translated "lust" is more often rendered "passion," and implies something which befalls a man, something done to him: "Not in the helpless passivity of concupiscence" or uncontrolled desire.

The Gentiles which know not God.—Note the punctuation. The readers of the letter were "Gentiles which knew God." Their brother Thessalonians are held up to them as melancholy examples of men who are trying in the wrong way to show their power over themselves. This is not one of the crimes which he alleges against Jews.

(6) That no man.—This is a final clause, expressing the purpose of such continence as has just been described. Men are to be chaste and self-possessed, not only for their own salvation's sake, but in justice to their brethren. In 3:12, 13 they were to love for the sake of becoming holy; here they are to be holy for the sake of charity—a blessed action and reaction.

Because that the Lord.—Again an anticipation of the Advent, for the vengeance meant is that of the Judgment Day, not the natural retribution which carnal sin brings with it. The "Lord," therefore, in this context probably means more particularly the Incarnate Son, who has a special claim upon men's bodies (I Cor. 6:13).

(7) Unto uncleanness, but unto holiness.—This implies not so much the definite end to which we are invited, as the terms on which the invitation will still stand, for the call is not yet accomplished.

Holiness is a mistranslation for "sanctification." The process, not the quality, is meant.

(8) Who hath also given.—The right reading is "**into you**"—i.e., "to enter into you, and dwell there" (John 14:17, etc.). The word "holy" in the original is emphatically placed, thus bringing out the startling contrast between such foul lives and the holiness which befitted and was possible (Rom. 6:14; 8:3, 4) for men in whom the

Holy Ghost, communicated by the laying on of hands, condescended to dwell.

(9) Brotherly love.—Not love of men at large, but of Christians in particular. Paul in this place does mean the sentiment rather than the practice, but has especially in view the exercise of liberality toward fellow Christians. The feeling of community can be known only by acts that prove it.

To love.—In the Greek the infinitive expresses the result and issue of God's teaching. This love is not actually contrasted with the "brotherly kindness" above, but means more.

(10) Toward.—The Thessalonians' charity has traveled a long way already from its starting point at home, extending over all northern Greece. As Thessalonica had been the center of evangelization (1:8), so also of the maintenance of the churches. The words need not necessarily (though they do probably) imply a number of missionary stations besides the three places where the apostles had preached.

(11) And that ye study to be quiet.—"And that ye make it your ambition to keep quiet"—their ambition having formerly been to make a stir among the churches. The warnings in this verse are not directed against defiance of the law of brotherly love, but against a thoroughly wrong mode of showing that love: the meddlesomeness with which it was accompanied is not so much an instance of unkindness to the brotherhood as scandal to the heathen. It is commonly supposed that the unsettlement arose from belief in the nearness of the Advent.

Do your own business.—Not merely was each individual to do his own work, but the whole church was to refrain from interfering ostentatiously with other churches. The statement signifies the negative idea of ceasing to meddle rather than the positive idea of industry. The words "with your own hands" are supposed to indicate that most of the Thessalonian Christians were of the artisan class.

(12) The heathen were certain to be watching the conduct of the members of the new religion, and it would bring down political suspicion if they were seen to be acting more like agitators for a secret society than honest citizens who worked at their handicraft and calling. It seems as if they had been reduced to begging of other churches in return for their own expensive charities.

(13) But.—We pass to the share of the Christian dead in the Coming of Christ. Possibly an association of ideas may have caused Paul to join the two subjects of quietude and Advent so closely.

Which are asleep.—The image of sleep is a mere metaphor, drawn from the outward phenomena of death, and is used as a euphemism for death. That the soul still retains consciousness after dissolution is clear from other places; but when the metaphor of sleep is used, it is used of the whole man, describing the peaceful appearance of the dead and the rest from labor. At the same time it suggests a continued existence, and the possibility of a reawakening. The word cannot be limited to the Christian dead; but on the mention of "the dead," the Thessalonians will at once think of their own brethren departed, so that there is no ambiguity.

(14) For if ... —A reason for thinking that if the Thessalonians knew and believed the truth, they ought not to be so miserable. The "if" implies no doubt, but merely clears the ground for a logical deduction. The writer does not care to prove so well-known a fact as the Resurrection of Christ; he only argues from the clear faith of the Thessalonians with regard to it.

Jesus died and rose again.—Notice the human name; though it is true that as God He raised Himself (John 10:18), as man He was no less dependent upon the Father than we are (Acts 17:31). His resurrection is a real argument for ours.

Which sleep in Jesus.—The simpler words in Rev. 14:13 mean "dying in full communion still with Him." Our present phrase (literally, "through Jesus") makes Him, as it were, the way, or door, by which they journeyed to death.

Will God bring with him—i.e., with Jesus. In the Greek the word God stands in an unemphatic position, implying that it was God also who had raised Jesus from the dead. But the thought of the Advent is so supreme with Paul that he passes at once to a moment beyond resurrection.

(15) By the word of the Lord.—A most direct claim to plenary inspiration: "**By way of** a divine revelation." In what way apostles and prophets became conscious of supernatural inspiration we cannot tell; but elsewhere also Paul speaks of possessing the consciousness sometimes and not at others. (See I Cor. 7:10, 12, 25, 40.) It must be remembered, with regard to the details, that it is the very idiom of prophecy to express by material imagery spiritual facts.

We which are alive and remain.—There is not the least necessity for supposing from these words that Paul confidently expected the Advent before his death. His converts are strongly under the impression that they will be alive at the Coming, and that it will be the worse for the departed; therefore, Paul identifies himself with them—assumes that it will be as they expected—and proves the more vividly the fallacy of the Thessalonians' fears.

Shall not prevent—i.e., "be before." If it were not for these words, we might have speculated that the Thessalonians had not been taught to believe in a resurrection at all, which would have been a strange departure from the usual apostolic Gospel (I Cor. 15). We here learn what was the exact nature of the Thessalonians' anxiety concerning the dead. They were full of excited hopes of that Coming which had formed so prominent a part of the apostles' preaching there (Acts 17:7), and were afraid that the highest glories would be engrossed by those who were alive to receive them. They thought that the dead, not being to rise till afterward, would have less blessed privileges. This would make them not only sorry for their dead friends, but also reluctant to die themselves.

(16) With a shout.—The Greek word means a "shout of command or encouragement," such as a captain gives to his soldiers, or a boatswain to his crew. The intention is only to convey the notion of the stirring noise, in the midst of which the Lord will descend. It is, however, somewhat particularized by what follows. Probably the shout of command is uttered by the leader of the angels, and the trump of God is blown to summon the mustering hosts. It suits the dignity of the scene better to imagine the loud sound to come from one of the heralds of the great army, rather than from the Lord Himself. The prepositon "in" is more effective than "with," for it calls attention to the long blast. (For the order of resurrection, see I Cor. 15:52.)

(17) Shall be caught up.—"Our Assumption," as one well calls it. The spiritualizing of our natural bodies without death, as described in I Cor. 15:50, seq., will enable us to be "caught up" equally well with, and in company with, the resurgent dead. The absolute equality, then, of living and dead is proved.

To meet the Lord in the air.—The word "air" in itself properly signifies the lower, denser, grosser atmosphere, in which the

powers of darkness reign (Eph. 2:2); but here it is used only in contrast with the ground, and means "on the way from heaven whence He comes." Thus, having once rejoined the Lord, they would never be parted from Him.

(18) Comfort one another.—Here is a balm for the "sorrow" of verse 13.

5

(1) But of the times.—Here begins the bearing of the doctrine of the Advent upon the Christian's own life. "Times and seasons" seem to mean the different periods at which men might conceive the Advent likely to come.

Ye have no need.—The next verse shows that this paragraph is not so much intended for an answer to a false theory about the time of the Advent, as practically to cure the restlessness common at Thessalonica. With scrupulous care Paul had instructed them on that topic.

(2) The day of the Lord.—Here "the Lord" (as usual in the New Testament) means Jesus Christ; and this day can mean nothing else than the great day of His return to judgment. The expression is taken from the Old Testament, where, of course, it does not primarily mean what we call "the Day of Judgment," but the set time which God has fixed for any great visitation.

As a thief in the night—i.e., unexpectedly (Matt. 24:43), and under cover of darkness. The frequency of the simile throws light on the words "know perfectly," making it apparent that it was the ordinary formula in which the doctrine was universally taught by the apostles.

(3) "They" will mean "the world." They are taking their repose in security, without dreaming of any interruption to their slumbers. (Comp. Matt. 25:1-13; Luke 21:34.)

(5) Ye are all.—Paul recognizes no exceptions, no inner distinctions among the members of the church: all stand alike as far as grace, privileges, and duties are concerned. The following exhortation shows that it was a matter of each man's free will whether he would sustain his character as a "child of light" or not.

Children of light.—The expression is an enthusiastic Hebrew poetical turn for intimate vital connection with anything; thus, "children of the light" are persons to whom darkness is an alien thing, whose natures ave a kinship, an intuitive responsiveness or whatever may be called "light." To such ersons the "light," the "day," can never ome as an unwelcome, startling apparition.

(6) Let us not sleep.—The metaphor here xpresses not so much actual sin (Eph. 5:14) s carelessness in spiritual and moral hings. Paul (as always) indicates that it vas possible for "children of light" to be onverted back into "children of darkness."

Watch and be sober.—The comparison of ight now suggests to the writer another hought besides that of sloth, namely, that f dissipation. Christians are not to turn lay into night by debauchery any more han by sleep.

(8) Putting on.—A curiously abrupt tran- ition, suggested by the sober vigilance just dvocated. The Christian must be careful to vatch, not only because the Lord is coming ack at some unexpected hour, but also ecause there are enemies all around. He is ot only the porter, sitting up to let his _ord in at any hour when He may return rom the wedding (Mark 13:34; Luke 2:36), but also the soldier standing sentry, iable to be surprised by the foe. (Comp. ph. 6:11 seq. for the aggressive Christian oldier.)

(9) To obtain salvation.—The Greek neans "acquire" by one's own efforts. God loes not predestinate men to "salvation" vithout laborious acquisition on their part, ut predestinates them to occupy a position n which they will be able to "work out heir own salvation" by placing them "un- ler grace" in the Church. The same word is ised of the Christian's way of securing alvation, and of Christ's way of securing it or him; both are "purchasing," "earning."

(10) The mention of Christ's death at nce brings back the recollection of the Advent and the questions concerning the lead in their relation to it. The words wake or sleep" seem distinctly suggested y the previous metaphor. Christ's dying lestroyed the power of death (Heb. 2:14); herefore it is only a matter of being awake or asleep. Those who sleep quite as truly ive, and live with Him, as we who wake see Luke 20:38; Rom. 14:8). The word together" must be separated from the with": "we should live with him together," .e., we, the living, and our brethren the lead. Paul has entirely reverted from the effect of the Advent doctrine on Christian ife to the subject of the last chapter—the equality of the two classes at Christ's com- ng.

(12) Here begin minor details of instruc- tion, no doubt suggested by observation of many defects in the Thessalonian Church. These details show us still further the mix- ture of restless ungoverned zeal with gloomy forebodings and discontents.

The command is to enter into the spirit of ecclesiastical discipline. The persons meant are not simply the hard-working lai- ty, contrasted with the idlers (4:11; II Thess. 3:11), but those who performed the laborious office of the ministry. The Greek word "know" indicates "appreciation"; they are bidden to acquaint themselves thor- oughly with the presbyter and his work, and to endeavor to understand his teaching and to value his example. It is especially inter- esting to notice how much power is given to the presbytery in this earliest writing of the New Testament, and how carefully Paul seems to have organized his churches, and that at the very foundation of them. It is only "in the Lord" that the presbytery are over men, that is, in spiritual matters.

(14) The writers turn to the presbytery, and explain their duty in the administration of discipline to the flock. The flock will be more apt to receive the discipline when they see with what apostolic authority their pastors are armed. Several special parts of the clerical office are then enumerated. The "unruly" or "disorderly" are those who in- fringe good discipline— said of soldiers who leave their ranks, here notably of those mentioned in II Thess. 3:11.

Feebleminded.—Or, "fainthearted." Such persons, e.g., as were overburdened with sorrow for the dead, or afraid of the perse- cutions, or the like.

(15) None render evil for evil.—Like the prohibition of fornication, abstinence from revenge is practically a new thought for Greeks, among whom feuds were frequent and undying. (Comp. Rom. 1:31; Tit. 3:3.)

That which is good—i.e., that which is kind. This duty is to be made an object to be pursued eagerly. There is not one stan- dard of morals toward the brethren and another toward the world.

(17) Pray without ceasing.—Though a man cannot be incessantly praying in words, the mind may be held continuously in an attitude of prayer, even in sleep (S. of Sol. 5:2).

(18) In every thing give thanks.—To the Christian who really trusts his Father's providence, and believes that his prayers are heard, every moment's occurrence will be just that for which he has prayed—the fulfillment of our Father's will. It is for this reason that thanksgiving is so inseparably joined with prayer. (See Phil. 4:6; Col. 4:2.)

In Christ Jesus.—This kind and loving will of God for our good was most abundantly manifested in the life, death, and resurrection of Christ Jesus, and even to this day it is chiefly manifested in what Christ Jesus still is for us (e.g., Heb. 6:19, 20).

(19) Quench not the Spirit.—The "Spirit" here must not be taken too sharply to mean the Person of the Holy Ghost, who may be grieved (Eph. 4:30), expelled (Ps. 51:11), neglected (I Tim. 4:14), but never extinguished. The word here again (as in 1:5) is in that intermediate sense which expresses the effect of the Holy Ghost's personal working upon our spirits. He kindles in us a fire (Matt. 3:11), that is, a consuming ardor and enthusiasm, of love to God and man, which ardor may be dampened, quenched, by not giving it free air and play. Gloom (verse 16), neglect of prayer (verse 17) which is the very feeding of the flame, discontentment with the answer which God chooses to give to prayer (verse 18), will in the end reduce us to the condition in which we were before we were proved (Rom. 8:9).

(20) Despise not prophesyings.—The despondency of the Thessalonians led them not only to quench the fervor of the Holy Ghost in their own bosoms, but also to turn a cold and disparaging ear to the inspired and inspiring preaching (I Cor. 12:28; 14:1, 5, 39). It is because of this double effect of gloominess that the command, "Quench not," occurs between the exhortation to thanksgiving and the warning not to despise prophecy.

(21) Prove all things.—That the warning was needed, or would be needed soon, is shown by II Thess. 2:2. It is couched in general terms, but, of course, has special reference to all things purporting to be manifestations of the Spirit. And how were these revelations to be tested? If they were not in accordance (1) with the original tradition (II Thess. 2:2), (2) with the supernatural inspirations of the other prophets who sat as judges (I Cor. 14:29), (3) with enlightened common sense (I John 4:1), they could not be "good" in the sense of "genuine" (see John 10:11).

(22) Abstain from all appearance of evil.—The word "evil" is here used in the moral sense, and does not constitute an exact antithesis to the "good" of the preceding verse.

(23) The very God of peace—"the God of peace Himself." The contrast is between the futile efforts after holiness of which they in themselves were capable, and the almighty power of sanctification exercised by God. This sanctification is here ascribed to the First Person of the Trinity. He is called (as in Heb. 13:20) the "God of peace," not in reference to any dissensions between the Thessalonians (verse 13), but because of the peace which His sanctification brings into the soul, so that it fears neither temptation's power nor persecution's rage.

Sanctify you wholly.—The idea is that of leaving no part unsanctified, rather than that of doing the work completely so far as it goes. Thus it serves to introduce the next sentence, which explains it.

Spirit and soul and body.—This is Paul's fullest and most scientific psychology, not merely a rhetorical piling up of words without any particular meaning being assigned to them. Elsewhere, he merely divides man according to popular language into two parts, visible and invisible, "body and spirit"; the division into "body and soul" he never uses. The "spirit" (**pneuma**) is the part by which we apprehend realities intuitively, i.e., without reasoning upon them; it is the inmost consciousness of the man, the part of him which survives death. The "soul" (**psyche**) includes the intellect, the affections, and the will; and it is of the essence of the Gospel to force sharply upon men the distinction between it and the spirit (Heb. 4:12). The soul belongs altogether to the lower nature, so that when Paul uses the twofold division "body and spirit," the soul is considered as part of the body; and when Paul describes the "works of the flesh," he includes among them such distinctly soul-sins as "heresies" (Gal. 5:20). Sanctification preserves all these three divisions entire, and in their due relation to each other; without sanctification, the spirit might be overwhelmed by the other parts gaining the predominance, which would, of course, eventually be the ruin both of "soul and body in hell" (Matt. 10:28).

Unto the coming.—A mistranslation for "at the coming." The idea is not so much that of their preservation from sin during the interval, but rather the writers hasten in eager anticipation to the Coming itself, and hope that the Thessalonians at the Coming will be found to have been preserved. "Blameless" should be "blamelessly." Verse 24 offers a reason for hoping confidently that they will be blamelessly preserved.

(26) Greet all the brethren.—It is concluded from the manner in which some are told to greet all, instead of all being told to greet one another (as in the parallel passages), that the "brethren" to whom the letter was sent especially were the ministry of Thessalonica (comp. verse 27). If so, the "holy kiss" had hardly become the fixed church ceremony which it afterward was, for the practice (according to the **Apostolical Constitutions**) was for the church members to pass the kiss from one to another, men kissing men, and women kissing women, not for all the people to be kissed in turn by the minister. This kiss, however, is no doubt intended by Paul to be given at a solemn assembly of the church, i.e., at the Holy Communion, which was the only fixed meeting of the Primitive Church. This kiss was to differ from the ordinary Greek salutation by being distinctly a holy kiss, i.e., a ceremonial, religious kiss.

(27) I charge you.—What is the cause of such awful solemnity? It certainly seems as if the contempt of discipline and partial alienation of clergy and laity implied in verses 12 and 13 might suggest to Paul a doubt whether his epistle would reach all the Thessalonian Christians. At any rate, the adjuration marks his sense of the extreme importance of the letter; and perhaps the fact that this was his first pastoral letter may have made him more anxious to insure its reception and success. It amounts to a claim to inspiration. (Comp. 4:15.) The reading is a public reading in the celebration of the Communion, at which we know from several early Fathers that the writings of the apostles were read aloud. (Comp. Col. 4:16; II Pet. 3:15, 16.)

SECOND THESSALONIANS

1

(1) Paul, and Silvanus, and Timotheus.—The company which dispatched the First Epistle is not yet broken up. This proves that the Second Epistle was written before the end of the second missionary journey, for after that time we do not read of Silvanus being in the company of Paul.

(3) We are bound to thank God always for you, brethren.—The thanksgiving is regarded as a positive debt incurred, which it would be a dishonesty not to pay.

Groweth exceedingly.—An enthusiastic word in the original: "is out-growing all bounds." It is a metaphor from vegetable or animal growth. This was one of the points about which Paul was anxious the last time that he had written; then there were deficiencies in their faith (I Thess. 3:10).

Charity.—Here, too, Paul remembers what he had said to them in the last epistle, in which he had devoted a whole section to the love of the brethren toward each other. The differences which had called forth such passages as I Thess. 3:12; 4:6-10; 5:12-14, had apparently all ceased, and mutual love was multiplying.

(4) Your patience and faith.—The apostolic labors had not been in vain (I Thess. 3:5). "Patience" in the New Testament does not mean a meek submissiveness, but a heroic endurance. The "faith" here becomes almost equivalent to "hope," except that it introduces the ground of such hope as confidence in the living God; it also includes the notion of faithfulness.

Persecutions and tribulations.—While "tribulation" is quite general, and implies no personal enmities, "persecution" means that a certain set of persons were organizing active measures for the annoyance of the church. Such persecution they were still "enduring" when the letter was written.

(5) The kingdom of God.—This had formed a prominent feature of the first preaching at Thessalonica. The Thessalonian Christians are in the kingdom of God, but only as its subjects; hereafter they are to be counted worthy not merely of admission into it, but to inherit it.

For which ye also suffer.—"Also" brings out more clearly the vital connection between suffering and reigning. They suffer "for the kingdom," not merely for the sake of winning it, but on its behalf, in defense

of it, in consequence of being its citizens, to extend its dominion.

(7) Rest with us.—"With us" shows sympathy in their present trials, for it implies that the writers themselves had earned or were earning (see Acts 18:12) that rest by the like trials. The "rest" is the opposite of the "strain" at which the persecution kept them. Such "rest" is not to be expected in its fullness until the judgment day.

(8) Many critics change the punctuation by omitting the comma after "angels" and inserting it after "fire." The "flaming fire" here is not the instrument of the vengeance— i.e., hellfire—but the common pictorial attribute of the divine Presence (Ex. 3:2; 19:18; Dan. 7:9). "Taking vengeance" would seem to be "assigning retribution": appointing, that is, to each man what satisfaction of justice he must make.

On them that know not God.—According to the Greek, the word "them" should be repeated also in the next clause. The effect will then be to mark off two classes: "them that know not," and "them that obey not." By the first class are meant Gentiles (comp. Eph. 4:17, 18; I Thess. 4:5); disobedience was the characteristic of the Jews (comp. Rom. 10:16, 21). The Greek negative particle shows that the ignorance of the one set and the disobedience of the other were just the points for which they were to be punished. Here, as the context shows, Paul is thinking chiefly of those Gentiles and Jews who actually persecuted the truth.

(9) Punished with everlasting destruction specifies the "vengeance" to be taken. But the word "destruction" does not stand absolutely and alone as a synonym for "annihilation." The lost are to be cut off from His presence and power for ever. The metaphor is from the courts of Oriental kings, where only honored courtiers are admitted to spend their time in the immediate presence of the sovereign. Familiar contact with Christ hereafter, accorded to all the saved, was God's ideal intention for the lost as well; therefore it is a positive "destruction" to be banished from it. But to the Jews, who looked for a Messiah who should keep regal state, the punishment was peculiarly appropriate.

(10) To be glorified in his saints.—This is not exactly the purpose, but the effect of His coming. The saints are the objects on which and by which the glorious perfection of Christ is exhibited (comp. John 13:31, 32; 14:13; 17:10; II Thess. 1:12). As the persecutors were divided into two classes to be punished, so the saved are described under two aspects: they are fully consecrated to God; they accepted the Gospel.

(11) Count you worthy of this calling.— The "calling" of which Paul is thinking is the calling "in that day" (see verse 5). They had been called to glory already, and had obeyed the call; and God was still calling them hourly. But that was no security that they would remain worthy of that last decisive call. "Many are called, but few chosen."

(12) That the name... —This verse gathers up what has been said in verses 8-10. Seeing the favors bestowed upon the Christians in the last day, all, the lost as well as the saved, will be forced to acknowledge the divine perfection of the Jesus whose Christship had been rejected, and the true dignity of the Christians who had been despised for their allegiance to Him.

2

The first chapter had encouraged the Thessalonians under persecution by the thought of the reality of the Advent. The author has not in the least changed his opinion about the Advent since writing the First Epistle. It is still a matter of most practical comfort. But now, in clear tones, he warns the Thessalonians against supposing that the "end" was "by-and-by" (Luke 21:9). He had, in fact, taught them so from the outset, and had even then pointed out to them a sign, unaccomplished as yet, which they must see accomplished before the Advent should come.

(1) Our gathering together.—The peculiar Greek word is the same as that used again only in Heb. 10:25 of the assembling to the Lord's Supper. In verb form it is used in I Thess. 4:17. The close connection between the two "gatherings together" may be seen in I Cor. 11:26. The "our" means the meeting of the dead and the living together.

(2) Not soon shaken.—The meaning would be clearer if we inserted "so" before "soon," for they had already been shaken, and that in an unconscionably short time since their first teaching on the subject. (Comp. Gal. 1:6.)

Be troubled.—The tense of the verb "be troubled" differs in the Greek from that of "be shaken"; for the "driving out of their wits" is regarded as a single act, the "agitation" as a chronic condition into which there was fear of their falling. These proba-

bly brought about the disorders spoken of in chap. 3. The instruments by which men had partly driven the Thessalonians out of their wits already were three: pretended manifestations of the Holy Spirit's power; word of mouth, as some persons misrepresented what they had heard the apostles say on the topic, or pretended to have been intrusted with a message from them; forged letters, purporting to be from Paul.

As that the day of Christ is at hand—the contents of the pretended revelation. The word for "is at hand" implies a close proximity to come, the participle, in fact (like our word "instant"), being used for "present" (see Gal. 1:4). Probably the form which the false doctrine at Thessalonica was beginning to take was that the day of the Lord had already set in, thus confusing the whole idea of a personal, visible Advent, just as, at a later period, Hymenaeus and Philetus confused the true doctrine of resurrection by affirming that it was already past (II Tim. 2:18). Paul not only denies vigorously that the day is come, but proceeds to show that the signs of its approach are not yet exhibited.

(3) A falling away.—In the original both "falling away" and "man of sin" are preceded by the article. In both cases the purpose is by no means to utter a new, strange prophecy, but to remind them of careful teaching given during the first few weeks after their conversion. "Falling away" must undoubtedly imply that the persons so apostatizing had formerly held the Christian faith, for men cannot fall from ground which they never occupied. Of this revelation of Antichrist the same word (**apocalypsis**) is used which is often used of Christ, so that we may expect to recognize him when he comes as clearly as we shall recognize Christ. The conception of the Antichrist is not merely that of an opponent of the Christ, but of a rival Christ; there is a hideous parallelism between the two.

That man of sin.—The context makes it reasonably clear that the Man of Sin is the head and center of the apostasy itself, and does not form a separate movement from it. The "Man of Sin," then, will have at one time formed part of the Christian Church, and the apostasy will culminate in him. (Thus, for instance, the requirements of the passage would not be fulfilled by interpreting the apostasy to mean the early Gnostic movement, followed up by the independent appearance of Nero as the Man of Sin.— The genitive is like a forcible epithet: "A man so wicked that, bad as other men are, wickedness should be his mark by which he is distinguished from all others; a man who **belongs** to sin, in whom the ideal of sin has become realized and incarnate." The context points clearly to that which is the crowning sin—spiritual pride and rebellious arrogance (Eph. 6:12).

The son of perdition.—The phrase (John 17:12) suits the description of the Man of Sin, who, like Judas, will have "fallen away" from high Christian privileges. It signifies one who belongs by natural ties to perdition—who from his birth chooses evil, and in such a sense may be said to be born to be lost (Matt. 26:24; II Pet. 2:12). Both his malignity and his doom are thus implied in it.

(4) Who opposeth and exalteth himself.— Comp. the description of Antiochus in Dan. 11. The word for "the opposer," or "adversary," is a close rendering of the name "Satan," and passed, in ecclesiastical Greek, into a synonym for it. The acts here attributed to the Man of Sin are peculiarly Satanic. (Comp. Isa. 14:12-14; II Tim. 3:6.) But we must not confound Satan himself with his human minister.

So that he as God.—The words "as God" are not part of the original text. In several other points, however, the Greek brings out more clearly the profanity of the act. "Himself" expresses the spontaneous arrogance of the deed; the Man of Sin does not merely yield to servile flatterers. The "sitting" is not in the tense of habitual custom, but indicates one expressive act of taking possession. "In" (literally, into) brings out the idea of actual intrusion; and the word for "temple" is not the general name for the whole group of buildings with their courts, but the sacred house itself.

The temple of God.—Paul did not expect the Antichrist as a prose fact to take his seat in that edifice. Rather, the whole phrase is a poetical or prophetical description of usurping divine prerogatives generally. Though the prophecy might be fulfilled without any symbolical act, yet the spontaneousness and the openness seem so essentially parts of the prophecy as of necessity to imply that the Man of Sin will make formal claim—identical with his apocalypse—to occupy that central seat in men's minds and aspirations which is acknowledged to be due to God alone.

Shewing himself.—It does not mean that he makes any attempt to prove that he is God; the word only carries on the pictorial

representation of the Man of Sin enthroning himself upon the Mercy Seat, and by that act of session parading his pretended divinity. It is hard to believe that anything avowedly atheistic would be spoken of as explicitly claiming or receiving divine honors. It seems, therefore, most probable that the great apostasy will not become avowedly atheistic, but will be an apostasy within the Church, and that the Man of Sin, who heads that apostasy, will make special claim upon the Christian Church to accord consciously the very honors which she pays to the living God.

(5) Remember ye not.—A rebuke of the same character as Rom. 6:3; I Cor. 6:19, and, like those, leveled at ignorance of what in apostolic days were thought the six fundamental points of Christian teaching (Heb. 5:12; 6:1, 2). The doctrine of antichrist would naturally form part of the course on resurrection and judgment.

(6) And now ye know.—The word "now" is not used exactly in a temporal sense, but as introducing another item. Knowing not only that Antichrist's apocalypse must precede Christ's, but also that Antichrist could not reveal himself yet, because the way was blocked by something still unremoved, the Thessalonians were absurd in acting as if the day of the Lord had come.

What withholdeth.—Unlike the Man of Sin himself, who was a dim figure in the mysterious future, the obstacle was present and tangible. Paul stirs their memory by telling them that they well know the thing itself. It must needs be a marked and mighty power which can prevent the development of the great Antichrist. At the same time, Paul's doctrine is that this marked power is destined after a while to be removed (verse 7).

(7) The mystery of iniquity doth already work.—The word "mystery" stands in sharp contrast with the word "revealed" in verses 6 and 8; the time for publishing, openly avowing, the secret has not yet come. Those who are contributing to the ultimate manifestation of lawlessness are deceived by it (verse 10), and, while sharers in the apostasy, still believe themselves members of the church. Though the mystery is said to work (the verb expresses an inward activity), it is not a personal thing; it is solely the unavowed design which is gradually gaining influence over men's hearts—the same movement as the "falling away" of verse 3. Here the "lawlessness" seems not so much o mean ordinary antinomianism as insubordination to God—rebellion.

Only he ... —The English "letteth" has obscured the meaning; the new word is precisely the same as in verse 6, the only difference being that there it was neuter, while here it is masculine. Evidently to Paul's mind there was a great obstructive power gathered up in, and wielded by, the person so described. How this potentate would disappear Paul gives no hint; but obviously it would not be by death, for unless the power itself were to disappear with him, his successor would equally be he that now withholdeth." We may therefore say that the prophecy would be satisfied if "he that withholdeth" proved to be a whole succession of persons; but we have hardly the same right to say so of the Lawless One."

(8) And then.—When the obstructor is gone, two things shall happen: (1) the Lawless One shall be revealed, and (2) then the Lord (the best text adds the name Jesus, which serves more clearly to contrast Him with His rival) will come and destroy him. (See Isa. 11:4.)

(9) Even him, whose coming.—The purpose of the verses following is not merely to describe Antichrist more fully, but to compare word for word his coming with that which will annihilate him.

Is ... with all power.—The advent of Antichrist will be accompanied by all kinds of miracles, not only wrought by Satan, but up to the full capacity of Satan to work them. The word "lying" should go with all three names. The words heighten the terror of the description, meaning that there will be a display of power to attest Antichrist's doctrine (signs) and to keep men spellbound in admiration of him (wonders).

(10) In them that perish.—These are not the persons who exercise the fraud, but the objects of it. Paul adds the words as a consolation to "them that are saved"; it will not be possible to seduce the elect (Mark 3:22). "They that perish" is a phrase which contains no reference whatever to the doctrine of predestination, but merely describes the class of men who let themselves thus be duped.

(11) And for this cause—i.e., because they did not care whether things were true or not. Antichrist's coming, then, is a judicial visitation. This verse is not a mere repetition of verses 9 and 10. There were told of external dangers which would attend Antichrist's coming for them that

perish; here is set forth the effect upon their own selves of refusing to accept God's gift of love of truth: God takes from them (by His natural law) their power of discerning the true from the false. Every wilful sin does this double mischief: it strengthens the power of the temptation without; it weakens the power to resist within.

(12) That they all ... —This is God's purpose in making them believe the lie. But God did not begin to will the sinner's judgment until after He had offered him freely the love of His own blessed truth, and had been rejected. When once the sinner is incurable, the only way to vindicate truth and righteousness is by hastening on his condemnation, whatever that condemnation may mean.

(13) To salvation.—This "salvation" is in contrast with the "destruction" (1:9), "perdition" (2:3), or "perishing" (2:10), all of which represent the same word in the Greek. Out of the wreck of a world, God had from eternity chosen these Thessalonians to come off safely.

Through sanctification of the Spirit and belief of the truth.—This teaches us the apostolic idea of election. It is not absolute irreversible predestination to a particular state of happiness on which the elect is to enter after death. The "salvation" is present, begun in this life (Eph. 2:5, 8), and carried on along fixed lines. If, therefore, God chose the Thessalonian Christians to salvation by a course of sanctification and belief, one thing is clear: that if any of them should leave that course, and fall into the errors and sins denounced in the foregoing verses, then, in the apostle's mind, they would have forfeited their salvation in spite of God's choice of them. "Sanctification of spirit" seems to mean "spiritual sanctification"—an inward process, not merely outward change of conduct. This is wrought by the action of the Holy Spirit on our spirits; but the omission of the definite article in the Greek is difficult to explain if the "spirit" mentioned be other than the spirit acted upon. "Belief of truth" is opposed to "believing the lie" of verse 11. (Comp. John 17:17.)

(14) Whereunto ... —From the neuter gender of the relative in the Greek we see that the antecedent in Paul's mind is the general state of life which is compounded of these three notions. The election takes place in eternity (verse 13); the call at that point of time when the men first hear the Gospel.

(See Rom. 8:30.) For "obtaining of the glory," see notes on 1:11, 12.

(15) Therefore brethren, stand fast.—Such an exhortation is, in itself, conclusive against a theory of irreversible predestination. If it were impossible for them to quit their ground, it would be needless to exhort them to maintain it. If it were possible for them to quit their ground, and yet be as well off after all, it would be needless also. The "therefore" sums up the whole burden of the Advent doctrine.

Hold the traditions.—The context shows that the particular traditions which were most consciously in Paul's mind at the moment were his eschatological teachings, given to them while he was among them. At the same time, he speaks generally, and we must not limit his words to that particular tradition. Whatever can be traced to apostolic origin is of the essence of the faith. Paul can speak on occasion as contemptuously of the "traditions of men" as our Lord did (Col. 2:8). Of course, it depends entirely on the individual character of any tradition whether, and to what extent, it is to be held. Any tradition, "by word" or written, which is in disagreement with the Scripture stands necessarily condemned.

By word, or our epistle.—Unless Paul had written them some other letter, now lost, this proves that the First Epistle was in reality the earlier written.

(17) The verbs "comfort" and "stablish" are singular in number. It is by these little incidental touches, still more than by express doctrinal statements, that we learn what was the real belief of the apostles concerning the divinity of Christ; and we may say the same with regard to many other great doctrines.

3

(1) Pray for us.—Paul leaves people praying for him everywhere (Rom. 15:30; II Cor. 1:11; Eph. 6:18, 19; Col. 4:3; I Thess. 5:25; comp. Heb. 13:18). In all these cases the request is for active help in his work of evangelizing. "That" stands for "in order that," and does not introduce merely the subject of the prayer.

Even as it is with you.—Such praise would motivate the Thessalonians to pray for him with greater fervor and assurance. People had only to look at Thessalonica, and they were forced to recognize the character of the Gospel.

(2) From unreasonable and wicked men.—Paul wishes the Thessalonians to pray for his deliverance from these "monstrous and depraved people." He is evidently meaning some particular foes whom he fears, for the original has the definite article. From Acts 18:5, 9, 12—where we are given the circumstances in which the letter was written—we can hardly doubt that they are the unbelieving Jews of Corinth. From these Jews he was, though narrowly, delivered. It was, perhaps, in direct answer to the prayers for which Paul here asks that he received the vision and assurances of our Lord, and that Gallio was moved to suppress so abruptly the proceedings of the Jews.

(5) Direct your hearts into the love of God.—This prayer in itself implies that they had not yet reached the point which Paul would have them reach, and were perhaps not taking the most direct course. The "love of God" meant here is that practical love which consists in keeping the commandments (John 14:21). This "patience" includes both the thought of bearing up under their present persecutions and also the thought of continuance as opposed to the fitful restlessness which had begun to prey upon the Thessalonian Church.

(6) In the name of our Lord.—This mention of the name in performing an action implies an invocation or attestation of the person, and a claim to the authority of the person—i.e., to act officially as his representative with full powers. The Thessalonians are not to think that in disobeying Paul's injunctions they are rebelling against a mere human authority; Christ Himself speaks to them through Paul's lips.

Withdraw yourselves.—This is a metaphor from the language of strategy: a cautious general shrinking from an encounter and timidly drawing off under cover. A social excommunication rather than ecclesiastical seems chiefly meant, though the latter might perhaps be involved.

Disorderly.—The word is rendered "unruly" in I Thess. 5:14, and is possibly suggested by the military metaphor above. It means properly "out of rank." The kind of irregularity which is meant is made clear by verses 10, 11.

The tradition.—See note on 2:15. The word must imply systematic and definite teaching; and we note here again that a clear code of ethics was part of the apostolic catechism. (See I Thess. 4:1.)

(7) To follow us.—The word means "to imitate"; then follows the historical justification of the statement that their example was a trustworthy model. The description of the apostles' conduct at Thessalonica is similar to that in the First Epistle, thus giving us a clearer understanding why they dwelt so long and so passionately on the topic there—namely, in order by force of tacit contrast to shame the disorderly brethren into imitation. (See I Thess. 2:9-12.)

(8) There is a flavor of scorn in Paul's disclaimer of such a parasite's life. To "be changeable" means more than "to make you pay": it contains the notion of burdensome expense.

(9) Power.—Rather, "authority," which is power plus legitimacy. How jealously Paul guards the rights of the Apostolate!

An ensample.—Literally, "a model." The argument is a strong **a fortiori.** Whatever reason these Thessalonians might have for giving up work, Paul had the same, and more.

(10) If any would not work.—The word "would" stands for "is not willing." To any weakness or incapacity for work, except in himself, Paul would be very tender. The Thessalonians are not to be misled into a false charity, giving food in Christ's name to persons who are capable of working and able to get work, and are too indolent to do so. The support which is here forbidden to be given to these disorderly persons might come either directly from the private liberality of individuals, or from some collected church fund administered by the deacons. This Thessalonian Church may have copied its model (I Thess. 2:14) in adopting some form of communism, or some extensive use of the **agape** which we see to have been in use at Corinth, established by the apostle at the time of writing this letter (I Cor. 11:21).

(11) For we hear.—Heretofore Paul has only been giving directions, without saying why. News had been brought back, no doubt, by the bearers of the First Epistle.

Working not at all, but are busybodies.—This is what constitutes the disorderliness. There is a scornful play of words here in the Greek, the word for "busybodies" being merely a compound form of the word "working." It comes to signify doing useless things, things which concern no one, and might as well be left alone; also meddling with matters which do not concern the doer, but do concern other people. Paul's readers had been over-busy in theorizing about the position of the departed at Christ's coming (I Thess. 4:15), and had been so eager over their idle doctrines of

the Advent as to forge communications from Paul. Such false inquisitiveness and gossiping discussions might well be described by the Greek word with which we are dealing. There was, too, a more practical form of the same disposition to mask idleness under cloak of work. (See 2:2.)

(13) Be not weary in well doing.—Now the writer turns to the orderly brethren, as quite a distinct class. The phrase takes for granted that they had been heretofore engaged in acting honorably. Paul is anxious to preserve them from slipping into like idleness and bringing scandal upon the church.

(14) And if any man.—An appeal to the right-minded, not only to persevere themselves, but to join with the overseers of their church in enforcing discipline, as in I Thess. 5:12-15.

Note that man.—The reflexive voice of the verb implies common agreement in warning against him. The best text goes on abruptly, without conjunction: "Note that man; have no company with him." This social extrusion from good men's conversation, not to speak of the sacraments, would, to a Christian in a heathen city, be indeed a delivering to Satan, a thrusting into outer darkness.

(15) Admonish him as a brother.—Perhaps the presbyters, to whom the work of "admonishing" especially belonged (see I Thess. 5:12, 14), were to visit them in private with that object; or, possibly, the admonition was to consist in the act of separation, and not in verbal reproof at all.

(16) The words "by all means," or, more literally, "in every shape and form," show that the apostle is extending his glance over all the subjects mentioned in the epistle now finished. Paul has spoken with strong censure of some; but he wishes to show that he bears no ill will to any, and to leave off by blessing all, as he began by giving thanks for all (1:3).

(17) The salutation.—At this point Paul takes the pen out of his secretary's hand and adds the closing words himself. The actual salutation does not begin until the benediction of verse 18.

Which.—Namely, the autograph addition of a salutation, or valedictory prayer, not the special words in which it was couched.

The token—i.e., a mark by which to tell an authentic epistle of his from those forged letters with which false brethren had troubled the Thessalonian Church (2:2). Here we must recollect several points: (1) Paul's genuine First Epistle, in spite of its claim to inspiration (4:15), could not yet have acquired in the eyes of the Thessalonians the sanctity it wears for us; they had no notion of such a thing as Holy Scriptures. (2) Such literary forgeries were common in that age, and scarcely considered reprehensible, unless they were framed to inculcate with authority some heretical teaching. Apocryphal gospels soon after abounded, under false titles, and works fathered by Clement and other great church teachers. (3) There need not always have been a direct intention to deceive the readers as to the authorship, but the renowned name acted as a tempting advertisement for the work. Such points must be borne in mind before we accept as genuine any of the early Christian writings.

In every epistle.—It seems necessary to suppose that Paul had already made a practice of concluding letters with his autograph, though only one letter of his is now extant of an earlier date than our present epistle. There is no reason whatever to suppose that all the letters ever written by Paul have been preserved to us, any more than all the sayings and acts of Jesus Christ (John 21:25); and even when he wrote his First Epistle to Thessalonica he had seen the necessity of giving careful directions about his letters (I Thess. 5:27), and of rousing his correspondents to a reasonable scepticism (ibid. 5:21). The same solicitude reappears in I Cor. 16:21; Gal. 6:11. And the rule which Paul had already made he always observed, as far as we can test, for all his extant epistles contain his "salutation" at the end.

So I write.—"Such is my handwriting." It need not mean that the Thessalonians heretofore were unacquainted with his hand; he only calls their attention closely to it. The great bold handwriting (comp. Gal. 6:11) would not easily be mistaken.

(18) The grace.—The Greek secular salutation, at greeting and parting alike, was **chaire** (literally, "rejoice"); so Paul, alike at beginning and ending, uses a word of kindred origin, **charis** ("grace").

FIRST TIMOTHY

1

(1) Paul, an apostle of Jesus Christ.—The letter to Timothy, though addressed to a very dear and intimate friend, was sent with a twofold purpose. It was an affectionate reminder from his old master, "Paul the Aged," to his disciple to be steadfast in the midst of the many perils to which one in the position of Timothy would be exposed in the city of Ephesus; but it was also an official command to resist a powerful school of false teaching which had arisen in the midst of that Ephesian Church over which Timothy was then presiding. So Paul prefaces his letter by designating himself an apostle according to the commandment of God. The commandment especially referred to is to be found in Acts 13:2.

God our Saviour.—This designation is peculiar to the Pastoral Epistles, but frequently occurs in the Septuagint. It is fitly ascribed to the first Person of the Trinity in reference to His redeeming love in Christ.

(2) My own son in the faith.—Timothy was Paul's very own son. No fleshly relationship existed between the two, but a closer and far dearer connection. Paul had taken him while yet a very young man to be his companion and fellow-laborer (Acts 16:3).

Mercy.—Between the usual salutation "grace and peace" in these Pastoral Epistles he introduces "mercy." The nearness of death, the weakness of old age, the dangers, ever increasing, which crowded around Paul, seem to have called forth from him deeper expressions of love and tender pity.

(3) That thou mightest charge some.—Some time **after** the first imprisonment at Rome, and consequently beyond the period included by Luke in the Acts, Paul must have left Timothy behind at Ephesus while he pursued his journey toward Macedonia, and given him this solemn charge.

That they teach no other doctrine—i.e., other than the truth. Unless these deadening influences were removed, the faith of the Ephesian Church threatened to become utterly impractical. The **doctrine** these restless men were teaching, and which Paul so bitterly condemns, seems to have been no settled form of heresy, but a profitless teaching, arising mainly, if not entirely, from Jewish sources. It had found its way during the apostle's long enforced absence

into the restless, ever-changing congregations at Ephesus.

(4) Neither give heed to fables.—These fables were, no doubt, purely Rabbinical. It was said in the Jewish schools that an oral Law had been given on Sinai, and that this Law a succession of teachers, from the time of Moses, had handed down. For centuries this code supplementary to the written Law in the Pentateuch was preserved by memory or in secret rolls, and doubtless was constantly receiving additions. This strange collection of tradition and comment was committed to writing in the second century by Rabbi Jehuda under the general name of the Mishna, or repetition (of the Law). Around this compilation a complement of discussions (the Gemara) was gradually formed, and was completed at Babylon somewhere about the end of the fifth century of our era. These works—the Mishna and the Gemara, together with a second Gemara, formed somewhat earlier in Palestine—are generally known as the Talmud. The influence of some of these traditions is alluded to by our Lord (Matt. 15:3).

Endless genealogies.—Genealogies in their proper sense, as found in the Book of the Pentateuch, and to which wild allegorical interpretations had been assigned. Such purely fanciful meanings had been already developed by Philo, whose religious writings were becoming at this time known and popular in many of the Jewish schools. Such teaching, if allowed in the Christian churches, Paul saw would effectually put a stop to the growth of Gentile Christendom.

Which minister questions.—Disputings, questions of mere controversy, inquiries, which could not possibly have any bearing on practical life.

(5) With the false teachers' sickly "fables," which only led to disputing, Paul contrasts that healthy practical teaching ("commandment"), the end and aim of which was love, or charity. And the root of this "charity" must be sought in "a faith unfeigned," a faith rich in works rather than in words.

(6) The error of the teachers of whom Timothy was warned consisted not so much in false doctrines as in an utter neglect of inculcating the necessity of a pure, self-denying life. They preferred curious questions and speculative inquiries to the grave, simple gospel teaching which led man to live an earnest, loving life. These teachers, still reckoned among the Christian congregations of the Ephesian Church, had once been in the right direction, but had not kept in it.

(7) Desiring to be teachers of the law.— They coveted the respect and influence which was ever paid to the acknowledged teachers of the Law of Moses; but these men utterly failed to understand the real spiritual meaning of that Law which they pretended to teach. (Comp. Rev. 2:9.)

(8) That the law is good, if a man use it lawfully.—The Law is good, should a man use it so as to make men conscious of their sins, conscious that of themselves they deserve no mercy, only punishment. To press this sorrowful knowledge was the Law's true work upon men. It was never intended to supply materials for casuistry and idle, profitless arguments. It was never meant as a system out of which man might draw material for self-deception. It was never meant as a system through which a man might imagine that by a compliance, more or less rigid, with its outer ritual he was satisfying all the higher requirements of justice and truth.

(9) That the law is not made for a righteous man.—The stern Mosaic Law was enacted centuries before the Messiah had given to men His new Law. The Law of Moses was not, then, enacted for a Christian in the true sense of the word, who has sought and found justification by faith in Jesus, and who, sanctified by the Holy Ghost, is living a new life.

But for the lawless.—The Law had been designed as a great protest against the everyday vices which dishonored Israel in common with the rest of mankind. The terrible enumeration of sins and sinners in these ninth and tenth verses, while following the order of the ancient Tables of Sinai, seems to allude pointedly to the vices especially prevalent in that day in the great centers of the Roman empire.

(11) Which was committed to my trust.— This precious deposit, this "trust," the gospel of the glory of God, was perhaps, in Paul's eyes, his truest title to honor. When we inquire more closely what was exactly meant by "the gospel committed to his trust," something more definite seems to be required than the general answer that he was a minister of the Church. Was it not possibly that gospel of "Luke," which Irenaeus, Origen, and Jerome tell us Paul was accustomed to mention as the gospel written by him? It was, perhaps, this privilege of having been judged worthy to compile, under the direction of the Holy Ghost—

or, at all events, largely to furnish materials for—one of the precious records of his Master's earthly life, work, and suffering which Paul loved to tell as his proudest title to honor. But though Paul knew his work was for all the ages, the true humility of the noble servant of Jesus appears in the substitution of "Luke" for "Paul"—the scribe's name in place of that of the real author.

(13) Who was before a blasphemer, and a persecutor, and injurious.—In these words of bitter self-accusation, Paul sums up the characteristic features of his brilliant career as a young Pharisee leader, as a popular Jewish patriot. The **object** of his intense hatred and of his burning antagonism during these never-to-be-forgotten days was **that very Lord**, from whom later he had received such unspeakable gifts. (See Acts 9:1; 22:4; 25:11.)

Because I did it ignorantly in unbelief.— From such scanty teaching as is contained in these words, and in such passages as Matt. 12:31, 32; Luke 23:34, we gather that there is an ignorance which at least greatly modifies the guilt of unbelief. We learn at least this much—such a sinner is not out of the pale of the operation of divine mercy. But in spite of these hints of the almost limitless area of the divine mercy, great care must be taken not to press too much these intimations of the **possibility** of a mercy far more extended than the usual interpretation would lead us to expect.

(14) The Greek word translated "was exceeding abundant" is very rare, and possesses a superlative force.

(15) This is a faithful saying, and worthy of all acceptation.—This striking formula in the New Testament, found only in the Pastoral Epistles, and the somewhat similar expression "these sayings are faithful and true" (Rev. 21:5; 22:6), were formulas expressing weighty and memorable truths, well known and often repeated by the brotherhood of Christians in the first ages of the faith. They were, no doubt, rehearsed constantly in the assemblies, until they became well-known watchwords in the various churches scattered over the Mediterranean provinces of the Roman empire; and in these "sayings" we see, perhaps, the germs of the great creeds of Christianity.

(16) Howbeit for this cause I obtained mercy.—In spite of this deep consciousness of his guilt, faith and confidence in his own salvation seem never to have wavered. He speaks of **this** with all certainty, and proceeds to tell us with great clearness why

Christ saved him, the chief of sinners (verse 15; see Eph. 3:8).

For a pattern to them which should hereafter believe on him.—If Christ could show mercy to him, surely in after times the greatest of sinners need never doubt the Redeemer's power and will to save. Thus to all sinners was Paul a pattern—an example of the Lord's longsuffering, of His patient waiting.

(17) This doxology is addressed to no one Person of the Trinity, but is a grand testimony to the monotheism of Paul: the Godhead, the Trinity of His worship, is a sublime unity.

(18) This charge I commit unto thee, son Timothy.—The nature of the charge which he committed to Timothy must be gathered from the solemn words and thoughts of verses 15 and 16. The charge was the last precious heritage, the priceless treasure which the old master, feeling that for him the end was not far distant, would leave to his favorite disciple, his own dear son in the faith.

According to the prophecies which went before on thee.—See Acts 16:1, 2. The prophecies in question were uttered, no doubt, over him at his ordination, and, possibly, some of them at his baptism. Special reference is made to doctrine and teaching.

(20) Of whom is Hymenaeus and Alexander.—Hymenaeus is probably identical with the heretic of that name, charged in the Second Epistle to Timothy with teaching that the resurrection was already passed, thus undermining the great hope on which Christian faith so firmly laid hold. The name "Alexander" was a very common one. Of the Alexander of Acts 19:33 we know nothing; from the circumstances in connection with which he is there mentioned, which took place some ten years before this epistle was written, he seems to have been a Jew. (See also II Tim. 4:14, 15 for "Alexander the coppersmith.")

Whom I have delivered unto Satan.—This is a solemn excommunication or expulsion from the church, accompanied with the infliction of bodily disease or death. In ordinary cases, the offender was quietly expelled from the Christian society. But an apostle seems to have possessed the awful powers of inflicting bodily suffering in the forms of disease and death, e.g., in the case of Ananias and Sapphira, Elymas, and the incestuous person at Corinth. (See Acts 8:24.) It is, however, noticeable that this punishment was not necessarily, in the case of disease, an irrevocable sentence. The true end and purpose of this, as of all divine punishments, was not revenge for the sin, but the ultimate recovery of the sinner.

2

(1) Supplications, prayers, intercessions, and giving of thanks.—The Greek word translated "supplications" signifies a request for particular benefits, and is a special form of the more general word rendered "prayers." The expression "intercessions" suggests a closer and more intimate communion with God on the part of the one praying. It speaks of drawing near God, of entering into free, familiar speech with Him. The Greek word suggests prayer in its most individual urgent form. "Giving of thanks" expresses that which ought never to be absent from any of our devotions—gratitude for past mercies.

(2) That we may lead a quiet and peaceable life.—The special object of prayer for those in high authority and power is, first, that through **their** wise rule the Christians might enjoy peace; and, second, that the temper of the people who prayed thus for the ruling powers might be so affected by the constant repetition of such prayers that all thoughts of revolt and resistance would be gradually stamped out.

Paul knew whom he was addressing. The Christian congregations of his age were largely made up of Jews. An intense longing to throw off the yoke of Rome pervaded the whole nation. The terrible events of the year 70 (only four or five years at most from the time of writing this epistle) show how deep-seated was their hatred of the stranger. No Christian, however, was implicated in that fatal rebellion, so thoroughly had the teaching of Paul and his fellow apostles done its work among the Jewish followers of the Crucified. And both Tertullian and Polycarp attest the same in later Christian history.

(4) Who will have all men to be saved, and to come unto the knowledge of the truth.—This great statement of Paul's is not to be used as a proof of universal redemption. We must remember the position it occupies in the argument, it being only introduced as a reason for the exhortation to pray for all. Through the sacrifice and the death of Christ **all** are rendered capable of salvation; that some are indisputably not

1091

saved is not due to any outward circumscription or inefficacy of the divine will, but to man's rejection of the special means of salvation which God has been pleased to appoint and to which it is His divine will that man's salvation should be limited. Redemption is universal, yet conditional—all **may** be saved, yet all **will** not be saved, because all will not conform to God's appointed condition.

(5) Paul with special emphasis speaks of the "one Mediator between God and man" as "the man Christ Jesus," no doubt wishing to bring into prominence the true humanity of the Lord. It is also a silent refutation of the docetic errors of some of the false teachers, of whose doctrines Timothy was to beware. These would have persuaded men that the Christ Jesus who was nailed to the cross was no man, but simply a phantom.

The human nature of Christ is also specially mentioned because in this state He performed His office as Mediator. In the statement of verse 6 we find another reason for Paul's allusion here to the fact of the Mediator being a man. The Messiah must have taken the human nature upon Him before He could have suffered that death which was the ransom of all. Again, the human nature of the Mediator is brought forward to show that the mediatorial office extended over the **whole** human race.

(6) **Who gave himself a ransom for all.**—The Mediator performed His office and work of His own free sovereign will, yielding up Himself to death as the price of the redemption of all mankind—His life in exchange for their forfeited lives. Paul's teaching here is very definite and utterly irreconcilable with the theology which rejects this great Christian doctrine of a **satisfactio vicaria.**

To be testified in due time.—Jesus Christ in the eternal counsels gave Himself to death as the price of the redemption of fallen man; at the appointed and fitting season He endured this death in witness to the truth of the counsels of the eternal Trinity.

(7) **I speak the truth . . . and lie not.**—The warmth with which Paul here asserted his divinely conferred commission as preacher and apostle was not called out by any desire on his part to seize an occasion of asserting in the presence of the false teachers of Ephesus his special rank and prerogatives. These earnest words had no private reference to **him** or to **his** special claims to be heard, but were uttered solely in view of the

surpassing magnitude of the message with which he was charged—that the Gospel of Jesus Christ was a message of glad tidings, an offer of salvation, not to a **people**, but to a **world**.

(8) **That men pray every where . . .**—The greater liberty which women, under the teaching of Christ, had enjoyed, and the distinguished services many of them had been permitted to accomplish in the Master's service, had no doubt contributed to a certain self-assertion on the part of female converts in the Ephesian congregations which threatened grave disorders in the conduct of divine worship. Paul, in his directions respecting divine service in the Christian assemblies, follows the custom here of the Jewish synagogue, where women were forbidden to speak.

Lifting up holy hands.—It was the Jewish practice, not only in taking a solemn oath—or in blessing—but also in prayer, to lift up the hands. (Comp. Pss. 28:2 and 63:4.) This seems to have been generally adopted by the early Christians as the attitude in prayer (See Clem. Rom., **To the Corinthians**, chap. 29.)

(9) **In like manner also, that women.**—The apostle continues his official injunctions in reference to public prayer. While the men were directed to conduct and lead the public prayer, the women who worshiped with them were enjoined, as their part of the solemn service, to be present, adorned with neatness of apparel, modesty of demeanor, and holy reputation of kind deeds.

Adorn themselves in modest apparel.—This direction to Christian women was not intended to apply to their ordinary dress in the world, but simply explained to the sisters of the Ephesian flock that their place in public worship was one of quiet attention. Their reverence and adoration must be shown not by thrusting themselves forward with a view to public teaching or public praying, but by being present and taking part silently, avoiding anything which would be likely to distract the thoughts of others.

With shamefacedness and sobriety.—The first word signifies the innate shrinking from anything unbecoming. The second includes the idea of self-restraint—the conquest over all wanton thought and desire.

Or gold.—The "gold" is supposed to be twined among the plaits of the hair. These elaborate adornments, so likely to catch the eye at divine worship, were quite inconsistent with Christian simplicity, besides being calculated to distract the attention of their fellow-worshipers, male as well as female. (See I Cor. 11:10 and I Pet. 3:3.) Comp. verses 10 and 11 with Acts 9:36; I Cor. 14:35.

(12) The whole purpose of these weighty admonitions relegates Christian women to their own legitimate area of action and influence. Paul raised forever the women of Christ out of the position of degradation and intellectual inferiority they had occupied in the various pagan systems of the East and West, and taught with all the weight of an apostle that woman was a fellow-heir with man of the glories of the kingdom. But while teaching this great and elevating truth, he shows what is the only proper area in which woman should work: while man's duties lay in the busy world without, woman's work was exclusively confined to the quiet stillness of home. The apostle then proceeds to ground these injunctions respecting the duties in public and private of the two sexes upon the original order of creation and upon the circumstances which attended the fall (verse 14).

(15) **Notwithstanding she shall be saved in childbearing.**—Rather, "she shall be saved by **the** childbearing" (the Incarnation), by the relation in which woman stood to the Messiah in consequence of the primal prophecy that her seed (not man's) should bruise the serpent's head (Gen. 3:15). The peculiar function of her sex, from its relation to her Saviour, shall be the medium of her salvation.

3

(1) **If a man desire the office of a bishop.**— In the Pastoral Epistles the Greek words rendered "bishop" and "presbyter" or elder (**episcopos, presbuteros**) are applied indifferently to the same person, for up to this period (A.D. 65-6) no necessity had arisen in the constitution of the Church for the appointment of a **special order** of superintending presbyters. The numbers of the members of the brotherhood, though every year showing a vast increase, were still, comparatively speaking, small. Peter, Paul, James, and John, and certainly the majority of the apostolic college, were still living. Until A.D. 70 the Jerusalem congregation still acted as the central authority of the Church, and grave questions continued to be referred to the Fathers resident there.

But during the last thirty years of the first century, a great change in church organization must have been effected. The Catholic Church in its episcopal character arose, no doubt, out of the needs of the **diaspora.** From notices in Eusebius, Irenaeus, and Clement of Rome, Rothe concludes "that immediately after the fall of Jerusalem, a council of the surviving Apostles and first teachers of the gospel was held to deliberate on the crisis, and to frame measures for the well-being of the Church. The center of the system thus organised was episcopacy, which at once secured the compact and harmonious working of each individual congregation, and, as the link of communication between the separate brotherhoods, formed the whole into one undivided Catholic Church. Recommended by this high authority, the new constitution was immediately and generally adopted."

He desireth a good work.—The office of a presbyter of the church in the days of Paul was a difficult and dangerous post; yet, from the Christian's standpoint, it was a work, if faithfully performed, of all toils the most honorable.

(2) **A bishop then must be blameless.**— The second chapter had treated of the duties of **congregations collectively** in the matter of public prayer; the third chapter speaks of the special character and qualities necessary for the **rulers** of these congregations. These "elders" must, in the first place, be men whose character is unimpeachable. Even those outside the brotherhood of Christ must respect the life and conversation of these prominent and conspicuous members of a society which, from the nature of things, would be sure to provoke distrust and jealousy.

The husband of one wife.—Most ancient writers tell us in general terms that the opinion of the Church from the earliest times interprets this saying of Paul as a declaration against second marriages in the case of those seeking the office of presbyter or deacon. There seems, however, good reason for doubting the accuracy of this popular interpretation, which appears to urge a spirit of asceticism on all Christian society very foreign to Paul's usual teaching. Inspired Christian teaching was careful not to distract the everyday life of men and women by insisting on sudden and violent changes. (The behavior of the great Christian teachers in the matter of that terrible and universal practice of slavery should be especially noted.)

What, then, did Paul mean by these words? We must picture to ourselves the state of society in the empire at the time when the apostle wrote to Timothy. The period was especially marked by an extreme depravity: polygamy, deterioration of family life, materialism. Paul, fully conscious of this low and debased moral tone which then pervaded all society in the empire, **in these few words** condemned all illicit relations between the sexes and directed that in choosing persons to fill holy offices in the congregations of Christians those should be selected who had married and remained faithful to the wife of their choice, and whose life and practice would thus serve as an example both to the flock and to the heathen world. This direction of course does not exclude those men who, while contracting no marriage ties, still were known to lead upright, moral lives.

Given to hospitality.—In the early days of Christianity, Christians traveling from one place to another were in the habit, when it was possible, of resorting to the houses of their brethren in the faith to avoid consorting with idolaters in the public inns. It was of no slight importance that the presiding elders in a congregation should be men who loved to entertain strangers and others, from whom nothing could be expected in return.

Apt to teach.—The elder should possess something more than a readiness to teach the less instructed the mysteries of the faith. He ought also to have the far rarer qualification of a power to impart knowledge to others. Zeal is not by any means the only, or even the principal, qualification to be sought in a minister of the Word.

(3) Not given to wine.—Drunkenness is scarcely alluded to here. It is rather a warning against choosing for the sacred office one given to frequenting noisy banquets, where wild and imprudent words are often spoken.

Not greedy of filthy lucre.—The Greek word thus translated does not occur in the older MSS in this place. But see 3:8 and Tit. 1:7.

(4) One that ruleth well his own house.—The life of the officer in the Church of God must be a pattern life for those without, as well as for those within, the Church's fold to copy and imitate. He must be pre-eminent in nobility of life and aims; but the life and the aims must belong to ordinary everyday life. His high standard must be no inimitable one; the example must be one

that all honest men may follow and copy, if they will. This will be at least a good test of a man's fitness to rule the large family gathered together in the form of a congregation, if his own home is gently yet firmly ruled.

(6) Not a novice.—The word "novice" here refers to want of experience and standing in the Christian brotherhood rather than to youth. Timothy himself was at the time, comparatively speaking, still a man young in years, although old in trials and in Christian experiences.

Lest being lifted up with pride he fall into the condemnation of the devil.—"Being lifted up" would better be rendered "being clouded" or "deluded." It marks the pride or vanity engendered by the finding himself in a position of authority for which no previous training and experience had fitted him. Such a "novice" would be in imminent danger of falling into the judgment passed by God upon the devil, whose fall was owing to the same blinding effect of pride.

(8) Likewise must the deacons.—See Acts 6:1-6. We possess scattered and casual notices of this lower order of deacons dating from the very first days of the faith. The order clearly sprang out of the needs of the rapidly increasing church. Some two years after the Ascension (A.D. 34-35) the seven deacons were appointed to assist the apostles. As the church's life developed, the functions of these primitive subordinate ecclesiastical officers were enlarged. The history of the career of Stephen and Philip supply ample evidence of this.

In the first half of the second century we find the order regularly and apparently universally established, constituting an acknowledged part of the Christian system of ecclesiastical government. The differences between the deacon of the Pastoral Epistles and the deacon of the writings of Justin Martyr are exactly what we should expect would result from the seventy years of gradual but progressive organization under men like John and his disciples and the immediate successors of the apostles.

Not given to much wine.—The professed minister—the advocate for the cause of the poor and needy—must show an example of the strictest sobriety. How well Timothy aimed at showing in himself a self-denying example to the flock we see from 5:23, when Paul deemed it requisite to warn his earnest disciple from an asceticism which was positively weakening his power of work and endurance.

Not greedy of filthy lucre.—Those entrusted with the care of the church's alms surely must be especially careful of their reputation in the matter of covetousness. Among the "chosen" of Timothy there must be no Judas.

(13) It was with good reason that the apostle laid great stress on the many varied qualifications necessary for one undertaking the duties of a deacon of the church, for very great indeed was the reward reserved for the true, loyal deacon when his work was over. The "good degree" they are now purchasing by earnest, patient work may refer to advancement to the higher ministries of the church, but, more probably, has reference to their future position in the blessed life to come.

(15) But if I tarry long.—Paul felt that dangers were pressing closer and closer. The hoped-for visit to his loved church at Ephesus might not, probably never would, be accomplished. Thus these foregoing solemn directions respecting the choice of colleagues in the ministry had been written to Timothy, that, in the event of Paul's never coming to him again, men should know how to conduct themselves in the congregation.

Which is the church of the living God.—The house of God is here plainly defined to be the "Church of the **living** God," who was working in its midst actively and personally, in strong contrast to that well-known graven image of the Diana of Ephesus, throned in that fair temple which glittered in its white and lifeless beauty over the roofs of the city where Timothy's charge lay.

The pillar and ground of the truth.—This peculiar aspect of the church was dwelt upon probably by the apostle as defining—with indirect allusion to nascent and developing heresies—the true note, office, and vocation of the church. Were there no church, there would be no witness, no guardian or archives, no basis, nothing whereon acknowledged truth could rest.

(16) God was manifest in the flesh.—Here, in the most ancient authorities, the word "God" does not occur. The Greek of the most trustworthy MSS must be translated **He who was manifested in the flesh.** The difference is to be attributed to probable scribal substitution of the abbreviation for **theos** ("God") for **hos** ("he who"). The Greek pronoun thus rendered is simply relative to an omitted but easily-inferred antecedent—**Christ.** The whole verse is a

fragment of an ancient Christian hymn, embodying a confession of faith well known to, and perhaps often sung by, the faithful among the congregations of such cities as Ephesus, Corinth, and Rome—a confession embodying the grand facts of the Incarnation and the Resurrection, the preaching of the cross to, and its reception by, the Gentile world, and the present session of Christ in glory. Fragments of similar hymns to Christ are found in II Tim. 2:11, and perhaps also in Eph. 5:14.

4

(1) Giving heed to seducing spirits.—This expression must not be watered down by explanations which understand it as referring to false teachers. The "seducing spirits" are none other than evil powers and spirits subject to Satan, and which are permitted to influence and to work in human hearts. (See Eph. 2:2; 6:12.)

Doctrines of devils.—These are doctrines and thoughts suggested by evil spirits. The personality of these beings is clearly taught by Paul. Of their influence in the heathen world and their antagonism to Christ and His followers, see I Cor. 10:20, 21.

(2) Speaking lies in hypocrisy.—The lies refer to their teaching that it was pleasing to the eye of the Creator for men and women to avoid certain meats and to abstain from marriage. Their hypocrisy consisted in their assumption of a mask of holiness, which holiness they considered was derived from their false asceticism and their abstinence from things which the apostle proceeded to show were lawful.

Having their conscience seared with a hot iron.—The image is drawn from the practice of branding slaves and certain criminals on their forehead with a mark. These men tried to teach the efficacy of a substitution of certain counsels of perfection in place of a faithful loving life. They based their teaching on wild Oriental speculations about the evil nature of all matter. This strange and unnatural counsel would, as time went on, grow into the impious dogma of certain of the great Gnostic schools. The Jewish sects of Essenes and Therapeutae had already taught that abstinence from marriage was meritorious. They were often themselves evil-livers, who, conscious of their own stained, scarred lives, strove with a show of outward sanctity and hypocritical self-denial to beguile and to lead astray others, and in the end to make them as vile as themselves.

And commanding to abstain from meats.—These false teachers, while they urged such abstinence as a likely way to win God's favor, would probably base, or at all events support, their arguments by reference to certain portions of the Mosaic law, rightly understood or wrongly understood. These points might have risen into the dignity of a controverted question between the (Pauline) Gentile and the Jewish congregations. So Paul at once removed it to a higher platform. All food was from the hand of one Maker; nothing, then, could really be considered common or unclean without throwing a slur upon the Creator.

(4) For every creature of God is good.—To teach that anything created was unclean would be an insult to the Creator. The very fact of its being His creation is enough. If made by God, then it **must** be good, notwithstanding men's arbitrary restrictions.

(6) Thou shalt be a good minister of Jesus Christ.—Timothy would by such apposition to the ascetic school earn the "title to honour," for Paul well knew how great was the danger of a comparatively young and ardent disciple like Timothy being attracted by such mistaken teachings of perfection. Asceticism is too often an attractive school of teaching to ministers, as, at a comparatively easy price, they win a great but thoroughly unhealthy power over the souls of men who practice these austerities, which tend necessarily to remove them out of the stream of active life.

Nourished up in the words of faith and of good doctrine.—The Greek present participle rendered here "nourished up in" marks a continuous and permanent process of self-education. Christian ministers of every age must never relax their efforts for self-improvement. The education of the good minister of Jesus Christ is never to be considered finished. Teachers of others, they must ever be striving after a higher knowledge in things spiritual.

(7) But refuse profane and old wives' fables.—Around the grand old Jewish history all kinds of mythical legends grew up. For a Jewish student of the Rabbinical schools the separation of the true from the false became in many cases impossible through all this elaborate and careful but almost profitless study. The minister of Christ was to avoid these strange and unusual interpretations. He was to regard them as merely profane and old wives'

fables, as being perfectly useless and ever harmful in their bearing on practical every day life.

And exercise thyself rather unto godliness.—Instead of the painful, useless ascet icism on the one hand, and the endless and barren Rabbinic studies of the Law on the other, Timothy, as a good minister of Jesus Christ, was to bestow all his pains and labor to promote an active, healthy, practical pie ty among the congregation of believers.

(8) For bodily exercise profiteth little.—Paul here, no doubt, was thinking of those bodily austerities alluded to in verse 3. This kind of victory over the flesh, in very many instances, leads to an unnatural state of mind, for the rigid ascetic has removed himself from the platform on which ordinary men and women move. For practical everyday life such an influence, always limited, is at times positively harmful, as its tendency is to depreciate that home life and family life which to raise and elevate is the true object of Christian teaching.

(10) Who is the Saviour of all men, specially of those that believe.—It must be borne in mind that there were many Hebrews in every Christian congregation who still adhered with passionate zeal to the thought that Messiah's work of salvation was limited to the chosen race. This and similar sayings were especially meant to set aside forever these narrow and selfish conceptions of the Redeemer's will. Still, with all this guarded consideration, which serves to warn us from entertaining any hopes of a universal redemption, such a saying as this seems to point to the Atonement mystery as performing a work, the consequences of which reach far beyond the limits of human thought.

(12) Let no man despise thy youth.—If Timothy desired that his teaching should be received with respectful earnest attention, let him be very careful that his comparative youth prove no stumblingblock. To Paul the aged, his son in the faith seemed still youthful. (At this time Timothy could not have been more than forty years of age.) The old master would have his young disciple supply the want of years by a gravity of life; he would have him, while fearless, at the same time modest and free from all that pretentious assumption. Paul proceeds further to explain his solemn warning by instancing the special points in which Timothy was to be a pattern to the other believers.

In conversation.—This rendering might

mislead. The Greek word signifies rather "manner of life" or "conduct."

(13) Till I come, give attendance to reading.—The words evidently imply a hope, perhaps even an expectation, on the part of Paul that he would one day be enabled once more to visit the church of Ephesus. But as long as that absence lasted, Timothy was to attend carefully to three special points in the public ministry in which he was, in the apostle's absence, the chief officer. The "reading" was that public reading of Scripture in the congregation, a practice borrowed from the synagogue service, when publicly the Law and the Prophets were read to the people assembled. (See Luke 4:16; Acts 13:15.) In these early Christian assemblies, about the year 66-67, it is probable that one at least of the older gospels (probably Mark) was already known and used in the Christian churches and read along with the Scriptures of the old covenant. That the reading of the "gospels" very soon became a part of the regular service in the congregations of Christians is evident from Justin Martyr (**Apologia** 1:67) in the first half of the second century. "Exhortation" and "doctrine" probably refer to the public ministry in the congregation. The first particularly applies to the **feelings**. The reading of the Scriptures must be followed by an earnest practical application of their teaching to the affairs of life. The second suggests a public teaching directed rather to the **understanding** of the hearers. The idea of exposition, or even of dogmatic teaching, seems here included.

(14) Neglect not the gift that is in thee, which was given thee by prophecy.—Here Paul reminds his representative in the Ephesian congregation of the special gift of teaching and exhortation which had been conferred upon him at his solemn ordination long ago, when designated for the post which John Mark had once held with the apostle. It was in many respects a similar office to that which in old days Elisha had held with Elijah; and, as in the case of the Hebrew prophet, so here the choice of Paul had been divinely guided.

With the laying on of the hands.—This was a symbolic action—the outward sign of an inward communication of the Holy Spirit for some spiritual office or undertaking—and was derived from the old solemn Hebrew custom. (See Num. 8:10; 27:18; Deut. 34:9.)

Of the presbytery.—There appears to have been such a body of elders in each particular city or district. The presbytery in this instance would seem in all probability to have belonged to the district of Lystra, Timothy's native city; but an old ecclesiastical tradition speaks of Ephesus as the place of this ordination.

(15) Meditate upon these things.—Rather, "be diligent in these things." "Profiting" is better rendered "advance" or "progress," and reminds all occupying any position of authority in the congregations that there must be a restless striving after the acquirement of new stores of knowledge, ever deeper and more accurate, and a ceaseless endeavor to attain to a higher eminence in the spiritual life. If the minister or teacher would be successful, the **result** of these efforts must be observable to the brethren with whom his lot was cast.

(16) Take heed unto thyself, and unto the doctrine; continue in them.—The apostle in these words sums up the two chief pastoral requisites, and then points out the mighty consequences which will result from faithfully carrying them out. Without true and efficient teaching the pure and upright life of the Christian pastor will fail to win souls for his Master; and, on the other hand, the most efficient instruction will be of no avail unless the life corresponds to the words publicly uttered.

5

(1, 2) Two-thirds of Paul's first letter to Timothy have been taken up with directions, warnings, and exhortations respecting the public duties connected with the office of presbyter, or bishop, of a church like that of Ephesus. From these directions in connection with the public teaching and the official life in the church the apostle passes on to speak of the private relations which one in Timothy's position ought to maintain with individual members of the congregation. To the elderly he is to use, instead of open rebuke, respectful and affectionate entreaties, after the manner of a son, not of an official. His relations with the younger members of the family of Christ ought to be rather those of a brother and a friend than of a superior in rank and dignity. In the case of the younger women, he is urged to add this self-denying, loving friendship a ceaseless watchfulness in all conduct, so as not to afford any ground for suspicion.

The novel prominence (see note on 2:8) of females in such great centers as Ephesus not only necessitated some organization which should administer the alms, and generally watch over and direct the self-sacrificing labors of the female portion of the community, but also required special vigilance on the part of the pastor and his presbyters and deacons to prevent the charities of the church being misused. She who is in every sense a widow and has no one to whom to look for aid always has a claim on the church. Not merely is she to be honored by a simple exhibition of respect, but she is to be assisted and supported out of the alms of the faithful. (See Exod. 22:22; Deut. 24:17; 27:19; Isa. 1:17, 10:2.)

(6) But she that liveth in pleasure is dead while she liveth.—The widow who could so forget her sorrow and her duty is spoken of as a living corpse, and is sharply contrasted with her far happier sister, who, dead to the pleasures of the flesh, living a life of prayer and of self-denial, in the true sense of the word, may be spoken of as **living**.

(8) But if any provide not for his own.—This repeated warning was necessary in the rapidly widening circle of believers. Men and women were attempting to persuade themselves that the hopes and promises of Christians could be attained and won by a mere profession of faith without any practice of stern self-denial or loving consideration for others.

And specially for those of his own house.—The circle of those for whose support and sustenance a Christian was responsible is here enlarged to include distant relatives and even dependents connected with the family who had fallen into poverty and distress.

And is worse than an infidel.—The rules even of the nobler pagan moralists forbid such heartless selfishness. For a Christian, then, deliberately to neglect such plain duties would bring shame and disgrace on the religion of the loving Christ, and, notwithstanding the name he bore, and the company in which he was enrolled, such a denier of the faith would be really worse than a heathen. (See Gal. 5:6.)

(9) These widows were a distinct and most honorable order, different from both deaconesses and the destitute widows to which allusion has just been made. Their duties, **presbyteral** rather than **diaconic**, apparently consisted in the exercise of superintendence over, and in the ministry of counsel and consolation to, the younger women. See verse 14, and note on 3:2, for the marital regulation.

(10) If she have diiligently followed every good work.—This sums up the beautiful character to be sought in the candidates for membership in this chosen woman's band: one who is a faithful wife and mother (or keeper of orphans), one given to hospitality, one ready with a word of encouragement and comfort.

In the **Shepherd of Hermas**, written about A.D. 150, some eighty years after Paul wrote this letter to Timothy, we have probably an example of one of these honored widows in the person of Grapte, whose task it was to teach the widows and orphans of the Roman Church the meaning of certain prophecies.

(11) The younger women,—younger used in a general sense—must positively be excluded from, and held ineligible for, this presbyteral order. This direction by no means shuts them out from participation in the alms of the church, if they were in need and destitute; but it wisely excluded the younger women from a position and from duties which they might in their first days of grief and desolation covet, but of which, as time passed on, they frequently wearied. And to forsake the toil begun, especially if the reasons be unsatisfactory, will bring condemnation (not "damnation," verse 12).

(15) After Satan.—They had swerved from the narrow, thorny road of self-denial which they had chosen for themselves, and perhaps dreading, after their public profession, to form afresh any legal marriage ties, had followed that downward path of sensuality which surely leads to Satan.

(17) The elders (presbyters) to whom Timothy was to accord some special honor were those who, in the congregations and Christian schools of so great a city as Ephesus, in addition to the many duties which were theirs, were distinguished by their preaching and teaching. The "double honor" seems to comprehend rank and position as well as remuneration. Timothy is here directed to confer on the more distinguished of the order of presbyters official rank and precedence as the reward of faithful and successful work.

(18) For the scripture saith, Thou shalt not muzzle the ox that treadeth out the corn.—See Deut. 25:4. If in the law of Israel there was a special reminder to God's people that the **very animals** that labored for them were not to be prevented from enjoying the fruits of their labors, surely **men** who with zeal and earnestness devoted themselves as God's servants to their fellows should be treated with all liberality and even dignified with special respect and honor.

And, The labourer is worthy of his reward.—Comp. Luke 10:7. The words "For the Scripture saith" is always applied by Paul to the writings of the Old Testament. It is better to understand these words as simply quoted by Paul, as one of the well-remembered declarations of the Lord Jesus, not as from any gospel yet written.

(19) Against an elder receive not an accusation, but before two or three witnesses.—Charges—owing, possibly, to jealousy, party feeling, suspected doctrinal error—will frequently be brought against a presbyter. Such an accusation is to be received by Timothy only when the evidence is perfectly clear. Every possible precaution against simply vexatious charges brought against one occupying the hard and difficult position of a presbyter must be taken by the presiding minister. (See Deut. 17:6.)

(20) Them that sin rebuke before all, that others also may fear.—The errors and sins of teachers of the faith are far more dangerous than in those who make up the rank and file of congregations. As the sin, whatever has been its nature, has been committed by man entrusted with a responsible and public charge, so the rebuke and punishment must also be in public, that the warning may then spread over the whole of the various congregations composing the church.

(21) I charge thee before God, and the Lord Jesus Christ.—Paul now reminds Timothy of the ever present unseen witnesses of his conduct. In that awful presence Timothy would guide and rule the congregations of Christians in Ephesus. They had been built up and consolidated by the personal presence and influence of Paul, resident there some three years; and at the time when Paul wrote to Timothy it was second in numbers and in influence to none of the early groups of congregations (except, perhaps, to the Christian communities of Syrian Antioch). Placed by an apostle as the first head of such a community, entrusted with one of the greatest and most important charges in Christendom, Timothy indeed needed to be watchful. Well might Paul remind him of the tremendous witnesses who would be present in his hour of trial.

Doing nothing by partiality.—Although these words, and those immediately preceding, were written with special reference to

the judicial inquiry Timothy would be constrained to hold in the event of any presbyter being formally accused either of a moral offense or of grave doctrinal error in his teaching, yet they must be understood in a far broader sense. The presiding elder in Ephesus must never forget that he bears rule, not only over one school of Christian thought, but over **all** men who acknowledged Jesus as Messiah and Redeemer. He must be above all party feeling.

(22) Lay hands suddenly on no man.—This command refers primarily to the solemn laying on of hands at the ordination of presbyters and deacons. It no doubt also includes the "laying on of hands" customary on the re-admission of penitents to church fellowship.

Neither be partaker of other men's sins.—By thus negligently admitting into the ministry unfit persons—by carelessly admitting persons to a church fellowship, which by their evil life they had forfeited—Timothy would incur a grave responsibility, and in fact "be a partaker" in the sins and errors committed by those men.

(23) Drink no longer water, but use a little wine for thy stomach's sake and thine often infirmities.—That Timothy possessed—as did his master Paul—a feeble body is clear from the words "thine often infirmities." He was, above all things, considering his great position in that growing church, to remember "to keep himself pure," but not on that account to observe ascetical abstinence and so further to weaken the body. Abstinence from wine was a well-known characteristic feature of the Essene and other Jewish ascetic sects. The practice of these grave and ascetic Jews, many of whom became Christians, no doubt affected the habits and tone of thought of the Ephesian congregations. Hence the necessity of Paul's warning against allowing the bodily power to be weakened through abstinence and extreme asceticism.

(24, 25) The judgment (**krisis**) here mentioned is that of Timothy as shown in the careful selection of candidates for ordination, in determining what sinners are fit for restoration to church fellowship, and in pronouncing sentence in the matter of accused presbyters. Paul also bids him take courage in the thought that in many a case self-sacrifice, generosity, and stern principle will be sufficiently manifest to guide him in his choice of fit persons for the holy calling; and in those rarer cases where the higher virtues are hidden, he may be sure that in

God's good season these too **will** become known to him.

6

(1) Let as many servants as are under the yoke count their own masters worthy of all honour.—Slavery was perhaps the most perplexing of all the questions Christianity had to face. It entered into all grades and ranks; it was common to all peoples and nations. The very fabric of society seemed knit and bound together by this miserable institution. It was indeed the curse of the world; but the Master and His chosen servants took their own course and their own time to clear it away. They left society as they found it, uprooting no ancient landmarks, alarming no ancient prejudices, content to live in the world as it was, and to do its work as they found it, yet trusting, by a new and lovely example, slowly and surely to raise men to a higher level. Paul here is addressing, in the first place, Christian slaves of a pagan master. Let these, if they love the Lord and would do honor to His holy teaching, in their relations to their earthly masters not presume upon their own knowledge, that "in Jesus Christ there was neither bond nor free, for all were one in Christ."

(2) And they that have believing masters, let them not despise them, because they are brethren.—This being in servitude to Christian masters would happen less frequently. Let those Christian slaves who have the good fortune to serve "believing masters" not presume on the common brotherhood of men in Christ, on their being fellow-heirs of heaven, and on this account deem their earthly masters their equals and so refuse them the customary respect and attention.

(3) If any man teach otherwise.—In the days of Paul, when the foundation-stones of the faith were being so painfully laid, there seems to have been a life-and-death contest between the teachers of the true and the false. In this passage Paul lays bare the secret springs of much of this anti-Christian doctrine. There is little doubt but that at Ephesus there existed then a school, professedly Christian, which taught the slave who had accepted the yoke of Christ to rebel against the yoke of any earthly lord.

And consent not to wholesome words, even the words of our Lord Jesus Christ.—The apostle, no doubt, was referring to well-known sayings of the Redeemer, such

as "Render unto Caesar the things that are Caesar's," or "Blessed are the meek, for they shall inherit the earth," or "But I say unto you, resist not evil." It was upon such sublime sayings as these that Paul, unlike his opponents, based his teaching and grounded his advice to the slaves in the flock of Christ.

(5) Supposing that gain is godliness.—Paul, here adding his command to Timothy to have no dealings with these men, dismisses the subject with these scathing words of scorn and contempt. This was by far the gravest of his public charges against these teachers of a strange and novel Christianity. We read elsewhere (I Cor. 3:12-15) men might go wrong in doctrine, might even teach an unpractical, useless religion, if only they were trying their poor best to build on the one foundation—Christ. Their faulty work would perish, but they would assuredly find mercy if only they were in earnest. But **these**, Paul tells Timothy and his church, were not in **earnest**. Their religion—they traded upon it; their teaching—they taught only to win gold.

(6) But godliness with contentment is great gain.—The monstrous thought has been that these worldly men dare to trade upon his dear Master's religion; they dare to make out of his holy doctrine a gain. The hateful word suggests to him another danger, to which many in a congregation drawn from the population of a wealthy commercial city like Ephesus were hourly exposed. Yet, though **they** were terribly mistaken, still there **is** a sense in which their miserable notion is true. True godliness is always accompanied with perfect contentment. In this sense, godliness **does** bring along with it great gain to its possessor.

(7) For we brought nothing into this world, and it is certain we can carry nothing out.—Comp. Job. 1:21. Every earthly possession is meant only for this life. If we could take anything with us when death parts soul and body, there would at once be an end to the "contentment" (of verse 6), for the future then would in some way be dependent on the present. This sentence is quoted by Polycarp, in his letter to the Philippians, written early in the second century. Such a reference shows that this epistle was known and treasured in the Christian Church even at that early date.

(9) But they that will be rich.—Here Paul guards against the danger of his words being misinterpreted by any dreamy, unpractical school of asceticism, supposing that voluntary poverty was a state of life peculiarly pleasing to the Most High. Yet those longing to be rich will fall into the temptation to increase their worldly goods, even at the sacrifice of principle. The "snare" is a tangle of conflicting motives— each fresh gratification of the ruling passion, perhaps excused under the plausible names of industry and healthy enterprise, entangling the unhappy soul more completely.

Destruction and perdition.—"Destruction" refers to wreck and ruin of the body, while "perdition" belongs to that more awful ruin of the eternal soul.

(10) For the love of money is the root of all evil.—Paul means, not that every evil **necessarily must** come from "love of money," but that there is no conceivable evil which can happen to the sons and daughters of men which **may** not spring from covetousness. The man coveting gold longs for opportunities in which his covetousness (love of money) may find a field for exercise.

And pierced themselves through with many sorrows.—The imagery seems to be that of a man who wanders from the straight path of life to gather some poisonous, fair-seeming root growing at a distance from the right road on which he was traveling. He wanders away and plucks it; and now that he has it in his hands he finds himself pierced and wounded with its unsuspected thorns. (See Ps. 16:4.)

(12) Fight the good fight of faith, lay hold on eternal life.—With the old stirring metaphor of the Olympic contests for a prize (I Cor. 9:24; Phil. 3:13, 14), he bids the "man of God," rising above the struggles for things perishable and useless, fight the noble fight of faith to lay hold of the **real** prize— life eternal. "The good fight" is the contest which the Christian has to maintain against the world, the flesh, and the devil. It is styled the "good fight of faith," partly because it is waged on behalf of the faith, but still more because from faith it derives its strength and draws its courage.

(15) Which in his times he shall shew.— Here the language of fervid expectation ("the appearing of our Lord Jesus Christ," verse 14) is qualified by words which imply that in Paul's mind then there was no certainty about the period of the "coming of the Lord." It depended on the unknown and mysterious counsels of the Most High. The impression is that Paul had given up all hope of living himself to see the dawn of that awful day, but he deemed it more than probable that his son in the faith would live to witness it.

Who is the blessed and only Potentate.— The stately and rhythmical doxology with which the solemn charge to Timothy is closed was probably taken from a hymn loved by the Ephesian Christians, and often sung in their churches. Possibly already in Ephesus the teachers of Gnosticism had begun their fables of the mighty aeons, and their strange Eastern conception of one God the source of good and another the source of evil.

(16) The Eternal is here pictured as dwelling in an atmosphere of light too glorious for any created beings (not only men) to approach. (See Ps. 104:2; Dan. 2:22.) It is noteworthy that the sublimest epithets the inspired pen of Paul could frame to dignify his description of the First Person of the Trinity, God the Father, are used again of the Son (Rev. 17:14; 19:16).

(17) Charge them that are rich.—In the congregations of Ephesus there were many, owing to birth or to other circumstances, already rich and powerful, already in the possession of gold and rank, in varied degrees. Before closing the letter to the chief pastor, Timothy, Paul must add a word of encouragement and special warning to these. The **wish to be rich** was a sure root of evil, but the **being rich** was a very different thing. This class was surrounded, indeed, with special perils, but still even **as rich** they might serve God faithfully. So in his charge to them he commands them not to strip themselves of the wealth, but to use it wisely and generously. This is the burden of verse 18.

(19) That they may lay hold on eternal life.—This is **the end** the wise, rich Christian proposes to himself when he orders his earthly life and administers his earthly goods, and Paul has just showed Timothy how this "end" is to be reached by such a man.

(20) O Timothy, keep that which is committed to thy trust.—It is a beautiful thought which sees in these few earnest closing words the very handwriting of the worn and aged Apostle Paul. The epistle, no doubt dictated by the old man, was in the handwriting of some friend of Paul and the church, who acted as his scribe; but, as seems to have been sometimes his habit (see especially the closing words of the Galatian letter), the last pleading reminder was added by the hand of the apostle himself. This

1101

"sacred trust" was the doctrine delivered by Paul to Timothy to preach, the central point of which, we know from the apostle's other writings, was the teaching respecting the atonement.

Oppositions of science falsely so called.— Rather, "of knowledge falsely so called." There is little doubt that the seeds of much of the Gnosticism of the next century were being then sown in some of the Jewish schools of Ephesus and the neighboring cities. (Comp. the allusions to these Jewish and cabalistic schools in Paul's letter to the Colossian Church.) The "oppositions" here may be understood as referring generally to the theories of the false teachers, who were undermining the doctrine of Paul as taught by Timothy.

(21) Grace be with thee.—The public nature of so many of the directions and instructions contained in this epistle account for the absence of those private greetings which we find in the Second Epistle of Paul to Timothy.

SECOND TIMOTHY

1

(1) Paul, an apostle of Jesus Christ by the will of God.—As in the epistles to the Corinthians, the Ephesians, and Colossians, he ascribes his apostleship to the sovereign will and election of God. It was that sovereign will that guided him all through that eventful life of his, and which brought him to the prison of the Caesar, where, face to face with death, he wrote this last letter to his friend and disciple Timothy.

According to the promise of life which is in Christ Jesus.—The object or intention of his appointment as apostle was to make known the promise of eternal life. Almost the first words of the epistle, written evidently under the expectation of **death**, dwell upon the promise of **life**. The central point of all evangelical preaching was life eternal, that life which, in the person of the Redeemer, was revealed to man, and which, through the Redeemer, is offered to the sinner.

(2) To Timothy, my dearly beloved son.—The words used in the address of the First Epistle were "my own son." The change was probably owing to Paul's feeling that, in spite of his earnest request for Timothy to come to him with all speed, these lines were in reality his **farewell** to his trusted friend.

(3) I thank God.—Paul's expression of thankfulness was for his remembrance of the unfeigned faith of Timothy, Lois, and Eunice (see verse 5).

Whom I serve from my forefathers.—Paul was here referring not to the great forefathers of the Jewish race—Abraham, Isaac, and the patriarchs—but to the members of his own family, who, he states, were religious, faithful persons.

(4) Being mindful of thy tears.—It is likely that the clouds of danger which were gathering thickly around Paul toward the close of his career had oppressed the brave-hearted apostle with a foreboding of coming evil, and had invested the last parting with Timothy with circumstances of unusual solemnity. Paul had affected others besides Timothy with the same great love (see Acts 20:37, 38).

(5) When I call to remembrance the unfeigned faith that is in thee.—It is probable that some special instance of this unfeigned faith on the part of the chief pastor of Ephesus had come to the apostle's knowledge, and cheered that great loving heart of his while he languished in prison.

Which dwelt first in thy grandmother Lois, and thy mother Eunice ... —In the course of his second missionary journey (Acts 16:1-3) Paul was brought into contact with this pious family at Lystra. It has been suggested that Lois, Eunice, and Timothy were kinsfolk of Paul, hence his intimacy with the family. Lystra is no great distance from Tarsus, Paul's native city. The supposition is just possible, but there is no data to support it.

(6) Wherefore I put thee in remembrance.—It seems, from the general tenor of the epistle, that Timothy was deeply despondent at the imprisonment of Paul. The heart of the younger man sank under the prospect of having to fight the Lord's battle at Ephesus—that famous center of Greek culture and of Oriental luxury—against enemies without and within, alone, and without the help of the great genius and the indomitable courage of the man who for a quarter of a century had been the guiding spirit of Gentile Christianity. So Paul now, persuaded that faith burned in his disciple's heart with the old steady flame, was minded, if possible, to cheer up the fainting heart and to inspire it with fresh courage to fight the Master's fight when he (Paul) had left the scene.

That thou stir up the gift of God, which is in thee by the putting on of my hands—literally, "to kindle up, to fan into flame." (See note on I Tim. 4:14.) Paul frequently uses for his illustrations of Christian life scenes well known, such as the Greek athletic games. Is it not possible that the apostle, while here charging Timothy to take care that the sacred fire of the Holy Ghost did not languish in his heart, had in mind the solemn words of the Roman law, "Let them watch the eternal flame of the public hearth"? (Cicero, **de Legibus**, 11:8.) The failure of the flame was regarded as an omen of dire misfortune, and the watchers, if they neglected the duty, were punished with the severest penalties.

(7) For God hath not given us the spirit of fear—or better, **the spirit of cowardice**, which manifests itself by a timidity and shrinking in the daily difficulties which the Christian meets in the warfare for the kingdom of God. (Comp. John 14:27; Rev. 21:8.) "Hath not given us," in this particular case, refers to the time when Timothy and Paul were chosen for the ministry; but it does admit, too, a far broader application.

But of power, and of love, and of a sound mind.—"A sound mind" is better translated "self-control." The Spirit works in us that power which, in the man or woman living in and mixing with the world, and exposed to its varied temptations and pleasures, is able to regulate and to keep in a wise subjection the passions, desires, and impulses.

(8) This "testimony" of which Timothy was not to be ashamed includes the sufferings and the shame of Christ; but "the testimony" signifies much more than what relates only to the Passion story. The Christian, instead of being ashamed of his "profession," must before the world show fearlessly that its hopes and its promises are his most precious treasure. Nor must Timothy be afraid of confessing before men that he had been the disciple and friend of the prisoner Paul, who had paid so dearly for the courage of his opinions. But, on the contrary, Timothy should rather be ready to suffer, if need be, with Paul, ready to bear some shame with him, ready to incur, perhaps, some danger for the Gospel's sake.

(9) Who hath saved us.—This is an inclusive word, and comprehends all God's dealings with us in respect to our redemption. Again, as so frequently in these Pastoral Epistles, the First Person of the Trinity is referred to as the Saviour.

Not according to our works, but according to his own purpose and grace.—We are told in the next clause that "the grace" was given from all eternity; therefore "our works" could have had nothing to do with the divine purpose which was resolved by God. The "grace" here is almost equivalent to the "mercy" of Tit. 3:5.

(10) Who hath abolished death.—The Greek signifies that by the action of the Lord, death was rendered inoperative—its sting was removed. "Death" has a far more extended meaning than separation of soul and body. It signifies that awful punishment of sin which is best described as the exact opposite to "eternal life."

And hath brought life and immortality to light through the gospel.—"Immortality" is more accurately translated "incorruption." Paul says Christ "brought to light" life and incorruption, not only from having imparted to His own these glorious and divine attributes, but chiefly because He has displayed the life and incorruption in His own resurrection body. In the Greek text, "death," being then a known and ruling power, has the article, while "life" and

"incorruption," being then only recently revealed and unknown powers, except to few are written without the article.

(12) That which I have committed unto him—more exactly, "my deposit." Paul has entrusted his deathless soul to the keeping of his Heavenly Father, and having done this, serene and joyful he waited for the end. His disciple Timothy must do the same. The language and imagery was probably taken by the apostle from one of those Hebrew Psalms he knew so well (Ps. 31:5).

Against that day, the day of the coming of Christ. He will keep my soul—"my deposit"—safe against that day when the crown of life will be given to all that love His appearing.

(13) Hold fast the form of sound words which thou hast heard of me.—Perhaps in the heart of Paul lurked some dread that the new glosses and specious explanation which the school of false teachers, so often referred to in these Pastoral Epistles, chose to add to the great doctrines of Christianity would be more likely to be listened to by Timothy when his old master had died. So he urged upon him to hold fast those inspired formularies he had heard from Paul's lips—such, for instance, as those "faithful sayings" which come before us so often in these epistles to Timothy and Titus. The frequent reference to the "sound, healthy words" in these epistles by Paul, and from which he urges his disciples and successors never to depart, indicate to us the deep importance Paul and the first generation of believers attached to the words and expressions used by the apostles and those who had been with the Lord. False doctrines so easily might creep in, and a lax life, too, Paul knew, was the almost invariable accompaniment of false doctrine.

(14) That good thing which was committed unto thee.—The "deposit" of verse 12 was something committed by Paul to God, while in verse 14 a trust committed by God to Timothy is indicated. (See note on I Tim. 6:20.)

(15) All they which are in Asia.—Large numbers of Christians, if not whole churches, repudiated their connection with the great father of Gentile Christianity, and possibly disobeyed some of his teaching. What, in fact, absolutely took place in Asia while Paul lay bound, waiting for death in Rome, had been often threatened in Corinth and in other centers. Party feeling ran high in those days, and one of the most sorrowful trials Paul had to endure in the agony of is last witnessing for his Lord was the knowledge that his name and teaching no longer was held in honor in some of those Asian churches so dear to him. The geographical term Asia is rather vague. But since a widespread defection from Pauline teaching seems improbable, and there is no tradition that anything of the kind ever took place, Paul probably wrote the term more in the old Homeric sense, and meant the district in the neighborhood of the river Cayster (*Iliad*, 2:461).

Of whom are Phygellus and Hermogenes.—These names would at once suggest to Timothy the men and the congregations of "Asia" to whom Paul was alluding, names well known especially to persons in the position of Timothy. But no tradition has been preserved which throws any light on the lives and actions of these traitorous friends of Paul.

(16) The Lord give mercy unto the house of Onesiphorus.—In striking contrast to those false friends who turned away from him was one, also well known to Timothy, probably an Ephesian merchant. Onesiphorus had, early in this last imprisonment of Paul, arrived in Rome on matters connected probably with business. There he heard of the arrest of that great master whom he had known well in Asia, and sought him out in his prison. There is but little doubt that when Paul wrote this epistle Onesiphorus' death must have recently taken place (see verse 18).

(17) He sought me out very diligently.—This must have been a much more rigorous captivity than the one alluded to in the last chapter of the Acts, when Paul dwelt in his own hired house with the soldier who guarded him. Now he was rigidly imprisoned ("my chain," verse 16), and the very place of his captivity was not, apparently, easily found.

2

(1) Thou therefore, my son, be strong in the grace that is in Christ Jesus.—Paul, after the reference to the faithless Asiatics and the true loyal Onesiphorus, with which he interrupted his exhortation, turns again to Timothy. It is as though he said, Imitate the one loyal follower, and make up to me for the faithless conduct of so many false friends.

(2) And the things that thou hast heard of me.—"The things" were, no doubt, the sum

of Paul's teaching, the general conception of Pauline theology, which Timothy, so long the apostle's intimate and confidential friend and disciple, was to give out to another generation of believers. It was, in fact, the "Gospel of Luke"—"my Gospel," as we love to think Paul termed that matchless summary of the life and teaching of Christ.

Who shall be able to teach others also.—Not only must the Christian teachers to whom Timothy is to give the commission of teaching be trustworthy men, but they must also possess knowledge and the power of communicating knowledge to others. Although the divine help was to be prayed for and expected in this and all other sacred works, yet it is noticeable how Paul directs that no ordinary human means of securing success must be neglected. Paul's last charge in these Pastoral Letters directed that only those shall be selected as teachers of religion whose earthly gifts were such as fitted them for the discharge of their duties. The words of Paul here point to the duty of not only himself to keep unchanged and safe the treasure of the Catholic faith as taught by the apostle, but to hand down the same unimpaired and safe to other hands.

(4) No man that warreth ... —Under three different pictures the apostle paints the duties and rewards of a Christian's life. The first picture is suggested by the last simile (in verse 3). It was one familiar to the numerous peoples dwelling under the shadow of the Roman power. None of the sworn legionaries have anything to do with buying or selling, with the Forum, or any of the many employments of civil life. So should it be with the earnest and faithful Christian; paramount and above any earthly considerations ever must rank his Master's service. But beneath the surface a solemn injunction may surely be read: and so the catholic Church has generally understood this direction to Timothy as warning her ministers from engaging in secular pursuits, either connected with business or pleasure.

But what of Paul's own example and that of other early Christian teachers, such as Aquila? Did not **they**, from time to time, pursue a secular calling—that of tentmakers? The Jewish life in those days contemplated and even desired that its rabbis and teachers should be acquainted with and, even, if necessary, practice some handicraft. The well-known Hebrew saying, "He that teacheth not his son a trade teacheth him to be a thief," is a proof of this. In Paul's case, and also in the case of the presbyters of the first and second age, especially if missionaries, it was impossible always to insure subsistence, unless by some exertions of their own they maintained themselves. It was, too, most desirable that these pioneers of Christianity should be above all reproach of covetousness, or even of the suspicion that they wished for any earthly thing from their converts. That, however, it was not intended that any such combination of work should be the rule of ecclesiastical order in coming days, can be seen in I Cor. 9:1-15.

(5) And if a man also strive for masteries.—Another picture is drawn, a well-known one to all the dwellers in the great cities of the empire. An athlete is chosen to represent the professed servant of Christ, one of those who, after long and careful training, contends in the public games—in wrestling or running, in chariot-racing, or in hand-to-hand contests.

Except he strive lawfully—i.e., according to the prescribed conditions of the contest. He must, of course, submit himself to the strict rules of the theater where the games are held, and must besides—if he hopes for a prize—go through all the long and severe training and discipline necessary before engaging in such a contest.

(6) The husbandman that laboureth must be first partaker of the fruits.—Again the picture is painted from everyday life: the successful tiller of the ground. It is the enduring, patient, self-sacrificing toil that is rewarded in the affairs of common life—and as in the world, so in religion.

(8) Timothy was to remember two great facts. They were to be the foundation stones of his whole life's work Remembering these in the hour of his greatest trouble, he was ever to take fresh courage. The two facts were that Jesus Christ, for whose sake he suffered, was born of flesh and blood, and yet He had risen from the dead. Two facts, then, are to be ever in Timothy's mind: the Incarnation and Resurrection of his Lord.

According to my gospel.—Jerome's remark, "As often as Paul in his epistles writes 'according to my Gospel,' he refers to the volume of Luke," appears on the whole substantially correct. (See Rom. 2:16; 16:25, and note on I Tim. 1:11.)

(10) Therefore I endure all things for the elect's sakes—that is, for those whom, in His infinite mercy, God has been pleased to choose as His people, for those who, in His unfathomable love, are yet to be brought into the one fold. Thus the "elect" include

both believers and unbelievers. The firs would in all ages be built up by the contem plation of the steadfastness under suffering of Paul; the second would be won to the faith by the divinely-inspired arguments and exhortations which the brave old man ceaselessly spoke or wrote down in prison just as when free (verse 9).

(11) For if we be dead with him, we shall also live with him.—There is high probability ity that the words and rhythmical character of verses 11-13 formed part of a liturgy in common use in the days of Timothy. If no as a hymn—which seems, on the whole, the most likely supposition—we can well con ceive them as part of the tapestry of a primitive Christian liturgy.

(13) Yet he abideth faithful: he canno deny himself.—The passage is one of dis tinct severity, for it tells how it is impos sible even for the Redeemer to forgive in the future life. He cannot act as though faithfulness and faithlessness were one and the same thing. The Christian teacher mus remember that, sure and certain as are the promises of glory and happiness to those who love the Lord and try to live His life so surely will fall the chastisement on al who are faithless and untrue.

(14) Of these things put them in remem brance.—A new division of the epistle be gins here. Paul now proceeds to charge Timothy respecting the special work he ha to do. First he deals with his duties as a teacher of truth brought face to face with teachers of error. He prefaces his direction by bidding him put his Ephesian flock in remembrance of those great and solemn truths set forth in verses 11-13: fellowship with Christ in suffering will be succeeded by fellowship with Christ in glory.

(15) Study to shew thyself approved unto God, a workman that needeth not to be ashamed.—Timothy, and those in the position of Timothy, were to show themselves approved unto God, by turning others, over whom they possessed influence, from the pursuit of vain and unprofitable things. His own words in the First Epistle to the Corinthians (3:10-15) were evidently in Paul's mind when he wrote down this direction to Timothy.

Rightly dividing the word of truth.—better rendered "rightly laying out the word of truth." The Greek word literally signifies "cutting a straight line." It seems most correct to regard it as a metaphor from laying out a road (see Prov. 3:6, LXX), or drawing a furrow, the merit of which consists in the traightness with which the work of cutting r laying out is performed. In the third entury, Clement of Alexandria (**Stromata**,) uses the word in a sense in which the dea of "cutting" has been lost, when he vrites **orthotomia** (a substantive) as an quivalent for **orthodoxia**—orthodoxy. It is robable that the use of the word here by *aul gave the word a fresh starting-point, nd that gradually the original meaning assed out of sight.

(17) And their word will eat as doth a anker—better rendered "as doth a gangrene." "Cancer" is adopted by Luther. The ife of the sufferer afflicted with cancer may ie prolonged for many years; a few hours, iowever, is sufficient to terminate the life if the patient attacked with "gangrene," inless the limb affected be cut away at once. Paul expresses his dread of the fatal influence of the words of these teachers on the lives of many of the flock of Christ. The close connection between grave fundamental errors in doctrine and a lax and purely elfish life is constantly alluded to by Paul.

Of whom is Hymenaeus and Philetus.—Regardless of the severe action which had been taken against him (I Tim. 1:20), Hymenaeus was apparently still continuing in his error.

(18) Who concerning the truth have erred.—The resurrection of the body, grounded upon the Lord's own words (John 5:28, 29), and experience, was one of the articles of the Christian faith upon which Paul especially loved to dwell. With this "resurrection of the body" Paul taught men that the future state of rewards and punishments was intimately bound up. This doctrine appears, in very early times, to have been questioned by some in the Christian community. Elaborated, but still scarcely disguised, the same denial of a bodily resurrection was a characteristic of the widely-spread Gnostic systems of the second and third centuries. These early Christian followers of men like Hymenaeus and Philetus had much in common with the ascetic Jewish sects of Essenes and Therapeutae, and especially with the famous Sadducean school, which attracted then so many cultured and wealthy Jews.

(19) Having this seal.—It was a custom from the earliest times to inscribe upon a building or a monument an inscription which told of its origin and purpose. In some cases, as in the oldest monuments of Egypt, the engraved writing told the name of the royal or priestly builder. On this "foundation storey" of the work of God, of which Paul was now speaking, was carved a legible inscription in two sentences. The one told of comfort and hope, reminding men God would always know "His own"; the other told of duty, reminding men that "God's own" had no share in unrighteousness. It is called "a seal" here instead of an inscription, for a seal best conveys the idea of the solemn binding character of the writing. (See Deut. 6:9; 11:20; Rev. 21:14.)

(20) But in a great house there are not only vessels of gold and of silver.—The apostle goes on with the same thought of the "Church of God on earth," but he changes the imagery. In a great house, argues Paul, are always found two distinct kinds of vessels—the precious and enduring, and also the comparatively valueless, lasting but a little while. The first kind are destined for honor, the second for dishonor. By these vessels the genuine and spurious members of the church are represented as forming two distinct classes. The enduring nature of the metals gold and silver are contrasted with the perishable nature of wood and earth. The former will remain a part of the church forever; the latter will endure only until the end of the world.

(21) If a man therefore purge himself from these.—The good and faithful must separate themselves from the evil and faithless. The thought of those deniers of the resurrection of the body was uppermost in Paul's mind. There must be no communion on the part of God's servants with impugners of fundamentals.

(22) Flee also youthful lusts.—But there was an **inner** work to be accomplished, as well as an outer and more public protest to be made. He must fight with and conquer those lusts, passions, and desires which are more peculiarly tempting to those who are still in the meridian of life. Timothy was at this time probably between thirty and forty years of age.

Out of a pure heart.—These words contrast those holy and humble men of heart who serve God without any ulterior motive, with those false teachers who dare to make their religion a gain, a source of profit.

(24) The exhortation is to be quiet and kind, not only to those belonging to the brotherhood of Christ, but **to all**. It is noteworthy now, in these Pastoral Epistles—which contain, so to speak, the last general directions to believers in Jesus as to life as well as doctrine of perhaps the greatest of the inspired teachers—so many careful suggestions are given for the guidance of Christians in all their relations with the great heathen world. **Conciliation** may be termed the keynote of these directions. Paul would press upon Timothy and his successors the great truth that it was the Master's will that the unnumbered peoples who sit in darkness and in the shadow of death should learn, by slow though sure degrees, how lovely and desirable a thing it was to be a Christian.

(25) By "those that oppose themselves," Paul alludes to those led away by false teachers. In verse 21, and in Tit. 3:10, the pronounced heretics were to be shunned. These, however, were evidently to be dealt with in a different manner.

(26) Who are taken captive by him at his will.—These words represent the captive to sin waking up ("recover") from his deathly slumber and escaping the toils of the evil one, for the purpose of carrying out for the future the will of God. The first personal pronoun in this clause, referred here to the devil, and the second, referred here to God, are represented in the Greek by two distinct words.

3

(1) In the last days.—Paul now, having told Timothy that although there was no reason to fear, yet warns him that grave dangers to the church **would** surely arise, and that God's servants, like Timothy, must be prepared to combat.

The majority of commentators have referred "the last days" to the period immediately preceding the second coming of the Lord—a day and an hour somewhere in the future but hidden, not merely from all men, but from the angels, and even from the Son (Mark 13:32). It seems, however, more in accordance with such passages as I John 2:18, where **the present**, and not an uncertain future is alluded to, to understand "the last days" as that period, probably of very long duration, extending from the days of the first coming of Christ to His second coming in judgment. The Jewish Rabbis of the days of Paul were in the habit of speaking of two great periods of the world's history—"this age" and "the age to come." The former included periods up to Messiah's advent; the latter included all periods subsequent to the appearance of Messiah. This latter period is often alluded to by the Hebrew prophets under the expression "in the end of days." (See Isa. 2:2; Hos. 3:5;

Mic. 4:1.) The words of verse 5, "from such turn away," would require certainly strained interpretation if we are to suppose that the "last days" referred to a time immediately preceding the end, or, in other words, the last period of the Christian era. The sad catalogue of vices is one with which all ages of the Church of Christ have been too well acquainted.

(2) Lovers of their own selves.—Selfishness well heads the list. It is the true root of all sin.

Blasphemers.—The two vices just mentioned refer to man's conduct to his brother man; this alludes to his behavior toward his God. The pride with which he looks down on his fellows develops itself into insolence in thought, if not in word, toward his God.

(3) Without natural affection.—Careless and regardless of the welfare of those connected with them by ties of blood.

Incontinent—having no control over the passions.

(4) Traitors—or "betrayers," probably of their Christian brethren. (Comp. Luke 6:16; Acts 7:52.) In those days, to inform against the believers in Jesus of Nazareth, to give information of their places of meeting in times of persecution, was often a profitable though a despicable work.

(5) Having a form of godliness, but denying the power thereof.—This means keeping up a show of observing the outward forms of religion, but renouncing its power and its influence over the heart and the life. These, by claiming the title of Christians, but by their lives dishonoring His name, did the gravest injury to the holy Christian cause.

From such turn away.—The pagan was to be courteously intreated, for in God's good time the glory of the Lord might shine, too, on those now sitting in darkness and in the shadow of death. The heretic, seduced by false men from the school of the apostles, where the life as well as the doctrine of Jesus was taught, was to be gently instructed; perhaps God would lead him once more home. But **these**, who, while pretending to belong to Jesus, lived the degraded life of the heathen, were to be shunned. No communion, no friendly intercourse was possible between the hypocrite and the Christian.

(6) For of this sort are they which creep into houses, and lead captive silly women.—The corrupting influence of these hypocritical professors of the religion of Jesus must have been already great, and the danger to real vital godliness in Ephesus imminent,

r Paul here specifies perhaps the most
ccessful work of these toilers for Satan.
hese men busied themselves in securing
)pularity among the female portion of the
)ck in the Ephesian Church by supplying
ιcification for the guilty consciences of
ese women, laden with sins. They showed
em, no doubt, how in **their** school they
ight still be Christians and yet indulge
eir diverse lusts. The expression "which
eep into houses," although perfectly natu-
ιl, acquires an increased force when we
:member the comparative state of seclu-
on in which women usually lived in Eastern
nds. Special fraud and deceit was needful
»r these false teachers to creep into the
omen's apartments in Asia. The Greek
ord translated "lead captive" is a peculiar
ιe, and represents these women as wholly
nder the influence of these bad men, to the
tter destruction of all true, healthy home
fe. "Silly women" is simply a diminutive,
xpressing contempt. There is no doubt but
ιat the older heresiarchs made great use of
'omen in the propagation of their new and
:range systems. They worked more easily,
erhaps, on the impulsive and emotional
:male mind; but what must be taken into
:count is the reaction which was **then**
ιking place among women, so long rele-
ated to an inferior and subordinate posi-
on, and now, by the teaching of Christ and
I is apostles, raised to a position of equality
'ith men as regards the hope of future
lory. In many instances, in the first ages of
'hristianity, there is no doubt but that they
ιisunderstood their position. According to
erome, Simon Magus, Nicolas of Antioch,
ιe Gnostic Marcus, Montanus, Donatus,
larcion, Arius, Priscillian, and other here-
archs famous in the annals of the early
hurches were intimately associated with or
upported by female influence.

**(7) Ever learning, and never able to come
) the knowledge of the truth.**—A morbid
)ve of novelty, and a hope to penetrate
ιto mysteries not revealed to God's true
:achers, spurred these female learners on.
'hat some of these false teachers laid claim
) occult arts is clear from the statement
ontained in verse 8, where certain sorcer-
rs of the time of Moses are compared to
ιem. (See Exod. 7:11-22.) The names "Jan-
es" and "Jambres," though not given in the
ιcred text, are preserved in the oral tradi-
on of Israel.

**(10) But thou hast fully known my doc-
rine.**—Here Paul recalls to Timothy's mind
'hat had been his—Paul's—life, words, and

works. No one knew the history of this life
like Timothy, the pupil and the friend, who
had been long trained to assist in carrying
on his teacher's work after Paul was removed. This appeal to Timothy's recollection of the past has two distinct purposes:
(1) it was to contrast that life of Paul's with
the lives of those false men who were poisoning the stream of Christianity at Ephesus; and (2) the memory of the master was
to serve as an incentive to the young teacher to suffer bravely in his turn.

(11) Persecutions, afflictions.—Why, out
of the pages of the closely written diary of
his life's experiences, does Paul select the
events which took place at Antioch, Iconium, and Lystra? Was there anything special
in what he endured in these places? The
most satisfactory answer seems to be that
what happened on that first journey would
never be forgotten by Timothy. Some of the
incidents were among his first experiences
with Paul of the work; others had taken
place just before Paul took him as his
associate, and, no doubt, had been often
discussed in Timothy's hearing in those
anxious hours which preceded his choice of
the calling of a missionary. Hearing of these
deeds of endurance perhaps contributed to
Timothy's resolve to emulate these acts.

(12) Yea, and all that will live godly.—
But Paul would not allow it to be thought
for a moment that in the fact of his enduring persecution and suffering there was anything remarkable or singular. To the statement "all that will live godly" it is noticeable that the apostle adds "in Christ Jesus,"
thus telling us there can be no true piety
except in communion with Him.

(15) The holy scriptures.—Literally, "the
sacred writings." The Scriptures of the Old
Testament are here exclusively meant. Paul
appealed to Timothy's own deep knowledge
of those Old Testament Scriptures. His disciple would know that the great Christian
doctrines respecting the Messiah were all
based strictly on these Old Testament writings.

**Which are able to make thee wise unto
salvation.**—The present participle rendered
"which are able" is noticeable, being here
used to express the ever-present power of
the Scriptures on the human heart. The
Holy Scriptures had not completed their
work on Timothy when, in his boyhood, he
first mastered their contents. It was still
going on.

**(16) All scripture is given by inspiration
of God.**—This verse declares positively the

inspiration of all the Old Testament Scriptures, for this is what the apostle must have had in reference. The New Testament at this period was certainly not all written; for instance, John's gospel, John's epistles, the epistle to the Hebrews, and the Apocalypse, with several of the Catholic Epistles, probably were composed at a later date than that assigned to this letter to Timothy. Paul spoke of the Jewish Scriptures, the "canon" of which was then determined. Thus he exhorted Timothy to show himself a contrast to the false teachers—ever shifting their ground—by keeping steadily to the old teaching of doctrine and of life.

Inspiration of God.—Comp. II Pet. 1:20, 21. The various uses of Holy Scripture in the training of the man of God are set forth in the enumeration which closes this verse. These sacred writings must be the one source from which he derives those instructions which teach the Christian how to grow in grace.

4

(1) I charge thee therefore before God, and the Lord Jesus Christ.—Probably Luke (verse 11), the faithful friend, was writing to the apostle's dictation. Paul would have the last words introduced by a most impressive preface. So before he sums up his directions and exhortations, he appeals to Timothy in these stately and solemn words.

At his appearing and his kingdom.—The "kingdom" here spoken of is to begin at Christ's glorious epiphany or manifestation. Timothy was charged by the "appearing" of Christ when he would have to stand before Him and be judged; he was charged, too, by "His kingdom," in which glorious state Timothy hoped to share, for was it not promised that His own should reign with Him (2:12)? There seems in this solemn ringing adjuration something which reminds us of "a faithful saying."

(2) Preach the word.—The language of the original here is abrupt and emphatic, written evidently under strong emotion and with intense earnestness. Paul charged his friend and successor with awful solemnity to proclaim, loudly and publicly, as a herald would announce the accession of his king. The exact opposite to what Paul would urge on Timothy is described by Isa. 56:10.

In season, out of season.—In other words, "For thy work, set apart no definite and fixed hours, no appointed times. Thy

work must be done at all hours, at all times. Thy work has to be done not only when thou art in church, not merely in times of security and peace, but it must be carried on in the midst of dangers, even if thou art a prisoner and in chains, even if death threatens thee."

With all longsuffering and doctrine.—He must reprove, rebuke, exhort, with all gentleness and patience; and in all this he must take care that "teaching" accompanies his rebuke and his words of comfort.

(3) For the time will come when they will not endure sound doctrine.—Errors now just apparent would attain more formidable dimensions. The thirst for novelties in doctrine, the desire for a teaching which, while offering peace to a troubled conscience, would yet allow the old self-indulgent life to go on as before, would increase. In full view of this development of error, and the thought that more and more of the so-called Christians would dislike the preaching of the "sound doctrine," Timothy and his brother teachers must indeed be wakeful, watchful, and earnest in their preaching and ministrations.

(4) And they shall turn away their ears from the truth.—This was the punishment of those who would only listen to what was pleasing to them, and which flattered instead of reproved their way of life. They became involved in the many various errors in doctrine which were then taught in the schools of the heretics, and they ended by turning away from every Christian truth. On the "fables" which they substituted, see I Tim. 1:4.

(5) Make full proof of thy ministry.—In other words, "Fully carry out the many duties imposed upon thee by thy great office." The office of Timothy in Ephesus included far more than merely those of a preacher or evangelist. He was the presiding presbyter of the church, to whom its government was entrusted; in fact, the many-sided life of Paul was now to be lived by Timothy.

(6) For I am now ready to be offered.—In his first imprisonment in Rome Paul looked on to a martyr's death as probable (see Phil. 2:17); in this second captivity at Rome he writes of the martyrdom as already beginning. The Greek word rendered "I am being offered" points to the drink offering of wine which, among the Jews, accompanied the sacrifice (see Num. 15:1-10). Among the heathen this wine was commonly poured upon the burning vic-ims. The allusion here is to Paul's bloody death.

And the time of my departure is at hand.—The Greek word rendered "departure" signifies the raising of the ship's anchor and the loosing of the cables by which the vessel was hindered from proceeding on her destined voyage.

(7) I have fought a good fight.—Paul changes the metaphor and adopts his old favorite one, so familiar to all Gentile readers, of the athlete contending in the games. First, he speaks generally of the combatant, the charioteer, and the runner. "I have fought the good fight," leaving it undetermined what description of strife or contest was in reference. The tense of the Greek verb—the perfect—"I **have** fought" is remarkable. The struggle had been bravely sustained in the past, and was now being equally bravely sustained to the end. His claim to the crown (verse 8) was established.

I have finished my course.—Or "race," for here the image of the stadium, the Olympic race-course, was occupying the apostle's thoughts. Again the perfect is used: "I **have** finished my course." (See Acts 20:24.)

I have kept the faith.—Here, again, the metaphor is changed, and Paul looks back on his life as on one long, painful struggle to guard the treasure of the catholic faith inviolate and untarnished (see I Tim. 6:20). And now the struggle was over, and he handed on the sacred deposit, safe. (Comp. Phil. 3:12.)

(8) Which the Lord, the righteous judge, shall give me.—As a righteous judge will the Lord award him the crown, recognizing him as one who had the prize of victory. Probably the expression "the righteous judge" was written in strong contrast to that unrighteous judge who had condemned Paul, and in accordance with whose unjust sentence he would presently suffer a painful death. (See note on 1:12.)

(10) For Demas hath forsaken me.—This once faithful companion of Paul had been with him during the first imprisonment of the apostle at Rome (Col. 4:14; Philem. 24); but now, terrified by the greater severity and the threatened fatal ending of the second imprisonment, he had forsaken his old master. The tradition which relates that he became in later days an idol priest at Thessalonica is baseless. Demas is probably a shorter form for the common Grecian name of Demetrius. The "present world" is the present (evil) course of things.

Is departed unto Thessalonica.—Chrysostom suggests that Thessalonica was apparently the "home" of Demas. It has been supposed, however, by some, that Thessalonica was chosen by Demas as his abode when he left Paul because it was a great mercantile center, because his business connections were there, and because he preferred them, the rich and prosperous friends, to Paul, the condemned and dying prisoner. Thessalonica was, at this time, one of the great cities of the empire.

Crescens to Galatia.—Nothing is known of this friend of Paul. One tradition speaks of him as a preacher in Galatia, and another of his having founded the Church of Vienne in Gaul. There is a curious variation in some of the older authorities here, "Gallia" being read instead of Galatia.

Titus unto Dalmatia.—Dalmatia was a province of Roman Illyricum, lying along the Adriatic. Nothing is known respecting this journey of Titus. It was, most probably, made with the apostle's sanction.

(11) Only Luke is with me.—He was the "writer" of the third gospel, the gospel which was possibly the work of Paul—"my Gospel." Luke, "the beloved physician" of Col. 4:14, of all Paul's companions, seems to have been most closely associated with the apostle. Most likely this close intimacy and long-continued association was owing to the apostle's weak and infirm health. Luke was with Paul in his second missionary journey, and again in his third; he accompanied him to Asia, and then to Jerusalem; and he was with him during the first time Paul was imprisoned in the capital (Acts 18). After Paul's death, Epiphanius speaks of him as preaching chiefly in Gaul. A general tradition includes him among the martyrs of the first age of the church.

Take Mark, and bring him with thee: for he is profitable to me for the ministry.—There is something touching in this message of the aged master to Timothy to bring with him on that last solemn journey one whom some quarter of a century before Paul had judged so severely, and on whose account he had separated from his old loved friend, Barnabas. (See Acts 15:38.) Since that hour when the young missionary's heart had failed him in Pamphylia, Mark had, by steady, earnest work, won back his place in Paul's heart. (See Col. 4:10; Philem. 24.) He is mentioned (I Pet. 5:13) by the endearing term of "my son," and the unanimous traditions of the ancient Christian writers represent him as the secretary or amanuensis of Peter. It was his office to commit to writing the orally delivered instructions and narrations of his master. These, in some revised and arranged form, probably under the direction of Peter himself, were given to the church under the title of Mark's gospel. A later and uncertain tradition says he subsequently became first Bishop of Alexandria, and there suffered martyrdom.

For he is profitable to me for the ministry.—He was such, according to Grotius, because of his knowledge of the Latin tongue. But it is more likely that he was serviceable as an assistant who was well acquainted with the details of Paul's many-sided work.

(12) And Tychicus have I sent to Ephesus.—Tychicus was evidently one of the trusted companions of Paul. He had been with him on his third missionary journey, and had, during Paul's first Roman imprisonment, some six or seven years before, been charged with a mission by his master to Ephesus. (See Eph. 6:21; Col. 4:7.) It has been suggested with considerable probability, that Tychicus had been the bearer of the first epistle to Timothy. Between the writing of these two letters no great interval could have elapsed.

(13) The cloak that I left at Troas.—Some have wished to understand by "the cloak" a garment Paul was in the habit of wearing when performing certain sacred functions. But such a supposition would be precarious, for nowhere in the New Testament is the slightest hint given us that any such vestment was ever used in the primitive Christian Church. We understand it to be simply a thick cloak, or mantle, which Paul had left. Probably, when he left it, it was summer, and he was disinclined to burden himself in his hurried journey with any superfluous things. Winter was now coming on, and the poor aged prisoner in the cold damp prison, with few friends and scant resources, remembered and wished for his cloak. Then too, Paul, by his wish here expressed, hopes against hope that yet a little while for work in the coming winter months was still before him.

And the books.—The books were, most likely, a few choice works bearing on Jewish sacred history. Others were probably heathen writings, of which we know, from his many references in his epistles, Paul was a diligent student. These—if God spared his life yet a few short months—he would have with him for reference in his prison room.

But especially the parchments.—These precious papers, above all, would Paul have with him. They were, most likely, commonplace books, in which the apostle—evidently always a diligent student—had written what he had observed as worthy of special notice in the reading of either the Scriptures of the Old Testament, or the other books bearing on Jewish or pagan literature and history. These precious notes were probably the result of many years' reading and study.

(14) Alexander the coppersmith did me much evil.—It has been suggested that this Alexander, an influential Ephesian Jew, had done much injury to the cause of the Christians generally, and to Paul personally, with the imperial authorities at Rome. (Comp. I Tim. 1:20.)

(15) Of whom be thou ware also.—This Alexander was evidently then at Ephesus. It is an interesting suggestion which refers the connection between Paul and Alexander back to those days when Saul and Alexander were both reckoned as belonging to the strictest Pharisee party, determined foes to the "Nazarenes." Saul—if we adopt this supposition—became the Apostle Paul of the Gentiles; Alexander remained a fanatic Jew—hence the enmity.

(16) At my first answer no man stood with me . . .—After the mention of what his **enemy** had done out of hatred to the cause of Christ, the old man passed on to speak of the conduct of his own **familiar friends** at that great public trial before the Praefectus Urbi, a nominee of the Emperor Nero. The position of a well-known Christian leader accused in the year 66-67 was a critical one, and the friend who dared to stand by him would himself be in great danger. After the great fire of Rome, in A.D. 64, the Christians were looked upon as the enemies of the state, and were charged as the authors of that terrible disaster. Nero, to avert suspicion from himself, allowed the Christians to be accused and condemned as encendiaries. A great persecution, in which, as Tacitus tells, a great multitude of the followers of Jesus perished, was the immediate result of the hateful charge. It is most probable that Paul, as a famous Nazarene leader, was eventually arrested as implicated in this crime and brought to Rome.

(17) That by me the preaching might be fully known.—Before the highest earthly tribunal in the capital city of the world, Paul pled not only for himself but for that great cause with which he was identified. He spoke possibly for the last time publicly we know nothing of the final trial, when he was condemned) the glad tidings of which he was the chosen herald to the Gentile world. It is probable that this great trial took place in the Forum; it is certain it was in the presence of a crowded audience.

And I was delivered out of the mouth of the lion.—Who is to be understood under the figure of the lion? The church fathers mostly believe the Emperor Nero; others have suggested the lions of the amphitheater. It is, however, best to understand the expression as figurative for extreme danger. Such figurative language was not unusual; comp. the **Epistle of Ignatius to the Romans** 2:8.

(18) And the Lord shall deliver me from every evil work . . . —This last letter of the great Gentile teacher reads in many places like a triumphant song of death. We supply after "every evil work" the words "of the enemies," and understand the deliverance which the Lord will accomplish for him, not as a deliverance from any shrinking or timidity, but as the Lord Jesus' delivering him from all weariness and toil, and bringing him safe into His heavenly kingdom, **through this very death.**

(19) Salute Prisca and Aquila.—These were two of Paul's earliest friends after he had begun his great work for his Master. Originally of Pontus, they had taken up their abode at Rome, where Aquila exercised his trade of a tent-maker. Driven out of Rome by the decree of Claudius, which banished the Jews from the capital, they came to Corinth, where Paul became acquainted with them. But they were evidently Christians when Paul first met them, about A.D. 51-52. We hear of them in company with Paul in Acts 18:2; I Cor. 16:19; and Rom. 16:3.

They were, evidently, among the many active and zealous teachers of the first days of the faith. That they possessed great ability as well as zeal is evident from the fact that it was from them that the eloquent and trained Alexandrian master, Apollos, learned to be a Christian (Acts 18:26).

And the household of Onesiphorus.—See note on 1:16.

(29) Erastus abode at Corinth.—There were among Paul's friends two men of this name: one was a resident official personage at Corinth, the other of that band who journeyed here and there for the propagation of the faith. (See Acts 19:22; Rom. 16:23.)

But Trophimus have I left at Miletum sick.—Trophimus, a Gentile Christian, was with Paul on his third missionary journey when the apostle was accused of defiling the Temple at Jerusalem. It was this accusation on the part of the Jews which led to Paul's arrest which preceded his first long imprisonment. The event here alluded to must have taken place some time **after** the apostle's release from the first imprisonment, A.D. 63, and, probably, in the course of his last journey, shortly before his second arrest and imprisonment at Rome, about A.D. 66.

Miletus (not "Miletum"), a seaport about thirty miles from Ephesus, once was a city of great renown. But in the days of Paul its glories were already on the wane. (See Acts 20:15.)

(21) Of these persons, Linus was, no doubt, the first of the long line of bishops of Rome. The date of his consecration corresponds with the year of Paul's martyrdom, A.D. 66. We know, from this greeting, he was one of the few "faithful" to his old master. It has been suggested, though of course there is no certainty of this, that the consecration of Linus to the government of the Roman Church as its first bishop was one of the dying acts of the Apostle Paul.

Some commentators identify the other two with "Pudens and Claudia" mentioned by Martial (**Epigrams** 4:13; 11:54). Pudens was the son of a Roman senator; Claudia (Rufina) was a Briton.

TITUS

1

(1) Paul, a servant of God, and an apostle of Jesus Christ.—In the other two Pastoral Epistles addressed to Timothy, Paul simply styles himself "an Apostle of Jesus Christ." Possibly, the longer and more formal title is adopted here because his relations were seldom of so intimate a character with Titus as with Timothy.

According to the faith of God's elect.—The rendering should be, "for (the furtherance of) the faith." Such election in no case seemingly affects our position here as free agents; surrounded with the most precious privileges, gifted with much knowledge, it is possible, as we too often see, deliberately to refuse the good and to choose the evil. All such allusions to the "elect" are intended not as a stumbling block for the believer but as a comfort for the faithful, struggling man of God, for it tells him how the eternal God "before the ages" had chosen him to be His servant.

And the acknowledging of the truth which is after godliness.—Here the further purpose of Paul's apostleship is specified. Paul was appointed an apostle that through him the elect of God might believe and heed "the truth"—that truth, the knowledge of which produces as its fruit in the individual a holy, useful life.

(2) Which God, that cannot lie.—Possibly, this singular and strong expression was chosen with reference to the peculiar vice of the Cretans, over whose church Titus was then presiding. (See verse 12.)

(3) According to the commandment of God our Saviour.—Paul dwells with emphasis on the thought that he was entrusted with the preaching of the Gospel according to the commandment of God. The First Person of the Trinity fitly possesses the title of "our Saviour," because through the death of His Son He redeemed us from death and made us heirs of eternal life. The Second Person of the Trinity is likewise a possessor of the title, because He shed His blood as the price of our redemption. The epithet of "Saviour"—the title just given to the Father, in the next verse ascribed to the Son—is one of the many indications we possess of Paul's belief that the Son was equal to the Father as touching His Godhead.

(4) To Titus.—We know comparatively little of Titus' earlier career. In the Acts he

is never mentioned; for what knowledge of him we possess we are entirely dependent upon a few casual allusions to him in the epistles. This presbyter, in charge of the Cretan Church, was a Greek, the son of Gentile parents, and uncircumcised. He owed his conversion to Christianity to Paul with whom ever after he seems to have been connected by ties of intimate friendship, though he was by no means the apostle's constant companion, as was Timothy, Silas, or Luke. He was with Paul and Barnabas when they went up together to Jerusalem to plead for Gentile liberty; but in no other of the journeys of Paul is he directly mentioned as one of the companions of the apostle. Only during the apostle's long residence at Ephesus (nearly three years) Titus appears to have been, for at least part of the time, closely associated with Paul, and his confidant in his complicated relations with foreign churches.

From the several casual notices in the Second Corinthian epistle, we gather considerable insight into the character and administrative powers of the Gentile convert. The church of Corinth was perhaps the largest and most wealthy of all the churches founded by Paul. Delegated apparently by Paul to restore order and to introduce a severer discipline in this great and turbulent Christian center—the example for good or for evil to so many smaller and less important churches—Titus seems to have fulfilled with rare tact, and with admirable prudence and wisdom, his difficult mission. We know nothing of his work and employment from this period, A.D. 57, until the date of this epistle, A.D. 65-66, early Christian history being silent respecting him. In these nine years of restless activity and burning zeal on the part of the Christian leaders, Titus, no doubt, did his part without falling short of his early promise. We find him again, in the last years of his old master, occupying in the Christian community a post so high and responsible as that of chief presbyter of the churches of the wealthy and populous Mediterranean island of Crete.

Mine own son.—Paul converted Titus to the faith, and ever after Titus stood to Paul in the position of a son in the faith. Titus evidently filled with Paul the position of one of his most trusty disciples, one who knew the inmost thoughts of his master.

(5) Crete.—We identify it with the Caphtor of the Old Testament (Deut. 2:23; Jer. 47:4; Amos 9:7). Very early it was the scene of an advanced civilization. In the **Odyssey**

it is mentioned as possessing ninety cities, in the **Iliad** as many as one hundred. In the days of Augustus it was united into one province with Cyrene. It abounded with Jews of wealth and influence; this we learn from the testimony of Philo and of Josephus. It probably received the Gospel from some of those of "Crete" who were present when the Spirit was poured on the apostles on the first Pentecost after the Resurrection (Acts 2:11).

We are ignorant of the circumstance which summoned the old apostle from the scene of what seems to have been most successful labors. He left behind him one of the ablest of his disciples, Titus, to organize the church life and to regulate the teaching of the powerful and numerous Christian community of Crete. The epistle addressed to Titus contains the formal credentials of his high office, stamping all his acts with the great name and authority of Paul. Paul wrote the letter when on his way to Nicopolis to winter. Soon after his arrival there he was arrested and sent to Rome to die. The date of this letter, then, would be A.D. 65 or 66, and was probably written from some place in Asia Minor—perhaps Ephesus.

That thou shouldest set in order the things that are wanting.—The "things that are wanting" were what Paul meant, no doubt, to have done himself, but was prevented by being hurried away. These "things" were want of church officials, lack of church government, want of cohesion between the churches of the island—in a word, there was plenty of Christian life, but no Christian organization as yet in Crete.

And ordain elders in every city.—In some churches there were several of these presbyters (see Acts 14:23; 15:22). The words "in every city" point to the wide extension of Christianity at that early period in Crete.

(6) See notes on I Tim. 3:2. In searching out these presbyters, whose charge would involve so many and such responsible duties, Titus must look for men of ripe age. There were even grave objections to the appointment of the comparatively young to this office. Timothy must have been at least approaching forty years of age when Paul warned him so earnestly of his behavior and his life, "Let no man despise thy youth." These presiding Cretan elders should be married men, with children already, so to speak, grown up.

These requirements evidently show that Christianity had been established in Crete

for a considerable period. Some thirty-three years had passed since that memorable Pentecost feast of Jerusalem, when "Cretes" were among the hearers of those marvelous utterances of the Spirit. Besides the children of the candidates for the presbyter's office being professing Christians, they must also be free from all suspicion of profligacy.

(7) For a bishop must be blameless.—There is no doubt that the "bishop" here must be identified with the presbyter of verse 6. In the Pastoral Epistles these terms are clearly applied indifferently to the same person. The title presbyter refers to the gravity and dignity of the office; the title bishop suggests rather the duties which belong to an elder of the church. (See note on I Tim. 3:1.) While the presbyter is not to be chosen on account of any stern austerities or rigid asceticism he may have practiced, he must be known as one temperate, moderate, self-denying.

(8) But a lover of hospitality.—This hospitality would be especially shown in the early centuries of Christianity, when Christians traveling from one place to another were received kindly and forwarded on their journey by their brethren.

A lover of good men.—"A lover of good" or benevolence generally; the appellation points here to that large heart which finds room for sympathy with all that is good and noble and generous.

Sober.—That self-command which wisely regulates pleasure and passions.

Just.—The man who is just is one who tries to perform his duties **towards men,** duties which integrity and justice seem imperatively to ask from him in his relations with his neighbor.

Holy.—The man who is holy strives to be true and faithful in his relations to God, duties which largely consist in keeping pure our bodies, the temple of the Holy Spirit.

Temperate.—This virtue is not to be understood in the usual and more limited sense which already has been specified in "not given to wine" of the preceding verse, but signifies being moderate in all things. The model presbyter, the ruler of a congregation of Christians, must be able at all times to command himself—to perform that most difficult of all tasks, tempering zeal with discretion.

(9) To exhort and to convince the gainsayers.—Two special purposes are specified for which the "sound doctrine" which the elder will acquire by steadfast application may be used. First, he is to exhort the adversaries; second, he is to confute their arguments. Chrysostom well remarks "that he who knows not how to contend with adversaries, and is not able to demolish their arguments, is far from the teacher's chair."

(10) Specially they of the circumcision.— Here Paul points out to Titus where he must look for the origin of this hostility. These men evidently were of the number of those sleepless opponents of Paul and his school—the Judaizing Christians.

(11) Teaching things which they ought not, for filthy lucre's sake.—It was no longer individuals that their poisonous teaching affected, but they were undermining the faith of whole families. Here Paul goes to the root of the evil, when he shows what was the end and aim of these "teachers'" life. It was a mean and sordid ambition, after all—merely base gain. When this is the main object of a religious teacher's life, his teaching naturally accommodates itself to men's tastes. He forgets the Giver of his commission, and in his thirst for the popularity which brings with it gold, his true work, as the faithful watchman of the house of Israel, is forgotten and ignored.

(12) One of themselves, even a prophet of their own, said.—Paul now supports his own condemning words by a reference to a well-known Cretan poet, one who, according to tradition, was even honored by them as a god. The verse quoted was written by the famous Epimenides of Gnossus (c. 600 B.C.), who died, allegedly, at 150 years of age. He appears to have deserved the title of prophet in its fullest sense, Plato speaking of him as a "divine man," and Cicero coupling him with the Erythaean Sibyl. The first three words were well known, and even used by Callimachus in his hymn to Zeus, "Cretans always liars." Paul's knowledge of the poem where the verse occurs is one of the several instances which we meet with in his writings indicating his familiarity with profane literature. Calvin calls superstitious those who decline to avail themselves of the learning of profane writers. Nothing wise and learned, he says, should be rejected, even though it proceed "ab impiis."

The Cretians are always liars.—This terrible estimate of the national Cretan character is amply borne out by the testimony of many profane writers, such as Callimachus, Plato, Polybius, Ovid, etc. The very word "to Cretize" (**kretizein**) was invented as a word synonymous with "to deceive," "to

utter a lie," just as **corinthiazein** signified to commit a still darker moral offense. Some writers suggest that this despicable vice of lying was received as a bequest from the early Phoenician colonists.

Evil beasts.—These words refer to their wild, fierce nature, their ferocity, their love of cruelty.

Slow bellies.—These terms paint with sharp accuracy another of the evil characteristics of the Cretan peoples—their dull gluttony, their slothful sensuality. The words are used especially of those who, by indulging their bodily appetites, become corpulent and indolent.

(14) Not giving heed to Jewish fables such as we now find embodied in the Talmud. (See I Tim. 1:4.) The oral law and traditional interpretations and glosses had to a great measure, obscured the original simple text. The Israelite of the time of Paul, trained in the stricter Jewish schools, was taught that the way to win the approval of the Most High was through the observance of countless ceremonies and the practice of an elaborate ritual.

(15) Unto the pure all things are pure.— The spirit of this famous saying of Paul, occurring almost in the same language in Rom. 14:20, was the groundwork of much of the Gentile apostle's teaching. The words of the Lord Jesus (Matt. 15:2, 11) contain the same grand truth. "All things" include much besides mere food—in a word, all acts connected with everyday life which in themselves are neither right nor wrong, neither good nor evil, but which derive their coloring of good or evil solely from the doer of the act.

But even their mind and conscience is defiled.—Here Paul defines exactly the sphere over which the moral defilement of these hapless ones extends—the mind and conscience. Defilement of the mind (**nous**) means that the thoughts, wishes, purposes, activities, are all stained and debased. The conscience (**suneidesis**) is the moral consciousness within, that which is ever bringing up the memory of the past. When this is defiled, then this last safeguard of the soul is broken down. The man of the defiled conscience is self-satisfied, hard, impenitent to the last.

(16) They profess that they know God; but in works they deny him.—These bitter foes to the truth will present themselves under the guise of friends. They will rank themselves in the Christian company openly, but in their way of life will deny the things they were so careful to affirm with their lips.

2

(1) But speak thou the things which become sound doctrine.—To introduce a regular organization and the principle of a central church government into the numerous but scattered Christian congregations in Crete was Titus' first work. The second and equally weighty mission the Apostle Paul charged him to execute was the refutation of a school of professed Christian teachers, who were promulgating doctrines at variance with the teaching of Paul and his brother apostles, and were also, by their example and lives, fatally lowering the tone of Christian life. It was to the latter point—the evil moral influence of these teachers—that the attention of Titus was especially directed. False doctrinal teaching was bringing forth already its sure fruit in the form of a life utterly unlike the pattern life of the Master.

(3) The aged women likewise.—Paul, faithful to what had now become one of the guiding principles of Christianity—the equal position of women in the city of God—proceeds to remind the elder women of Crete of their own high duties in the company of believers. They now—the women—must remember that the position which Christ and His disciples had claimed for them in the world was not without its grave responsibilities. These aged women of the flock, like the elders just exhorted, also had much to do for Christ.

That they be in behaviour as becometh holiness.—The Greek word rendered "in behaviour" includes an outward deportment dependent on something more internal. The elder Christian woman in her whole bearing should exhibit a certain dignity of sacred demeanor; there should be something in her general appearance, in her dress, in her speech, in her everyday behavior, which the younger and more thoughtless sister could respect and reverence—an ideal she might hope one day herself to reach.

(4) To love their husbands, to love their children.—There was evidently in Crete a feverish longing for excitement, for novelty in religious teaching (comp. 1:14). Women as well as men preferred rather to **do** something for religion and for God, and thus to wipe out past transgressions, and perhaps to purchase the liberty of future license. Paul's method of correcting this false and unhealthy view of religion was to recall women as well as men to the steady, faithful performance of those quiet everyday duties to which God had, in His providence, called them. The first duty of these younger women was the great home duty of loving their husbands and children.

(5) Keepers at home.—Home duties, cares, pleasures, sacrifices of self—these God-appointed duties ought to fill the mind and the heart of the young wife. There should be no desire, no attempt to go around to the other houses, and so contracting idle, gossiping habits.

Obedient to their own husbands.—In a church like that of Crete, made out of divided houses often, where the Christian wife was married to a pagan husband, such a charge as this was especially needful.

That the word of God be not blasphemed.—These words refer to all the exhortations from verse 2 onward, but more particularly to those clauses enforcing home duties immediately preceding. There was the fear that wives, carried away by religious fervor, might neglect the plainer everyday duties for the seemingly loftier and more self-denying occupations included under the head of religious works. Such failure in everyday tasks would, of course, be bitterly charged on the religion of Christ, and the Gospel would run the danger of being evil-spoken of, even in other than purely pagan circles.

(6) Young men likewise exhort to be sober minded.—The task of influencing the young men belongs especially to Titus. Among them, in respect to age, he still must be reckoned; as regarded their peculiar temptations, none could be found so fit as the still young Christian disciple of Paul (he was probably about forty years of age when he was placed over the Cretan Church) to set out vividly before them both the peril and the only means of guarding against it. It will be, he proceeds to show him, most effectually done by the sight of the example of his own manly, self-restrained religious life.

(8) Sound speech, that cannot be condemned.—Between the lines of verses 7 and 8 we can read the anxiety of the apostle that his representative in Crete should take all possible care that the matter of his teaching and preaching was studied and prepared with all the attention and thought so important a duty demanded. He should remember, too, that the words as well as the works of the Christian teacher will be subject to a sharp and often hostile criticism.

(9) Exhort servants to be obedient unto their own masters.—Paul now turns to the question of the instruction of another large class, among whom were to be found many Christians—the slaves. Probably these "words" to be addressed particularly to slaves were called out by some particular instances of insubordination and of impatience under their unhappy condition among the Cretan slaves. Paul knew it was a hard matter to persuade the bondman, fellow-heir of heaven with the freeman, to acquiesce patiently in his present condition of misery and servitude. Hence these repeated charges to this class. (See Eph. 6:5; Col. 3:22; I Tim. 6:1.)

And to please them well in all things; not answering again.—The apostle, in verse 10, gives them a noble inducement for this brave patience he would have so earnestly pressed upon them. Such conduct on their part would serve greatly to help the Master's cause; it would prepossess many hostile minds in favor of a religion which could so powerfully influence even the slave. Chrysostom comments thus: "Greeks form their estimate of doctrines not from the doctrine itself, but from the actions and the life" (of those who profess the doctrine).

(10) Not purloining, but shewing all good fidelity.—Many of the slaves in the Roman empire were employed in other duties besides those connected with the house or on the farm. Some were entrusted with shops, and these being left often quite to themselves, of course great opportunities for dishonesty and fraud were constantly present. Others received an elaborate training, and as artists, or even physicians, worked in part for their masters. A slave in the days of Paul had a hundred ways of showing to his owner this true and genuine fidelity, opposed to mere assumed surface obedience and service.

(11) For the grace of God that bringeth salvation hath appeared to all men.—Comp. Isa. 9:2, 60:1; Mal. 4:2. The thought of these passages was probably in Paul's view while he wrote the words to Titus telling him to exhort his flock, for God's grace had appeared to all men. The Greek word translated "appeared" occurs in Luke 1:79 and Acts 27:20, and in each of these passages it is used to express the shining of the sun. The "grace of God" here spoken of is that divine favor to and love for men

upon which the whole work of redemption was based, the object of which redemption was the ultimate restoration of man. The epiphany, or manifestation of this grace to the world, commenced with the Incarnation of our Lord. The "grace" alone brings salvation to all men—in other words, it is that grace of God whereby alone it is possible for mankind to be saved. The expression by no means asserts that all men will be saved by it, but that it is the only means by which salvation is possible.

(13) The manifestation of the "grace of God," in the first coming of the Lord **in humiliation** (verse 11), teaches us to live our lives in expectation of the manifestation of His glory in His second coming **in power** (verse 13). We must—in this great passage contained in verses 11 to 14—bear in mind that there is a twofold epiphany spoken of: the one, the manifestation of the "grace of God"—**that is past**; the other, the manifestation of the "glory of God"—**that is to come.**

Of the great God and our Saviour Jesus Christ.—The translation here should run, "of our great God and Saviour Jesus Christ." Taken thus, it is a declaration of the divinity of the Eternal Son. The word "manifestation" (**epiphany**), too, the central thought of the sentence, is employed by Paul in his epistles five times, in every one of them to describe the manifestation of Christ, and in four of them to designate the future manifestation of His coming in glory, as here. The term epiphany is never applied to the Father.

(14) And purify unto himself a peculiar people.—The expression "a peculiar people" is taken from the LXX (see Ex. 19:5; Deut. 14:2); the idea is also purely an Old Testament one. Jehovah had wished to establish a people which should belong to Him ("peculiarly His," "His very own"), submitting to His laws, in contrast to the rest of mankind, lawless, idolatrous; so Jesus would set apart and purify for Himself a people, which for His sake should devote itself to God, in contrast to the rest of humanity sunk in selfish sins.

(15) Titus is to remember now to exhort, now to rebuke, and all this "with authority," as chief pastor of the flock of Crete formally commissioned and appointed. And in the background of this stirring admonition of the aged master to his disciple, placed in so difficult and responsible a position, there is anxious warning again.

3

(1) Put them in mind to be subject to principalities and powers.—Paul's words, to his point, have been written with a reference generally to Christian life among Christians. But how were the people of Christ to regulate their behavior in their dealings with the vast pagan world outside? Paul goes to the root of the matter at once. Needful in Crete was such a reminder respecting obedience. The island had, when Paul wrote to Titus, been some century and a quarter under Roman rule. Their previous government had been democratic; and historians, like Polybius, who have written of Crete, have dwelt particularly on the turbulent and factious spirit which animated their people. The Greek words translated principalities and powers" are better rendered here by "rulers and authorities." The terms include all constituted governors and officials, Roman and otherwise, in the island.

To be ready to every good work.—Ready cheerfully to aid all lawful authority, municipal and otherwise, in their public works undertaken for city or state. The flock of Titus must remember that the true Christian ought to be known as a good citizen and a devoted patriot.

(2) To be no brawlers . . .—These characteristics were not common virtues in Crete, then the resort and mart of so many different nationalities, and singular in its situation in the Mediterranean midway between Europe, Africa, and Asia. Surely, Paul urges, the professed followers of the Crucified among the Cretans should aim at a nobler standard of life than was common among these rough and often selfish traders. These things charged here by Paul were new virtues to men. They are held up to admiration by no heathen moralists.

(5) God has saved us by His own act, independently of any work of ours. The Greek should be rendered, "by the laver of regeneration," etc. Regeneration is spoken of by John in his words, "Ye must be born again" (John 3:7); renovation ("renewing") is alluded to by Paul when he writes, "the inward man is renewed day by day" (II Cor. 4:16).

(6) The Father is ever pouring out upon us the Holy Ghost. It is because of the Son's atonement and intercession that this blessed outpouring takes place at all. Here the "Son" is given the same title of "Saviour,"

which, in the preceding verse, was applied to the "Father."

(7) "Being justified" is being freed from the future punishment and consequences of sin, and received into the favor of God, which favor had been, through sin, forfeited. "By his grace" means that by the kindness of God the Father are we restored to His love and friendship. For "heirs," see Rom. 8:17. "According to the hope of eternal life" means that this life eternal is still for us in the future, though ever present in respect of hope.

(8) And these things I will that thou affirm constantly.—Hearing this "faithful saying," thought the old man Paul, my children in Christ will surely be disposed to be more loyal subjects, more faithful citizens, more loving neighbors, though their civil magistrates, their fellow-citizens, their neighbors, be still idolaters, living without God in the world. Men, too, would see that they owed all their glorious Christian privileges to God's free grace.

Careful to maintain good works.—Paul's ideal Christian must be a generous, public-spirited man. In the eyes of this great teacher the cloistered ascetic would have found but little favor.

(9) But avoid foolish questions, and genealogies.—See note on I Tim. 1:4. The "contentions" were disputes and wranglings which arose out of arguments advanced by different teachers upon the "questions" and "genealogies." The "strivings about the law" were probably arguments suggested by disputed and intricate points connected with the law of Moses. Such wranglings had, cancer-like, eaten the life out of Judaism; it should not, if Paul could prevent it, poison in like manner the young life of Christianity.

(10) A man that is an heretick.—The Greek word translated "heretick" in the New Testament occurs here only. The term "heresies" occurs twice (I Cor. 11:19; Gal. 5:20). In neither of these passages does the word signify a fundamental or doctrinal error. This sense belongs to a usage of later times. The "heretic" of the church in Crete appears to have been a man who, dissatisfied with the organization and discipline introduced by Titus into the Christian community—probably considering himself in some way slighted—withdrew himself from the common body, and gathering around him other discontented spirits, established what might be termed a rival church in Crete.

After the first and second admonition reject.—There was, no doubt, some self-willed factious party leader in Crete well known to Paul to whom he referred here; but partly out of a loving hope that Titus would win him to his side, partly from the knowledge that this letter was a public instruction to many a church besides that of Crete, the disturber remained nameless.

(11) He is "thoroughly perverted"—the espression is a strong one, and signifies literally "hath been turned inside out." Without the excuse of ignorance he sins on in the full consciousness of his wilful and seditious life. His perverse conduct in stirring up party feeling in the church publicly convicts him of doing the wrong which in general he professes to condemn.

With these words the public or official portion of the letter to the residing presbyter in Crete closes.

(12) When I shall send Artemas unto thee, or Tychicus, be diligent to come unto me.—Titus is here reminded that he is only the temporary ruler of the Cretan Church, on a special commission of the great missionary apostle. Probably one of these two was intended to supply the place of Titus when this favorite and trusted assistant of Paul was recalled to his master's side. Of Artemas nothing certainly is known. Tradition, however, makes him subsequently Bishop of Lystra. Tychicus is mentioned also in Acts 20:4; Col. 4:7; II Tim. 4:12. He seems to have been one of the most esteemed of Paul's friends.

To Nicopolis.—There are cities bearing this name in Cilicia, in Thrace, and in Epirus. Considerable doubt prevails as to which the Apostle has been referring. On the whole, the Nicopolis in Epirus seems the most likely spot. This city was built by Augustus after the battle of Actium, from which it derived its name, "the City of Victory."

(13) Bring Zenas the lawyer.—It is likely that the law in which he was an expert was that of Moses. Hippolytus numbers him among the seventy disciples and relates how in later years he was Bishop of Diospolis. He is mentioned by name in the New Testament only in this place.

And Apollos.—This famous teacher appears often in the New Testament records. A distinguished Alexandrian scholar and a disciple of John the Baptist, he was converted to Christianity by the agency of the devoted Priscilla and Aquila, the tentmakers. He became the friend and intimate associate of Paul, and might, had he chosen, have rivalled or even superseded Paul in his supreme authority over the churches planted along the Mediterranean seaboard. Paul always seems to have treated the learned and eloquent Apollos as an equal power in the Church of Christ, classing the Alexandrian with Peter and himself. Luther's suggestion that Apollos was the unknown writer of the Epistle to the Hebrews has been adopted, though with reserve, by many.

Attention has been called to the somewhat remarkable fact that the names of the three friends of Paul, classed among his most faithful adherents in this almost the last epistle he wrote, were derived from three of the most famous heathen deities—Zenas from Zeus; Artemas from Artemis; Apollos from the wellknown sun god.

(14) And let ours also learn to maintain good works for necessary uses.—In the short compass of the Pastoral Epistles, in all only thirteen chapters, there are no less than eight special reminders to be earnest and zealous in good works. There was evidently a dread in Paul's mind that some of those who professed a love of Jesus, and said that they longed after the great salvation, would content themselves with a dreamy acquiescence in the great truths, while the life remained unaltered. It is noteworthy that these epistles, containing so many urgent exhortations to work for Christ, were Paul's last inspired utterances. (Comp. 1:16; 2:7, 14; 3:14; I Tim. 2:10; 5:10; 6:18; II Tim. 2:21.)

(15) All that are with me salute thee.—It is uncertain where Paul was when he wrote this letter. Those journeying in his company are not named, because the individuals composing the immediate following of Paul would be likely to be well-known to Titus.

Amen.—The greater number of the ancient authorities omit "Amen."

PHILEMON

(1) A prisoner of Jesus Christ.—It is interesting to note the substitution of the name "prisoner," appealing to sympathy, for the usual title of "apostle," embodying a claim to authority. In the other epistles of this period (see Eph. 3:1-13, 4:1; 6:20; Phil. 1:12-20; Col. 4:18) the apostle's captivity is dwelt upon mainly as a ground of glory and thankfulness, only secondarily as a cause for sympathy. Here, on the contrary, in this personal epistle, the latter aspect assumes an almost exclusive prominence.

Timothy.—Comp. Phil. 1:1; Col. 1:1. Here, as in the other epistles, the salutation includes Timothy, as desiring to imply in him a closeness of connection and sympathy with the apostle not found in others. But in all cases, and especially in this, the letter is emphatically the letter of Paul alone.

Philemon.—All we know of Philemon is gathered from this epistle. It is nowhere actually said he was a Colossian; but this is inferred from the fact that Onesimus, his slave, is described as of Colossae (Col. 4:9). It is clear that he was Paul's convert; but, as the apostle had not visited Colossae (Col. 2:1), we may probably conjecture that he had been brought under his influence during his long stay at Ephesus. Possibly, like Epaphras (Col. 1:7), he had been, under Paul's auspices, an evangelist of his native place. He is evidently a man of means: "the Church" gathers "in his house"; he is able, by his love, "to refresh the hearts of the saints," probably by temporal as well as spiritual gifts; to him Paul entrusts the charge of preparing a lodging for his hoped-for visit, and describes that visit as "being granted," "through his prayers," to him and his. We note also that the apostle treats him as almost an equal—as a "brother" (not "a son"), as "a fellow-labourer," and as a "partner."

(2) Apphia.—There seems little doubt that Apphia was Philemon's wife.

Archippus our fellowsoldier.—From this mention of Archippus we may certainly conclude that he was a member of Philemon's family; the ordinary conjecture makes him his son. The name "fellowsoldier" appears to denote ministerial office in Archippus (Col. 4:17). Comp. Phil. 2:25; II Tim. 2:3.

Church in thy house.—See note on Col. 4:15. The specially domestic and personal character of the epistle need not induce any limitation of the phrase to Philemon's own family.

(5) Thy love and faith, which thou hast toward the Lord Jesus, and toward all saints.—This description of a faith directed not only to the Lord Jesus, but to all the saints, has called out various explanations. The idea which runs through the letter is Philemon's "love to the saints." In writing of that love Paul cannot refrain from referring it to its true origin—the faith toward the Lord Jesus Christ. The sense seems therefore to be that which in some MSS has been brought out by a natural correction, "thy faith toward the Lord Jesus, and thy love to all the saints."

(6) That the communication of thy faith . . .—The general idea of Paul's prayer for Philemon is clear. (See Eph. 1:17; Phil. 1:9; Col. 1:9.) It describes the true order of Christian life, so fully and beautifully drawn out in Eph. 3:17-19, beginning in faith, deepened by love, and so growing to knowledge. That all such growth must be "towards Christ Jesus," dependent on unity with Him and serving to deepen such unity, is the characteristic doctrine of all the prison epistles, especially of the Colossian epistle, of which Onesimus was one of the bearers.

(7) The bowels of the saints are refreshed by thee.—"The bowels" means "the hearts." The word "refresh" is the word used by our Lord in His own gracious promise (Matt. 11:28). Paul frequently uses the word "refresh" to express the relief and rest given by Christian fellowship on earth. (See verse 20; comp. I Cor. 16:18; II Cor. 7:13.) In the Apocalypse it is applied to the rest with Christ in heaven (Rev. 6:11; 14:13).

Brother.—The name is given to Philemon here and in verse 20 with a marked emphasis of affection, evidently implying some special intimacy of friendship, not apparently at Colossae (see Col. 2:1), but perhaps at Ephesus, during Paul's long stay there. Probably Philemon was Paul's equal in age, and actually his convert, although not addressed (as usual) as his "son in the faith." In this place, moreover, the title "brother" has a peculiar appropriateness: the apostle has been speaking of the love of Philemon, which made him a brother indeed to all in the family of Christ.

(8-20) Here Paul enters on the main subject of his letter—the recommendation to Philemon of his runaway slave, Onesimus.

All thoughtful readers of the epistle must recognize in this a peculiar courtesy and delicacy of tone, through which an affectionate earnestness shows itself, and an authority all the greater because it is not asserted in command. The substance is equally notable in its bearing on slavery. Onesimus is doubly welcomed into the Christian family. He is Paul's son in the faith; he is to Philemon a brother beloved in the Lord.

(9) Paul the aged, and now also a prisoner of Jesus Christ.—At this time Paul must have been between fifty and sixty, and after a life of unexampled labor and suffering he might well call himself "aged," not, perhaps, in comparison with Philemon, but in relation to his need of ministry from his "son" Onesimus.

(10) My son.—Properly, "my own child . . . , Onesimus." The name is withheld until Philemon's interest is doubly engaged, for one who is the apostle's "own child" (a name of endearment given elsewhere only to Timothy and Titus), and for one who was begotten under the hardships and hindrances of imprisonment.

Onesimus.—Of Onesimus we know absolutely nothing, except what we read here and in Col. 4:9. Tradition makes him Bishop of Berea, in Macedonia, or identifies him with the Onesimus, Bishop of Ephesus, mentioned in the Ignatian "Epistle to the Ephesians" (1:2-6). The name was a common one, especially among slaves.

(11) In time past . . . unprofitable, but now profitable.—The name Onesimus means "useful," or "profitable." It is hardly possible not to see in this passage a play on words. Paul seems to say, "He belied his name in days past; he will more than deserve it now."

To thee and to me.—Paul says "to thee," for he was sending back Onesimus. He adds "to me," in affectionate notice of his kindly ministrations already rendered to his spiritual father.

(12) Mine own bowels.—See note on verse 7.

(13) In thy stead.—Here there is a certain delicacy of suggestion. A slave was his master's property; he could act only on his master's behalf and by his consent. Paul is sure that Philemon's love for him would have gladly given that consent, and so made Onesimus an instrument of willing service to Paul.

(14) That thy benefit should not be . . .—The benefit derived from the service of Onesimus Paul acknowledges as coming from Philemon, because given with his consent. He will not keep Onesimus and ask that consent by letter, lest it should convey even the semblance of constraint.

(15) For perhaps he therefore departed.—This is a further reason for sending Onesimus back. Paul now touches on Onesimus' "being parted" from Philemon, suggesting that his running away was, however unconsciously, overruled by a higher hand. God, in His wisdom, "parted" him from Philemon "for a season, that he might receive him for ever." The contrast might be satisfied here by the merely relative sense of perpetual or life-long service; but, considering that the phrase is used in direct reference to the brotherhood of the communion of saints, it is better to take it in its absolute sense of fellowship in the life eternal.

(16) Not now as a servant, but . . . a brother beloved . . . in the Lord.—In these words we have the principle which is absolutely destructive of the condition of slavery—a condition which is the exaggeration of natural inferiority to the effacement of the deeper natural equality. The slave is bought by Christ's blood, made a son of God, and therefore a brother to all who are members of the family of God. To reject and to outrage him is a rejection and outrage toward Christ. Comp. I Pet. 2:18-24.

Specially to me, but how much more unto thee?—Paul first emphasizes his own love for Onesimus, which, indeed, breathes in every line of the epistle; but then he goes on to infer in Philemon a yet greater affection—a natural love toward the nursling of his house, a spiritual love toward the brother "in the Lord," lost and found again.

(17) A partner.—Here the word can hardly refer to general Christian fellowship. It must indicate some peculiar bond of fellowship between Paul and Philemon. Philemon was his convert (see verse 19); yet we notice that he writes to him not as a son, but as a brother. Evidently he was a leader in the church at Colossae. Tradition makes him its bishop. He must have been Paul's partner in some common work or special communion of familiarity.

(18) If he hath wronged thee evidently refers to the time of Onesimus' escape. "If he oweth thee ought" is probably an allusion to some theft at the same time.

Put that on mine account.—Comp. Phil. 4:15-17.

(19) I Paul have written it with mine own

hand.—Paul actually introduces here a regular bond couched in legal form. In so doing he still continues the idea of the preceding verse; but the following words show that, though willing to stand to his bond, he knew Philemon too well to suppose that he would accept it.

It is clear from this passage that the apostle had money which he could rightly call his own. At Ephesus, where he probably first knew Philemon, it would probably be earned in the work with Aquila and Priscilla, as at Corinth, and it is possible that some of it might still remain. In Rome now, it could hardly be from any other source than the offerings from the church at Philippi.

Albeit I do not say to thee . . . —Here Paul escapes from the business-like promise of the last verse to the freer atmosphere of spiritual relations. He knew that this promise it was right for him to offer, but wrong for Philemon to accept. Philemon owed his own self—his new self in Christ—to the apostle. In that was a debt which he could not repay, but would rejoice even in this smaller matter to acknowledge.

(20) Let me have joy of thee.—Paul puts himself forward to plead for Onesimus what he himself could not plead. Nor can it be accidental that the word "profit" is the root of the name Onesimus. Paul says, in effect, "May I find thee (as I have found him) a true Onesimus."

(21) Do more than I say.—This can hardly refer to anything except the manumission of Onesimus, and possibly his being sent back again to Paul. Exactly in this way Christianity was to work out the release of the slave—not by command, but by free and natural inference from its emphatic declaration of his true brotherhood in Christ.

(22) I shall be given unto you.—If he were so, it would be by Caesar instrumentally, by God's overruling will ultimately. The passage, like Phil. 2:24, but even more definitely, expresses Paul's expectation of a release which might enable him to visit the East again. It is curious that there is no similar allusion in the Colossian epistle, sent with this.

HEBREWS

1

(1) God, who at sundry times... —The writer's object is to place the former revelation over against that which has now been given. To the fathers of the Jewish people (comp. Rom. 9:5) God's word was given part by part and in diverse manners. It came in the revelations of the patriarchal age; various truths were successively unveiled through the varying ministry of law, of prophecy, and of promise ever growing clearer through the teaching of experience and history. At one time the word came in direct precept, at another in typical ordinance or act, at another in parable or psalm. We must not unduly limit the application of "prophet"; besides those to whom the name is directly given, there were many who were representatives of God to His people and interpreters of His will.

(2) Hath in these last days... —The manifold successive partial disclosures of God's will have given place to one revelation, complete and final. The whole stress lies on these last words—literally "a Son"— designed to show the supreme dignity of Him who is God's latest Representative on earth. The prophet's commission extended no farther than the special message of his words and life; "a Son" spoke with His Father's authority, with complete knowledge of His will and purpose.

Whom he hath appointed.—In the divine counsels He was constituted "heir of all things." The clauses which follow describe the successive steps in the accomplishment of this purpose. (Comp. John 1:3; Col. 1:16.)

(3) Who being the brightness... — Rather, "Who being the effulgence of His glory and the exact image of His substance." In the Old Testament the token of the divine presence is the Shechinah, the "cloud of glory"; here it is the divine nature itself that is denoted by the "glory." Of the relation between this word and that which follows ("substance"), we say that the latter is internal and the former external—the latter the essence in itself, the former its manifestation. Thus the "Son" in His relation to "God" is represented here by light beaming forth from light, and by exact impress—the perfect image produced by stamp or seal.

Sat down on the right hand of the Majes- **ty on high.**—This figure, which we meet more than twenty times in the New Testament, is throughout derived from the first words of Ps. 110, which are descriptive of the exaltation of the Messiah. Jehovah's investiture of the Son of man with unlimited dominion (Dan. 7:14) and supreme dignity (Eph. 1:20, 21), the Saviour's rest after the accomplishment of His work on earth (8:1), and His waiting for the complete and final subjection of His enemies are the ideas signified.

(4) Being made.—Better, "having become." These words must be closely joined with the last clause of verse 3; they speak, not of the glory which was ever His, but of that which **became** His after He had "made purification of sins."

Name.—The verses which follow show that we are to understand by this all the dignity and glory contained in the name "Son of God." The glory which "became" His is proportionate to and consonant with the name which is His by essential right (verse 2).

(5) For unto which of the angels... — "God has spoken of the Messiah as His Son, a title which no angel ever receives from Him." The appellation "sons of God'" may be used in an inferior sense, but in these quotations "Son" is used of One, and in a sense that is unique. The two quotations are taken from Ps. 2:7 and II Sam. 7:14, depicting David's troublous times. At what period the people in general, guided by prophetic teaching and the discipline of history, learned in how secondary a sense such words could be used of any human king, we do not know; but we have clear evidence, both from the New Testament (5:5; Acts 4:25-27; 13:33; Rev. 2:27) and from Jewish tradition, that the Second Psalm was understood to be a distinct prophecy of the Messiah. Indeed, this very name "Messiah" and the appellation "Son of God" (see John 1:34, 49) may be traced to this Psalm. The declarations of verses 6, 7, are typical of the enthronement of the Messiah, the seed of David established forever. Paul (Acts 13:33) refers the words quoted here to the period of the Resurrection.

(6) The speaker ("He saith") is God, speaking in the word of Scripture; in this epistle quotations from the Old Testament are usually thus introduced. Psalm 97:7 belongs to a cycle (Pss. 93, 95-99), whose theme is the triumphant announcement of the coming of God's kingdom. When the

Messiah, reigning as the Firstborn of God (see verse 5), shall appear for judgment—that is, when God leads a second time His Firstborn into "the world of men" (see 2:5), that He may receive full possession of His inheritance—He says, and let all angels of God worship Him.

(7) The parallelism in these two lines of Hebrew poetry is complete, "angels" answering to "ministers," "winds" to "a flame of fire." The meaning appears to be that God, employing His messengers for His varied purposes, sends them forth in what manner He may please, clothing them with the appearance of the resistless wind or the devouring fire. (Contrast such ministers with the Son seated at the right hand of God.) The quotation is taken from Ps. 104:4.

(8) See Ps. 45:6, 7. Originally writing in celebration of the marriage of a king of David's line (perhaps Solomon), the inspired psalmist uses words which bear their full meaning only when applied to that Son of David of whose kingdom there shall be no end. With the promise of a divine sonship (Ps. 2) in his thought, he suddenly addresses the king as Elohim (verse 7), a divine king who receives from God the reward of righteousness (verse 8).

(9) **Thy fellows.**—In the first application, probably, these words point to other earthly kings. (Comp. Ps. 89:27.) But Eph. 1:21 will be the best commentary upon them in their higher meaning.

(10) **And.**—Verses 10-12 are by this word linked with verse 8 as presenting the second part of the contrast between angels and the Son. As there we read of a divine sovereignty, so here of the work of creation, the power to change all created things, the divine attribute of changeless existence. This quotation is from Ps. 102:25-27. In these verses the writer discovers a testimony to the supremacy of the Son in words which, as they stand in the Psalm, would appear to be directly addressed to God as Creator.

(13) **But to which of the angels.**—Ps. 110 was regularly understood by the Jews of our Lord's time to be a Messianic Psalm (see Matt. 22:43, 44). Most probably, it stands alone among the Psalms as being simply prophetic; the words of verse 1 have never been addressed either to angels or to an earthly king.

(14) **Are they not all ministering spirits?**—In this verse and the preceding is repeated, in reversed order, the contrast of verses 7-9. The last word, "salvation," expresses the divine purpose indicated by all the prophecies that have passed under review. The chapter has been occupied with promises of the Christ; the last word brings before us Jesus, the Saviour.

2

(1) **Lest at any time we should let them slip.**—The words must be rendered, "lest possibly we drift away." Unless the mind be held closely to the words that God has spoken, it must drift away from them and from the salvation which they promise.

(2) **The word spoken by angels.**—In accordance with the tone of the whole passage—in which the thought is not the reward of obedience, but the peril of neglect of duty—"the word" must denote divine **commands** delivered by angels, and especially the commands of the Mosaic law. (See 10:28, 29; Deut. 33:2; Ps. 68:17; Gal. 3:19.)

(3) **How shall we escape?**—Here are placed in contrast the command and threatening which came through angels and the salvation "spoken through the Lord"; while the one "word" is thus wholly unlike the other in substance and in form of proclamation, each is a **law** in that neglect is visited with penalty. On the intrinsic greatness of the salvation the writer does not dwell; it is implied in the unique dignity and commission of Him through whom it was given.

Which at the first began to be spoken.—In two other passages Jesus receives the name "our Lord" (7:14; 13:20), but nowhere else in this epistle (unless perhaps in 12:14) is He spoken of as "the Lord"; the dignity of the title here heightens the contrast. It is evident that the writer here classes himself with those who had not immediately heard the word from Jesus. Such language as this stands in striking contrast with Paul's claim, repeatedly maintained, to have received his doctrine directly from the Lord Himself (Gal. 1:12; I Cor. 9:1).

(4) **God also bearing them witness.**—We have here (as in Acts 2:22; II Cor. 12:12) the full threefold description of miracles as "signs," "wonders," and "powers"—as wonderful works that are wrought by divine power and are thus signs of the divine presence and symbols of a corresponding spiritual work. The last words remind us (1:1) that as it is God who speaks to men in His Son, it is He who works with those who

proclaim the word that they have heard, attesting their message by gifts according to His will.

(5) The world to come.—Here, as in 1:6, the meaning is "inhabited earth," "world of man." Is "the world to come" still future, or is it here looked at from the Old Testament point of view? The following verses (especially verse 9) make it clear that the period referred to is that which succeeds the exaltation of Christ. We ourselves cannot but markedly distinguish the present stage of Messiah's kingdom from the future; but in the perspective of prophecy the two were blended. The thought of this kingdom among men has been present from the first verses of the epistle.

(6) But one in a certain place.—As a rule, the words of Scripture are in this epistle quoted as God's own utterances; and though the nature of the quotation (which is an address to God) made this impossible here, the writer seems gladly to avoid the mention of the human prophet, perhaps as distracting the thought from the divine prophecy.

The quotation which follows (from Ps. 8:4-6) agrees verbally with the LXX. The Greek translation here faithfully represents the Hebrew, except in one point. For "a little lower than the angels," the Hebrew text has "a little less than God." The change was probably introduced by the translators on a principle which we may often trace in their work—a wish to tone down expressions relating to the Deity which seemed strong or bold. The argument of this section would not be affected materially if the true rendering of the Hebrew were restored. The Eighth Psalm is an expression of amazement that God should remember man. Not only is He "mindful of man," but He has made him but "little less than God," "crowned him with honour," given him "dominion over" all His works. (See Gen. 1:28.) The last clause bears the stress of the quotation. (That the same words are the groundwork of I Cor. 15:24-28 is one of the most interesting coincidences between this epistle and Paul.) David had in mind the words of the primal blessing, and probably did not himself think of more than those words seemed to imply. But the complete meaning of God's words can be learned only when they are fulfilled in history. To Him who speaks in Scripture the material dominion was the symbol of a higher and a universal rule, to be fulfilled in the Son of man when the fullness of time should come.

(9) But we see Jesus...—In one point we note an apparent departure from the sense of the Psalm, since words ("a little lower") which there denote dignity here denote humiliation. There is peculiar fitness in the use of the human name "Jesus" for Him in whom the psalmist's words concerning man are literally fulfilled. This exaltation of One is not a substitute for, but involves (Rom. 8:17, 29), and renders possible, the exaltation of the many. In the midst of this application of the words of Scripture to Jesus, the writer introduces his first reference to His death. The offense of the cross (Gal. 5:11) was an ever-active force among Jews; this is present to the writer's mind throughout the epistle. How can it be said that Jesus has been crowned with glory in order that He may "taste death for every man"?

It is impossible for the Christian to separate, even in thought, the sufferings from the certain triumph. In the gospel of John for example, we are taught that **in His crucifixion** Jesus is exalted (comp. verse 14). This clause, then, brings us back to the thought of the glory reserved for man.

(10) Captain.—"Author" (denoting origination) is the best rendering; but in a context which so distinctly presents our Lord as taking on Himself the conditions of man's lot, and so passing into the glory which He wins for man, the primary thought of **leading the way** must not be entirely set aside.

(11) For both he that sanctifieth...—The special meaning of "sanctify" in this epistle seems to be "bringing into fellowship with God," the Holy One. "They who are sanctified"—literally, "are being sanctified"—are those whom the Captain of their salvation, in fulfillment of the Father's purpose (verse 10), is leading unto glory.

Are all of one.—Of one Father. This is the connecting link between verses 11 and 10. Though His sonship is unique and infinitely exalted, He is not ashamed to own them as brethren.

(12) I will declare thy name...—Ps. 22 is remarkable for its close connection with the narratives of the Passion of our Lord. Notwithstanding certain difficulties (See note on Ps. 22), we must certainly regard it as descriptive of actual experience and as typically prophetic of Christ. Each division of this verse is in point as a quotation: (1) those to whom the Messiah will declare God's name He speaks of as "brethren"; (2) not alone, but in the **congregation** of God's people will He sing the praise of God. The latter thought—community with men, as attested by a like relation to God—is brought out with still greater prominence in verse 13 (see Isa. 8:17, 18).

(13) As Isaiah is taken as representing Christ, so those who, being of the same blood, are joined with him in his work and in the promise of salvation, represent those whom the Son calls "brethren." Thus the association of Jesus with His people contains three elements of thought—His essential superiority, His sharing the same nature with His people, His brotherhood with them.

(14, 15) These words bring into relief the former misery and the present freedom. They were prompted by the intense sympathy of the writer with the persecuted and tempted Christians whom he addresses. He writes throughout as one who knows well the power of the motives, the allurements, and the threats employed to lead them into apostasy. The crushing power of the "fear of death" over those who had not grasped the truth that, in Christ, life and immortality are brought to light, perhaps no thought of ours can reach.

(16) The words "take hold" distinctly suggest laying hold for the sake of giving help. It is probable that the language used here is derived from Isa. 41:8, 9. Even apart from the natural fitness of such words addressed to Jews, we may doubt if any other language would have been equally expressive. As to the **means**, it was by becoming a child of Abraham that the Saviour "took hold of" our race to raise it up; and as to the **purpose**, Paul teaches us that "the seed of Abraham" includes all who inherit Abraham's faith.

(17) In all things.—Like His "brethren," He must be liable to, and must suffer, temptation, sorrow, pain, death.

That he might be.—One who has not so understood the infirmities of his brethren as to be "compassionate" ("merciful") cannot be their "faithful" representative before God. But the word "faithful" is still more closely connected with the following words. It is through "the suffering of death" (verse 9) that He makes reconciliation (or rather, **propitiation**) for the sins of the people. The characteristic function of the high priest was his presentation of the sacrifice on the Day of Atonement that expiation might be made for the sins of the whole people, and that the displeasure of God might not rest on the nation on account of sin. (Comp.

verse 11.) The subject receives its full treatment in chaps. 9 and 10.

3

(1) The Apostle and High Priest of our profession, Christ Jesus.—The best MSS omit "Christ"; and it is impossible not to feel how fitly the personal name "Jesus" is used after the later verses of chap. 2. Here only is the name apostle directly given to our Lord. There is very little difference between **apostle** and **prophet**, thus applied; but the one brings into relief the mission, the other the office and position. Each presents a thought complementary to that contained in "high priest." The next verse renders it probable that the two terms contain a reference to the special mission of Moses and the priesthood of Aaron; our Christian confession looks to **One** mediator.

(2) As also Moses.—These words, which give the key to the following verses, are quoted from Num. 12:7, where Moses is placed in contrast with prophets in Israel to whom the Lord will make Himself known by vision or dream. The "house" or household is God's people Israel.

(3) Inasmuch as.—This is, "in proportion as." It is not said that Jesus is the Builder; but the relation in which He stands to the Builder of the house is compared with that of Moses to the house. (See verses 5, 6.)

(5) As a servant.—Verse 3 associated Moses with the house, Jesus with Him who built it. Moses was "in God's house"; however exalted his position, he was in the house as a servant ("attendant," "minister"). See Num. 12:7, LXX. Moses' "testimony" relates to the things spoken "in these last days"; of these, by his writings, his acts, his life, Moses bore constant witness.

(6) But Christ as a son over his own house.—The antithesis is complete: the one is a servant for witness, the other a Son having a natural right to rule. The name Christ (which here occurs for the first time) is in this epistle never a mere name; it contains implicitly the thought that all that to which Moses bore witness has reached its fulfillment now.

If we hold fast the confidence.—The exhortation differs from that in 2:1-4, in that it more distinctly implies that those who are addressed have a possession which they may lose. "Boldness" ("confidence") properly means "freedom of speech," denoting the demeanor connected with the free utterance of thought.

(7) To day if ye will hear his voice.—See Ps. 95:7-11. The entreaty "Harden not your hearts" is at once the utterance of the divine voice and the expression of his own urgent prayer. Other passages in which the hardening of the heart is spoken of as the work of man himself are Exod. 9:34; I Sam. 6:6; Prov. 28:14.

(8) In the day of temptation.—As in the LXX, so here, two words which in the Hebrew are proper names ("as at Meribah, and as in the day of Massah") are translated according to their intrinsic meaning. (See Exod. 17:7; Num. 20:13.) These places are here chosen for reference partly on account of their significant names; but it is noteworthy that the rebellions recorded in the names belonged to the beginning and to the close of the years of wandering.

(11) It is with these as it was with their fathers, the generations that came out of Egypt (Num. 14:21-24). "My rest" means the land where Jehovah shall dwell with them. (See Deut. 12:9; Ps. 132:14.)

(12) In departing.—The heart of unbelief will manifest its evil in apostasy. The Greek word **apistia** stands in direct contrast to "faithful" (**pistos**), verse 2, and combines the ideas of "unbelief" and "faithlessness."

(14) A different word for "confidence" from that used in verse 6 is found here. The former is "boldness"; the latter is applied to men who make a firm stand when attacked, who stand firmly under pressure. In the first energy of the new life such firm constancy had been shown by them—but would it be maintained "unto the end"? Verse 14 is parenthetical, so verse 15 emphasizes the reference to "to-day" in verse 13.

(16) The connecting link is the thought of "the provocation." The sense is: "For who when they had heard did provoke? Nay, was it not all that came out of Egypt through Moses?" Those who were disobedient were the people whom God, through Moses, had but now delivered from bondage! The two exceptions (Num. 14:30) are left out of account in the presence of the multitude of rebels.

(19) So we see.—As in verse 18 we read of the **oath** of exclusion, this verse records the **fact**, and also states the cause under an aspect which is most suitable for the exhortation which is in the writer's thought. There is force in "could not enter": not only

disobedience, but cowardice and weakness, sprang from "unbelief."

4

(1) Lest, a promise being left us.—Such a promise remains unexhausted, waiting for complete fulfillment. No Hebrew Christian would doubt this. As in chap. 1, the writer's aim is not to establish a truth absolutely new, but to show that in various parts of the Scriptures a received truth lies contained.

(2) How fitly the good news of the promise might, alike in their case and in ours, be designated as the "gospel." The words "the word preached" signify what was heard by those who declared the promise to the people, especially the message which Moses received from God.

Not being mixed with faith.—The Greek compels us to connect these words, not with the message, but with the people. That the word of Moses and those associated with him in declaring God's promise (perhaps Aaron, Joshua, Caleb) might benefit the people, speakers and hearers must be united by the bond of faith.

(3) The emphasis is twofold, resting both on "believed" and on "we enter." The former looks back to verse 2; the latter looks forward to the remainder of the verse. If in the Scripture (Ps. 95:8) God warns men of a later age not to imitate the guilt of those whom He excluded from His rest, it follows (verse 10) that the time for entering into the rest of God was not then past and gone. Nor is the rest into which God will enter with His redeemed people that which succeeded the works of creation. (See Gen. 2:2, 3; Ps. 95:11.)

(7) In David.—This is equivalent to saying, "In the Book of Psalms." In the LXX, Ps. 95 is ascribed to David.

After so long a time.—The period intervening between the divine sentence on the rebels in the wilderness (Num. 14) and the time of the psalmist.

(8) Had the promise been fulfilled in Joshua's conquest, God in the Psalm would not be speaking of another day. (In one other place in the New Testament the Greek form of the name Joshua is preserved. See Acts 7:45.)

(9) There remaineth therefore.—It is tacitly assumed that no subsequent fulfillment has altered the relation of the promise. Few things in the epistle are more striking than the constant presentation of the thought that Scripture language is **permanent** and at all times **present**. The implied promise, therefore, repeated whenever the "to-day" is heard, must have its fulfillment. The rescued people of Israel did indeed find a rest in Canaan; the true redeemed "people of God" shall rest with God.

(10) Hath ceased.—Man's sabbath-rest begins when he enters into God's rest (Gen. 2:2); as that was the goal of the creative work, so to the people of God this rest is the goal of their life of "works."

As the whole argument is reviewed, the question may naturally be asked, To what extent is this wide meaning present in Psalm 95 itself? The apparent expansion of the meaning of the Psalm relates to verse 11 alone. There, in the first instance, an historical fact is mentioned—the exclusion of the rebels from the Promised Land (Num. 14:28-30). That verse 8, when placed by the side of verse 11 (of the Psalm), shows the higher meaning of the words to have been in the psalmist's thought, and implies that the offer of admission to the rest of God was still made, it seems unreasonable to doubt. As the people learned through ages of experience and training to discern the deeper and more spiritual meaning that lay in the promises of the King and the Son of David, so was it with other promises which at first might seem to have no more than a temporal significance. The argument of this section, therefore, is no "accommodation" of Scripture.

(12) As in 3:12 the warning against the "evil heart of unbelief" is solemnly enforced by the mention of the "living God," so here, in pointing to the peril of disobedience, it is to the living power of the Word of God that the writer makes appeal. Outside the writings of John there is no passage in the New Testament in which the Word of God is as clearly invested with personal attributes as here. The word "living," "mighty in operation." (Although these and many other resemblances adduced may prove the writer's familiarity with the Alexandrian philosophy, they are wholly insufficient to show an adoption of Philo's doctrinal system in regard to the divine Word.) In this epistle reference is repeatedly made to the word of God in revelation. The key to the language of this verse is found in the habitual thought of Scripture as a **direct** divine utterance. And the **whole** Word of God is brought before us—mainly the word of threatening and judgment, but also the word of promise.

And is a discerner ... —It is quick to judge the thoughts, reflection, conceptions, and intents of the heart. Man's word may be lifeless, without power to discriminate; but the Spirit of God is never absent from His Word.

(13) Opened.—The Greek word literally means "to take by the neck." It is usually applied to a wrestler who by dragging back the neck overthrows his adversary; thus "prostrate" has been suggested as the meaning here. Another explanation refers the word to the drawing back of a criminal's head, so as to expose his face to public gaze.

(14) That is passed into the heavens.— Rather, "that hath passed through the heavens." As the high priest passed through the Holy Place to enter the Holy of Holies, Jesus "ascended up far above all heavens," and sat at the right hand of God. This thought is developed in chaps. 8-10.

(15) But was in all points ... —Better, "but One that hath in all points been tempted in like manner, apart from sin." These words show the nature and the limits of this sympathy of Christ. He suffers with His people, not merely showing compassion to those who are suffering and tempted, but taking to Himself a joint feeling of their weaknesses. He can do this because He has Himself been tempted. Whatever belongs to the necessary limitations of that human nature which He assumed is included in that truth. He was Himself tempted in like manner, except that in Him sin had no place (7:26). These last words supply the limit to the thought of weakness and temptation as applied to our High Priest. Not only was the temptation fruitless in **leading** to sin, but in the widest sense He could say, "The prince of this world cometh and hath nothing in me" (John 14:30).

(16) Obtain mercy.—If the last verse brought evidence that our High Priest has perfect knowledge of the help required, this gives the assurance that the help shall be given as needed, and in the time of need.

5

With this chapter begins the longest and most important division of the epistle, extending (with one break, 5:11-6:20) as far as

10:18. The general subject is the nature of the High Priesthood of our Lord.

(1) Gifts and sacrifices.—The former is in itself general; but when thus contrasted with "sacrifices" it denotes the "unbloody offerings" of the Law. The Day of Atonement is almost always in the writer's thoughts as he refers to the functions of the high priest. On that day all offerings, as well as all sacrifices, had relation to "sins."

(2, 3) The law of the Day of Atonement required a sin offering of a bullock and a burnt-offering of a ram for the high priest himself, and for the congregation a sin offering of two he-goats and a burnt offering of a ram. Over his own sin offering the high priest made confession of sins, first for himself and his household, then for the priests; over the goat sent into the wilderness the sins of the people were confessed.

(5) Christ.—In the one designation "the Christ" are united the two testimonies of Scripture which follow. He is the Anointed King (Ps. 2:7), addressed by Jehovah as His Son (see notes on 1:2, 4, 5); by the same Jehovah He is addressed as Priest forever after the order of one who was both priest and king (Ps. 110:4).

(6) Thou art a priest for ever . . .—Psalm 110:4 supplies the theme for a large portion of this epistle, especially chap. 7. As the promise of II Sam. 7 was the prelude to the revelation of the Second Psalm, the divine declaration recorded in Exod. 19:6 may have prepared the way for the promise of Ps. 110:4. The king of Israel was the type of the Son of David; and in the consecrated people, who, had they been faithful, would have remained the representatives of all nations before God, was dimly foreshadowed the Anointed Priest.

(7, 8) Who in the days of his flesh . . .—Of the two essential conditions mentioned in verses 2 and 4, the latter is first taken up in its application to Christ (verses 5, 6). These correspond to the general thought of verses 1 and 2, as far as it is applicable to "him who knew no sin."

No words could be more suitable where the relation of the Son of man to His "God and Father" is expressed; and it would be difficult to find any other word which should be suitable to this relation and yet contain no implication of sin to be acknowledged with humility and shame. The object of the "prayers and supplications" was to save Him "out of death," not "from death." The prayer was not that death might

be averted, but that there might be granted deliverance out of death. This prayer was answered; His death was the beginning of His glory (2:9). The word "offered," of frequent occurrence in this epistle, in every case except one has a sacrificial sense; it seems certain, therefore, that these prayers— a token of His suffering, an example of His reverent fear—are included in the sacrifice which comprised His whole life and death.

(8) Though he were a Son.—"The disposition of obedience Jesus possessed before He suffered, but the proof that this disposition existed must be shown in deed; this progress from the disposition to the deed of obedience is a practical learning of the virtue of obedience" (Lünemann).

(9) And being . . .—Rather, "and having been made perfect." This was the mode in which He who "glorified him to be made high priest" (verse 5) led Him into the possession of this office. (Comp. 2:9, 10; Phil. 2:6-13.) He presents to all the model of the obedience to be rendered to Him, and through Him to the Father.

(10) In 5:11-6:20 the writer is led to reflect on the inability of his readers to receive the teaching which befits their Christian standing. If we remember the practical aim that is predominant in the epistle, we can hardly call this a digression, so powerfully is every portion of it made subservient to one great purpose.

(11) Hard to be uttered.—Rather, "hard of interpretation, seeing ye have become sluggish in hearing." Their faculty of "hearing" had once been acute, and then few words and little explanation, even on such a subject as this, would have sufficed. Now there has come upon them a lack of interest, and with this a want of power.

(12) For the time—i.e., taking into account the time that had elapsed since they became Christians.

Ye have need.—These first rudiments, which they need to learn again (but which he himself is not about to teach), it may seem natural to identify with what the writer in 6:1 calls "the doctrine of the first principles of Christ." Yet there is good reason for regarding "the oracles of God" as synonymous with the Scriptures of the Old Testament.

(13) Those who are addressed had lost interest in the deeper truths of Christianity, those truths which alone expressed and explained its proper nature. Their temptation apparently was toward mingling a rudimen-

ary Christian doctrine with the teaching of
he synagogue. Yielding to this they would
ose all real knowledge of the very elements
of Christian truth, and with this all true
knowledge of the Old Testament itself. The
connection between this verse and the last
may probably be, "Ye have come to need
milk, for—making it any choice your sole
food—stand self-confessed as babes."

(14) Strong meat.—"Solid food belongs to
full-grown men." If they occupied themselves with the rudiments alone, their spiritual senses could not be trained by habit in
distinguishing between truth and falsehood
in the various systems of teaching which
men offered as the doctrine of Christ.

6

(1) The principles of the doctrine.—See
note on 5:12.

Let us go on.—There is an urgency in the
words. "Perfection" (**teleiotes**) answers to
that rendered "full grown" (**teleios**) in the
preceding verse, and expresses maturity,
fullness of growth. There is the contrast
with "babes," and the whole context relates
to Christian instruction—the elementary
and the complete. But the following verses
show clearly that teaching and learning are
not alone in the writer's thoughts. The relation between verses 3 and 4 proves that he
assumes a necessary union between learning
and practice; indeed, the connection between immaturity or apprehension of Christian truth and the danger of apostasy is a
thought present throughout the epistle.

Not laying again the foundation.—The
particulars which follow are intended to
illustrate the nature of the elementary
teaching which will not be taken up in this
epistle. It will be observed that there is no
disparagement of these subjects of teaching,
and that the subjects here specified are not
in themselves distinctively Christian. One
and all they belonged to the ancient faith,
though each one became more or less completely transformed when Jesus was received as the Messiah. We have many indications that the tendency of Jewish converts
was to rest satisfied with this class of truths.

Repentance from dead works.—See 9:14.
No man can show more than partial obedience, but the law exacts the whole. The first
step toward Christianity involved the acknowledgment of this truth, and the separation by repentance from all "dead works."
The Hebrew doctrine of faith connected

itself closely with a cardinal passage of
prophecy (Hab. 2:4), "the just shall live by
his faith."

(2) Of the doctrine of baptisms.—The
repetition of a rite seems to be intended.
Both the word itself and the use of the
plural are remarkable. The word perhaps
denotes the ceremonial washings of the
Jews, these washings in the Levitical law
being important as one of the appointed
modes of removing that uncleanness which
excluded from every sacred place. Both
John's baptism and that of Christ, therefore,
would, from the Hebrew point of view, be
"washings"; and the teaching which every
new convert must receive would include
instruction on the symbolical purification
of the Old Covenant and the New.

And of laying on of hands.—This ceremony is repeatedly mentioned in the Old
and New Testaments. Besides the sacrificial
use of the symbol, we find imposition of
hands connected with blessing, with works
of healing, with ordination, and with the
gift of the Holy Spirit. In every case the
figure denotes either a transfer or the communication of a gift from the person who
lays his hands upon another.

"Resurrection of the dead" and "eternal
judgment" would place no obstacles in the
way of a convert to the Christian faith. We
know (Acts 23:8) that, though the Sadducees
denied that there was any resurrection of
the dead (and the Alexandrian philosophy
seems to have held only the immortality of
the soul), yet by the most influential among
Jewish teachers these doctrines were held
and enforced, as indeed it was plainly
taught in their Scriptures (Dan. 12:2).

(4) For it is impossible for those ... —
The connection of thought extends from
verse 3. The greater part of this long sentence is dependent on the word "renew" in
verse 6.

Those who were once enlightened.—This
metaphor is introduced again in 10:32. This
inclusive application of the term (familiar
from prophecy, from our Lord's own
words, from apostolic usage; see Acts 26:18;
Eph. 1:18, I Pet. 2:9) throws light on the
construction of the verse before us. "Enlightened" is but the first term of a series; it
is probable that the clauses which follow
should be regarded as explanatory of the
enlightenment itself.

Tasted of the heavenly gift.—From the
clear parallelism which exists between these
verses and 2:3-5, we may infer that the
"salvation" offered in the gospel (2:3) is

intended by this "gift." It is a gift bestowed by Him from whom has come the "heavenly calling" (3:1; 2:10). The following words at once recall 2:4.

(5) Tasted the good word of God.—The Greek suggests that the words rather mean, "tasted that God's word is good."

Powers of the world to come.—See 2:5. The same **future** is contemplated in both places, namely, the age of the Messianic reign. In the earliest days of the church little account was taken of the period separating the pre-Christian age from that of the full manifestation of the kingdom of God; the "powers" received from God by those who believed (2:4) belonged to no earthly state, but were as truly anticipations of a future age of glory as was the "heavenly gift" an anticipation of the "heavenly fatherland" (11:16).

(6) If they shall fall away.—Rather, "and (than) fell away." The contrast with the preceding description is presented in the fewest possible words. The successive clauses have shown that all the marks of the divine working in and with His word (2:4) have been found in these men, who, notwithstanding, "fell away."

To renew them again—i.e., a second time to make "the old" into a "new man." There is no thought of human power acting by itself, but of the human appropriation of divine power, in accordance with the laws of the kingdom of God. The verse before us is often read as an assertion that men who have thus fallen **cannot be renewed**. It is the more necessary, therefore, to lay stress on the simple meaning of the words, as relating neither to the absolute power of God, nor to the efforts of the Christian teacher in unassisted human strength, but to the economy of God's spiritual kingdom, in which Christ's servants achieve every great result by claiming and obtaining the "fellow-working" of their Lord.

Seeing they crucify.—The apostasy was indicated by a single word; these added clauses describe the depth of the fall, while they explain the futility of all effort toward recovering the fallen. Both the writer and his readers knew well what was involved in "falling away" in such a case as this. To go back to Judaism implied an acceptance of all that Jews had said and done against the Son of God; yet the highest evidence for Christianity—that of true and deep Christian experience—had been given to them. Again, the words used clearly describe a continuing state. Not the punishment for a past act, but the hopelessness of an existing state, is brought before us here. It is therefore of those who, with a distinct conviction of the divine mission of Jesus, have deliberately denounced Him, that the writer says "it is impossible to renew them again unto repentance."

(The passage, together with 10:26-29; Matt. 12:32; I John 5:16, occupied an important place in early controversies, as those of the Montanists and Novatians, who, in misapplication of it, refused absolution to those who, after baptism—or, in the language of the Early Church, after "illumination"—fell into heinous sin.)

(7) For the earth.—Land which not only receives but also drinks in abundance of rain (Deut. 11:11), in such a climate as is here thought of, must either "bring forth herbage" or be condemned as irretrievably barren.

(8) But that which beareth.—See Gen. 3:18. The presence of briars is a sure evidence of a poor soil, on which labor will be wasted. If that land which has drunk in the abundant rain and received careful culture still proves unfruitful, it is rejected. Man can do no more; the curse of God is near. The connection with the preceding passages is that in the case of the apostates described there, man is helpless; God's curse is "nigh."

(9) Better things—that is, the alternative spoken of in verse 7. He has not written in despair but for warning only, believing that to them belongs, not the state which is "nigh unto a curse," but that which borders on salvation (5:9).

(12) Followers.—Better "imitators." They are not the first to whom "hope" has been given, and who have needed zeal that they might not fail of their hope. As in chap. 11 the writer appeals to precursors of **faith**, so here of **hope** to men who, having lived in hope, passed to the actual possession of the promised blessings by means of faith (which laid claim to the promise) and patience.

(13-15) Abraham is chosen for special mention as the most illustrious example of those who "inherit the promises" (comp. John 8:58) because the assurance given to him was confirmed by oath, and in it lay included the promise of the Christ. The promises made to Abraham were essentially one, with various parts progressively fulfilled. (See Gen. 12:3; 22:17.)

(17) Of promise.—The promise made to Abraham was substantially and really that which embraced all Messianic hope; of this promise not Abraham's sons only, but all "they which are of faith" (Gal. 3:7, 29), Abraham's spiritual seed, are the heirs.

(18) Two immutable things.—The promise and the oath (verse 17).

(19) Which hope we have as an anchor of the soul.—This beautiful image is introduced for a moment only to set forth the security of the soul, though tossed by the waves of trouble. This symbol of hope, so familiar in Christian art, is not mentioned in the Old Testament, but is found in Greek proverbial sayings and appears on ancient coins.

Both sure and stedfast.—These words relate to the hope itself—a hope unfailing, firm, which enters where no human sight can follow, even into the Most Holy Place, into heaven itself. The hope becomes personified, leading the reader's thought to Him who is Himself our hope.

(20) Whither the forerunner.—The Jewish high priest entered the Holiest Place by himself—a representative but not a leader. Jesus has entered the true sanctuary (9:24) that He may give His people entrance there (10:19; John 14:2, 3). With this renewed mention of the great high-priestly act (4:14), the writer returns to the words of Scripture on which he was about to dwell (5:10), when the painful thought of the unpreparedness of his readers for higher Christian teaching forced itself upon his mind.

7

(1) For this Melchisedec.—The sentence is completed in the last words of verse 3. Of Melchizedek we know nothing beyond what we learn from the brief narrative of Gen. 14. It may be that the result of many speculations has been to invest this chapter with a mystery which does not belong to it. The object of the writer is, in reality, very simple—to deal with the question, What is the import of the divine utterance that David's Lord is a "Priest for ever after the order of Melchizedek"? The first part of this sentence (verses 1 and 2, as far as "... tenth part of all") enumerates the known facts of the history of Melchizedek; the following clauses are occupied with the interpretation of the history and inferences from it.

King of Salem.—Jewish tradition (Josephus and Targums) affirms strongly that this Salem occupied the site on which Jerusalem afterward stood; and certainly

Salem is a poetic name of Jerusalem (Ps. 76:2). This agrees well with the circumstances of the narrative and seems to deserve acceptance.

The most high God—a title characteristic of the narrative (Gen. 14:18-20, 22). Melchizedek is the first who in Scripture is spoken of as priest, and the name is given without explanation. As in the earliest times this office was held by the head of a family (Job 1), it is not unusual to find a union of regal and sacerdotal functions in the same man.

(3) Not because we find no mention of the parents of Melchizedek is he thus spoken of as fatherless and motherless, but because he is suddenly introduced as priest without any token whatever that he held the office by right of genealogy, the only claim familiar to Hebrew readers. Careful inquiry was made into the pedigree of him who would be a priest (Lev. 21:13, 14; Neh. 7:64); it must descend from Aaron, and contain no doubtful link. But He who is a priest "like Melchizedek" holds a priesthood that rests on no such rights or claims. As the Scripture is silent as to his reception of the office, so also is it as to any transmission to another. In these respects "made like (as a divinely ordained type) unto the Son of God," he bears perpetually the character of priest. (See Ps. 110:4.)

(5) Here the thought is that Melchizedek received tithes even from Abraham the patriarch; in verse 4 he has been thus honored, though no enactment of law invested him with superior rights. The authority to exact tithes was in strictness vested in the priests, the supreme guardians of the laws relating to all religious duties and observances, and the Levites were but their assistants. The Levites themselves paid tithes to the priests, who therefore stood alone in receiving tithes but paying none. It is the positive ordinance of the law, and nothing but this, that raises brethren above brethren, and gives to the priest this claim upon men who would otherwise be on an equality with himself through common descent from Abraham.

(6) Received tithes.—In Melchizedek we see a man who, though no law gave him pre-eminence, takes tithes of Abraham and therefore appears in Scripture as holding a position of inherent and acknowledged superiority. This superiority is presented still more strikingly in connection with the **blessing** (verses 7, 8).

(8) Here men enter by birth into a state

with which this right is associated, and by death again pass out of it. No special significance, therefore, attaches to the men themselves. But the narrative of Genesis gives no other basis for Melchizedek's priesthood than the mere fact of his life. What he holds, he holds by **personal** right.

(9) And as I may so say.—The principle which prevailed throughout was that pre-eminence depended upon descent alone. Had Judah possessed an inherent superiority over his brother Levi, the descendants of Judah might have claimed the like pre-eminence over the descendants of Levi. The position of Melchizedek toward Abraham involves of necessity his superiority to Abraham, and to Levi also and his descendants, so that "the order of Melchizedek" is altogether different from, and higher than, "the order of Aaron." This being so, how could this other priesthood take the place of the Levitical if this latter had answered its full purpose (or "perfection," verse 11)?

In verse 11 the "other priest" is spoken of as not connected with Aaron; verse 12 is interposed to show the serious significance of such a fact; in verse 13 the assertion of verse 11 is substantiated—not, however, from the words of the Psalm, but from their fulfillment in Jesus, who was from a "different" (not merely "another") tribe.

(16) A carnal commandment—one that is limited to the sphere of man's nature of flesh. As such, it is bound up with distinctions of race, tribe, and family; it is limited by human infirmity; it accomplishes only the purifying of the flesh. In contrast to all that is temporary and limited is placed an indissoluble life. Because He of whom Melchizedek was the type lives—in virtue of what He **is**—He is Priest **for ever**.

(18, 19) These two verses point out with great fullness and clearness what is involved in the statement of verse 16. The commandment is weak and unprofitable because the priesthood it creates cannot attain the end of its institution, which is to bring men into fellowship with God—"for the Law made nothing perfect." But when the earlier commandment is annulled, in its place there is brought in a better hope. The "better hope" stands connected with the "better covenant" (verse 22) and the "better promises" (8:6). And by this better hope we draw near unto God. The end of the priesthood, therefore, is attained. (See verse 11.)

(21) For those priests.—Rather, "For they indeed have been made priests without an oath."

By him that said unto him.—The last fiv words of the verse are absent from the be authorities. They were not needed for th part of the argument, and are therefor omitted from the quotation. (See 6:13-18 c confirmation by oath.)

(22) By so much was Jesus made.—Se 1:4. As the priest whose appointment confirmed by the oath of God is raise above all former priests, in the same pro portion is the covenant of which Jesus i surety better than the former covenant.

This is the first occurrence in this epistl of the word **diatheke**, which hereafter wi occupy an important place in the argumen Throughout the LXX it is used to represen the Hebrew word rendered **covenant**, anc like the Hebrew word, it is applied both t mutual agreements between man and mar and to engagements into which God enter in regard to man. In classical writers **dia theke** commonly denotes a **testament**, an thus in the Old Latin translation of th Scriptures **testamentum** became the com mon rendering of the word. As, howevei this rendering is often found where it i impossible to think of such a meaning a **will**, it is plain that the Latin **testamentun** was used with an extended meaning, an swering to the wide application of th Greek word. (Paul's designation of th Jewish Scriptures as "the Old Covenant"— II Cor. 3:14—thus became familiarl known as **The Old Testament.**) In the Nev Testament, through the influence of the Lat in, **testament** is retained in several places But there is a general agreement of opinior that "covenant" must be the true meaning in all passages of the New Testament excep Heb. 9:15-20; and even in that place ther are strong reasons for retaining the same rendering. In this present verse only is Jesus spoken of as Surety, elsewhere as Mediator (8:6; 9:15; 12:24). As through the Son o man the covenant becomes established, se in Him it remains secure; the words ad dressed by God to Him as Priest and King contain the pledge of its validity and per manence.

(25) Wherefore.—Since His priesthood is inviolable, His power of saving is **complete** (The writer's thought is resting on the firs section of chap. 5.) The connecting link between the priestly office and "salvation" appears to be the prevalent intercession of which this verse speaks—an intercession which implies all that has preceded in His priestly ministration. With the high priest's confession of the sins of the people on the

Day of Atonement was joined fervent intercession on their behalf; this intercession was also symbolized in the offering of the incense.

Verses 26-28 look back on all that has preceded since the beginning of the fifth chapter and prepare the way for the subsequent sections. The type afforded by Melchizedek has yielded its lessons, and to this there is no further reference. The abrogation of the Levitical priesthood and the infinite elevation of the "other Priest" above those of the order of Aaron have been so clearly set forth that it is possible now to concentrate attention on the types and lessons furnished by the Jewish ritual itself.

(26) Holy, harmless, undefiled.—The three words, denoting personal purity, innocence, and freedom from all pollution of sin, present the idea of which the ceremonial purity of the high priest was the type. Seven days before the Day of Atonement the high priest left his house and took up his abode in the Temple, that, thus separated from men and things unclean, he might when the day arrived be found free from all defilement; five washings and ten purifications were required of him on the day itself.

Separate from sinners.—These words, if they extend the idea expressed by "undefiled," point to the perfect sinlessness of our Lord, who lived among sinners and yet was ever separated from their sin, not needing external separation to preserve Him from pollution. If they are joined with the following, it points to the complete severance which now exists: our exalted Lord is forever removed from a life in the midst of transgressors.

(27) As those high priests.—The high priest's offering up sacrifices first for himself and then for the people constituted a chief part of his duty upon the Day of Atonement. (See note on 5:3.) The **annual** ("daily," i.e., on each Day of Atonement, known by the Jews as "the day") recurrence of that day is distinctly referred to more than once in this epistle (see 9:25; 10:1, 3).

(28) In these closing words are united the two cardinal predictions of Pss. 2 and 110 (comp. 5:5, 6): "Thou art my son," "Thou art a priest for ever."

8

A new division of the argument begins here. There is a clear difference between the topics discussed before and after this point. Heretofore the personal characteristics of the High Priest have occupied the chief place; from this point to 10:18 it is His ministration that is brought before us, together with a comparison of the covenants to which the ministries belong.

(1) Who is set.—Twice before have the words of Ps. 110:1 been referred to Jesus (1:3, 13). The last verse of chap. 7 united the two predictions which pointed to Jesus as Priest and King, and the same thought is contained here. (See 10:11, 12.) The next verse must be closely joined with this, for the contrast does not imply that He no longer "ministers" on behalf of men (see 7:25; 9:24); on the contrary, it is as "a minister" of the sanctuary that He sat down on the right hand of God.

(2) Of the sanctuary.—The "sanctuary" will probably be the heavenly counterpart of the Holiest Place, the "true Tabernacle," the counterpart of the sacred Tent of Moses, containing both the Holy Place and the Holiest of all (9:2-4). The Holy of Holies is the place of God's immediate presence, the Tabernacle that of God's appointed service. The latter is expressly mentioned here because special reference is to be made to its typical representation upon earth; this is shown by the following words, which point to Exod. 33:7. "True" denotes that which is contrasted with everything shadowy or imperfect or merely typical. It is a word especially characteristic of the gospel of John. (See John 1:9.)

(5) Who serve unto . . . —That every part of God's earthly house might be a fitting emblem of spiritual truth to be afterward revealed, Moses was charged in all respects to follow the pattern which had been shown him in the mount (Exod. 25:40). Jewish tradition understood these words to imply the presentation of a heavenly tabernacle to the sight of Moses, as a model to be imitated with exactness (see Acts 7:44). But whether we think of a pattern shown in vision, or merely of explicit direction received by Moses (see Exod. 25:9), the meaning of "the heavenly things" remains the same. The view presented here of the Jewish tabernacle involves no depreciation, except in comparison with "the good things to come."

(6) As He is Mediator of a better covenant, in the same proportion does His ministry excel that of priests on earth. The verb "was established" properly means "to legislate." Here, then, a word which refers to the passing of a law is applied to a covenant. The explanation must be sought in the special nature of the covenants of God with man (see 7:22), which are not compacts between equals, but arrangements offered by the divine goodness and made dependent upon conditions. Hence such a covenant may be spoken of as enacted on the basis of promise. On the promises (see verses 8-12) which are given by God is based the "covenant" which becomes the law of His kingdom and the declaration of His procedure. The idea of Jesus as Mediator and Surety (7:22) of a better covenant is expanded in 9:15-18.

(8) Finding fault with them.—Not "with it," but "with them" through whom the covenant had failed. The following quotation (verses 8-12) is taken from Jer. 31:31-34. It is the crowning point of that collection of his prophecies which is brought together in chaps. 30-33, descriptive of the hope and salvation of Israel. Of this new covenant, "ordained" on the three promises of an inward revelation, universal knowledge of God, and free pardon of sin, Jesus is the Mediator.

The essential promises of the new covenant were not unknown under the old. But in regard to the nation there was failure. The rites of the Law did not lead to the perception of spiritual truths; ordinances which were intended to teach the divine intolerance of sin became mere ceremonies; external sanctions did not preserve the nation in true obedience to God's law. To all, the former covenant was a parable, explained only when the new covenant was "ordained."

9

(1) The verse attaches itself to 8:5, 6. The words so emphatically standing at the close of the verse are probably descriptive not of the "sanctuary" only, but also of the "ordinances." Both place and ministrations belonged to **this world**, and thus stand in contrast with "the heavenly things," of which the Tabernacle was a token and shadow.

(2) The first, wherein was . . . —The golden candlestick, the table, and the showbread were in the Holy Place as it is described in the Law. The writer plainly implies that none of the parts and arrangements of the Tabernacle were without significance. On the golden candlestick, see Exod. 25:31-37;

on the table and the showbread, see Exod. 25:23-30; Lev. 24:5-9 (I Kings 7:48; II Chron. 4:8). It is remarkable that the table should here be so distinctly mentioned, for usually no special importance appears to be assigned to it apart from the offering which was placed on it.

Sanctuary.—Or, "holy place." The same word is applied to the Holy of Holies in 8:2; 9:8, 12, 24, 25; 10:19; and probably in 13:11. This verse and the next give the proper names of the two parts of the Tabernacle, which must be used when the one is to be distinguished from the other. Where there is no risk of mistake, the simpler designation is sufficient. (See Lev. 16:2, 17, 20.)

(3) The tabernacle.—The inner chamber of the Tabernacle is in a few passages only mentioned separately in the Pentateuch as the "Most Holy Place" (Exod. 26:33, 34), or "the Holy Place" (Lev. 16:2, et al.). The veil separating the two divisions (Exod. 26:31; 36:35) is here called the second veil, by way of distinction from the "hanging for the door" of the Tabernacle (Exod. 26:36; 36:37).

(4) Had the golden censer.—The Pentateuch makes no mention of a special censer for the use of the high priest on the Day of Atonement (Lev. 16:12); but, as we learn from the Mishna, the later law not only prescribed a censer of gold, but laid stress on the particular kind of gold. In Philo and Josephus, however, the word used here is the regular designation of the **altar of incense** (comp. Exod. 40:5). Though "censer" has (mainly through the influence of the Vulgate) been the more familiar rendering, many eminent commentators have adopted the latter view. The incense-altar and the Ark are coupled together, and the word which describes their relation to the Holiest Place is that which, a little later in this verse, distinctly signifies "containing." Not only are the notices in Exodus perfectly plain, but passages in Philo and Josephus show how customary in the writer's own age it was to speak of the three sacred objects in the Holy Place—the candlestick, the table, and the golden altar. There must exist some special reason for this connection of the altar with the Most Holy Place—a connection which would have been otherwise expressed had the writer held it possible that readers, familiar with the facts, could regard his language as even ambiguous. (See Exod. 30:6; I Kings 6:22.)

Ark of the covenant (Num. 10:33; Deut.

1:26, **et al.**), often called "the ark of the testimony," i.e., the Ark containing the tables of the Ten Commandments, which were the symbol of the covenant of God with the people. (See Exod. 25:10-16.)

Wherein was ... —See Exod. 16:33, 34; Num. 17:10, 11; I Kings 8:9.

(5) Cherubims of glory.—See Exod. 25:18-22; 29:43; Num. 7:89; Ezek. 10:19, 0. As these passages will show, the reference is to the glory which appeared above the mercy seat. This is the only express mention of the cherubim in the New Testament (but see Rev. 4:6).

The mercy seat (literally, the **propitiatory**) is the rendering adopted in the LXX for the Hebrew **Capporeth**, signifying the golden covering of the Ark (Exod. 25:17). The act of expiation with which the Greek name stands connected is that of Lev. 16:10-14. It is noteworthy that in I Chron. 28:11 the Most Holy Place itself is called "the house of the mercy seat."

(7) By "once every year" we must understand on one day of the year—the tenth day of Tisri. On that day (Lev. 16) it was the duty of the high priest to enter the Holy of Holies twice: (1) with the incense and with the blood of the bullock, his own sin-offering (Lev. 16:12-14); (2) with the blood of the same bullock and that of the goat, the sin-offering for the people (verses 15-19).

(8) "The first Tabernacle" is the Holy Place as distinguished from the Holiest of all. This outer Tabernacle was the place from which (as well as from the inner sanctuary) the people generally were excluded, and it was the place beyond which the ministration of the priests in general might not extend. The contrast between the body of priests and the people meets us in the whole epistle only in a small number of general statements (7:14; 8:4, 9:8); the contrast intended here is between the one Priest or High Priest and all who approach unto God through Him. Not the Jewish economy, but that to which it pointed: Christ's people are now the priests, who offer through Him their constant sacrifice. Those who ministered in "the first Tabernacle" (representing the people) were excluded, not from entrance only, but even from sight of the place of God's presence.

(9) Which was a figure ... —In full accordance with the parabolic character of the first Tabernacle is the presentation of offerings which have no power to accomplish the perfect end of worship in the case of any worshiper. The priests offered sacrifices to God, but were limited to the outer sanctuary, which was not the place of God's manifested presence. This was a fit symbol of offerings which cannot purify the conscience (see verse 14; 10:1).

(11, 12) Now the Mediator of the New Covenant (8:6), "Christ," whose name brings with it the thought of the satisfaction of all hope and fulfillment of all promises, has appeared as High Priest; and entering into the true Holy of Holies He has accomplished once for all what the earlier ministrations typified. And as it was by passing through "the first Tabernacle" that the high priest reached the Holiest Place, so it was by means of the blood of the sin-offering that he was enabled to enter into that place of God's presence. In 10:20 the veil is spoken of as symbolizing "the flesh" of our Lord. Here we have in all probability an extension of the same thought, "the more perfect Tabernacle" being the human nature of our Lord. Through the sacrifice atonement has been made and sin expiated; the blessing has won, which in 5:9 is called eternal salvation, is here "eternal redemption." The latter figure enlarges the former by the additional thought of the payment of a price.

(13) For if the blood of bulls and of goats.—The sacrifice is mentioned here in words slightly different from those of verse 11; but in each case the writer's thought is resting on the sin offering of the day of Atonement—a bullock for the high priest himself, a goat for the people. (There is no distinct reference in this epistle to the "scapegoat" sent into the wilderness.)

And the ashes of an heifer.—See Num. 19:17-19. It is said that on the third and seventh days of the high priest's week of preparation for the Day of Atonement (see note on 7:26), he was sprinkled with this water of purification, lest he should inadvertently have contracted defilement.

Sanctifieth to the purifying of the flesh.— The sacrifices and rites of purification could not cleanse the conscience (verse 9); but they could and did remove what the Law accounted "uncleanness," and disabilities connected with the outward life and religious worship of the commonwealth.

(14) Through the eternal Spirit.—There seems to be no foundation in the usage of the New Testament for referring this to the Holy Spirit, nor is such indicated by anything in the context. The explanation of the words must rather be sought in the nature

1137

of our Lord, or in some attribute of that nature. The **pneuma** of Christ is not here the Holy Spirit, but **the higher principle** of spiritual life, which was not the Divinity (this would be an Apollinarian assertion) but especially and intimately united with it. (See Rom. 1:4; I Tim. 3:16; I Pet. 3:18.) Through this spirit, a spirit of holiness, a spirit of indissoluble life, He offered Himself to God. This made such a self-offering possible; this gave to the offering infinite worth beyond that of passive animals.

Without spot.—The sinlessness of Jesus is expressed under the same metaphor in I Pet. 1:19.

Purge your conscience from dead works to serve the living God.—The works are dead because they had no share in true life, which is the life of God. (See note on 6:1.) From the whole number of Jewish rites had been selected (verse 13) the two which most fully represented the purification from sin and from pollution through death, in order that this completeness of antithesis might be attained.

(15) And for this cause.—This verse looks back to the great truth of verses 11 and 12, which the last two verses have served to confirm and place in bolder relief. For "the new testament" we must certainly read a "new covenant"; whatever may be the force of the following group of verses, the rendering "testament" has no place here. The leading thought of chap. 8 is the establishment of a new covenant, and the former covenant has been referred to three times in this chapter (verses 1 and 4).

That by means of death.—The first covenant had been broken by "transgressions"; unless there be redemption from these—that is, from the bondage of penalty which has resulted from these—there can be no promise and no new covenant. In respect of this bondage, this penalty, the death of Christ was a ransom—an offering to God in payment of debt, service, or penalty due. When debt and payment are changed into the corresponding idea of sin and punishment, the **ransom** gives place to the **sin-offering**, of which the principle was the acknowledgment of death deserved, and the vicarious suffering of death. The offering of Christ's life (Matt. 20:28) was a ransom or an offering for sin; it was also a sacrifice inaugurating a new covenant, which contained the promise of the eternal inheritance. See verses 16-18; Gal. 3:13, 14, where the thought is very similar.

(16) Testament.—See note on 7:22.

Though to us this verse may present a familiar thought, we must not forget that to Jews dispositions by will were almost altogether unknown. Were it granted that a writer might for illustration avail himself of a second meaning which a word he is using might happen to bear, this liberty would only be taken if by that means familiar associations could be reached, and the argument or exhortation could be thus urged home. In an epistle steeped in Jewish thought any transition from "covenant" to "testament" would be inexplicable. Thus, in spite of difficulties of interpretation that may arise, we must not seek to remove them by wavering in the rendering of **diatheke** as "covenant" in these verses. We are reminded at once of the words of Jesus Himself, "This cup is the new covenant **in my blood**" (I Cor. 11:25). It is this thought which the writer proceeds to develop: a covenant cannot be established without death. The sacrificial death of Jesus in man's stead ratified the covenant forever, the former state of separation being brought to an end in "the reconciliation" of the Gospel. The peculiar character of verse 15, moreover, seems to suggest that, as Jesus is set forth as High Priest and sacrifice, so He is both the Author of the covenant and the sacrifice which gives to it validity. In this case we see represented in His sacrifice the death of the "covenanter." (See Ps. 50:5.)

(19) With water, and scarlet wool, and hyssop.—In Exod. 24 there is no mention of these details, but similar notices are found in other parts of the Pentateuch, where the ceremony of sprinkling for purification is described (Exod. 12:22; Lev. 14:4, 6; Num. 19:6, 17, 18). The precise notices in the Law forbid us to doubt that each of these substances had a definite symbolical meaning, but to us the subject is involved in obscurity.

Both the book and all the people.—We must suppose that, as the blood was divided into two portions (Exod. 24:6) in token of the two parties to the covenant, and part "cast upon the altar," the book of the covenant was associated with the altar as representing the presence of Jehovah.

(21) He sprinkled with blood.—See Exod. 40:9-15; Lev. 8:10-12. Whatever was connected with the covenant which God made with His people must be sprinkled with the blood, which at once typified purification (verses 14 and 24) and ratified the covenant (verses 15 and 17).

(22) And almost all things.—To the first

ule an exception is found in the various
urifications by water or by fire (see Num.
1:22-24); to the second in the remarkable
aw of Lev. 5:11-13. On "cleansed" (1:3), see
.ev. 16:19, 30; on "forgiveness," Lev. 4.
he second clause of the verse is founded
n Lev. 17:11.

(23) Everything relating to the covenant
f God with sinful man must be brought
nder the symbol of expiation, without
vhich he can have no part in that covenant.
he "heavenly things" are not defiled by
in; but the true heavenly sanctuary cannot
e entered by man—the new fellowship
etween God and man "in heavenly places"
annot be inaugurated—until the heavenly
hings themselves have been brought into
ssociation with the One atoning sacrifice
or man.

(24) Now to appear in the presence of
God for us.—On the Day of Atonement
igh priest came before what was but a
ymbol of the divine Presence. He did not
lare to delay his return, even by prolonging
is prayer, lest he should "excite terror in
srael." In the heavenly sanctuary the High
riest is made manifest before the face of
God. The form of the Greek verb "appear"
night seem to imply a single appearance
nly; but by the added word "now," the
vriter corrects or enlarges the thought, and
hows that the true meaning is a manifesta-
ion which is both one and unceasing.

(26) For then must he often have suf-
ered.—The repeated presentation of Him-
elf to God would imply, as a necessary
ondition, a repeated "suffering" of death,
s the high priest's offering of the blood of
xpiation in the Holiest Place implied the
revious sacrifice of the victim. The writer's
oint of view is the time when "Christ
ntered into heaven itself." In speaking of
he repeated "suffering," he marks the limits
vithin which it must lie, reaching back to
he "foundation of the world."

(28) So Christ was once offered.—The
vork of redemption is so ordered as to
orrespond to the course of man's history:
s man must die once, and what remains is
he judgment which he must abide (verse
27), so the Christ has died once, and what
emains is His return for judgment—a judg-
nent which He Himself administers, giving
alvation to His people. When the Christ
hall appear the second time, it shall be
'apart from sin"—no longer bearing sin,
but "separate from sinners" (7:26). The last
words, "unto salvation," declare the purpose
of His appearing, in a form which at once

recalls the teaching of earlier verses in the
epistle, and which brings to mind the name
of Him for whom we wait, the Saviour
(Phil. 3:20).

10

(1) Can never with those sacrifices.—See
8:5 and 9:11. By the annual sacrifices,
which were the same as those which the
priests were offering for the people every
day (for the sacrifice of the Day of Atonement did not in itself differ from the ordinary sin offering), they cannot make the
worshipers perfect. The very repetition of
the annual ceremonial was a testimony to
its imperfection (verse 2).

(4) This verse explains those which
precede. No inconsistency really belonged
to these sacrifices and this ceremonial,
though so often repeated, for it was impossible that any such sacrifice should really
remove sin. The offering was necessary, and
it answered its purpose; but it could not
remove the necessity for another and a
better offering.

(5) He saith—i.e., Christ, in the prophetic
word of Scripture. The words which follow
are a quotation from Ps. 40:6-8, and agree
substantially with the LXX. Like Pss. 50
and 51, Ps. 40 is remarkable for its anticipation of the teaching of the prophets on
the inferior worth of ceremonial observances when contrasted with moral duties.
It seems probable that the psalm is David's,
as the inscription relates, and that its keynote is to be found in the words of Samuel
to Saul (I Sam. 15:22). David has learned
that the true mode of displaying gratitude is
not by offerings of slain animals, but by the
sacrifice of the will. As far as the latter
excel the former—so truly is the sacrifice of
will in accordance with the will of God—
that the value of the legal offerings is in
comparison as nothing. Thus, in his understanding and his offering of himself, he is a
type, while his sinfulness and weakness render him but an imperfect type, of Him that
was to come. The words of David, only
partially true of himself, are fulfilled in the
Son of David.

But a body hast thou prepared me.—The
words of the psalmist in the Hebrew text
are, "In sacrifice and offering thou hast not
delighted: ears hast thou digged for me." As
in Samuel's words sacrifice is contrasted
with hearing and with hearkening to the
voice of the Lord, the meaning evidently is,

"Thou hast given me the power of hearing so as to obey." A channel of communication has been opened, through which the knowledge of God's true will can reach the heart and excite the desire to obey. All ancient Greek versions except the LXX more or less clearly express the literal meaning.

(9) He taketh away the first, that he may establish the second.—In making these words His own, Christ declares the sacrifices of the law to be in themselves without virtue; Jehovah seeks them not from Him, but, having prepared a human body for Him, He seeks only the fulfillment of His will. But included in that will of God was Christ's offering of Himself for the world; and it was His perfect surrender of Himself that gave completeness to that offering. His death was at once the antitype of the sacrifice for sin; He takes away the sacrifices of slain animals that He may establish the doing of God's will.

(10) By the which will we are sanctified.—In this will of God which He accomplished (verse 9) lies our sanctification, effected "through the offering of the body of Jesus Christ once for all." In 9:14 the efficacy of the blood of Christ to cleanse the conscience is contrasted with the power of the offerings of the law to "sanctify in regard to cleanness of the flesh"; here the real sanctification is joined with "the offering of the body of Jesus Christ." The body (verse 8) is looked upon as the instrument of obedient service, but the word "offering" still preserves its sacrificial character and contains an allusion to the presentation of the body of the slain victim. As this offering has been presented "once for all" (7:27; 9:12), so "once for all" has the work of sanctification been achieved.

(11) And every priest.—The writer brings us back to 8:1, 2—to that which he there declared to be the crowning point of all his words. The accumulation of words which point to the ceaseless repetition of the offerings of the law (verse 1) is noteworthy. The last words point to verse 4.

(12) But this man.—The contrast to verse 11 is strongly marked. The sacrificial work has been performed, and the High Priest no longer "standeth ministering." The words "sat down" (Ps. 110:1) add to the priestly imagery that of kingly state.

(13) Expecting.—Once before in this context (9:28) our thought has been thus directed to the future consummation. There it consists in the Second Coming of Christ for the salvation of "them that wait for him" here it is He Himself who is "waiting," and the end is the attainment of supreme dominion. (See 1:3 and 13.)

(14) No repetition of His offering is needed. See 7:11, 19, 25. The last word of this verse has occurred before (see note on 2:11). It literally means those who "are being sanctified," all those who, from age to age, through faith (verse 22) receive as their own that which has been procured for all men.

(15, 16) See notes on 8:8-12.

(18) Here the argument reaches its triumphant close. At this point we enter on the last great division of the epistle (10:19-13:25), which is occupied with earnest exhortation, encouragement to perseverance alternating with solemn warning against apostasy.

(19) By the blood of Jesus.—It is not that we enter with the blood, as the high priest entered the Holy of Holies (9:25); no comparison is made between Christ's people and the Jewish high priest. But as when he entered within the veil the whole people symbolically entered with him, so do we enter with our High Priest, who by means of His own blood entered for us (and as our "Forerunner"—6:20) into the immediate presence of God. In that through which He entered we have our "boldness to enter."

(20) By a new and living way.—As the veil concealed from the high priest the place of God's presence, which he could enter only by passing through the veil, so a our representative Jesus could not enter the heavenly sanctuary until He had passed through and out of His life of flesh (see 9:11). There is probably a covert allusion to the rending of the temple veil in the hour when Jesus passed through the rent veil of His flesh. This way is living, for in truth it is living union with Christ (John 14:6).

(21) An high priest.—The Greek words properly signify a "great priest." It may seem strange that the writer should here make use of a new word in the place of that which has occurred so frequently. But there is strong reason for believing that the language of Zech. 6:11-13 is here before his mind. In verses 12-14 he has used words which united sacerdotal and kingly imagery. This, no doubt, led his thought to that prophecy. In 3:6 the meaning of the last words is enlarged, but only so that under "the house" is also comprised the **household** of God. Here the two thoughts are combined. Into the house of God we may enter over it Jesus rules as "the great Priest." The family of God subject to His rule includes the whole community of "the people of God" in heaven and upon earth.

(22) "Sprinkled from an evil conscience" means freed by means of the "sprinkling" from a conscience defiled by guilt. In the last words there may be an allusion to baptism, as the symbol of the new life of purity.

(25) As the manner of some is.—Some members of this community had persuaded themselves that the relation of Judaism to Christianity, of the "synagogue" (the Greek word used here seems to allude to this technical name, and yet intentionally to avoid it) and the church, was such as to permit them to avoid close intercourse with Christians and direct association with Christian assemblies. This neglect was the first step toward apostasy.

The day.—As the writer gave these warnings, the day when the Son of man should come in His kingdom, bringing judgment upon Jerusalem (Matt. 16:28), was close at hand—that day which is distinctly presented to us in the New Testament as the type of His final coming.

(26) For.—The connecting links are the thought of the consequences to which such sinful neglect (verse 25) may lead, and the awful revelation of judgment which the final day will bring. Even more clearly than in 6:4-6 the state described is one of willful and continued sin, which is the result and the expression of apostasy from Christ. The descriptive words are few as compared with those of the former passage, but they teach the same lesson. The observances and ceremonies of Judaism, which had been full of meaning while they pointed to Him that was to come, have lost all their virtue through His coming. For the sin of knowing and willful rejection of the only Sin offering, God has provided no other sacrifice.

(27) But a certain fearful looking for.—In the prophetic imagery of the Old Testament the destruction of the enemies of Jehovah is but the other aspect of His zeal or jealousy for His people. This imagery was familiar to every Hebrew; and no words could show more powerfully than these that to forsake Christ for Judaism was to **abandon** "the people of God."

(28) He that despised Moses' law.—See Deut. 17:2-7. There the subject is apostasy from Jehovah to the worship of idols. That sin which, by the acknowledgment of all, had in ancient time robbed Israel of the name of God's people is tacitly placed by the side of the sin of those who forsake Christ.

(29) Shall he be thought worthy by God the Judge of all, when "the Day" shall come. The principle of this act becomes the principle of the whole succeeding life. That "blood" by which the new covenant was established (9:15-17)—the blood in which he himself had received the sanctification which the law could not give—he has esteemed an unholy thing.

Hath done despite—i.e., hath treated with outrage and insult the Spirit of whose gifts he had been partaker (6:4), for "grace" returning arrogant scorn.

(30) See Deut. 32:35; Rom. 12:19. As in Pss. 43:1, 135:14, "to judge" here signifies to maintain the right of one who is exposed to wrong. "The Lord shall judge his people" (see verse 27) when He shall appear to establish their cause by taking vengeance on His enemies and theirs.

(32) From warning the writer now turns to encouragement (as in chap. 6), and he thankfully recalls the earlier proofs which his readers had given of their Christian constancy and love. Let them call to mind and ever keep in remembrance what the grace of God had already enabled them to endure. As Theophylact has said, he bids them imitate, not others, but themselves.

Fight of afflictions.—Rather, "conflict of sufferings"; the last word in this epistle (2:9, 10) associations too sacred to be lost. The former word (akin to that used by Paul in II Tim. 2:5 of the contests in the public games) recalls the intense struggles of the contending athletes; it occurs nowhere else in the New Testament. Comp. Phil. 1:27; 4:3; (Phil. 1:30; Col. 1:29; 2:1; I Tim. 6:12; Heb. 12:1.) This struggle they had manfully endured.

(34) In the last clause two remarkable changes in the Greek text are made necessary by the testimony of the best authorities. The words "in heaven" must certainly be removed; they are evidently an explanatory comment which has found its way into the text. There is little doubt that we must read "yourselves" instead of "in yourselves." The most probable translation will now be, "perceiving that ye have your own selves for a better possession and one that abideth." See Luke 9:25, 21:19; so in verse 39 the writer speaks of "the gaining of the soul." They could accept with joy the loss of possessions for the sake of Christ, perceiving that in Him they had received themselves as a possession, a better and a lasting possession.

(37) A little while.—The subject of Isa. 26:20, from which the one expressive phrase is taken, is the coming of Jehovah "to punish the inhabitants of the earth for their iniquity"; in "a little moment" shall the indignation consume His foes, then will He give deliverance to His people.

Paul's citations are limited to a few words of Hab. 2:4, "But the just shall live by faith"; here, and at the end of verse 37, are the whole of the fourth verse and part of the third from the prophet. The only difference between the LXX and the words as they stand here consists in the substitution of "He that cometh" for "coming." Now the reference to the Deliverer and Judge is made plain. No designation of the Messiah, perhaps, was more familiar than "He that cometh"; but it is here employed with a new reference—to the second advent in place of the first. The salvation of Israel from present danger is throughout the prophets the symbol of the great deliverance.

(38) Now the just shall live by faith.— The translation of the verse in Greek probably should be, "But my righteous one shall live by faith." (In the Hebrew the first part of the verse is altogether different: "Behold his soul is lifted up, it is not upright in him; but the righteous shall live in his faithfulness." The first words seem to refer to the haughty Chaldean invader.) It is clear that in the passage before us the writer has taken the words as they stood in his text of the LXX, changing only the order of the clauses. Though the Hebrew word usually rendered "faith" in this passage occurs more than forty times in the Old Testament, in no other case has it this meaning; it almost always signifies faithfulness or truth. The thought of faithful constancy to God, however, is inseparably connected with trustful clinging to Him. Hence the accepted Jewish exposition of the passage seems to have taken the word in the sense of "faith." "My righteous one" means the man who will not be seduced into wickedness; he shall live by his faithful trust, for salvation and life shall be given him by God Himself.

11

(1) The last verses of chap. 10 have taught the necessity of faith for the attain-

ment of the promise. Now we begin to read of men to whom, through their faith, the promise has been made sure.

It has been debated whether that which follows is a definition of what faith is, or in reality a description of what faith does. The "things hoped for" are not mere figments of the imagination; their basis is **the word of God.** If we keep this in mind, the words, still remaining general in their form, agree with all that has led up to them and with all that follows. The exact meaning of the special terms used here is not easy to ascertain. The word rendered "substance" has already occurred twice in the epistle. In 1:3 it meant the essence which underlies ("stands under") the qualities possessed (see note on 3:14). Thus we may translate the first part of the verse: "Faith is the giving substance to things hoped for." Such a translation does not represent the things hoped for as being **without substance,** for **in regard to ourselves** these objects of our hope do not yet exist since they still belong to the future (Rom. 8:24, 25). The Greek word for "evidence" denotes putting to the test, examining for the purpose of proof, bringing to conviction. And now passing away from the general aspect of the words to that in which they are presented by the context, we have as the meaning: Faith, holding to God's Word, gives substance to what the Word promises, investing the future blessings with a present existence, treating them as if already objects of sight rather than of hope.

(3) So that things which are seen.—The writer intends to state the divine **purpose** in relation to that first creation and all subsequent acts that are included in the preparing of the ages—"In order that what is seen should not have come into being out of things which appear." In the narrative of the first chapter of Genesis God would have us learn a lesson for the whole course of human history and development. As the visible universe did not take its being out of what was apparent, so what from time to time is seen does not arise of itself out of what is manifest to man's natural perceptions. Not only is the eternity of matter denied, but from the beginning a warning has been given against a materialistic philosophy. The first page of Scripture is designed to teach the constant presence and work of the Creator. This lesson we learn and apply by faith; and the result of its application is seen in many points of the history which follows, the writer's obvious design being to call attention to the faith

ossessed by "the elders" (verse 2) and its
onderful triumphs.

(4) A more excellent.—In the narrative of
en. 4 the offerings of Cain and Abel are
esignated by the same name, both in the
ebrew and in the Greek. Thus, apart from
ie words "by faith," there is nothing said
ere to explain the superiority of Abel's
fering. But one who believes sacrifice to
ave been of divine institution, and who
otes the close connection between God's
'ord and the actions of the men whose
ith is here recorded, may hold it probable
at Abel's obedience was manifested in his
ode of approaching God.

By which he obtained witness.—Such ac-
ptance implied Abel's righteousness, and
ius testified to his faith (see Matt. 23:35; I
hn 3:12). In later Jewish tradition the
others are represented as types of faith
d unbelief.

(5) The word rendered "translated" is a
mple one, denoting merely change of
ace. The words "walked with God" are
ndered in the LXX "was well pleasing to
od." (See Gen. 5:24.)

(6) But without faith.—The statement
iat Enoch pleased God is an assertion that
ith was found in him. No one can be the
ibitual worshiper of God (this is what the
irase implies) if his faith does not grasp
ese two truths.

(7) See Gen. 7:5. Noah's obedience to the
vine warning was an evidence at once of
s godly fear and of the faith which gave
ibstance and present reality to "the things
ot seen as yet." By the same faith Noah
ecame an heir of the righteousness which
according to faith." He is the first to
ceive in Scripture the name "righteous"
Jen. 6:9; see also Ezek. 14:14, 20; II Pet.
5). There is no important difference from
auline thought, but the idea of a continu-
us inheritance answering to continuous
ith is strikingly presented here.

(8) Which he should after receive.—
braham, when "called," did not receive
ie promise that the land to which he would
e directed should in the future be his
iheritance. This promise is not found in
en. 12:1-3, but was bestowed when he had
beyed (Gen. 12:7; see also Acts 7:5).

(10) A city which hath foundations.—The
eneral thought is that which we find ex-
ressed in verses 14-16. All these verses
early teach that the promise as apprehend-
d by the patriarchs was not bounded by
ie gift of Canaan. Of what nature their
xpectations of the future life may have

been we cannot tell; but this they knew, that
their fellowship with God and their interest
in His promises would not cease with this
transient life. What they saw of earthly
blessing was but the earnest of some greater
gift still future, and yet present through the
power of their faith.

(11) Through faith also Sara herself.—
Sarah was the joint recipient with Abraham
of the divine promise, a promise in which it
might at first seem that she had no part.
(See Gen. 16:1, 2.) On verse 12, see Gen.
15:5; 22:17.

(13) These all died in faith.—What is said
is, "In accordance with faith all these died";
faith had been the support and guide of
their life, and their death was in accordance
with the same principle. They did not die in
possession of what had been promised
(verse 39), but saw at a distance the blessings of which God had spoken (verse 1).

(16) If they had sought nothing more than
an earthly home, there is one already,
which was once theirs and to which they
might return; hence it is no earthly but a
heavenly country that they desire. (See note
on verse 10.) Through faith the Patriarchs
were willing to connect their whole life and
that of their children with waiting at God's
bidding for the fulfillment of a promise,
wandering and sojourning until God's own
time should come when He would grant a
home in a country of their own. And yet
each of these servants of God recognized
that relation to God in which lay the
foundation of the promise to him to be
personal and abiding. Because of this lofty
desire, or rather, because of the faith and
love toward Him in which the desire was
founded, and of which therefore the longing
for a heavenly country was the expression,
God is not ashamed to be called their God.
Before the desire existed the home had been
provided. (Comp. Matt. 25:34.)

(17) The patriarchs displayed their faith
in the attitude of their whole life, and in
their death. The writer now passes to the
lessons taught by particular actions and
events. Abraham (see Gen. 22:1) stands before us in the permanent record of Scripture
as having offered his son. The offering is
spoken of as if consummated. As regards
faith the sacrifice was indeed complete; the
perfect surrender of will had been made,
and the hand was stretched out for the
deed.

(20) Concerning things to come.—Not
having regard to things present only, or
things almost at hand, but looking far into

the future, through the divine revelation which opened to him the meaning of the promises received by Abraham, Isaac gave to each son the blessing designed by God (Gen. 27:27-29, 39, 40).

(21) Both the sons.—The separate character of the two blessings is thus brought out (Gen. 48:14-19). In the case of the two events mentioned in this verse the order of time is reversed, probably that the blessing of Jacob may immediately follow the similar record of verse 20. The last clause recalls Israel's thankful and devout satisfaction when assured that he should rest with his fathers in the land of Canaan; by this, at the point of death, he expressed his faith in the promise by which Abraham and his seed received Canaan as their inheritance. So Joseph also did cling to that hope (verse 22; see Gen. 50:26; Exod. 13:9).

(25) Choosing.—Moses' act, at age 40 (Acts 7:23), was an expression of his deliberate choice. He joined his people because it was "the people of God." To stand aloof for the sake of ease and pleasure would for him have been apostasy from God. The faith of Moses had brought "conviction of the things not seen." See Exod. 2:11.

(26) The reproach of Christ.—The words are almost exactly a quotation from one of the chief of the Messianic Psalms (Ps. 89:50, 51). Throughout the whole of their history the people of Israel were the people of the Christ. Their national existence originated in the promise to Abraham, which was a promise of the Christ, and their mission was to prepare the way for Him. The reproach which Moses accepted by joining the people of the promise was, therefore, the type of that "reproach" which in later days His people will share with Him (13:13).

For he had respect unto the recompence of the reward.—He habitually "looked away" from the treasures in Egypt and fixed his eye on the heavenly reward. On verses 27-29, see Exod. 12-15.

(30-31) See Josh. 6.

(32) With a brief mention of names which would call up before the minds of his readers achievements almost as wonderful as those on which he has been dwelling, the writer passes from the elders who received witness from God by their faith, and (verses 33-38) speaks in general terms, but all the more distinctly, of the triumphs which faith has won.

The time would fail me.—To the exploits of Barak (Judg. 4, 5), Gideon (6-8), Samson

1144

(13-16), and Jephthah (11, 12) there is clear reference in the words of verses 33, 34. There seems to be no design in this arrangement of the names. (Comp. also the history of the Maccabaean times.)

(35, 36) See I Kings 17; II Kings 4; Macc. 6.

(37) They were stoned.—As Zechariah (II Chron. 24:20-22), and—according to Jewish tradition mentioned by Tertullian and others—Jeremiah. (See Matt. 23:35, 37.)

They were sawn asunder.—An ancient tradition, mentioned both by Jewish and by early Christian writers, relates that Isaiah was thus put to death by order of Manasseh. On the latter part of the verse see Macc. 2:28, 29; II Macc. 5:27; 6:11.

(39) Having obtained a good report.—Now that the history is concluded, the word of verse 2 is resumed. To the saints of the Old Testament the promised blessing was future; they obtained it, but not within the limits of this present life. To us the promised blessing is present, revealed to us in its true nature and obtained for us once for all through the work of Christ.

12

(1) Wherefore seeing we also are compassed about.—Here again we have the thought which the writer is never weary of enforcing—the need of faith and patience for all who would inherit the promises. As those who have preceded us reached the goal (chap. 11), each one for himself, by faith and patient endurance, so must we. The thought of persevering effort crowned by a recompense of reward naturally suggested the imagery of the public games (by this time familiar even to Jews), to which Paul in his epistles so frequently alludes. (See I Cor. 4:9; 9:24-27; Phil. 3:12-14; I Tim. 6:12; II Tim. 4:7, 8; comp. 10:32, 33.) In these passages are called up the various associations of the great national festivals of Greece—the severe discipline of the competitors, the intenseness of the struggle, the rewards, "the righteous judge," the crowd of spectators. Those who encompass us, a countless host (a "cloud" of witnesses), have had witness borne to them through their faith, and in turn stand forth as witnesses to faith, bearing testimony to its power and works. One and all they offer encouragement to us in our own contest of faith. The idea of the presence of spectators may be in oint here, but no interpretation must be allowed to interfere with the chief thought—that the runner's steadfast gaze is fixed on Him who has Himself traversed the course before us, and is now the Judge and Rewarder.

Every weight.—The Greek word was sometimes used by Greek writers to denote the excessive size and weight of body which the athlete sought to reduce by means of training, but may also signify the encumbrance of any burden—unnecessary clothing and the like—that renders the athlete less fitted for the race. In the interpretation we think of the "divers and strange teachings" (13:9), in which would be included the Judaizing practices which they were taught to observe.

And the sin which doth so easily beset us.—The prevailing opinion is that the word "beset" signifies "easily surrounding," and that the writer is comparing sin with a garment—either a **loosely** fitting garment by which the runner becomes entangled and tripped up, or one that clings **closely** to him and thus impedes his ease of movement. It is likely that the writer speaks of sin generally as an obstacle to the race, rather than of what is known as a "besetting sin"—the sin which in the case of any one of us is proved to possess special power.

(2) Looking unto Jesus.—The runner looks away from all other objects and fixes his gaze on One. Jesus is not directly cited as the Judge (II Tim. 4:8); but He has Himself reached the goal, and His presence marks the point at which the race will close. Of our faith this Jesus is the Author and the Perfecter. The former word has occurred in 2:10; here, as there, **origination** is the principal thought. There the idea of leading the way was also present, but here "Author" stands in contrast with "Perfecter." The example of our Lord is the subject of the clause which follows, where the shame of the death of the cross is set over against the joy that lay before Him. (See Phil. 2:9, 10.)

(3) Him that endured such contradiction.—Rather, "Him that hath endured such gainsaying from sinners against themselves." The word "gainsaying" ("contradiction") is so frequently used in the LXX for the rebelliousness of the people of Israel that we need not here limit it to contradiction in words. The change of "himself" into "themselves" (the reading of the oldest MSS) is important—the sin or the opposition manifested against Him was really against

themselves, since it was for their salvation that He came upon earth. To all His other sorrows were added the pain of their ingratitude and His grief over their aggravated guilt.

(4) Ye have not yet resisted unto blood.—For the foot-race is substituted the contest of the pugilists. In verse 1 sin was the hindrance which must be put aside; here it is the antagonist who must be subdued. (See I Cor. 9:26.) The contest has been maintained but feebly, for no blood has flowed in their struggle with temptation and sin; they have not deserted the arena, but have shrunk from the suffering which a determined struggle would have caused.

(5) In this cowardly avoidance of trouble and persecution they have been shrinking from that chastening which every son receives from the Lord. (See Prov. 3:11, 12.)

(9) Furthermore we have had fathers.—The thought of the former verses has been, "He chastens as a father." From likeness we here pass to contrast. The contrast drawn is between our natural parents and "the Father of spirits," the Giver of life to all.

(10) After their own pleasure.—Rather, "as seemed good unto them." The contrast is continued here between human liability to mistake and the perfect knowledge of our heavenly Father, who seeks our profit and cannot err in the means which He employs.

(11) The peaceable fruit of righteousness.—This stands in contrast with the unrest and trouble which have preceded during the time of "chastening." But there is more than rest after conflict, for the object of the conflict is attained. (Comp. Isa. 32:17; Prov. 11:30; Phil. 1:11; Jas. 3:17.)

(12) Wherefore.—As in 10:24, the writer passes from the thought of personal risk and duty to that which is binding on all members of a community. Comp. Isa. 35:3, where those who have lost heart and hope are encouraged by the promise of the coming of their God bringing recompense and salvation.

(13) Be turned out of the way.—The difficulty in these words is concealed to some extent when they are separated from the following clause, as in the Authorized Version; this separation, however, the Greek will not allow. The verb here bears the meaning which it frequently has in medical writers: **be put out of joint.** The words are a warning against the shifting courses of men who are ready to turn aside from strict duty when persecution threatens, and seek to avert the danger by compliance with what they do not in heart approve.

(14) Follow peace.—See Ps. 34:14. This charge is general (Rom. 12:18), and must not be limited to peace with fellow Christians (Rom. 14:19). The two admonitions of this verse were admirably suited to a period of persecution. Let all make peace their aim, yet not so as to sacrifice purity. (Comp. Jas. 3:17.)

And holiness.—Better, "and the sanctification without which no man shall see the Lord." In 9:28 we have the promise that "Christ . . . shall be seen" by them that wait for Him; thus it might be supposed that "the Lord" is here, as in 2:3, a designation of our Saviour. As, however, this epistle especially brings Him before us as the Sanctifier (2:11; 3:12), who leads us into the presence of God (10;19), we must rather look on these words as akin to Matt. 5:8, "Blessed are the pure in heart, for they shall see God."

(15) Lest any man fail.—The defection of one member of the community brings loss and danger to the whole body. The last words of 10:26 will show what is implied in this "falling back from the grace of God."

Any root of bitterness.—It is clear that Deut. 29:18 is before the writer's mind. Again, therefore (see 10:27, 28, 30), the apostasy to which the Hebrew Christians were tempted is compared with the sin committed by those who by idolatry fell away from God's ancient covenant; and as one idol-worshiper in a community might bring into it a root of bitter poison, so one apostate from the Christian faith would bring trouble and defilement on the church. (Comp. Acts 8:23.)

(16) Lest there be.—Though Jewish tradition affirms that Esau was a man of impure life, it is not probable that he is so represented in this verse. Here he is mentioned as a type of "the profane," who care not for divine things, but only for the gains and pleasures of this world. (See Gen. 25:29-34.)

(18) The exhortation to faithfulness now begins to be enforced most impressively by means of a comparison between the earlier revelation and that which is given in Christ. (See Exod. 19; Deut. 4.) "Israel's drawing nigh was at the same time a standing afar off. The true and inner communion with God had not yet been revealed; first must the Law lead to the painful consciousness that sin prevents such communion, and intensify the longing that sin may be taken out of the way. Under the New Covenant,

no longer is a tangible mountain the plac of a divine revelation made from afar; bu heaven is thrown open, and a new super sensuous world in which God is enthrone is opened to admit us, opened through th Mediator of the New Covenant, accessibl in virtue of His atoning blood" (Delitzsch).

(23) And to God the Judge of all.—Th order of the Greek seems to require th rendering, "and to a Judge (who is) God o all." Up to this point the thought has reste on the heavenly world and those who from the time of their creation have been in inhabitants. Men who have passed throug this earthly life have no essential right t citizenship in the "heavenly Jerusalem." They come before a Judge (comp. 9:27 who severs between His servants and Hi foes (Mal. 3:18; 4:1), condemning the wick ed and receiving the righteous to His ow dwelling place.

(24) In all other places in which we rea of the New Covenant a word is used which implies newness of kind and quality; here i is a covenant which is newly made— literally "young," having all the freshness o youth in comparison with that which lon since was growing old (8:13). Jesus is Mediator of a new covenant through the shed ding of His blood, typified by the blood o the covenant with which Moses sprinkle all the people. This blood speaks with greater power than Abel's, and speaks no for wrath but for purification and atonement. I John 2:1, 2 completes the contrast.

(25) For if they escaped not who refused.— The terrors which accompanied the givin of the Law were designed to impress all hearts with the fearful peril of disobedience In shrinking from the voice of Him who warned they could not escape the declaration of the Law or the terrible penalties which awaited all transgressors.

If we turn away.—The argument is similar to that of 2:2, 3. He from whom they turned aside on earth is He who now speaks to us. Then His voice was heard amid earthly terrors; now His revelation comes through His Son who is exalted in heaven.

(26-28) The terrors of Sinai were a typ of a more terrible revelation of judgment. when not only shall the earth tremble, bu the earth and the heaven shall be moved. and all that is transitory and mutable shall pass away. The words of Hag. 2:6 are taken as a prophecy of this consummation. Bu that which "cannot be shaken" is the king dom which we receive.

13

(2) To entertain strangers.—Hospitality to Christian brethren at a distance from their homes is especially intended (I Pet. 4:9). This was one manifestation of the "love of the brethren" (verse 1). On the latter clause, see Gen. 18, 19.

(4) Marriage is honourable in all.—Rather, "Let marriage be held in honour among all, and let the bed be undefiled; for fornication and adulterers God will judge." The precept is directed against impurity, and also against the false asceticism of men "forbidding to marry" (I Tim. 4:3). The laxity of morals among Gentiles (Acts 15:20) and the prevalence of divorce among Jews (Matt. 5:32) explain the sudden introduction of such warnings.

(5) Conversation.—Literally, **way** of thought and life, character, disposition.

For he.—The appositeness of these words (see Deut. 31:6) and those in verse 6 (see Ps. 118:6) will be seen if we remember the trials which the Hebrew Christians had already endured (10:32-34).

(8) Jesus Christ the same . . . —Their earlier guides (see chap. 11) have passed away (verse 7); their Lord and Saviour abides the same forever. What the Saviour was to them, that will He be to their survivors. He who is the subject of all Christian teaching is the same, therefore (verse 9) "be not carried away by divers teachings." Thus, this verse stands connected both with what precedes and with what follows.

(9) The contrasts expressed in the second part of this verse and in verses 10 and 11 throw light on the nature and source of the erroneous doctrine. Its subject was not "grace," but "meats"; its promoters were connected with those who serve the Tabernacle. As the whole system of ceremonial observance is alluded to under the one term "meats," so the blessings of the Christian faith are comprised under "grace," a word used throughout this epistle with peculiar significance. The writer is probably speaking of doctrines and practices similar to those censured by Paul in Col. 2:16-23.

(10, 11) For us there is but one sacrifice for sin, the efficacy of which endures forever (10:12); Jesus entering the Holiest Place for us in virtue of His own sacrifice has fulfilled the type contained in the high priest's sprinkling of the blood (Lev. 4:3-21; see note on 9:2). But whereas those priests might not eat of their sin-offering, to us greater privilege is given; we feed on Him

who was slain for us, whose flesh was for the life of the world (John 6:51-56).

(12) The bodies of those beasts serving as sin-offerings were burned **without the camp.** Jesus, who in all other points fulfilled the law of atonement, fulfilled it in this point also, in that He suffered "without the gate" (Matt. 27:32; John 19:20).

(13) The suffering "without the gate" was a symbol of His rejection by the Jews. All who would be His must share the reproach which came upon Him, who was cast out by His people and crucified (11:26); they also must go forth "without the camp" (even Jerusalem, literally—verse 14), forsaking the company of His foes.

(15) Let us offer the sacrifice.—The sacrifice that we as priests may bring is that symbolized by the thank-offering of Lev. 7:12. (See Ps. 50:14, 23.) "We will render the fruit of our lips" is the Greek version of Hos. 14:2; the Hebrew text has, "We will render our lips as bullocks"—i.e., as sacrifices. (Comp. Ps. 119:108; Isa. 57:19.)

(16) And yet another offering may we bring. With thankfulness to Him must be joined acts of well-doing to men, these too being presented as sacrifices to God.

(17) No words could more powerfully present to members of the church the motives for obedience to their spiritual guides. (See note on verse 8.)

(18) The following verses contain personal notices relating to the writer himself and to his readers (verses 18, 19, 22, 23), a prayer on their behalf (verses 20, 21), a doxology (verse 21), and brief salutations (verses 24, 25).

We trust.—Some prejudice against the writer, or some mistrust of his motives, must have existed in the church; that among Hebrew Christians a disciple of Paul should be misrepresented or misunderstood causes no surprise. But whatever suspicion might be cherished by a few, the next verse is proof that he knew himself to be beloved by the many.

(19) But I beseech you.—We infer from this verse that the writer had formerly been associated with those whom he now addresses, and that he is at present hindered from returning to them. (See verse 23.)

(20) Now the God of peace.—The writer here has in thought those divisions of thought and feeling which have been hinted at in verses 17-19, and which in truth were the expression of the deep-seated mental unrest which it is the object of the epistle to remove.

Our Lord Jesus.—The first of the blessings of the covenant ratified by His blood, and that in which all blessing lay included, was that God raised Him up from the dead to be "the great Shepherd of the sheep." If these prophetic words respecting Him who brings peace to the world (Zech. 9:10) were in the writer's mind, how natural is his appeal to the God of **peace.** This is the only passage in the epistle in which we read of the resurrection of our Lord apart from His ascension; elsewhere His exaltation is contemplated as one act.

(21) Make you perfect.—To "make perfect" is the translation of two different words in this epistle. In the one "perfect" stands contrasted with that which is immature, which has not attained its end and aim. The other, which is used here, rather conveys the thought of complete equipment or preparation.

(22) If we take into account the subjects with which the writer has been dealing, we shall not wonder that a letter which might have been read to the assembled church in less than an hour should be described as brief. (Comp. I Pet. 5:12.)

(23) The Hebrew Christians knew of the imprisonment of Timothy, but had not heard the news of his release. (See II Cor. 1:1; Col. 1:1; Philem. 1; I Thess. 3:2.)

(24) They of Italy salute you.—These much discussed words are consistent with either of two hypotheses: (1) that the writer is in Italy, and salutes "the Hebrews" in the name of the Christians of Italy; (2) that the writer is addressing a church of Italy, and sends greeting from Christians who have their home in Italy, but are now with him.

(As in the other epistles the subscription is destitute of authority, not being found in any MS of the epistle earlier than the ninth century. No ancient MS contains more than the simple notice, "To the Hebrews," except the Alexandrian, which adds "written from Rome.")

JAMES

1

(1) James, a servant of God and of the Lord Jesus Christ.—James was bound to Him in devotion and love. In like manner Paul (Rom. 1:1), Peter (II Pet. 1:1), and Jude, brother of James begin their letters. The writer of this has been identified with James the Just, first bishop of Jerusalem, the brother of our Lord.

To the twelve tribes which are scattered abroad.—Or, **to the twelve tribes in the dispersion**, the remnants of the house of Israel. (See Deut. 28:37; Jer. 29:18.) Strictly speaking, at the time this epistle was written, Judah and Benjamin, in great measure, were returned to the Holy Land from their captivity, though numbers of both tribes were living in various parts of the world. The remaining ten had lost their tribal distinctions, and have now perished from all historical record, though it is still one of the fancies of certain writers, rather pious than learned, to discover traces of them in the aborigines of America, Polynesia, and almost everywhere else. While the Temple stood, these scattered settlements were colonies of a nation, bound together by varied ties and sympathies, but ruled in the East by a rabbi called the Prince of the Captivity, and in the West by the Patriarch of Tiberias, who, curiously, had his seat in that Gentile city of Palestine. The fall of Jerusalem, and the end therewith of national existence, rather added to than detracted from the authority of these strange governments; the latter ceased only in the reign of the Emperor Theodosius, while the former continued in the royal line of David until the close of the eleventh century, after which the dominion passed wholly into the hands of the rabbinical aristocracy, from whom it has come down to the present day.

(2) Count it all joy when ye fall into divers temptations.—How can we feel any joy under such? Do we not pray in our Saviour's words, "Lead us not into temptation"? James here is following the same line of thought as that expressed in Heb. 5:14. Innocence is a grace indeed, and yet there is a higher stage of the same virtue—the purity which has been won by long and often bitter conflict with the thousand suggestions of evil from without, stirring up the natural impurity within. Temptation is not sin; and the soul victorious is by that very triumph

stronger and better able to undergo the next assault (verse 3). The interpretation of our Lord's prayer is rather the cry for help to God our Father in the trial than for actual escape from it. (Comp. I Cor. 10:13.)

(5) If any of you lack wisdom.—The apostle passes on from patience to the thought of heavenly wisdom, not the knowledge of the deep things of God but that which is able to make us wise unto our latter end (Prov. 19:20). God gives wisdom fully and directly, never reproving such a prayer.

(6) But let him ask in faith, nothing wavering.—Surely this verse alone would redeem James from the charge of slighting the claims of faith. It is here put in the very forefront of necessity; without it all prayer is useless.

Nothing wavering.—Or, **doubting nothing**. This doubting is the halting between belief and unbelief, with inclination toward the latter. Faith, in its first sense, is the direct gift of God; but it must be tended and used with love and zeal, or its precious faculties will soon be gone. Intellectual is not moral doubt; nevertheless, intellectual doubt may spring from an evil habit of carping criticism and self-opinion, for the foundation of which, insofar as a man himself has been either the willful or the careless cause, he must bear the curse of its results.

(9) Let the brother of low degree rejoice in that he is exalted.—There is no praise from the plain James for the pride which apes humility, nor the affectation which loves to be despised. Willingness for Christ's service, whether it be great or little, is the right condition of mind for all disciples. Pleasure will be naturally felt by most at the prospect of a rise in the world. But there are some finer spirits who shrink from anything like exaltation; and to these the kindly James writes that they may take heart and not fear the greater dangers which of necessity accompany a higher call.

(10) But the rich, in that he is made low.—There is an antithesis between the humiliation of the rich and the humility of "the brother of low degree." But there is a more spiritual significance underlying, which would teach the poorest that he may be "rich toward God" and win from the most wealthy the acknowledgment of his own deep poverty. (Comp. Matt. 6:30.)

(11) For the sun is no sooner risen . . .—Often must James have seen such an effect of the fiery Eastern sun, scorching with its pitiless glare the rich verdure of the wilderness. (Comp. Isa. 40:6-8.) But notice that it is not the rich brother who is to fade thus, though his wealth will so pass away. The warning is rather (as in Mark 10:24) "for them that **trust** in riches." Even "the mammon of unrighteousness" may be well used (Luke 16:9).

(12) Blessed is the man that endureth temptation.—The words that James uses in the original are the same as those which are expressed in verses 2-4 by "patience" and "trials," and mean a firm endurance, steadfastness, tenacity of purpose, and quenchless enthusiasm. (Comp. Matt. 5:3-11.) The "pride" and "beauty" of the worldling are as "a fading flower" (Isa. 28:1) under the scorching sun; but the unfading, ever-living crown is for the spiritual, the true lovers of their Lord.

(13) Let no man say when he is tempted, I am tempted of God.—Far be it from the true Christian either to give way to sin "that grace may abound" (Rom. 6:1), or to suppose for one moment that God is drawing him from righteousness. Almost every reflection upon the nature of sin leads up to an inquiry as to its cause; and the enigma will hardly be solved in this life. The very facts of the presence of evil among God's creatures, and its continual attraction even for the best, have often driven men to doubt His supremacy. The Manichees settled the difficulty (better than the Deists) by declaring the existence of a good God and a bad one, and appealed to the daily strife between virtue and vice in witness of their simple creed. Thanks to the Gospel, a nobler theology is our Christian heritage, whereby we are persuaded that good will triumph at the last, and by which we are taught humility withal to own that God's ways in so permitting and overworking evil are beyond man's comprehension.

Neither tempteth he any man.—The tempter is allowed but so far, and no further. We may be assured that trials and temptations are permitted to strengthen us— if we will—for His mightier service. And, as compulsory homage would be worthless to the Lord, voluntary homage must be found instead, and proved and perfected. Herein is the Christian conflict, and the secret of God's way with man.

(14) So far James has spoken of the outward part of temptation; now he lays bare the inner, for we suffer the twofold evil. Satan has learned too well the deep corruption of the heart and knows what gaudy bait will most attract the longing and licentious eyes.

(15) Then when lust hath conceived . . . —The image well depicts the repellent subject: the small beginning, from some vain delight or worldly lust and pleasure; next from the vile embrace, sin, growing in all its rank luxuriance, until it bear and engender, horribly, of itself, its deadly child. The progress is frightful in the sense it would convey, as of some monstrous deformity, a hideous progeny tenfold more cursed than its begetter. "The wages of sin is death" (Rom. 6:23), and their paymaster is the devil.

(17) Every good gift and every perfect gift is from above.—This beautiful sentence, more musical still in the Greek, is thought to be the fragment of some Christian hymn. Two words are translated by our one "gift"; the first is rather the act of giving, the second the gift itself, and the effect of both together is a climax to the statement of God's benevolence.

Cometh down from the Father of lights.— Great difference of opinion is found concerning these "lights," whether the term be figurative, as of goodness or wisdom; or a reference to the mysterious Urim (Exod. 28:30); or spiritual, as of grace and glory; or material, the "lights" set in the firmament of heaven (Gen. 1:14, 15). It were not amiss to take the whole of these interpretations. But that the mind of the sacred writer was mainly on the lights of the material universe may be seen from his next thought.

(18) Of his own will begat he us with the word of truth.—There is a greater witness to God's goodness than that which is written upon the dome of heaven, even the regeneration of man. As the old creation was "by the Word" (John 1:3, 10), the new is by Him also, the Logos, the Word of Truth, and that by means of His everlasting Gospel, delivered in the power of the Holy Ghost.

That we should be a kind of firstfruit of his creatures.—The longing for a future perfection is shared by all created beings upon earth, and their discontent at present imperfection points to another state freed from evil (Rom. 8:18-22). And the fruition of this hope is foreshadowed in the words above.

(21) Wherefore lay apart all filthiness and superfluity of naughtiness.—The defilement here referred to seems common to the whole natural man. The superabundance of evil will occupy the heart, if care be not taken to root it out, and, like the thorns in the parable of the sower (Matt. 13), spring up and choke the good seed.

Naughtiness is maliciousness. The badness implied in the original is unmistakably positive (see verses 19, 20).

Receive with meekness the engrafted word —engrafted, like a good olive tree, or rather implanted, in you. The term is peculiar to this place, and means "innate" in its first intention. If taken so, "the innate Word" will be Christ Himself formed within us. (Comp. Gal. 4:19.)

Able to save your souls.—The idea of salvation thus conveyed by the implanted word is so potentially and not actually. Tended and cultured, it will grow into a tree of life, the fruit whereof may heal the wounds of sin; but the after-growth of this plant of God is largely in the hands of man.

(22) Doers of the word—acting up to the full of their knowledge, whether gained by the spoken or the written Word of God. The term "deceiving" is the contrary of that rendered "word," and means its corruption; the Word which is the source of knowledge and life may be so handled as to cause error and death. No acquaintance with the Bible, apart from the practice of its precepts, will avail the Christian any more than it did the Jew.

(23) He is like unto a man beholding his natural face in a glass.—James points grimly to an example of this self-deception. This is not a "glass," but a mirror of polished steel such as are still used in the East. "His natural face" is the real appearance which the reflection of the Word of God, properly looked into, will afford the inquirer.

(25) But whoso looketh . . . —The earnest student of the Scriptures stoops down in humility of body and mind to learn what the will of their Author may be. He finds therein a law of liberty and not slavery, life and not death.

(26) If any man among you seem to be religious . . .—i.e., to himself, and not to others merely; the warning is not to the hypocrite, but the self-deceived. If such a one deceive his own heart, as he may, and give to those around him the proof of his self-delusion in not curbing his tongue, vain and useless is all his religious service. The first mark of true religion is gentleness of tongue, just as the contrary, blasphemy, is the most damning fault of all (Matt. 12:37). The text is more a guide for self-examination than a stone to be cast at a neighbor.

(27) Pure religion . . . —By religion here is meant religious service. Here is the double proof of the perfect life of holiness. The help afforded to the helpless, put thus in the first place of the two requirements, will often bring about the second, namely, the spotless condition of unworldliness which marks the true servant of the Lord Jesus Christ. Deeds of benevolence may be and are often done by those who are not His; but all who truly belong to Him must live a life which praises Him continually in good works.

2

(1) My brethren.—The lesson here is distinctly addressed to believers, and its severity appears to be caused by James' consciousness of its need. What were endurable in a heathen, or an alien, or even a Jew, ceased to be so in a professed follower of the lowly Jesus. And this seems to be a further reason for the indignant expostulation and condemnation of verse 14. Thus the whole chapter may really be considered as dealing with faith; and it flows naturally from the foregoing thoughts upon religious service.

If the central facts of the faith are believed—see, e.g., II Cor. 8:9; Phil. 2:4-7—how could there be among Christians such folly and shame as "acceptance of persons" according to the dictates of fashionable society and the world? True reverence and submission are in no way condemned by this Scripture, but rather their excess and gross extreme, the preference for vulgar wealth, the adulation of success, the worship, in short, of some new golden calf.

(2) For if there come unto your assembly (literally, synagogue).—This is the only place in the New Testament where the Jewish word is used for a Christian congregation, and suggests an early date for this epistle.

A man with a gold ring, in goodly apparel.—Roman satirists had much to say about the "dandies" of their time, with "all their fingers laden with rings"—some, if we may trust the sneer of Martial, having six on each. No doubt, the fashions set in Rome extended to Jerusalem. "Goodly apparel" are the same two words translated "gay clothing" in verse 3.

(3) Comp. Matt. 23:6. The elder in charge of the church finds a stall for the person of substantial presence, while anything does

for the poor one. He can stand, or, if he prefers, sit under the great man's footstool, that is, on the floor beneath. How then can there be escape from condemnation on the charge which follows?

(5) Hearken, my beloved brethren.—With complete change of manner James writes now as if he were speaking, in brief quivering sentences, in appeal to the hearts which his stronger words may not compel. The world must always measure by its own standard and consider poverty a curse, just as it looks on pain and trouble as evil. But the teaching of God, especially through His Son, is the direct opposite to this. In a worship which demands of its votaries costly gifts and offerings, the rich man has a golden pavement to his future bliss. It is no wonder, therefore, that again and again the Spirit of God has pointed out the narrow way and the eternal excellency of truth, faith, and love, the riches easiest of acquisition by the poor.

(6) Do not rich men oppress you? or **lord it over you** as a class. This cannot be said, of course, of each wealthy individual. It is the man trusting in his riches (comp. Matt. 10:24) who makes them a power for evil and not for good. Here is presented the other side of the argument, used on behalf of the poor, viz., observe first how God regards them (verse 5), and next, judge their adversaries by their own behavior.

Draw you before the judgment seats?— The purse-proud litigious man is the hardest to deal with. No body of laws could on the whole be more equitable than the Roman, but their administration in the provinces was frequently in venal hands; and besides, the large fees demanded by the **juris consulti** barred the way of the poorer suitors, such as, for the most part, were the Christians to whom this letter was written.

(7) Do not they blaspheme . . . —To "blaspheme" is to hurt with the tongue, and includes all manner of evil speech; but a more exclusive use of the word is with regard to things divine. It was the scorn and contempt visited upon His Name which changed mere abuse into a perilous likeness to the deadliest sin (Matt. 12:31). Most commentators thus restrict the Name here to that of Christ. If their view be correct, the blasphemy would probably be linked with that epithet of "Christian"—then so dishonorable—coined first in Antioch (Acts 11:26). But there were far more insulting terms found for the poor and struggling

believer—"Nazarene," "Atheist," and even worse.

(8) If ye fulfil the royal law.—The "royal" or "kingly law" is God's, in its highest utterance; and it may be taken as an illustration of what a law really consists: a command from a superior, a duty from an inferior, and a sanction or vindication of its authority. The sovereign law of love thus expressed by James is one so plain that the simplest mind may be made its interpreter; and the violation of it is at once clear to the offender.

(10, 11) The point which James urges is that sin, as sin, involves the curse of the law, and that "respect of persons," with its unloving and unlovely results, must bring its deceived possessor into condemnation before God. Just as our Lord referred the sixth and seventh commandments (Matt. 5:21-32) to the first issues of the angry or lustful heart, and by no means confined them as did the rabbinical teachers to the very act, so now in like manner James takes his stand upon the guiltiness of any breach whatever of the Law. Love is its complete fulfillment (Rom. 13:10), but in that startling briefness lies comprehended all the decalogue, with its utmost ramifications; and men of the world would find a rule of the most minute and rigid ceremony easier to be followed than this simple all-embracing one.

(14-26) We now enter on the most debatable ground of the epistle. Many have seen James and Paul at variance here; but the truth is that they regarded the same object with a different motive, and aimed at a dissimilar result—just as in medicine, opposite treatments are required by various sicknesses and in the several stages of disease. The besetting error of the Jewish Christians to whom James appealed was mystical speculation; and, as it wandered by slowly from the furthest East, it had not yet reached the churches of Europe, at least sufficiently to constitute a danger in the mind of Paul. But the divine lesson stands forth: faith must be embodied in acts. And no better tonic for the enervating effect of any perverted doctrine of faith could be found than a consideration of the nobler life of Abraham. What example could be upheld more likely to win back the hearts of his proud descendants? And so with him would James join the lowly Rahab, that he might, as it were, plead well with all men of every degree or kind.

(14) What doth it profit, my brethren,

though a man say he hath faith, and have not works?—Some allusion is made here most probably to the Shema, the Jewish creed, "Hear, O Israel, the Lord our God is one Lord" (Deut. 6:4). It was the daily protest of the devout Israelite in the midst of idolaters, and the words of his morning and evening of life, as well as of the ordinary day.

Can faith save him?—The stern inquiry comes like a prophecy of woe upon the wretched man—saved, as he fancied, by covenant with God, and holding a bare assent and not a loving faith in Him.

(16) Perhaps this was a scene in James' own experience during that famine foretold by Agabus (Acts 11:28-30). There would, however, seem to be a worse interpretation of the words. It is the rebuke of cool prosperity to importunate adversity. No amount of faith could clothe the shivering limbs and still the hunger pangs; what greater mockery than to be taunted with texts and godly precepts, the usual outcome of a spurious and cheap benevolence.

(17) Even so faith, if it hath not works, is dead, being alone.—If to be childless among women were a curse in Israel, so to be barren among God's graces is the condemnation of faith in Christendom. See Paul's substantial harmony with this assertion in Rom. 2:13. There had been no lack of charity under the earlier Jewish teaching; in fact, "righteousness" in many passages of Holy Writ, and in the paraphrases for the unlearned, called the Targums, was explained to be "almsgiving." But the whole system of rabbinism seems gradually to have destroyed the spiritual life of its scholars, and among them now was fast spreading the doctrine of a sterile faith.

(18) Yea, a man may say . . .—The words are those of scorn, uttered probably by some enemy of the faith—Jewish or pagan—and are another instance, like that of the unruly tongue, by which those outside the pale of Christianity may and will judge us within. Verses 18 to 22 are all the speech of this practical observer. The sense is obvious; and whether the speaker be Christian or not, he lays claim to faith in God, the Father of all, as the efficient cause of his good deeds.

(19) The devils also believe, and tremble.—They **shudder** in the belief which only assures them of their utter misery; literally, their hair stands on end with terror of the God they acknowledge. Assent, opinion, knowledge—all are thus shared by demons

of the pit; call not your joint possession by the holier name of faith. "I believe" is said in the full sense only by those who love God, and who are not only Christians in name, but in deed and in life.

(20) But wilt thou know, O vain man, that faith without works is dead?—"vain," i.e., empty and useless. Works are the natural fruit of faith; and without them it is evident the tree is dead, perhaps at the very roots, ready to be cut down and cast into the fire.

(21) Was not Abraham our father justified by works . . . ?—James now addresses his two examples from familiar history in force of his plea for active faith. The first is the marvelous devotion and trust of Abraham (Gen. 22) when he offered Isaac his son upon the altar. Isaac was the type of God's dear Son, who bore, like His meek ancestor, the sacrificial wood up the long weary road of death.

(23) Abraham believed God, and it was imputed unto him for righteousness.—See Gen. 15:6. He proved his faith by obedience when he freely gave back to the Giver his son, the heir of all the promise.

(24) Ye see then how that by works . . .—Observe that James says a man is not justified "by faith **only**," putting the adverb in the last and most emphatic position. He never denies justification by faith, but that fancied one of idle, speculative, theoretic faith, with no corresponding acts of love.

(25) Likewise also . . .—The second example is brought forward in strange and complete contrast to Abraham. Rahab the harlot received and sheltered in her house at Jericho the two spies sent out from the camp of Israel (Josh. 2). The evil name of the poor woman's trade cannot truthfully be softened down to "innkeeper," nor even "idolater."

Clement, Bishop of Rome, one of the Apostolic Fathers, in his first letter to the Corinthians, sees in the scarlet thread which Rahab bound in her window a type of our Redeemer's blood. And it is most remarkable, as showing the mercy of God, that this outcast of society was not only saved alive and brought into the fold of Israel, but became a direct ancestress of her Saviour, by marriage with Salmon, the great-great-grandfather of David (Matt. 1:5).

(26) As the body without the spirit . . .—Some take works to be like the body and faith its animation. But James' view seems to be that faith is the body, the sum and substance of the Christian life, and works (obedience) the moving and quickening of that body, just as the spirit is the moving and quickening principle of the natural body (Alford).

3

(1) Be not many masters.—The condemnation is of those who appoint themselves, and are as "blind leaders of the blind" (Matt. 15:14). No man had a right to exercise the sacred functions of the appointed teachers ("masters") in Israel, and none might take the honor of the priesthood unto himself, "but he that was called of God, as was Aaron" (Heb. 5:4). We know from our Lord's own words that the Scribes and Pharisees loved respectful "greetings in the markets, and to be called of men 'Rabbi, Rabbi' " (Matt. 23:1-12). Nevertheless His disciples were not to be acknowledged thus: for "one is your Master, even Christ; and all ye are brethren." The neglect of this wholesome caution perplexed the early Church.

The greater condemnation.—Rather, **the greater judgment**—more strictly searching and severe. If this be true of common Christian life, how deep is the responsibility incurred in the attempt to teach others! The test of all ministry must come at last in the day of trial and fiery inquisition of God; this and not the world's opinion will be the real approval (I Cor. 3:11-15).

(2) If any man offend not in word, the same is a perfect man.—To "offend" means to stumble over something and fall, and in this sense we get the exact meaning of "offending" by an unguarded allusion to a subject painful in the mind of another. (See Ps. 39:1.) Because the work of ruling the one rebel (the tongue) is so great, a much less corresponding effort will keep the others in subjection.

(3) Behold.—Three comparisons of the tongue are now introduced: the bit (verse 3), the rudder (verse 4), and a fire (verse 6). The two former show what mastery may be gained by self-discipline, while the latter warns us of a danger which may quickly spread beyond our power to quell.

(4) The governor—i.e., the "helmsman," from the Latin **gubernator**. James, remembering the storms of the Galilean lake, could well rejoice in a simile like this.

(5) Even so ... —**Thus**, like the tiny rudder of the mighty ship, whereon its course most critically depends ... The verb

translated **boasteth** is peculiar to this place, but occurs so often in the works of Philo that we may be almost certain James had read them. And many other verses of our epistle suggest his knowledge of this famous Alexandrian Jew.

Behold, how great a matter a little fire kindleth!—It would be more in the spirit and temper of this imaginative passage to render it, "Behold, how great a **forest** a little spark kindleth!" Thus it is expressed in the Latin Vulgate, and this in illustration of the far-reaching mischief resulting from a single cause.

(6) And the tongue is a fire.—"The course of nature" is literally the "wheel," the "orb of creation." The Jewish word for the place of torment, the accursed side of Hades, should be thus preserved; it was from there that the rich man of the parable prayed for water to cool his tongue (Luke 16:24). Three temptations "to smite with the tongue" are especially powerful of evil: as a relief from passion, as a gratification of spite, as revenge for wrong. (See Hos. 14:2; Eph. 5:4; I Pet. 2:23.)

(8) James does not mean that no one can tame his own tongue, for so he would hardly be responsible for its vagaries; and later it is written expressly, "these things ought not so to be." The hopeless savagery of the tongue, excelling the fury of wild beasts, must be that of the liar and the blasphemer. (Comp. Ps. 140.)

(9) Therewith bless we God, even the Father.—The more ancient manuscripts make it, **Therewith bless we the Lord and Father.** It may serve to remind us of the oneness of our God, that thus He may be termed Lord and Saviour. His worship and praise are (verse 6) the right use of the tongue, but, most inconsistently, **therewith curse we man.** The "likeness of God" assuredly remains in the most abandoned and fallen, and to curse it is to invoke the wrath of its Creator.

(11) This is a vivid picture, probably of the mineral springs abounding in the Jordan valley, near the Dead Sea, with which might be contrasted the clear and sparkling rivulets of the north, fed by the snows of Lebanon. Nature had no confusion in her plans, and thus to pour out curse and blessing from the same lips were unnatural indeed.

(13) Let him shew out of a good conversation—i.e., **right conduct.** "Conversation" has slipped from its original meaning, which exactly represented the Greek, and is often misapprehended by the English reader. Literally, "turning oneself about," it changed to "walking to and fro," and the talking while engaged in these peripatetics, and then to its limited present use. There is to be general **good conduct**, and particular proofs of it in noble acts of a holy habit.

(14) But if ye have bitter envying and strife in your hearts.—Rather, **bitter zeal and party-spirit**. That against which James inveighed had caused Jerusalem to run with blood, and afterward helped in her last hour to add horror upon shame. The Zealots were really assassins, pledged to any iniquity (see Acts 23:12). Some of these desperadoes escaped the swords of the Romans, and fled to the fastnesses of Mount Lebanon. They were probably the nucleus of a still more infamous society, known in the middle ages as that of the Old Man of the Mountain. In fact, our word "assassin" comes from "Hassan," their first sheik. They were at length exterminated by the Turks.

(17) But the wisdom that is from above ... —In contrast to all this repulsive foulness and riot, true wisdom is chaste, easy to be won, not double-minded. Comp. with this beautiful description Paul's list of the fruit of the Spirit (Gal. 5:22) and his discourse on love (I Cor. 13).

4

(1) From whence come wars ...?— Perfect peace, capable in some ways of beginning here below (3:17, 18), has by inevitable reaction led James to speak suddenly, almost fiercely, of the existing state of things. He traces the conflict raging around him to the fount and origin of evil within. (Comp. Rom. 7:23; I Pet. 2:11.)

(2, 3) It is interesting to notice the sharp, crisp sentences, recollecting at the same time that James himself fell a victim to the passions he thus assails, probably at the hands of a zealot mob. Is it objected that prayer is made but not answered? The reply: **Ye ask not** in the true sense; when ye do ask ye receive not, because God is too loving, even in His anger. What greater curse could fall than an eternity of avarice to the miser, of pollution to the sensual, or murder to the violent? Many a man of quiet Christian life will thank God finally that not a few of his prayers were unanswered, or at least that they were not granted in the way which he had desired. Safety is only to be found in our Lord's own manner of petition (Luke 22:42).

(4) Ye adulterers and adulteresses.—It should be, **ye adulteresses!** as accusing those who have broken their marriage vow to God. The sense is familiar from many passages in the Old Testament in which God speaks of Israel in a similar manner. (Comp. II Cor. 11:2.)

Know ye not that the friendship of the world is enmity with God?—i.e., the state of being an enemy to God, not one of simpler enmity with Him. There cannot be a passive condition to the faith of Christ (Matt. 12:30). Renunciation of the world, in the Christian promise, is not forsaking it when tired with its delights, but the earliest severance from it; to break this vow, or not to have made it, is to belong to the foes of God, and not merely to be out of covenant with Him. The forces of good and evil divide the land so sharply that there is no debatable ground.

(6) But he giveth more grace—i.e., because of this very presence of the Holy Ghost within us. He, as the author and conveyer of all good gifts, aids the weakest in his strife with sin, resisting the proud, lest he be led to destruction (Prov. 16:18); and helping the humble, lest he be "wearied and faint in his mind" (Heb. 12:3).

God resisteth the proud ... —Comp. Prov. 3:34, LXX. It is again brought forward by Peter (I Pet. 5:5), and seems to have been a common saying—a maxim of the wise that had become, as it were, a law of life.

(7) The hardest advice of all, to a man reliant on himself, is submission to any, more especially to the Unknown. But, as a correlative to this, James shows where pride may become a stimulant for good in contest with the Evil One. "The Devil," says **The Shepherd of Hermas**, "can fight, but he cannot conquer; if, therefore, thou dost withstand him, he will flee from thee, beaten and ashamed." The text is another proof of the personality of Satan; no amount of figures of speech could otherwise interpret it.

(8-10) Wretchedness, sorrow, and tears are the three steps of the homeward way to peace and God. And in proof of real conversion there must be the outward lamentation, as well as the inward contrition. (See II Cor. 7:10.)

(11) Speak not evil ... —See Matt. 7:1; Rom. 1:30. James reproves the setting up of our own tribunals, in which we are at once prosecutor, witness, law, law-giver, and judge, not to say executioner as well. **Praejudicium** was a merciful provision under Roman law, and often spared the innocent a lengthier after-trial; but **prejudice**—our word taken from it—is its most unfortunate opposite.

(12) There is one lawgiver ... —The ultimate source of law is God, and all judgment really is delegated by Him. To usurp such functions is to provoke the offended sovereign. "It is not our part," said Bengel, "to judge, since we cannot carry out our sentence." (Comp. Rom. 14:4.)

(13) Ye that say ... —The apostle would reason next with the worldly—not merely those abandoned to pleasure, but any and all absorbed in the quest of gain or advancement.

(14) For what is your life? It is even a vapour.—The rebuke is sharp and piercing—**Ye are even a vapour:** ye yourselves and all belonging to you, not merely life itself, for that confessedly is a breath. And many a man, acknowledging so much, counts of the morrow that he may lay up in store for other wants besides his own.

(16) How different is the case with you, cries James. Instead of reposing in the sovereign will of God (verse 15), you actually glory and delight in your own self-confidence and presumption, and every such rejoicing is evil. The word for "boastings" is the same as that translated "the pride of life" in I John 2:16—i.e., braggart boastfulness, not the innocent gladness of living. It is the trust of the "ungodly" (Ps. 10:6) and the mistaken confidence of even godly men (Job 29:18) before the Almighty instructs them by trouble, loss, and pain.

(17) The converse to the evil of vainglory in life is the good which may be wrought by every one. Occasions of well-doing lie at our doors, and the pleadings of pity in our very hearts. And thus it is that omission is at times worse than commission; and more souls are in jeopardy for things left undone than for things done.

5

(1) Go to now, ye rich.—"Go to" is a picture word imitating the cry of anguish, and peculiar to this place in the New Testament. Doubtless by this was meant primarily the pillage and destruction of Jerusalem, but under that first intention many others secondary and similar are included. (See

Prov. 23:5). In the sense that all prophecy, whether evil or good, is conditional, there is sufficient room to believe that no irrevocable doom was pronounced by "a Christian Jeremiah."

(3) Your gold and silver ... —The precious metals themselves do not corrode, but the base alloy which has been mixed with them for worldly use and device. The rust shall be a witness against them in the day of judgment, and a sign of the fire which shall consume them.

Ye have heaped ... —Some expositors have seen in this verse an instance of James' belief that he was living in the last days of the world's history, and compared his "delusion" with that of Paul and John (I Thess. 4:15; I John 2:18). But there was no mistake on the part of the inspired writers; freedom from error in their sacred office must be vindicated, or who shall sever the false gospel from the true? The simple explanation is the **potential** nearness of Christ. (See II Pet. 3:18.)

(4) Behold, the hire of the labourers.—The indignant remonstrance of the text is "a swift witness" against those whose God is self, whose religion political economy, and whose one great object in life is to buy in the cheapest market and sell in the dearest. These actions of niggardly masters were contrary to Lev. 19:13; Jer. 22:13; Mal. 3:5.

The Lord of sabaoth.—A sublime and awful picture is in the mind of James. **The Lord of Hosts,** the name by which He is called, especially by the last of the prophets, is seated as a judge on His throne to hear the right. The charge is laid, the guilty called, the witnesses heard. Bede reflects that James thus speaks of the Lord of Sabaoth, or **armies,** to terrify those who suppose that the poor have no helpers. (Comp. Pss. 9:12; 72:12.) Thus a Hebrew is writing to Hebrews respecting their particular sin of covetousness.

(5, 6) As they had dealt to others, so the vengeance of God dealt with them. The Passover called together the richest Jews from all parts of the earth, and they themselves were the victims in their last sacrifice. No words can overdraw the fury of the Roman onset under Titus, when the Temple floors ran with blood, and the roofs raged in fire till all was utter desolation.

(7) Be patient.—If there be wrath laid up in store for the oppressor, great is the coming peace of the oppressed. Through several verses (7-11) James repeats his advice, emphasizing it with various reasons:

the nearness of deliverance; the Judge standing at the gate; the example of the prophets; the hope of those who endure; the faithfulness and tender mercy of the Lord bringing all things to a perfect end. The King is patient, and has greater need of patience than His subjects. He is patient, because He is strong. Impatience is a sign of weakness. God can afford to wait. We can be strong in His strength, and wait also in patience. Insofar as James' hearers were earthly minded, they could not learn this lesson.

The early and latter rain.—There were only two seasons of rainfall in the Holy Land, and, if long delayed, famine was a certain result. With the change of the Israelites from pastoral life to agricultural, the malignity of these dearths was lessened; but they were still severe. The "early rain" fell during the autumn sowing—in October, November, and December; "the latter" in March and April.

(8) The coming of the Lord draweth nigh.—See note on verse 3.

(9) Grudge not.—Read in preference, **Murmur not**. "Grudge" has curiously changed its meaning from an outward murmur to an inward feeling. (See I Pet. 4:9; Ps. 59:15.)

Lest ye . . . —Rather, **lest ye be judged**, repeating the exact words of the original in Matt. 7:1.

Behold, the judge standeth before the door.—Comp. Rev. 3:20. One of the mocking questions put to James by his enemies as they hurried him to death was, "Which is the **door** of Jesus?" And failing to receive an answer to their mind, they said, "Let us stone this James the Just!" That they did, after they had cast him over the Temple wall.

(12) Let your yea be yea . . . —Your word be as your bond, needing no strengthening by any invocation of God or holy things, "lest ye fall into **judgment**"—not "condemnation," though certainly such might follow.

(14) The elders of the church—i.e., literally, **the presbyters**. The identity of "bishop" and "presbyter" in the language of the apostolic age seems conclusive. (See note on I Tim. 3:1.) In fact, organization of the early Church was much more elastic than many have supposed.

(14, 15) Anointing him with oil.—Or, **unction**—some precious and mysterious ointment obtained in most of the ancient nations, especially the Eastern. The Jews

themselves were by no means originators of the habit, although they carried it to its highest ceremony and significance. Apart, too, from the regular performances of the rite, as upon the accession of a king or the consecration of a high priest, it often occurred in private cases. Some striking instances are recorded in the gospels: Luke 7:36-50; John 12:3-9. These were not unusual acts, but chiefly worthy of note because of the persons concerned. Nor, again, was it a new ordinance with which the apostles were first commissioned (Mark 6:13). This use of a known form with a diviner import was the cause of astonishment; and clearly it was to such a practice, with simply its common intention, that James refers. "The prayer of faith shall save the sick"—i.e., shall **heal** him; the faithful prayer shall be that which God will answer, and so "raise up" the sufferer. And even if that affliction were occasioned by some sin, that sin shall be forgiven him. Such is the simple and undeniable sense of James, arguing for the efficacy of prayer.

(16) Confess your faults one to another.— Here we have a **general injunction** arising out of a circumstance necessarily to be inferred in the preceding example (verses 14, 15). There, the sin would of necessity have been confessed to the elders, before the prayer of faith could deal with it. And seeing the blessed consequences in that case, James urges the wider pursuit of the same salutary practice of confessing sins.

There can be little doubt that, strictly consonant with the apostolic charge, open confession was the custom of old. Offenders hastened to some minister of God, and in words, by which all present in the congregation might take notice of the fault, declared their guilt; convenient remedies were as publicly prescribed, and then all present joined in prayer to God. But after awhile this plain talk about sins was rightly judged to be a cause of mischief to the young and innocent, and such confessions were relegated to a private hearing. The change was in most ways beneficial, and hardly suspected of being a step in a completely new doctrine. It needed centuries to develop into the hard system of compulsory individual bondage that it became. The meaning attributed to the words of this verse by many devout Catholics cannot be established either from the opinion of antiquity or a critical examination of the Greek text.

The effectual fervent prayer . . . —Better, **The prayer of a righteous man availeth**

much in its working. The prayer of the just, pleading, striving fervently, has power with God, even like Israel of old, and shall prevail (Gen. 32:28). Some divines trace a literal force in the passage, finding in it an allusion to the Energumens of the first century (the "mediums" of that age), who were possessed by demons. Just as these beings strove in their bondage, so infinitely more should Christians "wrestle with the Lord."

(17) Elias.—James supplies a gap in the story of Elijah. (See I Kings 17.) The prophet "prayed earnestly"—literally, **prayed in his prayer**, a Hebraistic form of emphasis. He was no demi-god; we even learn how he shrank from his prophet's yoke, and longed to die. No one, therefore, may despair in his petitions, but rather let his "requests be made known unto God."

It rained not on the earth.—This Orientalism need not be a snare to the most literal of readers. The punishment, because of Ahab and Jezebel, fell on their own kingdom and not the whole world. For a similar hyperbole, see I Kings 18:10.

(19) If any of you do err... —It is not the willful error so much as the being seduced by others, who draw the unwary from their proper course. As the leading away was an act prompted by the devil, so the bringing home is the service of God, and each will have its fit reward. The sinner is galloping, as it were, headlong to destruction, when a friend lays hold upon the rein, and literally "converts" him, i.e., turns him around.

(20) Let him know.—Rather, **Know ye** be absolutely sure of this, in a knowledge better than all the gnostic and agnostic learning of the day. The sins hidden are not, of course, his own, but those of the penitent, brought back by this good servant into the fold. So is it possible to be a fellow-worker with Christ (II Cor. 6:1) and a sharer in His work of salvation, as, in another sense, we too vicariously suffer for the sins and faults of others.

FIRST PETER

1

(1) Peter, an apostle.—The authoritative tone of this epistle is shown at the outset. The writer assumes his full titles, not (as in the Second Epistle) his merely human name of Simon, nor his humble capacity of "servant," but the Rock-name which Christ had given him, and the official dignity of an "Apostle of Jesus Christ"—i.e., one charged with full legatine authority from Christ (John 17:18; 20:21). While Paul constantly adds "by the will of God," or some similar phrase, by way of justifying his assumption of the title, Peter has no need to do more than mention it; his claim was never questioned. And yet, with all this quiet assumption of dignity, Peter knows no higher title to bestow on himself than that which he held in common with the other eleven—"an apostle," not "the apostle," nor "bishop of bishops."

To the strangers scattered throughout... —Literally, "to the elect, sojourners of the dispersion of Pontus." The persons for whom the letter is destined are clearly specified. They are those of the dispersed Jews who live in Pontus. In Jas. 1:1 the same word—"dispersed" ("scattered")—is used, and, in fact, it seems to have been the recognized name for all Jews who did not live in Palestine. The word rendered by "sojourners" means people who are resident for a time among strangers. The addition of the words "the blood of Jesus Christ" is the only thing which shows that they are Christian Jews.

Pontus, Galatia... —The provinces which between them make up the whole, or nearly so, of what we call Asia Minor, are named in no order that can be assigned a meaning, or that indicates the quarter from which the letter was written. Possibly the circumstances which had called for the writing of the epistle may have been most striking in Pontus. The churches of Galatia and Asia owed their origin to Paul. Of the founding of the rest we know nothing; but Jewish settlers from Cappadocia and Pontus had heard Peter's first sermon after Pentecost (Acts 2:9). A few years later Pliny found the whole upper shore of Asia Minor overrun by Christians.

(2) Elect.—A true chosen people. This word marks them off from the rest of the Jewish settlers in those parts. God selected these particular Hebrews out of the whole number, and made them Christians; but what He elected them to is abundantly shown in the next words. For all their election they are not certain of salvation, and their title of "elect" implies no more than the fact that God has put them into the visible church.

According to the foreknowledge of God... —The origin of this election, the aim, and the means employed are now touched upon, and connected with the three divine Persons respectively. Their election is not accidental, nor yet an afterthought of God, but in execution of His forearranged scheme. The word implies not simply a perception of the future, but the forming of a decision. The preconcerted scheme of God embraced not only the choice of these particular persons for a blessing, but the lines on which the choice was to work itself out—in a course of sanctification by the Spirit. That to which God had elected them was not in the first instance the participation of the joys of the post-resurrection life, but the benefits of redemption on this side of the grave.

Sprinkling of the blood.—This seems to mean "selected for admission into the new covenant inaugurated by the sprinkling of Christ's blood." Whereas the old covenant was inaugurated by sprinkling the people collectively and once for all, the new is inaugurated by individual application and repeatedly. Doubtless the participation of the Holy Communion is the act of "sprinkling" here before Peter's mind, it being the one act which betokens membership in the new covenant-people, the new Israel. Of course the application of blood in both covenants rests on the notion of a death-forfeit being remitted. There is nothing in Paul's writings to compare with it.

Of Jesus Christ.—He does not say "of the new Testament," but substitutes the name of the Victim in whose blood the covenant is inaugurated—Jesus—as though Israel at Sinai had been sprinkled with the blood of Moses.

Be multiplied.—Comp. II Pet. 1:2; Jude 2. It contains an exhortation to progress. There are some good things of which we cannot have too much.

(3) Here begins the apostle's thanks to God for the resurrection of Jesus Christ. That fact assumes our regeneration and a pledge of future glory, in view of which such afflictions as beset the Asiatic Hebrews were seen to serve a purpose—the very salvation which had formed the theme of the Old Testament.

Hath begotten us again, the historical moment being here given as that of the resurrection of Christ. This great word, which is Peter's own, seems to indicate that it makes a complete change not only in the condition and prospects of the man, but in the man himself. (See John 3:3; II Cor. 5:17; Tit. 3:5; Jas. 1:18.) It is no metaphor when the change from the natural man to a man united with the incarnate God is described as an act of creation, for, according to Peter's teaching, we are thus actually made "partakers of the divine nature" (II Pet. 1:4).

By the resurrection of Jesus Christ.—We must not confine the meaning of the words to the effects of a conscious realization. Peter is viewing the transaction theologically, i.e., from God's point of view, not phenomenally, from man's. To God, with whom, according to Peter, time does not exist (II Pet. 3:8), there is no interval between His begetting of Christ again from the dead (Acts 13:33; Rev. 1:5), and His begetting of us again by it.

(4) To an inheritance.—This is structurally parallel to, and explanatory of, the clause "into a living hope." We are born to an estate. This notion of an inheritance is particularly Hebrew, occurring frequently in the Old Testament. The Pontine dispersion had lost their inheritance in Palestine, but there is a better in store for them. The three following epithets are exuberant descriptions of the excellencies of the new "Canaan."

(5) Kept ... through faith.—The apostle is fearful lest the last words should give a false assurance. God can guard none of us unless there is a corresponding exertion on our part—which is here called "faith"—combining the notions of staunch fidelity and of trustfulness in spite of appearances.

Unto salvation.—The thought of the perdition of the lost does not enter at all into the passage. Salvation here is primarily a deliverance from all the trials and persecutions, struggles and temptations of this life, an emergence into the state of peace and rest.

Ready to be revealed in the last time.—The tense of the word "revealed" implies the suddenness of the unveiling. It will be but the work of an instant to put aside the curtain and show the inheritance which has been kept hidden so long behind it. This, however, will not take place till the **exact** period (so the word for "time" suggests); and that period will be the last of the world's history.

(7) That the trial of your faith.—This is the purpose of God's providence in sending the griefs. The word "trial" here does not mean the same as in the passage of James. In that passage it signifies the active testing of faith; here it has rather the meaning of the cognate word translated "assurance" in Acts 17:31; "proof" in II Cor. 2:9, Phil. 2:22, i.e., the attested worth, the genuine character. You cannot compare an act or process with gold, but you can compare the genuine character brought out by the process of refinement properly enough. "Praise" is the language that will be used about these men's faith; "honor," the rank in which they will be placed; "glory," the fervent admiration accorded to them. The three words correspond to the regions of word, act, and feeling.

At the appearing of Jesus Christ.—"Revelation" would have been better, as the word in the Greek is the same as in verse 5. This gives the date at which the trial will have done its work; it is the same as the "last time" when the "deliverance" will be revealed.

(8) Whom, having not seen.—This is said in contrast to the word "revelation" in the last verse. There seems to be a kind of tender pity in the words, as spoken by one who himself had seen so abundantly (Acts 4:20; 10:41; II Pet. 1:16). In this and the following verse we return again from the sorrow to the joy, and to the true cause of that joy, which is only to be found in the love of Jesus Christ.

Ye love.—The word of calm and divinely-given attachment, in fact the usual word in the New Testament, that which Christ used in questioning the writer (John 20:15), not the word of warm human friendship with which Peter then answered Him.

In whom.—Peter, whose own faith gained him his name and prerogative, is as much the apostle of faith as Paul is, though his conception of it, perhaps, slightly differs from Paul's. Our present verse gives the leading thought of "faith" as being the opposite of sight, rather than as the opposite of works. (Comp. Heb. 11:1.) The main object of both Hebrews and I Peter is to keep the Hebrews from slipping back from internal to external religion, i.e., to strengthen faith. The apostle is full of admiration for a faith which, unlike his own, was not based on sight. (See John 20:29—an incident which may have been in the writer's mind.)

(9) Receiving the end of your faith.—The accent of the sentence falls on "end," not on "faith," and the whole clause is added to justify the statement that we rejoice with a joy which has already attained its full perfection (verse 8). The reason is that we receive already, in the present life, the object of all this trusting without sight; we need not wait until the next world to attain our glorification.

The salvation of your souls.—Our Lord fully recognizes the instinct of the higher self-preservation as that to which the ultimate appeal must be made (Matt. 16:25, 26). We are bound to make that our first object, if it were only to gratify Him who has no pleasure in the death of him who dies, even if we could possibly divest ourselves of all "selfish" interest in the matter. "Salvation" here seems to have widened its meaning since verse 5; while there the main thought was final deliverance from the afflictions of life, here the salvation is said to be received in the midst of all these afflictions. Salvation, then, is the restoration of man to the ideal excellence from which he was fallen. It contains here no allusion to damnation as an opposite.

(10) Have inquired and searched diligently.—Calvin rightly says: "When he states that the prophets inquired and examined, this refers not to their writings or teaching, but to the private longing with which each was fired." In fact, Peter goes on to say that the writings which the Holy Spirit impelled them to make were actually the text on which their longings were the comment: they endeavored to understand what they themselves had written. The two Greek words give a lively picture of the intense eagerness of the search, and of the depth to which it penetrated.

Who prophesied of the grace.—This is a description of the prophetic Scriptures. The whole subject of the Old Testament is the bounty of God under the New; and this was what the prophets tried to realize.

(11) Searching.—This particularizes the object of the inquiry. They knew that they spoke concerning a salvation, but they did not know the details. The present passage is perhaps the most striking in the whole New Testament in regard to the doctrine of prophetic inspiration. Assuming that the prophets did not speak simply of their own human calculation, but somehow under the influence of the divine Spirit, we are brought to face the question, how far their utterances were their own, and how far suggested to them from on high. It would seem that the prophets find themselves impelled to say words which they are conscious of choosing and using, but which they feel to have a deeper meaning than they themselves were conscious of intending. It is clear to them (verse 12) that what they meant primarily as applying to present circumstances was in reality being overruled by the Spirit to apply more fully to the future.

What, or what manner of time.—The simplest translation would be, "to whom, or what period, the Spirit of Christ in them was pointing." This would give new significance to the sentence. They were aware that they were speaking of a Messiah; but who the man should be who would hold that office, or at what period of their history he would arise, this was what they longed to know. They foresaw a Christ, but they could not foresee Jesus; they could give to their Christ no definite position in future history.

The Spirit of Christ which was in them.—Observe that a change has come over Peter's way of speaking. Heretofore he has always said "Jesus Christ," his object being to keep constantly before the eyes of these Hebrews the truth which he was the first man to enunciate, "Thou art the Christ" (Matt. 16:16), that Jesus was the person who fulfilled all that was expected of the Messiah. "Christ" is not once used by Peter (as it is often by Paul) as a proper name; it always marks the office, not the person. Neither the pre-existence of our Lord, nor the procession of the Holy Spirit from Him as well as from the Father, is expressed here. "The Spirit of Messiah" when applied to the ages before Christ came, means "the Messianic spirit." The prophets wondered to whom this Messianic inspiration which they felt within was pointing. Peter himself, again, was the first person who fully knew the answer.

The sufferings of Christ.—Beware of treating the title "Christ" as a proper name. Eight out of the ten times that Peter uses the word by itself it is in direct connection with suffering (here, and in 1:19; 2:21; 3:18; 4:1, 13, 14; 5:1). Conversely, he never speaks of the sufferings of **Jesus** Christ. That is to say, he dwells on the Passion of our Lord, not in its **personal** but in its **official** aspect. The striking point is that the Messiah should have suffered in this way. It

1161

was especially necessary to show this in any effort to retain the faith of the Hebrews. And we can see a reason of the insistence in Peter's history. The whole epistle may be said to be an expansion of what Jesus said in Matt. 16:23-27.

And the glory that should follow.— Literally, the plural "glories" corresponds to the plural "sufferings," the one as multiform as the other; reference is to resurrection, ascension, reassumption of the divine glory, triumphs of church history, restitution of all things.

(12) Unto us.—Better, "unto you." It is a distinct characteristic of this epistle that "we," "us," "our," are so seldom used (in the best text) where they might have been expected. Where Paul injects his own sympathy, and puts himself on a footing with those whom he addresses, Peter utters his lofty pastoral from above.

By them that have preached.—Peter is referring to the first bearers of the Gospel to those parts, not to all who from that time to the date of the letter had preached. This is a point well worth noticing. The phrase seems to show that Peter himself was not of the number. Perhaps half the churches which received the letter looked to Paul as their founder. (See note on verse 1.) Here, then, we find the Rock-Apostle authoritatively setting his seal to the teaching of his junior colleague, just as he does in the Second Epistle (3:15). It seems to imply that these Jewish Christians were beginning to feel a reaction (comp. Rev. 2:9; 3:9) from Paul's evangelical teaching, and that Peter is called in to enforce what Paul had taught. Peter's perfect concurrence with Paul here is a sufficient contradiction to the theory of their irreconcilable divergence.

With the Holy Ghost sent down from heaven.—Undoubtedly some of the recipients of the letter (see note on verse 1) were eyewitnesses of His being "sent" to Peter and the rest on the Day of Pentecost. Peter, then, here claims for Paul the same inspiration with which he was furnished. And as here he claims full inspiration for Paul's **preaching,** so he does afterward for his **writing** (II Pet. 3:15).

Which things the angels.—The "which things" here is grammatically parallel to the "which things" of the last sentence, and therefore would mean "the sufferings of Messiah and the glories after." But logically we have to go back to the beginning of verse 10. The word "to look into" means really "to bend aside to see." It seems to mean a strained attention to something which has caught your eye somewhat out of your usual line of sight. Here then, the intention is to show that we are in a better position to understand the mysteries of redemption, not only than prophets, but also than angels; and they covet to stoop from their own point of view to ours. And why so? Because they are incapable of fully understanding human nature, flesh and blood, with its temptations and pains, its need of a Savior.

(13) Gird up the loins of your mind.—A metaphor from persons gathering up the flowing Oriental dress (which had been let down for repose), so as to be ready for energetic action. A "mind," rather than "soul" or "heart," seems to bespeak practical intelligence.

(14) The former lusts in your ignorance.—"Ignorance" is surely not an unnatural word to represent the contrast between the state of unregenerate Jews and the same persons when they have attained to knowledge higher than that of prophets or of angels. Even Jews were men of flesh and blood, and therefore not exempt from the temptations of the flesh, from which mere legalism was quite insufficient to protect them.

(15) So be ye holy.—Perhaps the imperative would come out stronger thus, "Do ye also show yourselves holy in every part of your conduct." Leighton says, "He hath severed you from the mass of the profane world . . . for this end, that you may be holy to Him, as the Hebrew word that signifies 'holiness' imports 'setting apart,' or fitting for a peculiar use; be not then untrue to His design."

(16) Be ye holy; for I am holy.—The better reading here is, "Ye shall be holy"; it is still, however, a command, not a promise—except that all God's commands are promises.

(17) Who without respect of persons judgeth.—"Judgeth" has a forensic sense of lodging an appeal. Every time we lodge our appeal to the Father on the ground of His Fatherhood, He decides the case, but decides it without favor. He makes no allowance to our wrongdoing on the ground of being His regenerate children, and certainly none on the ground of being of the Hebrew race.

(18) Redeemed . . . from your vain conversation.—"Redeem" means to ransom a person out of slavery or captivity. The leading notion here is not that of paying an equivalent, but to call closer attention to the tate in which the readers were before. Vhat then was that condition? "Conversaion" or "manner of life" is far too wide a vord to be limited, and at the same time 'tradition" implies something purposely ianded down from father to son as an neirloom, so that it could not be applied to he careless, sensual life of Gentiles, learned by example only. Among the Jews, on the other hand, "tradition" entered into the ninutest details of daily life or "conversaion." (See Mark 7:3, 4—the Petrine Gospel.) Judaism itself, then, in the form it had hen assumed, was one of the foes and oppressors (see Acts 15:10) from which Christ came to "ransom" and "save" His oeople.

(19) With the precious blood of Christ.— "Precious" means "costly," opposed to perishableness of gold and silver. Notice hat it is not "Jesus," but "Christ," i.e., the Messiah. No price short of the "blood," i.e., the death of the Messiah could free the Jews from the thraldom of their "vain conversation." The following verses show that again Peter is thinking more of the theological than of the phenomenal side of the occurrence. (See note on verse 3.)

As of a lamb without blemish and without spot.— In Peter's mind the notion of a "sacrifice," in reference to the atonement, was only a simile, or metaphor, just as it was with the notion of "ransom." Once more observe that the sacrifice was offered to effect a redemption which for the readers had already taken place. (Comp. Heb. 9:14.) The primary thought in mentioning a "lamb" is, of course, that of sacrifice.

(20) Who verily was foreordained.— God knew from all eternity who was to be His Messiah and His Lamb, but for their sakes the particular and personal declaration of Him was reserved until now. For them has been kept the revelation of a secret which underlay the whole Old Testament system. The grammatical antecedent of the relative "who verily" is not "lamb," but "Christ"; and the word for "foreordained" is, literally, "foreknown," only with the additional notion of coming to a decision. (See note on verse 2.) Peter's doctrine has not changed since the great day of Pentecost (Acts 2:23). The foreknowledge includes not only the knowledge and decision that Jesus should be the Christ, but that the Christ's history should be what it was; and this seems to involve not only the doctrine that the Incarnation was no mere episode, consequent on the Fall of man, but also, the doctrine that,

"before the foundation of the world," God had foreknown, and predecided to allow, the Fall itself.

Was manifest—i.e., unambiguously shown, pointed out. The context shows that it does not simply mean the visible life of the Incarnate Word among men, but that the Messiah and Lamb of God was pointed out as being identical with the Man Jesus. (Comp. John 1:29.)

(22) Truth has a claim not only to be accepted intellectually, as truth, but to alter moral conduct in accordance (comp. John 17:17). That doctrine lies at the bottom of the Socratic maxim, "Virtue is knowledge." But the Socratic maxim does not sufficiently take into account the inertness of the will to act on principle. The first effect of such knowledge of the truth, under the Spirit's influence (although reference to the Spirit does not occur in the original), is to "purify" the soul of selfish aims and to give it that altruism, or desire for the benefit of the community rather than self, which is here described as "love of the brethren."

Unfeigned love of the brethren.— The epithet "unfeigned" would suggest that Peter was uneasy about the depth of their brotherly kindness. Is it not possible that some coolness had arisen between the Jewish and Gentile members of the church, and that Peter finds it necessary to remind the former that they are truly brethren?

(23) This is the argument: "You must learn not to be selfish, or arrogant, as being of the chosen race, but to have a true brotherly feeling and earnest love for the Gentile converts, and for those who, like Paul, are especially working for the Gentiles, because your inheritance of the promised 'salvation' is grounded, not on your Abrahamic descent, but on your spiritual regeneration, in which matter the Gentile converts are your equals." (See Acts 15:9, 11.)

The "seed" of all existence is the spoken Word of God, the expressed will and meaning of creative thought (Ps. 33:6); and so here, even when spoken mediately, it is that which begets men afresh. The "Word of God" here is, no doubt, the preaching of the Gospel, but especially, as it would seem, the preaching of the Resurrection (verse 3), or of the sufferings and glories of Messiah (verse 12), the "truth" of the last verse.

(24) For all flesh is as grass.— The citation is from Isa. 40:6-8, and varies between the Hebrew and the LXX in the kind of way which shows that the writer was familiar with both. But the passage is by no means quoted only to support the assertion that the Word of the Lord abides for ever. It is always impossible to grasp the meaning of an Old Testament quotation in the mouth of a Hebrew without taking into account the context of the original. Nothing is more common than to omit purposely the words which contain the whole point of the quotation. These sentences in Isaiah stand in the forefront of the herald's proclamation of the return of God to Zion, always interpreted of the establishment of the Messianic kingdom. This proclamation of the Messianic kingdom comprises words which Peter has purposely omitted, and they contain the point of the quotation. His Hebrew readers would at once understand the Hebrew method and see that he was calling attention to the absolute equality of Jew and Gentile proclaimed there. Generation of the corruptible seed, physical descent from Abraham, was "the glory of the flesh." On this "the Spirit of the Lord" had breathed (Ps. 104:30); and the merely fleshly glory had withered like grass. But "the word of our God," which Peter purposely changes into "the Word of the Lord," i.e., "of Jesus Christ," incidentally showing his Hebrew readers that he believed Jesus Christ to be "our God"—this "abideth for ever." The engendering by this is imperishable.

2

(1) Wherefore.—That is, because the Pauline teaching is correct which brings the Gentiles up to the same level with the Jews. Notice that this newly enunciated principle is called by Peter in the previous verse of the last chapter, a "gospel," or piece of good news, for all parties.

Laying aside.—This implies that before they had been wrapped up in these sins. There had been "malice" (i.e., ill will put into action) on the part of these Hebrew Christians against their Gentile brethren, and "guile," and "hypocrisies," and "jealousies," which are all instances of concealed malice. Of these three, the first plots, the second pretends not to plot, and the third rejoices to think of the plot succeeding. The word for "all evil speakings" is literally, "all talkings down"—this is "malice" in word. All these vices (natural vices to the Jewish mind) are contrasted with the "unfeigned (literally, 'un-hypocritical') brotherly kindness" of 1:22.

(2) As newborn babes.—The birth meant is the new birth of 1:23. They are said to be newborn because they are still so far from maturity in Christ, as these sins testified.

Desire the sincere milk.—The word for "desire" here is a strong word—"get an appetite for it." Peter here again seems to lend a thought to the writer to the Hebrews (Heb. 5:12-14). In both places Jewish Christians are beginning to rebel against the gospel instructions, and in both places they are warned that they have not yet outgrown the need of the simplest elements of the Gospel. The epithet "sincere" should have been rendered "guileless," as it contains a contrast with "guile" in the verse before.

Of the word.—This translation of the original adjective cannot possibly be right. The only other place in the New Testament where it is used (Rom. 12:1) will show clearly enough its meaning here. There it is rendered "your **reasonable** service"; so here, "the reasonable guileless milk." (Comp. I Cor. 3:2.) The apostle calls it "mental milk," just as he explained the metaphor in 1:13 by adding "of your mind." The apostle is pressing his readers to cling with ardent attachment to the evangelical religion taught them by the Pauline party.

That ye may grow thereby.—The best manuscripts and versions add "unto salvation," which may confidently be adopted into the text. "Grow" is said in reference to the infant state of the converts as yet, and the maturity set before them is spoken of as "salvation."

(3) If so be ye have tasted.—It should rather be "ye tasted," looking back to a past time, probably that of the first conversion, when the taste of spiritual things is the most delicious. How sad to be past the relish for evangelical truth! Peter is here applying to Jesus Christ a passage which otherwise we might not have thought of applying to Him in particular. It gives quite a new complexion to the Thirty-fourth Psalm, when we see that in Peter's view the psalmist was speaking prophetically of our Lord. (See 3:10.)

(4) To whom coming.—The apostolic writers do not contemplate the possibility of a difference between the visible and invisible church. From this point the regeneration idea, which colored the whole of the preceding portion of the epistle, suddenly disappears. The thought is no longer that of a spiritual seed instead of a carnal seed, but of a spiritual Temple instead of the stone temple at Jerusalem.

A living stone.—The substratum (**petros** and **petra**) is not thought of at all; Jesus Christ is a carefully selected and hewn stone (**lithos**), specially laid as the first act in the work of building. The only thing which is common to this passage and Matt. 7:24 is the simple thought of the Christian Church being like a building. Our present verse gives no direct help toward finding how Peter understood the famous name passage Matt. 16:18). All we can say for certain is that he did not so interpret it as to suppose an official connection with his own person to be the one essential of the true Church, or else in again using the metaphor of building the Church he could hardly have omitted all mention of himself. He is, apparently, thinking only of the Messianic interpretation of Old Testament sayings as expounded by our Lord.

Disallowed indeed of men.—Comp. Ps. 118:22. The word "disallowed," or "rejected," implies a form of trial or probation which comes to an unsatisfactory conclusion. The human builders examine the stone, inspect all its qualifications, and find it unsuited to the edifice which they have in hand, and refuse it not only the place of honor, but any place at all, in their architecture. Peter wishes to bring out strongly the absolute opposition between God and the Jews.

But chosen of God, and precious.—Comp. Isa. 28:16. While the human builders saw the qualities of the stone, and rejected it because of its not fitting in with their ideal, on the other hand, in God's counsel and plan, it had been selected for His building purposes. It was also singled out for the place of honor, i.e., for that of cornerstone. The designation of this stone as "elect" brings out again the eternal predestination of Jesus to the Messiahship (1:11, 20).

(5) **Ye also, as lively stones, are built up.**—The rendering "lively," instead of "living," as in verse 4, is arbitrary, the Greek being precisely the same, and the intention being to show the complete conformation of the believers to Him who is the type and model for humanity. "Built up," too, only expresses a part of the Greek word, which implies "built up **upon** Him."

A spiritual house.—These Hebrew Christians are treated **collectively**, along with the Gentile Christians, as so many stones, incomplete and unmeaning in themselves, by arrangement and cemented union to rise into an ideal **house of God**. The reason for introducing this figure seems to be to console the Hebrews for their vanishing privileges in the Temple at Jerusalem. They are being taught to recognize that they themselves, in their union with one another, and with Jesus Christ, are the true abode of the Most High. The Christian substitution of something else in lieu of the Jerusalem Temple was one of the greatest stumblingblocks to the Hebrews from the very first. (See Mark 14:58; John 2:21; Acts 7:48; 21:28; comp. Heb. 9:8, 11.)

An holy priesthood.—They not only compose the Temple, but minister in it. But the apostle is not dwelling on the individual priesthood of each, though that is involved; he stresses the hierarchical order of the whole company of Christians. They are an organized body or college of priests, a new seed of Aaron or Levi. (See Isa. 66:21.)

To offer up spiritual sacrifices.—None is a priest who does not offer sacrifices (Heb. 8:3). But the sacrifices of the new hierarchy are "spiritual," not material. If our priesthood is modeled on that of Jesus Christ, as is here implied, it consists mainly of the sacrifice of self, of the will; then, in a minor degree, of words and acts of worship, thanks and praise (Calvin). (See Heb. 13:10-16.) And these sacrifices are offered up on behalf of others. (See Heb. 5:1; I John 3:16.) The first notion of the priesthood of all believers is not that of a mediatorial system being abolished, but of the mediatorial system being extended.

By Jesus Christ.—We all help to present one another's prayers and praises, which pass through the lips of many priests; but for them to be acceptable, they must be presented finally through the lips of the Great High Priest. He, in His perfect sympathy with all men, must make the sacrifice His own. (See Heb. 10:19-25, especially verse 21.)

(6) **Wherefore also.**—The mention of Jesus Christ brings the writer back again to his theme—that the whole system to which his readers belong has undergone a radical change, and is based on Jesus and His fulfillment of the sufferings and glories of the Messiah.

Behold, I lay.—See Rom. 9:33. Gesenius, on Isa. 28:16, shows that the early Jewish explanation, current in our Lord's time, referred it to the Messiah; the later Rabbinical expositors, probably by way of opposition to the Christians, explained it to mean Hezekiah. In order to gain a clear conception of Peter's aim in the quotation, it is necessary to glance over the whole section

1165

contained in Isa. 28 and 29. "The prophecy here cited, if we look upon it in its own place, we shall find inserted in the middle of a very sad denunciation of judgment against the Jews" (Leighton). Comp. our Lord's prophecy of the destruction of Jerusalem with Isa. 29:3, 4; Matt. 15:7-9 with Isa. 29:13; Rom. 9:21 with Isa. 29:16. Peter's quotation here, therefore, calling attention as it does to the context, is at least as much intended to show his Hebrew readers the sweeping away of the carnal Israel as to encourage them in their Christian allegiance.

In Sion.—In Isaiah it means that the people do not have to look for any distant external aid, such as that of Pharaoh, but all that they need is to be found in the city of David itself. Here, it seems to impress upon the Hebrew Christians that they are not abandoning their position as Hebrews by attaching themselves to Jesus Christ. It is they who are really clinging to Sion when the other Jews are abandoning her.

Shall not be confounded.—Our version of Isaiah translates the Hebrew original by "shall not make haste." It really means "shall not flee." While all the Jewish rulers, who had turned faithless and trusted in their **finesse** with Egypt, would have to flee from the Assyrians, those who preserved their faith in God would be able to stand their ground. In the Messianic fulfillment the faith or unbelief of the individual makes all the difference to him; the overthrow of the many does not affect the few. The general quality of "faith" of which the prophet spoke becomes faith in Him in whom the promises are fulfilled. Peter prefers the LXX "be ashamed" to the Hebrew, there being (except at the Fall of Jerusalem) no opportunity for actual flight. It means the same thing: "shall not find his confidence misplaced."

(7) The stone which the builders disallowed.—The apostle inserts (by a quotation) the historical fact which brought the shame—the disappointment of their own design, and the glorious completion of that which they opposed. The words are quoted directly from the LXX, and properly represent the Hebrew. The best critics consider the Psalm (118) from which this verse is cited to be a late Psalm, written subsequent to the return from Babylon, in which case it is most probable that the composer was thinking directly of the prophecy of Isaiah quoted before. In its first application the passage seems to mean as follows: The speaker,

1166

Israel, has been a despised captive. The great builders of the world empires had recognized no greatness in him; they were engaged in aggrandisement of self alone. Yet, after all, Israel is firmly planted once more in Zion, to be the first stone of a new structure, a new empire. In the fulfillment Christ takes the place of Israel, as is the case with Isa. 53. The builders are the rulers of the Jews (Acts 4:11). They had been intent on building a fabric of their own, and had despised Jesus, yet, without any intention of doing so, had been the means of advancing Him (Acts 4:27, 28). He had been made the basis of a new spiritual structure, in which faith, not fleshly lineage, was the cement and bond; and the believing Israelites, united to Him in both ways, shared the honor of being cornerstone.

(8) And a stone of stumbling and a rock of offence.—Here there is no thought whatever of the stone as a material for building; the thought is that of a mass of rock on the road, on which the terror-stricken fugitives stumble and fall. The words are taken from the Hebrew of the great Immanuel section of Isaiah (chap. 7), and immediately involve like the quotation in verse 6, the sharp contrast between the Jews who trust in Immanuel (the presence of God with Israel) and the Jews who do not, but rely on "confederacies." (Comp. 3:14.) In the flight of terror before the Assyrians the stone which afforded right of sanctuary to those who recognized and trusted it was a dangerous obstacle, a trap full in the way to those who did not. Once more, therefore, the Hebrews of the Dispersion were obeying the warnings of the Immanuel prophecy, which every Hebrew recognized as Messianic. Though the coupling of these passages of the Old Testament together certainly seems to show traces of the influence of Paul (comp. Rom. 9:32, 33), yet Peter must have been present and heard the Lord Himself put them together (Luke 20:17, 18).

Whereunto also they were appointed.—When Peter says that these Jews were appointed to stumble, he primarily means that the clear prophecies of the Old Testament which he has quoted marked them for such a destiny. It was no unforeseen, accidental consequence of the Gospel; it had never been expected that all who heard the Gospel would accept it. Thus the introduction of the statement here has the direct practical purpose of confirming the faith of the readers by showing the verification of the prophecy. Still we must not shirk the fur-

:her point that, in a certain sense, it was God Himself who appointed them to stumble. It will be observed, however, from the outset, that our present passage casts not a glance at the condition of the stumbling Jews after death. With this caution, we may say that God puts men sometimes into positions where, during this life, they almost inevitably reject the truth. This is implied in the doctrine of election. (Comp. II Thess. 2:13.) These things remain as a trial of faith. It suffices that we know for certain that God is Love. We have but to prize more highly our own present salvation and to trust His love for that fuller harvest of which we are but the firstfruits (Jas. 1:18). In some way even their stumbling will ultimately prove His love, to them as well as to us.

(9) A chosen generation.—Better, "an elect race." As originally the clan of Abraham was selected from among "all the families of the earth" (Amos 3:2), so out of the clan of Abraham after the flesh were these men selected to be a new race. They are not merely individuals selected one by one and left in isolation, but a tribe consolidated, only the bond from now on is not merely one of common physical descent.

A royal priesthood.—See Exod. 19:6 (LXX). The Hebrew has a "kingdom of priests." The word "royal" describes belonging to the King. The substitution, therefore, of "royal priesthood" for "kingdom of priests" brings out more clearly the personal relation to the personal King.

A peculiar people.—Comp. Exod. 19:5; Isa. 43:21; Mal. 3:17. This phrase is literally, "a people for a special reservation." The word rendered "peculiar" means properly "making over and above," and would be represented in Latin by **peculium,** which means a man's private pocket money. When children speak of a thing being their "very own" it exactly expresses what we have here. The word comes in other places to mean "earning by hard work," in such a way as to establish peculiar rights of property over the thing acquired (Acts 20:28). Here the thought is "a people to be his very own." (Comp. I Thess. 5:9; Eph. 1:7.)

That ye should shew forth the praises.— The Greek means "virtues," "powers," or "excellencies," a rare word in the New Testament (see II Pet. 1:3). And the word for "shew forth," which is found nowhere else in the New Testament, means by rights "to proclaim to those without what has taken place within." This strict signification

is suitable here. Those of the old Israel were not elect for their own sake, but to act as God's exponents to the world. This function they abdicated by their selfish exclusiveness, and it has descended to the new Israel. Peter and Paul are at one.

Of him who hath called you out of darkness.—The act of calling (by the Father) was that of sending the preachers of the Gospel to them, i.e., Paul and his followers (comp. 1:12, 25). Here again Peter speaks in praise of Paul's mission. The state of the Jews immediately before Christ and without Him is often described as "darkness." (See Matt. 4:16; Luke 1:79.) This passage is quoted a few years later by Clement of Rome (chap. 36), as applying to himself among others, and Lightfoot has established that Clement was a Jew.

(10) Which in time past were not a people.—See Hos. 2:23. Who were Lo-ruhamah and Lo-ammi? Types of Israel left unpitied, and rejected from their covenant with God. Peter means that in his Hebrew readers and the brethren from among the Gentiles, who by the Gospel of Paul had adhered to them, this promise does not say "which in time past were not God's people," but "were not a people." This was the effect of the dispersion, or "scattering." (See note on 1:1.) The Hebrews had not only ceased to be in covenant as "God's people," but had ceased to be "a people" at all. But in Christ, that "scattering" becomes a "sowing"; their dispersion becomes the means of their multiplication by union' with the Gentiles in Christ, and thus spiritually they recover the lost unity and become once more "the people of God."

(11) As strangers and pilgrims.—Comp. Pss. 39:12; 119:19. The word "pilgrim" does not imply journeying, but simply residence in a foreign country. Though no longer "scattered," but gathered mercifully once more into "a people," they were still far from home—unprotected residents in an alien and hostile world, which scrutinized their conduct and was anxious to get rid of them.

Abstain from fleshly lusts.—Although **all** bad desires might be described as fleshly, the word seems here to mean the lusts which lead to drunkenness, gluttony, and uncleanness. Though such sins are usually characteristic of the Gentile, Jews were not impeccable in such matters; and here the apostle has a special reason for insisting on the observance of the seventh commandment. These Hebrew Christians needed to be more

1167

than ever vigilant, because of the slanders which the heathen were beginning to circulate about the Christians.

Which war against the soul.—This clause is a description of the way in which all fleshly lusts alike act. It means not merely a general antagonism between soul and body, but that the lusts are on active service, engaged in a definite campaign against the immortal part of the man.

(12) Conversation.—A favorite word with Peter, occurring as often (ten times) in his two epistles as in all the other New Testament writings put together. It means the visible conduct of the daily walk in life. "Honest" is the ordinary Greek word for "beautiful," and implies the attractiveness of the sight, the satisfaction afforded by an approach to ideal excellence.

They speak against you as evildoers.— Peter asserts distinctly that slanders were really rife about some particulars of the Christian morality at the time that this letter was written. It is a mark of a late date, for at first the Christians had not attracted sufficient notice, as a body, to be discussed either in praise or blame. The heathen at first regarded them as merely a Jewish sect (Acts 18:15; 25:18-20), and as such they received from the Roman government a contemptuous toleration. The first state recognition of Christianity as a separate religion, with characteristics of its own, was the persecution of Nero in the year 64. It so happens that we have almost contemporary heathen documents which bring out the force of this passage. Comp. Seutonius' life of Nero, Pliny's famous letter to Trajan, and the apologists of the second century.

Glorify God in the day of visitation.— This means not only the great last day, but on whatever occasion God brings matters to a crisis. The visitation is a visitation of the Christians and the heathen alike, and it brings both grace and vengeance, according as men choose to receive it. (See Luke 1:78; 19:44.)

(13) To every ordinance of man.—Comp. John 19:11; Rom. 13:1, where the reason assigned for submission is that ultimately the authority proceeds from God Himself. Here, however, the thought is quite different. They are to submit because of the practical consequences of not submitting. It must be done in order not to bring discredit on Christ's teaching and persecution on His Church. This difference of treatment, in the midst of so much resemblance, shows that at the date of Peter's letter there was much

more immediate cause for laying stress on political subordination. Paul, writing to the Roman Church, urges submission to Claudius, because the Roman Jews were often in trouble and expelled from the city of Rome (Acts 18:2); Peter, writing in all probability from the Roman Church, urges submission to Nero and the provincial governors because "ignorant and foolish men" were beginning to misrepresent the Christian Church as a kind of internationalist conspiracy.

(14) For the punishment of evildoers.— Peter credits Roman imperialism with having as its aim the promotion of moral behavior among its subjects. The "praise" (comp. Rom. 13:3) must mean the solid praise of preferments, which is hardly so marked a feature of government as the foregoing. Neither Peter nor Paul lays down any exceptions to the rule of complete obedience. They refuse to contemplate, at least to formulate, the occasions when disobedience may be necessary. Obedience is the first thing to learn, and when they have learned it, they will know of themselves when to disobey. Peter himself stands to all time as the type of magnificent disobedience (Acts 4:19).

(16) As free.—This points at once to what was the gift of the accusation. The Christian took up a position of complete independence within, and professed himself in a certain sense to be above the laws, by virtue of being a member of Christ's kingdom. This position of independence the heathen state resented, and looked upon the Christian Church as a dangerous organization. Here, therefore, Peter both insists upon and defines that independent position.

(17) Honour all men.—Paul had said that this honor was to be paid to those to whom it was due; Peter says that this includes all men. There is not one who can be entirely despised, not one who had quite lost the likeness of Christ; Jews are not at liberty to despise even the idolatrous Gentiles.

Love the brotherhood.—The brotherhood means all Christian men who formed a single confraternity. "All men," Christian or heathen, are to be "honored," but there is a special sense in which love is possible only between fellow Christians.

Fear God.—This enforces reverence for every law and ordinance of God, and therefore serves fitly to introduce the next precept. Rebellion against Nero is rebellion against God (Rom. 13:2).

(18) Servants.—This word brings forward

e family or household relation of servant slave to master, and not the mere fact of vnership. We need not be surprised at rections for household servants, or slaves, a letter addressed to Jewish Christians, r there were large numbers of Hebrews in is position. Clement, for example, was obably both.

The froward.—Literally, "the crooked." s meaning is made clear by the contrasted djectives. A "froward" master is one with a arped nature, who is unreasonably capri- ous, one who will deal with his servants in ιe manner spoken of in the following ver- ·s.

(19) For conscience toward God endure ·ief, suffering wrongfully.—Rather, "the ınsciousness of God," thrown in to guard ;ainst any false theory that patience by self is a thankworthy thing. A resignation hich comes from stoical fatalism, or from ıe sense that it is no good to seek redress, sinfully defective. The two necessary ıalifications, before patience can become ι any sense meritorious, are that the suffer- ιg should be undeserved, and that the man ιould recognize in it the hand of God.

(20) This is acceptable with God.— Acceptable" should be translated "thank- ·orthy" here as well as in verse 19, and ıust be taken in precisely the same sense.)bserve that the apostle does not continue, this is glory," as we might have expected; a `hristian is not supposed to care for such ·ash as fame. But a Christian may well care ɔ win the thanks of God! And such endu- ance of griefs for God's sake is not dis- inctly said to be "thankworthy" from God's oint of view.

(21) For even hereunto were ye called.— Jamely, to the combination of suffering nd well-doing. It was a special point in *aul's preaching to forewarn fairly of the ·ibulations attending all who wished to nter the kingdom of God. (Comp. I Thess. ·:3, 4; Acts 14:22, which latter passage efers to preaching in the homes of some of he recipients of this epistle.)

Christ also suffered.—Christ's experience ιust be that of every Christian. It is to be ·arefully observed that Paul does not say 'Jesus suffered"; the whole point is that hese Hebrew Christians have given in their ιdhesion to a **suffering Messiah.** (See note ɔn 1:11.) Christ is said to have suffered "**for** ·ou"; this does not mean "in your stead," ɔut "on your behalf, for your good." `hrist's atonement for us is not represented ιn this passage as vicarious. He did not,

according to Peter's teaching, die as a sub- stitute for us, any more than He rose again as our substitute.

Leaving us an example.—This clause seems added as a kind of explanation of the abrupt "because" just before. The curious word for "example," used nowhere else in the New Testament, means primarily the "copy" given to a child to write from, or a "plan" suggested for carrying out in detail, a sketch to be filled in. (See II Macc. 2:28, 29; I Clement 16.) The leaving of us of this copy was one of the benefits of His passion implied in "suffered **for you.**"

(22) Who did no sin.—This verse is not to be taken by itself, but in the closest conjunction with the following. It is not the sinlessness of Christ by itself that is set here as an example before the servants, but His sinlessness in combination with His ill- treatment. (See Isa. 53:9.) The word there was one of violent transgression; Peter sub- stitutes the simple word which he has used in verse 20, "fault."

(23) The writer was not thinking exclu- sively of any one occasion, but of our Lord's constant habit, though naturally there would be uppermost in Peter's mind the hours while he stood warming himself at Caiaphas' fire, with the denial on his lips, and saw the Messiah blindfolded and buffeted. He is also thinking of Isa. 53:7. Note that God is described in the aspect which is most reassuring to men who are suffering unjustly (II Thess. 1:5).

(24) Bare our sins . . . on the tree.—Peter does not say "the **punishment** of our sins." He asserts that Christ, in His boundless sympathy with fallen man, in His union with all mankind through the Incarnation whereby He became the second Adam, ac- tually took, as His own, our sins, as well as everything else belonging to us. He was so identified with us, that in the great Psalm of the Messianic sacrifice, He calls them "My sins" (Ps. 40:12), sinless as He was. (See Matt. 8:17.)

That we being dead.—Just as the former part of this verse is an expansion of "Christ suffered for us," so the latter part is an expansion of "that ye should follow his steps." (Comp. Rom. 6:2, 8, 11; II Cor. 5:14; Col. 1:22.) Peter's word for "dying" in this place is not elsewhere found in the New Testament, and is originally a euphemism for death; literally, "to be missing"—i.e., when sin comes to seek its old servants it finds them gone.

By whose stripes ye were healed.—The

1169

purpose of the clause seems to be once more to make the good and ill-used servants feel, when the weals were smarting on their backs, that the Righteous Servant of Jehovah had borne the same, and that it had served a beneficial purpose, as they knew to their everlasting gratitude. The "stripes" (in the original singular number) do not refer merely to the scourging. The words form a paradox.

(25) For ye were as sheep going astray.—The "for" introduces an explanation of how they came to be in need of "healing." Jew and Gentile take different ways, but both alike fulfill the prophecy, "every man to his own way." The metaphors of healing and going astray both are quotations from Isa. 53. We must notice how deeply that prophecy (the interpretation of which was probably learned from John the Baptist) had sunk into Peter's mind. (See 1:19.)

But are now returned.—The tense of the original verb points to the actual historical time at which it took place, rather than the position now occupied. "Returned" is the word that is often rendered "were converted," and only indicates that they turned around and moved in a contrary direction.

The shepherd and bishop of your souls.—Undoubtedly this means Christ. The first of the two titles is, of course, suggested by the simile of the sheep. (Comp. Ps. 23:3.) To the Hebrew mind the thought of superintendence and ruling, not that of giving food, was uppermost when they spoke of shepherds. Thus it will here be nearly synonymous with the second title of bishop. This name suggests not so much overseeing as visiting—i.e., going carefully into the different cases brought under the officer's notice. (Comp. 5:2, 4; Acts 20:28.) Both words were familiar, although not stereotyped, as ecclesiastical words already, and, as such were especially appropriate to Christ, the Head of the Church. It is interesting how Peter arranges almost every section of the epistle so as to end with some encouragement to the readers to cling to Jesus as the Messiah, and to their Christian state, from which they were in danger of receding into Judaism. He makes even the special exhortations lead up to that which is the main exhortation of the letter.

3

(1) Likewise ye wives ... —Whether this imposes for all time upon Christian wives

as complete a submission toward their husbands as is here enjoined might perhaps be questioned, because the special reason for the command in this place was to allay suspicions engendered by the boldness with which Christianity proclaimed the freedom of the individual. Peter has just been giving injunctions for absolute submission, even to injustice, on the part of slaves; and the progress of Christianity abolished slavery. The measure of the Christian wife's submission may safely be left to her own enlightened conscience, guided by other passages of the New Testament not written, like this, for a special emergency.

They also may ... —It is probable that the case here supposed is that of Hebrew (Christian) women, married to men of their own race who reject the Gospel. The point is spoiled by inserting the definite article before "word." (Peter was himself a married man.) What he means here is not that those who have resisted the public preaching in the synagogues should even without that public preaching be won; rather, that though the Gospel as uttered verbally only provokes them to opposition, the Gospel as submissively acted by their wives, without a word said on the matter, ought to convert them.

(2) On "chaste conversation" Leighton says, "It is a delicate, timorous grace, afraid of the least air, or shadow of anything that hath but a resemblance of wronging it, in carriage or speech, or apparel, as follows in the third and fourth verses."

(3) Whose adorning let it not be ... —The passage shows that the Asiatic Christians were not all of the poorer classes (Comp. I Tim. 2:9; Rev. 3:17.) Many of the wealthy Jewesses had joined them. Two things are to be noted about the advice given here. (1) It is not intended directly as a corrective of vanity. The main thought is How are the husbands to be attracted? Not, says Peter, by any external prettiness of adornment, but by inward graces. (2) The apostle is not forbidding the use of gold etc. Leighton says, "All regard of comeliness and ornament in apparel is not unlawful, nor doth the apostle's expression here, rightly considered, fasten that upon the adorning he here speaks of. He doth no more universally condemn the use of gold for ornament than he doth any other comely raiment, which here he means by that general word of "putting on of apparel," for his 'not' is comparative; 'not this adorning, but the ornament of a meek spirit,' that

ther, and as much more comely and pre-
ous. ..." We may be sure, however, that
ter would have spoken with abhorrence
any adorning which partook of the
ture of lying. (Even in one of Xenophon's
orks there is a passage where an Athenian
ntleman expostulates with his wife on the
lly of hoping to attract him by wearing
gh-heeled shoes and painting her face
ith rouge and white.)

**(4) Which is in the sight of God of great
ice.**—The thing which is valuable in the
ves of God is the having such an inward
aracter. Such a possession will be not
ly attractive to the husband for the time,
ut has a permanent value as being es-
emed by God.

(5) For after this manner.—Here we have
ot only the ground of the foregoing pre-
pts, but also of the assurance that God
ts a value on such embellishments. It had
een accepted by Him in the holy women
f old who hoped in Him, and would be
cepted again. Their subjection was their
dornment. (See Gen. 18:12.)

(7) Likewise, ye husbands.—The subjec-
on is not to be all one-sided, though the
usband's subjection to the wife will be of a
ifferent kind from the wife's to him. This
added to correct a false impression that
ight otherwise have been conveyed.

With them.—We must remember that Pe-
r's object throughout these instructions is
commend Christianity to jealous watch-
rs without. Here, therefore, we may well
uppose that he is thinking chiefly of the
ase of believing husbands (Jewish) married
o unbelieving wives (Jewish also), thus
resenting the counter-picture to that of
erse 1. And the first thing is that they are
o "dwell with" these wives, not to divorce
hem, nor to cease from conjugal cohabita-
ion with them; such harshness would lend
ttle attractiveness to the Christian religion
mong the Jewish homes to which the di-
orced wife would turn. (See I Cor. 7:12
eq.—a passage which must almost have
een in Peter's mind.)

Unto the wife, as unto the weaker vessel.—
This explains the saying "according to
nowledge." The thing which the husband is
specially to understand and take into ac-
ount is that he is dealing with a thing less
trong than himself. Weakness itself, by
eing weakness, has a claim upon the strong
nan's deference and self-submission. The
veakness here ascribed to the female sex is
rimarily that of the body. (For "vessel,"
ee note I Thess. 4:4.)

Giving honour.—The word for "giving"
implies rendering a portion which is due.
And what is here called "honour" is not to
be understood only of the wife's maintenance, nor is the wife only to be honored
by being consulted in affairs of importance
and put in charge of the household. The
"honour" is to be accorded to wives "as to
joint heirs of a grace of life."

The grace of life.—To interpret this as
eternal life neither gives sufficient force to
the conjoint nature of the possession, nor
does it take into account the possibility of
such a case as a believing husband and
unbelieving wife. It seems better, therefore,
to suppose that the "grace" of life is life in
the natural sense. This mysterious and divine gift—not apart from one another, but
conjointly—they are privileged by the
Creator's primeval benediction (Gen. 1:28)
to transmit. They have the power to bring
human beings into existence. And in consideration that such is the dignity and the
intention of marriage, a man may well be
called upon to revere his partner in the
great prerogative.

That your prayers be not hindered—i.e.,
the husbands' prayers, not necessarily their
prayers with their wives. Their conversion
is probably what Peter chiefly meant. Likely he had in view what Paul writes in I Cor.
7:5.

(9) Finally, be ye all.—A return from the
special to the general. Peter has not, however, forgotten the purpose with which the
former rules were given; his thought is still
how to produce a right impression on the
unbelieving world, although some of these
injunctions touch only internal relations between members of the church.

(9) Not rendering.—So far Peter has been
speaking of internal conduct. The two last
adjectives—"evil" (in act), "railing" (in
word)—however, lead gradually into the
wider field of conduct, and probably now
he is thinking solely of relation to the
adverse world.

But contrariwise blessing.—No doubt a
reminiscence of Matt. 5:44. (From the
traces of the earliest Christian literature, no
part of our Lord's discourses seem to have
taken so rapid and so firm a hold on the
Christian conscience as the Sermon on the
Mount.) Though the word "blessing" is chosen as the exact opposite of the bad language used against the Christians, it may
perhaps involve the opposite of unkind action as well.

(11) Let him eschew evil.—The two

former clauses dealt with the domain of word, these two with the domain of action. It suits Peter's intention better to take the verse, not as an exhortation to virtue in general, but as an instruction how to behave under provocation and in danger.

(12) For.—The sense that the Lord's eyes are over you is a sufficient reason for self-restraint under provocation, especially, perhaps, when we see that by "the Lord" Peter understands Jesus Christ. That this is the case is clear from his use of the same Psalm (34) in 2:3 (see note). If Christ, the model of meekness under persecution (2:23), is watching, we not only need no passionate self-defense, but should be ashamed to use it. Was Peter thinking how once, while he himself was cursing and swearing at those who accused him of being a Christian, he felt the eyes of the Lord turn upon him?

Against them that do evil.—This is sufficient comfort when men injure us (2:23), sufficient warning not to injure in return. See Ps. 56 for the historical circumstances in which Ps. 34 was composed. Peter deemed Psalm 34 so appropriate to his readers, misjudged and suspiciously watched by unbelievers, who only waited the opportunity to shed their blood (Ps. 56:1, 2, 5, 6). But the striking change is that, whereas David's trust in Jehovah was a trust simply in the Eternal Being without distinction of Persons, Peter bids the Hebrews of Asia read that Psalm into an act of faith in Jesus.

(14) But and if ye suffer.—What he means by this "suffering," which is so much more than being "harmed," may be seen from 2:21; 3:17; 4:1, 15. He means the horrors of capital punishment. He does not speak of this as something that was already occurring, nor as though it were something immediately and certainly impending, but as a case highly probable. There had then as yet been no martyrdoms in Asia. The letter is therefore earlier in date than the Apocalypse (Rev. 2:13).

(15) But sanctify the Lord God in your hearts.—The tense of this and the two preceding imperatives shows that Peter meant this for advice to be acted upon at the moment of being called on to suffer. The passage from Isaiah becomes striking when we note, without a shadow of doubt, the right reading here is "But sanctify the Lord the Christ in your hearts." This passage immediately precedes that which was quoted in 2:8, and (like that) is not caught

1172

up at random, but as coming in the gre Immanuel passage. That presence of G which was the palladium of Israel in t days of Hezekiah has found fulfillment "the Christ" now given. To "sanctify" H means to recognize, in word and deed, H full holiness, and therefore to treat H with due awe. This not only substitutes t fear of God for the fear of man (since th mutually exclude each other), but enforc purity of life, thus catching up again "th which is good" and "for righteousnes sake." This, adds Peter, is to be done " your hearts." The words "in your heart purposely call attention to the differen between Isaiah's use of the name Immanu and the Christian meaning of it. To Isaia God dwelt in the midst of a people in corporate capacity; Peter knew tha through the Incarnation, each individu Christian has God in him, united with him.

Ready always to give an answer.—This the consequence of sanctifying Christ with by the worship of a pure life, that at r moment any questioner find us unprepar to speak with freedom of our hope in Hi The word for "answer" here is **apologia**, defense, the reply of an accused person. does not mean that every person is boun to be able to state intellectually the natu and grounds of the Christian creed, thoug such a duty may, perhaps, be fairly deduce from the text; but that every Christian own life ought to be so free from taint, conscious of Christ enshrined within, as cause him no misgiving in defending th faith from the slanders (see 2:12) broug against it. The constant readiness, or fre dom from encumbrance of sin, is the ma point. Consciousness of impurity of li shuts a man's mouth from defending Chri tian morality.

That asketh you a reason.—It mea those who call Christians to account f their profession of the gospel hopes. Thoug it must not be exclusively so taken, Pet evidently means chiefly the being calle into the law court to give account. (Com Matt. 10:5, 16, 19; Luke 12:11.) Christianit is here called a hope, rather than a fait because, especially in times of persecutio so much of our creed has a future tinge. B the readiness of the Christian's defense himself and the Church from all mor aspersions is not to be marred by an self-exaltation or improper confidence.

(16) In Christ.—This is the nearest a proach in Peter to a use of this word as proper name. Other Hebrews, he remin

em in this word, were safe from persecu-
on only by rejecting the national hope of a
essiah. The phrase "in Christ," i.e., as
embers of the Church, occurs again in
10, 14; the thought is common enough in
ohn, but it does not occur in II Peter,
ebrews, James, or Jude. Of course, Paul's
ritings teem with it. It contains the con-
erse side of the Incarnation doctrine to
at involved in verse 15; we not only have
e whole Christ dwelling in us, but He
mbraces us all (see John 14:20).

(17) If the will of God be so.—This is to
e taken only with the word "suffer," which
self means, as in verse 14, to suffer capital-
. Peter is thinking of the legal process of
erses 15 and 16, coming to a verdict of
guilty." He was himself daily expecting
uch a death.

(18) For sins.—When the apostle says
Christ **also**," he raises a comparison be-
ween Christ and the Christian martyr. The
arallel does not merely consist in the fact
hat both "suffer" or are put to death. Both
re put to death but once; both are put to
eath innocent; both are "sin-offerings."
his is a fresh encouragement to Peter's
irst readers to meet death bravely.

That he might bring us to God.—The
ubstantive derived from this verb appears
s "access" in Rom. 5:2; Eph. 2:18; 3:12.
Peter says nothing about the Atonement in
ts effect upon the mind of the Father
oward man. It is a side on which the New
Testament writers do not much dwell. The
New Testament never speaks of the recon-
iliation as mutual. The quarrel is treated as
ne-sided, so far, at least, as in connection
vith the Atonement: "in order that He
night bring you to God," not "in order that
He might bring God to you." The voluntary
leath of a righteous man upon the cross, in
he calm calculation that nothing else would
o attract sinful men to Himself, and thus to
he Father who sent Him (John 12:32), is
he aspect of the Atonement which Peter
sets forth. He is still thinking of the effect of
Christian conduct on the outer world, and
his object is to make the Christians feel that
they too can, in their measure, bring the
unjust, the persecuting heathen and Jews, to
God by innocent and voluntary deaths.
Thus their deaths are carrying on the work
of reconciliation.

Quickened by the Spirit.—This refers not
to the resurrection of Christ, but to something which took place between His death
and His resurrection. The doctrine seems to
be that the spirit, set free from the body,

immediately receives new life, as it were,
from the body. To purely spiritual realities
it becomes alive in a manner which was
impossible while it was united to the flesh.
The new powers are exemplified in what
follows immediately. As long as Christ, as
long as any man, is alive in the flesh, he
cannot commune with spirits as such; but
the moment death severs flesh and spirit,
the spirit can deal with other spirits, which
Christ proceeded to do.

**(19) He went and preached unto the spir-
its in prison.**—To interpret this passage of
our Lord, in and through the person of
Noah, preaching repentance to the old
world, is altogether to dissociate it from the
doctrine of the descent into hell. Practically
all the Fathers, Calvin, Luther, Bengel, and
other scholars refer the passage to what our
Lord did while His body was dead. This is
the most natural construction to put upon
the words "in which also" (i.e., in spirit).
The "spirits" here will thus correspond with
"in spirit" there. We take it, then, to mean
that, when Christ's human spirit was disen-
gaged from the body, He gave proof of the
new powers of purely spiritual action thus
acquired by going to the place, or state, in
which other disembodied spirits were, and
"preached" unto them. What was the substance of this preaching we are not here
told; the word itself (which is not the same
as, e.g., in 1:25) means only to publish or
proclaim, like a crier or herald. (See note
on 4:6.)

(20) Which sometime were disobedient.—
Our Lord preached to the whole class of
spirits in prison, of all times and races; and
then, to magnify the bounty of this act,
Peter paints out a particular group of them,
who were the most marked criminals of
any, and whose case suggested a useful
application. He has a reason for using the
word "disobedient." It would not describe
all sinners, but those who had heard and
been convinced by the word of God, but
refused to accept it. This was the case with
those to whom Noah preached (II Pet. 2:5).
Peter's object through the whole of this
section is to encourage the Hebrew Christians to be ready, through a good conscience, for a brave martyrdom, if need be.
They are to think how their deaths, like
Christ's, may bring their persecutors to
God.

**When once the longsuffering of God
waited.**—The clause serves to heighten the
guilt of the poor sinners to whom Christ
preached in prison. These abandoned

Antediluvians sinned in spite of the long ministry of Noah, and died impenitent. Both their wickedness and God's longsuffering with them were embodied in Hebrew proverbs, which Peter's readers would know, and yet Christ had a Gospel for them.

(21) The like figure whereunto even baptism doth also now save us.—The word "water" in the preceding verse leads on to this thought. The thing it represented is Christian baptism. The main thought, however, is not of the Christians, as a body or family (like Noah's), being saved while others are lost. For each individual by himself there is a meaning in his baptism which is prefigured by the Flood; and the explanation of baptism which follows, and the opening of the next chapter, show that the apostle was thinking chiefly of this individual application.

Not the putting away of the filth of the flesh.—The apostle is not cautioning his readers against the thought that baptism acted **ex opere operato**, as a charm, but he is telling them, on the contrary, that it is no external rite. He was writing to Jews, who were familiar with ceremonial washings, or "baptizings," which, though they symbolized a cleansing from sin, really effected nothing but to make the skin less dirty.

By the resurrection.—This is properly joined with "doth save." As humanity died to the flesh in the bad Antediluvians, and rose again, washed clean, in Noah, so to the believer there was in baptism a death to the flesh, and he rose again, with a conscience washed clean through union with the crucified and risen Christ. Note that when the apostle speaks of glories he uses, for his purpose, the name of Jesus; when of sufferings, it is the title of Christ.

(22) Who is gone into heaven, and is on the right hand of God.—This verse, which partakes of the character of a doxology, serves two purposes. First, it carries on the history of Jesus Christ to His perpetual session with the Father. Second, it teaches the entire conformity of the believer to the Lord. The notion of being "on the right hand of God," taken, probably, from Ps. 110:1, seems to be that of occupying the highest post of honor possible, next after that of the Father Himself.

Angels and authorities and powers being made subject unto him.—There can be no doubt that this whole verse is colored by recollection of the circular letter which Paul had sent to the churches of Asia, which we call the Epistle to the Ephesians. Perhaps the heresy which Paul lamented in that epistle may still have lingered in existence, in cabalistic Jewish circles, among those same churches when Peter thus wrote to them. In favor of such an opinion one might appeal to the vivid picture of licentiousness in the next chapter, and the development of the same, clearly under Gnostic influence, in the Second Epistle and in the Apocalypse.

4

(1) For he that hath suffered in the flesh . . .—Rather, "that he that hath suffered to the flesh is at rest from sin." This is the "mind" which we are to take. The thought is probably derived from Rom. 6:7. The death of the body puts a stop to any further possibility of sin. Welcome, then. A slight difficulty is caused by the implied fact that Christ, too, in dying "ceased from sin." But the Greek word for "hath ceased" literally means "hath been caused to rest," meaning not a voluntary cessation from what one was doing before, but a pause imposed from without. (Comp. Rom. 6:10.)

(3) For the time past of our life.—There are two words in the English here which do not stand in the true text, and sadly impede the sense. They are "of our life," and "us."

The will of the Gentiles.—Just as in verse 2 there was a contrast between man's manifold and conflicting lusts and God's unity of will, so there is a contrast now between God's "will" and (for the Greek word is quite different) the heathen's "wish." "To have perpetuated the heathen's wish" means to have done the bad things of which the heathen wanted them to be guilty.

When we walked.—The participle in Greek does not directly state that they had so proceeded, but explains the foregoing verb: "The past is sufficient to have done what the heathen want you to have done."

Lasciviousness should be plural, expressing the repeated acts of sin. The word in Greek means any outrageous debauchery, so that it may be said to include all the words that follow.

Abominable idolatries.—It is not as idolatries that they are called abominable, but because of the abominable adjuncts of the idol festivals. This clause is the main support of those who think that the letter was written to converts from heathenism and not from Judaism. But Peter does not say

at they ever **had** lived in those sins. Quite
the contrary, he says (verse 4) that the
athen found, to their surprise, that the
hristians would **not** go with them in these
ings; and that, finding it to be so, they
lasphemed" or slandered them in this
spect.

(5) To him that is ready to judge.—This
rries on the history of Jesus Christ a step
rther still. The last thing was His sitting
the right hand of God. This is the order
the Apostles' Creed.

**(6) For for this cause was the gospel
reached also to them that are dead.**—Peter
carrying us back to his teaching of 3:19,
d is explaining further the purpose of
hrist's descent into hell.

**That they might be judged according to
en in the flesh, but live according to God
the spirit.**—In order to obtain a clear
otion of this hard saying, it will be neces-
ry once more to survey the course of the
hole passage. The apostle's readers must
ke their choice as to which kind of suffer-
g they would have. It was not indeed
rtain that in case they chose to do well
ey would suffer for it; and if they did,
ere was the history of Christ to encourage
em. But in case they chose to be evildo-
rs, it was certain that they would suffer.
And you had better," he says, "suffer in
ell-doing than in evil-doing." He then
ives an instance of persons who suffered in
vil-doing—the fleshly Antediluvians,
hom God cut short in their crimes by the
lood, and to whom Christ went to preach
their prison-house. The simplest explana-
on of our present text is that these Antedi-
vians were to be deprived of resurrection
f the flesh which they had so foully cor-
pted, but in God's mercy, through accep-
ng the Gospel preached to them by Christ
fter their death, were to be allowed a
urely spiritual existence. And what is the
oint of this dread warning, if in the end
ese Antediluvians attain to the same bliss,
both in body and soul," as other men?
here is a whole set of passages which
eems to teach that resurrection—i.e., the
ermanent restitution of life to the body—is
gift which does not belong to all.

(7) The end of all things is at hand.—It is
ut a repetition in other words of verse 5,
serted again to give weight to all the
xhortations which follow. Probably, if Pe-
r had thought the world would stand
venty centuries more, he would have ex-
ressed himself differently; yet see II Pet.
:4-10.

**Be ye therefore sober, and watch unto
prayer.**—These words sum up the cautions
given in verses 1-6, before passing on to the
next subject. The tense of the imperatives in
the Greek carries out the notion that the
persons addressed had slipped into a careless state, from which they needed an
arousal.

**(8) And above all things have fervent
charity among yourselves.**—Peter assumes
that the charity is there, but insists on its
not being allowed to waver in outward
expression.

Shall cover.—It far better suits the context to take the proverb in the same sense as
in James 5:20, without any reference to the
Old Testament passage (Prov. 10:12). Peter
is urging charity as something which will be
found advantageous when the "end of all
things" comes; and the advantage he mentions is, "because charity covereth a multitude of sins," i.e., the exercise of this grace
makes up for a great many other shortcomings in the man.

**(10) As every man hath received the
gift.**—They are reminded, as in I Cor. 4:7,
that the gift was **received**, and for the same
purpose. At what period these gifts were
received it is hard to say, as in some
instances the gift was of a spiritual nature,
in others of a temporal nature. Each, however, has a gift of some kind for the benefit
of the community.

(11) Peter proceeds to speak of two particular forms taken by this "manifold grace
of God"; (1) the power to speak; (2) the
power to minister. The speaking is, of
course, public preaching in the church; and
the man who does so is not to trust to his
own natural powers and wit, or to seek
applause for himself, but to act as one
possessed of powers not his own. The "ministering" is giving the good things of this
life for the benefit of the poor. The word
rendered "ability" frequently expresses a
sufficiency of wealth; and "giveth" is the
same which is used of supplying material
blessings in II Cor. 9:10. The original classical meaning of the word is to pay the
expenses of putting a play on the stage,
which at Athens was a public burden borne
by the wealthier citizens in turn. Thus the
wealthy Christian who supports the church
and relieves all the poor is not really the
church's patron. He is a responsible manager, but the paymaster is God.

(12) The fiery trial which is to try you.—
This rendering conveys a false impression,
for the fiery trial was not future, but actual-

1175

ly present. Already the Asiatic Christians are enduring a fierce persecution.

(13) But rejoice.—The opposite of being bewildered ("strange," verse 12) at it, "rejoicing" implies a recognition of its character and purpose.

(14) For the name of Christ.—Literally, "**in** the name of Christ," i.e., on the score of being Christians only. (Comp. verse 16.) Again, Peter presses the Messianic title; surely they will not abandon the hopes of Israel!

(15) But let none of you.—In order to understand this caution, we must recollect how largely the first converts were drawn from actually criminal classes, and how easily they were admitted. In the persecution of Diocletian, Mensurius of Carthage found it necessary to expose those who drew persecution on themselves to cloak their crimes under pretense of Christian faith. It is conceivable that Peter may have had some such danger in view.

(16) Yet if any man suffer as a Christian.—Peter purposely uses the name which was a name of derision among the heathen. It is not, as yet, one by which the believers would usually describe themselves. It occurs only two other times in the New Testament—in Acts 11:26 and 26:28. So contemptible was the name that "well-bred people avoided pronouncing the name, or, when forced to do so, made a kind of apology" (M. Renan). Tacitus says; "Those who were **vulgarly** known by the name of Christians."

(17) Begin at the house of God.—It seems as if Peter meant at first only to say, "Thank God that you **are** 'Christians,' for the judgment is just about to begin," as something which only concerns the unbelievers; then, as an afterthought, he adds, "and begin, too, at the house of God," by way of making the believers also feel the need of care.

That obey not the gospel of God?—The recipients of the letter, we must remember, were Jewish Christians, who were in a twofold danger—either of relapsing sullenly into Judaism, or of plunging into heathen excesses, under the notion that such things could not hurt the spiritually-minded. To meet these two forms of danger the apostle hints darkly at the punishment of the two classes in this phrase and in verse 18.

(18) And if the righteous scarcely be saved.—Comp. Prov. 11:31 (LXX). The apostle is thinking of the final judgment rather than of the life of trial; and he means that there was but little margin left—a few

more falls, a few more refusals to follow the calls of grace, and they would have been lost.

The ungodly and the sinner.—This is the Gentile character. "Ungodly" denotes open irreligion—contempt of God and all that belongs to His worship. "Sinner" goes more to the moral side of the nature, pointing most of all to sins of the flesh. "Sinners" was almost a synonym for "Gentiles."

(19) Commit the keeping of their souls.—The verb is a technical term for depositing a deed, a sum of money, or other valuable with any one in trust. The words which Peter probably has ringing in his ears when he thus writes are those of our Lord on the cross (Luke 23:46, where the same verb is used).

5

(1) The elders which are among you . .—In view of these hopes and threats, of the present persecution, and of the coming judgment, Peter gives his solemn charge to those who shared with him the responsibility of office in the church. The word rendered "exhort" includes encouragement and entreaty, and even consolation, as well as exhortation.

Who am also an elder.—Peter is giving no irresponsible advice. He knows by experience the dangers which beset the office. The head Christian of the world, and writing from the thick of the persecution already begun in Rome, he gives advice which the Asiatic elders cannot disregard as that of some easy layman who is untouched by the difficulty. It can hardly be said, therefore, that this is an example of Peter's humility, as though he recognized in himself no higher office than that of these presbyters. The effect is, on the contrary, to make the recipients of the letter feel that he is using a strong argument **a fortiori**.

(2) Feed the flock of God which is among you.—By the word "feed" here is meant not merely the giving of pasture, but the whole government. (See John 21:16.) There can be hardly any doubt that Peter was thinking of that scene when he issued these directions. Our Lord had committed into his hands all His sheep and lambs, without restriction of age or country, to be fed and shepherded; and now the time was approaching when he would have to "put off this tabernacle" (II Pet. 1:14), and he here takes order that "after his decease" the harge committed to him may be fulfilled. He still shepherds the flock by proxy. (Comp. Acts 20:28.)

Not by constraint, but willingly.—Why should this exhortation be given so prominently? By this time the word "bishop" had not become a fixed title of one special office, though the office itself was in existence. Probably he is thinking of the actual danger to life and property of being "ringleaders of the sect" (Acts 24:5), which would lead cowardly bishops to give up their office. He is not treating of the motives which should lead a man to accept the position. He speaks to persons who already hold the office, and urges them not to leave the flock, like hirelings, when they see the persecution imminent.

Not for filthy lucre, but of a ready mind.—The opposite vice to that on which he has just passed sentence. Some, who had no fears, might be tempted to retain the office by the good salary which the church gave, or might threaten to resign if their salaries were not raised in proportion to their risk. Love of the work itself should be the sole motive in seeking, or performing, the gospel ministry.

(3) Over God's heritage.—The heritage ("lots") over which the clergy are not to lord it are the different congregations, districts, parishes, dioceses, which had been allotted to them. Even in the apostle's days cowardice, greed, and self-assertion were not unknown.

(4) The beautiful word for "chief Shepherd" seems to have been invented by Peter, and it has been apparently imitated in Heb. 13:20. How could an office be more honored than by speaking of Christ as the chief bearer of that office?

(5) Likewise, ye younger.—Self-submission has been, at least tacitly, inculcated on the pastors in verse 3; so the writer can say "likewise" in turning to the rest. In comparison with the presbyters or elders, the lay people are styled "younger," or "juniors"; although in point of natural age, or of baptismal seniority, they might be the older.

Be clothed with humility.—There was a peculiar kind of cape, well known by a name taken from this verb (we might call it a "tie-up"), worn by slaves and no others. It was a badge of servitude. Thus Peter bids them all gird themselves for one another in a slave's "tie-up" of humility. None are to be masters in the Church of Christ. And the humility is to be the first thing noticed

about them, their outward mark and sign. (Comp. Prov. 3:34; Jas. 4:6.)

(6) In due time.—Peter probably means, in the day of judgment, which seemed so instant.

(7) Casting all your care upon him.—Comp. Ps. 55:22. Anxiety implies not only some distrust of God's providence, but also some king of belief that we may be able to manage better for ourselves. Confidence in God cannot be misplaced, for God is not forgetful of us.

(8) Peter is not calling attention to the fact that Satan is always prowling about, but he warns the sleeping shepherds that he is especially doing so now. This season of persecution was just his time for picking off one here and another there.

(9) Whom resist stedfast in the faith.—"Stand and face him," instead of running away from posts of duty (verse 2), or lying still and letting things take their course (verse 8). Not only is each individual to stand firm, but they are to present all together a solid front to the lion.

(10) Make you perfect.—Strictly these are futures. This verb implies the reduction to order and fitness for work of what is disordered or broken. The others, which are all similar in meaning, are heaped up after Peter's manner. All this is to take place at the close of the short season of suffering which is the means to it. Peter seems, therefore, to contemplate the passing of the persecution before the end of the world, for these verbs could hardly be so naturally used to express our education in the world to come.

(12) By Silvanus, a faithful brother unto you, as I suppose.—There is no reason for doubting that this is the same as the Silas of the Acts and the Silvanus of II Cor. 1:19; I Thess. 1:1; II Thess. 1:1. That the bearer of this letter was a personage of great consideration may be seen from the fact that Peter speaks of him as well known throughout the whole Hebrew population of Asia Minor. Silas being of the circumcision himself (Acts 15:22), Peter can without any risk, writing to the Jews, call him "brother." The words "as I suppose" imply the most complete confidence in Silas, which the writer is not at all ashamed to declare. This shows that Peter had not altered his opinion either of Silas or of the relative positions of Jew and Gentile in the church, since that great council in which he took so prominent a part, when Silas was selected, no doubt because of his uniting liberal views with steadfast allegiance to the Law, to bear the apostolic mandates to the Gentile metropolis of Antioch. The same qualifications which fitted him for that work would now again serve him in good stead to bear to the Jews of Asia Minor Peter's countersignature to the doctrine of Paul.

Briefly.—So Heb. 13:22. The writer hints that if this present letter is not enough to effect its purpose, it is not because there is any lack of matter or weakness of conviction. (See also John 20:25.)

Exhorting, and testifying that this is the true grace of God wherein ye stand.— These words give Peter's own account of the object and contents of the epistle. Nothing is to drive them or entice them from the ground which the Pauline preachers have marked out for them.

(13) The church ... elected together with you.—Comp. 1:2. It was becoming a frequent mode of designating a church to personify it under a female title (see II John 1, 4, 5, 13); it seems therefore natural to suppose that the salutation is from this church of "Babylon" to her sister churches in the provinces of Asia Minor. The modesty with which this church at "Babylon" is spoken of, as being only one of many "co-elect" ones, is noteworthy.

That is at Babylon.—The established interpretation is that the place meant is Rome. We never hear of Peter being in the East. Everything in the letter points to such a state of things as was to be found at Rome about the date when we believe the letter to have been written. The symbolism in the name is quite in keeping with the context Peter has just personified the church of the place from which he writes, which seem quite as unprosaic a use of language as to call Rome "Babylon." And it seems clea that the name was quite intelligible to Jewish readers, for whom it was intended The Apocalypse (17:18) speaks of Rome under this title. There were reasons o prudence, too, for not speaking too plainly about the presence of a large Christia society in Rome. The police were still more vigilant now than when Paul wrote in guarded language about the Roman empire to the Thessalonians. It might provoke hos tilities if the epistle fell into the hands of ar informer, with names and places too clearly given.

Marcus my son.—The particular word used here does not occur elsewhere of spir itual relationship, but the other thought is improbable. We should have heard of it in other places had Mark been his son in the flesh. (See Acts 12:12.) Mark was, of course, well-known in Asia Minor (Acts 12:25, Col 4:10, II Tim. 4:11).

(14) Kiss of charity.—See note on I Thess. 5:26.

SECOND PETER

1

(1) Simon Peter.—The reading "Symeon" is to be preferred. "Simon" has probably been substituted as being more usual. "Symeon," of Peter, occurs elsewhere only in Acts 15:14, a speech of the strongly Jewish James. As being the more Jewish form of the name, it points to a Jewish Christian as the author; as coming from Peter, the apostle of the circumcision, it is natural enough. The differences between this opening and that of I Peter are instructive. There, as approaching communities which might seem to belong to Paul, he carefully suppresses everything personal; he calls himself merely "Peter," the name which Christ Himself had given him along with his high commission (Matt. 16:18), and "apostle," the title which stated his commission. Here, as coming a second time to those who now know him better (both through his former epistle and through Silvanus), he adds personal designations. There, as if not venturing to depart greatly from his own peculiar field, he addresses himself mainly to the Jewish converts. Here, with more boldness, the natural result of increased familiarity, he addresses Gentile converts chiefly.

To them that have obtained.—The Greek word implies that they have not won it or earned it for themselves, but that it has been allotted to them. Comp. Acts 1:17; 1:17; 15:8-11, remarkable parallels to this.

Like precious faith with us.—All believed the same precious mysteries. (Comp. I Pet. 1:7.) "Us" may mean either the apostles, or (more probably) the first Christians, as distinct from those converted later, i.e., Jewish as distinct from Gentile Christians. This shows that Gentile converts are chiefly addressed in this epistle, as Jewish in the First Epistle. Gentiles would be more likely to be doubters respecting Christ's return to judgment, than Jews well-acquainted with Hebrew prophecies on the subject. Gentiles also would be more likely than Jews to fall into the excesses denounced in the second chapter, which bear a strong resemblance to the catalogue of heathen vices given by Paul in Rom. 1. The idea that Christians are the antitype of the chosen people is prominent in Peter's writings. (Comp. 2:1; I Pet. 1:10.) Note that no particular churches are mentioned. The Second Epistle is more

"general" or "catholic" in its address than the First.

Of God and our Saviour Jesus Christ.—Here, as in Tit. 2:13 (comp. II Thess. 1:12), we are somewhat in doubt as to whether we have one or two Persons of the Trinity mentioned. Rigid grammar would incline us to make "God" and "Saviour" both apply to Christ. But the next verse, independently of other considerations, seems to determine that both the Father and the Son are mentioned here. The mode of expression which causes doubt on the subject perhaps indicates the writer's perfect belief in the oneness of the Father with the Son. The addition of "Saviour" to the name of Jesus Christ shows how completely "Jesus" had become a proper name, the exact meaning of which was becoming obscured.

(2) Through the knowledge.—"Knowledge" is not quite strong enough. In the original we have a compound word, which implies fuller, riper, more minute knowledge. The same compound recurs in verse 3. It is rare in Paul's ealier letters, but is more common in the later ones. This fact, coupled with its appearance here, agrees well with the more contemplative aspect in which the Gospel began gradually to be presented, a change which finds its fullest expression in the transition from the first three gospels to the fourth. The word is introduced here with telling emphasis; "in the fuller knowledge of God" anticipates the attack that is coming upon the godless speculations of the "false teachers" in chapter 2.

And of Jesus our Lord.—These false teachers "denied the Lord that bought them" (2:1), and promised all kinds of highsounding benefits to their followers (2:18). The apostle assures his readers that only in fuller knowledge of their Lord can grace and peace be multiplied to them. The combination "Jesus our Lord" is unusual, elsewhere only in Rom. 4:24.

(3, 4) Verses 3 and 4 are a brief introduction to the direct exhortations contained in 5-11. The eagerness with which the writer goes directly to his subject is characteristic of Peter's temper.

(3) Godliness.—The Greek word belongs to the phraseology of the later books of the New Testament. "Godliness" is the realization of God's abiding presence, the fruits of which are reverence and trust. It is introduced here, perhaps, in opposition to the godlessness and irreverence of the false teachers. (Comp. II Tim. 3:5.)

(4) Promises.—They are "the greatest" because they contain an earnest of the completion and perfection of the Christian life; they are very "precious" because this earnest is in itself something real, and not mere empty words. Not the promises of the Old Testament are meant, that Christ should come; but those of the New Testament, that Christ should come again. The certainty of Christ's return to reward the righteous and punish the wicked is one of the main subjects of the epistle.

(5) Giving all diligence—i.e., making your contribution in answer to His. He has made all things possible for you; but they are not yet done, and you must labor diligently to realize the glorious possibilities opened to you.

Add to your faith virtue.—The notion of rendering a service that is expected of one in virtue of one's position fits in admirably here. God gives; His blessings and promises come from His free undeserved bounty; man renders, supplies, furnishes that which, considering the benefits which he has received, is fairly required of him. Note that we are not told to supply faith; that comes from God (Eph. 2:8), and the apostle assumes that his readers possess it.

And to virtue knowledge.—Virtue for each individual is the excellence corresponding to the talents committed to him. The word for "knowledge" here means knowledge that still admits of growth, not yet ripe or complete. Here it probably meant spiritual discernment as to what is right and what is wrong in all things.

(6) And to knowledge temperance; and to temperance patience; and to patience godliness.—Virtue and knowledge are energetic and progressive; they are exercised in developing the powers implanted in us. Self-control and patience are restrictive and disciplinary; they are exercised in checking and regulating the conflicting claims of many co-existing powers, so as to reduce all to harmony. There is special point in "self-control" being placed as the consequence of "knowledge." The false teachers would insist that knowledge led to liberty, which with them meant emancipation from all control whatever. Self-mastery is to the world at large the opposite of liberty; to the Christian it is another name for it—that service which is perfect freedom. Patience to the world is to accept loss and suffering; to the Christian it is to win the best of prizes—"in your patience possess ye your souls."

(7) And to godliness brotherly kindness; and to brotherly kindness charity.— Godliness must not be selfish and solitary, but social and Christian, for he who loves God must love his brother also (I John 4:20, 21). The translation "brotherly kindness" obscures the exact meaning of the word, and also the fact that the same word is used in I Pet. 1:22. "Love of the brethren" means love of Christians as such, as members of the same great family, as God's adopted children. "Charity" means love of men as such, as creatures made in the likeness of God, as souls for which Christ died. The word for "charity" is emphatically Christian love, not mere natural benevolence.

Each in this noble chain of virtues prepares the way for the next and is supplemented and perfected by it. But we must not insist too strongly upon the order in the series, as being either logically or chronologically necessary. It is a natural order that is given here, but not the only one. These three verses are the First Epistle condensed: virtue (1:13); knowledge (3:15); self-control (1:14; 2:11); patience (1:6; 2:21); godliness (1:15, 16; 3:4); love of the brethren (1:22, 3:8); charity (4:8). The slight amount of similarity affords no ground for supposing that the writer was acquainted with II Peter.

(8) First reason for the preceding exhortation—the benefit of having these graces.

Neither be barren nor unfruitful.—The two adjectives "idle" (barren) and "unfruitful" exactly correspond to the two verbs "be in you" and "increase." If these things be in you, you will be morally active; if they increase, you will be morally productive.

(9) Second reason for the exhortation to furnish all these graces—the evil of not having them.

Cannot see afar off.—The point seems to be not willful shutting of the eyes (those who **won't** see), but involuntary and partial closing, as in the case of shortsighted people; in a spiritual sense, those who have only a hazy apprehension of the objects of belief and of the bearing which their beliefs should have on their conduct.

And hath forgotten.—The phrase does not necessarily imply that the forgetfulness is voluntary; it is the inevitable result of willful neglect—the neglect to cultivate Christian virtues. The forgetfulness is not the cause of the shortsightedness, but a phase of it.

(10) Wherefore the rather.—The direct

address, "brethren," is a mark of increased earnestness, and also assures those addressed that they are not included among the mere nominal Christians described in the preceding verse.

Calling and election.—One of the best MSS and several versions insert "by means of your works," which gives the right sense, although the words are wanting in authority. It is by following the injunctions given (verses 5-7) that our election is made secure. God calls us to salvation (verse 3), selects us from the heathen; it is for each one of us to respond to the call, and thus ratify His choice.

Never fall.—The word means to knock one's foot and stumble. The man who has acquired these graces has his path freed from many stumblingblocks, and his vision cleared to see and avoid the rest.

(11) Thus ends the first main section of the epistle, which contains the substance of the whole. Its obvious harmony with the First Epistle has made some critics ready to admit its genuineness, who throw doubt on much of the rest. Change of style is amply accounted for by change to a new and exciting subject; and the links between the parts are too strong to be severed by any such considerations.

(12) And be established in the present truth.—"The present truth" is not the truth that we are now discussing, the truth before us, but the truth of the Gospel that is come to you (Col. 1:5, 6), and is present with you: "the faith once for all delivered unto the saints" (Jude 3).

(13) In this tabernacle.—The comparison of the human body to a dwelling is common in all literatures, and the temporary nature of a tent makes it especially appropriate. (Comp. II Cor. 5:1.)

(14) Knowing that shortly I must put off this my tabernacle.—Rather, "Knowing as I do that the putting off of my tabernacle will be done swiftly" (comp. 2:1)—i.e., will soon be over when it once begins. The point is not that the writer believes himself to be near his end, but that his end would be such as to allow of no death-bed exhortations; what he has to say must be said in good time, for Christ had told him that his death would be a violent one (John 21:18).

Hath shewed me.—The substitution of perfect for aorist is here objectionable, as it obscures the reference to a definite moment in the apostle's life. If the reference is to the event narrated in John 21:18, then that narrative confirms what is said here, this

being a prior and independent allusion to the same occurrence. In this case we have strong evidence of the authenticity of Peter.

(15) To what does this declaration point? The simplest answer is, to his writing this letter, which they might keep and read whenever they liked. (Comp. verse 13.) Other suggestions are: to his having copies of this letter distributed; or, writing other letters; or, instructing Mark to write his gospel; or, commissioning "faithful men" to teach these things. There seems to be nothing either for or against these conjectures. It is a coincidence worth noting that, with the Transfiguration in his mind (verses 16-18), he uses, in close succession, two words connected in Luke's account of the Transfiguration (Luke 9:31, 33)—"decease" and "tabernacle."

(16-21) The certainty of Christ's coming again is the basis of these exhortations; and that certainty is proved (1) by the Transfiguration, which was an anticipation of His coming again in glory, and (2) by the utterances of the prophets who predicted it.

(16) Cunningly devised fables.—Various things have been suggested as possibly indicated—heathen mythology, Jewish theosophy, Gnostic systems, Apocryphal gospels, the doctrine of the false teachers. There is reason for believing that the particular elements in the teaching of the latter thus incidentally condemned were of Jewish origin. If this conjecture be correct, then Peter is here dealing with errors similar to those condemned by Paul (I Tim. 1:4; II Tim. 4:4; Tit. 1:14—the only other passages in which the word "fables" occurs). And in this case much light is thrown on some of the marked peculiarities of this epistle and that of Jude, viz., the fondness of both writers for the oldest, and sometimes the most obscure, passages of Old Testament history, as well as for some strange portions of uncanonical and apocryphal tradition.

The power and coming.—The power conferred upon Christ after being glorified in His passion and resurrection, and His coming again to judgment. In this power He will come again. His first coming at the Incarnation would neither be the usual meaning of the word nor would suit the context.

Eyewitnesses of his majesty.—At the Transfiguration, which was a foretaste and an earnest of the glory of His Second Coming. This is Peter's view of it; and that it is the correct one is perhaps shown by the gospels themselves. Comp. Matt. 16:28;

Mark 9:1; Luke 9:27. Apparently the Transfiguration was regarded by Christ Himself as in some sense the coming of the Son of man. The kindred verb, "to be an eyewitness," occurs in I Pet. 2:12; 3:2, and nowhere else—a coincidence worth noting.

(19) We have also a more sure word of prophecy, as a second proof of the truth of my teaching respecting Christ's coming. The expression, "the prophetic word," occurs nowhere else in the New Testament, but in II Clement 11. The quotation in both cases is probably from some uncanonical book of prophecies. Here the expression means the whole body of prophecy respecting the subject in hand; but the meaning of the whole sentence is not quite clear. It may mean that in the prophetic word we have something more sure than the voice from heaven. Here a simple "and" is natural enough; and the **word** of prophecy is suitably compared with the **voice** from heaven. But how can the word of prophets be more sure than the voice of God? In itself it cannot be so; but it may be so regarded in reference to those who did not hear, but only heard of, the voice from heaven, and in reference to the subject in hand. If this interpretation is right, we have another mark of authenticity. A forger would be likely to magnify his own advantage in hearing the voice from heaven over the ordinary proofs open to every one. (Comp. Acts 3:20, 21; I Pet. 1:10-12.)

In a dark place.—This translation is somewhat doubtful. The word rendered "dark" occurs here only in the New Testament, and its usual meaning is "dry." "In a **waste** place" would perhaps be safer; and the image would then be that prophecy is like campfires in the desert, which may keep one from going utterly astray, until sunrise frees one from difficulty. The "waste place" is either the wilderness of this world or the tangled life of the imperfect Christian.

Until the day dawn.—The meaning may be Christ's return in glory to illumine the wilderness of this world, to clear off its obscurities, and show the way through its mazes. (Comp. Rev. 22:16.)

In your hearts.—These words belong with "take heed": "and ye do well in giving heed to it in your hearts"—i.e., let it influence your lives, not receive a mere intellectual attention.

(20) Is of any private interpretation.—The main question is the meaning of the word rendered "private," which may also mean "its own." Two explanations are possible. The term may refer to the recipients of the prophecies—that we may not expound prophecy according to our own fancy; or to the utterers of the prophecies— that the prophets had not the power of expounding their own prophecies. Verse 21 gives the reason **why** "no prophecy of the scripture," etc. If prophecy came "by the will of man," then it might be interpreted according to man's fancy. But it did not so come; consequently the interpretation must be sought at the same source from which the prophecy itself proceeded. If the prophets spoke just as they pleased, they would be the best exponents of what they meant. But they spoke under divine influence, and therefore need not know the import of their own words. (Comp. I Pet. 1:10-12.)' The whole body of prophecy, "the prophetic word" (verse 19), is our lamp in the wilderness, not the private dicta of any one seer.

(21) The rendering should be "not at any time." The word for "moved" is a strong one, meaning "borne along," as a ship before the wind (Acts 27:16, 17). Some have suggested that verses 19-21 savor of Montanism, and are evidence of the late origin of the epistle. But what is said here of the gift of prophecy is not more than we find elsewhere in the New Testament (Matt. 1:22; 2:15; Acts 1:16; 3:18) and in the Old Testament (Num. 11:17, 25, 29; I Sam. 10:6, 10; 19:20, 23; Jer. 1:5-7). Montanists used much stronger language, as readers of Tertullian know. With their prophecy was ecstasy and frenzy; prophets ceased to be men—their reason left them, and they became mere instruments on which the Spirit played. The wording of these verses points to an age previous to Montanism.

2

(1) By a perfectly natural transition, we pass to an entirely different subject—from exhortation to show forth Christian graces to a warning against corrupt doctrine. True prophets (1:21) suggest false prophets, and false prophets suggest false teachers. The fervor and impetuosity with which the writer attacks the evil before him are thoroughly in harmony with Peter's character. (Comp. Justin Martyr, **Trypho**, 82, and Shepherd of Hermas, **Sim.**, 8.6. 5.)

Heresies.—The term in the New Testament points rather to divisions than doctrines, and always to parties inside the

Church, not to sects that have separated from it.

Even denying the Lord that bought them.—See note on Jude 4. The phrase is remarkable as coming from one who himself denied his Master.

And bring upon themselves.—The two participles, "denying" and "bringing," without any conjunction to connect them, are awkward, and show that the writer's strong feeling is already beginning to ruffle the smoothness of his language.

Swift destruction—i.e., coming suddenly and unexpectedly, so as to preclude escape; not necessarily coming soon. The reference, probably, is to Christ's sudden return to judgment (3:10), scoffing at which was one of the ways in which they "denied their Master."

(2) Shall be evil spoken of.—By the heathen, who will judge of the way of truth by the evil lives of the many who have really been seduced from it, though they profess still to follow it. The connection between false doctrine and licentiousness was—and is—often real. In Second Clement 13 there is a remarkable amplification of this statement. Our epistle was probably known to the writer of the homily, who to a considerable extent preaches against similar evils.

(3) And through covetousness.—Comp. Acts 8:18; I Tim. 6:5. These false teachers, like the Greek Sophists, taught for money. A bombastic mysticism, promising to reveal secrets about the unseen world and the future, was a very lucrative profession in the last days of Paganism, and it passed over to Christianity as an element in various heresies. (Comp. Shepherd of Hermas, Sim. 9. 19. 3.)

(4-8) We now pass on to see how it is that this judgment "of a long time" has been working. It was pronounced against all sinners, such as they are, from the first beginning of the world. The three instances here are in chronological order (wanton angels, Flood, Sodom and Gomorrah), while those in Jude are not (unbelievers in the wilderness, impure angels, Sodom and Gomorrah). See note on Jude 5-7.

(4) For if God . . . —The sentence has no proper conclusion. The third instance of God's vengeance is so prolonged by the addition respecting Lot that the apodosis is wanting, the writer in his eagerness having lost the thread of the construction.

The angels that sinned.—What sin is meant? Jude is somewhat more explicit (see note on Jude 6).

Cast them down to hell.—The Greek word **Tartarus** occurs nowhere else in the Old or New Testament. It probably is the same as Gehenna. (See Matt. 5:22.)

(5) The fact that the Flood is taken as the second instance of divine vengeance gives us no clue as to the source of the first instance. In the Book of Enoch the Flood follows closely upon the sin of the angels, as in Gen. 6 upon that of the sons of God, so that in either case the first instance would naturally suggest the second. The coincidence with I Pet. 3:20 must not pass unobserved, especially as there the mention of "spirits in prison" immediately precedes, just as here, the angels in "caves of darkness."

(7) And delivered just Lot.—Better, "righteous Lot." Here, as in the case of the Flood (verse 5), the destruction of the guilty suggests the preservation of the innocent. Is it fanciful to think that these lights in a dark picture are characteristic of one who had himself "denied the Master who bought him," and yet had been preserved like Noah and rescued like Lot? This brighter side is wanting in Jude, so that in the strictly historical illustrations this epistle is more full than the other; it is where apocryphal books seem to be alluded to that Jude has more detail.

The judgment on Sodom and Gomorrha forms a fitting complement to that of the Flood as an instance of God's vengeance, a judgment by fire being regarded as more awful than a judgment by flood, as is more distinctly shown in 3:6, 7, where the total destruction of the world by fire is contrasted with the transformation of it wrought by the Flood.

(8) For that righteous man.—"Righteous" is a relative term; and in this case we must look at Lot both in comparison with the defective morality of the age and also with the licentiousness of those with whom he is here contrasted. Moreover, in the midst of this corruption he preserves some of the brighter features of his purer nomad life. Note Gen. 18:32; 19:2, 3, 8, 21; Heb. 13:2; and we must then admit that the epithet "righteous" as applied to Lot is by no means without warrant.

(9) The Lord knoweth.—This is the main sentence to which the various conditional clauses beginning verse 4 have been leading. What the writer especially wishes to prove is that the Lord knows how to reserve the ungodly to the day of judgment under punishment.

(10) Despise government.—The word translated "government" here and "dominion" in Jude is the same in the Greek, whereas the words translated in both places "despise" are different.

Presumptuous are they.—A fresh verse should begin here. From "the unjust" to "government" the reference is to ungodly and sensual people in general; here we return to the false teachers in particular. Audacious would be more literal than "presumptuous."

Speak evil of dignities.—The exact meaning of "dignities," or "glories," is not clear, either here or in Jude 8. The context in both places seems to show that spiritual powers alone are intended, and that earthly powers, whether civil or ecclesiastical, are not included, much less exclusively indicated. These men deny the existence of, or irreverently speak slightingly of, those spiritual agencies by means of which God conducts the government of the world.

(11) Whereas angels.—Only when compared with Jude 9 does this allusion become intelligible; but even so, it does not necessarily attest the priority of Jude. The writer of this epistle might possibly count on his readers at once understanding his allusion to a tradition that may have been well known, while Jude thought it best to point out the allusion more plainly. It is possible that the contest alluded to is not that between Satan and Michael about the body of Moses, but that between Satan and the angel of the Lord about Joshua the high priest (Zech. 3:1, 2). It is also possible that it does not refer to any contest with Satan at all, but merely to angels not denouncing these false teachers before God, but leaving them to His judgment.

Railing accusation against them.—"Against them" may mean "against the false teachers," i.e., they speak evil of angels, yet the angels bring no denunciation against them, but leave all judgment to God (Deut. 32:35, 36; Rom. 12:19; Heb. 10:30).

(12) Comp. the superior literary form of Jude 10. The force here is that these animals cannot help themselves—it is their nature to rush after what will prove their ruin; but the false teachers voluntarily seek their own destruction against nature. The word for "destruction" and "corruption" is the same in the Greek, the destroying being literal in the first case, moral in the second.

Moreover, the word for "perish" is from the same root.

(13) As they that count.—Though "rioting in the day time" makes good sense—revelry even among professed pleasure seekers being usually confined to the night (I Thess. 5:7)—the meaning is, perhaps, "for the day," without thought for the morrow, **counting luxury for the moment a pleasure**—the doctrine of the Cyrenaics and the instinct of "brute beasts."

With their own deceivings.—Both here and in Jude 12 (see note) the reading is uncertain, authorities being divided between **agapai**, "love feasts," and **apatai**, "deceits." In Jude the balance on purely critical grounds is decidedly in favor of "love feasts"; here (though much less decidedly) in favor of "deceits." In Jude the context confirms the reading "love feasts"; here the context is neutral, or slightly inclines to "love feasts," to which "while they feast with you" must in any case refer. But if "love feasts" is right in Jude (and this is so probable that we may almost assume it), this in itself is strong support to the same reading here. Whichever writer is prior, so strange a change from "deceits" to "love feasts" would hardly have been made deliberately, whereas, in copying mechanically, the interchange might easily be made, the words being so similar.

(14) Beguiling.—Strictly, "enticing with bait." We have the same word in verse 18, Jas. 1:14, and nowhere else. The metaphor from fishing, twice to this epistle and only once elsewhere, may point to a fisherman of Galilee. (Comp. Matt. 17:27.)

(15) Are gone astray.—In the historical incident of Balaam, as in that of Sodom and Gomorrah, our epistle is more detailed than Jude (see note on verse 7). The past tenses in this verse are quite in harmony with the view that this chapter is a genuine prediction. The future foretold with such confidence as to be spoken of as already past is a common form for prophecy to assume.

Balaam the son of Bosor.—The resemblance between these false teachers and Balaam consisted in their running counter to God's will for their own profit, and in prostituting their office to an infamous purpose, which brought ruin on the community. A comparison of this passage with Rev. 2:14, 15, gives countenance to the view that among the false teachers thus stigmatized the Nicolaitans may be included.

(16) Forbad the madness.—Thus the trivial discrepancy which some would urge

as existing between this passage and Num.
22 disappears. It has been objected that not
the ass but the angel forbad Balaam from
proceeding.

(17) **These are wells.**—These men are like
dried-up watering places in the desert,
which entice and mock the thirsty traveler,
perhaps leading him into danger also by
drawing him from places where there is
water. (Comp. Jer. 2:13; 14:3.) The parallel
passage (Jude 12, 13), is fuller than the one
before us, and is more like an amplification
of this than this a condensation of that.

Clouds that are carried with a tempest.—
These mists promise refreshment to the thirsty soil (Gen. 2:6), and are so flimsy that
they are blown away before they do any
good. So these false teachers deceived those
who were thirsting for the knowledge and
liberty promised them by raising hopes
which they could not satisfy.

(18) **Were clean escaped.**—Both verb and
adverb require correcting: "those who are
scarcely escaping," viz., the "unstable souls"
of verse 14.

(19) **Brought in bondage.**—Or, "enslaved." (comp. John 8:34; Rom. 6:16-20.)
There is nothing improbable in Peter being
well-acquainted with the epistle to the Romans during the last years of his life; the
improbability would rather be in supposing
that he did not know it.

(20) **Through the knowledge.**—The
knowledge is of the same mature and complete kind as that spoken of in 1:2, 3, 8 (see
note on 1:2), showing that these men were
well-instructed Christians. (Comp. Matt.
12:45.)

(21) **The way of righteousness.**—The life
of the Christian. That which from a doctrinal point of view is "the way of truth"
(verse 2), from a moral point of view is "the
way of righteousness." So also "the faith
delivered to the saints" of Jude 3 is the
doctrinal equivalent of "the holy commandment delivered unto them" of this verse.

(22) **But it is happened unto them according to the true proverb.**—The first
proverb is found in Prov. 26:11; and if that
is the source of the quotation, we have here
an independent translation of the Hebrew,
for the LXX gives an entirely different
rendering, "dog" being the only word in
common to the two Greek versions. The
LXX adds, "and becomes abominable,"
which has no equivalent in the existing
Hebrew text; and it has been suggested that
these words may misrepresent the Hebrew
original of the second proverb here. But it
is quite possible that both proverbs come
from popular tradition, and not from Scripture at all. If, however, the Book of Proverbs is the source of the quotation, it is
worthwhile noting that no less than four
times in as many chapters does Peter recall
passages from the Proverbs in the first epistle (1:7; 2:17; 4:8, 18).

3

(1) **This second epistle, beloved, I now
write.**—Rather, "This epistle, already a second one"—implying that no very long time
has elapsed since his first letter, and that
this one is addressed to much the same
circle of readers. There is no indication that
the first two chapters are one letter, and
that this is the beginning of another, as has
been supposed.

Pure minds.—The word for "pure" means
literally "separated"—according to one derivation, by being sifted; according to another, by being held up to the light. Here it
probably means untainted by sensuality.
The word for "mind" means the faculty of
moral reflection and moral understanding.
These two words are found together in a
beautiful passage in Plato's **Phaedo,** 66a.

(2) **By the holy prophets.**—Comp. Jude
17. In this verse the apostle commends the
warnings of the Old Testament and the New
Testament, as to the coming of Christ, to
Christians throughout all ages.

**The commandment of us the apostles of
the Lord.**—"Of us" should be "of you," or
"your"—"the commandment of your apostles (or rather) of the Lord and Saviour."
The commandment is at once a commandment of the apostles and of the Lord. The
expression "your apostles" may be taken as
a mark of genuineness rather than of the
contrary. It is at least probable that a true
apostle, having once stated his credentials
(1:1), would merge his own personality with
the group of his colleagues from a feeling of
humility and of delicacy toward those
whom he was addressing, especially when
they owed their Christianity mainly to other apostles than himself.

What commandment is meant? Probably
what is the main subject of this epistle, to
be ready for Christ's coming (Matt.
24:36-39; Mark 13:35-37; Luke 12:40; I
Thess. 5:2-4).

(4) **Of his coming.**—What has come of it?
Where is there any accomplishment of it?
"His" instead of "the Lord's" indicates not

merely that only one Person could be meant, but also the irreverent way in which these scoffers spoke of Him.

Since the fathers fell asleep.—Probably nothing more definite than our remote ancestors is intended. The thoroughly Christian term "cemetery" (sleeping-place), in the sense of a place of repose for the dead, comes from the same Greek root as here.

(5) The earth standing out of the water and in the water.—"Standing" is the same word translated "consist" in Col. 1:17. The notion is that of coherence, solidarity, and order, as distinct from chaos. "Out of water" indicates the material out of which the earth was made, not that out of which the earth rose, like an island from the ocean. In both clauses the article should perhaps be omitted—"the earth consisting out of water and through water." (Comp. Pss. 24:2; 136:6. In the Greek "by the word of God" comes last, not first; emphasis is obtained either way: "by the word of God," not by a fortuitous concourse of atoms.

(6) Whereby.—The original literally signifies, "by means of which things," i.e., the heavens and the earth. Both the heavens and the earth contributed to the deluge (see Gen. 7:11).

The world that then was, ... perished.— So it is absurd to say that all things continue unchanged since the Creation. The world was so transformed by the deluge that the world previous to that catastrophe perished, chaos for the moment returned, and a new world issued from the crisis.

(7) By the same word.—The sense is that the universe is preserved for judgment by the same power that created it. Just as "the world that then was" was destroyed by water, so the present world is being treasured up to be destroyed by fire. Christ Himself, in a discourse which Peter heard (Mark 13:3), had made the Flood a type of the Judgment (Matt. 24:37-39).

(8) This is another answer to the sceptical argument. Time is the condition of man's thought and action, but not of God's. His thoughts are not as our thoughts, nor His ways as our ways; what seems delay to us is none to Him. (Comp. Ps. 90:4.)

(9) This is still another answer—a practical one: Make good use of what to you seems to be delay.

The Lord is not slack.—In verse 8 "the Lord" certainly means God the Father; and this is in favor of the same meaning here. On the other hand, "concerning his promise" naturally refers to Christ's promise that

He will return. By "is not slack" is meant "does not delay beyond the time appointed." There is no dilatoriness; He waits, but is never slow, is never late.

But is longsuffering.—As Augustine puts it, God is **patiens quia aeternus**— longsuffering because He is eternal. He who is from everlasting to everlasting can afford to wait. (Comp. the **Shepherd of Hermas, Sim.** 8: 11.1.)

To us-ward.—The true reading is "towards you." It is natural here that Peter should not include himself among those whom he addresses, for he is writing mainly to Gentile Christians (1:1), and this longsuffering of God had been conspicuous in His dealings with the Gentiles (Rom. 11:11-36.)

(10) As a thief in the night.—Suddenly and without warning. Comp. Matt. 24:43, a saying which Peter certainly heard (Mark 13:3), and I Thess. 5:2, which may easily be included in the epistles referred to in verse 16. The words "in the night" are here wanting in authority.

The heavens shall pass away.—Comp. Matt. 24:35. This repeated reproduction of words and ideas from one of the most impressive of Christ's discourses, which only Peter and three others seem to have heard, may fairly be added to the evidence in favor of the authenticity of the epistle.

The elements shall melt with fervent heat.—Probably the various forms of matter in the universe, such as water and air, are intended, without any thought of indicating what they are precisely. But it is possible that the heavenly bodies are meant here, all the more so, as the mention of these "elements" immediately follows that of the heavens. "Shall melt" should rather be, as in the next two verses, "shall be dissolved." This dissolution is the opposite of the consistency spoken of in verse 5. In verse 12 "melt" is correct, and suits the heavenly bodies better than the four elements.

The earth also and the works that are therein.—A comprehensive sense for products both of nature and art. The moral work of each individual is not meant; consequently, a reference to I Cor. 3:13 is misleading. The two passages have little in common. In this passage the apostle is stating plainly and in detail what some of the prophets of the Old Testament had set forth in general and sometimes obscure language— that a judgment by fire is in store for the world (Isa. 66:15, 16, 24; Mal. 3:1-3; 4:1).

(11) What manner of persons.—Not so much a question as an exclamation. In any case, the sentence should run on to the end of verse 12.

In all holy conversation and godliness.— Literally, "in holy behaviors and godlinesses." The plurals indicate a variety of acts, hastening Christ's coming (verse 12).

(13) Nevertheless we, according to his promise.—"Nevertheless" is too strong, and the emphasis is on "new," not on "we." The promise of the new heavens and new earth is given in Isa. 65:17; 66:22. There are two words for "new" in Greek; one looks forward, "young" as opposed to "aged"; the other looks back, "fresh" as opposed to "worn out." It is the latter word that is used here and in Rev. 21:1, 2.

(14) Be found of him in peace, without spot, and blameless.—The pair of epithets, "spotless and blameless," should be noticed as coinciding with I Pet. 1:19, and also as forming a marked contrast to the false teachers, who are called "spots and blemishes" (II Pet. 2:13). "In peace" has no special reference. It expresses at once the condition and the consequence of being "spotless and blameless."

(15) The longsuffering of our Lord.— Again, as in verse 9, we are in doubt as to whether God the Father or the Lord Jesus is meant. In verse 8 "the Lord" certainly means God, and not the Lord Jesus. In verse 18 "our Lord" is expressly stated to be Jesus Christ. The fact that "our" appears in this verse before "Lord," as in verse 18, inclines the balance here toward the meaning in verse 18. If this is correct, and "our Lord" means Jesus Christ, then throughout this weighty passage the Lord Jesus is invested with the full attributes of deity. The message is to make use of His longsuffering for working out your own salvation in fear and trembling, instead of criticizing it.

As our beloved brother Paul.—This may possibly mean something more than that Paul was a fellow Christian and a personal friend—viz., that he was a fellow worker and brother evangelist. It is doubtful whether there is any allusion to the dispute between Peter and Paul (Gal. 2:11), although an expression of marked affection would be quite in place as evidence that all such differences were now forgotten. In any case the familiarity and equality which the expression implies should be noticed. It is in marked contrast to the way in which Clement of Rome, Ignatius, Polycarp, and Clement of Alexandria speak of Paul, and in this way is a decided note of genuineness. A writer of the sub-Apostolic age would not easily be able to free himself from the feeling of the age in this respect.

Hath written unto you.—More literally, "wrote to you." What epistle, or epistles, are meant here? Few points in this epistle have been more debated. But when we consider Rom. 2:4; 9:22, 23; that Romans appears to have been an encyclical letter; that in Rom. 3:8 Paul himself tells us that he was grossly misunderstood; that 9:3 might easily cause serious misunderstanding; and that Rom. 6:16 seems to be recalled in II Pet. 2:19—it will perhaps be thought that on the whole Romans best answers to the requirements of the context.

(16) As also in all his epistles.—All those known to the writer. The expression does not necessarily imply that Paul was dead, and that his epistles had been collected into one volume. That each church made a collection of them as they became known to it, and that in the great centers they became known soon after they were written, are conjectures of great probability. Polycarp, in his Epistle to the Philippians (3:2), seems to show that Paul's letters, in his day, had become the common property of the churches.

Speaking in them of these things—viz., of the return of Christ and of the destruction of the world. Some, however, understand the words as meaning the exhortations to holiness given here.

Some things hard to be understood.— Some contend that certainly the difficulties with which II Thess. 2 bristles are well described by this expression, and that they relate to the point in question—the time of Christ's coming. Moreover, scoffers could easily turn them to account by arguing that "the man of sin" had not yet appeared, and that therefore there was no likelihood of the end of the world coming just yet. But in admitting that II Thess. 2 is among the passages alluded to here, we are not committed to the theory that I and II Thess. are alluded to in verse 15.

Unlearned and unstable.—The word in Acts 4:13 signifies "without special study"; this means "without ordinary instruction." Ignorance naturally produces instability; those who have no clear principles of Christian doctrine easily fall victims to seductions of all kinds.

Wrest.—Literally, "torture by means of the rack"; therefore, "strain," "distort." That Paul's doctrine of Christian liberty, as opposed to the bondage of the Law, was seen by himself to be liable to great abuse, and had already begun to be abused, we learn from his own writings (I Cor. 6:12-20; Gal. 5:13-26). Many refer these words to Paul's doctrine of justification by faith as wrested to mean "faith without works." So, again, Eph. 2:5, 6 and Col. 2:12 might be wrested to mean that "the resurrection is past already" (II Tim. 2:18).

The other scriptures.—The Old Testament cannot well be meant. Peter would scarcely have placed the writings of a contemporary side by side with the Scriptures of the Old Testament (the canon of which had long since been closed) without some intimation of a grouping which at that time must have been novel and probably was quite unknown. It is much more probable that Christian writings of some kind are intended, but we can only conjecture which, many of the canonical writings of the New Testament then in existence, and perhaps some that are not canonical. That an apostle should speak of the writings of a brother-apostle in the same terms as the books of the Old Testament—viz., as Scripture—need not surprise us, especially when we remember the large claims made by Paul for his own words (I Thess. 2:13; II Thess. 2:15; Eph. 3:3-5. Comp. Acts 15:28; Rev. 22:18, 19. In I Pet. 1:12 evangelists are almost made superior to the Old Testament prophets—a statement indicating a view which harmonizes well both with II Pet. 1:15-19 and with the view set forth here; for in 1:15 he assigns to this epistle much the same purpose as in 1:19 he assigns to the Old Testament prophets.

Unto their own destruction.—The Greek is emphatic as to its being "their own." The inference drawn from this by Peter is not, "Do not read Scripture," nor even "Pass over what seems to be hard," but "Be on your guard against being led astray by interpretations contrary to the spirit of the Gospel."

(17) Fall from your own stedfastness.—This "steadfastness" will be based on belief in Christ's coming, and on the hope of entering into His kingdom, and thus will be in marked contrast to the unbelief of the "unstable" in verse 16.

The entire absence of directions—which Jude gives rather elaborately—as to how these evil men and their victims are to be treated by sound Christians is in favor of the priority of this epistle. When evil men begin to arise, the first impulse is to avoid them and their ways, and to this course Peter exhorts his readers. When such men have established themselves and gained proselytes, people begin to consider how to deal with the seducers and to win back the seduced, and to these points Jude directs his readers.

(18) But grow in grace, and in the knowledge of our Lord.—"The grace of our Lord" must mean the grace of which He is the giver, while "the knowledge of our Lord" must mean the knowledge of which He is the object.

Doxology.—The epistle comes to a most abrupt conclusion, without any personal remarks or greetings. This is so unlike the first epistle, so unusual in apostolic letters generally, that an imitator would scarcely have omitted so usual and natural an addition. But as to his death, which cannot be far off, Peter knows that it will come swiftly at the last, and his chief fear is lest it should come upon him before he has left on record these words of warning and exhortation (1:13-15). Therefore, at the opening he hurries to his subject at once, and presses on, without pause or break, until it is exhausted; and now that he has unburdened his heart he cares to say no more, but ends at once with a tribute of praise to the Master that bought him.

To him be glory.—There can be no doubt that in this doxology homage is paid to Jesus Christ as true God. It is, perhaps, the earliest example of that "hymn to Christ as God" which Pliny tells Trajan the Christians were accustomed to sing before daybreak.

And for ever.—Literally, "and to the day of eternity." It means that day which marks the end of time and the beginning of eternity, the day which not only begins but is eternity. The expression is quite in harmony with the general drift of the chapter.

Amen.—Comp. Jude 25. Here the word is of rather doubtful authority. Being usual in doxologies, it would be likely to be added by a copyist.

FIRST JOHN

1

(1-3) The profound emotion, the hearty sympathy, the tender anxiety which John feels as he begins his counsels to his friends, mark off this introduction distinctly from the parallel passage in the gospel. There it was calm contemplation of the height and depth of Christ's existence; here he vehemently insists on the personal relation between the Word and those to whom He had been revealed.

As in the gospel, he starts with the grandeur of an indefiniteness beyond which no eye can pierce: at the beginning of all that concerns us, be it world or universe or all creation, there was that which we are announcing. "That which," not "Him who," because it is not merely the Person of Christ which he is going to declare, but also His Being, all that relates to Him, His Gospel, the treasures of wisdom that lay in Him, His truth, all that could be known about Him by human knowledge.

The vibrating eloquence of the passage makes the construction at first sight obscure. But take "that declare we unto you" (verse 3) as the principal verb, set aside verse 2 as a parenthesis, notice the rising climax of verse 1 (heard, seen, etc.), pause at the end of verse 1 to sum up the results in the words "of the Word of life," and at the beginning of verse 3 resume the thoughts interrupted by the parenthesis, and all is at once clear.

The verbs of sensation might be directed against Cerinthus, and the Doketists, who held that Christ was only a phantom.

(5) That God is light.—Here is the essence of Christian theology, the truth about the Deity as opposed to all the imperfect conceptions of Him which had embittered the minds of the wise. To the heathen, Deity had meant angry, malevolent beings, worshiped best by the secrecy of outrageous vice; to the Greeks and Romans, forces of nature transformed into superhuman men and women, powerful and impure; to the philosophers, an abstraction either moral or physical; to the Gnostics it was a remote idea, equal and contending forces of good and evil, recognizable only through less and less perfect deputies. All this John, summing up what the Old Testament and our Lord had said about the Almighty Father,

sweeps away in one simple declaration of truth.

Light was God's garment in Ps. 104:2; to Ezekiel (1:4), the appearance of the likeness of the glory of the Lord was brightness; to Habakkuk (3:3), His brightness was as the light; Christ had called ths sons of God children of the light (John 12:36), and announced Himself as the Light of the World (8:12); in the Hebrews (1:3), Christ was the refracted ray of the Father's glory, "the express image of his person"; to James, the Almighty was the Father of all lights (1:17); to Paul, He dwells "in the light that no man can approach unto" (I Tim. 6:16); to Peter, the Christian state is an admission "into his marvellous light" (I Pet. 2:9). These ideas John comprehends: God is Light.

God is Light physical, because it was He who called everything first out of darkness, and from whom proceeds all health and perfection; light intellectual, because He is the source of all wisdom and knowledge, and in His mind exist the ideals after which all things strive; light moral, because His perfection shows that the difference between good and evil is not merely a question of degree, but fundamental and final, and the life of Christ had exhibited that contrast sharply, once for all.

Thus, on this declaration depends the whole doctrine of sin: sin is not merely imperfection; it is enmity to God. There can be no shades of progression, uniting good and evil: in Him is no darkness at all. Good and evil may be mixed in an individual: in themselves they are contrary.

(6) That we have fellowship with him ... —Some of the Gnostics said that on account of their spiritual knowledge they were free to act as they liked, without committing sin. For walking as a description of the spiritual state, comp. 2:6; II John 6; Rom. 6:4, 8:4; Eph. 4:17; Phil. 3:17.

Darkness would include any conscious habit which was opposed to God's example of perfection.

(7) Fellowship and cleanşing constitute the antithesis to "lying and doing not the truth," presented under the twofold aspect of the brotherly result of walking with God, and its purifying influence. Each human being that comes near us becomes the object of our friendly sympathy; and the sacrifice of Christ has both put away the sin of the world and prevents sin from reigning in our mortal bodies; it obtains forgiveness for us, and by reminding us that it was sin that brought Jesus to the cross, has a continually purifying power over us, through the Spirit of Christ and of the Father.

(8) If we say that we have no sin.—The preceding words had reminded John that even mature Christians, though certainly not "walking in darkness," yet have sinful tendencies in themselves: sensuous impulses, non-spiritual inclinations, lack of self-knowledge, a lowered standard, principles and views borrowed partly from the world, wavering of will, and even graver faults. Not to admit this would be to mislead ourselves, and in us the power and energy of light, searching the very corners of the heart, would not be working. (See Rom. 7:18-23; Gal. 5:17.)

(9) If we confess our sins.—An advance in the thought from the general "having sin." Confession to God must recognize and measure each particular fault.

He is faithful and just . . . —He, from the context, cannot possibly be any other than God. Here another grand progression of thought meets us: not merely "we are in the truth," but the actual and glorious result on God's side; faithful and just is He on account of Christ's sacrifice and our repentance.

(10) John is here repeating, in a more emphatic form, the thought of verse 8. Our foolish presumption is regarded in its worst aspect: an impiety against God, whose word, revelation, appeal to our conscience, and witness by the Spirit, are thus blasphemously contradicted.

2

Another idea, already suggested in 1:7, that arises from the great fact that God is Light is the doctrine of reconciliation and redemption. John does not wish them to contemplate with complacency the probability of sinning, but to remember gratefully, in spite of falls, that the Author and Restorer of light has provided a remedy both for the offense before God and for its effect on themselves. First come the principle that we must not sin; second, the admission that we do sin; third, the consolation for actual sin when it is in spite of sincere zeal for sanctification.

(1) My little children.—Six times in the letter this diminutive of tender and caressing love occurs (2:12, 28; 3:18; 4:4; 5:21). He was aged, he felt a fatherly care for them, and he was their spiritual progenitor.

The thought of the shame and misery of sin melted his heart.

That ye sin not.—Another side of the object of the teaching was that their joy could not be full unless they were earnest against sin. And yet the most holy would not be perfect.

We have an advocate with the Father, Jesus Christ the righteous.—The word here translated Advocate was translated Comforter in John 14:16, 26; 15:26, 16:7. It has two meanings: he who comforts, or exhorts; and he who is appealed to—a proxy, or attorney. (Comp. Rom. 8:26; Heb. 4:14-16; 7:25.) The Redeemer, the Word made flesh, and reascended with His human nature, is that part of the Deity which assures us of the ever-active vitality of divine love. If the justice of God is connected most with the Father, the mercy is pledged by the Son. He has exalted our nature, undertaken our interests, presents our prayers, and will one day be surrounded by the countless millions of His human brothers whom He has rescued, wearing the same nature as Himself. He is represented as continuing our advocate, because otherwise His work might appear a mere separate earthly manifestation. Christ, the only blameless example of human nature, can alone intercede for it with God (Heb. 7:25; I Pet. 3:18; John 16:8-10).

(2) And he is the propitiation for our sins.—By the satisfaction which the voluntary sacrifice of the Saviour offered to that divine order which requires the punishment of rebellion, both for its own correction and for a universal warning, the whole Deity has been rendered propitious, His graciousness has been called out, the righteousness of Rom. 3:26 has been set in motion, that wills not the death of a sinner, and is higher than mere retributive justice.

And not for ours only, but also for the sins of the whole world.—This statement must not be limited. Its scope is that Christ's redemption was offered for the whole of mankind, from Adam to the last man. Who lay hold of the redemption must be determined on other considerations. Multitudes may be saved through this redemption who never heard of Christ (Acts 10:34, 35; Rom. 2:14, 15). John's object in introducing this truth here is to rebuke the arrogance of those Christians who looked down on the non-Christian world as outside the Fatherhood and mercies of God.

Yet another inference from the doctrine that God is Light analyzes more accurately the general expression of 1:7. If Christ is, as in verses 1, 2, the Paraclete and Propitiation of the world, it becomes necessary to ascertain whether He is this to us, lest, when this salvation is offered, we condemn ourselves by rejecting it. The test is obedience to the commandments, especially in brotherly love.

(3) If we keep his commandments.— Comp. John 14:15. "Keep" like a precious heirloom, watching them against the inroads of our lower nature. If each man's conscience was the standard of practice, confusion would again reign in morals as it reigned in the days of the Sophists at Athens. A code and an example fitted for all times and all circumstances have been given by our Lord.

(4) He that saith . . . —In particularizing the general proposition according to his custom, John rejects the first person plural as shocking, unreal, and artificial, and throws the blasphemy on some third person. So "is a liar" is stronger than "we lie."

(5) In him verily is the love of God perfected.—John has before his mind an ideal of a man so filled with the Spirit that in all things he embodies the will of God; the love that such a man has for God is indeed complete. But he knows that the best of the human race can only approach such an ideal in different degrees, at a great distance; and the perfection of the love which they bear to God will vary in the same degree.

Hereby know we that we are in him.— Without such a test there could be no happiness in religion. "In him" implies that we are saved by His grace, with certain access to the divine throne, and heirs of the heavenly kingdom.

(6) Ought himself also so to walk, even as he walked.—Abiding in Christ is an evident reference to John 15:4-11. In the terms of verses 3-5 there is a double gradation: on the one hand, knowing Him, being in Him, remaining in Him; on the other, keeping His commandments, keeping His word, walking even as He walked. The last expression is the strongest of the latter three, as it views the Christian in action. In verses 7-11 brotherly love is introduced as the special manifestation of this obedience that springs from the walk in the light.

(7, 8) The commandment might have remained "old," i.e., confined to the definite point of time of its promulgation, had it not been embodied for ever (1) in the living example of Christ during His life on earth;

(2) in His active presence and power since His resurrection; (3) in the conduct and character of His people, radically renewed by His Spirit and continually growing after His image. A visible change, a notable renovation, is going on: gross darkness is being rent away in the circle of the apostolic preaching; the life of the Lord is now bursting far and wide into ever-increasing brightness; multitudes in every known land are gathered into His kingdom.

(9) He that saith . . . —The whole history of religious rancor has been a deplorable illustration of these words. Controversy for principles honestly and reasonably held is one thing; but prejudice, spite, private censures and condemnations, harsh words, suspicions, jealousies, misunderstandings and misrepresentations are the chief props of the kingdom of darkness among Christian churches and nations. (Comp. John 13:34; 15:12; I Cor. 13:2; I Pet. 1:22; II Pet. 1:7-9.)

Hateth means not merely the absence of love, but the presence, in ever so small a degree, of dislike or any of the feelings already described, or those kindred to them. This love is the pure disinterested seeking for another's welfare, of which Christ was the great example. It is that which the non-Christian world is trying to make its religion; but without the Christian motive, and cultivated for its own sake instead of by the working of the Spirit of God, it seems artificial and powerless. When love such as Christ's is the ruling principle of life, then the stumblingblocks of human nature are removed.

(11) But he that hateth.—Verse 10 was an antithesis to verse 9; verse 11 is, after John's manner, an antithesis again to verse 10, putting the matter of verse 9 more strongly and fully, and forcibly concluding the section which describes the walk in the light.

(12-17) The apostle will warn his "little children" with the most tender affection against the wicked one, the world, the flesh, the follies and vanities of the human heart; but first he shows them frankly what he thinks of them, what he hopes of them, the trust he places in them, the grounds which he takes for granted in writing to them.

(Some have thought the second triplet an explanatory note that has crept into the text; others that "I write" refers to what he is doing at the moment, "I wrote" ("I have written") the view they would take when they read what he had written. It seems better, however, if we allow the Gospel to have been written first, to refer "I am writing" to the epistle, "I did write" to the Gospel.)

(13) Him that is from the beginning.—There can be little doubt that this means the same Person as the subject of "His name's sake" in verse 12. Knowledge of Christ is assigned in both cases as the reason for addressing the elder members of his audience, because fully to understand the work, the doctrine, the example of Christ, is a work fitted for mature thought.

Young men.—They might be regarded more as still engaged in the work of settling their character, forming their habits, disciplining their inclinations, confirming the choice which all must make for themselves between good and evil. (Comp. II Tim. 2:22.) John is here addressing those who had gotten the better of temptations, or are in process of getting it.

Little children.—The word here is different from that used in verses 1 and 12, meaning children in age.

(15) Love not the world.—Having thus affectionately expressed his hopes about each class of them, the last of the apostles is freer to express that warning which was suggested to his mind by the mournful picture of verse 11. If they would not walk in darkness, then they must not love the world. What does "the world" mean? In Acts 17:24 it meant the universe; in John 1:9, perhaps more distinctly, the earth; in I John 2:2 the sum total of mankind; in John 8:23 that moral order, to be found in this spot of creation, which is antagonistic to God. Thus it became a phrase for all such inventions, plans, customs, thoughts, and estimates of mankind as are not in harmony with the will and purpose of God. This world—the sphere of rebellion—is that which is not to be loved.

(16) The lust of the flesh—i.e., that proceeds from the earthly nature; all desire taking possession of the soul as a motive for thought and action which does not arise from principles in harmony with the will of God.

The lust of the eyes—i.e., of which the eyes are the seat; all delight in objects living or inanimate apart from their moral and religious importance.

The pride of life.—The Greek word is used again in the New Testament only in Jas. 4:16. The phrase means a boastful, ostentatious attitude in regard to the good things of this life allotted by God to be

spent in His service. All living up to a supposed social position instead of as the responsible steward of undeserved bounties is hereby condemned.

(17) The world passeth away.—No reasonable man can set his affections on what is in its very essence perishable. It is passion, the madness of folly, the contagion of accumulated examples that influence the soul toward what can only create the agonizing ache of a growing void.

But he that doeth the will of God abideth for ever.—There is no permanence but that of defeat and failure in what is in rebellion to the Supreme Author and Ruler of all things. Everything that is good is a part of Him, and can no more fade than He can. It is by being in harmony with this undeviating tendency of righteousness to victory that real happiness discovers its own secret.

After cheering his readers by stating the grounds of his writing, and the opinion which he has of them, he reminds them of the momentous epoch at which they are living, of the discriminating effect which it has had on mere nominal Christians, and of the signs by which such might be known. The train of thought is appropriate to the treatment of the general subject of light as it brings the manifestation of its contrary.

(18) The last time.—Until the visions of the Apocalypse, John naturally thought from Christ's words (John 21:22) that he would see the last days before the Second Advent. Our Lord, in Matt. 24:36, distinctly asserted that not even the angels knew the day and the hour; and on this subject accordingly the apostles were evidently left to their own conjectures. Paul expected a speedy return (I Thess. 4:17); so did Peter (II Pet. 3:12-15). In the same way John thought that he recognized in the serious signs of his time that final period spoken of in Isa. 2:2; Mic. 4:1; Acts 2:17; I Tim. 4:1; II Tim. 3:1; and II Pet. 3:3.

Antichrist.—Of the terrible personage or power prophesied in II Thess. 2:1-12; Rev. 11, 13, and 17, the "liars" already mentioned in 1:6, and afterward in 4:3, 20, are regarded as forerunners. So might Hymenaeus and Philetus (II Tim. 2:17), Diotrephes (III John 9) the Nicolaitanes (Rev. 2:6), or Simon Magus, Cerinthus, Ebion, any who opposed the teaching of Christ from within or without. (Comp. Jude 4.)

(19) They went out.—The special instances in his mind were of men who had seemed to belong to the body of Christ, but were never really penetrated by His Spirit.

(Comp. Matt. 13:3-7, 24-30, 47-50.) John is not pronouncing a general law that grace is indefectible"; but in looking back on each case of apostasy he sees there must have been some element in the character not subdued to Christ. (Comp. Heb. 6:4-6.) Safety lies in the continual appeal to Christ.

(22) Who is a liar?—Rather, "the liar," the enemy of light above all others. All who err from Christ's teaching are liars; the greatest of all, he who may be called actually Antichrist, is he who denies that the Crucified is the Son of God. And a God who cannot be revealed, who has no Son, who cannot be heard or seen, is at best a cold abstraction.

(25) Eternal life.—The life which cannot be measured by days and years, but is the enjoyment of the blessedness of virtue. This is a present fact, begun as soon as the believer begins to be in Christ, growing more and more unto the perfect day as he walks more closely with God, secured for ever when he enters into his rest, and perfected in the glory of heaven.

(27) But the anointing.—He reverts to verses 20 and 21 as a favorite ground of consolation and encouragement. Anointing played a great part in the physical life of Eastern races. The climate was dry, sultry, and enervating; unguents restored freshness, elasticity, and life to the parched and feeble frame. So the healing, soothing influence of the divine Spirit breathes about the children of God, unfolds the meaning of what they have heard, brings all things to their remembrance, and guides them into all truth. They needed not the pretended discoveries of false teachers; all they wanted was the unction of God to bring home what they had heard from the beginning.

(29) In passing on to think of God in His character of love rather than of light (this, with several interludes, is the leading thought up to 5:12), John is led to pause for a moment on the idea of righteousness, which, as it was the main object of the earlier dispensation, so is the final cause of Christianity. This suggests to his mind the new idea, "The righteous are born of God."

He is righteous.—John looks at the Father and the Son as so essentially one that from his use of the pronoun merely it would not be clear which Person he meant. Here "born of him" shows that he thinks of the Father, or of the Deity in its oneness, not especially of Christ.

3

(1) Sons.—Rather, "children." The asserted relationship is no mere empty rhetorical title. It is not only a comparison to point to origin, dependence, sympathy, care, union, love; it is a fact. As our spiritual life comes from God, we have but to be conscious of it, and to claim its privileges.

(2) When we are able to see Him, by entering on the glorified life hereafter, our likeness will have grown complete, and it will never again be able to be defaced. A true knowledge must be convincing; when we are permitted to see the actual truth in God Himself, it will be impossible for any corner of the soul to remain unconvinced, unwarmed, unrenewed.

(3) John, as usual, turns gently to the practical side of his thought. If we really hold this glorious hope of the future likeness, it cannot help having a correlative force in our present life. Such a hope must be the source of the determination to be purified here, the resolve to be rid of all pollution in body or soul and to struggle free from the chains of sins. John probably thought of Matt. 5:8 in thus connecting the future vision with present purity.

(4-10) Here is an expansion of the thought of verse 3, which was the practical conclusion of the meditation on the divine love as seen in the new birth. In thinking of the nature of righteousness, of the new birth, and of purity, the apostle is led to dwell on their opposite, lawlessness, the synonym and essence of sin. His object being to bring purity and righteousness into relief, and to determine who are the children of God and who of the devil, he pursues the contrast by a series of antitheses, introducing, after his manner, reflections suggested by particular stages of the thought.

(4) The transgression of the law.—He is not thinking of the law of Moses, but defining and analyzing the nature of sin in general: it is acting from caprice instead of on principle, disobeying the conscience, neglecting the will of God, rebelling against His commandments.

(5) And ye know . . .—The Incarnation is mentioned here with the purpose of strengthening the appeal to purity. The object of Christ's coming was to take away our sins by atonement, and their power in us by reformation. He is Himself sinless. Those who really rest firmly in Him cannot be habitual sinners, nor, on the other hand, can habitual sinners be really in Him.

To take away our sins.—The idea of sacrificial substitution was uppermost in 2:2. Here it is rather that of sanctification; but the other is not excluded. The two are always connected in John's mind. (Comp. 1:7; 4:9, 10, 11.) The purpose of Christ's coming was not so much to teach a new doctrine as to produce a new life; the first was the means to the second.

(6) Sinneth not.—Although the Christian does not always do what is best, he does not willingly commit sin; his real self is on the side of God's law.

Whosoever sinneth—i.e., adopts the lawless disposition deliberately. A real saving sight of Christ is when our mind becomes conscious of the convincing truth, beauty, perfection, love, and power of His existence. The corresponding knowledge is when that sight has become experience, the soul having learned the effect of His strengthening, purifying grace; having proved the happiness of intimate spiritual union with Him; and having meditated continually on the records of the sayings and doings of His earthly manifestation. There may be here a reference to the Gnostics, who said that their "knowledge" was so great that they had no need to work righteousness: grace would be enough, without works.

(8) Of the devil.—Not that the devil has created the sinner, but that the sinner has allowed him to generate his evil nature, until gradually the whole nature may have become evil, to the exclusion of any elements of goodness. By making the devil the antithesis to Christ, John insists as strongly as possible on the moral importance of remembering the existence and kingdom of an allowed power of evil. The work of the Messiah cannot be fully understood without acknowledging this fact of human consciousness.

For the devil sinneth from the beginning.—"For" states the reason why sinners are of the devil. By "from the beginning" we understand, not the date of the devil's existence, or of the creation of the earth, or of human history, or of the devil's fall, but the beginning of human sin. As soon as human sin began, then the devil was at work and claiming his parentage.

The Son of God was manifested.—The devil is not honored by being placed over against the whole almighty Deity, but is

regarded as the special antagonist of the Son. In taking away our sins Christ would be destroying the works of the devil, which are every possible variety of sin. The consequences of sin—affliction, death, condemnation—are rather the wholesome discipline of God.

(9) We have seen that the birth of the new nature is not complete until we enter into our rest; so also the freedom from sin is progressive. "His seed" is the Holy Spirit, that influence proceeding from God, imbued with divine vitality, regenerating, renewing, refreshing, causing the nature of holiness to spring, to grow, to bloom, to bear fruit. The Christian does not say, "I have the seed of God within me, so I need not mind if I am betrayed into sin." That would alone be enough to prove that the seed of God is not there. He struggles to free his permanent will from all participation in what was wrong. He claims the help of the Spirit in his struggle; and his sincerity shows that it was a genuine bona fide betrayal, not a preconceived moral choice. "Sinneth not," therefore, looks rather to the Christian's course as a whole. "He cannot sin" means that if he is really born of God, it is an impossibility for him deliberately to choose evil. If he deliberately chooses evil, he is not born of God. "A child of God in this conflict receives indeed wounds daily, but never throws away his arms or makes peace with his deadly foe" (Luther).

Verse 10 sums up the matter in a terse distinction: all mankind are either children of God or children of the devil—they who try to do good, and they who deliberately and consciously choose evil. It is not even for an apostle to judge which man belongs to which class; at any rate, the true Christian can never be a willful rebel. Brotherly love, the most prominent part of Christian righteousness, may well be mentioned in the contrast between sin and holiness, as it is the most comprehensive of all virtues.

(11-18) Justice will become sternness without love; love will be weakness without justice. The two thoughts are introduced and connected in both halves of the epistle. (See 2:3-11.) Here the duty of love is still more strongly urged, as the general subject is the love of God, as in the first half of the epistle it was the light of God.

(12) Not as Cain . . . —Cain is introduced as the prototype of envy, jealousy, and the inward hatred which the evil feel at the good.

(14) This is a characteristic instance of John's logic. Another ground of assurance has been stated in 2:2: keeping the behests of Christ, of which love is the most prominent. "The brothers" means all the members of the human family; the love of Christ which, in verse 16, we are bidden to imitate, was for the whole world of sinners. (Comp. Matt. 5:44; I Cor. 4:12.)

(15) Regarding the absence of love as of one class with the presence of hatred, John here puts more prominently forward the active member of the class than the quiescent. The statement is intended as an illustration of the fact that where no love is there can neither be eternal life. (Comp. Matt. 5:21-26.)

(16) Hereby perceive we the love of God, meaning that perfection of love which is God Himself. Christ, the Word made flesh, is regarded as identical with this love, so only the pronoun is used. The highest proof of love is the sacrifice of that which is most precious: nothing could be more precious than the life of the Word made flesh.

And we ought.—The reason of this consequence is that we are to be like Christ in everything; even His unparallelled act of self-sacrifice must be reproduced in us, at however great a distance. For the good of our fellowmen we must be ready even to die.

(17) But implies a progress from the greater duty to the less; if the less is neglected, far more completely is the command disobeyed.

World is not used here in a bad sense, but merely of such elements of existence as are not spiritual.

The word translated "bowels of compassion" is used in the LXX for "tender mercies." It is used in the New Testament as we use "heart," and has nothing to do with bowels. It should be translated "compassion."

(19-24) Here the reality and sincerity of the brotherly love which John has been urging reminds him of the happy consequences of it: security in God, answers to prayers, the continuing presence of God, and the demonstrable transformation of our aims and thoughts by the Holy Spirit.

(19) Are of the truth.—"The truth" means all of the eternal nature, purpose, and will of God which it concerns us to know—revealed in Christ, brought home by the Spirit, exemplified in Christian lives. "The heart" means the affections (comp. John 14:1, 27; 16:6, 22), the seat of the moral feelings, as distinct from the intellect; the emotional side of the moral nature, of which the intellectual side was called by Paul "the conscience." (Comp. Acts 24:16; Rom. 2:15; 9:1; 13:5; I Cor. 8:7; II Cor. 5:11.)

(22) Whatsoever we ask.—If this sounds unlimited, we should remember that it is said of us in our character as children of God; as far as that is true of us, we cannot ask anything contrary to His will. (Comp. John 16:23, 24.) Our prayers are heard through the merits of Christ; but if we do not keep the commands of God, prayer must be fruitless.

(23) And this . . . —The sum of God's commandments, and the compendium of the life that pleases Him, is stated shortly in two spiritual facts indissolubly connected: belief on the name, and brotherly love. Belief is the root of the matter, because the recognition of Jesus as Messiah is the essential foundation of the Christian fellowship. (Comp. Gal. 5:6-14; I Tim. 1:5.)

(24) Up to this point the thoughts have been chiefly about the Father and the Son where any direct reference was made to Persons in the Trinity. Here the divine Spirit comes into prominence; formerly He had been alluded to only in the anointing (2:20, 27).

The mention of faith in verse 23 suggests to John the necessity of a still further discussion of truth and error, lest it should be thought that all religious fervor is of the truth. The mention of the Spirit enables him to make the transition distinctly, and he treats of the various phases of religious life, true and false, under the corresponding name of spirits.

4

The mention of God's Spirit gives John a form in which to clothe the discussion of truth and falsehood—intellectual as well as moral error—in its human manifestations. By "spirits" he means those tendencies toward good and evil which may be considered as coming from the supreme power of God, on the one hand, and from the inferior power of the devil, on the other. For Christians there was but one standard by which to measure all claims on their religious allegiance: confession that the man Christ Jesus was the Word. All that demurred to that plain fact, and the loyalty implied by it, belonged to the spirit of antichrist. His hearers, however, if he understood them rightly, need not fear. By virtue of their adherence to the truth, God was in them. In Him they had conquered the spirits of the world, and had but to claim their victory. The false teachers might be known, and must be condemned by the savor of the world that was in their method and their message, and by their popularity with what was opposed to God.

(1) Prophets, in the New Testament, preach rather than predict. (Comp. I Cor. 14:1-4, 24; Eph. 4:11.)

(2) Jesus Christ is taken to imply all His history. (Comp. 3:23 and verse 6.) The real humanity of the Saviour is the truth here especially emphasized.

Come is used of Christ in John's language for His mission and manifestation. (Comp. John 5:43; 6:14; 7:28, 29; 8:42; 16:28; 18:37.)

(3) Every spirit that confesseth not.—It is clear that this verse presupposes an evangelistic presentation of Christ before refusal to confess His historical person could be made. (Comp. 2:18.)

(4) This consolation is in the same manner as that in 2:12, and is introduced by the same endearing phrase. He is sure they have held to the truth, and have the Sonship. Although they may still have to struggle, they have only to claim Christ's strength, and they have won. In making their choice between light and darkness, love and hate, good and evil, God and the devil, they became of the victorious party.

(6) We are of God.—"We" is substituted for "ye," and means "the apostles and those who taught with them." John feels the grave duty, in condemnation of Cerinthus and other opponents, to assert the genuine truth and divine authority of the apostolic gospel. There could be no spiritual pride in this; it was a conscientious obligation. God spoke in them, and their loyalty forbade alike disclaimer and accommodation. (Comp. John 18:37.)

(7-21) This may be considered the central portion of the second half of the epistle. Nothing could be more significant of John's teaching. Here many trains of thought which have occurred before are gathered together in one grand treatise on love, divine and human—the complement of I Cor. 13. The connection with the paragraph on the trial of the spirits is obvious: the quality and quantity of our affection will be the best gauge whether we have the spirit of truth or of error. The absence of love is

ignorance of God, for real knowledge of Him imparts His nature. And if any ask how we know of His love, the answer is that it was seen in His Son. And these spiritual emotions and developments are not illusory, for they are guaranteed by the ocular and oral evidence of the apostles to the historical Person of Christ. So the result of all this will be perfect and fearless confidence.

(7) One another.—As God loved the world, so we are to love mankind, not merely Christians. (Comp. 3:13.)

(8) Knoweth not.—Rather, "never knew." Real knowledge of God has a convincing practical effect; without such an effect it is not knowledge, but a mere mental deception.

God is love.—In the early part of the epistle John had defined God as light, and the thoughts had been grouped in relation to that central idea. It would, of course, be impossible ever to exhaust all the definitions of God; but when we have thought of God as light, we shall not have traversed in outline all that we can know of His nature until we have also thought of Him as love, the author and source of all true affection, kindness, and pity.

(11) We ought.—As God has bestowed His affection so gratuitously on us (comp. John 15:16; Rom. 5:8, 10; Tit. 3:4), and we benefit by it in such an inconceivable degree, and can make Him no return, we can only **pay the debt** by bestowing our poor equivalent on our fellow men. Although our happiness depends strictly on God, still He has allowed us to be stewards for Him in some small degree for the happiness of those about us.

(12) No man . . . —John quotes his gospel (1:18). This is simply the general proposition, "God is invisible," and has no reference to spiritual sight. (Comp. Ex. 33:20; John 6:46; I Tim. 6:16.) The appearances of God to Abraham or Moses would be like the Shechinah in the Temple, but no material glimpse of Him who is Spirit. John mentions the fact as an admission of the limits of human nature and the condition of faith, but only in order to state the richness of the substitute, which is the presence of God within the soul, verified and substantiated by the historical Person of Christ.

His love is perfected in us.—Its operation in us has full scope and sway.

(13) Hereby know we.—The apostolic witness to the person of Christ is again and again insisted on as the foundation of

Christian theology. (Comp. 1:1-3, and verse 5; John 1:14.)'

(16) God is love.—In this meditative recapitulation John cannot help summing up everything again in the boundless formula of verse 8. Knowledge is here the process that leads to conviction; belief, the result of conviction. John's whole purpose is none other than to raise man to his highest possible development by demonstrating the reality and nature of fellowship with the Divine.

(17) Because as he is, so are we in this world.—If we live in this serene atmosphere of pure sympathy with God and man, Christ is in us and we in Him, because God is Love itself. Sharing His nature, therefore, we must be like Him, and the more completely we allow this divine love toward our Father and our brothers to transform our whole being, the more we shall be like our Judge, and the less cause we shall have for dread.

(18) There is no fear.—When love is perfect, fear dwindles to nothing, is absolutely expelled. Love, seeking to be perfect, and finding fear alongside of it, will diligently seek out the cause of the fear, perfect itself by getting rid of the cause, and so get rid of the fear. Fear in such a connection implies some ground for alarm, and suffers punishment (not "torment") by anticipation. The presence of such a ground for alarm would imply a proportionate imperfection of love. (Comp. 3:19-21.)

(19-21) These last three verses are a recapitulation in a vivid form of the truth and the duty contained in verses 10 and 11. God made it possible for us to love Him, and the first result of our feeling this power within us, and allowing it to put itself into force, will be seen in pure and devout sympathy for all whom we can help. As usual, hating, and not loving, are put as interchangeable members of the class of malevolence. John argues on the ground that it is much easier for human nature to be interested by what comes before its eyes than by that about which it has to think. However this may be, there is a still stronger position: the simple command of God in Christ.

5

(1-12) John has been setting love in the supreme place which it held in our Lord's teaching and in Paul's. But there is another faculty which has to regulate, purify, direct,

and stir up our weak and imperfect loving powers, and that is faith. Without faith we cannot be certain about the quality of our love. He begins simply with a position already laid down: genuine faith in Christ is the genuine birth from God. From that faith, through that birth, will come the proper love of our spiritual brothers and sisters. Then, having left the discussion about the effect of faith on love with the same thought which began it—belief in Jesus Christ—John is led to state the grounds on which that faith rests. These are here stated to be three: Christ's baptism, His meritorious cross and passion, and the Spirit. Finally, the contents of the record which God has thus given us are at once most simple and most comprehensive: the gift of eternal life in His Son.

(2) By this we know . . . —Love and obedience to God will assure us of the truth of our love to others. In 2:3 and 4:20, 21, obedience to God and love to our fellowmen were the signs of knowledge of God and love to Him. The two are really inseparable. If love of God is absent, then our love of our fellowmen is not genuine—it is earthly, a mockery. If love of our fellowmen is absent, then we have no love for God. All friendship must be tested by loyalty to God; all love to Him must be tested by charity.

(3) And his commandments are not grievous.—God has commanded us nothing for His own sake, but everything for our own highest profit and happiness. Were we perfect, we should not find them commands at all, for they would be our natural impulses. The more sincerely we serve God, the more enjoyment we shall derive from them. Only to those whose inclinations are distorted, perverted, and corrupted by sin can God's laws seem irksome.

(4) God overcame the world in Christ, and is still ever conquering through Him in His sons. As the conquest that is overcoming the world is wrought by human instruments, its agent may be regarded as our faith, which appropriates Christ's work, and carries it out for Him and through Him.

(6) This is he that came by water and blood, even Jesus Christ.—"Water" and "blood," two of the three great witnesses for Christ, are symbols, and look back to two of the most characteristic and significant acts of His personal history. Baptism in water was His outward sign and seal to the Old Testament: that He had not come to destroy but to fulfill the Law, not to supersede the prophecies but to claim them. It was to show that in Him the righteousness and purification which the Law intended was to be a reality, and through Him to be the law of His kingdom. "Blood," in the same way, refers to the special work of reconciliation and atonement by His death and passion, the realization of all that the sacrifices and types of the former state of religion had meant.

And it is the Spirit that beareth witness.—The Holy Spirit had descended on Jesus at His baptism, had proved Him to be the Son of God in every word and act of His life, and had raised Him up on the third day. He had, too, made new men of His disciples on the Day of Pentecost, laying far and wide the foundations of the new kingdom.

(7) These words cannot be retained in the text, as they are wanting in all the Greek codices and in all the ancient versions as late as the eighth century.

(8) This verse is a repetition of verse 6 for the purpose of emphasis. The fact that the three that bear witness are in the masculine gender bears out the interpretation given in verse 6, that they imply the Holy Spirit, the author of the Law, and the author of Redemption. It also explains how verse 7 crept in as a gloss.

(9) The witness of God is greater.—Any message that clearly comes from God is to be accepted by us with a readiness infinitely greater than in the case of mere human testimony. John considers the threefold witness from God to convey a certainty which no human evidence could claim.

(10) He that believeth on the Son of God hath the witness in himself.—To the real believer the threefold testimony of God no longer remains merely an outward object of thought to be contemplated and grasped: it has become part of his own nature. The water has assured him that he is no longer under the Law, but under grace, and has taught him the necessity of the new birth unto righteousness (John 3:5; Tit. 3:5). The blood has shown him that he cannot face God unless his sins are forgiven; and it has enabled him to feel that they are forgiven, that he is being daily cleansed, and that he has in himself the beginnings of eternal life (1:7; 2:22; John 6:53). And the Spirit, which has had part in both of these, is daily making him grow in grace (Gal. 5:22; Eph. 5:9).

He that believeth not God hath made him a liar.—The negative contrast, as usual, strengthens the affirmative. John regards

the evidence as so certain, that he to whom it is brought and who rejects it seems as if he were boldly asserting that what God had said was false.

(13-21) John, thinking perhaps of the close of his gospel, where he states the same purpose (John 20:31), and reminded by verse 11 of the supreme importance of having eternal life, and of the necessity of finding this in the Son, sums up the object of the letter in these two ideas. He tells his friends again that he writes to them because they believe on the name of the Son of God, and explains his wish to be that, by the thoughts which he has put before them, they may feel certain that the eternal life which ought to be theirs is theirs already, and that their belief may not cease, but may be really vital.

(14) And this is the confidence.—The assurance intended in verse 13 implies confidence, and confidence means the conviction that God is not deaf to our prayers. But these must not be contrary to His will. The Lord's Prayer reminds us that the Person referred to here is the Father.

(16) If any man see his brother sin a sin which is not unto death.—Here are meant such stumblings as do not imply any distinct, willful, deliberate severance from the faith of Christ.

There is a sin unto death.—The limit of intercession is now given: such conscious and determined sin as shows a loss of all hold on Christ. Such a state would be a sign of spiritual death. At the same time John is careful not to forbid it categorically; he says only that in such cases he does not recommend intercessory prayer.

(17) All unrighteousness is sin.—Here John reminds them that all Christians might, at one time or another, stand in need of intercessory prayer because every declension from the perfect righteousness of God is sin. Nothing that was not hopelessly deliberate need be considered a sign of absolute spiritual death. (Comp. 3:4.)

In verses 18-20 John refers back to "that ye may know" in verse 13, and sums up three points from former portions of the epistle, describing the true consciousness of the Christian. Each begins with "We know."

(18) Sinneth not.—There is no reason to supply "unto death." (Comp. note on 3:9.) John means strongly to insist, in this the solemn close of his letter, that the true ideal Christian frame is the absence of willful sin. Stumbles there may be, even such as need the prayers of friends, but intentional lawlessness there cannot be.

But he that is begotten of God keepeth himself.—Rather, "he that is begotten of God keepeth him": that is, the Son of God preserves him. (Comp. John 6:39; 10:28; 17:12, 15.)

(19) Next after the cardinal point that righteousness is the characteristic of the new birth comes the necessity that the Christian should make up his mind that he has been, or is being, born again, and is really different from the world. The proofs would be seen in 1:6; 2:3, 5, 29; 3:9, 14, 19, 24; 4:7, 13, 15; 5:1, 10.

(20) Him that is true.—Amid all the deceptions and fluctuations of the world, John felt, with the most absolute and penetrating and thankful conviction, that the followers of Christ were rooted and grounded in perfect, unshakable, unassailable truth. This could not be unless they were resting on the living Son and holding fast to Him.

(21) Little children, keep yourselves from idols.—This parting word is suggested by the thought of "the true God" in verse 20. "This idea is a general and very comprehensive one: it embraces all things and everything which may be opposed to the God revealed in Christ and to His worship in spirit and in truth. Pre-eminently, therefore, it embraces the delusive and vain idols of the Corinthian Gnosticism . . . , but it includes also the idols and false mediators of superstition, to whom the confidence is transferred which is due only to God in Christ—be their name . . . saints, or Pope, . . . or good works . . . The holiest things may become a snare if their letter is regarded and not their spirit. Every Christian Church has a tendency to worship its own brazen serpents. Happy are they who have a Hezekiah to call them Nehushtan!" (Ebrard) (See II Kings 18:4.)

SECOND JOHN

(1-3) A man so well-known to his correspondent that he calls himself only "the old man," or "the elder," writes to a mother, whose name is possibly Kyria, and to her children. Her sister's children are in the same place as the writer (verse 13). The two mothers are both honored with the religious title "elect." The writer (we assume from the introduction that he is the Apostle John) loves the family with true Christian love. All who are in the way of truth have the same feelings for them, for the truth is a bond of union between all such.

(1) The elder.—The word is used in the New Testament with reference both to age and to office.

Unto the elect lady.—Paul uses "elect" in exactly the same way (Rom. 16:13). (Comp. also I Pet. 1:1, 2.) The use of the epithet for the sister in verse 13 shows that it is impossible that the word should be the correspondent's name. The Greek word, however, for "lady," (**Kuria**, or **Kyria**) was a proper name; so that those who think that John addresses "the elect Kyria" are at liberty to do so.

If the name of the matron is not given, it is not absurd to suppose that the dangers of the times, or family persecution, may have made it advisable that both her name and that of the writer should be withheld. The messenger would supply both deficiencies.

(2) Shall be with us forever.—If Christ is once in our hearts, He will not leave us unless we deliberately leave Him. The expression is therefore equivalent to saying, "We will not let Him go."

(3) Grace be with you, mercy, and peace.—"Grace" is the favor of God conveying fully every spiritual blessing; "mercy" is the pitifulness which sympathizes with man, is longing to forgive his sins, and is more ready to hear than he to pray; "peace" is the result of the reception of these two gifts in the heart, the untroubled calm of a conscience void of offense before God and men.

In truth and love.—To be joined with "grace, mercy and peace." Truth was to absorb and regulate all their intellectual faculties; love, all their emotional.

(4-11) John proceeds to state the chief thing which he desires of her: the pure Christian love which implies every other grace and virtue; in other words, walking after the divine commandments. That this love should be pure, that these commandments should be unimpaired, it was necessary to remember that nothing new could be added to the original message of Christ. This warning was timely, because many errors had already appeared, especially that greatest error which denied the Incarnation.

(5) Love is the Christian's moral disposition of mind, which embraces all other virtues and graces. It implies faith, because it is founded on Christian principle, and can only be tested by a right belief. It implies purity, because it is modeled on the love of God, and has renounced the old man. It implies unselfishness, because it desires the good of the other for his own sake and God's. It implies humility, because it distrusts itself, relies on God, and thinks more of the other than of itself.

(6) The attitude of love in general, whether toward God or man, is best defined and described as "walking after God's commandments." It might have been thought that love would be a vague immeasurable feeling, differing chiefly in intensity; but the Christian dispositon which is described as love is that practical and enlightened result of faith which naturally acts and expresses itself by following God's will in all things. (Comp. I John 4:7, 16.)

(7) The ground of his love for the matron and her family was that they held to the truth. He is proportionately anxious that they should not go beyond it through evil influences.

(7) Confess not that Jesus Christ is come in the flesh.—The Greek implies the idea only, without reference to time. (Comp. I John 4:2, 3.) The expression would include both those who denied that Jesus was the Messiah, and those who, for Gnostic theories, held Him to be only a phantom, declaring the Incarnation to be an impossibility.

This is . . . —Rather, "the deceiver, and the antichrist"—i.e., among all the human errors by which the influence of the Evil One is manifested, this is the most destructive. Those who adopt such errors are the most fatal deceivers and opponents of Christ and truth.

(8) The result of the error would be loss of the fellowship with the Father and the Son in truth and love. The diminution of the reward would be in proportion to the gravity of the error. The reward would be he peace, stability, firmness, and joy which truth and love communicate.

(9) Progression beyond Christ's teaching is a sign of the absence of God, refusal to go beyond His lines a proof of the presence of Father and Son.

(10) This doctrine.—See verse 9. He is not speaking of those who had never heard or been instructed in the doctrine of Christ; they would be less dangerous. He means those who deliberately altered the apostolic teaching. The case supplies an important instruction in the theory of Christian social conduct. Although it would be possible to love unbelievers, in the sense of earnestly desiring that they might come to a knowledge of the truth, it would be wrong—for sincere Christians it would be impossible—to hold out to them the right hand of fellowship. Especially dangerous would it be for the matron and her family.

Receive him not into your house, neither bid him God speed.—These are no terms of ordinary politeness, which the apostle does not forbid, but terms of close Christian intimacy and spiritual communion, the deliberate cultivation of personal acquaintance. The highest sort of Christian brotherly love—love, that is, in its fulness and truth—can only find reciprocity in the same atmosphere of Christ, on the same basis, and in the same characteristics. (Comp. II Cor. 6:16.)

(11) Is partaker of his evil deeds—i.e., condones his false doctrine; puts himself in a position to accept it; shares the guilt of his disloyalty by sympathizing with him; and in this way lowers his whole moral standard. If any interpret the exhortations to love in the epistles of John too liberally, or by too low a measure, this passage is a wholesome corrective. In applying this teaching we should remember that, while John is speaking of those who deliberately deprave the doctrine of Christ in its great outlines, still there may be much in ourselves, in our systems, in our quarrels, in our incrustations of divine truth, in our want of the sense of proportion in dealing with divine things, which may have hindered others from receiving Christ.

(12) Having many things to write unto you.—This verse shows that the letter to the matron and her family was not a mere accompaniment of a copy of the first epistle. His heart is full of things to write, but he hopes soon to have unlimited conversation.

Paper and ink.—The papyrus-tree grows in the swamps of the Nile to the height of ten feet and more. Paper was prepared from the thin coats that surround the plant. Pliny describes the method (13.23). The different pieces were joined together by the turbid Nile water, as it has a kind of glutinous property. One layer of papyrus was laid flat on a board, and a cross layer put over it; these were pressed, and afterward dried in the sun. The sheets were then fastened or pasted together. The writing was in columns, on one side only. When the work was finished it was rolled on a staff, and sometimes wrapped in a parchment case.

Of the ink used by the Romans, Pliny says that it was made of soot and water in various ways, with burnt resin or pitch. The Jews seem to have used lampblack dissolved in gall juice, or lampblack and vitriole, for ink. The pen was a reed, sharpened with a knife, and split like a quill pen.

That our joy may be full.—Comp. I John 1:4. It would be the deep satisfaction of the interchange of spiritual thoughts and aspirations without the limitations of a monologue or of writing materials.

(13) The children of thy elect sister.—He may have been staying at this second matron's house; at any rate, the family knew he was writing.

THIRD JOHN

(1) The elder.—See II John 1.

Gaius.—The common Roman name Gaius. A Gaius is mentioned in Acts 19:29, 20:4; Rom. 16:23; I Cor. 1:14. The difference in date between these and John's correspondent would alone be sufficient reason against any attempt at identification. There is nothing to show whether he was a presbyter or not.

(2) Beloved.—John's affection is founded on the high merits of Gaius as a Christian (see verse 3).

Be in health.—An ascetic would be surprised that one of the greatest of the apostles should be so earnest on such a point. But the better a man's health, the more thoroughly he can do the work of God. Sickness may be allowed to chasten the erring or rebellious heart, but a Christian whose faith is firm and character established can ill afford to despise the inestimable blessing of a sound body. Functional and organic disorder or enervation proportionately lessen the capacity for thought, resolution, and activity.

Even as thy soul prospereth.—The word "prospereth" is literally "makes good way," and so links on to the idea of walking (verses 3 and 4). The health of the soul came first in the apostle's mind; when there is that, he can wish for bodily health to support it.

(4) My children means the members of the churches especially under the care of John.

(5) Thou doest faithfully—i.e., worthily of a faithful man, consistently with the Christian character. Whatever form the activity of Gaius might take, so high was the apostle's opinion of his character, that he was sure it would be done wisely and well.

And to strangers.—The strangers would be Christians; the brethren would be more or less acquaintances of their host. The duty of entertaining Christians on their travels was of peculiar importance in early times from the length of time which traveling required, from the poverty of the Christians, and from the kind of society they would meet at public inns. The duty is enforced in Rom. 12:13; I Tim. 3:2; Tit. 1:8; Heb. 13:2; I Pet. 4:9.

(6) Charity might be translated "love."

Before the church.—That where the apostle then was, and from which they had probably been sent forth as missionaries or, at any rate, with some definite religiou object (see verse 7).

Whom if thou bring forward.—Perhaps while they were still staying with Gaius, the emissaries sent back a report to the church from which they came. John seems to imply that there was still something which Gaiu could do for them.

After a godly sort.—Comp. Tit. 3:13; Cor. 16:11. It would imply journey money provisions, love, care, encouragement, prayer, a humble and reasonable imitation of God's providence to Gaius, proportional to his means, the occasion, and the recipients.

(7) Of the Gentiles.—Probably the heathen among whom they were preaching. From settled churches, or wealthy Christians of long standing, there would be nothing inimical to the interests of the message in receiving material support. Among those who were hearing for the first time, it would be highly prejudicial if there were any appearance of selling the truth. (Comp I Cor. 9:18; II Cor. 11:7, 12:16; I Thess. 2:9.)

(8) That we might be fellowhelpers to the truth.—The principle of cooperation was one of the earliest and leading ideas of the kingdom of Christ. Those who try to work alone lose the mighty force of sympathy and run the risk of a spirit of self-will, self-confidence, and spiritual pride. Those who do not care to help the good works of others are at best cold Christians, feeble believers; they fail in the great critical testing virtue of Christian love; they limit the operation of God, who has chosen to work by human means.

(9) I wrote unto the church.—This may either have been a copy of his gospel or his first epistle, or a lost letter of no special importance. The church was that of the place where Gaius and Diotrephes lived. Nothing whatever can be said of Diotrephes, except that his personal ambition led him into the grievous sin of rejecting the authority of the apostle; that he talked malignantly against him and his friends; that he refused to entertain the emissaries of the church in which John was residing; and that he actually went so far as to eject from the local congregation those who were willing to entertain them. We may conjecture that, on account of the loyalty of Gaius to John, there was so little exchange between him and Diotrephes that he would not even hear that John had written; that the greater part of the people of the place adhered for the present to Diotrephes, so that in addressing Gaius John calls them "the church," and "them"; and, from verse 11, that even now John did not think it superfluous to urge Gaius not to follow the example of Diotrephes or submit to his influence.

(10) **If I come.**—Comp. I John 2:28. John was evidently expecting in both letters to set out on the same journey.

(11) **Follow not that which is evil.**—This is one of those simple exhortations so characteristic of John, which derive an intense meaning from the circumstances and the context. There was probably every reason why Gaius should follow Diotrephes: peace, good-fellowship, the dislike of singularity, popular example, and the indolent indifference which ordinary men feel for truth and right. But the difference between right and wrong is eternal and irreconcilable. The conduct of Diotrephes was of the devil; and mighty moral consequences might follow if Gaius gave way from good-natured pliability.

He that doeth evil hath not seen God.—Comp. I John 2:3; 3:6, 10; 4:2, 3, 4, 6, 8; 5:19.

(12) **Demetrius** may likely be the bearer of the epistle.

And ye know that our record is true.—There is no arrogance or egotism in this; it is solely the appeal to the loyal fidelity of Gaius, to the simplicity of Christ's Gospel as set forth by John in accordance with the other apostles. The personal experience of believers would convince them of the truth of the last of the apostles. (Comp. John 19:25; 21:24.)

(13) Comp. II John 12.

(14) **Peace be to thee.**—The best wish which the apostle can form, instead of the usual Greek ending, "Be strong," or "Farewell!" It was our Lord's resurrection greeting: the internal peace of a good conscience, the external peace of universal friendship, the heavenly peace of future glory begun even in this life. (Comp. John 20:19, 26.)

Greet the friends by name.—Gaius would know who they were as well as if John wrote them down. In a short private letter it would be unsuitable to have a long list of special messages as in a Pauline epistle, especially as the apostle hoped shortly to see them. John perhaps thinks of his Master's ideal in John 10:3.

JUDE

(1) Jude.—As to the Jude who here addresses us, see Matt. 13:55; Mark 6:3; He is not the one to whom reference is made in Luke 6:16; Acts 1:13.

The servant of Jesus Christ.—There is nothing to show that these words indicate an evangelist, although it is more than probable that he was one; his writing this epistle is evidence of the fact. The words may have a side reference to the ungodly men against whom he writes, who are **not** "servants of Jesus Christ." As he does not say that he is an apostle, the inference is that he is not one. Excepting John, whose characteristic reserve accounts for it, apostles proclaim themselves to be such in stating their credentials.

And brother of James.—This is added not merely to explain who he is, but his claim to be heard. It is almost incredible that an apostle should have urged such a claim, and yet not have stated the much higher claim of his own office. The inference again is that the writer is not an apostle. Only one James can be meant. After the death of James the brother of John, only one James appears in the Acts (12:17; 15:13; 21:18)—James the Just, brother of our Lord (Matt. 13:55). The brother of so saintly a man, one of the "pillars" of the church (Gal. 2:9), and holding so high an office, might claim the attention of Christians.

To them that are sanctified.—A reading of great authority compels us to substitute "beloved" for "sanctified"; and the whole should probably run thus: "to those who are called, beloved in God the Father, and preserved for Jesus Christ."

(2) Mercy unto you, and peace, and love.—Another triplet, which possibly looks back to the one just preceding: called by God's mercy, preserved in peace, beloved in love. The addition "and love" is peculiar to this epistle. "Mercy" and "peace" occur in the opening greetings of I and II Timothy, Titus, and II John.

Be multiplied.—By God. The word, as used in salutations, is peculiar to I and II Pet., and Jude.

(3) Beloved.—Very unusual at the beginning of an epistle; III John 2 is the only other example. It indicates, possibly, the writer's wish to be brief and get to hi subject at once; and, as his subject is a ver unpleasing one, he hastens to assure hi readers of affection for them, to prevent hi strong language from offending them.

It was needful for me to write unte you.—Jude had intended to write on gener al gounds; then the circumstances stated i verse 4 made him write immediately for th special purpose of warning them against a pressing danger. The sense of urgency comes from the tense, which is present i the first clause, aorist in the second. Tha Jude had intended to write a longer letter i pure conjecture, for which there is no evi dence.

Contend for.—The word is a graphic one, implying standing over a thing to figh in its defense. You must fight as well a build (Neh. 4:16, 18).

The faith—i.e., that which is believed by Christians: not the expression of the doc trine, nor the holding of it, but the sub stance of it.

Once delivered.—Rather, "once for all delivered." No change in it is possible (Comp. Gal. 1:8, 9.) By "the saints" are meant all Christians. The word is used advisedly here, in marked contrast to the libertines now to be denounced.

(4) Certain men crept in unawares—viz., into the church. The "certain" shows that these men are a decided minority, and has a tinge of depreciation, as in Gal. 2:12 "Crept in unawares" is similar to Gal. 2:4 and II Pet. 2:1. It is this insidious invasion which constitutes the necessity for writing stated in verse 3. Unfaithful Christians are sometimes regarded as an emergence from within, rather than an invasion from without (I John 2:19).

Close similarity to II Peter begins here and continues down to verse 18. In this epistle the first three and last seven verses are the only portions not intimately related to II Peter.

Who were before of old ordained to this condemnation.—Comp. Rom. 15:4; Eph. 3:3. "Ordained" may be "written up," the metaphor perhaps coming from the practice of posting up the names of those who had to appear in court for trial. "Of old" cannot refer to the eternal purposes of God, but to something in history. It is doubtful whether it can refer to the recent warnings of Paul and Peter that false teachers should arise; otherwise one would be tempted to refer it to II Pet. 2. Something more remote from the writer's own day seems to be required, either the Old Testament prophets or the Book of Enoch.

To **this condemnation.**—The context shows that the judgment is an adverse one. "This condemnation" is the one stated in the denunciations which follow, and illustrated by the fate of those mentioned in verses 5-7. Note the threefold description of the men thus written down for judgment: they are ungodly; they pervert God's grace; they deny Christ.

Turning the grace of our God into lasciviousness.—Turning Christian liberty into unchristian license. Note "**our** God," not theirs.

Denying the only Lord God, and our Lord Jesus Christ.—"God" is an addition to the original text, and must be omitted. "Lord" represents two words in the Greek quite different one from the other. We are in doubt whether one or two Persons of the Trinity are mentioned here. (Comp. II Pet. 1:1.) Certainly II Peter 2:1 suggests our taking "the only Master" as meaning Christ; and the fact that the article is not repeated with "Lord" is in favor of only one Person being meant. But Luke 2:29; Acts 4:24; Rev. 6:10 suggest the Father; and the absence of the article before "Lord" is not conclusive. The insertion of "God" is, perhaps, a gloss to insist on this latter interpretation. If it be right, the clause is closely parallel to I John 2:22. Note the emphatic insertion of "our" once more. They will not have Him for their Lord; His divine authority was precisely what they denied.

(5-7) Three instances of God's vengeance: the unbelievers in the wilderness; the impure angels; Sodom and Gomorrah.

(5) How that the Lord.—There is strong evidence in favor of substituting "Jesus" for "the Lord," a most remarkable reading, showing how, in Christian language, the Man Jesus had become identified with the Eternal Son. The use of "Christ" in I Cor. 10:4, though less striking, is similar.

Having saved the people.—The order of the three examples of signal punishment is in II Peter chronologically: impure angels, flood, Sodom and Gomorrah. But the order here is quite intelligible. Jude's main object is to warn his readers against that party in the Christian community who, by its abuse of Christian liberty, transformed the Gospel of purity into a gospel of wantonness, and to give them a safeguard against such. And the safeguard is this: to hold fast the faith once for all delivered to them, and to remember the consequences of unbelief.

Afterward destroyed.—The reference is almost certainly to Num. 14:35; Deut. 1:35; etc. The destruction of Jerusalem can scarcely be meant, whatever date we assign to the epistle. The most obvious meaning is that the people destroyed were those who, in the first instance, were saved.

(6) And the angels which kept not.—This instance of the impure angels has nothing to do with the original rebellion of Satan, or "fall of the angels." The reference is either to Gen. 6:2, or (more probably) to passages in the Book of Enoch.

Their first estate.—The term belongs to the Jewish classification of angels, and here refers rather to their power over things earthly than to the beginning of their state. The two meanings are but two views of the same fact: their power or dignity was their first estate. (Comp. Milton's **Paradise Lost,** Book 5.)

He hath reserved.—Better, "He hath kept," in ironical contrast to "which kept not" just above; the same Greek word is used in both cases. This ironical contrast does not exist in the parallel passage, II Pet. 2:4. Would a writer, quite willing to copy, have failed to copy this?

In everlasting chains.—The reality of powers of evil may be inferred, apart from Scripture, from their effects. That some of these powers are personal, some not, some free, some not, and that all are to be defeated at last, seems to be implied in Scripture; but its silence is a rebuke to curious speculation. Enough is told us for our comfort, warning, and assurance. It consoles us to know that much of the evil of which we are conscious in ourselves is not our own, but comes from without. It puts us on our guard to know that we have such powers arrayed against us; it gives us confidence to know that we have abundant means of victory even over them.

(7) We must read, "Even as Sodom and Gomorrha, and the cities about them, giving themselves over to fornication in like manner to these. ... Who are meant by "these"? Not the ungodly men of verse 4, which would anticipate verse 8; nor the inhabitants of Sodom and Gomorrah, which would be somewhat clumsy in the Greek; but the angels of verse 6. The reference is again to the impurity of certain angels in having intercourse with the daughters of men, of which there is so much in the Book of Enoch. This sin of the angels was similar to that of the people of Sodom. The punishment of the submerged cities is perpetual;

moreover, there are appearances as of volcanic fire under them.

(8-10) Application of these three instances to the libertines who are now provoking God.

(8) These filthy dreamers.—"Filthy" is not in the original Greek, but is supplied from the next clause; not rightly, for "dreamers" goes with all three clauses, not with "defile the flesh" only. The word for "dreamer" is found in the LXX version of Isa. 56:10, of dogs that dream and make a noise in their sleep. Jude perhaps has this passage in his mind. "Dreamers" may perhaps refer to the empty speculations of these men.

Defile the flesh.—Like the inhabitants of the cities of the plain. Some of the earliest forms of Gnosticism, on its antinomian as distinct from it ascetic side, exhibit the licentiousness inveighed against here, e.g., the Simonians, Nicolaitanes, Cainites, Carpocratians.

Despise dominion.—Like the impure angels. The "dominion," or "lordship," is that of Almight God. "Set aside," or "reject," would be better than "despise," to mark the difference between this and II Pet. 2:10.

Speak evil of dignities.—Like the murmurers in the wilderness. By "dignities," or "glories," are meant unseen powers worthy of reverence.

(9) Yet Michael the archangel.—These libertines allow themselves to use language against celestial beings which even an archangel did not venture to use against Satan. In the Old Testament Michael appears as the guardian angel of the people of Israel (Dan. 10:21; 12:1); in the New Testament he is mentioned only here and in Rev. 12:7. In the Book of Enoch he is "the merciful, **the patient**, the holy Michael" (40:8).

He disputed about the body of Moses.—This is to be understood quite literally; to make "the body of Moses" into a metaphor for the people of Israel, or the Mosaic law, is most unnatural. This passage is the only evidence extant of any such incident or tradition. The nearest approach to it is the Targum of Jonathan on Deut. 34:6, and Origen's **De Princip.** 3.2.1. Evidently it is something supposed to be well known to those whom Jude is addressing, and it appears to be given as a fact which he believes, though we cannot be sure of this. In any case it does not follow that we are to believe in it as an historical fact. Reverent, and therefore cautious, theories of inspiration need not exclude the possibility of an unhistorical incident being cited as an illustration or a warning (comp. I Cor. 10:4).

The Lord rebuke thee.—It is probable that the tradition here given by Jude is derived from Zech. 3:2, or from a source common to both. There is another reminiscence of Zech. 3:2 in verse 23.

(10) But these ...—In strong contrast to the scrupulous reverence of the archangel. "Fools rush in where angels fear to tread."

What they know naturally.—The two halves of the verse are in emphatic contrast. What they do not know, and cannot know, they abuse by gross irreverence; what they know, and cannot help knowing, they abuse by gross licentiousness. The word for "know" is not the same in both clauses. The word used in "which they know not" is the most general and common word of the kind in Greek, expressing mere perception; that used in "what they know naturally" is more definite, and expresses practical experience productive of skill and science.

(11-19) Three examples of similar wickedness—Cain, Balaam, Korah—and their corresponding descriptions.

(11) Woe unto them!—The past tenses immediately following are owing to the writer's placing himself in thought at the moment when these men reap the consequences of their sins. Their punishment is so certain that he regards it as having come.

The triplet in this verse, like that in verse 8, is parallel to the three examples of God's vengeance (verses 5-7). Cain, like the inhabitants of Sodom and Gomorrah, outraged the laws of nature; Balaam, like the impure angels, despised the sovereignty of God; Korah, like those who disbelieved the report of the spies, spoke evil of dignities.

(12) These are spots in your feasts of charity, when they feast with you.—It is possible that as **spiloi**, Peter's word (II Pet. 2:13), may mean either "spots" or "rocks" (though more commonly the former), so Jude's word (**spilades**), may mean either "spots" or "rocks" (though almost invariably the latter). Here "rocks" is the safer translation. Peter is dwelling on the sensuality of these sinners, and for him "spots" is the more obvious metaphor. Jude, in tracing an analogy between them and Cain, would be more likely to select "rocks." These libertines, like Cain, turned the ordinances of religion into selfishness and sin: both, like sunken rocks, destroyed those who unsuspectingly approached them. Possibly the name **Agapae** for such feasts come from this passage. Had it been common when Paul wrote I Cor. 11, he would probably have made a point of it: love-feasts in which there was no love.

Feeding themselves without fear—i.e., feeding themselves" instead of the poorer members of the flock; whereas feeding the poor was one great object of the love-feasts. The scandal was similar to that described in Cor. 11:21. (Comp. Isa. 56:11.)

Clouds ... without water.—Comp. Prov. 25:14. The meaning is not that these men bring much food to the love-feasts and give nothing away, for there is no longer any allusion to the love-feasts. Rather, these men are ostentatious generally, and yet do no good: inflated and empty.

Twice dead.—Spiritually these men were utterly dead in having returned, after baptism, to the death of sin. The writer piles up metaphor on metaphor and epithet on epithet in the effort to express his indignation and abhorrence. The epithets here are in logical order: in autumn, fruitless, dead, rooted up.

(13) Foaming out their own shame—Isa. 57:20 is probably in Jude's mind: "The wicked are like the troubled sea, whose waters cast up mire and dirt.

Wandering stars.—The image is that of stars leaving their place in the heavens, where they are beautiful and useful, and wandering away (to the utter confusion of every one who directs his course by them) into sunless gloom, where their light is extinguished. This simile suits the "false teachers" of II Peter better than the "ungodly" of Jude. Would the writer of II Peter have neglected to avail himself of it?

(14) The seventh from Adam.—This is not inserted without special meaning. It either points to the extreme antiquity of the prophecy (in the Book of Enoch), or else to the mystical and sabbatical number seven. Enoch was a type of perfected humanity, and therefore the notion of divine completion and rest is perhaps suggested here. Comp. Augustine's reply to Faustus the Manichaean 12. 14).

(16) Complainers.—Men who shape their course according to their own lusts can never be content, for the means of gratifying them are not always present, and the lusts are insatiable. Such was eminently the case with Balaam. There is a possible reference to this verse in the Shepherd of Hermas (**Sim.** 9. 19.3).

Having men's persons in admiration—i.e., having regard to people of distinction, as Balaam to Balak. These ungodly men were courtiers, flatterers, and parasites, "because of advantage."

(17) Spoken before of the apostles.—Jude implies that this warning of the apostles is well known to those whom he addresses. This appeal to the authority of apostles would be more naturally made by one who was not an apostle, but cannot be regarded as decisive. (Comp. II Pet. 3:2.) There is nothing to show that the author of our epistle regards the apostles as considerably removed in time from himself. "In the last time" is their expression, not his; and by it they did not mean any age remote from themselves.

(18) There should be mockers.—The quotation is direct, introduced formally in the Greek. This, however, scarcely amounts to proof that the quotation is from a written document. The word for "mockers" here is the same as that translated "scoffers" in II Pet. 3:3. The translation should be the same in both passages.

(19) Who separate themselves.—"Themselves" must be omitted, the evidence against it being overwhelming. "Who separate"; who are creating a schism, like Korah and his company, claiming to be the chief and most enlightened members in the community to which they still profess to belong, though they turn upside down its fundamental principles.

Sensual.—The Greek word is "psychic," and has no English equivalent; "sensuous" would perhaps be best. "Carnal" and "spiritual" speak for themselves—the one bad, the other good. "Psychic," which comes between, is much closer to "carnal," and with it is opposed to "spiritual." This is more clearly seen in the Latin equivalents—**carnalis, animalis, spiritalis.** The carnal man is ruled by his passions, and rises little above the level of the brutes. The psychic man is ruled by human reasoning, and human affections, and does not rise above the world of sense. The spiritual man is ruled by his spirit—the noblest part of his nature—and this is ruled by the Spirit of God. He rises to and lives among those things which can only be "spiritually discerned."

Having not the Spirit.—The Holy Spirit may be meant, but more probably spiritual power and insight is what is meant. These men had allowed the spiritual part of their nature, of which they talked so much, to become so buried in the mire of sensual indulgence and human self-sufficiency, that it was utterly inoperative and practically non-existent.

Each of these three descriptions (verses 12-15, 16-18, and 19) is shorter than the preceding one. The writer hurries through an unpalatable subject to the more pleasing duty of exhorting those faithful Christians for whose sake he is writing.

(20) Building up yourselves.—The notion is not so much that of increasing and completing an edifice as of strengthening its foundations. Faith and its object are here almost identified. To have faith as one's foundation is the same as having Christ as one's foundation.

Praying in the Holy Ghost.—Only in this way can Christians make firm their foundation. The expression is not found elsewhere. It means that we pray in His strength and wisdom; He moves our hearts and directs our petitions. (See Rom. 8:26.)

(23) Pulling them out of the fire.—Comp. Amos 4:11; Zech. 3:1-3. The fire of judgment to come is probably not meant; rather the imminent danger (as of one who is asleep in a burning house) in which the fire of their sins keeps them. This is the second class: those who can still be rescued, but by strong measures.

After the words "out of the fire" we must insert another clause omitted from the inferior Greek texts used by our translators: "and on others have compassion in fear." This is the third and worst class: those on whom profound pity is all that we dare bestow, and that in fear and trembling, lest by contact with them we may be brought within the influence of the deadly contamination that clings to all their surroundings. Abhorrence must be shown to the externals of pollution.

(24) Now unto him that is able.—Comp. Rom. 16:25. It would be rash to infer from the similarity that Jude must have known the Epistle to the Romans, although there is nothing incredible in the supposition that he was acquainted with it. The epistle had been in circulation probably for some ten years before Jude wrote. Doxologies no doubt became elastic formulas almost from the first.

To keep you from falling.—Better, "to keep you unfallen." From his own warnings, denunciations, and exhortations, which have been severe and somber throughout, Jude turns in joyous, exulting confidence to Him who alone can make them effectual. "Keep you," or "guard you," indicates "protection" against the great perils just pointed out.

Before the presence of his glory.—The meaning is, "Who can bring it to pass that you stand blameless before the judgment seat" (Col. 1:22; I Thess. 3:13.)

(25) To the only wise God our Saviour.—The coupling of "Saviour" with "God" is common in the Pastoral Epistles (I Tim. 1:1; 2:3; Tit. 1:3; 2:10; 3:4). "Wise" must be omitted as wanting in authority. (See Rom. 16:27.) Doxologies became well-known forms with many variations; changes to something more familiar to the copyist might easily be made in transcribing. After "Saviour" must be inserted, on the highest MS authority, "through Jesus Christ our Lord."

Glory and majesty, dominion and power.—The Greek words represented by "majesty" and "power" occur here only in the New Testament. After "power" we must supply, on overwhelming authority, "before all time."

Both now and ever.—Thus we have a most comprehensive phrase for eternity—before time, time, after time.

REVELATION

1

(1) The Revelation of Jesus Christ.—The book is a revelation of the things which are and the things which shall be. "John is the writer, but Jesus Christ is the author," says Grotius; and consistently with this the action of Christ is seen throughout. Thus we learn that only a living person can be the Alpha and Omega, the starting point of creation and its final rest. The testimony of Jesus is the spirit of this prophecy, as of all others.

Shortly.—The force of this word—"speedily"—affords a plausible groundwork to the praeterist school of interpreters, who hold that the whole range of apocalyptic predictions was fulfilled within a comparatively short time after the apostle wrote. The truth, however, seems to be that the principles which are enunciated by the prophet, though "shortly" fulfilled, are not exhausted in the immediate fulfillment, but carry still lessons for the succeeding generations of mankind.

John—i.e., the apostle and evangelist. It seems natural that John, the beloved disciple, should be the recipient of this revelation. Those who have been nearest to God learn most of His will.

(3) Blessed is he that readeth . . . prophecy.—Any declaration of the principles of the divine government, with indications of their exemplification in coming history, is a prophecy. Sometimes the history which exemplifies these principles is immediate, sometimes more remote; in other cases the events are both immediate and remote. The word "keep" is in itself a proof that the whole fulfillment of the Apocalypse could not have been exhausted in the earliest times, nor reserved to the latest times of the church's history, but that its predictions are applicable in all eras.

The time is at hand.—In the apostolic mind this was always true. The spirit of vigilance for both the providential advents and the final advent of the Christ was enjoined. (Comp. Rom. 13:12; Jas. 5:9; II Pet. 3:8, 9.)

(4) JOHN to the seven churches which are in Asia.—The Asia here is not to be regarded as co-extensive with what we know as Asia Minor. It is the province of Asia (comp. Acts 2:9, 10; 16:6, 7), which was under a Roman proconsul and em-braced the western portion of Asia Minor. In John's time it consisted of a strip of seaboard some 100 square miles in extent. Its boundaries varied at different periods; but roughly they may be regarded as the Caycus on the north, the Maeander on the south, the Phrygian Hills on the east, and the Mediterranean on the west.

It has been maintained by some that the epistles to the seven churches are prophetic and set forth the condition of the church in the successive epochs of its history. The anxiety for circumstantial and limited fulfillments of prophecy has been at the root of such attempts. We stand in no need of such desperate efforts at symmetrical interpretations, for the truth is that words addressed to one age have their fitness for all. These epistles are the heritage of the church in every epoch; the churches are types and representatives of the whole family of God. "By the seven," writes Augustine, "is signified the perfection of the Church universal, and by writing to the seven he shows the fulness of one." And the words, "He that hath an ear, let him hear what the Spirit saith unto the churches," are a direct intimation that some universal application of their teaching was intended.

From him which is, and which was, and which is to come.—The expression must not be separated from what follows. The greeting is triple: from Him which is, and which was, and which cometh; from the seven Spirits; and from Jesus Christ—i.e., from the triune God. The first phrase would therefore seem to designate God the Father—personal, eternal, self-revealing—who is, who was, and who **cometh**. The words "He that cometh," used in the gospels, and applied by the Jews to the Messiah, may be designedly employed here by the apostle. The implication is that we are always to be looking for Him whose "comings" recur in all history as the earnests of the fuller and final Advent.

From the seven Spirits.—The greeting which comes from the Father and the Son comes also from the Holy Spirit sevenfold in His operations, whose gifts are diffused among all the churches, and who divides to every man as He will. The recurrence in this book of the number seven is selected to support the thought of completeness and variety. The dramatic unit is preserved, though the scenes which are unfolded are amply diversified.

(5) The prince of the kings of the earth.—The message does not come from One who will be, but who is the true ruler of all earthly potentates. The disposition to dwell on the future and more visibly recognized reign of Christ hereafter has tended to obscure the truth of His present reign.

Unto him that loved us, and washed us.—John remembered clearly that our Lord had said, "If I wash thee not, thou hast no part with me." The thought of the "cleansing blood," intensified by the recollection of the water and blood which he had seen flowing from Christ's pierced side (John 19:34; see verse 7), often recurred to his mind (7:13, 14; I John 1:7; 5:6-8).

(6) Kings and priests.—The symbol of washing naturally leads to the thought of consecration, accompanied by blood-sprinkling by the priest (Exod. 19:6, 10; 24:8; Heb. 9:21). The book will declare the kingship and priesthood of the children of God—a sovereignty over human fears and sufferings, and consecration even unto death. The doxology here is twofold: glory and dominion. The doxologies in which the Redeemed Church takes part grow in strength in the earlier chapters of this book. It is threefold in 4:9-11, fourfold in 5:13, and reaches the climax of sevenfold in 7:12.

(7) Shall wail because of him.—See Zech. 12:10. He toward whom they now direct their sorrow is the One over whom they shall have wailed when He was laid in His tomb.

(9) Patmos.—The position of the apostle in Patmos was probably that of an exile, free to roam where he would within the limits of the Mediterranean island. There was no limit of chains or guard, as in the case of Paul (Acts 28:16, 20). The cause of his exile was his faithfulness in proclaiming **the word of God and the testimony of Jesus.** Thus John struck a blow at the worship as well as the polity of the Roman empire. He opposed the God-man to the man-god.

(10) The mind, drawn onward by the contemplation of things spiritual, is abstracted from the immediate consciousness of outward earthly forms of life. The mouth which persecution closes God opens, and bids it speak to the world. (Comp. Paul and the epistles of his captivity.) There is no ground whatever for the futurist interpretation that this expression refers to the "Day of the Lord," as in II Thess. 2:2. The phrase in this latter passage is totally different.

(11) The seven churches.—There were more than seven churches in Asia Minor, but the number selected indicates completeness. Thus, though having special reference to the conditions of those churches, the epistles may be regarded as epistles conveying appropriate lessons to the churches of succeeding ages. The names of the seven churches are enumerated, as they would naturally be by a person writing from Patmos. First, Ephesus is addressed, as the Asiatic metropolis, and as the nearest church to Patmos; then the other churches on the western coast of Asia; then those in the interior.

(12) Seven golden candlesticks.—Comp. the vision in Zech. 4:2-11. John saw the old familiar seven-branched candlestick, identical in form with that which has been rendered familiar by the Arch of Titus. But as the mention of the seven churches was then fresh in his mind, his eye fell rather upon the seven limbs and seven lights than on the whole candlestand, especially as the figure of the Christ concealed part of the main stem. Thus to his view the separate individuality of the churches (see verse 20), and their real union in Him who was the Light, would be symbolized. And, too, the external teachings of the earlier symbols are now disturbed; the new revelation illumines the types and shadows of the older.

(13) He was present the same as He had been known on earth, for He is seen as Son of Man; yet He is different, for He is arrayed in the apparel of kingly and priestly dignity. He is robed to the foot with the long garment of the high priest. John uses the same word as the LXX version of Exod. 28:31 to describe the robe of the Ephod. (Comp. Zech. 3:4.) It has been understood by some, however, to indicate the "ample robe of judicial and kingly power." He is the King-Priest who is seen by the evangelist, the Melchisedec whom the epistle to the Hebrews had so gloriously set forth (Heb. 5:9, 10; 6:20; 7:1-17). The girdle is not around the loins, as though ready for action and toil (Luke 12:35), but it is worn as by one who rests from toil in the repose of sovereignty. The girdle is of pure gold, the emblem of a royal presence.

(14) His head and his hairs were white . . .—The whiteness here is the token of the transfiguration in light of the glorified person of the Redeemer. But there is, too, a hint of age. Age and youth alike have their glories. The glory of young men is their strength; the hoary head, the token of experience, dignity, wisdom, and authority, is the glory of age. Physically, white hair may be a sign of decay; typically it never is.

His eyes were as a flame of fire.—The eyes of the Lord, which are in every place beholding the evil and the good, are here described as like fire to express not merely indignation against evil but determination to consume it. Our God is a consuming fire, purging away sin from those who forsake sin, and consuming in their sin those who refuse to be separated from it.

(15) His feet like unto fine brass.—Many authors take **chalcolibanus** ("fine brass") as a hybrid word, half Greek, half Hebrew—**chalcos**, brass, and **labân**, white, to whiten—and understand it to signify brass which has attained in the furnace a white heat. "Such technical words were likely enough to be current in a population like that of Ephesus, consisting largely of workers in metal, some of whom . . . (Acts 19:34; II Tim. 4:14) were, without doubt, Jews. I believe the word in question to have belonged to this technical vocabulary" (Plumptre).

His voice as the sound.—The voice of a multitude (Dan. 10:6) was in earlier Hebrew writings compared to the sound of the waves of the sea, which the voice of the Lord alone could subdue (Pss. 65:7; 93:4). This image the evangelist adopts to describe the voice of Christ—strong and majestic amid the Babel-sounds of earth. That voice, whose word stilled the sea, sounds as the waves of the sea, which John heard Him rebuke.

(16) And he had in his right hand seven stars.—The stars are the emblems of the angels of the seven churches (see verse 20). They appeared perhaps as a wreath, or as a royal and star-adorned diadem in His right hand. It expresses their preciousness in Christ's sight, and the care He takes of them.

And out of his mouth went a sharp two-edged sword.—The sword of the Spirit, even the Word of God, is described here (Eph. 6:17; Heb. 4:12). This is the weapon with which Christ will subdue His enemies; with this He lays bare the hidden hypocrisies of men, cuts off the diseased members, and wounds that He may heal.

His countenance was as the sun shineth in his strength.—It is the spiritual truth which gives the splendor to such descriptions as these. The dazzling glory of Him who is the Sun of Righteousness is intolerable to human eyes (I Tim. 6:16; Heb. 1:3). It is the luster of holiness and righteousness which is signified here.

(17) I fell at his feet as dead.—The consciousness of unworthiness seems to have overcome the evangelist. (Comp. Exod. 33:18, 20, "Thou canst not see my face; for there shall no man see me and live.") For every man it is a dreadful thing to stand face to face with God. Yet the consciousness of this unworthiness to behold God, or to receive a near revelation of His presence, is a sign of faith and is welcomed as such.

(18) I am he that liveth, and was dead.—This verse must be carefully kept in connection with the preceding, as the description should go on without pause. He is the living One, who has life in Himself and is fountain and source of life to others. Translate, "I have the keys of death and of Hades." The true order is the more appropriate order. It is not of the second death that He speaks; our Lord is seen here as the conqueror of that clouded region, and that resistless foe which man dreaded. The whole verse affirms the undying power and the inalienable authority of our Master (see Matt. 16:18; I Pet. 3:19), and is a fitting prelude to a book which is to show the inherent divine tenacity of Christianity. The church lives on because Christ its Head lives on (John 14:19).

(20) Having bidden him write the meaning of this mystery, He gives to John an explanatory key. The angel is the ideal embodiment of the church. The generally adopted view is that the angel is the chief pastor or bishop of the church. The description of them as stars favors this view. Similar imagery is applied elsewhere to teachers, true and false (Dan. 12:3; Jude 13. Comp. Rev. 8:10; 12:4).

2

(1) On the word "angel," see note on 1:20. To those favoring an early date for writing (i.e., Nero's time), the "angel" is Timothy.

Ephesus.—The chief city of Ionia, and at this time the most important city in Asia. It possessed commercial, geographical, and ecclesiastical advantages. It was a wealthy focus for trade, reaching out one hand to the East, while with the other grasping Greek culture. Its magnificent temple was one of the seven wonders of the world, but the religious tone induced by its pagan worship was of the lowest order. Spiritual opportunities, however, were proportioned to its needs. It had been the scene of three years' labor of Paul (Acts 20:31), of the captivating and convincing eloquence of

Apollos (Acts 18:24), and of the persistent labors of Aquila and Priscilla (Acts 18:26). Tychicus, the beloved and faithful, had been minister there (Eph. 6:21); Timothy was its chief pastor.

These things saith he . . . —The titles by which Christ is described at the opening of the seven epistles are drawn mainly from chap. 1. The vision is found to supply features appropriate to the needs of the several churches. The message comes in this epistle from One who "**holdeth**" firmly in His grasp and "walketh" in their midst. The church at Ephesus needed to remember their Lord as such. The first love had gone out of their religion; there was a tendency to fall into a mechanical faith, strong against heresy but tolerant of conventionalism.

(2) I know thy works.—This phrase is probably common to all the epistles. It expresses the way in which all actions are naked and open before those flame-like eyes of Him with whom we have to do (1:14).

And thou hast tried them . . . and hast found them liars.—Paul had warned the Ephesian elders of the appearance of false teachers (Acts 20:28-31). Zeal for pure doctrine characterized the Ephesian Church. It is commended by Ignatius in his epistle (**ad Eph.** 6). The false apostles here spoken of are not to be identified with the Nicolaitanes of verse 6; that verse is introduced as a further ground of commendation, mitigating the censure of verses 4 and 5.

(3) And hast borne.—In this last word there is a recurrence of the word (**kopos**) translated "labour" in verse 2. They had toiled on to weariness without wearying of their toil (Gal. 6:9), just as they could not **bear** the evil and yet had **borne** reproaches for Christ's sake.

(4) Nevertheless I have somewhat against thee.—It is no trifle which is blamed, for the decay of love is the decay of that without which all other graces are as nothing (I Cor. 13:1-3). It is impossible not to see some reference in this to the language of Paul (which must have been familiar to the Ephesian Christians) in Eph. 5:23-33, where human love is made a type of the divine.

(5) Remember therefore from whence thou art fallen, . . . and do the first works.— It has been argued that we have here evidence that the Domitian date of the Apocalypse is the true one, since it describes a fall in spiritual life which might have occurred in thirty years, but would hardly have taken place in the few years—ten at the most—which elapsed between the visit

of Paul (Acts 20:29, 30) and the reign of Nero. Yet in Ephesus there is at present little outward sign of decay. They have resisted evil and false teachers; they have shown toil and endurance; but the great Searcher of hearts detects the almost imperceptible symptoms of an incipient decay. Further, it must not be forgotten that the apostle did express his presentiments of coming danger, and especially warned the elders (Acts 20:28) to take heed unto **themselves**; and in his epistle (Eph. 6:24) he gives in his closing words the covert caution that their love to Christ should be an incorruptible, unchanging love. The advice now given is threefold: remember, repent, reform.

(6) But this thou hast, that thou hatest the deeds (better, **works**) **of the Nicolaitanes.**— The Nicolaitanes were the Antinomians of the Asiatic Church. The life and conduct were little considered, and the faith professed was everything. Some hold that the name is symbolical, signifying "destroyer of the people," and that it is the Greek form of Balaam. (See notes on verses 14, 15.) The existence of a sect called Nicolaitanes in the second century is attested by Irenaeus, Tertullian, and Clement of Alexandria.

(7) He that hath an ear . . . —These words—an echo from the gospels—recur in all the seven epistles. In the first three, however, they are placed before the promise; in the remaining four they follow it. The heart which is hardened is the precursor of the ear that is deaf (Jer. 6:10; John 12:37-40).

(8) Smyrna, a mercantile center, has always been considered one of the most beautiful cities in Asia. It was situated in the ancient province of Ionia, a little north of Ephesus. In olden times it commanded the trade of the Levant, besides being the natural outlet for the produce of the Hermus valley. The neighborhood was peculiarly fertile, and there are indications that intemperance was prevalent among the inhabitants. Servility and flattery may be added, for the people of Smyrna seem to have been astutely fickle, and to have been keen in preserving the patronage of the ruling powers. In one of their temples the inscription declared Nero to be "the Saviour of the human race." Smyrna contested with six or seven other cities the honor of being the birthplace of the poet Homer.

The angel of the church in Smyrna.—We have no means of determining for certain who was the person addressed here. Many who accept the Domitian date of the Apocalypse argue that Polycarp was at this time the bishop or presiding minister at Smyrna. If so, the episcopate of Polycarp extended over sixty years. Polycarp was martyred A.D. 156. Ignatius addresses him in A.D. 108 as Bishop of Smyrna. Smyrna was a church whose trial was persecution.

(9) Tribulation.—If persecution brought upon them poverty, it was the means also of unfolding to view their possession of the "true riches" of being counted worthy to suffer.

Jews.—"It was in the synagogue that they heard words which reproached them as Nazarenes, Galileans, Christians, Disciples of the Crucified" (Plumptre). (Comp. Jas. 2:7.) It is interesting to notice that this characteristic hostility of the Jews was illustrated in the martyrdom of Polycarp. The Jews were foremost in bringing logs for the pile.

(10) Tried.—On the part of the adversary, the intention was that they might be **tempted** from their allegiance to Christ. The real effect would be that they who endured would come forth tested and approved. "Ten days" means that the test would be thorough.

A crown of life.—A crown was given at the Olympian Games, which were held at Smyrna and to which an allusion may be made. Some hold, however, the crown— though the word is **stephanos**, not **diadema**— is rather that of royalty than of victory. It is interesting to note that the narrative which tells of the death of Polycarp closes with words which it is difficult not to believe to be an allusion to this promise.

(11) The second death.—This phrase clearly points to a death which is other than that of the body; it stands in contrast with the crown of **life**. The expressions of 20:14 and 21:8 exclude the idea that a cessation of conscious existence is intended. The life of the spirit is the knowledge of God (John 17:3); the death of the spirit, or the second death, is the paralysis of the powers by which such a knowledge was possible.

(12) Pergamos.—Unlike Ephesus and Smyrna, Pergamos was not distinguished as a commercial city. Its importance was due to other causes. A striking cone-shaped hill rose from the plain which bordered the northern banks of the Caicus. The hill was considered sacred. Its value as a strong natural fortress was recognized early, and it was used as a treasury where local chieftains deposited their wealth. It has been described as a city of temples, a sort

of union of a pagan cathedral city, a university town, and a royal residence, with a library which rivalled that of Alexandria. It was declared by Pliny to be a city unrivaled in the province of Asia.

Sharp sword with two edges.—See note on 1:16.

(13) Why should this pre-eminence in evil be assigned to Pergamos? Plumptre suggests that the general character of the city, its worship and customs, in addition to the persecutions which the Christians had encountered, may well account for the description. The symbol of the serpent must have been conspicuous among the objects of adoration in the temple of AEsculapius. Curious arts were practiced; lying wonders were claimed; persecution had extended to death. Such evil in such a city may have led to its being regarded as the very headquarters of the enemy.

Antipas—short for Antipater. Nothing is known of Antipas beyond fanciful traditions.

(14) But I have a few things against thee.—Those who had been brave unto death in the days of persecution had been less temptation-proof against more seductive influences. The church tolerated without remonstrance men holding "the teaching of Balaam. . . ." Israel could not be cursed, but they might be made to bring a curse upon themselves by yielding to sin; so the counsel of Balaam was to tempt them through the women of Midian. A similar temptation was endangering the Pergamene Church. (See Num. 31.)

(15) So hast thou also them that hold the doctrine of the Nicolaitanes—i.e., thou, as well as those of old, hast such teachers. Opinions are divided whether we are to identify the Balaamites with the Nicolaitanes, and to suppose that both names point to the same sect. The simplest meaning of the passage seems to be that the temptation to which the Israelites were exposed is used to illustrate the temptations of the Pergamene Church, through the teaching of the Nicolaitanes. Both temptations lead in the same Antinomian direction. Such a tendency was seen early (comp. Rom. 6:4; Gal. 5:13; Jude 4).

(17) To him that overcometh.—Israel ate manna in the wilderness, and died; the Father gives the true bread from heaven that a man may eat thereof and not die. The Son is that Bread of Life (John 6:35, 48, 57). But the promise is of **hidden** manna. Is the allusion to the pot of manna which had

1213

been laid up in the Ark? The Jews long cherished the belief that the Ark and sacred treasures of the Temple had not perished. There was a fondly-held tradition that they had been buried by Jeremiah in a safe and secret spot on "the mountain where Moses climbed and saw the heritage of God, until the time that God shall gather his people again together, and show them his mercy" (II Macc. 2:4, 7). This "hidden manna," so longed for by an afflicted race, may have suggested the use of the word "hidden"; but the sacred writer would become anxious to bring out the spiritual truth that the fountains of Christian life are hidden (Col. 3:3); the world knoweth us not. Some see in the white (i.e., **shining**) stone an allusion to the Urim and Thummim, and therefore take it to indicate the "priestly dignity of the victorious Christian." Another suggestion is that the reference is to the stone of friendship, called **tessera hospitalis**, graven with some legend or device and giving to its possessor a claim of hospitality from him who gave it. The "new name" expressed the step which had been taken into a higher, truer life, and the change of heart and the elevation of character consequent upon it.

(18) Thyatira was situated between Pergamos and Sardis, a little off the main road which connected these two cities. It was a Macedonian colony, founded by Alexander the Great after the overthrow of the Persian empire. The Macedonian colonists appear to have introduced the worship of Apollo, honored as the Sun-god, under the name of Tyrimnas. Close commercial intercourse connected the daughter colony with its mother city. The dye-trade was, perhaps, the most important of all trades. (Lydia, the seller of purple, was in all likelihood connected with the guild of dyers; and her appearance in Philippi is an illustration of the trade relations of Macedonia and Thyatira. The Christian community at Thyatira may have owed its beginning to her.) The population was of a mixed character, including Asiatics, Macedonians, Italians, and Chaldeans. The message which is sent to the Christians dwelling among them is from **the Son of God**. The term **Son of Man** is used throughout the Book of Revelation; here only is the phrase "Son of God" used. But it suits the message which breathes the language of sovereignty and righteous sternness.

(20) Jezebel.—There was some personal influence at work for evil in Thyatira. The sin alleged against her is the same for which

the **Nicolaitanes** are condemned—fornication, and the eating of things sacrificed to idols. The leader of the exorcists is a woman regarded by her followers as a prophetess, but viewed by the Lord of the churches as a Jezebel, teaching and seducing the servants of God. The chief minister is rebuked for paying too much deference to her spiritual pretensions.

(23) Her children.—This is to be understood of her followers. The so-called prophetess, leading the way in looseness of morals, under the pretense of some deeper knowledge, had her disciples.

(26, 27) The promise is of authority to share in the shepherdlike sovereignty of the anointed King. (Comp. the Messianic prophecy of Ps. 2.) Those who refused to stoop to the customs around them, and to gain influence by crushing or ignoring their convictions, would share the nobler sway which He now established.

3

(1) Sardis was once the capital of the old Lydian monarchy, and associated with the names of Croesus, Cyrus, and Alexander. The art of dyeing is said to have been invented here; gold and silver coins were first minted at Sardis, and resident merchants first became a class there. An earthquake destroyed it in the reign of Tiberius; a pestilence followed, but the city seems to have recovered its prosperity before the date of this epistle. The worship of Cybele was the prevailing one; its rites, like those of Dionysos and Aphrodite, encouraged impurity. The faith of the angel of the Sardian Church, and the faith of the church around him, had sunk into a superficial, though perhaps ostentatious, state. Living with the credit of superior piety, it was easy to grow satisfied with the reputation and to forget to keep open the channels through which grace and life could flow.

(4) The case of the Sardian Church was bad, yet there were a few who had not defiled their garments. These had not succumbed to the oppressive moral atmosphere around them. This "white" is not the white of the undefiled robe; it is the lustrous white of glory, as in the promise in verse 5.

(7) Philadelphia.—The town of Philadelphia derived its name from Attalus Philadelphus, the king of Pergamos, who died 138 B.C. It was situated on the slopes of Mount Tmolus, some 900 feet above sea level. The whole region, however, was volcanic, and few cities suffered more from earthquakes; the frequent recurrence of these considerably reduced the population. But its favorable situation and fertile soil preserved it from entire desertion. And of all the seven churches, it had the longest life as a Christian city.

True is a favorite word with John, expressing more than the opposite of "false." It implies that which is perfect in contrast with the imperfect, the reality in contrast with the shadow. Christ, then, in calling Himself the True, declares that "all titles and names given to Him are realized in Him; the idea and the fact in Him are, what they can never be in any other, absolutely commensurate" (Trench).

The key of David.—Jesus Christ is the true Steward of the house of David. The faulty, self-seeking stewards of Philadelphia vainly claimed a right of exclusion from synagogue or church. But though in a sense the keys of spiritual advantages are in the hands of His servants, He still retains the highest administration of them in His own hands. The power of the keys entrusted to apostles gave them no right to alter the essentials of the Gospel, or the fundamental principles of morality. The absolution given by them can only be conditional.

(8) Behold, I have set before thee an open door.—Comp. Acts 14:27; I Cor. 16:8, 9; II Cor. 2:12, 13; Col. 4:3. The open door was not simply a way of escape from difficulties, but an opening for preaching the Gospel, an opportunity of doing good, as well as an abundant entrance into the kingdom.

For thou hast a little strength . . . —The tenses used point back to some epoch in the history of this church when some heavy trial or persecution arose, which tested the sincerity, fidelity, or Christian love of the faithful. "The reward then of a little strength is a door opened" (Vaughan).

(9) Of the synagogue of Satan.—We have here a reappearance of the same troubles which afflicted the Church of Smyrna: the fixed and contemptuous exclusiveness of the Judaizing party was their trial. But there was a time coming (see verse 10) when these faithful ones, now abused and excommunicated by the fanatical synagogue, would be acknowledged.

(12) Will I make a pillar, and an unshaken one. This may be a reference to the frequent earthquakes which had shaken down buildings in their city. Those who overcome will prove real supports to the great Christian temple. (Comp. Gal. 2:9.)

Write upon him.—The allusion is to the golden frontlet inscribed with the name of Jehovah. (Comp. 22:4.) He will reflect the likeness of God; and not only so, but he will bear the tokens of his heavenly citizenship (Phil. 3:20; Heb. 12:22, 23).

(14) Laodicea was situated half way between Philadelphia and Colossae, and not far from Hierapolis. It received its name from Laodice, wife of Antiochus the second king of Syria, by whom it was rebuilt and beautified. It shared with Thyatira and Sardis in the dye trade and enjoyed prosperity in commerce generally. The language of Col. 2:1 is most generally understood to imply that the apostle had never personally visited either Colossae or Laodicea. But it was a church in which Paul took the deepest possible interest; the believers there were constantly in his mind. He knew their special temptations to the worship of inferior mediators, and to spiritual paralysis springing from worldly prosperity and intellectual pride. He had great heart-conflict for those of Laodicea (Col. 3:1), and in proof of his earnest solicitude he addressed a letter to them (Col. 4:16), in all probability the epistle we call the Epistle to the Ephesians.

Unto the angel of the church of the Laodiceans.—By the "angel" we understand the presiding pastor. There is some ground for identifying him with Archippus (Col. 4:17).

These things saith the Amen, the faithful and true witness.—The "Amen" is used only here as a personal name. It is the Hebrew word for "verily." He who so often thus prefaced His solemn utterance now reveals Himself as the source of all certainty and truth (II Cor. 1:20).

The beginning of the creation of God.— See Col. 1:15-18. The "beginning" does not mean that Christ was the first among the created, but that He was the origination or **primary source** of all creation. Not **with** Him but **by** Him creation began (John 1:1-3). The word "beginning" (like the word "faithful") must be understood in an active sense. He has originating power (Acts 3:16) as well as priority of existence. The appropriateness of this use is seen when we remember that the Laodicean Church was exposed to the temptation of worshiping inferior principalities.

(15, 16) Neither cold nor hot.—The "hot" here is the glowing, fervent zeal and devotion which is commended and commanded elsewhere (Rom. 12:11). It is self-sacrifice, an earnestness which does not know itself earnest, being all too absorbed in its work. It is kindled of God and sustained by converse with the divine One. The "cold" describes the state of those who are as yet untouched by the Gospel of Love. An intermediate state between these is the "lukewarm"; such are neither earnest for God nor utterly indifferent to religion. They are best described as those who take an interest in religion, but who regard enthusiasm as illbred, and who have never put themselves to any inconvenience, braved any reproach, or abandoned any comfort for Christ's sake.

I would ... —The wish is not that they might grow cold rather than remain in this lukewarm state; it is more a regret that they are among those who are in a condition which is so liable to self-deception.

(17) I am rich.—The words should be taken as an amplification of the reason for their rejection—that tepid state which, beginning with self-satisfaction, led on to self-deception. Their wealth led them into a quiet unaggressive kind of religion; they were self-complacent because in comfortable worldly circumstances. There is a touch of irony in verse 18, where gold represents love (the currency of the kingdom of God), raiment the clothing with honor, and eye-salve genuine spiritual enlightenment.

(20) Behold, I stand at the door, and knock.—The life of Christ on earth abounds with illustrations which may well have suggested the image (Luke 10:38; 19:5, 6; 22:11-13; 24:29, 30; John 1:39. Comp. Cant. 5:2-6.)

4

From the world below, and the struggling churches, we are brought to see the Eternal who is ruling over all. A vision like this must dwarf our sense of life's sorrows and temptations, and prepare for the scenes of conflict, failure, and persecution which are about to be unfolded. Whatever painful sights the seer is called upon to behold, this vision will remain in the background as the constant witness that in all the vicissitudes of the church's history, God is her refuge.

(1) The first voice.—The **first** voice here spoken of is the one which the apostle had heard in the opening vision (1:10); he heard and recognized that trumpet-like voice again. This is the voice of Christ.

(3) The sardine is a stone of fiery red color; the emerald is a bright green; the jasper—the last stone in the high-priest's breastplate and first of the twelve foundations of the New Jerusalem (Exod. 28:20; Rev. 21:19)—is a dark, opaque green. The union of brightness and flame is understood of the holiness and righteousness of God. The emerald-colored bow is the evident symbol of the divine mercy. It was a covenant token (Gen. 9:12-16), bearing witness to God's faithfulness in dark times, God's care for the Ark of His church, and His mercy shining forth after storm.

(4) In the similar vision in Ezekiel no human beings are seen; their appearance here is significant. They are the representatives of Christ's church. The twenty-four elders represent the complete church of God in the Jewish (Patriarchs) and Gentile (Apostles) worlds, the true spiritual successors, as priests to God, of those twenty-four courses (I Chron. 24:1-19) arranged by David. (Comp. 15:3; 21:12, 14.)

(5) The Spirit of God in His manifold powers is described under emblems of fire. The vision of this chapter reminds us that God is ever mindful of His covenant: the rainbow, the token of the covenant with Noah; the flaming torches, tokens of the covenant with Abraham; and the thunderings and lightnings, tokens of the covenant at Sinai.

(6) Waters represent the unguided, unreasoning, and unprincipled thoughts of men. By analogy, the calm glass-like sea, which is never in storm, represents the counsels of God, those purposes of righteousness and love, often fathomless but never obscure. The position of the crystal sea is analogous to that of the molten sea in front of Solomon's Temple (II Chron. 4:9, 10). "And in the midst of the throne" means between the seer and the throne. The apostle saw the crystal sea, and beyond it the living creatures encircling the throne.

(7) These are **living beings**, not "beasts." The rendering "beasts" introduces confusion of thought and violates the laws of apocalyptic imagery. The evil powers are described under the emblem of wild beasts, for thus brute force, unrestrained passion, and self-will are symbolized. But these "living beings" do not represent the evil element in the world. They are representative of animated nature. There are **four** beings which hold a primacy in the world: among created beings, man; among birds, the eagle; among cattle, the ox; among untamed animals, the lion. The characteristics of these four chiefs of creation unite to make a perfect picture of the spirit of true service, which should be brave as a lion, patient as the ox, aspiring as the eagle, intelligent as man. (The number "four" in the Apocalypse is almost always associated with the earth.) Multiplicity of eyes may symbolize vitality and vigilance; the eyes are always observant of God's will, fixed on Him, as the eyes of a servant on his master.

(8) The resemblance to Isaiah's vision (6:1-4) may remind us that the voice of God's creation has in every age proclaimed His eternal holiness. The "six wings" are taken to express reverence (with twain he covered his face), humility (with twain he covered his feet), and obedience (with twain he did fly). The twenty-four elders represent the regenerate church (verses 9, 10). The new creation in Christ Jesus joins in praise with all created things (verse 11).

5

(1) And I saw in the right hand ... —The book is in the form of a roll, written not on the inside only, as was the usual way, but rather within and without (Ezek. 2:9, 10). The overflowing writing indicates the completeness of the contents; there was no room for addition to that which was written therein. If we say it is the book which unfolds the principles of God's government—in a wide sense, the book of salvation (comp. Rom. 16:25, 26)—the interpretation of life, which Christ alone can bestow (see verses 3-6), we shall include the practical truths which underlie a number of interpretations—Old Testament and New, man's heritage and destiny, God's purposes and providence. He who is the Light unfolds those truths which shed a light on all. The roll was fast sealed, so that even those who were wise and learned enough to read it, had it been unrolled, could not do so.

(2) Who is worthy ... —"Worthy" seems to imply moral fitness, which is the true strength in the heavenly world. It was not lack of intellectual capacity as much as the taint of moral unworthiness which hindered the reading of the book. It is not simply as divine Son of God, but also as victorious Saviour and King of His people, that Christ

opens the book; His worthiness has been established in conflict and temptation.

(5) The right to open the roll turns upon His victory; He conquered, and so opens the secret purposes of God to His church. The lion was the ancient symbol of the tribe of Judah. The symbol of strength, courage, and sovereignty, it also represented the royal house of David. He who is the Branch is also the Root (Isa. 11:10); He is the one who was David's Lord (Matt. 22:41-45).

(6) The evangelist is told of the **Lion** which will open the seals; he looks, and lo, it is a (little) Lamb! There is deep significance in this. When we read of the Lion, we think of power and majesty; but it is power manifested in apparent weakness. The Lamb is as one that had been slain. The woundmarks are there, but it is not dead; it is standing, for it represents Him who, though He died, is alive for evermore. The signs of suffering and death are visible, for it is not the Lamb, but the suffering Lamb, which is exalted. From the tokens of suffering the seer passes to the tokens of strength and wisdom which he saw in the Lamb. The horn is the strength of the animal which carries it. The seven horns denote completeness or fullness of strength. The seven eyes, like the seven lamps (4:5), represent the Holy Spirit in His manifold gifts of grace; but as they are described as eyes of the Lamb, they represent the omniscience of Him who is in heaven and yet, by His Spirit, everywhere (Matt. 28:20).

(8) The four living beings, who represent creation, join with the elders, who represent the church, in the adoration of the Lamb who holds the secret of life's meaning in His hand. Here we have the praises (represented by the harps) and the prayers (represented by the censers) of the world-wide and age-long Church of Christ. These comparisons are in strict accordance with Old Testament language.

(9, 10) It is the great victory in suffering and death which inspires the song. The suffering Saviour has died, has broken the bond of the oppressor, and has claimed, by right of purchase, mankind as His own; and the price was His blood. The kingdom and reign is the outcome of Christ's work. The redeemed reign with and in Christ, but they also reign on the earth. Christ gives them a kingship on the earth among men, for they are exerting those influences, promoting those principles, and dispensing those laws of righteousness, holiness, and peace which in reality rule all the best developments of life and history.

(11) And I beheld ... —The chorus of the redeemed is followed by a chorus of angels. If the Revelation is true, there can be no breach in the sympathies of any part of God's voluntary and intelligent universe. The numbers are not to be taken literally; they are simply employed to express the countless throng of that "innumerable company of angels" (Heb. 12:22) which raised the song.

(12) Saying with a loud voice ... —The doxology is sevenfold. (See note on 1:6.)

(13) And every creature ... —The third chorus is the chorus of the universe. The song of the redeemed, echoed by the hosts of angels, is now merged in the utterance of all. The song of praise rises from all quarters and from all forms of creation. The whole universe, animate and inanimate, joins in this glad acclaim. (See Rom. 8:23; Phil. 2:10.) The two preceding songs were in honor of the Lamb; in this last the praise is addressed to the Throned One and to the Lamb. This linking of the Lamb with God as the Throned One is common throughout the book. Here they are linked in praise; in 6:16 they are linked in wrath; in 7:17 they are linked in ministering consolation; in 19:6, 7, they are linked in triumph. In the final vision of the book the Lord God and the Lamb are the temple (21:22) and the light (21:23), the refreshment (22:1) and sovereignty (22:3), of the celestial city.

6

This section relates Christianity to great universal evils. The extinction of war, disease, death, persecution will not be immediate. The mission of Christianity is not to abolish these evils at once and by compulsion, but to undermine them. Her work is not coercion, but conviction, and is primarily to individuals, and only secondarily and indirectly to nations.

The seals which are opened by the Lamb seem to speak a double message. There are two lines of thought in the Bible, and these give rise to two apparently contradictory sets of pictures. There are the pictures of what would be the state of the world were the principles of Christ fully and universally accepted; and there are the pictures of the world as it will be because men do not fully accept them. The first set are the ideal, and include the abolition of war, social injus-

tice, and poverty. But between this grand possibility and its realization stands the wayward, tortuous, and weakened human will, which either rejects or fatally but half adopts the teachings of God. In earlier Christian times the hope of an ideal kingdom, soon to be realized in the immediate establishment of Christ's kingdom, was very strong. The first disciples yearned to see it set up immediately. They thought the day of the Lord, in the sense of the perfecting of His reign, was at hand; they forgot that the heavenly Bridegroom must gird His sword upon His thigh, and that His arrows must be sharp in the heart of the King's enemies (Ps. 45:3, 5). The vision of these seven seals is the repetition of the warning against such forgetfulness. The ideal Kingdom might come if mankind would receive it, but it must be established by conviction, not by coercion; and so the actual history of the growth of the Kingdom would be different from the ideal. The seals unfold, then, the general aspects of the world's history after Christ's ascension. Certain features would continue; war, famine, disease, death would remain. The Church through the seer is warned to prepare for her mission of suffering; and in this way the vision stretches on until the close of earth's history.

But this is not all. The visions of the book may have preliminary applications, because the principles on which they are constructed are eternal ones. Our Lord's own language in Matt. 24 is our guarantee that we may look for such preliminary applications. The story of the overthrow of many nations presents these features of war, famine, misery, convulsion. The fall of Jerusalem, as well as that of the Roman empire, was preceded by such. On this principle, other interpretations of the vision have a truth in them, as long as they are confined to broad, general principles. The mischievous affection for trivial details has been the bane of more than one school of interpreters.

(1) The living beings cry "**Come,**" and their cry is responded to by the appearance of the several riders. The living beings represent the nature and creation of God which groans and travails in pain, waiting for the manifestation of the sons of God. These summon the emblems of war and pestilence to come on the scene, for these things must necessarily be, and through these lies the way for the final coming of God's Christ, for whom creation longs.

(2) Conquering, and to conquer.—This

rider represents victory. The emblems—the crown and white horse—are obviously those of victory. The crown (**stephanos**) is the crown of triumph. The horses used in Roman triumphs were white. On the white horse of triumph the crowned rider goes forth conquering. But who or what is represented here? Some take it to be a mere emblem of conquest, as the next rider represents war. The description, however, seems to demand something more. Is not the vision the reflex of the hopes of early Christian thought? It is the symbol of Christian victory. They were right in their faith, and wrong in their expectation: right in their faith—He would conquer; wrong in their expectation—the visions of war, famine, death must intervene. It was through these that the conqueror would be proved more than conqueror.

(3, 4) The second seal.—This seal is the distinct and unmistakable declaration to the Church that they must look for wars, even after the Prince of Peace has come. The advent of the highest good does not work peace, but only because the hindrance is in man. Man's resistance to good turns the Gospel of peace into an occasion for the sword. So our Lord declares, "I came not to send peace, but a sword." The reign of peace, the beating of swords into plowshares, is not yet. The vision may help to fix the Christian position about war. It is to be expected; it is an evil, but often an inevitable evil. Those who take part in war are not condemned; those who occasion offenses are.

(5, 6) The third seal.—The balance is the emblem of scarcity; food is not weighed out thus in times of abundance. The denarius ("penny") was the usual daily pay of the laborer and the soldier. It is difficult to speak of this as other than terribly high prices for food. The whole of a man's pay goes for food, and even the coarser bread is so expensive that it takes a whole day's wages to supply food for three adults. There is a kind of irony in times of urgency, when the necessities are scarcely to be had, and the luxuries remain comparatively low in price. The splendors and comforts of life are held cheap, when hunger is showing that the life is more than meat and the body than raiment.

(7, 8) The fourth seal.—The color is that deadly greenish hue, which is the unmistakable token of the approach of death. The rider is Death—not a particular form of death, but Death himself. Attending him,

ready to gather up the slain, is Hades. The fourth seal is the darkest and most terrible. Single forms of death (war and famine) were revealed in the earlier seals; now the great King of Terrors himself appears, and in his hand are gathered all forms of death. These forms of death correspond with God's four sore judgments—the sword, famine, pestilence, and the noisome beasts of Ezek. 14:21. The seal, therefore, gathers up into one all the awfulness of the past seals. The pale horse of death, spiritually, is the parody of the white horse of victory; the form of godliness remains, but the power is gone.

(9-11) The fifth seal.—The voice which is now heard is not the cry of the groaning world, but of the oppressed and troubled Church. In the fourth seal the climax of world-sorrow seemed to be reached in the accumulation of war, famine, pestilence, and noisome beasts. Worldly policy, selfishness, and the untamed passions of mankind would still trouble humanity. Then if such troubles and disorders remain, what has the Church been doing? Where is the promise of that early vision of victory? The answer is given in the fifth seal. The Church has been following her Lord. The glowing dream of a quick conquest over all evil passes away, and the picture of an agonizing, persecuted Church takes its place. The four seals proclaim the Church's apparent failure; she has not brought peace and social and political harmony to the world. The fifth seal shows her suffering.

(10) How long ... ?—By a dramatic figure the persecuted and slain ones are represented as crying for retribution on their oppressors. The forgotten or ignored wrongs of generations come forth from oblivion and cry for vengeance. It is a poetical description, but it is not fiction. The righteous blood shed does fall upon the world in retribution; the laws of God avenge themselves, though the victims do not live to behold the reward of the ungodly.

(12-17) The sixth seal.—The seals follow the lines laid down by our Lord in Matt. 24. These features are described by our Master as preliminary to His Coming and the end of the world. But it is not to be forgotten that our Lord wished us to regard certain great culminating epochs as in a secondary sense His advents. The features indicated in the seals have a sequence which has been reproduced in the history of nations and churches.

The writer of the Apocalypse has kept

closely to Old Testament imagery. Events such as great calamities, changes, and revolutions in the world's history are described by emblems similar to those used in Isa. 34:3, 4; 50:3; Joel 2:30, 31; Hag. 2:6. Thus it seems right to regard the language here as figurative, and to bear in mind that, though its fullest application belongs to the final advent, there may be many anticipatory advents. The judgment is often rehearsed before the day of judgment. The **untimely** figs are the winter figs, which grow under the leaves and do not ripen at the proper season, but hang upon the trees until the winter. They are a fit emblem of those who have not used the opportunity and season to ripen for God. The crisis thus puts the feeble, timid, and negligent to the test, and also proves the vanity of those who make any world power their confidence.

Thus in the final day of judgment the revealing of the spiritual order of all life will confound men whose minds have been blinded by their entire absorption in world splendors and world powers. Nor is it merely the unveiling of the forgotten spiritual order which will confound them. The advent is of a Person—it is the revealing of God's Son from heaven. In that day of His wrath, it is not as a Judge who has laid aside the tokens of His humiliation and suffering; it is as the Lamb. He from whom they now shrink is He who came as a lamb, gentle, pure, and suffering on their behalf, and whose love they spurned.

(17) Who shall be able to stand?—Comp. Mal. 3:2. Whether it be His advent in the flesh, He tested men; or whether one of His advents in Providence, He still tests men; and much more, then, in the closing personal advent, when these visions will receive their fullest illustration, will He try men.

7

(1) And after these things.—This chapter answers the solemn question of the last chapter: "Who is able to stand?" The winds are clearly emblems of days of trouble or judgment; as the winds sweep away the chaff and clear the atmosphere, so do judgments try the ungodly. The winds of judgment are ready to blow from all quarters of the earth, but they are restrained until the servants of God are sealed.

(2) And I saw another angel . . . —Angels appear as carrying out the purposes of God. This angel rises into view from the door of the dawn. In the midst of the dark symptoms of coming storm and judgment, there springs up a light for the righteous. This angel carries a seal of the living God. The seal is the emblem of security. The seal, on the one side, is dependence on, and communion with, God; on the other side, it is holiness of life. (See Eph. 1:13, 14; Phil. 3:9.) The cry of the angel (verse 3) is, Injure not the sea nor the trees. These are mentioned as the objects which would be most disturbed by a storm of wind. Trees are used as emblems of real and of pretended religionism. (See Ps. 1:3, 4; Jude 12.)

(4-8) There are three questions which these verses suggest. (1) Who are these one hundred forty-four thousand? Some have thought that the sealed ones must be Jewish Christians: i.e., they are disposed to take the twelve tribes literally. The scope of the previous verses seems decisive against this view. Nor is there any necessity for so limiting (see Rom. 2:28, 29; Gal. 3:28). The Christian Church absorbs the Jewish, inherits her privileges, and adopts, with wider and nobler meaning, her phraseology. (2) How are we to understand the numbers? As we cannot adopt the literal interpretation of the tribes of Israel, still less can we admit a literal interpretation of the numbers mentioned here; but there is an appropriate symbolism in the numbers of the Apocalypse. Twelve is used as the number of those who in every age have been called out to witness for some truth which the world needed. Thus the twelve tribes of Israel were the appointed witnesses of a pure theology and a pure morality in the days of idolatry and license; and later, the twelve apostles became the inheritors of a similar, though higher, spiritual work in the world. The fruits of this world witness is a wide and sustained success: the twelve multiplied by the twelve a thousandfold. (3) Does the change in the order and names of the tribes symbolize anything? The alterations are not without significance. The number twelve is maintained to show that in all changes God's purposes stand. The omission of one tribe (Dan) and the changed name of another (Ephraim to Joseph) are designed to show that in the Church, as in Israel, the most splendid opportunities may be lost. The order of the names is altered: Judah, lion-like, resolute, and strong, wins the foremost place; from him springs the true Ruler, the Lion of the tribe of Judah, to unfold the counsels of God and to rule the world with a righteous scepter. The changes are the result of the actual history of the tribes, and illustrate how in the Christian Church, as in the Jewish, privileges may be lost, opportunities seized or cast away, offices and functions used for a time and then laid aside when their work is accomplished; but in all and through all changes, God's unchanging purpose runs onward to its certain close.

(9) After this I beheld . . . —We have just had the picture of the sealing of a multitude which could be numbered; now we have the picture of a countless throng. Who are these? Are they the same as the one hundred forty-four thousand, or are they others? This vision gives the climax of the previous one. The sealing represented the Passover of the Church; this vision represents its Feast of Tabernacles. The sealing assured us that God's hidden ones would be safe in trouble; this tells us that they have come safely out of great tribulation (verse 14). This latter vision is of the expanding prospects of the Church and her final repose. White robes and palm branches are the emblems of victory.

(11) The sevenfold form of the doxology, which implies a divine completeness, is appropriate to this vision. The vision shows us the close of the Church's agony, and is in itself a slight indication that the view which would limit the seals to some short period of church history is incorrect, as it is assuredly inadequate.

(14) The elder anticipated the seer's thoughts. The saints of God are continually passing into the unseen world and taking their place among the spirits of just men made perfect. They come out of **the** great tribulation. Are we to limit the expression to the special and peculiar afflictions of the last great trial? (There is no doubt about the emphasis which the Greek definite article gives.) While there may yet be in store for the Church of Christ trials so great that they may be called, in comparison with those which went before, **the** great tribulation, it yet seems out of harmony with the spirit of the Apocalypse and the complexion of this vision to limit the phrase. The vision here is not of those who will come safely out of some particular trials, but of the great multitude from every age and every race who waged war against sin, and who, in the midst of that protracted conflict, endured the great tribulation which is to continue until Christ's return. The imagery is found in John 13:8-11 and I John 1:7. The emblem of the **blood which washes**

white, or cleanses, is not used with such distinctness elsewhere in the New Testament.

(15) Therefore °are they before the throne . . . —The life is not simply one of joy or safety; it is one also of service. Reference to His temple can only be figurative, for in the heavenly city there is no temple (21:22). It serves to teach us that the servant will find his fitting work of service there as well as here. **Tabernacle**, or "dwell," alludes to the Shechinah, the symbol of the divine Presence, which rested over the mercy seat. Comp. Paul's expression in II Cor. 12:9, where there is a similar reference to the symbol of the divine Presence in the Holy of Holies.

(16, 17) None of the privations which they have endured for Christ's sake shall trouble them; none of the dissatisfactions and weariness of life shall afflict them. The writer told in 5:6 that he had seen a Lamb in the midst of the throne. When he looked toward the throne he saw the Lamb as the central object immediately in front of it. He who would draw near to the throne must pass the Lamb. For a further allusion to the Feast of Tabernacles, comp. Isa. 12:3.

8

(1) And when he had opened the seventh seal . . . —This verse is connected with that which goes before, not that which follows. The second verse of chapter eight introduces a new series of visions; this first verse gives the close of the visions which follow the opening of the seals. Here John evidently associates the visions of the seals with the contents of the roll. The book represents God's purposes and principles of His government in relation to world history; the seals show us some typical scenes in world history. But not all that is in the roll is ever unfolded. Such portions are made manifest as the seer could hear, and as the Church of Christ needed; and thus it may well be that the half hour's silence signifies that all God's purposes and revelations are not exhausted—that there is something behind which it is not well that we should know. But the stillness of this half hour, if it reminds us of what is yet untold, also proclaims to us a time of deep, unbroken tranquility, when the cries and groans of the earth, and even the grateful doxologies of heaven, are hushed into calm. It is the rest of the troubled on the breast of God.

(2) The series of visions which is now introduced extends to the close of the eleventh chapter. There is a marked correspondence of arrangement between these and the visions of the seals. As there, so here, there are introduced two subordinate visions toward the end of the series. The general intention in both cases is to give us an insight into the life of Christ's Church. The main visions give us more external aspects; the interposed visions show the inner and more spiritual aspects. Another structural similarity between the seals and the trumpets is to be found in the separation between the first four and the last three. But the general import of seals and trumpets is very different. We reach in the seventh seal the eternal quiet of God's presence; the assurance which we gather from the trumpets is that the Lord still fights for His Israel. The seals close with peace; the trumpets close appropriately with victory (11:15). The visions are not scenes of events which chronologically succeed one another. The one set shows us the way through trouble to rest; the other shows the way through conflict to triumph. The one set shows us the troubles which befall the Church because of the world; the other shows us the troubles which fall on the world because the Church advances to the conquest of the world.

And I saw the seven angels . . . —Who are these? The usual answer is that they are seven angels distinguished among the myriads around the throne (see Tobit 12:15; Luke 1:19). But seeing that the number seven is to be taken throughout the book as symbolical, it is perhaps better to view the seven angels as representatives of the power of God over the world. They are the seven, the complete circle of God's power in judgment.

Seven trumpets.—For assembling, for journeying, and for war, the sound of the trumpets was heard in the Old Testament. The judgments which follow the blowing of the trumpets in this series of visions here are the trumpet-toned calls of God, summoning mankind to assemble to the true tabernacle, bidding His people go forward, and announcing the overthrow of His adversaries. Every judgment on earth, sea, or river, by war or invasion, is a call which bids men listen to the still small voice, which they have resisted. Every judgment should rouse the true servant to greater vigilance and further advance; it is an alarm sounded on the great battlefield of life. The

land of promise is to be rescued from the tribes and peoples who corrupt it. We may hear, then, in each blast of the symbolical trumpet a promise and installment of the victory for which the groaning and travailing creation yearns, and which will be the banishment of earth's destroyers and the manifestation of the sons of God.

(3) And another angel . . . having a golden censer.—The symbolism of the Apocalypse is so largely built up out of Jewish materials that we need not be surprised to find the altar of incense introduced here. This altar was of gold and was situated in the holy place. Here the priest burned incense, while the people outside were praying (see Luke 1:8-11). The incense was to be mingled with the prayers of the saints. The incense was added to give a fragrance to the prayers and render them acceptable before God. The whole is symbolical of the truth that the prayers of all the saints need to be rendered acceptable by the infusion of some divine element. The best prayers of the best saints are imperfect at best. (See Eph. 5:1, 2.)

(5) The prayers have gone up, and the sprinkling of the ashes earthward is the symbol of the answer descending from heaven. The hot ashes are the tokens of the coming judgments.

(7) The first angel.—See Exod. 9:23-25. This resemblance to the history of Israel in Egypt gives us the hint of the true meaning. It carries us back to the past, and asks us to remember the mighty works of God in old times. But this plague differs from the Egyptian in the introduction of **blood.** This variation carries it out of the possibility of literal interpretations. We think of the strongly figurative language of Joel 2:30, and we call to mind that Peter announced that the fulfillment of this prophecy of Joel began with the Pentecostal effusion of the Holy Spirit. Then the war trumpet of deliverance had been sounded, and the process of the earth's emancipation had begun; then began the series of sorrows and judgments which the obstinate love of men for darkness rather than light would bring upon themselves, and through the operation of these the kingdom of Christ would be established. It matters little in what way this humbling of human pride takes place. The world is full of illustrations. The loftiness of Jerusalem was lowered when the weakness of her self-sufficient religiousness was revealed and her Pharisaic pride was exposed; the loftiness of Rome was humbled when the Gothic invaders, like a storm of hail (so they were described by Claudian), devastated the empire. These are illustrations; but the prophecy is for all time, for the day of the Lord is upon all that are proud. The phrase "the third part" clearly is designed to remind us that in wrath God remembers mercy, and that while He humbles all He does not utterly destroy.

(8, 9) And the second angel.—See Exod. 7:20, 21. The force of the vision is that certain gigantic forms of evil will be overthrown, but the overthrow will be accompanied with the development of new evils; the advance is made, but the step forward unveils the subtle force of evil. Every corrupt institution is destroyed with the risk of the evil elements diffusing themselves elsewhere, just as the political victory of Christianity was followed by the infusion of certain pagan elements into the Church. The vanquished always manage to impose some laws on the victor. Even the advance of the Church is accompanied by some such experience.

(10) And the third angel... —The flaming star seems to symbolize the fall of a potentate; the trumpet-blast proclaims that the mighty who have been, as luminaries, admired, and perhaps worshiped, will fall (comp. Obad. 4). The advancing progress of Christianity is to be marked by many such falls.

(11) And the name of the star... —The bitter, nauseous plant known as wormwood (**apsinthos**) is used to represent troubles and calamities (comp. Deut. 29:18; Jer. 9:15). Some have thought that this falling star signified some false teacher, whose evil influence poisoned the pure currents of the gospel and perverted the minds of men of original genius, who are represented here as fountains. The thought may be included in the general meaning of the vision; but the main point seems to be to give us hints of those stages which will mark the advance of Christianity. The fall of the great men, the rulers and leaders, will take place, and their fall will bring misery to mankind. Doubtless the appearance of false teachers in the Church is one of the evidences and an unavoidable accompaniment of a progressing faith (Matt. 13:26).

(12) And the fourth angel... —See Exod. 10:21-23. Times of darkness and sorrow must come. It is through seasons such as these, when the lights of human wisdom and of spiritual guidance seem alike obscured, that the Church must go forward.

(13) And I beheld... —The best MS authority is against the reading "angel" and in favor of **eagle.** It was an appropriate emblem: high-soaring as the spirit of the seer, the eagle-glance scanned the borders of the earth, and caught sight of the coming troubles and gave warning. Swift and strong as the judgments of God, its very form gave emphasis to the warnings of its voice.

9

(1) And the fifth angel... —Some great power or ruler is represented by this fallen star. He is said to have fallen from heaven, and he is represented as having been given the key of the abyss (see Luke 8:31). This leads us to expect the working of some evil spirit and diabolical agency (see verse 11; 12:8-12), for the abyss is the lowest spring of evil, from where the worst dangers arise. The verse before us suggests the picture of a vast depth approached by a pit or shaft, the top, or mouth, of which is covered.

(2) And he opened... —These visions, it must be remembered, are descriptive of that great war which the Church is waging with the world—which good is waging with evil—but the end of which, we are assured, is the victory of good. The kingdoms of this world become the Kingdoms of the Lord and of His Christ (11:15); but during the progress of the war the issue will often appear doubtful. The faith of Christ has come to give light to the world, but in her progress many lights fall—the false lights of world-power, world-wisdom, false religionism, and heresies. The enemy, too, is at work, and this obscuration is surely the diffusion on earth of evil thoughts and ideas, the spirit of falsehood and hate, hostility to truth, and enmity against God and man.

(3) And there came... —(See Exod. 10:12-15.) The outcome of the gloom is the power of devastation and pain. The scorpion-like power seems to depict a malicious energy, as the locusts depict a devastating multitude.

(4) And it was commanded... —The locusts are clearly not literal locusts. Whatever the plague be, it is one which cannot injure God's children. (See Luke 10:19.) It is interesting and suggestive to notice that this promise of our Lord was given immediately after the saying, "I beheld Satan as lightning fall from heaven," as the safety of the sealed ones is mentioned here after the vision of the star fallen from heaven. The sense in which we understand the danger from which Christ promised His disciples protection may afford us a guiding meaning here. No real injury can happen to Christ's disciples; pain and death might be encountered, but all things work together for their higher good (see 7:1-3).

(5) And to them . . . —"As the natural locusts commit their ravages only for five months, so the ravages of these symbolical ones will be only for a short period" (Stuart). Their power is to inflict torment, not death, upon those who do not have the seal of God in their foreheads. The wound of a scorpion occasions intense suffering; we have in it the symbol of the malicious cruelty of the merciless. Men will seek for death in vain.

(7-10) The resemblance is more distinct when the horses are made ready for battle, the hard shell or scales of the locust having the appearance of armor. It seems doubtful that in this or any of the other descriptions here there is any reference to the anatomical features of the locust. (See Jer. 51:27; Joel 2.) Like the description of the divine Presence in chap. 4, most of the visions of the book are incapable of pictorial realization without incongruities which would be grotesque and profane; nor need we be surprised, since the principles and truths are the main points with the writer. The exigencies of the symbolism are quite beyond the features of the ordinary locust: the sacred writer shows us a plague in which devastation, malice, king-like authority, intelligence, seductiveness, fierceness, and strength meet together under one directing spirit to torment men. The locust-like army has characteristics partly human, partly diabolical, partly civilized, partly barbarous. There is good ground for taking the vision to prefigure the hosts of a fierce invading army. And these were themselves types of still future scourges; so may we see here a vision which neither the history of Zealots, Gothic hordes, nor Saracens has exhausted, but one which draws our thoughts mainly to its spiritual and moral bearing. In the history of advancing truth there will come times when confused ideas will darken simple truth and right, and out of the darkness will emerge strange and mongrel teachings, with a certain enforced unity, but without moral harmony, which enslave and torment mankind.

(11) And they had a king . . . —The great movement is no mere undesigned or instinctive one, but the offspring of a hidden, spiritual force. The great battle is not on the surface only; the invasions, revolutions, and tyrannies which trouble mankind involve spiritual principles and are but tokens of the great conflict between the spirit of destruction and the spirit of salvation. The king of these locust hordes is named in Hebrew Abaddon, or Perdition, a name sometimes given to the place or abode of destruction (Job 26:6). In Greek his name is Apollyon, or Destroyer; the spirit of the destroyer is the spirit that inspires these hosts. It is not necessary for us to seek some great historical personage for the fulfillment of this portion of the prophecy, any more than we ought to accept any great historical event as an exhaustive fulfillment of the vision. But the vision should teach us to remember always the earnest way in which the sacred writers describe the subtle, venomous power of all sin and the merciless destructiveness of its work.

(13) The plague under this second woe trumpet resembles the last, though it is one of much more aggravated nature. Again we have vast hosts with powers at command, but the destructive elements are increased, the multitudes are more numerous, the horses' heads grow lion-like. They can deal forth not torment only, but death itself to a vast proportion of the human race. To aid in this new desolation new forces are released. Even more directly than before, we are reminded that the moral and spiritual aspect of these visions should claim our thought. The aim of the plague is to exhibit the death-working power of false thoughts, false customs, false beliefs, and to arouse men to forsake the false worships, worldliness, and self-indulgence into which they had fallen (verses 20, 21). Nor must another feature be overlooked: the historical basis of the Apocalypse is the past history of the chosen people; God's dealings with men always follow the same lines. The Apocalypse shows us the same principles working in higher levels and in wider arena. The Israel of God, the Church of Christ, with its grand opportunities, takes the place of the national Israel. Its advance is against the world, and the trumpets of war are sounded.

(14) The sixth angel . . . —The voice is represented as rising from the surface of the altar, at the corners of which were the four projections known as horns. The command is to loose the four angels bound at the Euphrates. Their number represents powers influencing all quarters. What is meant by

the Euphrates? The two cities Babylon and Jerusalem are the types of two radically different sets of ideas, two totally antagonistic views of life; and the meaning and mystical import of the river Euphrates must be determined by its relation to these two cities. It is out of all Scriptural analogy to interpret Jerusalem and Babylon allegorically, and then to claim the privilege of understanding Euphrates literally. Nor are those necessarily wrong who consistently hold all three to be literal. There are tokens that a revival of the East may change the whole political center of gravity of the world; but no such literal fulfillment would annul the more important mystical aspect of the Apocalypse. The conflict between a literal Babylon and a literal Jerusalem either in the past or the future can never vie in interest with prolonged and widespread conflict between the spirit of Christ and the spirit of Belial, which is waged along the whole line of history over the arena of the whole world, and plants its battleground in every human heart.

Here and in 16:12 the river Euphrates appears, each time in connection with some warlike demonstration or invasion. The basis of interpretation, as with Jerusalem and Babylon, must be sought in the history of Judah and Israel. The loosing of the four angels (or, **powers**) bound at the Euphrates can only signify changes analogous to disturbances on the great frontier line, as the drying up of the Euphrates signifies the annihilation of the protecting boundary. Such a frontier line between the spiritual city and the world city does in practice exist. There is a vast stretch of intervening territory which neither the Church nor the world really possesses, but over which each desires to possess power. There is a great neutral zone of public opinion, civilized habits, and general morality, which is hardly Christian, hardly anti-Christian. It is out of this that the worst aspects of trouble and danger arise. The loosing of these four angels, then, seems to indicate that the issues at stake have become more distinct; the conflict which has gone on under veiled forms begins to assume wider proportions and to be fought on clear issues.

(15) The temporal expression is not to be taken to imply that such was the duration of the plague, but rather that the loosing of the angels would take place at a definite period, the year, month, day and hour of which were known. It reminds us that there is a period—unknown but certain—at

which the latent powers of retribution wake and begin to avenge themselves, at which the restraints which have withheld the long-deserved scourges are removed. Happy only are they who are ready for the hour of the Lord's return.

(16) The number of this vast army of horsemen was twice ten thousand times ten thousand—i.e., two hundred millions. This utterly bewildering number simply stands for an immense host, and may serve to point out the prolific powers of retribution.

(17) See note on verse 13.

(18) We have here forces which are mighty, malicious, and relentless, and which are bidden forth against mankind for their sins of worldliness. The main teaching is the never-failing truth that this spirit provokes its own punishment, wherever it may exist, and its retribution is in a form which serves to reveal what latent power of destruction lurks behind every sin, and what hidden spiritual foes there are to intensify human passions and to increase human misery.

(20, 21) And the rest . . . —Whatever the nature of the plague might be, they were afflictions designed to bring about repentance, and to arouse men from the lethargy into which long indulged sin had plunged them. But these men did not repent out of their sin. Their sins are enumerated, and the enumeration again takes us back to the history of Israel as to the historical basis which the sacred seer enlarged and vivified, for the sins are just those against which Israel was warned and into which Israel fell (Deut. 4:28; Ps. 106:34-40; Acts 7:41). If we bear in mind that the series of visions describes features which will accompany the advance of Christianity in the world, we shall remember that it is against worldliness, wherever found and of whatever kind, that the true genius of Christianity makes war. Heavy woes must inevitably await the society, Christian or otherwise, which tolerates such works; but the worst omen of the coming doom is seen when society has lost the power to repent because it has lost the power to hate evil. Such an incapacity is invariably significant of advanced moral decay.

10

As between the opening of the sixth and seventh seals there was interposed a twofold vision—the sealing of the one hundred forty-four thousand and the glimpse of the great multitude (chap. 7)—so is a twofold vision interposed here between the sounding of the sixth and seventh (11:14) trumpets. The similarity of situation of these interposed visions suggests that there must be some corresponding value in their interpretation. This appears to be found in the answer to the question, What becomes of the Church, the bride of Christ, during these trials? We are answered by the interposed visions of the seventh chapter that they are sealed, and will be safe. Similarly, the scenes disclosed by the trumpets are spread before us, and we see the features which mark the advance of Christianity in the world—the pain, the confusion, the devastations and slaughters, the bringing to light of hidden evils, which are the necessary accompaniments of this prolonged war. The work of the Church is not to be measured by results now. It does achieve results, but her best work is the work of which she will know afterward; and there is a Church within the Church which is carrying on this work.

(1, 2) The angel here, if he does not represent Christ Himself, descends with the evidences of Christ's power. He comes to remind the secret ones of God that Christ is with them always, and that He will not hide His commandments from those who are living as strangers and pilgrims upon earth. The value of this vision is best seen by calling to mind the vision of the fifth trumpet. As an answer to it comes this angel, bearing the witnesses of Christ's power, and clothed with the token of the divine Presence. (Some call this the Angel of Time, because of his utterance in verse 6.) The open book that he carries contains none of those secret things which were the contents of the former book (5:1-5). The closed, sealed book pointed to the hidden springs of future history; this points to what is open to all. That book was comparatively large and filled with writings, as the visions of oncoming history were great; this book is small, and contains what all may master. The vision is a representation that he who comes armed with the witnesses of Christ's presence comes also with that ever open proclamation of God's love and righteousness. The little open book is that Gospel which is the sword of the Spirit, the weapon of the Church. Thus three books are associated in the Apocalypse: the first is the book of the course of this world (5:1); the last is the Book of Life (20:15; 21:27). Between these two comes another book, which is the

link between the other two, the ever open book of God's righteousness and power. The attitude of the angel with the Word, with one fiery foot planted on the sea and the other on the land, is that of a conqueror taking possession of the whole world.

(4) The seven thunders.—They are called the seven thunders to bring them before us as another order of sevens, and into harmony with the seven seals, the seven trumpets, and the seven vials. These thunders may have been more terrible judgments still, the sealing of them signifying the shortening of the days of judgment (Matt. 24:22).

(5-7) The oath in the passage under consideration is to the effect, not that time should cease and eternity begin, but that there shall be no longer any delay. The suffering saints had cried, "How long?" (6:9-11), and they had been bidden to wait a little time. Now the close of all such waiting time is announced: when the seventh trumpet shall have blown the mystery of God will be finished. "The mystery of God" means the whole of His plan and of His counsel concerning this earth in its present state of discipline and imperfection, and all that He means to do upon it and toward it.

(8, 9) The image of eating the roll is derived from the Old Testament (Ezek. 3:1-3; Jer. 15:16). The eating of the roll, or the words of the roll, is the complete mastering of the contents of the book—the digesting, as we say, its meaning, until the principles and truths are thoroughly familiar and loved. But the after effect of the sweet-tasting roll is bitterness (verse 10). We know how much the evangelist's fidelity to the words he loved so well must have cost him; but there come moments when men are tempted almost to turn back, and to think that they have undertaken a hopeless task, when they find how slow is their progress and what new and unexpected difficulties arise.

(11) He is told that the bitterness will arise in connection with his prophecies regarding peoples and kings. The end, indeed, will come; the Church will be victorious; the kingdoms of this world will become the kingdoms of Christ: but it will be through persecutions, apostasies, judgments. This is the sad vision he must describe.

11

The measuring of the Temple signifies its protection from profanation. The outer court given to the Gentiles indicates that practical heathenism and corruption have invaded the Church. Against corruptions and profanities, witnesses, who draw their strength from divine help, are raised up to protest. The vision therefore declares that, whatever corruptions invade the Church, the kernel of the Church will never be destroyed, but out of it will arise those who will be true to the Master's commission, and whose words will never be void of power. As Jerusalem and Babylon are symbolical names, so the Temple and the court of the Temple are to be understood as symbols.

(1) And there was... —Probably, the vision of Zechariah was in the seer's mind (Zech. 2:1, 2), for the vision there of the man with the measuring rod to measure Jerusalem is followed (Zech. 4:1-6) by the vision of the two olive trees, which are distinctly identified with the two witnesses in the present chapter (see verses 3, 4). The measuring, like the sealing of chap. 7, is a sign of preservation during impending dangers. The Temple proper, the **naos**, the house of God, is measured, together with the altar. The gist of the measurement is the preservation of the true, invisible Church, the Church within the Church; and everything necessary to the worship—Temple, altar, worshipers—all are reserved.

(2) But the court ... —The outer court—meaning, perhaps, all that lies outside the Temple itself—is to be omitted. He is not only not to measure it, but he is to pass it over, as though considered profane. The reason for this is that it was given to the Gentiles. Our Lord had said that Jerusalem should be trodden down of the Gentiles (Luke 21:24). The sacred seer catches the thought and the deeper significance. There is a treading down worse than that of the conqueror: it is the treading under of sacred things when the world-power in men tramples, like the swine, the pearls of grace under their feet and turns fiercely upon those who gave them. Such an experience must the Church of Christ undergo. But there is a limit to this desecration: it is to last forty-two months. The same length of time is expressed in different forms in verse 3, 12:6, 14; 13:5, though it is not, of course, necessarily the same period. (Comp. Dan. 7:25, 12:7, 11.) This incorporation of the expressions used by Daniel is one of those hints which remind us that the principles which receive illustration in one set of historical events are likely to receive similar illustra-

tions in after times. Thus the words of Daniel were not exhausted in the age of Antiochus, nor the visions of the Apocalypse in the overthrow of any one nation or the corruptions of any one church. The period of forty-two months, the equivalent of three and a half years (the half of seven, the complete and divine number), is the symbol of a period limited in length and under the control of Him who holds the seven stars and lives through the ages. It is the pilgrimage period of the Church, the period of the world's power, during which it seems to triumph.

(3-14) In the great progress toward victory the Church itself will suffer through corruptions and worldliness, but the true Temple—the kernel, so to speak, of the Church—will be unharmed and kept safe in her Master's hands. But the position of this hidden Church will not be one of idle security. To exhibit the nature of their work and its results is the apparent aim of the vision. The witnesses can scarcely be literal individual men. The vision in Zech. 4 is designed to encourage the weak and restored exiles in their work of rebuilding the Temple; they are shown that, weak as they are, there is a hidden strength which can make them triumph over all their difficulties. In both visions our minds are turned to the hidden sources of divine strength. This is the grace which made Zerubbabel and Joshua strong to achieve their work; this is the grace which can make the two witnesses strong to do their part in the building of that more glorious spiritual temple which is built on the foundation of apostles and prophets, Jesus Christ Himself being the chief cornerstone. The witnesses, then, stand as the typical representatives of those who, in the strength of God, have through the long ages borne witness for Christ against all wrong and falsehood.

(3) My two witnesses.—Two witnesses were required for competent evidence (Deut. 17:6; 19:15). The word **prophesy** must be allowed a much wider meaning than merely to predict future events. Their witnessing extends over forty-two months, a symbolical period corresponding to that during which other witnesses had worked for God. They bear testimony during the period that the world-power seems dominant. They are clad in the emblem of mourning (II Kings 6:30; Jonah 3:5).

(4) This verse refers us to the vision of Zechariah (chap. 4) for the basis of the present vision. The explanation is supposed to refer to Zerubbabel and Joshua, or, as others think, to Zechariah and Haggai. At that time these men were the witnesses for God in their land and among their people. But the vision is general and age-long; it shows us that such witnesses are to be found in more than one era, for it is not Zerubbabel and Joshua who can exhaust the fulness of a vision which is the representation of the eternal truth that the oil of gladness and strength from God will rest on those who rely, not on might or power, but on God's Spirit. Just as in the early chapters of this book we had seven golden candlesticks, which, though one in Christ, yet are spoken of as separate, so here the double aspect, the diverse though united efforts of the two witnesses, are brought into prominence.

(5, 6) Again the Old Testament basis becomes evident; the histories of Elijah and Moses supply the illustration. As from the mouths of the great Sixth Trumpet host there went forth fire and smoke and brimstone to kill the third part of mankind, so out of the mouths of these witnesses there goes forth a purer but mightier flame. The word which is like a sword to lay bare man to himself may become a consuming fire to those who resist or oppose it.

(7) The beast.—The beast will have his hour of triumph; he rises out of the abyss, as the locust horde did (9:1-3). There is, then, a beast-spirit which is in utter hostility to the Christ-spirit (chap. 13); here he is seen to be a spirit of irreconcilable antagonism to Christ. The image here is not new; Daniel made use of it (Dan. 7), though in a much more limited sense. This beast-power vanquishes the witnesses. If the witnesses are those who have taught the principles of a spiritual and social religion, the death of the witnesses following their overthrow signifies the triumph of opposing principles, the silencing of those who have withstood the growing current of evil.

(8-10) Their corpses remain unburied, while congratulations and rejoicings go on; it is the millennium of evil. They are said to lie in "the street of the great city." The city is described also as Sodom, Egypt, and Jerusalem. It is Sodom, for it is the place where, through pleasure and luxuriousness, the worst forms of immorality take root; it is Egypt, for it is the house of bondage, where the wages of sin become tyrannous; it is Jerusalem, for it is the apostate place where the presence of Christ is hated. The

same spirit which slew their Lord is alive to persecute His servants.

(11, 12) There is a resurrection power in even rejected truth. The cause that seemed dead is found to be possessed of a renewed power and life. The resurrection of the witnesses is followed by their ascension. It is the token that in this too they shall have a portion with their Lord; rejected and slain, there is welcome and honor for them. In verse 13 the visible Church of Christ is stirred; there is a reaction from the spirit of worldliness.

(14) The second woe ... —The eagle flying in mid-heaven had announced the three woe trumpets. A voice now reminds us that two of these had passed, just as at the close of the fifth trumpet a voice proclaimed that the first woe was past. The angel which descended from heaven declared that the end should not be delayed beyond the sounding of the seventh trumpet; the last woe trumpet, therefore, is the trumpet which will usher in the closing woe and the finishing of the mystery of God. Whatever view we adopt concerning the interpretation of the Apocalypse must be governed by the plainly declared fact that the seventh trumpet brings us to the very end.

(15) And the seventh angel ... —It is the kingdom—not "the kingdoms"—of the world which has become Christ's possession. (Satan was willing to surrender the **kingdoms** of the world to our Lord on condition of an homage which would have left him still in possession of the **kingdom** of the world.) The close of the contest is the overthrow of the kingdom of evil and the establishment of the kingdom of good.

(16-18) The four-and-twenty elders represent the Church of God in all ages; they sit with Christ in heavenly places, even while they are toiling and sorrowing on earth. We can catch the echo of the Second Psalm throughout this chorus of grateful praise. The prophets, the saints, and those who fear God's name, the small and the great—every class and rank of the true servants of the King—are included here.

But where, we may be disposed to ask, is the "woe" in all this? We are led to expect that the seventh trumpet as a woe trumpet will bring in some period of pain and trouble, as the others have done; but all we hear is the chorus of glad voices uttering praise. The answer is that we must not overlook all that this song of rejoicing implies. The chorus we hear is the thanksgiving to God that the hour has come for the overthrow of the kingdom of evil, the manifestation of the sons of God, and the acknowledgment throughout the world of the sovereignty of the Lord and of His Christ. The overthrow of that evil kingdom, which is now to take place, brings with it woe to those who have supported it.

(19) And the temple of God ... —At the beginning of the chapter the temple building proper (the **naos**) was measured off. Now it is opened to its inmost recesses, and there the Ark of the covenant of God is seen. The meaning of this, when read by the light of the measuring of the Temple, seems to be that now the secret abode of the safeguarded children of God was revealed. Now that the end has come there is no need that these should be hidden any more.

12

We now enter upon the third group of visions (or, the fourth section of the book, if we include the epistles to the seven churches), which occupy chapters 12-14. The close of each series of visions is in harmony with their general intention, and, as such, affords a key to their meaning. The seals end in peace; the trumpets end in victory; the present visions end in harvest. This set of visions deals with the spiritual conditions of the great war between evil and good— between an evil spirit and the Spirit of God. The issue is not between Christianity and unChristianity, but between Christianity and antiChristianity. We see no longer the battle under human forms, as the struggle for the possession of the Temple; but we see clearly and unmistakably the real spiritual work which the Church is designed to accomplish in the world.

(1) A woman.—This is the picture of the bride, the Church. (Comp. Cant. 6:10.) The beams of the divine glory clothe her; she rises superior to all change, and lays all lesser lights of knowledge under tribute. A crown of twelve stars represents the illustrious members of the Church, rejoicing in the day of Christ.

(2) It is the law of the Church's life that she must bring forth Christ to the world; she cannot work deliverance without knowing suffering. This, then, is the picture, the Church fulfilling her destiny even in pain.

(3) A great red dragon.—But there was to be opposition; the enemy is on the watch to destroy the likeness of Christ wherever it was seen. The dragon stands for some dread and hostile power. That fabulous monster of whom ancient poets told is intended here to describe him who, in verse 9, is also said to be that old serpent, called the Devil and Satan. Red is the color of flame and blood, and the symbol of destruction and slaughter. The dragon is the emblem of the evil spirit, the devil, the perpetual antagonist of good, the persecutor of the Church in all ages (comp. Ps. 74:13). The dragon is sometimes employed to represent the Egyptian power, the ancient foe of Israel (Isa. 51:9; Ezek. 29:3). The dragon is one, yet diverse: one, as an evil spirit; diverse, in the varieties of his power. The woman is but one, while her foe is multiform. She has one work to do, and can but fulfill it in her Master's way; evil is bound by no law, regards no scruple, and exerts its power by every means. The number seven is the representation of the great and world-wide power which he exercises as the prince of this world, whose kingdom is in much a parody of the true kingdom. The whole description should be compared with the account given of the beast in 17:3, 7, 10, 12. The picture represents, as concentrated into a single hostile form, all the varying forces and successive empires which have opposed or oppressed the people of God and sought to destroy their efforts for good. All evil has its root in a spirit at enmity with God; hence the dragon appears armed with all the insignia of those sovereignties and powers which have been animated by this spirit.

(4) And his tail ... —The stars are the light-bearers, the illustrious of earth, who were given by God high place that they might be burning and shining lights for Him. A large proportion of these are drawn away in the train of evil. They are dragged down from the height of the grandest possibilities of good to the low level of a life enslaved to evil.

And the dragon.—The spirit of evil is represented as ever on the watch to destroy the first tokens of better things. The mission of the Church is to bring forth in her members the life of Christ before men; the aim of the wicked spirit is to destroy that life. The same hostility which was shown to the infant Christ is active against His children.

(5) And she brought forth ... —The fact that this child is Christ must not cause us to limit the meaning of the vision to the efforts of the evil one to destroy the infant Jesus, for it is also the Christ in the Church which the wicked one hates. Though the basis of

1229

the vision is in the historical fact, the power of the vision reaches over a wider area and forcibly reminds us that as there are irreconcilable principles at work in the world, so all these, when traced to their original forms, are the Spirit of Christ and the spirit of the devil.

And her child was caught up unto God, and to his throne.—After death and resurrection, Christ ascended up where He was before. The vision is designed to assure us that, precisely because of this, so all life in Christ is beyond the power of the evil one, and that the forces hostile to good are powerless against that life which is hid with Christ in God.

(6) And the woman fled . . . —See verse 13. The woman, the representative of the Church, sojourns in the wilderness twelve hundred sixty days, a period corresponding in length to the forty-two months during which the witnesses prophesied. It is the period of the Church's witness against predominant evil.

(7) And there was war in heaven . . . —The narrative of the woman's flight into the wilderness is suspended that this passage may be inserted. Could we have a clearer indication of the anxiety of the sacred writer to connect this war in heaven with the birth and rapture of the man child? The powers of the foe are not confined to the material and historical world. The dragon is a tower in the world spiritual; but the man child is to be entirely a conqueror. There is unexplained mystery, perhaps, about this war in heaven, but there need be none about the general occasion to which reference is made. It is the overthrow of the evil one by Christ—the death-blow given by the Lord of Life to him who had the power of death. The name **Michael**—the meaning of which is "who is like unto God"—is a general name applied to any who for the moment represent the cause of God in the great conflict against evil. It may thus belong not to any one angel being, but be a kind of type-name used for the champion and prince of God's people, and so employed in this passage to denote Him who is the Captain of our salvation.

(9) On this verse see Gen. 3:15; Luke 11:21, 22; John 8:44; 16:11; I Pet. 5:8.

(10) And I heard a loud voice . . . —The words of this doxology are like an echo of the close of the Lord's Prayer. The prayer "Thy kingdom come" seems answered. But it is not the full establishment of the king-

dom which is described here; it is rather the manifestation of it.

(13) The wrath of the defeated dragon is manifested in persecution of the woman. This verse explains the reason of the flight into the wilderness mentioned in verse 6.

(14) And to the woman . . . —The way that seems hard is the way that is most blessed. The opposition of the dragon brings her blessings that she never would have received except in persecution; neither the eagle power nor the heavenly sustenance had been hers without the serpent's hate. She is given eagle's wings. God had spoken of the deliverance of Israel under a similar emblem (Exod. 19:4; comp. Deut. 32:10-12). The length of her sojourn is called here a season, seasons, and half a season; it was called twelve hundred sixty days in verse 6. The period is in both cases the same in length, three years and a half— i.e., the season (one year), the seasons (two years), and the half season (half a year). This is the period of the Church's trouble and persecution. It is not to be sought by any effort to find some historical period of persecution corresponding in length to this. The period is symbolical of the broken time (the half of the seven, the perfect number) of the tribulation of God's people. There may be some future period in which the vision may receive even more vivid fulfillment than it has thus far received; but the woman has been nourished in the wilderness in the ages that are gone. Her sustenance there by God is an experience of the past, and will be in the future.

(15) And the serpent . . . —The first attack on the woman is pictured as persecution by the dragon; from this she escapes by flight. But the subtlety of the enemy finds another device; the foe (now described as a serpent) pours forth water as a river to sweep away the woman. The emblem is not uncommon in the Bible, as the floods, the rivers, the waves of the sea, are employed to express popular movements. The woman that cannot be destroyed by positive persecution may be swept away by a hostile public opinion. But some earthly power is raised up to protect the Church against persecution (verse 16). Yet the foe will not give up his attacks (verse 17).

13

(1) The way in which the dragon carries out his plan of war is described. Like Milton's "superior fiend," he stands upon the shore and summons his legions (**Par. Lost,** Book I) to another form of war. Two monsters (verses 1 and 11), one distinguished by more brutal, the other by more subtle, power rise at his bidding. (On the whole of this section the parallel vision in Dan. 7 ought to be read.)

A beast.—The sea represents the great, restless mass of human kind. The individuals, like larger and smaller waves, make up this great ocean-like mass of men, swayed by impulse or passion. Out of the sea rises a wild beast. The word, not the same as that used in 4:7, implies the predominance of the beast nature. The wild beast is always the figure of the kingdoms of this world— i.e., the kingdoms which are founded on passion or selfishness. They are seven in number, as the beast had seven heads. We read afterward of seven mountains. These world-powers are spoken of as mountains for their strength and stability; as heads of the wild beast because, though separate, they are inspired by the dragon spirit, the spirit of utter enmity to the rule of the Righteous King. In 17:10 we read that five are fallen, one was in possession of power, and the seventh had not yet arisen. The key is thus placed in our hands. The sixth head is imperial Rome, the successor of those great world-powers which were founded in unrighteousness. The heads carry the names of blasphemy. The spirit of arrogant self-sufficiency characterized all the world-powers.

Ten horns are explained (17:12) as "the kings which have received no kingdom as yet," but which, when they rise, will draw their strength from the dragon and be members of the wild beast. The wild beast combined (verse 2) the features of three wild animals because it is a representative of all forms of world-power, which have been swift to shed blood. (Comp. Dante, **Inferno,** 1:10-74.)

(3) This is the historical point from which the vision starts. The death-blow has just been dealt: the seed of the woman has bruised the serpent's head. The blow which casts down the dragon inflicts a deadly wound upon the wild beast, which is his agent. When Christ overthrew the wicked one He gave the deathblow to all systems founded on passion, self-sufficiency, or inhumanity. But the death-blow is apparently healed. What is this but telling the Church of Christ that the fruits of Christ's victory will not be seen without delay?

(5) And there was given . . . —There is consolation in these words. He has no power beyond what is given; behind his reckless and apparently irresistible power there stands the veiled but real power of God. **Forty-two months** again represent the limited time of the world-power.

(8) This is the climax of his triumph. He is worshiped; but the saints, though conquered, conquer. There is some doubt about the connection of the words "from the foundation of the world." Some connect them with the word "written." But it is connected in other parts of the Bible with certain aspects of the work of Christ (I Pet. 1:19, 20; John 17:24), and it seems more natural to take the words in their simple order. Whatever view we take, the verse proclaims that the security of God's saints is based on the eternal love of God.

(11) Another beast.—The second beast is less monstrous in appearance. He somewhat resembles a lamb; he rises from the earth and not from the sea; his power lies in deception as well as violence; he seems to possess more supernatural power. Yet the whole of his work is directed to magnifying the first beast. Do not these features lead to the conclusion that the principles which the second wild beast supports are the same as those on which the former wild beast acted, but that he supports them with more subtlety, intelligence, and culture? He is called in later chapters (16:13; 19:20; 20:10) the False Prophet. The second wild beast is that change which is a change of mode, but not of spirit—a change of manners, but not of heart. There is more refinement, but it is still the world-power which is worshiped. Some see in this second wild beast the pagan priesthood aiding the imperial power, the embodiment of the first wild beast; others see in it the papal sacerdotal power, the heir of pagan rites. Though there is truth in these views, they are too narrow. All who use their knowledge, their culture, and their wisdom to teach men that there is nothing worthy of worship except what they can see, touch, and taste are acting the part of the second wild beast.

(16, 17) We read of the sealing of the servants of God in their foreheads (7:3; 22:4); the power of evil also has its mark or stamp. As slaves received a brand or mark in their flesh, betokening to whom they belonged, so in the spiritual conflict there is on the side of good and of evil a brand or mark. The subtle false prophet, the abettor of world-power, seeks to impress a mark on all, on the penalty of complete social exclusion. It is utterly unnecessary to take this brand of evil literally, any more than we took the seal of Christ literally. That seal we understood as spiritual; this evil brand we must interpret in like manner. It surely means the acquiescence in character (the forehead) and action (the right hand) to the principles of this tyrannical world-power.

(18) The number of a man.—The number is the combination of three sixes. With all its vaunted strength, the beast is but weak; with all its vaunted perfection, it is imperfect. It will never attain even the appearance of that perfect heavenly number symbolized by seven. This "six hundred and sixty-six," then, is a symbolical number, expressing all that it is possible for human wisdom and human power, when directed by an evil spirit, to achieve, and indicating a "golden age" when men will begin to say that faith in God is an impertinence, and the hope of a future life a libel upon the happiness of the present. Then will the world-power have reached the zenith of his influence.

Two other interpretations are based upon the theory that the letters of the name, when added together, according to their numerical value, will make up six hundred sixty-six. The first of these finds the word in Nero Caesar. The second, and more ancient, finds it in Lateinos. It will be seen that both these solutions make the number point to the great Roman power; and this was the great embodiment of the terrible spirit of self-sufficiency, tyranny, and utter godless worldliness with which John was familiar. These interpretations are interpretations in example, and as such probably true; but they are only types of that fuller and deeper view.

14

We have seen the power of evil rise to its blasphemous climax. But what has the Church of Christ been doing? The sealed ones of God have suffered; but have they done more than suffer? Has theirs been only a passive endurance of evils? Have they wielded no weapons against these foes, and used no counter-influence for good? In this chapter the seer takes us from our survey of the powers of evil and shows us the powers of good. We have seen the strength of the wild beast; we may now see the followers of the Lamb.

1232

(1) The Saviour, the Lamb, in whose blood the saints have found their victory, is seen standing on the citadel of the heavenly city. Babylon is to be introduced (verse 8). In contrast, Zion, the type of the spiritual city whose citizens are true to the King, is introduced. The sealed ones, 144,000 in number, represent the full growth of the choice ones of God, the true Israel of God. (See note on 7:4.) Amid the world-noises of Babylon they can neither hear nor sing aright the Lord's song (Ps. 137:4); but the redeemed of the Lord (verse 3) can come with singing unto Zion (Isa. 51:11).

(4, 5) The characteristics of the servants of the Lamb are given here: purity, obedience, separation, truthfulness.

(7) These words declare what ought to be the effect of the Gospel. Those to whom it is preached are sitting inactive on the earth. They must be aroused to fear God and give Him glory. They must realize that there is an hour of judgment at hand, which will discriminate between the worshipers of the world and of God.

(8) Babylon.—The second angel follows on the first; the doom of the world-city, the metropolis of the empire of the world-power, follows the proclamation of the Gospel. The principles of Christ's Gospel must undermine the world-power; the fall of some Babylon principle has almost always succeeded the age of spiritual revival. Babylon belongs not to one age, yet pagan Rome was Babylon to John.

(9) And the third angel ... —The powers which are in conflict are the word of God and the Babylon of the world. The Gospel will triumph; Babylon is doomed. Thus comes the warning that men should not identify themselves with the city of worldliness, falsehood, and sin. The reference to the wild beast, the image, and the mark shows us that Babylon is the city of the world-power. The warning not to receive the mark is a declaration that man, individual man, is responsible.

(11) For ever and ever.—Sin, which is first embraced as a delight, soon becomes an inexorable tyrant. Sin has the power of stamping its indelible features upon the human character, and giving to habit the force of a destiny.

(14) And I looked ... —There can be little doubt that Christ Himself is intended here. The "crown" is the crown of victory; the hour of conquest is at hand. The sickle shows that the harvest has come.

(15) And another angel ... —What harvest is this? It is the gathering of the good seed, the full corn in the ear, into the celestial garner (Mark 4:26-29). The angel who announces that the harvest is ready comes forth from the Temple, whereas the angel who calls for the vintage comes forth from the altar (verse 18). (See John 4:35.)

(18-20) The vintage symbolizes a harvest of judgment; the words respecting Babylon (verse 8) confirm this. The treading of the winepress was a figure representing vengeance; the red juice of the grape strongly suggested the shedding of blood. (Comp. Isa. 63:2-4.) The winepresses stood usually outside the city. It is so represented here, alluding to those who fall under the weight of this judgment because they have refused the defense of the true city and sanctuary. The distance (sixteen hundred stadii), i.e., four multiplied into itself and then multiplied, is symbolical of a judgment complete and full, and reaching to all corners of the earth.

15

(1) And I saw another sign in heaven.— This sign introduces a new set of scenes. The same characters will reappear, but we must start with fresh attention. The statement that these are the **last** plagues seems to show that the set of visions now beginning carry us down to the end of the age; the vials, like the seals and the trumpets, run up to the final consummation. They are plagues, because they are sent forth, not like the trumpets to warn men to repent, but upon those who have obstinately refused to return and who are deliberately hostile.

(2) And I saw as it were a sea of glass mingled with fire.—The wild beast rose out of the sea (13:1); the evil-hearted woman sits upon many waters (17:1). They draw strength from the wild, ungoverned, and shortsighted impulses of human passion. In opposition to this, near the throne of God is the calm and translucent sea of God's counsels of righteousness and love. The seer saw also those that are victorious over the wild beast. They come off conquerors out of the struggle, and they escape from the temptation to worship his image and wear the badge of his service. The life which has been a discord to the world rises into true music before God; those who will make their life a melody must take it first as a conflict.

(3, 4) See Exod. 14:26-31; 15:1-21. Israel

stood on the margin of the Red Sea and saw the tokens of the overthrow of the great world-power of that day; so these saints stand by the border of the fire-blent sea of glass, and sing the song of triumph over the doom of the great world-powers of every age. The cases are parellel; the songs are alike. They sing the song of the Lamb as well as the song of Moses. The Apocalypse is full of Christ. The Lamb is the axis on which the world of its scenery moves. He is the key of earth's history.

The word rendered "holy" in verse 4 is not that which is usually employed when the holiness of God is meant. It is a word which, when applied to men, denotes one who reverences the sacred obligations of natural and moral order, apart from the thought of mere law or custom. The word is applied here, and in 16:5, to God, and denotes the recognition of those sacred obligations which the character of God imposes upon Himself. It is the remembrance that God will, as Judge of all the earth, do right, and will vindicate the expectations of those who stay themselves upon His character, which generates a holy fear of Him.

(6) And the seven angels . . . —Out of the rejected temple the angels of wrath come. It is ever true that out of rejected mercies the heaviest of plagues are forged. The angels are clad in a garb resembling that of Christ (1:13); they come forth to do His bidding.

(7) Seven golden vials.—The vials are the shallow bowls which were used for incense. They now are filled with the wrath of God. These vials are given by one of the living creatures who represent creation; it is thus through creation that the wrath of God can visit the rebellious. That wrath of God is simply the operation of God's righteous law against sin.

(8) And the temple . . . —Comp. Isa. 6, where the prophet beheld the vision of God. The general drift of the present vision is similar. The days of warning are over; the plagues which now fall will fall on those who have trifled with convictions; the sanctuary which was opened as a refuge is now closed; none can enter until the plagues have descended.

16

(2) And the first . . . —The first angel pours his vial forth upon the earth, that is, the dry land. The plague falls on those who carry the mark of the beast, and who worship it. (Comp. Exod. 9:8-12; Deut. 28:27.) Egypt is one type of the world-power; and the plagues are used as types also, and are not to be understood literally. The plague of the "evil sore" denotes some throbbing and hateful sore, perhaps spiritual or mental, which distracts attention and disturbs the personal serenity and self-complacency of the worshipers of the world-power.

(3) And the second angel ... —Comp. Exod. 7:20. The sea, out of which the wild beast rose, from which the world-power drew strength, is turned to blood, the blood as of a dead man, corrupt and loathsome. The sea represented the tumultuous impulses and passions of the masses; there is a certain healthy force in these, but under certain conditions, when devoted to selfishness and earthliness, they become corrupt and deadly.

(4) And the third angel ... —This plague is acknowledged by heavenly voices as a just retribution (verses 5-7). The streams and rivers feed the sea; they are the powers and influences which go to the making up of the great popular sentiment. These are smitten by the same corruption. Men cannot worship worldliness or earthliness without degrading even those who contribute to their instruction. The fresh and bright gifts of God are polluted when the ocean of public thought is unwholesome.

(8, 9) And the fourth ... —This is another example of the way in which the things full of beneficence are turned into powers of sorrow to those who follow evil. The very source of light and knowledge becomes a power to destroy. There is a knowledge which withers while it illumines. The whole series of these judgments illustrate the awful truth that there is a stage in personal, national, and world life in which suffering loses its remedial force, because the character has become set, and even an occasional desire after higher things is no longer felt.

(10) And the fifth ... —The vials of judgment gradually dissolve the integrity and organization of the kingdom of the wild beast. The result of the principles on which it has been based begin to show themselves: moral disease in individuals; a corrupt tone of national morals spreading into the higher orders of society; the fierce pride of vaunted light which scorches. The retribution comes home; the throne of the world-power, the very head and center of its authority, is smitten. (Comp. Exod. 10:21-23.)

(12) And the sixth ... —For the symboli-

cal meaning of the Euphrates, see note on 9:14. In the great age-long struggle between the kingdoms of Christ and the world, the Euphrates represents the separating boundary, as the literal Euphrates formed the barrier between Israel and the hostile northern and eastern kingdoms. It is the great impediment to war. But there may come a time, after false principles have been taught, corrupt manners tolerated, and the light of better things darkened, when public sentiment loses all sense of shame, and the decorums of life, which have acted as a breakwater against the tide of outrageous evil, are swept away. Then is the Euphrates dried, and then may the hostile powers of evil, unrestrained by any considerations, unchecked by the popular conscience, cross boldly over and invade the whole sacred soil of human life. The "kings of the east" represent the forces of rude and open evil which have been long restrained.

(13, 14) The two hostile kingdoms are being brought slowly into open antagonism. The situation becomes so strained that it is useless to keep up the appearance of a respectable neutrality, for forces have been at work which are gradually bringing all powers into the conflict. All this points to the final mobilization of the hosts of evil for an attack upon the kingdom of Christ. Three evil spirits go forth for the purpose of motivating men. There are three radical foes of Christ and His righteousness: the dragon, representing the hate of evil spirits; the wild beast, representing the hostility of world-power; the false prophet, representing the antagonism of world-culture and intellectualism. These three send forth each their emissary, appealing to the pride and passions of men.

(15) Behold, I come as a thief.—It is the oft-repeated Scripture warning (3:3; I Thess. 5:2, 3; II Pet. 3:10; comp. Luke 12:35-40). It reminds us our Lord may come unexpectedly. Blessed are they who are ready, watching. But vigilance is not enough. The earnest watcher desires, like Paul, to be found in Christ, clad in the true righteousness of faith (Phil. 3:9).

(16) Armageddon is the mountain of Megiddo. It is the high table-land surrounded by hills which was the great battlefield of the Holy Land. There the fortunes of dynasties and kingdoms have been decided; the old battleground becomes the symbol of the decisive struggle. It is raised in meaning: it is a type, not a locality. The war of principles, the war of morals, the war of fashion

culminates in an Armageddon. The progress of the spiritual struggle in individual men must lead in the same way to a mountain of decision, where the long-wavering heart must take sides, and the set of the character be determined.

(17) And the seventh . . . —The results of the outpouring of this vial are described in the following verses; but before these are seen, God's own voice (see verse 1) proclaims, as though rejoicing in the near approach of the happy end, "It is done." The close of these scenes of sin and suffering is now at hand, for the last of the last plagues has been sent forth.

(18-20) The earthquake, which is the shaking down of the kingdom of evil, completes the overthrow of which the earlier judgments have been precursors. Now the metropolis of the wild beast's empire is about to fall. The three evil spirits endeavored to unite all powers in one grand assault, but there is no natural cohesion among those whose only bond is hatred of good. The fall of pagan Rome is but one illustration of the overthrow of Babylon.

(21) Such an overthrow awaits every confederacy that sets itself in array against the kingdom of the righteous King. The discomfiture and the plague works no repentance; the men blaspheme God because of the hail. The unrepentant state of those upon whom the vials are poured is to be contrasted with the different result of the earthquake in 11:13, when men gave glory to the God of heaven.

17

Chapters 17 and 18 give the more minute account of great Babylon, the metropolis of the wild beast's empire, the great city hostile to Jerusalem, the city of the saints. She is seen clothed in splendor, intoxicated with her own power and cruelty, hostile to the cause of the righteous King, but doomed to fall amid the wonder of the world and the rejoicing of the saints (18:17-21).

(1) The great whore.—In her greatness and her hostility to Jerusalem, Babylon became a type of later world-powers; and in John's vision, Babylon, in her purple and her pomp, in her luxuriousness and her tyranny, takes her place. It is explained in the vision that Babylon is no longer the literal Babylon, but the power which has taken her place of pride and empire. That power was Rome. Rome was in John's day just what Babylon had been in the days of the prophets. Yet the Babylon of the Apocalypse, while undoubtedly pagan Rome, cannot be limited to it. Insofar as Papal Rome has wielded tyrant power, turned persecutor, withheld the truth, sought aggrandizement, and been a political engine rather than a witness for the righteous King, she has inherited the features of Babylon. (Comp. Dante, **Inferno**, Cant. 19:109-117.)

(3, 4) Now the wild beast carries the woman, for she draws her support from the great world-power. The wild beast teems with tokens of lawlessness and self-sufficiency. The woman's appearance is one of imperial splendor.

(5) And upon her forehead . . . —It was usual with harlots to wear their name on the forehead; but here it is more than a name. Like the name impressed upon the foreheads of the saints, it is the expression of her nature.

(6) And I saw the woman drunken with the blood of the saints.—The cruel spirit of persecution marked old pagan Rome. She was drunk with their blood, as is spiritually true of papal Rome. Just as all the blood from righteous Abel to Zacharias was required of Jerusalem, so also of Babylon, for the spirit is the same spirit of hatred of holiness and love of worldliness. It is the Babylon spirit, wherever dominant, that kills the good.

And when I saw her, I wondered . . . —The wonder probably rose from the strange alliance of the woman with the wild beast. It was not astonishing to see the vision of a wild beast dealing out death and slaughter, but to see a woman allied with the monster and drunken with the blood of the holy, provoked astonishment. The woman, too, was a harlot. Did John read in the form of the vision the hint that in the lapse of years the Church of Christ, like Israel of old, might fall from her high calling and become the ally of the world-power?

(7) The angel identifies the wild beast which carries the woman with the wild beast of chap. 13. It has received its death wound from the dying and risen Lord. But though he is to be reckoned as doomed, yet he will show signs of vitality; he will rise into temporary power.

(9) Seven heads.—The description seems to be drawn from Rome, the seven-hilled city; but at the same time the further explanation (verse 10) widens our thoughts, and shows us that the literalism on which the imagery is based is used to convey a broader symbolical meaning. The woman rides on the seven-headed beast; even so Rome dwells on her seven hills, and so also the world-city, seen in vision, sits among the various empires which have risen, like great mountains, in the history of the world.

(10) Seven kings.—These kings represent world-kingdoms. The wild beast belongs to no one age, but is a power which has risen in every age. The seven heads represent the successive culminations of the world-power. The language used here, and the passages in the earlier prophets, which may be called the parent passages of the present vision, favor this interpretation. (It is said that the "kings fell." The word is the one which has been used for political catastrophe.) Daniel (chap. 7) saw four wild beasts rise from the sea. They represented the then great world-power Babylon, and its three successors, Persia, Greece, and Rome. This is a guide to us here. But two great world-powers had preceded Babylon: Egypt and Assyria. These figure in the ancient prophecies as forces hostile to the righteous King. John, whose visions took the range of the world's drama, could not see the representative of the ever rising spirit of worldly hostility to God's chosen without seeing Egypt and Assyria included. (The voices of Moses and Isaiah called to him across the centuries that in these the world principle of their day found its clearest and strongest manifestation.) In succession three kingdoms fell, only to be succeeded by another— Rome. Five fell; the one is. But what is the seventh, the other who is not yet come? We must recall the appearance of the wild beast. The seventh head was ten-horned. It did not have the same unity of appearance as the others. The ten horns are explained as ten kings or minor powers (verse 12). The conclusion, therefore, is that the seventh head must be rather an aggregation of monarchies than a single universal empire. This agrees with Daniel's prophecy that out of the fourth kingdom, which corresponds with the sixth head of the wild beast here, ten kings should arise (Dan. 7:7, 23, 24). The "short time" is probably the same as the "one hour" in verse 12.

(11) And the beast...—No eighth empire shall rise, but the wild beast, now smitten in all the seven heads of his power, will, in the convulsive death-throe, seem an eighth power in which the ebbing life of all the seven finds expression. This fierce and last assertion of the doomed power of evil is dwelt on again in 20:7-10.

(12) And the ten horns...—See note on verse 10. They are kingdoms or nationalities; as they are on the seventh head, the hour of their power is not yet, but comes at the fall of the sixth head. Then they receive power one hour. But though these are sundered powers, they are one in their subjection to the wild beast. The universal empire idea may disappear, but the spirit and principle of mere earthliness will remain. The ten horns are united in one mind. They shall make war with the Lamb; and the Lamb shall conquer them because He is Lord of lords and King of kings. When do these powers make war with the Lamb? They make war when the direction of their policy and morals is in favor of oppression, wrong, worldliness; whenever nations or peoples allow the secular spirit to breathe through all they do, they are against Him. There are hints that some "special outbreak" of hostility may take place on the eve of the full manifestation of the righteous King and His kingdom (19:16-19). It is not necessary to define the number "ten," for in Hebrew, "when a whole was to be divided into parts, ten was the number commonly adopted" (Bähr).

(15) The wild beast and the harlot both draw much of their power from the people. "Men never so much need to be theocratic as when they are most democratic" (De Tocqueville). They need most to recognize God as their King when their newly discovered strength is likely to be made the tool of unscrupulous ambition.

(16) The woman in the days of the Evangelist was Rome (verse 18), but great and resistless as her power seemed, it was doomed. The day would come when other kingdoms would rise who would hate her for her tyranny, envy her splendor, and covet her wealth. Then the great Babylon would fall. But they are only preparing for the crisis when the foes of the righteous King shall fall (19:19). Thus does the wrath of man ever turn to God's praise (verse 17).

18

(2) The description in this verse is drawn largely from Isa. 13:21, 22. It is a picture of desolation and degradation, but it has its moral counterpart.

(4) The coming forth is not to be under-

stood of a bodily exodus from Rome. It is
rather the warning, which is so needful in
every corrupt state of society, to have no
fellowship with the unfruitful works of
darkness. This duty of separation may
sometimes lead to a literal exodus, but the
jeopardy lies in attachment to the world-
spirit (I John 2:15).

(7) The thought of retribution is carried
on from verse 6. The words are echoes of
prophecies against old Babylon (Isa. 47:7-9)
and Tyre (Ezek. 28:2).

(9-19) Kings (verses 9, 10), merchants
(verses 11-17), and shippers (verses 17-19)
join in lamenting the overthrow of the great
city. The picture is designed to show the
corrupt luxury and voluptuousness of society in great Babylon. The various wares are
for her use and consumption. All the avenues from every distant spot of the earth
found their focus in Rome; her existence,
her political supremacy, and her luxuriousness of living created and sustained all the
commercial activity described here.

(20) Rejoice over her . . . —The saints are
summoned to rejoice because the law of
retribution has worked on her. The judgment which Babylon wrought on the holy is
now exacted from her. The covetous and the
worldly mourn; their minds were set upon a
material glory, which has slipped away
from their grasp. The wealth of holiness is
imperishable, and the fall of Babylon is the
removal of one vast hindrance to holiness.

(21-24) The irremediable overthrow of
Babylon is symbolically declared. (See Jer.
35, 51; Matt. 18:6.)

19

(1-7) The word Alleluia occurs in this
passage no less than four times (verses 1, 3,
4, 6). It is used nowhere else in the New
Testament; but it is familiar to us in the
Psalms, as fifteen of them begin or end with
"Praise ye the Lord," or "Hallelujah." The
song here is the echo of the ancient utterance—"Salvation belongeth unto God."
It is the triumphant affirmation of the truth
by which the children of God had sustained
their struggling petitions, as they closed the
prayer which Christ Himself had taught
them, saying, when too often it seemed to
be otherwise, "Thine is the Kingdom, and
the power, and the glory." All nature's tones
seem mingled in this voice of praise.

(8) And to her was granted . . . —The

song closes with the announcement that the
Lamb's wife made herself ready. Now follows the explanation of this readiness. Her
apparel is in contrast to the harlot: "the fine
linen is the righteousness of the saints." It is
pure and stainless white, the token of those
high, moral, spiritual qualities by which she
has been known. The source of these right-
eousnesses is divine.

(9) The marriage supper of the Lamb.—
This is one of the six benedictions of the
Apocalypse (comp. 1:3; 14:13; 20:6; 22:7,
14). It is founded on our Lord's parables
(Matt. 22:1; 25:1). The imagery is varied to
give fullness and force to truths which no
emblems can adequately express. The
Church of Christ will rest, feast, and reign
with her Lord; and in all the peace, gladness, and triumph of that joy-time God's
servants will share.

(10) The immediate checking of the impulse to worship the messenger here and in
22:8, 9 supplies an indirect evidence of the
genuineness of the whole book, and gives it
a moral tone immeasurably superior to the
vision-books of pretended revelations. The
angel is his fellow-servant, as he and the
apostle were engaged in one common work—
"the testimony of Jesus."

(11) And I saw heaven opened . . . —The
early vision of a conquering Christ had
been first a hope and then a despair, as age
after age interposed its obstacles to the
manifestation of the sons of God. But now,
with added splendor, the vision is renewed.
Once more the victorious rider appears. His
name combines two characteristics: fidelity
to promises, and power to satisfy every
legitimate desire which has been awakened
in the hearts of His people. Here is comfort
on the threshold of a vision of deliverance.

(12, 13) See notes on 1:14-16. There is no
doubt who is before us in this vision. He
wears many crowns—diadems—crowns
rather of royalty than of victory. He is truly
King—King of history, King of life, King of
human hearts. The blood-red vesture is a fit
token of the work. (See Isa. 63:2.) He comes
to destroy those that destroy the earth—to
tread the winepress of the wrath of God;
but we cannot forget that He who comes for
this came first to shed His own blood. "The
Word of God" is a name significant of
Christ's mediating work.

(14) And the armies . . . —The saints who
have fought the good fight here, and who
loved not their lives unto the death, will
share the triumph of their king. The hue of

triumph is here, but it is the triumph of righteousness (see verse 8).

(15) In 1:16 it was called the two-edged sword. The omission of the epithet in this passage, which describes the Word of God as the conqueror and the judge, is significant. The sword is now wielded for but one work—the **word** that Christ spoke will judge men at the last day (John 12:48). And we have again the figure of the vintage used. (Comp. 14:20.) It is the harvest of retribution. The wicked are filled with the fruit of their own doings.

(16) And he hath on his vesture . . . —On His robe, where it spreads out from the waist, His title is inscribed. Inscriptions on the outer garments were sometimes used by distinguished personages. The title anticipates the final victory; His power is irresistible, his Kingship universal.

(17, 18) The supper here is in contrast with the marriage supper of the Lamb (verse 9). All classes are mentioned. Those who follow the world-power, and array themselves in hostility to the true King, belong not to one class, but may be found among all. The vision is a great figurative representation of the defeat of the anti-Christian powers and principles in the world.

(20) The false prophet is the second wild beast of chap. 13. He succeeded in deceiving those who received the mark. The wild beast and the false prophet, who are the anti-Christian leaders, are cast into the fiery lake. These leaders are not to be regarded as particular individuals. It has, indeed, often happened, and will doubtless again happen, that an individual personage places himself at the head of a great anti-Christian movement; yet, in the eye of the seer, such would be but subordinate leaders. The world-power, whether coarse, ignorant and brutal, or cultured and intellectual, is seized and consigned to the lake of fire. The imagery here is based upon the Old Testament.

(21) And the remnant were slain . . . — No human being is described here as being cast into the lake of fire; only the two great leaders, the ideal representatives of evil principles, receive that punishment. The sword which goes out of the King's mouth slays the human allies of evil. That word which is mighty and life-giving, as well as death-giving, wins at the last.

20

The millennium vision is, like so many of the apostolic visions, an ideal picture; it exhibits a state of things which is possible to mankind at any time. Like the vision of the first seal, it shows us that the victory of Christ was a real victory, and has put into man's hand the promise of security against the wicked one's devices. The defeat of Satan (inflicted by redemption) is described as "a fall from heaven" (Luke 10:18), as "a casting out" (John 12:31), as a judgment passed (John 16:11). The ideal picture corresponds. But the rejection of Christ's power and victory postpones the realization of this picture. The vision has its approximate fulfillment as the Church of Christ, in the faith of the reality of her Lord's victory, carries on her warfare against the prince of this world and spiritual wickedness in high places. To an Irenaeus, a Polycarp, a Justin Martyr, a Tertullian, the picture of the world during the Christian centuries would have the aspect of a millennium, when contrasted with the age of pagan domination and persecution. But the Church today looks for a further and higher fulfillment in a future age. She can accept the firstfruits of God's promises, but she will not mistake them for the harvest; she can rejoice in the growth of her Lord's kingdom, but she looks for the day when the powers of evil will be more effectually curbed, and the Gospel will have freer course. Then the fullness of Christ's victory will be more clearly seen.

(1, 2) See notes on 1:18; 9:1; 11:7; 12:2; comp. Matt. 12:29; 25:41.

(3) That which in the vision is described as the work of a moment may in the fact and fulfillment be a very gradual work. To fix it to any incident is to fall into a vicious realism. The same applies to the duration of the imprisonment. It is not to be understood literally any more than the other numbers in the book, for it symbolizes a lengthened period. This period is followed by the loosing again of the devil for a short time.

(4) And I saw thrones.—Those who in the latter part are said to reign with Christ are clearly those who sit upon the thrones which first caught the prophet's eye; these are all the real servants of God. They appear before the seer in two great classes: the martyrs who have been faithful unto death, and those who have been faithful in life.

The triumph and sovereignty, whatever they be, are shared by all the faithful. These things are stated as constituting their privileges. The phrase "judgment was given" means that judicial powers are given to the saints as to those who occupy thrones. Those who lived for God, and refused the mark of earthliness, reign and judge us in our worldliness and weakness. This is their sovereign honor here, besides the glad reign in the unseen world.

(5) But the rest of the dead lived not again.—If the words "lived not" necessarily mean that the rest of the dead did not enjoy physical life on earth, then the living with Christ of the saints and the first resurrection must be understood as giving physical life on earth to the saints. But the "lived" of verse 4 and the "lived not" of verse 5 need not be understood literally. Are we to picture saints with glorified resurrection bodies living on the earth, which at the same time is tenanted by men and women still in the natural body? (See verse 8.) There is a resurrection, which surely is the second resurrection, described in verses 12 and 13; this last is a general resurrection of the dead, small and great. There seems no adequate reason to affirm that this first resurrection, then, **must** be physical. Our notions of life and death are so circumscribed by the geography of earth that we seldom give to the word "life" in our thoughts its true richness and fullness of meaning. The second death (verse 6), moreover, is not the mere physical dying; it is rather that more awful death which lies outside the region of the things seen and temporal. Whatever it means, and whatever the conditions which surround it, it is spiritual rather than physical.

(7) And when the thousand years are expired.—The binding of Satan implied restraint put upon his power and freedom of action; the loosing means the removing of these restraints. The reign of Christ with His saints has been a witness to the power of our Master over the wicked one. This witness has been an opportunity also to the world. It was the earthly approximation to the ideal picture. But the time of opportunity must end. The vision pictures to us how Christendom will be invaded by the influences of the evil one, when mankind has let slip this splendid opportunity of a really golden age.

(8) And shall go out to deceive the nations.—The nations deceived and led astray are designated as Gog and Magog. (See notes on Ezek. 38 and 39.) In rabbinical books the names were used to describe the nations who would rise against the reign of the Messiah. The names are to be understood figuratively for the great hosts of the nations, and their leaders, who would break forth into unwarranted hostility against the people of the Lord. When the restraints of the millennium are removed, the long-suppressed evil breaks forth, and the reluctantly submissive nations are gathered together to the war spoken of in chaps. 16 and 19. All the restraints which Christ and Christian teaching had supplied to the world are gradually removed. The Euphrates is dried, the Devil is loosed, the unclean spirits have gone forth, and the last phase of the long war between good and evil, between Christ and Belial, has been entered.

(9) The "beloved city" is the figure of the true spiritual Zion and Jerusalem which has been faithful to her king. The prophet is using here the incidents and actions of the past as imagery. The present vision is figurative, though of course not mere empty figure, for Christ will thoroughly purge His floor (Matt. 3:12).

(11) And I saw a great white throne...—The throne is so described as to set it in strong contrast to other thrones mentioned in the book, and in token of the purity of the judgment which follows. Some physical revolutions do in all probability await our earth, but the eye of the prophet looks more to the moral and spiritual regeneration of the world—more to the spiritual well-being of mankind than to any physical changes which may synchronize with the culmination of the world's moral history.

(12, 13) And I saw the dead, small and great...—These verses assure us that the dead, in whatever quarter, must appear before the judgment throne. It has been said by some that the dead spoken of here as coming forth from the grave are not all the dead, but only "the rest of the dead" mentioned in 20:5. Those who believe that the first resurrection mentioned there is a literal physical resurrection are compelled to limit the resurrection here to the resurrection only of the remainder of the dead. But the verses before us suggest no limitation, and the language most assuredly tends to the idea that saints and faithful servants of God take part in this later resurrection. If all the saints and righteous men of old are raised prior to the millennium, and take no part in this last judgment scene, then only the faithless and wicked are left to be judged before the great white throne, and as none of these can be found written in the book of life, the bringing forth of the book becomes meaningless. The real significance of the scene lies in the vivid picturing of that great and solemn truth that **all** must stand before the judgment seat of Christ, to be judged according to whether they have any life toward God. The works and the life toward God must be combined.

(14) And death and hell were cast into the lake of fire.—It is clearly figurative language, implying that Death, the last enemy (I Cor. 15:26) is destroyed, together with Hades, who was personified as Death's escort (6:8). So we read in 21:4 that "there shall be no more death." The second death is a death of which the first death—the physical death, now destroyed—was but a faint figure. It is a condition which needs no coarse exaggeration or literalization of the prophetic imagery to heighten its horror.

21

(1) And I saw a new heaven ... —The hope of the renewal and restitution of all things had been long cherished by prophets, apostles, and Christ Himself, e.g., Ezek. 40-48; Matt. 19:28; II Pet. 3. The characteristic word which runs throughout the description is the word **new. Kainos,** relating to quality, rather than **neos,** relating to time, is the word which is used throughout this chapter, and, indeed, throughout the Book of Revelation. The newness which is pictured is the newness of freshness; the old, decaying, enfeebling, and corrupting elements are swept away. The description is figurative, but the spirit of it implies that in the restitution age the sweetness of things loved and familiar will blend with the charm of all that is fresh and new.

And there was no more sea.—The **sea** has played an important part in the symbolism of the book (see notes on 13:1; 17:1; comp. Isa. 48:18; 57:20).

(2) And I John saw the holy city ... —Both images—the "city" and the "bride"—are familiar to the Bible student. The sacred city appears linked to God by a sacred bond. We know what her ornaments are, now that He is about to present her to Himself a glorious Church. She is seen, not rising from earth, or sea, like the foes of righteousness, but coming down from heaven. The world will never evolve a golden age or ideal state. The new Jerusalem must descend from God.

(4) And God shall wipe away all tears ... —We should translate "every tear," and so possess the promise in its true and tender form. The splendid array of negatives comes as a herald of the positive peace of the new Jerusalem: no sea, no tears, no death, no mourning, no crying, no pain; with the former things these six shadows pass away from life. On the whole passage, comp. Isa. 25:8; 65:19.

(7) He that overcometh shall inherit all things.—The general promise of verse 3 is in part repeated, and this time more individually. Again we catch, as it were, the echo of the promises to the Seven Churches: the blessing is for him who conquers. The idea of the war and the conquest is a favorite one with John.

(8) The list given here points to those classes of character which cannot find a place in the Holy City. The abominations cited here have reference to those mentioned in 17:4. The characters form four pairs: fear and unbelief go hand in hand; the workers of abomination and the murderers, and the fornicators and the sorcerers, are united as those who sin in secret; the idolaters and the false are listed as those who change God's truth into a lie.

(9) The descriptions beginning here are not to be understood literally. One of the seven angels which had the seven vials of wrath had shown to the seer the scarlet-clad harlot, the great and guilty Babylon. Now one of the same company shows him the pure Bride of the Lamb, the new and holy Jerusalem.

(10, 11) The glimpse of God's coming glories is best gained from the consecrated heights of self-surrender and prayer. The light of the city is the light which she gives. (See note on 4:3.)

(12, 13) On this arrangement of gates, comp. Ezek. 48. The gates lie open to all quarters; there is no refusal of admission to any people.

(14) The wall of the city.—The whole Old and New Testament Church is represented in the appearance of the city, but the work of the apostles receives its special recognition. It is on their teaching and witness for Christ that the great spiritual Jerusalem is built. (Comp. Matt. 16:18; Eph. 2:20; I Pet. 2:4-6.) The argument that ohn the apostle could not be the writer of he Apocalypse because he includes himself among the foundation-stones of the celestial :ity betrays a misapprehension of the meaning and value of symbols. Historically and doctrinally the Church of Chrish is built upon the foundations described here; our creeds declare an acknowledgment of a catholic and **apostolic** Church.

(16) And the city lieth foursquare... —The length, breadth, and height are equal; the city thus presents the symbol of perfect symmetry. The city is not designed, any more than the vision of chap. 4 or the vision of Ezek. 1, to be represented by painting to the eye. The main thought is to realize the harmony and proportion of that community in which broad and low and high will meet, and in which no truth will be exaggerated or distorted; in which no disproportioned adjustments will mar its social order; in which all those who are inbuilt as living stones will be measured, not by the false estimates of worldly thoughts, but by the golden reed of the sanctuary. The recurrence of the number one hundred forty-four (verse 17) recalls the figurative character of the description. (Comp. note on 7:4.)

(18) Pure gold.—The wealth of heaven is love. Love is the circulating medium of all holy activity and of all holy work. All who dwell within the heavenly city are encompassed by it; all who tread the streets of that city move along the ways of love. No dimness or obscuring motives of self-interest mar its luster—the "gold" is clear as pure glass.

(19) The harlot's robe was decked with gold, precious stones, and pearls. The Bride, the Lamb's wife, has her beautiful ornaments, richer and rarer than those which adorned the world-mistress. He who is content to pass by the dazzling attractions of the world, refusing splendor from the outstretched hand of Babylon, will win the true spiritual riches. The foundationstones are twelve. "As twelve, they indicate their numerical completeness (chaps. 7 and 14); as shining with a common luster, their unity; as stones of different hues, their manifoldness; as brilliant stones, the glorification of this earthly life through the light of heaven" (Lange).

(21) Each gate was made out of one pearl. The foundations are diverse; the gates are alike. All find entrance through one new and living Way (John 14:6; Acts 4:11, 12; I Cor. 3:11; Heb. 10:20). The pearl was esteemed of the greatest value among the ancients. It is an appropriate emblem of the highest truth, and so of Him who is the Truth as well as the Way of Life. And it is the only precious stone which the art and skill of men cannot improve. So is it with the truth, which sets men free.

(22) And I saw no temple therein... —Ezekiel's vision (Ezek. 48:8-20) declared that the literal temple would be replaced by a far more glorious spiritual temple. The age of the Christian Church succeeds the age of the Jewish temple-worship; the age of the Church triumphing will succeed the age of the Church toiling. And there the external organizations, helps, and instrumentalities required for the edifying of the body of Christ will no longer be needed (I Cor. 13:9; Eph. 4:11-13). Churches will disappear, absorbed in the one glorious Church.

(23) And the city had no need of the sun... —The Shechinah is cited again. Light is the emblem of knowledge and holiness—God is light, and in Him is no darkness at all (I John 1:5). The imagery is drawn from Isa. 60:19. No more will there be needed subsidiary or intermediate luminaries. Notice again that the emblem of the Lamb is used to describe our Lord in this verse, as also in verse 14. The memory of Christ's work on earth is never obliterated.

(25-27) As men find that every good gift and every perfect gift is from above, and that their strength is in Christ, without whom they can do nothing, so will their lives bring back to Him the luster of all their achievements.

22

(1) And he shewed me a pure river... —Water is the emblem of life; it is the beautiful symbol of life in its gladness, purity, activity, and fullness.

(2) The tree of life.—The hunger as well as the thirst of the spirit is to be satisfied (Matt. 5:6). The tree of life, as well as the river of life, is to be found in the new and better Eden (Gen. 2:9, 10; 3:22). The vision of Ezek. 47:7-12 is exactly parallel to the present. The twelve manner of fruit are to be noticed, for here, too, as well as in the foundations and gates of the city, we have variety allied with unity: the knowledge of life which makes the knowledge of things available to the highest good.

(3, 4) We turn from the city to the

1241

inhabitants. They are described as serving Him, seeing Him, and resembling Him. They shall serve Him; they shall offer Him the service of the priesthood—the word employed is that used of temple service—encouraged by His immediate presence. The **name** stands for what God is in holiness and righteousness, purity and love. The name on the forehead indicates their resemblance to their Master.

(5) And there shall be no night there ... —Twice is it said (21:25) that all darkness shall cease; the darkness in which the saints and sorrowing walked shall be dispelled, when God gives them light. No artificial light is needed, since He who is Light is their light. With this utterance regarding light and priesthood the visions of the Apocalypse close.

(6) The epilogue deals with practical exhortations, warnings, and blessings. The reference is to the whole book.

(7) Behold, I come quickly.—The words of Christ Himself follow (perhaps quoted by the angel) to confirm the declaration of the last verse. These confirming words are an embodiment of the spirit of the whole Apocalypse. The Apocalypse is the revelation of the coming One; it reveals the dealings of Him who came, who comes, and is to come. (Comp. note on 1:3, 4).

(11) Two pairs are selected to stand as representatives of the good and of the bad. In these four are included all classes of godly and ungodly: those who sin against society, and those sin against themselves; those who act honorably, and those who keep themselves pure. The verse is the declaration of the ever terrible truth that men are building up their destiny by the actions and habits of their lives. It is in this law of our nature that the key to many of the darkest problems of the future may lie. But the eternal laws of God, though righteously ordered, are not God. The refuge from the eternal laws which we invoke against ourselves by our sin is to be found in the Eternal God, the Alpha and the Omega. The

next verses set the way of refuge and safety before us.

(14) Blessed are they that do his commandments ... —The reading of two of the best MSS is, "Blessed are they that wash their robes." There is in Him, who is the First and the Last, refuge from the power of sin and law against which such solemn warning has been given.

(15) For without are dogs and sorcerers ... —The allusion to the dogs outside the city is hardly appreciated by westerners. In the East, however, troops of hungry and semi-wild dogs used to wander about the fields and streets of the cities, devouring dead bodies and other offal, and thus became such objects of dislike that fierce and cruel enemies are poetically styled **dogs** (Ps. 22:16, 20). This verse is the reiteration of the warning that those who would enter in must break off their sins by righteousness (verse 9).

(16, 17) The warning is followed by the voice of our Lord Himself testifying of the truth of the revelation made. Then follows the cry of all creation for its true Lord.

(18, 19) Comp. Deut. 4:2; 12:32. The words are a solemn protest against the spirit which handles rashly or deceitfully the Word of God; which adds its own thoughts or makes its wishes the parent of its interpretations; which dilutes the force of its warnings or impoverishes the fullness of its promises. In a minor degree, it is true that those who leave this book unstudied and unprayed over lose much spiritual sustenance and comfort.

(21) The grace of our Lord Jesus Christ ... —The grace or free pardon of the Lord Jesus is the last word left in our ears. It reminds us that whatever be the dangers or difficulties, the afflictions or persecutions, which have been pictured in the book, there is strength and love in the Lord to carry out the spiritual teachings and laws of that kingdom whose progress this book so vividly portrays.